NEW DICTIONARY *of*
CHRISTIAN
ETHICS &
PASTORAL
THEOLOGY

NEW DICTIONARY of CHRISTIAN ETHICS & PASTORAL THEOLOGY

EDITORS

David J. Atkinson

*Canon Chancellor of Southwark Cathedral, London;
formerly Fellow of Corpus Christi College, Oxford*

David H. Field

*Director of Professional Ministry, Church Pastoral Aid Society, Warwick;
formerly Vice-Principal and Lecturer in Christian Ethics, Oak Hill College, London*

CONSULTING EDITORS

Arthur F. Holmes

Professor of Philosophy, Wheaton College, Wheaton, Illinois

Oliver O'Donovan

*Regius Professor of Moral and Pastoral Theology, Oxford University;
Canon of Christ Church, Oxford*

INTERVARSITY PRESS
DOWNERS GROVE, ILLINOIS, USA
LEICESTER, ENGLAND

INTER-VARSITY PRESS
38 De Montfort Street, Leicester LE1 7GP, England
P.O. Box 1400, Downers Grove, Illinois 60515, USA

Inter-Varsity Press, England, is the publishing division of the Universities and Colleges Christian Fellowship (formerly the Inter-Varsity Fellowship), a student movement linking Christian Unions in universities and colleges throughout the United Kingdom and the Republic of Ireland, and a member movement of the International Fellowship of Evangelical Students. For information about local and national activities write to UCCF, 38 De Montfort Street, Leicester LE1 7GP.

InterVarsity Press®, USA, is the book-publishing division of InterVarsity Christian Fellowship®, a student movement active on campus at hundreds of universities, colleges and schools of nursing in the United States of America, and a member movement of the International Fellowship of Evangelical Students. For information about local and regional activities, write Public Relations Dept., InterVarsity Christian Fellowship, 6400 Schroeder Rd., P.O. Box 7895, Madison, WI 53707-7895.

Typeset in Great Britain by Action Typesetting Limited, Glouster

Printed in the United States of America ⊗

British Library Cataloguing in Publication Data

A catalogue record for this book is available from the British Library.

UK ISBN 0-85110-650-1

Library of Congress Cataloging-in-Publication Data

New dictionary of Christian ethics & pastoral theology/editors,
        David J. Atkinson . . . [et al.].
            p.   cm.
        Includes bibliographical references (p.).
        ISBN 0-8308-1408-6
            1. Christian ethics—Dictionaries.   2. Pastoral theology—Dictionaries.
    I. Atkinson, David John, 1943-   .
    BJ1199.N495   1995
        241'.03—dc20   94-40802
                                                            CIP

17	16	15	14	13	12	11	10	9	8	7	6	5	4	3	2	1
09	08	07	06	05	04	03	02	01	00	99	98	97	96	95		

Contents

Preface

In bringing together articles on Christian ethics and pastoral theology, the editors hope that this Dictionary will provide a major resource for pastors, social workers, doctors and counsellors working in a Christian context, as well as for clergy, ordinands, teachers, religious-studies students and interested lay people. We have attempted to integrate as far as possible, within the terms of the subject matter, both moral theology and pastoral and practical theology. Decision-making often raises questions of pastoral psychology, individual temperament, social and personal factors, and determinants of various psychological, sociological, economic and ideological kinds. Behind these lies a certain moral framework, centred on the general question 'What should be done?', and implying a network of values, duties and moral principles. And behind these again lies a certain set of basic assumptions about the way the world is, and the way people are – in other words, a certain 'theology'.

Our theological stance derives from the fundamental conviction that God has made himself known in Jesus Christ, his Son, and that he continues to disclose himself to us through the Holy Spirit within the life of his church. The Bible is our authoritative guide to God's self-disclosure: the Word of God in written form. The traditions of Christian thinking throughout the centuries illuminate for us ways in which God has guided his people in interpreting the Bible in different contexts, and in discerning his truth and his will. The Holy Spirit, who is given to guide us into truth, informs and sanctifies our reason, so that with our minds, as well as our hearts and souls, we can find appropriate expressions for our love of God and love of neighbour, and for manifesting justice in all human affairs.

One unique feature of this Dictionary is that in Part One we have drawn together eighteen major 'keynote' articles. These articles are arranged not in the traditional alphabetical order but in a theological order (numbered one to eighteen, and for ease of reference the numerals appear in tinted blocks down the outer edge of the pages). They give a basic introduction to the main themes of Christian ethics and pastoral theology – like a main river, from which many smaller rivers flow. Their theological order illustrates our method. We begin, as all Christian thinking ought, with God, and then explore the implications of his character of love and justice. Our attention is drawn next to the nature of the human moral agent, and the gospel themes of sin and salvation. After general historical surveys of Christian ethics and of practical and pastoral theology, we focus on particular areas of interest. Old Testament and New Testament ethics are treated in separate articles, and then follow specific discussions on issues such as sexuality, medical ethics and economic concerns. We conclude the keynote articles with a major essay from Professor O'Donovan illustrating method and meaning in Christian moral reasoning.

Our hope is that these keynote articles may be used as a textbook, offering the reader a broad survey of the field, and inviting further exploration of specific and detailed issues through cross-referencing to the many articles in Part Two.

A reader of 'Economic Ethics', for example, may be referred for more detail to articles in Part Two on such subjects as banking, monetarism, multinational corporations and taxation.

The Dictionary may also be used in reverse order, moving from the specific to the more general. Readers may turn to an article in Part Two on remarriage, to find that they wish to explore more fully the Christian theological traditions of thinking on marriage and divorce; and then be referred back to the major keynote article on 'Sexuality' in Part One.

In any selection of articles, gaps are inevitable. The task of weighing the interests of our readers against the need to keep this volume to a manageable size has not been easy. With one or two justifiable exceptions, we have not included biographical articles on persons who are still living.

Though the editors are aware that some users of this Dictionary prefer the term 'Two-Thirds World' to 'Third World', the latter is so well established in popular usage (*e.g.* in the phrase 'Third World aid') that it is difficult, if not impossible, to displace it from the public consciousness. They have therefore preferred the term 'Third World' in spite of the criticisms some have of it.

We are very grateful to the many authors who have contributed their expertise. We have been greatly helped by the editorial staff at IVP, and in particular by the Theological Books Editor, the Revd David Kingdon, and by Jane Horner, who has been a very efficient administrative co-ordinator for this ambitious project. Hazel Medcalf has contributed much expertise and not a little patience as copy-editor, and Dr Philip Hillyer has checked bibliographies and supplied many missing dates of persons. Jo Bramwell and Simon Fox have been diligent proofreaders. Our consulting editors, Professors Oliver O'Donovan and Arthur Holmes, have greatly helped us by their wisdom and counsel. Thanks are also due to Action Typesetting Limited, Gloucester, for their skills and ready co-operation in undertaking what has proved to be a complex volume.

It is our hope that this Dictionary will prove to be a useful resource to a wide circle of Christian people, to aid them in the mission and ministry of the kingdom of God.

David J. Atkinson
David H. Field

How to use this Dictionary

This introduction provides some guidance on how to use this Dictionary to the best advantage.

Arrangement

As soon as its pages are turned, it is obvious that this Dictionary is arranged differently from others. Instead of following the usual alphabetical order throughout, it is in two parts.

Part One, as the Preface explains, is arranged in a theological order, beginning with **GOD** and ending with **CHRISTIAN MORAL REASONING**. Each of the eighteen major articles in Part One provides a reasonably comprehensive overview of a major subject area in Christian ethics or pastoral theology, and a list of subjects is given on the Contents page. So, if you want to gain an overall grasp of the topic **HUMANITY**, for example, you should begin here in Part One with the article on page 21. Having read through the article, you will find at the end a list of references headed '*See especially*'. This alerts you to the presence of related articles in Part Two. Thus, in connection with **HUMANITY**, you may want to explore such matters as ADOLESCENCE, WORK, MARRIAGE, RETIREMENT, and DEATH AND DYING, to mention one possible sequence.

Part Two of the Dictionary contains shorter articles, arranged alphabetically and ranging in length from 2,000 to 250 words. In many of these articles you will find cross-references that include boxed numerals, which refer you to the eighteen major articles in Part One. So, for example, the article on **BIRTH CONTROL** contains on page 194 the reference '. . . sexuality (see ⑪) . . .'. This refers you to the eleventh article in Part One on the subject of **SEXUALITY**, and for easy access you will find the numeral 11 on the outer edges of pages 71–77.

Cross-references

It has been editorial policy in this Dictionary to group smaller topics together and treat them in a single larger article. For example, 'industrial action' is dealt with in the article on **STRIKES**, and 'closed shop' in the article on **TRADE UNIONS**. Some of the major articles in Part One also group together a number of topics. For example, **PASTORAL CARE, COUNSELLING AND PSYCHOTHERAPY** covers a wide range of subjects.

Cross-referencing is therefore an important feature of this Dictionary. Six methods are in use:

1. Numerous one-line entries refer you to the title of the article or articles where the topic is treated: *e.g.*

> **CONSERVATION**, see ENVIRONMENT.
> **MOURNING**, see BEREAVEMENT; GRIEF.

2. An asterisk after a word or phrase indicates that further relevant information will be found in the article under that title. It is equivalent to the abbreviation *q.v.* You should note:

    a. The *form* of the word asterisked will not always be precisely the same as that of the title of the article to which the asterisk refers. For example: 'teleological*' directs you to the article on **TELEOLOGY**, 'alcohol*' to **ALCOHOLISM**, and 'surrogacy*' to **SURROGATE MOTHERHOOD**.

    b. The asterisk sometimes applies to two or three words rather than to the word asterisked. Thus 'kingdom of God*' sends you to the article **KINGDOM OF GOD**, not 'God', and 'Thomas Aquinas*' to the entry **THOMAS AQUINAS**, not 'Aquinas'.

3. A reference in brackets in the body of an article such as '(see Consequentialism*)' is self-explanatory.

4. A reference including a boxed numeral refers you to one of the eighteen major articles in Part One. For example, '(see ②)' or '(see Love②)' refers you to the second major article in Part One, entitled **LOVE**.

5. Cross-references at the end of the eighteen articles in Part One are headed '*See especially*'. These refer you to articles in Part Two, though just occasionally they may also refer you to another major article that is of particular relevance.

6. Cross-references at the end of articles in Part Two are headed '*See also*'. These usually refer you to other articles in Part Two, and sometimes to one of the major articles in Part One.

Abbreviations

A list of abbreviations used in the Dictionary will be found on pp. xii – xv.

Authorship of articles

The authors of articles are indicated by their initials at the foot of each article. A full list of contributors will be found on pp. xvi – xxiii in alphabetical order of initials, not of surnames.

Bibliographies

Guidance for further study has been provided in most articles, sometimes in the body of the article itself, but in most cases in the bibliography at the end. The works listed in a bibliography may include studies which take up a different position from that of the contributor of the article. In biographical articles, writings by the subject of the article are placed first, followed by any studies.

Bible versions

Quotations from the Bible are from the New International Version, unless specified otherwise.

Transliteration

The following systems have been adopted throughout the volume:

Hebrew

א	=	'	ד	=	ḏ	י	=	y	ס	=	s	ר	=	r
ב	=	b	ה	=	h	כ	=	k	ע	=	'	שׂ	=	ś
ב	=	ḇ	ו	=	w	כ	=	ḵ	פ	=	p	שׁ	=	š
ג	=	g	ז	=	z	ל	=	l	פ	=	p̄	ת	=	t
ג	=	ḡ	ח	=	ḥ	מ	=	m	צ	=	ṣ	ת	=	ṯ
ד	=	d	ט	=	ṭ	נ	=	n	ק	=	q			

Long Vowels			Short Vowels		Very Short Vowels	
(ה)ָ = â	ָ = ā	ַ = a	ֲ = ᵃ		
ֵ = ê	ֵ = ē	ֶ = e	ֱ = ᵉ		
ִ = î		ִ = i	ְ = ᵉ (if vocal)		
וֹ = ô	ֹ = ō	ָ = o	ֳ = ᵒ		
וּ = û		ֻ = u			

Greek

α	=	a	ι	=	i	ρ	=	r	ῥ	=	rh
β	=	b	κ	=	k	σ, ς	=	s	'	=	h
γ	=	g	λ	=	l	τ	=	t	γξ	=	nx
δ	=	d	μ	=	m	υ	=	y	γγ	=	ng
ε	=	e	ν	=	n	φ	=	ph	αυ	=	au
ζ	=	z	ξ	=	x	χ	=	ch	ευ	=	eu
η	=	ē	ο	=	o	ψ	=	ps	ου	=	ou
θ	=	th	π	=	p	ω	=	ō	υι	=	yi

Abbreviations

1. Books and journals

ACPAN
Association of Christians in Planning and Architecture Newsletter, published by UCCF (Leicester, 1983–)

ACW
Ancient Christian Writers (Westminster, MD, and London, etc., 1946–)

AJP
American Journal of Psychiatry (Washington, DC, 1844–)

AJS
American Journal of Sociology (Chicago, IL, 1895–)

AJSMF
Australian Journal of Sex, Marriage and Family (Concord, NSW, 1980–)

AJTP
American Journal of Theology and Philosophy (West Lafayette, IN, 1980–)

Anv
Anvil (Bristol, 1984–)

ASR
American Sociological Review (Washington, DC, 1936–)

AV
Authorized (King James') Version, 1611

BCP
Book of Common Prayer

BDCE
Baker's Dictionary of Christian Ethics, ed. C. F. H. Henry (Grand Rapids and Glasgow, 1973)

BMJ
British Medical Journal (London, 1832–)

CC
Carer and Counsellor (originally *The Christian Counsellor*; Farnham, 1991–)

CD
Church Dogmatics, Karl Barth, 4 vols. in 13 + index vol. (ET, Edinburgh, 1936–81)

CDP
A Critical Dictionary of Psychoanalysis, C. Rycroft (London, 1968)

CH
Church History (Scottdale, PA, etc., 1932–)

Con
Contact (Edinburgh, 1960–)

CQR
Church Quarterly Review (London, 1875–1968)

Crim
Criminology (Columbus, OH, 1963–)

CT
Christianity Today (Washington, 1956–)

CTJ
Calvin Theological Journal (Grand Rapids, 1966–)

DCE
A Dictionary of Christian Ethics, ed. J. Macquarrie (London and Philadelphia, 1967)

DCS
A Dictionary of Christian Spirituality, ed. G. S. Wakefield (London, 1983) = *The Westminster Dictionary of Christian Spirituality* (Philadelphia, 1983)

DME
Dictionary of Medical Ethics, ed. A. S. Duncan, G. R. Dunstan and R. B. Welbourn (London, 1981)

DPC
A Dictionary of Pastoral Care, ed. A. V. Campbell (London and New York, 1987)

DPCC
A Dictionary of Pastoral Care and Counselling, ed. R. J. Hunter (Nashville, TN, 1990).

DSp
Dictionnaire de spiritualité, ed. M. Viller *et al.* (Paris, 1937–)

DSt
Death Studies (New York, 1977–)

DTC
Dictionnaire de théologie catholique, ed. A. Vacant *et al.*, 15 vols. (Paris, 1903–50)

EBio
Encyclopedia of Bioethics, ed. W. Reich, 4 vols. (New York, 1968)

ECJ
Encyclopedia of Crime and Justice, ed. S. Kadish (New York, 1983)

EcR
Ecumenical Review (Geneva, 1948–)

EP
Encyclopedia of Philosophy, ed. P. Edwards, 8 vols. (New York, 1967)

ER
The Encyclopedia of Religion, ed. M. Eliade, 16 vols. (London and New York, 1987)

ERE
Encyclopaedia of Religion and Ethics, ed. J. Hastings, 13 vols. (Edinburgh, 1908–26)

Eth
Ethics (Chicago, 1890–)

FP
Faith and Philosophy (Wilmore, KY, 1984–)

FT
Faith and Thought (London, 1866–)

HS
Handbook of Sociology, ed. N. J. Smelser (Newbury Park, CA, 1988)

IDB
The Interpreter's Dictionary of the Bible, ed. G. A. Buttrick, 4 vols. (New York and Nashville, TN, 1962)

IESS
International Encyclopedia of the Social Sciences, ed. D. E. Sills, 17 vols. (New York, 1968)

ILR
International Labour Review (Geneva, 1921–)

Int
Interpretation (Richmond, VA, 1947–)

Inter
Interchange (Surrey Hills, NSW, 1967–)

ISBE
International Standard Bible Encyclopedia, ed. J. Orr, 5 vols. (Chicago, ²1930); new edition, ed. G. W. Bromiley (Grand Rapids, 1979–)

ISM
In the Service of Medicine, now *Journal of the Christian Medical Fellowship* (London, 1952–)

ISQ
International Studies Quarterly (Stoneham, MA, 1957–)

JAP
Journal of Analytical Psychology (London, 1955–)

JB
Jerusalem Bible, 1966

JBP
The New Testament in Modern English, J. B. Phillips (Collins, 1958)

JCH
Journal of Christian Healing (Narberth, PN, 1979–)

JCP
Journal of Consulting Psychology, now *Journal of Consulting and Clinical Psychology* (Washington, DC, 1968–)

JETS
Journal of the Evangelical Theological Society (Wheaton, IL, 1969–)

JFCJ
Juvenile and Family Court Journal (Reno, NV, 1949–)

JJS
Journal of Jewish Studies (Oxford, 1948–)

JPalC
Journal of Palliative Care (Toronto, 1985–)

JPC
Journal of Pastoral Care (Decatur, GA, 1948–)

JPCo
Journal of Pastoral Counselling (New Rochelle, NY, 1966–)

JPP
Journal of Pastoral Practice (Laverock, PA, 1978–)

JPT
Journal of Psychology and Theology (La Mirada, CA, 1973–)

JR
Journal of Religion (Chicago, 1921–)

JSOT
Journal for the Study of the Old Testament (Sheffield, 1976–)

JSSR
Journal for the Scientific Study of Religion (Wetteren, *etc.*, 1961–)

JTS
Journal of Theological Studies (Oxford, 1899–)

JTSA
Journal of Theology for Southern Africa (Braamfontein, 1972–)

LCC
Library of Christian Classics, 26 vols. (London and Philadelphia, 1953–70)

MI
Medicine International (Oxford, 1981– ; n.s. 1984–)

Miss
Missiology (Denver, CO, *etc.*, 1953–)

NASB
New American Standard Bible, 1963

NCE
New Catholic Encyclopedia, ed. W. J. McDonald, 17 vols. (new York, 1967–79)

NDCE
A New Dictionary of Christian Ethics, ed. J. Macquarrie and J. F. Childress (London, 1986)

NDT
New Dictionary of Theology
(Leicester and Downers Grove,
IL, 1988)

NEJM
New England Journal of
Medicine (Waltham, MA,
1812–)

NIDNTT
The New International
Dictionary of New Testament
Theology, ed. C. Brown, 3 vols.
(Exeter and Grand Rapids,
1975–86)

NIV
New International Version of
the Bible, 1973, 1978, 1984

NovT
Novum Testamentum (Leiden,
1956–)

NPNF
A Select Library of Nicene and
Post-Nicene Fathers of the
Christian Church, first series,
ed. P. Schaff, 14 vols. (New
York, 1886–90); second series,
ed. H. Wace and P. Schaff, 14
vols. (New York, 1890–1900);
new ed. (Grand Rapids, 1980)

NRSV
New Revised Standard Version,
1989

OED
Oxford English Dictionary
(Oxford, ²1989)

PalM
Palliative Medicine (London,
1987–)

PP
Pastoral Psychology (New York,
1950–)

Psy
Psychiatry (New York, 1937–)

PsyM
Psychological Medicine
(Cambridge, 1970–)

PTR
Princeton Theological Review
(Philadelphia, 1903–29)

REB
Revised English Bible, 1989

RRR
Review of Religious Research
(Washington, DC, *etc.*,
1959/60–)

RSV
Revised Standard Version, NT
1946, ²1971; OT 1952

SJT
Scottish Journal of Theology
(Edinburgh, *etc.*, 1948–)

STh
Summa Theologiae, Thomas
Aquinas, 60 vols. + index vol.
(1265–73; ET, London and
New York, 1964–81)

TDNT
Theological Dictionary of the
New Testament, ed. G. W.
Bromiley, 10 vols. (Grand
Rapids, 1964–76), ET of
Theologisches Wörterbuch zum
Neuen Testament, ed. G. Kittell
and G. Friedrich (Stuttgart,
1932–74)

TDOT
Theological Dictionary of the
Old Testament, ed. G. J.
Botterweck and H. Ringgren
(Grand Rapids, 1974–); ET of
Theologische Wörterbuch zum
Alten Testament

TE
Theological Ethics, H. Thielicke,
vol. 1 (²1958; abridged ET,
Philadelphia, 1966, and London,
1968); vol. 2 (²1959; abridged
ET, Philadelphia and London,
1969); and 3-vol. ed. (Grand
Rapids, 1978)

Th
Theology (London, 1920–)

Them
Themelios (Lausanne, 1962–74;
n.s. London, *etc.*, 1975–)

ThW
Third Way (New Malden, 1977–)

TOS
The Other Side (Philadelphia,
1965–)

Tr
Transformation (Exeter, 1984–)

TrinJ
Trinity Journal (Deerfield, IL,
1971–78; n.s. 1980–)

TWOT
Theological Wordbook of the Old
Testament, ed. R. Laird Harris *et*
al., 2 vols. (Chicago, 1980)

TynB
Tyndale Bulletin (London, *etc.*,
1956–)

VE
Vox Evangelica (London, *etc.*,
1962–)

VTSupp
Vetus Testamentum Supplements
(Leiden, 1953–)

WTJ
Westminster Theological Journal
(Philadelphia, 1938–)

2. Biblical books

Books of the Old Testament
Gn., Ex., Lv., Nu., Dt., Jos., Jdg., Ru., 1, 2, Sa., 1,
2 Ki., 1, 2 Ch., Ezr., Ne., Est., Jb., Ps. (Pss.), Pr.,
Ec., Song, Is., Je., La., Ezk., Dn., Ho., Joel, Am.,
Ob., Jon., Mi., Na., Hab., Zp., Hg., Zc., Mal.

Books of the New Testament
Mt., Mk., Lk., Jn., Acts, Rom., 1, 2 Cor., Gal.,
Eph., Phil., Col., 1, 2 Thes., 1, 2 Tim., Tit.,
Phm., Heb., Jas., 1, 2 Pet., 1, 2, 3 Jn., Jude, Rev.

3. General abbreviations

ad loc.	*ad locum* (Lat.), at the place
Arab.	Arabic
Aram.	Aramaic
b,	born
c.	*circa* (Lat.), about, approximately
cf.	*confer* (Lat.), compare
ch. (chs.)	chapter(s)
col. (cols.)	column(s)
d.	died
Ecclus.	Ecclesiasticus (Apocrypha)
ed. (eds.)	edited by, edition, editor(s)
Eng.	English
ET	English translation
et al.	*et alii* (Lat.), and others
EVV	English versions
f. (ff.)	and the following (verse(s), *etc.*)
fl.	*floruit* (Lat.), flourished
Fr.	French
Ger.	German
Gk.	Greek
Heb.	Hebrew
ibid.	*ibidem* (Lat.), the same work
idem	*idem* (Lat.), the same author
It.	Italian

Lat.	Latin
lit.	literally
loc. cit.	*loco citato* (Lat.), in the place already quoted
LXX	Septuagint (Gk. version of OT)
Macc.	Maccabees (Apocrypha)
mg.	margin
MS (MSS)	manuscript(s)
n.d.	no date
n.s.	new series
NT	New Testament
op. cit.	*opere citato* (Lat.), in the work cited above
OT	Old Testament
par.	and parallel(s)
1QS	Rule of the Community (Qumran Text)
repr.	reprinted
Syr.	Syriac
tr.	translated, translation
v. (vv.)	verse(s)
viz.	*videlicit* (Lat.), namely
vol. (vols.)	volume(s)
W.	Welsh

List of Contributors

A.B. A. Brown, B.A., M. Ed., teacher and freelance writer.

A.B.C. A. B. Cramp, B.A., M.A., Ph.D., Fellow of Emmanuel College, Cambridge.

A.C. A. Chaplin, M.Phil., freelance writer.

A.C.B. A. C. Berry, M.B., B.S., Ph.D., Consultant Clinical Geneticist, Guy's Hospital, London.

A.C.P.S. A.C.P. Sims, M.A., M.D., F.R.C.Psych., F.R.C.P.E., Professor of Psychiatry, University of Leeds.

A.C.T. A. C. Thiselton, B.D., M.Th., Ph.D., D.D., Professor of Christian Theology and Head of the Department of Theology, University of Nottingham.

A.D.V. A. D. Verhey, B.D., Ph.D., The Evert J. and Hattie E. Blekkink Professor of Religion, Hope College, Holland, Michigan.

A.E.McG. A. E. McGrath, M.A., D.Phil., B.D., Research Lecturer in Theology, University of Oxford; Research Professor of Systematic Theology, Regent College, Vancouver; Lecturer in Historical and Systematic Theology, Wycliffe Hall, Oxford.

A.F.H. A. F. Holmes, B.A., M.A., Ph.D., Professor of Philosophy, Wheaton College, Wheaton, Illinois.

A.F.K. A. F. Kreider, B.A., M.A., Ph.D., Theologian-in-Residence, Northern Baptist College, Manchester.

A.G.V. A. G. Vos, B.A., M.A., Ph.D., Professor of Philosophy, Western Kentucky University, Bowling Green, Kentucky.

A.H.A.C.E. A. H. A. Crum Ewing, B.A., M.Th, self-employed artist and etcher.

A.J.H. A. J. Hartropp, B.Sc., Ph.D., Anglican ordinand at Oak Hill Theological College, London; formerly Lecturer in Financial Economics, Brunel University, Uxbridge, Middlesex.

A.J.T. A. J. Townsend, M.B., B.S., M.R.C.S., L.R.C.P., psychodynamic counsellor; Dean for Ministers in Secular Employment, Diocese of Southwark; honorary curate.

A.J.W. A. J. Wing, M.A., D.M., F.R.C.P., Consultant Physician, St Thomas' Hospital, London.

A.N.S.L. A. N. S. Lane, M.A., B.D., Senior Lecturer in Christian Doctrine, London Bible College.

A.O.I. A. O. Igenoza, B.A., Ph.D., Senior Lecturer in Biblical Studies, Head of the Department of Religious Studies, and Vice-Dean, Faculty of Arts, Obafemi Awolowo University, Ile-Ife, Nigeria.

A.P.F. A. P. Foster, B.Sc., B.V.Sc., Cert.S.A.D., M.R.C.V.S., Cats' Protection League Scholar, University of Bristol Veterinary School.

A.P.P. A.P. Parkinson, Pastor of Leeds Reformed Baptist Church; Chairman, Caring for Life, Leeds.

A.R.W.D. A. R. Wingfield Digby, B.A., Cert.Theol., Director, Christians in Sport, Oxford.

A.S. A. Storkey, M.Sc., M.A., Dip.Ed., Ph.D., Lecturer in Sociology, Oak Hill Theological College, London.

B.A.C. B. A. Clouse, B.A., M.A., Ph.D., Professor of Educational and School Psychology, Indiana State University, Terre Haute, Indiana.

B.B. B. Batson, B.A., M.A., Ph.D., Coordinator of the Special Collection in Shakespeare (Shakespeare and the Christian Tradition) Wheaton College; formerly Professor and Chair of the Department of English, Wheaton College, Wheaton, Illinois.

B.H. B. Harris, B.Sc., M.B., B.S., F.R.C.Psych., D.P.M., Senior Lecturer, University of Wales College of Medicine, Cardiff.

B.K.W. B. K. Waltke, A.B., Th.M., Th.D., Ph.D., Marshall Sheppard Professor of Biblical Studies, Regent College, Vancouver.

B.L.S. B. L. Shelley, B.A., M.D., Ph.D., Senior Professor of Church History, Denver Seminary, Denver, Colorado.

B.S. B. Stanley, M.A., Ph.D., Lecturer in Church History, Trinity College, Bristol.

B.T.A. B. T. Adeney, B.A., B.D., Ph.D., Professor of Ethics and Cross-cultural Studies, Graduate Program in Religion and Society, Satya Wacana Christian University, Salatiga, Java, Indonesia.

B.W.R. B. W. Reynolds, B.A., M.A., Ph.D., Professor of History, Asbury College, Wilmore, Kentucky.

C.A.B. C. A. Brown, B.D., M.A., Ph.D., S.Th., Academic Dean, Spurgeon's College, London.

C.E.H. C. E. Hart, B.A., M.A., M.Th., M.Phil., Lecturer in Practical Theology, St John's College, Nottingham.

C.F.A. C. F. Allison, B.A., M.Div., D.Phil., formerly Bishop of South Carolina.

C.F.G. C. F. Green, F.C.I.B., F.B.I.M., F.L.C.M., formerly Director and Deputy Group Chief Executive, National Westminster Bank.

C.G.K. C. G. Kruse, B.D., M.Phil., Ph.D., Senior Lecturer, Ridley College, University of Melbourne.

C.H.S. C. H. Sherlock, B.A., Th.L., M.A., B.D., Th.D., Senior Lecturer, Ridley College, Melbourne.

C.J.H.H. C. J. H. Hingley, M.A., Chaplain, Whitestone School, Bulawayo, Zimbabwe.

C.J.H.W. C. J. H. Wright, M.A., Ph.D., Principal, All Nations Christian College, Ware, Hertfordshire.

C.M.N.S. C. M. N. Sugden, M.A., M.Phil., Ph.D., Principal, Oxford Centre for Mission Studies.

C.P. C. Partee, A.B., M.A., B.D., Ph.D., P. C. Rossin Professor of Church History, Pittsburgh Theological Seminary.

C.S.E. C. S. Evans, B.A., Ph.D., Professor of Philosophy and Curator, Howard and Edna Hong Kierkegaard Library, St Olaf College, Northfield, Minnesota.

C.Y. C. Yeats, M.A., M.Th., M.B.A., Solway Fellow and Chaplain, University College, Durham.

D.A.L. D. A. Lyon, B.Sc.,

Ph.D., Professor and Head of Sociology, Queen's University, Kingston, Ontario.

D.A.N.F. D. A. N. Fergusson, B.Sc., M.B., B.S., M.R.C.G.P., General Secretary, Christian Medical Fellowship, London.

D.A.S. D. A. Stone, M.A., B.M., B.Ch., Vicar of St Jude's Church, South Kensington, London.

D.A.W. D. A. Westberg, B.A., M.A., M.Div., D.Phil., Assistant Professor, Department of Religious Studies, University of Virginia, Charlottesville, Virginia.

D.B.F. D. B. Fletcher, B.A., M.A., Ph.D., Associate Professor of Philosophy, Wheaton College, Wheaton, Illinois; Adjunct Professor of Bioethics, Trinity Evangelical Divinity School, Deerfield, Illinois.

D.B.G. D. B. Garlington, B.A., M.Div., Th.M., Ph.D., Professor of New Testament, Toronto Baptist Seminary.

D.B.W. D. B. Winter, B.A., Priest-in-Charge, Ducklington, Oxfordshire; formerly Head of Religious Broadcasting, BBC, London.

D.C.S. D. C. Spanner, B.Sc., Ph.D., D.Sc., F.Inst.Biol., Emeritus Professor of Plant Biophysics, Bedford College, University of London; Anglican non-stipendiary minister.

D.D.B. D. D. Burke, B.Sc., M.Phil., Minister of Knighton Evangelical Free Church, Leicester.

D.F.W. D. F. Wright, M.A., Senior Lecturer in Ecclesiastical History, New College, University of Edinburgh.

D.G.B. D. G. Bloesch, B.A., B.D., Ph.D., Emeritus Professor of Theology, University of Dubuque Theological Seminary, Dubuque, Iowa.

D.G.J. D. G. Jones, B.Sc., M.B., B.S., D.Sc., Professor of Anatomy and Structural

Biology, University of Otago, Dunedin, New Zealand.

D.H.F. D. H. Field, B.A., Director of Professional Ministry, Church Pastoral Aid Society, Warwick; formerly Vice-Principal and Lecturer in Christian Ethics, Oak Hill College, London.

D.J.A. D. J. Atkinson, B.Sc., M.Litt., Ph.D., M.A., Canon Chancellor of Southwark Cathedral, London; formerly Fellow of Corpus Christi College, Oxford.

D.J.E.A. D. J. E. Attwood, M.A., B.A., Ph.D., Director of Studies, Trinity Theological College, Bristol.

D.J.P. D. J. Pullinger, B.A., M.Sc., Ph.D., Electronic Product Manager, Institute of Physics, Edinburgh.

D.J.T. D. J. Tidball, B.A., B.D., Ph.D., Head of Mission Department, Baptist Union of Great Britain, Didcot, Oxfordshire.

D.L.M. D. L. Mathieson, B.A., LL.B., B.C.L., LL.D., Q.C., formerly Professor of Law, Victoria University of Wellington, New Zealand.

D.L.O. D. L. Okholm, B.A., M.Div., M.A., Th.M., Ph.D., Associate Professor of Theology, Wheaton College, Wheaton, Illinois.

D.L.P. D. L. Parkyn, B.A., M.Div., Ph.D., Professor of Religious Studies, Messiah College, Grantham, Pennsylvania.

D.M.C. D. M. Cansdale, M.Sc., Assistant Chief Constable, Hertfordshire Constabulary.

D.P.K. D. P. Kingdon, M.A., B.D., Theological Books Editor, Inter-Varsity Press, UK; formerly Principal, Irish Baptist College, Belfast.

D.P.N. D. P. Negus, LL.B., Senior Partner, Ellis-Fermor and Negus, Solicitors, Nottingham.

D.R. D. Ratzsch., B.A., M.A., Ph.D., Professor of Philosophy, Calvin College, Grand Rapids, Michigan.

D.R.G. D. R. Groothuis, B.S., M.A., Ph.D., Assistant Professor of Philosophy of Religion and Ethics, Denver Seminary, Denver, Colorado.

D.R.L.P. D. R. L. Porter, B.A., A.L.A., freelance author and editor.

D.R.S. D. R. Shell, B.Sc., M.A., Senior Lecturer in Politics, University of Bristol.

D.W.A. D. W. Augsburger, B.D., Ph.D., Professor of Pastoral Care and Counseling, Fuller Theological Seminary, Pasadena, California.

D.W.Be. D. W. Bebbington, M.A., Ph.D., F.R.Hist.S., Reader in History, University of Stirling.

D.W.Br. Dale W. Brown, A.B., B.D., Ph.D., Emeritus Professor of Theology and Director of Peace Studies, Bethany Theological Seminary, Oak Brook, Illinois.

D.W.Bro. David W. Brown, M.A., M.A., Ph.D., Van Mildert Professor of Divinity, University of Durham; Canon of Durham Cathedral.

D.W.G. D. W. Gill, B.A., M.A., Ph.D., Professor of Applied Ethics, North Park College, Chicago.

D.W.P. D. W. Parish, M.C.I.T., Facilities Development Manager, British Airways.

D.W.V. D. W. Vere, M.D., F.R.C.P., F.F.P.M., Professor of Therapeutics, University of London; Consultant Physician, the Royal London Hospital.

D.W.V.N. D. W. Van Ness, LL.M., J.D., B.A., Visiting Assistant Professor, University of Detroit Mercy School of Law.

E.D.C. E. D. Cook, B.A., M.A., Ph.D., M.A., Director, the Whitefield Institute; Fellow

and Chaplain, Green College, Oxford.

E.J.M. E. J. Muskus, B.Sc., Dip.Th., Tutor in Contemporary Theology, Evangelical Theological College of Wales, Bridgend, Mid Glamorgan.

E.M.B.G. E. M. B. Green, M.A., M.A., B.D., D.D., Advisor in Evangelism to the Archbishops of Canterbury and York.

E.M.S. E. M. Smith, B.A., Senior Pastoral Administrator, Caring for Life, Leeds.

E.R.M. E. R. Moberly, M.A., D.Phil., Director of Psychosexual Education and Therapy, BCM International, Upper Darby, Pennsylvania.

F.C. Sir Frederick Catherwood, M.A., F.C.A., President of the Evangelical Alliance; formerly Member of the European Parliament.

F.L. F. Lyall, M.A., LL.B., LL.M., Ph.D., Dean of the Faculty of Law, University of Aberdeen.

F.S. F. Schäfer, B.A., B.A., M.A., D.Phil., psychologist; Chief Human Resources Officer, South African Post Office.

F.V.W. F. V. Waddleton, B.Sc., B.D., Academic Dean, Glasgow Bible College.

F.W.B. F. W. Bridger, M.A., Dip.Th., Ph.D., Vicar of Woodthorpe, Nottingham; Associate Lecturer at St John's College, Nottingham.

G.A.C. G. A. Cole, B.A., B.D., M.Th., Th.D., Principal of Ridley College, University of Melbourne, Australia.

G.B.McG. G. B. McGuinness, B.Sc., M.Sc., G.M.E.C., Associate Minister, Christ Church, Chilwell, with St Barnabas, Inham Nook, Nottingham.

G.C.M. G. C. Meilaender Jr, B.A., M.Div., Ph.D., Professor of Religion, Oberlin College, Oberlin, Ohio.

G.D. G. Davies, M.B., B.S., F.R.C.Psych., M.Phil., D.P.M., formerly Consultant Psychiatrist, King's College Hospital and the Maudsley Hospital, London.

G.D.S. G. D. Skinner, T.Cert., D.A.S.E.(R.E.), M.Phil., Lecturer in Education, Centre for Ethnic Studies in Education, University of Manchester.

G.H.T. G. H. Twelftree, B.A., M.A., Ph.D., Minister of the Uniting Church in Australia, Adelaide.

G.J.J. G. J. Jenkins, B.A., B.A., Curate of St Luke's Church, West Norwood, London.

G.J.P. G. J. Pigott, B.D., M.Phil., Vicar of St Paul's, Wilford Hill, West Bridgford, Nottingham.

G.J.W. G. J. Wenham, M.A., Ph.D., Senior Lecturer in Religious Studies, Cheltenham and Gloucester College of Higher Education, Cheltenham.

G.K.S. G. K. Smith, I.Eng., M.I.Elect.E., M.I.Hosp.E., Postgraduate research student, De Montfort University, Leicester.

G.L.B. G. L. Bray, B.A., D.Litt., Professor of Anglican Studies, Beeson Divinity School, Samford University, Birmingham, Alabama.

G.O.S. G. O. Stone, M.A., M.A., P.G.C.E., Cert.Theol., Team Rector, Bucknall Team Ministry, Stoke-on-Trent.

G.R.C. G. R. Collins, B.A., M.A., Ph.D., Executive Director, American Association of Christian Counseling.

G.S. G. Smith, Research Officer, Aston Charities Community Involvement Unit, Newham.

G.S.F. G. S. Forster, M.A., Dip.Soc.Anth., Rector of Northenden, Manchester; Convenor of the Editorial Group for Grove Ethical Studies.

G.S.T. G. S. Tomlin, M.A., M.A., Tutor, Wycliffe Hall, Oxford; Chaplain, Jesus College, Oxford.

G.W.G. G. W. Grogan, B.D., M.Th., Principal Emeritus, Glasgow Bible College.

H.A.G.B. H. A. G. Blocher, B.D., D.D., Professor of Systematic Theology and Dean at the Faculté Libre de Théologie Evangélique, Vaux-sur-Seine, France.

H.C.H. H. C. Hendry, B.A., P.G.C.E., M.A., Lecturer in Pastoral Counselling and World Religions, Oak Hill Theological College, London.

H.H.D. H. H. Davis, B.A., Ph.D., Reader in Sociology, University of Kent at Canterbury.

H.K.J. H. K. Jacobsen, B.A., M.A., Ph.D., Minister, Northwest Covenant Church, Mt Prospect, Illinois; Adjunct Professor, North Park College, Chicago.

I.D.B. I. D. Bunting, M.A., M.Th., Diocesan Director of Ordinands, Diocese of Southwell, Nottingham.

I.H.M. I. H. Marshall, B.A., B.D., M.A., Ph.D., Professor of New Testament Exegesis, University of Aberdeen.

I.R.D. I. R. Davis, Dip. Arch. R.I.B.A., F.R.G.S., Ph.D., Director, Oxford Centre for Disaster Studies.

I.R.W. I. R. Wallace, M.Sc., M.Sc., Lecturer, Agricultural Extension and Rural Development Department, Reading University.

J.A.H.F. J. A. H. Francis, B.Sc., M.A., C.Q.S.W., psychotherapist and freelance writer.

J.A.M. J. A. Mathisen, M.A., Ph.D., Professor of Sociology, Wheaton College, Wheaton, Illinois.

J.A.R. J. A. Ross, B.A., B.A., M.Phil., Associate Minister, Trinity Baptist Church,

Bexleyheath, Kent; visiting lecturer, Spurgeon's College, London.

J.A.T. J. A. Temple, B.Sc., Ph.D., A.E.P., Group Managing Director, Plessey Tellumat SA Ltd, South Africa.

J.A.V. J. A. Vale, M.D., F.R.C.P., F.F.O.M., F.A.A.C.T., Director, National Poisons Information Service (Birmingham Centre), West Midlands Poisons Unit, Dudley Road Hospital, Birmingham.

J.B.G. J. B. Green, B.S., M.Th., Ph.D., Associate Professor of New Testament, American Baptist Seminary of the West and Graduate Theological Union, Berkeley, California.

J.B.W. J. B. Webster, M.A., Ph.D., Professor of Systematic Theology, Wycliffe College, University of Toronto.

J.C.D. J. C. Doggett, C.B.E., Barrister (Middle Temple); formerly Assistant Solicitor, Inland Revenue.

J.D.H. J. D. Healey, H.N.C., LL.B., L.R.P.S., Marketing Manager, Anthony Collins Solicitors, Birmingham.

J.D.M. J. D. Mason, B.A., Ph.D., Professor of Economics, Gordon College, Wenham, Massachusetts.

J.E. J. Evans, B.Sc., Ph.D., D.Sc., F.I.C.For., Chief Research Officer, Forestry Commission; Director, TEAR Fund, Teddington, Middlesex.

J.E.H. J. E. Hare, B.A., Ph.D., Professor, Department of Philosophy, Calvin College, Grand Rapids, Michigan.

J.G.C. J. G. Child, B.A., B.D., M.Th., Minister of Christ Church, La Lucia, Durban, South Africa.

J.G.McC. J. G. McConville, B.D., M.A., Ph.D., Lecturer in Old Testament, Wycliffe Hall, Oxford.

J.H.C. J. H. Court, B.A., Ph.D., F.B.Ps.S.,

C.Psychol.Dip.Clin.Hyp., Professor of Psychology and Director, the Psychological Center, Graduate School of Psychology, Fuller Theological Seminary, Pasadena, California.

J.H.G. J. H. Gillespie, B.A., Ph.D., Dip.Th., Senior Lecturer in French, University of Ulster.

J.H.O. J. H. Olthuis, B.A., B.D., Ph.D., Senior Member in Philosophical Theology, Institute for Christian Studies, Toronto; psychotherapist in private practice.

J.H.S. J. H. Sailhamer, Th.M., M.A., Ph.D., Associate Professor of the Old Testament, Trinity Evangelical Divinity School, Deerfield, Illinois.

J.I.P. J. I. Packer, M.A., D.Phil., Sangwoo Youtong Chee Professor of Theology, Regent College, Vancouver.

J.K.C. J. K. Cundy, M.A., solicitor in private practice.

J.M.S. J. M. Sentamu, B.A., LL.B., M.A., Ph.D., Vicar of Holy Trinity and St Matthias, Tulse Hill, London.

J.M.V.B. J. M. V. Blanshard, M.A., F.I.F.S.T., Professor of Food Science and Dean of the Faculty of Agricultural and Food Sciences, Nottingham University.

J.N.D.A. Sir Norman Anderson, O.B.E., M.A., LL.D., D.D., F.B.A., Q.C., Emeritus Professor of Oriental Laws, University of London; formerly Director of the Institute of Advanced Legal Studies.

J.N.H. J. N. Hall, B.A., M.Sc., Ph.D., F.B.Ps.S., Consultant Clinical Psychologist and Lecturer in Clinical Psychology, Warneford Hospital, Oxford.

J.P.C. J. P. Chaplin, B.A., M.Phil., Ph.D., Tutor in Politics, Plater College, Oxford.

J.R.G. J. R. Guy, B.A., M.S.W., formerly Assistant Director, Central Council for Education and Training in Social Work, London.

J.R.McG. J. R. McGrath, M.A., M.Phil., Principal Clinical Psychologist, Rivermead Rehabilitation Centre, Oxford.

J.R.P. J. R. Peck, B.D., A.L.B.C., Minister of Earl Soham Baptist Church, Suffolk; Senior Project Worker, College House, Cambridge.

J.S.E. J. S. Escobar, B.A., M.A., Ph.D., Thornley B. Wood Professor of Missiology at Eastern Baptist Theological Seminary, Philadelphia; Visiting Professor, Orlando E. Costas School of Missiology, Lima, Peru.

J.W.G. J. W. Gladwin, M.A., Dip.Theol., Provost of Sheffield.

K.E.Y. K. E. Yandell, B.A., M.A., Ph.D., Professor of Philosophy and South Asian Studies, University of Wisconsin, Madison, Wisconsin.

K.F. K. Ferdinando, B.A., M.A., Ph.D., Lecturer at the Institut Supérieur Théologique de Bunia, Zaïre.

K.G.E. K. G. Elzinga, B.A., M.A., Ph.D., Professor of Economics, University of Virginia, Charlottesville, Virginia.

L.B.K. L. B. Keeble, J.P., B.D., M.Th., Minister, Hillhead Baptist Church, Glasgow; formerly Tutor and Director in Pastoral Studies, Regent's Park College.

L.E.A.G. L. E. A. Gladwin, M.A., C.Q.S.W., independent social work consultant; formerly Director of Social Work, London Diocesan Board of Social Responsibility.

L.H.O. L. H. Osborn, B.D., M.Sc., Ph.D., Templeton Fellow, Ridley Hall, Cambridge.

L.M.-Y.C.-J. L. M.-Y. Cheung-Judge, B.Sc., M.A., Ph.D., Director of Quality and Equality Training and Consultancy Services, Oxford.

L.R. L. Ryken, B.A., Ph.D., Professor of English, Wheaton College, Wheaton, Illinois.

M.A.B. M. A. Bourdeaux, B.D., M.A., Director, Keston Institute, Oxford.

M.A.J. M. A. Jeeves, C.B.E., M.A., Ph.D., Hon.D.Sc., C.Psychol., F.B.Ps.S., F.R.S.E., Honorary Research Professor, School of Psychology, University of St Andrews, St Andrews, Fife.

M.A.N. M. A. Noll, B.A., M.A., Ph.D., McManis Professor of Christian Thought, Wheaton College, Wheaton, Illinois.

M.A.R. M. A. Reid, B.A., M.Div., Ph.D., Professor of Philosophy and Chairman, Department of Philosophy, Gordon College, Wenham, Massachusetts.

M.A.S. M. A. Swann, M.D., D.C.H., Senior Clinical Medical Officer, Belfast.

McC. Professor the Lord McColl, M.S., F.R.C.S., F.A.C.S., F.R.C.S.E., Chairman, Department of Surgery of the United Medical and Dental Schools of St Thomas' and Guy's Hospitals, London.

M.C.G. M. C. Griffiths, M.A., D.D., Minister at Large, International Fellowship of Evangelical Students; formerly Professor of Mission Studies, Regent College, Vancouver.

M.C.-J. M. Chave-Jones, Dip.Soc.Sci., formerly psychotherapist in private practice, and founder, Care and Counsel, London.

M.D.J. M. D. Jenkins, M.A., M.A., formerly Central Area Manager, Prison Service, UK.

M.E.A. M. E. Alsford, B.A., Ph.D., Senior Lecturer in Theology, University of Greenwich, London.

M.F.G. M. F. Goldsmith, M.A., Lecturer and International Representative, All Nations Christian College, Ware, Hertfordshire.

M.G.B. M. G. Barker, M.B., Ch.B., F.R.C.P.Ed., F.R.C.Psych., D.P.M., Consultant Psychiatrist and Medical Director, Heath House Priory Hospital, Bristol.

M.G.G.S. M. G. G. Schluter, B.A., Ph.D., Director, the Jubilee Centre and the Keep Sunday Special Campaign, Cambridge.

M.J.B. M. J. Bartel, B.A., M.Div., Ph.D. candidate at Princeton Theological Seminary, Princeton, New Jersey.

M.J.D. M. J. Dowling, B.A., B.D., M.Th., Ph.D., Tutor in Church History and Historical Theology, Irish Baptist College, Belfast.

M.J.E. M. J. Evans, B.Ed., B.A., M.Phil., Lecturer in Old Testament Studies, London Bible College.

M.J.H.A. M. J. H. Allison, M.A., Member of Parliament and Second Church Estates Commissioner, London.

M.J.M. M. J. Moss, S.R.N., C.Q.S.W., Principal Officer, Residential Care Services for Older People, Social Services Department, London Borough of Richmond-upon-Thames.

M.J.N.-A. M. J. Nazir-Ali, M.Litt., Ph.D., Bishop of Rochester; formerly General Secretary, Church Missionary Society, London.

M.K.B. M. K. Batchelor, B.A., freelance author.

M.M. M. Moynagh, M.A., Ph.D., Team Rector, Wicton, Taunton, Somerset.

M.P.C. M. P. Cosgrove, M.S., Ph.D., Professor of Psychology, Taylor University, Upland, Indiana.

M.S.L. M. S. Langley, B.D., M.A., Ph.D., H.Dip.Ed., F.R.A.I., Director of Training, Diocese of Carlisle, and Director of Carlisle Diocesan Training Institute.

M.T.N. M. T. Nelson, B.A., M.A., Ph.D., Associate Professor of Philosophy,

Hampden-Sydney College, Hampden-Sydney, Virginia.

N.J.B. N. J. Biggar, B.A., M.A., Ph.D., Master of Christian Studies, Chaplain and Fellow, Oriel College, Oxford; Lecturer in Christian Ethics, Wycliffe Hall, Oxford.

N.J.S. N. J. Smith, B.A., B.D., D.Th., Lecturer at the University of South Africa; Pastor of a black Dutch Reformed Church in Pretoria, South Africa.

N.L.G. N. L. Geisler, B.A., M.A., Th.B., Ph.D., Dean, Southern Evangelical Seminary, Charlotte, North Carolina.

N.M.deS.C. N. M. de S. Cameron, B.D., M.A., Ph.D., Associate Dean of Academic Doctoral Programs and Chair, Department of Systematic Theology, Trinity Evangelical Divinity School, Deerfield, Illinois.

N.P.H. N. P. Harvey, M.A., S.T.L., freelance writer and lecturer on moral theology; formerly Lecturer in Christian Ethics at Queen's College, Birmingham, and Lecturer in Moral Theology at Downside Abbey.

N.P.W. N. P. Wolterstorff, Ph.D., Noah Porter Professor of Philosophical Theology, Yale University, New Haven, Connecticut.

O.M.T.O'D. O. M. T. O'Donovan, M.A., D.Phil., Regius Professor of Moral and Pastoral Theology, Oxford University; Canon of Christ Church, Oxford.

O.R.B. O. R. Barclay, M.A., Ph.D., formerly General Secretary of the Universities and Colleges Christian Fellowship, Leicester.

P.A.H. P. A. Hicks, B.D., M.A., Ph.D., Lecturer and Director of Ministry, London Bible College.

P.A.M. P. A. Marshall, B.Sc., M.Sc., M.A., M.Phil., Ph.D., Senior Fellow in Political

Theory, Institute for Christian Studies, Toronto, Ontario.

P.A.Mi. P. A. Mickey, B.A., B.D., Ph.D., formerly Associate Professor of Pastoral Theology, Duke University Divinity School, Durham, North Carolina.

P.D.H. P. D. Hill, B.A., Minister-in-Charge, Pantygwydr Baptist Church, Swansea; Baptist Chaplain to Swansea University College.

P.D.McK. P. D. McKenzie, LL.M., B.D., Barrister and Chairman of the New Zealand Securities Commission.

P.D.W. P. D. Woodbridge, B.A., Ph.D., Tutor in Biblical Studies, Oak Hill Theological College, London.

P.E.H. P. E. Hodgson, M.A., D.Sc., Ph.D., A.R.C.S., D.I.C., C.Phys., F.Inst.P., Senior Research Fellow, Corpus Christi College, Oxford; Head of Nuclear Physics Theoretical Group, Department of Physics, University of Oxford.

P.F.S. P. F. Sims, M.B., B.Ch., F.R.C.S., M.R.C.O.G., Consultant Obstetrician and Gynaecologist, Hexham General Hospital, Northumberland.

P.H. P. Helm, M.A., Professor of the History and Philosophy of Religion, King's College, London.

P.H.deV. P. H. deVries, B.A., M.A., Ph.D., Ethics Chair, the King's College, New York; President, International Research Institute on Values Changes.

P.H.L. P. H. Lewis, Senior Pastor, Cornerstone Evangelical Church, Nottingham.

P.J.C. P. J. Clarke, B.A., Senior Chaplain at the Mildmay Mission Hospital (AIDS Hospice), London.

P.J.H.A. P. J. H. Adam, B.D., M.Th., Ph.D., Vicar of St Jude's, Carlton, Melbourne, Australia.

P.M.C. P. M. Clifford, B.A.,

B.D., D.Phil., Lecturer, Magdalen College, Oxford.

P.M.F. P. M. Fackler, A.B., M.A., M.A., Ph.D., Associate Professor and Chair, Department of Communications, Wheaton College, Wheaton, Illinois.

P.N.H. P. N. Hillyer, B.D., Ph.D., freelance theological author and editor; formerly Lecturer in Theology, Bishop's College, Calcutta.

P.N.P. P. N. Palmer, D.Comm., Professor in the Department of Business Economics, University of South Africa, Pretoria.

P.T. P. Toon, M.A., B.D., M.Th., D.Phil., Professor of Theology, Philadelphia Theological Seminary.

P.W.T. P. W. Timms, M.R.C.Psych., Senior Lecturer in Community Psychiatry, the United Medical and Dental Schools of St Thomas' and Guy's Hospitals, London.

R.A.B. R. A. Burridge, M.A., Ph.D., Dean of King's College, London.

R.A.Hig. R. A. Higginson, M.A., Dip.Th., Cert.Ed., Ph.D., Lecturer in Christian Ethics and Director of the Ridley Hall Foundation, Ridley Hall, Cambridge.

R.A.Hin. R. A. Hines, B.Sc., M.Th., Ph.D., Lecturer in Christian Worship, Oak Hill Theological College, London; Vice-Principal, North Thames Ministerial Training Course, London.

R.A.R. R. A. Russell, B.A., M.A., M.A., M.Ed., P.G.C.E., Dip.H.E.Theol., Vicar of Widcombe, Bath; Director of the Christian Studies Unit, Widcombe, Bath.

R.C.B. R. C. Baldwin, B.Sc., B.M., M.R.C.P., M.R.C.Psych., Consultant in Old Age Psychiatry, Manchester Royal Infirmary.

R.C.C. R. C. Chewning, B.S.,

M.B.A., Ph.D., Chavanne Professor of Christian Ethics in Business, Baylor University, Waco, Texas.

R.C.M. R. C. Macaulay, B.D., M.A., member of L'Abri Fellowship.

R.C.R. R. C. Roberts, B.A., B.D., M.A., Ph.D., Professor of Philosophy and Psychological Studies, Wheaton College, Wheaton, Illinois.

R.E.N.O. R. E. N. Oake, LL.B., Chief Constable, Isle of Man Constabulary.

R.E.P. R. E. Parker, B.A., M.Th., Deputy Director, Acorn Christian Healing Trust, Bordon, Hampshire.

R.F. R. Fowke, M.B., B.Ch., M.R.C.Psych., D.P.M., D.P.A., Consultant Psychiatrist.

R.F.H. R. F. Hurding, M.A., M.B.B.Chir., D.R.C.O.G., counsellor, psychotherapist, retired medical practitioner; Visiting Lecturer in Pastoral Studies, Trinity College, Bristol.

R.G.C. R. G. Clouse, B.A., B.D., M.A., Ph.D., Professor of History, Indiana State University, Terre Haute, Indiana; Minister of First Brethren Church, Clay City, Indiana.

R.G.T. R. G. Twycross, M.A., D.M., F.R.C.P., Macmillan Clinical Reader in Palliative Medicine, University of Oxford.

R.J.B. R. J. Bauckham, M.A., Ph.D., Professor of New Testament Studies, University of St Andrews, Fife.

R.J.Sh. R. J. Sheehan, B.D., Minister, Welwyn Evangelical Church, Welwyn, Hertfordshire.

R.J.Si. R. J. Sider, B.D., M.A., Ph.D., President of Evangelicals for Social Action, USA; Professor of Theology and Culture, Eastern Baptist Theological Seminary, Philadelphia, Pennsylvania.

R.J.So. R. J. Song, B.A., M.A., D.Phil., Tutor in Ethics, St John's College, Durham.

R.J.T. R. J. Toyn, LL.B., circuit judge (retired).

R.J.W. R. J. Whiteley, B.A., M.A., theological student, Ridley College, Melbourne, Australia.

R.K.McC. R. K. McCloughry, B.Sc., M.Sc., Director of the Kingdom Trust, Nottingham; Lecturer in Social Ethics at St John's College, Nottingham.

R.L.P. R. L. Purtill, B.A., M.A., Ph.D., Professor of Philosophy, Western Washington University, Bellingham, Washington.

R.L.S. R. L. Sturch, M.A., D.Phil., Rector of Islip, Oxfordshire.

R.M.H. R. M. Hanson, B.A., M.Phil., formerly Honorary Senior Research Fellow, Department of Psychiatry, University of Leeds.

R.P.L. R. P. Loy, A.B., M.A., Professsor of Political Science, Taylor University, Upland, Indiana.

R.P.M. The late R. P. Moss, B.Sc., Ph.D., Dip. in Soil Science, latterly Research Professor in Human Ecology, University of Salford.

R.S.A. R. S. Anderson, B.S., B.D., Ph.D., Professor of Theology and Ministry, Fuller Theological Seminary, Pasadena, California.

R.T.F. R. T. Forster, M.A., Leader, Ichthus Christian Fellowship, Forest Hill, London.

R.V. R. Vincent, B.Sc., M.D., F.R.C.P., A.K.C., F.E.S.C., Consultant Cardiologist, Royal Sussex County Hospital, Brighton, East Sussex; Professor of Medical Science, University of Sussex, Brighton.

R.W.G. R. W. Green, B.A., Member of the Springboard Team (the Archbishops' Initiative for the Decade of Evangelism).

R.W.H. R. W. Heinze, B.S., M.A., Ph.D., College Dean,

Oak Hill Theological College, London.

S.D. S. Dex, B.A., M.Sc., Ph.D., on secondment from the University of Keele to Research Professorship at the University of Essex, ESRC Centre for Micro-Social Change.

S.E.Al. S. E. Alsford, B.A., Ph.D., Senior Lecturer in Theology, University of Greenwich, London.

S.E.At. S. E. Atkinson, B.Sc., A.K.C., primary school teacher and education lecturer.

S.L.J. S. L. Jones, B.A., M.A., Ph.D., Professor and Chairperson, Department of Psychology, Wheaton College, Wheaton, Illinois.

S.M. S. Motyer, M.A., M.Litt., Ph.D., Lecturer, London Bible College.

S.N.W. S. N. Williams, M.A., Ph.D., formerly Professor of Theology, United Theological College, Aberystwyth, Dyfed.

S.S.H. S. S. Harakas, B.A.Th., B.D., Th.D., Archbishop Iakovos Professor of Orthodox Theology, Holy Cross Greek Orthodox School of Theology, Brookline, Massachusetts.

S.W. S. Webley, M.A., Director, British–North American Research Association, London.

T.A.D. T. A. Dearborn, B.A., M.T.S., Th.M., Ph.D., Executive Director of the Seattle Association for Theological Education and Assistant Professor of Practical Theology, Fuller Seminary, Pasadena, California, and Regent College, Vancouver.

T.D. T. Dean, Senior Producer, Religious Programmes, BBC World Service; formerly Editor, *Third Way*.

T.D.K. T. D. Kennedy, B.A., Ph.D., Associate Professor of Philosophy, Valparaiso University, Valparaiso, Indiana.

T.E.C.H. Sir Timothy Hoare, M.A., M.A., Director, Career Plan Ltd, London.

T.E.E.G. T. E. E. Goodacre, B.Sc., M.B.B.S., F.R.C.S., Consultant Plastic and Reconstructive Surgeon; Radcliffe Infirmary, Oxford.

T.J.Ch. T. J. Chester, B.D., Public Affairs Officer, TEAR Fund, Teddington, Middlesex.

T.J.Co. T. J. Cooling, B.A., Dip.Th., M.A., Ph.D., Projects Officer, Association of Christian Teachers, Nottingham.

T.O.K. T. O. Kay, A.B., M.A., Ph.D., Associate Professor of History, Chair, Department of History, and Coordinator, Interdisciplinary and General Studies, Wheaton College, Wheaton, Illinois.

T.O.W. T. O. Walker, M.A., Archdeacon of Nottingham.

T.R.A. T. R. Albin, B.A., M.A., Instructor in Christian Spiritual Formation, University of Dubuque Theological Seminary, Dubuque, Iowa.

V.G. V. Griffiths, B.A., M.A., P.G.C.E., formerly Sessional Lecturer, Regent College, Vancouver.

V.K.S. V. K. Samuel, B.Sc., B.D., M.Litt., D.D., Executive Director, International Fellowship of Evangelical Mission Theologians, Oxford.

V.M.S. V. M. Sinton, M.A., Cert.Ed., Dip.H.E.Theol., Director of Pastoral Studies, Wycliffe Hall, Oxford.

W.A.S. W. A. Strange, B.A., B.A. D.Phil., Vicar of Llandeilo Fawr, Dyfed.

W.F.S. W. F. Storrar, M.A., B.D., Ph.D., Lecturer in Practical Theology, Department of Divinity with Religious Studies, University of Aberdeen.

W.J.D. W. J. Dumbrell, B.A., M.A., B.D., M.Th., Th.D., Director of Post-Graduate Studies, Moore Theological College, Newtown, New South Wales.

W.R. W. Riggans, B.D., M.A., Ph.D., General Director, Church's Ministry Among the Jews, St Albans.

Z.G.L. Z. G. Lindblade, B.A., M.A., Ph.D., Professor of Sociology, Wheaton College, Wheaton, Illinois.

PART ONE

ONE

God

Christian moral theology (see Christian Moral Reasoning[18]) and pastoral theology (see Practical and Pastoral Theology[7]) are decisively shaped by Christian convictions about the nature of God. The primary determinant of our understanding of Christian action (moral and pastoral) is properly the gospel of God, proclaimed and embodied in Jesus* Christ. The gospel summons is enacted amongst a community of agents who are shaped by their confession of God's redemptive gift of himself in the life, death and resurrection* of Jesus and in Jesus' presence in the Holy Spirit.* Moral theology and pastoral theology reflect on the acts of the gospel community in the light of their divine source and norm.

1. Historical considerations

Classical Christian theology accords with the opening definition, in that it generally does not treat moral or pastoral questions in isolation from its exposition of the doctrinal substance of Christianity. Such questions receive only relatively independent coverage in works of ethical exhortation (often in a catechetical context), in treatments of disputed questions (such as the propriety of Christian attendance at the Greek games or of military service by Christians), and in controversial writings against pagans or heretics in which ethical polemic often figures large. Similarly, scholastic theology treats ethical and practical issues as an integral part of its *Summae* or *Sentences* (though commentaries on Aristotle's* *Ethics* flourished in the scholastic period). The magisterial Reformers continue this integration of doctrine and morals, as in John Calvin's* account of Christian action in the course of his exposition of the sanctifying work of Christ and the Spirit. Seventeenth-century Protestant scholasticism operates somewhat differently: the wider scope of the biblical account of God's dealings with humanity tends to fall away in favour of a formalized understanding of divine revelation as doctrinal or moral propositions, from which recommendations about human action are deduced by a casuistical* method largely derived from Aristotelian logic (enjoying renewed popularity in the European Protestant academies). Thus the Basel theologian Wollebius (1586–1629), in Book II of his *Compendium Theologiae Christianae* (tr. in W. Beardslee, ed., *Reformed Dogmatics*, Oxford and New York, 1965), outlines moral and pastoral theology by expounding the Decalogue* (construed as 'precepts') in such a way that God comes to be understood as 'the heavenly legislator' (II.xi.1). This goes along with an understanding of pastoral practice as extended application of principles for Christian conduct, derived by logical deduction from the biblical text. Whilst this method was often a form for articulating much biblical and practical wisdom – notably in English divines such as Richard Baxter* or John Owen (1616–83) – its formalism threatened to reduce the trinitarian and Christological dimensions of Christian teaching about God to an abstract dogmatic scheme.

It is arguable that this construal of the connection between God and human action as one between precept and obedience prepared the way for the contention of Immanuel Kant* that good moral action can never take its law from outside itself (from, *e.g.*, divine commands) since the moral self is essentially autonomous. For Kant, language about divine law, grace, *etc.*, corrupts our sense of ourselves as moral agents whose freedom from external determination is essential to the attribution of responsibility. Kant's immensely subtle critique of divine 'heteronomy' has largely shaped discussion and critique of Christian moral theology in the modern era. This can be seen in persistent criticism of the politically and psychologically alienating potential of the notion of obedience* to God's will, as articulated in the protest atheism of Ludwig Feuerbach (1804–72), Karl Marx,* Friedrich Nietzsche* and Sigmund Freud.* In a somewhat different vein, mid-20th-century analytical ethicists argued forcefully for the independence of morals from theological commitments (see the representative collection in Ian Ramsey, ed., *Christian Ethics and Contemporary Philosophy*, London, 1966). In pastoral theology, a parallel development in the present century can be seen in preference (especially in N. American Protestantism) for social scientific rather than theological analysis of the pastoral situation, and for clinical and therapeutic models of pastoral care (see Pastoral Care, Counselling and Psychotherapy[12]), often relegating the theological content of pastoral action to posterior 'theological reflection'.

Some more recent writing in moral and pastoral theology, however, shows considerable interest in the reintegration of these disciplines with Christian doctrine, crucially with the Christian doctrine of God. A major model here is provided by the work of Karl Barth,* whose monumental *Church Dogmatics* constitutes the most significant attempt since the Reformation to make ethics an essential component of the exposition of the Christian doctrine. The dogmatic basis for this attempt is Barth's understanding of covenant,* in which God elects from all eternity to be God with humanity in a relation of reciprocal agency, the action of divine grace* evoking the corresponding human work of gratitude. Extending Barth (and sometimes in criticism of his apparently inadequate moral psychology), some propose an analysis of human action in terms of the agent's convictions about God and the world, especially as those convictions are embodied in narratives which shape the identity of the moral agent (see the works of Stanley Hauerwas in the Bibliography). In a quite different direction, others (such as T. Rendtorff, in *Ethics* 1, ET, Philadelphia, 1986, and J. Gustafson), continue to urge the independence of ethics from dogmatics, and to locate Christian moral theology alongside the human and social sciences in contributing its particular analysis of common human reality. These different approaches to the theological content of moral and pastoral theology often reflect different accounts of the relation of Christianity to its cultural setting. Those who see significant correlation between faith and its context stress the necessity of integrating secular learning with Christian doctrine; others, unwilling to surrender heavy theological content, tend towards opposition to prevailing cultural trends or modes of knowledge, on the grounds that Christian faith in God proposes a radically distinct account of reality.

2. The Christian doctrine of God

a. Father, Son and Spirit. The Christian doctrine of God is the doctrine of the Trinity. This point is often obscured by treating some questions about 'God' (such as proofs of God's existence) in isolation from questions about the Trinity, a process which results in a reduction of trinitarian doctrine to a particular version of more general theistic ideas, failing to see trinitarian teaching as *the* distinctively Christian understanding of God. Although sometimes regarded as the fruit of inappropriate metaphysical speculation, trinitarian doctrine is best seen as the attempt to reconstruct the concept of God as creator, redeemer and perfector of all things, on the basis of God's self-gift in Jesus Christ. Trinitarian doctrine condenses the scriptural account of the acts and being of God and the church's experience of salvation (see Sin and Salvation[5]), furnishing an analysis of the divine identity as subject and agent in those acts.

The biblical writings do not yield explicit trinitarian doctrine, though there are formulae and patterns of argument (especially in the NT epistles and John's Gospel) through which later trinitarian constructs could be warranted. Trinitarian categories are an implication of the primary Christian confession that the contingent human person Jesus is Lord, that is, he is one whose historical particularity embodies the universal presence and effectiveness of God's saving rule. Confession of Christ's lordship accords him more than provisional, partial or local significance: as Lord, he constitutes the most comprehensive framework within which all things are to be known and judged. His person and acts, supremely his death and resurrection, reorder the relation of the entire creation* to God in a fashion so radical and completely effective that it can only be understood as divine in character. Hence

Jesus occupies the absolute, *i.e.* non-relative, place characteristically occupied by God and attracts to himself, in the NT and elsewhere, language characteristically reserved for God alone.

This confession clearly leads to a reconstruction of the concept of God, since severe strain is placed upon received language and concepts by this bringing together of the transcendent (God) and the contingent (Jesus). This does not mean straightforward identification of 'God' and 'Jesus' in which those terms become interchangeable (though passages in early writers like Ignatius of Antioch, *c.* 35–*c.* 107, come close to this). In developed patristic thought, the doctrine of God incorporates affirmations of a distinction within the Godhead between Father and Son. This distinction was bound up with a further distinction in incarnational theology between the divinity and humanity of Christ. This latter distinction rooted the man Jesus in the being of God, whilst at the same time preventing unqualified literal ascription of the history of Jesus to God and affirming the unity of the two 'natures' in the one historical 'person' or subject, Jesus of Nazareth. The differentiation between Father and Son was characterized by the awkward notion of the 'begetting' or 'generation' of the Son by the Father. This term identifies the Father as absolute origin or founding purpose, fulfilling his eternal resolve in relation to the Son who is distinct and derivative from, but (against Arius, *c.* 250–*c.* 336) in no way subsequent or subordinate to the (ingenerate) Father. Behind these distinctions lies the prime soteriological intention of retaining the divinity of Christ as agent of salvation, without compromise to the freedom or completeness of the being of God. Trinitarian language accomplishes this by making the relation of Jesus to the Father into the embodiment of an intrinsic 'relatedness' within God's very being.

The doctrine is completed by affirmations of the divinity of the Spirit, which stem from an understanding of the radically creative power of Christ present as Spirit in the Christian experience of regeneration. Since the Spirit effects union with Christ and the church's adoption into the divine life, the Spirit's being and agency are divine. For the Western tradition, this third trinitarian distinction has been less secure (partly because of heavy concentration on Christology, partly because Augustine's* interpretation of the trinitarian 'persons' as 'substantial relations' emphasizes unity rather than differentiation). In the East, a more richly elaborated theology of Spirit has encouraged a more pluralistic understanding of the Trinity.

The overall thrust of trinitarian doctrine is thus that the Christian meaning of the term 'God' is established out of the history of Jesus Christ, understood as the embodiment of God's saving will, activity and being, and as presently effective in the Spirit. So defined, God is not an undifferentiated self, but intrinsically relational; God's essential unity consists in the 'relation' of the 'persons' of Father, Son and Spirit (the metaphorical force of 'relation' and 'person' is not to be elided). Crucially, this intra-trinitarian relatedness is the ground of God's relation as creator, redeemer and perfecter to what is outside himself. Hence trinitarian language interprets God's acts towards the creation as the expression of his very being, rather than as external acts conducted through intermediary agencies.

Trinitarian doctrine is, then, fundamental to Christian reflection on ethical and pastoral practice. As an account of the identity of God, the doctrine of the Trinity also establishes the main lines of a Christian understanding of the way the world is and the ways in which human agents are to act in the world. Both the moral field and the moral agent are to be construed out of God's self-manifestation as creator, redeemer and sanctifier. Thus, from a trinitarian perspective, the world will be seen as created by, and related and unconditionally obligated to, God the Father who is the one from whom its purposive ethical order derives. The world will, further, be seen as caught up in and transfigured by the redemptive activity of the Son in which creation's original purpose is renewed and consummated. Finally, as the sphere of the operation of the Spirit, creation (and above all the church* as new creation) will be seen as realities in process of transformation through reorientation towards the purposes of God which they are newly empowered to serve.

b. The attributes of God. Language about God's attributes seeks to characterize God as *this particular* being in his self-manifestation. The subject of such attribution (God) defines the predicates, and vigilance against inappropriate carry-over from the human contexts of our language is necessary. The attributes have been classified in a large number of ways of greater or lesser elaborateness. Most accounts work with a core distinction between those attributes which display God's absolute freedom and those which display God's unreserved love. As free, God is utterly self-originating, possessing aseity (lit. 'from himself'), undetermined by any reality beyond himself (and hence 'impassible'), governed only by his own will in shaping his intentions and acts, unresolvable into any prior state of affairs. As such, God's relation to creation is gracious, the fruit only of his own disposing of himself, and one in which he retains his absolute majesty, sovereignty, glory and holiness. In his freedom, God transcends the conditions of creaturely existence, such as time, space and contingency, and so God is eternal, unchanging, omnipresent and omnipotent. This transcendence, however, is not such that God is unrelated to contingency or incapable of freely assuming those conditions when the Word becomes flesh. Above all, God's freedom is not to be thought of as absolute lack of constraint but as the liberty in which as Father, Son and Spirit he chooses, creates, sustains, redeems and sanctifies his creation. God's freedom is his freedom to love; his sovereignty is his undefeated rule in favour of his creation; his holiness is his power to sanctify; his righteousness is his act of upholding his cause (and therefore the cause of his creatures) against the disorder of sin; his glory is known in his sharing of his glory with humanity; his unity as the triune God is displayed in his establishment of fellowship with himself by the creation and election of humanity into covenant. God's attributes thus do not describe a divine reality anterior to God's saving self-manifestation, but point to his purposive acts in creation and covenant, sealed in Jesus Christ, as the locus of his being.

3. God, ethics and pastoral theology

a. God, belief and action. Fundamental to Christian conviction about reality is the proposal that 'God is'. Accordingly, any account of Christian moral and pastoral action has to be simultaneously an account of God and God's action: moral theology and pastoral theology are modes of the doctrine of God. Christian *agenda* cannot be detached without irreparable loss from Christian *credenda* concerning God's character and purposes. Reflection on Christian action is thus informed by the basic belief-structure of the Christian community. That belief-structure is articulated in a variety of activities, credal, cultic and practical, but above all in Scripture, which furnishes the normative and critical account of

Christian identity as it is shaped by the creative and redemptive activity of the triune God. Christian beliefs, encoded in this way, give rise to a certain understanding of self and world on the part of Christian believers. These beliefs characterize the field within which moral and pastoral action take place, and also characterize agents within that field, above all by reference to convictions about God. Belief in God, then, though it has a primary objective reference to God's transcendent reality, also has 'self-involving' aspects intrinsic to it: it describes the world in which Christian agents act, prescribes moral roles, and enjoins or dissuades from certain practices, habits and patterns of deliberation and action (see D. D. Evans, *The Logic of Self-Involvement,* London, 1963). An account of the connection between belief in God and moral action must go beyond the formal precept-obedience model by filling out the connections between belief-structure, self-understanding and practice.

b. The field of action. The Christian doctrine of God issues in a particular understanding of reality. That understanding is not merely 'theistic' in a generic sense, but more properly an understanding of reality as the sphere of God's creative and redemptive action. Above all, the Christian understanding of reality is specified by Jesus' resurrection from the dead as the anticipation of the re-creation of all things. His resurrection, and the gracious participation in that resurrection by the people of God through the power of the Spirit, constitute the 'new creation' which is determinative of the creation's very being. Out of Jesus' resurrection, creation can be seen as in process of transformation into glorious perfection (Rom. 8:19–23). The 'newness' of the creation means that its eschatological transfiguration is not the realization of latent possibilities, but the entire alteration of creation, precisely so that it can reach its consummation by becoming what God intends.

This eschatological process constitutes the *order* of reality as creation. The order of creation is not determined primarily by reference to its original ordering 'in the beginning', but by its redemption through Christ in which its true end is accomplished. Thus the moral order of creation – its meaningfulness or orderliness as a sphere for human action – is a divine accomplishment and gift. This means, first, that moral order exists: reality is not mere random process. Secondly, it means that moral order is *discovered* by obedient action rather than *imposed* by autonomous agents. Here the Christian faith diverges from existentialist (see Existentialist Ethics*) understandings of moral value as the pure creation of the human will, as well as from exclusively technological understandings of reality as having no order apart from that which is given to it by human purposes. Hence in ethical deliberations concerning the status of the human foetus, for example, the Christian doctrine of God opposes attempts to define (and thereby circumscribe) that status by sole reference to the life-project of either or both parents. Or in approaching ecological issues concerning the use of nature, the doctrine of God will prevent us from locating the meaning of nature simply in its status as raw material for human mastery. Intrinsic, then, to Christian affirmations concerning God is a further affirmation that the human agent is not the point at which moral order is created, but rather the *mediator* of an order established through God's transcendent acts (see T. F. Torrance, *Divine and Contingent Order*, Oxford, 1981, pp. 128–142).

As a reality in process of transformation towards its eschatological goal, the new creation exists in antithesis to the old order of sin and death,* which has been decisively set aside in God's work in Christ. Accordingly, Christian theology understands the field of human action as one in which disorder, unrighteousness and opposition to the purposes of God are already 'disarmed' (Col. 2:15), and in which the triumph of God's purposes is securely established. This both limits the scope of Christian action and gives it a distinctive shape. Christian action is limited, in that the triumph of God's new order requires no human actions for its completion, activation or realization, since it is already secured in Christ and effective in the Spirit. This does not mean that Christian action is superfluous, however, but that it takes its generative power as well as its distinctive patterns from God's own achievement, into which it is graciously drawn and to which it exists as humble, provisional but truthful testimony. Moreover, it again requires a different set of categories through which to construe the moral field, interpreting the world and its history and human actions in that history as in correspondence or opposition to the coming reign of God's good order. God's rule in Christ – in which the community of believers participates by grace as it is 'seated . . . with him in the heavenly realms' (Eph. 2:6) – constitutes *the* context in which all reality is to be interpreted. And so in the area of moral action, too, 'The church precedes the world epistemologically' (J. H. Yoder, *The Priestly Kingdom*, Notre Dame, IN, 1984, p. 10).

c. The agent. Human mediation of the moral order of reality is not a matter of simple intellectual perception of order, but rather of the obedient disposition of the moral self in all its habits, practices and modes of existence, individual and social, to God's saving rule in Jesus Christ. Accordingly, the Christian doctrine of God yields a specific understanding of the nature of the self* and it acts as existing in response and responsibility to God. In formal terms, this means that a Christian account of moral selfhood will be less concerned than some styles of moral philosophy with particular acts, with the will or with the process of deliberation, but more interested in the convictions about reality which are expressed and transmitted in the agent's way of life, amongst which convictions about God are fundamental.

The primary implication of the Christian doctrine of God for an understanding of the human agent is that human persons are creatures of divine grace. Over against the insistence since the Enlightenment* on the dynamics of self-making as basic to moral selfhood, Christian theology views the self as essentially dependent upon the creative and redemptive word and act of God. Hence faith* and gratitude are fundamental to the definition of the human person: faith in its widest sense as openness and receptivity towards and trust in divine determination, and gratitude as the orientation of the total life-act of the person to God's grace and goodness. In a redemptive context, this stress on passivity as proper to humanity is worked out in terms of the centrality of God's acts of justification* and sanctification* as primary to the moral psychology of the believer. Both justification and sanctification have deep roots in trinitarian belief: in the eternal saving will of the Father, in the reconciling work of the Son, in the Spirit's subjective realization of reconciliation.* The effect of making these soteriological concepts basic to the definition of the human person is to de-emphasize the significance of human acts in the estimation of human value. Human acts effect neither justification (acceptability in the divine judgment) nor holiness; instead, such acts are properly means whereby the person in Christ corresponds to God's prior act in making the person new. This clearly separates Christian anthropology from that stemming from the Marxist tradition (often expressed in the ethics of some contemporary theologies of justice and liberation; see Liberation Theology*), according to which human labour is the point at which reality is constituted as purposive (see G. Lukacs, *The Ontology of Social Being 3: Labour*, ET, London, 1980). The Christian doctrine of God relieves the human agent of responsibility for the creation of ultimate moral meaning and order, or for the final establishment and maintenance of the self's identity (since that identity is secured through the sequence of God's acts of election, calling and glorification).

Nevertheless, because as a creature of grace the human person is restored to the covenant broken by sin, he or she re-enters the sphere of covenantal obligation. Grace is teleological: its end is not simply the eradication of sin but the evocation of a life of obedient action in conformity to the will of God. The fundamental passivity of the human creature is thus complemented by a no less fundamental activity as partner to the covenant established by grace. As covenant partner, the moral agent exists under the command of God, the Lord of the covenant. The term 'command' needs careful definition if it is not to suggest mere tyranny by an absolutely superior power. God's absolute commands, as the commands of the creator and redeemer, are the expression of God's loving purposes for his creatures; their goal is not our diminishment or bondage but our liberation to flourish within the good order of the covenant. 'Law' (in the sense of the command of God) is thus a form of grace, and testifies to the mutuality of the covenant in which God's agency calls forth patterns of responsive human action (see C. H. Dodd, *Gospel and Law*, Cambridge, 1951, and Barth, *CD* II/2). The command of God, because it is the command of *God*, claims unreserved obedience. This does not, however, entail a complete rejection of moral deliberation but rather a shift in the meaning of deliberation. Deliberation is not wilful submission of divine commands to human judgment: Dietrich Bonhoeffer's* picture of this as the essence of human sin through the image of 'the Pharisee' who orders all life as good or evil around the self as the point of moral discrimination is entirely apt (see his *Ethics*, pp. 16f.). Properly speaking, deliberation is the conscious ordering of the self in giv-ing trustful assent and allegiance to the command of God as our ultimate good.

God's election of human partners to the covenant, accomplished in Jesus Christ (Eph. 1:5, 11–12) is thus the source of moral obligation.* God's act in Christ also specifies the shape of human life in obedience to God. This is the force of language about 'the imitation of Christ'. Imitating Christ is not a matter of slavish mimicry, or of collapsing the all-important distinction between the finished work of Christ and Christian ethical action. Imitation is a consequence of God's redemptive action, not its continuation or the realization of its effectiveness. Thus it is a matter of envisaging Jesus as a pattern of human moral agency, following which demands both prior conformity to Christ effected by the Spirit, and stringent demarcation of the distance between Christ's acts and those of the Christian. It is as 'analogies' to Jesus' humanity that human persons come to exist in God's image. Moral and pastoral theology will accordingly be concerned with human virtue,* not as an immanent set of qualities or natural teleology in the human creature, but as the Spirit-produced fruit of participation in the paschal movement of the death and resurrection of Christ.

4. Conclusion

The fate of Christian moral and pastoral theology lies largely in its capacity to articulate its own specific grounds (which, in the end, means its doctrine of God, construed through Christological and trinitarian categories). Only on that basis is it likely to adhere to its own vocation, for both in its content and its method it is – like all Christian theology – determined by reference to the first commandment, supremely manifested in the Word made flesh.

See especially: ATONEMENT; AUTHORITY; BLASPHEMY; BLESSING AND CURSING; CHURCH; CONSCIENCE; CONVERSION; COVENANT; CREATION; DECALOGUE; ESCHATOLOGY AND ETHICS; FAITH; FOLK RELIGION; FORGIVENESS; GODLINESS; GOODNESS; GOSPEL AND ETHICS; GRACE; HEALING; HEAVEN AND HELL; HOLINESS; HOLY SPIRIT; HOLY WAR; HOPE; HYPOCRISY; IMAGE OF GOD; ISLAMIC ETHICS; JESUS; JEWISH ETHICS; JUDGMENT AND THE JUDGMENT; JUSTIFICATION, DOCTRINE OF; KINGDOM OF GOD; LAW AND GOSPEL;

MERCY; MISSION, MORALITY OF; NATURAL LAW; POWER; PRAYER; PSYCHOLOGY OF RELIGION; RECONCILIATION; RELIGIOUS EDUCATION; REPENTANCE; RESPONSIBILITY; RESURRECTION; REVELATION; RIGHTEOUSNESS; SANCTIFICATION; SPIRITUALITY; SUNDAY; TEMPTATION; THEOCRACY; THEODICY; VOCATION.

Bibliography

On the doctrine of God: K. Barth, *CD* I/1; H. Berkhof, *Christian Faith* (ET, Grand Rapids, 1979); C. Braaten and R. Jenson, *Christian Dogmatics* 1 (Philadelphia, 1984); E. Jüngel, *The Doctrine of the Trinity* (ET, Edinburgh and Grand Rapids, 1976); W. Kasper, *The God of Jesus Christ* (ET, New York, 1983; London, 1984); J. N. D. Kelly, *Early Christian Doctrines* (London, ⁵1977); K. Rahner, *The Trinity* (ET, New York, 1970); T. F. Torrance, *The Trinitarian Faith* (Edinburgh, 1988); O. Weber, *Foundations of Dogmatics* 1 (ET, Grand Rapids, 1981).

On moral theology: K. Barth, *CD* II/2, III/4, IV/4; D. Bonhoeffer, *Ethics* (ET, London, ²1971); J. Gustafson, *Theology and Ethics* (Chicago and Oxford, 1981); S. Hauerwas, *The Peaceable Kingdom* (Notre Dame, IN, 1983; London, 1984); *idem*, *Against the Nations* (Minneapolis, MN, 1985); J. W. McClendon, *Systematic Theology* 1: *Ethics* (Nashville, TN, 1986); O. O'Donovan, *Resurrection and Moral Order* (Leicester and Grand Rapids, ²1994); H. Thielicke, *TE*.

On pastoral theology: D. Browning (ed.), *Practical Theology* (New York, 1983); L. Mudge and J. Poling (eds.), *Formation and Reflection* (Philadelphia, 1987); T. Oden, *Pastoral Theology* (San Francisco, 1983); M. Thornton, *The Function of Theology* (London, 1960); E. Thurneysen, *A Theology of Pastoral Care* (ET, Richmond, VA, 1962).

J.B.W.

T W O

Love

'This is love,' wrote John, 'not that we loved God, but that he loved us and sent his Son as an atoning sacrifice for our sins. Dear friends, since God so loved us, we also ought to love one another' (1 Jn. 4:10–11).

1. Biblical teaching

These two sentences in the NT encapsulate the four most distinctive features of the Christian love ethic. It is theocentric, because the origin of genuine loving lies in God's gracious initiative. It is Christocentric, in that the Son is the focal point of the Father's love. It is active and self-sacrificial, reaching its peak in the death of Christ. And it demands a reciprocal, imitative response from those who are its beneficiaries.

a. God's love. 'God *is* love', John states in the same context (1 Jn. 4:8, 16b). This is the bottom line. The true meaning of love is comprised in the relationship which binds the three Persons of the Godhead together. 'Beloved' is a word the Synoptic Gospels reserve to express the Father's love for the Son (especially at crucial points of Jesus' ministry, see Mk. 1:11; 9:7), thus underlining the supreme significance of that bond.

The Son loves the Father, too (Jn. 14:31). The hallmark of his love is obedience,* and the

Holy Spirit exhibits the same loving subservience in his relationship to the other two Persons of the Trinity (Jn. 16:13–15; *cf.* 12:49).

The Bible paints in the warm, supportive, forgiving nature of God's love, in a series of vivid word pictures. He cares for his people like a farmer for his vineyard and a shepherd for his sheep (Is. 5:1–7; Jn. 10:11–16). His concern is similar to – and greater than – that of parents for their children (Ps. 103:13; Is. 49:15; 66:13; Ho. 11:1). The warmth of his feeling can be compared to a totally committed friendship (Jn. 15:13–17), or even to the passion of falling in love (Is. 54:6–8; Ezk. 16).

It is within the framework of the covenant* that the most striking feature of God's love is displayed. He will always be faithful to his covenant promises, so his love can rightly be described as 'everlasting' (Je. 31:3). His people's commitment to him may be fickle (Ho. 6:4), but the power of his love will conquer the most outrageous unfaithfulness (Ho. 3:1; 11:8–9).

Paul picks up the same theme in a Christocentric fashion. He lists the most powerful forces which may prompt Christians to desert their Lord, and concludes that the embrace of Jesus' love will overcome everything (Rom. 8:35–39).

God's love is practical. This is a note sounded repeatedly in the OT. Israel owed her redemption from Egypt to his loving, mighty intervention (Dt. 4:37–38; 7:8; Ps. 106:6–12). Minority groups, like widows, orphans and immigrants, benefited from his powerful support (Dt. 10:18). And when, for their sins, his people were exiled, their loving Lord exercised his prerogative of mercy and restored them to their homeland (Is. 43:4ff.).

The story of God's love in action gathers momentum in the NT. It was the Father's committed concern for his world that prompted him to give the Son (Jn. 3:16). It was the Son's love for the sinner which led to his own act of self-giving (Gal. 2:20). And the gift of the Holy Spirit is further evidence of divine love 'poured out into our hearts' (Rom. 5:5).

Christ's death and resurrection* provide the supreme practical demonstration of God's love. Jesus showed his disciples 'the full extent of his love', as he led them forward to the cross (Jn. 13:1; 15:13; *cf.* 1 Jn. 3:16). In his love, he became an atoning sacrifice (see Atonement*) for their sins (1 Jn. 4:10). And the wealth of God's loving mercy makes them – and all

fellow believers – alive with him in his resurrection (Eph. 2:4–10).

The Bible summons men and women again and again to live a life of love. But the model and dynamic of such radical loving are not to be dredged up from the depths of human nature. They pre-exist already in the nature and activity of God.

b. Love for God. Jesus echoed the OT's plain command that people must love God with the whole of their human being (Dt. 6:4–5; Mt. 22:37–38). And if such love for the Father is genuine, he taught, it will inevitably embrace the Son, too (Jn. 8:42; *cf.* 1 Pet. 1:8).

The cold edge of this demand is softened by the assumption that such love is not coerced. It is the spontaneous response of humankind's overwhelming gratitude to God for his amazing grace.* 'Christ's love compels us', Paul confesses, with the cross in the front of his mind (2 Cor. 5:14). In verses like this, it is hard to decide whether the original meaning is 'Christ's love for us' or 'our love for Christ' (*cf.* Jn. 5:42). The two merge. Once a person grasps the gospel of redemption, believing leads straight to loving (Gal. 5:6; 1 Thes. 1:3; 3:6; 1 Tim. 1:14). Nevertheless, God's demand is frighteningly exclusive. The divine lover will tolerate no rivals, whether human or material (Mt. 6:24; 10:37). He insists on his people's loving loyalty with a jealous ferocity (Ex. 20:4–5). This is not obsessional possessiveness, but the righteous fury of a devoted husband who finds his wife in bed with another man (Jas. 4:4–5, NIV mg.). And he himself provides the inner resources to enable his human partner to stay faithful (Dt. 30:6; Rom. 5:5).

Humankind's devotion is a response to God's prior love. But the story does not end there. Human, responsive love is merely a link in a chain reaction. The Father loves those who love him and his Son (Pr. 8:17; Jn. 16:27). They, in turn, will come to know God more intimately (Jn. 14:21; Eph. 3:17–19). And that itself is part of a 'benign circle' which brings inconceivable benefits (1 Cor. 2:9–10).

c. Love for people. The Bible's teaching on love for others displays the same creative tension between clear-cut command and grateful response.

The Father's love stimulates a loving reaction from his children (1 Jn. 4:11; *cf.* Lk. 7:47). The Son's self-giving spurs his brothers and sisters to live a life of love like his (Eph. 5:1–2). And the Holy Spirit, alive in the believer, produces such love as his fruit (Gal. 5:22).

Jesus was not the first to highlight the two 'great commandments' (Dt. 6:5; Lv. 19:18; Mt. 22:34–40; cf. Jas. 2:8). But the way he brought them into dynamic relationship was certainly distinctive. Love shown to God's people is love shown to him (Heb. 6:10; cf. Mt. 25:34–40; 1 Jn. 4:20); while the proof of genuine love for others is obedient love for their heavenly Father (1 Jn. 5:2).

In OT times, the neighbour to be loved was the fellow member of the covenant people. The resident alien must be loved too (Lv. 19:34), so it would be wrong to suggest that covenant ethics encouraged racism (see Race*), but the law* made a clear distinction between neighbours and foreigners when it came (for example) to granting financial concessions in hard times (Dt. 15:1–11; 23:19–20; Ex. 22:25).

Under the covenant law (which contrasts sharply with other Near-Eastern law codes at this point), the weakest members of the community were targeted for preferential, loving treatment. Love demanded that these vulnerable neighbours be treated with fairness on pay days and with special generosity at harvest time (Ex. 22:21–27; Lv. 19:9–10; Dt. 24:14–15). The physically handicapped must be shown special consideration, too (Lv. 19:14).

The NT insists that love must be the distinguishing feature of church life. To love your brother or sister in Christ is both a mark of obedience to the Lord and an appropriate response to the way he already loves you (Jn. 15:12, 17; 1 Jn. 3:11; 4:11, 21). Love must be practical, not sentimental (1 Jn. 3:17–18); yet it must be deeply heartfelt and sincere as well (Rom. 12:9–10; 1 Pet. 1:22). It has evangelistic power, because when outsiders see such love at work they will recognize the Lord who enables its expression (Jn. 13:35).

In any Christian congregation, love is the principle which protects unity and encourages growth. It binds believers together in a common purpose as they progress in their knowledge of Christ (Phil. 2:1–2; Col. 2:2; cf. Jn. 17:22–23). The Christian body is built up, its work smoothly co-ordinated, as its members deepen their love for one another (1 Cor. 8:1; Eph. 4:16; see Fellowship*).

As far as individuals are concerned, love sometimes demands the surrender of personal rights and interests. Some activities which are blameless in themselves must be abandoned if they offend others (Rom. 14:13–23). Insults will not be returned (1 Pet. 3:8–9; Eph. 4:32; cf. 2 Cor. 2:5–11 and Mt. 18:21–22). Gentleness, patience and restraint are love's marks on a healthy Christian fellowship (Gal. 5:13; Eph. 4:2).

Most of the NT's teaching on love is directed at relationships in the church, but neighbour-love (see Neighbour*), as Jesus taught it, has much broader dimensions. In his parable of the good Samaritan he knocked down the fences which limited the concept of 'neighbour' to someone within the covenant community (Lk. 10:29–37). The story's punch-line ('Go and do likewise') underlines the Christian's obligation to show practical, sacrificial love to anyone in need – whether insider or outsider.

Nowhere is this strand of Jesus' teaching more startling than in his insistence that love does not discriminate in favour of the deserving. Distinctive Christian loving means doing good to those who have no intention of returning your gesture, just as God lavishes his gifts on the deliberately ungrateful (Lk. 6:32–36; cf. 14:12–14).

And God went even further than that. Christ loved his enemies, and Christians must do the same (Rom. 5:8–11; Mt. 5:43–48). The right way to counter hostility, said Jesus, is to respond with aggressive love (Mt. 5:38–42). In such circumstances, willed love must substitute for (and sometimes anticipate) felt love. Here Jesus openly clashed with religious teachers (like those at Qumran) who told their followers to balance their love for those inside the community by hatred for those outside it. He also practised what he preached (Lk. 23:33–34).

2. Ethical and pastoral discussion

Debate highlights four main issues: the meaning of the word 'love' itself; and the relationships between love and law, love and justice, and neighbour-love and self-love.

a. The meaning of 'love'. The Gk. word agapē dominates the Bible's ethical understanding of 'love'. It is the headline over all other virtues* (Col. 3:14; cf. 1 Cor. 13:13). In the NT it is a theocentric word describing the Father's nature (1 Jn. 4:8), the Son's example (Jn. 15:12) and the Spirit's fruit (Gal. 5:22). And the response it demands covers every aspect of human experience – disposition (1 Cor. 13:4–7), thought life (Phil. 2:1–5) and behaviour (1 Jn. 3:18).

2

It is all the more remarkable that the meaning of the verb *agapaō* and its derivatives is relatively colourless and obscure in pre-biblical literature. The noun *agapē* itself is virtually unknown. So *agapē*'s rich significance in Christian ethics is not an import from pre-Christian philosophical sources, but an amalgam of biblical usage.

In the LXX, *agapaō* usually translates the Heb. *'āhēḇ*, which is an umbrella term for physical attraction and delight in things like food and sleep (Gn. 29:18; 27:4; Pr. 20:13), as well as love in interpersonal and God–man relationships. In the NT, the revealed characteristics of God's love set *agapē*'s ethical parameters (although its exact meaning varies, depending on its subject and object in context).

The NT writers seem surprisingly reluctant to use other popular Gk. words for 'love'. *Erōs* (acquisitive love) does not feature at all, while *storgē* (family love) only appears rarely in compounds. The exception is the verb *phileō* and its derivatives (show friendly affection), which are relatively common.

Many commentators see a clear difference between *agapē* and *philia*, especially when the two words appear in the same biblical context (*e.g.* Jn. 21:15–17). *Philia* is selective, emotional and dependent on the lovable qualities it sees in its object. *Agapē* is universal; a love of the will which operates when it is neither attracted nor reciprocated. Other scholars prefer not to press the distinction, suggesting that the two words are either synonymous (especially in John) or complementary (the 'philic' note of warm affection resonating with Jesus' compassion and rescuing *agapē* from sterile altruism*).

In *Agape and Eros*, Anders Nygren* argues that *erōs* and *agapē* are two distinct motifs in theological ethics. Basically, he maintains, they are two contradictory theories of love. *Agapē* is theocentric, while *erōs* is anthropocentric. *Erōs* strives to climb the rungs of a ladder to God, while *agapē* describes God's loving initiative in descending to man. *Agapē* is sacrificial giving, while *erōs* is the desire to get and possess. *Erōs* is egocentric love (often of the highest kind), while *agapē* is unselfish love. *Agapē* creates value in its object, while *erōs* responds to some value already there.

Nygren claims that the NT writers deliberately rejected the *erōs* motif, which was dominant in Gk. philosophy, in favour of *agapē*. But Augustine,* with his neo-Platonic background, confused matters by importing *erōs* ideas into his exposition of Christian love (*caritas*). Until the Reformation (when Luther* reinstated *agapē* in its unadulterated form), the Western church languished in ethical as well as theological heresy.

Nygren's thesis remains influential, but has been criticized on three grounds. 1. Some would say that he has overplayed the discontinuity between *agapē* and *erōs*. He appears to ignore the order of creation by locating 'legitimate' love wholly within the order of redemption. 2. Others point to the difficulty Nygren has in giving biblical content to the notion of human love for God. To talk about loving God is obviously inappropriate if *agapē* creates value in its object. 3. Yet others fault him for attempting to build the Christian ethic on love alone.

b. Love and law. The relationship between a love ethic and law is a matter of sharp controversy.

Paul Ramsey,* borrowing William Frankena's (1908–) terminology, labels the two ends of the spectrum *act-agapism* and *rule-agapism*. The former, holding that each fresh situation is unique, judges every act by the criterion of *agapē*; rules have either no place at all in decision-making, or (at most) a merely advisory role. *Rule-agapism* maintains that moral cases are similar enough to categorize. Love-embodying rules can be formulated, and the decision-maker's business is to discern how to apply them.

Situation ethics* is an *act-agapistic* approach, though its best-known advocates – Joseph Fletcher* and J. A. T. Robinson (1919–83) – both deny charges of antinomianism.*

Situationists believe that the ruling (and only) norm of Christian decision-making is love. Its decisions must be made situationally, not prescriptively. This approach, they argue, is superior to a rule ethic on two grounds. It sets helping people above obeying laws; and it yields higher moral standards by tearing down law's false ceilings of obligation.* A loving end also justifies the means necessary to achieve it.

Fletcher claims Augustine as an ally, citing his homily on 1 Jn. 4:8 (*Dilige et quod vis fac* – which Fletcher is careful to translate, 'Love with care and then what you will, do'). Augustine was not, however, a straightforward act-agapist. Although his ethical system was based on love, he recognized the force of other absolutes* (*e.g.* the duty to tell the truth).

Those who favour *rule-agapism* are among the strongest critics of situation ethics. A. M. Ramsay (1904–88) in *Image Old and New* (London, 1963) believes that love is simply the headline which highlights the law's true meaning. J. I. Packer (1926–) in *Keep Yourself from Idols* (London, 1963) claims situationists devalue all law-keeping under the label of legalism* and accuses them of naïvety in suggesting that sinful people can find and follow the way of love unaided.

Paul Ramsey adds that *act-agapism* is antisocial. We need laws to tell us what love requires of us as a social practice, even when this does not seem to square with love's leading in a particular situation. Careful casuistry* is the way to deal with exceptional cases, not disregard for law in the name of love.

The interpretation of Jesus' summary of the law (Mt. 22:37–40) is clearly crucial, as is the use Paul makes of it (Rom. 13:8–10; Gal. 5:14). The *act-agapist* sees the summary as a distillation (an extraction of law's value from its external dross). To the *rule-agapist*, the summary is more of a compendium (a conflation of many laws which still retain their normative thrust).

Certainly the Bible gives no indication that love and law are on a collision course. In the OT, *tôrâ* lacks the cold, legalistic overtones 'law' often carries today. God's law was seen as both the expression of his love and the explanation of what loving relationships meant in practice. Love supplied both the context of the law's demands (*cf.* Ex. 20:2), and the chief motive for obeying it (Dt. 4:37–40; Lv. 19:33–34).

In the NT, as in the OT, obeying God's commandments is inseparably linked to the fostering of a good, loving relationship with him (1 Jn. 2:3; 3:24; *cf.* Pss. 19:7–10; 119:33–36). And Jesus apparently saw no inconsistency in bracketing love and obedience (Jn. 14:15, 21, 23–24, 31).

c. Love and justice. Christian ethicists have described the relationship between love and justice (see Justice and Peace③) in a variety of ways.

At one extreme, some divide between the two very sharply. Nygren, for example, banishes justice to his *erōs* category, in contrast to true Christian love which is *agapē*. And Tolstoy* sees conflict as inevitable. Justice, he asserts, concerns itself with groups, determines their rights, dispenses the rewards* and punishments* that are strictly due, and achieves its goals by force.* Love, as epitomized by Jesus, targets the individual 'neighbour', sets out to meet his or her personal needs, blesses the totally undeserving, and operates by gentle persuasion.

At the other end of the spectrum, Fletcher maintains that 'love and justice are the same, for justice is love distributed, nothing else'. He hotly disputes the view that love's operations must be limited to personal relationships. To say that love is for individuals and justice for groups is to sentimentalize love and to dehumanize justice. Justice, in fact, is simply love under another name – 'love coping with situations where distribution is called for'. So far, then, from keeping the two separate (or, worse still, assigning one priority over the other), Fletcher understands justice's role as finding absolute love's relative course in different situations.

Mediating positions abound. Emil Brunner,* for instance, sees a clear distinction between love and justice, but insists that the two are both compatible and necessary. In his view, love supplements justice.

The sphere of love and the sphere of justice 'lie as far apart as heaven and hell', Brunner explains. But love 'always presupposes justice and fulfils the claims of justice before setting about its own business, which consists in transcending those claims'. The business of living in the world's nexus of systems and institutions makes the structures of justice indispensable. Yet giving a group of people their rights and dues is not the summit of Christian social ethics* (see also Community Ethics⑯). The Christian is called to supplement the fight for social justice with a love for undeserving individuals which matches the grace of God.

Other representatives of the tradition acknowledge a far closer relationship between love and justice, without going as far as Fletcher did in identifying them. So Paul Tillich (1886–1965) compares love without justice to 'a body without backbone'. Nevertheless, though justice is immanent in love, love transcends it (in his view) because it is always possible to achieve justice without creating a loving relationship.

Reinhold Niebuhr* struggled with this tension throughout his prolific writing ministry. His eventual conclusions are broadly in line with Tillich's. He labels all efforts to build God's kingdom* on earth by means of love as hopelessly naïve. In this sin-soaked world only proximate ethical solutions are possible, and to achieve those the Christian must accept justice as love's best possible expression. But that is no mean compromise,* because in Christian ethics the love principle is an essential criterion both to inform justice's distributive decisions and to expose their limitations and failings.

d. Neighbour-love and self-love. Jesus' command, 'Love your neighbour as yourself', has been understood in many different ways. Fletcher (*Situation Ethics*) lists four possible interpretations of the word 'as' in this context: 1. 'just as much as'; 2. 'in addition to'; 3. 'in the way that you ought to'; or 4. 'instead of'.

A strong body of Christian tradition has supported the first and fourth of those options. Jesus meant, 'Love your neighbour as much as – *by nature* – you love yourself', says Nygren. He was simply drawing attention to an unfortunate fact of fallen human nature and teaching a lesson from it. 'The commandment', Karl Barth* concludes, 'is not a legitimation but a limitation of this reality.'

The continental Reformers (especially Luther and Calvin*) saw all attempts to rehabilitate self-love (see Self-esteem*) as directly antithetical to Jesus' teaching on self-denial* (Mk. 8:34–35; Jn. 15:13; Lk. 14:26–27; *cf.* Phil. 2:5–8). Paul, they pointed out, contrasted 'self-lovers' with 'God-lovers' (1 Tim. 3:2, 4) and characterized Christian love as 'not self-seeking' (1 Cor. 13:5). So self-love is a 'vicious love' (*vitiosus amor* – Luther's expression).

The Thomist tradition (see Thomist Ethics*), with its more optimistic view of human nature, leads the way in affirming the ethical legitimacy of self-love. Joseph Butler* expresses this conviction more strongly than most. Humankind, though fallen, retains the dignity of being made in God's image.* It is illogical to think that we can best love our Maker by hating what he has made, and faithless to deny the value of the self which bears his likeness.

Christians, it is argued, should be especially open to the merit of loving themselves because they are overwhelmingly aware of being the objects of God's redeeming love. Failure to love self puts us in the false position of despising what God loves.

Both Christian and secular psychologists stress the value of self-love in promoting personal well-being and good relationships. Only the person who loves himself, Erich Fromm* maintains, can be truly self-forgetful, because

only he can escape from the trap of self-preoccupation. And because concern for others is an integral part of a satisfying personal lifestyle, self-love is the only effective basis for neighbour-love.

This is why Jesus linked the two concepts in his second great commandment, suggests Norman Geisler (1932–) in *The Christian Ethic of Love*. How can a husband care for his wife if he has not first learned how to care for himself (*cf.* Eph. 5:29–30)? Jack Dominian (1929–) expresses himself equally strongly: 'There is not the remotest hope of really succeeding in loving our neighbour in a sustained manner until we first have learned to know the meaning of loving ourselves' (J. Dominian and A. R. Peacocke, *From Cosmos to Love*, London, 1976).

A third strand within the tradition approves self-love, but with qualifications. Augustine, for example, condemned fallen humankind's addiction to self-love. An act of God's grace is essential, he insisted, to redirect the sinner's love of self to the Christian's love of God and neighbour. But once this radical, redemptive refocusing has been achieved, a degree of self-love becomes legitimate.

Bernard of Clairvaux (1090–1153) suggested that moving from wrong to right expressions of self-love is like climbing a ladder. We begin by loving self for self's sake (wrong); move on to loving God for self's sake; climb another rung by learning how to love God for God's sake, and reach the top when we love self for God's sake (right).

Fletcher substitutes 'neighbour' for 'God' in Bernard's formula. He quotes Søren Kierkegaard* with approval: 'The command "Love thy neighbour as thyself" means "Thou shalt love thyself in the right way".' So the pregnant woman best exhibits care for her child when she takes extra pains to safeguard her own health.

Paul Ramsey (*Basic Christian Ethics*) makes the same point by importing the concept of vocation.* God calls Christians to develop and use all the talents he has given them, Ramsey writes, in order to love their neighbours more effectively (*cf.* Eph. 4:28). He, too, quotes Kierkegaard – this time, an expanded version of Jesus' second great commandment: 'You shall love yourself as you love your neighbour when you love him as yourself.'

This third, mediating position highlights a vital difference in the way the expression 'self-love' is used. If it is taken to mean self-centredness, self-assertion or selfishness, few Christian ethicists would approve. But if it stands for self-respect, self-esteem or self-acceptance, few would dispute its value.

See especially: ACCEPTANCE; ATONEMENT; BENEVOLENCE; CARE, CARING; CHARACTER; [10] CHURCH; COMPASSION; COVENANT; EMOTION; EMPATHY; FAMILY; FELLOWSHIP; FRIENDSHIP; GIVING; GRACE; GROUP THERAPY; HANDICAPPED, CARE OF; HOLY SPIRIT; HOMOSEXUALITY; HOSPITALITY; HUMANITARIANISM; JESUS; KINGDOM OF GOD; LAW AND GOSPEL; LUST; MARRIAGE; MERCY; MOTIVE, MOTIVATION; NEIGHBOUR; NON-VIOLENCE; OBEDIENCE; PATRIOTISM; RACE; RECONCILIATION; RESPONSIBILITY; SELF-ESTEEM; SERMON ON THE MOUNT; SEXUALITY; [11] SICK, CARE OF; SITUATION ETHICS; SOCIETY; THIRD WORLD AID; VIRTUE, VIRTUES; WELFARE STATE.

Bibliography

K. Barth, *CD* IV/2; E. Brunner, *The Divine Imperative* (ET, London and New York, 1937); J. Burnaby, *Amor Dei* (London, 1938); J. Fletcher, *Situation Ethics* (London and Philadelphia, 1966); N. L. Geisler, *The Christian Ethic of Love* (Grand Rapids, 1973); S. Kierkegaard, *Works of Love* (ET, New York, 1962); C. S. Lewis, *The Four Loves* (London and New York, 1960); J. Moffatt, *Love in the New Testament* (London, 1929); L. Morris, *Testaments of Love* (Grand Rapids, 1981); R. Niebuhr, *An Interpretation of Christian Ethics* (New York, 1935; London, 1936); A. Nygren, *Agape and Eros* (ET, London and Philadelphia, 1953); O. O'Donovan, *Resurrection and Moral Order* (Leicester and Grand Rapids, [2]1994); G. Outka, *Agape: An Ethical Analysis* (New Haven, CT, and London, 1972); P. Ramsey, *Basic Christian Ethics* (New York and London, 1950); N. H. G. Robinson, *The Groundwork of Christian Ethics* (London, 1971).

D.H.F.

THREE

Justice and Peace

It was practice among the Christian theologians of the West during the Middle Ages to think of justice as a personal virtue,* *i.e.* as one of those habits which are meritorious features of the character (see [10]) of a person. They typically classified justice as one of the four so-called 'cardinal' virtues, the others being prudence, fortitude and temperance; to these they added the three so-called 'theological' virtues of faith,* hope* and charity.

But justice is not only a meritorious character trait. Justice is also a meritorious dimension of social relationships. A social practice or arrangement, as well as some specific social interaction, may be just or unjust; justice may prevail in a certain regard within a certain group of people, or may fail to prevail.

Though the medieval theologians gave far more prominence to justice as a meritorious trait of character than they did to justice as a meritorious dimension of social relationships, the latter is the more fundamental concept. For the just person is the person whose habit it is to pursue justice in social relationships. The

3

fundamental question to be considered thus is this: What constitutes justice in social relationships? What is it for a person or group of persons, or for a social institution of one sort or another, to be treated justly?

1. The concept of justice

Ever since classical antiquity, the answer has been that it is when a person receives what is *due* to him or her that the person is treated justly. The same holds for groups of persons and social institutions. It has also been traditional to distinguish between *retributive* (see Retribution*) and *distributive* justice. When something is due to a person on account of some wrongdoing on that person's part, and the person receives what is thus due to him or her, then retributive justice is rendered that person (see Punishment*). By contrast, distributive justice is rendered a person when that which is rendered is not due to the person on account of wrongdoing on the person's part. (Naturally the same distinction applies to justice rendered to social groups and institutions.) The word 'distributive' is a bit misleading, however. It suggests fairness in distributing some good – or some evil! – among the members of a group of persons. But non-retributive justice, or injustice, need not involve fair distribution of goods or evils among the members of a group. When the officials at a race refuse to award the first-place prize to the person who comes in first because that person is black rather than Caucasian, and when also they do not give the prize to anyone else, they are acting unjustly, even though no unfair distribution has taken place.

In the traditional formula of justice as *receiving what is due to one*, there is an ambiguity, at least as it pertains to distributive justice. The formula might mean 'enjoying or undergoing *what someone has an obligation to render to one*', or it might mean 'enjoying or undergoing *that to which one has a legitimate claim*, be that claim grounded in morality, law, or practice'. In other words, someone else's obligation, versus one's own legitimate claim. If understood in the second sense, then (non-retributive) justice is the same phenomenon as enjoying one's rights; since to have a right to something, in at least one important sense of the phrase 'to have a right', is to have a legitimate claim to that something.

Admittedly, not everyone who writes about justice is willing, in this way, to connect justice with rights (see Rights, Human*). Alasdair

MacIntyre (1929–), for example, regards the concept of rights as a modern invention but regards the ancient Greeks as working with the concept of justice. His argument seems to be that before the modern era there was no *language* of rights, from which he infers that there was no concept of rights; and throughout his argument he seems to identify rights with that list of negative rights enshrined in modern liberal political theory. But rights – legitimate claims to some good or other – are vastly more extensive than such rights; the person who wins the Tour de France has a right to the first-place prize. And the fact that a writer lacks a distinctive language for rights does not establish that he or she lacks the concept. Ancient peoples had the concept of a legitimate claim to something; it did not take us moderns to bring that concept to birth.

It should also be mentioned that not everyone would concede that there is an ambiguity in Aristotle's* formulation. Some philosophers have held, for example, that the right to some good is always a right *against* someone for the granting of that good; a legitimate claim to some good is always a legitimate claim *against* someone. And then it is said that to have a right or legitimate claim *against* a person for some good is just for that other person to have the *duty* to grant one that good. Duties and rights are thus the mere converse of each other.

This position has proved attractive to a good many Christians. It is said to be incompatible with evangelical humility* to suppose that we have rights, if those are understood as anything other than the correlative of duties (see Duty*). Speaking of rights is a sign of, and a rationale for, the self-assertiveness which the gospel condemns; it encourages and expresses an individualistic way of thinking which is deeply alien to the Bible. The situation is rather that we are responsible to and for one another (see Responsibility*).

This is not the place to show in full detail that there are rights to which no duty corresponds; one example will have to suffice. Suppose I have the right to walk in the public gardens until 8 p.m.; the law book clearly says so. Suppose you are appointed keeper of the gardens. And suppose that, in your orientation sessions, you are falsely and deceptively told that it is your duty to keep people out after 6 p.m. I then appear one day at 7 p.m. and try to enter; and you prevent me from doing so. Your doing so is a violation of my rights. Yet you are morally innocent in preventing me; indeed, you would be morally culpable if you did not try to hinder me. You would be failing to do what you justifiably believed you ought to do. Here then is a right to which there is no corresponding duty. Rights do not alter in situations of ignorance in the way in which duties alter in situations of ignorance.

As to duties to which no rights correspond, charity provides us with a multitude of examples. There is a long line of Christian thought which holds that charity is not just notable and admirable but obligatory. Yet charity, though it often takes the form of rendering to someone some good to which that person has a legitimate right, also often takes the form of going beyond that; and sometimes it takes that form when it is obligatory to go beyond.

If these considerations are correct, then we must think of duties and rights as two distinct dimensions of our moral existence, both of fundamental importance. All of us are so situated before God and our fellow human beings as to have rights; and those of us capable of intentional action are also so situated before God and our fellow human beings as to have duties. One person's rights interact in complex ways with other persons' duties – and, indeed, with that person's duties. But the structure of rights is distinct and independent from the structure of duties; one is not merely the mirror image of the other. The other in my presence is someone to whom I have responsibilities; but the other in my presence also comes bearing claims. If my rights are not honoured, more is at stake than just that someone's moral character is besmirched for having failed to do his or her duty by me. *I am injured, morally* injured. The failure to do one's duty makes one guilty (see Guilt*); the failure to receive one's rights makes one injured. To the former, repentance* is appropriate; to the latter, lament, and perhaps outrage. Justice, distributive justice, is intrinsically connected with rights: justice is present among persons, groups and institutions when their rights, their legitimate claims, are honoured.

2. The biblical ground and contours of justice

More could be said about the concept of justice; but let us move on to the contours and the grounds of justice. It is here that most of our disagreements concerning justice are to be located – not so much over the concept of justice as over what is as a matter of fact due to persons (and groups and institutions) and why it is due to them. It is on these two points that both the OT and NT offer a distinct perspective.

a. The grounds of justice. Over and over the biblical writers say that God *loves* justice. 'I, the LORD, love justice' (Is. 61:8) and 'The LORD loves justice' (Ps. 37:28, RSV) are but two examples from a multitude.

Furthermore, God's love for justice is declared to be an active love: God *does* justice. For example, 'The LORD works righteousness and justice for all the oppressed' (Ps. 103:6); 'I know that the LORD secures justice for the poor and upholds the cause of the needy' (Ps. 140:12); and in Ps. 146 it is the Lord 'who executes justice for the oppressed; who gives food to the hungry. The LORD sets the prisoners free; the LORD opens the eyes of the blind. The LORD lifts up those who are bowed down; the LORD loves the righteous. The LORD watches over the sojourners, he upholds the widow and the fatherless; but the way of the wicked he brings to ruin' (Ps. 146:7–9, RSV).

An ancient, enduring, and prominent strand of Christian theology sees God's justice as exhibited in God's anger with those who disobey God's commands. God's justice is exhibited in God's practice of *retributive* justice. And the Bible does indeed speak of God's retributive justice. But the many passages which speak of God's *love* of justice are not pointing to God's delight over the suffering of those who are justly punished. God's love for justice is grounded in God's love (see 2) for the victims of injustice – for those who are morally violated, morally injured.

This love leads God to enjoin *us* to do justice. 'Follow justice and justice alone', says Moses in his farewell speech, 'so that you may live and possess the land the LORD your God is giving you' (Dt. 16:20). And in a passage which by now has entered deep into the consciousness of humanity, God says through Amos: 'Let justice roll on like a river, righteousness like a never-failing stream' (Am. 5:24).

Not only are we to see God's love for the injured and suffering behind God's injunction to us to do justice (*cf.* Mi. 6:8); we are also to see God's invitation to image God as lying behind it. As God is just, so are we to be just. We are to be icons of God, imaging God's justice in our justice. Again the farewell speech of Moses makes the point: God 'executes justice for the fatherless and the widows, and loves the sojourner, giving him food and clothing. Love the sojourner therefore; for you were sojourners in the land of Egypt' (Dt. 10:18–19, RSV). 'Do not deprive the alien or the fatherless of justice, or take the cloak of a widow as a pledge. Remember that you were slaves in Egypt and the LORD your God redeemed you from there. That is why I command you to do this' (Dt. 24:17–18). As God has heard our laments and satisfied our longings, so in imitation we are to hear the laments of the poor, the weak, and the oppressed.

Deep in the tradition of Christian reflection is the conviction that the requirement to do justice is rooted in the requirement to respect the image of God* in persons; honouring that image requires honouring the legitimate claims of that person. This theme is profoundly important; and is surely a legitimate extrapolation from Gn. 9: 'Whoever sheds the blood of a human, by a human shall that person's blood be shed; for in his own image God made humankind' (Gn. 9:6, NRSV). But more prominent in the Scriptures themselves than the theme of doing justice as a *manifestation of our respect for* the image of God in persons is the theme of doing justice as *constituting (part of) our imaging* of God.

b. The contours of justice. A clue to the prophetic understanding of the contours of justice is the fact that when justice is spoken of in the OT, over and over again it is widows, orphans, aliens, and the impoverished who are brought into view. Justice is intimately connected with the fate of these groups. The citations given above provide just a few examples. Reflection on the significance of these references leads one deep into the biblical understanding of the contours of justice. To become just, a society must bring into community all its weak and defenceless ones, its marginal ones, giving them voice and a fair share in the goods of the community. It is thus no accident that the holiness code in the Torah includes prescriptions concerning justice, since holiness requires wholeness, or integrity. By contrast, when Plato* in *The Republic* spoke of the just society, widows, orphans, aliens and the impoverished were nowhere in view. The fundamental contour of justice was identified by Plato with a certain kind of 'law and order': a society is just when authority is exercised by wise persons and is pervasively obeyed. So too John Locke (1632–1704), in his classic *Second Treatise on Civil Government* (1690) nowhere gives special attention to the marginal members of society. The liberal notion of the just society, in whose genesis Locke plays a pivotal role, is, roughly speaking, that a society is just when each person is free to pursue the good life as he or she sees fit, provided that a similar liberty is accorded to others.

It is often said that the OT concern for justice disappears in the NT. But if the OT picture of the just society has the contours suggested, that thesis is indefensible. For not only were the actions and parables of Jesus pervasively concerned with bringing the outsiders into community, these being the actions and stories which brought him constantly into conflict with the Pharisees who preached and practised the exclusiveness of the 'holy community'; Jesus' own self-identification as it occurred in the famous synagogue episode in Lk. 4 was an identification which consisted of saying that *he* was that harbinger of justice of which Isaiah and the other prophets spoke: 'The Spirit of the Lord is on me, because he has anointed me to preach good news to the poor. He has sent me to proclaim freedom for the prisoners and recovery of sight for the blind, to release the oppressed, to proclaim the year of the Lord's favour', and 'Today this scripture is fulfilled in your hearing' (Lk. 4:18–19, 21). It is true, of course, that Jesus did not engage in politics* in the usual sense: he was not concerned with reforming and reinforcing the practices of his society by means of State law. But it should be clear from the foregoing that it is mistaken to think that justice is exclusively the concern of politics.

It may be added that it would never occur to anyone reading the NT in its original Gk. that it did not speak of justice; it is our Eng. translations that encourage this thought. The Gk. words *dikaios* and *dikaiosynē* occur regularly in the NT, these being the words which, in classical Gk. anyway, are almost always translated as 'just' and 'justice' respectively. Yet seldom are they thus translated in our Eng. NTs. Customarily they are translated as 'righteous' and 'righteousness'. It cannot be said that these are mis-translations – not, at least, if one allows to come into prominence the notion of *going right* rather than the connotations, from contemporary Eng., of self-righteousness and private morality. But when none of the occurrences of *dikaios* and *dikaiosyne* are translated as 'just' and 'justice', when all are translated as 'righteous' and 'righteousness', then connections to the OT proclamations concerning justice are obliterated and a seriously false impression is given. One example will have to suffice here. In the Beatitudes* as recorded by Matthew, we read: 'Blessed are those who hunger and thirst for righteousness, for they will be filled', and 'Blessed are those who are persecuted because of righteousness, for theirs is the kingdom of heaven' (Mt. 5:6, 10). In both verses the word translated as 'righteousness' is *dikaiosynē*. Jesus is speaking of justice; he blesses those who long and struggle for justice.

3. Types of rights

A distinction is sometimes made, by rights theorists, between negative or freedom rights, and positive or benefit rights: a *negative* right is the right to be allowed to do something; a *positive* right, the right to receive some benefit or other. And it is regularly argued, by those of libertarian tendencies, whether Christian or other, that there is something incoherent or unacceptable in the notion of benefit rights. For example, it is argued that acknowledging benefit rights unavoidably infringes freedom rights; if a society is to secure the subsistence of its members, it will sometimes have to take property from certain of its members against their will (*e.g.* in the form of taxation) and give it to the impoverished for their sustenance, thus infringing their freedom rights.

This libertarian claim is clearly in conflict with the biblical contour of justice outlined above, according to which the fate of the impoverished and the marginal is central to the justice or injustice of social arrangements. In fact very many of the great theologians of the church have explicitly affirmed the right of the involuntarily and avoidably impoverished to fair access to means of sustenance: Basil of Caesarea (*c.* 329–379), John Chrysostom,* Ambrose,* Thomas Aquinas* and John Calvin* are examples. To cite just one of these, Basil said: 'Will not one be called a thief who stole the garment of one already clothed, and is one deserving of any other title who will not clothe the naked if he is able to do so? That bread which you keep, belongs to the hungry; that coat which you preserve in your wardrobe, to the naked; those shoes which are rotting in your possession, to the shoeless; that gold which you have hidden in the ground, to the needy. Wherefore, as often as you were able to help others, and refused, so often did you do them wrong' (quoted in C. Avila, *Ownership*, p. 50).

Nothing has been said in our discussion up to this point about *natural* rights, or about *human* rights – deliberately so, since calling attention to such rights at the beginning tends to obscure from view the wide diversity of rights. None the less, natural human rights are obviously of fundamental importance.

The two concepts should not be identified. The idea of a *natural* right to something is the idea of a right grounded in the nature of things rather than in some social arrangement. Medieval political theorists sometimes thought of the right of certain persons to be monarchs as a *natural* right of theirs; John Locke regarded one's right to possess that with which one has mixed one's labour as a *natural* right; and probably most of us think of parents and children as having certain rights with respect to each other which are grounded in the very nature of their relationship. The idea of a *human* right, by contrast, is the idea of something to which one has a right merely by virtue of being a human being. The natural rights cited above are not human rights. Even if someone has a right to be monarch, he or she does not have that right merely by virtue of being human; and the rights a person has by virtue of being a parent go beyond those that person possesses merely as a human being.

It appears that no-one in classical antiquity defended, or even considered, the view that there are *natural human* rights. The view emerged in late antiquity. And it appears to have had two sources: the biblical idea, already mentioned, that all human beings are created in the image of God; and the Stoic* idea, that all human beings are alike in having the divine principle of Reason present within each. Emil Brunner's* summary of the evidence concerning the origin of the concept of natural human rights, in his *Justice and the Social Order*, is judicious: 'Let us admit that it was the Christian view of life blended with the Stoic which created the conception of the equal dignity of all human beings' (p. 35).

4. Justice and shalom

It has already been mentioned that justice is closely connected in the Bible with holiness. It is just as closely connected with peace* – or, better, with what the Heb. writers called *shalom*. Shalom, however, is perhaps better translated into contemporary Eng. as 'flourishing' than as 'peace'. To experience shalom is to flourish in all one's relationships – with God, with one's fellow human beings, with the non-human creation, with oneself. Such 'flourishing' naturally presupposes peace in the usual sense, absence of hostility. But shalom goes beyond the absence of hostility, to fulfilment and enjoyment. A nation may be at peace with all its neighbours and yet, because of its impoverishment, not experience shalom.

There can be no doubt that justice was seen by the biblical writers as an indispensable component of flourishing in one's social relationships. Again, only an indication of the connection can be given here. Isaiah says that only when 'justice will dwell in the desert and righteousness live in the fertile field' will it be true that 'the fruit of righteousness will be peace [shalom]; the effect of righteousness will be quietness and confidence for ever' (Is. 32:16–17). And the psalmist says that, in shalom, 'Love and faithfulness meet together; righteousness and peace kiss each other. Faithfulness springs forth from the earth, and righteousness looks down from heaven' (Ps. 85:10–11).

5. Justice and love

The relation of love to justice has been a persistent theme of reflection by the theologians and philosophers of the church, from antiquity down into the 20th century. As to the relation of love to justice in *God's* case, the Augustinian view has been more influential than any other in the Western church: the sins of human beings make punishment something due to them; God's punishing human beings for their sins is thus a matter of retributive justice. Indeed, the sins of humankind merit everlasting punishment. However, God, out of a love which goes far beyond justice, has 'elected' certain human beings for salvation. The two principal difficulties which this view must confront are the fact that arbitrary 'election' to salvation seems unfair, hence unjust; and that justice and love are presented as if they were two unconnected attributes of God. On this last matter, Karl Barth,* in his *Church Dogmatics*, devoted a great deal of time to arguing that God's love is basic, and that God's anger must be seen as anger against all that injures those whom God loves.

As to the relation between love and justice in human beings, the standard view has probably been that love is something other than justice; and that, if we compare their deeds, the deeds of charity can be seen to *go beyond* deeds satisfying the demands of justice. That is the basic position taken by Brunner in *Justice and the Social Order*. To show that love and justice are two different things, Brunner emphasizes the personal character of love and the impersonal character of justice. As to the relationship between deeds of love and deeds of justice, Brunner concedes that there are difficulties in the 'going beyond' view, which none the less he embraces, since the coerciveness which the doing of justice sometimes requires seems incompatible with love.

It has been especially characteristic of the Lutheran tradition to see love in tension with justice rather than merely going beyond it. The tension was most vividly emphasized in our century by Reinhold Niebuhr* in *An Interpretation of Christian Ethics*. Niebuhr argued that the best we can and should expect out of social arrangements is justice, that the ethic of love preached by Jesus is in conflict with justice, that that ethic is thus an 'impossible ideal', but that we are none the less called to embrace it and live in the tension. It was characteristic of Niebuhr in his later writings to emphasize that the insertion of love into political and economic affairs is typically *destructive* in its consequences.

We cannot probe these issues further here. But it is worth recalling a point made earlier: in the Bible, God is represented as loving justice. That love is grounded in God's love for the victims of injustice. Perhaps it should be no different for us human beings. Love is a trait of character, whereas justice is a feature of social arrangements and interactions; so love and justice are indeed different. But doesn't charity require as a minimum that we struggle for the honouring of the rights of our fellow human beings? And doesn't love require, accordingly, an understanding of justice, and its practice? Perhaps, then, love is not entirely incompatible with coercion, specifically with coercion (see Force*) of the doer of injustice.

LAW, CIVIL AND CRIMINAL; LIBERATION
THEOLOGY; MERCY; NON-VIOLENCE;
PACIFISM; PEACE; POLICE; POLITICS;
POWER; PRISON AND PRISON REFORM;
PROFESSIONAL ETHICS; PROTEST;
PUNISHMENT; REBELLION; RECONCILIATION;
RETRIBUTION; REVENGE; RIGHTEOUSNESS;
RIGHTS, HUMAN; SECURITY; SENTENCING,
PRISON; SOCIAL CONTRACT; STATE;
STRIKES; TERRORISM; TORTURE; TRADE
UNIONS; VIOLENCE; WAR.

Bibliography
C. Avila, *Ownership: Early Christian Teaching* (Maryknoll, NY, 1983); K. Barth, CD II/I; E. Brunner, *Justice and the Social Order* (ET, New York and London, 1945); A. MacIntyre, *After Virtue* (Notre Dame, IN, ²1984; London, ²1985); R. Niebuhr, *An Interpretation of Christian Ethics* (New York, 1935; London, 1936); N. Wolterstorff, *Until Justice and Peace Embrace* (Grand Rapids, 1983).

N.P.W.

FOUR

Humanity

For the purposes of this article, the term 'humanity' refers to the human race or humankind. Previously, writers have spoken of 'the doctrine of man', but recent awareness of difficulties associated with gender-specific language has rendered the term 'man' problematic when used in reference to male and female alike. For this reason, the term 'humanity' is preferred.

1. Method

Theological discussions of humanity (theological anthropology) have conventionally followed an analytical approach. The phenomenon of being human is broken into its constituent theological parts which, when added together, are reckoned to provide a theological description of the whole. To be human on this account is to be understood as the sum of individual aspects.

Traditional analyses have consequently tended to abstract particular concepts such as the image of God* (*imago Dei*), conscience,* reason* and so on, and proceeded to expound their theological and historical development as individual components. Whilst the advantage of this method lies in its analytical clarity, its disadvantage is that it is essentially atomistic in its view of human beings. Moreover, such a method, in presupposing that humanity consists in a series of separable aspects, is necessarily ahistorical. The result is that a theology of human identity is rooted not in the formation of individual or corporate *persons* through social interaction and historical development, but in the ways in which *conceptual abstractions* have been understood over time.

An alternative approach (which will be followed here) is suggested by insights drawn from narrative theology. The question 'What does it mean to be human?' is accordingly answered by investigation of the human narrative supplied by biblically informed theology. Within this framework, it becomes possible to identify distinctive theological characteristics of humanity (such as the *imago Dei*) but to locate their significance within the unfolding theological story of the human race. They therefore cease to be logical abstractions and become instead narrative

21

4

themes grounded in theological space and time.

2. Alternative human narratives

It is worth noting in passing that all world-views rely upon human narratives to shape the meaning of experience for whole cultures and to provide the framework within which the 'mundane' stories of our individual lives can develop. Both liberal humanism* and Marxism (see Marx;* Marxist Ethics*) – the two most powerful philosophies of the modern westernized world – propose alternative narratives to that supplied by Christianity. In the case of humanism, the essential focus is the progessive rise of the autonomous, rational individual exemplified in Descartes' (1596–1650) famous dictum 'I think, therefore I am'. In the case of Marxism, individuals are submerged in the development of the society from which they take their identities. Society, in turn, is divided into classes, the development of which is determined by the operation of the historical dialectic. In both humanism and Marxism, the words of Pierre Simon de Laplace (1749–1827) about God are assumed: 'I have no need of this hypothesis.'

In contrast to these, the Christian narrative (in which history figures so prominently because Christianity is a historically revealed religion) takes its meaning not in the first instance from anthropology but from theology. Its primary reference point is God and only secondarily humanity. Human beings are not regarded as autonomous individuals but as social beings dependent upon the grace* of God. Autonomy and atomism are categorically ruled out. On a Christian account, therefore, the human narrative is derivative from, and contingent upon, the divine narrative, without which it would not exist.

3. The unfolding theological narrative

In theological terms, the narrative of the human race is structured by three decisive events: the original creation,* the incarnation (see Jesus*) and the consummation at the end of time. Such a narrative has its source in the creative determination of the persons of the Godhead to create humanity in their own image (Gn. 1:26). It must be noted, moreover, that human beings take their origin and destiny from the threefold God (see ☐) of trinitarian theology, not the singular god of the deists: 'Let *us* make man in *our* image.' The entire Godhead is involved in humanity's creation.

This trinitarian narrative takes specific Christological form in the first chapter of John's Gospel. Structurally, Jn. 1 echoes Gn. 1, but of particular significance is v. 3: 'Through him all things were made; without him nothing was made.' Thus the original narrative of human origins is filled out in terms of Christ and its trinitarian basis made plain.

Likewise, the Spirit is portrayed as central to the work of creation, not least of humankind: in Gn. 1:2 he hovers over the waters. In 2:7 he is breathed into the first human being so that only with the inbreathing of God's Spirit does Adam become a living being. The composite picture of humanity that emerges is one in which human beings individually and corporately are the creation of Father, Son and Spirit acting together. This has profound implications for the social nature of humanity.

Such a trinitarian understanding receives further support from the doctrine of the *imago Dei*. First, as we have noted (following Calvin*), the plural form of Gn. 1:26 suggests that the image is fundamentally trinitarian rather than unitarian, as is commonly supposed. Humans are not made in the image of God the creator but in the image of God the Holy Trinity. Secondly, Pauline references to the image emphasize that the original image was provisional rather than permanent: that it was only a prototype of that which was to come – namely the image of Christ who is viewed as the paradigm human being.

This is brought out in the 'two Adams' language of Paul. In contrast to the first Adam who was made in the divine image but who was not God (having been created from the dust), Christ as the second Adam is the beloved Son of the Father who, although equal with God, did not count equality a thing to be grasped but humbled himself and took the form of a man (Phil. 2:5–8). As such, he is 'the image of the invisible God' (Col. 1:15) who mirrors the glory of the Lord (2 Cor. 3:18). This means that through faith* in Christ, believers are renewed in the image of their creator (Col. 3:10) as they are transformed after the image of Christ the paradigm human being. 'Christ in his person fulfilled what God willed to make of man, an image of himself' (B. Rey, in J. Malatesta, ed., *A Christian Anthology*, Wheathampstead, 1974, p. 18). The centrality of the *imago Dei* as the defining characteristic of humanity is thus invested with a Christological and trinitarian significance.

In this way, biblical writers spell out the

primacy of theology in constructing the human story. The narrative begins with the sovereign creative will of the Godhead and, as it unfolds, is given definitive shape by the incarnation. Jesus is prototypical humanity precisely because he is the God-Man. A doctrine of humanity based on the Genesis account of creation would thus be incomplete. The narrative centre of the human story is Christ and it is he who gives it theological continuity.

In what does the *imago Dei* and subsequently the *imago Christi* consist? Broadly speaking, theologians have divided into two schools on this issue: *Substantialists* such as Irenaeus (*c.* 130–*c.* 200), Clement of Alexandria (*c.* 150–*c.* 215), Athanasius (*c.* 297–373), Augustine* and Thomas Aquinas* identified the key component as rationality: 'in the rational creature alone do we find a likeness of image' (Aquinas). As a consequence of this emphasis on reason and the mind, there developed a pronounced dualism* in which the mind or spirit came to be viewed as superior to the body (though in fact Augustine vigorously contended against a body–soul dualism).

Similarly, the image has been associated with the operation of conscience understood as an inner faculty, informed by reason and revelation, which informs the will. On this account, the combination of reason and conscience marks out humans as distinctive bearers of the *imago*. According to the Scottish theologian James Orr (1844–1913): 'The image of God . . . is a mental and moral image. It is to be sought for in the fact that man is a person – a spiritual, self-conscious being; and in the attributes of that personality – his rationality and capacity for moral life, including in the latter knowledge of moral law, self-determining freedom, and social affections . . .' (*God's Image in Man,* pp. 56–57).

The second school of thinkers, following Luther* and Calvin and represented among modern theologians by Barth* and Brunner,* identifies the image not in substantialist but in relational terms. These *relationalists* thus hold that the original image consisted in a threefold 'being in communion' established by God between humanity and himself, between human beings one to another and between human beings and the created world. 'The image of God . . . is to be understood as a relationship within which man sometimes stands, whenever like a mirror he obediently reflects God's will in his life and actions' (P. Ramsey, *Basic Chris-*

tian Ethics, New York and London, 1950, p. 255).

In the view of the present writer, the relational understanding is to be preferred for a number of reasons. First, it fits more adequately the trinitarian theology outlined above. If humanity is created in the image of the Trinity, it follows that the relational nature of the Godhead which is its central feature must be reflected in the structure of the *imago*. Secondly, to describe the image in terms of attributes is essentially to adopt a static conception of the Godhead. Yet the fundamental characteristic of the Trinity is its *dynamic* nature. Thirdly, it is questionable whether a substantialist view does justice to the notion of personhood, either divine or human. The substantialist view of God looks suspiciously like the god of the Greeks or the deists rather than the Three-Persons-in-One of Christianity. Finally, the relational view takes far more seriously the social, I–Thou, nature of the *imago*; the image is not to be understood primarily in individualistic but in corporate terms. The danger of the substantialist view is that it reduces the *imago* to a series of atomistic individual images of God located in individual human beings. On this interpretation, it becomes difficult to offer a coherent theology of the corporate *imago*.

An absolute opposition of substantialist and relational interpretations is not, however, strictly necessary. In principle, it is possible to synthesize the two provided that the language of attributes is cast within a relational framework. That characteristics such as reason, conscience and will* define the uniqueness of humanity can be agreed. Their role, none the less, should be understood as instrumental: they provide the structural aspects of human nature by which the distinctive threefold relationality of the Trinity can find expression. In this way, relational and substantialist interpretations of the *imago* can be brought together but only once the primacy of the former is accepted: the foremost defining characteristic of the image of God in humanity is its relationality.

How is the *imago* to be understood within a narrative framework? The Bible presents a story which begins with a wholly good original creation in which humanity in perfect fellowship with God is given responsibility over the created order. Human rebellion, however, brings the entry of sin and the unravelling of creation's original integrity. Yahweh's promise

4

to Abraham and subsequently his salvation of Israel act as signs of his universal intention to save the whole of humanity. Israel itself is to be the vehicle of this salvation.

However, it is the incarnation which opens the second act of this narrative drama. The coming of Jesus* Christ demonstrates the universal love (see ②) of God but at the same time paradoxically speaks of his judgment.* The cross witnesses to both sides of this paradox: it judges human sin but at the same time deals with it so that only through faith in the Christ of the cross can humanity find salvation. The incarnation, furthermore, anticipates the resurrection* of Jesus, which in turn establishes a new order of God's rule and vindicates his original creation. It is the firstfruit of a new order of creation.

The third act is prefigured in the second but does not unfold until the consummation of all things at the second coming of Christ. Then God will re-create a new heavens and a new earth (Rev. 21), which will include the resurrection of the dead to spiritual bodies after the pattern of Christ's resurrection body. Between the resurrection and the consummation, the church lives as the sign of this new creation. The Holy Spirit* in giving gifts and fruits to the people of God in Christ supplies a foretaste of God's re-creation. Christians thus experience something of the future kingdom* now but not wholly so. The period between the resurrection and consummation is an interim.

Within this entire narrative, the *imago* is to be understood relationally in terms of perfect fellowship* between humanity and God prior to the Fall,* followed by alienation* and distortion subsequently (though not obliteration, as Gn. 9:6 makes clear). The incarnation (including the death of Jesus) portrays an *imago* refashioned after the image of the Son of God by virtue of a restored relationship with God through the death of Christ. The resurrection symbolizes both the future consummation and the restoration of the threefold image through believers' relationship with Christ. It is not without significance that Paul envisages the consummation as encompassing the whole of creation (Rom. 8:18–22).

Whilst the image understood in trinitarian terms thus forms the theological centrepiece of humanity's constitution, three further aspects must nevertheless be noted: a. human somatic identity; b. social identity; c. sexual identity. All are closely interrelated within the human narrative.

a. Somatic identity. The human narrative is to be understood somatically (Gk. *sōma*, body). As we have observed earlier, the creation narratives make it clear that human beings are neither wholly spirit nor wholly matter but rather a combination of both. It is significant that a dualistic view of body and spirit is supported by neither the Genesis creation narratives nor the Pauline discussion of eschatological re-creation. The creation of Adam and derivatively Eve as representative human beings points to an integrated view of human existence. Body, mind and spirit comprise an interrelated whole, not separable parts. Thus Adam is made from dust but does not become a living being until the Spirit of God breathes into him. Likewise, Eve is a fleshly creation from the pre-formed man. The beginning of the human narrative is thus firmly anti-dualist.

By the same token, the incarnation underscores the structural integration of body, mind and spirit and affirms the significance of the human body. Against the docetic heresy which portrayed Jesus as a spirit masquerading as a man, the NT writers and early Christian theologians urged the full humanity of Christ. Thus 1 Jn. 4 speaks of the test of true faith as the acknowledgment that Jesus has come in the flesh. Since he is the paradigm human being, moreover, it follows that any theology which degrades or relegates the human body to an inferior place is anti-incarnational.

If the Christian theological narrative places great emphasis on the body as central to human identity, Paul's writings are of especial significance in this respect. We have noted that creation, incarnation and consummation mark the critical points in a narrative theology of humanity. Within Paul, however, the eschatological aspect is brought to the fore. Two observations are relevant.

1. We should note Paul's doctrine of the resurrection. In 1 Cor. 15 he stresses that the resurrection will be a resurrection of the body. This will entail each person at the *parousia* (the second coming of Christ) receiving a new body which, while resembling the first body in important respects, is nevertheless identifiably different. The pattern for this is the resurrection of Jesus whose post-Easter appearances made clear that the resurrection body is neither wholly like the previous body nor wholly unlike it. The risen Christ, for example, ate normal food but could dematerialize and appear in closed rooms.

The exact nature of the resurrection body,

therefore, must remain a mystery. What is important to recognize is that the NT knows nothing of immaterial souls or spirits persisting through eternity. Rather, the consummation will see a remaking of creation which will include the resurrection of human beings as unified somatic beings.

2. Paul's use of body language in 1 Cor. 12 and 14 suggests that the identity of human beings is to be found not in terms of individual development in isolation from others but rather in relationship to others. This clever play on the word 'body' thereby emphasizes once more the theological importance of viewing humanity corporately as well as individually and thus leads to the question of social identity.

b. Social identity. We have seen that on a trinitarian interpretation of the *imago* it follows that to conceive of humanity as a collection of individuals, all possessing their own separate image, is fundamentally misleading. The interrelationship of the Father, Son and Spirit as Three-Persons-in-One suggests that the image of God and therefore the nature of humanity is to be found in the constitution of human beings as *social* beings. As created imaging God, the human creature 'is at once and fully a relational being, a partnership, a co-existence'. The solitary, thinking individual posited by Descartes finds no place in Christian theological anthropology. To be human is to be-in-relation. In Heidegger's words, 'Being-in-the-world is a being-with.'

Once more, a narrative understanding of humanity illuminates this idea. The original creation established the social identity of humanity. The creation of woman is portrayed as the completion of humanity's creation. The solitary Adam is incomplete and inadequate to fulfil the purpose of God. Moreover, when the relationship between humanity and the rest of the created order is considered, it becomes clear that there is a qualitative difference between the kind of relationship that exists between human beings and, say, trees, and that which is established between humans one to another. Human beings stand in relation to the rest of the created order in terms of personal-impersonal; or as a number of writers put it (following Martin Buber, 1878–1935), 'I–It.' The creation of man in relation to woman, however, establishes an 'I–Thou' relationship in which human beings relate to one another in a different and greater way. In the words of

Helmut Thielicke,* 'This means that the relationship of fellow-humanity, represented by the man–woman relationship, is emphasized and given privileged status over against all I–It relationships' (*The Ethics of Sex*, New York and London, 1964, pp. 4–5).

The social character of human identity is consequently far from accidental or merely a facet of anthropological development. From a theological perspective it is fundamental. As Barth contends: 'The man who, because he is without his fellow man, has not become human, has not discovered the relationship of I and Thou, and therefore himself has not become a real I. He may be engaged in the most forceful action both intensively and extensively and yet he lacks everything for true humanity if he lacks the one thing – that he is not in encounter and is not therefore human and has no real part in humanity' (*CD* II/2, p. 261).

The meaning of society* is thereby rooted in the social nature of the Trinity and the creative will of the Godhead. The 'existence-in-community' of which Brunner speaks is constitutive of both the divine and human communities alike.

When we turn to insights from the doctrines of incarnation and redemption, the corporate nature of humanity is once more given central place. Just as Adam represents the whole of humanity, so with Christ. In taking flesh, the Word does not simply become a representative individual human being – he becomes representative of the human race. The incarnation is thus much more than an individual event. It is a corporate identification of the Godhead with humanity.

By the same token, salvation (see Sin and Salvation ⑤) is a corporate affair. The human narrative consists in the redemption not of isolated individuals but of the people of God. Both the OT and NT portray faith as a corporate encounter with God which includes, but cannot be reduced to, a collection of individualistic relationships with God.

This is nowhere more clear than in Paul's discussion of the church* as the body of Christ (1 Cor. 12:12). Here, believers are described in terms of a metaphor which leaves no room for atomism. Each part of the body (*i.e.* each believer) has an integral part to play within the body as a whole: 'The eye cannot say to the hand, "I don't need you!" And the head cannot say to the feet, "I don't need you!"' (1 Cor. 12:21). The fact is that all parts are linked by a relationship of mutual interdependence, for

4

'the body is not made up of one part but of many' (12:14).

The social implications of this are threefold: 1. Human beings are inextricably interrelated within a conception of society based on mutuality. 2. This interrelationship implies equality of status between members – to extend Paul's language, the eye is not superior to the hand. 3. There exists an irreducible responsibility between members of society to care for one another, notably the weak for the strong. The integrity of the whole body is such that what affects one affects all: 'If one part suffers, every part suffers with it; if one part is honoured, every part rejoices with it' (12:26).

The Christian church is therefore called to act as a model for renewed relationships within the redemptive purpose of God. Human society without God can only hope to imitate feebly the quality of relationships within the body of Christ indwelt by the Holy Spirit, but it nevertheless, through the *imago*, is not left without hope. The model offered by the Spirit-indwelt church cannot be copied but it can challenge and inspire. Only with the consummation, however, will society be renewed under the lordship of Christ.

c. Sexual identity. Increasingly since Freud,* Christian theology has come to recognize the centrality of sexuality (see [11]) to human self-understanding and to theological anthropology. Sexuality is now seen as constitutive of human identity (see Human Development*) and as a central component in the construction of individual and corporate narratives.

In terms of *theological* narrative, the origin of human sexual identity is to be found in creation. Adam and Eve are created as complementary sexual beings who together reflect the creative image of God. Humanity is therefore bi-polar in that it is created male and female. Moreover, since this bi-polarity is the outcome of divine creation, gender differentiation is not accidental, pragmatic or a matter of social convention. It must be seen as ontological, *i.e.* rooted in the very nature of human being.

This point is reinforced by further consideration of the *imago*. In Gn. 1:27, the *imago* is pictured both in corporate terms and in terms of the male–female relation. This relation is expressed in the term 'one flesh', which is not only a reference to the unitive character of sexual intercourse but also a powerful metaphor for the intrinsic complementarity of the sexes. As Ray Anderson (1925–) has put it, 'Human being is a polarity of being expressed as complementarity.' The sexual-relational nature of the *imago* is thus underlined. It is through the interrelationship of the sexes that humanity discovers its corporate identity.

When we turn to the incarnation, we find that although Christ was male, he represented in his person both male and female. His humanity, in other words, was *inclusive*. He saved humankind by virtue of identifying fully with humanity and in so doing brought us to God because he *is* God. Such a humanity, however, must logically be a common humanity shared by men and women alike as human beings, irrespective of gender. This is what it means to say that Christ's humanity is inclusive.

The kingdom* of Christ, however, relativizes human sexuality. By inaugurating the kingdom, Jesus established the beginnings of a new order of things in which the male–female relationship was put on a new basis. 1. In his discussion of marriage* he established that marriage is a provisional form of human relationship which will not exist in heaven: 'When the dead rise, they will neither marry nor be given in marriage; they will be like the angels in heaven' (Mk. 12:25). The present form of human sexuality is therefore not ultimate but penultimate. 2. As Paul indicates in Gal. 3:28, in Christ 'there is neither Jew nor Greek, slave nor free, male nor female.' In the kingdom of Christ, the old temporal order which governs the male–female role relation gives way to a new order of being-in-relation.

The key point here is that of temporality and provisionality. The period between Pentecost and the second coming of Christ represents an interim when the old is not yet dissolved and the new not yet fully in being. Thus marriage continues as part of God's purpose for humanity but not eternally. The breaking down of male–female role relations is a foreshadowing of the kingdom to come.

4. Conclusion

The narrative method offers a coherent way of understanding the character of humanity and its development. By focusing on the critical theological points in the theological story, it is possible to discover the interweaving of both the human and divine narratives. In this the pivotal character is Jesus Christ, who is the hermeneutical key to understanding how the two narratives are intertwined. It is in him that true humanity is found.

See especially: ADOLESCENCE; AGEING; ALIENATION; CHILDREN; CHURCH; CONSCIENCE; CONVERSION; CREATION; CULTURE; DEATH AND DYING; DEHUMANIZATION; DISABILITY AND HANDICAP; DISCRIMINATION; DUALISM; EDUCATION; EMBRYOLOGY; EMOTION; EQUALITY; FAITH DEVELOPMENT; FALL; FAMILY; FELLOWSHIP; FEMINISM; FLESH; FREE WILL AND DETERMINISM; FRIENDSHIP; GENOCIDE; GOVERNMENT; HEALING; HEALTH AND HEALTH CARE; HOLY SPIRIT; HOMOSEXUALITY; HUMAN DEVELOPMENT; HUMAN EXPERIMENTATION; HUMANISM; HUMANITARIANISM; IMAGE OF GOD; JESUS; LEISURE; LONELINESS; MARRIAGE; MATURITY; MENTAL HEALTH; MID-LIFE; MORAL DEVELOPMENT; MOTIVE, MOTIVATION; NATURAL LAW; NEIGHBOUR; PARENTHOOD, PARENTING; PERSONALITY; POLITICS; POPULATION POLICY; POVERTY; PRAYER; QUALITY OF LIFE; RACE; REASON AND RATIONALISM; RECONCILIATION; RESPONSIBILITY; RESURRECTION; RETIREMENT; RIGHTS, HUMAN; SANCTIFICATION; SCIENCE; SELF; SELF-ESTEEM; SEXISM; SEXUALITY; [11] SLAVERY; SOCIETY; STATE; STEWARDSHIP; TEMPERAMENT; UNEMPLOYMENT; VOCATION; WIDOWHOOD, WIDOWERHOOD; WILL, HUMAN; WORK.

Bibliography

R. S. Anderson, *On Being Human* (ET, Grand Rapids, 1982); G. C. Berkouwer, *Man: The Image of God* (ET, Grand Rapids, 1962); E. Brunner, *Man in Revolt* (London and Philadelphia, 1939); D. Cairns, *The Image of God in Man* (London, 1953); G. Carey, *I Believe in Man* (London, 1977); D. J. Hall, *Imaging God: Dominion as Stewardship* (ET, Grand Rapids, 1986); H. D. McDonald, *The Christian View of Man* (Basingstoke and Westchester, IL, 1981); E. Malatesta, *A Christian Anthropology* (Wheathampstead, 1974); R. Niebuhr, *The Nature and Destiny of Man*, 2 vols. (London and New York, 1941, 1943); J. Orr, *God's Image in Man* (London, 1905); J. A. Ziesler, *Pauline Christianity* (Oxford, 1983).

F.W.B.

5

FIVE

Sin and Salvation

Throughout Scripture and the Christian tradition, a constant theme recurs: there are two states, or ways of being, open to human beings. One is a state of inauthentic existence (to borrow a term from the existentialist philosopher Martin Heidegger, 1889–1976), in which humans are alienated from their true being and destiny; the other is a state of authentic existence, in which humans are enabled to achieve their full potential through fellowship with the living God. The first such antithetical state corresponds to the Christian idea of sin, and the second to that of salvation. For Christian theology, the full human potential can be understood (as being brought to completion in God through the consummation of all things in Jesus Christ) only in the light of the doctrines of creation and redemption, and achieved only through faith in Jesus* Christ.

Scripture uses a range of terms to refer to sin, embracing such meanings as 'falling short of a goal', 'breaking a relationship' and 'rebellion'. The common feature uniting these terms is the notion of a falling short of what God intends, a turning away from God to something lesser. Thus for Irenaeus of Lyons (c. 130–c. 200), sin may be thought of as the loss of our God-given identity in Adam, a process reversed (or 'recapitulated', to use Irenaeus' characteristic term) through Christ. The doctrine of original sin* gives formal expression to the biblical teaching that all human beings are born into a state of sin. This view, vigorously opposed by Pelagius (fl. c. 383–424) on account of its quietist* overtones, soon became the common currency of the Western church. Pelagius argued that sin arose through consciously deciding to imitate Adam, rather than sharing in his corporate primordial disobedience. In refuting this view, Augustine* pointed out that if Christ was the potential saviour of all human beings, it followed that all human beings require to be saved. For Augustine, the universality of the gospel promise of salvation implied the universality of sin – in all human beings, including infants. The natural human state is that of alienation* from God, in which love of self takes the place of love of God. Martin Luther* spoke of human nature as being 'curved in on itself' (incurvatus in se), as he stressed the egocentricity of sin. John Calvin* emphasized that sin was a 'hereditary corruption of our nature'. The implications of sin will be considered later in this article.

The Christian gospel centres upon the proclamation that, through the death and resurrection of Jesus Christ, believers are enabled to break free from this state of sin. Although the NT suggests that salvation is inaugurated, but not completed, in this life, it is clear that a decisive transition is envisaged. Through faith,* the believer begins to break the power of sin. The story is told of a little girl who asked a bishop whether he was saved. 'I have been saved from the penalty of sin, I am being saved from the power of sin, and one day I shall be saved from the presence of sin,' he replied. Christians are 'those who are being saved' (2 Cor. 2:15; cf. Acts 2:47; 1 Cor. 1:18).

Salvation and sin are both complex notions. The NT tends to understand salvation as the total package of benefits gained for and bestowed upon believers through God's actions in Jesus Christ. The ethical and pastoral implications of the Christian doctrine of sin and salvation are best (and most conveniently) explored by considering four of the primary images of salvation found in the NT, which have become major components of the classical Christian teaching on the matter. Each of these four foundational approaches to the concepts of sin and salvation has significant ethical and pastoral consequences, which will be considered below.

1. Salvation as wholeness

The Gk. verb sōzein, 'to save', is notoriously difficult to translate, reflecting the broad range of ideas associated with it. It can refer to any situation in which a person is delivered from a threat, such as from illness (Mk. 5:28) or from mortal danger (Mt. 8:25). Especially in the Synoptic Gospels, the verb sōzein is used to refer to both physical and spiritual healing* (Mk . 5:28; Lk. 7:50; 9:24). To be saved is to be made whole – that is, for individuals to be in a right relationship with God, with themselves, with their fellow humans, and with their environment. There is a fundamental link between 'health', 'wholeness' and 'salvation', which the Eng. language obscures through the post-Norman Conquest use of a Lat. term (salvation) in place of the Old Eng. term hoel. (This vital link is maintained in many modern European languages, such as Ger., Fr., and W. However, in Tyndale's NT translation, Lk. 19:9 is translated as 'Today health has come to this house'.)

Thus understood, salvation is about the achievement of wholeness, with sin understood as its absence. To be sinful is to exist within an incomplete or distorted set of relationships with God, with oneself, with others and with the environment.* Salvation centres upon the restoration of the whole person (rather than some fragmented portion of that person, such as the 'soul') to a proper network of relationships, embracing forgiveness* (restoration to fellowship with God and neighbours), healing (restoration of personal physical and psychological integrity) and a proper attitude to the world. On account of its broad scope, salvation can never be permitted to degenerate into purely individualist concerns. To be 'saved from sin' is not a private matter, but embraces the development of a series of right relationships.

Pastorally, this approach to salvation involves the recognition of the importance of a holistic approach to the person. The theologically informed pastor will recognize the need to minister to the spiritual, social and physical well-being and needs of the individual. Salvation is not, and cannot be, regarded simply as an initial act of commitment to Christ; it explicitly includes the process of working towards achievement of personal wholeness in the key areas just noted, for which pastoral support will be needed. Preaching, the ministry of healing, and a heightened awareness of the Christian's ethical and personal responsibilities towards others and towards the environment will be essential components of such an approach to sin and salvation.

2. Salvation as liberation

A cluster of biblical images for salvation centres upon the idea of liberation. Christians are those who are 'ransomed' (see Mk. 10:45; 1 Tim. 2:6) by Jesus Christ. The Gk. verb traditionally translated as 'redeem' (*exagorazein*) literally means 'remove from the market place' – in other words, purchase the freedom of a slave. For Paul, sin is to be understood as human bondage – *e.g.* enslavement to sin (Rom. 7:14) or to earthly powers (Gal. 4:3) – salvation as our deliverance from this slavery through appropriation of the action of God in Jesus Christ. Thus Paul is able to speak of the 'glorious freedom of the children of God' (Rom. 8:21).

Theologically, this idea has found particular expression in the great patristic motif of *Christus Victor* – the approach to the death and resurrection of Christ which lays especial stress upon a victory being gained over sin, death* and Satan.* Although especially associated with the early church, this theme has been reworked with great skill by writers such as Luther and, more recently, Gustaf Aulén (1879–1977). The basic theme is that Christ's death and resurrection are able to liberate us from the tyranny of hidden and unseen spiritual forces, which would otherwise exercise a baleful influence over us.

Pastorally, this concept of salvation is of considerable importance. Many Christians retain a sense of oppression by forces (psychological, social, economic and spiritual) which threaten to disrupt or destroy their faith. One such example is a fear of death. In his celebrated work *The Denial of Death* (New York, 1973), Ernest Becker pointed out how a fear of death threatened to tyrannize human existence. The coping mechanism devised by many people, he pointed out, was a simple *denial* of death: death is something that happens to someone else. The NT proclaims that the tyranny of this force has been broken. Through his death, Christ is able to 'free those who all their lives were held in slavery by their fear of death' (Heb. 2:15). Through faith, we are liberated from enslavement to this force. The Pauline stress upon the 'givenness' of Christ's victory over death (1 Cor. 15:56–57) echoes this point.

The pastor or counsellor will be aware of a network of forces which pose a threat to the fullness of the Christian life. Some individuals will find themselves coming under the influence of the occult* or Satanism, and will require to be delivered (see Deliverance Ministry*). Others will find themselves enslaved to debilitating habits, and require counselling and support if they are to break free from them. Martin Luther spoke of Christians being 'at one and the same time righteous and sinners', thus pointing to the potential continuing influence of sin in the Christian life, with patterns of bondage resulting. The pastor's task here is to enable individuals to identify areas of their lives in which such patterns of bondage remain, in order that the process of salvation may be continued by liberating them from this continuing spiritual oppression.

It must, however, be pointed out that there are oppressive forces confronting believers which are of a more or less directly social, political or economic nature. Latin American liberation theologians (see Liberation Theology*) helpfully refer to this as 'structural sin', thereby making the point that sin is expressed and embodied in the social structures created and erected, whether by intent or default, by human beings. Many individuals languish under appalling social conditions. Others are oppressed politically, through irresponsible and autocratic government. And others find themselves hopelessly entangled in economic difficulties. This serves to remind us that salvation has a strongly political and social dimension, especially in the OT prophetic writings. To be concerned for salvation is to be politically and socially aware, and committed to attempts to liberate people from such oppressive conditions. Once more, salvation is seen to extend far beyond individualist concerns, and to embrace a much wider range of issues (see Politics;* Social Ethics*).

3. Salvation as forgiveness

A central biblical theme concerns sin as guilt,*

5

and salvation as forgiveness (Eph. 4:32; Col. 2:13; Jas. 2:10). This notion of 'guilt' has been criticized by those committed to secular theories of legitimation and personal fulfilment – such as behaviourists, Freudians and Marxists – as perpetuating unhelpful patterns of submission* and introspection. It is thus important to stress that in this context 'forgiveness' is primarily a theological, rather than a moral, concept. While there is often an implied forensic or legal context to these concepts, their primary reference is not to moral behaviour, but to a broken and unfulfilled relationship.

The full implications of this approach to sin and salvation were developed by Anselm of Canterbury,* in his *Cur Deus Homo* (*Why God became Man*), written at some point during the 1090s. In this work, Anselm stresses the moral dilemma facing God in relation to human redemption. God cannot simply forgive sin by declaring it to be cancelled; he is obliged to take its moral guilt seriously, by acting in certain quite definite ways. The reality of human moral guilt is such that God cannot simply deny, cancel or overlook it. He must engage with it, and ensure that it is *justly* forgiven. Anselm argues that this involves a 'satisfaction'. Scriptural anticipations of this technical term, meaning 'a price paid as compensation for an offence', may be seen in the Heb. word *koper* (Nu. 35:31). A satisfaction for sin is required, if God is to be able to forgive human sin with integrity.

Anselm argues that, although sinful humanity ought to make satisfaction to God for the guilt of its own sins, God, in his mercy, has allowed Christ to make it in our place. It is we who owe the satisfaction; it is, however, only God who has the ability to make it. Therefore, in the incarnation of the Son of God, a God-man results who possesses both the obligation (as man) and the ability (as God) to make the necessary satisfaction, and thus gain full forgiveness for the guilt of human sin.

The central theme of Anselm's argument is the need for sin to be *justly* forgiven. This was developed by a number of later writers, such as Philip Melanchthon (1497–1560) and Calvin, who stressed the justice of God in dealing with sin through the cross. Christ's obedience was such as to merit, purchase or gain the forgiveness of human sins. Such approaches to the death of Christ are often collectively designated 'legal theories of the atonement'.

The death of Christ and the believer. A ques-

tion which demanded further consideration was the manner in which the 'benefits of Christ' (Melanchthon) affected the believer. How is the believer implicated in the positive consequences of the death of Christ? Three main schemes have been proposed, each resting securely upon scriptural foundations.

a. Christ as our Representative. According to this approach, Christ is seen as a covenantal representative of his people. A covenant* exists, established through the graciousness of God, by which Christ's benefits are shared by those whom he represents. To become a Christian is to enter within the sphere of this covenant, and to share in the benefits which Christ gained for his people. For Paul, the condition of entry to the sphere of this covenant is not 'works of the [Jewish] law', but faith (Rom. 3 – 4). It is not nationality, but faith, which establishes individuals as belonging to the people of God, and hence sharing in the benefits gained for that people by Christ as their representative.

b. Participation in Christ. One of the most significant phrases to recur within Paul's letter is 'in Christ' (*e.g.* Rom. 6:23; 8:1; 2 Cor. 5:17). This is a strongly participational idea, suggesting that the believer has been 'incorporated into Christ' (Calvin). Through faith, the believer's existence is caught up with that of the risen Christ. The believer participates in the life of Christ; he or she is 'in Christ'. As a result, he or she shares in all that Christ is, including the benefits he gained by his obedience upon the cross. Faith unites the believer with Christ, and all his benefits. To become a Christian is to share and participate in the life of the risen Christ through faith, and thus to have full access to his grace and righteousness.

c. Christ as our Substitute. A number of biblical passages suggest that it is appropriate to think of Christ taking our place (*e.g.* 2 Cor. 5:21). According to this way of thinking, our moral guilt was such that we ought to have been crucified upon the cross;* in his mercy, God allowed Christ to take our place. Important anticipations of this idea of 'vicarious suffering' are found in Is. 53:11–12, and echoed in 1 Pet. 2:24.

The moral and personal aspects of forgiveness. Each of the three approaches above aims to demonstrate the connection between Christ's act of obedient suffering upon the cross, and the life of the individual. But what of the pastoral and moral consequences of this forgiveness?

a. The moral aspects. In his highly influential work *Religion within the Limits of Reason Alone* (1793), the German philosopher Immanuel Kant* pointed out that the guilt of past moral sin posed a serious threat to the moral regeneration of individuals. The striving for moral perfection (a central theme of Kant's ethics) can be paralysed through a sense of the intrusion of the moral inadequacies of the past. It is therefore necessary, Kant concluded, for an individual to be assured that past moral guilt has been cancelled and wiped out, in order that the process of moral renewal might begin. Although Kant's work has a strongly rational and moral flavour, he scores an important point: moral renewal is impossible without the assurance of forgiveness.

b. The personal aspects. The significance of forgiveness for personal relationships is well established. The biblical injunctions to forgive others, as God has forgiven us, both stress the theological importance of forgiveness and give expression to the profoundly destructive psychological effects of unresolved tensions within personal relationships. Forgiveness is not about pretending that hurt has not been inflicted and offence not given: it is about acknowledging the reality of the hurt and offence, and allowing them to be handed over to and cancelled by God.

Two persistent themes may be detected within both the Synoptic Gospels and the Pauline letters: the *disproportion* between human and divine forgiveness, and the pressure which the latter brings to bear upon the former. It is far more costly for God to forgive us than for us to forgive our fellow human beings (Mt. 18:23–35). And the reality of that divine forgiveness places us under an obligation to forgive others (Mt. 6:14–15; Lk. 6:37). The demand that we forgive others 'not seven times, but seventy times seven' (Mt. 18:21–22, NIV mg.) is fundamentally a demand to *be of a forgiving nature*.

This point can be developed theologically, either through an application of the 'analogy of being' (Thomas Aquinas*) or the 'analogy of faith' (Karl Barth*). According to the former, the difficulties which we experience in genuinely forgiving others should bring home to us how difficult it is for God to forgive us. This reinforces the biblical stress upon both the costliness and the reality of God's forgiveness. According to the latter, the reality and cost of God's forgiveness of us (brought home by reflection upon the passion and death of Christ) provide a model for the patterns of forgiveness which should characterize Christian existence and behaviour.

4. Salvation as personal affirmation

One of the more tender insights into the Christian doctrine of salvation concerns the love (see ②) of God. The death of Jesus Christ makes plain the fullness of the overwhelming love of God for sinners (Jn. 3:16; Rom. 5:7–8; Gal. 2:20). An essential aspect of the Christian doctrine of salvation is that God acts in order to affirm his love for us, and to evoke a loving response from us.

In the period of the Enlightenment,* this insight was seriously abused. It was suggested by writers such as Hastings Rashdall (1858–1924) that the death of Christ did nothing other than demonstrate the love of God. This purely exemplarist approach to the cross (which Rashdall erroneously alleged to characterize the writings of the 11th-century theologian Peter Abelard*) treated human sin as little more than ignorance or confusion concerning the benevolence of God, which could be remedied by educational means. Nevertheless, this deficient account of this aspect of salvation must not be allowed to obscure the fact that it is an essential component of the total biblical portrayal of salvation.

The pastoral importance of this approach lies in its affirmation of individual believers. We are confronted with the paradox that God criticizes us in order to affirm us. The cross of Christ simultaneously exposes and judges us as sinners, and affirms the astonishing extent of the love of God for us. Richard Crashaw (1612–49) captures this insight in his poem *The Deare Bargain:* 'Lord, what is man? why should he cost thee / So deare? what has his ruine lost thee? / Lord, what is man, that thou hast over-bought / So much a thing of nought?' The cross affirms that God loves us, while we are still sinners. This insight brings dignity and meaning to belivers. In the midst of a dark, lonely and frightening world, God has affirmed them as individuals. The death of Christ is a striking and moving demonstration of the personal worth of believers. If God was prepared to go to such lengths to redeem them, they may assume that they are of value to him.

5. Categories of sin

Especially within Roman Catholic moral theology,* it has become increasingly common to distinguish between different types of sin.

The four categories most commonly encountered are the following:

a. Material sin. An action which is in itself contrary to the will of God, but which arises through ignorance or through coercion.

b. Formal sin. An action which is in itself contrary to the will of God, and which is committed in the full knowledge that it is so.

c. Venial sin. On the basis of 1 Jn. 5:16, Roman Catholic moral theology* recognized a distinction between sins which were 'deadly' or 'mortal', and those which were of lesser importance. These latter, referred to as venial sins, are not regarded as destroying the believer's relationship to God.

d. Mortal sin. A radical turning away from God to his creation, the extent of which threatens the believer's relationship to God. The traditional 'seven deadly sins', each of which represents a rejection of God in favour of some aspect of his creation, are pride,* covetousness,* envy,* lust,* gluttony, anger* and sloth. According to traditional Catholic moral theology, mortal sins can be expunged only by full confession* and contrition.

6. The ethical dimension of sin

Human beings are *sinners*. There is a flaw in human nature. We are fallen creatures in a fallen creation (see Fall*). The radical realism of the Christian view of sin has devastating consequences for our understanding of human beings as moral agents. Robert Browning (1812–89) expressed some such insights in *Gold Hair*: ''Tis the faith that launched point-blank her dart / At the head of a lie – taught Original Sin, / The corruption of Man's Heart.'

Luther and Calvin were among many writers to address the ethical implications of a radical doctrine of original sin. Luther pointed out that Christian ethical reasoning had to be based upon an attempt to minimize the sinfulness of human actions, rather than the utopian ideal that one can somehow act in such a way as to avoid sin altogether. Calvin stressed the need for appropriate social and political structures, capable of placing restraint upon human sinful actions, if the destructive effects of sin were to be minimized. The recognition of the reality of sin does not abolish human responsibility* for our actions; rather, it forces us to acknowledge that natural human instincts and attitudes cannot in themselves be regarded as right. As Calvin stressed, the gospel exposes sin for what it is, obliging us to concede that the law of nature (see Natural

Law*) is not necessarily the law of God.

The bland assumption of the natural goodness of human nature, so characteristic of much modern Western liberal thought, is called into question by this doctrine. The myth of human perfectability and inevitable progress has been shown up for what it is by the savagery and cruelty of the 20th century. As the American ethical writer and theologian Reinhold Niebuhr* stressed, the doctrine of original sin tells us that morality concerns weak, self-centred and exploitative human beings – *real* humans, not the perfectionist angels of wishful liberal thinking. Power,* capital (see Capitalism*) and force* – all can be, and will be, abused and exploited for personal ends, unless the political and moral will exists to control them. Niebuhr's 'Christian realism', which has had such a powerful impact upon 20th-century American social thought, laid emphasis upon the need to deal with human nature as it really is, rather than an abstract, idealized and utopian liberal concept of human nature.

The ethical implications of the doctrine of original sin,* touched upon by Calvin, have been further explored by Charles Curran (1934–), with particular reference to the concept of 'natural law'. Curran is especially critical of the natural-law doctrine to be found in recent papal encyclicals, such as *Humanae Vitae* (1968; see Papal Encyclicals*). For Curran, the 'disrupting influence of sin' affects both human reason, and the so-called 'nature' upon which natural law is grounded. Natural law has been used too often, in his opinion, in thoroughly sinful ways to deny human dignity, and thus it cannot be allowed to pass unchallenged. For such reasons, Curran rejects the optimistic and uncritical appeal to natural law which he regards as characteristic of many of his fellow Roman Catholics.

Curran also highlights the ethical implications of sin by his stress upon the ethical importance of compromise.* In sin-filled situations, it is often necessary to adopt a line of action which would be quite improper if sin were not present. There are circumstances in which the reality of human sin forces an ethical decision which is in itself sinful. As Helmut Thielicke* argues, Christians must frequently expect to encounter situations in which the outcome is not between a sin-free and sinful decision, but between decisions of varying degress of sinfulness. In such situations, Thielicke argues, the only appropriate course of action is to adopt the least sinful option, and, recognizing that it is sinful, ask God for forgiveness. It is this insight which underlies Luther's often misunderstood remark, 'Sin boldly, but believe more boldly still.'

The pastoral and ethical implications of the Christian doctrines of sin and salvation will thus be seen to be considerable. Christian ethics and pastoral theory and practice must be firmly grounded in doctrine, if they are to retain their distinctively Christian character, and not collapse into religious equivalents of secular ideas and practices.

See especially: ABUSE; ALIENATION; ATONEMENT; CAPITAL PUNISHMENT; CHURCH; COMPROMISE; CONFESSION; CONSCIENCE; CONVERSION; COVETOUSNESS; CREATION; CRIME; CROSS; CRUELTY; DEADLY SINS; DEATH; DEHUMANIZATION; DELIVERANCE MINISTRY; DEMONIC; DISCRIMINATION; EVIL; EXPLOITATION; FALL; FAITH; FORGIVENESS; FRAUD; FREEDOM; FREE WILL AND DETERMINISM; GENOCIDE; GOSPEL AND ETHICS; GRACE; GUILT; HATRED; HEALING; HEAVEN AND HELL; HOLY SPIRIT; HOPE; HYPOCRISY; INNER HEALING; JESUS; JUDGMENT AND THE JUDGMENT; JUSTIFICATION, DOCTRINE OF; JUVENILE DELINQUENCY; KINGDOM OF GOD; LAW AND GOSPEL; LIBERATION THEOLOGY; MANIPULATION; MATERIALISM; MATURITY; MERCY; MORTIFICATION; MOTIVE, MOTIVATION; NATURAL LAW; OCCULT; ORIGINAL SIN; PEACE; PORNOGRAPHY; POVERTY; PRIDE; PUNISHMENT; RACE; RAPE; RECONCILIATION; REPENTANCE; RESPONSIBILTY; RESURRECTION; RIGHTEOUSNESS; SANCTIFICATION; SACRAMENTAL HEALING; SATAN; SEXISM; SHAME; TEMPTATION; TERRORISM; THEFT; TORTURE; VICE; VIOLENCE; WAR; WASTE.

Bibliography

G. Aulén, *Christus Victor* (ET, London, 1931); J. P. Baker, *Salvation and Wholeness* (London, 1973); G. C. Berkouwer, *Sin* (ET, Grand Rapids, 1971); C. E. Curran, *Themes in Fundamental Moral Theology* (Notre Dame, IN, 1977); F. W. Dillistone, *The Christian Understanding of Atonement* (London and Philadelphia, 1968); E. M. B. Green, *The Meaning of Salvation* (London, 1965); A. E. McGrath, *Iustitia Dei: A History of the Christian Doctrine of Justification,* 2 vols. (Cambridge, 1986); J. R. W. Stott, *The Cross of Christ* (Leicester, 1986; Downers Grove, IL, 1987); H. Thielicke, *TE*; D. F. Wells, *The Search for Salvation* (Leicester and Downers Grove, IL, 1978).

A.E.McG.

SIX

History of Christian Ethics

The history of Christian ethics will be considered in this article as a history of engagement with philosophical ethics. Philosophical ethics starts in the Western world with the ancient Greeks.

1. Greek ethics

For the ancient Greeks, the primary authority in ethical questions was the Homeric poems, written down in the mid-8th century BC after a long oral tradition. These narratives of the Trojan War and the Return of Odysseus give a picture of heroic society and the virtues it praised, and of the proper (and improper) relations between humans and gods. The authority of Homer came under increasing challenge, however, in the succeeding centuries. In particular Socrates (470–399 BC) had difficulties with many of the Homeric stories about the gods, and with the traditional account of the virtues of piety, courage, moderation, justice and wisdom. He was condemned to death on the charges of corrupting the youth and not believing in the city's gods. In his defence, he urged that the real charge was that he had conducted his life asking uncomfortable questions about the nature of the good life and the virtues, asking people who were supposed to know the answers but did not. Socrates did not claim to know anything himself except that he knew nothing; he accused the Athenians of wanting to kill him in order to get rid of the irritation of having to think hard about these questions themselves. He did, however, have settled convictions, such as that it is always wrong to harm a man, even if he has harmed you first, and that it is worse to do wrong than to suffer it. He left no written work, but Plato,* his disciple, wrote up into dialogues the conversations he had heard.

Plato departed progressively, in the middle and later dialogues, from what Socrates had actually said. For example, he developed a theory of Forms out of Socrates' quest for definitions. According to this theory, we perceive in this world things which are, *e.g.,* red or beautiful or good; but these things have these properites by participating (though defectively) in the Forms, redness-itself or beauty-itself or goodness-itself, which exist in their own immutable world. We see the Forms directly only when our immortal souls are separate from the body; when joined with the body (in this life) we learn by being prompted to recollect the Forms by the right kinds of questions or experience. We can participate in the Form of justice if the highest part of the soul (and the highest class in the State, the rulers) recollects the Forms, and the other parts of the soul (and hence the other classes in the State) obey it.

Aristotle* was Plato's student. He said, unlike Plato, that the Forms are *in* particular things, directing their development towards mature exemplification of the species, which are (like the world itself) eternal. In ethics this immanence can be seen especially in his emphasis on the ends given to human beings by their biology and their culture. Human souls have the (plant-like) functions of growth and reproduction, and the (animal) functions of perception and movement, as well as the functions of feeling and thinking. The 'ethical' virtues* are the excellences of that part of the soul that listens to reason,* although it does not reason itself, and must be trained by habituation; the 'intellectual' virtues are the excellences of the reasoning part. Practical wisdom (an intellectual virtue) requires the perception of particulars as having or not having value, and links this to the agent's vision of the good, resulting in action. Aristotle's detailed discussion of the ethical virtues gives a somewhat nostalgic ideal of the Athenian gentleman. There is no attempt to revise or criticize this ideal. But he ends (surprisingly) with the claim that the chief good for human beings is a life of contemplation or study. This is the life closest to the divine, since Aristotle's God is 'thought thinking itself'. Aristotle does not seem to have a place for personal immortality.

After Aristotle, there were several schools of Gk. philosophy, of which the most influential was the Stoic.* For the Stoics, the highest instance of reason is God, who governs all events including human activities by an all-pervading 'law' or order (see Natural Law*). The human task is then to submit to that law.

2. The New Testament

The OT and the NT differ from the Gk. tradition in three major themes: 1. human beings are in the hands of a personal God (see ①), the God of Abraham, Isaac and Jacob, who chooses to save first his people (the Jews) and then those he will graft on to this vine by his own sovereign grace;* 2. this grace is a response to the Fall,* in which the first humans chose to disobey God's will and passed on this tendency towards disobedience to their descendants; and 3. this Fall was a departure from the order of creation,* in which God created all things, including human beings, good. These three themes (Redemption, Fall, Creation), are distinctively different from the Gk. tradition, and the rest of the story in this article is the history of the relations of these two traditions. Not all the story involves Christianity, however. In the Middle Ages, especially, we will see an important role played by Judaism and Islam. Within Christianity God's redemption of the world is by restoring creation through the death and resurrection of his Son Jesus* Christ, and eventually by the creation of a new heaven and a new earth.

The ethics of Jesus (see New Testament Ethics⑨), as portrayed in the NT, centres around the notions of love (*agapē*) and the kingdom* in which this love (see ②) is lived. The first commandment, says Jesus, is to 'Love the Lord your God with all your heart and with all your soul and with all your mind'; the second is to 'Love your neighbour as yourself' (Mt. 22:37–39). This love will require (as it did for Jesus) self-sacrifice. The kingdom* which he announces is one which brings peace* and righteousness, lifting the burdens especially of the poor and the oppressed. The early church responded to this teaching with a lifestyle of radical generosity, pacifism,* sexual abstinence and evangelical fervour.

3. The early Fathers

The early Fathers of the church were faced with the task of making Christianity accessible to the Graeco-Roman world. They did this in part by using the tools provided for them by Gk. philosophy. In the Western Roman Empire, the most influential figure in the carrying out of this task was Augustine,* who used especially the tools provided by the version of Platonism which he encountered. For Augustine, the Forms are in the mind of God, and God uses them in his creation of the world. Human beings were created for union with God, but they have the freedom* to turn towards themselves instead of God. If they turn to God, they can receive divine illumination, through a personal intuition of the eternal standards (the Forms). If they turn towards themselves, they will lose the sense of the order of creation, which the order of their own loves should reflect. Especially towards the end of his life, Augustine emphasized the tension between the world we are in as resident aliens, 'groaning with inexpressible groaning in our distant wandering', and our citizenship in the heavenly Jerusalem. Primacy is given by Augustine to the virtue of loving what ought to be loved, especially God. 'Love, and do what you will' expresses his view that humans who truly love God will also act in accord with the other precepts of divine (see Law*) and moral law; though love not merely fulfils the cardinal virtues, but transforms them.

The influence of Augustine in the subsequent history of ethics results from the fact that it is his synthesis of Christianity (the official religion of the Roman Empire after 325) and Gk. philosophy that survived the destruction of the Western Roman Empire. In the eight centuries that followed him in the West, there are several significant figures, such as Boethius (*c.* 480–524), Eriugena (810–*c.* 877), Anselm* and especially Abelard;* but for the history of ethics the more important developments are in the East. The Eastern Roman Empire survived Constantinople until it was finally taken by the Muslims in the 15th century. Knowledge of the ancient philosophers, especially Aristotle, disappeared in the West, but re-entered by a circuitous route. Aristotle was translated into Syr. and Arab., and was studied by Muslim scholars, most notably Avicenna (980–1037), after the Muslim conquests which eventually extended over N. Africa as far as Spain. In Spain, Maimonides (1135–1204), who eventually moved back to Cairo as chief rabbi, distinguished between the natural moral law, which can be known to people who have not received divine revelation, and the divine law, which is given in revelation, and which Maimonides analysed exhaustively. In Spain, Aristotle was translated from Arab. into Lat. and re-entered Christian Europe in the 12th century, accompanied by translations of the great Arab. commentaries. This new learning gave rise to a crisis, because it threatened to undermine the harmony established from the time of Augustine between the authority of reason, as represented by Gk. philosophy, and the authority of faith, as represented by the doctrines of the Christian church. There were especially three 'errors of Aristotle' which seemed threatening: his teaching that the world was eternal, his denial of personal immortality, and his account of God as 'thought thinking itself', which seemed to deny an active providence. These three issues (the world, the soul, God) continued to be the focus of philosophical thought for the next 600 years.

4. The late Middle Ages

Thomas Aquinas* denied that there was an irresoluble conflict. He set himself to show that Aristotle, properly understood, was consistent with the teaching of the church, and he used both Muslim and Jewish philosophical traditions in this task. We can think, then, of the differences between Plato and Aristotle as

6

recapitulated at least roughly in the differences between Augustine and Aquinas. Aquinas, like Aristotle, emphasized the ends (vegetative, animal and typically human) given to humans in the natural order. He emphasized the virtues (theological as well as cardinal), but he also talked of principles or rules. The rules governing how we ought to live are known, some of them by revelation, some of them by ordinary natural experience and rational reflection. But these rules are consistent in the determination of our good: 'God is not offended by us except by what we do against our own good.' God's will is not exercised by arbitrary fiat; but what is good for some human being is what may be understood as fitting for this kind of agent, in relation to the purpose this agent intends to accomplish, in the real environment of the action, including other persons individually and collectively. The rules of natural moral law are the universal judgments made by right reasoning about the kinds of actions which are morally appropriate and inappropriate for human agents. Aquinas was not initially successful in persuading the church to embrace Aristotle. In 1277 the Bishop of Paris condemned 219 propositions (not all Thomist), including the thesis that a person virtuous in Aristotle's terms 'is sufficiently disposed for eternal happiness'. But in the long run, the synthesis which Aquinas achieved became authoritative in Roman Catholic education.

Aquinas was a Dominican. Bonaventure (1221–74), his contemporary, was a Franciscan. One difference is that Bonaventure emphasized the unity and simplicity of the human soul (refusing to make radical distinctions between powers such as intellect and will), but held nevertheless that volitional activity and affective experience is more distinctive of humanity than is any cognitive activity. Another Franciscan, John Duns Scotus (1265/6–1308), held that the human will is free and rational by nature and superior to the human intellect, though it is the intellect by which practical principles are known and by which judgments are made about the conformity of concrete actions to those principles. A third Franciscan, William of Ockham (1284/85–1349), denied the reality of universals, asserting that the only realities are individuals, material or immaterial. He said that the will of God is the ultimate source of morality. 'Every right will is in conformity with right reason,' but reason is right because God has willed it to be so.

5. Reformation and Counter-Reformation

The two main figures of the Protestant Reformation are Martin Luther* and John Calvin.* Luther was an Augustinian friar, and it was his excommunication in 1521 that marked the formal break with Rome. He disputed the authority accorded to Aristotle ('that stinking philosopher') by Aquinas. Faith* alone, he said, is the instrument of salvation, and Scripture alone is the source for our knowledge of the faith. Luther was probably influenced (though the extent is controversial) by the followers of Ockham. He drew a radical distinction between the two realms of human existence (earthly and heavenly): reason rules properly in the first, but is constantly tempted to claim improper authority in the second. Calvin's emphasis is slightly different. He said that there is 'written, even engraved, upon the hearts of all' an inward law that asserts what the ten commandments assert. It is true that the knowledge of this inner law is corrupted by sin; our knowledge of God and his will is now so incomplete and distorted that nothing can be built upon it. But Calvin held that the main purpose of the law is not, as for Luther, 'to bring us to our knees', but to guide our grateful response to God's grace. A larger place is accordingly given to the possibility (through grace) of the Christian renewal of human social institutions. The source to which Calvin and Luther return, in their emphasis on the primacy of grace in human life, is the work of Augustine.

The Reformation was succeeded by the Counter-Reformation in Roman Catholic Europe. This had an influence on ethics through the attempt to formulate explicit rules for spiritual direction,* and through the encouragement this gave to casuistry* (the application of ethical rules to particular kinds of concrete cases). Thomism has a notable representative at this period in Francisco de Suarez.* Suarez claimed that the precepts of the natural law can be distinguished into those (like 'do good and avoid evil') which are known immediately and intuitively by all normal human beings, those (like 'do no injury to anyone') which require experience and thought to know them, but which are then self-evident, and those (like 'lying is always immoral') which are not self-evident but can be derived from the more basic precepts. A contemporary Protestant theorist of natural law was Hugo Grotius.*

He distinguished natural law both from human law and from 'voluntary divine right' which is revealed by God. Natural law is 'the dictate of right reason, showing the moral turpitude or moral necessity of any act from its agreement or disagreement with a rational nature' (*The Rights of War and Peace*, I.1.10, in B. Rand, tr., *Classical Moralists*, Oxford, 1897, pp. 208–209).

6. Rationalism and empiricism

The next two centuries in Europe can be described in terms of two lines of development, both of which resulted in the growth of an autonomous or secular ethics.

a. The history of rationalism on the continent of Europe, from Descartes to Leibniz. René Descartes (1596–1650), often described as the first modern philosopher, was not primarily interested in ethics. He accepted that traditional Aristotelian science had been undermined by Copernicus (1473–1543), Johann Kepler (1571–1630) and Galileo (1564–1642), and he proposed to re-establish knowledge on the foundation of rational principles that could not be doubted. The most important rationalist in ethics is Benedict de Spinoza (1632–77). He was a Jew, but was not regarded by his contemporaries as orthodox. Like Descartes, he attempted to duplicate the methods of geometry in philosophy. Substance, according to Spinoza, exists in itself and is conceived through itself; it is consequently one, infinite, and identical with God. There is no such thing as natural law, since all events in nature ('God or Nature') are equally natural. Everything in the universe is necessary, and there is no free will (see Free Will and Determinism*) except in as far as Spinoza is in favour of calling someone free who is led by reason. Each human mind is a limited aspect of the divine intellect. The human task is to move towards the greatest possible rational control of human life. Gottfried von Leibniz (1646–1716) was, like Descartes, not primarily an ethicist. He said, however, that the true good is 'whatever serves the perfection of intelligent substances', and the nearer creatures approach to this, the nearer they approach to perfect happiness.* The rationalists were not denying the centrality of God in human moral life, but their emphasis was on the access we have through the light of reason rather than through sacred text or ecclesiastical authority.

b. The development of empiricism* in Britain, from Hobbes to Hume. Thomas Hobbes (1588–1679) was impressed (like the rationalists) with the model of geometry, and also wanted to establish knowledge on firm foundations. But he wanted to do this, so to speak, from the bottom, from experience (especially the experience of the senses), rather than from the top (from indubitable principles of reason). All reality, he said, is bodily, and all events are motions in space. Willing, then, is a motion, and is merely the last act of desire or aversion in any process of deliberation. His view is that it is natural, and so reasonable, for each individual to aim solely at his own preservation or pleasure. In the state of nature, humans are selfish, and their lives are 'solitary, poor, nasty, brutish, and short', a war of all against all. The first precept of the law of nature is then for every man (or woman) pursuing his (or her) own interest, 'to endeavour peace, as far as he has hope of obtaining it; and when he cannot obtain it, that he may seek, and use, all helps, and advantages of war' (*Leviathan*, 1651; ed. A. R. Waller, Cambridge, 1935, p. 87). The second precept, given that every person has a right to everything, is that he (or she) should be willing to lay down this right to the extent that others are also willing. Twelve more precepts follow, including, 'Do not that to another, which thou wouldst not have done to thyself.' Right reason, which is the law, is thus made right by our approbation of it and voluntary subjection to it, but it is the same as what has been revealed as God's will.

The deists, especially William Wollaston (1659–1724) and Bernard Mandeville (1670–1733), believed that humans can reason from their experience of nature to the existence and some of the attributes of God, that revelation* and the mysteries of the faith may be unnecessary, and that the good life for humans finds adequate guidance in philosophical ethics. An example of such guidance is provided by Bishop Joseph Butler,* who argued that while both self-love and benevolence* are to be found in human nature, there is a superior faculty, reflection, which adjudicates between them. Francis Hutcheson (1694–1746) distinguished between objects which are naturally good, which excite personal or selfish pleasure, and those which are morally good, which are advantageous to other persons. He thought that God has given us a moral sense so that when intending the good of others, we undesignedly promote our own greatest private good. He concluded that 'that Action is best, which procures the greatest Happiness for the greatest Numbers'.

The most important figure in British 18th-century ethics is David Hume.* One basic principle of Hume's is that reason cannot command or move the human will. Since morals have an influence on the actions and affections, 'it follows that they cannot be derived from reason; and that because reason alone, as we have already proved, can never have any such influence' (*Treatise of Human Nature,* III.1, ed. L. A. Selby-Rigge, Oxford, 1951, p. 563). For Hume an action, or sentiment, or character, is virtuous or vicious 'because its view causes a pleasure or uneasiness of a particular kind'. The idea of morality implies that there is some sentiment of sympathy or (he later says) humanity, which is common to all human beings, and which 'recommends the same object to general approbation'. We should be careful, however, not to derive any proposition connected with an *ought* or an *ought not* from premises containing only *is* and *is not* (see Naturalistic Fallacy*). There is, that is to say, a gap between fact and value, and we must be suspicious of any ethical theory (*e.g.* any natural-law theory) that does not recognize one.

Finally, Thomas Reid (1710–96), the proponent of 'common sense', objected to what he held to be Hume's scepticism. He held that in morals, as in other parts of experience, there are universally accepted principles which need no philosophical proof; conscience* is the faculty which, on the basis of these common principles, dictates our duty.*

7. Kant and German idealism

Immanuel Kant* was brought up in a pietist Lutheran family and his system retains many features of Lutheranism. He belongs in the rationalist tradition from Descartes to Leibniz, but he was also, as he says, 'awoken from his dogmatic slumbers' by reading Hume. Kant's project was to 'deny knowledge in order to make room for faith'. He meant that our knowledge is restricted to the concepts of the understanding, whose domain he thought, following Hume, was confined to what could be experienced by the senses (namely, things as they appear to us, not things as they are in themselves). On the other hand, Reason and what Kant called its 'ideas' are not so confined. 'God', 'the soul' (and its freedom and immortality) and 'the world' are ideas of Reason.

Believing in God (as a rewarder of virtue) is required, he thought, if we are to lead a moral life. Starting from the fact of our experience, that we are bound unconditionally by our moral duty, Kant concluded that the authority of duty cannot derive from our desires or from the results of our actions. He reached several formulations of what the 'categorical imperative'* of duty must be. The most important are the first, 'Act only according to that maxim through which you can at the same time will that it should become a universal law,' and the third, 'Act in such a way that you always treat humanity, whether in your own person or in the person of any other, never simply as a means, but always at the same time as an end.' Kant wanted to translate, as far as he could, the tradition given us by revelation into a set of beliefs within the limits of reason alone, and he treated in this way the doctrines of creation, fall and redemption.

Kant's system was reinterpreted in different ways by his successors. Johann Gottlieb Fichte (1762–1814) presented an account of three 'moments'; the 'thesis', when the ego or self first posits itself and thereby exists; the 'antithesis', when the ego sets up the non-ego in opposition to itself; and the 'synthesis', when the ego without limitation (the Absolute) becomes aware that it must posit a certain limitation (or finitude) in both ego and non-ego. G. W. F. Hegel (1770–1831) also had a system with these three moments, but they are repeated again and again in a narrative or dialectic of development, which is the concrete evolution of mind or spirit as the realization of the Idea (God). The ethical life is, for Hegel, the idea of rational freedom; but it is realized in a set of customs and institutions, especially the family and the State. There is thus an absolute obligation to the State, as the embodiment of the Idea, and therefore of God. F. D. E. Schleiermacher* also emphasized the necessary sociality of thought, but he held that feeling is a form of self-consciousness not derived from other people, and that religion is the most highly developed mode of feeling, the feeling of absolute dependence. Arthur Schopenhauer (1788–1860) claimed that the fundamental energy which evolves in all things and produces all events is will: as individuals, humans are part of the world of appearances, but as things in themselves, they are united in the eternal will. In Britain Hegelianism was developed by T. H. Green (1836–82) and F. H. Bradley (1846–1924).

8. The nineteenth century

Søren Kierkegaard* saw himself as making a specifically *Christian* response to Hegelianism. He distinguished a number of 'stages on life's way', especially the aesthetic, ethical and religious stages. An individual becomes an individual by despairing of meaningfulness within his (or her) finiteness (within the aesthetic stage); if he then *chooses* that despair, he can find in this choice a self beyond the finite which has eternal validity, and he can then re-enter the finite by choosing it (this is the ethical stage). Kierkegaard is different from Kant in thinking that the ethical stage must itself be transcended ('the teleological suspension of the ethical'). It cannot itself be lived without self-deception, because of the irresoluble tension between the universal and the particular, what one ought to be and what one is. If a person will take Christ as a pattern (the perfectly divine and perfectly human), that person will see that by this standard he or she is always in the wrong (this is the 'leap' to the religious stage).

In England, Jeremy Bentham* adopted Hutcheson's principle that one ought to aim at the greatest happiness of the greatest number. The name 'utilitarianism' is given to the various kinds of theory which organize ethics under this principle (see Consequentialism*). Bentham held that we could determine what action this principle required by determining what pleasures and pains would result from that action for all the parties affected, counting each person as one and no person as more than one, and then measuring these pleasures and pains by their intensity, duration, certainty and propinquity. John Stuart Mill* carried the doctrine further by distinguishing qualities as well as quantities of pleasure; the ranking of quality was to be done by persons who had experienced all the types to be ranked. Mill saw himself as finding a way to apply the theory of Kant, rather than as providing a replacement, though many ethics textbooks deny that this is what he was doing. Henry Sidgwick (1838–1900) held that utilitarianism and egoism* would sometimes conflict, and that since both are reasonable, the only way to achieve a coherent system of our practical beliefs is to assert the existence of a moral power that will repay self-sacrifice and punish transgression. Unfortunately, he saw no evidence for the existence of such a power, and he therefore concluded (though he later questioned the need for

'evidence' in any standard sense) that the effort to frame 'a perfect ideal of rational conduct' is 'foredoomed to inevitable failure'. Sidgwick also objected to Mill's attempt to found utilitarianism on empirical principles of motivational psychology; no such attempt to derive an 'ought' from an 'is', he thought, had yet been successful.

Up to the middle of the 18th century there was a consensus, with various degrees of qualification, that there is an order of nature, which corresponds to an order within God's reason or will, and which it is the duty of humans to realize in their actions. In the 19th century this consensus was threatened by three intellectual developments outside philosophy, but within 'science' (though relying on premises not themselves in any narrow sense 'scientific'). Karl Marx,* following Hegel at some distance, claimed that ethical and religious systems are the by-product of political and economic relations. Charles Darwin* saw nature itself as developing over time, along with its species, thus making it difficult to hold to the fixity of natural law as traditionally conceived. Sigmund Freud* opposed traditional religion and ethics (*e.g.* the Kantian ethic that makes acute the tension between duty and desire) as repressive dictates from the super-ego. Much of 20th-century ethics bears traces of the influence of dialectical materialism, the theory of evolution (see Evolutionary Ethics*), and psychoanalysis.* Certainly, the antecedent consensus position became more exposed in this environment.

9. The twentieth century

There has been, nevertheless, a tension between those who welcome the progress of science and its model of clarity and rigour for ethics and for philosophy in general, and those who do not welcome it. This tension can be found within both major schools of Western 20th-century philosophy, the 'analytic' and the 'continental'. The difference between these two can be expressed geographically (like the earlier split between empiricism and rationalism) between on the one hand British philosophers and those in Scandinavia, Australia and certain schools of N. America, and on the other hand the rest of Western Europe and the Americas. Sometimes the divergence is said to be between those who do not and those who do read Hegel. Protestantism has tended to the first, and Catholicism to the second.

On the continent, ethics has been shaped

significantly in response to the attack on tradition by Friedrich Nietzsche* 'that God is dead'. Nietzsche wanted to get beyond the morality of the Jews, who exalted the values of slaves and the poor, beyond the 'old ladies' morality' of the Christians, in fact 'beyond good and evil' altogether. But it is a mistake to think of him as therefore a nihilist* about values, though his positive doctrine is hard to articulate. He preferred 'good and bad' to 'good and evil', admiring the values of Homer's heroes. The 'overman' is the human being who has organized the chaos of his passions, given style to his character, and become creative. Martin Heidegger (1889–1976) undertook as his quest to find what Being is; but before he could determine this, he had to ask about the nature of the being who alone among beings engages in this quest. Like Kierkegaard in his treatment of the ethical stage, Heidegger found the route to authentic human being leads through despair or dread (*Angst*), when a person's life as a whole loses meaning, but that loss is then chosen or appropriated as 'being-to-death'. This brings human being to its proper freedom, to make the decision that it cannot get beyond the norms into which it has been thrown by the contingencies of its birth. Jean-Paul Sartre* distinguished between being-in-itself and being-for-itself (again language from Kierkegaard), which is human consciousness, where the self (as in Fichte) generates its own nothingness by self-detachment. There is, for Sartre, no human nature or human essence to limit the openness of being-for-itself. The great virtue is authenticity, the acceptance of this freedom; the worst vice is bad faith, which is the individual's negation of this freedom (see Existentialist Ethics*). Though he does not belong in this tradition, John Dewey (1859–1952) also thought that there were no fixed final ends; and that we should therefore look for 'ends in view', proximate goals all of which may become means for further 'ends in view'. He emphasized education* in school as the place where this reconstruction of experience can be imbued with creativity* and intelligence.

To turn now to analytic ethics, G. E. Moore (1873–1958) objected to what he called 'the naturalistic fallacy', which is to identify 'good' with any natural property. He held that 'good' itself is a simple, indefinable quality, like 'yellow'; but unlike 'yellow' it is non-natural, and is known directly in itself by an 'intuition'. If we now ask, 'What are the pre-eminent goods attainable by human beings?', Moore's answer is, 'It is obvious that personal affection and aesthetic enjoyments include by far the greatest goods with which we are acquainted.' Analytic ethics, like analytic philosophy in general, was much impressed with the theory of meaning that confined meaningfulness to tautologies and assertions that could be in principle verifiable or falsifiable by sense experience. This theory put the meaningfulness of ethical judgments in question. One possibility, embraced by C. L. Stevenson (1908–78), was to analyse ethical language as having 'emotive meaning', which is dynamic rather than descriptive, having the function, *e.g.* of inciting people to action (as in oratory). This account had the disadvantage, pointed out by R. M. Hare,* of making it unclear how there could be ethical argument. Hare has proposed that there are three defining conditions of a moral judgment: 1. it must be universalizable (a condition which derives from Kant's first statement of the categorical imperative); 2. it must be prescriptive (if we assent to the claim that we should do something in some situation, and then we do not do it, we must logically be assenting insincerely); and 3. it must be (when considered reflectively) overriding, which is to say that we treat it as overriding all other prescriptions, including non-universalizable ones. Hare's view is that moral thinking, defined in this way, will be a kind of utilitarianism. There is, however, much analytic ethics that is not utilitarian. One prominent example is John Rawls (1921–), who has proposed a theory of justice which is also Kantian in inspiration. He asks us to imagine making judgments about what should be done as though we were behind a 'veil of ignorance', not knowing which roles in the situation we would play. He thinks that behind this veil we would agree on certain principles for the adjudication of disputes, and he thinks that these principles, unlike utilitarianism, have the merit of respecting the difference between persons.

Within Roman Catholicism Henri Bergson (1859–1941), though not primarily an ethicist, derived prescriptions about religion and morality from his theory of the *élan vital* (vital impetus) which underlies evolution. He distinguished societies that are closed, where morality and religion are an obstacle to human evolution, from those that are open. A follower of Bergson, Pierre Teilhard de Chardin (1881–1955), thought of evolution towards 'a point which we might call Omega', the integration of all personal consciousness. Jacques Maritain (1882–1973) was a student of Bergson, and developed a form of Thomism which retains the natural law, but regards ethical judgment as not purely cognitive but guided by preconceptual affective inclinations. Gabriel Marcel (1889–1973), like Heidegger, was concerned with the nature of being as it appears to human being, but he allowed more room for encounter with God. One recent movement has been liberation theology,* of which a leading spokesman from Latin America is Gustavo Gutiérrez (1928–). There are related movements in black theology and feminist theology. What these movements have in common is a commitment to relieving the condition of the oppressed; some of them believe a Marxist revolution is the only means to achieve this. Roman Catholic ethics has retained the tradition of casuistry, the detailed practical consideration of reasons for actions (*e.g.* the consideration of war,* and abortion*).

Within Protestantism, Karl Barth* reacted against the subjective 'religion of experience' of the tradition from Schleiermacher, and set himself to reassert the transcendence of God, the absolute lordship of Christ and the objective 'givenness' of revelation. He rejected all human ethics, and especially natural law theory, as merely 'the prolongation of the Fall'. This is not by itself to reject ethics, since 'the doctrine of God is at every point ethics'. Barth rejected also the Lutheran doctrine of the two realms, and put the State in the order of reconciliation, under the control of Christ. Paul Tillich (1886–1965) presented God as a practical answer to the anxieties of death,* meaninglessness and guilt.* He did not, however, think of God as personal, but rather as an ultimate reality, 'being-itself'. He defined faith as 'ultimate concern', which has being-itself as its object; but every human being has such ultimate concern, and it may be focused on different concrete objects which serve as more or as less adequate symbols of the Ultimate itself. Reinhold Niebuhr* distinguished sharply between love (*agapē*), which is by its nature sacrificial and seeks nothing in return, and justice which requires reciprocity and acknowledges the claims of self-interest. This tension gives rise to a 'Christian Realism' which simultaneously calls for a 'frank dualism' of ethics and politics, and holds the politician 'under the influence of the foolishness of the moral seer'. Paul Ramsey,* a student of Reinhold Niebuhr's brother H. Richard Niebuhr,* continued the tradition in his application of Christian ethics to warfare in the nuclear age (see Deterrence, Nuclear*) and to the new technologies of medicine (see Ethics of Medical Care[14]).

See especially: AMBROSE; ANABAPTISTS; ANGLICAN MORAL THEOLOGY; ANSELM; ARISTOTLE; AUGUSTINE; AYER, A. J.; BARTH, KARL; BAXTER, RICHARD; BENTHAM, JEREMY; BONHOEFFER, DIETRICH; BRUNNER, EMIL; BUCER, MARTIN; BULTMANN, RUDOLF; BUTLER, JOSEPH; CALVINISTIC ETHICS; CAROLINE DIVINES; CASUISTRY; CATHOLIC MORAL TRADITION; CHRISTIAN SOCIALISTS; CHRYSOSTOM, JOHN; CHURCH; CLAPHAM SECT; CRUSADES; DEVLIN–HART DEBATE; DISPENSATIONALISM; DOOYEVEERD, HERMANN; ECUMENICAL ETHICS; EDWARDS, JONATHAN; ELLUL, JACQUES; ENLIGHTENMENT; FLETCHER, JOSEPH; HARE, RICHARD M.; HIPPOCRATIC OATH; HOLY SPIRIT; HUME, DAVID; JESUITS; JESUS; KANT, IMMANUEL; KIERKEGAARD, SØREN; KING, MARTIN LUTHER; KIRK, KENNETH E.; KUYPER, ABRAHAM; LEWIS, C. S.; LUTHERAN ETHICS; MALTHUS, THOMAS ROBERT; MARXIST ETHICS; MAURICE, F. D.; MENNONITE ETHICS; MENNO SIMONS; MILL, JOHN STEWART; MORAL REARMAMENT; NIEBUHR, REINHOLD; NIEBUHR, H. RICHARD; NYGREN, ANDERS; ORTHODOX ETHICS; PAPAL ENCYCLICALS; PATRISTIC ETHICS; PHILOSOPHICAL ETHICS; PLATO; POLITICS; PROSELYTISM; PURITAN ETHICS; QUAKER ETHICS; RAMSEY, PAUL; RIGHTS, HUMAN; ROMAN CATHOLIC MORAL THEOLOGY; SCHAEFFER, FRANCIS; SCHLEIERMACHER, F. D. E.; SCIENCE; SECULARIZATION; SITUATION ETHICS; STATE; STOICISM; TAWNEY, R. H.; TAYLOR, JEREMY; TEMPLE, WILLIAM; TERTULLIAN; THIELICKE, HELMUT; THOMAS AQUINAS; THOMIST ETHICS; TOLSTOY, LEO; VIRTUE, VIRTUES; WILBERFORCE, WILLIAM; WITTGENSTEIN, LUDWIG.

Bibliography

V. J. Bourke, *History of Ethics* (Garden City, NY, 1968); R. J. Cavalier (ed.), *Ethics in the History of Western Philosophy* (New York and London, 1989); W. D. Hudson (ed.), *New Studies in Ethics*: vol. 1, *Classical Theories*, vol. 2, *Modern Theories* (New York, 1974); A.

MacIntyre, *A Short History of Ethics* (London and New York, 1967); H. Sidgwick, *Outline of the History of Ethics for English Readers* (London, ⁶1931); M. Warnock, *Ethics since 1900* (Oxford, ³1978).

J.E.H.

SEVEN

Practical and Pastoral Theology

7

'Pastoral theology' is a wide term admitting of many different definitions, whereas 'practical theology' has traditionally been used in a more restricted sense, especially in Scottish theological education, of the relating of theology to the practice of ministry.

1. Practical theology

The view that practical theology applies to the work of ministry owes much to F. D. E. Schleiermacher,* who analysed the tasks of theology into philosophical theology (the root), historical theology (the body) and practical theology (the crown). Practical theology studies the means by which the community of faith preserves and protects its identity. Within practical theology, the term 'pastoral theology' was used to discuss that aspect of the church's practice which was particularly concerned with the cure of souls, including a theology of ministry. In Schleiermacher, it focused largely on the functions of preaching and administration of the sacraments.

Although there are those who still use the term 'practical theology' in this way, there has been a considerable revolution in the concept in recent decades, and a more fundamental interpretation of practical theology advanced which sees it not as the practice of theology but as the theology of practice. Given a particular direction through the work of Anton Boisen,* who exercised considerable influence on the development of Clinical Pastoral Education in the USA in the middle of this century, and

whose approach had a large effect on such post-war teachers of pastoral theology as Seward Hiltner,* Wayne E. Oates (1917–) and Carroll Wise, the focus of interest in practical theology shifted from the application of doctrine in pastoral settings, to a critical dialogue between theology and praxis.* This new-style practical theology is concerned with the way in which the faith of the church works out in practice in the world and raises questions about what it sees, addressing them back to theology. One of the leading contemporary exponents is Don Browning (1934–) of the Chicago University Divinity School, who has drawn heavily on the recent recovery of the tradition of 'practical wisdom' in philosophy, to argue that all theological thinking, including systematic and historical theology, is essentially practical. The social and intellectual context in which theology is put into practice is brought into conversation with the vision implicit in pastoral practice itself, and with the normative interpretations of the faith handed down in the traditions of the church. Theology thus arises from practice, moves into theory, and is then put into practice again.

2. Pastoral theology

Pastoral theology (what Browning calls 'strategic practical theology') primarily concerns the church disciplines of religious education,* pastoral care, preaching, liturgy, mission, evangelism* and social ministries. There is still a wide spread of meanings in the term 'pastoral theology', however.

Eduard Thurneysen* uses the term to describe a theology of pastoral care which is part of the task of proclamation of the Word of God. Thomas Oden (1931–), perhaps too broadly, speaks of the task of pastoral theology being 'to reflect upon the self-disclosure of God witnessed by the Scriptures, mediated through tradition, reflected on by critical reasoning, and embodied in personal and social experience' (*Pastoral Theology*, p. 311). David Deeks gives a much less focused approach. For him, pastoral theology is concerned with the conversations that people have which betray their search for meaning in life. The pastoral theologian is to enter into those conversations, at first as if there were no God, but fully convinced that there must be more to life than meets the eye. From this starting-point, the pastor is like an artist who uses a wide range of sources to encourage reflection – including the Bible – in order to help people discover the meaning and sense of their experience, and to connect it with the Christian tradition. Probably Seward Hiltner's approach in *Preface to Pastoral Theology* has been as influential as any. The traditional concerns of discipline, edification and comfort were replaced in Hiltner by a case-study approach to healing, sustaining, guiding, communicating and organizing. He defines pastoral theology as 'that branch or field of theological knowledge and inquiry that brings the shepherding perspective to bear upon all operations and functions of the church and minister, and then draws conclusions of a theological order from reflection on these observations' (p. 20). Hiltner and others have been criticized for focusing too much on the rural metaphor of 'shepherd', and for the loss of an adequate historical and moral dimension to pastoral theology, which was increasingly becoming identified with Rogerian (see Rogers, Carl*) approaches to non-directive counselling.

Three major concerns have been expressed about this period of 'psychological captivity'. 1. Browning and others noted that the moral basis for much pastoral theology was inadequate. Non-directive counselling often lacked any ethical input. 2. Alistair Campbell (1938–) and others voiced the concern that the social and political dimensions had been neglected at the expense of the purely individual and personal dimension. 3. As

Thomas Oden has recently written in his major work, *Pastoral Theology*, pastoral theology has lost touch with its classical theological roots and may be in danger of rejecting its heritage.

Perhaps James Lapsley's (1930–) definition of pastoral theology is the clearest: 'the study of all aspects of the care of persons in the church, in a context of theological inquiry, including implications for other branches of theology' ('Pastoral Theology Past and Present' in W. B. Oglesby, Jr., ed., *The New Shape of Pastoral Theology*, Nashville, TN, 1969, p. 43).

Biblical and historical roots. The history of pastoral care in the Christian church is illustrated elsewhere (see Pastoral Care, Counselling and Psychotherapy[12]). It is important to remind ourselves, though, that much of this history is rooted in the view that the biblical documents themselves are in many cases written as pastoral documents.

The Old Testament is a rich mine of pastoral theology and repays careful excavation. Some of its pastoral deposits are obvious. The book of Job not only grapples with the problem of suffering* but demonstrates, through the role given to Job's friends, how easy it is to engage in careless pastoral theology and mistaken pastoral approaches to suffering people. The Psalms frequently give voice to human experience and bring that experience into the light of knowledge about God. Ecclesiastes gives vent to the existential *Angst* felt by many in the face of life's apparent meaninglessness. It hints at answers which lead to a different perspective on life, but treads cautiously so as not to trespass on the depth of the anguish felt.

Other parts of the OT have pastoral deposits which require deeper excavation. The story of the people of Israel is not recorded for barren historical purposes but so that future generations may know both their own identity and the identity of the God of the covenant* (Dt. 6:1–25). The prophetic writings often address the complex pastoral dilemmas of God's people. Habakkuk confronts the question of the holiness of God in the light of the injustice experienced by his people. Hosea speaks in rich pastoral tones concerning the unquenchable love of God for his people in spite of their waywardness. Isaiah 40 – 66 speaks to the people troubled by their experience of exile and of the seeming defeat of the dynasty of David. Isaiah's answer is to lead the people to a more splendid understanding of God –

7

whom they thought to have hidden himself from them – than anywhere else in the OT. Haggai addresses a people struggling to discover the glory of God as they settle back in the land God gave them and battle with all the disappointments which that entailed. He points them not only to the requirements of practical action but to hope for the future. These examples demonstrate that the pastoral dimension is a major aspect of the intention of these documents.

The Gospels have traditionally been seen as historical, theological or evangelistic documents, but contemporary approaches have shown a much greater awareness of their pastoral dimensions. This awareness owes much to redaction criticism and the consideration of the audiences to which they might have been addressed.

Matthew's Gospel addresses the problems thrown up by a rapidly expanding church, composed of a mixture of Jews and Gentiles, some of whom would have argued for a strict adherence to Jewish inheritance and law,* and others of whom would have sat loose to traditions and the law. This raised issues of the meaning of discipleship and called forth a pastoral strategy which emphasizes the teaching of Jesus. The law's demands remain in force (Mt. 5:17–20) and must be obeyed. But its demands are intensified and internalized (*e.g.* Mt. 5:21–48). At the same time, and standing in tension with such high demands, there is to be a rejection of legalism* and a concern for the little and vulnerable ones. Jesus, the one who fulfils OT prophecies, is shown to have commanding authority, and his disciples are cast in the role of learners. The true test of their learning was their obedience (Mt. 21:28–32).

Mark's strategy is to portray the actions of Jesus, particularly in regard to the theme of suffering. Throughout he displays a realism about the cost of discipleship and points to an identity between disciples who experience conflict as a result of their faith in the 'Son of Man'. Such an approach would have provided those being persecuted as Christians in Rome, or elsewhere, with strength to endure until their final vindication and reward (Mk. 10:29–31; 13:16–27).

Luke's pastoral agenda finds its focus in Theophilus, who appears to be full of doubts and uncertainties about the faith. Among the items which can be identified are questions concerning the place of the church in the plan of God and the sweep of history; uncertainty caused by the delay in the return of Christ; disappointment caused by failures in the church and by its lack of progress and questions about the nature of its socially mixed composition. Luke responds to the questions by telling stories, which recount the ministry of Jesus and the life of the early church, letting them speak for themselves.

John 20:31 defines the purpose of John's Gospel as to encourage belief. The belief may not refer, as has often been assumed, to initial belief so much as to continuing belief – the tense of the verb, although disputed, indicating this. With the passing of the original eyewitnesses to Jesus Christ, hostility shown to the early Christians by those in the synagogues, and differences emerging over the nature of Jesus Christ, this Gospel speaks to those pastoral situations by deep reflection on the life of Jesus Christ by one who claims to have been an eyewitness.

The Gospels, then, may be read as pastoral documents which use a variety of pastoral techniques to address the real-life pastoral situations of their recipients.

The letters are more explicitly pastoral documents, usually addressed to destinations and situations which are apparent. Thus, for example, 1 Thessalonians is addressed to a young congregation facing bewilderment in its early days because the apostle had been torn away from them (1 Thes. 2:17). Galatians is written to those whose freedom in Christ is under threat by those who would impose the cultural and legal requirements of the Jewish law on them (Gal. 5:1–6). Most of them contain instruction as to how to live in situations where they are surrounded by unbelievers.

Paul's pastoral approach is a didactic one which always relates the experience of his readers to the doctrines of the faith. So, to take but one issue, in seeking to address the question of division in the otherwise happy fellowship of Philippi (Phil. 2:2–4; 4:2–3), Paul relates their behaviour to the incarnation of Christ (2:5–11). In Ephesians the same issue is dealt with in relation to the unity of the Godhead (Eph. 4:1–6). Wherever possible Paul's teaching is set in the context of warm encouragement (*e.g.* Col. 1:3–14; 1 Thes. 1:2–10). But he is equally capable of open rebuke when the occasion demands (*e.g.* 1 Cor. 11:17; Gal. 1:6).

In addition to dealing plainly with pastoral issues the letters of Paul reveal something of the deep structures of pastoral relationships. Throughout his writings Paul refers to his aim of producing mature believers (Eph. 4:13; Col. 1:28) and of 'building up' the communities of believers (Rom. 15:2; 1 Cor. 14:12; Eph. 2:22; 4:29). Any authority he has is only for use towards these constructive ends (2 Cor. 10:8; 13:10). It is contradictory for the servants of Jesus to claim inherent rights. In all their dealings with others pastors must be aware that they, like them, are accountable to their master (1 Cor. 3:10–15; 9:24–27; 2 Cor. 5:9–15). Pastoral progress, then, depends on the quality of the relationship and on mutual trust, openness and love (2 Cor. 7:2–4, 10–13).

The other 'general' letters are equally pastoral in their intent but more varied in their approach. Hebrews engages in a careful exposition of the superiority of the new covenant to the old for those who are tempted to give in to the pressures of believing and revert to worship in the Jewish synagogue. James, with its direct and blunt approach, may be described as pastoral first-aid for believers who suffer, among other things, from economic oppression. 1 Peter excels as a pastoral letter in both its content and its style, and gives much encouragement to those starting out on the journey as Christians, and suffering for it, by a closely woven texture of doctrine and practice. John's letters are marked by a thoroughness of teaching style, gentle sympathy, strong warnings and Christ-centredness. 2 Peter and Jude adopt the more unusual approach of apocalyptic, which can equally be effective in providing a strong dose of pastoral medicine.

3. Theology of ministry

A substantial component of pastoral theology concerns a theology of ministry.* Any consideration of ministry must be much broader than the official and ordained ministry of the church. Ministry is simply service (*diakonia*), and takes place when the gifts of God's grace (*charismata*) are employed in the service of others, and when the functions of ministry are fulfilled (1 Cor. 12:1–11). The NT stresses that Christians should mutually minister to one another (Gal. 5:13; 6:2; Eph. 4:2, 32; Col. 3:16; 1 Thes. 3:12; 4:9, 18; 1 Pet. 4:9; 5:5; 1 Jn. 3:23). This may happen in formal or informal settings and involve those who are ordained or lay.

Yet the church also has regular ministers who are set apart to serve the church as their primary occupation, and it is the privilege and duty of the church to support them (1 Cor. 9:7–14; Gal. 6:6).

a. The task. A succinct statement of the pastoral task is first outlined in Ezk. 34:16, which, though originally directed to the political leaders of Israel, none the less can be applied to the work of pastors. The shepherd engages in searching, guiding, healing, nurturing and governing. Contemporary pastoral theology often defines the task of the pastor in similar terms as that of healing, sustaining, guiding, reconciling and nurturing.

In the NT, the goal of pastoring is to facilitate maturity* in the believer (Col. 1:28–29; Eph. 4:15). Maturity is to live fully as a person released from 'the dominion of darkness' and under the kingship of Christ (Col. 2:12–13). It is to live freely as a son of God (Gal. 3:26 – 4:7; 5:1), and faithfully in step with the Holy Spirit (Gal. 5:16 – 6:5; Eph. 5:1–21). It is to work increasingly through the implications of the gospel. The constant call is for believers progressively to realize their position in Christ and to live in a manner which is congruent with it (Eph. 4:1ff.).

In seeking to 'build up' the Christians (2 Cor. 10:8; Col. 2:6–7), Paul constantly relates their experience of life, the world and the church to the revealed doctrines of God (see ▣), Christ, the Holy Spirit,* creation,* salvation, *etc.* It is a correct understanding of truth that will lead them not only to live in an ethically correct way but also to experience true wholeness (shalom). Earle Ellis (1926–) has recently questioned whether the traditional picture of the minister as a minister of the Word and sacrament is quite accurate in biblical terms, since the NT does not indicate the sacraments to be a significant part of ministry. There is, however, greater emphasis on the teaching role of the pastor.

b. Dimensions of ministry. A fuller understanding of the nature of ministry can be acquired by an examination of the various titles applied to those who minister.

Among the many which highlight one aspect of the ministry or another are: Paul sees himself as the *servant*, even slave, of Christ (Rom. 1:1; Gal. 1:10; 2 Cor. 11:23), of God (2 Cor. 6:4) and of the gospel (Eph. 3:7; Col. 1:23), for the sake of the church. The word *diakonos* also comes to be used in the more defined sense of leaders within the church who have practical responsibilities in their care for the fellowship

(Phil. 1:1 and 1 Tim. 3:8–13). The title *steward* (1 Cor. 4:1; Tit. 1:7) stresses that the minister's responsibility is to manage the resources and fulfil the commission of his master rather than to create any basis for ministry in himself or herself. A related development of this word group emphasizes that the stewardship* is a stewardship of the gospel (Eph. 3:8–9).

A number of titles highlight ministry from the perspective of government. The pastor is an *overseer* (*episkopos* or *presbyteros*, Acts 14:23; 20:17, 28; 1 Tim. 3:1–7; 5:17–20; 1 Pet. 5:1–4), *pilot*, or leader (1 Cor. 12:28), or *president* (Rom. 12:8). The work of the ministry from this perspective is to give direction to the community of Christ's people and to individuals within it. Whilst evidently referring to a recognized position within the church, the greater stress of NT teaching lies not on the authority of their role but on the spiritual responsibility which falls to them in their role (1 Cor. 9:27; Heb. 13:17; 1 Pet. 5:1–4).

Three particular names draw attention to the specific functions of the ministry. *Priest* draws attention to the liturgical dimension of pastoring. But it is surprisingly little used, Rom. 15:16 being the only time Paul uses it to refer to a leadership role. Even there, what makes it 'priestly' is the 'duty of proclaiming the gospel of God'. Priesthood, in the new covenant, is devolved on all the people of God (1 Pet. 2:9; Rev. 1:6; 5:10). The leadership of worship is not explicitly referred to as the task of the priest or president (1 Cor. 14:26; Col. 3:16; 1 Tim. 2:1). *Teacher* and its cognates is a much more frequent concept (Rom. 12:7; 1 Cor. 12:28; Eph. 4:11, 20–21; Col. 1:28) and receives special emphasis in the pastoral letters (1 Tim. 2:7; 3:2; 4:11; 6:1–2; 2 Tim. 1:11; 4:3; Tit. 2:1, 15). It involves the learning of right doctrine (2 Tim. 1:13). Teaching is undertaken both by verbal instruction and the imparting of example (1 Tim. 4:11–14), and is dependent for its effectiveness on the ministry of the Holy Spirit.

There is no exact equivalent in the NT to the contemporary term 'counsellor', the accepting listener who enters into the problems of another and gives encouragement and possibly direction. The task of the counsellor is, however, related to the work of the Holy Spirit (*paraklētos*, Jn. 14:16, 26; 15:26; 16:7), is an extension of the ministry of exhortation (*paraklēsis*, Rom. 12:8; 1 Cor. 14:31), and can be seen as a frequent aspect of Paul's own ministry (Rom. 12:1; 2 Cor. 10:1; Phil. 2:1, *etc.*). The contemporary emphasis on individual counselling may owe more to an absence of corporate teaching and a lack of agreed doctrinal consensus in our churches than to an exact role model within the NT (note 1 Cor. 12:28). Others would refer to 'confronting' or 'setting right' (*nouthesia,* Eph. 6:4; Col. 1:28; Tit. 3:10) as a neglected aspect of biblical counselling, but Col. 1:28 and 3:16 both clearly link admonition to teaching. The doctrinal understanding and theological orientation of the counsellor has a marked effect on the method and style of counselling adopted.

c. The method of ministry. No systematic statement of the method of ministry is given, but some methodological consequences arise from the terms reviewed and a number of other key principles are evident. The quality of relationship, implicit in the shepherding motif, is vital in determining the success of pastoring. The long-running and variable relationship between Paul and the Corinthian church is an illustration of this. In all his relationships he tries to compliment, remind believers of what they know, build on what is good and encourage, but he is not afraid to offer blunt criticism and correction when they are needed.

The approach to individuals is never stereotyped but always sensitively takes account of their needs, situations and personalities (1 Thes. 5:14). Sometimes Paul instructs the ignorant, sometimes he encourages the weak and fearful, and sometimes he warns the wayward and stubborn.

All this is done in the context of Paul modelling the gospel in his own life and setting an example which serves both as an incentive and standard for others (1 Cor. 4:16–17; Phil. 3:17; 1 Thes. 1:6; 2:14; 1 Tim. 1:16).

4. The church as a therapeutic community

Human beings were made in the image of God* and for relationships with each other, but sin has marred, distorted and damaged both (see Fall*). Good relationships, however, of all kinds, may be therapeutic and cause a person to know healing or facilitate progress towards wholeness.

The church* should be the best therapeutic community in the world. Unlike any therapeutic community built around a psychological counsellor for his clients, it is not an artificial community. It emphasizes acceptance (Rom.

15:7), forgiveness (Eph. 4:32), compassion (Phil. 2:1; Col. 3:12) and grace – an unconditional and divine love (Jn. 13:34–35; Rom. 12:9–10; 1 Cor. 13; Gal. 5:13). These qualities arise because all have received acceptance,* forgiveness,* compassion* and grace* from Christ themselves. A true fellowship* (*koinōnia*) is therefore created. Fellowship is not the sharing of a common interest but a participation in the receipt of grace. This makes for an equality of love. Fellowships which are formed on the basis of a common interest in race, colour, sex, class, status, age or even moral background are illegitimate (Col. 3:11). True fellowship should provide security and be an ideal soil in which hurts can be healed and maturity reached. Furthermore, relationships within the fellowship are not hierarchical but brother to brother and sister to sister. They differ therefore from the doctor/patient or therapist/client relationship. All members, pastor no less than others, stand in a common need of grace and should stand in common submission under God's Word. Many contemporary structures within the church have failed to model this adequately, as hierarchical, patriarchal, and other structures of respectability have come to dominate. In so far as these exist, the church needs to repent and discover afresh the true basis for its community.

Some tension inevitably arises because the church is a purposeful community. Christ not only accepted the sinner unconditionally but commanded him or her to 'Go, and sin no more' (Jn. 8:11, AV). Grace does not render law obsolete but rather releases a person from his or her own failures and problems to begin to be liberated by keeping the law (Mt. 5:17–20; Gal. 5:13–15; Jas. 2:8). The accepting community of the church therefore must help its members to be released from the scars left by the sins of the past (either their own sins or sins done to them) and to grow towards maturity and wholeness (see Inner Healing*). Mutual encouragement, rebuke and discipline* are therefore permissible and even necessary if we are to overcome sin in our lives (1 Cor. 5:1–5; 2 Cor. 7:1; Heb. 10:25; 12:1–3, 14–17; 1 Jn. 1:9 – 2:11).

Maturity has many different dimensions to it but will include having a settled relationship with God, an ethical obedience* to his commands, a freedom* from self-preoccupation in order to live an other-directed life, an understanding of right belief, an endurance of faith* in spite of obstacles, and a real experience of God's presence through the Holy Spirit. Ephesians 4:15 sets maturity before us as the goal for the Christian, and the surrounding context (4:1 – 6:20) may be seen as an exposition of the meaning of maturity.

Healing and progress take place within the church in the normal course of the whole range of relationships as well as through worship, the administration of the sacraments, pastoral counselling and the preaching of the Bible. These are all 'means of grace'.

See especially: ACCEPTANCE; ACCIDIE; ACCOUNTABILITY; ADOLESENCE; ANXIETY; AUGUSTINE; BAXTER, RICHARD; BEHAVOURISM; BEREAVEMENT; BOISEN, ANTON; BURIAL AND CREMATION; CALVIN, JOHN; CASUISTRY; CHARITIES; CHURCH; CLINICAL THEOLOGY; COMPASSION; CONFESSION; CONFIDENTIALITY; CONVERSION; CULTURE; DEATH AND DYING; DEBT; DELIVERANCE MINISTRY; DISCIPLINE; DIVORCE; DRUGS; EDUCATION; EMPATHY; FAITH; FASTING; FELLOWSHIP; FORGIVENESS; GIVING; HANDICAPPED, CARE OF; HEALING; HILTNER, SEWARD; HOLY SPIRIT; HOPE; HOSPICE; HOSPITALITY; HUNGER, WORLD; INNER HEALING; JESUS; KINGDOM OF GOD; LEADERSHIP; LIBERATION THEOLOGY; LUTHER, MARTIN; MARRIAGE AND FAMILY COUNSELLING; MATURITY; MENTAL HEALTH; MINISTRY; MISSION, MORALITY OF; MONASTICISM; MORAL BEHAVIOUR; MORTIFICATION; NEIGHBOUR; NON-VIOLENCE; ORPHAN; PARENTHOOD, PARENTING; PIETISM; POVERTY; POWER; PRAYER; PRISON AND PRISON REFORM; PROSELYTISM; PROTEST; PSYCHOLOGY OF RELIGION; RECONCILIATION; RELIGIOUS EDUCATION; REPENTANCE; RETIREMENT; SANCTIFICATION; SCHLEIERMACHER, F. D. E.; SICK, CARE OF; SINGLE PARENTS; SOCIOLOGY OF RELIGION; SPIRITUALITY; STEWARDSHIP; STRESS; SUFFERING; THOMAS AQUINAS; UNEMPLOYMENT; VIOLENCE; VOCATION; WIDOWHOOD, WIDOWERHOOD; WORLD; WORLDLINESS.

Bibliography

E. Best, *Paul and his Converts* (Edinburgh, 1988); D. S. Browning, *The Moral Context of Pastoral Care* (Philadelphia, 1976); *idem*, *A Fundamental Practical Theology*

7

(Philadelphia, 1991); A. V. Campbell, 'The Politics of Pastoral Care', *Con* 62, 1979, pp. 2–14; *idem*, *Rediscovering Pastoral Care* (Philadelphia, 1981; London, ²1986); W. Carr, *The Pastor as Theologian* (London, 1989); D. Deeks, *Pastoral Theology: An Inquiry* (London, 1987); E. E. Ellis, *Pauline Theology: Ministry and Society* (Grand Rapids and Exeter, 1989); S. Hiltner, *Preface to Pastoral Theology* (Nashville, TN, 1958); C. Kruse, *New Testament Foundations of Ministry* (London, 1983); J. T. McNeill, *A History of the Cure of Souls* (New York, 1951; London, 1952); H. R. Niebuhr and D. D. Williams (eds.), *The Ministry in Historical Perspective* (New York, 1983); T. C. Oden, *Care of Souls in the Classic Tradition* (Philadelphia, 1984); *idem*, *Pastoral Theology* (San Francisco, 1983); S. Pattison, *A Critique of Pastoral Care* (London, 1988); E. E. Shelp and R. Sutherland (eds.), *A Biblical Basis for Ministry* (Philadelphia, 1981); E. Thurneysen, *A Theology of Pastoral Care* (ET, Richmond, VA, 1962); D. Tidball, *Skilful Shepherds: An Introduction to Pastoral Theology* (Leicester and Grand Rapids, 1986); J. A. Whyte, 'New Directions in Practical Theology', *Th* 76, 1973, pp. 228–238; F. Wright, *The Pastoral Nature of Ministry* (London, 1980).

D.J.T.

EIGHT

Old Testament Ethics

8

Biblical faith is theistic. It assumes the existence of one living personal God and sets the whole of human life in response to him. OT ethics, therefore, is primarily response to God (see ⒈), who he is and what he has done. That response is set first in the context of God as creator (see Creation*), and thus has a universal force. Secondly, OT ethics is set in the context of the God of covenant* purpose, whose commitment to bless the human race leads him to initiate a special relationship with Israel within which her ethical response is a central feature. Thirdly, we find that Israel's ethical response was shaped by the God of redemptive action (see Sin and Salvation⒌), who delivers his people and then gives them land to live in and law to live by.

1. Responding to the God of created order

Ethical simplicity. The assumption of mono-theism in the opening chapters of the Bible is so obvious that we easily miss its ethically revolutionary character. The creation narratives exclude polytheism and dualism,* and the pervasive ethico-cultural edifices that go with them. Only one God created the heavens and the earth. Human beings are answerable only to that one God. This immediately introduces a fundamental simplicity into biblical ethics. Commitment to love (see ⒉) and obey the one living God rescues us from the fear of offending one god by trying to please another with resulting conflict of moral requirements (*cf.* Dt. 6:4–5).

For Israel, the fear of Yahweh (EVV, the LORD) was the first principle not only of wisdom,* but of ethics. In Ps. 33 the thought moves directly from the sole creative word of Yahweh to the universal challenge to all human beings to fear him (33:6–8), since he is the moral adjudicator of all human behaviour (33:13–15; *cf.* also Ps. 96:4–5, 10–13).

To say that ethics in the OT was simple is not to say that obedience* was easy or that ethical decision-making faced no dilemmas. It is to say that the task of living in this world is not complicated by divided allegiances to competing gods, or by obscure philosophies which demand religious or 'expert' élites to interpret them. This essential simplicity was an incentive to act in accordance with God's will (Dt. 30:11–14; Mi. 6:8).

Moral order. Genesis 1 presents creation as a place of order, system and structure. We live in a cosmos, not a chaos (*cf.* Is. 45:18ff.). This provides an objective basis and authority for the exercise of moral freedom and sets limits to moral relativism. Whatever the culture* or historical context, we all have to live in God's created world as his human creatures. There is a basic shape to that world which we did not invent, and therefore a corresponding shape to the moral response required of us if we are to live within it with the kind of freedom which, by God's so ordering, it authorizes. Morality, in biblical terms, therefore, is preconditioned by the given shape of creation, which underlies the relativity of cultural responses to it within history.

The established order of creation also generates confidence in the reliability and predictability of life in this world. This does not, of course, rule out the unexpected apparent misfortunes of life (*cf.* Ecclesiastes). Nor is it fatalism. It is simply to note that the Heb. Bible does move from the observation of regularity, consistency and permanence in creation itself (*e.g.* in Je. 31:35ff.), to affirmations of the same characteristics in God, and thence to the assumption that certain consequences will always follow from certain actions. There are causes and effects in the moral realm, as in the physical, and it is part of wise living in this world to take note of them and behave accordingly.

Such ethical consequentialism* is found in the Wisdom literature, which tends to be grounded in a creation rather than a redemption theology. Much of the advice and guidance given in Proverbs is prudential: 'Think what will happen if . . .'. Behavioural cause and effect are repeatedly linked. The Wisdom tradition's sexual ethic illustrates this. Whereas the law simply prohibits adultery,* on penalty of death, Wisdom warns against it by describing the appalling consequences the adulterer exposes himself to, personally and socially. Moral rules and moral consequences actually reinforce one another in this way of thinking (*e.g.* Pr. 5; 6:24–35; 7). Wisdom's consequentialism, however, is thoroughly personal and theistic. Behind all the prudential advice of the sages stands their own foundational axiom: 'the fear of the Lord is the beginning of wisdom'. Whatever result follows from our actions is not mechanical cause and effect, but the outworking of God's own order in his world. The consequentialism of Wisdom is thus based on what we would theologically call God's sovereign providence and justice (see Justice and Peace③).

The image of God. Perhaps the most familiar of all the implications of the creation material for biblical ethics is the affirmation that God made human beings in his own image.* This has two primary ethical effects.

a. The sanctity of human life. As early as the texts of the Noah covenant (Gn. 9:8–17) the principle was stated that human life was to be treated as inviolable on the grounds of the image of God. Even animals would be held to account by God for the killing of humans. The influence of this principle can be seen in Israel's law. Laws about domestic animals that injure or kill humans are common in ancient Near Eastern legal corpora. All of them prescribe various degrees of compensation and punishment of the owner. Only the Heb. law prescribes also that the 'guilty' ox was to be stoned to death (Ex. 21:28–32). It seems most likely that this was because the law was influenced by the religious principle of the sanctity* of human life, as crystallized in Gn. 9:5 (*cf.* C. J. H. Wright, *God's People in God's Land*, pp. 156–160). Empirically, this high value shows itself in the narratives in several places where there is an abhorrence for the shedding of innocent blood (*e.g.* 1 Sa. 19:4–6; 25:26; 2 Sa. 2:22; 3:28, 37).

b. The equality of human beings. The OT did not eliminate all social distinctions, *e.g.* the subordinate social and economic status of the slave. It did, however, go a long way in mitigating the worst effects, by a theology of essential human equality* based on our common createdness in God's image. In its law, the OT knows nothing of the graded penalties for crimes against different ranks of victim, as is common in ancient Near Eastern law. There was equality before the law for the native and alien (Lv. 24:22). The slave was given human and legal rights unheard of in contemporary societies (Ex. 21:20–21, 26–27). This is reflected in Job's great ethical self-defence in

8

which he bases his claim to have treated his slaves with justice, in any case which they brought against him, upon an unambiguous statement of created human equality between master and slave: 'Did not he who made me in the womb also make them?' (Jb. 31:15). Once again it is in the Wisdom literature that we find the broadest outworking of this creation theology in the social ethos of Israel. There are several texts in Proverbs which affirm the equality before God of rich and poor (22:2; 29:13), and others which so identify God with every human being, regardless of status, that what we do to them we do to God himself (14:31; 17:5; 19:17). This is not the only place where we can hear distinct echoes of the Wisdom tradition in the ethical teaching of Jesus.

2. Responding to the God of covenant purpose

The God who created our world and then watched us spoil it chose to destroy neither it nor us, but instead to commit himself under covenant to a project of ultimate redemption and re-creation that would involve the whole of the rest of time and space. This is the scope of what God initiated through his dealings with Abraham, beginning in Gn. 12. It is the covenant of grace,* which stands behind all subsequent acts of God in history, for it represents God's commitment to the ultimate good of humanity. 'In you all the families of the earth shall be blessed' (Gn. 12:3, NASB). The universal scope of this promise echoes throughout the patriarchal narratives (Gn. 18:18; 22:18; 26:4–5; 28:14) and then on through the rest of the Heb. Bible. This commitment to a covenant purpose of redemption on God's part injects an element of hope and purpose into biblical ethics. Otherwise the uncertainties of history could reduce us to cynicism about the value of moral choices, as Ecclesiastes observed. But with the ultimate perspective of redemption and new creation, ethics has a firm foundation and is not just short-term expediency.

The people of God. A significant dimension of the covenant with Abraham for biblical ethics was the promise of a people. God's answer to a world of nations scattered in arrogance and strife (as portrayed in Gn. 11) was to create a new community. It would be a people descended from Abraham and blessed as he was, but who would ultimately be the vehicle for blessing to the whole world of na-

tions. And it would be a people whose contribution to that purpose would be by their ethical distinctiveness. Simply being Israel meant having an ethical agenda and mission in the midst of the world. To be an Israelite was to be called to respond to God's covenant purpose for the nations by living as the people of God in their midst.

The clearest expression of this is Gn. 18:19: 'I have chosen [Abraham], *so that* he will direct his children and his household after him to keep the way of the LORD by doing what is right and just, *so that* the LORD will bring about for Abraham what he has promised him.'

The context of this verse is God's imminent judgment upon Sodom and Gomorrah. Sodom's evil is causing an outcry that can be heard in heaven itself (see Gn. 18:20–21; ṣeʿāqâ, twice, is the technical term for the crying out of those suffering from oppression and cruelty). In the midst of a world characterized by Sodom, God wants a community characterized by his own values and priorities, *i.e.* righteousness* (ṣedāqâ, Gn. 18:19; one wonders if the word play between these two Heb. words is intentional here, as it certainly is in Is. 5:7) and justice (mišpāṭ, Gn. 18:19). The presence of these two phrases, 'the way of the LORD' (*i.e.* Yahweh) and 'doing what is right and just' (*i.e.* 'doing righteousness and justice', Gn. 18:19, NASB) here in the patriarchal narratives shows that Israel's identity as a distinct ethical community comes well before the Sinai covenant and Mosaic law. It was something written into Israel's genetic code, so to speak, while she was as yet in the loins of Abraham. In fact, such ethical distinctiveness is put forward here by God himself as his motivating purpose for the election of Abraham: 'I have chosen him, so that . . .'. The sense of purpose is very strong in Gn. 18:19. Abraham was chosen, not *because* of his righteousness, but *in order to* be the fountainhead of a righteous community. Election means election to an *ethical* agenda in the midst of a corrupt world of Sodoms.

But that ethical agenda is itself only part of a still wider purpose. The goal of the verse moves on into a third purpose clause: ʻ. . . so that the LORD will bring about for Abraham what he has promised him'. That is a clear reference, in the light of the preceding verse, to God's ultimate intention to bring blessing to all nations through the descendants of Abraham. That is God's mission, God's universal agenda. That too was the reason for the election of

8

Abraham. What is therefore highly significant in the structure of this verse, syntactically as well as theologically, is the way ethics stands as the middle term between election and mission. The distinctive quality of life of the people of God, committed to his way of righteousness and justice, stands as the purpose of election on the one hand and the means to mission on the other. It is the fulcrum of the verse.

Ethics and eschatology. Israel, then, was called to specific forms of ethical life in order to facilitate God's purpose of bringing the blessing promised to Abraham to the nations. OT ethics is thus set in a universal and eschatological framework, linked to the mission of being the nation for other nations. This universal context for ethical response is apparent in several significant places.

a. Davidic kingship. One of several links between the Davidic and the Abrahamic covenants is the awareness of the universal scope of what God was doing (*cf.* 2 Sa. 7:25–26; 1 Ki. 8:41–43). God's ethical demands on the house of David were written into the covenant from the start in the sonship response of obedience (2 Sa. 7:14–15). They had in any case been spelt out in the law of the king in Dt. 17:14–20, which unmistakably put the king under the covenant law of Sinai, with its demands for justice and protection of the weak. This was precisely what so many kings failed to do. Towards the end of the monarchy, Jeremiah stood at the gate of the royal palace itself to declare the ethical requirement on the incumbents of David's throne – a declaration which clearly subordinated Zion to Sinai (Je. 22:1–3).

The clearest link between the universal scope of the Davidic ideal and the ethical demand is found in Ps. 72. In the form of a prayer for the king, it concentrates strongly on the various forms of moral government that should flow from him, emphasizing yet again the socio-ethical combination of 'righteousness and justice' which he, as the embodiment of Israel, should manifest *par excellence.* And in 72:17b it looks beyond Israel to the rest of the world, with a clear echo of the Abrhamic covenant of blessing to the nations. 'All nations will be blessed through him [*i.e.* in this context, the royal son of David, ruling in justice] and they will call him blessed.'

The main thrust of this psalm is that if the king leads the nation in line with God's moral requirements then, first of all, the nation itself will enjoy peace* and prosperity. But beyond

that, by linking the king's rule to the Abrahamic covenant, the psalmist makes the point that God's purpose of blessing for the nations is inseparable from the ethical quality of life among his own people.

b. Jeremiah 4:1–2. Jeremiah first urges the people to renounce idolatry and to conduct their worship and general social life 'in truth, in justice, and in righteousness' (Je. 4:2, NASB). Then he goes on to spell out the results that would flow from such radically ethical repentance. He takes for granted that God's judgment on Israel itself would be averted, and skips forward to a more universal vision, and another clear allusion to the Abrahamic covenant: 'then the nations will be blessed by him and in him they will glory' (Je. 4:2b). Clearly Jeremiah believed that the quality of Israel's ethical life was not just an end in itself, but was supposed to have far-reaching consequences for the nations as well. Much more was at stake in the matter of Israel's moral and spiritual repentance than just saving Israel's own skin from judgment.

c. Isaiah 48:1, 17–19. The generation in exile hears the almost wistful voice of God ruefully pondering on what might have been the case if they had only obeyed his law. In Is. 48:1, the prophet Isaiah, like Jeremiah above, accuses the people of a nominal faith which was contradicted in their practical life by the absence of truth and righteousness. Then, in 48:17ff., in a kind of 'unrealized eschatology', God effectively says that if only Israel had been the community of obedience and righteousness that he desired and planned for her, then the promise to Abraham could have been fulfilled! The point is rhetorical and hypothetical, of course, and not to be pushed literally. But it does very strongly bind together again the link between God's redemptive purpose for humanity, as signalled in the Abrahamic covenant, and his ethical demand on Israel as the people of God. OT ethics had a missionary purpose.

3. Responding to the God of redemptive action

The God who declared his covenant purpose to Abraham went on to act in accordance with it in the historic deliverance of Israel from Egypt. The Exodus is explicitly said to be motivated by God's faithfulness to his covenant with Abraham. And within three months of the event, God introduced Israel to the ethical implications of what had happened to them.

Priestly and holy (Ex. 19:4–6). This is a

8

crucial text. It is a hinge between the redemptive history of the Exodus and the law* and the covenant texts that follow. In these verses God gives to Israel an identity and a mission, which are the basis for the ethical demands of the law. And behind both stands the redemptive action of God himself. So by way of preface to all the detailed legislation to follow, the fundamental ethical principle is that God's requirements depend a. on what God himself has done, and b. on who Israel is.

a. God's initiative and universal interest. 'You have seen what I did . . .' (Ex. 19:4). Just as he would later do when introducing the Ten Commandments (see Decalogue*), so here God begins with a historical reminder of his own action. Israel was now a free people because of God's initiative of redemptive grace and promise-keeping. Whatever moral demands she now faced could never be more than a response to what God had already done for her. The priority of grace over law was not a NT discovery or revolution, but was built into the nature of divine–human encounter from the beginning. It was an explicit part of the covenant with Israel and remains a fundamental principle of biblical ethics as a whole.

Although at this point in the canonical story the focus is primarily on Israel and the unique redemptive and covenant relationship between her and God (as his 'treasured possession'), the universal scope of the Abrahamic covenant has not been lost sight of. God's vision is still as broad as 'all the nations' and 'the whole earth'. Even in Egypt he had demonstrated that to Pharaoh (Ex. 9:14, 16, 29). Whatever ethical demands follow must be set not only in the light of the immediate historical act of redemption, but also in the context of God's universal goal.

b. Israel's identity and moral obligation. Having laid this dual foundation, God goes on to spell out the role and mission of Israel in two phrases which are echoed elsewhere in the OT and are also applied to the church in 1 Pet. 2:9: 'You will be for me a kingdom of priests and a holy nation' (Ex. 19:66).

1. Priestly. A priest in OT Israel was someone who stood in between God and the rest of the people. He was a mediator in both directions. On the one hand he represented God to the people, both in his life and example, but especially through his responsibility for teaching the law (Lv. 10:9–11; Dt. 33:8–10; Je. 18:18; Ho. 4:6; Mal. 2:1–9). Through the priest, then, the people *could*

know God. On the other hand, he represented the people before God, since it was his task to bring the sacrifices and to make atonement* for the people at the altar. Through the priest, then, the people *could come to God.*

So it is with this double significance that God says to Israel *as a whole community,* 'you are to be my priesthood in the midst of the nations of the earth'. On the one hand, Israel would represent the true God to the nations – revealing his will, his moral demands, his saving purpose, *etc.* Through Israel, other nations *would know Yahweh.* But also, it would be through Israel that God would eventually bring the other nations to himself in redemptive, atoning, covenant relationship. Through Israel, other nations *would come to Yahweh.* Later prophets pick up both ideas: the law of God going out from Israel to the nations, and other nations coming up to God to or through Israel (or Jerusalem; see Is. 2:3–4). The priesthood identity of Israel thus gives to OT ethics yet another dimension of 'missionary' relevance. Right at the start of Israel's historical journey, God sets her ethical agenda in the context of her mission in the midst of the nations (the same thrust is found in Peter's application of the priestliness of the people of God, 1 Pet. 2:9–12).

2. Holy. The word has the sense of distinctiveness and difference. Israel would be a nation as other nations, but she was to be holy – different from the rest of the nations (Lv. 18:3). This is the practical implication of the priestly doctrine of Israel's election from among the nations (Lv. 20:26). Even the foreigner Balaam recognized this conscious sense of distinctiveness about Israel (Nu. 23:9).

The outworking of this characteristic affected every dimension of Israel's national life, including her religion, but it also permeated her social, economic, political and personal affairs. This is most clearly seen in Lv. 19, a chapter full of very practical laws for daily life, all under the theme 'Be holy because I, the LORD your God, am holy' (Lv. 19:2). Holiness affected more than the ritual area of life. Holiness dictated generosity with agricultural produce (Lv. 19:9–10; *cf.* Dt. 24:19); fair treatment and payment of employees (19:13; *cf.* Dt. 24:14); practical compassion for the disabled and respect for the elderly (19:14, 32; *cf.* Dt. 27:18); the integrity of the judicial process (19:15; *cf.* Dt. 16:18–20); safety precautions (19:16b; *cf.* Dt. 22:8); ecological

8

sensitivity (19:23ff.; *cf.* Dt. 20:19–20); equality before the law for ethnic minorities (19:33–34; *cf.* Dt. 24:17); honesty in trade and business (19:35–36; *cf.* Dt. 25:13ff.). In short, to love your neighbour (and even the stranger) as yourself (19:18, 34), is not a revolutionary love ethic initiated by Jesus but the fundamental ethical demand of OT holiness (*cf.* J. G. Gammie, *Holiness in Israel*, pp. 33f.).

It is important to bear in mind this positive nature of holiness in Israel, since so often the concept of Israel's separateness from the nations has been construed as embryonic racism, especially when coupled with an over-emphasis on the wars of the OT (see Holy War* and Race*). Even in the OT period itself, Israel yielded to the temptation of feelings of national superiority and exclusiveness – though emphatically warned against it (*cf.* Dt. 7:7–8; 9:4–6) – and could find God's mercy towards the nations an embarrassment (Jon. 4). But careful study of the texts that refer to the nations shows a balance of, on the one hand, awareness of their rebellion, idolatry and wickedness, for which they stood under the judgment of God both historically and eschatologically, and on the other hand, amazing openness to their ultimate inclusion in the people of God. And alongside the fact of the intended driving out of the Canaanites (an event interpreted quite clearly within the category of moral judgment – Gn. 15:16; Lv. 18:24–28), we must place the special concern that the Torah displays for the rights and protection of aliens in the midst of the Israelite community once they had settled in the land.

Obeying the law. The first response, then, to God's redemptive action was for Israel to recognize her own identity and mission in the world, as God's priesthood, called to be holy – distinctive in every area of life. That having been grasped, it was then given detailed and specific content in the law itself.

Settling the OT law in this perspective, of God's redemptive action and human response to it, is helpful in softening the otherwise starkly deontological* flavour of the law – *i.e.* the predominance of divine command as the basis for behaviour. The covenant relationship between Israel and God entailed obedience to 'laws, statutes and ordinances'. Ethics certainly involved rules,* not just results. But the important thing is that the OT's deontology was as theistic as its consequen-

tialism. The authority of the law was not that of abstract ethical absolutes but the authority of the personal God whom Israel knew as creator and redeemer. Obedience to the law was thus not just conformity to the rules *per se* but personal loyalty to the God who gave them.

For that reason the law itself contains a large number of 'motive clauses', giving reasons why particular laws should be obeyed. These fall into several categories (*cf.* C. J. H. Wright, *Living as the People of God*, pp. 21–32).

a. Gratitude. The Decalogue itself begins with the statement of redemption, to underline the point that obedience to the following laws is a matter of grateful response (Ex. 20:2). The sermonic form of Dt. 4 – 11 reinforces it. The God who loved Israel's forefathers enough to rescue their descendants from slavery is a God to be loved in return, with a covenant love expressed in obedience. Significantly, the area of law where this motive of gratitude for historical deliverance is most pressed is that which concerned the poor, the stranger, the debtor, the slave – the very conditions from which God had rescued Israel (*e.g.* Ex. 22:21; 23:9; Lv. 19:33–36; 25:38, 42–43, 54–55; Dt. 15:15). There are narrative examples of the same principles at work (*e.g.* 1 Sa. 11:12–13; 30:22–25).

b. Imitation of Yahweh. God's action for Israel was not just the motive for obedience, but also the model for it. Obedience was 'walking in the way of the Lord'. In Dt. 10:12–19 this motive of imitation (10:17b–19) is added to the motive of gratitude (10:15). In the narratives, *cf.* David's imitation of the 'kindness' of Yahweh (2 Sa. 9:3). In the psalms, imitation of God's ethical characteristics was inculcated through regularly celebrating them, and occasionally by direct comparison of the ethical qualities of Yahweh with those of the righteous person (*cf.* in the parallel Pss. 111 and 112; note vv. 3, 4, 5 and 9 in each).

c. Our own good. Obedience to the law is not an inexplicable duty, but is constantly buttressed by the 'utilitarian' consideration that it will produce the greatest happiness of the greatest number. This is the thrust of the exhortations in Deuteronomy (*e.g.* 4:40; 5:33; 6:24–25; 30:15–20, *etc.*). The king's social justice will bring blessing and prosperity to the whole nation (Ps. 72). Conversely, endemic social evil will produce economic, ecological and political disaster (Ho. 4 and prophets *passim*). The psalms which praise the law are far removed from legalistic rule-book morality. Rather they rejoice in obedience as the means of maintaining and enjoying that righteous relationship with God which leads to the greatest personal freedom and social health (Pss. 1; 19; 119). Wisdom breathes the same spirit.

The values of the law. Set in this context, we can see the Ten Commandments, not as a code to be obeyed for the purpose of achieving righteousness, but as the heartbeat of a response to a righteousness already established by God's redemptive action. The liberties won for Israel in the Exodus were not to be squandered, but to be protected by social responsibility based on exclusive loyalty to Yahweh.

Within the Decalogue we can see a scale of priorities in the order of the commandments. God comes first (commandments 1 to 3). The sabbath commandment is for the good of the whole of society (commandment 4). Then comes the authority and integrity of the family (commandment 5), followed by individual life (6), sex and the integrity of marriage (7), property* (8 and 10), and judicial integrity (9).

The centrality of the family* in the list reflects the importance it had elsewhere in Israel's social and moral system. The 'father's house', which was an extended family of up to three generations, was the basic unit of Israel's land tenure system and also had significant religious, judicial and military responsibilities. Its economic viability was protected by laws of inalienability and inheritance of land, its authority protected by laws upholding parental respect, and its sexual integrity protected by strict laws relating to marriage, adultery and unlawful sexual relations. (See Wright, *God's People in God's Land*.)

The OT's strict sexual ethic must be seen in the context of this primary concern for preserving the stability of the larger family structure, since that in turn was an essential part of Israel's understanding and experience of the covenant relationship between the nation and Yahweh. It must also be set within the context of the way OT faith 'desacralized' sex (see Sexuality [11]). That is, it kept sex firmly within the created order, not as in any sense linked to the divine order or imbued with sacred power. Sex played no part in the process of the creation of the world, but is simply one feature internal to creation. Human sexuality is part of the image of God, but not in itself part of God. It is a gift within creation, to be enjoyed with God's

blessing, but not a means of manipulating either God or nature, as it is within the fertility cults that usually exist symbiotically with polytheism. The laws that carefully regulated sexual relations should not therefore be seen as arising from a view of sex as something sinful and dirty in itself. The unrestrained freedom of the Song of Songs' exaltation of the joy of sex under God's blessing counters any such view. Nor should Israel's sex laws be regarded as mere ritual taboos, or a devaluation of women. In Leviticus, sexual activity and emissions from the sexual organs render a person (male and female – not just the woman) temporarily unclean (Lv. 15). Uncleanness, it is important to remember, was not the same as sinfulness. It was a ritual state that temporarily prevented participation in worship at the sanctuary, normally only for the day or week that it lasted. Sexual activity could therefore never be a legitimate part of the worship of Yahweh, thereby excluding all the typical features of fertility cults, such as ritual prostitution.

As well as this emphasis on the integrity of the family, the rest of the laws show some definite priorities in their scale of values. Life matters more than property. So no offence involving property (theft, fraud, *etc.*) was punishable by death in normal Israelite judicial procedure. Nor could a murdered life be 'cashed' by a fine on the murderer (Nu. 35:31–34). Persons matter more than punishments. Contrary to popular belief, the *lex talionis* ('an eye for any eye', *etc.*) was designed to limit vengeance and protect the criminal from excessive punishment.* It was probably a principle stated in stark terms that was not meant to be literally applied. Physical punishment (beating) was strictly controlled to preserve the dignity of the offender (Dt. 25:1–3). Imprisonment was not prescribed for any offence. Physical mutilation is almost entirely absent (Dt. 25:11 being the single, remote exception). Needs matter more than rights and claims. There is an ethos in Israelite law, clearest in Deuteronomy, that even in a matter where one has a legal right or claim, one must act with consideration for the needs and feelings of the other party. Sometimes this ran counter to the whole custom of the ancient world, as in the granting of asylum to runaway slaves (Dt. 23:15–16). Sometimes it protected the dignity of the weakest and most vulnerable, such as debtors (Dt. 24:10–13) or female captives (Dt. 21:10–14). It put human physical need above strict property rights (Dt.

23:24–25; 24:19–22). It was even extended to animals (Dt. 22:1–4, 6–7; 25:4). There is, in short, within the overall social and economic system of Israel, a strong ethical thrust towards upholding the rights and needs of the weaker sections of society, not just by exhortations to charity, but also by structural mechanisms, such as sabbatical release of debt and slaves and the jubilee* year (*cf.* C. J. H. Wright, 'The Ethical Relevance of Israel as a Society').

A community ethic. There is evidence that apart from the periods of rampant paganism and moral decadence (such as the reign of Manasseh), average Israelites shared a common ethos which was substantially informed by the major distinctiveness of the Mosaic law.

Part of the evidence for this view is found in the great prophets. There can be no doubt that the prophets sharpened and deepened Israel's ethical awareness, but scholars no longer take the view (as they once did) that the great ethical insights of the OT were *innovated* by the prophets. They were not innovators but reformers. That is, they were calling people back to acknowledge and live by the ethical standards that were already present in the 'constitution' and ethos of Israel. Even those scholars who would be uncertain whether the specific legal texts of the completed Torah as we now have it were circulating as early as the ministry of the 8th-century prophets still recognize a strong legal and ethical foundation underlying the prophetic charge and challenge. Indeed, in the 9th century, the way Elijah challenged Ahab over his behaviour towards Naboth(1 Ki. 21) shows that he had flouted known standards of Israelite economic and legal justice. Amos attacks the injustice of the wealthy and the corruption of the courts in a way that presupposes the awareness that Israel's relationship to Yahweh demanded very different behaviour. Hosea bemoans the absence of the knowledge of God in the land – not because it had never been given, but because the priests were failing in their duty to teach the law to the people. The land was therefore full of social, economic and moral abuses which echo the Ten Commandments (Ho. 4). Isaiah's ringing woes (Is. 5:8ff.; 10:1–4) condemn economic greed, social debauchery, moral perversity, judicial corruption and legalized oppression. In the 7th century, Jeremiah condemned the behaviour of people who came enthusiastically to worship in the temple and to trust in its alleged security while all the time their social life trampled on the Decalogue (Je. 7:1–11). This last is just one example of a number of very powerful texts in which the prophets condemned Israel's worship when it was carried on in the context of social abuses. Ethics took priority over ritual. God cares more about justice than religion (*e.g.* Is. 1:10–17; 58:1–14; Ho. 6:6; 8:11–14; Am. 5:21–24; Mi. 6:6–8).

Further evidence of a broad consensus on ethical requirements is to be found in the ethical 'typologies' that are found here and there (*i.e.* portraits of typically righteous or unrighteous behaviour). These are very revealing precisely because they are not in a legal context, but reflect the extent to which the values of the law penetrated the commonly accepted values of society. Examples of such lists are found in the narratives (*e.g.* 1 Sa. 12:1–5), in the Psalms (Pss. 15; 24), in the Wisdom tradition (*e.g.* Jb. 31), and in the prophets (*e.g.* Ezk. 18). (See Wright, *Living as the People of God*, ch. 9.) The most notable feature of all these lists is the extent to which they combine what we would call private and public morality – everything from inward thoughts to civic duty.

See especially: ATONEMENT; BLESSING AND CURSING; CORPORATE PERSONALITY; COVENANT; CREATION; DECALOGUE; FALL; FAMILY; HOLINESS; HOLINESS CODE; HOLY WAR; HOSPITALITY; IMAGE OF GOD; JEWISH ETHICS; JUBILEE; LAND AND LAND REFORM; LAW; LAW AND GOSPEL; MARRIAGE; NEIGHBOUR; ORIGINAL SIN; POLYGAMY; PRAYER; PROCREATION; PROPHECY, OLD TESTAMENT; RESTITUTION; RETRIBUTION; RIGHTEOUSNESS; SABBATH; SLAVERY; STATE; THEOCRACY; WAR; WISDOM.

Bibliography
J. Barton, 'Understanding Old Testament Ethics', *JSOT* 9, 1978, pp. 44–64; W. Brueggemann, *The Land* (Philadelphia, 1977; London, 1978); V. Fletcher, 'The Shape of Old Testament Ethics', *SJT* 24, 1971, pp. 47–73; J. G. Gammie, *Holiness in Israel* (Minneapolis, MN, 1989); B. Gemser, 'The Importance of the Motive Clause in Old Testament Law', *VT Supp* 1, 1953, pp. 50–66; J. Goldingay, *Approaches to Old Testament Interpretation* (Leicester and Downers Grove, IL, ²1990), esp. ch. 2; W. C. Kaiser Jr., *Toward Old*

8

Testament Ethics (Grand Rapids, 1983); D. Patrick, *Old Testament Law* (Atlanta, 1985, and London, 1986); W. M. Swartley, *Slavery, Sabbath, War and Women* (Scottdale, PA, 1983); G. J. Wenham, 'Law and the Legal System in the Old Testament', in B. N. Kaye and G. J. Wenham (eds.), *Law, Morality and the Bible* (Leicester and Downers Grove, IL, 1978); C. J. H. Wright, 'The Ethical Authority of the Old Testament: A Survey of Approaches', *TynB* 43.1, 1992, pp. 101–120, and 43.2, 1992, pp. 203–231; *idem*, 'The Ethical Relevance of Israel as a Society', *Tr* 1.4, 1984, pp. 11–21; *idem*, *God's People in God's Land: Family, Land and Property in the Old Testament* (Grand Rapids and Exeter, 1990); *idem*, *Living as the People of God: The Relevance of Old Testament Ethics* (Leicester, 1983) = *An Eye for an Eye: The Place of Old Testament Ethics Today* (Downers Grove, IL, 1983).

C.J.H.W.

NINE

New Testament Ethics

9

New Testament ethics belong to a tradition of moral reflection which began with the announcement that the God of Abraham and of Moses raised the crucified Jesus of Nazareth from the dead. That good news was celebrated as the vindication of Jesus and his message, as the disclosure of God's power and purpose, and as the guarantee of God's good future. The resurrection* was a cause of great joy – and the basis of exhortations to live in memory and in hope, to see choices in the light of Jesus' story and in the promise of God's cosmic sovereignty, and to discern conduct and character and a common life 'worthy of the gospel of Christ' (Phil. 1:27).

1. Jesus and the ethics of the kingdom

The resurrection was the vindication of Jesus and his message. He came preaching that 'the kingdom of God is near' (Mk. 1:15). Against the background of the apocalyptic expectations of the 1st century, the kingdom of God* is neither an ideal social order whose coming is contingent upon human moral effort, nor simply God's sovereignty in the mysterious region of the soul. It is the future, unchallenged, cosmic sovereignty of God, and it is contingent finally only upon the world-shattering and world-renewing power of God. Jesus never made the kingdom contingent upon human morality, and he nowhere narrowed its scope to the mystical or pious or 'existential' surrender of an individual heart to God.

Jesus was not, however, like an apocalyptic seer, preoccupied with the discovery of epochs and the calculation of times; he rejected such speculation and calculation (Mk. 13:32; Lk. 17:20). He simply announced that the kingdom was 'near', made its power felt in his works and in his words, and called for repentance,* for a radical and joyful turning to God. Breaking through the pessimistic determinism of apocalypticism, his calls to 'watch' for the kingdom and to pray for it were joined to calls to 'repent', to welcome it as already present, and to form character and conduct in anticipation of God's good future and in response to the ways in which that future was already making its power felt in him.

Jesus also broke through the nationalistic* dreams of the seers for Israel's revenge against 'the nations'. In the great reversal of God's good future, the blessings of God would fall first not on Israel but on those in Israel conventionally thought to be least likely to receive them: the poor, women, children and 'sinners'. The announcement of such a future was captured in axioms like 'Many who are first will be last, and the last first' (Mk. 10:31; Mt. 19:30; Lk. 13:30; *cf.* 20:8). The call to welcome such a future, to repent before such a kingdom, was captured in commands like 'If anyone wants to be first, he must be the very last, and the servant of all' (Mk. 9:35; *cf.* 10:44).

Such was the eschatological shape of Jesus' ethic. To welcome here and now a future where the last will be first, a future already signalled by Jesus' presence among them 'as one who serves' (Lk. 22:27; *cf.* Mt. 20:28; Mk. 10:45; Jn. 13:2–17) was to be ready then and there humbly to serve (*e.g.* Mk. 10:44). To delight already in a coming kingdom in which the poor are blessed was even now to be carefree about wealth (Mt. 6:25, 31, 34; Lk. 12:22) and to give generously to help the poor (Mk. 10:21; Lk. 12:33). To repent before a kingdom which belongs to children (Mk. 10:14), which is already signalled by Jesus' open conversation with women (*e.g.* Mk. 7:24–30; Jn. 4:1–26), and which makes its power felt in Jesus' fellowship with sinners (*e.g.* Mk. 2:5; Lk. 7:48), was immediately to turn from conventional protocols of power* and to care for children, to treat women as agents, and to forgive 'sinners'.

Such, too, was the eschatological urgency of Jesus' ethic, for while human decisions remained decisions about this or that concrete possibility, in the light of Jesus' proclamation and in response to his commands human decisions were then and there also eschatologically charged decisions about whether to submit to God's coming sovereignty or to the standards and powers of the present age: whether, for example, to love God or 'Mammon' (see Mt. 6:24, RSV mg.).

a. Jesus and the law. Jesus spoke 'as one who had authority,* not as the teachers of the law' (Mk. 1:22). Here was not simply a pious interpreter of the law* but one who announced God's coming sovereignty and made known God's sovereign will. Jesus spoke of and from God's good future, and he set his own eschatological authority over against the authority of the past, even including the past of Sinai's revelation. Even so, Jesus did not destroy the law but brought it to its own eschatological fulfilment, for in God's good

future God's work and word as creator and covenantor would be fulfilled.

God's future demanded here and now a response of the whole person, not merely external observance of the law. Jesus condemned a legal casuistry* which left attitudes and dispositions unchanged (Mt. 15:17–20; 23:25–28; Lk. 11:39–41). He placed a claim on the whole person, not just some limits on their external behaviour. The legal casuistry about oaths,* for example (Mt. 5:33–37; 23:16–22; Mk. 7:9–13), might limit deceit, but it could also simply hide it and indeed be used in self-serving ways by the deceiver who knew the law. Jesus announced the coming sovereignty of God, an end to the power of the one who is 'the father of lies' (Jn. 8:44), and he called for truthfulness: 'Simply let your "Yes" be "Yes", and your "No", "No"' (Mt. 5:37; *cf.* Jas. 5:12). External observance of sabbath* legislation was set aside to welcome God's good future, the triumph of God's mercy and goodness and rest for those who are sick or oppressed or weary (*e.g.* Mk. 2:23 – 3:6; Jn. 5:1–18). Casuistry about ritual cleanliness was set aside to welcome the rule of God who desires inward purity (Mt. 15:1–20; Mk. 7:1–23). Casuistry about divorce* was a mark of a hardness of heart; to welcome God's good future is to honour God's initial intention with marriage, to be ready not to divorce even when the law would permit it (Mk. 10:2–11). The coming kingdom is welcomed not just by limiting anger by the legal prohibition of murder but by a readiness to 'be reconciled' (Mt. 5:21–26), not just by limiting revenge* by the *lex talionis* but by a disposition to forgive (Mt. 5:38–42), not just by limiting lust* by the prohibition of adultery but by not viewing women as sexual objects (Mt. 5:27–30). In none of this did Jesus legislate or provide the basis for a new and more rigorous casuistry; he announced the kingdom and invited people already to celebrate it, to welcome it, and to be formed and re-formed by it.

To be a disciple of this Jesus was not simply, like a pupil of a great rabbi, to study Torah and its interpretation; it was to study Jesus, to be apprentice to his works, to hear Jesus' words, spoken with authority, and to do them (Lk. 6:47; *cf.* Mk. 8:34–38). In his works and deeds disciples caught a glimpse of the coming kingdom, and they struggled to welcome it.

b. The love commandment. The love commandment (Mk. 12:28–34) summarized the fitting response to God's coming sovereignty

9

and so also summarizes and fulfils the law. Love (see 2) is, of course, no mere sentiment; it is the active celebration of God and of the neighbour, the disposition to delight in God and in the neighbour, and so, the willingness to honour God and to help the neighbour. The ethic of Jesus was hardly an ethic of obedience to law, however, even the law of love. The love command was not used as a basic principle from which subsidiary rules might be deduced. Jesus' ethic was rather an ethic of response to the coming rule of God – and perhaps the clearest example of this is what Jesus did with Lv. 19:18.

The commandment to love one's neighbour had not always been judged within legal casuistry to be relevant to enemies, but Jesus said, 'Love your enemies' (Mt. 5:44; Lk. 6:27, 35). The justification was that God 'is kind to the ungrateful and wicked' (Lk. 6:35; *cf.* Mt. 5:45), and the implicit assumption, of course, was that God's rule is 'near' and making its power felt. The conventional pattern of this age is reciprocity, loving 'those who love you' (Mt. 5:46; Lk. 6:32) while seeking the limit of lawful revenge against an enemy (Mt. 5:39–40; Lk. 6:29–30). But the power of that pattern is broken by trust in the coming rule of God, and in response to that good future the neighbour, even the enemy, may be and must be loved (Mt. 5:36–48; Lk. 6:27–36).

c. The politics of Jesus. Jesus was no Zealot. He rejected the vengeful nationalism of some apocalyptic seers and the violence which it nurtured. The enemy was to be loved, not destroyed. He entered Jerusalem riding no war horse but a donkey, and the self-conscious fulfilment of Zc. 9:9–10 pointed to no nationalistic 'holy war' but to 'peace to the nations'.

But he was no Saducean collaborator either. The temple-cleansing (Mk. 11:15–18; Jn. 2:13–17) was surely – even if not merely – a political act in protest against those who used their authority in the temple to make themselves rich at the expense of pious pilgrims and the poor. The proclamation of God's coming cosmic sovereignty hardly left collaborators with Roman colonialism with an easy conscience.

There was no political programme in Jesus' announcement of the kingdom, but there was a political posture, a posture ready to condemn the pride of power of those who 'lord it over' their subjects (Mk. 10:42–44), a posture that seeks peace and turns against the Zealot's

desire for revenge, a posture that seeks justice (see Justice and Peace 3) and turns against Saducean collaboration in exploitation* and extortion, a posture that is here and now blessing to the poor and powerless.

2. The Gospels

The Gospels tell the story of this vindicated Jesus – each in its own way, each creatively and faithfully bringing the memory of Jesus to bear upon the concrete problems faced by a particular community, each with its own distinctive focus of moral exhortation.

a. Mark. Mark was probably the first Gospel to be written. After Peter's death by Nero's command, the Gospel was written to preserve his preaching and to encourage the Gentile Christian community at Rome. It was a call to heroic discipleship.

Mark's account of the ministry of Jesus opened with the call to discipleship (Mk. 1:16–20), and by the central section of the Gospel, with its three passion predictions, it is clear how heroic and dangerous an adventure discipleship is: 'If anyone would come after me, he must deny himself and take up his cross and follow me' (8:34). Mark told the story of a Christ who was rejected, betrayed, denied, deserted, condemned, handed over, crucified and mocked – but also chosen and vindicated by God. The meaning is clear: to be his disciple is to be ready to suffer with him and even to die with him. (There are clear allusions to martyrdom in 8:35 and 10:38–39.)

This heroic discipleship was enabled and required by the call to watchfulness with which it was joined (13:33–37). A readiness to suffer for the sake of God's cause in the world, still hidden in mystery and proclamation, could be and had to be sustained – in spite of Nero's apparent power – by the expectation of the final triumph of God and of God's Christ.

Mark's ethic of watchful discipleship was applied to topics besides suffering,* and it illumined even the most mundane of them with the same heroism. Discipleship was not a matter of obedience to any law or code; it was a matter of freedom and integrity. Fasting* (2:18–22), sabbath observance (2:23 – 3:6), the distinction between 'clean' and 'unclean' (7:1–23), all belonged to the past, not to a community oriented to the coming of the Son of Man. The final norm was no longer the precepts of Moses but the Lord and his words (8:38). And, in a stunning collection of pronouncement stories (10:1–45), issues of

9

marriage,* children,* possessions and power are dealt with, not on the basis of law or conventional righteousness but on the basis of God's intention at creation* (10:6), the coming kingdom of God (10:14–15), the cost of discipleship (10:21), and the integrity of one's identification with Christ (10:39, 43–45).

Mark's eschatological ethic provided no code, but it did nurture a moral posture at once less rigid and more demanding than any code. It called for an ethos distinctively different from the ethos of either Jewish scribes or Roman rulers.

b. Matthew. Most of Mark's Gospel was repeated in Matthew, but by subtle changes and significant additions the focus of exhortation shifted to a call for a surpassing righteousness.

Matthew insisted for his largely Jewish Christian audience that the law of Moses remained normative. Jesus came not to 'abolish' the law, but to 'fulfil' it (Mt. 5:17). The least commandment ought still to be taught and still to be done (5:18–19; 23:23). Matthew specifically warned against the spiritually gifted 'false prophets' who dismissed the law and nurtured lawlessness (7:22–23; 24:11–12). To Mark's controversies about sabbath observance Matthew added legal arguments to prove that Jesus did only what was 'lawful' (12:1–14; *cf.* Mk. 2:23 – 3:6). From Mark's controversy about ritual cleanliness Matthew omitted the interpretation that Jesus 'declared all foods "clean"' (Mk. 7:19; *cf.* Mt. 15:17); even the kosher regulations were still normative. The issue of these controversies was no longer whether the law still held but who was its best interpreter (see also Mt. 9:9–13; 19:3–12; 22:34–40).

The law held for Matthew's ethic of a surpassing righteousness,* but it was not sufficient. The teachers of the law, with their pettifogging legalism, were 'blind guides' (23:16, 17, 19, 24, 26); they were blind to the real will of God in the law, and their quibbling interpretations hid it. Jesus, however, made it known – especially in the Sermon on the Mount.* There the call to a righteousness that 'surpasses that of the Pharisees and teachers of the law' was made explicit (5:17–20). The Beatitudes* (5:3–10) described the character traits that belong to such a righteousness. The 'antitheses' (5:21–47) contrasted such a righteousness to the concern of the teachers of the law with external observances of laws while the dispositions of anger, lust, deceit,

revenge and selfishness (see Self*) were left unchanged. This surpassing righteousness is next described in contrast to the preening piety of the Pharisees (6:1–19) and finally as a righteousness nonpareil, as a confident and expectant longing for God's 'kingdom and his righteousness' (6:33).

Matthew's community played an important role in the continuing task of interpreting the law; they were vested with the authority to 'bind' and to 'loose' (18:18), to make legal rulings and judgments. These responsibilities for mutual admonition and communal discernment were set in the context of concern for the 'little ones' (18:1–14) and forgiveness* (18:21–35) and were to be undertaken prayerfully (18:19). But in this way Jesus continued to be present among them (18:20), still calling for a surpassing righteousness.

The ethic of Matthew was no calculating 'works-righteousness'. It was rather a self-forgetful response to Jesus' announcement of the kingdom (4:12–25). The law held – but not as a basis for making claims on God's mercy. God's mercy was shown – but not to be presumed upon. Matthew remembered Jesus and his message of the kingdom and called for a surpassing righteousness, a righteousness which might not be reduced to 'scribal' righteousness or distorted into 'Christian' lawlessness.

c. Luke–Acts. The memory of Jesus nurtured Luke's concern for the poor and oppressed, and that concern shaped the story of Jesus that Luke told, modifying and adding to Mark. At the beginning of that story Mary's song celebrated God's action on behalf of the humiliated and hungry and poor (Lk. 1:46–55). The infant Jesus was visited by shepherds in a manger (Lk. 2:8–16), not by magi in a house (*cf.* Mt. 2:11–12). John the Baptist's preaching of repentance* included an admonition to share with the poor (Lk. 3:10–14). Jesus' ministry began in a synagogue at Nazareth when he read from Isaiah, 'The Spirit of the Lord is on me, because he has anointed me to preach good news to the poor' (Lk. 4:18; *cf.* Is. 61:1). And Jesus, the 'anointed' one, did exactly that throughout his ministry (see Lk. 7:22). In the Beatitudes (Lk. 6:20–26), for example, and in numerous parables (*e.g.* 12:13–21; 14:12–24; 16:19–31) Luke's Jesus proclaimed good news to the poor and announced judgment upon the anxious and ungenerous rich. Luke did not legislate in any of this; he gave no social

9

programme; but he made it clear that to acknowledge this Jesus as the Christ was to care for the poor and powerless (see Poverty*). The story of Zacchaeus (19:1–10) made it clear that to welcome Jesus 'gladly' was to do justice and to practice kindness. The story of the early church, that 'they shared everything they had' so that 'there were no needy persons among them' (Acts 4:32–35; *cf.* 2:44–45), made it clear that to acknowledge this 'anointed' one as Lord formed community and character into something fitting 'good news to the poor'.

The poor and oppressed included women, and the Gospel of Luke was good news for women, too. By a wide variety of additional stories and sayings (*e.g.* Lk. 1:28–30; 2:36–38; 4:25–27; 7:11–17; 10:38–42; 11:27–28; 13:10–17; 15:8–10; 18:1–8), Luke represented Jesus as remarkably free from the chauvinism of patriarchial culture. He rejected the reduction of women to their reproductive and domestic roles and welcomed women who, like Mary of Bethany, would learn from him as equals in the circle of his followers (10:38–42; 11:27–28). Luke's story of Jesus formed a community and a character whose attitude towards women was not determined by the patriarchalism around them but by Jesus' unconventional behaviour, a community and a character ready to recognize the new place Jesus gave to women and ready to insist that 'it will not be taken away from her' (10:42).

d. John. John's Gospel differs from the Synoptic Gospels in a number of ways, and not least in its distinctive ethic. The law 'given through Moses' (Jn. 1:17) was presumably still a guide to conduct for the Jewish Christians to whom John wrote (9:22; 12:42; 16:12). The focus for John, however, was not the law but 'life in his name' (20:31; *cf.* 10:10; 12:50; *etc.*).

Life in Christ's name was inalienably a life formed and informed by love. Christ is the great revelation of God's love for the world (3:16). The Father loves the Son (3:35; 5:20; *etc.*); the Son 'abides' in the Father's love and does his commandments (15:10); Jesus loves his own (13:1) and instructs them to abide in his love (15:9) and to keep his commandments; and his 'command is this: Love each other as I have loved you' (15:12; *cf.* 15:17). This 'new commandment' (13:34) was hardly novel, of course, but it rested on a new reality: the love of God in Christ and the love of Christ in his own.

That reality was secured at the cross,* uniquely and stunningly described by John as Christ's glorification. The Son of Man was 'lifted up' – on a cross (3:14; 12:32–34). Jesus was exalted not after, but precisely in, the self-giving love of the cross. Moreover, that glory of humble service and love was the glory Jesus shared with his disciples as gift and demand (17:22). They, too, were lifted up to be servants, exalted in self-giving love.

The love that constituted life in Christ's name was a mutual love. The commandment was always to love 'each other' (*e.g.* 15:17), never to love the 'neighbour' or the 'enemy'. The emphasis was undeniably on relations within the community, but an emphasis was not a restriction. The new reality established in Christ was enacted in the mutual love of those who abode in him. The focus was on the Christian community, but the horizon was the whole world (see Community Ethics[16]). 'God so loved the world' (3:16) that he sent his Son – and Jesus sent his followers – 'into the world' (17:18; *cf.* 20:21). The mission of the Father's love seeks a response, an answering love; it seeks mutual love, and where it finds it, there is 'life in Christ's name'.

3. Paul and his interpreters

Before the Gospels put the memories of Jesus into writing, Paul was addressing pastoral letters to his churches. He always wrote as an apostle (*e.g.* Rom. 1:1; 1 Cor. 1:1; *etc.*), never as a philosopher or a code-maker. And he always wrote to particular communities facing specific problems. In the letters, as in person, Paul was always proclaiming the gospel of the crucified and risen Christ.

Paul's proclamation of the gospel was sometimes in the indicative mood and sometimes in the imperative mood. Both were appropriate, and both were required, to announce the 'righteousness from God' (Rom. 1:17) made known in Christ. In the crucified and risen Christ, God has acted to end the reign of sin (see Sin and Salvation[5]) and death* and to begin the coming age of God's unchallenged sovereignty. Paul's indicative mood described the power of God to provide the eschatological salvation of which the Spirit was the 'firstfruits' (Rom. 8:23) and 'a deposit, guaranteeing what is to come' (2 Cor. 5:5). But the present evil age continued; the powers of sin and death still asserted their doomed reign, and the susceptibility of whole persons to these powers was 'the flesh'. Paul's imperative mood

9

acknowledged that Christians were still threatened by these powers and implored them to hold fast to the salvation, the righteousness, already given them in Christ. So, 'since we live by the Spirit, let us keep in step with the Spirit' (Gal. 5:25).

Reflection about morality was to be radically qualified by the gospel. Paul called upon the Christians in Rome, for example, to exercise a new discernment,* not conformed to this age but 'transformed by the renewing of your mind' (Rom. 12:1–2). There is no Pauline recipe for this new discernment, no checklist or wooden scheme, but some features of it are clear. The new discernment involved a new self-understanding of the moral agent; they were identified with Christ (Rom. 6:11; Gal. 2:20). It involved a new perspective on the moral situation, an eschatological perspective, attentive both to the ways in which the power of God was already effective in the world and to the continuing assertiveness of the doomed powers of sin and death. Paul's discernment also invoked some fundamental values, most notably, freedom* (*e.g.* 2 Cor. 3:17; Gal. 5:1) and love (*e.g.* 1 Cor. 13; Phil. 1:9), which were intimately associated with the work of the Holy Spirit.*

The new discernment was not simply a spontaneous intuition granted by the Spirit, nor did it create rules and guidelines *ex nihilo*. Existing moral traditions were utilized by Paul and his communities in discernment, but the moral traditions of Judaism and Hellenism and even of the church were never normative for discernment in the way that the gospel was. They might be good and useful for discernment, but they had to be tested and assimilated and criticized and qualified by the gospel. The law of Moses was 'good' (Rom. 7:16), but it was a secondary and provisional word, and as such it could not be allowed either the first or last word in Christian discernment. The moral traditions of Hellenistic philosophical schools provided certain elements of style (*e.g.* the diatribe) and certain concepts (*e.g.* 'conscience'* and 'contentment'; note the list of Hellenistic terms in Phil. 4:8), but both style and concepts were put into the service of Paul's mission and message as an apostle – and modified by that mission and message. The churches' tradition of Jesus' sayings was accepted as morally authoritative (*e.g.* 1 Cor. 7:10–11), but not as the basis for a new Christian code. Existing traditions were used but were also always qualified by the moral ident-

ity, the eschatological perspective, and the fundamental values formed by the gospel. By means of such a discernment the gospel was brought to bear on the wide range of concrete problems faced by the Pauline churches.

One problem was the relations of Jewish and Gentile Christians. Paul did not require Jewish Christians to act like Gentiles, or Gentile Christians to keep the law of Moses, but he did require them both to 'accept one another' (Rom. 15:7), not to repudiate or condemn each other. Indeed, the unity and equality of Jew and Gentile in Christ and in the church were closely related for Paul to 'the truth of the gospel' (Gal. 2:4, 14), to 'the obedience that comes from faith' (Rom. 1:5), and to 'the mystery of Christ' (Eph. 3:4–6). The power of God made of Jew and Gentile one new humanity, 'thus making peace' (Eph. 2:14–18).

A new discernment was also called for in the relationships of free and slave and of men and women. Paul did not lead a slave revolt or proclaim a women's year, but he did not simply accept without qualifications existing social roles and relationships either. He could not create *ex nihilo* new social traditions or new role assignments, but he did not accept existing traditions as the last word either. Paul qualified existing traditions in the light of a new identity in Christ, in whom 'there is neither Jew nor Greek, slave nor free, male nor female' (Gal. 3:28). This new identity was an eschatological reality, to be sure, but its firstfruits were harvested when Onesimus was received 'no longer as a slave, but . . . as a dear brother' (Phm. 16), and when Priscilla and other women were 'fellow-workers' (*e.g.* Rom. 16:3; 1 Cor. 16:9; Rom. 16:1; Phil 4:2). This mutuality and equality in Christ qualified and limited the acceptance of existing traditions even where they did not immediately destroy them (*e.g.* 1 Cor. 11:3–16; and notably the *Haustafeln* [see Household Codes*], *e.g.* Eph. 5:21 – 6:9).

There were still other problems calling for a new discernment: the question of the relationship of rich and poor in the churches (1 Cor. 11:22; 2 Cor. 8:8–14); the question of the appropriate attitude towards sexual intercourse (see Sexuality[11]) when the claim of some that they were already fully 'spiritual' had led to libertine behaviour (*e.g.* 1 Cor. 6:12–20) or to asceticism* (*e.g.* 1 Cor. 7:1–7; *cf.* 1 Tim. 4:1–5); the question of political responsibility (Rom. 13:1–7, where Paul put the political wisdom of Hellenistic Judaism in the context of the duty to love the neighbour in a world not yet fully submissive to God's unchallenged sovereignty); the question of eating meat sacrificed to idols (1 Cor. 8–10); and others.

In none of this did Paul provide a timeless moral code and simply demand obedience to it. Rather, he brought the gospel to bear upon the particular question of specific congregations and upon the moral traditions and resources they had for dealing with them. He addressed the communities as capable of the discernment he called for, as 'full of goodness, complete in knowledge and competent to instruct one another' (Rom. 15:14).

The ethic of the *Pastoral Epistles* is in the Pauline tradition but rather less radical, aiming at 'peaceful and quiet lives in all godliness and holiness' (1 Tim. 2:2). The eschatological situation was never quite forgotten (1 Tim. 4:7–8; Tit. 1:1–2; 2:12–13), but the ethic was less concerned with a new discernment than with establishing godly lives of moderation and sober good sense, avoiding the enthusiastic foolishness of others who claimed the Pauline tradition, whether ascetic or libertine.

The 'Pauline' epistle to the *Hebrews* described itself as 'a word of exhortation' (Heb. 13:22), and so it was. The subtle theological arguments did not exist for their own sake, but for the sake of the exhortations to acknowledge the truth and to act on it (2:1–4; 3:7 – 4:16; 5:11 – 6:12; 10:19–39; 12:1 – 13:19). The theological basis for this 'word of exhortation' was the 'new' and 'better' covenant (8:8, 13; 9:15; 12:24; 7:22; 8:6). The response fitting to covenant* was to 'be thankful, and so worship God acceptably with reverence and awe' (12:28). Cultic observances, priestly duties, temple service were all, however, things of the past; the new worship involved 'sacrifice', to be sure, and 'continually', but 'with such sacrifices God is pleased': 'to do good and to share with others' (13:16). Such general exhortations were made somewhat more concrete by the exhortations in chapter 13 to brotherly love (13:1), hospitality* to strangers (13:2), sympathetic identification with the imprisoned and oppressed (13:3; *cf.* 10:32–34), respect for marriage (13:4), and freedom from 'the love of money' (13:5). Hebrews 13 is a traditional Christian parenesis, *i.e.* a didactic collection of miscellaneous moral instructions.

4. The Catholic Epistles

The letter of *James* is really a parenesis. James's interest was not a theological one; the author was a moral teacher, not a theologian, but he surely wrote as a Christian, as 'a servant of God and of the Lord Jesus Christ' (Jas. 1:1), even as he gathers an eclectic assortment of moral instructions.

James contains, of course, the famous polemic against a 'faith without deeds' (Jas. 2:14–26). There can be little doubt that James had in mind a (perverted) Paulinism, but James was hardly interested in defending a different theology of justification.* Indeed, he acknowledged the important priority of God's grace* (1:17–18). It was not authentic Pauline theology that he opposed as much as the use of Pauline letters and slogans to rationalize indifference to one's moral obligations (2:14–17; see also 2 Pet. 3:14–17). James, like Paul, called for a faith* that acts (2:22). For Paul a faith that was not actively 'expressing itself through love' (Gal. 5:6) was inconceivable, but the behaviour of certain Paulinists had made it conceivable, and James's response was to insist that a faith that did not issue in deeds was reprehensible.

The 'law' was important to James (1:25; 2:8–12; 4:11), but it can be neither identified with the commandments of Torah nor reduced to the single command of love. It was simply the moral law as it was known through Scripture and 'wisdom' and borne by the traditional moral instructions which James gathered and handed on.

There is no single theme in James, but there is an unmistakable sympathy with the poor (1:9–11; 2:1–7, 15–16; 4:13 – 5:6) and a consistent concern about the use of that recalcitrant little bit of flesh, the tongue (1:19, 26; 3:1–12; 4:11; 5:9, 12).

The ethic of *1 Peter* was fundamentally a call for integrity with the identity one had owned in baptism. The 'new birth into a living hope through the resurrection of Jesus Christ from the dead' (1:3; *cf.* 1:23) was a cause for great joy (1:6, 8), but it was also reason to 'prepare your minds for action' (1:13). Between the resurrection of Jesus and the revelation of Jesus, descriptions of the new identity Christians have in Christ are always subtly imperatives as well. For example, 'Now that you have purified yourselves by obeying the truth so that you have sincere love for your brothers, love one another deeply, from the heart' (1:22; *cf.* 2:9–10).

1 Peter made extensive use of early Christian moral traditions: to 'abstain' (1 Pet. 2:11;

cf. Acts 15:20, 29; 21:25; 1 Thes. 4:3; 5:22), not to retaliate with evil for evil (1 Pet. 3:8–12; *cf.* Rom. 12:3–20; 1 Thes. 5:12–22), and to 'submit' to civic, domestic and ecclesiastical authorities (1 Pet. 2:13, 18; 3:1, 5; 5:5; *cf.* Rom. 13:1; Eph. 5:21–24; Col. 3:18; 1 Tim. 2:11; Tit. 2:5, 9; 3:1).

The mundane duties of this world in which Christians are 'aliens and strangers' (1 Pet. 2:11) were not disowned, but they were subtly and constantly reformed by being brought into association with the Christian's new moral identity and perspective. It was in terms of one's baptism, finally, one's dying with Christ and living in hope, that 1 Peter understood the moral life, emphasizing a new moral identity, an eschatological perspective, the duties of moral love and patient endurance of unjust suffering, and encompassing civic, domestic, and ecclesiastical relationships.

2 Peter and Jude defended sound doctrine and morality against heretics who 'promise them freedom' (2 Pet. 2:19) but 'change the grace of our God into a licence for immorality' (Jude 4). The abandonment of orthodoxy and sound morality reduced the heretics to 'creatures of instinct' (2 Pet. 2:12; Jude 10) and rendered them liable to God's judgment (as OT examples made clear). 2 Peter added to Jude a carefully-wrought catalogue of virtues,* beginning with faith and ending with love and including a number of traditional Hellenistic virtues (2 Pet. 1:5–8). It also added the unique note that 'holy and godly lives' not only were appropriate to the expectation of God's final triumph but might 'speed its coming' (3:11–12), and a warning against distorting Paul's letters into an excuse for lawlessness (3:15–17).

Like the Pastoral Epistles and 2 Peter and Jude, the *Epistles of John* defended sound doctrine and morality – but these epistles made their defence in ways clearly oriented to the Johannine perspective and, so, to the duty of love within the Christian community (*e.g.* 1 Jn. 2:9–11; 3:11, 14–18, 23; 4:7–12, 16–21; 2 Jn. 5–6).

Orthodoxy and morality were as indivisible here as in the pastorals and Jude, but here the connection was not only presumed but disclosed. To believe in Jesus – in the embodied, crucified Jesus! – was to stand under the obligation to love. Jesus' death on the cross was the way that 'we know what love is' (1 Jn. 3:16).

5. Revelation

The context for most apocalyptic literature – and for Revelation – was a group's experience of alienation* and oppression. Revelation was addressed (in the format of a letter, 1:4–5) to churches of Asia Minor which suffered the vicious injustice and the petty persecution of the emperor. It encouraged them and exhorted them by constructing a symbolic universe which made intelligible both their faith that Jesus is Lord and their daily experience of injustice and suffering.

The rock on which that universe was built was the resurrection. 'The Lamb, who was slain' (5:12) was raised from the dead and enthroned. He will come again and will rule. Now there are sovereignties in conflict; on the one side are God, his Christ, and those who worship them; on the other side are Satan,* his regents, the beasts and 'the kings of earth', and those who obey them. The victory has been won, but the eschatological struggle goes on. That, very briefly, was the background of intelligibility for their suffering and for their obligation of 'patient endurance' (1:9; 2:2–3, 10, 13, 19; 3:10; 13:10; 14:12).

The conflict of sovereignties is not a cosmic drama that one may watch as if it were some spectator sport; it is an eschatological battle for which one must enlist. And Revelation's account of the conflict called for courage,* not calculation; for watchfulness, not computation.

The churches were already participating in the hymnic acclaim given to the Lamb in its worship. They were already heralds of the Lamb's reign and a token of its realization. They were in Domitian's empire a counterempire. They were then the voice of all creation, until 'those who destroy the earth' (11:18) would be destroyed, until the sovereign Christ would make 'everything new' (21:5). The 'beasts' used political power (13:5–7) and economic power (13:16–17) to persecute and to oppress; but the defeat of the beasts was announced as good news to the whole world.

'Patient endurance' is not passivity. To be sure, Christians in this resistance movement, this counter-empire, did not take arms to achieve power. They did not plot a *coup* to seize economic power and political control. But even in their style of resistance they gave testimony to the victory of the Lamb who was slain. They were to defend the Lord's claim to the whole earth – and to its politics and

9

economics. They were to live courageously and faithfully, resisting the pollution of the cult of the emperor, including its murder, fornication, sorcery, idolatry, and especially its lie that Caesar is Lord (*cf.* the vice lists in 21:8; 22:15; also 9:20–21). They were to live their life under the sovereignty and to the praise of the one true Lord.

6. Conclusion

The moral tradition which the NT received, and of which it is the normative expression, was diverse and pluralistic, not simple and monolithic. To force this variety into one systematic whole is impossible and impoverishing. Nevertheless, these many and various voices do converge in the proclamation that Jesus of Nazareth, who was crucified under Pontius Pilate, was raised from the dead, and they converge in the exhortation to form conduct and character and community into something 'worthy of the gospel of Christ' (Phil. 1:27).

See especially: ATONEMENT; BEATITUDES; CHURCH; COMPASSION; CONSCIENCE; COVETOUSNESS; CROSS; DEMONIC; EQUALITY; ESCHATOLOGY AND ETHICS; EVIL; FAITH; FAMILY; FASTING; FELLOWSHIP; FORGIVENESS; FREEDOM; FRIENDSHIP; GIVING; GODLINESS; GOODNESS; GOSPEL AND ETHICS; GRACE; HEALING; HEAVEN AND HELL; HOLINESS; HOLY SPIRIT; HOPE; HOSPITALITY; HOUSEHOLD CODES; HUMILITY; HYPOCRISY; JESUS; JUDGMENT AND THE JUDGMENT; JUSTIFICATION, DOCTRINE OF; KINGDOM OF GOD; LAW; LAW AND GOSPEL; LOVE; 2 MARRIAGE; MATURITY; MERCY; MONEY; MOTIVE, MOTIVATION; NEIGHBOUR; PARENTHOOD, PARENTING; PEACE; POVERTY; POWER; PRAYER; PRIDE; PROPERTY; RECONCILIATION; REPENTANCE; RESURRECTION; REVELATION; REWARD; RIGHTEOUSNESS; SANCTIFICATION; SATAN; SERMON ON THE MOUNT; SLAVERY; SPEECH AND THE TONGUE; STATE; STEWARDSHIP; SUFFERING; SUNDAY; TEMPERANCE; TEMPTATION; TRUTH; VIOLENCE; VIRGINITY; WAGE; WIDOWHOOD, WIDOWERHOOD; WORK; WORLD; WORLDLINESS; ZEAL.

Bibliography

B. Chilton (ed.), *The Kingdom of God in the Teaching of Jesus* (Philadelphia and London, 1984); V. P. Furnish, *Theology and Ethics in Paul* (Nashville, TN, 1968); idem, *The Love Command in the New Testament* (Nashville, TN, 1972); J. L. Houlden, *Ethics and the New Testament* (Harmondsworth, 1973); R. N. Longenecker, *New Testament Social Ethics for Today* (Grand Rapids, 1984); W. A. Meeks, *The Moral World of the First Christians* (Philadelphia, 1986); S. C. Mott, *Biblical Ethics and Social Change* (New York and Oxford, 1982); idem, *Jesus and Social Ethics* (Bramcote, Nottingham, 1984); T. W. Ogletree, *The Use of the Bible in Christian Ethics* (Philadelphia, 1983; Oxford, 1984); J. T. Sanders, *Ethics in the New Testament* (Philadelphia and London, 1975); R. Schnackenburg, *The Moral Teaching of the New Testament* (ET, New York, 1967; London, 1975); W. Schrage, *The Ethics of the New Testament* (ET, Philadelphia and Edinburgh, 1988); A. Verhey, *The Great Reversal: Ethics and the New Testament* (Grand Rapids, 1984); R. E. O. White, *Biblical Ethics* (Exeter and Atlanta, 1979); J. H. Yoder, *The Politics of Jesus* (Grand Rapids, 1972).

A.D.V.

TEN

Character

Our word 'character' comes from the Gk. *charassein*, which means to scratch or engrave. Thus we still call the letters of the alphabet 'characters'.

1. Character and integrity

When we say something 'has character', we imply definite, striking and perhaps excellent features. The word often suggests age and permanence; an old village or human face may have character, but new ones do not, and even the best children do not have moral character. A person has character if he or she is 'characterized' by such traits as truthfulness, courage,* justice and compassion,* especially if that person is able to maintain virtuous action, emotion and thought despite pressures to slacken his or her measure. An associated word in our moral vocabulary is 'integrity', which comes from the Lat. *integer*, meaning whole or entire. A person is said to have integrity if he or she is a complete and definite self* and has powers to resist 'disintegration' in the face of temptation,* suffering,* peer pressure, and other adverse moral influences. To have moral integrity is to be, and to be able to remain, a moral entirety – that is, a person in the fullest and deepest sense.

2. Ideals of character and moral traditions

What it is to be a person in the fullest and deepest sense is a matter of controversy between different moral traditions. The *Stoic* (see Stoicism*) will say that the complete person is one whose mind is conformed to the inevitable processes of nature and thus possesses the virtue of 'apathy' or imperturbability. Such a one is detached from (*i.e.* unconcerned about) all things and persons, in so far as their natural destiny could be emotionally upsetting to that person were he or she attached to them. The ideal of personhood is invulnerability to frustration. To such a Stoic, Paul's grieving over fellow Jews who refuse the gospel (Rom. 9:1–3) is weakness and a failure of true humanity, while in the Christian view Paul's grief betokens the virtue of brotherly love.

To an *egoist* of Ayn Rand's (1905–82) stripe, a person of character is industrious, shrewd and proud, who considers, ultimately, only his (or her) self-interest. He looks out for others in so far as their prosperity serves his own, but has no sympathy for those who cannot survive the competition; such compassion is a form of weakness and bad character. Thus what is strength to the egoist is vice to the Christian, whose Lord models concern for the weak and wayward (Mk. 8:2–3).

To the *hedonist* a pleasant life is the human end; to the extent that hedonism* has a notion of what it is to be a person of proper character, it is to be a person whose traits tend to promote pleasure in himself and his fellow human beings.

The *Christian* believes that the goal of human life (the kingdom of God*) is glorious, the most properly pleasant state that persons can be in. However, it is not the pleasantness of the kingdom that is the goal, but the kingdom itself, its very character as the kingdom of God. Were some state of affairs other than the kingdom to be more pleasant (say, being on an eternal cocaine high), the kingdom would still be the only right choice. In the Christian picture the human being is not essentially a pleasure-seeker, but most fundamentally a child of God, a member of the kingdom. From this fact derive all the Christian virtues, which thus have a distinctly social or communal character. They can be summed up as love (see ②) of God and neighbour* (Lk. 10:25–28).

3. What is a virtue?

A virtue* is a learned personal trait, of one or another psychological type, which in some moral traditions is regarded as a form of human perfection.

In some psychological literature, 'trait' denotes supposedly genetically fixed personal tendencies such as introversion or extraversion. But virtues, as discussed in ethics, are learned traits resulting from moral and religious upbringing, from interaction with God and fellow humans, and from individual choices and self-discipline.

Since particular virtues such as patience or humility* are always embedded in some moral tradition, we should not speak simply of the virtue of hope, or courage, or self-control; instead we should index virtue-ascriptions to some tradition or other. Some things that are true of Christian hope* may not be true of Marxist hope; what is true of Christian peace* may not be true of Stoic equanimity; what is true of Christian courage may not be true of Aristotelian courage. The way a mature Christian handles his fear* (namely, his courage) will essentially involve his belief that God is personally present and trustworthy; thus it will depend on the practice of prayer* and the experience of the Holy Spirit.* Since the Aristotelian neither practises prayer, nor believes that God is present, nor has any experience of the Holy Spirit, his courage is not the same trait as the Christian's. The mature Christian and the mature Stoic both have a peace of mind, a lack of anxiety about the things that make most people anxious, *e.g.* money,* death,* reputation. But they do not have the same virtue. The Stoic's peace is won through calculating self-management, in response to an observation about the nature of frustration. The Christian's peace is a response to a message declaring a war to have ended (Eph. 2:11–22). Stoic peace results from learning not to care about *anything* – except, perhaps, one's own project of self-detachment and the wonderful order of nature; while the Christian's peace is based on hungering and thirsting for righteousness and finding it satisfied in a personal relationship with Christ.

The recent return of ethicists and theologians to an interest in character has caused us to rethink some divisions that once went unquestioned. In the thought of the classical virtue ethicists (Plato,* Aristotle,* the Stoics, the Church Fathers) there was no very clear distinction between moral goodness and mental health, between doing good and faring well, between living righteously and flourishing, between being moral and being happy. In this tradition a virtue is a realization or actualization of some aspect of human nature. It is proper and healthy for a hare to develop large and sensitive ears. It is in the *nature* of a hare to develop this way, and if an individual hare fails to develop this trait, it is to that extent *defective as a hare*. Similarly, it is in the nature of a human being to develop wisdom,* humility, self-control, gentleness and faith.* These traits and others are simply what it takes to be an excellent, flourishing, healthy and fully functioning specimen of humanity. Of course the biological analogy has limits: First, there is controversy about what human nature is, and thus about what the human virtues are, but none about whether it is natural for hares to have large, sensitive ears; secondly, merely biological developments occur without the organism's practising the trait or making any choices, while someone who develops a virtue must practise it and make the relevant choices; and thirdly, virtues require culture and tradition, but biological actualizations do not.

For Christians, another division that breaks down when we make character central to ethics is that between ethics and spirituality.* The spiritual disciplines of meditation, prayer, fasting,* almsgiving (see Giving*) and the rest, are just essential ways of developing and practising the Christian virtues. In the Christian tradition, ethics and spirituality are two angles on the same thing: the Christian life.

4. Psychotherapies

Character's connection with health also raises a question about the various psychotherapies (see Pastoral Care, Counselling and Psychotherapy ⑫) and the forms of pastoral counselling based on them and particularly their value in the development of (Christian) character. For many Christians, therapeutic techniques and concepts have come to play a significant role in their personal formation. How do these fit with the practices of Christian nurture? Most psychotherapies go far beyond being merely medical technologies for helping heal *bona fide* diseases, and are full philosophies of life offering ideologically-based ways of dealing with human 'problems' and general guidance in the conduct of life. In the present age psychotherapists have taken over the role formerly played by philosophers of supplying frameworks that supplement, clarify, and sometimes distort church teaching and nurture. Like Christianity, the therapies have their views of human nature, character ideals, ways of diagnosing failures of human functioning, and strategies for changing people in the direction of the ideal.

Assertiveness training, a therapy in the cognitive-behavioural mode (see Cognitive Behaviour Therapy*), regards assertiveness as a key to being a properly adaptive person (thus a cardinal virtue). Seeing that our lives go better if we are neither wimps nor bullies, this therapy trains clients in something like an Aristotelian mean between the extremes of passivity and aggressiveness. The training mostly takes the form of getting the client to 'practise' assertive behaviours in a variety of settings.

According to the *rational-emotive therapy* (RET) of Albert Ellis,* a human being is a calculating, satisfaction-maximizing individual, but for some reason we are beset by what he calls 'nutty ideas'. We tell ourselves we can't stand some of the circumstances we're in, we 'demand' that they be otherwise, we infer from our failure in this or that that we are a failure in general – and predictably we get depressed and anxious, and hate ourselves. Therapy consists of correcting our nutty ideas and thus our emotions. The RET virtues are rationality, equanimity, self-acceptance and mutuality (this last is a sort of policy of 'I'll scratch your back if you scratch mine, but I won't be anybody's martyr-servant').

The *client-centred therapy* of Carl Rogers* holds up as the ideal of character a kind of congruence of self-concept and actual self. Rogers think that neurotic people are basically fakes, trying to be somebody they really aren't, trying to satisfy the 'conditions of worth' imposed on them by their parents, lovers, teachers, customers, employers and society in general. Therapy consists in getting clients to talk (and thus to think) honestly about themselves, to let down their masks and get in touch with their real feelings. The therapist accomplishes this through warm empathy and a non-judgmental attitude called 'unconditional positive regard'.

The *analytical psychotherapy* of Carl Jung* also majors in self-insight and its transformative powers, but now the self in question is an unconscious psyche highly structured by universal forms of images called 'archetypes'.

Consciousness is only a small part of the human being, and true health, balance and virtue are to be found in listening to the unconscious. The unconscious psyche (which he calls 'the self' and sometimes identifies with God – for it is quite different from the ego) is wise about life and understands much better than the ego, or conscious self, what the individual needs. Psychotherapy thus aims to put the patient in touch with his unconscious, a goal typically pursued by having the patient report his dreams,* which are taken to be communication from the unconscious. The central virtue in the Jungian system is self-insight, and from it flow such other virtues as a detached and equilibrious sense of the terror and sweetness of life, wisdom, a sense of belonging to the eternal ages, equanimity about death, and willingness to let nature take her course.

The *family therapies,* unlike any of the therapies previously described, tend to see us as 'members one of another', as constituted in significant part by our relations with other important people, especially our families. The family-therapy virtues are trustworthiness, justice, generosity, loyalty, gratitude and mutuality (not Ellis' policy of 'you scratch my back and I'll scratch yours', but a sense that you and I belong ontologically to one another, that our destinies are inseparable). That the fundamental concepts of relational health are ethical is made especially explicit in the approach of Ivan Boszormenyi-Nagy (1920–) (called 'contextual therapy'). In their deeply communal conception of human nature, the family therapies are more congruent than other therapies with the Christian vision of persons, though some of them push our communal nature so far that they tend to lose sight of the individual.

All the above therapies and many others have been used by Christians. But they are not ideologically neutral (as one might think that psychotherapy, as a branch of medicine, ought to be). Instead they are, like Christianity, virtues-systems in their own right. Many of these are just as different from Christianity as stoicism or the egoism* of Ayn Rand. A completely successful therapist (if there ever were one) would turn out people, not with Christian character, but with RET character, or Rogerian or Jungian character. In the interest of Christian character, secular therapies must be structurally understood as virtues-systems and their techniques and diagnostic models carefully detached from any ideological

10

commitments incompatible with Christian thought and practice. This is a difficult and important task, requiring theological and philosophical skill as well as a knowledge of the psychotherapies.

5. Psychological types

Virtues come in different psychological types, playing different roles in the economy of character and serving different purposes in the pursuit of the moral life. Some virtues are mainly dispositions to behave in one way or another: thus gentleness, hospitality, generosity and truthfulness are evidenced chiefly in behaviour. Others seem to be in large part emotion-dispositions, *e.g.* gratitude,* hope and peace. Such virtues as self-control, courage, patience, forbearance and perseverance* are in large part self-management skills that enable us to think and act properly despite adverse emotions and desires. Others, like discernment and wisdom, are powers of thought and perception. Still other virtues seem to be primarily attitudes or ways of regarding ourselves and others: Christian humility is regarding ourselves and others as equal before God; Christian confidence consists in regarding all situations as 'manageable' because we are in God's fellowship; and Christian mercy* regards the offender in the light of universal sin (see Sin and Salvation [5]) and the atonement* of Christ.

Once we have observed these differences, we must also see the similarities and connections along the virtues. Compassion is an emotion-disposition, but it very clearly issues in compassionate behaviour: a person does not have Christian compassion if he only 'feels sorry' for sufferers. It is expected that gratitude for salvation and hope for the kingdom will issue in work for the kingdom. Self-control and perseverance will not be Christian virtues unless they are exercised in Christian hope and out of Christian gratitude, and aimed at the justice and peace of the kingdom of God; and none of the virtues can be exercised without a modicum of discernment and wisdom.

Like the features of a face – eyes, nose, mouth, forehead and cheeks – which by their juxtaposition give a face its *general* character, so the virtues form an interconnected configuration making up the recognizably Christian personality. But also like the individual face, which is distinctive in virtue of the *particular* shape of the eyes and other features, and the particular distances between them, so

the virtues of the individual and the specifics of their interrelationships constitute this individual's particular Christian character. She (or he) may have her own style of compassion, in which gentleness is minimized; a protruding sense of justice, though her courage is a bit recessive; her self-control may be more oriented upon the desires of the body than upon her anger; she may be insightful into personalities but fairly blind to the intricacies of 'political' situations; her humility may take the form of a special sense of humour about herself.

6. Vice and sin

If our ethical thinking is oriented upon the virtues, we will think of sin not just as sinful actions, but more basically as vices:* forms of failure to be the creatures God created us to be. For each of the virtues there will be one or more traits of corruption: corresponding to truthfulness is deceitfulness; to peaceableness, hostility and belligerence; to gratitude, ingratitude to God; to gentleness, roughness and violence; to hope, despair; to peace, anxiety;* and so forth. Just as virtues are forms, not only of moral goodness, but also of well-being, vices are not just moral evils, but at the same time modes of failure to flourish – forms of 'death' (Eph. 2:1).

In the Christian framework this 'death' which we have in Adam (Rom. 5:12) is fundamentally relational, because our life is basically communal – a life of fellowship with God and neighbour (see Humanity [4]). To be in Adam or to live according to his flesh (Rom. 8:5) is to be blind to God's goodness and deaf to his voice, unappreciative of his grace* and in disregard of the commandments which reflect his gracious will for us. It is to be blind also to the neighbour's nature as a beloved child of God and one for whom Christ died, and deaf to the call voiced by the neighbour's needs. In being out of 'communion' (in modern parlance we might say 'out of touch') with God and neighbour in these ways, we are also at odds with ourselves (since we are defined by these communal relations). We fail to be the human image* (Gn. 1:26) that God projects of himself (for he is 'love', 1 Jn. 4:8), as his intention in creation. All vice, Christianly interpreted as sin, is the failure to image God's nature as he projects it for us. For example, deceitfulness as a trait of character (a vice) is a failure to see, in the ones we are prone to deceive, the dear and respectable brothers and sisters of the kingdom that they are. It is a failure to see with the heart realities that can only be perceived with the heart, because the heart is corrupt. As such it is to be out of conformity with our own true selves as images of God, and thus to be in this sense 'sick' or 'dead'.

In this life, we are always spoiled in some degree. Though it is not impossible to display some compassion, some gentleness and patience and truthfulness and generosity, our virtue is always compromised by vice. This is why another central Christian virtue is contrition, the heartfelt perception of our own shortcoming enlightened by God's unspeakable mercy; and another is hope, by which we look beyond our present corruption to a time when, by that mercy, our character will be complete. The struggle for virtue is uphill and characterized almost always by suffering – by the inward suffering of frustration and disgust as we behold the contraventions of God's will in ourselves and our communities; by the outward suffering occasioned by our circumstances, which is almost always needed to impel us into serious efforts to take the path of sanctification;* and by the suffering occasioned by our Christian witness, which deepens us by casting us back on the resources of grace in the gospel, in the Christian community, and in ourselves (Rom. 5:3–5).

7. Christian virtues and the gospel

The Christian virtues, like those in other classical traditions, are aspects of the actualization of what is taken to be human nature. However, Christianity differs from other traditions in holding that what humans are has been revealed by God in the story of his dealings with humankind first as Israel, and then as the body of Christ. We are defined, as human beings, in terms of how God has dealt with us as a community. A theory of human nature can be formulated for Christianity, but if this is done it must be remembered that the theory was distilled from a story, and that the virtues are formed and maintained in us not by an inculcation of the distilled theory, but by remembering the original story. How is Christian character determined and formed by this story? In two ways: a. as a response to grace; and b. as imitation of God.

a. A number of the Christian virtues – notably the *emotion-virtues* of hope, gratitude, peace, contrition and joy* – are quite directly a response to the message that in Christ (*i.e.*

through his incarnation, life, death and resurrection) we are forgiven, reconciled and given access to God, and invited to the banquet of his eternal kingdom. We respond in *hope* because of the future good that is in store for us; with *gratitude* because God is our gracious benefactor and we are eternally indebted to him; with *peace* because this story is about the end of the war; with *contrition* because the story tells us of the unimagined magnitude of our transgressions. *Joy* does not, perhaps, designate a separate emotion, but is a summary term for all these emotions (except for contrition) in that they are happy emotions. Obviously one does not respond with these emotions simply upon hearing the gospel, even if one 'believes' it; one's heart must be prepared by a yearning to which the gospel can speak, a 'hungering and thirsting after righteousness' (Mt. 5:6), a 'seeking' of the kingdom of God (Lk. 12:31). When one becomes deeply and habitually disposed to respond with such emotions as these to the gospel and to the presence of God construed as the one who is active in this story, then one has these virtues. The emotion-virtues occupy an especially central and basic place in the Christian system of virtues, since they are so directly a response to the Christian message. *Virtues of will-power* – such as *self-control*, *patience* and *perseverance* – are less directly responses to the gospel; but calling to mind aspects of the gospel is what gives Christian distinctiveness to the Christian versions of these virtues. For example, to control anger* at his (or her) neighbour, the Christian reminds himself who he and his neighbour are, in gospel terms.

Significantly, though, the NT does not call the Christian virtues fruit of the gospel, but instead fruit of the Spirit (Gal. 5:22). This suggests that in the Christian view even the story of God's actions is not the ultimate or most important target of the Christian's joy, gratitude, peace and so forth. Essential as the story is, it is finally a vehicle for the activity of God himself, with whom the Christian virtues are forms of interaction. The word is not just *about* God and his kingdom; it is a word *of* God himself. Joy is joy in the Lord, gratitude is gratitude to God, peace is peace with God, contrition is contrition before God, hope is hope in God. If these central Christian virtues are dispositions to direct communion with God, it is not surprising that prayer is a central activity of the life of virtue. Christian character is not just shaped by a theory of human nature, or even stories about a paradigm individual, or

10

promises of a kingdom to come; it is a responsiveness to a living word of the living and present God. In this respect Christian character differs formally from Stoic character, Aristotelian character, and all the therapeutic characters we have reviewed. Indeed, if the Fall* is fundamentally a falling away from fellowship with God (and the neighbour specifically as a creature of God), all these virtues-systems can be regarded as in part products of the Fall.

b. The Christian story also determines character by enabling Christians to imitate God. We imitate God perhaps most notably in our *mercy* (forgiveness); but also in our *compassion, kindness, generosity, gentleness, humility, hospitality,* * *peaceableness, truthfulness* and *forbearance* we show ourselves to be children of our Father, adopted sisters and brothers of Jesus Christ. These are largely virtues by which we relate properly to our neighbours or, within the church, to our brothers and sisters. They are various dimensions of siblinghood or – if we may Christianize the word – of friendship to humanity. Only by violating their grammar as Christian virtues can the virtues of friendship* be possessed in abstraction from the virtues that are directly a response to God's grace. The reason is that to have the attitudes required for the virtues of friendship it is necessary to take a certain attitude towards the other members of the 'family', so to speak – towards oneself and God. And the proper attitude is established in such virtues as gratitude, peace and hope.

The reader may wonder why we have said so little about two of the major virtues in the Christian tradition, faith and love. If we take *faith* to be assent to the essential Christian teachings, then faith is presupposed by all the Christian virtues; for they are shaped by the story from which those teachings derive. But faith may also mean, more richly, the Christian's entire, trusting relation to God, thus his or her joy, peace, confidence, gratitude, hope. That is, 'faith' may not denote a separate virtue; it may be a summary term for those virtues that are directly responsive to the gospel. *Love* seems likewise to be a summary term for a broad range of virtues. In so far as love is directed to God, it encompasses the virtues we have just mentioned as summarized by 'faith'; in so far as it is directed to brother, sister and neighbour, it summarizes what we have called the virtues of friendship: compassion, kindness, gentleness, hospitality,

generosity, peaceableness, mercy and forbearance. 'Holiness' seems to be another such summary term.

8. The formation of Christian character

How does one acquire the Christian virtues? The short answer is: by practising the Christian life. If that life is communion with God, then a significant part of practice in the virtues will be *prayer*, for that is our central means of communicating with God. We have argued that the most fundamental Christian virtues are the emotion-virtues of gratitude, hope, joy, peace and so forth, because these are the most direct response to the gospel which shapes the entire life of Christian virtue. But if so, then *meditation*, or attentive thinking about the gospel and God's goodness and one's own place in the kingdom – *i.e.* setting one's mind on the things of the Spirit (Rom. 8:5) – would seem fundamental to deepening one's Christian character. Meditation is apropos of attitudinal virtues such as humility and mercy, as well. A number of the virtues – compassion, truthfulness, hospitality, gentleness – are behavioural, and here the obvious strategy is to *perform actions* exemplifying these virtues. *Fasting** and similar spiritual disciplines of self-deprivation seem to function primarily as aids to meditation and prayer, as they remind us of our dependency on the Lord; but in themselves they, like other actions done explicitly for God, also bind us to him in friendship. Fasting also may be training in self-control. The self-management virtues (patience, forbearance, self-control, perseverance) are often put into practice in Christian actions, while prayer and meditative attention are strategies by which they are pursued. Just as Christian character is an intricate web of the different types of virtues, so training in the Christian life involves an interconnected variety of disciplines.

See especially: ANGER; BENEVOLENCE; BLESSEDNESS; CHASTITY; COMPASSION; COURAGE; COVETOUSNESS; CRUELTY; DISCIPLINE; EVIL; FAITH; FAITH DEVELOPMENT; FEAR; FORGIVENESS; FREE WILL AND DETERMINISM; GODLINESS; GOODNESS; GRACE; GRATITUDE; HAPPINESS; HATRED; HOLINESS; HOLY SPIRIT; HONESTY; HOSPITALITY; HUMILITY; HYPOCRISY; INNOCENCE; JESUS; LUST; MATERIALISM; MATURITY; MERCY;

OBEDIENCE; PATRIOTISM; PEACE; PERSONALITY; PESSIMISM; PRIDE; REPENTANCE; RESPONSIBILITY; REVENGE; RIGHTEOUSNESS; SANCTIFICATION; SELF; SELF-ESTEEM; SHAME; SPIRITUALITY; SUFFERING; TEMPERAMENT; TRUST; VICE; VIOLENCE; VIRTUE, VIRTUES; WISDOM; WORLDLINESS.

Bibliography

Aristotle, *Nicomachean Ethics* (ET, Indi- anapolis, IN, 1985); S. Hauerwas, *A Community of Character* (Notre Dame, IN, 1981); A. MacIntyre, *After Virtue* (Notre Dame, IN, ²1984; London, ²1985); R. C. Roberts, *The Strengths of a Christian* (Philadelphia, 1984); *idem*, *Taking the Word to Heart* (Grand Rapids, 1993); *idem*, 'Therapies and the Grammar of a Virtue', in R. H. Bell (ed.), *The Grammar of the Heart* (San Francisco, 1988), pp. 149–170; Thomas Aquinas, *STh* 1a2ae 55–67, 2a2ae 1–170.

R.C.R.

ELEVEN

Sexuality

'God created man in his own image . . . male and female he created them' (Gn. 1:27). In man and woman God creates not two different kinds of beings but one: humankind, created as sexually differentiated. Because this differentiation constitutes our human nature, we cannot come fully to know the significance of being human without reference to it. And although Jesus says that 'at the resurrection people will neither marry nor be given in marriage' (Mt. 22:30), we have no warrant to suppose that the bodily resurrection* will be anything other than a resurrection of those who continue to exist within the differentiation of male and female.

If humankind is to praise God with one voice, our creation as male and female sets before us a task: realization of the community within which and for which we are created. Only as men and women together, in harmony and oneness, do we become fully human and realize the divine image. This happens – in part and paradigmatically – in the marriage of a man and a woman. But the task extends beyond the marital union; it belongs to men and women who together are to form one body that shall be the bride of Christ.

Human beings are created from the dust of the ground, but, unlike the other animals, they also have within them that God-breathed spirit that orients them towards God and causes them to transcend earthly life. They are both finite and free – located in the natural world of time and space, but freely transcending it as historical beings who shape their own existence. Nowhere is this union of nature and history in human beings more apparent or more puzzling than in the realm of sexuality.

The sexual differentiation is, initially and fundamentally, biological. In order that the image* of God may come to its fruition in a community of those who are united yet different, we must be male *or* female (Karl Barth,* *CD*, III/4, p. 118). The biological foundations for such differentiation can sometimes be disturbed, but ordinarily our sexual identity is grounded from the outset in the chromosomal configurations that distinguish female from male (XX or XY). Out of that initial distinction others develop:

differences in dominant hormones, in gonads (ovaries or testes), and in external genitalia.

In human beings, however, nature is never untouched by history, and the sexual differentiation is more than biological. It extends also to gender identity, where the distinction of masculine and feminine may be far more difficult to describe. For Christian theology, which thinks of human beings not simply as free spirits but as embodied creatures, gender identity must be grounded in biological sexuality without being reduced to it. Rigid role distinctions between men and women would reduce gender to sex, construing human nature as all finitude and no freedom. A denial that any gender distinctions may have an innate basis in our sexuality would lose the grounding of culture* in biology, construing human nature as all freedom* and no finitude. The importance of human 'embodiedness' for Christian theological reflection 'militates against any "new dualism" in which physical forms and differences have no correspondence with cognitive or affective characteristics. Arguments that the sexes must in principle be identical in all characteristics and capacities seem to presuppose that sexual differentiation is merely accidental in relation to some human essence abstracted from the physical forms in which it invariably must be realized' (L. S. Cahill, *Between the Sexes*, p. 84). In short, for men and women to be equal they need not be identical.

Granted this, it remains difficult to specify gender differences with anything like the precision that can be used in stating sexual differences. Certain differences may be innate – *e.g.* verbal ability in females and mathematical ability in males; aggression in males and nurturing behaviour in females (Cahill, p. 90). Some have argued that males and females have characteristically different modes of moral reasoning – with females tending more towards a morality of 'caring' that emphasizes webs of attachment, and males tending more towards an abstract morality of individualized 'justice' (C. Gilligan, *In A Different Voice*).

Certainly we inherit a set of culturally learned roles and expectations. These may be inculcated by those with authority to socialize us – parents and, perhaps, teachers. They may also be learned by imitation, as we turn quite naturally to those who share our biological sex. Biological differences alone cannot account for gender, and gender identity does not grow inevitably out of one's biological sex, but there may be predispositions connecting the two. The fit is not tight enough, for example, to prescribe rigid role distinctions within a marriage; yet, the difference between the reproductive roles of men and women suggests that we need to respect gender distinctions tied to those roles. In their freedom a husband and wife must take up the task of building a union in which they remain distinct but united, equal but not identical.

1. Marriage*

'It belongs to every human being to be male or female. It also belongs to every human being to be male in this or that near or distant relationship to the female, and female in a similar relationship to the male. . . . But it certainly does not belong to every [human being] to enter into the married state. . .' (Barth, CD, III/4, p. 140). Nevertheless, it remains true that within human history the community of man and woman is ordered towards the marital bond, which is the most intimate form of this community. Marriage is the lifelong union of a man and a woman, entered by their mutual and public consent.* As such it is the gift of God, who sees that 'it is not good for the man to be alone' (Gn. 2:18) and who wills that the human species should be sustained through offspring. Hence, marriage is a divine institution, though one that is worldly rather than ecclesiastical in its essential nature. It is established not by the declaration of priest or pastor, but by the consent of the partners.

For the Judaism from which Christianity first took root, marriage was a *mitzvah*, a religious duty, the means by which God preserved and sustained his elect people. Despite the high praise accorded marriage by Christians, especially when they were faced by gnostic systems of thought that disparaged the created world, it never became for them a duty. In the earliest centuries of the Christian era there were, side by side with affirmations of marriage, strong ascetic* currents of thought that refused to place the body in service of society (by bearing children) and sought even within history to live the unmarried life of the eschatological age (P. Brown, *The Body and Society*). This viewpoint is grounded in the desire for a life without division, oriented wholly towards God, a desire expressed already by Paul (1 Cor. 7:32–35). It gradually took shape in the view that, although marriage was a God-given and praiseworthy estate, the celibate life was a higher form of Christian faithfulness. Protestant thought in particular broke with that view, exalting marriage and refusing to distinguish higher from lower forms of Christian life. But even then marriage was not proclaimed to be a Christian duty, and the unmarried believer belongs equally to the eschatological family of God realized even now in the worshipping church. At any rate, the Christian norm has been that the deepest mysteries of one's self,* which involve being male or female, are to be reserved for expression within marriage or, for those who understand celibacy (see Singleness*) as their calling, for dedication to God.

Many features of marriage – e.g. the way that intention to marry is determined, and the roles of husband and wife – may vary from one society to another. Nevertheless, Christian thought over centuries of development has tended to discern three purposes in marriage, which we may term procreative, relational and healing. These purposes are ultimately God's, who uses us to care for others in the marital bond and uses that bond to shape and form our character in accord with his will.

a. The procreative purpose of marriage. Having created humankind as male and female, 'God blessed them and said to them, "Be fruitful and increase in number . . ."' (Gn. 1:28), a blessing* repeated to Noah and his sons after the great Flood (Gn. 9:1). This is a blessing, not precisely a command; yet, it stipulates for humankind a task. God intends to preserve humankind towards the end he has appointed, and to that end children* are the natural fruit of marriage. To take up this task is to align oneself with God's creative work, with the blessing embedded in the created order. In marriage a man and a woman step out of their separateness into community; they turn towards each other. But the union they form is also, by God's blessing, to turn outwards in the child.

This norm does not come to fruition in the life of every married couple, some of whom may be without children because one or both of the spouses is infertile (see Childlessness*). Their marital bond is not therefore incomplete, since procreation* is not the only purpose of marriage. Understandably, however, they may be saddened by their infertility. Because they have no child to manifest their oneness, they will need to use their historical freedom to seek some other common work in which their shared life can turn outwards and be fruitful.

The family* formed when a marriage gives rise to children is itself both a biological and a historical community. Through the family we are embedded in the world of nature, are marked by lines of kinship and descent, and are from birth individuals within a communal bond. Hence, our sense of self is deeply involved in the biological bond. Parents are not simply reproducing themselves. When from their oneness they beget a new human being, equal to them in dignity, that act testifies to the truth that by God's blessing such mutual love can be creative of community. With the biological bond come obligations. Parents have the responsibility to serve before their children as God's representatives. Children are to honour and esteem those who gave them life.

The family is also a community upon which is laid a cultural, historical task: transmission of a way of life. Parents are to 'tell the next generation the praiseworthy deeds of the LORD' (Ps. 78:4). Similarly, the apostle Paul writes that fathers should not exasperate their children, but should 'bring them up in the training [paideia] and instruction of the Lord' (Eph. 6:4). That task of paideia, of nurture and inculcation of a way of life, is the calling of parents.

b. The relational purpose of marriage. According to the story told in Genesis, when the beasts of the field and birds of the air have been created and the man has ordered the creation by naming them, he finds no-one who answers to his own need for companionship. God therefore provides the woman as one who will stand over against him, in relation to whom he will come to know himself. She is brought to him and, in their sexual differentiation, they become 'one flesh' (Gn. 2:24). This bond and the companionship it provides – a bond used in Scripture as an image of the relation between God and his people – is of great value even if a marriage is not blessed with children (1 Sa. 1:8). Christian thought has generally emphasized faithful companionship as one of the purposes of marriage. Only in modern times, however, have the tenderness and passion of romantic (erotic) love (see 2) been emphasized as integral to marriage.

Although our natural sexual appetites may lead us to this relation, they alone cannot create or sustain it. The satisfaction of biologically-given appetite alone need not involve a personal bond. At the level of appetite sexual partners might be nearly interchangeable, for it is their functions and

11

capacities – not their person – that is desired. Erotic love, however, is personal love, desire not simply for a man or a woman but for a particular person. *Erōs* desires not simply the pleasure* the other person can give, but union with that person. Hence, our sexual appetites are humanized and personalized only when taken into a personal bond of love (C. S. Lewis, *The Four Loves*, New York and London, 1960, pp. 134–135).

Christian thought has, therefore, opposed 'casual' sexual encounters in which partners become essentially interchangeable. In such an encounter no true relation of persons is established. Such an encounter is dehumanizing because it treats the giving of the body as if the person were not thereby involved, as if persons entirely transcended their bodies and were free to use the body simply as a pleasure-giving mechanism. By contrast, the Christian concept of the 'one flesh' union has reaffirmed the natural insight that personal significance must be discerned in our giving of the body-self.

Erotic love makes sexual appetite human; yet, *erōs* itself must also be transformed if the relational purpose of marriage is to be fully achieved. Love must be joined with commitment of the will to fidelity. Thus, neither appetite nor erotic love has been sufficient to form what Christians call the institution of marriage. It requires permanent commitment. Such permanence – though its goodness may not always be obvious and though it may be difficult to achieve – is grounded in the will of the creator (Mt. 19:3–10). But for Christians it is also grounded in the gospel, which assures us that we may commit ourselves to the spouse as Christ has committed himself to his bride, the church (Eph. 5:25–32). As *erōs* personalizes appetite, so *agapē* – a God-given and Christlike love – commits one to keeping *erōs* faithful.

Among the difficulties attending our understanding of the relational purpose of marriage is the relative importance of consent and consummation in formation of the marital bond. Paul does write (1 Cor. 6:16) that one who has intercourse with a prostitute (see Prostitution*) becomes 'one with her in body,' and he cites the 'one flesh' language of Gn 2. This seems, however, to be less a theory of what constitutes marriage and more an exhortation against unholiness, an argument that there are bodily actions incompatible with membership in Christ's body. In the development of Roman Catholic thought in the high Middle Ages, theologians tended to emphasize the centrality of consent in the making of a marriage. By contrast, canon lawyers (who needed to be able to specify circumstances under which a marriage might be annulled) tended to emphasize the necessity of consummation (E. Schillebeeckx, *Marriage*, p. 287). The issue retains contemporary significance in those rare cases when two people wish to marry but will be unable to consummate their union. Can the relational purpose be realized under such circumstances and a marriage undertaken? It is probably best to emphasize consent of the partners, to hold that they consent to all that is involved in marriage (including sexual intercourse), but that the relation itself involves a sharing of the whole of life and is possible even in rare cases in which the union will exist without intercourse.

Christians have generally presumed that the marital bond should be monogamous, despite the polygamy* of some of the OT patriarchs. The Bible neither prohibits polygamy nor precisely enjoins monogamy. The apostle Paul does write that 'since there is so much immorality, each man should have his own wife, and each woman her own husband' (1 Cor. 7:2). Spiritual leaders (variously termed *episkopoi*, *diakonoi*, and *presbyteroi*) are required to be the husband of only one wife (1 Tim. 3:2, 12; Tit. 1:6). Other factors may have been more important, however, in the general requirement of monogamy. The relational purpose of marriage may be difficult to realize fully and the 'one flesh' union almost impossible of realization unless the marital bond is monogamous. Moreover, the fact that marital imagery is used in Scripture to picture both the relation of Yahweh and Israel and the bond between Christ and the church reinforces tendencies towards a monogamous union.

The procreative and relational purposes are held together within marriage. The relation of mutual love is not incomplete if a marriage is childless, nor is the marriage of those past childbearing years or the sexual intercourse of those who are infertile improper. Such couples still take up the task of forging a lifelong bond between those who need the companionship of one who is 'other' in sex and gender, and they must still seek ways for their union – as a union – to turn outwards. They conform, therefore, to the Christian understanding of marriage.

More questionable, however, have been instances in which the procreative and relational purposes are deliberately severed – not by the (divinely governed) accidents of nature, but by the decision and will of the partners. One of the reasons fornication* and adultery* have been condemned in Christian thought is that the partners in such unions cannot will that their intercourse be fruitful. But the procreative and relational purposes can also be deliberately severed in other ways. Spouses can aim at enjoying sexual relations while deliberately avoiding conception (contraception), and they may aim at producing children apart from their physical union in sexual intercourse (artificial reproduction). The former possibility has given rise to a long history of Christian discussion (see Birth Control*); the latter is, for the most part, a recent concern (see Reproductive Technologies*).

c. The healing purpose of marriage. Christians have often had to struggle against their own tendency to regard the sexual act as peculiarly sinful (see Concupiscence*). But even while struggling against such tendencies they have also needed to say that sexual appetite, like all appetites of sinners, needs discipline* and control.

Appetite, uncontrolled by mutual love, constantly threatens to disrupt and damage human lives. Erotic love, pursued even at the cost of broken promises and unfaithfulness, becomes an idol. Marriage functions to provide needed restraint and discipline as the God-given place of healing for our sexual nature. Although in the modern era this has received far less emphasis than the relational and procreative purposes of marriage, healing also is one of the ends towards which God works through the marital bond. This is essentially what Paul means by writing that 'it is better to marry than to burn with passion' (1 Cor. 7:9), and it is what theologians mean by the 'quieting of concupiscence'. In learning the meaning of faithful love to one other person, a spouse, we gradually become more able to devote ourselves to the good of others. Our self-serving impulses begin to be healed. And in being loved in this way by a spouse, we find that some of our deepest anxieties – our fear of loneliness* and desertion* – are quieted.

Understanding marriage as a place of healing, we can see why Christians have characterized the marital bond not as a contract but as a covenant. The commitment is made by free human choice but is not to be terminated in the same way. For the institution cannot sustain and discipline us, cannot heal our sinful passions, if it rests on our feelings alone. Hence, for Christian thought there can be no such thing as a trial marriage (see Cohabitation*). Continued commitment to the bond is not to depend on what our desires may be at any given moment. Instead, the institution of marriage itself is to discipline, shape and transform those desires. In short, marriage serves to heal us when it begins to form our own love in the shape of God's steadfast faithfulness.

2. Divorce*

The marital vow is a commitment, not a prediction. If it were the latter, no honest person could make it when considering the statistics about marital failure. As a commitment, however, it announces an intention to attempt a permanent union. We may sometimes fail to carry out our intentions, but that should not happen because we understood ourselves merely to be making a prediction (which has now been falsified); it should happen only with the realization that we have failed in a commitment. The difference between these two attitudes will have an enormous impact on the way we approach the threat of failure in marriage.

That divorce must be a serious matter for Christians is evident from the three purposes of marriage. Through procreation a child is born as the embodiment of the union of a man and woman. The child's very identity and person are involved in their union. A divorce that ruptures the union must have profound consequences for the child's sense of self. Likewise, marriage as a relation in mutual love answers to very deep human needs: to be able to give ourselves completely to another; to trust that we will not be abandoned whatever the future may bring; to know that we are not interchangeable with anyone else. Hence, marriage gives rise to a set of expectations that ought not be disappointed. Finally, marriage cannot function as a place of healing if we refuse its constraints and reject its disciplines. It begins to heal us only as we give ourselves to the bond and let it shape our character.

It is evident, therefore, that Christians could not regard divorce as good. But could it be permitted? And could remarriage follow? The church has always found it difficult to hold up God's steadfast love as the norm for marital commitment and simultaneously to speak that same word of steadfast love and acceptance to all penitent sinners (including those who have

11

dissolved their marriages and may wish to remarry).

Biblical texts have not been decisive here. The sayings of Jesus reported in the Synoptic Gospels lead in several directions. Neither Lk. 16:18 nor Mk. 10:2–12 allows any ground for divorce. But Mt. 5:31–32 and 19:2–9 allow divorce on the ground of *porneia* (a term whose translation is disputed; rendered 'marital unfaithfulness' in the NIV). Paul, while permitting a Christian to acquiesce in an unbelieving spouse's desire for divorce and, presumably, thereafter to remarry a fellow believer (the so-called 'Pauline privilege' in 1 Cor. 7:12–15), appears to establish (though on his own authority and not on the basis of a dominical saying) a stricter rule for believers. In 1 Cor. 7:10–11 he seems to deny the permissibility of divorce and remarriage* for a Christian couple. Although this passage has been interpreted to permit divorce in cases of desertion by one partner, that is not its probable meaning. Paul seems to permit a separation from 'board and bed,' but since he makes clear that no remarriage is permitted, he can hardly have in mind an actual dissolution of the marriage.

Is no more than a separation from bed and board permitted? Or, if this marriage has in effect ended, might not remarriage be permitted? Christian opinion (at the churchly level) remains divided on this question. For Roman Catholic moral theology* the actual bond of marriage cannot be dissolved, and, hence, no remarriage is possible for Christians. For others who hold that, although the bond ought not to be broken, it can sometimes break down, the answer will seem less obvious. The grounds for sanctioning remarriage, if there is to be remarriage, must obviously be the three purposes towards which marriage is ordered: the good of children, the companionship of mutual love, and the healing of sexual appetites and passions.

3. Homosexuality*

It is generally held that many people have a measure of flexibility in the direction of their sexual drive and that 2% to 5% of the population is predominantly homosexual in orientation. Modern science and medicine have reached no consensus about the causes of homosexual orientation. Among the factors proposed as possible causes are genetic determination, pre-natal hormone levels, disturbances in family relationships (*e.g.* a distant father), and culturally transmitted learning. It may well be that more than one factor is involved.

Biblical texts demonstrate an awareness of homosexual activity but pay relatively little attention to the topic. Most important is probably Rom. 1:26–27, where Paul uses as his example of God's wrath upon idolaters the fact that God has given the Gentiles up to 'shameful lusts' – both women and men exchanging 'natural relations for unnatural ones'. It is clear that Paul does not here make the modern distinction between an invert (for whom a homosexual orientation seems natural) and a pervert (who knows himself or herself to be constitutionally heterosexual but, none the less, engages in genital sexual activity with others of the same sex). But he does seem clearly to regard homosexual behaviour as contrary to the will of God; for he regards such behaviour not simply as contrary to the constitution of particular individuals engaging in perversion but as contrary to the nature shared by humankind.

Because there is relatively little direct attention paid in the Bible to homosexuality, some have argued that the general tradition of Christian thought condemning homosexual behaviour should be rethought (J. Nelson, *Embodiment*). We should, it is argued, judge homosexual behaviour by the criterion appropriate for evaluating heterosexual behaviour: namely, whether it is characterized by mutual love. Not the bodily structure of the act but its inner spirit is what should count morally. (One might also carry the analogy with evaluation of heterosexual behaviour further and say that such mutual love should be enacted within a monogamous union dedicated to permanence.)

Despite such arguments, and despite the little attention given to homosexuality in the Bible, there is a large biblical context of thought about sexuality which clearly regards heterosexuality as the ideal and norm for human behaviour. The relation of Yahweh and his elect people Israel, and the relation of Christ and the church, are both characterized with marital imagery. Still more, the creation of humankind as male and female is the fundamental form of human community and is closely related to humankind's creation in the image of God. To men and women the sexual differentiation is given not simply as a blessing but as a task: to forge a harmonious community that unites them without obliterating their

11

differences. As the central and typical expression of male–female community, marriage calls one to that task. The first and second purposes of marriage discussed above provide the larger context that explains why heterosexuality has been the Christian norm. The homosexual relation is non-procreative, not by accident but in its very constitution. It cannot therefore be a sign that mutual love is, by God's blessing, creative and fruitful. And the homosexual relation resembles too closely the love of self that is forbidden. It does not seek to create community between those who encounter the beloved as 'other' even and especially in his or her body. From the perspective of this larger understanding of sexuality within Christian theology, any justification of homosexual behaviour – even in a stable, loving union – will have to recognize that it falls short of the Christian norm. Such justification might, however, still attempt to claim for its support the third purpose of marriage: healing and the 'quieting of concupiscence' (H. Thielicke, *The Ethics of Sex*, pp. 277–287).

4. Sexual variations

Unless one adopts the view that even within marriage all genital sexual activity must be open to the transmission of life, there is little reason to forbid husband and wife considerable scope for experimentation and play in their sexual relationship. The general rule will be that whatever nurtures and fosters the relational purpose of mutual love and companionship should be permitted, and whatever hinders or harms the growth of mutual love should be prohibited. Such a rule would, for example, prohibit a sado-masochistic relation in which one's pleasure depended on the infliction of pain. Sado-masochism is a subtle – but all the more dangerous therefore – perversion of the genuine giving and receiving that should characterize mutual love. Even consent of a spouse cannot justify the intent to harm. Such intent is, in any case, inappropriate within a relation that ought to enhance the equal dignity of a man and woman who together are to realize the image of God in which they have been created. Consent is also insufficient to justify paedophilia,* since no truly mutual love is possible when one of the partners is a child who cannot give and receive as an equal. Bestiality, in which one seeks gratification from an animal, must also be forbidden; for such behaviour is a flight from, rather than a search for, true human community between those who

can make claims upon each other.

Christian thought has often condemned masturbation,* and the fundamental theological ground is clear. In its very nature masturbation separates sexual satisfaction from the giving and receiving that ought to characterize the mutual love of spouses. We know, however, that the sexual development of adolescents is often characterized at certain points by masturbation as a temporary form of sexual experimentation. The nature of the act is different in such contexts. It is not a rejection of the sexual partner who is other than the self but a step on the way towards that partner. To go farther, however, and argue that for an adult the practice of masturbation may usefully provide knowledge that one's 'wholeness need not depend absolutely upon a relationship with another person' (Nelson, *Embodiment*, p. 172) is to lose sight of the fact that Christians believe our sexual nature to be oriented toward male–female community.

Incestuous* sexual activity is that which takes place between persons who are relatives either by blood (consanguinity) or by marriage (affinity). Obviously, only those fairly closely related are prohibited from marrying, though the precise degrees of kinship are ordinarily specified in law. Prohibited degrees in ancient Israel are specified in Lv. 18:6–18 and 20:11–12, 14, 17–21. Today we know that children born from incestuous relationships may face increased risk of genetically recessive disorders or congenital malformations, but, of course, such knowledge does not lie behind the prohibitions in ancient Israel. In part, these prohibitions – and certainly those dealing with relationships of affinity – seem to aim at 'the avoidance of domestic discord by precluding the possibility of wedlock between persons likely to be members of the same household' (D. S. Bailey, *Sexual Relation in Christian Thought*, p. 144). This alone, however, will not explain the depth of feeling associated with incest between, for example, a parent and child. The taboo* captures something central to human identity. A daughter, who embodies the union of her mother and father, is not sufficiently 'other' to be her father's object of sexual love. In *Summa Contra Gentiles* (III.125), Thomas Aquinas* builds upon such an insight with a suggestion which, though certainly not the reason for the original biblical prohibitions, explores their deeper theological rationale: 'In human society it is most necessary that there be friendship

11

among many people. But friendship is increased among men when unrelated persons are bound together by matrimony. Therefore, it was proper for it to be prescribed by laws that matrimony should be contracted with persons outside one's family and not with relatives.'

See especially: AIDS; ASCETICISM; BIRTH CONTROL; CHASTITY; CHILDREN; CREATION; DISCRIMINATION; DIVORCE; EQUALITY; FAMILY; FEMINISM; FRIENDSHIP; HEADSHIP; HOMOSEXUALITY; INCEST; LOVE;[2] LUST; MARRIAGE; MARRIAGE AND FAMILY COUNSELLING; NUDITY; NULLITY; PARENTHOOD, PARENTING; POLYGAMY; PORNOGRAPHY; PROCREATION; PROSTITUTION; RAPE; REMARRIAGE; REPRODUCTIVE TECHNOLOGIES; SEXISM; SEXUAL COUNSELLING AND THERAPY; SEXUAL DEVIATION; SEXUAL HARASSMENT; SINGLENESS; SINGLE PARENTS; STERILIZATION; SUBMISSION; TRANSSEXUALISM; TRANSVESTISM; VIRGINITY.

Bibliography
D. S. Bailey, *Sexual Relation in Christian Thought* (New York, 1959); K. Barth, *CD*, III/4; E. Batchelor, Jr. (ed.), *Homosexuality and Ethics* (New York, 1980); P. Brown, *The Body and Society* (New York, 1988; London, 1989); L. S. Cahill, *Between the Sexes* (Philadelphia and New York, 1985); C. Gilligan, *In a Different Voice* (Cambridge, MA, and London, 1982); P. K. Jewett, *Man as Male and Female* (Grand Rapids, 1975); C. S. Lewis, *The Four Loves* (New York and London, 1960); W. E. May, *Marriage and Chastity* (Chicago, 1981); J. B. Nelson, *Embodiment* (Minneapolis, MN, 1978); J. T. Noonan, Jr., *Contraception* (Cambridge, MA, and London, ²1986); O. O'Donovan, *Begotten or Made?* (Oxford, 1984); P. Ramsey, *Fabricated Man* (New Haven, CT, and London, 1970); E. Schillebeeckx, *Marriage* (ET, New York and London, 1965); S. Terrien, *Till the Heart Sings* (Philadelphia, 1985); H. Thielicke, *The Ethics of Sex* (ET, New York and London, 1964); P. Turner (ed.), *Men and Women* (Cambridge, MA, 1989).

G.C.M.

TWELVE

Pastoral Care, Counselling and Psychotherapy

12

It is important to see the 20th-century phenomena of counselling and psychotherapy in the context of the origins and history of pastoral care.

1. Pastoral care

Pastoral care is the practical outworking of the church's* concern for the everyday and ultimate needs of its members and the wider community. That concern has its mainspring in the love (see [2]) that God (see [1]) has for his people and for his world. There have been many attempts to place pastoral care in the overall calling of God to and through his people. For example, Jacob Firet's analysis of pastoring comprises *kerygma*, *didachē* and *paraklēsis*, terms derived from the Gk. NT and emphasizing the activities of preaching, teaching and practical application respectively. It is in the paracletic ministry (where the term *paraklēsis* includes encouragement, exhortation and consolation) that we see the focus of pastoral care; this in turn may be subdivided into elements of the prophetic, pastoral (or shepherding component), priestly and physicianly. It is important to remember that under each of these perspectives, Christian caring will always have a missionary thrust: *e.g.* under the 'prophetic', see Jn. 4:15–42; in 'shepherding', see Lk. 15:4–7 and Jn. 10:16; in the 'priestly', see 2 Cor. 5:18–21; and in the 'physicianly', see Mk. 2:1–12. Each of these elements has both individual and corporate aspects.

a. Prophetic care. The twin call of the prophet was to warn of personal, communal and national judgment as well as to give promise of restoration and renewal. Jeremiah, for instance, anticipated captivity and exile for Judah in the near future and, in generations to come, the return to the Promised Land (Je. 13:19; 23:7–8; 30:3). Moses heard tell of a prophet who would come with godly authority (Dt. 18:18–19), and this promise was fulfilled in the life and teaching of Jesus (Lk. 7:16; 24:19; Acts 7:37). We can see this prophetic role in Christ's encounters in the elements of declaring, exhorting, challenging, confronting and calling to repentance. This function also pervades the early church and is picked up, for example, in the Pauline use of the word *noutheteō* ('to admonish, warn, advise or instruct'), in the context of Christian fellowship (Rom. 15:14; Col. 3:16; 1 Thes. 5:12).

b. Shepherdly care. One of the cardinal pictures of God in the OT is that of shepherd (Gn. 48:15; Pss. 23:1; 80:1; Is. 40:11) and this imagery of practical caring is carried over into his call to military and political leaders to act as 'under-shepherds' (2 Sa. 7:7; Je. 23:1–4). In the context of the faithlessness of the latter there is promise of a Messiah-shepherd in Ezk. 34:23–24; 37:24; Zc. 11:7–11 and 13:7. The fulfilment of this expectation is clear in the portrayal of Christ as the one who gathers the 'lost sheep of Israel' (Mt. 9:36; 10:6; 15:24) and who is the good shepherd (Jn. 10:11–18), anticipated in Ezk. 34:11–16. In Jn. 10 the shepherding metaphor carries a picture of a leader whose relationship with his followers is

intimate, trustworthy, self-sacrificing, guiding, protecting and nurturing. The pastoral concern couched within this description is picked up at a number of points in the NT (see, *e.g.*, Jn. 21:15–17; Heb. 13:20; 1 Pet. 2:25; 5:1–4). Further, we see something of this pastoral commitment carried over into the consoling, comforting and encouraging actions of the early Christians, implied in certain uses of *parakaleō* (2 Cor. 1:3–7; 7:4–7; 2 Thes. 2:16–17; Heb. 6:18), in the guidance offered in the Pastoral Epistles and in the tender remonstrations of the Johannine letters. Again, it is important to see here the mutuality of the call to encourage, care for and shoulder burdens amongst the people of God (see, *e.g.*, Gal. 6:2; Heb. 10:24–25).

c. Priestly care. The priestly strand in overall pastoral care has its precursor in the ancient company of the Levites, whose go-between function has been superseded by the high-priestly work of Christ, 'in the order of Melchizedek' (Heb. 7:1–28). Here, Jesus stands as the representative of the people before God, displaying, as fully human, his solidarity with the needy and, as Son of God, his divine calling. This aspect of his caring for humanity is seen in his identifying, mediating, forgiving and reconciling ministry. Without undermining the uniqueness and efficacy of Christ's death and resurrection, God's people are also required to live lives of sacrifice and service as the 'priesthood of all believers' (Ex. 19:6; Is. 61:6; Rom. 15:16; 1 Pet. 2:9; Rev. 1:6; 5:10). In this perspective, the faithful, motivated by the love of Christ, are committed to reconciliation* within the new community (2 Cor. 5:17–21; Eph. 5:1–2; 1 Pet. 1:18–23; 1 Jn. 4:13–19). The church has handled the consequent issue of individual and corporate sin (see Sin and Salvation⑤) in a variety of ways, including an emphasis on the accessibility of forgiveness* directly through prayer; the public acknowledgment of sin within the body of Christ; and the place of private confession,* absolution* and penance in the more Catholic and sacramentalist traditions (Mt. 16:19; 18:15–20; Jn. 20:23; 1 Cor. 5:1–13; 2 Cor. 2:5–11).

d. Physicianly care. The Lord God is shown to be the supreme healer (Ex. 15:26; Dt. 32:39; Jb. 5:18; Ho. 6:1) and his concern for the sufferings of humanity is lived out in the compassionate acts of mercy of Jesus Christ. The comprehensiveness of the Son's ministry to the needy is manifest in the Messianic declaration of Lk. 4:18–19 (see also Is.

12

61:1–2). Here we find a level of care* which is relieving, liberating and restoring, and which seeks to bring wholeness, often through miracles of healing (*cf.* Mt. 11:5), to every aspect of personal and corporate life. As with other strands of pastoral care, God's physicianly activity is mirrored in the healing* work of his followers (1 Ki. 17:17–24; 2 Ki. 20:1–11; Acts 5:12–16; 14:8–10; Rom. 15:18–19; 1 Cor. 12:9). This work has been experienced in a host of ways within the church, including co-operation with medical practice, the use of means such as the laying on of hands and anointing with oil, the setting apart of individual healers, and the release of God's power to heal through his gathered people.

2. The history of pastoral care

The prophetic, pastoral, priestly and physicianly functions of pastoral care are demonstrated in the exhorting, sustaining, reconciling and healing activities of the people of God down through the centuries. Within that history, it is a truism that the church, in its ministry of care, is affected by the mind-sets of contemporary cultures, including the perspectives of current psychologies. Christian response may yield to, resist or enter into debate with the pervasive views of the day, and that response will colour pastoral emphasis. Further, pastoral outreach is always influenced by pastoral theology (see Practical and Pastoral Theology[7]) so that examples of the church's care for the troubled are expressed from and through the range of Christian traditions.

In the pre-Constantinian period mention can be made of the *Shepherd of Hermas*, written in the mid-2nd century and addressing the problem of post-baptismal sin, and the letters of Cyprian (*c.* 200–58), Bishop of Carthage, penned to discipline and encourage the faithful during the Decian persecution. After Constantine,* the medical knowledge and hospital-founding of Basil the Great (*c.* 329–79), the preaching and letter-writing of John Chrysostom* and the influence of Gregory the Great's (see Gregory I*) *Pastoral Rule* were outstanding examples of pastoral care.

Although within the Middle Ages pastoral care was tied to a superstitious sacramentalism, the practical spirituality* of Bernard of Clairvaux (1090–1153) and Hildegard of Bingen (1098–1179), and the commitment to the poor and outcast which characterized the mendicant orders of Dominic Guzman

(*c.* 1170–1221) and Francis of Assisi,* were godly beacons in a dark world.

The Reformation, with its rediscovery of a biblically-based pastoral theology, saw a renewed emphasis on the various strands of pastoral care. For example, in the *Fourteen Consolations* of Martin Luther,* *On the Cure of Souls* by Martin Bucer* and the teaching of John Calvin,* we see the elements of reconciling, shepherding and church discipline respectively.

In the 17th century, key exemplars of pastoral care included Jeremy Taylor* and his practical manuals *The Rule and Exercises of Holy Living* (1650) and *Holy Dying* (1651); George Herbert (1593–1633), whose *Country Parson* (1652) stresses the importance of parish visiting; and, supremely in this context, Richard Baxter* and his *Reformed Pastor* (1656), with its aim to instruct and guide in order to 'acquaint men with that God that made them'.

During the Evangelical Revival, John Wesley,* influenced by Count von Zinzendorf (1700–60) and the Moravians, introduced class meetings, offering advice and comfort which, in turn, spilled over into relief for the poor, and 'bands', small groups of Christians who met to confess their sins and thus find forgiveness and renewal. If we include Wesley's best-seller on practical medicine, *Primitive Physick* (1747), we observe the full spectrum of pastoral care in his work: exhorting, sustaining, reconciling and healing.

Pastoral care during the Industrial Revolution, as well as stressing individual piety, turned a great deal of attention to relieving the disadvantaged, both directly and through social reform: the compassion and campaigning of William Wilberforce* and the Clapham Sect, amongst evangelicals, and the practical acts of mercy carried out by newly founded religious communities in the Catholic tradition, are examples of this emphasis within the 19th century. It was towards the end of this century that the 'pastoralia' of Baxter's day was further systematized into the emerging discipline of pastoral theology.

3. Counselling and psychotherapy: definitions

Before continuing the story of pastoral care into the 20th century we need to examine the rise of the secular psychologies, for it is the influence of these on the church that is the key to the current debate on counselling, psychotherapy and pastoral care. For our purposes, 'counselling' may be defined as that activity which seeks to help others towards constructive change in any or all aspects of life within a caring relationship that has agreed boundaries. It is important to see that there is overlap and continuity between counselling and psychotherapy. The term 'psychotherapy' is more readily used where the aim of 'constructive change' makes more deliberate and consistent use of psychological mechanisms and processes, and where the 'caring relationship' is put on a more professional basis (implying education, expertise, dedication, responsibility and membership of a relevant institution on the part of the therapist). Contemporary counselling is concerned with issues of training, supervision and accreditation,* and so the distinction between psychotherapy and counselling is becoming less sharply defined.

4. The rise of the secular psychologies

By the beginning of the 19th century, metaphysics was dividing into two strands: mental philosophy, concerned with the human functions of the 'mental faculties' – reason,* will,* memory and the emotions;* and the empirical sciences, which sought to examine the natural order by careful observation and controlled experiment. The rise of the secular psychologies – behaviourism,* psychoanalysis,* personalism and transpersonalism – reflect four broad systems in which various attempts have been made to come to terms with how to view the inner and outer aspects of human nature.

a. Behaviourism. Behaviourism seeks to solve the mystery of humanness by majoring on the external and measurable. Its origins lie in an assumptive basis characterized by monism,* a belief that the natural world is made up of one impersonal reality; an extreme determinism (see Free Will and Determinism*) which sees all behaviour as rigidly tied to its cause; and materialism,* in the sense of regarding human beings as simply higher animals. Ivan Pavlov (1849–1936), John B. Watson (1878–1958) and B. F. Skinner,* important proponents of a purist form of behaviourism, have pioneered an understanding of learning theory through such concepts as the reflex arc, conditioning and the reinforcement of behaviour through rewards and punishment. Other experimental psychologists, like Hans Eysenck (1916–) and Joseph

Wolpe (1915–), have built on this earlier thinking useful theories for understanding and treating neurosis.* Much of this work has been turned to good use in behavioural therapy through relaxation techniques, the desensitizing of phobias, modelling so that feared tasks can be achieved, and training in assertiveness. More widely, a number of methodologies utilize cognitive as well as behavioural approaches, for example William Glasser's* reality therapy and Albert Ellis'* rational-emotive therapy. Attempts to change behaviour often lead to directive styles of counselling. As an overview, it is essential that the atheistic and reductionist* assumptions of behaviourism are not confused with research into behaviour and the use of behavioural methods in psychotherapy.

b. Psychoanalysis. In contrast to behaviourism, classical Freudianism investigates a person's inner life, assuming that the individual is the sum of his or her instincts. This time-consuming 'talking cure' seeks to be non-directive, although the analyst is undoubtedly a powerful and influential figure. Sigmund Freud,* the pioneer of psychoanalysis, stressed, in particular, that personality is based on biological drives that are mainly sexual in nature and that it develops through a series of inevitable stages during the first five years of life. Freud's views have been variously altered by subsequent analysts: his daughter, Anna Freud (1895–1982), amplified them, majoring on a greater importance for the ego and defence mechanisms;* Melanie Klein* and her followers modified them, developing object-relations theory and its emphasis on the first year of life; and, among those dissenting from them, Alfred Adler,* stressed aggression and the 'will to power', Carl Jung* openly acknowledged the supernatural in human psychology, and Otto Rank (1884–1939), argued that the trauma of birth is the origin of neurosis. Neo-Freudians, such as Karen Horney (1885–1952) and Erich Fromm,* see people as social beings and aim to help achieve inner strengths and improved relationships, adopting more 'here-and-now' and directive techniques. The late 20th century has seen the emergence of more eclectic approaches, combining Freudian, Jungian and Kleinian insights.

c. Personalism. Secular personalism can be broadly divided into humanistic* and existential psychology.* The first of these is prefigured in the 'understanding' psychology of

12

the German philosopher Wilhelm Dilthey (1833–1911). Carl Rogers* and Abraham Maslow* are well-known advocates of a humanistic psychology which reflects Dilthey's emphasis on personal integration, besides insisting that people have all the inner resources needed for change. Rogers' non-directiveness and client-centredness, avowedly a reaction to behaviourism and Freudianism, have been hugely influential on the rise of the counselling movement in the 1940s and 1950s.

Existential psychology has also been strongly influenced by European philosophy. For example, Søren Kierkegaard* has contributed to the thinking of Viktor Frankl,* whose logotherapy stresses meaning and the 'spiritual core' in human life, and Jean-Paul Sartre* has been a key mentor in the work of R. D. Laing (1927–89), with his anti-psychiatric stance and critique of schizophrenic behaviour.

As an overview, personalism emphasizes both the intrapersonal – the need for the client or patient to find self-esteem and a new autonomy – and the interpersonal – both in the counselling relationship and in a greater sense of responsibility toward others.

d. *Transpersonalism.* In recent decades, a number of humanistic and existential thinkers, seemingly discontent with human nature's inability to set its own house in order, have turned to transpersonalism. Here fulfilment is sought beyond the personal in the realms of the higher Self, Unity Consciousness, the Cosmos or God. This mystical search, aided by forms of meditation and deep-breathing exercises, ultimately encompasses a loss of a sense of self. Rogers, Maslow and Laing have all embraced transpersonalism; other exponents include George Gurdjieff (1874–1949), Peter Ouspensky (1878-1947) and Oscar Ichazo (1931–), each influenced by a range of religious traditions, including Yoga, Sufism, Buddhism and Christian monasticism;* and Roberto Assagioli (1888–1974), whose psychosynthesis, using techniques of imaginative journeying and music therapy, seeks ever-increasing peace and harmony at personal, interpersonal and transpersonal levels. Jung, although within the psychoanalytic tradition, is a transpersonalist of great significance to many Christian counsellors.

Although it is true to say that these four secular psychologies, in various admixtures, have contributed to the so-called 'newer' therapies (such as transactional analysis,* Gestalt therapy,* psycho-drama, primal therapy,*

bioenergetics, cognitive therapy,* neuro-linguistic programming and co-counselling), the influence of transpersonalism, in particular, has been a powerful force throughout the later part of the 20th century, not only in counselling and psychotherapy but in the wider fields of complementary medicine and the alternative therapies.

5. Christian responses

Thomas C. Oden (1931–), the American theologian, has noted a failure of nerve on the part of pastoral care, from the end of the 19th century onwards, in the face of the rise of the secular psychologies. Broadly, Christian response to this rise has been one of assimilation, reaction or dialogue. More specifically, and depending on how the interplay between theology and psychology is seen, we can discern five positions in pastoral care and counselling: assimilative, eclectic, excluding, perspectivalist and integrational. There is, inevitably, some overlap between certain of these positions: for example, one who seeks integration will often exercise a circumspect eclecticism for pragmatic reasons.

a. *Assimilative.* In the early years of the 20th century, pastoral carers in the USA increasingly looked towards scientific psychology for fresh insights, while academic psychology, influenced by William James,* turned its attention to Christianity, thus spawning the discipline of the psychology of religion.* In the 1930s Anton Boisen,* who pioneered the training of ordinands in the setting of psychiatric hospitals, warned the emerging Clinical Pastoral Education (CPE) movement of the dangers of an uncritical assimilation of Freudianism. In the following decades pastoral counselling grew from a blending of mainly liberal theology and secular psychology. Seward Hiltner* has been an important figure in this new psychologically-based pastoral care, with his 'shepherding perspective' on healing, guiding and sustaining. The transatlantic influence of pastoral counselling, both through CPE and the work of key individuals, has been strong: the London-based Leslie Weatherhead (1893–1976), for instance, encouraged by his North American links, in turn backed William Kyle (1925–80), a Methodist minister who eventually founded the Westminster Pastoral Foundation in 1970.

b. *Eclectic.* Eclecticism involves a borrowing from a number of sources and is a widespread stance among counsellors and other members of the caring professions. For many, eclecticism is essentially pragmatic: methods that seem to work are readily employed, each approach being tailored to the client's particular needs. For others, the borrowing is a more circumspect affair where each methodology considered is carefully weighed from Christian perspectives. Examples of eclecticism include Paul Tournier,* who looked to Freudian, Jungian, Rogerian and existential insights, Howard Clinebell (1922–), influenced by cognitive, personalistic and transcendental views, and Frank Lake,* turning to a wide range of the 'newer' therapies.

c. Excluding. In contrast to the assimilative tendencies of the first two groupings, other Christians have adopted a theological position which rejects, ignores or plays down the value of psychological insight. There is an inclination so to emphasize God's special revelation in Christ that the wider concept of a God who reveals himself through the created order is neglected (*cf.* Gn. 1; Pss. 19; 29; 93; 104; Jn. 1:9; Acts 14:17; Rom. 1:20; 2:15; Rev. 4:11, as well as the Christological passages in Eph. 1 and Col. 1). There is a range of emphasis among those who have reacted to the rise of the secular psychologies, extending from one of general dismissal through to more particularizing views that point out the subversive aspects of alien methodologies. Examples within this spread include the Barthian Eduard Thurneysen,* who powerfully stressed the centrality of the Word of God in all pastoral conversation, and Jay Adams (1929–), whose nouthetic counselling (from the Gk. word *noutheteō*, 'to warn or advise') acknowledges debt to O. Hobart Mowrer,* the neo-behaviourist, and Cornelius Van Til (1895–1987), the 'presuppositionalist' theologian.

d. Perspectivalist. Many Christian counsellors, psychotherapists and pastoral carers hold views that see theology and psychology as two valid disciplines which bring complementary understandings to human nature. Both are respected, but there is felt to be little or no overlap between them – either for pragmatic reasons, because life is inflexibly divided between the workaday world of psychology and the disconnected world of Christian belief, or for theoretical reasons, in that each stance is seen as mutually useful but disparate. There has been a great deal of productive thought given to this latter, 'perspectivalist' position as, for example, in the writings of Malcolm Jeeves (1926–) and Donald MacKay (1922–87), in the worlds of psychology and neuroscience respectively.

e. Integrational. Here there is a deliberate attempt to bring together psychological and theological insight into specifically Christian methodologies. The thinking behind this enterprise acknowledges that all statements of truth, whether moral, propositional or ontological truth, are descriptive of God-given reality. Further, it is argued that all disciplines, including theology and psychology, handle the raw material of that same reality and are therefore open to at least a degree of synthesis. In practice, the approach may be one of finding as much common ground as possible, or one that seeks to subsume psychology within the wider orbit of theological reflection. The quest is an ambitious one, and efforts to synthesize range through the complex theories of Lake's primal integration, the more discursive observations of Tournier's dialogue counselling, and the overtly biblical concepts of such as Gary R. Collins (1934–), John D. Carter and Bruce Narramore (1941–) in the USA. Oden, who later moved from liberalism to 'postmodern Christian orthodoxy', has been a particularly important bridge-builder between theology and psychology since the 1950s.

6. Christian approaches

In our survey of Christian responses to secular psychology we have suggested five broad categories. However, methodologies of Christian counselling are not merely the outcome of reaction to what is secular. As unthinking forms of assimilation and the more severely excluding views give way, one hopes, to dialogue and discernment, we can begin to see the pattern of distinctively *Christian* counselling more easily. There are a limited number of ways of viewing human nature, so it is not surprising to find Christian methodologies mirroring something of the emphases of behaviourism, psychoanalysis, personalism and transpersonalism. Although the atheistic and agnostic assumptions of these systems are plainly rejected, Christian thinking in the area of counselling can be looked at in terms of certain parallels. We can examine these trends under the headings of behavioural/cognitive, analytic, Christian personalist and Christian transpersonalist. In the wider context of pastoral care, we see the strands of exhortation, healing, sustenance and reconciliation coming to the fore in many of these methodologies.

12

a. Behavioural / cognitive. Among evangelical Christians there is a significant range of counselling approaches that attract the title 'biblical'. Although, under this broad heading, there are key practitioners, such as Collins and Lawrence J. Crabb, Jr. (1944–), whose styles are more integrational, there are many, whose methodologies have been hammered out in relation to secularism and liberalism, who tend towards an 'excluding' position. Examples of this latter trend include the nouthetic counselling of Adams, the spiritual counselling of Martin Bobgan (1930–) and Deirdre Bobgan (1935–), and the biblical counselling of Scope Ministries, Oklahoma City. A number of these approaches have been gathered into membership of the International Association of Biblical Counsellors. By and large, these methods are behavioural and cognitive, stressing the replacement of wrong patterns of action and thinking with those based on scriptural principles. It is here that the exhortative and confrontational components of prophetic caring are most evident. To this end, many in this group use biblical texts prescriptively.

b. Analytic. A number of therapists have taken analytical theory and practice very seriously and have sought a measure of integration between these and Christian theology. Such practitioners include Fritz Kunkel (1889–1956), who attempted a synthesis of Freudian, Jungian and Adlerian thinking; Ronald Fairbairn (1890–1964) and Harry Guntrip (1901–75), who put forward less deterministic forms of Kleinian theory; and Ian Suttie (1889–1935), who pioneered a style of psychoanalysis which linked Christian love and forgiveness with healthy social interaction. More recently, it is the analyst's fascination with the 'journey back' that has stirred parallels among Christian counsellors. There is variety as the search for earlier and earlier traumata is made, ranging from the methods of prayer counselling,* healing of the memories and faith imagination, through Lake's primal integration, with its attention to birth and intra-uterine experiences, to Kenneth McAll's healing of the family tree.* It is in this subgroup of Christian approaches to caring and counselling that we find the greatest emphasis on certain gifts of the Spirit as an aid to discernment and direction. Although elements of exhortation, sustenance and reconciliation may be present, it is the pastoral perspective of healing – physical, 'inner' (see Inner Healing*) and through deliverance* – which

predominates. These approaches are experiential and creative, rather than behavioural and cognitive. Besides Lake and McAll, proponents include Agnes Sanford (1897–1976), Anne White, Francis MacNutt (1925–) and Michael Scanlan (1931–).

c. Christian personalist. Although all Christian methodologies take note of human specialness in God's eyes, it is the personalists who help remind us most of our privilege as divine image-bearers. In making this crucial corrective there can be a tendency to be too optimistic about human nature, and thus a playing down of individual and corporate sin. Whereas 'excluding' approaches are inclined to neglect a theology of common grace, Christian personalism can be tempted to universalism. However, this development is by no means inevitable and is most readily avoided by a well-reasoned biblical theology. Christian personalism focuses on the relationship in counselling and, at its best, looks to scriptural models of encounter between one person and another. Further, this subgroup is the most representative of the paracletic tradition, where comfort, encouragement and sustenance are integral. In terms of method, the influence of the Bible is often formative rather than prescriptive: Oden, for example, has argued a parallelism between Christ's identification with fallen humanity and the counsellor's empathy;* and Donald Capps (1939–) has looked to the insights of form criticism for guidance in the shape and substance of the counselling process. Other well-known Christian adherents to personalism include Clinebell, and his growth counselling, and Tournier, one of the originators of *Médecine de la Personne.*

d. Christian transpersonalist. All Christian caring and counselling has its transpersonal dimension, but there is an important stream of methodologies which parallels the mystic quest of non-Christian proponents. Here the idea of an 'inner journey' towards union with God is fostered. As a guide on this pilgrimage towards maturity in Christ, the ancient Celtic practice of the 'soul friend' has been re-established in spiritual direction,* whereby a fellow Christian, lay or ordained, is available for regular advice and support. The priestly strand of pastoral care, with its bridge-building and reconciling work, is seen most clearly in this subgroup. The traditions of silence and contemplation, coupled with the reflective and imaginative use of Scripture, are crucial aids to devotion and spiritual growth. For the less discerning Christian transpersonalist, there are dangers of wandering towards Eastern monism* in one direction and occultic* contamination in another. As well as the writings of such Christian mystics as Julian of Norwich (c. 1342–1420) and John of the Cross (1542–91), the *Spiritual Exercises* (completed by 1535) by Ignatius of Loyola* and, most recently, the insights of Jung, are all important influences. Ignatian retreats and Myers-Briggs* workshops, based on Jungian personality types, are further tools for the inner journey. Among Christian transpersonalists who have sought a Christ-centred approach to Jung, Morton Kelsey (1917–) and Christopher Bryant (1905–85) are significant. The psychologist David Benner has contributed a valuable analysis of Christian transpersonalism from a broadly evangelical viewpoint.

7. Current trends in Christian caring and counselling

Whereas the 1960s and early 1970s were marked by a tendency to polarize concerning the links between counselling and Christian caring, and between psychology and theology, the late 1970s and 1980s have seen a much more rigorous critique emerge: assimilation and reaction have been giving way to dialogue. Four cardinal aspects are considered: professionalism, ethics, social concern and spirituality.

a. Professionalism. In 1963 the American Association of Pastoral Counsellors (AAPC) was founded with a firm commitment to professionalized ideals (see Professional Ethics*): pastoral counselling was to be the domain of the clergy and their training was to parallel that of other caring professionals. The concern expressed by Hiltner at that time re-emerged in the objections raised in 1971 by Robert Lambourne,* psychiatrist and theologian, who argued against the institutionalization of pastoral care in Britain. Lambourne's emphasis that Christian caring should be 'lay, corporate, adventurous, variegated and diffuse' was countered by Clinebell, who stressed the need also for professionally trained and accredited clergy as pastoral counsellors. Alastair Campbell (1938–), the pastoral theologian, has carried the debate into the 1980s, seeking to rescue pastoral care from 'professional captivity' and release it into the practical love expressed by the body of Christ. This discussion had earlier been influential on the founding

of the Association for Pastoral Care and Counselling (APCC) in Britain in 1975, in that the APCC is an affiliation of individuals and organizations rather than a regulatory body. In contrast, the Association of Christian Counsellors was set up in 1992 to encourage accreditation* and accountability.* The different views continue in the burgeoning number of training schemes within the churches and in parachurch counselling organizations. In this interchange, it is important that counselling is seen in the context of pastoral care, rather than that counselling is elevated as primary.

b. Ethics. Another aspect of the secularization of pastoral care has been the loss of an ethical cutting-edge: the pastoral and paracletic have been emphasized at the expense of the prophetic and nouthetic. In recent years, however, a better balance between consolation and confrontation has been achieved in a wide range of Christian methodologies. Here, the counselling encounter is more open to values, standards and meaning in encouraging responsibility and right choices. Ethical considerations for the pastoral counsellor include those of confidentiality,* the primacy of what is in the client's best interest (unless conflicting seriously with appropriate societal restraints), the avoidance of abusing a sense of power over the client and the discouragement of continuing dependency. Don Browning (1934–), in his commitment to dialogue between moral theology* and the social sciences, is perhaps foremost in recovering 'practical moral reasoning' in pastoral care.

c. Social concern. Individualism* has been a hallmark of many of the secular psychologies, and the neglect of social and political realities has also been widespread in pastoral caring and counselling. However, from the 1980s onwards many Christians have rediscovered the corporate and structural perspectives of biblical revelation, and a greater awareness of human context has entered the counselling relationship. Issues of justice (see Justice and Peace ③) and mercy* in employment, living conditions, income, language and cultural background, and their impingement on the lives of those seeking counsel, have been more clearly seen. Questions of racism (see Race*), sexism,* classism and ageism have been exposed and challenged within the orbit of a pastoral care which aims to 'satisfy the needs of the oppressed' (Is. 58:10) in the name of Christ.

d. Spirituality. Paralleling, perhaps, trends

in secular counselling where there has been a shift towards the transcendent, the later decades of the 20th century have witnessed a widespread revival of interest in Christian spirituality.* This phenomenon has many facets, including the charismatic and renewal movements, a fresh confidence in a biblical theology among evangelicals, and a reawakening of many in the Catholic and Orthodox traditions to the Word and the Spirit. This focus on spirituality has done a great deal for the quality of pastoral care and counselling in, for example, its stress on the call to Christian maturity, its opening up of a wide range of aids to devotion, and in a renewed emphasis on spiritual direction. Proponents as diverse in theological background as Kenneth Leech (1939–), Martin Israel (1927–), Gerard Hughes, Richard Lovelace (1930–) and Benner have all influenced this trend of exposing the theory and practice of care, counsel and therapy to the searching light of a Christ-centered spirituality.

See especially: ABUSE; ACCEPTANCE; AGEING; ANGER; ANALYTICAL PYCHOLOGY; ANXIETY; BEHAVIOURISM, BEHAVIOUR THERAPY AND MODIFICATION; BEREAVEMENT; BIBLICAL COUNSELLING; BRAINWASHING; CHILDLESSNESS; CLINICAL THEOLOGY; COGNITIVE BEHAVIOUR THERAPY; CONFIDENTIALITY; CONTRACTS IN THERAPY; CROSS-CULTURAL COUNSELLING; DEFENCE MECHANISMS, PSYCHOLOGICAL; DELIVERANCE MINISTRY; DEMONIC; DEPENDENCE; DEPRESSION; DREAMS; DRUGS; EATING DISORDERS; EMOTION; EMPATHY; EXISTENTIALIST PSYCHOLOGIES; FAMILY THERAPY; FEAR; FORGIVENESS; FRANKL, VICTOR; FREUD, SIGMUND; GENETIC COUNSELLING; GESTALT THERAPY; GROUP THERAPY; GUILT; HABIT; HEALING; HOSPICE; HUMAN DEVELOPMENT; HUMANISTIC PSYCHOLOGY; HYPNOSIS; INDIVIDUAL PSYCHOLOGY; INHIBITION; INNER HEALING; INSTITUTIONALIZATION; JUNG, CARL; LAKE, FRANK; LEARNING DISABILITIES; LONELINESS; MANIPULATION; MARRIAGE AND FAMILY COUNSELLING: MENTAL HEALTH; MINISTRY; MORAL BEHAVIOUR, PSYCHOLOGY OF; NEUROSIS; PAIN; PSYCHIATRIC CARE, ETHICS OF; PSYCHOANALYSIS; RAPE; RETIREMENT; ROGERS, CARL; SELF-ESTEEM; SEXUAL COUNSELLING AND THERAPY; SINGLE PARENTS; SUFFERING; SUICIDE; SUPERVISION; TOUCH; TRANSFERENCE; TRANSACTIONAL ANALYSIS; WELFARE STATE; WIDOWHOOD, WIDOWERHOOD.

Bibliography

R. Baxter, *The Reformed Pastor* (1656; Edinburgh, 1974); D. G. Benner, *Psychotherapy and the Spiritual Quest* (Grand Rapids, 1988; London, 1989); D. S. Browning, *Religious Ethics and Pastoral Care* (Philadelphia, 1983); A. V. Campbell, *Paid to Care?* (London, 1985); *idem* (ed.), DPC; D. Capps, *Biblical Approaches to Pastoral Counselling* (Philadelphia, 1981); D. E. Carlson, 'Jesus' Style of Relating: The Search for a Biblical View of Counselling', *JPT* 4, 1976, pp. 181–192; J. D. Carter and B. Narramore, *The Integration of Psychology and Theology* (Grand Rapids, 1979); W. A. Clebsch and C. R. Jaekle, *Pastoral Care in Historical Perspective* (New York, ²1975); H. J. Clinebell, *Basic Types of Pastoral Care and Counselling* (London and Nashville, TN, 1984); G. R. Collins, *The Rebuilding of Psychology: An Integration of Psychology and Christianity* (Eastbourne and Wheaton, IL, 1977; Milton Keynes, 1987); R. A. Duffy, *A Roman Catholic Theology of Pastoral Care* (Philadelphia, 1983); J. Firet, *Dynamics in Pastoring* (ET, Grand Rapids, 1986); S. Hiltner, *Preface to Pastoral Theology* (Nashville, TN, 1958); R. J. Hunter (ed.), DPCC; R. F. Hurding, *The Bible and Counselling* (London, 1992); *idem, Roots and Shoots: A Guide to Counselling and Psychotherapy* (London, 1986) = *The Tree of Healing* Grand Rapids, 1988); M. A. Jeeves, *Psychology and Christianity: The View Both Ways* (Leicester, 1976); S. L. Jones and R. E. Butman, *Modern Psychotherapies: A Comprehensive Christian Appraisal* (Downers Grove, IL, 1991); F. Lake, *Clinical Theology* (London, 1966); R. A. Lambourne, 'Objections to a National Pastoral Organisation', *Con* 35, 1971, pp. 24–31; K. Leech, *Spirituality and Pastoral Care* (London, 1986); R. F. Lovelace, *Dynamics of Spiritual Life* (Exeter and Downers Grove, IL, 1979); J. T. McNeill, *A History of the Cure of Souls* (New York, 1951; London, 1952); H. R. Niebuhr, *Christ and Culture* (New York, 1951; London 1952); T. C. Oden, *Kerygma and Counseling* (New York, 1978); *idem*, 'Recovering Lost Identity', *JPC* 1, 1980, pp. 4–18; S. Pattison, *A Critique of*

Pastoral Care (London, 1988); E. Thurneysen, *A Theology of Pastoral Care* (Richmond, VA, 1962); D. Tidball, *Skilful Shepherds: An Introduction to Pastoral Theology* (Leicester and Grand Rapids, 1986); H. A. Van Belle,

Basic Intent and Therapeutic Approach of Carl R. Rogers (Toronto, 1980); P. C. Vitz, *Psychology as Religion: The Cult of Self Worship* (Grand Rapids, 1977; Tring, ²1981).

R.F.H.

THIRTEEN

Life, Health and Death

The Nicene Creed speaks of the Holy Spirit 'as the Lord, the giver of life', underlining the Christian conviction that all life is a gift from God.

1. Life

God himself is described in both the OT and NT as 'the living God' (*e.g.* Dt. 5:26; Ps. 84:2; Heb. 10:31). As such, God gives life to his creatures. He himself gives to all people life and breath and everything else (Acts 17:25). When he takes away their breath, they die (Ps. 104:29). God is therefore the creative source of all life; all that lives receives its life from him.

The OT uses two Heb. words in particular (*ḥayyîm* and *nepeš*) which can both be translated 'life' in relation to human beings. They come together in Pr. 8:35–36, in which Wisdom says: 'For whoever finds me finds life (*ḥayyîm*) and receives favour from the LORD. But whoever fails to find me harms himself (*nepeš*); all who hate me love death.'

Though sometimes synonymous, *ḥayyîm* can be thought of mostly in terms of human existence – the life referred to in Ec. 5:18 ('the few days of life God has given him') – whereas *nepeš*, often translated 'soul', refers to humans as 'living beings'. When God breathed on his clay creature in the Garden 'man became a living being' (Gn. 2:7). (The Heb. *nepeš* often corresponds with the Gk. *psychē* – the human self* or soul.)

In the NT, the Gk. word *zōē* corresponds with the Heb. *ḥayyîm*. Alongside mere biological life (*bios*), *zōē* refers to life and vitality in the physical sense. *Zōē* can also refer to the supernatural life belonging to God which believers in Christ can receive and enjoy in some measure here and now, but in its fullness hereafter. The *zōē aiōnios* ('eternal life', 1 Jn. 5:20) is also the gift of God (1 Jn. 5:11–12). All life is thus God's gift. So all human life has a sacredness and value.

The sacredness and value of life are also an implication of the biblical view that human beings, male and female (see Sexuality [11]) are made to reflect the image of God* himself. It was this conviction which lay behind the legal requirements in the OT story of Noah, in which God sets out the conditions for life in a fallen, post-Flood world. That story illustrates the value to be placed on both animal and human life, but also the distinctions to be drawn concerning the degrees of protection appropriate to animals and to humans. The blood of animals is not to be needlessly shed; even when animals are used for food 'you must not eat meat that has its lifeblood still in it', for the life of the animal belongs to God. But innocent human life must not be taken at all. The reason given is that human beings are made in God's image (Gn. 9:3–6).

From such passages and from the widespread prohibition against murder (see Ex.

13

20:13), the principle is established throughout the Scriptures that innocent human beings have an absolute right not to be deliberately killed. In the prophets we find reference to the heinous crime of shedding innocent blood (Is. 59:7; Je. 22:3; Ezk. 22:4, *etc.*) and the NT also appeals in strong terms against those whose feet are 'swift to shed blood' (Rom. 3:15 quoting Is. 59:7). Judas' conviction was that he 'betrayed innocent blood' (Mt. 27:4). Human life is to be protected and respected because it is precious, and because ultimately it belongs to God. When Cain kills his brother as recorded in Gn. 4, Abel's blood cries out to God from the ground, because it belongs to God.

The sanctity* of human life is clearly not an absolute principle in the Bible, because of the requirements of capital punishment* at certain stages of the history of the people of God, and the permissibility, indeed requirement, of war* in some instances. But what does seem to be an absolute* is the sanctity of *innocent* human life: that innocent human beings have an absolute right not to be deliberately killed.

It was this principle which underlay the doctrine of non-combatant immunity in the just war theory.* However hard it is to speak in categories of innocence* and guilt* in wartime, a distinction – certainly in the days before the possibilities of global technological warfare – could be made between combatants and non-combatants. The just war criterion of discrimination sought to give expression to this distinction. It was this to which Bishop G. K. A. Bell (1883–1958) appealed in the House of Lords in 1944 in his condemnation of the Allied saturation bombings of Hamburg and Berlin.

The right of innocent human beings not to be deliberately killed is also a key component in the difficult decisions concerning abortion.* Whatever other values need to be weighed in moral decisions concerning abortion, this has to be one of them. The human foetus (see Embryology*) from the beginnings of its life is indisputably human, and indisputably a distinct genetic being. Whatever personal status society chooses to accord to it, it is a living human being – and not only innocent, but voiceless. It seems therefore that it has a prima facie right to protection and to life. Any possibly acceptable decisions to terminate pregnancy* with the death of the foetus would in this light have to be understood within the category of justifiable homicide (see Killing*).

The respect to be accorded to human life also means that no individual may choose death, or seek to cause his or her own death or that of another. This is not to blame a suicidally* depressed* person who, in the darkness of one of the worst pains a human being can face, attempts to take or succeeds in taking his or her life. It is to say that the appropriate response to a suicidal mentality is not assistance in doing the deed (as some of the advocates of voluntary euthanasia* might propose), but the provision of medical and spiritual support to enable the person once again, for as long as God gives life, to choose life. To choose death,* whether one's own or another's, is not an option open to the Christian. It is a denial that the Lord of life is trustworthy in trusting us with life, and it is an assertion of human autonomy* which cannot be justified in the light of the biblical view that human life is dependent on God.

Jesus' statements that he came that his followers might have life 'abundantly' (Jn. 10:10, RSV), and that it is not possible to 'live' by bread alone (Mt. 4:4) suggest a quality of life lived in relation to God which is God's gift, over and above natural physical life. This is the 'eternal life' of which the Fourth Gospel speaks. However, we need very great care in moving from this understanding of life's quality to the 'quality of life'* distinctions which are sometimes made in discussions about the beginning and ending of life. It is sometimes argued that because a person no longer has what is perceived to be a 'worthwhile quality of life', their life is no longer to be protected. However, such a person remains God's image-bearer, and in any case no one of us is in a position to judge the worthwhileness of another's life. As long as we are in the presence of a living human being, we are in the presence of someone whose life is precious and normally to be protected. That is not, of course, to deny the difficulties which sometimes surround the definition of death.

2. Health

Health,* according to Karl Barth,* is the strength for life. This definition needs, however, to be unpacked. Some people view health in contrast to 'disease', a pathological condition usually understood in physical terms. This leads to a minimal and physical understanding of health. Others contrast health with 'illness', a word used to describe a person's subjective perception of the disorder within themselves. Yet others define health in relation to 'sickness', which is defined socially in terms of a deviation from what society accepts as normal. This leads to a range of approaches to the definition of health, from the minimal physical aspects, to the maximal understanding of health as complete well-being at all levels of life, physical, mental, social, environmental and spiritual.

The maximal definition of health can be readily related to the biblical concept of 'shalom'. Often translated 'peace',* shalom means much more than the absence of conflict. Essentially a social rather than an individual term, shalom means wholeness, well-being, vigour and vitality in all the dimensions of human life. There are many places in the OT where shalom is linked to health. For example, Jeremiah writes: 'We hoped for peace [šālôm] but no good has come, for a time of healing, but there was only terror' (Je. 8:15). The Suffering Servant of Isaiah suffers for the healing and atonement of the people: 'Upon him was the chastisment that made us whole [šālôm], and with his stripes we are healed' (Is. 53:5). In the NT also the concepts of shalom and health are linked (Lk. 10:5–9; Heb. 12:13–14). In the Synoptic Gospels, the exorcisms and healings of Jesus demonstrate that he is the Messiah, the Prince of Peace, anointed to preach good news to the poor, to proclaim release to the captives, recovering of sight to the blind, and to set at liberty those who are oppressed (Lk. 4:18). Indeed, the NT word usually translated 'salvation' can also mean 'health'. Jesus is the bringer of shalom. Concern for an individual person's health and well-being needs to be set within this more social and corporate context.

The Bible points us to a holistic and dynamic concept of health which covers individual and social, physical and mental, temporal and spiritual life.

If this is coupled with a view that humanity (see [4]) is made to reflect the image of God, and that human beings are 'on the way' to true personal human life as they are in Christ, being renewed by his grace through the Holy Spirit, then Barth's definition of health as the strength for life – or, as Jürgen Moltmann (1926–) puts it, 'health is the strength to be human' – can be accepted.

If human life is God's gift, and health is the strength to be human, then a person's right to his or her health is a basic right (see Rights, Human*) which lays on each person for himself or herself and for others the duty of respecting and facilitating health. Just as God may

withhold life, so he may withhold health – but we may not make such judgments on one another. Rather, there is laid on each of us an obligation to ensure as far as possible that we and others are able to live healthy lives.

This will need to be expounded in the light of our theology of the *body* as a temple of the Holy Spirit,* which lays upon us the responsibility for bodily care: nourishment, clothing, hygiene, housing, recreation, sports,* sleep and appropriate use of medication. It will take seriously a theology of *community* (see Community Ethics[16]), and the need to combat social structures which may impede health by fracturing community. The creation mandate of Gn. 1:28 leads to a theology of the *environment** and the significance of the natural order which requires us to take seriously the implications for health of environmental pollution, ecological devastation and climate change. There is need for popular understanding of the need for clean drinking water, the avoidance of toxic gases in the air, the enforcement of speed limits. All this needs to be set in the context of a theology of *vocation*,* which may involve in some circumstances the risk to an aspect of health in the service of God. Concern for the health of the self has to be brought into line with a proper sense of self-denial, and a willingness to suffer and even forego health for some greater good.

The great costs of contemporary technological medicine require the involvement of *government** in the allocation of resources, and indicates the importance of government, local and national, as a limited and temporary provision of God for the furthering of justice in human society. The allocation of health care* resources is at once a *global* question (see Global Ethics[15]), related to economic structures and international co-operation, a *national* question in the allocation of priorities in national budgets between health care and other social priorities, and a *local* question (which medical needs shall take priority?). Who may benefit when not all can benefit because resources are limited? Are resources to be allocated on the basis of quality of life judgments (see QALY*), or on the basis of medical indications, or random distribution, or first come, first served, or what? The role of the *family** in health care is also important, especially in the Third World.

3. Disease, handicap and suffering

The biblical picture of shalom needs to be

balanced by the biblical picture of a fallen world (see Fall*). Since the Garden of Eden, this world has displayed an ambiguity of beauty and brokenness. The harsh realities of struggle in this world are related in the biblical account to the alienation* between human beings and God which has led to alienation of human beings from each other, from their environment, and within themselves.

Sometimes ill health is related to specific sin (Miriam in Nu. 12; Uzziah in 2 Ch. 26:19). In other places we are warned not to assume that a person's suffering is necessarily related to his or her sin (Jn. 9:2; Lk. 13:2). Sometimes the sins of the fathers are visited on the children (Ex. 20:5). Disease, suffering* and death are part of the way things are in a sin-infected world. Our attitude to such distortions can itself be healthy or sick.

If health is the strength for human existence, even those who are seriously ill can will to be healthy without any optimism or illusions about their condition. They are, argues Barth, to will to exercise the power that remains to them in spite of every obstacle. Sickness is a forerunner and messenger of death. It serves to remind us, as Dr Robert Twycross (1941–) has put it, that 'a doctor practises medicine in the knowledge that eventually all his patients will die'. The same applies to the Christian ministry of healing.* Sickness is the 'inevitable encroachment of the realm of death upon the living space squandered and forfeited by man' (Barth). In other words, handicap (see Disability and Handicap*), disease and illness are painful and visible reminders that we live in a fallen world. Conversely, sickness can also be a messenger and forerunner of life beyond death. Christian faith takes the sting out of death, and opens up the hope of resurrection.* We need a view of suffering which acknowledges both its pain* and its goal. There can be a pain which heals, a suffering which is a sharing in the suffering of Christ. Part of the Christian understanding of growth to maturity* in Christ involves an acknowledgment that 'suffering produces perseverance; perseverance character; and character hope' (Rom. 5:3–4). Sometimes God's power is made known in our weakness (2 Cor. 12:9).

This reminds us that, though it is part of our human responsibility to live healthily, health cannot ever be thought of as an absolute. Nor is the absence of suffering life's most important goal. This side of the Fall and this side of heaven, the ambiguity of the human situation is such that handicap, pain and disease are part of the limitations of life. Responsibility in health care thus needs to find an appropriate balance between the encouragement, protection and preservation of life, and the relief of suffering. Natural physical life is not an absolute.

It is well to recall Bonhoeffer's* insistence that natural life is at one and the same time a means to an end and an end in itself. To absolutize life only as a means to an end (whether that be the common good, or the vision of God) leads to the 'mechanization' of life, in which the person's physical life is seen of value only as a means to some social or spiritual goal. Physical life then loses its significance. On the other hand, to absolutize life as an end in itself (which Bonhoeffer calls 'vitalism') separates life from the ultimate goals which give it meaning and significance. There is a tension and paradox to life both as means and as end; and our view of life, and of the medical practice appropriate to it, must avoid the extremes which make an absolute of one of the other.

Sometimes medical decisions are based on the belief that natural physical life is an absolute before which all else must be sacrificed. Because of increasingly sophisticated technology it is possible to extend life's length in a way which simply prolongs the processes of dying (see Death and Dying*), effectively mechanizing and so dehumanizing both life and death. It is not a doctor's duty to prolong life for as long as possible at whatever cost. A point of decision is reached when further treatment of a patient is no longer curative, and medical responsibility then shifts from sustaining life and making available the resources for living, to that of allowing a dying person to die, and making his or her dying as comfortable as possible. This is not a distinction between 'to treat' and 'not to treat', but rather a question as to what form of treatment is appropriate.

Christian concern for health care is seen also in a wide range of church-based ministries, from the provision of hospices* for terminal care to the exercise of charismatic or sacramental healing* ministries. All are ways of responding to the prayer of John 'that you may be in health' (3 Jn. 2, RSV).

4. Death

In one sense, death is the most natural, and in another sense the most unnatural, of events.

We all have to face the moment when death brings us to the edge of our existence in this world. 'In the midst of life we are in death' says the Burial Service in the Book of Common Prayer. 'There is a time for everything . . . a time to be born and a time to die' (Ec. 3:1–2). Death is a part of the way it is with living beings in this world (*e.g.* Jos. 23:14; 1 Ki. 2:2). In some parts of the OT, death is depicted simply as a natural part of human existence. Yet other strands in the Bible speak of death as a symbol of divine judgment.* There is something evil about death; it has a negative and unnatural component. When God said to the man in the Garden, 'When you eat of it you will surely die' (Gn. 2:17), the indication is that death is the divine judgment on human sin. For Adam death was not the end of physical life – it was a change of situation before God. The blessing, freedom and vitality of life in the Garden give way to curse, bondage, toil and alienation outside the Garden, with the way back barred by cherubim with a flaming sword. This biblical imagery foreshadows the way in which, in later writings, death puts on the clothing of a powerful ruler who holds sinful humankind in his thrall. Death becomes a power which can dominate the present life of an individual. Thus for Paul 'the wages of sin is death' (Rom. 6:23), and 'through Christ Jesus the law of the Spirit of life' sets believers 'free from the law of sin and death' (Rom. 8:2).

Death, then, functions as a sign of the judgment of God against all that is disordered and ungodly in life. Barth comments: 'The man who fears death, even though he contrives to put a somewhat better face on it, is at least nearer to the truth than the man who does not fear it, or rather pretends that there is no reason why he should do so. Since it is a sign of the divine judgment of human sin and guilt, it is very much to be feared.'

However, in the ministry of Jesus we see him confronting sickness, disease and death. His snorting indignation at the grave of Lazarus indicates his sense that death is an alien intrusion into the goodness of God's world (Jn. 11:33). Yet, paradoxically, Jesus himself dies, and so in himself suffers death as the judgment of God. The NT faith affirms that those who by faith are 'in Christ' are freed from experiencing this judgment. For the Christian the 'sting' of death is drawn. He is no longer under threat of divine judgment. The last enemy is overcome. Death, in the death of Christ, is seen to be God's enemy, and God 'treats it as such by placing Himself at the side of man in the verdict there pronounced, and snatching man from its jaws by the death of Jesus for him' (Barth). Death remains for us as a sign of divine judgment. We no longer have to suffer the judgment itself.

Christian faith sees death, then, as ambiguous. There is a negative, evil and symbolic side to death, even when death's power is broken through the life of the Holy Spirit, but there is also a sense in which for the believer, death simply becomes 'falling asleep' in Jesus (1 Thes. 4:13).

Physical death is an enemy whose sting is drawn, though in physical experience we still all have to die.

This ambiguity is seen in the processes which are common in the experiences of those who know that they will soon die. Elisabeth Kübler-Ross's (1926–) studies of dying patients in Chicago illustrated the phases of emotional change from anger,* through bargaining and depression to acceptance, which are typical attitudes in terminally ill patients. The pastoral care of the dying and bereaved has recently been increasingly informed by such studies, recognizing the importance of the processes of grieving, both in the terminally ill as they contemplate their own death, and in the bereaved* as they come to terms with the loss of a loved one. The rituals associated with rites of passage can be powerful pastoral moments in the status transitions of life (baptism and marriage) and death (funerals).

The ambiguity associated with our understanding of death is also reflected in the perplexities surrounding the definition of death for the purposes of clinical practice. In the majority of cases, the cessation of respiration and the stoppage of the heart still remain valid criteria for determining death. But, particularly with the increasing sophistication of intensive care techniques, the possibilities of sustaining organ functioning through artificial means are now widespread in the developed world, and give rise to the need for careful criteria in the decisions whether and when to turn off machines.

Various criteria have been proposed. Joseph Fletcher* lists certain 'Indicators of Personhood', the minimum features which need to be present by which to affirm the presence of a living human person. Richard McCormick (1922–) offers the concept of 'relational potential', suggesting that life is to be preserved not for its own sake, but for the sake of other

13

values such as personal relationship. When the potential for relationship is no longer present – such as in some severely handicapped people – the need to preserve physical life ceases. Other writers draw on the distinction between 'ordinary' and 'extraordinary' means (see Ethics of Medical Care[14]) as a way of deciding on appropriate medical treatment in the case of the seriously ill, and yet others, notably Paul Ramsey,* argue for a 'medical indications policy' which concentrates on a comparison between different forms of treatment available, and does not consider questions of a person's putative 'worthwhile quality of life'.

As we have said earlier, the choice of death, for oneself or for another, is not a choice that is open to Christian morality, with its belief that life is on trust from God, and that we are not merely autonomous agents. The pressure from the Voluntary Euthanasia Society in the UK, the Hemlock Society in the US, and similar groups elsewhere, however, coupled with the growing practice of terminating life in places like Holland, keep the question of the choice of death high on the social agenda (see Euthanasia*). As Twycross notes, the strength of the argument in favour of euthanasia seems to be based on two assumptions, both of which he challenges. The first is that terminal pain cannot be relieved – which is countered by the experience of the hospice movement. The second is that doctors must preserve life at all costs – a view we have already questioned.

Both life and death are in the hands of God. 'I have come', said Jesus, 'that they may have life.' Christian moral judgments and Christian pastoral care need to be based on the fundamental assumptions that life is God's gift and therefore good, and normally to be protected, and that death is not open to human choice.

See especially: ABORTION; AGEING; AIDS; BIRTH CONTROL; BURIAL AND CREMATION; COMA; CONSENT; DEATH AND DYING; DEMENTIA; DEMONIC; DEPENDENCE; DEPRESSION; DISABILITY AND HANDICAP; DRUGS; EATING DISORDERS; HANDICAPPED, CARE OF; HEALING; HEALTH AND HEALTH CARE; HOSPICE; HUMAN DEVELOPMENT; INTENSIVE CARE; KILLING; LEARNING DISABILITIES; MATURITY; MENTAL HANDICAP; MENTAL HEALTH; NEGLIGENCE, PROFESSIONAL; PAIN; SELF-POISONING; SICK, CARE OF; SUFFERING; SUICIDE; TRIAGE; WELFARE STATE.

Bibliography

R. Anderson, *Theology, Death and Dying* (Oxford and New York, 1988); D. Atkinson, 'Care of the Family in Dying and Grieving: A Pastoral Approach', in R. Spilling (ed.), *Terminal Care at Home* (Oxford, 1986); K. Barth, CD III/2 and III/4; A. Fergusson (ed.), *Health: The Strength to be Human* (Leicester, 1993); E. Kübler-Ross, *On Death and Dying* (New York, 1969; London, 1970); H. Thielicke, *Living with Death* (ET, Grand Rapids, 1983); R. G. Twycross, 'Euthanasia', in *DME*.

D.J.A.

13

FOURTEEN

Ethics of Medical Care

thical reflection on the practice of medicine pre-dates Christianity. It can be traced back to the school of thought associated with Hippocrates (c. 460–c. 377 BC), who gave his name to the Hippocratic Oath.* In its original form the Oath involved swearing by pagan gods, but it has proved readily adaptable to other religious settings. Christians, along with Jews and Muslims, saw much to commend in this tradition, and the Hippocratic Oath has had an enduring effect upon Western medicine.

Despite the biblical reproach of King Asa, that 'even in his illness he did not seek help from the LORD, but only from the physicians' (2 Ch. 16:12), and notwithstanding the statement by a 2nd-century rabbi that 'the best of doctors will go to hell', Judaism has generally had a very positive appreciation of the art of medicine. It has seen medicine as an example of creative partnership between God and humanity. Some distinguished rabbis were themselves physicians.

Similarly, from its outset Christianity showed a keen interest in the practice of medicine. This is not surprising, given the prominence of healing* in the ministry of Jesus. Jesus presented his miraculous curing of the sick, exorcizing of the possessed and raising of the dead, along with the preaching of the good news to the poor, as signs of his Messianic authority and indication that the kingdom of God* had come (Lk. 7:18–23; 11:14–20). The concern shown by Jesus for the restoration of physical and mental health is consistent with the holistic view of humanity found in the OT, where God's blessing usually includes a sense of earthy well-being and, not least, living to a good old age (see, e.g., Is. 65:13–23). Moreover, though the Bible preceded scientific medicine, it is not silent on the art of healing,

and there are frequent allusions to the use of plants, oil, balm, wine, etc., for therapeutic purposes. Christians therefore readily recognized the worthiness of medicine's goals, and from the 4th century AD onwards Christian medical institutions became widespread.

Attitude to the taking of life

The church soon found itself forced to reflect on aspects of medical ethics, particularly issues relating to the taking of life. Despite the Hippocratic Oath's disapproval of the practice, abortion* was common in the Graeco-Roman world, as was infanticide* by exposure. The Church Fathers were united in condemning both. Despite this, they were not entirely agreed about the precise status of the foetus: we see in their writings the beginnings of two divergent views still reflected today. One strand of opinion insists on the full personal status of the unborn child from the time of conception, while the other strand makes a distinction roughly corresponding to that between embryo and foetus. Exodus 21:22–25, which refers to the hypothetical situation of a pregnant woman being accidentally hurt in a brawl between two men, with the result that a child 'comes forth', has played a significant part in this debate. It is not clear how this passage should be interpreted. If a premature birth is meant (see NIV), the implication is that the possible resulting death of the child is as serious as the death of the mother, both being covered under the penalty 'life for life'. But if a miscarriage is meant (see RSV), the implication is that the life of the pregnant woman ranks more highly than that of the child, the loss of the latter warranting only a fine.

The LXX translators actually complicated interpretation of this passage further by introducing an extra detail: they made a distinction between the 'formed' and the 'unformed' foetus, only the death of the former deserving the ultimate punishment. This distinction fitted with Aristotelian views about the nature of the soul and the time of 'ensoulment', which were assimilated by important Christian theologians including Thomas Aquinas.* He believed that the embryo was 'animated' successively by a vegetative, animal and finally a human soul. Nevertheless, those who took such a view did not thereby believe early abortions to be justified. They simply thought abortions which took place before animation of the human soul warranted less severe punishment than those which occurred after that stage. Until very recent times, there was basic agreement that life both at the embryonic and foetal stage was sacred and worthy of respect.

The impact of Christian ethical thought upon the history of medicine has very often been in terms of proscribing and opposing new developments. With regard to the advent of certain techniques like anaesthesia, narcotics in childbirth and vaccination, this has been misguided and unfortunate. But it has had a crucial and salutary role in affirming the conviction that the intentional killing* of innocent human beings is always wrong, and comprises no proper part of medical care. The word 'innocent' is important. Following exceptions to the sixth commandment implicitly made in the Bible, mainstream sectors of the Christian church have defended the taking of life in the circumstances of war, or as punishment for the most serious types of crime. The shedding of innocent blood, however, is consistently condemned in Scripture (see, e.g., Ex. 23:7; Pr. 6:17; Je. 7:6). Human beings are created by God, made in the image of God,* and redeemed by God: their lives should be held in precious regard by the rest of humanity (see Sanctity of Human Life*). While it is true that attempts to justify ending life within a medical context usually have the welfare of the patient in view, Christian ethicists have not traditionally regarded this beneficent motive as sufficient ground for overturning a deep-seated moral presumption.

Double effect

The fact remains that application of the principle that human life is sacred raises as many questions as it answers, especially in the modern context of fast-changing medical developments. Roman Catholic moral theology, which has provided the most systematic approach to medical ethics in the course of church history, has not been lacking in sophisticated concepts to deal with problematical situations. For instance, it has allowed the *indirect* killing of human beings through use of the principle of double effect.* In essence, this principle says that one is justified in permitting incidental evil effects from one's good actions if there is a proportionate reason for doing so.

A situation to which double effect is often applied is that involving a pregnant woman who has cancer of the uterus. Are doctors justified in removing her womb, knowing that such an action will result in the death of the foetus contained within it? The answer Catholic moralists have usually given is 'yes', because it meets the principle's fourfold conditions, *viz.*: 1. the action of removing the womb is not itself evil; it may be described as morally neutral; 2. the intention of the act, that of saving the life of the mother (the only life which can be saved in the circumstances), is a good one; 3. the good effect, relief to the mother, occurs at the same time as the evil effect, death of the foetus, so the latter is not being used as means to an end; 4. the life-or-death situation is grave enough to satisfy the criterion of proportion.

The principle of double effect has much to commend it. It attempts to steer a moral path which is neither unbendingly absolutist* nor thoroughgoingly consequentialist.* It has the virtue in this instance of retaining an important rule (against the direct taking of innocent life) while allowing action which achieves the limited but significant good which can be achieved in a tragic situation. But it is difficult to avoid some impression of artificiality about double effect. What if the woman's medical condition is such that the only way to save her life is through a direct assault on the foetus (e.g. where the wall of her aorta is so weakened that it balloons out behind her uterus)? The mother's life exercises a moral claim which surely justifies such action, however regrettable it may be in terms of damage done to the foetus.

Another situation where double effect has been applied is in relation to the care of terminally ill patients (see Death and Dying*). Catholic moral theologians have defended the use of large doses of analgesic where the intention is to reduce pain, even though such drugs may have a suppressive side-effect on the respiratory system and possibly shorten the patient's life. Neither they nor other Christian thinkers who oppose the direct taking of life believe this commits one to the corollary that all possible steps to keep a patient alive as long as possible should always be taken. They recognize that there comes a time when the patient should be allowed to die, notably when the struggle to cure a fatal illness has been lost and imminent death seems certain.

Ordinary and extraordinary means

Another influential concept in the Catholic tradition has been the distinction between *ordinary* and *extraordinary* means. According to this a sick person is obliged, as are those who care for that person, to employ all the obvious available means of preserving life and restoring health. If a woman is diagnosed as having a malignant lump in her breast, it denotes an irresponsible attitude to her body not to have the lump removed. Ordinary means are all treatments which offer a reasonable hope of benefit and can be obtained and used without undue expense, pain or other inconvenience. But a patient need not feel bound to incur or impose on his or her family an impoverishing expense; nor feel bound to submit to treatment which would cause great expense and distress, and of which the benefits are uncertain. A man dying from acute leukaemia need not feel obliged to submit to chemotherapy if that holds out the possibility of extending life by no more than a year and there is a less than 50% chance of it doing that. He may accept such treatment if he wishes but others should not force him to do so.

The distinction between ordinary and extraordinary means is one which can be defended on theological grounds. It does seem to correspond in an approximate sort of way to a Christian attitude which consists of a readiness to accept both life and death (see Life, Health and Death[13]) in a positive spirit. Paul looked forward to life beyond the grave, but was determined to serve God as best he could all the days left to him on earth: 'For to me, to live is Christ and to die is gain' (Phil. 1:21). On the one hand, Christians regard life as a gift from God, a state of being which we should hold sacred and seek to preserve. Inspired by the example of Christ, they are able to see redemptive possibilities in suffering: God's strength can be made perfect in our weakness (2 Cor. 12:9), and his presence can lighten the darkest hour. The state of death is more ambiguous. Because it represents the 'wages of sin' (Rom. 6:23), death has negative and hostile connotations, yet these are 'swallowed up in victory' (1 Cor. 15:54) when a believer claims the resurrection promise of Christ. Where that is the case, death need not be viewed as an enemy to be averted at all costs; it too can be a gift from God, a merciful release to a life beyond suffering. A balanced view of this sort points to the appropriateness of a medical policy which seeks to save life whenever the prognosis gives cause for hope, but is ready to accept death when the prospects are dire.

However, the distinction between ordinary and extraordinary means also has its limitations. First, the issue is complicated by the fact that in some cases patients are incapable of communicating whether they wish extraordinary means to be used to prolong their lives. Decisions have to be made for the comatose (see Coma*) or mentally retarded. Secondly, the line between ordinary and extraordinary means is a sliding one which changes with the passage of time. At one time amputation of a limb was clearly an extraordinary medical procedure, but anaesthetics, disinfectants and artificial limbs have moved it from one category to the other. What would one say now about kidney and heart transplants? Thirdly, the distinction begs the question of whether the fact that death is diagnosed as imminent makes a difference. A course of antibiotics for pneumonia would generally be considered an ordinary means, yet for centuries the illness has been described as 'the old man's friend'.

Care of the dying and the handicapped new-born

A more helpful concept is arguably that provided by the American Protestant ethicist Paul Ramsey* in *The Patient as Person*. He commends a policy of only *caring* for the dying. 'Dying' means someone in an irreversibly dying condition. It is not enough simply to say that a patient has cancer. If detected in its early stages cancer can be arrested, and even where it persists may, with the aid of appropriate medical treatment, permit an individual several years of life. But when a patient is in the final stages of a terminal illness, and doctors know that they can now do nothing to arrest its progress, it is right that medical objectives switch from saving life to providing the best possible quality of care.* This will probably include the

14

administration of drugs to relieve the pain caused by the illness; it may also entail not administering remedial treatment for a secondary illness which brings a certain death closer. The emphasis should be on care, on filling the final days of a patient with as much companionship and as little suffering as is practical (see Hospice*).

Another highly contentious issue is the treatment of severely handicapped new-born babies. Should their situation be seen as analagous to that of the dying, so that a policy of not intervening to supply corrective treatment is equally appropriate? Ramsey would say not necessarily. Certainly, where the extent of a baby's handicap is so severe that its death can be predicted as imminent, there is no point in carrying out futile operations. But the fact that a baby is handicapped should not be used as an excuse for neglecting routine operations and feeding procedures without which a child born with, e.g., Downs Syndrome or spina bifida will starve and die.

If an operation to remove a bowel obstruction is indicated to save the life of a normal infant, it should also be applied to a Downs infant. In an age when elimination of handicapped life is becoming an increasingly routine procedure at the foetal stage, Christians should be in the vanguard of those affirming the value of children born with severe handicap. But it has to be acknowledged that decisions about whether or not to treat are often extremely difficult because of the uncertainty of knowing how long a child might survive. At this and at the other end of life, it is perhaps more difficult than Ramsey concedes to identify when a patient is in a dying process. Nevertheless, his approach stands out as an attempt to apply rigorously medical criteria to decisions about treatment. He finds speculation about the future happiness of the children concerned invidious, in sharp contrast to another Protestant ethicist, Joseph Fletcher,* who takes an unashamedly utilitarian approach to such issues. Fletcher thinks that all Downs children would be better off dead and seems curiously blind to the fact that such children are renowned for their happy disposition, and often bring joy to their parents and others.

Commission and omission

In the work of Ramsey we see a Protestant engaging with a tradition of Christian writing on medical ethics which had been dominated by Roman Catholics, criticizing it, refining it

but essentially emerging with some fairly cautious, conservative positions. Certainly he stands by the traditional view that, while allowing a patient to die may in some circumstances be right, active killing of the patient is wrong. However, this view has come under serious attack in recent years, mainly (but not entirely) from secular philosophers and medical practitioners. The criticism focuses on the moral distinction commonly thought to prevail between acts of commission and omission.

Critics of the traditional view argue that in taking a decision not to pursue a particular course of action (such as saving life) one can be as responsible for the consequence which follows (the death of an individual) as if one takes a decision actually to cause it. If a father who desired the death of his son discovered him drowning in the bath and omitted to rescue him, we adjudge his behaviour just as reprehensible as if he had pushed his son's head under the water. In a similar way (though now assuming the absence of any evil motives), a doctor should be prepared to accept responsibility for the fact that a decision to withdraw support or withhold treatment is likely to bring forward the timing of a patient's death. Moreover, it is arguable that a readiness to let die but not kill will lead in some cases (where pain cannot be controlled) to an increase in the patient's suffering. Arguments such as these have fuelled the demand for the right to voluntary euthanasia* over recent decades. In Holland, the traditional ethic no longer holds sway and the practice of deliberately inducing death by the use of barbiturates and other drugs is now widespread.

However, most Christian writers (and indeed the majority of senior figures in Western medical circles) stand by the distinction between acts of commission and acts of omission. A doctor who withholds treatment does carry some responsibility for whatever ensues, but it is unlikely that he actively seeks the death of the patient, and he does not usually know with any certitude that the patient will die imminently. His motive is not so much to hasten the time of death as it is to prolong life no longer. The nuance is a fine one, but the evidence is that it matters, psychologically, both to the medical profession themselves and to the public's perception of them. If the sphere of medical care comes to include the deliberate inducing of death, this involves a radical reshaping of the task of medicine. Fortunately,

14

recent improvements in the quality of terminal care, especially the greater sophistication which hospices have developed in the use of pain-killing drugs, mean that few patients are now left to die in conditions of extreme suffering. One strong argument against legalizing euthanasia is that it might lead to a loss of impetus in the current movement towards better care for the dying.

Use of the Bible

The Roman Catholic contribution to the ethics of medical care is substantial. But it is open to criticism for being over-formal and too dependent on abstract principles derived from a rather narrow interpretation of natural law,* as evidenced by the way in which papal disapproval of artificial means of birth control has been maintained. A number of present-day Catholic writers on medical ethics, Bernard Häring (1912–), Charles Curran (1934–) and Richard McCormick (1922–), criticize their own tradition on this score. If Protestant and in particular evangelical Christians are to make a significant contribution to medical ethics (and thus far their record has been patchy), in what direction should they be moving? One hopes they will look to the Bible with confidence. But too much should not be expected from a straightforward appeal to biblical texts, partly because there is a scarcity of material dealing with the issues that are of most concern to us today, and partly because individual verses should not be wrenched out of context. The issue of abortion aptly illustrates the need to use the Bible carefully, imaginatively and sensitively.

Abortion was practised in biblical times, but the biblical writers do not explicitly address it. This is explained more satisfactorily by the likelihood that they regarded the practice as unthinkable than by any notion that they viewed it as tolerable. Jewish writers such as Josephus (c. 37–c. 100 AD) and Philo (c. 20 BC –c. AD 50) interpreted the thrust of OT law as forbidding abortion. There are certainly several passages in the Bible which indicate a high view of life in the womb. In Ps. 139:13–16, Jb. 10:8–12, Is. 49:1, Je. 1:5 and the nativity stories of Lk. 1, children in the womb are seen as objects of God's creative activity, loving care and special calling. Pre-natal experience is viewed as a crucial and continuous part of individuals' personal history. However, in view of the uncertainty surrounding the Ex. 21 passage (cited earlier) it cannot

be said that the Bible unequivocally or directly states that the unborn child is of equal status to the child or adult. We are not told whether the early embryo has or is a human soul, or whether it awaits an eternal destiny. Claims made by some evangelical thinkers that the Bible demands an absolute anti-abortion stance go too far. Nevertheless, three factors taken together do suggest a strong biblical presumption against abortion, while allowing some room for flexibility in hard cases such as where the mother's life is at risk: the high view of life in the womb stated above, the strictures against the taking of innocent life, and God's concern for the weak, defenceless and those whom society considers of no account. But the latter factor is two-edged: it also directs concerns toward vulnerable women who may have been left unsupported in pregnancy by the heartlessness of others.

Principles in creative tension

It is in the development and careful application of theological themes present in the Bible that Christians can contribute most helpfully to the ethics of medical care. Often this will lead not to simple permissions or prohibitions but to recognition of a delicate balance of responsibilities, a weighing of respective duties. Take, for instance, the main themes of Gn. 1 – 3, that God is creator, men and women are made in the divine image, they are called to fill the earth and subdue it, but that there is a temptation to be eschewed which is to 'be like God' (Gn. 3:5). On the one hand, Genesis reminds us of our creatureliness and warns us against the assumption of God-like powers over life and death. This has definite relevance to current debates over artificial fertilization (see Reproductive Technologies*) and genetic engineering,* where the creation of an embryo in a glass dish can easily become a cause of human pride in technological* achievements, and where some would like to see the gametes of outstanding men and women brought together in order to improve the quality of the human race. On the other hand, the Bible makes clear that humans do share in God's creativity, and are called to act as responsible stewards in the world, harnessing its resources, improving its conditions and reducing human suffering. The development of a technique such as *in vitro* fertilization may well fall within the sphere of legitimate stewardship.* But it certainly poses some hard questions. How, for instance, should we feel about

14

the malformed 'spare' embryos which are never inserted into a prospective mother's womb? Should they be taken as a sign that we are here meddling with matters we have no business to meddle with, or should we regard the death of such embryos as acceptable because it parallels the high wastage of embryos in natural reproduction? To possess a dual sense of humankind both as creature and as steward is helpful; it will not necessarily lead us to a cast-iron solution.

Consent and confidentiality

Another area where two worthy principles co-exist in tension is that of consent.* On the one hand, doctors need to remember that someone who is sick usually still has the gift of intelligence, and deserves to have sickness and its possible cure *explained*. The principle of 'informed consent' expresses the conviction that patients should be informed about and consent to whatever medical treatment they receive. It is particularly important as a safeguard against their being used unknowingly in medical experiments, and finds theological justification in notions of human dignity and respect for human freedom (displayed, after all, by God). On the other hand, the urgent requirements of a person's body can render his or her status as a moral agent secondary. Concern about respecting the patient's *wishes* may sometimes fly in the face of what the doctor judges to be attending to the patient's *needs*. (A Jehovah's Witness refusing a life-saving blood transfusion provides a classic example of this.) It is to be hoped that the doctor has a certain professional competence, and so his or her medical judgments should be better than the patient's; and the doctor is bound by a certain professional ethos (see Professional Ethics*), and so is not free to do whatever the patient demands. There is thus a proper element of paternalism present in the relationship. This should be grounded in the biblical principle of love for neighbour, a love which stands by and continues to treat a despairing patient even when that patient cannot see that this is to his or her benefit.

Like consent, professional confidentiality* has become a revered axiom in modern medicine. It is certainly important. A mutual understanding that information divulged in the course of treatment will not be passed on helps to establish a relationship of trust between doctor and patient, and is crucial to the medical task of ascertaining all relevant information and making a correct diagnosis. A promise that

has been made – either explicitly or implicitly – to keep information secret should be honoured, almost invariably. However, this prima facie duty could be overridden if its observance might seriously endanger others whom the patient has power to harm. Consider the cases of a mass murderer who confesses to a doctor but will not go to the police, or an AIDS patient who refuses to tell his sexual partner that he has contracted the disease. Exceptions to the general rule condemning dishonesty (failure to keep a promise being an extension of this) are permissible where human life is endangered: Ex. 1:15–21 gives an example of midwives who lied in order to save lives, yet received God's blessing.

Love and justice

In medical care, as in every other area of human life, the Christian should be guided by the primary principles of love (see ②) and justice (see Justice and Peace③). The imperative to love constitutes a perennial challenge to improve standards and maintain commitment to patient welfare in our health services. Love implies both a warmth of relationship and a commitment to seek what is best for another, even when he or she makes that difficult. The imperative to be just, conversely, constitutes a demand to give others their 'due'. Of course, there are different models of justice: the egalitarian, the differential, the meritocratic, and the redistributive are perhaps the most common, and each are valid in the appropriate context. Which model of justice should be applied to the issue of the allocation of resources, where individuals and groups compete for services which are necessarily limited? This is a topical question with regard both to issues of micro-allocation, where, *e.g.*, patients with renal failure compete for the same scarce resource (kidney dialysis), and to issues of macro-allocation, where different categories of patient (*e.g.* the mentally ill, those suffering from arthritic hips) compete for much larger but still finite resources.

With regard to the micro issue, most Christian writers who have written on this subject are agreed that considerations of wealth, status, occupation and family situation should not hold decisive sway in a medical context. Extremity of need is a valid criterion (though one that is not always easy to evaluate), but if that fails to decide the question, patients should be regarded as having an equal claim to treatment. It is then better to decide between

14

them randomly rather than evaluatively, because that attests to their fundamental equality before God. Questions of macro-allocation are more complex: a random distribution of resources (see Health and Health Care*) between different types of sufferers is clearly inappropriate if these groups are of widely differing size. But the valid model of justice remains the same: one which prioritizes those in special need but has an egalitarian thrust in its concern that members of different groups throughout society receive adequate care. In particular, it is sensitive to the needs of minority groups who wield little social influence, *e.g.*, the elderly, the seriously handicapped, the severely demented, and racial minorities suffering from illnesses distinctive to them.

A final example of the need for balanced theological emphases lies in the area of human possibilities and limitations. Human beings are sinful, and so naïve optimism regarding medical progress and society's capacity to control dangerous developments is unwarranted. The 1967 British Abortion Act is a salutary example of a piece of legislation which was intended to be both progressive and restrictive, but is exploited in the direction of an all-too-casual disregard for unborn life. A clause which allows abortions to take place where continued pregnancy poses significant risk to a woman's physical or mental health was worded so loosely that anyone who finds her pregnancy undesirable and therefore stressful stands a fair chance of having it terminated – certainly in the private sector. In the USA, a 1973 Supreme Court decision (*Roe* v. *Wade*) has led to the widespread practice of an indiscriminate 'abortion on demand'. But alongside attitudes which regard human life as cheap, there are others which seem to defy the inevitability of death. In the words of Ecclesiastes, this is a 'chasing after the wind'. Nevertheless, the sober realism which ought to be the province of the Christian should be matched by joy in the many good things that medicine has delivered and is delivering. Where people are healed of apparently incurable illness and vaccinations are discovered

to prevent diseases which once ruled in epidemic proportions, Christians can rejoice to see God's saving hand at work amidst human endeavour and ingenuity.

See especially: ABORTION; AIDS; COMA; CONFIDENTIALITY; CONSENT; COSMETIC SURGERY; DEATH AND DYING; DOUBLE EFFECT; DRUGS; EMBRYOLOGY; ENDS AND MEANS; EUTHANASIA; GENETIC ENGINEERING; HEALTH AND HEALTH CARE; HIPPOCRATIC OATH; HUMAN EXPERIMENTATION; IMAGE OF GOD; INSTITUTIONALIZATION; INTENSIVE CARE; KILLING; MEDICAL CODES OF PRACTICE; MEDICAL MALPRACTICE; PSYCHIATRIC CARE, ETHICS OF; QALY; QUALITY OF LIFE; REPRODUCTIVE TECHNOLOGIES; SCIENCE; STERILIZATION; TECHNOLOGY; TRANSPLANT SURGERY; TRIAGE; WELFARE STATE.

Bibliography

A. V. Campbell, *Moral Dilemmas in Medicine* (Edinburgh, ²1975); D. Cook, *Patients' Choice: A Consumer Guide to Medical Practice* (London, 1993); A. S. Duncan, G. R. Dunstan and R. B. Welbourn (eds.), *DME*; J. Fletcher, *Humanhood: Essays in Biomedical Ethics* (Buffalo, NY, 1979); B. Häring, *Medical Ethics* (Slough, ³1991); R. Higginson, *Dilemmas: A Christian Approach to Moral Decision-Making* (London and Louisville, KY, 1988); D. G. Jones, *Manufacturing Humans: The Challenge of the New Reproductive Technologies* (Leicester, 1987); S. E. Lammers and A. Verhey (eds.), *On Moral Medicine: Theological Perspectives in Medical Ethics* (Grand Rapids, 1987); R. A. McCormick, *How Brave A New World? Dilemmas in Bioethics* (Washington, DC, and London, 1981); O. O'Donovan, *Begotten or Made?* (Oxford, 1984); J. Rachels, *The End of Life: Euthanasia and Morality* (Oxford and New York, 1986); P. Ramsey, *The Patient as Person* (New Haven, CT, and London, 1970).

R.A.Hig.

14

FIFTEEN

Global Ethics

Global ethics defines moral responsibilities across political, social, economic and geographic boundaries to encompass the entire earth. The term assumes a transcendent commitment to care for human beings, nations and the environment throughout the world. Christians base a global ethic on God's creation* of the whole world and his declaration that it is very good (Gn. 1:31). All human beings are made in the image of God* and all of nature shows God's glory. The creation mandate to have dominion over the earth is God's command to steward (see Stewardship*) both the human and non-human creation.

Negatively, global ethics begins with the recognition that human sin has corrupted not only individuals in personal relationships, but communities, nations, the international order and nature itself. According to Paul, hope for redemption encompasses all creation because all creation is in bondage to decay (Rom. 8:19–23). Sin produces individual moral decay, social antagonisms, political conflict, economic injustice, international anarchy and environmental destruction. Global ethics seeks to understand the nature and causes of international moral problems and to find ways for individuals and communities to address them.

Global ethics and world evangelization

Some Christians argue that global ethics can safely be ignored because the only real responsibility of the church is to evangelize the world. Evangelization is understood to mean the proclamation of the gospel of repentance* and personal salvation (see Sin and Salvation⑤) through Jesus Christ. In contrast, other Christians suggest that global ethics is the gospel. God loves the whole world, and the coming reign of Christ is God's rule over all creation.

Christians are to work now for the kingdom of God* all over the world, so that God's will is done on earth as it is in heaven. The work of God in history is understood as the progressive defeat of social sin all over the world leading to the triumph of justice and peace on earth.

These two views are extremes along a continuum. Global ethics includes both personal evangelism and social transformation. Personal evangelism should not ignore God's love for whole people in a global environment. Nor can those who work for social and environmental reform afford to ignore the personal need of individuals for forgiveness* and reconciliation* with God. The Bible knows no such dichotomy between personal and social ethics. Love (see ②) knows no barrier between good news for the soul and good news for people who live in communities and the material world.

Global ethics is theologically grounded in the concepts of creation, covenant,* stewardship, redemption and hope* for the coming kingdom. It neither assumes nor denies the imminent destruction of the present world order. Hope is sustained by confidence in God's sovereign activity in the world. Work for global preservation, for justice and peace (see ③), embodies the good news of salvation and reconciliation. It is obedience to the command of God to love our neighbour; it is respect for the earth that belongs to the Lord; it is a response to the love of God for us; it is an integral part of the proclamation of God's love for the world.

The causes of international conflict

Global moral problems have been variously attributed to the nature and activities of individual human beings, the nature and activities of modern nation-states, and the structure of the international political and economic order (*cf.* Kenneth N. Waltz, *Man, the State and War*). These three approaches each seek to define where international moral problems come from. In so far as they illumine the nature and source of the problems faced by global ethics, they provide a framework out of which moral responses can arise.

1. The problem rooted in individuals. Some see international conflict as rooted in the fundamental character of the human person. Whether the problem is defined as lack of knowledge (Plato*), instinct for aggression (Social Darwinists), lust for power (Bertrand Russell, 1872–1970; F. Meinecke, 1862–1954), greed (Erich Fromm*), or sin (*cf.* Jas. 4:1–4), global crisis is located in the individual decisions of human beings. Augustine* argued that war and injustice stemmed from human pride and lack of worship. He wrote: 'It is thus that pride in its perversity apes God. It abhors equality with other men under him; but instead of his rule it seeks to impose a rule of its own upon equals' (*City of God*, Bk. XIX.12). From the curse of male domination of women in Gn. 3:16 and the fratricide of the first brothers (Gn. 4:8), to the battle of Armageddon – where Babylon, 'drunk with the blood of the saints', is thrown down (Rev. 16:16; 17:6) – human beings have sought to dominate each other.

If individuals are the source of international exploitation and conflict, then it is individuals who must be changed or restrained to solve the problem. The world must be changed from the bottom up. Suggestions for how this may be accomplished cover a broad spectrum. Psychologists suggest conditioning and therapy (especially for world leaders), academics suggest education, and theologians suggest conversion. Some Christians see sin as an exclusively spiritual problem that can only be addressed spiritually.

Schemes for changing human nature range from Maoist attempts at massive indoctrination to capitalist hope in unfettered free trade. Erich Fromm indicates the scale of the problem when he suggests that the whole orientation of humanity (see 4) which has existed for the last 6,000 years must be changed 'from having and hoarding to being and sharing' (*The Anatomy of Human Destructiveness*, San Francisco, 1973, p. 435). Only half in jest, someone has suggested that universal brain surgery is the only remedy for rooting out human aggression.

Pessimism over the possibility of changing human nature may lead to the rationalization of the *status quo*. But the luxury of accepting the current state of world affairs is possible only for those who benefit from the massive inequalities which characterize the world today. Reinhold Niebuhr* grappled with a pessimistic view of human nature and concluded that the only force which could counter an individual or group's selfishness was the self-interest of another individual or group. He saw the balance of power against power as the task of government. Thus, while the problems of global ethics were rooted in human nature, the solution lay in the restraint of selfishness by the State.

2. The problem rooted in nation-states. If solutions to global problems can be brought about only by national governments, then it is imperative to have the right kinds of governments. Indeed, many writers have attributed global conflict to flaws in the structure of individual states. It is undeniable that many international problems, from global warming, to a Palestinian homeland, to Third World infant mortality, can be addressed only by the concerted decisions of nation-states. Are there good States and bad States? If so, what kinds of States are good?

Operating from a faith in the all-powerful sovereignty of God, the Heb. prophets attributed the well-being of Israel and Judah to the level of justice practised in the States' social institutions. For example, Isaiah declared to Judah that her attempts to balance the power of Assyrian imperialism by alliance with Egypt were in vain because her own lack of social justice made her ripe for judgment (Is. 10:1–4). Not only security from enemies, but the well-being of the whole world was at stake. Isaiah also believed that social injustice affected all of nature (Is. 24:4–6).

In ancient times, writers as diverse as Plato and Confucius (551–479 BC; see Confucian Ethics*) identified the well-being of the people with the justice of their rulers. More recently the structure of government has been identified as the key to global peace and justice. Immanuel Kant* believed that the spread of democratic or republican States would lead to the agreement of all States to be governed by a common code of just laws. Many 19th-century social reformers believed that when working-class people got the vote, all politics would be changed because aristocrats and capitalists would be voted out of office. Karl Marx*

15

affirmed that when all States were socialist, governments would wither away and conflict would disappear.

The spread of democracy was the key to peace according to Woodrow Wilson (1856–1924), and the First World War was the war to end all wars. But from the perspective of rising nationalism* in the Third World, it was Western imperialism that threatened the emerging nations. The Second World War embroiled the world in a conflict with the racist powers of Fascism. But with the defeat of Fascism and the unravelling of the Western colonial empires, communism* was seen as the new evil that threatened to engulf the earth. In 1953, Richard Nixon (1913–) said, 'If it were not for the communist threat, the free world could live at peace.'

With the break-up of the Soviet empire, many in the West express hope that the spread of free-market capitalism* will lead to justice and peace. But in many poor nations, capitalist development has increased the grinding poverty* of the many while enriching the few, and led to unprecedented environmental destruction. While capitalism seems to have won the Cold War in the East–West conflict, the majority of the world remains trapped in poverty.

It is the perceived exploitation of the poor by the rich nations of the world which adds fuel to the political crisis in the Middle East. The accident of oil divides the rich Arab nations from the poor and allies the rich with the West. In this context, many Muslims see 'Christian' or godless capitalism as the major opponent to justice and peace. It is the Northern powers who extract wealth from the South and greedily consume most of the world's resources.

The second half of the 20th century has seen a continuing decline in the earning power of the poorest countries of the world (the South), while the economies of the industrialized Northern countries have continued to grow. This is commonly referred to as the 'North–South Divide'. The Brandt Commission (see Brandt Report*) summarized the plight of the poor countries as follows: 'The developing countries today are, with few exceptions, in a desperate plight. With the prices of commodities – the main exports of many countries – at their lowest level for over thirty years, recession and protectionism affecting their exports of manufactures, a slowing up in the flow of commercial capital and aid, their balance of payments problems have reached intolerable proportions. Cutting back on growth is the

order of the day – for those countries which have been growing. For numerous countries – especially in Sub-Saharan Africa, where there has been no growth in recent years – lack of capacity to import translates directly into increased hardship, even threatened starvation, for tens of millions of the most vulnerable people' (W. Brandt [chairperson], *Common Crisis, North–South: Co-operation for World Recovery*, London and New York, 1983, p. 18).

The war between Iraq and the USA and its allies provoked strong emotions in the Muslim world, because Saddam Hussein (1937–) is seen as the only Muslim strong enough to stand against the dominance of the decadent West. Many Muslims around the world perceive Israeli possession of Palestinian lands as of far greater significance than Iraq's annexation of Kuwait. While Saddam may be feared, he is also admired for his ability to challenge what is seen as an unjust *status quo*. Successive characterizations of American presidents as 'Satan' indicate that many Muslims see the West as an evil power arrayed against the godly forces of Islam.

In contrast, Western writers are more likely to see Saddam Hussein simply as a brutal dictator, whose aggression threatened all nations too small to defend themselves. Control of oil resources is important but secondary to the maintenance of a world order (see International Order*) in which States are sovereign and a free market regulates the flow of resources. Militant Islam is seen as an irrational (fanatical) opponent to peace and world order. The USA, even when acting under the authority of the UN, was perceived during the Gulf crisis as a global police officer, defending world order against the chaos of the law of the jungle.

The dispute over whether the world is evolving towards democratic capitalism or some form of socialism used to dominate the East–West conflict. Neither system has demonstrated an ability to overcome conflict, poverty or the environmental crisis (see Environment*). The resurgence of Islam, which began with the Iranian revolution in 1979, opposes both systems and suggests a theocratic alternative. But Islam holds little attraction outside of Muslim countries.

It is doubtful whether there is any one, 'good', political system that is appropriate for all countries. A Christian understanding of the universality of sin underlines the presence of evil* in even the best political systems. Similarly, the conviction that all human beings are made in the image of God should lead us to look for good in the most unlikely places. Nevertheless, the conviction that it is evil governments who make war, exploit the poor, and degrade the environment is not without basis. The totalitarian impulse toward self-deification has brought immeasurable suffering in the 20th century.

3. The problem rooted in the international system. Many political scientists believe that conflict in international relations is predominantly caused not by the characteristics of individual people or States, but by the international system. Three different theories account for global problems in the international system. These theories are referred to as political realism, complex interdependence and dependency theory.

a. Political realism. The dominant metaphor in political realism (see Realpolitik*) is the security dilemma. Political realism begins with the observation of Machiavelli (1469–1527) that politics is not dominated by the search for justice, but is the art of survival, by any means necessary.

Thomas Hobbes (1588–1679) suggested that the natural state of humanity is the law of the jungle, 'the war of every man against every man'. To escape that 'state of nature', human beings form a social contract* and create a 'leviathan', a government which rules by law with sufficient power* to enforce the contract on all members of society. Submission to a powerful government is the cost of escaping the state of nature, according to Hobbes. In international relations, however, there is no social contract, no powerful government and no enforceable law. International relations is still in the state of nature where nations face each other like gladiators and survival is the ultimate value. Raw power determines the division of resources.

Jean-Jacques Rousseau (1712–78) suggested that conflict between nations is inevitable, even between good States with ideal forms of government. He argued that the will of a State,* which is the general will in relation to its subjects, is only a particular will in relation to other States. Rousseau's parable of the stag hunt illustrates his point. Five starving people band together to hunt a stag. When they have the stag surrounded, one of the men sees a hare. By catching the hare to ensure his own survival, he abandons the stag hunt and the

stag escapes. The point is that where survival is at stake, rational self-interest takes precedence over the interests of the group.

According to political realism, international relations is a self-help, anarchic system. Hobbes argued that where there is no law, there is no morality, there is only survival. Without an enforceable law between States in the international system, nations exist in a 'state of nature' where each must survive by any means necessary. According to Hobbes, the state of nature is a condition of war. Rousseau advocated the formation of a world government to enforce a social contract between all nations, thus doing away with the state of nature. This idea has proved politically impossible because of the dangers it imposes and the lack of any global consensus on the form it should take. The UN is only a pale shadow of what it would take to eliminate the international state of nature.

Before the Treaty of Westphalia (1648), the Wars of Religion were fought to try to enforce a universal definition of Christianity which could unify the nations of Europe. Westphalia brought a new international order by recognizing the sovereignty of each State to rule without interference within its own boundaries. The idea of sovereignty as a basis for international order was a great step beyond the horror of absolute war between militant ideologies. But it did nothing to allay the perception of global politics as a state of nature. According to realism, the behaviour of sovereign nations is best explained by balance-of-power theory.

The dominant metaphors of political realism have been extensively criticized as overly abstract, pessimistic and simplistic. Moreover, its perspective on the world may be self-fulfilling; if enough people think about the world from a 'realist' perspective, that is the way nation-states will behave. At least in the realm of politics, global ethics will have no meaning except as a language of rationalization for activities that are really ruled by self-interest. Social problems such as racism, sexism and over-population; economic problems such as poverty and injustice; political conflicts over religion, human rights (see Rights, Human*), control of resources and forms of government; and world-wide environmental problems are all subordinated to the individual self-interest of the nation-state.

From the perspective of global ethics, important distinctions should be made between

15

political realism as descriptive, as explanatory, and as prescriptive theory. Structural realism is not an accurate description of international politics. The actual behaviour of nations is far more complex than the model of realism. As explanatory theory, realism fairs better. Some of the behaviour of nations can be explained in reference to the realist metaphors (*e.g.* the state of nature, the anarchic self-help realm, the security dilemma, *raison d'état* and *Realpolitik*; for a more detailed exposition and critique of structural realism, see B. T. Adeney, *Just War, Political Realism and Faith*). The Iraqi invasion of Kuwait in 1990 and the response of the Western powers may be seen as good examples of 'realist' behaviour. But realism claims that the structure of international relations is ultimately determinative. If States do not follow the dictates of self-help they will not survive in an anarchic system. At this point the theory becomes prescriptive.

Global ethics assumes that there is a freedom to act against selfishness and even against self-interest on the basis of transcendent values. But in realism, selfish behaviour is requisite. Balance-of-power theory attempts to explain not only why nations act the way they do, but why they must. If assertion of power against power is necessary and inevitable then there cannot be anything morally wrong with it. If national interests and necessity are always the ultimate or dominant determiners of international behaviour, values that contradict them are ultimately suicidal.

b. Complex interdependence. Two other structural theories have been proposed as alternatives to realism. The first takes 'complex interdependence' as its ruling metaphor (see R. Keohane and J. Nye, *Power and Interdependence*). In this model, the most significant factor determining how nations relate to each other is not military power, but interdependence. Multiple channels connect societies. Even the State is not a single coherent unit but a complex of organizations, each of which has its own agenda. Social, economic, religious and environmental relations often bypass government altogether and may eclipse political relations in importance.

It is not possible to infer a fixed hierarchy of issues. As Henry Kissinger (1923–) remarked, 'The problems of energy, resources, environment, population, the uses of space and sea now rank with questions of military security, ideology and territorial rivalry which have traditionally made up the diplomatic agenda'

(quoted in Keohane and Nye, *op. cit.*, p. 26). The revolution in communication technologies (see Information Technology*) and the global marketplace have created a new international order in which political and military power are often irrelevant for solving complex problems of interdependence. Interdependency theorists acknowledge that in times of war, national behaviour may descend into an Hobbesian state of nature. But even in the Middle East war of 1991, they would argue that military power was only one of the factors that determined its outcome. The historical, cultural, economic, political and moral perspectives of people all around the world also controlled the flow of events.

Complex interdependence as a structuring concept for global ethics is an improvement over realism. As descriptive theory it is like realism, an abstract selection of certain facets of international behaviour which are considered dominant. Nevertheless it accounts for more factors in present international realities and leaves more room for ethical input in facing them. Unlike realism, complex interdependence defines a world in which we need each other in order to survive and prosper.

As explanatory theory, interdependence is like realism in positing a morally neutral structure which determines international behaviour. Without discounting the importance of power, interdependence stresses the necessity of co-operation for survival. Self-interest is assumed to be the most significant factor in motivating interdependence. But interdependence theory masks the degree to which some nations are dependent and others are dominant. Interdependence is a misnomer where exploitation of the weak by the strong is the reality.

Global moral problems are sometimes exacerbated by interdependence. Environmental and economic destruction is often fuelled by the international market. International economic co-operation may lead to more efficient exploitation of the poor by those with power. The idea of interdependence suggests the need for mutually beneficial problem-solving rather than radical change. As morally prescriptive theory, interdependence supports the *status quo* as given, while advocating co-operation to make it better. Where relations between nations are fundamentally unjust, it has little to say.

c. Dependency theory. A more radical struc-

15

tural alternative to both realism and interdependence is dependency theory. Drawing from Marxist analysis, dependency theory suggests that the primary characteristics of the international structure are economic dominance and dependence. The 'core' States at the centre of the system, *i.e.*, the rich capitalist States, dominate the poor countries at the periphery, who have little power to determine their own destiny.

Like realist and interdependency theory, dependency theory does not suggest that evil politicians or bad States have created this system. The villain is international capitalism. The 'laws' of the international marketplace reward those who have the power, capital and resources to determine the terms of trade. Capital tends to follow cheap labour and resources and moulds the local economy to the needs of the international market. Both the technology* introduced and the products produced may be inappropriate to the local community. Meanwhile, the price of commodities produced by the poor countries tends to sink, while the price of manufactured goods produced by the rich countries goes up.

International institutions of this marketplace, such as the World Bank, reward those who participate in the system through specialization in the products needed by the international market. Many poor countries specializing in the products that are easiest to export have lost the ability to feed themselves. Dependent on trade but with little ability to influence the terms of trade, they are left economically and politically powerless. The result is a process of under-development whereby the rich get richer at the expense of the poor. Environmental degradation also follows as poor countries desperately strip their resources in an attempt to keep up with a declining balance of payments.

Dependency theory considers multinational corporations* (MNCs) especially culpable for this process of under-development. The budgets of MNCs often exceed the budgets of the nations in which they operate. Because they invest huge amounts of money, bring new technology and expertise, and provide significant employment, often at higher salaries than are available locally, poor countries are usually more than anxious for their business. Because of the power they wield, they are often able to dictate the terms of their investments. MNCs often enrich the ruling élites of poor countries and raise the gross national product through

their development efforts. But dependency theorists argue that their net effect is loss of food self-sufficiency, dependency on an international economy, impoverishment of the poor, depletion of unrenewable natural resources and mounting national debt.

From the perspective of dependency theory, the Middle East conflict of 1990–91 was about oil and the preservation of an international order dominated by the 'core States'. The goodness or evil of Saddam Hussein or George Bush (1924–) is secondary to the rational determination of the rich countries to control Middle Eastern energy resources. Saddam's gamble with Kuwait was seen as a rational attempt to regionalize the control of oil under his leadership. To do so he had to overthrow puppet governments of the West such as Kuwait.

As prescription, dependency theory advocates regional and national control of resources in order to rescue them from an international market controlled by the rich. This does not mean that dependency theorists support the means of Saddam Hussein. Most advocate a New International Economic Order (NIEO), under the aegis of the UN, which would stabilize the terms of trade or tilt them in favour of the poor. Dependency theorists are opposed to the General Agreement on Tarriffs and Trade (GATT; see International Trade*), which promotes the global economy by removing trade barriers. Fears are also expressed that GATT would promote a multinational rape of the environment. Other prescriptions include advocating food and energy sufficiency as far as possible for poor countries, and urging cooperation between poor countries in order to resist a global market that is geared for the rich. Regional and national economies should take precedence over the international market.

From the perspective of global ethics, dependency theory is attractive for its implicit commitment to the needs of the poor, the protection of local cultures and the preservation of the environment. The huge gap between rich and poor nations is convincing evidence of injustice in the world. The unequal distribution of resources in the world is not based on the virtue, hard work or even good fortune of the Northern countries alone. It is also a fruit of colonialist* and neo-colonialist expoitation of the poor by the rich. Western Christians need to listen to the convincing connections drawn by dependency theorists between the wealth of the North and the poverty of the South

15

(see North–South Divide* and Economic Development*).

As with the other two theories, it is important to note that this is a model and not literal description. Like the state of nature and interdependence, the global market is an abstraction based on the selection of certain factors among many. Like the other two theories it is reductionist* and fails to account for many aspects of international relations. Dependency theorists ignore the many causes of poverty and conflict which cannot be attributed to international injustice. Inequality and poverty are caused by complex historical, cultural, gender, religious, demographic, political, social, economic, geographic and military factors. Liberation theologians* and social ethicists sometimes write as if dependency theory were literal description. Not only does that overrate the power of the international economy, it obscures the positive effect of the market on some poor countries.

Conclusions

We have seen that global ethics can be informed by analysis which locates the key to global problems and moral action at three different levels. Christians have always had sympathy for the view that much of the problem lies in individual human beings. The doctrine of the Fall* indicates that all human beings are sinful and that evil originates in the human heart. A Christian approach to global ethics begins with the view that individuals have great significance, both for good and evil. All human beings contribute to global problems, through pride, racism, mistreatment of women, over-consumption of limited resources, hatred,* envy (see Jealousy and Envy*), greed, violence,* carelessness and the like. Personal transformation of individuals can therefore make a difference.

Jesus' commands to love God and our neighbour and to seek first the kingdom of God* are also urgently relevant to the task of global ethics. There is a social and corporate dimension to the Fall. Not only personal transformation, but the efforts of individuals to resist evil and care for its victims are also relevant. Exposure of evil that is structured through the institutions of society is part of this task. Both personal transformation and individual resistance to evil occur in communities. The significance of individual change for global ethics is directly related to the degree in which it is nurtured and extended through the work of a community.

Recognition of the importance of individuals should not be understood as downgrading the critical role of institutions and nations, as both perpetuators and restrainers of evil. Global problems are so vast that many can be addressed only at a national level. Political institutions which protect the value of the individual, restrain the exploitation of the weak, conserve creation, resist the violent and promote justice are crucial to the tasks of justice and peace. In the Bible, God is portrayed as active in the history of nations, supporting the weak and pulling the mighty from their thrones (Lk. 1:52). God uses individuals, such as Moses, Deborah, Amos, Esther, Daniel and Cyrus, to change the history of nations.

Today it is recognized that structures of good and evil exist beyond the borders of nations in the international order. All three structural theories provide an important contribution to global ethics.

In so far as there is a state of nature in international politics, Christians must understand the role of power and work to reduce the anarchy of the international system. A realist understanding of power combined with a Christian perception of the reality of evil can prevent a simplistic idealism which ignores the pervasiveness of conflict. As Reinhold Niebuhr observed, the assertion that if only people would love one another, all the complex problems of the international order would disappear, ignores the most basic fact of history: that most people and groups do not love one another. Christian realism recognizes that costly action must sometimes be taken to resist the spread of totalitarianism and tyranny.

But political realism can also be a faulty guide to behaviour. The assumption of an anarchic international realm ruled by power can lead to the justification of war* as the only means of settling conflict. It can lead to a devaluing of many potent ways to address injustice that are short of war. All of the major problems that concern global ethics are exacerbated by war. Not only does war divert attention and funds from other pressing issues, it virulently increases poverty and violence, ignites hatred and racism, and plants seeds for future conflict. In war it is the poor and the weak who often bear the greatest suffering. War destroys the environment on a scale which dwarfs the normal concerns of the environmental movement. Christians who benefit from the insights of realism must nevertheless oppose war as a means of settling disputes.

15

In so far as there is interdependence, Christians need to strengthen forms of co-operation which benefit the common good. Complex interdependency theory emphasizes the importance of a community of nations. God did not create a state of nature in which individuals fight tooth and claw. As Amos understood long ago, the dominance of one nation by another is not natural but sinful (Am. 1 – 2). Interdependency theory has the merits and drawbacks of most reformism. It rejects the extremes of war and revolution by recognizing that we live in a flawed and sinful world in which there are no final solutions, only graded improvements. By seeking co-operative solutions it accepts realities that are necessarily disappointing. This can shade into an acceptance of injustice in so far as it does not upset the theorists' own interests or the international order.

In so far as poverty is perpetuated by an international economic order which benefits the rich, we need to resist participation in structures which enrich the West at the cost of perpetuating poverty in the Third World. Western Christians can decrease their consumption of non-renewable resources, simplify their lifestyles, support domestic and foreign policy decisions which respect local and regional economies, boycott* luxury items produced in countries which cannot feed their own people, and oppose their own government's support for Third World élites which repress their own people while growing rich on international trade.

The problems which plague our world are overwhelming. Passionate social concern is easily burned out unless it is sustained by deep faith in the love and presence of God in history. Five tasks await Christians who are concerned about global ethics.

1. *Prayer*. Prayer is a moral act in so far as it reflects a hunger and thirst for the righteousness of God to prevail in the real world. It is an act of dependence and trust. It recognizes that only the power and goodness of God can bring shalom (see Peace*) to sinful communities.

2. *Knowledge*. Individual global problems are enormously complex. Simplistic slogans, unfounded optimism and apathy are all symptoms of unwillingness to study carefully the evils which threaten our neighbours and our planet. No-one can know everything, but everyone can explore one area (such as recycling programmes in their community), and share their knowledge with others.

3. *Modelling*, or being an exemplar. Actions are always more powerful than words in ethics. Lifestyle choices range from riding a bicycle instead of driving a car, to living with the poor in Manila. The knowledge we gain about global issues is dangerous. If we refuse to allow it to change our lifestyle, it may harden our heart.

4. *Action by groups and communities*. Corporate action is more powerful than that done by individuals. The church should model the values of the kingdom of God. As we become individually concerned, *e.g.*, about racism against Arabs in our community, the most effective response may be to invite Arabs to participate in our church programmes. Only as the church expresses the love of God for the world can it expect the world to listen to the gospel.

5. *Politics*. Christians too often ignore the political task. Community organizing, voting, writing, lobbying, demonstrating, contributing to political causes and running for local office are a few of the ways in which Christians can address moral problems through political means. Political solutions to moral problems must be found at every level of the human community: in families, in corporations, in hospitals, schools and banks, as well as in national governments and the UN. Just as the Jewish prophets gave voice to God's anguish over political injustice, so Christians need to recognize that love of neighbour* must include opposition to oppressive structural evils wherever they are found. The task of global ethics is well summarized in the words of the Lord's Prayer, 'Thy Kingdom come; thy will be done, on earth as it is in heaven.'

See especially: APARTHEID; ARMAMENTS; BRANDT REPORT; COLONIALISM; COMMUNISM; CREATION; CULTURE; DEBT; DEFENCE, MILITARY AND CIVIL; DEFORESTATION; DETERRENCE, NON-NUCLEAR; DETERRENCE, NUCLEAR; DISARMAMENT; DISCRIMINATION; ECONOMIC DEVELOPMENT; ECONOMIC SANCTIONS; EMIGRATION; ENERGY; ENVIRONMENT; EQUALITY; ESPIONAGE; FORCE; FREEDOM; GENOCIDE; GROSS NATIONAL PRODUCT; HUNGER, WORLD; IMMIGRATION; INTERNATIONAL ORDER; INTERNATIONAL TRADE; INVESTMENT; LAND AND LAND REFORM; LIBERATION THEOLOGY; MEDIA; MIGRANT LABOUR; MISSION, MORALITY OF; NATIONALISM; NATURAL LAW; NEIGHBOUR;

15

NORTH–SOUTH DIVIDE; PATRIOTISM; POLITICS; POPULATION POLICY; POVERTY; POWER; RACE; REBELLION; RIGHTS, ANIMAL; RIGHTS, HUMAN; SCIENCE; SECURITY; SLAVERY; SPORT; STATE; TECHNOLOGY; TERRORISM; THIRD WORLD AID; TRADE; VIOLENCE; WAR; WASTE; WORLD.

Bibliography

B. T. Adeney, *Just War, Political Realism and Faith* (Metuchen, NJ, and London, 1988); L. R. Brown *et al.*, *State of the World 1990* (New York and London, 1990); W. Byron, *The Causes of World Hunger* (New York, 1982); W. Granberg-Michaelson, *Tending the Garden: Essays on the Gospel and the Earth* (Grand Rapids, 1987); R. Keohane and J. Nye, *Power and Interdependence* (New York, 1977); R. Niebuhr, *Moral Man and Immoral Society* (New York, 1932); L. Osborn, *Guardians of Creation* (Leicester, 1993); R. J. Sider, *Rich Christians in an Age of Hunger* (Downers Grove, IL, 1977; London, ²1990); K. Waltz, *Man, the State and War* (New York, 1954); M. Walzer, *Just and Unjust Wars* (New York, 1977; Harmondsworth, 1980).

B.T.A.

SIXTEEN

Community Ethics

The word 'community' usually refers to a group of people living together in one locality who inhabit a culture of shared values.* When its use is purely descriptive, it may be enough that people live in the same geographical area. However, the word is often used to imply more than mere description. In this sense it does not refer to a collection of people, but only to those who have an identity as a group. It is possible for people to live in proximity to one another but not in community with one another. In a society in which undue emphasis has been placed on the autonomy* of the individual leading to the dominance of individualism* as a social philosophy, the word 'community' has also become a normative expression for those wanting to stress interdependence. It can also be used to express nostalgia, as in 'the quest for community'. This nostalgia, most recently articulated by some elements of the Green Movement, is itself a hallmark of the desire to change the fragmentation implicit in the modern world. It can also be used in a futuristic sense to point to a Utopia which might exist if certain conditions apply.

The fact that defining 'community' is more difficult than building a brick wall round a patch of fog is interesting, given that the allusion to community is so frequent in popular discourse. Whether we are noting its breakdown, as in the analysis of urban poverty, or warning of the environmental (see Environment*) threat to a quality of life summed up in allusions to 'global community' (see Global Ethics 15), or whether we are talking of the norms to which Christians are corporately subject, 'community' is a word in transition from being merely descriptive to becoming normative. However, Christians, who are called to a realism* based on the fact that they serve a God who works in history, must beware of the utopianism and nostalgia inherent in modern allusions to community.

16

But if the church is to be 'the city set on a hill' (see Mt. 5:14), a normative place of refuge to which a fragmented world looks for hope, it must itself rediscover the concepts of justice (see Justice and Peace③), inclusion and interdependence which are at the heart of the biblical view of community.

1. Key contributory factors

In assessing the different influences on current expressions of community, several key factors have contributed over the modern period to a decrease in the quality of association between people which is at the heart of community life.

a. The pace of change. Where technological (see Technology*) knowledge is changing very rapidly, the received wisdom* of former generations can be seen as useless. In stable societies, the elderly may be treated as wise people whose advice is sought and heeded. In early Judaism, to be 'full of years' was to be wise. The elderly are isolated when it is the young who are relevant and the elderly who are out of touch. The rapid pace of change makes a primary division between generations. One could conclude from this that where such change is not felt there will be greater inclusiveness across the generations.

Sociologist Alvin Toffler (1928–) has talked of the way in which the rapid pace of change dislocates us in time. Raymond Aron (1905–83), the French sociologist, has commented that 'no man is a contemporary of his own generation'. By this he means that all education depends on the received wisdom of a previous generation, but it cannot prepare us for that which is unknown and yet to come. In a world of constant change, the virtue which is prized above all is flexibility, and this is the primary quality required of labour in the postmodern world where change is endemic. Mining communities which are becoming victims of economic circumstances, and factory communities which have been dispersed because of the advent of robotics, all enjoyed stability as communities while their skills were in demand. Community is therefore very sensitive to the pace of change, and those social groups which are familiar with contemporary practices have an edge over those which are not.

b. The increase in mobility. Community is very sensitive to mobility.* Surveys of local communities show that the local neighbourhood is used most intensively by the elderly and by young parents (often women) with young children. Such people can be seen as those with restricted mobility who are most sensitive to the degree of provision and the quality of association in their local area. Other groups which have more access to transportation may not identify so closely with the local neighbourhood but travel widely throughout the urban space to find appropriate work,* entertainment or sport.* Churches are used to seeing themselves as drawing their support from the local community. This was certainly applicable in days where the parish system combined with restricted mobility to make the local area the important focus of social identity. In the modern world, the concept of the individual's right to choose, together with increased mobility, has meant that people are willing to travel across cities to support a church which more nearly conforms to their choice than the church in their locality. This frequently leads to a tension between large 'gathered' churches and community-based churches.

Mobility also puts great strain on family life. 'Rootedness' is at a premium in contemporary culture, and people may live at a distance from other members of their family. This can lead to pressure on the family* and ultimately to family breakdown. The anonymity of large cities can also lead to increased delinquency as people feel that they do not know others and are not known by them. This may in turn lead to a lack of accountability,* which fuels antisocial behaviour.

c. Materialism. Materialism* creates problems for human community because it emphasizes 'having' rather than 'being'. Relationships between people can flourish only where people treat each other as human subjects rather than as human objects. When materialism is mediated through a consumer (see Consumerism*) culture, it creates a series of masks which people can hide behind, rather than an emphasis on the uniqueness of each person. Advertising* and marketing create a series of images which are widely disseminated through the mass media. The ownership of such images can become regarded as a sign of success. But there is often no correspondence between success in terms of ownership and the inner psychological or spiritual state of the person.

It can then become difficult for those who live in wealthy communities to admit to the existence of major problems in personal or family life. Such an admission can be seen as a

16

109

betrayal of the idea that increased wealth solves problems. Yet wealthy neighbourhoods often exhibit problems which are to do with the absence of community. Loneliness,* alcoholism,* tranquillizer addiction (see Dependence;* Drugs*) and high divorce rates can be as much a hallmark of wealthy communities as of poorer communities. This problem can be characterized as a confusion between a high *standard of living* and a high *quality of life.*

Materialism also increases the desire for privacy.* Money* gives people the power to control their own lives. One of the hallmarks of poor people is that they frequently have important decisions made for them by other people (*e.g.* officers of the Welfare State*) or have no choices available to them. The requirement that the poor (see Poverty*) and the unemployed (see Unemployment*) 'get on their bikes' to look for work may not be feasible if the waiting lists for council properties mean that mobility is restricted, if the council stock of housing is so run down that the prospects of moving are not appealing, or if there is a general shortage of affordable, privately owned, rented accommodation. This is an expression of powerlessness. In contrast, wealthy communities are characterized not only by the power to choose as well as the freedom* to choose (see Choice*), but also by the ability to choose with whom one will associate.

Architecture* reflects this difference. In terraced housing, one is forced to live closely with other people through no choice of one's own, but in wealthy communities there are large detached houses with space around them and gates which keep others out. Wealth increases privacy and homogeneity as people choose to associate with like-minded people who share their values. This can raise a question mark about the homogeneity of wealthy churches which then do not have to face trying to form relationships with those who are very different from themselves. Terraced accommodation, such as the 'back to backs', are often remembered in our society for being places where there was a strong emphasis on human community and where people 'looked out for one another'. It is still the case that communities of poor people are often characterized by greater interdependence and an emphasis on close relationships than are wealthier neighbourhoods.

d. The use of time. The rich and the poor are divided not only by monetary wealth but also by different attitudes to time. We live in different time zones. Some people spend money to save time while others spend time to save money. The concept of 'convenience', so important in contemporary life, assumes that people will be able to spend money to save time. The modern kitchen with its labour-saving devices is an important metaphor for a particular attitude to the values implicit in being a human community. Busy people regard 'busy-ness' as an important commodity to own, even though it generates stress.* To be busy or in demand is as important a sign of status in the community as monetary wealth.

Unemployed people have all the time in the world. They are not busy. They may have no work and little by way of social conversation when they meet others, because of the absence of work-generated conversation. Busy people, on the other hand, have little time for the space and commitment necessary for intimate relationships. But people who have 'all the time in the world' often feel so devalued by this that their relationships also break down. The new materialism is to do with our attitude to time. A full Filofax is as important as a full stomach in a culture where being too busy gives high status. Professionalism adds to this problem by demanding everything from talented people who find that they have little time for committed relationships of any sort. One of the most important issues which must be addressed within our communities is how we can change attitudes to time within the church so that everybody can enjoy a higher quality of life.

e. Physical space. Architecture can serve the community, dominate it or destroy it. At its best, architecture is meant to express ways of being human. If it is the quality of being human that we wish to focus on, then it is important that the architecture around us serves that end. Where architecture focuses on values derived from the possibilities given by technology or a view of aesthetics which is internal to the profession, it may well be that architecture moves away from the service of human community.

The most obvious example of this is the British tower blocks of the 1960s, which were built because of the need for cheap housing for large numbers of people at a time when the technology of pre-stressed concrete had made tall buildings possible at low cost. Many of these buildings are no longer functional and are being demolished. The dark corridors, lift spaces and general anonymity of such buildings led to abuse and violence rather than the enhancement of human community. People were living in confined boxes behind anonymous doors opening on to public spaces which were badly lit and which did not belong to them. This meant that, quite often, people did not venture out or get to know one another.

We are currently learning that human community is enhanced by how we design physical space. There is a great deal of difference between a community which is oppressed and de-humanized (see Dehumanization*) by its architecture and people who are enabled to express their sense of community through the architecture of the space where they live.

2. Theology and community

The idea of community is at the heart of biblical theology. Theological reflection on contemporary life is important if we are to regain a perspective on issues which have become distorted, either because they have fallen prey to false *thinking* or because our world has stressed historical *processes* which have led us off course. In recent times, theologians have used a simple fourfold scheme to summarize a biblical perspective on a particular issue. In some ways this is reductionist* and can only be an indication of the richness of the biblical perspective. Nevertheless, it remains helpful when looking at a theme such as community. The four perspectives used are creation,* Fall,* redemption (see Sin and Salvation⑤) and consummation (see Eschatology and Ethics*).

a. Creation. Our post-Enlightenment tradition emphasizes the concept of the individual, but this is only a recent development. Cartesian philosophy ('I think, therefore I am'), based on the thought of René Descartes (1596–1650), emphasizes the individual as the basic unit of society. The Enlightenment* also gave impetus to the philosophy of individualism, which has been reasserted in the remark by the then Mrs Thatcher (1925–) that there is no such thing as society. The modern idea of the autonomy of the individual does not express the biblical view of personhood.

The creation narrative asserts that the person made of dust was an incomplete expression of humanity (Gn. 2:18). Creation of woman is important not only in terms of mutuality, complementarity and equality expressed in gender terms, but also in terms of the biblical concept of personhood. In making humanity (see ④)

God states, 'Let us make man in our image . . .' (Gn. 1:26). We are made in the image of a trinitarian God who is three persons in one Godhead. In being made in the image of God we reflect a God who is person in community. God is love (see ②) because within the Trinity God is both the subject and the object of love.

We too are 'persons in community', and interdependence rather than individual autonomy is the basic starting-point for an understanding of human community. We find our human destiny in words which have an inescapable dimension of community. Words such as 'love', 'worship' and 'justice' – which describe humanity's highest personal and social ideals – are all words of relationship. The image of God* is not only something I reflect personally but something which is found in those relationships between people which are characterized by love, justice, mercy* or peace.* It is for this reason that Western society is beginning to react against an over-emphasis on individualism and is talking about community values again. State collectivism has also broken down in many countries because it had too low a view of the human person and frequently resorted to coercion to maintain the *status quo.* The creation perspective illustrates God's original intentions for the created world. It enables us to reject views of human community which are either excessively individualistic or excessively collectivist. 'Person in community' expresses the creation insight about people.

b. Fall. The introduction of evil into the world is portrayed in three instances in Scripture. Genesis 3 focuses on personal sin; Gn. 11, the Babel incident, introduces the idea of corporate evil; while in Rom. 1, Paul outlines his own picture of the universal Fall, focusing on the idea of social evil. All of these are a disruption of community.

The personal fall disrupts the relationship of trust* between humanity and God. It also has the result of introducing power* into the equal partnership between men and women. Men now rule over women, though this was not the creator's original intention (Gn. 3:16b). The worlds of work and the environment both suffer from frustration and do not reward the arduous labour that goes into them (Gn. 3:17–19).

In the building of the Tower of Babel (Gn. 11:1–9), people conspire anonymously together to create an identity for themselves corporately which is independent of God but

16

which ultimately invites the judgment of God. In this incident we see the difference between sin and evil.* In the former, people are personally responsible and accountable to God for what they have done. In the latter, it is the group which provides the dynamic towards evil in which people are implicated. Babel warns us that communities can be corporately guilty of evil, either because they conspire to do so, or because their lack of protest and resistance mounts to a guilty collusion. There is evil in the world which cannot be laid at the door of any one person.

Paul's description of an entire culture living under judgment* of God in Rom. 1:18–32 shows that when a society turns its back on God's norms, evil takes over. These people suppress what they know of God, investing their longing for God in other things which are unworthy of it, making these things falsely sacred as a result. The result is a culture where disobedience to parents competes with distorted sexuality (see 11), slander and envy (see Jealousy and Envy*) in order to promote evil* as good and to glory in things which are shameful. This trinity of evil, in its personal, corporate and social dimensions, leads to a fragmentation of a community which can be maintained only as long as God is at the heart of its life.

c. Redemption. In early Israel, the economic dimension of community life was based not on self-interest or on an appeal to altruism* such as are present in modern ideological systems, but on the worship of the God of justice. If one takes the regulations covering debt* and loans, it becomes plain that no commercial motivation existed for wiping out debts in the sabbath year (see Jubilee*), only that of obedience to God. Worship and obedience* were the motivating drive for socio-economic life (see Old Testament Ethics 8). In a secularized society such as ours, we do not have such a vertical dimension to maintain our life together, and we therefore resort to managing our community life either according to a principle of self-interest, which at least appeals to our fallenness, or according to altruism, which appeals to the ideals that we strive for but which frequently shows itself to be too weak to correct injustice in our communities. The Bible holds both together in tension at the heart of community life because it believes that, although people are fallen, they are also made in the image of God. Biblical realism therefore expects community life to be a mixture of sin

and righteousness,* loyalty* and betrayal, hope* and despair.

At the heart of the vision of the OT community is a picture of justice which focuses on economic life. While modern concepts of justice are all on a spectrum from individualism to collectivism, the biblical picture focuses not on the autonomy of the individual, nor on the sufficiency of the State, but on relationships between people informed by the themes of sin and righteousness. God is a God of justice, and his justice defines the nature of human community. It is not that we decide what justice is and measure God up to our own criteria, but that God's character provides the framework for our life together.

The perspective of inclusiveness is pervasive throughout the OT. Economic life focuses on the needs of the poor rather than on the self-interest of the rich. The people of Israel are to remember their equality as slaves in Egypt and the fact that their freedom and nationhood exist only because of the grace* of God. This emphasis that rich and poor are to act on the memory of their common roots in slavery is in stark contrast to our society, where becoming wealthy is seen as an expression of difference from the poor rather than of solidarity with them. This common foundation is to provide the motivation for their attitude to the widow, the orphan and the minority ethnic group. The regulations governing economic life – *e.g.* gleaning, sabbath,* and lending at zero interest,* as well as the great theme of jubilee – all serve to maintain the position of those who do not have the means to preserve their place in community. When Israel becomes distracted from God by idolatry, she loses this distinctive economic perspective. This in turn leads both to exile and to denunciation by the 8th-century prophets for dividing the worship of God from the practice of justice.

Jesus in his teaching builds on this inclusiveness. He does not need to lay again the foundations built in the OT. He upholds the authority of the OT and declares that he has come to proclaim the year of jubilee ('the year of the Lord's favour', Lk. 4:19). The economic foundations for the kingdom (see Kingdom of God*) community have been laid; what is needed is the radical message which addresses social rather than economic justice.

The kingdom had been defined by the Pharisees to exclude certain categories of people who were powerless. Prostitutes, women and children, the lepers and the poor were all outside the boundaries of the kingdom. Jesus crossed boundaries maintained by religious bigotry and deliberately drew those outside them into the heart of the kingdom community. He thus reversed the values at the heart of religious life. The kingdom is an inclusive community because God has appeared again in Christ and has made his own character and mission the model for Christian justice. Human relationships within community are to be characterized by love, mercy, peace and justice, which draw in those who have been marginalized.

This perspective of inclusiveness is thus underwritten by both OT and NT. It results in the early church ordering its life around this breakdown of division between people. A summary of this ethic in the life of the Christian church is found in Gal. 3:28, which states, 'There is neither Jew nor Greek, slave nor free, male nor female, for you are all one in Christ Jesus.' The Christian church* is the community which reflects the breaking down of barriers between people. It is a model of the extended family where belonging rather than having, and fellowship* rather than autonomy, are the norm. Church life is therefore meant to reflect this perspective of inclusiveness. Jesus says in Lk. 6:32–36 that mutuality and reciprocity are not the basis for the public display of the love of God: 'If you love those who love you, what credit is that to you? Even "sinners" love those who love them' (Lk. 6:32). It is when Christians reach out to those who are least like them that they need to draw on the character of a God who is inclusive in loving those who are enemies. We are thus called to participate in the stream of God's self-revelation as the God of Israel and God in Christ, reflecting justice in our relationships.

This kind of justice creates community where there was none. Those who were estranged are brought near, and those who were powerless are given the means to sustain their life. Secular concepts of justice do not normally deal with the state of individuals before some 'injustice' is done to them. A poor person may receive redress for some wrong but he or she is still poor even after justice has been done. Biblical justice sees such persistent poverty as a denial of the character of God. Through the creative powers of biblical justice, however, the individual's ability to contribute to the community is not merely preserved but actually created by justice.

Christopher Wright (1947–) has pointed out that not only is the biblical concept of justice inextricably tied up with the concept of community, but that the way the Bible thinks about community is very different from contemporary Christianity. He comments: 'We tend to begin at the personal level and work outwards. Our emphasis is to persuade people to live a certain kind of life according to this and that moral standard. If enough individuals live up to such-and-such morality, then, almost as a by-product, society itself will be improved or at least maintained as a healthy, happy, safe environment for individuals to pursue their personal goodness. *This* is the kind of person you must be; *that* kind of society is a bonus in the background. The Old Testament tends to place the emphasis the other way round; here is the kind of society God wants. His desire is for a holy people for his own possession, a redeemed community, a model society through whom he can display a prototype of the new humanity of his ultimate redemptive purpose. Now if that is the kind of society God wants, what kind of person must you be once you belong to it?' (*Living as the People of God*, pp. 197–198).

Although the church is meant to be a normative community which demonstrates how people from different backgrounds of race, class and nationality relate to one another, we can see that, to the extent that modern Christianity has capitulated to individualism, it has lost this distinctive approach both to community and to justice as inclusion within the community. The loss of this identity is particularly strange among those Christians who self-consciously look to Scripture for the principles on which they base their life together. So many of the descriptions of God's people throughout the Scriptures are corporate, whether it be the nation of Israel, the body of Christ, the city of God, or the fellowship of believers. It is because of this quality of life together as the people of God that discrimination such as racism (see Race*) or sexism* is so repugnant within the institutional church. God's community is to glory in unity-in-diversity, bringing together peoples, classes, ideologies and backgrounds that remain polarized in the world. Such a remarkable community can exist only because of the work of grace mediated through the Holy Spirit's* mission to the church.

d. Consummation. Throughout the Scriptures, the idea of hope* is often attached to the

16

future of the human community and particularly of those who find their identity in God. The most potent expression of this is found in the book of Revelation, where a great multitude which no person can number is gathered before the throne of God, and it is explicitly stated that it is drawn from every nation and tribe (Rev. 7:9). This is the consummation of the ethic contained in Gal. 3:28 that the gospel is the foundation for a gathering which defies human boundaries, whether they be boundaries of gender, race, class or any other human condition. This eschatological perspective provides a motivation within history for us to work towards that end. The dynamic within Christianity to create community therefore comes not just from interpersonal love, nor just from the inclusivity of biblical justice, but also from the hope that the church as counter-community is a sign of the new community to come when the kingdom of God is consummated.

One of the reasons community has a normative quality in its modern usage is that people want in some way to live in a perfect community characterized by love and justice. Our own world is an indictment of such a dream, characterized as it is by war, famine and injustice. The longing for human community, so prevalent in contemporary life, is powerful because it encapsulates within it something of the eschatological hope which has faded from our world with the onset of secularization.* The idea of a new world coming, in which people will do by nature that which pleases God, is important for the church to hold up before the watching world. It is for this reason, among others, that there has recently been a resurgence of theologies based on the idea of hope.

3. The mission of the church

The theme of community, then, is present throughout Scripture, and if we are to maintain a biblical perspective rather than succumbing to the nostalgia of modernity (see Modernity and Postmodernity*) or to the distortions of individualism or collectivism, it must be viewed from these four perspectives which Scripture provides: namely creation, Fall, redemption and consummation. The role of the church is to be a 'new community' which witnesses to the coming of the kingdom of God in the midst of the world. Relationships between Christians are to be characterized by love, justice, mercy and peace as these reflect the image and character of God and also the coming community of the city of God. This counter-community is not just involved in the ethereal. It is a visible sign of the presence of the kingdom of God and a demonstration of the lordship of Jesus Christ over every aspect of human community. Christianity is therefore a challenge to all aspects of our life together, whether they be economic, political, cultural, social or personal. The pietism* of the early part of the 20th century left Christianity with very little to say about the theme of community because it had capitulated too far to a version of Christianity which owed too much to individualism and privatization of faith. At the end of the 20th century there has been a resurgence of interest in 'holistic mission' and in the concept of the Christian mind, with encouraging signs that the Christian church is beginning once more to recover its courage to challenge the powers which adversely affect community life.

Much of the new thinking about community has been set in theological reflection on life in the city and, more recently, in rural areas. The publication of the reports *Faith in the City* and *Faith in the Countryside* has re-emphasized the need to grapple with the way in which these contexts affect the lives of millions of people. In turn this has led to renewed interest in the church's role in the community, and thousands of projects have been started by local churches who have recovered a sense of responsibility for the plight of those who live around them. Many of these projects emphasize community *service* which 'meets the needs' of people in the local area. The emphasis on service is person-centred, and alleviates the symptoms of distress. Sometimes this leads on to community *action* in which biblical categories are used to scrutinize the causes of poverty and oppression. Some churches are involved in a further stage of community *development* in which the church empowers the people in the locality to equip themselves with the tools to tackle their own problems, expressed in their own way. All of this work is a very welcome demonstration that the mission of the church to the community must reflect both word and deed, proclamation and demonstration, as equal partners.

See especially: ADVERTISING; ALIENATION; ARCHITECTURE; AUTHORITY; BUREAUCRACY; CAPITALISM; CHRISTIAN SOCIALISTS; CITY; CIVIL DISOBEDIENCE;

16

COMMON OWNERSHIP; COMMUNISM; COPYRIGHT; CRIME; CULTURE; DATA PROTECTION; DEBT; DEFENCE, MILITARY AND CIVIL; DEMOCRACY; DICTATORSHIP; DISCRIMINATION; EDUCATION; EMPLOYERS' CONFEDERATIONS; ENERGY; ENVIRONMENT; EQUALITY; EXPLOITATION; FAMILY; FORCE; FREEDOM; FRIENDSHIP; GOVERNMENT; HOMELESSNESS; HOSPITALITY; IMMIGRATION; INDUSTRIAL RELATIONS; INDUSTRIALIZATION; INFORMATION TECHNOLOGY; INVESTMENT; LAND AND LAND REFORM; LAW, CIVIL AND CRIMINAL; LEISURE; LIBERALISM, POLITICAL; MAGISTRATES, MAGISTRACY; MANAGEMENT; MEDIA; MOBILITY; MULTICULTURAL EDUCATION; NATIONALISM; NEIGHBOUR; PATRIOTISM; PLURALISM; POLICE; POLITICS; POP CULTURE; POPULATION POLICY; POVERTY; POWER; PRISON AND PRISON REFORM; PRIVACY; PROFESSIONAL ETHICS; PROPERTY; PROTEST; PUNISHMENT; RACE; RELIGIOUS EDUCATION; SECURITY; SENTENCING, PRISON; SLAVERY; SOCIAL CONTRACT; SOCIAL ETHICS; SOCIALISM; SOCIETY; SOCIOLOGY OF ETHICS; SPORT; STATE; STRIKES; TAXATION; TECHNOLOGY; TRADE UNIONS; UNEMPLOYMENT; URBANIZATION; VIOLENCE; WELFARE STATE; WORK.

Bibliography

Archbishop of Canterbury's Commission on Urban Priority Areas, *Faith in the City* (London, 1985); Archbishops' Commission on Rural Affairs, *Faith in the Countryside* (London, 1990); A. Hake, 'Theological Reflections on "Community"', in A. Harvey (ed.), *Theology in the City: A Theological Response to 'Faith in the City'* (London, 1989); R. McCloughry, *The Eye of the Needle* (Leicester, 1990); S. C. Mott, *Biblical Ethics and Social Change* (New York and Oxford, 1982); idem, *Jesus and Social Ethics* (Bramcote, Nottingham, 1984); N. Wolterstorff, 'Why Care About Justice?', *ThW* 10.11, 1987, pp. 22–25; C. J. H. Wright, *Living as the People of God* (Leicester, 1983) = *An Eye for an Eye* (Downers Grove, IL, 1983).

R.K.McC.

SEVENTEEN

Economic Ethics

Natural ethics is the doctrine of conduct judged according to ultimate principles. Christian ethics, claimed Emil Brunner,* 'is distinguished from natural ethics by the fact that in it God's action is always regarded as the basis of human action' (*The Divine Imperative*, London and New York, 1937, p. 86). In the economic sphere, to ground human action in God's action is to recognize that humankind takes resources divinely provided, to use for purposes divinely ordained, and responds properly to the divine call only by consciously acting as steward.

God calls; we respond. 'Response-ible' stewardship,* or trusteeship, is our key and our theme. How might we (the trust is clearly collective) so order our economic activity as to make a proper response to God's gracious provision and purpose? We cannot begin to answer the question without careful reading of God's Word, and due deference to those who have read and formulated its teaching before us: our main shared resources are Scripture and (orthodox) theology.

17

Scripture and theology

Economic guidance in Scripture (D. A. Hay, *Economics Today*, chs. 1 and 2) is more evident in the OT than in the NT. Arguably, Christians in the modern era have paid inadequate attention to it, but the Jewish communities of the dispersion never ceased to search their sacred writings. Their conclusions have been summarized recently in M. Tamari's *With All Your Possessions*, and we shall draw on this portrayal of 'Jewish economic man', half-brother at least to the Christian counterpart.

Theologically-based social ethics were argued by William Temple* in *Christianity and Social Order* to yield the principles of *freedom*, *fellowship* and *service*. Naturalistic analyses, severing these principles from their theological foundations, have divided into two main branches, finding the inspiration of the market economy in Temple's first principle, and that of socialism* in his second and third.

The attractions of freedom* emerged first in modern thought in the guise of religious toleration, *i.e.* freedom from externally imposed beliefs. Since beliefs govern actions, the notion gained ground that real freedom consisted in the absence of any external constraint on individuals' activities, at least in such measure that freedom's exercise was consistent with equal liberty for all. This notion of freedom, adopted by liberal thought in the wake of John Locke (1632–1704), was made the basis of liberal economics by the classical writers of the following centuries.

From a Christian viewpoint, this type of economics is based on the false conception of human ethical autonomy (something which Locke himself discussed), and needs substantial modification to make it acceptable. Stewardly service of God is perfect freedom. Freedom *from* needs to be complemented by freedom *for*. The freedom conferred by salvation includes being set free from the obligation to seek one's own good, for the purpose of serving God and neighbour.

Love of neighbour fulfils the law of God (Rom. 13), and has been the motivating force behind most non-Marxist brands of socialism. The British Labour movement, it was famously said, owed more to Methodism than to Marxism. Temple himself developed a defence of the mixed economy and the Welfare State* which saw freedom as realizable in fellowship and service. He would of course have sympathized with the claim of V. A. Demant in *Religion and the Decline of Capitalism* that more is needed for human fulfilment, since man does not live by bread alone. However, he perhaps wrote too early to perceive the force of Evan Luard's argument (in *Socialism without the State*) that State action necessarily corrupted socialist ideals, rather than providing a channel for their realization.

However, neither the market capitalist* thesis, nor its state socialist antithesis, represent a valid response to the divine call in the economic sphere. Though both have elements of useful insight, the idea of Christian stewardship calls for a new synthesis, uniting these by-ways which have, in isolation, proved to be dead ends. We find the key to this synthesis in an important but neglected strand of Christian ethical thought which has explored the notion of 'persons-in-relationship' (see, *e.g.*, I. Fairweather and J. McDonald, *The Quest for Christian Ethics*). Work emanating from the Jubilee Centre in Cambridge, UK, has coined the term 'relationism' (*contra* capitalism, socialism) as an apt descriptive label for the biblical paradigm for society (see C. J. H. Wright, *Living as the People of God*).

The implications of this approach are symbiotic with those of E. F. Schumacher's *Small is Beautiful*. The ethical imperative to combat giantism surfaces ever and again, and it is heartening that modern technical changes are tending in a variety of ways to undermine the attractions, too easily accepted as inexorable, of scale economies in production.

So we join the necessary debate with modern secular thought where the action is, with focus on the free-market economy, whose virtues are widely regarded as prevailing over its vices. Christian stewardship cherishes freedom, but not as an absolute in the manner of liberal economics (especially but not exclusively the economics of the Austrian School). Rather, freedom is seen as a means towards wider objectives, notably good relationships in fellowship and service, ideals inherently communal (see Community Ethics[16]) rather than individual in orientation.

Freedom within limits

The implications of this perspective, of 'limits' to freedom enabling the quest for true freedom, are:

1. *Owning and using.* Property* in economic resources is perfectly legitimate by Christian criteria, but it is not strictly private,

17

and it is not absolute. Near the heart of the OT story is the allocation of land,* the principal productive resource in an agrarian society, to (extended) family groups (Wright, *op. cit.*). These owners, or rather stewards, possessed circumscribed powers. They could not sell their land outright, but could lease it out until the next year of jubilee* (Lv. 25).

Moreover, the use of the land for productive purposes was subject to quite strict limitations. For one thing, during the sabbatical year of rest the land must be left fallow. For another, fields were not to be stripped during harvesting, but rather the poor were to be allowed to glean round the edges (Lv. 19) to satisfy their needs (see Old Testament Ethics[8]).

Starting from this basis, it is common ground in Christian and Jewish discussion that human stewardship of resources implies responsibilities as well as rights. The precise form taken by the former (self-discipline, communal arrangements) is in essence a secondary matter, though sound economic organization will both permit adaptable response to changing ideas and methods, and cause different forms of sanction to reinforce one another.

The concept of legitimate but limited property rights can properly be extended from the 'given' productive resource of land to 'produced' means of production such as tools, machinery, buildings; such physical capital, and financial claims thereto, will be considered below. It will be convenient at this point, however, to take account of immaterial knowledge and ideas. Even during OT times productive methods changed, and Judaism's search for wisdom* was based partly on the dissemination, in oral and/or written form, of rabbinic reflection on the law* (Torah). Questions thus arose concerning matters we now call patent* and copyright,* protecting the property rights of inventors and teachers. Jewish thought (Tamari, p. 109) has consistently recognized the legitimacy of legal protection of this kind, representing a balance between the goods of encouraging inventiveness on the one hand, and cheap spread of the fruits thereof on the other. However, in the modern era in which rapid technical changes tend to disrupt established economic relationships faster than adverse effects can be easily salved, the law probably should lean against too strong an encouragement of scientific and technological* change. Good fruits mature slowly, by and large.

2. Buying and selling. Trade* by merchants operating on their own account is morally legitimate. Qualifications must come, but it is necessary initially to be clear about this. Patristic and medieval Christian thought, influenced often by Gk. philosophy, tended to display suspicion of mercantile operations, viewing them with disfavour compared with production and transport of commodities. Jewish thought, based on the OT as interpreted by rabbinic authorities, held more firmly to what would now be widely accepted as a proper Christian endorsement of market activity.

Mainstream Judaeo-Christian doctrine, however, has never embraced an unqualified free-market ideology, or anything close to it. It has called for restraint on three counts:

a. Trading relationships should be properly governed by rules of morality and kindness, inculcated in the course of education based on community values, not by naked self-interest. Christian thought should not follow Hayek (*The Fatal Conceit*) in arguing the essential and beneficial amorality and anonymity of an 'extended order' of trade in modern large-scale societies.

b. Trade should in principle be subject to various kinds of communal action to protect the weak and ignorant, who often receive harsh treatment from free-market forces.

c. Legal regulation of trade should embrace not simply regulation and enforcement of contracts, but also control of prices and profits in some circumstances, notably when the supply of basic commodities is subject to interruption. Two types of modern development bear on such regulatory activity:

1. Occasions for special intervention in the community's interest to relieve shortages have diminished close to vanishing point in all save the poorest countries. This is because the geographical expansion of trading links, and development of intra-market rules and procedures, have greatly reduced the probability of serious local scarcities.

2. The second type of development works strongly in the opposite direction, in at least three ways. The expansion of wealth has facilitated vast trading in commodities that are not on any count 'basic' to true human needs. So, first, trade in 'bads' is not legitimate: there is no blessing on buying and selling pornographic literature, and there are large questions about trade in drugs, even of kinds generally accepted like alcohol.

Taking this point further we note, secondly,

17

that many of the so-called 'goods' of modern life make at best marginal contribution to the true welfare of consumers, while their transport over great distances exacerbates adverse environmental effects. Quantification of these opposing influences, to establish mathematical judgment of what is on balance beneficial, is a delusion of utilitarian welfare economics, but decisions must be made. Free (international) trade is not a Christian slogan (A. B. Cramp, 'The Economic Systems').

Thirdly, community regulation of trade cannot avoid greater emphasis, in some measure, on the welfare of near neighbours than on that of distant ones. For example, destruction of local enterprises cannot without most serious consideration be excused by reference to presumed, but often nebulous, advantages to producers and consumers world-wide (Tamari, p. 103).

At this point there seems no escape from wrestling with the intractable problem of finding grounding for ethical attitudes towards 'the global economy' (see Global Ethics[15]). We could take note of the debate between two schools of thought which are in opposition both to each other and to narrow economistic perceptions (N. Wolterstorff, *Until Justice and Peace Embrace*, ch. 2). *Modernization* theorists led by Talcott Parsons (1902–79) see the world as consisting of distinct societies, each at a certain point in the ubiquitous transition from traditional to rational modes of action, so that economic development* is both desirable and possible for all. *World-system* theorists led by Immanuel Wallerstein (1930–) see the world as consisting of one society (albeit a multiplicity of peoples). This society is rendered interdependent by the international division of labour, capitalistic in varying degrees, and its mechanics are such that the developed 'core' necessarily dominates the 'periphery', so that attaining tolerably equal levels of development (with equitable distribution of income and wealth) is an impossibility.

Evidence on which to judge between these two schools is still emerging, but in the interim the cries of the wretched of the earth support Wallerstein, and challenge the complacency of market economists, many of whom claim Christian affiliation. That complacency being rejected, urgent measures of amelioration are called for. Save in emergencies like famines, international political action faces near-insuperable obstacles, laid bare long ago by Reinhold Niebuhr* (*Moral Man and Immoral Society*). Fundamental restructuring of economic organization to strengthen more localized relationships at the expense of impersonal global ones faces 'only' the problem of achieving a clear vision and impetus. It is, in this writer's view, the main Christianly defensible way forward.

3. Growing and making. So we come to the sphere of production, with the awareness that it meshes closely with trade, that there is a testing balance to be struck between freedom and guiding restraint, and that the difficulties are compounded to the extent that economic activity is organized by agents lacking full commitment to the communities (local, regional, national) to which worker-consumers feel ready allegiance.

Discussion may be organized round the role of *profit** (A. B. Cramp, 'Pleasures, Prices and Principles') in guiding economic activity. Chicago-style economic theory treats profit as the fruit of satisfying consumer needs. Especially when on the defensive, it is wont to extend its support for market freedom from constraint, by arguing that such freedom is in effect also for the purpose of improving the economic welfare of the poor, in absolute if not in relative terms. Christian stewardship, accepting some measure of validity in the argument, is again strong to contend for limitations of superficial freedom, to serve the goals of fostering fellowship and service in fulfilment of the divine purpose.

In the Christian conception, profit reflects divine blessing on the efforts of humankind. In the husbandry of OT times, it was God who gave the increase, through what early modern economists were to call 'the gifts of nature'. If in more capital-intensive agriculture, and in industry and commerce, the increase derives more clearly and proximately from entrepreneurial effort, none the less valid profit can be earned only in ways which respect God's will. Three seeming restrictions on market freedom are readily seen to follow:

a. Production should supply to consumers genuine goods (as already argued), made available on the basis of good work. Products resulting from paying workers insufficient to support dignified living, and from employing them in degrading working conditions, are therefore clearly excluded. So, however, more searchingly, is 'profitable' production flowing from boring, alienating jobs which do not contribute to (and may often derogate from) the use and development of workers' true gifts and powers. Admittedly, work post-Fall cannot be pure joy. Yet 'Who sweeps a room as for thy laws / Makes that and the action fine' (George Herbert). But the assembly-line workers of Charlie Chaplin's film *Modern Times* can hardly perform their tasks of mind-numbing monotony making 'drudgery divine', and they are not without counterparts today. Humble tasks can, and ought to, be done in an organizational context which gives them some transparent meaning.

b. Production guided by the norm of stewardship should seek to minimize adverse effects on the natural environment, and regard the preservation *and restoration* thereof as a proper charge before true profit is struck. Community action may be helpful in enforcing good stewardship and creating 'a level playing-field' for competition, but producers should encounter it in co-operative rather than adversarial spirit. Public bodies could perhaps properly act by selling 'licences to pollute', or similar market-mimic devices, but in that case their trading too will be governed by an ethical code, not by desire to maximize public revenues regardless of consequence.

c. Production based upon the criteria of stewardship should act to prevent the exploitation of monopoly positions. Thus natural monopolies (*e.g.* water supply) call for regulation in the interests of, if not indeed for ownership by, the community being served. Artificial monopolies* whether in the form of cartels* of producers, or of unions of workers, call for close examination. The greater the economic power of such combinations, the more heavily will legal regulation fall upon them. Usually this will involve more restriction of the operation of cartels rather than of trade unions* – though circumstances can arise, and have arisen, in which the implied bias favouring the poor and weak is neutralized by the growth of excessive union power.

4. Borrowing and lending. Concentrations of productive economic power, however, do not in general arise except in the context of capital market processes. Financial institutions provide services which are essential to production, which ought to be subsidiary and subordinate to it, but which in today's large-scale economy constantly threaten to abandon the role of useful servant in favour of the role of tyrannical master.

To recognize this is implicitly to accept the continuing relevance of the biblical prohibition of usury (*e.g.* Ex. 22; Lv. 25; Dt. 23). The term has often been interpreted, since the prohibition's relaxation in Calvin's* era, to refer to 'excessive' interest* or profit rates on loans. Further, a friendlier attitude has been adopted to loans to producers, the interest on which can be met from profits presumed to reflect success in socially useful work, than to consumer loans more prone to lead to unmanageable debt burdens.

These ethical judgments have been maintained without adequate testing during an era in which the financial channels linking lenders to borrowers have been utterly transformed in scale and complexity. The local mutual building society or savings bank has given way to giant institutions – first national, then international, in scope. Small savings are fused into vast parcels of finance, allocated to borrowers by impersonal 'rational' criteria of profitability. Meanwhile, the principle of limited liability has facilitated the development of stock markets which permit the use of borrowed funds to finance takeover bids which all too frequently raise problems of the kind adumbrated above.

The time has come to re-examine the foundations of the prevailing ethical code, to discover just why and how the superficial freedom of capital needs to be limited in the interests of true freedom for fellowship and service. The biblical prohibition seems to have been directed towards preservation of social bonds in tribe and extended family. Any system which operates on the principle of wealth-owners drawing income from activities in which they have no vestige of personal involvement stands under threat of condemnation for actively discouraging the responsible stewardship to which biblical doctrine calls us.

Laws may need adaptation, *e.g.* to cement relationships by limiting speedy resale of financial assets once acquired, and by limiting takeover bids by strangers. More importantly, more locally-orientated institutions need to be developed (*e.g.* credit unions, regional savings banks) which may facilitate, if not the abolition of interest, at least its automatic limitation by virtue of the inherent mutuality of more nearly neighbourly, communal relationships. The Spanish model of the Mondragon group of worker co-operatives, whose capital is provided from the community's savings, may depend for its success less on coherence deriving from Basque nationalism, as has been alleged, than on coherence with biblical norms, reflected in the principles of solidarity and

17

subsidiarity (A. McKee, *Economics and the Christian Mind*) and espoused by its Roman Catholic priest-initiator (R. Oakeshott, *The Case for Workers' Co-ops*). (See also C. Schumacher, *To Live and Work*.)

This example illustrates a vital point. Modern Roman Catholic social thought, epitomized and energized by papal encyclicals* from *Rerum Novarum* (1891) to *Centesimus Annus* (1991) constitutes, like the Jewish corpus already touched upon, a living and active tradition. Academic investigations, pursued in the cloister, can have practical fruits that affect the life of the world in a profound way – though not necessarily so. The Anglican-based Christian political economy of the early 19th century, re-explored recently by Anthony Waterman (*Revolution, Economics and Religion*), was to be fatally weakened by capitulation to secular presuppositions, especially those bearing on the nature of 'scientific' method in reasoning about society. Recent efforts to resurrect the corpse of Protestant thought on social issues are heartening (an example from the Kuyper*-Dooyeweerd* Calvinist school is N. Wolterstorff, *Until Justice and Peace Embrace*); but progress depends on the emergence of more groups of thinkers willing explicitly to ground their writings in Christian fundamentals, come what may. A chaotic world is increasingly desperate for guidance, and willing to listen.

The success of Mondragon ought to inspire renewed experimentation with the idea that the way forward for property-owning democracy is ownership by people, not so much of houses and general financial claims, as of capital stakes in the enterprises to which their working lives are committed. Given the will, risk-spreading could be provided for.

5. Spending and giving. The OT promised prosperity as reward for collective obedience to God's laws (Dt. 28); Paul claimed for himself, and by implication advocated for his followers, individual contentment with much or little (Phil. 4). Confusion and tension can scarcely be avoided by modern Christians, subject to intense and manifold pressures from a secularized society inspired by the vision of unlimited expansion to satisfy (mainly individual) human desires.

While the desires fostered by society remain predominantly materialistic, the vision is illusory. 'Concordes and castles for everyone' is a goal impossible of realization – if only because of population growth and environ-mental constraints. Economic theory supposes the goal to be founded on the rock of individual insatiability, treated both as axiom and as proposition backed by powerful empirical support. The fact that sociological theory often sees the same behaviour as evidence of willingness to sacrifice for the good of family or community (Cramp, 'Pleasures, Prices and Principles') should induce caution. Contentions by some medical specialists that the quest for material plenty conceals an existential vacuum in the heart of modern man strengthen doubts.

Attempts to provide *limited* desires with rational foundation, typified by Gandhi's dictum that 'There is enough for everyone's need, but not for everyone's greed', founder on the impossibility of distinguishing clearly between 'needs' and 'wants' (M. Starkey, *Born to Shop*, ch. 2); and anyway they must contend with the claim, not totally lacking in justification, that greed in the market economy causes trickle-down benefits even to the poorest.

There seems no escape from the Pauline standard for Christian individuals, families and groups, accompanied by struggle to reassert for society's guidance the imperatives of divine law. Only good stewardship of God's gifts offers a road towards true and enduring prosperity, free from gross inequality and strife. Journey's end depends on God's gracious action, its beginning on human submission to providential guidance. Society's goal must shift from 'more' to 'enough'. The implications for the manner in which market activity mobilizes human effort are profound and far-reaching. They inspire hope, and they elide with some of the aspirations of the Green movement.

It is worth emphasizing that 'enough' as a goal may well in practice result in 'more', but the latter's composition, and the manner of its gathering and use, will change. Meanwhile, asset-holders must be retaught to have regard to obligations towards communal as well as individual needs. Social as well as legal influence must be mobilized to stimulate fulfilment of responsibilities in the provision of collective goods like affordable housing, schools and hospitals. The social obligations accompanying wealth-ownership, far from being a feudal relic, need to be reinterpreted for application in a society with far more wealth, more widely spread. The modern era espoused the alternative route of abolishing the obligations after payment of a compulsory tax tribute to the

17

poor, but this has proved a blind alley. It eventually produced the mixed economy and the Welfare State, which appeared in Temple's era to be capable of fusing the goals of freedom, fellowship and service in a manner congenial to Christian conscience. However, these institutions today are, if not moribund, certainly struggling for survival. A new way forward is needed. Christians must seek it in picking up the old route, from which society wandered in pursuit of a mirage.

Conclusions

This recovery of reality founded on divine law calls for individual effort, embedded firmly in a group context; for it rests on trinitarian belief in a God who is one in three and three in one, who has called human beings into a church which is the body of Christ, with the eucharist both as nourishment and as model for relationships (C. Schumacher, *To Live and Work*). Much of the work must fall to groups of Christians (not to the institutional churches) banding together to research, to influence ideas and legislation, to establish pilot-plant institutions; much will involve co-operation with people and groups open to Christian guidance even though not claiming explicit Christian allegiance.

Profound humility is required, recognizing that Christians past and present have perceived blurred individualistic or socialistic visions. Yet the modern era in Western culture is but a few centuries old; that is to say, it is very young: semi-Christian thesis, confronted by semi-Christian antithesis, may yet result in less un-Christian synthesis. There is hope, and Christians with their anchorage in its true foundation, in God's objective moral guidance of God's world, should be at the forefront of its clarification and outworking.

The kingdom of God* is coming. It is already among us.

See especially: BANKING; CAPITALISM; CARTELS; COMMON OWNERSHIP; CONSUMERISM; DEBT; ECONOMIC DEVELOPMENT; ECONOMIC SANCTIONS; EMPLOYERS' CONFEDERATIONS; FRAUD; GIVING; GROSS NATIONAL PRODUCT; INDUSTRIAL RELATIONS; INSIDER DEALING; INSURANCE; INTEREST; INVESTMENT; JUST PRICE; LAND AND LAND REFORM; MANAGEMENT; MARXIST ETHICS; MONETARISM; MONEY; MONOPOLIES; MORTGAGES; MULTINATIONAL CORPORATIONS; POVERTY; PROFIT; PROPERTY; REWARD; SOCIALISM; STEWARDSHIP; STOCK MARKET; TAXATION; TRADE; WAGE; WASTE; WELFARE STATE; WORK.

Bibliography

A. B. Cramp, 'The Economic Systems', in N. Wolterstorff (ed.), *Justice in the International Economic Order* (Grand Rapids, 1978); *idem*, 'Pleasures, Prices and Principles', in J. G. Meeks (ed.), *Thoughtful Economic Man* (Cambridge, 1991); V. A. Demant, *Religion and the Decline of Capitalism* (London, 1952); I. C. M. Fairweather and J. I. H. McDonald, *The Quest for Christian Ethics* (Edinburgh, 1984); D. A. Hay, *Economics Today* (Leicester, 1989); F. A. von Hayek, *The Fatal Conceit: The Errors of Socialism* (London and New York, 1989); E. Luard, *Socialism without the State* (London, 1979); A. McKee, *Economics and the Christian Mind* (New York, Atlanta, Los Angeles, Chicago, 1987); R. Niebuhr, *Moral Man and Immoral Society* (New York, 1932); R. Oakeshott, *The Case for Workers' Co-ops* (London, 1990); C. Schumacher, *To Live and Work: A Theological Interpretation* (Bromley, 1987); E. F. Schumacher, *Small is Beautiful* (London, 1973); M. Starkey, *Born to Shop* (Eastbourne, 1989); M. Tamari, 'With all Your Possessions': Jewish Ethics and Economic Life* (London and New York, 1987); W. Temple, *Christianity and Social Order* (Harmondsworth, 1942; London, 1976); A. M. C. Waterman, *Revolution, Economics and Religion: Christian Political Economy, 1798–1833* (Cambridge, 1991); N. Wolterstorff, *Until Justice and Peace Embrace* (Grand Rapids, 1983); C. J. H. Wright, *Living as the People of God* (Leicester, 1983) = *An Eye for An Eye* (Downers Grove, IL, 1983).

A.B.C.

17

EIGHTEEN

Christian Moral Reasoning

Christian moral reasoning involves the exercise of two kinds of thought together: 1. reflection; and 2. deliberation. Reflection is thought *about* something; when we reflect, we ask 'What is the truth?' Deliberation is thought *towards action*; when we deliberate, we ask 'What are we to do?' The metaphors contained in the two words illustrate the difference: reflection is 'turning back' on something; deliberation is 'weighing up' alternative courses of action.

An alternative pair of terms, derived from Aristotle,* is often used to make a similar distinction: '*theoretical* reason' and '*practical* reason'. But if we describe reflection as 'theoretical' as opposed to 'practical', we may obscure the point that moral reasoning, too, has a stake in reflection on reality. Practical reasoning,* or deliberation, depends upon a reflective grasp of some truth. We must, of course, distinguish moral reasoning from purely theoretical disciplines of thought which involve *only* thinking-about, and especially from theoretical disciplines which involve thought about human action: *e.g.* history, or the behavioural sciences. For it is possible to think about human action without projecting it. Not until what was, or is, or will be done becomes a factor in our thinking towards what *is to be* done, are we engaged in moral reasoning. Nevertheless, though reflection unharnessed to deliberation is not moral reasoning, deliberation cannot happen at all without reflection. Thinking-towards always supposes some thinking-about. We can, precipitately, act without thinking. But we cannot think towards acting without some propositional or 'theoretical' elements in our thought.

There is one important theological account of moral responsibility which apparently denies this linking of deliberation and reflec-

tion. Karl Barth* argued that moral knowledge is different from factual knowledge in that it is 'unconditioned', *i.e.* we are not at an observer's distance from it but immediately challenged by it. Because we are touched by the good immediately, it is a 'concrete individual command' to us, not a general rule waiting to be filled with content. It tells us, 'Do *this* and do not do *that*' (*Ethics*, pp. 64–78). Barth suspected that the space allowed for discursive thought, reflection on the one hand and deliberation on the other, was a way of trying to 'master' ethical knowledge, to make it a 'conditioned' truth over which we might have a scientist's distance.

His primary concern, an entirely fitting one, was to guard against the idea that the exercise of the will* in choosing between alternatives is its own justification. Decision can be moral only as it answers to the reality that confronts us, and supremely to the unconditioned reality of God's command. That point is safeguarded by insisting that deliberation cannot stand on its own, as though the acting subject were unconditioned. It must follow from reflection on reality that does not lie within the subject's control.

But what is that reality? Solely the commanding God (see ①) who meets us, argued Barth; while our account intends to allow *created* reality, provided it is real and not the distorted construction of sinful imagination, to command our reflection and direct our deliberation. Here there is a difference of theological emphasis, centring on the question of creation.* Nevertheless, the command of God, for Barth, is one and the same with God's promise. It does not only tell us what to do and not to do, but it tells us about ourselves, that we are created as mankind, reconciled in Christ and redeemed. It gives us knowledge of ourselves which is part and parcel with our knowledge of what we must do. In judging what to do we must, said Barth, 'guard against caprice . . . by seeking to grasp and structure the concept of man in terms of the Word of God directed to man' (*Ethics*, p. 119). There is, then, a created reality, the structure of human existence, which determines our knowledge of what God, creator, revealer and commander, requires of us here and now. If that is not saying precisely the same as has been said by speaking of moral reflection and deliberation, it is saying something parallel to it.

1. Reflection

Reflection, if it is to provide a ground for deliberation, must describe the elements of *teleological order* which make deliberation intelligible and necessary. 'Teleology'* means the rational account of purpose. But purpose is a notion with two poles, a subjective and an objective. On the one hand there are the purposes of the agent's mind which, in its aspects as 'will', directs our action; on the other, there are the purposes implicit in the world which is so ordered as to make our active purposing intelligible. Teleology traces the correspondence between the purposes we form and the purposedness of reality.

But not *every* feature of reality evokes intelligible purposes. Most of the information in a scientific textbook, for example, engages us only at the level of disciplined curiosity; and, indeed, science* as an intellectual endeavour abstracts systematically from teleology. Yet we need to see the teleological order in the world if it is to appear to us a place that we can act into. That is why moral deliberation cannot begin immediately from the findings of the human sciences. Those findings, to be a useful part of moral reasoning, must first be integrated into an understanding of reality which can ground deliberative freedom; and that requires the teleological insight of philosophy or theology.

But how can claims to discern objective purposes in the world be tested? Such claims may often reflect cultural prejudices and are usually contentious. Why should we not agree, to take the famous comic example, that if we had not been meant to eat each other, we would not have been made of meat? From a formal point of view there is nothing to choose between that and the claim that we have brains for understanding and hands for manipulation. A powerful philosophical tradition has sought to rule out all such teleological judgments on formal grounds, but this is a mistake. There are true and false ones; and those that are false fail simply because what they discern falls short of what is there to be discerned.

Christian believers maintain that the purposes of God, disclosed by revelation,* are the only final measure against which to prove our claims to find purposive order in the world. It is not that God's purposes sweep our human discernments aside, replacing them with simple bare commands to be obeyed. From our point of view they may sometimes seem to do that, because they challenge our prejudices and perceptions, so that there are times when we must simply hear God's word and obey, without fully understanding why. But if that were all there was to it, God's purposes would simply be imposed upon the world; and in that case he would not be the God who created the world and then redeemed what he had created. God's purposes interpret the teleological structures of the world, for they uphold it and affirm it, though they also judge it. Moral reflection attends to what is shown us of God's purposes in creation and redemption (see Sin and Salvation ⑤), on the one hand, and to the order of the world, in the light of God's purposes, on the other.

In the first place, we reflect upon the history of God's dealings with the world: in creation, in the coming of Christ and in the promised fulfilment. Each area of moral interest must be viewed in the light of the whole of this history. For example, marriage* is not only a gift of creation; it is taken up into the reconciling fellowship of Christ, and is superseded in the eschatological kingdom (see Kingdom of God*). Telling the truth* is a task entrusted to Adam, in the Genesis story, as he names the animals; it is also a responsibility of redeemed mankind, who has been told the truth about itself in Jesus Christ and is summoned to confess it; and the full disclosure of the truth is promised in God's final act of judgment. Work* is a gift of creation; it is ennobled into mutual service in the fellowship of Christ; it gives place to the sabbath* rest of the kingdom. And so on. But this understanding of God's purposes in salvation-history can be won only through reading the story of Christ and its interpretation by prophets and apostles. Scriptural authority is foundational for Christian ethics, as for all Christian thought, because it is the means through which Christ is made known to us.

In the second place, we reflect upon the

immanent purposedness of the world itself, as it is shown in the light of revelation: the significance of fellow humanity (see ④), the 'neighbour' with whom we are destined to various forms of community (see Community Ethics ⑯); the significance of non-human nature, placed under our protection and serving our benefit but with its own dignity before God; the significance of the human body as the mode of personal presence to others, and of the conscience* as the place where we become aware of ourselves before God. The knowledge that we gain of the purposes implicit in these structures is theological knowledge and cannot simply be taken as self-evident; yet it may coincide with the fragmentary, but not negligible, moral perceptions which all human beings share (see Natural Law*). Christian reflection can appreciate these perceptions positively and can learn from them, but without supposing them to be autonomous or self-sufficient. They reflect to us the light that God has shed upon the world through his disclosure of himself, like the moon which reflects the light of the sun.

2. Deliberation

To say that deliberation is thought towards *action* is not the same as saying that it is always towards *decision*. A number of writers in recent years (*e.g.* James McClendon, 1924– , and Stanley Hauerwas, 1940–) have protested against the idea – christened 'decisionism' or 'quandary ethics' – that moral reasoning is solely a discipline of decision-making, as though nobody had any use for it until some quandary arose that had to be solved. Deliberation is not a form of thinking to which we have only occasional resort when we find ourselves, by accident, caught out with a divided mind and something needing to be done. Thought towards action is not restricted to thought towards some particular act, but includes, more embracingly, the whole of our active existence. Our deliberative agenda is not exhausted by the question, 'What shall we do next?' We also ask, 'How shall we live our lives?' and 'What attitudes shall we take to specific areas of practical concern?'

The question 'How shall we live our lives?' invites an answer in a kind of moral language quite different from the language we use in reporting our decisions, 'I ought' or 'I ought not'. This is the language of the virtues* and dispositions, much used in the NT and especially the epistles to sketch a general outline of the quality of Christian life. What is the relation of these two kinds of language? Is a virtue merely a disposition to repeat acts of a certain kind, so that when Paul says, 'Be kind to one another . . .' (Eph. 4:32), it is shorthand for the advice that we should first perform one kindly action, then a second, then a third and so on? But that would mean that we could never deliberate about the shape of life as a whole, but only about the next particular thing we have to do. Yet we do, at least, *reflect* about our own and others' conduct as a whole, finding general terms for the ways in which we behave ourselves: love, joy, peace, patience . . ., or contrariwise impurity, superstition, hostility . . . and so on (*cf.* Gal. 5:19ff.). But if such reflection is supposed to lead to any practical result, there must be a corresponding form of deliberation, so that we think how to shape the way we live, not only how to shape the next thing we do. We can frame policies for the conduct of our lives, and that is what the writers of the epistles are teaching us how to do well.

But besides framing policies for our conduct as a whole, we deliberate on our attitudes to specific areas of practical concern. What attitude, for example, should we adopt towards nuclear weapons (see Deterrence, Nuclear*)? That question demands an answer quite apart from any particular decision we may have to make. Comparatively few people, indeed, deal closely enough with nuclear weapons for particular decisions to arise; yet a thoughtful attitude to them is necessary if we are to chart a course responsibly through life in the late 20th century. To form that attitude rightly is part of the obedience we each owe God. And as with nuclear weapons, so with every other area: we must form a policy about the right and wrong of sexual self-disposal, for example, quite apart from any particular occasion of sexual opportunity (see Sexuality ⑪); we must have attitudes to the possession and use of wealth before we inherit an estate. We need to approach concrete decisions with moral policies already formed.

These policies include not only our handling of the matter directly, should occasion arise, but our dealings with those who do handle it. Deliberative questions about specific moral topics arise in more than one form: there are pastoral and political questions as well as questions of personal self-determination. 'How should I act?' is followed by 'How shall I advise others to act?' and 'How shall I use such public authority as I have to constrain the community to act?' The answers we give to these different questions may be interestingly contrasted. On the matter of abortion,* for example, one person might reply: 'I shall never have an abortion; I shall try to discourage those who see abortion as their only way out; I shall support policies of greater legal restriction.' That is one possible combination of consistent answers, not the only one and not necessarily the best. But not every combination of answers would be consistent. Their coherence must depend upon their all being compatible with the same set of reflective judgments on the meaning of abortion, the reasons for which it is performed, its effect on society, and so on.

*Moral rules.** In formulating these policies we depend upon *generic moral rules.* Lying behind the question 'What shall I do?' there is the more basic question 'What shall *we* do?' in which the subject is undifferentiated. If what I propose for myself does not correspond to what we human beings, faced with such questions, ought to propose, then I have proposed wrongly.

A terminology I have adopted and defended elsewhere (see *Resurrection and Moral Order*) uses 'generic' as the opposite of 'particular', meaning 'to do with a kind'. 'General', on the other hand, is the opposite of 'specific', and means 'imprecise'. A judgment may be more or less general: more general than some other judgment and more specific than a third. But between 'generic' and 'particular' there is no more or less. Either one makes a judgment about a particular case, as if pointing to it: '*This* war is criminal.' Or one makes a judgment about a *kind* of thing: 'War is criminal' – to which one may or may not add specifications: 'aggressive war is criminal', 'aggressive nuclear war is criminal', *etc.* English-speaking moral philosophers sometimes use 'universal' in place of 'generic'; while German-speaking writers often use 'universal' very widely, to cover what is meant both by 'generic' and 'general'. But the term 'universal' has another important sense – referring to the universe, or whole of things – and it is more convenient to avoid it altogether in this context.

a. When we deliberate about our moral rules, we aim to make them less general and more specific, *i.e.* to give them the clarity and precision that they need in relation to distinct kinds of circumstance. This sometimes, but not always, means noting 'exceptions'. If we say 'Murder is wrong, but killing in just war is not murder' – or, alternatively, 'Killing is wrong except in just war' – we are positing an exception to a general rule (see Just-War Theory;* Killing*).

Two difficulties, from opposite points of view, are commonly raised to the idea that valid general rules may have exceptions: 1. that if we recognize any moral laws as authoritative and God-given, then introducing exceptions to them is simply illegitimate; 2. that finding exceptions disproves the general rule, and so makes it invalid.

1. To the first difficulty, we reply that if we are to obey any rule, we must understand the scope and meaning of its terms; and that applies no less to God-given rules such as those in the Decalogue.* Does 'honouring' one's father and mother include acquiescing in unreasonable senile whims, even when one is an adult? And does 'father and mother' extend to grandfathers and aunts? Such questions can be given sensible answers, of course; the point is, they may need to be. If we do not see that such questions may arise, then we are underestimating what the command may require of us.

2. To the second difficulty it can be said that the exception proves the rule, since the question whether this or that exception is appropriate cannot be put unless there is a rule to make an exception to. Who would ever wonder about indulging tyrannous parental whims unless it were understood that parents have prerogatives? The command determines the shape our moral questioning shall take, what cases we shall find problematic, and so on. A moral rule is interestingly and helpfully general. It marks the terms of the moral discussion, and so assists us to chart a course through unfamiliar circumstances.

Exceptions to rules are not 'made' so much as 'found'. It is not a matter of arbitrary preference that moralists permit killing in just war while the Decalogue forbids murder; it is an implication of the requirement to do justice and defend the innocent. Furthermore, the specification of general rules does not always consist in finding exceptions and, as it were, whittling the rule away, as a third-rate casuistry* may sometimes make it seem. It also consists in finding unexpected moral suggestiveness in rules, as when Jesus found implications for the conduct of desire within the law forbidding adultery.* The purpose of deliberating on moral rules is to discern their *real* application to distinct circumstances.

18

'Exceptions' are no more than cases to which the rule, properly understood, does not apply. Some rules are sometimes said to be 'exceptionless'. If this is taken to mean that there are rules demanding or forbidding specific types of action about which it is impossible to ask in any case whether they apply or not, it is obviously a mistake. But in another sense that term may be appropriately applied to those basic moral rules which identify claims that must always be respected somehow, even when the respect required is paradoxical. Nobody may kill in a just war, for example, who is not defending innocent lives and who does not regard the lives of the guilty, too, as precious. Thus the command 'Thou shalt not murder' shapes the principles of just-war conduct. No moral rule is complete in itself; it is a kind of chapter-heading for moral deliberation, an organizing principle on which our reasoning must proceed.

b. *Particular* moral judgments, or 'decisions', involve bringing the particular instance under a generic moral principle or rule that has been grasped independently. If killing *this* person is wrong, it is because it would be a case of murder; and murder can be seen to be wrong irrespective of this case. The wrongness of the instance derives from the wrongness of the class. The logic of saying otherwise was explored to its irrationalist conclusions by the short-lived fashion called 'situation ethics',* represented by Joseph Fletcher.* Situation ethics is best understood as a proposal to construct moral deliberation solely in terms of particular decisions and one very general allembracing moral virtue, with nothing in between. Its tenor was punctiliar and individualist, an expression of that unqualified attention to the 'concrete' which was a fruit of late idealism* and existentialism.

What is required for a particular judgment, then, is that the case be lined up with the moral rule that it instantiates; but this demands a kind of leap of *recognition*: 'But *this* would be an act of murder, an instance of the kind of thing we meant when we said murder was wrong!' No amount of subtle specification of the general condemnation of murder will tell us whether what we are about to do is, in actual fact, a case of what we have been talking about. A particular moral decision is never derived directly from a generic rule; an act of recognition must intervene. There can be no rule for performing this act of recognition; if there were one, it would be a part of the moral rule itself. Recognition must just happen; it depends on 'insight'. That is the element of truth in situation ethics; but it is only one element of the truth, since no-one could recognize a case as being an instance of a kind unless there were rules that distinguished kinds of case.

Most of the time, it appears, recognition is no problem. Someone who acknowledges that lying (see Truth*) is wrong, but fails to see that a favourite politician's untruth was actually an instance of lying, usually strikes us as obtuse or prevaricating. This appearance, however, is misleading. Even the most obvious recognitions have to be learned in childhood, and there are, furthermore, recognitions that are genuinely difficult even for morally educated adults.

Let us press the example of the so-called 'justified lie'. The secret police are searching for an honest dissident, and only an elaborate subterfuge, involving outright deception, will protect him. Apparently it would be a case of lying, generally condemned. What account can we give of our intuitions, if we have them, that a falsehood in this case could not be blameworthy?

Three theories have been advanced: 1. There are cases which simply lie outside the scope of any rule – 'exceptional' not merely in the sense that they are unusual, but in that they are not capable of being encompassed in any generic formulation at all; 2. some cases arise at points where two moral rules conflict in the claims they make on us, the point of 'dilemma'; and 3. any moral rule may, in some specifiable circumstances, *not* demand of us what on the face of it it might *seem* to demand.

1. The difficulty with the first of these theories is that if the situation lies outside all moral rules, no appreciation of the moral claim it makes can ever be reached. We have no more reason to think that mercy* is appropriate than that truthfulness is.

2. The difficulty with the second is how we are to decide which of the two conflicting demands – mercy or truthfulness – should be decisive for our action. We seem to need some third rule to arbitrate between the two conflicting rules. But that rule-to-order-rules will either be a formal one (as in the 'proportionalism' advocated by Richard McCormick, 1922–), applicable to all conflicting rules regardless – though there can be no such rule; or it will express an insight into what *these* specific rules demand in *this kind* of conflict-

18

126

situation, and then we end up with the third account after all.

3. The third theory, represented by Paul Ramsey* and Helmut Thielicke,* is the best. If we decide that a demand to know the truth is weakened when it is asserted with a hostile and illegal purpose, then we have discerned something important about what truth itself demands of us and the conditions for the exercise of truthfulness. We have not merely decided that mercy should prevail in this case; we have gained an understanding of the law of truth itself.

See especially: ABSOLUTES; ATONEMENT; BENEVOLENCE; BLESSEDNESS; CASUISTRY; CHOICE; CONSCIENCE; CONTEXTUAL ETHICS; CREATION; DECALOGUE; DOUBLE EFFECT; DUALISM; DUTY; ENDS AND MEANS; ESCHATOLOGY AND ETHICS; EVIL; FAITH; FALL; FORGIVENESS; FREEDOM; FREE WILL AND DETERMINISM; GODLINESS; GOODNESS; GOSPEL AND ETHICS; GRACE; HAPPINESS; HEAVEN AND HELL; HOLINESS; HOLY SPIRIT; HOPE; HYPOCRISY; IDEALISM; IMAGE OF GOD; INTENTION; INTUITIONISM; JESUS; JEWISH ETHICS; JUDGMENT AND THE JUDGMENT; JUSTIFICATION; KINGDOM OF GOD; LAW; LAW AND GOSPEL; LAW, USES OF; LIBERATION THEOLOGY; MEAN, DOCTRINE OF THE; MELIORISM; MERCY; MERIT; MORAL AGENCY; MOTIVE, MOTIVATION; NATURAL LAW; NEIGHBOUR; NORMS; OBLIGATION; PHILOSOPHICAL ETHICS; PIETISM; PRACTICAL REASON; PROPHECY, OLD TESTAMENT; PROSELYTISM; REASON AND RATIONALISM; RECONCILIATION; REPENTANCE; RESPONSIBILITY; RESURRECTION; REVELATION; RIGHTEOUSNESS; RULES; SANCTIFICATION; SERMON ON THE MOUNT; TEMPTATION; THEODICY; VALUES; VICE; VIRTUE, VIRTUES; WILL, HUMAN; WISDOM; WORLD.

Bibliography

Augustine, *On Christian Doctrine*, in NPNF, 1st series, vol. 2; K. Barth, *Ethics,* tr. G. W. Bromiley (Edinburgh and New York, 1981); J. M. Finnis, *Fundamentals of Ethics* (Oxford, 1983); S. Hauerwas, *The Peaceable Kingdom* (Notre Dame, IN, 1983; London, 1984); J. W. McClendon, *Systematic Theology 1: Ethics* (Nashville, TN, 1986); R. McCormick and P. Ramsey (eds.) *Doing Evil to Achieve Good: Moral Choice in Conflict Situations* (Chicago, 1978); O. O'Donovan, *Resurrection and Moral Order* (Leicester and Grand Rapids, ²1994); G. H. Outka and P. Ramsey (eds.), *Norm and Context in Christian Ethics* (London and New York, 1968); H. Thielicke, *TE* 1, ch. 27.

O.M.T.O'D.

18

PART TWO

A

ABELARD, PETER (1079–1142). Born in Brittany, Abelard studied and then taught at various schools in France, and in 1113 became the head of the cathedral school of Notre-Dame in Paris. His account of his rise to fame and his humiliation because of his love affair with Héloise is found in his *Historia Calamitatum.* Abelard turned to theology only later in life, using the same dialectical skills that had made him so incisive as a philosopher to treat of such problems as the Trinity. Although criticized by Bernard of Clairvaux (1090–1153) for putting faith on the level of human opinion, it is fairer to say that Abelard employed a new, dialectical method for the understanding of faith,* a method that advanced theological method significantly.

In his ethical theory Abelard distinguishes between defect (or vice) and sin. Because of defect one consents to do evil and not do good. Such consent is sin. The wish or desire to do wrong is not sin, but only the consent. Also, sin is not increased by the action. Abelard, then, makes morality consist in intention* alone, and actions, apart from intention, are morally neutral.

Intention is not to be called good just because it seems good, but because it is what is pleasing to God. Persons who do not know the gospel cannot be held responsible for what they do not know, and so Abelard is unable to explain why those who die not knowing the gospel are none the less condemned (*cf.* Rom. 1:18–23).

In his *Theologia Christiana* (1123–24) Abelard argues that non-Christians also have access to God's laws and that those pagans and Jews who followed them were saved. Christianity is the total truth that contains the teachings of the pagans and Jews within it.

Bibliography

Peter Abelard's Ethics, tr. D. E. Luscombe (Oxford, 1971); *The Story of Abelard's Adversities*, tr. J. T. Muckle (Toronto, 1954).

J. R. McCallum, *Abelard's Christian Theology* (Oxford, 1948).

A.G.V.

ABORTION is an emotive issue. Varied descriptions of the same act carry different emotive contents. Evacuating the uterus sounds very different from 'scraping out the baby'. Spontaneous and natural abortion is distinguished from human intervention to end a pregnancy. Such intervention may be by drugs or surgical procedures. Some contraceptives like the intra-uterine device or coil and the RU486 drug act as aborto-facients (causing abortions) expelling fertilized eggs. From the Roman Catholic perspective, all contraception (see Birth Control*), even what prevents fertilization, is unnatural. In many countries, abortion is legal under specified circumstances.

Usually permission from at least two physicians is required, and some time-scale, *e.g.* 24 or 28 weeks, is set as the upper limit for performing abortions legally. The age limit varies, and in India may be up to 40 weeks. Specific conditions often refer to risks to the mother's life, to her social and psychological well-being, to the social, psychological and economic well-being of other children, and when the foetus is thought to be abnormal. This last category will grow as we are better able to diagnose congenital abnormalities. In such cases, abortion prevents the suffering of the abnormal individual and of the family and carers. While this may be true, it also implies a particular view of human worth, *i.e.* that handicap and abnormality make life not worth living, and calls in question society's view of normality. Doctors are thus permitted to perform abortions legally. There is a conscience clause which allows doctors and nurses to refrain from taking part, but this creates great problems in a medical unit and has discouraged many from becoming specialists in obstetrics and gynaecology. In practice, this legal permission has become almost abortion on demand, and doctors find it very difficult to refuse requests for abortions.

The language used to describe the foetal life itself can carry value. Some talk of embryos (potential humans), as opposed to foetuses (people with potential). Part of this is disagreement about when life begins. For some it begins at *fertilization,* when the sperm and the egg unite and the full genetic potential is in place, but the possibility of twinning and the over 40% loss of fertilized eggs in the normal monthly cycle without any suggestion of pregnancy are adduced as evidence against this. Research in embryology* and infertility uses 14 days as a cut-off point for experimentation on embryos, on the grounds that the individual is formed near that point as the primitive streak develops with the capacity to register pain. *Implantation,* when the fertilized egg fastens on the wall of the womb, is the next option, which allows the use of the coil – which many argue is vital for population control in the Third World, where it is the most effective contraception. Then *quickening,* when the child moves within the womb, or viability, when high technology medicine can preserve life, are selected. Medical practitioners favour *viability* as the point when a clear patient becomes the responsibility of the doctor. With advances in intra-uterine surgery, this line will not only continue to be reduced from 24 to 21 weeks, but be questioned as genetic engineering* and manipulation* become more viable. In practice, many doctors adopt a developmental life of the unborn, recognizing that as the foetus develops there is greater claim made on the rest of us by the foetus. When viable, the foetus can be considered as a patient to be cared for in the same way as the mother. Others, however, suggest *birth,* stressing that the Genesis account links life with the breath of God, and some claim that *genuinely independent existence* is necessary before we have human life in its fullness. This latter view links with moves to define human life in the having of certain fundamental capacities rather than in biological terms. The modern debate rejects all discussion of ensoulment, which was the traditional basis for asserting the value of foetal life. The arbitrariness of the moment of animation and the alleged difference between male and female ensoulment make the traditional view difficult to propound in a secular society. Even if we could agree about when life begins, that would not in itself solve the dilemma of the value implicit in or attached to human life at its various stages.

The heart of the abortion debate seems to rest on a decision between the rights (see Rights, Human*) of the mother and the rights of the child. The status of the child thus does have significance for there to be rights involved. Legal decisions about inheritance *in utero,* and the awarding of damages for accidents which happened *in utero,* seem to suggest that the foetus does have legal rights. In contrast, the women's movement in particular has argued that every woman has the right to do whatever she wants with her own body. It is hard to accept such claims, for society limits the freedom of all its members and their autonomy by restricting what people are

allowed to do with their bodies. Laws about seat-belts, motor-cycle helmets, pornography and prostitution embody such limits. The lesser claim is that in a situation of conflict of interests, the rights of the woman should have precedence over the rights of the father or of the child. Courts have usually found in favour of the mother rather than the father and the foetus. This would justify the rare occurrence of aborting the foetus when the life of the mother was at risk. More commonly, in situations of crime or incest,* abortion has been legally justified on the grounds of the woman's right over that of the foetus. Those opposed to abortion stress the need to protect the innocent and the principle of the sanctity of life.

The Christian perspective

The principle of the sanctity of life* is clearly established in Gn. 9 and in the Ten Commandments. The OT does picture God as permitting and requiring the taking of human life in terms of warfare and the death penalty for specific crimes. Some see this as justifying the killing only of the guilty and not of the innocent; others as a basis for a consistent, 'seamless robe' of the sanctity of life in every situation. The Bible as a whole clearly states that life comes from God as his gift and that we are answerable to him for what we do with our own and other people's lives. Such responsibility means that we shall all answer before the judgment* seat for our actions and failures to act. Thus, any and every taking of life is a most serious business and requires justification to God. Some suggest that in a fallen world there may be situations where no matter what we do it will be evil. Thus, in extreme settings, the taking of life may be the 'lesser of two evils', remaining an evil which needs confession and repentance. This may be reflected in Ex. 21:22–23, where a distinction is drawn between the loss of a woman's life and a baby's as a result of an accident. In the one case, the legal requirement is a life for a life, but in the case of foetal life, a fine is required. Though exegetically ambiguous, at most this shows a distinction between foetal and fully developed human life, but does not in itself justify abortion. Indeed, it is clearly seen as a wrongdoing requiring recompense, even though this is in the setting of accidental death and not, as in modern abortion, where death is the intention.

The calling of the prophets Isaiah and Jeremiah while in the womb, and the detailed description of foetal life as portrayed in Ps.

139, offer a clear picture of God's concern for and intimate involvement with human beings from before conception. While there is no doubt about God's role in the creation of life, these passages are all written from the perspective of psalmist and prophets looking backwards. All of their life has been in God's hand, and they testify to that. Whether we are able to look forwards from every embryo to the person they would be, if other things were equal and nothing else happened, is less certain.

In the NT, after the annunciation by Gabriel to Mary, the now newly pregnant Mary goes to visit the six-months-pregnant Elizabeth. She describes how the child in the womb (John the Baptist) leapt at the coming of the Saviour's mother (Lk. 1:39–45). This seems to point to foetal awareness in John and the foetal identity of both Jesus and John. The same note of backwards-looking reflection matters here, for the physician Luke records what happened to those who were known as John the Baptist and as Jesus. Whether the forwards projection or the generalization from such a unique, doubly miraculous event can in itself justify a high view of foetal life is more debatable.

The early church and its successors firmly held to the need to defend the unborn and the inviolability of the foetus, once it was ensouled. The modern debate has moved on, and Christians may disagree, but not about the central need to preserve the principle of the sanctity of life, and limit the idea that people are free to please themselves with regard to their own bodies regardless of the impact on others. This is not a patriarchal imposition, but a recognition that the vulnerable need to be protected. Within the Catholic community, abortion has sometimes been justified on the basis of the double-effect* argument. If the aim of an operation (e.g. an abortion) is to save the life of the mother, then that primary effect and intention* are morally acceptable; the second or double effect is the death of the child. While still ultimately responsible, if the doctor's primary intention was to preserve the woman's life and there was no alternative, then a doctor may be considered to be morally justified in ending foetal life.

Current issues

With increasing technological and genetic advances, the problems will continue to grow in this area. Selective reduction, where healthy implanted embryos are destroyed to avoid multiple births in infertility treatment, is now common. The use of foetal tissue from aborted foetuses raises moral questions about the integrity of the foetus and who should give permission for such work, if it should be permitted. Some regard this as a means of bringing some good result out of an evil situation, while others regard this as 'playing at God' and reducing the value and integrity of human life. As our capacity to measure and manipulate foetal and embryonic life grows, so will the moral dilemmas. Christians must remember that behind the dilemmas are real people facing unwanted pregnancies, bringing up handicapped children, or coping with the long-term results of rape* and incest. The need to offer genuine assistance to the unmarried mother, to the mother who already has a large family and no proper means of support, to the parents of handicapped children, and to those who have been criminally assaulted should be part of the Christian response regardless of our own attitude towards abortion. Such loving care may well decrease the number of abortions. Likewise, Christians must reflect on their responsibility in a society where human life is regarded cheaply. It is proper to ask what kind of society we become when human life is regarded as disposable; all of us may then be vulnerable. The prophetic proclamation of the principle of the sanctity of life must be matched by concern for those who do not and cannot accept that standard. Practical help with practical alternatives must be produced. In political terms, Christians are free in a democracy to work for a change in the abortion laws and to persuade society of the evil of abortion on demand. They do not have the right to inflict their morality on society. This creates a tension for politicians and law-makers who are Christians. Do they refuse to accept anything but the ideal they believe in, or are they willing to work by a process of compromise at reducing the conditions and time-scale for abortions, thus killing the abortion law by a series of reductions? As part of restraining evil in a pluralist society, many will feel that saving the few is better than saving none, and that, in time, science will show the integrity of human life from its earliest stages.

See also: ETHICS OF MEDICAL CARE. 14

Bibliography

D. Cook, *The Moral Maze* (London, 1992); R. F. R. Gardner, *Abortion: The Personal*

Dilemma (Exeter, 1972); O. O'Donovan, *Begotten or Made?* (Oxford, 1984).

E.D.C.

ABSOLUTES. When used in an ethical context, the word 'absolute' usually refers to a rule which maintains obligatory force under all circumstances. It allows no exceptions.

Ethical absolutism has a variety of roots. Some religious thinkers root it in the holy and unchanging nature of God (see ☐), who has revealed his will in propositional, prescriptive statements which are valid for all time. Some Enlightenment* thinkers (notably Immanuel Kant*) root it in the dictates of human reason,* which posits unconditional imperatives of a universal nature. Some 20th-century thinkers root it simply in human intuition: we simply know that a duty* such as keeping a promise should always be kept, even if we cannot fully explain why.

In some ways the Bible appears to support ethical absolutism. The Mosaic law* is presented as absolute and inviolable. In the narrative sections of the OT God is often portrayed as intolerant of the slightest disobedience to his commands, an attitude apt to be conveyed through acts of spectacular divine punishment (see, *e.g.,* Lv. 10:1–2; Nu. 15:32–36; 2 Sa. 6:6–7). Jesus affirmed the law down to its last jot and tittle, and said that his would-be followers must exceed the righteousness of the scribes and Pharisees, who were known for their precise observance of the law (Mt. 5:18–20). Paul lists various practices which seem to be forbidden absolutely, being seen as incompatible with inheritance of the kingdom of God (see, *e.g.,* 1 Cor. 6:9–11).

Good grounds exist for making certain rules absolute. The prohibition of rape* is an example. By very definition, rape is an unloving act; it forces another person into the most intimate of human behaviour against his or her will. It invariably humiliates, hurts and damages the victim, mentally and physically. There is no need to hedge qualifications and possible exceptions round a rule against rape; there is everything to be said for forbidding it absolutely.

Most of the rules which have strongest claims for being accorded absolute status have something important in common. Rape, bestiality, torture, 'framing' an innocent person, performing potentially lethal experiments on someone without his or her consent: all are serious violations of human dignity. They fail to respect the special value inherent in human beings which comes from the fact that we are made in God's image.*

But even from a biblical perspective, it may be argued that ethical absolutes are fairly few in number. The fact is that different God-given commands can come into conflict. One might think that the most fundamental violation of human dignity is the taking of human life. Certainly, the Bible forbids that in general terms. But the commandment not to kill (Ex. 20:13) is clearly qualified by express permission to kill in the circumstances of war* and capital punishment.* It appears that human beings can act in such a way that they forfeit the right to life. It is only killing of the innocent which receives absolute condemnation in the Bible.

As far as the duty to *preserve* the lives of innocent people is concerned, this can be an obligation which outweighs other moral duties which normally hold sway, *e.g.* telling the truth. Although some biblical commentators, notably Augustine,* have argued an absolutist line on truth-telling, lying to save life seems to receive clear biblical sanction in the stories of the Heb. midwives (Ex. 1:15–21), Rahab (Jos. 2) and Elisha at Dothan (2 Ki. 6:8–23). Again, the justification would seem to be that, in exceptional cases, human beings can forfeit their right to know the truth because of their malicious intent.

Conflicts of moral duty do occur, most often in times of war and political upheaval, but in many more everyday situations as well. Human beings are then obliged to rank one duty higher than another, to disobey one rule in order to obey another. This raises a question-mark about the absolute status of the vast majority of rules. Any rule that might, in some circumstance, be set aside in favour of another can no longer, strictly speaking, be called an absolute. However, there are many rules* (like truth-telling) which are not absolute, but which have a strong prima facie case for being obeyed.

It is also important to note that, despite Mt. 5:18–20, Jesus often adopted an attitude of radical reinterpretation of the law. He interpreted the sabbath* not in terms of a prohibition of all work but as an opportunity for doing good. He directed people's attention towards 'the more important matters of the law – justice, mercy and faithfulness' (Mt. 23:23) and, of course, love. These are moral obligations of perennial significance, which are rooted in the heart and character (not merely the will) of God. As such they are perhaps more deserving of the description 'absolute', but that would be to use the word in other than its usual sense.

See also: CHRISTIAN MORAL REASONING; [18] TRUTH.

Bibliography
J. A. Baker, *The Foolishness of God* (London, 1975); N. L. Geisler, *Christian Ethics: Options and Issues* (Grand Rapids, 1989; Leicester, 1990); R. Higginson, *Dilemmas: A Christian Approach to Moral Decision-making* (London and Louisville, KY, 1988); J. Murray, *Principles of Conduct* (Grand Rapids and London, 1957); P. Ramsey, *Deeds and Rules in Christian Ethics* (London and Edinburgh, 1965; New York, 1967); H. Thielicke, *TE* 1.

R.A.Hig.

ABSOLUTION is the expression to penitent believers that God for Christ's sake forgives them their sins. For example, English Anglican prayer books (1662 and 1980) offer congregations a declaration of, and prayers for, absolution, but avoid an indicative absolution ('I absolve you') except in illness if someone 'cannot quiet (his) own conscience' (*Book of Common Prayer*).

In Scripture, sin is not the last word (Lk. 23:43; Acts 9:10–19). God's mercy, expressed in Christ's supreme priestly sacrifice, secures release (Tit. 3:5; Heb. 4:14–16; Jas. 2:13b). Ministry (*e.g.* adult mutuality, Jas. 5:16) according to Christ's pattern, sensitive to the Spirit (Jn. 20:22–23), can help mediate the assurance of God's forgiveness* and acquittal (Mk. 2:5; Jn. 8:11; Rom. 5:1; 8:1; 1 Jn. 1:9–10).

Personalized absolution provides confidentiality and can assist the discrimination of real from imaginary guilt.* A traditional pattern of absolution can be understood theologically in this context. (Some ministers conclude: 'Please pray for me. I also am a sinner.') The 'crisis' of absolution encourages the 'process' of self-controlled life in the Spirit. Absolution reunites brethren in the bond of peace (Calvin), reminding Christians that personal relationships need continual attention.

An awareness of the moral dimension in pastoral care is expressed through a sensitive use of absolution. In corporate worship, for example, people can be helped to face failure, resolve occasions causing feelings of guilt, and overcome personal insecurity. However, opportunities for self-discovery and greater self-understanding are lost if absolution is offered too quickly. Thus the carer may select from this and other approaches when caring for those in need.

See also: CONFESSION.

Bibliography
M. Dudley and G. Rowell, *Confession and Absolution* (London, 1990); G. Oliver, 'Model and Myth in Pastoral Care', *Anv* 6.3, 1989, pp. 211–222.

G.O.S.

ABSTINENCE is refraining from certain practices, such as eating, drinking or sexual intercourse. It may be total (such as an absolute fast, see Est. 4:16; Acts 9:9), or partial (such as avoiding certain foods proscribed by the dietary laws of the OT, see Lv. 11; Dn. 10:3; also Acts 15:29). It may be perpetual (such as celibacy), or for a specific time or occasion (such as abstinence from sexual intercourse to devote oneself to prayer, 1 Cor. 7:5; fasting* for religious observances, Lv. 23:2; Zc. 8:19; or fasting in the context of a worship gathering, Acts 13:3; or the appointing of elders, 14:23). It may involve one person or a whole nation (see 2 Ch. 20:1–4).

Reasons for abstinence may be spiritual (Lk. 4:1–2), cultic (Lv. 11; Nu. 6:1–4; Je. 35:6), economic, medical or out of consideration for others (Rom. 14; 1 Cor. 8; 10); however, biblical abstinence focuses on spiritual purposes, such as gaining mastery over one's appetites (Mt. 4:3–4; 1 Cor. 6:12). Wrong reasons for abstinence include an attitude towards the body as inherently evil, atoning for sins, and acquiring merit with God and humans (see Zc. 7:5; Mt. 6:16–18; Rom. 6:19). In any case, all is to be done to the glory of God (1 Cor. 10:31).

Partial abstinence (such as fasting) seems to be expected by Christ (Mt. 6:16; 9:15) and was practised by the NT church (Acts 13:2–3). While the Bible does not command perpetual total abstinence, it does proscribe indulgence, such as drunkenness (*e.g.* Pr. 20:1; 23:29ff.; Is. 5:11, 22; Rom. 13:13; 1 Cor. 6:10). Ethical arguments in favour of total abstinence (of alcoholic beverages or of sexual intercourse, for instance) focus on the risk of injury to the individual who is intemperate or to the surrounding community.

In modern times abstinence (see Temperance*) has been directed at alcoholic beverages in Britain and the US (especially since the 19th century and particularly in the Wesleyan tradition), at the eating of meat or fish (see Vegetarianism*), and most recently at sexual relationships in light of the AIDS* epidemic. While abstinence is not exclusive to Christianity and has not been popular in modern society (which is biased against depriving any appetite) or among evangelicals (perhaps in reaction against the excesses of medieval asceticism), practices such as fasting have received much attention recently.

Bibliography

R. Foster, *Celebration of Discipline* (San Francisco, ²1988; London, ²1989); A. Wallis, *God's Chosen Fast* (Eastbourne and Fort Washington, PN, 1969).

D.L.O.

ABUSE. Person-abuse refers to the perversion / misuse of the privilege of caring for another person, *e.g.* a child, elderly relative or spouse.

In the NT, the Lord Jesus shows a deep concern for children and their care (Mt. 18:5–6; 21:16; Mk. 10:16; Lk. 18:15–16; Acts 2:39). His desire to 'release the oppressed' (Lk. 4:18) could be taken to include the defenceless and others who are abused in various ways.

In defining abuse, secular texts in the main only cite examples, but some authors have suggested that it is characterized both by the abuse of power and by behaviours that are not acceptable to a given society.

Examples of abuse

Non-accidental injury includes bruises, cuts, fractures, burns, internal haemorrhages, unconsciousness and brain damage. Any object to hand may be used as an instrument. Methods include suffocation, shaking, punching, burning, throwing down or against a wall, or pushing downstairs. Lesser assaults are repeated and escalate. The younger the child the more likely is this latter type of abuse. The perpetrator may be the mother, cohabitee, father, or other relative or minder. Husbands are the more usual instigators of spouse abuse; sons more usually abuse the elderly. The possibility of accidental injury must be recognized and a hospital diagnosis of abuse should be made by two senior doctors.

Physical neglect consists of inadequate warmth, cleanliness or nourishment, resulting in disease, starvation, hypothermia, retarded development or death.

Emotional abuse is typically verbal, including belittling, teasing or terrorizing, but might include partiality towards other siblings or physical restraint.

Munchausen-by-proxy submits a child to unnecessary medical procedures by fabrication of symptoms.

Abuse of the unborn child is rarely considered as such; destruction of the inconvenient unborn is often accepted, whereas smacking of infants is not.

Sexual abuse of children is perpetrated by adults or much older children. Spouses and the handicapped may also be sexually abused. Child sexual abuse includes exhibiting pornographic material, indecent exposure, inappropriate touching, deliberate sexual arousal, and oral, anal or vaginal penetration. Risk increases with age but can occur from the first day of life. The usual setting is the home, and incestuous abuse (see Incest*) by the father of a daughter is the common form, but adults of either sex may abuse boys or girls. Organized child prostitution is included, and abuse may occur in residential care and schools. It is claimed that ritual sexual abuse is practised to produce offspring for ceremonial mutilation or sacrifice, but, whatever the motivation, young people seduced into such communities suffer rape* among other traumas.

Prevalence

Child labour, child murder, exposure of newborn girls, *etc.*, have a long history, but recent discovery of a syndrome of injuries attributable to 'baby battering' has led to systematic concern and public attention.

Quoted rates vary widely with the design of the investigation: sample, type of problem, control group (unfortunately rarely obtained), quality of questioning, *etc.* Claims such as '1 in 10 sexually abused' are always inadequate. Many rates include cases where abuse either has not actually occurred or was fairly insignificant. Child Protection Registers also include non-abused siblings and 'at risk' children.

There *has* to be a low threshold of suspicion for abuse, but also wariness of 1. desire to help on the grand scale, and 2. ignorance of alternative explanations for weaknesses. Overreaction, including some intrusive forms of spiritual ministry, can traumatize clients.

Increasing prevalence may be an outcome of permissiveness. 'Safe sex', abortion,* divorce* and single parenthood* ultimately leave many carers unsupported. Media display of violence and sex and fascination with the occult* may also contribute. The registered increase in cases of abuse is undoubtedly also related to accepting attitudes, better detection and reporting.

Intervention

Diagnosis is rarely easy. Fantasy may occasionally produce claims of sexual abuse. Older children with other problems sometimes use false accusations to harm adults. Much has been done to enable children to tell the truth. The use of video-recording and restriction to one specialist interview help to minimize repetition and courtroom appearances. Nonprofessionals should ask sympathetic and few questions before reporting their concerns.

If a friend or relative is suspected, a direct approach is desirable as a first step. Showing genuine interest in the family's life can prepare the way for sensitive enquiries about any difficulties with the child or other family member. If denial persists and the victim's safety is in any doubt, reporting must be explained as the best course for all concerned, and must be carried out. Protection of a helpless and suffering person must override misgivings.

Much help with child abuse is now available in the UK. Out of classic disasters and their careful recording (*e.g.* Maria Colwell, 1972 and Cleveland, 1988), procedures have been developed for inter-professional teamwork. Social Services or the National Society for the Prevention of Cruelty to Children are contacted first, or the police if agency help is unobtainable. Indication of concern should elicit careful Social Services investigation, and removal from the home may not be necessary. The 1989 Children Act allows parents, grandparents, children and their assigned legal guardians more involvement in the investigation, and will reduce periods of separation. A key worker from the Social Services usually co-ordinates the crucial update and communication of information required. In spouse-abuse and elder-abuse, help may be sought at an even later stage. It is sometimes effective to summon the police, and often supportive to help the victim arrange a safe haven and establish a temporary separation with conditions spelt out for her (or his) return. These should include therapy.

Serious emotional abuse provokes many kinds of behavioural or mental disorder, and often psychotherapy for offenders and victims is a sufficient course of management.

Causes

Physical injury is seldom deliberate. Persistent crying, unresponsiveness, provocation or naughtiness are precipitants only. Self-control in the carer may be poor because of childhood trauma, bad role-models, succumbing to irresponsible partners, parenthood while very young, desertion, parental rejection, difficult accommodation and poverty,* unhelpful relatives, loneliness,* poor learning ability, depression* or anxiety.* Absence of partner or lack of partner's support are crucial features, being the factors most closely related to frequent resort to physical punishment of a small child. Severe physical injuries (which ultimately reach hospital and can therefore be counted) are particularly common among manual and unskilled workers' families, contrary to many claims that abuse is indifferent to socio-economic class. Adult victims of physical injury are often isolated, avoiding social contact or being kept away from it; at home they may be anxious and manipulative. With the elderly, unforeseen deterioration adds to other stresses. In any adult relationships, unresolved independence issues are often at work. Perpetrators are also insecure, communicating and asserting their needs with difficulty.

Alcohol and other disinhibitors sometimes feature in sexual abusers, but more prominent are a poor sense of being needed (see Self-esteem*), early sexual experience as victim, and current opportunity for illicit intimacy. Marital rape can express a need to dominate or a rigid view of marriage-roles which the wife resists.

Therapy

The causal factors suggest therapies. Once 'found out', abusers may lose reputation, carer, child or spouse, but can begin to admit difficulties. Although sometimes requesting and needing better circumstances, abusers also need effective means of communication, companionship, someone to love them loyally, control of their own thought patterns, forgiveness* from God and neighbour, and a stronger sense of responsibility for the future rather than of helplessness because of the past.

The sexually abused need to work on their perceived personal guilt* and shame* (their experiences having involved pleasure as well as pain, even in children). Both hatred and love for the abuser often co-exist in the victim; she (or he) has to deal with memories which do not go away and hopes, which may not be fulfilled, for regret and respect from the abuser. Contempt for self may find expression in a sexually immoral life.

Therapy is conducted with individuals, groups, families or family dyads. For serious sex-offending, treatment may be legally enforced. A well-trained therapist, using cognitive* with other methods carefully selected from a wide spectrum of psychological thought, can be constructive. A Christian friend can complement or correct aspects of the process with a realistic and balanced biblical perspective.

Prevention

Prevention ideally rests in the upbringing of children to maturity. Where home has failed, young people can still be helped to understand the needs of the children for whom they will eventually care. The small-group situation, with enthusiastic, imaginative adults leading, develops truth and involvement. If Christians teach, there is hope that a scriptural vision will be applied, which regards children from infancy as growing persons, as God's gift, as equally precious to him as are their carers, as made in God's image* for companionship, each called uniquely to learn to enjoy and steward the creation, and needing to have happy parents.

Conclusion

Abuse is an extreme sign of unhappiness in relationships. Its intergenerational transmission seriously affects capacity for learning. Recovery calls for work which is honest, humble, down-to-earth and costly.

Bibliography

F. G. Bolton and S. R. Bolton, *Working with Violent Families* (London and Newbury Park, CA, 1987); J. V. Cook and R. T. Bowles, *Child Abuse* (Toronto, 1980); P. Dale, *Dangerous Families* (London and New York, 1986); F. Finkelhor, *The Dark Side of Families* (London and Beverly Hills, CA, 1983); N. Frude, *Understanding Family Problems* (Chichester, 1991); M. Grant, *Counselling for Family Violence and Abuse,* vol. 1, in G. R. Collins (ed.), *Resources for Christian Counselling* series (Waco, TX, 1987); R. Hanson, 'Key characteristics of child abuse', in A. W. Franklin (ed.), *Child Abuse* (Edinburgh, London and New York, 1978); C. Lyon and P. De Cruz, *Child Abuse* (Bristol, 1990); P. Johnson, *Child Abuse* (Rainsbury, Wiltshire, 1990); P. Maher, *Child Abuse* (Oxford, 1987); W. S. Rogers, *Child Abuse and Neglect* (London, 1989).

R.M.H.

ACCEPTANCE. The word 'acceptance' in everyday Eng. usage has a wide and often ill-defined range of meanings. To accept things, words, ideas or people includes the concepts of resignation, accommodation, acknowledgment, agreement, approval and welcome. More generally, acceptance means both a taking, receiving or responding to what or who is offered, and the state or situation of being favourably received.

Acceptance in the Bible

Apart from the more everyday use of acceptance, such as receiving gifts, the term is widely distributed in the OT with respect to God's relating to humankind, especially in the prophetic and Wisdom literature. Within the Heb. word group, the words *lāqaḥ* (take, receive), *rāṣâ* (accept, be pleased with) and *raṣôn* (acceptable, giving pleasure) frequently point to the reality and conditions of this relationship. The prime mover is God, in his acceptance of his repentant and obedient people (Ps. 49:15; Ezk. 20:40–41), his reception of their prayers (Ps. 6:9; Ho. 14:2) and his offer of a time of favour and restoration, thought by some to be linked with the concept of jubilee* (Lv. 25:10; Ps. 69:13; Is. 49:8; 56:7; 58:5; 61:1–2). In turn, the people of God are called to receive and take to heart God's words and instruction (Pr. 2:1; 4:10; 10:8; Ezk. 3:10).

In the NT, the Gk. verbs *dechomai* and *lambanō*, in its more passive usage, and their compounds, cover the main range of meanings of receiving and accepting. We can discern five main uses of these various words with respect to acceptance:

1. As in much of the ancient world, the giving and receiving of hospitality is highly valued in the NT record, particularly in the wandering ministries of Jesus, Paul and the other apostles. Jesus sets the example in his warm receptivity of others (Lk. 9:11), and his openness to their welcome in turn (Lk. 8:40; Jn. 4:45). Similarly, the apostles respond to the acceptance of those they meet (Acts 21:17; Gal. 4:14),

readily receive others (Acts 28:30), and urge their fellow-Christians to obey the call to hospitality (Acts 18:27; 2 Cor. 7:15; Col. 4:10).

2. At a deeper level, there is clear teaching in the Gospels that to receive and accept other people is to receive and accept Jesus and, in turn, God himself. This principle, of welcoming God in a practical acceptance of others, is seen in a loving response to many whom society dubs as the 'least': Christ's disciples (Mt. 10:40–42; Jn. 13:20); little children (Mt. 18:5; Lk. 9:48); and anyone with unmet basic human needs (Mt. 25:31–46).

3. Just as we accept God by accepting others, so we are to accept others because God accepts us (see Justification, Doctrine of*). This principle comes through most clearly in the verb *proslambanō* where it means 'to admit into fellowship'. We are to follow the divine example in welcoming a brother or sister whose 'faith is weak' (Rom. 14:1) and, more widely, we are called to 'accept one another . . . just as Christ accepted [us]' (Rom. 15:7).

4. Another dimension of our acceptability in Christ is found in the use of *dektos* (acceptable, welcome, favourable) and its compounds. In contrast to the cultic sacrifices of the OT (Lv. 22:18–25), the new covenant declares God's acceptance of lives laid down and lived out in his service (Rom. 12:1; 15:16; Phil. 4:18; 1 Pet. 2:5).

5. Finally, the idea of accepting and receiving God's message is closely linked with faith* in Christ. The receiving of Christ is at one with the affirmative acceptance of his words and rule (Acts 2:41; 1 Thes. 1:6–8; 2:13).

Acceptance in counselling

The tide of optimistic humanism* and American pragmatism,* which gathered force during the first half of the 20th century, strongly influenced the rise of 'third force' psychology (see Humanistic Psychology,* and Pastoral Care, Counselling and Psychotherapy[12]) and, in turn, the emerging counselling movement of the 1940s and 50s. Within the individualism* and quest for autonomy* of these worldviews, counselling fostered the widespread use of the word 'acceptance' to demonstrate an attitude of affirmation towards the client in every aspect of his or her inner or outer life. A number of synonyms for this brand of acceptance have become common currency in personalistic counselling (see Client-Centred Counselling*), including 'respect', 'prizing'

and 'non-possessive warmth'. Following Stanley Standal (1922–) in *The Need for Positive Regard,* Carl Rogers* popularized the phrase 'unconditional positive regard', whereby the counsellor communicated a 'deep and genuine caring' for the client, a caring 'uncontaminated by evaluations of [the client's] thoughts, feelings, or behaviors' (C. Rogers, *The Therapeutic Relationship and its Impact,* p. 102; G. Egan, *The Skilled Helper,* p. 123). Such an approach in counselling reasons that it is this quality of non-judgmental acceptance which encourages self-acceptance (see Self-esteem*) in the person in need. Because previously unacknowledged feelings, thoughts and actions are disclosed and yet uncondemned by the counsellor, the client begins, it is argued, to value and face the self's realities.

The notion of unconditional acceptance can be misunderstood and mishandled. It is important to see that the concept concerns valuing the personhood of the client, and his or her capacity to make choices and live out their consequences. Such acceptance of another, rightly understood, steers a path between condoning and condemning. The counsellor's respect for the client, rather, seeks to encourage a climate within which the client can gain insight and begin to make more responsible decisions. Within this process, the counsellor's critical faculties need to be continually applied and there may be the need for challenge and confrontation. Where the counsellor's acceptance of another becomes undiscriminating and gullible, there are the twin dangers of collusion with the client or manipulation by the client.

Acceptance in pastoral care

It is important that the biblical principles of receiving and welcoming others are reflected on and applied in the church's pastoral care and counselling. This enterprise should include a discernment which avoids assimilating, on the one hand, a humanistic gloss on the concept of acceptance and, on the other, a reactionary approach that lapses into judgmentalism (Mt. 7:1–5). Pastoral carers are called to follow Christ's example in an acceptance of others that crosses the barriers of sex and gender, class, race, health and age, without losing sight of people's need for repentance* and forgiveness* (Mt. 9:9–13; Mk. 1:32–34; Lk. 17:11–19; Jn. 4:7–18; 8:2–11).

One example where the term 'acceptance' has sometimes been taken over uncritically by pastoral care is in the area of bereavement,* where Elizabeth Kübler-Ross (1926–) uses this word of the fifth and final stage of the grief process. Walter Brueggemann (1933–) questions whether Kübler-Ross signifies affirmation or resignation in her stage of acceptance. He contrasts this apparent ambiguity with the form of the lament in the Psalms, where the outcome of the psalmist's complaint moves towards 'words of assurance' and the 'vow to praise'. He criticizes the modernist's tendency to omit the dimension of a sovereign God who can 'powerfully intrude to transform' in the life of the grieving or dying person. In fairness to Kübler-Ross's analysis, a number of the Psalms do not conclude their lament so positively, although the final note may be a cry for help or of anguish rather than a resigned form of acceptance (see, *e.g.* Pss. 38; 88).

See also: LOVE. 2

Bibliography

D. W. Augsburger, *Pastoral Counselling Across Cultures* (Philadelphia, 1986); D. Bonhoeffer, *Life Together* (ET, London, 1954; San Francisco, 1976); W. Brueggemann, 'The Formfulness of Grief', *Int* 31, 1977, pp. 263–275; G. Egan, *The Skilled Helper* (Monterey, CA, ²1982); E. Kübler-Ross, *On Death and Dying* (New York, 1969; London 1970); H. J. M. Nouwen, *Reaching Out* (New York, 1975; London, 1976); C. R. Rogers, *On Becoming a Person* (Boston, MA, 1961; London ²1967); *idem*, (ed.), *The Therapeutic Relationship and its Impact* (Madison, WI, 1967); S. Standal, *The Need for Positive Regard: A Contribution to Client-Centred Theory*, unpubl. doctoral thesis (Chicago, 1954); C. Truax and R. R. Carkhuff, *Toward Effective Counselling and Psychotherapy* (Chicago, 1967).

R.F.H.

ACCIDIE. A state of lethargy attested by monks, especially hermits, engaged in intense spiritual warfare. The word derives from the Gk. *akēdia*, which means 'weariness' and is usually written in its Medieval Fr. form, giving it a somewhat exotic appearance in Eng. This may reflect the fact that the concept is little understood today and does not figure at all in most manuals of Christian spirituality.* Accidie was defined by Nilus of Ancyra (d. *c.* 430) as a weariness of the soul, rendering it incapable of having spiritual interests and unable to resist temptations (*De octo spiritibus malitiae* 13).

Its earliest exponent was Evagrius of Pontus (346–99), who contrasted it with 'patience' (*hypomonē*), and linked it to the concept of the midday plague or 'demon' (Ps. 91:6, LXX), because its pressure was most keenly felt in the midday heat (*De octo vitiosis cogitationibus* 7). Accidie would tempt the monk to abandon his devotions, and sometimes even his calling itself. It is fully described by John Cassian (*c.* 360–435, in *Institutes*, Book 10), John Climacus (*c.* 570–649, in *Scala Paradisi* 13) and Thomas Aquinas* (*STh* 2a2ae 35). The main cures for accidie are given as hard labour, constant prayer and contemplation of the nearness of death.

Though not a feature of Protestant spirituality, something very like accidie is experienced in the form of spiritual dryness or depression. The terminology is different, but the phenomenon is well understood and studied by evangelical exponents of the Christian life, notably the late Dr D. Martyn Lloyd-Jones.*

Bibliography

G. Lampe (ed.), *A Patristic Greek Lexicon* (Oxford, 1961), pp. 61–62; D. M. Lloyd-Jones, *Spiritual Depression* (London and Grand Rapids, 1965); S. Wenzel, *The Sin of Sloth: Acedia in Mediaeval Thought and Literature* (Chapel Hill, NC, 1967).

G.L.B.

ACCOUNTABILITY. Most therapists cherish the independence of their own particular discipline, although this state is not always compatible with the extent and direction of their responsibilities. All have more than one area of accountability, and some of these areas may be in conflict with one another. Every truly professional therapy is founded on the twin principles of confidentiality* and accountability. The first must be complete, but it cannot always be absolutely and totally so to the particular individual therapist concerned, and therein lies a frequent source of tension, especially for the more junior therapists. The second principle has until recently been accorded far less attention and is in general inadequately explored.

Who are the people and the institutions to whom the doctor or other health-care professional owes this duty and this obligation of being accountable? First and foremost it is of course to the one receiving their therapy, the patient or client. The therapist is responsible to his or her patient for keeping all professional matters confidential between the two of them for all time. Note that this very particular and personal responsibility does not pass away with the death of the patient; it remains intact when the person has ceased to do so, a fact which is not always appreciated by relatives and friends.

As well as the issue of confidentiality there is the expectation that each individual practitioner will always provide appropriate treatment to a consistently high level, and that he or she will at all times maintain proper professional standards. These extend to the whole matter of personal relationships and there may sometimes be a rather fine line between private and professional behaviour. Practitioners are answerable to their own conscience* for their private behaviour, although this may also come under the scrutiny of their professional bodies, and they are expected always to keep their conscience well honed. There can never be a 'day off' regarding moral behaviour in a professional setting. As well as being responsible to themselves and to their patients for their professional and private integrity, practitioners are also ultimately accountable to God – who created both them and their patients, together with all the resources of whatever kind that are used in the therapy, and who cares for all his creation, especially for people and their hurting areas.

When the patient is a minor, there is additional accountability to the parent or guardian, the extent and nature of this varying with the age, capacity for responsibility, and expressed preferences of the child. The nature and type of therapy also affect the degree of accountability to the parent(s) where this apparently conflicts with that of the minor. The older the minor the greater the difficulty experienced in working out the details of accountability in each particular instance.

Accountability is far more than the concern of the individual practitioner and it is of greater extent than a private matter between therapist and patient. For a salaried person there is always accountability to the employer for both quality and quantity of service, an increase in one frequently resulting in a decrease in the other. Therapists have the progress of individual patients as their paramount concern, while employers are preoccupied with wider issues of overall service provision, stressing such things as cost-effectiveness, turnover, occupancy rate and numbers of patients seen per session or annum. These differing parameters are a potential source of conflict in the provision of psychological therapies, much remedial work and all other time-consuming treatments.

Therapists also have the obligation to restrict their services to those categories of people for whom their employer has an expressed responsibility, which may conflict with their individual preferences. They are not self-contained systems; each is likely to have some responsibility to the person who referred the patient as well as to their colleagues. There is a duty of communication within professional bounds, having regard to the necessity for preserving confidentiality. Some therapists have administrative functions in addition to their clinical work, perhaps being head of department as well as clinician, which involves them in other areas of accountability. Every role, every responsibility carries with it accountability for each duty undertaken.

As well as being accountable to the individual patient, to their employer, to their own conscience and to their professional body, therapists as members of society also have a responsibility to the society of which they and their patients form a part. The only way to hold all these issues in balance is as part of the ethical, moral and theological framework of their lives. Societies can be mistaken, individuals can be misled. Behind the general accountability to society is the bedrock on which all else rests, accountability to God.

See also: PROFESSIONAL ETHICS; RESPONSIBILITY.

R.F.

ACCREDITATION. There is currently a rapidly increasing demand for counselling and psychotherapy but absolutely no standard training, qualifications or formal accreditation. Most people needing help with emotional and relationship difficulties approach voluntary organizations, some of which may specialize in particular areas of work, *e.g.* bereavement,* marital problems (see Marriage and Family Counselling*), eating disorders,* *etc.* These organizations, however, can no longer meet the demand, and they themselves are not subject to any uniformity or accreditation, relying simply on reputation and the upholding of their own published values.

The public is often confused about the meaning of the terms 'counselling' and 'psychotherapy', although practitioners would usually agree that counsellors tend to focus on specific current problems while psychotherapists would expect to work with long-term patterns of behaviour and those hoping to restructure their lives. Clearly, without adequate accreditation or protection, abuse and exploitation can occur.

Pressure to regulate this morass is being exerted by the EU on training institutions and practitioners in the UK, and from July 1992 the UK Standing Conference for Psychotherapy, acting as an umbrella organization, is compiling a register of practitioners but, like the list of those accredited by the British Association of Counselling, it has no legal status. The youthful Association of Christian Counsellors also aims ultimately to train practitioners eligible for recognition. Even so, the uneven distribution of resources in terms of quality and quantity will continue for some time to come.

In short, the situation remains very fluid, but most recognize the urgent need to clarify the private-sector muddle with the least possible delay, for the sake of consumers' protection.

J.A.H.F.

ACTS OF COMMISSION AND OMISSION, see ETHICS OF MEDICAL CARE. 14

ADAMS, JAY, see BIBLICAL COUNSELLING; REPENTANCE.

ADDICTION, see DEPENDENCE.

ADLER, ALFRED (1870–1937), the founder of 'individual psychology', grew up in the outskirts of Vienna as one of six children within a Hungarian Jewish family. A sickly child and experiencing a poor relationship with his elder brother, Adler's own story illustrated his later emphases on a sense of inferiority that stems from childhood and on sibling rivalry. His early acquaintance with illness and the death of a younger brother were instrumental in his choice of a career in medicine. As a young doctor he developed an interest in the sociological aspects of socialism, and a sense of community and a concern for social justice became lifelong characteristics. He was influenced by the French psychiatrist

Pierre Janet (1859–1947), whose observation of a 'sense of insufficiency' in his neurotic patients predated Adler's notion of 'inferior feeling' as the basic factor in every neurosis.

Working in private general practice in Vienna, Adler became a devoted follower of Freud,* joining the psychiatrist's inner circle of colleagues in 1902 and being made president of the Vienna Psychoanalytic Society in 1910. However, Adler soon diverged from Freud's more mechanistic and reductionist* approach: Adler's emphasis on social and environmental factors in disease, his work in 1907 on 'organ inferiority' (the idea that developmental abnormalities in children* lead to compensatory behaviour), his stress on aggressive drives and ego mechanisms, and his crusading interest in education* were all seen as a betrayal of 'depth psychology' by the psychoanalytic traditionalists. In 1911, two papers presented by Adler were quickly and publicly rebuffed by Freud, who saw Adler's approach as speculative rather than 'scientific'. Adler resigned as president of the Viennese group, and shortly after formed the Society for Individual Psychology. The rift between Adler and Freud was lifelong.

In 1912 Adler's *The Neurotic Constitution* was published, encapsulating his methodology of individual psychology. The assumptive basis of Adler's approach saw human nature as purposive unity which finds ways of compensating for childhood's disadvantages by establishing a 'life-plan', whose 'guiding fiction' serves as the individual's reality. Although, like Jung,* Adler rejected Freud's exclusive emphasis on sexuality (see 11) as the source of human motivation,* he acknowledged the encultured realities of sex and gender and argued that a fear of femininity within the nurturing family leads to the 'masculine protest', a compensatory quest for superiority. Adler regarded neurosis* as a deliberate ruse to avoid life's tasks, and saw the aim of therapy as one of active intervention in order to help patients with their feelings of inferiority, to lead them away from egoism* and towards a 'social feeling' that engages with society's needs. Adler's method was, ultimately, one of synthesis rather than analysis and, as a result, offered encouragement and support through a face-to-face approach, with less frequent sessions and a shorter span of therapy than classical Freudianism.

After the First World War, Adler founded child guidance clinics in Vienna, Berlin and Munich, and an experimental school, run on the principles of individual psychology, in Vienna in 1931. Following the first international Congress of Individual Psychology in Vienna in 1924, he began a series of lecture tours in Holland, Britain and the US up till his death in Aberdeen in 1937.

During his visits to Britain in 1936 and 1937, Adler's emphasis on social justice aroused the interest of Anglican and Roman Catholic clergy. However, his stance was essentially that of an optimistic humanist, as was made clear in *Religion und Individualpsychologie* (1935), a joint publication with a Protestant pastor. Here he criticized the attempts by Fritz Kunkel (1889–1956), a former colleague, to integrate Christianity with the psychologies of Freud, Jung and Adler himself. Adler insisted on the 'scientific nature' of his work and, although he conceded the social value of religion, he saw the idea of God as arising from 'the ever-present feeling of inferiority of necessitous mankind'. As well as in the fields of child and parent* education ('parent effectiveness training' is a movement in N. America which emphasizes Adler's notion of the child as a moral equal), Adlerian emphases are found in the parallel humanistic challenge to Freud in such neo-Freudians as Karen Horney (1885–1952), Harry S. Sullivan (1892–1949) and Erich Fromm.*

Bibliography
The Practice and Theory of Individual Psychology (London, ²1929).

T. Gordon, *Parent Effectiveness Training* (New York, 1970); P. Roazen, *Freud and His Followers* (London, 1976); L. Way, *Alfred Adler: An Introduction to his Psychology* (Harmondsworth and Baltimore, MD, 1956).

R.F.H.

ADOLESCENCE (a word in use in Eng. since the 15th century, from the Lat. *adolescere*, to grow up) is the transition period in normal human development between childhood and adulthood. The duration of adolescence has varied throughout history and from one culture to another for cultural, sociological and nutritional reasons.

The phenomenon of adolescence as an extended 'in-between' state is difficult to discern in the biblical record, since early betrothal and marriage* (and, for some, lives of extramarital sexual activity, such as prostitution, concubinage or serving the inheritance needs of the childless, as in Gn. 16 and 30) were com-

mon. Among Jews at the time of Christ, for example, girls under the age of twelve could be married off by their fathers. In the Bible, a range of Heb. and Gk. words that denote 'youth' or the comparatively young occur in verses which warn about the sins of youth (Jb. 13:26; Ps. 25:7; 2 Tim. 2:22); express gratitude to God for his teaching and sustenance in life's earlier stages (Pss. 71:5, 17; 119:9); urge the young to make wise choices (Ec. 11:9 – 12:1); and offer them encouragement in the face of divine calling (Je. 1:6–8; 1 Tim. 4:12).

There is strong evidence that the hormonally-controlled bodily transformation of puberty (from the Lat. *pubertas*, 'the age of manhood'), which marks the onset of adolescence, has speeded up over the last century or so where young people have reaped the benefits of better health, nutrition and living conditions. It is established that the onset of periods, for example, has come sooner by about four months every ten years since 1850, so that a menarche at the ages of sixteen or seventeen in the Victorian era has been replaced by one in the twelve- to fourteen-year-old age range since the early 1970s. The combination of earlier physical and sexual maturity, a trend towards later marriage, and the prolongation of educational opportunity, has led to protracted adolescence in more affluent countries.

Whereas early adolescence strongly features adjustment to bodily change and late adolescence sees the entry into the 'age of coping', it is the middle period of adolescence that witnesses the clearest shaping of a sense of identity – an awareness of inner cohesion and self-respect. Although Erik Erikson,* writing in the late 1960s, saw the 'identity crisis' as normative for adolescents, more recent research suggests, according to John Coleman, that only 25% to 35% of teenagers suffer from an experience of such intensity. Coleman sees it as probable that the majority of young people adapt 'very gradually over a period of years to the changes in identity experienced by them' (*The Nature of Adolescence*, ¹1980, p. 56). This adaptation involves the acceptance of a newly developing body-image, a period of 'adolescent egocentrism', in which the teenager is acutely self-conscious towards an 'imaginary audience' (see David Elkind, 'Egocentrism in Adolescence') and the gradual emergence of a clear sexual identity.

Pastoral care and counselling of teenagers has many distinctive features relating to the transitional nature of adolescence. Of particular importance is the process of 'identification', whereby the young person, for good or ill, incorporates the values, attitudes and styles of other significant people, including parents, other adults and peers. Where, for example, parents or parent-figures, instead of adopting a democratic approach to child-rearing, are autocratic or permissive, the consequently inadequate role-models may lead to suppressed personalities, low self-esteem,* rebelliousness, hedonism* or rootlessness. The rising tide of teenage petty crime* from the late 1980s onwards, to take one instance, has been attributed to anti-social attitudes in parents and general emotional conflict at home, as well as to group pressures and social deprivation. Parental role-modelling may be not only poor in quality but positively destructive, as when teenage children are physically or sexually abused (see Abuse*). In such instances, it may take sufferers till their thirties before the roots of suppressed anger* or self-disgust can be faced.

Relationships with contemporaries are at their most formative in the teen years and often serve to enhance both a sense of personal identity and of group belonging. In many ways, the rapid changes in adolescent subcultures (see Pop Culture*), expressed through music, clothes and lifestyle, help foster a sense of connectedness and solidarity that is all the more effective where the parental generation is, to some extent, excluded and even outraged. Adolescence is an age of experimentation, and this testing out of the environment is often powerfully reinforced by peer pressure. Although the use of tobacco and alcohol* amongst adolescents is commoner where parents are also smokers and drinkers, both these potential addictions* and the extension of pleasurable experience to illegal drugs* are influenced strongly by the habits and lifestyles of other young people. Further, susceptibility to peer pressure and the urge to experiment, coupled with the quest for sexual identity, an increasingly early sexual maturity, a decline in sexual mores and the exploitation of teenage sexuality by the mass media, have led to a great increase of sexual activity, unwanted pregnancies,* abortion* and sexually-transmitted diseases amongst the young since the 1960s. The links between the sexual transmission of hepatitis B virus and HIV (see AIDS*), the intravenous use of illegal drugs, criminality and social deprivation are well documented.

The transitional nature of adolescence is also linked with a number of maladaptive conditions, which may require psychotherapeutic (see Pastoral Care, Counselling and Psychotherapy[12]), psychiatric (see Mental Health*) or medical intervention. One example is the eating disorder* of anorexia nervosa, whose causation may relate to any of a range of factors, including slimming for the 'ideal' figure, a rejection of developing sexuality,* a bid for excessive control over one's own body at the expense of others, a fear of separation from a much-loved mother, and disappointment in an emotionally distant father. Anxiety* states, phobias, a tendency to depression,* and an incidence of suicide* and attempted suicide that has risen since the 1960s, are other elements that can point to disruption in the teenager's domestic, relational, educational and communal world.

Pastoral work amongst young people is both demanding and rewarding. The formative nature and emotional liability of the adolescent years, not least where teenagers are caught up in delinquent behaviour, feel trapped by poor living conditions and the bleak prospect of unemployment,* or are the victims of racist (see Race*) or classist attitudes, can lead to a great deal of frustration amongst parents, teachers, youth workers and church leaders. Particularly where parental role-models are lacking, the friendship and example of other significant, caring adults can provide a bridge into the future. Similarly, where there is unresolved conflict,* emotional disturbance or the danger of mental breakdown, a counsellor or psychotherapist, experienced in working with the young, may provide a stable and healing relationship through which the adolescent can regain confidence and hope. It is the fluidity and flexibility of adolescence, coupled with its idealism* and intense loyalties,* that can facilitate and encourage within the pastoral care of young people.

See also: Human Development.

Bibliography

E. Cashmore and B. Troyna (eds.), *Black Youth in Crisis* (London, 1982); J. C. Coleman, *The Nature of Adolescence* (London and New York, ²1989); D. Elkind, 'Egocentrism in Adolescence', *Child Development* 38, 1967, pp. 1025–1034; E. H. Erikson, *Identity: Youth and Crisis* (London and New York, 1968); P. Everett, *You'll Never Be 16 Again*

(London, 1986); L. J. Francis, *Teenagers and the Church: A Profile of Church-going Youth in the 1980s* (Glasgow, 1984); M. Herbert, *Living with Teenagers* (Oxford, 1987); R. F. Hurding, *Understanding Adolescence: A Time of Change* (London, 1989); L. Smedes, *Sex in the Real World* (Grand Rapids, 1976; Tring, 1979); J. White, *Parents in Pain* (Downers Grove, IL, 1979; Leicester, 1980).

R.F.H.

ADOPTION is the legal act in which at least one adult, not the biological parent of the child to be adopted, undertakes the responsibilities of parenthood* and is recognized as that child's parent. Traditionally, the norm has been for married couples only to adopt, although the adoption of children by single parents or unmarried couples is not generally prohibited in Western nations.

Christians are, in principle, well disposed to the practice of adoption for a number of reasons:

1. In his letter to the Galatians, Paul uses the metaphor of adoption to describe the relationship of the Christian to God (Gal. 4:4–5). As we, whatever our heritage, have been welcomed into the family of God by adoption, so we welcome others into our families.

2. Love of neighbour is a second reason for support of adoption, *i.e.* the Christian responsibility to care for the needy, in this case the biological or birth-mother as well as the child. This motivation for adoption is most relevant in situations in which adoption is understood as an alternative to abortion,* the birth-mother offering her child up to God and to a Christian family, and the Christian community supporting both the birth-mother who makes this wrenching decision and the adoptive parents who will nurture and raise the adopted child. Understanding God as the creator and giver of life, the church affirms the welcoming of new life into its midst as vastly preferable to the destructive act of abortion.

3. An additional basis for the Christian embrace of adoption is the recognition of the goodness of the family* and the natural desire of couples to parent and raise children. To be sure, Christians recognize in the teaching of Jesus a relativization of the family. 'Whoever does God's will is my brother and sister and mother' (Mk. 3:35, RSV). The family, while good, must be made new by Christ and find its proper place in the service of God. The church as the extended family of God displaces the household family as the primary community of God's people. Nevertheless, the family remains a good institution, created and blessed by God, a worthy context in which to offer and to receive love and care and to be trained in the love of God and neighbour. Thus, many infertile couples, desiring children and feeling a gnawing emptiness in their absence, appropriately turn to adoption as a means for creating a family (see Childlessness*). The widespread practice of abortion in many countries, however, has made it increasingly difficult to find children to adopt.

It can be argued that adoption is, for the infertile, a morally superior means of creating a family compared with most means of technological reproduction. Although the similarities between adoption and surrogate motherhood* are frequently alluded to by supporters of the practice of surrogacy, a great gulf divides the two practices. In surrogacy a new child is created for the purpose of being adopted by an individual or a couple. But many would say that the intention to create a child independent of a context of the union of a man and woman is not warranted in light of Christian understandings of sexual union and the family. In adoption no attempt is made to put a monetary value on the conception of the adopted child. Rather, recognizing the presence of the gift of new life in her womb, the birth-mother attempts to respond faithfully to God by securing the conditions under which she and her child can live humbly and in service to God.

The moral preferability of adoption to artificial insemination by donor (see Reproductive Technologies*), while more difficult to establish, may lie in the fact that in adoption kindness and relief are offered to an already existing child and birth-mother, while at the same time the adoptive parents benefit. The desire for artificial insemination with donor sperm may suggest that there is a moral significance to the genetic relationship between mother and child that a Christian understanding of the biological family as a relativized good cannot support. Furthermore, the financial costs of adoption, while not non-existent, may well be lower than the expenses of artificial insemination, and thus adoption may be better stewardship* for Christian couples.

This is not to suggest that the moral and pastoral problems of adoption are few. There are good prudential and legal reasons for arranging adoption through a reputable agency, although private adoption is not, of itself, morally questionable. Christians will view the adoption of a child into a family as morally and emotionally superior to adoption by a single parent, although adoption of special needs children and older children to a single parent is often preferable to institutionalization. The church rightly has reservations about the adoption of children to same-sex couples or un-married parents, not because we know of damaging psychological effects of such adoptions, but because these relationships do not comport well with Christian understandings of the family.

Given the decision to adopt, many of the questions adoptive parents must ask themselves are the same as any prospective parents will ask; other questions will be unique to the adoptive parents. A first question may be whether the adoptive parents will accept a 'special needs' child, i.e. a child with some mental or physical defect. There is no guarantee that biological parents will produce a 'perfect' child. Prospective adoptive parents must consider whether a refusal of a 'defective' child would be warranted.

The contemporary prevalence of bi-racial and international adoption raises several questions. Adoptive parents will want to be certain that the available children in international adoptions are not offered under duress, and that their birth-mothers freely offer them for international adoption. Adoptive parents of bi-racial and international children have a responsibility to be well-informed about the cultural heritage of their children, and will want to raise the children with an understanding and respect for their own cultural backgrounds as well as that of their parents.

It is generally agreed that it is in the best interests of both adopted children and their parents that there be candid recognition that a child is adopted from its earliest years. Secrecy about adoption is far more likely to damage a child's self-esteem than the open admission and delight in an adopted child's participation in the family.

At this point we know little about what sort of contact between birth-mother, adoptive parents and adopted child may be best for all individuals involved. Often the pain of offering a child for adoption can be mitigated by a meeting between the birth-mother and prospective adoptive parents. As they mature, adopted children will be curious about their biological parents and the circumstances of their adoption. This information may be gradually revealed and should be available to them in full upon the age of maturity. Assuming that confidentiality* is not violated, adoptive parents should not discourage their adopted child from seeking out and meeting the birth-mother. Such a meeting may be critical for the adopted child's self-understanding and appreciation for his or her birth-mother as well as the adoptive parents.

Bibliography

H. Bouma III *et al.*, *Christian Faith, Health, and Medical Practice* (Grand Rapids, 1989), pp. 195–202; T. Whaling, 'Adoption', *PTR* 21, 1923, pp. 223–235.

T.D.K.

ADULTERY is marital infidelity, the breaking of the marriage* bond. Adultery is usually seen as sexual intercourse between a married woman or married man with someone other than his/her partner in marriage. In fact adultery covers all the ways infidelity can take place in a marriage.

Adultery is specifically prohibited in Ex. 20:14. In the OT, it is intercourse by a married woman with another man, but a married man is not guilty of adultery if he has sexual intercourse with an unmarried girl. In the NT this inequality is corrected (*cf.* Mk. 10:12) in the light of the relationship which exists between Christ and the church (Eph. 5:27–33). Although traditionally the focus has been on the physical act of adultery, Jesus shows the way to a wider interpretation when he declares that a lustful look is already adultery (Mt. 5:27–28). Moreover, adultery in the OT is used as a metaphor for the faithlessness of Israel in respect to God. 'You shall not commit adultery' teaches us that marriage will be a blessing only when the partners 'keep the troth'.

Although a graphic form of adultery, physical adultery is often symptomatic of the fact that the marriage has already been in serious disrepair. Marriage is a total troth communion which can be broken by any kind of prolonged infidelity, whether through the squandering of monies, unwillingness to share of self, breaking of confidences, or other betrayals of trust.

Although a most serious offence, adultery is first of all something to be worked through, repented of, and forgiven. At the same time, when a marriage is irretrievably broken, divorce* may be the only alternative.

See also: REMARRIAGE.

J.H.O.

ADVANCE DIRECTIVE, see COMA; CONSENT; DEMENTIA; EUTHANASIA.

ADVERTISING. Long before the printing press and telegraph, and perhaps coincident with humankind's initial experiences with trade and services, there was advertising. Today, advertising is a social science and basic to competitive capitalism. In early commerce it was the woodcut of a large shoe outside a cobbler's shop, or the sing-song of a knife-sharpener rolling his cart past village homes. As long as people have tried to persuade others to buy, barter or believe, some form of advertising has been part of the process.

The development of modern communications technology merely altered the form and cost-effectiveness of advertising. Early English and American newspapers were frequently called 'Advertiser', to signal their appeal to merchants and coverage of trade. In 1840 Volney Palmer opened the first advertising agency in Philadelphia. He bought space from rural and frontier newspapers, sold it at a premium to manufacturers, and thus became an important conduit between coastal industrial centres and the country's interior. In 1870 N. Y. Ayer and Son began to provide marketing surveys and media strategies for clients, while mail-order merchants, entertainers such as P. T. Barnum (1810–91), and patent medicine-sellers discovered the riches to be won through demographics and hype – all part of the advertising mystique.

Advertising raises a number of ethical issues. 1. It can be used to manipulate people into purchasing goods by appealing to a desire for status ('keeping up with the Joneses'), acquisitiveness, feelings of insecurity or guilt. Subliminal advertising is the supreme example, now banned in many countries. Children may be manipulated so as to put pressure on parents to purchase expensive toys, *etc.* 2. Advertising may make inflated claims for a product, or draw false inferences (*e.g.* 'Nine out of ten housewives prefer . . .' when the sample is too small to be significant statistically). 3. Advertising is frequently guilty of the exploitative use of women (*e.g.* using scantily clad models to sell cars, *etc.*) and of stereotyping them in such a way as not to address them as intelligent persons.

From a Christian perspective, manipulation is prohibited by the gospel (*cf.* 1 Cor. 2:1–3), inflated claims by the commitment to truth-telling (Eph. 4:25), and the exploitative use of women by seeing them not as sex objects but as persons made in the image of God (Gn. 1:27).

Because of the recognized ability of advertising to create expectations which disappoint purchasers, many governments have sought to check its power. In the US, the Food and Drug Act of 1906 and the Federal Trade Commission Act of 1914 asserted federal authority over product-labelling, puffery and false claims.

In the UK, such measures as the Trade Descriptions Act (1968), the Consumer Credit Act (1974) and the Independent Broadcasting Authority Act (1973) regulate the ways in which products and services may or may not be advertised. Statutory bodies such as the Office of Fair Trading and the Advertising Standards Authority administer the law and implement agreed codes of practice. Associations of advertisers have also adopted their own regulatory codes.

Grassroots efforts in the US have led to restrictions on TV advertising to children, while Denmark, Sweden and Belgium ban all such advertising. Protecting the poor from exploitative advertising becomes legally more complex, yet casino gambling advertisements, restricted in Puerto Rico (to protect a vulnerable public), are completely legal elsewhere in the US (to lure mainland trade).

Advertising is clearly not a value-free exercise. It uses creativity,* one of God's gifts, to sell products which may either benefit or exploit the user or consumer (see Consumerism*). It also helps to harm the environment* by creating demand for products which are wastefully (see Waste*) packaged or sold in non-returnable, non-biodegradable containers. Yet advertising can also be used to create public awareness of conservation issues.

Churches and parachurch organizations need to be awake to the power and ambiguity of advertising and to watch that their own use of it comports with the gospel they profess. The Christian movement is inextricably part of the cultural web of advertising, seldom setting but often copying successful trends, frequently decrying advertising's influence but rarely witnessing to alternative communication systems.

Bibliography

C. G. Christians *et al., Media Ethics: Cases and Moral Reasoning* (New York and London, 1991); K. Rotzoll *et al., Advertising in*

Contemporary Society (Cincinnati, OH, ²1990).

P.M.F.

AGEING. The whole process of ageing is a highly individual one, and there is a wide variation in how it manifests itself. The age of a person is normally measured chronologically, but gerontologists have tended to be dismissive of this reckoning of age: some people are old at 50 years and others young at 80 years.

J. E. Birren (1918–) and V. J. Renner set out four concepts of ageing: 1. biological age, judged by the condition of one's life-limiting organ system; 2. psychological age, referring to a person's adaptive capacities and relating to learning, intelligence and motivation; 3. functional age, reflecting the individual's practical capacities for coping; and 4. social age, determined by how much and how well one performs within the social community (see 'Research on the Psychology of Ageing', in *Handbook of the Psychology of Ageing*, New York, 1977).

Aspects of ageing

There is often an association between old age and poverty, in that the oldest tend to be the poorest. Throughout Scripture emphasis is placed on the need to care for widows, the poor and deprived (*e.g.* Jas. 2:16).

In the UK and US there is a growing tendency, which increases with age, for elderly people to live alone. This tendency can be seen as social policy in practice, in that it is now widely recognized that most elderly people prefer to remain in their own homes and should be enabled to do so as long as they wish. Such a policy has implications with regard to the responsibility to provide adequate and appropriate services within the community, tailored to the individual's needs and desires (see Health and Health Care*).

The most common mental health problem in elderly people is depression,* which is often unrecognized and untreated. However, dementia,* which is based on brain cell loss, is the most significant and serious problem affecting family, neighbours and carers (see Care, Caring*), and making demands on health and social service resources.

Quality of life in old age

Factors which determine good quality of life for elderly people are not intrinsically different from those which apply to other age groups.

In the UK, the Social Services Inspectorate of the Department of Health (1989) has set benchmarks for measuring quality in residential care for elderly people. These values could be seen as universally relevant: choice; independence; dignity; privacy; rights; and fulfilment.

Age Concern's Manifesto in 1984 advocated that elderly people should be encouraged to continue to develop their full potential.

S. Jones states: 'Mental health can be considerably improved after retirement if a sense of purpose and of belonging to the whole community can be found' (*Liberation of Elders*, Keele, 1976, p. 68). In 1984 a Danish Government Commission, set up to produce a policy to enhance the quality of life of elderly people, stated three basic principles: 1. that a sense of continuity in the life span should be created; 2. that elderly people should have self-determination; and 3. that the resources of older people themselves should be used.

In social relationships there is a need to give as well as receive. P. Townsend (1928–) says that old people are 'members of families and whether or not they are treated as such largely determines their security, their health and their happiness' (*The Family Life of Old People*, p. 227).

Contributory factors to mental health are self-esteem* and a sense of identity and of being valued by others. In the development of education for older people in the USA, David A. Peterson states: 'Older persons are seen as individuals with potential who can contribute and serve as well as cope and survive' ('The Development of Education for Older People in the USA', in F. Glendenning, ed., *Educational Gerontology*, p. 94).

Values, rights and responsibilities

To protect the rights and civil liberties of elderly people it is necessary that the values outlined are actively promoted. Where a degree of dependency has to be accepted, it will be important to identify and safeguard the areas that the person can still manage, so that they remain in control and as independent as possible.

Where there is mental impairment 'the principle of self-determination has to be practised in a manner which acknowledges the person's limited capacity for decision-making and self-care but which preserves those areas of decision-making of which he is still capable' (C. Rowlings, *Social Work with Elderly People*, p. 50). The fact that people have lost certain faculties does not mean they have lost their adulthood.

Giving elderly persons time to answer for themselves, and not talking about them in their presence as though they were not there, demonstrates respect for them. The use of language will contribute to or detract from the person's dignity. Referring to 'the elderly' rather than 'elderly people' stereotypes them as an homogeneous group, thus denying their individuality.

Ageism

The term 'ageism' was coined by R. N. Butler in 1968 (see *Educational Gerontology*, p. 12). It signifies prejudice or discrimination against people on account of their age. It is a process of systematic stereotyping, associating age with an inability to contribute anything of value and involving many negative assumptions.

Ageism demeans old age; it insinuates that people who have lived a certain number of years become different from and inferior to people younger than themselves; it subtly encourages younger people no longer to identify with their elders as human beings. However, in both the OT and NT old people are honoured for their wisdom (*e.g.* Dt. 32:7). Their discernment is recognized (Jb. 12:12) and lack of respect for them is condemned (La. 5:12; *cf.* 1 Tim. 5:1).

Though ageing can bring with it disability and weakness, for the Christian there is a future hope through the resurrection of Jesus (2 Tim. 1:10) and the present reality of being renewed daily in the inner self (2 Cor. 4:16–18).

See also: HUMAN DEVELOPMENT; RETIREMENT.

Bibliography

D. B. Bromley, *Human Ageing* (London, New York, ³1988); F. Glendenning (ed.), *Educational Gerontology: International Perspectives* (Keele, 1985); J. and C. Hendricks, 'Ageism and Common Stereotypes', in V. Carver and P. Liddiard (eds.), *An Ageing Population* (London, 1978; New York, 1979); S. M. Pearce (ed.), *Researching Social Gerontology* (London, 1990); M. Puner, *To the Good Long Life* (London and New York, 1978); C. Rowlings, *Social Work with Elderly People* (London, 1981); A. Tinker, *The Elderly in Modern Society* (London, 1984); P. Townsend, *The Family Life of Old People* (London, 1963); B. Wade *et al.*, *Dependency with Dignity* (London, 1983).

M.J.M.

AGGRESSION, see ANGER; WAR.

AIDS. One of the greatest challenges the church has had to face in the moral and pastoral arena in the past decade has been caused by the rapid spread of the disease known as AIDS (Acquired Immune-Deficiency Syndrome). The virus that causes the illness was first identified and described almost simultaneously by scientists on both sides of the Atlantic in 1981, and the incidence of AIDS has been reported in many countries around the world. The dramatic spread of the virus, named Human Immuno-deficiency Virus (HIV), has been called 'a global epidemic' by the World Health Organization. The early reporting of the spread of HIV by the media of the Western world gave rise to a frightening mythology producing irrational fears and prejudicial attitudes towards infected individuals by some people. Early Christian comment could have been clearer, calling for compassion and a commitment to care in the face of an illness that strikes at the heart of humanness and leads to a fatal illness. The absence of literature from the church was remedied around the mid 1980s with a number of helpful leaflets published by most denominations.

The term 'AIDS' comes from the fact that the illness is *acquired* from some other person, rendering the body's *immune* system *deficient* so that a *syndrome* or group of illnesses takes hold of the person and results in the progressive disease. HIV is blood-borne, and the main route of infection is sexual. As the disease spread from individual to individual, it became clear that blood or blood products from infected people could pass on HIV. Intravenous drug-abusers have been infected through sharing injecting-equipment contaminated by infected blood. Babies have become infected from their HIV-positive mothers during pregnancy or birth and occasionally through breast milk.

HIV is a frail virus and does not survive long outside the body. It is not contagious through normal social contact. It has a long incubation period, when the carrier is virtually symptom-free but is able to infect others. This latent phase can last up to ten years or more, after which most HIV-positive people become unwell with a debilitating generalized illness or present to their physicians with one or more of the specific diseases which categorize AIDS. There is much that can be done for patients as HIV progressively weakens the immune system. The skills and compassion of health-care professionals in controlling symptoms can make life bearable and assist the person with AIDS to live life to the full. Patients prefer to speak of themselves as 'living with AIDS' and not dying of AIDS. None like to be referred to as 'victims'. Research scientists have made some headway in discovering helpful anti-viral drugs that slow down the rate of physical decline in patients but the pharmaceutical challenge to find a cure for AIDS remains. During the next decade, progress is needed that calls for close co-operation between all concerned, so that people infected with, or affected by, HIV can be supported compassionately and the spread of the disease arrested.

Pastoral opportunities

AIDS presents the pastoral worker with the opportunity of coming alongside people who are HIV-positive, or have AIDS, and their families and friends. Many people in the churches who work directly with the public may be anxious about possible infection, and could present the pastoral worker with a complex emotional, social and practical problem. There are informed policies in place in many institutions, like schools and factories, to guide in circumstances where staff or pupils are suddenly ill or injured. Pastoral support may be to refer those concerned to these policies, or to aid those responsible for others to seek advice from their local public-health experts.

A diagnosis of HIV or AIDS may accompany a lifestyle of intravenous drug* abuse, homosexuality* or sexual promiscuity. However, infection could result from a single sexual encounter, or from having only one regular partner. The pastoral worker needs to be clear in these situations about how to respond, in order to reflect something of the Christ who came alongside the sick, the weak, the desperate and the disadvantaged to bring the good news of help and hope. For the pastoral worker, opportunities arising from people with HIV/AIDS demand the greatest exercise of pastoral skills, where a non-judgmental attitude, with an approachable and compassionate disposition, will help to bring appropriate support to enquirers. The individual concerned could be deeply anxious about many issues but especially the issues of confidentiality.* The pastor may be faced with a person seeking comment about a number of deeply disturbing questions, *e.g.* euthanasia* or suicide.*

As the disease progresses, issues about taking powerful drugs to control troublesome symptoms and pain may arise. A frequent question asked by people with AIDS nearing the terminal stage of their illness is whether or not to continue with active treatment. The pastoral worker may be consulted to clarify the choices to be made, and will need to stand with the person as he or she chooses. Help may be requested to explain to family and friends a decision to stop treatment. The pastoral worker's attitudes to the individual's decision will have a profound effect. Sensitivity should be exercised, and wisdom will be called for as to how deeply to engage in personal and private areas. The temptation to be intrusive, beyond consent, ought to be resisted.

Death comes with its own challenges to all who support the dying, and carers should be appropriately cared for themselves. Pastoral workers with a firm, vital and personal commitment to Jesus Christ, the Resurrection and the Life, will be sustained and able to share their faith mainly by their presence. At the right moment, the spoken word could bring a sense of hope and comfort to those who are near the end of life.

Moral challenges

The AIDS epidemic has confronted the church with a complex of ethical issues that cannot be avoided. It is important for the pastoral worker to face these issues in order to develop a non-judgmental attitude to, and compassionate care for, those affected or infected by the virus. An approach based on a biblical ethic but offered with pastoral sensitivity is possible, where human nature can be honestly acknowledged with all its problems and positive possibilities. A view of human nature as created with rights and responsibilities, in which there is a balance between personal preferences and public needs, is presented in Gn. 3. Here the male and the female are created as people of value and the objects of God's love and concern. The first humans, according to Genesis, are viewed as social beings set in a relational context of family where mother and father are committed to each other in a lifelong bond of responsibility. This view of humanity (see 4) is set against the theological framework of creation/Fall/forgiveness/reconciliation, where the central purpose of God in Christ is to seek and save the lost.

In the literature addressed to Christians about AIDS, the concept of God's judgment* is often the moral and theological starting-point. However, the justice of God is sometimes almost dismissed in the effort to discourage a thoughtless judgmentalism. Judgmentalism is a grave disqualification for work in AIDS care. But the word 'judgmentalism' is also used in such a way as to suggest that the pastoral worker should abandon all notions of justice and personal judgments of any kind in AIDS care. The Bible portrays a pattern around events of judgment that involve warnings before and mercy* after. Divine judgment is the reluctant response of a God intensely concerned for justice, compassion and mercy. The cross* of Christ is the ultimate point where God's justice and mercy meet.

The apostle Paul's inspired commentary on humanity is found in Rom. 1:18–32. Humanity is pictured in moral and spiritual chaos. Judgment is a releasing from God's protective care and a giving-up to sinful personal choices, resulting in injustice, sexual confusion, family disintegration and violence. God's wrath is his response to those who destroy humanity through their greed and self-will. It is matched by God's love (see ②) in his personal involvement to rescue and reconcile through faith in Christ. Here all are seen as deserving of God's judgment, but all are seen as loved by him. All are seen as in need of reconciliation. AIDS does not seem to be a specific judgment on certain individuals but has come about due to a complicated mixture of medical, social, moral and sexual factors. Some people have been infected through contaminated blood products; some by an unfaithful partner; newborn babies have been infected by HIV-positive mothers. However, HIV has life only if given an environment in which to live and reproduce itself, *i.e.* our bodies.

No right-minded person deliberately acquires HIV and no-one needs to contract AIDS, so there is an urgent need to inform. Moral difficulties and pastoral challenges arise in the area of information-gathering and strategic planning in health care (see Health and Health Care*) and education. The Department of Health refrained from moralizing during the first ten years of the epidemic in the UK, and based its major efforts on reduction of infection rate through campaigns of preventive advice and information. These campaigns included the commendation of condoms to provide 'safer sex' practices, and the encouragement of schemes to issue free, sterile injecting-equipment to intravenous drug-abusers. Running parallel with these campaigns has been a movement to bring the claims of homosexual people to the public's attention. The pastoral worker needs to face the challenge of sensitive support for those with a homosexual orientation. Safe-sex practices and free issue of syringes are another challenge to pastoral engagement where the worker is seeking to maintain traditional Christian values. Here is an opportunity to show by example, supported by convincing argument, that sexual fidelity before and sexual faithfulness within the bond of marriage* not only guarantee freedom from HIV infection but are beneficial to the individual and society. Pastoral workers can also make a positive contribution in their congregations by helping to create an accepting and welcoming attitude to people who are HIV-positive. Thereby, the stigmatizing and rejection of people with AIDS will be reduced, and this will enable a greater freedom to develop so that HIV-infected people can feel safe and supported in our churches.

Adequate planning of the use of available resources for AIDS care needs accurate information about trends in the spread of HIV, so pastoral example and education of congregations will promote openness, which will be important and helpful. The general public are still frightened by HIV after ten years. Clear and compassionate pastoral input will help reduce the incidence of scapegoating. Intravenous drug-abusers, homosexual people, prostitutes and the promiscuous have all been blamed and persecuted by a resentful or ignorant but frightened public. It is not individuals but behaviour that needs to be challenged. It is more helpful to focus on risky behaviour than on specific groups.

AIDS is a problem for us all. A sensible and sensitive pastoral approach that takes hold of opportunities to support the anxious and that cares for the sick will reflect a gospel of hope* from a God of love and grace.*

See also: CARE, CARING; ETHICS OF MEDICAL CARE; ⑭ HOSPICE.

Bibliography

AIDS Care Education and Training (ACET), *HIV: It's Your Choice* (teacher-pupil resource pack; London, 1991); I. Ainsworth-Smith and P. Speck, *Letting Go: Caring for the Dying and Bereaved* (London, 1983); S. Cassidy, *Sharing the Darkness: The*

Spirituality of Caring (London, 1988; Maryknoll, NY, 1991); M. J. Christensen, *The Samaritan's Imperative: Compassionate Ministry to People Living with AIDS* (Nashville, TN, 1991); P. Dixon, *The Truth About AIDS* (Eastbourne, 1987); R. McCloughry and C. Bebawi, *AIDS: A Christian Resource* (Bramcote, Nottingham, 1987); Salvation Army, *AIDS Care: Practical and Pastoral Guidelines* (London, 1988).

P.J.C.

ALCOHOLISM is one form of drug dependence,* which has many features peculiar to itself. Alcohol drinking is a social habit in most cultures, so that alcohol dependence is facilitated by cultural norms and social connections (*e.g.* meeting friends, business deals). There are several different patterns of alcoholism; drinking may be social or solitary, steadily continuous or intermittent (bout drinking).

The psychological and social damages associated with habitual drinking are those of any drug dependence, with the added feature that alcohol behaves as a nervous-system depressant (an anaesthetic). The features of depression* of the nervous system include release of inhibition, leading to garrulous, indiscreet or violent behaviour, and then to loss of consciousness (drunkenness). Physical consequences of long-term drinking include malnutrition, when someone drinks instead of eating food, and target-organ damage; the target organ may be the liver, pancreas, brain or peripheral nerves, or heart; there is marked variation among individuals as to which organ sustains the impact. The behavioural features of heavy chronic drinking include times when individuals may find themselves inexplicably at a distant destination without realizing how they got there ('blackouts'), episodes of tremor and sweating ('the shakes') or of great fear ('the terrors'). These episodes (which have no relation to ordinary faints or 'blackouts', or to the sweating which can accompany them) are signs of nervous-system damage and alcohol withdrawal reaction; they indicate the onset of irreversible brain damage, and soon progress to episodes of wild nightmares and hallucination (delirium tremens) and dementia.* The dementia of chronic alcoholism often comprises socially damaging features; the alcoholic fills in gaps in conversation with imaginary material (confabulation), often of a very plausible kind.

Social deterioration in alcohol behaviour is often insidious, and family and colleagues often notice it only after alcohol dependence is well developed, and then find it very hard to know whether or how to intervene with help. The most difficult decision is whether to continue to tolerate the alcoholic's destructive company, or to exclude him or her. Domestic violence to property and persons is a common feature, plus the financial drain caused by a drinking habit.

Alcoholism may be associated with sexual violence, promiscuous behaviour and homosexuality, with reckless choices or with bouts of psychiatric depression.

Attempts to help alcoholics to relinquish their habit involve all the steps needed in countering any form of drug dependence. The outlook for success is no better than in any other form of dependence. A period of 'drying out' (detoxification) is followed by residential care with a regular programme of activity, including occupational therapies. Forces which militate against success include the social nexus which drinking occupies, and the constant availability of alcohol in the community. There is intense temptation, when sorrows are recollected, to seek the immediate release of alcohol, only to suffer the consequent return to the habit.

Some regular stepped method is undoubtedly useful to help dependent people to recognize their need in a way which also leads them directly to the next goal in the process of release. The 'Minnesota Model' is one such ladder of progressive recognition, and organizations like Alcoholics Anonymous have made successful use of such structures, used in a group setting. But the environment in which this is done, in particular its spiritual nature, the practical help provided, and the step to which the person moves on at the end of a successful programme are all extremely important elements. Not only can spiritual experience not be prescribed, but also breaches of disciplined growth cannot be accepted in such programmes. This is a narrow ethical path with many problems and lapses.

The pastoral concerns are for the drinker, and for his or her family and colleagues. Pastoral care is made very difficult by the untruthful and confabulative nature of alcoholic communication, by the hurts suffered by those who might normally be the chief carers among the alcoholic's social group, and by failure to recognize psychiatric depression in the alcoholic, especially amongst bout drinkers. Crime* by alcoholics adds the frequent dimension of legal constraints, imprisonment and fines. Counselling is essential, but requires long, time-consuming contact, with the need for patience with the frequent relapses that occur. The gospel of Christ has great power in practice and in perception, both to displace alcoholism and to restore that self-esteem* which is so essential for the alcoholic to gain. But the hurts and fears which lead to alcoholism are very deep, and the gospel cannot be prescribed or enjoined for anyone (see Inner Healing*). No-one is relieved from alcoholism without the inner will to emerge from the habit, and this cannot happen until all hurts are opened and dealt with and self-respect has been recreated.

See also: ADDICTION.

Bibliography

P. W. Brunt, 'Alcoholism as a Medico-social Problem', in D. W. Vere, *Topics in Therapeutics*, vol. 4 (London, 1978), pp. 124–135; S. Carroll, 'Spirituality and Purpose in Life in Alcoholism Recovery', *Journal of Studies on Alcohol* 54.3, 1993, pp. 297–301; A. L. Klatsky *et al.*, 'Alcoholism and Mortality', *Annals of Internal Medicine* 117.8, 1992, pp. 646–654; K. Nakamura *et al.*, 'Family Involvement for Improving the Abstinence Rate in the Rehabilitation Process of Female Alcoholics', *International Journal of the Addictions* 26.10, 1991, pp. 1055–1064; J. R. Peteet, 'A Closer Look at the Role of a Spiritual Approach in Addictions Treatment', *Journal of Substance Abuse Treatment* 10.3, 1993, pp. 263–267.

D.W.V.

ALIENATION is a common theme in any analysis of the condition of people in the modern world, especially the West. It has been the basis for thoroughgoing critiques of a contemporary society unable to provide an emotionally and psychologically satisfying existence to its members. The concept has been used, with significant variation, by Marxists, humanistic psychologists, Freudians, existentialists (see Existentialist Psychologies*) and sociologists. Karl Marx* is credited with contemporary awareness of the topic, particularly in his *Economic and Philosophic Manuscripts* of 1844, which were discovered in 1932.

Alienation is the state of being estranged, at odds with other individuals, society and oneself. It has been taken to mean any and all of the following: a sense of powerlessness, the experience of lack of meaning and purpose in life, the absence of commitment to standards of behaviour, an antagonism to the values of one's culture, a sense of being socially excluded, and the condition of being out of harmony with oneself (M. Seeman). Of course, these distinct meanings are not unconnected, and might well be found together or to have a common etiology.

While alienation is ancient, the modern understanding of the phenomenon owes much to 19th-century German idealism, and particularly to G. W. F. Hegel (1770–1831). Hegel took alienation to be an essential feature of the human condition, since human beings are both subject and object and their creations become objects outside of them. The concept was developed by the Hegelian Left, including Ludwig Feuerbach (1804–72) and Marx. Feuerbach saw religion as the source of alienation, because in religion people project human qualities on to a God who stands over and above them. Marx believed that religion is a creation of alienated people, but not the root cause of human alienation. Its cause is alienated labour, *i.e.* work done under the control of another and for the other's purposes. Since the essence of being human is to work, humanity will be frustrated and distorted in a social situation in which this labour is unfree. Alienated labour alienates the worker from himself, his product, the capitalist who is owner of his work, and from humanity at large (his 'species being'). In short, for Marx capitalism* is the cause of modern alienation, accounting for the worker's experience of powerlessness, meaninglessness, poverty and misery, and for social antagonisms. However, Marx believed that alienation could be overcome, not by an internal adjustment within the worker, but by a radical restructuring of socio-economic structures.

With the rise of urbanization,* regimentation in the workplace, the loss of traditional family and social ties, and the decline of religion in many segments of society, the 20th century has been called the era of alienation. Books with such titles as *The Organization Man* (W. H. Whyte, New York and London, 1957) and *The Lonely Crowd* (D. Reisman, *et al.*, New Haven, CT, 1950) have depicted modern life as a struggle to find meaning in relationships, society and a universe in which the individual seems to have no genuine significance.

Existentialist thinkers regard alienation as the state in which all individuals must find themselves, under the weight of mass society which imposes on them group values that they find themselves accepting uncritically. To be unalienated and 'authentic', we must realize that we are indeed alienated, however comfortable and complacent we may feel (in fact the more so, as we unthinkingly accept more and more our socially imposed false identity). According to existentialists, human beings have a tendency to create 'false consciousness', to accept and even defend these externally imposed norms and mores. Søren Kierkegaard* located alienation in the tendency to gravitate toward unauthentic existence as a member of the crowd rather than finding one's true identity, purpose and meaning as an individual, which he believed is possible only in an individual and personal relationship with Christ. This stress on individual authenticity, if not in its essential connection with Christ, is seen in secular existentialists such as Jean-Paul Sartre.* Sartre saw alienation as the condition of being both a free, self-conscious being and an object in the world. Reminiscent of Hegel's subject–object dichotomy, Sartre's analysis stresses the incongruity between our freedom, self-awareness and lust for transcendence, and our limited, determined and 'given' nature created by our personal history and social condition and physical limitations. In his extensive treatment of this dichotomy, Sartre discussed phenomena such as 'the Look', the experience of noting that in being observed by others we become an object to them. In social terms, we are alienated in that our relationships with others are characterized by a need to dominate them or be dominated by them, a theme reminiscent of Friedrich Nietzsche.* For Martin Heidegger (1889–1976), alienation stems from our inability to face the fact of our own imminent and inevitable death, a true realization of which would oblige us to take seriously the fact of our own individual responsibility for our lives.

Psychologists who have identified the problem of alienation include neo-Marxist Erich Fromm,* who combines psychological insight with existentialist analysis to stress the tendency of capitalist society to force people into economically useful roles rather than to allow their creativity* to flourish. For Freud,* alienation is a creature of the repressed subconscious, with its wild urges and drives which are denied even to oneself.

Although now out of favour among sociologists, the term was widely used and the phenomenon studied by a variety of social scientists, including Max Weber (1864–1920), who saw it as a reaction against a society viewed as corrupt and bureaucratized, and against which one was powerless. In the 1950s and 60s, sociologists like Seeman and R. Blaumann saw it as dissatisfaction with life and social experience, and devised tests to measure it and correlate it with antisocial behaviours.

Alienation has been blamed on economic factors by the Marxists, on the tension between subjective existence and objective existence by the existentialists, and on the structure of mass technological society by sociologists such as Talcott Parsons (1902–1979) or David Riesman (1909–). Recently the sociological version has been influential in the work of philosopher Alasdair MacIntyre (1929–). In his widely-read *After Virtue* (Notre Dame, IN, ²1984; London, ²1985) he depicts modern bureaucratic society as unable to provide meaning or shared values and as treating problems of human meaning as ones to be managed by professional specialists such as managers and bureaucrats. Modern society and its intellectual resources are incapable of providing genuinely meaningful, unalienated life, and MacIntyre's solution is to find meaning in small communities of shared vision, a new Benedictine* movement to preserve what is left of the Western heritage.

Alienation theorists differ as to whether the problem is created by external conditions or by internal philosophical-psychological conditions, whether it is accompanied by feelings of alienation or is an objective state in which one finds oneself unknowingly, and whether it is capable of being overcome or not.

Christians will find elements of truth in many of the major accounts of alienation, yet perhaps will be particularly drawn to Kierkegaard's insistence that alienation is overcome by a relationship with Christ, who alone can give meaning and purpose in any age or society. Alienation theorists certainly are correct in linking social dislocation to disordered individual life. Christ gives true meaning and significance to the life of the individual (Jn. 10:10) and brings reconciliation not only between people but between 'alienated' humanity and God (Col. 1:21–23).

Bibliography

D. B. Fletcher, *Social and Political Perspectives in the Thought of Søren Kierkegaard* (Lanham, MD, 1981); R. F. Geyer and D. Schweitzer, *Theories of Alienation* (Leiden, 1976); E. Josephson and M. Josephson (eds.), *Man Alone: Alienation in Modern Society* (New York, 1962); B. Ollman, *Alienation: Marx's Critique of Man in Capitalist Society* (Cambridge and New York, ²1976); R. Schacht, *Alienation* (London, 1970); M. Seeman, 'On the Meaning of Alienation', *ASR* 21, 1959.

D.B.F.

ALMSGIVING, see GIVING.

ALTERNATIVE MEDICINE, see HEALTH AND HEALTH CARE.

ALTRUISM (from It. *altrui*, of or to others) is generally understood as unselfish concern for the good of others. Since acting for the good of others is thought to be an important part of personal ethics, considerations of altruism raise two important ethical questions: 1. Is genuine altruism possible? 2. Is altruism always required?

Since Thomas Hobbes (1588–1679), many have denied that genuine altruism is even possible. Human action is always selfish, they argue, since it is always motivated by desire, and an agent's desires are all ultimately for his or her own well-being. Given this egoistic* conception of human nature, apparently altruistic action must be explained away in terms of selfish ulterior motives. Hobbes may relieve the distress of a beggar by giving him alms, but his motive for doing so is to relieve his own distress at seeing the beggar's distress. Similarly, Christian egoists such as William Paley (1743–1805) argue that it is in our self-interest to benefit others, since God will reward those who do and punish those who do not.

Critics have argued against the egoistic analysis of human action in various ways. Joseph Butler,* for example, denies that all desires are selfish, holding that we may at times desire the well-being of others for its own sake. Alternatively, Immanuel Kant* denies that all actions are motivated by desire alone, arguing instead that some actions may be motivated by the will to do one's duty out of respect for the moral law. Moreover, many Christian thinkers reject Hobbes's egoism because of its roots in a secular, naturalistic world-view. These Christians never doubt that altruism is possible; the question for them is instead whether there are times when we are permitted, but not required, to be altruistic.

This question arises because the NT, especially in the teachings of Jesus, urges a concern for the well-being of others and an attitude of self-sacrifice (*e.g.* Mt. 25:31–36; 10:37–39). In view of this, it might be thought that sacrificial regard for the well-being of others is the whole of Christian morality. To balance this view, other Christians have noted that the NT also allows a place for proper self-regard (*e.g.* 'Love your neighbour as yourself,' Mt. 22:39; 'What good will it be for a man if he gains the whole world, yet forfeits his soul?' Mt. 16:26).

In conclusion, it may be noted that the above discussion is couched in terms of personal ethics, since it is a matter of some controversy whether altruism can or should be present at the level of the nation. It might be argued, for instance, that national governments are specially ordained to promote *justice* rather than well-being, or even that only *persons* can be altruistic, so that the concept of altruism cannot apply to non-personal entities such as nations.

For historical sources of the debate over altruism and egoism, see Joseph Butler, *Fifteen Sermons* (1726), ed. T. A. Roberts (London, 1970), esp. Sermon XI; Thomas Hobbes, *Leviathan* (1651), ed. M. Oakeshott (Oxford, 1947); Immanuel Kant, *Foundations of the Metaphysics of Morals* (ET, Indianapolis, IN, 1959); and William Paley, *The Principles of Moral and Political Philosophy* (London, 1785; repr. New York, 1977). For a contemporary introduction, see Alasdair MacIntyre, *EP*, pp. 462–466. For a detailed contemporary study, see Thomas Nagel, *The Possibility of Altruism* (Oxford, 1970).

M.T.N.

AMBROSE (*c.* 339–97), bishop of Milan from 374. After a very rapid transition from provincial governor and unbaptized catechumen to bishop of a strategic see, Ambrose became an outstanding church leader and preacher, whose sermons were an important factor in the conversion of Augustine.* He successfully made Roman emperors subject, as 'sons of the church', to ecclesiastical teaching and discipline, thus influencing the course of church–State relations in the medieval West.

Ambrose was a pioneer of congregational hymnody, and a champion of monasticism* and virginity.* His most significant work was *On Duties,* addressed to clergy and loosely modelled on Cicero's (106–43 BC) similarly-named *De Officiis.* It is the first thorough account of Christian ethics, rather than a handbook of ministerial practice. It discusses virtue and expediency and concludes that neither is attainable without the other. It distinguishes between 'ordinary' requirements binding on all and the 'perfection' attained by few. Stoic* influence is obvious, *e.g.* in the guidance on living 'according to nature' and in the subjection of appetite to reason. Ambrose seeks to show that Christian morality is superior to pagan philosophy's counsel. He maintains a constant reference to eternal life, a corporate dimension (what is expedient for others) and a practical concern (*e.g.* in disapproving of profit in business). Despite many scriptural examples, Ambrose's thought remains largely in a Graeco-Roman orbit.

Bibliography

On Duties, tr. H. De Romestin, *NPNF,* 2nd series, X.

I. J. Davidson, *A Commentary on the De Officiis of St Ambrose,* unpubl. PhD dissert. (Glasgow, 1992); F. H. Dudden, *The Life and Times of St Ambrose,* 2 vols. (Oxford, 1935).

D.F.W.

AMNIOCENTESIS is the withdrawal of fluid that surrounds the foetus (see Embryology*) in the womb, by inserting a needle through the mother's abdomen. The risk of harming the mother is negligible, but there is a risk of about 1 in 150 that the procedure will precipitate a miscarriage.

The fluid, which is largely derived from the foetus, can be taken late in pregnancy to ascertain whether or not the infant's lungs are mature. More frequently, however, the test is done at about sixteen weeks into the pregnancy to test for the presence of foetal abnormalities. The results, which may take up to four weeks to obtain, can identify chromosome disorders (most frequently Down's syndrome) and many rarer genetically determined conditions.

Amniocentesis is offered to women who have some increased risk of giving birth to a child with handicap (see Disability and Handicap*) and it is usually done with a view to abortion* of the pregnancy* if the abnormality is detected. Parents need to inform

themselves about the conditions being tested for and think through their views about abortion *before* having the test undertaken. Those Christians who believe the foetus to be inviolate from conception will consider all such testing wrong.

Other Christians believe abortion to be permissible (though distressing and disruptive) in certain circumstances, and will see amniocentesis as providing information which is part of the basis upon which they can make a prayerful decision whether or not to continue the pregnancy.

An earlier test, the chorion biopsy, is now also available. Carried out at ten weeks, it has a slightly higher miscarriage risk, but if abortion is indicated it can be undertaken at twelve weeks, rather than at twenty weeks as with amniocentesis.

A.C.B.

ANABAPTIST ETHICS, see ANABAPTISTS; MENNONITE ETHICS.

ANABAPTISTS. Taken from the Gk. expression for one who 're-baptizes', the term 'Anabaptist' refers to the radical expression of the 16th-century European Reformation movement which reacted to the contemporary social, political, economic and religious context. Early Anabaptist leaders in Zurich included Conrad Grebel (*c.* 1498–1526) and Felix Mantz (1498–1527).

The first 're-baptism' took place on 21 January 1525, at which time selected believers were baptized *on confession of faith.* Anabaptists claimed not to baptize a second time, since they discounted the validity of infant baptism. Fierce persecution followed, and within two years Mantz was executed by drowning (a 'third baptism' it was called by the civil authorities), becoming one of the early martyrs of the movement. Anabaptists were persecuted by both Roman Catholics and other Protestants, with thousands of adherents killed in the early years.

Affirming that Scripture is authoritative for the church and should consequently be held above church tradition and civil authority, Anabaptists agreed with much of the Protestant Reformation. Anabaptists asserted, however, that the true church comprised those adults who freely and voluntarily expressed faith in Christ and submitted to baptism as an outward sign of their inward commitment. In addition, they maintained that the civil government existed only to hold evil in check, and that Christians should remain separate from the State and should thereby not wield the violent sword (see Violence*). Today, Anabaptists are represented by various groups, including the Amish, Brethren and Mennonites (see Mennonite Ethics;* Menno Simons*).

Characteristic of Anabaptist thought is the prescription that how one lives one's life is more important than how one systematizes one's faith. Within this tradition, theology has been formulated principally as an avenue through which to understand how Christians are to live. Anabaptist theology, and thereby Anabaptist ethics, is guided by five assertions: 1. Jesus is the model *par excellence* presented in Scripture; 2. the life of Jesus must be followed and his commandments obeyed by the Christian; 3. when obedience is activated, discipleship becomes the norm; 4. discipleship is best attained when the Christian is in community with fellow disciples; and 5. discipleship in the community of God's people requires a critique of and mission to the world. Contemporary emphases within Anabaptist ethics include concerns relative to militarism, issues of wealth (see Money*) and poverty* and nationalism.*

Bibliography
R. Friedmann, *The Theology of Anabaptism* (Scottdale, PA, 1973); W. Klaassen (ed.), *Anabaptism in Outline* (Scottdale, PA, 1981).

D.L.P.

ANALYTICAL PSYCHOLOGY. Unlike psychoanalysis,* analytical psychology is a methodology that is difficult to systematize, since its founder, Carl Jung,* both majored on the unmeasurable world of the unconscious* and argued for a fluid, dynamic understanding of the human psyche. We can, none the less, consider his approach and later modifications under the three headings 'Jungian concepts', 'Jungian analysis' and 'the Post-Jungians'.

1. Jungian concepts
Philosophically, some of the main influences on Jung's understanding of the human mind were: Plato's* concept of original Ideas, immaterial forms from which all material experience flows; the innate categories of perception put forward in the writings of Immanuel Kant;* and the pessimistic theodicy* of Arthur Schopenhauer (1788–1860) with its picture of

a 'blind world-creating Will'. Such considerations fostered Jung's archetypal theory and his emphasis on opposites, including that of a God who evokes 'not only man's bright and positive side but also his darkness and ungodliness' (*Memories, Dreams, Reflections*, p. 88). We can sample something of the complexity and, at times, amorphous nature of Jung's concepts by looking at four pairs of opposites. It is important to remember in Jungian bipolarity that the opposites are linked and that psychic energy is said to flow between them.

The most fundamental bipolarity in Jungian psychology is that of the 'conscious' and 'unconscious'. Consciousness is seen as that aspect of human nature which discriminates, controls the instincts, and enables the person to adapt to life's demands. In contrast, the unconscious, comprising both the 'personal unconscious' and 'collective unconscious' (a hidden repository of instinctual and inherited mythological material), is undifferentiated and acts in a compensatory way to balance any one-sidedness in the conscious.

The 'ego' and 'self'* in Jungian terminology are a source of confusion, since Jung used these terms in a variety of ways. However, his prime concept of the 'ego' is as an executive entity at the centre of consciousness whose main functions are those of establishing personal identity and a sense of continuity. Whereas Freud* saw the ego as the prime mover in human development,* Jung maintained the notion of the 'self' as *the* integrating force within the personality* – both its centre and, mysteriously, its entirety. This latter notion led Jung, at times, to lay claim to the concept of the self (the 'Self' in some post-Jungian writing) as indistinguishable from the 'God-image' within the human psyche.

The 'persona' and 'shadow', although not strictly opposites, are two further aspects of the polarity between consciousness and the unconscious respectively. Jung coined the term 'persona' from the Lat. for 'mask', as worn by actors, and saw it as 'a complicated system of relations between individual consciousness and society' (*Collected Works* 7, para. 305). The persona acts as a bridge between the ego and the outside world, through which gender and social roles are expressed. The 'shadow' represents the darker side of human nature, the thing we have 'no wish to be' (*CW* 16, para. 470). Whereas over-identification with the persona leads to a vulnerable superficiality, the shadow, when unfaced, may project (see

Defence Mechanisms*) powerfully on to others, leading to prejudiced and destructive behaviour.

Fundamental to all Jungian concepts lies the theory of the 'archetypes', inherited structural patterns within the collective unconscious which may be expressed through 'archetypal images' within the life of the individual. Of particular importance among these images are those of the 'anima' and 'animus', contrasexual archetypes which form a bridge between the unconscious and consciousness. Jung argued that the anima gives 'relationship and relatedness' to a man's self-awareness and the animus gives 'to woman's consciousness a capacity for reflection, deliberation and self-knowledge' (*CW* 9ii, para. 33). Various writers have questioned Jung's views on gender and sexuality (see ⑪), acknowledging both that his apparent sexism* was intrinsic to Swiss patriarchal society in the first half of the century, and that his emphasis on anima and animus can be seen as an integrating contribution to an understanding of human nature (see, *e.g.*, Wehr, *Jung and Feminism*, pp. 1–25).

2. Jungian analysis

The aim of Jungian analysis, and of life itself, is for the person to embrace the process and goal of 'individuation' (see Self-actualization*), an 'at-one-ment with oneself and . . . with humanity' (*CW* 16, para. 227). Individuation is a progressive integration and, at the same time, differentiation, of the conscious and unconscious, the collective and uniquely individual, of the spiritual and instinctual.

Jung anticipated many of the emphases of humanistic psychology* and the counselling movement (see Pastoral Care, Counselling and Psychotherapy⑫). He saw the method of analysis as 'an art', which stressed the individual's uniqueness, sat loose to theory and technique, emphasized the therapeutic relationship as one of equals (or, better, of 'assymetrical mutuality'), and engaged in a 'dialectical process' at every level (between analyst and patient, conscious and unconscious, ego and shadow, *etc.*). Such principles contrast Jung's approach with Freud's: Jung engaged the patient face to face, eschewing the Freudian couch; he was more positive about regression (see Defence Mechanisms*); and was more tolerant of the 'fantasy relationships' between analyst and patient, including that of counter-transference (see Transference*). Using the analysis of dreams* (which

Jung saw as 'compensatory' towards the conscious life, with both causal and purposive perspectives) and 'active imagination' (allowing a picture, mood or event to stimulate fantasy images which, in taking on a life of their own, can speak to the conscious) to explore the patient's unconscious, Jung saw the analytic process in four stages: 'catharsis', a 'cleansing' brought about by the patient's confession* and unburdening; 'elucidation' in which unexamined ties to the unconscious are revealed and conscious attitudes begin to change; 'education', a 'drawing forth' into the lengthy process of integration; and 'transformation' – not only of the patient but of the analyst too.

3. The post-Jungians

Unlike the post-Freudian tradition, with its clearly defined schools of systematized methodology, post-Jungians, influenced by the less doctrinaire approach of Jung, form a more diffuse body. None the less, there have been a number of attempts to classify post-Jungian forms of analytical psychology into broadly orthodox and innovative strands. Andrew Samuels (*Jung and the Post-Jungians,* pp. 1–22) has reviewed these attempts and puts forward his own schema: the 'Classical School' which follows Jung's theory and practice closely; the 'Developmental School', influenced most by such psychoanalysts as Donald Winnicott* and the object-relations theories of Melanie Klein* and her successors; and the 'Archetypal School' which emphasizes the importance of highly differentiated archetypal imagery and plays down the interpretative aspects of analysis.

See also: PASTORAL CARE, COUNSELLING AND PSYCHOTHERAPY. ⑫

Bibliography

C. G. Jung, *The Collected Works* (London and Princeton, NJ, 1953–1978); *idem*, *Memories, Dreams, Reflections* (London and New York, 1963); A. Samuels, *Jung and the Post-Jungians* (London and New York, 1985); A. Samuels *et al.*, *A Critical Dictionary of Jungian Analysis* (London, 1986); A. Stevens, *On Jung* (London and New York, 1991); D. S. Wehr, *Jung and Feminism: Liberating Archetypes* (London, 1988).

R.F.H.

ANALYTICAL PSYCHOTHERAPY, see ANALYTICAL PSYCHOLOGY; CHARACTER. ⑩

ANARCHY (lit. 'no ruler') denotes a range of conditions, from lawlessness and social chaos to a co-operative system of voluntary associations as the preferred structure of society. Common to all these usages is a rejection of authoritarian government* in favour of voluntary organization, to ensure the utmost individual freedom* compatible with the existence of society. Legal structures, including democratic institutions and political parties, are all suspect.

Anarchist trends are a recurrent historical phenomenon. Examples include Zeno (d. 263 BC), the Gk. Stoic* who repudiated dependence on the trappings of culture; the ancient Essenes; some early Anabaptists;* the Doukhabors, the 18th-century Russian sect; the Levellers in the Eng. Civil War; and other groups emphasizing that Christ has freed us from the evils of this world and bondage to the law. On similar religious grounds Leo Tolstoy* denounced the State and its rule of laws, renouncing even his own property and social status. The American writer Henry Thoreau (1817–62) adopted kindred ideas on romanticist grounds, and some Russian revolutionaries repudiated Marxism's 'dictatorship of the proletariat' in favour of a syndicate of voluntary labour groups. More recently, student activists of the 1960s in various countries revolted against the political and social establishment. A more right-wing American expression of anarchist ideas appears in Robert Nozick's (1938–) *Anarchy, State and Utopia*, with his insistence that individuals have the freedom to acquire whatever they can provided only that they do not take it illegally from others. An individual's acquisition rights are the centrepiece of society.

Anarchy's preference for voluntary rather than legal structures assumes that human beings are naturally good, that coercion (see Force*) is unnecessary, and that governmental authority tends to cause more harm than good. The Bible, by contrast, speaks of civil authority as ordained by God for the restraint of evil and the promotion of good (Rom. 13:1–7; 1 Pet. 2:13–17).

Bibliography

R. Nozick, *Anarchy, State, and Utopia* (New York, 1974; Oxford, 1975).

A.F.H.

ANGER is an emotion or passion directed towards self* or others in response to a real or perceived wrongdoing. Anger as emotional energy, and aggression as its physical expression, emerge in all humans, either in covert and subtle or in overt and confrontive forms. Anger should be differentiated from hostility, which is a state of animosity or antagonism and a negative orientation; anger may be either negative or positive, unloving or loving. Anger must also be distinguished from aggression, which is an action of invasion or injury towards another which may or may not be motivated by anger.

1. Anger theory. Theories of anger and aggression have emerged from three major perspectives: a. The psychoanalytic, instinctual, ethological group finds its most influential roots in Freudian theory. From his earliest formulations of anger and aggression arising from desire, to his final formulation of a self-destructive death instinct, Sigmund Freud* saw anger in terms of a hydraulic model of accumulating instincts which require tension discharge. Although the majority of psychoanalysts refuse the theory of a death instinct (*thanatos*), they acknowledge a destructive drive which is the reverse pole of the sexual instinct (*erōs*). b. The behavioural and social-learning theorists, such as J. Dollard, J. B. Rotter (1920–) and Albert Bandura (1925–), saw anger and aggression as environmentally induced, and invariably a consequence of frustration. These responses were seen as both innate and learned, so the focus of causal analysis included external instigations, stimulus events, and learned internal responses. c. The existential and phenomenological theorists, such as Rollo May,* Carl Rogers,* Abraham Maslow* and Frederick Perls (1893–1970), saw the individual's reactions to the environment as shaped by the perceptions which form the subjective reality of the person.

2. Anger dynamics. Anger is an emotional response with four component parts. a. Arousal: a physiological state of bodily arousal, with autonomic, facial, respiratory and metabolic manifestations, lies beneath the anger emotion. b. Appraisal: a cognitive state, appraising and defining the arousal, makes internal demands on both internal and external events. c. Approval: a moral-cultural approval process directs the anger emotion, censoring and filtering the response according to cultural expectations and the local moral order. d. Action: an energizing state with drive properties intensifies aggressive or assertive actions while also disorganizing concentration, attention and impulse control.

3. *Anger and theology.* The capacity for anger is a basic human endowment which is morally neither positive nor negative in and of itself. Its ethical value is found in the constructive or destructive impact of its effects on self and others. Anger may be either redemptive or destructive in its purposes. This is evident in both OT and NT. The anger of Cain, of Esau, of Joseph's brothers, of Moses, and God's own anger offer opening models of both destructive and constructive styles of anger management. The Bible treats anger as a neutral emotion, judging its causes, behaviours and effects by the communal standards of Israel and later by the context of the early church. Jesus expressed anger in various circumstances, yet forbade its destructive forms. Paul and James express both criticism and approval of properly controlled and directed anger (Eph. 5:26; Jas. 1:19).

4. *Anger management.* Anger is a crucial emotion in the pastoral counselling process. For the therapist, anger must be owned, appreciated, channelled and utilized to summon the inner resources of feelings, both positive and negative, into the counselling encounter. For the counsellee, anger must be welcomed, its impact weighed, its dignity prized, its demands clarified, cancelled or negotiated. In the therapeutic process, anger is a signal that growth, maturation and autonomy from the therapist is occurring. (When there is no negative transference, there is little or no therapeutic progress or growth.)

Destructive forms of anger management can be unlearned and creative patterns learned. Behavioural theory differentiates between styles of non-assertive (passive or internalized responses), assertive (appropriate caring and confronting responses) and aggressive behaviour (explosive or exploitive reactions). Modelling, rehearsing and reinforcing assertive behaviour patterns is an effective way of teaching constructive anger behaviours.

Anger training which combines theoretical, ethical and theological perspectives can assist the person in moving from being emotionally reactive to becoming emotionally responsive. The therapeutic goals are to facilitate differentiation between the thinking processes and the emotional processes. The capacity to think about one's experience and feel congruent emotions can be separated from the automatic emotional process which dominates or overwhelms thoughts and filters or blocks percep-

tions. As the person is able to separate anger and self-esteem,* anger and goal-orientation, anger and self-instructions, anger and power needs, anger and self-evaluation, then anger does not lower esteem, distract from goals, flood with negative self-instructions, exaggerate power needs and end in guilty negativism in review of the episode. Instead, the anger functions as increased arousal, heightened concern, deepened intensity of passion and more powerful expression of needs and wants. Anger management training has moved from the ventilationist process of flooding, which was used in mid- and late-20th century, to channelling, differentiation and cognitive clarification of boundaries between thought and emotion which permits control and direction of feelings and more effective relating in life.

See also: DEADLY SINS; HATRED.

Bibliography

D. Augsburger, *Anger, Assertiveness and Pastoral Care* (Philadelphia, 1979); A. V. Campbell, *The Gospel of Anger* (London and Philadelphia, 1986); M. Chave-Jones, *Living with Anger* (London, 1992); C. Tavris, *Anger, the Misunderstood Emotion* (New York, 1982).

D.W.A.

ANGLICAN MORAL THEOLOGY.

In Book I of his *Treatise of the Laws of Ecclesiastical Polity* (1594), Richard Hooker* established Anglican moral theology on foundations that owe much more to Thomas Aquinas* than to Martin Luther.* As a consequence, the Anglican tradition of ethical thought has tended to esteem more highly than its Lutheran,* Reformed (see Calvinistic Ethics*), or Anabaptist* (see also Mennonite Ethics*) counterparts the power of natural reason to discern what is good and right, without the aid of the grace of special revelation. Accordingly, it has been more ready to accredit sources of moral wisdom other than Scripture. This is evident, for example, in the confidence that Joseph Butler* placed in common moral sense and in the moral philosophical character of his influential writings. It is also evidenced by the respect with which William Temple* regarded the contributions to ethical debate of experts in the social and natural sciences, and by the Church of England's post-war proclivity – applauded by Ian Ramsey (1915–72) – for multi-disciplinary working parties on ethical issues.

Anglicanism has inherited from Thomist* moral theology a comparatively high regard for natural reason. It has also inherited a similar regard for moral reasoning (see Christian Moral Reasoning [18]). This has found expression in an Anglican tradition of casuistry,* which flourished in the 17th century in the hands of divines such as William Perkins (1558–1602), Robert Sanderson (1587–1663), Joseph Hall (1574–1656), and Jeremy Taylor,* and which Kenneth Kirk* sought to revive in the 1920s. Anglican casuistry has differed from its Roman counterpart in two respects. First, it has been set loose from the confessional (see Confession*). This means that its aim has not been to reach a retrospective judgment about the gravity of sins confessed, so that an appropriate penance might be imposed. Instead, it has sought to aid the formation of prospective judgments about the right course of action to be taken. Secondly, out of a high regard for the liberty of individual conscience* it has sought to aid the layperson directly, and not mediately through the priest. For this reason Anglican casuists have tended to write in the vernacular rather than Latin. On more than one occasion in the history of Anglican moral theology the high value placed upon liberty of conscience has combined with the high esteem of natural reason to erode belief in the need for moral reasoning. As examples of this take the confidence of Butler in the sufficiency of the intuitions (see Intuitionism*) of common moral sense, and of Joseph Fletcher* in the sufficiency of love's insight (*Situation Ethics*, London and Philadelphia, 1966).

A more fundamental point at which the Anglican ethical tradition has diverged from its Roman counterpart after the Council of Trent (1545–63) is in its location of moral considerations within the larger context of spiritual ones: Anglican moral theology stands firmly in the context of spiritual (or ascetical*) theology. This has had the salutary effect of checking the tendency of moral theology to degenerate into a legalistic preoccupation with the observance of rules, by making its aim not merely the avoidance of sin but also the pursuit of holiness. Anglican moral theology has thus been blessed with a positive orientation towards the cure of souls. This Anglican connection between the moral, the spiritual and the pastoral is well illustrated in the case of

Kirk, whose most famous work in the moral field is entitled *The Vision of God* (London, 1931), and for whom the Regius Chair of Pastoral Theology at Oxford was renamed the Regius Chair of Moral and Pastoral Theology in 1932.

Anglicanism's relatively high estimation of 'nature', its corresponding tendency to affirm the persistent goodness and redeemability of the world by paying more attention to the divine incarnation (see Jesus*) than to the cross, and its public responsibility as the established Church of England all combined with the prominence of the 'social question' in the second half of the 19th century to produce an Anglican tradition of socialism.* This flourished vigorously under the leadership of such eminent figures as F. D. Maurice,* Charles Gore (1853–1932) and William Temple up until the 1950s. Unlike the liberal Protestant social gospel* movement in America, this Anglican socialism has retained a strong and characteristic interest in spiritual formation, especially through the eucharistic liturgy, as necessary to sustain Christian political commitment (see, *e.g.*, Kenneth Leech, *The Social God*, London 1981).

Bibliography

P. Elmen (ed.), *The Anglican Moral Choice* (Wilton, CT, 1983); H. R. McAdoo, *The Structure of Caroline Moral Theology* (London, 1949); J. Oliver, *The Church and Social Order* (London, 1968); M. B. Reckitt, *Maurice to Temple* (London, 1946); T. Wood, *English Casuistical Divinity* (London, 1952).

N.J.B.

ANIMAL EXPERIMENTATION, see Rights, Animal.

ANIMAL RIGHTS, see Rights, Animal.

ANIMAL WELFARE, see Rights, Animal.

ANOINTING, see Sacramental Healing.

ANOREXIA, see Eating Disorders.

ANSELM (1033–1109). Born at Aosta, Italy, Anselm studied at Bec in Normandy and later became prior of Bec (1063) and abbot (1078). He was made Archbishop of Canterbury in 1093.

The spirit animating Anselm's thought is the

Augustinian* goal of faith seeking understanding. As he addresses God in the opening chapter of the *Proslogion:* 'I long to understand in some degree thy truth, which my heart believes and loves. For I do not seek to understand that I may believe, but believe in order to understand.' Anselm is perhaps best known for his argument for the existence of God, the so-called 'ontological argument' of the *Proslogion,* which moves from the idea of God to God as a reality.

In theology Anselm made a major contribution to the doctrine of the atonement* in his work, *Cur Deus Homo* (*Why God Became Man*). Anselm rejects the view, known as the ransom theory, that the devil, by virtue of man's sin, had 'a rightful ownership of man'. Sin is 'nothing else than not to render to God his due', with the result that God is dishonoured. It would not be proper for God to cancel sin without compensation or punishment;* rather, the one who sins must suffer the punishment of sin. Since humanity is created by God, we owe everything to him and cannot atone for our sin. Only Christ, by willingly assuming human nature and dying, can render God his due. Christ, by freely offering the Father payment for that which he did not himself owe, makes atonement for mankind.

Bibliography
Basic Writings (La Salle, IL, 1962).

A.G.V.

ANTINOMIANISM. The word 'antinomianism' derives from two Gk. words, *anti* (against) and *nomos* (law). In general it designates those who reject moral law as binding on conduct. This view has made its impact both inside and outside the Christian church.

Non-Christian forms of antinomianism include the ancient Epicurean saying 'eat, drink and be merry', and 2nd-century gnosticism, whose followers claimed that, since the law came from the Demiurge (a demonic being in opposition to God) and not from the loving Father, Christians had no obligation to obey it. In modern times, many existentialists have been considered antinomian, since they encourage individuals to 'do their own thing'. French existentialist Jean-Paul Sartre* claimed that it made no difference whether one decided to lead the nations or get drunk (*Being and Nothingness*, 1943; ET, London, 1957). The German philosopher Friedrich Nietzsche* claimed that God had died and all absolute values died with him. Situation ethicists, such as Joseph Fletcher,* have also denied all contentful ethical absolutes, and they are thereby open to the charge of lawlessness, though Fletcher distances himself from antinomianism.

Antinomianism has not been limited to non-Christians. Even in NT times Paul warned against it when he opposed the cry 'Let us do evil that good may result' (Rom. 3:8). Later, the Adamite sect in N. Africa condemned marriage and worshipped in the nude. A tract by Augustine* (*Against Adversaries of the Law and the Prophets*) reveals the presence of an antinomian element. During the Reformation, Martin Luther* opposed Johannes Agricola (1494–1566), who that denied that Christians owe obedience to any part of God's moral law, even that expressed in the Decalogue.* Traces of antinomianism were also found among Anabaptists,* High Calvinists in the Commonwealth, New England Puritans (*e.g.* Anne Hutchinson, 1591–1643) and even some Wesleyans. The latter elicited a strong response from John Fletcher (1729–85) in *Checks to Antinomianism* (1771). Antinomian trends still exist today among certain Christian cults and sects.

See also: LAW.

N.L.G.

ANTI-SEMITISM. While the term 'anti-Semitism' was not coined until 1879, the reality of anti-Jewish racialism has a long history. Because the Jews often remained a distinct community and refused participation in emperor-worship, they faced persecution under such emperors as Nero and Domitian.

In the 1st century the church and synagogue competed for the souls of those who were increasingly disillusioned with current immorality and decadent polytheism. Theological disputes concerning the person of Jesus, the role of the law/Torah and the position of Gentile believers fanned the hostility. The Gospels of Matthew and John reflect the tensions, although accusations of anti-Semitism in them seem unfounded, for both their authors were Jews.

With the shift in political power after 321 AD, Christian anti-Semitism became institutionalized. Despite the fact that Jesus and the apostles were Jewish and the NT teaches against racial discrimination, the church has been guilty of continuous anti-Semitism. High points were the Crusades, the fourth Lateran Council (1215), the Inquisition (1232 onwards), the Dreyfus affair in France (1894), Russian pogroms and supremely the Nazi Holocaust. While Islam, and more recently anti-Zionism, Marxism and the formerly Communist-bloc countries of Eastern Europe, have also exhibited anti-Semitism, the Christian church has particularly contributed to this ugly phenomenon.

An early stimulus towards anti-Semitism was the accusation that it was the Jews who killed the Messiah Jesus, ignoring the guilt of Pilate and the Roman authorities. Later Jews were accused of plotting against Christians as agents of the angel of death. Christian painters and cartoonists popularized this accusation, as also the idea that Jews sucked the blood of Christian babies and seduced Christian maidens. The Nazis inherited these prejudices and linked them with Richard Wagner (1818–83), Friedrich Nietzsche* and German nationalism to reduce Jews to sub-human non-Aryan vermin. Perhaps jealousy of Jewish financial expertise also played its part in fostering anti-Semitism.

Luther's* anti-Jewish writings encouraged Lutherans to follow in Roman Catholic anti-Semitic footsteps. Calvinism (see Calvinistic Ethics*), however, with its work ethic and its emphasis on the Heb. Scriptures and on the church as the new Israel, was less inclined to anti-Semitism.

See also: RACE.

Bibliography

J. G. Gager, *The Origins of Anti-Semitism* (Oxford, 1983); M. Gilbert, *The Holocaust* (London, 1986); C. Klein, *Anti-Judaism in Christian Theology* (London, 1978); R. S. Wistrich, *Anti-Zionism and Anti-Semitism in the Contemporary World* (London, 1990); Bat Ye'or, *The Dhimmi: Jews and Christians under Islam* (Cranbury, NJ, 1985).

M.F.G.

ANXIETY is part of the human condition from which no-one (including Christians) is exempt. It is an unpleasant emotion,* caused by external events and/or internal conflict which are experienced as presenting an actual, imagined or potential threat to one's equilibrium. Anxiety can be positive when it is seen as an amber light warning of danger ahead. For some people it acts as a positive stimulus to creative action (*e.g.* working hard for an examination), and they are able to take it in their stride. For others it produces some degree of paralysis (*e.g.* not being able to work at all for the examination). Both these reactions depend upon the complicated network of emotional, mental and biological structures which constitute the personality.

Anxiety is always an uncomfortable emotion with its physical accompaniments: pounding heart, tension headache, sweating palms, overactivity of the intestines, nausea, dilated pupils, *etc.* These reactions are the responses to increased adrenalin in the bloodstream, which prepares the body for fight or flight in the short term. If anxiety continues unabated over a long period, this increased adrenalin can produce biochemical changes and instigate various physical illnesses.

Some people live in a state of inner anxiety-producing conflict. For some it is a permanent state of dread and fear* of impending disaster, out of proportion to reality, which slows them down and diminishes their effectiveness severely. This is usually referred to as an 'anxiety state' or 'morbid anxiety'. It is often about a fear of nothingness, annihilation and non-relatedness (ultimate death).

Separation anxiety is always present in healthy children to whom separation from parents would represent real danger. However, its excessive manifestation in adults is usually related to some other anxiety-producing factor, probably traumatic events in childhood which have never been satisfactorily resolved and live on in the active memory or the unconscious (see Loneliness*).

There is a variety of defence mechanisms* which people use to shield themselves from the pain of awareness of the cause of the anxiety. This is not a conscious operation; it is an activity of the unconscious mind. These defences do not abolish the anxiety; they merely divert it. People then do not complain of the anxiety but of the headaches, the nausea, trembling hands, abdominal symptoms, *etc.* The defences are called 'neurotic anxiety'.

These defence mechanisms can take various forms: 1. Constant physical pain of no organic origin, which can involve endless medication and even multiple surgery. 2. Paralysis of a limb or impairment of a physical function which would be required in a threatening situation (*e.g.* an inexplicable and crippling pain in the arm before a written examination, with no conscious association). Any part of the body may be involved in the 'mysterious leap from mind to body' (Freud). This is referred to as 'hysterical conversion'. 3. Various phobias such as school phobia (the child's anxiety about going to school is usually not about what may happen at school but what may happen at home while the child is at school); agoraphobia; claustrophobia; arachnophobia (fear of spiders or other insects which dash about unpredictably and represent instincts which are hard to keep under control). 4. The obsessional performance of certain ritual behaviour, *e.g.* handwashing or not stepping on the cracks in the pavement. This has to do with an attempt to control excessive free-floating anxiety about dirt or some other 'contaminating' substance or idea and reduce its terror by making it manageable. In all these phobias the basic anxiety is hidden underneath some crippling social inability.

Another reaction to anxiety can be a complete emotional withdrawal from active participation in normal life. Depression* often results from prolonged anxiety.

Stress* is very similar to anxiety in its physical manifestations, including changes in sleeping patterns, timekeeping, personal organization, proneness to accidents, tiredness, loss of interest and efficiency at work, over-reaction and irritability. It is usually connected with external events which impinge too heavily on the limits of the personality. Thomas H. Holmes and R. H. Rahe produced a Social Readjustment Rating Scale which measured forty-two stressful events. The death of a spouse (see Bereavement*) is the highest (100), minor violations of the law the lowest (11), with marriage,* pregnancy,* and environmental change graduating between. Any change in the known routine is stressful to some extent. We can do various things to reduce our anxiety-level or prevent it from becoming abnormal, *i.e.* try to know ourselves, decide priorities and clarify boundaries where possible; have adequate relaxation and physical exercise; secure enough personal space; ensure enough support from others; not repress internal or interpersonal conflict. When the anxiety is high, all efforts to help oneself are of no avail until the level has been reduced, probably with medical help, so that we can start working at problem-solving again.

There are various therapeutic approaches to the treatment of severe anxiety. The behaviourist* school aims to submit the patient's symptoms to gradual, prolonged exposure, with support, to the external manifestation of the anxiety (*e.g.* fear of spiders) until the patient is able to tolerate its presence. This can be successful, but there is always the danger that the underlying anxiety, if not itself treated, will present in some other form. The psychodynamic approach takes much longer and works at the unconscious activity in the anxiety rather than the observable symptoms. Neurotic anxiety is sometimes helped by the support of prayer and a 'healing ministry', provided this is done with patient understanding of the whole problem.

Christian belief is totally relevant to one's sense of perspective. The providence of God includes his fatherly care for his children; thus they need not panic in their reactions to anxiety and stress. They need actively to remind themselves that 'underneath are the everlasting arms' (Dt. 33:27); they are not alone; and nothing can separate them from God's love (Rom. 8:38–39). It is sometimes hard to hold on to this knowledge in the face of some enigmatic situations, and then believers need the solidarity of Christian friends. However, the ultimate perspective for all of life, including anxiety, is eternity (2 Cor. 4:18).

Bibliography

J. Bowlby, *Separation: Anxiety and Anger* (London, 1973); G. Davies, *Stress* (Eastbourne, 1988).

M.C.-J.

APARTHEID (lit. 'apartness') particularly designates the policy of racial separation and discrimination pursued by the National Party government from 1948 till 1991 in the Republic of South Africa. (Apart from the introduction of a new Constitution, with voting rights for all races, all apartheid laws were scrapped by mid-1991.) Apartheid was characterized by the *hierarchical* ordering of economic, political and social structures on the basis of race, by political and economic *discrimination* against the 'non-white' races, and by the *segregation* of the races in most spheres of life. This system was legalized, institutionalized and enforced by the government (M. Lipton, *Capitalism and Apartheid*, pp. 14–15).

Historical roots

The roots of apartheid are complex and date back at least to the early 19th century. A major strand of apartheid thinking developed within the Dutch Reformed Church (DRC). Successful missionary work resulted in 'coloured' persons being added to the church. Presbytery and Synod decisions in 1829 and 1834 upheld their right to partake of the Lord's Supper together with 'born Christians' (whites), but in practice this was ignored. Then, in 1857, in a bid to gain support for its mission work, the Synod 'as a result of the weakness of some' permitted separate places of worship for the 'coloured' converts. This historic resolution paved the way for the 1881 decision to form the Dutch Reformed Mission Church. Racial prejudice, at least in part, had led to church 'apartheid'. While this development was more pragmatic than ideological, it nevertheless set a precedent which helped create a climate receptive to the idea of racial separation as a solution to racial prejudice or friction.

Apartheid as an *ideology*, however, only really developed in the 1930s. According to J. Kinghorn (in M. Prozesky, *Christianity Amidst Apartheid*, p. 61) the major factors in growth of the apartheid philosophy were economic and ideological, theology following their lead, though other scholars assign a more formative role to theology.

The Afrikaners were humiliated in the Anglo-Boer War (1899–1902) and subsequently impoverished and urbanized (see Urbanization*). Many were unemployed and lived in slums with blacks. It was into this situation that the ideological factor entered in the 1930s. 'A racially defined nationalism imported from Germany, Spain, Portugal and Italy penetrated Afrikanerdom like a veld fire' (J. Kinghorn, in M. Prozesky, *Christianity Amidst Apartheid*, pp. 61–62). Afrikaner nationalism developed in sympathy with these views and there were widespread calls for black/white separation. Even the Afrikaans churches joined in.

The Afrikaans churches believed that such a separation would restore the self-respect of the Afrikaner and save him from the slums. It did, but at the cost of denigrating and subjugating other races. In a number of delegations to the government, the DRC pressed for separate suburbs, schools and industries and for an end to racially mixed marriages. In 1942 the DRC told the government they were in favour of 'racial apartheid' and racial purity. No wonder they could claim with pride after the National Party victory in 1948: 'As a Church, we have always worked purposefully for the separation of the races. In this regard apartheid can rightfully be called a Church policy' (J. de Gruchy, *The Church Struggle in South Africa*, p. 59).

Identification with the plight of the Afrikaner was not the only factor that led the Afrikaans churches to support apartheid. The way was also prepared by the wide influence of Abraham Kuyper's* theology in the 1930s. Kuyper had emphasized the God-given diversity of the races and the right of each race to maintain its identity. His views were then modified and used to provide a theological justification of apartheid. This backing of apartheid by the churches gave it a *moral legitimacy* in the eyes of the Afrikaners, a church-going nation, and it was only after the DRC withdrew its support of apartheid in 1986 that ideological apartheid began to crumble.

Apartheid legislation

Before 1948 a number of discriminatory Acts were already on the statute books. The 1913 and 1936 Land Acts reserved 13% of the country for the 70% black majority, and in 1923 urban blacks were confined to segregated townships. There was discriminatory labour legislation, and only coloureds in the Cape and whites had the vote.

The victorious Nationalists soon began to turn their apartheid vision into reality, ushering in an all-embracing programme of social engineering. 'Within less than three decades, a total reconstruction of South African society, politics and the economy enabled the poverty of the poor whites to be converted into great affluence' (J. Kinghorn, in M. Prozesky, *Christianity Amidst Apartheid*, p. 63). The fulfilment of their dream, however, became a nightmare for millions of blacks.

Few areas of life were left untouched by the host of discriminatory laws that followed. Racially mixed marriages were prohibited in 1949 – later, even sex between whites and other races was forbidden. In 1950 the Population Registration Act classified all people racially, and via the Group Areas Act (1950) they were residentially segregated. The Influx Control Act of 1952 ('pass laws') denied freedom of movement to blacks. Reference books ('passes') had to be carried at all times and were bitterly resented. Rural blacks could work in the cities only by becoming migrant labourers* – this meant they only spent one month a year with their wives and children in the 'homelands'. Four of these homelands became 'independent' states – 8.5 million blacks thereby losing their South African citizenship – while another six opted for self-government.

Labour discrimination was extensive – skilled jobs were reserved for whites, blacks could trade only in their own areas, could not own property, and were even removed from the Unemployment Insurance Fund. The Bantu Education Act of 1953 effectively transferred the control of black education from the State-aided mission schools to the State, and funds for black education were deliberately kept very low to prevent them rising above their station as unskilled labourers. At its height, in 1970–71, the State spent over eighteen times more per capita on the education of white children.

The implementation of apartheid resulted in the forced resettlement of 3.7 million people, 17 million pass-law convictions (1916–81), 78,000 political detentions, many without trial, and 73 deaths in detention since 1960.

The effects of such laws and their enforcement were devastating. Psychologically, blacks suffered a loss of dignity and self-esteem.* The older generation developed a dependence mentality, while many youth rebelled. Without hope of change, despair, bitterness and anger set in, though a surprising degree of goodwill remained between the estranged races. Sociologically, there was a breakdown of family life, a loss of parental authority, increased sexual immorality, a rising culture of violence, and the development of separate institutions from churches to sporting bodies. Judicially, apartheid resulted in a loss of respect for the law and its enforcers, the police and defence force. Economically, poverty was entrenched, especially in the rural homelands, with its consequences of malnutrition, a high infant-mortality rate, poor health and lower life-expectancy. In the end, factors such as poor black education, the mismanagement of economic resources, the high cost of apartheid (10% to 20% of the annual budget) and finally disinvestment and economic sanctions* proved too much for the economy, pressurizing the government to move away from apartheid.

Theological evaluation

Fundamental to the biblical doctrine of the State is that it should exercise *justice* (Rom. 13), that it should show neither partiality to the poor nor favouritism to the rich, but judge fairly (Lv. 19:15). Under apartheid, the whites in South Africa were legally favoured economically, educationally, medically, socially and politically. Consequently, in all these areas there were massive inequalities.

By pursuing justice the State is also to seek the *good* of all its subjects (Rom. 13:4). Under apartheid, however, the welfare of the whites was continually promoted to the detriment of the other races.

Apartheid also discriminated between people on the basis of *race*, a category J. B. Root argues is foreign to Scripture (see 'Race', in *NDT*, pp. 555–556), judging people on the basis of external appearance or genetics rather than on character and obedience to God.

Apartheid, based as it was on the fundamental *irreconcilability* of the different races, in effect denied the reconciling and uniting power of Christ to overcome human divisions through the cross (Eph. 2:11–22).

Anthropologically, Scripture stresses the absolute unity of humanity in Adam, and the relativity and fluidity of the nations, while apartheid absolutized ethnic diversity and relativized human unity. This made it easy to regard some races as intrinsically superior to others and so devalue their dignity.

While ecclesiastical apartheid was never enforced, the country's policies led to racially separate churches and the failure of many churches to demonstrate their unity in Christ. Further, for many Afrikaners, race or nationality took precedence over their covenantal commitment to Christ. They found their identity first in their race and then in the people of God. Nationalism* thus became idolatrous, and the church's integrity and unity were denied.

Ethically, apartheid violated the fundamental moral principle of *neighbour love*, to love others as yourself and to treat them as you would be treated. Love for one's own people was stressed, and since power was in the hands of whites, white interests usually came first.

For reasons like these, the Alliance of Black Reformed Christians in Southern Africa in 1981 rightly declared that the moral and theological justification of apartheid was a heresy, while the dehumanizing aspects of apartheid led the mainline churches to oppose apartheid vigorously. The smaller evangelical churches, however, because of their pietistic heritage and individualistic emphasis, were very late in their public criticism of apartheid, with the gospel losing credibility as a result.

When ideas of ecclesiastical racial separation were first mooted in the DRC, Andrew Murray (1828–1917) had warned: 'The danger exists that the voice of blood, the voice of passion, of partisanship, of group interest will overpower the voice of the Gospel!' (C. Villa-Vicencio, *The Theology of Apartheid*, pp. 10–11). Tragically, the church failed to hear his prophetic voice and a whole nation suffered the consequences.

See also: EVANGELICAL WITNESS IN SOUTH AFRICA; KAIROS DOCUMENT; RACE.

Bibliography

M. Cassidy, *The Passing Summer* (London, 1989); J. W. de Gruchy, *The Church Struggle in South Africa* (Grand Rapids, ²1986); J. W. de Gruchy and C. Villa-Vicencio (eds.), *Apartheid is a Heresy* (Cape Town, 1983); M. Lipton, *Capitalism and Apartheid: South Africa, 1910–1986* (Aldershot, 1986); J. A. Loubser, *The Apartheid Bible* (Cape Town, 1987); D. J. Morphew, *South Africa: The Powers Behind* (Cape Town, 1989); M. Prozesky (ed.), *Christianity Amidst Apartheid* (London, 1990); C. Villa-Vicencio, *The Theology of Apartheid* (Cape Town, n.d.).

J.G.C.

AQUINAS, see THOMAS AQUINAS.

ARCHETYPAL THEORY, see ANALYTICAL PSYCHOLOGY; JESUS.

ARCHITECTURE. In 1624, Sir Henry Wooton (1568–1639) suggested that there was a moral imperative in the art of architecture: 'The end is to build well . . . well building hath three Conditions: Commodity, Firmness and Delight.' These conditions still relate to the challenge facing any designer to satisfy and integrate social, technological and aesthetic requirements, in order to produce a holistic approach to architecture and physical planning.

Potentially, such criteria relate closely to the application of Christian ethics in social, economic, legal, political, environmental and philosophical terms, both in the design process and in building performance. However, 'potential' is an appropriate word in view of the fragmentary attention to ethical matters, aside from a continual and frequently self-serving debate on professionalism and the contractual obligations and liability of architects to their clients and builders. In the UK, the issues of professional responsibility and ethical concern (see Professional Ethics*) came into sharp focus in 1993, when the Government declared its intention to abolish the legal protection of the description 'architect'. If this change had occurred, then anyone, trained or not, qualified or not, would have been entitled to use this designation. A fierce debate followed on a wide range of themes: professionalism, élitism, the demands of a free market relative to public service, and an ethical concern for public protection. As a direct response to pressure from architects and consumer groups, the Government unexpectedly abandoned the proposal. This result highlighted conflicting ethical issues: 1. it was seen as a victory for the consumers of architecture, who would continue to enjoy protection from charlatan designers; and 2. it was seen as an example of the power of professional self-interest, masquerading as ethical concern for the public good.

Ethical issues

The symptoms of the disregard of ethical issues can be found in the areas of writing, education and the assessment of competitions. 1. Until 1994 at least, no book has been specifically devoted to 'ethics and architecture'. 2. There is a major educational gap, since the subject rarely figures directly in the curriculum of architectural schools, although it is more prominent in planning education. 3. When a major architectural competition is assessed, whilst there is no shortage of comment on technological, stylistic and conceptual issues, it would be an exceedingly rare event for an assessor to comment on relevant ethical dimensions. This omission could include such 'incidentals' as the selection of non-renewable building materials, the social consequences on the population displaced by the proposed new building, or even the likely well-being of the occupants of the proposed entry.

However, despite this apparent neglect, there is no doubt that architectural ethics has been considered by many responsible designers since the mid-19th century, particularly within the arts and crafts movement (see P. Davey, *Arts and Crafts Architecture*). This tradition still continues in the work of certain responsible architects. (See B. Mikellides, *Architecture for People*, and R. Maguire, 'In Defence of Modernism'.) But in the absence of detailed documentation, or effective patterns of accountability of architects to their public, the concern remains fragmentary.

An incentive for a new awareness of the subject has come through the recent barrage of criticism (much of it coming from a broadly ethical position). This has assailed architects from various directions: from the Prince of Wales (1948–), planning officers, unsatisfied occupants of new buildings, and their vocal, unhappy neighbours. Such critics share a conviction that the consumers of architecture and physical planning deserve much better service from the relevant professions (C. Caddy, 'A Christian Planner and Development Control', and P. Dearnley, 'No Mean Cities').

There is one area of planning and architecture where ethical issues have been central: the debate on urban planning and public housing policy. In Europe and N. America, a series of influential studies was produced from the 1960s which challenged many utopian architectural and planning ideologies for the provision of new towns and mass housing with a strong social and ethical critique.

These culminated in the UK in 1985, when Professor Alice Coleman (1923–) of King's College, London, developed a hypothesis, tested through the analysis of 10,000 dwellings, that linked social malaise (expressed in urban vandalism, criminal activity, litter and children in care) to the design and layout of public housing estates (A. Coleman, *Utopia on Trial*). Since the underlying philosophy that influenced planning concepts and the design of high-rise and low-rise dwellings was heavily dependent on the ideas of leading architects and planners of the day, her study was inevitably vigorously opposed by the professional establishment. However, criticism from lay persons, official sources and academic researchers was influential, and it is clear that social concerns are now much higher on the agenda of the design process. The critique may have contributed to the sharp decline in the creation and maintenance of the public housing sector, which has been vigorously opposed in policies of successive Conservative governments with a commitment to the virtues of home ownership and growth in the private sector.

Architecture and Christian ethics

The roots of an understanding of Christian ethics and its relationship to architecture lie deep within three great biblical doctrines.

*1. Creation.** God has created a world of abundant resources for our well-being and aesthetic delight.

In recent years, there has been a renewed concern to promote a 'green architecture' that avoids wasting precious natural resources (see Environment*). Christians believe that God has provided and continues to sustain his creation with adequate provision (land, energy sources, building materials, skills and labour) for all habitation needs. But this abundance does not offer a licence for profligate waste. In practical terms, the desire to apply Christian ethics may need to exercise increasing influence on decisions about the specification of non-renewable materials, on how to avoid wasting land in locating a building on a site, on land-use planning and energy conservation.

As well as conserving and managing God's creation (see Stewardship*), designers will continue to recognize the wonder and diversity of creation as a primary inspiration for fertile design ideas in terms of colour, tone, form, texture, structural strength, *etc.*

The concept that 'Man does not live on bread alone' (Mt. 4:4) is not only a reminder of the spiritual dimensions of life; it can also refer to the realm of aesthetics, beauty and delight, since the giving of pleasure* is an essential part of Christian loving (see ②). Goodness* is concern expressed in action; action without love is morally meaningless, and love without action corresponds to faith* without works (see Good Works*). Christian architects should therefore be even more concerned than any designer coming from a humanist* stance to create wonderful structures that bring joy to their users and viewers, as well as to designer colleagues (G. Carey, 'Finding Security in an Insecure World').

But an important question concerning Christian ethics remains to be resolved in the complex field of beauty and taste. This concerns the 'accessibility' to the untrained eye of the architectural language that is used.

Thus, the doctrine of creation embraces the goodness of a loving God as he gives gifts to men and women, including all creative gifts necessary to design, build and manage the built environment for the good of present and future generations.

*2. The image of God.** The doctrine that humanity is made in the image of God has some important implications for architecture. The design and ambience of buildings need to reflect this truth.

Vital links need to be established between

designers (including the expanding range of professionals involved in the production of buildings), the 'producers' of buildings (including builders and persons with craft skills), and the occupants of buildings. Such relationships need to lead to mutual trust, the sharing and delegation of creative gifts, the development of patterns of accountability, and the detailed participation of users with the producers of their physical environment (R. Macleod, 'Christian Belief and the Built Environment').

There are encouraging signs of a more positive approach towards a socially responsive architecture. For example, the rapid growth in the community-architecture movement in Europe and N. America indicates that many architects (often motivated by a humanist rather than Christian concern) care deeply about the needs of disadvantaged people. They perceive their role to be 'enablers' to their clients, as opposed to assuming a passive acceptance of what they are perceived to need. The biblical understanding of humanity also relates to the demands of such disadvantaged groups, including the physically and mentally handicapped, and their access to appropriate architecture.

Human comfort, safety and health can all be affected for better or worse by building design. Christian designers and planners will need no reminder of this, not just with regard to homes, but also offices, studios and factories. Our Lord's demanding injunction 'Do to others what you would have them do to you' (Mt. 7:12) has its application in such areas.

3. Sin. Architecture does not operate in a spiritual and moral vacuum. It is designed to serve the needs of sinful humanity in a world contaminated by evil.

Powerful people and institutions have always promoted structures (including buildings) which can serve their own sectional interests to the detriment of the needs of other less influential groups. Effective legal action, 'citizen action groups' and mediating structures are thus needed to curb such vested interests, and to ensure that justice is promoted in the planning process in order to make certain that buildings and cities are not manipulated for the satisfaction of private greed as opposed to public good.

In addition, there is a need to design with an awareness of sin (see Sin and Salvation [5]). Much architectural writing glamorizes human behaviour with a heavy dose of utopian optimism. Christian ethics applied to architecture will lead towards practical design measures that may reduce crime and vandalism (O. Newman, *Defensible Space*). Such measures need to be regarded as a realistic rather than a pessimistic response to human needs.

Through considering the implication of basic doctrines, a 'Christian mind' needs to be developed in order to shape architectural and planning values in the time of uncertainty that grips the professions. To fulfil this noble aim, three exacting demands have to be met: 1. to design and build in harmony with the natural and human environment;* 2. when selecting spaces, forms and materials, to regard design as an act of service to others, especially vulnerable groups; and 3. to retain a realistic awareness of evil,* avoiding any utopian tendency to idealize social behaviour.

Ethical dimensions, and more specifically Christian considerations, need to be developed, documented, shared, applied and tested through design and contractual experience. This is needed in order to create a more responsible architecture and well-planned environment that celebrates a Creator God and his created world and brings joy* and satisfies the practical need of all sections of human society.

See also: COMMUNITY ETHICS. [16]

Bibliography

A. Coleman, *Utopia on Trial: Vision and Reality in Planned Housing* (London, 1985); P. Davey, *Arts and Crafts Architecture: The Search for Earthly Paradise* (London, 1980); B. Mikellides (ed.), *Architecture for People: Explorations in a New Humane Environment* (London, 1980), esp. P. Aldington and J. Craig, 'Understanding People and Developing a Brief', pp. 27–33; O. Newman, *Defensible Space* (New York, 1972; London, 1973).

The *Association of Christians in Planning and Architecture Newsletter* is a valuable source of Christian discussion of ethical issues relating to physical planning and architecture. See esp. C. Caddy, 'A Christian Planner and Development Control', *ACPAN* 13/14, 1988/89, pp. 19–31; G. Carey, 'Finding Security in an Insecure World', *ACPAN* 11, 1987, pp. 4–14; P. Dearnley, 'No Mean Cities: A Christian Perspective on Urban Planning and Policy', *ACPAN* 15, 1989, pp. 7–17; R. Macleod, 'Christian Belief and the Built Environment', *ACPAN* 1, 1983, pp. 6–17; *idem*, 'The Idea of a Christian Architecture', *ACPAN*

24, 1993, pp. 11–14; R. Maguire, 'In Defence of Modernism', *ACPAN* 24, 1993, pp. 15–19.

I.R.D.

ARISTOTLE (384–322 BC), the student of Plato,* the tutor of Alexander the Great (356–323 BC) and the founder of the Lyceum. His ethical writings (*Nicomachean Ethics, Eudemian Ethics* and, sometimes attributed to him, *Magna Moralia*) need to be understood against the background of his work in metaphysics, politics, biology and psychology.

Aristotle starts in his ethical writings with the search for the chief human good. He suggests that people agree in calling this 'happiness', but they do not agree on what happiness is. He himself ties happiness to human functioning, saying that the chief good is the activity of the soul which expresses virtue (or excellence in functioning). For Aristotle, the ethical virtues are the virtues* (or excellences) of that part of the human soul which listens to reason although it does not reason itself. They are acquired by habituation of character. They are stable dispositions to feel the appropriate amount of some passion in the appropriate circumstances and to act appropriately (where what is appropriate is decided by practical reason). Each virtue lies in a mean between two vices, one of excess and one of defect.

Practical wisdom is, for Aristotle, an intellectual virtue, or an excellence of the part of the human soul which reasons. It requires the perception of particulars as having or not having value, and links this to the agent's vision of the good, resulting in action.

He concludes that the chief human good is study or contemplation, since this is the most divine kind of life.

See also: HISTORY OF CHRISTIAN ETHICS. [6]

J.E.H.

ARMAMENTS. In a general sense, the term 'armaments' refers to the military and naval equipment and forces of a nation. In a more limited sense, it indicates the weapons with which these forces are supplied, such as guns, planes and missiles. Early armaments made from wood and stone evolved during prehistoric times until the development of bows, arrows, spears and slings. The use of metal during the third millennium BC gave one group technological superiority, thus forcing the disadvantaged to achieve or surpass the technology of the oppressors. This practice has led to a constant development of superior armaments through the ages.

Early Roman craftsmen looking for more plentiful metal produced iron, and by the end of the first millennium AD Chinese and Islamic workers made heat-forged steel. In Western Europe this harder metal made possible the replacement of wooden shields and leather protective garments with armour. As long as weapons were this simple the arguments for a 'just war'* based on a distinction between defensive and offensive weapons were quite persuasive. Using the example of ancient warfare as described in the Bible, the just-war theorists referred to body armour and shields as defensive and the sword and spear as offensive. During the Middle Ages, the use of cavalry led to the heavily armoured horsefighter or knight becoming the supreme offensive weapon, and castles the best means of defence.

In the late medieval period, gunpowder revolutionized warfare. Cannon were decisive in the Hundred Years War and the Italian Wars (1494–1559). By the mid-16th century, in addition to artillery, small arms were widely used. Further developments occurred in the 17th and 18th centuries, but the major change in armaments came with the increased productive capacity of the 19th-century Industrial Revolution.

The ideology for the use of modern armaments came from a Prussian military instructor, Karl von Clausewitz (1780–1831), who devised the concept of 'total war'. To him warfare was to be pushed to the 'utmost bounds' of violence in order to win. His ideas were accepted in most European military academies during the latter part of the 19th century.

The First World War made it possible to test these new weapons. Modern artillery, machine guns, poison gas, tanks, submarines and aerial bombardment gave war* a terrifying three-dimensional character that had never been known before. The invention of new armaments continued after the conflict. It can be argued that the Second World War was actually won by the Allied scientists who were better organized than their Axis counterparts. The British and Americans developed electronic gear such as radar, submarine detection devices and new types of long-range aircraft. However, the Germans and Japanese contributed more efficient torpedoes, submarines, jet planes and rockets to the advancing technology. Further development of armaments was continued during the Cold War, with the result that it became difficult for Christians to support the idea of a 'just war'.

The distinction between offensive and defensive weapons could no longer be maintained when armaments were produced for the express purpose of indiscriminately destroying civilian populations. This became apparent during the Second World War with the escalation of aerial bombardment. When the Nazis bombed innocent civilians, both President Franklin D. Roosevelt (1882–1945) and Prime Minister Winston Churchill (1874–1965) denounced such attacks. Yet by the end of the war, Allied air raids had destroyed 40% of the developed areas of sixty-six Japanese cities. Prior to this they had rained death on dozens of German cities with 'obliteration bombing', culminating in fire storms which turned both Hamburg and Dresden into huge furnaces where hundreds of thousands of innocent people died.

In addition to the horror visited on humankind by these conventional armaments, the war ushered in a new type of weapon, the atomic bomb. This was first used in 1945 on Hiroshima and Nagasaki, and since that time the power of nuclear weaponry has been greatly increased. At the present time, if several hundred nuclear weapons in the range of 100 kilotons were used, they would deplete the ozone layer, spew deadly radiation and cause a nuclear winter. This last phenomenon refers to lofting soot and smoke into the stratosphere and thus blocking the sun's rays so effectively that the average land surface temperature would cool by 10–20°C, causing crop failure and environmental damage in areas far removed from the explosion.

In addition to these nuclear armaments, several nations have developed chemical and biological weapons. The former consists of the deliberate use of chemical substances to kill plants, animals or humans, and the latter biological organisms to produce disease or death. Modern chemical warfare began during the First World War when both sides experimented with agents such as mustard gas and various ways to release these on the enemy. By the conclusion of the conflict, artillery shells filled with gas were being fired on the enemy. The heavy casualties resulting from these convinced military leaders that toxic chemicals were effective in warfare.

Research during the Second World War led to the manufacturing of more lethal nerve agents. The Germans produced these, and when the Soviets seized their war plants they became part of the Communist arsenal. However, no major power used gas in Europe during the war, largely because of the fear of massive retaliation. The development of chemical armaments has continued to the point where the US has vast stocks of toxins, such as VX, which are so lethal that one drop on a person's skin will result in death in less than four minutes. Although the major powers are hesitant to unleash these weapons, States such as Iraq have used them.

By the end of the Second World War, several nations had worked on the technology for large-scale use of biological warfare agents. These include toxins that cause food-poisoning symptoms, anthrax, tularemia, and various fungus agents. In addition, scientists have devised a large number of anti-animal and anti-plant substances that cause foot-and-mouth disease, potato blight, cereal rust, and destruction of other economically important crops. Biological weapons have never been used in any major war, although the Japanese experimented with them in China during the Second World War.

The 'ABC' weapons as they are often termed (atomic or nuclear, biological, and chemical) make the categories of the just war difficult to maintain. It is hard, if not impossible, to rationalize the use of these weapons of mass destruction with a 'just cause', a 'just goal' and respect for non-combatants. Such misgivings have led many to adopt a 'nuclear pacifist' position and to work for agreements among the nations to dismantle this gruesome arsenal of destruction.

Many non-pacifist Christians have come to regard nuclear and biological weapons as intrinsically evil on the ground that their use is utterly indiscriminate. Many also refuse to participate in the manufacture of armaments, because there is no guarantee that they will be used in a just cause. Moreover, there is widespread concern over the huge sums spent on armaments by many countries to the general impoverishment of their populations.

Bibliography

J. Adams, *Engines of War: Merchants of Death and the New Arms Race* (New York, 1990); T. J. Gander, *Nuclear, Biological, and Chemical Warfare* (London and New York, 1987); R. E. Lapp, *The Weapons Culture*

(New York, 1968); W. H. McNeill, *The Pursuit of Power: Technology, Armed Force, and Society Since AD 1000* (Chicago, 1982; Oxford, 1983).

R.G.C.

ART AND THE CHRISTIAN CHURCH. Historically, the role of the Christian church with respect to the arts has oscillated between that of patron and persecutor. Both negative and positive attitudes can be traced back to before the beginnings of the Christian era, in the writings of the OT. The prohibition against the making of graven images as one of the Ten Commandments (Ex. 20:4–5) has been an extremely influential text at particular moments of church history. Other OT books, *e.g.* the Song of Songs, have been equally important in their affirmation of the natural creation and a rich use of verbal images. The NT itself is silent on the specific issue of the visual arts. However, there is a strong 'imaginary' and visionary content in the NT writings themselves, particularly the parables of Jesus, the metaphors of Paul and the book of Revelation. Christian art *per se* began with the use of simple symbols, such as the fish and the cross. The use of symbol has subsequently played a great part in its development.

The first great period of Christian art came about through the use of icons in the Eastern Orthodox and Russian churches. Painted on wood, and adapted from ancient Egyptian funeral rites, icons became a highly sophisticated and precise art-form; they were made originally for public liturgies, but were subsequently also extremely popular as aids to private prayer. However, in the mid-8th century they became the centre of ecclesiastical and political controversy. The fierceness and prolonged length of the controversy bore witness to the ambiguous and ambivalent attitudes towards image-making in the OT and NT. Icons were condemned by some as idols and upheld by others as valuable means of worship. The controversy also points to the way in which early Christian thought concerning the arts had been heavily influenced by the distrust of the material and imaginary in Platonic Gk. thought.

The medieval period saw a flowering of Western Christian art under church patronage. The church was then at the pinnacle of its political power, with the ability to command the services of the greatest artists and craft-workers of the day. Gothic cathedrals such as that of Chartres, frescoed church walls, and intricate, vividly coloured illuminated manuscripts still survive as monuments to the era when virtually all art was religious. During the Renaissance, Christian art still predominated: major works were made on biblical themes. However, there was also a movement towards increased classical, historical and secular subject matter, which eventually gave rise to the modern art movement.

The Protestant Reformation saw a renewal of iconoclastic ideals, with many churches being stripped of perceived idolatrous images; church interiors were drastically simplified and purified. The growth of Protestantism and increased secularization have often combined to divorce church or religious patronage from the arts in the modern era. Modern art itself was conceived as a rejection of 'bourgeois' society and the implicit conservative Christian ideals which were seen to underpin such society. The Protestant tradition has historically incorporated within itself a distrust of artistic images as a part of worship; the Catholic tradition has historically relied on repetitive and stale images which frequently fail to convey the eternal newness and challenge of the Christian message.

There are indications of the beginnings of a rapprochement in the late 20th century between the church and the arts, particularly with the growth of the ecumenical movement. However, this often remains on the level of individual thought and enterprise. It is in no way a coherent movement. There are on the one hand comments and perceptions of individual modern artists who are not strictly affiliated to a particular Christian denomination, concerning the essentially religious or 'spiritual' nature of art. Then there are also secular artists who have used classic Christian themes in their work as a way of addressing the issues of war, violence and suffering in the 20th century. These include well-known artists such as Picasso (1881–1973), Epstein (1880–1959), Otto Lange (1879–1944), Stanley Spencer (1891–1959), Elisabeth Frink (1930–93) and Craigie Aitchison (1926–). There are also artists who incorporate a wider spectrum of Christian belief into their work to give expression to the lordship of Christ in themes of resurrection and renewal. Often a strongly calligraphic element is incorporated. These include artists such as Norman Adams (1927–), Ann Clark, Conwy Evans and John Poole.

Within many churches there has also recently been an increased interest in art as a means of self-expression, which can be used for creative healing and spiritual renewal.

See also: CENSORSHIP.

Bibliography
P. Burmansa and K. Nugent (eds.), *Prophecy and Vision* (Bristol, 1982); T. Talbot-Rice, *Icons* (London, 1990); N. Usherwood (ed.), *The Bible in Twentieth Century Art* (London, 1987).

A.H.A.C.E.

ARTIFICIAL INSEMINATION, see REPRODUCTIVE TECHNOLOGIES.

ARTIFICIAL INTELLIGENCE, see INFORMATION TECHNOLOGY.

ASCETICISM is derived from the Gk. word *askēsis*, which in pre-Christian usage referred to exercise, practice or training for some aspired goal, such as that undertaken by an athlete or soldier.

In the Christian tradition

Early patristic sources use the world with reference to *spiritual* exercise or training to attain Christian perfection. Given the obstacles to reaching this end, asceticism included struggle, self-denial* and renunciations (*e.g.* celibacy and poverty) in order to discipline the senses and free the mind for the contemplation of higher things. It soon came to be associated with the eremitic and monastic* life of withdrawal from a worldly Constantinian church. Some of these ascetics went to extremes (such as the Stylites), buttressed by a dualism* inherited from Gk. and oriental philosophies. Heretical forms of asceticism were also found among Gnostics, Montanists and Manicheans.

Old Testament precursors. For the most part, the Hebrews in the OT did not practise the self-denial and renunciations characteristic of the asceticism described above, perhaps due to their rejection of any dualism* and their reception of God's good creation. They did practise rites of purification and penitential fasting* (*e.g.* Lv. 15:16–18; Jdg. 13:4–5, 7, 14; Dn. 9:3). Abstinence* was practised in later Judaism, particularly among sectarian groups such as the Essenes and in Pharisaic schools.

New Testament asceticism. The NT excludes a legalistic asceticism (Col. 2:16–23; 1 Tim. 4:1–5). Fasting is retained from OT practices, particularly in association with prayer (*e.g.* Lk. 2:37; Acts 13:2). But NT asceticism is characterized as: 1. watchfulness, vigilance and sobriety in the Christian life (*e.g.* Mt. 24:42–44; 1 Thes. 5:5–11; 1 Pet. 1:13–16; 2 Pet. 3:11–12); 2. fulfilment of Christ's call to deny oneself, take up one's cross and follow him (*e.g.* Mt. 16:24–26; 19:16–22); 3. part of the moral struggle by which one gains victory over the 'old self' or the flesh (*i.e. sarx*; not *soma*, the physical body) and walks by the Spirit (Rom. 8:1–17; Gal. 5:16–25; Eph. 4:22–24); and 4. the discipline necessary to bring the body into subjection as an instrument of righteousness (1 Cor. 9:25–27). Success in the disciplined struggle of the Christian life is ensured by God's grace (Rom. 7:24–25).

Medieval ascetical theology. The early church (*e.g.* John Cassian, *c.* 360–435) produced literature that detailed this process of discipline, often using the metaphors of steps on a ladder or stages in a journey. In medieval theology, associated largely with monasticism and mysticism, this culminated in a spirituality* outlining three stages of the ascetic life in the quest for perfection: purgation, illumination and union with God. Ascetic practices were especially pertinent to the first step. This medieval asceticism was developed in connection with a soteriology grounded in a system of penances and works of satisfaction. Some saw asceticism as the way to imitate the poverty and sufferings of Jesus (*e.g.* the Desert Fathers and Francis of Assisi*).

A healthy asceticism

Asceticism must be seen as a response to God's call and therefore to God's offer of enabling grace to live the Christian life. As a step of faith in obedient submission to God's will, Christian asceticism conversely involves a renunciation of the self (see Self-denial*) – the daily exercise of bearing one's cross. This is done in the knowledge that one is sharing in the life of 'the author and perfecter of our faith' (Heb. 12:2; Mk. 8:34). And it is done in hope. As mentioned, the ascetic life is one of watchfulness and vigilance for Christ's coming. Thus, this life is one of pilgrimage, open to the future, not attached to human conceptions of what fulfils us.

A healthy asceticism must be seen as part of

the process of salvation, specifically sanctification,* in which one engages in the struggle of overcoming the self-centred desire to possess and to be in control – a discipline that leads in the end to true freedom (Rom. 8:19–23; 1 Cor. 7:29–31) and which will result in the edification of the church and loving service to God and neighbour (Phil. 2:1–13).

Such a chastened asceticism will avoid the un-Christian dualistic hierarchies of soul over body and of will over emotions, as well as sinful pride and austere otherworldliness. Instead, a holistic emphasis will see that ascetic practices help one in the struggle to achieve mastery over natural powers and processes, habituating one's nature to do God's will, and opening up clogged channels in one's life through which God's grace can be experienced. In this way, like the athlete who practises for the main event, one trains to overcome sin and perform good works.

The modern era. The Protestant Reformers criticized the double standards of contemporary Catholic ascetic practices whereby more was demanded of the religious (monks and nuns) than either the secular clergy (priests) or lay people. They also saw many ascetic practices as reinforcing the idea of salvation through meritorious works.

The Reformation took asceticism in several directions, including Lutheran pietism (*e.g.* Philipp Jakob Spener, 1635–1705), Calvinist Puritanism (*e.g.* John Owen, 1616–83), Anabaptist community discipline and primitive purity (*e.g.* Menno Simons*), and Catholic severity (*e.g.* Ignatius of Loyola*). Today it is difficult to find agreement on a definition of asceticism.

Contemporary misgivings

Actually, asceticism is not valued highly by most contemporary people. There may be good reasons for this. As mentioned above, asceticism has often been associated with a dualism that disparages the body in relation to the soul. Also, at times it has disguised misgivings about the affective dimension of life, training the will to achieve a dispassionate repose.

This contemporary evaluation is welcomed and may actually lead us to a healthy asceticism in keeping with emphases we have noted in the NT. Modern psychology, for instance, has uncovered pathological aspects of asceticism, such as masochism, unhealthy repressions and unconscious defence mechanisms.* But to deal with gluttony or sloth simply

through psychotherapy to the exclusion of ascetic practices may be a modern pretension. A healthy asceticism will take into account the observations of modern psychology and strive to be faithful to categories of Christian theology.

Bibliography

L. Bouyer, *Introduction to Spirituality* (ET, New York, 1961); O. Chadwick, *Western Asceticism* (London and Philadelphia, 1958); R. Foster, *Celebration of Discipline* (San Francisco, ²1988; London, ²1989); K. E. Kirk, *The Vision of God* (London and New York, 1931; repr. New York, 1966); R. Williams, *Christian Sprirituality* (Atlanta, 1979) = *The Wound of Knowledge* (London, 1979); D. Willard, *The Spirit of the Disciplines* (San Francisco, 1988).

D.L.O.

ASSERTIVENESS TRAINING, see CHARACTER. ⑩

ATONEMENT. First appearing in the 16th century as two words, 'at onement', this term signifies a making of amends and rendering of satisfaction for wrong done that brings an end to alienation and restores good relations. Through being used in AV for 'reconciliation' (*katallagē*) in Rom. 5:11 and for the regular covering of Israel's sin by the shedding of sacrificial blood (Lv. 16; 17:11; 23:27), the word came to connote comprehensively the death of Christ in its many-sided saving significance. Languages other than Eng. have no single word that covers so much.

In the New Testament

Atonement in this broad sense is the main theme of the entire NT. Salvation (see Sin and Salvation ⑤) is often said to be the NT's main theme, and is itself a large reality, embracing rescue from the jeopardy of guilt* for the past, and of enslavement to sin and death* in the present, and from hell (see Heaven and Hell*) to come; but *all* of salvation rests on and flows from Christ's atoning death. His cross* – *i.e.* his shameful and scandalous judicial execution – is the climactic centrepiece of each of the four Gospels; and as a sacrifice for sin, the cross is set forth as the object of faith, the focus of worship, the basis for living the saved life, and the reality signified by both sacraments, throughout the apostolic writings. Christ's resurrection,* we are told, demonstrated the efficacy of his death as an atonement for sin (1 Cor. 15:3, 17), and his present kingdom (see Kingdom of God*) was entered via, and on the basis of, this atoning death (Mt. 1:21; 20:28; 28:18; Phil. 2:5–11; Heb. 1:3; 2:9; 10:19–22; 12:3; Rev. 1:5b; 5:6–14). Biblical Christianity is cross-centred and atonement-oriented throughout. Life in Christ risen is life through Christ crucified; every aspect of the relationship of Christians with God is ultimately determined by the atonement.

Scripture depicts all human beings as needing to atone for their sins but lacking power and resources for doing so. No acceptance by, or fellowship with, the holy creator, who hates and punishes sin (Ps. 5:4–6; Hab. 1:13; Rom. 2:5–9), is possible without atonement, and we who need it cannot make it, since sin spoils everything we do. Paul in particular makes way for his proclamation of atonement in Rom. 3:21–26 by explaining at length that all humans live under the power of sin (Rom. 3:9) and so are guilty before God, with nothing but 'wrath and anger . . . trouble and distress' to look forward to (Rom. 2:8–9; see 1:18 – 3:20; Eph. 2:1–3). But against this background of human hopelessness, the gospel declares that out of love, grace,* mercy, pity, kindness and compassion, God, the offended creator, has provided the atonement that human sin made necessary. The cost of so doing was great: he 'did not spare his own Son, but gave him up for us all' (Rom. 8:32); 'God demonstrates his own love for us in this: While we were still sinners, Christ died for us' (Rom. 5:8; cf. Jn. 3:16; 2 Cor. 8:9; 1 Jn. 4:9–10). This amazing grace is the focal centre of all NT faith, hope, ethics, spiritual life, doxology and devotion.

God established in Israel as part of his covenant* a sacrificial system whereby the blood of unflawed animals was regularly shed and offered to God to make atonement (Lv. 17:11). These sacrifices set a pattern that would be fulfilled in the one all-sufficient sacrifice of Jesus Christ, the sinless Son of God, who was both high priest and victim in this atoning transaction (Heb. 9:11 – 10:14). Though sins were indeed 'left . . . unpunished' (Rom. 3:25) when the prescribed OT sacrifices were faithfully offered, it was not the animals' blood, but Christ's, that atoned for them. His death was for all the sins that were remitted before the event, as well as for sins committed after it (Rom. 3:25–26; 4:3–8; Heb. 9:11–15). Most NT references to the *blood* of

Christ are theological affirmations fitting into this frame of salvation through sacrifice.

In the NT Paul is the master theologian of atonement, welding into a single scheme all the insights into the cross that are developed separately by other writers such as Peter and John and the author of the letter to the Hebrews. Paul explains Christ's achievement in a series of linked categories. As a perfect *sacrifice* for sin (Rom. 8:3; Eph. 5:2), his death secured *redemption, i.e.* rescue by ransom, liberation of captives from helpless enslavement through payment of a price (Rom. 3:24; Gal. 4:4–5; Col. 1:14). This redemption was God's act of *reconciling* sinful humans to himself (2 Cor. 5:18–19), overcoming the hostility to us that our sins had provoked (Rom. 5:10; Col. 1:20–22). Thus the death of Christ *propitiated* God, *i.e.* quenched his judicial anger against sinners by expiating the sins that caused it (Rom. 3:25; *cf.* Heb. 2:17; 1 Jn. 2:2; 4:10). Christ's cross had this effect because Christ himself, as the 'second man' and 'last Adam' (1 Cor. 15:47, 45), *represented* sinners, taking their place under divine judgment ('the curse of the law', Gal. 3:13) and enduring the retribution due to them, so that he truly died as our *substitute,* with the damning record of our transgressions nailed to his cross as the God-appointed reason for his death (Col. 2:14; alluding to the written statement of the crime or crimes that was always attached to a felon's cross, see Mk. 15:26). Hereby, in a way that sounds paradoxical, he not only broke the power of satanic hosts that had assaulted him, evidently seeking to disrupt his obedience in accepting the predestined agony, but actually made it apparent that their power was gone (Col. 2:15).

Benefits

Paul sees three benefits flowing from Christ's death to believers, who are united to Christ risen by faith from the human side and by the Holy Spirit from the divine side.

1. Through their faith, believers receive reconciliation and the gift of righteousness (Rom. 5:11, 17), and thus they are *justified – i.e.* pardoned for the past, accepted in the present, and instated for the future (see Justification, Doctrine of*). The thought here is of the final verdict at the last judgment being pronounced now, and of the judge declaring that their sin is no longer counted against them, so that in and through Christ they have now become 'the righteousness of God' (2 Cor.

5:18–21; *i.e.* right with God relationally: the unexpected use of the abstract noun 'righteousness', like 'enmity' in Rom 8:7, AV, is an idiom of intensity). With this gift of justification comes the further gift of adoption: justified sinners are now children in God's family, sealed as his by the indwelling Holy Spirit* who prompts them henceforth to call on their creator as their Father (Rom. 8:15; Gal. 4:4–6). Thus their personal relationship with God is restored and renewed.

2. In receiving justification through their faith, believers are themselves received into the reality of *God's covenant commitment* to Abraham and his seed (Gal. 3:6–29). They are now 'all one [Gk., 'one man', the new humanity] in Christ Jesus', and as such 'the Israel of God' (Gal. 3:28; 6:16), the community that from God's standpoint is at the centre of this world's history as well as being the corporate inheritor of the world to come. Thus their communal identity is established.

3. Believers live henceforth in *liberty*, freed and indeed debarred from legalism* in all its forms, and so no longer exposed to the inward bondages of pride* or despair that legalism begets (Gal. 5:1). Our inbred legalistic mentality constantly prompts the feeling that for a good, or a better, relationship with God we must do more, sweat more, and merit more, and teaching on discipleship in the churches is often legalistically skewed as a result, as was already happening in the 'Christ-plus' legalisms of Galatia (Gal. 3:1–5; 4:8–11; 5:2–6; 6:12–16) and Colosse (Col. 2:16–23). But Christ's death fully secured the present and future salvation that is ours in him, and our only task now is to receive and keep receiving this inexpressibly wonderful gift – which is Christian liberty in full childlike expression, and is truly a life's task, and is actually what each discipline of the Christian life is about. Thus the authentic Christian temper is fostered and internalized.

Theories of the atonement

What are called 'theories' of the atonement are so many attempts by thinkers who already know something of trust, love, adoration and gratitude Godward through Jesus Christ to reason back from the benefits they see reaching them to a coherent rationale of how these benefits became available. Different theories highlight different elements in the complex weave of biblical analogy and affirmation about the atonement. Thus, patristic writers, viewing salvation as primarily deliverance from the devil and death, celebrated the cross as Christ overcoming these powers on our behalf. Anselm,* focusing on absolution, and Martin Luther,* appreciating justification, saw the cross as satisfaction to the world's offended Lord and judge, Anselm rating it as a compensatory sacrifice and Luther as a substitutionary bearing of the judicial retribution due to us. Hastings Rashdall (1858–1924), following Abelard* and various liberals, saw the cross as meant simply to make us forgivable through melting our rebel hearts by showing us God's love for us. Other theories have other emphases, and each has some truth in it. The Bible will not, however, permit elimination of the objectivity of God's judicial wrath against sin, wrath that only the cross could quench.

The Christian life

The atonement has regulative significance for the whole of the Christian's life with God. It is striking to see how many moral and pastoral problems the NT writers resolve by invoking it in one or another or both of its two aspects, as a marvellous achieving of peace with God on humankind's behalf and thus as a marvellous expression of love for sinful humans on the part of the Father and the Son. The death of Christ, we are told, deals with the problem of our guilt in both its objective and its subjective dimensions (objective: propitiation through Jesus' blood leads to just, *i.e.* justified, justification, Rom. 3:23–26; subjective: Christ's blood cleanses consciences* that knew themselves defiled and deathbound through moral failure, Heb. 9:14). The atonement deals too with the problem of hopelessness, unveiling and guaranteeing a sure hope of glory (Rom. 5:1–11; Eph. 2:11–22; Col. 1:19–27). As 'the measure and the pledge of love' (Thomas Kelly, 1769–1854), Christ's cross dispels doubts as to whether our creator is really concerned about us (Jn. 3:16; Rom. 5:8), and counters fear of loss in God's service by assuring believers that every other good gift that God can devise will be given them too, however much the world may take from them in the short term (Rom. 8:32).

Alongside these assurances, the atonement provides motivating restraint and constraint (1 Cor. 6:20; 2 Cor. 5:14), plus a standard of active, self-denying goodwill and humility by which believers must henceforth live (Eph. 5:1–2; Phil. 2:3–8; 1 Jn. 3:16). It models for them quiet acceptance of human hostility and life's rough treatment (Heb. 12:1–14; 1 Pet. 2:21–22), and enforces the forgiving spirit that Jesus taught was so important (Mt. 6:14–15; 18:21–35; Lk. 17:3–4, *cf.* 23:34; Eph. 4:31 – 5:2).

Finally, by terminating 'the curse of the law' (Gal. 3:13) for believers and opening to them the door into adoption and heirship in the Father's family (Gal. 4:4–5), the atonement solves in advance the very modern problems of stubborn self-hatred and low self-image (see Self-esteem*). If God has accepted us, we must not decline to accept ourselves, and if he has raised us up by adoption to be joint-heirs of his glory with Christ (Rom. 8:17), we must not put ourselves down and cast ourselves for losers, but must learn instead to walk tall, as infinitely privileged royal children.

As determining the mind-set, character and conduct of the Christian, as the foundation for the fellowship of the new multi-racial reality called the church (Eph. 2:14–22), and as the centrepiece in the grateful praise of God in both earth and heaven (Rev. 5:9–14), the praise that goes on for ever, the atonement is truly the focal point of the NT and the fulcrum of Christianity.

Bibliography

G. C. Berkouwer, *The Work of Christ* (Grand Rapids, 1965); S. Clark, *Redeemer* (Ann Arbor, MI, 1992); J. Denney, *The Death of Christ* (London, 1902; ed. R. V. G. Tasker, London, 1951); F. W. Dillistone, *The Christian Understanding of Atonement* (London and Philadelphia, 1968); R. S. Franks, *The Work of Christ* (London, 1962); L. W. Grensted, *A Short History of the Doctrine of Atonement* (Manchester, 1920); A. A. Hodge, *The Atonement* (New York, 1867); L. Morris, *The Apostolic Preaching of the Cross* (London, ³1965); *idem*, *The Atonement* (Leicester and Downers Grove, IL, 1983); *idem*, The Cross in the New Testament (Exeter and Grand Rapids, 1965); J. R. W. Stott, *The Cross of Christ* (Leicester and Downers Grove, IL, 1986); V. Taylor, *The Atonement in New Testament Teaching* (London, 1940); *idem*, *Forgiveness and Reconciliation* (London, 1946); R. S. Wallace, *The Atoning Death of Christ* (London and Westchester, IL, 1981); B. B. Warfield, *The Person and Work of Christ* (Phillipsburg, NJ, 1950).

J.I.P.

AUGUSTINE (354–430), the greatest of the Latin Fathers of the church. The story of Augustine's early life and conversion as told in his *Confessions*, his work as a bishop in N. Africa, and his many philosophical, theological and pastoral writings contributed to his vast influence on the Western church.

Born in N. Africa, Augustine received the usual schooling of his time, an education that focused narrowly on a few pagan classics. Through reading Cicero (106–43 BC) he acquired a desire for wisdom. The influence of his Christian mother Monica led him to seek his wisdom where the name of Christ was found. He read the Bible but found it lacking both in style and content – style because of its bad Latin, and content because of the morality of the patriarchs. Rejecting the church's understanding of Scripture, he became a Manichee, and remained a follower of his heresy for more than a decade.

After Faustus, a Manichaean leader, was unable to resolve the inconsistencies in Mani's (*c.* 216–76 AD) science, Augustine began to lose faith in his view. He had also found that the Manichaean ritual did not make him a better person. After moving to Rome and then Milan, Augustine discovered through the preaching of Ambrose* that Christians did not hold the simplistic view of God that he had been attributing to them, and that the offensive OT stories could be interpreted spiritually.

In the summer of 386 Augustine became a Christian. He gave up his teaching position, retired to the country with friends, and returned to Milan at Easter to be baptized. A year later he returned to Africa, planning to live a contemplative life with friends. However, in the spring of 391, while visiting in Hippo, he was forced by the congregation to be their priest, and in 395 he succeeded Bishop Valerius (d. 396). There, in the second largest city in Africa, Augustine worked tirelessly, becoming the most prominent bishop in the African church. Through his writings his influence rapidly extended to the far reaches of the Roman world.

The major themes in Augustine's theology arise out of his life. After the Manichees' claims on behalf of reason failed him, Augustine insisted that one must first believe and then seek to understand. All of his major works are efforts to articulate this understanding of faith. God is truth, and happiness is found in loving him. Such love is a gift of God. Through divine illumination – a teaching which reflects the influence of the Platonists – our minds are able to share in divine truth. Similarly, through the conscience we are aware of the moral law, which flows from the eternal law of God. Our will must be set right so that we can do the right. Prudence, justice, fortitude and temperance are present in God and establish a similar order in our souls.

God created Adam and Eve good, but through disobedience, they fell. The consequences of the Fall* extend to all humankind in the form of original sin.* Before the Fall, humans possessed all that was necessary to be good, but afterwards sin manifests itself primarily in ignorance and concupiscence. Not only is reason blinded by its ignorance, but human beings are dominated by their appetites. As love of God grows, the hold of concupiscence* or lust* is lessened, but complete freedom from it will be gained only in the future life.

Christians now must live in a world that, though disordered, still retains much that is good. Human nature retains the capacity for friendship,* a great natural good. The first natural social tie is that of man and wife. Although the woman was taken from the man, so indicating the priority of the man, still they are to walk together, partners in a friendly union. Three goods come from marriage:* children, fidelity and sacrament. With 'children' Augustine has in mind also nurture and education. 'Fidelity' refers to the right each spouse has to the other's body. 'Sacrament' refers, for Christians, to the indissolubility of marriage, as Christ is faithful to the church. Following Paul, Augustine holds that continence is best. Marital fidelity is good in that it brings concupiscence under control. To have children is a great good and so intercourse for the purpose of generation is without fault. Sex 'for the purpose of satisfying concupiscence' is a venial sin, but sex outside of marriage – fornication* or adultery* – is a mortal sin. This view of the place of sex dominated the West until Thomas Aquinas.*

After the sack of Rome in 410, its fall was blamed on the Christians. In *City of God* (413–26) Augustine responds to these charges, arguing that it is not Christian virtues which caused the ruin of the empire, but rather the vices of the pagans. In the last half of this work, Augustine sketches the origin, development and ends of two cities, the heavenly and the earthly city. The two cities are two societies which are inextricably intermingled, but which are distinguished by their love. The members of the earthly city have the goods of this life as their goal, as things to be enjoyed; but for the members of the heavenly city, the city of God, these same goods are merely to be used to reach the true end. Any conflicts that arise between the two cities stem from their different attitudes towards the same things.

The earthly city is not to be identified with the State,* for the members of the city of God are also citizens of the State; nor is the church composed only of citizens of the heavenly kingdom. As long as society is just, members of the city of God will respect this order and do their part to maintain it. However, when the earthly city fails to observe civil laws, then members of the city of God are to correct what they can, and endure what they cannot change.

Christians are not a threat to civil society, therefore, but will do their part to uphold the laws. All nations desire peace, and a society may even go to war to secure peace (see Just War*). Peace in society is 'the ordered harmony of authority and obedience between citizens'. The highest peace is that of the heavenly city where is found the 'harmonious communion of those who find their joy in God'.

See also: HISTORY OF CHRISTIAN ETHICS. 6

Bibliography

Confessions (ET, Harmondsworth, 1961); *The Writings of Saint Augustine*, 14 vols. (New York, 1948–52).

P. Brown, *Augustine of Hippo* (London and Los Angeles, CA, 1967); E. Gilson, *The Christian Philosophy of St Augustine* (ET, New York, 1960; London, 1961); F. Van der Meer, *Augustine the Bishop* (New York, 1961).

A.G.V.

AURICULAR CONFESSION, see CONFESSION.

AUTHORITY. Much moral thinking in the modern era has been fundamentally hostile to the notion of authority and the correlative notion of obedience.* The 17th century witnessed the culmination of a profound mutation in Western culture, in which authorities such as Scripture, church tradition or inherited social custom ceased to function effectively as a sufficient ground for knowledge or action. Truth or rightness, that is, could no longer be established by arguing *from* authorities; rather, claims to authority are themselves subject to critical appraisal, so that authority comes to be the *conclusion*, rather than the premise, of argument. This rejection of appeal to authority as a vehicle of rational persuasion is bound up with a certain understanding of the human self as fundamentally autonomous. The self, that is, is authentic or rational only in so far as it is unencumbered by prejudices derived from religious tradition or social convention. Rational selfhood consists therefore in the exercise of judgment. In the moral sphere, this means that authority may not be appealed to as a basis for action; authority has rather to be validated by a judgment of rightness on the part of one to whom an appeal for obedience is made. To be a free moral agent (see Moral Agency*) is thus to act in accordance with norms which are contingent upon my 'authorization' (even my creation).

This profound suspicion of authority is deeply embedded in Western moral thought, as well as in political and legal practice. Its persuasiveness depends upon the extraordinary success of its exposure of the pathological or oppressive character of many conceptions of authority and their social embodiment. Christian moral theology (see Christian Moral Reasoning[18]) has developed at least two strategies in response.

1. One strategy has been the deployment of a range of arguments to accommodate Christian understandings of moral authority to the climate of modernity. Thus, for example, the liberal Christian tradition has in many respects maintained a critical stance towards such norms of Christian moral discourse as the Bible and the Christian tradition, suggesting that they can no longer be considered as axiomatically authoritative since they are themselves subject to criteria of evaluation such as human experience or developing moral consciousness. Or again, the notion of the autonomy of the moral self has found a place in modern Christian thought, most frequently through the association of a (philosophical and political) notion of undetermined moral freedom with a (theological) notion of conscience* – though conscience no longer 'informed' by the Bible and Christian tradition. It is noteworthy that Christian moral thinking of this variety is largely indistinguishable from its non-Christian counterparts, since it shares common assumptions about the nature of moral actions and moral agents.

2. A quite contrary theological response to modernity's critique of authority has been to propose that both the nature of authority and the proper exercise of authority are defined by reference to the gospel of Jesus Christ. The task of a Christian account of authority is thus primarily one of describing the contours of Christian conviction, rooted in revelation* and testified to in the corporate life of the Christian community. Such an approach can acknowledge the justice of much of the critique raised by modernity, whilst proposing that Christian moral theory (if not Christian practice) is exempt from critique to the degree to which Christians have been faithful to the logic of the gospel.

Such a theology of authority would exhibit a number of distinct characteristics. a. Rather than analysing all authority in terms of the dynamic of arbitrary or irrational force, Christian theology could propose a view of authority as the givenness of a certain order within reality. Such an ordered structure within the creation is authoritative in that it elicits and sets limits to appropriate responsive human action. Authority is thereby conceived, not as a restriction of human autonomy* but as the formation of the moral self in response to a given context for moral growth. b. Accordingly, authority is essentially a moral concept in that it addresses itself to free, personal agents. On this account, to be 'under' authority is not to be subject to domination by an alien will, but to be required to become a responsive agent. Authority invites assent and decision, not simple compliance to superior power. For Christian anthropology, to be a full human person is to enter into the liberty of the children of God. But such liberty is God's gift, not the fruit of self-assertion over against external constraints. Thus, for Christian theology, obedience to authority is more a matter of glad acknowledgment of the possibilities and limits set by a person's status as a contingent creature than it is a matter of submission to threats or suppression of criticism. c. The authority of persons and social institutions is in important respects a function of the professed vision and goals of the community. Authority, again, is not arbitrary or abstract, but a means of promoting patterns of action which express and further the community's ends. In this way, authorities serve the community by inviting it to adhere to its fundamental commitments; they are, therefore, not to be isolated from the process of the reception of their claim by the community as a whole. d. Authority must consequently be exercised in accordance with the professed goals of the community. For

Christian moral theology, this will mean that the manner of the exercise of authority will always be subject to criticism by the model of Jesus Christ, the servant Lord. e. Finally, human and creaturely authority is subservient to the authority of God declared in the gospel of Jesus Christ. Human authority is never final, always relative. Its significance consists in its fragmentary mediation of or witness to divine authority. In Christian moral theology this is a principle of criticism by which contingent, creaturely authorities are subject to the final authority of the risen and ascended Jesus Christ, 'the Head over every power and authority' (Col. 2:10) in whom God's authority is definitively embodied and exercised.

See also: COMMUNITY ETHICS. 16

Bibliography
P. T. Forsyth, *The Principle of Authority* (London, 1952); N. Lash, *Voices of Authority* (London, 1976); O. O'Donovan, *Resurrection and Moral Order* (Leicester and Grand Rapids, ²1994, chs. 6 and 7; J. Stout, *The Flight from Authority* (Notre Dame, IN, 1981); J. M. Todd (ed.), *Problems of Authority* (London, 1952).

J.B.W.

AUTOCRACY means unrestrained and arbitrary rule by one person. Executive power is thus entirely concentrated in the autocrat, who is not subject to any constitutional or legal constraint. Autocracy may be thought of as the opposite of democracy* because of the absence of limitations on the power of the ruler, the lack of any forms of accountability,* and the requirement that the people merely submit to the ruler.

The term 'autocrat' is a strong one. Few genuine autocrats have existed, though the Russian Tsars may be cited as examples, as may some modern military rulers. Totalitarianism is a form of autocracy where an attempt is made to legitimize rule through the use of ideology. Traditionally autocrats maintained their rule by keeping people in ignorance and fear.

The word 'autocrat' is used loosely to describe someone who wields power within an organization but who flouts rules and procedures and refuses to acknowledge accountability. Those who behave like this in, *e.g.* schools, churches, trade unions or companies may be said to be undermining the values on which a democratic way of life is based, and by so doing are failing to recognize the intrinsic worth and dignity of every person. Thus it may be said that in contrast to autocrats strong leaders develop genuine authority* through their willingness to accept procedures ensuring accountability, because by this means the reasons for their decisions become better understood and support is thereby generated for their leadership.*

Bibliography
C. J. Friedrich and Z. K. Brezinksi, *Totalitarianism, Dictatorship and Autocracy* (New York, 1956).

D.R.S.

AUTONOMY refers to the free, sovereign exercise of an individual's rational will choosing self-determined, self-regulated moral rules. These should be universalizable as a check against self-centred judgments.

In medicine, there has been a shift from medical paternalism to patient autonomy. Autonomy depends on the free, unforced volition of the individual. It implies that the individual is able to understand not only what is happening, but the likely outcomes of the decision and the refusal to decide. This is part of an existentialist view that individuals are free to do whatever they want with their own bodies.

However, universalizability means that almost anything and everything could be universalized and offers no specifically moral content. The existential stress exaggerates freedom of choice and ignores the dependency of the will on reason and emotion, and of the individual on community. It also exaggerates our capacity to grasp what is involved, for example, in our medical care, when we may be in pain and unable to understand what is involved in treatment outcomes.

In reality, autonomy is always limited in a society. People are not free to do whatever they want with their own bodies, as legislation on seat belts, motor-cyclist helmets, prostitution, surrogacy and pornography indicates. Autonomy is limited, where the best interests of another are at stake. This may be part of the proper exercise of a professional responsibility.

Human freedom is always limited as we are responsible to the God, who created, redeemed, and has an eternal purpose for us.

Bibliography
R. S. Downie and E. Telfer, *Respect for Per-*

sons (London, 1969); S. Hampshire, *Freedom of the Individual* (London, 1965); I. Kant, *Fundamental Principles of the Metaphysics of Morals* (ET, New York, 1949).

E.D.C.

AXIOLOGY is the theory of values, or things which are worthwhile in themselves. Strictly speaking, 'axiology' is a wider term than 'ethics', as something may be valuable even when it is outside our power to bring it about; but axiology also forms a part of teleological* ethics, as the end to be pursued is presumably seen as worthwhile in itself.

Axiological ethics can be traced back to Plato,* but is especially associated with a series of thinkers beginning with the Austrian Franz Brentano (1838–1917). Brentano held that the mind, besides being conscious and forming beliefs, valued things as good or bad, and when it did so its valuations might have an intrinsic rightness we could not ignore. His fellow-Austrian Alexius Meinong (1853–1920) added that valuation must consider a thing as a contribution to reality as a whole, and distinguished between two kinds of valuation: desiring a thing and delighting in it.

In Britain, the philosopher G. E. Moore (1873–1958) and the theologian Hastings Rashdall (1858–1924) developed a theory of 'ideal utilitarianism' (Rashdall's term) which entailed axiology. According to this view one's duty is to act so as to produce the greatest good one can (see Consequentialism*). Moore claimed that 'goodness' was so basic a notion as to be indefinable, and that it inhered in many different states of affairs; hence it was necessary to evaluate the goodness in these to determine the best course of action. According to Moore, a state of affairs might be good even if no-one were aware of its existence; in this he differed from Rashdall, who thought only states of consciousness could be good (or bad) in themselves. Virtuous states of consciousness were, he held, the highest form of good; then, what might be called cultured states; and lastly, pleasurable states: but all three were necessary for the human or social ideal. For Rashdall (not for Moore) this ideal was part of God's purpose for the universe, and love for God and love for others combine, meeting above all in the love of Christ.

The last major figure in axiology was the German Nicolai Hartmann (1882–1950). Our feelings of approval or disapproval (which may be of things wholly beyond our power to af-fect) reveal the intrinsic nature, the value, of that of which they approve or disapprove. There are many kinds of value and disvalue, which Hartmann discussed at some length. Some are higher than others – we feel a greater deference towards them; but the absence of a lower one has a greater disvalue than that of a higher. (Thus appreciation of art* is nobler than freedom from pain;* but lack of appreciation is a less serious disvalue than the presence of pain.) Values* by their nature demand realization; hence the sense of duty* or obligation.*

Axiology lost much of its popularity during the 1930s. Its appeal to feelings opened the way to theories which saw ethics as entirely subjective and denied the real existence of any values except those we create for ourselves, though a theistically-grounded axiology might be better protected against this defect than others.

Bibliography

F. Brentano, *The Origin of our Knowledge of Right and Wrong* (ET, London and New York, 1969); *idem, The Foundation and Construction of Ethics* (ET, London and New York, 1973); J. N. Findlay, *Axiological Ethics* (London, 1970), also published in W. D. Hudson (ed.), *New Studies in Ethics,* vol. 2 (London, 1974); *idem, Values and Intentions* (London, 1961); N. Hartmann, *Ethics* (ET, London, 1932); G. E. Moore, *Principia Ethica* (Cambridge, 1903); H. H. Rashdall, *The Theory of Good and Evil* (Oxford, 1907).

R.L.S.

AXIOM. In logic and mathematics, an axiom is a basic principle which is not argued for, like Euclid's (*c.* 300 BC) 'Things equal to the same thing are equal to each other'; similarly, in ethics, it is an unargued principle of action. A 'middle axiom' is an ethical principle which is obvious in itself but can also be derived from one more fundamental (which may on occasion override it); thus the commandment 'Thou shalt not kill' needs no argument to prove it, and can be used as the basis for more detailed guidance in personal life or social policies, but still derives from the more fundamental commandment to love one's neighbour as oneself. The term has been criticized on the grounds that an axiom should be basic, not 'middle'; but even principles derivable from others can be described as axioms if they are treated in practice as basic.

R.L.S.

AYER, A. J. (1910–90). Sir Alfred Jules Ayer, professor at the University of London from 1946 to 1959 and Wykeham Professor of Logic at the University of Oxford from 1959 to 1978, was the leading figure of the 20th-century British philosophical movement of logical positivism.* His most influential work is *Language, Truth and Logic* (London, 1936). Ayer attempts to bring the insights of the logical theories of Bertrand Russell (1872–1970) and Ludwig Wittgenstein* to bear upon the empirical philosophical tradition of David Hume.*

Ayer's most important doctrine is his principle of verification. According to this, a statement is meaningful only if tautological or capable of being empirically verified. Tautological statements, *e.g.* 'All bachelors are unmarried', provide no information about the world, but only information about the meanings of the terms of the statement. Statements are capable of empirical verification only if they can be confirmed by sense-perception. Thus, 'Few Scots are bigamists' is meaningful because the number of Scottish bigamists can be determined by observation.

The implications of the verification principle for theology and ethics are startling. Theological statements such as 'God exists' and moral judgments such as 'Euthanasia is wrong' are literally meaningless when the verification principle is applied to them. This is not to say they are unimportant, only that they should be considered merely the subjective verbal expressions of individual feeling or commitment.

Few philosophers today identify themselves as logical positivists; indeed Ayer's own views were modified in his revised edition of *Language, Truth and Logic* (London, ²1946). The challenge to identify a principle of verification which is itself meaningful has proved more difficult than Ayer and his followers expected.

T.D.K.

B

BANKING has become a highly complex industry, comprising large and small, generalist and specialist, international and domestic institutions. For the purpose of this article, banking will be regarded as essentially a service industry receiving deposits from the public, and utilizing these deposits by lending or by other forms of facility, in order to add value to the life of the communities within which the operations take place. This broad definition will embrace advisory services, which complement the basic business of providing a safe home for the customer's money and lending it productively.

The ethics of banking

Banking is an ethical activity provided it issues in value added for the benefit of the community. The essential element of value added is in the management and transformation of *risk*. Typical customers leave their money with the bank at interest because they want it kept safely. Probably their funds are not large enough to sustain a risky enterprise; probably they themselves lack the skill or courage to undertake such enterprise. They know that the bank has this skill, and that it can combine their funds with others to 'spread' the risk and (in common with insurance* and equity investment*) enable activities to take place which otherwise would not be possible.

Borrowers take out loans on terms and conditions agreed in advance (unauthorized overdrafts are another matter!). Provided the terms are adhered to, borrowers can undertake their enterprises without being at the mercy of arbitrary or distress claims for repayment, to which they might otherwise be vulnerable if the money were borrowed from an individual.

This activity of taking and lending money is a legitimate one under the divine command to develop and improve the creation in harmony with the divine purposes for it (see Gn. 1:28 and 2:15).

The banking industry shares with the corporate sector generally a set of obligations* which stem from its relationships, both with its customers (*i.e.* borrowers, lenders and recipients of advice) and also with its employees, shareholders, and the community as a whole. These relationships require integrity of dealing, transparency (*i.e.* renouncing obscurity in contractual agreements), and adherence to the law in both letter and spirit. Such obligations are not merely those of the individuals employed by the bank, but apply to the corporate entity itself by reason of its existence as a legal 'person' under the provisions of the law.

In the UK in 1990 and 1991, codes of conduct were prepared by the major banks in consultation with consumer representatives, in order to give more detailed expression to these obligations as far as customers are concerned. A revised Code of Banking Practice, according to which banks are required to pre-notify customers of interest and debit charges, came into effect in March 1994.

Company ethics, in historical terms, is a topic no more than 150 years old, although corporate ethics in a broader sense is familiar from Scripture. The 19th century saw the introduction of the joint stock company, which enabled people to group together to undertake an enterprise with limited liability: in other words, only their subscribed capital was at stake, and no further financial obligation rested upon them as shareholders if the enterprise failed. The morality of this was much discussed at the time (see J. W. Gilbart, 'The Moral and Religious Duties of Public Companies', 1856) and is under review again today. J. W. Gilbart in particular draws parallels between the corporate accountability required by God of nations, tribes and families as evidenced in the OT, and the position of public companies today. He stresses their obligation to God in recognition of the created gifts which they receive from him, particularly in the ability of their employees or workforce.

The obligations by a bank to its customers, shareholders and the general public are paralleled by the obligations owed to it by its customers and staff. All need to exhibit the integrity that they expect to be displayed by the bank itself, and to exercise care in the handling of their duties and responsibilities.

Usury

One particular issue arising within banking is that of the validity of the rate of interest.* Current opinion on this is divided. Until the Reformation, OT strictures on usury were the basis for universal condemnation by the church of the charging of interest. But since Western economies developed sophisticated financial systems, the concept of money as a commodity, carrying a price, has become generally accepted, except in the Islamic world, though there is now emerging criticism by certain commentators (*e.g.* at the Cambridge-based Jubilee Centre) regarding the practice of charging interest (see P. Mills, *Interest in Interest*). The OT strictures seem to be limited to transactions within the nation of Israel, and specifically exclude transactions within the nation of Israel, and specifically exclude transactions with 'strangers'. But in today's world the concept of exclusion that this

implies is less sustainable, and concerns prompted by the burden of debt* on Third World countries (see Global Ethics;⑮ Third World Aid*) have raised this question again. Attempts to distinguish between actually committing money as a partner (good) and merely lending it (bad) envisage a financial system of much simpler structure than that pertaining in the modern Western economies, and do not present viable options. Islamic banking practices, while abjuring interest as such, at least find substitutes which are closely analogous with it; though these practices too do not obtain in dealings with non-Muslims. The problem of Third World debt needs to be studied in a global context, bearing in mind that some nations have accepted, and overcome, similar burdens by quality of government, though others are too weakly resourced for quality of government to be a decisive factor.

Bibliography

G. W. Goyder, *The Just Enterprise* (London, 1987); B. Griffiths, *Morality and the Market Place* (London, 1982); P. S. Mills, *Interest in Interest: The Old Testament Ban on Interest and its Implications for Today* (Cambridge, 1990).

C.F.G.

BARNARDO, THOMAS JOHN (1845–1905), founder of the children's charity that bears his name. The son of a Dublin furrier, he was converted to Christ in 1862 at a Brethren hall and four years later moved to London with the intention of serving with the China Inland Mission. While undertaking medical training, however, in 1868 he launched the East End Juvenile Mission, which was to become the basis of his life's work. Vigorous evangelism created a non-denominational church which from 1872 occupied the Edinburgh Castle in Limehouse in E. London, a former gin bar that was turned into a coffee palace. Meanwhile homeless boys were given shelter, elementary education and training in a trade. From 1876 girls were accommodated in cottages at Ilford in Essex.

Barnardo's success as a money-raiser aroused envy and his autocratic methods gave pretexts for criticism. His unauthorized use of the title 'doctor' before 1876 and his refusal to concentrate on the deserving poor also attracted censure, though in a protracted unofficial court of arbitration in 1877 he was declared worthy of public confidence. He sponsored child emigration to the colonies and, from 1886, organized extensive boarding-out of his charges. Barnardo's enterprise was less remarkable for innovation than for scale. He acted on the principles that no destitute child should be refused admission and that race, creed and handicap should never be dis-qualifications. Since the State was not pro-viding remedies for a major social problem, his evangelical faith drove Barnardo to take action.

Bibliography

G. Wagner, *Barnardo* (London, 1979).

D.W.Be

BARTH, KARL (1886–1968). Often hailed as the most influential and prolific theologian of the 20th century, Barth served as a pastor in the Swiss Reformed Church, and then held teaching positions at the universities of Göttingen, Münster, Bonn and Basel. The theological world began to take notice of him after the publication of his commentary on Romans (1919). Besides his theological con-tributions, he is noted for his prominent role in the German church's struggle against Hitler (1889–1945), being the principal author of the Barmen Declaration (1934).

Barth's theological pilgrimage can be traced through various stages: a neo-liberal phase in which Immanuel Kant* and Wilhelm Herr-mann (1846–1922) are influential; an existen-tialist phase, where he leans heavily upon Søren Kierkegaard;* a neo-Calvinist phase, in which church and sacraments are viewed as means of grace; and a position that approaches Christomonism, which envisages the whole of salvation (see Sin and Salvation⁵) as enacted and completed in the life, death and resurrec-tion of Jesus* Christ. Barth does, however, make a noteworthy place for the Holy Spirit* as the one who reveals and conveys the saving work of Christ to humanity, and therefore the Christomonistic label is not altogether ac-curate. His last phase is better described as a Christocentric triumphalism, for he sees Christ enacting a cosmic redemption in which the whole of creation* is caught up in the forward movement of the history of salvation.

Barth's emphasis is on the reconciling and redeeming work of Jesus Christ; justification,* sanctification* and calling are included within reconciliation.* While affirming justification as a forensic imputation of the righteousness of Christ to those who believe, he insists that

justification contains within itself the demand for sanctification. Sanctification, like justifica-tion, is a completed work outside us, for we – the whole of humanity – are reconciled and sanctified in the sacrificial, atoning work of Jesus Christ. Justification needs to be re-ceived by faith; sanctification must be appre-hended and manifested in works of love. Our human righteousness* is only a reflection and witness to the divine righteousness that alone justifies and saves. Through the grace* of God it can be made to correspond to God's righteousness, but it cannot duplicate or com-plete it.

The theme that runs through Barth's writings is that divine action is always some-thing different from human action. Human ac-tion can bear witness to divine action, but it is not the necessary instrumentality for divine ac-tion. This is why the later Barth prefers to speak of the Bible, the sermon and the so-called sacraments as signs of grace rather than means of grace.

Barth shows his distance from Lutheranism by affirming the priority of gospel over law (see Law and Gospel*). The law* is not a necessary preparation for the gospel, but the gospel prepares the way for a new understanding of the law. Just as grace is prior to works and revelation* prior to reason,* so the divine promise precedes the divine command. Yet this command is never a universal principle but always a concrete and specific word addressed to individual believers standing in a particular socio-historical context. The written com-mandments in Scripture testify to the divine commandment, but they cannot be extracted from their original historical context and con-verted into universal principles. They do serve, however, as guidelines that direct us to the Word of God and enable us to hear and understand it when it comes to us.

An emphasis on the inseparability of freedom* and obedience* is also characteristic of Barth. We are made free by grace to believe and obey, and works of obedience are not simply an appendage to faith but the crown and fruition of faith. These works do not pro-cure reparation for sin but instead demonstrate our gratefulness for Christ's atoning work, which is already enacted and completed. In an apparent break with Reformation theology, Barth insists that we can do works that are pleasing to God – yet only because of the work of the Spirit within and upon us. These works do not justify us because in and of themselves they are imperfect and deficient, but they attest the justification and sanctification already accomplished for us by Christ.

The witness of the church,* Barth insists, will have a political dimension, since the lordship of Christ pertains to the whole of life. Not only the church but also the State* is under the rule of Christ, though it does not yet know this as such. The political service of the church consists in setting up signs and parables of the coming kingdom of God.* We cannot bring in or build the kingdom, but we can witness to it by working for peace, justice and political liberation (see Justice and Peace ③). We are called, Barth believes, not so much to moral excellence as to the service of the downtrodden and needy. His focus is not on a pious and holy life but on a responsible and obedient life under God. Barth is adamant that we cannot make ourselves saints, but we can live out our vocation* as joyful servants and ambassadors of Jesus Christ.

Because of his stress on the solidarity of the church with the oppressed of the world, Barth has been accused of upholding a purely cultural Christ – the advocate of the oppressed and disenfranchised. Yet Barth is emphatic that our striving for human justice will always bring us into conflict with the vested interests that control society. We cannot create the kingdom of God, but we can work for human justice in the light of the promise of this kingdom. Christ and his gospel comprise the transforming leaven within society, the hope and goal of humanity.

Barth came to identify himself as an evangelical theologian, and he can be regarded as such because of his emphasis on salvation by grace rather than works; the universal crippling effects of sin; the vicarious, substitutionary sacrifice of Christ on the cross,* which makes God's forgiveness* available to us; the primacy of holy Scripture over church tradition and religious experience; and the call to discipleship as a demonstration of our gratitude for God's reconciling work on our behalf.

See also: HISTORY OF CHRISTIAN ETHICS. ⑥

Bibliography

The Christian Life (ET, Edinburgh and Grand Rapids, 1981); *Ethics* (ET, Edinburgh and New York, 1981); *Church Dogmatics*, I/1–IV/4 (ET, Edinburgh, 1936–81).

D.G.B.

BATTERY FARMING is a description for intensive livestock husbandry systems which house indoors large numbers of animals in cages, crates or stalls. The building environment is carefully controlled to maintain lighting, temperature, ventilation and humidity. The animals are fed diets formulated to maximize growth and to promote efficient food conversion into meat or eggs. The standards of stockmanship demanded are high and there is a reliance on vaccines and drugs to prevent disease outbreaks.

The factors which originally encouraged the development of battery farming were partly the result of post-Second World War food shortages and included the demand for cheap food,* the reduction of food imports and the high costs of labour.

It has been stated that the welfare of an individual animal is its state with regard to its attempts to cope with its environment (A. F. Fraser and D. M. Broom, *Farm Animal Behaviour and Welfare*, London, ³1990); but the scientific assessment of that state can be very difficult. Such an assessment may be based on five factors: freedom from thirst, hunger and malnutrition; appropriate comfort and shelter; prevention, or rapid diagnosis and treatment, of injury and disease; freedom to display most normal patterns of behaviour; and freedom from fear. The close confinement of farm animals may be associated with abnormal behaviour patterns which have been interpreted as indicative of poor welfare. Such animals have behavioural needs or freedoms which we are obliged to fulfil. Indeed some would contend that these animals have rights (see Rights, Animal*).

In the UK and some other countries there has been a move away from intensive battery farming methods towards extensive husbandry systems. Hens, for example, instead of being cooped in battery cages may be seen in large flocks, walking around a barn or aviary flapping their wings, or even outdoors freerange. Even so, in advocating alternative systems one has to be aware of the problems, including risk of disease, aggression (especially in pigs), the need for good observant stockmanship, and the fact that not all customers are prepared to pay the higher cost of the product.

It is important that Christians are at the forefront of the animal welfare debate, raising issues of priorities and values in the use of animals for food.

Bibliography

R. Ewbank, 'Intensive Livestock Production and Animal Welfare', in *Food and Farming Issues* (London, 1989), pp. 9–19; A. Linzey, *Christianity and the Rights of Animals* (London, 1987); T. Regan, *The Case for Animal Rights* (Berkley, CA, 1984).

A.P.F.

BAXTER, RICHARD (1615–91). Puritan clergyman, and author of doctrinal, apologetic, evangelistic, ethical, pastoral, ecclesiastical and devotional books. After an outstanding ministry at Kidderminster, Worcestershire, in 1641–42 and 1647–61, Baxter with almost 2,000 others declined the oath attached to the 1662 Act of Uniformity – which required the clergy of the Church of England to give unfeigned assent and consent to all and everything contained in the Prayer Book of 1559 – and he withdrew from parish ministry. Thereafter he wrote tirelessly and became the most voluminous British theologian ever.

Self-taught but well-read in medieval and patristic as well as 16th- and 17th-century theology, Baxter thought himself a mainstream Puritan, and in most things he was. However, he taught an Amyraldean universal redemption as a basis for the universal gospel invitation, an Arminian view of justification* as an amnesty conditional upon sustained obedience to a new law ('neonomianism'), and an implicitly Socinian view of the coherence of Christianity with natural theology which led to unitarian rationalism after his death.

On practical Christianity, however, Baxter is peerless. His huge work of 1673 – *A Christian Directory . . . in Four Parts: I. Christian Ethics (or Private Duties), II. Christian Economics (or Family Duties), III. Christian Ecclesiastics (or Church Duties), IV. Christian Politics (or Duties to our Rulers and Neighbours)* – claims to tell Christians how to use their knowledge and faith; how to improve all helps and means, and to perform all duties; how to overcome temptations, and to escape or mortify every sin. Standing on the shoulders of William Perkins (1558–1602), William Ames (1576–1633), Robert Sanderson (1587–1663) and Jeremy Taylor,* Baxter fulfils the promise of his title amazingly fully.

Other devotional classics from his pen (*e.g. The Saints' Everlasting Rest*, 1650; *The Life of Faith*, enlarged ed. 1670; *The Divine Life*, 1664; *Self-Denial*, 1659) amplify aspects of the analysis contained in this compendious overview, while *The Reformed Pastor* (1656) is a supreme statement, enormously energetic and energizing, of the spiritual demands of ministry to a congregation. Baxter-readers over three and a half centuries have unanimously acknowledged his mastery as a guide to the Christian life.

Bibliography

Practical Works, ed. W. Orme, 23 vols. (London, 1830); 4 vols. (Ligonier, PA, 1990–91).

C. F. Allison, *The Rise of Moralism: The Proclamation of the Gospel from Hooker to Baxter* (Wilton, CT, 1965; London, 1966); H. Martin, *Puritanism and Richard Baxter* (London, 1946); G. F. Nuttall, *Richard Baxter* (London, 1965).

J.I.P.

BEATITUDES are a literary form used to describe an individual whose life is consistent with what God expects, and to indicate that 'reward', or blessing, is to be anticipated. Beatitudes are used in Scripture to hold up the character or action of the person for others to see. In doing so, the beatified individual is praised and the hearer or reader is encouraged to emulate that person's character.

Beatitudes are found in both testaments. Examples from the OT are numerous, particularly in the Psalms (see Pss. 1:1–3; 40:4; 112:1; 128:1; and 32:1–2, which is quoted in Rom. 4:7–8). The form was, consequently, a familiar one for Jesus and the Hebrew community of his day. Most NT examples are from the teaching of Jesus.

The best-known collection of beatitudes is to be found in Mt. 5:3–10 and Lk. 6:20–22. Their context is the kingdom of God;* their meaning is best appreciated, and they are realized most fully, within the context of God's reign. They are both a present reality and an eschatological promise, for in them Jesus both proclaims the kingdom and extends future hope in the fully realized kingdom to those who are already part of it.

The beatitudes in Matthew and Luke reflect the paradox of understanding the kingdom of God in human terms. Here the poor, those who mourn and weep, the meek and merciful, those who hunger, the peacemakers, the pure in heart and the persecuted, are all considered blessed.

The Lukan beatitudes are set within

references to Is. 61, a prophecy about the Messiah which Jesus claimed as a reference to himself (see Lk. 4:18–21 and 7:22). The inclusion of parallel curses, or woes, in Lk. 6:24–26 illustrates the theme of reversal prominent in the Isaiah prophecy.

The beatitudes throughout Scripture deal both with personality and lifestyle. Each beatitude looks to the implementing of the righteousness of God within the world around us. To live the beatitudes is thus to reflect something of God's character.

D.L.P.

BEHAVIOUR CONTROL, see
BEHAVIOURISM, BEHAVIOUR THERAPY AND MODIFICATION; MANIPULATION.

BEHAVIOURISM, BEHAVIOUR THERAPY AND MODIFICATION.

Behaviourism is a metaphysical theory, which has had a very substantial influence on academic psychology and the development of psychological therapies in the 20th century. Its chief characteristics are the views that human beings are no more than higher primates whose behaviour is ultimately determined by evolutionary selective factors; that complex 'higher' psychological processes can be explained by multiple combinations of simple reflexes or conditioned responses (psychological *reductionism**); that the exclusive immediate determinants of behaviour are its environmental antecedents and consequences (the conditioning history); and that human behaviour is amenable to study using paradigms similar to those employed in natural science.

This radical behaviourist position was first articulated by J. B. Watson (1878–1958) in 1913, and represents a reaction to the mentalism and method of introspection characteristic of the contemporary psychology. He was influenced by the work of I. Pavlov (1849–1936) on the *classical conditioning* of appetitive and aversive responses in animals (*i.e.* the learning of associations between neutral and biologically meaningful stimuli). Watson's ideas were developed by B. F. Skinner* into a full-blown metaphysical theory, culminating in 1948 in a utopian novel (*Walden Two*) which describes a society based on behaviourist principles. Skinner's experimental work, which almost exclusively used animal subjects, investigated the properties of *operant conditioning* (*i.e.* the learning to connect responses with their consequences in order to achieve rewards or avoid/escape punishment by processes of *positive* or *negative reinforcement* respectively).

The epistemological implication of the radical behaviourist theory for the study of humans is a requirement that the subject of study should be amenable to reliable measurement and rigorous experimental test procedures. Any concepts which are not amenable to these methods should be *operationalized* (*i.e.* translated into behavioural terms). Explanations of behaviour should not be given in terms of inferred, irreducible mental concepts (*e.g.* 'he went to bed because he felt tired'). Thus precision is achieved and tautology avoided. The aim of this empirical approach is the prediction and control of behaviour rather than the understanding of the mind.

Many psychologists would value the methodology of the behaviourist approach for pragmatic reasons, while not being committed to the metaphysical theory from which it developed. For example, it might be useful to employ a paradigm where humans are viewed as machines, under certain circumstances, without accepting that humans are 'nothing but' machines. However, it has been argued that there is both logical inconsistency and psychological difficulty in accepting methodological behaviourism while rejecting metaphysical behaviourism (M. S. van Leeuwen, *The Person in Psychology*).

Behaviour therapy arose from Watson's early attempts to condition classically fear in naïve subjects. In the 1950s the first reports of successful treatment of specific phobias using *systematic desensitization* were reported (*e.g.* J. Wolpe, *Psychotherapy by Reciprocal Inhibition*). The technique involved graded exposure of the subject to the feared stimuli paired with an activity such as muscular relaxation (thought to be incompatible with anxiety responses). Its well-documented success led to a burgeoning of related therapeutic techniques in the 1960s and 1970s, used to treat a variety of neurotic disorders, though the link to the principles of learning theory had become more tenuous. These techniques include flooding, modelling, response prevention used to treat anxiety and obsessive compulsive disorders. The degree of success obtained has been variable, but, in general, high. More recently there has been a re-emergence of mentalistic concepts (although often operationalized into verbal responses) in the development of an integrated Cognitive Behaviour Therapy.*

Behaviour modification employs the operant conditioning paradigm to manipulate behaviour such that adaptive behaviour is increased and maladaptive behaviour reduced. Examples of the former are the enhancement of social, motor or life-skill acquisition in subjects with learning difficulties or suffering mental disorder, or in children. Examples of the latter are the control of habit disorders or violent or socially deviant behaviours in similar subjects. *Positive reinforcers* (rewards) may be primary, such as cigarettes or sweets, or secondary, such as tokens or stars. Secondary reinforcers may be exchanged for primary reinforcers or certain privileges. Aversive stimuli may be the removal of positive reinforcers, including brief temporary removal from the whole community in a side room (*time out*), or, in unusual cases, active punishment in various forms.

There is no doubt that specific behaviours can be brought under control where the environment is closed and the reinforcers sufficiently potent; but, like many other therapies, the gains achieved do not automatically generalize to other related behaviour or to other environments. Both behaviour therapy and behaviour modification share the characteristics of having developed out of learning theory research: both are applied directly and experimentally to the treatment of specific maladaptive behaviour patterns (being little influenced by more global diagnostic categorizations), and they focus on current maintaining factors rather than temporally or psychologically remote origins of the problem.

The advantages of the behavioural approach to problems are that treatment is usually of relatively brief duration; the technological quality of the approach enables it to be taught to primary carers and relatives and avoids mystique; the procedures are rigorously evaluated; even the most cognitively impaired person can benefit from the techniques; it aims to deal with specific problems without requiring the client to participate in the more threatening process of examining his or her whole life; on ethical grounds, it may be a preferable approach to sedating medication or physical restraint.

The disadvantages of the approach are that it may over-simplify complex problems. The role of language and verbal learning is almost entirely neglected by the behavioural approach (N. Chomsky, 'Review of "Verbal Behaviour"'). It also places little emphasis upon social and developmental issues. It is open to abuse, or can be used to maintain the *status quo*, particularly where the clients are of limited ability; the use of aversive stimuli and deprivation are ethically questionable, and in fact illegal in certain parts of the world (G. La Vigna and A. Donnellan, *Alternatives to Punishment*).

The fact that therapeutic procedures based loosely on learning theory show a relatively good degree of success in their own terms is not sufficient either to confirm or to discredit metaphysical behaviourism; it is essentially a belief system. As such it has some attractions when viewed from a Christian perspective: it is realistic about the tendency of humans to gratify desires and pursue self-interest; it does not offer a spurious quasi-spiritual alternative to the biblical description of our inner experience – rather, it ignores it; and it draws attention to the importance of the environment in shaping behaviour (see Fall* and Sin and Salvation[5]). For these reasons, and because of the efficacy of behaviour therapy and modification, many Christian counsellors (*e.g.* James Dobson, 1936–), adopt a methodologically behaviourist position in the context of a broader scriptural perspective. However, it must be noted that, in its most extreme form, behaviourism is fundamentally atheistic: God's direct influence upon behaviour is denied; humans are viewed as no more than complex animals; and the spiritual aspect of the individual is dismissed as having no reality.

See also: PASTORAL CARE, COUNSELLING AND PSYCHOTHERAPY. [12]

Bibliography

N. Chomsky, 'Review of "Verbal Behaviour" ', *Language* 35, 1959, pp. 26–58; G. Davey, *Applications of Conditioning Theory* (London, 1981); J. Dobson, *Dare to Discipline* (New York and Eastbourne, [2]1975); G. La Vigna and A. Donnellan, *Alternatives to Punishment: Solving Behavioural Problems with Non-Aversive Strategies* (New York, 1986); M. S. van Leeuwen, *The Person in Psychology* (Grand Rapids and Leicester, 1985); I. Pavlov, *Conditioned Reflexes* (Oxford, 1927); B. F. Skinner, *Walden Two* (New York and London, 1976); J. Wolpe, *Psychotherapy by Reciprocal Inhibition* (Stanford, CA, 1958).

J.R.McG.

BENEDICT OF NURSIA (*c.* 480– *c.* 550), known as 'the father of Western monasticism', was born in the Umbrian region of modern Norcia, Italy. Most of what is known about his life derives from the *Dialogues* of Pope Gregory I.*

Alarmed at the profligate lifestyle of fellow students in Rome, Benedict withdrew for three years into solitary life in a cave at Subiaco. Once discovered by local inhabitants he quickly attracted many followers, whom he subsequently organized into twelve monastic communities. However, Benedict eventually settled at Monte Cassino, south of Rome, where his most famous monastery was founded.

Much more can be deduced about the character of Benedict from the monastic 'rule' with which his name is ever associated; for, as Gregory put it, Benedict 'cannot have taught otherwise than as he lived'. Benedict's Rule – a comparatively short compilation drawing on the best of earlier monastic 'rules' – provides a flexible framework for daily life within which members of a stable community governed by an abbot undertake to learn obedience and humility, 'following the guidance of the Gospel'. The focus of community life is the *opus Dei* ('the work of God'), a daily pattern of praise and prayer comprising seven day 'offices' (*cf.* Ps. 119:164) and one night 'office' (*cf.* Ps. 119:62), each compiled almost exclusively of psalms (sung 'that mind and voice may be in harmony') and Scripture readings.

The influence of Benedict's Rule upon Christian spirituality* in Western Europe is incalculable, the rule having been officially adopted as the norm for monastic and religious life, and the daily office, likewise, as an obligation of prayer for secular clergy.

Bibliography

J. McCann, *Saint Benedict* (London, ²1979); *idem* (ed.), *The Rule of St Benedict* (ET, London, ²1972).

R.A.Hin.

B ENEVOLENCE is an attitude of good-will towards others, a desire to promote their well-being.

It is clearly seen in God (see ☐1) as an expression of his love (see ☐2) and grace.* He longs for the good of his creatures, and is committed to bringing it about as far as is possible. His benevolence is universal: he makes the sun rise on the evil and on the good (Mt. 5:45), he desires that all should be saved (1 Tim. 2:4).

Benevolence in men and women can be viewed in a number of ways. Some have argued that it is an innate quality, a natural bent towards desiring the well-being of the people we encounter. Others would contest this, suggesting that we are in essence self-centred: any apparent concern for the well-being of others can be traced back to our own self-interest; we express kindness to others so that they will be kind to us; we feed the hungry to salve our own consciences, and so on (see Altruism*). It could be that benevolence is a learned attitude; the growing child is taught to replace his basic self-centredness with a developing concern for the well-being of others.

A case can be made from the Bible that true benevolence is the fruit of the Spirit: unless God plants his character in us, any expressions of benevolence will be at best pale reflections of the real thing; true benevolence springs from *agapē* love; only those filled with the love of God can truly, selflessly, love their fellow women and men. Yet even in Christians it is still the case that benevolence never manages to become wholly altruistic.

Benevolence is a matter of the mind and the will, our attitudes and volitions, though the word is sometimes used to refer to the acts of kindness to which benevolence gives rise (*i.e.* beneficence). The Bible teaches that the relationship between attitude and action, well-wishing and well-doing, is a very close one indeed. The two must always be integrated. Kind thoughts and good wishes without corresponding action are valueless (Jas. 2:15–16); and good deeds that are not rooted in true benevolence are equally useless (1 Cor. 13:3).

Right action must be determined by right attitude. Deeds to others that are truly pleasing to God must spring from benevolence. Just as murder, adultery, immorality, theft and the like come 'out of the heart' (Mt. 15:19), so loving and caring and beneficial deeds must come from that inner spring of thought and will that the Bible calls 'the heart'. The story of the Good Samaritan (Lk. 10:25–37), however, makes it clear that a truly benevolent attitude is not necessarily one of smiling benignity and warm feelings. The Samaritan presumably found the wounded Jew at least superficially repulsive, yet he was at heart committed to his well-being.

Modern society has made virtues out of competitiveness, aggression and self-assertion. While these may seem to leave little room for benevolence, they at least provide a backdrop against which benevolence can stand out more clearly. Christians, especially, are called to 'do nothing out of selfish ambition or vain conceit, but in humility consider others better than yourselves. Each of you should look not only to your own interests, but also to the interests of others. Your attitude should be the same as that of Christ Jesus' (Phil. 2:3–5).

The task of recalling Western Christians to a true attitude of benevolence is a major one. Emptying ourselves for the sake of others, giving away all we have to the poor, or even sacrificing half our wardrobe (Phil. 2:5–7; Mk. 10:21; Lk. 3:11) are largely alien concepts; even our largesse is often little more than the disposal of our excess. Additionally, the sheer volume of the demands made on us makes the task seem impossible: the world's billions press in on us on every side; how can we feel or express benevolence to so many?

It may be that besides focusing on the commands and exhortations to benevolence in Scripture, and on the needs of the people of the world, the most fruitful ways of encouraging benevolence are to seek to look on others as Jesus sees them, and to ponder the truth that in showing benevolence to others we are in fact showing it to him (Mt. 25:31–46).

P.A.H.

BENTHAM, JEREMY (1748–1832), regarded as the father of classical utilitarianism (see Consequentialism*). For Bentham utilitarianism was primarily a theory to undergird progressive social policy and reform in the light of what he took to be the failure of natural rights* and social-contract theories.*

Bentham's version of utilitarianism was developed in his *Introduction to the Principles of Morals and Legislation* (1789; London, 1970). While asserting that 'Nature has placed mankind under the governance of two sovereign masters, pain and pleasure', he also maintains that humans feel pleasure* upon increasing the sum total of happiness in the universe, and pain upon the failure to accomplish this. Thus the principle of utility is foundational for Bentham's theory: we ought to perform only those actions which will bring about the greatest amount of pleasure for all involved.

Recognizing the difficulty in identifying which of the possible actions would increase the sum total of pleasure for all involved, Bentham presented a 'hedonic calculus' as an instrument of moral analysis (see Hedonism*). In estimating the value of a pleasure or pain,

the moral agent should consider such factors as the intensity, duration, certainty and propinquity of respective pleasures and pains, as well as their likelihood to lead to additional sensations of the same kind or of the opposite kind. This calculation was to be performed not only with reference to oneself, but to all those affected by the action in question. Bentham's quantitative utilitarianism was later revised by John Stuart Mill.*

See also: HISTORY OF CHRISTIAN ETHICS.[6]

T.D.K.

BEREAVEMENT is the experience of losing a loved person or loved object. Typically 'bereavement' describes a person's reaction to the death* of a spouse or close relative, although the term may also be used to describe the experience of other losses such as the amputation of a limb, moving house, going abroad, losing a job, or divorce. 'Grief' is the emotion of bereavement; it is part of the cost of having loved, a normal response to the loss of a significant loved person or object.

For a dying person, all his or her losses come together, and they are coupled with the fundamental further loss, namely the finality of death.

In the 1960s, Dr Elisabeth Kübler-Ross (1926–) established a seminar at the University of Chicago to consider the implications of terminal illness for patients and for those involved in their care. Her classic book *On Death and Dying* documents the attitudes she found among her terminally ill patients, which came to light during many conversations. She indicates that a patient may pass through several stages in coming to terms with his or her own death: denial and isolation; anger; bargaining; depression;* acceptance and hope. These are frequent, but not invariable, phases in the grief-work (see Grief*) of the dying (see Death and Dying*).

There is a growing literature concerned with the processes of grief and mourning, much of it written to help society relearn that death is an inescapable part of life, and that freer discussion of the processes of grieving might contribute to a more acceptable social attitude towards mourning. Following on from Freud's* early work 'Mourning and Melancholia' (see *Sigmund Freud: Collected Papers*, vol. 5, New York, 1917), Erich Lindemann published a major paper in 1944 ('The symptomatology and management of acute grief',

AJP, Sept 1944, pp. 7f.) in which he argued that a clear 'grief syndrome' can be described: sometimes this may appear immediately after a crisis; sometimes it may be delayed; sometimes it may apparently be absent. Bereavement, and the 'grief-work' which has to be undertaken during bereavement, are processes of coping, involving emancipation from bondage to the loss of the deceased, readjustment to the environment in which the deceased is missing, and the formation of new relationships. In 1972, Colin Murray Parkes (1928–) published his acclaimed study *Bereavement*, in which he isolates four main phases of normal grieving: a phase of numbness, shock and partial disregard of the reality of the loss; a phase of yearning, with an urge to recover the lost object; a phase of disorganization, despair and gradual coming to terms with the reality of the loss; a phase of reorganization and resolution. Often there will be physical reactions: stress symptoms, loss of appetite, change of sleep patterns, various somatic disorders. This is not necessarily a tidy process. Grief is complex, and different for each person. For some it continues for a long time, or may never seem to be completed; for others, there can be gradual progress back to stability and to a good resolution of the grief so that life can proceed normally. Typically, after a major bereavement such as the death of a spouse, the phase of shock may last up to two weeks, while the rest of the grief-work until satisfactory resolution may take two to four years. As C. S. Lewis* graphically illustrated in *A Grief Observed*, grief-work is not necessarily a linear progression: 'Tonight all the hells of young grief have opened again; the mad words, the bitter resentment, the fluttering in the stomach, the nightmare unreality, the wallowed-in tears. For in grief, nothing "stays put". One keeps on emerging from a phase, but it always recurs. Round and round. Everything repeats. Am I going in circles, or dare I hope I am on a spiral? But if a spiral, am I going up or down it?' (p. 46).

At each phase of grief, a positive resolution can enable the bereaved person to work back to normality. But things can also go wrong: the reality of the death may be denied, either by 'mummifying' the deceased's room or belongings, or by the superspirituality which refuses to face the pain of death; the normal depression may become chronic; the bereaved may become a recluse, or overdependent, or irresponsibly helpless. Abnormal grieving may need skilled intervention.

Grieving young children can often best be helped by helping the bereaved parent, as much of a child's grief may be a reflection of the parent's. If the adult can express feelings, and be advised that it is not harmful for the child to do likewise, both can be helped.

The Christian pastor, sometimes more than the family doctor or other helpers, may have a special ministry in assisting a bereaved family cope with loss. He or she is permitted by social convention to break through the taboos associated with death, in a way that is not open to many others. Many people think that helping at a time of death is in some way part of what the clergy are for. The pastor is a *representative* figure. His or her personal presence can give permission for those in need to share religious concerns and talk seriously (sometimes angrily) about them. The pastor represents the community of faith, and can serve as a bridge for grieving persons to get back into contact with their wider community. The pastor bears a shared tradition of interpretation about death and resurrection, within which the grieving person can be gradually helped to make some sense of the loss. The pastor can also be a *reconciling* figure, bringing the resources of divine grace. He can stand with the bereaved in their loneliness* and uncertainty, and his (sometimes silent) presence can support the grieving person as processes of reconciliation are undertaken towards God and towards others. It will sometimes be important for the pastor to help a grieving person come to terms with feelings of guilt* and find ways of handling this appropriately through forgiveness.* The pastor also serves a *ritual* function, sometimes in sacramental ministry to the sick or dying, and also in the funeral. The funeral can serve a most important social and psychological, as well as a spiritual, function for the bereaved person. It helps him or her to face the reality of the death, to interpret the changes that are happening, to focus the choices that are open and to recognize the status transitions going on. It offers the pain and the sorrow of the living, as well as the one who has died, to the mercy and grace of God, and provides an opportunity for the community of faith to surround the bereaved with their prayers and their support. The value of the funeral ritual is reinforced through monuments and memorials, which provide a focus for feelings, and through subsequent pastoral ministry, especially at significant times like the first anniversary. The pastoral task in relation to the bereaved is to seek to help them understand and use their experiences of loss in a way that enables them to let go appropriately, and build creatively for the future.

See also: BURIAL AND CREMATION.

Bibliography

E. Kübler-Ross, *On Death and Dying* (New York, 1969; London, 1970); C. S. Lewis, *A Grief Observed* (London, 1961); C. M. Parkes, *Bereavement* (Harmondsworth, ²1985; Madison, CT, ²1987); Y. Spiegel, *The Grief Process* (London, 1977); A. Stedeford, *Facing Death* (London, 1984); H. Thielicke, *Living with Death* (ET, Grand Rapids, 1983); P. Tournier, *Creative Suffering* (ET, London and San Francisco, 1982); N. Wolterstorff, *Lament for a Son* (Grand Rapids, 1987).

D.J.A.

BIBLICAL COUNSELLING. Within the range of Christian responses to the rise of the secular psychologies (see Pastoral Care, Counselling and Psychotherapy[12]), there have been a number of strands which have laid claim to the Bible as a basis for pastoral counselling. These have been outlined by the N. American pastoral theologian Donald Capps (1939–), and include: the open use of biblical passages in hospital chaplaincy work by Richard C. Cabot and Russell L. Dicks (1906–65); a more cautious approach in handling specific texts by Seward Hiltner;* the diagnostic use of the Bible by Wayne E. Oates (1917–); the Barthian stance of Eduard Thurneysen;* and the thematic style of William B. Oglesby (1916–), which looks to such biblical themes as 'fear and faith' and 'risk and redemption'; and to the work of OT theologian Gerhard von Rad (1901–71). Capps, in turn, develops his methodology by referring to form criticism, allowing the literary genre of the psalms, proverbs and parables to shape non-directive, directive and indirective styles of counselling respectively.

Parallel to such explorations of the use of the Bible in pastoral care and counselling, there has been a more conservative strand, whose various methodologies have been summed up in the generic term 'biblical counselling'. Under this banner can be grouped a number of approaches which maintain a high view of the Bible's inspiration and accuracy – ranging from 'excluding' positions, strong on special revelation* and tending to dismiss the validity

of psychiatry and the allied disciplines, through to 'integrational' stances, stressing general as well as special revelation and open to dialogue between a biblical theology and the insights of psychology. In the US, this range includes: the 'nouthetic counselling' of Jay Adams (1929–); the 'spiritual counselling' of Martin Bobgan (1930–) and Deirdre Bobgan (1935–); the 'biblical counselling' of Scope Ministries (and the International Association of Biblical Counselors, also based in Oklahoma City and founded in 1987); the more integrational 'biblical counselling' of Lawrence Crabb (1944–); and Gary Collins' (1934–) 'discipleship counselling' with its openness to dialogue. In the UK, mainstream biblical counselling is represented by the 'Christian counselling' of Selwyn Hughes (1928–), influenced by transatlantic contact with Crabb and with Clyde Narramore and Bruce Narramore (1941–), and forming the Institute of Christian Counselling out of a training programme launched in 1975. In 1981 and 1982, Adams (and, subsequently, John Bettler and Wayne Mack, also from the US) held courses in biblical counselling at Hildenborough Hall, Kent. One outcome of these enterprises was the setting up of the British Association of Biblical Counsellors in 1984.

Amongst others who look to the Bible as foundational in their counselling theory and practice, the influence of the London-based Care and Counsel (1974–90) has been important in fostering a more integrational approach. In 1992, the Association of Christian Counsellors (with a Statement of Faith and Practice that refers to counselling 'according to biblical assumptions, aims and methods') was launched in the UK to encourage recognition and accreditation* of Christian counsellors, supervisors and training courses.

Within the spread of biblical counselling approaches, nouthetic counselling, introduced in 1969, has held a unique and controversial position. Jay Adams, its founder, influenced by the anti-Freudianism of O. Hobart Mowrer,* has produced a methodology with an assumptive basis that looks solely to the special revelation of the Bible: 'All that is needed to form values, beliefs, attitudes, and behavioural styles is in the Scriptures' ('Nouthetic Counselling', in G. R. Collins, *Helping People Grow*, p. 158). From this stance, Adams has argued a 'duplex' view of human nature (the visible 'outer' and the 'inner', or 'heart') which sees all malady as either sin* or bodily disorder: there is no 'non-bodily psychological area' which is either unaffected by sin or is not a source of further sin (*More than Redemption*, pp. 110ff., 141–142). Within this framework, the place of psychotherapy becomes irrelevant and the focus of human need lies with the biblical counsellor or physician. Adams has centred his attention on the use in the NT of *noutheteō* (to warn, advise) and *nouthesia* (admonition, warning, exhortation) and is, thereby, faithful to the biblical contexts of their use, *i.e.* within the fellowship of believers, in propounding that his nouthetic counselling is suitable only for Christian clients. The aim is 'biblical change', whereby the Holy Spirit works through God's Word to effect new, Christ-centred patterns of thinking and action. The style is directive, exhortatory and confrontational, and the cognitive-behavioural* approach includes the 'two-factored process' of 'dehabituation' and 'rehabituation' (see, *e.g.*, Eph. 4:22–32) and the assigning of carefully monitored 'homework'. Criticisms of nouthetic counselling have included comment on Adams' apparent neglect of the much more widely used NT words *parakaleō* (to exhort, encourage, comfort) and *paraklēsis* (encouragement, exhortation, consolation), and a questioning of his use of the book of Proverbs as a blueprint for directive counselling (Capps, *Biblical Approaches to Pastoral Counselling*, pp. 101, 144ff.).

The debate continues on the relationship between the Bible and the theory and practice of Christian counselling. Crabb, for example, wrestles with what it means to be 'biblical' in the province of counselling and makes a plea for openness and non-defensiveness amongst biblical counsellors (*Understanding People*, pp. 14–15). Roger Hurding (1934–) has given a detailed critique of biblical counselling (*Roots and Shoots*, pp. 275–306) and argues for a more comprehensive model for the use of Scripture in pastoral care and counselling, in which the *prophetic* in so-called 'biblical' counselling, the *therapeutic* in the healing methodologies, the *pastoral* in 'relationship' counselling (see 'Christian personalism' in Pastoral Care, Counselling and Psychotherapy[12]), and the *priestly* in spiritual direction, can all develop their distinctive understanding and handling of Scripture (*The Bible and Counselling*, pp. 147–173).

Bibliography

J. E. Adams, *Competent to Counsel* (Grand Rapids, 1970); *idem*, *More than Redemption: A Theology of Christian Counseling* (Grand Rapids, 1979); D. Capps, *Biblical Approaches to Pastoral Counseling* (Philadelphia, 1981); D. E. Carlson, 'Jesus' Style of Relating: The Search for a Biblical View of Counselling', *JPT* 4, 1976, pp. 181–192; G. R. Collins (ed.), *Helping People Grow: Practical Approaches to Christian Counseling* (Santa Ana, CA, 1980); L. J. Crabb, *Effective Biblical Counseling* (Grand Rapids, 1977); *idem*, *Understanding People: Deep Longings for Relationship* (Grand Rapids, 1987; Basingstoke, 1988); R. F. Hurding, *Roots and Shoots: A Guide to Counselling and Psychotherapy* (London, 1986) = *The Tree of Healing* (Grand Rapids, 1988); *idem*, *The Bible and Counselling* (London, 1992); W. B. Oglesby, *Biblical Themes for Pastoral Care* (Nashville, TN, 1980).

R.F.H.

BIGAMY, see POLYGAMY.

BIOETHICS, see ETHICS OF MEDICAL CARE. [14]

BIRTH CONTROL, or contraception, is the restriction of procreation by human choice and control. Long practised, birth control was known in Egypt in 1900 BC and throughout the ancient world. Medical technology's recent achievement of effective contraception, beginning in the 19th century, has been called 'the most significant and far-reaching advancement produced by the new biology' (C. E. Curran, 'The Contraceptive Revolution and the Human Condition', p. 42).

The process of conception can be interrupted at several points. Mechanical methods of contraception prevent the introduction of sperm into the uterus and Fallopian tubes and include the condom, the diaphragm and the intra-uterine device (IUD). Chemically, contraception can be achieved by means of the 'Pill', in use since the 1960s, and the more recent Depo-Provera (DMPA) injection, particularly used in the Third World. Sterilization* is a more permanent means of achieving control over conception, and includes in females tubal ligation, or deliberate occlusion of the Fallopian tubes, which usually is permanent, and in males the partially reversible vasectomy. Less technological and less reliable methods include coitus interruptus (withdrawal by the male before ejaculation) and the 'rhythm' method in which intercourse is restricted to infertile periods. Technological contraception is known as 'artificial contraception' and has been received slowly, or not at all, by various Christian traditions and moralists. Abortion* has also come to be seen, in some quarters, as an acceptable means of contraception.

Historically, supporters of contraception could scarcely appeal to the people of Israel, who placed a high value both on childbearing and on chastity.* Greeks and Romans favoured high rates of reproduction to produce population for the State, and contraception was specifically condemned by the Stoics and by Philo (*c.* 20 BC – *c.* AD 50).

Scripture seems to say little directly about the issue, and it is to Augustine* that the church owes its traditionally negative attitude towards contraception. He believed that the use of contraception even within marriage* introduced moral corruption into the conjugal act, turning it into something akin to prostitution.* Contemporary Roman Catholic teaching holds that while responsible family planning is an important objective, it can be pursued only within the context of the moral law, which teaches that there is an unbreakable union of the unitive (or relational) and procreative 'meanings' of marital sexuality. This view, as elaborated by Pope Paul VI in *Humanae Vitae* (1968; see Papal Encyclicals*), sees 'artificial' contraception as intrinsically immoral and as having among its negative consequences the encouragement of fornication* and adultery,* the reduction of the woman to the status of an object (much as Augustine had taught), and the potential for political abuse. Negative social phenomena such as the dramatic rise in pre-marital sex, the rise in sexually transmitted diseases including AIDS, and the serious side-effects of the Pill can be cited as evidence by those who hold this view. Regarding political abuse, it is instructive that in the mid-1940s, thirty of the United States allowed mandatory non-voluntary sterilization of various groups in society, including the retarded, the deviant, the criminal and racial minorities.

Protestant thought and contemporary social attitudes departed from Roman Catholic teaching in the 20th century. In the late 19th century various laws in the US, influenced by Protestant morality, suppressed contraception. The Comstock Act of 1873, passed as the result of lobbying by the Young Men's Christian Association (YMCA), prohibited the distribution of contraceptives or birth control information. It was not until the 1960s that the US Supreme Court overturned a Connecticut law that prohibited the use of contraceptives in private by married couples. The birth control movement grew in the late 19th and early 20th centuries, led by Marie Stopes (1880–1959) and Margaret Sanger (1883–1950), often using Malthusian* arguments about the need to limit population growth (see Population Policy*) to keep within resource limitations. In the 'baby boom' period following the Second World War, governments began to advocate contraception both for their own populations and in their foreign aid policy for developing nations. Protestant thinking, led by the Anglicans in the early part of the century, gradually came to accept birth control as a legitimate means of limiting family size and population growth. Karl Barth,* in particular, gave theological backing to couples who wished to engage in marital sexual life without procreation, arguing that unprotected intercourse is impermissible in cases where there is concern for the mother's physical and psychological health, or where other problems are present which make it impossible to see a child as God's blessing. Barth's position has been echoed by theologians such as Jacques Ellul* and Reinhold Niebuhr,* and significantly in practice by many millions of Protestants who have used contraception and sterilization to limit the size of their families.

Christian thinking about contraception will have to take account of several factors. First of all, it must be admitted that contraception has encouraged sexual promiscuity, and that this is incompatible with fundamental Christian teaching about sexuality (see [11]) and its role in the family. In this sense, it has contributed to personal unhappiness and social disturbance. None the less, an important question today is the provision of contraception and advice to unmarried teenagers. Is the provision of contraception to teenagers a realistic concession to the practices already extant in society, or is it a sign of encouragement to immorality?

Secondly, contraception may well have a place in the Christian marriage when it is mutually agreed upon and seen as a method of postponing, spacing and limiting the bearing of children* in order to provide opportunities to complete education and similar commitments, to develop the personal relationship between spouses, and to enable the couple to provide better nurture and support to those children they choose to have. The biblical injunction to reproduce (Gn. 1:28) must be taken in context with the NT principle that other concerns, particularly the demands of faithfulness to God's call to service, can take precedence over both marriage and reproduction (1 Cor. 7). This seems to suggest that we are not under a divine call to produce as great a quantity of offspring as possible, but to bear children who can be nurtured and given appropriate attention, instruction, love and material resources.

Should a Christian couple use birth control to be permanently childless by choice? While official Catholic teaching refuses to allow any severance of the link between the unitive and the procreative aspects of reproduction and insists that this union be present on every occasion of sexual intercourse, others have argued that the link can be respected more generally by insisting that marital love be open to the bearing of children at some point, even if not in every instance of sexual activity. Perhaps, however, the decision to be childless, like the decision to remain celibate, is one that can be seen by some as a calling, a freeing for service in other ways, rather than mere selfishness. In any case, in view of the high infertility (see Childlessness*) statistics (one in seven couples), it is unwise to assume that couples who have not had children have chosen to be childless.

Bibliography
K. Barth, *CD* III/4, pp. 357–363; C. E. Curran, 'The Contraceptive Revolution and the Human Condition', *AJTP* 3, 1982, pp. 42–59; R. A. McCormick, *How Brave a New World? Dilemmas in Bioethics* (Washington, DC, and London, 1981); J. T. Noonan, *Contraception: A History of Its Treatment by the Catholic Theologians and Canonists* (Cambridge, MA, and London, ²1986); W. O. Spritzer and C. L. Saylor, *Birth Control and the Christian; A Protestant Symposium on the Control of Human Reproduction* (Wheaton, IL, 1964).

D.B.F.

BITTERNESS is an entrenched attitude of unresolved angry resentment. The bitter person sees himself or herself as the innocent victim. This attitude is a projection of unacceptable parts of the self* on to some external person or object. It is easier to contain these feelings if they are perceived as coming from 'out there' rather than 'in here'. Resolution involves taking personal responsibility*

and recognizing that when there is a victim within, there is also an aggressor, and they cannot be divided. The bitter person concentrates on being wounded and finds it painful to acknowledge his or her own destructive wishes, preferring to regard them as a justifiable defence against unreasonable injustice (real or fantasied).

Bitterness is found in people who are basically angry with life in general. Probably there has been some lack of adequately warm and generous parenting (see Parenthood, Parenting*); this has led to deep-seated frustration.* Some perceived repetition of this deprivation in adult life will reactivate the sense of grievance which is already there: this new outrage then becomes the focus for hitherto non-specific resentment. Change is likely to occur only within an atmosphere of acceptance* and consistently loving care* which was lacking in the foundational experiences of parental relationships. Within such an atmosphere it may become possible for the bitter person to begin to grieve over lost opportunities and regret pain* received and inflicted, rather than feel victimized. Criticism and condemnation are unlikely to thaw the hurt and angry heart. The task of the church is to offer the quality of care which will facilitate change (see Heb. 12:15).

See also: FORGIVENESS.

Bibliography
M. Chave-Jones, *Living with Anger* (London, 1992).

M.C.-J.

BLASPHEMY. Since it was Israel's special duty to hallow the name of God (Ex. 20:7), the blaspheming of that name was a special sin and was therefore to be punished most seriously by stoning (Lv. 24:13–16). By a supreme irony which pierces to the heart of biblical religion, the charge of blasphemy is levelled against the Messiah himself as a ground for his death (Mk. 14:64).

The Eng. term 'blasphemy', itself a transliteration from Gk., is used variously for the abusive or careless profaning of God, or the causing of grave offence to believers (and, by extension, for other severe but non-religious insults). Through the Christianizing of Roman law, and then the canon law of the medieval church, a tradition of civil penalty for blasphemy has been carried down to our own time. In the US, that tradition was ended by the Supreme Court. In the UK it continues, and – though it has been rarely employed – the common law preserves an attenuated version of Lv. 24. However, here, as in most historical jurisdictions, the law is intended less to protect God's sensibilities than to protect those of his followers: either directly (necessary to the preservation of the peace), or indirectly (reflecting the dependence of the *corpus* of law on the Christian religion, and therefore demanding respect for that religion). In 1977–79, the law was tested by a successful private prosecution for 'blasphemous libel', brought against the publication *Gay News* for having published in 1976 a poem which depicted Jesus as a homosexual. It is unlikely that Western jurisdictions will long retain such privileged protection for the Christian religion, but it is more than likely that blasphemy against the Qu'ran will be increasingly proscribed in a number of Muslim countries. The option of extending legal protection to other religious traditions has been canvassed, and attracted some support in the context of the supposedly pluralist identity of these societies. Yet the danger of general legal regulation of religious discourse is real, since it could so easily disallow the particularist and universal claims of the gospel.

The NT underlines the OT's especial regard for the holiness of the name of God: 'Hallowed be thy name' is the first petition of the Lord's Prayer (Lk. 11:2, AV). The dis-hallowing of the name in blasphemy can take many forms beyond the cursing specified in Lv. 24. The term is used of Paul's persecution of the church (1 Tim. 1:13), of the fruit of religious hypocrisy (Rom. 2:24), of the eschatological opposition of the beast and the harlot (Rev. 13:1; 17:3), and of the perplexing 'blasphemy against the Holy Spirit', a sin singled out in Mk. 3:29 (and par.) as unforgivable – and which seems to refer to persistent and conscious rejection of the light of the gospel rather than to some particular act for which forgiveness would be sought in vain (Mk. 3:28).

Bibliography

L. W. Levy, *Treason against God* (New York, 1981); F. L. Smith, *Blasphemy and the Battle for Faith* (London, 1990).

N.M.deS.C.

BLESSEDNESS. The state of blessedness refers to the joy and happiness promised to the individual who lives in the kingdom of God.* Since blessedness is humanly realized in the kingdom of God, it is only perfectly achieved in the future when the kingdom is fulfilled, yet it is already approachable by the children of God as the kingdom* is now present among us.

The presence of such joy is attained both psychologically, through an attitude based on an understanding of one's being blessed by God, and presently, through an acknowledged realization of the blessing of God in this life. The Scriptures reflect the varied nature of blessedness: it is both material and spiritual, present as well as future, human and divine, both personal and social.

This varied nature of blessedness is reflected in contrasting paradigms presented in three parts of the biblical text. In the OT, particularly the Psalms, blessedness is closely connected with following God. The blessed person is one who finds refuge in God (Pss. 2:12; 34:8), is forgiven by God (Ps. 32:1–2), trusts in God (Ps. 40:4), and fears God (Pss. 112:1; 128:1). These activities, characteristic of one who follows God, are collectively referred to in the person of one who 'walks' with God ('Blessed are those who have learned to acclaim you, who walk in the light of your presence, O LORD', Ps. 89:15; 'Blessed are they whose ways are blameless, who walk according to the law of the LORD', Ps. 119:1).

In the NT, the Matthean paradigm implies that blessedness is a result of spiritual maturity. The Beatitudes* which introduce the Sermon on the Mount* affirm the blessedness of the person who is poor in spirit, mourns, is meek, hungers and thirsts for righteousness, is merciful, is pure in heart, is a peacemaker, and is persecuted because of righteousness (Mt. 5:3–10). This spiritual sensitivity is affirmed in Jesus' words to the disciples following the telling of the parable of the sower: Jesus states, 'Blessed are your eyes because they see, and your ears because they hear' (Mt. 13:16). While many people may have access to the kingdom of God, and thereby to the state of blessedness, only the spiritually sensitive will see and hear as necessary, and thereby be blessed.

Blessedness is also present in the midst of injustice and wherever God's justice is practised. The Lukan statement of the Beatitudes ('Blessed are you who are poor, . . . you who hunger now, . . . you who weep now, . . . you when men hate you, . . . exclude you and insult you', Lk. 6:20–22) asserts that even those who suffer injustice will be blessed. Furthermore, the one who gives a banquet and invites 'the poor, the crippled, the lame, the blind' rather than 'your friends, your brothers or relatives, or your rich neighbours' is the one who 'will be blessed' (Lk. 14:12–14). Both living in the context of injustice and responding according to the rule of God in the presence of injustice are means to blessedness. This interpretation of blessedness reflects both Ps. 41:1 ('Blessed is he who has regard for the weak') and more generally Ps. 106:3 ('Blessed are they who maintain justice, who constantly do what is right').

Blessedness, therefore, is both an attitude and a present reality; it reflects both understanding and action. The integration of these in the state of blessedness is ascribed in Jas. 1:25: 'The man who looks intently [*i.e.* with the proper attitude and understanding] into the perfect law that gives freedom, and continues to do this [*i.e.* makes it a present reality, an action], not forgetting what he has heard, but doing it – he will be blessed in what he does.'

In the Catholic moral tradition,* the concept of blessedness is closely linked with the beatific vision of God. As such, it replaces pleasure* (see Hedonism*) and happiness* as 'man's chief end', when ethics are viewed teleologically* from a Christian perspective.

D.L.P.

BLESSING AND CURSING. To bless somebody is to express a hope or prayer that good, desirable things will happen to that person. Such prayers and the good things which result are both described as blessings. Similarly, to curse somebody is to call down evil upon him or her, and both the prayers for evil and evil happenings can be described as curses. The most common use of blessing and cursing in Scripture is associated with the covenant.* Israel and individuals within Israel call upon themselves blessings or curses dependent on whether they obey or disobey the covenant commands (*e.g.* Dt. 27 – 28; Jos. 23 – 24).

The blessing and cursing of others (Ne. 13:2; Mal. 2:2) does not control God or limit his freedom, but it is a way by which human beings can act as mediators of God's power and as facilitators of God's purposes. It is vital however to avoid misuse, which does not take God and his character seriously but tries to ensure that one's own desires are carried out (Ex. 20:7; Nu. 24:13).

It seems that blessing can have greater effect than cursing, and although cursing is used on occasion even in the NT (Acts 13:9–11), we are encouraged to use blessing rather than cursing in dealing with those who do us harm (Pr. 25:21–22; Lk. 6:27–36; Rom. 12:14, 19–21). The blessing of children, congregations, bride and groom, *etc.* is common today, but perhaps the deliberate and meaningful use of blessings by individuals calling for God's goodness to be shown to others including 'enemies' should be more widely used and encouraged.

M.J.E.

BOISEN, ANTON (1867–1966). Best known for the development of the Clinical Pastoral Education (CPE) movement in the USA in the 1930s, Boisen is a significant figure in the rise of modern pastoral theology (see Practical and Pastoral Theology[7]). He originally studied linguistics, did graduate work on William James,* and then undertook theological training for the ministry, during which time he studied the psychology of religion under the direction of George Coe (1862–1951). He used his time as a rural pastor to conduct social and religious surveys. At the age of forty-four, Boisen passed through 'a brief but extremely severe period of mental illness'. He then undertook further study at Harvard, and spent eight years as a hospital chaplain, which he claims 'was the first attempt to bring to such a position any special training for the service of the mentally ill'. He later served as chaplain at the Elgin State Hospital in Illinois, combining the work with research and a lecturership in psychopathology at Chicago Theological Seminary. It was from this work that the CPE movement was developed. In 1936 Boisen wrote a major treatise, drawing on his own and others' experiences: *The Exploration of the Inner World: A Study of Mental Disorder and Religious Experience.* He brought together the worlds of psychiatry and religion, hypothesizing that there is a relationship between acute mental illness – in which he sought theological meaning – and certain forms of religious experience, both being attempts at personal reorganization. Boisen's case-study method of writing practical theology made a major impact on Seward Hiltner,* who took Boisen's method into the more academic setting of post-Second World War pastoral theology.

Bibliography

Out of the Depths (New York, 1960); *The*

Exploration of the Inner World (New York, 1936).

S. Hiltner, *Preface to Pastoral Theology* (Nashville, TN, 1958).

D.J.A.

BONHOEFFER, DIETRICH (1906–45), theologian and church leader in Germany until his martyrdom, deeply influenced contemporary Christianity by both his writings and his example. His early work from his period as a teacher at Berlin, notably *Creation and Fall* (ET, London, 1959) and the *Christology* lectures (ET, London, 1978), is much under the influence of Karl Barth.* In the mid-30s, Bonhoeffer emerged as a leader of both the Confessing Church in Germany and the early ecumenical movement. Until its enforced closure by the Nazis, Bonhoeffer ran a seminary for the Confessing Church; during this period he produced some of his well-known writings on spiritual formation and pastoral theology, in particular *The Cost of Discipleship* (ET, London, 1948) and *Life Together* (ET, London, 1954).

Bonhoeffer's life and work in their entirety are concerned at a very deep level with questions of the relation of the Christian faith to moral practice – a concern most graphically shown in his involvement in the German resistance movement and the plot against Hitler. Until his imprisonment in 1943, he was at work on his major ethical work, the *Ethics*, published posthumously. The *Ethics* is not a finished treatise but a collection of substantial fragments which would have formed the basis for the work Bonhoeffer regarded as his major theological contribution. Though the material is sometimes difficult to date, the rearranged sixth Ger. edition (the basis of more recent Eng. editions) gives probably the best sense of the development of the text. The opening section proposes a radically theocentric and Christocentric account of both the moral situation and the moral agent, in which divine action is the primary focus. Other sections use central theological motifs such as conformity to Christ or justification,* and contain hints of the reflections on the gospel and the autonomy of the world which preoccupied Bonhoeffer in his *Letters and Papers from Prison* (ET, London, ²1971). Even in its fragmentary state, the *Ethics* is a work of acute spiritual and moral sensitivity. Together with the ethical sections of Barth's *Church Dogmatics*, his *Ethics* remains a serious challenge to accounts of ethics which focus on moral deliberation or which root Christian ethics in more general considerations of the human moral sphere.

Bibliography
Ethics (ET, London, ²1971).
E. Bethge, *Dietrich Bonhoeffer* (ET, London and New York, 1970).

J.B.W.

BOOTH, WILLIAM (1829–1912), founder of the Salvation Army, was also noted for his advocacy of social reform. Converted in 1844 while apprenticed to a pawnbroker in Nottingham, Booth served as a lay preacher among the Wesleyans and then as a Methodist New Connection minister. Accepting the teaching of the American Phoebe Palmer (1807–74) about entire sanctification, he determined in 1861 to be an independent evangelist and holiness teacher. A Christian Mission he founded in Whitechapel, London, in 1865 expanded and, in 1878, took the name of the Salvation Army. Booth, as General, tried to sustain a red-hot fervour that ignored respectability in order to attract converts among the poor. The Army insisted on total abstinence, and in the 1880s established homes for reformed prostitutes, discharged prisoners and the homeless of London. The economic depression of the late 1880s persuaded Booth to publish *In Darkest England, and the Way Out* (London, 1890), urging that the urban destitute should be transferred to farm colonies or overseas colonies. Only a few parts of the scheme were implemented, but an institutional commitment to social work thenceforward marked the Salvation Army. Yet in his last years, as in his first, Booth's overriding aim was to save souls from sin.

Bibliography
H. Begbie, *Life of William Booth*, 2 vols. (London, 1920); K. S. Inglis, *Churches and the Working Classes in Victorian England* (London, 1963).

D.W.B.

BOYCOTT. Though an individual can engage in a boycott, the term is best understood as an *organized* refusal to deal with a party with whom there is disagreement, generally accompanied by efforts (*e.g.* a picket* line) to induce others not to deal with this party as well. Such action is called a 'primary' boycott. A 'secondary' boycott describes a refusal to deal with a party with whom there is no disagreement directly, but because this party in turn deals with the party with whom there is a disagreement.

Boycotts have occurred throughout history, though the term was coined in the 1880s growing out of actions in Ireland. The historian Josephus (*c*. 37–*c*. 100 AD) records several sit-down strikes by 1st-century Jews in Jerusalem protesting against the nature of Roman occupation. The commonest modern form of primary boycott finds trade-union members withholding their labour from an employer (encouraging other workers to do the same and consumers not to purchase the employer's product). Boycotts of products (often sponsored by churches) have marked recent decades, such as the action against the Nestlé company to protest against its promotion of infant-formula milk in poorer nations.

For many years leading to the 1940s, Jewish residents in several European nations were subjected to social and economic boycotts, and the Arab nations have practised primary and secondary boycotts against Israel since its formation in 1948. Nations frequently engage in boycotts against other nations, such as the US boycott of the 1980 Olympics protesting against Soviet military occupation of Afghanistan, or the action of many nations protesting against apartheid* in South Africa.

Assessing the boycott ethically compels examining both the objectives and consequences of the action. A Christian cannot participate in (indeed should work against) a boycott having unjust objectives. Deciding this may have been easier when the target was Jewish residents of Europe yesterday, or recent immigrants there today. Things become muddier with trade-union* action for higher wages. Is this not largely self-serving? Will not jobs be lost in the long run (along with economic harm to some not parties to the original boycott)? On the other hand, are the owners and managers of the enterprise depriving workers of a fair wage? The church (and society at large) requires the insights of knowledgeable Christians in helping it discern where the objectives of boycott actions are just or unjust.

Given just objectives, the use of otherwise non-violent and non-coercive boycotts as the best means of protesting against an injustice is far from clear. As long recognized, the boycott is a blunt instrument, harming many 'innocents' while seeking to harm those with whom disagreement exists (including the very

ones the action is intended to help). Many opposed to apartheid in South Africa were unwilling to support an economic boycott (see Economic Sanctions*) out of concern that black South Africans would bear terrible costs from this.

The arena receiving the greatest social and legal attention over the last century is employment and trade-union activity, and Christian voices have spoken here. In his 1981 encyclical *Laborem Exercens* (*On Human Work;* see Papal Encyclicals*), Pope John Paul II grants the need for a struggle to achieve justice in the workplace, allowing the use of the strike (employment boycott) under appropriate conditions and suitably limited: an extreme means that must not be abused. Numerous Protestant conference statements affirm similar sentiments.

Scripture systematically expresses concern for exploitative work situations (Ex. 5; Lv. 19:13; 1 Ki. 12:4ff.; Is. 58:3; Jas. 5:4), and is concerned that justice (see Justice and Peace[3]) and righteousness* be worked out in society (Is. 59:9, 14) – a process that may allow the use of boycotts. One might see God's call through Moses for the Israelites to leave their distressful employment in Egypt as a permanent boycott. God desires that employees receive what is right and fair (Col. 4:1), and it may be that private actions (suitably constrained) to this end may well be less troublesome to the social order than either outright prohibition (with attending suppression of what is right and fair) or extensive bureaucratic oversight of labour relations.

Bibliography

E. B. Bruland, 'Voting With Your Checkbook', *CT* 35, 19 Aug 1991, pp. 18–21; L. Ranke (ed.), 'Studying the Church's Use of the Economic Boycott', *Engage/Social Action* 14, Dec 1986; John Paul II, *Laborem Exercens* (ET *On Human Work*, London, 1981).

J.D.M.

BRAIN DEATH. It is possible for vital functions (breathing, circulation, excretion) to persist, or to be sustained artificially, despite the destruction of the higher brain by disease. The problems which then arise are: 1. how to be certain that the brain is dead, and so incapable of sustaining the functions of a living person; and 2. given that certainty, when and how to discontinue vital support (the 'switching-off' problem). The answers to the first question are medical: brain death is diagnosed only after a set of rigorously prescribed tests are made. In Britain these tests are repeated once after a suitable interval, and are made only by two doctors of adequate seniority (*BMJ* 1976, 2, pp. 1187–1188 and 1157–1158).

The forebrain, which contains the cerebral cortex, is the structure essential for thought and the coherent expression of the features of personality. The hindbrain contains the brain stem in which reside those functions which maintain life, especially the 'vital functions' of breathing and circulation. The term 'brain death' implies the loss of at least the cortex irrecoverably. The term 'brain-stem death' implies irrecoverable loss of vital functions. Even when vital functions are for the time being maintained by machine aid, neither 'brain death' nor 'brain-stem death' is compatible with return of conscious function. It is in this situation that life support is withdrawn under conditions of rigorous proof. Neither brain death nor brain-stem death should be confused with the very rare 'locked-in state', where a patient is conscious and can comprehend but is unable to respond to others.

Theological and ethical problems arise in relating the concept of a person made in God's image to the existence of a patient without a functioning forebrain. Pastoral problems are concerned with informing relatives, gaining their acceptance of withdrawal of vital support, and relating to their concerns about how an apparently living, if unconscious, person can be dead. This acceptance may take time. Often there are feelings of guilt,* inadequacy and hopelessness which accompany the normal grieving over the death, and a sense that in some way switching off the machines may have killed the patient. It may be thought mistakenly that the decision to withdraw active therapy was occasioned by medical concerns for cost, for the needed bed, or just unwillingness to try. There may even be concerns in some that the person who has died may have been denied an opportunity to repent or to believe as a result of withdrawing life support. They may be helped to see how the prolongation of vital support, for those who can never again decide, brings only needless suffering to all who are involved.

See also: DEATH AND DYING; ETHICS OF MEDICAL CARE; [14] INTENSIVE CARE.

D.W.V.

BRAINWASHING. The term 'brainwashing', scarcely heard of fifty years ago, has now passed into everyday language. The basic ideas behind it are not new. It describes a coercive process of thought control in which a person's beliefs are, against his or her will, brought into line with another's. Coercion of people for the purposes of extracting confessions was in use in the time of Napoleon (1769–1821). The understanding of why such methods were effective took major steps forward when the relevance to human behaviour of the work on animals by the Russian Nobel Laureate in physiology, Ivan Petrovich Pavlov (1849–1936), became evident. Following the flooding of his laboratories, Pavlov noted that some tasks learned by his experimental animals prior to the trauma of flooding and near-death, were, seemingly, forgotten when the animals were tested in new laboratories. This observation raised the question of how such stress and trauma might result in the disappearance of previously established conditioned responses. It further raised the question of whether similar mechanisms might be at work following externally imposed trauma and stresses in humans.

Brainwashing was used during the Purge Trials in Soviet Russia in 1936 and developed during the Second World War by the Nazis to produce betrayals of loyalties. It gained most prominence when used by the Chinese Communists during the Korean War of 1950–53. The experiences of large numbers of American servicemen led to intensive study of the Communists' techniques by psychiatrists and psychologists in the USA. As a result, the basic component processes of the techniques were identified and it became apparent that there were superficial linkages with what happens in some religious communities. Robert J. Lifton (1926–), for example, identified several of the factors involved. These included assault upon personal identity, the establishment of guilt,* the compulsion to confess, and the final confession followed by rebirth and release.

William Sargant (1907–88), a British psychiatrist, noted that 'it is ordinary, normal people who are most susceptible to "brainwashing", "conversion", "possession", "the crisis" or whatever you wish to call it, and who in their hundreds or thousands or millions fall readily under the spell of the demagogue or the revivalist, the witch doctor or the pop group . . .' and he believed that 'the root of this all-too-common human experience is a state of heightened suggestibility, of openness to ideas and exultations, which is characteristic of subjects under hypnosis . . .' (*The Mind Possessed*, p. 31).

Brainwashing and evangelistic crusades

It has been claimed that aspects of suggestion and brainwashing operate in large evangelistic gatherings. The typical ingredients at such meetings include a speaker, already given considerable prestige through media build-up, who communicates with great fervour, conviction and seeming authority. The occasion is frequently one where there are large crowds and emotional hymns are sung repeatedly before and after the address. There are bright lights, massed choirs and stirring music, often with a strong repetitive rhythmic beat. Taken together, it is argued that such factors result in a significantly raised state of emotional arousal and thus facilitate the preacher's attempt to increase feelings of guilt and make more pressing the acceptance of the offered way of escape from these feelings, resulting in sudden conversions. The case is cogently argued and graphically illustrated by Sargant in *Battle for The Mind* and *The Mind Possessed*.

That some of these factors are at work in such meetings seems likely. The extent of their influence, however, remains to be clarified. It is probable that personality factors, whether a person is introverted, extroverted or neurotic, will interact with the external circumstances to influence the outcome at such meetings. Certainly physical and psychological stresses skilfully applied can produce dramatic changes in behaviour and beliefs. Sargant illustrates this graphically from his observations in many cultures. One of the most dramatic examples is the snake-handling sects of the southern States of America. There he observed emotional exhaustion, leading to the heightened suggestibility evident in extreme forms in political brainwashing and in some large evangelistic meetings still held today (see Psychology of Religion*).

A Christian perspective

From a Christian perspective there can never be any justification (see Justification, Moral*) for treating people like things to be manipulated. According to the Christian gospel, it is the unfathomable love and generosity of God who was in Christ dying for the sins of all humankind that evokes a genuine response. The whole person, and that includes emotions* and feelings as well as the mind, is involved in conversion.* Thought, emotion and will are all intrinsic parts of human nature and are all involved in religious commitment and the religious life. The accounts of conversions in the NT, *e.g.* in a few chapters of the Acts of the Apostles, illustrate the range of different circumstances within which Christian conversions occur. To read these is to explode the myth that only one stereotyped type of conversion is true and constitutes 'the real thing'.

Christians who are psychologists work for a deeper understanding of the many ways in which people are converted and come to faith in Christ. That knowledge, however, can never, with justification, be used to manipulate people through brainwashing or any other technique in order to increase the numbers of converts. It is, however, entirely proper to use such psychological knowledge in order to present as clearly as possible the love of God in Christ, the historical basis of the Christian gospel, and the demands it makes upon the unconverted, and to make unmistakably clear the way of escape offered in Christ. Persuasion and exultation, yes; manipulation* and brainwashing, no. This is the balance that must be maintained.

Bibliography

R. J. Lifton, *Thought Reform and the Psychology of Totalism* (New York and London, 1961); W. Sargant, *Battle for the Mind* (London and New York, 1957); *idem*, *The Mind Possessed* (London, 1973).

M.A.J.

BRANDT REPORT, THE. Named after Willy Brandt (1913–92), the former West German Chancellor and winner of the Nobel Peace Prize in 1971. Brandt is revered in his country for the policy of Ostpolitik, which contributed to the ending of the Cold War and to the reunification of Germany. Internationally, he is possibly better known for his part in the development debate (see Economic Development*).

In 1978, the Independent Commission on International Development Issues was set up under his chairmanship to look into the critical state of relations between the rich and poor countries and to make proposals for a more just international order.* The Commission's report was published in 1980, under the title *North – South: A Programme For Survival*. Three years later, worsening economic conditions and the lack of global co-operation compelled the Brandt Commission to publish a sequel, *Common Crisis, North – South: Co-operation for World Recovery* (see North – South Divide*).

The importance of the Brandt Report is that its detailed proposals have set a global agenda for world development. The main theme of the Report is that everyone stands to gain from the expansion of trade (see International Trade*) which would result from the North assisting the South to develop. This theme reflects Brandt's personal experience of Ostpolitik, in which he saw how important it is for the peaceful resolution of conflict to appeal to the self-interest of both sides. The theme is also a product of the depressed economic conditions of the late 1970s, when the rise in oil prices, in particular, had thrown the richer countries into recession, and when it looked as if calls for substantial increased aid to the Third World would go unheeded unless there was some benefit for the First World.

The main criticism of the Report is that it places too much faith in the enlightened self-interest of the North and overlooks the realities of political and economic competition between the major world groups. This criticism, which reflects the liberationist – realist division in Christian ethics, goes beyond Brandt to urge the radical transformation of existing international economic institutions and arrangements.

If not all Christians will be united behind the Report, at least all can unite behind Brandt's commitment to the flourishing of the whole human family, because central to the Christian faith is the belief that God is the one creator of all, whether we live in the North or the South.

See also: GLOBAL ETHICS. 15

Bibliography

W. Brandt (chairperson), *North – South: A Programme for Survival* (London and Cambridge, MA, 1980); *idem, Common Crisis, North – South: Co-operation for World Recovery* (London and New York, 1983); C. Elliott, *Comfortable Compassion? Poverty, Power and the Church* (London, 1987); J. P. Wogaman, *Economics and Ethics; A Christian Enquiry* (London and Philadelphia, 1986).

C.Y.

BRIBERY. Consider a public undertaking that provides, *e.g.*, goods for sale or services to others, and that is presumed free of secretive and special pleading. A bribe is an offer (typically covert) of money, goods or services to influence the performance of this undertaking in an improper way. Bribery then encompasses both the offer and the receipt of the bribe, along with the reciprocal impact upon the undertaking.

The Bible and Christian tradition consistently condemn bribery as detestable and to be proscribed. God accepts no bribes (Dt. 10:17). We are not to accept bribes (Ex. 23:8; Dt. 16:19). To accept bribes and to extort are detestable practices (Ezk. 22:2, 12). Most biblical references are to judicial settings, but the condemnation is general. Passages dealing explicitly with bribery make its 'acceptance' the offence. Naboth's contrived conviction (1 Ki. 21) and the rebuke of Simon the sorcerer (Acts 8:9 – 25) suggest that making the inducement is detestable. J. T. Noonan (1926 –), in his comprehensive and masterful work *Bribes*, systematizes the (sometimes tortuous) development of Christian tradition over the centuries, and finds it consistent with biblical instruction – also noting in careful detail the salutary effect of Christian teaching upon Western societies.

In elaborating biblical instruction, Noonan observes how OT gifts and sacrifices as well as Christ's sacrificial death can appear as bribes designed to extract reciprocity from God. 'How, then, does a [gift] to God to liberate us from sin differ from a payment to a judge to release a guilty prisoner?' (p. 64). Ambiguity resides here, he concludes – albeit his eventual resolution is the correct one. OT gifts and sacrifices, when not a reflection of a pleasing life and expressions of thanksgiving, become a stench to the God who desires mercy and obedience more than sacrifice (1 Sa. 15:22; Is. 1:11ff.; Ho. 6:6; Mt. 12:7).

To view Christ's sacrifice as affecting a lighter sentence fails to grasp both the horror and the wonder of the atonement.* Our sins were not excused; the sentence was paid in full. Jesus Christ 'was pierced for our transgressions, he was crushed for our iniquities' (Is. 53:5). Whatever difficulties surround the mystery of the atonement, bribery is not one of them. Our part here is to acknowledge our unworthiness, seek God's forgiveness, and accept Christ as saviour and Lord: hardly the makings of a gift (or bribe) – and something the poorest person can do as easily as the richest.

If bribery then so clearly is wrong, wherein lies the ethical issue for us? Difficulties arise in discerning where legitimate gift-giving becomes bribery, and where the offer of money, goods or services is a bribe to be condemned or a case of extortion (maybe resulting in lighter moral consequences). Some examples make clear the dilemmas: parents who volunteer in their children's school may well expect better treatment for their children as a result; an undesirable but ethically allowable payment may be made in the face of implicit (if not explicit) extortion; or a company may offer free consulting to some existing and potential buyers.

The type of bribery currently attracting the greatest attention is alleged extortion: a business feeling compelled to make a substantial 'gift' in order to have its product receive proper consideration. Does the Bible's general condemnation of accepting, rather than making, bribes implicitly acknowledge (and maybe pardon) the difficulty here? Note should be taken, however, of Paul's failure to 'bribe' Felix (Acts 24:26) – presumably to be set free (which surely would have enhanced his ministry). How freely should we engage in ethically problematic means to achieve what appears to be a desirable end?

As with so many practices (pride, slander, theft, *etc.*) the line between right and wrong is often subtle and requires vigilance. Bribery is wrong! We can write laws against the practice in its more blatant forms. But too many cases exist where otherwise innocent gift-giving bleeds over into efforts to extract obligations and favours, and thereby becomes bribery. No State can police against this. The health of a nation requires its citizens to discipline themselves in such cases.

Bibliography

T. L. Carson, 'Bribery, Extortion, and "The Foreign Corrupt Practices Act" ', *Philosophy and Public Affairs* 14, Winter 1985, pp. 66–90; J. T. Noonan, Jr., *Bribes* (New York and London, 1984); M. Philips, 'Bribery', *Eth* 94, 1984, pp. 621–636.

J.D.M.

BROADCASTING, see MEDIA.

BRUNNER, EMIL (1889–1966), Swiss pastor and professor of theology, was prominent in neo-orthodox circles. Accordingly, he advocated 'dialectical' or 'crisis theology' with its Kierkegaardian emphasis on God's existential confrontation of the individual through the Word of God revealed in Christ as uniquely witnessed to in Scripture and by the inner testimony of the Holy Spirit.

Brunner developed the idea of Jewish theologian Martin Buber (1878–1965) that God and truth are known in life-changing personal encounters with the One who chooses to reveal himself to humans – an 'I–Thou' rather than an 'I–it' relationship. This avoided Roman Catholic and fundamentalist 'objectivism' which equated revelation* with truths found in the Bible or church dogma, and the 'subjectivism' of classical Protestant liberalism which found truth in experience and feeling. But Brunner argued against Karl Barth* that there is a revelation of God in nature, and that fallen humans retain some 'point of contact' with God by virtue of being in the image of God,* both of which are necessary assertions if humans are to be held accountable for their sin.

Brunner insisted that there is no Christian faith apart from Christian conduct. Christian ethics is 'the science of human conduct as it is determined by Divine conduct' (*Divine Imperative*, p. 86). Divine conduct is characterized by *agapē* love (see ②), reflected in God's commands, obedience to which is determined by particular circumstances in the context of the 'orders of creation' (family, the State,* church,* culture* and economic life; see Economic Ethics ⑰) that God has established to maintain a stable common life. While the Decalogue* and the Sermon on the Mount* are prime indications of the shape that God's commands of love take, we relate to God and to our neighbours in a free act of love, not out of a sense of duty or case law. Brunner was critical of Nazi and communistic totalitarianism, which he argued was ultimately based on positivism.

Though he was overshadowed by the more prolific Barth, Brunner's significance in the English-speaking world of the post-Second World War years should not be underestimated. Evangelicals have appreciated his thought, while wishing that he had better safeguarded the objective normativity of Scripture. Some critics have argued that he was closer to liberalism (see Liberalism, Theological*) than other neo-orthodox theologians.

Bibliography

The Divine Imperative (ET, London and New York, 1937); *Dogmatics*, 3 vols. (ET,

London and Philadelphia, 1949, 1952, 1962); *Man in Revolt* (ET, London 1939); *The Mediator* (ET, London, 1934); 'Nature and Grace' in *Natural Theology* (ET, London, 1946); *Truth as Encounter* (ET, London and Philadelphia, 1964).

D.L.O.

BUCER, MARTIN (1491–1551). Born at Schettstadt (now Sélestat) in Alsace, Bucer became a Dominican friar at the age of fifteen and was also influenced by Erasmian humanism. He was won over by Martin Luther* at the Heidelberg disputation (1518), but went on to pursue a more independent path, attempting to mediate between Luther and Zwingli (1484–1531). He settled in Strasburg in 1523 and become one of the leaders of the church there. In 1549 he became Regius Professor of Divinity at Cambridge, during the Edwardian reformation, and died there in 1551.

Two of Bucer's works are of especial importance here. His *Von der waren Seelsorge ...* (*On the Care of Souls*, 1538) is one of the most important 16th-century works on pastoral care. Bucer stresses the need for a plurality of leadership* within each church, since no one person can have all the gifts. These leaders should be chosen from across the social spectrum. He also discusses strategies of pastoral care to different groups within the church.

His last work was his *De Regno Christi* (*The Kingdom of Christ*), which he wrote in the final few months of his life. It was a comprehensive blueprint for the reformation of England, dedicated to Edward VI. In it Bucer covers not just ecclesiastical matters but ethical, social and political issues. These include poor relief, marriage* and divorce,* public education, employment policy and the penal system. By the 'kingdom of Christ' he understood a 'Christian commonwealth' in which the State is as concerned for the first as for the second table of the law (see Decalogue*).

Bibliography

Von der waren Seelsorge ..., in R. Stupperich (ed.), *Martin Bucers Deutsche Schriften*, vol. 7 (Gütersloh and Paris, 1964); *The Kingdom of Christ*, in W. Pauck (ed.), *Melanchthon and Bucer*, LCC 19. Selections in D. F. Wright (ed.), *Common Places of Martin Bucer* (Appleford, 1972).

W. P. Stephens, *The Holy Spirit in the Theology of Martin Bucer* (Cambridge, 1970).

A.N.S.L.

BUDDHIST ETHICS. The ultimate Buddhist value is *achieving nirvana*; to this religious value all moral value is subservient. Desire or craving is viewed as typically inherent in human existence until nirvana is achieved. Moral conduct (not to do evil, to do good, to purify the mind) serves as a means to nirvana. The layperson is expected to follow a morality that forbids such things as lying, stealing, killing and doing violence; the monk, male or female, is required also to practise chastity, abstinence from alcohol, and eating only what is offered in alms.

How nirvana itself is conceived varies from one Buddhist school to another. Interpretations of nirvana range from identifying it with sheer annihilation to saying that it is ineffable. If nirvana is the desired goal of persons, it is relevant to ask what a person is thought to be. Typically, a person *at* any one point in time is conceived as a bundle or collection composed of five sorts of states (matter, sensation, perception, predisposition and consciousness); *over* time a person is conceived as a series of bundles. There is often said to be a pre-nirvanic state that one obtains in this life (nirvana-with-residue), achievement of which guarantees attaining permanent nirvana (nirvana-without-residue) upon death. If craving is inherent in all of the states that comprise a person, and craving is inherently unsatisfactory, then nirvana is escape only if it is the annihilation of the person. The only question that then remains is whether what *was* the person in any sense survives. The early Theravada tradition seems typically to answer in the negative. Even so, the goal here is to become an *arhat* – one who has achieved enlightenment, which includes accepting the Buddhist account of personhood. The later Mahayana tradition countenances nirvana-with-residue states that are not viewed as inherently involved with craving and so as not intrinsically unsatisfactory. Here, the ideal is not the *arhat* but the *bodhisattva* who, upon achieving nirvana-with-residue, deliberately postpones achieving ultimate nirvana out of compassion for others whom one then strives to help to achieve nirvana-with-residue. For those varieties of Mahayana that view ultimate nirvana as identical to cycle of birth and rebirth, the final conclusion concerning personal survival seems the same as that to which Theravada came, but other Mahayana schools deny the identity of nirvana with this cycle.

Bibliography

E. Conze, *Buddhism: Its Essence and Development* (Oxford and New York, 1951); C. Humphreys, *Buddhism* (Harmondsworth, ²1990).

K.E.Y.

BULIMIA, see EATING DISORDERS.

BULTMANN, RUDOLF (1884–1976), professor of theology at Marburg in Germany, was widely influential, during his lifetime, as a NT historical critic, exegete, and theologian.

Bultmann's theology

Strongly associated with the early, existentialist, philosophy of Martin Heidegger (1889–1976), Bultmann was perhaps most famous for his proposal that theologians 'demythologize' the NT. In his own work, demythologizing amounted to reading the NT documents as embodying, on the one hand, an antiquated world-view from which they must be delivered if we moderns are to understand them and, on the other hand, a message that we desperately need if we are to become authentic human beings. Thus demythologizing was regarded as a deeply practical and pastorally important activity. Through such an interpretation the NT documents would become able to speak to modern people who do not believe in a three-tiered universe, or miraculous divine interventions in natural processes, or the takeover of personalities by spirits (holy or otherwise). Once the mythological husk had been removed, the essential NT message of salvation – the 'kerygma' – could address modern people, calling them to decision and enabling them to become 'open to the future'. According to Bultmann's theology, such openness is what the NT calls faith.*

It may fairly be said that Bultmann's 'theology' is little more than a hermeneutical rationale for reading the philosophy of the early Heidegger into the NT. That philosophy is primarily a theory of human nature, and it says that we are essentially decision-makers. Of course it is banal to say that we make decisions, but what Bultmann's Heidegger has in mind is controversial: if we are decision-makers, then we *betray* ourselves to the extent that we identify with anything that is fixed, given, past, established, permanent or objective. For example, if we think of God as a being

who is really there, who hears our requests and has a plan for us, then identifying ourselves with this God – *e.g.* understanding ourselves as his children – is 'unauthentic'. Or if we identify ourselves in terms of Jesus' objective biography, pointing to that historical man as our saviour, then we have betrayed our true nature as decision-makers. Or again, whatever permanent virtues we may have – patience, compassion, courage, faith, hope or love – cannot be the true 'us'; we eixst not in our dispositions, but only in our actions, and thus in the 'moment'. It is of course endemic to human beings that we violate our nature by thinking of ourselves in terms of what is fixed, enduring and past; this is what the NT calls sin. To be authentic is to be radically open to the 'future' understood as an arena of pure 'possibility' where nothing is given, established, fixed, *etc.* – where nothing is metaphysical, historical (in the standard sense of past) or psychological.

Ethical and pastoral implications

What consequences would a consistent implementation of Bultmann's theology have for the ethical and spiritual life of a congregation? A Bultmannian pastor would do nothing aimed at instilling Christian character-traits in his or her parishioners, nor would he attempt to mobilize the congregation in the interest of social change. As Bultmann remarks, 'God's demand . . . aims neither at the formation of "character" nor at the molding of human society' (*Theology of the New Testament*, vol. 1, p. 19). The reason for this is obvious from what was said above: Christian spirituality,* on Bultmann's account, is a matter of *dissociating* oneself from one's character-traits or from any objective results that one's actions may achieve. It is found purely in affirming oneself as a decision-maker and thus transcending any such 'actualities'. The pastor does not aim at any permanent transformation of persons, but instead presents the kerygma moment by moment to elicit 'decisions' which in the next moment must be remade on pain of slippage into unauthenticity. The classical Christian view, that pastoral work consists in fostering the Christian virtues* in the members of the congregation, and the Calvinist view, that the pastor is to lead the congregation in the transformation of the social order, are quite directly denied, on the principles of this theology.

Bibliography

Kerygma and Myth: A Theological Debate (ET, London, 1962 and 1964; New York, 1964); *Theology of the New Testament*, 2 vols. (ET, New York, 1951 and 1955; London, 1952 and 1955); R. C. Roberts, *Rudolf Bultmann's Theology: A Critical Interpretation* (Grand Rapids, 1976; London, 1977); W. Schmithals, *An Introduction to the Theology of Rudolf Bultmann* (ET, London and Minneapolis, MN, 1968).

R.C.R.

BUNYAN, JOHN (1628–88), tinker, preacher and author, was born in Elstow, near Bedford. Although his formal education was slight, he possessed an inquiring mind and a lively imagination. During the early 1650s he underwent various spiritual crises which he later graphically described in one of the classics of Puritan autobiography, *Grace Abounding to the Chief of Sinners* (1666). The author of more than sixty books, Bunyan published in 1678 his famous allegory *The Pilgrim's Progress*, which for generations was the work, next to the Bible, most deeply cherished in English-speaking homes, and earned for him a unique place in Eng. literary history. The allegory also channelled the Puritan spirit into the main stream of the English tradition.

In theology Bunyan adhered essentially to the Calvinist tradition, but he was also indebted for various insights to the writings of Martin Luther* as well as to ideas from the Separatist tradition. Bunyan has been frequently called a Particular (*i.e.* he believed that Christ died for the elect only) Open Communion Baptist. In line with one strand of the Separatist tradition, he was open-minded about different modes of baptism and was prepared to admit persons to church membership on the basis (only) of a credible profession of faith (hence 'Open Communionist'). Bunyan gave a clear exposition of his theology in *The Doctrine of the Law and Grace Unfolded* (1659).

His prose writings focused primarily on theology, doctrine, church government and church worship, but showed equal concern with the implications of biblical teaching for personal living. *Christian Behaviour* (1663), belonging to a group of numerous, popular 17th-century manuals of conduct (see Puritans, Pastoral Counselling of*), emphasized the need for strong families and the role of fathers and their relation to all family members, including servants. It also stressed a view of economics which attacks the profit motive.

The Life and Death of Mr Badman (1680) unfolded Bunyan's most detailed treatment of ethical concerns (see Puritan Ethics*). Without discussing complexities, he pointed up numerous problems, such as abused women, sexual promiscuity, deception in business ventures, cultural mores as standards for living, greed, extortion, inequity in distribution of goods, hypocrisy and compromise, and books that set 'fleshly lusts on fire'. For Bunyan, godly living grounded in sound theology embodies transformation in society.

B.B.

BUREAUCRACY AND ORGANIZATION. Organization is the central concept for groups of people who are working together to realize goals. It includes as subsidiary concepts bureaucracy, management,* business, operations research and automation. It has gone through stages of development which reveal different priorities and frames of reference.

The idea of bureaucracy was first used in the late 18th century and was understood as rule by officials. The most famous historical example was in China, where from the Emperor downwards a vast educated army of officials ordered the society throughout many dynasties. An oft-noted characteristic of political bureaucracies was that, far from just administering orders, they accrued responsibility and executive power to themselves. Rulers came and went, but administrators carried on. This raised the underlying spectre of bureaucracy: officers who are self-serving make rules for their convenience, thus creating institutionalized behaviour. Centralized states, like those of Socialist Eastern Europe, have faced this problem acutely.

Max Weber (1864–1920) pushed the analysis of bureaucracy further. He used the concept to describe not just political organization, but also industrial and business complexes. They all, he argued, had a common structure: tight job descriptions specifying duties, an office hierarchy, the use of files, specialized training, meritocratic appointment, the primacy of administrative concern, and a specialized system of rules. He saw it as the central modern 'rational' way of responding to any large-scale task. This model at first seemed to dominate the development of modern organizations.

However, it had limitations. Adolf A. Berle (1895–1971) and Gardiner C. Means (1896–1988) – who developed the idea of managerial capitalism (see *The Modern Corporation and Private Property*, New York, ²1968) – pointed out that businesses may have more than one goal, *e.g.* both expansion and the maximization of profit, which compete within an organizational structure. The famous Hawthorne Works studies, carried out by Elton Mayo (1880–1949), showed that workers often did not share management aims at all. This led to a recognition of formal and informal structures within organizations, often working at cross-purposes. A deeper challenge came at the Nuremburg War Crimes Trials, which underlined officials' responsibility for all orders carried out. Later, W. H. Whyte's (1917–) book *The Organization Man* graphically posed the problem of conformity. This raised deeper questions about the values and principles which are supported by all members of an organization, not just by those at the top.

As management studies developed, they also moved away from a rigid bureaucratic model. P. F. Drucker (1909–) and others showed that the central directive model was not applicable to many kinds of production and service industries. Hierarchies were reversed. Often the unit providing the service or developing the product had to lead the managers. Also called into question was the assumption of organizational economies of scale. Charlie Chaplin (1889–1977) in the film *Modern Times* (1936), and E. F. Schumacher (1911–77) in the book *Small is Beautiful* (London, 1973), popularized the idea that intimacy in industry might be good, and now Volvo, ICI, and many other companies have built smaller work units into their structures. The personal meaning of work* was accorded respect, rather than just functional output.

Another critique of organizational development came from Jacques Ellul.* He argued that technique, the process of realizing goals, came to dominate organizations to the extent that it transformed the goals. The means became the end. Organizations could be wrapped up in efficient production to the exclusion of considering the value of what they were producing. Arms manufacturers could generate wars, not prevent them. This brought out the importance of the deeper values and commitments of organizations, and moved critique beyond efficiency to Christian and other faith commitments.

At the same time, much organizational theory developed in supposedly neutral scientific ways, which established criteria for efficiency which were objective and could be measured. Some of these were behavioural, and in the late 20th-century systems of incentives have supposedly created the best basis for maximizing efficiency. Yet alongside intense career structures are patterns of stress,* burnout and relocation, which suggest that many of the issues which arise in organizations are wider than considered by those who organize them. Relating them to families, community (see Community Ethics[16]), environment* and the wider economy requires the kind of awareness which few organizations handle well. Feminist* critiques have showed how male-centred many conceptions of organizations have been.

Finally, postmodernist (see Modernity and Postmodernity*) critics like Michel Foucault (1926–84) argue that organizations which believe they are operating on rational terms can be seen from other perspectives as irrational or mad. Military élites think in terms of efficiently killing millions of people, the prison service in terms of making people passive and docile, and industrialists in terms of selling people things they would otherwise not want. This opens up a more radical questioning of the purposes of organizations.

Christian contributions and systematic work in organization theory have been limited, with the noted exception of Ellul and Schumacher.

Bibliography

M. Douglas, *How Institutions Think* (Syracuse, NY, 1986; London, 1987); P. F. Drucker, *The Practice of Management* (San Francisco, 1954; London, 1955); J. Ellul, *The Technological Society* (1954; ET, New York, 1964, and London, 1965); M. Foucault, *Madness and Civilisation* (ET, London, 1967); M. Savage and A. Witz (eds.), *Gender and Bureaucracy* (Oxford and Cambridge, MA, 1992); D. Silverman, *The Theory of Organisations* (London, 1970); M. Weber, *Economy and Society* (Berkeley, CA, 1978); W. H. Whyte, *The Organization Man* (New York, 1956; London 1957).

A.S.

B URIAL AND CREMATION. Along with burial at sea, inhumation (placing a corpse in the humus or earth) and cremation (burning up a corpse and reducing it to ash) are ways to dispose reverently of the body of a deceased person.

Historical and cultural variations

Homer's Gk. heroes (like Buddhist priests and Tibetan high lamas) were cremated as a sign of great honour, whereas in ancient Egypt the honoured corpse was preserved for the after-life by embalming. First-century Rome (like 11th-century Scandinavia when the gospel arrived there) saw a change from cremation to burial. Since cremation became legal in England in 1884, there has been a growth in the numbers of cremations, especially since the 1940s. In 1988, in Britain 70% of deceased people were cremated, 57% in Switzerland, 15% in the USA, and 1% in Catholic Italy (D. J. Davies, *Cremation Today and Tomorrow*, p. 6). Variation within a nation was as marked as differences between nations (in the USA: Nevada 56%, Alabama 2%), reflecting different experiences of community (T. Walter, *Funerals and How to Improve Them*, ch. 2).

Burial places in city or country alike have become 'shrines'. Graves in English country churchyards (D. L. Edwards, *Christian England*, p. 27) and in Japanese rural cemeteries are alike decorated for special religious festivals (Walter, p. 197). Urbanization* and secular modernity threaten this close connection between the living and their dead, and between our physical existence and spiritual meaning.

Burial and Christian origins

Death followed by burial (perhaps in a family tomb, Gn. 35:29) is the usual biblical pattern (*e.g.* Gn. 35:20). To be unburied is undignified (Na. 3:3; Rev. 11:9). The 'cremation' of Saul and his sons was exceptional (1 Sa. 31:12) and the burning of bodies and bones was a shameful abuse (Am. 2:1). The burials of Lazarus (Jn. 11) and Jesus (Jn. 19:38–42) seem to have followed common practice. The demand upon descendants to bury the dead is relativized by the demands of the kingdom (Lk. 9:60), and no attempt is made to honour the place where Jesus was buried, because his resurrection* (and the resurrection of the believer) became the controlling hope (1 Thes. 4:14a).

The historically 'accidental' fact that Jesus was buried (and raised to life), reinforced by the sacraments of baptism and communion (*e.g.* Rom. 6:1–4), was a factor initially prejudicing Christians towards burial. Early Christians were buried together (sometimes near the tomb of a martyr), reflecting the solidarity of the new family 'in Christ'.

Perspectives for pastoral practice

1. The finality of death (see Death and Dying*) is emphasized as a body is lowered into a grave, symbolism which has important ritual functions for grieving relatives. However, at the crematorium, the body usually disappears at the 'committal', to await incineration. The symbolism of destroying fire is thereby hidden. Do traditional funeral liturgies (designed for burial) 'fit' this new symbolism, especially as the ashes are interred on a separate occasion? The whole process of cremation may suggest Gk. ideas of an immortal soul (Davies, pp. 30–35) rather than the Christian doctrine of the resurrection body. Davies (pp. 42–45) offers a revised liturgy with this in mind, though ambiguity in how people interpret events almost inevitably remains (Walter, p. 282).

2. Obituaries in city newspapers, or epitaphs in a country graveyard, also illustrate this ambiguity. Three common epitaphs are: 'He only takes the best'; 'Until we meet again re-united'; and 'Requiescat' (short for *Requiescat in pace* [or RIP], meaning 'May he [or she] rest in peace'). All three express the need to understand why a death has occurred, the hope of a future reunion and the (Christian) assurance that the dead lie at rest 'in Christ'. However, such popular sentiment may overlook the heart of the gospel, so that 'judgment', being 'at home' in the presence of God, and even the finality of death (albeit at present being asleep, 1 Thes. 4:13ff.; 'cemetery' in Gk. means sleeping-place) are overlooked.

3. Pastoral care treasures the memory of life and seeks hope* while facing the mystery of death. The choice between cremation and burial (including having access to adequate information, and overcoming any fear of fire that may prejudice a decision) can be made in advance. Thus energy can be focused on death's significance rather than on its form.

Bibliography

A. Billings, 'Obituaries and Pastoral Care', *Con* 1, 1989, pp. 25–39; D. J. Davies, *Cremation Today and Tomorrow* (Bramcote, Nottingham, 1990); D. L. Edwards, *Christian England*, vol. 1 (London, 1989), pp. 27, 50; T. Walter, *Funerals and How to Improve Them* (London, 1990).

G.O.S.

BURN-OUT, see STRESS.

BUSINESS ETHICS, see ECONOMIC ETHICS. [17]

BUTLER, JOSEPH (1692–1752). From a Presbyterian family, Butler became an Anglican and entered Oriel College, Oxford, in 1714. He was ordained in 1718 and his preaching won him a reputation for unusual scholarly ability. Moving to a parish near Durham he lived quietly insulated from all but his pastoral duties as he prepared his famous *Analogy of Religion, Natural and Revealed, to the Constitution and Course of Nature* (1736).

He was made Bishop of Bristol in 1738 and is said to have declined an offer to be Archbishop of Canterbury on the grounds that 'it was too late for him to try to support a falling church'. Later he did accept the appointment as Bishop of Durham (1750). His writings, especially the *Analogy*, became the outstanding work against the Deists, and the moral philosophy contained in his sermons was even more lastingly effective, as it became part of the curriculum at both Cambridge and Oxford.

The *Analogy* is free from any polemical bitterness and is characterized by a cautious and admirably restrained logic. It shows nature to contain precisely the same kind of difficulties that are found in revelation; thus the Deists' confidence in nature and their discarding of revelation is unfounded. Butler's argument assumes the validity of theism and the immortality of the soul (*a priori*). He argues from this that on the grounds of empirical evidence there is a governance of the world which encourages virtue, discourages vice, and implies the logical probability of ultimate congruity between moral duty* and self-interest. Both nature and revelation* are seen by analogy to proceed from the same Author.

Butler's rational and philosophical defence of orthodoxy against the Deists was in remarkable contrast to his contemporary, John Wesley,* to whom he complained, 'Sir, the pretending to extraordinary revelations and gifts of the Holy Ghost is a horrid thing, a very horrid thing.' Wesley's reply was to insist that there were no *extra*ordinary revelations but only 'what every Christian may receive and ought to expect and to pray for'.

Butler's appreciation of the imperfect apprehension of human knowledge of truth was much more realistic than that of the Deists but the tragic human capacity for positive evil is unacknowledged. This may explain his confidence in reason* and nature rather than in redemption (see Sin and Salvation [5]) and grace.* He once asked his chaplain, Josiah Tucker, if public bodies might not go mad as well as individuals, adding that nothing else would account for most of the transactions of history.

It has been remarked of Butler's teaching that such a gospel will never save a sinner, and it is true that his sermons are largely characterized by the absence of biblical exegesis, kerygmatic content and soteriological concern. However, given Butler's assumptions (not always acknowledged), the ability of conscience,* religiously informed in its role in establishing virtue under orderly supervision of Providence, is still able to evoke confidence in Christian moral teachings as it did for John Henry Newman (1801–90).

Bibliography

A. A. Carlsson, *Butler's Ethics* (The Hague, 1964); W. E. Gladstone (ed.), *The Works of Joseph Butler*, 3 vols. (London, 1896); E. C. Mossner, *Bishop Butler and the Age of Reason* (New York, 1936); I. T. Ramsey, *Joseph Butler* (London, 1969).

C.F.A.

C

CALLING, see VOCATION.

CALVIN, JOHN (1509–64). Born in France on 10 July 1509, Calvin became the chief Reformer of Geneva, where he died on 27 May 1564. His major contribution was the exposition of a type of Protestant theology which is called 'Reformed' or 'Calvinistic'.

Calvin's theology is a permanent resource for Christian reflection. Its pastoral context is Geneva, where Calvin laboured from 1536 to 1564 (except for the important Strasburg years 1536–41) as pastor, preacher, teacher and writer. The reformer of both church and city life, Calvin emphasized the vocation* of all people, with their variety of gifts, to glorify God in every area of life, and he worked to transfer the governance of the church into the hands of pastors and elders.

Unfortunately, the popular view is that Calvin was a 'theo-logician' who taught the absolute sovereignty of God with such conviction that he did not shrink from deducing the corollary doctrine of double predestination. In the latter, human freewill and responsibility virtually disappear before the divine decrees of eternal election for some and eternal reprobation for others. Calvin certainly believed salvation is directly attributable to God's grace alone, but predestination is not his 'central dogma'. Calvin's exposition of 'union with Christ' may be taken as a more basic and comprehensive standpoint from which to evaluate his theological contribution.

The final edition of his masterwork, the *Institutes of the Christian Religion* (1559), contains four books. In Book One, entitled 'The Knowledge of God the Creator', Calvin rejects speculation about the 'being' of God in favour of what God reveals concerning his will. God is known to us as the creator of all things visible and invisible. Moreover, God continues to care for all that he has made. Therefore events do not occur by necessity or fate, nor do they happen by fortune or chance. Instead, Christians are to understand, and be comforted by, the fact that God governs everything. Thus God's all-encompassing providence requires the firm assertion that in both prosperity and adversity we deal with the God who loves us and became incarnate to save us.

Since Calvin believes that God is revealed first as creator and secondly as redeemer, Book Two deals with the knowledge of Jesus Christ, the mediator and redeemer. The opening five chapters describe human sin. Calvin accepts the traditional doctrine of original sin,* but his primary focus is on actual sin which results in our 'total depravity'. Calvin did not teach that we are as evil as we could possibly be, or that there is no goodness in us. Total depravity means that even our virtues are not exempt from the encroachment of sin.

According to Calvin, the fact of sin is evident, and redemption from it is provided in Jesus Christ, but no theoretical explanation of sin is possible. The cause of sin is unbelief, but, in the light of God's omnipotence and omniscience, the origin of sin is 'adventitious', which means that no reason can be given for its existence. Having rejected the concept of chance in his doctrine of providence, Calvin seems to assert it in his doctrine of sin!

Following the section on sin, Calvin deals with the scriptural disclosure of redemption in the OT and NT under the themes of law and gospel (chapters 6 to 11), insisting that salvation was always to be sought in Christ alone, and that God's grace precedes the promulgation of the law* and the recognition of human inability to fulfil God's commandment.

In addition to a description of the threefold work of Christ as prophet, king and priest, Calvin expounds the traditional view of Jesus* Christ as one person in two natures: human and divine. However, while affirming the deity of Christ, Calvin also places a strong emphasis on the eternal humanity of Christ. His commentary on Gal. 3:13 states that in Christ's human nature there are two things to be considered: 1. that in himself Christ was the sinless Son of God; and 2. that he took our place and became a sinner.

Having dealt with what God does for us as creator (Book One) and redeemer (Book Two), Calvin maintains that what God has done for the world is useless unless the Holy Spirit* applies salvation to us. Thereupon Calvin explains what God does in us as individuals (Book Three) and as a community (Book Four).

According to Calvin, the principal work of the Holy Spirit is the gift of faith,* which is chiefly explained in terms of two interlocking sets of 'double graces': regeneration and justification; and prayer and predestination. 1. Regeneration (or sanctification) means that on the basis of faith, the individual is both encouraged and enabled to do good works and to become more Christlike each day. Justification means that in Jesus Christ our sins are forgiven once for all. Good works are not the cause of justification. Rather, because of our justification, God expects good works from us. 2. The second set of 'double graces' contains prayer, which Calvin defines as 'the chief exercise of faith' (see his commentary on Eph. 6:18) and predestination (or eternal election), the humble exposition of the believer's experience of the gift of faith.

Each of these doctrines exalts the sovereign grace of God but in different ways. Regeneration and prayer have a 'humanly active' component, while justification and predestination are 'humanly passive'. In Book Four, Calvin treats the redeemed community: the church's ministry, sacraments and relation to civil government.

At the beginning of the *Institutes*, John Calvin declares that wisdom consists of the knowledge of God and of ourselves. However,

Calvin does not develop a doctrine of the 'separate self'. We know ourselves truly only in terms of our union with Jesus Christ. Calvin did not produce a system of theology in which all the doctrines are logically consistent and may be rationally defended. Rather, he expounded a systematic theology where each doctrine receives careful reflection in terms of Scripture for the purpose of Christian understanding and obedience.

See also: HISTORY OF CHRISTIAN ETHICS. 8

Bibliography

The Institutes of the Christian Religion, LCC 20–21.

E. Doumergue, *Jean Calvin: Les hommes et les choses de son temps*, 7 vols. (Lausanne, 1897–1927); R. Stauffer, *The Humanness of John Calvin* (ET, Nashville, TN, 1971); W. Walker, *John Calvin: The Organizer of Reformed Protestantism, 1509–1564* (London, 1906; repr. New York, 1969); F. Wendel, *Calvin: The Origins and Development of his Religious Thought* (ET, New York and London, 1963).

C.P.

CALVINISTIC ETHICS. John Calvin* did not prize novelty. He cared less for originality than for fidelity to the gospel. He celebrated the veracity and authority of Scripture and acknowledged his indebtedness to Augustine,* Martin Luther,* Martin Bucer* and others. But his achievements as a theologian, biblical commentator, pastor and churchman left such a distinctive mark that the tradition sometimes called Reformed or Presbyterian is also sometimes called simply Calvinism, and contemporary Calvinistic ethics continues to find in his work a source and standard.

Among the distinctive features of Calvin's account of the moral life are his emphasis on piety or the religious affections, his positive assessment of the role of the law* as a guide for gratitude, his account of the Christian life as sharing in Christ and in his cross* and resurrection,* his concern for discipline in the church, his representative polity for the church, his positive but limited approval of a civil government* independent of the church, and his acceptance of economic change in the 16th century.

Piety, Calvin wrote, is 'reverence joined with love of God' (*Institutes* I.ii.1). It is evoked by the presence and power of God. Piety was central to Calvin's theology and to his ethics. Without it there is no genuine knowledge of God; with it people willingly serve God. Piety is not the pretentious display of religion or 'great ostentation in ceremonies' (I.ii.2), which Calvin despised as much as anyone; it is an attitude of reverence and trust, a sense of dependence and gratitude, a readiness to 'observe his authority . . ., advance his glory, and obey his commandments' (I.ii.2).

'The natural order was that the frame of the universe should be the school in which we learn piety' (II.vi.1), but rebellion had dulled human senses, and the law was given as a schoolmaster to lead sinners to repentance and to provide for civic righteousness, to lead the proud to humility, and to restrain the licentious (II.vii.6–11). 'The third and principal use' of the law, however, is to teach believers 'a purer knowledge of the divine will' and to arouse them to obedience (II.vii.12; see Law, Uses of*).

The moral law is dependent upon God and upon the meaning and value built into the world by God's creative and sustaining power. And the law is instrumental; it leads to confrontation with the righteousness of God and so, finally, to Christ.

Precisely because it is instrumental, there must be – and is – some natural awareness of the law, an 'inward law' or 'natural law' (II.viii.1, see also II.ii.12–13). God has provided us with a written law as a remedy for 'our dullness and our arrogance' (II.viii.1).

In his treatment of the Decalogue,* Calvin begins with that natural awareness, with particular prohibitions of actions so 'frightful and wicked' that 'our senses might shudder' at the hearing of them (II.viii.10), and he moves by a series of inferences involving synecdoche, intention and contraries (II.iii.8) to other prohibitions and other prescriptions until he reaches finally the dispositions to love God and the neighbour.

The moral law is never disowned or abrogated for Calvin: the gospel *holds us to* the moral law. But Calvin's treatment of the Christian life in 'The Golden Booklet' (III.vi–x) is not simply identical with the Decalogue. There he begins with our participation in Christ's cross and resurrection by faith. Mortification* and vivification train the Christian for self-denial (III.vii), for cross-bearing (III.viii) and for meditation on the future life (III.ix). These traits enable us to live in the present world with a certain nonchalance, with moderation, and with love for the neighbour (III.x). This account of the Christian life holds Christians to their natural duties in conduct while it surpasses and transforms them by formation of character (see ⑩) according to the pattern of Christ.

For Calvin discipline* was not one of the 'marks of the church', but a discipline which functioned firmly, kindly and equitably was necessary lest the head of the church be dishonoured, the good be corrupted, and the offenders be complacent in unrighteousness (IV.xii.1–13).

In ecclesiastical and in civil government, Calvin rejects both anarchy* and tyranny. He prefers plural authorities and representative governments, insisting on 'the consent of the people' (IV.iii.15, IV.iv.10) in ecclesiastical offices and recommending 'a system compounded of aristocracy and democracy' (IV.xx.8) for civil governments.

Calvin affirmed the legitimate authority of civil government, distinguishing it from spiritual governance, but expecting it not only to maintain 'humanity' (IV.xx.3), 'freedom' (IV.xx.8) and 'equity' ('the goal and rule and limit of all laws', IV.xx.16) but also 'to cherish and protect the outward worship of God, (IV.xx.2). He calls civil authority 'the most honourable of all callings' (IV.xx.4) and calls upon the authorities to fulfil their vocation as 'deputies of God' (IV.xx.6). Citizens are to obey their rulers, even unjust ones (IV.xx.23, 24), but Calvin calls upon 'lower magistrates' to oppose the corruption of tyrants and to 'restrain the willfulness of kings' (IV.xx.31).

In the economic order, Calvin broke with the ancient tradition – both biblical and Aristotelian – which prohibited interest* on loans. He prohibited excessive interest, however, and regarded any interest on loans to the poor as excessive. The inner-worldly asceticism* of Calvin and the dispositions of diligence in one's calling and moderation in one's consumption prompted the development of modern capitalist economies in Calvinistic societies (according to Max Weber [1864–1920] at any rate).

No Calvinistic ethic simply repeats Calvin; there is always, however, some selective retrieval from his work. The emphasis on piety was developed in different ways by Jonathan Edwards* and F. D. E. Schleiermacher* (and recently by James Gustafson, 1925–) and virtually ignored by some others. The account of the law has been retrieved in a variety of ways. Some Calvinists of the Enlightenment* so emphasized the natural and rational moral order that Scripture became nearly expendable, while some others so emphasized the positive law of Scripture that both natural moral wisdom and commitment to the law-giver might be ignored. Some Calvinists have interpreted Calvin's account of civil government along authoritarian lines, but many more (e.g. Theodore Beza, 1519–1605, and Samuel Rutherford, 1600–61) interpreted it in ways which contributed to the development of constitutional democracies.

In spite of Weber's account of the link between Calvinism and capitalism,* many Calvinists have found grounds to challenge not only the autonomy of the economic order but also the assumption about an invisible hand and any single-minded devotion to profit* as economic goal in Calvin's notions of stewardship* and distribution, tested as they are by 'the rule of love' (III.vii.5, III.x.5).

See also: STATE.

Bibliography

J. Calvin, *The Institutes of the Christian Religion*, LCC 20–21; J. Leith, *John Calvin's Doctrine of the Christian Life* (Philadelphia, 1989); A. E. McGrath, *A Life of John Calvin: A Study in the Shaping of Western Culture* (Oxford and Cambridge, MA, 1990); J. T. McNeill, *The History and Character of Calvinism* (New York, 1954).

A.D.V.

CANNABIS, see DRUGS.

C ANNIBALISM, the killing and eating, in part or in whole, of the flesh and vital organs of fellow human beings, has occurred in different societies for different reasons. In many cultures it has been part of the practice of *warfare*. The Iroquois Indians, after torturing their prisoners, killed them and ate their remains in cannibalistic feasts. This terrible practice seems to have rested on the belief that to eat the enemy is to derive strength from his annihilation.

Cannibalism was often the outcome of *ritual sacrifice* to the gods. The Aztecs ritually slaughtered great numbers of prisoners, offering the heart to the sun, before they were eaten.

In other cultures, cannibalism has been practised in times of *famine*. In central Australia

Ngali and Yumu women have aborted foetuses in order to feed children, or have killed small children in order to feed older siblings. Cannibalism has also been resorted to in cities under prolonged siege (cf. 2 Ki. 6:26–29).

Cannibalism involving murder is clearly ruled out by the sixth commandment (Ex. 20:13); less clear, from the ethical standpoint, is the eating of bodies of persons already dead as a result of starvation or accident (as in the famous case of sixteen Uruguayan survivors of a plane crash in the Andes in 1973). It could be argued that in principle the only difference between such a situation and the use of organs of a hopelessly brain-damaged person in transplant surgery* is that the consent of near relatives is not involved (though survivors of the Andean plane crash have said that they gave consent for their bodies to be eaten should they die). Yet respect for the mortal remains of the deceased, engendered by centuries of Christian teaching, must not be easily set aside, extreme though circumstances may be.

Bibliography

M. Harris, *Cannibals and Kings: The Origins of Cultures* (Glasgow, 1978); R. Tannahill, *Flesh and Blood* (New York, 1975).

D.P.K.

CAPITALISM. The term 'capitalism' relates to a system of organizing economic life and production. Its definition and use tend to vary with the biases of the user. It is treated by some historians as a historical category (Max Weber, 1864–1920; R. H. Tawney; Karl Marx*), which emerged in a time sequence, after feudalism, around the 16th century in Europe.

Weber made the now famous link between the rise of Protestant Christianity and the development of new forms of economic organization called 'capitalism'. The change in world-view which accompanied Protestant Christianity encouraged hard work, diligence, the notion of vocation (that people could serve God in their everyday work), the virtue of saving, and the prudent use of gifts and resources. These were in contrast to the asceticism of Catholicism. Weber argued that these characteristics laid the foundation for business and profit-making to show enormous increase in countries where Catholicism was displaced. More recent historians have debated the timing of capitalism's emergence (K. Tribe, *Genealogies of Capitalism*) and have found its origins much earlier. There is also a debate over what is the essence of capitalism. Such work has implications for the priority given to Protestantism as a prime cause of introducing capitalism. However, on the whole, there is agreement that Protestant Christianity contributed to the enormous economic growth under capitalism in subsequent centuries.

Karl Marx has probably had the most influence on the definition of capitalism, and it is the Marxist link with capitalism which has made it value-loaded. For Marx, capitalism was a mode of production in which there were two main classes: the owners of the means of production, and wage labourers who were dependent on their labour power for subsistence. Capitalism, in Marx's theory, was an intermediate stage of economic organization before socialism and communism, which were deterministically predicted eventually to emerge. Authors influenced by Marx can differ with him on what is the essence of the capitalist mode of production: it can be the separation of consumption and production, or the rise of a dominant class supplying the capital necessary to employ a large number of workers. It is from Marxists that the idea has come that capitalism is a bad way of organizing economic life, and is unfair, unequal and in need of overthrow.

These historical writings form the background for the contemporary debates which occur over capitalism. Twentieth-century capitalism clearly rests on the freedom of individuals to produce and sell and to buy goods and services in markets which are largely cleared by allowing prices to fluctuate. On the one hand, there are those who think this is an ideal system such that they want to prevent any interference with it, especially State regulation. These libertarians often claim allegiance to Adam Smith's (1723–90) writing in *The Wealth of Nations*. This camp values, above all, the freedom of the individual which an unfettered capitalism brings. The inequalities which this system also entails are thought to be no bad thing and partly the outcome of people taking up the opportunities to prosper to varying degrees. Also, it is argued, everybody benefits from freely allowing those with exceptional entrepreneurial talents to exercise them. On the other hand, those who stress equality want to regulate markets to prevent those with more money oppressing those with less money and less power. They would like to see much more equality in resource ownership. In the extreme this regulation becomes a planned economy of the sort that used to exist in Eastern Europe. The obvious failure of planned economies to prosper or to remove gross inequalities has removed one of the extremes and a whole wing in this debate. It is now difficult to imagine anyone arguing for a planned economy and there is a universal acceptance that free markets need to be introduced into the former Soviet Union countries. However, the argument over the necessary level of State regulation in market economies will continue.

Judging the economic merits of these arguments is complex. It is possible to find Christian economists who align themselves to one or other of these camps. A useful discussion of these alternatives can be found in D. A. Hay, *Economics Today*, which seeks in chapter 4 to judge the arguments with a set of scriptural principles which Hay has previously outlined. Capitalism can be criticized for failing to have a concept of care for the natural order which the Scriptures mandate (see Environment*). It does allow individuals to exercise stewardship* through the rights attached to private property, but it fails to encourage the responsibilities which should go alongside, *e.g.* sharing the product with the poor. Capitalism fails to allow all to exercise stewardship through work opportunities or through influencing the running of their firm, and it encourages the idol of pursuing wealth for its own sake. No doubt market economies which also tried to build on Christian social values would come closer to fulfilling scriptural principles than do the contemporary examples; but then so would the other ways of organizing our economic life. There is clearly much scope for Christians to advocate changes which would improve the capitalist system. Both Hay in *Economics Today* and Alan Storkey in *Transforming Economics* have suggested some of these ways.

Bibliography

D. A. Hay, *Economics Today* (Leicester, 1989); A. Storkey, *Transforming Economics: A Christian Way to Employment* (London, 1986); R. H. Tawney, *Religion and the Rise of Capitalism* (London, 1926); K. Tribe, *Genealogies of Capitalism* (London, 1981); M. Weber, *The Protestant Ethic and the Spirit of Capitalism* (1904–05; ET, London, 1930).

S.D.

CAPITAL PUNISHMENT is execution under legal authority as the penalty for a crime. It is an ancient form of punishment,* which has been applied to crimes* ranging from burglary to homicide to treason. It is currently used by few Western countries outside the US.

Christians are divided on whether biblical teaching supports use of this sanction. For some, OT provisions establishing the death penalty demonstrate its acceptability. Others look to the words and deeds of Jesus, and conclude that it is forbidden. Still others emphasize the importance of the practical dimensions of deterrence (see Deterrence, Nonnuclear*) or risk of mistake.

It is perhaps helpful to consider this issue by addressing three questions, each of which leads logically to the next:

1. Is capital punishment mandated, prohibited or permitted?

a. Those who believe that biblical teaching mandates the death penalty do so on the grounds that life is sacred (see Sanctity of Human Life*), and that those who take another life, or place it in great peril, must lose theirs. They cite the divine command of Noah after the Flood: 'Whoever sheds the blood of man, by man shall his blood be shed; for in the image of God has God made man' (Gn. 9:6). This principle was reflected in the law of Moses, which ordained execution for eighteen offences (including several which did not involve homicide, *e.g.* rape, *cf.* Dt. 22:25–27). Several NT passages (*e.g.* Rom. 13:1–7) imply its continued appropriateness.

b. Those who conclude that biblical teaching prohibits the death penalty argue that the OT arguments supporting this sanction are superseded by NT developments. (i) They note that Israel was a unique nation, a theocracy* ruled directly by God, with unique laws. When Israel ceased to be a nation, its law was nullified. (ii) Christ's death and resurrection ended the requirement for blood recompense and blood sacrifice. His incarnation made it unnecessary to execute murderers in order to establish human dignity and value. (iii) Christ's teaching emphasizes the need for forgiveness* and for suffering evil rather than resisting it by force. His behaviour towards the woman taken in adultery (Jn. 8) does not appear to be consistent with the belief that the death penalty is mandated.

c. There are those who argue that the Bible neither mandates, nor prohibits, but permits the death penalty: (i) They note the presence of the death penalty in OT law, and that its existence was assumed in the NT. Passages such as Rom. 13 are cited as evidence that the government has the *authority* to impose the death penalty, but not necessarily the *obligation* to do so. (ii) Both Testaments give illustrations of capital criminals who were not executed, clearly with divine approval. Examples include Cain, Moses, David and the woman taken in adultery. This suggests that use of the death penalty is discretionary, not mandated.

2. Under what conditions may a legal authority exercise capital punishment?

A review of OT law reveals that evidentiary and due-process protections were established to govern death-penalty cases. These include *proportionality* (Ex. 21:23–25); *certainty of guilt* established by two witnesses (Dt. 17:6; Nu. 35:30); *intent* (Nu. 35:22–24); *due-process* provisions including the cities of refuge which protected an accused until trial (Nu. 35); *individual responsibility* (Dt. 24:16); *fairness* of legal proceedings regardless of economic standing in the community (Ex. 23:6–7); and *restraint* in imposing the death penalty (Ezk. 33:11).

Each of these is a principle, which means they must be implemented in a contemporary context different from that found in the OT. The principles are universal even though the specific applications found in the Mosaic law may not be.

3. How should legal authorities be guided in determining whether to impose the death penalty?

If the death penalty is permitted (not mandated or prohibited), and if the government has established procedures which comply with the principles noted above, should it exercise this power? Three reasons are typically given for doing so: a. General deterrence, the theory that when one person is punished other potential offenders will be discouraged from committing similar crimes. Whether capital punishment in fact deters in this way has been hotly contested. b. Specific deterrence, the theory that the executed offender will commit no further crimes. c. Retribution,* the theory that a proportionate penalty must follow an offence.

These issues must be weighed against the fact that death is irreversible. If an innocent person is mistakenly executed there is no remedy. Life's value is the very reason that the death penalty raises such troubling questions.

Bibliography

G. Archer, *The Encyclopedia of Bible Difficulties* (Grand Rapids, 1982); I. J. Kazis, 'Judaism and the Death Penalty', in H. A. Bedau (ed.), *The Death Penalty in America* (New York, 1964); O. O'Donovan, *Measure for Measure: Justice in Punishment and the Sentence of Death* (Bramcote, Nottingham, 1977); V. Poythress, *The Shadow of Christ in the Law of Moses* (Brentwood, TN, 1991); R. J. Rushdoony, *The Institutes of Biblical Law* (Nutley, NJ, 1973); E. van den Haag and J. Conrad, *The Death Penalty: A Debate* (New York, 1983); D. W. Van Ness, *Crime and Its Victims* (Downers Grove, IL, 1986; Leicester, 1989).

D.W.V.N.

CARDINAL VIRTUES, see CHARACTER; [10] VIRTUE AND VIRTUES.

CARE, CARING, stemming from Lat. *cura*, has a range of meanings which include grief, lament, concern, interest, attention, solicitude, cure, management, administration and guardianship. Recent popular use refers less to 'cares' as a noun with the sense of anxieties; it assimilates 'care' and 'affection'; it speaks of 'in care,' meaning under offical oversight and protection; and it understands 'caring' increasingly to describe cherishing or helping, especially by charitable agencies or professional helpers such as medical practitioners, social workers and counsellors.

Government policy has focused attention on the relationship of care provided by the State and by voluntary bodies. With more attention given to training and literature informed by behaviourial and social sciences and to the need for support for carers, voluntary carers have begun to shed their 'tea and sympathy' image and are now becoming better informed, more aware of potential problems in caring relationships, and alert to the dangers of stress* and 'burn-out'.

Old Testament social instructions – particularly Deuteronomic concern for the poor, widows, orphans and strangers, and for almsgiving, harvest gleaning and the year of jubilee – and prophetic calls for social justice, belong to a context which emphasizes that Israel, graciously chosen by God, is to be a caring society. Love of God, who is persistently just, good, merciful and full of loving-kindness, means love of neighbour.

In the life of Jesus, his compassionate attitude, healings and other acts, and in his total, sacrificial self-giving, the character of God as gracious is revealed with new depths of meaning. The parables of the good Samaritan, the last judgment and other parables, and sayings of grace,* underline the connection between grace and care. This helps to explain why the first Christians sought to express care through evangelism, communal worship, sharing possessions, daily food distribution, a collection for those suffering from famine, and the ability to weep and to rejoice together. Their caring extended to the complete person, consistent with the integrated view of the person found in Scripture, and to all of life, in keeping with the wholeness of healing and salvation.

The Christian community is to 'love each other as I have loved you' (Jn. 15:12). The Fourth Gospel explains this love as the love the Father and the Son have for each other which extends to 'those who will believe' (Jn. 17:20, 23). Grounded in the love between Father and Son, caring becomes a comprehensive and enduring covenant.* This suggests that, though support for those in need is very important, and although there are specific individuals, problems or needs which require specialist contract care by professionals, caring begins at the basic, everyday level vital for personal worth. Caring belongs within loving, persisting relationship. It expresses the love and grace of God which both helper and helped experience and of which they both remain in constant and common need. It is mutually involving and supportive, encompassing life's normality as well as life's difficulties. It is of a piece with the love of Jn. 3:16 – costly, giving for the world, and loving to the end (Jn. 13:1).

L.B.K.

CARE OF THE HANDICAPPED, see HANDICAPPED, CARE OF.

CARE OF THE HANDICAPPED NEWBORN, see ETHICS OF MEDICAL CARE. 14

CARE OF THE DYING, see DEATH AND DYING; ETHICS OF MEDICAL CARE; 14 HOSPICE.

CAROLINE DIVINES. The term 'Caroline' is applied in Anglican studies to those theological writers who lived during the reigns of Charles I (1625–49; b. 1600) and Charles II (1660–85; b. 1630).

Their writings include the magisterial sermons of Lancelot Andrewes (1555–1626); the metaphysical poetry of John Donne (1571/2–1631), George Herbert (1593–1633), Thomas Traherne (1636–74) and Henry Vaughan (1622–95); the moral theology of Ralph Cudworth (1617–88), Robert Sanderson (1587–1663) and Jeremy Taylor*; and the doctrinal works of William Beveridge (1639–1708), John Cosin (1594–1672), Joseph Hall (1574–1656), John Pearson (1612–86) and James Ussher (1581–1656). Together these formed a tradition of Anglican thought that has been widely regarded as manifesting the essence of Anglicanism (see Anglican Moral Theology*).

The Carolines' voluminous writings were characterized by appeal foremost to Scripture, to the early Church Fathers, and to reason,* in order to express the Christian faith in the 17th century. The beginnings of toleration and the roots of the Enlightenment* can be found especially in the second generation of Caroline divines, but there is a departure from the doctrinal and confessional commitments of the earlier generation.

The Tractarian experience of the 19th century gave great impetus to the study of these theological writers who, along with the patristic age, were seen as normative for Anglicanism, more so than the Anglican Reformers of the 16th century or the evangelicals of the 18th century. *The Library of Anglo-Catholic Theology* (Oxford, 1841–) reprinted and translated scores of volumes of Caroline divinity.

Bibliography
C. F. Allison, *The Rise of Moralism: The Proclamation of the Gospel from Hooker to Baxter* (Wilton, CT, 1965; London, 1966); H. R. McAdoo, *The Spirit of Anglicanism* (New York, 1965); P. E. More and F. L. Cross (eds.), *Anglicanism* (London, 1951); D. A. Scott, *Christian Character: Jeremy Taylor and Christian Ethics Today* (Oxford, 1991); B. Willey, *The Seventeenth Century Background* (London, 1946).

C.F.A.

CARTELS. A cartel is an agreement among competing enterprises to regulate competition in some way: *e.g.* among professional associations (architects, physicians, *etc.*); in establishing recommended prices and advertising standards; and as seen in OPEC (Organization of Petroleum Exporting Countries), where a uniform price is set for oil pro-

duction quotas assigned among its members. An important historical antecedent is the medieval guild system, and the ethical difficulties surrounding the guilds apply to contemporary cartels.

Competition generally provides benefits to society – lower prices, better service, wider selection and improved quality. The pressure of competition can lead to socially troubling realities, however: unjust working conditions, inappropriate advertising* and harm to the surrounding environment.* How then can the socially beneficial outcomes be obtained without incurring the harmful realities? Every society has opted for government oversight. Aggressive oversight in one direction, however, may create problems in the other, and thus reliance upon self-governance by members of some professions (see Professional Ethics*) or industries (i.e. cartels) therefore seems prudent. This train of analysis can explain the otherwise confusing reality of generally outlawing cartels but de facto allowing them in certain cases.

Whatever their professed intentions, cartels effect a concentration of economic power. The Mosaic legislation (and prophetic appeal) clearly finds dangers in such concentration (e.g. Dt. 17:16–20, Ezk. 45:7–12 and 46:16–18 restrict the power of the king; and Mi. 4:4 and Zc. 3:10 see the ideal economic order as free from the oppression that results from the concentration of economic power in few hands). The Bible also calls for just employment conditions and warns against misrepresentation in commercial dealings – realities often used to justify the necessity for common standards among members of a profession or industry (i.e. cartels).

The long historical experience with cartels however, from the Middle Ages (at least) to the present, is that self-regulation risks abuse of the public interest. Adam Smith's (1723–90) warning in 1776 rings true today: 'People of the same trade seldom meet together, even for merriment and diversion, but the conversation ends in a conspiracy against the public, or in some contrivance to raise prices.' Therefore, when cartels are allowed to function, they should be made accountable for their behaviour to the public in some well-defined way.

J.D.M.

CASTI CONNUBII, see PAPAL ENCYCLICALS.

CASUISTRY is a term derived from the Lat. casus ('case'), and refers to that part of moral theology which seeks to apply abstract moral principles to particular concrete cases. Thus it attempts to 'make real' Christian ideals in all spheres of human life, individual, social or professional.

While abstractly formulated moral principles can be readily understood intellectually, the problem arises when they have to be applied to individual cases which are essentially unique and complex. This is a necessary process if moral principles are to have any validity or meaning in informing and governing human behaviour. Casuistry seeks to bridge the gap between the abstract norm and the concrete act.

Casuistry is to be found in the NT (though Pharisaic casuistry had its origins in the inter-testamental period). For example, in Mk. 2:23–28 Jesus' disciples, plucking ears of corn as they went through the cornfields, were accused by the Pharisees of working on the sabbath. In their defence, Jesus quoted the example of David who, in the time of Abiathar the high priest, entered the Temple and ate the shewbread which only the priests could eat.

In Lk. 20:20–26, when Jesus was questioned as to whether it was lawful or not to pay tribute to Caesar, he replied, 'Give to Caesar what is Caesar's, and to God what is God's.' Paul had to deal with cases of conscience* when, for example, he was asked by the Corinthian Christians whether it was lawful to eat food sacrificed to idols (1 Cor. 8). In the patristic age, cases of conscience arose frequently in connection with the issues involved in military service, and persecutions. In all these cases attempts were made to apply general principles to particular situations.

With the development of auricular confession,* casuistry came to be formulated more specifically so that it could become a guide for confessors. Through typical cases, whether real or fictional, future confessors and counsellors were taught the correct way to handle moral principles. When the fourth Lateran Council in 1215 made annual confession and communion obligatory, a new impetus was given to casuistry as clerics had to be initiated into the solving of cases of conscience.

This gave rise to the need for written works, which was met by the production of manuals such as the Summae Confessorum. Later, it was obligatory for all clerics to take a course in casuistry, and other works were produced to fulfil this need. As a result casuistry was put on a more scientific basis as the principles of morality had to be analysed and clarified. The *Institutiones Theologiae Moralis*, produced in the 16th century, was the result of this process.

The great weakness of all these productions is that they arose out of a specific practical need and were designed to meet it. They enabled priests to be better prepared, but the inherent danger was that a rigid system could evolve which would deflect from personal reflection and undermine the very basis for casuistry as an aid to conscience. Whilst it guided the confessor in the process of administering forgiveness* and absolution,* it could easily limit itself to that without encouraging the desire and resolve to aim at a higher level of moral behaviour.

Protestant casuistry developed in the 17th century. Such books as Richard Baxter's* *Christian Directory* reflect this aspect of English Puritanism.

Casuistry degenerated in the mid-17th century when it separated itself in thought from concrete reality and sought to establish itself as an independent system. The failure to recognize that casuistry must form part of a total moral system led in the 18th century to a situation where moral theology was contained exclusively in predominantly casuistic manuals.

The renewal of moral theology since the Second World War has reinstated casuistry in its legitimate position as a valuable aid to conscience and not its replacement. It has to be recognized that it must remain part of moral theology to retain its usefulness and, even more important, it cannot divorce itself from concrete situations.

On the other hand, the advocates of situation ethics* have rejected it altogether since, by definition, case law refers to what was decided in a particular historical circumstance which excluded the personal details that made that case unique. Nevertheless, some would argue that it is still valuable since it can give some guidance to present and future cases of conscience. Others think that casuistry belongs to the sphere of jurisprudence* rather than to morality and is therefore inappropriate in decisions of conscience in the moral sphere.

See also: CHRISTIAN MORAL REASONING. [18]

P.T.

CATEGORICAL IMPERATIVE. Immanuel Kant* calls what he holds to be the supreme principle of duty* a 'categorical imperative'. This principle provides a test for maxims (the prescriptions from which an agent acts), such that if a maxim can be willed in a way which satisfies the categorical imperative, then it is morally permissible for an agent to will that maxim. The principle is categorical, because it does not (unlike hypothetical imperatives) depend for its legitimacy upon any other ends we have. It is objective in the sense that a rational agent would necessarily act upon it if reason had full control over inclination.

Kant gives various formulations of this imperative, which he holds to be equivalent, but the most important are the following: 1. 'Act only on that maxim through which you can at the same time will that it should become a universal law.' 2. 'Act in such a way that you always treat humanity, whether in your own person or in the person of any other, never simply as a means, but always at the same time as an end.' Kant holds that agents are autonomous to the degree that they will in accordance with the categorical imperative, since they are then themselves (in their rational nature) making the law under which they are then bound.

Bibliography

I. Kant, *Groundwork of the Metaphysic of Morals* (ET, London, ³1958), ch. 2.

J.E.H.

CATHOLIC MORAL TRADITION. The word 'catholic' means 'universal'. So in theory our phrase means the moral tradition of the universal church. In practice, the phrase 'Catholic moral tradition' often stands for a particular strand of moral thinking within Christianity: Catholic as opposed to Protestant.

The first Christian centuries made no cut-and-dried distinction between theology, spirituality* and morality. Perceptions of the wisdom and desirability of prayer, fasting and almsgiving, and of virginity, arose at least at the conscious level from images of God and traditions about Jesus. The Fathers' moral concerns had a mystical base (see Patristic Ethics*). The monastic pioneers sought to create an alternative world in which people could pursue oneness with God in Christ without being overwhelmed by the distractions and temptations of the world (see Monasticism*). This approach made headway in the

Middle Ages, though in tension with the more reason-centred strand called 'scholasticism', which flourished with the recovery of Gk. philosophy and the rise of universities.

The patronage of Pope Leo XIII (1878–1903; b. 1810) at the end of the 19th century gave to the thought of Thomas Aquinas* (though often in a debased form) a status which his work had not enjoyed in medieval times. Nevertheless, the strength of the scholastic tradition which Aquinas represents was its rigorous pursuit of difficult questions in the conviction that reason aided by faith could illuminate them. In this connection it is noteworthy that the concept of natural law* is sometimes seen as the linchpin of Catholic moral tradition. Yet this concept has not had a uniformly central role. In Aquinas it occupies an insignificant place compared to his extended treatment of the virtues,* and yields in practice very modest results.

A quite different strand, the development from the 6th century onwards of the penitentials and the later growth of a highly sophisticated casuistry,* shows the extent to which the church's thinking about morality came to centre on confessional practice, and specifically on the role of the confessor as judge of the gravity or otherwise of the sins confessed. This could be criticized for perpetuating infantilism in the penitent, and for fostering a sin-centred and juridical picture of Christian moral living.

It is often assumed that Catholic moral tradition is characterized by continuity and consistency (see Roman Catholic Moral Theology*), but even if the enquiry is confined to Roman Catholicism the reality is kaleidoscopic. Current mainstream teaching about the unequivocal goodness of human sexuality (see [11]) has not been the dominant view, despite Genesis and the Song of Songs. It was only at Vatican II (see Second Vatican Council*) that the principle of religious liberty, hitherto strongly denied, was espoused. To call these and other shifts developments rather than changes of mind strains credulity.

A factor militating against appropriation of the richness and diversity of Catholic moral tradition is the expansion since Vatican I of 'creeping infallibility' or infallibility by association. The moral teaching of the Catholic Church has come to be almost equated with detailed statements by recent popes.

A vital dimension of the Catholic tradition is the rooting of Christian behaviour in a perception of created reality as sacramental. Awareness of an awesome harmony and purposiveness, in all that is, founds a distinctive moral response – mystery-encountering rather than problem-centred. In contrast to a mechanistic view of sacramental grace, which evades moral responsibility, this approach concurs with John Wesley's* view of the eucharist as 'a converting ordinance'. Those who in eucharistic worship 'proclaim the Lord's death' look to, and are fashioned and sustained by, the hope of that consummation towards which all creation is moving.

Catholic moral tradition is a developing commentary, necessarily inadequate and fragmentary, on human maturing in the light of Christian faith. This is the world of theological virtue rather than that of static moral principles and fixed authorities. Awakened sacramental perception and practice focus on horizons far beyond dependence on these things for the shaping of our personal identity as we become attuned to the resonances of the life, death and resurrection of Jesus in our own story.

See also: CHRISTIAN MORAL REASONING; [18] HISTORY OF CHRISTIAN ETHICS. [6]

Bibliography
J. Fuchs, *Christian Morality: The Word Becomes Flesh* (ET, Dublin and Washington, DC, 1987); J. Mahoney, *The Making of Moral Theology* (Oxford, 1987); S. Moore, *The Inner Loneliness* (London, 1982); P. Brown, *The Body and Society* (New York, 1988; London, 1989).

N.P.H.

CELIBACY, see SINGLENESS.

CENSORSHIP is the procedure whereby publications are examined prior to publication, and banned if they contravene certain legally defined criteria.

Censorship is a two-edged sword, which when used wisely can establish the boundaries of decency and acceptability within a community, and when used capriciously, or more often, for political ends, can be a destructive and oppressive force at variance with principles of democracy as well as Christian respect for freedom.*

Historical accounts most commonly attend to the excesses and abuses which have arisen. Politically, censorship has been an instrument of totalitarian States wishing to impose conformity on its members, and this contrasts with the freedom-of-speech principles of democracies. In the religious tradition, strict censorship continues to be a feature of fundamentalist Muslim countries. In the Christian tradition, in the name of protecting orthodoxy against heresy, it was most evident in the Catholic development from the 16th century of the Index of Prohibited Books, revoked after Vatican II.

In more recent times the boundaries of obscenity in the depiction of sexuality (see 11) and violence* have become the targets for change, with the case for moral restraint being set over against the desire for complete freedom of expression.

Where to draw the line

Because there are conflicting principles underlying the censorship debate, there will continue to be differences over where the line should be drawn between the acceptable and the unacceptable – how the distinctions shall be drawn, and who shall be empowered to decide. What needs to remain is the conviction that a line *does* have to be drawn somewhere, and the recognition that past (or even present) abuses of censorship do not provide a sufficient basis for its abolition. The novelist James Michener (1907–), whose novels have often been banned, is committed to free speech yet still maintains that 'freedom of speech has limits', and exemplifies this by reference to libel* laws, lying under oath, and production of child pornography.*

The long history of censorship by responsible governments would suggest that it *can* have a valuable role in the preservation of an orderly society, and the protection of individuals. The existence of what we now see to be oppressive decisions, as with the Roman called 'Cato the Censor' (234–*c.* 148 BC), the suppression of Tyndale's translation of the Bible in 16th-century England, the burning of the works of Confucius in the Chin dynasty in China (250 BC), and the suppression of *Dr Zhivago* in Russia, highlights the dangers of abusing censorship for particular political ends.

When it comes to sexual obscenity, a series of 'landmark' decisions by the UK courts, such as 'Lady Chatterly's Lover' (1960), 'Fanny Hill' (1963), and 'Tropic of Cancer' (1965) led to redefinition of the criteria for censorship and increasing pressure for its abolition.

The changing context

Pressures to push back or abolish the boundaries have increased in recent years, fuelled by several concurrent forces.

A loss of respect for authority* in favour of personal freedom of choice has flowed from developments in theology and psychology, and resulted in the 'permissive society'. The concept of a socially unifying norm of belief and behaviour has been challenged by increasing invocation of a 'pluralist' society with no one defining set of norms, and hence no clear criterion for decision-making. This has been amplified by the undoubted change in the ethnic and religious mix of most Western countries. While the Christian tradition remains, it is surrounded by many vigorous alternatives demanding recognition. The abuse of censorship by totalitarian groups has caused many to see it as inimical to a free society and hence to become willing to throw out the baby with the bath water. Technological advances in the mass production of books, magazines, films, videos and other media have produced an unprecedented situation: control of the sources of information is no longer possible, and dissemination into every home can be achieved in a manner inconceivable only fifty years ago.

Censorship can best be seen as a means of last resort, while other strategies pose fewer problems. The guidelines proposed by S. V. Monsma in 1990 are helpful: 1. freedom of artistic expression does not mean the right to produce anything without any restrictions whatsoever; 2. legally imposed restraints should be distinguished from withholding of public funds. Refusal to fund is different from censorious restriction; 3. legally imposed restraints should be distinguished from economic and social pressures. Demonstrations, lobbying and buying elsewhere are powerful forms of expression; and 4. in some situations, the extreme step of government restriction (*i.e.* censorship) may be needed.

Changing responses

In determining how to respond to such principles in the light of major social changes, one shift has been towards establishing the principles which might govern rational censorship decisions. The concept of *harm*, derived from the utilitarianism (see Consequentialism*) of John Stuart Mill,* served as a focus for the Williams Report on Obscenity and Pornography (1979). The debate then rages around what we mean by harm, and to whom, and how to balance degrees of harm over against potential benefits. The result has been to turn away from philosophy or religion as sources, to be guided by scientific evidence on harmful effects. The approach, attractive in its apparent objectivity, is fraught with the dangers of inexact science, value-laden interpretations, and a reductionism* that misses much that is of truly human value. Moral and spiritual values are readily relegated or dismissed.

A second shift has been towards replacing censorship by classification. Seeking to avoid the absolute constraints of total prohibition, governments have favoured systems of ratings for films, television, magazines and books, with committees established to create ratings to indicate levels of restriction. This seeks to make some materials available to adults while protecting children from that for which they are unprepared. Although some activists would wish to abolish all restrictions, some degree of censorship is retained even with classification. There is, at present, almost universal support for the complete censorship of child pornography, and increasing evidence of the harmfulness of portrayals of sexual aggression. In the US, with its strong commitment to constitutional protection of free speech (the First Amendment), it remains true that pornography is not protected.

While classification seeks a compromise between the needs of children and the desires of adults, it deals at best only with point-of-sale concerns and fails to prevent classified materials reaching juveniles in many devious ways. Complete censorship is more effective in achieving protection for minors, but it can never operate completely effectively in a free society, and any system needs the active support of the community.

A third recent shift relates to who makes the decisions about censorship. From the fiat of the church, or the opinion of the judge, there is increasingly an active participation by community groups seeking to represent their own standards. Libertarians, conservatives, radicals, financial vested interests all now lobby for their own view to prevail. The debate about censorship has become more audible, and often polarized, as groups seek to represent 'prevailing community standards'.

Christian involvement

Christian groups have been prominent in this movement, with the recognition that silence will simply allow alternative world-views to prevail. Participation in the shaping of community standards assumes the legitimacy of being active on issues of social justice, especially care for the weak, and a belief that there are normative standards of behaviour worth defending against those who would seek their abolition. As Monsma observes, we operate 'under the assumption that both *art* and *freedom* are God-given gifts that should be honored and protected'.

The danger for Christians of advocating censorship are many: of lacking artistic sensitivity or cultural awareness and simply defending the status quo; of stridently pursuing self-serving ends without sensitivity to the needs of others; of expecting more from censorship as a moral containment mechanism than it can ever deliver; of appearing to be anti-everything rather than *for* that which is good; and of seeking to promote orthodoxy by silencing dissent.

The dangers of vacating the field are greater, if the potential for exploitation,* degradation and harm is allowed to proceed unchecked. Paradoxically, many have found that religious freedom falls an early victim to those who, in the name of freedom of speech, become oppressively willing to censor alternative viewpoints. Advocacy of civilized boundaries of expression is a necessary part of stability in society. True freedom of expression exists only when the parameters are adequately defined.

Bibliography

S. V. Monsma, 'Yelling Fire in a Crowded Art Gallery', *CT*, 22 Oct 1990, pp. 40–41; B. Williams, *Report of the Committee on Obscenity and Film Censorship* (London, 1979).

J.H.C.

CENTESIMUS ANNUS, see PAPAL ENCYCLICALS.

CHANGE, PERSONAL, see DEPRESSION; STRESS.

CHANGE, SOCIAL, see COMMUNITY ETHICS; [16] TECHNOLOGY.

CHARITIES have a special interest in Eng. and US law, giving them exemption from both income and succession or inheritance taxes. To qualify for this special status, they must be set up for the promotion of religion or learning, or the relief of poverty or suffering, though these main criteria are fairly widely interpreted. They must also be non-profit organizations, and any surplus must either be retained, or, if the founding deed of trust allows it, be given to other recognized charities. To obtain legal recognition, a charity in England or Wales must be registered with the Charity Commissioners, who receive annual accounts. Charities in Scotland must be registered with the Inland Revenue.

Political parties cannot register as charities, nor can any body set up to promote a sectional interest. A trade union, for instance, is not a charity. A body set up to research the medical and social effects of abortion could be a charity, but an anti-abortion body could not be. A body set up to promote better management through seminars, lectures and literature could be a charity, but not a body set up to promote the interests of managers. Sometimes there can be a fine line between the charitable investigation of an unacceptable activity and the non-charitable campaign against the activity based on the study. But money raised for a study cannot be used for a campaign.

All charities must have trustees, and the trustees cannot gain financially from the charity. The trustees are legally responsible for the activities of the charity, which, in England and Wales, are supervised by the Charities Commission. Scottish charities are supervised separately.

A great many Christians wish to support overseas activities. To gain tax exemption, contributions have to be made to a home-registered charity whose purposes allow it to use its funds on the overseas activity.

Churches are, of course, charities, though no distinction is made between (say) the Church of England and the Unification Church. But if a church runs a non-charitable activity, then it should pay tax on the profits of that activity.

Since British charities can reclaim tax on regular donations under deed of covenant, most charities, and especially churches, like to receive as much giving as possible in this way. Since it is a commitment to pay a particular charity for a number of years (at present four) it gives the charity a secure income. But, since donors may not want to fix the pattern of their giving too rigidly over a period of years, many give to an intermediate charity under covenant and then ask that charity to allocate the funds to the charitable causes they nominate. Those

with substantial funds can set up their own charity, but the simplest way for most donors is to make a covenant to the Charities Aid Foundation, which will reclaim the tax and allocate the funds according to the donor's direction.

Those who want to donate casual fees they receive to charity can also ask that these fees be sent to the Charities Aid Foundation, which then allocates them as the donor requests.

Since 1990, UK donors may give substantial single gifts to charities tax free, using the Gift Aid scheme. The necessary Revenue forms are available from most charities including the Charities Aid Foundation. Those in employment may use the Give As You Earn payroll deduction scheme if their employers agree to operate it.

Donors are faced with a bewildering variety of charitable causes, and it is not easy for the average citizen to know where their giving will do most good. There is, regrettably, some expensive fund-raising, which cuts heavily into the donations income, so donors should ask to see accounts and look at the proportion of income devoted to fund-raising and administration. There is also a temptation to appeal to sentiment rather than real, but less appealing, need.

For these reasons many Christians confine their giving to churches and to missions at home and overseas which they know well, but this puts a heavy onus on churches to make sure that their giving also includes the wider needs of the community in which they live.

A new idea which is being tried in England in the Diocese of Salisbury is a diocesan cheque-book account. A standing-order payment goes to the parish whilst the cheques are available for use for other charitable purposes. Not all churches would have the staff to operate donor accounts, but it could be used by large churches or groups of churches as a mini-Charities Aid Foundation, more geared to the needs of church central giving.

In a Welfare State* many question whether churches and other charities can or should meet the welfare needs of the community. But the Welfare State is also a secular State which cannot help those whose material problem has a moral cause. Nor does bureaucratic welfare have the adaptability and flexibility which is often needed, and the Christian church, above all, should be ready to go the extra mile and help in ways which are outside the State's more rigid rules.

F.C.

222

CHASTITY refers to the morally responsible exercise of human sexuality (see 11) in the human community. To be chaste is to be morally blameless, to treat with honour, respect, troth and integrity ourselves and our neighbours as persons, image-bearers of God. Chastity is often viewed in a more narrow and restricted sense as abstinence* from forbidden sexual lusts and actions: virginity* for the unmarried, sexual fidelity for the married, continence for the widowed. However, it is important that a broader, more positive understanding of chastity be nurtured, which sees chastity not merely as the reponsible exercise of physical sexuality within relationships of mutuality, troth and commitment, but as the purity of heart and integrity of person which we owe to ourselves and each other as children of God, called to do everything in the name of love.

Originally chastity meant purity, especially ritual cleanliness in regard to things connected with deity. Then, as in the Scriptures, it came to have the deeper ethical sense of 'morally blameless', 'pure', 'sincere' in all actions (Gk. hagnos, 'pure', 'holy'). In the NT, Christians are encouraged to purify themselves (2 Cor. 6:6; 1 Jn. 3:3), and to seek 'pure' wisdom (Jas. 3:17). Office-bearers are to keep themselves 'pure' (1 Tim. 5:22; Tit. 2:5), wives are to exercise 'purity' (1 Pet. 3:2). Paul chides those who do not preach Christ 'sincerely' (Phil. 1:17), commends those who prove themselves 'innocent' (2 Cor. 7:11), exhorts his readers to think on whatever is 'pure' (Phil. 4:8), and is concerned that the Corinthian church have a 'pure devotion' as a 'pure virgin' to Christ (2 Cor. 11:2–3).

In the early Christian church, chastity came more and more to mean sexual purity, often in the sense of resisting sexual passions. Against the laxity of the pagan world, chastity was considered especially virtuous. Virginity, voluntary abstinence from sexual intercourse out of devotion to God – a dedicated virgin, taught Thomas Aquinas* in the 13th century, was 'wed to Christ' – became the highest form of chastity.

This distorted ideal of virginity and chastity, developed from the view that sex is a lower passion unworthy of intelligent persons, was not wholly overcome by the Reformation. The Reformers did stress the legitimacy of marriage – for Luther 'a remedy against sin' – and it was no longer considered inferior to virginity. But the church's suppression of sex as something lower and base continued – surfacing especially in movements such as Puritanism (see Puritan Ethics*) and Pietism,* and even on into the present – sometimes consciously, but more often unconsciously, affecting thought and action. The harm and frustration caused by the notion that sex always has an element of lust* is still not uncommon.

In reaction to the suppression and devaluation of sexuality, the modern sexual revolution laughed at chastity, and divorced sex from the contexts of love and commitment which give it meaning. However, in the late 20th century we are discovering that such attitudes – 'sex is candy' or 'sex for the fun of it' – can themselves be as harmful and frustrating as the earlier devaluations of sexuality.

In this context Christians are called to avoid both the undervaluation and overvaluation of sexuality. The male–female difference, sexual attraction, and sexual feelings are good, and ought to be celebrated. But our sexuality needs to be exercised appropriately in the contexts of personal commitment, love and sharing.

In its full meaning, to be chaste is to be a person of integrity, true to self and other persons, devoted to love of God and neighbour in all things. The call to chastity is the call to receive, affirm, exercise and celebrate our ways of being human together, including sexual ways, so that respect, love, trust, mutuality and commitment towards ourselves and our neighbours will grow and abound in the human community.

J.H.O.

CHILD ABUSE, see ABUSE; INCEST.

CHILDLESSNESS. Difficulties in childbearing are experienced by 10% to 15% of married couples; of these, approximately one in ten is described as 'inexplicably infertile'.

These statistics often come as a surprise to those who have had no problems in having children, and herein lies just one of the stresses which childless couples have to bear: not fitting in to the accepted norm.

Experience

Childlessness is often experienced as bereavement* for a person who has never existed. It is acutely felt by the woman, shared by her husband to a certain degree, and often incomprehensible to others who have not had a similar experience. Consequently, relationships are put under enormous pressure. The couple feel isolated from their contemporaries, and they feel isolated from each other, as one or other partner will often feel responsible for the predicament, and in any case, it is almost impossible for the man to appreciate the depths of the desire in his wife. And, tragically, they feel isolated from God, either because their childlessness is seen as a punishment, or because they see it as evidence of the absence of God's love. To be childless is often to feel terribly alone.

Yet the Bible teaches that childlessness is not inevitably related to sin, and that God cares for those in this situation (Ps. 113:9; Lk. 1:5–7); God's salvation plan is worked out through the children of childless couples, children brought about by divine intervention, who played their part in the foundation of Israel (Isaac, Jacob and Jacob's sons) and in the proclamation of the Messiah's coming (John the Baptist). The pattern of family life in the OT, and the church family in the NT, provide a support structure for childless couples, which should mean that this burden is never borne alone. And in declaring that people are made in God's image* and are valuable to him for this reason, the Bible holds out comfort to those who feel incomplete, failures or misfits simply because they have never had a child.

The isolation of the childless within both the secular and Christian communities is a moral issue. Exclusion is discrimination in democratic societies, and within the body of Christ is a denial of the gospel and flies in the face of Jesus' example. He associated with social misfits and called them friends. As with many other people who don't fit, the childless need love and acceptance, and above all, people who will listen to their story and share their burdens.

Support

The need for a support structure is made more acute by the technological means that modern science has provided for overcoming childlessness for many couples. D. Gareth Jones (1940–) lists thirteen 'technological' means of providing a child to a couple. Yet none of these methods is ethically neutral, raising such issues as the sanctity of the marriage bond (surrogacy,* AID), the rights of the embryo* (IVF in its various forms; see Reproductive Technologies*); and the dignity and humanity of a carrying mother (surrogacy). They are often costly, never 100% successful, and can subject the couple, particularly the woman, to indignity and emotional stress. If Christians desire that couples make the right ethical choices, then they must be prepared to stand alongside those whose choosing has painful consequences, and be prepared to share their sorrows.

For Christians, the issues of God's sovereignty and plan for his people's lives are real issues. Recourse to technological means, even where ethically acceptable, may not be in God's plan for some couples. Sarai's turning to 'representational begetting' as a solution to her barrenness was a socially acceptable practice, but was not God's will for her or Abram, and had far-reaching consequences (Gn. 16:1–12; 17:19–21). The Bible also encourages God's people to look beyond their own circumstances to God's wider purposes. If Jesus came at just the right time, then so did John the Baptist. The cost to Zechariah and Elizabeth, both of them 'upright in the sight of God' (Lk. 1:6), was years of barrenness, and social disgrace.

The biblical picture would not be complete, however, without the recognition that God can and does intervene in the lives of childless couples, or without the acknowledgment that the experience of childlessness for some couples brought them nearer to God. The gift of children to the barren brings joy and blessing, not only to the parents but to the wider community, and many of the heroes of the Scriptures (Isaac, Jacob, Samuel, John the Baptist) are children of the childless.

It is possible that God has 'called' a couple to childlessness; it is equally possible that he has not. In the latter case, the couple may legitimately pursue medical means of help, having first honestly examined the ethical legitimacy of the means on offer, and having been guided by the Holy Spirit through prayer. However, for some (including this writer) the call may be, like Abraham's, to wait on the Lord, and trust his promises.

Like all other issues of life, childlessness is a faith matter, requiring that we involve God and God's people. The willingness to share the pain of childlessness with one's partner, one's friends, one's church and one's God is the means by which understanding and acceptance, and ultimately fulfilment, are gained.

See also: ADOPTION.

Bibliography

G. R. Collins, *Christian Counselling* (Milton Keynes, 1985, and Waco, TX, 1980); D. G. Jones, *Manufacturing Humans: The Challenge of the New Reproductive Technologies* (Leicester, 1987); D. Prior, *Living by Faith: Abraham's Example for Today* (London, 1986).

G.B.McG.

CHILDREN. In her recommendations contained within the 1988 Cleveland (UK) Inquiry Report on child abuse, Lord Justice Elizabeth Butler-Sloss (1933–) states that 'the child is a person, not an object of concern' (*The Report of the Inquiry into Child Abuse in Cleveland*, London, 1988, p. 245).

Only just over a century earlier in New York, a child's right to legal protection from ill treatment by her adoptive parents was granted on the grounds that she was 'a member of the animal kingdom'. Laws existed at that time to protect animals from cruelty, but not children (P. Dale, *Dangerous Families*, p. 1).

Much has changed since then, with the formulation of child-care legislation and various organizations to protect children's interests. The UN Convention on the Rights of the Child, 1989, declared the necessity for States to take all possible measures to protect children (P. Newell, *The UN Convention and Children's Rights in the UK*, p. 69). In the UK, the Children Act of 1989 was heralded as the most far-reaching reform of child law this century. Yet despite all these efforts to safeguard the welfare of children, it has to be admitted that children are far from safe within our world.

This is the case not only in poorer countries; within comparatively prosperous Western societies children are known to be increasingly at risk, not only from unscrupulous individuals, but also tragically from other children and from highly sophisticated organizations trading in child pornography* or prostitution.*

In this disturbing scenario it is vital that the true basis of a child's right to protection is fully grasped and also promoted and acted upon by the Christian church. The important reminder in the Cleveland Report that a child is actually a person must be expanded upon with the full biblical statement that each human being is created by God in his image (Gn. 1:26–27; see Image of God*).

As the most vulnerable bearers of God's image, children have a special right to protection. They must be seen not as the property of their parents or guardians, but as individual unique human beings who are themselves responsible to God and who are entrusted to the care of their parents (see Parenthood*) for a time. As such, children must be accorded the dignity which is richly and equally deserved by every human being, created in God's likeness.

The example which Scripture portrays of Jesus Christ's relationship with children is sensitive and beautiful, his acceptance of and tenderness towards them (Mk. 10:13–16), with their trust of him and loyalty to him (Mt. 21:15–16) demonstrating the relationship which existed between them.

Jesus' words in Mt. 18:5 and the severe warning which follows against harming little ones are often interpreted as referring solely to young ones in the faith, but the overall NT picture of Jesus' care for children, and the fact that he spoke these words with a child by his side, make it difficult to deny any reference to children themselves (W. Hendriksen, *The Gospel of Matthew*, Grand Rapids, 1973, pp. 686–690).

The dignity and protection which Christ accorded to children must be mirrored in the church. Sadly, the closed nature of some church communities, the teaching of children implicitly to trust their 'aunties' and 'uncles' in the church, plus a reticence to believe that church members can be perpetrators of child abuse in one form or another, has created within some congregations a secluded, impenetrable environment in which abuse, to the shame of the church, can flourish, and has flourished.

The recognition that children are not appendages of their parents but are entrusted to their care under God calls for courageous, compassionate and infinitely wise pastoring of children.

The dilemma of how to protect children effectively when they are found to be at risk is a continuing one, particularly as increasing incidences of children being abused by other children or by adults in residential and foster care come to light. The importance of the church's role in preventive work and in family support cannot be overestimated.

As part of the promotion of children's rights, some societies are seeking to end all corporal punishment of children. This tendency has to be balanced against the biblical view of humankind as not only created by God but also responsible to him. The removal of corporal punishment as one means of disciplining children may lead to an inability to control and thus protect children, or to children failing to develop the self-discipline necessary for their own safety.

The protection of the rights of a child cannot be safely based on changing trends in thinking but only on the biblical view of true humanity.

Men such as Dr Barnardo,* Lord Shaftesbury* and C. H. Spurgeon* championed the cause of child protection in the past. The need for God's people the world over to do the same is as acute as it ever was.

Bibliography

P. Dale, *Dangerous Families* (London and New York, 1986); P. Newell, *The UN Convention and Children's Rights in the UK* (London, 1991); R. White, P. Carr and N. Lowe, *A Guide to the Children Act 1989* (London, 1990).

E.M.S.

CHOICE is the term used in ethics to describe an agent's selection of a particular action or course of action; it may be as trivial as deciding to take a rest or as important in choosing a career.

Various types of determinism (in philosophy, psychology and theology) have tried to dismiss choice as an illusion, arguing that we only think we choose our actions when actually we are 'programmed' or otherwise determined beforehand to do certain things. While this approach is contrary to ordinary experience and to biblical morality, it also usefully illumines errors in the modern notion of choice as subjective preference, as if life were a kind of cafeteria offering us a range of choices from which we have absolute freedom to pick.

Our freedom* and responsibility* to choose are determined not by the number of options available or by the control we have over a situation and its outcome, but by the characters (see [10]) we bring to a situation – our desires, beliefs and attitudes. Fundamentally, it is by giving meaning and purpose to what we do that we choose. When Luther said, 'Here I stand, I can do no other', he had few options open to him (we might even say that he had 'no choice' but to take the course he did); but in that decision he was expressing most characteristically what his purpose and faith required in that situation.

Aristotle* in the *Nicomachean Ethics* set the foundation for analysis of the psychology of action (philosophical and theological) in ancient and medieval thought and in much current discussion. In his analysis, choice (*prohairesis*) is: 1. a combination of intellect and affect, which he called 'reasoned desire'; and 2. an expression of a person's character – his outlook, principles, values and the quality of his emotional life. Just as our actions reveal our characters, so the pattern of choices we make in turn shapes our characters.

A major difficulty facing the interpreters and adapters of Aristotle has been to describe the relationship between reason* and will* in the act of choice. A common way of describing this process is to split the process into a stage of reason and deliberation, followed by a decision made by the will. This seems right, since deliberation is a matter of rational analysis, and because it accounts for error and sin, *i.e.* the agent knows what is right and decides against it because of a faulty will.

The problem with this sequential view of deliberation by intellect and choice by will is to make the intellect more of an instrument of the will rather than a full participant in the process of choice as it should be. It also implies that in cases where no deliberation takes place, then reason is not very involved.

If one of your children is in danger (*e.g.* wandering into traffic), you react immediately. You do not need to deliberate (delay might be fatal), and you see immediately the action that is required. This should not be explained, however, by instinct or an act of will; rather, you instantaneously size up the situation, see the action that is required (which involves cognition), and decide to move quickly to protect your child. Both reason and desire are involved.

Many decisions do require deliberation, such as taking a holiday, or making a change of career. But whether a decision is made quickly or after long reflection, common to the process are the sizing up of the situation and the decision to act. The choice or decision which results in action should be seen as expressing a judgment of the mind which understands the nature and purpose of the action, as well as an affirmation of the will that this is what is wanted.

When the act of choice was reduced to an act of will in the later Middle Ages (*liberum arbitrium* for Thomas Aquinas* and most of the earlier tradition involved both reason and will), the notion of 'free choice' was confused with the problem of 'free will'. This meant that it became difficult (for Protestants and Catholics alike) to discuss the operation of the human mind without discussing the relation to grace* and providence. But if the distinction is made, and choice is considered a part of normal human agency, then it is possible to affirm the freedom of the agent to make decisions *for the goals and purposes he has*, and at the same time say that without grace that person has no will for the true good, and that all his decisions reflect the disorder of a mind out of touch with God. We may also see that a person may make a genuine choice to become a disciple of Christ and yet understand the truth of the Lord's statement that 'You did not choose me, but I chose you' (Jn. 15–16).

See also: FREE WILL AND DETERMINISM.

Bibliography
A. Donagan, *Choice: The Essential Element in Human Action* (London, 1987); A. Gardeil, DTC 4, cols. 2242–2256; J. I. Packer, 'Conscience, Choice and Character', in B. N. Kaye and G. J. Wenham (eds.), *Law, Morality and the Bible: A Symposium* (Leicester and Downers Grove, IL, 1978); V. S. Poythress, *The Shadow of Christ in the Law of Moses* (Brentwood, TN, 1991); J. O. Urmson, *Aristotle's Ethics* (Oxford, 1988).

D.A.W.

CHRISTIAN RECONSTRUCTION MOVEMENT.
This movement essentially seeks to bring all areas of life under the lordship of Christ. It owes its origin to Rousas John Rushdoony (1916–), an American theologian, whose book *The Institutes of Biblical Law* (1973) effectively launched the movement. Other important thinkers include Greg Bahnsen (1949–) and especially Gary North (1941–).

A number of theological emphases have come together in Christian Reconstructionism: 1. the sovereignty of God (Calvinism); 2. the theological and sociological significance of the covenant;* 3. the application of biblical law* to modern society (theonomy); 4. the presuppositional apologetics of Cornelius Van Til (1895–1987); and 5. the triumph of the cause of Christ in the world (post-millennialism).

The movement has been influential in theologically and politically conservative circles, though not without controversy. The questioning of critics has focused on the issues of theonomy and post-millennialism. Can laws given to Israel be mandatory for nations not in the covenant relationship with God? How can laws integral to the Mosaic covenant survive the abolition of that covenant? What bearing does Christ's fulfilment of the law (Mt. 5:17) have on its contemporary application? Answers to such questions have not been entirely satisfactory and a more precise understanding of biblical law is still necessary. Eschatologically, the welcome emphasis on victory and dominion needs to incorporate a greater appreciation of the church's suffering and weakness to be fully biblical.

By forcing Christians to grapple with the OT's contribution to Christian ethics and a just society, and by offering insightful biblical solutions to the problems of the modern world, the Reconstructionists have enriched the church.

Bibliography
G. L. Bahnsen, *Theonomy in Christian Ethics* (Phillipsburg, NJ, ²1984); W. S. Barker and W. R. Godfrey (eds.), *Theonomy: a Reformed Critique* (Grand Rapids, 1990); G. North and G. DeMar, *Christian Reconstruction: What it is, what it isn't* (Tyler, TX, 1991); R. J. Rushdoony, *The Institutes of Biblical Law* (Nutley, NJ, 1973).

J.G.C.

CHRISTIAN SOCIALISTS.
Utopian visions of a future society of peace, community and justice have influenced Christian thought throughout its history. In all traditions – Catholic, Protestant and Anabaptist – there have been those who have kept alive the vision of a better world. This hope has been kept alive in the theology and spirituality of the monastic tradition and in the communal experience of Anabaptist movements.

The great economic changes of the late 18th and 19th centuries in Europe moved social experience into an urban and industrialized culture. The development of market economies after the theory of Adam Smith (1723–90) replaced the feudalism of an agrarian order. The divisions of feudalism gave way to the class structure of mass industrialized societies.

There were many Christian responses to these changes. There were those who, encountering the human damage of the move to industrial life, worked hard to get the law to protect its victims. Clergy were prominent in early 19th-century campaigns to protect women and children in industrial employment and to restrict hours of working. Others began to question some of the the fundamental assumptions of a capitalist economy.

The work of F. D. Maurice* and his friends J. M. F. Ludlow (1821–1911), Charles Kingsley (1819–75) and Thomas Hughes (1822–96), in the middle of the 19th century, set in train a way of thought which brought together Christianity and the emerging ideas of socialism.* Maurice and Ludlow both formed co-operative movements and sought to develop a corporate and communal understanding of human life. The kingdom of Christ was a universal reality which was to be the guide for all endeavours.

The Christian Socialist movement had many sides to it as it grew. The tradition which grew directly from Maurice's theological work continued in a long line of Christian leaders who were sympathetic to socialist ideas because they seemed to make sense of important aspects of Christian thought and spirituality. Bishop Westcott (1825–1901) in the 19th century, J. H. Oldham (1874–1969) and William Temple* in the 20th century, were important figures in this tradition. They were all interested in Christian models and themes for contemporary urban society. They felt the need to find new ways of responding to the pervasive problems of poverty and social division. Christianity had much to say in the reconstruction and reform of the social order.

Others took a more radical line. These, following on the work of Stewart Headlam (1847–1924) rooted their socialism in their pastoral experience of ministry to the poor and excluded. Combining a revival of Catholic theology and practice, especially within the Church of England, they found inescapable connections between Jesus of Nazareth and the struggle for a socialist society. These were the campaigners and activists who assisted in the trade-union movement, joined in protest movements and were founders in the early years of Labour political organizations.

Parallel things were happening on the other side of the Atlantic. In different ways Reinhold Niebuhr* and Paul Tillich (1886–1965) both espoused socialist ideas at different points in their ministry. Niebuhr's theology was well suited to the demands of corporate political and economic action.

Those who brought Christian life to the new urban and working-class communities often played a critical role in the formation of working-class political and industrial structures. In the north-east of England, as in other places, there were close links between the growth of Methodism with its training of lay leadership and the development of trade unions. In East Anglia the struggle for better conditions for agricultural workers was often supported from within the Baptist movement, whose roots went back into generations of protest against both agricultural and ecclesiastical power.

The last quarter of the 20th century has witnessed a major decline in both socialist thinking and socialist organization. The failures of Marxism in the former Soviet Union and the collapse of command economies has raised deep questions about the whole socialist movement. Whether Christians committed to socialism can help in turning it to a future contribution is yet to be seen. What is not in doubt is the persistence of those who hold a vision of a better future and who believe that the gospel demands its support.

Bibliography

T. Christensen, *Origin and History of Christian Socialism 1848–54* (Aarhus, 1962); E. R. Norman, *The Victorian Christian Socialists* (Cambridge, 1987); P. Tillich, *The Socialist Decision* (1933; ET, New York, 1977).

J.W.G.

CHRYSOSTOM, JOHN (*c.* 347–407). Born of noble parents, Chrysostom was destined for the law. Under the influence of Meletius of Antioch (d. 381) he turned away from secular affairs, was baptized in 367, and shortly afterwards withdrew to the desert as a monk. When his health failed, he returned to Antioch where in 386 Flavian (bishop 381–404) ordained him priest and appointed him to the special duty of preaching in the cathedral. Here he systematically expounded the literal method of interpreting Scripture – which was characteristic of the Antiochene school – and he earned the title 'golden-tongued'.

In 398 he was unwillingly appointed patriarch of Constantinople. There his leadership was uncompromising and sometimes diplomatically naïve. Although having little time for speculative theology, he opposed the Arians, antagonized Bishop Theophilus of Alexandria (d. 412) and the Empress Eudoxia (d. 404), among others. The first time he was deposed and exiled, the crowd ensured his rapid recall. But he died on his second journey into exile.

Chrysostom had entered into an agreement with a friend, in 386, to let their names go forward for election as bishops. In the event Chrysostom fled and then wrote a lengthy work in justification called *On the Priesthood*. The work displays a very high view of the priesthood but is marred by a male chauvinism. It is full of practical wisdom about the duties and pitfalls of a pastor, sets out excellent advice about preaching, details the high spiritual standards required of leaders and the enormous demands and responsibilities, as well as joys, laid upon them. It remains one of the great classic works of pastoral theology (see Practical and Pastoral Theology[7]).

Bibliography
On the Priesthood, NPNF 9.
D. Attwater, *St John Chrysostom* (London, 1939); C. Baur, *John Chrysostom and His Time* (Vaduz, ²1988).

D.J.T.

CHURCH. The Christian church is that collection of human societies which is inspired by, and seeks to represent, the significance of Jesus. Hence Paul's description of it as the 'body' of Christ (*e.g.* Eph. 1:22–23). Because Jesus was deemed by early Christians to be the epitome of Israel, the church is described in the NT as 'the people of God' (*e.g.* 1 Pet. 2:10). Further, since it was believed to be the people among whom God is present to an unprecedented and decisive degree, the church is referred to as 'the temple' of God's Spirit (*e.g.* 1 Cor. 3:16; 2 Cor. 6:16). When attention focused upon the sanctifying effects of the Spirit, it is spoken of as the new, re-created humanity (*e.g.* Rom. 5–6; 1 Cor. 15). The ethical and pastoral significance of this society varies according to the terms in which it is conceived, and the history of Christian reflection upon the church – *i.e.* the history of ecclesiology – has given rise to a variety of typical conceptions.

1. Some have emphasized the institutional dimension of the church. With respect to those who regard its institutionalization as symptomatic of its loss of charismatic vitality, it is inevitable that it should have such a dimension: for the cohesion of any large and continuous society requires the distribution of authority,* the ordering of roles, and the establishment of procedures. It is not inevitable, however, that the institutional dimension should be given primary emphasis, or that it should take a rigidly hierarchical form. This happens when the main task of the church is seen to be that of maintaining unity in the face of internecine conflict, or of guarding right doctrine and practice – *i.e.* when the need for communal discipline is reckoned paramount, and when the exercise of political authority is thought to be the most appropriate implement. So, for example, Cyprian (*c.* 200–258), when faced with the Novatianist schism in the 3rd century, developed an ecclesiology which founded the church's unity on the episcopate. In its Counter-Reformation phase, Roman Catholicism virtually regarded divine grace as the property of the church's dominically established hierarchy, to be dispensed by its ordained officers pre-eminently in their performance of the seven sacraments.

The ethical and pastoral implications of this model of the church are several. Here moral and pastoral wisdom is made the special preserve of the priesthood, whose job it is to instruct, judge, and guide the laity according to the official teaching of the church. The moral life tends to be thought of in terms of conformity to law, with the priest-confessor playing a judicial role in his assignation of penance to transgressors. It follows that docility and obedience rank high among lay virtues, and responsible discernment ranks low. Further, although the morally and spiritually formative function of the sacraments is not logically tied to a predominantly institutional view of the church, it acquires a distinctive prominence here where the sacraments are regarded as the institutionally controlled outlets of grace. Finally, when the authority of the ecclesial institution, its officers, and its sanctions, are highly regarded, moral and pastoral discipline acquires a gravity it otherwise lacks.

2. Martin Luther* reacted against the authoritarian and hierarchical character of the predominantly institutional ecclesiology of the late medieval church, which he regarded as unbiblical. He offered an alternative account of the church in terms of its objective, divine basis: the Word of God addressed to humankind in Jesus Christ. For Luther the church is constituted not by a divinely established political authority, but by common acceptance of the Word. This ecclesiology has been made to yield some general moral implications. According to Karl Barth,* for example, one of the

basic characteristics of right (*i.e.* Christian) conduct is the yielding of precedence to the Word, pre-eminently as it appears in Scripture. Stanley Hauerwas (1940–) has recently underscored the primacy of the biblical 'story' in forming the moral identity of the Christian community.

But this classically Protestant concept of the church has also been made to yield more specific moral material. If the church is thought to be constituted by the declaration and acknowledgment of God's Word, then it follows that the first duty of its members is to affirm that Word. What form such affirmation should take has been variously conceived by different Protestant traditions. Pietists and evangelicals have emphasized its verbal form, stressing the importance of proclaiming the redeeming acts of God, pre-eminently in Jesus Christ. Here the Word of God enjoins evangelism upon its hearers. But others have entertained a more practical concept of affirmation. Barth, for example, speaks of 'bearing witness' to the Word, and argues that such attestation usually takes the form of acts rather than words. Moreover, he contends that the basic form of all Christian (re)action is invocation, and that the central Christian acts of invocation are the corporate liturgical ones of baptism and the Lord's Supper. The Anabaptist* tradition, however, identifying the Word of God very closely with the Jesus of the Gospels, understands practical attestation primarily in terms of the abjuration of all forms of violence.

3. This last tradition exemplifies another characteristically Protestant concept of the church (though characteristic also of the Augustinian tradition) – *i.e.* as a community which displays a distinctive (or, at least, definite) Christian spirit or ethos. Here the emphasis shifts from the objective ground of the church – God's Word – to its subjective character; from Christ as the head of his body to the body itself. Common to all Protestant ecclesiologies, and following from the Pauline metaphor of the church as a body (Rom. 12 and 1 Cor. 12), there has been an emphasis on the ethos of mutuality with a correlative qualification of – if not opposition to – hierarchy. Accordingly, Protestantism has spawned presbyterian and congregational ecclesial polities, and where it has maintained an episcopal polity (as in its Lutheran and Anglican expressions), it has at the same time reduced episcopal authority. Thus the Protestant conviction that the Christian church is a community characterized by an ethos of fraternal mutuality has led to institutional reform on the ground of a moral conception of human relations.

For some, the distinctive Christian ethos is the property of a confessing community: *i.e.* a community which shares specifically Christian religious beliefs and practices. The church here is held to be a quite discrete society, whose primary duty is to perform a prophetic ministry by representing the kingdom of God* more or less indirectly in itself, its ethos and its institutions. This is the line typically taken by the Anabaptist tradition, whose foremost representative today is John Howard Yoder (1927–), and whose stance has largely been adopted by Hauerwas. This ecclesiology, finding biblical precedent in the Johannine literature of the NT, presupposes a sharp opposition between the church and the world, and prescribes as the first duty of church members 'love for the brethren' (*e.g.* Jn. 15:9–17; 1 Jn. 3 – 4). It is not the case that such an ethos is necessarily introverted or socially irresponsible, as has sometimes been supposed, in so far as the point of paying primary attention to the life of the Christian community is to enable it to address the world effectively.

The classic Lutheran and Calvinist ecclesiologies also distinguish between the ethos of the church and that of the world, but they contrapose them less. More unequivocally than Augustine,* Luther affirmed that both the kingdom of God, where the gospel of Christ reigns, and the kingdom of the world, which is governed by the civil law, are ordained by God; and, against the Anabaptists, he maintained that Christians must operate in the latter. Like Augustine, however, Luther was modest in his hopes for the Christian gospel to qualify the secular administration of justice. John Calvin,* on the other hand, was much more sanguine, and in his attempt to create a theocracy* in Geneva he displayed a remarkable confidence in the power of the church to absorb and transform the world.

It is not the case that to understand the church primarily in terms of its ethos necessarily leads one to distinguish it sharply from the world. Sometimes, the Spirit of God is believed to be redemptively effective outside the church as well as in it. Barth, for example, on the one hand adamantly emphasizes the duty of the church to remain faithful to its peculiar identity by placing the precedence of God's Word and the acts of invocation at the heart of its life.

But, on the other had, he argues that the ascendant Christ is Lord of the whole world, that the final boundaries of the church are eschatological and hidden, that Christians should regard all human beings as virtual brethren, and that the church might therefore discover moral wisdom and virtue outside its own walls.

Further along the spectrum lies the liberal Protestant tradition, stemming from Immanuel Kant* through Albrecht Ritschl (1822–89) to the social gospel* movement in America. Here the boundary between the church and the world becomes least distinct, for the church's identity is reduced to the ethos of its secular relations (worthwhile religious beliefs being regarded as reducible to moral ones, and specifically religious practices as immoral distractions from the real moral business of inter-human relations), and its members are held to comprise all who are committed to the cause of just community. The logic of this eccesiology reaches its apogee in the social gospel of Walter Rauschenbusch (1861–1918), for whom the Christian church is little other than a 'religious' species of the socialist movement. Some liberation theologies* reach the same point when they identify the mission of the church simply as that of lending its support to a particular struggle for economic, social or political liberation.

The ethical significance of the church as community is not exhaustively described in terms of its display of a distinctive communal ethos. As Hauerwas has recently emphasized, it should also be described in terms of its role as the social context of the formation of moral character and the making of moral decisions. The Christian community plays its part in character-formation by means of the socially transmitted traditions of morally exemplary stories and moral practices, in which the individual grows up. It plays its part in moral decision-making by presenting the individual with paradigmatic cases of right and wrong behaviour, moral rules, and the possibility of moral criticism.

The sanctificatory or therapeutic importance of small Christian communities as schools for the moral and spiritual cure of souls has, of course, long been recognized in practice – as witness cenobitic (communal) monasticism, the Pietist collegium pietatis, the Methodist 'class', Bonhoeffer's* community at Finkenwalde, and the liberationist 'base communities'. It is the small community that plays this role because it provides a suitable environment for the growth of intimate friendship, and so for the exercise of fraternal accountability, confession, and aid.

This is the ecclesial model that many contemporary evangelicals have primarily in mind when they refer to the church as a 'family'. The virtue of this metaphor is that it holds forth appropriate ideals of intimacy, care and responsibility. However, in so far as the picture of the family is romanticized, it makes it harder for members of a church to acknowledge the serious conflicts that afflict their community, and thus hinders them from developing realistic and responsible responses.

See also: COMMUNITY ETHICS. [16]

Bibliography

Augustine, The City of God; P. Avis, Anglicanism and the Christian Church (Edinburgh, 1989); idem, The Church in the Theology of the Reformers (London and Atlanta, 1981); K. Barth, 'The Christian Community and the Civil Community', in Community, State and Church (Gloucester, MA, 1946); D. Bonhoeffer, Life Together (ET, London, 1954; repr. San Francisco, 1976); A. Dulles, Models of the Church (Garden City, NY, 1974; Dublin, ²1988); S. Hauerwas, A Community of Character (Notre Dame, IN, 1981); H. Küng, The Church (ET, London, 1967); H. R. Niebuhr, Christ and Culture (New York, 1951; London, 1952); J. H. Yoder, The Priestly Kingdom (Notre Dame, IN, 1984).

N.J.B.

CITY. A 'city' is a settlement where a large number of people (there is no general agreement as to how many) is concentrated for residential and economic purposes into a relatively small geographical area. The word has associations with the idea of politics and civic independence (via Gk. polis) and with the idea of civilization (via Lat. civitas), although the common use of another Latin-derived word 'urban', along with such words as 'decay', 'crisis', 'jungle', 'problem' or 'unrest', suggests a more negative view of cities. The claim of smaller historic towns to city status, because of their ancient cathedrals or town walls, reminds us of a world where most important settlements were tiny by modern standards. Indeed it takes us back to the OT where 'cities' (Heb. 'îr) were little more than fortified villages.

Cities today

Already there are 300 cities of over a million people and in most parts of the world cities are rapidly growing. Before long the Third World will be predominantly urban. For over a century in Europe, N. America and Australasia the majority of people have lived in cities. Despite negative attitudes, flight from inner areas, and the decentralization of economies as transport and telecommunications networks grow, most Western people will continue an urban lifestyle for years to come. Even those who move out to greener pastures will remain dependent economically and culturally on the life of the great urban cities.

Modern cities are far more than a place plus people. We need to understand the complexity of their structures and systems and the variety of their functions. Some cities are mostly industrial (e.g. Sheffield), some financial and cultural (e.g. New York), some governmental (e.g. Canberra), and others combine many functions (e.g. London). There are still cities which have a religious function and symbolic importance (e.g. Rome, Jerusalem, Varanasi). However, most modern cities operate on secular assumptions.

Social conflicts, ever present in this sinful world, become sharply polarized in large cities. As a result there are ethical issues with a distinctive urban flavour. Wealth (see Money*), poverty* and economic justice (see Economic Ethics[17]) are high on the agenda, whether we look at the favelas of São Paolo, the obscene wealth of Malabar Hill in Bombay or the juxtaposition of the City of London with the deprived East End. Money usually means power* and the powerlessness of many urban people has rightly led urban Christian leaders to campaign alongside the poor, for basic human rights (see Rights, Human*) and an end to oppression. Often struggles centre around issues of land* and housing, even in today's wealthy London, where thousands sleep on the streets, in hostels and in bed-and-breakfast hostels.

International migration adds ethnic and religious plurality to the pluralism* of values and lifestyle which is always a feature of large cities. Housing becomes segregated, community networks (including religious ones) are based on ethnicity, and the economy is stratified on racial lines. Racial justice thus becomes an important issue for urban Christians.

Cities in the Bible

The Bible speaks of an urban past and urban future. According to Stuart Murray in City Vision, there are over 1,400 scriptural references to cities. These range from the small fortified settlements of the Promised Land (e.g. Jos. 21) to the megalopolises of Nineveh (Jon. 3:2–3) and Rome (Acts 28:14–15). The Bible is a surprisingly urban book, and the first churches flourished in cities like Corinth, Ephesus, Philippi and Antioch. Ancient cities obviously differ from modern ones in size, structure, architecture, transport systems and government. While this makes hermeneutics difficult, there are a number of underlying biblical themes which should shape our attitudes to the cities in which we live.

Personalities and principalities. According to Ray Bakke in *The Urban Christian* (London, 1987), cities in the Bible are portrayed as having a (usually female) personality. Jerusalem (eventually a bride) has sisters in Sodom and Samaria (Ezk. 16:44–58) and a rival in the prostitute Babylon/Rome (Rev. 17:1 – 18:24). Throughout Scripture Babylon is the symbol of an evil city system, and of an unjust and oppressive empire. Indeed in certain circumstances God's people are called to flee. In contrast Jerusalem – 'the foundation of šālôm (peace)' – although repeatedly and tragically falling, and even murdering the prophets, becomes the symbol of what is possible for a city if redeemed. The vision of Is. 65:17–25, taken up in Rev. 21:1 – 22:5, is a model on which to build our urban hopes and dreams.

Charismatic urban theology (e.g. Pieter Bos, as reported by Greg Smith in City Cries 18, 1989) has developed the biblical ideas of city personalities alongside a theology of angels, powers, principalities and ruling spirits. Such writers see an intimate connection between places, history and spiritual oppression. They offer strategies of spiritual warfare to help bring in the kingdom of God* in urban areas.

Judgment, mercy and transformation. Many events recorded in Scripture show that God is merciful to cities and their people, far more than they deserve. God would have spared Sodom if only ten righteous people had lived there (Gn. 18:26–33). He sent Jonah to Nineveh by special delivery to preach repentance, and much to the prophet's chagrin was merciful not only to adults who repented, but to infants and cattle as well (Jon. 4:11). In the

NT many cities from Jerusalem to Rome were blessed, and eventually changed for the better by the preaching of the gospel and the 'salting' of the believers.

Some Christian writers such as Jacques Ellul* (and probably the majority of Western evangelicals) take a pessimistic view of cities, emphasizing the depravity which they see as gathering there. For them hope resides mainly in the salvation of individuals out of the evil city. Other modern radicals such as Harvey Cox (in *The Secular City*) have held an essentially optimistic view of the urban. For them the city offers freedom, choice and the chance to exercise human responsibility in a secular setting. More recent writings by radical evangelicals such as David Lim (*e.g.* 'The City in the Bible') and Stuart Murray present a more balanced view of the city as a place where good and evil conflict, but where God's purposes for personal and social transformation can be worked out, usually by the children of the kingdom, and sometimes without or even despite them.

Incarnation. To some extent the welfare of any city is connected with the willingness of God's people to live there and follow the pattern of incarnation and service which Jesus showed. In one sense Christians should be pilgrims like Abraham with no abiding city (Heb. 11:10, 16), stressing instead their citizenship of heaven (Phil. 3:20). Yet like the exiles in Babylon (exemplified in the lives of Daniel and his colleagues, Dn. 1 – 6) they are called to settle down and work for the welfare (shalom) of their cities as instructed by Jeremiah (Je. 29:4–7). For us today this commitment involves both a verbal witness to Jesus Christ, and a life of full community involvement, compassionate service, social action and political passion for justice and truth.

The role of the church

Many observers have noted that large cities in the West, and especially the poorer districts, have been 'stony ground' for the growth (or even survival) of the traditional Protestant churches. Certainly the middle-class culture of the church, masquerading as the gospel, when imposed on working-class believers has led to what the American writer Gibson Winter has described as 'the suburban captivity of the churches'. In England, Anglican concern for the plight of communities and churches in 'urban priority areas' led to the publication of the influential *Faith in the City* report in 1985.

Since then there has been a renewed thrust in urban mission activity throughout the UK, and there is now some evidence, from inner London at least, that the trend of numerical decline in church attendance has been reversed (MARC, *Prospects for the Nineties*, London, 1991). Certainly the inner-city church in the UK is a community of life, hope and vibrancy in the midst of oppression, struggle and despair.

In many large cities neighbourliness and a sense of community are notably absent. Therefore the first great specifically urban calling of the church is to neighbour-love and community-building. Small base community groups, on the pattern of those now common in Latin America, are proving very effective in this context. In multi-ethnic cities there is a special challenge to break down barriers in the church (Gal. 3:28), to express the gospel in more than one culture.

A well-rounded urban church, as a result of its social setting and biblical faithfulness, should therefore display most of the following characteristics: a body of diverse people, striving for unity; an evangelizing and church-planting mission; a community with meetings at cell, congregation and celebration level; one small minority group among many; a prophetic and political witness; a serving and suffering presence; a force standing for justice alongside the poor; an accepting, compassionate, healing, praying and praising community.

See also: DISCRIMINATION; RACE.

Bibliography

Archbishop of Canterbury's Commission on Urban Priority Areas, *Faith in the City* (London, 1985); H. Cox, *The Secular City* (New York and London, 1965); J. Ellul, *The Meaning of the City* (Grand Rapids, 1970); D. S. Lim, 'The City in the Bible', *Evangelical Review of Theology* 12.2, April 1988; S. Murray, *City Vision* (London, 1990); D. Sheppard, *Built as a City* (London, 1975); G. Smith, 'God's Heart for the City: A Few Tips from Amsterdam', *City Cries* 18, Spring 1989 (a report of P. Bos's lectures); *idem, Christianity in the Inner City: Some Sociological Issues* (Bromley, 1988); G. Winter, *The Suburban Captivity of the Churches* (New York, 1961).

G.S.

CIVIL DISOBEDIENCE is a form of political protest, distinguished by the fact that it openly breaks the law (see Law, Civil and Criminal*) for conscientious reasons. Civil disobedience campaigns have been mounted for a variety of causes, *e.g.* against war, racial segregation, forms of taxation and abortion. Normally such campaigns break relevant laws or challenge particular institutions. Methods may involve sit-ins, illegal marches or protests, tax boycotts or demonstrative attacks on, say, military bases or abortion clinics.

Civil disobedience is usually distinguished from certain kindred actions, namely conscientious objection involving violence,* and legitimate forms of protest. Conscientious objection is not always illegal, for many States make provision for it. Even when it is illegal, it is not usually directly political in intention; its primary concern is the refusal to be actively involved in military service. Campaigns of violence are typically not open to public approbation, and not submissive to the rule of law as a whole. Therefore violent campaigns, such as those engaged in by some animal rights (see Rights, Animals*) activists and some anti-abortionists, are seen as more akin to campaigns of insurgency, like those waged at varying levels by nationalist movements. On the other hand, lawful protests, *e.g.* orderly demonstrations and marches, which do not break the law, are on occasion a proper part of political life and raise no special moral issue. Civil disobedience openly breaks the law in order to draw attention to political injustice, or to change the law or public policy. Even in its law-breaking, it remains submissive to the rule of law as a whole and is willing to accept the proper legal punishment.

Modern theories of civil disobedience are able to claim authority in Christian tradition. Peter and the apostles argued, 'We must obey God rather than men' (Acts 5:29) when refusing not to teach in the name of Jesus. Much later, Thomas Aquinas* argued that justice was so essential to law that an unjust law was no law, from which it would follow that it cannot command obedience. More commonly, however, the church has more cautiously taught the duty of obedience even to an unjust regime. In this it has followed a clear strand of NT thought (*cf.* Rom. 13:1–7; 1 Pet. 2:13–14). The points at which Christian thought has reached widespread agreement on the duty of disobedience to the State and its laws are: 1. when believers are required to deny their faith in Christ, or explicitly disown their Lord; and 2. when the State has required Christians to take part in action which is in clear conflict with their Christianly formed conscience.*

Political philosophers gave considerable attention to the question in the late 1960s, and have continued to discuss it. Two movements in the 1960s brought it to prominence: the civil rights movement led by Martin Luther King,* and the anti-Vietnam War protests. It raises points of great interest for political theory. Its paradoxical quality is of obvious interest, but more fundamentally it raises basic questions about the nature of civil law and civil obedience. Naturally, different philosophers answer these questions in different ways. But there would be a general consensus for the view that, though civil disobedience cannot be ruled out on every occasion, it must be carefully justified. It must meet a number of relatively strenuous criteria. These criteria would supply a good starting-point for any Christian view of the matter. The following criteria follow from the nature of civil disobedience as outlined above: 1. All constitutional and democratic means must genuinely be exhausted. It is far preferable to persuade people by democratic argument. Some argue that in practice one can never exhaust the possibilities of lawful democratic methods, and conclude that in practically every case civil disobedience diverts energy and resources from proper democratic channels. 2. Civil disobedience should be open and public. It should be submissive to arrest and punishment, ready to take responsibility for its illegal actions. 3. It should strongly prefer non-violent methods; some would say that it must insist on non-violence.* 4. Actions of civil disobedience should display a good knowledge of the law, and a full respect for it. 5. Actions should be appropriate to the cause. 6. Civil disobedience should have a specific and realistic end in view. It should not be designed or undertaken in ways that are politically counter-productive. Fundamentally it remains only an extreme form of protest and persuasion, and it is not a form of coercion.

Bibliography

H. A. Bedau (ed.), *Civil Disobedience in Focus* (London, 1991); D. Bonhoeffer, *Ethics* (London, ²1971); J. F. Childress, *Civil Disobedience and Political Obligation* (New Haven, CT, 1971); C. Gans, *Philosophical Anarchism and Political Disobedience* (Cambridge, 1992); J. Rawls, *A Theory of Justice* (Cambridge, MA, 1971; Oxford, 1972).

D.J.E.A.

CLAPHAM SECT, THE. A group of politicians, mainly evangelicals and mainly resident in and about Clapham, who acted with William Wilberforce* in his campaigns against the slave trade and other social evils at the turn of the 19th century.

Clapham at that time was a separate village, some five miles from London, that was home to a growing community of businessmen from the City. Among them was Henry Thornton (1760–1815), a banker and MP for Southwark, who erected a house for his fellow evangelical Charles Grant (1746–1823), a director of the East India Company. Wilberforce lived with Thornton from 1793 until 1797, when, on his marriage, he set up a separate household in the village. Others attracted by the group and by the evangelical ministry of John Venn (1759–1813), rector of Clapham from 1792, included James Stephen (1758–1832), a fiery barrister; Lord Teignmouth (1751–1834), a former Governor-General of India; and Zachary Macaulay (1768–1838), a former Governor of Sierra Leone who in 1802 became editor of the evangelical Anglican *Christian Observer*. The only non-Anglican member of the group was William Smith (1756–1835), a Socinian dissenter, who was also a Foxite Whig. Most, however, were followers of the Prime Minister, William Pitt (1759–1806).

Their powerful political connections enabled the Claphamites to bring about the abolition of the slave trade in 1807, to exert pressure for the stricter enforcement of legislation against disorderly behaviour, and to open India to Christian missionaries. They were also generous to the British and Foreign Bible Society, to Sunday schools and to many charitable causes.

Bibliography
E. M. Howse, *Saints in Politics: The 'Clapham Sect' and the Growth of Freedom* (London, 1953).

D.W.Be.

CLASS CONFLICT, see INDUSTRIAL RELATIONS; LIBERATION THEOLOGY.

CLIENT-CENTRED COUNSELLING. Carl Rogers,* with his conviction that the individual has all the inner resources needed for innovation and change, was the initiator of client-centredness in the developing counselling movement (see Pastoral Care, Counselling and Psychotheraphy[12]). In the 1940s, he stressed the technique of non-directiveness in order to facilitate the client's uninhibited expression of feelings, the gaining of personal insight and the making of constructive choices. During the following decade, Rogers shifted his emphasis to the more dynamic notion of client-centredness, in which the therapeutic process is enhanced by the counsellor's basic trust in the client's capacity for insight and personal growth. This trust, to be effective, needs to be demonstrated by the counsellor's genuineness, empathic* understanding, and unconditional acceptance* of the client's thoughts, feelings and actions. Catalysed by the exercise of these therapeutic qualities in the counsellor, the client becomes aware of the distortions and denials (see Defence Mechanisms*) in his or her self-understanding (see Self*), learns to reflect more realistically on and assimilate life's experiences, and thus begins to move towards a more integrated personality.*

In the 1970s, Rogers' stance widened to a more fully developed personalism which has been termed 'person-centredness', a perspective which has extended its influence beyond the realm of individual and group counselling and psychotherapy into the fields of education, management and cross-cultural communication. In this development, Rogers argued that the welcoming and non-judgmental acceptance of the individual releases not only therapeutic change but a process of 'changingness' in every aspect of the person's life. To quote Van Belle's summary of Rogers' person-centredness: 'One becomes an experiential organismic process, and thus a more fully functioning person' (*Basic Intent*, p. 51).

The influence of client- and person-centredness is widespread too in Christian personalism, since, although humanistic presuppositions will be rejected, the valuing of the person in his or her uniqueness is fundamental in a biblical anthropology. Paul Tournier,* the Swiss medical practitioner, in his dialogue-counselling and co-founding of *Médecine de la Personne*, established a person-centredness which gave full reign not only to the intra- and interpersonal aspects of the therapeutic relationship but to a Christ-centredness which kept that relationship open to a dialogue with God.

Bibliography

R. F. Levant and J. Shlien (eds.) *Client-Centered Therapy and the Person-Centered Approach* (New York, 1984); D. Mearns and B. Thorne, *Person-Centred Counselling in Action* (London and Beverly Hills, CA, 1988); C. R. Rogers, *Client-Centered Therapy* (Boston, MA, 1951); *idem*, *On Becoming a Person* (London, ²1967); P. Tournier, *The Meaning of Persons* (ET, London and New York, 1957); H. A. Van Belle, *Basic Intent and Therapeutic Approach of Carl R. Rogers* (Toronto, 1980).

R.F.H.

CLIENT-CENTRED THERAPY, see CHARACTER;[10] CLIENT-CENTRED COUNSELLING; ROGERS, CARL.

CLINICAL THEOLOGY. In the 1950s a missionary doctor, Frank Lake,* retrained as a psychiatrist, and developed a radical synthesis of theological and psychological ideas, which he called 'clinical theology'. Influenced particularly by Søren Kierkegaard,* John of the Cross (1542–91), and the 'object-relations' theories of psychoanalysis,* Lake explored the pain* that living brought to many people, from these differing perspectives. He wanted those suffering from psychological problems to find help in the Christian faith.

Through the use of the drug LSD (lysergic acid diethylamide) to recover repressed memories, Lake discovered that birth and early life produced significant psychological trauma. Looking for a theological understanding of this, Lake produced his 'dynamic cycle'* based on the life of Jesus. He thus brought together a clinical psychiatric and psychoanalytic understanding that made theological sense, and an existential theology that made psychological sense: hence 'clinical theology'. Lake's ideas were never fully accepted in psychiatric, psychoanalytic or theological circles.

From 1958, Lake established clinical theology groups in various Anglican dioceses. These groups proved successful and in 1962 the Clinical Theology Association (CTA) was formed to develop this work, with other colleagues joining Lake. The significance of these groups was threefold: there was little training in psychology at theological colleges and many clergy felt ill-equipped to meet the demands of parish life; by including doctors and psychiatrists, these groups enabled clergy to be ac-cepted where their traditional 'helping' role had been marginalized; and the groups encouraged self-awareness and helped the personal growth of many clergy.

Throughout the 1960s, the work of the CTA continued to expand. Its theoretical basis was published in 1966 in Lake's *Clinical Theology*; it helped sponsor *Contact*, an influential journal discussing psychological, pastoral and theological issues; and as the numbers attending the courses grew, a base was established at Lingdale in Nottingham.

In the 1970s Lake became more influenced by experiential-style groups and he came to see the origins of emotional pain as being the first months in the womb (mother–foetal distress syndrome). The CTA became more experiential with the main focus becoming primal therapy.* Lake found support for his ideas in the 'inner healing'* of the charismatic movement and the writings of Pope John Paul II, developing these ideas in *Tight Corners in Pastoral Counselling* (London, 1981). On Lake's death the CTA went through considerable trauma in trying to resolve the two foci of Lake's work, and still maintains a difficult balancing act. The CTA's influence in the church lessened in the 1970s, although, among secular psychotherapists, Lake is regarded as pioneering primal therapy in Britain.

Lake had a passionate desire to help those in mental pain, and was known for his intensive involvement with people and his huge capacity for work, sadly at no small cost to his family. Because of his own needs, Lake was difficult to work with and the CTA never developed to its full potential. Out of his struggle to relate his deep faith to his inner pain, Lake produced a creative but flawed synthesis of psychological and theological ideas. His search for new ideas hindered a fully worked integration of his existing ideas. However, the CTA played an important part in developing pastoral counselling in Britain.

See also: PASTORAL CARE, COUNSELLING AND PSYCHOTHERAPY.[12]

Bibliography

C. Christian, *In the Spirit of Truth: a reader in the work of Frank Lake* (London, 1991); F. Lake, *Clinical Theology* (London, 1966), abridged version by M. H. Yeomans (London, 1986); J. Peters, *Frank Lake, the Man and his Work* (London, 1989).

J.A.R.

CLONING, see MANIPULATION.

CLOSED SHOP, see TRADE UNIONS.

CODES OF PRACTICE, see PROFESSIONAL ETHICS.

COERCION, see FORCE.

COGNITIVE BEHAVIOUR THERAPY is a form of structured psychological therapy which has been developed since the late 1960s, developing from the ideas of behaviourism and behaviour therapy to emphasize centrally the role of cognitions and feelings in psychological disturbance. It now constitutes a distinctive form of secular psychological treatment, contrasted with the other main forms, which are psychodynamic, humanistic and behavioural treatments. It is a more liberal form of behaviour therapy in the recognition paid to thoughts and beliefs in understanding and changing psychiatric and psychological problems, and thus is of special interest pastorally. It is also linked to the more cognitive approach adopted in academic psychology generally, illustrated by a recent study of religious belief from a cognitive perspective (see F. N. Watts and J. M. G. Williams, *The Psychology of Religious Knowing*).

The extension of the behavioural paradigm essentially proposes a three- or four-systems approach to psychological problems, suggesting behavioural, cognitive and/or affective, and physiological systems. This alternative to a unitary behavioural view is important, because it helps to account for a wider range of symptom patterns which patients report, and leads to a more appropriate evaluation of treatment outcome. In therapeutic practice, cognitive behaviour therapy (CBT) concentrates on the here-and-now, as opposed to the attention paid to developmental issues in more psychodynamic approaches, and it utilizes three major categories of procedures – problem-solving, cognitive restructuring and coping skills – as an integral part of treatment. All aspects of therapy are made explicit to the patient, and therapist and patient work openly and collaboratively towards agreed goals, and to that extent the patient has more control over treatment than in some other forms of psychological treatment. Along with other forms of brief focused therapy, CBT may also offer an effective alternative to the so-called minor tranquillizers, which do have some potential for creating dependency.

Some distinctively Christian approaches to pastoral counselling have been developed within a cognitive-behavioural framework, using terms such as biblical counselling,* misbelief therapy and inner healing.* The steps used in such approaches employ such terms as encouragement, exhortation and enlightenment, and in their detailed identification of problem feelings, behaviour and thinking may closely parallel secular approaches. These specifically Christian approaches may be particularly helpful with people who are depressed (see Depression*). It is not uncommon for the thoughts of such people to focus on their real or imagined guilt,* or to be related to perfectionist characteristics, and the cognitive approach can then integrate the patient's concepts of God, of sin and of judgment, with their present problem, while respecting the patient's own theological position. Inner healing approaches may be helpful for those with problems arising from past events or abuse.*

The Christian pastoral community has not yet fully absorbed the significance of cognitive treatment methods. Along with any other treatment modality, they have their own assumptions and methods. Positively, from a professional point of view they offer well-validated effective treatment for a range of mood- and anxiety-related conditions. From a Christian point of view they may contribute to setting Christians free from erroneous or unbiblical cognitions and beliefs (1 Cor. 12:1–2; Eph. 4:22–24). They view people as active partners in treatment, able to contribute rationally and emotionally to understanding their problem, and they are able fully to integrate the person's own beliefs into treatment. On the other hand, cognitive methods may neglect issues of early relationship and other contextual factors, they can be seen as essentially pragmatic without a coherent underlying philosophy, and can be viewed as denying the experiential and revelational parts of a person's Christian faith. Cognitive approaches have at least as much potential for integration with pastoral practice as other primarily secular approaches that have been welcomed within the pastoral fold, and deserve close attention by pastoral counsellors and theologians.

See also: BEHAVIOURISM, BEHAVIOUR THERAPY AND MODIFICATION; ELLIS, ALBERT;

Bibliography

L. J. Crabb, *Effective Biblical Counselling* (Grand Rapids, 1977); K. Hawton *et al.*, *Cognitive Behaviour Therapy for Psychiatric Problems* (Oxford, 1989); F. N. Watts and J. M. G. Williams, *The Psychology of Religious Knowing* (Cambridge, 1988).

J.N.H.

C OHABITATION. A cohabiting couple may be defined as 'any unmarried heterosexual couple who consistently share a common residence and regularly engage in sexual intercourse'. Cohabitation can be very temporary and casual (more like 'steady dating'), or it may be a preparation for marriage* or a substitute for it. Since the 1970s the incidence of cohabitation has increased sharply in many Western societies (D. Dormer, *The Relationship Revolution*, pp. 7–20). In Britain, for example, cohabitation before marriage had become the majority practice by 1992.

Some of the perceived advantages of cohabitation are: 1. it is easier to begin and end than marriage; 2. it can be cheaper; 3. it seems to be more loving because it does not depend on the external prop of the marriage bond; 4. it provides the opportunity to try out a relationship prior to making the full commitment of marriage; 5. it offers a relationship where sex roles are less stereotyped; and 6. it combines the sexual and emotional closeness of marriage with the autonomy of singlehood.

Cohabitation and the Bible

Marriage is presented in the Scriptures as the normative sexual relationship. Although there is no specific mention of cohabitation in Scripture, all sexual relationships (see Sexuality [11]) can be measured against the norms governing marriage. A number of key areas of biblical teaching are relevant to cohabitation.

Love. Permanence is at the heart of the biblical understanding of the committed reliable love that should characterize marriage. Cohabitation, however, rarely involves a commitment to permanence because: 1. it is often chosen in preference to marriage precisely because no such commitment is involved; 2. it often begins in a casual and indefinite way with no discussion about the likely duration of the relationship; and 3. there is a bias against permanence in the surrounding culture (it is seen

as idealistic and impracticable). It is ironic that many people opt for cohabitation as a trial for marriage because the one thing that you can not have a trial for is a *permanent* relationship such as marriage.

Vows. Though vows are not explicitly mentioned in Scripture, they are implicit in the idea of 'cleave' (AV) or 'be united' (Gn. 2:24). Wedding vows have two functions: 1. to define the nature of the relationship; and 2. to declare future intent. Whilst marriage is a commitment for the future as well as for the present, cohabitation tends to be a relationship just for the present with the future left deliberately open-ended. Some cohabitants *have* defined their relationships and future intentions with written contracts, but these write impermanence and, sometimes, unfaithfulness too into their very heart.

Sex. The Bible views sex in the context of the union of lives. This is the meaning of 'one flesh' (Gn. 2:24). Cohabitation involves sexual union without the full committed union of lives. Sex without a lifelong commitment 'violates the inner reality of the act; it is wrong because unmarried people thereby engage in life-uniting acts without a life-uniting intent' (L. Smedes, *Sex in the Real World*, Grand Rapids, 1976, p. 122).

Community. Marriage in the Bible is more than a private contract between individuals. It unites families. It is something that society recognizes and respects. The community offers married couples certain protections and places certain responsibilities on them. Cohabitation, however, is an essentially private relationship, and is largely blind to this community dimension.

Children. Couples in Scripture have a general duty to care for children* and educate them. Children need to grow up in the security that a constant permanent married relationship, at its best, affords.

Freedom. Cohabitation appears to be freer than marriage, but the freedom to leave introduces fear* into the relationship. Fear is destructive of real freedom, which grows best in the security of a loving, committed, permanent relationship.

Cohabitation and the church

What practical steps ought the church to take in facing the challenge posed by the present increased incidence of cohabitation? Here are some suggestions: 1. Beware of generalizations. All cohabitation relationships are different. Some are closer to the biblical norms than others, and this needs to be acknowledged, as does the fact that many marriages fall short of them. 2. Be sensitive to those who have opted for cohabitation as a result of painful experiences of marriage (whether their own or others'). 3. Take marriage preparation for cohabitants seriously. A wedding will not automatically *regularize* a relationship if it is founded on unbiblical ideas that have gone unchallenged. 4. Develop a convincing apologetic for marriage, and be prepared to teach and commend a Christian marriage to a sceptical generation.

The church's approach to cohabitation needs to be rooted in the convictions that 1. marriage is created by God; 2. it is *good;* and 3. it is for all humankind.

Bibliography

D. Dormer, *The Relationship Revolution* (London, 1992); G. Forster, *Marriage before Marriage?* (Bramcote, Nottingham, 1988); G. Jenkins, *Cohabitation: A Biblical Perspective* (Bramcote, Nottingham, 1992); E. Pratt, *Living in Sin?* (Southsea, 1992).

G.J.J.

COLLECTIVISM, see COMMUNITY ETHICS.[16]

COLONIALISM. Narrowly defined, colonialism may be described as that form of imperialism in which the imperial power imposes formal governmental control on a people or territory, usually without having to resort to large-scale human settlement or colonization. In this sense, the term is most commonly used by historians today to refer to the expansion of Western political control into the non-Western world, such as the substantial empires constructed by Spain and Portugal in South America in the 16th century or the tropical empires acquired by the European powers during the 1880s and 1890s, and dismantled only during the 1950s and 1960s. In much Marxist thought, this late 19th-century efflorescence of colonialism is seen (developing a theory of Lenin's) as a result of the evolution of capitalism* towards its final or monopolistic phase, in which the controlling financial forces of capitalism dictated the partition of the globe between the capitalist powers.

More loosely, colonialism is frequently employed in popular parlance as a synonym for imperialism, being applied to any tendency on the part of powerful nations and peoples to dominate and exploit the economy, life and culture* of less powerful nations and peoples.

Whatever definition is adopted, colonialism should properly be recognized as a recurring feature of human political behaviour throughout history, and not the peculiarity of any one period, economic system or ideology.

From the perspective of Christian ethics, colonialism poses two primary questions. The first relates to the appropriate moral judgment to be passed on the phenomenon itself. In so far as colonial states have existed to serve the interests of the colonial power, and not for the sake of the colonized population, political and economic exploitation of the subject peoples is an inescapable ingredient of colonialism. To that extent, unequivocal moral censure of colonialism seems the only response appropriate to a Christian. However, such exploitation does not necessarily mean that in every case the colonized people were left in a worse condition than before the advent of the colonial power; it means only that any material good accruing to the subject people from colonial rule was ultimately outweighed by the economic or political benefit extracted by the colonial power from the connection.

The issue needs to be seen in the wider context of debates about the function and legitimacy of political power.* In the modern world, made up as it is of sovereign nation-states, colonialism may be more easily differentiated from other forms of political rule than in the past, where political units were less clearly defined and concepts of nationhood often weak or non-existent. Thus neither the OT nor the NT makes any principled distinction between political rule exercised within the boundaries of a nation-state and that exercised over subject peoples beyond those boundaries. The only distinction which matters for the biblical writers is that between nations which seek to reflect the divine values of justice (see Justice and Peace[3]), righteousness* and compassion,* and those which pay scant regard for such values. Large colonial empires, such as those of Assyria or Babylon, may be intrinsically less likely to exhibit divine values than smaller political units, but they are condemned, not because they are empires rather than nation-states, but because the manner of their rule is unrighteous and arrogant. However, any censure of colonialism has to come to terms with the fact that many colonialists (often animated by religious faith) have genuinely believed themselves to be serving the best interests of the colonized peoples.

The second issue raised for Christian ethics by this subject is thus the ambiguous relationship which has frequently existed between Christian missionary endeavour and colonial powers. Most British Christians regarded the British empire in the 19th and 20th centuries as an instrument of God's purposes for the temporal good and eternal salvation of the subject peoples. This conviction lay behind the general readiness of missionaries and their supporters to espouse the general aims of British colonialism, even though they persistently challenged the repeated failure of colonial policy-makers and administrators to act in the best interests of the subject peoples. Christians today who wish to regard such convictions as fundamentally misguided are surely obliged to attempt to construct a theology of divine providence in history which balances the fact that God can never approve of exploitation* with a recognition that empires can be part of God's purposes of judgment and salvation for the world.

Bibliography

D. K. Fieldhouse, *Colonialism 1870–1945: An Introduction* (London, 1981); S. C. Neill, *Colonialism and Christian Missions* (London, 1966); B. Stanley, *The Bible and the Flag: Protestant Missions and British Imperialism in the Nineteenth and Twentieth Centuries* (Leicester, 1990).

B.S.

COLOUR, see RACE.

C OMA is a deep loss of consciousness in which vital functions (breathing, circulation, waste elimination, temperature control) are maintained either naturally or artificially. A person in coma does not respond to stimulation outwardly. There is growing evidence that in some cases stimuli, even spoken words, may be perceived unconsciously, and may alter subsequent behaviour. An anaesthetic is medically induced coma.

The higher brain (cerebral cortex) is depressed in coma; the presence of coma does not itself show whether or not higher brain function can or cannot return.

Natural sleep resembles coma, but a sleeper can be awakened.

Coma can be caused by a wide variety of factors: low or high body temperature, chemical poisons, biochemical imbalances of many kinds, brain injury (*e.g.* 'knockout'), lack of oxygen or accumulation of carbon dioxide, inflammations of the brain and brain tumours.

Recoverable coma can be very prolonged, even weeks or months in exceptional cases. But coma carries its own secondary dangers such as infections, vascular problems, and skin and stomach ulcers, which can be fatal.

Recovery from coma can reveal brain damage, witnessed by loss of intellect, emotional lability or personality change.

On rare occasions, though expressive consciousness is not regained since the damage to the higher forebrain has been too severe, the hindbrain is able to sustain control of breathing and circulation and the eyes are open so that the patient appears to be awake, though entirely unresponsive. This is called 'persistent vegetative state'; it raises extreme ethical difficulty because there is no sign that the patient has true consciousness, though this cannot be proven. In the early stages of this state careful nutrition and continuous stimulation have, in a few cases, resulted in a return to full awareness. In chronic cases, however, this has not succeeded. It is then that the difficult decision to discontinue treatment has had to be addressed; such cases have on occasion endured for over three years, with immense stress to all involved. (See C. Dyer, *BMJ* 305, 10 Oct 1992, pp. 853–854; see also R.V. Rakestraw, 'The Persistent Vegetative State and the Withdrawal of Nutrition and Hydration', *Journal of the Evangelical Theological Society* 35.3, 1992, pp. 389–405.)

Many pastoral problems arise, including: 1. family support during a prolonged, distressing illness; 2. concerns about the spiritual state of the unconscious person; 3. concern about the extent and duration of active medical and nursing measures: How long should efforts be made to save life? What will be the mental condition of the patient given recovery of consciousness? If there is brain death,* should active care be withdrawn?; 4. can any stimuli or messages reach the unconscious person, even if he or she cannot respond? and 5. in coma, patients may move or appear to respond to others for purely reflex (lower brain) reasons. This may lead relatives to draw quite false inferences about their likelihood of recovery or their expressed wishes.

When coma is prolonged, feelings of real or imagined guilt* often appear within families, which add to an already very stressful time; such factors can evoke unhelpful behaviour and reopen old tensions amongst relatives. The prolonged visiting involved is also very tiring and emotionally taxing.

A considerable problem of autonomy* arises. In most illnesses patients are able to express their wishes about their illness, its treatment, and what should happen if they do not recover. If unconscious, patients cannot express such autonomous choices. Relatives are not necessarily reliable guides to a patient's wishes. They cannot give consent* for another. To cover such circumstances, some advocate drawing up a 'living will' or 'advance directive', which indicates what patients want to happen or not happen at such time as they are unable to express their wishes.

It is very important to take care about all that is said near someone who is in coma. Not only is there evidence that spoken thoughts may influence those who are unconscious but there are well-recorded examples of people hearing and remembering things said near them when they seemed to be unconscious.

A central medical duty is to communicate adequately and with sympathy with the family of a comatose patient; much of the distress arises from the uncertainties which inevitably accompany coma, and which are markedly increased by lack of information. Because the outlook is so uncertain, unless there is demonstrable brain death, patients in coma must be treated as if they were going to recover and be accorded the status of those who are potentially conscious.

The 'locked-in syndrome' is a very rare, but extremely difficult, situation in which someone appears to be unconscious but can in fact perceive their surroundings without being able to respond.

It is often difficult to know how hard to try to treat comatose patients after the first few days. Decisions are varied by several considerations: age, outlook for the causal disorder, outlook for brain damage, and how many and how severely body systems are broken down all contribute to the decision. It is important, if efforts to cure cease and only care remains, to remove the paraphernalia of medical technology, so as to restore dignity and calm to an otherwise distressing environment.

See also: ETHICS OF MEDICAL CARE. [14]

D.W.V.

COMMERCE, see ECONOMIC ETHICS. [17]

COMMON OWNERSHIP. Although it is self-evident that we bring nothing into this world and can take nothing out of it, humankind is instinctively acquisitive and individuals naturally tend to assert the right to possess land or goods to the exclusion of others. A person will not willingly labour to till the soil except in expectation of its crop, or build or manufacture except to earn a livelihood. If people are entitled to benefit from their own labour, society must offer some protection for that benefit. Some have argued with Proudhon (1809–65) that all ownership is theft, but in practice organized society will not long endure without some concept of property.* Most societies have been able to survive and advance only by facilitating the exchange of property by means of a common coin. Normally ownership can be transmitted on death either to heirs of the testator's choice or according to regulations made by society. The tension between what an individual may justifiably treat as his or her 'own' and what ought to be regarded as the common rights of all has led to various schemes of proprietorship.

Invariably in order to regulate the conduct of members of a society for the mutual good, its governments (of whatever sort) must be financed by transferring a percentage of the property in individual ownerships into a fund at the disposal of the government intended to be used for the common benefit (see Taxation*). This revenue in fact represents a form of common ownership, although frequently not recognized as such. Societies differ in the extent to which individuals have any influence or control over the destination of such revenue.

Historically various attempts have been made to create not merely a common purse of *some* of the wealth of society but an equal sharing in *the whole* of that wealth. Such common ownership has been mainly confined either to fairly primitive rural societies or else it has been only partial and short-lived. Common ownership is more easily managed over grazing or hunting land than over arable land, buildings or movable property. Common ownership of the means of production and public utilities was fundamental to the ideology of socialism.* Whilst theoretically such industries and services belonged to everyone in the State, in practice they came to be operated bureaucratically and it was sometimes doubtful if they were being run for the benefit of anyone, let alone everyone. Therefore such public ownership is increasingly falling out of favour in the West and Westernized countries.

Although forms of ownership vary in different legal systems, the common elements are control over the property owned and responsibility for it. Where more than one person 'owns' the same property, mechanisms must be provided for resolving internal disputes between the various 'owners' of the same thing. A small group (or an individual) may emerge which is able to impose its will on the use of the property. Thus the group members' 'rights' or enjoyment of ownership tend to bring more benefit to them than to their theoretical co-owners. Commonly owned property has often ended up being parcelled out amongst the individual owners, who thereby assumed exclusive rights over their divided share. For instance, in England lands which had from Anglo-Saxon times been common lands enjoyed by the residents of a particular village were mostly 'enclosed' as private land by a series of Acts of Parliament during the 17th to 19th centuries.

Externally, third parties dealing with common property have found it inconvenient to have to deal with every one of a multiplicity of owners. Most legal systems have therefore evolved methods for making a few representative owners responsible vis-à-vis the rest of society, leaving them to resolve the consequences internally amongst all the owners.

Theocratic Israel represented a limited type of common ownership in that the land belonged to God and no-one was able to alienate in perpetuity his tribal inheritance. The most that could be sold was the right to the crops for however many years remained until the next jubilee, when the land reverted to its original tribal family. In essence this was a commonwealth in which every native-born Israelite owned an inalienable (albeit unequal) right to a part of the land.

The famous NT instance of the early Jerusalem church (Acts 2:44–45; 4:32–35) is not strictly an example of common ownership at all, but rather a sale of individual assets (Acts 5:1–4) resulting in the proceeds being placed into a common purse and disbursed for the collective good. No attempt appears to have been made to control and manage jointly owned assets for the long-term support of the group, so that in fact within a matter of a few years the collective purse was empty and they

became reliant upon the support of other churches (Rom. 15:26). The fall of Jerusalem (AD 70) meant that little was lost by the earlier sale of property within the city, but the Jerusalem experiment does not appear to have been copied in any other NT churches.

See also: OLD TESTAMENT ETHICS. [8]

D.P.N.

COMMUNISM. The idea of communism as a social system in which members resign their rights to ownership and share possessions in common has recurred throughout history. Early Christians are described as having 'everything in common' (Acts 4:32, RSV), surrendering their possessions for redistribution by the apostles according to the principle of need (Acts 4:34–35). There are strong echoes of this in Christian communities which adopted this early Christian communism as a model (e.g. the Anabaptist* group called the Hutterites and their Bruderhof communities which are based on the common ownership of property).

In the 20th century the dominant meaning became detached from the communitarian ideal and utopian socialism and became synonymous with the political and social system of the State socialist countries under Communist Party rule. These countries had similar ideologies, political structures and economic systems despite continuing to have distinct national characteristics. The ideology of communism is in direct line of descent from Karl Marx* and Friedrich Engels (1820–95) who, in the Communist Manifesto of 1848, saw communism as the final stage in the history of class societies. Their utopian vision of a society free from material necessity, private property and social exploitation inspired the revolutionary working-class movements which eventually led to the 1917 Bolshevik revolution and to the rule of the Communist Party in the Soviet Union under Lenin (1870–1924). The subsequent development of State socialist societies expressed the tension between two interpretations of revolution: one based on the Paris commune of 1871 in which the citizens of Paris rejected State authority in a popular participatory movement, and another which created a new centralized authority – the 'dictatorship of the proletariat'. Marxism-Leninism in the Soviet Union, like the regimes of post-war Eastern Europe and Maoist China, took the latter course. The common ideological features of the communist world are scientific materialism, atheism and authoritarianism. The political regimes consist of a combined Party–State structure with a monopoly of power which permeates all institutions and levels of society. Economic production and distribution are subject to a centrally controlled command system which, over time, may be modified to include elements of market regulation, but which is still subject to the inefficiencies of planning.

The status and meaning of religion in communist societies is quite clear. It is identified as a reactionary force, either tolerated as a residual phenomenon in the transition to socialism and communism, or deliberately repressed as a form of counter-revolutionary activity. In practice, there have been great variations in the tolerance and intolerance of religion in the history of communism. At the times when communist parties needed internal allies or were under threat from external enemies, as in the Soviet Union in the 1940s, religious institutions and expressions of belief were granted more space, especially if they provided a useful focus for patriotic sentiment. At other times, official recognition for religious groups was withheld or granted with extreme reluctance, thus driving many believers into a shadow or underground existence. The history of attempts to tame or abolish religion under communism are well documented by a number of authors including Trevor Beeson (1926–), Michael Bordeaux (1934–) and the publications of Keston College, Kent.

Communism challenges Christian belief and practice in two quite different ways. 1. Communism is a system of ideology which, despite its atheism, contains a certain structural resemblance to religion. It has a vision of a future kingdom of harmony, the proletariat is like a chosen people, and the revolutionary movement invites total commitment in the ideological struggle. This encouraged the view, popular in some quarters at the height of the Cold War, which identified communism with Antichrist, and attitudes of total hostility which at times have even been used to justify the threat of military annihilation. In sharp contrast to this was the response of the Christian–Marxist dialogue (most active in the years of *détente*) which explored the areas of convergence as well as divergence between Christian and Marxist communist beliefs, so as to create the basis for co-operation in the building of socialist society. Such dialogue was never officially recognized, and the main practical consequence of communist ideology in Eastern Europe, the former Soviet Union and China has been to deny religion any public role, although the unintended consequence has been to give it inner strength through persecution.

2. Communism as a form of revolutionary praxis* challenges Christians to express their solidarity with the poor. The experience of Latin America and Third World countries is most pertinent here. Some earlier traditions of Christian theology and ethics were prepared to justify resistance to or rebellion* against unjust powers provided that it could be shown by reference to natural law* that the fundamental moral community had been violated (see Civil Disobedience*). Liberation theology,* however, recognizes that class struggle and the violence of the oppressor are endemic and unavoidable facts. The problem for Christian involvement in proletarian revolution is not that it needs to be justified as a special case. Rather, it is the problem of the relationship between means and ends in a world which is in constant transformation. A communist revolution leading to the dictatorship of the proletariat is not committed to justice and peace as primary goals. History shows that the pattern of the communist rise to power is through cynical manipulation of the coercive apparatus of the State, and that revolutionary thinking often becomes trapped by the dualistic conception that through revolution evil can be overcome.

Can one be a Christian and a communist? Most would answer this question in the negative. Membership of communist parties is normally denied to those professing religious beliefs, while active involvement in an atheistic movement is clearly incompatible with Christian witness. But this clear antithesis does not offer any easy way out of the characteristic dilemmas of being a citizen in a communist country where, for example, party membership may be a condition of practising one's profession or any public service.

The events in Eastern Europe in 1989 were hailed as the end of communism. While communism is no longer a force in that region or in the former Soviet Union, except as a burden of history, China and some other countries have yet to follow the same path. Even where communism has ceased to play an active role, its legacy will persist in a number of forms: through continued dependency on the authority of the State, habits of suspicion and secrecy, and ignorance of spiritual teaching. As an idea, the utopian aspect of communist ideology – an end to human alienation* and social divisions based on private property – is likely to remain as one of the key motifs in speculation about the future destination of modern societies.

Bibliography

T. Beeson, *Discretion and Valour* (London and Philadelphia, ²1982); M. Bordeaux, *Gorbachev, Glasnost and the Gospel* (London, 1990); D. Lane, *Soviet Economy and Society* (Oxford and New York, 1985); J. Lawrence, *The Hammer and the Cross* (London, 1986); V. I. Lenin, *The State and Revolution* (Moscow, 1974).

H.H.D.

COMMUNITY, see COMMUNITY ETHICS;[16] SOCIETY.

COMPASSION. As popularly conceived, compassion means both the emotion experienced when a person is moved by the suffering of others, and the act of entering into the suffering of another person with the purpose of relieving it. The first conceptualization may include a *desire* to relieve suffering; the second requires *action* to relieve it. In Christian ethics the former is an insufficient response to suffering; the expression of compassion must include an active involvement on the part of the one who shows compassion.

Compassion, consequently, involves 'doing' rather then just 'saying'. A compassionate response to suffering requires that one be moved by the suffering of the other, act to remove the immediate effects of the suffering, and respond at length to correct the structures which may have given rise to the suffering itself. The person who shows and lives compassion, therefore, accepts responsibility to heal, bring hope and minister justice. Compassion is the avenue by which God's grace and Spirit – spiritually, emotionally and physically – come to those in need.

Compassion is demonstrated in the life of Jesus, and it is also part of the instruction he gave to those who inquired how they might follow him. The Gospel narratives indicate that as Jesus travelled throughout the towns and villages 'he had compassion' for the people

'because they were harassed and helpless, like sheep without a shepherd' (Mt. 9:36; see also 14:14; Mk. 1:41; *etc.*).

In the parable of the good Samaritan, Jesus indicates that he who acted uprightly was the one who, upon seeing the wounded man by the side of the road, 'had compassion on him' (Lk. 10:33, RSV). The compassion of the Samaritan was, furthermore, reflected in the specific actions he took to help him recover (Lk. 10:34–35).

Other parts of Scripture as well regard compassion as an essential virtue* of the ethical life. As we fulfil the command to love one another (see 1 Jn. 3:11–18), we express compassion; this is the case also when we 'carry each other's burdens' (Gal. 6:2). The instruction of Jesus, and that of the rest of Scripture, teaches that: 1. compassion centres on the need of the other, rather than on one's own need; 2. it is not obligation to every neighbour, *i.e.* to all persons in need; and 3. it is not just an emotion or passive feeling, but an active response to need.

Compassion, further, must not be limited to personal relationships. It must also be directed to social problems. Where there is hunger,* compassion requires the feeding of the hungry. Where there is poverty,* compassion requires economic justice (see Justice and Peace[3]). Where there is oppression, compassion requires social and political reform.

Repeatedly, the Psalms indicate that God is a 'compassionate and gracious God' (Ps. 86:15; see also 111:4 and 145:8). Because God is one who suffers with those who suffer, it is in compassionate action that we encounter God. When we fulfil the command to 'show mercy and compassion to one another' (Zc. 7:9) we find God.

In biblical imagery, the antithesis of compassion is 'hardness of heart'. Here compassion is dried up; the person characterized by hardness of heart can no longer see and feel the pain and suffering of others. The Pharaoh of the Exodus is the clearest biblical example of this attitude (Ex. 8:15).

See also: MERCY.

D.L.P.

COMPETITION, see CAPITALISM; CARTELS; MONOPOLIES.

COMPROMISE. A compromise is basically the accommodation of an ethical rule or principle to the exigencies of life in the real world. Within that definition, however, important distinctions need to be made.

At one extreme, compromise may represent evasion of duty,* when a clear obligation is avoided on ethically inadequate grounds for the sake of personal advantage. At the other extreme, a compromise may express an intention to discover God's will in an ethically ambivalent situation, especially when two or more principles dictate courses of action which are incompatible.

In between the two extremes, some compromises are made in a serious effort to adapt principles to life's circumstances. A strike,* for example, may be resolved by a mediating compromise which does some justice to both sides in the dispute, without fully meeting the claims of either.

However a compromise is evaluated, the use of the word implies that deontological* concerns are paramount. Compromises imply the existence of absolutes.* This contrasts with the teleological* language of utilitarianism (see Consequentialism*). The utilitarian evaluates means relatively in terms of their ends. Those who embrace compromise (reluctantly, perhaps) tacitly accept that there are some things which are always right or wrong in themselves.

By his teaching and example, Jesus condemned the kind of evasive compromise which exempts a believer from obvious obligations. If there is a clear choice between the Lord's will and personal gain, Christians are left in no doubt where their duty lies; there is no scope for negotiation between God and money, when both claim mastery (Mt. 6:24). Similarly, Jesus rejected any suggestion that the calls of physical or social security should be allowed to deflect the force of his demand for radical discipleship (Mt. 10:37–38; 18:8–9). In this sense, Jesus' temptations in the desert were the devil's attempts to get him to compromise, and the cross was the logical outcome of his refusal to comply.

Jesus was especially critical of Pharisaic casuistry.* In principle, casuistry aims to construct a logical network of compromises by analysing difficult cases and by categorizing degrees of certainty with which conflicting ethical principles can – in a modified way – be applied (see Probabilism*). Jesus' criticisms (echoed by Blaise Pascal, 1623–62, in countering 17th-century Jesuit casuistry) were aimed not so much at the system but at its abuse. Systematic compromise had led, in his

day, to ingenious evasion of clear-cut duties, which he condemned unequivocally (Mk. 7:9–13).

If casuistry accepts the inevitability of compromise when rules and principles are applied to difficult cases, the school of moral philosophy associated with Immanuel Kant* firmly denies it. For Kant, the call of duty allows for no compromising exceptions. In his treatise 'On a Supposed Right to Lie from Benevolent Motives', he explains that both truth-telling and life-saving are aspects of the categorical imperative.* Any clash between their demands can therefore only be apparent, not real. It can never be right to compromise the truth by telling a lie, even if telling the truth (e.g. to a murderer) results in the loss of a life.

Some moral theologians take a similar stance. John Murray (1898–1975), for example, echoes Kant's refusal to justify a lie told to a murderer, by encouraging Christians to trust in God's providence. The Lord will provide a 'third way' out of such dilemmas, as he did for Daniel (in different circumstances) in OT times.

Helmut Thielicke* is typical of other moral theologians (the majority) who reject this view as unrealistic. 'Compromise', he maintains, 'is a tribute that must be paid to a fallen world.' Appealing to Luther's 'two kingdoms' doctrine (see Lutheran Ethics*), he defends the necessity of telling diplomatic lies (for example), because the secular structures of a sinful world make this and similar compromises essential. To deny the necessity of any compromise at all is fanatical radicalism, he complains, not Christian realism but a denial of the world as it is.

To Thielicke, however, the necessity of compromise does not justify it. Our sinful environment may make lesser-evil choices inevitable, but their inevitability does not make them good. Necessary compromise is simply 'gauze in the wound'. God may require us to 'sin bravely' (pecca fortiter), in the assurance that forgiveness is available in Christ, but we must never lose sight of the fact that all compromise is wrong. 'Compromise does not mean that we have an excuse. It means that we participate in the suprapersonal guilt of this aeon' (H. Thielicke, TE 1, ET, Philadelphia, 1966; London, 1968, p. 500).

Norman Geisler (1932–), among other ethicists from the Reformed tradition, is unhappy with Thielicke's claim that necessary compromises are sinful. Jesus, he points out, faced moral conflicts that necessitated compromise (in deciding, for example, whether or not to disobey the authorities in order to perform acts of mercy). But the Bible assures us that he never sinned (Heb. 4:15). Moreover, people in Scripture who compromised by telling lies in order to save lives, like the Hebrew midwives and Rahab the prostitute, are praised, not called to repentance (Ex. 1:15–21; Jos. 2:1–7; Jas. 2:25).

Geisler therefore prefers to speak of choosing the greater good (rather than the lesser evil) when describing the kind of compromise Christians may legitimately make in situations of conflict. On such occasions, the Christian is exempt from the lower obligation by virtue of the higher. 'Exemption' is the proper way to describe such a compromise, because it affirms the lower obligation while temporarily shelving it in the interests of repecting the higher.

This hierarchical approach is attested by Scripture, maintains Geisler. In various ways, the Bible arranges duties in a league table of obligation. Loving God is a higher Christian duty, for example, than loving parents. Obeying God must be set above obeying the government. And the demands of showing mercy outstrip the demands of telling the truth.

Moreover, contrary to Luther, Geisler believes that no guilt attaches to the kind of compromise which expresses the choice of a greater good. 'One is not morally culpable if he fails to keep an obligation he could not possibly keep without breaking a higher obligation' (*Christian Ethics*, p. 120).

The Christian ethical consensus, therefore, is that compromise may be in line with God's will when it is necessitated either by a clash of principles or by a set of circumstances where mediation is essential, but not when it masks an evasion of reponsibility for trivial or selfish purposes.

Bibliography

N. L. Geisler, *Christian Ethics: Options and Issues* (Grand Rapids, 1989; Leicester, 1990); K. E. Kirk, *Conscience and Its Problems* (London, 1927); H. Thielicke, *TE 1*.

D.H.F.

COMPUTER ETHICS, see DATA PROTECTION.

CONCEPTION, see EMBRYOLOGY.

CONCUPISCENCE is a dated word meaning immoderate desire, usually sexual, which comes from the Lat. *con* + *cupere* (to desire wholly). The AV used 'concupiscence' as one of the translations of the Gk. *epithymia* in Rom. 7:8; Col. 3:5; 1 Thes. 4:5. *Epithymia* itself may have the positive connotation of legitimate desire as it does a number of times in Scripture, but more frequently it bears the negative connotation of inordinate desire or lust.*

According to Augustine,* before the Fall* sexual organs and sexual intercourse were subject to the voluntary control of reason in humankind. After the Fall the genitals are no longer under voluntary control, but are subject to the lust of concupiscence. This view, which makes every act of intercourse an act of lust (only the goal of procreation* stops it from becoming debauchery), helped to set the stage for many centuries of negative Christian thinking about sexuality (see 11).

Warnings against concupiscence can serve a function in condemning sexual desire (or any form of desire) which covets satisfaction of needs without regard for the other person as person, without concern to be involved in a relationship of mutual giving and sharing. As such, concupiscence is an overwhelming desire to obtain and immorally possess another person.

It is not sexual urges or sexual intercourse which are wrong or sinful, but their improper use. In this context repression of desires as well as their inappropriate expression is equally bad. Concupiscence, then, is not restricted to sexual matters, but is a deeply spiritual problem of the human heart: the obsession to possess. Put in modern terms, sexual concupiscence (inappropriate sexual desires with or without acting them out) is sexual addiction.* As in treating substance abuse, it is important to treat the underlying personal-emotional-spiritual issue of which the addiction is symptomatic.

J.H.O.

CONFESSION involves the acknowledgment of responsibility* and an admission of guilt,* in relation to God and neighbour. A 'ministry of reconciliation' (in some denominations and under appropriate circumstances) offers a means of making this confession individual and specific. 'Christ crucified' is the 'confession of faith' upon which confession and reconciliation* are based. Debate continues about how confession relates to psychological understandings of human maturing.

Confession and culture

There is a widespread human longing for reconciliation, expressed in public ritual and internal disposition. Traditional Catholic confession is in decline, and reasons can be marshalled to explain this, *e.g.* the anti-clericalism of a society that often suspects authority figures. No single moral code acts as an 'umbrella' to unite a culture seeking individualistic self-fulfilment, and since Freud* and Jung* human behaviour is understood (at popular and academic levels) to be significantly affected by aspects of the unconscious.* Jung (quoted in Dudley and Rowell, *Confession and Absolution*, p. 176) said, 'Through confession, I throw myself into the arms of humanity again, freed at last from the burden of moral exile'. 'Confession' is a first stage in psychotherapy (see Pastoral Care, Counselling and Psychotherapy[12]). Roger Hurding (1934–) notes the importance of knowing one's faults and owning them (*Roots and Shoots*, p. 354), but also suggests criteria whereby 'revealed theology' may evaluate such insights (p. 264). Such an evaluation will discriminate between theological and neurotic guilt, so that pastoral care may (as appropriate) offer the grace of God's forgiveness* and/or encourage the owning of hitherto hidden aspects of the unconscious self.

Confession in Christian tradition

OT prophets confess personal sin (Is. 6:5) and national sin (Ne. 1:6; Dn. 9:4ff.), in the expectation of God's covenant mercy. The seven 'penitential psalms' (Pss. 6, 32, 38, 51, 102, 130 and 143), integral to Israel's worship, form a bridge into Christian worship. Jesus never confessed sins on his own behalf (Heb. 4:15) but had a unique authority over sin (Mk. 2:5) and the sinner (Jn. 8:11). His teaching expressed the universal need for confession (Lk. 11:4) which Luke records in vivid penportraits (the surprised apostle, 5:8; the taxcollector's 'Lord, have mercy', 18:13; the prodigal's proposed confession 'Father, I have sinned', 15:18–19; and the woman weeping at his feet, 7:38). Lest sin deceive (1 Jn. 1:7–10), confession within the congregation (Jas. 5:15–16) is depicted as a normal part of the mutuality of NT Christian relationships.

In the post-apostolic church, confession was a second baptism, allowed only *once*. By 1215, an *annual* confession was required in the Western church. According to G. E. H. Palmer (1904–) the Orthodox Desert Fathers of the Eastern church commended confession within the pursuit of holiness. Medieval misuse led to criticism of private confession as unnecessary by John Wyclif (*c.* 1329–84). John Calvin* (*Institutes* III.iv.11 and 14) later commended general confession as the norm. (For how Jesus' authority to forgive sins has been understood as delegated to the church, see Dudley and Rowell, pp. 15–132.) Kenneth Leech (1939–), in *Soul Friend* explores how confession relates to spiritual direction.*

Confession today

1. Confession must be placed doctrinally and pastorally within the wider context of conversion,* discipleship and healing.* Confession is 'daily baptism' (Augustine, *Sermon* 213:8), reassuring the believer of God's grace in Christ. It leads to fellowship in mutual prayer,* service and shared life with other justified sinners.

2. To hear confessions requires discernment (Palmer *et al.*, *The Philokalia*, p. 359) and the humility to receive direction oneself. 'Too much reliance' on confession can encourage scrupulosity, but 'too little opportunity' for reconciliation and guidance can leave people coping with 'unresolved guilt feelings' (*cf.* John Macquarrie, *Principles of Christian Theology*, London, ²1977, p. 484).

3. The Holy Spirit brings conviction (Jn. 16:8) and new joy (Ps. 51:11–12). Grace cannot be restricted to 'sacramental' structures (*cf.* Dudley and Rowell, ch. 7). However, the warning to Anglican priests in the *Canons* of the Church of England 'not, at any time [to] reveal ... any ... offence ... committed to his trust' (Canon B 29), reminds all who practise this ministry to seek self-control (2 Tim. 1:7).

4. Responsibility for guilt must be balanced by an awareness of factors beyond a person's control, both in the self and in society (see Campbell, *Rediscovering Pastoral Care*, ch. 6). In a world that needs to know both its fallibility and its forgivability, the church can show that confession and reconciliation constitute good news.

See also: ABSOLUTION.

Bibliography

D. Bonhoeffer, *Life Together* (ET, London, 1954; repr. San Francisco), ch. 5; A. V.

Campbell, *Rediscovering Pastoral Care* (London, ²1986), chs. 1, 3 and 6; M. Dudley and G. Rowell, *Confession and Absolution* (London, 1990); R. F. Hurding, *Roots and Shoots: A Guide to Counselling and Psychotherapy* (London, 1986) = *The Tree of Healing* (Grand Rapids, 1988); K. Leech, *Soul Friend* (London, 1977); G. E. H. Palmer *et al.* (eds.), *The Philokalia*, vol. 1 (London and Boston, MA, 1979).

G.O.S.

CONFIDENTIALITY characterizes one important aspect of a relationship based upon mutual trust,* enabling one or all parties to disclose to others matters which, if generally revealed, would embarrass or compromise those concerned. A confidential relationship is thus one in which one or more secrets are shared. Confidentiality is stronger than confidence, for confidence is a general requirement for the establishing or continuing of any relationship between people, *e.g.* in business. Confidentiality is closely related to privacy* and might be regarded as a controlled extension of it. It is a feature of close friendship* and an important ingredient in certain kinds of professional relationships, *e.g.* those between doctor and patient, and lawyer and client (see Professional Ethics*).

Its basic justification lies in the right of an individual to decide whether, and to whom, personal information is to be disclosed. Willingness to disclose such information to anyone usually presupposes the existence of a relationship of mutual respect, whether personal or professional. The existence of such a justification creates a presumption in favour of the maintenance of confidentiality which may, however, in certain circumstances be overridden.

Confidentiality raises several interesting and important ethical issues, in particular over the limits of confidentiality, and the purpose of it.

Given that one is told a matter in confidence, is one ever bound to disclose it? A confidential relationship is a special case of promise-making and the same general considerations apply. One may only break a confidence under very exceptional circumstances: *e.g.* if through growing incapacity one of the parties does not recognize markedly changed circumstances; or if some grave and unanticipatable injustice would result if confidentiality were kept. The law recognizes certain privileged confidential relationships, *e.g.* that between a priest and his client, and that between husband and wife. A more controversial relationship is that between a journalist and his or her sources of information, journalists arguing that both present undertakings and future sources of sensitive information would be compromised if their sources were to be disclosed in court; the courts arguing that the public interest in some cases requires such disclosure. Similar problems arise in connection with police informers, private detectives and a national secret service (see Secrecy*).

One important justification of confidentiality is to preserve human integrity, and to allow the formation of close human bonds. Other justifications are the integrity and security of the State and the gaining or preservation of commercial advantage. Where only a breach of confidence would prevent the undermining of the public good, or the harming of the innocent, that breach is at least permissible and may, it is arguable, be obligatory. Similar qualifications are necessary in the case of professional confidential relationships established with children, or with those otherwise weak and immature, for such relationships may conflict with other obligations.

The importance of maintaining confidentiality once it is established, coupled with the fact that any such relation cannot be absolute, would appear to caution against entering into a confidential relationship lightly (*cf.* Pr. 11:13; 20:19b), without due consideration of its responsibilities and the potential conflicts that may arise. Scripture cautions against passing on confidential information ('talebearing'), and in view of this a distinction should perhaps be drawn between listening to confidences in the context of a request to provide counselling and other assistance, and listening to them for personal gratification.

English law has recently placed greater emphasis upon a client's or patient's right to know what is kept on file about him or her. These are all cases of the legality or otherwise of confidential relationships: it may be argued that the legal question is irrelevant to morality. Clearly, if one were bound generally to disclose to a court or some other body what one is told in confidence then the whole relationship would break down, as has frequently happened in totalitarian regimes with a large and active secret police.

The question has also been raised as to whether those in public life can expect the same degree of privacy, and hence confidentiality, in their family and other personal relationships, as others enjoy. Such intrusiveness, *e.g.* by the media (see Media Ethics*), is regarded by some not only as distasteful but as a violation of a basic right. Political liberals, in particular, wish to make a sharp but not always clear distinction between what is private and confidential (what J. S. Mill* called 'self-regarding acts'), and what is public and professional ('other-regarding acts').

Confidentiality takes on a questionable aspect when it is used by professionals and professional organizations to protect themselves against investigation, especially in cases where their decisions affect many lives. It is perhaps possible to make a distinction between the confidentiality of procedures, including those procedures necessary for the formulation of policy and the making of decisions, and the confidentiality of the policies thus formed. The former have a greater degree of justification than the latter, which is hard to justify unless there is some larger overriding purpose, *e.g.* the defence of the State from terrorism or external threat.

The purpose of confidentiality in a bureaucracy cannot be to deprive people of information to which they are entitled, but rather (as with journalism) to help the flow of such information by ensuring its reliability. But the more general reason for confidentiality has to do with human vulnerability and fallibility. Advice may need to be sought, the psychological comfort of telling a confidence to a trusted friend may be needed, ideas (*e.g.* in business or in government) may need to be tried out. Without the assurance of confidentiality many people would be deprived of access to professional, expert help which they need and to which they are entitled, and would be less willing to give expression to untested ideas.

In addition, the complexity of modern society is such that it becomes important that certain interpersonal relations (involving, *e.g.* employment) are merely transactional, for which information about the personal lives of the participants (*e.g.* their marital or family status, or their political or religious opinions), may not in general be relevant. Where confidentiality is the basis for immoral and illegal activity it becomes conspiracy.

There is little direct teaching in Scripture about the ethics of confidentiality, but it is presupposed in a number of places. Gossiping and talebearing are condemned (*e.g.* Pr. 18:8;

20:19a) and wisdom* is frequently linked with restraint in behaviour, including speech. Jesus praises those whose giving is in secret (Mt. 6:4), and confidentiality is linked with possessing a charitable disposition (1 Cor. 13:4–6). But there are no confidences from God, who knows the secrets of hearts (Rom. 2:16).

See also: DATA PROTECTION; ETHICS OF MEDICAL CARE. [14]

Bibliography

S. Bok, *Secrets: On the Ethics of Concealment and Revelation* (New York, 1983; Oxford, 1984).

P.H.

CONFLICT is inevitable as people interact with one another. They come with different experiences, expectations and interests that have to be lived with or resolved in everyday life. The important issue is not whether or not there is conflict, but how the conflict is handled. Christians sometimes think that all conflict is to be avoided and that harmony must reign. But this is not a scriptural view; it is more of a personal, subjective view born of unsatisfactory handling of conflict. Conflict is not only inevitable; constructive conflict can be invaluable in strengthening character and deepening understanding.

Conflict exists in *group situations* and institutions where different factions have differing interests which are in deep opposition to one another. If each party fears that it may lose something that is vital to its cause in the antipathetic struggle, there is probably little room for negotiation or fair bargaining. The vexed question of 'the just war'* – on a minor or major scale – has its roots here (*cf.* Jas. 4:1–2).

Conflict within communities is a large-scale reflection of *interpersonal conflict*. Each person has his or her own values and expectations. It may seem very threatening to be required to moderate or abandon them if they represent the totality of the inner self. It is important that people should be operating from their own inner still centre (genuine self-possession), so that they are not easily threatened by external differences. They are then in a position to decide whether the conflictual issue is of sufficient absolute importance to take a firm stand or whether to give way graciously. (Consider Jn. 13:3–5, where Jesus was so secure in his own identity and self-esteem born of his relationship with his Father that he could do the menial task of washing the disciples' feet without losing face.)

Marriage and family life is a major arena for conflict, as people with different backgrounds, expectations and experiences try to blend together and learn how to make their needs and views known effectively. Sometimes this involves toleration of strong conflict and painful acknowledgment that some of these cherished values, views or habits need to be reviewed. Effective conflict-resolution can take place only within an atmosphere of love (see 2) and trust* where both parties know that there will be no winners or losers but each is respected for his or her own value. There is an opportunity for personal growth within this type of conflict. The approach to conflict which seeks to get its own way and prove the other person wrong is destructive of both parties and of the relationship. It can lead eventually to much frustration* and bitterness.*

Everyone experiences *intrapersonal conflict*, to some degree. There are two sorts of internal conflict.

1. The first category of internal conflict is caused by the imbalance between various parts of the ego structure – some parts being overdeveloped, *e.g.* conscience,* and some foundational needs being unmet, *e.g.* the basic need for affirmation and approval which contribute to self-esteem* and internal wholeness. Such conflict is largely resolved when some integration of the self* has been achieved. Conflict which is loaded with morbid guilt* usually belongs in this category. Maturity* is about relief from the sense of drivenness or imprisonment by these unmet needs, and the balance between being able to give and to receive emotionally. The sense of internal conflict can never be resolved until those legitimate loveneeds have been met satisfactorily in a personal relationship of some sort. The Christian faith is addressed to this very situation, since the internal conflict is basically about the need for love, unconditional acceptance,* personal value and affirmation.

2. The other type of internal conflict occurs in the spiritual journey into personal holiness,* as new areas of living are discovered and the old egocentric parts of the self are gradually handed over to the love of Christ.

There is often confusion in people's minds between these two different types of conflict. For instance, when a person cannot overcome some addictive habit in spite of much wrestling

in prayer* and effort, it is usually because the area of struggle is in the first category of internal conflict. In a general sense, though, the first category is obviously subsumed under the second.

The entire story of redemption is based on conflict on a grand scale and is reflected in a personal way. The great assurance of the Christian is the ultimate resolution of this conflict in the peace (shalom) of the final kingdom of God (*cf.* Rev. 22:2).

See also: CROSS-CULTURAL CONFLICT MEDIATION.

Bibliography
M. Chave-Jones, *Living with Anger* (London, 1992); A. Storr, *Human Aggression* (Harmondsworth, ²1970).

M.C.-J.

CONFUCIAN ETHICS. K'ung-fu-tsu, meaning 'Master Kung', Latinized as Confucius, China's first philosophic genius (551–479 BC), was tutor to aristocratic sons of a city-state. He was the first demythologizer.

Confucius reinterpreted the primary religion of China from magic and superstition into an ethical system: thus *te*, 'magical force', became moral 'virtue', and *li* is converted from 'rites' into 'gentlemanly conduct'. The Japanese word for *shitsu-rei*, meaning 'rudeness', means literally 'lack of *rei*' (*li* in Chinese). This greatly honoured philosopher changed a superstitious people believing in good and bad 'luck' into moral people concerned with right and wrong behaviour. *Jen* means to be authentically human, to have achieved ideal sainthood through virtue.

Confucius died despairing of persuading the ruler of his own city-state to put his teaching into practice. Not until the great Emperor Wu of the Han dynasty (140–87 BC) did Confucianism become State orthodoxy in China. No other single person, or for that matter no religion, has so deeply influenced the cultures and society not only of China, but of Korea and Japan as well.

China was a meritocracy, and success in examinations in the Confucian classics (*Wu-ching*) qualified the brilliant student to become a mandarin. Both Korea and Japan accepted Buddhism to provide the philosophy, and Confucianism the ethics, which were lacking in both Korean Shamanism and Japanese Shinto.

Confucius was agnostic about 'God', referring to impersonal 'heaven' (*tien*) and only once to *shang ti*, 'the emperor above'. He did have to come to terms with ancestor worship, but even there he transformed *hsiao*, 'filial piety', from respect/fear of the spirits of the dead into obedience towards them while they are still living. This principle extends to all relationships – the junior respects his senior, the mentor who reciprocates with affectionate responsibility towards his protégé. In Japan this principle, known as *oyabun-kobun* (father part, child part), governs many other areas of life – in business, education and even in the relationship between pastor and his flock.

The 'Five Relationships' (Lord and retainer; father and son; older and younger brother; husband and wife; and friend and friend) provide a sequence of moral priorities for life, as well as for the moral dilemmas of literature and drama. Interestingly 'teacher–disciple' is not one of the five, possibly because Chinese bureaucracy was always fearful to the point of paranoia that a new teacher would gain a following which might result in a revolution overthrowing government.

Though China, Japan and Korea are strongly influenced by Confucian relationships, their emphases are now different. The Japanese tend to emphasize the vertical hierarchical relationship with the feudal lord (or company president!); the Chinese stress the familial relationships; whereas the Koreans particularly stress the friend–friend bond between classmates and peer group. Thus military *coups* are carried out by classmates at the military academy, and even church growth in Korea may owe something to Confucius, as classmates join the same churches.

M.C.G.

CONSCIENCE is the inner aspect of the life of the individual where a sense of what is right and wrong is developed. Our conscience prompts us to react according to the code of morality it has learnt either with a sense of guilt* or of well-being to proposed or past courses of action. Christians understand conscience as the guardian of the integrity of the person.

There are three basic biblical principles in understanding conscience: 1. Conscience is universal and is given to us by God (Rom. 2:12–16). This explains why those who have no knowledge of God's law may still obey its requirements. Those who have no other guide should obey their conscience. 2. Consciences have been affected by the sinfulness of human nature. Although the conscience is a gift of God, it is not perfect and may be corrupt (Tit. 1:15). Thus it may accuse where there is no reason for accusation and remain silent when it ought to speak. 3. The saving work of Jesus cleanses guilty consciences (Heb. 9:14). The blood of Jesus can both cleanse us from the blight of a guilty conscience and also liberate us for the service of God.

Conscience therefore needs instruction, so that it may be trained to alert us to what is genuinely right and manifestly wrong, and it also needs the liberating experience of forgiveness. The dynamic of conscience in the Christian life is explained by these two things: education and liberation.

Conscience requires educating against a sense of false guilt (such as that of a child who feels somehow responsible for his or her parents' divorce), and against scrupulosity* (an obsession with the minutiae of conduct which destroys all joy* in the Christian life).

Because conscience needs educating, it is a mistake to equate it with the voice of God, as has sometimes been done. That God addresses the conscience is clear from Scripture (*e.g.* 2 Cor. 4:2), but conscience can either be so stifled as to become utterly insensitive (1 Tim. 4:2) or become so morbid as to refuse the forgiveness promised in the gospel.

Conscience has been the subject of controversy over many centuries. Thomas Aquinas* saw it as the place of moral judgment in human life – the place where a Christian exercised reason in working out what to do. Kant* saw conscience as the faculty of judgment where the person turns the 'is' of the universal law into the 'ought' of what should or should not be done. Freud* understood it as the super-ego developed in the individual in childhood whereby we internalize the prohibitions imposed upon us by those who parent and educate us. For Freud it was a repressive force, capable of doing great damage to the psychological health of the person. He had no time for religious belief which seemed to give universal validity to this deeply damaging aspect of our personality. Jung,* accepting the truthfulness of the psychoanalytic approach, turned these understandings to a more positive understanding of religious experience. He understood the liberating possibilities of the spiritual side of living and recognized that Freud had been too restricted by his preoccupation with sick people. If Thomas

Aquinas and Kant relate more to the educative task in relation to conscience, Freud and Jung relate to the liberation aspects. Thus the Christian tradition is able to encompass all serious knowledge about conscience. The experience of conscience is therefore one of the most fundamental aspects of what it means to be a human being made by a creating and redeeming God (see Image of God*).

Bibliography

J. W. Gladwin, *Conscience* (Bramcote, Nottingham, 1977); C. G. Jung, *Modern Man in Search of a Soul* (London, 1962); C. A. Pierce, *Conscience in the New Testament* (London, 1955); I. T. Ramsey, 'Towards a Rehabilitation of Natural Law', in *Christian Ethics and Contemporary Philosophy* (London, 1966).

J.W.G.

CONSCIENTIOUS OBJECTION, see CONSCIENCE; JUST-WAR THEORY; WAR.

CONSCIENTIZATION, see LIBERATION THEOLOGY.

CONSENT. People consent when they give voluntary agreement to something done to them and comply with that decision. Consent may be clearly expressed in written or oral form: implied, as when a patient visits a doctor and offers an arm for an injection, and when someone fails to indicate dissent when a reasonable person would have been expected to do so; or presumed, as when someone is unconscious and a doctor acts assuming that the person would have given consent if it were possible. It rests on the integrity and autonomy* of the individual who has the right to self-determination, which is expressed in giving or withholding of consent.

Most commonly, consent is important in sexual activity and marriage, where the absence of consent is tantamount to rape.* A marriage may be annulled if consent is lacking. The age of consent of male and female to marriage and sexual intercourse varies throughout the world. In politics, many regard the consent of the governed as necessary for democracy to flourish. The clearest example of giving or withholding consent is the doctor–patient relationship.

To be valid, consent must be voluntary and free from pressure and duress. This is shown by the fact that the degree of responsibility varies according to the force and coercion a person was under in making a decision. Consent must also be fully informed. People are to know the facts and likely outcomes of the choices they make. Volition thus is matched by a careful assessment of the facts. For some, this might mean knowing all the facts; for others, knowing all the relevant facts. In the USA, a doctor is obliged to reveal all the facts of conditions and treatments. In the UK, only relevant facts are required and that is defined by what any reasonable doctor would provide. This difference rests on a distinction between all that there is to know, as opposed to all that a patient might want, or that was in his or her best interests, to know. Failure to gain consent is, in law, an assault or battery, and the doctor may be found negligent if he or she fails to gain consent. Defensive, contract-based medicine would have to give all information about a disease, its likely outcome and the risks of treating and not treating. Covenant-based medicine stresses the quality of relationship between doctor and patient and that consent is a process which requires trust,* checking, and continuing involvement of the patient in deciding what happens. Both systems require doctors to be able to communicate difficult information to vulnerable people, allowing them the freedom to reject treatment as well as to accept it. People are free to withdraw consent as and when they wish.

Consent also assumes competence. In the case of children, they are required to give consent. While there is no universally agreed minimum age of consent, a child must be, and parents may be, consulted. The doctor must decide whether the child is competent, and that involves assessing the personal and mental maturity of the child. In difficult areas like contraception for under-age girls, the doctor's first loyalty is to the girl and confidentiality.* Parents do not own their children, and, as with competent adults, no-one is able to give consent for another.

With the mentally incapacitated, no-one is legally empowered to provide consent. Consent forms have no legal standing and are at best indications of a process of consultation. The confused state of British law is likely to be resolved in the direction of advocacy or guardianship. Proxy consent is likely to grow as situations where people are unable to express their own wishes may increase. Those in prison are still entitled to give or withhold consent for medical treatment. This may be difficult for the doctor to safeguard, as in the case of members of the armed forces.

In clinical research, the patient's consent is crucial. The elderly and other dependent groups may be pressurized by family or society to do what they do not wish. Even governments may put individuals under pressure to consent to various immunization and testing procedures. This is often justified by the greater benefit for society as a whole. The need for justification is the mark that consent is important. In situations of organ transplants, living donors may be under pressure to consent to donation. Doctors must protect the donor and ensure that consent is valid. While a willing donor may leave organs to be used after death, the current practice of medicine tends to allow the wishes of the family priority over those of the deceased. In the USA, there have been sad cases where families and medical authorities have had to resort to the courts to establish what is construed as in the best interests of an individual, whether keeping the patient on a life-support machine or the removal of feeding tubes. Technological advances mean that consent will be harder to establish in a wider variety of situations. This has led to 'living wills' or 'advance directives', in which someone indicates what kind of treament or none that they wish if they develop specified diseases or require extraordinary medical support. This is a natural extension of the consent and autonomy of the individual, but must be seen as an indication of the person's wishes at that time. The doctor must retain the professional freedom to judge whether or not circumstances have changed so that the patient might express a different desire now.

God's creation of humankind so that we are free to accept or reject God's commands is fundamental to human nature. Christ never forced himself or his salvation on people, but allowed them the freedom to reject him and his way. Consent means that in evangelism, pastoral counselling and care, as well as in the formalized areas of sexuality, marriage and medicine, respect for the willing, informed, free consent of others is both a Christian and a moral responsibility.

See also: COMA; ETHICS OF MEDICAL CARE. [14]

Bibliography

S. Horner (chairperson), *Medical Ethics Today* (London, 1993); D. Cook, *Patients' Choice* (London, 1993); S. E. Lammers and A. Verhey (eds.), *On Moral Medicine* (Grand Rapids, 1987).

E.D.C.

CONSEQUENTIALISM is a type of theory of obligation* according to which the rightness or wrongness of an action is completely determined by the action's consequences. Theories of obligation are systematic accounts of what makes actions morally right or wrong, and these accounts usually are of two types. 'Backward-looking' theories hold that actions are made right or wrong by something *before* the action, such as the agent's motive* for performing the action. 'Forward-looking' or consequentialist theories, on the other hand, hold that actions are made right or wrong by something *after* the action in time, *viz.* the action's good consequences. By 'consequences' is usually meant the actual and causal (rather than intended and merely conceptual) consequences of the action.

Consequentialist theories typically differ in two ways. 1. They differ over which good consequences right actions produce, with various theories holding that the good is, *e.g.* pleasure,* enlightenment or biological survival. Such theories need not require the maximization of this good, but most do. 2. Consequentialist theories also differ over whose good we are to produce. Consequentialist theories range between egoistic* theories, according to which right actions produce good for the individual agent, and universalistic theories, according to which right actions produce good for every being affected.

Universal ethical hedonism,* or utilitarianism, is the most widely discussed consequentialist theory. Championed by Jeremy Bentham,* John Stuart Mill* and Henry Sidgwick (1838–1900) in the 19th century, this theory holds that right actions are those which produce the greatest total pleasure for everyone affected by their consequences and wrong actions are those which fail to produce this greatest total pleasure. The later 'ideal utilitarians', such as G. E. Moore (1873–1958), agreed with earlier utilitarians that right actions were those which maximized the good, but held that some things other than pleasurable experiences were intrinsically good. Contemporary consequentialists have often dropped the term 'pleasure', because of its ambiguity, in favour of 'preference satisfaction', which is more amenable to analysis in terms of contemporary economic theory.

Consequentialism in general, and utilitarianism in particular, have been advocated on several grounds. 1. Some consequentialists have argued that moral choice can be rational only if it is based on an evaluation of the consequences of actions; *i.e.* in the absence of consequentialist considerations, moral choice devolves into personal preference or arbitrary fiat. 2. Utilitarian theories in particular accord with certain widely held convictions that human well-being is intrinsically good, and that actions should be judged according to their effect on this well-being. Christian consequentialists have extended this second point, arguing that Jesus preached an ethic of love requiring us to work for the well-being of all humanity (*e.g.* see the Sermon on the Mount,* Mt. 5 – 7; the Great Commandment, Mt. 22:37–40).

Consequentialism has also been criticized on several grounds. 1. Its practical application seems to require the ability to predict accurately the long-range consequences of our actions, something we are rarely able to do. 2. Many versions of consequentialism require that goods and ills be measured, added, and subtracted according to some common scale, but a satisfactory account of such measurement and calculation has proven elusive. 3. Many consequentialist theories have reductionistic* tendencies, and seem overly willing to sacrifice goods they ignore, such as justice, for goods they happen to favour, such as utility. 4. Finally, although there have been Christian consequentialists such as William Paley (1743–1805), other Christian thinkers have had particular complaints about consequentialism, *e.g.* that consequentialism arrogates to humans God's reponsibility for ensuring best overall results in the universe.

For classic statements of consequentialist theories see William Paley, *The Principles of Moral and Political Philosophy* (London, 1785), Jeremy Bentham, *An Introduction to the Principles of Morals and Legislation* (1789; London, 1970) and John Stuart Mill, *Utilitarianism* (London, 1863). For a contemporary discussion of consequentialism, see J. J. C. Smart and Bernard Williams, *Utilitarianism: For and Against* (Cambridge, 1973). For discussion of consequentialism from a Christian point of view, see Gilbert Meilander, 'Eritis Sicut Deus: Moral Theory and the Sin of Pride', *FP* 3.4, 1986, pp. 397–415, and James Keller, 'Christianity and Consequentialism: A Reply to Meilander', *FP* 6.2, 1989, pp. 198–205.

M.T.N.

CONSERVATION, see ENVIRONMENT.

CONSERVATISM

CONSERVATISM is a short-hand term for a body of political attitudes which tends to prefer the established order rather then the new and untried, and which emphasizes the importance of law and order, continuity and tradition. Premised upon the imperfectibility of human nature, it is distrustful of political philosophies which expect more good from it than is warranted by experience.

In English history

Toryism, as Conservatism was originally termed, gave priority to the established church, the family* and private property. The term 'Conservative' seems to have first been used in the British political context by J. W. Croker (1780–1857) in an article in the *Quarterly Review* for January 1830. He referred to 'what is called the Tory, and which might with more propriety be called the Conservative party'. The coining of this new title was, according to J. C. D. Clark (1951–), a response to the crucial political changes of 1828–32, which resulted in the sweeping victory of the Tories' Whig opponents. The repeal of the Test and Corporation Acts in 1828, which opened the door to nonconformist participation in government, and Catholic emancipation in 1829, broke the exclusive link of church and State, which had been hitherto defended in Parliament 'by a loose and unstructured governing coalition assembled by the crown' (J. C. D. Clark, 'Conservatism before Conservatism', in M. Alison and D. L. Edwards, eds., *Christianity and Conservatism*, pp. 117–118).

From this period, 'Conservative' began to supersede 'Tory', though inevitably continuities both in membership and in political thought existed between the old Tory coalition and the newly emerging party. For those like Benjamin Disraeli (1804–88), who carried the unfurling banner of Conservatism through the latter years of the 19th century, evolution from earlier Toryism, not revolution, was the natural way forward.

It can be argued that 20th-century Conservatism still has its roots in the old Anglican political theology of Toryism. This conceived of England as a Christian nation, answerable in its spiritual life to the established church and in its secular life to the State, both being ruled by the monarch.

In American history

In the US, the alignment of conservative political philosophy with the Republican party can be traced back to the Jacksonian era. Between 1810 and 1830, the pietists (NT-oriented, anti-ritualistic, congregational in governance, committed to individual conversion and societal reform to usher in the millennial reign of Jesus Christ) began to enter the political world to influence society. They helped develop reforms to eradicate slavery,* saloons, sabbath* desecration and other social ills. In the 1830s they entered the political mainstream and gravitated to the Whig and Republican parties. However, from the 1850s until the early 1870s, the political agenda of the Republicans seemed to be headed by Protestant anti-Catholic concerns rather than conservatism. In the 1870s and 1880s, the Republicans returned to a conservative platform partly out of a concern for moral decline and partly because of political desperation. During the 1950s, William F. Buckley (1925–) was a key force in American conservatism by developing forums for conservative voices. He founded the *National Review*, a bi-weekly journal designed to express conservative opinions, news and views. He later started a television show dealing with politics and public affairs.

Later, after evangelical and fundamentalist activists helped Ronald Reagan (1911–) defeat Jimmy Carter (1924–) in 1980, a new Christian right was seen emerging in national politics. Events in previous decades set the stage for the new conservatism to rise. The late 1960s and early 1970s became a polarizing time between the New Left (whose aims were to assure equality for women, African Americans and homosexuals) and the cultural conservatives (who affirmed traditional values). Conservatives felt they were watching their country's values 'decline' steadily as legalization of abortion, the availability of sexually explicit material, and prospective ratification of the Equal Rights Amendment loomed. Secular humanism was seen as an encroaching threat. In 1980, Ronald Reagan aligned himself with conservatives and their hopes. His tenure gave conservatives a voice in the White House. Reagan's successor, George Bush (1924–), likewise aligned himself with conservatism.

In the modern world

The market economy of today, operating in an environment of democratic capitalism,* serving an increasingly secular and multicultural society, might seem to prosper precisely to the extent that it leaves the old ways and values of Anglican political theology. But in reality many of its insights find an application today. Thus the assertion of Article 9 of the Thirty-nine Articles, that 'man is very far gone from original righteousness, and is of his own nature inclined to evil', finds a ready echo in C. S. Lewis'* espousal of democracy*: 'I am a democrat because I believe in the Fall of Man . . . Mankind is so fallen that no man can be trusted with unchecked power over his fellows' (C. S. Lewis, *Present Concerns: Ethical Essays*, London, 1986, p. 17).

The Anglican insistence that 'the individual had the freedom and power, despite his sinful inclinations, to hear and obey divine injunctions' (Clark, p. 150) has been utilized by advocates of democratic capitalism. Michael Novak (1933–), for example, has taken the notions of the individual and conscience as the key to 20th-century capitalism and wealth creation.

Brian Griffiths (1942–) has argued that the success of the market economy can be traced back to the influence of Jewish and Christian teaching: '. . . the physical world as God's world, the mandate to subdue and harness the earth, the significance of work in a context of vocation and calling, the need for private property rights and the rule of law, a recognition by the state of the creative and innovative character of people, and the importance of government's role in enforcing justice' ('The Conservative Quadrilateral' in *Christianity and Conservatism*, p. 233).

Critics of Conservatism sometimes charge that its emphasis on law and order can lead to Fascism, but the Conservative emphasis on the individual is inimical to all forms of statist political theory. Others claim that modern Conservatism is so individualistic as to have no real place for a concept of community in its social philosophy, but this criticism overlooks Conservatism's predilection for continuity.

Bibliography

M. Alison and D. L. Edwards (eds.), *Christianity and Conservatism* (London, 1990); M. Novak, *Will it Liberate?* (New York, 1986).

M.J.H.A.

CONSTANTINE (*c*. 274–337), Roman emperor from 306 in the West, and from

324 in the East. Following his capture of Rome in 312, he issued the Edict of Milan, which made Christianity a legal religion for the first time. Constantine presided at the First Council of Nicaea (325) and favoured Christians in the empire, but was baptized only on his deathbed. His reputation as a Christian saint is based largely on the biography by Eusebius of Caesarea (*c.* 265–*c.* 339), but nowadays the reality of his conversion is hotly disputed. However, there is no doubt that he passed a number of laws which formed the basis of Christian Europe in later centuries. Because of this, he is frequently credited as the founder of the so-called 'Constantinian Era' of church–State relations, which lasted until 1918. In fact, however, it was Theodosius I (*c.* 346–395) who made Christianity the State religion (27 February 380) and not Constantine himself.

The main items of legislation for which he was reponsible were the payment of clergy salaries (313), the exemption of clergy from public office (313), and the establishment of Sunday as a public holiday (321).

Bibliography

A. Kee, *Constantine versus Christ* (London, 1982); J. Stevenson and W. H. C. Frend (eds.), *A New Eusebius* (London, 1987).

G.L.B.

CONSUMERISM. Economically speaking, consumption refers to the using of goods, whether natural resources or human-made, and of services by people, *i.e.* the consumers. Consumerism, then, is a particular focusing of social and personal life on the processes of consuming. Today, in fact, the world's rich countries are often called consumer societies.

Although at the end of the 19th century Thorstein Veblen (1857–1929) described the practice of buying and displaying expensive items to demonstrate wealth and enhance social status as 'conspicuous consumption', only since the Second World War has this theme been reworked to apply to society at large. This is because the post-war years heralded an era of mass consumption on an unprecedented scale. The productive boom, increasingly enhanced by new technologies,* meant that capacity to supply goods and services far outstripped demand. The only way to cope with the resulting gluts was to stimulate demand, or consumption.

Thus marketing ploys such as advertising* were intensified (witness Vance Packard's famous *Hidden Persuaders*, London, 1957; repr. New York, 1984), goods were designed with built-in obsolescence, and governments encouraged consumption by reducing taxes. Consumer organizations were formed to protect people from sharp practices and to give advice on the best buys. New markets, such as lucrative teenage fashion and music (see Pop Culture*), were opened up. By the 1980s credit cards further extended the capacity to consume.

On the other side of the coin is the way people have become more and more market-dependent. Shopping skills replace older arts such as cooking and laundry as signs of competence. New 'needs' are constantly created, whose satisfaction is imperative. Competition occurs between consumers: 'keeping up with the Joneses' becomes a necessary part of normal life. Not only is entertainment now something to buy rather than do, but buying itself has become entertainment. Shopping malls are theme parks for family outings. The effortless McDonald's culture of fast foods and false smiles epitomizes the world of consumerism.

The implications of consumerism have yet to be fully understood; the phenomenon continues to expand at an accelerating pace. Three major aspects deserve attention, however.

1. Consumer society is highly unequal; mass consumption does not mean that all benefit. Indeed, within the world's wealthier nations, a widening gap exists between those with and without the means to consume. Today it is non-consumers, not necessarily non-producers, who are stigmatized and shunned. Consumption integrates people into society, seduced by the promise of market freedom and affluence. Those who fail the consumer test for whatever reason slip into more or less punishing regimes of 'welfare'. Meanwhile the gap between wealthy and poor nations is ever more marked.

2. The second consequence of consumerism relates to waste,* and the rate at which creation's resources are used. On the one hand, say critics, such resources are finite. There are limits to the ever-increasing expansion of production and consumption. On the other hand, they observe, such expansion does not seem to have increased the happiness promised in consumption. Perhaps fulfilment lies elsewhere than in amassing possessions? Unfortunately,

of course, consumerism has established such a hold that alternatives to it appear rather quirky.

3. Even more profoundly, in Western societies our outlook and lifestyles have come to be dominated by consumerism (indeed, 'lifestyle' is a consumerist term). The consumer is the antithesis of the ascetic, disciplined, industrious, rational Puritan (see Puritan Ethics*) who supposedly gave birth to modernity. Consumers are concerned above all about comfort and convenience; virtue and joy lie in spending. Social status, personal success and well-being may be found in buying and owning goods. Consumerism is a meaning-system of great power, if also great banality. Its signs and symbols relate to fashions and trends, grocery coupons and cash dispensers. The T-shirt tells all. The 'new' must be sampled, non-stop fun is both ethic and goal. As we saw, consumerism is also a means of maintaining social order.

All of this makes it hard to present any alternative, just because consumerism is so thoroughly out of kilter with Christian commitment – or should be. Needless to say, consumerism has infected the church, which turns to marketing strategies to promote its unique product, and thus, for example, encourages its members to shop around for the congregation in which they feel most comfortable. At base, consumerism derives its power from a systematic and flagrant denial of the commandment prohibiting covetousness.* Its consequences are thus predictably and universally bad. Following Christ entails a sharp break with consumerism, that emphasizes, on a personal level, contentment (and a grateful enjoyment of creation's good things). On the political-economic plane, it emphasizes restraint and a commitment to fairness, and careful stewardship* with regard to created resources.

Bibliography

Z. Bauman, *Freedom* (Milton Keynes, 1988); M. Featherstone, *Consumer Culture and Postmodernism* (London and Newbury Park, CA, 1991); M. Starkey, *Born to Shop* (Eastbourne, 1989); J. White, *Money isn't God* (Downers Grove, IL, and Leicester, 1993).

D.A.L.

CONTEXTUAL ETHICS refers broadly to that class of ethical theories which emphasizes moral context as a most critical element in the determination of moral responsibility. There are, however, a number of different types of contextual ethical theories, so the identification of a moral theory as a contextual ethic may be less illuminating than at first appears.

1. The most straightforward form of contextual ethics is the 'situation ethics'* of Joseph Fletcher.* Abjuring moral 'legalism' and 'rule-worship', Fletcher identifies love (see ②) as the only moral principle binding at all times and in all places. Our obligation is always to bring about the most loving consequences for all involved in a particular situation. Exactly what love requires will, of course, vary from one moral context or situation to the next.

2. A more complicated form of contextual ethics is the moral theory of H. Richard Niebuhr.* Although it is seldom obvious, God is at work in the world, creating, governing and redeeming it. The Christian's moral calling is to respond appropriately to the particular activity of God in a given context. In order to respond in a fitting way one must first discern how God is present in that context, and what type of activity God is engaged in at that place and at that time. Then, drawing upon a variety of moral sources and moral norms, the moral agent attempts to identify the particular response which is appropriate to God's activity in that moral context.

3. Closely related to Niebuhr's contextual ethic is the koinonia (see Fellowship*) ethic of Paul Lehmann (1906–). Lehmann insists upon the importance of the context in which 'ethical insights and practices are nourished', identifying the relevant context for Christians as the koinonia or community established by Jesus Christ. In this koinonia, we see most clearly God's activity in the world; here we discover that God is acting in the world to 'keep human life human'. God is 'humanizing' our world, bringing about wholeness and maturity for all persons through the Messianic activity of Jesus. What actions will best contribute to human maturity cannot be specified in advance, for God values humanization more than consistency; God is free to act and free to call Christians to act in whatever way the immediate context requires. Christians, mindful of God's aims in history and of God's final victory, are able imaginatively to engage in moral situations and to discern in them God's specific humanizing will.

4. Another type of contextual ethic is developed within and alongside contemporary 'contextual theologies'. This type of contextual

theological ethic emphasizes the location or context from which one speaks about God and God's actions in the world. The differing experiences people have in the world may lead to differing theological insights and emphases. The experience of being female differs from the experience of being male. There is, therefore, a feminist* or 'womanist' contextual theology and theological ethic. Likewise, the experience of the African, the Asian or the Latino (see Liberation Theology*), differs from the experience of the white male, so there may be African contextual ethics, Asian contextual ethics, *etc.* This type of contextual ethics refers not to the particular moral context to which some response is required, but rather to the moral context from which one deliberates and articulates one's moral and theological beliefs.

5. A final type of contextual ethic, sometimes referred to as moral particularism, is prominent in some contemporary neo-Aristotelian moral philosophy. As in the situation ethics of Joseph Fletcher, moral particularism rejects the construction of a significant body of moral rules or principles. In fact, moral particularists believe that the moral properties of each particular context differ so much as to rule out the possibility of even one universal moral principle such as love. The correct moral response requires not moral principles but moral discernment. Moral discernment is analogous to aesthetic discernment. Just as there are good judges of beauty – people who have (or who have developed) an ear for music or an eye for visual art – so there are excellent judges of the morally good. These individuals are disposed to consider carefully the moral context and, upon moral consideration, they perceive the moral properties of the context and what a fitting feeling or action would be in that particular context.

What unifies these quite diverse types of contextual ethics is their agreement that context is critical for the identification of the articulation of what is morally required. Because moral context is so important a factor in the moral life, excellence in the moral discernment of the context plays a most visible and significant role in these theories.

In light of the diversity of contextual ethics, apt critical generalizations of them all are few. The greatest weakness of these contextual ethics is, in fact, their particularism, their reluctance to generalize. In their emphasis upon moral contexts they minimize the general moral knowledge we have of God's will. While we cannot move without reflection from biblical injunctions to moral decisions, we are able to glean from Scripture general moral principles which should inform our decisions, whatever the moral context. We enter each new moral context with more moral knowledge than contextual ethics recognize. A failure to recognize this fact leads to a more parsimonious ethic than Christian revelation warrants.

Bibliography

J. M. Gustafson, 'Context Versus Principles: A Misplaced Debate in Christian Ethics', in M. E. Marty and D. G. Peerman (eds.), *New Theology*, vol. 3 (New York, 1966); P. Lehmann, *Ethics in a Christian Context* (New York, 1963; London, ²1979); H. R. Niebuhr, *The Responsible Self* (London and New York, 1963); P. Ramsey, *Deeds and Rules in Christian Ethics* (London and Edinburgh, 1965; New York, 1967); C. West, *Prophesy Deliverance: An Afro-American Revolutionary Christianity* (Philadelphia, 1982).

T.D.K.

CONTRACEPTION, see BIRTH CONTROL.

CONTRACTS IN THERAPY. A contract is an indispensable tool in any working arrangement. It defines what is expected, what can be delivered, the terms on which delivery can take place, and the conditions necessary to facilitate the operation. This contract is binding on both parties who engage in the work.

In a professionally therapeutic situation, the overt contract refers to the place, duration and regularity of the meeting, the time of day, fees and confidentiality.* Both therapist and client are expected in such a situation to give these commitments priority over other demands in their life. The contract also includes the degree of professionalism which the client may expect, and it may specify areas for concentrated work or a particular period of time. The relationship excludes mutuality and reciprocity on a functional level, though, of course, not on a feeling level. It is important that the professional therapist and client do not meet socially outside the therapeutic situation, because that would blur the therapeutic boundaries of the relationship. The therapist and the client/patient both need to be protected from dynamics other than those which operate within the working relationship.

The purpose of these conditions is to make a safe ambience for both client and therapist. The client begins to feel secure and to experience reliability, continuity and dependence without being suffocated by too much closeness and intimacy. Clients can use this space however they wish, and this is not possible in an ordinary social situation. At times they may feel frustrated by the limitations imposed by the clock, the payment, the regularity and the restricted social contact. Frustration,* dependence, love (see ②), anger,* envy,* greed (see Covetousness*) and other dangerous and powerful feelings are typical of the constraints of ordinary life and, within this therapeutic relationship, there is a safe place in which to explore unsatisfactory and hurtful situations of the past in a healing and protected environment. The boundaries protect the therapist from being unduly 'invaded' by the demands, dependencies and pains of the client/patient. Thus the therapist will be able to be more genuinely available to the person with whom he or she is working.

The expectation of professional therapists is that they must also have their own personal therapy and that their current work must be supervised.* Thus, the standard of work is maintained, and the therapists ensure that they are not working out some of their own problems, unconsciously, on their clients/patients. A contract as binding as this is required only when the work is of professional standard. Christian professionals in this field are very dependent on the Holy Spirit to use their training and expertise. This is very costly incarnational work, which gives some damaged people a first-time experience of *agapē*.

Many pastors and others engaged in the ministry of encouragement, helping and counselling also need a contract, though it may be much more flexible. Many a sincere helper has become exhausted by or inappropriately entangled emotionally with a person in need, because there have been no protective contractual boundaries. It is vital for both parties to know what is appropriate to give or expect in terms of the time and quality of contact or relationship which is available, and to adhere to these terms fairly conscientiously. Helpers need to know how to respond to their own difficulty in saying 'no' on occasions, and not to confuse this difficulty with some false sense of guilt* about not being endlessly available (consider Mk. 6:30–32). Helpers must be aware of their own emotional needs, which must be met outside the helping relationship, so that they are not feeding their own egos on the gratitude, love or neediness of the person they are trying to help. They also need to be able to handle constructively the outraged reactions that legitimate non-availability sometimes produces. By observing these boundaries and caring for themselves, helpers are more genuinely able to care for others and thus, both benefit.

Helpers are wise to limit the one-to-one social contact during the counselling period as much as possible, so that a dispassionate attitude can be maintained. It is also very beneficial for pastors to have some person or group with whom they can share some of their pastoral problems (with suitable confidentiality safeguards). This acts as a personal support as well as a check, and could usefully be included in their employment contract.

See also: PROFESSIONAL ETHICS.

Bibliography

M. Jacobs, *Psychodynamic Counselling in Action* (London, 1990).

M.C.-J.

CONTRITION, see REPENTANCE.

CONVERSION.

In the West today, non-Christian religions and cults within the Christian religion have an increasing impact. Consequently stories of conversion become commonplace. A student is captivated by the teaching of an Eastern guru, a young person joins a cult, there is a dramatic change of allegiance from one political party to another. All may, with some justification, be called a 'conversion'. In each there has been a dramatic change of belief, allegiance, outlook and, frequently, way of life. But they are not Christian conversions. Christ is not their cause or their centre, nor is his service their outcome. There has been no decisive *turning from* and *turning to* within the Christian context.

The necessity for conversion

In the NT, the Thessalonians 'turned to God from idols to serve the living and true God' (1 Thes. 1:9). The Lycaonians were exhorted to '*turn from* these worthless things *to* the living God' (Acts 14:15). The apostle Paul's mission to the Gentiles was summed up as 'to open their eyes and *turn them from* darkness *to* light and *from* the power of Satan *to* God, so that they may receive forgiveness of sins and a place among those who are sanctified by faith in me [Jesus]' (Acts 26:18). These passages highlight two distinct elements in conversion: conversion is *from* an old way of life, and *to* a new and different allegiance. In Scripture, the fundamental nature of the transaction between humankind and God is basic to the notion of conversion. Interest in any mechanisms that are at work in that transaction are ignored or totally secondary. As David F. Wells (1939–) wrote recently, 'Christianity without conversion is no longer Christian, because conversion means turning to God' (*Turning to God*, p. 27). And it is not only within the NT that the concept of conversion applies. Within the OT, people were called upon time and again to a fresh understanding of what it meant to be a person in covenant* with God. Those outside the covenant needed to discover a filial relationship with God for which all humankind was created. That relationship, destroyed by sin, has been re-established in the new covenant. There will therefore be differences in the process of turning to God, depending upon whether the turning is as an outsider or as an insider.

The diversity of biblical accounts

Within the span of a few chapters of the Acts of the Apostles we meet people with vastly *different* backgrounds who come to faith in Christ in *different* ways and under *different* circumstances and yet all of them share a common faith. An Ethiopian leader eager to learn (Acts 8:26–40); Saul of Tarsus, already deeply immersed in Judaism and the Jewish Scriptures, and doubtless knowledgeable about the beliefs of those he was persecuting (Acts 9:1–30); a religious army officer, worshipping God as best he knew (Acts 10:1–48); a prison keeper, subject to acute stress, making a sudden profession (Acts 16:16–34). The people all differ, the circumstances differ widely, but all come to faith in Christ.

Noting these five episodes within a short span of the NT, it is very difficult to see how one can maintain that there is only one stereotyped form which every Christian conversion must fit if it is to be accepted as genuine. But in every case the outcome was the same: belief in God and faith in Christ. As we study the text carefully, it is important to note that it is made absolutely clear that the conversion was the work of God. The Protestant Reformation was precipitated by the conviction that God's saving grace* could be neither

triggered nor augmented by anything that we do. God did not merely accomplish part of our salvation and leave us to complete the rest through obedience and good works. The Reformers were clear that God's salvation in Christ is free, perfectly complete, and to be accepted by faith* alone.

A diversity of psychological mechanisms

The diversity of conversions recorded in Scripture is paralleled by the diversity of mechanisms of conversion proposed by psychologists, sociologists and physiologists. As new psychological theories are put forward, it is not long before someone applies them to understanding the process of conversion. Some accounts gain wide currency and much publicity. For example, with the holding of large evangelistic crusades it was an easy move to apply the psychophysiological theories of brainwashing* current in the 1950s and 60s to the events occurring at such gatherings. The psychiatrist William Sargant (1907–88) did so with insight and, at times, provocatively. He linked psychological accounts of brainwashing with similar processes supposedly at work in some religious conversions (see also Psychology of Religion*).

Today it seems that Sargant's particular psychophysiology was insecurely based and his theories probably wrong. Nevertheless, others will be proposed which bring us a little nearer to understanding the neural substrate of conversion. Recently, some neuropsychologists have attempted to link particular brain events with religious conversion.

Other putative mechanisms have been proposed to underlie conversion. Social psychologists, for example, have explored the configuration of social circumstances within the family and larger social groups which combine, as they would put it, to facilitate conversion. Psychologists interested in personality theories study whether some personality types, *e.g.* the more extroverted or the more introverted, are more likely to be converted in large evangelistic crusades.

Experimental psychologists have confirmed that when information is presented repeatedly, spaced over time, it is seen as more credible. Speakers, including preachers, and especially evangelists, capitalize on this, finding that spaced repetition makes messages more memorable and appealing.

In so far as conversion involves radical changes of attitude, it should be noted that social psychologists find that passive exposure to information affects people's attitudes less than active participation in group discussion. This is a finding perhaps unknowingly put to good effect by some religious cults, with their concentration on small-group sharing of experiences. Something learned passively is unlikely to change attitudes very much. William James* made this point: 'No reception without reaction, no impression without correlative expression – this is the great maxim which the teacher ought never to forget' (*Talks to Teachers on Psychology; and to Students on Some of Life's Ideals*, New York, 1922, p. 33). He thus anticipated how active listening facilitates attitude change.

Social-psychological research has also established convincingly that our actions influence our attitudes. It seems that we are as likely to believe in what we have stood up for as to stand up for what we believe. Thus, effective evangelism* that leads to conversion will not leave the hearer wondering what to do about what has been said.

Evaluating psychological accounts of conversion

There are many different explanations of conversion in psychological and physiological terms to choose from. Each tells us something of the mechanisms that may be at work when a person is converted. This gives us a deeper insight into the ways in which God brings about his divine purposes in the lives of men and women. Nothing in the psychological or physiological accounts can, however, help us to decide one way or the other the truth or falsehood of the beliefs that are acquired by the person being converted. We shall not decide whether there was a man called Jesus Christ who lived, died and rose again, by understanding the psychology of conversion. Neither shall we understand the historicity or the significance of the great salvation events of history, such as the crossing of the Red Sea and the giving of the Ten Commandments, by a little more psychology.

Scripture illustrates the diverse paths by which people come to faith in God and in Christ. Such diversity is parallelled by the possible scientific mechanisms, psychological and physiological, at work when conversions occur. The outcome of conversion in terms of beliefs held and personal relationships formed is not to be judged by the mechanisms at work in arriving at that destination. The contem-porary danger is of trivializing the whole process of conversion by presenting it in slick media-motivated forms aimed at achieving 'results', but this has little to do with the Bible's account. Psychologizing about what is happening in conversion can divert attention from the great events of salvation history, which demand a response, a *turning from* and a *turning to*.

Christianity is not primarily about gaining inner contentment or freedom from stress,* though these are often advocated by TV evangelists as the primary reason for accepting Christ. The early disciples knew much inner anguish as they strove to spread the gospel. They certainly knew no freedom from stress as they sought faithfully to follow the One in whom they had put their trust. The apostle Paul was concerned with objective truth and with historical events, not with subjective needs. Ultimately, the test of true conversion is the evidence of a life of convertedness.

Bibliography

C. B. Johnson and H. N. Malony, *Christian Conversions: Biblical and Psychological Perspectives* (Grand Rapids, 1982); D. F. Wells, *Turning to God* (Grand Rapids, 1989).

M.A.J.

COPYRIGHT. Not until printing technology made literary plagiarism a viable enterprise did governments begin to guarantee to authors and publishers the rights of property that other fungible goods had enjoyed for centuries. Copyright protections have sought to guarantee to their creators the fruits of literary and artistic labour, and through economic incentive to stimulate creative work for the enrichment of the public.

Copyright protections originated in Venice in 1469 with the grant of a five-year monopoly on printing and a prohibition on imports. In Germany the privilege existed in 1501, in France in 1503, and in England by 1518. In 1556 the Stationers' Company, a guild of London printers, was given monopoly rights on book publishing. Unauthorized printing and failure to register were punishable by the Court of Star Chamber. Thus the protection of intellectual property and government censorship found common purpose in copyright.

While England overthrew and then reinstated monarchy in the 17th century, printing acts were allowed to expire. Immediate relief from censorship accompanied a rapid growth in pirated books. Finally Parliament enacted, in 1709, a remarkable law which gave rights to authors rather than publishers, extended protection through two terms of fourteen years, and set the stage for American copyright, guaranteed in Article 1 Section 8 of the US Constitution.

The first US Congress (1790) enacted a parallel statute, but limited protection to US citizens and required published notice in newspapers. Several changes in the 19th century led to the 1909 extension of protection to 56 years (two terms of 28 years), and finally to the Copyright Act of 1976 (effective 1 January 1978). Current US law, like that in the UK, bases protection on life of the author (lifespan plus 50 years) rather than date of publication. Anything fixed in tangible form is protected (pantomimes, sound, sculpture, *etc*.), though registration is required for successful suit for infringement (but this is not the case in the UK).

Unpublished works were brought under Federal protection, and the distinction between 'idea' (not protected) and 'expression' was established. The controversial 'fair use' doctrine (Section 107) provides exceptions to the 'exclusive use' provisions of Section 106.

Fair use in US law permits reviewers, scholars, teachers and researchers limited rights to quote without permission. Without specifying quantitative ranges of this right, Section 107 sets four criteria by which to judge an infringement, the most important of which is impact on the original's market. Extensive litigation has followed the use of direct quotations in a review published in advance of the book's publication (*Harper & Row* v. *Nation*, 471 US 539, 1985); use of quotations and paraphrases of unpublished material in a biography (*Salinger* v. *Random House*, 13 Med L Rptr 1954, 1987); a motion picture's use of the ideas contained in published research (*Hoehling* v. *Universal City Studios*, 618 F.2d 972, 1980); use of historically unique yet protected material (the 8mm film of John Kennedy's motorcade in Dallas); home video recording of copyrighted broadcast material (*Sony* v. *Universal City*, 464 US 417, 1984); and cases involving parody and trademark infringement (marks are protected under the Lanham Act of 1946).

In the UK, copyright law is at present governed by the Copyright, Designs and Patents Act of 1988. This Act, among other matters, defines the types of work protected by copyright, specifies things which can or cannot be done without the copyright owner's permission, and introduces new legislation relating to the rental of sound recordings and films. Overall the Act seeks to take account of developments in technology. These undoubtedly pose an increasing problem for the upholding of copyright law, especially with respect to multimedia products. For example, a purchaser can, by exploiting digital technology, run off perfect copies of a product without further payment to the producer.

Regarding copyright royalties, it can be argued that, if a wage is regarded in a narrow sense as a previously agreed sum to be paid for so many hours of work done, then the payment of copyright royalties does not seem to constitute a wage. However, in the wider sense of a return on effort expended, royalties can be regarded as a wage. To deprive authors of royalties by infringing copyright therefore in effect amounts to theft* (*cf*. Mal. 3:5; Lk. 10:7).

Some argue that certain articles, such as translations of the Bible, ought to be regarded as gifts of God on which copyright charges are immoral. The premiss on which the argument is based, however, is open to question. Water is a gift of God, yet charges are imposed for its supply to homes without any suggestion that they are immoral.

Churches are seldom litigants in copyright actions, since market impact of churchly infringements rarely warrants a suit. Yet religious organizations confront copyright regularly: copying popular religious art in church publications; using texts of closely guarded Bible translations (the NIV especially); showing in church meetings rented video material which carries a 'For Home Use Only' implied contract; photocopying music and other materials for choirs or their teaching curricula. In the UK, a licensing arrangement permits the photocopying of choruses and songs, or their use by means of an overhead projector, on the payment of an annual fee. Churches and Christian organizations which profess to uphold the Ten Commandments need to be particularly sensitive to infringing copyright.

An increasing problem is the printing of pirated editions of books (especially textbooks) in various developing countries. For the sales of these, authors receive no royalties and the original publishers no rights income. Such a practice would seem to be outright theft, depriving both authors and publishers of income justifiably earned, though it could be argued that the high cost of importing books helps to create pressure to produce pirated editions. It is often difficult to enforce copyright in such situations, and frequently an attempt to do so would not justify the expense involved.

Another problem is the photocopying of sections (often considerable) of books for study purposes, thus avoiding the purchase of actual copies of the book. Again, authors are deprived of income by what amounts, in some cases, to theft.

Themes of justice, creativity and national development are engaged in international copyright law, where two competing theories of protection have now found their synthesis. The International Copyright Union (ICU) was born at Berne in 1886. It required member nations to protect foreign authors to the same degree that it protected its own citizens. The US declined membership in the Berne Convention, insisting on its own registration formalities and a term based on first publication. That position, coupled with needs of developing nations for access to protected materials, set the stage in 1952 for a second international treaty, the Universal Copyright Convention, adopted in Geneva. Under its provisions, foreign works are protected by the symbol © with name of copyright owner and year of publication, other formalities notwithstanding. In 1967, India led Berne members to adjust regulations in favour of developing countries; from that conference the United Nations' World Intellectual Property Organization was born.

As technology advances, copyright protections are certain to fall behind. The rise of computer-aided graphics has already raised conundrums for the 1976 Act. What degree of change constitutes an original product in text or visuals? Answers will depend on a comprehensive social ethic, a field where Christian scholarship will never exhaust the need for great wisdom.

Bibliography

J. M Cavendish and K. Pool, *Handbook of Copyright in British Publishing Practice* (London, ³1993); V. M. Helm, *What Educators Should Know about Copyright* (Bloomington, IN, 1986); A. Kohn, *The Art of Music Licensing* (Englewood Cliffs, NJ, 1992); J. S. Lawrence and B. Timberg (eds.), *Fair Use and Free Inquiry: Copyright Law and the New Media* (Norwood, NJ, 1980); J. K. Miller, *US Copyright Documents: An Annotated Collection for Use by Educators and Librarians* (Littleton, CO, 1981); F. S. Siebert, *Freedom of the Press in England, 1476–1776* (Urbana, IL, 1965).

P.M.F.

CORPORAL PUNISHMENT, see Punishment.

CORPORATE PERSONALITY is the view that the basic units in society are groups, not individuals. H. Wheeler Robinson (1872–1945) applied the idea to the OT, finding in it an explanation of instances in which the guilt of individuals led to the punishment of whole groups, as in the cases of Achan (Jos. 7) and the sons of Saul (2 Sa. 21:1–6; see *The Religious Ideas of the Old Testament*, pp. 87–89). In his understanding (based on the anthropological theories of L. Levy-Bruhl, 1857–1939), the idea was more than the basis of legal process, but a primitive mentality, according to which people did not distinguish clearly between themselves as individuals and the group to which they belonged.

Corporate personality, however, gave way under the influence of the prophets to the rise of individual consciousness in religion, and therefore of individual moral responsibility (*op. cit.*, pp. 89f.; *idem, The Christian Doctrine of Man*, p. 11). Yet in Robinson's view, the older way of thinking retained a certain influence, so that it even affected NT Christology.

In reality, the idea that the Hebrews had a 'primitive mentality' is highly suspect. Instances which an older generation might attribute to 'corporate personality' are explicable on other grounds. In particular the idea that the OT exhibits a transition from the primitive idea to individualism* in religion and morality fails to notice either that OT laws (and punishments) are typically addressed to individuals (see Ex. 21 – 23), or that the prophets understood the social dimension of life (Jeremiah's vision of the future is still a *covenant*,* albeit a new one, Je. 31:31; contrast Robinson, *Religious Ideas*, pp. 89–90).

The OT can reflect on the relation between an individual's sin and its effect on others (*e.g.* David and his family, 2 Sa. 11:1ff.). Yet if guilt can be extensive in its effects (*cf.* Ex. 20:5–6), this idea is always tempered by the call to each individual and generation to repent (Ezk. 18).

Bibliography

H. W. Robinson, *The Christian Doctrine of Man* (Edinburgh, 1911); *idem*, *The Religious Ideas of the Old Testament* (London, 1913); J. W. Rogerson, 'The Hebrew Conception of Corporate Personality: A Re-examination', *JTS*, n.s., 21, 1970, pp. 1–16; *idem*, *Anthropology and the Old Testament* (Sheffield, 1984).

J.G.McC.

COSMETIC SURGERY. Ever since primitive surgeons in India reconstructed noses using forehead skin around 600 BC, the art of surgery has been used to improve appearance as well as to save life and ameliorate the more physical consequences of disease. Surgery for appearance covers a wide spectrum, from the repair of very obvious bodily anomalies such as cleft lips and improving burn scars, to the use of surgery to enhance beauty in bodies which do not deviate from the 'norm' in any medically definable sense. Between these two extremes lies a range of conditions which includes visible body parts of a size outside the range which society accepts as 'normal' (*e.g.* very large or small noses, breasts, 'bat' ears and the like); lesser deformities which still affect the patient in some significant way or other; unacceptable sequelae of pregnancy, surgery, trauma, weight loss; and the signs of ageing which a person might desire to have removed in the quest for eternal youth.

To date, there has been no rational approach to the use of surgery for these conditions in any society. Rather, the availability and acceptability of treatment at any given time has depended more upon a complex and vague web of social values. The shifting sands upon which such judgments are based becomes obvious when one sees how rapidly they change from decade to decade, and across different cultures.

What cosmetic surgery, then, if any, is justifiable from a Christian ethical viewpoint? A Christian perspective must take into account Christ's approach to the whole person, one of enormous *care* for all aspects of well-being, from physical health to feelings and emotions. He also approached each person as an *individual*, and in maintaining this attitude in our medical care, we should refuse the inexorable contemporary trend to categorize conditions for treatment with standardized methods. Thus, two patients with a hooked nose might have wholly differing psychological responses to that condition. One might be utterly socially disabled by the inhibitions that the condition imposes, becoming reclusive and depressed, whilst the other is able to integrate fully into society. By far the best 'cure' for the former patient is to remove the hook from the nose.

It may be that the social pressure to appear 'normal' is a manifestation of evil in this world; it is certainly becoming more difficult year by year for the individual with features which are unusual to achieve worldly success, other than as a freak. It is therefore manifestly unjust for the majority of society, who are blessed with appearances which fall within the 'norm' (by definition), to judge the corrective surgery sought by the few to be unjustified, frivolous, or even morally unacceptable.

The doctor faced with such requests should attempt to determine whether the root of the problem is a physically correctable deformity which, when corrected, would lead to restored wholeness of the body and greater integration of the individual into society in order to fulfil his or her functions more fully. The fine line between patients who request cosmetic correction of 'abnormal' appearance and those who request 'beautification' is sometimes thin, requiring wisdom in discernment. In this area, the Christlike attitudes of responsible stewardship, wisdom, care, and an overriding love for the total needs of the whole person are critical elements in making judgments on use of precious resources. It is not within the scope of this article to discuss the Christian ethic of the use of cosmetics for adornment, but the debate on cosmetic surgery for beautification hinges on precisely the same ground; those who use any form of cosmetic should be careful about being the first to cast stones at cosmetic surgery.

If the value of such surgery is accepted, where does it rank in the scale of values for resource allocation? This difficult area can be looked at from various scales of 'quality of life improvement', and it scores remarkably highly compared with many surgical procedures for the seriously ill, which might be heroic but have poor overall outcomes. Many patients seeking cosmetic surgery will be young and have many years ahead in which to experience the improved quality of life that the surgery might give them.

It is unlikely that any society will ever possess adequate resources (see Health and Health Care*) to provide all the appearance-restoring operations that might be requested by all its population at any one time. Therefore an equitable distribution of what can be provided to the most needy (for improved appearance) must be considered by those in a position to ensure it.

T.E.E.G.

COUNSELLING, see PASTORAL CARE, COUNSELLING AND PSYCHOTHERAPY. [12]

COURAGE belongs to a class of virtues* that we might call the virtues of will-power or strength. They equip us to resist desires, emotions, urges and impulses that are, in some circumstances if not in all, adverse to the moral and spiritual life. Self-control, for example, is the ability to manage the urges of sex and palate, as well as emotions like anger, envy and contempt. Patience and perseverance* enable us to act, think and feel properly, despite the adversities of boredom and discouragement. Courage enables us not to be derailed by fear.*

The virtues of will-power seem to be *instruments* of the moral and spiritual life, rather than its very substance. In this way they differ from justice (see Justice and Peace[3]) and love (see [2]). Justice would still be a virtue in a world without psychological adversities (though it would certainly be less noticed in such a world), but courage loses its point if nothing evokes fear. Furthermore, courage does not seem to be, in itself, a specifically moral trait. Mentioning courage along with some other traits of character, Kant* says 'they can also be extremely bad and harmful . . . if the will is not good'. Courage renders a thief or tyrant or seducer even more effective in his or her perversity. Thus the virtues of will-power become morally good only if enlisted in the service of the moral and spiritual life – used in the interest of holiness,* love, justice and obedience to God. Another way to see this is to note that the virtues of will-power do not by themselves supply any motivation: one acts *with* courage and self-control, but not *out of* courage and self-control. In contrast, one does act out of – *i.e.* with the motive of – generosity, compassion* and honesty.* In acting courageously, one needs to be motivated from elsewhere, *e.g.* by a concern to defend one's family or save one's life or further God's kingdom or line one's pocketbook.

Courage differs from rashness and daredevilry. The rash person rushes into danger without fully counting the cost and perceiving the danger; but to the extent that a person does not reckon with the danger, courage, which is the ability to manage one's fear, is not even called into play. Daredevilry seems to be the positive enjoyment of dangers, or perhaps the enjoyment of displaying oneself to others as confronting and overcoming dangers. If it is the former, it seems to involve, like rashness, a failure to reckon with the dangerousness of the danger; in any case, the *enjoyment* of danger is certainly no criterion of courage. If the enjoyment of self-display is taken to be essential, this is, again, a feature not characteristic of courage.

If courage is an ability to manage fears, the question arises: how does the courageous person do it? What kind of ability is this? It seems to be something like a skill, but this is not superficial 'technique' or self-management, because the resources that the skill calls upon are quite deeply involved in one's sense of identity and one's view of the world. The courageous Christian, faced with the danger of persecution and even death, will manage his or her justified fear of these things by reminding himself or herself who he or she is – a child of God, a recipient of God's unspeakable grace* – and by considering the danger of losing his or her life in the larger context of the losses and gains associated with unfaithfulness or faithfulness. This person will also reckon with the presence of God with him or her in the danger, and so will find strength in prayer, and in meditation on God's presence and power. Since these resources are not to be acquired in the course of a weekend retreat, we can see how dependent the development of Christian courage is on the general development of the Christian personality (see Character[10]). There is a reciprocity between the development of a sense of self and the exercise of courage: in exercising courage, one trades on the sense of self; but the sense of self is tested and deepened and confirmed as one faces dangers in the distinctively Christian ways. Traditions other than the Christian one also have virtues of courage – *i.e.* they involve a different sense of self and thus partial differences in the skills by which fear is managed. Thus Christian courage differs from other courage in two ways: in the strategies of fear-control that it employs, and in the ends that it serves as an instrument.

Bibliography
P. T. Geach, 'Courage', in *The Virtues*

(Cambridge, 1977), ch. 8; R. C. Roberts, *The Strengths of a Christian* (Philadelphia, 1984); Thomas Aquinas, *STh* 2a2ae 123; P. Tillich, *The Courage to Be* (New Haven, CT, and London, 1952).

R.C.R.

COVENANT. The biblical notion of covenant is first introduced by God at Gn. 6:18, a passage which Gn. 9:9–13 takes up and develops. The use of the word 'covenant' (Heb. b^erît) in the OT refers to steps taken to affirm a set of relationships already in being by further quasi-legal arrangements (D. J. McCarthy, 'Berit and Covenant in the Deuteronomistic History'). The covenant thus confirms existing relationships and does not call them into being. Thus the reference to 'my covenant' at Gn. 6:18 implies an existing set of relationships divinely established. It is significant then that after the Flood Noah is called upon to reinaugurate the relationship of dominion established initially in Gn. 1:26–28. The Flood represented the general undoing of creation (*cf.* Gn. 7:11, and the structure of the narrative) so that after it, in Gn. 9:9–13, the divine covenant is re-established with humankind, animals and the whole earth. It can be argued, then, that the covenant of Gn. 6:18 refers to a specific set of relationships with humankind and creation that God had pledged himself to by the very fact of creation* itself.

Because the Abrahamic covenant, through which the whole world was to find blessing, was a reply to Gn. 1 – 11 and the problem of the Fall,* this movement of redemption though Abraham presumably had in mind the work of finally re-establishing the relationship of God to humankind and creation. It is to be noted that the relationship with Abraham begins in Gn. 12:1–3 but that the covenant itself which confirms it does not come into existence until Gn. 15:18. At that point the Heb. idiom 'cut a covenant', which refers to contractual obligations between two parties, is used as it could not be used at Gn. 6:18, since that reference had concerned a divine undertaking independent of human participation.

A further series of biblical covenants divinely imposed is made between God and Israel. By them the theology of redemption (see Sin and Salvation[5]) intended through Abraham is specified. The Sinai covenant is a further movement whereby: 1. the Abrahamic covenant is now to operate through Israel; and 2. the creation mandate given to Adam now devolves upon Israel (W. J. Dumbrell, *Covenant and Creation*, pp. 84–90). The reason given for the conclusion of the Sinai covenant with Israel is because 'the whole earth is mine' (Ex. 19:5). Through this particular covenant with Israel, Abraham's descendant, God's concern for the whole world was expressed. The political model given to Israel (as a 'kingdom of priests and a holy nation') is thus a model of the kingdom-of-God* government that was to come for all humankind. Though access to Israel by neighbouring peoples was always theoretically available, the OT emphasis on Israel's world mission to be the Israel of God and her failure at that level meant a certain national exclusivity arose, a situation which the NT would redress.

The purpose of the Davidic covenant (2 Sa. 7, though the actual word 'covenant' is missing in that chapter; *cf.* 2 Sa. 23:5 and Ps. 89:3) is to add Messiahship to the Sinai covenant with Christ in view. Jeremiah's new covenant has in mind the renewal of the people of God and the great interior blessing of conformity to God's will by its members by putting the law* in the hearts of his people. It envisages a time when this will be possible, when sin will have been removed as a factor in human experience. This removal constitutes the 'newness' of the new covenant. This new covenant presupposes the work of the cross* but looks beyond it to the final gathering of the people of God, and to the erection of the kingdom of God. Jesus inaugurates this new covenant at his last supper with the disciples.

The covenant relationship formed the basis of Israel's ethic (see Old Testament Ethics[8]), which was at all times responsory as prophetic preaching always presupposes. Given the set of relationships with God in which Israel existed, the prophets required conduct appropriate to the relationship. The demand the prophets made was a demand for a proper reaction within a context of grace, an appeal to an indicative state in which an imperative could be imposed. Israel was called upon to demonstrate her response to the grace of her Exodus redemption by freely conforming to the covenant expectations. Her keeping of the covenant was the proper response to what God had done in redemption. Moral and social faults which characterized the Israel of Amos' day were not criticized for their own sake merely, but as manifestations which would not have otherwise occurred had covenant relationships been correctly exhibited. The final failure of Israel to rise to covenant expectations meant that Jesus, as the embodiment of Israel, assumed Israel's necessary servant role.

Biblically, humankind stands with a more generalized covenant relationship, that which was instituted by creation itself, and implicit within this relationship is a morality which may be expected to demonstrate it. This moral demand later found concentrated expression in the Ten Commandments (see Decalogue*), all of which, however, were in existence as general demands before Sinai. Correspondingly, where social aberrations and injustices or social inequalities appear, they are continuing manifestations of the broken set of relationships between God and humankind and are to be addressed by Christians as such.

Bibliography

W. J. Dumbrell, *Covenant and Creation* (Exeter, 1984); E. Kutsch, *Verheissung und Gesetz: Untersuchungen zum sogenannten 'Bund' im Alten Testament* (Berlin, 1973); D. J. McCarthy, 'Berit and Covenant in the Deuteronomistic History', *VTSupp* 23, 1972, pp. 65–85; *idem*, 'Covenant Relationships', in C. Brekelmans (ed.), *Questions Disputées d'Ancien Testament*; E. W. Nicholson, *God and His People: Covenant and Theology in the Old Testament* (Oxford and New York, 1986).

W.J.D.

COVETOUSNESS is a form of distorted, misplaced or unlawful desire focused on another's possessions or property, or even on another person (Ex. 20:17; Dt. 5:21).

In the OT there are three different Heb. words which can be translated 'covet', each having a different emphasis in meaning:

1. *hāmad* is inappropriate desire (Ex. 20:17) which can lead to the taking of another's possessions (Jos. 7:21), or social injustice in the plotting and seizing of another's house or lands (Mi. 2:2).

2. *'āwâ*, to desire for oneself (Dt. 5:21; Pr. 21:26), expresses the personal greed or craving which is present, so the REB translates Dt. 5:21 as 'lust' in relation to a neighbour's wife.

3. *bāṣa'* emphasizes distorted or misplaced desire which issues in dishonest gain, or the greed for more which has become a common social disposition (Je. 6:13; 8:10; 22:17). This can lead to a deeper distortion at the centre of a person's being (Ezk. 33:31). Such unlawful gain occurred especially in the aftermath of

war (Hab. 2) or in periods of substantial social injustice, and attracted prophetic denunciation (Is. 57:17).

A cycle can develop whereby a person's distorted desires lead to a greed which will unlawfully dispossess another in order to satisfy cravings and in turn these can become more insistent, compounding the initial desire.

In the NT there is a variety of examples of coveting, including positive and well-channelled expressions of desire. The key words are as follows:

1. *Epithymeō*, to fix the mind on, identifying the intense focus of a person's attention rather than the disordered cravings that can be experienced. Paul recognized this danger in himself when he cited the command not to covet as stirring in him 'every kind of covetous desire' (Rom. 7:7–8). This may be one reason why he chose to support himself, as a protection against desiring the possessions of those he sought to serve (Acts 20:33). When summarizing the law (Rom. 13:9), Paul includes not coveting as an expression of loving one's neighbour as oneself. To covet is to maltreat one's neighbour. By implication, not to covet is a form of respectful care (Rom. 13:10).

2. *Zēloō*, to be zealous for, or eagerly desire, (AV, 'covet'). This is used very positively by Paul to encourage the seeking for the spiritual gifts, especially prophecy (1 Cor. 12:31; 14:1, 39).

3. *Oregomai* and *philargyros*, two words used to convey covetousness in relation to money.*

Oregomai, lit. 'a hankering after', means to extend the arms for anything (1 Tim. 6:10). The NIV translates it 'love'; RSV is stronger, 'craving'; REB, 'pursuit'. These highlight the strength of the orientation.

Philargyros, a lover of silver, is used to describe the Pharisees (Lk. 16:14) and is a danger into which people can be enticed through a lack of personal discipline leading to a highly disordered personal life and anti-social behaviour (2 Tim. 3:2–5). For this reason the counsel for Christians is very direct: 'Keep your lives free from the love of money' (*aphilargyros*, Heb. 13:5). The positive virtue to cultivate is contentment (1 Tim. 6:6; Heb. 13:5).

4. *Pleonexia*, the wish to have more, is associated with the excesses resulting from covetousness, a greediness and preoccupation with possessing which Jesus warned could take a variety of forms (Lk. 12:15), and was

evidence of evil desires in a person's interior life (Mk. 7:22). Such covetousness is also linked with a variety of forms of sexual immorality, swindling and possibly prostitution. Identifying covetousness as idolatry indicates a ruthless form of greed, intent to get whatever one desires without regard for the rights, feelings or welfare of others: a disposition that can come to dominate a person's life, till satisfying one's own needs becomes a god. 'Hearts trained in greed' (RSV, 2 Pet. 2:14) can prevent people from sharing in the kingdom of God (1 Cor. 5:10–11; 6:10; Eph. 5:3–5).

Covetousness is descriptive, not diagnostic, of human behaviour, evidence of disordered desires or primary needs which have not been appropriately met or personally integrated.

See also: JEALOUSY AND ENVY.

G.J.P.

CREATION. The doctrine of creation is one of the major theological themes that informs a Christian ethic. That God repeatedly declared his creation to be good, that it is purposely ordered to attest the perfections of its maker and to contribute to the development of faith and righteousness in human beings created in his image, and that they are entrusted with responsibilities in and for the creation – all of this has far-reaching ethical implications.

Biblical evidence

Some of these implications are indicated by Scripture itself. Genesis 1 records the mandate to 'be fruitful and increase in number; fill the earth and subdue it' (Gn. 1:28), while Genesis 2 places limits on human autonomy in those tasks and sets them in context of an instituted marriage* relationship. The narrative that immediately builds on this account tells of the Fall* of Adam and Eve and the piling up of moral failure on moral failure by their posterity. When murder is denounced, it is because God created human beings in his own image, entrusting to them the care of his creation. Yet the promise of salvation also runs throughout the narrative, so that from the outset the concepts of creation, sin and redemption (see Sin and Salvation⁵) underlie everything the Bible says or implies about ethics.

The OT Wisdom literature ponders the meaning of life's vicissitudes in God's creation: the book of Proverbs spells out sage advice about friendships, marriage and work,* about

resisting temptation and taking advice, about controlling the tongue and avoiding foolishness of various kinds: all of this is the responsibility of God's creatures living in the presence of their maker and Lord. The book of Ecclesiastes, contrasting the lifestyle of a self-absorbed secularist with that of a God-fearing person, urges readers to remember their creator before their years relentlessly bring senility and they finally must face God.

Jesus himself based some of his moral teachings on the creation. What is the point of our anxiety about earthly goods when God so lavishly provides for birds and flowers (Mt. 6:19–34)? And when asked about divorce, Jesus referred to God's original intention for marriage at its creation, attributing Moses' allowance for divorce to human sin (Mt. 19:3–12). To those with the Gnostic tendency to regard physical things as evil, who advocated celibacy and rigid asceticism,* Paul responded that everything God created is good (1 Tim. 4:1–5).

The most significant NT passage is Rom. 1:18 – 2:16, where Paul argues that those without the Mosaic law are morally reponsible to God because the moral law is engrained into human nature. While he refers to a wide range of sins which result from worshipping created things while ignoring the creator, he specifically calls homosexual behaviour 'unnatural'. He plainly regards the male/female physical and emotional nature with which God originally endowed us as still in evidence, and as good.

Advantages of a creation ethic

These biblical passages have throughout church history encouraged Christians to draw ethical implications from the doctrine of creation, a procedure which also has practical value in a relativist* and pluralist* context. Just as Paul argued that all people of whatever cultural or religious background are accountable for the witness of creation to God and his moral law, so it may still be asserted that since all people are equally his creatures, made in his image (see Image of God*), human nature bears the imprint of his purposes. Whatever the individual and cultural differences, generic human characteristics of a biological, psychological and rational sort persist. The good which God purposed is to that extent the same for all, and appeal can accordingly be made to universal moral law evidenced in universal human needs and potentials, despite cultural or religious pluralism. Likewise Christian and non-Christian can often support a common cause, even though on different ultimate bases.

By the same token a creation ethic stands against any ethical subjectivism* that reduces moral beliefs to subjective feelings or attitudes devoid of objective basis. The immediate basis for moral values (in contrast to its ultimate basis in God's character and will) is in the created nature of things that is as it is independently of whether we recognize it or not. Ethical discussion can therefore be a rational debate of the ethical implications of objective features in human nature and societal relationships, rather than a pitting of purely subjective feelings one against the other.

The universal and objective grounds of a creation ethic also explain why historically Christian ethicists developed versions of ethical theories that began in the Gk. or Rom. world. Plato* initiated a tradition that it is possible to gain an intuitive knowledge of universal moral ideals, something which has had ongoing appeal. Eighteenth-century 'moral sense' philosophers, for example, claimed that we all have a natural capacity for making intuitive moral judgments, a capacity which Bishop Joseph Butler* identified as 'conscience'. Twentieth-century intuitionist theories, like that of W. D. Ross (1877–1940), continue to attract others. Analogously the Rom. Stoics developed a natural-law* ethic based on their belief that all of nature is orderly and law-governed. Thomas Aquinas* adapted this to his more Aristotelian philosophy, so that natural law is the revelation in the natural order of God's eternal law, and natural tendencies and potentials indicate good ends that God purposed for his creation: the drive to survive indicates a natural moral law of self-preservation; the sexual drive has reproduction as its natural purpose, its good; human rationality points to the good of an ordered society and of coming to the knowledge of God. Natural-law ethics understandably attracted both Catholic and Protestant ethicists, athough it is more common in the former tradition.

Among contemporary Protestant ethicists, Lewis Smedes (1921–) speaks of morality woven into the fabric of our humanness, in that God sets us in broad channels where we are free but must respect the boundaries (*Mere Morality*, pp. vii, 7; also pp. 250–251, note 18). Oliver O'Donovan (1945–) distinguishes two concepts of order, as 'end' (teleological order) and as 'kind' (generic order) (*Resurrection and Moral Order*, ch. 2). Both are discernible within the overall created order, but the only pure teleological relation is between creature and creator: creation is for God, for his purposes and honour. He is the only purely intrinsic good, and his will commands. A Christian ethic therefore finds its source of obligation* in God, and it conceives what is good in terms of God's perfect will (Rom. 12:2). While it finds indications in what God has made of what ought to be, it is not merely a deontological* ethic, stressing duty* for duty's sake, but rather also a teleological* ethic affirming a purpose that embraces yet transcends all the lesser ends we properly seek in God's creation.

Practical implications

What ethical implications then can be drawn from the doctrine of creation?

1. There are implications for moral knowledge: if nature somehow bears witness to our responsibility to the creator, then some natural moral knowledge is to that extent possible. Ethical intuitionism* and natural-law theories may be overly optimistic in this epistemological regard, in underestimating the effects of human sinfulness on moral vision and ethical sensitivity, but they are on the right track in asserting that natural moral knowledge is at least to some degree possible by virtue both of God-given human capacities and of the good possibilities inherent in our God-given abilities and tasks.

2. There are implications of a substantive sort. John Calvin,* for example, regarded the Ten Commandments (see Decalogue*) as a re-promulgation of the natural moral law (see *Institutes* II.viii.2), a view reiterated by Presbyterian theologian Charles Hodge (1797–1878): 'The law is revealed in the constitution of our nature, and more fully and clearly in the written Word of God' (*Systematic Theology*, vol. 3, Grand Rapids, 1960, p. 266). Hodge's reference is to Rom. 2, while he is introducing the Ten Commandments. More recently John Murray (1898–1975) finds creation ordinances regarding marriage and procreation,* replenishing and subduing the earth, labour and the sabbath* referred to in Scripture and reaffirmed in the Decalogue and its application. These ordinances relate to human instincts and interests and to all that engages human thought and action. They are not abrogated or modified after the Fall, but are more expressly enunciated in *Principles of Conduct*, chs. 1 and 2. On the other hand,

some Lutheran theologians such as Helmut Thielicke* claim that the command of God in creation is modified after the Fall, as in Moses' allowance for divorce. But Thielicke joins Reformed theologians in regarding marriage, work and government as 'spheres' (others call them 'orders') inherent in the nature of things (*TE* 1, ch. 9).

3. The goodness of creation is also significant. As Baptist theologian A. H. Strong (1836–1921) states it: 'At the first creation, the world was good in two senses; first as free from moral evil . . .; secondly as adapted to beneficent ends, – for example, the revelation of God's perfection, and the probation and happiness of intelligent and obedient creatures' (*Systematic Theology*, Philadelphia, 1907, p. 402).

Plainly also it means that God loves and appreciates his creation, and that it was as he intended. Consequently as his creatures we too should love and respect what he made and what he intended, and this has broad implications regarding ecology and environmental ethics (see Environment*), respect for future generations, the identification of priority goals for society and for individual life, and the basis for self-respect and personal worth.

Karl Barth* develops this more fully and in doing so sums up much previous ethical thinking of the church (*Ethics*, ch. 2). By creating human beings, God commands them to live, for they exist distinct from God, specific individuals with freedom,* experiencing both the continuity and the change which time brings. God called this kind of life good, and it is to be lived in obedience to the creator. We must therefore affirm life, resist death, reject suicide.* To affirm life means to attend to such necessities as food and rest, to accept our sexuality (see [11]), enjoy life's pleasures, respect the distinctiveness of individual human beings and other living things as well. It implies that we may appropriate creation's resources to meet our needs, but it places limits on competition and acquisitiveness.

In addition to these general ways of affirming life, creation gives individuals more particularized callings as sexual beings, and in friendships, family relationships and nations, callings related to one's age, gifts, particular guidance and even to dying. Each person has particular callings to fulfil in God's creation, and needs the kind of regulation provided in the orders of creation, work, marriage and the body politic, as well as in the church itself. In sum, then, by his act of creation God commands us to affirm life, fulfilling individual callings within the orders he has chosen for governing human freedom.

But if a creation ethic is a teleological ethic, then duties are not the whole story. If redemption's purpose is to bring about God's purpose for creation, then it means an ethic of virtues,* character (see [10]) and social justice (see Social Ethics*) amid a creation blossoming in every way that glorifies its maker.

Finally, by affirming as it does the goodness of what God made, creation promises his continued care and offers hope in the face of moral evils that tear apart both human lives and society as a whole.

Restoration or re-creation?

Theologians differ on whether God will finally restore his creation to its original perfection or whether he will transform it into something far better, but in either case the biblical story is of a good creation twisted and marred by sin, yet to be redeemed by God's grace and power when his kingdom (see Kingdom of God*) is fully realized (Rom. 8:18–25). Creation, sin, grace and kingdom are inseparably joined in God's purposes. The eschatological vision in the OT prophets and the book of Revelation is of a creation in which God's good purposes for creation are brought finally to fulfilment. For individuals struggling with evils of various sorts, and for human society as a whole, this hope inspires courage and effort, knowing that our labours are 'not in vain' (1 Cor. 15:58).

See also: CHRISTIAN MORAL REASONING. [18]

Bibliography
K. Barth, *Ethics* (ET, Edinburgh and New York, 1981), ch. 2; J. Murray, *Principles of Conduct* (London and Grand Rapids, 1957), chs. 1 and 2; O. O'Donovan, *Resurrection and Moral Order* (Leicester and Grand Rapids, ²1994), ch. 2; L. Smedes, *Mere Morality* (Grand Rapids, 1981; Tring, 1983); H. Thielicke, *TE* 1, ch. 9.

A.F.H.

CREATION ETHICS, see CREATION; COMMUNITY ETHICS; [16] POLITICS.

CREATIVITY. The emphasis on creativity as a core concept for artistic production is essentially a romantic concept. The artist is seen as an especially gifted visionary of spiritual truth: the creative genius. The roots of this concept as related to producing art* can be traced back to the 17th and 18th centuries, when humankind sought to emancipate itself from a created cosmos governed by divine law and replace it with the creative power of the human mind.

This desire found its philosophical expression in the writings of Immanuel Kant,* who said that 'man', as an autonomous centre of consciousness, should no longer derive laws from nature but rather prescribe them to nature. Before that time, any comparison between God's *creatio ex nihilo* and the work done by artists would have sounded irreverent and preposterous. To the Greek, the artist imitated an already perfect world. Only the poet (Gk. *poieō* means 'to make') was free to produce his own (fictional) world. It was also in connection with poetry that, in the 16th century, the first connections with creativity were being made.

In the second half of the 20th century, the word 'creativity' has acquired a wider scope of reference so that it now includes, for example, creative thinking, creative cooking or creative management. Instead of focusing on art, the emphasis is on the use of imagination in any possible field.

Throughout the 20th century, Christians have tried to christianize the concept of artistic creativity by interpreting it in the light of Gn. 1:26: humankind being made in the image of God* means that humankind too is bestowed with the gift of creativity. The best-known exponent of this view is Dorothy L. Sayers (1893–1957), who elaborates on the analogy between artistic and divine creation by referring to the way God expresses himself in his Son, the visible image of himself as (invisible) divine Idea. This she applies to the artistic process. As well as having Hegelian overtones, Sayer's aesthetics are thus largely based on the concept of art as self-expression.

The argument that humankind is creative because God is creative is a form of analogical reasoning which has its origin in Thomistic scholasticism (see Thomas Aquinas*). A similar form of arguing is frequently employed to identify other distinctive human capacities such as 'rationality', 'morality' or 'personality'. In Gn. 1:26, however, the emphasis is put on God's delegation of responsible stewardship* in general rather than on any particular capacity with which to fulfil this task, a theme which recurs in Ps. 8:4–6.

One weakness of an aesthetic theory based on the concept of creativity is that it singles out what one takes to be an aspect of image-bearing and relates this to one particular form of human action, *i.e.* artistic production. This risks giving the false impression that artists resemble God more closely than people involved in more mundane or routine professions.

The idea of image-bearing in the Bible is both more universal and more religiously oriented than the mere singling out of one (or more) human capacities.

Another weakness of the romantic concept of creativity is its inherent leanings towards idolatry, *i.e.* the worship of what is created instead of the creator himself (Rom. 1:25). Even if the artworks themselves are not idols in the narrow sense (see *e.g.* Is. 44:9–20), a cult of creativity can still turn them and their human makers into objects of idolatry.

A more rounded biblical approach to the question of creativity would be to see it in the context of the cultural mandate and of stewardship. Whereas we are all called to develop the potential inherent in God's creation, artists – in distinction from, *e.g.*, scientists, agriculturalists or homemakers – unfold the specifically aesthetic dimension of this world. They use their artistically creative talents to that end.

Bibliography

D. L. Sayers, *The Mind of the Maker* (London, 1941); *idem*, 'Towards a Christian Aesthetic', in *Unpopular Opinions* (London, 1946); W. Tatarkiewicz, *A History of Six Ideas* (The Hague, 1980); N. Wolterstorff, *Art in Action* (Grand Rapids, 1980).

A.C.

CREDIT is the sum of the money value the supplier has extended, or will extend, to the borrower or buyer. Personal credit is extended to people in many forms, such as the aggregate amount they may charge up on their credit cards, the mortgages they have on their homes, or the monthly payments they agree to when they purchase a car. Businesses borrow money from banks by negotiating and drawing against what is called 'lines of credit'; they sell bonds to institutions and individuals whose purchases extend them credit; and their suppliers offer them 'terms of credit' (*e.g.* you may take a 2% cash discount if you pay your bill in ten days, but regardless of whether you take the discount or not, the full balance is due within thirty days).

When credit is offered and used, it results in the creation of a loan or debt* which in turn bears an interest cost that the borrower must pay. The OT offers a number of warnings to those who would accept and use credit (*e.g.* Pr. 22:7; Hab. 2:6–8). It also provides many instructions to those who extend credit (*e.g.* Lv. 25:35–38; Dt. 15:1–11).

Credit, as offered in the Western hemisphere by banks and retailers in the last fifty years, has taken a form that was unheard of in earlier days. Those who extended credit to those of prior generations were deeply concerned with: 1. the character of the person to whom credit was extended; 2. the capacity of the borrower to repay the credit balance; and 3. the collateral available to repay the debt balance should it be necessary. Much credit has been offered in the past half-century, however, on what is called the 'law of large numbers' – the 'faith' premise that the vast majority of people are honest and will repay their debts. Little attention has therefore been paid recently to matters of character or people's capacity to repay. The wide distribution of credit cards by financial and retail businesses illustrates this new impersonal form of granting credit. Obtaining credit has become quite easy, and this has encouraged many people, who otherwise would probably have forgone the purchase, to purchase on credit. This has led to an explosion of personal debt over the past half-century, and more and more of people's income is being spent to service their debt. It is hard to believe that those extending such credit really have the best interests of the ordinary consumer in mind. And those who take advantage of this easy credit are not following the clear admonition to 'let no debt remain outstanding, except the continuing debt to love one another' (Rom. 13:8). The practical outcome of this is that many families have reached for a standard of living that is years ahead of their income and savings. They have thereby become, in some real financial and psychological ways, servants of their possessions and slaves to their creditors.

R.C.C.

See also: INTEREST; MONEY.

CREMATION, see BURIAL AND CREMATION.

CRIME. A crime is an act committed or omitted in violation of a law, but this rather simplistic definition needs to be qualified in the light of the distinction between criminal and other law.*

Criminal law is derived from the protection of a person's or group's natural rights,* *e.g.* the right to life, to property, to be free from assault and to be at liberty. Rules of conduct in any society, be it primitive or sophisticated, are agreed either formally or informally by prohibiting actions which might harm another person; it is from these rules that clearly defined law has been derived.

Of the laws for humanity's benefit contained in the Ten Commandments, only two are seen today as concerned with crime: 'Do not murder,' and 'Do not steal.' Adultery,* in some jurisdictions still regarded as a criminal act, has been transferred generally to the civil code in many countries.

Much debate has taken place as to whether acts of immorality, in the widest sense, are in themselves crimes. Criminal acts are generally restricted to the domain of public wrong; as Sir Carleton Allen (1887–1966) writes, 'Crime is crime because it consists in wrongdoing which directly and in serious degree threatens insecurity or well-being of society' ('The Nature of a Crime', *Journal of Comparative Legislation*, Feb 1931). However, some have argued that a criminal act also defies public morality (see Devlin–Hart Debate*). In the case of *Shaw* v. *Director of Public Prosecutions*, Lord Simmonds (1881–1971) asserted that 'there remains in Courts of Law a residual power to enforce the supreme and fundamental purpose of the law, to conserve not only the safety and order but also the moral welfare of the state' (see (1962) A.C. 220 (1961) 2 All ER 446). On the other hand, H. L. A. Hart (1907–92) maintains that 'it is not proper for the state to enforce the general morality' (*The Listener*, 30 July 1959, p. 162).

Range of crime

Some crimes are common to all nations and societies. Perhaps the most common is theft,* or stealing in its many facets. Dishonesty and deceit damage community life, and have led to 'white-collar crimes' – fraud,* tax evasion, insider dealing,* *etc.*

Assaults, ranging in severity from slight injuries to manslaughter and murder, are also a feature of most societies. They are frequently committed in the home as well as in public places. Research shows that much violence* follows abuse of alcohol.*

The use of prohibited drugs* inflates crime figures, not only because of the offence itself, but also because of the means often used to obtain money to purchase the drugs, *e.g.* robbery and blackmail. The use of offensive weapons (knives, firearms, *etc.*) in the furtherance of crime has increased significantly, as has the employment of explosives in connection with the international crime of terrorism.*

Sexual offences, both within the home and elsewhere, especially indecent assaults on children and women, including rape,* have shown alarming increases in recent years, and are perhaps a reflection of the permissive society which now conditions the Western world.

Proof of crime

When a crime has been committed, it must be proved beyond reasonable doubt that not only has the person charged been involved in the event which is against the criminal law (the *actus reus*) but also that that person either intended the act or that the result of his or her actions could be reasonably expected (the *mens rea*). Both elements are essential to conviction in court.

Defence of the accused

A person accused of crime, provided the elements of *actus reus* and *mens rea* are present, has general defences available to him or her to plead that the intention* was not possible.

Generally, a child under the age of ten is assumed to be incapable of committing a crime and, although many such infants are used as accomplices (*e.g.* in shoplifting with a parent), the child may not be charged.

A defendant may plead that his or her actions were justified (*e.g.* in assaulting a burglar), and therefore that the result is not criminal.

Another may plead insanity at the time the offence was committed or even at the time of trial. A plea of diminished responsibility* may also result in the reduction of a murder indictment to one of manslaughter.

Though many defendants claim to have been under the influence of alcohol or drugs at the time an offence was committed, courts are wary of such defences, especially if the alcohol or drug was self-administered.

Occasionally, a defendant may assert that his or her actions were attributable to orders from a superior, either in a military or disciplined service context or even in civilian life.

This is not normally regarded as a valid excuse although, in a similar vein, a person committing criminal actions under duress* or coercion (see Force*) may be acquitted, depending on the seriousness of the threat or the crime.

Reasons for crime

While the range of crimes given above is by no means exhaustive, it will be seen that much crime represents a wrongful desire for something which another has. Some children are raised in an environment where pressure from either family or peers induces the youngster to commit crime. It is thought that poverty* and deprivation are the catalysts for some basic crimes, but this view does not explain why the majority of impoverished people live honest and law-abiding lives despite their needs.

Crime is often committed when reason and rationality have been suspended (due, perhaps, to the influence of alcohol and other drugs). Criminal damage or vandalism is said to be the culmination of boredom or an expression of jealousy, although that does not explain every instance which could simply be described as mindless.

Prevention

Crime prevention is the primary objective of any police force, and it is normally a high priority and essential ingredient of both short- and long-term policy. Some crimes defy prevention (*e.g.* crimes of passion, fraud, sexual abuse in homes, *etc.*), although a good detection rate and subsequent punishment* may in itself be a deterrent. Such prevention as is possible mainly comprises home, vehicle and personal security; anti-drink and anti-drug campaigns; and systems of Vehicle and Home (or Neighbourhood) Watch, where residents assist each other and local police by vigilance and reporting.

Bibliography

P. Devlin, *The Enforcement of Morals* (Oxford, 1965); C. S. Kenny, *Outlines of Criminal Law* (Cambridge, [15]1936); J. C. Smith and B. Hogan, *Criminal Law* (London, 1988).

R.E.N.O.

C RIMINAL JUSTICE is both the procedure by which a person is convicted of a crime* and the subsequent process through which the official organs of civil society work out that form of justice, the outcome of which is the infliction of punishment upon someone found guilty of the commission of a crime. The element of punishment* distinguishes criminal justice from civil justice.

In civil justice the authorities seek to restore civil relationships to what they were before they were broken, or, in cases where restoration is impossible, they seek to ensure that an injured party is compensated for the injury done to him (*e.g.* by the award of damages). In other civil cases (*e.g.* divorce*) new legal relationships may be established and the old altered.

In criminal justice the infliction of its hallmark, punishment, is authorized by official organs of the State and may be carried out either by some official generally authorized or by someone particularly authorized in the given instance. The OT 'avenger of blood' is not now found in most civilized societies (*cf.* Dt. 19:4–7, 11–13).

In Christian thinking about the organization of civil society, the doing of justice in criminal cases is lawful. 'The authorities that exist have been established by God' (Rom. 13:1). The civil authority within a State* 'does not bear the sword for nothing. He is God's servant, an agent of wrath to bring punishment on the wrongdoer' (Rom. 13:4). The purpose is that 'we may live peaceful and quiet lives in all godliness and holiness' (1 Tim. 2:2). Although Paul wrote before the days of the modern company, few would dispute the application of the criminal law to modern legal entities, or that they may generally invoke the legal protections available to individuals.

In most civil societies a crime is defined as the wilful commission of an offence. What constitutes an offence is a matter for the legal system involved. Whatever disturbs the ability of the citizenry to 'live peaceful and quiet lives in all godliness and holiness' clearly comes within consideration. But the precise parameters of 'crime' remain a matter for definition in any legal system. This is open both to variance and to abuse. While all States consider murder, which is prohibited by the Ten Commandments, as criminal, few (some Muslim societies excepted) now hold adultery as criminal, although that also is prohibited by the Ten Commandments. Some States use their criminal law to impose through sanction religious requirements, to ban religions of which they disapprove, and otherwise to mould their societies in ways approved of by those holding power for the time. 'Christian' potentates have used the law to encourage 'Christian' behaviour and discourage conduct of which they disapprove.

All legal systems consider it criminal for a citizen to attempt their displacement by force (treason) and many hold it criminal to encourage others to do so (sedition). None the less, the duty of citizens to oppose by all necessary means a civil authority which has forfeited its position by failing properly to discharge its divine function has been argued by some theologians, *e.g.* in Scotland by John Knox (*History*, 1560–71), George Buchanan (*De Iure Regni apud Scotos*, 1579) and Samuel Rutherford (*Lex Rex*, 1644). (*Cf.* John Calvin, *Institutes*, 1536 ed., VI.35–36; 1559 ed., IV.xx.1–2.) In modern times and following such reasoning, some have considered that a law prohibiting the preaching of the gospel is not a true 'law' requiring obedience by Christians. Short of that, questions arise as to the obedience owed to a regime that seeks to suppress civil liberties, dissent or opposition (see Civil Disobedience;* Rebellion;* Tyrannicide*).

That a criminal offence shall be 'wilfully' committed is another common general requirement. All modern societies have found it expedient in certain instances to dispense with the element of volition, and make simply the occurrence of a prohibited action (or inaction) criminally punishable. The connection between the event and the 'criminal' is held to be sufficient to justify the imposition of the criminal sanction. For example, a company may be held criminally liable for committing an environmental offence, although it would be impossible to prove that the artificial legal 'person' had any intention at all in the matter. (Similarly a company may be held civilly liable in damages, say, for loss caused by 'its negligence'.)

Again, while most societies have adopted the Mosaic requirement of two witnesses (Dt. 17:6), all societies have made exemptions from that general principle in cases where the finding of two witnesses may be difficult or unnecessarily expensive (*e.g.* in the UK certain traffic offences may be proved by the evidence of a single police officer). This is sensible, although if one surveys the legislation of States round the world such reasoning can be abused.

Punishment has a variety of functions, which vary in their balance in different instances: it is retribution for wrong; marks society's disapproval; allows the wrongdoer to expiate his or her crime; can assist in his or her reformation; and deters others from committing similar crimes.

See also: JUSTICE AND PEACE. ③

F.L.

C ROSS, THE. As the central symbol of Christianity, the cross has played a unique role in Christian spirituality* (see Forgiveness*) and ethics. It has often played a major role in discussions concerning suffering.* The need to 'bear one's cross' in imitation of Christ, an idea which can be traced back to the NT (Mt. 16:24), has played an important role in monastic* spirituality. It has also loomed large in the concept of spiritual warfare, as can be seen in the signing with the cross in baptism. The Crusades too, manifested this idea, albeit in a somewhat secularized and debased form. In the spirituality of the individual, bearing the cross is clearly connected with the principle of self-denial, though the traditional interpretation, which is that Christians should bear their sufferings patiently, is not always accepted today.

From the time of the Reformation, it is possible to trace the existence of the *theologia crucis* ('theology of the cross'), which understands suffering and persecution as central to Christian experience on earth, and contrasts them with the triumph and bliss of heaven (*theologia gloriae*). In recent years, these two theologies have often separated from each other and taken extreme forms. On the one hand is the belief, born of the experience of mass persecution, that only the doctrine of a crucified God is adequate to make Christianity credible today. According to this way of thinking, there is a cross at the heart of God, which alone gives meaning to the sufferings of the universe. At the other extreme is a prosperity gospel which tries to eliminate suffering from authentic Christian experience, and regards it as a sign of lingering sin and disobedience.

The former view may be criticized for its failure to appreciate fully the reality of Christ's victory, and for glorifying suffering as an end in itself. But the latter view is a much more serious distortion of the gospel, since it denies a fundamental aspect of the Christian life, and attributes what belongs to God to the devil.

See also: ATONEMENT.

Bibliography
J. Moltmann, *The Way of Jesus Christ* (ET, London and San Francisco, 1990); J. R. W. Stott, *The Cross of Christ* (Leicester and Downers Grove, IL, 1986).

G.L.B.

C ROSS-CULTURAL CONFLICT MEDIATION. Conflict,* a universal, a cultural and an individual process, is essential to, ineradicable from, and inevitable in human life. It is a universal phenomenon, with cultural pathways and patterns which shape the behaviours of individuals in dispute. Mediation practised within a culture* must be contextually congruent with that culture's views and values; mediation between persons of two cultures must honour expectations from both and recognize the third culture that is formed at the boundary by mediating persons who act as a bridge.

The variations and contrasts in understanding of conflict from culture to culture challenge virtually all basic beliefs about conflict. Traditional cultures see conflict as a communal concern; the group has ownership of the conflict and context; whereas urbanized (Westernized) cultures focus on individual issues and insist on personal and private ownership. Traditional cultures deal with conflict in preferred patterns of third-party mediation which achieve resolution in indirect, lateral and systemic ways; urbanized cultures prefer direct, one-to-one encounter between disputants drawing in third parties only in legal processes which are more often adversarial than mediating. Traditional cultures follow conflict patterns embedded in the mores and customs of the group (high context); urbanized cultures see the patterns for conflict as situational (low context), pragmatic and open to wide variation of choice and strategy. Women tend to utilize the more private styles, men the more public; women tend to utilize relational networks, men tend to own the dominant power structures of the society.

The common pool of cultural assumptions which come into play in our negotiation of disputes expresses the cultures' preferred paths for conflicts. In strongly individualistic cultures, the conflict belongs to the disputants, and advocates are involved by invitation; in more traditional societies the conflict does not belong to the disputants but to the community, and third parties are participants from the outset. In every culture conflict is triangular in origin (two persons and an issue or a problem person) and is best resolved triangularly with mediation or adjudication. A go-between person (traditional), a process (urban-Western), or a combination of the two is needed.

Key variations in conflict patterns also include: high context, in which relationships are primary, versus low context, in which issue is predominant; honour and face as a significant factor versus dignity and satisfaction; anger* as an instrumental process for community; activation versus anger as an agent-focused emotion; forgiveness* as an individual process of forgetting and forgoing versus forgiveness as a responsible, mutually repentant process of reconciliation.*

Culturally sensitive and culturally congruent processes are of crucial importance and maximum effectiveness.

Bibliography

D. W. Augsburger, *Conflict Mediation Across Cultures* (Louisville, OH, 1992); P. H. Gulliver, *Disputes and Negotiations* (New York, 1979).

D.W.A.

CROSS-CULTURAL COUNSEL-LING. Therapeutic effectiveness is dependent on its contextual congruence, so counselling and culture* have an intimate relationship and an intricate dialectic. The counsellor must be sensitive to what is universal – true of all humans; to what is cultural – true of some humans; and to what is individual – true only of this particular human. The *universal* includes the biological and general elements of social and psychological dimensions, but these are filtered through cultural values and views so that the culturally aware therapist sees universals as shaped by and selected by cultural processes. The *cultural* includes all these processes of human behaviour, association, institutions and traditions which provide both context and content for much of the counselling agenda. The *individual* includes the personality* formation, its developmental journey, and the unique configuration of traits, abilities and preferences that define the person (see Character[10]). The realm of the individual is also shaped by the cultural, thus all counselling is a cultural experience and exploration. When the counsellor and counsellee come from different primary cultures, the task of building a cultural bridge falls primarily to the therapist, and, as the relationship progresses, is gradually shared by both.

1. *Sympathy, empathy, interpathy.* Three processes of understanding the other person mark the movement to cultural competence. *Sympathy* is the spontaneous affective reaction to another's feelings based on perceived similarity between observer and observed; *empathy* is an intentional affective response to another's feelings based on perceived differences between the observer and the observed; *interpathy* is an intentional cognitive and affective envisioning of another's thoughts and feelings from another culture, world-view and epistemology. Cultural competence is marked by the counsellor's developing ability to seek to learn a foreign belief, take an alternative perspective, base thought on another assumption, and feel the resultant feelings and their consequences in a foreign context. Interpathic understanding seeks to experience a separate other without common cultural assumptions, values and views.

2. *World-view, values and life patterns.* The cross-cultural counsellor holds several assumptions which equip the person to be self-critical of the therapeutic process. These include the following. a. Cultural assumptions shape all clinical applications. b. Clinical practice is grounded in cultural depths of family history, communal tradition, social history, ethos and values. c. All claims to 'know' must be justified; all theories must be seen as tools, not ultimate truths. d. All therapy must be contextually grounded, all healing processes culturally connected, and all reconciliation processes congruent with the world of the client. e. We must hold all our assumptions tentatively, provisionally, heuristically, and remain open to challenge and changes. f. We must learn to move rhythmically between universal assumptions and cultural translations, between our own meanings and the client's world of meanings, in a constant dialectic. g. We must confess that for every perspective on doing therapy there are colleagues within our own cultures who hold an equally supported and opposite position. Other cultures possess equal variation to our own diversity, and a willingness to respect this wide spectrum can inform our work in assisting the counsellee to sort out views, values and life choices.

3. *Individualism,* collectivism and community* (see Community Ethics[16]). The commitment of Western psychology and psychotherapy to the understanding and treatment of

the individual must be balanced by awareness of collective personality processes in cultures which place solidarity and community in an equal value with personal destiny and choice. Promotion of Western individualism at the expense of familial and social accountability violates both person and community in many traditional settings. A balance between inner and outer controls and a union of internal and external responsibility in relationships is characteristic of more collective cultures, as well as desirable in Western contexts of individualism and of privacy in decision and self-definition.

4. *Training of cross-cultural counsellors.* Two central issues in training intercultural counsellors are: a. the paradigmatic primacy of seeing all individual development as embedded in and inseparable from its social and cultural context; and b. the development of counselling models and training programmes which appreciate the validity of 'the second culture' equally with that of the dominant culture of the training or care delivery context. In a multicultural world, such priorities and such skills are invaluable and essential.

See also: PASTORAL CARE, COUNSELLING AND PSYCHOTHERAPY. [12]

Bibliography

D. W. Augsburger, *Pastoral Counseling Across Cultures* (Philadelphia, 1986); D. W. Sue, *Counseling the Culturally Different* (Boston, MA, 1965); P. Pederson, *Counseling Across Cultures* (Honolulu, HI, 1981).

D.W.A.

CRUELTY is the wilful infliction of suffering. It may operate or be perceived within many human activities; those practised for political, scientific or economic purposes will not be considered here.

Conduct which imposes suffering on children (including child neglect, which does not readily fit the element of intent in cruelty) is now described as child abuse (see Abuse*) rather than cruelty. This is probably to allow for the complexity of motives, such as the role of the unconscious, the victim as an agent (even in infancy), the agent as a victim of his own circumstances, two-way interaction patterns and family and societal systems. Recognition of such factors may engender compassion* towards perpetrators of cruelty in general. The danger is that, with diminishing use of the word, responsibility* and culpability are disregarded.

'Being cruel to be kind' introduces the idea that some forms of cruelty may be less harmful than abuse, since abuse can never be seen objectively as having a good (loving) purpose. A measure of pain or distress, *e.g.* in discipline or surgery, can be justifiable as a means to a good end.

Cruelty within marriage is no longer a ground for divorce* in the UK but may be used as evidence of irretrievable breakdown of marriage. Cruelty is clearly condemned in Scripture, both within the covenant people of Israel (Pr. 12:10) and in other peoples (*e.g.* Am. 1:13). It is regarded as particularly reprehensible when visited upon weak and defenceless members of society (*e.g.* Ex. 22:22; Lv. 19:14).

R.M.H.

CRUSADES. The Crusades, which took their name from the cross which the Crusaders had emblazoned on their clothing, captured the imagination of many European people from 1100–1300. Although the Council of Clermont (1076) is usually regarded as the initiation of the Crusades, there were many longstanding factors of papal policy, theology, politics and social expansion that contributed to their development. These notions survived afterwards as political and ecclesiastical leaders used them to motivate people for a variety of causes.

The Crusades sought to reconquer the Holy Land from Islam after the capture of Jerusalem by the Seljukian Turks (1071). The First Crusade (1096–99), in spite of diversions, was the most successful. A territorial base, including Jerusalem, was established. Although the Holy City was lost in 1144, some territories on the mainland remained in Christian hands until 1291 when Acre fell.

The undergirding concept of crusade was commitment to God and the church under the papacy, and this was regarded by medieval Christians as their premier ethic. It is ironic that such a lofty ideal was twisted to justify excessive violence as recorded in the accounts of the capture of Jerusalem in 1099, to motivate Christian against Christian as in the sack of Constantinople in 1204, and to encourage the use of violence against pagans and heretics in Europe.

The enmity established by Holy War between Muslims and Christians continues to endure. Sensitive evangelism among Muslims thus avoids the term 'crusade' because of its associations. However, this is not the only legacy of the Crusades. The ideal of commitment to a cause, spiritual or temporal, remains in evangelistic crusades, social enterprises, and even the 'Crusade for Europe' which focused the efforts of the Allies in the Second World War.

Bibliography

P. M. Holt, *The Age of the Crusades* (New York and London, 1986); H. Mayer, *The Crusades* (New York and Oxford, ²1988); J. Riley-Smith, *The Crusades* (New Haven, CT, and London, 1987); S. Runciman, *A History of the Crusades* (Cambridge, 1951–54); K. M. Setton (ed.), *A History of the Crusades* (Philadelphia, 1955– ; Madison, WI, 1967–).

T.O.K.

CULTURE consists of the institutions, technology,* art,* customs and social patterns that a society evolves. Culture is the context within which every person inevitably lives his or her daily life.

The problem of 'Christ and culture' is ordinarily taken to mean the relationship between Christians and the prevailing culture in which they live. But this obscures an important point: even when Christians reject their surrounding culture, culture itself remains the medium of their existence as they create a Christian *subculture*. There is no such thing as a cultureless Christianity.

The historic positions

H. Richard Niebuhr's* classic book *Christ and Culture* outlines the five attitudes that Christians have historically taken to the question of culture. Both in history and in a Christian's individual life, there is no single response to culture.

The radical position is that Christ is *against* culture. Here culture is viewed as being hostile to Christianity in principle as well as practice. Regardless of the society in which Christians find themselves, they are called to oppose the customs and achievements of society. Commitment to Christ requires an either/or decision.

A second position is the Christ-*of*-culture attitude, which avows a fundamental harmony between Christ and culture. Christ himself is viewed as a supreme hero of culture. His life and teachings are the highest human achievement. Followers of Christ can accordingly trust culture to be essentially congruent with their own ideals, and they need not renounce their surrounding culture.

A third possibility is that Christ is *above* culture. This synthesist position affirms both Christ and culture while keeping them distinct. Christ is more than simply the hero of culture. He is higher and greater than culture and worthy of a greater allegiance. But culture also demands a Christian's participation. As citizens of two realms, Christians can live with a clear conscience in both worlds, even as Jesus, the God-man, did.

Fourthly, theologians like the apostle Paul and Luther* have held Christ and culture *in paradox*. This position is based on a duality that accepts the authority of both Christ and culture. Christians accordingly live in uneasy tension, trying to meet the demands of both authorities and longing for an eventual transhistorical salvation that will resolve the tension.

Finally, Christ can be viewed as the *transformer of culture*. The tradition of Augustine* and Calvin* has claimed that despite the fallenness of human culture, commitment to Christ allows a person to transform culture into a godly pursuit. Because Christ converts people and social institutions, Christians can carry on the work of God through their ordinary cultural activities.

Doctrinal underpinnings

A Christian endorsement of culture begins with the doctrine of creation.* This obligates Christians to claim the world for God and feeds their outrage over the degree to which God's world has been counterclaimed by Satan and evil. Christians have a cultural mandate as well as a creation mandate and missionary mandate.

A second key doctrine is the Fall* and the consequent evil for human nature and social institutions. For a Christian, culture is always on trial. It tends toward depravity (though more so in some times and places than in others). Like everything else in a fallen world, culture possesses a permanent tendency to cross the line from being good to being evil.

The Bible, however, does not locate evil in external forms *per se*. The world and human culture are capable of being turned to good use or bad use. The abuse of something does not invalidate the thing itself. The result is the need for moral responsibility in the pursuit of culture.

Christ's aphorism enjoining his followers to 'render to Caesar the things that are Caesar's, and to God the things that are God's' (Mt. 22:21, RSV) sums up the biblical theme that the institutions of society are part of God's design of human living and as such are worthy of their legitimate allegiance. But at the heart of Christianity is the conviction that 'the things of God' have a higher claim than the things of Caesar. Culture is always a secondary good.

The doctrine of vocation* – the belief that God calls people to specific tasks and gives them the abilities required to perform them – likewise feeds a Christian affirmation of culture. The Bible takes for granted (*e.g.* Gn. 4:20–22) that God calls some people to be farmers, others to be musicians, others to be homemakers – all of them callings with cultural connections.

The Christian conviction that for a redeemed person all of life is God's is summed up in the NT injunction that 'whether you eat or drink or whatever you do, do it all for the glory of God' (1 Cor. 10:31). For a Christian, even the most ordinary cultural pursuit can be part of living the God-centred life.

Bibliography

C. H. Kraft, *Christianity in Culture* (New York, 1979); H. R. Niebuhr, *Christ and Culture* (New York, 1951; London, 1952); L. Ryken, *Culture in Christian Perspective* (Portland, OR, 1986); J. R. W. Stott and R. T. Coote (eds.), *Down to Earth: Studies in Christianity and Culture* (Grand Rapids, 1980; London, 1981).

L.R.

CURSING, see BLESSING AND CURSING; OATHS.

D

DARWIN, CHARLES (1809–82). Darwin's great work *On the Origin of Species by means of Natural Selection, or the Preservation of Favoured Races in the Struggle for Life* (1859) was a landmark in the relationship between science* and the Christian faith. His theory was the first theory of organic evolution to give a plausible explanation, in terms of purely natural processes, of how living creatures had diversified into highly complex and beautiful forms by gradual changes over immense periods of time. In so doing it challenged at once the argument from design (that design implies a Designer), and also the idea (very widely held to represent the biblical teaching) that all species of plants and animals had been individually created as such, and at a time not more than a few thousand years ago. This was especially upsetting to many in the case of the human species, whom it seemed to deprive of the 'image of God'* and to reduce to purely animal status. The biblical concepts of sin (see Sin and Salvation⑤) and the Fall* seemed to lose their validity, as did any idea of a pre-ordained goal for human life. God had apparently been replaced by chance and necessity.

Darwinism has had a considerable impact on private morality, and also, in league with Herbert Spencer's (1820–1903) dictum of the 'survival of the fittest', on the spheres of business (see Economic Ethics;⑰ *e.g.* ruthless competition) and of political* ethics (*e.g.* racism). The issues raised by Darwin's theory are still very live, and the biblical doctrine of creation* is far from having succumbed to its challenge. In fact, in many ways the theory has been forced on the defensive, even if it has succeeded in causing interpreters to think again (as also did Copernicus' heliocentric theory) about some time-honoured but superficial understandings of the biblical text.

Bibliography

A. Desmond and J. Moore, *Darwin* (London, 1991); R. Forster and P. Marston, *Reason and Faith* (Eastbourne, 1989).

D.C.S.

DATA PROTECTION. Information which has been prepared so that it can be processed automatically by equipment (*e.g.* a computer), in response to instructions given for that purpose, is called 'data'. When data relates to an individual who can be identified from the data, or from the data in conjunction with other information in the possession of the data user, it is termed 'personal data'.

'Data protection' (or 'information privacy') involves persons and organizations which use and maintain personal data in accordance with ethical practices which promote the privacy* of individuals ('data subjects').

Personal privacy

In the days before personal computers had been invented, the British Government recognized that data held on powerful computers was becoming increasingly open to abuse in ways that posed threats to individual privacy. It appointed a committee, chaired by Sir Kenneth Younger (1941–), 'To consider whether legislation is needed to give further protection to the individual citizen and to commercial and industrial interests against intrusions into privacy by private persons and organizations or by companies and to make recommendations'. The committee's investigations were explicitly limited to the private sector (*The Report of the Committee on Privacy*, London, 1972).

Three years later, a Government White Paper was issued on *Computers and Privacy* (London, 1975), together with the supplement *Computers: Safeguards for Privacy* (London, 1975). These papers responded to the Younger Report relative to the private sector, and provided evidence that a parallel, but unpublished, study of confidentiality* in State computer installations had also taken place. In the White Paper, the Government proposed legislation, both to set standards governing the use of computers that handle personal information, and also to establish a permanent statutory agency to oversee the use of computers in both the public and private sectors, in order to ensure that they are operated with proper regard to privacy, and with the necessary safeguards for the personal information which they contain.

A further committee, chaired by Sir Norman Lindop (1921 –), was set up in 1976. Its terms of reference focused upon the narrower concern of computers and data processing. This committee reported in 1978, recommending various measures including the establishment of a Data Protection Authority (*Report of the Committee on Data Protection*, London, 1978).

The adoption by the British Government of the Council of Europe's 'Convention for the Protection of Individuals with Regard to Automatic Processing of Personal Data' (1981) led directly to the passing of the Data Protection Act (1984). A White Paper in 1982 had endorsed the Council of Europe's principles and proposed the establishment of the Data Protection Registrar. A Bill was brought before Parliament, and received the Royal Assent on 12 July 1984.

Concern over personal privacy, however, was probably not the only consideration in the minds of the legislators. Greville Janner (1927 –) described the main object of introducing the UK's Data Protection Act as 'to ensure that the UK is not excluded from various trade deals which involve the transport or transmission of personal data' ('Data Protection', in *Chemistry and Industry* 22, 18 November 1985, p. 747). This fear of losing contracts for lack of data protection legislation possibly played a decisive role in the Bill's progress: some Third World countries are now using such legislation to create non-tariff barriers around indigenous data processing companies. Such actions suggest that the main driving factor behind legislation is creation of corporate wealth, rather than protection of the individual citizen.

The Data Protection Act

The Council of Europe's 1981 Convention had two objectives: 1. to protect individuals in circumstances where information about them is processed automatically; and 2. to facilitate a common international standard of protection for individuals, such that the free flow of information across international boundaries can proceed properly. The Data Protection Act is therefore concerned with information about individuals which is processed by computer (personal data). It introduced significant new rights for data subjects. Such individuals generally have the right to: claim compensation for damage and any associated distress arising from the loss or unauthorized destruction or disclosure of personal data relating to him or herself, or arising from the inaccuracy of such data; have a copy of the information about himself or herself which is held on computer (the 'subject access' right); and challenge the information if he or she believes it to be wrong and, where appropriate, have it corrected or erased.

The Act obliges data users to be open about their practices (through the Data Protection Register) and to follow sound and proper practices (the Data Protection Principles). Computer bureaux have more limited obligations, mainly concerned with maintaining security around personal data. The Act established the Data Protection Registrar in a position of independence, reporting directly to Parliament. The Registrar is charged with administering the Act and supervising its operation.

Principles

The Act was designed to ensure that 'personal data' are used only in accordance with eight general principles, which are themselves intended to accord with the Council of Europe's Convention. All eight principles apply to data users, and the eighth applies only to data bureaux.

1. The information to be contained in personal data shall be obtained, and personal data shall be processed, fairly and lawfully.
2. Personal data shall be held only for one or more specified and lawful purposes.
3. Personal data held for any purpose or purposes shall not be used or disclosed in any manner incompatible with that purpose or those purposes.
4. Personal data held for any purpose or purposes shall be adequate, relevant and not excessive in relation to that purpose or purposes.
5. Personal data shall be accurate and, where necessary, kept up to date.
6. Personal data held for any purpose or purposes shall not be kept longer than is necessary for that purpose or those purposes.
7. An individual shall be entitled:
   a. at reasonable intervals and without undue delay or expense:
      i. to be informed by any data user whether he holds personal data of which that individual is subject, and
      ii. to access to any such data held by a data user; and
   b. where appropriate, to have such data corrected or erased.
8. Appropriate security measures shall be taken against unauthorized access to, or alteration, disclosure or destruction of, personal data and against accidental loss or destruction of personal data.

(For a more detailed discussion see D. Campbell and S. Connor, *On The Record: Surveillance, Computers and Privacy – The Inside Story*, London, 1986, p. 32.)

Proposals for a new European law of privacy

In 1992, the European Commission published an amended proposal for a Council Directive, to strengthen individuals' rights of information privacy and self-determination (*Amended Proposal for a Data Protection Directive*, 15 October 1992).

Changes from the current UK position are being proposed, principally widening the definitions of what constitutes 'personal data' and 'processing' so as to remove many existing restrictions, and requiring that the data subject's consent* must normally be obtained to his or her information being processed. The aim is to achieve a link between securing free flows of personal data within the European Union, and acknowledging the potential for abuse of personal information, both in the private and public sector, by unrestricted data flows.

Challenges in the information age

The ubiquitous 'chip' has now become an integral part of our daily lives, enhancing the storage and communication of data and information in many ways, *e.g.* personal computers, fax machines, wireless digital networks, cellular phones, cable TV, direct mail, telephone calling line identity (CLI) and credit cards. These and other cultural changes are now moving us towards a global economy. For example, information-gathering for taxation purposes which previously required whole populations to move across countries (*e.g.* Lk. 2:1 – 4), can now be accomplished by electronically harvesting individual data records from disparate sources (*e.g.* Inland Revenue records, bank and credit-card account data, supermarket EPOS [electronic point-of-sale] systems, immigration records, telephone call-billing systems, petrol-station sales records, credit reference agency data banks), and by using 'fuzzy logic' techniques to identify matching data items, thus building up a composite record of an individual's lifestyle. Never before has it been possible to undertake such wholesale monitoring of people's activity using multiple data records which, although not ordinarily sensitive on their own, become so in combination. Some have argued (*e.g.* see L. Ellis, ed., *Privacy and the Computer: Steps to Practicality*, London, 1972) that if each type of data is protected against deliberate theft and careless disclosure, regardless of whether held on computer or other files, the extent of extra precautions necessary to prevent combinations would be minimized.

Problems arise, however, when attempting to link records which have been collected at different times and for different purposes. Credit-card companies need to have very fast access to account details using the card number alone, but nevertheless want to be able to know which cards have been issued to an individual. They might allocate a unique code which, although it may suffice for a small credit-card company, could result in a number of individuals sharing the same code. To avoid such problems, most data users key their data on existing codes (*e.g.* employees' National Insurance numbers), which they hope will reduce the likelihood of duplications. Various government attempts at uniquely numbering individuals (*e.g.* the 'Australia card') have met with stoic resistance. Current initiatives are therefore carried out in a more covert manner, and have even been marketed as beneficial (*e.g.* the proposed UK NHS number, which will allow any doctor in the country to gain 'immediate access to a patient's computerized medical history').

This revolution in electronic digital communication brings with it a disturbing erosion of privacy. In the past, if the government wanted to violate the privacy of ordinary citizens, it had to expend a certain amount of effort to intercept letters and monitor spoken telephone conversations. Philip R. Zimmermann (1954–), in his evidence to the US House of Representatives Subcommittee for Economic Policy, Trade, and the Environment in October 1993 (reported in the electronic publication *Computer Underground Digest* 6.30, 1994), likened this approach to catching fish with a hook and a line, one fish at a time. He contrasted it with the process of gathering information from electronic mail: 'Today, electronic mail is gradually replacing conventional paper mail . . . Unlike paper mail, E-mail messages are just too easy to intercept and scan for interesting keywords. This can be done easily, routinely, automatically, and undetectably on a grand scale. This is analogous to drift-net fishing – making a quantitative and qualitative Orwellian difference to the health of democracy.'

What can be done to limit further large-scale abuses? One of the most effective strategies seems to be the swift and massive expression of public disapproval. In 1991, 30,000 complaints were received by Lotus Development Corporation against its proposed *Lotus Marketplace: Households* database, resulting in its demise (see T. Forester and P. Morrison, *Computer Ethics*). This product was to have contained a vast amount of data on 120 million N. Americans, including their names, addresses, estimated incomes, consumer preferences and other personal details. In effect, anyone with a suitable personal computer could purchase a copy for $750 and use the information to his or her own ends (*e.g.* searching for the names and addresses of all single women over seventy years of age would be useful for aspiring burglars).

To create a greater awareness of the dangers inherent in computer use, there is much to be said for ensuring that discussion of the broader ethical issues forms an integral part of all professional computing courses (D. B. Paradice, 'Ethical Attitudes of Entry-level MIS Personnel', *Information and Management* 18, March 1990, pp. 143–151). It seems all too easy to limit such discussions to the issues of virus propagation and software copyright protection. However, it needs to be appreciated that there are much weightier ethical matters, which need ongoing consideration as the technology evolves.

Clearly the information age has taken us by surprise: standards of personal privacy that had become enshrined in law and tradition are seen to be inadequate to meet the challenges that technological change is forcing upon us. Everyone who is involved with processing personal data has a responsibility to become involved in shaping the way that data can be used. It is not enough simply to leave the setting of limits to our legislators. As Zimmerman says: 'When making public policy decisions about new technologies for the Government, I think one should ask oneself which technologies would best strengthen the hand of a police state. Then, do not allow the Government to deploy those technologies. This is simply a matter of good civic hygiene' (*Computer Underground Digest* 6.30, 1994).

Bibliography

J. E. Ettinger (ed.), *Information Security: An Integrated Approach* (London, 1993); T. Forester and P. Morrison, *Computer Ethics: Cautionary Tales and Dilemmas in Computing* (London, ²1994); W. Madsen, *Handbook of Personal Data Protection* (Basingstoke, 1992); R. A. J. Middleton (ed.) *Guidelines on Good Security Practice* (Swindon, 1990).

G.K.S.

DEACONS, see MINISTRY.

DEADLY SINS. Originating probably among the Egyptian Desert Fathers of the 4th century, lists of central or leading ('capital') sins were, throughout the Middle

Ages and beyond, a much-used device for organizing reflection about spiritual psychology and ordering the life of the confessional. Although the lists vary in content and length, the following catalogue of seven is fairly standard: pride,* envy (see Jealousy and Envy*), anger,* sloth, greed (see Covetousness*), gluttony and lust.*

These sins are thought to be grounds, or types, of a number of other sins, so that in its elaboration the list of seven can cover quite a wide variety of wayward attitudes, motives and deeds, and help to identify diagnostically interesting connections between sins. Although the seven are popularly called 'deadly sins', not all instances of sins going by these names would count as mortal, rather than venial, among theologians who countenance this distinction. A sin is *mortal* only if the agent treats some creature as an end more glorious than God, thus dishonouring and disobeying God and alienating himself or herself from God, the source of his or her life. *Venial* sins, by contrast, do not involve inordinate exaltation of created things. For example, a sin of gluttony might be committed through weakness of will, rather than through considering pâté de fois gras as more glorious than God. Or a person might love riches more than he or she ought to, yet without loving them so much that they compete with God for his or her allegiance. Roman Catholic and early Lutheran theologians accept the distinction between mortal and venial sins, but Reformed thinkers reject it, holding that all sins alienate the sinner from God, and thus are mortal.

Whether or not all sins are mortal, it seems that the kind of careful and detailed psychological description of them and their consequences, that is occasioned by pastoral preoccupation with the lists, can deepen the life of faith and our appreciation of Christ's grace in overcoming our sins and restoring us to fellowship with God. It can heighten our understanding of the Christian virtues* and our zeal for cultivating them, as well as our understanding of how to cultivate them, through co-operation with the indwelling Holy Spirit.*

Pride is a perverted attitude towards one's own excellence. As defined with God in view, it is a perception of oneself as self-sufficient with respect to one's life and righteousness.* As defined with other humans in view, pride is a perception of oneself as having special personal worth because of one's superiority, in some respect, to others. Humility* is the counterpart virtue, namely the perception of oneself as dependent on God for righteousness and life, and as equal before God (and thus equal in personal value) with one's human brothers and sisters.

Envy is a disposition to be displeased at another person's excellence because it seems to demean one. Thus, in the struggle for self-worth (see Self-esteem*) the envious person wishes to 'put down' others who seem to be doing well. The perverted logic of envy is that others' doing less well means that I am worth more, since personal worth is an essentially competitive prize. Envy is usually largely unacknowledged by the envier, as it constitutes an admission of being the loser in this important competition. As a form of hostility to the alienation from my brother and sister, envy is a violation of my created nature as bonded to him or her in love, and a rejection of the God who created me so. In its competitive logic, envy is closely related to pride, and its counterpart virtue, like pride's, is humility: the heartfelt acknowledgment that, whatever differences of excellence may exist between us, this brother and I are equally glorious before God, being his beloved children.

Anger, unlike envy, is not an essentially perverse type of emotion. It is the concerned perception that another person has culpably offended in some way and deserves punishment, and such a perception may very well be true and just. It is, however, 'judgmental': the angry person 'judges' the other to be in the wrong, and takes himself or herself to be occupying the moral high ground. Such an attitude, in a sinner, must always be a provisional, passing state of mind. When it is heightened into contempt for the offender, or hardened into grudge-bearing against him or her, or permitted to issue in significant vengeful behaviour, it is a denial of one's place in God's economy – namely, the place of a forgiven sinner and brother or sister to the offender. Forgiveness* is the most obvious counterpart virtue.

Sloth is a lack of enthusiasm for God and his kingdom. It is a spiritual torpor, a faintheartedness for the life of faith (see Accidie*), an unwillingness to venture much if anything for God. It is a carelessness about one's duties of worship and service, a willingness to settle for spiritual mediocrity, triviality and banality. It is not the same as ordinary laziness or boredom; one can be slothful and yet quite enthusiastic about one's art, career, wealth, fame and health. The ill effects of sloth can, however, be expected to manifest themselves in a despair that is detectable by spiritual directors and that may lead to more publicly observable symptoms. The virtue counterpart of sloth is full-hearted love for God.

Greed is inordinate love of possessions. This is an especially clear case of 'capital' sin, since it so obviously begets other sins such as stinginess, injustice, treachery, fraud, lying, restlessness, violence and callousness to the needs of others. The chief counterpart virtue is perhaps generosity.

Gluttony and *lust*, unlike the other sins in the list, are carnal, *i.e.* perversions of physical appetites. But it is in our attitude to these appetites, and in the appetites as affected by our attitudes, and in our voluntary behavioural response to the appetites – rather than in the simple physical appetites themselves – that the sin may reside. Our appetites can be shaped, to some extent, by our 'view' of them and of their objects. For example, we can see the sexual appetite as a gift by which God bonds us to our spouses and encourages us to beget children – or we may see it just as a source of pleasure for ourselves as individuals. And we may see persons to whom we are not married as children of God who to us are sexual aliens, or we may fantazize about them as 'fair game'. The assimilation of such alternative views into our appetites and our habitual behavioural responses to our appetites make the difference between sin – alienation from God's order and thus from God – and the life of growing holiness in Jesus Christ.

Bibliography

K. Barth, *CD* IV/2, pp. 403–483 (on sloth); Thomas Aquinas, *STh* 1a2ae 84 (the list of capital sins), 1a2ae88 (venial and mortal sin), 2a2ae 118 (greed), 2a2ae 153–4 (lust), 2a2ae 162 (pride), 2a2ae36 (envy), 2a2ae 158 (anger), 2a2ae 35 (sloth).

R.C.R.

DEATH AND DYING. The Christian view of death and dying is so at variance with a secular view, and indeed that of most other faiths, that conflicts often arise about this within individuals and families, and both within and between societies. To the secular mind, death is an ultimate disaster, to be averted or postponed as far as possible. The Christian view is that death happens to all (Rom. 5:12), and is to be accepted where the dying process makes it inevitable (2 Pet. 1:13–14), but averted where this is not the case (Lk. 10:30–37). For the Christian, death is not the ultimate disintegration, though it is in a sense a 'sacrament' or outward sign of universal sinfulness (Rom. 5:12b). The endowment of a new body of a kind foreign to this present age (1 Cor. 15:35–54) renders death an essential preparation for resurrection* in Christ (1 Cor. 15:49). So, what matters most is not death, but a person's union with Christ (2 Cor. 5:17).

Further, secular views are strangely contradictory. On the one hand, death is seen as the ultimate terror to be avoided or postponed, even by exaggerated medical means which are doomed to fail (*cf.* the technological prolongation of the life of General Franco). On the other hand, a life can be regarded as so broken, disabled or fading as to be not worthwhile, or of no social value, and hence it may be neglected or even extinguished by voluntary or involuntary euthanasia.*

The Christian view is that exaggerated medical means ought not to be employed to prolong life unnecessarily, especially when used out of consideration for a dying person's wealth or status. Furthermore, to neglect the needs of the poor, the disabled or the disadvantaged is evil, even if it is 'economical'; life is not ours to extinguish, since it belongs to God (see Sanctity of Human Life*). These arguments relate to all kinds of human life, whether it be the unborn child (see Abortion*), the infant (see Infanticide*), the disabled or the dying. To relieve the suffering of the dying is, however, a Christian aim.

Global ethical (see ⒂) issues of resource allocation (see Health and Health Care*) abound. Christian mission has been in the forefront of medical aid and famine relief to refugees, the underprivileged, epidemic victims and prisoners, for the kinds of spiritual and ethical reasons just given; health care always accompanies the gospel as a matter of Christian integrity (*e.g.* Mt. 11:4–6).

Death and dying are the ends of a process which begins in everyone from conception; even our bodily form is shaped in part by the death of some of its proliferations before birth. Ageing* is a part of dying, and leads to death whether by accident or disease. Hence the Christian church has never sought to disguise or feign the absence of this normal process, but rather to look forward to the vital nature of the life beyond (Mt. 16:25–28).

It is inevitable that stress* within and between individuals and families will occur in relation to death; this is reflected in medical choice, in cosmetic activities, and in the types and styles of funerals. It is essential and right to allow sorrow for separation from loved ones, and for a normal bereavement* reaction. This usually takes from six to nine months or more, and may begin after the period of brave bearing (or even denial) is over, some time after a death has occurred. Equally, before death, it is essential to understand and allow for natural reactions of denial, anger,* acquiescence or distress, as these occur successively in a terminal illness. It is also important to remember how an illness may itself modify even normal reactions, or a person's habitual temperament, to face death. Even so, a Christian reaction to these sad events is changed qualitatively by the hope of the resurrection (e.g. Jn. 11:21–27; 1 Thes. 4:13).

The discussion of spiritual topics with the dying is a vital pastoral concern; many dying people are too confused or toxic to grasp abstract or new ideas, though lucid intervals often occur. It is best to approach such topics through the sufferers' own immediate concerns, through what is at the top of their agenda. This may be fear,* pain* or concern for those who will remain. Often it is simplest to encourage prayer,* and assure them of its being made for them; then to point to the worthiness of the one to whom the prayer is made, and the special characteristics which fit him uniquely to be the Saviour, ours and theirs. Many dying people need only to be reminded of a trust* which they have ceased to exercise, or of which they have never seen their need to use before. No-one can help a dying person, or their near and dear ones, who has not faced and come to terms with his or her own dying, for pretence is no comfort. Particular problems which may arise include when and if attempts at spiritual healing* are sought, the disposition of the patient's property* and wills,* and the need for reconciliation* with alienated friends or family.

A time of dying evokes many reactions within relatives and friends, not all of them helpful. Some evince guilt* about past events, or what they might have done to help; often this takes the form of exaggerated blame for others, even for the dying. Others distance themselves, because they do not know what to do or say, or because their own distress is their chief concern. So pastors find themselves caring not only for the dying, but for their circle as well. It is essential to be able to listen, and to find time for this; to decide who to meet together or separately, and how far to go with each.

In general, as in the hospice* movement, it is essential to move so as to lessen fear and isolation, to aid people to meet rather than to remain apart, to encourage, explain and interpret the numerous small incidents which may cause needless fear or distress. Medical help should aim for care and comfort, not cure; to be open in its reasons rather than secretive; to respect the wishes of the sufferer the most wherever it seems right and reasonable so to do, rather than to impose traditional approaches as to 'what we do'.

It is essential for pastor and medical carers to collaborate in 'shared care', not to compete or to deny others their proper place in caring; carers must aim to treat problems in the interests of the dying person and their relatives, not to serve themselves. Perhaps the greatest element of Christian care is love (see [2]), which is not replaceable by even the most otherwise-competent medicine or care. The Good Samaritan is the Lord's example of loving competence; as 'purchaser' he channelled the 'provider' function of the innkeeper, monitoring its performance (Lk. 10:33–36); this seems to be the best model for a Christian view of resource allocation for the seriously ill. The things that happen when someone dies, or nearly dies, shape the emotions and living of those about them who must live on with those memories.

See also: ETHICS OF MEDICAL CARE; [14] LIFE, HEALTH AND DEATH. [13]

Bibliography
E. Kübler-Ross, On Death and Dying (New York, 1969; London, 1970); S. E. Lammers and A. Verhey (eds.), On Moral Medicine (Grand Rapids, 1987); C. M. Parkes, 'Bereavement', MI 94, 1991, pp. 3928–3929; P. Ramsey, Ethics at the Edges of Life (New Haven, CT, 1978).

D.W.V.

DEATH, DEFINITION OF, see BRAIN DEATH; LIFE, HEALTH AND DEATH; [13] TRANSPLANT SURGERY.

DEBT is an obligation to pay for prior receipts of goods, services or money. The assumption of personal debt (not commercial debt) is clearly discouraged in Scripture, though not forbidden. Most of the biblical references to debt focus on the relationship between prosperous creditors and financially weak debtors, but Scripture also warns against the practice of using 'borrowed' funds to enhance one's standard of living (Hab. 2:6–8). Just as God desires people to be free from sin (1 Jn. 2:1–6), he also wants his people to be unencumbered by debt (Dt. 15:1–2). Both sin and debt are enslaving and destructive if they are not covered and eliminated. The more important concerns regarding debt are:

1. *Duration of debt.* When personal debt is deemed necessary, how long should the loan remain outstanding? The law placed a seven-year limit on debt (Dt. 15:1–11; 31:10–11). In fact, specific 'seventh years' were to be designated throughout the land as the time for cancelling debts. Cancellation was to take place during the Feast of Tabernacles (Dt. 31:10). This was to provide a time for community-wide celebration when everybody was to be released from their debt burdens (see Jubilee*). These instructions regarding debt were given to limit the lenders, not the borrowers, for they were in the positions of financial power. In this arrangement, the lender knew that if he loaned a sum of money that could not reasonably be repaid by the year of release, then the balance of the obligation was to be forgiven. This required the lender to care for the long-term best interest of those who were financially distressed. This principle of the prosperous and powerful being under obligation to care for the long-term best interest of the weak and needy overflows into every area of the Bible's teaching, not just creditor/borrower relationships (Pr. 29:7; 31:8–9; Je. 5:28).

Are these OT financial principles (a seven-year limit on debt; forgiving all debts not repaid in seven years; the financially strong being obligated to act in the best financial interest of the financially weak) practical or useful in modern society? They are clearly ignored today, and our debt burdens and the percentage of our income used to service our debts would be much less if God's wisdom were heeded. It is ignored to our own harm.

2. *Commands to give and lend.* We are called upon by God to both 'give' and 'lend' to our neighbours (Mt. 5:42; Lk. 6:30–35).

When are we to give, and when should we lend? We give to those who have legitimate authority to ask for our money. For example, taxing authorities have this right (Rom. 13:5–7). We are to give to those who have immediate, acute needs – the hungry, naked and cold (1 Jn. 3:16–18). There are times, however, when lending and not giving is the loving response to a genuine need (Dt. 15:7–8; Lk. 6:30–35). It is in everyone's best long-term interest for individuals to assume the full responsibility, and its accompanying obligations, for the well-being of themselves and their dependents. Lending to the needy, when there is no real chance of repayment, positions the act of lending (without expecting to get it back) as one of true charity. By this act, though, the recipients are enabled both to maintain their self-respect and to acknowledge the basic truth that they should, if at all possible, care for themselves. It allows the borrowers to affirm their desire and hope to be able to meet their obligations. It allows the lender to emulate God who forgives our debts, as we are expected to forgive our debtors (Mt. 6:12–14; 18:21–35).

3. *Guaranteeing another's debt repayment.* We are on occasions asked by friends or acquaintances to help them secure loans. Should a person endorse or co-sign a debt obligation for the benefit of another person? Scripture provides strenuous and explicit warnings against doing this, *e.g.* 'Do not . . . pledge . . . if you lack the means to pay' or else you will find yourself suffering unaffordable losses (Pr. 22:26–27; see also 11:15). The reasons for caution are deeper than a potential financial loss, though. The relationship between a borrower and the endorser or co-signer is altered when such a financial arrangement is entered into. An adverse outcome can easily damage the theretofore friendly association. And, finally, the inability of the primary borrower to be able to secure the loan as an independent party is clear evidence that he or she is not yet in a position to assume such a financial risk independently. The borrowers are trying to reach beyond their current financial ability in such situations.

4. *Obligation to repay debts.* Is there a moral defence for a debtor declaring bankruptcy? There is no such defence if the borrower has a cavalier attitude from the time the money was borrowed, reasoning that, if things turn financially sour, the money will not need to be repaid because the obligation is avoidable in

bankruptcy court. Seeking voluntary bankruptcy under the civil law is not prescribed in Scripture. However, the Bible instructs us to seek release directly from those for whom we have entered into guarantees if we need to do so (Pr. 6:1–5). The righteous also give their word and honour it, even when doing so creates personal hurt (Ps. 15:4). Scripture defines borrowing and not paying back as wickedness (Ps. 37:21). Suppose, however, the creditors force the borrower into involuntary bankruptcy, and the court, after distributing all assets, declares the debtor absolved from the unpaid balances. Is a Christian in such a case still morally obligated to pay? In such a situation, continuing to repay a legally excused debt is a powerful testimony to the unbelieving world of the integrity of the debtor, and in doing this the Christian emulates the unchanging character of God who honours his word in all circumstances (Nu. 23:19; Tit. 1:2; Heb. 6:13–20). Are we not called to be like our heavenly Father?

5. *Speculative borrowing.* The world tells us that borrowing is good, especially if we hope to profit by it. But is it morally defensible: a. to borrow money that is not needed, for the purpose of using it in the hope that it can be repaid later in cheaper monetary units (currency that is devalued through inflation); or b. to plan on selling assets purchased with the loan money at a hoped-for higher price in the future in order to make a profit and repay the loan (*e.g.* buy stock with borrowed money and hope it will appreciate)? Scripture warns us against such speculation which may fail and cause us to lose more than the value of the assets we acquired (Pr. 22:7; Hab. 2:6–7). Why does one desire to speculate with borrowed money in the first place? Scripture calls us to examine our hearts to see if greed and covetousness* are present. Beware of them (Pr. 11:6; Is. 56:11; Lk. 12:15; Rom. 1:29; 2 Pet. 2:14)!

6. *National debt.* Biblically, a nation that maintains a creditor (lending) position, rather than a debtor (borrowing) position, is seen as bearing the mark of God's special blessings (Dt. 15:6; 28:12–13). This is so, for nations that borrow must accept controls on their economic policies and thereby become subject to the restraints imposed by the creditors. And a portion of their wealth is soon transferred out of the nation to one's foreign creditors. This eliminates the opportunity to use the wealth (interest and principal repayment) in one's own nation. Thus the capital used to repay the borrowings, both interest and principal, must be less than the returns earned on the borrowed funds, or else the borrowing nation will be weakened financially. Nations, as individuals, should avoid debt whenever possible.

7. *Other topics related to debt.* In addition to the aforementioned topics there are others in which God expresses an interest, such as: a. the differences to be observed when lending to 'believers' and 'non-believers' (Dt. 15:3); b. questions of usury (Lv. 25:35–38); c. special external hardships (*e.g.* famine) that force borrowing (Ne. 5:1–13); d. restoring borrowed collateral (Lv. 25:35–38; Dt. 24:10–13); e. choosing servitude as a means of avoiding welfare (Lv. 25:47–48); and f. the issues surrounding banking* and commercial lending (Mt. 21:12; 25:27; Lk. 19:23).

See also: INTEREST.

R.C.C.

DECALOGUE. The Ten Commandments (or the Decalogue) have been widely observed throughout church history as a summary but comprehensive exposition of God's requirements for right behaviour (sometimes called the 'moral law'). Tertullian* declared that they were written on human hearts long before they were engraved on stone. Thomas Aquinas* called them God's reminders to human beings of duties which sin has obscured. And John Calvin* described the process of sanctification* as 'ever more complete obedience to the Ten Commandments'.

Old Testament scholars debate the origin and literary history of the Decalogue (which is recorded twice, with minor differences, in Ex. 20 and Dt. 5), but do not dispute its centrality. It forms the basis of the Pentateuch's civil and criminal law codes (see Law, Civil and Criminal*), together with their penology.

The Decalogue's place in Christian decision-making is subject to all the hermeneutical considerations which arise whenever the relevance of OT law* is considered (see Old Testament Ethics[8]). Apart from the culture gap which is exposed in the wording of the second, fourth and tenth commandments, most of the Decalogue is cast in a negative form and addressed to the individual – thus obscuring (some would say) the roles of positive values and social morality. Moreover, the emphasis on actions and words in all but the tenth commandment needs supplementing by Jesus' stress on attitudes and motives.*

The Decalogue does, however, display continuity with Jesus' ethical teaching. Both are theocentric, rooted in the related concepts of covenant* and kingdom,* and their demands are presented as right human responses to God's prior acts of grace. When read in this light, with its principles exposed, the Decalogue still retains its Christian ethical bite.

D.H.F.

DECEPTION, see FRAUD; TRUTH.

DECLARATION OF GENEVA, see HIPPOCRATIC OATH.

DEFENCE MECHANISMS, PSYCHOLOGICAL. The literature contains many different definitions. Charles Morris defines defence mechanisms as 'the way people react to frustration and conflict by deceiving themselves about their real desires and goals in an effort to maintain their self-esteem and avoid anxiety' (*Psychology*, p. 439). Others say that defence mechanisms are essential to help cope with failure and are a way of maintaining a positive self-image. However, in some situations the defence mechanism may stop a person from doing the appropriate thing.

Sigmund Freud,* the first person to focus on defence mechanisms, studied the subtle ways that people try to deceive themselves and others. His work was developed by Anna Freud (1895–1982). The classic studies of ego-defence mechanisms are rooted in the Freudian tradition. Defence mechanisms protect from anxiety,* which occurs when individuals' desires clash with the image they have of themselves. Behavioural psychology views defence mechanisms as psychological and verbal activities which protect people from unpleasant experiences. These occur when a person's actual behaviour clashes with the way in which he or she has learned to behave from 'significant' people.

There are at least forty different types of defence mechanisms, the main ones being:

Denial. Personal responsibility is rejected for actions. Reality is denied. The person may deny things that are known to be true, *e.g.* refusing to believe that a loved one has just died.

Distortion. A person reshapes the external reality to suit his or her inner needs. This can frequently involve some grand delusion; it may even involve 'hearing' voices from God.

Repression. * Feelings, impulses or motives that are unacceptable are pushed into the unconscious* and prevented from becoming conscious, *e.g.* a memory of being attacked, which is too painful to deal with, is 'forgotten'. This mechanism is often seen as the primary defence mechanism upon which all the others are based.

Regression. The person faced with conflict returns to an earlier stage of emotional immaturity at which he or she felt safer and protected, *e.g.* a child of six may regress to infancy and start bed-wetting.

Rationalization. A person justifies unacceptable attitudes, beliefs and behaviour by trying to explain his or her actions or blaming other people for the problems.

Projection. A person will not come to terms with his or her own attributes, and so instead accuses someone else of that attribute. Angry people do not see their own anger but accuse someone else of being angry.

Displacement. An individual transfers an emotion from its original object to something which may seem less threatening, *e.g.* a man who cannot be angry with his boss takes his anger out on his wife.

Suppression (similar to repression). People postpone dealing with conscious conflict. They fool themselves into thinking that they will deal with the conflict later, but never do.

Intellectualization. This can look very like rationalization. A person avoids difficult feelings, such as severe feelings of inferiority, by use of intellectual language, discussions and philosophizing.

Attribution of blame. People shift the blame away from themselves. The fault is said always to lie with someone else, with circumstances or with God.

D. Powlison challenges the traditional view of defence mechanisms. He argues that to view them as a set of intrapsychic mechanisms totally misses out the interpersonal component. A person's defence mechanisms can affect the people with whom he or she is in contact. How one views defence mechanisms is important. If one holds the view that they are thought to be unconscious and therefore people cannot be held accountable for them, then there is the danger of Pelagianism (refusing responsibility before God for whatever the person is not in complete control of). In reality, unconscious and conscious behaviour are not easy to distinguish. In Scripture people are held accountable for their actions whether they are aware of them or not. So even if a defence mechanism is unconscious, the person is accountable for it and for its effect upon other people.

Scripture illustrates certain defence mechanisms, *e.g.* Saul projects his own hostility on to David (1 Sa. 19:9–10). Defence mechanisms are basically a form of deceit and therefore sinful. This is addressed in Pr. 14:8, 'The folly of fools is deception.' Jeremiah, too, avers that 'The heart is deceitful above all things, and desperately wicked: who can know it?' (Je. 17:9, AV). Since defence mechanisms involve people in being deceitful to themselves and to others there is often a need gently to peel them away and replace them with truth: this is often part of the task of therapy or counselling.

Bibliography

A. Freud, *The Ego and Mechanisms of Defence* (London, 1937); C. Morris, *Psychology: An Introduction* (Englewood Cliffs, NJ, 1973); D. Powlison, 'Human Defensiveness: The Third Way', *JPP* 8.1, 1985.

H.C.H.

DEFENCE: MILITARY AND CIVIL.
'Military defence' is the deployment of armed forces to protect a nation against attack, or the threat of attack, by another nation. 'Civil defence' means the non-military precautions taken to reduce loss of life and property in the event of attack.

1. In *military defence*, no hard-and-fast line can be drawn between preparation for defence and for attack. In order to defend oneself, it may be the best policy to attack enemy forces. Defence includes not only measures to meet attack, but measures to prevent attack by attacking first. The need for deterrence* is also included in defence.

The system of military defence comprises not only the armed forces and their weapons, but also a large infrastructure of research, communications, supply, administration, *etc.* The maintenance of a defence force that is appropriate to a nation's political situation is an important obligation if it be allowed that one of its functions is to restrain evil-doers (Rom. 13:3–4). In a world of armed nation-states, each nation has a duty to maintain forces that are adequate in order to deter and prevent the possibility of armed conflict, by so ensuring that there is little or nothing to be gained from initiating it. However, this is not to justify any and all defence measures.

It is also a nation's political duty to act so as to build international trust and to reduce the chances of war. It is important to maintain only forces which are appropriate, neither too weak nor too large. Inadequate forces may give the wrong signals (as, for instance, British naval reductions before the Argentine invasion of the Falkland Islands). Excessive forces may be maintained out of anxiety or a misplaced concern for total security, in ways that do little to build international peace and security.

Christian attitudes to participation in military defence obviously depend on the individual's attitude to war.* Pacifists* who see no Christian justification for participating in war will not be able to participate in good conscience in the majority of defence preparations. There may be exceptions, *e.g.* in areas of preserving life and civil society, such as researching and preparing antidotes for new weapons. Those who accept the just-war theory* will be ready to be employed in the work of defence. But they too will wish to consider the nature of their involvement with care. Some, for instance, might question the justification for nuclear deterrence (see Deterrence, Nuclear*) and with it work on nuclear weapons. The same could be said about chemical and biological warfare, while recognizing that one has to understand the nature of the offensive weapons in order to be able to take adequate precautions against them.

2. The need for *civil defence* is a response chiefly to aerial warfare. The idea is to take precautions to protect populations against bombs and rockets, whether carrying conventional explosives, nuclear bombs, or chemical or biological weapons. It dates back effectively to the Second World War. Since then, attempts have been made in some countries to take precautions against nuclear bombs. These include the USA and the UK, but the most systematic work appears to have been carried out in the former Soviet Union.

There are a number of measures characteristic of civil defence. They include: blackouts; provision of shelters, gas masks and first aid; evacuation of cities; the provision of warning and communication systems; firefighting measures, including the reduction of fire hazards and designing firebreaks; strengthening buildings; and providing duplicate and emergency services. The need for, and extent of, civil defence provision obviously varies with the international political climate; but many physical aspects, such as design of cities or building underground shelters, require long-term planning.

Some pacifist groups have opposed civil defence, arguing that defence against nuclear attack is futile and that such defence encourages the acceptance of war as inevitable. These arguments do not seem compelling, and to some extent they run in opposing directions. It is widely agreed that large-scale nuclear war would be destructive on an unprecedented scale. But more limited kinds of war may take place, and there seems no good reason not to take some reasonable precautions to save life and property in such an eventuality if we can. It is hard to believe that civil defence could encourage anyone to go to war, or in any way make war more likely. Of course, a nation determined on war would very likely take civil defence more seriously, but the logic does not run the other way.

D.J.E.A.

DEFORESTATION may be defined as clearance of forest or woodland for another land use. Such clearance is now occurring in most tropical countries at an even faster rate than in recent years. In 1990 deforestation in the tropics was estimated to average 16.8 million hectares per year or rather more than 1% per year of the whole tropical forest resource (Dembner, 'Provisional Data from the Forest Resources Assessment 1990 Project'). In temperate regions forest clearance and forest creation are more or less in balance, with most countries now promoting policies leading to net increase in forest cover.

Consequences

Deforestation in the tropics has three serious consequences: 1. destruction of some of the richest ecosystems in the world and the inevitable extinction of some plant and animal species; 2. release of huge amounts of carbon dioxide, from the carbon stored in wood and organic matter, which is an important 'greenhouse' gas contributing to global warming; and, most importantly, 3. displacement of many tribal peoples, shifting cultivators and other forest dwellers and users. Lesser, but still locally significant, consequences of clearance are increased risk of soil erosion and flash floods, desertification, and changed microclimate. Taking together these consequences and the scale at which deforestation is occurring, the resultant, continuing destruction is a calamity.

Over the centuries some deforestation has been necessary to provide land for farming as populations have risen, but today the great bulk of remaining forest is on land ill suited to settled agriculture. Indeed, all the richest volcanic and sedimentary soils of the tropics have long been cleared of their natural vegetation for cultivation. However, timber and other forest products are valuable commodities, the realization of which cannot be wholly denied a nation or country. The challenge is to devise ways of sustainable management that will make forests a genuinely renewable resource: experience has shown the exceeding difficulty of this in the tropics (M. E. D. Poore, No Timber without Trees).

Causes

Tropical deforestation is a complex phenomenon. The immediate causes may be listed as shifting cultivation, clearance for agriculture, logging, developing mineral exploitation and other industries, wars, transmigration and urbanization, wildfires and, especially in the drier tropics, overgrazing and overcutting of woodland and savanna for firewood, poles and fodder. However, the pressures which precipitate these quintessentially human activities mostly flow from economic dictates, such as North–South* trade flows and excessive Western consumption, corruption and nepotism realizing forest wealth for personal gain, and from land laws and land policies that are environmentally bad, such as transmigration in Brazil and Indonesia, and villagization in Tanzania and Ethiopia.

Increasing population is largely not to blame. Although population growth rates in tropical countries are rising, unavailability of food, fuel and other needs, leading to pressure on dwindling forests, has more to do with enormous inequity in land ownership, inadequate means of distribution of food and other resources, and selfish profiteering and environmental disregard. The earth is so blessed that it is easily able to feed its present population, as agricultural surpluses testify.

Responses

Deforestation issues are high on political agendas owing, in large part, to pressure from environmental groups. This increased awareness grew in the 1980s and, as far as it goes, is to be applauded. The international response has been less encouraging, with the main initiative being the *Tropical Forestry Action Plan* of the Food and Agriculture Organization. This programme has brought donors and other agencies together and further focused attention, but has not yet seriously addressed the prime causes of deforestation. Under consideration is a proposal for an international forestry instrument to regulate forest use world-wide, but any agreement is remote. All these inadequacies are not surprising, since the causes of deforestation are overwhelmingly the product of human nature. Addressing this fundamental issue of sin, greed and selfishness is, of course, what the gospel of Christ confronts and is where, ultimately, the only solution lies.

On a practical level increased tree-planting can help deflect pressures from natural forest, but can never substitute all the values of such forest or, so far, produce the high-quality timbers sought from tropical forests, with the important exception of teak (J. Evans, *Plantation Forestry in the Tropics*). Planting does offer ways of alleviating domestic needs for fuel and building materials through programmes of social forestry, and can aid food production through agroforestry. It is not a panacea, but is undoubtedly a legitimate development objective.

Relief of poverty* is the broader aim which will most ease deforestation pressures, but this can be achieved only once bad policies and laws and other inequities are themselves tackled.

Ultimately deforestation is a matter of stewardship* of an important but fragile resource. Biblical stewardship is care, and involves husbandry that conserves and makes forests productive for humankind. It does not permit wanton destruction, even if for apparently legitimate ends (*e.g.* even when laying siege, the Jews were enjoined not to fell trees because they are useful, Dt. 20:19).

The imagery of trees as figures of beauty (Gn. 2:9), strength and certainty of faith (Ps. 1:1–3), and of healing of the nations (Rev. 22:2) is not merely poetic reflection, but points to a living reality essential to our environmental well-being.

Bibliography

S. Dembner, 'Provisional Data from the Forest Resources Assessment 1990 Project', in *Unasylva* 164, 1991, pp. 40–44; J. Evans, *Plantation Forestry in the Tropics* (Oxford, ²1992); Food and Agriculture Organization, *Tropical Forestry Action Plan* (Rome, 1985); M. E. D. Poore, *No Timber without Trees* (London, 1989).

J.E.

DEFORMITY, see DISABILITY AND HANDICAP.

D EHUMANIZATION refers to the loss or suppression of characteristically human traits such as dignity, freedom,* spontaneity, creativity,* love (see ②) and the capacity to worship. There are many forces at work that oppress and destroy human personality.* Contemporary existence in the urban, industrial environment has been said to be dehumanizing, since it so often can lack opportunities for significant attachments, creative work and meaningful involvements. Particularly in the post-Second World War period, writers have called attention to the effects of conformist, regimented society and its consumerism* which suppresses individual integrity in the process of providing a remarkably high standard of material comfort.

An aspect of contemporary Western society that is singled out for criticism is its overriding involvement with technology.* The technological servant has become the master, moulding human beings in subtle ways. Automation* threatens to make people expendable in many occupations, while television supplants conversation, reading and imagination with lowest-common-denominator entertainment. The automobile has shaped the modern city to its service while increasing both our isolation and our physical lethargy, while the computer has multiplied our capacity for information beyond that of wise control. Technological medicine, while providing dramatic remedies for many illnesses and injuries, has created for many the spectre of long-term existence in a diminished, dehumanized state, prompting the call for 'death with dignity' (see Euthanasia*).

With our modern technological society come pollution (see Environment*), abject poverty,* global malnutrition and other ills that have perhaps a mixture of human and natural causes. Many millions in the Third World suffer the disastrous effect of such phenomena, which make it impossible to have even a semblance of fulfilled, truly human, lives.

Totalitarian societies have dehumanized their members by suppressing their free activity in the interests of State ideologies. The comprehensive oppression of Jews and other groups by Adolf Hitler (1889–1945) began with public harassment and humiliation, and resulted in the ultimate dehumanization of the mass extermination camps with their efficient means of gassing and cremating millions. The Stalinist persecution of political opponents included the gross misuse of psychiatric hospitals and therapies and appalling work camps and prisons, the 'Gulag'.

C. S. Lewis* believed that dehumanizing tendencies exist in modern cultural life. Current philosophical and educational views, which he finds even in a seemingly innocuous school textbook, have helped shape modern people into 'men without chests', by severing the essential link between the rational head, the feeling, emotional chest, and the appetitive bowels, so that only the intellect and appetites remain and full human existence as an integrated whole becomes impossible. Such truncated individuals are ripe for manipulation* by a controlling élite, using the latest manipulative methods of the social sciences.

For the Christian, the source of our truly human characteristics and capacities is the God (see ①) who created us in his image* and acted in his Son to redeem and reconcile us to himself (Gn. 1:27; Rom. 5:10–11). God wishes his creatures to live in fulfilment of their divinely imaged human potential, enjoying work,* social life and cultural involvements. Dehumanization is a consequence to be expected when people reject God and his revealed will. While dehumanizing forces have always been at work, the immensity of 20th-century dehumanization in the forms mentioned above seems not unrelated to our living in a post-Christian era in which the theological basis for respect for human individuals in all of their particularity has been undercut (Rom. 1:21–32). Christians must discern the times and identify and resist any dehumanizing tendencies they find in their immediate circumstances. This may well involve them in political activity, relief work for the needy at home and abroad, as well as in looking at their own lives to locate and remove any aspect of their interpersonal relationships that distorts or denies the full human dignity of others.

See also: RIGHTS, HUMAN.

Bibliography

J. Ellul, *The Technological Society* (1954; ET, New York, 1964, and London 1965); C. S. Lewis, *The Abolition of Man* (London, 1943); J. Macquarrie, *In Search of humanity* (London, 1983); H. Marcuse, *One-Dimensional Man* (Boston and London, 1964).

D.B.F.

DELIBERATION, see CHOICE.

DELINQUENCY, JUVENILE, see JUVENILE DELINQUENCY.

DELIVERANCE MINISTRY is a term currently used to describe the ministry of exorcism, which was practised by Jesus and his followers, and which has been exercised within the discipline and life of the church since apostolic times. Exorcism is a ministry of binding and releasing, performed on a person or place believed to be demonized.

Whilst the ministry of deliverance embraces exorcism, it covers a much wider field and is used for acts of minor deliverance from any form of satanic bondage. Whereas in most branches of the Christian church there are clear rules for conducting an exorcism, which must be observed, deliverance ministry is often a matter of simple prayer by one Christian or a group of Christians, for a troubled person seeking deliverance from affliction. In this sense it can be part of a wider ministry of prayer,* counselling and healing.*

Inner healing*

Deliverance ministry is often a significant factor in helping needy people to wholeness of body, mind and spirit, whether or not they have been involved with the occult or with demonic powers. There can be inward hurt and damage of character (see ⑩) and personality* due to painful childhood experiences or traumatic instances of bereavement,* rejection or breakdown, which blight a person's being and open the door to satanic attack. When Jesus was led by the Spirit to be tempted by Satan* in the desert, his enemy chose the time immediately after his baptism, with its assurance of his sonship and the time of hunger following fasting,* to launch his severest temptations at Jesus. Similarly, Satan, 'the accuser of our brothers' (Rev. 12:10), will choose key moments and elements in human experience to bring people into personality bondage and fear through his temptation to doubt and to believe lies about themselves. The prayer of deliverance, ministered in love, frequently frees people from a false view of themselves which is due to Satan, 'the father of lies' (Jn. 8:44), seizing on to some negative aspect of life and using it to a person's disadvantage and sometimes destruction.

Occult involvement

A more specific deliverance ministry is required for someone who has engaged in occult* practice. This may be at an apparently light-hearted level of playing with a Ouija board or being fascinated with horoscopes or occult literature, or it may be at a serious level of commitment to black magic, witchcraft or satanism.

In such cases careful counselling (see Pastoral Care, Counselling and Psychotherapy⑫) is required from those who, if possible, have had some experience in deliverance ministry. It is important not to induce fear through a wrong sensationalizing of the issue, and it is vital that the counsellor should not impose his or her categories of thought on the one seeking help. The task is to listen, discuss, give wise scriptural counsel and to pray for deliverance as the person repents and believes in Jesus Christ. Counselling in the course of deliverance ministry will affirm that 'the one who is in you [*i.e.* in the child of God] is greater than the one who is in the world' (1 Jn. 4:4). All such ministry that sets people free from the power of Satan affirms the power of victory of Jesus Christ over sin and evil through his life, ministry, death and resurrection.

Christian exorcism

The casting out of demons is the work of God through his church, and is a sign of the coming of God's kingdom.* As part of the overall healing ministry, exorcism is best undertaken, if the demonized person is willing, in consultation with the appropriate medical practitioners. If the case demands more than a prayer of blessing or a low-key prayer for deliverance, it is important to observe the discipline of the church and seek help from those authorized in the ministry of exorcism. Although it is rare to find people completely 'possessed' by evil spirits, it is clear from the NT that such cases occur.

If a person has been deeply involved in an occult group they must: 1. renounce membership; and 2. confess past sin and receive forgiveness in Christ as they repent.

A battle with the evil forces gripping such a person's life will then ensue. The exorcist will: 1. bind in Jesus' name (Mt. 12:29; Lk. 11:17–26; Acts 16:18); 2. command the spirit or spirits to leave that person and harm no others (Lk. 8:29a); and 3. command the spirit to go, under the authority of Jesus, to the place of God's appointing (Lk. 8:29, 31; Rev. 20:10).

A person from whom evil is cast out must be encouraged in worship, prayer, Bible study and public teaching of God's Word, and must be helped to sustain a life of sacramental fellowship as he or she grows in the life of the Spirit in the company of God's believing people.

Bibliography

M. Harper, *Spiritual Warfare* (London, 1970); K. E. Koch, *Demonology Past and Present* (Karlsruhe, 1973); M. Perry (ed.), *Deliverance* (London 1987); J. Richards, *But Deliver us from Evil* (London and New York, 1974); *idem*, *Exorcism, Deliverance and Healing* (Bramcote, Nottingham, 1976); G. H. Twelftree, *Christ Triumphant: Exorcism Then and Now* (London, 1985).

T.O.W.

DEMENTIA. The Lat. word *demens* ('being out of one's mind') was historically a general term for insanity. Dementia is now defined as 'an acquired global impairment of intellect, memory and personality' (A. Lishman, *Organic Psychiatry*). Thus, marked forgetfulness occurs, followed by increasing difficulties with reasoning, judgment, communication and daily living skills, along with a change in temperament. It has a number of causes, of which Alzheimer's disease, a condition of unknown origin, is the commonest. The incidence of dementia is approximately 5% of all those above retirement age, but 20% of those aged over 80. However, AIDS frequently involves the brain, so that an increase in dementia in younger people is also anticipated.

The *practical care* of people with dementia is informed by the same compassion* which motivates Christian care in any illness. The prejudice of ageism (see Ageing*), loss of autonomy* and neglected spiritual needs are special difficulties encountered by those with dementia. Given the profound difficulties of empathizing with people with advanced dementia, a theological perspective becomes essential in determining attitudes, ethics and practical care.

A *theology* of dementia must encompass both an understanding of the unchanging relationship of God towards humanity, and of the demented person's relationship to others. An important theological concept is the *imago Dei* (see Image of God*). In this respect contemporary Christianity often ascribes particular importance to rationality and activity. W. H. Vanstone argues in *The Stature of Waiting* that the image of God may be manifest as much in passivity as in activity, and that Jesus' later ministry was characterized by divinely ordained passivity. Thus, Vanstone argues, the word for 'betrayal' (*paradidōmi*) used by Jesus in Gethsemane (Lk. 22:48) can also be understood as 'handing over', *i.e.* a voluntary submission to the activity of others. This passivity or 'waiting' suggests a way of understanding the predicament of people with dementia. H. M. D. Petzsch believes this to be an inadequate model for dementia, as this kind of 'waiting' still depends on an intact intellect (see 'Does he know how frightening he is . . .?'). He proposes a model based on Jesus' ministry which he calls 'dominical acceptance without condition': an active, unconditional reaching out to the dementia sufferer. A related concept is *diminishment*. Thus Teilhard de Chardin reflects that 'God must in some way or other make room for Himself, hollowing us and emptying himself if He is finally to penetrate us' (*Le Milieu Divin*, p. 89) – a situation not dissimilar to those in the later stages of dementia. A development of this is the paradox of creativity which may arise from diminishment, as when a sufferer's helplessness becomes a catalyst which draws out the best in those around them.

The *ethics* of caring for those with dementia are closely linked to the *value of life*. The life of one who is made in God's image is always to be respected and is independent of intellectual awareness or personal usefulness. The Nazi programme of genocide was founded on the premise that some lives are not worthy to be lived, and the inroads into this value system were through attitudes to the sick and the disabled (L. Alexander, 'Medical Science under Dictatorship').

The value of the individual informs discussion of *quality of life*, upon which arguments for euthanasia* often rest. Relevant themes include a respect for *individuality, choice* and meaningful *activity* (A. Norman, *Severe Dementia*). Proponents of assisted suicide argue on the grounds of maintaining autonomy in the face of serious disease, which makes it an especially dubious notion in relation to dementia. Related issues are 'living wills' and 'advance directives' (see Age Concern's publication, *The Living Will*). They are advocated when 'mental competence' is lost, and so may be suggested in cases of dementia. However, dementia does not produce a uniform or wholly predictable degree of mental incompetence, nor is a precise prognosis, which is also required, usually possible in dementia.

The *spiritual needs* of people with dementia are unfortunately largely ignored (Petzsch). Sufferers vary in their awareness of God. The sacrament of the present moment is particularly important, for happenings will soon be forgotten. Thus, birdsong, a happy conversation or well-loved music may be very poignant. Services must be kept short, using words and liturgy familiar to the person. Non-verbal cues can be especially important in ministry – touch, smell and vision. If using music, familiar hymns should be chosen. For the carer the question 'why?' will be important, but also guilt* and a bereavement* reaction ahead of actual death are common feelings which must be acknowledged.

Bibliography

Age Concern, Institute of Gerontology and the Centre of Medical Law and Ethics Working Party, *The Living Will* (London, 1988); L. Alexander, 'Medical Science under Dictatorship', *NEJM* 241, 1949, pp. 39–47; W. A. Lishman, *Organic Psychiatry* (Oxford, 1987); A. Norman, *Severe Dementia: The Provision of Longstay Care* (London, 1987); H. M. D. Petzsch, *'Does he know how frightening he is in his strangeness?': A study of attitudes to dementing people* (Edinburgh, 1984); P. Teilhard de Chardin, *Le Milieu Divin* (ET London, 1960); H. Vanstone, *The Stature of Waiting* (London, 1982).

R.C.B.

DEMOCRACY. The idea that power rests with the people in any given society, and that it is they who delegate or entrust power* to those who govern, goes back at least as far as classical thought in the Gk. tradition. In the Athenian form of democracy, citizens of the Republic (which did not include slaves) possessed power. Where there is division of opinion among the people, systems of voting determine the wishes of the majority. Democratic traditions are, therefore, made up of a concept of power which gives predominance to the people and to systems of political life which enable the wishes of the people to be carried out. It is in contrast to dictatorships, oligarchies and those monarchies which exercise real political power.

It is important to realize that the Christian religion is not the parent of democracy. Democratic ideals and systems are not necessarily Christian. Down the centuries the church has encouraged support for a variety of political systems. The NT recognizes the necessity for the exercise of power but provides no blueprint for any one political system. The submission of the church to those who rule is genuine but not uncritical. Both governments and governed have duties under God.

The spread of democratic ideals and systems in the modern era has encouraged the church to see connections between Christian faith and democratic life. In practice, churches in the 20th century have been involved in movements opposing tyranny and the exclusion of people from power. There has been a growing and deepening attachment in the church to the importance of democracy as a bulwark against the abuse of power. The classic 20th-century definition of this is to be found in the work of Reinhold Niebuhr.* His book *Children of Light and Children of Darkness* (New York, 1944; London, 1945) offers a principled Christian apology for democracy: 'Man's capacity for justice makes democracy possible; but man's inclination to injustice makes democracy necessary.' Though we know no other system which is better fitted to keep a check on power and offer the hope that we may be protected from a propensity to injustice and even to tyranny, it needs to be recognized that democracy can sometimes marginalize groups which can command only a minority vote. There are three crucial elements to democracy:

1. *The exercise of power.* In all democratic thought, those who exercise power in the political forum do so as trustees on behalf of the people. Governments* do not have either a divine, or any other, right to the unrestricted use of the power they possess. Power belongs not to governments but to the people.

In practice, there is a clear recognition that the possession of power contains within it the temptation to corrupt and abuse.

The dilemma of democracy is to be found in its need for a commitment to fundamental social values of justice (see Justice and Peace[3]) and equality.* If power is to rest with the people, the people need a sense of corporate identity and responsibility.

2. *Accountability.* Democratic ideas affirm the importance of the people's ability to call to account those who exercise power. The notion of accountability is vital to democracy. It is the lack of effective accountability by the people in other systems of political life which has led many to see democracy as basic to a principled political order. In democratic societies the people have mechanisms for removing from power those whom they have put there. In every truly democratic society, every government has to account to the people for its stewardship of the trust the people have placed in them.

3. *Representation.* The old political slogan 'No taxation without representation' sums up an important element in democratic practice. If the people are to submit to the government to whom they entrust their power, then that government must be representative of their interest. Thus democracy has become a way in which the multiple interests which make up any society find representation at the heart of power. Usually this means that governments are formed from parliaments made up of elected representatives of the people. Only when there is this representative element are people prepared to submit themselves to the demands made by governments upon them. Especially does this concern the right of governments to tax the people.

How far democracy extends has been a subject for discussion over a very long period. Some see democracy as concerned only with political systems. Others want to include every form of power to which people are subject. This latter group would include economic order, recognizing the great importance to the lives of people of the forces of economic life, be they agrarian or industrial. Questions about control and distribution of land and of corporate economic power are included in the demand for democratic reform of the structures of society.

For some in the Christian church there has been a concern for democracy. Some Christians lay great stress on the belief that the church should be governed by the will of its members. Anabaptist* traditions are often committed to such methods of church government and ministry.

If we accept the fundamental equality of all human beings as both created by God in God's image (see Image of God*) and as being the object of his love in Christ, there is much to be said in favour of church support for systems of social and political life rooted in this perception. A truly democratic society affirms and upholds the equality of all, both before the law and in the responsibility for the exercise of power.

J.W.G.

DEMONIC, THE. In Christian theology, this term is generally used to describe the evil* which is neither the direct responsibility of God nor under immediate human control. It is understood to be incoherent, mutually conflicting and self-assertive, especially against God and his creation, yet self-concealing to guard its identity so that there is not always clear evidence to identify the presence of the demonic. Occasionally collective human evil is referred to as demonic.

1. Background

The OT expresses relatively little interest in the demonic, for both good and evil were seen as the responsibility of Yahweh (1 Sa. 16: 14–23). Probably under Eastern influence, belief developed in evil spiritual beings independent of God, and Satan* became the chief of an army of demons opposed to God and his angels (1 QS 3:13 – 4:26). For Greeks in the NT period, the distinction between a good and an evil demon (*daimonion*) was determined by its activity (Josephus, *Antiquities* 13.415; 16.210). For NT writers, the demonic, which was not limited to demon possession (Acts 10:38), was the responsibility of Satan or the devil and his messengers who could speak through those they possessed; cause suffering (Mk. 5:1–20; 2 Cor. 12:7); become objects of worship (1 Cor. 10:20–21), and therefore needed to be withstood (1 Pet. 5:8–9). The most obvious meaning of Paul's phrase 'principalities and powers' (*e.g.* Col. 2:15) is that behind the pagan world order stood supernatural motivating powers (Dn. 10:13, 20). Potentially, these powers were also able to separate people from the love of God (Rom. 8:38–39). Jesus' ministry of exorcism (Mt. 12:28) and the crucifixion (Jn. 12:31; Col. 2:14–15) were seen as the first stage of the defeat of the demonic, to be completed in the end time (1 Cor. 15:24).

2. The demonic and the contemporary world

Increasing and often bizarre speculation about the demonic was checked by the rationalism of the Enlightenment,* so that with a few exceptions (notably Barth, *CD* III/3, pp. 519–531),

most contemporary theologians have ignored or demythologized the biblical notion of the demonic. Paul Tillich (1886–1965) said the demonic participates in a distorted way in the divine, and is experienced in the claim to divinity or infinity, and in a state of mind when elements of the self aspire to be the whole mind and destroy it (*Systematic Theology* 3, Chicago, 1963; London, 1964). For psychotherapist Rollo May,* the 'daimonic', which he equates with psychosis,* is any natural function, such as sex, hunger, anger and craving for power, which becomes evil when it takes over the whole person (*Love and Will*, New York, 1969; London, 1970). However, human experience of evil requires the biblical categories of good and evil to be remythologized rather than demythologized.

3. Sickness and the demonic

Freud* considered that what were thought to be evil spirits are repressed evil wishes originating in the inner life of a person (*Collected Psychological Works* 19, London, 1961, p. 71). And, in Jungian* thought possession is the control of the total personality by a particular state of mind (C. G. Jung, *Collected Works* 18, London and Princeton, NJ, 1977, p. 648). Thus, 'cacodemonomania' is used for those considered as having the delusion of being possessed by demons.

Despite advances in medical science there is a continuing debate on the demonic as an albeit rare explanation for some sickness. In recent years the debate has focused on the place of the demonic in the rare dissociative and Multiple Personality Disorders (MPD) in which complex behaviour takes place outside the awareness of one's predominate consciousness. Symptoms include anxiety,* dizziness, trances, blackouts, auditory hallucinations and self-mutilation in severe cases. Depression* is the most common symptom, and amnesia is considered the pathogenic sign of MPD. In almost all cases, there is a history of physical or sexual abuse in childhood, about half being through satanic ritual abuse. Some clinicians maintain psychiatric models for MPD in which treatment involves the integration of alter, or secondary, personalities, while others list distinctions between MPD and demon possession. (In the latter case exorcism is required.) For example: 1. spirits are arrogant and devious, and there is no sense of relationship with them; alters can evoke empathy; 2. the patient does not experience spirits as part of the self; 3. spirits stir up confusion; 4. a spirit pushes its way to dominance, performs its evil task, then blames the person; alters usually conform to their surroundings; 5. a spirit is experienced only as a voice; and 6. bickering alters give the feeling of internal sibling rivalry, but demonic voices provoke intense fear and hatred (J. Friesen, *JCH* 11.3, 1989, pp. 4–16).

The Gospel writers considered demonic possession to be involved in sickness when: 1. a sufferer exhibited physical symptoms such as changes in character and behaviour (Mk. 1:23; 9:22), preternatural strength and indifference to pain (Mk. 5:3–5); 2. the sufferer initially responded adversely to a confrontation with Jesus (Mk. 3:11; 5:6–7; 9:20); and 3. there was a change in the sufferer's voice (Mk. 1:26; 5:8). An increasing number of psychologists and therapists employ a multiple-causation approach, recognizing that mental illness and the demonic are not mutually exclusive but that either, both or neither may be the cause of illness. However, there are those represented by John White (1924–), who consider that science is helpless in diagnosing the presence of the demonic: 'I can conceive of no demonic state which cannot be "explained" by a non-demonic hypothesis. I can likewise conceive of no experiment to give conclusive support to demonic rather than para-psychological hypotheses' (in J. W. Montgomery, ed., *Demon Possession*, p. 253). Therefore, because of the subtle, incoherent and devious nature of the demonic, the pastor or healer requires a God-given facility to discern the possible demonic dimensions of an illness. Among those who practise exorcism it is generally agreed, and some churches require, that exorcism should be conducted in association with the medical profession, with the patient's consent and in the context of a team ministry (see Deliverance Ministry*).

See also: OCCULT.

Bibliography

American Psychiatric Association, *Diagnostic and Statistical Manual of Mental Disorders* (Washington, DC, ³1980); D. N. Augsburger, *Pastoral Counseling Across Cultures* (Philadelphia, 1986); R. K. Bufford, *Counseling and the Demonic* (Dallas, TX, 1988); F. S. MacNutt, *Healing* (New York and London, ²1990); J. W. Montgomery (ed.), *Demon Possession* (Minneapolis, MN, 1976); S. Peck, *People of the Lie* (London, 1983); M. Perry (ed.), *Deliverance* (London, 1987); J. Richards, *But Deliver Us From Evil* (London and New York, 1974); L. Sperry, 'Dissociation, Multiple Personality, and the Phenomenon of Evil', *JPCo* 25, 1990, pp. 90–100; G. H. Twelftree, *Christ Triumphant: Exorcism Then and Now* (London, 1985); *idem*, *Jesus the Exorcist* (Tübingen, 1992); *idem*, 'The Place of Exorcism in Contemporary Ministry', *Anv* 5, 1988, pp. 133–150.

G.H.T.

DENIAL, see BEREAVEMENT; DEATH AND DYING; DEFENCE MECHANISMS.

DEONTOLOGY (from Gk. *deon*, that which is obligatory) is in general the study of moral obligation,* and in particular a specific kind of theory of obligation. In contrast to consequentialist* theories of obligation, deontological theories hold that actions are *not* right or wrong simply because of their good or bad consequences. Rather, actions are right or wrong to the extent that they are, or are not, fulfilments of duty,* where duty is not determined wholly in terms of consequences.

Deontological theories differ over what are the grounds of duty: for some, it is the will of God; for others, it is rationality as such; for still others, duties are groundless, brute facts. Theories also differ over how far obligation is independent of consequences. Immanuel Kant* held that consequences were irrelevant to obligation – 'Do your duty though the heavens may fall!' – while W. D. Ross (1877–1940) held that consequences were just one factor among many relevant to obligation. Deontological theories have been praised for their congruity with the moral intuitions of ordinary persons, including the intuition that 'the ends do not always justify the means'. They have been criticized for making moral obligation appear arbitrary or inexplicable, and for vitiating incentive to act morally.

See also: CHRISTIAN MORAL REASONING. [18]

Bibliography

B. Blanshard, *Reason and Goodness* (London, 1961); A. Donagan, *The Theory of Morality* (Chicago, 1977); I. Kant, *Foundations of the Metaphysics of Morals* (1785; ET, Indianapolis, IN, 1959); W. D. Ross, *The Right and the Good* (Oxford, 1930).

M.T.N.

DEPENDENCE. The term 'dependence' means behaviour focused by craving for a substrate (*e.g.* drug, alcohol, nicotine, food) upon gaining it in harmful ways. The harm can be personal or social, or both; it disrupts social relationships.

'Addiction' is dependence behaviour contrary to law; the substrate may be unobtainable legally, or illegal acts are used to obtain it.

Dependence, and therefore addiction, can be physical or psychological or both. In physical dependence, drug withdrawal makes someone ill. In psychological dependence, withdrawal worsens craving. In both, a person returns to the substrate to relieve his or her symptoms.

In dependence, complex changes occur in behaviour which pose many pastoral problems. The central features are: 1. loss of self-esteem* and self-worth ('There's no point', 'I deserve punishment' or 'harm'); 2. denial: evading or avoiding what is true because it evokes fear and is denied at the conscious level; 3. hence deceit, evasion, lies and misrepresentation, often very plausible, lead to a world of image and fantasy; 4. blame of others; 5. damage to persons and property, through neglect, denigration, or sale to gain drugs.* This often involves theft or violence even to relatives and friends. Abusive, disinhibited behaviour is frequent; 6. rejection of social norms; identification with alternative society; and 7. in some cases association with (but not necessarily causation of, or by) mental disorders or deviations of other kinds: psychoneurosis, depression,* schizophrenia, personality disorder, or loss of sexual identity and libido.

Behaviour swings are frequent, sometimes deeply disordered, and at other times making a promising struggle towards the positive, even as if two persons were within one. 'I must try again' alternates with 'What's the point of trying?'

It is a common belief that the central problem in dependence is the substrate. That this is at the least too simple is shown by the following factors. 1. When a substrate is not to hand, conversion to another occurs readily. 2. When newly released into a society, substrate use grows rapidly at first, but soon levels off; only a proportion of those exposed use it. 3. Patterns of use for almost all drugs of dependence are similar. 4. A stronger desire can displace addiction – the 'expulsive power of a higher affection' – in a non-specific way. 5. Dependence is often linked to psychological damage (*e.g.* past hurts or rejection). 6. Decisions made in open society are often painful for the dependent person. Behaviour is much easier to control in an institution, whether hospital, prison or managed hostel (the 'four walls effect'). Dependent persons in institutions often complain that others are deciding for them, but outside they complain that they cannot bear the pain of taking decisions for themselves. 7. Many dependent persons eventually come to an end of themselves and abandon their habit (getting 'round the corner'). 8. Effects relate closely to the social context, and the expected effects of drug-taking. 9. Slow drug withdrawal may not evoke symptoms, but removal of the social contexts of drug use (*e.g.* injection, tobacco-pipe rituals, or drinking routines) can evoke severe effects. 10. Other compulsive behaviours (*e.g.* gambling, emotional overeating) strongly resemble drug-dependence behaviour.

The family impact of dependence affects everyone, though the numbers of dependent persons within a family may be several or one. Antecedent factors often seem to be rejection, actual or perceived, or some wounding experience so deep that it cannot be admitted to self or to others (see Inner Healing*). But the problem often presents to outsiders as some new and critical incident, when in fact there is a long, hidden story of years of increasing dependence, often with episodes of hostel, detoxification unit, or prison life. Families are often forced into tragic distortions in their efforts to cope with this problem: the hardest decision is often whether to let someone remain in the home, or to send them away.

The outlook for lasting relief is not good, even in cases with the most favourable features: five-year abstinence* is found in some 5% to 15%. Yet the aims of care* must remain as abstinence, talking out to a counsellor every wounding experience, and the practical steps needed to improve self-esteem, so proving that other satisfactions exist than the self-destructive drives of dependence. Unless the behavioural drives to dependence can be opened up and dealt with, abstinence is merely followed by re-addiction, conversion to another substrate or deception.

Other key aspects are that carers must be constant, despite repeated relapse. Addictive behaviour recurs readily, with returning sorrowful memories and social contexts. Dissociation and denial lead to behaviour swings which seem inexplicable and tax a carer's patience to the limit. Families and friends need support, as well as the index sufferer. Self-harm can amount to actual mutilation; hence warnings about the harmful effects of addiction can be counter-productive, even attractive. Blame of others is only a part of demanding manipulative and bargaining behaviour, usually at a blatantly self-contradictory level.

It is important to know some of the care agencies to which referrals can be made at helpful times and places. The stages of care are: 1. detoxification: a heavily drug-affected person cannot accept or understand counsel; and 2. voluntary institutional rehabilitation: this must have a carefully worked out and informed programme of activity and counselling with means of social reorientation. Siting this can be difficult: it is best within the dependent person's general culture, but away from unhelpful contacts; many promise, yet default.

Addiction and dependence are evils for the following reasons. 1. Men and women are meant to relate to God; to become subject to another controlling influence cannot be good (1 Cor. 6:12). 2. People need to relate to one another in families (Ps. 68:6) and by marriage (Gn. 2:18, 24; Mt. 19:8–9) in trustworthy social bonds. The community is built and strengthened by honourable dealings and love (Ex. 18:21; 2 Cor. 8:21; Eph. 6:1–4), whereas drug dependence is above all else focused upon self. 3. Body and mind are not ours to use as we please, to damage or to destroy (Pr. 23:19–21; 1 Cor. 6:19–20); they are the vehicles of God's work on earth (Eph. 5:18). 4. Loss of self-respect is evil, and addiction leads to contempt of persons (Joel 3:3). Humankind has a place of unique dignity and privilege amongst creatures (Gn. 1:26; Ps. 8:4–9; Lk. 12:7); humans forgiven, as children of God, recover their lost worth (Rom. 8:11–17; 1 Jn. 3:1–3), but worthless feelings are a sign of depression or of alienation* from God, from his plan and purpose. 5. The 'satisfaction' gained through dependence is illusory (Pr. 20:1; 21:17). 6. Denial is an unreal escape (Pr. 14:12–13; cf. Rom. 1:21).

The use of drugs to bring repressed fears to consciousness ('abreaction') is dangerous and has been abandoned. Counselling is more helpful: sometimes repressed material can be dealt with by asking, 'Suppose the most feared threat were to happen, what then?' Training is desirable for carers, but these problems are so prevalent that every pastor and carer is likely to encounter them many times. Many parents painfully encounter them first in their own child. For all these reasons, it is important for knowledge about these problems to be diffused.

See also: ALCOHOLISM; PASTORAL CARE, COUNSELLING AND PSYCHOTHERAPY;[12] EATING DISORDERS; MENTAL HEALTH.

D.W.V.

DEPENDENCY THEORY, see GLOBAL ETHICS.[15]

DEPRESSION covers a wide spectrum of experience, from short-lived gloom to a deep, prolonged immobility of spirit and body (or a feeling of being pressed down).

Adults, adolescents* and children, both Christian and non-Christian,* are all susceptible to depression, because it is part of the general atmosphere of emotional pollution in which everyone lives in this world. It can be a painful emotional* illness in which the sufferer feels hopeless and in despair, isolated, preoccupied with the depression, worthless and unable to make even small decisions, and full of anxiety.* In this case, it is accompanied by such features as constant and prolonged weeping, diminished sexual interest, under- or over-eating (see Eating Disorders*) and disturbed sleep patterns. The mood is particularly black on waking, but this often lightens as the day wears on. The depressed person may have murderous feelings towards others and / or entertain suicidal* thoughts. Children show their depression in listlessness, inability to do school work properly and other physical symptoms, because they do not have the verbal skills with which to articulate their distress. Adolescents also express themselves in listless purposelessness, and their depression is often the result of their search for identity and sometimes the pressure of expectations put upon them.

Depression arises from several main causes, though they are always interrelated. They are chiefly:

1. *Heredity.* It may be useful to some people to realize that depression can be a handicap which is traceable along the family line.

2. *Chemical imbalance.* Sometimes this is a result of an illness, childbirth, menopause, *etc.*

3. *The after-effect* of a prolonged period of emotional or physical stress* can cause

depression. This will right itself after appropriate rest.

4. *Reaction* to a major change in life experience is another cause, *e.g.* loss or change of job, bereavement,* divorce,* change of house, retirement* especially when it involves loss of status and friends, loss of a limb or faculty, *etc.* In fact, change of any sort, even though it is not a disaster, may precipitate a depression, because change represents a loss of the familiar in which a part of the self has been invested. There is anxiety lest the reduced self will not be able to meet the demands of the new situation and it therefore tries to withdraw. It is a well-established fact that a person who has lost a parent, for whatever reason, before the age of about seventeen, is liable to depression in adult life.

5. *Cause unidentifiable*, known as 'endogenous depression'. This is the hardest to tolerate because, in addition to the pain of the depression, there is the apparent irrationality of it. Endogenous depression is the result of some deep life-long anger* which the sufferer has turned in on himself or herself because it is not safe to direct it against the people whom he or she feels may have caused it. This anger is usually buried too deeply to be easily accessible to comfort or exhortation. It is often associated with a sense of insecure dependence on some significant person and the persistent yearning for that person's approval, without which there is a feeling of self-doubt and guilt.* A depressed person has often experienced a marked degree of maternal / parental deprivation, hence the consistently low self-esteem* and intense need for affirmation. People sometimes regard depression as a spiritual attack. It may be, but, obviously, a person's vulnerable area is likely to be the first that collapses under strain.

Manic depression is a condition in which there are periodic mood swings between depression and euphoria. A severely depressed person is in need of medical help, particularly if there is risk of self-injury (see Hospitalization, Involuntary*). There are therapeutic drugs* which can be of great benefit. However, in endogenous depression, anti-depressants will only help to moderate the symptoms; they cannot alter the underlying cause. In this case, treatment is required. This may be from a professionally qualified therapist, who will be able to accept the patient's feelings of worthlessness without necessarily sharing them; and will be able to explore with him or her the fearful,

buried experiences of the past and enable them to be held in the present within a trustful relationship, thus diffusing the anger and enabling the patient to move into a more constructive attitude to himself or herself. Treatment may include different forms of spiritual ministry.

The pastoral care of depressed people is important and demanding. It is necessary to remember that depression is infectious. The carer (see Care, Caring*) may pick up the submerged anger and become impatient, wanting the patient to 'pull himself together' or 'snap out of it'. Alternatively, carers themselves may become depressed. The most useful way of helping is just to be there, quietly undeterred by the difficulties in communication; not giving exhortations or verbal reassurances which may sound hollow to the sufferer; not being offended by overt indifference or hopelessness and resisting the temptation to give little homilies, but just quietly and consistently waiting for it to pass. This is no easy task.

Depression, for a Christian person, is particularly difficult to endure because, in the generalized sense of isolation, it seems as though God has forgotten or deserted him or her. The sufferer's own Christian faith comes into question; he (or she) feels a failure; he has not managed to secure God's much-needed approval in spite of conscientious efforts, and the supports on which he relied previously seem to have given way. (He may forget, temporarily, that he is in the company of Job, David of the many depressed psalms, Elijah, and others.) This accentuates the already-depressed sense of being unloved and unlovable. A sense of guilt also compounds the misery. Thus prayer becomes impossible and Bible reading meaningless by the very nature of the illness, not necessarily because of any spiritual failure. The sufferer needs people to be the go-between for him until he rediscovers his ability to make personal relationships and sense of worth. The carer may offer very short prayers or read short Bible verses, *e.g.* Rom. 8:39 – '. . . nor anything else [not even my depression] will be able to separate us from the love of God . . .' – which is a statement about God holding on to us, not about us trying unsuccessfully to hold on to God (*i.e.* justification* by faith, not by good works and effort to win approbation). Like most other pain,* depression is giving a clear message that something is amiss and needs attention. It is important to try to discover what this depression is saying for this person, and what adjustments need to be made in his or her lifestyle and relationships, and not simply to wait until the pain has passed, imagining that when the pain ceases the illness is necessarily cured. Depression is cyclical in nature, especially when it is treated only by drugs with no attempt to search for the root cause. Some people think that seeking professional help is 'lack of faith', and that makes them guilty, so the cycle continues.

See also: PASTORAL CARE, COUNSELLING AND PSYCHOTHERAPY. 15

Bibliography
S. Atkinson, *Climbing out of Depression* (Oxford, 1993); J. Bowlby, *Attachment and Loss*, 3 vols. (London, 1969–80); M. Chave-Jones, *Coping with Depression* (Tring and Batavia, IL, 1981); J. Dominian, *Depression* (London, 1976); J. White, *The Masks of Melancholy: A Christian Psychiatrist Looks at Depression and Suicide* (Leicester and Downers Grove, IL, 1982).

M.C.-J.

DESCRIPTIVISM is the position which holds that the meaning of a term can be given by specifying when descriptions using that term are true and when they are false. For example, we can give the meaning of 'red' by specifying when a description of something as 'red' is true and when it is false.

J. L. Austin (1911–60) used the phrase 'the descriptive fallacy' for the view that the meaning of *all* words can be given this way. Descriptivism about moral words holds that the meaning of 'good' is like the meaning of 'red' in this respect. Prescriptivism is the position that the meaning of ethical terms is unlike the meaning of purely descriptive terms in that it contains a prescriptive component. To give the meaning of 'good', for instance, requires specifying that the term is used to commend. To commend something is not merely, according to a prescriptivist, to attribute to it certain descriptive properties; it is to express a preference of some kind for it. One natural linguistic form for such expression is the prescision, in the imperative mood rather than the indicative. For a prescriptivist, if we assent orally to the judgment that we should do something in some situation, and then we do not do it, we logically must be assenting insincerely.

Prescriptivists do not, however, claim that the meaning of all moral words is exhausted by their prescriptive component; and even moral words whose prescriptive meaning is dominant may have descriptively specified criteria for their application.

See also: PHILOSOPHICAL ETHICS.

Bibliography
R. M. Hare, *Moral Thinking* (Oxford, 1981), ch. 4.

J.E.H.

DESERT, see PUNISHMENT.

DESERTION is the act of abandoning those closest to us. It commonly refers to a husband's or wife's withdrawal from their marriage or, increasingly, to one live-in partner pulling out of the relationship. It is used of a parent leaving a child and of children abandoning their parents. By its very nature, such an action implies a sudden and often irrevocable breaking-off of a relationship and cannot fail to be the cause of considerable distress to those left behind. In the past, desertion has been grounds for divorce,* and a deserting parent is still likely to be regarded unfavourably by the courts when there is a question of custody of children.

Desertion seems to spring primarily from an inability or unwillingness either to cope with responsibilities or to withdraw from them by using normal channels of communication. Sometimes a deserting person may be suffering from a depressive illness; in other cases a simple lack of maturity may render that person incapable of handling tensions or crises in a responsible way. These may range from falling in love with someone outside the marriage or outside of the cohabiting partnership to being unable to handle the normal stresses and strains of family life: the upheaval of a new baby, the problems of teenagers or the demands of an elderly relative. Whatever the obvious or immediate cause of desertion, some breakdown in normal communication is likely to lie behind it.

People who are deserted not unnaturally fall prey to some very strong emotions. Foremost among these may be anxiety* or fear,* particularly if there has been no advance warning of trouble or if a young person is involved. Pastorally there may be a real need for reassurance that God cares for all those involved in the situation: 'Cast all your anxiety on him because he cares for you' (1 Pet. 5:7);

such reassurance may be greatly helped by simple expressions of love from Christian friends.

Then, as in bereavement,* anger* is likely to be present whatever the circumstances. 'Why has this happened to me?' is a cry that needs to be expressed if those abandoned are eventually to make a healthy recovery from their experience. If there have been communication problems within the past relationship, people may need help in articulating this. It is not wrong to ask 'why?' or 'how?': it is simply to echo the despairing cry of Job, 'Why did I not perish at birth?' (3:11), and the anguish of Jesus quoting Ps. 22, 'My God, my God, why have you forsaken me?' We need to cry out for God to help us because, as the psalmist says to him: 'You hear . . . the desire of the afflicted; you encourage them, and you listen to their cry, defending the fatherless and the oppressed' (Ps. 10:17–18).

Other feelings which need to be handled may include guilt* (often unfounded, but very real to those who seek an explanation and end up blaming themselves), loneliness* and depression* – feeling that no-one understands. Yet Jesus himself knew what it was like to be deserted by those closest to him (Mt. 26:56). The Bible's insistence on God's care for people who lose an important family relationship is remarkable, *e.g.* 'Leave your orphans; I will protect their lives. Your widows too can trust in me' (Je. 49:11), and Jesus' promise: 'I will not leave you as orphans; I will come to you' (Jn. 14:18). Similarly, God's faithfulness whatever disasters may occur is borne out by the whole story of the OT and its record of his promises to his people: 'I will never leave you nor forsake you' (Jos. 1:5).

Pastoral care in cases of desertion may also need to extend to the practical step of seeking police help if the person's whereabouts are unknown. Every disappearance is treated very seriously and the police can be contacted as soon as there is cause for concern. Once a missing adult is found, the police have no authority to tell the family or partner where he or she is, but they will convey the message back that the person is alive and well. While it is hard to come to terms with the news that a loved one is refusing all contact, there is at least the reassurance that the person is unharmed and even a glimmer of hope for the future. Like the police, the Salvation Army are committed to confidentiality* if a missing person contacts them, but they too will reassure the family that he or she is safe, and can convey back to that person the message that those left behind still care.

P.M.C.

DESERTIONS, SPIRITUAL. 'Desertion' or 'spiritual desertions' were terms commonly given by the Eng. Puritan pastors to describe times when the believer's spiritual life seems to be dying, God seems far away, joy in the Lord gives way to aridity, and the soul even doubts its salvation. Mystics of a previous age called it 'the dark night of the soul'. Puritan 'practical' writers diagnosed it closely and treated it superbly in such treatises as *A Child of Light Walking in Darkness* by Thomas Goodwin (1600–80), and *A Lifting Up for the Downcast* by William Bridge (1600–70). (See P. Lewis, *The Genius of Puritanism*.)

These Puritans recognized that sin unconfessed and not dealt with could be a major reason for the experience. However, they also realized that the best of Christians could be taken through such times by God to prove their utter dependence on him: to develop such graces as faith, humility, assurance and prayer; to weaken the attraction and hold of sin; or to qualify them to help others in such a condition. They recognized as well the effect of 'false reasonings' and strong emotions unregulated by Scripture, as well as the distinct but often confusing effects of 'melancholy' (depression) which was wisely seen as a medical rather than a spiritual condition. They saw too how Satan can make devastating use of times of desertion.

Their 'remedies' included directions to 'fly to God' (tell your Father *everything* – he knows and understands and cares); trust in God (in his Son, in his providence, in his promises, *and in nothing else*); put convictions of sin into balanced perspective; seek to live for God's praise more than spiritual experiences; value holiness, more even than happiness; and appreciate that 'times of refreshing' will return in God's time.

Bibliography

W. Bridge, *A Lifting Up for the Downcast* (1649; Edinburgh, 1990); P. Lewis, *The Genius of Puritanism* (Haywards Heath, 1979); M. Lloyd-Jones, *Spiritual Depression* (London, 1965).

P.H.L.

DESIRE, see ALTRUISM; LUST.

DETERMINISM, see FREE WILL AND DETERMINISM.

DETERRENCE, NON-NUCLEAR.

To deter a person, group or nation from some wrong or aggressive action is to restrain them from such action by a clear threat of punishment.* The hope is to make potential wrongdoers aware of the likely consequences of their behaviour, and so prevent them from carrying through their plans. Deterrence is the system of punishment, or maintenance of armed force, which embodies this concern to protect society against those who threaten its well-being.

There are two main aspects to deterrence. Internally, it takes the form of law enforcement and judicial punishment, to deter criminal activity; externally, it involves the maintenance of standing armies to deter military aggression (or the threat of it; see Defence*).

Deterrence is one of the justifications for punishment. Many studies make clear that both the prospect of being caught and the prospect of punishment are needed in order effectively to deter the would-be criminal. The particular punishment prescribed for a crime seems of less importance for purposes of deterrence. Effective deterrence also presupposes a certain type of rationality on the part of the criminal, and it should be noted that the emotional roots of some crimes in fact display a different kind of rationality.

It is important to note that deterrence alone cannot provide sufficient grounds either for penal policy or for specific punishments. Punishment must always be in some way appropriate to the offence; that is, it needs to contain some element of retribution. Failure to recognize this can result in unjust sentences for purposes of deterrence or treatment. In particular, judges are sometimes under pressure to pass deterrent sentences, for the social good, but which exceed the appropriate retribution for the actual offence committed.

Deterrence is one of the main reasons for maintaining armies in times of peace. Here also much depends on convincing a potential wrongdoer or aggressor that the likely response will be both forthcoming and effective.

See also: CRIME; DETERRENCE, NUCLEAR; PUNISHMENT.

D.J.E.A.

DETERRENCE, NUCLEAR.

Deterrence in general aims to prevent war by the maintenance of a military force sufficient to dissuade potential enemies from hostile action (see Defence*). Defined like this, deterrence is a perennial feature of the history of nations, which always need to defend their security and prevent warfare. If this were a definition which adequately covered all that goes under the name deterrence, there would be little need for specific moral analysis (as distinct from the morality of warfare). However, there are features of nuclear deterrence in the present age which do demand a distinctive moral analysis. Nuclear deterrence involves both the arsenals of weapons, and the patterns of strategic thought which require and design those arsenals. Some of the moral approaches to nuclear deterrence are outlined below.

The complexity and technicality of some of the moral debates spring from the difficulties inherent in theories of nuclear deterrence. Any moral analysis first requires an understanding of the strategic theories. The various paradoxes at the heart of such deterrence make this a complex business, quite apart from the technologies involved. For instance, nuclear deterrence insists that the more dangerous the deterrent, the more effective it is, and the less likely it will ever be used. The more dangerous, the safer. This and other paradoxes have convinced some theologians that the theory of deterrence is fundamentally flawed. On the other hand, others have been convinced by the view that deterrence is effective in practice, and sufficiently stable. They have argued that nuclear deterrence is justified by its results. We can select only a few representative approaches of the differing moral analyses of nuclear deterrence. Just-war theory* relates to several of these approaches.

1. One approach accepts the claim that nuclear deterrence is the best and only practical way of preserving peace and security. The argument cuts in two directions. On the one hand, it is claimed that the threats of nuclear war are so devastating that the chances of it actually happening are vanishingly small: the fear of nuclear destruction will effectively maintain peace. On the other hand, to disarm would be highly unsettling politically, and at the worst might even risk war itself. The best that can be hoped for is arms control – the maintenance of a 'nuclear balance' at reasonable and mutually agreed levels. By arguing that deterrence will thus prevent war, this approach aims to avoid having to handle the tests of just-war theory as they apply to the just means of war (*jus in bello*). All that needs to be

said is that the dangers involved in deterrence are outweighed by the benefits it confers.

2. Another approach seeks to correct this view by drawing attention to the moral importance of threats. It is argued that what is threatened must be justifiable, just as much as what is actually done. In particular, nuclear deterrence makes huge threats of destruction. These threats must be truly intended in some real sense, however remote or conditional they may appear. (If they were merely bluff, and not really intended, that would soon become clear to potential enemies.) These threats themselves must therefore meet the tests of just-war theory, of *jus in bello*: a. nuclear weapons may be targeted only on military forces, not on civilian populations (the test of discrimination, *i.e.* that there should be no direct attack on non-combatants); and b. any use of nuclear weapons could be justified only if there were a reasonable prospect that to use them would do more good than harm (the test of proportion). This approach considers that there could be circumstances, albeit extreme, in which the use of nuclear weapons could meet these moral requirements. Given that, it is reasonable to design and possess such weapons in the belief (as in the first approach) that the weapons will effectively deter war. But (proponents of this approach would usually say) only a much lower capability than that currently possessed by the superpowers could be justified along these lines.

3. A third type of approach makes the point that it would be highly desirable to move away from nuclear deterrence, because nuclear war itself could never be justified. Typically, this type of analysis denies that there can be any morally legitimate use of nuclear weapons, and also draws attention to their inherent dangers. Nevertheless, it accepts that at present nuclear deterrence in practice maintains a certain balance and stability. While urging continuing moves towards disarmament,* this approach considers that deterrence is for the time being morally acceptable. Arguments along these lines are often urged by Roman Catholic leaders (*e.g.* Pope John Paul II [1978– ; b. 1920] in his Message to the UN in 1982, or the US Catholic bishops in *The Challenge of Peace*).

4. Yet another approach also depends on just-war theory. This approach considers that just-war principles forbid all use of nuclear weapons, and also their possession and use. The question is raised against the second ap-

proach: can there ever really be any discriminate use of nuclear weapons? Further, given the dangers of escalation, can there ever be any reasonable prospect that using nuclear weapons could ever do more good than harm? Neither of these questions can be answered satisfactorily. There is therefore no moral alternative to disarmament. Advocates of this approach do not always say that disarmament must necessarily follow immediately and unilaterally. The key moral point is that there should be a clear unequivocal commitment to seeking and finding better ways of ensuring peace. Given such a commitment, it is imperative to disarm in ways that are not themselves politically dangerous and unsettling.

Apart from those who work from just-war principles, there are also many who would condemn nuclear deterrence on pacifist grounds. This is obvious enough, but an important rider can be added here: the abhorrence of nuclear weapons has undoubtedly been a key factor in the rise of pacifism in our times.

The commitment to nuclear deterrence has had unseen effects upon political morality, which should not be overlooked. It is impossible to know what the effects may have been of living in the knowledge that the destruction of the inhabited world is technically possible in all-out war. Apart from that, deterrence has done much to make us all moral cynics. For living with deterrence has appeared to leave us with an unanswerable moral dilemma. It has seemed that we must either be ready to will the deaths of many millions of enemy citizens, or give up the concern to preserve world security and peace. Neither alternative seems morally acceptable, and consequently many have become convinced that whatever we do, we must do wrong. Nuclear deterrence has thus played its part for many in the loss of confidence in the reality, and objective rightness, of moral truth itself.

See also: WAR.

Bibliography

Church of England Board for Social Responsibility, *The Church and the Bomb: Nuclear Weapons and Christian Conscience* (London, 1982); J. M. Finnis *et al.*, *Nuclear Deterrence, Morality and Realism* (Oxford, 1987); National Conference of Catholic Bishops, *The Challenge of Peace: God's Promise and*

Our Response (London and Washington, DC, 1983); Oliver O'Donovan, *Peace and Certainty: A Theological Essay on Deterrence* (Oxford, 1989); H. Thielicke, *TE 2*.

D.J.E.A.

DEVELOPMENT, ECONOMIC, see ECONOMIC DEVELOPMENT, ETHICS OF.

DEVIANCE, see SEXUAL DEVIATION.

DEVIL, see SATAN.

DEVLIN–HART DEBATE. The protracted controversy between Lord Devlin (1905–92, latterly Lord of Appeal in Ordinary) and H. L. A. Hart (1907–92, latterly Emeritus Professor of Jurisprudence in the University of Oxford) provides the outstanding example of a recent debate about the problem of whether, and in what circumstances, morality may properly be imposed by criminal sanctions (see Criminal Justice*).

The starting-point of the controversy was the second Maccabean Lecture on Jurisprudence of the British Academy, given in 1959 by Mr Justice Devlin (as he then was) on 'The Enforcement of Morals'. Though he had largely agreed with the 1957 report of the Wolfenden Committee on Homosexual Offences and Prostitution (before which he had given evidence), he challenged its basic assumption that there is a sphere of private morality which should lie altogether outside the purview of the criminal law (see Law, Civil and Criminal*). Instead, he argued that a society is held together not only by its political structure but also by a shared morality, so, just as every community has the right to protect its political integrity by the law of treason, so it has the right, in suitable circumstances, to safeguard its ideological integrity by criminal sanctions. But 'Nothing should be punished by the law that does not lie beyond the limits of tolerance ...; there must be a real feeling of reprobation ... No society', he insisted, 'can do without intolerance, indignation, and disgust; they are the forces behind the moral law, and indeed it can be argued that if they or something like them are not present, the feelings of society cannot be weighty enough to deprive the individual of freedom of choice' (*cf. The Enforcement of Morals*, pp. 16f.; and see p. viii for Devlin's defence of the phrase 'intolerance, indignation, and disgust').

This thesis, and the detailed arguments by

which Devlin had supported it, was almost immediately challenged by Hart in an article in *The Listener* (30 July 1959) on 'Immorality and Treason' (reprinted in L. Blom-Cooper, ed., *The Law as Literature*). He strongly supported the contention of the Wolfenden Committee that there 'must remain a realm of private morality and immorality which in brief and crude terms is not the law's business' (p. 201) – largely on the basis of John Stuart Mill's* famous words in his essay *On Liberty*: 'The only purpose for which power can be rightfully exercised over any member of a civilized community, against his will, is to prevent harm to others. His own good, either physical or moral, is not a sufficient warrant. He cannot rightfully be compelled to do or forbear ... because, in the opinion of others, to do so would be wise, or even right' (p. 73). While 'most previous thinkers' who had repudiated this classic formula of liberalism had 'done so because they thought that morality consisted either of divine commands or of rational principles of human conduct discoverable by human reason', Devlin had based his definition of those breaches of morality which could rightly be punished by law not on 'the mere adverse judgement of society', but 'one which is inspired by feeling raised to the concert pitch of intolerance, indignation, and disgust' (*The Law as Literature*, p. 222). Hart did, however, concede that Mill's formula 'may well be too simple. The grounds for interfering with human liberty are more various than the single criterion of "harm to others" suggests: cruelty to animals or organizing prostitution for gain do not, as Mill himself saw, fall easily under the description of harm to others' (p. 224). It would be dangerous, on the other hand, to 'mount the man in the street on the top of the Clapham omnibus' (these words pick up expressions used by Devlin to describe a typical member of a jury) 'and to tell him that if only he feels sick enough about what other people do in private to demand its suppression by law no theoretical criticism can be made of his demand' (p. 227).

In 1963 Hart expanded his views in three lectures published under the title *Law, Liberty and Morality*. Mill's doctrine, he insisted, was 'to apply to human beings only "in the maturity of their faculties": it is not to apply to children or to backward societies' (pp. 4f.); but, apart from these two examples, Mill was utterly opposed to legal 'paternalism'. He had even cited 'the example of restrictions on the sale of drugs, and criticises them as interferences with the liberty of the would-be purchaser rather than with that of the seller'. Today, however, we have 'an increased awareness of a great range of factors which diminish the significance to be attached to an apparently free choice or to consent . . . Underlying Mill's extreme fear of paternalism there perhaps is a conception of what a normal human being is like which now seems not to correspond to the facts' (pp. 32f.). But Hart still insisted on making a sharp distinction between paternalism and what he terms 'legal moralism' (pp. 33f.), particularly in the sphere of sexual morals. Examples of the latter which he cites include 'bestiality, incest, living on the earnings of prostitution, keeping a house for prostitution, and also, since the decision in Shaw's case [1961], a conspiracy to corrupt public morals, interpreted to mean in substance, leading others (in the opinion of a jury) "morally astray"' (p. 25). It is significant, however, that Hart considers it perfectly consistent to 'insist on the one hand that the only justification for having a *system* of punishment is to prevent harm and only harmful conduct should be punished, and, on the other, agree that when the *quantum* of punishment for such conduct is raised, we should defer to principles which make relative moral wickedness of different offenders a partial determinant of the severity of punishment' (p. 37).

Two years later Devlin replied in his book *The Enforcement of Morals*, a collection of lectures and addresses on the subject of law and morality. In these he comments on morality and the law of tort, of contract and of marriage, respectively, together with its relationship to democracy and contemporary social reality. In his address on 'Democracy and Morality' (pp. 86–101) he focuses on, and discusses the implications of, *Shaw* v. *Director of Public Prosecutions* (1962) A.C. 220, in which the House of Lords found Shaw guilty, in publishing a magazine called *The Ladies' Directory*, of three offences: 1. publishing an obscene article; 2. living on the earnings of the prostitutes who paid for the insertion of their advertisements in *The Ladies' Directory*; and 3. conspiring to corrupt public morals by means of *The Ladies' Directory*.

The first two of these charges were straightforward, under the Obscene Publications Act, 1959, and the Sexual Offences Act, 1956, respectively. The charge of 'conspiring to corrupt public morals' was much more controversial, and the defence insisted that there was, currently, no such offence known to English law. But Lord Simmonds (1881–1971) asserted that there 'remains in the courts of law a residual power . . . to conserve not only the safety and order but also the moral welfare of the State', and that Lord Mansfield's (1705–93) statement, two centuries before, that 'the Court of King's Bench was the *custos morum* [keeper of morals] of the people and had the superintendency of offences *contra bonos mores* [against good morals]' was still valid. Only Lord Reid (1890–1975) dissented from the contention that a conspiracy to corrupt public morals was still an offence. Professor Hart was, of course, horrified (*Law, Liberty and Morality*, pp. 6–10), and Lord Devlin observed that 'one of the most interesting features in *Shaw's* case is that (in cases of uncategorized immorality contrary to common law as distinct from offences defined by statute) it . . . makes the jury a constitutional organ for determining what amounts to immorality and when the law should be enforced' (*loc. cit.*, p. 91).

In the past what was regarded as 'divine law' was the arbiter. Today, in Hart's view, 'rationalist morality' should assume that role, while Devlin argues, in effect, that in a democracy* it is what the majority of its duly appointed representatives shall enact as its statue law and what its courts shall duly embed in its case-law.

See also: PUNISHMENT.

Bibliography

P. Devlin, *The Enforcement of Morals* (Oxford, 1965); H. L. A. Hart, 'Immorality and Treason', in L. Blom-Cooper (ed.), *The Law as Literature* (London, 1961); *idem*, *Law, Liberty and Morality* (London, 1963).

J.N.D.A.

DICTATORSHIP is the concentration of power* in a single ruler or small group and the often arbitrary use of that power by those who rule, including the reduction of civil liberties, and aggressive control of all social and political institutions by the State.

Dictatorship entails both a particular structure of government* and a special orientation to power. As a structure of government, dictatorship is defined often as the domination and control of the State by a single individual or a small group of individuals. It is immediately apparent, however, that that definition is far too inclusive. Contemporary scholars do not regard as dictatorships all governments dominated and controlled by a single individual or small group of individuals.

In *The Politics*, Aristotle* helps to clarify the nature of contemporary dictatorships. Aristotle defined a constitution as the arrangement of offices in a *polis* (city) and in particular the office which was thought of as sovereign. He argued further that right constitutions are ones in which those who rule do so out of a concern for the common interest. Bad constitutions are ones in which those who govern do so with the purpose of advancing personal or group interest, often at the expense of the common good.

Following Aristotle, contemporary political theorists view dictatorship as more than a form of government. The motives and style of those who govern are as important as structure. A more comprehensive definition of dictatorship is that it is the domination of the state by a single individual or group of individuals who use the State's coercive power to advance their self-interest without any effective constitutional limitations on their exercise of power.

Carl J. Friedrich (1901–84) and Zbigniew K. Brzezinski (1928–) refined further our understanding of dictatorship. They distinguished the new form of twentieth-century dictatorship, which they called totalitarian dictatorship, from earlier forms of tyranny, monarchy and autocracy.*

Although totalitarian dictatorships share some characteristics with earlier forms of centralized political power, modern totalitarian dictatorships also consciously create an ideology, means of political coercion, and carefully controlled structures of mass political participation as instruments by which the rulers control the ruled.

If dictatorship is singularly thought of as a structure of government, little in it concerns Christians. Clearly, Christians can live, and have lived, under the authority of diverse structures of government. Scripture neither condemns nor condones any particular structural arrangement of political authority.*

Scripture, however, is not silent about the ruler's orientation to power or his proper use of political authority. Political authority used primarily for the personal enhancement of the ruler, which denies or seriously denigrates human rights (see Rights, Human*) and which is so centralized that it inhibits human interaction and creativity, is contrary to the biblical mandate.

In Rom. 13, Paul teaches that government, while established by God, is given specific tasks as well as specific tools – the sword, for example – by which to fulfil its role within the created order. The authority and power of rulers are limited by their tasks (Rom. 13:1–7).

Furthermore, the OT makes clear that when God consented to a monarchy for Israel, he established a limited monarchy, not one of unlimited power as existed in the pagan societies surrounding Israel. Saul and David, the first two kings of Israel, covenanted with the people, and each understood his rights, duties and responsibilities to the people as well as the limits God placed on his authority (1 Sa. 10:25 and 2 Sa. 5:3).

When David's adulterous relationship with Bathsheba went beyond those limitations, God punished David not only because he was immoral, but because David violated his agreement with the people. His indirect murder of Uriah is further evidence of one of those traits Aristotle highlights, namely that rulers ought not to be self-seeking (2 Sa. 11).

Even after the division of the kingdom, many of the apostate kings of Israel understood the limited nature of their rule. Ahab, for example, would not, on his own, seize Naboth's garden because he knew that he, Ahab, had no right to do so (1 Ki. 21).

In his book, *Democracy and Its Critics*, the American political scientist, Robert A. Dahl (1915–), distinguished democracy from two other forms of authority, anarchy and guardianship. Anarchy,* the absence of any form of political authority, is clearly contrary to the created order. That does not mean, however, that the Bible mandates democracy. Guardianship, the belief that government ought to be left to a minority which possesses special knowledge, virtue or social attributes, has existed far longer as a form of authority than has democracy.

Christians can live obediently under, and even advocate, some form of guardianship as long as it respects basic human rights and seeks the common good. When guardianship, in whatever form, violates human rights and sacrifices the common interest for those of the rulers, it moves closer to totalitarian dictatorship. And the later is clearly contrary to biblical prescription.

See also: COMMUNITY ETHICS. [16]

Bibliography

H. Arendt, *The Origins of Totalitarianism*, new ed. (New York, 1966); E. Baker, *The Politics of Aristotle* (New York, 1962); R. Dahl, *Democracy and Its Critics* (New Haven, CT, and London, 1989); C. J. Friedrich and Z. K. Brzezinski, *Totalitarian Dictatorship and Autocracy* (Cambridge, MA, and London, 1956).

R.P.L.

DISABILITY AND HANDICAP. In common usage the two terms 'disability' and 'handicap' are often used interchangeably. Dictionary definitions often suggest equivalent meanings, as something that hampers or hinders, or as an inability to perform a task because of a mental or physical impairment.

In contemporary medical terminology, there is a logical link between the three related concepts of impairment, disability and handicap. An impairment is any stable and persisting defect at the organic level. It may or may not lead to a disability, which is the stable and persisting loss of an ability to perform an activity, such as feeding oneself. Then, most importantly, the extent to which a disability leads to a handicap is influenced by, on the one hand, social and material resources (see Health and Health Care*), such as the availability of helping relatives or a prosthetic aid, and on the other hand, personal resources, such as appropriate coping strategies. Handicap is then a social role assumed by the impaired and disabled person that is assigned from the expectations of society. This sequence is now enshrined in the 1980 World Health Organization's International Classification of Impairment, Disability and Handicap (ICIDH). A number of estimates suggest that 10% of the adult population have a significant handicap.

Disability and handicap are primarily associated with chronic diseases (which may be congenital), or with traumatic injury. By definition, chronic diseases are those which do not remit, and hence individuals' ability to cope with the disease, their emotional reactions to the disease, their ability to adapt to their condition and to control further threats to their health, are all important. The impact of a disease will vary according to the nature of the disease, *e.g.* whether it involves complete sensory loss, or loss of voluntary movement.

Different causes of disability have different ages of onset, and may thus have different developmental implications; cerebral palsy, with early onset, will have implications for development of the child, while cerebrovascular accidents tend to occur in older people, and have their main impact on the ability to function independently. World-wide estimates of numbers of disabled people suggest that malnutrition and non-communicable somatic diseases are now the two most common medical causes of handicap. The probability of disability is thus related to access to basic health care: many disabling conditions in developing countries (*e.g.* trachoma and leprosy) are easily treated in their early stages.

Disabling conditions were clearly recognized in Egyptian and Babylonian texts as well as in Hebrew sources. In the OT, lameness is referred to on several occasions, as in the case of the lameness in both feet of Mephibosheth (2 Sa. 4:4; 9:3, 13). While on the one hand the lame were recognized as helpless (2 Sa. 5:6–8) and thus deserving of mercy and social justice, the deformed were precluded from the priesthood (Lv. 21:18–20; but note the prophetic expectation, Is. 56:3–5), as their defect would detract from the wholeness (holiness) of God. Physical deformity is referred to in the NT, *e.g.* the woman 'bent over' for eighteen years (Lk. 13:10–17). Blindness was common, as a consequence both of disease and of old age (Gn. 48:10).

Leprosy is probably the chronic condition most frequently mentioned in the Bible (*e.g.* 2 Ch. 26:19–21; Lk. 17:11–19). The conditions referred to as leprosy refer to several different medical conditions, but it is significant that Jesus on several occasions superseded Mosaic prohibitions about touching not only the leprous, but the dead (Mt. 9:25), and his example towards the leprous has been a major contributor to Christian concern for leprosy sufferers.

A key NT passage with reference to handicap is Jn. 9:1–7, where Jesus heals the man blind from birth. This passage includes the denial that sin has anything to do with the handicap; and that God uses people in specific ways to fulfil his intention for the world. The parable of the householder (Lk. 14:11–14) illustrates how the kingdom of God* is not complete without the blind and the maimed. To the extent that we safeguard an image of ourselves as healthy and free from all defect, we may minimize the part of the handicapped have to play within the membership of the church.

There are many pastoral implications of

concern for those with disabilities. Because of the duration of the disabling condition, helpers may grow lax, patients may continue to comply with prescribed medical regimes, pain and weakness may persist. The role of the pastor is clear in acute illness and injury, where shared Christian assumptions can enable the resources of faith to be brought to bear on the healing process. Where the duration of disorder is both lengthy and uncertain, there is a recurring challenge to faith. The simple issue of the physical and psychological accessibility of public worship to the physically limited and the mentally limited is a challenge to many congregations. The two main elements of the pastoral challenge of disability are the affirmation and congregational acceptance of disabled people within the mainstream of congregational life, and the ability of a congregation to translate into contemporary practice the challenge of response to the needy and the confined (Mt. 25:34–45).

See also: LEARNING DISABILITIES.

Bibliography

G. Muller-Fahrenholz, *Partners in Life: The Handicapped and the Church* (Geneva, 1979); B. Palmer (ed.), *Medicine and the Bible* (Exeter, 1986); World Health Organization, *International Classification of Impairments, Disabilities and Handicaps* (Geneva, 1980).

J.N.H.

DISARMAMENT. The term 'disarmament' refers to: 1. the reduction of armaments of a defeated nation, such as Germany under the Versailles Treaty of 1919; 2. bilateral understandings, such as the Rush–Bagot agreement which since 1817 has kept the border between Canada and the US demilitarized; 3. the attempts in the 20th century through the League of Nations and the United Nations to limit and reduce arms by general international agreement; and 4. the complete abolition of all weapons as taught by certain pacifist* and utopian groups.

The Christian revelation and the teaching of many churches, such as the Friends (Quakers*), the Mennonites* and the Church of the Brethren, emphasize the need for a peaceful life. These groups have stressed NT texts such as the Sermon on the Mount (Mt. 5:39, 44) which seem to forbid the use of armed force by Christians. They point out that Jesus taught that the cause of God was never to be advanced by physical force (Jn. 18:36), and that he condemned Peter for using a weapon to defend him (Mt. 26:51–54; Jn. 18:10–11). This testimony was continued by the early church, but during the 4th and 5th centuries the Germanic invasions and the legalization of Christianity by Constantine* led to the acceptance of violence.* During the Middle Ages, this was carried out to such an extreme that the church even authorized the Crusades to rid Europe of heretics and to conquer the Holy Land.

The Reformation accepted the use of arms, and new developments such as gunpowder, when combined with religious zeal, led to the bloody wars of religion (c. 1550–1648). However, even in that brutal and coarse age the Christian humanist, Erasmus (c. 1469–1536), and many of the Anabaptists* opposed a resort to arms. With the growth of modern States and the technological advances of the Industrial Revolution, total or absolute war became possible. The horrors of such campaigns caused Christians who accepted the idea of a just war* to encourage attempts to limit arms on an international scale.

These individuals, and many who took a more secular approach, supported attempts at humanitarian co-operation among the nations. A series of international gatherings, such as those held at the Hague in 1899 and 1907, agreed that certain weapons (including poison gas and dumdum bullets) would not be used, and that projectiles ought not to be thrown on the enemy from balloons. These decisions, although negligible, were important because they came from the first general meetings of nations to deal with armament problems.

Despite these hopeful signs, total or absolute war was waged by both sides in the First World War (1914–18). Conflict became three-dimensional for the first time and struck at civilian population in an inhumane way. Modern artillery, extensive use of mines, machine guns, poison gas, submarine warfare and aerial bombardment broke the spirit of the pre-war peace conferences. After the conflict it was decided by many that there was a causal link between armaments and war.* The goal of disarmament 'to the lowest point consistent with domestic safety' was among the Fourteen Points proclaimed by the President of the US, Woodrow Wilson (1856–1924), as the basis of the peace treaties.

The armistice stripped Germany of its armaments, and it was expected that the League of Nations (1920) would inaugurate the principle of universal collective security. Despite the pacifist attitudes of the victors in the war and peace assemblies such as the Washington Conference of 1921 and a world-wide disarmament meeting in 1932, this did not happen, and the forces of totalitarianism in Germany, Italy, and Japan rearmed. The result was the Second World War (1939–45) and the development of even more frightful weapons. Out of this maelstrom came the UN (United Nations), organized in 1945 to replace the defunct League of Nations. One of its basic goals was to establish 'a system for the regulation of armament'.

New characteristics of weaponry in the field of rocketry, nuclear, chemical and biological warfare have stimulated a fresh concern for disarmament in the post-war decades. The state of technology* has given the advantage to the offensive power. The fear of so-called 'first-strike capability' has encouraged continuous peace discussions at the UN and, in addition, the superpowers have negotiated the Strategic Arms Limitation Talks (SALT) of the 1970s and the Strategic Arms Reduction Talks (START) of the 1980s and 1990s.

Despite these achievements, many conservative Christians remain sceptical and support 'peace through strength'. They believe that the Western democracies could be tricked into giving up too many armaments and that some neo-totalitarian powers would attack them. Then the very thing feared by those who advocate disarmament would come about.

Bibliography

R. H. Bainton, *Christian Attitudes toward War and Peace* (Nashville, TN, 1960) = *Christian Attitudes to War and Peace* (London, 1961); R. G. Clouse (ed.), *War: Four Christian Views* (Downers Grove, IL, 1991); Department for Disarmament Affairs, *Disarmament: A Periodic Review by the United Nations* (1978–); A. Geyer, *The Idea of Disarmament!: Rethinking the Unthinkable* (Elgin, IL, 1982); E. Regehr, *Militarism and the World Military Order* (Geneva, 1980).

R.G.C.

DISCIPLINE. The noun 'discipline' has various meanings: 1. a branch of instruction (*e.g.* physics); 2. the enforcement of order; and 3. the sanctions associated with keeping order (*e.g.* being under church* discipline). The verb, which has the meaning of 'to train to obedience', suggests that discipline is as much a process as a set of sanctions or a particular state.

In Christian spirituality,* various disciplines are seen as means of aiding spiritual growth in a life of committed discipleship (see Asceticism;* Disciplines, Spiritual*). In ecclesiology, discipline, particularly in the Reformed tradition, has embraced a range of concerns generally subsumed under the term 'polity': issues of church order, including church courts, and the moulding of a Christian society in which the laws and social order reflected, and were sustained by, Christian principles. A notable expression of the latter concern is the *First Book of Discipline* (1560) and the *Second Book of Discipline* (1578) of the Reformed Church of Scotland. These dealt not only with the polity of the church, the responsibilities of ministers and the enforcement of morals, but also with the establishment of schools and the reform of the universities. Discipline in this sense is thus intimately connected with the vision of a Christian society.

Biblical teaching

In the OT, the verb *ysr* can range in meaning from 'admonish' (*e.g.* Ps. 94:10; Pr. 9:7), and 'discipline' (*e.g.* Dt. 4:36; Pr. 3:11), to 'chastise' (*e.g.* Lv. 26:18, 28; Pr. 19:18). The associated noun *mûsār* is used of correction ('instruction', Pr. 15:33, NASB) which leads to wisdom, and of education or instruction (Ps. 50:17). The disciplining of his son by a father provides an analogy for God's disciplining of his covenant people (Dt. 8:5; Pr. 3:11–12; *cf.* Heb. 12:4–11).

In the Wisdom teaching the educative function of discipline is prominent. Thus to heed discipline is to gain understanding (Pr. 15:32); indeed wisdom and discipline are inseparably linked (Pr. 1:2–3). According to Proverbs, education cannot dispense with corporal punishment (13:24; *cf.* 29:15). Such correction when necessary gives hope of amendment (19:18), drives out folly (22:15), and gives life to those who receive it (4:13). But it must be done in love (13:24), not anger.

In the NT, the verb *paideuō* and noun *paideia* have a similar range of meaning to *ysr* and *mûsār*. Thus Moses was 'educated in all the wisdom of the Egyptians' (Acts 7:22) and children are 'disciplined' by their parents (Heb. 12:8). The word *paideuō* is also used of divine discipline (Heb. 12:6), exercised in love that we may share in God's holiness (Heb. 12:10).

Pastoral perspectives

The fact that, biblically, discipline is educative as well as punitive has important pastoral implications. God's education or training of his people involves much more than punishing them for their wrongdoing, as the story of Job shows. The suffering that Job endured by God's permission brought him to a deeper trust in God (Jb. 13:15) and a greater humility before him (40:3–5). It was Job's friends who wanted to read his sufferings as punitive – not Job, or indeed God! It is therefore pastorally wise to work with this distinction in mind, otherwise those who suffer may easily conclude that suffering* is always due to sin.

In Christian families the upbringing (*paideia*) of children (Eph. 6:4) is to reflect God's fatherly dealings with his people. It is to be 'of the Lord', *i.e.* the education which God gives through the father (taking *kyriou* as a subjective genitive). Though firm, it is not to be harsh or unbalanced, not thundering wrath to the neglect of encouragement, otherwise children will be made angry and resentful (*cf.* 'exasperate', NIV). Great wisdom is needed as children grow to maturity lest prohibitions appropriate to early childhood are still insisted upon in early adulthood.

In the West in the last two generations, the pendulum has swung from authoritarianism to permissiveness in the upbringing of children. Neither is a valid option for Christian parents if their nurturing (as indeed all Christian nurture) is to be 'training in righteousness' (2 Tim. 3:16). For righteousness is not permissive, since it is in antithesis to self-centredness and sin. Nor is it purely authoritarian, since new-covenant righteousness is brought about not by the thunderings of the law, but through the internal work of the Spirit (Rom. 8:1–4).

From a biblical perspective, the whole of the Christian life is to be seen as training for eternity under the fatherly discipline of God. In this the Scriptures (2 Tim. 3:16–17), person-to-person exhortation (Eph. 4:25), and the corporate life and sanctions of the church (*cf.* 1 Cor. 5:1–5), each have important parts to play.

D.P.K.

DISCIPLINES, SPIRITUAL, have been practised in religions from the beginning of human history, and are found in Judaism and Christianity. Christians are called 'disciples' and embrace 'disciplines' in order to 'Offer your bodies as living sacrifices, holy and pleasing to God – this is your spiritual service of worship' (Rom. 12:1). These disciplines are called *your* righteousness, (Mt. 6:1) and are to be distinguished from *God's* righteousness, which is a gift (Rom. 5:17) and in which a believer seeks to be found right with God and living in right obedience (Phil. 3:9; Rom. 6:16).

Disciplines are the believer's activities in sowing to the Spirit (Gal. 6:8). They are not in themselves the harvest of the Spirit, which is Christ's life being brought forth as fruit (Gal. 5:22), but are our provision of right conditions for its growth. John Wesley* said, 'It was a common saying among the Christians of the primitive church, the soul and the body make a man, the Spirit and discipline make a Christian, implying that none could be real Christians without the help of Christian discipline. But if this be so, is it any wonder that we find so few Christians, for where is Christian discipline?' ('Causes of the Inefficacy of Christianity', in *Sermons on Several Occasions*, vol. 1, London, 1836, p. 437). Richard Foster's (1942–) more recent advocacy of spiritual disciplines says that they are 'classical', but 'not classical merely because they are ancient, although they have been practised by sincere people over the centuries. The disciplines are classical because they are *central* to experiential Christianity.' (See *Celebration of Discipline*, London, 1980, p. 1.)

Jesus accepts the three most important disciplines of Judaism (*giving, prayer* and *fasting*, Mt. 6:2, 5 and 16), and purifies them from self-display and self-righteous Pharisaism. The following further sixteen disciplines at least are affirmed in the Scriptures, and appear throughout the history of the church. These are not, as sometimes has been misunderstood, meritorious works; neither are they acts of penance to pay for the soul's misdoings, but rather a means for hungering after God (Ps. 42:1).

Individual disciplines

1. *Meditation* is where the objective is not monistic oblivion, but the object is Christ himself and his works, or indeed whatever is true, noble, right, pure, lovely, admirable, excellent or praiseworthy (Phil. 4:8). 2. Closely aligned to this is *study*, which is primarily of the Scriptures and God's work in creation (Ps. 19), but also of the works and lives of men and women of God. 3. *Simplicity*, 4. *frugality* and

5. *sacrifice* all serve to build a life-style free from materialism, the heart of which is the discipline of 'giving' mentioned above, but they add the dimension of freedom for the disciple to be available to God. 6. Jesus often practised *solitude* (Mk. 1:35), giving an example to follow, and 7. *silence*, which takes one further into isolation and tongue-control, that we might be 'slow to speak' (Jas. 1:19). 8. *Secrecy* involves taking steps to prevent our good deeds being known; Thomas à Kempis (*c.* 1380–1471) in *The Imitation of Christ* speaks of the great tranquillity of heart that comes by rising above praising and blamings. 9. *Chastity** is not just the discipline of celibacy (see Singleness*) to which some give themselves with the enabling of the Holy Spirit, but also mutual abstention to give oneself to prayer (1 Cor. 7:5–7).

Corporate disciplines

10. *Service* includes being salt and light in society, so that our good works glorify our heavenly Father (Mt. 5:16), and it also means doing our work well, 'with all your heart, as working for the Lord, not for men' (Col. 3:22–24). 11. *Celebration* is the enjoyment of life, following the example of Jesus who enjoyed another's wedding, though he himself would never marry, and was accused of being a glutton and a drunkard (Mt. 11:19). Francis of Assisi* taught his followers that they must always be happy, so cultivating the habit of happiness. This too is a discipline, as indeed is 12. *worship*, which has been described as the art of love-making with God. 13. *Fellowship** is the essential benefit which comes from the mingling and sharing of our lives together in many of the activities that have already been spelled out. There is a negative side to this particular discipline, namely the loss of fellowship's privileges where church discipline is administered (Mt. 18:15–20). 14. *Submission* (Heb. 13:7, 17) demands a high degree of fellowship and loyalty, and also involves 15. *confession** (Jas. 5:16), and 16. *guidance*, not only the daily concerns of an individual's Spirit-led life, but a submission to the corporate mind (Acts 13:1–3; 15:28).

Leo Tolstoy* said, 'Everyone thinks of changing humanity and nobody thinks of changing himself.' The aim, however, of all disciplines, whether we classify them as inward or outward, or individual and corporate (see R. Foster's *Celebration of Discipline*), or whether we see them as abstaining from certain things and engaging in others (see D. Willard, *The Spirit of the Disciplines*, p. 158) is that we might succeed in guarding our heart, 'the wellspring of life' (Pr. 4:23), so that from it might flow a pure, unadulterated stream of God's life (Jn. 7:38).

Bibliography

R. Foster, *Celebration of Discipline* (San Francisco, ²1988; London, ²1989); J. Owen, 'Of the Mortification of Sin in Believers', *Works*, vol. 6 (1656; repr. London, 1966), pp. 5–86; Thomas à Kempis, *The Imitation of Christ* (1418; many eds.); D. Willard, *The Spirit of the Disciplines* (San Francisco, 1988).

R.T.F.

DISCRIMINATION.

The 1968 UK Race Relations Act (amended in 1976) and the 1975 Sex Discrimination Act (amended in 1986) define 'discrimination' as treating one person 'less favourably than s/he treats or would treat other persons'. The Race Relations Act also has a separate subsection which includes segregation. The focus of the legal definition of 'discrimination' is therefore on behaviour rather than attitude. Discrimination can be either a deliberate wrong perpetrated by one individual against a specific victim, or the result of the inaction of an individual or organization. In either case it is the action or inaction, irrespective of motive, *e.g.* malice, fear or dislike, which has a 'disproportional adverse impact' on a certain individual/group/community. Through time, discrimination creates substantial inequality and unequal life chances between groups in the areas of education, employment, housing, health, access to various services, and socio-economic status. Examples of this 'substantial inequality' and unequal life chance are prevalent, if one chooses to see and hear them. Even with an equal level of education, women still earn only two thirds of what their male colleagues earn on both sides of the Atlantic. Blacks suffer worse housing and an unemployment* rate three times higher than whites, and only 31% of disabled (see Disability and Handicap*) people of working age are in employment.

As a result, in the UK, the State, taking full recognition of the nation-wide problem in discrimination, took on the responsibility for setting the legislative framework for employers, local authorities, service providers and public statutory bodies. The Race Relations Act (1968) outlined the legal responsibilities of these agencies to ensure non-discrimination. It made direct and indirect discrimination and victimization on the grounds of race,* colour, ethnic origin, nationality and national origin to be illegal. The Race Relations Act was followed by the Sex Discrimination Act in 1975, which forbids discrimination on the grounds of gender and marital status. Both Acts have since been amended, and there are now certain statutory regulations that all organizations have to observe. They cover virtually all employment practices including recruitment, promotion, transfer and training, as well as access to benefits, facilities and services. They also cover dismissal.

These, together with other items of legislation (*e.g.* regarding equal pay and the employment of disabled persons) have set a legislative requirement by which all who employ staff and provide services must abide. Other countries, *e.g.* the USA, have also provided a legislative framework which goes beyond forbidding discrimination and actually allows reverse discrimination (*i.e.* affirmative action) whereas other European countries are also beginning to consider tackling societal discrimination via the legal route.

The legislation testifies to the reality of discrimination among many groups and communities who are denied the basic civil rights (see Rights, Human*) to which they are entitled. Discrimination, especially institutional discrimination, does not affirm that differences between people are simply differences, something to be reckoned with, accepted and celebrated. Instead these differences are seen as a tool for stratification – degradation or elevation depending on the groups to which one belongs. Features of the differences become signs and symbols for marking out those who are 'acceptable' and those who are 'unacceptable'.

Such destructive discrimination does not reflect the kind of distinction that the Sermon on the Mount* draws (*i.e.* between good and bad attitudes and behaviour, between the narrow and wide gates for life's journey, Mt. 7:6, 13–16). Instead, Jesus firmly rebukes discrimination when we judge others in a censorious way and set ourselves up over them on some standard of goodness or acceptability. Of course there are differences between people. The Christian church, as the body of Christ, includes the rich variety of different personalities, different gifts, different races, different genders. The task of the body is mutual ministry and mutual acceptance (Eph. 4) so that there can be growth in all the diversity towards harmony in Christ.

The history of the human race, and all too often of the Christian church, is a history of the sort of discrimination that either judges in a censorious way, or makes discrimination between people on the basis of human preferences or human fears, and fails to acknowledge that all of us are creatures of the same God, and bear his image (see Image of God*). The church as an institution has often failed to be salt and light in the area of fighting against inequality. Either it all too frequently participates in the history of various forms of discrimination, or it lifts no hands in correcting the wrongs of injustice, despite brave individuals such as Lord Shaftesbury* and Martin Luther King.*

In the creation account in Gn. 1, male and female together are made in the divine image, and in Gn. 2 the gender complementarity reflects something of God's purpose for human sexuality. However, the story of sin from Gn. 3 onwards is the story all too often of male dominance and female subservience – a story which is rectified in the NT, not only by Jesus' affirmative attitude towards women, but also by Paul's affirmation that in Christ 'there is neither . . . male nor female' in terms of difference of human status (Gal. 3:28).

Racial discrimination, whether in a subtle form or the extreme form of apartheid,* is also a denial of God's creative purposes for humanity. There are real difficulties in using the discrimination between Israelite and foreigner in the OT as a basis for contemporary Christian action. The loose and irresponsible use of the doctrine of election to imply that certain races are superior to others in the purposes of God fails to acknowledge that 'from one man God made every nation of men, that they should inhabit the whole earth' (Acts 17:26), and it fails to recognize that discrimination based on race is also subverted by the gospel, together with the prejudice that feeds it. The early church had to come to terms with the inclusion of the Gentiles within the people of God (see Acts 15:1–21), and Paul's letters to the Romans and Galatians in particular discuss the practical decisions required by the gospel statement that in Christ 'there is neither Jew nor Greek' (Gal. 3:28).

It is clear from the total message of Scripture

that one cannot speak of God's love for us and Christ's sacrifice on the cross without speaking of his righteousness and justice. God's love for his people is never sentimental. It is always practical and concrete. As Allan Boesak (1946–) puts it: 'Yahweh takes the side of his people against the oppressor, the pharaoh . . . Yahweh comes openly to the aid of his downtrodden people for all the world to see and know that . . . he is the liberator of the oppressed and the One who uprightly defends the poorest, who saves the children of those in need and crushes their oppressors' (see Ps. 72:4; *Black Theology, Black Power*, p. 19). As people redeemed by this only true God, our moral and ethical response to discrimination is not just 'feeling' how terrible it is that precious lives and talents are wasted because certain members of society are branded less acceptable than others. The minimum duty of Christian people is to take a clear moral and ethical stand in the church, workplace and any other institution – be it political, educational, economic or voluntary – that discrimination is unacceptable and that Christians are ready to work with others towards a fairer and more just world.

At the institutional level, questions could be asked about workforce statistics, implications of past practices that affect the 'access' of those people who have been discriminated against in the institution; meaningful and implementable 'equal opportunities' policy and practice could be suggested; the ethics and value of treating everyone fairly, in accordance to equal values, needs to be modelled in roles and relationships.

And at the societal level, demands could be made of political representatives, in the name of social justice, about equality issues in the political arena; individuals can join or get involved in local communities to understand how deprivation affects individuals and learn from them what programmes of action are desirable.

Bibliography

L. Abdela, *Breaking through the Glass Ceilings* (Solihull, 1991); A. A. Boesak, *Black Theology, Black Power* London and Maryknoll, NY, 1978); M. Davidson and J. Earnshaw, *Vulnerable Workers: Psychosocial and Legal Issues* Chichester, 1991); R. Jenkins, *Racism and Recruitment* (Cambridge, 1986); L. Lustgarten, *Legal Control of Racial Discrimination* (London, 1980); *idem, Women Managers: The Untapped Resource* (London, 1990).

L.M.-Y.C.-J.

DISHONESTY, see FRAUD.

DISINVESTMENT, see ECONOMIC SANCTIONS.

DISPENSATIONALISM. A system of scriptural interpretation, which teaches that God has dealt with humans in unique ways during the different eras of biblical history. As C. I. Scofield (1843–1921), one of its leading exponents, explained: 'A dispensation is a period of time during which man is tested in respect of obedience to some *specific* revelation of the will of God' (*Scofield Reference Bible*, note 4, at Gn. 1:28 – 3:13).

Although many claim that the movement started much earlier, modern dispensationalism began with the ministry of J. N. Darby (1880–82) and the Plymouth Brethren. Their work inspired a series of interdenominational Bible teachers and evangelists, including D. L. Moody (1837–99), H. A. Ironside (1876–1951) and Scofield. The *Scofield Reference Bible* (1909) was especially important because the notes made dispensationalism an integral part of the interpretative scheme. Within fifty years, three million copies of this Bible were printed in the US. In more recent times, works such as *The Late Great Planet Earth* (Grand Rapids, 1970; London, 1971) by Hal Lindsey (1930–) have sold tens of millions of copies and served to popularize the view to an even greater extent.

There are differences among dispensationalists, and many do not agree with Scofield's outline of seven ages. However, they all make distinctions between the OT period of the law,* the NT age of grace,* and the coming era of the millennial kingdom (see Kingdom of God*). They also distinguish between Israel and the church* and the Bible passages which apply to each of them. Because of a literalist emphasis on most parts of Scripture and a penchant for applying troublesome verses to future or past dispensations, it is difficult to find a carefully articulated ethical theory among them. Certain characteristics of this belief do have moral implications. One of the more obvious is a pessimistic attitude towards society.* Dispensationalists believe in a supernatural social theory which limits God's ability to affect change in society in the present age. Christians who follow this theology tend to feel that it is useless to support social programmes that try to ameliorate the conditions of the poor, despite clear statements such as those found in Mt. 25 and Rom. 12:20. They narrow the task of the church to 'saving souls' rather than working for the moral betterment of humankind.

The church, rather than being central to the cause of God, is thought to be no better than Israel, and its main purpose is to be a promotional or sales organization for the gospel. High-pressure tactics are used to foster an emphasis on 'winning the last soul to Christ', so that he will return and 'rapture' the church.

Dispensationalists also take a very negative view of culture.* They encourage Bible colleges and seminaries to train individuals for 'full-time' Christian service. A thorough knowledge of the liberal arts and an understanding of the history of Christian thought are not considered important. This pessimistic view extends to the arts* and entertainment* media as well, and consequently they ignore and condemn these aspects of expression. Rather than encouraging meaningful participation by Christians in such activities, they develop their own counter-culture. Because of this, their preaching seems irrelevant to those who have not been initiated into dispensationalism.

Another aspect of this theology that has ethical implications is the effort to identify the signs of the times. Such occurrences as wars, the rise of authoritarian political leaders, technological advances, natural disasters and apostasy in the churches are cited as proof that the end of the age is near and that the second coming of Christ is about to take place. Attention is focused on the Zionist establishment of the State of Israel as the focus for these signs. This not only encourages attempts to set the dates for the return of Christ but it also leads to an uncritical support of Israel in the Middle East. Accepting a belligerent foreign policy in that area could lead to wider international conflicts. In fact, many such as Hal Lindsey identify nuclear warfare with biblical statements describing the second coming.

These positions would not characterize all dispensationalists, however, because their social ethic is extremely individualistic. The OT law in its civil, ceremonial and moral function, they claim, belongs to another age. The principles of the Sermon on the Mount* apply primarily to the millennial kingdom and any application to the present is purely secondary. Thus one is left with moral and ethical statements drawn from the letters of the apostles in the NT.

There is one sense in which dispensationalism is quite helpful. Many Christians tend to ignore the eschatological passages of the Bible. They tacitly accept the view that the world will continue as it is for ever. Those who concentrate on the second coming constantly remind the church that the gospel is a message of hope and openness to the future. The end is coming and, however one interprets Scripture, 'the blessed hope' that Christians will live and reign with their Lord for ever must never be absent from Christian preaching.

Bibliography
R. G. Clouse (ed.), *The Meaning of the Millennium: Four Views* (Downers Grove, IL, 1977); C. C. Ryrie, *Dispensationalism Today* (Chicago, 1965); E. R. Sandeen, *The Roots of Fundamentalism* (Chicago, 1970).

R.G.C.

DIVORCE. The OT, like the rest of the ancient Orient, presupposes the right of divorce, but it never explains under exactly what circumstances it may be exercised. So here, as in other areas of family* life, the OT picture must be supplemented by data from surrounding cultures.

Though divorce was allowed, it was discouraged by social convention, law and financial penalty. Both Gn. 2:24 ('a man will . . . be united [lit. "stick"] to his wife'), and the wedding vow ('I am her husband . . . for ever'), and the elaborateness of the wedding ceremony itself all express the hope that marriage* will be for life. To be divorced was to fall in social esteem (Pr. 30:23; see William McKane, *Proverbs*, London, 1970, p. 666), and to be debarred from marrying a priest (Lv. 21:7). However Mal. 2:16 ('I hate divorce') should be translated, it certainly expresses the prophet's antipathy to divorce.

In practice divorce must have been rare because it was expensive. On marriage the bride was presented with a large dowry by her father, often equivalent to several years' wages. The dowry was jointly owned by husband and wife, but if she was divorced for anything less than grave misbehaviour, she took the dowry with her. This must have made divorce exceptional.

There are few laws about divorce. It is prohibited in two situations (Dt. 22:19, 29), perhaps because the young man has shown himself hot-headed and liable to behave rashly. Other rules limit remarriage* after divorce.

The rules in Lv. 18:6–18 covering the choice of marriage partners would particularly affect divorcees and widow(er)s.

Deuteronomy 24:1–4 is primarily concerned with remarriage. A twice-married woman is forbidden after the death or divorce of her second husband to return to her first husband. The reason for this prohibition is obscure. But this law mentions two different grounds for divorce: the first husband divorces her because of 'something indecent', the second because he 'dislikes' her. 'Something indecent' suggests sexual misconduct. Though adultery,* if caught in the act, could be punished by death, this was not mandatory (*cf.* Pr. 6:29–35), so 'something indecent' may cover adultery as well as other sexual acts.

In the prophets, Israel's idolatry is often compared to spiritual adultery. The Lord therefore punishes her with divorce, *i.e.* exile, but he longs for her to repent and return to himself (Hos. 14:1–3).

The NT shares the OT's aversion to divorce. Asked to adjudicate between the liberal Hillelite Pharisees, who held that trivial grounds (*e.g.* bad cooking) warranted divorce, and the strict Shammaites, who allowed divorce only for 'indecency', Jesus pointed to God's original intention for marriage: 'the two . . . become one flesh. So they are no longer two, but one. Therefore what God has joined together, let man not separate' (Mt. 19:5–6). In other words, Jesus regards divorce as wrong. Furthermore he states that the OT permitted divorce only as a concession to human sinfulness: 'Moses permitted you to divorce your wives because your hearts were hard' (Mt. 19:8).

Thus far the teaching of Jesus is similar to that of the OT and the stricter Pharisaic party. But, according to Mark, Luke and Paul, Jesus went further than the OT in forbidding remarriage after divorce. In Mk. 10:11–12 and Lk. 16:18 he calls it adultery, and Paul paraphrases Jesus' teaching: 'A wife must not separate from her husband. But if she does, she must remain unmarried or else be reconciled to her husband. And a husband must not divorce his wife' (1 Cor. 7:10–11). Paul evidently understands Jesus to tolerate separation from one's spouse but not remarriage to someone else. This underlies the traditional Catholic view that the only kind of divorce allowable by the church is *a mensa et thoro* (*i.e.* from table to bed), not *a vinculo* (*i.e.* from the bond of marriage).

But according to Mt. 5:32 and 19:9, Jesus did allow divorce for *porneia* (NIV 'marital unfaithfulness'; RSV, REB 'unchastity'). The normal meaning of *porneia* and its present context demand that it is understood in a broad way of any sexual offences that are prohibited in the OT law: adultery, incest,* homosexuality,* *etc.*; anything that Dt. 24:1 might term 'something indecent'. It should not be understood to refer here just to premarital unchastity, or marriage within the forbidden degrees. A wider range of sexual misconduct is in view. This exception, allowing divorce for *porneia*, was probably a concession to the law of the day, since both Roman and Jewish law required that adulterous wives be divorced, though it may be seen as another concession to hard-heartedness.

However, it is unlikely that Jesus or Matthew allowed such divorcees to remarry. Grammatically it is possible to read Mt. 19:9 as permitting remarriage, but it is not required. In fact the context is against it. To suppose that Jesus allowed innocent divorcees to remarry would make him agree with the Shammaite Pharisees, whom he had just condemned. It also fails to explain the disciples' astonishment at his harsh novel teaching, 'If this is the situation . . . it is better not to marry' (Mt. 19:10), or the fact that Jesus goes on to speak of eunuchs who have renounced marriage (19:12). To suppose Jesus allowed divorcees to remarry also conflicts with the understanding of his teaching by Mark, Luke and Paul, and the early church, which for the first five centuries regarded remarriage after divorce as contrary to Christ's teaching.

On any reading, the NT poses great problems for an age where divorce and remarriage are commonplace. How is the church to bear witness to the permanency of marriage on the one hand and the forgiveness* of sins on the other? To move from exegesis to pastoral practice in this area is very difficult. Whatever stance is adopted to remarriage, all can agree that loyalty to biblical principles demands that all Christians, both individually and corporately, should work to maintain existing marriages and offer support and encouragement to those who are divorced.

In society as a whole Christians need to press for legislation and taxation policies that encourage partners to reconcile their differences rather than seek divorce. Modern British law, which allows divorce on trivial grounds within a year of marriage, is clearly contrary to biblical teaching. Lawyers should explore the possibility of reconciliation* before advising clients about divorce.

But once divorce has occurred and reconciliation is out of the question, the pastoral perspective alters. Now the Christian response is to bind up the broken-hearted and comfort those who mourn. Psychologically and financially, the trauma of divorce is often worse than bereavement, so that the divorcee will need all the support and encouragement that the Christian community can provide. All divorcees need open ears to listen to their griefs and hopes. Single parents* need to share their burdens with other families, especially when there are no grandparents nearby. For them the church family should provide an alternative network of care and support.

Spiritually, too, divorcees need complete assurance that God forgives them even when they cannot forgive themselves, and that the single are able to serve God with less distraction than married people and thus their ministry is particularly valued by Scripture (Mt. 19:11–12; 1 Cor. 7:32–38) and the contemporary church (see Singleness*). In all these ways, the church can bear witness to the love and forgiveness of Christ to those who are often most conscious of their need for it.

See also: SEXUALITY. [11]

Bibliography

D. J. Atkinson, *To Have and to Hold* (London, 1979); A. J. C. Cornes, *Divorce and Remarriage* (London, 1993); W. A. Heth and G. J. Wenham, *Jesus and Divorce* (London, 1984); D. Phypers, *Christian Marriage in Crisis* (London, 1985).

G.J.W.

DONATION, ORGAN, see TRANSPLANT SURGERY.

DOOYEWEERD, HERMAN (1894–1977), an outstanding Dutch Christian scholar, founder of the philosophy of the 'cosmonomic idea' or 'law idea', often referred to as the Amsterdam philosophy or reformational philosophy. He had a lifelong involvement with the (Reformed) Free University of Amsterdam, first as a student and finally as Professor of Jurisprudence (1926–65). The Free University had been founded in 1880 by Abraham Kuyper* as a Christian university in which all subjects were to be researched and taught from the perspective of a Christian worldview. Sharing in this vision, Dooyeweerd showed in detail the ways in which religious allegiances – pagan, Christian and humanist – had undergirded all human activity, including science, scholarship and education in the West. His seminal publication *De Wijsbegeerte der wetsidee* (1935–36) was revised and translated into Eng. as *A New Critique of Theoretical Thought* (4 vols., 1953–58).

In this encyclopedic work, Dooyeweerd sought to expose what he called 'the dogma of the autonomy of theoretical thought'. He argued that science and scholarship were religiously neutral not only in practice but also in principle. Every discipline was of necessity constituted by philosophical conceptions (ontological and epistemological) and behind these lay religious allegiances – ultimately for or against the kingdom of Christ. This formed the basis of Dooyeweerd's advocacy of the possibility and necessity of *Christian* scholarship as a strategic part of the obedience and renewal demanded by the gospel of the kingdom.

At first, English-speaking evangelical scholars displayed considerable hostility to such a viewpoint. The only Christian scholarship they were prepared to acknowledge was that of academic theology. Other disciplines were regarded as 'secular' rather than 'sacred' and therefore as religiously neutral. But the tide has now turned. Dualistic evangelicalism is now on the defensive, and mainline (humanist) philosophy itself has long since abandoned positivistic and objectivistic theories of knowledge. There is no doubt that the leaven of reformational philosophy has been a potent factor in the scholarly and cultural renaissance that is beginning in the evangelical world.

A number of works by Dooyeweerd are available in English. These include *In the Twilight of Western Thought* (Philadelphia, 1960); *Roots of Western Culture* (Toronto, 1979); *A Christian Theory of Social Institutions* (Ontario, 1986); and *A New Critique of Theoretical Thought* (Ontario, 1984). A vigorous programme of translation is now under way. The best introductions to Dooyeweerd available in English are L. Kalsbeek, *Contours of a Christian Philosophy* (Toronto, 1975), and R. A. Clouser, *The Myth of Religious Neutrality* (Notre Dame, IN, and London, 1991).

R.A.R.

DOUBLE EFFECT.

In carrying out a particular action or series of actions, a person may also be aware that such actions have side-effects, which, though they may be foreseen, may not be directly intended. If that person *is* aware of such side-effects, does he (or she), in virtue of that knowledge, actually *intend* to cause these side-effects? If so, may he therefore be said to be responsible for their occurrence even though he may not want them to happen and may even abhor and detest their occurrence? To take a typical example, a Second World War bomber pilot, in dropping bombs on a munitions factory, may be aware that some of the bombs will go astray and cause casualties among civilians not involved in munitions manufacture. He may not want these casualties to occur, but since he foresees them as the side-effect of the bombing, is he not also responsible for the deaths of the civilians? Or a drug may be given to a patient, with the intention of reducing pain but in the knowledge that administering it will shorten the patient's life. Is the physician responsible for killing the patient?

Many moralists would answer this question in the negative, and would cite 'the principle of double effect' as the reason. For them, the morally significant factor is the intention* of the agent, the precise effect that he intends by his action, and not the side-effect which, though he may be aware of it, he does not intend.

Those who uphold the principle of double effect do not endorse its use in every circumstance. If, for example, the action to be performed is an intrinsically wrong or immoral act, then the principle does not apply, since the action is forbidden in the first place. Further, the principle is not intended to allow an agent to 'get away with' what is otherwise to be regarded as immoral. Nor is it to be trivially applied; the good intended in the action must be of sufficient weight or strength to outweigh the evil of the side-effect which is foreseen and (allegedly) not intended. Finally, the principle is not to be confused with the view that it is permissible to do evil in order that good may come. The principle therefore does not maintain that the foreseen but not intended side-effect causally contributes to the intended good.

The issue raised by this principle is of considerable importance in the debate between utilitarians (see Consequentialism*) and others about the ethical rightness of actions. For the principle of double effect attributes a moral significance to intention (or to the absence of intention) irrespective of the consequences of the action. The principle maintains that the way in which an action is performed contributes to its moral character. So, if the principle is upheld, it undermines the utilitarian claim that the morality of an action is a function solely of the consequences of that action. For this reason those who are in any case opposed to utilitarianism may be less disposed to question the principle.

Critics of the principle tend to focus on two of its features. The first of these is the distinction between intended acts and acts that are merely foreseen (the side-effect), *i.e.* the difference between direct and oblique intention. It is argued, for example, that it is impossible to foresee a consequence of an intended act and not at the same time to intend that consequence, for it is an inseparable effect of the central act, and the agent knows this.

The second feature to which critics pay attention is the view that a person is not necessarily responsible for an effect of his action which he foresees but does not intend. While there are clear cases of such responsibility, these cases may depend upon a particular causal relationship between the action and its unintended effect.

The principle has been frequently invoked by Roman Catholic and other moralists in the context of the debate about abortion.* It is argued that a surgeon whose only recourse, in order to save the life of an expectant mother, is to perform an operation which he knows will result in the death of the foetus, is not performing an abortion if, in doing so, he does not intend the death.

There appears to be no clear teaching or example in Scripture which would settle the moral status of the principle of double effect decisively. But in so far as Scripture does not adopt a utilitarian ethic, its teaching may be said not to rule out an application of the principle in certain cases.

See also: ETHICS OF MEDICAL CARE. [14]

Bibliography

F. J. Connell, *NCE* 4, pp. 1020–1022; P. Foot, *Virtues and Vices and Other Essays in Moral Philosophy* (Oxford, 1978); J. Glover, *Causing Death and Saving Lives* (Harmondsworth, 1977).

P.H.

D **REAMS.** There are over 130 references to dreams in the Bible and almost 100 to visions, the bulk of them in the OT. This reflects the interest expressed in this subject in the ancient Near East.

The Heb. verb for dream is *ḥālam*, and like its Aram. counterpart it means 'to be healthy or strong'. The verb used for seeing a vision, a parallel experience to dreaming, is *ḥāzâ* and implies the ability to perceive with the inner eye. It is a word closely related to the term 'seer' (*ḥozeh*). The LXX and NT words for dream are *onar*, which refers to visions in sleep (*cf.* Mt. 1:20; 2:12; 27:19), and *enypiazomai* which indicates having visions in dreams (Joel 2:28 [LXX 3:1]; Acts 2:17; Jude 8). There is also a range of words for 'vision', all implying an ability to see, which are often used of dream messages as well: *horama*, whether asleep or awake (Acts 10:3); *horasis* (Acts 2:17; Rev. 9:17); *optasia* (Lk. 1:22; 24:23; 2 Cor. 12:1). Dreams and visions are brought close together by such expressions as 'vision of the night' (Gn. 46:2; Jb. 20:8; Is. 29:7) and 'visions of the head' (Dn. 2:28; 4:5; 10:14). It would appear that whereas dreams are generally the work and creation of the dreamer exploring his or her recent experiences, the vision is given directly by God and its content comes with authority and demands a response. It is clear from the Bible that God does communicate through dreams for a number of purposes.

According to Jb. 33:14–18 God uses dreams in various ways: 1. warnings: 'he may speak in their ears and terrify them with warnings' (33:16); 2. guidance: 'to turn man from wrongdoing' (33:17a); 3. discipline: 'and keep him from pride' (33:17b); and 4. deliverance: 'to preserve his soul from the pit, his life from perishing by the sword' (33:18).

Ability to understand dreams was regarded as evidence of God's favour and blessing (*e.g.* Gn. 41:16, 39). Understanding of dreams was regarded as a resource for spiritual wisdom* (Dn. 1:17), and it was in a dream that Solomon gained his extraordinary wisdom (1 Ki. 3:10–15). Knowledge of dreams was thought to give access to the word of God and this is principally demonstrated in the ability to prophesy.

The prophet was respectfully called a dreamer (Dt. 13:1–5) and dream messages are subjected to the same criteria as prophetic utterance. Jeremiah indicts the prophets of his day for claiming that their dreams came from God when in fact they were their own creations (Je. 23:25, 27). Though Nu. 12:6ff. compares how God speaks directly to Moses and via dreams to others, this in no way invalidates the dream as a means of revelation. Herman Riffel suggests that dreams in this context function like parables which contain picture clues to God's word (*Voice of God*, Wheaton, IL, 1978, pp. 73–74). The fact that dreams were acceptable as a vehicle for prophecy is tragically portrayed in the life of Saul who, on the eve of his last battle, finds that there is no word from God 'by dreams or Urim or prophets' (1 Sa. 28:6).

There are a number of examples of God speaking directly through dreams; the catalogues surrounding the nativity story are a case in point (Mt. 1:20; 2:12–13, 19, 22). In three of these accounts the term 'angel of the Lord' is used to convey the idea of direct encounter with the divine presence. Dreams are also used to bring the guidance of God whether directly or otherwise. Gideon received his final instalment of courage when he overheard a Midianite sentry share his dream of impending doom from the armies of Israel; he in fact based his use of fire and noise directly upon the symbols contained in the sentry's dream (Jdg. 7:13–21). We may conclude that the Bible, far from marginalizing the usefulness of dreams, in fact endorses them as a means to personal wholeness and a vehicle of divine guidance.

Dreams have been reappraised in 20th-century research both from a functional and a psychotherapeutic standpoint. Nathaniel Kleitman has pinpointed dreaming to the rapid eye-movement phase of sleep (REM) when most dreamers can recall their dreams in greater detail, and William Dement has demonstrated that without REM sleep there is considerable dysfunction within the person's behaviour.

There have been many theories as to why we dream. Freud* pioneered the way with his theory of wish-fulfilment whereby we disguise our true feelings behind dream symbols. Calvin S. Hall (1909–) has argued that dreams are a basic letter written to ourselves giving comment upon how we view our recent circumstances. He suggested that dreams followed up thoughts and convictions in waking life upon which we had not properly acted. If it is true that we write our own dreams, then we must look at the whole issue of nightmares and disturbing dreams. On the whole such dreams are about unfinished material in our lives, either recent or related to unhealed memories which we are not yet ready to work through, and this explains why the nightmare is abruptly terminated before it concludes.

There is no absolute method of interpreting dreams, and we must be careful not to impose our own interpretation upon another's dream. A helpful approach to working with a dream could be: 1. write down the dream; 2. share it with a friend but be careful to tell it in the present tense; 3. make a special note of any extra details which occur in addition to the original remembering; 4. write down any particular feeling words which strike you; 5. see if there are any related events or memories which correspond to these feeling words; 6. make a note of any insights or thoughts you have gained from this; 7. determine what action you wish to take in the light of what you have learned; and 8. commit this action to prayer.

Bibliography

R. Parker, *Dreams and Spirituality* (Bramcote, Nottingham, 1985); *idem, Healing Dreams* (London, 1988).

R.E.P.

DRUG ABUSE, see Drugs

DRUGS. Many people have a simplistic and inaccurate view of what is appropriate drug use and what constitutes misuse. In part, this is because 'drug' is defined by them only as a harmful, dangerous, addictive or illegal substance. However, the World Health Organization (WHO, 1966) has defined a drug as 'any substance or product that is used or intended to be used to modify or explore physiological systems or pathological states for the benefit of the recipient'. Under this wider and more comprehensive definition, not only are illicit drugs included, but so also are medicines, solvents and other volatile chemicals (*e.g.* as used in 'glue-sniffing'), alcohol (see Alcoholism*), tobacco, and beverages such as coffee and tea which contain caffeine and related substances.

It is appropriate that Christians are concerned about the misuse of illicit drugs, and they will want to support government action to warn of the health risks of opiates, and to endorse the action of the Customs in seeking to reduce illicit drug imports. Yet, it should be recognized that numerically the problem of non-illicit drug misuse is far greater than illicit drug use and, inconsistently, may be indulged in by those who are most vocal in their opposi-

tion to illicit drug use. In 1985 the UK population was sedated or tranquillized by more than 39 million prescriptions for psychoactive drugs (*i.e.* substances that alter the emotions or mental state) whereas in the same year there were only 26,596 convictions or cautions for offences under the Misuse of Drugs Act 1971. At the same time there was an annual toll of an estimated 100,000 premature deaths due to tobacco smoking and over 200,000 convictions for drunkenness and drink-driving offences. In an average Health District in the UK there are some 22,000 alcohol misusers (750,000 in the UK) and nationally some 16,000 hospital admissions each year for alcohol dependence. It has been estimated that in 1986 the total cost of alcohol misuse in England and Wales was £1,908m. This cost was offset, though not morally justified, by the £5,700m that the UK government received from excise duty and value added tax (VAT) levied on alcohol.

Drug-use statistics are also grim in the US. For 1985, 317,144 deaths were attributed to smoking. For 1989, there were 164,912 alcohol-related deaths and 374,437 alcoholics in treatment. Total annual loss to the economy related to alcohol abuse is estimated at 85.8 billion dollars.

Contrary to popular misconception, most drug misusers are not young people with a criminal record; they are middle-aged and elderly 'respectable' citizens. Consequently, there are few individuals who do not have one or more drug misusers in their immediate circle of family and friends, and, equally, drug misuse will be observed at work and in church life.

Drug use and misuse

Drugs may be prescribed by a physician or self-administered with a variety of intents, including the following: 1. to correct abnormalities, so that disease may be cured (*e.g.* the use of antibiotics to treat infection); 2. to relieve or suppress symptoms caused by disease which may or may not itself be curable currently (*e.g.* in the treatment of rheumatoid arthritis); 3. to relieve anxiety or mental distress caused by disease whether directly (*e.g.* depression) or indirectly (*e.g.* arising from the implications of a poor prognosis); 4. to prevent the onset of a disease that may be anticipated (*e.g.* the use of anti-malarials in an area where malaria is known to be endemic); 5. to interfere with normal physiological functions (*e.g.* to prevent pregnancy or to induce an abortion after conception); 6. for convenience (*e.g.* to delay menstruation and so permit swimming during a holiday; to lessen the harmful effects of sunbathing; to avoid a sleepless night in a noisy hotel); 7. as a prop to help an individual cope with life (*e.g.* 'pills for personal problems', such as psychoactive drugs, alcohol and tobacco); 8. as a substitute for self-control (*e.g.* drugs to control the appetite for food, nicotine or alcohol); 9. to produce a state of intoxication, to get 'high' with friends, to relax, to relieve 'pressure', to give ease in conversation, to give increased enjoyment while listening to music or dancing, to obtain temporary removal of inhibitions or to produce increased activity; 10. with intent to harm (*e.g.* the intentional administration of a drug by an individual either to himself or herself, *i.e.* suicide, or to another, *i.e.* murder); 11. to attempt to manipulate difficult and stressful personal and social circumstances by taking a drug overdose (para-suicide); and 12. to enhance performance either in sport or sexually. Some of these uses are appropriate both in a therapeutic sense and from a Christian perspective, but many suggest drug misuse and dependence.*

Regarding the sound, medical use of drugs, Duncan W. Vere (1971) has written that a doctor 'should, in general, offer treatment only when he has a precise diagnosis . . . he will want the diagnosis to comprise physical, mental and spiritual aspects. He can then direct his drugs, if they are needed, like bullets towards defined targets. These targets will be: (a) to restore towards normality, for that person, physical and mental function so as (b) to permit, but not influence, the emergence and relief of his spiritual problems.' Whilst the drugs administered will not solve the patient's spiritual problems, there is no hope of meeting those problems so long as body and mind do not function so as to permit them to be expressed. For a Christian perspective, 'the aim is to subdue mental disorder so that a man's real self, and its spiritual problems, can emerge'. Treatments which 'cultivate false attitudes to life', such as assisting the patient to evade problems, will be avoided in the interests of a healing which encompasses body, mind and spirit. (See 'Psychopharmacology and Moral Responsibility', *ISM* 67, 1971, pp. 8–15.)

Results of drug misuse

The misuse of drugs may have various harmful consequences, including the following:

1. Actual harm to the individual. Drug misuse may lead to damaged physical or mental health, as is the case with the alcohol abuser who develops liver and neuropsychiatric damage, or the smoker who develops lung cancer. Ultimately, drug misuse may impair that person's social functioning, resulting in an inability to get or hold down a job, or to find a place to live, and thus maybe leading to crime, such as theft and prostitution, in order to finance the habit.

2. Potential harm to the individual. Even if overt harm does not occur, the user's health or social well-being is put at risk. When under the influence of a hallucinogenic drug (*e.g.* LSD) the risk of actual self-harm is great.

3. Actual or potential harm to others. Passive cigarette smoking is now known sometimes to result in harm similar to that experienced by those who actively smoke. An individual who is intoxicated with drugs and who assaults another person has misused drugs as much as a person who kills himself or herself (deliberately or accidentally) while in the same intoxicated condition. In addition, the tensions resulting from drug misuse may lead to the break-up of relationships and estrangement from families and friends.

4. Harm to the interests of the community or State. Drug misuse may render the misusers incapable of themselves contributing to the public purse, so increasing the financial burden on the rest of society. The cost of the medical treatment of these misusers then further consumes public resources. Moreover, as drug misuse may lead to criminal activity, this will also impinge on society, which must then bear the additional costs of law enforcement.

Use and misuse of psychoactive drugs

Although in certain circumstances (*e.g.* treatment of depression* and schizophrenia) it is appropriate for doctors to prescribe psychoactive drugs and for patients to take them, an increasing proportion of the population enjoying good physical health is now demanding that such drugs are prescribed for them on a long-term basis in the belief that they will help individuals come to terms with themselves and their environment. In addition, approximately 100,000 patients are admitted each year to hospitals in England and Wales as a result of a self-poisoning* episode, and many of these patients have ingested a psychoactive drug. The majority are not attempting suicide* but are indulging in a conscious, impulsive, manipulative act undertaken to secure redress of an intolerable situation which, for the particular individual in question, cannot be or has not been relieved by more rational means. Yet such problems are incurable by drug therapy alone.

Should 'soft' and 'hard' drugs be available legally?

The widespread use of 'soft' drugs raises the question whether or not such mind-altering agents should be more freely available. In addition, there are those who advocate that even 'hard' drugs should be decriminalized and be made freely available. Fundamentally, this is a matter of whether or not an individual has real freedom to do what he wants. In our society at present, freedom is rightly constrained in many ways both to protect the individual from unacceptable risk (*e.g.* heroin misuse) and to benefit the community (*e.g.* payment of taxes). Society, through the various agencies to which it delegates responsibility, decides the constraints on this freedom and imposes them by legislation. Some would argue that because many smoke 'pot' (cannabis) in spite of current legislation, the law should be relaxed. This does not, however, follow. Mass law-breaking (*e.g.* petty thieving, exceeding the speed limit and tax evasion) is in itself no good reason for changing the law. If 'pot' smoking was completely harmless to the individual and society, then the law would be unjust and unreasonable. However, any drug that is capable of producing a pleasurable state of mind is subject to considerable use, and therefore misuse, with resulting psychological and physical effects. Society has to decide whether the individual and collective benefits outweigh the risk. Many believe they do not.

Biblical perspectives

There are no explicit biblical statements regarding the use of drugs, other than alcohol. Alcohol was frequently consumed with meals in the ancient world, though often in diluted form, which may have had the additional advantage of making the water safer (and more palatable) to drink. There were occasions in the OT when the provision of wine was considered a sign of blessing and a source of joy (Ps. 104:15), and times when abstinence was practised as a discipline (Lv. 10:8–9). It was recognized that alcohol imbibing could lead to immodest behaviour (Gn. 9:21), anger (Is. 5:11) and a befuddled mind (Is. 28:7). In the NT we read that Jesus himself drank wine, and on one occasion miraculously produced more than 100 gallons of quality wine (Jn. 2:1–11). However, misuse is linked to sexual immorality (Eph. 5:18) and to weaker Christians being offended or harmed (Rom. 14:21). Church leaders were warned against drinking excessively, as this could make them unfit for their divine task (1 Tim. 3:8; Tit. 2:3).

Wine was also used for medicinal purposes, particularly when mixed with spices or oil. Wine and oil were used by the good Samaritan to dress the wounds of the beaten man (Lk. 10:34), and Timothy was advised to take alcohol to help his digestion (1 Tim. 5:23).

God is the author and giver of life and has given us our bodies; we are answerable to him in our use of them. Those who misuse drugs are often questioning the nature of reality, the true nature of humanity and the existence of an objective moral order. Many are unable to cope with guilt,* and lack the power to discontinue drug misuse even if they appreciate its inherent dangers. Pastorally, individuals who have suffered through drug misuse may need to be shown that God gives them worth (see Self-esteem*) and that they are of such value that Christ died for them. They will need to be helped to reorder their lives in the light of God's purposes for humanity – which are for the good both of individuals and of society. Such a realization can lead to a new understanding of truth, reality and forgiveness. This can open the way to spiritual factors in dealing with the problem of drug misuse. To point individuals towards harnessing the spiritual resources of grace* is ultimately more important than simply offering social support and advice, let alone condemnation.

J.A.V.

DRUGS, TESTING OF, see HUMAN DEVELOPMENT; RIGHTS, ANIMAL.

DUALISM. Ethical dualism should be distinguished from other dualisms, *i.e.* between mind and body, God and Satan, or time and eternity. While ethical dualism is sometimes related to these or similar dualities, it holds that good and evil are both eternal, grounded in the contrasting natures of two opposing realities.

A tendency to regard matter as evil, and reason or spirit as good, appeared in a variety of forms during the first five centuries of the church, and has occasionally recurred since.

Plato's* depreciation of the body contributed, along with his assertion that matter was originally chaotic and the suggestion in his *Laws* that, in addition to the Demiurge who fashioned everything rationally for good, there may be another world soul, the Dyad, whose folly causes wild and irregular behaviour of physical things. Gnosticism developed this theme with the help of Eastern ideas so that a heavenly spirit, acting independently of the good God, formed the material world and trapped human spirits in material bodies. The moral life must therefore be one of asceticism,* denying the body and its desires. The classic form of dualism was in the 4th- and 5th-century Manichaeism, with its realms of light and darkness in eternal conflict with each other. Humans have two living souls, one rational, a fragment of light that came from the good God, and the other irrational, springing from the intercourse of demons in the kingdom of darkness. Matter is evil, a foul and mis-shapen mass devoid of reason or form, while spirit or reason is good. Bodily desires should therefore be denied; yet the common tendency according to Augustine* was to abandon that relentless struggle and give in to bodily indulgence.

Augustine was attracted to the Manichaeans before his conversion, but became disillusioned and later wrote extensively against them. He recognized that dualism undermined the positive implications of the doctrine of creation,* especially the eventual triumph of good and all hope for the future. Gnosticism had led to a denial of the incarnation, for if matter is evil then an incarnate God would have become evil: that would be impossible. Augustine, on the other hand, argued that the darkness was either made by God or not made by him. If made by God, then it is good and not evil. If made by another, then there are two eternal camps; we are but pawns in their battle and have no real will of our own. The moral life then becomes an empty charade.

The OT, on the other hand, displays a positive appreciation of the goodness of the physical creation with its worlds of sight and sound, food, drink and sex; it celebrates them as good gifts of God, while recognizing our sinful abuse of God's goodness. The NT explicitly rejects dualism. Paul's letter to the Colossians is the outstanding case, for the 'Colossian heresy' which he denounces apparently questioned the divine creation of earthly things and advocated a stringent asceticism. Paul therefore starts by praying that the Colossian Christians will gain the wisdom and strength they need, having already been delivered from the kingdom of darkness and transferred to the kingdom of God's Son (Col. 1:9–14). The Son is then presented as creator, sustainer and Lord of everything in heaven and on earth (Col. 1:15–19). The contrast with the tradition which is troubling Colosse becomes plain: self-abasement before supposed spirits and an ascetic denial of the body are useless in checking sinful desires. It is the living Christ who empowers the moral life (Col. 2:8 – 3:17).

Elsewhere similar themes emerge. Responding to advocates of asceticism and celibacy (see Singleness*), Paul affirms the goodness and acceptability of everything God created (1 Tim. 4:3–4). John's first epistle warns against those who deny the reality of Christ's incarnation. The epistle therefore begins by affirming that the eternal Son has been 'seen with our eyes . . . and our hands have touched' him (1 Jn. 1:1–3). He must really have come in the flesh. Fellowship with the Father and Son requires keeping his commandments, as summed up in Christ's command to love as he loved us, rather than indulging 'the lust of the flesh, and the lust of the eyes, and the pride of life' (1 Jn. 2:7–16, AV).

Both Paul and John speak of light and darkness, of spirit and flesh; it reads like the language of dualism, yet, in the context of the above passages which plainly reject dualism, the language is converted to a distinctively Christian use. 'Darkness' and 'flesh' sometimes still connote evil, but not in the sense of another eternal realm of being. Rather, they speak of sin ('sinful man', NIV) that transgresses against God's law and the kind of love he enjoins, an evil that perverts the good but which Christ has overcome. 'Light' and 'spirit' connote the good by which we should live. But 'spirit' is not the power of reason over against 'flesh' or body. God created the body, and it is his good gift of life to be received, enjoyed and employed out of love for him and our neighbours. Nor is human spirit inherently good, for sinfulness extends into every area of the person. It too needs to be enlightened and renewed in loving fellowship with God and his people.

Bibliography

R. M. Grant, *Gnosticism and Early Christianity* (New York, ²1966); G. Quispell, *ER* 5, pp. 566–574.

A.F.H.

DURESS as a word is derived from the Lat. *duritia*, meaning hardness or harsh treatment. In law, the word used is 'durance', implying forced confinement, imprisonment or constraint. Duress is thus constraint illegally exercised to force a person to do something. A person is said to be 'under duress' when he or she is acting not voluntarily but by constraint imposed by force.

There are a number of examples in Scripture of persons acting under duress. The Jews rebuilding Jerusalem after their return from exile in Babylon were 'compelled . . . by force to stop' (Ezr. 4:23). The apostle Paul was 'compelled to appeal' to Caesar because he would not have received a fair trial in Jerusalem (Acts 28:19). He himself, before his conversion, was prepared to sanction the use of force against Christians (Acts 26:11).

Though resorting to duress is not explicitly forbidden to Christians, there are a number of indications that clearly rule it out. Conversion* is to result from persuasion (Acts 18:4), not brainwashing.* Discipleship is to be freely and voluntarily embraced (Mt. 16:24). Giving is to be done willingly out of gratitude for God's grace, not under psychological pressure, for God loves cheerful givers (2 Cor. 9:5, 7).

In Eng. law, an act of duress is the commission of, or a threat to commit, a wrong. A wrongful act may include a threatened breach of contract, breach of trust, breach of statutory duty, a tort (*e.g.* inviting another to breach his or her contract) or a crime (*e.g.* blackmail). Therefore, actual or threatened violence to the person constitutes duress. This is generally directed against the plaintiff, but can also be employed against one's spouse or child as well as other relatives. Any deed, contract or transaction entered into under duress of this kind is voidable by the person concerned. Duress to the person constitutes both a crime and a tort, in which case the plaintiff will have other remedies for the recovery of things entered into under duress. So, in law, duress is the compulsion under which a person acts through fear of personal suffering, as from injury to the body or from confinement, actual or threatened.

The proper use of the legal process does not constitute duress. Everyone is free to invoke the aid of the law in a proper case: civil and criminal cases properly filed do not constitute duress. For example, a threat to commence bankruptcy proceedings, made in good faith, does not amount to duress, nor does a bona fide threat to institute criminal proceedings. This rule also applies to lawful arrest, imprisonment and the threat thereof. In each of these cases, the aid of the law is being invoked to bring pressure to bear on a person; provided the proceedings are regular, lawful and invoked in good faith, and not abused or calculated to cause error, then duress cannot be said to be exercised on the person against whom they have been brought.

However, where pressure has been brought to bear by the improper application of a legal process, this does amount to duress. The coerced party is not *in pari delicto*, *i.e.* it acted under duress (R. Goff and G. Jones, *The Law of Restitution*, London, ²1978, pp. 163–164). The effect of duress upon a marriage is the same as upon a contract, *i.e.* it renders it not voidable but void, for the right to a free choice of a partner is axiomatic. That is why, as in a contract, if there is no consent but one partner has acted under duress, the marriage is void (J. Jackson, *The Formation and Annulment of Marriage*, London, ²1969, pp. 282–289). If, therefore, owing to fear or threat, one of the parties is induced to enter into that which, in the absence of compulsion, he would never have contracted, the marriage will be void (P. M. Bromley and N. V. Lowe, *Bromley's Family Law*, London, ⁷1987, pp. 89–92).

Under criminal law, duress provides a defence to a charge of any offence other than murder and some forms of treason (*Halsbury's Laws of England*, vol. II (i), London, ⁴1990, p. 32, para. 24). Duress is regarded as a defence because it postulates the existence of threats of imminent death or serious personal violence so great as to overbear the ordinary power of human resistance to the doing of acts which would otherwise be criminal (*e.g.* as in a threat made by the accused to a woman living with him as his wife). A threat of such harm to another may suffice as a defence, but a threat to property is not sufficient to constitute a defence of duress. The defence is available only where the threat was operative and effective at the time of the act or omission alleged to constitute the offence.

The test of duress is not purely subjective but includes the objective test of whether a sober man (or woman) of reasonable firmness, having the accused's character, would have responded to whatever he reasonably believed was said or done by the other person taking part in the crime. Did that person voluntarily put himself under the duress of another, or could he have voluntarily withdrawn? Did he place himself under dominance of another? (*Halsbury's Laws of England*, *ibid.*)

J.M.S.

DURKHEIM, EMILE (1858–1917). Born in Epinal in north-eastern France into a Jewish rabbinical family, and early recognized as a promising scholar, Durkheim studied at the élite Ecole Normale Superieure in Paris, where he received his doctorate of philosophy. His initial teaching position was at Bordeaux in 1887 where he established his first sociology class. In 1902 he took a position at the Sorbonne in Paris, where he taught philosophy and sociology until his death. His writing included over 500 articles on subjects ranging from social change and sociological method to the sociologies of religion* and knowledge plus several books of continuing influence. Together with Karl Marx* and Max Weber (1864–1920), Durkheim is acknowledged as a key figure in classical sociological thought, and as the one who established both the methodology and theoretical bases for early sociology as an intellectual field.

Influenced by the French intellectual thought of Henri de Saint-Simon (1760–1825) and Auguste Comte (1798–1857), as well as by British utilitarianism (see Consequentialism*) and German idealism, Durkheim developed a sociology that was both eclectic and reductionistic.* He espoused the existence of irreducible social facts and the existence of society as a *sui generis* reality. He believed that shared values and beliefs form a collective consciousness which supersedes individual consciousness and which socializes persons into society by proscribing their actions. Historically, social cohesion evolves from the mechanical, unifying solidarity of simple societies to an organic, diversifying solidarity resulting from the increasing division of labour in complex societies (*cf. The Division of Labor in Society*).

In his famous work *Suicide*, Durkheim refined his ideas on anomie, a societal condition resulting from the inadequate integrative power of socially approved norms. Such norms operate differently among groups – Protestants versus Roman Catholics or singles versus marrieds. Then in *The Elementary Forms of the Religious Life*, Durkheim built on his familiarity with the Australian Arunta to argue that religion performs an essential integrative function for society by binding its members together. Society is god-like, and its members elevate to sacred significance the previously profane beliefs, rituals and totemic representations that have united them. Thus, in adhering to its beliefs and rituals, a society worships itself – an idea that has greatly influenced modern thinking about civil religions and their functions.

Bibliography

The Division of Labor in Society (ET, New York, 1933; Basingstoke, 1984); *The Elementary Forms of the Religious Life* (ET, London and New York, 1915); *The Rules of Sociological Method* (ET, Chicago, 1938; ⁸1964); *Suicide: A Study in Sociology* (ET, Glencoe, IL, 1951; London, 1952, ²1976).

S. G. Mestrovic, *Emile Durkheim and the Reformation of Sociology* (Totowa, NJ, 1988); W. S. F. Pickering, *Durkheim's Sociology of Religion: Themes and Theories* (London, 1984).

J.A.M.

DUTY. The concept of duty in its most important modern sense, that given it by Immanuel Kant,* plays little role in the biblical writings. The Stoics* are often considered the first philosophers to make duty a central moral concept, and Stoic conceptions of duty (what is fitting because in accord with nature) may have influenced the apostle Paul. Philosophers have sometimes distinguished between duty and obligation* – understanding duties as arising out of our station or role in life, and obligations as arising out of relations (*e.g.* contracts) into which we have voluntarily entered. This sort of distinction is unknown in the Bible; however, whereas moderns have found obligations easier to accept and understand than duties, biblical thought takes seriously duties that are not simply obligations (that are not the result of our own promises or contractual agreements). Thus, the duty of children to honour and obey their parents is affirmed in the Bible, even though no child has voluntarily undertaken such a duty from birth. Instead, the duty is understood to be embedded within a certain role. More fundamentally still, the duty to honour and obey God is assumed in the Bible, but it is not thought to depend for its binding quality on our own assent of will; the author of our being is presumed to have authority over us. Our ordinary sense of particular duties and obligations as actions we are obligated to undertake is present in the Bible, though without any systematic theoretical development. Biblical writers have a concept of 'owing' something to someone, or 'being indebted' to someone (the word group *opheilō*). The best known is probably the image of 'indebtedness' used in the Lord's Prayer (Mt. 6:12).

Because duties are grounded in our roles and relations (whether voluntarily undertaken or not), and because we may stand in a variety of roles at one time, duties may sometimes seem to conflict. Since W. D. Ross's (1877–1940) *The Right and the Good*, philosophers have used the language of 'prima facie duties' to describe these various, possibly conflicting, claims upon us. Little agreement exists about how we ought to decide what our actual obligation is when prima facie duties conflict. The Bible offers no hierarchy of duties to help us decide – except the assumption that duty to God is overriding (Acts 5:29) and that other-regard should take priority over self-regard (Mt. 5:38–42). The Christian life is, finally, less dedicated to drawing up a hierarchical code to solve conflicts of duties than to creating sanctified and virtuous people who will begin to have the capacity to discern what ought to be done when duties conflict or when there is no action possible that clearly recommends itself as our duty. Thus, Martin Luther* could view the place of 'works' in the Christian life as similar to that which 'models and plans have among builders and artisans. They are prepared not as a permanent structure, but because without them nothing could be built or made. When the structure is complete the models and plans are laid aside. You see, they are not despised, rather they are greatly sought after; but what we despise is the false estimate of them since no one holds them to be the real and permanent structure' (Luther, 'The Freedom of a Christian', *Luther's Works*, vol. 31 [ET, Philadelphia, 1957], pp. 375–376). Hence, although it is surely better to act in accord with duty than to fall short of what ought to be done, for Christians duty is not the centre of the moral life. In relation to God, fulfillment of one's duty gives one no claim (Lk. 17:10). And in relation to others, duty is finally transcended in love (see [2]), as the pun in Rom. 13:8 indicates: 'Let no debt remain outstanding, except the continuing debt to love one another, for he who loves his fellow-man has fulfilled the law.'

In his *Foundations of the Metaphysics of Morals*, Kant developed a very distinctive and influential theory that treats duty as the central concept of morality (see Christian Moral Reasoning [18]). For Kant 'duty' refers not so much to particular actions we are obligated to undertake as to the one morally acceptable motive for action. His programmatic statement is justly famous: 'Nothing in the world – indeed nothing even beyond the world – can possibly be conceived which could be called good without qualification except a *good will*' (p. 9). The good will* is good precisely in that it has no motive for acting other than respect for moral law. That is, to act from duty is not simply to do what we are inclined to do. It is not merely to aim at a worthwhile result, nor does the goodness of action depend in any way on whether a desirable result is attained. Moral goodness resides only in that 'principle of will' which acts from respect for law. This means that we act not simply in accord with the moral law but for the sake of the law. Only such action springs from the motive of duty.

Kant also has a concept of a holy will – a perfectly good will that would never experience any inclination contrary to the moral law's dictates. Such a will could feel no constraint in the face of duty, and Kant holds that it is inappropriate to apply 'ought' language to it. 'Thus, no imperatives hold for the divine will or, more generally, for a holy will. The "ought" is here out of place, for the volition of itself is necessarily in unison with the law' (p. 31). Hence, to act from duty seems to imply that one acts while also feeling the pull of contrary inclinations.

We can understand such a claim. There are, for example, some activities – *e.g.* eating and drinking for nourishment – which are right to do and which we would not ordinarily term duties (because we have no inclination to do otherwise). Nevertheless, to delimit the moral sphere in terms of duty as Kant does can be unduly restrictive. Quite different is a theory like Aristotle's,* which makes moral growth and development in virtue central. For Aristotle our aim ought to be virtue: a state in which we habitually and effortlessly do as we ought, not a state in which we are constantly torn by contrary inclinations. Similarly, a Christian emphasis on growth in righteousness* – while recognizing the continued presence of sin in human life – may be less inclined to make the experience of contrary inclination a test for the presence of the good will. Moreover, Christian emphasis upon virtues such as love has been intended to encourage spontaneity and whole-heartedness in desiring what is good. But to act because one is moved by a spirit of love is not the same as acting from respect for the moral law – and, according to Kant's programmatic statement, must therefore manifest something other than the good will. Kant recognizes that some may 'find an inner satisfaction in spreading joy, and rejoice in the contentment of others ... But I say that, however dutiful [*i.e.* in accord with the moral law] and amiable it may be, that kind of action has no true moral worth' (p. 14), since the agent is moved to act by love and not by respect for the moral law.

This makes clear that, for Kant, even a motive of obedience* to God taints the moral quality of action. He is clear that morality cannot consist in obedience to God's commands. Such heteronomous action would undercut the autonomous human being who, out of respect for the moral law, prescribes for himself maxims to direct his action. 'Even the Holy One of the Gospel must be compared with our ideal of moral perfection before He is recognized as such ...' (p. 25). Human beings can act from respect for the moral law without losing their autonomy only because such action is grounded in reason, which always prescribes the law universally (for all rational beings). The moral agent does not bow to the commands of God; instead, in respecting the moral law, he or she legislates for all people in similar circumstances, *i.e.* legislates in a godlike manner.

This emphasis on universality will leave little space for a part of morality that is permitted rather than required, a realm in which love discerns what law cannot command. It will leave no place for a supererogatory deed (*i.e.* an act which is praiseworthy if done but not blameworthy if left undone). And it will have difficulty with the moral 'ought' one might use to characterize a special calling – as when the monk says, 'Although marriage is good, I ought to follow the life of celibacy to which God has called me.' Nor can this emphasis on universality make place for Søren Kierkegaard's* 'teleological suspension of the ethical' in which, having teleologically suspended the universal, one simply loves each neighbour in his or her particularity.

The Kantian concept of duty has been and continues to be an extremely powerful depiction of much that is deeply embedded in our understanding of the moral life. For Christian thought, however, the good will that acts solely out of respect for the moral law is finally

to be transcended. If such holiness cannot be achieved entirely in this life, it is nevertheless the aim even here and now. The good will depicted by Kant is to be transcended and duty is to become delight.

Bibliography
I. Kant, *The Foundations of the Metaphysics of Morals* (ET, Indianapolis, IN, 1959); S. Kierkegaard, *Fear and Trembling* with *The Sickness Unto Death* (ET, Princeton, NJ, 1954); G. Meilaender, *The Theory and Practice of Virtue* (Notre Dame, IN, 1984); W. D. Ross, *The Right and the Good* (Oxford, 1930).

G.C.M.

DYING, see DEATH AND DYING.

DYNAMIC CYCLE, THE, is a central concept in clinical theology.* Dr Frank Lake* suggested that any true understanding of personhood (see Human Development*) is based on the relationship between God the Father and Jesus the Son. Jesus receives from his Father *acceptance* (Jn. 3:17) and *sustenance* (Jn. 14:11), which enables Jesus to have a sense of well-being marked by *status* (Jn. 1:14) and *achievement* (Jn. 4:34). As Jesus brings others into relationship with God the Father they experience this cycle of well-being.

Lake's 'object-relations' background suggested that these categories evidenced in the adult life of Jesus were present in his infant life. Jesus therefore gives us a model for the healthy development of personhood, and any interruption in this cycle of acceptance, sustenance, status and achievement could result in poor physical, psychological or spiritual health.

The dynamic cycle has a number of weaknesses. 1. It is theologically questionable whether one can establish a retrospective psychological understanding of Jesus. 2. There is little theological co-relation between the dynamic cycle and the death of Christ, another central concept in Lake's work. 3. At times Lake's forcing of complex psychological problems into the cycle destroys its simplicity.

One of the dynamic cycle's strengths is its creative and pioneering attempt at relating psychoanalytic* and psychiatric theory to theology, thus becoming a vital catalyst in this theologically neglected area. Another is that its cyclical nature and simplicity have found considerable application in pastoral counselling in the church in Britain.

See also: PASTORAL CARE, COUNSELLING AND PSYCHOTHERAPY. [12]

Bibliography

C. Christian, *In the Spirit of Truth: A Reader in the Work of Frank Lake* (London, 1991); P. J. van de Kasteele, *The Dynamic Cycle*, unpublished lecture available from the Clinical Theology Association (Oxford, 1986).

J.A.R.

E

EATING DISORDERS. 'Anorexia nervosa' and 'bulimia nervosa' are defined as disordered patterns of eating. Anorexia is characterized by startling weight loss, bulimia by recurrent eating binges and vomiting. They are commonly discussed as if they were separate and unrelated conditions. However, they are more usefully understood as two distinctive ways of expressing distress, sharing a common central feature – fear of fatness. Individuals often suffer from symptoms of both disorders, women being affected ten times as often as men.

1. Anorexia

Anorexia most often starts in the teenage years while the sufferer is still living at home, one fifteen-year-old girl in every 150 being affected. Girls from professional or managerial families are more at risk than girls from working-class backgrounds.

The symptoms are: under-eating/starvation; loss of weight to more than 15% below normal limits; fear of fatness, even when underweight; a self-perception of being fat, even when thin; absence of three or more consecutive menstrual periods; and vigorous exercising.

Anorexia typically starts with the everyday dieting that is so much a part of teenage life. However, the dieting and the loss of weight do not stop, but continue until the sufferer is well below the normal limit for her age and height. Paradoxically, sufferers with anorexia often take an avid interest in shopping and cooking for others. With time, the symptoms of bulimia may also appear.

2. Bulimia

This condition usually affects a slightly older age group, often women in their early to mid-twenties who have been overweight as children. Three out of every 100 women will be affected at some time in their lives.

The symptoms are: fear of fatness, even when weight is within normal limits; recurrent episodes of binge-eating; regular vomiting and/or excessive use of laxatives; normal weight; and menstrual irregularity.

Like anorexics, bulimics diet assiduously. Unlike anorexics, their weight usually stays within normal limits. The calories lost by dieting, vomiting or taking laxatives are made up for by the food eaten during 'binges', *i.e.* episodes of massive, uncontrollable eating, usually followed by vomiting. The self-disgust after a binge provokes further excessive dieting, resulting in further binges.

3. Physical consquences

Starvation leads to broken sleep and constipation, accompanied by the growth of fine hair all over the body. Concentration becomes impaired, and muscle-wasting makes ordinary activities progressively more difficult. Bones become brittle and more likely to fracture.

Vomiting causes the enlargement of the salivary glands, which produces a puffy facial appearance, and tooth enamel is dissolved. Although some sufferers can vomit at will, others need to stick their fingers down their throat, and they thus develop callouses on their knuckles. Loss of potassium in the vomit may produce heart problems, muscle weakness, kidney damage and epileptic fits.

Laxative abuse may cause persistent abdominal pain, swelling of the fingers and long-term constipation.

4. Causes

A whole range of emotionally distressing circumstances can cause anorexia or bulimia. For around 50% of sufferers, their disorder seems to have been triggered by a distressing event or major change, such as leaving home or getting married. It has been suggested that a failure to mourn, and particularly guilt over an abortion, may have a specific role in precipitating anorexia. However, no hard evidence has yet emerged to suggest that this is any more significant than other painful experiences.

Emotional distress may be expressed by disturbances of eating for a variety of reasons:

1. Western culture places a high value on appearance and particularly on being thin. Around 30% of fifteen-year-old girls diet, and those who do diet are eight times more likely to develop an eating disorder. It is easy to see how this social pressure can provoke the dieting that may tip over into anorexia, or provoke the see-sawing of bulimia. In societies where plumpness rather than thinness is culturally valued, eating disorders are rare.

2. Dieting can be a very comforting activity because it is a concrete, if limited, way of exercising control over one's world. This can be an extremely important issue for girls in their teens, still living at home, who may often feel that it is the only way in which they can exercise any autonomy.

3. The weight loss of anorexia stops or reverses the physical changes of puberty, and sufferers often look very young for their age. It can therefore be seen as a way of avoiding the emerging demands of sexuality (see ⑪). Unfortunately, it also makes it difficult for the adolescent to develop the maturity and self-awareness that come from facing problems and dealing with them.

4. Eating together is central to family life. It is therefore often the arena in which family difficulties surface, and a son or daughter may express difficulties by a refusal to eat.

5. Treatment

The earlier the problem is recognized, the easier it is to treat and the better the outlook. Help should usually be sought through a GP, but the treatment is mainly psychological and is carried out by psychiatrists and/or psychologists. It may involve family members (see Family Therapy*) as well as the individual affected and usually takes place on an outpatient basis, unless the weight loss of anorexia has become dangerous or has proved intractable. Some sufferers find self-help groups useful, and indeed for some this may be the only help that is needed.

Bibliography

Anorexic Family Aid, *A to Z of Anorexia Nervosa* (Norwich, 1986); M. Duker and R. Slade, *Anorexia Nervosa and Bulimia* (Milton Keynes, 1988); R. L. Palmer, *Anorexia Nervosa* (Harmondsworth, 1980).

P.W.T.

ECOLOGY, see ENVIRONMENT.

ECONOMIC DEVELOPMENT. Economic developments are human changes in living and working environments, including especially the goods and services available to people. Responsibility for such changes is a primary duty of humankind according to the biblical point of view, and methods and goals need to be responsibly directed.

The very earliest explicit commands of God designated man and woman as stewards* in charge of his many creatures on earth, with the initial responsibility to 'dress and keep' the Garden of Eden. God himself set a profound example by working in creation* to develop our environment* to be full of 'goods' and potential services. Not coincidentally, 'economic' and 'ecological' have the same linguistic root (Gk. *oikos*); they both concern the living environment in which we engage in both work and leisure.

The term 'economic development' is generally reserved for changes involving some plan and purpose, *e.g.* bringing a new industry to a country or region, building new housing or office complexes, exploiting an area's natural resources for human use, inventing or expanding a technology, increasing trade between groups of people, and such like. Economies create and distribute wealth, and economic development adds new tools, buildings, resources, or methods for the purpose of enhancing that process. For this reason, it can be used as a form of missionary or national 'aid' for depressed peoples and economies.

Unfortunately, the term 'economic development' frequently connotes an unjustified positive evaluation. People often blindly assume that the plans and purposes guiding an economic development project are beneficial and fair for all the people involved. Also, uncritically declaring an area 'underdeveloped' suggests that it is of low value, crude, primitive, undesirable, unappealing, *etc.* However, human failings and finitude both distort the best development plans and activities, and they limit even the best-intentioned purposes and results, overt and covert selfishness and greediness aside.

For whom, where, to what purpose, by what means, and with what results will it be done? These are among the enduring ethical questions that must be raised in evaluating any planned or completed economic development project.

1. *For whom?* Since economic activity necessarily affects both the environment and

other people's lives, the purposes and interests of many must be considered and understood: a. the creation itself; b. the planners, affected workers, potential customers and neighbouring people; c. future generations of planners, workers, customers and neighbours; and d. God.

a. The Bible teaches us to receive the creation as a gift to be enjoyed, used and even wisely exploited – and at the same time to revere it as God's priceless, irreplaceable handiwork. It can be utilized for human purposes because it is not divine, but it must not be abused or neglected either, because it is a masterpiece of God. Economic development must embrace both use and reverence.

b. The people who are affected all have interests and claims – as heirs of Adam and Eve, as citizens of nations, as images of God.* The only one with an absolute property* claim is God; all our other property claims must be negotiated through the guidance of biblical principles for accountability, justice (see Justice and Peace③) and care. Therefore, whenever an economic development project is proposed or defended, it is necessary to cut through the familiar rhetoric of what good will be produced for everyone, and to investigate whose interests are actually being satisfied. Will the whole community benefit? Who gains the most? – and who might suffer the most? Truly mutually beneficial economic development projects are possible (God commands us to pursue them), but they require skilled 'savvy', sensitive planning and meticulous monitoring.

c. The interests of future generations are intensely important but difficult to predict, plan and protect. How many future generations will there be? What alternative resources will they have available? How might present economic development benefit them?

d. Finally, how does this development serve God and his purposes? This question is all-encompassing. Responsibility to God should force even the most influential and powerful economic developers to examine the justice and real benefits of their projects.

2. *Where will the development occur?* Different sets of issues face different choices. Developments in other countries require deep comprehension of the culture* and people's real needs and wishes. Considerable losses can occur to the other country's residents or to the developer when comprehensive understanding is lacking. The destructive consequences of colonialism,* exploitive industrialization,* Third World debt, squandering of depletable resources, paternalism and suchlike are well known. Too often the foreigner, even under the pretence of Christian concern, has exploited the weaker and less informed and brought shame to the name of Christ.

Economic developers working within their own countries also must choose a location within the labyrinth of personal pressures, tax incentives, grants, zoning restrictions and concessions, and other community pressures. However, do these competing pressures produce fair site selections? For example, why are developments so frequently supported and encouraged in suburban areas, bypassing poorer regions of major cities where the employment needs are much higher? Why are new offices and factories built disproportionately in regions dominated by whites?

3. *To what purpose?* The distinction between greed and self-interest is especially significant. Probably nothing ever happens in an economy without strong self-interest motivations on all sides. God has created a world in which mutual benefit sustains economies. But greed always blinds: developers are blinded to their own best interest, and are also tempted to deceive others about their true interests. A biblical understanding of the purposes of creating wealth and producing goods and services helps counteract the distortions of greed.

4. *By what means?* The issues of justice, love (see ②)and stewardship* are essential in the selection of development methods. Do agreement and support of the development involve deception, coercion, oppression? How are the benefits distributed? Do the development processes contribute to the availability and dignity of work? Will the environment be polluted or resources depleted? Too often economic development has increased mechanization while reducing job availability and wasting energy. Who is benefited when a robot displaces the jobs of three people?

5. *With what results?* Both the planned results and the actual results need to be fruitfully assessed and evaluated. Plans are changed before they are implemented; and the new industries, buildings, technologies, and trade can be altered. Economic development is a central human task that affects other people tremendously, for good or evil. It requires comprehensive, prayerful, and scrupulous moral attention.

P.H.deV.

ECONOMIC ISSUES, see ECONOMIC ETHICS. [17]

ECONOMIC SANCTIONS are a form of coercion (see Force*) which uses economic penalties. These penalties can be various and of differing severity. The two main groups are trade and financial sanctions. Examples of trade sanctions are the embargoes on exports and imports. Financial sanctions place penalties on loans and investment.*

As a form of coercion, the use of economic sanctions raises the standard questions: 1. When is it justifiable to use coercion? 2. What kind of coercion should be used?

Answers to these questions are best sought in the Christian tradition of the just war,* because, although there are differences in the form of coercion they use, war and economic sanctions are in many respects similar: to adapt some words from the great theoretician of war, Karl von Clausewitz (1780–1831), imposing economic sanctions is war carried on by other means. The advantage of adopting this approach is that it roots ethical reflection on economic sanctions in an ecumenical Christian tradition, which is itself based on the 'love of neighbour' principle of the Bible.

Accepting that the tests of a just war can be used, then the tests of just cause and proportionality are the relevant ones in deciding when to impose economic sanctions. In connection with *just cause*, it is important to recognize that the traditional Christian understanding is far wider than the non-ideological test in international law. The limitations of the latter, which allows war only against an external aggressor, were exposed in the Kurdish crisis of 1991, in which the principle of national sovereignty was set aside in the interests of a 'duty of intervention', a principle which is much closer to the spirit of the traditional Christian test of just cause.

The test of *proportionality* is complicated by the difficulty of predicting the consequences of economic sanctions. In this connection, not only must the prediction be informed by complex economic factors, but also by even more complex political factors. A good example is the case of the oil sanction imposed against South Africa because of that country's apartheid policy. Reliable predictions of the economic impact were rendered virtually impossible because statistics on illegal oil imports and the oil stockpile were made a closely guarded State secret, and few could have predicted the political response, which was to develop one of the world's most advanced and extensive programmes for converting coal into oil. Nevertheless, because the test gives a rough guide as to whether more good than harm will be caused by economic sanctions, it is a very necessary safeguard against 'zealotism', the attitude which thinks that because justice 'is on its side', economic sanctions must be imposed regardless of the consequences.

The test of *discrimination* or *non-combatant immunity* is sometimes held to pose an insurmountable moral obstacle in the way of using economic sanctions. The difficulty with this objection is that the just-war doctrine has long accepted that civilians may be killed 'in virtue of collateral circumstance', as no policing operation can ever totally ensure against the possibility of civilian deaths. Rather than view the test of discrimination as prohibiting their use, therefore, it is more consistent with traditional Christian morality to understand this test as insisting on the targeting of economic sanctions in a way that minimizes the suffering of civilians. Furthermore, this test could also be legitimately interpreted as requiring the selective economic relief of civilians made to suffer.

A grave weakness of economic sanctions is the immense effort and diplomatic skill needed to sustain the long-term political consensus on which their effectiveness depends. It may have been this weakness which led the Western powers, fearing a breakdown of the international coalition against Iraq, to abandon economic sanctions in favour of war in the Gulf crisis of 1990–91. The creation of a supranational sanctions authority, with the legal powers to impose and enforce economic sanctions for violations of international law, might be a way of overcoming this weakness.

Another serious weakness is the ease with which economic sanctions appear to be evaded. While a sanctions-monitoring and enforcement unit may find it impossible to stamp out low-level smuggling where borders are easily crossed, the technology to detect sanctions-breaking in international trade, such as satellite surveillance of shipping, is already advanced, and suggests that the deeper problem is a lack of political will to make trade sanctions effective. Much more problematical are financial sanctions, given the secrecy of the international banking system.

Until measures are found to overcome these weaknesses, despite the prohibitive cost of modern warfare in terms of lives, resources and damage to the environement, it may be premature to conclude that economic sanctions have replaced war as the only moral alternative to diplomacy for settling international disputes.

Bibliography

J. Hanlon (ed.), *The Sanctions Handbook* (Harmondsworth, 1987); J. T. Johnson, *Ideology, Reason and the Limitation of War* (Princeton, NJ, 1975); P. Ramsey, *War and the Christian Conscience* (Durham, NC, 1961); C. Yeats, *Morality and Economic Sanctions* (Bramcote, Nottingham, 1990).

C.Y.

E CUMENICAL ETHICS. At the end of the 20th century, Christian ethics, like Christian theology, is increasingly an ecumenical endeavour, as ethical discussion engages, almost indiscriminately, thinkers and writers of different ecclesiastical traditions. This is not to deny that particular churches or confessions continue to maintain distinctive ethical stances (*e.g.* the disapproval of contraception* and abortion* by Roman Catholicism) or that churches pursue their own independent ethical projects (*cf.* the series of denominational reports on sexual issues in the 1980s and 1990s). But co-operation in doing Christian ethics by people who belong to different churches is commonplace, and by no means confined to the activities of formal ecumenical bodies.

Within the ecumenical movement proper, stemming from the Edinburgh World Missionary Conference of 1910, and from 1948 focused in the World Council of Churches (WCC), ethical concerns have been mainly social, political and economic, although a wider range of issues, including the family,* women's roles (see Feminism*) and the environment,* has more recently enjoyed attention. One of the two main streams (the other was Faith and Order) whose confluence created the WCC at Amsterdam in 1948 was Life and Work, which had held important conferences at Stockholm (1925) and Oxford (1937). Stockholm's 'Message' declared that 'The mission of the church is above all to state principles, and to assert the ideal [in] applying [the] Gospel in all realms of human life – industrial, social, political and international'.

Major themes at Stockholm were the Church and International Relations (the conference met while still in the shadow of the First World War) and the Church and Economic and Industrial Problems. The Oxford conference issued eight volumes of reports in a 'Church, Community and State' series, the first a basic study of *The Church and its Function in Society* (London, 1937), by W. A. Visser 't Hooft and J. H. Oldham. Experts and scholars aided understanding, and the result was a distinguished corpus of Protestant social ethics, aiming 'to define the points in the contemporary situation at which the specifically Christian understanding of life is crucially involved' (J. H. Oldham, ed., *The Churches Survey Their Task: The Report of the Conference at Oxford* . . . , London, 1937, p. 26).

Behind much Life and Work activity, framed as it was by two World Wars, lay the sentiment that 'doctrine (or dogma) divides, service (or action) unites'. As a justification for refusing to make ethical reflection wait upon interchurch agreement on Faith and Order it was understandable, but it presaged a deep-seated weakness of much subsequent WCC comment on 'church and society' – its lack of firm theological consensus as foundation.

Life and Work was perpetuated in the WCC's Department on Church and Society. The founding Assembly at Amsterdam (delayed as well as sobered by the Second World War) issued a report on 'The Church and the Disorder of Society' (in *The First Assembly* . . . , ed. Visser 't Hooft, Geneva, 1948, pp. 39–47), which identified two chief factors contributing to 'the crisis of our age': 'the vast concentrations of power – which are under capitalism mainly economic and under communism both economic and political', and the domination of society by 'technics'. It expounded the ideal of 'the responsible society' – a phrase which for a few decades summed up ecumenical ideals (*cf.* P. Bock, *In Search of a Responsible World Society*, Philadelphia, 1974). For Amsterdam it was a society 'where freedom is the freedom of men who acknowledge responsibility to justice and public order, and where those who hold political authority or economic power are responsible for its exercise to God and the people whose welfare is affected by it'. The church's social influence would take effect primarily through the conduct of its members in their occupations and political opportunities.

The second Assembly at Evanston, Illinois, in 1954 could assert that the 'responsible society is not an alternative social or political system ... Christians are called to live responsibly ... in any society, even within the most unfavourable social structures' (*The Evanston Report*, ed. Visser 't Hooft, New York, 1955, p. 113). But the Assembly marked a turning of the tide. Hitherto, the East–West/capitalist–communist divide set the context for ecumenical social ethics. Now the 'rapid social change' of the underdeveloped countries of Asia, Africa and Latin America would increasingly fix the agenda (*cf.* P. Abrecht, *The Churches and Rapid Social Change*, London and New York, 1961). In 1961 the New Delhi Assembly was the first to meet in 'the South' (see North–South Divide*). The shift in the WCC's priorities and preoccupations was manifest at the third (after Stockholm and Oxford) conference on Church and Society held at Geneva in 1966.

The Geneva conference's four preparatory volumes (published 1966) were entitled: *Christian Social Ethics in a Changing World* (ed. J. C. Bennett), *Economic Growth in World Perspective* (ed. D. Munby), *Responsible Government in a Revolutionary Age* (ed. Z. K. Matthews) and *Man in Community* (ed. E. de Vries). Lay people predominated ('theology was not the integrating universe of discourse', C. C. West in *DCE*, p. 97), and the quest for 'a new international economic order' and revolutionary political programmes took over. The often authoritarian nationalism* of newly independent states was affirmed as a vehicle of social integration (unlike the 'aggressive nationalism' of the West), and revolutionary violence was sanctioned as a last resort to overturn the falsely legitimized violence of the present order.

The conference spelt out the implications of these convictions in considerable detail (*e.g.* on tariff barriers, commodity prices and the Vietnam war), provoking allegations that it confounded the spheres of church and State. Paul Ramsey's* *Who Speaks for the Church?* (Nashville, TN, 1967) was a response to the Geneva conference.

The 1968 WCC Assembly at Uppsala devoted four of its six main sections to 'rapid social change', adopting many of the 1966 conference's positions. It was unable to agree in commending birth control as a contribution to population control (the Orthodox churches, members of WCC since 1961, objected), but called for full equality for women in every sphere. The justification (see Justification, Moral*) of revolutionary violence against 'inhumane structures' was viewed as one of the Assembly's main resolutions, although different sections were not agreed on the issue. By now WCC thinking had become deeply impregnated by liberation theology,* and Uppsala authorized the controversial Program to Combat Racism. Its grants to liberation movements and resistance groups were defended, in the face of bitter criticism and resignations, as serving the radical transformation of economic, social and political structures demanded by God's kingdom (see Kingdom of God*).

The Nairobi Assembly of 1975, the first south of the equator, witnessed the radical politicization of the WCC at its height. 'In essence, Nairobi proclaimed that poverty, racism, violations of human rights, and militarism (excluding military action by "liberation" groups) the world over result from unjust systems foisted upon humanity by the white-dominated societies of the Northern Hemisphere. "Liberation" meant changing or overthrowing unjust structures and replacing them with systems that serve rather than exploit people' (E. W. Lefever, *Amsterdam to Nairobi*, p. 43). To some extent, the keynotes of Nairobi's strident message found an echo in the WCC's mission conference at Bangkok in 1973, where concepts of salvation and mission were drastically de-spiritualized.

The Assemblies at Uppsala and Nairobi evoked growing protests from evangelicals, and subsequent Assemblies at Vancouver (1983) and Canberra (1990), as well as the world conference on mission and evangelism at San Antonio, Texas (1989), were more careful to heed dissenting voices. Ecological issues have inevitably come to the fore, and 'justice, peace and the integrity of creation' (JPIC) now summarizes the WCC's 'church and society' commitment. The 'integrity of creation' has been defined as 'the value of all creatures in and for themselves, for one another, and for God, and their interconnectedness in a diverse whole that has unique value for God' (quoted in T. F. Best, ed., *Vancouver to Canberra 1983–1990*, Geneva, 1990, p. 121). JPIC (the WCC is inordinately fond of initials), which draws together different threats to survival and harmony on the planet, was the theme of a major conference at Seoul in 1990. The previous year the WCC issued an impressive statement on ethical problems of bio-technology (*ibid.*, pp. 122–123).

Agencies of the WCC continue to be highly productive and stimulating in the ethical fields surveyed in this article. They have provoked evangelicals into recovering the conviction that socio-political action and reform are an essential part of Christian mission, and that biblical faith is concerned with the wholeness of human life (often expressed in the Heb. shalom). Nevertheless, valid criticisms may still be addressed to much of the World Council's ethical endeavours:

1. Scripture is too often neglected, or used selectively, or cited without regard for context, such that biblical realities like 'kingdom', 'salvation' and 'peace' are distorted.

2. Ethical engagement is frequently problem-led or campaign-led ('leapfrogging from one problem to another', to quote Paul Ramsey), without tarrying to lay solid theological and ethical foundations.

3. Fashionable 'secular ecumenicism' repeatedly confuses the distinctive roles, under God, of church and State, of Christian and citizen. Hence it presumes to speak on matters beyond the competence of the Christian faith as such. Robert McAfee Brown (1920–) commented that the Geneva 1966 conference 'was able to take it for granted that the place of the church is on the cutting edge of the major secular movements of the contemporary world'. 'The world sets the agenda for the church' may be a perilous half-truth, if the church's Lord is no longer allowed to set its agenda.

4. 'Selective indignation', justified on prudential or diplomatic grounds, has left the WCC silent on abuses and corruptions in socialist regimes that should, on its own terms, have atttracted critique. The recent liberation movements in the former Soviet bloc owed little to WCC-led thinking, and have left it – and some of its member-churches in the region – somewhat flat-footed.

Bibliography
E. Duff, *The Social Thought of the World Council of Churches* (London, 1956); H. E. Fey (ed.), *A History of the Ecumenical Movement*, vol. 2 (Geneva, ²1986), esp. P. Abrecht, 'The Development of Ecumenical Social Thought and Action'; J. M. Gustafson, *Protestant and Roman Catholic Ethics: Prospects for Rapprochement* (Chicago, 1978; London, ²1979); E. W. Lefever, *Amsterdam to Nairobi: The World Council of Churches and the Third World* (Washington, DC, 1979); R. Mehl, *Catholic Ethics and Protestant Ethics* (Philadelphia, 1917); R. J. Neuhaus, *The World Council of Churches and Radical Chic* (Washington, DC, 1977); A. J. Van der Bent, *Major Studies and Themes in the Ecumenical Movement* (Geneva, 1981); idem, *Six Hundred Ecumenical Consultations 1948–1982* (Geneva, 1983); J. A. E. Vermaat, *The World Council of Churches and Politics* (New York, 1989).

D.F.W.

EDUCATION. The meaning of education is open to debate. For some, the focus is on 'rearing' or 'nourishing', perhaps by 'drawing out' potential and gifts. For others education is concerned with seeing children as empty vessels to be filled with knowledge. Others include any process by which a person of any age grows in knowledge, awareness and life skills.

In focusing on the formal education of the young, in the context mainly of Western culture, we may ask such questions as: What is education for? Is it to produce adequate factory-workers to perpetuate the materialist society? Is it to encourage thinking, to teach the values of a loving community, and to help individuals develop their own potential as valuable human beings?

Christians vary in their responses to the definitions and purposes contained in these questions. The concept of 'Christian education' is not straightforward, though many parents want 'moral' education for their children, however that is defined. The Hebrew-Christian tradition is committed to moral education to enable people to love and serve both God and neighbour. The family in the OT is the context in which God's law is taught (Dt. 6:1–7). The Wisdom literature illustrates moral education (Pr. 3:1ff.). According to Jewish tradition, local schools were first organized systematically in Palestine by Simeon ben Shetah in the 1st century BC. In the NT, teaching and learning are of great importance: Jesus teaches his disciples (Mt. 5:2); and in the early church, teaching was regarded as a gift (Eph. 4:11; 1 Tim. 4:11–14). Learning is an important part of Christian pilgrimage, and learning is perhaps best understood in the light of the model Jesus gives of apprentices learning from the master in an active and personal way.

Public education in the West grew from this Christian tradition of teaching within the home and the church. In Europe and the USA the earliest schools were founded by Christians. Historically the Judaeo-Christian ethic underpinned most Western education. The 20th century has seen a dramatic shift towards a more secular approach, presenting problems both for parents desiring a 'Christian' education for their children and for Christian educators.

Education takes place in many different contexts, and the crucial home influence on learning is widely acknowledged. The Judaeo-Christian model emphasizes the importance of a partnership between home and school, but in reality parents often abdicate responsibility to schools and there is an unhealthy denigration of the role of parents on the part of some teachers.

In recent years there has been a growth in 'modern methods' that give greater attention to the ways children learn, and a move from the child being a passive listener, to the child being active learner. To some Christians this change is regretted as the unwelcome influence of humanism,* whereas others see it as a positive move towards acknowledging respect for the child as someone made in the image of God.* Related to this is the question whether there should be compulsory education at all, particularly for the very young. Many Christians campaign for nursery education for all who want it, in the belief that this offers everyone equal opportunity.

The choice of school can be problematic for Christian parents. Should they send their children to the local State school, where values may not be Christian but where they would play their part in the local community? (Indeed, in a pluralist society, there is a question whether pro-Christian education is in any case morally acceptable.) Can parents justify school fees when millions are starving in the Third World? Do fee-paying schools contribute to élitism and class divisions in society? When it comes to the needs of their own child, what people believe in is sometimes overriden. For some parents the secularization of education, or the belief that there is too little discipline, or the fact that their child's teacher is not a Christian, has led them to remove their child to a 'Christian school' or to offer education at home. Home schooling is growing in Western cultures, with a consequent growth of curricula for these children, many of them being specifically Christian. There has also been a growth in Christian schools (i.e. fee-paying schools outside the State system in the UK, as distinct from 'State-aided' or 'State-controlled' Church of England schools), but some argue that such schools give a child too restricted an outlook and fail to prepare him or her adequately for life in the world.

Other difficult choices for parents include those between Christian discipline and freedom, a Christian school ethic and a more liberal or multicultural one, and how to react to the 'hidden' curriculum (i.e. the priorities given to some subjects, and the values and ideologies assumed). Questions also arise such as: Who controls the curriculum? Politicians? Parents? The State? The school board? Furthermore, however much schools claim to be value-free, and whatever the schools' stated intentions, children are very susceptible to the 'hidden' messages (e.g. from the products the school permits to be advertised on the premises). The message of a British school since the Education Act of 1988 is that 'market forces' dictate decisions: choices have to be made, e.g. shall we have smaller classes, or more books, or mend the roof? Does this economic priority teach children that they matter less than the financial well-being of the school, or that, in a materialistic society, such financial choices affect many aspects of life? Schools may not be able to budget for children with special needs, and what would any concept of 'payment by results' do to schools in deprived areas? Resources are often so scarce that parents are asked to contribute towards basic books, which again raises questions of national budget priorities.

The crucial relationship between teacher and child is under threat. In an increasingly stressed society the role of the teacher has had to change to include that of social worker. The headteacher has had to become a manager, and some believe that the quality of what is taught has consequently suffered. Demands on educators increase, yet their status in society decreases, and any perception that teachers have of their 'selves' will clearly influence how they teach. As the belief grows that teacher-efficiency can be measured by testing children, the importance of the relationship between teacher and child may become submerged. For some teachers, it is that relationship of personal respect and love for the child that is the crucial means by which the child learns personal value and what it

335

means to be a member of the kingdom of God.*

Bibliography
M. Donaldson, *Children's Minds* (Glasgow, 1978); B. V. Hill, *That They May Learn: Towards a Christian View of Education* (Exeter, 1990); C. Martin, *Schools Now: A Parents' Guide* (Oxford, 1988); R. Pinder, *Why Don't Teachers Teach Like They Used To?* (London, 1987); M. Roques, *Curriculum Unmasked: Towards a Christian Understanding of Education* (Eastbourne, 1989).

S.E.At.

E DWARDS, JONATHAN (1703–58), best known as a promoter of the 18th-century Great Awakening and as a defender of traditional Calvinism. Edwards was also a profound moralist, whose ethical writings have become the subject of increasingly serious attention in recent decades.

The context for Edwards' ethics was twofold: his own effort to define morality in a biblical way; and the preoccupation of his age with the moral capacities of human nature. Though never summarized in one comprehensive statement, Edwards' most elaborate ethical writings constitute a subtle blending of scriptural themes and theocentric responses to the optimistic ethical views of the Enlightenment.* These works elaborate a cohesive ethical stance: a sermon series from 1738 on 1 Cor. 13, later published as *Charity and Its Fruits*; an analysis of genuine spirituality in *Religious Affections* (1746); the posthumous *Two Dissertations* (1765) that included *Concerning the End for Which God created the World* and *The Nature of True Virtue*; as well as extensive private notations.

Edwards felt, first, that moralists of the Enlightenment were partially correct. Because of God's benevolence in creation, all humans do have some reliable instincts about virtue.* But, secondly, these natural instincts do not constitute 'true virtue' since they are focused on the well-being of creatures. 'True virtue', by contrast, 'consists in benevolence to Being in general'. It 'must chiefly consist in love to God: the Being of beings, infinitely the greatest and best of beings' (*Ethical Writings*, ed. P. Ramsey, pp. 540, 550). Thirdly, a person oriented towards God as the source of all good is able to act benevolently to lesser beings because of the awareness that these lesser beings also depend upon God for existence and purpose.

Bibliography
N. Fiering, *Jonathan Edwards's Moral Thought and Its British Context* (Chapel Hill, NC, 1981); P. Ramsey (ed.), *The Works of Jonathan Edwards, Vol. 8: Ethical Writings* (New Haven, CT, 1989); J. E. Smith (ed.), *The Works of Jonathan Edwards, Vol. 2: Religious Affections* (New Haven, CT, 1959).

M.A.N.

EGO, see ANALYTICAL PSYCHOLOGY; PERSONALITY; PSYCHOANALYSIS; UNCONSCIOUS.

E GOISM. The word 'egoism' is derived from the Gk. *egōo and Lat. ego*, 'I'. Generally it means to centre in the self. Popularly, it is often used in the pejorative sense of being self-centred. Egoism is divided into theoretical and practical forms.

Theoretical egoism encompasses both subjective idealism and solipsism, which hold that one's own individual ego is the only one which can be known for sure to exist.

Practical egoism, such as that of Ayn Rand (1905–82; see *For the New Intellectual*, New York, 1961) believes that one's own good is the proper motive of human choice. On the opposite end of the spectrum is radical self-denial and asceticism* which debases the self,* especially in its material dimension. Asceticism is found in early Gnosticism, with shadows in certain forms of Christian mysticism.

By contrast to both extremes of egoism and asceticism, the Bible offers a balanced perspective on the self.* First, it affirms that each self (person) is made in God's image* and likeness and, hence, has God-given value (Gn. 1:27). Further, recognizing the self-centred propensity of fallen human nature, Paul warned against being 'lovers of self' (2 Tim. 3:2, RSV). Likewise, Jesus insisted one must 'deny himself' (Mt. 16:24) by sacrificing personal desires in order to become his disciple. None the less, there is a legitimate sense of self-love (see Self-esteem*) implied in Jesus' command to love one's neighbour* 'as [you love] yourself' (Mt. 19:19). Indeed, Paul declares that 'no-one ever hated his own body, but he feeds and cares for it . . .' (Eph. 5:29). That is, we should cultivate an attitude of self-sacrifice and concern for our neighbour that will at least equal the natural love that we have for ourselves. However, the ultimate check on egoism is that, while we should love other humans *as* ourselves, we must love God pre-eminently *with* our whole self, heart and soul (Mt. 22:37).

N.L.G.

ELDERSHIP, see MINISTRY.

ELECTRA COMPLEX, see PSYCHOANALYSIS.

ELECTROCONVULSIVE THERAPY (ECT), see MENTAL HEALTH; PSYCHIATRIC CARE, ETHICS OF.

ELLIS, ALBERT (1913–), founder of rational-emotive therapy (RET), is a self-described humanist* and atheist. Trained in the psychoanalytic* method, Ellis soon despaired of its inefficiency and ineffectiveness. He began to experiment with RET, called 'rational therapy' in its early stages.

The core postulate of RET is well summarized in the phrase of Epictetus (*c.* 55–135 AD), a Stoic philosopher, who said, 'Men are disturbed not by things, but by the views which they take of them' (quoted by Ellis and Whitely in *Theoretical and Empirical Foundations of Rational-Emotive Therapy*). RET is taught in an A–B–C format. People often assume that Activating Events (A) cause them to experience certain emotional Consequences (C): *e.g.* 'My wife left me and so I feel awful.' But Activating Events have Consequences only through the mediation of our Beliefs (B) about those events. Rational beliefs result in rational consequences; irrational beliefs result in irrational consequences. The main irrational beliefs that consistently trouble people are that others must approve of and accept one, and that the conditions of one's life should be in accord with one's wishes.

Counselling in the RET system consists of education in the basic premises of RET, understanding the irrational beliefs that are producing the subjective distress of the person, and assisting the person to change irrational beliefs through disputation of those beliefs. Ellis' therapeutic style is highly didactic and confrontational. Christian evaluation of RET (see S. L. Jones and R. E. Butman in *Modern Psychotherapies*) would note positively RET's high view of rationality and of client capacity for change, and its direct, problem-solving focus. Negatively: 1. RET has become a platform for the explicit promulgation of a humanistic, atheistic and hedonistic* life philosophy; 2. its definition of rationality is

pragmatic (rational is whatever makes one feel good), and ultimately circular because it has no objective, external referent for truth; and 3. RET so overemphasizes rationality that all other facets of human life (*e.g.* spirituality, emotional experience, intuition) are minimized or ignored. The empirical support for the efficacy of the approach is modest at best.

See also: CHARACTER. [10]

Bibliography
A. Ellis and J. Whitely (eds.), *Theoretical and Empirical Foundations of Rational-Emotive Therapy* (Monterey, CA, 1978); S. L. Jones and R. E. Butman, *Modern Psychotherapies: A Comprehensive Christian Appraisal* (Downers Grove, IL, 1991).

S.L.J.

ELLUL, JACQUES (1912–). A sociologist, historian and Christian ethicist, Ellul was born and raised in Bordeaux, France. During studies at the University of Bordeaux (Licence en Droit, 1931; Doctor of Law, 1936), he was first converted to Marxism, then to Christianity. He was dismissed from his Strasburg faculty post in 1940 because of his opposition to Pétain and the Vichy government. A participant in the Resistance during the Ger. occupation, he was appointed to the Bordeaux city government, in charge of public works projects, from 1944 to 46.

From 1944 until retirement in 1980, Ellul was Professor of the History and Sociology of Institutions in the Faculty of Law and Economic Sciences at Bordeaux and also taught regularly in the Institute of Political Studies. An active lay member of the Reformed Church of France, he served in local church leadership and from 1951 to 1970 on the National Council and its commissions; from 1947 to 1951 he participated in various commissions of the World Council of Churches.

Author of some fifty books and more than 700 published articles, Ellul is known best for *The Technological Society* (1954; ET, New York, 1964), *The Political Illusion* (1965; ET, New York, 1967) and other sociological and historical works in which he argues that 'technique' (the rule of rationalistic, quantitative analysis in search of measurably efficient means) is the increasingly dominant mode of thought and source of value not just in science* and technology* but in the politics, economics, pedagogy, art, religion, communications and popular culture of the modern world.

Parallel to this study of sociological reality, Ellul has produced many volumes of theological and biblical studies, such as *The Meaning of the City* (ET, Grand Rapids, 1970) and *The Ethics of Freedom*, 3 vols. (1973–84; ET, Grand Rapids, 1976), in which he promotes a radical Christian way of freedom, holiness and love for individuals who refuse to bow to the principalities and powers of our era, *i.e.* technique, rationalism, quantification and efficiency.

Bibliography

In Season, Out of Season (1981; ET, San Francisco, 1982); *What I Believe* (1987; ET, Grand Rapids, 1989).

D. W. Gill, *The Word of God in the Ethics of Jacques Ellul* (Metuchen, NJ, 1984); J. M. Hanks, *Jacques Ellul: A Comprehensive Bibliography* (Greenwich, CT, and London, 1984).

D.W.G.

E MBRYOLOGY is the study of development from fertilization until birth. In humans all the parts and organs are formed during the first three months of pregnancy* and during the remaining six months the embryo, usually known then as a foetus, simply grows and matures. Although the biological facts are relatively straightforward, their interpretation in a spiritual and philosophical sense is not, and opinions differ as to when 'life' begins.

Biological aspects

A new human being is initiated when egg and sperm fuse. The parents' body cells all contain twenty-three pairs of chromosomes, each of which contains thousands of genes or chemical messengers. When each egg or sperm is formed, it receives only one from each pair. In every generation, individuals inherit half their chromosomes from each of their parents, who in turn have inherited half *their* chromosomes from each of their parents, and so on. In this way the genetic material is continually passed from generation to generation. Errors in the genetic code (see below) give rise to inherited diseases which can sometimes be traced back through past centuries.

During the production of egg and sperm there is some mixing of the genetic information, and as there are about 100,000 items to be reshuffled during their formation, each egg and sperm, and therefore each individual, has a unique genetic make-up.

The genetic information itself is based on a simple code of four chemicals (bases): adenine (A), thymine (T), guanine (G) and cytosine (C), whose order determines the proteins to be formed. By varying the sequence of these four, the message received varies and different proteins and enzymes are produced. This code is virtually universal for the entire range of living organisms from virusus to elephants and humans. A lowly organism such as a virus can be characterized by its entire specific sequence of these bases, so that its genetic make-up would read GGATTAATTGC ... to 200,000 letters.

Humans have 3,000 million base pairs and at present the sequence is known for only a few portions, although by early next century it may well be that the order of all the bases will be known, and each person will be describable by his or her unique sequence.

At the time of conception, a sperm with its unique sequence fuses with an egg with its unique sequence and we have the genetic blueprint for a new person. During the next ten days, the single cell divides many times, forming two, four, eight cells, *etc.,* and ultimately a round ball of cells which floats freely in the mother's womb. At this stage, the ball of cells may split into two and each cell clump continue to grow independently. The two individuals eventually born will be genetically identical and are identical twins.

Also during this time, it is possible to remove one cell and the remaining cells regulate themselves to develop into a healthy embryo. The one cell removed can be tested to find its sex or whether a disease gene is present, and the result indicates the make-up of the embryo from which it came. At this early stage, known as the pre-implantation stage, the embryo has great flexibility; some cells will form the extra-embryonic membranes which will surround the growing foetus, and others will eventually become the embryo proper. It seems that many (perhaps 50%) of these embryos are imperfect and fail to develop.

After about ten days, a cavity appears in the ball of cells and some cells are seen to heap up in one area. From this time any attempt at division into two gives rise to conjoined or 'Siamese' twins. Individual cells can no longer be removed with impunity, as the different cells are becoming 'committed' to different functions. Soon a groove, the primitive streak, becomes visible, and it is cells around this which will give rise to the embryo itself. The remainder of the cells will provide the support system for the embryo, such as the placenta and membranes.

During this time, the embryo stops floating freely and becomes embedded in the lining of the womb. Now it can obtain nourishment from the mother for further development. A signal in the form of a hormone is released so that the mother's body is informed that implantation has occurred, and her next menstrual period is suppressed. It is only then that she becomes aware of the presence of the embryo.

Once implanted (by about day fourteen), the primitive streak continues to develop, and the different organs become differentiated. It is during these early weeks that normal development is particularly susceptible to disruption by harmful agents such as drugs or viruses. About 15% of conceptions which implant are lost as miscarriages during these next crucial few weeks.

Three weeks from the time of fertilization (which occurs about two weeks after the last menstrual period, and is the date usually used to age the pregnancy), the brain and nervous system begin to form; by four weeks the heart starts beating; by eight weeks the limbs, fingers and toes are all developed and the embryo is about 3cm long; and by ten weeks all organs are formed.

The embryo is now known as a foetus, and it continues to grow and mature in the shelter of the womb until about thirty-eight weeks after fertilization.

Theological aspects

The biological facts are straightforward and not disputed, but what is that status of this early embryo? Is the embryo, from the time of fusion of egg and sperm, my brother or sister for whom Christ died? Christians have differing views: some believe that as the unique blueprint is present from conception, the valued person is indeed there; others believe this comes later.

From such texts as Je. 1:5 and Gal. 1:15, Scripture teaches us that God knows and calls us from the womb, but Eph. 1:4 reminds us that God is outside time and knew us before the creation of the world. Ps. 139, often quoted to suggest that personhood is present from the moment of conception, is an exclamation of wonder at God's omniscience and all-pervading care for us as individuals with individual histories. The psalm does not actually address questions raised by modern embryology. Luke's account of the miraculous conception of Jesus shows that he was indeed known and named from the start, but Christ's origins and parentage cannot be extrapolated to every conception.

Gn. 1:27 tells us that God made humankind in his own image. Should we see the image of God* in a genetic blueprint for which in twenty years time we may have an accurate computer printout? It is humankind's relationship with God that makes us special, so it could be that its relationships make the embryo special. During the first fourteen days, only God knows whether or not egg and sperm have fused. The embryo has no other relationships, and it floats freely in the mother's passages. It may pass on and out into the sewer unknown and unmourned. If, however, implantation occurs, the mother (usually) becomes increasingly aware of her pregnancy, and ending it is a disruptive event. As the pregnancy continues, the bond continues to develop, and culminates in the birth of the baby who is infinitely precious.

Could imagehood be similarly progressive and in some way be mediated through the embryo's relationship with its mother?

Applications

These considerations are not merely academic. For those Christians who believe the embryo to be sacrosanct from the moment of fusion of egg and sperm, any agents which hinder implantation are forbidden, including several particular forms of contraception.

Eggs and sperm can be fused in the laboratory, and infertile couples can achieve pregnancies by having such conceptions returned to the mother's uterus. But there may be more embryos available than needed. Returning them all to the womb could jeopardize the success of the procedure. Some Christians believe the excess can be discarded, while others maintain that Christians should not be involved in such procedures. For those struggling with the problem of infertility, these are crucial issues (see Childlessness*).

See also: EMBRYO TRANSFER; REPRODUCTIVE TECHNOLOGIES.

Bibliography
A. C. Berry, *Beginnings: Christian Views of the Early Embryo* (London, 1993); N. M. Ford, *When Did I Begin? Conception of the Human Individual in History, Philosophy and Science* (Cambridge, 1988); T. Iglesias, 'What Kind of Being is the Human Embryo?', in N. M. de S. Cameron (ed.), *Embryos and Ethics: The Warnock Report in Debate* (Edinburgh, 1987).

A.C.B.

EMBRYO TRANSFER involves the production of an embryo, usually in the laboratory, and its transfer to the uterus (womb) of a recipient mother. Usually the embryo transferred has been made by bringing together the recipient woman's egg and her husband's sperm. The embryo may be transferred as soon as it is ready or, if there are more available than are needed (see Embryology*), some may be deep-frozen, and these may then be transferred many years later.

Where a couple are at high risk of having a child with a serious genetic disorder, it is theoretically possible to test the embryos to see if the disease gene is present or absent. Healthy embryos are transferred and the affected ones discarded. This type of pre-implantation testing is only just starting to become technically possible.

Christians disagree as to whether this type of embryo transfer is right or not. Those who believe that personhood starts when egg or sperm fuse could not discard embryos, while those who do not believe the pre-implantation embryo to be a person find it entirely legitimate.

Embryo transfer can, however, be more complex. It is possible for a couple to donate their spare embryos to another couple who are unable to produce their own. The recipient mother would then become pregnant and carry a child who was genetically unrelated to either her or her husband. Similarly embryos can be transferred which have either sperm or ovum donated while the other gamete comes from one member of the recipient couple. The issues here are similar to those considered under donor insemination, but more complex as there can be a genetic mother and father, a rearing mother and father and even a surrogate mother. The potential legal, social, emotional and moral problems are huge.

There are two other procedures used in the treatment of infertility which have some overlap with embryo transfer: 1. GIFT (gamete intra-Fallopian transfer): ova and sperm are together introduced into the woman's Fallopian tube, thus avoiding the problems of conception occurring in the laboratory and of the spare embryos; and 2. ZIFT (zygote intra-Fallopian transfer): fusion of egg and sperm is brought about with some external assistance, but the resulting zygote is then transferred to the woman's Fallopian tube.

The only moral concern that arises with these two techniques is that procreation has been separated from the sexual act. This is the reverse of contraception.

See also: REPRODUCTIVE TECHNOLOGIES.

Bibliography
D. G. Jones, *Manufacturing Humans: The Challenge of the New Reproductive Technologies* (Leicester, 1987); O. O'Donovan, *Begotten or Made?* (Oxford, 1984).

A.C.B.

EMIGRATION. What makes emigration, leaving the land of one's domicile, a moral issue? The position of the Vietnamese 'economic refugees' in Hong Kong poses the dilemma. They have fled at great risk from what they see as an oppressive regime, yet no countries are willing to receive them. The position of the Hong Kong Chinese, many of whom have already fled Communist China, poses a similar dilemma. Should they be prevented from leaving when Hong Kong returns to being ruled from Peking in 1997? Should other countries be morally obliged to receive them?

Emigration – both voluntary and forced – has taken place throughout history. It forms part of the biblical record. Abraham is called to emigrate (Gn. 12:1–3); the children of Israel 'emigrate' from Egypt (Ex. 12:31–42), which for the people of the Exodus generation was their place of birth. Amos 9:7–8 records a number of 'emigrations' for which God was responsible.

The biblical vision of a new land has formed a powerful motivation for those seeking to escape from what they perceived as oppression. The Pilgrim Fathers emigrated from England seeking a new land; the Voortrekkers in South Africa emigrated from the Cape Colony in search of a place where they could have political independence.

People have emigrated to avoid persecution.

The Mennonites emigrated across Europe after the Reformation; those Jews who could do so emigrated from Nazi Germany.

Emigration in contemporary situations presents a dilemma. On the one hand, those who can emigrate and are welcomed into other countries are people whose skills the host countries need. Such people are often the people with skills that their own poor 'motherlands' also need, in order to develop. Such emigration, while understandable in personal terms, is often a case of the wealthy countries reinforcing their strong positions by drawing off the best brains and people of those countries that could have become their competitors.

On the other hand, *émigrés* often see that there is no future in their own country. People of mixed British-Indian descent in India find themselves discriminated against in education and job prospects; people with wealth and skills in Vietnam find no future for themselves in their own motherland. Families who have emigrated to more prosperous countries have often provided economic support for their relatives left in their own countries. The economy of the Philippines took a severe jolt during the 1991 Gulf War, as many families no longer received income from their relatives working in Kuwait.

At the end of the 20th century, the concept of the nation-state, which is less than 400 years old, is being increasingly challenged. Within such States as (the former) Yugoslavia, ethnic groups call for their own political and economic autonomy. In the resultant conflict, large-scale involuntary emigration takes place, as elsewhere in the world.

The biblical injunction to remember the 'sojourner', the person who is an *émigré*, applies especially to those who have found a new home in a new land. It speaks to the very human tendency to decide that, even though their grandparents may have been refugees, and their presence in the particular country and its benefits is due to them being 'welcomed in', their own security and standard of living would be threatened if they accepted further emigrants.

The biblical teaching that members of the community who are unable to work must be assisted by the rest of the community means that any argument against emigration from 'poorer' countries must be accompanied by genuine practical and effective assistance to the people of those countries. This help might be given either individually, through churches and agencies, or by governments, to enable them to improve their economies and their records on human rights (see Rights, Human*).

The Christian understanding of human solidarity, that individual gifts are for the benefit of the community, means that any argument for emigration from such countries must be accompanied (as it often is) by genuine effective assistance for those left behind by the *émigrés*.

In those cases where there is substantial doubt of any improvement in the short term, especially for persecuted minorities, there must be effective and real assistance to those who are forced to emigrate. While it is clear now that assistance to the Jews in the 1930s was a moral imperative, it was not so clear at the time.

C.M.N.S. and V.K.S.

EMOTION. An emotion is an involuntary response of the personality to certain stimuli, either outside us or from within us, usually associated with bodily changes (in, for instance, facial expression, breathing, heartbeat, sweat), with more extreme feelings than usual, and sometimes with intense behaviour of either aggression (see Violence*) or flight. In very intense emotion, rational control of behaviour may be lost, but usually we remain responsible for our actions. In day-to-day conversation, to experience emotion means to experience such feelings as anger,* happiness, sadness, fear,* disgust and surprise. It is not easy to find an agreed psychological definition, however.

Various factors probably contribute to the pattern of a person's emotional responses, *e.g.* parental modelling or early learning experiences. These often lead to cultural differences in the ways emotions are expressed. In one culture, grief may usually be expressed through silent withdrawal; in another through public, demonstrative behaviour.

Some Christians are very wary of emotion, finding that feelings can too easily get out of hand, and the loss of rational control over life is taken to be unhelpful if not sinful. 'Faith not feelings' may describe their approach to spirituality. Such Christians may deny certain emotions (such as anger) within themselves, or may repress (see Repression, Psychological*) their feelings in an attempt to 'be at peace'. Sometimes the failure to express emotion appropriately can lead to disorders in other areas of life, such as psychosomatic illness. At other times, Christians have been criticized for too much 'enthusiasm', and certain strands of Christian spirituality have concentrated too much on the experiential and emotional side of religion to the exclusion of theological evaluation. In worship there can be an appropriate expression of emotion. There can also be symptoms of pathology, such as when the 'suggestibility' of certain people is manipulatively enhanced through certain stimuli (lights, music, drumbeat, massed choirs; see Brainwashing,* Conversion,* and Psychology of Religion*). This has led critics of mass evangelism to reject many conversion testimonies from such settings as 'mere emotion'.

The Scriptures portray the full range of human emotions, however, and the various writers of the psalms, for instance, were less inhibited in emotional expression than are some Christian people. The psalms include lament (Ps. 137), exultation (Ps. 47), despair (Ps. 88), longing (Ps. 42), bitterness (Ps. 73) and contentment (Ps. 23), to name but a few emotions. The prophets feel anger at injustice (Amos), and anger at God (Habakkuk). The Wisdom literature shows us depression* and anguish (Job), and searching frustration (Ecclesiastes). In the Gospels, the portrait of Jesus Christ shows us a human being expressing a wide range of human emotions, but always appropriately and responsibly. In his paper 'On the Emotional Life of Our Lord', B. B. Warfield (1851–1921) illustrates how Jesus Christ felt compassion, love, indignation, anger, sorrow and joy. His soul was 'troubled' (Jn. 11:33); he was distressed and despondent (Mt. 26:37). He expressed wonder (Mt. 8:10) and desire (Lk. 22:15). Once he was conceivably the subject of 'shame' (Mk. 8:38). Jesus' emotions led to physical reactions. He was hungry (Mt. 4:2), thirsty (Jn. 19:28), and weary (Jn. 4:6). He wept (Jn. 11:35), wailed (Lk. 19:41), sighed (Mk. 7:34) and groaned (Mk. 8:12). We read of his angry glare (Mk. 3:5), annoyed speech (Mk. 10:14), rage (Jn. 11:33, 38), agitation (Jn. 11:35), exultation of joy (Lk. 10:21), the unrest of his movements in the face of anticipated evils (Mt. 26:37), and his loud cry in the moment of desolation (Mt. 27:46).

Christian maturing includes learning how to express emotion appropriately, how to recognize and name the feelings within oneself, and how to be able to use feelings creatively. Expression of emotion is one component of non-verbal interpersonal communication. A certain level of emotional arousal is essential for carrying out certain tasks: too little and there is insufficient motivation or energy; too much and the loss of control diminishes effectiveness.

Christian therapy, counselling and pastoral care (see Pastoral Care, Counselling and Psychotherapy[12]) can all facilitate emotional maturity. Some approaches to therapy focus on the client's emotions, and work with the feelings in the client, and also with those generated in the 'transference' between client and therapist. The counsellor's own emotional response to the client can be used constructively in therapy, although in unskilled hands emotional 'involvement' between counsellor and client can be destructive. Psychodynamic approaches (such as that developed in a Christian context by Frank Lake*) and relational approaches (building on the client-centred work of Carl Rogers*), work with the client's emotions as a route towards personal healing. Other, more cognitive, approaches begin with the basic belief that much of our feeling derives from our thoughts, and that mistaken or irrational or ungodly thinking processes are at the root of much personal misery. Albert Ellis* argued, for example, that emotions arise in an A, B, C pattern: A = external or internal activating event; B = my beliefs about A; C = consequential emotion. While we naturally tend to think that A causes C, Ellis argued that it is in fact B (our fundamental pattern of thoughts) which causes C. Therapy, then, requires the isolation of irrational ideas which cause disturbances, and the deliberate development of new mental habits, if emotional healing is to be achieved. Archibald Hart developed Albert Ellis' 'rational-emotive therapy' in a Christian direction in *Feeling Free;* David Seamands also makes use of this approach in *Healing for Damaged Emotions.* Alongside such therapeutic approaches, there is a growing interest in and use of prayer for 'healing of memories', sometimes in the context of sacramental ministry, which are ways of casting our care on to God, for he cares for us (see 1 Pet. 5:7), by bringing painful memories into touch with the healing presence of the Holy Spirit.

See also: INNER HEALING.

Bibliography

M. Chave-Jones, *Listening to your Feelings* (Oxford, 1989); A. Hart, *Feeling Free* (Old Tappan, NJ, 1979); F. Lake, *Tight Corners in*

Pastoral Counselling (London, 1981); R. C. Roberts, *Spirituality and Human Emotion* (Grand Rapids, 1983); D. Seamands, *Healing for Damaged Emotions* (Amersham, 1981); B. B. Warfield, 'On the Emotional Life of our Lord', in Samuel G. Craig (ed.), *The Person and Work of Christ* (Phillipsburg, NJ, 1950).

D.J.A.

EMOTIONAL PAIN, see CLINICAL THEOLOGY; INNER HEALING; PRIMAL THERAPY.

EMOTIVISM, see LOGICAL POSITIVISM.

EMPATHY is an important concept for counselling. Most people understand it to mean 'putting yourself in the other person's shoes' or 'seeing the world as they see it'. Though therapists such as Sigmund Freud,* Theodor Reik (1888–1969) and Harry S. Sullivan (1892–1949) have discussed empathy, it is with Carl Rogers* that it has been most closely linked, because it is a major concept within his counselling theory. Rogers defined empathy as the 'accurate perception of another's internal frame of reference'. He believed that the therapist's attitude of empathy, genuineness and positive regard for the client is necessary for the client's change and growth. Empathy helps the client in his or her self-exploration and resolution of conflicting feelings.

Most definitions of empathy show that it involves comprehending what the other person feels without actually experiencing it. No-one can ever know exactly what another person feels or thinks, as we are all unique individuals, but to some extent we can understand. Empathy is about entering the other person's internal frame of reference, understanding the person's world and knowing the person's self-perception. It means understanding not only what the person thinks and feels, but also what are his or her values and goals in life. It is possible to help people without fully understanding them, but a person who can empathize is likely to be more effective.

Empathy is not just about understanding a person but also about communicating that understanding. The counsellor needs to listen to the verbal and non-verbal messages and respond in a way that communicates understanding. The responses must be at a level that is appropriate and use suitable vocabulary (*e.g.* for a child). The responses should help people in their exploration of their feelings and thoughts. It may be that as a person talks, the counsellor picks up that he or she is angry, even though he or she does not say so. The response, 'It sounds as though that made you angry', can help people get in touch with their feelings and help in their self-understanding.

R. R. Carkhuff suggests five levels of empathic response. At level one the verbal and behavioural expressions of the counsellor do not detract significantly from the verbal and behavioural expressions of the client, nor do they add significantly to the counselling; at level five the counsellor's responses do add significantly to the feeling and meaning of the client. They accurately express feeling-levels beyond what clients have been able to express, or, in the event of continuing deep self-exploration on the clients' part, they share fully with them in their deepest moments.

Some people are naturally empathic, but for those who are not, empathy is a skill that can be learnt. Counsellor training generally includes training in empathy skills. A counsellor learns how to reflect, paraphrase, restate and focus on what has been communicated, either verbally or non-verbally. Gerard Egan (1930–) examines what makes empathy effective in his training manual. He looks at ways of improving empathic responses, such as giving time to think before responding, using short responses, and gearing responses to the person.

Research suggests that empathy is correlated with the client's self-exploration and the improvement of the client, but some of the research is not very reliable. The sufficiency of empathy, positive regard and genuineness for client improvements has not been consistently demonstrated. Therefore totally to focus the whole counselling approach on empathy would be foolish.

Christ knew what people were like; he could read their hearts and respond to them accordingly. We do not have that ability in the same way, but if we are to help people effectively we need to understand them, to see the world through their eyes and choose the best approach for them. In 1 Thes. 5:14 Paul urges the early Christians to 'warn those who are idle . . . encourage the timid . . . help the weak'. Here one can see a variety of approaches to people with problems. A lack of understanding prevents the choice of the most effective approach. Elsewhere Paul tells us to rejoice with those who rejoice and weep with those who weep (Rom. 12:15). In order to be able to do so, we need to know what a person is feeling. Empathy is at the heart of Christian ministry.

Bibliography

R. R. Carkhuff, *Helping and Human Relations: A Primer for Lay and Professional Helpers*, vol. 1, 'Selection and Training' (New York, 1969); G. Egan, *The Skilled Helper: A Systematic Approach to Effective Helping* (Monterey, CA, ²1982); C. Rogers, 'The necessary and sufficient conditions of therapeutic personality changes', *JCP* 21.2, 1957, pp. 95–103.

H.C.H.

E MPIRICISM is the view that the source of all knowledge is sense-experience. The main proponents were John Locke (1632–1704), G. Berkeley (1685–1753) and David Hume.* They rejected the mind as the basis of knowledge. Reason provided only what was known already by deduction and definition and was absolutely certain. In contrast, the sense provided genuinely new knowledge which was synthetic, contingent, a posteriori and open to doubt. In empiricist thinking, the mind is like a white sheet of paper or wax tablet on which the senses write and leave their marks. Most empiricists distinguished between direct impressions and ideas, which were copies of impressions, to explain the different elements of our mental life. This led to the search for basic units of experience, which were directly experienced, and about which we could not be mistaken. It was a means of finding certainty in human knowledge.

With the Vienna Circle and the school of logical positivism,* metaphysics, religion and ethics were held to have no objective basis, but to be purely subjective preferences and expressions of emotion. The notorious principle of verifiability was the means of excluding all kinds of statements which could not be founded on sense-experience.

The failure to find a basic unit of sense-experience, *e.g.* a sense datum, the need to redefine verifiability to avoid self-contradiction, and the inability to find an adequate mathematical language to express all human knowledge blunted the effects of empiricism and led to a more commonsense and descriptive approach to philosophy, language and meaning.

See also: AYER, A. J.; WITTGENSTEIN, L.

Bibliography

A. J. Ayer, *Language, Truth and Logic* (London, ²1946); B. Russell, *Human Knowledge* (London, 1948).

E.D.C.

E MPLOYERS' CONFEDERATIONS. Employers' organizations, using the definition of J. J. Oechslin, are 'formal groups of employers set up to defend, represent or advise affiliated employers and to strengthen their position in society at large with respect to labour matters [*i.e.* relations with employees] as distinct from economic matters'. ('Employers' Organisations', in R. Blanpain, ed., *Comparative Labour Law and Industrial Relations*, p. 229.) They are composed of enterprises, not individual human beings. They may or may not conclude collective agreements in their own right. Their legal form varies considerably between different countries (employers' associations in the UK, the USA and several European countries are discussed by F. Schmidt in B. Aaron and K. W. Wedderburn, eds., *Industrial Conflict*, ch. 1).

The evolution of employers' organizations in anything like their modern form began after trade unions* of workers had been functioning for many years. In New Zealand, for example, the formation of employers' associations after the maritime strike in 1890 was essentially a defensive reaction to what employers regarded as a continuing threat from militant and increasingly international trade unionism. But even in the earliest years of the industrial revolutions of Western countries, Adam Smith (1723–90) warned that it would be 'ignorant' to imagine that 'masters rarely combine' (*The Wealth of Nations*, Harmondsworth, 1970, p. 169).

Membership of a federation is always voluntary, at least in theory. There is therefore no genuine employer counterpart to the issues which cluster around the closed or the 'union shop' or compulsory unionism, and which lead to the question whether it is a fundamental human right not to belong to a particular or any workers' trade union, and whether the law should admit conscientious objections. Many Christians over the years have exercised such a right, arguing that all unionism is wrong and (sometimes) that to join would mean an 'unequal yoking' with unbelievers (*cf.* 2 Cor. 6:14).

Another distinction is that, whereas trade unions are often linked, as in Britain, with political parties, employers' organizations do not have *formal* links with political parties. But they inevitably develop numerous personal contacts with politicians in power. In recent years most federations have been forced to move beyond their traditional roles of representing and advising employers into articulating coherent views of political and economic policy. Their comment is, for example, often sought when a government's budget is presented in Parliament.

The question whether it is morally right for a Christian employer to become a member of an employers' (con)federation is scarcely ever asked. The question itself is an unsatisfactory one if it is taken to imply that such federations always and everywhere share common objectives and perform essentially similar functions, regardless of the political system in which operate. The federations are in fact enormously diverse. Any merely general answer to the question would therefore involve extremely superficial moral theorizing. Rather we must take account of the objectives and practices of each national federation, and must ask: 'Does *this* federation in practice seek to oppress the poor, or deny the equality of men and women, or seek to manipulate its own members?' For if it promotes a morally evil aim (often hard to decide), it may become comparatively easy for the Christian employer to decide that he or she or the company one controls must not encourage or assist such a federation by joining it and helping to finance it.

Unfortunately, in this field, as in many others where tough moral decisions have to be made, there is a difference between the *Christian employer* and the *employer who is a Christian*. This may seem an unduly slick distinction, but what these labels help us to see is that whereas the former has integrated his faith and his business practices, and has reflected at some depth on the relation between them, the latter has not done either but has lodged Christian faith and business practices in different compartments: one of the products of the secularization* which has invaded the church.

Christian employers' federations exist in a small handful of countries and are very active. No survey as to their effectiveness or as to the respects in which they incarnate Christian love seems to have been attempted. Whether it is right to splinter the employers in a particular industry by forming a Christian organization,

and whether there is enough Christian consensus to enable such an organization to function in a thoroughgoing and principled way, are essentially the same problems that are faced by those contemplating the formation of a 'Christian' political party, especially in the context of a Westminster-type political system, which operates on the principle of confrontation rather than consensus.

Bibliography

B. Aaron and K. W. Wedderburn (eds.), *Industrial Conflict: A Comparative Legal Survey* (Harlow, 1972); R. Blanpain (ed.), *Comparative Labour Law and Industrial Relations* (Norwell, MA, [2]1981), ch. 12; J. J. Oechslin, 'Employers' Organisations: Current Trends and Social Responsibilities', *ILR* 121.5, 1982; R. M. Rudman, 'Employer Organisations: Their Development and Role in Industrial Relations', in J. M. Howells *et al.*, *Labour and Industrial Relations in New Zealand* (Melbourne, 1974).

D.L.M.

EMPLOYMENT, see WORK.

ENDS AND MEANS. The word 'ends' refers to the results of actions and 'means' to the instruments by which the ends are attained. Ends are willed for their own sake, but means are willed only for the sake of ends. Ends have intrinsic value, whereas the moral significance of means is to be judged by their relation to ends. (So, for example, the desired end of procreating a child could not be justified in terms of Christian ethics by the means of fornication or adultery.) Persons are ends; things are means. Thus, in deontological* ethics, such as the Judaeo-Christian tradition, persons should be loved and things should be used. But one should never love things and use people.

'I' am an end, but 'it' is a means. In this connection, some scholars (*e.g.* Martin Buber, *I and Thou*; ET, New York, 1970; Edinburgh, 1971) believe it is wrong to have an 'I-it' relation to others, as opposed to an 'I-thou' relation. Others should never be treated as an 'it'. For this reason Immanuel Kant's* categorical imperative involved treating others as a kingdom of ends (*Critique of Practical Reason*, ET, London, [6]1909). Ultimately, this is based on Jesus' statement that we should love others as we love ourselves (Mt. 22:39). That is, others are ends, they should be treated as persons too.

Most ethical debates concern means rather than ends. Both disputants, for example, could believe in justice for all (the end) but disagree as to which social programme (the means) is the best means of fulfilling it. Likewise, two opposed political parties may each believe we ought to have the best government (the end), but may disagree as to whose candidate will be the best person (the means) to achieve it. Thus, for deontologists, ends are absolute, whereas means are relative.

There are immediate ends and an ultimate End. Finite persons are immediate ends. For Christians, God alone is the ultimate End. Humans are willed for their own sake finitely, but only God is willed for his own sake infinitely. To will finite persons as ultimate is idolatry. But to deny that humans are ends with God-given value in themselves is dehumanizing.

N.L.G.

Energy comes in many forms: heat, light, sound, mechanical, electrical, chemical and nuclear. It was one of the great achievements of 19th-century physics to show that all the forms of energy known at that time could be converted into each other in definite ratios. Energy is essential for our life. Our bodies convert chemical energy in the form of food into heat and motion. We need energy to heat our homes and to cook our food, to travel and to communicate by telephone and radio. Energy is the basis of our manufacturing industries, and of our transport by land, sea and air. Our standard of living is directly proportional to the energy available.

In ancient times wood was the main source of energy, as it still is in much of the Third World. As time went on the forests of the Mediterranean lands and later on of central Europe were cut down to satisfy the needs of the growing populations. More recently, coal replaced wood as the main fuel, and together with deposits of iron ore provided the motive power of the Industrial Revolution. In the last century oil was discovered, and since it is easier to extract and to transport, it has gradually replaced coal in a wide range of applications.

The world demand for energy is rapidly increasing, due partly to the increase in population and partly to the rising standards of living in many countries. At present the world population is doubling about every forty years, and energy consumption about every twenty years (see Population Policy*). Do we have enough energy to supply these needs?

There is almost limitless energy available in the motions of the winds, the waves and the tides, and in the rays of the sun. It is however very spread out and not easy to harness in useful form. To be useful, energy must be concentrated, and that is why wood, coal and oil are widely used. There is not enough wood to meet our needs, so we have first to consider coal and oil. There are still vast deposits of coal, so that remains a possibility, but estimates show that world oil production is likely to peak some time in the early decades of the next century, and thereafter to fall.

This combination of rising demands and dwindling resources is the basis of the energy crisis. Where is the energy needed by future generations to come from? We certainly need all the energy we can get, and so the possible sources must be evaluated for their capacity, cost, safety, reliability and effects on the environment.*

In addition to the energy sources mentioned, hydroelectric and nuclear power must be considered. Hydropower is very important, especially in mountainous countries like Switzerland and Norway. The number of suitable rivers is, however, limited, and it is unlikely to provide more than about 10% of world energy needs. Nuclear power certainly has the capacity to satisfy our needs, and already provides more electricity in Western Europe than coal does.

The renewable sources – wind, wave and solar – have important small-scale applications, but are unreliable, costly and bad for the environment. Apart from oil, which is fast running out, that leaves coal and nuclear power as the main sources of future energy supplies. The experience of many countries is that their costs are comparable, with nuclear rather cheaper in most cases.

No energy source is completely safe; the mining of coal, the construction of power stations, the transport of fuel and the distribution to the consumer are all more or less hazardous activities. Detailed studies by Edward Pochin and Herbert Inhaber show that the deaths involved in the generation of 1,000 megawatt years of electricity in various ways are approximately: coal 40, oil 10, nuclear 1, gas 0.5, hydroelectric 3, wind and solar 5.

Coal-power stations emit large quantities of carbon dioxide that contribute to the greenhouse effect, and oxides of nitrogen and sulphur and other poisonous chemicals that form acid rain. Some of these poisonous emissions can be prevented, but only a great expense. In normal operation, nuclear power stations have practically no deleterious effects on the environment.

Despite these obvious advantages, nuclear power has encountered great opposition. The initial association with the atomic bomb, and accidents like those at Three Mile Island and Chernobyl, have undermined public confidence. The former accident was attributable to poor operating procedures, and the latter to a reactor design unacceptable in the West and to flagrant disregard of operating procedures.

There is also much concern about the disposal of nuclear waste. This consists of the highly radioactive fission products which remain in the fuel rods after the uranium has been burnt. The disposal of such waste is, however, a well-tried procedure. The radioactivity is first allowed to decay to a much lower level, and then the waste is fused into an insoluble ceramic, encased in stainless steel and buried deep in a stable geological formation where it can cause no harm. Radioactivity can easily be detected, and the whole process is carefully monitored. The radiation due to the nuclear industry is far lower than that due to natural sources.

Some studies have shown a small excess of leukaemia cases in the vicinity of nuclear plants, but many others have shown no excess. It is, however, unlikely that any excess could be due to nuclear radiation, because the amounts that escape from the plants are far lower than in the natural background. Furthermore, there are many leukaemia clusters in other places, and so it is likely that they are of viral or chemical origin. Recent work suggesting a link between paternal irradiation and leukaemic children is inconsistent with previous results, especially the absence of leukaemia among children of survivors of Hiroshima and Nagasaki, who received on average five times the dose of the Sellafield fathers. Studies of DNA instability show that a causal relationship is extremely unlikely.

Looking to the future, it is likely that the pollution due to coal power will be increasingly recognized, and that nuclear power will regain public confidence. When uranium supplies become depleted, fast reactors will enable the uranium 238 to be burnt, and this is about a hundred times as plentiful in natural uranium as the uranium 235 which is burnt at present. Still further ahead, we may hope that fusion power will eventually become available.

Energy in all its forms is a gift of the creator, to be harnessed and used responsibly. Many of the earth's resources are limited and should be used to satisfy real needs, and not irresponsibly squandered. Technology* provides the means to carry out more efficiently Christ's commands to feed the hungry and to clothe the naked and so it is good and indeed essential. It should, however, remain our servant and not become our master. In all its activities there is a duty to reduce its harmful effects, from inhuman working conditions to pollution of the environment.

See also: GLOBAL ETHICS; ⑮ STEWARDSHIP.

Bibliography

E. Boyes (ed.), *Shaping Tomorrow* (London, 1981); B. Cohen, *Before It's Too Late* (New York, 1983); P. E. Hodgson, *Our Nuclear Future?* (London, 1983); *idem*, *World Energy Needs and Resources* (Bramcote, Nottingham, 1981).

P.E.H.

ENLIGHTENMENT, THE (Ger. *Aufklärung*), is a historically ambiguous and politically contentious designation. In its most general sense, the term stands for new intellectual and social trends formulated in the late 17th century, expounded in the 18th and transformed in the 19th. At the end of the 20th century, the Enlightenment is regarded by some as a critical first step in the liberation of the human spirit, by others as a disastrous turn from God to idols, and by still others as a complex phenomenon understandable only through analysis of the most discriminating sort.

Because notions now associated with the Enlightenment developed over time, differed from country to country, and were capable of being used both to support and to attack Christianity, the Englightenment is best defined first of all as generically as possible. The historian Henry May (1915–) has provided an excellent example of such a definition: 'Let us say that the Enlightenment consists of all those who believe two propositions: first, that the present age is more enlightened than the past; and second, that we understand nature and man best through the use of our natural faculties' (*The Enlightenment in America*, p. xiv). A second necessary step is to differentiate among types of Enlightenment. Again, Henry May's designation of four different Enlightenments is a model: 1. 'moderate', as exemplified in the work of Isaac Newton (1642–1727) and John Locke (1632–1704), with an emphasis on rational and scientific explanations for natural and human phenomena; 2. 'sceptical', as illustrated by the arguments of David Hume* against epistemological certainty and by Voltaire (1694–1778) against inherited traditions in State, church and universities; 3. 'revolutionary', as propounded by a number of energetic iconoclasts during the second half of the 18th century, including Jean-Jacques Rousseau (1712–78), Thomas Paine (1737–1809), and William Godwin (1765–1836); and 4. 'didactic', developed most fully in Scotland and the US in a process where Scottish philosophers like Francis Hutcheson (1694–1746) and Thomas Reid (1710–96) pointed the way for several generations of American college presidents in restoring confidence and social cohesion to the ideals of the 'moderate' Enlightenment.

May's general difinition, combined with his attention to the varieties of the Enlightenment, make it possible to explain some of the theological anomalies of the 18th century. Enlightenment themes – e.g. the epistemic priority of reason* and experience as opposed to the deliverances of tradition – fuelled the anti-supernatural speculations of English deists like John Toland (1670–1722), supported the belief of G. E. Lessing (1729–81) that historical events could never constitute necessary truths of reason, underlay Rousseau's confidence in the natural moral capacities of uncorrupted children, and led some French *philosophes* to become atheists. But the same themes also could be exploited by those who desired to support the State church (as in the England of Sir Isaac Newton), who wanted to find new expressions for personal faith in Christ (as in the hymns of Charles Wesley, 1707–88), or who hoped to secure the faith through the use of natural theology (as in the apologetics of William Paley, 1743–1805, and numerous American imitators). Immanuel Kant* responded to the question 'What is Enlightenment?' with a justly famous answer that revealed a prejudice against traditional Christianity: 'Enlightenment is man's emergence from his self-imposed nonage. Nonage is the inability to use one's own understanding without another's guidance ... *Sapere aude,* "Have the courage to use your own understanding," is therefore the motto of the enlightenment' (P. Gay, ed., *The Enlightenment: A Comprehensive Anthology,* New York, 1973, p. 384). But equally characteristic of the Enlightenment was the affirmation by Kant's contemporary, the Presbyterian president of Princeton College, John Witherspoon (1723–94), that a Christian seeking to live a moral life would be greatly helped by 'treating moral philosophy as Newton and his successors have done natural [philosophy]. It is always safer in our reasonings to trace facts upwards than to reason downwards upon metaphysical principles' (John Witherspoon, *Works,* Philadelphia, 1802, 3:470).

Given these varied uses of intellectual themes from the 18th century, it is not surprising that the Englightenment underlay several different (even contradictory) ethical movements. For example, Kantian idealism, with its response to the moral implications of Hume's scepticism, as well as Benthamite* utilitarianism (see Consequentialism*), with its technical calculus of this-worldly probabilities, were both descended from Englightenment principles. The Enlightenment also serves as a shorthand designation for several general tendencies that influenced Christian ethics. Jonathan Edwards* wrestled with definitions of 'the moral sense' expounded by Hutcheson. John Wesley* exploited Lockean conceptions of human experience to define his doctrine of Christian perfection. The utilitarian ethics of Paley were both religiously conservative and rooted in Enlightenment conventions about human happiness. The Enlightenment, as a protean movement, had protean effects. Since the 18th century, all ethicists, both Christian and non-Christian, have been coming to terms with its multiform influences.

Bibliography

D. W. Bebbington, *Evangelicalism in Modern Britain* (London, 1989), pp. 20–74; P. Gay, *The Enlightenment: An Interpretation,* 2 vols. (New York, 1966, 1969); P. Hazard, *European Thought in the Eighteenth Century, from Montesquieu to Lessing* (ET, New Haven, CT, and London, 1954); M. C. Jacob, *The Newtonians and the English Revolution, 1689–1720* (Ithaca, NY, 1976); A. MacIntyre, *After Virtue* (Notre Dame, IN, [2]1984; London, [2]1985); H. May, *The Enlightenment in America* (New York, 1976); R. Porter and M. Teich (eds.), *The Enlightenment in National Context* (Cambridge, 1981); H. D. Rack, *Reasonable Enthusiast: John Wesley and the Rise of Methodism* (London and Philadelphia, 1989); R. B. Sher, *Church and University in the Scottish Enlightenment* (Princeton, NJ, 1985).

M.A.N.

ENVIRONMENT. The term 'environment' is an elusive one. It is most often used in contemporary society to indicate a whole range of issues which involve the relationships of humankind to the animate and inanimate world. Such issues raise problems which range from the largely individual, *e.g.* the effect of nuclear radiation or chemical pollution on the health of human beings, through the regional, *e.g.* the effects of over-fishing in the North Sea or the rapid clearance of tropical rain forest (see Deforestation*), through to those embracing the whole planet, notably global warming and the breakdown of the ozone layer. The preservation of 'endangered' species, the conservation of habitats and ecosystems, and the fragility of high-energy farming are also major issues for debate.

The scientific dimensions of these problems are generally understood, at least in broad terms. It is generally acknowledged, however, that mere understanding is not enough, and that there is an ethical dimension to these problems which requires fuller exploration. The common view, based on dubious exegesis of Gn. 1:26–28, that the 'Judaeo-Christian ethic of mankind's unfettered dominion over nature' is to blame, has now been generally refuted (see J. Passmore, *Man's Responsibility For Nature;* R. Attfield, *The Ethics of Environmental Concern*), but the search for an ethical basis is still seen as an urgent question (Church Information Office, *Our Responsibility for the Living Environment*). The new perspective on the natural world which has been provided by the science of ecology has often been advocated as a novel starting-point appropriate to modern thought. The scientific understanding so achieved is in itself, however, unable to bear the ethical burden, and is always, often implicitly, supported by the elevation of 'evolution' to the status of an ontological principle, or by the introduction of a mystical view of nature and its complexity.

Ethical perspectives

There are five broad ethical perspectives which are proposed or assumed.

1. Technological pragmatism. Relationships with elements in the environment, both animate and inanimate, are seen simply as aspects of management,* embracing both normal use and the solution of any problems which arise. The ethical questions are not faced explicitly; the solution to a problem consists in finding an appropriate technique to control or eliminate it. That technique may well involve legal prescriptions as well as technology* in the more restricted sense. This approach is common in much thinking in the developed world and underlies much contemporary political concern about environmental issues. It does not, however, face the questions as to whether or why the human species should be concerned about the environment in which it exists independently of any benefit or threat it may afford. Nor does it face the question why the human species itself should in any sense be 'worth' preserving, and it assumes an anthropocentric focus which considers human material advance as the paramount value.

2. Evolutionary humanism. The evolutionary-humanist view attempts to answer these questions by positing some inherent value in 'evolution' itself. Evolution is seen as an overriding ontological principle, in that the human species is the most complex product of that process so far; by virtue of its intellectual development, it is now able to 'determine his own evolution', and by its technological ingenuity can also control the course of development of other species and indeed the planet as a whole. This is typified by many prominent writers, *e.g.* David Attenborough (1926–) and biologists such as Edward Wilson (1929–). (See A. L. Caplan, *The Sociobiology Debate*.)

A. N. Flew (1923–) has discussed the problems of deriving an ethical system from such biological premises in *Evolutionary Ethics.* The fundamental dilemma is the equation of the development of increasing complexity with 'progress', which is a value concept (see Evolutionary Ethics*). This step in the argument has no demonstrable logical justification, and depends upon arbitrarily assigning 'value' to a sequence of events. Ethical concepts are linked intuitively to evolutionary knowledge and research by writers such as Richard Dawkins (1941–), *e.g.* in *The Blind Watchmaker.*

3. Ecological mysticism. It is therefore not surprising that an element of 'nature mysticism' insinuates itself into the argument, often implicitly. Such ecological mysticism takes various forms. An appeal is sometimes made to the philosophy of oriental religions, such as Buddhism, which are seen as being more 'nature-friendly' than the transcendent monotheism of Islam, Judaism and Christianity (F. Fraser Darling, 'Man's Responsibility For the Environment'). Others take the apparent self-regulation of the planet as a whole, which J. E. Lovelock (1919–) has advanced as an arguable scientific hypothesis in *Gaia: A New Look at Life on Earth*, and instil a mystical character into it so that it becomes a quasi-religious concept, termed the 'Gaia' hypothesis. This frequently leads to a deep reverence for nature, and even to the worship of the earth, sometimes as the Earth Mother. This underlying reverence and awe, even personification of nature itself, probably represents ancient beliefs whose origins are lost in the mists of prehistory. It now shows an active resurgence resulting from a developing dissatisfaction with the ecological consequences of 'scientism', *i.e.* naïve trust in and reliance on the methods and findings of scientific study to solve all problems and to direct human behaviour. This trust in science* and technology is undoubtedly supported by many valuable technological achievements, and has held intellectual sway for well over a century in the industrialized world.

The most rapidly growing element in this contemporary resurgence is the New Age movement.* This is a broad spectrum of related outlooks. At one end is the relatively innocuous desire to return to a closer, more wholesome, relationship with nature, which is supposed to have existed universally in the past, and is seen still to exist in aboriginal societies in Australia and the remoter recesses of the Amazon forests. At the other end there is an overt involvement with the occult.* Much New Age thinking explicitly embraces an astrological evaluation which sees the year 2000 as a passage from the age of 'Pisces', equated with the Christian era, to the age of 'Aquarius', an era of universal harmony and brotherhood between human beings and between humankind and nature. That New Age is to be actively anticipated now by those who are properly enlightened. It also sometimes emphasizes that this change will be achieved by a new recognition of the Earth Mother and the according of proper reverence and worship to her. The attraction of the movement in an age of disillusion with 'science' is very clear; it combines a degree of scientific understanding with a deeply religious dimension which is not in any sense transcendent, and which therefore can make no absolute moral demands on the whole of life. It internalizes religious aspirations within the universe itself.

4. Liberal Christianity. The 'liberal' Christian perspective also embraces a range of somewhat dissimilar views. Most assign a primary role to evolutionary thinking, and therefore implicitly relegate the idea of a unique revelation to a subsidiary position. Those which are 'evolutionist' in a broad philosophical sense generally produce an overt syncretism (as in the case of Matthew Fox, *Original Blessing: A Primer in Creation Spirituality*). Other contemporary Roman Catholic writers acknowledge a primary debt to P. Teilhard de Chardin (1881–1955), and adopt a more orthodox stance (*e.g.* Sean McDonagh, *To Care for the Earth* and *The Greening of the Church*). In Protestant writing there is a tendency to minimize the effects of the Fall,* and to think in terms of a 'cosmic Christ' at the expense of the historical Jesus of Nazareth (*e.g.* I. Bradley, *God is Green*). This usually leads to a neglect of the explicit link of the redemption of nature to the redemption of individual men and women into a new creation in Christ, made by Paul in Rom. 8:18–25. This view of the ethic of the use of nature by humankind does emphasize the important point that ethics are intimately interwoven with theology.

5. Conservative Christianity. More 'conservative' Christian views have been put forward. C. Derrick (1921–), from the Roman Catholic Church, argued that present problems are brought about by the heresy of Manichaeism, which supposed that matter was inherently evil, subtly infiltrating Christian thinking about nature (see *The Delicate Creation*). Francis Schaeffer* had already set out the biblical view that creation is good, but misused and damaged by humankind in self-centred disobedience to God (*Pollution and the Death of Man*). Other theologically conservative Christians have also made a contribution, arguing that a comprehensive biblical approach provides a workable and justifiable ethic for the use of the resources of the environment, and care for the natural world in itself (R. Elsdon, *Bent World*; R. P. Moss, 'Environmental Problems and the Christian Ethic').

The basic concept underlying such an approach is that of 'stewardship'* (D. J. Hall, *Imaging God*; W. Granberg-Michaelson, ed., *Tending the Garden*). Humankind is directly responsible to God for the use of the earth and its resources. As stewards or tenants people are responsible for the use they make of property which is not their own. This concept is derived largely from OT sources, but the redemption of the whole cosmos together with humankind is seen as a central element in the work of Christ. There is a further corollary. Failure to recognize divine ownership is disobedience and sin, not simply ignorance, and thus repentance is a primary requirement in seeking to solve the problems with which humankind is now so evidently confronted.

Environment and world community

It may be asked why it is that environmental problems now occupy so central a place in political and religious concern. This is clearly the result of the fact that the consequences of misusing the earth and its resources now directly affect humankind in an increasingly acute way. The further question is therefore: Why should that be happening now? A book containing the texts of a series of lectures given at Darwin College, Cambridge, in 1986, gives an excellent scientific overview of the major global problems (L. Friday and R. C. Laskey, *The Fragile Environment*).

These issues, however, relate to society as a whole and are not purely scientific. The accentuation of these problems has been attributed to a number of factors: 1. There is the numerical growth of the population of the world, which creates an additional demand for resources. 2. The development and spread of technology in itself increases the environmental pressure. 3. The growing sophistication of technology also makes a greater impact on the environment as new resources are exploited, as in the case of nuclear energy* and, increasingly, by genetic engineering;* more importantly they create new possibilities for damage to nature itself when they are extensively used. 4. There is the growing affluence of the developing world, which creates a greater demand for goods and energy, which has to be met from the resources of the earth. 5. Environmental damage has been seen as the product of capitalism,* an economic system which depends upon the operation of market forces which encourage the minimization of costs, including those of the prevention of environmental damage. It would now seem that the Marxist-Leninist socialism of Eastern Europe has led to no less damage, but some would see that as a form of State capitalism.

These suggestions raise the further question

whether there should be any limit to technological development. It would seem that the limits of human ingenuity have not yet been approached; questions remain concerning the availability of earth resources, but some would maintain that the only inevitable requirement for further development is an adequate energy supply, which is in practice potentially unlimited. The ethical dilemma posed by the question whether economic growth can continue without further significant environmental damage nevertheless remains. This leads into the debate whether environmental considerations should enter into economic and business decisions. It seems clear that practical environmental concern will involve increased costs, resulting in either higher prices or reduced profits, and that reduced consumption will lead to decreasing demand, which may in turn produce unemployment.*

Such ethical considerations inevitably raise the issues which surround the global economy, and the acute problems of famine and environmental degradation faced in the developing world which are closely linked to the operation of that economy. The poor, as individuals or communities or nations, have little environmental choice. The rich tend to make increasing environmental demands as greater affluence and an increase in material possessions are seen as overriding goods. This, in turn, leads on to the moral and practical problems of Third World aid* and investment.

The problems which relate to the relationship of humankind to the rest of creation thus pose many ethical questions. Furthermore, there are few other aspects of human behaviour individually or in society upon which such questions do not impinge. The formulation and justification of ethical norms in this area are therefore crucial, but the answers are not straightforward, either in theory or in their practical outworking.

See also: GLOBAL ETHICS;[15] POPULATION POLICY.

Bibliography

R. Attfield, *The Ethics of Environmental Concern* (Oxford, 1983); I. Bradley, *God is Green: Christianity and the Environment* (London, 1990); A. L. Caplan (ed.), *The Sociobiology Debate: Readings on the Ethical Issues concerning Sociobiology* (London, 1972; New York, 1978); Church Information Office, *Our Responsibility for the Living*

Environment (London, 1986); F. F. Darling, 'Man's Responsibility for the Environment', in F. J. Ebling (ed.), *Biology and Ethics* (London, 1969); R. Dawkins, *The Blind Watchmaker* (London, 1986); C. Derrick, *The Delicate Creation: Towards a Theology of the Environment* (London, 1972); R. Elsdon, *Bent World: Science, the Bible and the Environment* (Leicester, 1981); A. N. Flew, *Evolutionary Ethics* (London, 1967; New York, 1968); M. Fox, *Original Blessing: A Primer in Creation Spirituality, in Four Paths, Twenty-six Themes, and Two Questions* (Santa Fe, NM, 1983; Cambridge, MA, ²1990); L. Friday and R. C. Laskey (eds.), *The Fragile Environment* (Cambridge, 1989); W. Granberg-Michaelson (ed.), *Tending the Garden: Essays on the Gospel and the Earth* (Grand Rapids, 1987); D. J. Hall, *Imaging God: Dominion as Stewardship* (Grand Rapids, 1986); J. E. Lovelock, *Gaia: A New Look at Life on Earth* (Oxford, 1979); S. McDonagh, *To Care for the Earth: A Call to a New Theology* (Santa Fe, NM, and London, 1986); *idem*, *The Greening of the Church* (Maryknoll, NY, 1990); R. P. Moss, 'Environmental Problems and the Christian Ethic', in C. F. Henry (ed.), *Horizons of Science: Christian Scholars Speak Out* (New York, 1978); L. Osborn, *Guardians of Creation* (Leicester, 1993); J. Passmore, *Man's Responsibility for Nature* (London, ²1980); F. A. Schaeffer, *Pollution and the Death of Man: The Christian View of Ecology* (London and Wheaton, IL, 1970).

R.P.M.

ENVY, see DEADLY SINS; JEALOUSY AND ENVY.

EQUALITY is a contested concept: that is to say its meaning is far from clear and it is difficult to arrive at an agreed definition. The most common use of equality is in the economic sphere.

Two main approaches to equality

The quasi-mathematical sense of the term 'equality' has led to the advocacy of two main approaches:

1. Equality of outcome. On this view, egalitarian policies should minimize or eradicate differentials in wealth between individuals or households. Taxation* and other mechanisms should be used to redistribute wealth from the richer to the poorer.

Critics of equality of outcome point out that:

a. it is unrealistically utopian; b. human nature will always seek ways of restoring wealth differentials, whether overtly or covertly; c. history shows that all attempts to impose such equality have failed; d. equality of outcome could apply only to tangible forms of wealth (money, houses, goods, *etc.*), not to intangibles such as power,* which are just as important; e. the cost would be high in terms of freedom,* since equality could be achieved only by totalitarian means; f. the justice it seeks to achieve would be replaced by injustice; and g. the depressive effects upon economic incentive and initiative would reduce the total wealth available for redistribution and therefore would be counter-productive.

2. Equality of opportunity. Proponents of this view accept the criticisms outlined above, and argue instead that the purpose of egalitarian policies should not be to create equality of outcome, but to enable individuals and households to have fair access to the economic system and to be in a position to maximize their benefits from it. In the metaphor of an athletics race, the aim is not that all should finish in the same position but that all should be enabled to compete fairly.

Critics point out that, whilst avoiding some of the problems associated with equality of outcome, equality of opportunity presents its own difficulties: a. how far is it a theory of equality at all if it does not address the question of redistribution?; b. it is no less utopian since it assumes that all individuals can be enabled to gain access to the economic system; c. for those who remain unable to do so through disability, illness, lack of education, poverty, *etc.*, the problem of redistribution remains, so it becomes necessary to narrow wealth differentials as in equality of outcome; and d. the metaphor of the race is inadequate, since not all can run the race, and some of those who can, have the ability to reap only minimum rewards.

Equality therefore cannot be discussed in isolation. Any viable theory of equality must also address concepts of freedom and justice (see Justice and Peace③) and present a coherent relationship between all three.

The most recent major attempt to do this has been that of the American philosopher John Rawls (1921–). In *A Theory of Justice* (Cambridge, MA, 1971; Oxford, 1972), he argued that inequalities of wealth were acceptable only under three conditions: a. that each person should have an equal right to the most extensive basic liberties compatible with a like liberty for all; b. that inequalities of wealth, power, income and status must result in the maximization of benefit to the most disadvantaged (the principle of 'maximin'); and c. such inequalities must go with positions or appointments open to all under fair conditions of equality of opportunity (see Discrimination*).

From these principles it can be seen that Rawls attempts to bring together both approaches to equality cited earlier. Although criticized on a number of grounds, Rawls' theory has the virtues both of integrating ideas of freedom and justice with equality and of offering criteria by which these concepts may be evaluated. The notion of 'maximin' is especially useful (*i.e.* the choice of an action which has, as its worse outcome, a consequence which is better than the worst consequence of any alternative action).

Theological reflection

The concepts of equality, freedom and justice in the sense in which they appear in contemporary debate are distinctly modern. They are not to be found in the Bible or in early church writings. This does not invalidate them, but it does require that they be set in a critical theological context.

One approach would ground ideas of economic and political equality, freedom and justice in the Being of God (see ①) as Trinity and then derivatively in the model this provides for human society. Theologically and historically the Trinity has been held to function as a model of persons-in-relationship. In this social model, Father, Son and Spirit are co-equal in status and exist in a relationship of dialogue, reciprocity, self-giving and mutual love. The persons of the Godhead do not exist as independent persons for themselves but, in the words of Leonardo Boff (1938–): 'the essential characteristic of each person is to be *for* the others, *through* the others, *with* the others and *in* the others' (*Trinity and Society*, ET, London and Maryknoll, NY, 1988, pp. 127–128).

The significance of this paradigm for human society can be traced through: 1. the image of God,* which is given to human beings in plural form in Gn. 1:26–27; 2. the incarnation; 3. the metaphor of the body of Christ; and 4. the kingdom of God.* In all these, the life of the Trinity is to be imaged and shared.

Alongside this must be emphasized the biblical notion of differentiation. Although equal in status, neither the members of the Godhead nor human beings as the recipients of the image of God should be viewed as identical. This rules out secular theories of equality of outcome since differing gifts will lead to differing outcomes.

The concept of freedom likewise derives from Trinitarian theology. The freedom of the Godhead is to be 'for the others'. Similarly, as Richard Bauckham (1946–) has pointed out, biblical ideas of freedom have to do not with individualistic freedom to self-fulfilment but with corporate freedom for the service of others: 'My neighbour is not simply a restraint on my freedom but one whom I am to love as myself' (*The Bible in Politics*, London and Philadelphia, KY, 1989, p. 107). Freedom is thus a positive good arising out of our service to God.

Further theological light is shed on the notion of equality by the pattern of economic life envisaged in the OT (see Old Testament Ethics⑧). The land* formed the fundamental resource which required to be shared according to three theological principles: 1. it belonged to God so that Israelites held it leasehold not freehold; 2. it was a grace-gift to the whole nation in which all had a stake; and 3. it was to be used fairly, *i.e.* all households must have access to it as an economic resource. For these reasons, unjust accumulation of land and unfair dealing were condemned by the prophets. Equality of outcome was not demanded but fair access was, along with compassion for those who became economically marginalized. Thus Israel's 'own brand . . . of economic egalitarianism . . . did not obliterate differentials but attempted to confine them within the proper limits of functional necessity for the harmony and peace of society' (C. J. H. Wright, *Living as the People of God*, Leicester and Downers Grove, IL, 1983, p. 112).

A theologically-based theory of equality must therefore go further than that of any secular theorist, since it is grounded positively in the divine purpose for humanity. That purpose is to share in the life of the Trinity and thereby to create a community of reciprocal compassion and love. This is not dependent upon equality of outcome or opportunity but upon equal access to the grace* of God revealed in Christ.

Bibliography
R. Norman, *Free and Equal* (Oxford, 1983); J. D. Wogaman, *Economics and Ethics* (London and Philadelphia, 1986); B. Wren, *Education for Justice* (London, 1986).

F.W.B.

EQUAL OPPORTUNITIES, see
Equality.

ERIKSON, ERIK (1902–94). Born in
Germany of a Jewish mother, Erikson fled to Boston in 1933, where he worked as the city's only child-analyst. He later taught at Harvard and at Yale, and also at one time had a private psychoanalytic practice in California.

Erikson's contact with sociologists and anthropologists, as well as psychologists, contributed to his classic study *Childhood and Society* (1950). In this, Erikson explores the links between society's values and individual development, and provides the groundwork for his reconstruction of psychoanalytic theory. He called this an 'epigenetic' approach to psycho-social development, and opened up ways of linking psychoanalytic theory with questions of moral and spiritual values, and with the development of faith. His work has formed the basis for much subsequent pastoral psychology and pastoral theology (see Practical and Pastoral Theology[7]), and for James Fowler's (1940–) theories regarding the stages of faith development.* Each phase of Erikson's eight-stage scheme is a psycho-social crisis, which needs to be resolved satisfactorily if individual maturity is to be achieved, and personal identity established. The crucial phases are described as: 1. the critical decision between trust versus mistrust; 2. autonomy* versus shame and doubt; 3. initiative versus guilt;* 4. industry versus inferiority; 5. identity versus role confusion; 6. intimacy versus isolation; 7. generativity versus stagnation; and 8. integrity versus despair. The dynamics of identity formation were also explored in *Identity: Youth and Crisis* (1968).

In addition, Erikson wrote studies of various significant historic figures, including Martin Luther* and Mohandas (Mahatma) Gandhi (1869–1948).

See also: Psychoanalysis.

Bibliography

Childhood and Society (New York, ²1963; Harmondsworth, ²1965).

R. Coles, *Erik H. Erikson: The Growth of his Work* (London, 1973); M. Jacobs, *Towards the Fullness of Christ: Pastoral Care and Christian Maturity* (London, 1988); J. E. Wright, *Erikson: Identity and Religion* (New York, 1982).

D.J.A.

ESCHATOLOGY AND ETHICS.
Neither 'eschatology' nor 'ethics' formed part of the vocabulary of the NT writers but both words are heavily used by modern scholars to sum up certain aspects of the NT's teaching. Strictly speaking, 'eschatology' is 'teaching about the last things', and its content is the coming of the Son of Man/Messiah at the end of the age accompanied by the full inauguration of the kingdom of God,* the last judgment* and the 'age to come'.

The teaching of Jesus was largely concerned with these events. The kingdom of God was the key concept in his teaching. He certainly looked forward to its future coming, and urged people to prepare themselves to enter it. He also spoke of its coming as something that could happen at any time, and therefore there was an urgency about his references to it. For some scholars that was all he said: that the kingdom was future, and indeed, very near, so that nothing remained for mankind but to prepare for its coming (see Interim Ethic*). For others, the decisive element in Jesus' message was that the kingdom had already come or was in process of coming – and again this introduces the note of urgency into his preaching.

The first followers of Jesus recognized that he was the Messiah, God's agent in the coming of his kingdom, who had already come and was now ruling from heaven, and they looked forward to his future coming – which again they thought of as capable of happening at any time. But if the Messiah had come, then it follows that what was traditionally thought of as the subject of 'eschatology' – the last things – was already taking place (hence the phrase 'realized eschatology' to signify that the final intervention of God into world history has already begun to happen, and that the so-called 'last days' have already begun).

All this means that the proclamation of Jesus and his followers was dominated by the belief in the presence and imminence of the rule of God and its agent, the Messiah. Inevitably, therefore, the teaching of Jesus and of the early Christians about how people should live was fundamentally shaped by this basic conviction.

The term 'ethics' is normally used to signify how people ought to behave in relation to one another (and towards the physical environment*). It thus covers the social aspects of conduct. As applied to the teaching of Jesus, it includes this area – note his teaching about love (see [2]) for one's neighbours and enemies – but it is even wider in scope, covering the relationship of people to God as well. Biblical ethics is thus concerned with faith* and love towards God, as well as with moral repentance.*

The early Christian belief in the coming of the kingdom of God influenced the *motives* for living ethically. One of the main sanctions of biblical morality lies in the intervention of God in the life of the world in and through Jesus both now and in the future; the future judgment is a powerful stimulus to live ethically, and the fact that the kingdom of God has come and that the followers of Jesus are part of it means that they are to live the kind of life appropriate to its members.

As regards the *content* of the ethics, it is true that some biblical teaching rests upon the nature of the order imposed by God as part of creation,* and some teaching is of such a general kind that it would be acceptable to people of any religion or none. Some theologians want to distinguish between 'creation ethics' and 'kingdom ethics', but, since God is one and unchanging, the ethics of the kingdom are the same as those of creation; God's way of life for his people comes to sharper focus and more concentrated expression in the teaching of Jesus and his followers. Jesus gives instruction for his followers who accept 'the yoke of the kingdom', and does not make the concessions 'because of the hardness of your hearts' that were made in the law of Moses, but in principle his teaching is intended for all humankind. His followers are to live out the life of the kingdom of God here and now in this world, thus fulfilling his original purpose for his creation.

See also: NEW TESTAMENT ETHICS;[9] OLD TESTAMENT ETHICS.[8]

Bibliography

G. E. Ladd, *Jesus and the Kingdom* (New York, 1964; London, 1966) = *The Presence of the Future* (Grand Rapids, 1974); W. Schrage, *The Ethics of the New Testament* (ET, Edinburgh and Philadelphia, 1988); A. N. Wilder, *Eschatology and Ethics in the Teaching of Jesus* (New York, 1950).

I.H.M.

ESPIONAGE. The use of clandestine methods for obtaining accurate knowledge about others, whether industrial competitors or foreign nations, has long been regarded as necessary to effective policy-formation. Espionage is the covert side of the process of gathering and analysing secret information, which is itself one part of intelligence activity as a whole and should be distinguished from counter-intelligence (the protection of secrets from rival companies or hostile intelligence services) and covert political action (intervention by national intelligence agencies in the domestic affairs of other countries). Although this article concentrates on military, political and industrial information-gathering, analogous moral considerations apply in the case of undercover police work, investigative journalism, *etc.*

Espionage work is often portrayed as a morally distasteful but (in certain circumstances) necessary means to a good end, or, more radically, as a realm in which ethical norms do not apply. By contrast, a fully incarnational Christian ethic will reject the thought, whether prompted by high-mindedness or by cynicism, that morality and espionage occupy separate spheres of existence – though it will also accept that the task of discerning the right course of action may be difficult and at times demand exceptional courage and practical wisdom. Instead theological reflection starts from the keeping of secrets (see Secrecy*) as the context of espionage. While the promise in Mt. 10:26, that in the coming kingdom there is 'nothing concealed that will not be disclosed, or hidden that will not be made known', suggests that there should be a presumption in favour of openness and non-concealment, the world is nevertheless fallen, and some organizational secrecy may be justified for the sake of the common good. Some military secrets may be necessary for a nation's self-preservation; some administrative confidentiality* may be required to prevent premature disclosure of unformed policies; and without industrial secrecy companies may have reduced incentives to undertake creative research and development projects.

Such examples can be interpreted in terms of a limited right to secrecy, which may not be impugned without just cause. This notion of just cause forms the primary criterion for the morality of intelligence-gathering, making clear that the right to secrecy is not absolute but may be qualified by the requirements of the national and international common good which ground it. Thus satellite surveillance of a country trying to evade verification of its compliance with arms-control agreements might be justified by appeal to this principle, as might intelligence work against terrorist organizations, drugs cartels, and (within limits prescribed by an account of the morality of international relations) actual or potential enemies. In the case of industrial espionage, by contrast, although the rewards may be great (*e.g.* saving wasteful expenditure on research or new plant), it is not clear that they ordinarily amount to a just cause, though this depends in part on the nature of the business and the provisions made by the public authorities for the common good. It should be noted that even the bulk of routine intelligence work, which draws on published documents, the mass media and other overt sources, should be referred to this criterion, though the public availability of the information may be prima-facie evidence that the right to secrecy has been waived.

Even if the goal of gathering secret information is on occasions justifiable through this principle, not all means of obtaining it are moral. Apart from clearly unacceptable practices (*e.g.* blackmail, extortion and torture), the most prominent moral questions surround intelligence activities which are not merely covert (*e.g.* eavesdropping or interception of communications) but also deceptive. Informants and undercover agents may need to fashion elaborate webs of lies to maintain their cover, yet without them many kinds of criminal or terrorist behaviour would be effectively immune. If deliberately telling an untruth is wrong, regardless of one's intention, such disguises would be categorically inadmissible. If, however, it is possible for a hearer to lose the 'right to know the truth', they might under certain circumstances be justified (*cf.* Jos. 2:1–7, and see Lying*); though even here the primacy of truthfulness implies that non-deceptive alternatives should be used where available.

This emphasis on a proper but limited role for espionage work has implications for the place of the intelligence services in a democracy. Aside from questions about whether in general they make an effective use of money, organizations whose activities are hidden from public view by blanket appeals to 'national security' or 'executive privilege' are liable to corruption; this danger is vastly magnified if their powers are not limited by law, or if their corporate ethos is dominated by pragmatic notions that whatever is necessary for the public

good is honourable. To counter this, one important means of helping ensure that intelligence agencies remain sensitive to the requirements of democratic process lies in public scrutiny of their activities, based on statutory definition and limitation of their powers, together with the establishment of effective internal organizational checks. Such accountability need not be incompatible in practice with genuine security needs (to protect sources of information, *etc.*). But it is an important way of giving substance to the principle of open government, and thereby foreshadowing the future kingdom of God.*

R.J.S.

ETHICAL METHOD, see CHRISTIAN MORAL REASONING. [18]

EUDAEMONISM is an approach to ethics which sees happiness* as the greatest expression of good and the basis for moral obligation; whatever most promotes human happiness is right. Though the use of the term was largely limited to the 19th century, the concept underlies a good deal of contemporary ethical thinking. The rejection of the nature or the commands of God as a basis for morality makes it necessary to find an alternative basis in humanity or in the natural world. Happiness, whether individual or corporate (the greatest happiness of the greatest number) is an obvious possibility.

Much depends on the definition of happiness in this context. Aristotle* was able to use the word (Gk. *eudaimonia*) to include good deeds as well as the experience of happiness. Some forms of utilitarianism (see Consequentialism*), by contrast, have defined happiness simply in terms of what we desire.

Biblical ethical teaching certainly has a place for happiness; but happiness is seen as the fruit of goodness rather than its criterion. The Sermon on the Mount* starts with an exposition of happiness; but happiness here is seen as the outcome of holiness,* not the basis of morality. Most EVV therefore rightly, here and elsewhere, translate *makarios*, the standard NT word for happiness, as 'blessed', reflecting the fact that its origin is in God and not in us (Mt. 5:3–12).

P.A.H.

EUGENICS, see MANIPULATION.

EUTHANASIA is the intentional killing, by act or omission, of one whose life is deemed not worth living. Despite appearances, the word 'euthanasia' is originally Eng. and of relatively recent coinage (1646, according to *OED*), referring to a good or happy death. In its current sense (of such a death brought about by contrivance; so-called 'mercy-killing'), the first *OED* citation is as recent as 1869. Though in this latter sense the term is of such recent coinage, and though it has only lately been added to the agenda of serious ethical discussion in Western law and medicine, its practice was widespread in the ancient world and has been endemic in many primitive cultures. Most Christian ethicists have seen euthanasia as inimical to an understanding of the dignity of humanity and a trust in the providence of God (see also Vatican Statements*). Some, however, argue for it on grounds of compassion and autonomy. The emergence of medical and legal toleration of euthanasia in Holland during the 1980s is one of the most striking evidences of the development of the post-Christian society in contemporary Europe.

The question of euthanasia is complex. There are different ethical and practical permutations (active/passive; voluntary/non-voluntary/involuntary), and there are vital interfaces with a series of (mainly medical) debates (the nature of the so-called 'persistent vegetative state' [see Coma*]; definitions of brain-stem death [see Brain Death*]), and issues of patient autonomy (the 'living will' [see Consent*]), health economics and the allocation of scarce resources (see Health and Health Care*). Special questions have been raised in the case of handicapped new-borns (see Ethics of Medical Care[14]), where non-treatment decisions have become common and where the logic of euthanasia is scarcely distinguishable from that of abortion.*

Much popular support for euthanasia arises from two common misconceptions: that death is normally preceded by serious pain,* and that the application of modern medical technology is intended to draw out the dying process as long as possible (see Death and Dying*). Euthanasia is widely, and understandably, preferred. In fact, modern drug therapies free most terminal patients from serious discomfort, and good medicine, while rejecting euthanasia, has always also rejected futile treatment which merely prolongs the process of dying. In traditional Hippocratic medicine the priority in terminal care has always been the comfort of the patient, even if securing that comfort (by treating with pain-killing drugs) may also have the effect of shortening life. Treatment is not started or continued unless it is beneficial, *i.e.* likely to lead to a significant improvement in the patient's condition and life-expectancy, or if the discomfort it will cause is out of proportion to any such benefit. These and other such principles of good medicine are exemplified in the modern hospice* movement. In repudiating 'mercy-killing', they focus on what has been called 'mercy-dying', that idea of death with dignity which lies at the heart of traditional approaches to the care of the terminally ill.

Customary distinctions have been made between euthanasia which is 'active' (the result of positive action on the part of the attendant), and that which is 'passive' (involving the omission or discontinuation of life-sustaining treatment). In each case the intention is the same: to bring about the patient's death. There is a growing tendency to enlarge definitions of 'treatment' so as to include feeding by tube as well as more obviously medical procedures (such as mechanical ventilation), and in a series of celebrated cases in the US courts permission has been sought to 'withdraw treatment' and thereby cause death by denial of nutrition and hydration. In such circumstances, the cessation or withholding of 'treatment' is ethically indistinguishable from positive action to bring about death, for the medical attendant and others responsible have a duty to the patient, know the likely implications of their action, and may indeed have engaged in this management option intending to bring about the patient's death.

There is a fundamental ethical and clinical distinction between such 'non-treatment' decisions and those made in the context of the final stages of terminal illness, when the criteria of proportionate benefit apply and when death does not occur as a result of the physician's intention to bring it about.

A more fundamental distinction appears to lie between euthanasia that is 'voluntary' (requested by the patient) and that which is 'involuntary' (determined by another, whether physician, relative or the State) or 'non-voluntary' (in cases where the patient is incompetent, *e.g.* an infant [see Infanticide*]).

Most contemporary advocates of legalized euthanasia stress the voluntary character of their goal, and place considerable weight on the autonomy of the patient as the determining factor in the argument. The patient has the right to decide when to die. There are many difficulties with this superficially attractive view. For one thing, the 'voluntary' character of any decision for euthanasia is problematic: it will almost inevitably be taken either at a time of great distress or so far in advance (through an 'advance directive' or 'living will') that the decision is hypothetical; the patient may be suffering from clinical depression* (not uncommon in chronic or terminal illness); the influence of relatives and doctor may be great, though subtle (and their interests, emotional or financial, hard to disentangle). Again, if a request for euthanasia is to be distinguished from a desire for suicide,* some criteria of reasonableness must be applied, to give objective validity to the patient's assessment of his or her situation. All such criteria (whether referring to a level of pain, a degree of handicap or a particular prognosis) involve some conception of a life that is 'not worth living'; and that, in turn, has implications for euthanasia which is *in*voluntary. If A has made a reasonable or justified request for euthanasia, what is the standing of B, whose circumstances are the same, yet who has not made such a request? Surely B is *un*reasonable and *un*justified to refrain from requesting euthanasia. Moreover, once the essentially reasonable, objective character of such a decision is accepted, other factors come into play. B is using costly resources and placing considerable strains on relatives and medical and nursing staff. The 'non-voluntary' case adds to the problem of distinguishing between these two, since here some set of objective criteria must do duty for an expression of the patient's will; the judgment of someone other than the patient must be substituted, and that judgment must be supported by some kind of model of what it takes for a life 'not to be worth living'. The appeal of voluntary euthanasia as the final outcome of patient autonomy depends crucially upon its separability from euthanasia which is involuntary, and which represents the inversion of patient autonomy in a new and deadly paternalism. If this separation cannot be sustained, the case for voluntary euthanasia is fatally flawed.

The relation of (voluntary) euthanasia and suicide is often noted, as if euthanasia were essentially an act of assisted suicide. Yet euthanasia is not self-killing; it is the killing of the self by another. It may involve the will to self-destruction which characterizes the suicide, but it involves also the acquiescence in that will by another who then commits an act of homicide. The logic of patient autonomy would go further, and suggest that for the physician or nurse or relative there is a duty to kill, which raises further ethical and practical problems. Linguistic masking (the killing of the sick dressed up as 'aid-in-dying') fails to conceal the principle that is at issue and its extreme novelty in the Western medical tradition. If the idea that there are ascertainable criteria which can and should validate a euthanasia request is disowned, the idea of a life not worth living becomes entirely subjective ('I find my life intolerable at this point'). But if that subjective judgment places a duty to 'aid-in-dying' on others, what of the jilted teenager and the post-natal depressive? Unfettered patient autonomy leads straight into *reductio ad absurdum*.

A further complication is raised by the advance directive, the so-called 'living will', in which conditions are laid down for the refusal of future medical treatment in case of incompetence. Considered simply as an extension of the principle that patients must consent to treatment, these 'wills' seem unexceptionable – especially in a society such as the US, where they are widely used, and in which fear of litigation can lead to serious distortions in clinical management if patients' wishes are unclear. The 'living will' is problematic partly because of its origin, in that it was designed, as a Trojan horse, by lobbyists for legalized euthanasia. A major practical difficulty is that the general terms in which these 'wills' are couched can leave them open to abuse by relatives and others, and this draws attention to the fact that they are necessarily drawn up some time in advance of the situation in which they are intended to be applied; and may be signed in complete ignorance of the actual clinical circumstances in which they must be interpreted, *i.e.* by physician, relatives or the courts. The extent to which the 'consent' they purpose to give or withhold is truly 'informed' is plainly rather attenuated, so the claim that they carry the standard of patient autonomy requires qualification. At best they offer patients some choice in the kind of care they will receive after they can no longer give expression to their choices. In the process, they bear striking testimony to the break-up of the ethical consensus within which Western medicine has long been practised, which presupposed shared values in society and the profession. The 'living will' is the potent symbol of a medical culture in which every patient may, perhaps must, write his or her own ethical agenda; his or her own revision of the Hippocratic Oath,* which for so long guaranteed a particular ethical character for medicine.

The Christian understanding of human life takes as its point of departure the creation of humanity, male and female, in the image of God.* The special character of human life derives from its nature as God made it, a reflection in finite, creaturely form of his own nature. God has made us like him, and that is the ground of the Bible's insistence on the supreme value of life (see Sanctity of Human Life*). This basic biblical doctrine explains the congruence of Christian perspectives on medicine with the values of pagan Hippocratism which were early absorbed by the church and which formed the basis of the Western medical tradition. The Hippocratic refusal to prescribe lethal drugs for medically assisted suicide (evidently a common practice in the pre-Hippocratic medicine of Gk. antiquity) set the face of Western medicine against any variety of suicide or euthanasia.

Two exceptions may be noted in recent years. 1. In the years immediately before the outbreak of the Second World War, doctors in Nazi Germany consented to an extensive programme of State-directed and involuntary euthanasia which led to the deaths of hundreds of thousands of German civilians – handicapped children, First World War amputees, the mentally ill. Recent historical scholarship has revealed the extent of this horrific exercise, which pre-dated and helped prepare for the wartime extermination of Jews and others. The Declaration of Geneva, in which the substance of the Hippocratic values was reaffirmed by the world medical community in the aftermath of the War, commits post-war medicine to resist euthanasia afresh. 2. During the 1980s, the medical profession in Holland began to engage in an extensive programme of voluntary euthanasia. It has not been formally legalized, but its practice is with impunity since there is medical and general social acceptance. Campaigners for the legalization of ('voluntary') euthanasia point to Holland as their model and are embarrassed by the example of frankly eugenic and involuntary medical killing in Nazi Germany.

The example of Holland is unlikely to be followed in Great Britain, as an all-party committee of the House of Lords unanimously agreed, in February 1993, that there should be no change in the law to permit euthanasia. The committee argued: 'It would be next to impossible to ensure that all acts of euthanasia were truly voluntary and that any liberalization of the law was not abused.' It also rejected the suggestion that a new offence of 'mercy-killing' should be created: 'To distinguish between murder and mercy-killing would be to cross the line which prohibits any intentional killing, a line which we think it essential to preserve' (*Report of the Select Committee on Medical Ethics*). However, the committee supported the right of doctors to withdraw medical treatment from patients, particularly those in a persistent vegetative state. Treatment need not be given if it will 'add nothing to the patient's well-being as a person'. The report calls on doctors to draw up an agreed definition of this state, which should include the condition that the patient has shown no mental, verbal or physical responses for at least twelve months.

See also: LIFE, HEALTH AND DEATH;[13] QUALITY OF LIFE.

Bibliography
H. Bouma III *et al.*, *Christian Faith, Health, and Medical Practice* (Grand Rapids, 1989); N. M. de S. Cameron (ed.), *Death without Dignity: Euthanasia in Perspective* (Edinburgh, 1990); R. Proctor, *Racial Hygiene: Medicine under the Nazis* (Cambridge, MA, and London, 1988); J. Rachels, *The End of Life: Euthanasia and Morality* (Oxford and New York, 1986); *Report of the Select Committee on Medical Ethics* (London, 1994); R. Sherlock, *Preserving Life: Public Policy and the Life Not Worth Living* (Chicago, 1987); R. W. Wennberg, *Terminal Choices* (Grand Rapids, and Exeter, 1989).

N.M.deS.C.

EVANGELICAL WITNESS IN SOUTH AFRICA. In 1986, a statement by 133 'concerned evangelicals' was published under the title *Evangelical Witness in South Africa: Evangelicals Critique their own Theology and Practice*. The document (EWISA) was written as a response by a number of mainly black evangelical pastors and theologians who had reflected on *The Kairos Document** and decided that, instead of criticizing the more radical theological tradition which it expressed, they would rather

determine their own response to the crisis situation in South Africa at that time. In their response they pointed out that the theology and practice of the evangelical churches, groups and organizations in South Africa were totally irrelevant to the struggle against the injustice of apartheid.*

The EWISA document can be considered as a Third World statement which challenges the idea that evangelicalism is a Western form of understanding and expressing the Christian faith. It is a document expressing the reality of the experience of oppression by Black evangelicals in South Africa. The document therefore addresses the demands of a situation which called for a socially relevant form of faith. It criticizes the dualism* in evangelicalism which divorces spiritual experience from sociopolitical concerns. The basic character of the document reflects a holistic emphasis in evangelical theology which gives particular expression to the concerns, hopes and aspirations of Third World Christians where the experience of oppression calls for relevant answers from the Christian faith.

The EWISA document became a rallying point for a movement of Concerned Evangelicals (CE). After the publication of the document, CE organized themselves into a national movement which addresses the context from an evangelical perspective. One of its main projects is ETHOS (Evangelical Theological House of Studies). It is designed to provide formal theological education for progressive evangelicals. The movement also participates in an international network called INFEMIT (International Fellowship of Mission Theologians).

Bibliography

Evangelical Witness in South Africa: Evangelicals Critique their own Theology and Practice (Johannesburg and Oxford, 1986).

J. R. Cochrane *et al.*, *In Word and Deed* (Pietermaritzburg, 1991); C. A. Lund, *A Critical Examination of Evangelicalism in South Africa* (with special reference to the EWISA document and Concerned Evangelicals; unpubl. MA dissert., Cape Town, 1988); D. S. Walker, *Radical Evangelicalism and the Poor: A Challenge to Aspects of Evangelical Theology in the South African Context* (Pietermaritzburg, 1990).

N.J.S.

EVANGELISM is neatly defined by the 1974 Lausanne Congress on World Evangelization (see Lausanne Convenant*); 'To evangelize is to spread the good news that Jesus Christ died for our sins and was raised from the dead according to the Scriptures, and that as the reigning Lord he now offers the forgiveness of sins and the liberating gift of the Spirit to all who repent and believe' (The Lausanne Covenant, para. 4).

While *proselytism* is the recruiting activity of any religious group, and the word 'proselyte' could describe a convert to anything, *evangelism* is a uniquely Christian activity, communicating the story of Jesus and its implications for the world. Though all Christian traditions as well as the pseudo-Christian cults engage in evangelism, it is in the public mind one of the distinguishing features of the evangelical wing of the church, and most evangelism conveys a message rooted in evangelical theology.

Evangelism generates both enthusiasm and guilt in the churches. On the one hand, committed believers are highly motivated to share the good news, but many others feel guilty because their personality inhibits confident sharing. Others sense that to evangelize is wrong in a pluralistic* society. This last point prompts many outside the evangelical tradition to redefine evangelism as a quest for understanding rather than an attempt to convert others: *i.e.* an attempt 'to produce a climate conducive to open and free exchange of ideas, mutual respect, confidence in each other, and restraint in the divisive areas ... based on the firm confidence that no-one is seeking to convert or proselytize' (Neil Richardson, 'Evangelism's Diminishing Returns', *The Guardian*, 14 August 1990).

The advance of existentialism and secular thought, coupled with the new diversity of religious ideas found in modern society, have created an atmosphere where to claim exclusive truth for the gospel seems contrary to common sense. In addition to this, many of our cities* have large ethnic populations with deep social, racial and religious differences between them. Here, evangelism could be a dangerous spark to an already dry bonfire. So some would caution that preaching the gospel is undesirable in a pluralistic society.

Yet it is clear that the Christians of the NT boldly proclaimed the gospel in societies where there was both diversity of religion and the potential for violent opposition (Acts 17:1–9; 19:23–41). They employed both proclamation and dialogue to achieve this end. There was bold proclamation in the first evangelists' preaching and teaching (Acts 2:14–41; 7:2–53), as well as careful dialogue with those who did not yet believe (Acts 18:4; 19:8–10). It is also clear that this dialogue was intended to convert people from other faiths to the faith of Christ.

Again, the Lausanne Covenant expresses this well in para. 4: 'Our Christian presence in the world is indispensable to evangelism, and so is that kind of dialogue whose purpose is to listen sensitively in order to understand. But evangelism itself is the proclamation of the historical, biblical Christ as Saviour and Lord, with a view to persuading people to come to him personally and so be reconciled to God.'

'Friendship evangelism' has always been at the core of Christian witness. The majority of people coming to Christian faith have done so because a Christian befriended them first. Recent trends in evangelism have emphasized both this and the need to find methods of communication that will touch the unchurched. The work of the Willow Creek Community Church in Chicago has been very influential in stimulating the development of 'seeker-friendly' church services. At the back of both of these important models is the understanding that people need time to learn and evaluate the gospel before making a decision: evangelism is a process.

The process should not stop once a commitment is made. William Abraham (1947–) in his influential book *The Logic of Evangelism* extends the definition of evangelism to include initiation into the local church, as well as the acquiring of spiritual gifts and demonstration of real change in lifestyle. Responsible evangelism is pastorally sensitive and provides for the development of the new Christian.

Wise pastors need to find ways of encouraging their embattled flock to continue the work of evangelism in a relativistic culture. The first thing people need is a clear understanding of the *uniqueness* of Jesus* Christ. He is not merely the founder of one of the world's great religions, but the one-and-only Son of the one-and-only God, who came to reconcile lost humankind to the Father. Only those convinced of the uniqueness of Christ, and who are personally involved with him, will have the motivation to go out and share the good news.

Combined with this we need an appreciation of Christ's *character*. Seeing his boldness in tackling the rich young ruler (Mk. 10:17–23),

and his sensitivity in helping the woman caught in adultery back to her feet (Jn. 8:2–11), should influence the way we communicate the same good news. Healthy evangelism flows from an understanding of the uniqueness and the character of Jesus: his uniqueness gives us both the authority to evangelize and the content of our message; his character gives us the example of boldness with sensitivity that we ought to imitate in our methods.

See also: MISSION, MORALITY OF.

Bibliography

W. Abraham, *The Logic of Evangelism* (London, 1989); C. R. Padilla (ed.), *The New Face of Evangelicalism* (London, 1975; Downers Grove, IL, 1976); I. S. Rennie, *NDT*, pp. 239–240.

D.D.B.

EVIL. Like other primary notions, evil is most helpfully defined by context and by configuration. Evil is the antonym of 'good': what people 'wish not to happen' to those they love; what people feel they 'ought not to do'; the cause of fear, shame, remorse and indignation. Gottfried von Leibniz (1646–1716) distinguished between *physical* evil (mainly pain), *moral* evil (actions that entail guilt), and *metaphysical* evil (imperfections of finite beings). However, the distinction between 'evil done' (malignancy) and 'evil undergone' (wrongs) seems to be more basic and incontrovertible.

The topic of evil is a fertile field for symbolism. 'Evil' conjures up images of darkness, disease and destruction, and also of wanderings, twisting, filth, failure and conflict. The negative connotations are obvious, and use of language confirms them: the prefixes *a-* (*e.g.* amiss), *dis-* (*e.g.* disable), *in-* (*e.g.* inhuman), and *un-* (*e.g.* unjust) witness that evil is recognized in reference to the good, as the lack of it. Yet, it is also positive, not in the sense of value, but of effective reality. Humanity encounters evil as real in experience. The prefixes *mis-* (*e.g.* mischief, mishap) and *dys-* (*e.g.* dysfunction) may hint at both the 'reality' and the 'negative' affecting it, and even at the reality of the affection itself, a factor that brings about results; the metaphors of disfiguration and perversion lie near.

Biblical language differs little from ours in this respect. The negative slant is apparent (see Is. 41:29; Zc. 10:2; and words with privative a- in NT Gk., *e.g. anomia*, 'lawlessness', *cf.* 1 Jn. 3:4). No less so, the sense of the reality of evil is also apparent. Characteristic is the enormous space the topic occupies. The Bible relentlessly denounces evil and reinforces abhorrence of it: 'Hate what is evil' (Rom. 12:9); it would never blunt the antithesis: 'Woe to those who call evil good and good evil' (Is. 5:20). Biblical history revolves round the fact of sin, starting in Eden. Scripture also progressively unveils the activity of 'evil spirits' or 'powers' devoted to wickedness; their leader deserves the title 'the Evil One' and the name Belial (in the OT, 'worthlessness'). In relation to these spirits, the emphasis is on moral evil; Satan* is 'the accuser' (Rev. 12:10) and 'the tempter' (Mt. 4:3).

Human anguish asks about the origin of evil. The experience of horror bursts forth in the questions 'Whence?' and 'Why?' Augustine,* however, insisted that another question takes precedence: 'When one asks whence evil comes, one must ask first what it is' (*The Nature of the Good*, IV.4). Actually, the questions are interdependent.

What is evil?

The range of answers to this question extends from 'mere illusion' to 'ultimate reality'.

Monistic systems, in mystical/speculative passion for the purely One, tend to dissolve the reality of evil. So in India, but Albert Schweitzer (1875–1965) showed that, even there, ethical thinkers resisted the trend (*Indian Thought and its Development*, 1935; ET, 1936). Spinoza (1632–77) reduces evil to *subjective status*, showing a modern sense of the subject. Stoicism* emphasizes *assessment*: appreciating ills as goods; its motive is moral – adherence to the divine *logos* in everything, which requires Herculean self-mastery.

Neo-Platonism incorporated Stoic elements, but, after Plato,* attached evil to the metaphysical principle of *matter*. Such mitigated, asymmetrical, dualism* is common. Many Greeks interpreted matter as relative non-being (*mē on*). Transition is then easy to evil as the *privation of goodness*, the key concept in Augustinian theory. Moderns (influencing liberal theologians) reinterpret matter within the evolutionary scheme: vestigia, inertia. Ethical consequences follow: Platonism leads to disparagement of bodily life, severity for desire and possession; evolutionism excuses traces of animal descent, and condemns what hampers progress.

Even Zoroastrian-Manichean *dualism* comes short of perfect symmetry: evil, an eternal substance equally with the good, shall be vanquished. But 'how?' is the unanswered question. *Pessimism* is rarest: Schopenhauer's malignant 'Will' as the essence of the universe, Albert Camus' (1913–60) and Jean-Paul Sartre's* denial of any coherence or meaning – though they did not live accordingly! None the less, the tragic suspicion that malevolence lodges with Ultimacy still smoulders.

The biblical understanding of evil does not fit into this spectrum. Evil is no first principle or substance. Even the Evil One and his troop fell from prior righteousness (Jude 6). God is goodness unmixed (1 Jn. 1:5). Yet, evil is a real foe, a horrible corruption of the good. It stems from sin, the misuse of freedom* and the breaking of God's law (*anomia*, 1 Jn. 3:4). Evil is included in God's will of *decree* (otherwise it would not happen), but opposed to God's will of *precept* and *desire*.

Whence and why?

While extreme answers suppress the question, moderate dualism (Neo-Platonic, Hegelian) explains evil as *locally* negative but *globally* useful: a dissonance contributing to total harmony. Stronger dualism appears to take its evilness seriously, but it consolidates evil as the metaphysical partner of the good; symmetry brings evil into harmony. Both deprive indignation of any point, make guilt insignificant, and confront God with a necessity that is independent of him. Nevertheless, the Augustinian-Thomist tradition and Hegelian theology (with which Barth* has been compared) accommodate similar thoughts to Christianity: evil as the ransom-price of redemption enables one to sing *felix culpa!*

Many espouse the 'free-will defence'. God could not create a free creature without taking the risk of disobedience. Evil as the constitutive possibility of freedom is thus the price of that higher good.

Scripture does incriminate freedom: the Fall, being historical, as Paul Ricoeur (1913–) perceived, rules out a metaphysical source of evil. But is this a final answer? If God governs human choices (*e.g.* Pr. 21:1), why did he permit the Fall? The 'free-will' solution also imposes a necessity on God (*i.e.* God *could* not) and somehow roots evil in creation.

Job and Paul (Rom. 9:15ff.) call us to accept in faith the enigma, steadfastly believing the revealed truths of God's perfect goodness, God's total sovereignty, and the radical evilness of evil. We cannot bring evil, the alien, inexcusable, factor, into logical harmony with God's work.

Inability to comprehend means obligation to combat. Its reverse side is *hope*: only the sovereign God who hates evil assures us of evil ended (Rev. 21:4, 8), through the redemptive work of his Son (1 Cor. 15:24–28; Col. 2:15).

Bibliography

K. Barth, *CD* III/3; G. C. Berkouwer, *Sin* (ET, Grand Rapids, 1971); H. Blocher, *Evil and the Cross* (1990; ET, Leicester, 1994); E. Borne, *Le Problème du mal* (Paris, 1958); P. T. Geach, *Providence and Evil* (Cambridge and New York, 1977); J. Hick, *Evil and the God of Love* (London, ²1977); C. Journet, *The Meaning of Evil* (ET, London, 1963); C. S. Lewis, *The Problem of Pain* (London, 1940); P. Ricoeur, *The Symbolism of Evil* (ET, Boston, 1967); K. Surin, *Theology and the Problem of Evil* (Oxford, 1986); J. W. Wenham, *The Enigma of Evil* (Leicester, ²1985); C. Werner, *Le Problème du mal dans la pensée humaine* (Paris, 1944).

H.A.G.B.

EVOLUTIONARY ETHICS. The work of Charles Darwin* forms the base for evolutionary ethics. His *On the Origin of Species By Means of Natural Selection* argued that the history and biology of living things showed that evolution had in fact occurred. There are variations in plants and animals, some of which are more beneficial than others. These beneficial traits give advantages to progeny and form the basis of evolutionary development. Thus characteristics which favour survival create a means of nature selecting which characteristics will be carried forward in the preservation and development of a species.

Darwinism applied and critiqued

This biological theory was soon applied to social, economic and political change and development. It offered one account of how the structures and patterns of behaviour are historically conditioned. This social Darwinism, of which the British philosopher Herbert Spencer (1820–1903) was an early proponent, was applied to ethical, economic and political problems by both the Right and

the Left. Those of a capitalist turn of mind stressed that the ruthless, imaginative, frugal and industrious tend to do well. The survival of the fittest rests on inequality and liberty. There is, as Adam Smith (1723–90) held, an invisible hand at work in human history. This justified a *laissez-faire** attitude towards social change and reform. The Left followed a Marxist account of social and economic development leading to a stage when the State itself would wither away and all humanity would be free.

There are many who argue that the theory of Darwin in biological terms has yet to be proved, and that any empirical and inductive account must be open to disproof and revision. At most it seems that Darwin showed that some natural selection is at work, but not that it was the only means of modification. Likewise, there is no evidence that all species are descended from other species; thus the uniqueness of humanity remains intact.

The most telling critique of the application of Darwinism to ethics is that evolutionary ethics commits the naturalistic fallacy.* It offers a neutral statement about the alleged nature of nature, as if this could itself entail a conclusion about what is to be commended or approved. For many this is the wrong-headed attempt to derive an 'ought' from an 'is' – a moral imperative from a descriptive account. The validity of such a step is hotly debated in moral philosophy, but there is no clear way that we can deduce what is desirable from what is actually desired. Ethically, Darwinism has led to such directly contradictory moral and political conclusions, claimed to be from the same natural facts, that it seems that there must be more to morality than simply a recounting of certain natural features.

Evolutionary ethics

Evolutionary ethics is not merely a morality based on the 'survival of the fittest'. That would simply offer a description of whatever survives as good, defining 'good' as what makes for survival. Most of us are not convinced that life in itself is ultimately the most important thing. The martyr is not bound by a law of self-preservation and survival. Choices and reasons for those choices are more part of our moral armoury than any absolute law which forces us to act in certain ways. Even if we know what people are like and are sure that they will act in particular ways, that is not inevitable, and they are not forced by natural forces.

Julian Huxley (1887–1975) claims that realizing ever-new possibilities in evolution, respecting human individuality and encouraging its fullest development, and constructing a mechanism for further social evolution in keeping with these aims, is right and good. Humanity is the business manager for the cosmic process of evolution and should be guiding that process in positive directions.

Philosophers, following Bertrand Russell (1872–1970), recognize that from evolution itself it is hard to see that moral behaviour is more advanced than immoral behaviour. Whatever happens to evolve would on that basis alone be regarded as good simply because it had evolved.

The Christian perspective

While process theologians may look for support from evolutionary ethics, the Christian should be wary of any purely naturalistic account which is cut off from God and his divine activity. The reductionism* of evolutionary ethics belittles human beings as well as God and makes morality a closed, deterministic matter. Modern scientific thinking calls in question such an evolutionist account in itself and in its application to ethics. For the Christian, morality rests on the nature of God and his dealings with humankind and cannot be explained by a purely naturalistic account.

Bibliography

A. N. Flew, *Evolutionary Ethics* (London, 1967; New York, 1968); T. H. and J. S. Huxley, *Evolution and Ethics* (London, 1947).

E.D.C.

EXECUTION, see Capital Punishment.

EXHIBITIONISM, see Sexual Addiction; Sexual Deviation.

EXISTENTIALIST ETHICS. For some commentators it seems a contradiction in terms to talk about ethics in connection with existentialism, since it is seen as being merely a philosophy of life or a way of doing philosophy. Indeed, existentialism does not accept, because of the contingency and absurdity of the world, the foundational nature of any moral rights and duties or recommended courses of conduct. They are seen as being often in conflict and unable to take full account of the subjectivity of the individual. But, although there are different emphases in different thinkers (some are Christian, some religious and some atheist), there is a profound moral concern in their thought and writings. However, their ethics are not detailed moral doctrines, but rather outline a basic moral stance which may be adopted in different situations.

Existentialist ethics involves the rejection of all illusions about reality and a fundamental honesty about what is. As a first step this entails a recognition and unmasking of the emptiness of moral and other conventions, of habit and of custom. The existentialist tends to experience a radical moral conversion. He (or she) discovers that to be is to be free, to live an authentic life – that is honestly and sincerely without recourse to external values.

The emphasis is on the individual's situation, on his 'being in the world' (Martin Heidegger, 1889–1976; Jean-Paul Sartre*). The individual must choose. Choices and decisions are made in *angst*, in fear and trembling because the individual alone has responsibility for them and for the guilt or remorse which may ensue. Aware of his finitude, and the contingency of his existence, circumscribed by death, and surrounded by paradoxes and uncertainties, he cannot rely on anything outside himself. For Søren Kierkegaard* this stage of religious seriousness, which is beyond the ethical stage, beyond the rules of conventional Christianity, is the highest stage. The individual is higher than universal and collective rules.

Sartre emphasizes the individual as authority and law-giver, not as libertine; the whole man is involved in the concreteness of decisions, which are relative to each situation. Moral choice is a personal activity, not a functional or abstract one. The individual is dynamic, projecting himself in action. Surrounded by his possibilities, he is what he makes himself on the basis of his moral decisions. No-one can show him which direction he should take, he must make his own way. In this sense man is, in Friedrich Nietzsche's* phrase, beyond good and evil.

Those who fail to live this authentic life are viewed as being, in Sartre's phrase, in bad and faith, trying to escape the full consequences of their freedom.* This implies that freedom is a moral imperative as well as an ontological reality, and avoiding it is an existentialist sin. For Sartre freedom is absolute; and the individual is reciprocally free – in intuiting his own freedom he recognizes the value of freedom in others and acts to enable the other to retain it. In choosing for himself he chooses for all. He is not isolated, but free for others as well as for himself; indeed being for others is a basic element of an individual's identity. Bad faith is to relate in a conflictual manner to others, to try to subordinate their freedom to ours.

Existentialist freedom is not detachment. For Sartre and Simone de Beauvoir (1908–) it is commitment ('engagement'); for Albert Camus (1913–60) it is solidarity and complicity, a collaboration with others for relative, limited goals; for Gabriel Marcel (1889–1973) it is availability, community and fidelity. However, these similarities in interpersonal relationships disappear on the political plane where a great diversity of political imperatives are based on existentialism. Indeed, some existentialists move on to other positions such as Marxism (see Marxist Ethics*) or humanism.

Existentialist accounts of the individual as he makes moral choices in situation, the nature and importance of those choices, and the emotions involved, have much to offer. Their characterization of the difficulty of applying moral precepts to specific situations has cogency. Their analysis of human failings – moral cowardice, hypocrisy, *etc.* – is finely observed. Their emphasis on the virtues of courage, honesty, sincereity and integrity is admirable.

Yet existentialist ethics, because they reject moral norms, are open to abuse and provide little detailed moral guidance in vast areas of life. Individuals freely choosing must inevitably conflict unless they move to other moral systems, whether consciously or unconsciously. Existentialism is also unconvincing in dealing with wider political and social questions. It is fundamentally an ethic of individual freedom and authenticity rather than a source of detailed ethical analysis. It is also open to charges of being an élitist ethic which only the strong could sustain, since too many questions are left open for the individual. Moreover, it fails to recognize the importance of convention, habit and tradition in morality. And, most significantly, the normative character of God's laws and commandments as revealed in Scripture is rejected in favour of individual choice.

J.H.G.

EXISTENTIALIST PSYCHOLOGIES.
Although existentialist psychologies, like humanistic psychology and Gestalt* psychology, have been influenced by the personalism and holism of the 'understanding' psychology (see Humanistic Psychology*) of Wilhelm Dilthey (1833–1911), their origins lie, essentially, in the philosophies of phenomenology and existentialism.

The influences of the latter are complex, since there is no overarching philosophical methodology that has impinged evenly on the range of existentialist psychologies. The more foundational strands include the theistic quest of Søren Kierkegaard* for the authenticity of individual and subjective truth; the 'God is dead' stance of Friedrich Nietzsche,* with his bid for human freedom from moral restraint; the phenomenological insights of Edmund Husserl (1859–1938), who urged that human consciousness should lay aside all assumptions and prejudice in favour of an objective description of what is observed; and the application of Husserlian thinking by Martin Heidegger (1889–1976) to the meaning of being. Themes of authenticity, choice, freedom, responsibility and meaning have become the hallmarks of the existentialist psychologies. The seedbed for these themes has been the continent of Europe and we can see something of this origin, and the therapeutic variety engendered, in the work of Ludwig Binswanger (1881–1966), Viktor Frankl,* Rollo May* and R. D. Laing (1927–89).

The Swiss psychiatrist Ludwig Binswanger, a personal friend of Sigmund Freud,* was one of the first to bring phenomenological and existential insights into therapy. His 'existential analysis', pioneered with his patients at the Kreuzlinger sanatorium, became a widely-used model for existential therapy through the translation of his writings into English during the 1940s and 50s.

Viktor Frankl, indebted to Kierkegaard and Husserl, founded the so-called 'third Viennese school of psychotherapy', both linked with and seeking to supersede Freud's psychoanalysis and the individual psychology of Alfred Adler.* Frankl's 'logotherapy', introduced in 1926, stressed human responsibility, spiritual awareness and the 'will to meaning'.

Rollo May, who had begun his psychotherapeutic studies in Vienna, completed his doctorate and psychoanalytical training in New York and was greatly influenced by the philosophical theologian Paul Tillich (1886–

1965), introduced existential perspectives into the more humanistic tradition of the N. American counselling scene.

In Britain, Laing, looking to the existential ideas of Jean-Paul Sartre,* put forward his 'social phenomenology' – not as a complete methodology but as the groundbase for his 'anti-psychiatry' perspectives. During the 1960s, Laing, along with two other existential psychiatrists, David Cooper (1931–86) and Aaron Esterson, spearheaded an attack on traditional psychiatric theory and practice, reversing notions of mental illness (see Mental Health*), based on the medical model, and replacing these with ideas that saw schizophrenia (see Psychosis*), for example, as 'a natural psychic healing process' (Peter Sedgwick in R. Boyers and R. Orrill, eds., *Laing and Anti-Psychiatry*, p. 33). Laing's influence has extended through the foundation in 1964 of the London-based Philadelphia Association, a charity which set up therapeutic communities where no treatment was given without the individual's consent. In more recent years, this association is given to exploring the works of such philosophers as Ludwig Wittgenstein* and Michel Foucault (1926–84), and the French psychoanalyst Jacques Lacan (1901–81).

Although these examples of existential and phenomenonological emphasis are diverse, there are certain common themes which serve to distinguish the existentialist psychologies from other systems. Human nature is viewed as process: individuals are not seen to have fixed identities but to be in a state of flux and change. This perspective may lead to an awareness of inner emptiness, accompanied at times by notions of life's meaninglessness, and, consequently, may produce a pervasive sense of anxiety* (*Angst*). Such anxiety needs to be faced: responsible living will seek to create something constructive out of the ups and downs of the everyday world. Existential psychology sees four main dimensions to human existence and experience – the physical (*Umwelt*), the social (*Mitwelt*), the psychological (*Eigenwelt*) and the spiritual (*Uberwelt*) – and argues that in all these domains the individual needs release from habitual self-deception, and unreflective conformity to others, to an attitude that discovers an inner authority and the courage to see life's possibilities. This movement forwards may be spurred by 'existential guilt', in which the person acknowledges culpability at his or her neglect of the quest for individual 'authenticity'. Psychological disturbance may arise in the face of life's trials, where a sense of personal guilt and responsibility are resisted, where the stressed person is unsupported by friends and family, or where he or she feels overwhelmed by the apparent heedlessness of society and its institutions.

Existential psychotherapy and counselling build on these views, seeking to enable clients to be truthful with themselves, broaden their perspectives, and so learn from the past that they may live with commitment in the present and find meaning for the future. This goal of 'authenticity' is the achievement of a sense of 'being true' to personal insight and experience, rather than a bid for egoism. The focus in existential therapy is one-to-one rather than within a group,* and the therapeutic style is one of openness, flexibility and dialogue, in which there is a preparedness for insight and change within the therapist, as well as client. The therapeutic process is essentially free of specific technique, and the therapist seeks to foster a climate for the client's own journey of discovery. The enterprise is characterized by an exploration of and respect for the client's assumptions and values, an openness to clarify and, where appropriate, reinterpret the past, and a commitment to help the client face life's limitations and possibilities. This unstructured form of therapy can be adapted for cross-cultural counselling* and handling very young children, although it is especially well suited to clients who face questions of meaning in relation to pending loss or life's transitional stages, such as adolescence.* Where existential methodologies are open to the transcendent, as with Frankl's logotherapy, there can be a great deal within their assumptive insights, aims and methods that eclectic Christian therapists can sift and use profitably.

See also: PASTORAL CARE, COUNSELLING AND PSYCHOTHERAPY. [12]

Bibliography

L. Binswanger, *Being in the World* (ET, London, 1978); R. Boyers and R. Orrill, *Laing and Anti-Psychiatry* (Harmondsworth, 1972); A. Collier, *R. D. Laing: The Politics and Philosophy of Psychotherapy* (Brighton and New York 1977); V. E. Frankl, *The Unconscious God: Psychotherapy and Theology* (New York, 1975; London, 1977); J. N. Isbister, 'Anti-psychiatry: Christian Roots in the Thought of R. D. Laing', *FT* 106, 1979, pp. 23–49; R. D. Laing, *The Divided Self* (Harmondsworth, ²1965; New York, ²1969); *idem, The Politics of Experience* (Harmondsworth and New York, ²1983); R. May, *Love and Will* (New York, 1969; London, 1970); R. May *et al., Existence* (New York, 1958); D. F. Tweedie, *Logotherapy: An Evaluation of Frankl's Existential Approach to Psychotherapy* (Grand Rapids, 1961); E. van Duerzen-Smith, 'Existential Therapy', in W. Dryden (ed.), *Individual Therapy: A Handbook* (Milton Keynes and Bristol, PA, 1990); I. D. Yalom, *Existential Psychotherapy* (New York, 1980).

R.F.H.

EXORCISM, see DELIVERANCE MINISTRY.

EXPLOITATION. The term 'exploitation' came into use in the early 19th century to describe the more organized and efficient approach to harvesting the earth's natural resources (especially mining) which went hand in hand with the Industrial Revolution. Originally a quasi-technical term, it acquired its pejorative and political connotations as recently as the late 19th century, finding expression 1. in the rise of the international human rights (see Rights, Human*) movement, and 2. in Marx's more technical definition of it as an inevitable product of the class struggle.

Both these movements have their philosophical roots in the liberal humanism of post-Enlightenment thought, with its emphases on individualism,* materialism,* reason* and natural justice. However, the climate of concern for social justice in the 19th century, particularly in the English-speaking world, was significantly influenced by the largely evangelical movement for social reform. Secular historians attach particular importance here to the Clapham Sect.* In this way the emergence of human rights issues is the product both of Christian and humanist agendas.

A biblical critique of exploitation must address questions both of worth and of the limits of power* and authority,* as exploitation presupposes a worth contradicted and a power abused. The relevant themes are: 1. Creation* as the source of meaning, function and order, as much for material (Gn. 1:1) and animal (Gn. 1:21) as for human existence (Gn. 1:27), matters addressed profoundly by Gn. 1 – 11 as a whole. 2. OT jurisprudence* as the expres-

sion of covenant* society, where much attention is paid to protecting the weak (*e.g.* Ex. 21 – 22) and practising impartial justice (Ex. 23:1ff.), as expressions of God's perfect character (Lv. 19:22) and as a condition of God's continued favour (Dt. 4:2; 2 Ch. 7:14). 3. The developed view of prudent government in OT Wisdom literature (*eg.* Pr. 11:14; 16:10–12). 4. The prophetic call for justice and mercy (Mi. 6:8; Am. 5:14–15). 5. The kingdom* ethic proposed by Jesus (Mt. 5–7, *etc.*), which both reflects and radically develops the above OT themes, *e.g.* the creation ideal for marriage (Mt. 19:3–6), and God's favour towards the oppressed (Mt. 5:1–12). 6. Jesus' model of accepting outcasts (*cf.* his treatment of women, children, servants of the Roman occupation, *etc.*) and his servanthood as the source of moral authority (*e.g.* Mt. 11:29–30). 7. The Pauline vision of the church as a new society, bridging gaps of race and culture (Gal. 3:26–27; Eph. 2:11–22).

Christian attitudes toward exploitation are informed not only by biblical motifs, however, but by five main interpretative traditions: 1. For Roman Catholic thought, the concept of mutual obligation as the basis of a Christian society is still fundamental, as is its Thomist philosophical framework. 2. Classic Reformed belief, based on the idea of a society under God's law, sees a judicial basis in the permanence of the moral law and the example of OT civil law (supplemented by a churchly calling to 'works of mercy'). 3. Evangelical thought as a distinctive movement arising from the Methodist Revival places characteristic emphasis as a reason for social justice on the inherent value of the individual by virtue of having a (convertible) soul, and so both reflects and criticizes the individualism of the post-Enlightenment society in which it was born. 4. The Radical Reformation tradition, of which Anabaptist* life is the most enduring example, looks to a more literalistic acceptance of Jesus' kingdom teaching and thus proposes the 'realized eschatology' of a society not simply negatively free from exploitation but which positively realizes the kingdom here and now. 5. Finally, liberation theology* has emerged more recently, claiming a Christian justification for the Marxist understanding of exploitation.

Each of the above can be challenged either for lack of sufficient biblical foundations or for over-dependence on the ideological climate present at its birth (and often for both).

Nevertheless, there is a remarkable unity regarding two essential elements: 1. that creation in general and human life in particular have a spiritual worth beyond merely utilitarian considerations, which calls for a due order and mutual respect in human society on earth (if not more); and 2. that government is not merely or even primarily the possession of power but rather the service of God to promote good and resist evil. These convictions, though extremely broad, have far-reaching consequences not only for political but for personal attitudes towards the misuse of power for personal gain.

Bibliography

D. W. Bebbington, *Evangelicalism in Modern Britain* (London, 1989); D. D. Raphael (ed.), *Political Theory and the Rights of Man* (London and Bloomington, IN, 1967); C. J. H. Wright, *Living as the People of God* (Leicester, 1983) = *An Eye for an Eye* (Downers Grove, IL, 1983).

P.D.H.

EXTENDED FAMILY, see OLD TESTAMENT ETHICS.

EXTROVERSION, see JUNG, CARL; MYERS-BRIGGS TYPE INDICATOR.

F

FAITH. In the OT, faith is more often expressed by verbs, such as 'believe' ('*āman*), 'trust' (*bātan*) or 'hope' (*yhl*), but in the NT it is much more common as a noun (*pistis*). It is the leading biblical term for the relationship humans are to have towards God. It expresses an orientation of the whole person. For that reason, faith is not merely intellectual assent to orthodox doctrine (*fides*, often used in the Middle Ages to express mental assent), but confidence, trust* and assurance of the graciousness of God as revealed in Jesus Christ (*fiducia*, as the Reformers referred to it). Faith does have a cognitive dimension, but it also has an affective dimension. Medieval theology taught that the former (called *fides informis*) grew into the latter (called *fides caritate formata*). The Reformers rejected this, insisting that faith includes a pious, loving disposition from the beginning. Faith is an assured knowledge that changes the believer.

The object of faith is God and his promises. Faith in God's promises is based on the reliability of God's own character, demonstrated in the believer's experiences (see Ps. 78). This has two implications. 1. The content of faith (*fides quae creditur*) is as important as the act of believing (*fides qua creditur*), particularly since intensity of feeling does not make the object of belief true, and placing one's trust in what is false can have fatal consequences. And faith is more than just a state; it is belief in certain credal tenets implied in one's trust in the person of God revealed in Jesus Christ (*e.g.* that Jesus of Nazareth is the Messiah; that Jesus is the only way to the Father). 2. Since faith is placed in God's promises, faith has a future or eschatological dimension and is therefore closely related to hope for things not yet seen (Heb. 11:1).

Faith is the means through which we receive justification* (not that which itself justifies us) and is necessary for righteousness before God (Rom. 3:21–26; 4:1–8). It is also the means by which the believer continues to live the Christian life (Rom. 6); as such, faith is to increase. The Reformers emphasized this in their doctrine of *sola fides*. Furthermore, though faith is a free act of human response to the grace of God, the NT makes it clear that faith is paradoxically a gift of God (Eph. 2:8–9) – an interior act of God's grace, which John Calvin* referred to as 'the principal work of the Holy Spirit'.

The present dimension of faith is the life of obedience* in which the believer demonstrates his or her faithfulness to God out of gratitude and love for the one whom he or she unconditionally trusts. Refusal to believe and rebellion against God are often linked in Scripture. This dimension of faith raises the thorny problem of the relation of faith and works. It is clear that genuine faith is not without works of love; there is no such thing as genuine Christian faith without obedience (Gal. 5:6; Jas. 2:14–26).

Another controversy throughout the church's history has been the relation of faith and reason.* Positions range from understanding faith as a rational act to understanding it as a knowledge *sui generis* (see 1 Cor. 2:11–12; 2 Cor. 4:6). In any case, faith is not mere opinion, since one must have some warrant for believing; and faith is not scientific knowledge, since it is based on the infallible testimony of

God whom one wilfully chooses to believe. A related issue has involved the medieval notion of 'implicit faith', whereby one gives assent to what the church teaches without really knowing or understanding what it is that one believes. This comes close to Karl Rahner's (1904–84) contemporary idea of the 'anonymous Christian', which denotes the person who has a religious faith but who for reasons of ignorance is not aware of the God revealed in Jesus Christ. Placing one's faith in the God of the Bible does not preclude doubt (except for Cartesian methodological doubt and extreme scepticism). Perhaps this is best expressed as 'wondering' how God will carry out what he has promised; it can be seen in the examples of Abraham (Gn. 15:2–6) and Mary (Lk. 2:34). In this regard, faith has an existential dimension to it.

Much of the recent discussion has focused on faith development,* a social-science description of sanctification.* Drawing on various psychological theories that describe the stages of human growth, faith development refers to the growth that occurs in one's religious life from childhood to death. Based on theories like Erik Erikson's* or Jean Piaget's,* and using ideas drawn from H. Richard Niebuhr,* Wilfred Cantwell Smith (1916–) and others, these schools trace the stages of a person's changing construals of value and meaning in life. This has yielded helpful insights for understanding religious development and how best to facilitate growth to the next more mature stage. Some have criticized this developmental approach for making psychological theory normative vis-à-vis the individual's experience of God's grace.* Furthermore, some argue that the structure of the stages distorts the phenomenon of faith whose object is a living person, God. Others question the description of faith as an activity of 'meaning-making' whereby, following the lead of Paul Tillich (1886–1965), one composes a sense of the ultimate character of reality around a central value or 'ultimate concern', hopefully ending in a mature adult faith that is centred on a meaning comprehensive enough to embrace all experience (see S. Parks, The Critical Years).

Bibliography

D. M. Baillie, Faith in God (Edinburgh, 1927); J. Calvin, The Institutes of the Christian Religion III.2, LCC 20–21; J. G. Machen, What Is Faith? (Grand Rapids, Michigan, 1925); J. H. Newman, An Essay in Aid of a Grammar of Assent (1870; Oxford, 1985); S. Parks, The Critical Years (San Francisco, 1986); P. Tillich, Dynamics of Faith (San Francisco and London, 1957); A. Weiser and R. Bultmann, TDNT 6, pp. 174–228.

D.L.O.

FAITH DEVELOPMENT is the name given to a field of studies which seeks to understand faith* by constructing a synthesis between theology and developmental theories in psychology.

The two main theorists associated with faith development are the Americans John Westerhoff III and James Fowler (1940–). Working independently in the 1970s they produced two distinct models. Fowler's is the more scientific in form and method and has sparked a continuing academic debate among psychologists of religion and religious educators.

Assumptions common to both models include the following:

1. Faith is a universal human phenomenon. It must be understood as a mode of being and relating common to all people irrespective of specific religious allegiance or none. To be human means to have faith in something or someone. The content and object of faith are secondary.

2. Faith is a process of existential becoming. It is not static but dynamic. Because it is a mode of being rather than a set of beliefs, it is open to movement and change. Fowler speaks of faith as a verb as well as a noun.

3. Faith is concerned with constructing meaning. Its basis lies in relationships which enable the individual to make sense of experience and develop meaning. Hence the phenomenon of faith is universal though its content will be variable.

4. The faith process is capable of developmental analysis. Fowler uses concepts and methods drawn explicitly from developmental psychology. Westerhoff is less scientific in his approach. Both, however, use the idea of faith stages (Westerhoff calls them 'styles') to explain development.

The Westerhoff model

Westerhoff posits four styles of faith development which he likens to the rings of a tree. A tree with fewer rings is as complete and whole as one with more. The latter is simply an expanded tree, not a better one. Like trees, human beings expand in faith as they move from one style to another. Such movement does not result in discarding earlier styles but in incorporating them.

The first style is known as *experienced faith*. This centres on relationships of trust* established in the early months and years of life. The second is *affiliative faith*, which is the faith mode of the individual-in-community who accepts the faith of his or her peers and significant others without having yet arrived at a self-chosen, critical faith. It is typical of later childhood though it may well persist into adulthood. The third style, *searching faith*, is common in adolescence when the individual questions previous assumptions and begins to develop critical judgment. This leads to a growing crisis as he or she searches for a new way of making sense of the world and personal experience. The fourth style is called *owned faith*. It integrates the previous stages in a reconstructed faith through which individuals find meaning and a perspective which they are ready to own as theirs, *i.e.* a reconstitution of personal faith identity. The transition from searching to owned faith is marked by what Westerhoff calls 'the act of surrender', which can be likened to the evangelical idea of conversion.*

More recently, Westerhoff has reworked his original model, using the metaphor of three pathways or trails to God. Styles one and two are integrated into the *affiliative-experiencing path* concerned with developing a nurtured faith. This is contrasted with the *illuminative-reflective path* centring on the searching style and therefore much less secure. The third is the *unitive-integrating path* which combines the first two to produce something like owned faith.

The Fowler model

Fowler's model is much more scientific in orientation and method, drawing on the work of Jean Piaget,* Lawrence Kohlberg (1927–87) and Erik Erikson.* Based on considerable empirical research, Fowler has constructed a model comprising seven stages. Unlike Westerhoff, Fowler regards these as hierarchical, sequential and invariant. Individuals cannot skip stages and thereby progress through the hierarchy. Each stage must be experienced in turn. Successive stages are increasingly complex, building on and incorporating the operations of previous stages.

Fowler's developmental stages are well-defined, integrated units, incorporating observable empirical characteristics which mark out one stage from another. Movement from stage to stage is triggered by crises and challenges which threaten the equilibrium of a person's current stage of development. Life crises would typically bring about transition.

Fowler's seven stages are not rigidly tied to chronological age but none the less can be related to human growth and development through the life cycle.

Stage 0: Primal faith. Faith is experienced as simple pre-linguistic trust. It is the faith of babyhood engendered by an infant's trust in its mother.

Stage 1: Intuitive-projective faith. This is the stage of unordered yet powerful images. The child constructs meaning by using these images to interpret experience but no concepts are yet available to order them intellectually.

Stage 2: Mythic-literal faith. The child from six or seven up to eleven years develops thinking skills based on a literal interpretation of the world. Story-telling is crucial to development but abstract thinking is not yet a feature.

Stage 3: Synthetic-conventional faith. The adolescent develops abstract thinking abilities and so is able to create meaning beyond the literal. This is also the stage of conformity to peer-group beliefs and may continue well into adulthood.

Stage 4: Individuative-reflective faith. The young adult develops critical judgment and begins to choose faith for himself or herself: a 'critical distancing from one's previous value system'.

Stage 5: Conjunctive faith. The dissolution of previous certainties sets in. The adult (typically in mid-life) must rework the faith-meaning created in previous stages, often under the impact of a life crisis. The hallmark of this stage is critical openness.

Stage 6: Universalizing faith. A very rare stage attained by few usually later in life. Its central characteristic is the abandonment of self. Fowler cites Mother Teresa (see Teresa, Mother*), Dag Hammarskjöld (1905–61) and Martin Luther King* as examples.

Evaluation

Fowler's work has received critical welcome from educators, psychologists of religion and pastoral theologians. Its strength is twofold: 1. it offers a substantial model of human development which draws upon acknowledged theories and empirical studies; and 2. it attempts to integrate a theological understanding of faith with insights drawn from the human sciences.

Criticisms have included: 1. that Fowler offers a phenomenologically useful but theologically inadequate definition of faith; 2. that his method subordinates theology to psychology; 3. that his empirical basis is too restricted in being drawn mainly from middle-class Americans; 4. that he fails to allow for cultural and gender differences which might alter the model; 5. that his dependence on Piaget overestimates the significance of the rational in constructing and sustaining faith over and against the affective and imaginative dimensions of human development; and 6. that the model over-emphasizes individualistic psychology, failing to appreciate that individuals are formed by their social contexts.

Despite these criticisms, Fowler has contributed more than any recent figure to an integrated understanding of faith. In the words of a 1991 evaluation: 'It is possible to view the work of Fowler and others as a useful tool . . . while more careful empirical work is always needed, and theoretical criticism is absolutely essential, some of the central themes of faith development are too important . . . to be cavalierly ignored' (Church of England Board of Education, *How Faith Grows*, p. 50).

See also: HUMAN DEVELOPMENT.

Bibliography
F. Bridger, *Children Finding Faith* (London, 1988); Church of England Board of Education, *How Faith Grows* (London, 1991); Church of England Board of Education and Board of Mission, *All God's Children?* (London, 1991); C. Dykstra and S. Parks (eds.), *Faith Development and Fowler* (Birmingham, AL, 1986); J. W. Fowler, *Stages of Faith* (San Francisco, 1981); J. H. Westerhoff, *Will our Children have Faith?* (New York, 1976).

F.W.B.

FALL, THE. The image of a 'fall' has traditionally been employed within Christian theology to express a cluster of pervasive biblical insights concerning human nature. These could be summarized as follows. 1. The present state of things, supremely that of human nature, is not what it is intended to be by God. The created order no longer directly corresponds to the 'goodness' (Gn. 1) of its original integrity. It has lapsed. It has been spoiled or ruined – but not irredeemably, as the doctrines of salvation (see Sin and Salvation 5) and justification* affirm. The image of a 'fall', although not strictly biblical in itself, brilliantly conveys the idea that creation* now exists at a lower level than that intended for it by God. 2. All human beings are contaminated by sin from the moment of their birth.

In contrast to many modern existentialist philosophies (such as that of Martin Heidegger, 1889–1976) which affirm that 'fallenness (*Verfallenheit*)' is an option which we choose (rather than something which is chosen for us), the NT and Christian tradition (especially as represented in the writings of Augustine,* Luther* and Calvin*) portray sin as inherent to human nature. It is an integral, not an optional, aspect of our being. This insight, which is given more rigorous expression in the doctrine of original sin,* is of central importance to the doctrines of sin and salvation. In that all are sinners, all require redemption. The image thus points to the universal need for redemption – for restoration to the situation which pertained before the Fall. In that all have fallen short of the glory of God, all require to be redeemed.

The most significant theological debate concerning the Fall is the Pelagian controversy of the early 5th century. For Pelagius (*fl. c.* 383–424), it was only proper to speak of a 'fall' in an individual sense. An individual was not contaminated from birth by the original sin of Adam. Rather, individuals choose to imitate the sin of Adam, thus, in effect, contaminating themselves. For Pelagius, 'fallenness' is the outcome of individual acts of sin or disobedience; for Augustine (who here seems to reflect the NT more accurately), 'fallenness' is the state which gives rise to individual acts of sin or disobedience.

The more humanist writers of the 16th century (including Erasmus, *c.* 1469–1536, and Zwingli, 1484–1531) had serious reservations concerning the notion of an historical Fall, not least on account of its implications for human moral action. For Calvin, the Fall compromised human freedom,* but not human responsibility;* Erasmus held that these two could not be thus distinguished and separated. The advent of the Enlightenment* witnessed a sustained critique of the notion of the Fall, which was held to be detrimental to human dignity and autonomy. Especially in 18th-century France (*cf.* the writings of Voltaire, 1694–1778, and Diderot, 1713–84), the idea was held to be conducive to political and social oppression, in that it encouraged individuals to think of themselves as powerless to resist repression (see Repression, Political*) or change their situations. The French Revolution was seen by some critics of Christianity as representing the triumph of secular reason and human autonomy over the pessimistic view of human nature allegedly sustained by the notions of original sin and the Fall. A sustained critique of the notion, especially the related doctrine of original sin, gradually became typical of secular and humanist critiques of Christianity, especially in the later 19th century (partly in response to Darwin's* theory of biological evolution, which was seen as posing a serious challenge to traditional interpretations of Gn. 3). More recently, however, there has been renewed sympathy within secular thought for the notion of a defect or flaw within human nature, as the renewed interest in the notion of tragedy suggests, and especially in the aftermath of the decline of the humanist optimism of earlier rationalism.

The notion of 'the Fall' has significant ethical and pastoral implications, of which the most important may be noted. It exposes the futility of the utopian delusions of various human-centred philosophies. It cuts the ground from under shallow and superficial views of human nature, which insist upon uncritically affirming the goodness of humanity. The shocking events of the 20th century – such as the horrors of the First World War and Auschwitz – have drawn attention to the darker side of human nature, all too often overlooked by liberal writers, and given theological expression in the concept of 'fallenness'. Ethical and pastoral reflection which ignores the flawed character of human nature is liable to be vulnerable to the charge of being utopian, unrealistic and naïve. Perhaps the most influential exposition of this 'Christian realism' may be found in the writings of Reinhold Niebuhr.*

See also: COMMUNITY ETHICS. ⑯

Bibliography

G. C. Berkouwer, *Sin* (Grand Rapids, 1971); D. Cairns, *The Image of God in Man* (London, 1973); R. Niebuhr, *The Nature and Destiny of Man*, 2 vols. (London and New York, 1941, 1943); C. R. Smith, *The Biblical Doctrine of Sin* (London, 1953); F. R. Tennant, *The Origin and Propagation of Sin* (London, 1902); N. P. Williams, *The Ideas of the Fall and of Original Sin* (London, 1927).

A.E.M.

FAMILY. Much ink has been spilled on defining 'the family'. That is because it is so hard to find a definition which embraces the Western nuclear family, the African extended family, 'gay marriages' and heterosexual families, single-parent families and so on. Scripture has a very fluid definition. The OT word for family (*mišpāḥâ*) blurs the distinctions between family and tribe and between family and nation. The Bible keeps pushing out the boundaries of the family.

Modern families are under immense pressure. Social pressures include the separation of work* from home, often involving long working hours or shift work which cuts the time family members can spend with each other; the subordinate position of women, in spite of tremendous advances this century, which means that key family decisions are often still taken with the husband's interests uppermost in mind; the isolation of families because of the breakdown of community in many places; poverty,* which frequently leads to acute family stress; and the tendency for people to live longer, which means more older relatives for families to look after. Psychological pressures include the tendency for damaging 'rules' of behaviour within families to be handed down for generations. Moral pressures include the liberal, self-fulfilment ethic, which creates a moral atmosphere that can damage families: the self-fulfilment ethic comes too close to selfishness to prevent selfishness.

In the Old Testament

The OT contains a vision for families which can help to sustain commitment when family life becomes tough. Families are to help create a global family. Adam and Eve are given children so that their family can spread over the whole earth (Gn. 1:28). Children are given to Abraham so that his descendants can reverse the fragmentation of humanity at Babel: Israel was to become a planet-wide family by growing in size and attracting foreigners to Judaism. Individual families were to help build this family by procreation, by bringing foreigners into the nation (Dt. 21:10; Gn. 17:12–13) and by contributing to the community economically and politically (political power was to be centred on family 'elders'). Growing *through* families, Israel was to *become* a family. Each generation felt that it belonged to the same family as its ancestors and descendants (Am. 3:1).

Families were to pass on knowledge of God so that this global family would become a godly family. Parents were to do this by loving, teaching and disciplining* their children (Dt. 6:4–9; Pr. 13:24). This would benefit the nation (Dt. 6:2–3, 24–25). Children were to separate from their parents emotionally so that they could choose for themselves whether to adopt the faith (Gn. 2:24). They were to honour their parents so that the nation would benefit (Dt. 5:16).

As families created a godly family, God's glory would be reflected in the nation through relationships of equality, solidarity and liberty. The OT reflects the patriarchal assumptions of the surrounding cultures, but contains principles which would have encouraged partners to strain towards equality in marriage. In spite of a long tradition of exegesis to the contrary, the Adam and Eve partnership is one of equality in decision-making. The ideal of equality is celebrated in the Song of Songs. It is hinted at in Pr. 2:17 where the husband is described as 'partner', a term reserved for the closest of friends. Children were to honour their father *and* mother. Parental authority* was not absolute, since children were expected to separate from their parents – a move towards equality. Equality would encourage solidarity in the family – 'one-fleshness' in marriage (Gn. 2:24), for example, and the custom of gō'ēl whereby family members stood by each other if they were in trouble. This in turn enabled families to encourage liberty. The purpose of gō'ēl, which included the protection of relatives who had fallen on hard times, was to protect the family's economic freedom (*e.g.* Lv. 25:47–49). Families were to bring freedom from starvation and from enslavement to those outside the home (Dt. 24:19; Pr. 17:2). Families were to act as bastions of freedom by preventing the economic and political concentration of power (1 Sa. 8:10–18). Because families were pivotal to Israelite society, as their partnerships strained towards equality, solidarity and liberty, so these qualities would be displayed in the nation as a whole.

Families, then, were to create a global, godly and glorious family. But the OT is very realistic about their inability to do this on their own. Inter-marriage with foreign women became such a feature of Israelite society that the people were unable to escape the influence of foreign gods (*e.g.* 1 Ki. 16:31). Both the northern and southern kingdoms were exiled as a result. Far from drawing the world into a single family, God's family had been scattered into the world. The chain of faith between the generations was regularly broken. The book of Judges records the cycle of repentance by one generation and apostasy by the next. Spiritual leaders like Eli, Samuel and David all have sons who turn from God. It seems that the sons of Samuel's contemporaries turn away from God also, and then ask for a monarchy which they are warned will lead to the oppression of families (1 Sa. 7:2; 8:3ff.). Families abandon their defence of freedom. The failure of so many Israelite families to play their role in creating God's family (especially the shortcomings of David's family when David was in such close contact with God) is a great encouragement to modern families: God used Israel and David's family to create a society and a home fit for the Messiah. He still loves and uses families, in spite of their mistakes.

In the New Testament

Jesus is brought up in a home which models the parent–child relationship expected of families in the OT. His parents successfully pass on to him the faith: the religious authorities are amazed at his knowledge (Lk. 2:47). Jesus separates from his parents (Mk. 3:31), and honours them (Lk. 2:51). His upbringing equipped him for his work of saving that global family which human families had been unable to create on their own. The Son felt abandoned by the Father on whom he depended (Mk. 15:34); the Father saw his Son as a rebel (since Jesus bore our sins of rebellion, 1 Pet. 2:24); and the Son died as the family scapegoat (Father and Son colluded with the Son's brothers and sisters by not using their power to prevent the crucifixion). Father and Son experienced the rejection that often occurs in human families. It is important, however, to qualify the parallel between what happened on the cross* and human families. Often parent–child relationships cause pain because of a failure within the relationship: there was no failure in the Father–Son relationship. At the crucifixion, Father and Son were united by a common willingness to suffer for humanity (see Atonement*). Collusion in family scapegoating is usually unconscious: Father and Son colluded deliberately and consciously with members of their family who put Jesus to death, though for the Son's brothers and sisters the collusion was unconscious.

Nevertheless, by sharing the core hurt of human families, Father and Son saved their family from the failure of human families to bring it into existence. Individuals are adopted into this family by the Holy Spirit. NT language confirms that this community is indeed a family. Though Jesus announces the coming of the kingdom,* he instructs his followers to address God as Father rather than King. 'Kingdom' denotes the fact of God's authority: the nature of that authority is paternal. Paul uses the term 'brothers' on almost every page of his letters because he thinks of the church as a family. The godly nature of the family is assured by the Holy Spirit who writes God's laws in our hearts (cf. Je. 31:33). Thanks to the Spirit, the faith is successfully passed on from the Father to his 'sons'. This Father–Son relationship is primary in God's family, rather than marriage,* which is often seen as central. When marriage is central, single people often feel excluded (see Singleness*). By emphasizing the parent–child relationship, Scripture ensures that single people are not left out. Relationships in God's family are characterized by equality. The Father and Son are not exclusively masculine in character. They display so-called feminine qualities. So the Son is the 'image' of the Father (Col. 1:15). Since God's image was reflected equally in the man and the woman in Gn. 1:27, this may imply that Jesus reflects so-called 'masculine' and 'feminine' traits equally in himself, and that in so doing he also reflects the Father. This in turn suggests that God values the 'feminine' as much as the 'masculine', which implies that men and women will have equal value in heaven. The parable of the vineyard indicates that God has no favourites, which is the basis of equality (Mt. 20:1–16). The cross made possible the creation of a global, godly and glorious family.

This family contains models which can help human families realize the OT vision for family life. God's family is an extended family in which all can be included. This ideal was reflected by the first Christians, who made virtually no distinction between the family household and the 'household of God'.

Believers ate together, worshipped in their homes and shared their possessions. The Father models parenting by loving his Son (Jn. 5:20), teaching him (Jn. 8:28), and disciplining him, in the sense that on the cross the Son bore the punishment that should have been ours (2 Cor. 5:21; Col. 3:13). By delegating the kingdom to the Son (Mt. 28:18), he models how parents should allow their children to separate. By handing the kingdom back to the Father (1 Cor. 15:24), the Son models how children should honour their parents. The Son offers back to his Father what he has done, as a child might offer back part of his or her life to his or her parents by affirming them and looking after them when they are old. This model is reflected in Paul's teaching about parent–child relationships in Eph. 6:1–4. Similarly, God's family models equality. Christ's death on the cross provides something of a role model for husbands. Husbands are to put their wives first by making sacrifices for them. Wives are to respond by putting their husbands first. There is to be mutual submission (Eph. 5:21–33). The husband's headship consists not of authority, but of helping his wife to be fully herself in a relationship of mutuality (cf. Eph. 4:15). The unity of God's family, reflected in Paul's 'body' imagery, models family solidarity. The liberty of the children of God models the liberty that families are to bring both to their members and to those outside the family. As these models are imitated in the church, they become visible to families who can identify with them, and be challenged by them. They will be helped to achieve in the present what God has intended in the past.

Help for families

How can these scriptural themes help families to face the pressures upon them? 1. Their strong emphasis on the goal of family life provides a morality which is more able to resist selfishness than is the self-fulfilment ethic. Families are to put the future of God's family before their own immediate pleasure. They are to identify with role models within that family. This will create a moral atmosphere that will promote family well-being.

2. Scripture provides healthy family rules that can begin to change the damaging patterns of behaviour frequently passed on from one generation to the next. The OT portrays families on the move, which will encourage families to expect change. Scripture counters the despair which undermines the desire for

change by showing how the benefits of change outweigh the advantages of staying still. These benefits include the knowledge that through change families can become more like God's family, and that they will experience some of the joys of that family as a result. Role models within the heavenly family, as echoed in the church on earth, can show families how to change. Adoption into God's family can provide the psychic energy to change – as individuals know they are accepted in that family, that they belong to it and that they experience the Holy Spirit's power.

3. Scripture helps families to counter some of the social pressures upon them. It challenges the modern priority of work. The 'work' of the cross occurred in a family context (Father, Son and the Son's 'brothers'). It created a family rather than just a work community. Families have a key role in helping to create God's family, which means that work must not assume such importance that the task of families is neglected. Instead of the stereotyping of women's roles, which is still frequent in spite of the advances in this century, Scripture encourages spouses to relate on the basis of equality and mutuality. The role of families in building community will help to counter the isolation of individuals and families experienced so often today. OT families were to be a bulwark against poverty, and NT families shared their possessions with the needy. Modern families can combat the damaging effects of poverty on family life by sharing a little of what they have.

This theological model of the family can be described as 'eschatological' because it is forward looking. Families are to help create God's family and they are to be challenged by the nature of this family – what it will be like – when it is completed in the future. This eschatological model helps to round out the Catholic sacramental model which sees families as a vehicle of God's grace.* The sacramental model is weak on explaining how grace is mediated through families. The eschatological model suggests that grace is mediated as families are challenged by the future of God's family. It also rounds out the Protestant 'covenant' model, which suggests that family relationships should imitate God's relationship to his people. Though it need not be, often this covenant* model is presented in rather static terms. The eschatological model can bring into the covenant model a strong dynamic for change. Families are to raise their

sights as they help to build the home of tomorrow.

See also: CHILDREN; FAMILY THERAPY; MOBILITY; PARENTHOOD, PARENTING; SINGLE PARENTS.

Bibliography

R. S. Anderson and D. B. Guernsey, *On Being Family: A Social Theology of the Family* (Grand Rapids, 1985); M. Moynagh, *Home to Home: Understanding the Family* (London, 1990); E. Schillebeeckx, *Marriage: Human Reality and Saving Mystery* (New York and London, 1965).

M.M.

FAMILY THERAPY treats the family* as a unit as the primary patient, and the individual family member as a part of the dynamic system of relationships and persons. Many schools of family theory and therapy have emerged, largely from 1950 to 1980 (identified with persons such as M. Bowen, W. Toman, S. Minuchin, V. Satir, J. Haley, M. S. Palazzoli, H. Stierlin and R. Skynner, or with places such as New York, Palo Alto, Milan, Heidelberg and the Tavistock Institute in London). All these share the following points, although with differing theoretical language and formulations, and with contrasting emphases on the intrapsychic and the interrelational dynamics.

1. *The family system*. The individual is viewed within the family context as a part of its functioning and balance as well as of its dysfunctioning and skewed homeostasis. The system is a dynamic, changing network influenced by the surrounding social systems, pursuing its developmental stages throughout the family life-cycle. The family is not only a nuclear unit of one or two parents and children, but a subunit of the joint family with extended loyalties, obligations and enmeshments. The present family is only a manifestation of the multigenerational patterns, processes, rules, myths, secrets, emotional mortgages, gifts, graces and blessings.

2. *Principles of family therapy*. Although central principles vary among theorists, key issues are: a. *Power*.* The energy within each person presses forward growth and wholeness so the power to change, mature and grow lies within the family. As the family is set more free to express and exercise its own power, it will move forward in progressive stages.

b. *Symptoms*. Individual problems are symptoms of dysfunctional family transactions and the maladaptive behaviour changes as the family learns to relate in new ways. c. *The patient*. The identified patient is pointed to by the family as the cause of the family's problems, but the real patient is the family itself and as the focus is shifted to family stress,* the person is freed to change. d. *Sequences and structures*. The family as an organism functions in regular sequences and within consistent structures. As this organization of experience is modified, the stress level and symptom pattern also change. e. *Intervention*. The therapist is seen as an enabler or a coach, a person who joins with the family, becomes part of its processes, tracks its sequences and structures, assists in restructuring by challenging the symptom, the structure and the family reality, then separates from the family in a healthful leave-taking.

3. *Multigenerational family process*. The family possesses its own identity and process, which are visible in: a. the family collective mind, called the joint ego mass; b. relational triangles composed of two closely connected persons and a third person or issue in an outside position; c. the subsystems of spouses, siblings and parents with their own means of handling stress, conflict* and immaturity; d. the multigenerational transmission of traits which maps the past on to the future from generation to generation; e. emotional cut-offs by which persons avoid anxiety* by severing relationships; f. balanced and centred experience of separateness and connectedness which is called differentiation; and g. maintaining clear boundaries that are flexible and permeable. Good family boundaries are firm within the family but open to the community; dysfunctional families have rigid walls around the family and weak or absent boundaries between family members. All these concepts are interlocking and function not in cause-and-effect ways but as elements in the dynamic organism of the family system.

4. *Family therapy and pastoral care and counselling*. Pastoral care of families can invite healthy differentiation and nourish connectedness between persons in ways that respect personhood and invite growth of the whole family unit. The pastoral counsellor serves as a family advocate, consultant, educator and as needed therapist. Although the congregation is meant to be a community of faith with diverse and unrelated members which goes beyond the projections of the family

of origin, it still functions as a system with subsystems in ways that are parallel to the family organism. Many pastoral interventions in congregational confusion and conflict function in ways that apply family therapy practice.

See also: CHARACTER. [10]

Bibliography

M. Bowen, *Family Therapy in Clinical Practice* (New York, 1978); E. Friedman, *Generation to Generation* (New York, 1985); V. Satir, *Peoplemaking* (Palo Alto, CA, 1972); R. Skynner, *One Flesh, Separate Persons* (London, 1976); S. Walrond-Skinner, *Family Matters* (London, 1988).

D.W.A.

FAMILY TREE, see HEALING OF FAMILY TREE.

FASTING (Heb. *ṣûm*, 'to cover the mouth'; *'innâ napšô*, 'to humble oneself', lit. 'to afflict the soul'; Gk. *nēsteuō*, 'to fast'), a practice found in all societies, cultures and centuries, is prompted by a variety of objectives and rationales. Although it is a well-established spiritual discipline (see Disciplines, Spiritual*) occurring in both OT and NT and other religious literature, it is not confined to religious usage. The fasts of Mohandas (Mahatma) Gandhi (1869–1948) and the IRA hunger-strikes are well-known instruments of political pressure and protest against injustice, often evoking admiration, but morally questionable; whereas hunger lunches and abstention from food to identify with the poor and raise relief are clearly Christlike (Is. 58:6–7). Some health regimes use fasts to tone up the body.

The theology of fasting

Old Testament. In the OT, fasting is used to express repentance (Joel 2:12–13; Jon. 3:5–9) or a desperate plea for God's intervention when in peril (Est. 4:1–4). Consequently it was a sign of mourning and sorrow for sins, a stance of humility sometimes using sackcloth and ashes (Dn. 9:3), and in itself a petition, though often also accompanied by vocal prayer. (The natural abstention from food in bereavement may have been the origin of religious fasting, the historical roots of which are otherwise obscure.) On occasions it is resorted to for healing (1 Sa. 1:7–8; Ps. 35:13), protection, renewal and revelation, as when God spoke to Moses on Sinai (Ex. 34:28), but in essence in these cases fasting is also seen as a dramatic, serious appeal for God to act. This is the reason that God ordered the only fast for all the people under the law to be on the Day of Atonement, when he annually removed the nation's sin (Lv. 16:29–31).

Jesus' example and teaching. Jesus fasted (Mt. 4:2) and expected that his disciples would keep fasts also, along with the other two important Jewish disciplines, prayer and giving (Mt. 6:1–18). He inherits and therefore assumes all the OT understanding concerning this discipline, re-emphasizing the warning of Is. 58:1–5 against hypocrisy. Self-display and self-righteousness, as portrayed by the Pharisee in Jesus' parable (Lk. 18:9–14), are rejected, and consequently the Jewish practice of sackcloth and ashes (Mt. 6:16–18). The Day of Atonement with its compulsory fast and sabbath (Lv. 16:29–31; 23:26–32) is superseded by Jesus' 'sacrifice' of crucifixion and 'sabbath rest' of salvation without works.

Although some sections of the church, like Israel, have commanded compulsory fast days, these seem contrary to the spirit of Jesus' voluntary fasting, although a church or national fast would be acceptable as a corporate exercise if not enforced, as when Britain was threatened by Napoleon, or as in the case of Nineveh in Jon. 3. Even the four feasts mourning the end of the monarchy, the destruction of Jerusalem and the exile were destined to be turned into joyful feasts (Zc. 8:19). No doubt Jesus as a good Israelite would have fasted on the Day of Atonement, but his disciples were criticized for feasting and not fasting. Jesus' reply was that they would fast when he was taken away (Mk. 2:18–20; Lk. 5:33–35). The church age of the new wineskin is to be characterized by both feasting and fasting, since the kingdom is here but not in its entirety. Disciples will feast because they have met the bridegroom, but will also fast for his return.

The New Testament church. Since apart from the NT little is known about the 1st-century church, it is inadmissible to assert, as some do, that fasting was not practised or that Jesus' view on the subject is unclear (*e.g.* Johannes Behm, 'Fasting', in *TDNT* 4). What is clear is that: 1. Jesus gave both example and teaching in the Gospels, clearly indicating that it was an outward sign of an inner state; and 2. there are at least seven references to fasting in the best texts of the Acts and the epistles. Paul fasted (Acts 9:9; 13:2–3; 14:23) to receive light and power from God in the establishing of the church. 2 Cor. 6:5 and 11:27 have both been interpreted as references to involuntary hunger, but since the latter mentions both involuntary hunger (*limos*) and voluntary going without food (*nēsteia*), it is likely that religious fasting is also in view there.

Fasting in church history

The sub-apostolic church fasted, as Clement of Rome (*fl. c.* 96) indicates. The *Didache* (*c.* 2nd century), in ch. 8, teaches fasting twice a week (Wednesdays and Fridays, to differ from the Pharisees – 'hypocrites', who fasted on Mondays and Thursdays), and also in preparation for Easter. The *Shepherd* of Hermas (2nd century) in ch. 5, shows fasting in relationship to prayer for the Lord's return. The *Epistle of Barnabas* 3:1, Polycarp (*c.* 69–*c.* 155) and Justin Martyr (*c.* 100–165) in his *Dialogue* 15:1 all show fasting as a regular Christian discipline. However, by the 3rd century, Tertullian* clearly treats fasting as meritorious (*De Poenitentia* 13; *De Oratione* 18) as do the Apocrypha and Tobit 12:8, and later teachers till the Reformation suggest its value for atoning for sin. While most teachers of this period warn against asceticism,* the theology of works of merit takes precedence over that of fasting being a discipline and means of grace.

Outstanding Christian leaders through the centuries practised fasting for a variety of reasons. Origen (*c.* 185–*c.* 254), Jerome (*c.* 342–420), Augustine,* Thomas Aquinas,* Martin Luther,* John and Charles Wesley,* David Brainerd (1718–47) and Charles G. Finney (1792–1875) are but a few.

Types of fasting

There are various types of fasts: 1. supernatural fasts – sustained by God, since a human cannot live without water for more than three days (*e.g.* Moses and Elijah, Ex. 34:28 and 1 Ki. 19:8); 2. absolute fasts – no food and water for a maximum of three days (Est. 4:16; Acts 9:9); 3. normal fasts – including water, either long (forty days, *e.g.* Jesus, Lk. 4:1–2), or short (one day, *e.g.* Lv. 23:12–14); and 4. partial fasts (1 Ki. 17:6; Dn. 1:12–16; 10:2–3). There are, however, also hypocritical fasts (1 Ki. 21:9–12; Is. 58:3–5; 1 Tim. 4:3).

Moses, Elijah and Jesus, each fasting for forty days, introduced respectively the Law, the Prophets and the kingdom (*cf.* Lk. 16:16). Though the NT emphasizes the joy of the kingdom of God, it is none the less appropriate that on occasion, such as during a time of spiritual dearth, churches and individuals should choose to seek the restoring of God's favour by fasting.

See also: CHARACTER. ⑩

Bibliography

J. Behm, *TDNT* 4, pp. 924–935; R. D. Chatham, *Fasting* (South Plainfield, NJ, 1987); J. E. Hartley, *TWOT* 2, pp. 758–759; A. Wallis, *God's Chosen Fast* (Eastbourne and Fort Washington, PN, 1969).

R.T.F.

FATHERING, see PARENTHOOD, PARENTING.

FEAR may be defined as a state of mind, experienced in a threatening situation, and resulting in behaviour which is designed to escape or avoid the threat. In this state, unpleasant feelings prevail. The word is used in a multitude of other ways, many of which describe the state of the brain and nervous system when fear predominates. There is a high arousal, which is sometimes felt as anxiety,* with its well-known physical manifestations. Lovers of horror films will testify that the arousal is not always disliked.

In itself, fear and the reactions it triggers in our minds and bodies is a kind of signal of which we do well to take note, and then to act appropriately. Many fears seem *innate* in animals and humans, such as the fear of snakes or of birds such as a hawk. Ethologists, studying animal behaviour, have made major contributions to understanding the nature of fear as a biological process. Some fears are age-appropriate: fear of noises or strange objects may become much less in humans between the age of one year and six years. Other fears may be *acquired* in these early years by a process of conditioning.

Psychologists, studying both human and animal behaviour, have elaborated theories to attempt to explain *excessive fears*, and to help in their treatment. Thus, many phobias can be explained simply by a process of learning, though the method of becoming fearful may be very complex. The importance of these findings is that treatment of clinically severe fears and phobias may be based on *unlearning* what has been learned by faulty teaching, experience or conditioning.

Doctors have studied the clinical pictures of the neuroses* where fear is the predominant feature, as in anxiety states or phobic disorders. Symptoms such as a fast heart-rate causing palpitations, or gut symptoms such as nausea (sick with fear) or diarrhoea, and many others, may be the result of fear. Such fear may be appropriate in some situations, but in neurotic disorders it is almost always the result of poor adaptation to present needs. Since the physical effects of fear are mediated by adrenalin as well as other neuro-endocrine responses, the discovery of beta-adrenergic blocking drugs such as propranolol has proved of great value in such conditions as raised blood pressure, as well as many other more specific anxiety symptoms. In many depressive illnesses (see Depression*), fear in the form of severe agitation is often marked, and responds to treatment of the underlying illness, rather than to a direct approach to the fears involved.

The term 'anxiety' has often been used with exactly the same meaning as fear. In the theories which follow Freud* and others, the burying of a fearful experience by a process of repression (see Repression, Psychological*) has led to many treatment approaches. Thus, by a process of psychoanalysis* it was thought desirable to arrive at the painful experience that had been long-forgotten, and, by bringing the unconscious fear into the world of conscious awareness, it was hoped to cure the neurosis.

More simply, a man who had been injured in a burning tank in a war experience might, with the help of a therapist and a suitable amount of medication, be able to live through the past experience and recover from its harmful effects: this process of abreaction or catharsis is less used today. Post-traumatic stress* disorders may be treated by going over, with a trained listener in a safe place, the whole experience of mugging, near-drowning or whatever trauma gave rise to the disorder.

Fear may be wholly *proper* in relation to spiritual things, or the approach to God in worship (*e.g.* Ps. 86:11). This sense of the numinous is sometimes spoken of as awe or reverential fear (*e.g.* Acts 5:11).

Appropriate fear is what is meant by the fear of the Lord being the beginning of wisdom (Pr. 1:7); whereas it is the fear which has torment that is cast out by perfect love (1 Jn. 4:18).

Bibliography

J. A. Gray, *The Psychology of Fear and*

Stress (Cambridge, ²1987); I. M. Marks, *Fears, Phobias and Rituals* (London, 1984); S. Rachman, *The Meanings of Fear* (London, 1974).

G.D.

FELLOWSHIP. To have fellowship (Gk. *koinōnia*) is to have a share in, to participate in, and to be in communion with, someone in something. Its secular usage is seen in Lk. 5:10 where James and John are said to be 'fellow-shippers' (*koinōnoi*) with Peter in his fishing business. The Christian understanding of fellowship, however, has developed into a much deeper concept. Fellowship is not the mere sharing of a common interest or the working towards the achievement of a common goal. It is 'a common participation in God's grace in Christ' (Bruce Milne). The basis of fellowship is the believer's participation in Christ.

In the OT, fellowship with God was disrupted through the Fall* (Gn. 3:8–10), with the result that people became alienated from one another and true community became unobtainable. The covenant* with Abraham (Gn. 15:1–21) looks to the creation of a new community and, based as it was on faith, anticipates the work of Christ which restores fellowship with God. Furthermore, the wilderness period is used to portray an ideal picture of fellowship between God and his people (*e.g.* Is. 43:19–21; 48:21).

The NT portrays not only how fellowship with God can be restored, but the consequences of that restoration for human relationships. Although the concept is not limited to Paul's writing it is brought into sharpest focus there. He variously describes it as 'fellowship with his Son Jesus Christ' (1 Cor. 1:9); 'the fellowship of the Holy Spirit' (2 Cor. 13:14; *cf.* Phil. 2:2); a fellowship 'in the gospel' and 'in God's grace' (Phil. 1:5, 7). The book of Hebrews speaks of it as sharing 'in Christ' (3:14), Peter of participating 'in the divine nature' (2 Pet. 1:4), whilst John writes of the result of our fellowship as being 'with the Father and with his Son, Jesus Christ' (1 Jn. 1:3).

Fellowship is more than a theoretical idea. The believer experimentally takes part in the experiences of Christ. Thus he or she participates in Christ's suffering (Rom. 8:17; Col. 1:24), death (Rom. 6:6, 8), burial (Rom. 6:4; Col. 2:12), resurrection and ascension (Rom. 6:4; Eph. 2:6; Col. 2:12; 3:1) and glory (Rom. 8:18; 2 Tim. 2:12).

A chief expression of fellowship in Christ was to be found in the fellowship meal. Participation in Christ gave rise to the sharing of bread and wine together (1 Cor. 10:14–17; Acts 2:42). Participation in the meal implied that one accepted one's fellow-diners as valid participants in Christ. The issues of whom one could have 'fellowship' with at a meal was consequently to dog the early church until the principle of salvation by grace through Christ alone was thoroughly established. (See Acts 10:1 – 11:18, esp. 11:3; Gal. 2:11–21.) This issue highlights that fellowship can only be on the basis of truth (Gal. 2:14). The fellowship meal further points forward (1 Cor. 11:26), to the time of the Messianic banquet when perfect fellowship will be realized (Rev. 19:9, 17).

The quality of fellowship in the early church was not perfect. Hence there are frequent exhortations to improve it by accepting one another (Rom. 15:7) and forgiving one another (Eph. 4:32), and to serve one another by bearing each other's burdens (Jn. 13:1–17; Gal. 6:2). There is also a realistic recognition of the fact that care can degenerate into busybodiness and prayer into gossip under the guise of fellowship (Gal. 6:4–5; 1 Tim. 5:13). The task of pastoral leadership was to facilitate fellowship by exhortation, rebuke, counsel and by further exposition of the meaning of the gospel which they had come to believe. Individualism,* which ignored the fellowship implications of discipleship, was foreign to their thinking.

The vertical dimension of fellowship with God, rightly understood, cannot but lead to a true fellowship with fellow-believers. Through the new birth a person is initiated into an accepting, forgiving and healing community. Thus the isolation, alienation and loneliness which are the result of sin, and the sinner's cutting off from God, should be overcome at the deepest level. Unfortunately, the church is caught between 'the already' and 'the not yet' of God's kingdom and may well, therefore, fail to live up to its ideal.

Encouragement to attain the ideal is not to be gained by the organization of more communal activities, which may sometimes sadly have the opposite effect, but by a greater appreciation of the meaning of fellowship. To reduce a Christian understanding of fellowship to drinking coffee after a service, engaging in recreational activities or the fulfilment of a particular work project, is superficial, if not erroneous. Such activities may stem from fellowship but are not fellowship in themselves.

Bibliography

R. Banks, *Paul's Idea of Community* (Exeter, 1980); P. F. Esler, *Community and Gospel in Luke-Acts* (Cambridge, 1987); R. P. Martin, *The Family and the Fellowship* (Exeter, 1979); B. Milne, *We Belong Together: The Meaning of Fellowship* (Leicester, 1978); J. Schattermann, *NIDNTT* 1, pp. 639–644.

D.J.T.

FEMINISM. There are many diverse strands in feminist theory. Feminists differ in their explanations of the origin and nature of woman's oppression and how best to gain liberation. This reflects the complex history of feminism. Its course has been shaped by the interaction of various social, political and philosophical currents. Perhaps the single most powerful influence on feminist ideology was the 18th-century Enlightenment* theory about an individual's natural rights.* Mary Wollstonecraft's *A Vindication of the Rights of Woman* (1792) was foundational, applying the principle of natural rights to women, arguing that women have equal worth with men and therefore have the same rights.

An organized women's movement emerged in the 19th century. At first it was allied to the struggle for the abolition of slavery* and the temperance and moral reform movements. Later, women who were fighting for social justice for others realized the extent to which women themselves were subjected to social injustices, and a movement to obtain political, legal and educational rights for women developed. Nineteenth-century socialism* added another layer to feminist thinking. The emphasis shifted from the rights of the individual woman to the economic rights of women as a class. Socialist feminists provided a critique of the capitalist* system, in which women as a class are oppressed by the sexual division of labour.

The women's movement re-emerged in the 1960s. Radical feminism was born out of the civil rights movement and the New Left. The radical feminists moved beyond demands for equal rights and attempts to change the system to the revolutionary goal of removing patriarchy, *i.e.* the systematic oppression of women by men in social structures and institutions. They argued that patriarchy was all-pervasive in our culture and that women were owned and controlled through the tyranny of marriage, sex and child-bearing. They advocated abolition of marriage* and the nuclear family,* which should be replaced by alternative forms of reproduction and child-rearing. Radical feminism sometimes led to separatism and the exclusion of men. Changing the laws on abortion,* rape* and violence* against women became key issues in achieving women's sexual rights.

Christian women were prominent in the 19th-century women's movement, but the relationship between Christianity and feminism has often been one of mutual distrust. Feminists both within and outside the church have accused the church of propagating a negative view of woman. Those outside the church tend to regard Christianity as a patriarchal religion which has devalued woman, and they view the church as a powerful agent of oppression. Awkward questions have been asked about the maleness of church hierarchies, the exclusively male language employed in hymns, liturgies and sermon illustrations, and the restrictions placed on women. The bias in traditional interpretations of the Bible has been challenged. Modern feminist theology has developed as a reaction and a protest to patriarchal theology.

There are three main groupings of modern-day feminists:

1. The *post-Christian* feminists, believing that Christianity is irredeemably patriarchal, have abandoned the church and attempt to construct an alternative feminist religion (see, *e.g.*, M. Daly, *Beyond God the Father*, Boston, MA, 1973).

2. The *revisionists* are critical of the male-centredness of traditional theology, but they do not reject the Bible completely. Among this revisionist group are Elisabeth Schussler Fiorenza (1938–), Catharina Halkes (1920–), Rosemary Radford Ruether (1936–), Letty M. Russell (1929–) and Phyllis Trible. They believe that there are liberating elements within the biblical text. Their aim is to reinterpret the Bible and liberate it from patriarchy. The most distinctive feature of their theology is their emphasis on 'woman's experience' as the key to interpreting the Bible.

3. *Biblical feminists* do not believe that the Bible itself is misogynist, but they challenge some of the ways in which it has been interpreted. Among this group are Paul Jewett (1919–91), Myrtle Langley and Virginia Ramey Mollenkott (1932–), who tend to employ a hermeneutic of deculturization. Others, such as Mary J. Evans (1946– ; see

Woman in the Bible, Exeter, 1983; Downers Grove, IL, 1984) re-examine the biblical material but emphasize careful exegesis rather than the cultural conditioning of the Bible.

By means of careful exegesis, or by consideration of the cultural context, biblical feminists attempt to redress the balance. Fundamental to this perspective is the conviction that the Bible is God's Word, not merely men's words. Their contention is that both sexes were made in God's image* and shared the same place in the created order (Gn. 1:26–28; 2:18–25). Together they rebelled against God. They were found equally guilty and punished by hard labour, death and exile from God's presence (Gn. 3:1–24). After the Fall,* man's domination became oppressive (Gn. 3:16); the OT reflects this. But, there is no double standard in the way women relate personally to God. Jesus' attitudes were revolutionary and run counter to those of any culture. The good news of the gospel is for both sexes (Mt. 12:50). Women were included in Jesus' ministry (Lk. 8:1–3), received some of the most important revelations (Jn. 4:1–42; 11:17–27), and witnessed miracles (Mk. 5:24–34; Lk. 13:10–17). In a culture where women could not give evidence in a court of law, they were chosen as the first witnesses of the resurrection (Mt. 28:1–10; Mk. 15:47 – 16:11; Lk. 23:55 – 24:11; Jn. 20:1–18). Jesus' negative remarks about women were reserved for those who put domestic and maternal roles before obedience to the gospel (Lk. 10:38–42; 11:27–28). The inclusion of women continued in the early church as both men and women were empowered by the Holy Spirit to spread the gospel (Acts 2:1–21), and their fundamental equality with men was affirmed by the apostle Paul (Gal. 3:28).

At one extreme, the church's response to feminism has been reactionary and dismissive. Feminists have been caricatured and treated with deep suspicion. There has been a failure to take seriously any of the issues raised by the women's movement. At the other extreme, there has been an uncritical identification with the women's movement. Often this is because women have become disheartened and frustrated by the right-wing reaction of the church. They tend to drift into a more liberal theological position and liberal lifestyle. However, people sharing this biblical perspective have developed organizations which seek to educate Christians regarding the equality of men and women (*e.g.* 'Men, Women and God'

in Britain, and 'Christians for Biblical Equality' in the US).

Though the radical feminist movement has passed its peak, there can be little doubt that a revolution has occurred in the way women think. In fact, feminism as a social movement has profoundly affected both men and women. If the church is to be relevant, a range of issues must be addressed. These include the following:

1. Traditional theology needs to be more open to the feminist critique and must seriously evaluate feminist hermeneutics. Feminist theology is not for women only.

2. Feminists are right to point out that women's experience has been ignored. The church's teaching must engage with the real issues in women's lives. It must get inside the futility, anger, hurt, powerlessness and contradictions many women feel. Single (see Singleness*) and childless (see Childlessness*) women, for example, complain that instead of alleviating their pain, the church exacerbates it by emphasizing marriage and child-bearing as a woman's vocation.

3. Women need to hear a message that offers hope in a language that they understand. Focusing on Jesus' radical, liberating treatment of women may help to convince them that he is a saviour for women as well as men. One fruitful evangelistic and apologetic approach for women may be to explore the extent to which Western literature and religious art reflect a patriarchal, cultural image rather than a positive, biblical image of woman.

4. The church is also accused of alienating women by using exclusively male language. In this debate about linguistic discrimination, there are two separate issues to be considered: a. the language used to describe God's people, the church; and b. the language used to address God. (See A. E. Lewis, ed., *The Motherhood of God*, Edinburgh, 1984.) There is certainly scope for modifying the language that we use to describe God's people in hymns and prayers, and to make sermons more gender-inclusive. From the biblical perspective, we are not free to address God as we see fit, but reference to the female imagery used to describe God (Ps. 131:2; Is. 42:14; 49:15; 66:13) could help some women to see how closely God has identified with their experience.

5. Women need help to recognize their spiritual gifts and every encouragement to play an active part in the Christian community. This is a much broader issue than the debate on

the ordination of women. In that debate, we can lose sight of the NT teaching about the priesthood of all believers and the church as the body of Christ composed of people with different gifts (1 Pet. 2:5). For too long we have approached the role of women in the church from the wrong angle, emphasizing the restrictions that should be placed on women, when the real problem is how to help all believers to discover and use their gifts. Often church structures discourage both women and men from developing their gifts. The church has not always examined whether its practices are cultural, traditional or thoroughly biblical. The part played by women in biblical history and church history has been neglected. Those women could supply positive role models and provide inspiration for modern women.

6. The church community may mirror our society by dividing into sub-groups, and this can lead to the painful isolation of single women, single parents* and others who do not fit neatly into one of the groups. The caring Christian community will find creative ways of expressing its oneness as the family* of God and providing opportunities for relationships which are healing and enriching.

7. There is increasing confusion and uncertainty about gender roles and identity. People need help to reappraise their marriages, to think through their roles in parenting,* in domestic responsibilities and in the work place. Sexual problems may be linked to the confusion about gender identity. This is an area where the church could provide more sensitive teaching, counselling and support for those who struggle with their sexual orientation. (See M. S. van Leeuwen, *Gender and Grace*, Downers Grove and Leicester, 1991.)

8. The women's movement has led the way in objecting to the ways women are used in advertising,* pornography* and media violence. It has also provided practical help for women who are victims of violence. This must prompt some soul-searching in the Christian community about its silence on these issues and the extent of its social involvement.

See also: DISCRIMINATION; SEXUAL HARASSMENT.

Bibliography

O. Banks, *Faces of Feminism* (Oxford, 1981); A. Brown, *Apology to Women: Christian Images of the Female Sex* (Leicester, 1991); J. B. Hurley, *Man and Woman in Biblical Perspective* (Leicester and Grand Rapids, 1981); P. K. Jewett, *Man as Male and Female* (Grand Rapids, 1975); R. R. Ruether, 'A Method of Correlation', in L. M. Russell (ed.), *Feminist Interpretation of the Bible* (Oxford and Philadelphia, 1985); *idem*, *New Woman, New Earth*, (New York, 1975); E. Storkey, *What's Right with Feminism* (London, 1985; Grand Rapids, 1986).

A.B.

FEMINITY, see SEXUALITY. [11]

FETISHISM, see SEXUAL DEVIATION.

FLESH. The word 'flesh' (usually *bāśār* in the OT and consistently *sarx* in the NT) is often misunderstoood as referring to something inherently evil or as a part of the human being which contains, and is at odds with, the soul (ideas influenced by Hellenistic thought). On the contrary, it stands for the *whole* person from the perspective of his or her external and physical existence, in contrast to the internal and spiritual (Jn. 3:6; Rom. 2:28–29; 2 Cor. 4:11). It denotes the earthly life in its totality in a non-disparaging manner (Gal. 2:20; Phil. 1:22, 24); as such it is that aspect of humans which binds them to the whole created order (see Rom. 8:23) and it distinguishes the creature from God (who is spirit and not flesh), emphasizing the frailty, limitations and mortality of human existence (Mk. 14:38; Rom. 6:19; 1 Cor. 15:50; *cf.* 1 Cor. 1:26 and 2:5, 13).

Accordingly, the term 'flesh' can refer simply to meat or bodily tissue (Lv. 6:27; 1 Cor. 15:39); the whole body (Pr. 14:30; 1 Cor. 6:16–17); the self (Ps. 63:1; Rom. 7:18); human beings (Mt. 16:17; Rom. 3:20); the whole human race (Pss. 65:2; 145:21; Joel 2:28; Acts 2:17); racial or genealogical lineage (Rom. 1:3; 9:8); or the realm of ordinary historical existence and society (2 Cor. 10:1–3; Phil. 3:3ff.). Christ came 'in the flesh' (see Eph. 2:15; Col. 1:22; Heb. 5:7). It is obvious that being 'in the flesh' in this sense is not incompatible with being 'in the Lord' (see Gal. 2:20; Phm. 16).

But being *en sarki* can become incompatible with being a Christian. When one allows one's God-given form of earthly existence to govern thinking and conduct, the *sarx* becomes sinful. What is evil is not the flesh itself, but limiting oneself to it and trusting human resources and efforts apart from God (see Gal. 6:12–13; 2

Cor. 11:13; Phil. 3:3). (It is for this reason that relying on the Law* for one's salvation is as carnal as sensuality; see Gal. 3:3.)

This ethical dimension to *sarx* is distinctly (though not exclusively) Pauline and goes beyond OT conceptions. Paul speaks of it as living or walking 'according the flesh' (Rom. 8:4–9, 12–14) – *i.e.* orienting one's whole being around what is earthly, assuming that human life consists simply in the flesh, and maintaining a self-sufficiency apart from God. To do this is to accept the natural end of flesh – namely, dissolution and death (Rom. 8:13; Gal. 6:8).

The carnally minded person is not able to understand divine revelation, accurately assess the identity of Christ or carry on spiritual warfare (Jn. 3:6; 1 Cor. 2:14; 2 Cor. 5:16–17; 10:3–4). As flesh, humans are not able to inherit the kingdom of God (1 Cor. 15:50).

Paul further develops the ethical dimension of *sarx* by arguing that, when we orient our lives around *sarx*, it becomes a power (opposed to God's Spirit) that shapes us and enslaves us. Flesh (designating the whole person) becomes the willing instrument of sin, such that we disobey God in every area of our lives (as the list of 'works of the flesh' in Gal. 5:19–21 indicates). Only the power of God's Spirit is able to free us from servitude to the flesh. And even then the flesh continues to war against the Christian who has received God's Spirit (Rom. 7; 1 Pet. 2:11).

It is important to stress that Paul does not link flesh to sin on the basis of Gk. notions of the intrinsic and irremediably evil character of the material part of human existence, but only on the basis of a life-sustaining attitude of denial of the creature's relation to God.

The Christian is instructed not to walk according to the flesh, but to 'put on' Christ and the 'new self' (Rom. 13:14; Eph. 4:24; Col. 3:10, 12ff.). This does not mean denying our bodily existence. It requires a disposition that regards the flesh (in the ethical sense) as dead, having been crucified in believers who are now 'in the Spirit' (Rom. 6:11; Gal. 5:24). Again, this is still a physical (fleshly) existence, but one that now places ultimate confidence in Christ, not in self or earthly resources (Gal. 2:20). This is a powerful concept for us who are tempted to secure our lives through wealth, technology, good works, national power, and the like. Further, it requires the positive action of living according to the Spirit (Rom. 8:4; Gal. 5:16). This involves intentional behaviours – spiritual disciplines that allow God's grace to strengthen the flesh that is weak when the spirit is willing.

Bibliography

A. Hoekema, *Created in God's Image* (Exeter and Grand Rapids, 1986); G. E. Ladd, *A Theology of the New Testament* (Grand Rapids, 1974); J. A. T. Robinson, *The Body* (London and Chicago, 1952); D. Willard, *The Spirit of the Disciplines* (San Francisco, 1988); E. Schweizer *et al.*, *TDNT* 7, pp. 98–151.

D.L.O.

FLETCHER, JOSEPH (1905–91). Professor of Social Ethics at the Episcopal Theological School of Cambridge, Massachusetts, Joseph Fletcher created one of the most lively moral debates in American church circles in the 1960s and 70s with the publication of *Situation Ethics: The New Morality* (Philadelphia and London, 1966). Fletcher presented situationism (see Situation Ethics*) as an alternative to legalism* and antinomianism.*

The Christian situationist recognizes the love commandment as the only absolute moral principle and examines each situation carefully to determine what love requires then and there. Other moral rules are 'illuminators' indicating common wisdom about what usually results in the most loving consequences for all involved; unlike the principle of love (see ②), they have no universal significance, no absolute binding power.

Fletcher's moral theory is, thus, a form of act-utilitarianism, although Fletcher's version of utilitarianism (see Consequentialism*) is non-hedonistic (see Hedonism*). The situationist performs the action which will bring about the greatest good for all those involved. Fletcher, however, never clearly articulated what that good consists of and how it can be determined.

Joseph Fletcher's most lasting contribution to moral theology may be his early work in biomedical ethics rather than his popular *Situation Ethics* and its companion volume *Moral Responsibility: Situation Ethics at Work* (Philadelphia and London, 1967). His *Morals and Medicine* (Boston, MA, 1954) was groundbreaking as an attempt to apply moral theory to medical problems of contraception (see Birth Control*), sterilization* and euthanasia.* He continued his work in medical ethics with *The Ethics of Genetic Control* (Garden City,

NY, 1974) and ended his teaching career as a visiting lecturer in medical ethics at the University of Virginia.

See also: ETHICS OF MEDICAL CARE. [14]

T.D.K.

FOETUS, see ABORTION; AMNIOCENTESIS; EMBRYOLOGY; ETHICS OF MEDICAL CARE; [14] LIFE, HEALTH AND DEATH. [13]

FOLK RELIGION. Folk (implicit or popular) religion is a vague term, covering an unsystematic, non-organized, evolving collection of ideas and rituals more closely related to the experience of ordinary people in any culture* than the confessional statements of any institutional religion.

1. Aspects of folk religion

Rites of passage (baptisms, weddings, funerals) particularly focus any understanding of folk religion, because they reflect the human need for help in negotiating times of crisis. Folk religion is also about maintaining life as it is, hence for country people in Britain, annual festivals (Harvest, Remembrance, Christmas) are important, and even in cities church buildings symbolize continuity.

People derive important meaning from folk rituals and symbols. They learn ideas about God, fate, luck, merit and magic. Secularization* has not ended this religious 'search': many otherwise-secular Japanese turn to Shinto and Buddhism for births and deaths: the city of Liverpool wept and prayed after the Hillsborough football disaster; there is the recent growth in celebrating Hallowe'en.

P. G. Hiebert (1892–1987) uses an anthropological model to help understand the phenomena of folk religion, phenomena as diverse as seeking guidance for daily living, prayers for healing,* the practice of magic, and invocation of saints. He groups these phenomena in a middle zone (of 'human history'), bridging what in many Western cultures is a gap between an upper zone (of the God of truth, the creator and judge, the God of 'cosmic history') and the tangible world (of 'natural history') which we experience in daily life. He asserts that it is no wonder that folk or popular religion prospers when so much orthodox religion overlooks the presence of God in this middle zone of human experience.

2. Responses to folk religion

Folk religion must be taken with the utmost seriousness. John Habgood (1927–) likens it to the submerged part of an iceberg whose visible tip is represented by active church-goers. But, like natural theology, folk religion can be criticized for under-emphasizing grace* and revelation.* For example, an anthropological explanation of natural priesthood in folk religion is in conflict with a Christian theology of ministry. Some popular religious ideas are also pastorally dangerous, denying the reality of death,* or ignoring the needs of the poor (Mk. 10:17–31).

But accepting that religious rituals and symbols are often misunderstood, folk religion can be seen as the expression of a universal human need, the first stage in faith development.* In J. Westerhoff's terms, 'the faith of utter dependence' (the most elementary faith) can grow into 'adult owned faith' and full personal commitment. Such mature faith, arising out of a conversion of heart and mind, refuses to manipulate 'god', or make the satisfaction of human need (*e.g.* personal healing) central to religion, but recognizes God as Lord or cosmic, natural and human history.

3. Folk religion and evangelism

Apologetics, pastoral theology (see Practical and Pastoral Theology [7]) and popular religion alike are responses to human life *as it is*. H. Oppenheimer shows how folk religion (often strong on morality) remains undernourished and impoverished until surrounded by the grace of God – specifically until people have reason to be grateful to God the creator because of the cross* and resurrection* of Jesus Christ. Popular Christianity (the same is true in other religions) may bear little resemblance to orthodoxy, requiring discernment and continual christological reflection.

Growth into maturity of faith may be resisted particularly when such faith is focused on rites of passage. By definition, this religion is required only at times of crisis. The 'priest' is perceived as an unattainable ideal (a remote figure – like God), not as someone whose faith can be imitated. The symbols become 'ends' rather than signs to something greater. However, if aspects of life's continuity can be seen alongside these moments of crisis, and if our common humanity be recognized in the person of Christ, then the minister at a rite of passage may be both their helper and a bringer of good news.

To embrace and work with popular religion is demanding. If people in anger resist their world-view being challenged by something bigger it can be painful (as when penitence was expressed alongside thanksgiving at the service in London, following the end of war in the Falklands in 1982). But the pastor's call is to follow Christ's example and embrace people for God's sake with all their faults.

Bibliography

E. Bailey, *A Workbook of Popular Religion* (Dorchester, 1986); J. Bax, *The Good Wine* (London, 1986), ch. 3; C. Chapman, *Shadows of the Supernatural* (Oxford, 1990), pp. 142–147; D. Davies, 'Natural and Christian Priesthood in Folk Religiosity', *Anv* 2.1, 1985, pp. 43f.; C. Hart, 'Natural Priesthood, the Priesthood of All Believers and Parochial Ministry', *Anv* 6.3, 1989, pp. 243–250; P. G. Hiebert, 'Folk Religion in Andhra Pradesh', in V. Samuel and C. Sugden (eds.), *Evangelism and the Poor* (Oxford, 1982; Bangalore, 1983); M. Silversides, *Folk Religion: Friend or Foe?* (Bramcote, Nottingham, 1986); G. Smith, *Christianity in the Inner City: Some Sociological Issues* (Bromley, 1988), pp. 5–20; J. Williams, 'The Sociology of Religion and Contemporary Strategies for the Church', *Anv* 6.2, 1989, pp. 135–148.

G.O.S.

FOOD is a fundamental requisite for human life and, as might be expected, occupies an important role in the physical, social and commercial areas of human polity as well as in those areas that are explicitly religious. The biblical texts suggest four general principles which appear to have great relevance to present-day society and industry.

1. Food is a God-ordained provision for physical life

The supply of food, either directly, or indirectly as resources such as land,* which permits its production, is an expression of the goodness of God (Dt. 8:3, 7, 18; Ec. 2:24–26; 5:18–20). Both OT and NT illustrate God's concern for the physical needs of people: the divine insight and wisdom given to Joseph in handling the Middle Eastern famine (Gn. 41); provision for Israel's journey through the wilderness (Dt. 8:16); provision for individuals (1 Ki. 17:4; 18:4); and Christ himself both looked and acted with compassion towards the crowds of 4,000 and 5,000 men

(Mt. 15:29–39; 14:13–21). What is true for nations and individuals is also relevant for families and their children. However, humankind is not simply a beneficiary but also a steward (see Stewardship*) and tenant in God's creation (Gn. 1:26–28; Lv. 25:23), and we are under an obligation to use these resources wisely to provide for our continuing existence. We must not squander or destroy them, but rather ensure that every person receives a share in God's provision for humankind's basic bodily needs (Gn. 2:16; 3:2; Lv. 19:9–10; Dt. 24:19–22; Mt. 6:25–32; 1 Tim. 6:8).

2. Food should be safe, nutritious and palatable

The hazards of unpalatable or poisonous food are mentioned on several occasions in Scripture (Ex. 15:25; 2 Ki. 2:19–22; 4:39–41), illustrating how individuals and, implicitly, organizations are responsible for ensuring that their activities, their property and their products are not harmful to other members of their community (Ex. 21:28–36; 22:6). In contemporary terms, it is evident that the whole area of misinformation and misrepresentation is immensely important to both the food industry and the consumer.

For example, despite the view held by many in the Western world that the food industry is lax in attending to the safety of food products, the opposite is now largely the case. The activities of unscrupulous operators were notorious in the 19th century. Legal action to contain their activities commenced with the Sale of Food and Drugs Act in 1875 in the UK, and has been followed by further legislation culminating in the Food Act of 1990 which requires a manufacturer to exercise all due diligence to ensure the hygienic quality of a food product. The major food companies do pay close attention to such issues and, in practice, the most common reasons for food poisoning are inadequate understanding and control of the raw materials and processing procedures by small catering operations.

The two general statements identified above in fact represent the *principal driving forces* in the food industry:

a. The need to operate efficiently and profitably. That such an endeavour has had success and is beneficial to the consumer is seen in the fact that only 3%–4% of the working population in developed economies are involved in food production, whereas the major proportion of the population in developing countries is obliged to contribute to growing its own food. However, the majority of the staple food items which are produced with high efficiency in the Western world are sold with very low profit margins. There is therefore a tendency, even temptation, for the food companies to promote other products of relatively low raw-material cost and nutritional value (*e.g.* snack foods), which have a much higher profit margin. Undoubtedly such materials have an attraction because of their value in a social context, but their purchase is further stimulated by advertising. Other pressures, including convenience and cost, contrive to move such items in the diet from being peripheral, which is perfectly reasonable, to a more central role, especially in children's diet, which is not desirable.

b. The awareness that food should be nutritious. Companies are increasingly conscious of the need to provide foods of an appropriate nutritional plane. Consumer groups provide a valuable check for any companies where commercial considerations and pressurized selling outweigh nutritional issues. The 'baby-food story' is an example where initial good intentions by the industry led for a period to damaging results through the persistent pursuit of aggressive marketing strategies (A. Chetley, *The Baby Killer Scandal*). However, consumer demand may lead companies to manufacture products of whose nutritional value they are not wholly convinced, *e.g.* high-sugar cereals. Similarly, consumer demand for wheat bread in some tropical countries, where it is difficult to grow that cereal, has had deleterious social effects. Local cereals frequently are perfectly satisfactory nutritionally, but do not produce a product with the same cultural appeal. This unreasoned demand for wheat has, in practice, prompted local farmers to attempt to grow the crop. Subsequent failure led to bankruptcy, and the ensuing local famine resulted in the migration of rural families to the cities.

c. The requirement that foods should be non-toxic. In part, the sensitivity and publicity surrounding food quality and safety are a consequence of increased technology* and knowledge but limited understanding. For example, in the minds of the general public, 'natural' food is 'safe' food, but there is little awareness of naturally occurring toxicants, *e.g.* mycotoxins, cyanogens, protease inhibitors, lathyrogens, glucosinolates and alkaloids. Great efforts have been made by the food industry and its associated institutions to detect and eliminate these from food raw materials and to protect consumers from their harmful effects. Great effort has also been made to remove any additions or colorants with even a suspicion of toxicity. It is ironic that the new analytical methods and the exhaustive toxicological testing which have permitted the detection and evaluation of these materials have provided press and individuals, who are thirsty for defamatory detail, with the arguments and publicity weapons to vilify the food industry. Premature statements and judgments which are ultimately shown to be wrong can be extremely damaging to the perplexed consumer, as well as to the companies and public organizations who advise and legislate on diet/health issues.

3. Food has a social significance

In addition to satisfying hunger and providing for the needs of the body, it is acknowledged in the Bible that food brings pleasure to the consumer and is an important component of family and social activities. As is still sometimes the case today, a meal is an opportunity for people to gather together and converse, to interact in a relaxed fashion and to preserve, if not enhance, family cohesion. A welcome to a meal may be a sign of forgiveness (Gn. 26:30; 31:54; 43:31) or of esteem (Gn. 18:6–8). In the recent past, festive occasions were signalled in a very positive manner by the food that was served. The situation is now changing, in that the advent of mass-produced and/or fabricated food, which is 'convenient' when eaten at home or 'fast' when consumed in the dinette, is being accompanied by an increased tendency to eat casually. The decline of formal meals and the collapse of the social groups which used to eat together mean that food habits are becoming increasingly structureless, individualistic and anonymous (L. Gofton, 'The Rules of the Table'). The biblical injunctions concerning care of the poor and hungry are as pertinent now as in the time they were written.

4. Food can have a spiritual significance

It is not surprising that such an important and basic element in human life should be invested with religious symbolism and significance. In the OT, the food laws, *e.g.* in Lv. 11, describe those animals which may be eaten while others are proscribed. There is good reason to believe that their purpose was not so much based on considerations of hygiene but as a reminder to Israel of their special calling to holiness and a distinctive role in God's purposes (see G. J. Wenham, *The Book of Leviticus*). Within the NT, Jesus declared 'all foods clean' (Mk. 7:17–19). Within the early church this was reinforced by the vision given to Peter (Acts 10:11–16, 28) which was subsequently debated at the Council of Jerusalem. In the epistles, the use of food is referred to in a number of passages and Christians are advised to abstain from certain foods, not because they are 'unclean' (*cf.* 1 Cor. 10:26) but out of a principle of love which purposes to give no offence to a weaker brother and cause him to stumble. Food is not to be a cause for gluttony or excess (Pr. 23:2; 1 Pet. 4:3), selfishness or argument (1 Cor. 11:19–22), but rather its significance in the physical realm is accentuated by Christ describing himself in his ministry as the bread of life and even as flesh upon which the inner, spiritual man feeds (Jn. 6:35, 55). It is very significant that what Jesus asked his disciples to 'do . . . in remembrance' of him (Lk. 22:19) was to eat bread and drink wine – a sacramental action in almost all the Christian churches. It is fitting, then, that when we eat we should give thanks, not only for the food itself but also for Christ, of whom it is a reminder, and for the beneficent provision of our heavenly Father (Jn. 6:11; Acts 27:35; Eph. 5:20).

See also: VEGETARIANISM.

Bibliography
A. Chetley, *The Baby Killer Scandal* (London, 1979); L. Gofton, 'The Rules of the Table: Sociological Factors Influencing Food Choice', in C. Ritson *et al.*, The Food Consumer (Chichester and New York, 1986), pp. 127–153; G. J. Wenham, *The Book of Leviticus* (Grand Rapids, 1979).

J.M.V.B.

FORCE is the use of physical constraint to prevent someone from doing something, or to make them do something. Coercion, a wider term, includes force or the threat of force, and other actions or threats such as strikes,* lock-outs, economic sanctions* or boycotts.* This article will centre on the ethics of force as the prismatic case of coercion. It should be noted that some contemporary theologians (*e.g.* Juan Luís Segundo, 1925–) have maintained that all kinds of coercion should be thought of as violence,* a claim which, however, blurs important distinctions.

There are occasions on which force may and should be used, and occasions on which it certainly should not be. As an example of the former, we might think of a parent controlling a young child on a busy road; of the latter the tyrannical use of military strength by one country to overthrow and subjugate another. The range in between will include teaching, caring for the mentally handicapped or ill, policing and law enforcement, criminal punishment, peace-keeping and war-fighting. In all these tasks, and others, there will be proper and improper uses of force.

At least two major strands in the NT must be considered. One is exemplified by the saying of Jesus, 'Do not resist an evil person' (Mt. 5:39); the other by Paul's claim, 'The authorities that exist have been established by God . . . if you do wrong, be afraid, for he [*i.e.* the one in authority] does not bear the sword for nothing' (Rom. 13:1, 4). The former means, at the very least, that there have to be strong reasons for the Christian to use force rather than suffer it; the latter that the governing authorities work under God's hand for the social good. Both these strands are important and their implications must be followed through. The words of Jesus teach us that there is no absolute right of self-defence in the gospel, which rather demands that we should be ready on our own account to suffer at the hands of evil-doers. But this does not mean that we should stand by and see others suffer. The Christian may be called to play a part in maintaining social order as part of his or her service to the neighbour. In this way it can be understood how force may be employed in the service of others, for their protection. On this basis self-defence can also be justified in order to be able to protect others. The use of force can be a service of love (see [2]) and a witness to God's justice (see Justice and Peace[3]).

Love demands that force should be used only to meet the needs of others. For instance, policing includes protecting people for their own safety (traffic control, crowd control) and protecting society from the criminal plans of those who would endanger life and property* for their own gain. In addition, love and justice also demand that the claims of every individual person affected by the use of force should be respected. Force should be used directly only to prevent oppression by force, and proportionately (see Proportion*) to the oppressive force. Physical force must be used discriminately against those who themselves present or threaten physical danger to themselves or others. Love cannot will that third parties should be coerced and hurt, however great the good that is aimed at or the wrong to be prevented. For instance, a teacher cannot justly punish the best friend of a pupil who does wrong, whether or not such a punishment is effective in preventing and deterring the wrong.

The use of force, in other words, should be rightly motivated and subject to the control of moral reason. The meaning of moral reason in this connection has been most fully explored in examination of the morality of war* (and see Just-War Theory*). The moral limits on the use of force are determined precisely by the arguments which first justified that use of force. Since love and justice demand that force be only used to protect the weak, it can never be used directly to oppress others who are weak. This consideration gives rise to the principle of discrimination, which forbids the use of force directly against non-combatants in time of war. Analogous limits can and should be derived for other forms of coercion. Another moral limit is learned from the point that it is only the achievement of certain ends (the maintenance of justice, of law, of social order, etc.) that can justify the use of force. This means that any use of force must be proportionate to the ends to be achieved. More good than evil should be done; and if, in the nature of things, this cannot be assured, then the balance must be carefully and prudently weighed. This requirement rules out all use of 'violence', if violence is understood as 'the use of force which is not subject to the control of reason'. It also includes the point that minimum force should always be employed. This may mean that a particular injustice cannot be put right because the only means available are means which morally are simply too costly. Their use would do more harm than allowing the injustice to continue.

The scale on which force is used is not of itself the determining factor in deciding the moral question. For instance, some would claim that only non-lethal force may ever rightly be used. They would argue from the prohibition on killing* that no purpose can justify the taking of human life. Others would claim that other boundary lines should be drawn on the scale of force which can rightly be used, e.g. the size or kind of weapons to be employed. However, arguments based on the proportionate use of force could draw this kind of boundary relative only to particular circumstances. There are, for instance, occasions when life may be taken in order to save or protect other lives. By the same token, of course, life may not be taken simply to prevent theft; the police are not justified in killing a bank robber unless he directly threatens other lives, and then only when there is no other way to stop him.

The principle of discrimination is of cardinal importance in our day. The second half of the 20th century has seen the development or growth of various methods which attempt to achieve their ends by threatening or harming third parties. One thinks of nuclear weapons and deterrence,* terrorism,* and general strikes, to name but three. All these kinds of coercion, and others, work chiefly by acting on the wills of populations at large, placing the general public under some kind of duress.* Even if such means appear to be successful in gaining their ends, love and justice would place large moral questions against them. Those directly affected are people who are innocent of the political struggle; and such people, whether whole populations or not, are being made means by whom others try to get at the wills of the rulers, etc. To use people as means in this kind of way can never be loving or just, for it ultimately denies them the respect which they deserve as human beings. It can only be suggested here that this consideration might make us a little more cautious about the current enthusiasm for sanctions as a political weapon against an unjust regime. For sanctions are often likely to operate more against the poor than against the wealthy or the enforcers of such a regime.

Bibliography

J. Ellul, *Violence: Reflections from a Christian Perspective* (ET, New York, 1969; London, 1970); O. Guinness, *Violence: A Study of Contemporary Attitudes* (Downers Grove, IL, 1974); P. Ramsey, *War and the Christian Conscience* (Durham, NC, 1961); M. Walzer, *Just and Unjust Wars* (New York, 1977; Harmondsworth, 1980).

D.J.E.A.

FORGERY is the fraudulent creation or alteration of a document, or the fabrication of an article (such as a painting designed to be attributed to an old master), with the intent to deceive and misrepresent. Frequently it takes the form of signing another's name for the purpose of stealing. Forgery, of the type described here, is a blatant violation of the commandment not to steal (Ex. 20:15) and amounts to bearing false witness (Ex. 20:16). As well as the temptation to forge in order to steal for personal gain, there are other circumstances and conditions which probably offer a greater temptation to otherwise mature citizens.

Most people who become embroiled in forgery generally discover, in retrospect, that their journey into the problem took place over an extended period of time, and was paved with good intentions. The good intentions normally serve to cover and justify the inappropriate rationalizations that undergird the wrong behaviour. The chosen behaviour is frequently embraced at the start as harmless, or as a once-only event, or as a means to avoid an unnecessarily embarrassing problem, or as a reasonable approach to a temporary need. Furthermore, forgery is typically undertaken in an effort to deal with yet another and more basic problem.

To illustrate, a man has been experiencing considerable difficulty in his business over an extended period of time, and this has generated a lot of financial pressure for him. The local bank has been willing to extend some small unsecured bridging loans to help out in the short run. The passage of time, however, finds the bank officers becoming concerned, and they begin demanding that some collateral be put up to secure the loan and protect their depositors. At this juncture, the owner stalls for more time, but the business climate is not helping and the pressure is mounting. The bank finally demands that specific security be offered as collateral or it will begin court proceedings to recover the loan through the sale of general assets. The banker and the owner finally agree that the only solid asset in the man's net worth is his and his wife's equity in their home. The suggestion is therefore made that the owner secure his wife's signature, authorizing the establishment of a new mortgage on their home that will serve as collateral for the business loan. At this point the owner rationally acknowledges to himself that this is the correct line of action to take. Emotionally, however, he encounters a different set of realities. He is too embarrassed to share with his wife that things have come to this low point, and he fears that this will place a heavy emotional burden on a basically nervous wife.

What should he do? Should he tell his wife? Should he forgo making the new mortgage and let the bank take him to court? In fact, he signed his wife's name to the document and proceeded on as usual, telling himself that it would all be repaid in six months and that everything would be all right. He forged his wife's signature.

Actions of this type are taken daily by people who otherwise would never think of themselves as forgers. Most acts of forgery are related not to intended thefts but to rationalized, self-serving false justifications.

See also: FRAUD.

R.C.C.

FORGIVENESS is the mutual recognition that repentance* of either or both parties is genuine and that right relationships have been restored or achieved. The three requirements for forgiveness are: the restoration of an attitude of love (see 2), since wrongdoing is not a valid reason for not loving the wrongdoer; the working through of pain, anger* and alienation* until both parties perceive that the repentance process is mutually satisfactory; and the opening of the future to appropriate relating, with trust* and good faith which permits risk, spontaneity and the possibility of further failure or conflict.

All forgiveness, whether human or divine, proceeds in similar process. God has done all in Christ (see Justification, Doctrine of*) to move towards us in our brokenness, and he invites our repentant response. God's gracious love is unconditional, but the consequent forgiveness is conditional. It requires the repentant response which receives love, reappropriates relationship, and experiences reconciliation.*

Human forgiveness also is grounded in a non-conditional love, but it requires the working through of those conditions for constructive relating that are requisite to authentic reconciliation. The restoring of an attitude of love is a prerequisite to the forgiveness process. It is not in itself forgiveness, though love is a forgiving attitude which reaches towards restoration. Wrongdoing is not a valid reason for not loving another. Enemy-love is the nature of God and of God's children, and thus motivates a willingness to forgive and to work at the forgiveness process until authentic reconciliation is possible. Human love, though rarely if ever unconditional, can be enabled by divine grace* to love with as few conditions as possible, and to extend forgiveness against any injury.

See also: SIN AND SALVATION. ⑤

Bibliography
D. Augsburger, *Caring Enough to Forgive* (Ventura, CA, 1981); J. Patton, *Is Human Forgiveness Possible?* (Philadelphia, 1985); L. Smedes, *Forgive and Forget* (San Francisco, 1984).

D.W.A.

FORNICATION refers to sexual intercourse between unmarried persons. In the NT, the word commonly translated 'fornication' in the AV (*porneia*) is an umbrella term for extra-marital sex of all kinds, which NIV translates as 'sexual immorality' (*e.g.* Acts 15:20; 1 Cor. 6:13).

Christian ethicists agree that fornication is wrong, but there are important differences of interpretation. Many, taking their cue from a broad understanding of *porneia*, take the NT's ban on fornication to imply a total condemnation of all extra-marital intercourse.

Others, treating the term more narrowly as a synonym for promiscuity, believe the ethical veto does not extend to intercourse between committed but officially unmarried couples (see Cohabitation*) who are in a relationship of deep troth. Fornication (in the sense of promiscuous behaviour) is wrong, they argue, because it takes intercourse out of the contexts of personhood, love, sharing and commitment. Such behaviour, even if mutually welcomed, is exploitative because its primary goal is not the giving and sharing of self, but the gratifying of sexual desire.

J.H.O.

FOSTERING is the care and nurture, within a family, of persons who are not members of that family by birth. Definitions of fostering include, without exception, the tasks of rearing and encouragement by those who are not natural parents. It is essentially a fixed-term arrangement not characterized by permanence, which is the primary feature of 'adoption'.*

Fostering has become increasingly popular in the 20th century. Persons fostered include: young children, whose birth parents cannot for a period of time meet their needs; older people, whose families are unable to give them the level off support they require; and other individuals, who need a substitute family for a certain period in their lives. Such people may include those with physical disability or learning difficulties, those suffering psychiatric illness, young single mothers (see Single Parents*) needing family experience and support in learning to parent their babies, and young people without adequate housing or family support (see Homelessness*).

For young children who cannot remain within their own families, fostering has for many years been the preferred method of caring, particularly since the Children Act of 1948. The Curtis committee considered that, second to adoption, fostering is the best way of providing children with the experience of family life and personal care. Many would regard the provision of substitute parents as a basic human right of children who cannot be brought up within their own families. It can offer greater consistency and normality than care within a residential home.

For children, therefore, fostering may be arranged on two different bases:

1. *Private fostering*. This is an informal arrangement made by the child's parent(s) with another person. The child's parents take full responsibility for the placement and the agreed payment for the service. Private foster-parents have to be registered, and have to allow access to their homes for Health and Social Services personnel but are not selected by these officials. Private foster homes are often used by natural parents who wish to undertake further education courses, or whose demands in employment mean that they cannot fulfil their parental obligations for a period.

2. *Statutory provision*. The majority of foster homes in Britain are provided through a local-authority Social Services department or voluntary social-work agency working on behalf of such a body. The children who require fostering are normally 'placed in the care of' or 'looked after' or 'accommodated by' the authority. This responsibility is given to the authority either by the Courts or by a voluntary agreement between the parents and the Social Services department. The local authority then takes responsibility for 'fostering' the child with approved foster-parents. Social workers select, train and approve people who volunteer their services and who are considered suitable to take on the task of becoming foster-parents.

The demands of parenting* are always considered. Fostering and hence parenting other people's children require particular characteristics and commitment on the part of the caregivers. The majority of the children, young people and others for whom fostering is sought have special needs. Many have experienced breakdown, disruption and loss in their lives. Hence in their foster-families they need even more care, love, security and stability than others, and may make heavy demands on the families with whom they are placed. Although professional support and training are available to foster-carers, the quality of their own relationships in marriage and their family life patterns is crucial in providing 'good enough' parenting in the face of difficult and even hostile behaviour of children who are not their own.

When children are placed in foster homes there is usually an expectation that the arrangement will not be long term. The British law rightly requires that every possible effort be made to return children to their own families. Exceptions to this will include those who have been seriously abused (see Abuse*) by their own parents, those whose natural parents are not considered, on the basis of their proven lifestyles and past performance as parents, to be able to care adequately, and those who do not wish to resume caring for their children. Fostering therefore often includes contact with the child's natural parents and family. If plans for the child include rehabilitation with the birth parents, such contact will be regular and will increase as the return to their own families is achieved.

At the end of the 20th century, the formal requirements of fostering are necessary in order to protect those who need the nurture and security which substitute family care should provide. Such is the nature of our society that, even with stringent procedures required by legislation, the system is never without its failures, as human beings are tempted to take advantage of responsibilities entrusted to them. However, it does seem important to recognize that in God's pattern for meeting our emotional, physical and spiritual needs, the value of nurture within a family is clear.

L.E.A.G.

FOWLER, JAMES, see FAITH DEVELOPMENT; TRUST

F**RANCIS OF ASSISI** (1182–1226), founder of the Franciscan order, one of the two major mendicant movements of the 13th century. Born of a wealthy Italian mer-chant and a French mother, Francis received the typical education of his time. As a young man he participated in the local fighting between Assisi and neighbouring towns and was captured and imprisoned. In his early twenties he had a series of visions and dreams that resulted in his conversion.* He severed his relations with his father, renounced his possessions, and began to rebuild churches. In 1209 when at mass he heard Mt. 10:5–14, the instructions of Jesus to his disciples, and he took them as the guide for his life.

Soon others joined him. In 1210 Francis and his small band of followers gained papal approval of their life and mission. The original rule is lost, but it seems to have contained rules for their common life and the observance of the vows of poverty, chastity* and obedience.* The small band had a powerful influence, resulting in both a revival of piety and increased missionary activity. Francis himself travelled to Egypt during the Fifth Crusade and tried in vain to convert the sultan.

By 1217 his followers had become an order whose members were found in several countries of Europe. In 1221, 3,000 friars attended the chapter meeting in Assisi. Increasingly the organization of the order was left to others and Francis devoted himself to prayer and meditation. In 1224 he received the stigmata. He was blind and ill during the last years of his life. Two years after his death he was canonized.

The spirituality* that Francis taught is characterized by a focus on Christ, especially on imitating his words and deeds. Christ is encountered here and now in meeting the needs of others. God is present in all his creatures, and so all created things are to be revered. His spiritual ideal is still a model for today as is evidenced by the many books on his life and work.

Bibliography
J. H. Smith, *Francis of Assisi* (New York, 1972).

A.G.V.

F**RANKL, VIKTOR** (1905–). Frankl's *Man's Search For Meaning* was based on his own experiences of suffering and working with others, as a prisoner in Auschwitz and Dachau in the Second World War.

A Viennese psychiatrist influenced by Søren Kierkegaard,* Martin Heidegger (1889–1976), Karl Jaspers (1883–1969), and Edmund Husserl (1859–1938), Frankl developed an existential analysis of the human person, critical of mainstream psychoanalytic theories, focused on the three dimensions of the somatic, psychic and spiritual. The therapy derived from this approach he called 'logotherapy', which attempted to extend the scope of psychotherapy beyond the psyche, to include 'the spiritual', 'the meaning'. Where psychoanalysis* speaks of the *pleasure principle*, and individual psychology of the *will-to-power*, Frankl is concerned with 'that which most deeply inspires man', 'the innate desire to give as much meaning as possible to one's life, to actualize as many values as possible – what I should like to call the *will-to-meaning*' (*The Doctor and the Soul*, p. x).

Frankl's reflections on his prison experiences correspond with Friedrich Nietzsche's* dictum 'He who has a *why* to live for can bear with almost any *how*.' The way a person accepts suffering gives opportunity to add deeper meaning to life. The striving to find such a meaning is the primary motivational force in human beings. But Frankl sets this in a context of moral objectivity. The meaning of our existence is not invented but detected. Values do not push us, but rather pull us. Always there is freedom of choice; what all human beings need is a striving and struggling towards some goal of which they are worthy. What matters is not the meaning of life in general, but the specific meaning of a person's life at a given moment. Rather than speaking as Abraham Maslow* does of 'self-actualization', therefore, Frankl speaks of human existence being basically 'self-transcendence'. We find fulfilment through reaching out beyond ourselves. We can discover a meaning in life by giving something to life, *e.g.* in creative work, or by experiencing some value in nature or culture, and especially by suffering, the stand one takes towards what cannot be changed. Logotherapy functions as an educative approach to discovering the transcendent, the spiritual domain of human beings, their freedom of will, and their responsibility. It recognizes the value of the tension between what we have achieved and what we still should become, and seeks to help us towards that.

Frankl thus offers an interpretation of the human condition which avoids the pessimism of Sigmund Freud* and the inflated self-absorption of some humanistic psychologies. He points out that it is human beings who invented the gas chambers of Auschwitz; but that it is also human beings who have entered those gas chambers upright, with the Lord's Prayer or the Shema Yisrael on their lips.

Frankl understands the question of God's existence in terms of his existential analysis of Ultimate Meaning. There is in all authentic human life a basic religiousness, though this is often repressed or denied. Logotherapy can itself lead to religion, just as true religion may itself be logotherapeutic – *i.e.* it can help people towards meaning in their lives.

Bibliography

The Doctor and the Soul (New York, ²1965); *Man's Search For Meaning* (London and Boston, MA, ²1962).

J. J. Shea, 'On the Place of Religion in the Thought of Viktor Frankl', in J. R. Fleck and J. D. Carter (eds.), *Psychology and Christianity* (Nashville, TN, 1981).

D.J.A.

FRAUD may be defined as 'the perpetration of intentional falsehood in order to gain something from another'. Fraud is, thus, more than 'negligence' in that it involves positive, intentional deception. Fraudulent deception may be attempted through intentional omission or concealment of information, innuendo, gesture and the like, as well as through overtly false communication.

Fraud is thus a subset of the larger category of the lie (see Truth*), which could be defined as any intentional communication of a falsehood. It is a lie utilized to gain something from another or to induce someone to surrender a legal right. It is lying as a deliberate strategy to enrich oneself at the expense of one whose confidence has first been gained. Fraud is also a subset of the larger category of theft.* It is theft not by deeds or stealth but by means of untruthful communication. It is criminal deception, using false representations to get an unjust advantage or injure the rights or interests of another. Fraud is cheating or dishonestly tricking people out of their rights or their goods.

The term 'fraud' may be applied to a person who is an imposter, unqualified to provide a specialized service being offered. Most often, fraud refers to business and legal affairs (*e.g.* tax fraud, insurance fraud) because it has to do with goods, services and rights. The sale of merchandise or services that fall short of reasonable expectation and the promise of the vendor might be fraud. Deceptive advertising,* a misleading lure or bait held out to consumers, might also be fraud.

Fraud is motivated by a desire to obtain

something more easily and quickly than would be the case if the truth of the matter were known to all parties. The root of fraud is some combination of need and greed. Impatience or perceived urgency often plays a role in motivating fraud. In a highly competitive market environment, sales and advertising personnel may be led to provide an imbalanced if not fraudulent depiction of their goods or services.

Fraud must be prohibited or an unregulated predatory ('let the buyer beware') combat will rule, undermining all possibility of a peaceful or just society. Fraud is a challenging enough social problem where there is a face-to-face encounter of seller and buyer. The size, speed, complexity and impersonal nature of the modern economy make regulation slow, inconsistent and difficult. Thus, the integrity of the participants (individual and corporate), not just the existence of laws and agencies of enforcement, will determine the extent to which fraud is a problem in society.

The Bible condemns all forms of theft and dishonesty. Fraud, theft by means of dishonesty, is specifically prohibited in many texts (*e.g.* Lv. 6:1–5; Dt. 25:15–16; Pr. 11:1). The prophets, too, criticized fraud (Je. 5:26–28; Am. 8:5–6).

In an interesting Gospel episode, Jesus says to the rich young man, 'You know the commandments,' quotes the fifth, sixth, seventh, eighth and ninth commandments, and adds 'Do not defraud' to the list (Mk. 10:19)!

Jesus' linking of lies with the devil (Jn. 8:44–47), his emphasis on speaking and living the truth, his general concern for the poor and for freedom from the grip of 'Mammon', for living lives of simplicity, integrity and love of neighbour, rule out all possibility of fraud. So, too, Paul writes that 'thieves . . . the greedy . . . swindlers' do not inherit the kingdom of God (1 Cor. 5:11; 6:10). Christians are to put off falsehood and stealing, instead speaking the truth in love and giving to those in need (Eph. 4:25, 28). They are also to pay prompt and fair wages to their hired labourers (Jas. 5:4). Ananias and Sapphira's sudden deaths could be seen as an indication of the seriousness of fraud, in this case failure to live up to a financial promise to God (Acts 5:1–11).

A promising counterpoint to this canon-wide denunciation of fraud is the example of Jacob, his mother Rebekah and his wife Rachel. God chooses Jacob to become Israel, despite his fraud in deceiving his brother Esau, his father Isaac, and his father-in-law Laban (Gn. 27; 30; 31). Even a fraud can be chosen and transformed by God.

Fraud is not just illegal and criminal. 1. It is immoral and sinful, and it is wrong most of all because it is an offence against the God of truth, honesty and justice. 2. Fraud harms one's neighbour, directly as theft from him or her, indirectly in undermining the fabric of trust* in human relations and in setting a bad example, especially for children and the weak. 3. Fraud harms the self:* its integrity (the conflict between my action and what I know to be the truth), its dignity (stooping to such a low level), its freedom (it takes effort to cover up my fraud), and its relational health (fraud alienates me from God and my neighbours).

Christians might respond on four fronts to fraud in society. 1. It is important to formulate and enforce laws and rules setting civil, criminal and ecclesiastical boundaries to prevent fraud as much as possible. 2. People in church and society need better education regarding the multiple consequences of fraud and deceit, not only in socio-economic terms but in relation to the life with God. 3. Christians might address the fundamental problem of motivation, of the purpose of one's life and of one's business enterprise. Through evangelism and education, Christians might propose alternative and better life goals and corporate goals, other than the all-consuming desire to make a profit, and thus undermine the basic motivation of most fraud. 4. Christians might devote much more energy and thought to the positive articulation of honest business practice. Rather than becoming society's specialists in saying 'No' to fraud, Christians might specialize in saying 'Yes' to the creative and redemptive, entrepreneurial potential of truth, love and fidelity in economic life.

See also: ECONOMIC ETHICS;[17] FORGERY.

D.W.G.

FREEDOM is a complex concept, having metaphysical (see Free Will and Determinism*) and moral as well as political aspects. Beside the question whether a person's actions can be free from causal determination (and the consequences if they cannot) is the question whether, free from such determination or not, they are free in the sense that they are in accord with that person's true nature. In this sense it is possible to think of rational or moral freedom; the opposite of such freedom is not causal determination but irrationality or sinful action. In addition there is the further question whether freedom in that or in any other sense is sufficient for the ascription of moral responsibility* for actions.

Where freedom concerns human political or social relations, it may be thought of in negative or in positive terms: it is freedom *from* or freedom *to*. Understood negatively, the free person is one who is free from external impediment, free to do what he or she wants to do unconstrained by pathological compulsions or by other people or authorities. Laws against censorship* and in favour of toleration often rely upon freedom in this sense. This is the freedom of the political liberal or libertarian, and it is also one of the significant senses of freedom that is compatible with determinism. Freedom is held by many to be a human right; for others it is not meaningful to speak of freedom (in the abstract) as a right, only of particular freedoms enshrined in common or statute law.

But freedom (or freedoms), even if granted, do not ensure that a free person is free in the further sense that what he or she does is in accord with his or her true nature. For what that person wants to do may be immoral or misguided. Only in libertarianism, and in certain versions of existentialism, is such freedom exalted to the position of the supreme value. In such systems the fact of free decision is all-important for the maintaining of human authenticity.

While a contrast between a person's real nature, and what he or she in practice values, is an obvious one, the contrast itself is not free of difficulties. It carries with it the danger that someone other than the agent will claim to know what is best for that person. This has not only paternalistic but even, in a political context, totalitarian implications. For it may be held by those in commercial influence or political power, for example, that a person is truly free only when he or she buys a particular product, or subjects himself or herself to a particular political authority.

No metaphysical view of freedom should be adopted by the Christian which is at odds with the divine decree of whatever comes to pass, with the divine providential rule of the creation. Yet in Scripture, and particularly in the NT, greater prominence is given to freedom as a moral idea than to the metaphysical issues of freedom and determinism that have pre-occupied modern philosophers and theologians.

Two freedom-themes are given great prominence in the NT: the fact that Christ makes his people free, and the fact that freedom is not lawlessness but results in conformity to the moral law.*

As Scripture portrays the 'natural man', he is in bondage to sin, not a physical bondage but a way of thinking and acting that a person cannot, by his own powers, redirect ethically. He does not want to please God. Although actions may publicly conform to the moral law (Luther's 'civic righteousness'), this is as a result of various pressures and habits, not as a result of correct motivation, the love for God and desire for his glory. Outward conformity does not ensure inward conformity, and mere outward conformity is a sign of ethical bondage.

Christ frees, not by releasing such a person from his (or her) obligations* and by allowing him to do whatever he wishes, or by introducing randomness or indeterminism into human choices, but by providing, in conversion,* the motive and the inward strength of will to keep the commands of God. This is freedom, though it is not perfect or total freedom, since the one who is freed still also acts out of weakness and incorrect motives. Hence the Pauline struggle between 'flesh' and 'spirit', which is not a struggle between the body and the soul but between what a person is and what that person, in Christ, wants to be. This is the condition Augustine* characterized as *posse non peccare* ('able not to sin'), not *non posse peccare* ('not able to sin').

Augustine's phrases are significant. The freedom relates to sin, and since sin, in Scripture, is conceptually related to the law of God, the freedom in question is not freedom from the law or even freedom to keep it, but it is the freedom that comes from keeping it.

In the 18th century Immanuel Kant* provided a secularized version of this Christian teaching, according to which the free man is the moral man is the rational man, since freedom comes, for Kant, in the keeping of the moral law. This is a secularized version, because the law in question is not the divine law, but one which the human rational agent himself creates and endorses. None the less Kant's abstract conceptualizing preserves the formal linkage between freedom, morality and rationality that is to be found in the pages of the NT.

Ever since the apostle Paul raised the question 'Shall we continue in sin that grace may abound?' (Rom. 6:1, AV), the charge has been repeatedly levelled against the Christian doctrine of freedom that it implies, or at least permits, antinomianism* or libertinism. But this is not so, not only for the reasons already given but for the more central and compelling reason that as a Christian a person has died to sin and is united to Christ. So how could one who is united to Christ live a course of life that is completely contrary to the moral character of Christ and a total repudiation of his work as redeemer? How could a believer do those things the pardon of which required the offering up of his or her Saviour? The fact that individuals, either in real life or in fiction (as in James Hogg, *The Private Memoirs and Confessions of a Justified Sinner*, 1824), abuse the doctrine of grace* is not an argument against it.

Bibliography

H. G. Frankfurt, *The Importance of What we Care About* (Cambridge, 1988); A. J. P. Kenny, *Will, Freedom and Power* (Oxford, 1976); M. Luther, *The Bondage of the Will* (ET, London, 1957).

P.H.

FREE WILL AND DETERMINISM.

The positions on the nature of the human choice fall into three basic categories: determinism, indeterminism and self-determinism. In terms of their cause these fall, respectively, into actions caused by another, uncaused, or self-caused.

1. Determinism

Some believe that human choices are determined (or caused) by another. Proponents of this view believe that human choices are the result of antecedent causes, which in turn were caused by prior causes, and so on.

Naturalistic proponents of this position include B. F. Skinner,* who holds that all human behaviour is determined by genetic and behavioural factors. On this view, humans are like a brush in the hands of an artist. They are not the cause originating the action but simply the instrument through which it is expressed.

The philosophical argument in favour of determinism takes this form. All human behaviour is either uncaused, self-caused or caused by something else. However, human behaviour cannot be uncaused, since nothing occurs without a cause. Further, human actions cannot be self-caused, for no act can cause itself. To do so, it would have to be prior to itself, which is impossible. The only remaining alternative, then, is that all human behaviour is caused by something external to it.

In response, *opponents* make several points:

a. It is a misinterpretation of self-determinism to assert that actions cause themselves. For example, self-determinists do not believe that actions cause actions but that 'actors' cause actions. Self-determinism does not mean that one is determining oneself. Rather, the self (free agent) is causing its own free actions. In other words, 'self-caused' does not mean the cause of one's self but causing by oneself.

b. Determinism is self-defeating. A determinist insists that both determinists and non-determinists are determined to believe what they believe. However, determinists believe self-determinists are wrong and ought to change their view. But 'ought to change' implies they are free to change, which is contrary to determinism.

c. Other opponents (*e.g.* C. S. Lewis*) argue that complete determinism is irrational. In order for determinism to be true, there would have to be a rational basis for thought. But if determinism is true, then there is no rational basis for thought, since all is determined by non-rational forces. So, if determinism claims to be true, then it must be false.

Theistic defenders of determinism insist that God is the ultimate cause who determines all human actions. Both Martin Luther's* *Bondage of the Will* (1525) and Jonathan Edwards'* *Freedom of the Will* (1754) are examples of this theistic determinism. Edwards argued that all actions are caused, since it is irrational to claim that things arise without a cause. But for him a self-caused action is impossible, since a cause is prior to an effect, and one cannot be prior to oneself. Therefore, all actions are ultimately caused by a First Cause (God). 'Free choice' for Edwards is doing what one desires, but God gives the desires. Hence, all human actions are determined by God.

Opponents of theistic determinism respond as follows: a. Defining free choice as 'doing what one desires' is contrary to experience. For people do not always do what they desire, nor do they always desire to do what they do (*cf.* Rom. 7:15–16).

b. Edwards also misunderstands self-determinism as causing itself. Rather, it means simply that a self can cause something else to happen. That is, a free agent can cause a free action.

c. Edwards has a faulty, mechanistic view of human personhood. He likens human free choice to balancing scales in need of more pressure from the outside in order to tip the scales from dead centre. But humans are not machines; they are persons made in the image of God* and regarded as responsible for their actions.

d. Edwards wrongly assumes that self-determinism is contrary to the God's sovereignty. For God could have pre-determined things in accordance with free choice, rather than in contradiction to it. Even the Calvinistic *Westminster Confession* (1646) declares that 'Although in relation to the foreknowledge and decree of God, the first cause, all things come to pass immutably and infallibly, yet by the same providence he ordereth them to fall out, according to the nature of second causes, either necessarily, freely, or contingently' (V.ii).

2. Indeterminism

According to this view, at least some (if not all) human actions are uncaused. Thus, events and actions are contingent and spontaneous. Two *proponents* of this view were Charles Peirce (1839–1914) and William James.* Some contemporary indeterminists appeal to Heisenberg's (1901–76) principle to support their position. According to this principle, events in the subatomic realm (like the specific course of a given particle) are, to our present understanding, completely unpredictable.

Opponents of indeterminism offer several objections: a. They contend that Heisenberg's principle is misapplied, since it does not deal with the causality of an event but with its unpredictability. b. All forms of indeterminism fall shipwreck on the principle of causality, since they deny these events have causes. c. Indeterminism robs humans of their moral responsibility, since they are not the cause of these actions. If not, then why should they be blamed for evil actions. d. Indeterminism, at least on a cosmic scale, is unacceptable from a biblical perspective, since God is causally related to the world as both originator (Gn. 1) and sustainer of all things (Col. 1:15–17).

3. Self-determinism

According to this view, a person's moral acts are caused by himself or herself. The *arguments for* this view go like this: a. Moral actions are uncaused, caused by another, or caused by oneself. However, no action can be uncaused, since this violates the fundamental rational principle that every event has a cause. Neither can a person's actions be caused by others, for in that case they would not be that person's actions. Further, if one's acts are caused by another, then how can one be held responsible for them? Both Augustine* (in *On Free Will* and *On Grace and Free Will*) and Thomas Aquinas* were self-determinists, as are Arminians.

b. Human beings have moral responsibility.* But moral responsibility demands the ability to respond (= free choice).

c. The Bible insists that there are actions that people ought to perform (*cf.* Ex. 20). But 'ought' implies 'can' (= free choice).

d. Both the Bible and common understanding entails that some acts are praiseworthy (*e.g.* heroism), and some are blameworthy (*e.g.* cruelty). But if one is not free to perform the act, then it makes no sense to praise or blame one for doing it.

e. If God determines all acts, then he is responsible for the origin of sin, not Satan. For if a free choice is doing what one desires and God gives the desire, then God must have given to the devil the desire to rebel against him. But this is morally absurd, since it would be God working against himself.

Of the *objections to* self-determinism, one is that if everything needs a cause, then so do acts of the will, in which case they are not caused by oneself. In response, self-determinists claim this confuses the 'actor' (agent) who causes the act and the 'act' being caused. But the principle of causality does not demand that every thing (or person) has a cause but only that every *event* has a cause. That is, if a free agent (*e.g.* a human person) is the first cause of his or her own free actions, then it is meaningless to ask, 'What caused that person to do it?' In brief, God caused the *fact* of free choice (by making free agents), but free agents are the cause of free actions.

Others object that self-determinism is contrary to God's predestination. But self-determinists respond that God can pre-determine according to his 'foreknowledge' (1 Pet. 1:2), insisting that 'those God foreknew he also predestined' (Rom. 8:29). God, they insist, can determine the future by means of free choice, since he omnisciently knows how they will freely act. Still others insist that, regardless of what free choice Adam may have had (Rom. 5:12), fallen human beings are in bondage to sin and not free to respond to the gospel unless God works in them by the Holy Spirit to enable them to do so. But this view seems contrary to both God's consistent call on people to believe (*e.g.* Jn. 3:16; Acts 16:31), as well as to direct statements that even unbelievers have the ability to respond to God's grace (Mt. 23:37; Jn. 7:17; Rom. 7:18; 1 Cor. 9:17; Phm. 14; 1 Pet. 5:2).

Finally, some argue that if humans have the ability to respond, then salvation is not of grace (Eph. 2:8–9) but by human effort. However, this is a confusion about the nature of faith.* The ability of a person to receive God's gracious *gift* of salvation is not the same as working for it. To think so is to give credit for the gift to the receiver rather than to the Giver who graciously gave it.

Bibliography

D. A. Carson, *Divine Sovereignty and Human Responsibility: Biblical Perspectives in Tension* (London and Atlanta, 1981); R. Swinburne, *Responsibility and Atonement* (Oxford, 1989).

N.L.G.

FREUD, SIGMUND (1856–1939) was the initiator of the theory and method of psychoanalysis.* His ideas have influenced thought and culture well beyond the field of psychology. Born of Jewish (but not orthodox) parents in Freiburg, Moravia, the eldest of a family of eight, he moved when a few years old to Vienna, where he lived until the final year of his life. His father was a merchant of modest means.

As a young man, Freud had a sense of destiny and a confidence in his capacity to succeed which he attributed to his mother's 'special regard'. Financial constraints, from which he was hardly free throughout his life, made him abandon other early ambitions and become a medical student. His real interest was in scientific research, and he gained considerable recognition for his work in anatomy and physiology. Lack of money, however, prevented him from pursuing some very fruitful ideas further, and he qualified and practised somewhat unwillingly as a doctor.

Subsequently, Freud went to Paris to study under Jean Martin Charcot (1825–93), one of the first doctors to take the condition of hysteria seriously, and he was interested in the reproduction of their symptoms by hysterical patients under hypnosis.* The success obtained by a colleague, Josef Breuer (1842–1925), in obtaining symptom relief for a patient by letting her talk, encouraged Freud to experiment along the same lines, concentrating on the treatment of patients with neuroses.* From these beginnings the clinical practice and the theory of psychoanalysis developed.

Freud was impressed by Charles Darwin's,* work and shared the hope that scientific discovery would reveal the secrets of the universe, rendering religious 'explanations' unnecessary. He extended his strong deterministic beliefs (see Free Will and Determinism*) to psychology, postulating a biologically based theory of instincts, that human behaviour was meaningful, motivated and goal-seeking, and that much mental activity was unconscious.* This he deduced from what his patients revealed first under hypnosis, then through free association, and from his observations of the lapses of ordinary people. One of the main outcomes of his work was to break down the divide between normal and abnormal human psychology.

Many of Freud's theories developed from his own self-analysis, undertaken in an effort to understand some of his behaviour and mood-swings. His own early relationships had been complex: his mother was a second wife, only twenty-one when he was born, and he had a step-brother with a son a little older than himself, whom he loved, but of whom he also felt jealous. A younger brother died in infancy. As painful memories arose, he recollected, amongst many other things, murderous wishes against this infant usurper, and towards his father, whom in his fantasy he destroyed and replaced in possessing his mother. Theories of omnipotence of thought, of love–hate relationships, the Oedipus complex and infantile sexuality (see ⑪) resulted from the analysis (undertaken between the years 1897–99). The latter was one of the main reasons he was ostracized by most of the medical establishment, not only in Austria but also abroad, and he encountered considerable social opprobrium. At first, Freud believed that his patients had actually been sexually assaulted in childhood; later he concluded that for many the accounts expressed a repressed wish. The whole question has been reopened in the light of more recent findings of the extent of child abuse.*

Freud's own sexual life and conduct were on strictly ethical and moral lines. He was a faithful husband, a loving father and a generous and loyal friend, providing for the needs of this extended family, and an extremely hard and disciplined worker.

Freud revised and developed his theories throughout his life, confining himself to individual psychology, until his later years when he extended his ideas to social psychology. In 1913 he published *Totem and Taboo*, linking Darwin's notion of the primal horde to his own theories about the Oedipus complex and problems of guilt* and expiation. Other speculative works followed, on the struggle between an individual's libidinal wishes and the demands of society, the role and future of religion, and the connection between Jewish guilt, Christianity as wish-fulfilment and anti-Semitism. Freud was a life-long atheist; religion was an illusion from whose strictures and promises humans needed to be liberated by science. He alternated between profound pessimism* at the unhappy human condition, and some optimism over the possibility of progress through self-awareness and scientific advance.

For much of his life, Freud was somewhat isolated, though with a small, close-knit group of adherents (most of his inner circle were Jewish). He was happy for group members to develop their own theories, but these had to be consonant with his basic tenets, which he was convinced represented the truth, and he keenly felt any defection (such as that of Carl Jung*). International recognition came slowly, in the USA (where he lectured once) and in Europe. At the very end he was made a member of the Royal Society in England, the country in which he finally took refuge, finding it 'free and generous'. The last sixteen years were clouded by the loss of close family members and friends, the burning of his books by the Nazis, and threats to family safety, the loss of savings, and a painful and recurrent cancer of the jaw, though he continued to write and to see patients up to the time of his death.

Bibliography

The Complete Psychological Works of Sigmund Freud, 24 vols. (ET, London and New York, 1953–74, repr. 1978–81): *The Psychopathology of Everyday Life*, vol. 6; *Five Lectures on Psycho-Analysis*, vol. 11; *Totem and Taboo*, vol. 13; *The Future of an Illusion*, vol. 21; *Civilisation and its Discontents*, vol. 21; *Moses and Monotheism*, vol. 23.

J. N. Isbister, *Freud: An Introduction to his Life and Work* (Cambridge, 1985); E. Jones, *Sigmund Freud: Life and Work*, 3 vols. (London and New York, 1953–57).

J.R.G.

FRIENDSHIP. A new interest in the importance of friendship is beginning to emerge, in part because of the realization that the individualism* of Western culture has been damaging and one-sided. Recognition of the importance of community (see Community Ethics[16]) is paralleled in church life by emphasis on relationships and groups for support and encouragement. As welcome as this is, a theological recovery is also required, so that friendship may be moved from the sidelines back to the centre of a view of God and his relationship with us.

In classical times a great deal of emphasis was put on the importance of friendship (Gk. *philia*; Lat. *amicitia*) in the moral life, and important philosophical treatments were written by Plato,* Aristotle* and Cicero (106–43 BC). In Aristotle's analysis, friendship is based on a relationship in which something is shared – that is its essence. There are three categories of friendship, two of which are inferior: 1. a friendship based on pleasure (two or more people enjoying a common activity); and 2. a friendship based on usefulness (as when neighbours or business associates derive mutual advantage from a relationship). 3. True friendship, however, is based on virtue,* not profit or pleasure.* Such friendship is found when one loves someone for the moral qualities he or she has, and desires good for that person.

This tradition was carried into Christian thought through the writing of Ambrose* and Augustine,* and influenced later medieval thinkers, especially as they reflected on the qualities of the close spiritual relationships provided by the development of monasticism* and religious orders. Among these the most noteworthy is Aelred of Rievaulx (c. 1110–67), whose work *On Spiritual Friendship* draws on Cicero and Augustine, but is richly supplied with examples from the Bible. Aelred distinguishes between friendship for pleasure, worldly friendship and friendship based on true spirituality; true friendship is guided by charity, not by selfish interests. At one stage Aelred points to the theological significance of *amicitia* with his paraphrase of 'God is love' (1 Jn. 4:16) as 'God is friendship' (an anticipation of the insights of Thomas Aquinas*).

In the later Middle Ages and the Reformation, friendship becomes less important as the conception of morality and the Christian life moves from one of virtues and relationships to one of conscience,* obedience to authority,* and law. Friendship as a moral category was thought to be incompatible with an ethic based on duty* and obligation.*

The language of friendship did not disappear however; it blossomed in devotional literature and was applied to the mystical relation of the soul to God. But in both Catholic and Protestant contexts the notion of love (see [2]) was often sentimentalized or developed in terms of self-abnegation: the soul in union with God was to be absorbed in his Being. Friendship with God became a mystical category, not a theological or moral one.

One result of these various trends was to confirm the notion of love (agapē) as by definition opposed to any element of self; virtue comes to be defined as basically unselfish love, a denial of any element of any self-regarding motivation. Since the essence of friendship is a mutual relationship, friendship was thought to be excluded from the doctrine of Christian love which was described increasingly in terms of total self-giving and self-sacrifice. The fact that Anders Nygren's* Agapē and Eros (ET, London, 1932–39), which stresses this view, had no real analysis of philia indicates the vacuum in Western thought.

The NT does not support a substantial difference between agapē and friendship. Philia is used to describe Jesus' love for Lazarus (Jn. 11:36), but also for the love of the Father for the Son (Jn. 5:20). Agapē, too, is used in various relationships: in Jn. 3:16 it is the love of God for the world, but it is used as the friendship of Jesus for Mary, Martha and Lazarus (Jn. 11:5). It is also used for the unworthy love of the Pharisees for the praises of men (Jn. 12:43). In the usage of Paul, agapē is the term for the qualities of love in 1 Cor. 13; but also is used of Demas who deserted Paul because he was 'in love with this present world' (2 Tim. 4:10, RSV).

There is thus a strong biblical and theological basis for the approach taken by Thomas Aquinas that charity (agapē) is in essence a kind of friendship. He writes, 'There is a sharing of man with God by his sharing his happiness with us, and it is on this that a friendship is based. As Paul says [1 Cor. 1:9], "God is faithful by whom you were called into the fellowship of his Son". Now the love which is based on this sort of friendship is charity; thus it is clear that charity is a friendship of man and God' (STh 2a2ae 23:1). God's love to us is the sharing of his life with us, to enable us to enter a relationship of friendship love with him, made possible by the Holy Spirit making us more like Christ.

The notion of friendship can be seen as a good way of bringing out the meaning of the covenant* relation between God and his people, and of Jesus' love for his disciples (Jn. 15:15); but many Protestants (e.g. G. C. Meilaender) will remain sceptical about incorporating mutuality into agapē; even Catholic writers have noted the 'breathtakingly audacious' (F. Kerr) and 'almost blasphemous' (P. J. Waddell) conception that sinful man can be friends with God when Aristotle himself ruled that out because of the absolute inequality in such a relationship. But man brings to the relationship not himself as such, but what God gives him through grace: a self changed by the Holy Spirit. This makes possible a friendship where each loves the other for what he is: we love God for what he is, and God loves us for what we are and are to become, chosen and perfected in Christ.

The love which Christians are to have for their neighbour can also be seen as essentially a friendship. We love others not on the basis of their attractiveness or usefulness, or out of sheer benevolence,* but because we want them to share in God's happiness. The same love that we have for God is extended to others, namely seeing them as loved by God. This is also the only realistic basis on which to love our enemies – we do not love them for what we share on the human level, but because we know they are loved by God, and it is that love in which we all share.

Bibliography

J. Houston, The Transforming Friendship (Oxford and Batavia, IL, 1989); F. Kerr, 'Charity as Friendship', in B. Davies (ed.), Language, Meaning and God: Essays in Honour of Herbert McCabe (London, 1987); M. A. Macnamara, Friendship in St Augustine (Fribourg, 1958); G. C. Meilaender, Friendship: a Study in Theological Ethics (Notre Dame, IN, 1981); A. W. Price, Love and Friendship in Plato and Aristotle (Oxford, 1989); G. Vansteenberghe, DSp 1, cols. 500–529; P. J. Waddell, Friendship and the Moral Life (Notre Dame, IN, 1989).

D.A.W.

FROMM, ERICH (1900–1980). Born in Germany into an orthodox Jewish family (though he later renounced his faith), Fromm studied sociology and psychology, and trained in psychoanalysis.* He practised in Frankfurt before emigrating to the USA in 1934. His 'humanistic psychoanalysis' synthesized his studies of the Talmud and the OT with Freudian psychology, and with Marxist and Weberian social perspectives. In the first of many major books, *The Fear of Freedom* (London 1942), Fromm applied psychoanalytical tools to a critique of Western society, a theme further developed in later works, notably *The Sane Society* (New York, 1955). *The Art of Loving* (New York and London, 1957) was a very widely read exploration of the relation of love to the total personality; *To Have or To Be?* (New York, 1976; London, 1979) explores the choice for humankind between on the one hand material possessions and power, and on the other the pleasure of shared experience and human values. In *Man For Himself* (New York, 1947; London, 1949), Fromm offers a psychology of the moral life and human character, and in various other writings (*You shall Be as Gods*, New York, 1966; *The Dogma of Christ*, New York and London, 1963; and *Psychoanalysis and Religion*, New Haven, CT, and London, 1950) he explores the relationships between religious faith, moral and spiritual values, and psychoanalytic theory. He argues for a 'humanistic religion', being unhappy with the concept of God, but believing in the importance of spiritual reality, and the value in therapy of helping patients towards a 'religious attitude'.

Bibliography

D. Helminiak, 'Spiritual Concerns in Erich Fromm', *JPT* 16, 1988, p. 222; P. Morea, *Personality* (Harmondsworth, 1990), ch. 5.

D.J.A.

FRUSTRATION results when a course of action which would lead to the attainment a desired goal is thwarted. The way in which a hope is balked, or a design defeated, is endlessly variable, but the condition that follows is unpleasant, linked to feelings of disappointment and failure. It is frequently, in modern parlance, linked to sexual frustration, but this is only one special use.

A situation may be described as frustrating when there appears to be an insoluble problem, beset with barriers which seem to make a solution impossible in spite of a strong wish to overcome them. The capacity to tolerate frustration is usually seen as a measure of such a person's strong will or self-discipline.

Modern psychology has sought to explain frustration in terms of experimental studies. In 1939, J. Dollard and N. E. Miller (1909–) made a notable contribution by linking aggression to frustration. Their hypothesis was that frustration led to aggression (easily shown in pigeons or rats) and anger (as often observed in humans).

J. A. Gray argues that fear* and frustration are much the same thing and that non-reward (the essential feature in frustration) is the same as punishment* (which plays a large part in fear and anxiety*). Gray admits that equating fear and frustration runs counter to our intuitions. Both result in states of distress which can be relieved by drugs such as alcohol and benzodiazepines. Frustration and fear lead to conflicts which bring many to counselling and therapy (see Pastoral Care, Counselling and Psychotherapy [12]) and therapy.

In ordinary experience it is abundantly confirmed that 'hope deferred makes the heart sick' (Pr. 13:12). There is a clash between biblical and contemporary values over frustration. Expectations of fulfilment are among the hallmarks of modern hopes. This is true of the two strongest instincts in human life, the sexual and the aggressive drives. Children in most cultures are taught ways of learning to delay gratification of these basic impulses. Similarly, acquisitive impulses may be controlled, but the modern view is, 'I want it now.'

Counselling offers understanding and insight, shared with the person suffering from the consequences of frustration. Aid in problem-solving is built in to much casework, and is directed to helping the client to make his or her own decisions, which may resolve conflict. Medical and psychological consequences are legion. Hysteria was seen as a response where intolerably strong drives which could not be fulfilled might lead to a dissociative state, or a running away from the problem. Anxiety in many forms may result from frustration. Where anger,* as part of frustration, is turned inwards, severe depression* may result. There are many who show antisocial behaviour which is attributed to frustration.

Symptomatic treatment of the anxiety or depression may be needed, especially when there are physical symptoms caused by frustration. Frequently the remedy is neither medical nor psychological but social. Thus if work and earning money are the desired goal, and economic recession and unemployment prevent this, both suicide rates and depression increase. Only meaningful work will treat such frustration and restore self-esteem and well-being.

The higher the moral standards, the more frustration is likely. Coming to terms with the demands of the Sermon on the Mount* may require the metaphorical loss of eye or hand. The demands of chastity* are only one example of the way frustration hurts: handling anger and its related feelings is even more difficult for many.

It seems clear from the NT that raising the stakes with Pharisaical adding of burdens of rules and regulations is bad, partly because it increases the risk of frustrating failure. This should be borne in mind by parents, educators and Christian teachers, who should bear in mind that Christ's yoke is easy and his burden light.

Perhaps conflict is inevitable between a rigorist* or ascetic* interpretation of the NT and one which makes allowances for failure, forgiveness* and the need for tolerance of human weakness. Perfection is the goal, but we must not add burdens to people, often in matters which are morally neutral. The aim should not be to create unnecessary frustration.

Bibliography
J. A. Gray, *The Psychology of Fear and Stress* (Cambridge, ²1987); J. Dollard *et al.*, *Frustration and Aggression* (New Haven, CT, 1939).

G.D.

FRY, ELIZABETH (1780–1845), a pioneer in prison reform and women's philanthropic work. Born the daughter of John Gurney, a prosperous Quaker in Norwich, Elizabeth became personally convinced of the Quaker faith in her late teens. In 1800 she married Joseph Fry, a London merchant, and had eleven children.

Elizabeth first visited Newgate, a notorious London gaol near her home, in 1811. She discovered dirty, overcrowded conditions in which there was virtually no attempt at rehabilitation. In 1817 she organized a team of ladies to read the Bible to female prisoners each day while they were given sewing lessons. Monitors were appointed to supervise small classes of fellow-prisoners and soon the new approach proved so successful that it was imitated elsewhere. In 1812 Elizabeth established the British Society for Promoting Reformation of Female Prisoners to link various Ladies' Committees, and in 1827 published *Observations on the Visiting, Superintendence and Government of Female Prisoners*, which was bold enough to advocate the end of capital punishment. Although penal policy in the 1830s began to favour solitary confinement, which Elizabeth disliked, from 1838 she was able to propagate her views as a Quaker travelling minister in continental Europe. Elizabeth was an inspiration for ladies to take up Christian caring outside the home. She was eager to co-operate with other evangelicals in organizations such as the Bible Society, but she saw her activities as an outgrowth of the Quaker belief that all human beings deserve respect.

Bibliography
J. Rose, *Elizabeth Fry: A Biography* (London, 1980).

D.W.Be.

FUNERALS, see BEREAVEMENT; BURIAL AND CREMATION; DEATH AND DYING; LIFE, HEALTH AND DEATH. [13]

G

GAMBLING is 'an agreement between two parties whereby the transfer of something of value is made dependent on an uncertain event, in such a way that one party will gain and the other lose' (Churches' Council on Gambling, 1974).

Thus defined, gambling includes gaming (playing for money), betting (staking money on the uncertain outcome of an event) and participating in lotteries (when prizes are allocated at random). Skill may be involved, but the element of chance predominates.

Insurance* is not usually considered gambling, because clients intend to avert unavoidable risks by paying their premiums, not embrace artificial risks by parting with their stake money. Similarly, the practice of casting lots in the Bible (*e.g.* 1 Ch. 24:5; Acts 1:26) cannot be bracketed with gambling, because the intention was either to discern God's will or to ensure fairness. Business investment and speculation are harder to categorize, as they span a much broader spectrum of intent.

Thomas Aquinas* permitted gambling, providing it was not motivated by covetousness,* characterized by unfairness (loaded dice) or used to exploit the young and psychologically immature.

Following his lead, some modern Christians find gambling ethically acceptable. They point especially to the good material results achieved through State lotteries and church raffles. The building of the Sydney Opera House, the Montreal Olympics, and the London Metropolitan water supply were all financed through public lotteries. Moreover, they argue, gamblers may be well motivated. Many elderly people who go to bingo sessions do so to escape loneliness, not out of greed, and those who buy raffle tickets are usually more concerned to make a contribution to the good cause than to win the prize.

Nowhere, they point out, does the Bible condemn gambling. Indeed, the NT invites Christians to 'put their hope in God, who richly provides us with everything for our enjoyment' (1 Tim. 6:17). If the stewardship* principle allows for expenditure on leisure activities, surely those who find gambling enjoyable are as ethically correct as their neighbours who prefer to buy tickets for the theatre or pay for a meal at a smart restaurant.

Other influential figures from church history have a much more negative view. Tertullian* wrote bluntly, 'If you say you are a Christian when you are a dice-player, you say you are what you are not, for you are a partner with the world' (*De Spectaculis*, xvi). Hugh Latimer (1485–1555) preached his famous 'Sermon on the Cards' in 1529 to deter Christians from gaming.

William Temple* (*Essays in Christian Politics and Kindred Subjects*, London, 1927) listed four reasons why gambling is wrong in itself. 1. It glorifies chance. In the Bible, God is revealed as a God of order (*cf.* 1 Cor. 14:33). He leaves nothing to good fortune and provides for all his people's need. Because gambling glorifies chance, it encourages people to trust their luck rather than rely on God's providence. 2. Whatever its defenders may claim, said Temple, gambling disregards the stewardship principle. Christians accept that they are only caretakers of their property, not owners.

Gamblers are risking what belongs to God. 3. Gambling attempts to profit out of someone else's loss. That is the antithesis of Christian teaching on neighbour love. 4. Those who promote gambling (including governments who sanction State lotteries) make their appeal to human covetousness, a selfish approach to life which is condemned both by the Ten Commandments and by the teaching of Jesus (Ex. 20:17; Lk. 12:15). As Jeremy Taylor* put it in his famous 'Sermon on the Cards', preached in 1660: 'If a man be willing or indifferent to lose his own money and not at all desirous to get another's, to what purpose is it that he plays for it? If he be not indifferent, then he is covetous or a fool: he covets that which is not his own, or unreasonably ventures that which is.'

Those who oppose gambling point to the human disasters which sometimes follow in its wake. Once deeply ingrained, the habit can master its victims. They may steal for their stake money. They often lose their jobs. And marriage breakdowns may follow.

Whichever side of the argument is considered weightier, all agree that excessive gambling is wrong. Organizations like Gamblers Anonymous exist to help compulsive gamblers (see Dependence*) and their dependants.

Bibliography

National Council for Social Aid, *Christianity and Gambling* (Oxford, 1983).

D.H.F.

GAUDIUM ET SPES, see SECOND VATICAN COUNCIL.

GAY RIGHTS, see HOMOSEXUALITY.

GENDER, see SEXUALITY. [11]

GENEROSITY, see GIVING.

GENE THERAPY, see GENETIC ENGINEERING.

GENETIC COUNSELLING. As knowledge of genetic disease increases, more people need information about their risks and help in working out how to handle this information. Genetic-counselling centres, usually hospital-based, aim both to inform and to provide such help.

If an individual belongs to a family where several members are affected by a particular disease, he or she may want to know about their own possible future disability. Others may have a child with some form of handicap (see Disability and Handicap*) and wish to know the outlook for any future children, while yet others may have lost such a child or had a pregnancy aborted because serious abnormalities had been detected. The genetic counsellor will collate the family details and give the enquirer as accurate information as possible.

Where risks are high he or she will then discuss what courses of action are available or advisable. If, for example, an individual is at risk of developing a certain type of cancer, then a strategy for regular examination can be instigated so that early detection will allow optimum treatment. For other diseases, no such preventive measures may be possible, and the person concerned will need to think carefully whether he or she really wishes to know if the disease gene (or predisposition) is present.

Where parents are at high risk of having a handicapped child, the decisions before them may be more difficult. Possible options would include the use of reliable contraception (see Birth Control*) to ensure that they have no children themselves. This is a hard decision in our family-orientated culture, particularly if the couple have had a brief taste of parenthood through a child who died young.

For many conditions, pre-natal detection is possible using tests such as amniocentesis,* chorion biopsy or ultrasound scanning. Should the test show the foetus to be affected then abortion* would be offered, so couples facing this possibility need to weigh up whether or not this would be acceptable for them.

Another difficult option would be the use of artificial insemination (see Reproductive Technologies*) by donor or ovum donation (though at present donated ova are only rarely available). These techniques can enable a couple to avoid a high risk of having an affected child when no pre-natal test is available, but clearly are not to be undertaken lightly.

Having established the risk to be faced, the genetic counsellor will talk through the various options available to the couple and work out with them which course of action is the best for them. If a couple make it clear that they would not contemplate abortion, then the counsellor would explore other possibilities with them.

Thus this non-directive genetic counselling is largely informative and supportive, and decisions with moral implications are the choice of the individuals concerned since it is they who have to live with the results of their choices. Inevitably, though, the counsellors' views may have some impact on those seeking help.

There is no clear Bible teaching on genetic counselling, so general principles have to be applied. A first principle is that Christians seek *truth* and this includes ascertaining the facts about risks and what can be done about them. They are by no means committed to making use of the techniques they hear about.

A second principle is that of the value of the *family* unit. There may be a tension between the need for sharing what may be upsetting information within the family,* yet respecting confidentiality* where individuals wish to keep their knowledge to themselves.

Both the OT and NT stress the worth of *the individual*. Christians may disagree on the stage in development at which this great value becomes established (see Embryology*); but the command to love one's neighbour as one's self is fundamental.

Medical teaching in the UK and the USA maintains that the needs of the individual have priority over those of the State, but as materialism combined with scarcity of resources becomes commoner, this cannot be taken for granted. Whatever views may be held on the morality of the various techniques described, the prior concern must be for the individual or couple coping with grief and difficult decision-making.

A.C.B.

GENETIC ENGINEERING. The term 'genetic engineering' encapsulates people's fears regarding future abuses of science, since it is seen as having the potential to manipulate human nature. For some, it is 'playing God' in the most objectionable of ways. However, present-day human genetics is far less monolithic than this term suggests, ranging as it does from genetic screening and the use of DNA probes to pre-emptive intervention and selective abortion,* from genetic counselling* to somatic and germ line gene therapy, and from the human genome project (with its efforts to produce the complete nucleotide sequences of the human genome) to cloning and eugenics (see Manipulation*). This range of possibilities is made possible only because contemporary molecular genetics allows for the manipulation of the genetic content of human cells. Consequently, it holds out prospects both for dramatically extending the range of current medical therapies, and for effecting radical changes to the way in which medicine itself is practised. Hitherto intractable genetic diseases, such as cystic fibrosis and muscular dystrophy, are being unravelled, and the genes involved have been defined. Also, the nature of cancer as an acquired genetic disease is being clarified.

Genetic screening was revolutionized in the late 1970s by the advent of the recombinant DNA technologies, that in turn have led to the development of DNA probes for detecting large numbers of human genetic variants and genes with known functions. The amount of information stemming from these procedures is enormous, and its use demands serious ethical assessment. Criteria are required for determining who is to be tested, and what those with positive tests are to be told and whether their privacy* and confidentiality* can be maintained under all circumstances. The testing of people for susceptibility to a disease (*e.g.* severe arthritis or manic depressive illness) can be used sensitively and constructively, but it may serve to stigmatize individuals because of their genetic constitution. The consequence of genetic testing of the foetus is frequently abortion following a positive finding, although the prospects of treatment of afflicted foetuses are improving. The precision of genetic information is not always as great as some claim, and care needs to be exercised to ensure that it does not lead to genetic determinism.

Somatic cell gene therapy, which was first tested in humans in 1989, involves the correction of gene defects in patients' own cells, the cells in question being somatic cells (*i.e.* ordinary body cells). The strategy involves gene replacement, gene correction or gene augmentation, the genes being introduced via retroviral vectors. The aim of this form of gene therapy is to modify a particular cell population and so rectify a particular disease in a particular patient. As such, it is similar to procedures like organ transplantation (see Transplant Surgery*), but is far more powerful than any indirect genetic therapies. However, there are technical difficulties associated with the expression and appropriate regulation of new genes in somatic cells, and with its current limitation to disorders stemming from defective function of genes in the specialized cells from which blood cells are derived. For some

time it will be confined to attempts at correcting single gene defects, such as found in thalassemia and phenylketonuria.

Since its aim is the alleviation of disease, and not the improvement of the human species, it fits within Christian goals for health care.* Ethical issues of significance include the need to balance any potential benefits and harms, and assess the safety and effectiveness of new techniques. There must be unequivocal evidence from animal studies that the inserted gene will function adequately and have no deleterious effects; there needs to be assurance that the new gene can be accurately placed into the target cells and that it will remain there long enough to be effective, that it will be expressed in the cell at the appropriate level and only in that tissue, and that neither it nor the retroviruses will harm the cell or the patient. It is important to assess the benefits of gene therapy against current alternative therapies (such as bone marrow transplantation), and to ensure that the interests of the patients are paramount. For the foreseeable future, it should be viewed as the treatment of last resort.

It may be objected that somatic cell gene therapy is unethical since it represents the beginning of a slippery slope, its inevitable concomitant being germ line gene therapy and eugenics. Understandable as this objection may be, there is a considerable moral gulf between gene therapy to treat disease and gene manipulation to alter behaviour or morality.

Germ line gene therapy involves inserting the gene into the germ line (sperms, eggs and embryos), so that when the modified individual reproduces, all offspring will have the inserted gene instead of the original defective one. It is attempting to manipulate an early embryo so that the individual it will become is not afflicted with a fatal disease. Animal experiments have shown this form of gene therapy to be associated with high risks, since gene expression may occur in inappropriate tissues. Since the foreign gene is inserted randomly into the host DNA, some facets of normal embryological development may be disrupted with serious adverse consequences. Further, any damage to the DNA caused by this procedure will stay in the germ line and be passed on to subsequent generations. But what if it becomes a safe and effective procedure?

Were this to happen, there are various arguments in favour of germ line gene therapy. Some genetic disorders may be amenable to treatment only in this way (*e.g.* brain cells in hereditary central-nervous-system disorders, which are not open to genetic repair after birth). It would also dispense with the need to repeat somatic-cell gene therapy in different generations of a family with a genetic disorder, by eliminating the defective gene from the population and so improving the efficiency of gene therapy. In assessing these arguments, it is pertinent to point out that germ line therapy involves obtaining embryos via *in vitro* fertilization (see Reproductive Technologies*), determining which ones require treatment, and then carrying out the therapy. However, the far simpler procedure of refraining from implanting defective embryos achieves the same therapeutic aims without running the risks of inserting a new gene into a defective embryo. This simpler course of action requires the disposal of defective embryos, and may be rejected by some on the ground that it is unethical to select healthy embryos and reject defective ones. Neither would it satisfy those wishing to eliminate a defective gene from the population.

Enhancement genetic engineering involves the insertion of a gene in an attempt to alter a particular trait of an individual. This approach has ethical problems, since it aims to alter a healthy individual in a permanent manner. This is similar to providing growth hormone to normal individuals in order to improve their sporting prowess. The extra gene (whether normal or modified) may have adverse consequences resulting from protein imbalance. However, an alternative preventive use of enhancement genetic engineering can be imagined, such as altering the concentration of a protein that leads to heart disease. If the goal in this instance is the alleviation of disease, it may be ethically justified, representing a form of preventive medicine; the scientific situation would have to be clarified before this approach could be seriously contemplated.

See also: EMBRYOLOGY; EMBRYO TRANSFER.

Bibliography

W. F. Anderson, 'Human Gene Therapy', *Science* 256, 1992, pp. 808–813; C. K. Boone, 'Bad Axioms in Genetic Engineering', *Hastings Center Report* 18.4, 1988, pp. 9–13; H. Bouma III *et al.*, *Christian Faith, Health, and Medical Practice* (Grand Rapids, 1989); J. A. Bryant, 'Mapping the Human Genome: The Human Genome Project', *Science and*

Christian Belief 4, 1992, pp. 105–125; P. J. M. Van Tongeren, 'Ethical Manipulations: An Ethical Evaluation of the Debate Surrounding Genetic Engineering', *Human Gene Therapy* 2, 1991, pp. 71–75; L. Walters, 'Human Gene Therapy: Ethics and Public Policy', *Human Gene Therapy* 2, 1991, pp. 115–122.

D.G.J.

GENETIC SCREENING, see GENETIC COUNSELLING; GENETIC ENGINEERING.

GENEVA CONVENTION. This term is used to refer to a series of international treaties that codified the rules of war.* A major role in this work has been played by the International Committee of the Red Cross, founded in 1863 through the inspired Christian leadership of Jean Henri Dunant (1828–1910).

The first treaty, signed in 1864 by sixteen European powers, provided for the care of the sick and wounded soldiers, the neutrality of the medical corps, the humane treatment of prisoners, and the display of a distinctive emblem, such as the Red Cross, by persons and places involved in medical work. These articles were extended and amended in a series of meetings held at the Hague in 1899 and 1907, and at Geneva in 1906, 1929, 1949 and 1977. The most important of these meetings was held in 1949 in response to the horrors of the Second World War, and it drew up the most complete of the Geneva Conventions. The articles included the following: 1. provision for care of the wounded and sick in land warfare; 2. rules for the care of those who were injured or shipwrecked at sea; 3. laws guaranteeing the just treatment of prisoners of war; and 4. provisions that protected citizens of occupied territories by condoning such practices as deportation, taking of hostages, torture, collective reprisals, wanton destruction of property, and discrimination based on race, religion or nationality. In 1977 another conference supplemented these with two additional protocols that extended the protection of international law to wars of liberation or civil wars. Over 150 nations have signed the 1949 conventions, but far fewer have agreed to the 1977 protocols.

R.G.C.

GENOCIDE. The word 'genocide' was first widely used after the Nazi holocaust to describe the purposeful attempt to destroy a racial, religious or political group. The systematic elimination of six million Jewish men, women and children in Europe inspired the United Nations to draw up the Genocide Convention. The General Assembly approved the convention in 1948 and brought it into effect as Resolution 96 in 1951. The resolution departed from previously normal principles by declaring that State authorities as well as those who practise their commands are equally guilty. It also lays it down that genocide does not constitute 'a matter essentially within the domestic jurisdiction', but is of international concern.

Although the term 'genocide' immediately conjures up the image of the Nazi concentration camps and gas chambers, other horrific examples of deliberate genocide have darkened the pages of human history. In early history whole tribes were eliminated by their conquerors, as was later the case with the Mongol armies as they swept through central Asia. In 1915 the Turks sought to wipe out their Armenian population, and the Pol Pot regime in the late 1970s eliminated all professional classes of Cambodians.

The United Nations Genocide Convention outlines the specific activities which constitute genocide. In seeking to destroy a people, genocide may include: 1. killing members of the group; 2. causing serious physical or mental harm; 3. deliberately inflicting on the group such living conditions as will bring about its destruction; 4. imposing measures aimed at preventing reproduction within the group; and 5. forcing the group's children to be given to members of other peoples. It may be observed that all five of these activities were perpetrated by the Germans in Hitler's 'final solution' to the Jewish question.

In the definition of genocide the above activities are not carried out because the particular individuals or families are singled out as criminal elements or enemies of the State. The victims are destroyed purely because they belong to their racial, religious or political group. So in Nazi Germany even assimilated Jews were eliminated, although they were culturally identified with their German neighbours and were loyal servants of the German State. Totally harmless women and children suffered the same humiliating fate for no other reason than that they were Jews.

Nazi Germany's 'final solution' provides a clear example of the fact that genocide normally presupposes the idea that the victimized people is naturally inferior or even sub-human. Thus Spanish Argentinians in their genocidal hunting down of Chaco Indians believed that the Indians were more animal than human. Nazi propaganda likewise depicted the Jews as sub-human 'vermin', and this teaching was supported by highly sophisticated pseudo-scientific journals which purported to demonstrate that the Jewish brain resembles that of an animal more than that of human beings. Such teaching fitted the mood of German nationalism and the master-race philosophy of Richard Wagner (1813–83) and Friedrich Nietzsche.*

In this context the biblical teaching concerning the divine creation of all humanity becomes particularly significant. The Bible affirms that all humanity – all races and classes as well as both men and women – are made in the image and likeness of God (see Image of God*). The genealogy in Lk. 3 reminds us that God is the father of Adam and thus of all people. Jesus Christ traces his descent not just from Abraham, the father of Israel, but also from Adam, the father of all humanity. In Jesus therefore there can be no status distinctions between races, classes or genders.

Genocide may also stem from a genuine or imagined fear* of the other people. In earlier centuries Christians developed a fear of the Jews, believing that they were in league with the angel of death to plot for the destruction of Christians. Scandalous rumours spread that Jews captured Christian children in order to drink their blood, and maidens for their sexual pleasure. Fear can darken people's minds and prevent loving or rational discernment. Such fear played a major part in driving Christian peoples in Europe to destroy Jewish communities in their midst. 1 Jn. 4:18, however, declares that fear cannot co-exist with love. While John is primarily teaching that God's love casts out the human fear that God will destroy us in judgment, the principle applies more widely. Love for our neighbour precludes irrational fear.

In facing the sad realities of human and church history with its catalogue of examples of genocide, we are forced to confess the depth of human sin. Selfish pride, irrational fear, gullible acceptance of current propaganda and a stereotyping judgment of other groups which dehumanizes them – such depravity lies deep within all human beings. Genocide is therefore an ever-present danger.

M.F.G.

GERM LINE GENE THERAPY, see GENETIC ENGINEERING.

GESTALT THERAPY has its roots in the Gestalt and existential psychologies* of Germany in the first third of the 20th century and the humanistic psychology of the US in the 1950s and 60s. The figures of Frederick (Fritz) Perls (1893–1970) and Laura Perls (1906–90) are pre-eminent in the unfolding story. The conceptual contexts of Gestalt psychology included the 'understanding' psychology (see Humanistic Psychology*) of Wilhelm Dilthey (1833–1911), with its emphasis on the integrated whole, and the phenomenology of Edmund Husserl (1859–1938), whose philosophy argued the prerequisite of a scientific and descriptive approach to human consciousness.

The Ger. word *Gestalt* was first used within a psychological framework in 1890 by the Austrian psychologist and philosopher, Christian von Ehrenfels (1859–1932), who reasoned that there is a 'gestalt, or form' quality, present in the whole of a structure, which is absent from any of the parts that make up that whole. In 1912, three young German psychologists, Max Wertheimer (1880–1943), Kurt Koffka (1886–1941) and Wolfgang Köhler (1887– 1967), working in the vicinity of Frankfurt, founded the Berlin Gestalt school, which rejected both the reductionist* views of John B. Watson's (1878–1958) behaviourism* and the bid for a 'higher' mental process in constructing human awareness of the environment, as favoured by the Austrian Gestaltists. The Berlin school became the main trendsetter in Gestalt psychology. In time, many of its psychologists left for the US where, in spite of their earlier resistance, they capitulated to Watsonian 'objectivism' and, to quote Fritz Perls, gave priority to 'installing quantitative measures and excessive experimental restrictions' (F. S. Perls *et al.*, *Gestalt Therapy*, pp. 25–26).

Fritz Perls, working as a psychiatrist and psychoanalyst in Germany during the 1920s and 30s, became disenchanted with orthodox Freudianism* and, following the advice of the neo-Freudian, Karen Horney (1885–1952), sought analysis with Wilhelm Reich (1897– 1957). Reichian thinking, stressing that the body is as important as the mind in the development of resistances (see Defence Mechanisms*), was highly formative on Perls' later thinking and practice. In 1926, while working at the Institute for Brain-Damaged Soldiers in Frankfurt, under the directorship of Kurt Goldstein (1878–1965), Perls met his wife, Laura, a Gestalt psychologist. The influences of Goldstein's 'holism' and emphasis on 'self-actualization' and, in turn, the existentialism* of Paul Tillich (1886–1965) and Martin Buber (1878–1965), with whom Laura Perls also worked, were strong in the eventual establishment of Gestalt therapy. Added to these psychoanalytic, humanistic and existential strands, the optimistic cultural climate in the Germany of the 1920s, as expressed in the Bauhaus movement of architecture and applied art, and his personal friendship with the Austrian theatre director, Max Reinhardt (1873–1943), stirred in Fritz Perls a love of drama and theatricality which infused the workshops of his later years. In 1933, the Perls fled Nazi Germany and settled in South Africa, where they founded that country's first psychoanalytic institute. With the rise of the National Party after the Second World War, and the threat of a stricter form of apartheid,* the Perls emigrated to the US. In New York, they soon became the focus of a small group of therapists, writers and political activists, which settled on the term 'Gestalt therapy' as an approach that emphasizes that human perception sees the world as made up of coherent, intelligible configurations or 'gestalts'. In 1952, the first Institute of Gestalt Therapy was set up in New York.

While Laura Perls has remained a stable, and increasingly acknowledged, central figure in the development of Gestalt therapy, Fritz Perls, its avowed and charismatic leader in the earlier years, lived a restless existence through the 1950s and 60s. Eventually settling at the Esalen Institute in California, Perls became caught up in the so-called 'human potential movement' of the 1960s, a pot-pourri of open-ended approaches – psychoanalytic, existential, humanist and transpersonal – to therapy and personal growth. In 1969, the year before his death, Perls founded a Gestalt community at Cowichen, Vancouver Island.

Gestalt therapy, it is argued by many today, has been misunderstood and misrepresented as a result of the overly confrontational and anti-intellectual stance of its earlier protagonists. Latterly, the theory and practice of Gestalt therapy has been more clearly established and a greater professionalism encouraged through the training offered by, amongst others, the Gestalt Centre in London and the Scottish

Association for Gestalt Education, and the founding, in 1985, of the British-based Gestalt Psychotherapy Training Institute. The influence of Gestalt therapy has spread to the areas of organizational development and management training.

The assumptive basis of Gestalt therapy sees the person as an 'organismic' whole, functioning through the bodily, mental and spiritual dimensions of the total organism. Following some of the concepts of the early Gestalt psychologists, Gestalt therapists argue that, at any point of time, in healthy functioning, the individual's prior need (e.g. a pressing thirst) stands out as a 'figure' against the general 'ground' of what is being experienced. This overall configuration is the 'gestalt', of which, ideally, the person becomes aware (with the thirst as 'figure'), and then responds to it by action (taking a drink) and integration (the satisfaction of a quenched thirst). In creative adjustment, a series of gestalts emerge and dissolve as they are recognized and handled constructively. In disturbed functioning, the healthy cycle can be blocked at any stage: the need is not acknowledged, no action is taken to meet that need, the met need is not integrated or allowed to melt away. Gestalt therapy recognizes four main patterns (see Defence Mechanisms*) which can disrupt awareness of the self* and the environment, and thus lead to the 'unfinished business' of such 'incomplete gestalts': introjection, in which elements of the environment are taken into the self unreflectingly; projection, where there is displacement from the self into the environment; retroflexion, involving an unproductive inner dialogue rather than engagement with the outside world; and confluence, in which there is a merging of the self with the surrounds, avoiding distinctiveness.

In the face of such maladjustment, Gestalt therapy, through individual counselling or group therapy,* seeks to provide a context for the client to work towards a greater awareness of moment-by-moment experience, the cultivation of an inner strength, a fuller integration into everyday life and an increased ability to relate to others. With these aims in mind, the Gestalt therapist operates with a style that is unique to each therapeutic relationship. There is great emphasis on the 'here-and-now' experience within the counselling process. This immediacy is stimulated and fostered by the therapist's willingness to share something of his or her own feelings and re-

actions as the counselling progresses, and by the asking of 'what?' and 'how?', rather than the more analytical 'why?', questions. The holism of Gestalt theory is further expressed in creative experimentation in which clients, once relational trust is established, may be encouraged to act out what they are feeling, sensing or thinking through dramatization, re-enacting a dream, art work, dance or other physical movement. At such times, the 'empty chair' technique may be used, where a client is invited to express himself or herself to the imagined presence of someone significant or to enter into a dialogue, for example, between his or her 'stronger' and 'weaker' selves.

The holism, immediacy and quest for integration in Gestalt therapy have attracted a number of Christian counsellors and psychotherapists who have incorporated something of the aims, techniques and language of this methodology into their therapeutic work. One eclectic approach that assimilates some of the perspectives of Gestalt is that of Ian Davidson (1932–), who writes, 'Gestalt . . . is a tool, a way of seeing, a wholeness of perception, a method of personal growth, a grasping of hoped-for possibilities, like faith itself . . .' (*Here and Now*, p. 181).

See also: PASTORAL CARE, COUNSELLING AND PSYCHOTHERAPY. [12]

Bibliography

M. Buber, *I and Thou* (ET, New York, 1970; Edinburgh, 1971); P. Clarkson, *Gestalt Counselling in Action* (London and Newbury Park, CA, 1989); I. Davidson, *Here and Now: An Approach to Christian Healing through Gestalt* (London, 1991); M. Parlett and F. Page, 'Gestalt Therapy', in W. Dryden (ed.), *Individual Therapy: A Handbook* (Milton Keynes and Bristol, PA, 1990); F. S. Perls, *The Gestalt Approach and Eye Witness to Therapy* (New York, ²1976); F. S. Perls *et al.*, *Gestalt Therapy: Excitement and Growth in the Human Personality* (New York, ³1972; Harmondsworth, 1974); V. Van De Riet, M. P. Korb and J. J. Gorrell, *Gestalt Therapy: An Introduction* (New York, ²1985).

R.F.H.

GIVING can be understood as a demand or responsibility placed upon us, for almsgiving is an obligation common to many worldviews. This article also explores the overwhelming motivation for giving as response to the love of God.

1. The virtue of giving

Alms-giving is one of the five 'pillars' of Islam, and in Buddhism the laity are required to give food and alms to enable monks to fulfil their teaching role. Money is appropriately given to support ministers of the gospel (see Thomas Oden, *Ministry through Word and Sacrament*). Contemporary Judaism summons all humankind to act for the common good and to give to relieve the poor for God's sake. But anthropologists recognize gift-giving as a universal of human behaviour, often accompanied by an ethical concern about the inner attitude of the giver, which is sometimes expressed as 'the golden rule'.* This concern for motivation leads us to recognize with the psychologist that human maturity should always include elements of unconditional self-acceptance, decreasing self-centredness and a courage to take risks. In Christian spiritual writings, maturity has been expressed in terms of an attachment to God with a corresponding detachment from the pressures, fears and anxieties of the material world.

2. Christian giving

The NT (Mt. 6:1–4; Lk. 11:41; 12:33) encourages alms-giving (Gk. root *eleos*, 'mercy'), in continuity with earlier teaching (Ps. 41:1; Pr. 19:17; Dn. 4:27; Tobit 12:8). Jesus allowed himself to be interrupted by human need (Mt. 9:20; 15:22), and told the rich young man to 'Go, sell . . . give . . .' as a prelude to receiving treasure in heaven and starting a life of discipleship (Mk. 10:21). Christ, who gave his life for enemies (Rom. 5:8), taught love for enemies (Mt. 5:43–45). Giving can mirror the Father's love for all and be a doorway to sharing God's joy (Acts 20:35). As a joyful response to the love and forgiveness of God, kindness is done 'to Jesus Christ' (Mt. 25:40), and expresses self-giving devotion to God (Mt. 10:21). See the generosity of Zaccheus (to whose house 'salvation' had come, Lk. 19:9) and the lifestyle of the church in Acts (Acts 2:44–46; 4:32–35; *cf.* Phil. 4:10–20). It is culpable to ignore the opportunity for alms-giving (Lk. 16:19–31), because the rich are to express their security in God by such generosity. But charity alone is inadequate – God (in Jesus' parable in Mt. 20:1–16) gives both work and wages, reflecting the context for OT alms-giving, namely a covenant based on justice that protected the poor (Ex. 20:22 – 23:19).

3. Symbolic giving

Gifts are symbolic. They reveal priorities and express relationships. For example, in some group training exercises, the giving of some object represents the giving of self involved in group membership; or, in studies of people who have behaved in an altruistic manner, researchers have tried to identify the 'ethic of care or giving' that makes some people active 'rescuers' rather than passive 'bystanders'. Similarly, pastoral leaders need to reflect carefully on the meaning of anything they are given, and be ready to receive it in God's name. Oden shows how, in the history of pastoral care, gifts (money or kind offered within worship) both provide for ministry and express love for God, mirroring the way Jesus expressed *his* human dependence (Lk. 8:2–3; 5:29). The apostolic collection from the Gentiles offered to Jewish Christians in Jerusalem (Acts 11:29–30; Rom. 15:26–27) was highly symbolic in that it provided famine relief, but also expressed a radically new solidarity in Christ, a Christological basis for future giving (2 Cor. 8:9; 9:15), so that generosity and mutuality became recognized as authentic marks of the church. Such giving that arises out of love (1 Cor. 13:3; and in the OT this included loans, according to Pss. 37:26; 112:5; Pr. 19:17) finds expression not only in the 'conversion of the pocket', but also in giving time, energy, experience, skill or some other expertise – and more recently in giving blood, donating an organ for transplant and in giving one's life for another.

4. Giving and society

It follows that giving can have social and political dimensions. In European history, because the church was such a large landowner, monasteries and churches became channels through which society benefited from Christian giving. Expressing justice and advancing the 'common good' today, governments make fiscal provision for disadvantaged sections of society, and give economic aid to disadvantaged nations. But such 'giving' can easily lack integrity. Japan (the world's largest aid-giver) has wasted precious tropical hardwoods on building sites; other 'aid-givers' have often received a greater sum back from developing countries in interest on loans. So 'trade, not aid' has sometimes been advocated as the more generous policy. However, while trading commits the 'giver' to greater involvement with the receiver, the benefits of trade can be restricted to a small élite, from whom little extra wealth 'trickles down' to the poor. The 'gift' of education, to develop adult literacy skills, new socio-political awareness and a higher standard of managerial competence has been a way of 'giving power to the people' (see P. Freire, *Pedagogy of the Oppressed*).

5. Giving and the church

Strict integrity is also needed in handling financial gifts between churches. Figures show that when large sums of money have been given overseas from Britain and the USA, significant amounts have gone astray, and some donors refuse to give where there is no managerial accountability. But the danger of such commendable caution is that the self-sufficient, wealthy giver can retain inappropriate control over the recipient, and thereby deny the mutuality and common dependence on God that characterize Christian giving. At the small scale of personal giving, this interdependency can lead to involvement in and prayer for the lives and ministry of the recipients. An equivalent divesting of control is necessary on the larger scale.

6. The OT tithe and Christian giving

The payment of a tithe (a tenth) represented someone's whole life offered to the covenant God within the community's celebration (Gn. 14:17–20; 28:20–22; Dt. 7:12ff.; 15:15; 26:1ff.). Crops, fruit, animals and money were given (Lv. 27:30–33), and thereby provision was made for the poor, the Levite and the priests (*e.g.* Nu. 18). To omit to give God's tithe was 'robbery' (Mal. 3:8–10). Tithing was 'faith in practice', a generosity seen elsewhere in the OT (*e.g.* Ex. 25:1ff.; 31:1ff.).

Christ fulfilled the OT (*e.g.* Mt. 5:17–20; Heb. 7), and often in parables spoke of money as symptomatic of spiritual priorities. The tithe has enduring value today in so far as Christians a. give, pray and fast to the glory of God (Mt. 6:1ff.); b. give in a planned manner but also respond joyfully to God's gracious blessing (1 Cor. 16:1–2); c. are concerned for justice more than ritual practice (Mt. 23:23); d. pay attention to motive more than the amount of the gift (1 Cor. 13:3), so as to affirm the generosity of the poor (Lk. 21:4; 2 Cor. 8–9); e. aim through giving to express the grace of the gospel (Acts 11:29–30; Rom. 15:26–27); and f. use giving as a way to minister to their ministers.

Our Lord's total self-giving alone constitutes the basis for Christian giving: 'Freely you have received, freely give' (Mt. 10:8).

Bibliography

R. J. Foster, *Money, Sex and Power* (London, 1985), pp. 1–87; P. Freire, *Pedagogy of the Oppressed* (London and New York, 1972); T. C. Oden, *Ministry through Word and Sacrament* (New York, 1989), pp. 200–225.

G.O.S.

GLASSER, WILLIAM (1925–). Advertised as 'a new approach to psychiatry', Dr William Glasser's *Reality Therapy*, first published in New York in 1965, and rapidly a best-seller, was one of several severely critical responses to psychoanalytic* approaches to so-called 'mental illness'. Glasser rejected the concept of mental illness that 'People do not act irresponsibly because they are "ill"; they are "ill" because they act irresponsibly', and he also challenged all the other central postulates of psychoanalytic theory. He argued that the 'mentally ill' are unable to satisfy their basic needs of relatedness and respect in a responsible way, because they deny the reality of their world. His key words are reality, responsibility* and right and wrong.

According to Glasser, the human needs to love and be loved and to feel that we are worthwhile to ourselves and to others are bound up with maintaining a certain standard of behaviour. Morals, standards and values are all intimately related to the fulfilment of our need for self-worth (see Self-esteem*). The complicated business of acquiring responsibility thus becomes, for reality therapy, an essential ingredient, and this can be achieved through the development of an emotional relationship between the client and a responsible therapist. The responsibility for change rests with the client, and the skill of therapy is to facilitate a sense of responsibility in the client.

Glasser has also written *The Identity Society* (New York, 1975), *Mental Health or Mental Illness?* (New York, 1960) and *Schools without Failure* (New York, 1969).

D.J.A.

GLUTTONY, see DEADLY SINS.

GODLINESS is the ideal quality of a Christian's life, the sign of spiritual health and the means of glorifying God. The term itself, which is becoming ominously rarer in contemporary Christian speech, has for four centuries carried the thought of humble reverence for God expressed in devotion to him, desire to please him, conscientious conformity to his word, concern and compassion for those in need, and a capacity to endure, press on, and keep worshipping in face of all kinds of adverse pressure and discouragement. It is thus a weighty word, comparable in its breadth of meaning to *pietas* (piety), a key word in Calvin's* Latin. In the OT, 'the fear of the Lord' is a pantechnicon phrase that includes all aspects of God-centred, self-abasing, law-loving, worship-oriented living, in other words the whole substance of godliness in its pre-Christian form. In the pastoral epistles and 2 Peter, the Gk. word *eusebeia*, elsewhere a generic label for religiousness of any kind, signifies godliness in the full Christian sense: evidently by the sixties of the 1st century it was becoming a technical theological term.

In these texts the focus of godliness is the 'mystery' (revealed reality) of Jesus* Christ, the incarnate mediator, now risen and glorified (1 Tim. 3:16), and the formula for godliness is to turn resolutely from sin in order to live uprightly henceforth in readiness for Christ's return (Tit. 2:11–14). The 'sound' doctrine (1 Tim. 1:10; 6:3; 2 Tim. 1:13; 4:3; Tit. 1:9; 2:1) – *i.e.* the teaching that is healthful in the sense of health-giving – is the teaching that accords with (makes for, and leads to) godliness (1 Tim. 6:3; Tit. 1:1). Power, which here means the influence of the Holy Spirit inducing Christlike ways of behaving, is fundamental to godliness (2 Tim. 3:5; *cf.* 2 Pet. 1:3), and there is no genuine godliness without it. Godliness is to be added to faith, goodness, knowledge, self-control and perseverance, for godliness (living for God and to God day by day) synthesizes all these into a stable mix, and so becomes the immediate basis for the regular loving service of others that is to be added to godliness to complete the Petrine bouquet of virtues (2 Pet. 1:5–7). Godliness involves accepting one's responsibilities for others, *e.g.* in family support (1 Tim. 5:4, where the verb is *eusebeō*, meaning to express *eusebeia* towards another person). Godliness is God's will for all his people at all times (1 Tim. 2:2), even under the persecution and hostility that every Christian will meet in some shape or form (2 Tim. 3:12).

Godliness is exemplified and modelled most clearly by the psalmists, the Lord Jesus Christ, and the apostle Paul. The psalmists praise and pray, confess, complain, celebrate and rejoice from the heart, not concealing any feeling, and thus they display to us the motivational, perceptual, emotional and doxological impulses that make up the inside story of godly living. Though the psychology and inner life of God incarnate must obviously have dimensions and depths that are wholly beyond our ken, Jesus in the Gospel narratives exhibits all the character qualities that Paul calls 'the fruit of the Spirit' in believers – love, joy, peace, patience, kindness, goodness, faithfulness, gentleness and self-control (Gal. 5:22–23) – along with a single-minded zeal for his Father's will and glory that is so intense as to be almost terrifying (see Jn. 2:13–17; *cf.* Lk. 12:49–50; 13:31–35), which also believers are clearly meant to imitate (*cf.* Rom. 12:11). Paul, as one such imitator, consciously models godliness to guide his converts (1 Cor. 11:1; *cf.* 4:16; Phil. 3:17; 4:9; 1 Thes. 1:6; 2 Thes. 3:7–9), and his own real godliness is mirrored and profiled very clearly in 1 Corinthians 1 – 4, 2 Corinthians, Philippians, 1 Thessalonians, 2 Timothy and Philemon.

Three errors that recur in the church's thought and life are: focusing on ethical effort in disregard of faith, contemplation and worship (legalism*); focusing on faith, contemplation and worship in disregard of ethical effort (antinomianism*); and focusing on the externals of behaviour in disregard of motivation (formalism, exemplified by the Pharisees). The teaching that makes for godliness unites these concerns and never allows them to be detached from each other.

J.I.P.

GOLDEN RULE, THE. A term used for well over 200 years, it designates Christ's exhortation to his disciples, recorded in Mt. 7:12, 'So in everything, do to others what you would have them do to you, for this sums up the Law and the Prophets' (*cf.* Lk. 6:31).

The nearest parallel in Mark's Gospel is to be found in our Lord's quotation from Leviticus in Mk. 12:31: 'Love your neighbour as yourself.' This is also quoted by Paul, as summing up the law, in Rom. 13:9.

There are some parallel sayings in other religions, and in ancient Gk. philosophy. Most are negative, like this from a Hindu source: 'Let no man do to another any act he wishes not done to himself by others, knowing it to be painful to himself' (*Mahabharata*, Shanti parva, cclx.21).

Rabbinic parallels are also negative. Hillel the Elder (*fl.* 1st century BC) is reported as saying, 'Do not do to your neighbour what is hateful to you; this is the whole Law, all the rest is commentary' (*Shabbath* 31a).

The more positive Muslim statement, 'No man is a true believer unless he desires for his brother that which he desires for himself,' may itself have been influenced by the words of Jesus, although we cannot be certain of this.

As a maxim, the Golden Rule, in the form it takes in the teaching of Jesus, expresses the essential altruism, inwardness, homogeneity and positive character of his ethic.

G.W.G.

GOOD, THE, see GOODNESS; HAPPINESS; SUBJECTIVISM.

GOODNESS is excellence of quality, particularly the moral qualities of benevolence* (lit. wanting what is good), and it is thereby akin to love (see ②) and mercy.* God not only *does* good (beneficence), he *is* good (benevolence). While it is ascribed ultimately to God, it is used derivatively of his creatures in so far as they reflect the goodness of their maker.

The biblical picture

The psalmist says of God, 'How great is your goodness' (Ps. 31:19), and that men 'will celebrate your abundant goodness . . . The LORD is good to all; he has compassion on all he has made' (Ps. 145:7, 9). Again and again in praise to God for his mighty works, God's goodness recurs: 'Give thanks to the LORD, for he is good; his love endures forever' (Pss. 106; 107). Jesus picked up on this OT theme when he asked, 'Why do you call me good? No-one is good except God alone' (Mk. 10:18).

Yet the creation* is full of God's goodness (Ps. 33:5), and the Genesis narrative records God's own appraisal of what he made: 'it was good . . . it was good . . . it was very good' (Gn. 1:10, 12, 18, 21, 25, 31). On this basis the NT affirms the goodness of food and marital sex, over against some other-worldly ascetics (1 Tim. 4:1–5; *cf.* Ps. 107:9). God's goodness follows us throughout life (Ps. 23:6) and it leads to repentance (Rom. 2:4, AV). In the believer, goodness is a fruit of the Spirit (Gal. 5:22), the fruit of walking in the light (Eph. 5:9).

This biblical picture has been a major source of Christian ethical reflection. It affirms: 1. God alone is altogether good, so that morally he transcends everyone else; 2. every good thing we possess comes from God; 3. the goodness of creation derives from and is dependent on God; 4. creation's gifts are therefore to be received and enjoyed with thankfulness; 5. while sin has marred the goodness of creation, particularly human nature, God's goodness calls us to repentance and the good work of his Spirit creates moral goodness in his people.

God as the Good

The history of Christian ethics has been profoundly influenced by this relation of God's goodness to that of his creatures. Plato* had conceived of a form of the Good, but it was an impersonal ideal. His Demiurge (the maker of the physical world) fashioned things according to such ideals, desiring that everything be good, but he was limited by irrational forces in nature. Aristotle* wrote that the highest good for human beings must be something intrinsically good, something for the sake of which every other good is to be sought. But this highest good, a full human life lived virtuously under the rule of reason, is devoid of the resources of biblical faith in the visible incarnation of perfect goodness in Jesus Christ, and his saving goodness that creates the good in us. Augustine,* who came to Christianity out of his study of Platonism, saw that God is the good which Plato had sought, the God whose goodness fills the earth and surrounds our lives, and whom we know in Jesus Christ. Augustine's *Confessions* recounts this discovery. Other conceptions of the good, like Aristotle's, are anthropocentric, thinking of goodness only in terms of human good, but Augustine says God made us for himself and our hearts are restless until they rest in his goodness. Love for God must therefore replace all lower loves in governing the soul. As the Westminster divines put it later, the highest end (good) of man is to glorify God and enjoy him for ever.

Creation's goodness

Augustine also found in the biblical view of goodness a key to understanding evil.* If everything in creation has its exemplar in the mind of God, then evil must be a privation of that divinely intended goodness (like an apple that rots). Sin is just such a privation due to our failure to love God fully in all his goodness.

By the same token, since the human body God created is good, no neglect or abuse of it should be allowed. Augustine showed a deep appreciation of nature's beauty and disagreed with some Platonists who said we should flee from the sensory world. He advocated a broad education in mathematics, music, history and literature on the ground that all creation's resources are good. If pagans have said things that are true, even though they misused what they know, Christians can reclaim that truth for themselves and restore it to the whole of God's truth from which it was in effect torn. Love for truth is love for what is good. Of course, knowledge is not the highest good: God is, but in his goodness all creation participates. So love for God cannot preclude loving truth or loving the creation. We should love them because God loves them, delighting in them to his praise as the psalmist did. Love for the good God is the unifying virtue that gives other good things their proper place.

Thomas Aquinas* further developed this line of thought. God, he asserts, is the good of every other good, the one who makes every other good the good it is. This is because God introduces his own likeness into created things in varying ways and degrees, so that the whole array of creation together manifests his goodness. In that sense, all being is good; all things tend, if only implicitly, towards God. Not only the human heart, but everything in creation is made for God and is restless until it rests in his likeness.

Human goodness

That God is the highest good for all creation has implications for human goodness. God's goodness is the norm, so a person is good in so far as he or she is like God in benevolence and loving kindness. To 'be good' is not just to be 'on one's best behaviour': that might be a hollow façade, and in any case behaviour is a matter of what we do overtly rather than what we are inwardly. It can be beneficence without benevolence. The latter is a virtue, and as such it involves attitudes, intentions, desires, the will, an inner disposition to act in beneficent ways. A good person, truly virtuous, is thus one who in his or her heart desires what, and as, God desires. To be good is to be like God, to image his goodness in both the inner reality and the outward activities of one's life.

Virtue* finds outward expression as 'good works' flow from the inner virtue of goodness. By themselves they are not virtuous: 'If I give all I possess to the poor . . . but have not love, I gain nothing' (1 Cor. 13:3). But works of love done from the heart are what goodness is about. As faith without works is dead, so is goodness without good works.

To do good we direct our actions to beneficial ends. Beneficence and benevolence are teleological concepts; beneficence is a teleological principle for making ethical decisions. Thus the first precept in Aquinas' statement of the natural moral law is that 'good is to be done and ensued, and evil is to be avoided'. All other precepts of natural law,* he says, are based on this. Later ethicists see the principle of beneficence, that we have an obligation to do good and prevent harm, in the utilitarian's (see Consequentialism*) rule about maximizing the balance of good over evil. In this way, the biblical conception of goodness continues to influence Western ethical thinking, whether or not contemporary thinkers recognize it.

Locating perfect goodness in God alone, like Augustine's identification of God as the good, has suggested an argument for the existence of God. Anselm,* in his *Monologium*, argued from the degrees of goodness existing in creatures to a standard of perfect goodness by which they are measured, and which accordingly must exist. This was apparently the first of several forms of the moral argument for God's existence.

Bibliography

Augustine, *Confessions*, LCC 7; *idem*, *The Nature of the Good* in *Augustine: Earlier Writings* LCC 6; Thomas Aquinas, *STh* 1a 5–6.
A.F.H.

GOOD WORKS.

GOOD WORKS. The issue of 'good works' figured at the heart of the Reformation debate about justification.* Protestant theologians claimed faithfulness to Paul in teaching that justification is by faith *alone*, so that our 'good works' contribute nothing at all to our standing before God. On the other hand Roman Catholic theologians emphasized the eschatological nature of justification, and replied that our acquittal at the final judgment would depend on whether we had, by the grace of God and by faith in Christ, obeyed the commandments and atoned for our sins.

Although the disagreement was very sharp, recently attempts have been made to minimize the differences between these positions. Certainly, from the point of view of ethics and pastoral theology, we may say that both sides emphasized the necessity for 'good works' as the practical response of the Christian to the grace of God in Christ (*cf.* Jas. 2:17ff.). As far as Christian life is concerned, it is a matter purely of academic interest to discover the precise relationship between the death and resurrection of Christ as the objective foundation of our salvation, and our own response as its proximate cause. Protestants need to ensure that they take seriously the biblical teaching of final judgment* by works, and the emphasis on human reponsibility that follows from it (Mt. 25:31–46; Jn. 5:29; Rom. 2:6–10; 1 Cor. 3:10–15; 2 Cor. 5:10; 1 Pet. 4:17–19; Rev. 20:11–15), and Catholics need to be careful that the emphasis on this in their tradition does not rob them of a proper biblical assurance of salvation here and now (Jn. 5:24; 10:27–30; Rom. 5:1–2; 8:31–39; Heb. 6:16–20; 1 Pet. 1:3–9; 2 Pet. 1:3–4; 1 Jn. 5:6–13).

The expression 'good work(s)' is used thirty times in the NT, and typically refers to works of mercy and charity towards others in need. So Dorcas' practical care for the widows of Joppa is called her 'good works' (Acts 9:36), and Paul defines the 'good works' of the godly widow as 'bringing up children, showing hospitality, washing the feet of the saints, helping those in trouble and devoting herself to all kinds of good deeds' (1 Tim. 5:10; *cf.* 2 Cor. 9:8). Such practical service is probably the main content of the expression in other places where this is not immediately obvious from the context (*e.g.* Tit. 1:16; 2:7, 14; 3:1, 8, 14).

This fits with the overall structure of NT ethics, which does not focus on obeying the commandments, but on following the leading of the Holy Spirit in imitation of Christ and the apostles (Mt. 10:24–25; Jn. 13:13–17; Rom. 8:5–9; 1 Cor. 11:1).

S.M.

GOSPEL AND ETHICS. In the Graeco-Roman imperial cult, 'gospel' (Gk. *euangelion*) referred to announcements of the accession of an emperor, the birth or coming of age of his heir, or significant imperial actions and decrees. In the NT, 'gospel' vocabulary is used of God as king. The unique, historic events of the birth, ministry, death and resurrection of Jesus are a public, universal announcement of God's plan and action to save the world. This 'gospel' warns that human beings are sinful in the religious sense of arrogantly rebelling against God or of failing to trust in him. It offers forgiveness* to those who repent and turn to God in Christ, and proclaims hope of eternal, resurrected life beyond the grave.

At every stage the spiritual themes of sin (see Sin and Salvation⑤) and its counterpart, faith,* are inseparable from the ethical themes of evil and good. To be a sinner in relation to God is also to fall short of the character and behaviour which would be described as 'good', 'loving' or 'truthful' in relation to other people and the material world. Ethics comes before the gospel, in that ethics helps to focus the significance of sin and pin-point what needs to be forgiven. So some writers have seen Jesus' teaching in the Sermon on the Mount* as an 'impossible ethic' to drive the sinner towards the gospel. More emphasis is placed in the NT, however, on the fact that Christian ethics derives from the gospel. The NT scholar J. Jeremias (1900–79) suggests that the Sermon on the Mount should be described not so much as Christian morality but as 'lived faith'.

The connection of gospel and ethics assumes fundamental analogies between relationships in the material world and those in the mental or spiritual realm. When Paul, for example, argued for the importance of his fund to relieve poverty in the Jerusalem church, he appealed to gospel events. The Lord gave up the richness of his heavenly existence and became poor. Believers have become correspondingly richer in their experience of life in Christ. Therefore they should be willing to become economically poorer to help others become richer (2 Cor. 8:9, 13).

Forgiveness is another gospel theme at the heart of Jesus' ethics. God is merciful. As creator he allows his sun and rain to benefit the most evil or ungrateful person. As redeemer he has provided an atonement* available for the sins of the world. These salvation truths demand concrete ethical responses. Followers of Christ should take risks to love, lending money which may not be returned, and befriending people who have been hostile or violent (Lk. 6:34–36).

Attempting to define more closely how gospel and ethics relate has led to some deep divisions. The Reformation doctrine of justification* by faith stressed that God 'imputes' righteousness to the repentant believer in Christ's atoning death. Status or relationship with God changes and that permeates through other aspects of the believer's life as the Holy Spirit* leads to ethical change (sanctification*). The Counter-Reformation was suspicious of this language, fearing it might sever the vital connection between a right relationship with God and a quality of rightness or justice in human relationships. They continued to use the term 'justification' for an ongoing process including sanctification. Protestants argued that this could undermine the assurance in Paul's gospel and imply that our moral efforts secure God's favour. Since Hans Küng's (1928–) work on justification, the differences have narrowed but not disappeared.

Evangelicals this century have been suspicious of extending the connection between gospel and ethics from personal to social ethics.* Nineteenth-century criticism raised doubts about the historicity of gospel events such as the birth, miracles or resurrection of Jesus, or about belief in an end to history with the return of Christ. These were increasingly treated by the 'social gospel' school as powerful myths whose main role was to motivate social ethics. Liberal optimism about the fatherhood of God inspiring 'the brotherhood of man' has been replaced by many in the later 20th century with a liberationist model of God's bias towards the poor and oppressed as they struggle, perhaps violently, to be free (see Liberation Theology*).

Evangelicals have remained committed to the eternal importance of a personal response to Christ as Lord and saviour. Making the gospel known to individuals carries a high priority for the energy and resources of the church. There is a feeling that wrestling with complex social issues undermines the simplicity of the gospel and distracts energy from evangelism.

Despite these fears, since 1970 there has been much evangelical interest in social ethics. Biblical studies have highlighted the kingdom of God* not just as a collection of saved souls but as a community of persons with social relationships. Just as belief in resurrection of the body gives an ethical value to the physical side of mortal life (see Paul's argument in 1 Cor. 6:13–14), so belief in a future redeemed community gives an ethical value to relationships and structures in the communities in which we find ourselves now. Because the issues are complex and we do not have all the answers, we should not be deterred from putting them on the church's agenda. The gospel affirms the value of human life in this world and the next.

Bibliography

N. Biggar, 'Showing the Gospel in Social Praxis', *Anv* 8.1, 1991, pp. 7–18; T. Chester, *Awakening to a World of Need* (Leicester, 1993); J. Jeremias, *The Sermon on the Mount* (London, 1961); H. Küng, *Justification: The Doctrine of Karl Barth and a Catholic Reflection* (Philadelphia and London, ²1981); A. E. McGrath, *Justification by Faith* (Grand Rapids and Basingstoke, 1988); V. Sinton, 'Evangelical Social Ethics: Has it Betrayed the Gospel?', in M. Tinker (ed.), *Restoring the Vision* (Eastbourne, 1990); A. Verhey, *The Great Reversal: Ethics and the New Testament* (Grand Rapids, 1984).

V.M.S.

GOSPEL AND LAW, see LAW AND GOSPEL.

GOVERNMENT. In contemporary usage, 'the Government' refers to the executive branch of the State in distinction to its legislative and judicial branches. In this article, the term 'government' will refer more broadly to 'political authorities', whatever their precise institutional form.

The diversity of biblical material relating to government arises from the different political contexts in which biblical authors wrote, rather than, as is often supposed, from some fundamental scriptural ambiguity as to the nature and purpose of government. Amidst this undoubted contextual diversity, the divinely established nature and purpose of government nevertheless emerge clearly. Government is consistently seen as instituted, authorized and circumscribed by God, and its legitimacy as dependent upon the proper exercise of that authority, the purpose of which may be formulated as the establishment of justice (see Justice and Peace③) in the public realm of society.

The classic Pauline statement of this purpose in Rom. 13:1–7 has, rightly, been regarded in Christian tradition as of special normative significance, but it is necessary to interpret it in the light of the whole biblical narrative. In certain sections of the Bible, political authority is reflected upon from the perspective of the outsider (the patriarchal narratives), the subjugated (the Exile, the Gospels), the oppressed (the Exodus story, the Apocalypse), or the governed (Dt. 17:14–20). These essential perspectives highlight, in the first case, the limited and relative value of government, and in the second and third, its capacity, in a fallen world, for violent abuse and even idolatrous or demonic perversion. In the latter cases, the force of the denunciations of oppressive governments derives from the assumption of a divinely given purpose for government.

Israel's divine calling as covenant* community included the establishment of social, legal and political structures which displayed before all the nations the order of just relationships which God required. The distinctive content of these relationships was given in the Law,* of which one striking characteristic was concern for the rights of 'the poor'. To set Israel clearly apart from the Canaanite practice of ascribing deity to kings, Israel was to confess Yahweh alone as her king (*e.g.* Dt. 33:5), and, initially at least, to renounce the specific institution of kingship.

Political and judicial authority in Israel was, instead, first exercised by local elders, chosen by the people, constituting a rudimentary system of decentralized local government (*cf.* Ex. 5:6, 15, 19; Dt. 1:9–18; Nu. 1:16; 11:16). In merciful response to the incapacity of this system to deal with escalating injustice, God then appoints 'judges' to restore obedience to the just demands of the Law (Jdg. 2:16), though without dismantling the system of tribal eldership.

The people's subsequent cries for a king modelled on those of the surrounding nations reveal their disobedient desire to put a king in God's place, even though their appeal is also motivated by a legitimate desire for a more secure enforcement of justice (Jdg. 8:22–23; 9:1ff.; 1 Sa. 8; 9:16). Deuteronomy 17:14–15 ('When you enter the land . . . be sure to appoint over you the king the LORD your God chooses'), together with the subsequent blessing of the reigns of David and other righteous kings (*cf.* Ps. 72), suggests that there was no divine disapproval of monarchy *per se*. (No specific *forms* of government are either enjoined or prohibited in Scripture.) Rather, what is condemned is faith in human power rather than in God, as well as the unjust and arbitrary practice of kingship which is the unavoidable consequence of such misplaced faith (*cf.* Dt. 17:15b–20).

Prophetic denunciations of the abuse of political authority were trenchant (*e.g.* 1 Ki. 11:29–39; 14:1–16; 21:17ff.; Je. 22; Am. 7:7–17). That the same criteria of justice and righteousness were applied to the rulers of other nations (*e.g.* Is. 10:5ff.; Je. 19:15; 27:1–11; Dn. 2:37–38; 4:27) also points to the universality of the divine requirement for political authority. Just government was not merely a special obligation on the covenant people.

NT references to government are consistent with the OT vision in holding to the divine origin of and limits upon, political authority, and hence to the divine judgment merited by political rulers who perpetrate injustice – indeed the arrival of the Messiah testifies to a God who overthrows governments (Lk. 1:52). In the context of the subjugation of Palestine by the powerful Roman Empire, Jesus announces the imminent arrival of the kingdom of God.* This kingdom challenges Roman political authority by asserting its wholly derivative character (Jn. 19:11), and by exposing its authoritarian style of government (Lk. 13:32; 22:24–27). The injunction to 'give to Caesar what is Caesar's' (Mk. 12:17) presupposes the existence of definite limits on what Caesar may legitimately claim.

Apostolic proclamation of Jesus as Lord was perceived to be no less a challenge to the practice of Roman political authority; hence in Acts 17:7 Paul and Silas are charged with heralding Jesus as a rival king. The consistent apostolic position was already clear: 'We must obey God rather than men' (Acts 5:29). It is against this background that Paul's acknowledgment of the divine origin of Roman political authority in Rom. 13 (and Peter's in 1 Pet. 2:13–14) must be viewed. God has authorized the office of government as 'God's servant to do you good', specifically, to punish wrong and promote right conduct (Rom. 13:4; *cf.* 1 Pet. 2:14). The effect of declaring before Roman ears that government is a mere 'servant' is first to repudiate Roman claims to the deity of the Emperor, and secondly, by bringing government under the limits of divine law, to undermine the Roman concept of absolute political sovereignty.

The detailed practical meaning of the principle that the distinctive purpose of government is the establishment of justice in the public realm can be elucidated with reference to the substantial biblical teaching on what justice actually requires in numerous particular contexts. Further elucidation can be obtained from the Christian tradition, *e.g.* the works of Augustine,* Luther,* and Calvin* (see also Calvinistic Ethics*). Certain possible implications regarding the nature and operation of contemporary government can be suggested.

1. The idea that the authority of government is limited to its specific purpose points to the need for effective constitutional restraints on the exercise of that authority. An important one operative today in many Western democracies is making executives accountable

to independent and democratically elected legislatures. However, in view of the fact that democratic procedures are no guarantee of just outcomes, this is insufficient in itself; indeed non-democratic governments may also act justly.

2. Doing justice in the public realm may be understood as rendering to each person or institution in society what is their due, *i.e.* protecting the rights and duties of each. If so, then the role of government may be defined as the public guaranteeing of such rights and duties. By anchoring justifications of government activity in a coherent and comprehensive Christian conception of rights and duties, governments can be warned both against exceeding the competence attached to their office, and against rationalizing their passivity in the face of serious injustices.

See also: POWER; RIGHTS, HUMAN.

Bibliography

E. Brunner, *Justice and the Social Order* (London and New York, 1945); A. P. D'Entreves, *The Notion of the State* (Oxford, 1967); J. Maritain, *Man and the State* (ET, Chicago, 1951; London, 1954); P. Marshall, *Thine is the Kingdom: A Biblical Perspective on the Nature of Government and Politics Today* (Basingstoke and Grand Rapids, 1984); G. S. Smith (ed.), *God and Politics: Four Views on the Reformation of Civil Government* (Phillipsburg, NJ, 1989).

J.P.C.

GRACE. An adequate understanding of grace is indispensable in Christian ethics. Misunderstandings of grace as tolerance, or as amnesty, abound. The biblical definition of grace unites forgiveness* and moral absolutes.

1. The biblical redefinition of grace

The dominant meaning of the Gk. word (*charis*) was 'to find favour from a superior who bestows an undeserved gift'. Aristotle* defined *charis* as 'Helpfulness, towards someone in need, not in return for anything' (*Rhetoric* ii.7), *i.e.* 'charity', as we would say today. The LXX primarily uses *charis* to translate the Heb. *ḥēn*, which denotes the undeserved mercy* by which a stronger person aids someone weaker. Grace in this sense resolves the first aspect of the human moral dilemma: the need for mercy in response to failure to live with perfect love and obedience.

However, charity alone is insufficient in resolving the second dilemma: the capacity and power to live appropriately. The foundation for the more encompassing Christian understanding of grace is laid in the Heb. *ḥesed, i.e.* God's covenant* faithfulness. This conveys both aspects of grace: forgiveness, for Israel did not deserve God's love; and power to fulfil God's law.*

For Paul, who gave to *charis* its distinctively Christian meaning, grace always relates to the cross* and to Jesus* Christ (see Rom. 3:24–26; 5:1–21; 1 Cor. 1:18–19). Christ is the basis and even the content of its meaning (*e.g.* Rom. 5:15; 16:20b; 1 Cor. 1:4; 16:23; 2 Cor. 13:14). As T. F. Torrance (1913–) says, 'Grace is in fact identical with Jesus Christ in person and word and deed' (*The Doctrine of Grace in the Apostolic Fathers*, p. 21). Grace is God's being and action in Jesus Christ, both to forgive humankind's spiritual and moral failure, and to offer the perfect human response to God's moral demands.

2. Historical understandings of grace

Theologians have described many aspects of grace. 'Uncreated grace' is the being of God in triune communion. 'Created grace' is the action of God in people which empowers moral behaviour (Tertullian, *De Anima* 21; Thomas Aquinas, *STh* 1a2ae 108–109). The suggestion that grace heals human nature ('healing grace') led to the belief that the sacraments 'contained' grace ('sacramental grace') and enabled their recipients to perform meritorious deeds ('habitual grace').

Debate has raged throughout church history over whether grace actually enables one to be righteous, or whether it only accounts one as righteous. Augustine* rejected Pelagius' (*fl. c.* 383–424) insistence that God's grace gave people the capacity to live morally on their own (see *On Nature and Grace*, 53; *On Grace and Free Will*, 23–26). The Protestant Reformers asserted that believers remain sinful within themselves, and are righteous only in Christ. Otherwise, one risks believing that the source of moral goodness is within oneself, and Christ is functionally no longer necessary, except as an enabler and example. Martin Luther* denounced as blasphemous the assertion that 'our works create us or we are the creators of our works'. Such a view makes us 'our own gods' (*Works*, vol. 39.1). John Calvin* proclaimed, 'I renounce myself and my nature in which only shame and confusion are to be

417

found, but I come to Him in the name of the Lord Jesus Christ . . . He speaks for me, and it is in His name that I present myself, just as though I were He Himself' (*Sermon on Galatians*, 3:26–29).

3. Grace and law

There is no dichotomy between grace and law. Grace does not remove the imperatives of God's moral absolutes. In response to its salvation from slavery, Israel was called to observe the law of the covenant. Similarly, because of their deliverance from slavery to sin in Christ, believers are called to observe God's moral law. The imperatives of the law always follow, rather than precede, the indicatives of God's grace.

God's grace precedes and constitutes any response people make of faith,* obedience* and service. Karl Barth* asserts that God's will is *not* known in the 'guise of rules, principles, axioms, and general moral truth' (*CD* III / 4, p. 12). One discovers God's will in relationship with Christ. Apart from such a relationship, moral laws are inadequate, for through them people can seek dominion over God and rationalize their moral failure. Humankind's moral incapacity is not solved by moral pronouncements or by calls to obedience. The capacity to do the good that people know is pleasing to God results from their being brought into relationship with himself through adoption (Gal. 4:4–7). Thus they are enabled by the Holy Spirit,* on the basis of their life in Christ, to do works pleasing to him. Because of God's grace, relationship with God *and* a life of moral obedience are found in Christ rather than in one's own efforts. Emil Brunner* calls this 'the great inversion of existence . . . and it becomes manifest that the attempt to attain God by our own efforts rather than to base all our life on God, legalism, is the root of sin' (*The Divine Imperative*, ET, London and New York, 1937, p. 76).

Disobedience and unfaithfulness are not merely the violation of a standard. They are the defiling of a relationship. Scripture refers to unfaithfulness as whoring and adultery (Je. 2 – 3; Ho. 9:1; Mal. 2:11). Obedience to the commands of God is fundamental to the Christian life, but rather than being a strenuous human effort to comply with God's orders, it is the joyous living out of what Christians *are* in Christ. Christians are not to live like the Gentiles (Eph. 4:17–24) but are to show by their lives that they are in the light (Eph. 5:8); to live

like those who have been reconciled to God (Col. 1:22), who have been made alive in Christ (Col. 2:13) and clothed with him (Gal. 3:27). The old conduct has been put away, or more accurately, put to death (Col. 3:7–10).

4. Grace and freedom

Augustine summarized his ethical teaching in the often-misunderstood axiom 'Love and do what you will' (*oblige et quod vis fac* in the context of his defence of paternal chastisement means 'Love God, and what you then will, do'). He goes on to say, 'Let love's root be within you, and from that root nothing but good can come', and the root of love is Jesus Christ ('Homilies on 1 John' in *Later Works*, *LCC* 8, p. 316). This expresses the radical freedom of the Christian ethic. Moral obedience is a response to the salvation which is received by faith in Christ, rather than an obligation by which salvation is earned. Christians are freed to live with neither self-condemnation nor self-adulation.

Both grace and freedom are confused when too closely aligned with tolerance. To tolerate someone else's self-destructive behaviour because of the conviction that out of love people must be allowed to do as they please is not love but the antithesis of love. The moral indifference that dominates contemporary ethics under the banner of tolerance is in fact the insidious endorsement of anti-love. Human life cannot be merely tolerated as it is, for even the best human effort is insufficient to deserve God's favour. By God's grace in Christ, people are freed to live in his life which is pleasing to God, and actively pursue what is best and life-giving for their neighbours. Grace thus enables both humility* and hope* in Christians' encounters with their own as well as others' moral dilemmas.

Bibliography

H. Conzelman and W. Zimmerli, *TDNT* 9, pp. 372–415; J. Moffatt, *Grace in the New Testament* (London, 1931); J. Oman, *Grace and Personality* (Cambridge, 1917; ²1919); T. F. Torrance, *The Doctrine of Grace in the Apostolic Fathers* (Edinburgh, 1948); W. T. Whitley (ed.), *The Doctrine of Grace* (London, 1932).

T.A.D.

GRATITUDE is the appropriate response to a benevolently given gift, or to what someone is, or has done for one. It is a happy emotion, a gladness to have what is given, and to receive it in particular from the giver. One who dislikes the gift cannot be grateful for *it*, though he or she may be grateful for the 'thought', *i.e.* glad of the giver's benevolence.* If a person is glad to have the item given, but does not like to receive it from the particular person who has given it, then the receiver's emotion is not gratitude. Gratitude is the affirmation of a certain bond between the giver and the recipient. To the extent that what was given was owed to the recipient, or was required by duty to be given, gratitude is not appropriate, though it is appropriate for the recipient to be glad that his or her debtor has paid the debt. Gratitude also seems inappropriate to the extent that the giver is not motivated by benevolence towards the recipient. Gratitude also motivates actions – most notably giving thanks, returning favours, and doing kindnesses; but the truly grateful person does not see such actions as repayment of any debt.

It is clear from this definition why gratitude figures in the Christian life. The heart of the Christian message is about a gift (see Grace*) that God has freely and benevolently given to his people – the gift of eternal life, of liberation from sin and death, of admission to fellowship with himself and participation in his kingdom. The sense of glad dependency on the giver that characterizes Christian gratitude bonds the believer to God in love, and is a veridical perception of the goodness of the new life in him, his goodness (benevolence), and our dependency on him. For this reason gratitude is one of the central Christian virtues. As a virtue,* gratitude is not just an occasional feeling, but a well-confirmed trait of personality* or character (see ⑩), a reliable disposition to feel gratitude to God and to perform Christian actions out of gratitude to him.

Gratitude is by nature circumstantial: as a response to a gift, it is not appropriate where no gift is given. Thus in the ordinary circumstances of life, gratitude is only *sometimes* fitting. But Paul exhorts the Thessalonians: 'Be joyful always; pray continually; give thanks in all circumstances, for this is God's will for you in Christ Jesus' (1 Thes. 5:16–18). The reason that gratitude to God is always fitting, and can in principle be felt in all circumstances, is that *this* circumstance – that God has justified us through Christ's death and adopted us as his children – holds regardless of what the local circumstances of our lives may be. Thus Chris-

tian gratitude – like Christian hope* and Christian peace* – is a psychological foothold outside the temporal order. Gratitude also ties Christians to the temporal order, when they thank him for particular daily blessings – the health of their children, the spread of the church, the success of their work, particular answers to prayer. But this more circumstantial gratitude depends, for its Christian authenticity, on the readiness to give thanks in all circumstances; for it is this that ties us decisively to the Father of our Lord Jesus Christ.

Bibliography

F. Berger, 'Gratitude', *Eth* 85, 1975, pp. 298–309; P. S. Minear, 'Gratitude as a Synthesis of the Temporal and the Eternal', in H. A. Johnson (ed.), *A Kierkegaard Critique* (New York, 1962); R. C. Roberts, 'Virtues and Rules', *Philosophy and Phenomenological Research* 51.2, 1991, pp. 325–343; *idem, Spirituality and Human Emotion* (Grand Rapids, 1983), ch. 6; Thomas Aquinas, *STh* 2a2ae 106–107.

R.C.R.

GREED, see Covetousness.

GREGORY I (*c.* 540–604), influential pope and writer, also called Gregory the Great. After holding high civil office in Rome he became a monk. Recruitment to the ranks of the clergy issued in his becoming Bishop of Rome in 590. His achievements distinguished him as 'founder of the medieval papacy'.

His writings included the *Pastoral Rule* (*c.* 591) on the duties and qualities of the bishop as shepherd of souls, which for secular clergy had an influence almost as wide as Benedict's Rule for monks. Alfred the Great (849–*c.* 900) translated it into Old English. Preaching, spiritual direction* and the bishop's own example are prominent.

Gregory's massive exposition of Job, *Moralia* (finished *c.* 595), likewise became a standard manual of moral theology (see Christian Moral Reasoning ⑱) and asceticism* in the medieval West. Applying a threefold pattern of intepretation – historical, allegorical and moral – it considers the relationship between the active and the contemplative life. With his *Homilies on Ezekiel*, it made him a recognized master on mysticism (*cf.* C. Butler, *Western Mysticism*, London, 1922).

Gregory's theology was a moderated

Augustinianism. He ensured the continuing dominance of ascetic ideals in Latin Christianity, and fulfilled a remarkably energetic role as a pastoral administrator.

Bibliography

ETs of *Pastoral Rule*: J. Barmby, *NPNF*, 2nd series, XII; H. Davis, *ACW* 11; J. Bliss, 3 vols. in 4 (Oxford, 1844–50).

F. H. Dudden, *Gregory the Great*, 2 vols. (London, 1905); G. R. Evans, *The Thought of Gregory the Great* (Cambridge, 1986).

D.F.W.

GRIEF, see BEREAVEMENT; LIFE, HEALTH AND DEATH. 13

G ROSS NATIONAL PRODUCT (GNP) is one of the names for the total national income of a country, usually measured every year. It is a measure of a country's total economic activity. There are three ways of measuring total national income: by production, by income and by expenditure.

GNP, the *production* method, aggregates all of the firms' output. This is done by totalling up the value added by each firm's contribution to products. If the value added was not computed, there would be double counting of the value of output in instances where firms are engaged only in the intermediate production of goods which they pass on to other firms to finish off before they are sold. The *income* method aggregates all personal incomes (wages, rents and profits) but excludes transfer payments (*e.g.* State pensions, student grants) in order to avoid double counting. Lastly, the *expenditure* method adds up all items of final expenditure on goods and services by consumers and governments but excludes intermediate expenditure (*e.g.* payments for raw materials) by firms. When allowance is made for imports and exports, these three methods should give the same totals. In practice they are not precisely the same because errors creep in at every level of the information collection.

There is a range of other measures of national income which use gross value as their starting-point. Net national income is derived by subtracting depreciation, *i.e.* wear and tear of capital equipment, from the gross figure. It is possible to have national income measured at market prices or at factor costs: factor costs are obtained by subtracting any indirect taxes (*e.g.* Value Added Tax) from the prices which give the value of goods and services, and add-

ing in the value of any subsidies. GNP at constant prices has deflated the yearly values in order to control for inflation and to see if real growth has occurred. *Gross domestic product (GDP)* is a measure of the activity within a national boundary; imports and capital inflows are subtracted but exports and capital outflows are added. In some developing countries, GDP can be higher than GNP, whereas in most developed countries, GNP is higher than GDP. Per capita values can be obtained for any of these national income measures by dividing the total by the head of population. However, the most usual value to calculate is the income method per head of population.

These measures are often used to give an idea of a country's wealth and standard of living. They are used by policy-makers and governments, and general economic targets are set for the whole economy using these measures. This use started largely after the acceptance of Keynesian economic theories in the 1930s. If GNP at constant prices is increasing over time, it suggests the economy is growing. Comparisons of per capita income between countries are used to give a rough idea of comparative standards of living. For a number of reasons it is important to see these measures only as rough indicators. Within one country, some aspects of economic activity will not be counted because they are not paid for, and yet they affect our quality of life: *e.g.* housework or child care. Countries also have different accounting conventions. In the former Soviet Union, payments to government employees for personal services such as hairdressing and entertainment were not included in national income. Countries which have a private system of health or education will have a different base for their calculations from those which use public funds for these services, *etc.* Also, aggregate measures do not tell us anything about the distribution of incomes within a country, which can be very important for its social stability. Although aggregate measures are imperfect for representing standards of living, at a broad level, they do accurately reflect differences between developed and developing countries.

Underlying much of the use of national income measures is the idea that economic growth must be a good thing. However, an increasing group of economists and politicians are questioning this assumption, mostly because of the effects of economic growth on our global environment* and the way it uses up exhaustible natural resources. Donald Hay in *Economics Today*, ch. 8, contains a review of these debates. That growth is necessarily good, and that it is more important than issues of distribution, are clearly materialist assumptions which Christians would want to question. However, if a country were to advocate a no-growth option, there would be considerable resultant problems of unemployment and regional decline for a domestic economy to address.

Bibliography

D. A. Hay, *Economics Today* (Leicester, 1989).

S.D.

GROTIUS, HUGO (1583–1645) was born in Delft. Influenced by liberal ideas, he became a friend of Arminius (1560–1609) and a leader of the Remonstrants. At fourteen he graduated from Leiden and then occupied high legal posts, obtaining in 1613 a seat in the States of Holland. In 1618 he was imprisoned for life for opposition to the Gomarian Calvinism of the Synod of Dordt. In 1621 he escaped and fled to Paris, becoming from 1634 until his death the Swedish Ambassador to France.

His *De Veritate Religionis Christianae* (1627) was a widely used simple and direct apologetic work. His *Defensio Fidei Catholicae de Satisfactione Christi* developed a 'governmental' theory of the atonement* wherein the key was God's willingness to accept Christ's sacrifice. He also pioneered in historical-philological studies of Scripture and produced an equivocating work on predestination.

His greatest work was ethical and legal. He is, with reason, often regarded as the father of international law. While Francisco de Vitoria* and others had written previously, Grotius' work commanded wide assent and was accepted as authoritative. *De Jure Praedae* (1605) discussed rules for captured ships, while *Mare Liberum* (1609) defended freedom of the seas. His masterpiece was *De Jure Belli ac Pacis* (1625) which combined philosophy with reflection on current treaties (*jus voluntarium*). It elaborated just grounds and rules for war (see Just-War Theory*). He sought laws governing States, hence antecedent to institutions, and postulated a legal ground in a law of nature (see Natural Law*) mediated by an absolutist version of a social contract.* This law was independent of God. While firmly believing in God, he was an influence in separating ethics from theology.

Bibliography

De Jure Belli ac Pacis (ET, New York, 1964).

A. H. Chroust, 'Hugo Grotius and the Scholastic Natural Law Tradition', *New Scholasticism* 17.4, 1943, pp. 101–133; E. Dumbauld, *The Life and Legal Writings of Hugo Grotius* (Norman, OK, 1969); C. S. Edwards, *Hugo Grotius: The Miracle of Holland* (Chicago, 1981); W. S. M. Knight, *The Life and Works of Hugo Grotius* (London, 1962); H. Lauterpacht, 'The Grotian Tradition in International Law', *British Yearbook of International Law* 23, 1943, p. 51.

P.A.M.

GROUP DYNAMICS. All of us belong to various groups (family, church, college, union, *etc.*) which have some significance for us.

Although sometimes used more loosely, the term 'group dynamics' technically refers to the academic field of inquiry into the nature, development and maintenance of groups, their interrelationships with individuals, other groups and larger institutions with particular reference to their psychological and social factors. Group dynamics began as an identifiable field of inquiry in the 1930s, associated initially with Kurt Lewin's (1890–1947) work on field theory in the USA, and in the past few decades a considerable amount of empirical research has been published.

A 'group' in this sense is more than just an aggregate of people. It is typically defined as 'a collection of individuals who have relations to one another that make them interdependent to some significant degree' (D. Cartwright and A. Zander, *Group Dynamics*, p. 46). For instance, an aggregate of tourists separately looking round a church is not a group, but a collection of tourists with a guide, focusing together on specific tasks, is a group. A collection of people in a room may not be a group: if someone shouts 'Fire!', their interdependence and shared focus of interest constitutes them a group.

Groups are inevitable and ubiquitous; the dynamics they generate are powerful, and can have positive or destructive consequences.

Social scientists are concerned to ask what conditions are necessary for the formation of groups (*e.g.* spontaneous or deliberate), their selection, duration, maintenance or disintegration. Much research has centred on how groups establish norms ('What we, in this group, think, believe or behave'); the influence these have on members; group cohesion (external threats, dedication to task, *etc.*); conformity (fear of sanction, group disapproval, *etc.*); power and influence in groups; patterns of leadership* and factors affecting group performance; the structure of groups and the influence of size. Research methodology has posed problems. Some use observational methods, some use experimentation (sometimes with hidden manipulation – which raises ethical questions). Some theories draw on the psychology of interpersonal relations, some on Gestalt, field and psychoanalytic theories. All have their own hidden values and assumptions.

Training groups ('T' groups) to help leader and manager experience group dynamics, their own behaviour in groups, and others' response to them became popular in the 1960s, the groups varying with the theoretical perspective of the trainer. One approach which had a significant influence on pastoral training was that of W. F. Bion (1897–1979), who documented various patterns of relatedness within the behaviour of small groups (*i.e.* eight to ten people). He postulated two types of mental activity: 'work-group' activity, which is directed to the task for which the group exists; and the largely unconscious 'basic assumptions' activity, which can either assist or obstruct the group's task. The fundamental hidden desire of the group is to survive, and three common basic assumptions may guard against the anxiety that the group may disintegrate. These are what Bion calls: 1. *dependence*, in which group members place all their hopes in one of its number to solve all their needs; 2. *expectancy*, in which the group hopes that a new leader or circumstance will arise – sometimes related to the belief that the interaction of two of the members of the group (pairing) will produce the needed resolution; and 3. *fight-flight*, in which the group finds its cohesion in defending itself against some supposed external threat.

In 1978, Bruce Reed's (1920–) *Dynamics of Religion* drew on some group dynamics theory to provide a social study of the nature of religious activity.

The work on the functioning of management teams by R. M. Belbin (1926–) has been used within Christian communities in the understanding and management of differing gifts. Belbin's research and self-perception inventories have indicated the benefits for constructive task-oriented group functioning of a variety of different personality types. An understanding of personal attributes can facilitate an understanding of best team roles (*cf.* Myers-Briggs*). Belbin indicates that an ideal team might need a range of skills such as 'company worker' (loyal and dutiful); a 'chairman' (self-confident and controlled); a 'shaper' (outgoing and dynamic); a 'plant' (*i.e.* an 'ideas person'; individualistic, unorthodox); a 'resource investigator' (extroverted, curious); a 'monitor evaluator' (unemotional, prudent); several 'team workers' (socially oriented, mild, sensitive); and a 'completer/finisher' (painstaking, orderly, conscientious, anxious). Such a team would work more constructively than one composed of people with identical gifts. Others have drawn up alternative lists.

A knowledge of group dynamics can be particularly useful to pastors in helping identify different types of groups within congregations, suiting group size to the task and the capacity of its members, and developing awareness of the interaction of different groups within the church. There are dangers, however, in adopting any one model too enthusiastically, since the variables in the study of groups are many and interactive, and no one theory covers every situation. Especial care is needed to avoid transferring theories about small group (*e.g.* family) behaviour on to large groups (*e.g.* congregations) and introducing techniques from group therapy* into task-related friendship groups.

Bibliography

J. Adair, *Developing Leaders* (Maidenhead, 1988; New York, 1989); M. Argyle, *The Psychology of Interpersonal Behaviour* (Harmondsworth, 1967); R. M. Belbin, *Management Teams* (Oxford and New York, 1981); W. R. Bion, *Experiences in Groups* (New York and London, 1961); D. Cartwright and A. Zander, *Group Dynamics* (London, ³1968); C. B. Handy, *Understanding Organisations* (Harmondsworth, 1985); B. Reed, *The Dynamics of Religion* (London, 1978).

D.J.A.

GROUP THERAPY covers a range of activities which harness the properties of groups for therapeutic purposes: in particular for improving participants' interactional skills, increasing self-awareness and improving individual functioning. The therapist, leader, consultant or central person creates a climate and a context in which change can occur. A wide spectrum of beliefs, values, assumptions and theoretical formulations underlie the different experiences offered, involving short-term or long-term commitments, and requiring different qualifications and training in those who lead them.

A basic assumption underlying group therapy is that it is natural for people to live in social groupings, and that interaction with others is necessary for socialization and personal well-being. Since it is also within relationships that most problems arise, groups are seen as a natural and useful context for the resolution of difficulties.

Among groups formed for various purposes are those which are mainly recreational and educational, those which are life-enhancing and growth-promoting, those offering support in times of developmental stress, those focusing on a particular problem, and those which treat personality malfunction and pathological conditions. In some, an activity is in itself thought to be therapeutic; in others, activities such as art and music are specifically arranged for therapeutic purposes; in others, talking is the main or only medium.

The use of groups developed in a variety of settings, receiving considerable impetus with the development of group dynamics* as a discipline. Following the Second World War, the shortage of psychiatric facilities and the increase in patients needing such facilities encouraged the use of groups as an economy measure, but their positive advantages were soon discovered. Some hospitals and other institutions tried with varying degrees of success to develop therapeutic communities in which a conscious effort was made to involve all staff and inmates in an overall programme according to their training and capacity.

T-groups, or skill-training groups, developed in the USA under the leadership of Kurt Lewin (1890–1947) in the 1940s and 50s to help managers in industry improve their performance. Members learned to understand the dynamics of groups by studying their own processes as these were allowed to develop unhindered by the usual adoption of social roles (role strip). Educational in intention, T-groups had an essential research component, carried out by an observer, who gave immediate feedback on performance. This became the most-valued ingredient and subsequently the primary focus, other ways being found of dealing with task-related and organizational problems. T-groups lasted from a few days up to a week, and incorporated opportunities for observing subgroupings and inter-group behaviour; they were used in training a number of mental-health professionals and others preparing to lead groups. Encounter groups and sensitivity groups are now more generally used for this purpose.

The 1960s saw an explosion in group experiences on offer, in particular those associated with the Esalen Institute at Big Sur, California. These began largely in response to widespread disenchantment with the dehumanizing effect of an achievement-oriented culture, with its subsequent breakdown of family and community life, resulting in feelings of isolation and anomie. They were a reaction, too, to long-term psychotherapy and analysis, with its stress on the cerebral. These experiential groups were seen as life-enhancing 'therapy for normals', and usually lasted for short periods, frequently under charismatic leadership. They encouraged immediate interaction, the breaking-down of defences, and confrontation. Emphasis was on the 'here and now' of the encounter, rather than on gaining insight.

Marathon groups, involving almost continuous encounter and usually lasting from one to three days, stimulated intense emotional reactions and provided opportunities for the immediate trial of new ways of behaving. Groups of these types have proliferated under a variety of names, some with skilled and trained leaders, and some with enthusiasts with little training. Some participants have found them affirming and positive, but they have been very destructive for others. Key factors are the values embraced, views on the proper resolution of life's problems, and the ethics, integrity and competence of the leader.

Distinct from these are groups which focus on personality malfunction and on patients with a clearly diagnosed pathology. The main divisions in this category are groups based on psychoanalytic* and other psychodynamic theories, those based on group dynamic theories, on behaviourist* and cognitive* theories, on interpersonal theories, and those which emphasize particular techniques (e.g. Gestalt,* Transactional Analysis*). In groups based on psychodynamic theories, old conflicts are laid bare and brought into awareness, and old fixations in development are liquidated; in group analytic psychotherapy (see Analytical Psychology*), the group is seen as having the character of an individual, developing defences and resistances which it is the task of the therapist to analyse and to interpret the transference:* free-floating discussion takes the place of free association. Groups based on group dynamic theories typically highlight conflicts around dependence, aggression, competition and intimacy, and provide opportunities for members to fill roles, engage in power struggles, display deviance or conformity to group norms, or to scapegoat and form subgroups. The leader identifies these issues and encourages the group to work on them. Groups based on interpersonal theories stress the current, observable behaviour between group members; those on behavioural theories identify behaviours needing modification and devise a strategy for change and maintenance.

A key distinction is between those who treat individuals in the context of the group (*e.g.* Gestalt, behaviourist, psycho-drama) and those who relate to the group as a whole. Emphases also vary as to the interaction between group and individual, between therapist and group, and the level of therapist intervention. Some leaders of some types of group are less active than others; some vary their input at various points in group development. The size and composition and the frequency and duration of groups vary considerably with the aims and methods adopted. (For a useful table of comparison, see A. Stein *et al.*, 'The Group Therapies', in J. Lewis and G. Usdin, eds., *Treatment and Planning in Psychiatry*.)

With increased awareness of group processes, the categories of different groups tend not to be as discreet as they were, and more than one method may be used at different times in a group's life. Some writers (*e.g.* D. Whitaker and M. Lieberman, *Psychotherapy through the Group Process*) have attempted a rapprochement between psychodynamic and group dynamic theories, as for example in group conflict theory. Others (*e.g.* I. D. Yalom, *The Theory and Practice of Group Psychotherapy*) see the main role of the leader as exploiting the inherent therapeutic possibilities of the group to facilitate change.

Although not all characteristics are present in all therapeutic groups, the main advantages of group treatment have been described as: 1. universalization, *i.e.* the discovery that others share similar problems; 2. acceptance by others, aided by the phenomenon of group cohesion; 3. catharsis; 4. self-disclosure; 5. altruism,* *i.e.* discovering the ability to help others; 6. vicarious learning through observing the learning of others; 7. learning from interpersonal interaction; 8. gaining insight; 9. receiving direct information and advice; and 10. the instillation of hope through observing improvement and receiving encouragement. Some of these factors depend on the individual, some on the leader and some on the group (see B. Bloch and E. Crouch, *Therapeutic Factors in Group Psychotherapy*).

In order for a group to be effective, the following components have been identified: 1. sound composition and organization; 2. careful attention to pre-group screening, diagnostic assessment, and patient selection and preparation; and 3. active and responsible group leadership, based on a firm grounding in group theory and dynamics. The personal characteristics of the leader, particularly warmth and the ability to clarify and stimulate, have been identified as crucial to success, and more important than the theoretical position adopted. (See A. Stein *et al.* in *Treatment and Planning in Psychiatry*; for a full discussion of curative factors, see I. D. Yalom, *The Theory and Practice of Group Psychotherapy*.)

S. H. Foulkes (1916–76) in *Group Analytic Psychotherapy* highlights the qualities required by the leader of a psychotherapeutic group as of supreme importance, especially in the light of their popularity and proliferation. Among the qualities he cites are: ethical integrity, including intellectual honesty; interest and expertise in the subject matter, requiring high intelligence; skills in observation and communication; respect for the beliefs of others; a freedom from neurotic* disturbance; and insight into his or her own unconscious* motivations and transference. He stresses that the leader must not succumb to a wish for power, since groups provide rich opportunities for its exploitation.

Bibliography

B. Bloch and E. Crouch, *Therapeutic Factors in Group Psychotherapy* (Oxford, 1985); S. H. Foulkes, *Group Analytic Psychotherapy* (New York, 1975); W. H. Friedman, *Practical Group Therapy* (London, 1989); J. Lewis and G. Usdin (eds.), *Treatment and Planning in Psychiatry* (Washington, DC, ²1982); H. Mullan and M. Rosenbaum, *Group Psychotherapy* (New York, ²1978); D. Whitaker and M. Lieberman, *Psychotherapy through the*

Group Process (London, 1965); I. D. Yalom, *The Theory and Practice of Group Psychotherapy* (New York, ²1975).

J.R.G.

GUILT. The term 'guilt' may be used to refer either to the state of having transgressed the law, or to the emotion of feeling oneself to be in the wrong.

In his 1957 paper, 'Guilt and Guilt Feelings' (see *Psychiatry* 20.1, Feb. 1975, pp. 114ff.), Martin Buber (1878–1965) distinguished what he called 'civil guilt', namely an objective state of a person in relation to society's laws, from 'existential-religious guilt' on the one hand and 'psychologic guilt' on the other. The second of these (existential-religious guilt) is to do with our moral responsibility in personal relationships. Christians believe that objective moral guilt results from our sinful transgression of the divine pattern for human life. 'All have sinned and fall short of the glory of God' (Rom. 3:23; *cf.* Jas. 2:10). Such moral guilt can be dealt with by experiencing the forgiveness* of God. For the believer in Christ, there is no further condemnation from the divine law (Rom. 8:1), since Christ has himself carried the burden of his sin (see Sin and Salvation⑤), and God has declared him justified in Christ. Objective guilt also results from moral wrong in our relationships with other people, and can be dealt with by experiencing forgiveness from them.

The third of Buber's alternatives (psychologic guilt) refers to the subjective experience of guilty feelings, which may or may not be related to objective moral guilt. It is possible to be guilty without feeling guilty, and possible to feel guilty without objectively being guilty. To feel guilty is to experience a painful emotion,* which people often tend to repress in ways which can lead to neurotic* symptoms.

Psychologists have understood the genesis of guilty feelings in various ways. Melanie Klein,* for example, indicated that guilt feelings arise as a child is coming to terms with the ambiguity of the external world. Erik Erikson* argued that guilt feelings arise in relation to that phase of development (see Human Development*) in which a child is testing out his or her place in the social world in relation to other significant people. It is probable that guilt feelings grow from a number of different roots including biological factors, social expectancies and the development of moral capacity.

A number of writers, notably Bruce Narramore (1941–), have further divided subjective guilt feelings into two categories: 'self-condemning guilt' and 'constructive sorrow'. On the one hand, 'guilt feelings' can describe self-condemning emotions, which may be appropriately labelled neurotic or punitive. Sometimes these result from wrong that has been done by the person. Sometimes they are the expression of a false guilt which arises from a psychological state of anxiety or depression,* unrelated to objectively wrong attitudes or behaviour. There may also be 'delusional guilt', sometimes as a symptom of depression. Many psychologists (*e.g.,* Albert Ellis* in *Reason and Emotion in Psychotherapy*, Secaucus, NJ, 1977, including an expanded version of his paper 'There is No Place for the Concept of Sin in Psychotherapy') are unwilling to accept the concept of 'wrong' in this sense, and regard Christian focus on guilt as psychologically damaging. Many others (following, *e.g.,* Karl Menninger in *Whatever became of Sin?*, New York, 1973) have sought to recover a moral context for personal therapy, in which personal responsibility* can be affirmed and facilitated.

It is sadly the case that some Christian ministry has focused so heavily on sin and so insufficiently on grace* that it has increased rather than relieved guilt. Therapy, counselling and Christian pastoral care (in the broadest sense, including preaching and teaching as health promotion or illness prevention) can all be helpful in relieving troubled people of inappropriate feelings of false guilt, and in coming to terms with appropriately handling feelings of true guilt.

On the other hand, subjective guilt can sometimes be what Narramore calls a 'love-based' – rather than a punitive – emotion, which can serve a creative purpose in enabling people to make constructive changes in their lives. 'Constructive sorrow' is an appropriate Christian response to continuing sin in a believer's life. In contrast to the punitive approach to guilt, which leads to a self-centred punishing and essentially destructive attitude, 'constructive sorrow' is an approach to wrong directed lovingly towards others in an attempt to move beyond the wrong into a creative reshaping of future possibilities. Narramore refers to Paul's statement that 'Godly sorrow brings repentance that leads to salvation and leaves no regret, but worldly sorrow brings death' (2 Cor. 7:8–10). Christian ministry should not be focused on destructive feelings of punitive guilt, looking to the past, which can only be harmful. Rather, motivation for constructive change should arise from the other-directed 'godly sorrow', looking to creative new possibilities for the future with the grace of God. This is part of the meaning of forgiveness.

See also: PASTORAL CARE, COUNSELLING AND PSYCHOTHERAPY. [12]

Bibliography

H. McKeating, *Living with Guilt* (London, 1970); S. B. Narramore, *No Condemnation* (Grand Rapids, 1984); P. Tournier, *Guilt and Grace* (ET, Crowborough, ²1987).

D.J.A.

H

HABIT. A habit is an automatic response learned through repeated use or disuse of some capability. As learned, habits differ from reflexes, such as blinking in bright light, and instincts, such as the newborn's tendency to suck when presented with a breast. As automatic, a habitual response differs from a deliberate response, such as handing over a certain amount of change, after calculation, in a context of ordered monetary exchange. As learned through repeated exercise, a habit differs from a response learned suddenly, like a snake phobia acquired by a single bite. A habitual response may be behavioural (*e.g.* pronouncing one's r's in an American way), affective (*e.g.* reacting to minor irritations with a feeling of anger), or intellectual (*e.g.* thinking '25' in response to '5 × 5').

Habits are very basic to our functioning, and much of our education is a matter of behavioural, emotional and intellectual habituation. To act intelligently (*i.e.* not merely habitually, but with attention and deliberation), we must be supplied with a rich repertoire of habits. For example, to converse intelligently, measuring one's response appropriately to the unpredictable last comment of one's interlocutor, a person must make many logical inferences quite automatically ('without thinking'); he or she must be able to pronounce clearly the words of the language he or she is speaking, and follow the rules of grammar and syntax for that language, for the most part without thinking; and he or she may have to resist succumbing to various distractions, again for the most part without thinking. To the extent that a person has to deliberate about his or her inferences, about pronunciation or sentence construction, or about how to avoid being distracted by the music in the background, he or she will be disabled for carrying on an intelligent (that is, non-automatic) conversation.

Our moral and spiritual life is as much an arena of habits as our economic, ambulatory, conversational and intellectual dimensions. Aristotle* holds that we acquire the moral virtues by habituation – *i.e.* by repeated practice of the actions and states of mind that exemplify these virtues – and Thomas Aquinas* says that virtues,* such as faith, hope, love, wisdom, courage, temperance and justice, *are* 'habits' (Lat. *habitus*). While it was natural for Aquinas to call courage* and wisdom* habits, this is not natural English usage. We say that a person brushes his teeth or pronounces her r's in the American way as a matter of habit; it is not natural to say that the courageous person acts courageously as a matter of habit. *Habitus* is broader than our word 'habit', implying less strongly the automaticity and learned character of the response. *Habitus* (along with its Gk. near-equivalent *hexis*) is rendered better by the less-committal Eng. word 'disposition'. How, then, are virtues related to habits in our sense of the word?

Virtues are composed *in part* of habits. Someone who exemplifies the Christian virtue of hope* desires the kingdom of God* and believes it will one day come, and neither the desire nor the belief is a habit. But one can also transcend present circumstances, which sometimes militate against hope, feeling hope in God despite the circumstances. This ability may result from repeatedly setting one's mind on the things of the Spirit, developing thus the *habit* of seeing the world in terms of the kingdom when circumstances begin speaking the language of despair. For someone who has long practised the spiritual disciplines of Christianity, this particular hopeful turn of mind may have an automatic aspect while still not being fully automatic. That is, the individual may still have to turn his or her mind intentionally to the reasons for his or her hope, just as the cyclist intentionally peddles his or her bike and turns it in one direction or another.

But just as the cyclist makes these intentional movements against a developed background of automatic responses of shifting his or her weight and attention and managing small muscles of which he or she may not even be aware, so the Christian intentionally transcends the 'desperate' circumstances of life by reference to the promises of God only against a background of habits of Christian perception and Christian thought. Thus, while Christian character is not just a matter of habit, it is largely acquired through habituation and is constituted, in significant part, of habits.

Bibliography

Aristotle, *Nicomachean Ethics*, book 2; W. James, 'Habit', in *The Principles of Psychology*, vol. 1 (New York, 1890), ch. 4; Thomas Aquinas, *STh* 1a2ae 49–54.

R.C.R.

HANDICAP, see DISABILITY AND HANDICAP.

HANDICAPPED, CARE OF. Healthy adults mostly care for themselves. Most handicapped adults care for themselves, most of the time and in most areas. The need for special care occurs only when they cannot care for themselves in identified areas, or when the burden upon immediate family members cannot be sustained. Works of charity and of welfare to the disabled, of being the 'good Samaritan', have come to be closely associated with the Christian obligation of love for the neighbour.

Care* slips between the disciplines of psychology and sociology and is often used imprecisely, to describe the whole overview of care, specific care practices, or simply an attitude of concern. In medical terminology it is only one component of prevention, palliation and cure, as a response to a presented illness or condition. It is best thought of as a mix of attitudes, beliefs, practices and relationships. We may 'care for' someone emotionally, or be concerned about them, but unless that concern is translated into action, care has not taken place (*cf.* Mt. 25:35–40, 42–45).

To talk of care presupposes both a cared-for handicapped person, and a carer or carers. The cared-for are first and foremost individuals who usually have some awareness of their handicap, and who should be as actively involved as possible both in decisions about their care, and in the process of care. A positive view of the dignity of the handicapped person, and of the presence of the image of God* in them, is a pre-condition to maintaining care over a prolonged period. The cared-for are often seen as belonging to one of four groups: frail elderly people; mentally-ill people; people with learning difficulties; and people with physical disabilities. To categorize people in this way may not help in caring for them. It is more helpful to identify their individual needs accurately, and to respond to those needs.

While there are inspiring traditions of caring by the Christian monastic orders, and by Christian reformers in social legislation and establishment of hospitals in the 19th century (note especially the work of the Seventh Earl of Shaftesbury*), historically most carers have been women relatives of the cared-for, usually not otherwise employed, and living near their relative. In most Western European countries, with greater expectation of life, fewer school-leavers, and with greater population mobility and female employment, it is not possible to maintain traditional patterns of caring. A pastoral opportunity to demonstrate 'community care' in a specifically Christian manner then confronts most congregations. Apart from those who care for a handicapped relative, most congregations will contain members of the caring professions, who have their own pastoral needs for support and understanding, *e.g.* those working in a hospice.

Many of the NT healing miracles indicate the involvement of carers, *i.e.* people who brought the sick to Jesus (Lk. 4:40; 5:19; Jn. 5:7). Caring in this sense is an example of *diakonia*, both in nurturing brothers and sisters in the faith, and also in the outreach aspect of caring in missionary situations.

The task of care consists of a number of components. Presence, or being, is often important, before rushing on to doing. Alertness and vigilance is often called for. Apart from the obvious acts of physical support, dressing, washing, *etc.* there are the less tangible aspects of care, such as the sensitive use of touch,* and allowing self-determination and choice. Care is emotionally demanding – more so for those caring for a relative who was previously fit, than for those caring for a relative who has always been handicapped – so the families of those who are seriously handicapped may themselves need care and support. The role of carer and cared-for may be reversed, and may become a reciprocal relationship of concern and care.

Good care requires caring people, and may require special places: these have been called colonies or infirmaries, and are now variously called nursing homes and hostels. As a principle of caring it is usually helpful to allow the cared-for to stay at home as long as possible, as integrated as possible with normal rhythms of living, but the need for special equipment, or for space for the disturbed (recalling the very positive initial meaning of 'asylum') means that some people may best be cared for in specially designed environments, which can still be 'personalized' and open to the wider community. Bad care may sadly take place in poor institutions, and press accounts of assault on and exploitation of those 'in care' alert us to the need for continuing vigilance on behalf of the handicapped.

Contemporary pastoral involvement in care of the handicapped takes several forms. Christian ministry to handicapped people continues to be carried out through specialized chaplaincy work, as the 'sustaining' component of parochial and congregational pastoral care, through the establishment of pastoral and caring teams within individual churches or groups of local churches, and as one expression of the total life of the church community as a 'therapeutic community'. Special mention should be made of the current interest in the care of people with learning difficulties, as illustrated by the writing of Jean Vanier (1928–) and by the example of the L'Arche communities set up by him.

See also: DISABILITY AND HANDICAP.

Bibliography

British Council of Churches, *Christians and Community Care* (London, 1989); N. Kohner, *Caring* (Cambridge, 1988); J. Vanier, *Man and Woman He Made Them* (Paris and Montreal, 1984; London, 1985).

J.N.H.

HAPPINESS is desired universally, as Augustine* recognized in his *Confessions*: 'It is not I alone or even a few others who wish to be happy, but absolutely everybody' (x.21). However, there is by no means universal agreement as to what happiness consists in when it comes to defining it.

At the popular level, the pursuit of happiness is identified with hedonism,* *i.e.* pleasure is the supreme good and pain the supreme evil. However, in philosophy and ethics there are a number of theories of happiness, two of which have been particularly influential.

1. *Eudaemonism*. This is closely associated with Aristotle.* In his ethics, 'excellence' (*aretē*) is held to characterize both passions and actions. What makes for human happiness (*eudaimonia*) is excellence, which is understood not as the satisfaction of physical needs and desires but as the actualization of what human beings are capable of. This comes about as people are trained in the development of habit* in a society governed under right laws.

2. *Utilitarianism* (see Consequentialism*). This sees the ultimate good to be the greatest happiness of the greatest number. The rightness of actions is thus defined in terms of their contribution to the general happiness of society.

Both theories see happiness not as an end in itself but as the realization of an a priori good, the actualization of what human beings are capable of or the well-being of the greatest number. Yet they differ in that eudaemonism is strictly egoistic, thinking solely in terms of the good of the individual agent, whereas utilitarianism is universalistic, having in view the happiness of the greatest number. In the Christian tradition, happiness is very differently orientated. In the Beatitudes* (see also Sermon on the Mount*) happiness is 'not a mental state but a condition of life' (R. T. France, *The Gospel According to Matthew*, Leicester and Grand Rapids, 1985, p. 108). As members of the kingdom of God,* disciples reverse the values and standards of 'normal' society (Mt. 5:3–12). Their happiness (see Blessedness*) derives from living to please God by doing his will, seeking to be perfect as he is perfect (Mt. 5:48).

Christian theology has built upon this theocentric view of happiness. In the form of spiritual and pastoral teaching about the vision of God, God himself is seen as the ultimate good of human life. To know God in heaven, in an immediate relationship, will for the redeemed be an eternally satisfying experience, involving both the love of beauty and the love of truth. God will be their *summum bonum*, the object of all their desire and the sum of all their joy. Pastorally, in our hedonistic age, it is important that the process of discipling should correct secular (especially hedonistic) conceptions of happiness in terms of theocentric teaching of Scripture. If this does not happen, it is likely that pagan conceptions will simply be clothed in a Christian dress, leaving egocentrism basically untouched and a practical, if somewhat refined, hedonism as the dominant philosophy of life.

Bibliography

Aristotle, *Nicomachean Ethics* (Indianapolis, IN, 1985); Augustine, *Confessions* (Philadelphia, 1955); J. Piper, *Desiring God* (Portland, OR, 1986; Leicester, 1991); Thomas Aquinas, *STh* 1a2ae 1–5.

R.C.R.

HARE, RICHARD M. (1919–). Until 1984 White's Professor of Moral Philosophy in Oxford University, Hare is a leading figure in 20th-century ethics. A philosopher in the school of linguistic analysis, he argues that the chief task of ethics is the logical study of moral terms such as 'ought', 'right' and 'good'. A logical analysis of 'ought' sentences, for instance, reveals that their chief meaning is prescriptive rather than descriptive. That is, the sentence 'You ought not to lie' is more like the imperative 'Do not lie!' than it is like the statement 'Lying tends to exhibit such and such characteristics.' Logical analysis also reveals that these moral imperatives, unlike other imperatives, must be universalizable, action-guiding and overriding. In early writings, Hare suggested that different, even competing, moral judgments could satisfy these requirements, and that one's choice of ultimate moral principles was arbitrary. In recent writings, though, Hare states that these logical requirements on moral judgments yield a single justified method of moral judgment whose results are similar to those of a sophisticated form of utilitarianism (see Consequentialism*). Hare's critics have tended to argue that moral terms are primarily descriptive, that Hare's method does not lead to these utilitarian conclusions or that these utilitarian conclusions are unacceptable. Hare's views are presented in numerous articles and books, including *The Language of Morals* (Oxford, 1952), *Freedom and Reason* (Oxford, 1963) and *Moral Thinking* (Oxford, 1981).

See also: HISTORY OF CHRISTIAN ETHICS.⑥

M.T.N.

HATRED is the settled attitude of strong dislike or detestation generally of another person or group of people. In any strong form it means wishing the other not to be there, not to exist, or to be dead. It can also lead to the desire for punishment or revenge, or to the desire to inflict pain, or to humiliate in some way. Wishing someone dead is of course not the same as killing them, but there is a moral equivalence. Jesus pointed this out very clearly when he amplified the command not to kill. Anger* and hatred are morally forbidden by the commandment against killing: 'But I tell you that anyone who is angry with his brother will be subject to judgment' (Mt. 5:22). We may make two brief comments on this verse. It seems that Jesus is exaggerating to make a point, as he so often did. It is also true that some manuscripts have the extra phrase 'without cause' to allow for the need for righteous anger, *i.e.* anger against what is wrong. It does not seem possible, or helpful, to abolish anger altogether. It is when anger settles that it becomes morally dangerous, as the letter to the Ephesians puts it: 'Do not let the sun go down while you are still angry' (Eph. 4:26).

Anger can lead to hatred, especially to personal hatred of another individual. But there are other causes of hatred, emotions such as fear or jealousy. A person can also be full of hatred because he or she has known too little love. Both psychologically and morally it is important to be clear about the differences between the emotional cause and the attitude to which emotion can lead when it settles and hardens. Being angry, afraid, jealous, *etc.*, are natural emotions which arise in response to frustration, anxiety, the need for love, *etc.*

For instance, frustration* when one cannot get one's way gives rise to anger. It is important that the sense of frustration is admitted, and possibly expressed. If the frustration and anger are not admitted, but are denied or bottled up, then they can lead to various problems, such as hatred. The important thing is that the emotion is handled in an appropriate way. It needs to be kept in proportion, and it needs to be dealt with so that it is not stored up, becoming a fixed attitude. The full answer to anger is to be found in love or forgiveness,* as we see the one with whom we are angry as another child of God, loved and forgiven by him. But it is important in pastoral care not to move too quickly to this point, lest in so doing the depth of feeling is denied, and not actually handled properly at all.

Jealousy (see Jealousy and Envy*) can also give rise to hatred. Here love for another can lead to antagonism to others who are seen as rivals for that affection. In addition to this, the love for the other can also turn to antagonism and hatred. This alerts us to ask about the nature of the original love. The kind of love which leads to jealousy is a possessive love, a love which is too much centred on meeting one's own needs, and too little on valuing the loved one for his or her own sake. Human love must always strike a balance between loving for one's own sake, and loving others for themselves. Clearly, for human love truly to reflect something of divine love, it is love of others for who they are in themselves which must come to predominate.

In social groups, fear* is one of the emotions which leads to hatred. Other groups, which may be other races, religions or nations, or the opposite sex, can be feared as a threat, or because they are different. The roots of this fear are no doubt to be found in the quest for identity and security, on all sorts of levels. Whatever the precise cause, there is no mistaking the prevalence and importance of group and social hatred. It includes racial and religious hatred, misogyny (hatred of women), *etc.* Hatred is also a component of some forms of nationalism.* That it is so is not to deny the rightness of a proper love of country (see Patriotism*), but it is to warn against the wrong motives for that love. Those who believe it is their duty to fight or kill in the service of the State need to learn how they can carry out that role without learning to hate those who become their enemies. The duty to fight does not render irrelevant the command of Jesus: 'Love your enemies and pray for those who persecute you' (Mt. 5:44). This is not an impossibility, as can be seen from many sensitive accounts given by soldiers about their feelings in doing their job.

Hatred of persons is morally serious, and personally destructive. It is the diametrical opposite of love (see [2]). Instead of wishing the good of others, instead of valuing, respecting and caring for them, it is the opposite of all these things. It wishes for their harm, for their failure and suffering, and even for their death or non-existence. The cure, in the love of God and love of one another, is easy to prescribe but costly to administer.

Scripture, however, commends hatred of evil, which is inseparable from the love of righteousness (*e.g.* Heb. 1:9, quoting Ps. 45:6–7). The OT also speaks of God's hatred of wrongdoers, and the righteous person hates 'the assembly of evildoers' (Ps. 26:5). But the NT makes clear that hatred of evil should never spill over into hatred of evildoers themselves.

Finally, a word ought to be added about self-hatred. In its strongest form, it too can lead to the feeling that one ought not to be there. There is a close analogy with hatred of others. So it leads to the wish not to exist, and so to suicide.* It is also connected with the condition of anorexia (see Eating Disorders*). Again, the prescription is easy to name, but can be very difficult to receive, if the person lacks the foundations of self-esteem or self-love on which to build.

See also: KILLING; SELF-ESTEEM.

D.J.E.A.

HEADSHIP. Christian debates about headship primarily concern the interpretation and application of Paul's teaching that 'the husband is the head of the wife as Christ is the head of the church' (Eph. 5:23).

The conclusion that headship in marriage implies masculine authority (and feminine submission) has been strongly challenged. Exegetically, some scholars claim that 'head' should be understood as 'source' (as in 'head' of a river); so Paul is instructing husbands to be a source of love in their marriages, not authority figures. Moreover, he prefaces his instruction by a call to *mutual* submission (Eph. 5:21). Theologically, any suggestion that women are inferior to men cuts across the Bible's insistence that the sexes are of equal worth (Gn. 1:27; Gal. 3:28).

Other scholars point out that 'source' is only one of the meanings of 'head' in Scripture. In the immediate context of Paul's teaching on marriage in Ephesians, he has already used the word 'head' to mean the focal point of authority, as well as the source of growth and unity, in describing Christ's relationship with the church. Husbands should therefore (they conclude) take on themselves the responsibility of serving leadership in their marriages. Indeed, the blending of love and authority is a feature of all good relationships that the Bible describes (including the Godhead, 1 Cor. 11:3). Questions of status and role should be kept distinct.

The debate continues, but both sides agree that the NT's teaching on headship must never be used as a prop to support chauvinist sexism.*

See also: SEXUALITY. [11]

J.H.O.

HEALING. Concepts of healing and health* refer to the bringing of wholeness and soundness to any or every aspect of human life. We may talk of *natural* healing (through the body's intrinsic and environmental resources), *medical* healing (through preventative and therapeutic action) and *miraculous* healing (through spectacular divine intervention which sets aside or speeds up natural and medical processes). The term 'inner healing'* is sometimes used where the focus of restoration is on past psychological and emotional damage, both known and hidden. In all these phenomena, God is the source of healing.

1. Healing in the Bible

The OT reveals Yahweh as healer, both in his words and actions. As he declares to the Israelites: 'I am the LORD who heals you' (Ex. 15:26). His healing work can variously result in physical and material well-being (2 Ki. 4:32–35; 5:14; Jb. 42:12–17; Ps. 103:3), in forgiveness* (2 Ch. 30:18–20; Is. 57:18–19), and in forthcoming deliverance (Ps. 6:1–3; Je. 17:14; Mal. 4:2). At the same time, the Lord God is seen as one who brings affliction (see Suffering*): 'Plague went before him; pestilence followed his steps' (Hab. 3:5). This twin perspective is shown in the declaration: 'For he wounds, but he also binds up; he injures, but his hands also heal' (Jb. 5:18; see also Gn. 20:17–18; Dt. 32:39; Ho. 6:1).

The OT concedes that powers other than God's can produce 'signs and wonders',* but such miracles are seen as inferior (Ex. 7:10–12). Although the art of medicine is mentioned somewhat incidentally (Gn. 50:2; 2 Ch. 16:12; Jb. 13:4; Je. 8:22), the account of King Hezekiah's illness and recovery shows God to be the source of all true healing, whether by direct intervention or medical means (2 Ki. 20:4–7). In the intertestamental period, Judaism built up a rigid system of equating disease with specific sin, and yet we also find a greater compassion emerging, *e.g.*, in the words of the devout Jew Ben Sira (*c.* 190 BC): 'My son, when you are ill, do not be depressed, but pray to the Lord and he will heal you' (Ecclus. 38:9, JB).

In the NT we see that healing is an integral part of Christ's mission to a needy world. As Morton Kelsey (1917–) has noted, nearly one fifth of the gospel record is taken up with the incidents and debates surrounding the Lord's healings. This ministry is inextricably linked with his proclamation: 'Jesus went throughout Galilee, teaching in their synagogues, preaching the good news of the kingdom, and healing every disease and sickness among the people' (Mt. 4:23; see also Mk. 1:32–39; Lk. 4:16–21, 40–44).

The main Gk. verbs that are relevant (*therapeuō*, 'to heal or cure'; *iaomai*, 'to restore'; *hygiainō*, 'to make well again', 'to heal the whole person'; and *sōzō*, 'to rescue or deliver in order to heal the whole being') indicate the thoroughness and comprehensiveness of Christ's healing work. Further, the conditions healed are primarily those considered virtually incurable: blindness (Mk. 8:25; 10:52; Jn. 9:7), deafness (Mk. 7:35), dumbness (Mt. 9:33; Mk. 7:35), spinal deformity (Lk. 13:13), paralysis (Mk. 2:12; 3:5), chronic skin disease (Mk. 1:42; Lk. 17:14), menorrhagia (Mt. 9:22) and fluid retention (Lk. 14:4), as well as a complexity of mental and spiritual disorder that was implicit on those occasions when he 'drove out many demons' (Mk. 1:34; see also Mk. 1:26; 5:13; 9:26; Lk. 4:41; see Deliverance Ministry*). The power of Christ over death itself is manifest on at least three occasions (Lk. 7:15; 8:55; Jn. 11:44).

Ultimately, it is this divine power that dynamizes Christ's healing action; as Lk. 5:17 puts it: 'And the power of the Lord was present for him to heal the sick.' Even so, restoration is commonly mediated through touch* as well as word (Mk. 1:31, 41; 5:41; Lk. 13:13) and, on occasions, Jesus uses saliva, both directly and through the medium of clay (Mk. 7:33; 8:23; Jn. 9:6–7). Although the Jews had some belief in the medicinal efficacy of saliva, it is probably more appropriate to conclude, with Kelsey, that for Jesus the spittle was a 'carrier of his personality and power'.

The Gospels demonstrate that Christ healed out of love and concern: 'When Jesus landed and saw a large crowd, he had compassion on them and healed their sick' (Mt. 14:14). Beyond his immediate response to human need, though, there is the perspective of an 'inaugurated eschatology', to use the phrase coined by J. A. T. Robinson (1919–83), in which the 'last things' press in on the here and now. As Jesus declared to his opponents: 'But if I drive out demons by the finger of God, then the kingdom of God has come to you' (Lk. 11:20; see also Mt. 8:16–17 and Lk. 7:20–22). In this context, Robert Lambourne* has argued that Jesus' healings were not only 'effective signs' of the kingdom but '*public* effective signs' that demanded a verdict from all who witnessed them (see Jn. 20:30–31). His bringing of wholeness was a foretaste of the coming banquet when 'He will wipe every tear from their eyes' and 'There will be no more death or mourning or crying or pain . . .' (Rev. 21:4).

We see amongst the early disciples the continuance of a healing ministry, both through Jesus' commissionings of his followers (Mt. 10:1; Lk. 10:9) and, after Pentecost, in the demonstration of the power of the risen Lord (Acts 3:6–8; 5:16). As with Christ, the church's proclamation was a blending of word and action that demanded response, whether that of discipleship or rejection (Acts 3:6–8, 12–13; 4:2, 19–22; 14:3–4). Although there is little direct mention of 'signs and wonders' in the epistles (see Rom. 15:18–19; 2 Cor. 12:12), a few statements suggest the existence of the church's continuing call to heal (1 Cor. 12:9; Jas. 5:14–15).

Anointing with oil had been anciently associated with divine blessings and empowerment and, by NT times, the use of olive oil was seen to be medicinal as well as symbolic of God's healing (Jas. 5:14; see also Mk. 6:13 and Lk. 10:34). In Jas. 5 we also find the church's corporate responsibility to bring health ('call the elders'), the potential linkages between sickness and sin, healing and forgiveness, and the seeds of a sacramentalism (see Sacramental Healing*) which became, in time, the rites of chrism and unction.

2. Healing in the history of the church

Healing has always been a strand within the church's pastoral care (see ⑫) and, inevitably, its ministry to the sick and needy has been influenced by the history of medical care in wider society. The healings recorded in the Bible, for example, can be seen against the background of the origins of Western medical practice in Egypt in the 3rd millennium BC, and in the code of ethics introduced by Hippocrates (*c.* 460–*c.* 377 BC) in Greece in the 5th century BC (see Hippocratic Oath*). In spite of the valuable systematization of the Hippocratic school, the simplicity and effectiveness of the healings of Jesus by word and touch contrast strongly with the spells, conjurations and miracles of punishment cast by the physicians of ancient Greece.

Writing in 1940, Evelyn Frost examined the patristic literature of the ante-Nicene church and concluded that this period is 'full of evidence of healing of various degrees of value'. Amongst the more reputable documents, she quotes Irenaeus (*c.* 130–*c.* 200) who witnessed healing miracles in the name of Christ, 'which Name . . . cures thoroughly and effectively all who anywhere believe in Him'. Cyprian (*c.* 200–58) later recorded the concurrent increase of division and moral laxity in the church and the decline of healing power.

Although this deterioration continued with the rise of Constantine,* there were some pointers to a continuation of healing care during the next century or two. Basil the Great (*c.* 329–79), for example, had good medical knowledge, founded a large hospital outside Caesarea and knew of miraculous healings. Augustine,* though arguing initially against an expectation of the gifts of healing, later (in 424) appears to have changed his outlook.

From the 6th century onwards, superstition permeated the church so that by the 12th century healing was sought almost entirely through the relics of the 'saints'. In 1163 the Council of Tours prohibited clerics from working as surgeons, because 'the church abhors the shedding of blood', and this rift between Christendom and medical practice continued and deepened during the following centuries. The Council of Trent (1551) completed the shift away from the ministry of healing by limiting the age-old rite of anointing the sick to that of extreme unction, reserved for those in danger of death.

Within the Reformation, Calvin* stated that the gifts of the Spirit, including healing, were only temporary 'to make the preaching of the gospel wonderful', whereas Luther,* though earlier holding a similar view, seems to have become more open to the possibility of the miraculous in the face of the recovery from point of death of his friend Melanchthon (1497–1560). Times of revival in subsequent centuries saw outbreaks of more spectacular healing: John Wesley* not only wrote a treatise on medical practice, *Primitive Physick* (1747), but also documented a number of miracles of healing; in 1842, Johann Christoph Blumhardt, a Lutheran pastor working in the Black Forest, witnessed a fresh outpouring of the Spirit in widespread repentance and dramatic healings among the people.

The split between the church and medicine, fostered by medieval dualism (which followed ancient Gk. thought in divorcing the bodily from the spiritual), professional rivalry and the increasing rationalism of Western medical practice, began tentatively to lessen towards the end of the 19th century. One measure of this was the rapid increase in the number of medical missionaries sent out by the Church Missionary Society (13 in service in 1852; 650 by 1900). Spurred further by the rise of numerous cults and sects, such as Christian Science (founded 1879), with their heterodox views on health and healing, dialogue between Christian ministers and the medical profession took on a new urgency in the early years of the 20th century, and led to the foundations of the Guild of Health (1904), the Society of Emmanuel (1905; later, the Divine Healing Mission), and the Guild of St Raphael (1915), with its emphasis on anointing with oil and laying on of hands. At the same time, a series of Lambeth conferences debated relevant issues, recognizing, in 1930, the validity of the 'ministry of healing'. The Archbishops' Commission of 1958, comprising clergy, doctors and nurses, rejected the partial terms of 'divine', 'spiritual' and 'faith' healing, and concluded that the church's ministry of healing is 'an integral part of the Church's total work by which men and women are to become true sons and daughters of God's kingdom'.

3. Healing today

Along with the huge advances of conventional medicine, the 20th century has witnessed a widespread debate on healing through the claims of individual healers, the founding of healing communities such as Burrswood and Crowhurst in southern England, a renewed commitment to anointing with oil, the laying on of hands and the context of the eucharist for healing, the successive waves of pentecostalism, and the charismatic and 'signs and wonders' movements, and the emergence of alternative, or complementary, medical practice. Amidst this plethora of interest, three broad positions can be identified amongst Christians with respect to the ministry of healing: dispensationalism,* triumphalism and inaugurated eschatology.

a. Dispensationalism. Dispensationalism argues that God reveals himself through particular purposes within specific periods of time. The dispensationalist perspective on miraculous healing reasons that God has dispensed his healing gifts on humankind at certain crucial stages in biblical history, such as the time of apostasy during the days of Elijah and Elisha, and at the coming of the Messiah.

Although similar views were held by Augustine, at least initially, and by many of the Reformers, it is the names of J. N. Darby (1800–82) and C. I. Scofield (1843–1921) that are primarily associated with classical dispensationalism. B. B. Warfield (1851–1921), although not part of this mainstream emphasis, held parallel views with respect to the dispensation of God's gifts of healing. In his *Counterfeit Miracles* (later published as *Miracles: Yesterday and Today, True and False*), he wrote that the miraculous belonged 'exclusively to the Apostolic age', concluding that accounts of spectacular healing in later centuries show 'an infusion of heathen modes of thought into the church'.

Many who adopt a similar position to Warfield tend to argue, for example, that when Jesus spoke of his own activity and added, 'anyone who has faith in me . . . will do even greater things than these' (Jn. 14:12), it is solely the 'spiritual works' of repentance and regeneration that are referred to. By the same token, Paul's inclusion of 'gifts of healing' in 1 Cor. 12:9, and the injunction to seek healing through prayer and anointing with oil in Jas. 5:14–15, are seen either as linked exclusively with the apostolic period or as ambiguous to interpretation. In fairness, though, there are others who hold views similar to Warfield who do also obey James' call to anoint the sick and pray for healing.

b. Triumphalism. At the opposite pole to dispensationalism is a triumphalist view which claims that healing is the birthright of every Christian. There is a tendency to see the death of Christ as equally effective in overcoming sin and sickness, arguing this application from such texts as Is. 53:4–5, Mt. 8:16–17 and 1 Pet. 2:24. From this basis, the miraculous works of Christ and the apostles are viewed as a paradigm for all time, whereby the church, gifted and empowered by the Holy Spirit, shows forth the reign of God through 'signs and wonders', including miracles of healing. In the extreme forms of this triumphalism, the only limit to God's blessing is lack of personal faith.

c. An inaugurated eschatology. Whereas dispensationalism majors on a theology of suffering, and triumphalism on a theology of healing, an emphasis on an inaugurated eschatology ideally attempts to hold these two theologies together. The kingdom of God both has come and is to come and, within the 'now' and 'not yet' of this view, healing, whether natural, medical or miraculous, is seen as a foretaste of the final consummation when the victory of Christ over every mainfestation of evil, including sickness, is realized in the bodily resurrection (Jn. 6:39–40; 1 Cor. 15:50–57; 2 Cor. 5:1–5; Rev. 21:4). Within this perspective, God is acknowledged to be both healer and sovereign (Dn. 4:34–35; Rom. 9:14–21): at times he heals dramatically, as with Hezekiah (2 Ki. 20:5); at times he brings restoration slowly, as in Job's story (Jb. 42:12–17); and at other times he allows continuance of suffering to demonstrate his power in human weakness (2 Cor. 12:7–10). The implications for health and healing in the 'in-between' time, as Lambourne and others have pointed out, stretch beyond the individual to the communal, and beyond personal well-being to social, political and environmental conditions. We find the roots of this wider vision in the words and actions of Jesus and the early church (see, e.g. Mt. 25:31–46; Lk. 4:18–19; 6:20–26; Acts 4:32–35; Jas. 2:14–17; 5:1–6).

Bibliography

C. Brown, *Miracles and the Critical Mind* (Grand Rapids and Exeter, 1984); E. Frost, *Christian Healing* (London, 1940); H. W. Frost, *Miraculous Healing* (London, 1961); R. Gardner, *Healing Miracles* (London, 1986); P. L. Garlick, *Man's Search for Health: A Study in the Inter-relation of Religion and Medicine* (London, 1952); J. Goldingay (ed.), *Signs, Wonders and Healing* (Leicester, 1989); J. Gunstone, *Signs and Wonders: The Wimber Phenomenon* (London, 1989); R. F. Hurding, 'Healing', in B. Palmer (ed.), *Medicine and the Bible* (Exeter, 1986); M. T. Kelsey, *Healing and Christianity* (London, 1973; San Francisco, ²1988); R. A. Lambourne, *Community, Church and Healing* (London, 1963); D. C. Lewis, *Healing: Fiction, Fantasy or Fact?* (London, 1989); F. S. MacNutt, *Healing* (New York and London, ²1989); M. Maddocks, *The Christian Healing Ministry* (London, ²1990); B. Martin, *The Healing Ministry in the Church* (ET, London, 1960); S. Pattison, *Alive and Kicking: Towards a Practical Theology of Illness and Healing* (London, 1989); W. J. Sheils (ed.), *The Church and Healing* (Oxford, 1982); T. Smail, 'The Love of Power and the Power of Love', *Anv* 6.3, 1989, pp. 223–233; B. B. Warfield, *Miracles: Yesterday and Today, True and False* (Grand Rapids, 1965) = *Counterfeit Miracles* (London, 1972); J. Wilkinson, *Health and Healing:*

Studies in New Testament Principles and Practice (Edinburgh, 1980); M. Wilson (ed.), *Explorations in Health and Salvation: A Selection of Papers by Bob Lambourne* (Birmingham, 1983); J. Wimber (with K. Springer), *Power Healing* (London and San Francisco, 1986).

R.F.H.

HEALING OF MEMORIES, see INNER HEALING.

HEALING THE FAMILY TREE. This form of healing* has largely been associated with the work of Dr Kenneth R. McAll, who explored the relationship between the various illnesses of his patients and the known sicknesses or circumstances of their deceased relatives. He concluded that very often the pains and disturbances of the living are caused by the unquiet dead who, feeling earthbound, seek recognition and direction from their living relatives. He does in fact describe it as a 'possession state' of the living by the dead. A less radical explanation is that the sins of the fathers are being visited upon their children down to the third and fourth generations (Ex. 20:5; 34:7; Nu. 14:18; Dt. 5:9). Such generational effects will be disease, disasters and lingering illnesses (Dt. 28:18, 59; 30:1–2, 19). Another way of looking at this, which is more familiar to students of counselling and psychology, is that children have inherited unhealthy patterns of behaviour or have become bound to a form of life which is reinforced by familiar statements (or scripts) which parents used in order to enforce their way. For some, their parents are very much alive in the moment when someone else uses a familiar 'punch-line' or ('catch-phrase') of theirs. Such ingrained forms of bondage need to be recognized, challenged and changed. An example of the repeated family pattern can be seen in the family tree of Abraham, where the father-and-son dynamic was spoilt through favouritism (Gn. 16; 17:20–22; 25:27–34; 37:3–11).

Another area for healing is that of unacknowledged deaths. Where there have been stillborn children, miscarriages or abortions which have not been worked through, one form of therapy is to name such children in faith (as now being among the communion of saints) and bring them to a service of Holy Communion where they are included amongst the prayers of intercession. Once such an act of recognition has taken place, then the living are themselves prayed for and released from any emotional hurts that they may have trapped inside them.

See also: INNER HEALING.

Bibliography
I. Barclay, *Death and the Life to Come* (London, 1988) = *Death and the Life After* (Nelson, CO, ²1992); K. R. McAll, *Healing the Family Tree* (London, 1987); M. Mitton and R. Parker, *Requiem Healing* (London, 1992); D. A. Seamands, *Healing of the Memories* (Amersham, 1986).

R.E.P.

HEALTH AND HEALTH CARE.

In our world, health is seen as a positive aim for human beings. Good governments provide for the well-being of their citizens by systems of health care both in preventive and curative medicine. The World Health Organization defines health as 'the state of complete physical, mental and social well-being; not merely the absence of disease and infirmity'. While recognizing the ideal and even impossible nature of this definition, there is general agreement that health covers not only disease prevention and cure, but also care and supporting proper relationships of the whole person in the context of the community.

Healthcare systems

World-wide, there is obviously great disparity in the amounts that governments spend, and are able to spend, on health care and the services they provide. The gap between the First World and the Third World is vast, but so too is the varying amount spent by different Western countries. In Europe almost 6% of the gross national product is spent on health care, while the figure in the US is 12%. However, with a growing demand for more and better healthcare provision, criticism of how that money is spent and the results obtained is widespread. Almost 37 million Americans have no health insurance, and 14 million more are under-insured. Thus the quality of their health care is very different from that of those who are able to pay for adequate health care. That very ability to pay is under threat as medical technology, new and more expensive drugs, alternative therapies and consumer demand drive up the cost of health care. The role of malpractice suits (see Medical Malpractice*), insurance companies, hospitals and doctors' professional bodies has not helped limit the cost of health care in the US. In the UK, the growing expectations of patients that modern medicine will provide 'a pill for every ill', a cure for every disease, and prolong not only life itself but the quality of life,* is pushing up the cost of medicine. The delivery systems themselves are breaking down, and governments are engaged in radical restructuring and reorganization of hospitals, general practice, and allied health provisions.

Moral issues of the right to health care, the responsibility of governments to provide healthcare facilities for citizens, the appropriateness of demand-based medicine, the control of spiralling costs, the limits of technological medicine, the roles of professional bodies, the funding of health services, justice and the defence and limits of patients' rights, are all key areas in the continuing debate. The West seems committed to providing a basic level of care for those in need regardless of ability to pay. What constitutes healthcare needs and is genuinely basic is hotly and widely disputed. Generally, insurance schemes, whether private or public, play a key role in funding such healthcare provision. But rising demand and expectation are forcing healthcare authorities to take stock of how to measure the performance and delivery of health care, from the levels of systems to the particular treatments and units.

The context of health care

It is clear that health varies according to the wealth or poverty of people. Poor housing, malnutrition, lack of exercise and poverty are closely linked with the continuing existence and high levels of certain diseases like cancer, heart disorders, ulcers and strokes. Wealth brings its own health risks and lifestyles, which include lack of exercise, over-eating, smoking and drinking. Thus there is increasing awareness of the need for prevention of disease, dealing with causes rather than simply treating symptoms, greater taking of responsibility on the part of individuals and communities for their health and well-being, and generally dealing with the social factors which cause disease.

The practice of modern medicine itself can create its own problems. The doctor has become something of a scientific specialist expert in biological, materialistic, mechanistic and individualistic understandings of human beings. This has tended to reduce human beings and created a gulf between patients and doctors where personal skills on the part of the doctor are sacrificed for scientific excellence. Awareness of such problems has led to radical realignments in the selection and training of medical students, with increasing emphasis on personal relationships and communication skills.

As part of a reaction against technological (see Technology*) science, there has been a growing interest in alternative medicine and therapies. This must be distinguished from allied therapeutic skills such as physiotherapy and occupational therapy. Alternative medicine stresses holistic approaches and so-called 'natural' remedies. These range from homeopathy to aromatherapy and the use of crystals. This reaction to traditional medicine has gained little support from the medical community, and until and unless there is some kind of critical assessment and objective measurement of success, as well as some regulation of practitioners by professional criteria and standards, there will continue to be suspicion. Nevertheless, the holistic and natural emphases are important protests and correctives.

In the community, medicine and health have positive overtones. Sickness, disease and illness are some of the ways a society both assigns and relieves responsibility. Society sanctions certain patterns of dealing with the 'sick' in terms of hospitals, quarantine and health regulations. The law permits or refuses certain medical practices such as abortion* or euthanasia* and may require health warnings to be given on items like cigarettes.

Continuing advances in medicine and in disease patterns create new challenges. The rise of AIDS* and the problems of population growth (see Population Policy*), in a world where starvation, malnutrition and lack of hydration allow childhood diseases to wreak havoc, mean that medicine needs to come to terms with the basic needs of humankind. Western medicine is too concerned with high technological practices, whether in the form of genetic manipulation* (see Genetic Engineering*), transplantation, drug therapies or new diagnostic and treatment machines. The main health crisis in the world is survival. The main health crisis in the West seems to be financial. The allocation of scarce resources whether on a global or a national scale will require more medical and social decision-making. We cannot continue to expect or to have an unlimited rise in our standards of health and healthcare provision. Thus justice for all, the priorities of the needy, and taking more responsibility for our own health as we see the influence of diet, lifestyle and social conditions on well-being, must be the West's health agenda.

A biblical perspective

Illness, disease and sickness were not part of the original paradise Garden (Gn. 1 – 2). These came into the world as a result of the Fall.* With sin comes death* and disease in the broken relationships of human beings with God, each other, the world and one's own self (Gn. 3). In the fallen world, ill health and disease are real and genuine and cannot be denied as Christian Scientists claim. Such illness can be a punishment in terms of retribution and the inevitable reaping of what we sow. God's world is a moral realm where sin has consequences and disease and illness are part of that process. The Bible does not picture God as the author of disease, but rather as using those experiences as tests of our faith and as a means of growth (Rom. 5:3–5; 2 Cor. 7:11; 1 Pet. 1:6–7). Disease and illness often stem from the work of the devil and the demonic* realm.

It is in challenge of that realm that Jesus came as the Great Physician who brought healing* and wholeness to humanity. In his healing ministry the power of God was at work in Jesus over evil, disease and illness, restoring men and women to the health which God created them to enjoy. Likewise in the eschaton, illness and disease will disappear and have no part in that final restored realm (Rev. 21:3–4; 22:1–3; Is. 34 – 35; Rev. 7:13–17).

The biblical picture of health is that of *shalom* (see Peace*). It stands in sharp contrast to disease, disability, deformity and death. Shalom happens in the context of relationships and community (see Community Ethics[16]). It affects the whole of a person in every aspect of their lives, including mind, body, spirit and soul. Such shalom is promised to those who live properly in relationship with God and with each other. Shalom includes pleasure* and happiness,* peace and well-being, as well as overtones of justice. It is to live appropriately and to have harmony and balance in every aspect of one's life and relationships.

In recent theology, Jürgen Moltmann (1926–) has suggested that a suitable definition of health is 'the strength to be human', and that the role of the church is to create a setting and framework where men and women gain such strength through the grace* and power of God.

Certainly the apostles, following in the steps of Christ, brought healing and restoration to those who were sick. The charismatic movement has argued that such miraculous healing was not just intended for the apostolic age, but is available today for those who believe in the power of God and claim his promises. There are many claims to healing, which some dispute, but there can be no doubt but that God has the power to heal and to act miraculously in his own world. What is disputed is whether we can control or demand such miraculous interventions. The 'signs and wonders'* school of Christian thought stresses that such healings are part of the proof that God is at work. Miracles, if claimed, need to be open to rigorous testing if they are to be proferred as support for the truth of the gospel.

Death is feared by most human beings, for it is a step into the unknown. It seems the last enemy, even if to some who are ill it may come as a blessed relief. Death and dying were not part of God's original paradise, and are presented as the direct result of human sin. In that way death is unnatural, yet in our now-fallen world it has become natural and inevitable. Jesus Christ came to defeat death. In the cross* and resurrection* we see the very worst that the powers of evil could do to humanity as Christ bore the sin of the world. Yet he was raised from the dead by the power of God and Christians have nothing to fear from death. Jesus warned that we should not fear those who have the power to kill the body (Mt. 10:28). Death is not the worst thing that can happen to us. Sadly, modern medicine often refuses to accept the inevitability of death, and tries to resist it at all costs and by every means. This is sub-Christian. While it is proper to resist the evil of illness and death in general terms, it is wrong to refuse to accept death and to be unwilling to commit each other to the mercy and love of God in sure and certain hope of the resurrection of the body. The Christian hope* for life after death rests on Christ alone (1 Cor. 15).

In the meantime, the church has a ministry of healing. It is part and parcel of the declaration of the power of God as witness to the authority and authenticity of Jesus, his Son. The NT encourages those who are sick to call for the elders of the church that they may pray for them (Jas. 5:14). The history of the church reveals a deep commitment to prayer for healing and anointing with oil. This has also been expressed in the ministry of exorcism (see Deliverance Ministry*) where evil has been driven out by prayer* and fasting.* There can be no assumption that we control God like a coin in the slot machine, where we put in a prayer and out pops a healing miracle. But neither can we deny the power of God to heal and restore in his mercy and love.

It is no surprise that many nurses and doctors are Christians and that the church was crucially involved in the development of hospitals and hospices.* The motive of loving care and the desire to allow God's healing work to act are fundamental to Christian thinking and practice, especially as we face continuing health challenges with AIDS, genetic control and technological advances.

See also: ETHICS OF MEDICAL CARE; [14] LIFE, HEALTH AND DEATH. [13]

Bibliography

A. V. Campbell, *Moral Dilemmas in Medicine* (Edinburgh, [2]1975); A. Fergusson (ed.), *Health: The Strength to be Human* (Leicester, 1993); S. E. Lammers and A. Verhey (eds.), *On Moral Medicine* (Grand Rapids, 1987).

E.D.C.

HEAVEN AND HELL. In Christian tradition, the terms 'heaven' and 'hell' are powerful expressions of the immense privilege of fellowship with God and the appalling awfulness of eternal separation from his presence.

Heaven

The Bible speaks of heaven as God's home (thereby symbolizing divine transcendence) and as the abode of angels (Dt. 26:15; Ps. 2:4; Mk. 12:25; Lk. 2:15). But God is not restricted to heaven (1 Ki. 8:27), for his presence fills creation (Ps. 139:7–12). Heaven is the place of perfection where there is complete harmony and order (Lk. 12:33; 1 Pet. 1:4; Rev. 21:10 – 22:5), the realm in which God's will is perfectly done (Mt. 6:10). To it the glorified Christ returned (Acts 1:11) and from it he will come again for judgment (2 Thes. 1:6–10) and to renew the cosmos (2 Pet. 3:13; Rev. 21:1).

In its final form as 'the new heaven and new earth', heaven will be peopled by believers having resurrected bodies (2 Cor. 5:1–8). Heaven is thus the final, eschatological state (Is. 65:17; Rom. 8:18–25), the kingdom of God's glory, in which those who are in Christ will share in the beatific vision of God (Mt. 5:8; 1 Jn. 3:2).

Though future, the contemplation of heaven has profound present implications for Christian living. It reminds Christians that, as 'strangers in the world' (1 Pet. 2:11), they are to cultivate a certain sense of spiritual detachment from this present world; that as 'aliens' (1 Pet. 2:11) their citizenship is elsewhere (Phil. 3:20); and that as sufferers of present affliction (Rom. 8:18) heaven will bring release and rest. To contemplate heaven encourages heavenly-mindedness, not in the sense of earthly uselessness, but in preparation for enjoying 'a world of love' (Jonathan Edwards*).

Marxists criticize the hope* of heaven as an escape from confronting the grim realities of earth, but Scripture teaches that heaven is not gained at the expense of neglecting the practical demands of loving our neighbour (cf. 1 Jn. 3:16–18).

Others argue that the notion of heaven leads to apathy now, but the sense of the brevity of life which the idea of heaven encourages serves rather as a spur to action.

Hell

In Scripture hell is portrayed as separated from heaven by an unbridgeable chasm (Lk. 16:26), and as a place where stubborn unbelievers and the wicked are eternally punished (Mt. 23:33; 25:41; Mk. 9:43, 48; Jude 7). In the AV, the Heb. word *še'ôl* (Sheol) and the Gk. words *hadēs* and *Geēnna* (Gehenna) are all translated 'hell', but only the last is properly translated as 'hell'. Although there is no single picture of the afterlife in the intertestamental and NT periods, generally speaking *še'ôl* and *hadēs* had come to stand for the place where all the dead go to experience a disembodied, shadow-like existence where souls await their final destination, whether to life eternal or everlasting punishment. Gehenna – referring to *gē hinnōm* (valley of Hinnom), south of Jerusalem, where fires were kept continually burning to consume the city's rubbish – became the symbol word for the realm of eternal damnation.

Traditionally, hell has been understood to involve everlasting punishment,* its awfulness being depicted by such metaphors as a lake of fire (Rev. 20:13–15; 21:8), or a prison (Jude 6), or a place where there is 'weeping and gnashing of teeth' (Mt. 8:12; 25:30). Its

punishment is retribution* upon all who have rebelled against God, whereby God's honour is vindicated and his righteous rule re-established (Rom. 2:5–11; 1 Cor. 15:24–28; Heb. 10:26–31).

Like heaven, hell is an eschatological concept. It takes place at the consummation of salvation history when God's offer of salvation is no longer extended, and the impenitent are permanently confined to Gehenna. Again, as with the biblical concept of heaven, the existence of hell is meant to impress upon us the heinousness of sin (see Sin and Salvation⑤) and to encourage us to seek the grace* of God which delivers us from it (Mt. 5:29–30; 13:48–50).

Criticisms

Various criticisms are made of the traditional doctrine of hell. Usually these have to do with reconciling God's unconquerable benevolence and omnipotence with the notion of the everlasting punishment of the perpetually existing wicked. Universalists object that hell negates the love of God who wills to save all humanity (cf. 2 Pet. 3:9). Others, who reject universalism as without biblical basis and who take a high view of the authority of Scripture, object that the everlastingness of punishment does not justly comport with finite sins committed in time, and teach either the annihilation at death of all who are not 'in Christ' (conditional immortality) or a period of limited punishment followed by personal extinction (annihilationism). They find it hard to reconcile the traditional doctrine of unceasing, conscious separation from God with Paul's teaching that ultimately God will be all and in all (1 Cor. 15:28) and that God will unite all things in Christ (Eph. 1:10). Yet others regard hell as a place of ultimately successful remedial punishment from which all will emerge to leave it finally unpeopled.

Traditionalists reply that universalism seems to presuppose a determinism which saves despite freely chosen and obdurate opposition to God. Conditionalism sees punishment as non-existence, which would seem no discouragement to pursuing licentiousness in all its forms (cf. 1 Cor. 15:32). Annihilationism too readily assumes that we are in a position to determine what is the exact equivalent in terms of punishment of 'the godlessness and wickedness of men' (Rom. 1:18) and that the retributive punishment of hell is visited only upon sins committed in this life (though Rev.

22:11 suggests otherwise). The fact that here punishment is by no means always remedial suggests that it may not be so hereafter.

Bibliography

N. M. de S. Cameron (ed.), *Universalism and the Doctrine of Hell* (Carlisle and Grand Rapids, 1993); J. Cooper, *Body, Soul, and Life Everlasting* (Grand Rapids, 1989); C. S. Lewis, *The Problem of Pain* (London, 1940); T. Philips, 'Hell: A Christological Reflection', in W. Crockett and J. Sigountos (eds.), *Through No Fault of Their Own* (Grand Rapids, 1991); P. Toon, *Heaven and Hell: A Biblical and Theological Overview* (Nashville, TN, 1966).

D.L.O.

HEDONISM. The term 'hedonism' is derived from the Gk. word for 'pleasure', *hēdonē*. It is broadly applied to any view in which pleasure* is considered the ultimate good. Hedonism is customarily considered under two basic views: ethical hedonism and psychological hedonism.

Ethical hedonism holds that pleasure is intrinsically good and that displeasure is intrinsically evil. For something to be intrinsically good means that it is desirable in itself as an end, not as a means to something else. Ethical hedonism finds its roots in the early Gk. philosopher Aristippus of Cyrene (*c.* 435–366 BC), who founded the Cyrenaic School. Aristippus proposed that the ethical end for man must be pleasure. For the Cyrenaic School pleasure came to be viewed as bodily enjoyment which was held to be above intellectual pleasure. Epicurus (341–270 BC) proposed that pleasure is painlessness. The Epicureans taught that pleasure is morally right and displeasure is morally wrong.

Hedonism was revived in the utilitarianism (see Consequentialism*) of Jeremy Bentham,* who held that duty was to maximize the *quantity* of pleasure. Later, John Stuart Mill* maintained that we should bring about the greatest *quality* of pleasure. Most modern hedonists believe that it is our obligation to work for the greatest good for the greatest number of people over the long run.

Since the time of Plato,* ethical hedonism has been challenged by such questions as, 'What is meant by "pleasure"?' Are there criteria beyond pleasure itself which must be employed to determine which pleasures are more desirable than others? The hedonistic thesis depends upon what is meant by the term 'pleasure'. If what is morally right is that which brings the most pleasure, then what kind of pleasure should be used as the standard? If what is morally right is that which brings the most good, then either 'good' and 'right' are defined in terms of each other, or good must be determined by some standard beyond itself. Other critics note that some pleasures are evil (*e.g.* sadism), and some pain* is good (*e.g.* warning pains).

Psychological hedonism asserts that the natural and regular acts of humans are governed by the desire for pleasure. It operates on the circular assumption that people naturally seek pleasure, and that what people seek gives them pleasure. Many ethical hedonists endeavour to support their position by an appeal to psychological hedonism. Psychological hedonism is expounded by such writers as L. T. Troland and P. T. Young. Some modern psychologists believe that psychological hedonism provides a viable account of the motivation of human actions, and it is the basic assumption of therapists as diverse as Sigmund Freud* and Carl Rogers.*

Besides the difficulty in verifying or falsifying these psychological aspects, there is a tendency to confuse what is desirable with what is pleasurable. Something that is desirable may not necessarily be pleasurable at the present. This is especially evident in light of the Christian ethic of self-denial as Jesus taught in Mk. 8:34, and, indeed, as demonstrated at the cross.

The NT condemns the love of pleasure, but not pleasure itself, which the Bible as a whole affirms (*e.g.* in the Song of Songs). In 2 Timothy, Paul warns of the coming apostasy when men will become lovers of themselves and 'lovers of pleasure rather than lovers of God' (2 Tim. 3:4). In its place, the Bible exhorts the believer not to seek only his or her own good, but also to seek the good of others (1 Cor. 10:24). Ultimately, the goal of the Christian should not be pleasure, but to 'do all to the glory of God' (1 Cor. 10:31).

N.L.G.

HETERONOMY. Immanuel Kant* formulates what he holds to be the supreme principle of morality as a 'categorical imperative'.* He holds that an autonomous agent is one who wills the maxims of his actions (the prescriptions from which he acts) in a way that satisfies the categorical imperative in its various formulations. The categorical imperative is objective, according to Kant, in the sense that a rational agent would necessarily act upon it if reason had full control over inclination. Agents who respect the moral law thus are making it (prescribing it in accordance with their rational nature) and are bound by it at the same time. They have autonomy in the sense that they them*selves* (Gk. *autos*) are the *law* (Gk. *nomos*).

Opposed to autonomy* are the various kinds of *heteronomy* (in Gk. *heteros* means 'other' or 'different'), making the law governing human action depend, not on the rational will itself, but on objects other than the will. Empirical heteronomy is where agents prescribe their own happiness or some other feeling of satisfaction as the final goal of their actions. Rational heteronomy is where agents obey the moral law for the sake of realizing their own perfection or for the sake of obeying the perfect will of God. Morality, on Kant's view, leads to religion, since God is a postulate of practical reason; but morality cannot derive from religion without losing autonomy (and hence without ceasing to be morality).

Kant's argument derives from Plato's* *Euthyphro*, in which Socrates (470–399 BC) argued that the gods love the holy because it is holy, and it is not holy because they love it. If we suppose God is good (and so we should wish to obey his will) we must either derive the concept of his perfection from our own concepts (especially the categorical imperative), or we must suppose his will is independent of this standard. In the former case, the claim that we should obey his will is circular. In the second case, the only concept of God's will remaining to us is one drawn from his power; and our obedience will then be motivated by fear and will not be (in Kant's sense) moral at all.

Kant does not consider alternatives between the horns of this dilemma (and neither does Plato). It is possible, for example, that 'good' does not *mean* 'willed by God' (which would generate the circularity of which Kant complains), but that God wills the good because it is his nature to will it. In this case our desire to be like God might motivate our desire to be good without our motivation thereby becoming one of fear. We might hold that the categorical imperative is a partial, but not yet complete, account of God's goodness.

Bibliography

I. Kant, *Groundwork of the Metaphysic of Morals* (ET, London, ³1958), ch. 2; P. L. Quinn, *Divine Commands and Moral Requirements* (Oxford, 1978), chs. 1–3.

J.E.H.

HILTNER, SEWARD (1909–84). Ordained as a Presbyterian minister in 1935, Seward Hiltner became the foremost pastoral theologian of the American pastoral care movement in the years following the Second World War. Studying under Anton Boisen,* and an early proponent of the Clinical Pastoral Education movement (see Pastoral Care, Counselling and Psychotherapy[12]), he was one of the first to use verbatim transcriptions of patients' histories (Boisen's 'living human documents') as a teaching method for theological students. Along with Russell Dicks (1906–65), Hiltner also pioneered the setting of standards for chaplains in hospitals, prisons and other institutions. As professor of pastoral theology at the University of Chicago Divinity School in the 1950s and at Princeton Theological Seminary in the 1960s and 70s, Hiltner's teaching and prolific writing – not least through his articles in the journal *Pastoral Psychology* (founded in 1950) – helped to reshape the attitudes of American clergy towards a more widely informed pastoral commitment.

Although Hiltner's approach paralleled that of Carl Rogers'* client-centredness, he was also committed to ethical considerations and the centrality of the minister's role in pastoral counselling. In his *Pastoral Counselling* he laid out his 'eductive' method in which 'the creative potentialities of the person needing help' (p. 97) are drawn out. His *Preface to Pastoral Theology* proved to be a major contribution to the definition of the discipline of pastoral theology (see Practical and Pastoral Theology[7]). Given three overall 'perspectives' in pastoral activity – shepherding, communicating and organizing – he argued that it is the 'shepherding perspective' (comprising healing, sustaining and guiding) that both forms the focus of pastoral theology and illuminates *all* the church's doctrine and activity. In the 1960s, Hiltner and Wayne Oates (1917–) warned against the tendencies of pastoral counselling to dominate the church's pastoral care and of Christian ministers to emulate the role of the psychotherapist.

Hiltner has influenced the shape of pastoral care in a number of positive ways. These include: the value of critical theological reflection in the pastoral context; a concern for the whole person and for individual uniqueness; a challenge to coercive and simplistic approaches to pastoral care; and the encouragement of dialogue between the various social, psychological and theological disciplines. He has been criticized for his strong emphasis on the rural metaphor of the shepherd; for the selectivity and vagueness of his theological groundbase, influenced by Paul Tillich (1886–1965) and the more liberal forms of process theology; and for the tendency of his perspectival approach to obscure theological and psychological distinctions.

Bibliography
Pastoral Counseling (Nashville, TN, 1949); *Preface to Pastoral Theology* (Nashville, TN, 1958).

A. V. Campbell, *Paid to Care? The Limits of Professionalism in Pastoral Care* (London, 1985); D. Capps, *Biblical Approaches to Pastoral Counseling* (Philadelphia, 1981); R. J. Hunter (ed.), *DPCC*; J. N. Lapsley, *Salvation and Health* (Philadelphia, 1972); L. O. Mills (ed.), 'Pastoral Theologian of the Year: Seward Hiltner', *PP* 29, 1980, pp. 5–77; D. Tidball, *Skilful Shepherds: An Introduction to Pastoral Theology* (Leicester and Grand Rapids, 1986).

R.F.H.

HINDU ETHICS is developed within a conception of human life in which each person is caught in *samsara*, a beginningless cycle of births and deaths (reincarnation). Negatively, the point of life is to escape *samsara*. Each right or wrong action receives its own fruit, pleasant or unpleasant, in accord with laws of recompense that are conceived as natural laws (*karma*). Escape from the cycle requires putting an end to the process of accumulating the deserved fruit of one's actions. Positively, the point of life is to achieve enlightenment. Achieving enlightenment involves having an esoteric religious experience, called *moksha*, which guarantees that one will not be further reincarnated.

Enlightenment traditionally is conceived as available in the current lifetime only to male Brahmans. Four post-childhood stages of life set the ideal pattern for a Brahman male: student (of the sacred texts), householder (involving marriage and children), hermit (involving leaving home, meditating and doing penance in the forest), and wanderer (breaking all worldly ties, begging for food and seeking

enlightenment). This exhibits the way in which enlightenment, as the ultimate value, ideally determines the seeking of all other values.

Usually three ends of life are recognized: *artha* (gaining wealth honestly), *kama* (pleasure of all kinds); *dharma* (religious merit gained through following Sacred Law). The first two obviously refer to life within *samsara*. The last concerns life within *samsara* as preparatory to escape from *samsara*.

Hinduism has both monotheistic and monistic schools. For the monotheist, Brahman – conceived as the omnipotent, omniscient moral agent who sustains the world in existence – can release a repentant person from the otherwise inevitable fruits of wrong actions. Repentance of one's sins and trust in Brahman constitutes enlightenment; upon repentance, one is freed by grace from the cycle of rebirth. The worshipper is then released from evil *karma* or the unpleasant fruit of actions, and good actions, done unselfishly, do not accumulate positive *karma*. Hence one's life ends when all of one's old karmic accumulations run out. Since no further accumulation has occurred, one is not reborn but lives in communion with God. This is the monotheistic conception of enlightenment or *moksha* as the highest good.

For the monist, we must distinguish between the level of appearance (how things non-idiosyncratically seem to us) and the level of reality (how things are). As things are, Brahman – conceived as qualityless – is all that exists, and enlightenment consists in coming to see that all that seems to exist – one's physical environment, other persons and oneself, and even Brahman monotheistically conceived – only *seem* to exist. Having a *moksha* or enlightenment experience involves acceptance of this belief. Thus for a monist even the most minimal condition of morality – there being at least one moral agent – only appears to be met.

For monistic Hinduism, moral values serve the end of an ultimate religious value in which distinct human persons do not endure. For a monotheistic Hinduism, moral values are included within an ultimate religious value of total devotion to Brahman.

Bibliography
D. Burnett, *The Spirit of Hinduism* (Eastbourne, 1992); T. Hopkins, *The Hindu Religious Tradition* (Encino, CA, 1971); G. B. Walker, *Hindu World: An Encylopedic Survey*

of Hinduism, 2 vols. (London and New York, 1968); R. C. Zaehner, *Hinduism* (Oxford, ²1966).

K.E.Y.

HIPPOCRATIC OATH. Though Hippocrates of Cos (*c.* 460–*c.* 377 BC) was known in antiquity as the greatest of clinicians, we know little of his life. He died at a great age, and a massive literary legacy is attributed to him – the so-called Hippocratic *corpus*, a collection of medical treatises which address clinical, ethical and professional medical matters.

Central to his legacy is the Oath which bears his name and which, with remarkable moral power, lays out the values which have cradled the Western medical tradition. The Oath's formal ethics are well known: abortion* and suicide*/euthanasia* are forbidden to physicians, who are committed to confidentiality* and a refusal to exploit patients or their households for sexual purposes. One also takes on special obligations to one's teacher and the teacher's family. However, the context of these ethical demands is covenantal; unlike its imitators, the Oath is no naked code of ethics. There are three chief covenants: between doctor and patient, between doctor and teacher (and those whom he or she will in due time teach), and – underlying them both – between doctor and God. The ethical code arises out of these covenant obligations which demand, for example, that medical confidentiality be observed, since the patient's private affairs are nothing less than 'holy secrets'.

Despite its pagan origins, the Oath was early adopted by Christians as a summary of their own vision for medicine. Some attempts were made to remove the references to pagan divinites and to 'Christianize' the text of the Oath. These Christian versions did not last, though an Islamicized version was early devised and widely used.

Several contemporary statements follow the pattern of the Oath, most importantly the Declaration of Geneva (1949), which sought to re-state Hippocratic values in the aftermath of the Nuremberg 'medical trials' at the end of the Second World War. Though self-consciously Hippocratic in intention, the Declaration's post-Hippocratic character is curiously evident in its disavowal of the oath-form of the original. Though much of the Hippocratic content remains, the transcendent grounding of medical values beyond the

human situation is thereby lost. The Declaration unconsciously heralded the post-Hippocratic medicine of the late 20th century; seeking to reinstate the humane values denied by the Nazi doctors, it refused to give them any rationale. The Genevan ethic could only be transitional. It is no surprise that the Declaration was revised by the World Medical Association in the 1960s to permit liberal abortion (through an ambiguous rephrasing),

---

The Hippocratic Oath

'I swear by Apollo Physician, by Asclepius, by Health, by Panacea and by all the gods and goddesses, making them my witnesses, that I will carry out, according to my ability and judgement, this oath and this indenture.

'To hold my teacher in this art equal to my own parents; to make him partner in my livelihood; when he is in need of money to share mine with him; to consider his family as my own brothers, and to teach them this art, if they want to learn it, without fee or indenture; to impart precept, oral instruction, and all other instruction to my own sons, the sons of my teacher, and to indentured pupils who have taken the physician's oath, but to nobody else.

'I will use treatment to help the sick according to my ability and judgement, but never with a view to injury and wrong-doing.

'Neither will I administer a poison to anybody when asked to do so, nor will I suggest such a course. Similarly I will not give to a woman a pessary to cause abortion.

'But I will keep pure and holy both my life and my art.

'I will not use the knife, not even, verily, on sufferers from stone, but I will give place to such as are craftsmen therein.

'Into whatsoever house I enter, I will enter to help the sick, and I will abstain from all intentional wrong-doing and harm, especially from abusing the bodies of man or woman, bond or free.

'And whatsoever I shall see or hear in the course of my profession, as well as outside my profession in my intercourse with men, if it be what should not be published abroad, I will never divulge, holding such things to be holy secrets.

'Now if I carry out this oath, and break it not, may I gain for ever reputation among all men for my life and for my art; but if I transgress it and foreswear myself, may the opposite befall me.'
(See W. H. S. Jones, *Hippocrates*, vol. 1, London, 1923, pp. 299–301.)

reversing one of the most characteristic of Hippocratic doctrines.

The Hippocratic 'legend' was an enduring myth of antiquity, suffusing understandings of medicine in the Middle Ages and on into modern times with a model of ancient Gk. medicine as exclusively Hippocratic; a model which has proved illusory. Ludwig Edelstein's (1902–65) trenchant monograph of 1943 disposed of the myth by assigning the Oath a distinct origin in the Pythagoreanism of the later 4th century BC. Hippocratism was neither universal nor, as commentators had come complacently to suggest, self-evident: it rested on certain religious–philosophical assumptions which were the preserve of a small minority in Gk. antiquity, and while their compatibility with Christian (and some other religious) thinking was later to give Hippocratism very wide appeal, the Oath began as the 'manifesto' of a reforming minority of Gk. physicians who sought to displace the liberal ethical consensus of their day. Edelstein's re-pristination of the Oath has been regarded with suspicion by Christians, partly because the US Supreme Court used it to aid the marginalizing of Hippocratic values in the momentous *Roe* v. *Wade* abortion judgment (1973). Yet Edelstein's work freed the Oath from centuries of complacent familiarity. By uncovering its minority and reformist character he has given back to Christians and those who share their humane medical vision a manifesto for medicine in the post-Hippocratic (and increasingly post-Christian) society.

In the Hippocratic Oath's unconditional approach to the patient we see the origins not only of medicine, but also of a substantial tributary of the idea of a 'profession'; and we recognize a model of human obligation* which is peculiarly appropriate to the Christian who, like the pagan Hippocratic, believes that doctor and patient alike are made by God to whom finally both must give account.

See also: MEDICAL CODES OF PRACTICE; PROFESSIONAL ETHICS.

Bibliography

N. M. de S. Cameron, *The New Medicine* (London, 1991); L. Edelstein, *The Hippocratic Oath: Text, Translation and Interpretation* (Baltimore, MD, 1943); D. Gourevitch, *Le Triangle Hippocratique dans Le Monde Greco-Romain* (Rome, 1984); W. H. S. Jones, *The Doctor's Oath: An Essay in the History of Medicine* (Cambridge, 1924); M. Ullman, *Islamic Medicine* (Edinburgh, 1978).

N.M.deS.C.

HOBBES, THOMAS, see GLOBAL ETHICS; [15] HISTORY OF CHRISTIAN ETHICS. [6]

HOLINESS is a thoroughly religious word. It is a fundamental characteristic of God (see [1]), emphasized as frequently throughout Scripture as, for instance, righteousness and love. It is, however, a much harder concept for human minds to grasp. Justice and love we understand initially through our experience in human relationships, and we learn by analogy to apply the words to God. Holiness usually takes its definition from the presence of God.

The Heb. root *qdš* probably implies separation. Places and objects become holy when they are deliberately distinguished from the ordinary and set aside for symbolic use in the worship of God. The otherness of God and the numinous feelings of reverence and awe inspired by the thought of his presence are an important part of our concept of the holiness of God. The nearest human analogies range from the splendour and majesty of a national leader in a State ceremony to the wonder felt by parents with their new-born baby or by bride and groom at their wedding.

Holiness and purity

Those involved in the service of a majestic leader dress and behave in ways that indicate respect and add to the splendour of the occasion. The people who belong to God are called to be holy people. 'Be holy, for I am holy' is a recurring theme in Leviticus. Gordon Wenham (1943–) has pointed out that the three categories in Leviticus – 'unclean', 'clean' and 'holy' – are related in a progression. The unclean can be cleansed to become clean and the clean can be sanctified to become holy. Cleanness or purity is a normal state as opposed to the dirty, the diseased, the disordered or distorted. Holiness includes all that, but there is an extra dimension, the gift or grace of being infused with the presence of God. Israel is called to be a holy people. It is the Lord who sets them apart as holy (Lv. 20:8). Yet paradoxically they consecrate themselves (Lv. 20:7) by obeying the moral law,* observing the cleanness codes and carrying out rituals such as sacrifice. The so-called holiness code of

Lv. 17 – 26 contains behavioural imperatives for the holy people.

Holiness as wholeness

While the initial emphasis of holiness seems to be about separation and otherness, being cut off from all that is unclean and defiling, scholars such as M. Douglas (1921– ; *e.g. Purity and Danger*, London, 1966) have suggested that the underlying principle in the holiness code* is wholeness and completeness. The sacrificial animal must not be blemished. The priest must be physically entire (Lv. 21:18–21). The boundaries between different classes of things in God's creation should not be confused. Stock of different species are not to be mated together, and clothes are not to be woven with two kinds of material (Lv. 19:19).

These sometimes bizarre details in the pentateuchal law do not obscure the fact that it is the moral characteristics of justice/righteousness rooted in love for the neighbour and the alien which is the heart of the holiness of the people of God (Lv. 19:18, 34). The prophets stress how abhorrent to God is any attempt to achieve sanctity through religious ceremony without moral righteousness. Holiness is the shining brilliance of all God's attributes blended together into a whole. As light banishes darkness, it is directed in judgment and retribution against all that is evil and destructive.

Holiness and moral goodness

In the NT the language of holiness/sanctification* is frequently paired with justice/righteousness* or with purity/cleansing. The terms are often almost interchangeable. In Jesus' key saying of Mk. 7:21, the 'unclean' is defined by thoughts within human hearts that lead on to actions or words which damage people sexually, financially, physically or emotionally. This metaphorical dirt is sin (see Sin and Salvation⑤), and it is washed away in the forgiveness* that accompanies faith in the death of Christ (see Atonement;* Eph. 5:26–27; 1 Pet. 1:15–22). In the typology of Hebrews, the external ritual of sacrifices which made the worshipper clean and holy have been replaced by the Holy Spirit applying to the conscience of the believer the sacrificial blood of Christ (Heb. 9:13–14).

Holiness paired with righteousness is found in a number of NT writers. In Mt. 6:20 it is the character of John the Baptist. In Luke and Acts, God's salvation is a rescue which enables us to serve him in righteousness and holiness (Lk. 1:74–75) and Jesus is supremely the holy and righteous servant (Acts 3:13–14). Paul describes Jesus as our righteousness, holiness and redemption (1 Cor. 1:30). In Rom. 6:19 there is a progression from slavery to impurity to voluntary slavery to righteousness leading on to holiness. This is not a moralizing statement about achieving holiness through efforts at right living. Righteousness in Romans is predominantly about God's grace and power to put and keep his covenant people in a right relationship with him.

In one sense, Christians are holy people (saints) because they have been called by God, chosen and designated to be part of a holy community, the body of which Christ is the head (1 Cor. 1:2; Eph. 5:26; 1 Pet. 2:9). In another sense, they become holy as they become more distinctive as they are infused with the Spirit of God. Set apart from the world (but not by being socially separated or uninvolved), they stand out like lights on a hilltop. It is noticeable that the holiness of the Father and the Son is only briefly mentioned in the NT but that the word 'Spirit' is usually prefaced by 'Holy'.

Despite the overlap between holiness and righteousness words in the NT, Reformed theology has tended to emphasize justification* as the starting-point of our right relationship with God, and sanctification as a gradual process of becoming more like God, genuinely righteous and holy (Eph. 4:24). The process is not complete until history ends and we are in the presence of God (1 Thes. 3:13). The distinction is pastorally helpful in reminding those who have seen big changes in their lives at a time of conversion* or an experience of spiritual renewal that there is a long steady journey required in growth towards God's kind of wholeness.

See also: KESWICK MOVEMENT.

Bibliography
J. Murray, *Collected Writings*, vol. 2 (Edinburgh, 1977), pp. 277–317; J. I. Packer, *Keep in Step with the Spirit* (Old Tappan, NJ, and Leicester, 1984); J. C. Ryle, *Holiness* (1879; repr. Dartington, 1979); R. C. Sproul, *The Holiness of God* (Wheaton, IL, 1985); G. J. Wenham, *The Book of Leviticus* (Grand Rapids, 1979).

V.M.S.

HOLINESS CODE.

HOLINESS CODE. Critical scholarship usually refers to Lv. 17 – 26 as the Holiness Code, because of its great concern that the people of Israel should exemplify in their own lives the holiness of God: 'Be holy because I, the LORD your God, am holy' (Lv. 19:2). It is usually held that the Holiness Code is a distinct source within the Priestly Code (approximately Ex. 25 – Nu. 36) and somewhat earlier than other priestly material. However, the traditional definition and dating of the Holiness Code have been contested in recent commentaries on Leviticus (*e.g.* J. Milgrom, *Leviticus 1 – 16*, New York, 1991; G. J. Wenham, *The Book of Leviticus*, Grand Rapids, 1979).

The whole book of Leviticus is concerned with the idea that the people of God should imitate God, that human behaviour should reflect the divine holiness. The Holiness Code shows what a far-reaching demand this is. Holiness involves the correct and regular worship of God (Lv. 23) and the avoidance of pollution (Lv. 21 – 22). As God is pure and holy, life, death and associated phenomena must be shunned. Holiness thus expresses the intimate covenant* bond between God and Israel: her highest privilege is that the holy God lives and walks among his people (Lv. 26:11–12).

But holiness does not merely impinge on the God–man dimension. It should transform all inter-human relationships. It involves the right use of sex: the people of God must avoid incest,* adultery,* bigamy, homosexuality* and so on (Lv. 18; 20). It involves caring for the downtrodden, the poor, the oppressed and the immigrant (Lv. 19). The law of jubilee* is designed to ensure that no individual or family is irrevocably burdened with debt.* Every fifty years a fresh start is possible, when debts are waived, and land and financial independence are restored (Lv. 25). Generosity and a care for others are essential elements of holiness, summed up in the command, 'Love your neighbour as yourself' (Lv. 19:18; *cf.* Mt. 22:39).

See also: OLD TESTAMENT ETHICS. 8

G.J.W.

HOLY SPIRIT.

HOLY SPIRIT. So named in the NT above 100 times, the Holy Spirit appears there as the third person of the triune Godhead. ('Person' here means an 'I' to whom other persons are 'you'; 'Godhead' means the one complex reality that the three 'I's' form; 'Spirit' carries the thought of active energy; 'Holy' of divinity.) OT references to the Spirit of God point generally to the divine presence and power, variously exerted in creation,* providence and grace,* but the entire NT has moved beyond this. The Spirit's personhood becomes evident when Jesus introduces him as 'another' (*i.e.* a second) Paraclete (Jn. 14:16) who will replace Jesus on earth as counsellor, helper, strengthener, supporter, adviser, advocate and ally: all of which roles are involved in being a *paraklētos*, and all of which are indisputably personal. So, too, when the Spirit is said to speak, convince, testify, show, lead, guide, teach, prompt speech, command, forbid, desire, help, intercede with groans, and be grieved, lied to and blasphemed (see Mt. 12:31–32; Mk. 13:11; Jn. 14:26; 15:26; 16:7–15; Acts 2:4; 5:3; 8:29; 13:2; 16:6–7; 21:11; Rom. 8:14, 16, 26–27; Gal. 4:6; 5:17–18; Eph. 4:30; Heb. 3:7; 10:15; 1 Pet. 1:11; Rev. 2:7; *etc.*), personhood is clearly in view: only persons can act and suffer in this way.

The Spirit's personal deity is clearly implicit in all of this, as it is also in the 'triadic' passages on God's gracious activity in saving lost sinners (Jn. 14:16 – 16:15; Rom. 8; 1 Cor. 12:4–6; 2 Cor. 13:4; Eph. 1:3–14; 2:18; 3:14–19; 4:4–6; 2 Thes. 2:13–14; 1 Pet. 1:2; *etc.*). It becomes quite explicit when Jesus, instituting Christian baptism, declares the 'name' (singular) of the one God to be the Father, the Son and the Holy Spirit (Mt. 28:19); when John sets the Spirit (called 'seven spirits' because seven signifies divine perfection) in between the Father and the Son as the source of divine grace and peace (Rev. 1:4–5; *cf.* 3:1; 4:5; 5:6); and when lying to the Holy Spirit is interpreted as lying to God (Acts 5:3–4).

Though the NT has no technical trinitarian vocabulary and stops short at saying that Christians worship and pray to and fellowship with the Father and the Son through the Spirit (*e.g.* Eph. 2:17–22; 1 Jn. 1:3 with 3:21–24), the systematically tripersonal way in which the writers conceive God's work of saving sinners cannot be missed. The God whose solitariness (as against polytheistic systems) was stressed so strongly both in the OT and by Paul at Athens (Acts 17:24–31), and whose utterances recorded in the OT use unipersonal speech forms throughout (see Is. 45:5–7; 46:9; *etc.*), now stands revealed as three-in-one – a divine society – both the Son and the Spirit being distinct from the Father. Yahweh must henceforth be seen as 'they', and 'they' as 'he'. Such is the mystery – the unique, unfathomable revealed reality – of the one true God.

In forming a positive notion of the Holy Spirit's true place in the divine economy, certain pitfalls must be avoided. The unitarianism of 3rd-century modalists, who saw Father, Son and Spirit as three roles played by a single person, and of G. W. H. Lampe (1912–80) whose *God as Spirit* (London, ²1983) reduced the Holy Spirit to a name for the active presence of the transcendent creator, does not square with the NT witness to the Spirit's personhood; nor does the 'binitarianism' of Hendrikus Berkof (1914–), who in *The Doctrine of the Holy Spirit* (London, 1964) treated the Holy Spirit as a name for the exalted Christ active in his church and kingdom. Augustine's* assertion that the Trinity is reflected in the human reality of love (see ②) – where the lover corresponds to the Father, the beloved to the Son, and the love that unites them to the Holy Spirit – has had the unintended effect of depersonalizing the Spirit in Western minds (for love, as such, is obviously not a distinct person), so that Western theology and devotion outside the evangelical tradition (which has always been strong on the Spirit, though this is not always noticed) have repeatedly lapsed into legalism,* moralism, sacramentalism and formal 'churchianity' for want of appreciating the personal, life-giving ministry of the Spirit in those whom he indwells and empowers. Today's charismatic movement, previously execrated, as original pentecostalism was before it, as an unspiritual and perhaps demonic aberration, has vindicated itself as a practical corrective of the Augustinian shortcoming in places where such a corrective was needed. Yet it is in constant danger of separating the Holy Spirit too much from Christ and so opening the door to fresh deviances of an illuminist and gnostic sort, as some Anabaptists, early Quakers and others did in the past.

The true path is to grasp two things: 1. that the Spirit, no less than the Father and the Son, is (not *less* but) *more* fully personal – more aware, more integrated, more purposeful – than we are; and 2. that as the Spirit fulfilled a ministry of loving service to the redeemer – effecting his incarnation (Lk. 1:35), enriching him inwardly from birth onwards (*cf.* Lk. 2:52) and empowering him in a special way at and after his baptism (Lk. 3:22; 4:1, 14, 18), both for his teaching (*cf.* Jn. 6:63) and for his sacrifice (Heb. 9:14) and resurrection (*cf.* Rom. 8:11) – so he is now given and

sent by the risen Lord to fulfil a comparable personal ministry to the redeemed. He reveals to them the reality of the crucified and risen Christ of apostolic proclamation, so that they are brought to confess 'Jesus is Lord' (Jn. 16:8–11; 1 Cor. 12:3; 2 Cor. 4:6). He unites them to Christ in regenerative, life-giving co-resurrection so that they become members (living limbs and units) in the body of which he is head (Rom. 6:3–11 with 7:4–6 and 8:9–11; Eph. 2:1–10 with 4:3–16; Tit. 3:4–7). He assures them that they are God's children and heirs (Rom. 8:12–17; Gal. 4:6) and sustains them in conscious fellowship with the Father and the Son (1 Jn. 1:3 with 3:1–10, 24). He transforms their characters progressively into Christ's moral and spiritual likeness, by instilling new desires for God and godliness that issue in new patterns of behaviour (2 Cor. 3:18; Gal. 5:16–25). He prompts prayer (Eph. 6:18; Jude 20) and prays earnestly and effectively for believers who do not know to pray for themselves (Rom. 8:26–27). Also, he gives 'gifts' – *i.e.* witnessing and serving abilities for expressing Christ in a way that extends and edifies the church (Acts 1:8; Rom. 12:3–13; 1 Cor. 12; Eph. 4:7–16; 5:18–20; 1 Pet. 4:10–11).

All these are aspects of the Spirit's new-covenant ministry of glorifying the glorified Christ to and through Christians, the ministry that Jesus foretold (Jn. 7:37–39; 14:16 – 16:15) and that Pentecost began. In this ministry the Spirit is self-effacing: he is the hidden floodlight shining on the saviour, the secret surgeon of the heart who redirects love and desire to the living and true God, and to Jesus in particular, the unnoticed matchmaker who brings us to the feet of Christ, the 'intercom' channel that sustains communication between us and our Lord, and the hidden energizer guaranteeing perseverance in faith,* hope,* love and worship. Since the Spirit fulfils this many-sided ministry as Jesus' agent, it is not surprising that Jesus himself is sometimes said to do what the Spirit does in Christians (indwell, Col. 1:27; impart life, Col. 3:4; sanctify, Eph. 5:26; give strength, 2 Tim. 4:17) and through Christians (transmit the gospel, Eph. 2:17; secure conversions, Jn. 12:32; Rom. 15:18). The Christocentric focus of the Spirit's paraclete ministry is sustained throughout the NT.

The life generated by the Holy Spirit in Christians is one in which the behavioural uprightness and beauty lost at the Fall* of Adam begin to be restored. In this sanctifying process the Spirit exerts his power, not by suspending or overriding the ordinary operations of mind and body by ecstatic takeover, as non-human agencies are understood to do in shamanism, in the trances of spiritist mediums, and in New Age channelling, but in bringing about a directed use of our natural powers in obedient, creative service of God, motivated by gratitude and a purpose of glorifying him for the grace he has given. Life in the Spirit is therefore neither activism (self-reliant as opposed to self-distrustful and God-reliant activity) nor quietism (apathetic passivity till inwardly moved to do something specific). In both Testaments the individual's active consciousness – the mix of thinking, feeling, being aware, acting, relating and bearing responsibility, that makes up one's selfhood – is called not only the 'soul' (e.g. Pss. 23:3; 42:1; Mt. 11:29) but also the 'spirit' (e.g. Pss. 31:5; 32:2; 1 Cor. 2:11), and our spirit receives testimony from the divine Spirit (cf. Rom. 8:16), through the Word of God read, made audible in preaching and visible in sacraments, and applied by its author to mind and heart. But the directional, relational and habitual changes that the Spirit induces by thus applying the Word, however much they exceed what would be possible without him, are wrought with and through the believer's active co-operation in responsive and prayerful moral endeavour. The image of God* that is being restored – namely, Christlike holiness (Eph. 4:24; 4:32 – 5:2) – comes about without any violence being done to the rational, relational and reverential powers of the believer.

The epistles assume that receiving the Holy Spirit in adult conversion, when one is born again (Jas. 1:18; 1 Pet. 1:3, 23; 1 Jn. 3:9; 4:7; 5:1, 4; see Jn. 3:3–8) and becomes a new creation (2 Cor. 5:17; Gal. 6:15), involves an experiential change, so that one knows it has happened (see 1 Cor. 12:13; Gal. 3:2–5; Eph. 1:13–14; 1 Thes. 1:9; 1 Jn. 3:24; 4:13). The change, however, is essentially one, not of emotional temper (though this may well occur as a spin-off), but of altered purposes and quickened and augmented powers, which, far from diminishing personal selfhood or self-control, deepens both (cf. Gal. 5:23; 2 Tim. 1:7). Random and irresponsible behaviour, such as the freedom-flaunting Corinthians allowed themselves, and unwillingness to safeguard Christian unity by accepting accountability within the body of Christ (see Eph. 4:3–6), indicate deep-level resistance to the Spirit rather than co-operation with him, and in effect a preference for childishness above maturity in Christ.

Christians' moral lives, then, are the focus of the Spirit's transforming work. He leads believers to infer from Calvary the greatness and permanence of God's love to them (Rom. 5:6–8; 8:32–39; 1 Jn. 4:8–10), and to realize their new identity as children of God (Jn. 1:13) and heirs of glory with their Saviour (Rom. 8:15–17). He nurtures in them the filial instinct to view God as their Father when they pray (Gal. 4:6); saying 'Father' from the heart is where praying in the Spirit starts (Eph. 6:18; Jude 20). He gives them joy* by keeping them rejoicing and exulting in the privileges of grace and prospects of glory that are theirs (Rom. 5:2–3, 11; 14:17; Gal. 5:22; 1 Thes. 1:6; cf. Acts 13:52). He moves them, by concentrating on Christ and prayerfuly watching against particular lapses, to do to death (mortify) sin within them in its manifold guises (Rom. 8:13; Col. 3:5), and stirs them up to work at forming Christlike behaviour patterns, which, because his is the power that makes these endeavours effective, Paul speaks of as the Spirit's 'fruit' in their lives (Gal. 5:22–23; cf. 2 Cor. 3:18). Centrally, he moves them to practise love to the Father, the Son and all humankind – love being, quite simply, a resolve to serve and exalt the loved ones (Rom. 15:30; Col. 1:8). Christians feel tensions between conflicting desires (Gal. 5:16–17), and their moral reach constantly exceeds their moral grasp (Rom. 7:21–25), so that an element of distress marks their experience, yet they 'walk by' (Gal. 5:16, NASB) and 'keep in step with' (Gal. 5:25, NIV) the Spirit who indwells them (Rom. 8:9), and the resultant supernaturalizing of their natural lives (cf. Jn. 7:37–39) in moral reformation (Eph. 4:20–24; 5:8–21), bold witness (Acts 4:8, 13, 29, 31), and superhuman endurance (1 Pet. 3:1–4, 9–17; 4:1–4, 14), is such as to amaze the world (cf. Jn. 3:8–9).

Whatever problems of temperament,* emotional scarring, past victimization, and present bad habits Christians may have, a vital element of pastoral care is to hold before them the power of the Holy Spirit to change the most unpromising human material into the moral likeness of Jesus Christ, and to insist that the call to be thus transformed, however disruptive, may not be evaded. For this is true life in the kingdom of God, which is 'a matter . . . of righteousness, peace and joy in the Holy Spirit' (Rom. 14:17).

Bibliography

F. D. Bruner, *A Theology of the Holy Spirit* (Grand Rapids, 1970); J. D. G. Dunn, *Baptism in the Holy Spirit* (London, 1970); *idem, Jesus and the Spirit* (London, 1975); *idem, NIDNTT* 3, pp. 693–707; G. D. Fee, *God's Empowering Presence* (Peabody, MA, 1994); M. Green, *I Believe in the Holy Spirit* (London, 1975); A. I. C. Heron, *The Holy Spirit* (London and Philadelphia, 1983); A. Kuyper, *The Work of the Holy Spirit* (Grand Rapids, 1946); J. Owen, *The Works of John Owen*, ed. W. H. Goold (repr. London, 1965–66), vols. 3, 4, 6, 7; J. I. Packer, *Keep in Step with the Spirit* (Old Tappan, NJ, and Leicester, 1984); *idem, A Passion for Holiness* (Cambridge, 1992); T. Smail, *The Giving Gift* (London, 1988); *idem, Reflected Glory: The Spirit in Christ and Christians* (London, 1975); G. Smeaton, *The Doctrine of the Holy Spirit* (London, 1958); J. V. Taylor, *The Go-Between God: The Holy Spirit and the Christian Mission* (London, 1972).

J.I.P.

HOLY WAR denotes war* conducted under religious auspices. The term does not itself occur in the Scriptures, and covers various concepts.

1. Concepts of 'holy war'

a. Holy war can denote wars of religion fought to defend or propagate a faith (*e.g.* the Islamic *jihad*). This usage has little connection with biblical warfare: 'Israel did not fight for her faith but for her existence' (R. de Vaux, 1903–71). Neither OT nor NT supports offensive war to propagate faith, though they have been used to justify it (*e.g.* the Crusades). Christ's emphasis on doing good to enemies leaves no room for 'holy war' in this sense.

b. In ancient Gk. usage, 'holy war' referred to military action against members of the Delphic league (an amphictyony) who violated sacred rites. Following this model, Gerhard von Rad (1901–71) saw 'holy war' as a similar sanction operative within Israel. Yet only in Jos. 22 and Jdg. 20 is there intra-Israel military action (*cf.* Dt. 13:12–18). The use of force to uphold orthodoxy (*e.g.* Augustine's* advocacy of it against the Donatists) traces its roots to this understanding of 'holy war'.

c. In the ancient Near East, 'holy war' could describe the mythological presentation of war among deities. This literary tradition contrasts with the historical basis of divine involvement in war in Israel's experience. The Scriptures utilized the power of war imagery in similar ways (*e.g.* Is. 51:9–11), especially in cultic and apocalyptic texts.

'Holy war' thus has little place in Christian moral perspectives. This tradition has consistently rejected 'positive' views of war, regarding it in 'negative' terms, via the 'just war' theory.* This gives guidance regarding the conduct of war once it is unavoidable, but is distinct from the various notions of 'holy war'.

2. The moral problem of 'holy war'

Even so, biblical passages depicting God as allowing, commanding or taking part in warfare raise sharp moral questions. This particularly applies to the divinely commanded 'ban' (Heb. *herem*) of utter destruction (*e.g.* Dt. 7:1–5), which seems to legitimate genocide,* although the basic idea is that a whole city, inhabitants and property, should be devoted to God. Despite the rejection of war as an ideal by the prophets, and the peacemaking work of Christ, the moral problem of the ban raises many questions. Practically, can the ban be used today? Exegetically, what use do we make of texts which record its use? Theologically, how do we respond to the God who could command it?

a. In the Middle Ages, the ban was used to justify both the burning of heretics, and crusades against infidels. Could it justify the obliteration of a 'godless' enemy through nuclear attack? The ban is commanded only at a specific time in Israel's history, as a rationale for the conquest of Canaan: to apply it outside this time is illegitimate (as later prophetic metaphorical use of it shows). Today the people of God extends beyond one national entity, to include people of every nation. Advocacy of the ban would set Christian against Christian in wholesale obliterative conflict. Finally, pre-emptive war rejects the will of God as revealed in the teaching of Jesus.

b. How are the ban texts to be used? Legitimate appeal can be made to them to stress the radicalism of obedience (so 1 Sa. 15:22). Some have used the ban to argue that, within the limits of warfare which does not involve non-combatants, that strategy is most merciful which produced a decisive and swift outcome. Yet this has no relevance in an age of mechanical weapons: distinguishing combatants and non-combatants has become impossible. Others reject these texts, seeing them as either mistaken zeal (so V. Eller, 1927–), or literary inventions by later authors for cultic reasons (Gerhard von Rad) or for ideological reasons (T. W. Hobbs, 1942–). But difficult and problematic as they are, they still form part of the scriptural canon.

c. What do we make of the ban having been commanded by God? The Bible never countenances human sacrifice: why does God require human slaughter in warfare? The OT provides some mitigation in its insistence upon the corrupt nature of Canaanite society (*e.g.* Dt. 9:4). Further, as Lord of all, including warfare, God can dispose of nations according to the divine purpose. This is certainly the biblical context for the ban, although divine use of it may appear arbitrary.

Some therefore take a 'developmental' approach: the ban was a necessary stage in the progress from a 'creation-order' to a 'righteousness-order' in the fallen world (H. Junker, 1891–). This omits a Christological perspective, however: God's purpose includes the fulfilling and focusing of OT revelation in Christ. The divine plan required not only divine involvement, not only the keeping pure of a people from idolatry (the motive for the ban in Dt. 7), but also the taking of the consequences of that involvement and idolatry. The ban reflected what it meant to be the enemy of God, accursed. The NT teaches that God has in Christ taken the ban/curse due to humanity: Christ suffered the fate of the good when it enters a fallen world. Christ thus stands in the place of both 'friends' and 'enemies' of God.

In sum, the ban reveals something of the seriousness of opposing God, shown at its deepest level in Christ's work as the ban for us in his life and death. This still leaves the issue of how the God revealed in Christ could command the ban, but sets it in the context of the overall biblical story.

See also: WAR.

Bibliography

L. Barrett, *The Way God Fights* (Scottdale, PA, 1987); P. C. Craigie, *The Problem of War in the Old Testament* (Grand Rapids, 1976); V. Eller, *King Jesus' Manual of Arms for the 'Armless* (Nashville, TN, 1973); T. W. Hobbs, *A Time for War: A Study of Warfare in the Old Testament* (Wilmington, DE, 1989); M. Lind, *Yahweh is a Warrior: The Theology of Warfare in Ancient Israel* (Scottdale, PA, 1980); C. H. Sherlock, *The God Who Fights* (Edinburgh, 1991).

C.H.S.

HOMELESSNESS. The term 'homeless' conveys a picture of an alcoholic vagrant male, rummaging through dustbins, in a dirty overcoat, exhibiting antisocial behaviour. The reality is vastly different, for homelessness embraces both sexes, all age groups, and people from a surprisingly broad social spectrum.

Media attention from the late 1980s onwards increased public awareness of the problem, but its extent has never been fully known. That it has always been a social problem is an indisputable fact. During the 19th century, severe poverty, high parental mortality rates, increasing incidences of child abuse and increasing child prostitution compelled champions of true evangelicalism (*e.g.* C. H. Spurgeon* and Thomas Barnardo*) to implement radical social policies of compassion, in 'sharing the love of Jesus' with the many thousands of desperately needy people.

There are three factors which have always affected homelessness: poverty; abuse (both physical and sexual); and the neglect of those with special needs.

Homelessness must not be regarded as simply referring to 'street' dwellers, for it includes a huge number of people known as 'the hidden homeless', *i.e.* those no longer living in their parental homes or in the care of a local authority, but living on friends' floors, squatting illegally, or moving from one source of temporary accommodation to another.

Various current factors have caused an increase in homelessness since the 1980s. Poverty* is a principal cause, with a variety of factors causing individuals to be unable to maintain a home of their own. Government legislation regarding State benefits affects many. Unemployment* has been a major factor, resulting in a low sense of self-esteem* and an inevitable sense of failure, which in turn results in a lack of motivation. Unemployment has resulted in many house repossessions, adding to the large numbers of families coming into the category of the homeless. Other significant factors are reduced availability of local authority accommodation and financial stress.

From the 1980s onwards, child abuse* became widely publicized, resulting in complaints from abused children and adolescents being taken seriously, and victims finding that there were adults prepared to help. The realization of having a right to leave an abusive environment occasioned large numbers of children and young people leaving parental homes and care establishments.

Another vulnerable group is those with special needs, including those with moderate learning difficulties, who leave their family home through rejection or the break-up of the family. These people are unable to cope with independent living, sometimes even being incapable of filling out the standard claim forms of the UK's Department of Social Security. Those with psychiatric illnesses also form a significant number. Such people quickly find themselves with no adequate support and are especially vulnerable to exploitation and abuse. In 1990, the Centrepoint night shelter in London's Soho reported that one in three homeless young people had been approached to become involved in prostitution, as opposed to one in five just two years earlier.

Homelessness impacts the lives of its victims in very distressing ways: no future, no hope, no dignity and no home. It can precipitate psychiatric disturbance and ill health. Some admit to committing crimes in order to get custodial sentences, thereby ensuring 'a roof over their heads' and 'food in their bellies'.

The Christian view of humanity (see ④) contrasts sharply with the humanistic and evolutionary view which underlies the attitudes of governments, individuals and social theorists to the problem of homelessness.

The recognition of people as created by God demands that all human beings, irrespective of their circumstances, be treated with dignity as bearing his image (see Image of God*). The same recognition, however, obliges each person to recognize his or her own accountability to live before God in obedience to his laws and in community with each other.

The reality of homelessness and the existence of an underprivileged and neglected minority expose the absence of a commonly-held, Christian or biblical view of humanity.

The initial provision of a 'roof over one's head', whilst being vital 'first aid' to the homeless, will need to be accompanied by ongoing care. A vital second step is to introduce the homeless into a 'community', for only thereby can people live as God prescribed and intended. The existence of a community in which compassionate care and commitment play their part is a vital requisite in enabling persons who have experienced the deprivations of homelessness to realize their human potential and enjoy a life of meaningful fulfilment in God's world.

All the evidence points to the fact that few will achieve such a step without intervention, support and help.

These are the very issues with which Christ was concerned when he called his followers to face the challenge of the afflicted and the 'homeless' of his generation (Mt. 25:34–40). These are the same issues that Isaiah addressed when he directed his readers to the nature of true religion (Is. 58:6–7). The biblical challenge will always remain as an inescapable call to conscience,* demanding the church's response in every generation.

Bibliography

Association of Metropolitan Authorities, *Homelessness: Programme for Action* (London, 1990); Centrepoint, *Homeless and Hungry: A Sign of the Times* (London, 1989); M. Fearon, *No Place Like Home: Christians and the Scandal of Homelessness* (London, 1989); J. Greve, *Homelessness in London* (York, 1986); idem, *Homelessness in Britain* (York, 1990); Institute of Housing, *Who will House the Homeless?* (London, 1988); London Housing Aid Centre (SHAC), *The New Homeless* (London, 1990); National Children's Homes, *Housing: Vulnerable Young Single Homeless People* (London, 1989); B. Saunders, *Homeless Young People in Britain: The Contribution of the Voluntary Sector* (London, 1986); Single Homeless in London, *Move-on Housing* (London, 1989); West End Central Policy Community Consultative Group, *Report on Homeless in Central London* (London, 1990); Young Homeless Group, *Unsecured Futures* (London, ²1990).

A.P.P.

HOMOSEXUALITY is an ambivalent term. It may be applied to *people* who are sexually attracted to members of their own sex; or to same-sex genital *acts*. It comprises both men and women, though lesbianism is the word normally used to distinguish female homosexuality.

The difference between personal orientation and behaviour is important. Some people with a homosexual orientation never put their desires into practice; while others whose attraction is primarily heterosexual engage in homosexual acts occasionally.

The incidence of homosexual behaviour is notoriously hard to identify accurately. From his survey of white American adult males (1948), A. C. Kinsey (1894–1956; see Kinsey Reports*) found that 4% were exclusively homosexual in their behaviour after puberty, while 8% were exclusively homosexual for at least three years. His figures for females (1953) were lower and based on a smaller sample; he discovered that 13% had behaved homosexually at some point in their lives before the age of 45.

Kinsey identified a broad spectrum of sexual preference. His research revealed that homosexual activity is usually part of a life-pattern which includes heterosexual behaviour as well. This further blurs the meaning of the word 'homosexual' when applied to people rather than to acts.

At the homosexual end of the spectrum, there is no consensus about the causation of same-sex desires. Some trace the orientation to genetic or biochemical sources (as yet undiscovered). Others prefer a psychological aetiology. Among the latter, Elizabeth Moberly argues that a homosexual condition in adulthood may arise from an unresolved relational deficit with the parent of the same sex during childhood.

A point on which the majority of the experts agree is that a homosexual orientation is discovered, not chosen. This clearly has important implications when personal responsibility* is discussed.

1. Ethical considerations

a. *Homosexuality in the Bible.* The Bible says nothing about the homosexual orientation, but it does condemn homosexual behaviour forthrightly. Sodom suffered God's judgment for threatened homosexual rape (Gn. 19:1–25; cf. Jdg. 19:11 – 20:48); while the OT law labelled male homosexual practice as 'detestable' and prescribed the death penalty for convicted offenders (Lv. 18:22; 20:13; cf. 1 Ki. 14:24; 15:12; 22:46). In the NT, Paul censured homosexual practice (including lesbianism) as unnatural, incompatible with the lifestyle of God's kingdom and an affront to God's law and gospel (Rom. 1:18–27; 1 Cor. 6:9–11; 1 Tim. 1:8–11).

Some scholars, however, following the lead of Sherwin Bailey (1910–84; see *Homosexuality and the Western Christian Tradition*) and John Boswell (1947– ; see *Christianity, Social Tolerance and Homosexuality*), challenge the traditionally negative conclusions drawn from these biblical passages.

Exegetically, they argue that the key Heb. and Gk. expressions in the Bible's few references to homosexual behaviour cannot bear the weight usually put on them. The word 'know' in Genesis 19 shows that Sodom's sin was inhospitality, not homosexual perversion. 'Destestable' in Leviticus and 'unnatural' in Romans mean 'not according to Jewish law and custom'. And *arsenokoites* in 1 Corinthians and 1 Timothy means a male prostitute, not a homosexual person who seeks a lasting faithful relationship.

Hermeneutically, these writers point to the inconsistency involved in invoking the OT law against homosexuals, while turning a blind eye to those who transgress other regulations in the Holiness Code. And Rom. 1:26–27 is cited to argue that Paul, as a child of his age, was unaware of a settled homosexual orientation. His condemnation of same-sex intercourse cannot, therefore, be applied across the culture gap that separates his day from ours.

Boswell's historical survey of attitudes to homosexuality has been particularly influential, but the overwhelming weight of scholarly opinion contradicts these liberal conclusions about the meaning and interpretation of the biblical text. That much is agreed exegetically by the vast majority of commentators on the relevant passages. After a comprehensive, non-polemical survey of the evidence, Peter Coleman (1928–) concludes that if we ask what the biblical writers actually meant, the answer is clear. They intended to put a ban on all homosexual behaviour.

Conservative scholars have sometimes been guilty of dodging the hermeneutical issues, but the case in favour of applying the Bible's veto to homosexual behaviour today retains its congency.

David Atkinson (1943–) quotes the biblical scholar John Bright (1908–) to good effect. The interpreter's task, says Bright, is 'to detect behind every biblical text . . . that facet of theology which expresses itself there'. Judged by this standard, Atkinson maintains, the Bible's ban on homosexual acts takes on vital contemporary significance.

An important facet of theology expressed by the OT law's ban on homosexual acts is the 'one-flesh' pattern of heterosexual marriage in Genesis. That, no doubt, was why Paul bracketed homosexual behaviour with adultery in his updated application of the Ten Commandments in 1 Timothy. He hits the same note in Romans, where the context of his ban on homosexual acts is the doctrine of creation.* And when the 'kingdom' (see Kingdom of God*) context of 1 Corinthians is taken into account as well, the links in the theological chain (from creation to kingdom, *via* the

Decalogue*) are impressively strong in their contemporary relevance.

b. Nature and creation. Is homosexual behaviour unnatural? Not for those at the homosexual end of Kinsey's spectrum, it is suggested. For them, same-sex intercourse seems perfectly natural. Statistically, the homosexual person's preference is abnormal. But ethically, this abnormality is no more significant than left-handedness.

From Thomas Aquinas* to Karl Barth* and Helmut Thielicke,* prominent Christian ethicists have questioned this line of argument. Christians must relate their understanding of nature to the doctrine of creation, they insist. To ask whether homosexuality is natural is to ask whether God made it. And the answer to that has to be in the negative.

Barth refers his readers to the Bible's account of creation and points to the complementarity of male and female in the *imago Dei*. An individual can come to 'fellow humanity', he maintains, only through relating to a member of the *opposite* sex. A homosexual union is effectively denying the 'otherness' of the one-flesh relationship which the creator initiated between man and woman.

Aquinas (followed by orthodox Roman Catholic moral theology*) stresses the procreative end of heterosexual intercourse. To be natural, he argues, an act must serve the ends which are natural to it. Homosexual intercourse is by definition non-procreative in intention. It is therefore immoral, because it cannot lead to full, secure family life.

c. The criterion of love. While the Catholic disciple of Thomas Aquinas sees procreation as the chief end of sexual intercourse, the Protestant gives a higher profile to the unitive value of physical intimacy. And this has prepared the ground for a situationist approach to homosexuality, majoring on the application of *agapē* love (see 2).

Norman Pittenger's (1905–) criterion for evaluating homosexual acts is openly situationist (see Situation Ethics*): 'Insofar as they contribute to a movement of persons towards mutual fulfilment and fulfilment in mutuality, with all the accompanying characteristics of love', he writes, 'they are *good* acts' (*Time for Consent*, p. 103).

This approach effectively undercuts any ethical distinction between homosexual and heterosexual behaviour. Both are to be judged by the same standard. God's purpose for us all is that we should realize our humanity as lovers, so any act which takes us nearer that goal is morally justified.

The Anglican Report, *Homosexual Relationships* (1979), is sympathetic to the situationist approach, but notes two ethical drawbacks in it. First, it leads to a highly subjective approach to morality, depending on the individual's interpretation of love's demands in any particular situation. Secondly, when taken to its logical conclusion, it opens the door to far more than the homosexual counterpart of marriage.

In their 'Critical Observations', the Report's sponsors make an even more damaging criticism. Basically, they say, 'it is an error to reduce ethics to an undefined emotively elastic principle of "love" – and then to treat all other rules . . . as binding only insofar as they derive from that principle'. It is a particularly perverse use of Scripture which 'invites us to bring under the "love" principle actions expressly forbidden in the authorities from which the principle derives'.

In the US, mainline denominations (such as the United Methodist Church, the Episcopal Church and the Presbyterian Church USA) have also been vexed by the issue of homosexuality. In public statements, however, nearly all have refused to condone homosexual behaviour or the ordination of practising homosexuals.

2. Pastoral considerations

A statement in 1981 on *Attitudes to Homosexual People*, from a working party convened by the British organization called Care and Counsel, identified 'acceptance' as homosexual people's chief need. They must be reassured that God accepts them. They must learn to accept themselves (which implies an admission, not an endorsement, of their orientation). And they need to find acceptance from others.

a. Acceptance and celibacy. Most of those who believe that all homosexual behaviour is wrong conclude that a lasting same-sex preference is a *de facto* vocation to celibacy (see Singleness*).

Not all conservative scholars, however, take this view without qualification. Lewis Smedes (1921–) calls it a 'sledgehammer judgment', which may be ethically correct but is 'ineffective pastoral counsel'. Echoing Thielicke, he maintains that homosexual conduct is ethically unwarranted, so the homosexual person should actively seek change and seriously strive for celibacy.

But if both those options prove impossible, he or she should aim for an 'optimum homosexual morality', developing a faithful, loving association with one other person. Though falling short of God's ideal, this is 'preferable to a life of sexual chaos'.

Jack Dominian (1929–) extends this 'lesser evil' argument by applying it to the AIDS pandemic. If the alternative to a faithful homosexual relationship is a promiscuous lifestyle, with the constant risk of HIV infection, the Christian counsellor must encourage the former in order to deter the latter.

Others see this approach as the top of a slippery slope and a denial of the healing resources of the gospel. Richard Lovelace (1930–), for example, compares Paul's tolerance on some issues of conscience (in Rom. 14 and 1 Cor. 8) with his very strong stand against sexual sin (1 Cor. 5 – 6 and 2 Cor. 7). He concludes that permissiveness is an inappropriate response to sexual misbehaviour.

Paul's repeated injunction to shun *porneia* assumes that abstinence from sexual intercourse is at least possible, and the charismatic wing of the church (especially) claims many instances where the Spirit's healing power has led to a change of sexual orientation, as well as control of homosexual desire. While many Christian counsellors urge caution over claims to complete, instantaneous 'cures', the NT certainly bears witness to the gospel's potential for rescuing those trapped in ingrained lifestyles (*cf.* 1 Cor. 6:9–11).

It does not, of course, suggest that a shift from same-sex preference is the final solution for the homosexual's problems. The goal for homosexual and heterosexual alike is fulfilment and wholeness in Christ.

b. Acceptance and homophobia. Homophobia is the name given to the heterosexual's fear of homosexuality, which often leads to an emotional rejection of homosexual people. It is sometimes a defence mechanism triggered by the homophobe's own latent homosexual desires.

Homophobic hostility reinforces homosexuals' feelings of alienation, drives them more deeply into secrecy and deceit (or into defiant self-advertisement) and militates against their acceptance in church and society.

Informed Christian opinion is united in condemning homophobia. The homosexual person is a 'neighbour' and therefore as much a candidate for love as anyone else. It is particularly disturbing to find churches which intensify the homosexual's sense of loneliness and isolation by their judgmental attitudes. The existence of gay congregations, where homosexuals converge to find support and friendship, is in part a rebuke to main-line churches which fail to accept them.

Gay congregations do, of course, attract members who make demands which most other churches find it ethically impossible to meet. The two most controversial examples are requests for the blessing of homosexual and lesbian unions and the admission of homosexual ministers who make no secret of their intention to sleep with their lovers.

At the secular level, in spite of the relaxation of legal restraints, symptoms of homophobia are still evident, especially in stereotyping and (more occasionally) in the denial of civil rights.

Whenever men and women are victimized because of their sexual orientation, whether formally in the law courts or less formally through television humour and scapegoating (as in the labelling of AIDS as the 'gay plague'), the Christian duty is clearly to stand alongside the oppressed minority in their struggle for justice. As J. B. Nelson (1930–) comments, the homosexual 'problem' in such cases turns out to be a heterosexual one – just as the 'black problem' is really to do with white racism.

See also: SEXUAL DEVIATION; SEXUALITY. [11]

Bibliography
D. J. Atkinson, *Homosexuals in the Christian Fellowship* (Oxford, 1979); D. S. Bailey, *Homosexuality and the Western Christian Tradition* (London, 1955; repr. Hampden, CT, 1975); K. Barth, CD III/4; J. Boswell, *Christianity, Social Tolerance and Homosexuality* (Chicago, 1980); Church of England Board for Social Responsibility, *Homosexual Relationships* (London, 1979); P. Coleman, *Christian Attitudes to Homosexuality* (London, 1980); idem, *Gay Christians* (London and Philadelphia, 1989); J. Dominian, *Sexual Integrity* (London, 1987); D. H. Field, *The Homosexual Way* (Leicester, ²1979); R. F. Lovelace, *Homosexuality and the Church* (Old Tappan, NJ, 1978); E. R. Moberly, *Homosexuality: A New Christian Ethic* (Cambridge, 1983); J. B. Nelson, NDCE, pp. 271–274; L. Payne, *The Broken Image* (Westchester, IL, 1981); N. Pittenger, *Time for Consent* (London, 1976); R. Scroggs, *The New Testament and Homosexuality*

(Minneapolis, MN, 1984); L. Smedes, *Sex in the Real World* (Grand Rapids, 1976; Tring, 1979); H. Thielicke, *The Ethics of Sex* (ET, London and New York, 1964); D. F. Wright, 'Early Christian Attitudes to Homosexuality', *Studia Patristica* 18.2, 1989, pp. 329–334; *idem*, 'Homosexuality: The Relevance of the Bible', *Evangelical Quarterly* 61, 1989, pp. 291–300; *idem*, 'Homosexuals or Prostitutes? The Meaning of *arsenokoitai* (1 Cor. 6:9, 1 Tim. 1:10)', *Vigiliae Christianae* 38, 1984, pp. 125–153.

D.H.F.

HONESTY bears on the issues of truthfulness and deception. An honest shopkeeper accurately represents what he or she sells to the customers, and makes good any misrepresentations that may inadvertently occur. 'Honesty' seems to cover a family of virtues,* which we might call the virtues of truthfulness. The class includes *forthrightness*, the disposition to volunteer truth* that might with some justification have been kept to oneself, and *promise-keeping*, since the honest person wishes his or her words to concur with reality. *Intellectual honesty* is an inquirer's willingness to follow evidence and arguments wherever they may lead, even if they threaten to undermine his or her cherished opinions. *Sincerity* is expressive honesty, honesty about how one feels: the sincere person does not express grief unless he or she really feels it, does not give the impression of wanting to help if he or she does not want to help. *Self-transparency* is honesty about oneself, especially about one's emotions, desires and preferences, and is thus basic to self-knowledge and thus to mature selfhood.

Honesty is manifested in emotional response as well as in the behaviour of telling and pursuing the truth, rectifying inadvertent deception, and expressing oneself truthfully. An honest person rejoices in truth and truth-telling, and is angered, disgusted, sad, contrite (as the case may be) in the face of hypocrisy and falsehood. People sometimes are truthful in a superficial, behavioural way, without being honest *persons*. For example, in a court of law a person might tell the truth, but do so only out of fear of the consequences of being caught in perjury. He or she does not care that the truth be known, or that he or she should speak it, but only wishes to avoid embarrassment, a fine or a time in jail. By contrast, the honest person's truthful behaviour is rooted in the personality:

he or she loves truth, and so feels an affective compulsion to tell or know it, feels uncomfortable with sloppiness in telling, investigating or acknowledging truths and, in appropriate circumstances, takes positive pleasure in rigorous investigation, and precision of utterance and expression. Honesty is thus a trait of character,* a disposition.

But even persons who love truth can experience aversions that deflect them from it. People who hold power of security and life over us may not want the truth to be known. Publication of the truth may embarrass or otherwise hurt people we love. An investigation may threaten the tenability of ideas we hold very dear. We may become weary and disheartened in the face of difficulty, opposition and indifference. In such cases honesty requires supporting virtues that even become ingredients in it: patience,* perseverance* and hope* to counteract discouragment; courage* to keep our honesty from succumbing to fear; self-control to resist the appeal of easy answers. So important are these virtues of willpower in support of honesty that we hardly think a person honest at all if his or her love of truth is not fit to weather the storms of temptation.

When Paul enjoins the churches to speak the truth in love (Eph. 4:15), he seems to acknowledge that honesty must be tempered by (and not just be fitted to resist) other concerns. The truthful word should sometimes be withheld, and not just *any* way of speaking it is equally good. If a wayward brother or sister is in a fit of rage and defensiveness, the truth may be best postponed for a calmer, more receptive moment. And then it can be spoken in a spirit of gentleness, and the speaker can let the other know that the speaker acknowledges himself or herself to be a fellow sinner. Honesty needs to be supplemented not only with powers to resist its characteristic temptations, but also with the wisdom* to know when to speak and how much to say, and the gentleness, humility,* and contrition by which one's speaking becomes a grace to the hearer.

Discussions of honesty often focus on dilemmas in which only by lying will one avoid some great evil: Should I really tell the Gestapo about the Jews hiding in my attic? If we admit that a lie is sometimes the lesser of two evils, it will still be the mark of the honest person (the *lover* of truth) that he or she will not lie easily or without emotional distress.

The love of truth is one of the ways in which

we image God (see Image of God*). It is basic to our nature that we are able to represent states of affairs in speech and in states of mind such as perceptions, beliefs and emotions. In each case we can represent them truly or untruly, and to represent them as they are is a state of realization of our potential as representing creatures. To be concerned that our mental and linguistic representations be true is to love that state for which we were created – *i.e.* to reflect in our character the intention of God. And to express the truth, as far as in us lies, to others, is not only to expedite their practical affairs and foster the harmony of our life with them, but also to promote in them that same state of representational realization that we desire for ourselves.

Bibliography
Thomas Aquinas, *STh* 2a2ae 109–111.

R.C.R.

HOOKER, RICHARD (*c.* 1554–1600). The 'judicious Hooker' has been described as the Anglican theologian par excellence. He became successively a Fellow of Corpus Christi College, Oxford (1577–84) and Professor of Hebrew, rector of Drayton Beauchamp, Master of the Temple (1585–91), rector of Boscombe, Wilts., and, from 1595, of Bishopsbourne, Kent. The supreme apologist of the Elizabethan Settlement, he developed his 'via media' while he was Master of the Temple in opposition to aspects of Calvinist theology and he wrote the seminal *Treatise on the Laws of Ecclesiastical Polity* (Books I–IV, 1594; V, 1597; VI and VIII published posthumously in 1648; and VII in 1662).

Hooker understands our moral duties in the light of the law of reason,* the laws of the universe being grounded in the eternal law of God's being. This is confirmed and interpreted by the law of Scripture, which together with reason and tradition* is the source of authority* for faith* and practice. Human laws for society and for the church, both aspects of the one Christian social order, are to be derived from, or to be consistent with, this positive divine law. Hooker argues against the Puritans'* use of the Bible as simply a code of rules, and against the high churchmen and Rome concerning certain understandings of the church and priesthood. He emphasizes the organic nature of the Church of England, a reformed church though in continuity with the medieval church. His influential theology of political government was largely a contractual one.

Bibliography
The Works of Mr Richard Hooker, ed. J. Keble, 7th ed. rev. by R. V. Church and F. Paget, 3 vols. (Oxford, 1888).

D.J.A.

HOPE. In its most general sense, hope is a positive attitude or disposition towards the future. Broadly defined, then, hope could include wishes, dreams and fantasies, whether well grounded or not. In biblical terms, hope is confident expectation in God (see ①). The first distinctive of Christian hope is its confidence, grounded in a historical judgment (regarding Jesus Christ) and personal faith experience (of God's presence in life). Christian hope is not a wish or a dream but a confident expectation. The second distinctive is its object: Christian hope is placed in God – not in science, technology, evolution, progress, human nature, the nation or anything else. Christian hope is partly about what God will do in our own contingent, human experience during next week or next year; much more profoundly, Christian hope is about what God will do at the end (of my life, of human history), *i.e.* the 'eschaton'.

The OT often exhibits a strong sense of historical expectation, whether in hope of a bright future (the promises of God) or in dread of coming judgment* (the warnings of God). This is most clearly seen in the Prophets (*e.g.* Is. 65:17–25; Je. 33:1–9; Mal. 4:1–6). The Law itself is full of promises and warnings (*e.g.* Ex. 20:4–6). The Writings evidence hope or dread in their own distinctive ways (*e.g.* Ps. 130). In the NT, the Gospel portraits of our Lord continue and further develop this OT sense of expectation. The coming kingdom of God* is central to Jesus' teaching; Jesus' own promise to return looms large (Mt. 24; Jn. 14:1–4).

The apostles Peter and Paul give the theology and ethics of hope its full and comprehensive biblical articulation. God 'has given us new birth into a living hope through the resurrection of Jesus Christ from the dead'; 'God . . . raised him for the dead and glorified him, and so your faith and hope are in God' (1 Pet. 1:3, 21). In these phrases Peter shows that the *basis* of Christian hope is the fact of the resurrection* of Jesus Christ. If Jesus' crucifixion on Good Friday was followed by his resurrection on Easter Sunday, then all things are truly possible. To the extent that we are attached to Jesus Christ we might expect that an 'Easter' lies up ahead at the end of our own history. Of course, Christians bear witness to innumerable experiences of God's renewing intervention in daily life.

If the resurrection of Jesus is the basis, the ultimate *goal* of Christian hope is the return of Christ. 'Set your hope fully on the grace to be given you when Jesus Christ is revealed' (1 Pet. 1:13). Paul describes it in similar fashion: 'The grace of God has appeared . . . It teaches us . . . to live . . . in this present age, while we wait for the blessed hope – the glorious appearing of our great God and Saviour, Jesus Christ' (Tit. 2:11–13). Of course, according to Scripture, this return of Christ will mean judgment as well as reward,* destruction of evil as well as recreation of the heavens and the earth. For Christians this evokes not terror but hope, because the Christ who will return is the same gracious Saviour who has forgiven all our offences.

1. Hope as a theological virtue

Traditionally hope has been viewed with faith* and love (see ②) as 'theological', 'supernatural' or 'infused' virtue.* As such, these virtues are the gifts of God's grace: reasonable arguments can be made on behalf of faith, hope and love, but reason alone cannot create these virtues in our life. By contrast, the four classical, cardinal virtues (justice, prudence, courage/fortitude, temperance) have been regarded as 'natural', *i.e.* accessible, perceptible and trainable through the exercise of ordinary reason and will as they interact with nature and society.* Faith, hope and love, however, are spiritually bestowed upon us by God. One could say these are the virtues of grace and the 'new nature'. Over the centuries, debates have continued over the identity and status of the virtues. For example, should the 'natural virtues' be identified precisely and exclusively as the four listed above? Has sin so corrupted nature, reason and will that it is wrong to speak of any virtue independent of grace? Are the three 'theological virtues' merely affective, pious dispositions irrelevant to the demands of justice and ethics in the real world?

However one argues such questions, the NT itself promotes faith, hope and love as a very important description of Christian life and character (1 Cor. 13:13; 1 Thes. 1:3; Heb. 6:10–12; 1 Pet. 1:21–22; *etc.*). If *faith* is that faculty by which we attach ourselves (cognitively, volitionally, affectively, practically) to the living God whom we cannot now see, *love* is that faculty by which we are one with the Spirit of Jesus Christ, allowing him to fill and use us in loving God and loving our neighbour. *Hope*, then, is living this moment on my journey in confident expectation that God in Jesus Christ is up ahead on my pathway and (not just waiting for me to reach him but) moving towards me. Like faith, hope is exercised without benefit of sight; hope might be termed the 'future tense of faith'. By faith I attach my life to the unseen but spiritually real Jesus Christ in my present; by hope I live my life today in confident expectation that the day is coming when I will see this Jesus Christ fully and clearly. In faith I am related to a humble Saviour who accompanies me through the struggles of life in a world in revolt; in hope I live my life confident that the King of kings and Lord of lords will return in victory and power.

2. The ethics of hope

The ethical implications of hope may be summarized as follows: a. Christian eschatological hope *relativizes* this world and this present history. Absolute justice (or equality, or peace, *etc.*) will occur at the return of Christ and only then. This frees us in the present from idolatries, perfectionism, utopian schemes and absolutizing of positions, parties, nations or ideologies. Perfection comes only at the End. Thus, I can avoid taking myself or my projects too seriously. Hope leads to an ethics of freedom.* Hope frees us in the present by binding us to the End.

b. Hope *motivates* ethical behaviour in the present. To the extent that this hope is genuine, Christians take seriously the promise that the Christ who is coming says, 'I will bring my rewards with me' (Rev. 22:12, GNB). They are motivated by the promise that 'we will all stand before God's judgment seat' and 'give an account' of our life (Rom. 14:10–12). The Christ who will come is the same one who demonstrated concern for love and justice in his own sojourn on earth and who teaches his followers so to live. 'You ought to live holy and godly lives as you look forward to the day of God' (2 Pet. 3:11–12). 'Everyone who has this hope in him purifies himself' (1 Jn. 3:3). Motivated by hope (rather than dread), the servants of the coming Lord want to act in ways that will deserve a 'Well done, you good and faithful servant' (Mt. 25:14–30). Much as a bride lives now in active preparation for her forthcoming wedding, the servants of Christ are motivated by hope. Thus, while Christian hope relativizes the present, far from engendering apathy it gives absolute seriousness to that relativity.

c. Hope *guides* ethical behaviour in the present. Hope not only sanctions and motivates, it gives a distinct content to Christian character and action in the present. 'The night is nearly over; the day is almost here ... Let us behave ... as in the daytime' (Rom. 13: 12–13). Christian 'citizenship' is in heaven, in the coming kingdom of God. The Holy Spirit given to Christians is described as a 'downpayment' (Gk. *arrabōn*, Eph. 1:14) or 'pledge' (NASB; Gk. *aparchē*, lit. 'firstfruits', Rom. 8:23) of a future inheritance. Great care needs to be exercised at this point to avoid perfectionist or utopian mistakes. This present era remains fallen, and only the return of Christ can and will resolve the problem of the world as a whole. Nevertheless, it is our future hope which guides our present particular action. While we are not called upon to purge, reform and manage the world as a whole, we are called to find ways of acting as faithful 'signs' of God's promised future. It is this eschatological orientation which made Jesus' life so singular; it is this ethic of hope which alone will render Christian presence distinctive as true salt and light in our earth. The ethical question is, 'How can we in our character and action, as individuals and in social groups, creatively demonstrate and faithfully promote today the glorious reality of Christ's coming kingdom of truth, love, justice and peace?'

3. The psychology of hope

It remains to comment on the psychological and pastoral-care dimensions of hope. Certainly, hopelessness, anxiety,* pessimism,* discouragement, dread and despair are epidemic in our era. Growing numbers of suicides and widespread escapism into drugs* or other addictive (see Dependence*) or obsessive behaviour bear witness that not only outside but within the Christian church, hope is much needed. The manifold stresses and tensions of life in a frantic, noisy, complex, hostile, impersonal world are discouraging enough. At the same time as the social environment grows more difficult, however, the information, entertainment and advertising media perfect their propaganda* of every individual's absolute right to immediate and total gratification. Modern man and woman are caught between such harsh daily realities and a media environment of demonic lies.

In this context, one cannot do better than follow the counsel given to Titus: 'Say "No" to ungodliness' (including greed, perfectionism, narcissism, hedonism,* *etc.*) and strive to 'live ... godly lives ... while we wait for the blessed hope' (Tit. 2:11–14). Our pastoral counsel must include the 'No' to the lies and fantasies of our culture and a still more profound and vocal 'Yes' to a new way of life shaped by hope in Jesus Christ. Whether counselling individuals or leading groups toward recovery, the 'No' of identifying, understanding and banishing the addictions, obsessions and wounds of my past and present must be accompanied by the 'Yes' of formulating positive agendas shaped by hope in Christ. Lacking this twofold approach, the morass of despair cannot be conquered.

More broadly, hope is related to other prominent biblical virtues such as patience, perseverance,* longsuffering and self-control. These related virtues have to do, first, with a courageous persevering in the positive agenda, continuing to do the right thing without immediate gratification or reward because of hope's longer perspective. Secondly, such terms as longsuffering and self-control are the counterpart to perseverance in that they refer to a capacity and willingness to continue to absorb the negative (suffering, persecution, hardship) in the light of the promise and the hope that is expected ahead.

Finally, freedom* and joy* are two of the fruits of a life shaped by Christian hope. Hope binds us to the future and thus frees us in the present. And both by assuring victory and relativizing the present, hope produces true joy in our lives.

Bibliography
R. A. Alves, *A Theology of Human Hope* (New York, 1969); Augustine, *The Enchiridion on Faith, Hope and Love* (Chicago, 1961); J. Ellul, *Hope in Time of Abandonment* (ET, New York, 1973); J. Moltmann, *Theology of Hope* (London, 1967).

D.W.G.

HOSPICE is a programme of care for terminally ill patients and their families. In practice, most of the patients helped in this way have cancer. The name 'hospice', 'a resting place for travellers or pilgrims', was popularized by Dame Cicely Saunders (1918–), who founded St Christopher's Hospice, London, in 1967, and thereby launched the modern hospice movement. The choice was dictated by the desire to provide a type of care which incorporated the skills of a hospital and the more leisurely hospitality and warmth of a home. In the hospice, the centre of interest shifts from the disease to the patient and family, from the pathological process to the person.

The main goals of hospice care are to provide: 1. relief for patients from pain and other distressing symptoms; 2. psychological and spiritual care for patients so that they may come to terms with and prepare for their own death as fully as they can; 3. a support system to help the patients live as actively and creatively as possible until death, thereby promoting autonomy, personal integrity and self-esteem; 4. a support system to help families cope during the patient's illness and in bereavement (see R. G. Twycross, 'Hospice Care', and A. Stedeford, 'Hospice: A Safe Place to Suffer?').

Although hospice philosophy is not limited by 'the tyranny of cure', it is steadfastly opposed to euthanasia.* Hospice both affirms life and recognizes dying as a normal process. It therefore seeks neither to hasten nor to postpone death (see *Standards of a Hospice Program of Care*).

A concept of care

There are now few communities in the UK that do not have some access to a form of hospice care (see the *Directory of Hospice Services in the UK and the Republic of Ireland*, published annually by St Christopher's Hospice Information Service). An increasing number of other countries are developing similar services, which are now generally called palliative care. Because it has not always been possible or desirable to build a separate institution, other approaches have been adopted including home-care hospice programmes and hospital symptom-control teams. These alternatives emphasize that 'hospice' is a concept of care rather than a building.

Hospice seeks to prevent *last* days becoming *lost* days by offering a type of care which is appropriate to the needs of the dying. Although it has been described as 'low tech and high touch', hospice is not intrinsically against modern medical technology. Rather, it seeks to ensure that love and not science is the controlling force in patient care. 'High tech' investigations and treatments are used only when their benefits clearly outweigh any potential burdens. Thus, science is used in the service of love, and not vice versa. In summary, hospice care is an attempt to re-establish the traditional clinical role: 'to cure sometimes, to relieve often, to comfort always.'

Towards wholeness of care

Relief of pain* and other distressing symptoms is rightly seen as the primary goal of hospice care. Expertise in symptom control has reached a point where patients can expect to be almost free of pain (see the WHO report, *Cancer Pain Relief and Palliative Care*). A high measure of relief can also be expected with most other symptoms. No longer distracted and exhausted by unrelieved pain, patients may become distressed emotionally and spiritually as they contemplate their approaching death. Few do this with equilibrium.

In consequence, it has been suggested that a hospice should be thought of as 'a safe place to suffer': 'They need to know that their turmoil and distress is [sic] a sign that they are making a major adjustment, and not that they are going mad' (Stedeford, 'Hospice: A Safe Place to Suffer?'). It is necessary to offer fully personal care. The staff aim to help the patient to do his or her best given his or her personality, family, cultural background, beliefs, age, illness, symptoms, anxieties and fears. The patient and family form the unit of care. There is need of flexibility: patients must be met where they are socially, culturally, psychologically and spiritually, as well as physically. There is no such being as a typical dying patient.

Hospice roots

The modern hospice is historically rooted in Christian belief, although in practice it is more broadly theistic. A Jewish involvement has been evident from the early days, and there is now a Buddhist Hospice Association. To work with the dying demands a belief in life. Life is seen as having meaning and purpose throughout the terminal illness.

This conviction is manifested primarily by attitudes and deeds rather than by words; in how we respond to the dying and how we care for them, rather than by what we say. The unspoken message has been summarized by Cicely Saunders: 'You matter because you are you. You matter to the last moment of your life, and we will do all we can not only to help you die peacefully, but to live until you die.'

It is this unspoken message that brings a sense of security to those cared for. Many patients say, 'It is wonderful to feel safe.' This security enables the individual patient to consider within himself or herself fundamental questions concerning life, God and the hereafter. Such contemplation is facilitated by the physical comfort which hospices provide. Spiritual care, therefore, may well be non-verbal, but none the less real for all that.

When dying, many people take stock of their lives for the first time: 'I have lived a good life'; 'I never did anyone any harm'; 'Why should it happen to me?'; 'What have I done to deserve this?' Only a minority of patients discuss these matters with their doctor, although the majority do so with a nurse, a social worker, or with relatives and close friends. Regard for an individual as a person, however, means that the carer must not impose his own beliefs on the patient (J. Mauritzen, 'Pastoral Care for the Dying and Bereaved').

Teamwork

Hospice care can be administered only by a group of people working together as a team. The composition of the team may vary but includes first the patient and then the immediate family, friends, doctor(s), nurses, social worker, therapists, minister and, on occasion, lawyer. The team is corporately concerned for the well-being of the patient and the family – physical, psychological, spiritual and social. In this situation roles may become blurred, at least at the edges: 'When hospice workers function well as a team, pooling their skills and resources – caring for one another as well as for the patient and family – there seems to be almost inevitably a sense of rightnesss about it, a kind of joy and fulfilment that is all too rarely found in the workplace today' (S. Stoddard, 'Hospice in the United States').

See also: DEATH AND DYING; LIFE, HEALTH AND DEATH. [13]

Bibliography

S. du Boulay, *Cicely Saunders: Founder of the Modern Hospice Movement* (London, 1994); J. Mauritzen, 'Pastoral Care for the Dying and Bereaved', *DSt* 12, 1988, pp. 111–122; National Hospice Organization (USA), *Standards of a Hospice Program of Care* (Arlington, VA, 1981); A. Stedeford, 'Hospice: A Safe Place to Suffer?', *PalM* 1, 1987, pp. 73–74; S. Stoddard, 'Hospice in the United States: An Overview', *JPalC* 5.3, 1989, pp. 10–19; R. G. Twycross, 'Hospice Care', in R. Spilling (ed.), *Terminal Care at Home* (Oxford, 1986), pp. 96–112; World Health Organization, *Cancer Pain Relief and Palliative Care* (Geneva, 1990).

R.G.T.

HOSPITALITY. Although not a peculiarly Christian virtue, hospitality has a very high profile both in the Bible and in the history of the church. The fact that the root of the word (Lat. *hospes*) also gave rise to the words 'hospital' and 'hospice' is no linguistic accident, because most modern institutions of medical and social care trace their origins to Christian initiatives. In patristic and medieval times, especially, providing the sick with shelter and medical attention was seen as a natural extension of being hospitable.

In OT times, when travel was hazardous, hospitality was considered a prime duty, not least because the provider was also likely at some time to be a beneficiary. The host was responsible for his guest's safety as well as his welfare, and that could sometimes be a risky business (*cf.* Gn. 19:1–9; Jdg. 19:20–28).

The guest must be offered bread and water, at the very least (Dt. 23:4). Usually something rather more substantial was provided, such as meat and milk (Gn. 18:7–8). The traveller's dusty feet were washed (Gn. 18:4), and his animals looked after (Gn. 24:14).

Failure to be hospitable was treated very seriously (*cf.* 1 Sa. 25:1–39). Conversely, generous hospitality ('providing the poor wanderer with shelter') was regarded as an expression of practical religious commitment which the Lord approved (Is. 58:6–7). Those who responded hospitably to strangers might even find themselves welcoming God's messengers, human or otherwise (Gn. 18:1–8; Jdg. 13:9–16; 2 Ki. 4:8–10; *cf.* Heb. 13:2).

Jesus depended heavily on other people's hospitality during his ministry (*cf.* Mt. 9:10; Mk. 1:29; Lk. 7:36; 10:38). So did his first followers (*cf.* Acts 10:6; 16:15; 18:1–3). Indeed, giving hospitality to travelling preachers, sometimes at considerable risk to the hosts (*cf.* Acts 17:5–9), played a prominent part in the spread of the gospel during the first years of the church's life.

The NT demands hospitality no less strongly than does the OT. 'Practise hospitality', Paul tells the Christians at Rome (Rom. 12:13). And do it 'without grumbling', adds Peter (1 Pet. 4:9). Jesus even taught that a hospitable attitude on the part of others towards him and his followers was a sure indication of their acceptance of the gospel – and *vice versa* – with eternal consequences (Mt. 10:11–15; 25: 31–46).

The Bible only rarely specifies situations in which giving or receiving hospitality is to be refused. An invitation to a prostitute's room is best rejected (Pr. 9:13–16). And any impulse to welcome a false teacher into your home is to be resisted (2 Jn. 10–11). As a protective measure against the latter, Christian travellers were given letters of commendation by their local churches (*cf.* Rom. 16:1; Col. 4:10; 2 Cor. 3:1). Armed with one of those, a believer could be assured of food and shelter wherever a congregation existed.

The NT instructs church leaders to set an example in being hospitable (1 Tim. 3:2; Tit. 1:8), and the bishops of the early church accepted this responsibility conscientiously. Chrysostom,* for example, built seven different 'hospitality units' in Constantinople between AD 400 and 403, ranging from a hotel for fit travellers to shelters for the chronically ill and homes for orphans and the elderly.

In the Middle Ages, religious orders were the church's main agents of hospitality. The Benedictines were particularly prominent; their Rule demanded, 'Let all visitors who chance to arrive be welcomed as if it were Christ himself' (ch. 53). Few monasteries lacked *xenodochia* (for the care of travellers), and many boasted *nosokomia* as well (for the treatment of the sick).

With the arrival of the Welfare State, the blossoming of the hotel industry and the secularization of caring agencies, the church has lost its leading role as the main provider of institutional hospitality in the developed world. Elsewhere (*cf.* Mother Teresa's* work in Calcutta) it retains its high profile, as care for the stranger goes hand in hand with the preaching of the gospel.

The Bible's insistence that the Lord's people should be hospitable highlights several vital, lasting theological and ethical principles. One is *stewardship*:* showing hospitality is simply good caretaking, distributing the Master's resources where they are most needed. Another is *the imitation of God*: being

hospitable is being like God, who treated his people so generously when they were strangers in Egypt (Ex. 22:21; Dt. 10:19). And a third is *grace*:* as God lavishes his love on those who deserve none of it, so Christians must provide hospitality for those who cannot earn or repay their generosity (Lk. 14:12–14; *cf.* Rom. 12:13–14).

D.H.F.

HOSPITALIZATION, INVOLUNTARY.

This is bitterly argued about: some want to ensure proper care for the mentally ill, while others fear political abuse, loss of freedom* and human rights (see Rights, Human*). In England, the Mental Health Act (MHA) of 1983 defines the code of practice. Old words like being 'certified', 'committed' or 'put away' reflect the history of the trade in lunacy and the misuse of madhouses.

Legal provisions are aimed at ensuring proper care for those unwilling to be admitted informally. In practice this covers patients who lack insight, who may be a danger to themselves or others, or who require care for the sake of their own health and safety. Thus suicide,* homicide and arson may be prevented, and the miseries of severe depression* or psychosis* may be treated.

In England, the legal provisions are described under 'Sections' of the MHA: hence the patient hospitalized involuntarily is sometimes called 'a sectioned patient'. Some of the most significant sections are: Sec. 136, which enables the police to bring someone to a place of safety (hospital) if found in a public place and thought to need assessment and care; Sec. 4, which enables one doctor to sign the necessary papers applying for emergency admission involuntarily, with a relative or social worker applying for admission for a maximum of seventy-two hours; Sec. 2, which provides for a period of 28 days' assessment and limited treatment: two doctors (one approved, usually a psychiatrist, and one who knows the patient) must sign the form, and a relative or approved social worker signs the application; and Sec. 3, which extends the period for up to six months: similar procedures as Sec. 2 apply, but Sec. 3 is usually for known serious disorders requiring planned, prolonged treatment. Detention by nurse or doctor for up to seventy-two hours may be arranged under Sec. 5: a 'holding power' for patients already in hospital who attempt to leave when this is thought inadvisable.

The MHA may not be used when sexual deviation, drug or alcohol dependence is the reason for needing care. Criminal offenders are covered by other sections of the MHA and secure units, and other provisions may be made by court order.

In the USA, health law varies from State to State. In the last twenty-five years, the civil rights movement has resulted in changes from simple medical certification for committal to more rigorous criteria. Thus California required the patient to be found dangerous, to himself or others, and gravely disabled (*i.e.* unable to provide clothing, food or shelter), in order to be held for seventy-two hours. Suicidal patients had to be released within thirty-one days; patients dangerous to others might be held for three months. One State allows initial confinement for only twenty-four hours.

Treatment with medication has been hedged about with much restrictive legislation, but only some 10% of involuntary patients refuse medication. In about 90% of cases, medication is given in spite of such objection.

MHA Tribunals are provided, and MHA Commissioners (with wide powers) are appointed to provide monitoring of care, consent to treatment, and for patients to appeal against their detention. A Tribunal has a lawyer, a consultant psychiatrist and a lay member.

The multi-disciplinary team (doctors, nurses, psychologists, social workers, occupational therapists) plans and carries out formal, involuntary care. The provisions for community care are often poor, leading to the *abandonati*, patients who sleep rough without proper supervision – an increasing scandal in many countries.

Bibliography
R. Bluglass, *A Guide to the Mental Health Act 1983* (London, 1984).

G.D.

H OUSEHOLD CODES. This is the name first given by Martin Luther* (Ger. *Haustafeln*) to the passages in Eph. 5:22 – 6:9, Col. 3:18 – 4:1 and 1 Pet. 2: 18 – 3:7 where related pairs are addressed: in the fuller form (in Eph. and Col.), these pairs are wives and husbands, children and parents, slaves and masters.

It looks as though Paul and Peter took over a form of ethical instruction which was already current in Stoic and Jewish Hellenistic circles (J. E. Crouch, *The Origin and Intention of the Colossian Haustafel*), and they developed it considerably. In none of the previous examples were both halves of the pair addressed, merely the dominant half; so the direct address to wives, children and slaves – let alone addressing them first – is striking.

It has been argued (*e.g.* by J. T. Sanders in *Ethics in the New Testament*) that the household codes have little value for Christian ethics, because they represent a relapse into an uncritical acceptance of worldly hierarchical structures, over against the vision of Gal. 3:28 and 1 Cor. 12 in which earthly status and office are denied by the new life of the Spirit in the body of Christ. A close reading of the codes, however, reveals that worldly structures are indeed undermined, for instance by telling slaves that they serve God, *not* men (Eph. 6:7; Col. 3:23), and masters that they are slaves too (Eph. 6:9; Col. 4:1).

Similarly, the mutual self-giving of husband and wife in Eph. 5:22–33 radically undermines the patriarchalism of the surrounding culture.

See also: NEW TESTAMENT ETHICS. [9]

Bibliography
J. E. Crouch, *The Origin and Intention of the Colossian Haustafel* (Göttingen, 1972); S. Motyer, 'The Relationship between Paul's Gospel of "All One in Christ Jesus" (Gal. 3:28) and the "Household Codes"', *VE* 19, 1989, pp. 33–48; J. T. Sanders, *Ethics in the New Testament: Change and Development* (London and Philadelphia, 1975), pp. 73–78.

S.M.

HUBRIS, see PRIDE.

HUMANAE VITAE, see PAPAL ENCYCLICALS.

H UMAN DEVELOPMENT is the process of change and growth – psychological, biological, social and spiritual – over the human life span.

The idea of development over the life span is common in the biblical record, both directly and by analogy with plant growth (*e.g.* the reference to the fruit of the Spirit, Gal. 5:22). There is a recognition of developmental change in nutritional requirements (Heb. 5:12–14 uses the analogy of progressing from milk to solid food in our growth in grace).

There is on the one hand a recognition of the innocence and directness of a child's faith, by implication, as opposed to an adult's (Mk. 10:13–16). On the other hand there is the beautiful allegory of Ec. 12:1–7, 'the strong men stoop' (12:3), and 'desire no longer is stirred' (12:5, taken to refer to the loss of sexual desire), usually interpreted as recognizing the physical changes of later life. The effects of right childhood training are recognized (Pr. 22:6), as are the learning and experience that come from a balanced life within the family,* which is to be valued and used to the benefit of the church (1 Tim. 3:1–15). Development is seen not as a passive process, but as a process where individuals themselves have the capacity to respond to and change the environment within which they are growing.

In biblical times, average life expectancy was short – probably not more than twenty-five years in NT times. While the ideal expectancy of seventy or eighty years (Ps. 90:10) was not so different from the 20th century, and although these ages were attained (see 2 Sa. 19:32), childhood mortality was high, so the older individuals would not have been representative of the whole population. The old were venerated in biblical times, as opposed to more recent focus on the young in Western societies.

Chronological age is only one index of developmental progress through life. Different cultures impose responsibilities and offer opportunities at different ages, and so vary in the developmental opportunities open to their members. Progress is also marked by rites of passage, as represented by attainment of marital states – marriage and widowhood; by stages of family life – grandparenthood; by occupational achievement and retirement from work;* and by reaction to events in our own or other lives, such as bereavement,* and periods of illness or incarceration. Conversion* itself, as a 'new birth' (1 Pet. 1:3), suggests a spiritual development intertwining with physical and psychological development.

Psychological, biological and social aspects of development

Two basic questions underlie psychological and biological theories of human development. First, is development to be seen as a continuous process of change, or is it best understood as a series of distinct changes? For example, should pastoral importance be attached to the period of adolescence,* as a time of special ministry? Secondly, is development fundamentally determined by heredity (by the genetic programme fixed at the point of conception), or is it primarily guided by external environmental events? The assumptions that developmental theories make on these two questions shape their interpretation of what is observed and experienced.

The two major aims of developmental psychology are: 1. to describe what developments there are (and the limits of 'normal' development); and 2. to discover the causes of developmental differences. The ways in which development is studied influence understanding of it. If age differences are studied cross-sectionally, there is a risk of confusing age trends with secular trends, and therefore ideally a given group of individuals should be followed through as a cohort. By definition this is an extremely lengthy and expensive means of study. Identical twins are important to developmental studies.

A knowledge of the average or typical rate of development is important pastorally for the support, for example, of a parent in the congregation with a potentially developmentally delayed child who may be contemplating seeking professional help. Individual differences in ability and developmental attainment, e.g. intelligence and musical talent, are to be recognized positively as gifts from God, but should not bias our acceptance of the less gifted (1 Cor. 12:12–26). There is little doubt that better preventive medicine, nutrition, environmental health and child-rearing practices result in fitter and stronger children, better able to learn earlier, but there is less consensus on what constitutes either the 'best' pattern of child-rearing, or the 'best' relationship between the generations.

Accounts of development commonly involve an examination of particular aspects of human functioning, such as thinking, at particular life-stages. Until relatively recently the main life-stages studied were childhood and adolescence, with a secondary interest in ageing.* The most commonly identified life-stages are: infancy; childhood; adolescence; young adulthood; middle age; and old age. Attention has been paid to pre-birth emotional experience, as in the thinking of Frank Lake,* but it is extremely difficult to ascertain the relationship between such experiences and later development. Certainly attitudes towards the as-yet-unborn child will affect the love and affection with which it is received into the world.

Developmental changes are most obvious

during early childhood, and advanced age. Early physical development is marked by rapid skeletal and muscular growth and development of finely tuned motor movement, and is parallelled by psychological development, notably the remarkable phenomenon of language acquisition. Heredity affects not only the end result of growth, but also the rate at which it is achieved. Adolescence is a period marked both by the physical changes of puberty – the onset of menstruation for girls, and the achievement of fertility for boys, as well as the emergence of visible secondary sexual characteristics – and by the social transition from dependence to independence. The teenage years are the period when religious 'conversion' is most likely to occur, leaving aside the issue of the form of that conversion.*

The late twenties or early thirties are the peak period of physical development for most people (as indicated by peak performance in sport). Only recently has there been serious study of changes in middle age, significant pastorally since for most adults it is the period of greatest contribution to ministry and church life. While the menopause has known physiological correlates for women, there is no comparable male physiological change. It is simplistic to explain the long-term trends during middle life as 'mid-life crisis' or a 'male menopause'. More recent evidence suggests little change of interest in religion during adulthood, with probably increased interest from sixty onwards.

With the fifties and sixties comes noticeable ageing of cells and tissues, and ageing of body systems such as the reproductive system and sensory functioning. However, better health and maintenance of physical activity are now undoubtedly enjoyed by older people in developed countries, with corresponding changes in patterns of living, and changing pastoral demands and opportunities.

Social development begins within the natural or surrogate family, usually with parental – most often maternal – bonding, and school is for most children the beginning of social relationships with peers which are not controlled by parents. The book of Proverbs is full of examples of the consequences of right – and wrong – example and teaching within the family and neighbourhood. The formation of intimate and small-group relationships, and the accompanying development of social skills, continue during childhood and adolesence, and entry into the world of work*

is for most people an important means of learning differentiated role relationships. Opportunities for group membership and carrying out valued tasks within a church community are valuable means of social development and discovering gifts and talents.

Theories of personality development

Human development has been conceptualized in many ways, with Shakespeare's 'seven ages' being a popular model. Many contemporary theories have been derived from Sigmund Freud's* formulation of basic instinctual drives. Freud placed major emphasis on what he saw as a fixed sequence of early patterns of relationship between the child and mother, and the subsequent effect of those satisfactions and frustrations through into adult life. His thinking on defence mechanisms,* especially regression, alerts us to the fact that development can sometimes occur in reverse, as it were, so that earlier stages or patterns of living can recur, especially under stress. More recent theorists, while emphasizing early development, have reconceptualized it, as for instance in the object-relations theory of Melanie Klein.*

Freud, however, considered development only during the first twenty years or so of life. His early associate, Carl Jung,* was concerned to look at the second half of life, and at the process of 'individuation' that he considered characteristic of later life. Erik Erikson* also developed a model of development through the life span, which is influential in theological education – although it is not always recognized how speculative his theory is (especially in his thinking about later stages), or how his theory could be seen as reflecting specifically masculine ideas of maturity. Erikson's work is popular in the USA (see R. C. Fuller, *Religion and the Life Cycle*), and has influenced a number of more recent writers, such as Donald Capps (1939–).

Development of spirituality

The idea of sanctification* is a theological representation of a progressive spiritual development through the life span. Sanctification, seen as an ongoing and future work of God in the life of the believer, can be seen as a state in which believers find themselves (*e.g.* 2 Thes. 2:13), as a state to which they must strive (Rom. 6:19), and as a goal which they must pursue (Heb. 12:14). Thus conversion to Christian faith brings about not only spiritual regeneration but a potential change of lifestyle and motivation. Sanctification can then be seen as a process with believers being and becoming holy as part of the changing work of God in their lives, and as a process in which they actively participate. The continuing tension between the call to holiness and the continuing presence of sinful tendencies is an important contributor to the spiritual development of individuals in their personal Christian journey through this life, as illustrated by John Bunyan's* *Pilgrim's Progress*. Some forms of the holiness movement, as seen in early Wesleyan traditions and perfectionism* teachings, imply a state of motivational sinlessness, usually seen as heterodox.

Since the emergence of modern psychology there have been attempts to formulate theories of spiritual development. The Dutch pastoral theologian Heije Faber has based a theory of religious development upon the three early stages – oral, anal and genital – of Freudian theory, with a fourth adolescent stage. The theories of Jung are of major interest, as being the representative of classical psychoanalytic* thought most positively interested in religious thought, and as illustrated by his idea of middle age as the phase of the 'noon of life'. Gerard Hughes has been an important expositor of Friedrich von Hügel's (1852–1925) idea of three stages of development – infancy, adolescence and adulthood – corresponding respectively to the institutional, critical and mystical elements of religious development.

An issue of major pastoral significance is the relationship between intellectual or cognitive development, and the capacity to understand religious and spiritual truth. Most thinking in this area has been influenced by the French psychologist Jean Piaget,* and by his theory of an intellectual progression from concrete thinking to formal, abstract, logical thinking. Similar in its conception of a sequence of development is the work of Lawrence Kohlberg (1927–87) on moral development, and the later influential work of James Fowler (1940–) on stages of 'faith development'.* Kohlberg claims that a stage of moral development has to be reached before the equivalent stage of faith development can occur, and hence suggests that moral attitudes are not derived from faith, but from their stage of moral development. The later stages of moral and religious development of Kohlberg (such as his stage 6 – 'universal humanistic'), and of Fowler and others, can be seen as offering a model, or goal, of maturity. It is important to be critically aware of the speculative nature of aspects of these theories, especially in the goals they offer of 'maturity' and of the preoccupation with achievement of maturity which the acceptance of such theories may engender.

Development, whether physical, personality or spiritual, need not be seen as happening in separate stages or in rigid sequence, but should be seen multi-dimensionally and dynamically, depending upon external circumstances and internal responses. Our lives can be variously portrayed as a race (Heb. 12:1), or as a fight (1 Tim. 6:12), to achieve the biblical model of mature personhood. Christian maturity is understanding the wisdom of God revealed by the Spirit (1 Cor. 2:6–16), 'attaining to the whole measure of the fulness of Christ' (Eph. 4:13), following Christian rules for holy living (Col. 3:1–17).

Bibliography

L. B. Brown, *The Psychology of Religion* (London, 1988); R. C. Fuller, *Religion and the Life Cycle* (Philadelphia, 1988); G. W. Hughes, *God of Surprises* (London, 1985); M. Jacobs, *Towards the Fullness of Christ: Pastoral Care and Christian Maturity* (London, 1988); E. Rayner, *Human Development* (London, ³1986).

J.N.H.

HUMAN EXPERIMENTATION. There is a sense in which every treatment prescribed is an experiment, but the term 'human experimentation' is usually taken firstly to mean the physiological testing of new drugs or procedures on healthy human volunteers. However, because much of this work can be done *in vitro* on tissue culture or *in vivo* on animals (see Rights, Animal*), the second use of the expression 'human experimentation' relates to testing new drugs or procedures in patients suffering from the relevant condition.

This is done by what is called a 'controlled clinical trial', where in a statistically significant way the new drug is tested for benefit in comparison with an established drug and / or with a placebo (an inert substance without specific activity). There has been a great deal of discussion as to whether controlled clinical trials in themselves are ethical, but most ethicists agree that the only worthwhile way to try out a new treatment clinically is by a controlled trial, and furthermore that to introduce new treatments on a large scale without a controlled trial would be unethical.

Because of inability or failure to do this in the past, it is now known that in some fields of medicine only 20% of treatments are of proven value. For example, thousands of tonsils and wombs have been removed in many countries quite unnecessarily (see Medical Malpractice*), but it is confusing to ascribe this to pecuniary motives. It would seem that surgeons' capacity for work is more related to their 'work ethic' than to the method of remuneration, and the main factor correlating with the number of operations done is the number of surgeons available to satisfy patients' demands.

Controlled clinical trials are thus very necessary, and are the only acceptable way of deciding whether a promising new treatment should be adopted. The concept of the 'sanctity of human life'* means that any experimentation or trial on humans must be conducted on strictly ethical lines, and must be seen to be so conducted, and permission for experimentation or a trial must first be sought from a formally-constituted research ethics committee. This would include hospital and university personnel, and lay members.

The first question to be answered is whether the proposed work is necessary and worthwhile, and then a good working guide to experimentation is the maxim 'Do to others what you would have them do to you' (Mt. 7:12), or to ask the question, 'Would you do this to one of your own family?' This latter may be a safer approach, as there have been over-enthusiastic investigators who have taken too many risks in experiments on themselves.

Once the experiment or trial is established, the individual patient's permission should be sought, and in the UK this is usually readily obtained, perhaps because patients believe being part of a trial will ensure better attention and treatment. Permission must be sought in such a way that: 1. the implications are fully understood by the subject; and 2. the subject can refuse without embarrassment. The absence of any refusals should alert the investigator to the distinct possibility that permission is being sought in too overpowering a manner.

Particular caution is needed with dependent subjects who could easily imagine they might suffer if they did not consent. This category is recognized to include prisoners, members of the Armed Forces, and students, although the latter are usually carefully protected in universities by the ethics committees. Similarly, permission for research on patients is best sought by somebody other than a member of the medical team, so that the patient is under no sense of obligation. Consent* should always be 'fully informed', and subjects who would have difficulty in understanding the implications of the request should be excluded.

It is considered unethical to perform experiments on patients who are terminally ill and near death. If experiments are proposed on children, the parents' permission is mandatory, and the procedures must be conducted with the greatest sensitivity. Where possible, the children's own permission should also be sought, and it should be quite easy to explain the request in terms they can understand.

Financial rewards for subjects who volunteer for experiments and for those who conduct research pose an ethical dilemma. While it is proper to reimburse subjects for loss of earnings related to participation in the research, there should be no suggestion of bribery. There have been problems with the practice of some commercial companies giving financial rewards for the successful conclusion of research projects. Those engaged in such work are best paid a recognized salary by their employing authority, to whom any payments from the commercial firms should be made.

There are international and professional guidelines (see Medical Codes of Practice*) for medical research on human beings. Wartime abuse under the Nazi regime led to the Nuremburg Code of 1947. Medical concern over experimentation resulted in the various declarations of Helsinki, Geneva and Tokyo (1964, 1975, 1983). These stress that the health of the patient must be the first consideration, and proper care must be exercised over risk, benefits, consent and privacy. These recommendations are not legally binding on doctors, however, until and unless they have become part of the law of the land.

In summary, human experimentation demands the highest ethical and professional standards in order to ensure that the whole exercise is worthwhile, that every aspect is carried out as well as possible, and that no-one is disadvantaged in any way.

McC.

HUMANISM. In the broadest sense, humanism is any view that recognizes the value of dignity of human persons, and wants the human condition to improve. It has its roots both in the Graeco-Roman and the Judaeo-Christian tradition: on the one hand the famous dictum of Socrates (470–399 BC), 'Know thyself', was but a prelude to cultivating virtues and improving the soul; the Stoic* ethic commended a rational life and spoke of a kind of universal harmony. On the other hand the Bible speaks of human beings as created by God in his own image (see Image of God*) and as objects of his love, and the Christian church has therefore been concerned with the physical as well as spiritual well-being of people. This much both traditions have in common, resulting in common causes and parallel, even co-operative efforts. Augustine* and Thomas Aquinas* represent a medieval Christian humanism that concerned itself with economic, political and educational issues as well as the individual moral and spiritual life.

Renaissance humanism showed renewed interest in the literature and learning of the ancients, new social ideals emerged in writers like Machiavelli (1469–1527) and Thomas More (1480–1535), the feudal system began to break down and the ideal of human freedom came more to the fore. Freedom from the church's authority ballooned by the 18th-century Enlightenment* into a rejection of all tradition* and revelation* in favour of the supremacy of the individual's reason.* 'Free thinking' and the separation of ethics from its historical and religious roots secularized the culture.

The result has been a distinction and a growing conflict between two kinds of humanism: Christian and secular. The one is explicitly theocentric, affirming the theological basis for the dignity of persons and the centrality of love for God in every human endeavour. The other is explicitly naturalistic, denying any supernatural reality, and therefore anthropocentric in that there is no higher end to pursue than bettering the human condition. Persons are a part and product of the physical world with neither immortal soul nor hope beyond this life, and nature is entirely indifferent to human ideals and purposes. Values are what human beings find worthwhile in their experience so that, as Protagoras (c. 485–c. 420 BC) put it: 'Man is the measure of all things.' People must achieve for themselves a good life, deciding what they find 'good'; they must develop a just society and fulfil their own creative potentials.

Representative of this secular humanism was the instrumentalist ethic of John Dewey (1859–1952), for whom values, like all ideas, are just means for resolving particular problems, relative therefore to particular situations. Nothing is intrinsically valuable in itself, but only instrumentally valuable, as a means to some practical end in ongoing survival. There are no unchanging values. Thus marital fidelity may have value in avoiding conflicts and enabling the marriage to survive, but it has no value in and of itself.

A more recent example is the 'contractarian' ethic which avoids conflict between different individuals on the one hand, and the imposition of some fictitious 'absolutes' on the other, by grounding moral ideals and standards in a supposed social contract.* The values we live by are those on which our society has agreed.

Modern 'secular humanism' generally adds another claim to its naturalism and anthropocentrism, namely that scientific knowledge (see Science*) can solve our problems and best test our moral beliefs. Scientific knowledge is regarded as the most reliable knowledge available, and scientific methods the most reliable methods. So the social and behavioural sciences, with their understanding of human behaviour and social processes, should govern our goals and policies. It is today's version of the Enlightenment's 'rule of reason'.

Secular humanism claims to be thoroughly humanitarian, deploring the dehumanization* of a technological society and the tragic effects of war,* poverty and disease, and seeking to muster scientific means for resolving the problems we face. Its vision for the future is therefore one shaped by scientific knowledge and technological (see Technology*) possibilities, as are its beliefs and values in general.

Other varieties of secular humanism are less optimistic about vesting our hopes in science. The existential humanist, alert to the historical causes of many human alienations, finds scientism too optimistic about the amenability of science to human concerns, and too naïve about the limitations of scientific knowledge. We must create our own values and our own lives, rather than being ruled by some new authority or scientific tradition.

Marxism is also a kind of secular humanism in its concern about alienation* and its attempts to change the socio-economic order. While its original goals were subverted by political power and resorts to violent repression, and while it proved to be misguided and disillusioning, it is a worthy goal to transform society from one in which things rule people into one in which human beings are freed from the tyranny of impersonal forces to shape their own lives. Liberation is a thoroughly humanist ideal. From a Christian standpoint the problem is rather that human sinfulness perverts the best of ideals and tends to divert the process we contrive.

All these versions of secular humanism secularize values. Without respect for the image of God in people, the only limit on how people are treated is how those in power decide to limit themselves. So human foetal life, being only a biological phenomenon without any intrinsic worth other than the value we accord it, is easily considered disposable as a matter of choice (see Abortion*). Yet the same foetal life, with God-given promise of manifesting the divine image, has value independently of human choice.

The point is not just that particular decisions come out differently for Christian and secular humanists, and not just that sinful people fail in the pursuit of what is good. It is that *all* values are defined on very different premises and by very different methods, and that decisions are made by appeal to different authorities: the God of Scripture, or the science of our day, or perhaps the current consensus of a secular society.

On such a choice the Bible could hardly be more explicit. In one form or another it recurs throughout biblical history: the temptation in Eden, Jacob and Esau, Joshua's challenge to Israel to choose whom they would serve, and so forth, but most plainly the Colossians' choice between that philosophy which accords with human tradition and that which accords with Christ (Col. 2:8).

Bibliography

N. Geisler, *Is Man the Measure? An Examination of Contemporary Humanism* (Grand Rapids, 1983); P. Kurtz, *A Secular Humanist Declaration* (Buffalo, NY, 1980); G. MacGregor, *The Hemlock and the Cross* (Philadelphia, 1963); J. Maritain, *True Humanism* (ET, London and New York, 1938).

A.F.H.

HUMANISTIC PSYCHOLOGY.
Modern humanism,* with its roots in the Enlightenment,* has been a powerful factor in shaping contemporary psychology. In particular, humanistic psychology has been moulded by the God-demoting, humanity-idealizing notions initiated by thinkers like Ludwig Feuerbach (1804–72) and Auguste Comte (1798–1857) and by the emerging desire of certain German philosophers, at the end of the 19th century, to break free from the reductionism* of the experimental psychologist. Amongst the latter influencers, Wilhelm Dilthey (1833–1911), with his bid for an 'understanding' psychology that allowed for human uniqueness and sought personal integration, is outstanding. Dilthey, directly and indirectly, proved a humanizing influence on the personality theories of Edward Spranger (1882–1963) and Gordon Allport (1897–1967), the rise of existential* and Gestalt* psychology, and the shaping of humanistic, or third-force, psychology.

By the 1960s, the growing tide of reaction to the twin camps of the behaviourism* of experimental psychology and the psychoanalytic* theory of clinical psychology gathered into the 'third-force' of humanistic psychology. Like Carl Rogers,* Abraham Maslow,* the chief architect of the movement, though respecting behaviourist and analytic* insights, sought to move beyond the innate pessimism and reductionism of these approaches to an integrating perspective that acknowledges the individual's innate power to change. The American Association for Humanistic Psychology, in its brochure for 1965–66, described the third-force movement as having 'an ultimate concern with . . . the dignity and worth of man and an interest in the development of the potential inherent in every person'. It was Maslow, too, who, aware of the limited horizons of optimistic humanism, expressed the gathering momentum of humanistic psychology to turn its attention towards the transcendental: 'I consider . . . Third Force Psychology to be transitional, a preparation for a still "higher" Fourth Psychology, transpersonal, transhuman, centred in the cosmos rather than in human needs and interest' (*Toward a Psychology of Being*, pp. iii–iv).

See also: PASTORAL CARE, COUNSELLING AND PSYCHOTHERAPY. [12]

Bibliography

J. F. T. Bugental (ed.), *Challenges of Humanistic Psychology* (New York, 1967); G. R. Collins, *The Rebuilding of Psychology: An Integration of Psychology and Christianity* (Eastbourne and Wheaton, IL, 1977); F. Goble, *The Third Force: The Psychology of*

Abraham Maslow (New York, 1970); A. H. Maslow, *Toward a Psychology of Being* (New York, ²1968); H. P. Rickman, *Wilhelm Dilthey: Pioneer of the Human Studies* (London, 1979).

R.F.H.

HUMANITARIANISM. Though somewhat indefinite in meaning, humanitarianism is most usually taken to convey a love or concern for human beings, typically expressing itself in a desire for the betterment of the material conditions of human life as a paramount virtue. Humanitarianism may be part of a more general ideology of human improvement and progress, even of human perfectibility, or it may evidence itself in response to particular abuses and needs. A humanitarian attitude may spill over into a concern for other matters of great value and importance to human beings, such as animals and the physical environment. Such humanitarianism is to be contrasted both with an ethic of duty* in the abstract and with a vague sentimentality.

It may be thought that Christ's teaching, *e.g.* in the parable of the good Samaritan, would be sufficient to ensure that the Christian church places great emphasis upon humanitarian goals. But there have been alarming blindspots in the history of the church, not all of which can be justified in terms of Christians adopting the mores of the day. But the stance of the church has often been compromised by a vague sentimentalism which does not reckon with the realities of human suffering and tragedy.

The implementation of humanitarian policies and ideals has been effected in two different and contrasting ways: 1. through voluntary charity, the setting up of voluntary agencies to address particular abuses; and 2. (at the other extreme) through government action, including the passing of appropriate legislation, the setting up of State agencies, and the provision of State funding. In practice, in liberal democracies humanitarian aspirations are met by a combination of the two. In recent years there has been an increasing use made of free-market mechanisms, *e.g.* in pricing, even in areas where the establishing of a true market is impossible. At the root of these contrasting approaches is a conflict between those who hold that the government should be to some degree paternalistic, and those who hold, on libertarian grounds, that it should only be permissive and enabling.

The modern humanitarian movement may be said to have started in reaction to the blatant human abuses which were a by-product of the Industrial Revolution and of the colonial expansion from the end of the 18th century. Classic humanitarian campaigns were waged against slavery,* child labour, and bad housing and sanitation. In the contemporary world, humanitarian campaigning is mainly against drug abuse (see Drugs*), child abuse (see Abuse*) and, particularly in the Third World, poverty* and material deprivation. Environmental pressure groups may also have a humanitarian impetus.

Humanitarian thought and action have increasingly drawn their inspiration from human rights (see Rights, Human*) and alleged violations of those rights, *e.g.* by physical persecution or detention without trial, so that documents such as the United Nations Declaration on Human Rights may be said to embody pivotal humanitarian ideals and claims. However, the number of such rights has increased to the extent that a claim that a human right has been violated has only rhetorical effect.

The attitude of the Christian church to humanitarianism's needs and ideals has always been somewhat ambivalent. The church has those in it who favour a socialistic approach to meeting human need, and those who favour the market and private charity. Such differences are not only about means towards an agreed end, for sometimes there are sharp differences among Christians about social and political ends.

Nevertheless, it has been recognized that each person is made in the image of God* and has intrinsic worth, and has an obligation to love his or her neighbours and to meet their needs wherever possible. Yet there has also been a strong other-worldly emphasis in the church, a belief that a person's chief aim in this life should be to prepare for the next, and this has militated against the adoption of humanitarian programmes, and in particular against their identification with the coming of the kingdom of God.*

Sometimes the doctrine of divine providence has been invoked to preserve the *status quo*, at other times to promote change. But to whatever extent the church has been supportive of humanitarian goals, it has recognized that salvation does not lie in and through their achievement. Only in the anabaptistic* or perfectionist fringes of the church, or in modern liberal theology, has salvation been held to include a humanitarian goal, the establishment of the kingdom of God on earth by political means.

P.H.

HUMAN RIGHTS, see RIGHTS, HUMAN.

HUME, DAVID (1711–76). In Hume's moral philosophy, the purpose of moral judgments is to move us to action. The consequence of this is that, because in Hume's view reason* cannot do this, judgments of reason cannot give us moral judgments. Reason deals with facts or the relationship between ideas, but cannot offer us the necessary impulse to act morally. The significance of this is that Hume makes a general, though contentious, point, that factual truth logically can never be a basis for moral action, so that if we limit ourselves to considering any action rationally, we can never find virtue* or vice* within it. It is the passions, motives, volitions and thoughts that move us to act, and in particular the possibility of present or future pleasure* or pain.*

The essence of Hume's case is that moral judgments are formed from moral sentiments, so that when we consider an action in general and without reference to our own interests, and have a feeling of approval, *i.e.* of joy* and pleasure, the action is virtuous. The contrary is to be found in a feeling of disapproval, *i.e.* of disgust or pain or unease. Thus 'the impressions by which good and evil is known, are nothing but particular pains or pleasures'. This does not mean that an action or character is virtuous because it pleases, but rather that in the experience of feeling pleasure at an action or character, we feel that it is virtuous.

See also: HISTORY OF CHRISTIAN ETHICS. [6]

Bibliography
F. Copleston, *A History of Philosophy*, vol. 5 (London, 1961); A. MacIntyre, *A Short History of Ethics* (London and New York, 1967).

C.A.B.

HUMILITY. Contemporary use of the Eng. word 'humility', to signify dependence, lowliness and submissiveness, maintains fidelity to its etymological roots in the Lat. *humilis*, 'lowly', and *humus*, 'earth'. In many contexts, we use it and its cognates to refer to persons or things of little or diminished worth. For example, we speak of 'a person of

humble birth', or of a home as 'a humble dwelling'. More poignantly, we also use it when various kinds of harm are inflicted, as when the politically powerful publicly humiliate their rivals by coerced, self-serving confessions of wrongdoing. Here it is important to recognize that these uses of the word entail conditions opposed to its being understood as a virtue* or grace. In the latter usage, those who are virtuously humble are the agents of their own freely embraced humiliation, and their humbling is freely, even joyfully, entered into to bring about good for others. It is a misunderstanding of the virtue of humility (a misunderstanding in part occasioned by the previously mentioned use) to think that it must include any notion of the agent dishonouring or devaluing his or her own worth as a person, or of giving less than an honest estimate of his or her own gifts or achievements.

No grace of the Christian life better illustrates the value transformation effected by the life and ministry of Jesus than humility. In much contemporary usage, to be humble is to be abject, to debase oneself in a servile fashion. For example, some contemporary dictionaries define the verb 'to grovel' by using the phrase 'to behave humbly or abjectly, as before authority'. In the words and actions of Jesus, the sense of what it means to be humble is strikingly different. In washing his disciples' feet, he did enter upon the duties of a servant, much to the consternation of his disciples. But in so doing he clearly did not think of *himself* as servile or abject and he certainly did not think of *his disciples* as authorities (Jn. 13:13–14).

The close relationship between humility and poverty,* affliction and low social status, is a striking and characteristic feature of the situations in which humility is used in the Scriptures. In the OT, God shows a continuing, deep concern for the humble poor (Ex. 23:6; Dt. 15:4, 7, 11; 24:6, 10–15, 17–22; Am. 2:6–7; Mi. 6:8; Zp. 2:3; 3:12–13). The wealthy and powerful who treated them unjustly are portrayed as the enemies of Yahweh by all the later prophets (Is. 3:14–15; Je. 2:34; 5:28; Am. 2:6–7; 4:1).

The very existence of Israel as a people is never to be thought of as their own achievement, but always as a consequence of the covenantal initiative of God with the patriarchs. Learning to acknowledge Yahweh as the source of all power and wealth always proved difficult (2 Ch. 12:7–12), so he humbled his people in the desert (Dt. 8:2) and in exile (2 Ki. 17: 25).

In most NT references, humility (*prautēs*) refers to a trait of character independent of any conditions of poverty (*tapeinos*, *cf.* Lk. 1:52), political powerlessness or oppression. It appears in a number of lists of virtues (Gal. 5:23, frequently translated 'gentleness'; Eph. 4:2; Col. 3:12; Tit. 3:2; 1 Pet. 3:8). In the Pauline letters, humility is an essential feature of *agapē* (love) that preserves us from corruption into self-centredness (1 Cor. 13:4–7). It is also the self-forgetful, other-regarding quality that moved the Son of God to undertake incarnation as Jesus of Nazareth and his redemptive role as the servant Messiah (Phil. 2:5–11).

Among non-Jewish and non-Christian moralists in the West, this conception of humility as a virtue was unknown, neglected or confused with self-abnegation or humiliation. No trait of character could qualify as morally excellent except on the assumption that it fostered self-respect and self-esteem. And even where humility was understood as entailing submissiveness and the free renunciation of legitimate prerogatives, as with Benedict de Spinoza (1632–77) and David Hume,* it was rejected as a 'monkish virtue', one that required a devaluing of persons and their achievements.

If some Christian teachers, in their zeal to commend the self-emptying of Christ for emulation, have thought this required servile self-abasement on the part of the faithful, then they were clearly mistaken. It has no biblical warrant, no sound theological justification. Sin has sullied the image of God* in every person but it has not destroyed it. This means that even where honesty requires a modest opinion of our achievements, humility does not require self-abasement or self-loathing. Here it is helpful to mark a distinction between 'respect' and 'esteem'. The *respect* we have for ourselves or others involves only one value judgment and it admits of no degrees; we cannot have more or less respect for ourselves or others. The *esteem* we have for ourselves or others may involve many value judgments and it admits of degrees; we can have more or less esteem for ourselves or others. Observing this distinction should help Christians to avoid confusing humility with either the denial of a proper self-respect grounded in their creation in the 'image and likeness of God', or a dishonest lack of esteem for the relative gifts or achievements of themselves or others.

If we have helped to rescue 'humility' from uses that name a vice rather than a virtue, we have not yet fully explored its sense as a crucial Christian grace. Having identified the essence of sin as pride,* it is not surprising that Augustine* would declare that 'in humility is human life perfected' (*Sermon on Psalm 130*). Elsewhere he writes, 'this way [of Christ] is, in the first place, humility; in the second place humility; in the third place, humility . . . As often as you say to me about the Christian religion's norms of conduct, I choose to give no other answer than: humility' (*Letter* 118). Romano Guardini (1885–1968) illuminates an important aspect of the humility of Christ, seen in the foot-washing episode mentioned earlier (*The Lord*, Chicago, 1954, pp. 322–328). Humility, he argues, describes an attitude that the greater may take towards the lesser but not the lesser to the greater; it is present only where the great honours one who is not and the very unimportance of the inferior is itself unimportant. What Christians and others have generally taken it to mean, namely an unenvious, honouring of or submission to the superior by the inferior, is not humility but the important, yet different, virtue of honesty.* The popular idea that humility, whatever else it means, includes the notion of a self-forgetful interest in the honouring of, or even submission to, others is correct. It is incorrect in assuming it is a duty or virtue most generally related to the attitudes and actions of the inferior. Even if one were to disagree with Guardini and maintain that both the inferior and the superior should manifest this virtue, this difference needs to be acknowledged; the object to be respected and honoured in each case is not the same. The inferior honours without resentment the superior status, qualities or achievements of the superior, while the superior relinquishes any interest in having them so honoured so that they will not be a barrier to affirming and honouring the person of the inferior and serving his or her needs.

M.A.R.

HUNGER, WORLD. The face of hunger is typified by a hungry four-year-old, who gets a single meal a day of about 400 calories, only a third of its average needs, and who is chronically undernourished. The World Bank estimates of 1986 show 730 million people in the world suffering from chronic hunger. The number continues to rise, though the percentage in proportion to the population of developing countries and of the world continues to decline.

The chronically hungry, notes Susan George (1934–) in her study *How the Other Half Dies*, 'are physically less developed and mentally less alert than people who eat enough; they have far less resistance to disease and are far more susceptible to invasion by the parasites that proliferate in their poor countries' (p. 31).

It must be noted that significant progress has been made in meeting people's need for food on a global scale. 'Progress in providing food security for a major part of a much larger world population is one of the outstanding achievements of our times and further progress continues to be made,' writes Kirit Parikh of the World Institute for Development Economics Research.

Adequate food is produced regionally and globally; yet several hundred million people in the world suffer from chronic hunger, and in famines like the one in Sudan (1984–85) nearly 1,100,000 people died above the average rate in a small region. This apparent contradiction makes hunger an urgent ethical issue for the Christian.

The problem of hunger is the problem of poverty.* Hungry people have meagre incomes and are unable to buy all the food they need. Their incomes are small because they own insufficient productive resources of capital, land and skills. National government policies directly affect domestic prices of goods and services. In an interdependent world economy, policies of national government also depend on the policies of other governments. In 1991 the Dunkel draft of the General Agreement on Tariffs and Trade (GATT) proposed among other things a complete integration of the agriculture of the developing countries into the world economy (see International Trade*).

It would be right to conclude that the causes of hunger are both national and international. Cultural values, unjust systems, weather shocks and national government policies all contribute to the perpetuation of poverty and hunger. Richer countries also have a substantial influence as they protect their agriculture more and export domestic surpluses on the world market, making it difficult for poor countries. The European hungry of the 19th century found a major answer in emigrating to the more productive USA, Canada and Australia. Today's hungry have no such option.

The creation account (Gn. 1:26–31) describes humans as made in God's image* and therefore as his stewards, entrusted with authority and capacity to rule the earth, care for it, make it bear fruit and enjoy it for sustenance and growth. The Fall* brings a curse on the ground, making human food-producing activity frustrating and burdensome.

A powerful biblical image that sums up God's concern for the hungry is found in Is. 65:17–25. The prophet's vision of the new heavens and new earth that God promises includes restoration of the fruits of labour to the workers: 'they will plant vineyards and eat their fruits' (65:21). The prophets view hunger as a justice issue, God's righting of a wrong of human origin (Am. 5:11).

Each of the Gospels recounts the story of Jesus feeding the five thousand. They stress Jesus' compassion for the hungry (Mt. 14:13–21, and par.). In the book of Acts, Luke identifies the provision of the food needs of believers, the daily distribution of food to the widows (Acts 6:1–4; *cf.* 4:34–35), as a distinctive mark of the early church's life.

Matthew's Gospel stresses that feeding the hungry and giving drink to the thirsty are of eternal significance and are the evidence of serving Christ himself (Mt. 25:34–40). Christian response to hunger is seen as universal and unconditional; even a hungry enemy must be fed (Rom. 12:20).

Encouraging food aid from areas of plenty to areas of need is a Christian imperative. The story of Joseph, whose planning protected the people of Egypt from the effects of prolonged famine (Gn. 41:46–57), should encourage Christians to work for the elimination of hunger. Modern technology makes it possible for a small percentage of people to produce enormous quantities of food and for agriculture to be almost independent of weather shocks. Christian concern must work for the transference of such skills and technology to needy areas.

Christians have promoted aid for economic development* to poor countries since the 1950s. State development projects have received substantial support from the West and have rarely been successful. Aid has not addressed the problems of the rising cost of fertilizers, high-yielding seeds and irrigation projects, all tied to Western technology. A Christian response needs to take the above problem seriously. It must help poor countries to develop productive agricultural systems which can be sustained by indigenous skills and resources.

Hunger is also the result of short-sighted patterns of land use by local populations. Forests are cut down for firewood and to satisfy land needs of growing populations. This results in erosion of topsoil during the rains and consequent desertification (see Deforestation*). Some of the tragedy of widespread famine in sub-Saharan Africa in the 1980s was caused by such a process. The tension between immediate land use for exploding populations and long-term needs of conserving the environment is an ethical issue for Christians.

Kenya has the highest growth rate of population in the world. It is clear that the land cannot meet the needs of such an increasing population indefinitely. Population control and management are a necessity (see Population Policy*). This is primarily a cultural issue. Large families are seen as a sign of blessing* and success. It requires both political will and the education of the people to begin to address the problem. Improvement in the standard of living and democratization of the political system provide significant incentives for population control. Women are often the leaders in the acceptance of family-planning programmes (see Birth Control*).

Some Christians in the West have called for a simpler lifestyle among Christians in affluent countries, as a response to the needs of hunger and economic development in poor countries. The impact of such a response will be minimal unless it is combined with political action. Such action must influence the size of aid allocation by affluent nations, promote just trade relations and discourage the arms trade on which poor nations spend so much of their resources.

The right to food is not a universally accepted right (see Rights, Human*). The Christian view of God's concern for the hungry puts the elimination of hunger high on the Christian's social agenda.

Bibliography

T. Chester, *Awakening to a World of Need* (Leicester, 1993); S. George, *How the Other Half Dies* (Harmondsworth, 1976); P. Harrison, *The Third World Tomorrow* (Harmondsworth, 1980; P. Nürnberger (ed.), *Affluence, Poverty and the Word of God* (Durban, 1978); M. Olasky *et al.*, *Freedom, Justice and Hope: Toward a Strategy for the Poor and the Oppressed* (Westchester, IL, 1988).

V.K.S.

HYPNOSIS is a state of induced relaxation and drowsiness, associated with heightened suggestibility, voluntary suspension of initiative, restriction of attention to a narrow field, and reduction in self-consciousness and in critical appraisal. It is usually produced by a repetitive stimulus inducing a state in which suggestion, the process whereby an individual accepts a proposition put by another, is more effective than usual. The word, first used by James Braid (*c.* 1795–1860) in 1843, derives from *hypnos*, 'sleep', a misnomer, as the electroencephalogram shows hypnotic subjects to be awake and not asleep.

Suggestion in hypnosis is direct and obvious; the subject is not gullible or without willpower. Susceptible subjects may be predicted, *e.g.* by the body sway test. For hypnosis to be induced, subjects must be willing; they should be relaxed and able to exercise imagination. Possibly anyone could be hypnotized, but some are more susceptible than others. A good hypnotic subject is mentally normal with a capacity for involvement in aesthetic and imaginative experience in childhood, and susceptibility persists over time and is in part inherited genetically.

In hypnosis the subject ceases to make his or her own plans; attention is selectively directed towards the hypnotist; reality testing is decreased and reality distortion accepted; suggestibility is increased; the subject readily enacts unusual roles; and post-hypnotic amnesia is often present (*i.e.* a suggestion can be made under hypnosis that will be carried out after leaving the state).

Hypnosis is not powerful therapeutically; it cannot be used in all individuals, it takes time to induce, and its effectiveness is variable in the same subject. It therefore has only limited use in treatment. It has been used with varying efficacy in the following situations: 1. symptom removal, *e.g.* using post-hypnotic suggestion to stop smoking; 2. exploration in psychotherapy, revealing unconscious material, though most therapists find that hypnosis is unnecessary for this purpose; 3. as an adjunct to anxiety control, light hypnosis is used and autohypnosis learnt to produce relaxation in anxiety-provoking situations; and 4. relaxation, anaesthesia and analgesia by hypnosis during painful procedures have been used for burns dressings and with dental treatment. Analgesia can be achieved in only about 20% of cases.

Ethical dilemmas

Those with ethical doubts about the use of hypnosis raise the following questions: 1. What is the source of the 'power' of hypnosis? 2. Can it be right to hand over control to another person? 3. Is there a risk of acquiring symptoms as a result of hypnosis?

In response to these questions:

1. Some stage hypnotists *ascribe power supernaturally*, sometimes to demons. That, however, is unnecessary. The use of hypnosis by a doctor or a dentist as a part of treatment of a patient is ethically in no different position from other medical or surgical techniques.

2. There is some *loss of control*, in that suggestion implies suspension of critical evaluation. The question is therefore asked, Will persons under hypnosis do something against their moral code?

In fact, suggestibility varies between people, and varies for the same person at different stages of life and in different situations. Most people consider that subjects under hypnosis will carry out actions they find abhorrent, but that the hypnosis may 'legitimize' what they could not justify or usually do. A famous murder trial took place in 1890 in Paris in which Gabrielle Bompard, aged 22, was an accomplice. She claimed innocence and complete anmesia due to her having been hypnotized by her lover, who had made a post-hypnotic suggestion for her to assist him in the killing (R. Harris, 'Murder under Hypnosis', *PsyM* 15, 1985, pp. 477–506). This carries implications for law and psychiatry, and it has never been wholly resolved to what extent the individual loses self-control. Hypnosis should, therefore, be used only by qualified practitioners in their professional capacity and place of work, preferably with a chaperon. It is important to be aware of the power of suggestion in other supposedly non-hypnotic contexts, such as the general practitioner's surgery, or a preacher 'inviting' people 'to come to the front'.

Those recommending hypnosis in Christian counselling stress the importance of co-operation with the client in achieving mastery over a problem, rather than imposing their will (J. H. Court, 'Hypnosis Revisited', *Inter* 34, 1983, pp. 55–60). Such an approach is consistent with the call to renew our minds (Rom. 12:2); hypnotherapy seeks to return control to, rather than take it over from, those who have lost it.

3. There is some danger of *acquiring symptoms* as a result of oft-repeated hypnosis, especially in those with severe disturbance of personality who may show loss of feelings of responsibility. It may impair a sense of personal identity, and cause hypochondriasis or even multiple personality. Hypnosis may encourage the 'sick role', with dependence upon the hypnotist.

Conclusion

In summary, hypnosis is a distinct phenomenon that is difficult to define but has certain clear-cut characteristics. It is associated with wakefulness and not sleep, with increased suggestibility, the use of monotonous stimulation, and with fantasy. It has good and bad uses, but is essentially morally and ethically neutral. It has some limited place in medicine and dentistry.

A.C.P.S.

HYPOCRISY is a state of mind and life in which an outward appearance of truth or uprightness masks hidden untruth or wickedness.

The word 'masks' in this definition reveals how helpful it is, in this case, to bear in mind the etymology of the word in seeking its meaning. The Gk. word *hypokritēs* originally meant 'actor'. In the classical Gk. theatre, characters were identified by masks; so plays were often performed by only a handful of actors, who would change parts throughout the play by donning new masks. In biblical Gk. the word acquired a strongly negative connotation, as a potent metaphor for pretence and 'play-acting' in human relationships: but it is interesting that it never developed this negative sense in secular Gk. ethics, where the art of 'persuasion' was highly prized.

In the NT, 'hypocrisy' is in particular an accusation levelled by Jesus against the Pharisees. He calls hypocrisy 'the yeast of the Pharisees' (Lk. 12:1, *i.e.* something with which they infect the whole people) and denounces their hypocrisy at length in Mt. 23. Analysis reveals that the word is used of several different states.

1. Performance for applause. The original meaning 'play-actor' is close to the surface in some references, for instance in Mt. 6:2, 5, 16. Jeremias suggests that the 'hypocrites' in Mt. 6:5 are those who ensured that they were still in the street when the trumpet sounded for the hour of prayer, so that they could ostentatiously perform their prayers in public. *Cf.* also Mt. 23:5–7. Paul expresses a similar thought about the Galatian heretics in Gal. 6:12. This shades into the next category.

2. Pretence in devotion to God. This is the substance of the accusation in Mt. 15:7. The Pharisees are outraged by the disciples' flouting of 'the traditions of the elders' (15:2), but Jesus points out their deliberate scheme to avoid uncomfortable obedience to God's command. Their outrage is therefore pretentious. *Cf.* also Mt. 23:25–28.

3. Pretence in personal relationships. Those who ask Jesus about the payment of taxes to Caesar conceal their true motives: they present themselves as genuine inquirers after truth who recognize Jesus' authority (Mk. 12:14), but actually they want 'to catch him in his words' (Mk. 12:13; *cf.* Lk. 20:20). Jesus recognizes 'their hypocrisy' (Mk. 12:15; *cf.* Mt. 22:18).

4. Unconscious inconsistency between belief and practice. In the NT hypocrisy can be unconscious. Paul accuses Peter and Barnabas of hypocrisy in Gal. 2:12–14: when they withdrew from table-fellowship with Gentile Christians, their behaviour no longer matched the gospel they were seeking to obey – though they themselves felt that their action was God's will.

This is the essence of Jesus' charge against the Pharisees in Mt. 23: in their case it is the law to which they are supposed to be conforming their lives, but they fail to do so and are unconscious of the failure, because they interpret it wrongly (Mt. 23:23–24; *cf.* also Lk. 13:15). In particular they say they disapprove of the killing of the prophets by their fathers (Mt. 23:29–30), and yet they have rejected the Christ, who is their Prophet (23:10; *cf.* 21:45–46). They are unconscious of this inconsistency precisely because they do not recognize Jesus' authority.

5. Blindness towards the truth. In modern usage hypocrisy cannot be unconscious in quite the same way as in the last category. But the NT employs the idea even more widely. The accusation of hypocrisy in Lk. 12:56 refers to spiritual blindness allied to earthly 'savvy': the people are so clever in predicting the weather according to the time of year, but not the 'season' of the arrival of the kingdom (see Kingdom of God*). Such blindness is particularly reprehensible in teachers, who thus lead others astray: this is Jesus' charge against the Pharisees in Mt. 23:15–22, and Paul's against the false teachers in 1 Tim. 4:2. They are 'hypocritical liars, whose consciences have been seared as with a hot iron', and who thus

are unable to discern that the truth they think they know and teach is actually falsehood. 'Wolves in sheep's clothing' is a vivid metaphor for the same thing (see Mt. 7:15).

Defined in this broad way, 'hypocrisy' refers not just to deliberate pretence in relationships (with each other or with God), but also to any false claim to teach and follow the truth, because in this case, too, falsehood is masking reality.

S.M.

I

ID, see PERSONALITY; PSYCHOANALYSIS; UNCONSCIOUS.

IDEALISM. In the general use of the term, idealism is the pursuit of ideals, a striving after excellence, rather than a 'realistic' acceptance of more modest goals. The Bible would appear to advocate elements of both realism and idealism in this sense; we need to be aware that we fall short even of our own ideals, let alone God's; yet we press on to the highest goal (Phil. 3:10–14). The saving feature here is God's grace* which is willing to accept us as we are and, through the work of the Holy Spirit, move us towards what he wants us to be.

In philosophy and ethics the term 'idealism' has a wide range of more technical meanings. Grasping its main principles is made difficult not just by this range, but by the fact that the word can be used to refer to ideas as well as ideals.

Philosophical idealism is primarily concerned with ideas; it is the doctrine that ultimate reality is mental or spiritual as opposed to material or physical. Matter is derived from and dependent on mind (*e.g.* God creates the universe and holds it in being), not mind on matter (*e.g.* in the popular evolutionist view that mind has emerged from matter and is reducible to it). Christianity could thus be called a form of idealism, although traditionally idealists have chosen to play down the importance of the material world, something which Christianity does not do. Among the best-known philosophers who can be broadly classified as idealists are Plato,* G. Berkeley (1685–1753), Immanuel Kant* and G. W. F.

Hegel (1770–1831), although they disagreed considerably on the way their idealism was worked out.

All idealists accepted the existence of a mental or spiritual being, sometimes approximating loosely to the Christian concept of God. They also held that mind or spirit is the 'higher' part of human beings with which we apprehend what is truly real.

Idealism has held the centre of the philosophical stage, especially in Germany, until this century; remnants of it are still seen in existentialism. But the dominance of science and evolutionary theory, the influence of Marxism, the reductionist* desire to move from dualism* to a single-substance cosmos, and the general rejection of the reality of the spiritual or supernatural, have meant that, for much of the 20th century, philosophical idealism has been out of favour.

Idealist ethical theory varied from one idealist philosopher to another. Tenets generally held would be: 1. the existence of some ultimate spiritual/mental reality which is the source of ethical values; 2. the ability of individuals to know for themselves universal moral principles to which they ought to be subject; 3. any system, like utilitarianism (see Consequentialism*) or Marxism, which locates the basis of morals in the material world, is to be rejected (see Marxist Ethics*); and 4. women and men possess real freedom* enabling them to obey or disobey the moral imperatives with which they are confronted.

The rejection of idealist philosophy has meant that these principles are now largely unsupported in ethical theory, though they tend to linger on in popular thought. Universal moral imperatives rooted in ultimate reality have been replaced with utilitarian or situational* or relativistic* theories, most of which come with strong deterministic overtones.

Recent biblical theology has tended to move away from a strong dualism between body and mind or between matter and spirit. Though the two are to be distinguished, they are not to be set against each other; the concept that spirit or mind is more real than matter or body, and morally superior to them, is looked on as 'Greek' rather than biblical. Though God is spirit, he is also the God of creation and incarnation; an individual human being, rather than being seen as a (superior) imprisoned soul within an (inferior) body, is to be regarded as a psychosomatic unity. Because of this, the question whether mind/spirit or body/matter is primary seems less relevant today than to previous generations. While accepting that a basically idealist philosophy fits best with the biblical world-view, few biblical theologians would thereby wish to belittle the significance of the material; Christianity is concerned with bodies as much as with souls, with the material world as much as the heavenly realm.

Bibliography

A. C. Ewing (ed.), *The Idealist Tradition from Berkeley to Blanshard* (London, 1957); H. J. Paton, *The Categorical Imperative* (Chicago, 1948; London, [3]1958).

P.A.H.

IDENTITY, see ADOLESCENCE.

IDEOLOGY, see INDOCTRINATION; MARXIST ETHICS.

IGNATIUS OF LOYOLA (1491–1556). Ignatius was born into a wealthy family from the Basque region of northern Spain. In 1521, whilst fighting to repel a French invasion of the city of Pamplona, he was severely wounded and came close to death. During convalescence, without the books he usually enjoyed, he read and reflected deeply upon Ludolph of Saxony's (c. 1300–78) *Life of Christ* (1474) and a selection of biographies entitled *Lives of Saints*. The latter represented the saints (especially the founders of religious orders) as chivalrous knights in the service of Jesus Christ. Thus began Ignatius' dramatic conversion,* his desire to serve Christ wholeheartedly like the saints of old, and his intense interest in the 'discerning of spirits' – a fascination with the psychology of temptations to sin and impulses to virtuous living, and with moods he called 'consolations' of God's comfort and encouragement and the humbling 'desolations' of God's apparent absence (see Desertions, Spiritual*).

Soon after beginning a secret pilgrimage to Jerusalem he spent time alone at Manresa, where, following deep spiritual depression, he experienced a new peace and sense of God's presence and was delivered from tormenting doubts. He believed that through an experience of God's grace he had 'perceived and understood many things, both spiritual and touching matters of faith and learning'. A strong desire to share his insights with others prompted him to keep careful notes of his scriptural reading and prayers at this time and these formed the basis of his *Spiritual*

Exercises – a manual to direct others through several weeks of prayer and imaginative meditation on the life of Christ and thus to total consecration to God's purpose for their life.

During years of study in Spain and France, Ignatius made close and lasting friendships with many men of outstanding intellect – among them Francis Xavier (1502–52) – who came under the influence of his spiritual direction.* Often they too were dramatically converted, like the seven close friends who in 1535 bound themselves together by an oath to the service of God and were later ordained priest with Ignatius.

Ignatius subsequently claimed a vision of God at a small chapel in La Storta which confirmed his plans to form a 'company' of servants of Christ. In 1540 Pope Julius III (1487–1555) agreed the foundation of the Society of Jesus and Ignatius reluctantly accepted unanimous election as its first Superior General. Thereafter Jesuits* were active in catechizing children, in evangelism – especially among Jewish people – in preaching, and in serving as spiritual directors. Ignatius lived the remainder of his life in Rome, governing the Society through a vast correspondence and compiling its Constitutions. Colleges were established to train future Jesuits and 'the propagation of the faith', to which Pope Julius committed the Society, involved both Ignatius and his fellow priests in detailed and enlightened schemes for Jesuit missions in India, China, Brazil and central Africa.

Ignatius' *Spiritual Exercises*, which reflect the theology of Thomas Aquinas* and the teaching of the Roman Catholic Church concerning sin, the Virgin Mary and the saints, were of immense importance in forming the spirituality* of Jesuits, who in turn played a key part in the so-called Counter-Reformation of the 16th century. Currently the *Spiritual Exercises* (though never intended for general publication), Ignatian-style retreats and methods of imaginative meditation on the Gospels are popular and widely used by Protestants and Catholics alike.

Bibliography

P. Caraman, *Ignatius Loyola* (London, 1990); T. Corbishley, *The Spiritual Exercises of Saint Ignatius Loyola* (London and New York, 1963); D. Lonsdale, *Eyes to See, Ears to Hear: An Introduction to Ignatian Spirituality* (London, 1990); D. Mitchel, *The Jesuits: A History* (London, 1980); A. Netherwood, *The Voice of this Calling: An Evangelical Encounters the Spiritual Exercises of Saint Ignatius Loyola* (London, 1990).

R.A.Hin.

IMAGE OF GOD.

This important doctrine, relating as it does to the creation,* Fall* and re-creation of humanity (see ④) touches almost every aspect of Christian doctrine, both systematic and practical. It has important implications for a Christian approach to many disciplines, notably philosophy, psychology, social studies, ethics and law.

The biblical revelation was given in the context of a religious world. Rulers such as the Egyptian Pharaohs and later the Roman emperors were regarded as divine. The Greeks and Romans depicted their gods in human form (see Acts 14:11–13), as of course many peoples have done. Scripture rejects all such ideas along with their associated idolatry. There is only one God, and he is not to be represented by any visible form. He has, however, made human beings in his image.

1. The Old Testament

Gn. 1:26–27 uses 'image' and 'likeness' in reference to man's unique endowment by God. 'Likeness' stands alone in Gn. 5:1 (but see v. 3), and 'image' alone in Gn. 9:6. They are virtual synonyms, with the first slightly more concrete than the second. They certainly seem to occur together in Gn. 1:26–27 for emphasis, not for distinction.

What then, for Genesis, is the divine image? Is it physical, psychological, spiritual, or some combination of these? Scripture teaches God's spirituality, so the image must at least be inward. Yet a human being is a unity, and it is the physical body which is the means through which the image within finds outward expression.

Some writers relate it simply to man's God-given, 'God-like' dominion over creation, so that it designates a function rather than essential being. Here we detect modern theological nervousness about moving beyond functional to ontological considerations, due to widespread but highly questionable philosophical presuppositions. Certainly dominion is a function but in it a God-given nature reveals itself.

Some say that the creation of humanity as male and female expresses the divine image in some way, either in a community of persons (the Trinity) or in terms of masculine and feminine qualities in God. The Genesis statement is, however, more likely to be an addition to than an explanation of the words about the divine image.

2. The New Testament

Despite the Fall, the NT writers clearly accept the divine image as an abiding reality (1 Cor. 11:7; Jas. 3:9). Heb. 2, however, recognizes that the fullness of dominion celebrated in Ps. 8 lacks as yet practical realization, so implying some disturbance through sin. The main NT emphasis, however, is on the image as restored in Christ, and this itself presupposes its impairment.

In Col. 1:15–17, Christ the creator is called 'the image of the invisible God'. The same thought, differently expressed, occurs in Heb. 1:1–3. He is also God's image as the prototype of redeemed humanity (Phil. 3:21; Col. 3:10–11). He can therefore be called 'the last Adam' or 'the second man' (1 Cor. 15:45, 47; *cf.* Rom. 5:12–21; Acts 17:26, 31). Moreover, redeemed humanity would seem to be remade in Christ in God's image in a corporate, as well as an individual, sense (*cf.* 2 Cor. 3:18 with its stress on 'all' [*pantes*]).

The reference to Christ as 'being in very nature God' (Phil. 2:6) has been applied by scholars either to his divine nature or to the divine image in the perfect Man. The issue is not all-important, for, as we have seen, elsewhere Paul uses 'image' in connection both with his deity and his humanity.

3. The history of the doctrine

Tertullian,* probably influenced by his pre-Christian Stoicism, distinguished the image and likeness as man's physical and spiritual nature respectively, but the Fathers and schoolmen usually differentiated them by assigning reason to the image and original righteousness to the likeness.

The Reformers, however, rejected any distinction between the two terms. The image, Calvin* taught, was greatly defaced but not totally eradicated by the Fall, although original righteousness was lost.

Liberalism's* weak doctrine of sin led to the idea that the image is man's universal capacity for God. Barth's* reaction against liberalism caused him at first to deny any retention of the divine image by fallen man. Evangelical theologians have normally held to a view much like Calvin's, *i.e.* the image, though defaced, is not obliterated.

4. Contemporary issues

Modern philosophy, preoccupied since Kant* with epistemology, needed but lacked the notion of the divine image in man as a secure basis for knowledge, especially knowledge of God. Schools of psychology and systems of psychiatry vary in many ways, but rarely recognize a divine dimension to life.

For Christian ethics, the infinite value of each person rests on the divine image. This then must be an important consideration in any Christian outlook on issues of life and death, like war,* capital punishment,* abortion* and euthanasia,* and also on foetus experimentation (see Embryology*) and genetic engineering.* It has obvious relevance too to issues of personality violation, such as torture,* brainwashing,* rape* and child abuse,* as well as to racism and sexism. Clearly then belief in the divine image will influence Christians in their approach to changes in legislation relating to such matters.

God's goal for his church and so for every Christian is maturity in Christ (Eph. 4:13) and so conformity to his image (Rom. 8:28–29; 12:1–2; 2 Cor. 3:18). This should affect our whole perspective on the Christian life, the main goal of which should not be happiness or self-realization but holiness, likeness to Christ. This will also determine at every point the nature of the pastoral task, for, despite all our differences in background, temperament and vocation,* the Holy Spirit works to this end in every Christian's life.

See also: HUMANITY. [4]

Bibliography

R. S. Anderson, *On Being Human: Essays in Theological Anthropology* (Grand Rapids, 1982); G. C. Berkouwer, *Man: The Image of God* (Grand Rapids, 1962); D. Cairns, *The Image of God in Man* (London, 1953); J. Fichtner, *Man the Image of God: A Christian Anthropology* (New York, 1978); P. E. Hughes, *The True Image: The Origin and Destiny of Man in Christ* (Grand Rapids, and Leicester, 1989).

G.W.G.

IMITATION OF CHRIST (IMITATIO CHRISTI), see JESUS.

IMMIGRATION refers to the passage of people from one territory to make their home and seek work in another. Though in itself a neutral concept, it may be viewed both positively and negatively in different situations.

Indonesia, for instance, has numerous underpopulated islands and many overpopulated ones. The government has pursued a vigorous policy of promoting immigration into the underpopulated islands. This has had the support of the churches. In many countries, the lack of certain skills or numbers in the labour force has often led to incentives to people to immigrate.

Europe has until very recently been a net exporter of people. Since 1945 it has actively encouraged immigration, and cannot halt it now without forcing thousands of families to be separated. With a low birth-rate, there are good economic reasons for Europe to continue to allow people in. Immigration from the Third World will have little impact on the ethnic composition of countries in the European Union. Of 340 million residents of the EU, 9 million are non-EU nationals: 7 million are from Africa, Asia, Turkey and Latin America (with 1 million more legal immigrants expected by 1996); and nearly 2 million from E. Europe and the former Soviet Union, with 2 million more legal immigrants expected in 1991–96. Half a million illegal immigrants are also expected in this same time-span.

The biblical Christian view is that divisions between races* are the work of the principalities and powers of evil which have been defeated by Christ's cross;* that in the new humanity which Jesus Christ heads and creates there is neither Jew nor Greek, no division because of race (Gal. 3:28; Eph. 2 – 3). Thus harmonious racial pluralism is actively welcomed in the NT. It brings an important richness into society whereby the gifts and riches of each community make for a rich cultural diversity. There is therefore no biblical warrant for separation of people into separated countries so that they cannot 'migrate'. The OT continually pleads for the rights of the sojourner, the immigrant and the resident foreigner. This would particularly apply to refugees or asylum-seekers.

Immigration is viewed negatively when a group of people (a national or regional group) believes that the incursion of large numbers of people from elsewhere is depriving them and their children of resources they would have a right to expect. Often this is confused with issues of race and colour. Thus there is no restriction at all on the immigration into the UK of nationals from the Irish Republic, in order to reside or seek work. Yet there is restriction and resentment at the immigration of S. Asians, West Indians, and more recently people from Hong Kong. While European voters are not opposed to European immigrants, they oppose immigration by Africans and Asians.

Immigration is therefore often confused with issues of colour to reflect racism (a belief that certain racial groups are superior and therefore justified in discriminatory behaviour) and/or racial prejudice (where people are seen only as members of a group to be confronted with hatred, condescension or envy).

Immigration can also be confused with issues of religion, and the argument constructed that immigration would bring races with false religions into a country. Prejudice against their religious beliefs is used as a reason to reject racial groups. This view has been used by overseas governments in restricting the entry of Christian missionaries, which Christians would oppose. It has also been used by some Christians to reject the entry of non-Christian peoples into their country. The standing contradiction of this view is the presence of Christians among these coloured races.

It is therefore very important that Christians distinguish in discussions between issues of immigration which refer to a resident population's need to expand or limit its numbers for its own benefit and security, and issues of race which can reveal discrimination in immigration policy between races.

The very concept of a nation-state dates only from the French Revolution at the end of the 18th century. Most nation-states have naturally mixed populations. The concept of a homogenous racial group with its own national homeland is a myth, but the existence of a dominant culture within a national boundary is a reality.

Immigration from the Third World into economically prosperous countries raises a number of factors. Often the very people who are able to contribute much to the development of the Third World countries are able to migrate elsewhere. Their ability to do this often results in the creaming off of the better-qualified of the new generation to sustain the primacy of the economically prosperous countries. Any controls on immigration into these countries (or even encouragement of immigration) must therefore be accompanied by action to foster healthy economic growth in these other countries.

In contemporary discussions of immigration, reciprocity is an important issue for Christians. It is especially noticed that Islamic immigrants often quite properly request rights and freedoms in their adopted land (freedom of religion, segregated schools), but these same freedoms are not granted to immigrant minorities in Islamic countries.

C.M.N.S.

IMPLICIT RELIGION, see FOLK RELIGION.

INCARNATION, see JESUS.

INCEST. The legal definition of a person who commits incest is: 'Any male person who has carnal knowledge of a female who is, to his knowledge, either his granddaughter, daughter, sister or mother. Any female of or above sixteen who, with consent, permits her grandfather, father, brother or son to have carnal knowledge of her knowing him to be such' (Punishment of Incest Act, 1908).

This is a very narrow legal definition, and would only include those cases in which there was vaginal intercourse within the relationships stated. The people involved from both parties may be adults, but incestuous relationships occur not only across generations but within the same generation. It also applies to relationships with children. However, it is accepted by many that inappropriate sexual contact between family members is just as harmful to children, and could be viewed as incestuous. David Finkelhor (1947–), for the purpose of research reported in his book *Sexually Victimized Children*, used the term 'incest' to mean 'sexual contact between family members including not just intercourse but also mutual masturbation, hand-genital or oral-genital contact, sexual fondling, exhibition and even sexual propositioning' (p. 84). When family members are referred to, this can include step relations. Incestuous relationships can also occur within the same gender. This wider definition will be used for the purpose of this article.

In the OT, Lv. 18:6 states: 'No-one is to approach any close relative to have sexual relations. I am the LORD.' Some of these close relatives are defined in Lv. 18:7–16, *e.g.* mother, father's wife, sister, granddaughter, aunt, daughter-in-law, sister-in-law. These commands are given from a male perspective. The fact that these are close relationships is the only reason given for the practice being so firmly forbidden. This can be seen as a protection for those living in the close intimate proximity that is found within families.

The account of the rape* of Tamar by her half-brother Amnon is a poignant and tragic illustration of how a close relationship was exploited by Amnon, under the guise of Tamar caring for her 'ill' half-brother (2 Sa. 13).

Although the father–daughter incest is the most commonly reported type of incest, professionals involved in this field have for long felt that brother–sister incest is the most common (see D. Finkelhor, *Sexually Victimized Children*). For most cultures, incest is taboo.* Indeed, most cultures would accept that sexual relationships between adults and children are wrong.

In this there is a recognition that adults are responsible for children. Developing this further, parents (see Parenthood, Parenting*) have a prime responsibility towards their children. For any child, a sexual relationship with an adult, whether a relative or not, carries a high risk of serious consequences. So the incest taboo can be seen to protect not only the child but also family life.

Most people would accept that incest is wrong, but there seems to be a reluctance for society to accept that incest is more prevalent than is possibly assumed. Other assumptions can be made that such activities happen only in poorer, uneducated, lower social classes living in some isolated rural community. Incest occurs across all social classes, in town or country, educated or not.

In the first major epidemiological study of reported incidence of child sexual abuse* that was undertaken in the UK (see The Research Team, *Child Sexual Abuse in Northern Ireland*), the reported incidence rate for sexual abuse in Northern Ireland lies somewhere between 0.9 to 1.8 cases per 1,000 population. For the USA, a comparable incidence rate (issued in 1981 by the National Centre in Child Abuse and Neglect) is 0.7 cases per 1,000 per year. Incidence is defined as the number of new cases occurring over a specific time period, *i.e.* per year. It is accepted that for each reported case there will be many unreported cases. Of the cases considered in the Northern Ireland survey, 85.1% knew their abuser. Summarized in the table below are just some of the findings of that survey.

Father as abuser	10.9%	girls
	2.6%	boys
Stepfather as abuser	2.7%	girls
	7.7%	boys
Brother as abuser	5.2%	girls
	2.6%	boys
Mother as abuser	0.6%	girls
	3.8%	boys

These figures give an indication not only of the prevalence of sexual abuse by relatives but also of the differences between boys and girls.

For a victim, whether an adult or a child, there is a unique trauma associated with sexual abuse, no more so than for children. There is a further uniqueness when children are abused within the family. Not only are many of the problems compounded, but by very definition many family members may be involved.

The dynamics and the psychological impact for victims are both very well summarized by David Finkelhor and Angela Browne in *A Source Book on Child Sexual Abuse*, part of which is reproduced here with permission.

Traumatic sexualization
Dynamics
    child rewarded for sexual behavior inappropriate to development level
    offender exchanges attention and affection for sex
    sexual parts of child fetishized
    offender transmits misconceptions about sexual behavior and sexual morality
    conditioning of sexual activity with negative emotions and memories

Psychological impact
    increased salience of sexual issues
    confusion about sexual identity
    confusion about sexual norms
    confusion of sex with love and care-getting or care-giving
    negative associations to sexual activities and arousal sensations
    aversion to sex or intimacy

Stigmatization
Dynamics
    offender blames, denigrates victim
    offender and others pressure child for secrecy
    child infers attitudes of shame about activities
    others have shocked reaction to disclosure
    others blame child for events
    victim is stereotyped as damaged goods

Psychological impact
    guilt, shame
    lowered self-esteem
    sense of differentness from others

Betrayal
Dynamics
    trust and vulnerability manipulated
    violation of expectation that others will provide care and protection
    child's well-being disregarded
    lack of support and protection from parent(s)

Psychological impact
    grief, depression
    extreme dependency
    impaired ability to judge trustworthiness of others
    mistrust, particularly of men
    anger, hostility

Powerlessness
Dynamics
    body territory invaded against the child's wishes
    vulnerability to invasion continues over time
    offender uses force or trickery to involve child
    child feels unable to protect self and halt abuse
    repeated experience of fear
    child is unable to make others believe

Psychological impact
    anxiety, fear
    lowered sense of efficacy
    perception of self as victim
    need to control
    identification with the aggressor

When one applies any of these issues outlined in this model to a child being sexually abused by a close relative, the negative consequences for such a child becomes evident.

Hence the child who should receive unconditional love, appropriate affection, protection from all that is harmful, and a sense of mastery in his or her life is tricked or forced into a relationship that stigmatizes him or her, and places what can be an intolerable burden on the child's shoulders. All this can happen in a home or family within our society.

Bibliography
D. Finkelhor, *Sexually Victimized Children* (New York and London, 1979); *idem, A Source Book on Child Sexual Abuse* (Newbury Park, CA, 1986); National Center in Child Abuse and Neglect, *Child Sexual Abuse: Incest, Assault, and Sexual Exploitation* (Washington, DC, 1981); The Research Team, *Child Sexual Abuse in Northern*

Ireland: A Recent Study of Incidence (Antrim, 1990).

M.A.S.

INDIVIDUALISM is an approach to social and ethical theory which advocates the right and freedom of each individual to make decisions and implement actions independently of others. It is to be contrasted with approaches which stress the central role of the community or the State,* *e.g.* collectivism and socialism.*

Modern individualism has its roots in the humanism of the Renaissance, the Reformation's stress on each individual's personal relationship with God, the Enlightenment* teaching on the sufficiency of our individual reason,* and the search for personal and political freedom* which gave rise to Western democracies.

Few would wish to claim that there should be no limits on our individual freedom. Equally, few would admit to holding a view of the community or State which totally submerges the rights (see Rights, Human*) and freedom of the individual. All contemporary social, ethical and political theories have to adopt some position between excessive individualism, which leads to anarchy* or solipsism, and the total loss of the individual in the collective whole.

The Bible teaches that we are made in the image of God* and so are free and of great individual worth. But we are also fallen and sinful, so curbs need to be placed on our individual freedom lest we use it for evil.* Further, the principle of love (see ②) calls us to put others' interests before our own. God leads the individual Christian directly through the Holy Spirit; but he also chooses to use the State, the church* and the Scriptures as expressions of his moral authority. Individual wholeness comes not from unbridled freedom, but from willing submission to God in whatever way his voice is heard.

P.A.H.

INDIVIDUAL PSYCHOLOGY, see ADLER, ALFRED.

INDOCTRINATION is a form of teaching which is technically the opposite of 'education'. Whereas education is, strictly speaking, the bringing-out of the student's innate knowledge and capabilities with the intention that he or she might use these more effectively, indoctrination is the implanting in the mind of concepts and thought-patterns which are essentially alien to it.

Conscious awareness of this process is a modern phenomenon, and in this sense it had been employed as a technique mainly by totalitarian Fascist or communist regimes. These have sought to devise simple formulas and rituals, some of them modelled on Christian ceremonies, to convey their particular ideology. Christians have often been in the vanguard of opposition to this, particularly in Eastern Europe where the church is relatively strong. However, opponents of Christianity frequently claim that indoctrination is a main means of instructing and securing the allegiance of believers, so that the resulting faith cannot be regarded as genuine.

As evidence, one may cite the long tradition of catechesis, which reached the apogee of its development in the 17th century. Both Roman Catholic and Protestant children were expected to learn their catechism, often by heart, as a means of acquiring a knowledge of sound doctrine. The problem with this interpretation is that traditional catechesis understood Christian doctrine as a body of facts, not as an ideological position, and therefore thought of it as more akin to the sciences than to political opinions.

The modern battle against indoctrination in the religious sphere reached its zenith in the mid-20th century, as a result of the work of A. D. Nock and W. Sargant. Since that time, however, Christians have generally taken great care not to present their faith as a mindless form of learning by rote, and have stressed the need for a dialogue with other world-views in which the latter are treated with respect. Further research into the psychology of religious belief (see Psychology of Religion*) has also done much to discredit earlier theories, and to re-establish religious conviction and education as a legitimate form of instruction.

Another factor which has played an increasing role in recent years is the apparent failure of indoctrination when carried out by repressive governments. It is now clear that the main effect of this activity has been the exact opposite of what was intended, and that the most lively intellectual life, as well as much of the most vibrant Christian spirituality* can be found in places where formal indoctrination in a contrary value-system has been most profound. Of course it may also be the case that when Christianity has indulged in indoctrination techniques, it has provoked a similar reaction, as can be seen in the writings of many 18th- and

19th-century atheists. However, it is now obvious that Christian faith does not depend on indoctrination for its survival, and that use of the techniques associated with it is an aberration in Christian thought.

It now seems that indoctrination has been largely discredited as a means of persuading others to accept a particular ideology or belief structure, and that it will become less common (or, some would say, much more subtle) in the future.

Bibliography

H. N. Malony, *Current Perspectives in the Psychology of Religion* (Grand Rapids, 1977); A. D. Nock, *Conversion* (Oxford, 1961); K. R. Popper, *The Open Society and its Enemies*, 2 vols. (London, ⁵1966); W. Sargant, *Battle for the Mind* (London and New York, 1957).

G.L.B.

INDUSTRIAL ACTION, see STRIKES.

INDUSTRIALIZATION refers to long-term economic growth stimulated by applying inanimate energy to the production of goods. In the vernacular, machine-power replaces muscle-power. The early phase of European industrialization (*c.* 1750–*c.* 1850) is often thought of as the 'Industrial Revolution'. During this time, new machines were invented, *e.g.* for tasks such as yarn-spinning; new energy sources were tapped, especially water and steam; and science was used to improve methods of production. Creative imagination seemingly knew no bounds. People began to gain their livelihoods in new ways, and the pace of development quickened in contrast to the slow rate of change in traditional societies.

From the late 19th century, such technologically innovative situations were referred to increasingly as 'industrial societies', implying that the 'revolution' had instituted a new social order. Industrialization does have a certain intrinsic logic. But it is important to remember that the 'revolution' was not made by industrialization alone, but by how industry was *organized* within capitalism. During the 20th century, numerous experiments have been tried with 'socialist' alternatives to capitalist organization, with varying degrees of success. Today, industrialization, organized on predominantly capitalist lines, is a global phenomenon.

Changes of great magnitude are experienced in the process of industrialization. The proportion of people working the land diminishes as workers are absorbed into factory production and, at a later stage, offices. Whereas once the majority was involved in agriculture, in industrial countries this shrinks to only 2%–5%. Within the industry-oriented population, the division of labour becomes very complex, involving especially new categories such as owners of capital, managers and employees. New occupations appear, related to particular skills and qualifications, producing new kinds of inclusion and exclusion. For some, this spells fresh opportunities to engage meaningfully in work. For others, a sense of alienation* from tasks and fellow-workers can occur.

Cities* and towns grow tremendously and, in certain periods, at an accelerating pace. New energies are released and optimism soars. New geographical concentrations of industry and population appear, which, when industries eventually decline, may leave areas of depression and disadvantage. Urbanization* in turn means more impersonal relationships; a 'society of strangers' (Georg Simmel, 1858–1918) comes into being, and with it the challenge of discovering new modes of social cohesion. Lives are deeply affected by working within, and dealing with, large organizations. The sense of being cut off from traditional routines of day and night, seed-time and harvest, as well as the anonymity of life in urban-industrial societies, may help create what Peter Berger (1929–) calls 'homeless minds'.

Industrialization also coincides with political change. New forms of transport and communication make possible the co-ordination of governmental affairs within the nation-state. The same factors also enabled massive growth of trade between industrial and non-industrial countries, thus enhancing productivity, but bringing ambiguous consequences for the latter. And between nation-states, relations have been permanently affected by the industrialization of war. Superior weaponry, along with economic strength and political cohesion, has given power to the advanced societies, often contributing to the underdevelopment of non-industrial countries. Today's so-called North–South* divide is tightly bound up with this process.

Industrialization today represents a cause of major concern over the created environment.*

Many feel that the processes unleashed in the Industrial Revolution have had very negative impacts, seen in air, water and soil pollution, degradations of deforestation* and desertification (often caused by the attempted industrialization of agriculture), urban decay, the 'greenhouse effect', the depletion of the ozone layer, *etc.* Behind this, however, lies the typical Western instrumental approach to nature, that sees it only as the medium of material progress. Green movements, committed to curbing industrial excesses, often fail to appreciate a positive Christian contribution in the concept of stewardship.*

Much debate over the past twenty years has centred on the idea that the advanced societies are moving beyond industrialism into a 'post-industrial' era. Services rather than industrial production engage a bigger proportion of employed populations, new information technologies* enhance mental power rather than muscle power. While the idea of post-industrialism is flawed in many respects, it does seem that the key characteristics of industrial societies are undergoing change. Fresh opportunities are presented to articulate Christian vision in relation to these changes, in management,* education,* urban planning and local politics as well as within churches themselves.

To be effective, however, contemporary involvement relies on lessons from the past. Awareness of how industrialization affected social life grew slowly, and was retarded by at least three factors. 1. One factor was uncritical involvement by Christian people in the processes of technological innovation (see Technology*), factory life and urban development. On good grounds – the 'creation mandate' (Gn. 1:26) – the opportunites of industrialism were seized, but insufficient attention was paid to how Christians might speak on matters such as the use of nature or industrial relations. 2. Another factor was over-reaction against those trying to connect the gospel with modernity,* namely, the 'social gospel'.* Many evangelicals mistakenly confused a *personal* gospel with *individualism*,* thus denying the essential and inescapable sociality of the gospel. 3. A third factor was the social blindness of certain branches of the (especially established or mainline) church, regarding their position in capital ownership or status level, with the result that the church appeared distant from the concerns of those disadvantaged by industrialization.

See also: ECONOMIC DEVELOPMENT.

Bibliography
H. Davis and R. Scase, *Western Capitalism and State Socialism* (Oxford, 1987); K. Kumar, *The Sociology of Industrial and Post-industrial Society* (Harmondsworth, 1978); D. Lyon, *The Information Society: Issues and Illusions* (Oxford, 1988); *idem*, *The Silicon Society* (Tring, 1986).

D.A.L.

INDUSTRIAL RELATIONS. An employer's relationship with his employee has always been a matter of concern for the Judaeo-Christian ethic. The OT prophets inveighed against the oppressive employer (see, *e.g.*, Mal. 3:5). In the NT, Paul outlined the reciprocal duties of masters and slaves (Eph. 6:5–9; Col. 3:22 – 4:1); James condemns the exploitative rich in no uncertain terms (Jas. 5:4). In the Christian tradition, thinkers who are usually classed as socially conservative (*e.g.* Martin Luther* and Richard Baxter*) still encouraged a highly responsible attitude to relationships in the economic sphere.

The phrase 'industrial relations', however, is generally used only in relation to the period since the Industrial Revolution. It concerns both the personal attitudes and the structural arrangements which have characterized the relationship between different groups in industry. Christian thought about industrial relations has proved highly diverse, and tends to be linked to one's evaluation of the morality of the capitalist* system which has fuelled industrialization.* It is possible to identify various important strands of thinking.

1. Class conflict

The Marxist view (see Marxist Ethics*) of employer–employee relations under capitalism is that they are intrinsically exploitative. The employee is alienated* from his work and deprived of a proper reward for his labour. Regarding religious profession as subordinate to economic circumstances, Marxists have viewed Christianity as a tool of social control. Employers drew on the Christian faith to inculcate obedience in the work-place and to channel emotions in a non-subversive way at weekends.

Many Christians have recognized elements of truth in this analysis. They have sought to unmask the oppression which they believe to be endemic in the capitalist system and to proclaim a different, more radical understanding of Christianity. They had faced up frankly to the phenomenon of class conflict and have argued that the proper Christian response is to stand on the side of the powerless and exploited. Such was the thinking which underlay the involvement of many working-class people (especially nonconformists) in the early trade-union movement, and of the various Christian Socialist* groups which have been a feature of English church life since 1850. Trade unions* took on a representative role to bargain collectively for improved wages and working conditions on behalf of employees. Their formation was initially resisted by most employers, and the history of trade unionism has been a long and frequently bitter struggle for the recognition of various rights, not least the right to strike when the process of collective bargaining fails to produce agreement. Over the last century and a half Christians have been involved with others in Western society in a reappraisal of the legitimacy of strikes.* The withdrawal of one's labour, action which in the early stages of the Industrial Revolution was widely condemned as criminal, has come to be seen by many as a morally responsible weapon comparable in significant respects to the fighting of a just war – and to which the criteria of the just-war theory* (just cause, last resort, prospect of success, *etc.*) may also be applied.

There is a certain ambiguity in the Marxist analysis because, though Marxists have not hesitated to condemn the activities of capitalists, their theory actually purports to find the root of the problem in the economic system. Christians of a socialist* ilk have been willing both to attribute personal blame and recognize the possibility of personal redemption. But they too have proclaimed the need for fundamental economic change. Their problem has been that they have been unsure what the nature of this change should be. Workers' cooperatives and guild socialism attracted the interest of British Christian Socialists such as F. D. Maurice* and Maurice Reckitt (1888–1980). State socialism in the shape of nationalized industries eventually won the support of many during the Second World War period and after. Few today would claim that it proved a satisfactory answer. Nationalized industries scored poorly in terms of efficiency and wealth creation: they were subject to political interference which made pursuit of consistent strategies difficult; and they did not fundamentally alter the relationship between managers and the managed, proving even more prone to strike activity than the private sector of industry.

2. The neutrality of the market

A second strand of thought is much more hesitant about applying the categories of Christian moral thought to industrial relations. This is because its general tendency is to objectify economics as a science; how people behave in the economic sphere therefore has an inevitable, morally neutral quality to it. According to Adam Smith (1723–90) and many economic theorists and social psychologists since, human beings are inevitably guided by considerations of self-interest in the conduct of business. They buy as cheaply as they can, and they sell as dearly as they can: not, admittedly, in every individual case, but this is an unmistakable overall tendency, and it is foolish to try to erect an economic system on any other foundation. For an employer, wages* are one cost among many others which he wishes to restrain in order to maintain profit* margins. If these wages are low (in either relative or absolute terms), this does not necessarily mean that he is an oppressive employer. Such an economy may be crucial to the survival of the business, and in turn to the employment of his work-force; he is also acting according to a cost-reduction principle which informs his employees' behaviour in their own economic dealings.

Describing industrial relations in this matter-of-fact, morally neutral way has been characteristic of much recent thinking in the so-called New Right. The market economy with its laws of supply and demand is conceived as possessing an autonomous authority. As Brian Griffiths writes: 'In a market economy wage differentials are determined by scarcity and not the intrinsic moral worth of the job being done . . . The fact that a businessman may earn five times more than a nurse has nothing to do with the moral worth of the respective jobs' (*The Creation of Wealth*, pp. 77, 79). But those who stress the authority of the market system are not themselves neutral. They have a clear tendency to emphasize the system's beneficent effects. Adam Smith spoke in terms of an 'invisible hand' which brought common good out of the process he described: from the self-interest (not the benevolence*) of the butcher, brewer and baker, we can anticipate getting our dinner. There are present-day counterparts to this in the shape of the 'trickle-down theory' which speaks of the poor profiting in the wake of the rich.

With regard to industrial relations, economic theorists of this persuasion may be questioned on at least two counts: 1. It may be asked whether employers' freedom of action really is as constrained as is claimed. They do have choices about the size of their profit targets, and about their relative weighting of costs; these choices are complex and often made in uncertain and pressurized circumstances, but they contain an undeniable moral component. 2. In most Western countries, there is now an abundance of legislation governing the conduct of business, and this provides evidence that, left to itself, the results of the system cannot be trusted to be altogether beneficent. Some of this legislation protects the interests of customers, and increasingly the environment,* but some is directly concerned to protect employees (*e.g.* health and safety legislation).

3. The paternalistic employer

A third strand of thought resembles the second in adopting a generally positive attitude towards capitalism, but is far less complacent. It recognizes the need for reform and the taking of positive initiatives within the system. Many of those who take this view are business practitioners, not theorists.

The relationship between Christianity and capitalism is viewed rather differently from the Marxist understanding, on this way of thinking. The Christian ethic (in particular, its Protestant, Puritan* variety) is seen as a force for social change, not a tool of social control. Virtues inculcated by this ethic, notably the habits of diligence, thrift, and the careful stewardship* of time, money and talents, were indeed one factor in helping to fuel the Industrial Revolution. Business men and women who profited from the process believed that they were fulfilling a God-given mandate: they were seeking to develop their own talents and the earth's resources fully. Involvement in capitalism *per se* was not a matter about which they need feel shame. However, the best of them recognized that the way in which they treated their employees was very much an ethical concern. They felt a responsibility to see that their work-force was decently paid, clothed, fed and housed – and they were concerned too about the wider social environment in which their employees grew up.

In Britain, the late Victorian and Edwardian eras saw the rise of several notable Christian employers who created not just a work-place but villages or suburbs to house their workforce, *e.g.* Titus Salt (1803–76) in Saltaire, W. H. Lever (1851–1925) in Port Sunlight and George Cadbury (1839–1922) in Bournville. In the US, Thomas T. Watson (1914–) of IBM was a man in much the same mould. Such employers have been called 'paternalist', which is a much less complimentary description now than it used to be. Vividly inspired by a (generally nonconformist) faith, paternalist employers could be authoritarian in their sure assumptions about what was good for their employees. But they provided an impressive alternative to inner-city slums, and in many cases helped their workers to help themselves. Above all, they showed that individual segments of capitalism, informed by a Christian critique, were capable of self-reform.

Similar comment may be made about the many reforms which passed their way into the statute book in the 19th and early 20th centuries, shortening factory hours, improving safety regulations and introducing sanitation. In Britain Lord Shaftesbury,* an Anglican paternalist of unflagging energy, was the instigator of many. He was the 'working man's friend', who trusted his own judgment better than the working men themselves; it was a later generation which established the legal rights of trade unions.

The heyday of the Christian paternalist employer was short-lived. The demands of international competition meant that their firms had to expand way beyond their roots to survive. The 1862 Companies Act, which introduced the concept of limited liability for shareholders, made possible the transition from family-controlled business to multinational corporation.* The easiest way for companies to secure the needed infusion of risk capital was through ensuring that the risk was substantially reduced. Although companies with a distinctive ethos often tried hard to maintain it, there was an inevitable diluting of this distinctiveness as power passed effectively from the managers to the shareholders. In addition, the high degree of secularization* and emphasis on personal autonomy* which have characterized the 20th century make the paternalistic model a difficult one to copy.

4. Creative contemporary alternatives

Debate about economic systems and industrial relations have taken some interesting fresh turns in recent years. Private enterprise seems to have won the day over public enterprise, and the class-conflict model is being increasingly discarded. In contrast with the 1960s and 1970s, which were marked by an 'us and them' attitude between management and unions and a high incidence of strikes, the 1980s saw the establishment of much more harmonious industrial relations in Britain. Strike activity decreased, productivity rose, and conditions of work became more flexible. Management and union officials started to establish bridges of confidence and, sobered by experience of a major recession, recognized a common stake in working together for the corporate good. There was a considerable growth in non-unionized industry, especially in the high-tech area, where successful companies which have a record of treating their employees well say they do not provoke any demands for trade unions. In the US, many companies moved from the unionized North to the 'sun-rise' States of the non-unionized South.

From a Christian viewpoint, the fundamental question about industrial relations concerns not trade unions *per se*, but whether individuals throughout a firm or industry are respected and valued. The best firms have the knack of positively affirming the contributions made by employees at whatever level, and of recognizing wisdom and ingenious approaches to problem-solving wherever these are evident. They embrace, consciously or not, the idea of 'quality circles' where concern for quality in all aspects of the operation is a shared responsibility. There are Christian connotations here of the 'body of Christ', with each member having an important contribution to make and being valued for it. Interestingly, some of the companies which practise this most faithfully are Japanese; interdependence appears to come more easily to them than to Westerners with their stronger strain of individualism.*

The continuing role of trade unions is most apparent in industries where the lines between different types of job are clearly demarcated. Unions can provide a structural means for carrying out processes of consultation and negotiation which do not occur in the normal way more informally. Where there is a relationship of trust between managers and union leaders, this can take place in a constructive spirit without rancour. But the time has not yet come when the role of the union as a potential protector of the poor and exploited* can be said to have passed.

In the sphere of management, there are paradoxical trends at work. Alongside a greater emphasis on open communication with and genuine participation of the work-force, there is an affirmation that responsibility* should not be abdicated. It is notable that the idea of worker participation (*i.e.* employee representation on the board of directors), which has been a positive feature of the post-war German system of industrial relations, has caught on less in other Western countries: it has tended to be popular with neither management nor unions. There is evidence that employees wish to be consulted, but they do not wish to be saddled with a responsibility which they see managers as being paid (often very handsomely) to carry. The business heroes of the 1980s were leaders who were not afraid to take hard decisions after consultation. Significantly, the word 'manager' is being more and more replaced by 'leader', because leadership is seen as an inspirational role which demands the quality of communicating a vision to employees and carrying them along with you. The Christian notion of servant leadership* which is yet unafraid to lead from the front does not seem too far removed from this.

A question which is beginning to attract attention, both among Christians and more widely, is the future of the joint stock company. Offering shares to the public is a prolific way of raising money, but it does lead to a thoroughgoing separation between the roles of ownership and stewardship. Many of the shareholders (represented as they usually are by a financial institution) may have no long-term concern for the welfare of the company. Diligent managing directors who have put much time and energy into running a company can then be left rueing their dependence on shareholders' fickleness, especially in an atmosphere where takeover mania is rife. Some Christian writers like George Goyder (1908–) have validly questioned whether the notion of limited liability is compatible with a proper notion of responsibility; Goyder suggests that equity shares should in time be sold back to individuals working for the company. There are certainly some companies moving in this direction. Management buy-outs and employee share-ownership were increasing trends in the 1980s, and there are a few companies which have gone further still, the employees actually owning the company. It is to internal structural issues such as these, which raise very important questions about justice and responsibility, that evaluation of industrial relations may increasingly turn in the present era.

Bibliography

F. Catherwood, *The Christian in Industrial Society* (Leicester, ³1980); D. Clutterbuck and S. Crainer, *The Decline and Rise of British Industry* (London, 1988); J. Davis, *Greening Business* (Oxford and Cambridge, MA, 1991); G. Goyder, *The Just Enterprise* (London, 1987); B. Griffiths, *The Creation of Wealth* (London, 1984); D. J. Jeremy, *Capitalists and Christians: Business Leaders and the Churches in Britain 1900–1960* (Oxford and New York, 1990); R. H. Preston, *Religion and the Persistence of Capitalism* (London, 1979).

R.A.Hig.

INDUSTRY, see INDUSTRIAL RELATIONS.

INEQUALITY, see EQUALITY.

INFANTICIDE is the killing of an infant, whether by the mother (as in some technical usage of the term) or by another, from motives of mercy or malice. This practice was common in the ancient world and has been widely observed in many societies – whether in the case of handicap, for sex selection, or simply to limit family size (or hide illicit pregnancy). The classical practice of exposure sometimes, perhaps generally, led to the death of the child. Christianity is largely credited with the eradication of infanticide from the Graeco-Roman world, at least as a publicly acknowledged practice.

During the following centuries infanticide was seen as a serious crime; but in recent years – partly as a result of the spread of liberal abortion* in the 1960s and 1970s – a radically fresh climate of opinion has come about in which many paediatricians, and parents, regard the handicapped newborn as, in effect, a 'foetus *ex utero*'. He or she is therefore a candidate for neo-natal euthanasia,* since his or her life is burdensome and 'not worth living'. These cases are rarely exposed to public view, and generally take the form of decisions 'not to treat' and/or to withhold nutrition. Equally rarely examined are the complex motives of well-meaning doctors and distressed parents. When they are, it becomes evident that sympathy for the child is only one of many factors in a decision which essentially parallels that of people in ancient

societies in like circumstances. It should be added that good medical practice has always opposed futile treatment, and – as in all terminal care – if the prognosis is very poor the focus may move from active treatment to palliative. Yet in other cases, where the intention is to bring about death because of handicap (see Disability and Handicap*) or for some other motive, good medicine has given way to infanticide.

Bibliography

N. M. de S. Cameron (ed.), *Death without Dignity: Euthanasia in Perspective* (Edinburgh, 1990); H. Kuhse and P. Singer, *Should the Baby Live?* (Oxford, 1985); R. W. Wennberg, *Terminal Choices* (Grand Rapids and Exeter, 1989).

N.M.deS.C.

INFERTILITY, see CHILDLESSNESS; EMBRYO TRANSFER; REPRODUCTIVE TECHNOLOGIES; SURROGATE MOTHERHOOD.

INFORMATION TECHNOLOGY is a particularly significant technology* in today's world. It is concerned not only with the systematic, electronic organization of data and information associated with running everyday life (*e.g.* fax machines, word-processors, databases, computer networks, telephone systems) but also with the automatic functioning of machines at home and at work (*e.g.* washing machines, automated factories) and with the systematic collection and use of data in scientific research and technological development.

Information technology (IT) has both a direct impact on society through the industrial aspects (the number of jobs and skills required; what is researched and funded for production), and an indirect one through who owns and controls information and the attitudes perpetrated by IT. Conversely, IT emerges as part of 20th-century socio-political culture, and so has to be viewed as itself a product of underlying values.*

IT raises a whole range of issues. In particular, increasing automation has changed both the skills required in society and the nature of the jobs relating to information-storing (along with the danger that knowledge can be lost to society following the failure of information-storing machines). Other direct effects of IT are that things that are easier to channel (*i.e.* through an information route in data transmission) tend to get done; its use changes the structure of organizations; the domination of research and development by the military leads to the development of particular types of computer systems which are not always the best for the rest of society; and the government, in order to boost another manufacturing industry in chips, encourages increasingly sophisticated consumer products.

A second range of issues is associated with the information itself. A good starting-point is Kipling's six journalistic questions: What information? Why is it collected? How is it collected? Who is collecting it? When is it collected? Where is it put to use? The collection of information from satellites by the US on the growth of crops means that controllers can anticipate, far better than farmers on the ground in S. America and Africa, what the value of their crops will be, and can alter the market accordingly to US advantage. Although the promise of IT is often seen in terms of accessibility to information, it is frequently available to privileged groups. Thus there are a cluster of concerns to do with ownership, property, control and accessibility. Continuous surveillance on the location of people and objects is now comparatively easy with electronic tagging via radio or global positioning satellite systems (GPS). This can be restrictive, as when used to confine someone to a house instead of sending that person to prison, or supportive, as when used for sailors on ocean journeys.

A further cluster of concerns lie around the quality, truth and context of the data gathered and held. It may contain errors or be out of date, despite EU legislation binding owners to maintain quality (see Data Protection*), and information is often confused with truth. Although much collection is done in the name of Francis Bacon's (1561–1626) aphorism 'knowledge is power', he warned against distortions of knowledge, inaccurate data, taking words for the real world, and following the fashions of the day (Bacon, *Novum Organum*, 1620; ET, New York, 1960). To make meaning and hence truth requires discipline in maintaining quality and a context, which is often assumed or guessed at when processing data.

IT is a source of images, metaphors and language change. The pervasiveness of IT leads to new use of many general terms: programming, input/output (making the machine the centre), hardware/software, *etc*. These begin to change our thinking. This 'computer mentality' emphasizes programmability and information, in which there is a strong element of control. Sherry Turkle (1948–) in her survey *The Second Self* (London, 1984) points out the lure of personal computing as being 'small enough to control and big enough to surprise'. The message for both personal development and limitation is that 'good' means getting others to do your bidding and 'bad' means losing control. There is also a strong and coherently argued belief in artificial intelligence (AI) that there can be valid separation of intelligence from our constraining creatureliness, with the often explicit claim that 'God was not a very good designer'. Thus the 'computer mentality' does not restrict itself to IT but offers a definition of what life is like and is supposed to be like: manipulation of information towards bodiless intelligence. For Jacques Ellul* in *The Technological Society* (1954; ET, New York, 1964, and London, 1965) this change in thought and language leads to the danger of being trapped in our technosphere; for David Lyon (1948–) it reflects the fragmentation of postmodernity (see Modernity and Postmodernity*). However, a few AI experts are already seeing the shallowness of this approach and urge (following Ludwig Wittgenstein*) that meaning and understanding cannot be developed except in a context with sensory input and intentional interaction – in other words, some sort of feeling body, committed to action, in which Christians would immediately recognize the principle of incarnation. The best defence against the computer mentality at a pastoral level, as recommended by Allen Emerson and Cheryl Forbes in *The Invasion of the Computer Culture*, is maintenance of an incarnational approach to life, with acceptance of its relationships, nourished by reading both the Bible and other literature.

When IT practitioners design electronic systems, they have to make decisions, many of which have ethical components (*e.g.* in a hospital computer system, what information one requires and the measure chosen to determine the priority for hospital beds). Most do not recognize this, because one 'just does one's job'; the decision-making is implicit. Society thus seems to change without the opportunity for participatory discussion on its future. There appears to be no point at which it is easy for informed involvement, which means we wake up 'facing tomorrow in a world that we did not expect nor even want' (Langdon Gilkey, *Society and the Sacred*, New York,

1981). There is a need to look at how IT is shaping society and analyse the routes by which decisions are made and, conversely, at how values in society are shaping IT.

Ethical reflection, particularly from a Christian perspective, is very sparse. Why is this? The answer lies partly in the scarcity of work on technology itself and in the complexity of issues raised for a modern society: IT is embedded in every aspect of life. Work on descriptive ethics placed into the context of the biblical imperatives would seem a fruitful direction to take. Just as IT is not deterministic and is shaped by practitioners and the values of society, so this is true of personal and organizational ethics (as demonstrated by the development of the books of law in the Pentateuch). The development of what is, and what is not, appropriate behaviour has proceeded with a number of clashes between groups, resulting from the convergence of technologies that make up IT. Thus hacking and intellectual property rights, for example, become debates in resolving the ethics of different groups. It is clear that 'significant ethical learning occurs primarily in social interactions with real consequences for real actors' (A. Mowshowitz). Christian ethics can be introduced by Christians participating in IT in strategic ways, 'in the world, but not of the world'. Finally, ethics has to be developed from ideologies, in our case Christian theology. There is much work to do in the establishment of a new, socially aware, incarnational theology, opposed to the computer mentality; on the place and role of humanity on earth, faced with competing claims of being animal-like in terms of planet survival, but machine-like in AI; and in opposing the shift towards instrumental ethics developed, says Mowshowitz, from the expertise of computers in comparing means while being less concerned about goals.

Bibliography
General literature on IT and ethics: H. Burkert, 'The Ethics of Computing?', in J. Beleur *et al.* (eds.), *The Information Society: Evolving Landscapes* (New York, 1990), pp. 4–19; C. Dunlop and R. Kling, *Computerization and Controversy: Value Conflicts and Social Choices* (New York, 1991); D. G. Johnson, *Computer Ethics* (New York, 1985); D. Lyon, *The Information Society* (Oxford, 1988); A. Mowshowitz, 'Ethics and cultural integration in a computerised world', in A. Mowshowitz (ed.), *Human Choice and Computers 2* (Amsterdam, 1980), pp. 251–270; D. B. Parker, *Ethical Conflicts in Computer Science and Technology* (Arlington, VA, 1981); D. J. Pullinger, 'Religious-Cultural Contribution to IT', *Information Age* 12.4, 1990, pp. 245–254.

Christian approaches to IT and ethics: A. Emerson and C. Forbes, *The Invasion of the Computer Culture* (Downers Grove, IL, 1989; Leicester, 1990); D. Lyon, *The Silicon Society* (Tring, 1986); D. MacKay, *The Open Mind and other Essays* (Leicester, 1988); S. V. Monsma, *Responsible Technology* (Grand Rapids, 1986).

D.J.P.

INHIBITION is generally used to mean restraint of behaviour, movement, thought or feeling. The term when used in psychology can be a little unclear. It is often used to describe repression (see Repression, Psychological*). This is how Sigmund Freud* uses the term, which he developed when he was dealing with neurological problems. In some areas of psychology, 'inhibition' is used to refer to what happens when unconscious mental mechanisms restrain the free recognition or expression of feelings, thoughts, behaviour and desires. In physiology, inhibition is used to describe what happens when one bodily process blocks another.

Inhibition is often seen as a negative thing, something that must be worked through, so that the person can become uninhibited. However, without some elements of inhibition in our lives there would be anarchy if each person gave way to doing whatever he or she felt like, regardless of whether it was appropriate. Inhibition is a form of control mechanism. A child learns through socialization, for instance, not to tell his aunt that he cannot stand her. But inhibition needs to be distinguished from self-control, because the latter implies a conscious restraint, whereas inhibition is a more unconscious process.

When people have inhibitions this can prevent them being themselves. It may affect the maturity of their relationships. The inhibitions need to be uncovered and worked through so that people are able to make conscious decisions concerning their behaviour, thoughts and feelings rather than being affected by their unconscious. However, even if the inhibition is an unconscious process, people are still responsible before God for how they behave.

H.C.H.

INNER HEALING describes various approaches to counselling and healing* ministry which have developed within the charismatic traditions in the church, including 'the healing of memories', 'prayer counselling' and 'faith-imagination'.

Typically, such approaches seek for an experience of the risen Christ through the Holy Spirit in an individual's life to restore a sense of psychological well-being in deep areas of past hurt and personal pain. Ruth Carter Stapleton (1929–83) used a process of guided meditation in which Jesus Christ is invited in prayer to go back in steps into a person's memory to heal traumatic episodes. Agnes Sandford (1897–1976), Anne White, Francis MacNutt (1925–), Michael Scanlan (1931–), David Seamands and others minister (or ministered) in the belief that Jesus can heal us from past wounds, and fill with his love the places in our lives that have been drained of the poison of hurts and resentments. Prayer counselling,* within a supportive Christian community, may sometimes require sessions of several hours of 'soaking prayer' in a relaxed atmosphere, as a hurting person is enabled to bring his or her needs to God. Though many testify to profound psychological and spiritual renewal through such ministries, and they can be seen as ways of 'casting our anxieties' on to God (see 1 Pet. 5:7), such practices raise questions such as: What theology of prayer* and providence, of health and suffering,* is assumed? What level of dependency on the counsellors may be created? What expectancies for change are appropriate?

Bibliography

D. A. Seamands, *Healing for Damaged Emotions* (Amersham and Wheaton, IL, 1981); R. Carter Stapleton, *The Gift of Inner Healing* (London, 1976); F. S. MacNutt, *Healing* (New York and London, ²1989); A. Sandford, *Healing Gifts of the Spirit* (London 1966).

D.J.A.

INNOCENCE. The concept of innocence appears in various contexts in ethical discourse. It is not to be confused with sinlessness which, if one takes seriously the doctrine of original or birth sin, cannot be predicated of any human being save the incarnate Son of God, Jesus Christ. Innocence is, strictly, innocence of any offence which warrants deprivation of a particular good (*e.g.* loss of liberty because of a crime committed). Innocence in this sense stands in contrast to guilt.*

However, innocence is also related to status. According to just-war theory* (see also War*), non-combatant civilians are to be regarded as innocent of complicity in military action, and are not therefore to be killed. The morality of waging a just war is founded upon the assumption of their innocence, even though many civilians are in fact killed accidentally in modern warfare. Without such a moral distinction war would be difficult to justify under any circumstances (even when pursued to bring about justice); nor could it be prevented from becoming a total onslaught on the lives of all on the opposing side.

Very young children, before reaching the age of moral accountability (*cf.* Dt. 1:39; Is. 7:16; Jon. 4:11), have traditionally been regarded as innocent of personal guilt for sin and as not blameworthy before the laws of society. On the other hand, persons guilty of abusing young children, whether physically, sexually or psychologically, are rightly charged with destroying their innocence, *i.e.* their right to a childhood free of exploitation.

In many legal systems, including the British, persons accused of infractions of the law are presumed innocent until proven guilty, although in others the accused are faced with a much more difficult task of proving their innocence. The presumption of innocence is not an assertion of actual innocence but a declaration of present status before the law until guilt has been established.

Traditionally theology has tended to equate innocence with perfection. Thus the Scottish divine Thomas Boston (1676–1732) headed the first section of his classic work *Human Nature in its Fourfold State* (1720) as *The State of Innocence* (*i.e.* before the Fall). More recently, however, theologians have been inclined to distinguish between the two. F. R. Tennant (1886–1957) pointed out that 'the moral innocence of childhood is not the same thing as eternal perfection . . . There are heights of considerateness and courtesy, for instance, which are inevitably beyond the compass of a child's nature in that they involve knowledge of ourselves and of our fellows derived from experience such as cannot lie within the child's reach' (*The Concept of Sin*, Cambridge, 1912, pp. 37–38). Such a concept of innocence, by not equating it with perfection, clearly allows for moral growth.

Pastorally the concept of innocence is of considerable importance, as the book of Job shows. Job unfailingly protests his innocence to his 'comforters', who wish to make a causal connection between the losses and afflictions from which he is suffering and his personal sins (*e.g.* Jb. 4:7–8). According to Eliphaz, everything evil that befalls you must result from something sinful you have done, which is manifestly untrue (*cf.* Jn. 9:2–3). Significantly Job calls out to the Almighty for vindication, *i.e.* the establishment of his innocence in the face of his friends' well-meaning but erroneous charges (see Jb. 23:3–7). And, just as significantly, Job's friends are rebuked by God for their false and pitiless theology (42:7). Pleas for divine vindication are also a feature of the Psalms (*e.g.* Pss. 38:17–22; 44:20–26) and of the Apocalypse (Rev. 11:17–18). Such pleas presume innocence of charges made and undeservedness of treatment received, not in an absolute but in a none the less real sense.

The book of Job especially is a warning against making an all-too-easy connection between suffering and sin. That *some* suffering is due to personal sin is obvious; that *all* suffering is so caused is patently false, and it is pastorally disastrous to suggest as much.

Unjust (*i.e.* innocent) suffering is a particular theme of 1 Peter. Christians are often called to suffer for offences they have not committed. In such circumstances, their model and inspiration is Christ himself, the supremely innocent (because sinless) sufferer (1 Pet. 2:25) whom the Father vindicated by raising him from the dead (Acts 2:31–33; Rom. 1:4).

D.P.K.

INQUISITION, THE. Commonly understood to be a special church tribunal established to find, combat and punish heresy, the Inquisition was the product of the slow process of historical events. *Inquisitio ex officio* was the term for the universal method of trial procedure in all ecclesiastical courts. Church officials used this common mechanism to create an *Inquisitio heretice pravitatis* ('Inquisition of heretical depravity') to find and remove heresy as early as 1184. By the mid-13th century the papal bull *Ad extirpanda* (1252) had established most of common inquisitorial practice. But it was not until the so-called 'Spanish Inquisition', begun in 1478, that the Inquisition became regularized and enduring. By 1542, Pope Paul III (1534–49; b. 1468) authorized the extension of this model of Inquisition to all Catholic lands as a

response to the Protestant Reformation.

As with all historic courts, the Inquisition had the power to fine, imprison, scourge and confiscate property. As an ecclesiastical court, it could order penance, including the wearing of the family-stigmatizing garment called the *sanbenito*, and, since the Synod of Arles (314) had ruled that heretics may be executed, even impose the death penalty. It is in the means for discovering and convicting heretics that the Inquisition has earned its largest measure of infamy. Following Roman law practice, the Inquisition used torture to extract testimony, and could convict associates of known heretics as *fautors*, or accomplices in heresy. The accused had no counsel before the tribunal and could not know the exact charge against him or the identity of his accuser. All in all, the Inquisition served only to increase levels of tension and a type of sullen obedience in Catholic lands. Since it could not exist in Protestant countries, it proved useless in reversing the Reformation, but in Spain, where it was closely bound up with the State, it did succeed in virtually extirpating Protestantism. The last vestiges of the Inquisition were discontinued in Latin America in 1834.

In its declaration that 'the human person has a right to religious freedom' and that such freedom 'means that all men are to be immune from coercion on the part of individuals or of social groups and of any human power', the Second Vatican Council (1963–65) effectively rules out the use of the kind of force practised by the Inquisition (Walter M. Abbott, ed., *The Documents of Vatican II*, London and Dublin, 1966, pp. 678–679).

Bibliography

H. A. Kelly, 'Inquisition and the Persecution of Heresy: Misconceptions and Abuses', *CH* 58.4, 1989, pp. 439–451; H. C. Lea, *A History of the Inquisition of the Middle Ages*, 3 vols. (1888; repr. New York, 1909); *idem*, *A History of the Inquisition of Spain*, 4 vols. (New York, 1906–07); A. Murray, 'The Medieval Inquisition: An Instrument of Secular Politics', *Peritia* 5, 1986, pp. 161–200; E. Peters, *Inquisition* (New York, 1988); A. S. Turberville, *Medieval Heresy and the Inquisition* (1920; repr. London, 1964).

B.W.R.

INSIDER DEALING is the buying or selling of common stock, bonds, real estate or other assets by those who, because of their favoured position, had access to heretofore undisclosed facts that would change the value of marketable assets, and they and/or their friends acted on the information before the general public had access to the new facts. Is it ethically wrong to take advantage of such privileged information? If so, why? If there were no civil or criminal laws governing such behaviour, as is true in many parts of the world, are there still biblical principles governing such situations?

Insider dealing may take more than one form. It may involve managers or employees who have early access to their business's market-influencing information, which they use to benefit themselves or their friends. Outsiders, such as lawyers, investment bankers, contract printers and others who handle business information, also frequently obtain vital information before it is released to the public. They, too, face temptations regarding its use. The same issues also arise in connection with the work of government commissions, agencies and authorities whose plans and decisions, if known before the general public is privy to them, can offer substantial financial advantages to those with early access to the news of their decisions. The planned location of highways, or the forthcoming change in the interest rates to be charged by a government's central bank, are examples of this.

The OT speaks of God who 'comes to judge the earth. He will judge the world in righteousness and the peoples with equity' (Ps. 98:9). The theme of righteousness* (the character of God's conduct) is found throughout the Bible. And equity (fairness) is an integral part of that doctrine. God will hold everybody accountable for how they manage their 'special opportunities'. Using favoured positions for selfish ends, rather than to promote justice and to seek equity, is absolutely contrary to God's very nature.

The first reason, therefore, that insider dealing is unethical when it is stimulated by the receipt of undisclosed information is that such information conveys with it a 'time advantage'. Its possessors are enabled to reap benefits from others whose actions would have, in all probability, been different if the same information had been in their possession. There is no equity in such a situation. It is like letting one runner start a race ahead of another runner.

Where information technology* and rapid communications are an integral part of the forces of the market-place, reliable informa-

tion is equivalent to power. If God judges how kings and princes use their power, will he not judge those who buy and sell assets in the market-place? Does his interest not extend to managers, lawyers, stockholders and accountants?

It is not stretching the truth to categorize the deliberate use of insider-obtained information for personal profit as stealing, a violation of the eighth commandment (Ex. 20:15). The very fact that the possessors of 'early information' act on it is a clear testimony to the fact that they believe they will gain an advantage by doing so. In doing so, they steal other people's opportunities to re-evaluate and adjust both the timing of their decisions and the amount of money they might accept in trading the revalued assets.

In the last quarter of the 20th century there have been a number of well-publicized examples of insider dealing, and of conspiracy between parties to act in concert, to gain financial advantages over others who had no clue about the unannounced information that affected the value of their holdings. Conspiracy simply enlarges the problem and renders it all the more reprehensible.

This simply adds weight to the argument that most people who acted without the favoured information would have probably altered their economic decisions if they had had that information.

Those who claim to see nothing wrong with insider dealings, on the grounds that the parties who acted without the information were not really hurt but did only what they freely and independently decided to do for other reasons, fail to consider two points: 1. the information that was not available would have altered the decisions, in all probability; and 2. the intent and motives of the parties acting with the undisclosed information was to gain a market advantage that would not have otherwise been available. Insider trading is grounded on the hope of being able to capitalize on other people's ignorance and thereby robs them of an economic opportunity.

R.C.C.

INSTINCTS, see FREUD, SIGMUND; PERSONALITY; PSYCHOANALYSIS.

INSTITUTIONALIZATION. For people who are disabled, living as one of a group in an ordered setting that is physically and psychologically sheltered may have positive benefits. When the conditions of living in such a segregated setting are controlled by another group, and are not self-determined, the key conditions for negative consequences – for institutionalization, for institutional neurosis,* or for the 'social breakdown syndrome' – are set. At the centre of the problem of institution-alization are issues of power,* freedom* and human dignity, on all of which a Christian perspective exists.

Institutionalization is the end-point of a pro-cess, which begins whenever one person con-trols the life of another more than is necessary. The consequences of the process move from excessive dependency and loss of initiative, to the state found in 'total institutions' of marked apathy and social withdrawal, and the end-state of loss of self-initiated speech and normal self-help skills. This process may be aided by institutional procedures, such as 'strip-ping' – the removal of personal possessions and identity as part of the initiation or entry in-to the institution – and may interact with the particular vulnerability of individuals at risk, such as those suffering from chronic psychi-atric conditions.

The classic description of the effects of living in total institutions has been given by Erving Goffman (1922–). In his book *Asylums* he describes vividly the main types of total institu-tion, including homes for the blind, mental hospitals, prisons and concentration camps – also boarding schools and cloistered religious communities – and what he sees as the com-mon outcome of prolonged exposure to any of these institutions. Goffman writes as a sociologist, but essentially anecdotally, and his account is weakened by the selective nature of his evidence, and by the negative outcome he attributes to all institutional care.

What is now clear is that the negative conse-quences of over-protected living can appear even in small groups living in ordinary hous-ing, when the controlling group no longer see the protected group as people with normal feel-ings and status. There is then the opportunity for 'block routines' to occur, denying in-dividual abilities and need, and for exploita-tion and abuse to occur. Essentially the same process can occur where parents of a handi-capped child over-protect their child, and fail to give opportunities to encounter and con-front the wider world, and the process may also occur in cultic enclosed communities. For some, however, institutionalization may not be imposed but may be positively accepted, by those who see a long-term 'career' in hospital as meeting their needs.

There is no biblical account of what would today be called institutionalization. There are some biblical references to prisons, usually pits or underground dungeons, but prisoners would not survive long under such conditions, and many prisoners are recorded as being under 'house arrest' (Acts 28:16, 30). There is evidence from the Middle Ages of lunatics and idiots, as those with psychiatric and learning disabilities were then termed, being restrained under degrading conditions, and the exposure of such patients as a public entertainment in-dicates the lack of humanity in their care. A noticeable feature in the era of 'moral treat-ment' in the early 19th century was the increas-ing respect shown to mental patients, and the encouragement of normal patterns of living and social interaction.

Institutionalization is better prevented than reversed. Wherever a special place of care is needed, or wherever a person perceived as vulnerable or needy is helped, then that person has to be seen as being made in the image of God* and possessed of individual humanity. The aim of those who care in an institutional setting should be to reduce their own power, and to promote independence and choice,* and to encourage contact with and experience of the outside world. Other antidotes include provision of a personally meaningful pattern of daily life, and promotion of the positive pro-spects of relationships and achievements. Overcoming institutionalization lies not only in specific techniques, but in having an overall positive philosophy of care. This is expressed in secular professional terms as, for example, aiming for 'minimal restrictiveness', or in pro-moting 'maximum engagement'; in Christian terms it can be expressed as aiming for life more abundant (Jn. 10:10).

Bibliography

E. Goffman, *Asylums: Essays on the Social Situation of Mental Patients and Other In-mates* (New York, 1961; Harmondsworth, 1968); K. Jones and A. J. Fowles, *Ideas on In-stitutions* (London, 1984).

J.N.H.

INSURANCE is a means of reducing or eliminating risk. It is effected by the payment of a sum of money (a premium) to someone – normally an insurance company –

who undertakes to pay for specified losses should they occur. Thus, the losses of the few are met from the premiums of the many. Early references to insurance are found in the transactions of 17th-century merchants importing and exporting produce by sea. They offered to 'cover' risks of losing both the vessel and its cargo. By the 18th century, insurers were offering to cover fire-brigade bills and other losses.

The idea soon grew that all types of risk could be assessed and insured against. Today, fire and marine insurance still occupies a significant place in the insurance industry. In this century, motoring insurance has emerged as another major market helped by the legal necessity for drivers to be insured for fire, theft and claims by others who may be injured in some way by a vehicle. In the last few decades, aviation insurance has grown significantly as airlines seek to offset the risks of carrying an increasing number of passengers and amount of freight.

A similar but separate category of insurance is *life assurance*. Unlike 'insurance' which covers risks which *may* happen, 'assurance' covers eventualities which *must* occur, the most common being death. Companies specializing in this form of business are known as life companies, a number being run by Christian denominations. Their policies take a variety of forms, the most common being a fixed termly premium which, when invested, will produce a gross sum when the insured reaches a given age, such as retirement, or dies. It would seem virtuous to encourage this type of provision for old age or to help dependants if and when the main household earner is unable to work. In recent years, the idea of insurance to meet cost associated with old age has been extended, at least in the wealthier countries: some States have set up comprehensive national insurance schemes. They cover sickness, unemployment and retirement payments and are financed by premiums paid by both employees and employers and deducted at the time of earning. Though most schemes are subsidized by tax payers, they do ensure that the least well off can receive help when most needed.

Medical insurance is that which covers the risk of a person becoming ill or incapacitated by refunding the cost of expensive treatment. Some employers justify this benefit for employees to ensure their quick treatment. Medical insurers will not cover risks associated with conditions already diagnosed, and are becoming increasingly rigorous in their assessments before entering into contract, insisting, for instance, on blood tests to identify hidden conditions such as HIV or leukaemia. How far a person's privacy should be invaded to ascertain medical or other information is a matter of debate, but risk-bearers, such as insurance companies, are unlikely to expose themselves to undue uncertainty when it is possible to assess it. The community may be willing (through taxes or charities) to bear the cost of uninsurable risk, but demand for such resources usually outstrips supply.

The insurance industry, which takes in premium income of about £25 billion per annum, is regulated by legal statutes. The Insurance Acts of 1977 and 1982 as well as the Financial Services Act of 1986 serve as the foundation in the UK, and the McCarran-Fergerson Act is the basis for State insurance legislation in the USA. Most countries have similar laws. The general public is thus assured of a fair deal and has the means to have complaints heard, which is an important safeguard for those who enter into long-term contracts.

How far insuring against unexpected happenings undermines the Christian concept of living by faith has been raised by some. They cite Jesus' injunction to his followers, 'Do not worry about your life, what you will eat or drink; or about your body, what you will wear. . . . your heavenly Father knows that you need them' (Mt. 6:25–32). The context indicates that Jesus here was warning that a preoccupation with these matters showed a wrong priority; it was unlikely that he was advocating an irresponsible abandonment of duty.

While few risks can be foreseen and therefore guarded against adequately, it seems morally right that those who undertake responsibility for others – partner, children, parents, employees *etc*. – do have obligations to see that, should calamity happen, provision is made to ease the effects on others. While many may be unable to devote a proportion of their income to insurance premiums, it does not nullify the principle of prudence. Insurance is a means of protecting dependants from the adverse aspects of the unforeseen.

Bibliography
A. Gilpin, *Dictionary of Economic and Financial Markets* (London, ²1986); D. Wright and W. Valentine, *Business of Banking* (Plymouth, ³1992).

s.w.

INTELLIGENCE, ARTIFICIAL, see INFORMATION TECHNOLOGY.

INTENSIVE CARE. Intensive care units (ICUs; or intensive therapy units, ITUs) are aptly named. Patients who are endangered by severe and complex illness demand continuous and close observation and finely adjusted treatment. Many patients are totally unable to communicate, and recovery is in no way assured even after days or weeks of intensive care.

An ICU breeds high levels of activity and noise, and of emotional pressures on both staff and relatives. Intensity, complexity and uncertainty provide ample need for pastoral care.

The patient, if alert, may welcome the opportunity to talk over the alarms that his or her critical illness has triggered: the reality of death,* deep anxieties about future health, work, sexual or social status, guilt* over the events preceding admission. But the ICU is a place for an initial caring contact, not for extended counselling.

The unconscious patient may seem to invite silent prayer* more than direct contact. But an unresponsive patient may be much more aware than is obvious. Talking as though he or she were fully awake is recommended.

The relatives of a patient in an ICU will be subject to a variety of feelings. Bewilderment is common; and the first balm for its correction may be the simple expedient of seeking unhurried explanatory interviews with the medical or nursing staff. Anxiety* is universal and anger* is common. It may arise at the perceived losses brought by the illness to the patient and to his or her family, or it may cover an underlying feeling of guilt (justified or not). Anger may be clearly directed to the situation or can be focused aberrantly on the medical facilities or staff. Gentle listening is mandatory to give effective support in this situation (*cf.* Pr. 15:1).

The staff in ICUs will also experience psychological struggles. Fear may be based not on the patient's outcome, but on (often unnecessary) doubts of professional competence. Anger may sometimes be driven by others' therapeutic decisions. Disappointment and fatigue are common. Knowledge of these inner feelings may be helpful to those giving pastoral care.

Ethical challenges made on ICUs primarily concern the starting and stopping of treatment. ICU therapies are powerful and expensive – not only financially but in their adverse effects. Yet they include treatments without which some patients would undoubtedly die: artificial ventilation, cardiac pacing and renal dialysis. Whether or not to implement such treatment and when to withdraw it can be challenging. Starting treatment is easy; trying *everything* possible often seems an attractive plan for the individual patient, and relieves staff of the fear of criticism that necessary therapy has been omitted. But 'everything possible' may lead to long and costly treatment that gives false optimism, prolongs the *relatives'* suffering, increases nursing workload, and consumes limited financial resources. Most treatment is therefore introduced taking account of the overall chances of successful outcome, and the global 'cost' of the treatment concerned.

This is inevitably a grey area. If a patient with a 20% chance of full recovery develops a further complication, should additional high-cost treatment be introduced or should the battle be declared lost and dying with dignity become the chief therapeutic goal? Regarding the patient as a *person*, not as a utility or as a physiological system, affords a Christian perspective on this issue. The difficulty of decision-making is compounded by the frequent difficulty of assessing the chances of survival.

Withdrawing treatment poses no challenge if it is because the patient has recovered sufficiently, but where withdrawal of treatment may lead directly to deterioration or death, the decision becomes harder. Strict criteria to define 'brain death' can be used and are mandatory for any patient where organ donation is considered. Withdrawing life-support treatment in patients who do not fulfil these criteria completely is a medically allowable but a more agonizing decision, often taken after wide discussion with the medical team and with the relatives.

From a Christian perspective, the following seem mandatory for those working in ICUs: the highest possible level of medical and nursing skill; scrupulous but gracious honesty in dealing with data, relatives and staff; humility to recognize that though ICU treatments are powerful, the healing process extends beyond the technical; enthusiasm for research that allows better prediction of outcome; and vigour in arguing for adequate resources to be made available to all likely to benefit from them.

Bibliography

Conference of Medical Royal Colleges, 'Diagnosis of Brain Death', *BMJ* 1976, 2, pp. 1187–1188; S. E. Lammers and A. Verhey (eds.), *On Moral Medicine* (Grand Rapids, 1987); P. Ramsey, *The Patient as Person* (New Haven, CT, and London, 1970).

R.V.

INTENTION may be seen as a kind of desire – a desire for some result which is, or is thought to be, within one's power to produce. Typically, statements about intentions give to the question 'Why?' the answer 'In order that'. It is widely thought that praise or blame is due not so much to the results of our actions as to the intention with which they were performed: 'holy intention is to the actions that which the Soul is to the body', said Jeremy Taylor.* The king of Assyria did not intend to carry out God's judgment on Judah (Is. 10:5–7); on the contrary, his only intention was to destroy and pillage; and therefore, though he was in fact God's instrument, he in turn would be punished. Conversely, someone who meant well, but whose intentions did not in fact work out, may be excused, even praised (*cf. e.g.* Ezk. 33:9).

Cases of accident, or of actions done in ignorance, are special instances of the absence of intention, and hence of the inappropriateness of the praise or blame that might otherwise have attached to them. Our language contains in fact a number of quite subtle distinctions between such notions as 'intentional' and 'deliberate'; or, equally, between 'unintentional', 'accidental', and 'inadvertent'. These seem to refer to different ways in which intention may be present or absent, but in most cases the nuances are unlikely to be of great moral importance.

There are, however, certain qualifications which need to be made to the above. 1. Someone whose good intentions do not work out may well be blamed, not indeed for deliberately producing the unintended results of his or her action, but for failing to foresee that they would occur. (In Eng. and US law this principle is simplified, and one is *presumed* to intend the 'natural consequences' of one's acts even if in fact they were *not* intended. *Mens rea*, 'a guilty mind', is required for criminal guilt, but may take the form of recklessness or negligence as well as of malicious intent.)

2. A result may be foreseen and still not be intended. If I take my car into a busy city centre, I may well foresee that I shall be caught in a traffic-jam, but it would be absurd to say that I intended this. There seems to be a kind of half-way house between the intentional and the unintentional. This becomes important in considering the idea of a 'double effect',* where one particular result of an action is intended, and another (undesirable) one is foreseen though not intended; the agent is clearly responsible for the latter's having taken place (it is not 'unintentional'), but can hardly be said to have brought it about on purpose.

3. Whether an act was intended may depend very much on how we describe the act, for intention rests not in the act itself but in the mind of the agent. Thus, the authorities in Jerusalem certainly intended the execution of Jesus; equally certainly, they did not intend to execute the Son of God (*cf.* Acts 3:17; 1 Cor. 2:8). Although there were not two separate actions, the action could be described in more than one way, and the description 'executing the Son of God' did not occur in their thoughts.

4. Intention is relevant only to judging the moral worth of the agent. It is of no use in deciding between possible courses of action. The question 'Was A right to do such-and-such?' is ambiguous; it may mean 'Did A choose the correct course of action?' (where intention is not relevant) or it may mean 'Ought I to think well of A?' (where it certainly is). And I cannot escape the duty to weigh the rights and wrongs of alternative courses of action by telling myself that my intentions are good.

Bibliography

G. E. M. Anscombe, *Intention* (Oxford, 1956); J. L. Austin, 'A Plea for Excuses' and 'Three Ways of Spilling Ink', in *Philosophical Papers* (London and New York, ²1970).

R.L.S.

INTEREST is the charge paid for using borrowed funds. It is generally expressed as an annual percentage rate paid on the outstanding balance due to the creditor. Interest is therefore the 'rent' paid for using someone else's money.

The OT law forbade the Israelites to charge interest on loans to their needy fellow believers (Ex. 22:25; Lv. 25:35–38; Dt. 23:19–20). To do so was to become a usurer – a transgressor whose explicit offence was to add to the burdens and distress of a 'sister or brother' when it was in the lender's power to eliminate the added hardship. Those who had experienced the grace and mercy of God as he tended to their needs were to offer the same kindness and help to their needy neighbours.

Does this mean, then, that all interest is forbidden by Scripture? If not, then when and under what circumstances is it now legitimate? Is there a distinction between interest and usury in Scripture? Are commercial loans, institutional loans to individuals, and personal loans all to be treated alike in the light of Scripture?

1. *Interest as usury.* Biblically, interest and usury are synonymous. The root meaning of interest (usury) is 'to bite' and 'to exact' something from another. In other words, the lender has the legal right to take a bite out of the borrower's future income, over and above the repayment of principal. But the word 'interest' does not embody in itself the idea that a specific interest charge, when it moves from say 6% to 8%, suddenly crosses an ethical line that thereafter places interest in a negative category. In modern usage the word 'interest' is generally associated with acceptable charges, and the word 'usury' carries with it illegal or immoral connotations. No such distinction is found in Scripture.

When, then, is interest acceptable and when is it unjust or immoral? a. It is unacceptable when the poor in the family of God are in distress, and the wealthy 'bite' their future. b. When a governing body sets a legal limit on the interest that can be charged, in an effort to prevent the wealthy and powerful from exacting too much from the less fortunate, it is immoral to break that law. c. It is immoral to charge high interest when natural disasters create tough times for everybody. d. In addition, people who are not poor are warned against going into debt* in an effort to advance their standard of living beyond that which God has providentially provided for them up to that point in time. e. Moreover, a distinction needs to be made between immorality and mere foolishness, although foolishness itself can result in poor stewardship* and so become sin. When a person is not forced by circumstances to borrow money, yet decides knowingly to pay high rates of interest on borrowed money, that person has no ground later to complain of usury. On the other hand, all lenders will be judged for the attitudes of their hearts, and the presence and absence of greed in their character (Rom. 14:11–12; 1 Cor. 4:5).

2. *Lending to the poor.* When an individual Christian is asked by a poor fellow believer to lend him or her money, what interest charge should be placed on the loan? According to Scripture, no interest should be charged (Ex. 22:25; Lv. 25:35–38; Dt. 23:19). By not charging interest to such individuals, we manifest the heart of love that God has for us by not compounding their distress. In fact, the person who is gracious to the poor is said to be lending to the Lord, who will repay the lender for his good deed (Pr. 19:17; 28:8; 2 Cor. 9:6–8).

3. *Lending in the history of the church.* The medieval church, and many monastic orders and merchant guilds operating under its power and influence, condemned any charging of interest to anyone or any institution, rich or poor. Interest-taking was ground for excommunication from the church. Many of the economic practices of the Middle Ages, however, came under scrutiny during the Reformation. Its leaders, though, did not always agree on the appropriate interpretation of past practices. For example, Martin Luther* held to the condemnation of charging interest, no matter the economic context, but John Calvin* encouraged the lending of money at interest when the borrowed money was to be used in commerce. The Protestant movement gradually came to reflect the Calvinistic viewpoint in the market-place until the distinctions between lending for business purposes and personal reasons, or lending to the prosperous or the poor, have all but been forgotten in both institutional lending and individual or personal lending. Christians need once again to struggle with these distinctions; Scripture seems clearly to rule out the charging of interest to the poor in the church.

4. *Personal and commercial borrowing and interest.* The vast majority of biblical references to money, interest, borrowing, debt and lending are in the context of one individual dealing with another individual. Furthermore, the references are predominantly concerned with the plight of the poor, not the wealthy. It is clear, though, that banks (see Banking*) and institutional lending and borrowing were known (Mt. 21:12; 25:27; Lk. 19:23). Money-changers and bankers who made loans and accepted deposits were commonly understood. It is the modern phenomenon of establishing corporate institutions that are given the legal status of 'persons' (with those who manage them being shielded from many of the worst aspects of personal liability and accountability) that has given rise to the

assumption that God's principles governing debt and interest no longer apply. This is, however, mistaken, for individuals will be held accountable by God in the final judgment for every thought, motion, intention, word and action for which they are responsible, no matter the context – institutional or personal – in which they occur (Rom. 14:11-12; 1 Cor. 4:5). Those who work in corporate entities are simply stewards of other people's wealth, whatever the procedures by which lending and borrowing take place. Borrowing for commercial purposes, or borrowing for personal purposes when there is no hardship involved, is not forbidden. Such borrowing may be deemed unwise (Pr. 22:7; Hab. 2:6-7) but it is not the focus of biblical teaching. It is accurate, though, to say that all debt is discouraged in Scripture.

5. *Interest related to widespread hardships.* The account of Nehemiah caring for the poor, oppressed Jews (Ne. 5) reveals in a tangible, visible way God's concern for his children, and his view of justice, in the midst of widespread economic distress. It is clear in the Nehemiah account that it is unconscionable for one person to take advantage of another person's hardship by placing more burdens on him or her. Times of trouble are times of testing for both the rich and the poor. The poor are tested in their faith in God who has promised that he will never leave or forsake his children during economic distress (Heb. 13:5-6). The rich are tested to see if they will love their neighbours, even as God has loved them.

Interest, the price paid for borrowed money, is but one kind of price/commodity relationship that comes under the scrutiny of God's justice. The church, in the Middle Ages, was concerned with interest-rate issues, just prices* and just wages (see Wage*). We in the West today are likely to scoff at efforts by the government (or by the historic church) to regulate the prices of money, wages and commodities. We tend to put our trust in the forces of the free market and believe that these will set better prices than any individual or group can. This is economically defensible in many situations. But when natural disasters, and/or market interruptions, create monopolies,* acute shortages of necessities or other market irregularities, some form of regulation may well be needed. After all, the free market is itself a regulatory force that generally works, but when it stumbles, another mechanism may be needed if the market is to behave in a just man-

ner. This is so because the fallen nature of many individuals will show itself, as they perceive disastrous circumstances to be an opportunity to gain wealth through the distress of others (*cf.* Am. 8:5-6).

R.C.C.

INTERDEPENDENCE, see GLOBAL ETHICS. [15]

INTERIM ETHIC. According to J. Weiss (1863-1914) and Albert Schweitzer (1875-1965), Jesus proclaimed the coming of the kingdom of God* as a cataclysmic event bringing human history to an end. He expected this event in the very near future – in a matter of weeks or months rather than years. His ethical teaching was not intended for the period after the kingdom came (when it would no longer be required). Rather, he demanded repentance* as an 'interim ethic' during the brief period before its coming. Time was so short that the dominant factor in human life was the coming of the kingdom, and therefore people must make every effort in order to prepare themselves for it. The situation was like that in a time of war or in running a fast sprint where people can be called upon to behave in a concentrated and demanding way for a comparatively brief time. Jesus made intense demands (*e.g.* for self-renunciation) that could not be maintained over a long period as a pattern for normal life.

It follows that, since Jesus was wrong about the imminent coming of the end, this crisis-ethic is no longer required of his followers; the intense living demanded in the Sermon on the Mount* is not a viable option for Christians today.

This understanding of the ethics of Jesus rested on two shaky foundations: 1. a particular understanding of the imminent future coming of the kingdom of God which has been shown to be questionable by many scholars; 2. an understanding of Jesus' teaching as impracticable except for a short period of crisis.

See also: ESCHATOLOGY AND ETHICS.

Bibliography
A. Schweitzer, *The Mystery of the Kingdom of God* (London, 1914).

I.H.M.

INTERNATIONAL ORDER. The claim to sovereignty is inherent in the structure of

States,* and external or internal challenges to a State's sovereignty over a particular territory and particular peoples have always been a leading cause for conflict between and within States. For centuries, States have recognized the sovereignty of other States by treaties. The Treaty of Westphalia (1648) marks a watershed in relations between States. At Westphalia, the princes of Europe recognized that religious conflict could not be settled by military means and acknowledged each other's sovereignty over particular peoples and territories. Since Westphalia, the principle of sovereignty has increasingly been recognized as the principle on which international relations should be based.

This is not to say, of course, that it has never been challenged and even violated. Within Europe, it has frequently been challenged by political and military adventurism. The history of European imperialism, moreover, shows us how the European powers, for defensible and indefensible reasons, violated the sovereignty of other nations. One consequence of European imperialism has been the emergence of nation-states whose territories are defined by the areas of influence of the former imperial powers. Within such arbitrarily defined geographical boundaries, mutually antagonistic groups of people divided along religious, ethnic and tribal lines are often to be found. Conflict among such groups and the oppression of one group by another has become one of the great international problems of our time.

These problems have been greatly exacerbated by the dramatic and unprincipled expansion in international arms trade (see Armaments*) in recent years. During the Cold War period, each superpower and its allies justified this trade in terms of the geo-political interests of their own bloc. The trade has continued, however, and there are few signs of its abatement. The hardware that is being bought and sold is of increasing sophistication, and the trade often shows a disregard for the moral credentials of purchasers. Both the West and the former Soviet Union have been implicated in supplying arms to morally bankrupt governments. These arms have been used both in cross-border conflicts and in the suppression of legitimate movements within nations. Both powers have also supplied arms to guerilla movements with very dubious motives, and this has often caused significant regional destabilization.

Apart from the two world wars, this century has been witness to numerous regional and local conflicts. Many of them appear to be endemic and show few signs of resolution in the foreseeable future. Diplomacy, which for long has been regarded as an instrument for negotiation and the maintenance of peace, has to be complemented by the principle of accountability. Both the League of Nations and its successor, the United Nations, were established to provide recognition for the sovereignty of States *and* accountability for their behaviour in the international arena. The General Assembly of the United Nations and the International Court of Justice, although their powers are limited, both provide, in different ways, access for *nations* to the international community. It is the Security Council of the UN, and particularly its permanent members who have the veto, however, with whom real power resides. The Council can secure compliance of its resolutions by the use of mandatory sanctions (see Economic Sanctions*) and even the use of force.

Recent events, such as the Gulf War of 1991, have shown that when great-power rivalries can be set aside for international good, the Security Council is able to function relatively effectively. It is possible, however, that in the light of significant changes, both globally and regionally, its structure and composition need to be reviewed. The five permanent members, for instance, were chosen at about the time the Cold War was beginning and before the settling-in of the era of decolonization. It is notable that there is no permanent member from Africa, and that significant regional powers, such as India, are not permanent members. If the Council is to continue to have credibility in different parts of the world, it is important that its structure should reflect its international nature. At the same time, it is necessary to ensure that members, and especially permanent members, of a powerful Security Council should have representative and accountable governments.

While the UN has brought about a greater recognition and respect for the sovereignty of *States*, the doctrine of non-interference in the internal affairs of such States has prevented ethnic and religious groups and individuals with grievances from gaining access to its various forums. In this matter, the practice of the UN is at variance with regional bodies, such as the European Court of Human Rights, to which individuals and groups *can* gain access. Recent media attention to the genocidal* policies and human rights (see Rights, Human*) abuses of several authoritarian governments has demonstrated the need for the UN to be able to act constitutionally in these areas.

Cross-border conflicts, civil war and repressive regimes are all responsible for the large numbers of displaced people in the world today. The UN has had a crucial part to play in meeting the immediate needs of refugees and in the process of their settlement, either in the country to which they have fled or in a third country. The poorer countries of the world are currently bearing the greatest burden as far as refugees are concerned. There is a need to ensure that the richer countries do not shut their doors on refugees and that procedures for entry and settlement remain fair and within the scope of judicial review. In a highly mobile world, it is likely that the movements of people will continue. It is highly desirable that policies for immigration* and asylum should be fair and be seen to be fair. Many parts of the world, particularly the industrialized countries, will continue to experience shortages of labour, making some immigration necessary. In such cases, it would be important to ensure that immigration policies do not discriminate on the basis of caste, creed or colour. At the same time, immigrants and refugees will need to be made aware that they should respect the values of the host society, while at the same time making their own contribution to it.

Fair immigration and refugee policies, however, cannot be the panacea for all the world's ills. These are more likely to be addressed by the emergence of governments that are accountable both internationally and to their own people, and by fairer terms of trade. Stabilization of commodity prices, compensation for the victims of particularly sharp price fluctuations in the commodity markets, the lowering of tariff barriers, the prevention of 'dumping' of agricultural produce and good practice by multinationals* are some of the ways in which a more stable international order can be promoted by fairer trade policies.

See also: INTERNATIONAL TRADE.

Bibliography

W. Bello, *Brave New Third World* (London, 1990); W. Brandt (chairperson), *North–South: A Programme for Survival* (Report of the Independent Commission on International Development Issues: London and Cambridge, MA, 1980); Catholic Institute for International Relations, *States of Terror* (London, 1989); M. Frost, *Towards a Normative Theory of International Relations* (Cambridge, 1986); D. Joly, *Refugees in Europe* (London, 1990); H. de Soto, *The Other Path* (London, 1989).

M.J.N-A.

INTERNATIONAL TRADE.

The motive and justification of all trade* is that there is a benefit to both parties. International trade enables primary producers to exchange commodities for manufactures and manufacturing countries to specialize in what they do best. The whole process keeps down the cost to the consumer and promotes economic growth.

The long period of economic growth following the Second World War was the result of the progressive lowering of trade barriers between the leading industrial countries under the General Agreement on Tariffs and Trade (GATT), which enabled world trade to grow twice as fast as the growth of the national product in the main signatory countries. This was in sharp contrast to the disastrous trade wars leading up to the Second World War in which the leading countries erected tariff and quota barriers against imports.

The lowering of trading barriers does not solve all problems. There is still an imbalance between the rich North and the poor South (see North–South Divide*). The transnational companies, the main vehicle of technology transfer and world trade, are more powerful than some sovereign States (see Multinational Corporations*). But it needs the vigorous engine of expanding trade to raise the price of the commodities on which so much of the Third World depends.

Neither the Communist countries nor the Third World of developing countries have had the confidence to lower their tariffs and import quotas, and it is argued that the Japanese structure of interlocking company ownership has placed more effective barriers against imports than any tariffs or quotas. But the opening of the N. American and Western European markets to imports and the growth in world trade has done far more for the Third World than any direct aid could do. This has the added advantage of strengthening the trading sector in those countries and of avoiding the all-too-easy diversion of direct aid to less worthy causes.

The main exceptions to the GATT process

have been textiles and farm produce. The industrialized nations all had substantial labour-intensive textile industries in which the developing nations, especially South Korea, Hong Kong, Taiwan and Brazil, had a strong competitive advantage. To give the industrialized countries time to restructure their industries and redeploy their labour forces from textiles, they were allowed to place temporary restrictions on imports. By the 1990s this process had been substantially completed, and the 'Uruguay Round' of GATT negotiations put a terminal date on the restrictions on textile trade.

The removal of restrictions on farm products has been much more difficult. Following the Second World War, most countries believed in the strategic necessity for self-sufficiency in farm products and most subsidized their farms. The European Community's Common Agricultural Policy was matched by similar farm subsidies in the USA. As farming methods improved, these subsidies produced substantial surpluses which were dumped on world markets at prices which other countries could not match. This caused damage to food-exporting countries like Canada, Australia, New Zealand and Argentina, and especial damage to actual and potential exporters in the Third World, who need the hard currency from farm exports to expand production and feed their rising populations (see Hunger, World*).

For these reasons, the Uruguay Round proposed the mutual reduction of export subsidies, which should raise world prices for farm products, reduce food prices in Western Europe, and bring agricultural trade into line with the fair-trading rules of GATT. The Uruguay Round locked into place the agreement to phase out subsidies and the dumping which so harms the Third World producers, who should benefit substantially from better and fairer prices of temperate farm products on world markets.

GATT also regulates trading practices. It forbids 'dumping', *i.e.* the sale of goods in export markets at well below their price in the exporter's domestic market. It also prohibits government subsidies, which enable producers to export at less than the competitive cost. It does not prohibit 'social dumping', *i.e.* exports from countries which are cheap because their governments do not impose on their industries the high social security costs which they carry in most of the industrial democracies. In most

of the Third World, the cost of labour is, in any case, a fraction of the cost in the industrial democracies, but the productivity is correspondingly low. When productivity rises, so do wages, as has happened in the newly-industrialized countries (NICs) such as Singapore, South Korea, Taiwan and Brazil.

Despite the enormous and evident benefits of liberalized trade under the GATT system, governments are under constant pressure from protectionist lobbies. This is because the benefits of liberalized trade are general, while the perceived threat to particular industries is specific, and those who feel threatened (*e.g.* workers, companies and regions) are organized and articulate. So liberalized trade has to be supported by political policies which enable industries to restructure, workers to be retrained, and alternative investment to be encouraged. And where, as in the case of Japan, cross-ownership in industry, banking and commerce makes reciprocal trade difficult, it is sometimes necessary to meet the genuine threat from an industry whose exports are based on an effectively protected domestic market.

There are often demands for economic sanctions* against countries whose domestic human rights (see Rights, Human*) policies are offensive. If trade sanctions can be circumvented, as they so often can, then they harm only the countries imposing them. In Iran, following the imposition of sanctions when American embassy officials had been taken hostage in 1979, foreign trade went up by 50%. Sanctions against Rhodesia (now Zimbabwe) in the 1960s and 70s were circumvented by switching trade through South Africa. Some sanctions against South Africa's apartheid* policy do seem to have had some effect, as do the sanctions against Iraq following its invasion of Kuwait in 1991. So trade sanctions can be used only very selectively.

There is considerable concern about the trade in arms (see Armaments*), especially with those countries which can least afford this diversion of their very scarce resources. During the Cold War (1947–75), it was argued that if the Western countries did not supply, the Soviet Union would do it. But, following the end of the cold war, a mutual reduction of armament output seems possible. One of the problems of government-to-government aid is that it enables the receiving government to switch expenditure from the needs of its own people to armaments. A mutual agreement among the arms-producing countries to limit production and trade would not prevent all trade in arms, but it might help to reduce it and to divert some trade into more benign channels.

GATT is an 'agreement', not a treaty, and its rulings on disputes are implemented because the parties wish the agreement to continue. The agreement depends in particular on the two largest trading partners: first the European Union, which negotiates trade agreements on behalf of all member States; and secondly the USA. Both see it as in their interests and in the interests of the rest of the world that the agreement should continue.

See also: ECONOMIC DEVELOPMENT.

F.C.

INTROVERSION, see JUNG, CARL; MYERS-BRIGGS TYPE INDICATOR.

INTUITIONISM is both a philosophical and ethical theory concerning the direct and immediate apprehension of a concept, proposition or entity. In epistemology it refers to the direct knowledge of things about which there can be no argument. It implies a direct contact by the mind with reality. Truth is thus understood directly, though this may involve the use of accumulated experience and previous knowledge before that act or moment of intuition when the knowledge is directly achieved and known to be certain. In the same kind of way, in ethics, moralists have claimed that there is a direct knowledge of moral certainties and realities. In this way, intuition is the intellectual counterpart of instinct and offers an immediate grasp by the intelligence of moral reality.

This reality might refer to knowing intuitively that certain kinds of actions are right or wrong by direct intuition of their rightness or wrongness. It might refer to knowledge of the rightness or wrongness of specific actions in their particular contexts. In that sense, it might be seen as a moral skill or sense. It might refer to the knowledge that certain statements or propositions about what is right and wrong are true and reliable.

Behind and beyond these definitions is the desire to refute utilitarianism (see Consequentialism*) and all teleological* views of morality which make the rightness or wrongness of actions, individually or as a class, depend on the calculation of consequences. In this spirit H. A. Prichard (1871–1947), Henry Sidgwick (1838–1900) and W. D. Ross (1877–1940)

argued for there being prima-facie duties. These were obvious to the morally tutored, and once perceived, required, and could have, no other justification than themselves. Thus certain obligations were perceived as ultimate, underivative, primitive, unanalysable, simple, indefinable and unique. This gave a bedrock of objectivity to the process of moral discussion and argument and a court of last appeal where the sceptic could be pointed in the right direction, and, if the situation were fully and properly explained, then would 'see' what was morally correct with no further argument. The use of the metaphor of sight and vision is no accident, for the general epistemological thrust of intuition has drawn heavily on mathematical and geometric models which are directly seen. It is, however, not so easy to find some organ of moral insight which would enable the morally blind to see.

In opposition to the naturalist* and utilitarian schools of morality, Ross argued that there were certain prima-facie dutes which were immediately and directly obvious to all who considered them. In spite of then offering supporting arguments, Ross, however, claimed that promise-keeping, fidelity, reparation, gratitude, justice, beneficence, non-maleficence and self-improvement were such prima-facie duties. This meant that they were not only perceived as binding obligations but that they must be done, unless some other duties or circumstances intervened. This is the infamous *ceteris paribus* (other things being equal) clause, much quoted in modern moral philosophy. Things are not very often equal, and so people are provided with an escape by claiming some overriding obligation and significant change in circumstance. Ross did not think that the plain man would immediately perceive the moral correctness of these duties, but that after sufficient tutoring, explanation and clarification he would come to 'see' the truth. Critics responded that there is great variety in different cultures about which duties are binding, and the very variety shows the falsity of Ross's position.

G. E. Moore (1873–1958) argued that the 'goodness' is an indefinable, non-natural quality. Against the naturalists who committed the naturalistic fallacy* (*i.e.* explaining the nature of the good in terms of some qualities other than goodness itself), Moore offered a means of solving moral debates and resolving moral disputes. He believed that anyone with the necessary insight would know what goodness was when presented with it. The empiricists* rejected this as resting on hidden rational premises, requiring some unknown organ of perception, and failing to grasp that morality was about emotions and sympathy.

For the Christian, direct knowledge of God and his will is no surprise. When such knowledge is present, as in Abraham's call to sacrifice Isaac, then obedience is the only proper response. The direct awareness of the moral structure of reality and of human being is matched by an awareness of the validity of God's laws, which are universally valid, though they may find different expression in different settings, thus confusing the relativist. Bringing others to the direct awareness comes by faith and God's Holy Spirit.

Bibliography

A. C. Ewing, *The Definition of Good* (New York and London, 1947); G. E. Moore, *Principia Ethica* (Cambridge, 1903); W. D. Ross, *The Foundations of Ethics* (Oxford, 1939).

E.D.C.

INVESTMENT is thought to occur if there is an increase in the capital stock of a firm or a nation over a period of time, usually a year. An increase in a firm's stocks is also regarded as investment. In addition popular usage refers to the purchase of financial assets and stocks and shares as investment, but this is regarded by economists as having more in common with saving. Capital investment has the property that the spending does not add to consumption immediately, but does produce consumable goods and services in the future. Gross investment is the total spending on investment in a year, whereas net investment is the gross investment less the value of depreciation allowed for wear and tear.

Investment is important because it is thought to be a major source of increasing the productive capacity which underlies economic growth. Not all would see economic growth as a priority, but investment is in any case required to maintain a steady state because capital depreciates. Donald Hay in *Economics Today*, ch. 8, reviews the debates amongst economists over economic growth. Investment is also the major route through which technical progress can be achieved. Infrastructure investment is thought to be vital in facilitating the operation of the whole economic life of a country and usually takes place via public investment.

What determines the level of investment in an economy is not well established. A number of theories claim to capture the important elements of private-sector investment demand, but empirical studies suggest that none wholly explains it. The two main determinants of private-sector investment demand are thought by economists to be the rate of interest* and changes in national income. An increase in the rate of interest is thought to cause a decrease in the level of investment. Other factors which can influence investment, but in a less fundamental way, are those which affect the relative costs of capital and labour, *e.g.* wage and tax rates. Also important are the ability of a country's capital goods to produce industry in order to meet increased demand, and the availability and cost of imported capital goods. Businessmen and the Confederation of British Industry suggest that confidence is a vital factor determining firms' investment plans, but economists find this hard to measure or to include in empirical estimates of investment. Public investment has played an important role in theories of the economy that are based on the ideas of John Maynard Keynes (1883–1946). Keynesians have argued that public investment (*e.g.* in housing stock or infrastructure) can play an important catalytic role in stimulating an economy and leading it out of recession.

Christians are encouraged to view their whole life and decisions, as well as their stewardship* over money* and wealth, in terms of investment opportunities. Unlike the secular world, what is important is not the monetary rate of return but the contribution made to the eternal and undecaying kingdom of God: 'store up for yourselves treasures in heaven' (Mt. 6:19–21). In addition, if God has made an investment in Christians, through bestowing gifts or talents upon them, he will require some return (Mt. 25:14–30; Lk. 12:48). One aspect of the judgment over the stewardship of resources will be in terms of what wealth, capital or income has done for those who are in need (Ps. 41:1; Lk. 16:9). Given that poverty* is very much related to unemployment* and old age in our present economy, one might translate this biblical concern with stewardship and the poor into how far Christians have used their resources to provide stable jobs for the poor and hence an ability to support themselves through work. The absence of work* is demoralizing and limits people's ability to live in the image of God.*

For the elderly, a system which ensures an adequate pension is an important priority. Alan Storkey, in *Transforming Economics*, provides a range of other ideas for Christians who are concerned about investment and employment generation.

These prescriptions need not be only for the very wealthy; they can be enacted on a more humble scale by buying services instead of the increasing trend towards 'do-it-yourself'. There are also many applications of the investment paradigm in decisions about use of time, *e.g.* setting aside time to visit lonely or shut-in members of a congregation.

The OT has much instruction about making loans or investments without interest (*e.g.* Lv. 25:35–37), in particular within the people of God (Dt. 23:19–20). Some Christian economists think that Christians should be following these instructions today, and that there would be benefits from applying these principles more widely (M. Schluter, *The Old Testament Ban on Interest*; P. S. Mills, *Interest in Interest*).

Bibliography

D. A. Hay, *Economics Today* (Leicester, 1989); J. M. Keynes, *The General Theory of Employment, Interest and Money* (Cambridge, 1936); P. S. Mills, *Interest in Interest: The Old Testament Ban on Interest and its Implications for Today* (Cambridge, 1990); M. Schluter, *The Old Testament Ban on Interest: Its Relevance for Reform of Britain's Industrial Structure in the 1980s* (Cambridge, 1986); A. Storkey, *Transforming Economics: A Christian Way to Employment* (London, 1986).

S.D.

IN VITRO FERTILIZATION, see REPRODUCTIVE TECHNOLOGIES.

ISLAMIC ETHICS. The basis for all behaviour among Muslims is the *Sharī'ah* or Law of Islam. Literally, the word means a 'path' and is sometimes used interchangeably with *fiqh*, although this latter word can also denote specific schools of Law within Islam. In Sunnī Islam there are four schools of Law which are traditionally recognized: the *Ḥanafī*, the *Shāfi'ī*, the *Mālikī* and the *Ḥanbalī*. The *Shī'a* have their own school known as the *Ja'farī*. *Fiqh* is divided into the *uṣūl al-fiqh* (the roots or principles of the Law) and the *furū'al-fiqh* (the branches of the Law). The former are, in order of importance: the *Qur'ān* itself; the *Sunnah* or the practice of Muḥammad based upon the *ḥadīth* or carefully collected traditions about him; *ijmā'* or consensus in the community; and *qiyās* or analogical reasoning. The latter deal with the elaboration of the Law in particular areas and its application in specific cases.

It is basic to Islamic Law, as indeed it is to all law, that human beings are accountable for their actions. The earliest theologians in Islam, the *Mu'tazila*, held that human free will (see Free Will and Determinism*) is necessary if the Qur'anic view of God's justice is to be preserved. God cannot judge beings who are not free to act one way or another. Such a view was rejected by the extreme predestinarians who held that it compromised God's absolute power. A compromise was reached ultimately between these two positions, which taught that all was decreed by God but that human beings have the power to 'acquire' (*kasb*) what has been decreed and are thus accountable. 'Modernist' Muslims have sometimes interpreted this to mean that God has determined the total possibilities in this universe. It is for human beings to decide which they are going to make actual. It is this which makes them accountable.

Schools

It is perhaps worth noting that the first three schools of Sunnī Law all have a principle of movement within them which allows the jurists to limit or to extend the application of a particular law in view of the specific conditions existing at the time. Unfortunately, on occasion, this principle was abused and gave rise to excessive casuistry.* This, in turn, caused a reaction: all forms of juristic opinion (or *ra'y*) were rigidly excluded and greater and greater reliance was put on deduction from the Qur'ān and *ḥadīth*.

Ṣūfism (or Islamic mysticism) was yet another reaction to the emphasis on the letter of the Law in the schools. By contrast, the Ṣūfis were concerned with a personal experience of God and, therefore, with the interior life. They tried to give a spiritual meaning to the Law of Islam and often came into conflict with the orthodox. In extreme cases, a rejection of traditional interpretations of the Law resulted in antinomianism* which, at times, could be deliberately cultivated – allegedly so that one was not seen as flaunting one's sanctity! On the other hand, such a rejection could also lead to extreme forms of asceticism.*

Modern period

Generally speaking, the authority of the established schools was not challenged until the advent of the modern period. Towards the end of the 19th century, some Muslim scholars in Egypt, India and Central Asia who had, to a greater or lesser extent, come under Western influence, began to challenge the domination of the traditional schools and tried to recover for themselves the principle of movement in Islamic jurisprudence under the name of *ijtihād* (or free enquiry). During the colonial period, there was a particular need to recast laws which had to do with social and political relations with non-Muslims. There was a need also for a revision of penal laws in the light of modern conditions and for a commercial law which recognized the obligations of international trade which was increasing rapidly at the time. Changes in the place of women in society, marriage, divorce and questions of inheritance also led to revised codifications of Family Law.

The theological underpinning for this position was provided by a radical critique not only of the consensus of past ages but even of *ḥadīth* literature and the ways in which its compilation had affected Muslim estimates of the *Sunnah* of their Prophet. The net result of such an exercise was to reaffirm the supremacy of the Qur'ān as the primary source of Law. The 'modernists' did not rest here, however. They went on to distinguish between the 'eternal truths' in the Qur'ān and the conditions in which they were revealed and enforced. According to the 'modernists' these 'eternal truths', such as 'stealing and adultery are wrong', remain binding on Muslims everywhere and at all times but the particular ways in which their observance is enforced will change from culture to culture and from age to age.

Fundamentalism

The waning of Western influence in the world of Islām, the failure of secular ideologies such as nationalism* and socialism* to bring prosperity to the masses, and a growing sense of power which oil-wealth has brought, have all contributed to the rise of fundamentalism. Indeed, in some cases the very 'modernist' elevation of the Qur'ān above other kinds of authority has brought about fundamentalist 'back to the Qur'ān' movements.

Fundamentalist Islam, particularly in its Sunnī forms, is either very conservative, tend-ing to lend support to the *status quo*; or is very revolutionary, seeking the overthrow of existing rulers and their replacement by a theocracy.* Shī'a fundamentalism has tended to be revolutionary in character. While both Sunnī and Shī'a fundamentalists seek a return to the strict application of the *Sharī'ah* in its most primitive forms and oppose any accommodation to modernity, the Shī'a are also dependent upon the guidance of eminent religious leaders such as the *Āyatullāhs*, especially in matters of moment.

Although the *Sharī'ah* is dominant in Muslim thinking on moral issues, it is recognized that there *are* aspects of human behaviour which are beyond legislation. Negatively, a sense of shame will prevent people doing that which is disapproved of by the community. More positively, the concept of *akhlāq* is important. Matters such as generosity, keeping one's word, loyalty and fairness to those with whom there is no formal contract are governed by *akhlāq* or 'moral disposition', which enables people to behave honourably even when there is no legal requirement to do so. Indeed, it is widely recognized that the *Sharī'ah*, even in prescribed matters, can only govern only the external compliance of an individual. It is right disposition, however, which makes an act acceptable to Allah. Having such a disposition is part of being a Muslim, *i.e.* one who has surrendered to God. A right disposition cannot be created in an individual by the imposition of an external law, however total its demands. It must arise out of a free response to God's revelation of himself. It is here that Islāmic moral thought draws near to central Christian ideas about repentance,* inner transformation and personal experience of the divine.

Bibliography

A. A. Fyzee, *Outlines of Muhammadan Law* (Oxford, 1949); Muhammad Iqbal, *The Reconstruction of Religious Thought In Islam* (Lahore, 1971); M. Nazir-Ali, *Frontiers in Muslim–Christian Encounter* (Oxford, 1987); idem, *Islam: A Christian Perspective* (Exeter, 1983); idem, *Martyrs and Magistrates: Toleration and Trial in Islam* (Bramcote, Nottingham, 1989); F. Rahman, *Islam and Modernity: Transformation of an Intellectual Tradition* (Chicago, 1982); W. C. Smith, *Islam in Modern History* (Princeton, NJ, 1957); M. Youssef, *Revolt against Modernity: Muslim Zealots and the West* (Leiden, 1985).

M.J.N.-A.

J

JAMES, WILLIAM (1843–1910).

Born in New York, the eldest son of a profoundly religious father, James studied painting for a while before changing to chemistry and then graduating in medicine. He read widely in physiology, psychology and philosophy, himself struggling with depression and 'philosophic pessimism', as well as chronic physical ill health. He first taught physiology at Harvard, where from 1880 to 1907 he was subsequently professor of psychology and then professor of philosophy. His massive *Principles of Psychology* (1890) led to the invitation to give the Gifford Lectures in Edinburgh in 1901–02, published as *The Varieties of Religious Experience*. This book was essentially descriptive, drawing widely on biographies and self-reports. James was the first major psychologist to offer an academic study of religion, and much subsequent psychology of religion* takes its departure from his work. He defined religion as 'the feelings, acts and experiences of individual men in their solitude, so far as they apprehend themselves to stand in relation to whatever they may consider the divine' (*The Varieties of Religious Experience*, p. 31). James explored the nature of individual religious experience in relation to the 'healthy-minded' and the 'sick-souled' personalities; the latter may through a conversion* experience move from the 'once-born' to the 'twice-born'. His own faith was a pragmatic supernaturalism, recognizing the benefits of prayer and mystical experience in others, but not fully enjoying them himself. His attempts to develop an empirical approach to the study of religion have been carried forward recently by the Alister Hardy Religious Experience Research Centre in Oxford.

Bibliography

The Varieties of Religious Experience (1902; London, 1952).

A. Hardy, *The Spiritual Nature of Man* (Oxford, 1983); D. Hay, *Exploring Inner Space: Scientists and Religious Experience* (Harmondsworth, 1982); *idem*, *Religious Experience Today* (London, 1990).

D.J.A.

JEALOUSY AND ENVY.

Jealousy is a powerful emotion aroused in response to perceived disloyalty or rivalry, where love offered or desired is experienced as spurned or lost due to the attraction of another. It is triadic, *i.e.* involving a threesome, in contrast to *envy*, with which it can be easily confused, which is dyadic, *i.e.* involving only two. Jealousy arises out of the desire to be in significant relationship with another, sometimes in a possessive way. Envy issues from comparing oneself unfavourably with another who is perceived or experienced as better, having qualities or possessions one desires. It can lead to malice and begrudging resentment, *e.g.* Mt. 20:15: 'Are you envious [lit. "Is your eye evil?"] because I am generous?' Envy can be turned into a competitive stimulus to achieve (Ec. 4:4), with the inherent danger of becoming selfish ambition (Jas. 3:14, 16).

Both jealousy and envy can lead to abusive, violent, destructive or persecutory behaviour: the Philistines blocked up the wells Abraham had dug out of envy at Isaac's wealth (Gn. 26:14); the Jews were jealous of the successes of Peter and Paul and spoke abusively, imprisoned them, and stirred up a riot (Acts 5:17–18; 13:45; 17:5). The envy of the chief priests (Mt. 27:18) led them to hand Jesus over to Pilate, and stir up the crowds to cry for the release of Barabbas (Mk. 15:10–11), aware that the outcome would lead to Jesus being crucified; Paul was aware that envy could even be a motive in preaching (Phil. 1:15); and within the letters to the young church, jealousy is linked with quarrelling (1 Cor. 3:3; 2 Cor. 12:20), disagreements (Rom. 13:13; Gal. 5:20; 1 Tim. 6:4), malice, slander and hatred (Tit. 3:3; 1 Pet. 2:1), all essentially relationships involving three or more.

In the OT and NT, the same words are used in the original texts for both envy and jealousy: Heb. *qin'â*; Gk. *phthonos*, and occasionally *zēlos*. Translations in the different Eng. versions vary according to the meaning discerned in each context, related to contemporary Eng. usage: *e.g.* Rachel and Leah (Gn. 30:1); Joseph and his brothers (Gn. 37:11; Acts 7:9). This includes the translation 'zeal' as a form of jealousy, expressed positively or negatively: positive in Elijah (1 Ki. 19:10) and Paul (2 Cor. 11:12); destructive, legalistic and persecuting as Paul knew personally (Phil. 3:6).

Scripture is consistent in describing God as jealous, this characteristic being a compatible aspect of his covenant* love and faithful care of his people, expecting in return their trust and faithful allegiance, yet frequently being provoked into jealousy towards them (Pss. 78:58; 16:38, 42; 23:25; Joel 2:18; *etc.*), or into jealousy for Jerusalem (Zion) as his focal dwelling-place (Zc. 1:14; 8:2). Though jealousy is a disposition into which God can be provoked, he is never described as envious (*cf.* love described in 1 Cor. 13:4), for whereas jealousy is related to rivalry and loss, envy is related to greed and lack. The former can be attributed to God in his relationships with human beings, but the latter is inappropriate because God is the source of all that is good (Ps. 104; Jas. 1:17). This may be a clue to why jealousy has never been included among the seven deadly sins* originally identified by the early Desert Fathers, Evagrius of Pontus (346–99) and John Cassian (*c.* 360–435), whereas envy is consistently listed in their writings. The reactive patterns of both are formed in the primary stages of human development, and are rooted in experiences of the lack, loss, or frustration of physical and emotional needs when feeding and while dependent on parental attention and care. Jealousy can give rise to an enormous power to defend its interests (Pr. 27:4; Song 8:6). Envy is far more insidious. Jealousy is related to loving, having, hating and losing. Envy relates only to hating and not having, and can be both reactive and innate, destroying a person's life. Envy is best acknowledged (Ps. 73:3), and avoided (Pr. 3:31; 23:17), because it is so deeply and inwardly damaging (Pr. 14:30, 'envy rots the bones'). The humbling journey into self-awareness leading to personal honesty,* an experience of mercy,* and supportive human relationships, are the keys to both spiritual and emotional levels of healing from envy and jealousy.

Bibliography

J. Berke, *The Tyranny of Malice: Exploring the Dark Side of Character and Culture* (New York, 1989); M. Klein, *Envy and Gratitude* (London, 1957).

G.J.P.

JESUITS.

Founded by the Basque nobleman Ignatius of Loyola* in 1534, and receiving papal approval in 1540, the Society of Jesus was the most vigorous agent of the Counter-Reformation. Jesuit schools and colleges appeared across Europe, and their missionaries were in the forefront of evangelism in the new continents being discovered in the 16th century.

The Jesuits were a new type of religious order, with no distinctive dress and no obligation to recite the daily services of the church. Active involvement in, rather than withdrawal from, the world was advocated, and Ignatius' *Spiritual Exercises* used imaginative meditation rather than passive contemplation, aiming at practical resolutions and indifference to worldly circumstances.

Although known for its emphasis on unquestioning obedience to both the Pope and superiors, at the heart of the Society and the 'spiritual exercises' is a vision of the freedom of individuals within the grace of God, and a consequent flexibility towards individual cases, as Jesuits encountered the new discoveries of the 16th and 17th centuries and new moral dilemmas in new continents. Casuistry* became crucial to Jesuit moral thinking and training, being based on probabilism,* the doctrine that any action could be justified for which a reasonable case could be made, sometimes regardless of the strength of the opposite case. This attracted the fierce criticism, from the Jansenists' Augustinian doctrine of grace, that casuistry could be used to justify almost anything, and it engendered a consequent moral laxity. But it was at best an attempt to adapt traditional morality to a new world in a way which gave pastoral concern to complex issues, a characteristic Jesuit concern.

Bibliography

M. Foss, *The Founding of the Jesuits* (London, 1969); J. Mahoney, *The Making of Moral Theology* (Oxford, 1987); D. Mitchell, *The Jesuits: A History* (London, 1980).

G.S.T.

JESUS.

The subject 'Jesus' is of central importance in Christian ethics and pastoral theology. This is because Jesus is the Word of God, the only divine and universal saviour, the one who sustains all things by his word of power. Ethics and pastoral theology (see 7) which do not relate to Jesus could scarcely be called Christian.

The person and work of Jesus

It is Jesus' nature as both human and divine which qualifies him to be the universal saviour. He is one in his humanity with the human race he came to redeem, and his divine status means that he has the authority and power to bring salvation (see Sin and Salvation⑤). His *person* (his human and divine identity) enables his *work* (the salvation of humankind).

The centrality of Jesus and of his saving work provides the right context for any study of ethics or pastoral theology.

So, for example, any Christian ethical theories must be worked out in the context of the doctrine of Jesus as God and saviour. They must relate to Jesus' significance in this universe, his divine rule and authority. Obedience to Jesus and his teaching must be a part of Christian ethics. And Jesus' saving work also provides the right context for any evaluation of behaviour. Any good act may be good in intention* and content, but in Christian theology it is of itself a 'dead work', unable to win God's favour. This is the case because of the corrupt nature of the doer of the act. The only 'good' act is one done according to God's will and with a single-minded desire to honour God in the act, and done by one who is in a right relationship with God. So, in this sense, an unbeliever cannot do a good act. But one who has been saved by the mercy of God is then called to do 'good deeds', which are prepared by God and covered in their frailty by the goodness and grace* of Christ.

Christian pastoral theology must also relate to the person and work of Christ. Some areas of pastoral theology fall into the trap of treating the individual within his or her own private world of meaning, without reference to the external reality of Christ's rule. Then the resolution of internal guilt feelings replaces the receiving of forgiveness* and cleansing of objective guilt* by the sacrifice of Christ; coming to terms with personal goals and desires obscures the need to serve and obey the Lord Jesus; learning to love oneself becomes more important than knowing God's love in Christ's death. And whereas pastoral theology often concentrates on individuals, the role of pastor in the church* is primarily that of pastor of the whole body, the people of God. For some strange reason, pastoral theology as popularly conceived, does not often include the task of teaching and preaching the Bible, the Word of God, whereas teaching the Bible to the people of God is of prime pastoral importance.

Christian ethics will tackle both the significance of Christ's rule and authority for the individual and society, and also the implications for individual responsibility* and freedom.* Christian pastoral theology will cover both the objective significance of Christ's work of redemption, and also its health-giving impact on the people of God and individual Christians.

Jesus the human

The humanity of Christ means that the Son of God understands humankind not just because we are made in God's image* and likeness but also because he has experienced humanity himself in taking our flesh. He knows the joys, delights and frustrations implicit in human existence; he understands our temptations, pain and sorrow. He understands too the rigorous requirements of the moral law, not only because he gave it, but also because he has obeyed it. He suffered pain, and the anguish of death on the cross* as our saviour, and his resurrected body is a sign of hope to all humanity, the promise of restored and perfected human existence (see Resurrection*). So in his humanity Jesus can sympathize with human existence and provide a model of ethical obedience;* he suffered for our salvation, and in his risen life provides a sign of hope for humankind.

Jesus the Son

It is the divinity of Jesus, his status as the only Son of God, which is the basis for our hope of salvation. Because he is the eternal Son of God, his work of salvation is a divine work, with God's power, authority and eternal effectiveness. Jesus' divine status means that he is Lord of the human race, and indeed of the universe, that all things find their origin, present meaning and ultimate destiny in him. He has both human and divine authority and power. He is rightly addressed and worshipped as Lord and God. So Christian ethics and pastoral theology must relate to him, or they function in an unreal world, without meaning or effectiveness.

Jesus as example

The idea of Jesus as example, as a model to be copied, has been powerful both in pastoral theology and in ethics. Some different strands of this idea are best distinguished by the names of the writers who have expounded them.

Thomas à Kempis (*c.* 1380–1471) in *The Imitation of Christ* portrayed Christ as an example to us of suffering, self-deprivation, humility, patience, solitude and brokenness of will. The piety is that of denying the pleasures of the world, to take the 'royal way of the holy Cross'.

John Calvin* developed a theology of the imitation of Christ based on the work of God in transforming us into the image of God in Christ. So the practice of imitation is based on the prior work of God in salvation. This transformation will be completed at the last day.

Ignatius of Loyola* developed an imitation of Christ in his *Spiritual Exercises*. The imaginative following of the mysteries of Christ begins with the incarnation and stresses the events of the passion of Christ. The idea is of an internal meditation on Christ in order to love him better and follow him more closely.

Carl Jung* writes of the importance of Christ as an *archetype* (see *Memories, Dreams, Reflections*, London and New York, 1963). But for Jung there are other archetypes that are equally valid: and in any case the function of this archetype is not to give us a model to copy, but to encourage us to express our own uniqueness. And Jung's model of wholeness is amoral: self-realization means that we will come to terms with all aspects of our character (see ⑩), good and evil.

Leonardo Boff (1938–) writes of the need to follow Christ as example of liberation (see Liberation Theology*). Christ is the paradigm of what will happen to all human beings and to the whole of creation. The following of Jesus means putting Utopia into practice – and this will involve conflict, sacrificing love (see ②), hope,* faith,* cross and resurrection.

We see that the theme of the imitation of Christ is malleable. Our guideline will be the Bible's use of Christ as example.

Jesus the Christ

The Jewishness of Jesus – his particular ethnic, historical and theological context, his place in the saving purpose of God for humankind – is summed up in that familiar title and role by which Jesus is known: the Christ. For he is one anointed by God, who will fulfil the purpose of God that Abraham's descendant will bring blessing to all the nations. Jesus the Christ is the historical source of hope and salvation for Jews and Gentiles, as all God's promises find their 'yes' in him (2 Cor. 1:20). The pure revelation of God in Christ is not culturally limited or conditioned, but it is culturally expressed, in a theological, political and social milieu which God had prepared, and which manifested the working out of his long-term plans, promises and judgments. Abraham's descendant is born in Abraham's land; David's Son dies and rises again in David's city. Salvation is of the Jews, and then the Gentiles come to share in God's promises and covenant.* An ethical, or pastoral, use of Jesus which removes him from this historical context is of no value: it is as Jesus is the Christ that we can discover his God-invested meaning.

Jesus our substitute

Jesus is saviour through his death for us as our substitute (see Atonement*). Jesus is not only 'for us' in that his death was for our benefit, he is 'for us' in that he died in our place, he died the death we deserved. He served us in that he gave his life as a ransom in the place of many: as priest he offered the sacrifice which won our cleansing and acceptance, and enables us to approach God with boldness; he was himself that sacrifice offered in our place. He was God's atoning sacrifice and we are saved through faith in his blood. So if we confess our sins, God is then faithful and just in both forgiving us and making us clean.

Jesus' death in our place releases us from the quest for an unattainable moral perfection. For it is by Christ's act of righteousness that we are given the status of acceptability with God. This does not remove the demands of ethical obedience. In gratitude for our free acceptance, we are to serve God in glad obedience. And the power of God is seen not only in Christ's death for us, but in God's gradual transformation of us into the image of his Son.

The truths of Christ's salvation provide a rich resource for pastoral theology. For those who are lost there is the good news of the searching shepherd; for those who feel remote and alienated, there is the good news of God's acceptance of us by Christ's death; for those who feel dirty and defiled, there is the good news of cleansing by Christ's blood; for those who are shackled by sin and failure, there is the good news of Christ's powerful redemption. All of these imply a move from inner feeling to an awareness of outward reality, from a self-constructed world of meaning to the reality of God's world, in which he has acted to save.

Jesus and the defeat of Satan

An understanding of the power of Satan* within God's world ought not to lead to a fascination with evil power, or with a dualistic* view in which God and Satan are opponents of equal power, or to an idea that Satan has control of this world. But under the sovereign power of God, Satan has a sphere of influence, especially in promoting untrue ideas about God, in bringing death and disease, and in preventing humans from serving God. So we are not totally free agents – we are restricted not only by the sin which lies within us, but also by the power Satan has in our lives.

Christ's victory over Satan on the cross is of great significance. For it is in receiving that salvation power that we can become free to refute Satan's lies, can move from serving him to the kingdom of Christ, and can know freedom from Satan's power over our lives. Exorcism (see Deliverance Ministry*) is one way in which Satan's power is refuted and removed: less dramatic ways include the rejection of lies about God, and the acceptance of the truth that God is revealed through Christ. Jesus' rejection of Satan in the wilderness is a model for this stance of faith.

Jesus the coming saviour

An important element of the Bible's teaching about the saviour and our salvation is that of future salvation. Though the saving work of Christ was completed on the cross and we can now receive assurance of eternal salvation, based on an eternal verdict of 'acquitted', the working-out of Christ's salvation is still to happen. So the NT speaks of the return of Christ primarily as salvation, rather than as judgment.* Jesus Christ will return to this earth to save the elect (Mk. 13:26–27), to rescue believers from God's wrath (1 Thes. 1:10; 4:16–17; 5:9–10), to change our bodies to be like his body (Phil. 3:21), to bring about the resurrection of all, whether to salvation or judgment (1 Cor. 15:20–23) and to bring a new heaven and a new earth (2 Pet. 3:13).

The neglect of this strand of teaching has led to an impossible ethical perfectionism* and to a pastoral theology which is determined to see the fullness of salvation now, in healing* and personal fulfilment. We must learn to wait in patience for the return of Jesus our saviour.

See also: CHRISTIAN MORAL REASONING; [18] KINGDOM OF GOD; NEW TESTAMENT ETHICS.[9]

Bibliography

R. Baxter, *A Christian Directory* (1673; Ligonier, PA, 1990); *idem*, *The Reformed Pastor* (1656; Edinburgh, 1974); L. Boff, *Jesus Christ Liberator* (ET, Maryknoll, NY, 1978; London, 1980); W. H. Longridge, *The Spiritual Exercises of St Ignatius of Loyola* (London, 1919); O. O'Donovan, *Resurrection and Moral Order* (Leicester and Grand Rapids, ²1994); Thomas à Kempis, *The Imitation of Christ* (1418; many eds.); P. C. Vitz, *Psychology as Religion: The Cult of Self-Worship* (Grand Rapids, 1977; Tring, ²1981); R. S. Wallace, *Calvin's Doctrine of the Christian Life* (Edinburgh, 1959); D. F. Wells, *The Person of Christ* (Westchester, IL, 1984); *idem*, *The Search for Salvation* (Leicester and Downers Grove, IL, 1978).

P.J.H.A.

JEWISH ETHICS. The heart of ethics in the Heb. Scriptures lies in the character of God himself. Because God is utterly pure and holy, his people should become like him in holiness. Jewish ethics is based on the idea that religion and ethics cannot be separated. True worship includes both personal and social righteousness. Following Proverbs and some Psalms, this connection of religion and ethics was interpreted by Hellenistic Jewish teaching and by Palestinian rabbinics as emphasizing moderation. However, Job and Ecclesiastes show God opposing moderation, which the Talmud declares to be 'the way of Sodom' (Avot 5.13).

The heart of God's law is sometimes considered to lie in the threefold commandments of Am. 5:15 and Mi. 6:8, which in turn were summarized by the twofold command to love God and neighbour (see Mk. 12:30–31). The focus of all is summarized in the righteous living by their faith (Hab. 2:4).

While Hillel the Elder (fl. 1st century BC) maintained that ethics form the essence of Torah, others were influenced by Gk. philosophy and considered spiritual issues to be higher than material or ethical concerns. In the Heb. Scriptures, however, the spiritual and the material cannot be separated. Our relation to God in worship and prayer is manifest in such earthy commandments as the sabbath,* sexual ethics or patterns of agriculture. There can be no division between moral and ritual ordinances. Likewise, personal ethics for the individual goes together with requirements for social justice in the community of God's people.

Biblical ethics is taught not only through direct commandments of law (*Halakhah*), but also by the narratives of biblical history (*Haggadah*). The centre of Haggadah lies in the climactic event of the Exodus from Egypt. God's deliverance of Israel from slavery is remembered annually by all Jews and the Passover liturgy is often termed 'the Haggadah'. The passover event is the basis for the sabbath commandment (Dt. 5:15) which is the touchstone of the law.

Profoundly influential in all later developments of Jewish ethics was the 11th-century *Hovot ha-Levavot* by Bahya ben Joseph ibn Paquda (?*c*. 1050–*c*. 1120). He developed an ethical pattern based on three principles. Alongside his emphasis on practical commandments he taught *kavvanah*, the inner intention* or motivation of the doer which gave value to the external works of the law. Then he outlined a system of purely spiritual commandments which had no external or physical outworking.

In rabbinic teaching, ethics was founded particularly on *Haggadah* and the exposition of biblical thought in the development of Talmud. In later Ashkenazic circles (*i.e.* German Jews and their descendants), the Hasidim specially emphasized more specific moral commandments rather than abstract principles. Obedience to detailed laws became the test of devotion to God. The Hasidim tended to go beyond other Ashkenazim in teaching that behaviour which is contrary to human nature demonstrates a greater love for God. The high point of such obedience is seen in martyrdom.

Among the Ashkenazim, cabbalistic approaches (representing the mystical religious stream in Judaism) became increasingly influential. They combined the rabbinic emphasis on Haggadah and Talmud with the Hassidic promotion of specific ethical issues. To this they added the authority of the *Zohar* (the chief work of the Spanish cabbala) and a particular interest in the person of Satan and the reality of sin. As was also true of the Sabbatians (followers of Shabbetai Tzevi, d. 1676), they adopted the Hasidic teaching that the earthly law (*din Torah*) is inferior to and different from the heavenly law (*din shamayim*). The righteous should aim to go beyond the down-to-earth *din Torah* and follow the higher and more spiritual *din shamayim*.

Ashkenazic and cabbalistic ethics largely replaced S. European philosophical ethics in emphasis, because the latter had opened the door to the mass conversion of Jews to Catholicism in Spain in 1492. So also the Musar movement arose among Orthodox Jews in Lithuania in the latter part of the 19th century and spread through European *yeshivot*, the rabbinic training schools. This movement aimed to educate individual Jews in strict Halakhah ethics to counter the perceived moral degeneration due to the declining religious values of 19th-century European Jewry. This decline was particularly evident in the influence of the new Reform Jewry with its rationalist teaching and its desire for assimilation into the surrounding Gentile cultures. Alongside the Reform and ensuring Sabbatianism, secularism and Zionism were also gaining ground to the detriment of ethical values. To counter these influences, the Musar movement trained people to recite Bible verses and sections of Talmud in melody. Yeshivah students also spent about half an hour daily reciting texts from earlier Jewish ethical writers.

Since the traumatic destruction of middle-European Jewry under Hitler's Third Reich, such spiritually vibrant movements of Jewish ethics have largely disappeared, except among the Hassidic communities which tend towards separatist life and thus to minority status. In the mainstream of Jewish ethics today the Orthodox continue to uphold the traditional teaching of the Bible, rabbinics and Talmud.

Bibliography

L. Jacobs, *Jewish Ethics, Philosophy and Mysticism* (New York, 1969); L. G. Montefiore and H. Loewe, *Rabbinic Anthology* (New York, 1974); E. P. Sanders, *Jewish Law from Jesus to the Mishnah* (London, 1990); E. E. Urbach, *The Sages: Their Concepts and Beliefs* (Jerusalem, 1975).

M.F.G.

JOHN XXIII, POPE (1881–1963). Angelo Giuseppe Roncalli, of peasant origin, was influenced early in his life by the progressive leaders of the Italian Catholic Socialist movement. He became highly cultured and held important appointments abroad, yet was a humble man with a deep faith and unwavering trust in divine providence. As Bishop of Rome he exhibited great care of his diocese, making frequent visits to parishes, hospitals, and educational and charitable institutions. He worked for a highly educated priesthood, enhanced the sacred liturgy and encouraged missions. He became Pope in 1958.

It was his convocation in 1962 of the Second Vatican Council,* attributed to a sudden inspiration of the Holy Spirit, that has marked his pontificate as initiating a new era in the history of the Roman Catholic Church. To achieve his ultimate goal of Christian unity, he proposed that the Council should work for renewal of the religious life of Catholics and the updating (*aggiornamento*) of the Church's teaching, discipline and organization. A turning-point was reached when he intervened to set up a special mixed commission to handle the question of revelation, thus encouraging the mood for change.

During his pontificate, he issued seven encyclical letters (see Papal Encyclicals*), perhaps the most famous being *Pacem in Terris* in 1963, addressed to all men of good will, on peace among all the nations based on truth, justice, charity and liberty. For the first time, in November 1961 the Roman Catholic Church was represented at an assembly of the World Council of Churches in New Delhi. Out of consideration for Jews, the Pope commanded that words offensive to Jews in the Roman liturgy of Good Friday should be deleted. He was awarded the Peace Prize in 1962 by the International Balzan Foundation.

P.T.

JOURNALISM, see MEDIA ETHICS.

JOY. Few qualities of life are more universally desired and more widely misunderstood than joy. Typically, it is viewed as a fruit of one's circumstances and as an emotional condition. Biblically, joy has three distinctive characteristics which radically distinguish it from its circumstantial and emotional counterpart.

1. Rather than being dependent upon circumstances, Christian joy is a fruit of the Spirit and a condition of one's being (Gal. 5:22; Rom. 14:17). The only circumstance upon which joy depends is that of one's life in Christ. Jesus promised to give joy which no-one, not even any circumstance, could take away (Jn. 16:20–22). Christians are joyful because they are alive in Christ (Phil. 4:4).

2. Because of the independence of Christian joy from circumstances, Christians are commanded to rejoice in all things (Lk. 10:20; Jn. 14:28; 15:11; Jas. 1:2; 1 Pet. 1:6). This capacity to rejoice even in suffering (2 Cor. 7:4) and in weakness (2 Cor. 13:9) is the result of the Spirit's continued reassurance to believers of God's love for them in Christ and their assured hope that God can use even difficulties and suffering for the furtherance of his purposes (Rom. 5:3–5).

3. Christian joy does not isolate the jubilant

from those who weep and mourn. It holds a place for tears and enables compassionate participation in others' pain. Sharing in Christ's compassionate life, the believer is freed to extend God's comfort to those who are suffering (2 Cor. 7:4–7). In so doing, Christians manifest the firstfruits of the future joy, when God will dwell among his people and wipe away every tear and remove all mourning, crying and pain (Rev. 21:1–4).

T.A.D.

JUBILEE. The year of jubilee came at the end of the cycle of seven sabbatical years, i.e. probably in the fiftieth year. In this year there was a proclamation of liberty to Israelites who had become enslaved for debt,* and a restoration of land to families who had been compelled to sell it out of economic need in the previous fifty years. Instructions concerning the jubilee, and its relation to the procedures of land and slave redemption, are found entirely in Lv. 25:8–55. It was an economic institution designed to protect the viability of the households, which were the basic units of Israel's land tenure. It was not, as sometimes alleged, a *redistribution* of land, but a *restoration* to original owners of land which had been pledged as security for loans.

Although it is not known whether the jubilee was put into practice in ancient Israel (there is no record of it in the narratives, but equally there is no record of any observance of the Day of Atonement), its two main thrusts, liberty and restoration, were both easily transferred from the strictly economic provision of the jubilee itself to a wider metaphorical application. Many scholars see jubilary imagery in texts such as Is. 35; 42:1–7; 58 and 61. The jubilee could be used to portray God's final intervention for Messianic redemption and restoration; but it could also support ethical challenge for justice to the oppressed in contemporary history (see Justice and Peace 3). The same combined use of jubilary concepts is found in the NT, in the ministry of Jesus (*e.g.* Lk. 4:16–30) and in the preaching and socio-economic behaviour of the early church (Acts 1:6; 3:21; 4:34).

Without envisaging any literal enactment of its provisions, the jubilee still remains a powerful model in formulating Christian biblical ethics. Its primary assumptions and objectives can be used as a guide and critique for our own ethical agenda in the modern world.

Economically, the jubilee existed to protect a form of land* tenure that was based on an equitable and widespread distribution of the land, and to prevent the accumulation of ownership in the hands of a wealthy few. This echoes the creation principle that the whole earth is given by God to all humanity, who act as co-stewards of its resources. The jubilee thus stands as a critique not only of massive private accumulation of land and related wealth, but also of large-scale forms of collect-ivism or nationalization which destroy any meaningful sense of personal or family ownership.

Socially, the jubilee embodied a practical concern to protect and restore the family* unit. The jubilee aimed to restore social dignity and participation to families through maintaining or restoring their economic viability. The economic collapse of a family in one genera-tion was not to condemn all future generations to the bondage of perpetual indebtedness. Such principles and objectives are certainly not ir-relevant to welfare legislation, or indeed any legislation with socio-economic implications.

Theologically, the jubilee was based upon several central affirmations of Israel's faith. Like the rest of the sabbatical (see Sabbath*) provisions, the jubilee proclaimed the sover-eignty of God over time and nature, and obedi-ence to it would require submission to that sovereignty, hence the year is dubbed 'holy', to be observed out of the fear of Yahweh (Lv. 25:12, 17). Furthermore, observing the fallow year would also require faith in God's pro-vidence as the one who could command bless-ing in the natural order (25:18–22). Additional motivation for the law is provided by repeated appeals to the knowledge of God's historical act of redemption, the Exodus, and all it had meant for Israel (25:38, 42, 55). To this historical dimension was added the recurring experience of forgiveness in the fact that the jubilee was proclaimed on the day of atonement (25:9). To know oneself forgiven by God was to issue in practical remission of debts and bondages for fellow Israelites. And the inbuilt future hope of the literal jubilee blended with an eschato-logical hope of God's final restoration of humanity and nature to his original purpose.

To apply the jubilee model, then, requires that people face the sovereignty of God, trust his providence, know his redemptive action, experience his atonement,* practise his justice and hope in his promise. The wholeness of the model embraces the church's evangelistic mis-sion, its personal and social ethics and its future hope.

Bibliography

R. North, *Sociology of the Biblical Jubilee* (Rome, 1954); S. H. Ringe, *Jesus, Liberation, and the Biblical Jubilee: Images for Ethics and Christology* (Philadelphia, 1985); G. J. Wenham, *The Book of Leviticus* (Grand Rapids, 1979); C. J. H. Wright, *God's People in God's Land* (Grand Rapids and Exeter, 1990); *idem, Anchor Bible Dictionary*, vol. 3 (New York, 1992), pp. 1025–1030.

C.J.H.W.

JUDGMENT AND THE JUDGMENT.

Judgment is a prominent theme in the Bible, primarily associated with God. The Bible focuses its understanding of the judgment of God not on the future 'day of judgment', but on God's status and activity as the *present* ruler and director of the world. 'Will not the Judge of all the earth do right?' (Gn. 18:25) is echoed throughout the Bible as a cry for the vindication of God as the just creator of a world which seems not to reflect his being. In this theodicy,* the final judgment plays a vital role, and has profound implica-tions for Christian ethics and pastoral theology.

Judgment and evil

For the biblical tradition, the problem of evil* is not its bare existence, but its presence in a world under God's rule. In fact, in the Bible God's judgment is not the *answer* to the prob-lem of evil, but its *cause*: for his 'judgment' is that by which he decrees the shape and course of his world (*e.g.* Ps. 97). So Job's problem was to reconcile his belief about the power and wisdom of God's rule (Jb. 9:1–13) with God's apparent injustice in his case. If Satan had been on the throne, Job would have had no problem (or rather, a very different one!).

The biblical answer to this problem takes on its distinctive shape in the NT. The response of the book of Revelation is not to deny the real existence of evil (*cf.* Hinduism, Christian Science), or to make a capricious God the source of evil (*cf.* Islam), or to teach that evil and God / good are balanced and struggling against each other (*cf.* Zoroastrianism, Marx-ism). Rather, its response is 1. to insist that God rules from 'the throne', even though the world is in a mess ('the throne' is mentioned 46 times in Rev.); 2. to teach a final judgment, in which not only will the powers of evil be over-thrown (Rev. 20), but also the justice of God's 'judgments' will be revealed, *in retrospect* (*e.g.*

Rev. 15:3–4; 16:5–7; 19:1–2); and, most important of all, 3. to bring God himself into personal engagement with the evil of the world, first as victim of it, and then as victor over it. On the throne stands 'the Lamb who was slain' (see Rev. 5:6). It is as crucified, having shared and borne the evil of the world, that Jesus exercises God's judgment on God's behalf.

Government, destiny and revelation

It is thus necessary to distinguish in the Bible between three types of 'judgment' exercised by God: 1. the judgment by which the world is governed; 2. the final judgment by which the destiny of people, the world and the powers of evil is determined; and 3. the spoken revelation of his 'judgments', *i.e.* his will expressed for his people to obey. The Heb. word *mišpāṭ*, which is used 417 times in the OT, covers all three areas of meaning. It connotes the 'royal decree' which the King issues, his spoken judgments which shape his realm or call for the response of his subjects. In the NT, we find that all three 'judgments' are committed to Jesus Christ, who holds the world in being (1 Cor. 8:6; Col. 1:17; Heb. 1:3), will exercise the final judgment (Jn. 5:22, 27–30; Acts 17:31; Rom. 2:16), and is the agent and expression of God's 'word' of revelation (although the word 'judgment' is not part of the revelation vocabulary of the NT, unlike the OT).

The final judgment

The prophetic expectation of a coming 'day' of judgment (*e.g.* Is. 2:12ff.; Am. 5:18) is taken up in the NT, particularly by Jesus himself (*e.g.* Mt. 11:22; 12:36; Lk. 11:31–32; *cf.* Rom. 2:5; 1 Jn. 4:17). It is associated with the 'coming of the Son of Man' (Mk. 13:26–27), involves the whole world (Mt. 25:31ff.), and means rewarding each 'according to what he has done in the flesh, whether good or evil' (2 Cor. 5:10, RSV). In Revelation the event is expanded to itemize the destruction of the spiritual powers of evil (Rev. 19:19–21; 20:7–10), as well the judgment of mankind (22:11–14).

Paul does not hesitate to use the OT notion of 'the wrath of God' in connection with the day of judgment (Rom. 2:5; 5:9; Col. 3:6; *etc.*). Liberal scholars have tried to demythologize this idea, maintaining that 'wrath' refers to impersonal processes of retribution occurring within human society, rather than to final judgment by an angry God. Certainly in Rom. 1:18ff. Paul thinks of

'wrath' as revealed in the present, but within biblical thinking as a whole a final judgment is made necessary by the plain fact that retribution does *not* take place now: for some reason, under God's 'governmental' judgment, the wicked prosper (*e.g.* Je. 12:1–13; Ps. 73), and so the Day is necessary in order to iron out the inequities of present experience (Ps. 98:9; Am. 1:3 – 2:16). Paul's view is that the final judgment has been postponed to allow space for repentance (Rom. 2:4; 9:22–24; *cf.* 2 Pet. 3:9).

Ethical and pastoral implications

The moral universe. In contrast to secular world-views, Christians need to affirm the fundamentally moral structure, not just of humankind, but of the world itself, heading towards destruction and renewal (2 Pet. 3:7–13).

Personal accountability. Our accountability before God is viewed with enormous seriousness in the Bible. Our destiny hangs upon our response to him (Rom. 8:13); and our dignity as human beings is undermined if we seek to evade the consequences of our actions. But if we face up to our accountability, and find salvation in Christ, then our destiny and dignity are actually to reign with him (Rom. 5:17) and to share in the judgment (1 Cor. 6:2; *cf.* Mt. 19:28).

The provisionality of present judgment. Paul urges the Romans to make their minds up firmly about the matters concerning which he has written, but then tells them not to criticize each other if they come to different convictions. 'To his own master he stands or falls . . . why do you judge your brother? . . . we will all stand before God's judgment seat' (Rom. 14:4, 10; *cf.* 1 Cor. 4:3–5). In the light of God's judgment, all human judgment is provisional, even though we cannot live without exercising it.

Bibliography
S. H. Travis, *Christ and the Judgment of God* (Basingstoke, 1986).

S.M.

JUNG, CARL (1875–1961). Swiss psychiatrist and founder of analytical psychology,* Carl Gustav Jung ascribed a great deal of his subsequent beliefs and theorizing to the influence of his parents and grandparents. His mother's parents were spiritualists and she, although outgoing and loving, exhibited a dual nature: a 'day-time' personality marked by a 'hearty, animal warmth', and a more unnerving 'night-time' one which featured prescience and an awareness of the super-natural. In his autobiographical *Memories, Dreams, Reflections*, Jung wrote of his own 'number one' (conscious and rational) and 'number two' (unconscious and irrational) per-sonalities, and this latter aspect was expressed in a lifelong interest in the paranormal. His father, the son of an eminent physician and freemason in Basel, was a Reformed pastor whose doubt-racked faith and dismissive at-titude to his son's enquiries seemed to con-tribute to Jung's rejection of institutionalized and dogmatic Christianity.

In 1900, Carl Jung graduated in medicine at Basel University and, seeking an integration of his 'number one' and 'number two' per-sonalities by specializing in psychiatry, became an assistant to Eugen Bleuler (1857–1939), the renowned authority on schizophrenia, at the Burghölzli Mental Institute in Zürich. Marry-ing Emma Rauschenbach (1882–1955) in 1903, Jung was appointed two years later as lecturer in psychiatry at the University of Zürich and senior staff physician at the Burghölzli. Following his research into word-association (the use of stimulus words to evoke responsive associated words which, in turn, Jung later argued, indicate 'complexes' within the patient's unconscious*) and its publication in 1906, Jung made contact with Sigmund Freud.* At their first meeting, in March 1907, the two men appear to have been mutually im-pressed and a fertile correspondence was struck up between them. In 1909 they were both invited to lecture at Clark University, Worcester, Massachusetts, and a year later the International Psychoanalytic Association was founded, with Jung as its first president. Freud, nineteen years older than Jung, saw the younger man as his 'son and heir' within the psychoanalytic movement (see Psycho-analysis*). However, Jung became increas-ingly critical of Freud's emphasis on sexuality (see ⑪) as the prime source of human motivation,* his dismissal of the importance of religion, and his authoritarianism in their per-sonal relationship, and in 1914 their col-laboration was finally severed. Jung resigned from all his public commitments and retreated to his house at Küsnacht to private practice and his continuing research.

Over the four or five years following the break with Freud, Jung experienced a period of profound mental anguish (perhaps exacer-bated by his affair with a former patient, An-tonia Wolff, and consequent bitter rows with his wife, Emma) which he sought to resolve by his 'confrontation with the unconscious'. Within this process of self-analysis, Jung, recording his dreams* painstakingly and enter-ing into dialogue with his 'inner figures' (he first used the term 'archetypes' of these in 1919), further refined the concepts which underlie the methodology of analytical psychology.

In the years following his 'experiment with the unconscious', Jung continued his interest in world religions through various anthropo-logical expeditions and his study of gnosticism, mythology and medieval alchemy. He wrote prolifically; see his *Collected Works*, occupy-ing twenty volumes.

The expression of Jung's lifelong interest in religious and occultic matters, and its distinct-ive contribution to the psychology of religion,* is widely spread through his writings. Much of his work on the contrasts between the Western forms of the Judaeo-Christian tradition and Eastern mysticism is gathered together in *Psychology and Religion: West and East* (*Col-lected Works* 11), which includes his com-mentaries: *A Psychological Approach to the Dogma of the Trinity* (1942/1948) and *Answer to Job* (1952). Jung referred to religion as 'the *numinosum*, that is, a dynamic agency or effect not caused by an arbitrary act of will' (*CW* 11, para. 6), and it is essential to see his reflections on religious themes as springing from his own psychological understanding, especially that of archetypal theory. For example, his musings on the Trinity, influ-enced by Platonic* thought, postulate the psy-chological need for a 'quaternity', in which Christ the Son is opposed by Lucifer, the Anti-christ. Further, he bemoaned the lack of the feminine in conventional thinking about the Godhead, and felt that the papal proclamation of the Assumption of the Blessed Virgin Mary in 1950 was a significant step in redressing this perceived imbalance.

From considerations such as these it is not surprising that Christians polarize about Jung and his teaching. A number in the more con-servative traditions regard his dabbling with the occult and his engagement in dialogue with archetypes with great suspicion. Others of more liberal and catholic persuasions have sometimes seemed quite uncritical and even adulatory over Jung's insights. Undeniably, his emphasis on symbol, image, the shadow, the numinous and 'the God within' have attracted many in the more mystical and sacramentalist traditions, including Victor White (1902–60) and Christopher Bryant (1905–85) in the UK, and Morton Kelsey (1917–) and John A. Stanford in the US. In a more critical vein, David G. Benner has written that Jung's religious doctrine has rendered God completely 'interiorized', a process in which 'self is deified and God is psychologized' (*Psychotherapy and the Spiritual Quest*, p. 58).

At a more popular level, Jung's influence is probably best known through his work on personality types, a typology which postulates that each individual has a preference between the 'attitudes' of extroversion and introversion, between the 'rational functions' of thinking and feeling, and the 'irrational functions' of sensation and intuition. This schema was further refined in the US in the 1940s by Katharine C. Briggs and her daughter Isabel Briggs Myers. The resulting Myers-Briggs* Type Indicator (1975) is a psychometric test now widely used in education,* career guidance, communication skills, group dynamics* and in counselling and other pastoral contexts. The Jungian approach is also seen in the dream workshops and the use of 'active imagination' in many Christian retreat centres.

Bibliography

Collected Works, 20 vols. (London, New York and Princeton, NJ, 1953–1978); *Memories, Dreams, Reflections* (London and New York, 1963).

D. G. Benner, *Psychotherapy and the Spiritual Quest* (Grand Rapids, 1988; London, 1989); I. Briggs Myers, *Gifts Differing* (Palo Alto, CA, 1980); C. Bryant, *Jung and the Christian Way* (London, 1983); M. Kelsey, *Encounter with God: A Theology of Christian Experience* (Minnesota, MN, 1972; London, 1974); R. L. Moore and D. J. Meckel (eds.), *Jung and Christianity in Dialogue* (New York, 1990); C. Perry, *Listen to the Voice Within: A Jungian Approach to Pastoral Care* (London, 1991); J. A. Sanford, *Dreams: God's Forgotten Language* (San Francisco, 1989); A. Stevens, *On Jung* (London and New York, 1991); V. White, *God and the Unconscious* (London, 1952).

R.F.H.

JURISPRUDENCE is a term with several contents. The jurisprudence of a court is the body of its decisions, expressing its view of the law (see Law, Civil and Criminal*) and, through those decisions, developing the law. More usually, however, jurisprudence is the philosophy of law, the product of attempts to answer the question 'What is law?' These answers are many and various, and most, by concentrating on a particular interpretation of the question, are only partially successful.

A broad distinction may be drawn between analytic and normative theories. Analytic jurisprudence deals with the functioning of law. Analytic theories are mainly positivist. Their basis is all or any of the following: that laws are commands by human beings; that there is no necessary connection between law and morals, or between the law as it is and law as it should be; that legal ideas are worth studying; that a legal system is a complete, logical system within which correct decisions can be deduced without recourse to outside elements; and that moral judgments, however established, are independent of legal judgments. Analytic theories of law range from the analytical discussion of concepts (whether those of a particular legal system, or of concepts found to be common to legal systems such as law, act, responsibility and intention), to analysis of the way in which courts and legislatures, adjudicatory and law-making bodies function.

Positivism contains broad and narrow philosophies of law, and discussions of the nature of rules and how they interact to form a legal system. Proponents of analytical jurisprudence would say that the analysis and explication of law can and should be fully carried out without reference to its content, and that a clear distinction between law and morals is essential for a proper understanding of law. The function of jurisprudence is the analysis of law as it is, not as it should be. The purpose of the analysis is descriptive. From such a view a properly constituted or enacted law remains law, although it is immoral or unjust. A procedurally correct extermination order, for example, is as much law as a traffic regulation.

Within positivism are many schools of thought, most with useful elements to contribute to a full understanding of law and the legal process. The writings of John Austin (1790–1859) are historically influential within the Anglo-American tradition, and state clearly basic principles of positivism. More recently H. L. A. Hart's (1907–92) *The Concept of Law* usefully isolated the concepts of 'rule' and 'obligation', and drew attention to the way in which rules are recognized. Hans Kelsen (1881–1973) attempted with some success to show how a legal system could be analysed in terms of a hierarchy of norms,* although many find that the end (or summit) of the hierarchy is difficult to recognize within a living legal system.

By contrast, normative jurisprudence is not indifferent to the content of law. Without necessarily dismissing the insights of positivism, normative theories do deal with the questions whether and to what extent the morality of a rule is relevant to a consideration of its nature as law. Natural law* is a term often used in this connection, but there are many varieties of natural law, ranging from the exclusively theological to the sociological.

Historically, jurisprudential thinking in Western Europe was a subset of theological discussion, principles of law and of legal practice all being derived from Christianity. Law and the legal order constituted a gift of God, given for the proper regulation and functioning of society. Such theologians as Augustine* and Thomas Aquinas* were major influences. Much of the medieval discussion of the 'just price',* and of the 'just wage' (see Wage*) and the mechanisms to ensure that the principles of each were worked out in practice, can be analysed from the perspective of today as jurisprudential discussion. A theologically based 'natural law' was appealed to, and was a common ground between the proponents of different views.

The watershed between such theologically oriented jurisprudence and modern theories came with the writings of Hugo Grotius.* His *De Iure Belli ac Pacis* (1625) begins with a discussion of law, tracing the validity of law to the decrees of God. However, he also states that in considering law, right reason applied to the social order would arrive at the same conclusion, and that right reason would continue to justify law even if there were no God.

Liberated from theology, jurisprudence flourished. The way was open for positivism, as described above. Others contributed without becoming extreme in their disregard of moral and ethical questions. Thus utilitarianism (see Consequentialism*) could incorporate the notion of 'greatest good' in evaluating legislation and the legal process. Some would have regard to rights, intrinsic in or to humankind as a social organism, or even intrinsic to individuals. Yet others consider that common morality and expectations have a

role to play. The economic analysis of law, whether based on Marxist doctrine or otherwise, has also contributed to the discussion. In modern times the debate between H. L. A. Hart and Lord Devlin (1905–92) was instructive (see Devlin–Hart Debate*), and the writings of Ronald Dworkin (1931–) on Rights, of John Rawls (1921–) on Justice, and of John Finnis (1940–) on Natural Law, deserve study.

In the 20th century, various forms of critical legal studies have also developed. The American Realist school stressed the functioning of the law and the role of the judiciary in shaping the law through interpretation of legislation. The Scandinavian Realists, by contrast, show how the language of the law conceals both persuasion (even conditioning) and force in the inculcation of obedience to a particular legal system. Most recently a new form of critical legal studies has been influenced by deconstructionist ideas from other disciplines.

A balanced reply to the question 'What is law?' is difficult. Both major kinds of theory – positivism with its emphasis on what is, and normativism pointing to content as being an essential aspect of law – contribute elements to that reply, and have to be held in a creative, not a destructive, tension. A proper approach to legal philosophy requires the use of different approaches depending on the nature of the problem that is being considered. The last word has not yet been said.

Bibliography

P. Devlin, *The Enforcement of Morals* (Oxford, 1965); R. Dworkin, *Law's Empire* (Cambridge, MA, 1986); J. M. Finnis, *Natural Law and Natural Rights* (Oxford, 1980); H. L. A. Hart, *The Concept of Law* (Oxford, 1961); J. Rawls, *A Theory of Justice* (Cambridge, MA, 1971; Oxford, 1972).

F.L.

JUS AD BELLUM, see JUST-WAR THEORY; WAR.

JUS IN BELLO, see JUST-WAR THEORY; WAR.

JUSTICE, see CRIMINAL JUSTICE; JUSTICE AND PEACE;③ VIRTUE AND VIRTUES.

JUSTICE, DISTRIBUTIVE, see JUSTICE AND PEACE.③

JUSTICE, RETRIBUTIVE, see JUSTICE AND PEACE; ③ PRISON AND PRISON REFORM; PUNISHMENT.

JUSTIFICATION, DOCTRINE OF.

Justification is a central notion within the Pauline writings (especially Rom. and Gal.). The term is difficult to render in Eng., on account of the richness of its associations in Heb. and NT Gk. Ideas such as 'being put in the right', 'being declared to be in the right', 'restoration' and 'vindication' go some way towards indicating the richness of the themes brought together in this model for understanding what God has achieved for us, and in us, through Jesus Christ. It is, however, the fact of justification (rather than a specific doctrine of justification) which dominates the NT. The NT writers (especially Paul and James) are perhaps more concerned to explore the consequences of justification than to explore its preconditions. Given that Christians *are* justified (Rom. 5:1), what follows?

Pressure to clarify how justification takes place (that is, the *doctrine* of justification) developed at two major junctures in Christian history. The first debate to centre on its themes was the Pelagian controversy of the 5th century (see Sin and Salvation⑤), which saw the rejection of the idea that we are justified through our own attempts to obey the law (see Law and Gospel*), or to follow the moral example set for us by Jesus Christ. Perhaps the more important was the Reformation of the 16th century, especially as it centred upon Martin Luther.* Convinced that the church of his day had lapsed into Pelagianism or some form of 'Judaism' (by which he meant an outlook on life which regarded salvation as something merited or earned), Luther urged the church to recover the Pauline doctrine of justification by faith. He drew a sharp distinction between the 'alien righteousness of Christ', on the basis of which we are justified, and the righteousness which develops within believers in response to the renewing and restoring work of the Holy Spirit. We are justified on account of the former, not the latter.

Before exploring the pastoral and ethical implications of the doctrine, it is necessary to note two serious misunderstandings of the doctrine which still surface in popular writings. First, it must be stressed that by 'justification by faith', Luther did not intend us to understand that we are justified *on account of faith*, as if faith were some kind of human work or achievement.

Rather, faith was itself seen as God's work within us, the God-given channel by which the 'benefits of Christ' (Melanchthon) could be conveyed to believers. Secondly, justification by faith, rightly understood, does not devalue or discourage human ethical activity. The doctrine affirms that while we are not justified on account of our moral activities, good works are an entirely appropriate and natural response to the justification. Luther uses the image of a fruit tree to make this point: justification represents God's gracious establishment of a good root system (faith), on account of which fruit (good works) will naturally follow. The doctrine liberates us from the oppressive mind-set which declares that we must be high achievers before we can enter the kingdom of God;* but in no way does it discourage us from becoming high achievers for God after our justification.

Pastoral implications

Pastorally, the most important implications of the doctrine relate to the co-existence of sin and righteousness* in believers, an idea given theological expression in Luther's phrase 'at one and the same time righteous and a sinner (*simul iustus et peccator*)'. The grounds of our justification lie outside us, in the righteousness of Christ (which, for Luther, could be likened to a protective covering). We are shielded by the righteousness of Christ, as our own righteousness begins to develop, in much the same way as a person who is ill begins to recover, given good medical care. And just as that person is at one and the same time both ill (in reality) and well (in hope), so the justified believer is both a sinner (in reality) and righteous (in hope, grounded in the utter trustworthiness of the promises of God). For Luther, the persistence of sin in believers is thus to be expected, and should not be the cause for anxiety or despair. The grounds of assurance lie not in ourselves, but in the promises of God.

The second major pastoral implication of the doctrine relates to the self-esteem* of believers. The doctrine of justification affirms that our status in the sight of God is something given, not something earned. Our self-esteem is declared to be something which is, and should be, grounded in the grace* of God, and not in our own efforts or achievements. The doctrine invites us to temper Christian humility (the recognition that we contribute nothing whatsoever to our justification, save providing the problem which God has to solve) with the insight that God still deems us worth justifying. The doctrine affirms that we are valued – not on account of who or what *we* are, but on account of who and what *God* is. The whole trajectory of the doctrine of justification by grace through faith (to use the full terminology) is that God affirms and values us, despite the fact that we inherently possess nothing which could be the basis of such an astonishingly generous attitude on God's part.

Ethical implications

The ethical implications of the doctrine centre on the motivation for performing good works.* Unlike many secular theories of ethics, which tend to locate the motivation for ethical action in the value of the deed done, the doctrine of justification points to the basic motivation for ethical action as lying in the changed situation of the believer. A new life leads to a new lifestyle. Justification establishes the root system of the plant that naturally and spontaneously leads to good works. There is thus a tension between two ethical components of the doctrine of justification. On the one hand, the changed status and situation of believers naturally incline them to perform acts pleasing to God. On the other, sin remains within believers, and continues to exercise a negative effect upon them, inhibiting them from performing such acts. It is this tension which underlies the tendency within the NT to oscillate between the indicative ('You are righteous') and the imperative ('Be righteous!'). This tension is perhaps best resolved through the formula 'Become what you are' – that is, that believers should actualize in their lives their new status, given to them through their gracious justification by God.

Bibliography

H. Küng, *Justification: The Doctrine of Karl Barth and a Catholic Reflection* (ET, London and Philadelphia, ²1981); A. E. McGrath, *Iustitia Dei: A History of the Christian Doctrine of Justification*, 2 vols. (Cambridge, 1986); *idem*, *Roots that Refresh: Tapping the Spiritual Vitality of the Reformation* (London, 1992), chs. 8 and 9; G. Reid (ed.), *The Great Acquittal* (London, 1980); H. Thielicke, *TE*.

A.E.McG.

JUSTIFICATION, MORAL, is the supplying of an adequate explanation for the moral choices we make: why we oppose euthanasia, avoid CFCs, tell the truth, *etc.*

Specific moral choices are usually justified by referring to more general moral rules: *e.g.* I ought not to avoid paying my train fare because stealing is wrong. But the rules themselves also need justifying. This is done by referring to fundamental moral principles, such as 'Always act in love', or to the principle that the moral rules that we should follow are those that can be satisfactorily universalized. Thus the rule 'Do not steal' could be justified on the grounds that taking another person's property is an unloving thing to do, or that total anarchy would result if we made it a universal rule that anyone can help themselves to anything they want.

But appealing to fundamental moral principles only pushes the issue of justification one stage further back. Through the centuries a wide range of differing moral principles has been put forward. How do we justify the specific moral principles that we choose to adopt?

Even those ethical systems like emotivism,* situation ethics* and relativism,* which tell us there are no fixed moral rules, contain basic moral principles like 'You should always do what feels right to you', 'You should do the loving thing in each situation', and so on. Other ethical systems put forward alternative fundamental principles, claiming that we should always do what promotes pleasure* (see Hedonism*), or the greatest happiness of the greatest number (see Consequentialism*), or the well-being of society, or the survival of the human race, or the furthering of the process of evolution, or the ecological well-being of planet Earth. To these the Christian adds that our fundamental moral principle is that we should do what God commands.

It is generally accepted that it is not possible to provide definitive proof that any given moral principle or ethical system is true and that all others are false. This is not surprising; the same applies in most areas of philosophy and human knowledge. Even in the sciences certain and finally proven facts are hard to come by. But that does not mean that nothing can be done towards justifying the adopting of one particular philosophical or ethical system or, for that matter, scientific theory.

In the field of ethics it is possible to seek to justify the principles we adopt in a number of ways. We might support these principles by pointing out, *e.g.*, that we know them intuitively (see Intuitionism*), or through some innate or God-given ability. Or we could claim that those moral principles which seem to be held in common by the vast majority of the human race throughout history are the ones that have been shown to be right. Alternatively, we may approach the issue more pragmatically: the correct moral principles are those that work, enabling society to function well and smoothly. Yet again, we might make reason* the arbiter of the correctness of moral principles: is the system to which they give rise rational, coherent and consistent with what we know of the universe and life, and so on?

The Christian who accepts the Bible as authoritative in ethical matters can still be confronted with the question, 'Why should we accept the moral principles and commands we find there?' To this we can reply, 'Because they are the commands of God', or, better still, 'Because they express the nature of God.' Telling the truth is right not just because God commands it (though that would be a sufficient reason) but also because God is truth. In telling the truth we are acting in keeping with the creator and Lord of the universe.

That is not to say that the Christian should not make use of the other means mentioned above when seeking to justify Christian moral principles, especially when confronted with those who will not accept the authority of the Bible. We can certainly claim that some moral truths are intuitively known (Rom. 1:18–21) or discernible in society and history. Christian moral principles can stand the pragmatic test, and can be well defended by rational arguments.

In a society which is confronted with a bewildering array of approaches and principles in the ethical market-place, Christians have an opportunity to demonstrate that their system as a whole is superior to all of its rivals. If we are convinced of this, we need to go beyond the basic 'We do it because the Bible says so' (though this may well be a sufficient reason for us personally), and be willing to justify Christian morality to others both by argument and, perhaps even more importantly, by consistently putting it into practice.

Bibliography

B. Mitchell, *Morality, Religious and Secular* (Oxford, 1980); O. O'Donovan, *Resurrection and Moral Order* (Leicester and Grand Rapids, ²1994).

P.A.H.

JUST PRICE is the term coined by medieval churchmen to describe the idea that all economic transactions should be made at a price which both rewards the seller and satisfies the customer. They argued that justice required that exchange involves equivalent values. Although the concept of fairness in exchange-value originates in the ethical writings of Aristotle,* its most coherent exposition is found in Thomas Aquinas,* *STh* 2a2ae 77. His biblical basis was the statement of Jesus, 'so in everything, do to others what you would have them do to you, for this sums up the Law and the Prophets' (Mt. 7:12).

Aquinas developed the concept of just price against a background of a largely rural economy producing an increasing surplus of agricultural goods when cities were emerging as centres for manufacture and exchange. People were used to prices of goods and services, especially food, remaining stable; any major deviation from this norm often produced social disquiet. Rulers asked the clergy for a means to dissuade any who saw the chance of a quick profit by exploiting a temporary surplus or deficiency. The 'just price' was their answer.

As a practical means of determining prices, the concept of the just price rapidly became of theoretical use only. It was realized that price had to take into account incidentals in the cost of production, such as transport to and from market. Thus, a just price was soon defined as one arrived at by common evaluation; in other words, one agreed between a willing buyer and a willing seller, or what today would be called 'the market price'. The deeply held general desire for a stable value of the currency is still reflected today in the wish to rid a country of price inflation.

There is a special case within the concept of the just price which has continued to attract attention in the centuries since medieval schoolmen tried to extend their idea of moral order into economic life. This is the 'just wage' (see Wage*) or the price of labour. Economists have always recognized the unique characteristics of labour as a factor of production. The application of the just-price idea to wage determination was defined in terms of enabling the wage-earner to maintain his wife and children 'at the standard customary in his social class'. Michael Fogarty (1916–) has explored the application of this concept to contemporary wage determination and the debate concerning a national minimum wage (see *The Just Wage*).

The relevance of the just price today can

perhaps be seen in two areas of public policy: control of inflation; and protection of consumers from exploitation by monopoly* suppliers of goods and services. Significant increases in prices produce not only hardship for the thrifty (who see their savings dissipated), but unfairness to those who are unable to compensate for decreasing real value of income – people who have no marketable skills or who are on fixed incomes, *e.g.* pensioners. Rampant inflation can also lead to the collapse of stable government and is unjust and unfair to the majority of the population. It follows that the idea of a just price for an individual transaction also includes a moral obligation by the State to protect the value of the means of exchange, the currency.

Protection from using monopolistic power to set prices is also deemed to be a moral duty of the State. Three means are normally used: 1. The regulation of pricing policies of legal or natural monopolies by the appointment of regulators, for instance in those industries which provide public utilities (*e.g.* fuel and water). Such regulators can ensure both that the service is increasingly efficient, and that prices are kept below those which would have resulted from unfettered operation of markets. 2. The State's insistence on competition in the provision of goods and services. This is achieved by guaranteeing the right of entry to the market and by outlawing all uncompetitive practices such as price-fixing agreements. 3. The introduction by some governments of prices-and-incomes policies where changes in either are strictly controlled. These policies are most often found in wartime or other exceptional circumstances.

A price in a competitive environment will approximate to the cost of production plus an incentive (say 10%) to organize and take risk. A price which is widely different from cost is unlikely to be justifiable on moral grounds. Hopefully it will be undercut by additional suppliers who will provide the product or service at lower prices.

Bibliography

M. Blaug, *Economic Theory in Retrospect* (Cambridge and New York, 1988); M. P. Fogarty, *The Just Wage* (London, 1961; repr. Westport, CN, 1975); R. Kaulla, *The Theory of Just Price* (New York, 1941); E. Roll, *A History of Economic Thought* (London and Boston, MA, 1972); G. Routh, *The Origin of Economic Ideas* (London and Dobbs Ferry, NY, ²1989); R. H. Tawney, *Religion and the Rise of Capitalism* (1926; repr. Harmondsworth, 1969).

S.W.

JUST REVOLUTION, see JUST-WAR THEORY.

JUST WAGE, see ECONOMIC ETHICS; [17] WAGE.

JUST-WAR THEORY attempts to limit both resort to war* and the conduct of war to what justice allows. As an application of Christian love it gives priority to reconciliation, and seeks to prevent just punishment of an aggressor from deteriorating into vengeful retaliation.

Rules of war

The rules that govern going to war (*jus ad bellum*) are: 1. the only *just cause* is defence against violent aggression; 2. the only *just intention* is to restore a just peace to friend and foe alike; 3. the use of military force must be a *last resort*, after negotiations and every other resort have been tried and have failed; and 4. the decision must be made by the *highest governmental authority*.

The conduct of war (*jus in bello*) requires also: 5. a war must be for *limited ends* only, sufficient to repel aggression and redress its injustice; 6. the means must be limited by *proportionality* to the offence; 7. *non-combatant immunity* from intentional and direct attack must be respected; and 8. combat should not be prolonged when there is no *reasonable hope of success* within these limits.

Biblical and historical roots

Just-war theory was developed by Augustine,* (in contrast to the pacifism* of the first three centuries AD), Thomas Aquinas,* Francisco de Vitoria,* John Calvin,* Francisco de Suarez,* Hugo Grotius* and John Locke (1632–1704). Applications to modern warfare have been developed most notably by Paul Ramsey.* It is the traditional position of Roman Catholic, Presbyterian and Reformed churches, though rejected by Mennonites and other Christian pacifists. While an earlier version based on justice without love was formulated by Cicero (106–43 BC), biblical roots for the Christian tradition run throughout the OT and NT.

Christians are enjoined (Rom. 13:7; 1 Pet. 2:13–17) to respect governmental authority and pay taxes that support its God-given mandate to resist and punish evil, a theme abundantly illustrated in OT history. Jesus himself affirmed the OT concept of retributive* justice (Mt. 5:17–26; 7:13–23), while removing the *lex talionis* from the context of an individual's quarrels (Mt. 5:38–46). Loving one's enemies does not deny to government the responsibility of enforcing a just peace (*cf.* Rom. 12:17–13:8). While private parties should 'turn the other cheek', government may properly resort to force.

The *lex talionis* in both Mt. 5:38 and Rom. 13:1–5 refers not to taking personal revenge but to just punishment administered by governments. It provides a doctrine of proportion, protecting offenders from indiscriminate retaliation or excessive penalty. 'An eye for an eye' sets the limit (Ex. 21:18–25), and a fair trial was required in order to protect the innocent (Dt. 19:15–21) from unjust treatment.

Just-war theory extends this approach beyond the civil order to maintaining a just peace more generally. Justice requires that unjust violence be resisted and then punished proportionally. So the prophet denounced excessive bloodshed and massacre of innocents in times of war (Am. 1:11–15). Moreover, there is precedent for armed rebellion* in the history of Israel (*e.g.* 2 Ki. 9:1–10); requiring declaration of war by the highest authority does not rule out the possibility of a just revolution (see Violence*). The Scholastic theologians argue that a tyrant who violates the common good and represses the people for his personal benefit is guilty of sedition, and may therefore be overthrown (see Tyrannicide*). Locke likewise, invoking the consent of the governed, claims that the people may as a last resort establish a government themselves and, on its authority, evict the tyrant. Just-war rules apply to both the causes and the conduct of revolution.

The fact remains that war is a disastrous tragedy from which the innocent as well as the guilty suffer. The psalmist laments it (*e.g.* Ps. 46:8–11) and the prophet looks for a day when swords will be beaten into ploughshares and the kingdom of shalom appears (Is. 2:1–5; 9:1–7; 11:1–9). 'Just cause', however, eliminates war as an instrument of politics, ideological rivalry, geographic expansion, or for seizing economic resources. Cicero (106–43 BC) allowed war either for defence or to avenge a dishonour, but Augustine, knowing that love seeks no vengeance, limited just cause to defence alone. If all parties were to accept this limitation, there would be neither aggression nor war, and peace would indeed reign.

While biblical influences shaped this line of thought, a natural-law* ethic also undergirds it. Aquinas, Vitoria and Suarez, with their Aristotelian orientation, stress the natural ends to which the creator inclined humankind; hence the law of self-preservation and our need for a rationally ordered society forbid war for anything but defence. Locke and Grotius see natural law more in the tradition of Cicero and the Stoics, as grounding the rights of rational beings in a rationally ordered world. From these general principles just-war rules seem naturally to follow.

Should a Christian fight?

Granted the moral legitimacy of governmental uses of force,* the question of Christians participating in war still remains. Christians are called to be peacemakers, and to love their enemies. The question then is whether believers may participate in the morally just functions of governments. Christians of the just-war tradition believe that the OT provides abundant precedent in those who were called by God to rule, to judge and even to war. Jesus and the apostles never changed this, never advised a governor to resign, or disarmed a converted soldier. If God has entrusted to governments limited uses of force for just ends, and if believers may participate in just functions of government, then, it is argued, they may participate in just uses of force.

This, however, implies selective conscientious objection, for not every conflict a government engages in or every means it uses may be just. Vitoria and Suarez maintained that those in a position to have sufficient information should in love weigh things carefully and voice their judgments; those without such opportunity may in good conscience go to war, unless it is clearly unjust.

See also: JUSTICE AND PEACE. ③

Bibliography

D. C. Curry (ed.), *Evangelicals and the Bishops' Pastoral Letter* (Grand Rapids, 1984), sec. 2, 'The Just War in a Nuclear Age', pp. 49–75; A. F. Holmes (ed.), *War and Christian Ethics: Classic Readings on the Morality of War* (Grand Rapids, ²1991); J. T. Johnson, *Just War Tradition and the Restraint of War*

(Princeton, NJ, 1981); National Conference of Catholic Bishops, *The Challenge of Peace: God's Promise and Our Response* (Washington, DC, and London, 1983); P. Ramsey, *The Just War: Force and Political Responsibility* (New York, 1968); *idem, War and the Christian Conscience* (Durham, NC, 1961).

A.F.H.

JUVENILE DELINQUENCY. Before the distinctive character of social deviance in children was recognized, the *classical-punishment* views of Cesare Beccaria (1738–94) and Jeremy Bentham* advocated punishment* to fit the crime.* Since criminals exercise free will, punishment is both earned and deserved. The social or personal characteristics of the offender are irrelevant. C. S. Lewis,* in 'The Humanitarian Theory of Punishment', supported this retributive, or 'just deserts', view of justice as the appropriate response recognizing both free will and responsibility.

In contrast, the *positivist-rehabilitation* view focuses on punishment to fit the criminal. Individual characteristics and the social situation of the offender may limit the range of choices and diminish the level of individual responsibility. The mentally ill, the insane and children are to be treated differently from the fully responsible adult offender. Within the positivist perspective, the special needs of children come sharply into focus. Treatment and rehabilitation rather than punishment become the norm for juvenile offenders.

English common law has formed the basis for treatment of juveniles by American courts. Children under seven years are incapable of *mens rea*, or criminal intent, and cannot be convicted of a crime. Children aged seven to fourteen may be charged with crimes if evidence indicates their ability to distinguish between right and wrong. Adolescents over the age of fourteen are adults and may be adjudicated as criminal (W. Thornton *et al.*, *Delinquency and Justice*). In 1899 the first American juvenile court was established in Illinois. Both court adjudication and corrections for juveniles were separated from the adult justice system. When convicted of illegal behaviour, minors under the age of eighteen are defined as *juvenile deliquents*.

'Status offences' are violations structured by the unique social position of the minor and include school truancy, running away from family, engaging in lewd or immoral behaviour, using obscene language, incorrigibility and violating curfew. Many juveniles of both sexes have been introduced to the juvenile justice system as a result of status-offence behaviours. The federal Juvenile Justice and Delinquency Prevention Act of 1974 redefined this non-criminal activity and created separate categories for neglect, dependency and minors in need of supervision. Programmes are created to divert status offenders from correctional facilities to counselling or group foster homes. However, at least eleven States still place delinquents and status offenders together in maximum-security institutions (D. Shichor, 'Historical and Current Trends in American Juvenile Justice').

In addition to status offences, three other categories of juvenile behaviour are identified in the research literature. According to the annual National Youth Survey begun in 1976, 90% of all minors in the US engage in *occasional delinquency* typified by vandalism, petty theft, shoplifting and non-aggravated assault. Occasional deliquency cuts across social class, race and gender categories and is thought by many to be part of the norms-testing engaged in during American adolescence. A small percentage of those involved in occasional delinquency are adjudicated and sent to correctional institutions (D. S. Elliot *et al.*, *The Prevalence and Incidence of Delinquent Behaviour*).

The *chronic delinquent* is a repeat offender involved in breaking in to homes, robbery, vehicle theft and illegal gun possession. The National Youth Survey of 1983 finds that 7% of the occasional delinquents go on to become chronic delinquents, with about 3% of these engaged in violent crime. M. Wolfgang's (1924–) cohort studies ('Delinquency in a Birth Cohort II') found that less than 7% of a longitudinal sample of 14,000 boys born in 1958 commit most of the juvenile crimes. These are young males who begin their criminal careers early and continue into adult life. According to the Uniform Crime Reports, juvenile crime among girls under the age of eighteen more than tripled between 1960 and 1982, with most of the major increases in property crimes. Female delinquency generally declines or remains stable as girls move through adolescence (S. Ageton, 'The Dynamics of Female Delinquency').

Juvenile street gangs have a long history in both the US and Britain. During the late 19th and early 20th centuries, first-generation immigrant, migrant and poverty-stricken boys created defensive primary groups which provided 'family' and purpose for their lives. Irish, Polish, Italian and black gangs in New York City, Chicago and other American cities, and Borstal gangs in Britain, represent the traditional, usually non-violent, street gangs prior to the Second World War. Following the war, major urban centres of Europe, Britain and the US endured massive infiltrations of illegal hard drugs on a scale not experienced before. Motivated by their own drug abuse (see Drugs*) and by the lucrative market for drug sales, juvenile gang members have now become criminal and violent.

One response to the volatile situation is to move from rehabilitation to retribution with a 'get tough' court response towards juveniles who commit felony crimes. For a heinous crime or murder, or if the juvenile has been convicted of two previous felonies, or if a handgun has been used in a drug violation, the minor may be tried and sentenced under the adult criminal code. Controversy continues over this response of the law, particularly in the case of a juvenile charged with a capital offence. Under Eng. common law, no-one under the age of sixteen could be put to death for a criminal offence (F. Ludwig, *Youth and the Law*). Under what possible circumstances could contemporary society approve the execution of a juvenile who has been sentenced under the adult criminal code?

Correctional facilities are generally unprepared for the current influx of minors, or for the handling of juveniles under life sentences. Constructive response to delinquency is needed at both the micro and macro levels. Advocacy programmes for delinquents provide opportunity for pastors, youth leaders and caring adults within the church to develop healthy relationships with status offenders, delinquents and minors tried as adults. Trained social workers are present in every community to provide information, counselling and referral assistance to families. Since the juvenile court is closed to the general public for protection of the minor's privacy, communities have created 'guardian *ad litem*' groups to monitor court procedures and correctional facilities. In addition, church organizations offer redemptive justice to restore and reconcile the juvenile offender back into the community.

Without distributive justice at the macro level, however, individual advocacy and court monitoring are short-term responses. The educational system must provide necessary life-skills especially for those adolescents most likely to be abandoned by the system. Nuclear families are fragile; some cannot successfully socialize children into healthy adulthood, and require assistance. Social values which encourage greed, competitiveness and individualism* need to be re-evaluated. Media representations of violence, exploitive sex and drug abuse should be opposed. Among the many factors contributing to delinquency, criminologists highlight those reflecting poverty: substandard housing, inadequate nutrition, and health-care and familial economic stress. The Christian is commanded to do justice, to love mercy, and to walk humbly with God (Mi. 6:8). Juvenile delinquency presents opportunity to obey this command.

Bibliography

S. Ageton, 'The Dynamics of Female Delinquency, 1976–1980', *Crim* 21, 1983, pp. 555–584; C. Beccaria, *On Crimes and Punishments* (1764; ET, Indianapolis, IN, 1986); D. S. Elliot *et al.*, *The Prevalence and Incidence of Delinquent Behavior, 1976–1980*, National Youth Survey Report no. 26 (Boulder, CO, 1983); C. S. Lewis, 'The Humanitarian Theory of Punishment', in W. Hooper (ed.), *God in the Dock* (Grand Rapids, 1970) = *Undeceptions* (London, 1971); F. Ludwig, *Youth and the Law: Handbook on Laws Affecting Youth* (New York, 1955); D. Shichor, 'Historical and Current Trends in American Juvenile Justice', *JFCJ* 34.3, 1983, pp. 61–75; W. Thornton *et al.*, *Delinquency and Justice* (Glenview, IL, 1982); M. Wolfgang, 'Delinquency in a Birth Cohort II: Some Preliminary Results', in P. Langan and L. Greenfeld, *Career Patterns in Crime* (Washington, DC, 1983).

Z.G.L.

KAIROS DOCUMENT, THE. Published in South Africa on 25 September 1985, the Kairos Document was drafted by a group of black and white pastors and theologians ministering and teaching in the midst of repression, brutalities and atrocities committed within the black communities by the Security Forces in a last desperate attempt to consolidate white domination of the country.

The document basically consists of a critique of what is called 'State theology' and 'church theology', and as an alternative to these theologies it proposes a prophetic theology for South Africa. Under State theology, the God mentioned in the preamble in the South African constitution is identified as the 'god' of the South African State and therefore an idol. The political policy of apartheid,* implemented by the State,* is exposed as a heresy.

Under church theology, it points out the total failure of the churches in South Africa to have prevented or stopped apartheid as an ungodly system. The unwillingness of the churches to confront the State on its devastating political policy weakened the Christian witness and made it pathetically ineffective.

In its proposed prophetic theology, the document has a strong 'evangelistic' appeal. It calls the churches to conversion,* since the conversion of 'outsiders' to the Christian faith is severely obstructed by an unconverted and compromised church. It demands a faithful prophetic witness in what it sees as a demonic socio-political situation.

The document caused unexpected, overwhelming reactions from both inside and outside South Africa. It was immediately condemned by the government and by the churches neutral to, or in support of, the government's apartheid policy. Many conservative Christians labelled the document a Marxist document calling for revolution and violence.* To other conservative Christians the document was considered a serious challenge to their own faithfulness to the gospel. They responded to the document by publishing a document called *Evangelical Witness in South Africa:* Evangelicals Critique their own Theology and Practice* (Johannesburg and Oxford, 1986).

Many Christians, however, both ecumenical and evangelical, evaluated the document as a timely word of prophecy in a 'kairos' (decisive moment) in the history of South Africa. In February 1990 the government and the majority of the churches in South Africa rejected the policy of apartheid as an unjust and evil system.

Bibliography

The Kairos Document: Challenge to the Church – A Theological Comment on the Political Crisis in South Africa (Johannesburg, 1985; Johannesburg and Grand Rapids, ²1986); C. Green, 'The Kairos Debate: Christology and Tyranny', *JTSA* 55, June 1986; W. Huber, 'The Barmen Declaration and the Kairos Document: On the Relationship between Confession and Politics', *JTSA* 75, June 1991; J. N. J. Kritzinger, 'The Kairos Document: A Call to Conversion', *Missionalia* 16:3, 1988; W. Saayman, *Christian Mission in South Africa* (Pretoria, 1991).

N.J.S.

KANT, IMMANUEL (1724–1804), the son of a saddler, reputedly of Scottish origin, was for many years professor of logic and metaphysics at the university of Königsberg, East Prussia. His ethics is a systematic, theoretical presentation of some of the main principles of the Enlightenment.* Kant turned away from an ethic based upon natural law,* or divine command or any hedonic (see Hedonism*) principle. Instead he appealed to the moral law which any person, in so far as he or she was rational and free, would legislate in a dispassionate, universal manner. Kant provided several different renderings of this law, but perhaps the most famous and influential is 'Act so as to treat humanity never only as a means, but always also as an end'. True morality is the choice of individuals who form a community only in so far as they are rational, and what they 'legislate' is the moral law.

Kant envisaged human reason as the source of morality, and so autonomous. In this he was effecting a 'Copernican revolution' in moral thought comparable to that effected in his critical epistemological writings. Such morality has unconditional, categorical force (see Categorical Imperative*). Paradoxically, perhaps, Kant argued that such an account of morality requires God's existence to be postulated. Any other possible source of morality than human reason, including the law of God, was heteronomous, capable of generating an imperative that was 'hypothetical', suspended upon the choice of certain ends. Only the categorical imperative, willed unconditionally, is moral.

Kant believed that from this austere and abstract framework it is possible to derive substantive ethical rules, the most famous of which is the absolute prohibition against lying. The success of such derivations is controversial. But what is not in doubt is that Kant bequeathed to subsequent moral philosophy and to the wider culture certain key ideas, notably autonomy* and universalizability, and the ideal of an ethic of duties that holds, no matter what the consequences.

See also: HISTORY OF CHRISTIAN ETHICS. [6]

Bibliography

Groundwork of the Metaphysic of Morals (1785; ET, London, ³1958); *Prolegomena to Any Future Metaphysics* (1783; ET, Indianapolis, IN, 1977); R. Scruton, *Kant* (Oxford, 1982); A. W. Wood, *Kant's Moral Religion* (Ithaca, NY, 1970).

P.H.

KEBLE, JOHN (1792–1866). Born the son of a village clergyman, John Keble became one of the primary instigators of the Oxford Movement,* John Henry Newman (1801–90) citing Keble's Assize sermon on 'National Apostasy' in 1833 as the start of the Movement. Although a Fellow of Oriel College, Oxford, from 1811 and Professor of Poetry from 1831 to 1835, from 1823 he was occupied with assisting his ailing father's parochial work, afterwards remaining as the vicar of Hursley in Hampshire from 1836 until his death. He was best known for his immensely popular collection of poems, constructed around the fasts and feasts of the *Book of Common Prayer*, entitled *The Christian Year*, published in 1827.

Although no great original thinker, Keble provided the Oxford Movement with its strongest link with both the old High Church tradition of the Caroline Divines,* and the parochial clergy of the Eng. countryside. In response to the upheaval of the times he urged not radical social change, but the divine inviolability of the Church of England and the service of God in 'the daily and hourly duties of piety, purity, charity, justice'. He advocated daily services in the Church, more frequent Holy Communion and the revival of private confession,* arguing mainly on the grounds of its pastoral benefit for the priest, in enabling him to know the true needs of his people better.

For many in the Oxford Movement, Keble became a symbol of both resistance to State domination of the Church and the ideal of the saintly parish priest, labouring for moral and spiritual holiness in his people by means of the exaltation of the mind and spirit to the mysteries of God.

Bibliography

G. Battiscombe, *John Keble: A Study in Limitations* (London, 1963); J. R. Griffin, *John Keble: Saint of Anglicanism* (Macon, GA, 1987); G. Rowell, *The Vision Glorious* (Oxford, 1983).

G.S.T.

KESWICK MOVEMENT. An evangelical Protestant movement with a distinctive emphasis on personal holiness.*

Keswick teaching arose from the ministries of three Americans: William E. Boardman (1810–86), and Robert Pearsall Smith (1827–89) and his wife Hanna Whitall Smith (1832–1911). In the mid-19th century, after reading the testimonies of Charles Finney (1792–1875) and Asa Mahon (1799–1889), Boardman found 'rest of heart in Jesus for sanctification' and became an advocate of the 'Higher Christian Life'.

In the late 1860s Robert Pearsall Smith and his wife also began travelling in the interest of holiness. Mrs Smith traced her special experience to 1867, when she had learned through a Methodist dressmaker about a 'second blessing' which brought 'victory' to a Christian believer. She introduced her husband to 'the secret of victory'.

During evangelist Dwight L. Moody's (1837–99) London campaign of 1873, the Smiths joined Boardman for a series of breakfasts designed to promote the holiness experience. A series of conferences followed, including one at Oxford.

Under the inspiration of the Oxford meetings Canon T. D. Harford-Battersby (*c.* 1823–83) arranged for an open-air convention at Keswick. The town became the centre of holiness teaching in England and gave its name to the movement, which continues to this day.

Keswick teaching rejects the traditional evangelical doctrine that, though a believer can be justified in a moment, sanctification* proceeds through a life-long struggle. Keswick teaches instead deliverance from the power of sin. Conference speakers often urge their listeners to yield and trust Christ in an instant, but maintain that the believer's tendency to sin is not extinguished but merely counteracted by living victoriously in the Spirit.

Largely through Moody's ministry, Keswick teaching spread throughout the UK and N. America, and influenced many evangelical Bible schools and missionary agencies.

Bibliography

S. Barabas, *So Great Salvation: The History and Message of the Keswick Convention* (London, 1952); J. C. Pollock, *The Keswick Story* (London and Chicago, 1964); J. C. Ryle, *Holiness* (1879; repr. Darlington, 1977); B. B. Warfield, *Perfectionism*, 2 vols. (New York, 1931).

B.L.S.

KIERKEGAARD, SØREN AABYE

(1813–55), a Danish writer whose philosophical, theological and edifying works resist easy classification. Many of Kierkegaard's most important philosophical works were published pseudonymously, the pseudonymous 'authors' being like characters in a novel. Simultaneously, Kierkegaard published devotional and theological works under his own name. His writing culminated with an 'attack on Christendom', waged in newspapers and in a popular periodical which he had founded.

Kierkegaard saw his task as being 'to reintroduce Christianity into Christendom', helping people become Christians who assumed they were already Christians by virtue of being part of a 'Christian' society. Kierkegaard believed that Christianity provided the best answer to the problems of human existence; he thought his contemporaries did not understand Christianity because they had lost a sense of what human life itself is about. Thus a great deal of his work is psychological in character; he provides descriptions of human existence in light of the Christian understanding of human beings as spiritual creatures who stand before God and are responsible to God.

He stressed that Christian faith* is not merely intellectual assent that is the result of evidence, but is a 'passion' created in the person when the individual encounters God, a firsthand meeting with Jesus Christ that produces in the individual a consciousness of sin. Rather than altering Christianity to make it palatable to modern thought, as many liberal theologians of his day wished to do, Kierkegaard stressed that the content of the Christian revelation, ultimately the paradoxical incarnation of God in human form, is naturally repugnant to human thinking that is shaped by sin and consequently chafes at divine authority. When Christianity is rightly proclaimed, it always carries with it the 'possibility of offence'. However, this is only a possibility; in the 'happy passion' of faith,

reason* and God's revelation of himself in human form are on good terms. The true Christian is a follower of Jesus, not merely an admirer, and is willing to suffer persecution from the world for the sake of the gospel.

See also: HISTORY OF CHRISTIAN ETHICS.[6]

Bibliography

Kierkegaard's Writings, 26 vols. (Princeton, NJ, 1978–94).

C. S. Evans, *Søren Kierkegaard's Christian Psychology* (Grand Rapids, 1990); *idem, Kierkegaard's Fragments and Postscript* (Atlantic Highlands, NJ, 1983); M. Westphal, *Kierkegaard's Critique of Reason and Society* (Mercer, GA, 1987).

C.S.E.

KILLING.

The prohibition of the taking of human life is deeply rooted in Christian faith. It is one of the fundamental prohibitions in the OT: 'Whoever sheds the blood of man, by man shall his blood be shed; for in the image of God has God made man' (Gn. 9:6); 'You shall not murder' (Ex. 20:13), or in JB 'You shall not kill'. It is presupposed by Jesus: 'You have heard that it was said to the people long ago, "Do not murder, and anyone who murders will be subject to judgment"' (Mt. 5:21); and in the NT generally: *e.g.* '"Do not murder" . . . Love does no harm to its neighbour. Therefore love is the fulfilment of the law' (Rom. 13:9–10). From these and other passages it is easy to trace a number of reasons for this prohibition. Human life is created by God, but more than that, it is created in his image.* God loves his people, and commands them to love one another. Jesus Christ is the Word made flesh, and more than that, he died to bring life to the world. How can we kill another human being for whom Christ also died? The matter is summarized in the command to love our neighbour (Rom. 13:10). These themes provide the basis for the sanctity* of human life; there are others also relevant for some borderline cases.

The question arises whether there are any permitted exceptions, *i.e.* occasions when human life may be taken, and if so, on what grounds. Although modern translations of the Ten Commandments vary (some using 'murder', some 'kill'), there can be no reasonable doubt about what is intended. The OT clearly intends that some taking of human life is in fact required, for instance in punishment of the murderer (*e.g.* Gn. 9:6), and the adulterer (Lv. 20:10).

Genesis 9:6 offers us a strong clue for considering how we should approach the possible exceptions. The murderer's life is taken precisely because he has shed the blood of another. Killing is here required in order to defend the living and to protect the sanctity of human life. This strongly suggests the fundamental reason which can alone justify deliberate killing, namely, the protection of other lives.

The OT thus underwrites the sanctity of human life, and provides ground for the taking of life in defence of that sanctity. This is paradoxical, but it is not self-contradictory. The NT, however, provides even more cogent grounds for not taking human life. Christ lived in human form, and died to save humanity. How then can Christians ever kill? There have always been those who argue that Christians should never shed the blood of another; not even to uphold the law, defend one's country, or defend one's own life.

The seriousness of the crime of murder or homicide cannot be in question. Murder is the unlawful and deliberate killing of another. Killings commanded or authorized by the State,* such as those in war,* or in law enforcement, are not murder. Unlawful killings are murderous if done with deliberate intention. Deliberately causing serious injury which leads to death is also murder. This excludes killing by accident, and killing where it is not possible to ascribe a full degree of responsibility. Killing in self-defence is not usually murder; and there is a special category for the killing of babies *in utero* (see Abortion*), and in some circumstances for the killing of infants (see Infanticide*). In English law there is no special category for 'mercy-killings' (or euthanasia*).

The legal distinctions rest on moral grounds. The grounds for the possible lawfulness of killing are close to the grounds for moral justification. The basic Christian moral argument is that it may, in some circumstances, be both justified and a duty to take one life in order to save another. This can happen only where the life to be taken directly threatens the life of the other. The reasoning is clear in the case of ectopic pregnancy (a condition in which the growth of the foetus seriously jeopardizes the health of the mother). A different example is provided when a policeman has no alternative but to shoot a gunman in order to prevent him killing others. The logic of this example is easily extended to cover killing in warfare. A similar but not identical argument may support the case for capital punishment* (in continuity with Gn. 9:6). (In our day, most moralists urge that the sanctity of life can be best respected and protected by other less final forms of punishment.*)

The distinction between deliberate and unintentional killing is also essential. A death brought about by accident may still be culpable, *e.g.* if there was a lack of care or forethought (maybe, in a road accident). But the responsibility is a different one. Some moral authorities extend this distinction and subsume under it all cases of justifiable killing. They would propose that any justifiable killing must be indirect (not directly willed and intended). In the examples in the previous paragraph, the surgeon's direct intention is to save the mother's life; the policeman's to save the lives of the people threatened by the gunman. In both cases the deaths are willed only indirectly (see Double Effect*).

In the debate about what is directly intended, and what indirectly, it is important to distinguish between motive* and intention.* The motive refers widely to the general context of action, the intention to what is directly and actually done. For instance, the policeman shooting the gunman may well hate him, if he already knows him. If so, this would be a wrong motive, but it would not mean that the action itself is the wrong one, for the direct intention is the saving of others. To put an example the other way, there may be a good motive for a wrong action. Those who oppose the direct killing of terminally ill patients would say that this was a wrong action (the direct intention is to bring about death), although the motive is perfectly right, namely to save the patient from suffering.

Finally, a distinction must be made between the wrongfulness of an action and the degree of culpability. The extent of blame is not simply proportional to the results of action. One who kills under extreme provocation may be less morally blameworthy than one who fosters hatred without ever giving physical expression to it. This distinction is often important in reaction to those who take their own life.

See also: JUST-WAR THEORY; RIGHTS, ANIMAL; SUICIDE.

D.J.E.A.

KING, MARTIN LUTHER (1939–68).

The most prominent leader of the civil rights movement in the US, Martin Luther King, Jr., Ph.D., was born on 15 January 1939 in Atlanta, Georgia, the son and grandson of Baptist ministers. He was shaped intellectually by Augustine,* Henry Thoreau (1817–62), a variety of philosophers, social gospel proponent Walter Rauschenbusch (1861–1918), and above all by Mohandas (Mahatma) Gandhi (1869–1948), to whose thinking he had been exposed while an undergraduate.

Appointed in 1954 to the pastorate of Dexter Avenue Baptist Church in Montgomery, Alabama, he soon became embroiled in the civil rights struggle. Heading the ultimately successful boycott* against segregated public transportation in Montgomery, his home was bombed and he was indicted for conspiracy to obstruct business, the first of many jailings for his activities. King was prominent in his role as president of the Southern Christian Leadership Conference, a group of more than sixty black clergy formed to oppose racial discrimination. He was also involved in nationwide activities to extend voting rights to blacks, desegregate public facilities in the Southern States, remove educational, employment, and housing restrictions for blacks, and halt the Vietnam War. Near the end of his career, he focused on the economic needs of people of all races.

In 1964 he won the Nobel Peace Prize, and is credited with assisting in the passage of the Civil Rights Acts of 1964 and 1968, which provided legal guarantees and remedies for blacks. King was assassinated in Memphis, Tennessee, in 1968 while attempting to quell the violence of the sanitation workers' strike, leaving a wife and four children.

King's theology emphasized the personal nature of God who acts in history, and human persons as fallen creatures of God who retain value and dignity. He accepted Augustine's judgment that unjust laws are not true laws at all, and combined Christian love with the non-violent methods of the Hindu Gandhi to create a philosophy of non-violent but vigorous struggle against evil and injustice (see Non-violence*).

Bibliography

R. B. Fowler, *A New Engagement: Evangelical Political Thought 1966–1976* (Grand Rapids, 1982); E. S. Lyght, *The Religious and Philosophical Foundations in the Thought of Martin Luther King, Jr.* (New York, 1972); S. B. Oates, *Let the Trumpet Sound: The Life of Martin Luther King, Jr.* (New York and London, 1982); E. Smith, *The Ethics of Martin Luther King, Jr.* (Lewistown, NY, 1981).

D.B.F.

KINGDOM ETHICS, see COMMUNITY

ETHICS;[16] CREATION; ESCHATOLOGY AND ETHICS; KINGDOM OF GOD; POLITICS; SOCIAL ETHICS.

KINGDOM OF GOD. According to the

Synoptic Gospels, 'the kingdom of God' (*hē basileia tou theou*) is central to Jesus' mission and foundational to his ethics. His understanding of the nature of the kingdom, much debated in this century, borrows heavily from OT and Jewish views of the era of salvation (see Sin and Salvation[5]). Overlooked in many recent discussions of the apostolate of the church and the nature of the life of discipleship, Jesus' proclamation of the kingdom of God in word and deed is now being recovered as a source for rooting and expanding our understandings of both.

In the Synoptic Gospels, 'the kingdom of God' and 'the kingdom of (the) heaven(s)' (*hē basileia tou ouranōn*) are interchangeable (*cf.* Mt. 13:11 = Mk. 4:11 = Lk. 8:10; Mt. 19:23–24). The latter is a translation of the later Jewish expression *malᵉkût šāmayim*, where 'heaven' has replaced the divine name out of reverence. (For examples of this as well as other circumlocutions of the divine name, see Mk. 14:61–62; Lk. 15:21; 1 Macc. 3:50.) It is impossible to determine which expression was characteristic of Jesus; indeed, it is possible that his own usage varied. Sometimes in the Synoptics the absolute 'the kingdom' (*hē basileia*) is also used.

Kingdom-expressions are found more than a hundred times in the first three Gospels, but only twice in the Fourth Gospel (Jn. 3:3, 5; *cf.* 18:36) and rarely outside the Gospels. This alone bespeaks its importance to the historical ministry of Jesus. What is more, the authors of the Synoptic Gospels record a number of *summaries* of Jesus' message into which are incorporated references to his kingdom-proclamation (*e.g.* Mt. 4:17, 23; 9:35; Mk. 1:14–15; Lk. 4:43; 9:11; Acts 1:3).

According to the Gospels, both John the Baptist and Jesus initiated their ministries with reference to the imminence of the 'kingdom of God' without defining its meaning for their audiences. We can only assume from this that this idea was well known within 1st-century Judaism.

Indeed, though the phrase itself is missing from the OT, the notion of God's rule is everywhere present; moreover, in the centuries before Christ, the concept of the kingdom of God took a more concrete form in Judaism. G. R. Beasley-Murray (1916–) has illuminated the idea of God's rule in the OT and its relations to subsequent talk of the kingdom of God by grounding it in Israel's experience of the coming of God in the Exodus to bring judgment and salvation, to establish God's will. Hence, when God's people looked to the future in expectation of the coming of God's kingdom, they would focus pre-eminently on the coming of God himself. Then, God would inaugurate his universal rule, justice would triumph, and peace and salvation would be established in the world (see Justice and Peace[3]). Isaiah explicitly refers to this coming as 'good tidings' or 'good news' (cf. Is. 40:1–9; 52:7), a fact not overlooked by the writer of the second Gospel (Mk. 1:1–15).

Subsequent Judaism developed this notion of the kingdom of God away from its historical roots in the material world. For some, notions of the kingdom of God were placed in tandem with growing Messianic expectation, focused above all on a Davidic king who would overturn foreign domination and usher in a new epoch of peace. But under the influence of various strands of apocalyptic thought, others developed the view that the kingdom of God referred to God's cataclysmic intervention in history, perhaps through the agency of a transcendent Messiah, to draw history to a close and establish a new, transcendent and eternal era of God's rule. Of course, the lines between the nationalistic and apocalyptic perspectives should not be overdrawn, but they do give expression to the major tendencies of the kingdom-speculation of Jesus' day.

Recent study has shown that Jesus borrowed from and adapted both strands of this tradition. Though he moved away from the nationalistic tendencies of the former, he nevertheless proclaimed the reality of the presence of the kingdom of God in the here and now. In his ministry of healing and exorcism, announcement of the forgiveness of sins, ministry among the marginalized of society, and open-table fellowship, he demonstrated that, in him, the kingdom of God was already at work in the world. Likewise, while insisting on the this-worldly significance of the kingdom, Jesus also embraced the apocalyptic emphasis on the future and transcendent coming of the kingdom. The presence and future of the kingdom of God – God's coming to bring peace and justice to the whole world – were held in dynamic tension in Jesus' message.

Numerous attempts to modify or collapse this temporal dialectic have been proposed. The most influential of these has been the effort of N. Perrin (1912–76) to define the kingdom of God in Jesus' understanding with no time referent, as a symbol evoking the myth of God acting with sovereign power. On this reading, Jesus would have offered no vision of the future at all, for the real force of his message was the importance of making real the experience of God as king. However, as D. C. Allison, Jr., has observed, 'kingdom of God' might refer *both* to God's saving activity *and* to the reality of his present-and-future reign. Moreover, Perrin's view rests on a very sceptical evaluation of the authenticity of the sayings of Jesus in the Gospels.

Others have focused almost entirely on the future coming of the kingdom of God – either explicitly, by denying the contemporary relevance of Jesus' proclamation of the present kingdom during his ministry (as in Dispensationalism*); or implicitly, by overlooking the profound social and political dimensions of the demand of the kingdom. Thus, throughout most of the 20th century, Mary's song (Lk. 1:46–55), which contains a profound vision of God's activity in ushering in the age of salvation, has been interpreted as primarily or exclusively an eschatological or a spiritual reality not to be understood as having a referent in the material world of today. Others have assumed that the best we can do today is to pray for the future coming of the kingdom: only by the mighty intervention of God can the peace and justice of the kingdom be realized.

On the other hand, and in response to this other-worldly interpretation of Jesus' kingdom-proclamation, some have dispensed with any future dimension to the kingdom. For them, the kingdom must be realized here, in this world, or not at all. The Latin American liberation theologian* Juan Luís Segundo (1925–), for example, reacts against those who relegate fully the coming of the kingdom of God to divine activity and so deny their own present responsibilities in light of the in-breaking kingdom. For him, the kingdom of

God is especially 'here and now', and the 'not-yetness' of the kingdom does not speak of the need for apocalyptic intervention on God's part, but of the necessity of and call for human collaboration in establishing justice in the world.

According to the Synoptic Gospels, however, the dynamic tension of present and future is characteristic of Jesus, and it will not do to collapse one into the other. Indeed, the message of the NT as a whole underscores the present and future dimensions of God's redemptive work. For this reason, the description of Jesus' eschatology as 'inaugurated' rather than 'realized' or 'futuristic' is more to the point, as is evident in numerous parables of Jesus (*e.g.* Mk. 4:26–32) as well as his redemptive activity. In his mission we see the revolutionary, salvific presence of the kingdom of God breaking into the realm of the historical. To what end?

It has often been noted that Jesus' kingdom-proclamation included no political or social programme. This differentiated his message from the nationalistic Messianism of his day. Undoubtedly, this transformation of Jewish expectation was a source of misunderstanding in Jesus' 1st-century context: Jesus announced the arrival of the long-awaited time of God's sovereign rule, but, for many, the evidence for this phenomenon must have been disappointing. Jesus spoke to this – both by depicting the mysterious, small beginnings of the kingdom of God in parabolic form, and by describing the kingdom in terms of mercy* and blessedness,* forgiveness* and healing,* not punishment and wrath.

Jesus' refusal to interpret the kingdom along nationalistic or militaristic lines should not be taken as evidence that his message of the kingdom was without a social and political dimension, however. After all, we may recall, to speak of the coming of the kingdom is to speak of the coming of God to bring justice and peace for all creation,* and the socio-political orientation of this reality is transparent. Moreover, the shape of Jesus' own ministry underscores the nature of salvation as directed towards the whole person. Indeed, the preaching of the kingdom is an affirmation of creation, and the consummation of the kingdom is 'creation healed' (Hans Küng).

Jesus' intention that his followers share in this ministry of the kingdom is evident from the Gospels as well. During the course of his ministry, the disciples were sent out to preach and heal (Mk. 6:6–13, par.). More fundamentally, Mark's summary of Jesus' message makes clear that Jesus' proclamation of the kingdom puts men and women on notice that the in-breaking kingdom of God demands response: 'The time is fulfilled! The kingdom of God has drawn near! Repent and believe the good news!' (Mk. 1:15 [my translation]). As the subsequent narrative of the calling of the first disciples makes clear, this meant nothing less than a complete reorientation of life around the kingdom of God. All other loyalties and commitments are relativized by the demand of the kingdom, including those of family* and State.*

Not only would disciples share in the peace and justice of God, they would be challenged and empowered to act as its agents. As with his first apostles, his followers are called 'to be with him' – *i.e.* to join the community of disciples, share in his life, and learn in his company – 'and to be sent out to proclaim the message, and to have authority to cast out demons' (Mk. 3:14–15, NRSV). Accordingly, the mission of the church and the challenge of discipleship must not be focused too narrowly. Formative spirituality,* the experience of community, and partnership with God in the work of the kingdom – *e.g.* proclaiming justice in word and deed, communicating God's mercy to all, announcing God's salvation and inviting response – and more, define life in the service of the kingdom.

That means, as has been increasingly recognized by Protestants and Roman Catholics alike, that the community of Jesus' followers shares the fundamental, corporate call to serve the kingdom of God. It takes up the message of Jesus and continues his ministry of extending the grace of God beyond human-originated lines of demarcation – to women, those of other races, the sick, outcasts, the poor. It does so not *in order to* bring the kingdom near, but precisely *because* the kingdom is at hand. This reorientation of life is the prescribed response to the kingdom; the in-breaking presence of God's salvation determines the shape of the church's mission and human morality.

This is not to suggest that an ethic derived from and oriented around the kingdom is necessarily at odds with an ethic rooted in creation theology or common grace. After all, kingdom ethics are grounded in the coming *of God* to bring shalom *to all creation*. At the same time, Jesus' proclamation of the kingdom introduces a state of emergency. His message calls people to orient their lives around a new reality. This reality is the in-breaking kingdom of God, in the light of which life can no longer be the same. On the basis of this understanding and experience of God's redemptive activity, Jesus can build the sort of radical, seemingly impracticable ethic we find in the Sermon on the Mount* and elsewhere in the Synoptic Gospels.

Because of its overtly masculine connotations in certain cultures, the appropriateness of our continuing use of the term 'kingdom' is sometimes questioned, and various alternatives have been proposed *e.g.* 'reign', 'new age' and 'basileia' (a transliteration from Gk.). Precedent for innovations of this sort is found already in the NT. Thus, in their attempts to carry the good news across cultural boundaries, Paul and John have chosen to employ other terms and phrases: (eternal) life, truth, salvation, the lordship of Christ, *etc.* Similarly, given the centrality of the kingdom of God to Jesus' ministry, it is imperative that ways be found to communicate its dynamic present and challenge in the many contexts in which the church ministers today. When seeking alternative language, however, the church should take care to give expression to the richness of meaning associated with the kingdom of God in the context of Jesus' own mission.

Bibliography

D. C. Allison, Jr., *The End of the Ages Has Come* (Philadelphia, 1985); M. Arias, *Announcing the Reign of God* (Philadelphia, 1984); G. R. Beasley-Murray, *Jesus and the Kingdom of God* (Exeter and Grand Rapids, 1986); B. Chilton and J. I. H. McDonald, *Jesus and the Ethics of the Kingdom* (London and Grand Rapids, 1987); I. H. Marshall, 'The Hope of a New Age: The Kingdom of God in the New Testament', *Them* 11, 1985, pp. 5–15; N. Perrin, *Jesus and the Language of the Kingdom* (London and Philadelphia, 1976); J. Riches, *Jesus and the Transformation of Judaism* (London, 1980; New York, 1982); J. L. Segundo, *Jesus of Nazareth Yesterday and Today*, vol. 2: *The Historical Jesus of the Synoptics* (London, Melbourne, and Maryknoll, NY, 1985); H. A. Snyder, *A Kingdom Manifesto* (Downers Grove, IL, 1985); W. Willis (ed.), *The Kingdom of God in 20th-Century Interpretation* (Peabody, MA, 1987).

J.B.G.

KINSEY REPORTS. These nine studies, published in the USA by the Institute for Sex Research, were on men (1948), women (1953), pregnancy, birth, abortion (1958), sex offenders (1965), child molesters (1971), and homosexuality (1971, 1972 and 1974).

The early period of the institute began with Alfred Kinsey (1894–1956), a biologist, teaching a course on marriage at Indiana University. He used elaborate interviewing techniques on the sexual life of college students, hospital patients and prison inmates. The formative years, 1948–53, saw the publication of the reports on male and female sexual behaviour, based on interviews with 5,300 males and 5,940 females. The mature years, 1954–68, witnessed Kinsey's death, a leadership transition, increased research and teaching, more funding and international recognition. Since 1968 multiple research projects, with further staff specialization, and a focus on smaller studies, such as homosexuality, have occurred.

Kinsey himself trained as a biological positivist. His interests lay in the accurate description of sexual behaviour gained through elaborately conceived and carefully secured interview materials. During his lifetime he conducted nearly 100,000 interviews.

Bibliography

A. C. Kinsey *et al.*, *Sexual Behaviour in the Human Male* (Philadelphia, 1948); A. C. Kinsey *et al.*, *Sexual Behaviour in the Human Female* (Philadelphia, 1953); M. S. Weinberg, *Sex Research: Studies from the Kinsey Institute* (London, 1976).

P.A.Mi.

KIRK, KENNETH E. (1886–1954). The foremost Anglican moral theologian of this century, and described on his death as 'the greatest master of the spiritual life of our times', Kirk was influential in the revival of moral, pastoral and ascetical theology (see Asceticism*) within the Church of England. After being a Chaplain to the Forces during the First World War, Fellow of Magdalen College and then of Trinity College, Oxford, Kirk became Regius Professor of Moral and Pastoral Theology in 1932. He was appointed Bishop of Oxford in 1937.

Kirk is best known for his Bampton Lectures of 1928, expanded for publication as *The Vision of God* (London and New York, 1931), which, though weak on the Reformers and the Puritans, gives an otherwise magisterial historical survey of Christian spirituality.* He also wrote many articles and reviews as well as other books including *Some Principles of Moral Theology* (London, 1920), *Ignorance, Faith and Conformity* (London, 1925), *Conscience and Its Problems* (London, 1927), and *Marriage and Divorce* (London, 1933, ²1948), and he edited *The Apostolic Ministry* on the history and doctrine of episcopacy (London, 1946). Kirk described the theology of Thomas Aquinas* as having a value for the student of morals second only to that of the Bible and the Fathers, and he drew heavily also on the 17th-century divines, especially Richard Hooker,* Robert Sanderson (1587–1663) and Jeremy Taylor.* He was concerned to bring moral and pastoral theological traditions into conversation with current psychological understanding and practice, always with a view to assisting moral understanding, spiritual direction,* and the development of Christian character, and upholding the primacy of worship.

Bibliography
V. A. Demant, 'Kenneth Kirk as Moral Theologian', *CQR* 158, 1957, pp. 423–434; E. W. Kemp, *The Life and Letters of Kenneth Escott Kirk* (London, 1959).

D.J.A.

KLEIN, MELANIE (1892–1960). Born in Vienna, Klein emigrated to England in 1922 where her reputation soon grew as a psychoanalyst of children. Strongly influenced by Sigmund Freud* and Karl Abraham (1877–1925), she moved beyond Freudian emphasis on biological instincts to stress the significance of 'object relations', *i.e.* the emotional components of a child's relationships with his or her social environment.

In one of her major papers ('Our adult world and its roots in infancy'), Klein argues that the patterns of emotional response learned in childhood are repeated later in life. The child typically develops from a stage of 'omnipotence' (in which she is the centre of her world) into the 'paranoid-schizoid position', in which the external world is perceived to be split into 'part objects', some nourishing, others threatening. At this stage persecutory anxieties can arise. Normal development (see Human Development*) in a good environment enables the child to grow into the 'depressive

position', in which the external world can be perceived as ambiguous whole objects, and in which feelings of guilt* arise. A satisfactory growth through this stage enables the child to learn to express creativity and concern. Klein's work was always controversial, but it contributed significantly to British psychoanalysis, though relatively little in the USA. Klein led the way, taken up by Ronald Fairbairn (1890–1964), D. W. Winnicott* and Harry Guntrip (1901–75), in the 'object-relations' approach to personality development and related pathology. Through these later writers, as well as through her own work, Klein was an important influence on Frank Lake* in the early development of clinical theology.*

Bibliography
Collected Papers, 4 vols. (London, 1975): *Love, Guilt and Reparation*; *The Psychoanalysis of Children*; *Envy and Gratitude*; and *Narrative of a Child Analysis*.
H. Segal, *Klein* (London, 1979).

D.J.A.

KOHLBERG, LAWRENCE, see HUMAN DEVELOPMENT; MORAL DEVELOPMENT.

KOINONIA, see FELLOWSHIP.

KUYPER, ABRAHAM (1837–1920), the most prominent leader of the influential Dutch neo-Calvinist movement, which emerged during the late 19th century and which had a significant impact on Dutch society. Influenced by the Dutch Christian historian and statesman Guillaume Groen van Prinsterer (1801–76), Kuyper provided a highly original and forceful presentation of the Calvinist 'world-view', at the base of which was a confession of the universal sovereignty of God over all aspects of creation.

Kuyper became a minister of the Reformed Church (*Hervormde Kerk*) in 1863. After fully embracing Calvinist orthodoxy, Kuyper led a vigorous, though unsuccessful, struggle against its State-supported liberal establishment. In 1886 he led a secession and set up an independent Reformed church (*Gereformeerde Kerk*), which proved crucial to the subsequent successes of neo-Calvinism.

Kuyper's public life ranged across many spheres. He became a key figure in the movement to defend Christian schools, founded and taught at the Free University of Amsterdam, edited a newspaper and a journal which served as his principal channel of popular communication, and was active in support of the Christian trades union movement.

In 1878 he established the organization of the Anti-Revolutionary Party (ARP), the name indicating a repudiation of French Revolutionary secularism. The party's programme drew heavily on Kuyper's political vision, which can be seen as a distinctively Protestant source of Christian Democratic pluralism. The ARP eventually entered government in coalition with other Protestant and Catholic parties. Kuyper served as Prime Minister of such a coalition from 1901 to 1905.

Kuyper's extensive corpus includes many substantial theological, social and political writings. His translated works include: *Encyclopedia of Sacred Theology* (New York, 1898), *Lectures on Calvinism* (Grand Rapids, 1931), and *The Problem of Poverty* (Grand Rapids, 1991).

J.P.C.

L

LABOREM EXERCENS, see PAPAL ENCYCLICALS.

LAISSEZ-FAIRE, a Fr. expression for 'allow to do', was introduced by Fr. and Eng. 18th-century writers to designate the general policy of minimum government participation or interference in people's lives, especially in the economy. Its influence is seen in modern statements of human rights that frequently emphasize protection from government intrusion.

No *laissez-faire* theorist has advocated government's complete non-participation and non-interference in an economy. For example, modern government is always a significant employer and property owner, and the very existence of private property and monetary systems depends on government protections. In addition, all governments require taxes, but the way these are collected tremendously affects economic activity.

The *laissez-faire* approach has been supported by many Christian and non-Christian thinkers. It received a powerful endorsement by Adam Smith (1723–90), a Christian and the father of classical economics. In his intensely influential *Wealth of Nations* (1776) he provides a two-fold defence of free markets. He trusts the mechanisms of the natural economic order, and he knows that the people in a position to influence government regulations tend to be motivated by greed to protect or increase their own economic power. Nevertheless, Smith supports regulations on two grounds: regulations protecting justice are necessary for a free market to exist in the first place; and whenever workers or the poor request some regulation their cause is nearly always fair.

Other defences and criticisms of *laissez-faire* are important. For example, John Stuart Mill* and other secular individualists argue that every individual has a basic right to pursue personal ends without interference from others. *Laissez-faire* policies are criticized when they violate the needs of the group, neglect the rights of the weak, or depend on narrowly individualistic world-views.

P.H.deV.

LAKE, FRANK (1914–82), best remembered for his contribution to the development of Christian pastoral counselling in Britain in the 1960s and 70s. He was born in Lancashire, the son of Anglican parents. After graduation from Edinburgh medical school in 1937 he subsequently went to India with the Church Missionary Society, during which time he became interested in dynamic psychiatry.

Lake's return to England in 1951 was followed by a period of retraining in psychiatry and entry into clinical practice. In 1962 he moved to Nottingham, where he was to remain to the end of his life, to found the Clinical Theology Association (CTA). Encouraged by the then Bishop of Bradford, Dr Donald Coggan (1909–), Lake was convinced that clergy-training in pastoral care and counselling had failed to engage with the revolutions in psychiatry of the 20th century – hence the title 'clinical theology'.*

At its height, the CTA boasted that it had run courses in forty-one Anglican dioceses, eighteen theological colleges and several universities. In 1981, Lake himself claimed that some 12,000 men and women had undertaken CTA courses. This was later revised upwards to 20,000. The rapid growth of interest reflected the absence of any substantive, biblically-oriented, model attempting to integrate theology and psychology.

The theory of clinical theology, expressed in Lake's massive textbook of the same name, revolved around two theories. The first, derived from classical object-relations theory, stated that adult psychological disorders could be traced to a deficiency of interpersonal, essentially parental, relationships during the first year of life, especially the first trimester. In later years this was extended to cover the intra-uterine experience of the foetus (mother-foetal distress syndrome). At one point, Lake even claimed that individuals were capable of remembering the night of their conception and how far they were loved within the womb. Although the earlier part of the theory was defensible from widely accepted premises, this latter claim divided the CTA and brought ridicule from secular professionals.

The second theory was no less controversial. Based on a dubious theology of John's Gospel, Lake developed an 'ontological model' designed to achieve what he called 'a dynamic cycle',* in which the love of Christ is introduced into the client's experience as an antidote to the lack of love experienced in early life. Secular practitioners found this an impossible claim to verify, thereby undermining the scientific credibility of the clinical theology model. A less ambitious claim would have been to present Christian theology and symbolism as a cognitive framework to enable patients to interpret and reconstruct their inner and outer worlds of meaning. This would at least have placed clinical theology in a stronger theoretical position, since such a view would have had affinities with other approaches to therapy.

Although the CTA has declined in importance, Lake's achievement, as Michael Jacobs (1941–) commented in 1987, was to 'put the discipline [of counselling] firmly on the map', for which British pastoral counselling owes Frank Lake 'an enormous debt'.

See also: PASTORAL CARE, COUNSELLING AND PSYCHOTHERAPY. ☒12☒

Bibliography
Clinical Theology (London, 1966), abridged by M. H. Yeomans (London, 1986). D. Atkinson and I. Williams, 'Frank Lake, Explorer in Pastoral Counselling', *ThW* 5.9, 1982, pp. 25–28; R. F. Hurding, *Roots and Shoots: A Guide to Counselling and Psychotherapy* (London, 1986) = *The Tree of Healing* (Grand Rapids, 1988); J. Peters, *Frank Lake: The Man and His Work* (London, 1989).

F.W.B.

LAMBOURNE, ROBERT A. (1917–72). General practitioner, theologian and psychiatrist, Bob Lambourne has contributed significantly to the discipline of pastoral theology (see ☒7☒) in England. His major book, *Community, Church and Healing* (London, 1963), was a study of the theology of healing,* including a careful analysis of healing in the Gospels, arguing for a view of humankind as social beings, and that the healings of Jesus are as much community events (confronting the sufferer's social group with the demands of the kingdom*) as they are ministry to individual people. An edition of his other papers (*Explorations in Health and Salvation*, ed. Michael Wilson) was published posthumously in 1983 by the University of Birmingham where, from 1964 to 1972, Lambourne was a lecturer in pastoral studies at the department of theology. His wide perspectives and inter-disciplinary interests, his determination to integrate his Christian faith with medical and psychiatric practice, his sharp critique of the idolatry of certain ideologies underlying much secular psychotherapy and counselling, his concern for pastoral training for lay people and clergy, and his involvement in the World Council of Churches, all add up to a unique contribution to pastoral studies. Many of his research students have carried his insights further. Some of his writings have led to changes in hospital chaplaincy, and methods of training in pastoral care. Though not widely known, his contribution continues to grow.

D.J.A.

LAND AND LAND REFORM. The issue of land distribution and use has always been a major point in economic ethics (see ☒17☒), and has taken on a new ecological urgency with the added 'green' dimension. Biblical resources for Christian reflection on these issues include the teaching regarding the earth as a whole, and the more specific theology of the land of Israel.

The creation* basis of OT teaching gives us two complementary truths about the earth: on the one hand, it belongs to God who made it (Ps. 24:1); on the other hand, it has been given and entrusted to human beings (Gn. 1:28–30; Pss. 8:6; 115:16). God, as ultimate owner, thus retains the right of moral control over how the earth is used. Human beings, as stewards* and managers, are accountable to him for the care and use of the earth and all its resources. Since God gave the earth to humanity as a whole, it seems a reasonable conclusion that it was meant to be shared in such a way that all people have access to the use of its resources. Private ownership is legitimate, as OT law shows, but is not absolutized. Ultimate ownership belongs to God and human ownership has to be exercised subordinately to his moral requirements of sharing and justice. The creation ethic would regard the right to use as higher than the right to own.

Israel's system of land tenure embodies the same two principles. On the one hand, the land was God's gift to Israel, an essential part of the promise to Abraham and a tangible proof of his faithfulness. As their 'inheritance', it was at the heart of their covenant* relationship with Yahweh. On the other hand, the land was still owned by God (Lv. 25:23), so that as divine landlord he retained authority over how it should be used. Hence Israel's whole economic system was subject to God's moral critique.

When Israel established their control over the land of Canaan, they introduced a system of land tenure which was unmistakably different from what had gone before. The pre-Israelite Canaanite system was similar to 'feudalism'. The land was owned by the kings of each little city state, with the bulk of the population living on the king's land as tenant serfs, paying taxes and owing military service (as observed by Samuel in 1 Sa. 8:10–18). Israel's system was founded first of all on an equitable distribution of the land throughout the whole kinship system. The basic unit of land ownership was the extended family (the 'father's house'), which was the smallest social unit in the system of tribes and clans. The allotments of land were proportionate to the size of the tribes (Nu. 33:53–54), and the description of the division of territory after the conquest specifies that the land was shared out 'according to clans / families' (Jos. 13 – 19). The intention was clearly that every Israelite household should have access to economic viability through having a fair and sufficient share in the greatest national asset – God's gift of the land.

This objective was then protected by the principle of inalienability. Land was not to be bought and sold commercially outside the family (Lv. 25:23). It was to remain within the kinship allotment for the benefit of future generations. Where debt or other reasons for severe poverty forced a family to sell some or all of its land, the law of redemption laid the duty on more prosperous kinsmen to pre-empt

or buy back such land in order to keep it in the family (as illustrated in Je. 32 and probably also Ru. 4). And the jubilee* law prescribed that in the fiftieth year (*i.e.* approximately every other generation) there should be a restoration of land to the original owners and release of any persons who had entered into slavery because of debt poverty. The laws of redemption and jubilee in Lv. 25 are strongly based on theological principles. Both land and people belong ultimately to God and nobody has the right of absolute ownership, accumulation or disposal of either.

The story of Naboth in 1 Ki. 21 illustrates Israel's economic system at a point where it clashed with the non-Israelite attitudes and economic values of Jezebel. Her Canaanite view of political and economic power, still widespread today, was that the powerful could own what they could seize. Her clever manipulation of Israelite law showed her contempt for the system of economic justice that Yahweh had given under which a Naboth could withstand an Ahab on his own family land. Elijah's words of condemnation (1 Ki. 21:17ff.) were echoed by other prophets who showed their concern for God's idea of justice on the land by condemning those who accumulated large estates of land at the expense of the poor (Is. 5:8; Mi. 2:1ff.). This became a major social problem in Israel, from the time of Solomon onwards. If the prophets revealed the mind of God, then they show that the issue of justice in the distribution and use of the land is high on his moral agenda.

Agrarian discontent forms the background to some of the teaching of Jesus also. Palestine at the time of Jesus was beset by similar economic problems as the OT prophets lament, only made even worse by the imposition of Roman imperial government. There was intensive exploitation of the peasant farmers, the majority of whom were tenants, since the ownership of land was concentrated in the hands of few wealthy families. Tenant farmers were hard pressed trying to meet a variety of demands on what they could produce – rents, taxes, tithes, debt repayments. Out of what was left, they had to feed themselves and still find something to invest in the next year's sowing. Since many of the landowners lived in Jerusalem, there was antagonism between town and country. Villagers suffered many hardships and discriminations and there was much discontent. The pressures of debt and dispossession drove some into the extreme revolutionary camp of the Zealots, who attacked both the Roman power and the Jewish aristocratic collaborators. It was a tense and sometimes violent agrarian scene in which Jesus grew up.

In his 'Nazareth manifesto' (Lk. 4:16–21) Jesus declared his mission by quoting from Is. 61, a passage which draws on ideas connected with the jubilee year, with its twin pillars of release from debt and restoration of one's rightful inheritance. Some scholars have suggested that Jesus called for an actual jubilee year to be put into operation, *i.e.* a radical programme of debt cancellation and redistribution of land. In the context of Roman Palestine, that would have been essentially a call for revolution (see Violence*). Most scholars, however, point out that Jesus did not call for a literal operation of the Levitical law, but rather quoted from the prophetic use of jubilee ideas as a way of characterizing his own ministry. In other words, he was deeply concerned about the economic realities that the jubilee had tried to remedy, but his answer was not a straight return to that ancient legislation. Jesus did not announce a jubilee and hope it would inaugurate the kingdom of God.* Rather, he announced the arrival of the kingdom of God and then used jubilee imagery to characterize its demands.

Jesus, then, was not a revolutionary, in the usual sense of that word. There was no evidence that he sided with those who advocated violent seizure of land from absentee landowners and redistribution of it to tenant farmers. He was very much aware of the problem, though, and the feelings it generated. The parable of the so-called 'wicked husbandmen' (Mk. 12:1–9) shows his familiarity with the murderous bitterness of tenant farmers and their desire for ownership of vineyards for themselves. But he shows no sympathy with their actions or intentions, and rather uses the story (which may well have had a basis in incidents he himself witnessed) as a means of condemning the spiritual and political leaders of his people. On another occasion, Jesus refused to get involved in a dispute over land, using the occasion instead as an opportunity to hammer home the dangers of greed that possession of land can engender (Lk. 12:13–21).

A biblical basis for land reform, then, includes the following points: human accountability to God as creator for the sharing and use of the whole earth; God's preference, expressed through Israel's law and history, for widespread distribution of the land rather than concentration of ownership in the hands of a few; the paramount economic interests of the smaller units of human society, *i.e.* households and families; the importance of structural and legal instruments (such as OT sabbatical and jubilee legislation) for restoring justice in the field of agrarian poverty and indebtedness; the relevance of the values of the kingdom of God in the economic realm, but the rejection of violent revolution as a means of achieving them.

See also: OLD TESTAMENT ETHICS. [8]

Bibliography

W. Brueggemann, *The Land: Place as Gift, Promise and Challenge in Biblical Faith* (Philadelphia, 1977; London, 1978); D. A. Hay, *Economics Today* (Leicester, 1989); S. C. Mott, *Jesus and Social Ethics* (Bramcote, Nottingham, 1984); D. E. Oakman, *Jesus and the Economic Questions of his Day* (New York, 1986); S. H. Ringe, *Jesus, Liberation and the Biblical Jubilee* (Philadelphia, 1985); C. J. H. Wright, 'The Ethical Relevance of Israel as a Society', *Tr* 1.4, 1984, pp. 11–21; *idem, God's People in God's Land: Family, Land and Property in the Old Testament* (Grand Rapids and Exeter, 1990); *idem, Living as the People of God* (Leicester, 1983) = *An Eye for an Eye* (Downers Grove, IL, 1983).

C.J.H.W.

LAND RIGHTS, see LAND AND LAND REFORM.

LAUSANNE COVENANT. The Lausanne Covenant arose from the International Congress On World Evangelization held in July 1974 in Lausanne, Switzerland. Two thousand seven hundred evangelicals from 150 countries met under the leadership of Billy Graham (1918–). The Covenant was drafted on the basis of speakers' papers and revised during the Congress. The term 'covenant' was chosen to express the signatories' commitment not simply to a declaration, but to the task of world evangelization.

In its fifteen paragraphs, the Covenant affirms God's purpose in calling a people for himself, the power and authority of the Bible, the uniqueness and sufficiency of Christ, the importance of human rights, and the hope of Christ's return. Yet the main focus of the

Covenant is upon the nature and urgency of the evangelistic task. At the centre of this task is the church – marked by the cross* and empowered by the Holy Spirit.* Commitment is made to co-operation in evangelism,* to the training of indigenous leaders, and, by those in affluent circumstances, to the development of a simple lifestyle.

As with most ecclesiastical confessions, the Covenant was in part shaped by external factors. The previous gatherings of the World Council of Churches (Uppsala, 1968) and its Commission on World Mission and Evangelism conference (Bangkok, 1973) had seen the goal of mission primarily in terms of humanization and liberation (see Liberation Theology*). Many evangelicals felt that the pursuit of social justice had eclipsed evangelism in the ecumenical movement (see Ecumenical Ethics*). In contrast the Lausanne Covenant stated that political liberation was not salvation (see Sin and Salvation⑤) and emphasized the importance of the task of mission to the millions of unreached people in the world.

During the Congress John Stott (1921–) spoke of mission as the church's sacrificial service to the world which includes both evangelism and social action. This broader conception of mission was enshrined in the Covenant. At the same time speakers from the Two Thirds World, in particular René Padilla (1932–) and Samuel Escobar (1934–), had a tremendous impact upon the Congress. Padilla and Escobar were anxious lest the Congress would instigate a programme of evangelization using Western marketing techniques which, for the sake of numerical success, would ignore the social implications of repentance.* In the event, however, the Covenant warned against concealing the cost of discipleship and affirmed that socio-political involvement was part of a Christian's duty. It also acknowledged that 'churches have sometimes been in bondage to culture rather than to the Scriptures'. Despite suspicion of ecumenical theology, the Covenant declared that Christians should share God's concern for reconciliation* throughout human society and liberation from oppression.

The Covenant has had a tremendous impact upon the evangelical world. It has been a significant impetus to mission and has provided a framework within which evangelicals can co-operate. Its affirmation of social responsibility proved a turning-point in evangel-

ical attitudes to social action. Those whose social involvement had been viewed with suspicion by other evangelicals could now point to the Covenant as evidence that one could be socially active and still belong to the evangelical mainstream.

A number of N. Americans were subsequently critical of the Covenant. Although the Covenant affirmed that 'in the church's mission of sacrificial service evangelism is primary', they felt that the implication that other activities, i.e. social action, were also involved in mission would undermine evangelism. In contrast others, particularly from the Two Thirds World, have been critical of the language of primacy since they believe it creates a false dichotomy between the proclamation and demonstration of the gospel. An alternative statement, The Statement of Radical Discipleship, was produced during the Congress and accepted by John Stott (chairman of the Covenant-drafting committee) as an addendum to the Covenant. This proposed a holistic approach to mission.

A continuation committee, the Lausanne Committee for World Evangelization, was established to further the achievements of the Congress. Over the years it has sought to facilitate evangelical co-operation in mission on the basis of the Covenant. In July 1989, Lausanne II was held at Manila in the Philippines.

The Manila Manifesto (for which see J. D. Douglas, ed., *Proclaim Christ Until He Comes*, pp. 25–38), like the Lausanne Covenant, asserted the primacy of evangelism but added that 'Jesus not only proclaimed the kingdom of God, he also demonstrated its arrival by works of mercy and power. We are called today to a similar integration of words and deeds.' In a carefully balanced statement, it steered a middle course between the claim that signs and wonders* are to be expected as normal and frequent in the life of the church today, and the contention that they were confined to the era of the apostolic church. 'We reject', it declared, 'both the scepticism which denies miracles and the presumption which demands them, both the timidity which shrinks from the fulness of the Spirit and the triumphalism which shrinks from the weakness in which Christ's power is made perfect.'

Bibliography

J. D. Douglas (ed.), *Let the Earth Hear His Voice* (Minneapolis, MN, 1975), the Congress papers; *idem* (ed.), *Proclaim Christ Until He Comes* (Minneapolis, MN, 1990), the papers of Lausanne II; C. R. Padilla (ed.), *The New Face of Evangelicalism* (London, 1975; Downers Grove, IL, 1976); *idem*, *How Evangelicals Endorsed Social Responsibility* (Bramcote, Nottingham, 1985); J. R. W. Stott, *The Lausanne Covenant: An Exposition and Commentary* (Minneapolis, MN, 1975) = *Explaining the Lausanne Covenant* (London, 1975); *idem*, *Christian Mission in the Modern World* (London, 1975; Eastbourne, 1986).

T.J.Ch.

LAW. After redeeming the people of Israel from bondage in Egypt, the Lord gave them the law, a legislative system comprising many commandments and statutes, by which they were to order their lives. By obeying the law, they acknowledged their special relationship to God, continued to experience his blessing and protection, and became living witnesses to the goodness of God among the nations (Ex. 20:1–26; Dt. 4:5–8; 6:20–25). To deliberately throw off the law (especially its prohibitions concerning idolatry) would be tantamount to severing their relationship with their Lord (Dt. 6:10–15). We may say that the people of Israel kept the law, not that they might be accepted by God, but because that was what God required of those whom he had already accepted.

When Christ came, his purpose was not to destroy the law or the prophets, but to fulfil them (Mt. 5:17–18). Early Christians did not understand this to mean that all believers would obey the law given by God to Israel through Moses. It was agreed that such obedience would not be required of Gentile Christians, a fact exemplified clearly in the waiving of circumcision (a fundamental requirement of the law) as far as they were concerned (Acts 15:22–29). The NT reflects a difference of opinion concerning whether Jewish Christians were obliged to continue obeying the law in its entirety. The Jerusalem church, for the most part, continued to hold that this was obligatory (Acts 21:17–26). Paul taught that it was not, even rebuking Jewish Christians for being unwilling to give up observance of certain elements of the law for the sake of fellowship with Gentile believers (Gal. 2:1–21). Paul, more than any other NT writer, dealt with the issues relating to the role of the law in the lives of believers.

Issues relating to the law

Legalism. By legalism is meant reliance upon fulfilment of the requirements of the law in order to be accepted by God. This was not the teaching of the OT, for it was to a people already accepted by God that the law was given. Until relatively recently it was often assumed (especially in Protestant exegesis) that 1st-century Judaism was legalistic, and that it was this legalism which Paul attacked in Galatians and Romans. In more recent times it has been recognized that neither 1st-century Judaism nor the Jerusalem church was legalistic in principle. The disagreement between both these groups and Paul had more to do with the matter of nomism than legalism.

Nomism. By nomism here is meant the belief that, having been accepted by God on the basis of his saving grace,* his people are obliged to obey the Mosaic law. This was certainly the case in Israel before the coming of Christ, and it is therefore right to think of OT religion (and probably 1st-century Judaism as well) as nomistic. It is also true to say that the Jerusalem church was nomistic, for, as Acts indicates, members of this church continued to observe the hours of prayer (Acts 3:1) and Jewish food laws (Acts 10:9–16). They continued to circumcise their male children (Acts 15:1; 21:20–21) and to offer sacrifices in the temple (Acts 21:23–26). However, Paul taught that the Christian faith ought not to be nomistic. The role of the law as a rule of life had been brought to an end with the coming of Christ (Rom. 7:1–4; Gal. 3:23 – 4:7). Now life was to be lived by faith* in Christ and in the power of the Holy Spirit* (Gal. 2:18–21). Accordingly, Paul argued that Gentile believers need not submit to circumcision (Gal. 5:2–6), or observe food laws (*cf.* Col. 2:20–22) and sabbaths (Col. 2:16; *cf.* Gal. 4:9–11).

Antinomianism. Some of Paul's critics charged him with antinomianism, saying that his gospel invited people to dispense with moral restraints altogether. This charge the apostle vigorously denied, pointing out that people were freed from the law as a regulatory norm in order to live under the lordship of Christ and in the power of the Spirit, and that this does not lead to immoral living (Rom. 3:8; 6:15–19; Gal. 5:13–25).

The law as a paradigm. While Paul rejected law as a rule of life for Christians, he nevertheless continued to see the law as an important resource for instruction. Its authority was that of a paradigm. By showing how God related to Israel, and how Israelites were to relate to him and to one another, it provided a model which could guide Christians in their new situations. Thus Paul appealed frequently to the law to warn believers of the consequences of sinful behaviour, and to illustrate godly behaviour (1 Cor 10:1–11; Gal. 4:21 – 5:1).

The law as commandment. Paul's statement in 1 Cor. 7:19 ('Circumcision is nothing and uncircumcision is nothing. Keeping God's commands is what counts') appears to be giving back to the Mosaic law a function in the life of believers which he denies elsewhere. However, this is clearly not the case, because circumcision, one of the primary demands of the law, he says, is 'nothing'. What Paul means by 'God's commands' here is perhaps best understood in terms of the ethical imperatives of the gospel. These are summed up in the command to love one's neighbour, and that love is the fruit of the Spirit's work in those who believe in Christ (*cf.* Gal. 5:13–15, 22–26; 6:2).

While Paul dispensed with the Mosaic law as a rule of life for Christians, he upheld the binding character of the commands of Christ (1 Cor. 7:10). In addition he expected his own apostolic injunctions to be obeyed (1 Cor. 14:37–38), and the tradition established among all his churches to be observed (1 Cor. 11:16).

See also: NEW TESTAMENT ETHICS; ⑨ OLD TESTAMENT ETHICS. ⑧

Bibliography

R. Banks, *Jesus and the Law in the Synoptic Tradition* (Cambridge, 1975); E. E. Ellis, *Paul's Use of the Old Testament* (Edinburgh, 1957; Grand Rapids, 1981); E. P. Sanders, *Paul, the Law and the Jewish People* (Philadelphia, 1983); S. Westerholm, *Israel's Law and the Church's Faith: Paul and His Recent Interpreters* (Grand Rapids, 1988); C. J. H. Wright, *Living as the People of God: The Relevance of Old Testament Ethics* (Leicester, 1983) = *An Eye for an Eye* (Downers Grove, IL, 1983).

C.G.K.

LAW AND GOSPEL. 'The law' sets out the duties imposed by God on human beings as his creatures and servants. It requires perfect obedience and offers eternal life as its reward, but warns of death as the penalty for disobedience.

The gospel declares the good news of the salvation (see Sin and Salvation⑤) provided by God, for men and women as law-breaking sinners meriting death. It commands faith in the saviour to receive salvation and know eternal life.

God established his initial relationship with humanity on the basis of law.* His fundamental requirements are written on every human heart and constitute each person a religious and moral being with a sense of duty to love God and fellow humans (Mt. 22:37–40; Rom. 2:14–15). No-one has fulfilled this internal duty, and all are law-breakers or sinners.

To this internal law God has added explanatory statements of duty, the most important being the Decalogue.* Humanity's duty to God is explained in four of the Ten Commandments, and duty to fellow humans in six (Ex. 20:1–21). By the giving of this law, God exposed and emphasized the extent of human sinfulness and the need of a saviour (Gal. 3:19; 2 Cor. 3:7–11).

In addition, God gave Israel laws to regulate her life as his covenant* nation, distinct and separate from all other nations (Ex. 19:5–6; Est. 3:8). These laws determined Israel's political and civic structures, her religious activities and the behaviour of her citizens. Disobedience to these laws was a sin for every Jew.

Some people attained a high level of obedience to the demands of the law in its external requirements. In their civil, religious and moral duties they were blameless (Lk. 1:6; Phil. 3:6). However, as the law requires internal as well as external obedience, and regulates attitudes as well as behaviour, it stirs up sin, creates frustration and convicts of failure, thereby emphasizing the need of a saviour (Mt. 5:17–48; Rom. 7:5, 7–12).

Throughout the OT, the coming of a saviour was promised. There were implicit and explicit prophecies. The work of the saviour was foreshadowed in the religious system ordained for Israel. Its prophets, priests, kings, sacrifices, tabernacle and temple all taught the need for salvation. In the OT salvation was not attained by obedience to the law, because no-one accomplished this, but by faith* in the promises of God (Gn. 15:4–6; Rom. 4; Gal. 3:6–14; Heb. 11).

The arrival of the saviour, Jesus Christ, involved him in submission to all the requirements of God's law (Gal. 4:4–5). By his obedience he attained righteousness and eternal life for sinners. He gave to God's law the obedience no sinner had given (Rom. 5:18–21).

In his death (see Atonement*) the saviour brought the Jewish religious system to its fulfilment and rendered its continuance meaningless. The many priests of Israel found that fulfilment in the final priest, Christ. The numerous sacrifices were fulfilled and superseded by the ultimate sacrifice, Christ. Coming to God in a temple was replaced by direct access to God in Christ. OT shadows faded in NT substance (Heb. 7–10).

By his death the Lord Jesus paid the penalty the law requires for disobedience. He died as the substitute for sinners so that they might not die, but live reconciled to God through him (2 Cor. 5:17–21; Col. 1:21–22).

Through his death, the distinctive laws which made Israel a people apart were abolished. The new international community of the church was formed with its own structures and behaviour (Eph. 2:11–22). The people of God are no longer bound by distinctively Jewish laws, nor must a Gentile Christian adopt Jewish customs to become, or remain, pleasing to God (Acts 15:1–35; Gal. 2:11–21).

The obedient life and sacrificial death of the Lord Jesus Christ result in a gospel that offers to sinners a new relationship with God as part of his church, received by faith in the saviour. The saved sinner or Christian no longer has a relationship with God based on a duty personally to obey the laws, but a relationship based on God's gracious acceptance of Christ's fulfilment of the law, positively and negatively, for him. Hence he is 'not under law but under grace' in his relationship to God (Rom. 6:14).

To be 'not under law but under grace' does not mean that the Christian may sin or be lawless (Rom. 6:14–15; 1 Jn. 3:4). It is true that he is freed from all distinctively Jewish law, whether in the political, civic, religious or private realm, but he is not lawless.

The Decalogue is still binding on the Christian because it is written on his mind and heart as part of the benefit that the new covenant, sealed in Christ's blood, brings him (1 Cor. 11:25; Heb. 8:10). The interiority of the Decalogue means the Christian has not only the duty to obey but the desire also (Ezk. 36:26–27). The internationalization of God's people means that the Decalogue is obeyed in its essential moral principles, not in its culturally related detail. Hence, obedient children gain blessings on earth, not in Israel (Dt. 5:16; Eph. 6:1–3). The rigid, Jewish, Saturday Sabbath gives way to worship on the Lord's Day (Acts 20:7; Col. 2:16–17).

OT moral laws outside of the Decalogue also remain binding (e.g. Mt. 4:4, 7, 10). They are not tied to Jewish political or ceremonial structures but are applications of the foundational principles of God's law (Mt. 22:37–40). Love (see ②) does not replace the law but is the motivation for obedience to the commands, and the spirit in which they are obeyed (Rom. 13:8–10).

Each OT law has a moral principle at its centre that is to be obeyed, even when the Jewish application of the law is abrogated. Hence Christian workers are to be paid because God's law requires that oxen treading out corn must not be muzzled (1 Cor. 9:9–10; 1 Tim. 5:17–18). The moral principle is that he who works should benefit from his work.

The coming of Christ has not rendered the OT irrelevant, because the moral aspects of its law shape Christian behaviour. To these are added the legal obligations the Christian has to Christ as his or her law-giver and prophet (1 Cor. 9:21). It is by obedience to Christ's commands that Christians demonstrate their love for Christ and the reality of their relationship with him (Jn. 14:15, 23; 1 Jn. 2:3–4).

The gospel frees humanity from having to obey the law in order to gain righteousness (Rom. 10:4), and from the law as defined by Judaism (Eph. 2:11–21). The moral requirements of the law remain as a rule of Christian conduct in their new-covenant form, along with the commands of Christ and his apostles.

See also: Law; Law, Uses of.

Bibliography

W. Gutbrod, *TDNT* 4, pp. 1059–1091; D. Guthrie, *New Testament Theology* (Leicester and Downers Grove, IL, 1981), pp. 675–700; E. F. Kevan, *The Grace of Law: A Study in Puritan Theology* (London, 1964); J. Murray, *Collected Writings IV* (Edinburgh, 1982), pp. 132–141.

R.J.Sh.

LAW, CIVIL AND CRIMINAL. The word 'law' is used in a variety of senses to indicate the ordering or operation of some field of activity. Some uses are descriptive (*e.g.* the laws of physics or nature), and some are prescriptive.

Civil and criminal law is concerned with law as a system of rules which prescribe the ordering of human behaviour. Every society has, by appeal to recognized custom or precedent or recorded code, developed a system of rules for governing behaviour, and sanctions for breaches of such rules.

Criminal law is that body of law which the community or, in more developed forms of society, the State* acting through the police* and the court and penal system, prosecutes and penalizes offenders (see Punishment*). This body of law deals with crimes* or offences against the community or State.

Civil law is that body of law which governs the relations of persons to each other, and which provides remedies by way of compensation, by enforcement of promises (where these have effects as contracts) and by restraint of conduct in breach of the law. In its broadest sense, civil law covers all branches of domestic (*i.e.* local as distinct from international) law, including disputes between the individual and government (administrative law) and disputes of a matrimonial or domestic kind (family law). Civil law is concerned with providing the individual with a remedy for his or her grievance, rather than with penalizing behaviour, which is the province of the criminal law. The same conduct, *e.g.* an assault, can have both civil and criminal consequences, *i.e.* give rise to a claim for compensation by the injured person, and give rise to penalty under the criminal system.

In early legal systems such as OT law, the law has a strongly civil character. Although justice was administered through courts established by the king (2 Ch. 19:4–7), the law was concerned with resolving disputes, doing justice between individuals, and compensating the individual for the wrong suffered. Laws having this civil character are often prefaced by the words 'if' or 'when', followed by a description of certain conduct, and concluding with the form of compensation to be awarded to the injured party. OT law also had a criminal character in that certain serious offences were not only offences against the individual concerned but also offences against God, and so also offences against the community of Israel, which was dependent on him. The offences set out in the Decalogue are examples of law of this kind (see Old Testament Ethics[8]).

Law and morality

The relationship between law and morality has been debated by generations of legal philosophers. Their responses have included: 1. theories of natural law* (influential in Roman Catholicism through Thomas Aquinas* and later thinkers), which derive law from a set of universal moral principles which may be discerned by human reason (and a limited concept of natural law is found in Paul's reference to the witness of conscience in Rom. 2:14–15 but is not put forward as the basis for any system of law); 2. sociological and realist theories of law, which explain law in terms of societal response; 3. the historical school, which sees the law as the expression of the common consciousness of a people derived from their history; 4. positivist theories, which rigorously divorce statements of what the law is from statements of value – what the law ought to be – and see the basis of law in the rules issued or sanctioned by the State without intrinsic moral connotations; and 5. the current critical legal theorists who, in reaction to the inability of the positivist school to construct any basis for human rights (see Rights, Human*), have endeavoured to find in current value aspirations a basis for a variety of legal emphases, such as feminist jurisprudence and minority rights. The diversity of approaches among current critical theorists illustrates the absence of any common set of values in post-Christian society.

OT law was seen as dependent on the commands of God, and law was therefore almost coincident with morality. There were always some stipulations, however, which could not be enforced through the courts, such as the command to love one's neighbour. In the NT, God's commands are seen as fulfilled in Christ, the commands each being particular applications of love (see [2]) towards God and neighbour and fulfilled in the one who gave the new command to love one another as he has loved us (Jn. 15:12; Rom. 13:8–10; Gal. 5:13).

Sources of law

In the English-based systems, law may take the form of statute law issued by the legislature, or be in the form of common law derived from earlier decisions of the courts. Significant sections of law, such as contract law and the law of torts (civil obligations), remain in the form of case-law. Where the law is in statutory form, it tends to be prescriptive and detailed. The countries which have derived their law from this tradition are known as the common-law countries. The other major tradition of law is the Roman or civil law tradition, which has been adopted by most European countries. The major sections of law in countries having this tradition are codified. The function of the courts is to interpret and apply the more general provisions of the code to specific situations.

The rule of law

This phrase usually describes a state of society where an individual can appeal to a recognized body of law to determine a dispute with another, and particularly a dispute with the governing authority itself. In popular language it describes the situation where nobody (not even the government) is above the law. In the OT there are several examples of this rule in operation, *e.g.* Naboth and Ahab (1 Ki. 21) and David's condemnation by Nathan (2 Sa. 12). Behind this is the deeper recognition that both ruled and ruler come under the judgment of God, *e.g.* Jesus' statement to Pilate in Jn. 19:11.

See also: DEVLIN–HART DEBATE; LAW, USES OF.

Bibliography

J. N. D. Anderson, *Freedom under Law* (London, 1988); *idem*, *Morality, Law and Grace* (London, 1972); H. J. Berman, 'Towards an Integrative Jurisprudence', 76 *California Univ. Law Rev.* 131, 1988; J. Ellul, *The Theological Foundation of Law* (ET, New York, 1960); D. Lloyd, *The Idea of Law* (London, 1964).

P.D.McK.

LAW, USES OF. The Protestant Reformers, particularly Philip Melanchthon (1497–1560) and John Calvin,* identified a threefold use of the law (for Calvin, essentially but not exclusively expressed in the Decalogue,* Ex. 20:1–17). 1. For Calvin, the first use of law* is to exhibit the righteousness of God by acting as a kind of mirror to show humanity, impotence and the stain of sin (Rom. 3:20). 2. The second use is to denounce wrongdoing, to exercise discipline, and to set out punishment. The law curbs those who, unless forced, would otherwise have no regard for rectitude and justice. Christians have an obligation here to obey the law and to respect those who exercise legal authority as exercising a God-given role (Rom. 13:1–7; 1 Pet. 2:13–17). 3. The third and, according to Calvin, principal use of law relates only to believers. Though they have the Spirit of God in their hearts 'they are still weak in the flesh, and would rather serve sin than God. The law is to this flesh like a whip to an idle and balky ass, to goad, stir, arouse it to work' (Calvin, *Institutes*, 1536 edition, tr. and annotated by F. L. Battles, Grand Rapids and London, 1986, p. 36). The law in this sense is not abrogated for the Christian. From it believers learn each day what God's will is for their lives and how they may please him. The law is thus the instrument which the Holy Spirit uses in the sanctifying of the people of God. It is to an exposition of this third use of the law that Richard Baxter* devoted his monumental work on Christian ethics, *A Christian Directory* (1673).

One of the difficult questions which Christians face as members of a minority group within a pluralistic society is the extent to which Christian moral values should be enforced by civil law. Calvin's first two uses of the law find recognition within any society: 1. in the educative role which the law is seen to have in assisting the moulding of public opinion (whether directed by Christian or liberal sentiment, *e.g.* race relations legislation); and 2. in the protection of individuals or society from harm. The first is, however, dependent on the second: the justification for the law's educative role is that it is necessary in order that individuals or society can be protected by the law.

Should the law be used to promote and enforce all Christian moral values? The Puritans sought to align the law with morality by applying biblical law with very limited adaptation to contemporary circumstances. The theonomist school is currently renewing this emphasis in America and elsewhere (see Christian Reconstruction Movement*). In post-Christian society this question arises in relation to laws which are or have been on the statute book from an earlier time of Christian consensus, *e.g.* Sunday trading, censorship* of obscenity (see Pornography*) and blasphemy,* and laws against abortion* and homosexuality.*

The libertarian view, advanced particularly by J. S. Mill* in *On Liberty* (London, 1859), is that the only principle on which the use of force by way of legal penalties can be justified is to prevent harm to others. It is on that basis that the Wolfenden Committee in England in 1957 recommended that homosexual activity between consenting adults should not be the concern of the law. The same approach was advanced by H. L. A. Hart (1907–92) in a vigorous and influential debate with the Eng. judge, Lord Devlin (1905–92), in the early 1960s (see Devlin–Hart Debate*). Lord Devlin's response to Hart emphasized the need to protect society rather than the individual. Law is required to safeguard the shared morality which is foundational to a society's existence. The difficulty with this view is that in resting on a shared morality it depends on a precarious and shifting base. Better support for the use of the law in its educative and protective role lies in pointing out the narrow and negative view of 'harm' to the individual which the libertarian approach takes in matters such as obscenity and abortion, and the importance of providing support for institutions such as marriage* and the family* which give cohesion to society.

It is also necessary to recognize the limitations of law as a means of requiring adherence to moral standards. The law is powerless to make people good (Rom. 8:3–4). It can restrain evil but it loses its effectiveness if a particular law is widely disregarded, is difficult to enforce, and falls into disrepute, *e.g.* prohibition in the US in the 1930s.

Bibliography

J. N. D. Anderson, *Morality, Law and Grace* (London, 1972); G. L. Bahnsen, *Theonomy in Christian Ethics* (Phillipsburg, NJ, ²1984); J. Calvin, *Institutes of the Christian Religion*, II.vii; B. Mitchell, *Law, Morality and Religion in a Secular Society* (Oxford, 1967).

P.D.McK.

LAYING ON OF HANDS, see SACRAMENTAL HEALING.

LEADERSHIP gives vision and direction to a group, and enables its members to work together to fulfil its aims. Early studies of leadership observed the characteristics of 'born leaders', the need of groups for leaders, and how they emerged and were overthrown. As group dynamics* developed as a speciality, so too did methodologies for experimental studies in leadership; difficulties encountered in correlating results included the number of variables, and the value* preferences of researchers. Two main approaches developed: one regarded leadership as inherent in an individual; and the other as a function of a group, which throws up its own leader, leadership changing as members' contributions become relevant to the fulfilment of the group's task.

Trait studies endeavoured to find common factors in the personality of leaders, such as intelligence, initiative, capacity to take an overall view, self-assurance, dependability and social participation. Of these, the first two were found most frequently. *Style studies* looked at a continuum from autocratic to democratic leadership, relating this to outcome.

Contingency theories contain aspects of both, stressing a constellation of factors and their relationship to each other, especially that of leader with group, and with the requirements of the task. C. B. Handy's 'best fit' approach (see *Understanding Organizations*) suggests that the characteristics of the leader, the preferences of subordinates, and the requirements of the task should correspond, if there is to be a successful outcome. These are charted along a scale from 'tight' (structured) to 'flexible' (supportive). The way in which the fit is achieved will depend on the environment, which includes: 1. the power or position of the leader; 2. the relationship between leader and group; 3. organizational norms; 4. structure and technology; 5. variety of task; and 6. variety of subordinates. In addition to motivating and activating, the leader carries responsibility as ambassador for, and model to, the group. Good leaders will be characterized by a high tolerance of ambiguity, skill in differentiating, a clear self-concept, energy, standards which are moderately high, and the giving of feedback.

J. M. Burns, in *Leadership* (New York, 1978), contrasts transformative (inspirational) leadership, conveying a higher morality, with transactional leadership, focusing on task accomplishment. W. Bennis and B. Nanus distinguish, in their book *Leaders*, between leading and managing: 1. leaders have the vision of what they want, and total concentration on it; 2. they get the message across unequivocally at every level, by a variety of means; 3. they stick with the position adopted, so creating trust and a strong organizational identity; and 4. they have positive self-regard, recognizing strengths, compensating for weaknesses, a constructive attitude to failure and continuing self-development. They also tend to have stable marriages.

J. Adair, in a refinement of his previous formulations (*Developing Leaders*), sees leaders' and managers' functions as overlapping. Both have to handle the tension between task, team and individual needs by 1. setting objectives; 2. briefing; 3. planning; 4. controlling; 5. informing; 6. supporting; and 7. reviewing; but their emphases and special skills will vary. Leaders promote change and have a somewhat anarchic strain: managers excel in administration. An organization needs both.

Leadership implies power. This power may be based on: 1. the ability to reward; 2. having the power to punish; 3. possessing expertise; 4. holding a position of recognized authority; and 5. attracting and inspiring others, where any of these may be desired or feared by the person on whom the power is exerted (J. R. P. French and B. Raven, in D. Cartwright, ed., *Studies in Social Power*, Ann Arbor, MI, 1959). The more of these bases are possessed, the more powerful the leader, whose own self-regard raises the self-esteem of subordinates. Effective leadership moves beyond encouraging participation to actual empowerment of others. Leaders have a need for power, but will empower others if it is satisfied by the achievement of objectives rather than personal aggrandisement. An insufficient power-base can lead to the exercise of unduly coercive behaviour, with consequent poor results (W. W. Burke, *Executive Power*).

Though inheritance and early environment are important, leadership skills can be improved by the provision of learning opportunities, feedback on performance, evaluation, support, and crucially, an example to follow.

While no one theory of leadership is sufficient for the church, some findings illumine biblical principles. All authority* is delegated from God, and those exercising it are responsible to him. Those holding the office of overseer are required to have the highest standards of spirituality,* of conduct in family and public life, and emotional maturity; they lead by example and are to model themselves on Christ. Leaders are to serve and not to dominate. Leaders need a right, but not inflated, self-regard, and an appreciation of others. All members are linked to the head of the church, Christ, and to each other; all are empowered by the Holy Spirit. The gift of leadership is not confined to office-holders. Leaders have responsibility for ensuring the commission to make disciples is carried out by preaching, teaching and pastoring, recognizing and orchestrating the gifts of all so that all reach maturity.

The complexity of the interlocking factors demands flexible structures and allows for a variety of different styles. While leadership is essential, its various aspects are likely to be shared between a number of people characterized by an awareness of their accountability, and by diligence in carrying out the task.

See also: MANAGEMENT.

Bibliography

J. Adair, *Developing Leaders* (Maidenhead, 1988; New York, 1989); P. Beasley-Murray, *Dynamic Leadership* (Eastbourne, 1990); W. Bennis and B. Nanus, *Leaders* (New York, 1985); W. W. Burke, 'Leadership as empowering others', in S. Scrivaster *et al.*, *Executive Power* (San Francisco, 1986); C. B. Handy, *Understanding Organizations* (Harmondsworth, ³1985); N. Summerton, *A Noble Task* (Exeter, 1987); J. Tiller and M. Birchall, *The Gospel Community and its Leadership* (London, 1987).

J.R.G.

LEARNING DISABILITIES describes the range of difficulties in learning, evident from early life, which impair adaptive functioning and may limit the acquisition of basic and important skills. The terminology of the condition which has, until recently, been called 'mental handicap' or 'mental retardation', has been subject to change over the years. The present preferred term of 'learning disabilities' places the condition within an internationally accepted framework which distinguishes disability from the causal impairment, and from the potentially consequential handicap. Most people with mild degrees of learning disability have no identifiable physical cause for their disability, but there are a number of known physical or genetic causes, such as Downs syndrome. People with more severe learning disabilities are more likely to have some physical basis for their disability, and are also more likely to have some associated physical disability. It is also clear that improved early education and subsequent later training opportunities can substantially reduce the social and other handicaps conventionally linked with 'mental handicap'.

In standard intelligence tests, a score of 70 has been seen as a cut-off score, with scores below that indicative of a learning disability, but since some people with lowered test scores are totally independent, test scores themselves are not reliable indicators. A better basis for planning good care and education is early identification, careful assessment of individual skills, access to good health care to correct any physical conditions, and early access to special education with support and specialist guidance positively available to parents. Short-term respite care should be readily accessible, both to give family relief and to allow the young person the normal experience of separation from parents. For adults with learning difficulties, there are now a range of individual interventions available for any particular problems, and also a range of group settings which may offer either a positive day-care or residential-care environment. There is often a continuous need for pastoral care over the years, including support for caring parents and other relatives, not least because the statutory services may not be able to provide all the services which would be helpful.

The term 'fool' in Scripture (*e.g.* Pr. 1:7, and see NIV mg.; 26:1, *etc.*) does not refer to people with learning difficulties, but to those with moral understanding who behave irresponsibly or stubbornly. A number of other stigmatizing terms for those who are less intellectually able are common parlance, and one important pastoral issue for people with all disabilities is the affirmation of their significance and value, not least by the use of affirming terms.

With the results of better special education now available, it is clear that many people with moderate levels of learning disability can go through normal schools and can experience the full range of emotional, social and sexual aspirations as their peers. They will love and grieve, and should be offered support in finding appropriate expression for their emotions and creativity. Many can grasp spiritual realities and can participate meaningfully in sacramental and congregational worship, especially if worship is visually and action-oriented, and can join in other church activities, such as house groups.

The key to understanding people with learning disabilities is the establishment of reciprocal relationships with them. This is fundamentally forming friendships – being equal partners in the eyes of God and of each other, sharing the same humanity (Jn. 15:14), and growing through awareness, integration, and commitment to deep friendship. They show up our assumptions of 'normal' humanity, they challenge whether we really do feed the hungry and clothe the naked, and by their vulnerability and trusting they challenge a culture oriented to intellect and attainment. In recent years there has been a remarkable flow of theological reflection on the meaning of learning disability, and pastoral innovation in care by local congregations and by Christian agencies (such as the L'Arche communities set up by Jean Vanier, 1928– , and 'A Cause for Concern', a Christian organization for the mentally handicapped).

See also: DISABILITY AND HANDICAP.

Bibliography
S. Hauerwas, *Suffering Presence: Theological Reflections on Medicine, the Mentally Handicapped and the Church* (Edinburgh and Notre Dame, IN, 1986); S. Hollins and M. Grimer, *Going Somewhere: People with Mental Handicaps and their Pastoral Care* (London, 1988); F. Young, *Face to Face: A Narrative Essay in the Theology of Suffering* (Edinburgh, 1990).

J.N.H.

LEGALISM. In Christianity, salvation is obtained not by law-keeping but by relying upon Christ's righteousness. The importance of law-keeping is a *consequence* of commitment to God, a sign of covenant faithfulness, not a condition of obtaining the covenant.* So law-keeping has an important, but not the central, place in the Christian gospel. This important emphasis upon law-keeping has sometimes bred legalism an attitude of mind which gives excessive respect to the law and which seeks to enforce conduct of a similar kind in others. Quite apart from that unbiblical attitude of mind which seeks salvation through law-keeping, a legalistic attitude can express itself in a variety of other ways. 'Legalism' and 'legalistic' are almost always terms of reproach.

The law* of God, even in its Mosaic detail in the OT, was not all-embracing. There are enormous numbers of actions which the law of Moses neither commands nor forbids. One way in which a legalistic mind expresses itself is in seeking to extend those areas of life about which the law makes specific prescriptions. This was the attitude of mind which Paul encountered in Corinth, when those with weak consciences sought to make the eating of what had been sacrificed to idols a sin (1 Cor. 8:7–9). Paul countered this teaching by showing that there are matters which are morally indifferent. Another way in which legalism can show itself is in excessive emphasis upon what the law forbids as against what it enjoins.

The law deals with matters of differing importance. People may develop a particular fondness for or attachment to particular laws, and neglect others. Christ reprimanded those Pharisees who tithed mint and anise and cummin and who yet neglected the weightier matters of the law (Mt. 23:23). Christ did not condemn their tithing, however, only the imbalance.

The charge of legalism is sometimes unwarrantably brought against law-keeping as such. Paul's words 'the letter kills, but the Spirit gives life' (2 Cor. 3:6) are often used to argue that any principled observance of any law is 'legalistic', but in this and other passages Paul is not arguing against the observance of law, but contrasting the apostolic ministry (a ministry of righteousness) with that of Moses (a ministry of condemnation). The spirit referred to is not the spirit of law-keeping, but the Spirit who brings liberty from condemnation through Christ's righteousness.

The opposing of love (see ②) to law, and the use of the epithet 'legalism' to enforce it, is foreign to the NT and to mainstream Christian teaching, where love is not opposed to law but defined in terms of it (cf., e.g., 1 Jn. 5:3).

There have been periods of Christian history when a generation which has sought to uphold the law in society through a love for it has been followed by a generation which has retained the observance of the law but with a loss of inner conviction and motivation which makes that law a delight. In such circumstances the Christian gospel degenerates into moralism. Such an attitude, observable in England at the end of the Puritan period, and in aspects of Victorian life, has been aptly described as legalistic.

See also: LAW AND GOSPEL; LAW, USES OF.

Bibliography

C. F. Allison, *The Rise of Moralism* (London, 1966); B. N. Kaye and G. J. Wenham (eds.), *Law, Morality and the Bible* (Leicester and Downers Grove, IL, 1978); E. F. Kevan, *The Grace of Law* (London, 1964).

P.H.

LEISURE.

The etymology of the word 'leisure' defines its essential quality. The Eng. word can be traced back to two words (from which the Eng. verbs 'license' and 'school' are derived), both of which imply the idea of ceasing from work* and being free from obligation.

With this as a context, it is possible to define leisure in three complementary ways. The minimal requirement is that leisure is free time. More positively, leisure has traditionally been defined in terms of activities – cultural pursuits, recreation, entertainment, hobbies and social activities. At an even higher level, leisure is a quality of life – a state of soul or well-being.

Leisure has been a subject of neglect in the Christian church. Books and sermons on work have abounded, but not on leisure. The church has usually either condemned leisure as worldly (see Worldliness*) and unworthy of a spiritually minded person, or it has imitated the practices of a secular society.

A theology of leisure

A Christian view of leisure begins with the biblical account of creation. After God performed the work of creation, 'he rested, and was refreshed' (Ex. 31:17, RSV). We can find here a creation ordinance that prescribes periodic cessation from work as a necessary part of life.

The idea of the sabbath* reinforces this. According to the fourth commandment of the Decalogue, 'Six days you shall labour and do all your work; but the seventh day . . . you shall not do any work' (Ex. 20:9–10). Here is the God-intended balance – a harmonious rhythm in which work and leisure are equally important.

The command to cease from work also appears in the OT system of religious festivals. Society then, even though it was a subsistence society, followed a schedule of religious festivals that ensured days free from work (see, e.g., Nu. 28:18, 25, 26; Lv. 25). The idea of rest is deeply ingrained in the biblical consciousness, as are festivity and celebration.

The example of Jesus confirms all this. During his extraordinarily busy public years, Jesus found times of retreat. According to the Gospels, one of his favourite activities was attending dinner parties. On one occasion he commanded his disciples to stop ministering to the needs of the crowd and spend time refreshing themselves (Mk. 6:30–32). Jesus did not confine life to ceaseless work and evangelism. He took time to contemplate the beauty of the lilies and commanded his followers to do likewise (Mt. 6:28).

The Christian doctrine of stewardship* also undergirds a Christian view of leisure. Stewardship means honouring God with all that he had entrusted to a person – time, ability and materials. As stewards, Christians are as accountable for their leisure time as they are for their work.

Christian apologists for leisure have traditionally drawn a link between worship and leisure. While the two cannot simply be equated, the worship that God prescribes as part of life provides a rationale for seeing the value of leisure as well. The common ground between worship and leisure includes cessation from work, momentary renunciation of the acquisitive urge, contemplation, shared community, renewal, and the recovery of values.

A Christian leisure ethic

A theology of leisure informs one's thinking about leisure and declares its necessity. The ethics of leisure must inform the practice of leisure.

We can begin by positioning leisure in relation to some common ethical viewpoints. A strongly utilitarian (see Consequentialism*) ethic will either scorn leisure as being useless, or it will value leisure only as it contributes to work. An ethic of self-denial will discourage leisure because leisure is by its very nature a form of self-indulgence. On the positive side, leisure thrives in a context of hedonism* (in the loose sense of pleasure-seeking) and humanism* (in the traditional sense of affirming human fulfilment as a value). A Christian leisure ethic takes its place within this framework.

To begin with Christianity does not reduce life to the utilitarian. The world that God created is more than utilitarian. When God established the perfect human environment, he created trees that were not only 'good for food' (a utilitarian criterion) but also 'pleasing to the eye' (Gn. 2:9). Jesus warned against the tyranny of the utilitarian and the acquisitive spirit in his discourse against anxiety (Mt. 6:25–34).

An element of tension enters the picture when we consider the strong element of self-denial (Mk. 8:34) and the sense of duty* that are at the heart of Christianity. But the Bible equally embraces pleasure* and enjoyment. The most extended discussion comes in the book of Ecclesiastes. Although this book takes a dim view of the purely human pursuit of pleasure 'under the sun', it repeatedly praises the ideal of pleasure-seeking within a God-centred framework (e.g. Ec. 2:24–26; 3:11–13; 5:18–19).

The NT counterpart of this zestful endorsement of enjoyment is Paul's comment that God 'richly furnishes us with everything to enjoy' (1 Tim. 6:17, RSV). A Christian leisure ethic is rooted in an ethic of responsible pleasure. To live normally in the realm of leisure is to cultivate an ability to enjoy life outside of work and obligation.*

A Christian leisure ethic is also rooted in an affirmation of human creaturehood. Jesus' redemptive purpose is to enable people to have 'life . . . to the full' (Jn. 10:10). To be ethical, an activity must respect the end or *telos* of a thing – the purpose for which it was created and towards which it tends. If God's purpose for every person's life is a full life, the self-fulfilment that is at the heart of leisure will be zestfully and gratefully received as part of God's good provision.

Leisure did not escape the effects of the Fall.* In fact, a society's leisure seems often to provide heightened scope for its immoral tendencies. A Christian leisure ethic always subjects leisure to ordinary moral tests. The abuse of leisure occurs when people make an idol of it, when they fill it with immoral activities, when they transform it into selfish indulgence, and when they neglect duty.

The abuse of leisure should not lead Christians to reject leisure itself as worldly or immoral. Rather, a Christian's leisure is most completely moral when it is thoughtfully chosen, when it meets Christian goals, and when it fosters godly self-fulfilment in a person's life.

See also: PLAY.

Bibliography
R. K. Johnston, *The Christian at Play* (Grand Rapids, 1983); L. Ryken, *Work and Leisure in Christian Perspective* (Portland, OR, 1987; Leicester, 1989).

L.R.

LENDING, see CREDIT; DEBT; INTEREST.

LESBIAN RIGHTS, see HOMOSEXUALITY.

LEWIS, C. S. (1898–1963). Clive Staples Lewis, probably the greatest apologist for orthodox Christianity of the 20th century, was born in Belfast of Welsh and English ancestry but spent most of his life in England, chiefly at the University of Oxford. Resuming his undergraduate career at Oxford after service in the First World War, he took Firsts in Greats (which included a study of Gk. and Lat. historians and philosophers) and in English, tutored in philosophy for a year, and then was elected to a fellowship in Eng. at Magdalen College which he retained until his appointment as Professor of Renaissance and Medieval Literature at Cambridge in 1954. Lewis was married late in life (1956) to Joy Davidman, an American already seriously ill with cancer, though a remission allowed Lewis and his wife several years of happiness before her death in 1960. Lewis died a few years later, on 22 November 1963.

After his reconversion to Christianity in 1931, Lewis became increasingly well known as a writer on religious topics, his best-known early books being *The Screwtape Letters* (London, 1942), *The Problem of Pain* (London, 1940) and a series of BBC lectures eventually collected as *Mere Christianity* (London, 1952). These early apologetic works combined an incomparable prose style, a poet's imagination and a philosopher's devotion to argument.

Lewis also found a new way to share his Christian vision, by means of fiction. A trilogy of books in the science-fiction genre – *Out of the Silent Planet* (London, 1938), *Perelandra* (London, 1943) and *That Hideous Strength* (London, 1945) – and a series of seven books for children called *Chronicles of Narnia* (London, 1950–56) have given countless readers (and viewers) an imaginative grasp of Christian truths.

Lewis also wrote on other themes. His essay 'The Humanitarian Theory of Punishment' (in *God in the Dock Undeceptions*) continues to attract attention, and *A Grief Observed* (London, 1961), written after the death of his wife, is a major text in bereavement studies. *The Abolition of Man* (London, 1943) is an outstanding defence of human freedom and dignity.

Lewis' fame as a religious writer led to invitations to lecture on military bases during the Second World War and to a flood of letters from inquirers, which Lewis conscientiously answered, often with a brilliance equal to that of his published writings. The enthusiasm of his admirers had led to a reaction in some quarters, and there have been several attempts to downgrade his writing and even to distort his personal life in an effort to counteract his influence. These attempts have been largely unsuccessful; any serious inquiry into his life and writings shows a man and a writer worthy of great respect, admiration and gratitude for his contribution to teaching and defending the Christian faith.

Bibliography

Christian Reflections, ed. W. Hooper (London, 1967); *God in the Dock: Essays on Theology and Ethics*, ed. W. Hooper (Grand Rapids, 1970) = *Undeceptions* (London, 1971).

G. Meilander, *The Taste for the Other: The Social and Ethical Thought of C. S. Lewis* (Grand Rapids, 1978); P. Schakel, *Reason and Imagination in C. S. Lewis* (Exeter, 1984).

R.L.P.

LIBEL. The law recognizes a right on the part of the individual to have his or her reputation protected, so that the estimation in which that person stands is not injured by false statements to that person's discredit unless there exists some lawful justification or excuse. A libel is committed if the defamatory statement is written or is made in some permanent form or broadcast. A slander is committed if it is spoken or is in some other transient form. Libel and slander are both referred to under the general description of 'defamation'. Under Eng. law and the law of those countries deriving their system of law from England, a remedy in damages is awarded in civil proceedings, normally in a jury trial, to the injured party, which is designed to compensate for the harm done and injury to feelings. Libel is also a criminal offence because of its tendency to disturb public order, but in most jurisdictions special leave is required to bring a prosecution and very few cases are brought.

The law endeavours to preserve some balance between the individual interest in reputation and the public interest in freedom of speech and comment and the ability to assess the genuineness of a reputation. The law does this by providing a number of defences to an action in defamation. Truth, at least in civil proceedings, will always be a justification, but the burden of proving that the statement is true rests on the defendant. Fair comment on matters of public concern is permitted provided the comment is based on facts which are true and is not malicious (based on improper motive); a statement will be privileged if made on an occasion where there was a proper interest in making and receiving it and it is not malicious (*e.g.* reporting an alleged thief to an employer or to the police). Some statements, *e.g.* statements in court or in Parliamentary debate, are absolutely privileged whatever the motive.

In the US the courts, by reason of the First Amendment to the Constitution on freedom of speech, and from concern that public figures should not be immune from attack and enjoy a false reputation, have given much greater freedom to journalistic comment on persons in public life. The Eng. and Commonwealth legal systems have given public figures somewhat more protection leading to more restrained media comment. There is an important but difficult balance to be struck with widespread news media in modern open society between allowing the dissemination of libellous attacks on public figures and withholding information for fear of legal action and thereby allowing a false reputation to be maintained.

The ethical basis for laws on defamation is found in the ninth commandment forbidding false witness (Ex. 20:16). In a wider context, we are told to put off falsehood and to speak truth to our neighbour (Eph. 4:25). Slander and gossip are condemned in many places in the Bible (Nu. 14:36; Pss. 52:1–4; 101:5; Pr. 10:18; 20:19). We are to speak the truth in love (Eph. 4:15). As with the other commandments, the ethical injunction to love one another as Christ has loved us (Jn. 15:12) goes much beyond the letter of the commandment.

Bibliography

P. Lewis, *Gatley on Libel and Slander* (London, 81981); H. Street, *Freedom, the Individual and the Law* (Harmondsworth, 51982).

P.D.McK.

L IBERALISM, POLITICAL. Liberalism is often said, not least by liberals themselves, to be the governing political theory of the modern world, and many of its core ideas are taken for received truths by the dominant classes in Western societies. Although there is now much debate about whether any combination of ideas that can properly be termed 'liberalism' existed before the late 18th century, its centrality to the history of the self-understanding of democracies on the N. Atlantic model is beyond dispute.

Varieties of liberalism

Despite the baffling diversity of uses of the term 'liberal' and its cognates within political discussion, a number of broad types of liberalism are often picked out.

1. Classical liberalism. Partially exemplified in 19th-century Britain and revived during the 1980s, classical liberalism is closely connected with the economic and political doctrines of free-market capitalism.* Indebted in part to the classical political economists of the 18th and 19th centuries, it has been defended in the 20th century by writers such as Freidrich August von Hayek (1899–1992) and Robert Nozick (1938–). This variant of liberalism typically advocates *laissez-faire** policies in economics, freedom of trade internationally and minimal governmental intervention domestically, the right of individuals to freedom of contract, and justice in any distributions of wealth which result from free exchange.

2. Revisionist liberalism. As a response to the appalling social consequences of industrial capitalism, from the late 19th century revisionist liberalism recognized the need for social reform to accompany economic growth. This was instrumental in bringing about the New Deal in the US, and the post-war Welfare State* in Britain; at a theoretical level individual liberty and social justice have been coupled together by political philosophers such as L. T. Hobhouse (1864–1929) and John Rawls (1921–). Especially in N. America, revisionist liberalism has come to be associated not just with redistributionist economic policies and welfarist social policies, but also with, *e.g.*, support for the civil rights movement and the rights of minorities in general, suspicion of the power of central government and big business, opposition to religious fundamentalism and moral dogmatism, a preference for non-coercive measures to military force, *etc.*

3. Constitutional liberalism. Although classical and revisionist liberals often take differing stances in particular political debates, they find common ground in a general commitment to constitutional liberalism. This is frequently thought to articulate the underlying rationale of Western-style political institutions, and as such to express one of the defining features of the modern Western world. It is usually associated with the American and French revolutions, and (with varying degrees of historical accuracy) with writers such as John Locke (1632–1704), Baron de Montesquieu (1689–1755), Immanuel Kant,* and the authors of *The Federalist* (1787–88). In general, constitutional liberalism attempts to provide a theoretical justification for a set of practices clustered around the principle of limited government,* including most or all of the following: effective restraints on the arbitrary or tyrannical exercise of power;* constitutional definition of governmental powers; the rule of law; government legitimated by consent of the people; maintenance of the rights of individuals, especially their civil and political rights; official toleration of a plurality of religions and moral codes; and the legal protection of private property.

4. The liberal world-view. There is often asserted to be a liberal world-view which informs each of the above in different ways. While it is difficult to enumerate its different features precisely, it is typically held to be suspicious of the claims of religion, progressivist in relation to history, optimistic about the human capacity to reason, hospitable to the claims of science, committed to the futherance of democratic institutions, and universal in its ambitions for itself. These elements are held together by the supreme liberal principles of the centrality of the individual, over against the claims of tradition, authority,* hierarchy or community; the fundamental equality* of individuals, regardless of birth, status, gender, race* or creed; and, above all, the liberty of individuals, with a concomitant emphasis on consent, choice and human autonomy.*

Theological issues

Because of the all-embracing nature of liberalism as a general political doctrine, as well as its protean character, a critical analysis of liberalism is in good part a critical analysis of particular features of one version of liberalism or another. Thus the critic might wish to examine specific theoretical defences of liberalism (*e.g.* utilitarian [see Consequentialism*], contractarian or rights-based [see Rights, Human*]), specific concepts employed by liberalism (*e.g.* rights, consent, autonomy, neutrality, *etc.*), specific liberal values (notably the centrality of the individual, equality and liberty), or characteristic ways in which different liberalisms have failed to live up to their declared ideals.

However, Christian theological reflection on liberalism (see Liberalism, Theological*) has some more general questions, which relate particularly to the so-called liberal world-view. 1. In its universal aspirations and its affinity with doctrines of moral and social progress, there can arguably be glimpsed on occasions the spectre of liberalism as a surrogate religion offering a this-worldly eschatology; this is liable to engender inordinate expectations of what politics can achieve, and may potentially function as a substitute for Christian salvation. 2. The optimistic liberal view of human beings and their reasoning abilities may lead to sociological naïvety and a blindness about the nature of power, which are better recognized by Marxists and conservatives (see Conservatism*), as well as in the Christian understanding of human sinfulness. 3. Although religious unity is not evidently necessary for political unity in at least some modern countries, liberalism has not always been clear about what historical conditions make religious pluralism* possible; nor has it sufficiently addressed the possibility that a liberal social order may depend on individuals holding moral or religious beliefs which are not themselves sustained by liberalism. 4. Its general commitment to State neutrality with regard to the religious and moral beliefs of individuals raises questions about the meaning and possibility of neutrality; in particular, liberalism is often accused of lacking a sense of the common good, and of insensitivity to the shared values and collective goods that are essential to some non-individualistic understandings of human flourishing.

Nevertheless, certain important Christian truths about the political order are preserved in liberalism. Various aspects of liberal beliefs – *e.g.* about the value of the person, the need for concern and respect towards those who are not part of the majority, the limitations of the State's competence, the importance of private property, and the equality and freedom of individuals – all find cogent defenders within Christian thought. Most notably, the doctrine that religious belief and practice are not a matter of political obligation reflect the idea that political authority cannot secure salvation. The public realm comprises groups of differing beliefs and identities who are willing to co-operate concerning the this-worldly matters that they hold in common: it is not an instrument of saving grace. One fundamental corollary of this is that no particular social group, religious or otherwise, can demand as a matter of right that its values be enshrined as the public values.

Bibliography

J. Gray, *Liberalisms* (London, 1989); F. A. von Hayek, *The Constitution of Liberty* (London and Chicago, 1960); L. T. Hobhouse, *Liberalism* (1911; New York, 1964); J. S. Mill, *On Liberty* (1859; Cambridge, 1989); J. Rawls, *Political Liberalism* (New York, 1993); J. Raz, *The Morality of Freedom* (Oxford, 1986).

R.J.S.

LIBERALISM, THEOLOGICAL. The term 'theological liberalism' shares with other uses of the word (*e.g.* political liberalism*) a general reference to open-mindedness, freedom from tradition,* tolerance and humane respect for the individual. It also has more narrow reference to specific types of theology, where ethics is often given the utmost importance.

Historically liberalism dominated 19th-century European theology as a reaction – in the Enlightenment* tradition – against elements of orthodox Christianity which were seen as out of date, and as maintained only by unacceptable authoritarianism. There was also a positive concern to take account of the contemporary scientific world-view which seemed to raise questions both about Christianity's historical claims and about its claims to transcendent revelation.

As the historicity of the Gospel accounts was seemingly discredited by such work as that of H. S. Reimarus (1694–1768), G. E. Lessing (1729–81), D. F. Strauss (1808–74) and J. E. Renan (1823–92), and as the miraculous / supernatural elements of Christianity were seen by many as untenable, liberal theologians increasingly stressed the lasting value of Jesus' life and moral teaching. The pattern of salvation tended to be seen no longer in the three stages of Augustine* and the Reformers: 1. a perfect creation; 2. the Fall and original sin (which doctrines were also questioned); and 3. supernatural salvation through transcendent revelation and incarnation. The pattern was, rather, a single process of the progress of the human race – following the example and teaching of Jesus, but ultimately achieving salvation themselves.

The essence of Christianity came to be identified with subjective values – the sense of 'absolute dependence' – for F. D. E. Schleiermacher,* or with its ethical teaching for Adolf Harnack (1851–1930) and Albrecht Ritschl (1822–89). By the time of Ritschl the kingdom of God* is equated with the morally perfect human society founded by Jesus. With the optimistic view of human beings which characterized liberalism, this goal was seen as achievable within human history and by human effort.

These characteristics of 19th-century liberal theology – an optimistic view of human beings, emphasis on immanence, on the goodness of creation and on progress, and a view of Jesus as the perfect moral example – were carried into the 20th century especially by the social gospel school, which reached its height in the US early in the century with the work of Walter Rauschenbusch (1861–1918), and by the death-of-God theology of Paul van Buren (1924–) and Harvey Cox (1929–) in the 1960s.

Although liberalism is most often taken as referring to Protestant thinkers, a Roman Catholic social liberal movement also developed at the beginning of the 20th century, centred particularly around the teaching of John A. Ryan (1869–1945). In Catholic thought liberalism is rooted in the strong traditional emphasis on natural law,* affirming the availability of natural moral laws to the God-given reason of all human beings.

The theological emphases outlined above tend to stress the universality of ethics as based on values – such as love (see ②), and the freedom,* value and rights* of the individual – which are inherent or readily available to humanity through natural and rational means. Human responsibility* and ability to do the right are stressed and there is no great discontinuity between the kingdom of God and human history and society, or (in ethical terms at least) between Christian and non-Christian. This leads to a strong social concern and attention to the need to educate and to change society, and to co-operate with one another inside and outside the church for the good of all.

Liberalism is frequently criticized for its weak view of sin which is likely to be seen as apathy, as failure to take responsibility or as lack of knowledge, and its optimistic anthropology has always suffered serious damage in the light of events such as war. Reinhold Niebuhr,* while also expressing great social concern, was particularly critical of this weakness. Another focus for criticism has been liberalism's loss of the transcendent, neo-orthodoxy and particularly Karl Barth* bringing a devastating attack to bear on the liberal tendency to reduce Christian faith and ethics to purely human phenomena.

While these problems must be addressed, there is, none the less, much to be learned from liberalism, particularly with reference to ethics. Human beings are in the image of God,* and the ethical significance of this must be maintained alongside – even in tension with – a realistic account of sinfulness, Protestant theology having sometimes lost sight of the former in its emphasis on the latter.

Of particular value also is the stress of liberalism on the church's role as an ethical – and not a solely spiritual – community. This is a concept which has been developed recently, within very different theological frameworks, by Stanley Hauerwas (1940–) and John Howard Yoder (1927–).

Bibliography

P. D. L. Avis, *The Science of Theology* (Basingstoke, 1988); C. E. Curran, *Moral Theology: A Continuing Journey* (Notre Dame, IN, 1982); B. M. G. Reardon (ed.), *Liberal Protestantism* (London, 1968); A. Ritschl, *The Christian Doctrine of Justification and Reconciliation* (ET, Edinburgh, 1900).

M.E.A. and S.E.Al.

LIBERATION, see LIBERATION THEOLOGY; SIN AND SALVATION. [5]

L IBERATION THEOLOGY. Gustavo Gutiérrez (1928–) defines liberation theology as 'a critical reflection on Christian praxis in the light of the Word'. Liberationists maintain that reflection on the experiences of poor, exploited Latin Americans is at the heart of this theology. If social, political and economic concerns are ignored, theology is irrelevant in Latin America.

This methodology and classist perspective form the basis for other world-wide, inter-faith liberation theologies which have emerged in the last three decades. African, Black, feminist, Asian and Jewish liberation theologies all concur in the premise that they speak on behalf of minority groups who suffer oppression.

Within Latin American liberation theology, the strategy of action is set by the grassroots organizers or the organic intellectuals (a term coined by A. Gramsci, 1891–1937) who make the poor aware of their potential to transform their social, political and economic situation. This acquiring of the knowledge of their potentiality, which is termed *conscientization*, is rooted in the ideological notion that the poor as historical subjects are capable of removing the prevailing injustices. Once the exploited poor recognize their potential, they engage themselves in the process of liberation. This process permits what is termed 'second violence' as a response to the first violence committed against the poor. Not all liberationists subscribe to violence, although they agree with Gutiérrez when he says, 'The Latin American peoples will not emerge from their present status except by means of a profound transformation, *a social revolution* which will radically and qualitatively change the conditions in which they now live' (*A Theology of Liberation*, ET, 1973, p. 88). After making their action a political act, the theological moment occurs, which is critical reflection from within and upon concrete historical praxis.* This constitutes the first pillar of liberation theology.

The word 'liberation', not 'development', describes the real need of Latin America: liberation from sinful political and socio-economic structures. Such commitment to the process of liberation originates from such questions as: How do we speak about God who reveals himself in love in a reality marked by poverty and oppression? How do we announce a God of life to people who die prematurely and unjustly?

These questions lead liberationists to opt for the poor and to theologize their perspective; they regard this as a biblical approach. This constitutes the second pillar in the liberationist structure and is the key to an understanding of liberation. Leonardo Boff (1938–) affirms: 'Reading history from the position of the poor is the dominant perspective of the Bible.' This claim is based on the premise that God loves the poor preferentially. Liberation ethics is inseparable from what God is doing to free the oppressed. To find out what one can do, one can use the Bible and experience. Scripture, it is argued, shows that Jesus identified with outcasts not just because he felt pity for them, but in order to reveal God's judgment on political and religious structures which oppressed the weak. Furthermore, it is affirmed, this identification reveals the nucleus of the biblical message, namely the relationship between God and the poor; and Jesus Christ is therefore seen as God become poor. When the gospel is preached to the poor (Lk. 4:18), according to liberation theologians, it is preached to a social, marginalized, exploited group. Therefore, to spiritualize this biblical text (and others) to mean the spiritually poor, Gutiérrez submits, is to nurture the idea that God loves first and foremost the meritorious.

This conception, however, is built on the notion that God loves only those who are good and righteous on their own merits (*i.e.* the poor). This understanding betrays a 'salvation by works' framework and negates the biblical affirmation that all have sinned and are under the wrath of God, and that salvation from the guilt, power, and corruption of sin comes only through personal faith in Christ whose substitutionary death alone reconciles sinners to God.

Liberationists affirm that by taking the word 'poor' literally, God challenges us and will judge us on 'the basis of our concrete, historical actions toward the poor ("In so far as you did this to one of the least of these brothers of mine . . .", Mat. 25:40)'. The hermeneutic reveals an ideological determinant. The poor of Latin America match the oppressed in Karl Marx's* analysis of society. The poor are made pivotal in the Messianic practice of Jesus; he died the violent death of the oppressed as he opposed the *status quo*. The transformation of the historical condition of the poor is thus seen to have been the mission of Jesus Christ.

According to liberation theologians, a major contributory factor in producing social changes for the poor is their culture and popular beliefs. Such persuasion has an ideological root, and liberationists have adopted the 'religious myth' identified by the Peruvian J. C. Mariátegui (1895–1930), who believed that the proletariat (*i.e.* the poor) were the sole possessor of this myth. The poor are regarded as historical subjects, being the embodiment of this religious myth: although they have no prospect of real social improvement, yet they are seen as being capable of changing society. The Bartolomé Las Casas Centre, based in Lima, conducted a study to determine the implications of popular religion on liberative praxis. Tokihiro Kudó and Raúl Vidales (1943–) carried out this study, starting from the perspective that culture and religiosity have an inherent ability to raise historical and political consciousness. The findings of the Las Casas Centre revealed that religiosity is used as a defence mechanism primarily in the rural areas, and popular

religion is internally superstitious and externally Catholic. The implication for liberative praxis is that religiosity serves as a vehicle through which the poor can articulate their political consciousness and effect changes in society. Argentinian liberation theologian Juan Carlos Scannone (1931–) supports the findings as he maintains that popular Catholicism has a liberating effect. On the other hand, Uruguayan Juan Luís Segundo (1925–) perceives popular religion as a distortion of Christianity and having an adverse effect on liberative praxis.

Social changes being channelled by the effectiveness of liberation praxis find echoes in the 'Base ecclesial communities' (BECs). These groups are being identified as the true church. Boff writes: 'For us the [BEC] is the Church itself, the universal sacrament of salvation, continuing the mission of Christ as prophet, priest and pastor' (*Ecclesiogenesis: The Base Communities Reinvent the Church*, p. 12). This view of the nature of the church has a precedent in the Second Vatican Council* documents (*i.e. Lumen Gentium*).

Various questions have been raised about liberation theology, particularly the implicit paternalism observed in who determines the programme of conscientization. The grassroots organizers determine this programme. Their task, as trained leaders both in political analysis and theological education, is to tap the power present in the culture and belief of the poor in such a way that they point to the urgency of a revolutionary process. They also stimulate appropriate socio-political action on their behalf. These grassroots organizers are not the poor, and without them conscientization is impossible. Sociologist Madelaine Adriance separates them from the poor, and classifies them as professional people. They serve as pastoral agents; often they are nuns, priests and educated lay people. Liberationists recognize their important role, as Curt Cadorette indicates: 'The organic intellectual is a person passionately yet intelligently committed to the struggle for justice. She or he walks with the poor as a person skilled in expressing their collective wisdom. The finality of that wisdom is to sustain a vision of integral liberation' (*From the Heart of the People*, Oak Park, IL, p. 96). These individuals facilitate the process through which the oppressed will acquire a capacity to judge; he or she sifts out the people's real will, and is 'a tactician adept at planning and strategizing' (p. 97).

The claim that liberation theology is autochthonous, in the sense that it emerges from the poor of Latin America, is ill founded and is contradicted by what is revealed in the study of culture and popular religiosity. Other criticisms made are: 1. the inadequacy of liberation theology in articulating the primacy of the vertical dimension of salvation; and 2. the restricted view of sin held by liberationists promotes the idea that salvation is equivalent to liberation from poverty and oppression. The genuine concern expressed by liberation theologians via their lives and writings towards the plight of the poor is blunted by their submission to ideologies that run contrary to the gospel of Jesus Christ.

See also: SIN AND SALVATION;⁵ VATICAN STATEMENTS.

Bibliography
M. Adriance, 'Opting for the Poor: A Social-Historical Analysis of the Changing Brazilian Catholic Church', *Sociological Analysis* 46.2, 1985, pp. 131–146; L. Blowers, 'Ecclesiogenesis: Birth of the Church, or Birth of Utopia?', *Miss* 17.4, 1989, pp. 405–420; L. Boff, *Ecclesiogenesis: The Base Communities Reinvent the Church* (ET, Maryknoll, NY, 1986); E. Dussel, *Ethics and the Theology of Liberation* (ET, Maryknoll, NY, 1978); G. Gutiérrez, *The Power of the Poor in History* (ET, London and Maryknoll, NY, 1983); *idem*, *A Theology of Liberation* (ET, London and New York, ²1988); T. Kudó and R. Vidales, *Práctica Religiosa y Proyecto Histórico* (Lima, 1975 and 1980); E. Núñez, *Liberation Theology* (ET, Chicago, 1985); J. C. Scannone, *Teología de la Liberación y Praxis Popular* (Salamanca, 1976); J. L. Segundo, *The Liberation of Theology* (ET, London and Maryknoll, NY, 1976).

E.J.M.

LIBERTINISM, see FREEDOM.

LIBIDO, see FREUD, SIGMUND; PSYCHOANALYSIS.

LIFE CYCLE, see HUMAN DEVELOPMENT.

LIFESTYLE, see CONSUMERISM.

LIFE SUPPORT, see BRAIN DEATH; COMA; DEATH AND DYING; INTENSIVE CARE; LIFE, HEALTH AND DEATH;¹³ QUALITY OF LIFE; TRANSPLANT SURGERY.

LIVING WILL, see COMA; CONSENT; DEMENTIA; EUTHANASIA.

LLOYD-JONES, MARTYN (1899–1981). A magnetic and influential Welsh preacher and pastor, with commanding intellectual gifts, David Martyn Lloyd-Jones served a congregation of the Presbyterian Church of Wales in Aberavon, Port Talbot, from 1927 to 1938, and then the Independent congregation at Westminster Chapel, London, first as colleague and then as successor of G. Campbell Morgan (1863–1945). He retired in 1968, but continued itinerant preaching till shortly before his death.

'(The) Doctor', as he was always called, trained and qualified as a physician before moving into ministry, and his diagnostic way of exposing the needs of unbelievers, Christians and churches in clinical rhetoric was arresting. Self-taught in the Puritan, Calvinistic Methodist, and Princetonian streams of Reformed theology and spiritual life, he was a tireless expositor of the riches of God's grace* and power according to the Scriptures, and the tireless foe of whatever obstructed or undermined a clear grasp of these riches – facile rationalistic liberalism (see Liberalism, Theological*); hollow neo-orthodoxy; the barren sacramentalist legalism* of the Roman system as defined at Trent; and indifference to ecumenical pressures which seemed to him certain to lead to watered-down views of faith, an inadequate idea of what constitutes a Christian, and unconcern about authentic Christian unity. Pressing the latter point during his last years isolated him from many clergy and evangelical organizations that had previously viewed him as a mentor, consultant, and guide, outstanding for knowledge and wisdom.

Within the Reformed mainstream, Lloyd-Jones's ministry was distinctive for: 1. commitment to grand-scale expository preaching (*e.g.* eleven years on Rom. 1–14); 2. emphasis on the rational adequacy of biblical faith, and his common-sense, 'man-to-man', forthright style of pulpit persuasion; 3. deeply experiential presentation of the gospel, with sustained emphasis on pardon, peace, assurance, joy and hope in God; 4. stress on Spirit-baptism as a post-conversion event of direct assurance that all Christians should seek; 5. highlighting spiritual revival, understood in Edwardian (see Edwards, Jonathan*) terms as a fresh outpouring of the Spirit to bless the preached Word, as the contemporary church's only ultimate hope; and 6. highlighting preaching itself as a pneumatic and supremely significant activity.

All Lloyd-Jones' published works are transcribed sermons or lectures.

Bibliography
Ephesians, 7 vols. (Edinburgh, 1974–82); *Preaching and Preachers* (London, 1971); *Romans*, 6 vols. (Edinburgh, 1970–89); *The Sermon on the Mount*, 2 vols. (London, 1959–60); *Spiritual Depression* (London, 1965).
C. Catherwood (ed.), *Martyn Lloyd-Jones: Chosen by God* (Westchester, IL, and Crowborough, 1986); I. H. Murray, *D. M. Lloyd-Jones: The First Forty Years, 1899–1939* (Edinburgh, 1982); idem, *D. M. Lloyd-Jones: The Fight of Faith, 1939–81* (Edinburgh, 1990).

J.I.P.

LOGICAL POSITIVISM is the name given to a set of doctrines, derived largely from the empiricism of David Hume,* developed by the Vienna Circle in the decades immediately before the Second World War. Its tenets were brilliantly expounded and advocated by A. J. Ayer* in *Language, Truth and Logic*. Logical positivism is best known for the verification principle, according to which the meaning of a proposition consists in the method of its verification.

In ethics, the consequences of accepting the verification principle were of more importance than the principle itself. These consequences led in the direction of emotivism, though on balance the interest of the logical positivists in ethics was far outweighed by that in epistemology and the philosophy of science. The verification principle does not by itself entail emotivism, but it would appear to entail some version of non-cognitivism if it is also held, as the positivists held, that moral sentences are not verifiable by sense experience.

Thus although 'Stealing is wrong' appears to have the same logical form as 'Steel is strong', in fact, because it is unverifiable, it *states nothing*. It follows therefore that there are no moral facts, only scientific facts. What, then, is the function of moral utterances? They are expressive. To say that stealing money is wrong is, according to Ayer, 'as if I had written "Stealing money!!"' – where the shape and thickness of the exclamation marks show, by a suitable

convention, that a special sort of moral disapproval is the feeling that is being expressed. It is clear that there is nothing said here which can be true or false' (*Language, Truth and Logic*, p. 107).

What Ayer dealt with in a few short paragraphs was developed more thoroughly by the American philosopher C. L. Stevenson (1908–78), who argued that the language of ethics has not only an expressive but also a persuasive function.

It is sometimes asserted that emotivism trivializes ethics, even that it is antinomian.* But this is to forget that emotivism is a thesis in meta-ethics; it does not offer a set of moral values. Trivialization is inevitable only if human emotion is trivial. What stirs human emotion to utter expressions of value is a matter of empirical investigation. But what is undoubted is that emotivism renders both moral reasoning and moral disagreement impossible, since according to it moral differences are merely differences in emotional reaction. In *The Language of Morals*, R. M. Hare* retained the non-cognitivism (as 'prescriptivism') but attempted to reinstate moral reasoning with the use of the universalizability principle.

Bibliography
A. J. Ayer, *Language, Truth and Logic* (London, 1936; ²1946); R. M. Hare, *The Language of Morals* (Oxford, 1952); C. L. Stevenson, *Ethics and Language* (New Haven, CT, 1944).

P.H.

LOGOTHERAPY, see FRANKL, VIKTOR.

LONELINESS is a fact of life, known in some degree to everyone, even if unrecognized. Nevertheless, there has been little documented psychological or sociological investigation into this phenomenon. Mother Teresa* says that loneliness, not starvation, is the scourge of our present day. It can be a major cause of alcoholism,* promiscuity, depression,* behaviour difficulties in adolescents, psychosomatic problems and even suicide.* No doubt the widespread sense of alienation,* meaninglessness and lack of identity is a contributory cause.

Loneliness, which is to be distinguished from being alone, is common to all ages and strata of society. It is the experience of failure to satisfy the basic human need for deep personal relationships with other people. It is an intensely painful sense of exclusion, of rejection, of not mattering to anyone, and of being worthless, and it is accompanied by feelings of distress, restlessness and heightened self-concentration. Simultaneously, there is a strong fantasy that everyone else is enjoying unclouded love and fun, which adds poignancy to the loneliness. This is accentuated by media portrayal of idealized intimacy. Loneliness carries an unwarranted stigma in society, which makes lonely people reluctant to make their social and emotional needs known for fear of being regarded as peculiar in some way. The pain of inner loneliness can drive a person to find any distraction: busyness, shopping, television, computers, sport or noise of any sort. It often throws a person into the arms of some companion on life's journey: anybody is better than nobody. Thus people can find themselves in relationships which eventually turn out to be unsatisfying, boring or suffocating. If loneliness is the factor which brings people together in the hope that they, together, will no longer be lonely, then they impose unrealistic demands on each other.

Individual needs and lonelinesses vary at different stages and circumstances of life. Conditions which might cause some people to be lonely (*e.g.* old age, singleness,* mid-life changes) do not affect others. It is a subjective experience.

Behaviourists* regard loneliness as a defect in quality and type of social skills, which can be remedied by adequate learning processes. The analytic* schools of thought believe that the foundations of relationship-building are laid in early infancy. At that time, the child feels secure and able to be trustfully dependent in the parents' physical proximity. This trustfulness is gradually incorporated into the child's inner-life experience and he or she feels safe within himself or herself. For increasing lengths of time, the parents can be away but the child will not feel frightened or lost. He or she can be alone and yet, internally, together with them (= alone-together). People learn to be alone only by being together. However, if the parent disappears suddenly, or for longer than the child can tolerate, he or she will lose his or her security and *raison d'être*. The child will need to dull the intense fear and disorientation by demanding various distractions (often carried in some form into adult life). The pain is fear of abandonment and nothingness (= alone-alone).

Thus, the quality of adult relationships is formed. The alone-alone (abandoned) position is destructive and threatening to basic, personal emotional health and to relationship-making, in that any hint of dependency or personal exposure is inevitably experienced as the precursor to intense pain. The alone-together position enables a person to be centred in the self* (which is not at all the same as being self-centred) and makes possible satisfying personal relationships involving dependence, interdependence or independence.

In the view of some humanistic psychologists, it is essential to live with the deep loneliness which lies at the heart of existence rather than attempting to avoid it by distractions. Christian experience adds that a personal relationship with God speaks into this very void, in that while Christians do often feel lonely, they are not alone-alone. Jesus himself experienced this when he knew that all his disciples would leave him, and he would feel their desertion: 'Yet I am not alone, for my Father is with me' (Jn. 16:32). He promised that, similarly, in our inner self and the private depths of our aloneness, the Father will meet us through the Holy Spirit. Thus it is that, in our loneliness, there is potential for spiritual and personal growth, which does not exist when our life is crammed with distractions.

Bibliography

J. Bowlby, *The Making and Breaking of Affectional Bonds* (London, 1979); R. F. Hobson, 'Loneliness', *JAP* 19, 1974; R. Rolheiser, *The Restless Heart* (London, 1988).

M.C.-J.

LOSS, see BEREAVEMENT.

LOVE, see LOVE;② VIRTUE AND VIRTUES.

LOVE AND JUSTICE, see JUSTICE AND PEACE;③ LOVE.②

LOYALTY. If a person is loyal to another person, group or cause, then he or she can be relied on to defend, aid or support them. Thus loyalty to a friend is displayed especially where the friend is in some danger or need, and where the succour is rather costly to provide. Costliness is relevant as providing evidence of reliability: it is a 'test' of loyalty. But loyalty is not just reliability of behaviour. The trustworthiness of the loyal person stems from an attitude of attachment to the object of his or her loyalty, a heartfelt identification with it and love for it. Soldiers who are kept 'loyal' in battle by rifles of other soldiers aimed at the back of their heads are not really loyal. It is no accident that loyalty is typically to friends, family and country.

Loyalty can be regarded as a virtue* because, in addition to the benefits accruing to the object of loyalty and the social bonding that it betokens, as a reliability based in attachment it is an expression of personal integrity. A person with no firm identity, capable of no steady attachments but tossed about by shifting passions and subject to every change of environment, cannot be loyal. Neither can a utilitarian (see Consequentialism*) who must decide what to do on the basis of calculations of benefit that prescind from the particular identity of the persons involved; for loyalty is impossible without particular attachments. Loyalty might seem to be sometimes vicious, since one can be loyal to an evil person or cause; loyalty to Hitler or the principle of apartheid* is surely worse, morally and spiritually, than no loyalty at all. Such loyalties are doubtless evil, but the fact remains that true loyalty – even to something evil – shows an integration of personality without which no morality or spirituality at all would be possible. Despite this, however, the phenomenon of divided loyalties is generally recognized (*e.g.* to the demands of church and State).

The psychologist Ivan Boszormenyi-Nagy (1920–) has introduced the concept of 'invisible' loyalties in the context of a deeply relational theory of persons and psychotherapy. In his view, persons are naturally loyal, especially to members of their families, and much of human behaviour and emotion (both healthy and dysfunctional) can be explained in terms of the various ways this loyalty is satisfied and frustrated. The loyalty that binds us to our families is often invisible, both because we are so close to it and because it may be masked by behaviour that appears disloyal. In one example, a truant, drug-abusing youngest son turns out, on the loyalty-diagnosis, to be rescuing his mother from losing the last of her children, by making himself unfit to live outside the home. Articulating this diagnosis for the family is therapeutic, enabling both mother and son better to 'individuate' – *i.e.* to express their loyalty to one another in healthier, consciously chosen ways. In making loyalty so basic, Nagy is saying that our bonds with particular persons are essential to our development and existence as persons.

The psychology inherent in Christianity is also a strongly relational one, insisting on our bonds with one another ('each member belongs to all the others', Rom. 12:5), and with God ('Because you are sons, God sent the Spirit of his Son into our hearts, the Spirit who calls out "Abba! Father!"', Gal. 4:6). Although 'loyalty' is not an NT word, it seems that loyalty to fellow members of the church is a Christian virtue, for the love that is required of us is a reliable readiness to defend, aid and support our brothers and sisters in often costly ways, out of a heartfelt identification with them. The love of God to which we are called is likewise one that stands steadfastly 'with' him in his service, often through great difficulties. Just as in Nagy's psychology no-one can be a fully developed person unless he or she lives in a human context in which his or her tendency towards loyalty-attachments can be properly realized and expressed, so in the Christian psychology God has so structured our psyches as to find realization of our potential in the loyalties characteristic of God's kingdom.

Bibliography

I. Boszormenyi-Nagy and G. M. Spark, *Invisible Loyalties: Reciprocity in Intergenerational Family Therapy* (New York, 1973); J. Royce, *The Philosophy of Loyalty* (New York, 1908); B. Williams, 'A Critique of Utilitarianism', in J. J. C. Smart and B. Williams, *Utilitarianism: For and Against* (Cambridge, 1973).

R.C.R.

LOYOLA, IGNATIUS, see IGNATIUS OF LOYOLA.

L UST is inordinate passion or unintegrated desire for pleasure, often sexual pleasure. In the Christian tradition sexual lust has been generally seen as the paradigmatic form of lust, frequently as a metaphor for lust of power and money. Traditionally lust is one of the seven deadly sins* contrasted with chastity* and temperance.*

In the NT, the Gk. term *epithymia*, or 'strong desire', sometimes has a positive meaning (Mt. 13:17; Lk. 22:15; Phil. 1:23) translated by the NIV respectively as 'longed', 'eagerly desired', 'desire', but more often it bears the negative meaning of lust. 1 Jn. 2:16 refers to the 'lust of his eyes', Col. 3:5 to 'lust', Gal. 5:16 to 'desires . . . sinful'. In Mt. 5:28

Jesus forbids a man to look 'lustfully' at a woman. In general, *epithymia* is often used in Gk. writings to refer to sexual desire.

Lust seeks gratification for the moment. Lust exploits other people, turning them into objects. Lust is the obsession to possess, an exercise of domination and violence* rather than one of love. The vice of lust is its depersonalization, as much to its perpetrator as to its victim. The perpetrator loses his or her sense of self to some unbridled fixation. Instead of integrating one's energies (including sexual) in a personal reaching out for mutuality and connection, one becomes a victim of one's own energies and is driven in any way to have the needs met. Manoeuvre and coercion become second nature.

Fundamentally lust is a stance of hostility, alien to intimacy and an isolating, asocial attitude, which contrasts with the respect, mutuality and connection of love. Lust is so unhealthy because it can captivate a whole person and monopolize his or her energies to the exclusion of all interests unrelated to that particular passion. To lust is to be in the service of an idol.

As inordinate desire, lust needs to be clearly distinguished from strong desires or vital energies. Thus, it is good to feel a strong desire to make a difference in the world and exercise power. It is not the desire for power which is wrong, but the destructive way it is often exercised. When the desire for power becomes the desire to dominate others, it is troubling. And when it becomes an all-controlling desire to dominate to the exclusion of all other considerations, it becomes demonic.

Similarly, sexual feelings and sexual attraction are good gifts of God, normal and healthy (see Sexuality[11]). Sexual lust is wrong not because it is sexual or desire, but because it turns healthy desire for loving connection with another person into a depersonalized encounter in which the other person is reduced to an object who can satisfy one's desire. Indifferent to the personality of its object, lust is an attitude of abuse* rather than of care. In this form, lust is an assault on another person spiritually and emotionally, and can easily lead to physical violation. Sexual lust is interested only in taking pleasure,* and as such is contrasted with sexual love which is the mutual giving and receiving of pleasure in intimacy.

See also: CONCUPISCENCE.

J.H.O.

LUTHER, MARTIN (1483–1546). Born at Eisleben in Saxony of parents of modest but increasing means, Luther received elementary and university education which provided a focus for his spiritual and intellectual development. These influences emphasized the importance of the Bible as a guide to life and the significance of an individual's own spiritual and moral choices. They also laid the basis for a critique of the institutionalized religious life of the late medieval church. The Brethren of the Common Life, nominalist theology, eremitic Augustinianism, German mysticism (especially John Tauler, *c.* 1300–61) and early Christian humanism were all a part of the influences on Luther's formative years.

The ideas and convictions which were to demarcate Luther's theology matured in the context of the monastery and university at Wittenberg between his arrival there in 1508 and throughout the following years, and included the posting of the Ninety-five Theses of 1517, and his appearance before the Emperor, Charles V (1500–58; ruled 1519–56) at the Diet of Worms in 1521. Perhaps the strongest influence during these years came from his study of the Psalms, Hebrews, Galatians and Romans. These developing, seminal ideas included the supremacy of the authority of Holy Scripture, the priesthood of believers, justification* by faith, substitutionary atonement,* the theology of the cross,* the need for reform in the institutional church, the paradox of human freedom in the face of a sovereign God (*The Freedom of the Christian*, 1520), and the reduction of the sacraments to two (baptism and the eucharist) rather than the traditional seven.

Luther's life after 1525 was not exclusively that of the university study. He married Katherina von Bora (1499–1552) and raised a family. The Luther household was the scene for many lively discussions by students, visitors and family concerning the practical issues of daily life. Many of these ordinary applications, recorded in the notes of students and published in *Table Talk*, have left indelible images in the Lutheran tradition.

Luther clearly identified his paramount spiritual and ethical authority in his defence at Worms (1521): 'Unless I am convinced by Scripture and plain reason . . . my conscience is captive to the Word of God . . . to go against conscience is neither right nor safe.' Although standing his ground decisively before the emperor, Luther was not a radical. This was true not only for theology and ecclesiology, but also for his political and social thought. Luther's ethic was founded on this very high regard for all authority. It was with some reluctance that he attacked the leadership of the church and others who argued against him, until he realized the lack of commitment to biblical authority on the part of many of these people. It was the allegiance to the Bible as the Word of God and therefore as of supreme authority that provided the focus for the development of Luther's theology in both life and thought.

Such commitment to authority* was basic to Luther's political and social conservatism. It places in context Luther's social and theological criticism of radical Reformers such as Andreas Carlstadt (c. 1477–1541) and the social revolutionaries of the early 16th century, and supports Luther's recognition of civil authority as having a rightful role in the governance of the church, even serving the church in ridding it of its enemies.

Luther's theology gave rise to the articulation of a doctrine of passive obedience which meant that all persons were to give nominal obedience to temporal authorities even though citizens might not concur with the demands required by secular authority. For Luther there was no room for a doctrine of revolution. The implications of these ideas and the closely related 'two-kingdom theory' were very significant in German political ethics, especially in the 20th century. This theory has also tended to limit effective participation of Lutherans in the development of ideas and activities directed to implement political and social change.

Luther's conservatism was also seen in his thinking about the life of the church. Liturgy, clerical dress and church furnishings were all modified as little as possible while bringing them into conformity with his theology. 'That which Holy Scripture does not expressly forbid may be permitted' was the guideline for Lutheran ecclesiastical reform. In addition to biblical authority, Luther held the history and traditions of spirituality of the historic church in high regard. He considered them helpful guides for all Christians, although at times abused by misguided clergy and laity. The *Shorter Catechism* (1529), the *Augsburg Confession* (1530) and other writings of Luther and his supporters have captured the essence of Lutheran spirituality* and ethical thought and practice in a style that has endured.

See also: HISTORY OF CHRISTIAN ETHICS; [6] LUTHERAN ETHICS.

Bibliography
Luther's Works, ed. J. Pelikan and H. T. Lehmann, 55 vols. (St Louis, MO, and Philadelphia, 1955–86).

R. Bainton, *Here I Stand: A Life of Martin Luther* (New York, 1950); G. Ebeling, *Luther: An Introduction to His Thought* (ET, London, 1970); B. Lohse, *Martin Luther: An Introduction to his Life and Thought* (ET, Edinburgh, 1985; Philadelphia, 1986); D. Steinmetz, *Luther in Context* (Bloomington, IN, 1986).

T.O.K.

LUTHERAN ETHICS. The foundation for Lutheran ethics, Martin Luther's* understanding of justification* by grace through faith (Eph. 2:8), is theological. Salvation is a gift and not something achieved. For Luther, the purpose of the law* is to expose sin (Rom. 7:9) and thereby to lead a person to the gift of God, righteousness in Christ (Rom. 3:21–22).

From this principle Luther develops an ethical theory of paradox which was revolutionary to medieval ethical systems. The good will of God is done when a person accepts the gift of God with faith (Jn. 6:28–29). The will of God is not done by trying to keep the commandments, and certainly not by pilgrimages and by the purchase of indulgences. Indeed accepting righteousness as a gift entails confessing oneself to be a sinner. It is the purpose of the law to increase trespass (Rom. 5:20) and not to inform people how to be righteous.

Luther illustrates his point with the following analogy. Only a good tree can be assured of bearing good fruit, but good fruit does not make the tree good. Human beings must first become righteous before God by faith, then they are free to be good. To explain the union of these ideas Luther characterizes the Christian as simultaneously both sinner and justified.

For Luther, the Christian is a perfectly free lord of all, subject to no-one; and the Christian is a dutiful servant of all, subject to everyone (1 Cor. 9:19). In this paradox, freedom is available only by Christian faith, and the ethic which follows requires a life of service for the neighbour (Gal. 6:2). Only the truly free can truly serve.

The mature Luther expresses these thoughts in terms of two kingdoms. Unlike many two-kingdom ethics which teach that one kingdom is good while the other is evil, Luther's ethic claims that both kingdoms are from God and the Christian is obligated to live responsibly in both.

In the one kingdom God has established authorities for the sake of the human race (Rom. 13:1–7). In this kingdom the primary law is to love the neighbour. This love is expressed in terms of social relationships and maintained by some form of coercion. These social relationships are found in family, the work-place, government and church, and are constitutionally established in the Ten Commandments. All human beings find themselves called (see Vocation*) to one or more positions (stations) of responsibility in this kingdom.

The other kingdom is the kingdom of faith (1 Pet. 2:9). Love continues to be the primary law, but here the Christian has no authority over another as everyone is equal, and here one loves the neighbour by suffering on the neighbour's behalf (1 Pet. 3:17–18). This kingdom provides for the private ethic of self-denial as well (Gal. 5:24).

The critical features of Lutheran ethics are three: 1. justification by grace through faith; 2. the paradox of being sinner and justified at the same time; and 3. the concept of responsibility in two kingdoms. In the one kingdom coercion is the final authority and, in the other, forgiveness or suffering on another's behalf. In both kingdoms love is the motivating principle.

Bibliography

'Heidelberg Disputation', 'Treatise on Good Works', 'To the Christian Nobility', 'The Freedom of a Christian', 'Temporal Authority' and 'Admonition to Peace', in T. G. Tappert (ed.), *Selected Writings of Martin Luther*, 4 vols. (Philadelphia, 1967).

P. Althaus, *The Ethics of Martin Luther* (ET, Philadelphia, 1972); H. Thielicke, *TE*.

H.K.J.

LYING, see TRUTH.

M

MAGISTRATES, MAGISTRACY. Public officers fulfilling a legislative, judicial or executive role, the title referring to quasi-judicial officers, to judges, to governors, presidents or kings. More specifically, in countries influenced by the Roman legal system, it has come to be used of subordinate civil officers responsible for administering laws, some having jurisdiction over criminal matters. Status and duties vary from country to country and, in the USA, from State to State.

Justices of the Peace (JPs) were first appointed as magistrates in 13th-century Britain, though the title is earlier. In the USA they are normally elected, may solemnize marriages, but have less jurisdiction in criminal matters than in Britain. Britain has stipendiary magistrates and JPs (unpaid, lay magistrates) who serve as jury and judge in a form of people's justice. JPs are appointed, following recommendations from a local Advisory Committee, by the Lord Chancellor, to preside in specific petty sessional divisions. Ideally, though in practice it is not so simple, local magistrates' benches represent the whole spectrum of local society, with a balance between the sexes and between the political, social-economic, religious and age character of the locality. The basic qualities required are common sense, fair-mindedness and ability to weigh evidence. Training is given before serving, taking the chair in court or joining specialist panels. Annual retraining is now also a requirement.

Lay magistrates remain responsible for the conduct of the court and complete about 94% of the criminal jurisdiction in England and Wales. They are not intended to be experts in the law, relying for legal advice on qualified court clerks, but the decisions they make within the law are theirs alone. Lay magistrates are not permitted to sit alone, but confer, check and adjust their judgments against each other. In reaching decisions magistrates have to consider an individual's circumstances, local concerns, expectations of society, the requirements of the law, and to balance punishment* and rehabilitation. In sentencing they may, and in certain instances must, avail themselves of Social Enquiry Reports prepared by the Probation Service, and their powers range from full acquittal to up to six months imprisonment. A right of appeal against their decisions is referred to a higher court at a hearing at which a magistrate or magistrates sit with a presiding judge.

JPs may also serve on specialist panels: Youth Courts, dealing with offenders aged between ten and seventeen inclusive; and Family Courts, responsible for 'care proceedings' and with powers to ensure maintenance for a separated family, contact with children, and to prevent violence within domestic life. In these courts, magistrates are able to be more pro-active, and have a greater scope to exercise a caring role.

While lay magistrates retain popular support in Britain, human imperfections, constraints of the expense of court proceedings, curtailments in the provision of legal aid, problems over the letter and spirit of the law, and rulings which are remote from immediate circumstances impair the ideals of justice and of people's justice. The limited sentencing options available cause continuing concern among magistrates, and account for much of the public's criticisms against them.

Some question whether Christians should serve as magistrates. Exodus 18:13ff. has sometimes been used to support involvement. The debate during the Reformation and post-Reformation periods related mainly to whether Christians should enforce religious uniformity. Anglicans, Lutherans and Presbyterians supported enforcement according to their views. Congregationalists and Baptists opposed it, arguing for freedom of conscience.

Christian magistrates are likely to face additional tensions. While holding to the primary authority of God, they are bound by vow or affirmation to uphold the laws of the State. They live under the gospel of grace* and forgiveness,* yet are required to judge others and dispense punishment, and their role within the legal system restricts a desire to be agents of redemption. They are committed to the ethics of the kingdom,* yet have to relate to and work sympathetically within laws framed for a pluralist society with its widely varying views of what is right and just. They are called to the 'bias' of Lk. 4:18–19, yet they operate within a system of laws concerned with the ethics of protecting property, and they preside in courts dealing extensively with the less articulate and privileged, who may sometimes be more offended against than offending in the imbalances of our society. Through all this, Christian magistrates are to keep company with God, whose character holds together judgment* and compassion.*

L.B.K.

MALTHUS, THOMAS ROBERT (1766–1834), British economist, famous for his theories of population growth. Malthus entered Jesus College, Cambridge, in 1784 and was ordained in 1797. His famous book, *An Essay on the Principle of Population*, was published a year later, and represents an attack on the liberal ideas which were fashionable at the time. Malthus could not accept the prevailing doctrine, that the French Revolution heralded a new era of human progress, and instead propounded the theory that continued population growth would outstrip the food supply and gradually destroy the human race. Malthus presented his arguments with great learning and ingenuity, though it is generally recognized today that his claims to be empirically objective in his assessment are exaggerated. What we have instead is a brilliantly argued theory which is still influential, even though it by no means always coincides with the facts.

Most shocking to the modern mind, Malthus believed that vice should be encouraged and that charity should be refused, because morality and social concern both tended to favour population increase. It is true that 'vice' for Malthus included contraception (see Birth Control*), but even so, his ideas seem to be contrary to the Christian gospel, of which he was in theory a minister. Nevertheless, his influence on policy was very great during his own lifetime, and contributed to that indifference to human suffering which so inflamed the evangelical conscience of Victorian times. For a long time thereafter, Malthus went into eclipse, only to be revived as a serious thinker in the 1950s. Today it is generally agreed that he had a point in criticizing unrestrained population growth, much of which is admittedly due to improved health care and the like. His advocacy of contraception is now also generally accepted, though not by the Roman Catholic Church. But the modern mind still recoils from what it sees as Malthus' callous indifference and pessimism in the face of human misery, and it generally refuses to follow him in that approach to social problems.

See also: POPULATION POLICY.

Bibliography
D. E. C. Eversley, *Social Theories of Fertility and the Malthusian Debate* (London, 1959); D. V. Glass (ed.), *Introduction to Malthus* (London, 1953).

G.L.B.

MANAGEMENT.

The dictionary meaning of 'manage' or 'management' is wide, with the specific interpretation taken from the context. In this article, 'management' is used with a narrow meaning, namely to govern or control people, finance, means and materials in order to achieve some predetermined result or goal. In its widest application within this meaning, it covers the entire spectrum of human organizational structures (including government, military, social organizations, *etc.*), but in a narrower sense it applies to business, industry and commerce. It is in this sense that management is more generally understood.

The prominence given to the management of people requires assumptions to be made about the nature of men and women. Biblical and secular assumptions about people differ, leading to differing management theories. Biblically, men and women, made in the image* of God (Gn. 1:27), are entrusted by their creator with the responsible task of 'subduing' (*i.e.* stewarding or managing) the world (Gn. 2:15). Though humanity is now fallen (see Fall*), God continues to demand that stewardship of the created order be exercised with justice (Pr. 14:34; Mi. 6:8), diligence (Pr. 10:4), fairness (Am. 8:5–6) and faithfulness (1 Cor. 4:2).

Christian management principles that are soundly based on biblical theology assume certain positions. Because they are made in God's image, men and women possess dignity and must be treated with respect. Though fallen, they are blessed with traces of some attributes of God. These include creativity, initiative, personality, morality, individuality, intellect, knowledge, wisdom, power, authority, and the ability to work or act. Through sin, however, humans also tend to selfishness, pride, greed, lust (for power), and every form of evil.

Christian management is based on a realistic view of humanity because it acknowledges this ambiguity. It endeavours to utilize the positive attributes of people whilst acknowledging that their sinful nature does not permit trusting them with too much power. Results are acceptable, but may never take precedence over Christian values.

Secular management theories are based on humanistic presuppositions (see Humanism*) and on empirical results. They commence with the presupposition that humanity is good. All that is needed is to unlock and direct this goodness. The dynamics of management are often based on behavioural psychology (*e.g.* see B. F. Skinner*). Some writers have postulated that we are motivated by a hierarchy of needs (see Abraham Maslow*) and demotivated by the lack of what are defined as hygiene factors (*e.g.* F. Herzberg). Others have sought to place people into categories (*e.g.* G. D. Bell and D. G. McGregor). Appropriate management styles can then be applied to different individuals. This can be a sensitive form of managing, but it can degenerate into manipulation.* Secular management is therefore wholly pragmatic.

Secular theory based on empirical methods relies on extrapolating particular results into a general theory, which is not of necessity valid. Nevertheless, accurate observations of behaviour will be consistent with biblical teaching. This is because God as creator knows people and how they behave (Ps. 103:14). In practice, therefore, many conclusions of secular theorists are consistent with the Christian view. The difference is in the basis of the theory. This is important because extrapolations which commence from differing starting-points may lead to diverse conclusions. For example, persons may be motivated by concern because of God's common grace. Secular theorists may interpret this as a demonstration of humanity's goodness. They may also be motivated by selfishness, greed or lust. A Christian will understand the difference between the two and only encourage the former.

Management theory goes beyond human behaviour and incorporates economics, technology,* materials and values. The Bible speaks on these issues, and the presuppositions listed above apply to them as well. In this regard, the works of certain reconstructionists are useful (*e.g.* David Chiltern and Gary North; see also Christian Reconstruction Movement*).

According to Louis Allen, who is generally acclaimed as having formalized the theory, management in its simplest form comprises four functions: 1. planning; 2. organizing; 3. leading; and 4. controlling. Each of these can be expanded into subfunctions.

Examples of these functions are found in Scripture. It is generally accepted that the earliest recorded example of management theory occurred when Jethro advised his son-in-law Moses to organize the children of Israel into groups. He advised Moses to select leaders, train them, and delegate authority; all are components of leadership. He then proposed control of the process by exception and degree of difficulty (Ex. 18:13–26).

Planning, and one of its elements, budgeting, were condoned by Jesus, who taught: 'Suppose one of you wants to build a tower. Will he not first sit down and estimate the cost . . .? . . . Or suppose a king is about to go to war . . . Will he not first sit down and consider . . .?' (Lk. 14:28–31).

Leadership* is richly described in the Bible. The prime example is that of Jesus who, despite being true God, took upon himself the role of a servant. Peter, in writing to the elders, encouraged them to be 'eager to serve; not lording it over those entrusted to you, but being examples . . .' (1 Pet. 5:3). Modern secular theory of leadership also accepts elements of this view. It too stresses leading by example, coaching, encouraging, motivating, empowering and challenging. Goals are based on a shared vision and shared values. This is consistent with the Christian view, but presents a danger in that control may be overlooked. No person should be entrusted with too much power nor be left unchecked.

Christian goals focus on principles that regulate the inputs to the management process, *e.g.* righteousness, diligence, humility, compassion, *etc.* Christians believe that God honours such activities, and that results can be entrusted to him. Pragmatic management sets goals focused on the outputs, often justifying the means or inputs in terms of the results. This is only in order if pragmatism is limited to morally neutral issues. Actions that transgress biblical principles are never acceptable.

Bibliography

L. A. Allen, *Management Profession* (New York, 1964); G. D. Bell, *The Achievers: Motivational Analysis and Styles of Leadership* (Chapel Hill, NC, 1973); F. Catherwood, *The Christian in Industrial Society* (London, 1964); R. C. Chewning *et al.*, *Business Through the Eyes of Faith* (Leicester, 1990); F. Herzberg *et al.*, *The Motivation to Work* (New York, 1959); A. Maslow, *Motivation and Personality* (New York, ²1970); D. G. McGregor, *The Human Side of Enterprise* (New York, 1960); P. Rudge, *Ministry and Management* (London, 1968); B. F. Skinner, *About Behaviourism* (New York, 1974).

J.A.T.

MANICHAEISM, see AUGUSTINE; DUALISM.

MANILA MANIFESTO, see LAUSANNE COVENANT.

MANIPULATION. The notion of manipulation contains within it the idea of one individual controlling another, and in so doing infringing the autonomy* of the individual being manipulated. Of the numerous ways in which this can occur, biomedical means include those of genetic control and behaviour control.

Genetic control differs from behaviour control in that it can alter an individual prior to birth, and possibly prior to conception. Two areas of genetic control require discussion within the ambit of manipulation, namely eugenics (both negative and positive) and cloning.

Negative eugenics involves the elimination of defective genes, and hence of the prospective possessors of these genes, from the population. While negative eugenics does not actually change individuals, its potential for changing the genetic make-up of a community is considerable. Strictly speaking, negative eugenics is not an illustration of manipulation, since it does not modify individuals who will be born. However, it is a means of selecting healthy as opposed to unhealthy individuals, via the abortion* of foetuses thought to be carrying defective genes. In this sense, it is implicated in manipulation of the population (see Population Policy*), although viewpoints vary considerably regarding the ethical status of abortion in this context. Ethical considerations to be taken account of in decision-making (see Genetic Counselling*) include: the severity of the genetic disorder and its effect on the possibility of meaningful life for affected foetuses; the physical, emotional and economic impact on family and society of the birth of a child with the genetic condition; the availability of adequate medical management and special educational facilities; the reliability of the diagnosis; and the increase in the load of detrimental genes in the population resulting from the carriers of genetic diseases reproducing.

Positive eugenics has invited a great deal of idealistic support, with visions of improving attributes such as intelligence and personality. This emphasis on improving human design stands in stark contrast to conventional medical approaches with their emphasis on rectifying abnormalities and combating disease, and it is this emphasis that is the hallmark of positive eugenics. This form of eugenics has a long history, extending from 1883, when it was based on the notion of encouraging reproduction of the select. Although current emphases are on genetic approaches, the concept has changed little. The difficulty has always been to identify the select, and then to promote only those genes considered to be desirable. It is not surprising that eugenic approaches have proved disappointing, since traits, such as intelligence, are controlled by ten to one hundred genes, as well as by environmental factors. Quite apart from deciding which traits to promulgate, control of this order lies outside the realm of feasible science, and may always do so. Consequently, positive eugenics is both unscientific and unethical; any attempts to impose it on society (no matter how crude) would be at the expense of individual freedom* of choice.*

Cloning, in the sense of producing carbon copies of human individuals, is probably the best-known, and also most questionable, of genetic techniques in regard to social policy. It refers to asexual reproduction, with the result that the new individual or individuals are derived from a single parent and are genetically identical to that parent. It is brought about by the removal of the nucleus from a mature but unfertilized egg, and its replacement by the nucleus of a specialized body cell of an adult organism. The result is an unlimited number or clone of identical individuals. Once again, there are overtones of attempting to improve upon biological mechanisms, and of selecting individuals for particular abilities or characteristics. There is no evidence that this approach would prove successful, especially since it fails to account for environmental factors. A crucial ethical consideration is that, since the members of a clone would have been produced 'to order', their value in the eyes of their progenitors would appear to lie in the extent to which they replicated a previous person or were able to carry out certain predetermined tasks. The danger here is that they would not be valued as ends in themselves and as unique individuals, but simply in terms of their ability to perform specified functions or demonstrate specified traits. If this is not the case, why produce clones? In so far as cloning is used to treat human beings as solely of functional value to society or groups within society, it undermines the intrinsic worth and dignity of human beings.

Behaviour control is a change of environmental conditions in order to bring about a definite behavioural result in an individual. Various psychological techniques are central, although psychotropic drugs and psychosurgery may also have a part to play in altering the brain and, therefore, a person's behaviour. Three particularly powerful manipulatory devices are sensory deprivation, psychotherapy and conditioning. Particular problems occur when behaviour control is applied to the treatment of mental illness and crime, areas of social deviance that require value decisions about the respective importance of individual freedom of action and the dictates of society. A careful distinction has to be made between enslaving and liberating techniques. When aimed at enlarging an individual's ability to make decisions, exercise responsibility, relate to fellow beings, find fulfilment in human attributes and respond to God and other people, the techniques have a valuable part to play in promoting God's purposes. However, where there is no place for dialogue, and when used to further the cause of one group of people over another so that one will benefit at the expense of the other, manipulation is an inevitable end-result. A further distinction is that between behaviour therapy (see Behaviourism, Behaviour Therapy and Modification*) and behaviour management. Behaviour therapy can be legitimate if respect is maintained for personal liberty, and if it is carried out in partnership with the patient, ensuring that the patient's conscience, freedom and convictions are respected.

See also: BRAINWASHING; GENETIC ENGINEERING.

Bibliography
B. Häring, *Manipulation* (Slough, 1975).

D.G.J.

MARRIAGE is a mutual, exclusive, lifelong, one-flesh union between a husband and wife characterized by troth. Troth is an Old Eng. word for fidelity, truth, trust, love and commitment. Marriage is the ultimate human connection in which two people commit themselves fully and trothfully to each other in a lifelong journey of deep sharing, mutual respect and growing intimacy.

Troth holds the 'one-flesh' union together, the mutual bond that makes a marriage a marriage. At the same time, sexual intercourse and romantic connectedness are indispensable ingredients of being one flesh. In sexual intercourse, lovers celebrate their troth in a bodily joining of mutual surrender and ecstasy. In romance, there is the delight of feeling in touch and being emotionally connected. Without sexual passion and emotional connection, troth is thin, uninspiring and cold. But sex and romance without troth are capricious, fleeting and, finally, unfulfilling. Troth with sex and romance can mean compassion, connection and fulfilment.

'Therefore,' says Gn. 2:24, 'a man leaves his father and his mother and cleaves to his wife, and they become one flesh' (RSV). To 'cleave' is an Old Eng. word for keeping the troth, clinging to, holding fast. Keeping the troth is counting on each other, giving the utmost, sharing deeply from inside, sticking together through thick and thin. Husbands and wives are open and vulnerable together, not closed and defended. 'The man and his wife were both naked, and they felt no shame' (Gn. 2:25).

When the commitment is total, clear and unreserved, partners are encouraged freely and openly to share their inner struggles and fears as well as their joys and triumphs. Without the enduring commitment, the relationship is in a state of permanent crisis in which every unpleasantness, problem or disagreement can easily escalate into a heavy 'discussion' about whether the partners really belong together: if I do not please my partner's every whim, if I reveal my true feelings, and if I show my needy side, my partner may decide to leave. When a person cannot count on the fact that his or her partner will stand by, it is difficult, if not impossible, to share more and more of one's inner self. Without such assurance, partners tend to avoid differences and conflicts, closing down to protect against feelings of rejection, inadequacy, failure and shame.* The openness and sharing, which is crucial for the healing of hurts, deepening of self-esteem* and the enrichment of intimacy, is breached and gradually erodes. On the other hand, when partners hold fast to each other, an exhilarating troth-spiral of 'we-ness' can develop in which the partners have the room to be themselves, honour their differences, face their problems openly and, in the process, deepen their joining.

In marriage there is no room for superiority or inferiority. Husbands and wives are called to a co-partnership of equality in difference. Neither may lord it over the other. Genesis 3:16 is a curse on human sin, not a command

to be obeyed. Troth flourishes in a mutual relationship of belonging in which partners, secure in their own identities, commit themselves to sharing life together.

As a gift of God, marriage is also a calling (see Vocation*) which takes a great deal of energy and devotion. Husbands and wives are called to live together, not only physically, but on every level of life. Economically, aesthetically, socially, recreationally, in matters of faith, politics and lifestyle, they are to keep troth with each other. This is a monumental task. Since each person is unique, with his or her own idiosyncracies, likes and dislikes, it takes a great deal of sensitivity, commitment and work to develop a way and rhythm of being together which is not only enriching for them as a couple, but also individually.

Keeping the troth in marriage is not the merging of personalities or the obliterating of individual differences. Troth begins with and thrives on the uniqueness of the individuals in the relationship. Partners who do not allow each other their own expectations, feelings and identity may be enmeshed with each other, but they do not have a healthy troth-relation which depends on the mutual recognition and respect of their difference as persons. When husbands and wives respect, accept and understand each other as persons in their own rights, rather than as people who can meet respective needs, they are able to form a way of being together, a rhythm of affirming and being affirmed, of yielding to and receiving from. They learn to meet in the middle, 'with-promise' (the original meaning of 'com-promise') for the deepening of the relation. In troth there is no room for threats or manipulations. When each of the partners feels accepted and understood, they can safely open up more and more of themselves to each other and deepen their sharing. Then, individual differences in likes, attitudes and experiences add to, rather than detract from, the health, vibrancy and intimacy of the marriage.

Marriage and family

Even though marriage and family* are intertwined, it is important to recognize their distinctive features. Although in God's good design marriage is serviceable for the beginning of families, procreation* is not the special mark of marriage. For too long, that approach has made it difficult for the unique nature of marriage as a covenant* of troth between a husband and wife to come fully into its own. In contrast, a family has its own distinctive dynamic as a covenant of troth between parents (see Parenthood, Parenting*) and children.* Being mother and father differs from being wife and husband. A childless* couple is not an incomplete family; it is a marriage that did not generate a family even as it remained a marriage. This distinction is of particular help, for example, in alerting partners to the importance of not allowing their relationship as husband and wife to get lost in or subsumed in their roles as parents. And it makes clear, in situations of divorce,* that although a man and woman may no longer be husband and wife, they continue to be father and mother to their children.

Although in contemporary society marriage is as important as it ever was, it is more vulnerable than ever before, largely because it lacks the close intertwinements that supported it in earlier times. In most parts of the world, marriage is no longer closely linked with estates with their kinship ties, laws of inheritance and socio-economic pressures. In the West, most marriages are matters of personal choice and preference rather than concerns of clan and tribe. The fact that women as well as men are free to have their own careers, as well as the wide availability of restaurants, hotels, laundries, daycare centres, *etc.*, has loosened their dependence on the marital home for the sundries of daily existence. More than ever before, a marriage today must make it as a union of troth, or it does not make it at all.

This changing situation also means that it is more important than ever that modern couples consciously work on deepening their bond of intimacy. And, at the first signs of serious difficulties, it is particularly crucial that partners seek help. Today many communities have a variety of marital enrichment programmes, all the way from premarital courses and seminars on better communication through to marital counselling (see Marriage and Family Counselling*).

Marriage, State and church

As a pledging of troth between a man and a woman, marriage is neither basically a legal nor an ecclesiastical institution. In the period of the early Christian church, marriage, although of great concern to the community at large, was regarded as a personal and family affair. Augustine, however, spoke of marriage as a 'certain sacramental bond' (*i.e.* it *should* not be broken). It was not until the 11th and

12th centuries that the church obtained complete jurisdiction over marriage, including its civil aspect. By the 13th century, marriage had become a sacrament, with its implied indissolubility (*i.e.* it *cannot* be broken). The Reformers stressed that marriage is a covenant, and thought of marriage as a divine institution. In Protestant countries after the Reformation, there was reaction against the sacramental character of marriage, and marriage legislation reverted to the State. The French Revolution with its Constitution of 1791 initiated the beginning of the civil marriage proper. At present, in many countries people may choose between a civil or an ecclesiastical rite, both making the marriage legally valid. More recently, the State's concern to promote justice for all its citizens has led many nations to give legal status to so-called common-law marriages.

By means of a marriage licence (and bill of divorce), the State legally acknowledges the birth (and death) of a marriage. By means of a public blessing, the church community recognizes the marriage and pledges support. A wedding rite is a celebrative ceremony in which a couple, sharing their joy and seeking support, publicly pledge their troth in the presence of family, friends, church, State and God.

Divorce and remarriage

Sometimes the bond between husband and wife breaks down completely, and, despite intensive work and counselling, it is not restored. What ought to happen, *i.e.* a revitalized marriage, does not happen. What ought not to happen, *i.e.* a dead marriage, does happen. At such times, it is especially important for the Christian church to practise the gospel of grace and forgiveness. In the face of serious shortcomings in our lives, including failure in marriage, the gospel of grace* calls us to repentance* and assures us of forgiveness* and new opportunities. Although some people still question whether remarriage is a biblical option, many Christians today believe that God's grace is big enough to forgive divorce and open the way for the possibility of a new marriage.

Stages in intimacy

The development of intimacy in marriage is a process which appears to follow a sequence of stages and phases, each with its own dynamics.

Stage	Calling	Danger
1. Romance	grounding in reality	ungrounding
2. Power-struggle	adjusting to differences	competing and projecting
3. Shifting gears	renegotiating	retrenching
4. Mutuality	connecting	retreating and idling
5. Co-creativity	interconnecting	scattering

Although each stage has a unique calling which acts to give a characteristic flavour and colour to that stage, each of the callings shows up in some form in all the other stages. Similarly, naming the first stage 'romance' and the second stage 'power-struggle' in no way limits romance to the first stage or struggle to the second. What it does suggest is that, in a typical marriage, there is an initial stage where romance is the dominant tone, followed by a second stage in which acknowledging and working out of differences becomes the dominant feature. Moreover, although the stages seem to follow in sequence, the movement from stage to stage is more spiral-like than simple linear progression.

1. *Romance* seems to be the only appropriate name for the initial dreams-and-roses stage, in which two people experience total delight and abandon in each other. Without the delight of romance, a marriage is likely to be dreary and listless. However, when romance is not grounded in a robust sense of personal identities, lovers can easily lose themselves in an escapist romanticism.

2. *Power-struggle* is the adjustment stage in which partners need to come to terms with their differences in personality, style and idiosyncracies. The danger is that, in fear and anger, the partners will hide behind masks and turn to games of manipulation and intimidation in order to have their needs met. Competing and projecting begin to replace giving and sharing. Sooner or later, the pain and hurt of growing frustration* and disconnection force the couple to find a way out. Sometimes partners attempt to lose themselves in other activities or in affairs, sometimes they agree to settle for less, and sometimes they dissolve the relationship. The challenge in this difficult stage is to own fears and projections, acknowledge differences, and negotiate a new way of being together which affirms each partner as it nourishes their connection.

3. *Shifting gears* is the stage in which partners give up on their games of denial and deceit, desist from blaming each other, and own their own responsibilities. Learning to accept themselves more fully, they are empowered more fully to accept their partners. Shifting gears is a three-phase process: taking off masks; distancing to find one's own space; and meeting in the middle in a new way.

4. *Mutuality* is the stage in which giving and sharing become the settled and easy pattern. Deepest intimacy needs are met even as deepest identity needs are honoured. Partners are able to be close without fear of engulfment, and are able to be apart without fear of devastation.

5. *Co-creativity* is the stage in which the joy of mutuality flows over into the caring of and sharing with all of God's creatures. Partners become co-creators of newness in their children, with friends, in society at large, and in themselves.

See also: SEXUALITY. [11]

Bibliography

C. Clulow and J. Mattison, *Marriage Inside Out* (Harmondsworth, 1989); J. Dominian, *Marriage, Faith and Love* (London, 1981); J. H. Olthuis, *I Pledge you my Troth: A Christian View of Marriage, Family, Friendship* (San Francisco, ²1989); *idem, Keeping our Troth: Staying in Love during the Five Stages of Marriage* (San Francisco, 1986); H. Oppenheimer, *Marriage* (London, 1990); M. Scarf, *Intimate Partners: Patterns in Love and Marriage* (New York, 1987).

J.H.O.

MARRIAGE AND FAMILY COUN-SELLING seeks primarily to help persons modify their marital relationship or alter family* relationships which are conflictual (see Conflict*), oppressive or empty. Approaches vary from those focusing on the individual dynamics of the spouses or family members to methods designed to change communications, negotiation and resolution processes. This article focuses primarily on marital counselling. (For family counselling, see Family Therapy.*)

Couples come for marital therapy when the relationship has reached a normal passage in the stages of the marital developmental cycle, or when the relationship is in trouble so that one or both of the partners experience pain, or when the partners desire to make a good marriage* better by enhancing communication or enriching intimacy and mutual need satisfaction.

1. Presenting problems. The most common patterns of marital discord seen in marriage counselling are: a. The cold distant husband and the lonely dissatisfied wife – often called the workaholic married to the abandoned and love-starved. The personalities tend towards an obsessive man and a histrionic woman. b. The 'in search of a mother' marriage, with a histrionic dependent male and an obsessive female. He is dependent on her for emotional support and satisfaction and when threatened by change or children he seeks another mother figure. c. The interlocking histrionic conflictual marriage of two intensely dependent persons in 'conflict alternating with closeness' cycles. d. The addictive marriage, in which one is addicted to substances, career or sexual exploits, and the partner enables, covers and denies until exhaustion explodes the collusion. e. The abusive marriage, in which an abuser and a victim conspire together to go through cycles of closeness, accumulating grievances, explosion, violence, contrition, and a return to pseudo-closeness.

The more normal problems of adjustment, integrating patterns from the two families of origin, and dealing with the developmental crises of children, careers, teenage family and the empty nest, may also bring couples to counselling to deal with conflict, change, loss and grief work. In contrast, marriages in which one or both partners possess a significant personality disorder – the most common examples being borderline, narcissistic, paranoid, schizoid or histrionic – will usually require both marital and individual work simultaneously or in tandem. It is crucial that support be given to the marriage while one or both partners are in individual therapy, or the changes and threats of maturation are likely to sever or severely strain the marital bond.

2. Models of marriage counselling. Marital therapy takes many forms. The selection is often according to the availability of therapists, their preferences, or their assessment of the couple's needs and designing of an appropriate strategy. Commonly used models include: a. *individual* therapy, where each partner has a separate therapist and each works both on intrapsychic issues and on the part played in the marriage; b. *collaborative* therapy, in which each sees an individual therapist while giving permission for the

therapists to consult at regular intervals; c. *parallel* therapy, in which the same therapist sees both spouses in individual therapy only; d. *conjoint* therapy, where both spouses are present for all sessions with a single therapist; e. *tandem* therapy, where individual and conjoint sessions alternate with the same therapist; and f. *group* therapy, with multiple couples working with a therapist in group process.

The individual models, though concerned about and dealing with marriage issues, are not authentic marriage counselling or therapy. When persons are being seen individually, their personal agenda takes precedence over marital issues. Someone is needed to support the relationship as well as giving support to the persons who are in the change process.

3. Marriage counselling therapy. Although early psychoanalytic theory refused marital therapy as violating the transferent relationship by introducing truly social relationships, the contribution of analytic theory (see Analytical Psychology*) stands alongside behavioural, existential and systems theory approaches.

a. *Analytic* theory focuses on understanding the unconscious conflicts which distort the sense of self and thus damage the marital contract. The bilateral transference* from families of origin must be analysed as following the pattern of the partner's childhood responses to conflict with his or her parents. The defence mechanisms* of the person are explored as they impact on the intimacy and co-operation tasks. Analytic therapy is most frequently indicated when one or both partners is diagnosed with a significant personality disorder.

b. *Behavioural* theories (see Behaviourism*) provide a learning-theory approach to positive behavioural, cognitive and emotional change. It focuses on problem-solving, desensitization of phobic or aversive behaviours, assertive skills in conflict resolution, cognitive change in inner conversations called self-instructions, and positive accomplishment of tasks. Although the origins of behavioural marriage counselling utilized operant conditioning to build positive interactions through a social reinforcement reward system, the movement has shifted towards cognitive reorientation, constructive conflict training, and development of communication skills.

c. *Existential* (see Existential Psychologies*) marital counselling has applied Gestalt,* experiential, transactional* and rational-emotive (see Ellis, Albert*) techniques and experiences, to assist people to deepen awareness of, and achieve insight into, their ways of being in relationships (in that order). Experience always precedes explanation, meeting is stressed before any interpretation of meanings, awareness of how and what one does and feels is explored before insight into why and because is permitted. These approaches to therapy are equally useful in group counselling as in couples' therapy, and are often combined with other approaches such as systems or social learning forms of behavioural therapy.

d. *Systems therapy.* The dominant theory of marital therapy is based on general systems theory which addresses the couple as a unit within the larger unit of the whole family system. The persons are seen as parts of a dynamic pattern of interactions and interrelationships which create the organism of the family. It refuses linear explanations of cause and effect with their inevitable blaming or labelling, and focuses on the balance, homeostasis and interaction of behaviours with the development of systems therapy. Marital therapists are able to utilize elements of psychoanalytic, behavioural and existential theory to intervene in parts of the system, not in random eclecticism but in intentional application of systems analysis.

4. *The practice of marital therapy.* Couples come to therapy with many different complaints. Lack of communication, dysfunctional conflict, sexual discord, emotional distancing, financial disagreements, extended family conflicts, sexual infidelity, child conflicts, power issues, addictions,* abuse,* jealousy* and paranoid suspicion. The therapist must be skilled as a communications model and trainer, a conflict-resolution facilitator, a sexual educator, a family systems interventionist, and also as an individual therapist sensitive to intrapersonal conflicts. Addictions-counselling skills may be useful as well as the ability to collaborate with and refer to enrichment programmes, addictions treatment centres and other therapeutic and supportive resources. The marital and family therapist has access to the whole life of the couple or family and may offer wider resources than the individual therapist.

5. *The process of therapy.* Marital therapy begins with the therapist joining the couple or family. a. Establishing an effective alliance with people who are in conflict, under stress or in pain requires empathy, the ability to evoke trust and the capacity to undergird self-

esteem – all essential to bonding with the partners in initiating the therapeutic journey. b. Evoking the power within the marriage or family to heal itself is the second major task. If the system has the power to keep itself enmeshed against all pressures to meet each other's needs, it also has the power to welcome and work through change. c. The counsellor listens to both content and process. The couple is locked in struggle over the content while repeating dysfunctional, cyclical processes. The counsellor observes and intervenes in the sequences of behaviour and the structures that support the destructive spirals of negative communication and conflict. d. Movement from issues to persons can then be encouraged. Partners come to therapy being hard on persons and blind to process. The therapist invites them to become soft on persons and hard on process. As awareness of what they do to each other and how they do it grows, the marriage matures into a collaborative relationship with depth of feeling and esteem.

6. *Techniques.* Technique is always secondary to the personhood of the counsellor. The classic therapeutic triad of non-possessive warmth, accurate empathy and genuineness are central to the authenticity of the therapist and the effectiveness of the intervention. However, it is helpful for the counsellor to have a wide repertoire of skills in clarifying expectations, identifying issues for competing family-of-origin structures, reframing the problem into creative alternatives, sorting out values and priorities, refocusing perceptions, expressing feelings, developing mutual empathy, appreciating each other's spirituality, drive for meaning and ultimate commitments. Marriage counselling is not only release of intrapsychic pain and reconstruction of relationship, it is re-education for appropriate belief systems for living together and living in the world.

7. *Pastoral care and marriage counselling.* The pastoral counsellor as a marital therapist brings several unique advantages. The counsellor is not an isolated secular consultant but a representative of community who acts in accountability with the values of that context. The pastoral counsellor is an ethicist and does not avoid ethical issues in the denial process of pretending to be value-free. The client is more safe from moral imposition when counselled by a therapist who is willing to explore ethical concerns while guarding the moral agency of both counsellor and counsellee. Since virtually

all issues in marital and family therapy have ethical dimensions, the pastoral therapist meets the family with holistic care and authenticity. As a community representative, the pastor invites the family system to join with larger systems, to connect with other families and with groups of families within the congregation.

See also: PASTORAL CARE, COUNSELLING AND PSYCHOTHERAPY.[12]

Bibliography

H. J. Clinebell and C. H. Clinebell, *The Intimate Marriage* (Nashville, TN, 1970); S. Minuchin, *Marriage and Marital Therapy* (Cambridge, MA, 1974); V. Satir, *Peoplemaking* (Palo Alto, CA, 1972); R. Skynner, *One Flesh, Separate Persons* (London, 1976).

D.W.A.

MARX, KARL (1818–83). The philosophical ideas of Karl Marx constitute one of the leading contemporary alternatives to a Christian world-view. Marx was born on 5 May 1818 in the Prussian town of Trier to parents descended from lines of rabbis, but his father Heschel and the children were baptized into the Lutheran church in order to retain the family's position in the face of Prussian religious oppression. Heschel, now Heinrich Marx, a lawyer who held Enlightenment* views, had a very strong influence on his son.

After a year at the University of Bonn, Marx transferred to the more serious environment of the University of Berlin to study law and philosophy. There he came under the powerful sway of the thought of the recently deceased philosopher G. W. F. Hegel (1770–1831). Marx joined a group called the Young Hegelians or the Hegelian Left, who interpreted Hegel's views about historical progress and the role of criticism in a radical direction, unlike the more conventional Hegelianism which idealized the existing Prussian social order. Following Bruno Bauer (1809–92) and Ludwig Feuerbach (1804–72), Marx saw the Christian faith as founded on myth and as an expression of human psychological needs. Philosophically Marx became an atheist and a materialist, writing his doctoral thesis on the Greek materialists Democritus (*c.* 460–*c.* 370 BC) and Epicurus (*c.* 341–270 BC). After a Prussian crackdown on the Young Hegelians and the dismissal of Bauer, Marx was obliged to submit his thesis to the lax University of Jena from which he received his doctorate in 1841. Two years later he married Jenny, daughter of the Baron von Westphalen.

In the years following, Marx worked as a journalist, writing for newspapers in Prussia, Paris and Brussels and associating with international workers' movements. He also began collaborating with Friedrich Engels (1820–95), son of a Manchester industrialist who would provide financial support to Marx for many years. In 1849 Marx moved to London and undertook a study of the British economic theorists Adam Smith (1723–90) and David Ricardo (1772–1823), while living under such great hardship that only three of his seven children survived to maturity. In later years Marx became internationally known for his support of a workers' revolt in 1870–71 known as the Paris Commune, and was actively involved in controversies throughout Europe. Predeceased by his wife and eldest daughter, Marx died in London on 14 March 1883.

Marx left a large body of written work produced primarily between 1845 and 1876, culminating in his masterpiece, *Das Kapital*. Central to his thought is the idea that human beings are fundamentally transformers of nature by work;* humanity (see [4]) is *Homo faber*, man the maker, rather than *Homo sapiens*, man the knower. Since human nature lies in working, it is to the conditions of human labour that we must look if we are to understand history, culture and the human predicament. Capitalist society (see Capitalism*) requires workers to place their essential nature in the hands of capitalists, who pay their wages and in return purchase their creative, productive energy. Since capitalists control the means of production, the worker's success in production concentrates wealth and power in the hands of the capitalist to use against the worker. The more the workers produce, the poorer they become in spiritual as well as economic terms. Human beings are estranged from their fellow human beings, from nature, and from themselves in the fundamentally unfree economic situation in which they must earn their daily bread.

Economic relationships (see Economic Ethics[17]) determine the shape and nature of social, cultural, intellectual and religious life. Economic realities, or 'relations of production', are the 'economic base' on which the 'superstructure' of laws, consciousness, intellectual life and religious faith depend. This view, called 'historical materialism', implies that only by changing the concrete facts of economic life can society be changed, not by intellectual criticism of its superstructure. Furthermore, it enables ideas contrary to those of Marxian analysis to be discounted as mere capitalist 'ideology'.

Marx believed that human history is a series of clashes between economically antagonistic groups, or classes, a process seen today in conflict between the proletariat, or working class, and the bourgeoisie, or capitalist class. The bourgeoisie by its very nature extracts value from the proletariat, sapping its strength by removing from it 'the surplus value' produced by its labour and creating profit. The 'contradictions' of capitalism make it more and more unstable, until in the course of history the proletariat rises up and grasps the means of production. After a foreseeable brutish period of 'raw communism', true communism will emerge in which people will overcome alienation* and realize their true humanity in the brotherhood of a worker's paradise.

Marx's idea that consciousness, including all philosophical, ethical and religious ideas, is the product of economic factors lies behind his well-known view that religion is the 'opiate' of the workers. Religion plays a role in the oppression of humanity. Religion is created by alienation; humanity alienates its own best features and invests them in a fantastic deity. In turn, religion helps the oppressors maintain their position of privilege over the oppressed by justifying the existing situation. Marx never addressed religious claims head on by examining theistic philosophical claims or biblical evidence; rather, he assumed the falsity of Christian theism and then attempted to give an account of this illusion.

The relationship between Christianity and Marxism is controversial. Some believe that because of Marx's essential atheism, Marxism can never be an element in a Christian worldview. Others argue that Marx's vision of human liberation is religious in the sense that Marx simply secularized the prophetic biblical concern for the poor and oppressed and its hope for an eschatological kingdom. Further, his view of unalienated humanity, free to work, create, and share, resembles the biblical vision of shalom (see Health and Health Care;* Life, Health and Death[13]). Liberation theologians* use analyses derived from Marx, particularly the concept of class struggle, to challenge existing social conditions in the Third World and for minorities elsewhere. While many evangelicals believe that too much is conceded to Marxism by the liberationists, all must share their concern for the poor who suffer at the hands of the powerful (Jas. 5:1–6).

See also: COMMUNISM; MARXIST ETHICS; POVERTY.

Bibliography
J. M. Bonino, *Christians and Marxists: The Mutual Challenge to Revolution* (London, 1976); D. Lyon, *Karl Marx: A Christian Appreciation of His Life and Thought* (Tring, 1979); D. McLellan, *Karl Marx: Selected Writings* (Oxford, 1977); D. McLennan, *Marxism and Religion* (Basingstoke, 1987); P. Singer, *Marx* (Oxford, 1980); D. Turner, *Marxism and Christianity* (Oxford, 1983); N. Wolterstorff, *Until Justice and Peace Embrace* (Grand Rapids, 1983).

D.B.F.

MARXIST ETHICS. It is generally agreed that the writings of Karl Marx,* which range widely over economics, politics and philosophy, contain no fully developed ethical theory. Scholars of Marx have interpreted this lack in several different ways.

1. One interpretation (see, *e.g.*, E. Kamenka, *Marxism and Ethics*) emphasizes the lack of consistency in a body of work which begins in the *Economic and Philosophical Manuscripts of 1844* by giving fundamental ethical concepts like 'alienation'* a central place, and then later rejects ethical categories on the grounds that all ethical systems are historically conditioned.

2. Another interpretation accepts that the main thrust of Marx's work is anti-moral in its claim that morality is ideology but recognizes the paradox that the scientific analysis of class and capitalism* is expressed in highly moralistic terms. Thus S. Lukes (see *Marxism and Moralism*) attempts to reconcile Marx's anti-moral arguments with his obvious moral commitment.

3. A third interpretation is that Marx's critique of all religion, law and morality as ideology is essentially consistent, although there are shifts in emphasis and it is not fully eleborated anywhere in his writing. P. J. Kain (in *Marx and Ethics*), for example, describes how Marx's theory of historical materialism* has direct implications for ethics at every stage of its development.

4. Finally, there is the question of the relationship between Marx's writings and the various forms of socialism* and communism.* Scientific socialism has typically involved an instrumental view of ethics in which means are subordinated to ends. 'Morality is a function of the class struggle,' claimed Trotsky (1879–1940).

Debate continues between these different perspectives, but the main ethical features of Marx's own writing are the materialist critique of ethics and morality as ideology, the aggressive condemnation of capitalist exploitation, and (least developed of these) a utopian vision of communism as a higher, more 'real' form of human society based on the principle 'From each according to his ability, to each according to his needs'. This positive ethic of freedom through political struggle has powerfully motivated liberation movements for more than a century.

Marx's anti-morality is part of his general critique of philosophy, ideas, religion and law. These are forms of ideology which have social origins and which serve class interests. Their appeal to objective truth and universal principles, according to Marx, is an illusion. For example, while Marx agrees that bourgeois concepts of 'justice', such as those involved in wage contracts, may be just in a formal sense and are not simply a legitimate form of theft, he argues that these norms of justice operate at the level of appearances only. True ethical activity is not just a problem of capitalist society. It has not been possible in any society because the conditions for free, spontaneous and rational co-operation have never existed.

Marxist ethics are incompatible with Christian belief because of their atheism and their assumption that human nature is socially conditioned, and because of their assumption that morality does not transcend social conditioning. Moreover, the vision of a distant communist utopia has to be set alongside the record of Marxist-Leninist regimes which have attempted to put ethics on a 'scientific' footing. Whether as revolutionary movements or as State bureaucratic systems of the Soviet type, their record includes habitual contempt for legality and the arbitrary application of the Party's view of what is expedient in the circumstances.

This theoretical divergence should not be allowed to obscure the points of convergence. The Cold War which prevailed for forty-five years between 'communist' East and 'Christian' West underlined the incompatibility between ethical approaches and allowed each side to claim ethical superiority over the other: the West pointing to the neglect of human rights (see Rights, Human*) in the East, the East accusing the West of perpetuating the social injustices of capitalism. However, there are reasons for rejecting confrontation and adopting a more positive approach. Kamenka tempers his own criticism with the observation that Marx's ethical agenda stands as a reproach to excessive individualism* and scholasticism in moral philosophy. This was one of the themes of the dialogue which opened up between Marxist and Christian intellectuals in the 1960s, and it has continued to influence the development of social ethics. It had a profound impact on theologians such as Jürgen Moltmann (1926–), whose political theology and ethics were developed through a Christian critique of Marx and the Messianic Marxism of Ernst Bloch (1885–1977). Subsequently, the Latin American liberation theologians (see Liberation Theology*) accepted much of the Marxist ideology critique and drew ethical inspiration as well as analytical resources from Marx for their opposition to society based on privilege and exploitation. Just as Marx's concern was not just to interpret the world but to change it, so liberation theology is committed to praxis,* or engagement with the poor and the exploited in their struggle for liberation.

Marx's writings will outlive the collapse of communism in Eastern Europe and the Soviet Union which brought to an end the arid State-sponsored 'ethics' of scientific socialism. From the point of view of ethical theory, Marx will be an essential point of reference for questions about the ideological functions and sociology of ethics* as well as the possibility of a normative ethical theory. From the point of view of ethical conduct, Marx will continue to challenge Christians to demonstrate the practical value of their faith, for unless it can transform the world, it will be condemned as a myth and a merely illusory compensation for human suffering.

Bibliography

K. Bockmuehl, *The Challenge of Marxism* (Leicester and Downers Grove, IL, 1980); P. J. Kain, *Marx and Ethics* (Oxford and New York, 1988); E. Kamenka, *Marxism and Ethics* (London and New York, 1969); S. Lukes, *Marxism and Morality* (Oxford and New York, 1987); K. Nielsen and S. C. Patten (eds.), 'Marx and Morality', *Canadian Journal of Philosophy*, supplementary vol. 7, 1981.

H.H.D.

MASCULINITY, see SEXUALITY. [1]

MASLOW, ABRAHAM (1908–70). Having trained on a behavioural programme in psychology at the University of Wisconsin, Abraham H. Maslow became one of the prime theoreticians of humanistic* (or 'third force') psychology during the 1950s and 60s. Questioning the reductionism* of behaviourism* and psychoanalysis,* he argued for a 'holistic-dynamic' theory of human motivation* and personality,* which acknowledged the pragmatic functionalism of William James* and John Dewey (1859–1952; see also Carl Rogers*), the holism of Gestalt* psychology, and the psychodynamic perspectives of the psychoanalytic tradition, especially the social dimension of Alfred Adler's* psychology.

At a fundamental level, Maslow sought to challenge the 'value-free' stance of contemporary science,* arguing for the blending of objective and subjective in the need for 'experiential' and 'love' knowledge, as well as the 'spectator' knowledge of traditional science. In this quest he saw strong parallels in the epistemology of Michael Polanyi (1891–1976), with its commitment to an integration of faith* and knowledge at a personal level. Using the technique of 'iteration' (a process of refinement of a general notion through repeated stages of analysis, reappraisal and redefinition), Maslow is particularly renowned for his lifelong research into the concept of self-actualization,* with its attendant 'hierarchical-integrative' theory of human needs. In the late 1960s he modified this theory, declaring that the 'basic' needs (*i.e.* bodily needs, the need for safety, for a sense of 'belongingness', esteem and self-actualization) are, in reality, only partially satisfied, may vary in their experiential order, and should be seen alongside other aspects of life, such as cognitive and aesthetic needs.

Although Maslow's humanism* steered him away from Sigmund Freud's* pessimistic view of human nature, in time his search for a 'new image of man' included attempts to clarify a 'psychology of evil' (see Evil*) and humanity's need for transcendence. In the 2nd ed. (1970) of *Motivation and Personality*, for example, he says that the human being has weak 'instinct-remnants', or 'instinctoid tendencies', which are 'good, desirable, and healthy' rather than 'malign and evil', and yet are easily overwhelmed, and even turned towards destructiveness, by 'learned cultural forces' (p. 129). His perspectives on the transcendent, although conceding humanity's need for 'something "bigger than we are" to be awed by and to commit ourselves to' (*Toward a Psychology of Being*, p. iv), always kept to an essentially naturalistic base, where the human being needs 'a framework of values ... a religion or religion-surrogate to live by ... in about the same sense that he needs sunlight, calcium or love' (*ibid.*, p. 206).

Bibliography
Motivation and Personality (New York, ²1970); *Toward a Psychology of Being* (New York, ²1968).
R. F. Hurding, *Roots and Shoots: A Guide to Counselling and Psychotherapy* (London, 1986) = *The Tree of Healing* (Grand Rapids, 1988); M. Polanyi, *Personal Knowledge* (London, 1958).

R.F.H.

MASTURBATION is the stimulation of one's own sexual organs for pleasure with or without orgasm. Although very widely practised, it remains a highly guilt-ridden form of genital expression for many people.

Scripture does not forbid masturbation. However, Onan's act of *coitus interruptus* (withdrawal before ejaculation) in Gn. 38:6–10, by which he refused to impregnate his widowed sister-in-law, was long taken as such prohibition. The sin of Onan was not masturbation, but his refusal to raise up progeny for his brother as required by the Jewish law of levirate marriage (Dt. 25:5–10). Nevertheless, Christian tradition has by and large considered masturbation sinful if voluntary and deliberate, particularly by males. Official Roman Catholic teaching still rejects masturbation, because it is not directed toward procreation and conjugal love.

Although masturbation has long been seen as illness in itself, or as causing a variety of maladies all the way from pimples to suicide, modern medicine sees no physical or emotional harm from the act itself. Today masturbation is seen as an act of self-pleasuring, which is common from earliest childhood through youth into maturity.

The morality of masturbation is determined by its nature and role in a particular person's life. Masturbation can mean different things, as in the self-discovery of children or adolescents, in the sexual release in the absence or illness of one's partner, or simply for release of tension and pleasure of the moment. Mutual masturbation may be engaged in for variety in sexual play. But masturbation may also be a way to escape loneliness* or a preferred replacement for intercourse with one's partner. When accompanied by compulsive phantasizing about persons other than one's partner, it can be a form of 'committing adultery in the heart'.

Some people still regard masturbation as evidence of emotional immaturity, and at best a lesser evil. On the other hand, it is often neither encouraged nor discouraged. In this view, masturbation can range all the way from a healthy, pleasurable, comforting sensation of delight to a neurotic escape from facing one's inner problems or from being intimate with another person.

See also: SEXUALITY. [11]

J.H.O.

MATERIALISM is an underlying philosophy of Western culture which says that only the material world exists. It denies both the existence of God and that moral values have any grounding in God's law (which by definition is seen not to exist). In an extreme form, everything is ultimately to be explained in terms of the forces and material conditions that surround it. The popular idea, that it is money, not God, that makes the world go round, is derived from the more basic meaning of materialism.

Greek atomists of the 5th century, Leucippus (*fl. c.* 400 BC) and Democritus (*c.* 460–*c.* 370 BC) offered materialist explanations, but perhaps the greatest classical materialist was Lucretius (99 / 94–55 / 51 BC), who was influenced by Epicurus (341–270 BC). He sought to refute the religion of the day by explaining the origin of everything in Nature. This view was submerged by Christianity and Neoplatonism for much of the period up to the Renaissance, although Nature worship was a large part of the pagan religions of Europe. It re-emerged in the Renaissance and later, especially in the philosophy of science developed by Galileo (1564–1642), Thomas Hobbes (1588–1679), René Descartes (1596–1650), Julien de la Mettrie (1709–51) and Baron d'Holbach (1723–89). This posited material forces which caused movement as the basic description of the universe.

During the 18th century, there was a fundamental division, which defined materialism more closely. Mechanistic explanations posited mechanical laws, according to which the world runs like clockwork, whilst materialistic explanations thought in terms of causes which happened in much more chaotic and random ways. From that time onwards, materialism was associated with more radical and anarchic patterns of explanation. There were two key directions in its 19th-century development.

1. Karl Marx,* who studied Democritus and Epicurus in his doctoral thesis, espoused a form of materialism which he asserted against the rationalism of G. W. F. Hegel (1770–1831). Marx argued that the material conditions of life determined economic and political life, and he saw them as shaping history even by convulsive change as reality broke through on the ideological constructs which ruling groups had imposed on society. This 'dialectical materialism' defined the inner causal processes of history. Friedrich Engels (1820–95), Lenin (1870–1924) and other Marxist thinkers carried this tradition on into the 20th century.

2. Another development occurred with the growth of evolutionary theory. This posited that an underlying struggle for existence was the central reality of life. Social Darwinism further suggested that races were in a competitive struggle to survive. Aryans were the active, future-shaping race, which worked on a different principle from the old intellectualism of neo-Kantian Germany. This activism of marching boots and autobahns was another expression of materialist philosophy.

However, a deeper challenge to materialism was occurring within the natural sciences. The idea of basic atomic material was undermined by subatomic physics and relativity theory. The categories of the new physics moved beyond the possibility of expression in material terms, so that it was clear that the universe was not constructed out of little objects which were basic to existence. Since these changes at the beginning of the century, the natural sciences have moved further and further away from a materialist conception.

For a while, some theorists in other disciplines looked to materialist explanations. Eugenics (see Manipulation*) flourished as an explanation of national prowess in terms of a gene bank. W. McDougall (1871–1938) and others were worried that the intellectually gifted were less fecund, leading to racial deterioration. Phrenology examined bumps on the head as an explanation of character types. Later, psychologists looked to physiological explanations as basic to explaining psychological processes. Edward Titchener (1867–1927) and others developed approaches which tended towards experimental psychology. This developed into certain defined subdisciplines, like perception and memory, but its limitations in dealing with basic patterns of emotional and psycho-social life were evident from the start.

The popular meaning of materialism implies that money is the basic engine of human action, that the end of life is to buy goods. On this view, money is supposed to supply human values, when actually it represents them, albeit in an incomplete way. In fact, money cannot buy love or most of the activities which are part of the normal economy. Half of economic activity in the home, State, education, *etc.*, functions on the basis of gift.

The underlying problem is the way materialist explanations must explain personal phenomena in subpersonal terms, rather than acknowledging that the creator is the source of, and gives meaning to, all that is either personal or part of the natural creation. Even when the idea of physical objects as basic to reality is dropped and replaced by some concept of elementary forces and particles, these obviously do not function in a self-subsistent way, but bear witness to the coherence of the creation, so that the creation is made out of that which is not seen (Heb. 11:3). Materialism thus wrongly relies on the physical perception of 'stuff' and sees it as basic. Actually, our perception of 'material reality' is a very limited perception of the creation.

Bibliography

F. Engels, *Herr Eugen Dühring's Revolution in Science* (1877–78; ET, New York, 1939); T. Hobbes, *Leviathan* (1651; Oxford, 1947); V. I. Lenin, *Materialism and Empirio-Criticism* (ET, London, 1927); Lucretius, *On the Nature of Things* (ET, Cambridge, MA, ²1982); K. Marx, *A Contribution to the Critique of Political Economy* (1859; ET, New York, 1970; London, 1971); W. McDougall, *Modern Materialism and Emergent Evolution* (London, 1928; New York, 1929); *idem, Religion and the Sciences of Life* (London, 1934).

A.S.

MATURITY. The maturity of a living being is a state of completion, resulting from growth, relative to a standard established by its intrinsic teleology.* Thus an animal is regarded as mature when it has reached its full size as determined by its genetic potential, and when it has certain powers, *e.g.* of reproduction, food procurance and self-defence.

When we speak of Christian maturity, we also have reference to the realization of a potential through growth, but it is now the potential implanted in us, in creation and then in restoration through spiritual rebirth, to function as God's loving and beloved children, as proper brothers and sisters to one another, and as proper stewards of the creation. The process of growth towards Christian maturity is called santification.* Just as the growth of an animal towards completeness is a process of acquiring the traits or characteristics proper to whatever species is in question, so Christian sanctification is a process of acquiring those traits or virtues* that God has appointed in creation and redemption to be the distinctive marks of humanity. If fully developed coat, claws, teeth, sex organs, *etc.*, are the equipment of the mature animal, the spiritually mature human being is equipped with patience, kindness, forbearance, forgiveness, compassion, self-control, gratitude, hope and other Christian virtues.

In the key NT passages on human maturity, one (1 Cor. 13) seems to speak of the maturity of the individual, while the other (Eph. 4:1–16) speaks of the maturity of the Christian community. In both, the chief mark of maturity is love, conceived as emotional attachment to God and fellow church members, and harmony and co-operation in the work of the kingdom, empowered by the Holy Spirit. In the Ephesians passage Paul strongly emphasizes the unity of the Christian community: because there is just one Spirit, one Lord, one Father, one hope, one faith and one baptism, there cannot, in logic, be dissension, strife, party spirit, recrimination, envy, one-upmanship, grudge-bearing and other kinds of division and alienation in the church if it is functioning *as* the church – *i.e.* as the mature body of Jesus Christ. The church contains diversity, for Christ has given differential gifts to individual members for the church's prosperity, but these are to be dedicated to the work of ministry, which is the upbuilding of the body of Christ, 'until we all reach unity in the faith and in the knowledge of the Son of

God and become mature' (Eph. 4:13). Paul associates bodily growth with its members' being 'joined and held together by every supporting ligament' (Eph. 4:16).

Paul is clearly speaking of the maturity of the individual when he says, 'When I was a child, I talked like a child, I thought like a child, I reasoned like a child. When I became a man, I put childish ways behind me' (1 Cor. 13:11; almost consistently in this chapter he writes in the first person singular). What he gave up was jealousy, boastfulness, arrogance, rudeness and the other traits that are contrary to the bond of peace. Though this chapter is about the individual, it is sandwiched between two chapters about the unity and upbuilding of the church. Just as the maturity of the church is its unity, through love, in the one Spirit so, it is arguable, the maturity of the individual not only fits him or her to promote the unity of the church as one of its members, but is also an integration of personality wrought through loving God above all and seeking first his kingdom. We might paraphrase Søren Kierkegaard* and say that purity of heart is to love one God. Such singleness of mind would reflect the lordship and sovereignty of the God in whose image* we are created, as well as reduplicate, at the individual level, the unity that Paul so clearly makes the chief mark of maturity in the church. And corresponding to the diversity of gifts in the church would be the variety of Christian virtues in the individual, all springing in one way or another from the believer's love, but equipping him or her for the various trials and tasks of Christian life in the world.

See also: CHARACTER; [10] HUMAN DEVELOPMENT.

Bibliography
S. Kierkegaard, *Purity of Heart is to Will One Thing* (ET, New York, 1938); *idem*, *Works of Love* (ET, New York, 1962); C. S. Lewis, 'Beyond Personality', in *Mere Christianity* (London, 1952).

R.C.R.

MAURICE, F. D. (1805–72). English theologian, social reformer and educator, Frederick Denison Maurice's thought had a profound influence on future generations, and he is considered one of the founders of Christian Socialism.* The son of a unitarian minister, Maurice was distressed by the religious divisions which developed in his family. This resulted in a deeply-felt commitment to unity throughout his life. He joined the Church of England after some initial hesitation, and was ordained in 1834. In his most influential book, *The Kingdom of Christ* (1838), he denounced faction and argued that with Christ as 'Head and King' all human beings are united. The church ideally should provide deliverance from all sects and parties. He maintained that each of the main Christian traditions stood for something that was true, but their fault was insisting that they alone were right.

His belief in the application of Christian principles to social reform led him to join with J. M. F. Ludlow (1821–1911) and Charles Kingsley (1819–75) in advocating Christian Socialism. However, Maurice was not sympathetic with many of the beliefs of 19th-century socialism.* He viewed socialism as the natural economic outgrowth of his conviction that human beings under Christ should co-operate rather than compete. For him socialism was the opposite of individualism,* which he considered divisive and contrary to Christian principles. Although he had great sympathy for the working classes and many among them looked to him as a friend, he was largely unsuccessful in improving their economic conditions. He was, however, responsible for the establishment of the Working Man's College in 1854, which has continued to the present day.

Bibliography
The Kingdom of Christ (1838; ed. A. R. Vidler, London, ²1958).
O. J. Brose, *Frederick Denison Maurice: Rebellious Conformist 1805–1872* (Columbus, OH, 1971); A. R. Vidler, *F. D. Maurice and Company: Nineteenth-Century Studies* (London, 1966).

R.W.H.

MAY, ROLLO (1909–). A major American thinker associated with humanistic psychology, Rollo May is most accurately described as an existential psychologist or psychotherapist. The major intellectual influence upon May has been the existential theologian Paul Tillich (1886–1965).

In his early writings May addresses the problems of loneliness* and anxiety* and argues that a certain type of anxiety is emotionally healthy. In 1969 he published *Love and Will* (New York) in which he encouraged individuals to choose freely whom they would love and to take responsibility for those free choices. Most recently in *The Cry for Myth* (New York, 1991), May has contended that myth is critical in providing us with moral standards and he has decried the absence of myth in contemporary society. For May, Christianity is a helpful myth, helpful for the encouragement and support that Christianity provides in the search for serenity and in loving and serving our fellow human beings.

Throughout his career, May has insisted that therapists and counsellors address the real, 'deep' human problems about the meaning of life in a hostile world, the problems that all humans share, rather than the particular problems of an individual. In addition to the works mentioned above, May's most important books include *The Meaning of Anxiety* (New York, 1950), *Man's Search for Himself* (New York, 1953), *Power and Innocence: A Search for the Sources of Violence* (New York, 1972), and *The Courage to Create* (New York, 1975).

T.D.K.

MEAN, DOCTRINE OF THE.
Essential to Aristotle's* theory of moral virtue, or virtues of character, is his view that virtue* is a mean between vices of excess and deficiency.

A virtuous person makes correct choices about feelings and actions, choices which avoid inappropriate excess and deficiency of feeling or action. Sometimes we feel or do more than is morally fitting. I may become outraged when my daughter fails to clean her room. I may punish her by removing all her property and giving it away. Both my anger and my action in response to her rare negligence would be excessive. At other times we are deficient in our moral feelings or actions. Perhaps when I view the painting my son has laboured over for hours, I feel no gratitude but only irritation at one more thing to clutter my office; or, upon noticing a serious accident, I may say a short prayer but fail to report the accident to the proper authorities. In the former case, I feel less gratitude than I should; in the latter case I do something, but what I do is less than that which virtue demands. Thus, virtue requires, first of all, knowledge of moral context, of what the appropriate feeling or action and its extremes may be.

The morally wise person steers between these vicious extremes of excess and deficiency. He or she identifies the mean of the relevant feelings and actions and aims for it. The mean is not, however, equidistant between the two extremes of each feeling or action. Some virtues are more like their extremes of excess, others more like their extremes of deficiency. Courage, or right fearlessness, is more like foolhardiness or excessive fearlessness than like cowardice. On the other hand, a moderate person more closely resembles the ascetic than the epicurean.

Identification of the mean requires not only insight into the moral context and into the character of particular virtues, but also self-knowledge. Aristotle insists that the mean is relative to the individual, that virtue does not require identical feelings or actions of each individual. Some people are naturally shy. The virtue of friendliness does not require of the shy person the same actions in the same sort of way as these feelings or actions are required of the gregarious. There are some courageous people for whom the fear of men would be inappropriate, but there are others, say, victims of abuse, who do not fall short of the mean of courage despite having some fearful feelings toward men. What the mean is, relative to the individual, can be determined by a morally wise person only upon a careful inventory of the self.

Aristotle denies that there is a mean for every feeling or action. Some actions, *e.g.* adultery and murder, are intrinsically vicious. They cannot be performed in the right sort of way, for there is no right way with respect to these actions. The same can be said for certain feelings. There is no appropriate amount of shamelessness to feel, for the failure to feel ashamed in the presence of morally inferior actions or feelings cannot be other than vicious and blameworthy.

Identification of the mean, of what are the right feelings or actions 'at the right times, about the right things, towards the right people, for the right end, and in the right way', is a difficult matter, but there is a standard or norm to which appeal can be made as one attemps to discern the mean in a particular case. The standard for the correct identification of the mean is the morally wise person, the person who has the virtue of practical wisdom. The morally wise person 'sees' what feelings or actions are appropriate in the situation. He or she knows how much of a feeling is too much, then and there, and which action would be too little in the circumstances. The morally wise person knows his or her own character and temptations, and adjusts his or her aim accordingly. There can be no real virtue in the absence of this practical insight into situations, into the virtues, into oneself.

Aristotle does provide general advice to his students for achieving the mean. They should first identify and avoid the extreme that is more opposed to the relevant virtue. Secondly, they should attentively avoid the extreme which is the easier for them. Finally, they should be most circumspect about all those things they find pleasurable, outflanking the snares of temptation in order better to achieve the mean. Following this advice does not guarantee the attainment of the mean, but it does lessen the likelihood that one will go far wrong, and that one's deviation from the mean will not be excessive.

Bibliography

Aristotle, *The Nichomachean Ethics*, Book Two, chs. 6–9, in J. A. K. Thomson, *The Ethics of Aristotle* (ET, Harmondsworth, 1953), pp. 63–75.

T.D.K.

MEDIA. The term 'the media' is shorthand for 'the media of mass communication' and popularly refers to television, radio and newspapers. As a concept it is modern. Mass circulation newspapers date back to the second half of the nineteenth century, but radio broadcasting to the general public began in 1922 and television became significant as a mass medium in the 1950s. The impact of these new media on public attitudes and behaviour and their influence on political and social affairs have made them in a relatively short space of time enormously powerful organs of persuasion. In earlier days a *coup d'état* centred on the royal or presidential palace. In the modern world it typically centres on the capital's radio or television station. Those who control the media can be assumed to control the State.

Ethical issues

The ethical issues raised by the media can be categorized under three headings:

1. The issue of power. Because of the almost universal availability of the electronic media, those who control them wield enormous influence in the shaping of public opinion. In totalitarian States this has led to political indoctrination. In the liberal democracies it has tended to promote the ideas of the cultural establishment or the commercial interests of the proprietors. Some people believe that television, especially, has served to promote a 'permissive' attitude towards sexual behaviour. Others hold that broadcasting merely reflects the changing views of society, holding up a mirror to its shifting attitudes. However, even a reflecting mirror is an 'influence', in the sense that it repeats and sometimes magnifies what it reflects, and that seems to be true of broadcasting.

2. The media-saturated society. This description of modern Western society, coined by Wesley Carr (1941–) in *Ministry and the Media*, refers to the way in which the media tend to dominate people's lives. Watching television is by far the most popular leisure pastime, taking up about 28 hours a week of the average viewer's time in the UK, and more than 30 hours a week for the average US viewer. Consumer decisions, holiday choices, style (individual and corporate), as well as political preferences are largely determined by radio and television. Commercial interests can create demand by the manipulation of media opportunities. Political parties have learnt how to use the mass media. Indeed, in most countries of the world general elections are fought out almost entirely on television.

On the other hand, it has to be said that public opinion remains obstinately independent. Seventy years of incessant atheistic propaganda in the Soviet Union could not eradicate a widespread longing for religious faith, which surfaced the moment there was freedom for it to do so. In the really important issues of belief and behaviour people seem to be remarkably resistant to media influence. In other words, the media's influence is pervasive and important (especially in relatively trivial matters), but not irresistible.

3. The issue of truth. Malcolm Muggeridge (1903–90) argued in *Christ and the Media* that television cameras are 'the repository and emanation of all our fraudulence'. He saw them as lying witnesses, which by their very presence distorted the truth.* While this seems an extreme view, there is little doubt that the mass media's tendency to trivialization, sensationalism and confrontation does tend to oversimplify and distort issues. Walter Lippman (1889–1974) has written in *The Public Philosophy*: 'When distant and unfamiliar and complex things are communicated to great masses of people, the truth suffers a considerable and often a radical distortion. The complex is made over into the simple, the hypothetical into the dogmatic and the relative into an absolute.' It might be equally truly said that the absolute is made over into a relative, for the media in Western Europe have an almost palpable dislike of anything that smacks of an absolute truth, which they tend to categorize as 'fundamentalist' (whether Christian, Jewish or Muslim).

A Christian response

The Bible has nothing to say, of course, about modern mass media, but it has a good deal to say about idle or careless words, about bearing false witness and the value of truth (*e.g.* Mt. 12:36; Jn. 18:37). To trifle with the truth, to trivialize great issues and to spread falsehood are manifestly contrary to the will of God. A biblical and Christian critique of the media would call them to account in the areas of truthfulness and seriousness in handling great issues.

It would also ask serious questions about the saturation of our society and its culture with the values of the mass media, which are often implicitly, if not explicitly, those of the *cosmos* – society organized as though God did not exist. Development of discipline in the amount of time spent watching television and of a critical faculty on the part of its viewers deserves a place both in school curricula and in the teaching role of the Christian church.

The mass media have offered much that is positive to our society, including a broader knowledge of the world around us and a more informed insight into the process of democratic government. They have also, in many countries, provided significant opportunities for Christians to make their message more widely known and understood.

But their positive contributions should not blind us to the dangers inherent in mass communication, especially where effective control is in the hands of a very few wealthy and powerful individuals. The media like to see themselves as the guardians of the public conscience. But who guards the guardians?

By definition a 'medium' is simply that – a 'means' to do something, not the end itself. The media are morally neutral, just as a blank sheet of paper and a pen are neutral. It is what people do with the media that determines their moral values. The 'problem' of the mass media

is, as always, a 'problem' about fallen human nature.

In the entrance hall of the BBC's Broadcasting House in London these words were inscribed by the Corporation's first governors in 1931: 'It is their prayer that good seeds sown may bring forth a good harvest, that all things hostile to peace or purity may be banished from this house, that the people, inclining their ears to whatsoever things are beautiful, honest and of good report, may tread the paths of wisdom and righteousness.' A Christian ethic for broadcasting, or the mass media in general, could ask no more, and certainly should accept no less, than that.

See also: ADVERTISING; MEDIA ETHICS.

Bibliography

W. Carr, *Ministry and the Media* (London, 1990); M. Muggeridge, *Christ and the Media* (London, 1977); W. Lippman, *The Public Philosophy* (New York, 1955).

D.B.W.

MEDIA ETHICS. The world of mass communication covers the various media* of books, newspapers, magazines, radio, television, cinema, records, compact discs and the growing realm of computers and interactive visual and tactual systems. The media control and process masses of information, and provide education and knowledge, as well as entertainment. Ethical questions are raised about the nature of the various media. The impact of the visual and the images it portrays, as well as the new possibilities created by 'virtual reality' forms which allow us to participate and experience while remaining spectators, raise fundamental questions about abuses and necessary control.

The centrality of truth* and the danger of manipulating, oversimplifying or distorting truth to fit the medium, the time available, the producer's intention or the station-owner's wishes are proper concerns. The very variety of media and the differences in presentations of the same news or feature lend credence to allegations about the media's bias and lack of objectivity.

The purpose of the media may be to inform, educate or entertain. The limits appropriate to these purposes and which allow the viewer / listener / reader the freedom to make his or her own judgment about issues are crucial. It is important to consider whether the media are seeking to move and shape public opinion or merely to reflect it. In political and moral issues, this may lead to power residing in the hands of a few, unelected and unrepresentative media owners.

The law seeks to control the media, balancing the need for the freedom of the press with protection for the vulnerable in laws of libel* and slander. Invasion of privacy* can be legislated for, and in court settings, reporting or 'gag' restrictions protect the innocent, as when a rape victim's anonymity is safeguarded. Governments restrict the media when issues of national security are at stake.

Those who work in and for the media may face moral problems over conflicts of interests which might affect their objectivity and ability to report accurately and justly. Involvement with a news source or pressure from a superior to omit or add an item may create problems.

The impact of the media on social and political life raises the moral issue of how far they should support or question the *status quo*. Political campaigning has been fundamentally affected by television, with its emphasis on 'sound bites', personality politics and photo opportunities.

The 'gutter press and media' have been guilty of entrapment by creating settings and luring individuals into acting in criminal or offensive ways. This is paralleled by 'cheque book' journalism, which buys stories and is in danger of creating much ado about nothing, while pandering to the greed and vulnerability of people. The media often exercise self-regulation, as in life-threatening situations where the facts of kidnapping or details of crimes may be withheld. The use of unnamed sources raises issues of how information was obtained. The issues of bribery* and fees for service are moral concerns.

Governments may also abuse the media and seek to censor (see Censorship*) information. Society expresses its views on such issues in law and its enforcement, but secular societies are deeply divided over the freedom of individuals to make and watch pornography* and the need to control explicit sexual and violent material. Part of the concern is over their impact on the vulnerable and the young. There is disagreement about the extent to which people become hardened and desensitized as opposed to imitators and stimulated. The media often exercise restraint by having a 'not before nine o'clock' rule for the depiction of sexual and violent scenes and bad language. Various

viewer watchdogs and national broadcasting regulatory authorities deal with complaints by the public against the media, though the penalties often seem ineffective.

Advertising* issues of truth-telling, exaggeration, image creation and misrepresentation are moral areas where advertising regulatory authorities wage a constant campaign to maintain high standards of integrity.

Christians focus on the importance of truth as part of God's requirements and commands for humankind, as well as on truth in its full and final expression in Christ. Concern for the impact on the vulnerable and children by the media must be matched with unease about the images and portrayal of women, racial groups and the elderly. The way that advertising creates demand and leads to increasing debt* in a consumer-led, selfish society reveals the power of the media to create and reinforce values. These values must be made explicit and tested for their correspondence with the values that Christians are to have and live (Phil. 4:8).

Bibliography
J. R. Bittner, *Mass Communication* (Englewood Cliffs, NJ, 1983); L. Thayer (ed.), *Ethics, Morality and the Media* (New York, 1980).

E.D.C.

MEDICAL CARE, see ETHICS OF MEDICAL CARE. [14]

MEDICAL CODES OF PRACTICE. From ancient times, practitioners of medicine have had medical codes of practice to guide them. The most famous of these, the Hippocratic Oath,* emphasizes the need for high standards and confidentiality* in caring for patients and specifically forbids euthanasia,* abortion,* engaging in practices without proper training, and illicit sexual relationships. Contrary to popular belief, there are few medical schools in England where pupils actually take this, or indeed any other, medical oath.

In the Hippocratic writings dealing with medical ethics, doctors are warned against avarice (G. E. R. Lloyd, *Hippocratic Writings*, Harmondsworth, 1978, p. 19). They are advised: 1. to bear in mind the patient's means when charging them and to be prepared on occasions to charge them nothing (Hippocrates, *Precepts VI*, vol. 1, London, 1923, p. 319); and 2. never to begin a consultation with the discussion of the fee (Hippocrates, *Precepts IV*, vol. 1, London, 1923, p. 317).

A Christian version of the Hippocratic Oath was probably formulated in the first few centuries AD. It replaced the reference to Greek deities, and also omitted the 'restrictive practices' part of the Hippocratic Oath which obliged doctors to regard their medical teachers as equal to their parents, to teach medicine only to their teachers' sons, their own sons or those who subscribe to the oath.

Codes of medical practice are needed for several reasons. It has been suggested that medical ethics are simply applied good manners and that anyone with high moral principles does not need rules, but this is to take an overly optimistic view of human nature, and to overlook the fact that, in the Second World War, doctors in Germany and Japan were involved in human experimentation. In giving judgment against a group of physicians who had committed such crimes, in 1947 a tribunal laid down the Nuremburg code, to which physicians must conform. Doctors rise to great heights of human endeavour and high moral standards usually prevail, but the potential for evil demands a code of practice.

Another reason for such a code is to instruct persons entering the medical profession on matters where conscience may not immediately indicate the right way to behave. For instance, if a National Health Service (NHS) general practitioner refers a patient to an NHS consultant for an operation and the patient then changes to the private sector and has the operation done privately for a fee of, say, £1,000, it might seem a kind gesture for the consultant to give part of the fee to the general practitioner. A code would alert the doctor that such fee-splitting is unacceptable, and in the UK it may result in removal from the medical register. Codes of medical practice are regarded as yardsticks for professional self-regulation (see Professional Ethics*).

Further codes and declarations have been published since the Second World War. The Declaration of Geneva (1948; amended 1968) elaborates on the previous themes while the Declaration of Sydney (1968) is a statement on death to help especially those involved in transplantation (see Transplant Surgery*). The Declaration of Tokyo (1975) is a statement on torture* and other cruel, inhuman or degrading treatment or punishment, and the Declaration of Hawaii (1977) involves psychiatric medicine. The Declaration of Oslo (1970) is a statement on therapeutic abortion, which was precipitated by legislation in many countries legalizing abortion as a therapeutic measure. The great difficulty with abortion is that when it is illegal, the back-street abortionists flourish. Those countries that have legalized abortion have chosen what some regard as the lesser of two evils. Unfortunately, legalizing therapeutic abortion often leads to the practice of abortion on demand.

Discussion is under way on the question of changing the present law on euthanasia. Some try to change codes of practice by quoting the practices of other countries, where a euthanasia law is reputed to work well. However, legalizing euthanasia may well open the door to allow some citizens to be eliminated without their true permission.

Most codes of practice do not seem to emphasize the importance of the doctor having the right attitude to the patient, to the medical student and to other healthcare workers. 1. Patients should be treated not only expertly in medical terms, but also with the kind of courtesy, warmth and good humour which reduces the intimidation often felt by patients. 2. Most of the codes state early on that medical teachers should be held in respect by their pupils, and most would agree with this principle but might question whether they should not also emphasize that students should be treated with courtesy and understanding. 3. There should be mutual respect between all healthcare workers. This emphasis on attitude is in the interests of all patients, healthcare workers and students, and is in keeping with the high ethical standards which medicine demands.

What motivates people to have this right attitude to patients, to all healthcare workers and to those in training? The humanist is motivated by his or her belief that human life is intrinsically valuable, while the Christian, and adherents of many other religions, believe that human life is of value because it is the gift of God.

Our attitude therefore is conditioned by the value of *all* human life, and is supported by the experience that correct attitudes to the patient lead to better rapport between the cared-for and the carers, and to a more enjoyable working life for all involved.

See also: ETHICS OF MEDICAL CARE; [14] HEALTH AND HEALTH CARE.

McC.

MEDICAL MALPRACTICE is an emotionally laden and highly controversial topic in medicine today. The term 'medical malpractice' can be defined as deliberate wrongdoing or culpable negligence committed by healthcare providers, particularly physicians, in the course of their treatment of patients. Examples would include abandonment, assault and battery, use of procedures such as surgery without patient consent, failure to fulfil an agreement to produce a specified result, deception or fraud, wilful misconduct, breach of confidence, and failure to warn that a patient may be dangerous to others. Medical malpractice is legally actionable under tort law in the US, and the huge jury-awarded damages paid to malpractice victims is often cited as one of the major factors in the rise of healthcare costs there. To this is added the practice of expensive 'defensive medicine', in which physicians order extra tests and procedures to protect themselves from lawsuits.

In terms of deliberate wrongdoing, one important area of malpractice is surgery that is unnecessary and often incompetent. A study conducted by the US House of Representatives Committee on Interstate and Foreign Commerce in 1976 estimated that there were 2.38 million unnecessary surgical procedures performed in 1974, at a cost of $3.92 billion and almost 12,000 deaths.

A frequently discussed area of medical malpractice concerns failure to obtain informed consent* for medical procedures. Since the 1960s, patients have won judgments in malpractice suits that were based on the lack of informed consent. In *Mitchell* v. *Robinson*, a 1960 Missouri case, a judge awarded damages to a patient who received bone fractures during convulsions as a side-effect of insulin shock treatments, when the physicians had failed to notify him of the hazards. In *Natanson* v. *Kline*, in the same year, a Kansas judge awarded damages to a woman who had been injured as a result of radiation therapy after a radical mastectomy, because she had not been warned of the side-effects. These judgments led to a large number of malpractice suits based on lack of patient consent to treatment, estimated at one time as more than 14% of all malpractice suits.

A number of suits were filed by children whose births were affected by the use of the drugs thalidomide and DES during pregnancy. The thalidomide babies were born with very serious physical defects, and DES-affected girls developed malignancies as adults. Today, there are a number of suits based on 'wrongful birth', alleging that physicians failed to notify of potential hazards in conception and childbirth to parents judged at risk based on a variety of factors. As a result of the decision in *Tarasoff* v. *Regents of the University of California* (1976), in which a man under psychological care murdered a young woman after announcing this desire to his psychologist, physicians and other professionals can be held liable for not informing people of the risks posed to them by patients. A growing area of malpractice concern involves suits by those infected with the HIV virus, whether infected by a patient whose condition was known to a physician who might have warned the victim, by contaminated blood administered during medical procedures, or inadvertently by an infected healthcare worker (as in the case of Florida woman Kimberly Bergalis, who became infected in 1987 during the course of dental treatment).

Several proposals are being considered to limit the number of costly malpractice lawsuits, which consume time, energy and money, and lower physician morale. Proposals for reform of the malpractice litigation problem in the US include the use of compensation boards using an award schedule to assess compensation, no-fault statutes which permit compensation without the need for establishment of fault through litigation, payment under patient-purchased insurance, binding arbitration, the establishment of maximum awards, and more recently, the development of a set of practice guidelines which can be consulted to determine if the physician followed standard parameters of care, a plan recently introduced in the State of Maine.

While excessive lawsuits ought indeed to be discouraged, the genuine problem of medical malpractice needs to be addressed more seriously by the medical community, which all too often has been perceived as covering up for some of its members. Genuine incidents of unprofessional conduct represent a serious charge against a profession which holds high the principle of *primum non nocere* ('Above all, do no harm') and helps account for the shrinking respect of the public for that profession. Perhaps the public has superhuman expectations of the medical profession, but this is understandable when the life and basic welfare of patients are at stake.

Bibliography

K. L. Brown, *Medical Problems and the Law* (Springfield, IL, 1971); G. H. Hauck and D. W. Louisell, 'Medical Malpractice', in *EBio*, pp. 1020–1028; A. R. Holder, *Medical Malpractice Law* (New York, 1975); D. F. Stroman, *The Quick Knife: Unnecessary Surgery USA* (Port Washington, NY, and London, 1979).

D.B.F.

MEDICINE, see Ethics of Medical Care. 14

MEDITATION, see Character; 10 Disciplines, Spiritual; Ignatius of Loyola.

MELIORISM is the doctrine that humans can and should make the world a better place. It specifically rejects both the pessimistic doctrine that the world is so evil that nothing can be done about it, and the optimistic view that it is so good that nothing needs to be done. Rather, we are to take the world as it is and do what we can to improve it.

Essentially a humanistic, progressive and pragmatic viewpoint, with its roots in evolutionary theory, the concept was popular in the US in the later 19th century. The term is rarely found today, though the concept remains.

Recent Christian thought has tended to put a great deal of stress on our responsibility to be 'salt' and 'light' (Mt. 5:13–16) to the world, and thus to change it for good. Some elements of liberal Christianity have seen the betterment of society as the heart of the Christian message. Most evangelicals, while holding that the personal transformation of the individual is of primary importance, and that only the second coming of the Lord Jesus will truly solve the problems of the world, at the same time accept the responsibility of doing what we can in the name of Christ in order to change the social, economic and political orders of the world for the better.

See also: Social Gospel.

P.A.H.

MENNONITE ETHICS. It is difficult to describe in brief compass the ethics of an Anabaptist Mennonite tradition that is over 450 years old and whose members are now found in 60 countries. What follows represents some dominant ethical themes in N. American Mennonitism, which in 1993 represented over 40% of the world's 965,000 Mennonites.

Mennonites, for whom the Bible is the final authority in faith and practice, view their ethics as an expression of their discipleship of Jesus* Christ. Hermeneutically, Mennonites see Jesus as the key to all of Scripture: the OT finds fulfilment in Jesus the Messiah; the NT writings, written by his followers, continue and apply the Messiah's teaching and way. Jesus represented the in-breaking of God's kingdom (see Kingdom of God*); by word and example he revealed God perfectly; he called his disciples to respond to God's action by concrete acts of obedience and imitation. A programmatic Anabaptist ethical text is that of Hans Denck (d. 1528): 'No one can know Christ except by following him in life.'

Jesus' cross* is the paradigm of how God restores broken relationships. In the Mennonite view, ethics grows out of soteriology: Jesus' sharing, suffering, non-retaliatory example is the way his followers also will hunger for justice and make peace (see Justice and Peace 3). For some Mennonites this has led to political quietism; in their concern to maintain 'non-resistance' (and at times in response to persecution) they have avoided political and legal involvement. For other Mennonites, the way of the cross has led to varying forms of social engagement. Responding both to writings of scholars such as John Howard Yoder (1927–) and to their own experience of urbanization* and world-wide missionary and service activity, these Mennonites have sought to follow Jesus, whom they find to be 'non-violent' but political. Both strands of Mennonite ethical thinking emphasize practical service such as disaster relief and development work. The more activist strand, open to the use of physical constraint (but not violence), has pioneered new forms of justice-making. Some of these have received international attention, *e.g.* programmes of conciliation / mediation, victim–offender reconciliation and advocacy of oppressed people. An ongoing debate among Mennonites centres on the extent to which Christians, in their attempt to be 'faithful' to the way of the cross, must also renounce 'responsibility' for shaping the course of history.

Mennonite ethical thinking is corporate. Jesus' primary challenge, according to Yoder, was 'the creation of a distinct community with its own deviant set of values and its coherent way of incarnating them'. The primary vehicle for God's action in history, Mennonites believe, is neither the isolated believer nor the State:* it is the church* whose members, empowered by the Holy Spirit, live the life of God's kingdom in the midst of an old order that has not yet recognized the Messiah. The church is a 'lantern of justice', living in exemplary way personal and corporate shalom. Mennonites believe that congregations where *koinonia* (see Fellowship*) is real are the places to learn and to pass on to new members the practical meanings of following Jesus. Mennonite congregations emphasize strong family* life, mutual aid, simplicity of lifestyle and reconciled relationships.

In the 1970s and 1980s Mennonite ethics, which some critics had dismissed as slavishly adherent to Jesus' 'impossible ideal', have been discovered and elaborated by members of other traditions. Evangelicals in the 'radical discipleship' stream and ethicists such as Stanley Hauerwas (Methodist; 1940–) and James McClendon (Baptist; 1924–) have seen Mennonite ethical emphases as relevant to all Christians.

Bibliography

J. L. Burkholder, *The Problem of Social Responsibility from the Perspective of the Mennonite Church* (Elkhart, IN, 1989); S. Hauerwas, *The Peaceable Kingdom: A Primer in Christian Ethics* (Notre Dame, IN, 1983; London, 1984); G. F. Hershberger, *The Way of the Cross in Human Relations* (Scottdale, PA, 1958); D. Kraybill, *The Upside-Down Kingdom* (Scottdale, PA, ²1991); J. W. McClendon, *Systematic Theology 1: Ethics* (Nashville, TN, 1986); R. J. Sider, *Exploring the Limits of Non-violence* (London, 1988) = *Non-violence: The Invisible Weapon?* (Dallas, TX, 1989); J. H. Yoder, *The Politics of Jesus* (Grand Rapids, 1972); *idem*, *The Priestly Kingdom: Social Ethics as Gospel* (Notre Dame, IN, 1984).

A.F.K.

MENNO SIMONS (1496–1561), or more precisely Menno Simonszoon (*i.e.* Menno son of Simon). Menno was a priest in Friesland, Holland, who, in 1536, renounced the Catholic Church and entered the network of persecuted Anabaptist cells. He quickly emerged as a leader, preaching precariously 'in houses and in fields' and shepherding a sometimes turbulent movement towards peace and unity. The first Reformer of the Netherlands, Menno later came to be recognized as a father of the 'Mennonite' tradition and indeed of Protestant nonconformity in general.

Menno's ethics and pastoral theology were rooted in his experience and understanding of conversion; in an early pamphlet entitled *The New Birth* he enunciated a lifelong leitmotiv. According to Menno's understanding this regeneration, in which believers have died to sin and 'have received a new heart and spirit', would lead to specific changes. 1. The first change was believers' baptism, of which Menno was a pioneer in modern European history. 2. Another was entry into the persecuted church. Baptism for Menno was the threshold of entry into the community of obedient faithfulness, in which Christians support each other in a new family. 3. A third change was a transformed lifestyle. Menno was convinced that through the new birth, in which the believers were 'renewed in Christ', they must begin obediently 'to walk as Christ walked'. This search for a consonance of confession and praxis* led to a commitment to simplicity and sharing, in which believers 'serve their neighbours, not only with money and goods, but also . . . in an evangelical manner, with life and blood'. It also led to a commitment to non-violence:* God's people 'are children of peace who have beaten their swords into ploughshares'. And it involved a principled rejection of persecution, which places Menno among the earliest advocates of religious toleration.

Bibliography

Complete Writings, tr. L. Verduin, ed. J. C. Wenger (Scottdale, PA, 1956).

G. R. Brunk, *Menno Simons: A Reappraisal* (Harrisonburg, VA, 1992); H. J. Hillerbrand, 'Menno Simons: Sixteenth-Century Reformer', *CH* 31, 1962, pp. 387–399; I. B. Horst, 'Menno Simons', in H.-J. Goertz (ed.), *Profiles of Radical Reformers* (Kitchener, Ontario, 1982), pp. 203–213.

A.F.K.

MENTAL HANDICAP, see LEARNING DISABILITIES; MENTAL HEALTH.

MENTAL HEALTH. The World Health Organization in its International Charter in 1948 stated: 'Health is a state of complete physical, mental and social wellbeing.' This assumed an idealized state of normality which, if not immediately avail-

able, was theoretically attainable. Hitherto psychiatrists defined certain features of human behaviour and thought as 'mental disorder' or 'illness' and therefore potentially treatable. The popularization of psychoanalytic* theory with the pursuit of freedom from anxiety,* full achievement of one's potential and absence of unfulfilled drives, possibly linked with the 'pursuit of happiness' as a basic human right, gradually lent credence to the search for 'mental health'.

By the 1970s, not only was the concept of 'mental illness' denied but the antipsychiatry movement maintained that psychiatrists with their dependence on diagnoses, physical treatments and restraint in psychiatric hospitals were themselves the destroyers of mental health. Such polemics were not helped by the difficulty in translating writings emanating from the US into the context of psychiatry as practised in the UK. Terms such as 'schizophrenia' and even the word 'psychiatry' had a much broader application in the US. Also the British National Health Service provides a much more uniform and co-ordinated service, using the general practitioner as the point of entry and referring agent to the psychiatric services.

The debate moved on, and the UK Mental Health Act (1983) agreed that there is a category of individual who can be described as 'mentally disordered'; it brought extra safeguards in terms of strict criteria for the giving of treatment, and a regular review of all patients detained or treated against their will. The closure of the larger and more isolated psychiatric hospitals coincided with several other developments. The pharmacological advances in the use of antidepressants and major tranquillizers allowed more patients to be treated and maintained in their own homes or hostels. The growth of multi-disciplinary approaches to care allowed a much broader therapeutic effort, focused not only on the alleviation of symptoms but also on encouraging support and changes in a patient's family, work and social network. Psychiatrists became much less likely to take a purely organic approach to mental disorder, and were prepared to promote initiatives to lessen a person's 'dis-ease' in order to prevent 'disease'. Roughly similar developments have also occurred in the US. In the UK, the development of community mental health units has now been widely set up with government encouragement.

Mental illness

The concept of *mental illness*, although brought under scrutiny in recent years, has survived. It is based upon the observation that there is a recognized cluster of complaints and clinical observations which occur and lead to difficulties in a sufficiently predictable way to merit their being given a label or diagnosis. There is far greater agreement in determining diagnostic criteria today in view of the development of the international classification of mental disease. This facilitates the communication between doctors when talking about disease and the necessary research regarding causation and treatment.

Psychiatrists have divided mental disorder into those more serious conditions where the person may become 'psychotic' (see Psychosis*), and those conditions where the person is unlikely to become psychotic but is distressed or disabled by mental symptoms sufficient to interfere in some measure with a previously established pattern of life. The *psychoses* have been shown to have a significant hereditary influence, but may also be affected by physical and environmental changes.

The major tranquillizers have made a significant improvement in the supervision, compliance and long-term prognosis of schizophrenia. For most patients admission to hospital is briefer, thus allowing greater continuity in the person's domestic and support network. Such drugs are not without side-effects, and careful monitoring is necessary to achieve maximum benefit with minimal side-effects. Regular contact with a known nurse or doctor in giving and supervising treatment produces greatest compliance and least relapse. Antidepressants have dramatically reduced the severity and need for admission of patients with severe depression, but they may have to be taken for many months and sometimes longer in order to prevent relapse. Antidepressants are not addictive, but unhappily they have been confused with minor tranquillizing drugs, such as the diazepines, in the public mind. Lithium carbonate has produced dramatic improvement in patients with severe swings of mood or recurrent depression. Many patients hitherto unable to sustain themselves in employment have been able to pursue an active and highly effective career in the most demanding of professions because of this medication. Some patients, often of a rather creative, artistic nature, complain that they miss the creative surge associated with the early stages of becoming elated. The need for negotiation with a patient and weighing up the consequences of compliance or non-compliance can be a demanding and constant challenge. Electroconvulsive therapy is one of the few treatments which has withstood the test of time and much hostile publicity. There is no doubt as to its efficacy in depression* of a severe kind with considerable agitation or almost total withdrawal. Unfortunately, like most treatments which work, there is a tendency for it to be over-used and abused, giving substance to some of the complaints popularized in, *e.g.*, the film *One Flew Over the Cuckoo's Nest*.

The lesser disorders are known as *neuroses,** and include various conditions characterized by anxiety, phobias and compulsive acts and thoughts. The causation here is much less clear, and although there may be some constitutional influence, changes in a person's life situation and emotional conflicts would appear to be more significant. That small proportion of patients who are referred to the specialist psychiatric services are those whose complaints have not spontaneously remitted or whose lives have become particularly impaired. The use of psychological therapies has had an increasing importance in the treatment of these conditions.

The vast majority of patients who suffer from 'nerves' are never referred to a psychiatrist, and in the 1960s and 70s would often be given minor tranquillizers. There is no doubt that the increasing public awareness of 'health issues' as opposed to the treatment of illness has heightened the awareness of society regarding the psychological dangers of such medication, and made the medical profession more alert to the need to explore the broader issues of a person's goals in life and fundamental motivations. Such explorations between patient and doctor challenge both parties to look at their view of humankind, whether we are mere dust or 'dust with a destiny'. While the majority of people cope well with their minor psychological problems, one in eight of the population consult their general practitioner each year with a psychological problem or one which has a significant psychological component. Only 10% of these are referred to a psychiatrist. Even then only a very small proportion are admitted to a psychiatric unit, though some will expect to be referred to some helper, medical or otherwise, for counselling and help.

In the US the percentage of citizens seeking psychotherapy rose from 13% in the 1970s to 30% in the 1980s. The National Institute of Mental Health estimates that 15.5 million Americans undergo psychotherapy each year.

Mental health services in the UK

It required the Herculean efforts of the evangelical earl Lord Shaftesbury* and others to ensure that there was proper provision for the care and treatment of the mentally ill and an asylum in every county and major city in the land. Poor funding, the population explosion and medical nihilism led to these being increasingly overcrowded, and rightly, in some cases, earning the criticism of society. In this century psychiatric units within district general hospitals have become the more acceptable and fashionable locus of in-patient treatment. Here mental-health professionals are in close association with their colleagues in other disciplines, and mentally ill patients are expected to be 'cured' in the same way as physically ill patients. The units are often too small to cope with the demand laid upon them or to meet the needs of those patients who still require longer-term care. This means that the psychiatric hospitals cannot be closed, sometimes leading to unsatisfactory situations where acute patients are cared for in general hospitals and chronic patients in mental hospitals.

By the 1970s there was increasing pressure to provide a more comprehensive system of care for those with 'mental-health problems', based upon local communities and their special needs. These became known as 'community mental health centres', and it was intended that they would be linked to an in-patient unit for only the most disturbed patients requiring admission to hospital, on either a voluntary or a compulsory basis. The aim is to serve a population of 30,000 to 90,000, thus ensuring that the unit is much more locally based, accessible to the majority of the population, and served by a team of mental-health professionals who will get to know the population, its needs and the most effective and appropriate service provision. These teams include medically qualified psychiatrists, psychiatric nurses, clinical psychologists and occupational therapists, as well as staff from the local social services department. The service is based upon out-patient referrals, domiciliary consultation, case discussion, and focusing upon daily or sessional attendance according to the special needs of the 'client'. Close liaison and cross-referral are expected between the mental-health professionals and other agencies within the community. Self-referral by clients is also encouraged in some centres.

This is likely to be the established pattern of care in the next decade as the larger psychiatric hospitals continue to be reduced in size and closed. There has been a tendency for such units to over-expose themselves to the demands of the local population and to acquire a 'case load' which necessitated waiting-lists and delays in assessment. This clearly frustrated the aims of such units to give a quick, local and accurate appraisal with a view to preventing deterioration and more serious disability. This inability to meet expectations sometimes leads to a demand for more funding from health authorities or a return to more traditional methods of referral where they still exist. A more serious problem is that, without a clear limit to the cost of such broad developments, there is a tendency for the most disadvantaged, less vocal and most chronic patients being neglected in meeting the demands of the more vocal and demanding 'clients' or 'customers' of the health services. The increasing number of severely mentally ill patients maintained at home or in group homes and hostels as the larger psychiatric hospitals close is now causing concern, as there are fewer beds into which they can be readmitted during a relapse. Often such patients do not provide the satisfaction for those mental-health professionals who are keen to develop their skills in counselling and other psychological, and sometimes alternative, therapies among those who are less disabled.

There is increasing governmental pressure on health authorities to use their funds for the treatment of the more disabled. The development of a healthcare plan for each patient discharged from a psychiatric unit helps to identify those personnel responsible for supervision and support of each patient with continuing mental-health problems. As this has been a mandatory requirement since April 1992, there could well be a shift of emphasis towards maintaining the mental health of the more disabled.

In the US, beginning in the 1960s, widespread disenchantment grew against large State mental health hospitals designed to treat chronic psychiatric patients. Authorities in the field began to view the institutions as warehouses for the insane, unhelpful and inhumane. Reformers recommended that patients be returned to their families and communities. Incorporation into community life was the goal. Thus hospital populations decreased from 574,878 in 1970 to 276,138 in 1986. Inpatient hospitalization constituted 77% of all mental-health episodes in 1955, but was down to 27% in 1986. However, the influx of these people into society has been blamed for the increase in homelessness,* and even crime, as community mental-health programmes were ill equipped to handle the release of so many patients.

The pastoral scene

As fewer patients are admitted to hospital and more are maintained in some kind of community setting, churches may find that they have a group home or other community facilities within their neighbourhood. These could provide an opportunity for demonstrating care and support for those who are the most disadvantaged in our society. However, it is as well to remember that in the community mental-health team there will be recognized and designated official 'key workers'. Any initiative by a church should be carefully worked out and monitored with a responsible member of the clinical team. Unwise attempts at Christian counselling (see Biblical Counselling*) and healing* could be associated with undesirable and even dangerous consequences, however well-meaning may have been the attempt.

Over the past decades the Christian community's reaction to mental illness has tended to be somewhat ambivalent at best and frequently negative. This to some extent derives from the increasingly high profile given to the materialistic and atheistic views of some psychiatrists. There has also been a fairly recurrent theme among some Christians that they should not need to have recourse to a psychiatrist or to physical methods of treatment of emotional problems. In this they assume a dichotomy between brain and mind which is as misjudged as the attitude of the psychiatrist who would seem to equate brain with mind. There is also the added unhappiness in the minds of some Christians who may believe that all mental problems are derived from spiritual conflicts and are to be dealt with exclusively by 'spiritual' methods such as exorcism (see Deliverance Ministry*), inner healing* or specific Christian counselling. The refusal to subject such 'healings' to proper scrutiny and evaluation leads to further polarization as the medical profession encounters those who have not responded to such healing and may have been made worse, while the healers ascribe undoubted improvement in some individuals exclusively to spiritual processes.

The plethora of 'spiritual remedies', 'spiritual healings', and the range of 'How to overcome . . .' books does not indicate necessarily a Christian bias. Some even derive from a New Age* stable. There is a widespread demand for alternative therapies in all spheres, and many of the popular 'healing' and 'counselling' books purporting to come from a Christian viewpoint seem merely to reflect the secular world's similar quest for 'spiritual health' which is equated with the discovery of happiness,* self-actualization* and an absence of mental suffering. Such approaches are simplistic, and can deceive the Christian who has a theology of suffering* which looks beyond self-authentication and the acquiring of good feelings as an indication of health. It is well to research the provenance of some of the alleged Christian healing and counselling programmes (see Roger Hurding, *Roots and Shoots*).

The search for a Christian psychiatrist or counsellor can be a further problem. While the congruence of the world-view of counsellor and counsellee has been shown to promote feelings of well-being and can contribute to the relief of symptoms and improvement of function, this is not the only factor in promoting health and recovery. Accurate assessment and acknowledgment of the need for several therapeutic approaches and initiatives are equally important.

The pastoral worker who is likely to encounter people with mental problems would be well advised to purchase a simple medical student's textbook recommended by the department of psychiatry at the local regional medical school. The fact that someone is under psychiatric treatment does not mean relinquishing pastoral care. On the contrary, there almost certainly will be spiritual and relational issues requiring pastoral help during and after any psychiatric treatment. It is often after the more acute phase of an illness that friendship, counselling and a realistic goal worked through with a Christian friend or counsellor are most relevant in promoting mental health.

Bibliography

M. G. Barker, 'Psychological Aspects of Inner Healing', in N. M. de S. Cameron and S. B. Ferguson (eds.), *Pulpit and People: Essays in Honour of William Still* (Edinburgh, 1986), pp. 89–102; A. Clare, *Psychiatry in Dissent* (London, ²1980); R. F. Hurding, *Roots and Shoots: A Guide to Counselling and Psychotherapy* (London, 1986) = *The Tree of Healing* (Grand Rapids, 1988); S. L. Jones and R. E. Butman, *Modern Psychotherapies* (Downers Grove, IL, 1991); A. Lewis, 'Health as a Social Concept', repr. in A. Lewis, *The State of Psychiatry* (London, 1967), pp. 179–194; Office of Health Economics, *Mental Health in the 1990s from Custody to Care* (London, 1989); J. White, *The Masks of Melancholy: A Christian Psychiatrist Looks at Depression and Suicide* (Leicester and Downers Grove, IL, 1982); B. Wooton, *Social Science and Social Pathology* (London, 1959).

M.G.B.

MENTAL ILLNESS, see BIBLICAL COUNSELLING; GLASSER, WILLIAM; MENTAL HEALTH; MOWRER, ALBERT; PSYCHOSIS.

MERCY is firstly the deep heartfelt compassion* aroused, by the need or distress of another, in one who is in a position to relieve such need or distress but who has no requirement to do so other than the impetus of his or her own compassion; it is also the action taken to bring relief. Indeed, if the emotion does not result in action, it cannot be described as mercy.

Many different words and concepts are involved in explaining mercy. It is loving-kindness, pity, compassion coming from the very centre of the being of the one who is merciful. The earlier idiom which speaks of it as surging up from the 'bowels' (*e.g.* Col. 3:12, AV) is perhaps even more evocative than our term 'heartfelt'. Mercy is also the forbearance, grace,* forgiveness* and help inspired by those merciful feelings.

At the heart of the Christian understanding of mercy lies the conviction that God (see ☐) is merciful, and that mercy and compassion are fundamental to God's nature (Ex. 34:6; Ps. 116:5). He is the 'Father of mercies' (2 Cor. 1:3, RSV) who 'has compassion on all he has made' (Ps. 145:9). His mercy stems from his covenant love, but is also applied to all peoples (Dt. 4:31; La. 3:22; Rom. 9 – 11; 1 Pet. 2:10). It is inspired by human weakness, but independent of human will (Ps. 51:1; Dn. 9:8–9; Rom. 9:15–18). God's mercy is shown in bringing new life and in dealing with sin (Eph. 2:4; Tit. 3:5; Heb. 8:12; 1 Pet. 1:3); in relieving distress in 'everyday' situations like Elizabeth's barrenness and Epaphroditus' sickness (Lk. 1:58; Phil. 2:27); and in providing special gifts and callings (2 Cor. 4:1; 1 Cor. 7:25). Christ's mercy enables us to approach and receive God's mercy (Heb. 4:16).

God's mercy is presented in Scripture both as the basis of salvation and as the motivation for Christian behaviour. The essential response to receiving God's mercy is to pass it on (Rom. 12:1). As Helmut Thielicke* puts it: 'As one who was and is the object of the divine mercy, I am also summoned now as a subject to grasp and actualize that mercy, or better, to let it happen to me and in me' (*TE* 1, ET, Philadelphia, 1966, and London, 1968, p. 129). The believer is to be merciful because this reflects God's character (Lk. 6:36; 2 Cor. 1:3–4); because it is in line with God's purposes (Lk. 10:37); and because it provides the environment in which mercy can be received (Mt. 18:21–35). To be merciless is a total denial of knowing God (Rom. 1:28–31) and in some way prevents the receiving of mercy. Knowing his merciful character, it is possible to ask God for mercy, but that mercy can apparently be received only if the channel through which mercy is given out to others is open (Mt. 6:14–15; Jas. 2:13). Thus human mercy is presented in somewhat paradoxical fashion as both the result of, and the prerequisite for, receiving God's mercy. Mercy is expected to be shown within family relationships (Is. 49:15; Am. 1:11), and to neighbour and stranger alike (Jb. 19:21; Jude 21–23). In particular it is to be shown to the needy and the helpless (Ps. 72:12–14; Zc. 7:9–10), both within the church family and beyond (Lk. 10:25–37; Jas. 2:14–26).

However, there are certain problems with the concept of mercy. It is clear that to be merciful involves having compassion on undeserved affliction, giving help to those in distress, rescinding debts, and treating defeated enemies with kindness. But what about those whose affliction is deserved? How far is it right to show compassion to the guilty? Justice is equally a basic characteristic of God (*cf.* Mi. 6:8); what then is the relationship between mercy and justice? Individuals may forgive offences committed against them personally and God can deal with their sin, but

can a society allow criminal offences to go unpunished? Is W. C. Kaiser (1933–) right to argue in support of capital punishment that 'To extend love or mercy in exchange for justice at this level is to despise both the image of God in the one who has been suddenly felled and . . . the very basis by which we received new life in Christ' (*Toward Old Testament Ethics*, p. 148)? How does mercy apply in the judging of a claim between two needy appellants? Is it just or merciful to give out equally or to each according to their needs? It is clearly not merciful to provide handouts to the needy in a way that destroys their own decision-making or capacity for action, but where should the line be drawn? Yet mercy is not the opposite of justice – injustice is. Moreover, mercy is frequently exercised in the context of justice, *e.g.* when a recommendation of mercy is accepted in a court of law.

Bibliography
R. Daly (ed.), *Christian Biblical Ethics* (New York, 1984); H.-H. Esser, *NIDNTT* 2, pp. 593–601; W. C. Kaiser, *Toward Old Testament Ethics* (Grand Rapids, 1983); P. T. O'Brien and D. G. Peterson (eds.), *God Who is Rich in Mercy* (Grand Rapids, 1986); H. Thielicke, *TE* 1.

M.J.E.

MERIT is the entitlement to reward on the basis of virtue or good actions. The word has specialist applications both in ethics and theology.

The concept of merit plays an important role in discussions of the nature of justice (see Justice and Peace ③). According to the most commonly held view, criminal justice* is based on giving guilty people their deserts. Thus, some would argue, justice as a whole is a matter of giving people what they deserve, and specifically of rewarding merit. If people are good they should be rewarded; if a person works well he or she should get rich. Justice is based on merit.

Those who hold this view would promote a competitive society, with strong incentives to meritorious acts, and clear rewards for meritorious deeds, with lack of reward* forming a clear disincentive to inaction or socially unacceptable behaviour.

An alternative concept of justice rejects merit as a basis and replaces it with need. Justice demands that the weak, the failures, those who are at the bottom of the pile, should receive just as much as those who amass the most merit. All human beings have an equal right to the world's resources, whatever our apparent deserts or merit. This right rests on the fact that we are human and that we need both the basic and the good things of life, not that we earn them by our meritorious actions. Indeed, where the rewarding of merit results in the rich becoming richer and nothing being done for the poor, it is precisely injustice.

Both the merit concept and the needs concept of justice have been argued by pointing to passages of Scripture (merit, Dt. 11:13–17; Mt. 25:29; Rom. 2:6–8; needs, Ps. 82:3–4; Mi. 6:8; Lk. 3:10–14); but many would feel that it is the needs concept that is most in keeping with the general tenor of both OT and NT. God's people are called to express God's concern for those who are in need, and to work for a just and equable distribution of the world's resources.

The theological debate over the place of merit in our individual salvation and relationship with God arose first at the time of the Reformation. The Roman Catholic Church taught that certain acts, *e.g.* prayer and celibacy, merited a reward from God; merit could even be transferred from one individual to another. The Reformers, convinced that salvation was by God's grace* alone, and that even our best deeds fall short of God's standards, rejected this concept totally, stressing our inability to earn any merit with God through our own efforts.

In recent discusssions on this issue, Roman Catholic scholars have been ready to accept that salvation is a matter of God's grace, not our merit. Protestants, meanwhile, are able to agree that, as a result of the working of God's Spirit in our hearts, we are able to perform deeds which are pleasing to God and which will ultimately be rewarded by him in heaven. Such deeds do not earn us God's favour; that is freely given. But in that they express his character and purposes for the world they bring joy to his heart (Mt. 25:21, 23; 1 Thes. 4:1).

Bibliography

H. G. Anderson *et al.* (eds.), *Justification by Faith: Lutherans and Catholics in Dialogue* (Minneapolis, MN, 1985); P. C. Böttger *et al.*, *NIDNTT* 3, pp. 134–145; D. D. Raphael, *Moral Philosophy* (Oxford, 1981).

P.A.H.

MIDDLE AXIOMS, see AXIOM.

MID-LIFE, whenever it arrives, is a time of change. For women, the menopause may involve emotional as well as physiological changes. Men, in their turn, experience a lessening of physical powers.

There may also be changes in the pattern of relationships. Elderly parents become dependent rather than giving support, while children are seeking independence. There may be sons-in-law and daughters-in-law to accept and grandchildren to welcome. Some need to adapt to second marriage and new family situations. Change creates stress* but it can also positively refresh and enhance life.

Mid-life may be stressful. Demands of work are maximum while at home there may be pressures from a teenage family as well as from older relatives in need of care. Money may be tight. There may be fears of losing a job or losing a marriage partner. Christian faith is needed to provide stability and strength to endure.

Mid-life may be marked by loss. As well as loss of youth there may be children leaving home, the death of parents and separation from a partner. Early retirement* may mean loss of work. There may be a relinquishing of identity as accustomed 'labels' at home and work are outlived. Christian faith can give the assurance that people are valued for themselves and not their roles.

Mid-life can be a time of growth if spiritual needs are recognized and met. When storms are weathered, a second and gentler stage of life may follow, invested with hope* and purpose for the future.

See also: HUMAN DEVELOPMENT.

Bibliography

M. Batchelor, *Meeting the Mid-Life Challenge* (Oxford, 1989).

M.K.B.

MIGRANT LABOUR, which involves the temporary (but sometimes permanent) transfer of surplus labour (often the least skilled), usually from rural to urban areas – in search of job opportunities – is characteristic of many dualistic economies. It is both national and international in character.

Traditionally, the process of labour migration was viewed as the movement of rurally sourced labour in search of urban employment, but more recent studies suggest that this is not always the case, given the apparently inexplicable acceleration of rural–urban labour migration, even in the face of rising urban unemployment. This indicates not only that it is due to economic factors, on account of inequalities in the spatial distribution of employment opportunities, but also that it reflects social, psychological (perceptions of job expectations), and security considerations.

Although it is internationally pervasive, labour migration has been most noticeable in Africa and Asia. For years N. and W. Africa have supplied both Europe, the Gulf States and the Middle East with migrant labourers, while the Southern African regions have supplied the more developed South African economy with migrant labourers.

In the case of Asia, the oscillation of migrant labourers from mainland China to Malaysia, from the Phillipines to the US, and even within countries such as India (from rural areas to metropolises such as New Delhi), confirm its pervasiveness. Likewise, the perpetual oscillation of casual Mexican migrant workers (the 'wet-backs') to and from the US, as well as the ongoing influx of Turks into W. Germany ('*Gastarbeiters*'), has elicited international attention. However, lest the impression be created that this phenomenon characterizes Third World economies, labour migration is becoming an increasing phenomenon within the European Community countries, notably Portugal, Spain, France and Germany.

Economically, the problems associated with migrant labour are epitomized by the cost of labour turnover to the employer; the extent to which the migrant labour system prevents the acquisition of skills; inadequate, and often discriminatory, wages and social security benefits; and the displacement of local labourers, which frequently exacerbates unemployment. Implicit in these problems is the inequitable distribution of earnings, reflecting the injustices of migrant labourers actually subsidizing the true cost of labour. To this must be added the atypical cost of transport and administration, all of which distorts factor prices, notably labour. These deficiencies and distortions in turn often lead to poor management on the part of the employer.

Likewise, it is not uncommon for migrant labourers to be exploited due to their *political* 'footlooseness', which often deprives them of basic legal rights. The potential and frequent rejection of the humanity of migrant workers –

due to their alien status in the host region / country – is tantamount to emotional and psychological cruelty.

Sociologically, conjugal separation frequently leads to bigamy, prostitution and the breakdown of parental authority. Allied to this are the appallingly crowded living conditions which are often the lot of the migrant labourer. Moreover, the rising incidence of alcoholism* among migrant labourers further reflects the tragedy of their circumstances.

To compound matters, *medically* speaking, labour migration complicates the control of diseases such as AIDS, venereal infections, tuberculosis, malnutrition, beri-beri and alcoholism, which are all indisputable concomitants of the practice.

Biblically, the response to labour migration draws on Scripture's portrayal of God's love, righteousness and justice and his abhorrence of any form of oppression or exploitation.

Historically, the plight of Hebrew migrant labourers in Egypt (Ex. 2:11 – 5:21) and God's opposition to Pharaoh's oppression of these labourers bears this out, while the prevention of injustice(s), according to Mosaic law (Dt. 6:20–25), and the treatment of the poor, alienated and disadvantaged, constitutes the acid test of a community's life (Lv. 25; Jas. 2:1–7).

As victims of poverty and potential exploitation (Pr. 22:22–23), the transience of migrant labourers highlights the moral responsibility to protect them (Ps. 82:3–4) and care for their needs, both materially and spiritually (Ex. 22:21; 23:9; Dt. 10:19; 14:28–29; 15:4; 23:7; 26:12; Lk. 12:13–34; 16:19–31).

Christian ethics also recognizes the moral indefensibility of forced conjugal separation, which is a regular feature of labour migration. Indeed, the biblical imperatives underlying marriage and family life are blatantly contradicted through this practice, as expressed in passages such as Gn. 2:15, 18; Song 1:5–6; 4:1–7; Mt. 19:4–5.

Although the predicament of the migrant labourer is usually due to force of necessity, it calls for an informed and compassionate response, together with a practical, evangelistic concern for the well-being of those who, on account of their location in society, often escape our attention.

Bibliography

R. Holman, *Poverty: Explanations of Social Deprivation* (London, 1978); W. Molle, 'International Movements of Labour under Conditions of Economic Integration: The Case of Western Europe', *Journal of Common Market Studies* 26.3, 1988, pp. 317–339; S. C. Mott, *Biblical Ethics and Social Change* (Oxford, 1982); M. P. Todaro, *Economic Development in the Third World* (Harlow, ⁴1989); M. Voirin, 'Social Security for Migrant Workers in Africa', *ILR* 122.3, 1983, pp. 329–341; F. Wilson, *Migrant Labour in South Africa* (Johannesburg, 1972).

P.N.P.

MILL, JOHN STUART (1806–73), the most influential of 19th-century British philosophers. An empiricist and a utilitarian (see Consequentialism*), a major project of Mill's was the revision and defence of the utilitarian theory articulated by Jeremy Bentham.*

Mill embraced Bentham's 'greatest happiness principle', *i.e.* actions which increase the overall amount of happiness for all those involved are better than those which produce less happiness. Moral actions are, thus, to be evaluated solely in terms of their consequences. Mill, like Bentham, was a hedonist:* pleasure* being that alone which is desirable for its own sake, we, as rational agents, thus appropriately seek pleasure and the avoidance of pain. A good action brings about a greater amount of pleasure than other possible actions. Considering the objection that Bentham's hedonism treats human beings as though we are but swine, Mill distinguishes between 'higher', or mental, pleasures, and the 'lower', sensual pleasures which are qualitatively inferior to mental pleasures. Mill's utilitarianism, thus, requires that one performs those actions which will bring about not only the greatest sum of pleasure, but the greatest sum of the best type of pleasure.

Two additional works of Mill stand alongside his *Utilitarianism* (London, 1863) in terms of moral import. In *On Liberty* (London, 1859) Mill articulated the libertarian claim that the only morally justifiable grounds for interfering with the free choices of an individual are to prevent direct and immediate harm to others. In *The Subjection of Women* (London, 1869) Mill advocated that there are no grounds for treating women as less than equals of men.

See also: HISTORY OF CHRISTIAN ETHICS.[6]

T.D.K.

MINISTRY. The term 'ministry' is used in both a broad and narrow sense. Broadly, it refers to mutual acts of service performed by members of the church towards God and one another. Narrowly, the concern of this article, it has come to refer to the service of those recognized, usually by an act of ordination,* as leaders within the church.

Contemporary understanding of ministry varies across the churches. It is commonly seen as the ministry of the Word and the sacraments, and is believed to be derived from the ministry of Jesus and to be representative of him. For many, the emphasis lies on its priestly nature; hence it is the minister who presides at the eucharist. The ministry is considered to be composed of three orders, namely, bishops, priests and deacons. Ordination is the recognition and empowering of those duly trained and examined, and serves as a guarantee of apostolic tradition.

Substantiating these views of ministry from Scripture is difficult because the evidence of Scripture regarding ministry is meagre. Our understanding of the Bible often comes from reading back into it our present patterns of ministry. So, for example, Edward Schillebeeckx (1919–) argues that Phil. 2:17 is evidence of Paul having a certain concern for what might be called apostolic succession. The fact, however, is that the NT has little concern with the issue of ministry in its narrower sense at all.

The Bible

The Old Testament. The spiritual leaders of Israel consisted of prophets, priests and wise men (Je. 18:18). After Sinai, priests were given a clear place within Israel (Ex. 28:1 – 29:46; Lv. 8:1 – 9:24), in spite of it being God's intention that the people should be a nation of priests (Ex. 19:6).

Jesus and the Twelve. Jesus' own ministry was one of preaching and healing (Mk. 1:34, 45), leading to his sacrificial death on the cross. He chose the Twelve to be with him (Mk. 3:14–19) and sent them out to minister as he had done (Lk. 9:1–6). The Twelve were eyewitnesses of his ministry and resurrection (Acts 1:21–22) and, with Paul rather than Matthias as the replacement for Judas (Acts 1:15–26; 1 Cor. 15:8–10), they became foundational for the church (Eph. 2:20; 3:5; 2 Pet. 3:2).

The epistles show an almost entire absence of concern over the question of the apostles' successors. As Alec Motyer (1924–) has pointed out, not only does Rev. 21:4 imply that their position was unique and so unrepeatable, but 2 Timothy, where one would most expect to find it, shows no interest in the question at all.

There is, however, a concern for the preservation of apostolic truth and apostolic tradition (*e.g.* 1 Cor. 11:23; 15:1–8; 2 Tim. 1:13–14). The word 'apostle' is used both of the Twelve and in a looser sense of 'one who is sent' (Acts 14:4, 14; 2 Cor. 8:23; Phil. 2:25). In this sense it is possible that Rom. 16:7 alludes to a woman among the ranks of the apostles.

Other New Testament ministries. The concept of priesthood is not used with reference to what we know as ministers of the church. Priesthood is attributed firstly to Jesus* Christ, who through his sacrificial death is our great High Priest (Heb. 4:14–16; 7:26 – 8:2; 9:24–28), and secondly to all the people of God (1 Pet. 2:5, 9; Rev. 1:6; 5:10).

The stress of the NT writings falls on the functions of ministry, among which are those of the apostle, prophet, evangelist, pastor and teacher (Acts 21:8, 10; 1 Cor. 12:29; 14:29; Eph. 4:11; 2 Tim. 2:2; 4:5; Jas. 3:1). Teaching receives a special emphasis in the Pastoral Epistles, leading many to think that this was the chief pastoral task, but Rom. 12:8, 1 Cor. 12:28, and 1 Tim. 5:17 may well imply that pastors had a more general 'management' role in the church.

Little clear organizational pattern emerges from the NT writings. Leadership seems to have both reflected local, existing patterns of leadership and been responsible to local needs as is seen in James's role in the church at Jerusalem (Acts 15:13). The terms 'elders' (*presbyteroi*) and 'bishops' or 'overseers' (*episcopoi*) seem to be used interchangeably (see Tit. 1:5, 7), and their usage seems to depend on local circumstances. (For 'elder' see Acts 14:23; 1 Tim. 4:14; Tit. 1:5; for 'overseer' see Phil. 1:1; 1 Tim. 3:1–7; Tit. 1:7; 1 Pet. 5:2.)

Deacons were also among the leaders of the local church (Phil. 1:1). Their ministry was probably practical, concerning the administration of welfare, but they were still required to possess high spiritual qualifications (1 Tim. 3:8–13). The choosing of the seven (Acts 6:1–7) is now usually considered to be a one-off incident rather than the origin of the diaconate.

It is evident that solo ministry was not envisaged and that it was even discouraged (3 Jn. 9). Plurality always seems to be in view. Nor is there any sense of hierarchy involved, even if some, like Titus, seem to exercise an area oversight on behalf of the apostle.

Developments after the New Testament

With the writings of Ignatius (*c.* 35–*c.* 107), Tertullian* and Hippolytus (*c.* 170–*c.* 236), a more standard pattern emerges, giving a place to the role and authority of the bishop beyond that envisaged in the NT. The bishop's position comes to mature flower in Cyprian (*c.* 200–58). This led in time to a hardening of understanding of the ministry as composed of the three orders of bishop, priest and deacon.

Various theories have been advanced to explain the emergence of this pattern by the mid-2nd century, and especially the role of the bishop. Dom Gregory Dix (1901–52) believed the authority of the apostles to be parallel to that of the Jewish *shaliah* – a legal functionary appointed to represent the Sanhedrin and invested with full authority. But his argument cannot bear the weight he gave it. J. B. Lightfoot (1828–89) challenged the commonly acepted view that the bishops were the successors of the apostles and argued rather that they arose as an elevation from the presbyterate. B. H. Streeter (1874–1937) suggested that their position arose from the process of standardization. Adolf Harnack (1851–1930) has developed the idea of there being a distinction between local and translocal ministries.

Ordination

Ordination is the setting apart of a person for the work of the ministry, usually by the laying on of hands. In some churches this must be done by the bishop, to ensure apostolic succession. In others it is done by the local congregation. An area of dispute is whether such an act confers indelible status on the ordinand or not.

In the OT, the laying on of hands was used in various ways, with Nu. 27:23 unusually showing it as a means of commissioning for service. A similar diversity is seen in the NT, but a greater place is given to it as a means of recognizing persons called to service and of conferring on them, although not as a unique event, the Holy Spirit (Acts 6:6; 13:3). These acts do not amount to ordination services as such, although allusions to these may be found in 1 Tim. 4:14, 5:22 and 2 Tim. 1:6. The earliest evidence of a sacramental act of ordination, including laying on of hands, is found in the *Apostolic Tradition* of Hippolytus (*c.* 215).

The ordination of women

For many this is the most controversial issue. Catholics oppose it as inconsistent with their priestly view of ministry. They argue that Christ was male and chose male apostles and that females cannot form legitimate succession or play the crucial part in the sacrifical and sacramental acts of the eucharist. Evangelicals have also opposed their ordination, chiefly on the basis of Paul's apparently blanket ban on women speaking and teaching in the church (1 Cor. 14:34; 1 Tim. 2:11–15). Many contemporary evangelical exegetes would not understand these verses as imposing a fixed principle for all time but rather as a temporary measure, given the circumstances then. They note, for example, Paul's acceptance of women's participation in worship (1 Cor. 11:5, 13); their leadership role within the early church (Acts 16:15; 18:26; Rom. 16:1, 7); and Paul's stress on his personal practice as if in contrast to a fixed principle (1 Tim. 2:12). The debate over the meaning of Scripture is tied up with other issues such as the ideas of headship and submission.

The chief problem seems to lie in our concept of ministry and ordination which appears so far removed from the freer and more flexible approach we find in the NT itself. Above all else, ministry therein is service, not hierarchy, status or authority, and should be characterized by the attitudes Christ commands in Mt. 23:8–10 and Mk. 10:42–43. Its validity is judged by its function and spiritual worth, and it is always firmly ministry in partnership with others in the context of the priesthood of all believers.

See also: PRACTICAL AND PASTORAL THEOLOGY. [7]

Bibliography

C. K. Barrett, *Church, Ministry and Sacraments in the New Testament* (Exeter, 1985); E. E. Ellis, *Pauline Theology: Ministry and Society* (Grand Rapids and Exeter, 1989); J. A. Motyer, 'The Meaning of Ministry', in M. Tinker (ed.), *Restoring the Vision* (Eastbourne, 1990); E. Schillebeeckx, *The Church with a Human Face: A New and Expanded Theology of Ministry* (ET, London, 1985); A. Schweizer, *Church Order in the New Testament* (London, 1961); M. Warkentin, *Ordination* (Grand Rapids and Exeter, 1982); World Council of Churches, *Baptism, Eucharist and Ministry* (Geneva, 1982).

D.J.T.

MIRACLES, see HEALING.

MISSION, MORALITY OF. Of the world's major religions, Christianity, like Islam and unlike Judaism and Hinduism, is a missionary religion. As Jesus was *sent* (Lat. *missio*, 'a sending away'; Gk. *apostellein*, 'to send') by his Father into the world (Jn. 20:19–23), so the apostles and early Christians were commissioned to be witnesses 'in Jerusalem, and in all Judea and Samaria, and to the ends of the earth' (Acts 1:8; see also Mt. 28:16–20). If atonement* can be said to be the 'great saving act', then the incarnation itself is undoubtedly the 'great missionary act' at the very heart of Christian faith.

Nevertheless, the Christian church throughout the ages has not only used a variety of biblical texts and interpretations to understand and justify its mission but has sought to carry out its task within a wide diversity of social, cultural and political contexts. Not surprisingly, this has given rise to a number of differing theologies and methodologies of Christian mission. Neither the meaning of the gospel nor the best way to proclaim it has been obvious to all or agreed by many, from the very beginning.

Moreover, significant expansion of Christianity as a 'religion of the masses (or peoples)' from the earliest times to the present day has gone hand in hand with political conquests, socio-cultural movements, colonial adventures and imperial rule. Clearly, of such nature was the Constantinian expansion of Christianity within the Roman Empire, the spread of Catholicism into the Americas and to the East with the Portuguese and Spanish conquests, and the spread of Western Christianity, both Catholic and Protestant, into Africa with 19th-century colonization. But of similar nature, if not quite so clearly so, was the missionary expansion of the Celtic church, the Great Schism between the Eastern and Western churches, and the Reformation development of Protestant and Catholic States.

Through the centuries, during such periods of expansion as well as at times of consolidation and in the midst of decline, there were always people inside and outside the church who raised moral questions about the conduct of mission and missionaries. In the heyday of the 19th-century missionary movement from Europe and N. America their voices were heard, for instance, in relation to medical missions and polygamy,* issues concerned with the content and effect of mission and direct precursors of 20th-century doubts and misgivings about the very morality of mission itself.

Were medical missions an end in themselves because they provided medical care, or were they to be a means to the end of 'converting the heathen'? This puts simply the first of the two issues. It was variously resolved. For instance, the (Anglican) Church Missionary Society appointed a sub-committee in 1885 to consider the place of medical missions in the total mission of the church, and concluded in their minutes that they were of use only 'when the Gospel could not easily be preached by ordinary evangelists, or among aboriginal and uncivilised people likely to be impressed by the kindly influence of medical work'. In this spirit Bishop Tucker of Uganda took Dr (later Sir) Albert Cook on his pioneer journeys so that 'the preaching of the Word might be reinforced by signs and wonders'. Yet in 1886 the founders of the German Lutheran Evangelical Missionary Society incorporated in its constitution the humanitarian emphases of medicine and education, believing that they were following in the footsteps of Jesus who healed the sick out of love and compassion. And although they met with stiff resistance from leading German churchmen, they went ahead in the belief that medical work was an integral part of the good news.

Ought polygamists (usually men with more than one wife and strictly speaking polygynists) to be baptized, or ought they to be asked to put away all but one wife first? This puts simply the second of the two issues. Again, the resolutions were various. For instance, Anglican missionaries in the early and mid-19th century were not prepared to set hard and fast rules, and encouraged the baptism of polygamists under certain circumstances. Then in 1857, Henry Venn (1796–1873), General Secretary of the Church Missionary Society, issued a memorandum laying down the policy that polygamists should not be accepted into the church. With few exceptions, this became the prevailing view of all the mission churches until the mid-20th century, and it became one of the major factors in the emergence of African Independent Churches. Even then the mission churches differed as to what should become of the cast-off wives: some were given a house and a small plot of land for cultivation; others were abandoned, often to prostitution, a late arrival in the new townships brought about by colonialism.*

The late-20th-century debate surrounding the very morality of mission itself arises out of a number of movements, socio-cultural and political as well as religious and global in consciousness and extent. The *history of religions* school, especially the work of Ernst Troeltsch (1865–1923), believed that religions should confine themselves to their places of origin (and Christianity's was thought plainly to be the Western world!), and ought not to proselytize (see Proselytism*). *Marxists* of all shades believed religion itself to be 'the opiate of the people' and 'the tool of the ruling classes' and therefore without a role in a communist utopia. *Post-colonialists and anti-imperialists* of all kinds, within and without the churches and particularly in the countries which had just thrown off the colonial yoke, recognized the close relationship between Christianity and its message and the culture in which the message was wrapped. David Livingstone (1813–73) had set out 'to make an open path for commerce and Christianity' in Africa. Victorian Christians had understood Christianization and civilization to be synonymous terms. Yet many of the peoples colonized had perceived the white man to have come 'with the Bible in one hand and the Maxim gun in the other', and who could blame the Kikuyu of Kenya who observed, 'There is no difference between a white man and a missionary'? *Anthropologists* opposed the imposition of alien cultures and lifestyles on 'tribal' peoples. *Humanists* of all kinds, inside and outside the churches, emphasized humanization rather than missionization which was seen as proselytization.

These moral dilemmas are not easily resolved one way or the other. However, it is appropriate to conclude that because mission is of the essence of Christian faith, Christians will continue to be constrained to proclaim the gospel. But they ought to do so with love and compassion, sensitivity and humility. And if they do so consciously following the example of Jesus Christ, they will in the process respect the freedom and dignity of every human being, made in the image of God.*

See also: EVANGELISM.

Bibliography

D. J. Bosch, *Transforming Mission: Paradigm Shifts in the Theology of Mission* (Maryknoll, NY, 1991); S. Neill, *Christian Missions* (Harmondsworth, ²1986); D. Senior and C. Stuhlmueller, *The Biblical Foundations for Mission* (London and Maryknoll, NY, 1983).

M.S.L.

M OBILITY. The issue most often raised in Christian circles in relation to job mobility is the dilemma of determining the appropriate balance between the priorities of work* and family.* As a phenomenon, job mobility almost necessarily implies a family moving to a new home, and therefore implies the decision-making process involved in evaluating the priorities of work and family, as well as effects on the extended family, network of friends, and communities that the family moves to and leaves.

The issue of mobility raises the question of values for Christians today. Especially in higher-paying jobs, success and approval by the business institution have become society's definition of worth. Indeed, in many workplaces, whether they are high-paying or not, an employee's loyalty to the business is determined by the priority the job has in the employee's life. Seeing the worker as a whole person, *i.e.* with family and other interests and obligations,* has become *passé* unless these factors affect the productivity of the particular worker.

Job mobility does not just affect the individual. The employee along with his spouse must make the decision about the demands of job and the needs of the family. The employee, in addition, may undergo the potentially stressful situation of adjusting to a new work situation. The spouse of the relocated employee normally bears the burden of easing the separation of ties in the move and establishing new networks of support in the new area. Children must adjust to new schools and new circles of friends, which, especially for teenagers at their sensitive age, is often a difficult adjustment.

Job mobility also affects relational networks, especially in the extended family. The break-up of the extended family, most often caused by job mobility, strikes at the roots of relationships. As a cohesive and nurturing unit, naturally structured for sustenance, maintenance and growth both of the individual and the family group, the extended family forms a base that provides financial support from those who earn, wisdom and comfort from the elders who have experienced much of life, and peer support and companionship for family members of all ages.

Community structures are also affected by job mobility, both in the locality and in the church. Often mobility results from the economic decline of a region. Then, it is the young and more able who are generally the first to go, leaving behind the elderly, the less able and those least able to handle change. Local communities, deprived of leadership, often enter a spiral of decay.

A major cause of such regional decline is mobility of capital. As funds are deposited in financial institutions and transferred to other regions, or even overseas, new jobs are created in other growth regions and so the exodus of key personnel becomes inevitable. The biblical injunctions against the taking of interest (*e.g.* Dt. 23:19–20), and against centralization of political power (*e.g.* Dt. 17:14–20) may have been designed in part to prevent the outflow of key people (see 1 Sa. 8:10–18).

The larger question raised by consideration of the issue of mobility is how values are propagated within our society and our involvement in, contribution to, and challenge to those values. Christians must not accept the culture* of their society as given by God, but must be prepared to challenge their culture in the light of God's Word (Mk. 7:9–13). A sense of place, as the context within which our relationships takes place, is a central category of biblical faith. Mobility undermines the relational basis of daily life and must therefore be a key point at which Christians challenge contemporary Western culture.

See also: COMMUNITY ETHICS. [16]

M.G.G.S. and M.J.B.

M ODERNITY AND POSTMODERNITY. Only in the 1970s did Christian commentators, learning from social science, begin to characterize the social world as 'modernity'. The term was used to sum up some key features of an era that began in the 17th and 18th centuries in Europe, but that reached its climax only in the mid-20th century. Included was a reliance upon science* and technology* as the instruments of reason* and progress, the development of industrial production of commodities usually within a capitalist* economic system, the emergence of bureaucratic organizations (see Bureaucracy*), both to manage those industries and to run the increasingly complex government of nation-states, and the coming of total, mechanized war,* dependent on constantly upgraded technologies of transport and communication. Modernity came to be seen by many as the backdrop against which church life had to be understood, and for which 'secularization'* provided the complementary analytical tool. Questions of 'faith and reason', the relation of church and society, and the basis of morals and politics represented crucial questions under this rubric.

Not only one view of modernity is available, however. Modernity is seen positively and optimistically as the only human hope, or negatively and pessimistically as the root of all our problems. Opinions vary depending on time and place. During economic recession, for instance, modernity's blessings seem at best ambiguous. In a country crippled by poverty,* however, modernization may appear as a bright dream. Ambivalence towards modernity seems an appropriate stance, given the twin truths of Christian involvement in its inception and the Christian critique of its consequences. Such ambivalence should not be confused with complacency, however, with respect either to modernity or to its supposed demise.

Modernity may not last for ever. Since the 1980s the social sciences have engaged with a growing debate over 'postmodernity', a debate having close affinity with parallel ('postmodern/ist') discussions within the arts, including particularly architecture. While some make bold to announce the arrival of 'consumer', 'information', or 'programmed' society, other participants content themselves with the 'post-' prefix to suggest that the preceding kind of society is coming to an end. Hence, 'post-industrial', 'post-capitalist', and 'postmodern'. While such debates do sometimes degenerate into mere intellectual fads, there is also enough of substance to warrant careful attention from anyone who would discern the signs of the times.

1. What evidence suggests we are witness to a social transformation? Prominent among the various factors in question is the idea that new information technologies* permit extensive changes in the mode of production. Locally, this means flexible forms of manufacture, geared closely to consumption, quite different from the standardization and rigidity of modernity's mass production methods. Globally, capitalist enterprises penetrate every corner of the globe (see Multinational Corporations*), thus dwarfing old rivalries between nation-states in importance. However, the military-industrial complex still informs and galvanizes much technological development. A so-called 'new class' has appeared of white-collar and service workers who use their educational background to achieve mobility and who spawn new social movements such as feminism* and the greens (or environmentalists), all of which tends towards a restructuring of both production and politics.

2. As the debate over postmodernity meshes cultural with social questions, what yields the sense of an ending here? One sees postmodernity as the collapse of the 'grand narratives' of the Enlightenment* – reason, democracy,* progress, etc. Events of the 20th century have cast radical doubt on them all. The scepticism of the *philosophes* turns finally on to their own doctrines. The only certainty is that there are no certainties. Science softens. Truth is dismantled. Another theorist connects this with consumption (see Consumerism*) and communications technologies. The world of electronic media, especially TV, immerses us in signs or images, cut off from any 'reality' they may once have represented. The 'Levi' denim tag and the 'Coke' can label seen on TV ads are what we consume and what gives us our sense of social status, our identity. Eventually political and even religious choices are reduced to the consumption of signs. Universally binding standards dissolve. As Karl Marx* once said, 'All that is solid melts into air . . .'

3. All this generates big questions about whether any basis remains for political or moral life. Some within the postmodernity debate embrace the nihilism* of Friedrich Nietzsche:* his early doubts about the illusion of progress yield no alternatives. Others argue that in the demise of old hierarchies of gender, class and race we can see old oppressions crumbling; today not equality but 'difference' is the goal. Yet others fear that this simply opens the door to 'neotribalism', each group having its own story, but never able to agree on the 'common good'. If nothing else, the question of what kinds of normative fixed points might exist 'after virtue' is kept alive by the acutely risky environment bequeathed by modernity, visible in ecological crisis (see Environment*), famine and underdevelopment (see Economic Development*), and nuclear instability.

Christian contributors are not prominent in the debate over postmodernity, even though in a sense the issues cry out for such involvement. Part of the problem lies with ways that Christianity itself is entangled with modernity. It is all too easily associated negatively with the rise of predatory modern science and technology, with cultural domination through church-based education or missionary expansion, or with sexual oppression because of its unjust treatment of women or homosexuals.* An urgent task is to break the gospel free from false alliances with economic arrangements or rationalist arguments which, however laudable their original intentions, now constitute a millstone around the neck of any meaningful attempts to be 'salt and light' today. Even 'secularization', the supposed tool for understanding modernity, often concedes to the canons of social science.

That said, openings for Christian comment may not be as remote as some think. As the logic of postmodernity pushes beyond the constraints of modernity, what once was spurned as theological and metaphysical terrain seems unavoidable, as more than one participant has observed. Whether new groundings for postmodern social and political life are sought in revived Greek virtues, in New Age* deities such as Gaia, or in a rediscovery of the Logos as the original and unique 'meta discourse', remains to be seen. Christianity will certainly have to become aware of the extent of its collusion with (post-)modernity, and recover some lost nerve, for the latter possibility to become a real hope.

Bibliography

A. Giddens, *The Consequences of Modernity* (Cambridge and Stanford, CA, 1990); J. Milbank, *Theology and Social Theory: Beyond Secular Reason* (Oxford and Cambridge, MA, 1991); L. Newbigin, *Foolishness to the Greeks* (London and Geneva, 1986); B. Smart, *Postmodernity* (London, 1993).

D.A.L.

MODESTY is an attitude or pattern of behaviour which expresses restraint and avoids ostentatious display. In Aristotelian terms, modest people avoid excess. The obverse of modest conduct is anything shameful, so E. M. Brecher (1911–89) defines modesty as 'behaviour designed to forestall a blush' (*The Sex Researchers*, London, 1969, p. 13). It is protected (and sometimes dictated) by conventions and taboos* which may differ markedly from culture* to culture.

In the NT modesty characterizes those who model Christian virtues like love (see ②), humility* and self-control.* Women are encouraged to dress modestly, spending their money on care for others rather than on expensive jewellery, clothes or coiffures (1 Tim. 2:9–10). The church is not to tolerate men who parade their wealth immodestly in the congregation (Jas. 2:2–4). Modesty requires that conversation is restrained, with all mention of things which are 'improper' or 'out of place' carefully avoided (Eph. 5:3–4). And it dictates realism in refraining from proud pretence, whether in other people's company or in God's presence (Rom. 12:3; Lk. 18:9ff.).

The link between modesty, dress and sex is clear but complex. Both Clement of Alexandria (*c.* 150–*c.* 215) and Tertullian* complain that public, nude bathing is immodest. Such sentiments, which find many echos throughout church history, trace their biblical origin to Gn. 3, where sin's intrusion led Adam and Eve to cover their genitalia in a vain attempt to conceal their new sense of unease in each other's company.

The Bible does not, however, advocate modesty as a pathway to ascetic self-deprecation. Physical and material things are affirmed, not denied, in Scripture. Modesty simply encourages control on excess, in the interests of love for God and neighbour.

D.H.F.

MONASTICISM. Christian monasticism has been a foundational spiritual and ethical force throughout church history, individually and institutionally. The monk or nun has few rivals as symbols of high spirituality.* Although early ascetes (see Asceticism*) and later monks chose such a life to work out their own salvation and become a spiritual élite, service to the church and its people became a major component of their lives.

Drawing from biblical admonitions and examples of separation and self-denial in Jesus and Paul, Christians of the early church frequently drew away from society for the purpose of fasting, praying and mortifying the flesh. Syria and Egypt were the primary locations for early ascetics, such as Simeon Stylites (*c.* 390–459) and Antony (*c.* 251–356).

The increasing number of people engaged in these ascetic and spiritual practices led to the need for communities and rules. The many groups of the 4th and 5th centuries found in the Middle East, Greece, Italy, Africa, Gaul and Ireland observed a variety of rules. The rules developed by Basil of Caesarea (c. 329–379) in the East and Benedict of Nursia* in the West provided the pattern for the dominant forms of monasticism.

In Western Europe, Benedictine monasticism gradually replaced all other independent and institutional monastic alternatives by the 8th and 9th centuries when, under the leadership of Benedict of Aniane (c. 750–821), Carolingian monastic reform introduced a higher level of monastic uniformity.

The ideal and essence of Benedictinism is expressed in the terms 'poverty', 'chastity' and 'obedience'. Personal possessions were denied. Absolute celibacy was demanded. Obedience was required to Christ and to the abbot, and, for some orders, to the Pope. The unique characteristic of Benedict's rule was a strong work ethic. Each monk must do assigned manual labour daily. Later these responsibilities were delegated to lay brothers or tied in with the feudal social structure of the Middle Ages. In its place the *opus Dei* (work of God) came to be the regular, daily recitation of the Psalter and prayers. Monastic work, the work of God, thus became exclusively spiritual. This aspect of the monastic spiritual tradition is continued in the Daily Office, Morning Prayers and Vespers of the Anglican and Catholic Communions.

From its inception monasticism has been characterized by recurring reforms which developed from problems related to the corporate possessions of monasteries, the accumulation of wealth, and the need to enforce the rules more strictly. Reform often led to new orders with stricter, revised vows. The revived spiritual life attracted more monks and more gifts and hence more wealth, and the need for reform often developed again.

This pattern of reform and renewal found exception when some persons of high spiritual acuity discerned special needs in the church, in the laity or in evangelization and formed new monastic orders which had more narrowly defined or specified purposes than traditional monasticism. Such groups were the Franciscans, Dominicans and Jesuits. The followers of Francis of Assisi* were lay persons called to minister to lepers and social outcasts. The brothers (friars) were not to be conventicled but to live in the world moving from village to village, a significant departure from traditional

monasticism. Later, university education and more traditional monastic spirituality consumed their efforts. Dominic (1170–1221) founded the Order of Preachers (Dominicans), which focused attention on the evangelization of heretics in locations where churches had closed or were without orthodox clergy. They, like the Franciscans, originally were not endowed, did not build monasteries, and later served in the universities. The Jesuits (Society of Jesus) were founded as a response to Protestantism out of the personal religious experiences of several dynamic spiritual leaders of the 16th century, chief of whom was Ignatius of Loyola,* whose primary goal was unflinching service to the papacy. Since the 16th century, there have been additional monastic foundations directed towards education, social service and foreign missions in the Catholic Church. Monasticism is also found today in the Anglican Communion. The Lutheran Deaconesses resemble a women's order of social service.

Though concerned to develop their own spirituality, the lives of monks, friars and nuns became characterized by good deeds and love for others, their institutions known as centres of hospitality, care and education, and their reputation as the supreme spiritual, ethical and academic leaders (in spite of occasional, well-known aberrations) spread throughout Europe. Increasingly, monks desired to become priests. After the 8th and 9th centuries, all monks were required to do so. Estate administration, fulfilment of feudal responsibilities (even military), and response to calls from princes and monarchs for educated spiritual and temporal advisors kept much of the monastic leadership involved beyond the walls of the cloister during the Middle Ages. Although not as visible in the modern world, monasticism has still had a major influence within Christendom, especially in the areas of spirituality, ethics, mission and social service.

Bibliography

Benedict of Nursia, *The Rule of St Benedict* (ET, Garden City, NY, 1975); Ignatius of Loyola, *Spiritual Exercises* (ET, London and New York, 1963); D. Knowles, *Christian Monasticism* (New York and London, 1969); *idem*, *The Monastic Order in England* (Cambridge, ²1963); C. H. Lawrence, *Medieval Monasticism* (London and New York, ²1989).

T.O.K.

MONETARISM is the name given both to a theory and to a policy for regulating a national economy. It suggests a method of using a set of policy instruments for the control of a key function in any economy – the supply of money.*

It postulates that the quantity of money circulating in an economy (nation-state) determines the aggregate price level, thus linking the quantity of money available with the determination of the rate of inflation. It follows that controlling the supply of money has the effect of regulating the pace of economic activity. Closely allied with this theory is the belief that markets must be allowed to function freely so that economic resources may be allocated in the most efficient manner. It is argued that economies with large private sectors are likely to be more stable and less corrupt than those dominated by the State or private monopolies.

The origins of monetarist theory can be traced both to the anti-interventionist ideas of the Austrian-British economist Friedrich August von Hayek (1899–1992) and to the research and writing of Professor Milton Friedman (1912–) of the University of Chicago. Friedman was sceptical of the claim of John Maynard Keynes (1883–1946) and others that policies of demand management as a means of regulating an economy would produce the stable growth and full employment for which politicians asked. He pointed out that Keynes never dismissed the traditional view of the link between the supply of money and the price level. He argued that the history of discretionary actions by governments – tax changes, expenditure programmes, *etc.* – had tended to destabilize an economy rather than have the opposite effect. Only control of the money supply would produce the desired result.

Controversy about monetarism has arisen because economists disagree as to what particular types of money should be targeted for control. Money definitions range from 'M0', which measures visible currency, to 'M4', which includes bank and savings balances. The control of the supply of money via the banking* system is at the heart of monetarism.

Advocates of monetarism share the same policy objective as those of the Keynesian school, namely the control of the fluctuations of economic activity which have become a feature of the 20th century. Keynesians suggest that this can be achieved by demand management, while monetarists emphasize their belief that inflation – the progressive reduction in real value of the currency unit – is both an economic and a moral evil. They derive their fear of its social effects from the experiences of what happened in Germany in the late 1920s when the Deutschmark inflated to a point where it was unable to fulfil its monetary function. All those with savings (the middle classes) were left without any monetary assets and totally disillusioned with their political leaders. What infuriated them was the realization that what had been advocated as a virtue (saving) as a means of self-support turned out to be the means of their destitution. Similar experiences have been noted in some S. American republics in more recent years.

Some commentators (notably, C. Bresciani-Turoni and Thomas Mann) point out that the rise of Nazism can be traced directly to hyperinflation as experienced in Germany.

Monetarism was the principal economic policy followed by the US during the Reagan/Bush administrations (1981–93), and during the Thatcher era (1979–90) in the UK. Intellectual objections to the policy were voiced by some economists, notably in Cambridge in the UK; even Conservative politicians were unhappy with the apparent trade-off between low inflation and relatively high levels of unemployment.* Furthermore, most Treasury targets for money supply in the 1980s were consistently exceeded, and new sophisticated ways of holding money devised by the investment industry confounded the policymakers.

Monetarists maintain that monetary policies alone are not enough to produce a growing, non-inflationary economy; they must be supplemented by structural reform including effective competition policies and a reduction of State commercial activity.

From a moral standpoint, both inflation and unemployment must be considered to have evil effects. The former seems less odious as it is normally slow in its progress and lagging in its effects on any particular person or family; monetarism addresses this dilemma. On the other hand, unemployment is more dramatic and personally disruptive, and although the majority of those losing their jobs find another within a short time, ordinary families fear this more than the loss of value of their purchasing power. Monetarists have so far failed to address seriously the problem of long-term unemployment, which tends to follow from the application of their policies.

Bibliography
T. Congdon, *Monetarism Lost* (London, 1989); M. Friedman, *Monetarist Economics* (Cambridge, MA, 1990; Oxford, 1991); B. Griffiths, *Inflation: The Price of Prosperity* (London, 1976); D. A. Hay, *Economics Today* (Leicester, 1989); N. Kaldor, *The Scourge of Monetarism* (Oxford, 1985).

s.w.

MONEY is a means of payment, a method of exchange, a numeraire for measuring relative values and a store of value. It is the most liquid of the possible stores of wealth, since it is acceptable as a settlement for contracts and debts and in exchanges in a way that other assets are not.

Money has been in existence for a very long time, even in primitive economies that primarily used barter. In order to act as money, objects need to have certain properties: relative natural scarcity; easy and undisputed recognition; and, as John Maynard Keynes (1883–1946) pointed out, an elasticity of production which is zero or negligible, so that unemployed workers cannot go out and harvest money from the trees.

Metal money, most often silver or gold, has been the most popular form of money. Bank notes have also counted as money since at least 1700. In the 20th century cheques and credit cards have become increasingly common forms of money. Paper money initially had to be backed up by a certain reserve of bullion, but the fixed proportion was abandoned and since 1971 banks are left to make their own decisions about their levels and types of reserves. The introduction of cheques and credit cards has altered the speed of circulation of money round the economy and lessened the ability of governments to control the amounts of money in circulation. In most countries, the 20th century has seen a change from the private issue of bank-notes money by individual banks to State control over the definition and issue of money, usually through a central bank, *e.g.* the Bank of England, or the Federal Reserve Bank in the USA.

When countries attempt to measure their money supply, they must count not only the notes and coins in circulation but other forms of money. In practice this leads to a range of definitions of the money supply, according to what is included in addition to notes and coins: *e.g.* bank and building society instant-access accounts, time deposits, bank deposits, bank reserves, *etc.*, can all be added into the money supply.

Banks now have a major role in the creation of money through the credit* creation principle. A bank need only keep in reserve a small proportion of individuals' deposits for day-to-day liabilities. The rest it can loan out to borrowers at interest. Since part of these loans will end up becoming the bank deposits of others, further loans will be made after deducting the reserve proportion. The money supply is thus expanded on the base of the initial loans, to a multiple which is related to the amount of reserve kept back. The introduction of credit cards expands the money supply further in ways which are difficult to measure since the credit amounts have a less clear relationship to deposits.

Controlling the money supply has become a target of government policies since the Second World War because of the adoption of Keynesian economic theories and policies. The policy of printing money was advocated in the 1930s in Britain and the USA on the basis of Keynesian theories. More precisely, governments spent money on various projects in order to give people incomes and thus get the economy out of the 1930s recession. Though Keynes built upon earlier theories, particularly the quantity theory of money dating back to 1664 (Thomas Mun, 1571–1641), he introduced some novel elements in *The General Theory of Employment, Interest and Money* (Cambridge, 1936). The most notable idea was that people could hold money for speculative purposes as assets and not just as a means of exchange or method of payment.

The idea of restraining the money supply in order to contain and reduce inflation was argued extensively in the 1970s by monetarists,* following Milton Friedman's (1912–) earlier work (in *Studies in the Quantity Theory of Money*), although the idea claims to be linked back to the quantity theory. Monetarist policies were adopted in the 1970s and 1980s amid much controversy, in some advanced industrial economies (*e.g.* the UK), but not without some Keynesian policies also being used at the same time. A fuller discussion of these different approaches to managing the economy, judged from a Christian perspective, can be found in Alan Storkey's (1943–) *Transforming Economics* (chs. 1–3) and Donald Hay's (1944–) *Economics Today* (ch. 6). Both authors find things to commend and things to criticize in all the secular approaches when they are judged against the standard of scriptural principles.

Money raises a number of practical issues for Christians. Though it is one of the assets we are given by God to steward, Christians are warned that money can become an idol, competing with God (Lk. 16:12–13). The love of money (not money itself, as is often misquoted) is the root of all evils (1 Tim. 6:10; *cf*. Mk. 4:19). Money is not to be hoarded (Mt. 6:19–21; Lk. 12:16–21). We are to pay our taxes willingly (Mk. 12:13–17), and giving* is to be a major part of our stewardship* of money (1 Cor. 16:2; 2 Cor. 8:7; Heb. 13:16) based on tithing as a minimum (Mal. 3:10). The scriptural principles which apply to giving and the responsible stewardship of money are helpfully discussed by Simon Webley (1932–) in *Money Matters* (Leicester, 1978) alongside the questions as to whether Christians should save, borrow, lend, invest or gamble. The changes in the form of money which have occurred this century through the banking* system and the wider availability of credit and credit cards raise some practical ethical issues which Christians should address. The ease with which credit is now available means that it is possible for large numbers of individuals to get into serious debt, even apart from those who have over-extended themselves on mortgages (see A. Hartropp and R. McCloughry, *Debt*). Webley suggests that biblical teaching on debt can best be summarized by 'do without the thing or services that cannot be afforded' (*Money Matters*, p. 39). Crippling debt leads to poverty,* and biblical teaching on poverty suggests that institutions should try to avoid people being locked into this state. Allowing credit too easily therefore goes against scriptural principles. Credit cards raise other moral issues, since they involve a cost to the seller which will no doubt be passed on in higher prices for everyone, the poor included, and not just those who use the cards. Money can be used to make more money without engaging in any work, *e.g.* through buying stocks and shares or other financial assets. These practices also raise moral issues for Christians which require careful thinking about, since it is possible to argue that some such practices are little different from gambling.*

Bibliography

M. Friedman, 'The Quantity Theory of Money: A Restatement', in M. Friedman (ed.), *Studies in the Quantity Theory of Money* (Chicago, 1956); A. Hartropp and R. McCloughry, *Debt* (Bramcote, Nottingham, 1990); D. Hay, *Economics Today* (Leicester, 1989); A. Storkey, *Transforming Economics: A Christian Way to Employment* (London, 1986).

S.D.

MONISM. The activity of metaphysics aims to produce a grand theory of reality. One of the basic issues such a theory must address is whether the universe is made up of one substance (*e.g.* matter) or more than one (*e.g.* mind and matter). The term 'monism' was coined by philosopher Christian Wolff (1679–1754) from the Gk. word *monos* meaning 'single'. Any theory which suggests that the universe is made up of only one substance (mind) or one kind of substance (minds) is an example of monism. The former is sometimes called substantival monism, and the latter, attributive monism. Monism as a metaphysical theory contrasts with dualism* (two substances or kinds of substance make up reality) and pluralism (more than two substances or two kinds of substance make up reality).

Monism has had a long history both in Western and Eastern thought. Parmenides of Elea (b. *c*. 510 BC) believed that reality was one, static and indivisible. Sankara (d. 820 AD), one of the greatest Hindu thinkers, established the doctrine of *advaita* ('no twoness'). Monism, however, has little appeal for Christian thinkers. The Bible teaches there is a radical difference between the creator and the creation* (Gn. 1). Monism appears to blur this basic distinction. The Christian concepts of creation (*creatio ex nihilo*) and incarnation (the creator become creature) make much more sense against the backdrop of some kind of dualism. Indeed, the dualism of creator and creature is fundamental both to the Scriptures and the classic Christian creeds based on Scripture (*e.g.* the Nicene Creed). This scriptural dualism is a contingent one. As Samuel Taylor Coleridge (1772–1834) pointed out: the world minus God is zero, but God minus the world is still God undiminished. In philosophical terms the God of the Bible is externally related to his creatures. They, however, are internally related to him.

Monism shows itself at a popular level in Westernized versions of Eastern thought which suggests that reality is one or that human beings are manifestations of God or God substance. Not only do such views make the

Christian doctrines of creation and incarnation unintelligible, they also in some versions (especially substantival ones) threaten the very individuality of the person holding to the theory. Monism is tidy, but at the cost of personal reality. The Christian universe is personal. Without ontological distinctions it is hard to account for personal identity which arises out of reciprocation. The Christian doctrine of the Trinity also makes monist thinking unacceptable to the Christian. Unity and diversity are grounded on the reality of the triune God, who in his own nature is the resolution of the one and the many.

Bibliography

D. W. Hamlyn, *Metaphysics* (Cambridge, 1984); A. F. Holmes, *Contours of a World View* (Grand Rapids, 1983).

G.A.C.

MONOPOLIES. In common parlance, a monopoly is a single seller of a particular product or service. This definition is of limited use because it begs the question of how a product is defined, *e.g.* are cola drinks all soft drinks, all non-alcoholic beverages, or some other subset of potables? In economic analysis and public policy discussion, reference commonly is made to monopoly power (or its synonym, market power), which is the ability of a firm to control price and exclude rivals.

A seller facing many rivals in a market, or a seller unable to prevent the entry of new rivals or the expansion of existing rivals, would have no significant monopoly power. Most goods and services have some substitutes, so monopoly power is a matter of degree.

Monopoly power may be exercised collectively by more than one firm in a market. A cartel* is a group of rivals who collusively restrict output and collectively decide upon the terms of trade with their customers. An effective cartel, then, exercises some degree of monopoly power.

Objections to monopoly include: the monopolist's ability to restrict output in order to raise price, preventing some consumers from being able to make purchases even though they are willing to pay the full resource cost of the good or service; the lack of initiative that may come from a protected market position; and the profits a monopoly may earn that may unfairly enrich some people (owners, managers or workers) associated with the firm. Many cartels have been guilty of the sin of

bearing false witness, since members often purport to be competing for buyers' favour when, unbeknown to their customers, they are conspiring with one another to avoid competition.

Governments in the West have been ambivalent toward monopolies: in some cases promoting them, through exclusive grants and privileges; in some cases regulating them, through public utility commissions; and in some cases seeking to deter or undo them, through anti-trust and trade regulation laws. Another source of ambivalence is the hypothesis, associated with Joseph Schumpeter (1883–1950), that monopoly is the catalyst that motivates innovation and economic progress.

See also: ECONOMIC ETHICS. [17]

Bibliography

W. Adams and H. Gray, *Monopoly in America* (New York, 1955); F. M. Scherer and D. Ross, *Industrial Market Structure and Economic Performance* (Boston, 1990).

K.G.E.

MOORE, G. E., see HISTORY OF CHRISTIAN ETHICS. [6]

MORAL AGENCY is the power or ability to perform actions for which the agent is morally accountable. It is to be distinguished from natural processes, such as the processes of mental and physical decay and death, which may also have important moral consequences but for which it makes no sense to hold anyone morally accountable. Bacteria may be causally responsible for a death without being the moral agents of death. The assertion of moral agency in the case of human beings is one important way in which humankind's distinctness from physical nature is claimed. Moral agency is thus denied or severely attenuated by some kinds of determinism (see Freewill and Determinism*) as well as by fatalists.

If more is required for moral agency than mere causal agency, mere physical power, what more? Answers that have been offered to this question diverge widely. It is possible to distinguish at least four different kinds of answer.

1. Libertarians claim that moral agency is to be found only where agents have the power to act in a self-caused or uncaused manner. For it

is only under these conditions that sense can be made of the claim that the agent could have done differently than he or she in fact did. For the libertarian, a moral agent could have done differently had he or she chosen to do so, and if he or she *could* have chosen. Difficulties have been experienced in giving an account of such agency which satisfactorily distinguishes it from randomness or whimsicality.

2. A second kind of answer holds that moral agency consists in uncompelled choice* in accordance with a person's prevailing reasons and / or desires. A person is a moral agent when he or she does what he or she wants to do. Such a view is compatible with at least some versions of determinism, but it remains a matter of controversy whether it is sufficiently strong to support normal intuitions about responsibility.* There are sometimes difficulties in distinguishing causation from compulsion. Some determinists construe moral agency not in terms of liability for what has been done but as capacity for reform.

3. Moral agency is closely allied to the idea of a person, and some hold that personhood is itself a moral category. So while reason* and choice might be necessary for moral agency, and even necessary and sufficient for minimal moral agency, full moral agency is achieved only when an agent is delivered from the prevailing influences of sensual desire or selfish ambition and acts in accordance with true reason, or the will of God, when he or she acts so as to fulfil his or her true nature.

4. Finally, since in the view of some a person can be such only in a community of persons, moral agency is said to be possible only in relation with other people. For it is only in such circumstances that self-knowledge and self-identity are capable of development, and reciprocal relations of love and mutual dependence made possible. Some have used the divine Trinity as a model for the idea of persons in relation (see Humanity④).

The scriptural account of moral agency appears to contain both metaphysical and moral strands to it. At the metaphysical level any account of moral agency has to be consistent with God's sovereignty over his creation; but Scripture asserts that full freedom,* and also moral agency, consists in the service of Christ.

Despite widely differing accounts of moral agency it is agreed that the capacity for moral agency matures through human childhood (see Human Development*) and may be diminished in old age. Yet the recognition of such general conditions for moral agency ought not to be confused with its legal conditions. The fact that the law (see Law, Civil and Criminal*) recognizes a sharp distinction between minority and adulthood need carry no metaphysical implications any more than the fact that the law attributes moral agency to firms and clubs.

Who are, or who are capable of becoming, moral agents in the metaphysical sense? In Christian thought, not only human beings but also angels good and bad. Is God a moral agent? In a sense he is the supreme moral agent in that his actions are free and wholly good. He is not acted upon but is independent of all contingency. Yet in so far as moral agency carries with it the idea of moral assessment, it may be doubted whether God's actions are susceptible of such evaluation. For while he can be praised he cannot be blamed. And while in the incarnation (see Jesus*) God the Son becomes part of the human community, this is not at the expense of his creatorhood.

Bibliography
A. J. P. Kenny, *Freewill and Responsibility* (London, 1978); J. M. Fischer (ed.), *Moral Responsibility* (Ithaca, NY, and London, 1986).

P.H.

MORAL BEHAVIOUR, PSYCHO-LOGY OF.
The moral behaviour of people may be shaped by their own moral character which itself is affected by their genetic make-up, by their early learning experiences, by the life choices they make and by the ideals towards which they strive. It may be shaped also by the social context in which their behaviour is set, and by the nature of their relationships with significant other people in their lives.

Various psychological theories have been advanced to account for the development and maintenance of a person's capacity to be a moral being and to behave in a moral way.

Social influence

The various theoretical perspectives under this heading all assume that a person's experience and behaviour is strongly influenced by other people. Some social psychologists have used the analogy of a theatre to clarify 'social roles', 'social norms' and 'reference groups'. 'Social roles' describe the patterns of behaviour which are expected of people in particular positions in the social structure, *i.e.* the parts they play. 'Social norms' are the scripts which society writes for such parts. The 'reference groups' are the audiences to whom the actors play, from whom they value some response. Moral behaviour in an individual can then be understood in terms of conformity to the expectancies of others in that individual's group.

While it seems clear that social influence plays a significant part in moral behaviour, it cannot account adequately for the processes of independent moral judgment, adherence to conscience,* and rejection of social norms which are evident in some people. Nor does it account for the internal factors in a person's moral character.

Psychoanalytic theory

Sigmund Freud's* personality theory proposes the existence of the 'super-ego', a refinement of the 'ego' that includes a sort of internalized, critical, parental voice which then comes into conflict with the instinctive sexual and aggressive desires of the 'id'. The super-ego, like the traditional scrupulous conscience, acts as both a censor and a source of guilt,* both of which can motivate moral behaviour. Moral character then develops in a person as a defence against internal psychic conflict. Largely rejected in their original form by contemporary psychologists, Freudian concepts lie behind the much-used developmental approach of Erik Erikson,* and have been further developed in the humanistic approach to ethics in writers such as Erich Fromm.*

Behaviourism

Human personality and behaviour are explained by behaviourists largely in terms of conditioned reflexes, coupled with a system of rewards and punishments. 'Operant conditioning' describes the process whereby, after some trial and error, human beings come to discover the sorts of behaviour which lead to positive rewards for that person. Radical behaviourists like B. F. Skinner* do not work with 'moral' concepts such as value, choice and purpose. The social context in which all human behaviour is learned response (contingency-determined as opposed to rule-determined) is sufficient to explain 'moral' behaviour. Many critics reject such hard-line determinism as ignoring some of the irreducible features of human life (mind, consciousness, choice, freedom) and as failing to see that not only are human beings shaped by their environments,

but they can effect change in their environment themselves.

Cognitive development

Cognitive psychologists understand the human person as an originator of moral ideas. Jean Piaget's* theory suggests that children's cognitive capacities develop through various identifiable stages, and that doing and knowing belong together. Though subject to recent criticism, Piaget's study has been the basis for much subsequent work, not least Ronald Goldman's 1960s studies on religious education (*e.g. Readiness for Religion*, London, ²1969), and Lawrence Kohlberg's theory of moral development* (*e.g.* 'Moral stages and moralization', in T. Lickona, ed., *Moral Development and Behaviour*, New York, 1976, pp. 31–53). Kohlberg described three levels (of two stages each) of moral development in children: the 'pre-moral' (a prudential morality of keeping out of trouble); the 'conventional' (in which moral imperatives are followed out of obedience to external authority); and the 'principled' (in which a person chooses the principles which govern his or her choices). Kohlberg's approach has been criticized on philosophical grounds (that his understanding of morality is wrongly restricted to a concern with justice), on psychological grounds (that the capacity to organize information cognitively is not, as he believed, sufficient for moral maturity) and methodologically (that morality is more than responding to moral dilemmas, as Kohlberg's research assumed: it is also about character [see ⑩]). Kohlberg's work in an adapted form has been used in James Fowler's (1940–) studies of faith development,* *Stages of Faith*.

What is needed is a psychological interpretation of moral character which does justice both to the complexities of a person's social context and inner experience, and also recognizes that morality is about the ongoing life story to which a person's choices and behaviour contribute.

See also: FREE WILL AND DETERMINISM; HUMAN DEVELOPMENT.

Bibliography

C. Dykstra, *Vision and Character* (New York, 1980); C. Dykstra and S. Parks (eds.), *Faith Development and Fowler* (Birmingham, AL, 1986); J. C. Flugel, *Man, Morals and Society* (London, 1945); J. W. Fowler, *Stages of Faith* (San Francisco, 1981); M. Jacobs, *Towards the Fullness of Christ: Pastoral Care and Christian Maturity* (London, 1988); J. Piaget, *The Moral Judgement of the Child* (ET, London, 1932; Harmondsworth, 1977); D. Wright, *The Psychology of Moral Behaviour* (Harmondsworth, 1971).

D.J.A.

MORAL DEVELOPMENT

MORAL DEVELOPMENT is a technical term denoting an approach to moral reasoning, particularly associated with the American psychologist Lawrence Kohlberg (1927–87). Observing that most moral decisions are made when people are faced with moral dilemmas, Kohlberg set out to determine how such decisions are made. His work began in the 1950s by means of a series of longitudinal studies (*i.e.* studies of individuals over a period of time), designed to discover how the process of moral reasoning unfolds.

Taking the work of Jean Piaget* as his paradigm, Kohlberg constructed a model which falls within the structuralist-developmentalist approach to human maturation.

General features of Kohlberg's model

1. Moral development is understood to be a process which possesses a rational core. Judgment and action are not just the outcomes of feelings and values. In any moral dilemma, they involve analysis, interpretation, selection of relevant data, evaluation and choice. It is this which marks out the distinctive nature of morality as opposed to instinctive reaction.

2. It follows that, if moral reasoning lies at the heart of moral development, the reasoning process itself must be analysed. It is here that Kohlberg's debt to Piaget becomes most evident. Directly adapting Piaget's cognitive stage theory, Kohlberg posited a model in which individuals move through clearly definable stages of moral development, shaped by their movement through stages of cognitive development. Morality and reasoning are thus inextricably intertwined.

3. Each stage has it own structural features. These are determined by the interaction between the individual, his or her environment and the society in which he or she is set. Moreover, the features of each stage result in what Piaget calls 'formalized operations', by which individuals act to make moral decisions in the external world according to their stage of development.

4. The stages are: a. *hierarchical*, each stage building on the operations contained within previous stages; b. *sequential*, each following on logically from the previous one; c. *invariant*, each being located within a specified order so that stages cannot be jumped over or moved about; and d. *universal*, the sequence as a whole being the same across cultures. This last point especially has been the subject of controversy.

Kohlberg's six stages

The model of moral development proposed by Kohlberg follows six stages, grouped on three levels. Ideally, the individual progresses through all stages as he or she moves from very concrete to more abstract reasoning. However, in his later work, Kohlberg conceded that the model constitutes an ideal: in reality, very few people arrive at stage six.

1. The preconventional level. At this level, the individual (usually the young child) responds to culturally-given labels of good / bad, right / wrong, but evaluates these by reference to the consequences they produce: pleasure / pain, punishment / reward.

Stage 1: Right and wrong are defined by whether an action brings punishment. Rightness is a matter of avoiding punishment.

Stage 2: The right action is that which brings reward. Morality is understood instrumentally, as that which satisfies one's needs.

2. The conventional level. Here the essence of morality is loyalty to group expectations. Right and wrong are framed by reference to the conventions of whatever group is apposite (*e.g.* family, school, nation).

Stage 3: The individual conforms to the standards of others for fear of their disapproval. Right actions are those which are approved by others, and wrong actions are disapproved of. Intentions become important for the first time. Kohlberg calls this the 'Good Boy-Nice Girl' stage.

Stage 4: Morality is orientation towards authority.* Fixed rules and social order are regarded as crucial moral determinants. Rightness is concerned with doing one's duty towards authority for its own sake.

3. The postconventional, autonomous or principled level. At this level, the individual defines morality increasingly in terms of its inherent validity, rather than by reference to external norms or groups, or his or her identification with them.

Stage 5: Right actions are those which conform to rules agreed by some kind of social contract. Individual values and priorities are recognized as relativistic (see Relativism*), hence the need for social agreement. Rules can be changed by consent, but individuals may not break them unilaterally with impunity. Kohlberg sees the American Constitution as the embodiment of this type of morality.

Stage 6: Right and wrong are defined by the individual conscience* acting upon freely, self-chosen values and principles. These will appeal to logical comprehensiveness, consistency and universalizability. The central principles include justice, equality of human rights and respect for persons.

Comment

Kohlberg makes large claims for his model, not least that it is universally applicable. By this he means that although the content of morality will vary from culture to culture, the structures and process of development do not. This is perhaps the most contested of his claims, even though Kohlberg insisted that his research was based on empirical data from a cross-section of cultures and classes.

Four comments are relevant. 1. If universally true, it is remarkable that Kohlberg's model should happen to resemble late 20th-century Western social development and philosophy. It is as if all cultures ought to be viewed as latently Western in their structure of moral reasoning. 2. Since the most advanced stages (five and six) are clearly post-Enlightenment* in their concepts and values, what evaluation can be made of earlier societies? 3. From a theological point of view, the model sees morality as a purely human construct. All the major theistic religions, however, would require much greater consideration of the place of divinely-revealed ethics and morality derived from theological reflection. 4. As Carol Gilligan (1936–) has pointed out, in *In a Different Voice,* Kohlberg's methods and conclusions are essentially masculine, and fail to take account of evidence which might suggest a different model of psychological development for women. Gilligan's analysis itself has not passed without criticism, but needs to be taken seriously since it reinforces the conclusion that Kohlberg's work is very much a product of his own intellectual milieu and culture.

These considerations would suggest that, although useful as one model of the process of human moral development, Kohlberg's theory should not be taken as an inflexible guide to moral development, and must be seen as itself culture-relative.

See also: HUMAN DEVELOPMENT.

Bibliography
J. W. Fowler, *Stages of Faith* (San Francisco, 1981), parts 2 and 3; C. Gilligan, *In a Different Voice* (Cambridge, MA, and London, 1982); L. Kohlberg, *Collected Papers on Moral Development and Moral Education* (Cambridge, MA, 1973).

F.W.B.

MORALITY, see CHRISTIAN MORAL REASONING. [18]

MORAL LAW, see CHRISTIAN MORAL REASONING; [18] DECALOGUE; LAW; LAW AND GOSPEL.

MORAL ORDER, see CHRISTIAN MORAL REASONING. [18]

MORAL REALISM, see REALISM.

MORAL REARMAMENT originated through Frank Buchman (1878–1961), an America Lutheran. Converted at Keswick* in 1908, he visited Oxford and Cambridge universities in 1921, bringing his message of spiritual renewal to small groups of students. During a visit of a team of Rhodes and other scholars which he led to South Africa in 1928, the *Cape Times* labelled his movement 'the Oxford Group', but when Buchman launched his world programme of moral rearmament in Washington, DC, in 1938 it became known as Moral Rearmament (MRA).

At the heart of Buchman's personal philosophy was the conviction that modern man's technological advances needed to be matched by similar progress in character and spiritual growth. Four absolutes came to be emphasized: absolute purity, unselfishness, honesty and love. These, though drawn from the Christian tradition, could readily be fitted into other religious contexts such as Hinduism. Thus an MRA pamphlet described the movement as 'an expeditionary force from all faiths and races engaged in a race with time to modernize the character and purpose of man' (*What is MRA?*).

During the Second World War, MRA in the US emphasized patriotism* in a morale-building exercise and afterwards, in the Cold

War period, it waged a strong campaign against communism.* Also in this later period Buchman directed his message to highly-placed politicians and other people of influence in society, rather than to the masses. He was decorated by eight governments, all of them in the Western bloc, for services rendered to their countries by MRA.

On Buchman's death leadership passed to Peter Howard (1908–65), and MRA is now directed from the USA but with strong regional centres in Caux in Switzerland, in Japan and other countries.

MRA can be described as a movement which emphasizes the ethical standards of Christianity more or less detached (according to religious context) from the person and work of Christ. Its appeal has been, and continues to be, largely to people who desire some kind of religious experience without undue concern for Christian doctrine.

Bibliography

K. D. Belden, *Reflections on MRA* (London, 1983); F. Buchman, *Remaking the World* (New York, 1949); A. W. Gordon, *Peter Howard: Life and Letters* (London, 1969).

D.P.K.

MORALS, LEGAL ENFORCEMENT OF, see Devlin–Hart Debate; Law, Uses of.

MORAL THEOLOGY, see Anglican Moral Theology; God; ☐ Roman Catholic Moral Theology.

MORTGAGES. The mortgage is one of the oldest money-lending arrangements, and as the *hypothēkē* was common in the Gk. world of the 1st century. It is a form of debt* which, except in the case of failure to keep up payments, transfers the rights to the property to the person taking out the mortgage loan. The word itself is derived from Old Fr. (*mort*, dead; and *gage*, pledge). The most common use of the mortgage today is to purchase a house.

For the individual taking out a mortgage, it is important to realize that any loan taken with a pledge implies risk (Dt. 24:11). This is why advertisements for mortgage-lending should carry a 'wealth warning', to the effect that failure to keep up payments may result in the loss of the house. The ability to keep up payments must be taken into account when taking out the loan, and a safe multiple is twice annual earnings before tax.

Fluctuations in interest* rates will affect monthly payments, and when loans are taken out at a time when interest rates are low, thought should be given to the ability to meet these payments if the rate were to move up three or four percentage points.

The repayment mortgage, the most common form, allows the borrower to pay off both the principle and the interest over an agreed number of years. The longer the term, the lower the monthly payment, but more is paid in interest.

Another common type of mortgage is an endowment mortgage, where a life insurance policy is taken out. When the policy matures, it should cover the original capital cost of the house and only interest is paid to the lender. Most reputable insurance companies have a good record of not only covering the purchase cost but also earning bonus payments as well.

There is also a product called an investment-linked mortgage, but as this is geared to stock-market performance, it has a higher element of risk.

Low-start and low-cost mortgages may seem attractive, but in reality they build up larger payments for future years and depend on incomes increasing. Similarly, interest-only loans depend on the borrower having some other source of savings to meet the original capital cost payment when the term of the loan ends.

It is not for nothing that Scripture constantly warns against the dangers of debt. Paul writes in Rom. 13:8 that Christians should 'let no debt remain outstanding'. That implies that debt for essentials like a home is permissible, but that the debt should be within our means to repay.

The church in the Middle Ages banned lending at interest, and even John Calvin* considered that any interest rate charged should be equitable and not usurious, thus following the OT principle (Lv. 25:36; Ps. 15:1–5). However, the reality of modern life is that people are generally no longer able to save enough to build and buy their own house outright. For the majority the mortgage is a safe and simple way of obtaining a home so that they can obey the scriptural injunction to provide for their families. Churches should also exercise restraint in taking out large mortgages for ambitious building projects and leaving future generations with massive debt.

D.W.P.

MORTIFICATION.

M ORTIFICATION. The term 'mortification' arose in ascetic theology (see Asceticism*) and developed largely in service of the hermetic and the monastic movements in the church. For this reason the term, though by no means all of the spiritual disciplines covered by the term, may be unfamiliar to many contemporary Christians.

Mortification (Lat. *mortificare*) lit. means 'to put to death', and came into Christian usage from the Latin Vulgate translation of Paul's injunction to 'put to death whatever belongs to your earthly nature' (Col. 3:5). Here the apostle is reiterating the words of Christ: 'If anyone would come after me, he must deny himself and take up his cross daily and follow me' (Lk. 9:23). The Christian life is inseparable from this mortification of sin which the apostle boldly expresses as being 'crucified with Christ' (Gal. 2:20; *cf.* 5:24). However, mortification is not to be regarded as a goal of the Christian life but only as a practice made necessary in view of 'the flesh'. Living in obedience to Christ requires mortification of the inevitable attachment of any Christian in any age to those things, persons, habits or addictions of everyday life that prevent such obedience. Mortification of sin, by whatever means, has as its aim a sustained and systematic 'dying to' the pursuit of any pleasures, powers or possessions incompatible with love for God and delight in loving service for his sake. Thus, mortification of sin may be readily understood as every Christian's first responsibility upon experiencing the Holy One. All the great saints would agree with Simone Weil (1903–43) when she says that to know God is to know that the selfish aspirations of the soul are condemned not just to suffering but to death (*Gravity and Grace*, ET, London and New York, 1952).

The goals envisioned, and the means used, in following Paul's injunction to 'put to death whatever belongs to your earthly nature', have differed considerably in the history of Christianity. While there is clear support in the teachings and practice of Jesus and the apostles for a variety of spiritual disciplines (see Disciplines, Spiritual;* *e.g.* voluntary solitude and silence, Lk. 5:16; fasting,* Mt. 6:16–18; Lk. 4:2; chastity,* 1 Cor. 7:5; 1 Thes. 4:4), there is no support for the more extreme ascetic practices (*e.g.* not speaking a word for years, living in chains, stigmatization and flagellation). From the 12th century onwards, the variety, extent and severity of such mortifications of the body increased. A series of reform movements began from about the 9th century, but the purpose of ascetic practices seemed always to degenerate from spiritual disciplines necessary for breaking the power of attachments to lesser goods than Christ, to asceticism for its own sake.

Knowledge of these excesses in part explains why contemporary Christians tend to ignore or dismiss all practices that have as their aim to mortify our selfish tendencies. But only in part, for there are at least two other factors that together reinforce this neglect: 1. the Protestant theological principle of justification* by faith* alone, by definition, excludes any practices that have as their aim the meriting of forgiveness* through self-denial* and suffering;* and 2. while the Reformers taught that discipline* and self-denial should qualify every action of the believer, most of their heirs have tended in practice to ignore all mortifying disciplines as inessential to maturing in the new life in Christ. The tendency has been to think that hearing the Scriptures rightly interpreted and the sacraments faithfully administered was all that was essential to the formation of Christian character. The protest against ascetic practices as meriting salvation is fully justified by the clear teaching of Jesus and his apostles, but the ignoring of spiritual disciplines like solitude and meditative prayer,* fasting and frugality, chastity and self-denial is not. And even where the more punitive sorts of mortification of the body, like flagellation, were not intended to merit salvation but to demonstrate devotion, they are properly rejected as lacking scriptural warrant and as encouraging a contempt for the body and a self-obsessed pride in strenuous exertion for its own sake.

Recognition of the theological and moral errors associated with the mortification of sin in the history of the church invites a serious refocusing of the aim, and a rethinking of the means, appropriate to the injunction to 'put to death' selfish desires. It is of first importance, then, to emphasize that the goal of mortification of sin is neither the chastisement of the body nor the denial of all its pleasures* for their own sake. Nor does it require social separation from engagement in morally licit relationships, offices or activities in any culture. Rather, it has centrally to do with the voluntary renunciation of attachments to any object or condition that prevents growing identification with Christ (his vision, virtues and vitality) and faithful service for his kingdom (see Kingdom of God*). And since justification by faith does not by itself result in the extinguishing of all subsequent selfish desires and actions in the life of any believer, disciplines (like those mentioned earlier) that have this as their goal are required. Thus mortification should be regarded as a necessary ingredient in the Pauline injunction 'to work out your salvation with fear and trembling', while at each moment knowing that 'it is God who works in you to will and to act according to his good pleasure' (Phil. 2:12–13). The apostle Paul, and Augustine* later, particularly recognized that bodily appetites, covetous desires and anxiousness require habitual discipline if the believer is to attain whole-hearted love for God and others.

Christians, early and late, have too readily accepted the unbiblical notion that all that really matters in living the Christian life is the quality of the internal conscious states (feelings, ideas, beliefs and motives) that they have towards God. The consequence is 'a headful of vital truths about God and a body unable to fend off sin' (Dallas Willard, *The Spirit of the Disciplines*, San Francisco, 1988, p. 152). Mortification of sin requires not just discernment of the habitual ways in which selfish desires manifest themselves, but also continuous practice of those spiritual disciplines that do deaden them and free the soul to delight in God and his kingdom.

See also: SPIRITUAL DIRECTION; SPIRITUALITY.

M.A.R.

MOTHER–FOETAL DISTRESS SYNDROME, see CLINICAL THEOLOGY; LAKE, FRANK.

MOTHERING, see PARENTHOOD, PARENTING.

MOTIVE, MOTIVATION. Some of the most difficult theoretical and practical issues in ethics, Christian or non-Christian, centre on trying to understand the psychological and moral status of human motivation and the specific motives alleged to occasion actions or kinds of actions. Discussions of the nature of motivation have been part of: 1. the attempt of modern psychology to map systematically the causes of human behaviour; 2. theological and philosophical debates about human free will and divine or natural (hard) determinism; and 3. the claims of psychological and ethical egoism in ethics that all actions either are, or ought to be, motivated solely by self-interest. For example, an advocate of psychological egoism* may argue that the sole motivation for someone who paid back a debt was not a desire to pay a promised obligation but rather a self-interested desire not to be thought unjust for not paying the debt. This example also demonstrates how the question of motivation leads to, and may easily be confused with, the larger issue of justification. Motivation is what moves a person to act; justification is what makes the act morally right (see Justification, Moral*). If we assume (contrary to the dubious theses of psychological or ethical egoism) that morality essentially includes, at a minimum, respect for the needs and interests of other people, then the question of motivation in ethics might be put like this: Are there *moral* motives distinct from merely personal interests?

In the history of the church, both Scripture and rational moral reflection have emphasized distinct moral motives other than self-interest without concluding that every self-interested motive is a selfish motive. The Pauline injunction that each Christian should 'look not only to your own interests, but also to the interests of others' is typical (Phil. 2:4). It is important to note that Scripture nowhere supports pure altruism,* *i.e.* the view that the motivation for *every* action must be the desire to put the interests of others ahead of our own. The great commandment affirms the importance of a proper self-love: 'Love your neighbour as yourself' (Mt. 19:19; Gal. 5:14; Jas. 2:8). But since the needs and sufferings of others are often so much greater than our own, genuine love manifests itself as compassion.* The Gospels describe Jesus as 'moved with compassion' (*splanchnizomai*, Mt. 9:36; 14:14; 15:32; 20:34; Lk. 7:13), and it is the overriding motivation of the Samaritan and of the father in the two great parables of Jesus (Lk. 10:25–37; 15:11–32). Furthermore, just as Christian ethics rejects pure altruism as inhuman, so it rejects the claim of Immanuel Kant* that a morally good action requires a perfectly pure or disinterested motive (*Groundwork of the Metaphysics of Morals*, 1785; ET, London, 1948, pp. 8–13). In the Sermon on the Mount,* Jesus does not rule out secondary motives, like the desire for rewards, as necessarily incompatible with the primary motive of hungering and thirsting after righteousness (Mt. 5:3–11; 6:33). And even if someone were to argue, as did Augustine* and Thomas Aquinas* later on, that fellowship with God and with one another in God in the new heaven and earth is indistinguishable from the reward sought, nevertheless this principal motive is not incompatible with lesser motives like the desire to be free from guilt or to have peace of mind so long as it remains the principal motive (*The City of God*, ET, Harmondsworth, 1972, ch. 19; *STh* 1a2ae 18–19). But the noblest motive for Christians is gratitude or thanksgiving (*eucharistia*) for the reality of the grace (*charis*) of God in forgiving their sin through the atoning death of Christ (2 Cor. 9:10–15; Col. 2:6–7; 4:2; 1 Thes. 5:18).

The preceding general reflections on motives and motivation in Christian ethics invite further refinement by way of understanding important distinctions between 1. motives and desires; 2. motives and motivation; and 3. motives and consequences.

1. Desires may, but motives do not, exist apart from actual or intended actions. This is so because while every motive is a desire that moves a person to act, not all desires are motives. A person may desire the presence of a friend without envisaging or intending any action, but he or she cannot have any motive with respect to his or her friend without envisaging or intending some act.

2. There are reasons for thinking that the term 'motive' has a more limited use than the term 'motivation'. a. We typically find ourselves using the term 'motive' in close connection with any action done for morally dubious or unacceptable reasons. Thus, we might ask what A's motive was in attempting to corner the silver market or what B's motive was for murdering C. In the former case we may speak of an 'ulterior motive' and in the latter of a 'vengeful motive'. b. We are not typically concerned about the motive for unimportant actions like picking up a dropped button. Our use of 'motivation' and discussions of motivation as the question of how *any* desire (important or unimportant) moves a person to an action (moral or non-moral, good or bad) is not so confined.

3. Attention to motives and motivation arises when we find it necessary to distinguish the good or bad consequences of an action from the intention of the person responsible for the action. So a good motive (*e.g.* generosity) may have bad consequences (engendered envy), or a bad motive (*e.g.* vengeful plotting) good consequences (the plot fails).

Finally, in Christian ethics we are interested in motives and motivation not only as an important aspect of our understanding and evaluation of right and wrong *actions* but also of good or bad *character*. Important virtues* like justice, compassion and generosity should function as habitual moral motives. Just, compassionate or generous people always want to do just, compassionate or generous acts; they take pleasure in them when they succeed and are pained when they fail.

M.A.R.

MOURNING, see BEREAVEMENT; GRIEF.

MOWRER, O. HOBART (1907–82), a former president of the American Psychological Association, was representative of the second generation of behavioural psychologists who succeeded the 'founding fathers' of behaviourism,* theorists like Ivan Pavlov (1849–1936), John B. Watson (1878–1958) and B. F. Skinner.* This second wave, sometimes described as neo-behaviourism, brought a wider vision to the reductionist* views of the early behaviourists, acknowledging a greater complexity in human response to environmental stimuli.

During the late 1930s and 40s, Mowrer established a number of important links between laboratory research and clinical practice, including his work on a machine to help break the habit of bed-wetting and his two-factor learning theory, combining Pavlov's classical conditioning and Skinnerian instrumental conditioning. This latter theorizing led to practical insights into the avoidance response, and consequent reduction of anxiety,* in many people with neurotic disorders.

From the late 1940s and through the 50s, Mowrer, influenced by the concerns of Anton Boisen* at the assimilation of psychoanalytic assumptions by the pastoral counselling movement (see Pastoral Care, Counselling and Psychotherapy[12]), expressed strong anti-Freudian views which were widely disseminated in *The Crisis in Psychiatry and Religion* (1961). In this work, Mowrer, describing himself as an 'active churchman' (p. 110), sought to reverse Freud's* 'impulse theory', that anxiety arises out of giving way to a severe super-ego and is neurotic, by his 'guilt theory', that anxiety is the result of suppressing the voice of conscience and is culpable.

In the 1960s and 70s, Mowrer further

developed the perspective that the recovery of psychological health is closely allied to responsible and moral living. A distinctive extension to this view is found in his 'integrity groups', a form of group therapy* in which new entrants are interviewed by existing members who, in turn, model a high level of openness in sharing stories and difficulties. The groups, comprising eight to ten people, may be part of a wider community, and function according to three cardinal rules: 1. honesty over temptations and unkept promises; 2. individual commitment to counselling and relationship contracts;* and 3. a concern for one another in encouraging responsible living.

Mowrer's questioning of the medical model, with its emphasis on sickness ('mental illness'), and his provision of a moral model, which acknowledges sin and guilt,* has attracted a number of conservative Christians in the field of counselling, notably Jay Adams (1929–) and John W. Drakeford (1914–), whose 'integrity therapy' modified Mowrer's basic principles of group-work and introduced them into the life of the church.

Bibliography

The Crisis in Psychiatry and Religion (Princeton, NJ, 1961); *Learning Theory and Behaviour* (New York, 1960).

J. W. Drakeford, *Integrity Therapy* (Nashville, TN, 1967); O. H. Mowrer *et al.*, *Integrity Groups: The Loss and Recovery of Community* (Urbana, IL, 1975).

R.F.H.

MULTICULTURAL EDUCATION

is an imprecise term used to describe a range of educational responses to post-war increases in pluralism.* Although Britain and the US have always been to some degree multicultural and multiracial, immigration from African, Asian, Latin American and other countries in post-war years changed the multiracial nature of Britain and the US, particularly the large cities (though in the US there was already a considerable black minority, subject to much discrimination and frequent oppression). In the case of Britain, immigrants came not as 'guest' or 'migrant' workers but as British citizens, sometimes escaping from poverty or persecution. In the US, there was also a growing awareness that ethnic cultures long established in the country (*e.g.* the African-American culture) were suffering wrongful discrimination.

Initial educational responses sought to assimilate immigrant children into mainstream culture,* mainly through developing skills in the Eng. language. But social concerns also motivated some responses, including early experiments with 'bussing' children between schools in order to keep ratios of white and black pupils to acceptable sizes.

Multicultural education developed as a more creative and integrationist response to pluralism. In its early stages, the focus was on celebrating the culture of minority children in order to bolster their self-esteem and hopefully their achievement (a view strongly challenged by the black sociologist Maureen Stone). Many multiracial schools developed some form of multicultural education for *all* their pupils, seeking to promote mutual understanding and tolerance.* A later stage, strongly advocated by the Swann Report (1985), set up by the UK Department of Education and Science (DES), argued that multicultural ideals should permeate the school curriculum of pupils in all British schools. In the US, multicultural education also became an important concern in the 1980s, particularly at the university level.

Theories of multicultural education are usually underpinned by concepts of justice (*e.g.* J. Lynch, *Prejudice Reduction and the Schools*), equal opportunities (*e.g.* J. Rex, in G. K. Verma, ed., *Education for All*), and social harmony (*e.g.* see Swann Report). Practical developments have focused on both the specific needs of ethnic-minority pupils and the need for all pupils growing up in a plural society to have some understanding of other cultures and to develop skills in responding to pluralism. Of particular concern has been the apparent underachievement of children from Afro-Caribbean families. The interim report of the DES's Rampton Commission (1981) argued that multicultural education would help to combat the factors which contribute to such underachievement.

The debate about educational responses to pluralism has given birth to the concept of 'anti-racist education'. While sometimes used interchangeably with multicultural education, its focus (and often underlying philosophy) is different, highlighting the need to combat (white) racism in all its forms (including institutional and unintentional) rather than the celebrating of cultural diversity. In the US, this concern has often focused on university curricula, with institutions such as Stanford University striving to represent various minorities in texts and classroom instruction. While some educationists see anti-racist and multicultural education as complementary, others see it as stemming from a different and contradictory critique of society. Thus criticisms of multicultural education have come both from conservative postitions (fearful of a perceived threat to traditional British cultures) and radical positions which see multicultural education as more concerned with satisfying the liberal teacher conscience than with tackling deep-rooted racism.

The religious dimension

The relationship between religion and culture is complex and dynamic. T. S. Eliot's (1888–1965) definition of culture as 'the incarnation of religion' is true of many minority cultures. Thus the cultural relativism which underpins much multicultural education may assume religious relativism. Charles H. Kraft (*Christianity in Culture*) argues that Christians might adopt a position of 'relative cultural relativism'. That is, while all cultures perform equal functions in relation to their communities, the values which they reflect should not be relativized. Ultimately all cultures (including those drawing on Christian truths and traditions) stand under the judgment* of God. The presence of this religious dimension means that some of the issues raised by multicultural education are similar to those of multi-faith religious education.

Christian responses

Biblical principles relevant to the debate about multicultural or anti-racist education include those which speak of: 1. the treatment of 'strangers' in the community (*e.g.* Nu. 15:15), although in British schools the vast majority of ethnic-majority children are now British-born and are not 'immigrants'; 2. God's opposition to racism (*e.g.* Acts 10:34–35); 3. the call to love and respect neighbours, whatever their race, culture or religious convictions (*e.g.* Lk. 10:25–37); and 4. commitment to reconciliation* (*e.g.* Eph. 2:14–16). Christian parents may need help in distinguishing between genuine Christian principles and ethnocentric attidues inculcated as part of the formal and informal educational processes which still tend to reflect Britain's imperial past, and the American ideal of the 'melting pot' of assimilation. While Christians may not agree with the (often Marxist) critique of education and society which underlies much

anti-racist education, they will 'insist there is only one race, the human race, and . . . make this the proposition that governs all educational thinking' (M. Hobbs, *Teaching in a Multi-racial Society*, p. 41). However, the call to witness to the truth of certain fundamental Christian beliefs implies a reluctance to adopt models of multicultural education which reject absolute religious or moral values.

See also: ETHNICITY; RACE; RELIGIOUS EDUCATION.

Bibliography
Department of Education and Science, *West Indian Children in Our Schools: The Interim Report of the Committee of Inquiry into the Education of Children from Ethnic Minority Groups* (The Rampton Report; London, 1981); *idem, Education for All: The Report of the Committee of Inquiry into the Education of Children from Ethnic Minority Groups* (The Swann Report; London, 1985); T. S. Eliot, *Notes Towards the Definition of Culture* (London, 1948); M. Hobbs, *Teaching in a Multiracial Society* (Exeter, 1987); C. H. Kraft, *Christianity in Culture: A Study in Dynamic Biblical Theologizing in Cross-Cultural Perspective* (New York, 1979); D. Levesque, 'Multiculturalism, Christianity and Schools', *Spectrum* 23.1, 1991, pp. 17–28; J. Lynch, *Prejudice Reduction and the Schools* (London, 1987); J. Rex, 'Equality of Opportunity, Multi-culturalism, Anti-racism and Education for All', in G. K. Verma (ed.), *Education for All: A Landmark in Pluralism* (Lewes, 1989); M. Stone, *The Education of the Black Child in Britain: The Myth of Multiracial Education* (London, 1981).

G.D.S.

MULTINATIONAL CORPORATIONS, sometimes called MNCs or global corporations, are usually national firms which operate in a number of countries through separately incorporated enterprises that are linked and responsible to a central headquarters. Some authors have suggested that only companies that have operations in six or more countries should be called 'multinational' (see, *e.g.*, J. H. Dunning in *International Production and the Multinational Enterprise*). Their strategy for growth has been to undertake direct investment* in countries other than their country of origin, usually because of some benefit: such as reduced labour costs (*e.g.* Singer Sewing Machines in S. America); in order to integrate the different stages of their production (*e.g.* mining and oil companies); or to circumscribe national restrictions on imports of their products (*e.g.* Japanese car manufacturers' investments in Europe).

Companies which have engaged in this behaviour are undoubtedly world giants that originally had their base in one of the industrialized countries, the USA providing the greatest number in the post-Second World War period. This form of investment has been important since the 19th century: by 1897 Europeans were complaining about an American invasion, and in 1914 the value of US private foreign investment was 7% of US gross domestic product; interestingly, it was only the same percentage in 1966, when the attention of academics and policy-makers started to be drawn to this phenomenon.

By far the largest amount of this kind of investment has been by companies of one highly industrialized country investing in another such country. A sizeable amount of such investment has also taken place in developing countries. This growth in the scale of enterprises has relied upon technological developments in transportation and communication and in organizational and administrative coordination skills. Multinationals are a logical extension of long-term industrial and market trends which have been reducing the cost of consumer goods and simultaneously increasing the potential market, thus affecting the standard of living of the masses, especially in industrial societies. They dominate a range of industries, *e.g.* mining, oil, pharmaceuticals and electronics.

'At what cost?' is a question which is often asked. The enormous size of multinational enterprises is a feature which worries many commentators because of the power* that goes with it. On paper, they can adjust their trading in order to gain the best tax advantages from the countries in which they operate. They can move large amounts of capital around the world, and this can be used as a threat to national governments unwilling to give them favourable conditions. Large economic institutions will inevitably have political influence not extended to small-scale enterprise. Significant disruption to a national economy, even in advanced industrial countries, can be caused by multinationals closing down their operation.

In a developing country, the disruption caused by such a closure can be disastrous, since the multinational enterprise will often constitute a very large percentage of the gross national product of that country. The MNC's products may constitute most of the prized exports and foreign currency earnings of a small country. Profits can be shifted out of low-income countries (LICs) to countries with lower tax regimes, through under-invoicing the products which are being exported from the LIC. Additional problems for developing countries can come through the intrusion of 'inappropriate technology' and sometimes inflated wages upon the structure of indigenous production, and through the modification of the tastes of consumers. On the positive side, however, the MNCs can bring valuable expertise, technology and marketing skills, which improve the distribution networks of developing economies. Korea is an example of an economy which has benefited from MNCs. MNCs also have to risk being nationalized by nationalist governments in developing countries. These issues are reviewed by R. E. Caves (1931–) in *Multinational Enterprise and Economic Analysis*.

In attempting to evaluate the net effects of multinationals, commentators are faced with a problem. Their size and structures are so complex that it is usually impossible to determine whether, or to what extent, they are engaging in bad practices. This surely is a condemnation of this form of enterprise, since ineffective systems of accountability open the way to malpractice. M. Schluter (1947–) and D. Lee (1957–) maintain in *The R Factor* that large size is undesirable in industry because it often precludes relationships based on parity and mutual obligation; they argue that the importance and priority of healthy relationships is central to the Christian faith, and should be a prime criterion by which to evaluate economic structures, institutions and social and economic life in general.

See also: ECONOMIC ETHICS; [17] GLOBAL ETHICS. [15]

Bibliography

R. E. Caves, *Multinational Enterprise and Economic Analysis* (Cambridge, 1982); J. H. Dunning, *International Production and the Multinational Enterprise* (London, 1981); M. Schluter and D. Lee, *The R Factor* (London, 1993).

S.D.

MULTIPLE PERSONALITY DISORDERS, see DEMONIC, THE.

MURDER, see KILLING.

MYERS-BRIGGS TYPE INDICATOR.

This is a typology of human personality developed by two Americans, Katharine Briggs and her daughter Isabel Briggs Myers (1898–1980). At an early stage in its development they became familiar with Jung's* theory of psychological types and came to rely heavily on his insights.

The indicator uses a complex of carefully weighted questions to elicit people's preferences on four scales. *Extroversion–Introversion* (E / I) measures one's preference for one of two complementary attitudes to the world. The extrovert prefers to focus on the external world of objects and people, while the introvert prefers the inner world of ideas and feelings. *Sensing–Intuition* (S / N) measures one's preferred way of perceiving the world: either by direct use of the five senses, or indirectly, processing sensory information through the unconscious to produce intuitive responses. *Thinking – Feeling* (T / F) indicates one's preference for either of two complementary ways of making judgments or decisions; either by rational processes, or in a more subjective way. It is important to recall that, for Jung, feeling did not mean just our feelings and emotions. On the contrary, it was a very broad term which encompassed ethical and aesthetic judgments. The final scale, *Judging–Perceiving* (J / P), is the major modification which Briggs and Myers made to Jung's theory in order to give it practical expression. This scale indicates whether a person relates to the external world primarily by means of their judging (T / F) or their perceiving functions (S / N).

These four scales may be combined to produce sixteen distinct personality types. It is important to realize that a preference for one function does not indicate that an individual is unable to use its complement. On the contrary, Briggs and Myers, following Jung, insisted that a normal person was capable of using all of these functions. It is strictly a matter of preference rather than ability. An analogy with left- and right-handedness is often drawn to underline this.

Used sensitively the indicator can be an aid to greater self-understanding. It is also valuable in understanding others – what may have been regarded as irritating differences and inexplicable attitudes come to be seen as strengths which complement our own weaknesses. Attention to type can help us to be more tolerant and to communicate more effectively.

However, the approach does have limitations. Jung maintained that the functions at the heart of this system (S, N, T and F) were chosen arbitrarily – they happened to be helpful to him in understanding clients in a clinical context. It is not, and should never be taken as, a complete account of human personality. Nevertheless, some people have been tempted to use it to categorize people. For example, some businesses now use it to weed out people who are 'temperamentally unsuited' to particular jobs. At the other extreme, its very success in explaining previously puzzling disagreements or behaviour patterns may tempt users to reduce all our differences to matters of personality or temperament. The latter danger is particularly real when the indicator is applied to Christian life and practice. For example, we must beware of reducing genuine theological differences to the level of psychology.

However, provided its limitations are recognized, the indicator may be a useful tool for Christian leaders. It is already in widespread use as an aid for spiritual direction,* *e.g.* it may help the director find the most appropriate approaches to prayer for a particular individual. Since the theory on which it was based was developed as a tool for the psychoanalyst, it has obvious applications in the area of pastoral counselling (primarily as an aid to understanding more fully the people with whom one is working). Other fields in which the indicator has already been found helpful include teaching and team-building. Finally, its capacity to make us more sensitive to how we communicate suggests that it has considerable potential as a tool in training for preaching and evangelism.

Bibliography

C. G. Jung, *Psychological Types*, in *Collected Works*, vol. 6 (London and Princeton, NJ, 1971); I. B. Myers, *Gifts Differing* (Palo Alto, CA, 1980); *idem* and M. H. McCaulley, *Manual: A Guide to the Development and Use of the Myers-Briggs Type Indicator* (Palo Alto, CA, ²1985); L. H. and D. M. Osborn, *God's Diverse People: Personality and the Christian Life* (London, 1991); R. M. Oswald and O.

Kroeger, *Personality Type and Religious Leadership* (Washington, DC, 1988).

L.H.O.

N

NATIONALISM refers to those political ideologies and movements that foster national consciousness and advocate the right of nations to self-determination. Many different nationalist ideologies and movements are found in all parts of the world today, some arguing for statehood as the natural right (see Natural Rights*) of nations, while others offer utilitarian reasons for self-government. Nationalism remains a major political force, requiring informed analysis and ethical assessment. No one definition or historical account of nations and nationalism has been agreed by scholars. A nation is any group of people that considers itself to be such, based on shared characteristics like religion, language, history, territory, institutions, culture,* statehood or aspiration to statehood. Scholarly consensus has established, however, that nations are historical and not natural phenomena.

One view is that nations are 'imagined communities', in the sense that they share a common style of imagining their own identity and interests. There have been other ways of imagining social identity, such as the tribe, empire or 'universal' community of Christendom. A nation is seen as transcending internal social divisions, through images of a community with a common but limited membership and with some measure of sovereignty over its own affairs.

It is this use of 'image', with its biblical resonances, that opens up the moral ambiguity of nationalism. The Christian ethicist must ask if nations are one, valid, cultural expression of humanity created in God's image (see Image of God*), and, therefore, if nationalism is a legitimate defence of that identity. But he or she must also ask if nations and nationalism reflect the false worship of 'images' or idols, *i.e.* the idolatry of an absolute loyalty to the nation. Three factors must be considered in any ethical argument.

1. Biblically, the Scriptures offer theological insights into nationhood. While recognizing that there is no continuity between biblical and contemporary nations, some theorists recognize that the latter are often constructed out of earlier ethnic identities that reach back in recorded history to the peoples of that same ancient world. The biblical perspective, that the nations are an ambivalent historical phenomenon and not the created condition of the one human race, is not without significance for today. Genesis affirms the common humanity of all men and women, created in the image of God. It is only in the course of rebellious human history, and not in the creation,* that the different tribes, peoples and nations of the earth emerge with a dual theological meaning. After Babel, they are the bearers of divine judgment on sinful humanity, in their divisions and mutual incomprehension. But the diversity of nations within history is also seen as restraining human evil or hubris (see Pride*) on a global scale, and offering one historical context for humanity's rich cultural and linguistic diversity.

A Christian ethical approach must hold in tension these two biblical insights, that the nations are both historical bearers of human sin, and also one historical medium of a cultural mandate given by God to the one human race. In practice today, this may mean arguing in one context that a xenophobic nationalism stands under God's judgment, while arguing in another context that a democratic nationalism may legitimately pursue its cause within a universal framework of international law and human rights, and a biblical concern for justice, solidarity and global stewardship.

2. Historically, we must distinguish among distinct eras in the development of nations and nationalism, and their different attitudes to Christ. While many scholars link nationalism with the rise of modernity and the sovereign nation-state in the 18th century, pre-modern nationalism, articulating a developing sense of Christian nationhood, existed in Europe since at least as early as the 9th century. Pre-modern nationalism had an inseparable relationship with Christianity and with religious conflicts in medieval and Reformation Europe. It was the secular nationalism of the modern era, born out of the Enlightenment* and the French Revolution, that declared humanity and the nation-state absolute and sovereign against the claims of God in Christ. The turn of this century is seeing the emergence of a post-modern nationalism, where autonomous regions and nations, defined by cultural pluralism, a common civil society and citizenship rather

than ethnicity, seek autonomy within larger political communities like the European Union, on the principle of subsidiarity rather than sovereignty. This emerging post-nationalism may be compatible in some measure with Christian social doctrines of solidarity, justice and stewardship at local, regional and global levels, in ways that ethnic nationalism manifestly is not.

3. Theologically, we must set the nations within God's mission to the world in Jesus Christ. The eschatological vision of the coming reign of God (Is. 60; Rev. 21 – 22) affirms both the place of the nations in final judgment and the prospect that their cultural legacy for good may enter the new Jerusalem. No nationalism will survive its ambivalent historical role within this passing age, but the unity of the new humanity in Christ would not seem to efface the frail, national identities within which humanity has at times sheltered in its history.

It is through a critical assessment of these three factors that nationalism must be judged ethically in each particular instance. Too often, Christian responses have offered a qualified support for patriotism* while dismissing nationalism out of hand. In a world of genocidal ethnic conflicts, this is understandable but indiscriminate. In context, patriotism may cloak national aggression, while nationalism may express a just defence of universal civic and democratic rights for particular communities within one world. Morally, both are two-edged concepts. Imagined communities must serve, and not deny, the divine image in humanity.

Bibliography

P. H. Ballard and D. H. Jones (eds.), *This Land and People: A Symposium on Christian and Welsh National Identity* (Cardiff, 1979); K. Barth, *CD* III/4, pp. 285–323; F. Catherwood, 'Nationalism', *Christian Arena* 43.3, 1990, pp. 3–6; J. Habgood, *Church and Nation in a Secular Age* (London, 1983); D. Jenkins, *The British: Their Identity and their Religion* (London, 1975); O. R. Johnston, *Nationhood: Towards a Christian Perspective* (Oxford, 1980); W. Storrar, 'The Modern Judas: A Theology of Nationhood for Europe', *Christian Arena* 43.3, 1990, pp. 7–10; T. Sundermeier (ed.), *Church and Nationalism in South Africa* (Johannesburg, 1975); B. Thorogood, *The Flag and the Cross: National Limits and Church Universal* London, 1988); C. Villa-Vicencio, *A Theology of Reconstruction: Nation-building and Human Rights* (Cambridge, 1992).

W.F.S.

NATURALISTIC ETHICS. There is a long tradition of linking ethical concepts with what is natural and unnatural, which developed, from both Aristotelian and Stoic sources, into the natural-law* tradition. It is held that Stoic* views may underlie the apostle Paul's appeal to the moral significance of what is natural and unnatural (Rom. 1:26; 1 Cor. 11:14–15). More recently the theory of evolution promoted, in writers such as Herbert Spencer (1820–1903), the coupling of ethical rightness with evolutionary or developmental success. More recently still, attempts have been made to show the ethical importance of genetic inheritance. Where 'natural' means 'animal', ethical naturalism may be said to support instinct in ethics, as opposed to reason.

However, the phrase 'naturalistic ethics' has come to have a more precise meaning in moral philosophy than that of an association, however close, between nature and ethics. It often denotes a thesis about the *meaning* of ethical terms or, at the very least, a thesis about how ethical assertions are known to be true or false.

Thus it is asserted (and denied) that 'good', for example, is definable in terms, say, of 'fittedness for survival' or 'what God wills'. However, it becomes apparent that such a claim is in fact two separate claims: that ethical terms are *definable*; and that ethical terms are definable in terms of what is detectable by the senses alone. If the claims are not separated in this way it would follow that some versions of ethical supernaturalism commit the naturalistic fallacy.* It is possible to allow that moral terms are definable in non-moral terms, without allowing that they are definable in natural, *i.e.* empirical terms.

Alternatively, naturalism may be a thesis not about the meaning of ethical terms but about how the criteria of their application are to be identified, whether by some natural or non-natural process.

David Hume's* claim that it is not possible logically to derive a (moral) 'ought' from a (factual) 'is' – *i.e.* the claim that values do not follow logically from facts – presents a formidable challenge to naturalism in ethics. Yet even if values do not derive from facts, it does not follow that facts have no moral relevance whatsoever. In the present century, G. E.

Moore (1873–1958) held that all versions of naturalism committed the 'naturalistic fallacy', the fallacy of deducing statements about what ought to be the case only from statements about what is the case.

Accounts of how the non-naturalism of ethics arises have varied markedly. For Hume, ethical non-naturalism was the joint product of subjectivism* and his view that moral distinctions are derivable from passion. By contrast, G. E. Moore held that goodness is an indefinable non-natural property or quality directly experienced, discernible by something akin to intuition. For the Cambridge Platonists the goodness of honesty, say, is a metaphysically necessary state of affairs. Thus, while naturalistic ethics is by definition cognitivist, some non-naturalists have been non-cognitivists, while others have held to the metaphysical objectivity of moral judgments.

Well-known ethical positions may be neutral as between naturalism and non-naturalism. Thus there are two versions of utilitarianism (see Consequentialism*) according to whether or not utility or satisfaction is thought to be identifiable empirically.

Bibliography

P. Foot (ed.), *Theories of Ethics* (Oxford, 1967); G. E. Moore, *Principia Ethica* (Cambridge, 1903); M. Warnock, *Ethics Since 1900* (Oxford, ³1978).

P.H.

NATURALISTIC FALLACY. According to G. E. Moore (1873–1958), all attempts to define ethical terms in non-ethical (*i.e.* natural) terms commit the 'naturalistic fallacy'. For of any state of affairs it is possible to ask the 'open question', 'But is it good?' 'Naturalism' is a rather misleading title for what Moore was attacking, since any attempted definitions of moral terms, including definitions in supernatural terms, are 'natural'. Moore's views were part of his own non-naturalism according to which what is good, notably (in Moore's case) friendship, is discernible by immediate intuition (see Intuitionism*).

If Moore is correct, then all versions of ethical naturalism rest upon the mistake of treating matters of value as if they were straightforwardly factual. Yet it does not follow, even if Moore is correct, that facts have no bearing on values, only that they do not logically entail them. Nor does it follow that

one is committed to Moore's own rather Platonic, intuitionistic views about moral goodness. One may believe that the naturalistic fallacy is a fallacy and hold a subjectivist* or emotivist* account of the nature of moral value.

Even if Moore is correct, it does not follow that the so-called open-question argument is the way to demonstrate this. For one may sensibly ask of any state of affairs, such as friendship, 'But is it good?' Only of goodness itself it makes no sense to ask this.

Lying behind Moore's argument is David Hume's* claim that matters of value are not deducible from matters of fact alone.

See also: NATURALISTIC ETHICS.

Bibliography

P. Foot, *Theories of Ethics* (Oxford, 1967); R. M. Hare, *The Language of Morals* (Oxford, 1952); G. E. Moore, *Ethics* (London, 1912).

P.H.

NATURAL LAW. The moral law of God is sufficiently evident from the nature of human beings as accountable. This in brief is Paul's claim in Rom. 1 – 3: Gentiles who do not have the Mosaic law are guilty along with the Jews who do. Gentiles have the truth but suppress it (Rom. 1:18), worshipping not God the creator but created things, as their idols reveal (1:21–24). They thus violate the first two commandments of the Decalogue.* From this distorted devotion spring unnatural behaviours that pervert human sexuality (see ⑪), disrupt relationships, and breed self-centredness, greed, envy* and conflicts of every kind (1:26–32). On the other hand, Gentiles who by nature do what the law requires show that it is written in their heart (2:14–16).

Such language would have been well understood in Rome, where a Stoic* concept of natural law had taken root, emphasizing social harmony and a well-ordered personal life modelled on the law-governed nature of the physical world. Paul himself had probably met such thinking, since his home town of Tarsus was a major seat of Stoic philosophy, and it would have reminded him of his Jewish belief that God the creator orders nature well and governs his people with laws that are good.

The same idea is echoed in 1 Tim. 4:1–5 where the goodness* of creation* has ethical implications about food and sex, and in 1 Cor. 5:1, where even pagans are said to abjure incest.* Jesus pointed out that allowing divorce* is a concession to human sinfulness, and not part of the original order of creation (Mt. 19:3–8).

Similarly in the OT, the book of Proverbs gathers together the moral wisdom* of some ancients. Ecclesiastes likewise is a wisdom learned in the natural experiences of life. The prophets held pagan nations morally accountable for their needless violence (*e.g.* Am. 1). Plainly too, those before Moses were aware of the essential content of the Decalogue, and knew that not only idolatry but also murder (see Killing*), thieving (see theft*) and adultery* were wrong. There was and is available a natural moral knowledge apart from the specially revealed moral law (see Law and Gospel*) recorded in Scripture.

Historical development

Natural-law theory, which attempts to explain this natural moral awareness, emerged within two traditions, one developing from the Stoics and Roman jurisprudence,* the other from Thomas Aquinas'* work with Aristotelian* ideas. The former view emphasized that humans are rational beings who can adjust their behaviour and attitudes to conform to the natural order of things. Living in a law-governed world, we must abide by the natural laws that govern our lives, accepting our lot rather than being driven by irrational desire to buck the inevitable tide. Some Stoics accepted their fate with quiet resignation. Others ordered their affairs and those of their society by enacting laws that could be uniformly enforced. Enlightenment thinkers pursued this tradition: John Locke (1632–1704) in his *Second Treatise on Civil Government* (1690) and *Essays on the Law of Nature* (*c.* 1676) described our natural state in terms of individual rights to life, liberty and property, and conceived of a civil society as building on and enhancing those rights. Thomas Jefferson (1743–1826) stood in this general tradition, as did Hugo Grotius,* the Dutch jurist who laid foundations in natural law for international law and the laws of war.* The State* is not an artificial creation alien to nature, but a natural institution based on the consent of the governed.

As representative of the latter view, Thomas Aquinas' *Treatise on Law* distinguishes four kinds of law: 1. the eternal law as God's will

and wisdom, revealed in 2. divine law given in Scripture and through the church, but also revealed in 3. natural law, from which 4. human law (see Law, Civil and Criminal*) is to be derived. Natural law is inherent in the essence of created things, in the good ends that are natural for all humans to pursue, the potential that humans generically share. Since all beings naturally seek their good, and we are beings, we should do good and avoid evil. Since we exist as substances and all substances seek to preserve their existence, whatever preserves human life and wards off obstacles is in accordance with natural law. Like other animals, we have a natural sexual drive and want to rear our offspring. But the distinctively human is our rational potential, which naturally inclines us to know about God and to desire a rationally ordered society.

Natural-law theory gained renewed acceptance in the context of the Second World War because of the moral atrocities committed by the Nazis, and partly in reaction against the subjectivism of the 1930s. It continues to inform Roman Catholic ethical thinking (see Roman Catholic Moral Theology*).

Objections

The idea of a natural moral law faces a number of objections.

1. It is too optimistic to suppose we can logically derive specific moral rules unambiguously from generalizations about human nature. Is reasoning that objective and conclusive? Are the premises agreed on, and are there sufficient premises to require the specific kinds of decisions we seek? All this depends on one's assessment of moral epistemology. At least it must be said that human nature as God's creation affords indications of his good purposes for us, indications we ignore at our peril.

2. Is human nature uniformly and unchangingly the same? Some say that sin (see Sin and Salvation⑤) has radically changed what we were intended to be, so as to blur recognition of our natural good. Others insist that human nature is a product of evolution and is still in the process of change. Both objections pose metaphysical questions about the essence of humanness, as well as theological questions about the image of God* and the extent to which depravity distorts human nature. If we say the image of God is still present or that humans are still rational beings, and that our lives should in practice exhibit it, then to that extent a natural moral law still makes sense.

3. But is human nature the same in the new creation God is producing in Christ as it was in the old creation in Adam? Or is human nature being transformed by grace* into something very different? Is God's intention that we now act on what we were originally, or on what we shall be in his kingdom* that is yet to come? This raises questions about the relation of the OT to the NT, of creation to kingdom, and of law to grace. Anabaptist* theology tends to separate the two members of each of these pairs, and to point out fundamental ways in which they differ. On the other hand Reformed theology (see Calvinistic Ethics*) sees more continuity, so that God's kingdom, the new creation, will fully actualize for the first time the rich potential for good that God vested in the old creation. The law (see Law, Uses of*) was indeed propaedeutic to grace: it restrained evil and required a more humane society, pointing to the love and justice which God's grace brings. In this case, a natural-law ethic must go hand in hand with grace (as it did in Aquinas), and grace will lead us a second mile and more in love beyond what the law alone requires. Divine law, as Aquinas knew, goes beyond what natural law requires, and acts of supererogation exceed natural moral duties.

Human laws derive from natural law, sometimes by logical inference: natural law forbids murder, and so the law of nations in every realm should forbid it, too. Sometimes human law is a local application, rather than a necessary deduction that is universally valid: thus natural law requires that the law-breaker be punished, but does not specify how; so depending on the particular situation, forms of punishment* may legitimately differ.

Here arises objection 4: in a pluralistic society with no universal recognition of natural law, how can we expect it to be the basis for human laws? Plainly other legal philosophies exist, particularly the historicist view that law is shaped by historical processes rather than derived from some unchanging norm; or legal positivism, that the authority of law derives from the authority of those who legislate and enforce (see Jurisprudence*). But where a constitutional tradition is the only common point of reference, an ethical basis for formulating and critiquing legislation is of utmost importance. In so far as natural-law theory can inform the thinking of Christians and others involved, it can enable them to bear witness to a higher authority and at times to influence human law-making and policy-setting in directions that coincide with those which biblical morality also favours.

Bibliography

C. E. Curran, *Themes in Fundamental Moral Theology* (Notre Dame, IN, 1977); I. Ramsey, 'Towards a Rehabilitation of Natural Law', in *Christian Ethics and Contemporary Philosophy* (London, 1966); P. Sigmund, *Natural Law in Political Thought* (Lanham, MD, 1971); T. R. Simon, *The Tradition of Natural Law* (New York, 1965); H. Thielicke, *TE* 1, chs. 19–22; Thomas Aquinas, *Treatise on Law*, in *STh* a 2 ae 90–97.

A.F.H.

NATURAL RIGHTS are that category of claims in legal theory or jurisprudence* which are rights inherent in human beings by virtue of their very nature and of natural law,* rather than by the positive law of their state(s). Some writers (*e.g.* Arthur F. Holmes, 1924– ; John Finnis, 1940–) use the term interchangeably with 'human rights' (see Rights, Human*). The concept is inextricably interlinked with natural law.

Neither Gk. nor Rom. legal theory had well-developed concepts of natural rights, but parallel concepts existed. Though Thomas Aquinas* said that natural rights were disclosed through God's plan, there has always been a strong emphasis on natural rights as a rational foundation for moral judgment. A. P. d'Entreves (1902–85) in *Natural Law* says that the three distinctives of natural rights are rationalism, individualism and radicalism. John Locke (1632–1704) identified inalienable natural rights of life, liberty and estate (private property), ideas enshrined (*inter alia*) in the American Declaration of Independence of 1776 by the US founding fathers, who viewed natural rights as 'self-evident'. 'Happiness'* is often appended to this list of rights. The concept developed both in Roman Catholic and Puritan thought, but has most recently been influential in Catholic social philosophy (*e.g.* the writings of Jacques Maritain, 1882–1973).

The core issue is whether natural rights are simply self-evident to reason,* or specifically revealed by God. Whilst Thomas Paine (1737–1809) argued for the divine origin of the rights of man at creation, many use the concept without reference to any religious source. The Christian understanding of humans made in the image of God* provides the starting-point for analysis of the concept and its significance. If we accept natural rights as implied from, *e.g.*, Gn. 1:26–27; 9:6 and Jas. 3:9, there must exist parallel concepts of natural *responsibilities* (*e.g.* Gn. 1:28; 2:17). If we understand that the worth of humanity rests on our created nature, the concept is fundamental in the legal and moral regulation of humans' affairs (Mt. 22:35–40).

See also: JUSTICE AND PEACE. ③

Bibliography
G. Carey, *I Believe in Man* (London and Grand Rapids, 1977); J. D. Dengerink, *NDT*, pp. 594–595; A. P. d'Entreves, *Natural Law* (London, ²1970); J. M. Finnis, *Natural Law and Natural Rights* (Oxford, 1980); H. L. A. Hart, *Essays in Jurisprudence and Philosophy* (Oxford, 1983); H. Lauterpacht, *International Law and Human Rights* (London, 1950); Lord Lloyd of Hampstead and M. D. A. Freeman, *Lloyd's Introduction to Jurisprudence* (London, ⁵1985); J. R. W. Stott, *Issues Facing Christians Today* (Basingstoke, ²1990) = *Involvement* (Old Tappan, NJ, ²1990), ch. 8; R. Tuck, *Natural Rights Theories* (Cambridge, 1978); J. Waldron, *Oxford Readings in Philosophy* (Oxford, 1984); D. M. Walker, *Oxford Companion to Law* (Oxford, 1980).

J.D.H.

NATURISM, see NUDITY.

NEGLIGENCE, PROFESSIONAL.
Strictly, 'negligence' is a basis of liability for a legal action in tort (*i.e.* a non-contractual civil wrong), as opposed to a single nominate tort (*i.e.* a basis of legal action in a claim for civil wrong), although the term 'tort of negligence' is regularly used in common law jurisdictions such as England and Wales. Civil jurisdictions differ in their analysis of the concept, and are usually based more on underlying principles (as opposed to precedent) as a basis for defining negligence and its limits. In Scottish law any kind of delict (*i.e.* civil liability for unjustifiable harm or loss) may be done intentionally or negligently (*i.e.* by failing to exercise a standard of care), and an act of negligence is a wrong which is committed negligently as opposed to intentionally.

'Professional negligence' (or malpractice) is this area of legal liability when concerned specifically with professional persons or firms, and it must be distinguished from professional misconduct (*e.g.* the breach of a professional code of ethics; see Professional Ethics*). Though an act is regarded as professionally negligent, it is not necessarily professional misconduct, and vice versa.

An act (or omission) by a professional person resulting in loss or injury will, in general terms, give rise to a basis for an action founded on negligence within a common law jurisdiction if the following criteria are satisfied: 1. a duty* of care towards others directly or indirectly relying on his or her specialist skills (the concept of such a duty in commonwealth jurisdictions arose principally from judicial observations in a Scottish case on the NT concept of 'neighbour' in Lk. 10:25–29; Lord Atkin in *Donaghue* v. *Stevenson* [1932] AC 562 at p. 580); 2. failure to act in accordance with a reasonable standard of care consistent with his or her professional status, deeming him or her to be in breach of the duty – the 'negligent act or omission'; 3. material and / or (sometimes exclusively) economic injury – 'loss'; and 4. a connection between the negligent act and the loss – 'remoteness' or 'proximity'.

The category of 'professional' includes not only those usually understood to be 'professionals' (*e.g.* lawyers, medical doctors, accountants) but also generally anyone whose skill, trade, business or profession requires them in the normal course of events to perform acts, provide services, and make statements, give advice or information which they anticipate will be relied upon. The standard of care exercised by a professional person is critical in deciding whether or not negligence has occurred (Lord Clyde in *Hunter* v. *Hanley* [1955] S 200 at p. 206 and *Whitehouse* v. *Jordan* [1981] 1 All ER 267).

The duty of care extends both to those with whom the professional is in a contractual relationship (potentially giving rise to 'concurrent liability' in both contract and tort), and to those outside of that relationship whom the professional might reasonably foresee as being affected by or reliant upon his or her actions. The absence of a contract does not preclude tortious or delictual duty. For example, in Eng. law, if a lawyer incorrectly advises a client about the execution of his or her will, so depriving a beneficiary (with whom the lawyer has no contractual relationship) of his or her entitlement, the beneficiary may have a cause of action against the lawyer (*Ross* v. *Caunters* [1980] Ch 297; see also *Murphy* v. *Brentwood D.C.* [1990] 2 All ER 908, and *Caparo In-*

dustries PLC v. *Dickman* [1990] 1 All ER 568).

A claim for loss may be prejudiced in common-law systems by the acts or omissions of the injured party, *e.g.* by contributory negligence, voluntary assumption of risk and failure to apportion fault correctly in litigation. Professional negligence may also lead to criminal prosecution.

Within common-law systems, legal development as to the expansion or restraint of categories of negligence is generally a matter for the courts. Trends vary in different jurisdictions as to whether categories are expanding or contracting, and the severity of standards of care may vary from profession to profession. Member States of the EU are subject to supranational legislation, harmonizing consumer safeguards across the community in the light of the European Single Market.

The level of damages for the same level of loss varies according to jurisdiction, because of factors such as whether juries or the judiciary set damages, whether punitive damages constitute part of the quantum of damages, and whether lawyers are paid on a contingency fee basis. (Punitive damages were introduced in the USA over 200 years ago to penalize and deter professional negligence but exclude medical and legal malpractice cases.) One of the biggest factors influencing litigation is professional indemnity insurance; insurance premiums for some medical specialties are so high in some jurisdictions (*e.g.* Florida in the USA) that few new practitioners enter that specialty. The cost of indemnity insurance and the risk of litigation tend to force practitioners to engage in 'defensive practice', where the types of practice engaged in and the courses of action followed are chosen principally with a view to minimizing the risk of professional-negligence claims, rather than in the best interests of the client. Some jurisdictions have moved in part to no-fault damage systems, ombudsmen and arbitration mechanisms to limit litigation, all of which (as with insurance-based systems) have ethical merits and demerits.

Other considerations include the degree of access to legal services for the poor for complex cases, the delay in cases coming before the courts, the vested interests lobbying or influencing law-makers (*e.g.* professional-indemnity insurance providers) and whether an error of professional judgment made in good faith should automatically be adjudged to be profes-sional negligence. Heated debate also occurs on the social implications of the extension of categories of negligence, especially in medicine. Another controversial development was the attempts made in the USA in the 1980s to bring actions for 'clergy malpractice', *e.g.* where pastoral advice given to a church member was alleged to have resulted in his suicide (*Nally* v. *Grace Community Church of the Valley*, 47 Cal. 3d 278): the pastors of the church were alleged to be negligent in their role as a 'professional adviser'.

Bibliography

A. M. Dugdale and K. M. Stanton, *Professional Negligence* (London, ²1989); J. G. Fleming, *The Law of Torts* (London, 1987); R. M. Jackson and J. L. Powell, *Professional Negligence* (London, 1987); J. K. Mason and R. A. McCall Smith, *Law and Medical Ethics* (London, 1983); R. A. Percy, *The Law of Negligence* (London, 1990); W. L. Prosser, *The Law of Torts* (St Paul, MN, 1964); D. M. Walker, *The Law of Delict in Scotland* (Edinburgh, ²1981).

J.D.H.

NEIGHBOUR. The meaning of 'neighbour', as delineated in the Bible, is twofold. On one level, 'neighbour' represents anyone in need, particularly those with whom we come into contact. On a second level, we become neighbours ourselves as we reach out in compassion* and meet the needs of others.

In the Heb. Bible, two words are used frequently in reference to the neighbour. *Šāqen* indicates those people who live in adjacent areas. No differentiation is made between those nearby who are friendly to us and those who are not. *Rēa'* suggests any person with whom we come into contact. This refers both to those whom we meet because we live in the same area, as in *šāqen*, and to those with whom we have only occasional contact. *Rēa'* refers both to people within the covenant* and to those outside the covenant, including those who oppressed God's people. The distinction between the two is determined primarily through appropriation of the literary context of each reference. However, foreigners who by definition are outside the covenant could on occasion be treated differently from fellow Israelites (*e.g.* they could be charged interest, Dt. 23:20).

The most frequent usage of these terms comes in contexts directed to members of the covenant people (*e.g.* Lv. 25:25; Dt. 15:2–3, 7, 9, 11–12; 17:15; 22:1–4). Each person, within the covenant, has a moral obligation to aid other members of this group whenever necessary and possible.

In contrast to this, references in the Decalogue* (Ex. 20:1–17; Dt. 5:6–21) and the Holiness Code (Lv. 17 – 26) are more broadly directed. The Decalogue includes commands concerning honesty* towards one's neighbour (Ex. 20:16; see also Dt. 5:20) and respect for the possessions of one's neighbour (Ex. 20:17; see also Dt. 5:21). The commandment of honesty with neighbour is illustrated in Pr. 11:9 and 12, and Ps. 12:2 describes a context wherein honesty to one's neighbours is denied. The commandment related to a neighbour's possessions is highlighted in Ex. 22:7–9: what is taken from a neighbour must be returned in double portion.

The OT teaching is stated in summary form in Lv. 19:13–18, with the whole of the commandment encapsulated in the phrase, 'Love your neighbour as yourself'. This short summary expression from Lv. 19:18 is quoted on several occasions in the NT, by both Jesus and the writers of the epistles.

In the NT, *plēsion* is used most frequently for denoting the idea of 'neighbour'. This term parallels the Heb. *rēa'* and is always used in the NT when reference is made to the OT command to love the neighbour (Mt. 5:43; 19:19; 22:39; Mk. 12:31, 33; Lk. 10:27; Rom. 13:9; Gal. 5:14; Jas. 2:8). This term refers to a relationship having to do with another person; it is a general reference to every possible type of relationship between people, without limitation to blood relationship or geographical proximity.

Two important adjustments to the OT understanding of 'neighbour' are incorporated in the NT. The first of these is Jesus' summation of the law. In response to a question concerning which is the greatest commandment, Jesus replies with a twofold summation: 'Love the Lord your God with all your heart and with all your soul and with all your mind . . . [and] love your neighbour as yourself' (Mt. 22:34–40; also Mk. 12:28–31). In this text Jesus takes two distinct OT commandments – to love God (Dt. 6:5; 10:12) and to love one's neighbour (Lv. 19:18) – and places them together as parallel commandments.

The unity of these two appears to be significant to Jesus. In Christ, and in the followers of Christ, these two come together. As God's mercy and compassion – his neighbourliness – awaken love and compassion in us for others, so our neighbourliness will awaken like actions in others. Furthermore, we meet Christ in the other person, and in being a neighbour to the other, we are a neighbour to Christ.

The second NT adjustment to the concept of 'neighbour' expands its parameters so as to make it more inclusive. Many of the references in OT commandment passages refer exclusively to the covenant community. Jesus removes this exclusivity to include even one's enemies. He states: 'You have heard that it was said, "Love your neighbour and hate your enemy." But I tell you: Love your enemies and pray for those who persecute you' (Mt. 5:43–44).

There is no doubt that the *rēa'* of Lv. 19:18 is a member of the covenant community. Jesus' removal of this restriction prompts 'an expert in the law . . . to test' him by asking, 'Who is my neighbour?' (Lk. 10:29). In response, Jesus tells the parable of the good Samaritan (Lk. 10:30–35).

In this parable Jesus expands the parameters first by taking two people who are not in agreement – a Jew and a Samaritan – and brings them into relationship. It is the enemy, the Samaritan, rather than the traditional 'neighbours', the priest and Levite, who responds compassionately to the wounded man by the side of the road.

The parameters are also expanded when Jesus changes the question. The parable begins with the challenger's question, 'Who is my neighbour?' Jesus concludes it with a new question: 'Which of these three do you think was neighbour to the man who fell into the hands of robbers?' (Lk. 10:36). The first question suggests that the neighbour is a recipient, some one who receives the compassionate care of another. Jesus' question, however, implies that a neighbour is the person who acts on behalf of another. Jesus' articulation moves the understanding of neighbour from the other to one's self.

Jesus expands the notion of neighbour so fully that it becomes synonymous with 'humankind'. We cannot predict who will be in need of our being a neighbour. The course of life will reveal this to us. We cannot explicate who our neighbour will be; we can only be a neighbour. Jesus' injunction in this parable requires those who follow God to be neighbours: *i.e.* those who follow God must compassionately care for the needs of those in the world, whenever and however possible.

D.L.P.

NEIGHBOUR-LOVE, see LOVE.[2]

NEUROSIS can be defined as 'a psychological reaction to acute or continuous perceived stress, expressed in emotion or behaviour ultimately inappropriate in dealing with that stress' (A. Sims, *Neurosis in Society*, p. 3). The term was first recorded in 1769 by the Scottish physician William Cullen (1710–90), and was described as a 'general affection of the nervous system', a phrase that embraced such conditions as convulsions, coma and insanity. In time the word 'neurosis' was associated primarily with emotional and personality disorders. In 1895, Sigmund Freud* (acknowledging a previous description by E. Hecker in 1893 in the Ger. literature) first referred to anxiety-neurosis as a distinct syndrome. His listing of the constituent elements has given a broad picture that still tallies with the traditional view of neurosis: general irritability, anxious expectation, free-floating anxiety,* attacks of acute anxiety, night terrors, giddiness, various phobias, gastrointestinal disturbance, strange sensations of numbness and tingling, and a chronicity of the condition.

By the 1970s, the longstanding separation between the terms 'psychosis'* (mental disorders with a marked lack of insight and a clear loss of contact with reality) and 'neurosis' (psychological disorders where insight and a sense of reality are unimpaired) was being called into question. At the same time, particularly in the USA, there was sharp controversy between those who favoured a psychodynamic approach (seeing the roots of disturbance in early life and favouring the word 'neurosis') and the phenomenologists (who adhered to a descriptive approach and opted for the term 'neurotic disorder'). The trend towards demoting the word 'neurosis' is reflected in the classification of mental conditions in the 3rd ed. of the American Diagnostic and Statistical Manual (1980) and its revision (1987), and in the 10th ed. of the International Classification of Diseases (1992), published by the World Health Organization. In the latter, there is overlap between the 'neurotic disorders', the 'mood [affective] disorders', including the former categorizations of depression,* and the 'behavioural syndromes', which incorporate the eating disorders.*

Discussion about the causes of neurosis has centred on the contributory factors of stress,* personality* and biology. Broadly, the psychoanalytic* tradition has seen the roots of neurosis in the stresses of childhood: Freud postulated the primacy of infantile sexuality (see [11]) in generating neurotic conflict; Alfred Adler* emphasized feelings of inferiority as the driving force; and neo-Freudians (see Pastoral Care, Counselling and Psychotherapy[12]), like Karen Horney (1885–1952), saw neurotic trends as arising from a child's search for security. The 'traumatic neurosis' of classical Freudianism is now subsumed into today's well-recognized 'post-traumatic stress disorder'.

Although Hans Eysenck (1916–), writing in the 1960s and 70s, saw neurotic disorder as related to abnormal personality (his scale of 'neuroticism' argued a correlation with the factor of introversion), research in the 1980s suggests that there is no clear link between personality and neurosis. Another influential theoretician in this field, Raymond B. Cattell (1905–), an American psychologist, has argued that neurotic traits are spread continuously through the population and do not necessarily indicate abnormality. Biological factors – through the disciplines of genetics, physiology, pharmacology and the neurosciences – have come increasingly to the fore in the understanding of mental conditions, not least in the relation between certain neurotransmitter substances (including the 'indoleamine' and 'catecholamine' systems) and some mood disorders.

The neuroses, in contrast generally to the psychoses, are seen as particularly susceptible to relief from psychotherapy. Although each school of psychological treatment has its distinctive approach, the most crucial factors lie less in methodology and technique and more in the relationship of trust between therapist and patient. Methods range from the use of transference* and dream* interpretation in the psychodynamic schools, through the more 'here-and-now', briefer, experiential therapies of the humanistic* and existential* psychologies, through to behavioural* and cognitive* approaches which see the roots of neurosis in a process of conditioning and distorted beliefs and attitudes respectively. The complementary arm of treating neurosis is pharmacological. The traditional use of sedatives, such as the benzodiazepines, to reduce anxiety and induce sleep, has the major danger of tolerance and drug* dependence. From the late 1950s, it has been established that certain antidepressants (*e.g.* monoamine oxidase inhibitors for severe anxiety, and imipramine for panic attacks) can alleviate the symptoms of neurosis.

Bibliography

G. Davies, *Stress: The Challenge to Christian Caring* (Eastbourne, 1988); I. Marks, *Cure and Care of Neurosis: Theory and Practice of Behavioural Psychotherapy* (New York, 1981); A. Sims, *Neurosis in Society* (London, 1983); P. Snaith, *Clinical Neurosis* (Oxford, ²1991); P. Tyrer, *Classification of Neurosis* (Chichester and New York, 1989); World Health Organization, *The ICD-10 Classification of Mental and Behavioural Disorders: Clinical Descriptions and Diagnostic Guidelines* (Geneva, 1992).

R.F.H.

NEW AGE MOVEMENT. The New Age movement is best understood not as a sect, cult, denomination or conspiracy, but as an eclectic and diverse collection of like-minded individuals and organizations who hold to an essentially pantheistic, monistic,* relativistic, reincarnationist and spiritualistic world-view which positions itself as an antidote to both secular materialism* and orthodox Christianity. Although it is not an organized movement with one leader or a strict set of beliefs, the New Age movement has influenced psychology, business, politics, education, entertainment, medicine, and the church in both America and Europe.

New Age enthusiasts argue that the economic, military, ecological (see Environment*) and social crises of modernity (see Modernity and Postmodernity*) are rooted in wrong views of reality. Christianity, like all monotheistic religions, is viewed as dogmatic and alienating because it removes God (see ①) from creation and divorces humans from deity. Secular humanism* is likewise rejected as spiritually myopic and scientistic because it reduces reality to the empirically verifiable and scientifically manipulable. Drawing on diverse sources such as Hinduism, shamanism and avant-garde speculations in quantum physics, the New Age calls for people to tap into their unlimited potential through a number of consciousness-raising techniques including yoga, meditation, visualization, pagan rituals, self-hypnosis, and other forms of mind-expansion. Those involved in the New Age movement hope to see humanity realize its divinity and so evolve to a higher spiritual consciousness which will lead to a new era of unprecedented spiritual and political harmony, unity and peace.

A curious mixture of the modern and the ancient, the New Age strives to integrate traditional pantheistic and monistic beliefs with modern Western civilization. Thus reincarnation is stripped of its traditionally negative connotations and is viewed in terms of unlimited opportunity for fulfilment after death. Similarly, meditation is technologized through various devices claiming to alter brainwave activity and so to engender enlightenment more efficiently than traditional ascetic disciplines.

A Christian response to the New Age

Although the effect and extent of New Age activities have been overestimated by some apocalyptic prognosticators who uncritically correlate New Age aims with the rise of Antichrist and the end of the world, the New Age movement none the less poses a serious challenge to Christians.

In response to the New Age world-view, the orthodox Christian world-view offers an alternative both to materialism and to pantheism. The *universe* is neither divine, nor merely matter in motion, but is rather created by and contingent upon *the creator,* who is not an impersonal and amoral force but the Lord of heaven and earth.

Humans are neither sleeping gods nor naked apes but made in the image* and likeness of God (Gn. 1:26–27). Although more like God than anything else in the material universe, humans fall infinitely short of divinity. Besides the ontological gap between creator and creature is the ethical alienation between a holy God and fallen humans. While the New Age identifies the central problem of humanity as ignorance of innate godhood, Christianity affirms the reality of sin as the breaking of God's moral law and the cause of humanity's estrangement from its creator.

New Age teachings deem *Jesus** a spiritually attuned master, guru, swami, yogi or avatar; he is not accorded the worship due to the unique redeemer. He is rather an example of a God-realized or Christ-conscious human. Instead of being the Lord and Saviour, the Jesus of the New Age is deemed a model of what anyone can attain through proper self-development. Against this revisionist claim, the Bible presents a Jesus who singles himself out of the cosmic crowd through his sinless life, matchless teaching, multiple miracles, redemptive death and death-defeating resurrection. Neither his claim to be 'the way and the truth and the life' (Jn. 14:6) nor his credentials as the one and only Christ can be synthesized with New Age syncretism.

The New Age uses *terms* associated with Christianity to articulate a world-view incompatible with biblical faith. Biblically defined, being 'born again' means spiritual regeneration by grace* in this life, not reincarnation. The word 'God' does not refer to an impersonal force, principle, or power, but to the great 'I AM WHO I AM' (Ex. 3:14) who takes on human flesh to save a lost race and dies on the cross to prove his love (Jn. 3:16). 'Christ' is not a level of consciousness available to those who tap into an impersonal power, but a title applicable only to Jesus of Nazareth (Lk. 2:11). While the New Age may use Christian vocabulary, it does not use it in a Christian sense. New Age interest in divination and mediumship as connections to the paranormal or supernatural realm clashes with biblical vetos on *occult* activities (Dt. 18:10–12; Is. 8:19). Because Satan* masquerades as an angel of light (2 Cor. 11:14), the allure of occult power and knowledge is real but dangerous. Spiritual safety and satisfaction can be found only in Christ, who defeated the works of the devil (1 Jn. 3:8) and was declared the Son of God with power through his resurrection (Rom. 1:4).

The issue does not end with theology and apologetics. Many interested in New Age spirituality are seeking a *spiritual sustenance* they have not found in the church or in secular culture. They challenge the church to live up to its high calling to be 'the light of the world'.

Bibliography

R. Chandler, *Understanding the New Age* (Waco, TX, 1988; Milton Keynes, 1989); D. Groothuis, *Unmasking the New Age* (Downers Grove, IL, 1986; Leicester, 1992); *idem*, *Revealing the New Age Jesus* (Downers Grove, IL, and Leicester, 1990).

D.R.G.

NIEBUHR, H. RICHARD (1894–1962).

Pastor and Yale professor of theology and ethics, H. Richard Niebuhr is best known for his work on the relation between culture* and the Christian church, and between the relativities of historical life and the theocentric revelation of the radically monotheistic Christian faith. He was influenced by Karl Barth's* neo-orthodox understanding of revelation,* Ernst Troeltsch's (1865–1923) approach to the problem of Christianity's universal validity vis-à-vis historical relativism,* Kantian and existentialist* characterizations of the self* as radically free, and the social theory of the self espoused by Charles H. Cooley (1864–1929), George Herbert Mead (1880–1949) and Josiah Royce (1855–1916), in which identity is shaped in response to groups and persons.

The last two influences contributed to Niebuhr's 'social existentialism', which viewed the self always in relationship to others, yet responsible for others and to God. Niebuhr spurned two types of theories of the self with their corresponding ethic: 1. the Barthian view of the human as 'citizen', with the deontological* ethic that asks, 'What is the law?'; and 2. the Thomistic (see Thomist Ethics*) view of the human as 'maker, fashioner, or artificer', with a teleological ethic that asks, 'What is my telos [goal]?' He espoused instead a view of the human as 'answerer', employing an ethic of response and responsibility* in which the fundamental ethical question is 'What is going on?'

All of life has the characteristic of responsive action, argued Niebuhr, and our response is shaped by our interpretations of what is occurring. Thus, moral action is a response to *interpreted* action upon us. Christian theology provides us with an interpretation of the One who is ultimately acting upon us in all human and historical actions: 'Responsibility affirms: "God is acting in all actions upon you. So respond to all actions upon you as to respond to his actions"' (*The Responsible Self*, p. 126). This is the God known to Israel, known through the Bible as it reveals the living person of Jesus Christ, and known in the church community, which transmits its interpretations through language, and judges our response to what is happening as either fitting or unfitting, appropriate or inappropriate. To interpret adequately what is going on also requires a view of the totality of history and life; thus, ethical reflection must rely on philosophy, the social sciences, and awareness of the contemporary cultural situation.

Responsible moral action is the *fitting* response to the creating, governing, and redeeming God who is acting upon us. A fitting response might include restraining evil, promoting and evoking good, or demonstrating love. Sin (unfitting response) is defined as unfaithfulness and irresponsibility to God and to humans in one's historical and social existence.

Christian ethics therefore asks first of all, 'What is *God* doing?', and only secondly asks, 'What should *we* do?' The result is a 'contextualist ethic' (*e.g.* see Paul Lehmann, *Ethics in a Christian Context*, London, ²1979). This tries to avoid relativism* and situationalism (see Situation Ethics*) by placing the stress on doing what is right in relation to what is occurring, which is theologically reflected upon and existentially analysed in a continuing community of Christian agents. Nevertheless, critics have charged that this ethic leans too heavily on imagination, intuition and free response.

Niebuhr's social agenda was controlled by a Calvinist sense of transforming the kingdom of this world into the kingdom of God.* This transformative approach engages with other church-culture models, namely the Anabaptist* stance 'against culture', the Thomistic position of church 'over culture', the Protestant liberal church 'of culture', and the Lutheran (see Lutheran Ethics*) tension in which church and culture co-exist 'in paradox'.

Bibliography

Christ and Culture (New York, 1951); *Radical Monotheism and Western Culture* (New York, 1960); *The Responsible Self* (New York and London, 1963).

P. Ramsey (ed.), *Faith and Ethics: The Theology of H. Richard Niebuhr* (New York, 1957).

D.L.O.

NIEBUHR, REINHOLD (1892–1971). The Christian social thought of Reinhold Niebuhr has had a powerful and pervasive influence both in the church and in the world of politics. Leading politicians on both sides of the Atlantic have found help and inspiration in his work. The radical shape of his thinking broke upon the world with the publication in 1932 of *Moral Man and Immoral Society*, a text still studied by students of both social theory and Christian ethics. Rejecting the predominant liberal individualism* of previous eras, Niebuhr sought to come to terms with the realities of corporate power. Liberal individualism's understanding of charity and compassion* had not the intellectual

strength needed to make sense of the subtleties and pervasiveness of corporate power both in the political and in the industrial and commercial sectors. Niebuhr recognized that only a full doctrine of justice (see Justice and Peace ③ – which may fall short of the ultimate vision of love in the Christian tradition – could help us get to grips with power and bring it under human control. Niebuhr came to this conclusion from his own pastoral experience. His pastoring of a Presbyterian church in Detroit in the 1920s in the midst of economic depression made him face the nature of the power of the motor industry and the weakness of the individual when up against it. In Detroit he developed a reputation as a powerful preacher, able to give the people insight into the circumstances of their social experience.

The experience of the 20s and 30s provided the backdrop for the development of his thought. These were the years of the collapse of Wall Street and the slump. They were also the years which saw the rise of Fascism and Stalinism and the dreadful threat of Nazi ideology hanging over the world. A theologian able to comprehend the evils of power* and to find structures of thought which could shape a Christian contribution was bound to have a deep influence. His Gifford Lectures given in Edinburgh, published in two volumes as *The Nature and Destiny of Man*, have been criticized for having too gloomy a view of human nature. In those dark and troubled days they seemed to tell the truth as few others and to point the way forward to freedom through faith and grace.

In his early years Niebuhr played a part in socialist political movements in the States. He was particularly interested in the work of the post-war Labour government in Britain, and some of the younger generation of Labour politicians had studied his work and claimed to have benefited from it. In the States Niebuhr drifted away from the socialist movement and came to be more identified with the New Deal as furthered by Roosevelt.

After the Second World War the threat of Stalinism led him to seek to defend democracy.* His book *The Children of Light and the Children of Darkness* is a powerful and principled defence of democracy as a necessary and inescapable way of keeping power under a measure of control. He clearly thought it preferable to the Soviet, centralized, repressive system of unaccountable power.

Critics of his work suggest that his view of human life was too pessimistic and that he lacked joy in his approach. Those who had the responsibilities of power, however, found him in touch with the realities of political life. Those who knew the limits of choice, and who recognized that decisions had to be taken even when the perfect escaped them, found in Niebuhr a way of thinking which both came to terms with reality and preserved the vision of something better. His capacity to find models and structures of thought which connected with political experience made him the dominant figure of serious Christian social thought for the first half of the 20th century. Few who have come after him have been able to escape his influence.

Bibliography

The Children of Light and the Children of Darkness (New York, 1944; London, 1945); *Faith and History* (London and New York, 1949); *Moral Man and Immoral Society* (New York, 1932); *The Nature and Destiny of Man*, 2 vols. (London and New York, 1941, 1943).

K. Durkin, *Reinhold Niebuhr* (London, 1989; Harrisburg, PA, 1990); R. Fox, *Reinhold Niebuhr* (New York, 1985); R. Harries (ed.), *Reinhold Niebuhr and the Issues of Our Time* (London, 1986).

J.W.G.

NIETZSCHE, FRIEDRICH (1844–1900).

The son of a German Lutheran pastor, Friedrich Wilhelm Nietzsche became an atheist in his youth. After working for some years as a classical scholar at Basel, he resigned in 1879, and devoted himself for the next ten years to writing and to developing a highly idiosyncratic philosophy. This was never given definitive exposition, because of the insanity which ended his career in 1889.

Nietzsche held that the central feature of human living was the 'will to power'. (Indeed, he sought to take this principle beyond human life and to make it the basis of a metaphysics, though even his admirers have often had doubts about this.) Ethical systems merely express this 'will to power' in varying forms. The weak, who cannot put their will into power as individuals, seek to do so collectively; hence such 'herd-' or 'slave-moralities' as the Christian morality, which inculcate so-called virtues* like humility and gentleness, so as to enforce equality between unequals at the expense of stronger and higher personalities, whose superiority the herd resents. Christ himself Nietzsche regarded with respect, as an honourable opponent who stood for everything he himself rejected; but he had no use for Christians, and even less use for those who advocate Christian morals without the Christian God.

There is therefore, according to Nietzsche, no such thing as universal morality. The weak will, naturally enough, choose something which favours them and try to impose it as universal. The strong will seek out their own codes. Over against moralities of good and evil, Nietzsche set one of good and bad, or noble and base; a morality arising from self-affirmation rather than resentment of others. (Truly superior beings will handle the mediocre more gently than themselves or their equals. 'Only in their case is benevolence not weakness.') Such a code cannot be universal, because the selves to be affirmed differ. But there was an ideal, which could not be defined as it had yet to appear; what Nietzsche called the '*Übermensch*' or 'superman'. Such a being would combine the highest levels of intellect, culture, physical perfection, and above all strength of will and character.

Nietzsche frequently wrote, even thought, in aphorisms rather than in connected trains of argument, and it is possible to extract very different ideas from his writings. Hence his influence has been extraordinarily varied. He has been hailed as a source by existentialists, Nazis (though he repudiated anti-Semitism), some post-modernists (see Modernity and Postmodernity*) and psychoanalysts; and Christians have had to take care lest they approach too closely to his caricature.

Bibliography

Beyond Good and Evil (1886; ET, Winchester, MA, 1923); *The Birth of Tragedy* (1872; ET, New York, 1956).

F. C. Copleston, *Friedrich Nietzsche: Philosopher of Culture* (London and New York, ²1975); J. N. Figgis, *The Will to Freedom* (London, 1917); W. Kaufmann, *Nietzsche: Philosopher, Psychologist, Antichrist* (Princeton, NJ, ³1968).

R.L.S.

NIHILISM

is a term normally used only in condemnation of ideas with which the speaker disagrees. It implies a rejection as 'nothings' (Lat. *nihil*) of all standards of morality, in theory as well as in practice. A wide variety of views might be called 'nihilistic' in this sense, including some forms of existentialism and logical positivism;* but it is unlikely that their adherents would actually describe themselves as nihilists. Friedrich Nietzsche* distinguished between a 'passive nihilism', which despairs of life but goes no further, and an 'active nihilism', which seeks to destroy false moralities and may clear the way for something superior.

The word is often used of a Russian movement which flourished for a time in the mid-19th century (its adherents generally preferred to call themselves 'narodniks', from the Russian word for 'the people'). They professed a strictly scientific world-view, and rejected all such institutions as church, State and family. After a time, finding that 'the people' did not respond, the movement turned to violence, and after the assassination of Tsar Alexander II (1818–81) by nihilists, it was ruthlessly suppressed.

R.L.S.

NOMISM, see LAW.

NON-VIOLENCE,

NON-VIOLENCE, as used in contemporary ethical thought, is a philosophy and strategy that involves an activist, non-lethal confrontation with evil* that respects the personhood even of the enemy, and therefore seeks both to end social evils such as oppression, injustice and invasion, and to reconcile the oppressor.

The concept of non-violence requires a distinction between coercion (see Force*) and violence.* Power* is not innately evil. If used both for good ends and in non-lethal ways that respect the integrity of persons, coercion can be good. Coercion is violent and immoral when it becomes lethal or fails to respect the integrity of persons. Non-violence includes a wide variety of actions that extend from verbal and symbolic persuasion through social, economic and political non-co-operation (including boycotts* and strikes*) to non-lethal, loving, physical restraint of evil-doers. In his classic book on the varieties of non-violent action, Dr Gene Sharp distinguishes 198 different non-violent tactics (see *Exploring Non-Violent Alternatives.*)

Modern non-violent movements owe a great deal to pacifism.* Both Mohandas (Mahatma) Gandhi (1869–1948) and Martin Luther King* sought to develop effective socio-political movements to challenge oppression in a way that was consistent with their pacifist rejection of killing. Their astonishing successes have contributed greatly to a growing interest in non-violence.

Contemporary non-violence has two forms. 1. Many believe that killing* is always wrong; therefore, the methods for resisting and overcoming oppression, injustice and war* must always be non-violent. 2. Others are willing to entertain the 'necessity' of lethal violence as a last resort, but believe there are vast unexplored possibilities for non-violent methods.

The last few decades have seen increasing interest in non-violence. There are at least three reasons.

1. The increasing impact of lethal weaponry has nurtured the search for non-violent alternatives. In the 20th century – perhaps the most violent in human history – the sword has devoured at least one hundred million people. The ever-growing nuclear arsenals of the superpowers (until 1991), and the spread of nuclear weapons to more and more nations, raised the possibility of a nuclear catastrophe that might destroy much or all of the planet.

2. Another factor promoting the exploration of non-violent methods has been the inner logic of, and the debate between, the pacifist and just-war* positions. Pacifists have long claimed they had an alternative to the sword. Increasingly, just-war people have pointed out that the pacifists' verbal claims lack integrity unless they engage in a vastly increased non-violent, but vigorous, confrontation with the follies and tyrants that swagger through human history.

Just-war theorists have always demanded that war must be a last resort. That means that all realistic non-violent alternatives must be tried before one resorts to war. Pacifists here increasingly pointed out that in a century where Gandhi, King and many others have demonstrated that non-violence often works, just-war people cannot validly justify war as a last resort unless they have invested vast new energy and resources in a new sustained exploration of the unrealized possibilities of non-violent alternatives.

3. The astonishing success of non-violent campaigns in the 20th century is a third, and perhaps the most influential, fact in the increased interest in non-violence. Gandhi's non-violent campaign wrested national independence from the British empire. Martin Luther King's non-violent civil rights movement changed the US today. Deservedly, Gandhi and King have become the household

names of modern non-violent success.

But there are also many other, albeit less known, successes. Non-violent general strikes overthrew seven Latin American dictators in this century. Praying nuns, elderly women in wheelchairs, and hundreds of thousands of others, young and old, defied Ferdinand Marcos' tanks in early 1986, ending two decades of dictatorship in the Philippines.

The recent, stunning, non-violent victories in Eastern Europe and the Soviet Union have done even more to underline the possibilities of non-violence. Non-violence advocates have often been told that their techniques would never work against Communist dictators. In a patient, decades-long struggle in Poland, Solidarity proved otherwise, eventually toppling the Communist dictatorship and restoring democracy. In 1989 and 1990, non-violent movements accomplished the same results even faster in almost all other Communist countries of Eastern Europe. Most astonishing of all, perhaps, non-violent resistance successfully foiled the attempted coup by hardliners in the Soviet Union in August 1991.

Non-violence obviously works. And it is, at least sometimes, more effective in the specific sense that it accomplishes its objectives with fewer casualties. India's non-violent struggle for independence from Britain (1919–46) took longer than Algeria's violent victory over French colonialism (1955–61). But only 8,000 Indians died, whereas a million Algerians lost their lives. When one compares the casualties to total population, the figures are even more striking. Only 1 in 400,000 Indians died whereas 1 in 10 Algerians lost their lives.

For these and other reasons, and in an unprecedented way, an increasing number of people are exploring non-violence as a serious alternative to much if not all armed conflict.

Critics of non-violence allege that non-violence often fails to work; that it leads to a failure to defend the rights of oppressed and endangered neighbours; and that it assumes a naïvely optimistic view of human nature. Defenders of non-violence reply that when war kills 100 million people in one century, it cannot be labelled totally successful; that the activist non-violence of King and Gandhi does not neglect one's obligation to defend the neighbour; and that the long history of religious people regularly defending their current government's military adventures perhaps suggests that the hope that sinful people can successfully apply just-war criteria in the midst of the heated passions of wartime also reflects a naïvely optimistic view of human capabilities.

Bibliography
T. Ebert, *Soziale Verteidigung* (Waldkirch, 1981); A. P. Esquivel, *Christ in a Poncho: Testimonials of the Non-Violent Struggles of Latin America* (Maryknoll, NY, 1983); M. K. Gandhi, *An Autobiography: The Story of my Experiments with Truth* (ET, Ahmedabad, 1927; London, 1949); M. L. King, *Stride Toward Freedom* (New York, 1958); R. Niebuhr, *An Interpretation of Christian Ethics* (New York, 1935; London, 1936); G. Sharp, *Exploring Non-violent Alternatives* (Boston, MA, 1970); R. J. Sider, *Exploring the Limits of Non-violence* (London, 1988) = *Non-violence: The Invisible Weapon?* (Dallas, TX, 1989); G. Weigel, *Tranquillitas Ordinis* (New York, 1987); W. Wink, *Jesus' Third Way* (Philadelphia, 1987).

R.J.Si.

NORMS.

As used in ethics, a norm is a rule, law or standard for conduct.

How norms function in ethics can be seen in relation to the question whether it is right to lie in order to save a life. For example, in OT times, Rahab lied in order to save the lives of the Jewish spies in Jericho (Jos. 2); in modern times, Corrie ten Boom (1892–1983) lied in order to save Jews from the Nazi death camps. This issue of telling lies serves to focus the difference in the six basic, ethical positions with regard to norms.

1. *Antinomianism:* 'Lying is neither right nor wrong.' Antinomians deny that lying to save lives is either right or wrong. There are no objective moral principles by which the issue can be judged right or wrong. Decisions must be made on subjective or on other grounds, not on any objective moral ground.

2. *Generalism:* 'Lying is generally wrong.' Generalism, as proposed by John Stuart Mill* (in *Utilitarianism*, London, 1863; see also Consequentialism*), claims that lying is generally wrong. But in specific cases this general rule can be broken, depending on whether it brings good results. Most generalists believe that lying to save a life is right, because in this case the end justifies the means necessary to attain it.

3. *Situationism:* 'Lying is sometimes right.' As held by Joseph Fletcher* (in *Situation Ethics*, Philadelphia and London, 1966; see also Situation Ethics*), this view claims that

love is the only absolute, not truth-telling. Sometimes lying may be the loving thing to do. In fact, lying to save a life is the loving thing to do. Hence, lying is sometimes right; it all depends on the situation.

4. *Unqualified absolutism:* 'Lying is always wrong.' This position was embraced by Augustine* (in *Against Lying*) and Immanuel Kant* (in *On a Supposed Right to Tell Lies from Benevolent Motives*). They believed that there are many absolute moral laws, and none of them should ever be broken. Truth is such a law. Therefore, one must always tell the truth, even if someone dies as a result of it. Truth is absolute, and absolutes* cannot be broken. Therefore, there are no exceptions to telling the truth. Results are never used to break rules, even if the results are very desirable.

5. *Conflicting absolutism:* 'Lying is forgivable.' This view finds roots in Martin Luther's* two-kingdom view and is expressed by Helmut Thielicke* in *TE* 1. It recognizes that we live in an evil world where absolute moral laws sometimes run into unavoidable conflict. In such cases, it is our moral duty to do the lesser evil. That is, we must break the lesser law and plead mercy. For instance, we should lie to save the life and then ask for forgiveness for breaking God's absolute moral law. Even though moral dilemmas are sometimes unavoidable, we are culpable anyway.

6. *Graded absolutism:* 'Lying is sometimes right.' Graded absolutism has roots in Reformed theology. Charles Hodge (1797–1878) held a form of it (see his *Systematic Theology*, 1872; Grand Rapids, 1960) when he spoke of some commands based on God's nature being of greater weight than those based on God's will. Others see a hierarchy of duty in Jesus' claim that love for God is higher than love for humans (Mt. 22:36–37). This view holds that there are many absolute norms, and, in unavoidable conflicts, our duty is to follow the higher one. In such cases God exempts us from responsibility to follow the lower law in view of the overriding obligation to obey the higher law. Many graded absolutists believe that mercy to the innocent is a greater moral duty than telling truth to the guilty. Hence, they are convinced that it is right in such cases to lie in order to save a life.

These six views may be summarized by the following comparison. Antinomianism sets forth its view to the *exclusion* of all objective moral norms. Generalism claims that there are *exceptions* to moral laws, for they are general, not universal. Situationism holds one exclusive moral absolute: *love*. Unqualified absolutism insists that there is always an *escape* from the apparent conflict between absolute moral laws. Conflicting absolutism contends that when moral norms conflict, then doing the lesser evil is *excusable*. And graded absolutism holds that when moral laws conflict, God grants an *exemption* from the lower in view of our duty to obey the higher. In such a case, regret may be appropriate, but not repentance, for in obeying the higher law no sin has been committed.

Bibliography

N. Geisler, *Christian Ethics: Options and Issues* (Grand Rapids, 1989; Leicester, 1990), pp. 17–132; A. F. Holmes, *Ethics: Approaching Moral Decisions* (Downers Grove, IL, and Leicester, 1984).

N.L.G.

NORTH–SOUTH DIVIDE. The concept of the North–South divide has its basis in the work of the Brandt* Commission (1978–80). The Commission's striking division of the world, based on the Peters Projection of the world map, shows the far wealthier, high-energy-consuming 'North' as N. America, Europe, the former USSR and Australasia – and the remainder as the much poorer 'South'.

The origins of such divisions are ancient. Great centres of development have always tended to amass wealth by their power to draw resources from less-developed areas and nations on terms favourable to themselves. In Joseph's time (Gn. 39–47) Egypt was the 'North' and Canaan was part of the poorer 'South'. In NT times, Rome and the wealthy provinces of Greece and Asia represented the 'North' – Palestine was part of the 'South' (see Third World Aid*).

Today the divide is even starker, and raises great and complex moral issues which Christians need to address. In 1987 almost 4 billion people inhabited the 93 low- and middle-income countries, against 0.8 billion in the 25 high-income countries of the 'North' (World Bank). Average gross national product per capita in the former was US $290 against $14,430 in the latter. Average energy consumption per head was 12 times greater in the 'North', and there was one doctor for every 650 persons in contrast with 21,000 in the 'South'.

T. Whiston has accused the countries of the 'North' of seeing themselves as 'God's chosen children, ordained to gobble up materials and energy' at the unreal price of cheap products from the 'South'.

John Stott (1921–) has argued that the correct moral stance for Christians is not compassion but justice, which demands a drastic narrowing of the gap. For this to occur, radical changes in attitudes, consumption patterns and expectations are necessary. Concerted efforts are required from governments, churches, voluntary agencies and lobbyists. Every Christian ought to become 'a more committed internationalist', and universal education is likely to prove 'the shortest route to social justice'.

Bibliography

W. Brandt (chairperson), *North–South: A Programme for Survival* (Report of the Independent Commission on International Development Issues; London and Cambridge, MA, 1980); J. R. W. Stott, *Issues Facing Christians Today* (Basingstoke, ²1990) = *Involvement* (Old Tappan, NJ, ²1990); T. Whiston, *The Global Environment: Technical Fix or Radical Change?* (Brighton, 1990); World Bank, *World Development Report 1987* (published annually; New York, 1988).

I.R.W.

NOUTHETIC COUNSELLING, see BIBLICAL COUNSELLING; PASTORAL CARE, COUNSELLING AND PSYCHOTHERAPY. 12

NUCLEAR POWER, see ENERGY.

NUCLEAR WEAPONS, see DETERRENCE, NUCLEAR.

NUDITY. The first two references to nudity in the Bible aptly illustrate the ambivalence of Christian ethical attitudes towards it. The account of man and woman's creation in relationship ends with the comment, 'The man and his wife were both naked, and they felt no shame' (Gn. 2:25). But following their disastrous act of disobedience, the man says to his creator, 'I was afraid, because I was naked' (Gn. 3:10).

The first reference highlights the goodness of the human body. Biblical anthropology has no place for the Gk. dualistic contrast between the soul (pure and immortal) and the body (its corrupt, mortal prison). The naked body is one of those things God pronounced 'very good', not something so dirty that it needs to be hidden under clothes. As Calvin* comments (on Gn. 2:25), 'That the nakedness of men should be deemed indecorous and unsightly, while that of cattle has nothing disgraceful, seems little to agree with the dignity of human nature' (*Commentary on Genesis*, ET, London, 1965, p. 137).

The second reference illustrates the breakdown sin caused in all human relationships and anticipates the embarrassment and shame* with which nudity is usually presented in the rest of Scripture. Man and woman were now uneasy in each other's presence; anxiety to conceal their 'private' parts replaced the earlier stage of innocent openness when their attention was not riveted to their genitals. And it is only a short step from that fallen state to the compulsory exposure with which captured enemies and convicted adulterers were punished (Is. 20:2–4; 47:1–3; Je. 13:25–27).

Nudity itself is amoral. Whether it is good, bad or morally indifferent depends on the human context in which it is set.

In normal circumstances, undressing in a doctor's surgery today is as innocent as stripping for a practice session in a Gk. gymnasium used to be two thousand years ago. Morality simply does not relate to either situation (though corruption does and did enter into both occasionally).

Organized nudism can be regarded in the same ethical light. The nudist groups which multiplied in Western Europe at the beginning of the 20th century (and a decade or two later in the USA) governed themselves by strict regulations which were designed to rule out all erotic behaviour. Whether their aim was to build strong, healthy bodies, or simply to enhance the enjoyment of a summer holiday, most of these groups banned physical contact and made serious attempts to create an ethos in which awareness of members' sexuality receded.

There are certainly grounds for querying the presuppositions of nudism (often termed 'naturism'), especially the assumptions (spoken or unspoken) that taking your clothes off removes the inhibitions which impede good relationships and makes freedom from human problems possible. In biblical terms, there is no road back from the shame and shattered unity of Gn. 3 to the innocence and togetherness of Gn. 2 *via* nakedness. But it would be wrong to charge well-run nudist organizations with deliberate attempts to encourage sexual promiscuity. The same cannot be said of all displays of nudity. Some are deliberately prurient and sexually exploitative, and incur Christian ethical criticism for that reason.

John Chrysostom* condemned nude practices at Antioch for demeaning humanity. Slaves were exploited at two quite different levels. Upper-class women thought nothing of stripping before their male servants (ignoring their sexual vulnerability), while their husbands ogled female servants who were compelled to splash naked in public fountains for general amusement. In both cases, Chrysostom argued, the slaves were being treated as sub-human.

More modern critics point to the nudity (nearly always female) which features in sex magazines, strip shows, late-night films and suggestive advertising (see Pornography*). It is the context, they claim, which makes the practice immoral. Helmut Thielicke* draws a helpful distinction, as far as the arts are concerned, by distinguishing nudity as a *state* from nudity as *part of a process*. In the former case nakedness is not titillating to the average viewer, who sees it with 'disinterested delight' (Immanuel Kant*). In the latter case it is 'an unveiling, a violation, or an act of betraying the mystery' of sexual union, which is the end of the thought-process that is deliberately stimulated.

J. A. T. Robinson (1919–83) makes a similar point by contrasting *the erotic* with *eroticism*. In the context of marriage, nakedness can be beautifully erotic. But eroticism, by purveying naked sex as entertainment, abstracts it from 'the total relationship of human beings in love in which alone it is whole and true' (*Christian Freedom in a Permissive Society*, London, 1970, p. 76). In other words, the kind of nude display which stimulates sexual arousal is only ethically appropriate in a context where sexual intercourse is appropriate – in Christian terms, marriage.

D.H.F.

NULLITY. There are certain situations in civil law which indicate that a marriage* is *void*. In Eng. law (The Nullity of Marriage Act 1971), there is no valid marriage if the parties are 1. within the prohibited degrees of consanguinity or affinity or under the age of 16; 2. at the time of the marriage already married; and 3. not respectively male and female biologically. There are also grounds for declaring a marriage *voidable* in law if it is made with lack of valid consent; non-consummation through incapacity or wilful refusal; mental disorder, venereal disease, or pregnancy by another at the time of the marriage. Christians of all churches have recognized such grounds for annulment by civil law (excepting in some cases wilful refusal to consummate), and have allowed either party to contract another marriage (see Remarriage*).

Some Christians, particularly within the Catholic traditions, have gone further. Those who hold to the absolute indissolubility of marriage, and claim, therefore, that divorce* is not only impermissible but impossible, have sometimes sought ecclesiastical help in relief from intolerable marriages through the procedure of annulment. Medieval marriage law contained reference to many impediments which could give rise to dispensations and nullity suits. The Reformers believed that much of this practice brought the ideal of marriage into disrepute. Catholic churches today advocate the exploration of annulment after civil divorce, in order to demonstrate that in the eyes of the church there never was a true marriage at all. By such procedure, divorced persons may be brought back into the sacramental life of the church. The Church of Rome recognizes three elements to an indissoluble marriage: validity, consummation and sacramentality. A union which does not possess these three qualities 'may be said not to exist'. Non-consummated marriages between baptized people can be dissolved by the Pope. Marriages between two unbaptized people can be dissolved 'in favour of the faith' if one partner is baptized in a Catholic church. Various 'diriment impediments' indicate a lack of validity (age of consent, lack of capacity to give valid consent, impotence, a previous marriage, lack of baptism in the Catholic Church, having taken sacred orders or vows of chastity).

The Roman Catholic Church thus has a much wider understanding of nullity than other Christian denominations, or indeed than civil law. Other Christians have believed the Catholic position to be theologically or practically unacceptable. Kenneth Kirk* wrote that 'an easy suspicion lingers in many minds that nullity suits are still sometimes used as convenient substitutes for that divorce which Western Canon Law so stringently forbids'. The theological question concerns whether or not a valid marriage is brought into being through the consent of the partners, declared before witnesses, as many Christians have believed, in which case – apart from the situations recognized by civil law – to declare such marriages null and void on other grounds appears for the most part to be an attempt to provide for hard cases without having to recognize divorce.

D.J.A.

NYGREN, ANDERS (1890–1977). Lutheran clergyman, professor of theology and ethics at the University of Lund in Sweden, biblical commentator and leading ecumenist. Influenced by biblical criticism and Kant's* philosophy, Nygren argued that theology must have its own subject matter, language and method, over against science, ethics and art. Further, each religion is unique in its conception of God (see ①) and as a way to fellowship with God, along with ethical implications. This was most clearly demonstrated in Nygren's two-part classic *Agape and Eros* (ET, 1932; 1939), in which he uses 'motif research' to find the fundamental idea in systems of thought, specifically Christianity, Hellenism and Judaism.

The method of 'motif research' discovers in each religion the 'fundamental motif' which answers the 'fundamental question': 'How is fellowship with God conceived or realized?' The fundamental motif colours everything in the system, and its centrality can be traced through the history of a religion. The fundamental category of Christianity is *agapē*, seen especially in the NT and in Luther.* This religion is a 'theocentric' way of salvation: God comes to humans with a love (see ②) that is unprovoked, indifferent to the value of the loved object, creative of value in the beloved, and the initiator in divine–human fellowship; such a religion encourages a selfless human love of neighbour. This is contrasted with the *erōs* motif in Hellenism (especially in Plato* and Neoplatonism), an 'egocentric' way of salvation in which humans, who have an original divine dignity, seek God out of an acquisitive love. These two motifs existed side by side in the early church, were combined in Augustine's* *caritas* synthesis, which, in turn, was challenged by the Renaissance revival of Hellenism's religious ideas and the Reformation's revival of the biblical *agapē* motif.

Bibliography

Agape and Eros (ET, London and Philadelphia, 1953).

D.L.O.

O

OATHS. The swearing of an oath either 1. openly and solemnly expresses the deliberate and true intention behind human speech (promissory vows); or 2. expresses inner feelings in theological, sexual or scatological language (expletives). Oaths aim to promote truth in speech (Jas. 5:12) and are understood to reveal aspects of our true humanity.

1. The swearing of oaths

Quakers,* Mennonites* and others interpret Mt. 5:33–36 as forbidding all oaths. By contrast the *Book of Common Prayer*, Article 39, recognizes Christ's opposition as being only against 'vain and rash' (*i.e.* frivolous) swearing (R. A. Guelich, *The Sermon on the Mount*, Waco, TX, 1982, pp. 211–219). For legal regulations, see R. Cross and C. Tapper, *On Evidence*.

While oaths can be misused (1 Sa. 14:24; Mt. 14:7; Acts 23:12), the OT approves seriously taken oaths (Gn. 24:2–4; Ex. 13:19). God himself is described as swearing (Heb. 6:13–14) and Christ apparently took the oath at his trial (Mt. 26:63–64).

Helmut Thielicke,* writing in wartime Germany, recognizes ambiguity in oath-taking: an oath may strengthen social order but may also be misused to keep people from protest against injustice.

2. Expletives

Wilfrid Owen (1893–1918) in 'The Last Laugh' (see A. V. Campbell, *The Gospel of Anger*, London, 1986, pp. 68f.), wrote: '"Oh! Jesus Christ! I'm hit," he said; and died. / Whether he vainly cursed or prayed indeed . . .' Owen's poem reflects an association between prayers and oaths basic to any understanding of expletives.

Pastoral care can help people to acknowledge, understand and communicate the feelings behind expletives, lest their sound is heard but their meaning lost. Scatological and sexual expletives may reflect human longings for transcedence. However, self-control by the Spirit commits the Christian to restraint in expressing unkind, unnecessary or unholy words, and encourages true and God-honouring speech in the public realm (Mt. 5:33–37; Eph. 4:15, 25; 4:29 – 5:4; Col. 4:5; 2 Tim. 1:7).

See also: PRAYER.

Bibliography

R. Cross and C. Tapper, *On Evidence* (London, ⁷1990), pp. 220–223; H. Thielicke, *TE* 1 (ET, Philadelphia, 1966; London, 1968), pp. 531, 592, 607–680.

G.O.S.

OBEDIENCE. Basic to the concept of Christian obedience is a recognition of God's right to rule and to command, for basic to all obedience, as acknowledged by the Christian community, is obedience to God (see 1).

Without the existence of God's rights, obedience to the will of God becomes a matter of whim. The Christian claim is that God has such rights, in part because they derive from his supremacy in the hierarchy of creation* in that he ordered and constructed the created order by his word. In part they derive from his sovereign claims as the redeemer of humankind. To be God he must have such rights, and obedience is above all a response to the revealed wishes of the God who has the right to rule and command.

Biblically, obedience is a religious response either to truth (1 Pet. 1:22) or to Christ (2 Cor. 10:5), from which moral attitudes are derived (1 Pet. 1:14; Rom. 6:16–17). As such it is based on an acknowledgment that Christ is the supreme authority to whom obedience is due (see Jesus*). Christians are described as 'obedient children', a description which identifies part of their status in relation to the God who is sovereign. It is because of the authority of Christ that Paul described his apostolic purpose as being 'to call people from among all the Gentiles to the obedience that comes from faith' (Rom. 1:5). He speaks of his achievements in the gospel as being 'what Christ has accomplished through me in leading the Gentiles to obey God by what I have said and done' (Rom. 15:18). Such obedience is described as belonging to the truth (1 Pet. 1:22), leading to righteousness (Rom. 6:16–18).

Obedience has a further and wider implication, for obedience to Christ implies obedience to others. As an apostle of Christ, Paul expected to be obeyed by his fellow Christians (2 Cor. 13:2–3). Obedience to Christ is also to be expressed in our response to parents and masters (Eph. 6:1–9) and in recognizing the authority of kings and governors (1 Pet. 2:13).

The NT presents Christ as the supreme example of obedience, notably in Phil. 2:8 where it is said, 'he humbled himself and became obedient to death – even death on a cross!' The same thought is expressed in Rom. 5:19, 'through the obedience of the one man the many will be made righteous'. The obedience of Christ is the characteristic advanced by Paul as being instrumental in the redemption of humankind, yet in no way did his obedience limit his powers (Mk. 4:41).

Whilst obedience is a major concept in Christian morality, to give the fuller picture it must be placed alongside that of love (see 2). In Christ there was a linking of love and obedience such that in his death he exhibited both his love for the Father and his obedience to his Father's commandments (Jn. 14:31). In him, love implied obedience, yet transformed it from adherence to the letter of the law* to a willingness to respond to the Father's will.

The obedience of love goes beyond that entailed by the law, which by its nature effects the minimum requirements. Love produces an obedience which extends beyond the minimum in seeking to respond to the spirit of God's commands. It causes the Christian to desire to know the mind of God and to respond to the nuances of God's will. In his obedience of love there is a recognition of what grieves God and then a response to that grief.

In representing the minimum response to God's commands, the obedience to prescriptive laws is likely to come from a concern not to break such laws. It does not satisfy the one who obeys out of love. For such a person the law* points to an ideal which is fulfilled by love. Indeed, 'love is the fulfilment of the law' and for Christian obedience even to approach its full potential and significance, it must be in response to love and as an expression of love.

Nevertheless, the process of learning to obey requires a recognition of the place of law. It needs a framework of prescription to give substance to concepts such as the right to be obeyed, and rule, and it is difficult to understand how obedience will be learnt without concrete laws. It is when the basic conceptual work has been done that we are able to move on to an obedience of love.

Bibliography

B. Häring, *The Law of Christ*, vols. 2 and

3 (Cork, 1963 and 1967); W. Mundle, *NIDNTT* 2, pp. 179–180.

C.A.B.

OBJECTIVITY OF MORALS. To speak of the objectivity of morals is to say that moral qualities like right and wrong, good and bad, do not depend on what we may think or desire. Something is right or wrong independently of what people may say. Whether or not we think it to be so, adultery is morally wrong. Moral judgments are therefore true or false, analogously to other statements about factual matters. The objectivity of morals does not imply, however, that a moral judgment is either logically provable like a theorem in geometry, or empirically verifiable like a prediction about tomorrow's weather. It is a claim, not about our knowledge of right and wrong, but simply about right and wrong themselves. Moral knowledge then is more like discovering something that already exists than creating something for ourselves. We do not make something morally wrong by discovering it is wrong. Nor are we simply saying it appears to be wrong, for even if it does not appear wrong to us, it is still right or wrong independently of all our opinions. Moral objectivity in this sense is sometimes labelled 'ethical realism'.

The immediate question that arises is: what is this independent reality in which morals are grounded? Biblically, the answer is that they are grounded in God, his moral character, his will and purposes, his moral law, all of which are what they are independently of what we think. To say 'stealing is wrong', then, is to say it is incompatible with God's character or against his will, or that he intends that we respect other people and their property, and simply that stealing violates his law. To claim that these statements are objectively true is to affirm the objectivity of morals.

What God wills is in many cases revealed by means that also are objective. Biblical statements of the moral law, such as the commandment 'Thou shalt not steal', are objective enough, even though ambiguities might arise about some possible applications. Natural law* ethics follows Paul in Rom. 1 in appealing to human nature as manifesting God's eternal law: the natural inclination of all living things to survival is the premise for a moral law of self-preservation. Others appeal to the image* of God in us as an objective fact with far-reaching moral import: murder is forbidden on this basis (Gn. 9:6).

Biblical ethics is not alone in asserting the objectivity of morals. Analogous convictions are evident in ancient Sophocles (495–406 BC) and Aeschylus (c. 525–456 BC). Plato* grounded his ethic in three elements constituting the human self, each requiring its appropriate virtue:* temperance for the appetites, courage for the spiritual part, and wisdom for the intellect. Each of these virtues derives from an objective ideal form. Aristotle* derived the highest good from the essence of human nature universally, and the Stoic* ethic of reason was based on the Stoics' view of nature as governed by rational laws. In modern times, Immanuel Kant* laid aside desires and self-interest, building his categorical imperative* on the rule of reason.

Subjectivism, in this light, is a minority problem in Western ethics, and even then it does not necessarily imply relativism.* David Hume,* for instance, grounded ethics in moral feelings like sympathy, maintaining that such sentiments are universal rather than relative to different individuals. Yet a popular kind of subjectivism* sees moral judgments as expressions of personal feeling: 'It's wrong' means simply 'I disapprove' or 'I don't like it'. Such a translation, however, reduces moral statements about right and wrong to emotional autobiography. Yet there is far more to moral outrage than individual feelings, notably the expectation that *everybody* should disapprove for good reasons. Something was objectively wrong, and terribly so, about the Holocaust. Cases of that sort argue persuasively for the objectivity of morals.

Ethical objectivisms of a philosophical sort are often employed in developing a Christian ethic. Thus Augustine* adapted Plato's virtues, Thomas Aquinas'* natural-law ethic drew on Aristotle's thinking, Stoic natural law appealed to Christian ethicists in the Enlightenment,* and the commonly used principle of 'respect for persons' is drawn from Kant. Grafting them on to theological roots, however, frequently requires careful changes, for biblical concepts like goodness and justice and the biblical understanding of the human person are different from many of their philosophical counterparts. God's character and will are the norm, and his ways are not necessarily ours.

Bibliography

O. O'Donovan, *Resurrection and Moral Order* (Leicester and Grand Rapids, ²1994), chs. 1–4; K. Ward, *Ethics and Christianity*, part 1 (London, 1969).

A.F.H.

OBJECT RELATIONS, see ANALYTICAL PSYCHOLOGY; DYNAMIC CYCLE; KLEIN, MELANIE; LAKE, FRANK; PASTORAL CARE, COUNSELLING AND PSYCHOTHERAPY;⑫ TRANSFERENCE.

OBLIGATION. The notion of obligation refers to claims upon our conduct whose force is not dependent upon our perceived needs, our wishes or our understanding. That which it is my duty* to do properly transcends (though it may coincide with) that which I may wish or hope for myself or others, and is in this way an unconditional requirement.

The prominence of the notion of obligation in modern Western ethical theory derives by and large from Immanuel Kant's* ethical writings. For Kant, the apprehension of duty is morally fundamental. Hence for him the dignity of the human agent resides in the agent's capacity to obey the claims of duty without regard to personal preference or consequence. The goodness of human acts is therefore to be ascertained not by reference to their capacity to promote well-being or hinder its realization, but solely by reference to the agent's unconditional submission to the demands of the moral law. For Kant, therefore, attempts to justify the moral law, by seeking answers to the question '*Why* should we do our duty?', are subversive of the claim of duty, since, in effect, all such attempts undermine the axiomatic character of obligation.

An ethic of obligation (sometimes called a deontological* ethic) is thus to be distinguished from a utilitarian or teleological* ethic, in which conduct is judged by how actions contribute to the bringing about of certain ends which are held to be good. In terms of more recent ethical debate, therefore, an ethic of obligation is to be contrasted with ethical consequentialism.* A 'hard' type of consequentialism (such as found in some versions of 'situation ethics'*) makes acts themselves morally neutral, assessing acts only in the light of their consequences. An ethic of obligation is also to be contrasted with an ethic of virtue.* The notion of virtue draws attention to the character of the moral agent, the processes of character (see ⑩) formation and development, and makes intention* and motivation (see Motive*) primary factors in making judgments about human acts. Christian theological theories of ethics can often be distinguished by reference to the relative weight assigned to obligation or virtue. Thus, for example, a theological ethic focused on the notion of obedience to an unconditional divine command will make much of the notion of obligation; a theological ethic focused on analysis of the moral self and its world will make much greater use of the notion of virtue.

The force of the notion of obligation, in a theological context as elsewhere, derives from the way in which it highlights the moral situation in which we ought to undertake certain actions even though we may not desire to do so. In cruder expositions, a theological ethic of obligation can certainly be coarsened in such a way that moral conduct is reduced to quasi-mechanical, unreflective obedience* to authoritative precepts, with no reference to the true ends of human life or to the characters of human agents. However, the strength of the notion, properly construed, is that it sets human action within a divine order which requires that human beings act in certain ways. Obligation is both realist and anti-subjective: the good is determined by reference to a reality external to the self and its choices and decisions. To speak of moral obligation is thus to identify reasons for acting which transcend personal preference or social tradition and norm. In effect, this means that the notion of moral obligation has a critical force in an ethical context, since it articulates how moral requirements can run counter to personal or social intention. Thereby, obligation shows its incompatibility with moral voluntarism.*

However, a theory of obligation does not constitute a complete theory of morality, and it needs supplementing by attention to other considerations. Analysis of duty will inevitably involve analysis of the consequences of doing one's duty, for example. Much recent theory, especially amongst Roman Catholic moral theologians, has shown great interest in phrasing moral questions through analysis of proportionality (*i.e.* the idea that certain evil acts or effects may be warranted if they bring about a proportionate* good). Or again, recent Christian ethicists, both Protestant and Roman Catholic, have sought to reinstate the concept of virtue in the attempt to develop a more rounded moral psychology, supplementing (and occasionally supplanting) the notion of obligation by a theory of human character.

Whatever its interconnections with other

moral concepts, the notion of obligation stands in need of clear *theological* specification. It needs, that is, to be spelt out by reference to a Christian theological account of the nature and purposes of God (see ☐), of God's relations to his creatures, and of the ends to which human life is ordered by God as creator, redeemer and sanctifier. Like the closely related notions of divine 'command' or divine 'law', the notion of obligation can easily appear abstract or arbitrary unless it is carefully construed out of the history of God's dealings with humanity, which has its organizing centre in Jesus Christ. 'Obligation' in a Christian sense will not be a pure imperative requiring only the suppression of judgment and the submission of the will in obedience. Instead, it will be a term for identifying the unconditional requirements under which the subjects of God's creative and redemptive activity stand by virtue of God's covenant* allegiance to them and their responsive fidelity to God. Obligation, therefore, flows from the gracious activity of God, so that obedience to duty is a consequence of, not a condition for, acceptance by God. Obligation as imperative flows from grace* as indicative. Moreover, whilst obligations are not subject to appraisal by those who stand beneath their claim, duty is not antithetical to human flourishing. Indeed, obligation and fulfilment will coincide, since the function of obligation is to direct human lives towards their true end.

Bibliography

C. H. Dodd, *Gospel and Law: The Relation of Faith and Ethics in Early Christianity* (Cambridge, 1951); S. Hauerwas, 'Obligation and Virtue Once More', in *Truthfulness and Tragedy: Further Investigations into Christian Ethics* (Notre Dame, IN, and London, 1977), pp. 40–56; C. F. D. Moule, 'Obligation in the Ethic of Paul', in *Essays in New Testament Interpretation* (Cambridge, 1982), pp. 261–277; H. R. Niebuhr, *The Responsible Self* (London and New York, 1963); W. D. Ross, *The Right and the Good* (Oxford, 1930).

J.B.W.

OBSCENITY, see CENSORSHIP; PORNOGRAPHY.

OCCULT. The term 'occult' means 'hidden' (Lat. *occultus*) and it refers to something which is secret and beyond the range of ordinary knowledge. Occultists believe that there are hidden resources in the universe which can be revealed to those who inquire. Occultism is a way to tap the power of supernatural forces, to get in touch with the 'other side', to know and manipulate the future. A fascination with occult activity often begins with children's games, popular literature or horror films. It may lead to serious involvement in organized black magic or Satanist groups. Interest in the occult is a world-wide phenomenon in the latter part of the 20th century.

Some argue that occultism is more akin to science than religion because it does not involve worship and surrender to God. It involves gaining power for selfish and manipulative ends. Others speak of 'practising occult arts'. However it is viewed, dabbling in the occult is an attempt to discover supernatural knowledge and power in a way that is plainly forbidden in Scripture.

Biblical prohibitions

Moses warned of the dangers of the occultism as God's people prepared to enter the Promised Land (Dt. 18:9–13). Occult practices are defined in terms of human sacrifice to a heathen deity; divination or soothsaying in order to gain knowledge of future events; necromancy, which is the practice of extracting secret knowledge from the dead and disturbing their rest; augury, which interprets signs and omens in the sky; and sorcery, which uses magic powers obtained through occult formulae, incantations and rituals. Such acts are seen in Scripture as rebellion against God. Samuel said to the disobedient Saul, 'For rebellion is like the sin of divination, and arrogance like the evil of idolatry' (1 Sa. 15:23), and in the NT 'idolatry and witchcraft' are listed among the 'acts of the sinful nature' (Gal. 5:16–21). With the word against disobedience is the warning of judgment in both the OT and the NT: 'those who live like this will not inherit the kingdom of God' (Gal. 5:21).

Modern occult practices

Divination is a factor in the spiritist seance, as a medium seeks to gain knowledge by contacting departed spirits. Augury has its modern equivalent in fortune-telling, astrology, palmistry, divining with rods, pendulums or crystal balls and other forms of clairvoyance. Sorcery is expressed in forms of white and black magic and witchcraft too. White magicians claim that their power is from God, though they clearly ignore the warnings in Scripture about occult practices. Both black and white magic seeks power in order to control others, whether for good or harmful purposes. Witchcraft is basically worship of the forces of nature and is very mixed in its contemporary expression, linking Eastern religious thought with pagan or occultist ideas. The festivals of witchcraft are linked with the movements of the sun and moon, particularly with the solstices and equinoxes and with the full phase of the moon.

A particularly anti-Christian expression of the works of darkness is found in Satanism, a well-ordered movement that attracts many followers. Its sacred days are the nights of the new moon and specific feasts when the black mass is celebrated. Satanist groups are known to desecrate church buildings, steal consecrated wafers and if possible entice clergy to join a black circle.

Those who are trained in magic will involve their followers in developing powers of extrasensory perception, astral or out-of-body travel, psychokinesis and levitation.

Widespread occult interest is furthered by the followers of the New Age movement,* who believe that the day of covenant religion is over as the Age of Aquarius has dawned.

The source of evil

Behind the cosmic conflict between good and evil, the Bible sees a conflict between God and Satan* his adversary. Paul speaks of the spiritual warfare in which we are engaged: 'For our struggle is not against flesh and blood, but against the rulers, against the authorities, against the powers of this dark world and against the spiritual forces of evil in the heavenly realms' (Eph. 6:12). It is for this conflict that God provides armour for assault and for protection. Satan, whom Jesus described as falling 'like lightning from heaven' (Lk. 10:18), is presented in the NT as 'prince of this world' (Jn. 12:31) and 'god of this age' (2 Cor. 4:4), who with his demonic* agents deceives and grips as many as he can. Occult activity is to be seen as dabbling with demonic powers, often without realizing that Satan's purpose is always harm and destruction (1 Pet. 5:8).

The way of escape

The way to deal with Satan's onslaughts is to 'resist him, standing firm in the faith' (1 Pet. 5:9).

Many involved in the pastoral care of believers and unbelievers are asked to counsel those who have trouble because of past or present occult involvement, or who sense that they are under some threat or curse from an occult source. In such counselling, the following steps are important: 1. listen carefully; 2. help the occultist to renounce his or her occult dealings; 3. counsel repentance towards God and help the person to living faith in Jesus Christ as Lord and God; 4. pray for deliverance, resisting the devil; 5. pray specifically against any person who may have been used to harm the counsellee; and 6. arrange for friendship and ongoing counsel within the worshipping Christian congregation.

Final warnings

Never counsel such a person alone if it is possible to do so in partnership with a Christian friend or fellow counsellor.

Be aware of the discipline of your local church as far as the full ministry of exorcism is concerned.

Remember that 'The reason the Son of God appeared was to destroy the devil's work' (1 Jn. 3:8).

See also: DELIVERANCE MINISTRY.

Bibliography

K. E. Koch, *Between Christ and Satan* (ET, Grand Rapids, 1967); *idem*, *Christian Counselling and Occultism* (ET, Grand Rapids, 1965); F. S. Leahy, *Satan Cast Out* (Edinburgh, 1975); R. Parker, *The Occult* (Leicester, 1989); M. Perry, *Deliverance* (London, 1987); J. Richards, *But Deliver Us from Evil* (London, 1974); G. H. Twelftree, *Christ Triumphant: Exorcism Then and Now* (London, 1985); M. F. Unger, *Demons in the World Today* (Wheaton, IL, 1971); T. O. Walker, *The Occult Web* (Leicester, 1989).

T.O.W.

OEDIPUS COMPLEX, see FREUD, SIGMUND; PSYCHOANALYSIS; PSYCHOLOGY OF RELIGION.

OLD TESTAMENT PROPHECY, see PROPHECY, OLD TESTAMENT.

OPTIMISM. As a human phenomenon, the tendency to see or expect the best may be promoted by personal factors such as physical condition and temperament,* perhaps expressing a cheerful disposition or else reacting to a melancholic one, and by external considerations such as environment and experience. It will naturally reflect whatever the individual values as 'the best'.

Optimism may also describe a more formal belief in the prevalence of good in the world, (evil* being seen as limited or even illusory), or in a happy final outcome to history. Such views may rest on assumptions that are valid or false, appealing to some impersonal principle of progress, to faith in humanity or else in God. They would be less than Christian if they rested on an inadequate estimate of the existence, nature, seriousness and remedy of evil. For example, the argument of Gottfried von Leibniz (1646–1716) in his 'Theodicy'* and 'The Ultimate Origination of Things', holding this world with its imperfections to be the best possible for the maximizing of happiness, has been criticized as coming too close to legitimizing evil. Similarly defective false optimisms are challenged, e.g., by 1 Jn. 1:6, 8, 10.

The Christian will readily acknowledge that the present world order is compromised by sin. Such, however, is the redemption secured by the atoning work of Christ, entailing the decisive destruction of evil and the ultimate triumph of God, and such is the faith in God he encouraged in his disciples, that an underlying optimism can hardly be resisted, and this is best expressed in terms of hope* (e.g. Rom. 8:18–21).

Bibliography

G. W. von Leibniz, 'The Ultimate Origination of Things', in G. H. R. Parkinson (ed.), *Leibniz: Philosophical Writings* (London, ²1973); H. Oppenheimer, *The Hope of Happiness* (London, 1983).

F.V.W.

ORDINARY AND EXTRAORDINARY MEANS, see ETHICS OF MEDICAL CARE. 14

ORDINATION, see MINISTRY.

ORGAN TRANSPLANTS, see TRANSPLANT SURGERY.

ORIGINAL SIN. The notion of original sin is usually expounded in one of two senses. A tighter definition views original sin as a hereditary taint or guilt* on the part of the human race, which results from Adam's infection of humanity through his act of rebellion at the Fall. A looser construal uses the notion of original sin to speak of sin as a transpersonal phenomenon – as historical and social, and therefore as more than simply the accumulation of particular willed acts of worshipping. In this way, the broader definition speaks of human sinfulness as a given situation in which humanity finds itself, rather than as a mere malfunction of a neutral capacity to decide for or against God in particular circumstances.

This tighter construal is classically expounded by Augustine.* Adam, as the racial head, infects all subsequent human persons with the guilt of his sin, independent of any actual sins they may or may not commit. The propagation of the human race becomes the means whereby this inherited guiltiness is transmitted; baptism becomes the means of its remission. In much Western theology, the notion of an inherited taint has extraordinary imaginative power, especially when it functions alongside other components of a larger theological scheme: a vivid awareness of human corruption, a powerful sense of human solidarity 'In Adam', a dramatic, substitutionary Christology and soteriology. Moreover, the notion has considerable explanatory power in accounting for the fallenness of the human situation which appears to go far beyond particular sinful acts.

There remain, however, some acute difficulties in this account as it developed in the later Western Christian tradition. Its exegetical foundations are insecure, especially in Augustine's reliance on the Lat. mistranslation of Rom. 5:12 to read 'in whom all sinned', rather than 'in that all sinned'. More seriously, there is an incompatibility between the notion of guilt and that of inheritance. Our language of the guiltiness of human persons seems meaningful only in the context of decisions and acts in which we are ourselves in some manner involved. That which I inherit simply as the result of the situation into which I enter involuntarily cannot be my responsibility and therefore cannot render me guilty. Thus to speak of inherited guilt appears arbitrary or fatalistic, and to deny the fact that the relation between God and his human creatures is a moral relation, rather than a merely abstract relation. The tighter notion of original sin thus seems to require a notion of causality which is impersonal and which does not take sufficient account of human persons as intentional moral agents. Finally, talk of guilt as an inheritance may function as an alibi, a means of absolving ourselves of responsibility for our sins by blaming another, a progenitor through whom our situation was brought into being.

Nevertheless, the notion of original sin, used in its broader sense, has continued value. 1. It enables us to talk of sin as the situation in which we find ourselves as fallen human beings, rather than as simply specific culpable acts. It identifies, that is, our sinfulness as a truth prior to and beyond particular deeds, and it explains how sin ties us so that we act or fail to act in particular ways. In this way, it analyses the situation which the NT describes as 'the law of sin' – the way in which sin undermines our capacity to resist, since it attacks the well-spring of action in the intention and the will. 2. Original sin is closely tied to the notion of total depravity – to the notion that sin affects the totality of human existence.

For Christian moral and pastoral theology, the notion of original sin is important above all because it helps identify how the human situation requires that we be redeemed by an agent beyond ourselves, through whose activity the character of our situation can be entirely remade. Since we are sinners enslaved within a disordered situation and incapable of restoring ourselves, we require more than mere education towards better goals or encouragement to better performance. The notion of original sin is thus strongly incompatible with voluntarist* accounts of the moral life; original sin dramatizes human incapacity, and thereby throws into relief the sole competence of God in Christ to effect human moral renewal.

See also: SIN AND SALVATION. [5]

Bibliography

K. Barth, *CD* IV/1, pp. 499–512; H. Berkhof, *Christian Faith* (ET, Grand Rapids, 1979), pp. 203–209; G. C. Berkouwer, *Sin* (Grand Rapids, 1971), pp. 424–433; P. Ricoeur, '"Original Sin": A Study in Meaning', in *The Conflict of Interpretations* (Evanston, IL, 1974), pp. 269–286; N. P. Williams, *The Ideas of the Fall and of Original Sin* (London, 1927).

J.B.W.

ORPHAN, a person who has been deprived, through death, of both parents (though 'orphan' is often more loosely used of someone who has lost only one parent). The term may be taken to imply a person bereft, with no-one to care for him or her.

The OT emphasizes God's concern for widows* and orphans (*e.g.* Ex. 22:22–24; Ps. 146:9) and Israelite law accordingly made careful provision for both categories (*cf.* Dt. 14:28–29). There were times when this proved inadequate, but even so, the principle was firmly established that the rights and interests of such a vulnerable group should be protected, especially if no other kith or kin existed.

There are few direct biblical references to orphans, though probably the best known is Jas. 1:27: 'look after orphans and widows in their distress'. It is understandable, therefore, that throughout Christian history the care of orphans has continued to be a major part of social concern. Traditionally, orphanages have been part of the practical demonstration of Christian love, both on and off the mission field, and though in Europe and the Western world generally they have recently given way to more appropriate adoption,* fostering* or small-scale residential care provision, they continue in less-developed parts of the world. In Britain, the 19th-century witnessed a huge rise in the numbers of children taken in by Christian foundations, like the Muller Homes in Bristol, Dr Barnardo's* (as it was then called), the Stockwell Orphanage initiated by C. H. Spurgeon,* and the precursor of the Children's Society. All have since adopted a more sympathetic approach to the care of such children, including those rejected or abandoned by one or both parents and hence orphaned in a different way. Recent child-centred legislation has gone some way towards improving the status of these children and young people, with greater attempts being made to find the most appropriate individual long-term placement. Organizations such as the Voice of the Child in Care bring pressure to bear on charities, local authorities and government to shape social policy to the needs of youngsters in this situation.

Many natural parents, if they think about their children's security, make provision for their care in the event of a disaster. Other family members, god-parents and others may well be nominated as trustees or future guardians should both parents be rendered incapable, through death, accident or illness, of discharging their parental responsibilities. There will always be those, however, for whom no provision has been made, or those from families in which there is no available parental substitute. Then it remains up to the local authority, preferably in conjunction with other interested parties, to seek the best solution. This could, but need not necessarily, mean the assumption by the local authority of parental rights in some form.

The biblical attitude was one of care and concern for orphans, to assist in practical and legal ways, and to forestall the stigma of low status which accompanied a child's bereavement. Perhaps today such stigma is lessened, especially in the complex patterns of social behaviour now prevalent. Yet the need for protection and appropriate provision remains, and it should still be a concern of those within the Christian family to welcome the orphan and fatherless into the extended membership of the body of Christ, to share in his love, compassion and acceptance.

J.A.H.F.

ORTHODOX ETHICS. The ethical approach of Eastern Orthodox Christianity is rooted in its doctrinal, theological and ecclesial teaching and existence. Orthodox Christianity understands itself as the continuation of the undivided church of the first eight centuries. Its identity is rooted in Scripture, the Greek Fathers, the seven ecumenical councils and the Constantinopolitan Byzantine liturgy.

Major doctrinal themes inform Orthodox ethics. God as Holy Trinity is identified with the good. God is the source of every other good, both interpersonally and structurally. Evil* does not have ultimate reality: it is the absence or denial of the good, who is God. Nevertheless evil exists empirically, because rejection of the good which is God creates a distorted and incomplete state of existence.

God created everything to share in his goodness. Rational beings – angels and human beings – were created with a self-determining ability to either reject or accept communion with the good that is the triune God. This self-determining ability, together with a moral sense and drive and the conscience are part of the image* and likeness of God in human existence. The Orthodox patristic tradition distinguishes between 'image', understood as the complex of uniquely human characteristics, and 'likeness', understood as the goal towards which humanity is called through divine grace and human self-determination to grow. The goal of human existence is 'God-like living', often referred to in Orthodox literature as 'divinization' (Gk. *theosis*).

Sin (see Sin and Salvation⑤) is understood primarily as the breaking of the relationship between the good God and created reality, *i.e.* between self-determining beings (angelic and human) and the triune God. The consequences of sin are distortion, brokenness and fragmentation of life, though Orthodox ethics holds that basic moral capacities remain, though darkened and weakened.

For Orthodox ethics, the essential content of moral norms exists in the natural moral law* and the evangelical ethic. The natural moral law is understood as universally present in all societies and cultures, but expressed in different formulae. An excellent expression of the natural moral law according to the Greek Fathers is the Decalogue.* It is an expression of a moral standard essential for the functioning of any human society.

The evangelical ethic arises from the redemptive work of Jesus Christ for all of humanity and the cosmos which shares in the fallen human condition. While the natural moral law focuses on external actions, the evangelical ethic focuses on inner dispositions such as intents or motives engendered through the saving work of Jesus Christ. Through his incarnation, teaching, death on the cross and resurrection, Jesus* Christ has in principle conquered the forces that break the relationship of human beings with God, thus restoring to those who accept and participate in his saving work the potential to grow toward 'God-likeness'.

The ethical life consists of growing in the fulfilment of the God-like life. This takes place through a synergy between the leading of the Holy Spirit and the self-determination of each person. This requires that the ethical life be lived in the ecclesial context where the grace of God is manifested in the sacramental life and where others' needs and presence give specificity to the goal of God-likeness. Growth is expressed in character (see ⑩) formation (dispositions), in ethical decision-making (choices) and in overt implementation (actions).

God-likeness as a goal recognizes several important values that are emphasized in Orthodox moral, ethical and spiritual thought. Chief among these is love (see ②); *agapē* and *theios erōs*, understood both as selfless benevolence for the neighbour* and interpersonal communion with God, the neighbour and the created world, though the focus is on participation in divine life as the source of all other relationships. Related to this supreme virtue* of God-likeness are particular virtues such as humility,* self-sacrifice and patience.

Growth toward God-likeness requires a continuing struggle against evil and sin (*agōnia* and *askēsis*), through practices of spiritual discipline, constant repentance, ongoing sacramental and personal communion with God, and spiritual guidance.

In practice, the ethical life is manifested in three spheres, all of which interpenetrate and inform each other. In the personal dimension, the deepest forms of divine–human communion that makes possible growth in God-likeness ought to be cultivated. In the ecclesial dimension, the person finds that ethical living requires the presence of others, particularly the shared life of the people of God. In the outreach dimension the Christian ethical life is expressed in mission, philanthropy and social concern.

Orthodox Christianity has a long history of cultural involvement with personal, ecclesial and outreach dimensions present. However, for historical reasons, the past half-millennium has seen the ecclesial dimension dominate, followed by the personal, with outreach concerns least expressed. More recent events such as the diaspora to Western lands has begun to provoke a restored balance.

Bibliography
S. S. Harakas, *Contemporary Moral Issues Facing the Orthodox Christian* (Minneapolis, MN, 1982); *idem, Toward Transfigured Life: The 'Theoria' of Eastern Orthodox Ethics* (Minneapolis, MN, 1983).

S.S.H.

OVERDOSE, see SELF-POISONING.

OXFORD MOVEMENT. A movement within the Church of England which sought to combat the secular liberalism of early 19th-century England and revive a high doctrine of the church. It is usually said to have begun on 14 July 1833, when John Keble* preached his famous sermon on 'National Apostasy' in the University Church, Oxford. It moved into a new phase after 1845, when its leading exponent, John Henry Newman (1801–90), became a Roman Catholic and many of the others set about establishing what is now the Anglo-Catholic party in the Church of England.

The Oxford Movement published its views in a series of *Tracts for the Times*, of which the last and most famous was Tract 90, in which Newman tried to demonstrate that the Thirty-nine Articles of Religion were consonant with Roman Catholic teaching. At first the Tractarians, as they were called, were mainly interested in securing the independence of the church from the State, which they believed was not capable of determining matters of doctrine and church order. Gradually they sought to revive 'Catholic' practices like confession* to a priest and religious vows, but the main development of Catholic ritualism came in the second generation.

The founders of the movement were extremely conservative in matters of faith, but wanted to elevate the role of the clergy within the church. The Catholic idea of the priest set aside for a life of particular holiness was one which found great favour with them, and their particular pastoral concern attracted a wide following. Many later adopted fairly radical political views, and were prepared to work in deprived urban areas at a time when this was avoided in other parts of the church (see Christian Socialists*).

Bibliography
P. Butler (ed.), *Pusey Rediscovered* (London, 1983); R. W. Church, *The Oxford Movement* (London, 1891); I. T. Ker, *John Henry Newman: A Biography* (Oxford and New York, 1989).

G.L.B.

P

PACIFISM literally means 'peacemaking'. The fact that the Lat. root connotes political contexts may explain the more specific meanings which embrace its usage, for pacifism has come to signify movements that refuse to sanction wars* or participation in warfare. The word is also used to reject spiritual, psychological or physical violence* in all of its forms. Very often the word implies the advocacy of non-violent* instead of violent means in movements for social change. Though the word is rejected by many because of its negative implications, pacifists generally assume that to say 'no' to war is to say 'yes' to the things that make for peace.

Most church historians generally agree that pacifism was a prevailing attitude of Christians for the first three centuries. Scholars differ as to the extent of the exceptions to this view and whether admonitions against becoming a soldier were based primarily on the opposition to an idolatrous oath to the emperor. From the early writings, however, there are many statements which would support the avowal of Origen (*c*. 185–*c*. 254) that '. . . we no longer take sword against a nation, nor do we learn any more to make war, having become sons of peace for the sake of Jesus, who is our commander' (*Against Celsus* 5.33). Such sentiments are repeated in the oft-quoted statement of Tertullian:* 'Christ in disarming Peter ungirt every soldier.' One can discern both the pacifism and the presence of soldiers in early communities from early church canons found in the *Apostolic Tradition* of Hippolytus, originating from the early 3rd century: 1. anyone who is either Christian or catechumen is forbidden to join the army; 2. anyone who had been a soldier at the time of conversion may remain one, but only on condition that he refuse to become involved in warfare; 3. if in a responsible position [an officer], he must resign (see J.-M. Hornus, *It is not Lawful for me to Fight*, pp. 161–168).

Though Augustine* and the conversion of Constantine* marked the demise of pacifism, it continued to be a rule in monastic life, in Waldensian and Franciscan piety, and in later mystical and reform circles of the Middle Ages. A strong pacifist stream emerged out of the Reformation milieu in the testimony of the evangelical Anabaptists.* Tortured, drowned, and burned at the stake for engaging in rebaptism, a sizeable portion of this movement focused on texts such as 'Resist not evil' (Mt. 5:39, AV) and the commandment to love enemies (Mt. 5:44), due to their refusal to do to others what was being done to them (*cf.* Mt. 7:12).

Conrad Grebel (*c*. 1498–1526), a leader of the Swiss Brethren, said in 1524: 'True Christians use neither worldly sword nor engage in war, since among them taking human life has ceased entirely, for we are no longer under the Old Covenant. . . The Gospel and those who accept it are not to be protected with the sword, neither should they thus protect themselves' (quoted in G. F. Hershberger, ed., *The Recovery of the Anabaptist Vision*, Scottdale, PA, 1957). Three years later, Anabaptist leaders reiterated the above stance in what has come to be known as the Schleitheim Confession, named after the place of a gathering which met on the border between Switzerland and Germany. The confession of faith added a variation of Luther's* two-kingdom doctrine. For it allowed that outside the perfection of Christ the sword was ordained by God for the purpose of maintaining order.

In the Netherlands and northern Germany, Menno Simons* espoused the same non-resistance stance for the called-out people of God: 'These regenerated people . . . are the children of peace who have beaten their swords into plowshares and their spears into pruning hooks, and know war no more' (*ibid.*, pp. 51–52). But Menno often departed from the two-kingdom theory in calling magistrates who claimed to be Christian to refrain from using the sword.

As one who imbibed the spirit of radical movements in mid-17th-century England, George Fox (1624–91) reformulated the stance of the 16th-century Anabaptists in his oft-quoted statement to the rulers: 'I told the Commonwealth Commissioners I lived in the virtue of that life and power that took away the occasion of all wars and I knew from whence all wars did rise, from the lust, according to James's doctrine . . . I told them I was come into the covenant of peace which was before wars and strifes were.' Yet Quakers, in agreeing with Fox, have held to a one-kingdom view in which the way of the Sermon on the Mount* is regarded as normative and ultimately effective for all peoples and nations.

This has produced the difference in peace-church circles between principled pacifism, based on a literal following of the non-resistance stance of Jesus by believers, and what might be called apolitical pacifism, which proclaims the positive possibilities of goodwill, reconciliation and non-violence for all. For Anabaptists the non-resistant way of love may be possible only for the regenerate. Quakers have generally held to a Christian humanist stance, which appeals to the image of God,* or the light of Christ, which is universally present in every person. In applying the above, there has often emerged a polarity between what has been named as biblical non-resistance versus non-violent resistance.

An interesting historical incarnation of an attempt to bridge the above differences is found in the life and ministry of Adin Ballou (1803–90), an evangelical social reformer in New England in America in the context of the civil war in the mid-19th century. His importance may come from his book entitled *Christian Non-resistance* (1846; Englewood,

NJ, 1972), which circulated in Russia and is reputed to have influenced both Leo Tolstoy* and Mohandas (Mahatma) Gandhi (1869–1948). Like Anabaptists, he espoused a stance which refused to vote for or participate in a government whose constitution established violence. But he insisted that non-resistance does not imply passivity. To the 'Resist not evil' text he added his favourite text: '. . . do not be overcome by evil, but overcome evil with good' (Rom. 12:21). He refused to pay taxes, and was active in supporting underground railroads to help slaves on their road to freedom.

A similar legacy can be found in 20th-century non-violent resistance movements led by Gandhi and Martin Luther King.* Referring to the civil rights struggle, King said that 'Christ furnished the spirit and motivation, while Gandhi furnished the method.'

These movements knew a religious base, which nourished strong convictions as to the rightness of their cause. The focus was on destroying evil while effecting reconciliation with the enemy. Gandhi's tactics have been named as moral ju-jitsu, an activity which surprises opponents with unexpected actions. For example, Gandhi, in observing the sweat and discomfort of white soldiers in the mid-day sun, sent a message: 'In seeing how miserable it is for your troops, we are calling off our demonstration until evening.' Many respect the Christ-like behaviour of Gandhi, who preferred self-suffering to a desire to inflict suffering on adversaries.

Gandhi espoused what is consistent with Christian ethics, namely, that means should be kept consistent with ends (see Ends and Means*) as much as possible. In fact, means are more important, for they help shape ends. Wrong means lead to further conflict and to the common phenomenon that those who are freed through violent means often turn out to be the new oppressors.

Pacifists are criticized for having a non-biblical, naïve view of human nature. They have been said to imbibe the Marcionite heresy in their refusal to take seriously the holy-war passages of the OT. They have been accused of emphasizing God's love so as to neglect God's wrath and judgment. Peace, love and reconciliation have been stressed so as to neglect major biblical emphases on justice (see Justice and Peace③). Reinhold Niebuhr* repudiated the naïve optimistic pacifist stance of his early formation to become a major critic of pacifist movements. He argued that pacifists shirk responsibility in striving for greater justice by their refusal to compromise their love ethic. Consequently, they often have opted for tyranny rather than choosing the lesser of two evils. Niebuhr, nevertheless, believed that Jesus was a non-resistant kind of pacifist, one who uniquely embodied divine love. He further admired Anabaptist types who in their lives keep alive the ideal of agapē love which serves as an absolute whereby the lesser evil can be discerned in making ethical decisions. His critique was primarily of those who, like Quakers, were calling structures which were committed to the preservation of order and the self-interests of all, to the same impossible ideal in a world in which we all remain justified sinners. Niebuhr's reasoning sanctions what has been called vocational pacifism, a stance which involves a special calling for a few but not all people, even Christians.

Liberation theologians* differ concerning whether to sanction violence such as killing in struggles for greater justice. However, most advocates of liberation motifs would oppose the kind of pacifism which ignores the reality of structural or systemic violence. Unjust structures tolerate malnutrition, abject poverty, and lack of adequate housing and care, all of which result in death. Pacifists, thereby, participate in structures of violence. They enjoy products raised on lands which could be producing food for those who labour there. In our corporate life, pacifists share sins which violate others even unto death.

Though the issue of systemic violence is one which will continue to require prayerful discernment by pacifists, there has emerged a new category of pacifists. Many who theoretically might support revolutionary violence in particular struggles for justice and some conventional wars of the past can no longer sanction present wars. They have been named selective pacifists, nuclear pacifists, or more recently just-war pacifists. Modern weapon systems have become so destructive as to fail to meet criteria of just-war theory,* the traditional position of most Protestants and Roman Catholics. Neither can contemporary warfare satisfy the prohibition which forbids mass killings of innocent people. There will be fewer wars about which it can be reasoned that the good to be achieved will outweigh the evil which will follow. Such realization accounts for the growing convergence of traditional just-war advocates (including Niebuhrians) and pacifists in movements for peace and justice.

Whether or not one agrees with the pacifist witness, there are teachings which may contribute to ethical decisions and practical theology. Non-pacifists and pacifists need to agree that appeals for peace in the world will have more power when the witness is exemplified in caring and sharing communities of faith. A pacifist theology of the cross* can enrich understandings of the atonement.* Christ's death for us even when we were God's enemies leads to a grateful faith response which extends grace to those whom we regard as unworthy of our love. Christ's atoning death on the cross, then, is intimately related to the biblical commandment to love enemies.

Views differ about the millennium and the second coming of Christ. The contribution of pacifist theology is to propose that the now, the kingdom at hand, be added to the mix of our strong convictions about the future kingdom (see Kingdom of God*). If our hope affirms the ultimate victory of God's purposes, however we define it, we should consider the convictions of early Anabaptists that we are called to live in this world as if the kingdom has already come. As pilgrims and sojourners we can experience a foretaste of and testify to the first fruits of the kingdom of peace, justice and righteousness. The kingdom is both not yet, and now.

There are many varieties of Christian pacifism. The applications are often very different. Pacifists will continue to raise serious questions about the efficacy and validity of violence for Christians. At the same time they will increasingly recognize that they do not possess pat answers to difficult questions posed to them by other Christians.

Bibliography

R. H. Bainton, *Christian Attitudes toward War and Peace* (Nashville, TN, 1960) = *Christian Attitudes to War and Peace* (London, 1961); O. R. Barclay (ed.), *Pacificism and War* (Leicester, 1984); D. Brown, *Biblical Pacifism: A Peace Church Perspective* (Elgin, IL, 1986); J.-M. Hornus, *It is not Lawful for me to Fight: Early Christian Attitudes toward War, Violence, and the State* (ET, Scottdale, PA, 1980); G. H. C. Macgregor, *The New Testament Basis of Pacifism* (Nyack, NY, 1936; London, ²1953); H. Thielicke, *TE 2*.

D.W.Br.

PAEDOPHILIA involves sexual behaviour with children, whether boys or girls. For some paedophiles, this is their preferred or exclusive mode of sexual contact. For others, there is also sexual contact with adults. For instance, a man may act sexually with both his wife and his daughter or stepdaughter, in an incestuous situation. Incest* specifically involves sexual expression within the prohibited degrees of affinity. Paedophilia refers to sex with children both within and outside of the family. Such contact may be heterosexual or homosexual, though it should be noted that the majority of both heterosexuals and homosexuals are not paedophiles.

Sexual activity with children is developmentally inappropriate, and typically results in damage to the growing child's self-esteem and ability to trust adults. The damage is compounded if the child attempts to tell what has happened, and is not believed. Adults who were molested as children often experience major difficulties. These include: sexual dysfunction or sexual identity problems; poor self-esteem;* fear and problems of trust; promiscuity and sexual addiction;* substance abuse; and problems with intimacy and emotional bonding. In addition, some – though not all – victims will behave sexually with children in their turn, in an ongoing cycle of victimization. There is also increasing recognition that severe, early sexual abuse is typically the cause of multiple personality disorder (MPD) in adult life. In such instances, long-term therapy is required for reintegration of the personality.

In general, survivors of early molestation will benefit from appropriate therapy and support groups. They need help to break through secrecy; to get in touch with their feelings, such as unresolved anger; to mourn the loss of a normal childhood; and to rebuild self-esteem and satisfying adult relationships.

In addition to actual sexual contact with children, there is also the possibility of emotional incest. Typically, the child becomes a confidante for the parent, or is required to assume inappropriate adult responsibilities. The child becomes a surrogate partner for the parent, emotionally if not sexually. Whether or not accompanied by physical contact, this crossing of generational boundaries is also damaging to the child's development.

Children are not able to give meaningful consent to sexual contact with adults. In addition, there are important parallels in adult life. Sexual exploitation by therapists and other professionals is recognized as being psychologically comparable to incest. Adult patients are in a position of unusual vulnerability, and their dependency and trust are sometimes exploited by unethical professionals. As in childhood exploitation, there is a significant power differential between persons involved. Another point of comparison is the transference* that arises in therapeutic relationships, *i.e.* the patient transfers feelings from childhood into the current situation, and views the therapist as a surrogate parent. Sexual contact with patients not only destroys good therapy, but also typically creates psychological damage comparable to that arising from sexual contact in childhood. Sexual exploitation of children and adults alike should always be considered unethical.

Bibliography

L. Davis, *Allies in Healing: When the Person you Love was Sexually Abused as a Child* (New York, 1991); J. G. Friesen, *Uncovering the Mystery of MPD* (San Bernardino, CA, 1991); M. Hancock and K. B. Mains, *Child Sexual Abuse* (Wheaton, IL, 1987; Crowborough, 1988); P. Love, *The Emotional Incest Syndrome* (London and New York, 1991); W. Maltz, *The Sexual Healing Journey* (New York, 1991); G. Martin, *Please Don't Hurt Me* (Wheaton, IL, 1987); M. Mawyer, *Silent Shame: The Alarming Rise of Child Sexual Abuse and How to Protect your Children from It* (Westchester, IL, 1987); K. S. Pope and J. C. Bouhoutsos, *Sexual Intimacy between Therapists and Patients* (London and New York, 1986); F. W. Putnam, *Diagnosis and Treatment of Multiple Personality Disorder* (London and New York, 1989); V. R. Wiehe, *Perilous Rivalry* (Lexington, KY, 1991).

E.R.M.

PAIN is a form of suffering,* associated with specialized parts of the nervous system, and normally induced by some kind of damage to the body. The word is also extended to apply to 'mental pain', such as that of sufferers from depression. Its existence, apparently at random, has always been a major theoretical and practical problem confronting Christians. There is the theoretical problem, 'How can pain be reconciled with belief in a God (see ☐) who is all-wise, all-loving and all-powerful?'; and the practical problem, 'How can one cope in a Christian spirit with pain in one's own life, and encourage others to cope with it in theirs?' The problems are not of course confined to Christians, or to modern times; they were raised in OT times too. Several of the Psalms (notably Pss. 44 and 74) complain of God's apparent neglect of his faithful people; and the book of Job is both the classic expression of the innocent sufferer's demand to know 'Why?', and the classic rejection of the superficial answer that all suffering must have been merited by sin. (*Cf.* also Lk. 13:1–5; Jn. 9:1–3.)

Christian apologists have given various answers to the theoretical problem. It has been pointed out, correctly, that physical pain is of vital importance to warn organisms of danger; the great menace of leprosy, for instance, is that it destroys the sense of pain, leaving sufferers unaware of injuries that disfigure and cripple. Yet this says nothing of mental pain; nor of the fact that pain may continue when nothing further can be done to remedy the trouble that caused it.

It has also been pointed out that only if pain exists can there be triumph over it, just as only if danger exists can there be any courage. Again, this is true; but sufferers' characters (see ☑) may be destroyed as well as enhanced, and pain may fall on those ill-equipped to triumph over it. Nor does this explain the sufferings of animals who have no moral character to be ennobled or degraded.

Others argue that most suffering is caused by human sin or stupidity, not by God. The most vehement attacks on the divine ordering of the world often come from people who are more comfortably off than the average, not from the poor whose expectations are lower; for we cause ourselves to suffer by our excessive demands on life. (This probably leads to mental distress more frequently than to physical pain.) And much suffering is caused by human beings to one another. The evils of war,* crime,* injustice and oppression result directly from human sin; far from being the responsibility of God, they are in direct rebellion against his commandment to love (see ☑). The most that can be said against God is that he has allowed them by giving his creatures freedom.* Moreover, this applies to a vast amount of pain that might carelessly be supposed to be 'natural' rather than man-made: most of the hunger and much of the disease in the world could be eliminated if peoples and governments directed their efforts towards doing so, rather than towards self-satisfaction and self-aggrandisement. This too is true; but a residue of suffering still remains which cannot be explained in this way – pain resulting from disease which cannot be cured, or from such events as floods and earthquakes, not to mention the pains of animals (other than those caused by human cruelty or indifference).

Some see the cause of this evil, not in sinful human wills, but in a sinful superhuman will: they see so-called 'natural' evil as the work of Satan.* This may be so in particular cases (cf. Lk. 13:16), but it is difficult to see this as a general solution to the theoretical problem. For it seems that these evils arise from the workings of the laws of nature (earthquakes, for instance, arising from the way the earth's crust is composed of plates moving in relation to one another); and to ascribe the laws of nature to Satan rather than to God the creator seems nearer Manichaeanism than Christianity.

Yet the very fact that this residue of pain does seem to arise out of the workings of scientific laws may help towards a further answer. For that there are such laws is plainly a good thing for the inhabitants of the world, normally working for their benefit; that from time to time it should not do so is inevitable, as the laws can hardly include reference to the desires or feelings of those affected by them. It seems that not even divine omnipotence could create a world which both operated according to law and contained sentient beings, and yet which invariably avoided suffering to the latter.

Theoretical considerations are unlikely to be of great value in the practical pastoral handling of pain. Job's demands for an explanation were not met; instead, his persistence was rewarded with an encounter with the Lord, after which questions and answers seemed inappropriate. The sufferer's aim should be to let suffering draw him or her closer to God; we remember Paul's wrestling with the problem of his 'thorn in the flesh' (2 Cor. 12:7–9). (This is perhaps easier with physical pain than with mental, where the mind itself, which should do the drawing closer, is affected.) It may be worth recalling that, whatever reasons led God to allow suffering in the world, he has not left us to endure it alone, but has himself entered into and shared our pains, as well as promising their ultimate disappearance.

See also: THEODICY.

Bibliography

A. Farrer, Love Almighty and Ills Unlimited (London, 1962); J. Hick, Evil and the God of Love (London, ²1977); S. A. Kierkegaard, 'Joyful Notes in the Strife of Suffering', in Christian Discourses (ET, London and New York, 1939); C. S. Lewis, The Problem of Pain (London, 1940); idem, A Grief Observed (London, 1961); F. R. Tennant, Philosophical Theology, vol. 2 (Cambridge, 1930).

R.L.S.

PAPAL ENCYCLICALS. Some of the important papal encyclicals on matters such as marriage and birth control, the rights of workers, the value of human work, and capitalism, are outlined below chronologically. An encyclical is a formal pastoral letter addressed by the Pope to the whole (Roman Catholic) Church. Though encyclicals do not have the status of infallibility accorded to the ex cathedra pronouncements of the Pope on matters of dogma (e.g. the bodily assumption of the Virgin Mary to heaven, 1950), Catholics are nevertheless under obligation to give assent to their doctrinal and moral content. This must be given 'in such a way that his supreme magisterium is acknowledged with reverence, the judgements made by him are sincerely adhered to, according to his manifest mind and will' (Documents of the Second Vatican Council, Lumen Gentium, 25). Encyclicals are normally published in Latin, and their titles are taken from the first words of the document concerned.

Rerum Novarum

On 15 May 1891, Pope Leo XIII (1878–1903; b. 1810) issued the encyclical Rerum Novarum, in which he affirmed the Church's commitment to labour by recognizing the right of the workers to organize labour unions (see Trade Unions*) in order to redress their grievances. These arose out of the laissez-faire* capitalism* of the early Industrial Revolution, which created class conflicts between labour and capital, resulting in poor conditions for the working classes.

With the consolidation of capital in large corporations in the period following the Second World War, labour was able to organize itself into strong and powerful unions and force governments to adopt benevolent welfare programmes, such as social security, minimum wage and unemployment compensations.

Casti Connubii

Pope Pius XI (1922–39; b. 1857) issued an encyclical in 1930 on the nature and dignity of Christian marriage.* This restricted the right to have children to the marriage state, wherein alone the duty to educate children for life here and hereafter can be adequately fulfilled.

Through conjugal fidelity, the husband and wife sanctify each other and the marriage contract itself becomes an efficacious sign of sacramental grace. As such it is not to be degraded to the level of a mere civil contract, dissolvable by the State. All temporary, experimental or companionate human unions are evil and create an unhealthy society (see Cohabitation*).

Humanae Vitae

This encyclical letter on birth control,* issued on 29 July 1968 by Pope Paul VI (1963–78; b. 1897), restated the Roman Catholic Church's traditional teaching that 'each and every marriage act must remain open to the transmission of life or its possibility', thus enabling spouses to 'collaborate with God in the generation of new lives'.

Consequently, except for the utilization of the natural rhythms, the encyclical stated that all birth control techniques such as abortion, sterilization and the anovulant pill, which render procreation impossible, must be rejected as an intrinsic evil, unrectifiable by good ulterior motives or by other conjugal acts left open to procreation.

Although not claimed as infallible, this teaching commands 'religious submission of mind and will', and excludes the right of individual conscience*/judgment.

Laborem Exercens

An encyclical of Pope John Paul II (1978– ; b. 1920) on 'human work', *Laborem Exercens* was issued on 14 September 1981. Any human activity, whether intellectual or manual, constitutes work,* which is a fundamental dimension of human existence. It distinguishes human beings from other creatures.

A person's life derives dignity from work, and all situations in which that dignity is violated must be condemned. The basis for determining the value of human work is not primarily the kind of work done but the fact that the one who is doing it is a person, a conscious and free subject who realizes his or her humanity through it and fulfils his or her role as creature. A person is destined for work, not work for a person, although work has an ethical value of its own. On this view of persons, labour always has priority over capital.

Centesimus Annus

Issued by John Paul II in 1991, this encyclical addresses the issue of capitalism* in the light of the collapse of the centrally controlled economies of Russia and Eastern Europe. Private ownership (see Property*) of productive goods is the basis of a healthy economy, but the mechanism of the market is not the only criterion of the social good. Affluence is not to be pursued for its own sake to the exclusion of morality and religion. Trade unions* have a legitimate role in seeing justice is done.

The State's* function is to provide the institutional, juridical and political framework in which freedom* and responsibility* can flourish. Poverty and deprivation are to be remedied by social welfare according to the principle of subsidiarity: the State should interfere in a 'subsidiary' way by giving assistance to a lower level organization (*e.g.* the family) only if that organization cannot meet its obligations on its own.

See also: VATICAN STATEMENTS.

Bibliography

T. Herr, *Catholic Social Teaching*: *A Textbook of Christian Insights* (ET, London, 1991).

P.T.

PARDON, see RECONCILIATION.

PARENTHOOD, PARENTING, is usually thought to be the process of rearing children* who are the natural offspring of the father or mother. In today's complex social environment, with lone parents (see Single Parents*), reconstituted families, differing patterns of fostering* and adoption,* and ethnic mix, it is clear that child-rearing is a task which falls upon a far wider range of adults than was the case with the so-called 'nuclear family'.

'Parenthood' implies accepting responsibility for the physical care and emotional nurture of a child from birth. Some see it as a function which begins at conception with ante-natal care, or even before conception.

Physical care clearly involves protection from harm in terms of providing a safe home, coupled with adequate warmth, shelter, food and clothing. In the dependency of infanthood, such provision is more essential than for a growing child who has gained some control over his or her environment. For the latter, safety becomes, if anything, even more of an issue, not just physically but also in terms of providing protection outside the home. For many parents this sense of being a protector is lifelong, even when children have long since left the parental home.

The mothering aspect of parenting is complex. It involves the building up of secure emotional bonds, within which strong attachments are formed between parent and child and then, utilizing that good experience, between the child and others within the family and beyond. It is the security of knowing that needs will be met, and that he or she is loved, valued and accepted (see Self-esteem*), which gives the offspring confidence and interest to learn. Nurture may imply appropriate discipline* and training, so that eventually the parent(s) will have equipped sons or daughters to make their way in the adult world independently, able to look after themselves, to work, to sustain good personal relationships, and ultimately to prove good parents themselves.

Most parents, at some time, feel their role is an exceedingly onerous one. It was D. W. Winnicott* who coined the phrase 'the good-enough mother' in his analytical work with young children. 'Good enough' is a concept which relieves the pressure to be perfect, and encourages parents to permit the natural resilience of a healthy child to deal with life's difficulties, provided that the essence of his or her parental relationship is trustworthy, secure and largely consistent.

Societal norms in the 1990s are very different from those in the immediate post-war period, when much new understanding about childhood growth and development resulted from innovative work by Anna Freud (1895–1982), John Bowlby (1907–90), D. W. Winnicott, V.M. Axline (1911–), B. Bettelheim (1903–90)and others. In the UK today, 40% of marriages break down; at least 20% of children are reared by only one parent, and very many live in families which have second or third step-parents, with their children too. For a significant proportion, therefore, the making, breaking or stretching of affectional ties is an anticipated fact of life. Because it is so common, some see it as an acceptable cost of separation or divorce,* but most children do, in reality, suffer greatly.

In this context, it is therefore perhaps not surprising that all this can prove too much for some children to cope with. Within Western legal frameworks, recently increased emphasis on the primacy of children's interests has resulted in a few children taking action against parents who are deemed to have failed in their responsibilities. Children bear stresses in many ways, including the enduring of neglect, and sexual, emotional and physical abuse.* Some are received into care for their own protection. The substitute parenting required by foster children or those in residential care is consequently most demanding. Adoption may not be easy either, though the latter does carry with it the legal status (and responsibilities) of full parenthood. Other legal categories such as custodianship and guardianship may confer responsibilities without full legal parental status.

Fostering and adoption by single people, and sometimes also by couples other than those in a normal heterosexual relationship, are occasionally permitted. These candidates are usually required to convince authorities of their desire to care for a child through rigorous assessment procedures, thus providing parenting in a potentially non-familial context.

Many biblical references to parenthood relate to the concepts of protection and inheritance, often strictly codified. Yet parenting itself was clearly shared within the extended family or household, possibly with servants. There is no description of the nuclear family, considered so desirable recently in the West. Perhaps Christians adopted that model as it seemed a practical outworking of the NT teaching on sexual continence within marriage, as well as honouring the teaching on codes of conduct and respect between parents and children (1 Cor. 7 and Eph. 6:1–4). The criticism of muddled families often springs from that teaching, in so far as biblical descriptions of extended families sharing their caring is one thing, but widespread marital infidelity, breakdown and cohabitation* is quite another. Children, regarded as precious in the sight of God, may be seen as, and sadly often are, innocent victims of irresponsible adult behaviour.

The family* of Jesus himself is the only clear NT model: the son of Joseph and Mary, he is known to have had brothers and sisters (Mt. 13:55–56). The only extended family member referred to is Elizabeth, Mary's cousin (Lk. 1:36), and she was not local. Christians, therefore, may well also have tended to adopt this pattern as supporting the idea that the nuclear family is the norm in present times. They have generally paid less attention to the extended family, though worldwide there are, of course, cultural variations.

J.A.H.F.

PASTORAL CARE, see Pastoral Care, Counselling and Psychotherapy. [12]

PASTORAL COUNSELLING, see Pastoral Care, Counselling and Psychotherapy. [12]

PASTORAL THEOLOGY, see Practical and Pastoral Theology. [7]

PATENTS are intended to establish legal rights to proprietary claims on inventions, processes, or features of marketable or otherwise useful assets. They are intended to protect owners against a type of theft,* *i.e.* copying, and the selling of the copy. Patents provide a protected monopoly* for a specific period of time. There are nations where patents are not recognized as legally binding constraints against copying and marketing products, and there are many people who, while abiding by the patent laws, find fault with their restrictions and duration of restraint (either too little or too much).

Those who support patents advance the argument that the patent process protects small and financially weak individuals and organizations from the abuse that can emanate from financially powerful and technically sophisticated business enterprises. During these times of rapidly advancing technology* and expanding mass markets, an inventor who is not sophisticated in business matters, or who is not financially strong, is given time to seek an alliance with those who will reward equitably the creative efforts of the inventor. There is biblical justification for such a line of reasoning, for since the Fall the strong and wealthy have had an all-too-often ungodly interest in taking advantage of those who are less well-endowed than themselves.

Patents also represent an effort to put some outward constraints on the public demonstration of personal greed and covetousness.* In modern market-oriented societies, ideas with commercial value are prized, as were land, jewels, and precious metals in earlier times. So patents, and the body of law supporting them, are a legal/political/social means of publicly addressing the eighth and tenth command-ments: 'You shall not steal,' and 'You shall not covet . . .' (Ex. 20:15, 17).

See also: Copyright.

R.C.C.

PATRIOTISM is the love shown in loyalty to a native or adopted country. As such, it must be scrutinized in the light of that greater, agapic love (see [2]) that characterizes Christian social ethics.* No country can legitimately make an absolute moral claim on the loyalty* of the Christian or any of its members. Christians and the nations are called to a greater love and an ultimate loyalty to the Lord Jesus Christ. Countries and nations are not part of God's original creation* but have developed in the course of fallen human history as provisional and changing communities, bearing all the marks of moral ambiguity in their culture and institutions. It is identity in Christ and the gospel of the kingdom which offer hope and reconciliation in a divided world, not national identity and patriotism. And yet Christians and the one human race live in the context of a range of social, cultural and political communities. That is an integral part of a God-given humanity[4] as created social creatures. The gospel both judges and affirms social context and identity, including the context of country and nationhood. Patriotism may be a worthy disposition for Christians in their earthly citizenship within the wider loyalty and horizon of the heavenly city.

The love that Christians may show for their country must be discerning and discriminating. At its core patriotism must be an affirmation of what is best in a country's history and life, including the humane and creative achievements of its culture,* its struggles for greater justice (see Justice and Peace[3]) in human affairs at home and in the wider world, and the expression of certain moral values in its public life and institutions. The scale for assessing the worth of one's country does not lie in some innate national spirit or genius, as in the spurious claims of romantic nationalism*, but in that human creativity* and partial grasp of truth which is God's gift to all humanity even after its fall into sin and rebellious history. Each culture and country may express that creativity and grasp of truth in its own distinctive ways, but no mere country is endowed with a monopoly of wisdom or possesses some unique destiny. It is the church* of Jesus* Christ which is the herald of the coming kingdom of

God*, a community which draws its membership from every country and culture.

Nor must patriotism be confused with an ethnocentric or chauvinistic view of the world. The qualities and achievements that evoke a love for one's own country, however distinctive, should lead a true patriot to a respect and appreciation for other countries and cultures. No true love of country is blind to the failures, injustices and shameful episodes that mark the history and contemporary life of every country. A true patriotism will expose all that is evil or morally compromised in its own country, in the light of the gospel. Christian patriots like Dietrich Bonhoeffer* and Simone Weil (1903–43) show the cost, honesty and courage required for true love of God and country in Christ.

Bibliography

P.H. Ballard and D.H. Jones (eds.), *This Land and People: A Symposium on Christian and Welsh National Identity* (Cardiff, 1979); K. Barth, *CD* III/4, pp. 285–323; F. Catherwood, *A Better Way: The Case for a Christian Social Order* (London, 1975); idem, 'Nationalism', *Christian Arena* 43.3. 1990, pp. 3–6; K. W. Clements, *A Patriotism for Today: Love for Country in Dialogue with the Witness of Dietrich Bonhoeffer* (London, 1986); J. Habgood, *Church and Nation in a Secular Age* (London, 1983); D. Jenkins, *The British: Their Identity and their Religion* (London, 1975); O. R. Johnston, *Nationhood: Towards a Christian Perspective* (Oxford, 1980); W. Storrar, 'The Modern Judas: A Theology of Nationhood for Europe', *Christian Arena* 43.3, 1990, pp.7–10; idem, *Scottish Identity: A Christian Vision* (Edinburgh, 1988); B. Thorogood, *The Flag and the Cross: National Limits and Church Universal* (London, 1988); C. Villa-Vicencio, *A Theology of Reconstruction: Nation-building and Human Rights* (Cambridge, 1992); S. Weil, *The Need for Roots* (ET, New York, 1952; repr. London, 1978, and New York, 1979).

W.F.S.

PATRISTIC ETHICS. The ethical teachings of the Fathers (Lat. *patres*) of the early church varied considerably, according to their intellectual and religious formation, historical, geographical and social context, literary genres, methods of interpreting Scripture and other factors. For example, the emergence of the 'Christian empire' under Constantine* and his successors in the 4th century marked a significant watershed. In the earlier 'age of the martyrs', pacifism,* or at least anti-militarism, was the order of the day, but after persecution ceased, writers like Eusebius (*c.* 265–*c.* 339) and Augustine* argued the case for the holy war, the just war* and even the judicial coercion of schismatics and heretics. Even within the pre-Constantinian era, military service might be allowed for Christians in the ranks or in peaceful areas – *i.e.* in contexts where it carried no risk of shedding blood. And at least some anti-militarism was inspired not by principled refusal to kill but by avoidance of the religious paganism that pervaded camp life. Finally, plentiful evidence shows that Christians often served as soldiers, presumably in defiance of their teachers.

Regional differences in ethical outlook were sometimes unmistakable, *e.g.* between the Christian traditions of Carthage (near modern Tunis) and Alexandria in Egypt. In the former, Tertullian* and Cyprian (*c.* 200–58) demanded a more stringent distinctiveness, *e.g.* in dress, and even in social separation, whereas in the latter, Clement (*c.* 150–*c.* 215) and Origen (*c.* 185–*c.* 254) countenanced more liberal involvement so long as inner detachment garrisoned the soul. Or again, in the 'peace of the church' after Constantine, a double-standard ethic developed, with monks and clergy bound to more exacting standards – that had in some respects been binding on all pre-Constantinian Christians.

But if generalizations about early Christian ethics have frequently to be hedged about with qualifications, some common positions can be established. In the main, the Fathers were not as creative and productive in ethics, especially social ethics, as in theology, apologetics, spirituality* and liturgy. (No history of early Christian ethics has been written comparable to the great histories of doctrine.) This was partly because they were heirs to OT and Jewish ethics. Jews in the Roman world had centuries of experience in maintaining their identity in a pagan and often hostile environment – though not all Jews had responded to this challenge along identical lines. The 'two-ways' (of life and death, light and darkness) pattern of moral instruction found in several early Fathers was of Jewish derivation, and the lists of occupations forbidden to Christians given by Tertullian (in *Idolatry*), Hippolytus (*c.* 170–*c.* 236; in *Apostolic Tradition*) and others, had much in common with similar Jewish listings. Furthermore, patristic ethics was also powerfully influenced by secular traditions, chiefly Stoic* but also Platonic* and Pythagorean (as in *The Sentences of Sextus*).

Moreover, until the persecutions ended, dying like Christ was the most distinctive visible aspect of Christian existence. For Ignatius (*c.* 35–*c.* 107) it was martyrdom that made one a true disciple of Christ. In martyrdom all were equal, and slaves died alongside their masters and mistresses. Not only was the ethos of such Christianity profoundly other-worldly, but its ethics were mostly personal rather than social. Not until Augustine's *City of God* (413–26) did a Christian writer give extended critical attention to the socio-political realities of the Roman Empire. Most earlier Fathers, such as the apologists of the 2nd and 3rd centuries, were more interested in protestations of law-abiding, tax-paying loyalty to the emperors than in protests against such blatant injustices as slavery.

The asceticism* that was present from the teaching of Jesus onwards with ever-increasing appeal contributed to rigorous sexual and marital ethics. Hardly any Fathers allowed divorce (*cf.* H. Crouzel, *L'église primitive face au divorce*, Paris, 1971); most disapproved of the widowed remarrying; long before Augustine procreation was widely viewed as the only proper purpose of sexual intercourse; writers on all sides narrowly avoided denigrating marriage in their zeal to commend celibacy, virginity and sexual abstinence within marriage; homosexuality was universally condemned; and the ideals of family life were more assumed than vigorously developed – although Christians were distinguishable by their rejection of abortion and of the abandonment of unwanted children.

Basil the Great's (*c.* 329–79) *Moralia* (Gk. *ta ēthika*) is in reality an ascetic manifesto. This fact illustrates the remarkable pervasiveness of ascetic aspirations and practices in the church of the Fathers. Poverty, however, was less commonly advocated than chastity. Clement of Alexandria famously spiritualized Jesus' words 'Go, sell everything you have' (Mk. 10:21) – *i.e.* it was the wealth of passions that one must renounce – but patristic homilies repeatedly warned against the snare of riches. Most Christian moralists endorsed the right of private property but also remained faithful to the OT's condemnation of usury. Christians' generosity in providing for their own poor and orphans and widows was so conspicuous as to be almost a byword. Such sharing was inculcated partly by means of distorted notions of the meritorious character of almsgiving. In time Christians gained an equally impressive record for caring for others' sick and needy, *e.g.* during the plague at Carthage in Cyprian's episcopate. Institutions such as hostels, hospitals and refuges first came to the fore in the context of monastic communities in major cities.

The command to love (see ②) was perhaps the single most dominant motive in early Christian ethics. It received suggestive elaboration under Platonic influence in Clement of Alexandria. Basil the Great (also called Basil of Caesarea) insisted that only in community, not in hermitic solitude, could it be fulfilled. Augustine preached and wrote on the hierarchy of loves with great profundity, even at length on lawful self-love (*cf.* J. Burnaby, *Amor Dei: A Study of St Augustine's Teaching on the Love of God as the Motive of Christian Life*, London, 1938; O. O'Donovan, *The Problem of Self-Love in St Augustine*, New Haven, CT, and London, 1980). Augustine's maxim, 'Love and do what you will', meant something far different from its modern misappropriations: it justified the severity of loving discipline and even the corrective persecution of religious dissidents. Thus did orthodoxy have the edge over orthopraxis in the Fathers; in Ambrose's* portentous words, 'Justice must yield to religion' (*cedat censura religioni*).

Bibliography

C. J. Cadoux, *The Early Church and the World* (Edinburgh, 1925); G. W. Forell, *History of Christian Ethics*, vol. 1 (Minneapolis, MN, 1979); R. M. Grant, *Early Christianity and Society* (San Francisco, 1977; London, 1978); F. X. Murphy, *The Christian Way of Life* (Wilmington, DE, 1986); E. Osborn, *Ethical Patterns in Early Christian Thought* (Cambridge, 1976); H. H. Scullard, *Early Christian Ethics in the West from Clement to Ambrose* (London, 1907); R. E. O. White, *The Changing Continuity of Christian Ethics*, vol. 2 (Exeter, 1981) = *Christian Ethics: The Historical Development* (Atlanta, 1987); J. L. Womer (ed. and tr.), *Morality and Ethics in Early Christianity* (Philadelphia, 1987).

D.F.W.

PEACE. The Hebrew word for 'peace', *šālôm* (often transliterated 'shalom') abounds in meaning. It signifies salvation (see Sin and Salvation⑤), wholeness, integrity, community, righteousness,* justice (see Justice and Peace③) and well-being. Since by 'soul' the biblical writers mean 'the total person', the church is engaged in shalom business when it embraces any manifestation of the Spirit which brings persons into right relationships with God, others, and God's good creation. Whereas the Greeks were content to think of *eirenē* as inner peace, the NT writers were influenced by the place which shalom had in Judaism. Consistent with the relational nature of Hebraic shalom, *eirenē* was used often as a greeting (Jn. 20:19, 21, 26) or a departing salutation (Mk. 5:34).

In the Gospels, peace is primarily a gift of Christ, the bringer of shalom (*cf.* Eph. 2:14–18), rather than something we can attain. If we accept God's acceptance (see Justification, Doctrine of*) and loving forgiveness, we know the joy of children of God testifying to a peace which the world cannot give or take away (Jn. 14:27). In the spirit of thanksgiving, we then can do no other than be vehicles of this same grace towards others, even those whom we judge to be undeserving of our love. The church is called to be a caring and sharing community of God's peace.

It is difficult to critique humanistic philosophies that propose we should love others because of their natural goodness. But motivation based on the faith that others are lovable can quickly bring disillusionment when it is proven otherwise. If we love others because God loves them, however, we can keep on loving them even when we consider them to be undeserving of our love.

Paul and the Gospel-writers believe not only that we are channels of God's peace, but also that we are to make peace in our families, congregations, communities and nations. In this peacemakers do not avoid judgment. As a part of their covenant with the church, members of the historic peace churches (see Pacifism*) have promised to settle differences by practising Mt. 18:15–19. If you believe yourself to be sinned against, confront the person. If the person refuses to listen, take two or three others with you. And if this does not work, take the matter to the church. At its best, the contemporary pursuit of conflict* resolution simply appropriates what is basic in this teaching of our Lord.

Misunderstandings

Many wonder why Jesus seemed to disclaim the above good news of giving and making peace when he posed the question, 'Do you think I came to bring peace on earth? No, I tell you, but division' (Lk. 12:51). This signifies that Jesus, in claiming their primary allegiance, brings division into the lives of people.

Another misunderstanding of shalom occurs when Christians adopt a Stoic* view. For NT authors, peace is not detachment from the world, void of passion. Rather, peace comes out of deep feelings of concern, such as the lament of Jesus overlooking Jerusalem. In contemplating what might happen because of their disobedience, he wept, saying: 'If you, even you, had only known on this day what would bring you peace . . .' (Lk. 19:42). Christian compassion compels us to be concerned for peace on earth.

Some interpret hearing of 'wars and rumours of wars' in Mk. 13:7 to mean that wars* are the will of God. It is thus assumed that if Christians become peacemakers, they are opposing God. In weeping over Jerusalem, Jesus, rather than sanctioning war, was predicting what happens when people break their covenant with God. Have you ever heard the subsequent prediction in Mk. 13:12, that children will put their parents to death, used to maintain that we should cease striving for better relationships in the family?

Peace, justice and evangelism*

Christians continue to attempt to discern the relation of peace and justice. From Ps. 85:10 and Jas. 3:18 we learn that there is no peace without justice and no justice without peace. As peace should not be kept at any price, so justice should not be achieved by any means. Peacemaking is intimately related to setting at liberty those who are oppressed. The good news is for those who have been sinned against as well as for all who have sinned.

Another aspect of biblical shalom is emerging in the Christian conscience. Our concerns for personal salvation, peace and justice cannot be separated from a deep respect for everything that God created and pronounced as good. Ecological concerns (see Environment*) must become a part of the agenda of Christians. The insights of the psalmist's declaration that the earth is the Lord's invites us to relate to the creating, redeeming and sustaining activity of the Trinity.

Such insights would lead to holistic evangelism. We often too neatly separate concerns for personal, relational, political and ecological redemption, all of which are implied by biblical shalom. In the NT, God's shalom is the most elementary expression of what life is intended to be in the age inaugurated by Jesus' coming. In preaching the 'good news of peace through Jesus Christ, who is Lord of all', Peter did not neatly differentiate between evangelism and peace (Acts 10:36). In the Gospel of John, the golden text of personal salvation cannot be separated from the salvation of the world. If one emphasizes Jn. 3:16 without Jn. 3:17, Christianity can easily become but another mystery cult which ignores its Jewish heritage of historical redemption. But if one chooses Jn. 3:17 without Jn. 3:16, Christianity will become but another social movement without the power of personal commitment.

This Hebraic concern for what happens in history is found in Ephesians. The epistle heralds the beautiful news that the one who is our peace made peace between bitter enemies, Jews and Gentiles, by destroying 'the dividing wall of hostility' (Eph. 2:14). The church should exemplify in its own life the peace which God wills for the coming kingdom (see Kingdom of God*). Christians hold differing views about the nature and timing of the millennium. Whatever our belief, we all are called to begin now to imbibe a foretaste or firstfruits of that future kingdom. When Jesus announced the kingdom at hand or spoke of the kingdom in our midst, his listeners knew better than many contemporary Christians that he would include the vision of the prophets about how nations will not train for war any more (Mi. 4:3). Until the kingdom comes in God's time and the creation is liberated from its bondage to decay (Rom. 8:21), Christians are to experience a foretaste, receive the firstfruits, and participate in signs of the kingdom coming. As much as possible they are to live at peace with all, preach the good news of personal salvation, love their enemies, overcome evil with good, deeply respect God's creation and become ministers of reconciliation.

D.W.Br.

PENANCE, see Penitential Tradition.

PENITENTIAL TRADITION is concerned with the practice of penance and the forgiveness of post-baptismal sins. There is no definite evidence that a formal method existed in the first four centuries of the Christian era whereby sins were confessed to a priest and the absolution given. This practice gradually developed over the centuries.

In the early church, controversy arose over the question of the church's forgiveness of the grave post-baptismal sins of adultery, murder, idolatry and apostasy. While Tertullian* taught that only God could forgive these, Cyprian (c. 200–258) and Augustine* taught that there were no sins which the church could not forgive but insisted, like Clement of Alexandria (c. 150–c. 215) and Origen (c. 185–c. 254), that forgiveness should be preceded by a long and rigorous penance.

From the 6th century seven psalms (Pss. 6, 31, 37, 51, 101, 129, 142), called the Penitential Psalms, have established themselves as the classic prayers of repentance for sin. Psalms 51 and 129 are still popularly known and used as such.

In the 13th century, after much debate, it was decided that there were three kinds of penance, each requiring its own penitential act. Solemn penance was for those guilty of capital sins which hurt the church and required a special ceremony of absolution* given once only. Public penance took the form of ecclesiastical acts of prayer, fasting and almsgiving. Private penance was made daily before the priest.

When public confessions began to be replaced by private ones, the need became urgent for confessors to be given some guidance, and this was met by the production of manuals which allotted penances for specified sins. These manuals were normally produced by individuals, especially abbots of monasteries, who had gained a reputation for knowledge and holiness. Irish influence played a major role in this development, especially with its emphasis on the healing aspect of penance.

P.T.

PERFECTIONISM is a theory about perfection; more specifically the doctrine that moral and religious perfection can be attained in this life.

Christians have generally accepted that the Bible sets before us nothing less than the highest goal: 'Be holy because I, the Lord your God, am holy' (Lv. 19:2); 'Be perfect, therefore, as your heavenly Father is perfect' (Mt. 5:48). But differing views have arisen over the meaning of perfection, and whether or not we can reach it in this life.

Augustine* and the Reformers held that while we should set perfection, in the sense of sinlessness of life, before us as a goal, we will never achieve it while still in the body, so great is the power of sin in fallen humanity.

Others have felt that God would not call us to something intrinsically impossible; so by careful redefinition of perfection (*e.g.* emphasizing the root meanings of the biblical words such as 'maturity', 'wholeness', 'completeness') have argued that it is an attainable goal.

John Wesley,* for example, taught that Christians could and should attain perfection, not as sinlessness (he accepted that we all continue to fall short of God's standards all our lives), but rather as a perfect relation of pure love to God, resulting in a life of Christlikeness.

Pastorally, the call to perfection needs to be accompanied with a corresponding proclamation of God's mercy* and forgiving grace to us when we fall short. Whether we define perfection as attainable or as a goal we reach only in heaven, we need to avoid calling people to reach towards perfection by their own efforts (Gal. 3:3); whatever perfection may be attained, it is still God's work of grace (Gal. 2:19–21).

Bibliography
R. N. Flew, *The Idea of Perfection in Christian Theology* (Oxford, 1934); B. B. Warfield, *Perfectionism*, 2 vols. (New York, 1931); J. Wesley, *A Plain Account of Christian Perfection* (1765; London, 1968).

P.A.H.

PERSEVERANCE. The theme of perseverance may be approached from ethical or doctrinal directions. Each has considerable pastoral implications.

Ethically, the NT root (*proskartereō*) is used in Acts and the Pauline epistles to summon believers to show the quality of persistence in their Christian living. Constancy, zeal,* devotion and determination are the key ideas. Jesus' parable of the importunate widow provides the best illustration (Lk. 18:1–8). The usual objective, as that parable explains, is prayer which never gives up (Acts 1:14; Rom. 12:12; Col. 4:2), but the other means of grace – God's Word and sacraments – also feature prominently in the NT's call to perseverance (Acts 2:42, 46; 6:4).

Doctrinally, teaching on the 'perseverance of the saints' (*perseverantia sanctorum*) is linked most closely with Augustine* and John Calvin.* Highlighting the NT's teaching on election, justification* and union with Christ, they concluded that God's irresistible grace will ensure every genuine believer's eternal security. The NT's strong warnings against apostasy (especially Heb. 6:1–9; 10:26–31) were taken to refer either to temporary lapses on a Christian's part or to God's exposure of bogus believers.

Taken separately, these two approaches are not completely adequate. Perseverance as sheer moral effort can collapse into a humanistic self-reliance. And perseverance as a guarantee of eternal life (only) can lead Christians into complacency and careless irresponsibility.

Taken together, they display considerable ethical and pastoral strength. The call to moral endeavour strengthens believers in their fight against spiritual lethargy. And the focus on God's grace provides them with full assurance of his keeping, enabling power as they continue their struggle.

D.H.F.

PERSISTENT VEGETATIVE STATE, see COMA; EUTHANASIA.

PERSONA, see ANALYTICAL PSYCHOLOGY.

PERSONALISM, see PASTORAL CARE, COUNSELLING AND PSYCHOTHERAPY. [12]

PERSONALITY. After knowing someone for a while, one gets to know how that person will probably behave in some common circumstances (*e.g.* at a party with lots of strangers), and how he or she is likely to feel (*e.g.* comfortable, anxious but under control, or panicky). One can perhaps describe that person's response-tendencies, *e.g.* 'gregarious', 'self-confident', 'withdrawn', 'shy', *etc.* Those responses are not just a result of the circumstance, but of circumstance plus something else – *i.e.* personal qualities that are fairly permanent. The total configuration of motivated response tendencies of an individual – often called 'traits' – constitute that person's *personality.*

Psychologists often offer 'theories of personality'. A personality theory aims to answer two questions: 1. How do people get their personalities (*e.g.* why are some people more fastidious about details, or more empathic towards other people, or neater, or more

gregarious, or more carefree, than others)?
2. What configuration of traits makes for the
ideal, healthy, or fully functional, personality?
As a basis for answering these questions, the
psychologist advances an account of *funda-mental human nature*. This nature, unlike the
personalities that people display, does not dif-fer from individual to individual, but is postu-lated as universal among human beings. The
account of fundamental human nature will ex-plain how, in interaction with their social en-vironments, individuals come to have the traits
they have (*i.e.* it will provide an account of *per-sonality development*); and it also strongly
suggests what configuration of traits will be the
terminus of *successful development*.

According to Sigmund Freud,* people are
'driven' by three basic biological instincts: 1.
survival (the need to eat, drink, breathe); 2. sex
(the need for heterosexual genital intercourse);
and 3. death. These instincts (the id) are
universal, and ultimately, motivate everything
we do. But we can satisfy them only in a social
context which sets limits on our freedom to
satisfy them. We cannot eat whatever we want
whenever we wish, nor have intercourse
whenever and with just whomever our instinct
bids us. If we did, chaos would reign and our
instincts would be even less well satisfied than
they are. Condemned to frustration,* we must
settle for a compromise between instinctual
and cultural demands. In the interest of max-imizing instinctual satisfaction the individual
becomes a calculator (the ego), forming rules
regarding what behaviour does or does not
succeed. But case-by-case calculation to max-imize satisfaction is inefficient. It is better to
'internalize' in our emotions (the super-ego) the
societal punishments – *i.e.* to learn to feel
guilty when we behave in a disapproved way.
Thus we become (unconsciously) afraid of our
instincts, and defend ourselves against them by
intellectualizing them, denying them, project-ing them, *etc*. These defences form our traits of
personality.

As a personality theory, Freud's account of
the instincts and the mechanisms of their
socialization purports to be able to explain all
of any person's traits in terms of the par-ticularities of his or her upbringing. In Freud's
case, these are traits expressing some optimiz-ing compromise between instinctual gratifica-tion (especially genital sexuality) and social-ization.

Carl Jung* saw human nature as a synthesis
of two dimensions, the conscious or finite ego,
and the unconscious or infinite self. In the un-conscious are all the materials of religion,
which are essential to the proper formation of
personality, but in most people the conscious
and the unconscious are isolated from one
another. The goal of life is to become 'in-dividuated', *i.e.* the conscious ego is to become
aware of what is in the unconscious, and the
unconscious (which is otherwise universal and
unconcrete) is to become the possession of
this particular historical ego. Unindividuated
people have traits of restlessness, dependency
on others, and subjection to their emotions,
whereas individuated people are serene, self-possessed, and objective about emotions with-out being cold and rationalistic. Cognitive-behavioural psychologists (see Cognitive
Behaviour Therapy*) tend to think of human
nature as basically an open receptacle for
behavioural training or cognitive input. There
is no code written on the psyche that dictates
what fulfilment or maturity will be like,
though the organism is clearly capable of ex-periencing pleasure and pain. Since personality
is just whatever dispositions have been condi-tioned or cognitively learned, those traits
should be promoted, through training and
teaching, that 'adapt' the individual to
whatever environment he or she has to live in,
so that the individual experiences a minimum
of pain and frustration and a maximum of
pleasure and satisfaction.

A humanistic psychologist like Carl Rogers*
tends to think of the human individual as being
like a fertile egg. If it is just kept warm, the em-bryo will grow, of its own internal resources,
into what it was destined to be. If, on the other
hand, external conditioning (or indoctrina-tion) is imposed, development will be
distorted. Thus Rogers tends to think of all de-viant personality as resulting from 'conditions
of worth' imposed on the individual by his or
her social environment (*e.g.* 'I won't love you
unless you shape up!'), and all proper per-sonality development as a sort of flowering of
our innate potential for self-love, openness and
creativity.

Christianity can be said to have a personality
theory, or at least an incipient one, because it
has an account of fundamental human nature
from which a list of the ideal personality traits,
i.e. the Christian virtues,* can be derived.
Human persons are created in the image of
God,* for joyful obedience* and dependence
on him, and for loving fellowship with their
fellow human creatures. Theologians in the

Augustinian tradition posit something we might call a God-libido, or fundamental desire for God, which can explain some patterns of personality development. Furthermore, the Christian tradition contains rich articulations of the disciplines (see Disciplines, Spiritual*) by which a mature personality is formed. Its emphasis is less on childhood development than on development (see Human Development*) after the age of discernment, and it is perhaps a task for modern Christian psychologists to work out an account of early development that is felicitous for achieving Christian character (see ⑩). Christian psychology, as it exists, is also less detailed than many of the secular theories in its explanations of the etiology of deviant or immature personality traits. It would be interesting and worthwhile for Christian psychologists to try to extend their personality theory in this direction as well.

Bibliography

T. J. Burke (ed.), *Man and Mind: A Christian Theory of Personality* (Hillsdale, MI, 1987); S. Kierkegaard, *The Sickness unto Death* (ET, Princeton, NJ, 1980); M. van Leeuwen, *The Person in Psychology: A Contemporary Christian Appraisal* (Leicester and Grand Rapids, 1985); S. Maddi, *Personality Theories: A Comparative Analysis* (Homewood, IL, ⁴1980); P. Morea, *Personality* (Harmondsworth, 1990).

R.C.R.

PESSIMISM. As a human phenomenon, the tendency to see or expect the worst may be induced by personal factors such as temperament* and physical condition and by external influences such as environment and experience, *e.g.* the failure of a former object of hope. It will naturally reflect whatever the individual conceives as the 'worst' possible conclusion or outcome in the circumstances.

Such a cast of mind might be reinforced by a realism founded on the Christian predilection for honesty. Elements of Christian belief that may thus occasion a degree of pessimism especially include the Fall* and the resulting depravity of humanity, the sway of evil* or of the evil one, and the incidence of suffering.* The doctrine of hell (see Heaven and Hell*), rendering final the God-denying choice and eternally protracting the consequent suffering, would appear to extend part of the occasion for pessimism into eternity.

Pessimism may also refer to the more formal belief that nature is either meaningless or perverse or else that evil will ultimately triumph. Such conclusions are often associated with irrationalism or scepticism, *e.g.* in Arthur Schopenhauer (1788–1860), Friedrich Nietzsche,* Martin Heidegger (1889–1976) and Jean-Paul Sartre,* or with a non-progressive cyclic view of history.

Scripture itself, especially in Ecclesiastes, points out that, but for the more positive input of faith, a profound pessimism would be warranted. However, the goodness of God and of his creation, his providence and a sure hope in his ultimate triumph, all combine to prevent the Christian from embracing its most radical form.

Bibliography

M. L. Bringle, *Despair: Sickness or Sin?* (Nashville, TN, 1990); D. Kidner, *The Message of Ecclesiastes* (Leicester and Downers Grove, IL, 1976).

F.V.W.

PHILANTHROPY. The Gk. root word means 'love of humankind'. It is used of God's saving love (see ②) for us in Tit. 3:4, and of human acts of kindness in Acts 27:3 and 28:2. In the broadest sense, therefore, philanthropy is equivalent to that love of one's neighbour described by Jesus as the second commandment. In present-day usage, however, the word is normally confined to generous giving to causes like health, education and the relief of poverty, especially where a single large-scale donor is involved.

This has a long history in Christian teaching and practice (*cf.*, *e.g.*, Gal. 6:10; 1 Tim. 6:17–19), and before that in the OT (*cf.*, *e.g.*, Jb. 29; Ps. 112). It reached its heyday perhaps in the 19th and early 20th centuries, with the rise both of huge industrial fortunes and of social concern, the latter frequently of evangelical origin. Examples would be the Carnegie Libraries in America and the various Nuffield foundations in Britain. Often the work of philanthropists has been continued after their lifetimes by trusts, with the personal element naturally reduced.

In some countries, and in some respects, the growth of the 'Welfare State'* has made the older philanthropy seem obsolete, but as long as 'the poor are with you' (*cf.* Mt. 26:11) it will continue to be of value, and a challenge to Christians.

Bibliography
D. Owen, *English Philanthropy 1660–1960* (Cambridge, MA, 1965).

R.L.S.

PHILOSOPHICAL ETHICS. Current philosophical thinking about ethics divides moral theories into three broad camps: 1. deontological* ethics stresses the importance of principle-based morality, usually expressed by rules; 2. teleological* ethics emphasizes the role of consequences in moral decision-making; and 3. virtue or character ethics has regained popularity through the work of Alasdair MacIntyre (1929–), and makes the moral character of an agent who reveals the traditional virtues the basis for ethical thought and debate. This has shifted discussion from the descriptivist / prescriptivist focus on whether morality consists of 'brute moral facts' or is a function of the human rational will.

1. At the heart of *deontological* theories lies the idea of a moral imperative which ought to be done for its own sake. Things are right and wrong, and are so simply because they are right and wrong. No other level of explanation is needed or can be given. Intuition* is, for some, the means whereby we arrive at such moral absolutes. We intuit them directly and know them to be morally binding. For the person who cannot see that they ought to be done, we must explain the context and significance of the rule or principle, and then he or she will see. This seems to rest on a kind of naturalism or descriptivism, the assumption being that simply by describing the way the world is and functions, we will know certain things which are good for us and are to be encouraged, and those which do us harm and are to be avoided. Thus, human flourishing is the standard by which what is natural is to be judged. The vagueness of the actual content offered, and concern whether it is possible to derive an 'ought' from an 'is', or a moral imperative from a description of the ways things are in the world, lead many to reject all such approaches and to focus on consequences as the ground of philosophical ethics.

2. According to *teleological* theories, moral problems are resolved by working out the consequences of actions and omissions. If the results are good, then they are to be pursued; if bad, then avoided. The end is held to justify the means. The difficulty of predicting or controlling the consequences of actions makes this approach more difficult than it seems. So attention has focused on the pleasurable consequences of actions as found in moral theories like egoism* and hedonism* which emphasize individual pleasure-seeking. Clashes of different desires within a society caused Jeremy Bentham* and J. S. Mill* to found utilitarianism (see Consequentialism*), which bases moral decisions on calculating the greatest happiness of the greatest number. Bentham designed a pleasure calculus to measure pleasure and pain, and thus provided a simple tool by which to make moral and legal judgments. Problems over the actual units for the measurement of pleasure and pain, and the relative importance of avoiding pain before seeking pleasure, were added to the problem of justice. Mill tried to refine the theory, criticized as 'fit only for pigs', by introducing definitions of higher and lower pleasures and a principle of justice, where everyone counted for only one. This seemed to make the majority right, and make the apparently simple to be highly complex. Recent discussions of utilitarianism have tried to 'save' the emphasis by distinguishing act from rule forms. The act-utilitarian must calculate the consequences of every act; whereas the rule-utilitarian calculates only the rule, and then each action falls under a particular rule. This makes the theory more practicable, but ends up with different results from the act-utilitarian.

3. With the advent of Alasdair MacIntyre's *After Virtue* and subsequent writings which have emphasized the *character of the individual*, there has been a concern lest the struggle between emotivism* and utilitarianism, with its competing views of humanity, has failed to grasp the heart of morality. Like G. E. M. Anscombe (1919–), MacIntyre seems to suggest a recovery of psychology by going back to Aristotle's* concept of morality as teleological, in the sense of fulfilling a purposeful goal. The virtues* necessary to achieve the moral goals of humanity are the essence of the moral life. Thus MacIntyre argues for a return to rationality and justice, which he believes can be found only in an Aristotelian account of human virtues.

Recent theological writers such as Stanley Hauerwas (1940–) have broadened this theme to note how virtues are set in the context of communities with shared stories and values. Theological ethics thus can learn from philosophical ethics by outlining the kind of character and the virtues or characteristics of a community member.

This is a radical shift away from decision-making as the focus of morality to a morality of being. It seeks to develop and grow moral personalities, rather than skilled moral decision-makers. Moral judgment and conscience* are the inevitable, moral expressions of a moral personality, marked by the virtuous qualities of faith, hope, love, temperance, justice, *etc.*

Whether it is possible to return to an Aristotelian concept of morality is debatable. Many doubt MacIntyre's analogies and his critical assessment. They are even less convinced of his suggested replacement and focus on virtue.

The deontological approach stresses the objectivity of morals. Since the attacks of empiricism* on moral language, various theories have stressed the subjectivity of morals. The relativist* rejects moral absolutes* and claims that morality is relative to particular contexts. Morality depends on where, who, what, when and how you are. When in Rome, we do as the Romans. Relativists recognize that if each of us did what was right in our own eyes, anarchy would result. For society to survive, we must all be tolerant, living and letting live.

The denial of absolutes in morality raises a fundamental problem in that to state it is to fall into self-contradiction. While this does not prove its falsity, it must cast doubt on its logic. Furthermore, it contradicts the facts. Examination of moral, religious and legal codes reveal a common core of morality based on parent–children relationships, sexual roles, truth-telling, the sanctity of life, and what belongs or does not belong to me or to us. While varying in expression, the bases of these rules are common. The self-contradiction of relativism continues in propounding tolerance as a universal value, which must itself be limited in its capacity to cope with intolerance, especially intolerance of tolerance.

The emotivist is more standardly empiricist, arguing that morality is a matter of seeking to express and arouse feelings. Thus, it too is entirely subjective.

In light of the meaninglessness of the world, the existentialist (see Existentialist Ethics*) claims that human beings create morality by their will and choices. It does not matter what is chosen. All that matters is that we choose, and in choosing commit the whole of our being to that choice. Thus we create meaning and are authentic human beings! This stress on the will

separates both the will from the rest of our human being, *e.g.* our emotions and reason, and the individual from the community. In both it fails to do justice to the totality of humanity.

R. M. Hare,* impressed by such thinking, coined the term 'prescriptivism' as the basis of moral language. He claims that we are exercising our wills in an imperative form, presenting not simply what we ought to do, but what everyone in the same situation ought to do. This principle of universalizability, based on Kant,* guards against idiosyncracy and makes moral prescriptions rational.

Much debate has ensued over the '*ceteris paribus*' – other things having equal importance as well as the role of the universal will. The apparent failure for things ever to be exactly equal, the lack of specific moral content in the prescriptivist exercise, and the lack of integration of the will are key points of debate.

This debate has focused on promises. Here all the prescriptivists argue that we cannot get an 'ought' from an 'is' and that a promise is part of an agreed institution in which the words 'I promise' are equivalent to 'I ought to pay'. Thus, at best we derive an 'ought' from an 'ought' and not from an 'is', for morality is what we as human beings do. We create our morality.

Philosophical ethics will undoubtedly continue to pose challenges to theological ethics in terms of its epistemology and ontology, and especially in relation to the view of the sufficiency of human beings in moral terms.

See also: CHARACTER; [10] HISTORY OF CHRISTIAN ETHICS. [6]

Bibliography

J. Feinberg (ed.), *Moral Concepts* (Oxford, 1969); A. MacIntyre, *After Virtue* (Notre Dame, IN, 1984; London, ²1985); G. J. Warnock, *Contemporary Moral Philosophy* (London, 1967); M. Warnock, *Existentialism* (London, 1970).

E.D.C.

PIAGET, JEAN (1896–1980), Swiss biologist, philosopher and psychologist, was director of the J. J. Rousseau Institute and the International Center for Genetic Epistemology, and president of the Swiss commission of UNESCO (United Nations Educational, Scientific and Cultural Organization).

Piaget's interest in religion and ethics

appeared to be greatest during his teens and twenties, and his personal search for the highest good led him to the concept of the Idea. The Idea – though never defined – was linked to God, justice, personal suffering, selflessness and faith. 'In the beginning was the Idea,' Piaget wrote, and 'Jesus is the Idea made flesh' ('The Mission of the Idea', p. 27). Piaget condemned organized religion as restrictive of individual and societal attainment. Jesus was admired because he lashed out at an establishment considered to be respectable and legitimate yet one that treated people without compassion and justice.

The ultimate in ethical understanding is a concern for others. As Piaget stated: 'Life is good but the individual pursuing his self-interest renders it bad ... Self-interest may lead the individual to keep for himself some of the vital energy which he might bring to others' ('The Mission of the Idea', p. 29).

Piaget is best known for an interpretation of intellectual development from birth to adulthood. During the sensory-motor period until the age of two years, the infant observes the consequences of reflexive actions and learns by engaging in repetitious behaviour patterns. In the pre-operational period, from ages two to six, the child is able to see relationships and becomes adept at language but makes errors in that he or she believes what he or she sees, *e.g.* 'The moon follows me', and 'If I break a stick of gum into three pieces, I have more.' During concrete operations, between the ages of six and twelve, the child realizes that things are not always as they appear and is able to classify and form concepts. But these are known only as they are experienced. In the last stage of formal operations, the young person is able to think about his or her own thinking and looks to what is possible as well as to what exists in the here and now.

A person's stage of cognitive development determines his or her understanding of the moral and religious world as well as of the physical world. Lawrence Kohlberg's (1927–87) theory of six stages of moral reasoning (see Moral Development*), which in itself has fostered an estimated 5,000 studies, was directly influenced by Piaget's theory. James Fowler (1940–) links Piaget's concrete operational stage to his own mythic–literal faith stage in which the child identifies with the community of faith through stories and observances (see Faith Development*). Likewise, the adolescent at early formal operations

operates at the synthetic–conventional faith stage, in which the meaning of life and one's place within the larger society gives new direction and purpose. Piaget's theory has also been linked with Erik Erikson's* psychosocial stages (see W. E. Conn, 'Personal Identity and Creative Self-understanding'); with the words of Jesus in the Gospel of Matthew (B. Clouse, 'The Teachings of Jesus . . .'); and used by Ronald Goldman to determine the content of religious education among children (*Readiness for Religion*, London, ²1969).

Bibliography

B. Clouse, 'The Teachings of Jesus and Piaget's Concept of Mature Moral Judgment, in J. R. Fleck and J. D. Carter (eds.), in *Psychology and Christianity* (Nashville, TN, 1981); W. E. Conn, 'Personal Identity and Creative Self-Understanding: Contributions of Jean Piaget and Erik Erikson to the Psychological Foundations of Theology', *JPT* 5, 1977, pp. 34–39; J. W. Fowler, *Becoming Adult, Becoming Christian: Adult Development and Christian Faith* (San Francisco, 1984); J. Piaget, *The Moral Judgment of the Child* (ET, London, 1932); *idem*, 'The Mission of the Idea' (1916) in H. E. Gruber and J. J. Vonèche (eds.), *The Essential Piaget* (New York, 1977), pp. 26–37.

B.A.C.

PICKETING is the practice whereby a person or, more usually, a group of people attempts to dissuade others from entering premises with the intention of inflicting economic damage on the occupier. It is a principal weapon of organized labour without which simple withdrawal of labour in a dispute against an employer is often ineffective. It is also used by pressure groups, including pro-life groups against abortion clinics and environmentalist groups against polluting industries.

The underlying right to picket is rooted in freedom of speech and the liberty to inform other people of circumstances which may lead them to change their opinion or intended course of action. Moral conflict arises from several aspects of picketing. The occupier of the property picketed will generally assert his right to conduct his trade or business freely and alleges that the pickets are interfering with his liberty and livelihood. Accepting that the pickets themselves are at liberty not to work for him, to trade with him or to enter his premises, what liberty ought they to have to persuade others to assist their cause contrary to their original (uninformed) intentions? Pickets invariably consider that they occupy the moral high ground and that the justice of their case is very clear. This can lead to intolerance of those unable to see the matter with the same clarity and a tendency for pickets to believe that they are thereby morally justified in taking persuasion to the point of physically preventing anyone from entering the premises.

See also: INDUSTRIAL RELATIONS.

D.P.N.

PIETISM is a word which often denotes kindred evangelical awakenings led by John and Charles Wesley,* George Whitefield (1714–70) and Charles Finney (1792–1875), among others. More narrowly, however, the word had its genesis in the second reformation in Germany led by Philip Jakob Spener (1635–1705) and August Hermann Francke (1663–1727).

Though Johann Arndt's (1555–1621) book, *True Christianity* (1605; ET, New York and London, 1979), had constituted an influential corrective to the rigidity and rationalism of Lutheran scholasticism, it was Spener's preface to a book of sermons by Arndt (1675) which is regarded by historians as the spark which engendered pietism. The designation was at first a derogatory name employed by Spener's enemies. Spener's preface was reissued a year later under the title, *Pia Desideria: or Heartfelt Desires for a God-pleasing Improvement of the true Protestant Church* (ET, Philadelphia, 1964).

Pietism was a Spirit movement, articulating a theology of religious experience. However, it was equally a reform movement with strong ethical emphases. Professing to be true to Luther, Spener proposed that the earlier reformation of doctrine must result in reformation of life. Though we are saved by faith* alone, faith must become active in love. Justification* by faith must be joined with emphases on regeneration and sanctification.* Pietists believed that the God who is good enough to forgive us is powerful enough to change us. New birth meant a new person who would manifest the fruit of the Spirit (Gal. 5:22–23).

Spener believed that new persons would be leaven to reform the church. This was the intent of the proposals of his *Pia Desideria*. In the context of the prevalent state of morality, he advocated a regenerate clergy. Pastors should model exemplary lives and be shepherds of souls. Theological students would be educated accordingly. Preachers ought not to preach to display their knowledge but to edify the lives of believers. Instead of dogmatics, biblical theology would be central in the life of the church. Such a remedial programme would lead to personal relationships with parishioners, pastoral visitation, small groups for Bible study and catechetical instruction. (For the contributions of Pietism to pastoral care, see J. McNeill, *A History of the Cure of Souls*.)

Moreover, Spener radically interpreted Luther's doctrine of the priesthood of all believers. He desired to eliminate the chasm which separated clergy and laity. He sought a more democratic polity in which princes and clergy would relinquish some of their power to the third estate, the laity.

Holding fast to sound doctrine in essentials, Spener advocated love rather than coercion in dealing with heresy. Unlike radical pietists, Spener and Francke desired appropriation of, rather than rejection of, doctrine; participation in, and not repudiation of, the church.

Though Spener was the pastor-theologian of early pietism, Francke was the organizational genius. As pastor and professor in a newly-founded pietist university at Halle, he gave birth to many educational and charitable enterprises. He founded a home and school for orphans. Soon a residence was erected for destitute widows. There were many ministries on behalf of the poor. Pressures from the more affluent led Francke to establish a similar school for upper-class youth. A hospital and dispensary followed. A printing enterprise grew to constitute the celebrated Canstein Bible Institute which distributed three million Bibles by the end of the century. The university became the base from which many were commissioned as the first Protestant missionaries to the new and old worlds.

In addition to bequeathing an impetus on philanthropic activity to evangelical Protestantism, many of the pietists espoused a 'this-worldly' eschatology. Spener wrote his doctoral dissertation on various interpretations of the book of Revelation. He was open to the appearance of premillennial and dispensational views among the pietists. Personally, he struggled through to a non-literalistic interpretation, by which he characterized pietists as those who hope for better times for the church and the world. For Spener eschatological emphases were productive of, rather than antithetical to, ethical concerns. The kingdom (see Kingdom of God*) which will be realized only in God's time in the future must become a present reality in penetrating history through the renewal of the church, evangelistic endeavours, and philanthropic and social missions.

The pietists' pastoral and ethical stance as outlined above defies usual caricatures of a world-negating, escapist movement which stresses completely individualistic interpretations of personal salvation and retreats to a world of personal piety. A good knowledge and appropriation of the theology and ministry of Spener, Francke and the Wesleys will substantiate their emphases on personal salvation. At the same time their views can provide a corrective to many contemporary aberrations and degenerations of what has been best in the ethical heritage of pietism.

Bibliography
D. W. Brown, *Understanding Pietism* (Grand Rapids, 1978); P. Erb (ed.), *Pietists: Selected Writings* (New York and London, 1983); J. T. McNeill, *A History of the Cure of Souls* (New York, 1951; London, 1952); E. F. Stoeffler, *German Pietism during the Eighteenth Century* (Leiden, 1973); *idem*, *The Rise of Evangelical Pietism* (Leiden, 1965).

D.W.Br.

PLANNING, see ARCHITECTURE; MANAGEMENT.

PLATO (427–347 BC). A student of Socrates, Plato was concerned not only to transmit the teaching of Socrates (470–399 BC), which he does in such early dialogues as the *Apology*, the *Crito*, the *Meno* and the *Euthyphro*, but also to develop his own theories. Plato's mature philosophy, in which he integrates the moral concerns of Socrates into a broader philosophical foundation influenced most by earlier Pythagorean philosophy, is displayed in the works of his middle and later periods, the *Republic* being chief among these.

For Plato, as for Socrates, virtue* is knowledge; but to be virtuous is to know the Good, a changeless, immaterial, transcendent Absolute. Those who know the Good order their lives accordingly, with their appetites subordinate to the rule of reason assisted by the

honour-loving part of the soul. Knowledge of the Good is acquired not by diligent examination of the world around us but rather by a rigorous moral and intellectual training that enables the soul to recognize the knowledge it has from its previous disembodied existence. Distracted by desires and appetites, we require moral training in the discipline of the flesh before we can know the Good. But moral training is not sufficient, for the Good is immaterial, and knowledge of the Good requires excellence in those intellectual disciplines, notably abstract mathematics and philosophy, which direct the soul to that which is immaterial.

Aspects of Plato's philosophy have long been attractive to Christian thinkers, most notably Augustine,* who understood Plato's Good to be a veiled reference to God.

See also: HISTORY OF CHRISTIAN ETHICS.[6]

T.D.K.

PLAY impinges upon the Christian life in the same ways as does leisure.* It depends for its validation and enjoyment on a positive evaluation of pleasure* and the acceptance of the balance between work* and ceasing from labour that God has ordained. The keynote was sounded by C. S. Lewis* when he wrote (echoing 1 Cor. 10:31) that 'we can play, as we can eat, to the glory of God'.

Play in the sense of playfulness extends to virtually all of life, not simply leisure. Considered in this way, it is an attitude of mind – a spirit or mood – that includes as its distinguishing traits light-heartedness, high-spiritedness, enjoyment, celebration and (much of the time) community.

The psychoanalyst D. W. Winnicott* developed a theory of play with reference to the bonding relationship between mother and baby – a relationship of trust which is at the root of all healthy relationships and our capacity for creativity. On the basis of play, in this sense, 'is built the whole of man's experiential existence' (see D. W. Winnicott, *Playing and Reality*, Harmondsworth, 1971).

To understand play in the broader sense, we should note some of its appearances in the Bible. God's creation of the world, for example, was an exuberant and voluntary act done for God's own pleasure (Rev. 4:11, AV). Proverbs 8:30–31 describes God's personified attribute Wisdom as a playmate of the creator, delighting and playing in the created world.

According to Ps. 104:26, God created Leviathan to sport or frolic in the sea.

A similar note appears in the Bible's eschatological pictures of the coming kingdom. We read that 'the streets of the city shall be full of boys and girls playing in its streets' (Zc. 8:5, RSV). The city will resound with 'the voices of those who make merry' (Je. 30:19, RSV), and it will be a place of dancing and merry-making, joy and feasting (Je. 31:13–14).

Between creation and *eschaton* (*i.e.* the final, perfected state of existence) stands life in a fallen world, and here, too, biblical faith endorses a life of zest and playfulness. Employing ancient images of festivity and celebration, the writer of Ecclesiastes commands, 'Let your garments be always white; let not oil be lacking on your head' (9:8, RSV).

The supreme exemplar of playfulness in the Bible is Jesus. The Gospels record his fondness for attending dinners. At his first miracle he turned water into wine to keep a wedding party going. Elton Trueblood's (1900–) small classic on the subject of Jesus' humour shows the extent to which his language and dialogue show a playful bent. The most characteristic form of that humour was the giantesque – the hilarious exaggeration or preposterous fantasy.

It is apparent, then, how wrong has been the Christian church's suspicion of play. This tradition can be traced back to Augustine,* for whom conversion meant a conversion *from* play to the enjoyment of God only. Although the Puritan tradition theoretically found a place for spiritual joy and legitimate leisure, its prevailing seriousness about life and work made it an unpromising seedbed for play.

Christian thought in the last decades of the 20th century has made notable strides towards recovering a biblical play ethic. Such recovery begins with a conviction that play is at the heart of God himself, and further that God placed a spirit of play into his creatures. People at play express their God-implanted nature. God created people to play as well as work and worship. Play is part of the redeemed life – a celebration of God's gifts to the human race and a revelling in the believer's freedom in Christ.

The theologian J. Moltmann (1926–) argues that an appropriate theology of work must include an appropriate theology of play. Work 'must encompass freedom for self-presentation and thus playfulness ... In the seriousness of work also belongs, in a human sense, the relaxed joy of existence: "Let it be!"' (*On Human Dignity*, ET, London and Philadelphia, 1984, p. 41; *cf. Theology of Play*, ET, New York, 1972).

While affirming play in principle, Christianity's awareness of sin makes it watchful of the potential abuses of play. These include idolizing play (see Sport*), abandonment of duty, trivialization of life, addiction to play, compulsive competitiveness in play, desecration of the environment in the pursuit of play, excessive spending of money or resources, time-wasting, and a refusal to grant seriousness to serious issues.

The potential abuse of play does not, however, invalidate the Christian endorsement of play itself. There is a time for everything, including laughing and dancing (Ec. 3:4).

Bibliography

R. K. Johnston, *The Christian at Play* (Grand Rapids, 1983); L. Ryken, *Work and Leisure in Christian Perspective* (Portland, OR, 1987; Leicester, 1989); E. Trueblood, *The Humor of Christ* (New York, 1964).

L.R.

PLEASURE. The concept of pleasure has had a particularly high profile in ethical systems of the teleological kind, where it features as an 'end' to which human life should be directed. It is sometimes identified with – and sometimes distinguished from – other major ethical concepts like happiness* and well-being.

The 18th- and 19th-century utilitarians (see Consequentialism*) gave pleasure the central place in their philosophies. Jeremy Bentham,* building on the hedonism* of Epicurus (341–270 BC), asserted that 'nature has placed mankind under the government of two sovereign masters, pain and pleasure; it is for them alone to point out what we ought to do, as well as what we shall do' (*An Introduction to the Principles of Morals and Legislation*, New York, 1965, p. 1).

In order to calculate the surplus of pleasure over pain (or vice versa), Bentham proposed a hedonistic calculus which graded pleasures according to their intensity, duration, certainty, propinquity, fecundity (will they produce more?) and purity. And in order to counter the charge of egoism,* he added a seventh factor, extent, thus expressing the classical utilitarian goal of 'the greatest happiness for the greatest number'.

John Stuart Mill,* while affirming the centrality of pleasure, shifted the focus from quantity to quality. Intellectual pleasures, he maintained, are superior to those rooted in animal appetites. So, 'it is better to be a human being dissatisfied than a pig satisfied, better to be Socrates dissatisfied than a fool satisfied' (*Utilitarianism*, New York, 1961, p. 410).

Unlike Epicurus, Aristotle* was not a hedonist. But pleasure filled an important role in his moral philosophy, too. Humankind's goal, he taught, is well-being (*eudaimonia*). This is achieved when a person's natural capacities and energies are exercised and developed, under the control of reason, in a harmonious, consistent and socially integrated way. Pleasure is not the 'chief end' of life, but is normally the accompaniment of *eudaimonia* – taking life *as a whole*.

Both these ethical systems (the utilitarian and the Aristotelian) have come under philosophical fire, not least because of the central (or prominent) place they give to pleasure. And moral theology contributes an extra dimension of critique, by positing blessedness* as an alternative Christian definition of humankind's *summum bonum*.

As the goal of life, blessedness does not exclude pleasure. But, in accordance with the spirit of Jesus' declarations in the Beatitudes,* Scripture does define pleasure in a distinctively God-centred way. Lasting pleasure and full joy* are to be found only in God's presence (Ps. 16:11), through doing his will (Jn. 15:9–11). This is the criterion by which all pleasant experiences are to be judged. Negatively, 'pleasures' which are selfish or enslaving are bogus and deadly (Lk. 8:14; 1 Tim. 5:6; Jas. 5:5). Positively, Christians find their greatest pleasure in serving God and pleasing other people (Rom. 15:1ff.).

Paradoxically, this means that the pleasures of blessedness are entirely compatible with hardship and suffering (*cf.* Heb. 12:2). But Christians do not subscribe to any pleasure-denying form of asceticism.* They are liberated from the frustrations of hedonism to enjoy the wealth of all God's gifts – a pleasure which is all the richer because it is a by-product, not an end in itself.

D.H.F.

PLURALISM describes the situation where a society is marked by a variety and diversity of views and outlooks. Different moral, religious and political philosophies and ways of life compete with each other. This creates a smorgasbord effect, where those in the society find it hard to decide between the competing views. Different groups of people disagree over their understanding of truth, goodness, reality, and the nature, purpose and goal of human life. This situation may lead to a lack of consensus and agreement on basic moral issues, and society must develop some way of dealing with diversity and its effects. Doubt about the universal applicability of one's own view is not uncommon, and that may lead to a blind holding of traditional values or to its opposite, *i.e.* doubt about their validity. Tolerance* is often the way a society encourages its members to cope with diversity.

A State and its institutions may respond to pluralism in different ways. Neutrality about different views and moralities may be the agreed basis. This will lead to a stress on laws which allow each individual maximum freedom to pursue whatever goals and purposes he or she wishes. Diversity may equally be seen as a simple fact of life which has to be coped with, without any real hope of the resolution of conflicts. Different religious perspectives may offer different ways of life and belief systems. The problems arise when these come in conflict with each other, and so are mutually exclusive in terms of truth claims and lifestyles.

This is no new situation. In the OT, the constant threat to the distinctiveness of Israel was the impact of pluralistic society on its beliefs, outlook and behaviour. Holiness, in terms of being set apart for God and living according to the distinctive laws he gave, was the way to cope in a pluralistic society.

The gospel was proclaimed in a pluralistic world where different religions, philosophies and outlooks competed with each other for adherents. The NT account of the spread of the gospel is clearly set in challenging the false and idolatrous beliefs of the day and proclaiming the absolute and unique claims of Christ. There is an opposite trend in modern theology towards finding a basic minimum of faith within different religions. This has led, in the case of Christianity, to calls for rejection of the incarnation and the uniqueness of Christ. It is urged that these claims are offensive in a multi-cultural, multi-faith society. Humility, it is suggested, ought to set limits to such absolute, universal claims. The reality behind religions is fundamentally mysterious and no one religion can hope to encapsulate all truth in itself.

There is no fundamentally moral superiority between different religions, thus none can claim to have a monopoly on truth or what is moral.

While recognizing the failure of the church to live as it ought, and the gap between the truth proclaimed and the truth lived out, Christians are bound to find that the gospel makes fundamental claims about the uniqueness and finality of Christ as the full and complete revelation of God. He is the Way, the Truth and the Life. He is the one who alone brings people to God. The standards Christ proclaimed and lived are absolute and final standards which judge all others. In the life, death and resurrection of Christ, there is the implicit recognition of the uniqueness of Jesus in God's dealings with humanity. The church's success or failure in imitating and fulfilling that life and God's requirements does not affect the truth of Christ's unique role in human salvation.

Proclaiming Christ and the gospel in a pluralist world and society requires pastoral sensitivity to other religions and a theology of mission and evangelism* which does justice to the fact that all men and women are created in the image of God* and have some awareness of God's law written on their heart (Gn. 1 – 3; Rom. 1 – 3). It also requires creativity and sensitivity in expressing the message of salvation to those whose perception of salvation and religious outlook is very different (see Mission, Morality of*). But for those who wish to hold to the biblical and traditional understanding of faith there is no escape from Christianity's claim to be unique. This is no ground for pride of the part of Christians, but rather confers a greater responsibility to witness to and live out the reality of the gospel in such a way that people will be drawn to faith and not reject the message because of the messenger.

See also: PROSELYTISM.

Bibliography

M. Goulder (ed.), *Incarnation and Myth* (London, 1979); P. Knitter and J. Hick, *The Myth of Christian Uniqueness* (Maryknoll, NY, 1987; London, 1988).

E.D.C.

POLICE. The fundamental purpose of 'kings and all those in authority', according to 1 Tim. 2:2, is to enable members of society to 'live peaceful and quiet lives in all godliness and holiness'. Although the prime tasks of the police include prevention and detection of crime,* protection of life and property, service to the public and law enforcement (see Law, Civil and Criminal*), all these tasks can be summed up in the phrase 'keeping the peace'.

Most demands on police officers are not directly related to crime or the law, but to providing more general assistance and advice. Nevertheless, the law is central to their work, although the acceptance of other tasks may be seen as being essential in order to develop and maintain public support and consent.* The increasing emphasis on service as opposed solely to enforcement reflects this, although the very existence of law presupposes offences against it, many of which demand a police response.

In NT times, sanctions were applied by the priests and their officials or by the troops of the occupying Roman power, and both Jesus and members of the early church had contacts with the law in which the authorities acted partially and improperly. Despite this, Paul insisted that 'everyone must submit himself to the governing authorities' (Rom. 13:1), because the very concept of authority* derives from God and human authorities exist only with his blessing. As God's agents, the officers of the law are to be respected and obeyed. Only those who break the law have reason to fear and, implies Paul, it is right and proper that they should be afraid of 'the officer [who] is God's servant for your protection' (Rom. 13:4, JBP).

In the book of Acts, however, Peter and John faced a direct clash between God's will and the demands of the Sanhedrin, and saw no choice but to obey God rather than the human authorities (Acts 4:18–20). Such a dilemma could arise today, and a Christian would need to resolve it similarly, by disobeying civil authority out of obedience to God.

The Reformation saw attempts to rethink the role of the secular authorities, including peace-keeping and law enforcement. While Martin Luther* derived the need for policing from the Fall,* he expressed a high view of all civil authority as God's agents in governing his fallen world.

The most thorough restructuring of civil administration on Christian lines was undertaken by John Calvin* in Geneva in the 1540s. He saw the primary function of the secular powers as being to enhance the education, culture and welfare of the citizens, but considered that they should also ensure 'that the public quiet be not disturbed, that every man's property be kept secure'. To achieve the 'common peace and tranquillity' he said that the authorities should also have 'the power to take up arms in order to execute public vengeance' (*Institutes of the Christian Religion* IV.xx.3 and 11; see R. S. Wallace, *Calvin, Geneva and the Reformation*, Edinburgh, 1988, pp. 115–116). This reflects Paul's teaching that the appointed enforcer of the law 'does not bear the sword for nothing' (Rom. 13:4). The Anabaptists,* who took a pacifist position, forbade their members' involvement in law-enforcing agencies which employed force, beginning a tradition which continues to the present time.

England did not enjoy the benefits of the Reformers' attempts to improve the secular world. The Normans had strengthened the concept that each man was accountable for law enforcement within his own area of responsibility, be he the head of a family or the lord of a manor. The Anglo-Saxons had emphasized the rights of the victim of crime to restitution, but as early as the reign of Henry I (1100–35; b. 1068) this began to weaken, notably with his invention of the King's Peace, a device to generate funds for the royal coffers by making the king the prime victim if the peace was disturbed. Even Cromwell's (1599–1658) attempts to remodel England on Puritan lines from 1649 did not affect basic law enforcement, and by that time there was little effective peace-keeping. Crime and lawlessness increased, particularly with the growth of cities, until the first recognizable police forces were formed from 1829 onwards.

The wearing of non-military uniform and restrictions on the carrying of firearms were designed to make this a civilian body that would earn public acceptance and support rather than impose its will by force and fear. The earliest instructions emphasized both the primacy of crime prevention and peace-keeping, and the need for each officer to regard himself as 'the servant and guardian of the general public' in order to gain approval. With the advent of the 'modern' police force, citizens retained their ancient powers of arrest for felonies, and even today the same echoes of reliance on 'do-it-yourself' policing remain with us, although the risks of 'having a go' are frequently stressed.

Uniquely, each British police constable holds an independent office under the Crown with accountability to the law through the courts. Although local and national politicians control police budgets, the operational independence of a Chief Constable is a protection against partisan control of police operations.

The latter half of the 20th century has seen a marked decline in the acceptance of authority. The police, as the most visible interface between society and the law, have borne the brunt of this to the point of violence and riot, and now have little choice but to prepare and equip themselves to meet force with force where necessary. In these circumstances, the tasks which do not concern law enforcement may be seen as cost-ineffective distractions from essential policing functions, although they are actually important non-confrontational opportunities that can be used to earn the consent of the public for the total police role.

The late 1980s and early 90s have seen a rapid escalation in reported crime – particularly burglaries and thefts* of and from motor vehicles ('auto-crime'). Increasing pressure on resources has led to a concentration of police efforts on the more serious crimes (*e.g.* armed robbery, street crime and child abuse*), which has made the public aware of the limitations of the police. At the same time, a number of successful appeals against trial verdicts have highlighted the issue of the sufficiency and reliability of the evidence (especially forensic). Together with changes in prosecution and sentencing policies, these have increased public frustration with the effectiveness of the whole criminal justice system and have helped create a climate in which vigilantism can occur.

Other matters which have attracted attention include the accountability of the police to society in general and to locally elected authorities in particular. The 1993 Government White Paper, which seeks to some degree to re-centralize control over local Police Authorities, has provoked considerable debate. Racism and equal-opportunity issues are also being addressed, and determined efforts are being made to root out racism and discrimination, and to encourage the recruitment of more police men and women from ethnic minorities.

In the colonial period, the US police system was organized on the UK model. The sheriff, the constable and the night watch were the policemen of the 17th and 18th centuries. But by the mid-19th century, this system could no longer cope with the rising crime rate in growing cities such as New York and Boston. In response, a new system of law enforcement emerged. The new police officers, unlike the old enforcers of the law, worked both day and night, wore uniforms, patrolled the streets and carried firearms.

The US police force was largely inefficient until reforms in the early 20th century, because of control by politicians, poor equipment and poor pay, as well as corruption and brutality within the force. But a move to 'professionalize' the police in the 1920s, as well as strong leaders such as Theodore Roosevelt (1858–1919), gradually eliminated much politics and corruption from policing. Today, modern American police departments strive to prevent and combat corruption, brutality and racism, and programmes to promote and maintain high ethical standards and quality management are followed widely.

The current emphasis on quality of service and on the need for consultation with the public is being vigorously pursued by the police, and it is possible to hope that society may respond, not only with passive consent, but with active co-operation. This might even achieve a return to an acceptance of individual responsibility for crime prevention and law enforcement, and a situation in which the police officer is once again seen alongside the Justice of the Peace as the 'lay minister of the peace'.

D.M.C.

POLITICAL REALISM, see NIEBUHR, REINHOLD; REALPOLITIK.

POLITICS. Although the word 'politics' can be used in a broad sense to refer to the organized conduct of relationships in any form of human community (as in 'ecclesiastical politics' or 'sexual politics'), it will be used here in the more common sense in which it refers more narrowly to the government of human society in the State.*

The legitimacy of government

Christians have generally regarded political authority as a necessary feature of human society in this world, with a positive role in God's purpose for his world. This fundamental legitimacy of government* as such need not, of course, imply the legitimacy of any specific government in power, still less the uncritical acceptance of any specific policies or actions of government. Throughout much of Christian history there has been, on the one hand, a tendency to submissive acceptance of the

government in power and, on the other hand, a tradition of prophetic critique and principled opposition to unjust government.

Two NT texts have been especially important in Christian discussion of the legitimacy of government (Mk. 12:13–17, and par.; Rom. 13:1–7). Both have been used, not only to support the legitimacy of government as such, but also to require a Christian duty of uncritical submission to whatever government rules. In the first passage, Jesus refuses to identify himself with the position of Jewish religious nationalists who rejected the legitimacy of Caesar's rule over God's people (and therefore his right to tax God's people) on the grounds that God's people Israel may be subject only to God. Against this position, Jesus' saying (Mk. 12:17) makes the point that God's rights over his people do not exclude Caesar's legitimate rights. But the saying, with its emphasis on giving God his due, does not make an absolute demarcation between Caesar's sphere of authority and God's, as though political affairs were not subject to God. Jesus and his hearers would take it for granted that every area of life is subject to God. Hence Jesus' acknowledgment that Caesar has the right to collect taxes is by no means inconsistent with criticism of the oppression characteristic of actual Roman rule (Mk. 10:42).

In Rom. 13 Paul also asserts the legitimacy of the Roman government, probably again with Jewish theocratic* nationalism in view. The new people of God, composed of both Jews and Gentiles, are not, like the Jews, a political entity in themselves. They are subjects of the empire, with no special privileges, and must not expect to be exempt from Roman rule or from the ordinary duties of citizens to their government. So Paul's point is that government has a God-given role which even pagan rulers can fulfil, and is therefore entitled to the respect and co-operation of citizens, including Christians. The passage requires of Christians a positive attitude to government as such, but does not raise the question of a Christian response to injustice and abuse of power by governments.

It is an important biblical and Christian principle, expressed in Rom. 13, that government owes its legitimacy to God. But this means that its right to obedience is relative, not absolute (Acts 5:29). Rulers who, instead of implementing God's just rule, act with the flagrant injustice of those against whom Ps. 94 is written forfeit their God-given legitimacy

(Ps. 94:20), so that the psalmist can pray for their overthrow (94:1–2, 23). Alongside the account of the Roman government in Rom. 13, as appointed by God (Rom. 13:1–2) and acting as God's servant to execute justice (13:4), we must also place the vision of the Roman imperial power (the beast) in Rev. 13, where it is seen to derive its power and authority from the devil (Rev. 13:2). The evil of the beast is that it absolutizes itself, requiring of its subjects the absolute loyalty due only to God (Rev. 13:4–14). In the face of this kind of totalitarian claim, Christians must witness to the ultimate rule of God by refusing the absolute allegiance demanded by the State. Many of the martyrs of the early church died for this reason: because of their acknowledgment of the lordship of Christ they could not participate in the political religion which absolutized the Roman State.

Thus the legitimacy of governments is called in question when they set themselves against God's rule, either by unjust government, flouting divine justice, or by totalitarian claims, usurping divine rule. These alternatives are closely connected, but in modern times the latter especially provoked Christian opposition to government in the European context, while the former has been the focus of Christian opposition to government in the Third World. In the Barmen Declaration (1934), the Confessing Church in Germany rediscovered and reasserted the sole lordship of Christ as the basis for opposing the totalitarianism of the Nazi State. This has remained a foundational insight for modern Christian attitudes to politics, but, as expressed in the Barmen Declaration, it did not necessarily lead to resistance to Hitler (1889–1945) in the political sphere where his policies did not directly encroach on the church. It was the European political theology of the 1960s, and even more clearly and effectively the liberation theology* of Latin America and other parts of the Third World (together with the black theology of N. America and South Africa) in the 1970s and 80s, which brought to the fore the imperative for Christian opposition to unjust political structures, with the social and economic interests that support them.

Creation and eschatology

If government has a positive role in God's purpose for his world, then it is necessary for Christians to discern its place within an overall biblical-theological framework, in which God's purpose moves from creation* in the beginning to the final achievement of his kingdom* in the end. There have been two tendencies in Christian thought: one which sees government in the light of creation, as one of the 'orders of creation' established by God as permanent structures of human life (often with reference to Rom. 13:1); and another which views politics in the light of the coming kingdom, as potentially an instrument in bringing about God's eschatological purpose for human society (often with reference to the prophet's visions of the coming age of justice and peace, as well as to Jesus' proclamation of the kingdom). The former tendency has been the more common in the mainstream Christian tradition, while the latter, characteristic of some more radical Christian thinking in the past, has come into its own in recent political and liberation theologies. The former tendency, with its backward-looking perspective, favours a conservative view of politics, in which the role of government is to preserve the good already given, though it can also support a reformist critique of corrupt governments which neglect and pervert the standards of the past. The future-orientated perspective of the second tendency favours a more revolutionary outlook, in which the future can be expected to surpass the past and political action can effect radical changes for the better in human society. Another, related, difference between the two tendencies is that the first typically makes a sharp distinction between God's activity in creation, to which government belongs, and his redemptive activity in the church, whereas the second tendency sees the political and the spiritual as two aspects of God's redemptive activity to establish his universal kingdom.

Both tendencies can be given their due within a view of the kingdom of God as the renewal of creation. The kingdom does not replace creation but fulfils it. Political activity can participate in God's purpose for his world, both by conserving what is good from the past and by seizing the novel opportunities for good which come from the future. The purposes of God for human life are consistent throughout history, but changing historical circumstances offer differing occasions and possibilities for realizing them politically. To see political activity in this context is to see it in thoroughly historical terms, subject to certain permanent norms but also immersed in the dynamic of the historical process.

The direction of God's purpose from creation to the kingdom must not be understood abstractly, but discerned primarily from the biblical story of God's action in history. Especially paradigmatic are the Exodus, in which God liberated Israel from enslavement to be his people, establishing his kingdom over Israel, and the life, death and resurrection of Jesus, in which God definitively established his universal kingdom. Neither event should be reduced to the political dimension, but both touch the political along with other dimensions of human life.

In relation to the coming kingdom of God, political activity can be understood as seeking to anticipate the kingdom or to realize the values of the kingdom, as far as possible in any particular circumstances, within the radically imperfect conditions of this world. The hope of the coming kingdom can give political vision and direction. But for the sake of political realism,* it is also vital to remember that political activity cannot establish the eschatological kingdom of God itself. Its achievements are never more than fragmentary anticipations of the kingdom, whose transcendence beyond all such anticipations keeps political activity realistic, flexible and never satisfied with the *status quo*.

Political goals and political forms

Both in forms of political organization and in the nature and scope of political activity, the political is one of the most changeable aspects of human society. Christians cannot therefore expect to find in the Bible a static blueprint for human society. What they can find are the general principles, directions and concerns of God's purposes for human life, sometimes expressed in general terms, sometimes instantiated in paradigmatic examples, which relate to specific historical circumstances (such as those of ancient Israel) but can inspire appropriate thinking and activity in different circumstances. Both because the church in NT times had little scope for direct political involvement and because the functions of government have expanded considerably since biblical times, it is important not to reduce what is of modern political relevance in the Bible to what is explicitly political in the Bible. For example, the NT does not draw clearly political consequences from its principle of universal love (*i.e.* that the neighbour I must love is not just or even especially my compatriot, but whoever needs my help: Lk. 10:29–37; *cf.* Mt. 5:43–44), but this principle

does have far-reaching consequences for the conduct of international politics. It is also important to realize that the direction of biblical teaching may point beyond the practice of biblical societies, as the example of slavery* makes clear. If the direction of God's purpose can be seen in Scripture to be towards, for example, freedom and equality for all people, economic justice, and peace between nations, then contemporary political activity is not limited by the extent to which such ideals were realizable in the specific circumstances of biblical societies, but only by the extent to which they are realizable here and now.

The question of Christian support for democratic forms of government must also be seen in the light of the general directions and the historically changeable specifics of the biblical material. Forms of government are human inventions, not prescribed by God, and contemporary representative democracy is a recent invention, which became possible in specifically modern circumstances. However, although the Bible therefore does not anticipate democracy, there is much to be learned from the OT's highly ambivalent attitude to the dominant political form of its own time: absolute monarchy. Monarchy sat uneasily with the basic OT conviction that all Israelites, as God's freed slaves, subject to him alone (*cf.* Jdg. 8:23; 1 Sa. 8:7), had equal rights to life and liberty. So kingship was tolerable only if the king behaved as a brother to his brothers and sisters, a first among equals (Dt. 17:14–20). Furthermore, the only real justification for the king's supreme power was his ability to intervene to protect his most vulnerable subjects from his more powerful subjects (Ps. 72:4, 12–14; Je. 22:15–16). If the king's government was to be in the interests of all, then it must especially protect the rights of the weakest. Thus the institution of monarchy was critically evaluated in the light of two fundamental biblical political concerns: for the equal rights and freedom of all, and for justice for the most vulnerable. It is these concerns which, in modern conditions, may require a democratic political system, as best able to safeguard them. But for Christians the concerns will retain their priority over the system.

Bibliography

R. Bauckham, *The Bible in Politics* (London and Philadelphia, 1989); J. C. Bennett, *Christians and the State* (New York, 1958); O.

Cullmann, *The State in the New Testament* (ET, New York, 1956; London, 1957); G. J. Dorrien, *Reconstructing the Common Good* (New York, 1990); G. Gutiérrez, *A Theology of Liberation* (ET, London and New York, ²1988); K. Wengst, *Pax Romana and the Peace of Jesus Christ* (ET, London and Philadelphia, 1987); J. P. Wogaman, *Christian Perspectives on Politics* (Philadelphia and London, 1988); J. H. Yoder, *The Politics of Jesus* (Grand Rapids, 1972).

R.J.B.

POLLUTION, see ENVIRONMENT.

POLYANDRY, see POLYGAMY.

POLYGAMY. In popular parlance, polygamy is the practice whereby a man has many wives simultaneously. The situation is better described as 'polygyny'. When two wives are involved, it is bigamy. Polyandry exists when a woman has many husbands simultaneously. Extreme polygamy involving the sharing of many women by many men has been substantiated among the Todas of South India in which 'several brothers shared several wives' (Nida, *Customs, Culture and Christianity,* p. 104). Polyandry has been documented among the Tibetans, the Todas and some Eskimos. Female infanticide* was practised by the Eskimos, and in Tibet, the climate is particularly harsh on women. A type of polyandry occurred among the Lele of Africa who designated captured women or women refugees as 'wives of the village'.

In the OT a woman had to be faithful to one man, her husband, and adultery was punishable by death (Lv. 20:10). Though the death penalty was not enforced in NT times, adultery on the part of a woman remained sinful (Mk. 6:18; Jn. 8:3–11; Rom. 13:9). Polyandry was, therefore, out of the question. The episode of the Samaritan woman to whom Jesus said, 'You have had five husbands' (Jn. 5:18), does not suggest polyandry but rather that the woman was contracting loose liaisons one after the other. The abolition of female infanticide and the improvement of health care has ensured the survival of female children in erstwhile polyandrous cultures. Again modern interaction and communication has ensured that no society can remain closed, and cross-cultural marriages have become real possibilities. Thus polyandry as a result of the shortage of women ought not to threaten any society in contemporary times.

Polygamy (including bigamy) is a much more common phenomenon. It has 'reached its highest degree of development [in] Africa, in many parts of which the practice is so frequent and has so impressed itself upon the social organization that it has influenced the nomenclature of relationship, and special terms are used to distinguish from one another the children by the different wives of a polygynous marriage' (W. H. R. Rivers, *ERE* 8, p. 427). Polygamy is also found in many parts of Asia where Islam, which permits a man to have four wives at the same time, is the dominant religion. Most marriages in these cultures are monogamous, but there is no legislation, as in the Western world, to prevent them from becoming polygamous.

Statistics indicate that the number of male children born alive is slightly higher than that of female children. However, infant mortality is higher among males. Wars and occupational hazards tend to deplete male population faster than female. The net result is that there are more females than males, and this makes polygamy easier in those cultures that practise it. Then there is the factor known as 'the chronological age gap'. This arises because in many cultures men marry relatively late in life while women marry relatively early. According to E. Hillman in *Polygamy Reconsidered*, this age discrepancy, more than anything else, provides an adequate 'pool' of marriageable females. In such a situation, there are always men of wealth and status to whom women are ready to act as second or third wife.

Other factors and beliefs promote polygamy even among ordinary people. The value placed on children, particularly male children, in some societies, is such that barrenness or inability to produce male children on the part of a wife may make her husband contract another marriage. African tradition, for the safety of the child, discourages intercourse from conception (or birth) to weaning at the age of three years. A man could therefore contract another marriage when the first wife is pregnant or weaning a child. The prolonged illness of a wife and the practice of widow inheritance are other factors, as is urbanization which, particularly in Africa, has led to businessmen and others taking a 'town wife', while leaving the 'rural wife' on the family land in country districts.

Polygamy (including bigamy) was practised in ancient Israel. Lamech (Gn. 4:19), Elkanah

(1 Sa. 1:1–2) and Joash (2 Ch. 24:1–3) were bigamists. Gideon, also called Jerub-Baal (Jdg. 8:30), David (2 Sa. 3:2–5; 5:13–16) and Solomon (1 Ki. 11:3) were prominent polygamists, the practice being mainly the prerogative of kings and the powerful. Concubinage (*i.e.* the state of cohabitation without legal marriage) seems, however, to have been widely practised in the population at large (Gn. 16:3; 30:3, 9; Jdg. 19:1). Barrenness and the levirate provision mainly accounted for the marginal polygamy that existed among the common people in ancient Israel, and during intertestamental and NT times. From the pastoral regulation that a 'bishop' (overseer) or deacon in the church should be the husband of one wife, it may be inferred that polygamous Jews (or indeed Gentiles with extra-marital concubines) existed as full members in the church (1 Tim. 3:2, 12; Tit. 1:6).

The early church fully appreciated the significance of the one-flesh union between a couple (Mt. 19:4–6; Mk. 10:6–9; Eph. 5:31). Its exclusive nature ruled out polygamy as an option for the Christian. But when polygamists (or bigamists) become Christians, their situation needs an informed approach. Jesus was apparently careful not to condemn polygamists. There is no scriptural warrant to enforce the dissolution of polygamous marriages or to exclude believing polygamists from full church membership. The guiding principle should be, 'each one should remain in the situation which he was in when God called him' (1 Cor. 7:20). But such Christians are not free to keep mistresses or take additional wives. And if any of the wives voluntarily repudiates the union the husband should not compel her to remain. Some think that polygamy could die out in a few decades, but with no legislation against it in Muslim or traditional cultures, it is likely to assume a different pattern.

Bibliography

D. Gitari, 'The Church and Polygamy', *Tr* 1.1, 1984; *idem*, 'Rethinking Polygamy', *TOS* 24, 1988; A. Hastings, *Christian Marriage in Africa* (London, 1973); E. Hillman, *Polygamy Reconsidered: African Plural Marriage and the Christian Churches* (New York, 1975); S. Lowy, 'The Extent of Jewish Polygamy in Talmudic Times', *JJS* 9, 1958; E. A. Nida, *Customs, Culture and Christianity* (London, 1963); W. H. R. Rivers, *ERE* 8, pp. 426–427; R. de Vaux, *Ancient Israel: Its Life and Institutions* (ET, London and New York, 1961).

A.O.I.

POP CULTURE is the name given to an amorphous, continually changing subculture in modern Westernized society, characteristically reflected and fostered by the mass media.* It expresses itself through artefacts, clothes, group activities, visual art, vivid and fast-changing slang, cult personalities, and above all, music. It is the product of a number of factors:

1. A long education period has changed youth's self-assertive experiments in independent personality (which prepare adolescents for adulthood) from being episodes in family life into being a self-conscious subculture. Its ethos jealously fosters in its members an identity over which adults must have no control; its membership has unprecedented resources of spare purchasing power and leisure.*

2. A post-war generation reacted against the pursuit of affluence, which left it with no goal to strive for. (Torn jeans were a typical symbolic statement on this.) The cushioning effect of comfort aroused a craving to *feel* the 'rough male touch of reality', aggravated by a reaction against the depersonalizing effects of scientific rationalism. The call was for spontaneity and emotion. For this, drugs and the sheer physicality of rock 'n' roll offered some fulfilment.

3. Rapid technological change has eroded adult authority. Parents no longer teach the vital work-skills, and the demands of work in a competitive society lessened still further the areas of mutual contact. The resultant social changes have posed moral (especially sexual) issues apparently beyond the competence of the parental generation.

4. There is a common cause, with the powerless sections of society being in revolt against the authority of the adult establishment. Rock and rap music both arose from a marriage of white rebelliousness and black protest in a common struggle for power over personal identity and destiny.

In all this the mass media have played a special part. Their concern to gain the loyalty of the largest market has naturally focused on the youth subculture. They mirror and 'adopt' it: 1. by depicting its images, sounds, and stories; 2. by depicting world-wide structures of self-interested power before whose oppressions parents and other authority figures are seen as helpless or even in collusion; and 3. by offering experiences of identity and intimacy more universal and abiding than those offered by local social relationships in our highly mobile society.

The subculture's reactions to the media images vary. The devotees of pop music (as distinct from rock or rap) largely accept current styles and fashions in artefacts (though not necessarily indiscriminately), and social values: their heroes are conspicuously extravagant consumers. Other groups, however, seem to conduct what Professor Fiske calls 'a guerrilla warfare', constantly resisting any kind of conformism, and developing new 'outrageous' motifs (e.g. punk, rap) as each successive one becomes adopted.

The adult world reacts variously to the pop culture. Parents with a proper sense of order and respect for authority have often seen the rock and, more recently, 'acid-house' expressions of pop culture only as a threat. However, authority's rightful claims do not put it beyond criticism. Disorderliness is often the last resort of disfranchised critics.

Pop culture has often been identified as 'worldliness'.* But we all share some particular culture* in obedience to the creation mandate of Genesis. The Jerusalem Council's decision (Acts 15:19ff.) implies that the Christian gospel translates into every culture and can transform it in the process. Worldliness is an uncritical acceptance of *any* cultural values, in establishment or protest. Curiously, there has often been violent Christian opposition to rock music for its overt (predominantly male) sexuality, while sentimental pop-styles, often expressing typically female sexuality (love as adoring admiration, the ecstasy of surrender to the beloved) are acceptable. Such inconsistencies do not go unnoticed.

The revolt against rule-based morality is not entirely wrong-headed. Rules* are notoriously helpless before new situations. Youth's 'Why not?' is a plea for a *reasonable* morality, i.e. one expressive of a fully coherent philosophy of life. Conservative Christianity has tended to avoid the task of developing a distinctively gospel philosophy – largely because most modern attempts to formulate a Christian philosophy (using non-biblical motifs) have blurred its fundamental message. But without an integrated gospel vision, rules and their resultant casuistry* tend to make Christian morality seem irrational and unconvincing.

The commercial establishment sees the motifs of the pop culture as commodities to be tamed and marketed. Other adults with a pastoral interest often try to become a part of it. To these attempts its devotees develop their own strategies of avoidance. Paradoxical and contradictory as pop culture is, it seems that respect, rather than condemnation, patronage or exploitation, is a primary requisite.

Bibliography
J. Fiske, *Understanding Popular Culture* (London, 1989); J. Godfrey, *Decade of i-Deas: An Encyclopedia of the '80s* (Harmondsworth, 1990); E. Lucie-Smith, *Cultural Calendar of the 20th Century* (Oxford and New York, 1979); Q. Schultze and R. Anker (eds.), *Dancing in the Dark* (Grand Rapids, 1991); M. Wroe (ed.), *Dancing in the Dragon's Jaws* (London, 1988).

J.R.P.

POPE JOHN XXIII, see JOHN XXIII, POPE.

POPULATION POLICY is the attempt to control population, especially its size, but also such other characteristics as age, ethnic composition and proportions from certain social groups. Population is controlled by means of central planning and activity, which attempt to influence reproductive activity by couples that will result in an increase or decrease in the birth rate.

In the past, governments have encouraged procreation in order to offset losses due to wars and diseases, as did European nations as recently as the period after the First World War. Today, however, concern about population centres on huge rates of population growth on a global scale. The United Nations noted in 1958 that this century has witnessed an unprecedented explosion of population. In the period from 1850 to 1900 there was a 42% rise in world population to 1,500 million. By 1925 it rose another 23% to 1,907 million, and by 1950 another 31% to 2,500 million. Since then it has risen to 4,837.5 million in 1985, and is expected to rise to 6,267 million by the end of the 20th century. The effects of this dramatic population rise on available food and water resources, population density, standards of living and environmental* pollution levels are expected to be severe.

Overpopulation is not an empirical, value-free concept. When a country is judged to be overpopulated, this judgment reflects both empirical characteristics and value concerns, particularly about what is an acceptable standard of living, the available resources for meeting this standard, and the expected and acceptable levels of damage to the environment. Currently, death rates are low relative to birth rates, so modern societies are experiencing population growth which they see as a problem of overpopulation.

In the past, increases in population were welcomed as a sign of divine blessing. Jews and Christians regarded themselves to be under a divine mandate to 'be fruitful and multiply' (Gn. 1:28, RSV), and religious views of marriage,* sexuality (see 11) and the family* tend to favour higher reproductive rates. Support for expanding populations can also be found in traditional Chinese, Indian and Japanese cultures. Such an attitude also characterized 16th- and 17th-century European writers, who believed that a large population was economically advantageous to nations. The writing of Thomas Malthus* represented the first systematic treatment of population dynamics, coupled with alarm that population growth would rise geometrically at a much higher rate than would available food supply. For Malthus, the alternatives were to limit population voluntarily by having fewer children or to allow it to be limited by starvation. An optimum population size would be that which produces the best balance of numbers and economic productivity.

Christian thinking about population policy has been characterized by a concern for the theological character of marriage and the family* and a concern for the dignity of the individual, along with a healthy concern that government policies should not infringe on these. Contemporary Catholic teaching is traced to the work of Pius XII, John XXIII, Paul I, Vatican II and the Synod of Bishops. Best known, perhaps, is the Catholic teaching that artificial contraception (see Birth Control*) and abortion* are not to be used by the faithful (see Papal Encyclicals*), nor can any State legitimately require their use. Also characteristic, however, is a concern for the population problem, and an acceptance of a legitimate State role in addressing it, within moral guidelines. Protestant thinkers have stressed the companionship nature of marriage alongside its reproductive function, and have emphasized that the proper spiritual and emotional nurture of children* might require limiting the number of children in a family. Such emphases have allowed Protestants to accept voluntary limitations on the size of families as compatible with Christian obligations. Since the 1930s most Protestants have accepted contraception as morally legitimate

within Christian marriage. Protestant church statements from 1960 have accepted that population rise is excessive in view of the world's resources, and have called for governments to be involved in non-coercive and non-discriminatory birth-control policy, alongside other efforts at effecting a more just distribution of resources and opportunities.

Much Protestant thinking about population ethics has stressed the responsibility of the individual couple in planning their family. Decisions are made to limit the number of children voluntarily, with an eye not only to family resources but also to global concerns. Many such families are choosing to bear a few children and adopt others, particularly those with special social, emotional or physical needs.

Ethical dimensions of population policy that will concern Christian thinking about population policy will be the element of coercion, either of a government against its citizens or of First World aid donors to Third World recipients. Coercion can be either in the form of threats, as is the case in China, where children born over the government mandated limit are penalized, or in the form of coercive inducements to use contraception or sterilization.* Marriage and the family have a God-given integrity that ought not to be unduly encroached upon by outside authorities.

Bibliography

G. M. Berardi, *World Food, Population and Development* (Totowa, NJ, 1985); D. Callahan, *The American Population Debate* (New York, 1971); A. J. Dyck, *On Human Care* (Nashville, TN, 1977); J. P. Wogaman, *The Population Crisis and Moral Responsibility* (Washington, DC, 1973).

D.B.F.

PORNOGRAPHY. Although the term 'pornography' is used to express disapproval of violence, war, poverty and other social evils, its correct usage relates to sexual presentations. Following the broad Gk. meaning of *porneia* as sexual immorality, pornography is now used to refer to gratuitously explicit depictions of sexuality (see 11), whether in words or pictures, which debase sex and exploit the sexual passions.

Definition

It is not the degree of sexual explicitness which defines pornography, since much great art presents sexuality with explicitness, yet without debasing it. Nor is it simply the intent to generate a sexual response, as most recent studies and reports identify such materials as erotica (*Attorney General's Commission on Pornography*, 1986).

Its definition is in fact a shifting one, since pornography generates a response through its pairing of sexual themes with other arousal mechanisms, most notably aggressive or dehumanizing themes, and through the breakdown of long-established taboos. Such a pairing of the erotic with the aggressive is both powerful and dangerous, as much recent research testifies (N. M. Malamuth and E. Donnerstein, *Pornography and Sexual Aggression*; D. Zillman and J. Bryant, eds., *Pornography: Research Advances and Policy Considerations*).

This combination challenges the prevailing norms of our society, which respects the sexual relationship as one of loving intimacy. Instead, by fostering a dehumanized biological reactivity in which (predominantly) women are exploited by men, a significant social taboo is assaulted. Even without overt aggressive themes, there are significant psychological and moral dangers in those sexual materials which objectify and demean the sexual encounter.

Changing attitudes

The boundaries of tolerance have been progressively pushed back, notably over the years since 1970 when the US Presidential Commission on Obscenity and Pornography claimed to find no significant harm from such materials (a view vigorously challenged by *The Longford Report* of 1972). Successive legal actions have redefined the boundaries to allow increasingly obscene materials to be free from prosecution. Longitudinal studies of sexually explicit materials make clear the shift through increasing explicitness to gross presentations of illegal sexual conduct, in which hate and hostility outweigh the sexual themes.

These changes in some ways mirror the changes in society being advocated by the exponents of free expression, but also themselves contribute to the social climate and create a shift in public perceptions of what normative sexuality is, and how it should be expressed.

Pornography is typically reductionistic* in content, denying humanity and committed relationship to focus instead on transience, and bodily sensation, divorced from real human encounter. Its emphasis on biological gratifica-

tion is in sharp contrast to the experience of love.

Throughout history, and still today, the consumers of pornography are predominantly men. The objects of their attention are predominantly women presented verbally or graphically as available and ready to be exploited. More recent trends have included children as available sex objects. This trend has generated a strong negative reaction even from liberals, who now declare child pornography anathema.

The same degree of offence has not been registered widely at the abuse of women in pornography, except by groups of concerned Christians and by the feminist movement. Both, from different philosophical viewpoints, have perceived the sexist implications of pornography as portraying women as less than human, and to be used or abused by men. Feminists (*e.g.* L. Lederer, *Take Back the Night*) have emphasized the unequal power relationships implicit in pornography as an example of a wider social problem, while many Christians have focused on the affront to human dignity which denies the image of God* in creation (*e.g.* J. H. Court, *Pornography: A Christian Critique*; T. Minnery, ed., *Pornography: A Human Tragedy*).

Until the 1970s, little public attention and almost no scientific research were devoted to pornography, since it was an infrequent and non-intrusive phenomenon for most people. It had existed for centuries, but in small quantities and available only to those who sought it out.

Then the pressures of the 'permissive society' together with dramatic changes in capacity to mass-produce pornography in books, colour magazines, films and videos produced an explosion of material which has become a highly visible and indeed inescapable part of people's lives. The result has been a response at many levels – moral considerations from the churches, political reactions through commissions, legal judgments and changes in the law, and a massive increase in social science research (see F. M. Osanka and S. L. Johann, *Sourcebook on Pornography*) – all occurring in the context of a multi-million financial bonanza for producers.

Depending on one's world-view, there are those who argue that this explosion has been a refreshing emancipation from outmoded sexual restraints, and heralding a new, more honest society. This optimism is in contrast to those who argue that sex has been debased, and the social consequences are already tragically obvious.

Technical arguments abound regarding whether pornography *causes* such phenomena as increased sexual crimes, and the escalation of sexually transmitted diseases. This obscures the real issue that pornography is a major contributing factor, in the absence of which, these major sexual problems would be a great deal less. Proof of such relationships is at least as difficult as showing the smoking / cancer link, but none the less, increasingly the evidence supports the view that links do exist even though their modes of operation are diverse. The powerful combination of research studies of various kinds, together with anecdotal reports of personal tragedies, place the onus firmly on those who believe there is *no* harm to demonstrate their case.

The contrary view, that pornography might actually have some therapeutic value, is occasionally advanced, but the research base for this has been found to be inadequate and methodologically flawed (J. H. Court, 'The Relief of Sexual Problems through Pornography'). Popular confusion surrounds this myth, since explicit erotica have been found to desensitize some who have developed unhealthy inhibitions about sexual responsiveness.

The widespread attraction of pornography says something about the kind of relationships that exist in society, and the prevailing unhealthy attitudes to sexuality. Only when inadequate views of relationship or traumatic experiences of sex exist does pornography generate its addictive fascination. Our Western tradition, including Christian teaching, appears to have left many ill prepared to approach sex in a healthy way. Many Christian homes, and many pastors, are now reporting the inroads of pornography into family life. This not only erodes moral values of those involved, but it also affects the kinds of public response which are needed from those with Christian views of sexuality.

Christian responses

Pornography is now so prevalent that to ignore it would be as irresponsible as disregarding issues like race relations or poverty.

It is not sufficient simply to express outrage or personal distaste, or even to invoke moral platitudes. A serious response involves theological reflection on the nature of man and woman and the divine purposes of sexuality. It involves political sensitivity to the social context in which pornography has been marketed as an apparent, but deceptive, answer to human sexual longings. It requires an understanding of the insights now available from scientific research which, while still inadequate, increasingly demonstrates the personal, social and moral harm flowing from pornography. It calls for strong and unflinching social action to re-establish the social boundaries of healthy sexual expression without exploitation. It invites a strong and positive declaration of the beauty and wonder of human sexuality when experienced in healthy God-given relationships so that the pathological addictive attraction for pornography can be diminished.

Bibliography

Attorney General's Commission on Pornography (Washington, DC, 1986); J. H. Court, *Pornography: A Christian Critique* (Downers Grove, IL, 1980); *idem*, 'The Relief of Sexual Problems through Pornography', *AJSMF* 5.2, 1984, pp. 97–106; L. Lederer, *Take back the Night: Women on Pornography* (New York, 1980); Lord Longford, *The Longford Report* (London, 1972); N. M. Malamuth and E. Donnerstein, *Pornography and Sexual Aggression* (New York, 1984); T. Minnery (ed.), *Pornography: A Human Tragedy* (Wheaton, IL, 1986); F. M. Osanka and S. L. Johann, *Sourcebook on Pornography* (Lexington, KY, 1990); *idem*, *U.S. Presidential Commission on Obscenity and Pornography* (New York, 1970); D. Zillman and J. Bryant (eds.), *Pornography: Research Advances and Policy Considerations* (Hillside, NJ, 1989).

J.H.C.

POSSESSIONS, see PROPERTY.

POST-INDUSTRIALIZATION, see INDUSTRIALIZATION.

POSTMODERNITY, see MODERNITY AND POSTMODERNITY.

POVERTY. The poor are those who barely survive. They struggle to obtain the necessities of life. Such a definition of poverty, however, requires amplification. Some people may not be so poor that they go hungry or thirsty, and yet they are relatively poor when compared with others.

Humankind needs to be healthy and fulfilled as well as to be sheltered and adequately fed. We have to meet needs of a social and cultural sort. The poor are not therefore simply those who fall below a certain level of subsistence. Some also suffer from relative deprivation. Their quality of life is lower than that of others and can lead to hardship, by the community's accepted standards of well-being. So, for example, a family, in the comfortable world, may have sufficient food and shelter, and yet be unable to find employment (see Work*) which will bring the rewards leading to freedom of choice* about where to live or how to enjoy leisure.* In the developing world, by contrast, a family may barely scrape a subsistence and be totally excluded from the benefits which come from education* and paid work. In the eyes of the second family, the first family appears to be rich beyond imagination. Discussions of poverty, therefore, must include questions of inequality and fairness, and have a global reference (see Global Ethics[15]).

Poverty in the Bible

The Bible recognizes different types of poverty. The poor are those who are powerless to determine their own destiny and meet their own needs. They include those who suffer from adverse circumstances: the sick, the physically handicapped, the orphaned* and widowed,* immigrants,* slaves* and prisoners. Also, some categories of people are relatively poor because they are helpless when compared with others; the young and the old, women and single persons. In the NT, Jesus identifies with both kinds. In the parable of the sheep and the goats, the king of God's kingdom is served when the poor and oppressed are served (Mt. 25:40). At the same time, he describes the cost of discipleship in terms of embracing homelessness* (Mt. 8:20–22). Jesus favoured those who were absolutely and relatively poor. When Jesus sent his disciples to further his own work, he sent them in a style which would make them poor, relatively speaking, in comparison with those to whom they were sent (Lk. 10:3–4). God is with the poor. Those who are to receive the message of God must recognize that it comes from the poor disciples, and is for those who are prepared to receive from poor and humble people.

Poverty is not, however, a good. It isolates people from family and friends (Pr. 14:20; 19:4, 7). It puts people at the mercy of the rich and powerful (Pr. 18:23). Above all, it encourages the oppressive to dishonour the poor person's creator (Pr. 14:31; 17:5). There should be no poor in the land (Dt. 15:4). It is better for people to be neither rich nor poor, but to have enough and be content (Pr. 30:8).

Justice (see Justice and Peace[3]) is more important than wealth or poverty, and leads to security in the land (Pr. 29:14). God hates injustice (Dt. 25:16). Justice demands sharing. Paul sees this as obligatory (Rom. 15:26–27), and, when it comes to the spiritual and material needs of the believers, it is impossible to resist the egalitarian thrust at the heart of the gospel (Acts 2:44; 4:32; 2 Cor. 8:13–15).

The gospel is about justice for the poor. Without God they do not get it. God is not biased. That is why God favours the poor. Either are they the victims of injustice or they find themselves in a position in which they are powerless to resist the oppression of the powerful.

The gospel is received by those who are poor in spirit (Mt. 5:3). This is because they are not so self-sufficient as to imagine they can draw close to God in any other way. It is the same for poor and rich alike. So, for example, materially comfortable Zacchaeus receives salvation (Lk. 19:9). The wealthy ruler, on the other hand, does not enter the kingdom of God (Lk. 18:23–25). In this way, many Christians have come to see the dependence and receptivity of the poor as a paradigm of receiving salvation (see Sin and Salvation[5]) and entering the kingdom of God.* They display the character of faith* which is not reflected in the confidence of the rich. The poor are vulnerable, humble, patient when exploited, often forgiving when sinned against, and resilient when they become the victims of the powerful for trying to do the right thing.

There is a dignity in poverty. Those who are believers, albeit poor, appreciate and enjoy the riches of their inheritance in the kingdom of God. Poverty need not inhibit an exuberant and rich expression of Christian faith. In the developing world it rarely does.

Poverty in Christian history

The history of the Christian church reflects the biblical attitudes to poverty. In the early days, monks chose poverty, with an ascetic lifestyle, as an acceptable alternative to physical martyrdom on the road to union with God. The churches pursued the service of the poor as an outworking of Christian discipleship. The Reformation removed some of the mystique of poverty by establishing new grounds for self-esteem* in the grace of God, but only by continuing to underline the humility of humankind, standing under the judgment of God.

In the 19th and 20th centuries, Christians have become more aware of the scale of the injustices in the world at large. This has moved the debate about poverty on to a new level. We have learned that the traditional responses of the churches to poverty have become hopelessly inadequate: 1. personal and corporate charity, of the kind envisaged in the NT and the early church, is, of itself, powerless to address the needs of the poor world-wide; 2. self-help policies, often attributed to Protestant Christianity and arising out of convictions about a human being's potential for self-realization, barely begin to redress the inequalities under many repressive regimes; 3. even the organizing of local communities, sometimes considered a fruit of liberation theologies,* in order to take in hand the meeting of the community's own needs, cannot tackle the injustices which follow when global forces, at the end of the day, determine the destiny of the poor world-wide.

Of course, the Christian is not helpless in the face of poverty. A gospel of the generous God calls forth a generous spirit in even the poorest widow in the NT (Mk. 12:44), and wealth, where it is found, is to be shared with a view to equality. Christians have been much preoccupied with the practicality of such a goal.

Action against poverty

Many have slowly come to the conclusion that this can be approached only by spiritual and political action. Each human being who receives the gospel of Jesus Christ receives a spirit of affirmation of his or her worth as a person created by God and reflecting his creativity* and inventiveness. For some, the responsibility for addressing the challenge of others' poverty has to be exercised in the opportunity immediately to hand, if possible with others. For them, there is no resource upon which to call other than that which they do or do not possess, and no other opportunity. Even if, possessing nothing, the poor have only their poverty to give, it is a proclamation and opportunity for the gospel to be heard, and to call forth a response in others. The poor are thus a sacrament of the gospel to the rich, a sign of what it means to depend upon God and each other.

Most Christians in the comfortable world face a different challenge. 'Bread for myself is a material problem. Bread for my neighbour is a spiritual problem' (Nicholas Berdyaev, 1874–1948). Because of the scale of poverty in the world, which is hardly touched by personal generosity, funded schemes of one sort or another designed to help people to help themselves, or community organization designed to enable individuals to discover new strength in collaborative enterprise, it becomes a concern of global proportions which assaults narrow spiritualities. Poverty calls people to move beyond their own personal or community resources, to work for change with many different others. Where it addresses poverty on a world scale, action crosses the narrower boundaries, for example of gender, class, race* and religion, as well as wealth and political power. In so doing, it mirrors the self-giving of Christ (2 Cor. 8:9).

See also: NORTH-SOUTH DIVIDE; THIRD WORLD AID.

Bibliography

R. Holman, *Poverty* (London, 1978); D. Sheppard, *Bias to the Poor* (London, 1983); A. Smith, *Journeying with God* (London, 1991); J. Sobrino, *The True Church and the Poor* (ET, Maryknoll, NY, 1984; London, 1985); J. Vanier, *Community and Growth* (London, ²1989).

I.D.B.

POWER. The concept of power, and cognate terms such as ability, authority, cause, domination and control, is contested and controversial. The ways in which it is used in theology, in physics, in the social sciences and in everyday life frequently have little to do with one another. Even within these fields there is little agreement.

In political studies, explicitly from Aristotle* onwards, the type and location of power have been among the chief features used to distinguish good and bad regimes. This has also been extended to views of society generally. Forms of such power include appointed office, wealth, information, charisma, skill and military means. It can include power over things as well as power over people. Power over people need not be exercised contrary to the wills of those subject to it: many forms of power stem from leadership* abilities which win people over to a cause freely. Nor does power always exist only in large-scale social settings. We can speak of a powerful argument, a powerful book or a powerful sermon. Anything which is able to achieve its end can be regarded as a form of power.

The core sense in discussions of society is almost the equivalent of ability or potentiality to achieve a particular end: this reflects the Lat. origins of 'power' in *potestas* and *potentia*. While this is a fairly imprecise idea, it does seem to capture the element common to most uses, including those in theology. It must be remembered, though, that we never meet power as such but always a particular form of power such as political power, rhetorical power or physical power. Consequently, many assertions made about power would better be made about distinct types of power. Similarly, it is common to distinguish 'power' (understood generally as the mere ability to do something) from 'authority'* (understood generally as legitimate or official power). In the NT this corresponds roughly to the distinction between *dynamis* (*cf*. 2 Cor. 8:3; Eph. 3:16) and *exousia* (Mt. 21:23–27).

Biblically, all power comes from God and belongs to God (Mt. 26:64; Jn. 19:11). God upholds the world itself (Is. 40:10–20). The NT draws explicit attention to Jesus' power. He has power over all things and this power is a manifestation of his kingdom* (Lk. 4:14; 5:17; 11:20–22). It is shown especially in his overcoming death by his resurrection and in his bringing new life in the Spirit to those who follow him (Rom. 1:4; Eph. 1:19 – 2:7). Now he forgives sins, overcomes devils, heals, controls the natural order (Mt. 8:26–27) and raises the dead. He will vanquish his enemies, overcome sin and renew the heavens and earth (Rev. 21).

God's power is delegated to human agents in the form of authority or office (Gn. 1:26–28; Ps. 8:5–8). Such types of authority exist within and beyond the church and include priests, judges, rulers, apostles and elders. They are given to promote good and resist evil and are the means of carrying out God's will as God's representatives. Consequently power is a fundamental and indispensable feature of human affairs.

Christian ethics has sometimes treated the exercise of power *per se* as sinful. But this neglects the purpose and the diversity of types of power. Even political power is not intrinsically evil (Rom. 13:4; Jn. 19:11). While it is true, in Acton's famous dictum, that 'power

corrupts', it is also true that powerlessness or an unwillingness to use legitimate power can also corrupt.

However, the caution about power is well deserved. Power is easily perverted. It also provides greater temptation to sinful people and can give much greater scope and consequence to evil action. Those who are more powerful by definition can, and often do, bring about widespread destruction, pain and immorality. Power is frequently used to oppress and exploit those subject to it (Mi. 2:1–2; Jas. 5:1–6).

One particularly significant form of power, and of its perversion, is contained in what Paul called 'principalities and powers'. Especially since the Second World War this theme has received increasing attention and, for some theologians, has become a central theme for understanding the social order and even the gospel itself. In some instances the expression seems to refer to specific human authorities (Rom. 13:1–3; Tit. 3:1). But other instances, including 'principalities' (*archai*), 'powers' (*dynameis*), 'dominions' (*kyriotetes*), 'authorities' (*exousiai*), 'thrones' (*thronoi*) and 'rulers of this age' (*archontes*) have been held to be references to either angelic or demonic powers (Rom. 8:38; 1 Cor. 2:6; 15:24; Eph. 1:20–21; 3:10; 6:12; Col. 1:16; 2:10, 15).

These terms do not seem to refer to distinct, carefully defined entities. These powers find their origin in Christ but can also be turned against him. They seem to be necessary features of the world, but can pervert the mind, politics and religion itself (Gal. 4:3; Col. 2:8, 20–21). E. G. Rupp (1910–86) maintained that these expressions referred in a metaphorical way to social structures which had become corrupt and demonized. Hendrikus Berkhof (1914–) similarly believed that Paul had demythologized the apocalyptic Jewish notions of heavenly spirits and had reinterpreted them as social structures. John Howard Yoder (1927–) claimed that they were any structure of human life which had been idolized, thus demanding a commitment which can only properly be given to God. He argued that Jesus destroyed the basic source of power of these agencies, hence freeing the church to live a new life in whole-hearted commitment to Jesus Christ. The most thorough treatment of these issues is in the ongoing work of Walter Wink (1935–). He views the powers 'not as separate or ethereal entities but as the inner aspect of material or tangible aspects of power'. The '"angels of nature" are the patterning of physical things – rocks, trees'. Principalities and powers are 'the inner or spiritual essence, or gestalt, of an institution or state or system'. In turn '"Satan" is the actual power that congeals around collective idolatry, injustice, or inhumanity . . .' (*Naming the Powers* [vol. 1 of *The Powers*], p. 105).

This debate is ongoing and it would be premature to offer a definite conclusion. However, it would be unwise to stake too much of a biblical view of State,* economy and society* on these still somewhat tentative treatments when there are other teachings that address such matters more directly.

What is clear is that the power which comes from God may be easily perverted and so must be used cautiously. Jesus continually stressed the right types and use of power. He emphasized that power is servanthood, thus reversing the common understanding (Mk. 10:42–45; Jn. 10:17–18; Rom. 1:16; 1 Cor. 1:18). All forms of power must find their true place in a life of love lived in the power of Jesus Christ (Jn. 13:1; Phil. 2:5–11).

Bibliography

C. E. Arnold, *Powers of Darkness: 'Principalities and Powers' in Paul's Letters* (Downers Grove, IL, and Leicester, 1992); H. Berkhof, *Christ and the Powers* (Scottdale, PA, 1962); S. Lukes, *Power: A Radical View* (London, 1974); R. Niebuhr, *Christianity and Power Politics* (New York, 1940); T. Parsons, 'On the Concept of Political Power', *Proceedings of the American Philosophical Society* 107, 1963, pp. 232–262; K. Rahner, 'The Theology of Power' in *Theological Investigations*, vol. 4 (London, 1966), pp. 391–409; E. G. Rupp, *Principalities and Powers: Studies in the Christian Conflict in History* (London, 1952); W. Wink, *The Powers*, 3 vols. (Philadelphia, 1984, 1986, 1993); J. H. Yoder, *The Politics of Jesus* (Grand Rapids, 1972).

P.A.M.

PRACTICAL REASON is the intellectual factor in action, the process of applying thought to what one does; it is distinguished from theoretic reason, which aims at producing knowledge. Aristotle* (unlike Kant*) defined the process of human behaviour in terms of the combination of intellect and desire: a person has certain goals and wants, and then thinks about what to do to fulfil them.

While the ethical theory of Aristotle had its influence on Stoic and early Christian theology, it is mainly in the revival of interest in the 13th century that we see a serious attempt to work out a Christian version of practical reason, especially in the theology of Thomas Aquinas.*

In his account in *Summa Theologiae*, Aquinas describes the process of practical reason in different stages (*STh* la2ae). There is 1. an *intention** towards a certain goal, which is taken as a given in the process of action (since it is a function of the person's will and character); 2. in order to accomplish one's goal, *deliberation* is often required about the means to achieve it, and this will involve (depending on the complexity of the action) comparison of different ways of achieving it, and an analysis of the moral factors involved; then 3. a *choice** is made about a specific action; this is the decision to take action on what one has been deliberating about; and 4. the *execution* of the decision, the carrying out of the choices that are made. In a very real way the last stage is the most important, because good deliberation and decisions are useless if they are not carried out.

In many of our actions (especially normal, repeated ones) the stages will appear to coincide; but the separation into these stages allows us to see why some choices are poor because of a failure to think them through; while sometimes we may make the right decision, but fail to carry it through, or perform it in the wrong way. The key point in this analysis is that reason is not restricted to deliberation and analysis, but is involved in decision and awareness of the right way to execute the action.

On the other hand, it is important to realize that this description is not 'rationalist' in the sense that it considers actions to be the result only of knowledge, analysis and intellectual judgment. Full account is taken of the importance of the affections of the heart: the agent's goals and desires shape his or her intentions, and if his or her emotions* are disordered he or she will seek the wrong things; anger* or fear* may bring rash judgment or a failure to see the situation clearly; these emotional factors may result not only in poor decisions but also in failure to execute good ones.

For various reasons (including the very comprehensiveness and subtlety of the account) a shift towards a description of human action in terms of law and will* developed after

Aquinas. Practical reason became restricted to the stage of deliberation and was discussed under the heading of conscience,* so that choice and execution of action became a matter of the will.

In the Catholic tradition handbooks of legal morality came to dominate; in the Protestant tradition the Holy Spirit was assumed to provide direct instruction, or the instructed conscience was thought to provide knowledge of what to do, so that the scope of practical reason was reduced. Common to these approaches was the emphasis on the will and a tendency to neglect the role of intellect in the process of human action. The crux of morality became not so much a matter of wisdom* but a matter of having the right disposition of will to carry out the dictates of conscience.

The rediscovery of practical reason by a number of moral philosophers and theologians in the last generation has yet to be applied to a revision of general moral theories; this applies also to Christian thought, where either obedience to law or an ethic of love guided by some vague intuition often prevails. One way of understanding the term 'situation ethics'* is to see it as the final development of an exclusive emphasis on the will (love as benevolence) and an almost total abandonment of practical reason.

The theory of practical reason is not at all inconsistent with a biblical view of morality. The function of law is to provide a framework in which to judge the rightness and wrongness of the actions we deliberate about. The concept of the mind shaped by good purposes, able to see the relevant circumstances and decide on actions in accordance with the principles revealed to us in Scripture, and then to recognize how to carry them out properly, is really the description of wisdom in the OT and in the Pauline notion of having the mind of Christ.

Bibliography

S. Hauerwas, *Character and the Christian Life: A Study in Theological Ethics* (San Antonio, TX, 1985); R. McInerny, *Ethica Thomistica: the Moral Philosophy of Thomas Aquinas* (Washington, DC, 1982); J. Raz (ed.), *Practical Reasoning* (Oxford, 1978); D. Westberg, *Right Practical Reason: Aquinas on Prudence and Human Action* (Oxford, forthcoming).

D.A.W.

PRACTICAL THEOLOGY, see

PRACTICAL AND PASTORAL THEOLOGY.[7]

PRAGMATISM is a theory of meaning which seeks to establish the meaning of a notion with reference to its actual effects on human experience. With roots in the British empiricist tradition of John Locke (1632–1704) and John Stuart Mill,* pragmatism as a developed philosophy is found in the work of American philosophers Charles S. Peirce (1839–1914), William James* and John Dewey (1859–1952).

Inherent to pragmatism is a rejection of a priori truth claims. No truth can be regarded as self-evident; the truth of a notion is dependent solely upon its practical consequences. Thus truth and meaning are dependent upon empirical verification. The pragmatists were deeply committed to modern science's experimental method, which was proving to be so fruitful.

Pragmatism represents a rejection of rational idealism* where truth is seen as eternal and one. William James make this point: the world is characterized by change and truth, and meaning must be remade as we construct new concepts out of our new experiences of the world (*A Pluralistic Universe*, 1909). James regarded the world as ethically neutral but with potential for improvement. This orientation towards an improved future was taken up by Dewey, who was also influenced by the Darwinian evolutionary outlook.

Dewey referred to his own brand of pragmatism as instrumentalism: for him ideas were instruments for adjusting life in both its natural and social mode. It is here that we see the ethical implications of pragmatism most clearly. Ethics is seen as the adjusting of human behaviour towards more satisfying ways of living. This modification takes place at the natural and social level rather than at any metaphysical one. Dewey was dismissive of any system of thought, such as idealism and classical theology, which he saw as disengaging itself from the truly human environment: 'Philosophy recovers itself when it ceases to be a device for dealing with problems of philosophers and becomes a method, cultivated by philosophers, for dealing with the problems of men.' In this respect ethics is primarily concerned with the consequences of human actions and is thus teleological in character.

Bibliography

A. J. Ayer, *The Origins of Pragmatism* (San Francisco, 1968); R. J. Cavalier (ed.), *Ethics in the History of Western Philosophy* (London and New York, 1989); J. Dewey, *Reconstruction in Philosophy* (1920; New York, 1948; London, 1956); W. James, *Pragmatism* (1907; Cambridge, 1978); M. Warnock, *Ethics Since 1900* (Oxford, ³1978).

M.E.A. and S.E.Al.

PRAXIS (from Gk. *praxis*, 'action, activity') refers to human activity which shapes and fashions human beings and nature. Elaborated in the work of Karl Marx* and Friedrich Engels (1820–95), it is the practical movement towards revolution combining objective and subjective elements: 'In revolutionary activity, the changing of oneself coincides with the changing of circumstances' (*The German Ideology*, 1846; Moscow, 1968, p. 234). Marxist and other writers use the term in an attempt to reconcile the dualities of theory and practice, reason and faith, science and ethics.

In liberation theology* and political theology, praxis is the activity which leads to an understanding of oppressive social structures and identification with the progressive movement for change. It involves both knowledge and action. Thus true teaching (orthodoxy) stems from authentic, true praxis (orthopraxis), which is the faithful and obedient activity of the people of God. There are two distinct emphases in the interpretation of praxis which closely correspond to the fundamental tension between 'scientific' Marxism, which attempts to grasp objectively the essential social reality of knowledge and consciousness, and 'critical' Marxism, which is the attempt to interpret reflexively the dependency of knowledge on the historical development of human society through activism and political engagement. Praxis, therefore, is simultaneously a hermeneutic method which has general applicability and a source of interpretations which are highly specific and context-bound. This has led to the accusation that liberation theology has failed to deliver clear and realistic criteria for concrete praxis, or that it is simply a form of applied Marxism. The counter-criticism would be that understanding comes through the suspicions and questions raised by active commitment to liberation.

Liberating praxis is an essential component of Christian ethics. 'Knowing' and 'doing' the truth are inextricably linked (Jn. 3:21; Jas. 1:22, 25), and they combine in a process which is always incomplete and unfinished. Liberation theology's insistence on historical praxis as theology's vital milieu challenges other theologies to reflect on questions of method, especially their claims to universality. It is equally a reminder that theology and ethics are ancillary to the practice of faith.

Bibliography

C. Boff, *Theology and Praxis* (ET, Maryknoll, NY, 1987); G. Gutiérrez, *A Theology of Liberation* (ET, London and New York, ²1988); J. A. Kirk, *Liberation Theology: An Evangelical View from the Third World* (London and Atlanta, 1979); J. Míguez Bonino, *Toward a Christian Political Ethics* (Philadelphia and London, 1983).

H.H.D.

PRAYER. This article aims to explore prayer (human conversation responding to God) in relation to the concerns of (mainly Christian) pastoral care and ethical guidance.

1. A human phenomenon

Prayer is a universal phenomenon. It is found in all the world's religions. There is a human need for prayer, and, like human sexuality, prayer will find expression even if consciously suppressed. In a secular society we may recognize prayer-like behaviour in spontaneous applause, as when an aircraft lands safely after a turbulent flight, or an angry crowd in a refugee camp appeals for justice. David Hay documents people experiencing a 'connection with God', 90% of whom seldom or never went near a church (quoted in W. Carr, *The Pastor as Theologian*, p. 99). But in a 'new age', human reaching out for 'the Real' is expressed in more overtly 'spiritual' ways, just as in some churches there has been a new 'search' for charismatic spontaneity and a 'rediscovery' of older Christian traditions of prayer.

2. The Christian pattern

Jesus prayed as true Man, demonstrating how Christian prayer is an attitude of filial dependence, as opposed to magic where the prayer aims to manipulate the deity. Jesus' prayers approaching death (Lk. 22:40–46; 23:46; Jn. 17:1–26) supremely illustrate his obedient life and his challenge to would-be disciples. Humankind (*homo adorans*) is thereby offered its fulfilment 'in Christ' in a community which prays together (Mt. 6:5–15; Rom. 8:12–39; Rev. 21:22–27). Christ gives himself, praying in us as God responding to God in confession of need, confidence of faith or corporateness of concern (Rom. 8:26–27). God's will (Rom. 8:27) is explained as Christlikeness (8:29). Hence prayer and discipline are linked (Mt. 18:15–20).

3. Prayer and life

The Christian prays and lives 'through Jesus Christ Our Lord' (Rom. 5:21; 6:23; 7:25; 8:39), and so the connections can fruitfully be explored between prayer and work (*e.g.* Ecclesiasticus 38:34, JB), prayer and pastoral care (see K. Leech, *Spirituality and Pastoral Care*), and prayer and politics (see C. Elliott, *Praying the Kingdom*, and M. Williams, 'A Personal Reflection on Prayer and Politics'). V. Brummer in *What are we Doing when we Pray?* shows how we are affected by the prayers we pray and are thus sustained to live the moral life and live with others to our mutual good (*cf.* Jn. 15:7–8; Mt. 9:35 – 10:23). Indeed, the absence of a moral life to match the words uttered in prayer is a cause for concern (Jas. 3:9–12).

4. Prayer and maturity

Jesus 'grew in wisdom and stature, and in favour with God and man' (Lk. 2:52). In helping Christians toward *their* maturity in prayer, there is the need for guidance (see Spiritual Direction*) and discipline, so that the Spirit's resources can be appropriately received by each person (see G. E. H. Palmer *et al.*, *The Philokalia*, and A. Long, *Approaches to Spiritual Direction*). Christians can help each other persevere in prayer into old age towards 'the whole measure of the fulness of Christ' (Eph. 4:13). Anyone acting as a 'spiritual guide' to another needs to know his or her own weakness (see D. Bosch, *A Spirituality for the Road*, Scottdale, PA, 1979, ch. 5), and may find that the human sciences can complement the gifts of wisdom and discernment (Gk. *diakrisis*) to this end (M. Jacobs, *Towards the Fullness of Christ*, London, 1988, pp. 128–135; R. F. Hurding, *Roots and Shoots*, London, 1986, and Grand Rapids, 1988, chs. 14, 16).

5. Prayer and the human context

A different stage in the life-cycle may suggest a revised pattern of prayer, as (for example) the idealism of adolescence is replaced by adulthood (G. W. Hughes, *God of Surprises*, London, 1985, chs. 2, 13), or the busyness of adulthood moves into the stability and potential simplicity of old age (see G. Keyes, 'Prayer in the Second Half of Life'). The understanding of personality-type, or the recognition of factors of gender (L. Byrne, *Women before God*) can also illuminate both the pray-er's self-understanding and also the biblical texts. Choices can also be made for corporate prayer, drawing upon patterns as diverse as ecumenical adoration from Taizé, political protest from Iona, simple biblical meditation, or charismatic or liturgical celebrations.

6. Prayer and the psalms

The realism of the psalter (Jesus' own prayer-book) has been the church's lifeline in many generations. The psalmists discovered God's counsel and were able to share all life's experiences with God. Other great OT prayers (Ex. 32:11–14, 31–32; Ne. 1:4–11; Dn. 9:3–19) express a similar realism.

See also: PRAYER COUNSELLING; SPIRITUALITY.

Bibliography

V. Brummer, *What are we Doing when we Pray?* (London, 1984); L. Byrne, *Women before God* (London, 1988); W. Carr, *The Pastor as Theologian* (London, 1989), ch. 7; C. Elliott, *Praying the Kingdom* (London, 1985); G. Keyes, 'Prayer in the Second Half of Life', in D. J. Davies, *Studies in Pastoral Theology and Social Anthropology* (Birmingham, 1986), pp. 82–101; K. Leech, *Spirituality and Pastoral Care* (London, 1986); A. Long, *Approaches to Spiritual Direction* (Bramcote, Nottingham, 1984); Sr Margaret Magdalen, *Jesus: Man of Prayer* (London, 1987); G. E. H. Palmer *et al.*, *The Philokalia* (ET, London and Boston, MA, 1979), pp. 29–71, 199–250, *etc.*; M. Williams, 'A Personal Reflection on Prayer and Politics', *Anv* 4.3, 1987, pp. 215–219.

G.O.S.

PRAYER COUNSELLING. In this approach to Christian counselling, God is seen as an active participant in the whole counselling process, almost as a third person present with the counsellor and the client. Two-way prayer – talking to God and expecting him to communicate – is a vital ingredient of the session. This does not replace any of the normal aspects of the encounter between counsellor and client but it adds an extra dimension.

There is an extended time to talk, to explore the problem(s) in depth, to seek to understand the causes and implications, and to examine relevant biblical teaching. This is followed by a relaxed time of verbalized prayer. In this it is expected that God will give insight, which may come in a variety of ways: thoughts, memories, conviction of sin, biblical references, pictures and visions, new understanding of the problem and of the reality of God. Often the spiritual gifts of 1 Cor. 12:7–11 are in evidence: particularly tongues, with interpretation (by word or by picture), knowledge (divine revelation of facts that were not otherwise known by the people present), prophetic words, discernment of spirits. Times of silence allow the Holy Spirit to work. Counsellor and client are both active participants in this prayer, which must be wholly controlled by God, who often works in utterly unexpected ways. Prayer is not to be regarded as a technique, but as a channel for the Holy Spirit to act. The danger of it being used in a manipulative fashion, or dominated by the counsellor, should be recognized.

Prayer counselling can be used in various situations. It is not confined to *inner healing*,* where a person's present attitudes to life have been marred by past experience. God does not change past events, but in inner healing, prayer is used to invite God to heal the effects of those events, so that current attitudes can be changed.

Bibliography
R. Bennett, *How to Pray for Inner Healing* (Old Tappan, NJ, 1983; Eastbourne, 1984); R. Green, *God's Catalyst* (London, 1991); F. S. MacNutt, *Prayer in the Family* (Notre Dame, IN, 1983).

See also: PASTORAL CARE, COUNSELLING AND PSYCHOTHERAPY. [12]

R.W.G.

PREFERENTIAL OPTION FOR THE POOR, see LIBERATION THEOLOGY.

PREGNANCY. Gestation in the human female is traditionally counted as nine months, though more accurately 40 weeks, from the first day of the woman's last menstrual period. Pregnancy actually begins with fertilization of the egg and subsequent implantation in the uterine wall by the early embryo. The early conceptus contains all the genetic material required for the development of a new individual, whilst still in the womb, and after birth.

Enormous hormonal changes occur in the mother-to-be from early pregnancy onwards, resulting in circulatory, metabolic and emotional effects. These are suddenly interrupted if the pregnancy is halted by abortion,* spontaneous or induced. Grieving is as important for the woman suffering miscarriage as still birth.

The pregnant woman these days can be confident that new mothers and their babies have never been healthier. Antenatal care is aimed at treating common conditions such as anaemia and detecting early signs of 'toxaemia', affecting blood pressure and kidney function. Ultrasound scanning early in pregnancy checks on the size (and number) of babies and placental position. Sadly, antenatal testing for quite proper reasons merges into the more sinister aim of detecting the abnormal. Any pregnant woman over the age of 35 needs to be prepared for the offer of amniocentesis* (test for Down's syndrome) and its implication of abortion.

The birth of a first baby is for most women the biggest event of their lives so far. The average couple experiencing the 'miracle' of pregnancy and birth may be brought closer to acknowledging God than ever before.

P.F.S.

PRESERVATION OF LIFE, see ETHICS OF MEDICAL CARE; [14] LIFE, HEALTH AND DEATH. [13]

PRIDE (or 'hubris') is the inordinate desire to excel over others and God, often with malicious intent. In the NT and in Christian theology, the Gk. word *hybris* is usually translated as 'insolence', and is related to terms like loftiness, arrogance and haughtiness. It is the supreme vice over against humility.* Gregory the Great (see Gregory I*), Augustine,* Dante (1265–1321), Thomas Aquinas,* Luther,* Calvin* and others considered it to be the essence and root of sin, including the fall of the angels and of the human race. Among the 'seven deadly sins' (see Deadly Sins*), pride is one of the antisocial sins (with envy and wrath) over against individual moral failings (*i.e.* sloth, gluttony, avarice and lust).

Envy is usually associated with it, either as its fuel or one of its symptoms.

The arrogance of pride is a defiance against God which not only transgresses the limits imposed by God (a concept also found in classical Gk. mythology), but also refuses to acknowledge or fear God for who he is in relation to the creature (Ps. 10:4; Je. 13:9–11; Lk. 1:50–52). Hence, as Thomas Aquinas explains, the Lat. word for pride is *superbia*. In this sense, it is related to covetousness with reference to God – the inordinate desire to be like God (see *STh* 2a2ae 162 and 163.1–2). Thus, pride involves the denial of one's finitude, creatureliness and contingency – an illusion often sustained by human ingenuity and technology, but shattered by death (see Lk. 12:19–20). This denial is described by Paul in Rom. 1, which, as Reinhold Niebuhr* observed, makes clear that Christianity defines sin as self-glorification *vis-à-vis* the rationalist-classical identification of sin with ignorance or sensuality. And Paul argues that pride leads to disobedience against God. Pride, then, is an obstacle to salvation which requires an admission by the fallen creature of his or her impotence (Eph. 2:1–3), of the need for grace (Eph. 2:8) and of a shared predicament with the rest of the human race (Rom. 3:23). Pride is the antithesis of faith* – absolute trust in God as the source of goodness and fulfilment (Rom. 3:27; 4:2–5).

The theological sense of 'hubris' gives rise to moral and social injustice. It poisons human relations and consumes others (see Pr. 13:10; *cf*. 1 Cor. 13:4–5). Given the nature of pride, which C. S. Lewis* defined as 'essentially competitive' (because pride is always comparative – always an excelling *over* others), the quest to make self the central concern leads one to ignore other people or to use them for one's self-exaltation, depreciating them and often seeking deliberately to scorn, injure or humiliate them (see Ps. 10:2–4; Mt. 22:6; 1 Tim. 1:13). (The use of 'hubris' in classical Gk. literature consistently connoted harm and injury done out of arrogance or presumption.)

These social implications, epitomized in the Bible by the autonomous ruler who is hostile to God with idolatrous pretension, are often seen on a national scale – a 'collective egotism' (to use Niebuhr's phrase), against which the OT prophets railed (Is. 9:8–10; 47:10–11; Ho. 5:5; 7:10; Je. 13:17), and which often included exploitation of the poor and widows by the wealthy and the wicked (Pr. 15:25; 16:19; Am. 5:11–12). In any society the collective pride of a people can lead to racism, nationalism, class snobbery, *etc*. God finds such pride abominable and culpable (Pr. 6:17; 16:5; Lk. 1:51–52; 16:15); it leads to the proverbial fall of the proud individual or nation (Pr. 16:18; *cf*. Augustine's explanation of the fall of Rome in his *City of God*).

Pride manifests itself in the insatiable thirst for power, in arrogant knowledge, and even in the quest for virtue (in the form of self-righteousness and a pseudo-humility; see Lk. 18:11–14). Regarding the last category, Thomas Aquinas noted that the original sin in Eden consisted of a pride that coveted a spiritual good beyond the creature's measure.

The sin of pride is not to be confused with a legitimate self-love that recognizes one's rightful place in relation to others and God. Nor is it to be confused with rightful expressions of aggressiveness, assertiveness, initiative, self-confidence or self-esteem,* or with taking pleasure in praise.

Dealing with pride in one's life first requires a recognition of its presence, since self-deception is symptomatic of pride (see Je. 49:16). Because pride comes naturally to fallen creatures, one must work at 'putting on' humility (1 Pet. 5:5–6). This will necessitate an understanding of oneself as a creature made in God's image (see Image of God*), fallen, and redeemable; and it will mean establishing one's self-esteem, not on the basis of comparison with others, but on a realistic assessment of one's God-given abilities and calling. Rejoicing in the excellence of others, as Paul enjoins in 1 Cor. 13:6 and Phil. 2:3, is a spiritual discipline to counteract pride.

Bibliography

Augustine, *City of God* (ET, Harmondsworth and New York, 1984); G. Bertram, *TDNT* 8, pp. 295–307; C. S. Lewis, *Mere Christianity* (London, 1952); J. and A. McGrath, *The Dilemma of Self-Esteem: The Cross and Christian Confidence* (Wheaton, IL, and Cambridge, 1992); R. Niebuhr, *The Nature and Destiny of Man*, vol. 1: *Human Nature* (London and New York, 1941); R. C. Roberts, *Spirituality and Human Emotion* (Grand Rapids, 1983).

D.L.O.

PRIMAL INTEGRATION, see PRIMAL THERAPY.

PRIMAL THERAPY is the general title given to a therapeutic approach that sees psychological problems stemming from trauma occurring at birth or in the womb. This therapy aims to enable people to regress, experientially, to the point of trauma that has been retained in their unconscious. Through this cathartic experience and the ongoing work of a therapist or group, people are more able to integrate themselves as physical, emotional and spiritual beings. Frank Lake* developed these ideas in the 1950s but his emphasis became more marked in the 1970s, alongside Arthur Janov (1924–) and William Swartley.

Lake's theological perspective was that there is some correlation between being spiritually 'born again' and being psychologically 'born again' within the safe 'womb' of the Holy Spirit. Christ identifies with our most profound pain through his experience of crucifixion, but his rising to a new life holds out the promise that we can experience resurrection in a psychological sense. Lake tended to oversimplify the relationship between the theological and the psychological with his existential understanding of the crucifixion.

Various questions have been raised about primal therapy's reductionist* view of humanity, its scientific basis, the openness to suggestion in an emotionally vulnerable state, and the fact that some of its practitioners are part of the New Age movement.* Much of its popularity was based on Janov's books and its influence has waned in Britain in recent years, although Dr Roger Moss (1939–) is currently evaluating the continuing contributions of primal therapy.

See also: PASTORAL CARE, COUNSELLING AND PSYCHOTHERAPY. 12

Bibliography

F. Lake, *Studies in Constricted Confusion* (Oxford, 1980); *idem*, *Tight Corners in Pastoral Counselling* (London, 1981); J. Rowan, 'Primal Integration Therapy', in J. Rowan and W. Dryden (eds.), *Innovative Therapy in Britain* (Milton Keynes and Philadelphia, 1988).

J.A.R.

PRISON AND PRISON REFORM. When the Bible refers to prison, it is primarily to a place of control, as we read with reference to Joseph (Gn. 39:20), Jeremiah (Je. 38:6–13), John the Baptist (Mt. 14:3) and Christians generally (Acts 26:10). Debtors could also be 'thrown into prison . . . until you have paid the last penny' (Mt. 5:25–26). In the OT, prison is, in places, recognized as a fact of life, though an oppressive one, and its captives were classed as victims along with the poor, the widows and the blind (*e.g.* Ps. 146:7–9 and Is. 61:1–2). The Law of Moses, however, made 'no provision for imprisonment as a judicial sentence' (see A. Harvey, *Custody*), and punishments were 'not designed to deter potential criminals, nor as an act of retribution but as a means of preventing divine action by appeasing Jahweh's wrath' (A. Phillips, *Ancient Israel's Criminal Law*, p. 12). The use of imprisonment as a punishment* is once referred to (alongside death, banishment and confiscation of property) in the commission of Artaxerxes to Ezra (Ezr. 7:26).

Since Norman times in England, the 'peace' of the king or queen has been enforced by prison where finally necessary. Since an Act of 1361, Justices of the Peace have been commissioned 'To restrain the offenders . . . and to cause them to be imprisoned and duly punished according to the law and custom of the realm . . .' (J. P. Eddy, *Justice of the Peace*, London, 1963, p. 4). Prisons were supplemented by Bridewells (for petty offenders) and houses of correction, and all came under the Justices' authority. Conditions were bad and gaolers were often corrupt. John Howard (1726–90) was the first to publicize this effectively in 'The State of the Prisons' (1777). Conditions were improved, and during the 19th century the central government assumed increasing responsibility for inspecting, setting rules and expanding the system, in order to cope with the abolition of transportation and hulks and the reduction of capital punishment. Prisons were 'nationalized' in 1877 in one service for England and Wales; there are separate services for Scotland and Northern Ireland. The first commercially-run prison opened in 1991 and more are expected; they work under contract to the Home Office. The Prisons Act, 1952, provides the statutory basis for English prisons but has been modified by a series of Criminal Justice Acts.

The Prison Department of the Home Office publishes an annual report, and so does Her Majesty's Chief Inspector of Prisons. These describe the number of prisons and prisoners, the conditions, the costs, plans, problems, *etc.* There are 128 prison establishments, many with several functions. The total number of prisoners in England and Wales exceeded 50,000 in 1988 (Home Office, *Report on the Work of the Prison Service, April 1988–March 1989*, London, 1989). Compared with the general prison population, black inmates are over-represented in prisons (E. Genders and E. Player, *Race Relations in Prison*, p. 1). The projected number of prisoners in British jails for the year 2000 is 57,500 (Home Office, *Statistical Bulletin 10/92*, London, 1992). Prison populations in Council of Europe countries have generally risen over the past 20 years, but falls have been recorded in five (T. Mathiesen, *Prison on Trial*, p. 1). In 1988 the UK had 97.4 prisoners per 100,000 population, the highest proportion in Europe; Holland had 40 per 100,000 and Cyprus and Iceland slightly less (Council of Europe Prison Information Bulletin no. 15, Strasburg, June 1990). The average USA figure is 320 per 100,000 (T. Mathiesen, *Prison on Trial*). The problems of the English prisons were thoroughly explored by Lord Justice Woolf (1933–) and Judge Stephen Tumim (1930–) after the riot at Strangeways Prison in April 1990 (see Home Office, *Prison Disturbances April 1990*). The Home Office response to this, *Custody, Care and Justice*, sets an agenda 'for the rest of this century and beyond' (p. 3). Conditions in three large urban prisons in England were sharply criticized by the Council of Europe (*Report to the UK Government . . .*). There has been criticism also from researchers (*e.g.* K. McDermott and R. D. King, 'As Full a Life', and P. Scraton *et al.*, *Prisons under Protest*), and from former inmates (*e.g.* R. Caird, *A Good and Useful Life*, London, 1974, and A. Peckham, *A Woman in Custody*, London, 1985).

It may seem surprising that 'prison reform' has such a long and continuous history. Prison standards have undoubtedly risen, but many untried prisoners linger in custody on remand, several thousand cells are still shared, not every cell has a toilet (and toilets within cells are only one step better than chamber pots), regimes (especially in urban prisons) are very limited, and facilities for visits are improving only slowly. Woolf urged a better balance of security, custody and justice (in *Prison Disturbances April 1990*) and gave a broad definition to justice because he included humane standards of care. Suicides* in prison have also been increasing despite attempts to prevent them (Home Office, *Report of a Review . . .*). There is still a role for prison reform groups such as the Howard League for Penal Reform, the National Association for the Care and Resettlement of Offenders, and the Prison Reform Trust.

But on what grounds have prisons been justified? It seems certain that their justification has followed centuries of use. The classical bases of retribution,* deterrence* and reform were examined in 1934 by William Temple* in relation to penal action generally, and they were supported by him within this framework: '. . . it is true that though Retribution is the most fundamental element in penal action and Deterrence for practical reasons the most indispensable, yet the Reformative element is not only the most valuable in the sympathy which it exhibits and in the effects which it produces, but is also that which alone confers upon the other two the full quality of Justice' (*The Ethics of Penal Action*, pp. 39–40).

This optimistic statement needs modification in the light of research and criticism. N. Walker (1917–), in *Punishment, Danger and Stigma*, has considered the expectations of punishing, denouncing and reducing crime through imprisonment. Punishment looks back to the offence (the focus of the Criminal Justice Act, 1991) and can be unjust both through not regarding the offender and through the addition of stigma rather than restoration. Stigma attaches especially to prison. 'Denouncing' reinforces society's rules. 'Reducing' covers a range of utilitarian (see Consequentialism*) concepts about reducing future crime whether by deterrence, by rehabilitation or by 'incapacitation'. Several authors have effectively demonstrated that prison very seldom 'rehabilitates' and does not deter (*e.g.* R. Martinson, 'What Works?'; S. R. Brody, *The Effectiveness of Sentencing*; and T. Mathiesen, *Prison on Trial*). New programmes with amenable subjects and 'good' counsellors sometimes work (*e.g.*, see M. Shaw, *Social Work in Prison*, London, 1974). Charles Colson (1931–) confirms such assessments from his experience of prison in the USA ('Towards an Understanding of Imprisonment and Rehabilitation', p. 160). Imprisonment seriously disadvantages families (see R. Shaw, *Prisoners' Children*, and J. Blake, *Sentenced by Association*). Prison is now at the extreme end of the tariff; other court disposals can be more effective and cheaper; the Government looks to Area Criminal Justice Committees to work out sounder, less expensive means of reducing crime (*Prison Disturbances April 1990*, ch. 9).

The issues of tariff, justice and mercy have been discussed by Oliver O'Donovan (1945–) in *Measure for Measure* and, more recently, by A. E. Bottoms (1939–) in 'The Aims of Imprisonment'.

Christians will distinguish between 'conversion' and individual reform, and need not be blown off course by political rhetoric. Many Christians have described their conversion in prison (*e.g.* R. Catchpole, *Key to Freedom*, Guildford, 1974, and R. Nightingale, *Freed for Ever*, London, 1985). As far as the church's attitude to prisoners is concerned, the issues are excellently covered by D. W. Van Ness (1949–) in *Crime and its Victims*. The NT's approach is certainly clear: 'Remember those in prison as if you were their fellow-prisoners, and those who are ill-treated as if you yourselves were suffering' (Heb. 13:3). Note also the words of Jesus about visiting those in prison (Mt. 25:36).

All prisons have Chaplains (full or part-time) and many are linked to Prison Fellowship groups. Prisoners' Week each November focuses attention on those in prison – prisoners, staff and volunteers. Clergy have contributed to public debate (see C. Copley, *Report of the Working Party on Inmates' Marriage Relationships*; J. Cooke, *The Cross behind Bars*; R. Hardy, *The Meaning of Imprisonment* and *Respect in Prison*; J. A. Hoyles, *Punishment in the Bible*; and A. Speller, *Breaking Out*). Probation Services are committed to resettlement, and the Langley House Trust (based at Witney, Oxfordshire), provides homes for ex-offenders. There are many ways of responding (including prison visitors) and many self-help groups (*e.g.* Help and Advice Line for Offenders' Wives).

Remembering especially the requirement 'to act justly and to love mercy' (Mi. 6:8), we need to find ways of diverting potential offenders, of reinforcing pro-social tendencies, of minimizing re-offending, and of supporting victims, prisoners and their families.

See also: CRIME; CRIMINAL JUSTICE; SENTENCING, PRISON.

Bibliography
J. Blake, *Sentenced by Association* (London, 1991); A. E. Bottoms, 'The Aims of Imprisonment', in D. Garland (ed.), *Justice, Guilt and Forgiveness in the Penal System* (Edinburgh, 1990); S. R. Brody, *The Effectiveness of Sentencing* (London, 1976); C. W. Colson, 'Towards an Understanding of Imprisonment and Rehabilitation', in J. R. W. Stott and N. Miller (eds.), *Crime and the Responsible Community* (London, 1980); J. Cooke, *The Cross behind Bars* (Eastbourne, 1983); C. Copley, *Report of the Working Party on Inmates' Marriage Relationships* (London, 1979); Council of Europe, *Report to the UK Government on the Visit to the UK carried out by the European Committee for the Prevention of Torture and Inhuman or Degrading Treatment or Punishment* (Strasburg, 1991); E. Genders and E. Player, *Race Relations in Prison* (Oxford, 1989); R. Hardy, *The Meaning of Imprisonment* (Lincoln, 1990); *idem*, *Respect in Prison* (Lincoln, 1991); A. Harvey, *Custody: Its Necessity or Otherwise* (address to Prison Chaplains' Conference, July 1974); Home Office, *Custody, Care and Justice* (London, 1991); *idem*, *Prison Disturbances April 1990* (London, 1991); *idem*, *Report of a Review by HMCIP of Suicide and Self Harm in Prison Service Establishments in England and Wales* (London, 1990); J. A. Hoyles, *Punishment in the Bible* (London, 1986); K. McDermott and R. D. King, 'As Full a Life', *Prison Service Journal* 77, 1990, pp. 30–40; R. Martinson, 'What Works? Questions and Answers about Prison Reform', *The Public Interest* 35, 1974, pp. 22–54; T. Mathiesen, *Prison on Trial* (ET, London, 1990); O. O'Donovan, *Measure for Measure: Justice in Punishment and the Sentence of Death* (Bramcote, Nottingham, 1977); A. Phillips, *Ancient Israel's Criminal Law* (Oxford, 1970); P. Scraton *et al.*, *Prisons Under Protest* (Milton Keynes, 1991); R. Shaw (ed.), *Prisoners' Children: What are the Issues?* (London, 1992); A. Speller, *Breaking Out: A Christian Critique of Criminal Justice* (London, 1986); W. Temple, *The Ethics of Penal Action* (Rochester, 1934); D. W. Van Ness, *Crime and Its Victims* (Downers Grove, IL, 1986; Leicester, 1989); N. Walker, *Punishment, Danger and Stigma* (Oxford, 1980).

M.D.J.

PRISON SENTENCING, see SENTENCING, PRISON.

PRIVACY. The right to privacy is rooted in our understanding of the nature, value and integrity of the individual person. It suggests that, if society and the wider community are to be seen to respect the boundaries which protect the individual, then they will make provision for social norms which guard each person's right to privacy.

Privacy is related to, but not the same as, secrecy* and confidentiality.* Secrets are matters deliberately withheld from others for reasons which may or may not be morally justified. Confidentiality is the commitment to guard information concerning others and not to pass it on without their consent through agreed and accepted procedures.

The right of privacy is rooted in the conviction that crucial matters of individual experience belong to that person alone. No person has a right to enter into these areas in the lives of others without their consent.* Matters widely considered to be private include matters affecting our bodies, our minds and our souls. Thus medical treatment requires the consent of the person. Indoctrination* is unlawful. Enforced submission to religious beliefs and systems is immoral. Sexual relationships, provided they are lawful, are private matters belonging to the choices and consents of the individuals involved. No other person has the power to take away our life. For Christians many of these areas are matters for which each person is responsible to God. Others may offer advice and provide guidelines. Since, however, these issues touch the nature of our being as God has created us, they are personal and private.

Every society has to decide where the boundaries of privacy lie. Do they extend from the person to that person's property? Some would argue that the inviolability of the person extends to their property* and that this principle is a necessary guardian of liberty. Others would argue that the rights of the individual over property – and, therefore, their right to privacy in these matters if they so choose – is dependent upon such property rights being subject to the demands of justice. No-one can claim an absolute right to protection in this area when the social setting is one of manifest injustice. Nevertheless, respect for property, and people's privacy in relation to it, is a vital protection of the individual against the abuses of corporate power.

Similarly, all societies must have procedures for overriding the rights of individuals in certain extreme circumstances. If, for example, people are not capable of giving consent, there have to be processes for taking action for their own protection. When people have lost control of their own minds there have to be ways in which the community is able to make proper

decisions for their care and help. Such decisions must be demonstrably in the interests of the person and justified by agreed legal and moral criteria. Our duty to respect the life and property of others may have to give way to other demands in extreme situation such as war.* Even here both the conduct of the action and its purposes should be related to the protection of individuals and to the restoration of their rights in peaceful and free communities.

Privacy reminds us that there are boundaries which protect each person, and that other people – the law, the State, the church or whatever other corporate bodies with which we are involved – may not stray over them. Only in extreme and defined situations may these boundaries be breached without consent. It is the normal duty of all such persons and bodies to protect the right of privacy and the personal responsibility for one's own life which is inextricably bound to it.

See also: DATA PROTECTION; INFORMATION TECHNOLOGY.

Bibliography
J. B Young (ed.), *Privacy* (Chichester, 1978).
J.W.G.

PROBABILIORISM. One solution to an old problem in casuistry.* Suppose I can do either X or Y, and should personally prefer to do Y, but feel that it may possibly be my moral duty to do X. Probabiliorism is the view that I may do Y without sin, but only if it is more probable than not that it is morally preferable too.

This contrasts with probabilism,* which holds that Y may be done provided there is some 'probable' (here used in a specialized sense of 'reasonably solid') argument in favour of the action; there may be much stronger reasons for thinking it wrong, but according to probabilists it may still be done. If God has not made it absolutely clear that X is to be done, how can he demand of us that we do it?

Probabiliorism has been maintained by virtually all Protestant casuists, and by many Roman Catholic ones too. It seemed common sense: if it was more likely than not that one ought to do X, surely it was encouraging laxity to maintain that one could nevertheless do Y. That it is not absolutely certain that I should do X makes no difference, if I believe that in all probability I ought to; not to do it would be going against conscience and apparent truth.

Bibliography

K. E. Kirk, *Some Principles of Moral Theology* (London, 1920), ch. 8, §4; B. Pascal, *Provincial Letters*, ed. A. J. Krailsheimer (Harmondsworth, 1967), Letter 5.

R.L.S.

PROBABILISM. The view in casuistry* that an action (or inaction) may be done without sin provided that there is 'probable' reason to believe it legitimate. This does not mean 'more probable than not' (that would be 'probabiliorism'*), but simply that there is some fairly solid reason in favour of the action; there may be considerably stronger reasons for thinking it wrong, but according to probabilists it may still be done. For (it was argued) a law that is not made clear is not binding, and if there is fairly solid reason for thinking the action permissible, then there obviously is no clear law against it.

Probabilism was associated especially with the Jesuit casuists; virtually all Protestant casuists, and for a long time many Roman Catholic ones, rejected it in favour of probabiliorism. It was felt that probabilism encouraged laxity, especially as, according to some, the 'probable reason' might consist simply of one moralist's opinion. But probabilism became prevalent among Roman Catholic moralists in the late 18th and 19th centuries, and is still found in many conservative writings, though much recent ethical debate has been conducted in different terms altogether and has left this debate rather on one side.

Bibliography

K. E. Kirk, *Some Principles of Moral Theology* (London, 1920), ch. 8, §4; R. C. Mortimer, *Elements of Moral Theology* (London, 1947), pp. 86–99; B. Pascal, *Provincial Letters*, ed. A. J. Krailsheimer (Harmondsworth, 1967), Letter 5.

R.L.S.

PROCREATION is the family* process in which father and mother bring children* into the world. Parents procreate by acting on behalf of the creator to create offspring. In Gn. 1:28 ('Be fruitful and increase in number') humans are called by God to procreation. Although it is often limited to the biophysical process of generating children, procreation in its full meaning includes caring for and nurturing children, and providing them with a sense of belonging and security, identity and confidence.

The early church made procreation the chief aim of marriage* and approved of sexual intercourse only with the positive intent of procreation. Although officially procreation and nurture remain the primary end of marriage in the Roman Catholic Church, in the Protestant Church companionship and mutual help are generally considered the main aims of marriage as a 'one-flesh union' in terms of which procreation is also a valid purpose.

In other words, although parenthood* is still considered highly desirable, the Protestant ethos calls for responsible parenthood and rejects any notion of bondage to biological function. The emphasis is on *choosing* to procreate, *i.e.* on *choosing* to become a parent. The focus is on quality of family life rather than quantity of family. Procreation is not a one-dimensional biotic process, but a familial, multi-dimensional process in which decisions are made by couples as to how to deal with the powers of procreation and responsibilities are assumed about caring for the resulting children.

Such an idea of responsible parenthood gives married couples the ethical room to practise birth control* and, it is argued, to decide not to have children as well as the option to look for other ways to have children (*e.g.* by adoption*) when the normal procreative way is not available to them (see Reproductive Technologies*). Becoming a parent is only the start; being a parent through the nurture and care of one's offspring over the years remains the challenge.

Procreation is exciting and awesome. Children are a wonderful blessing of God (Pss. 127:3; 128:3–4). Since the early years of life are so significant in the shaping of identity and character (see ⑩), having and raising children is also a large, sometimes even overwhelming, responsibility. Parents are to teach God's ways diligently to their children 'when you sit at home and when you walk along the road, when you lie down and when you get up' (Dt. 6:7). Jesus underlines the importance of healthy nurturing (Mt. 18:5–6), and parents are warned not to 'exasperate your children; instead, bring them up in the training and instruction of the Lord' (Eph. 6:4).

J.H.O.

PROFESSIONAL ETHICS.

Ethical issues arise in all of the established professions, such as medicine, law, nursing, the clergy, science and education, as well as in such 'emerging professions' as librarianship, social work, engineering, police work, counselling, architecture, government and civic planning, computer science, journalism, healthcare administration and accounting. Contemporary professional ethics brings together the ethical insight and clarity of philosophers, theologians and other scholars with the practical wisdom of professionals.

The term 'profession' derives historically from the professing, or taking, of religious vows. This casts some light on the nature of professions, which are specialized forms of activity with unique goals, standards and institutional characteristics. A profession is distinguished from other occupations, including many that are highly skilled in their own right, by its involving a high degree of generalized and systematic knowledge in addition to any required skills. The role of a professional is to be a trusted adviser, a 'learned friend', by virtue of his or her specialized knowledge. A profession has a primary orientation to the community interest rather than to individual self-interest. Trust* is essential to the functioning of a profession, a trust earned by the profession's willingness to uphold and adhere to high standards of competence and practice. Professions also tend to have a process of certification and licensure, professional organizations, and a tradition of individual autonomy in the performance of professional duties. They follow a policy of self-policing of ethical impropriety and incompetence. Thus, a professional undertakes a period of study to master a substantial body of information, is socialized into the norms of the profession, and is then regarded as competent to give advice and other services to clients.

Given the nature of professions, certain ethical problems suggest themselves. The professional's superior knowledge, and the often highly important nature of his or her involvement with the client, create a number of ethically sensitive concerns. The obligation of the professional to obtain the client's informed consent* to any services to be provided, as for example in medical care, is well established, but are there limits on this requirement if the professional is convinced that it would not be in the client's interest to provide the necessary information or to leave the decision with the client? The broader question of paternalism arises: traditionally in some professions, the professional takes upon himself or herself decision-making in the interest of the client without gaining the full, knowledgeable participation of the client, a participation that becomes the harder to obtain the more the decision involves specialized expertise.

Many professions must also face the issue of confidentiality.* Since the professional is in a position to gain information about the client that the client would not wish to have made known to others, the professional is seen to be under an obligation to keep confidential any such information gained in the professional-client relationship. Is this bond of confidentiality capable of being overridden by other concerns, such as the prevention of harm to others or the punishment of wrongdoers in the interest of society? Some professions, such as the Roman Catholic priesthood, see confidentiality as absolute, but other professions (e.g. medicine or teaching) must face the question posed when other factors override the obligation to uphold confidentiality.

A related question is that of truthfulness. Is a professional ever justified in keeping the truth from a client for the client's good? Does this justify actively deceiving the client? In the legal profession, is the ordinary obligation to truthfulness overridden by the special nature of the adversary system, so that lawyers may mislead juries in order to gain the best results for their client? A broader question into which this issue falls is that of whether there is a special 'role morality' for the professional, distinct from the everyday morality binding on all people in their normal lives. It does seem that the moral obligations of professionals in the course of their duties are distinct from general, everyday obligations, placing special, stringent obligations on the professional while granting him or her certain special privileges and even exceptions from ordinary standards of conduct. The limits of role morality are the subject of much discussion.

Other issues in professional ethics derive from the role of the profession in society. Are those with essential professional duties, such as doctors, nurses and teachers, precluded from having recourse to remedies such as strikes* in negotiations with employers? Is there an obligation to see that professional services are available to those of low income, as is attested by the tradition of providing free, limited services in medicine and law for the public good? Are there circumstances in which concern for the public good overrides loyalties to clients, as when engineers inform authorities that public projects are hazardous? And are the profession's own self-policing mechanisms always an adequate protection for the public, or are they sometimes a way of shielding the profession from justifiable public scrutiny?

Christian professionals are strongly motivated to exhibit the highest standards of professional service, since they regard themselves as stewards under God of their gifts and training (1 Cor. 4:2). Professions are opportunities to serve others in love, and can be seen as a participation in the extension of Christ's ministry of healing, reconciliation and service. Christians have shown considerable leadership in professional ethical behaviour, and have begun to form their own Christian professional associations alongside the secular ones to which they belong. Christians could also take the initiative in guiding their professions to take more seriously their obligation to serve the disadvantaged and powerless in society, as for example in the provision of medical, legal and educational services.

See also: PASTORAL CARE, COUNSELLING AND PSYCHOTHERAPY. [12]

Bibliography

M. D. Bayles, *Professional Ethics* (Belmont, CA, 1981); J. Boyajian (ed.), *Ethical Issues in the Practice of Ministry* (Minneapolis, MN, 1984); S. M. Cahn, *Saints and Scamps: Ethics in Academia* (Totowa, NJ, 1986); J. C. Callahan (ed.), *Ethical Issues in Professional Life* (Oxford, 1988); T. Donaldson and P. H. Werhane (eds.), *Ethical Issues in Business* (Englewood Cliffs, NJ, ²1983); S. Gorovitz, *Doctors' Dilemmas: Moral Conflict and Medical Care* (New York, 1985); K. Kipnis, *Legal Ethics* (Englewood Cliffs, NJ, 1986).

D.B.F.

PROFIT is a residual, *i.e.* that which remains after a firm's costs have been deducted from its revenues. In the fields of both accounting and economics, there is a sizeable literature about the proper measurement of costs and revenues in order to calculate a firm's profits.

A distinction is often drawn between accounting profits and economic profits. Accounting profit is calculated using conventional accounting standards, which generally regard cost as the original acquisition or historical cost of the input. Accounting costs do not always include the cost of inputs supplied by the firm's owners.

Economic profit is the residual after the costs of *all* inputs are deducted from the firm's revenues. In economics, costs reflect an input's highest valued use elsewhere in the economy (*i.e.* 'opportunity cost'). Thus, a firm earning only zero *economic* profit can be self-sustaining over time. The same firm may have a positive accounting profit because accounting measures may ignore the cost of owner-supplied management, financial capital or land, or may ignore the increase in value of some inputs since their time of acquisition by the firm.

When profits are portrayed as a percentage, they are generally called a rate of return. For example, a firm's profits divided by its sales revenues would yield the firm's rate of return on sales. Owners of a firm may be interested in the profitability of their investment,* *i.e.* the firm's rate of return on owners' equity.

In economics, there is a sizeable literature about the beneficiaries of the profit residual. Possibilities range from: 1. a return to entrepreneurs for bearing risk (*e.g.* to an innovator who invents and markets a new pharmaceutical product); 2. a reward to those firms which demonstrate superior skill, foresight and industry (*e.g.* to a firm which builds a better mousetrap); 3. a financial benefit to firms with monopoly* positions (*e.g.* to a firm able to restrict output and raise price because its customers have no suitable alternative supply sources); and 4. the gains to firms who defraud their customers or input suppliers (*e.g.* to a firm that reduces its costs by giving short weight).

Most individuals would find no difficulty with profits going to the first two beneficiaries, but many would object to the latter two. Many disagreements about the role of profits involve disputes about the recipients of a firm's profits. The actual magnitude of the profit stream may be a point of debate too.

Not all business enterprises receive profits. If revenues fall short of costs, profits are negative. Enterprise economies are sometimes called profit-and-loss economies, reflecting the possibility of negative profits. Negative profits may be due to factors outside the firm's control, such as economic recession or a change in buyer preferences; or due to a firm's shortcomings, such as failure to control costs or product quality.

Under conditions of market competition, high profits serve as a lure to business expansion, thereby attracting more resources to a sector where consumers currently value output higher than the cost of producing it. Losses have the opposite effect: provoking the exit of sellers and thereby reducing the amount of society's scarce resources allocated to a sector where consumer preferences are low relative to the value of the resources utilized there. Shifting resources in response to changes in consumer demand is one of the most difficult problems faced by economies that do not have a profit-and-loss system.

In addition to its technical usage in economics and accounting, the word 'profit' has an ethical connotation. The profit motive is the motive of self-interest, and at root it is no different from the motive of the consumer in finding the best buy or the worker in looking for the best job (Pr. 14:23; 21:5). The Scriptures warn against obsession with the pursuit of profit when it swamps the practice of charity and piety, or in instances when the profit is secured through dishonest tactics (Pr. 20:10). The Scriptures are disposed favourably to the pursuit of profit when it entails good stewardship* over society's scarce resources, be this in the business or in the home, when the Lord is honoured by the returns (Pr. 3:9–10).

The most famous reference to profit in the Eng. Bible (and probably in the Eng. language) is: 'For what shall it profit a man, if he shall gain the whole world, and lose his own soul?' (Mk. 8:36, AV). To pursue profit too avidly was the sin of the rich fool (Lk. 12:16–21). Yet the Bible does not condemn the receipt of profits that are the result of diligent endeavour (Ec. 11:6). For example, the virtuous woman of Proverbs sells merchandise that is not only good but profitable (Pr. 31:18).

The word 'profit' must be used discriminately, since it is asked to wear so many hats in the Eng. language.

See also: ECONOMIC ETHICS. [17]

Bibliography

B. S. Kierstead, *IESS* 12, pp. 547–552; F. H. Knight, *Risk, Uncertainty and Profit* (New York, 1921); J. F. Weston, 'The Profit Concept and Theory: A Restatement', *Journal of Political Economy* 62, 1954, pp. 152–170.

K.G.E.

PROMISES. A promise is a form of self-binding obligation, according to which an obligation to perform an action arises from the act of communicating an intention to assume an obligation to perform it. Inasmuch as promises create an obligation* in this way, they may be distinguished from mere statements of intent, which imply no such obligation to perform, although in practice the distinction may be difficult to draw. Promises are usually thought to require acceptance by another party to be properly constituted.

How promises bind has been much disputed. One account, arising in the 17th century under the influence of Hugo Grotius* and Samuel Pufendorf (1632–94), explains their binding force in terms of an act of the will obligating itself to a future action. But this voluntarist* approach (apart from its apparent implication that an uncommunicated promise would still be binding) mistakenly regards the act of the will, which is in truth one of the conditions of a promise, as the source of its obligation.

Utilitarian theories by contrast claim that promise-keeping should be adhered to because it promotes trust and social co-operation, and thereby maximizes welfare. But, amongst other problems, consequentialist* approaches do not explain convincingly why a promise may not be violated even when it would lead to the best consequences to do so. A similar objection may be raised against David Hume's* attempt to explain the obligation of promises in terms of an individual's long-term self-interest.

A third approach, reflecting the Eng. common-law notion that promises are in general legally binding only if they have benefited the promisor or have been relied upon by the promisee, argues that the moral obligation of promising is based on the duty not to harm others by letting them down. But this line of thought, while it rightly recognizes that the duty* to keep a promise is stronger if others have relied on it, cannot account for the residual binding force which promises have independently of their being relied upon.

Perhaps the most persuasive theory of promise-making starts from an acknowledgment of promising as a social practice. Promise-making is at one level an institution governed by (maybe tacit) rules, which generate the expectation that those who make promises will perform what they have promised. Such a practice encourages predictability of behaviour and furthers co-operation in joint projects; individuals participate in it because they have reason both to value for its own sake the common good which the practice fosters, and (as a part of that common good) to respect the principle of impartiality which requires that one undertakes the responsibilities owed to others as the result of making a promise. In this way the intuition that there is an obligation inherent in promise-making can be acknowledged, as can the contribution that promising makes to the common welfare, and yet a plausible account can also be given of the place of the reasonings of individual agents within the practice as a whole.

For Jews and Christians, the setting of human promising is fixed by the biblical understanding of a steadfast God whose righteousness* is expressed in his faithfulness to his promises, a fidelity which is sustained even when his human covenant-partners are unfaithful. God has power to do what he promises (Rom. 4:21), and the faithfulness to carry it out (Rom. 15:8, his 'truth'). Fulfilled in Christ (Acts 13:32–33), guaranteed by the Spirit (Eph. 1:13–14), and oriented to a new heaven and a new earth (2 Pet. 3:13), God's promises are the ground of Christian hope and the context of Christian obedience.

Correspondingly, human promise-making should be characterized by faithfulness and constancy, seeking a climate of trust* that encourages human community and flourishing. One should promise only what is within one's power to fulfil, and may not promise to do what is immoral. Promises are properly constituted only if made voluntarily, without coercion, and in circumstances which are in general terms fair; a promise may fail to be binding if to fulfil it would clash with other higher obligations, if circumstances change significantly and unexpectedly, or if the claim on the promisor is waived by the promisee. Above all, as God's promise of grace* stands despite human faithfulness, so within the human community the response to a neighbour's failure to keep a promise should be marked by the commitment to forgive.

Vows

In biblical usage and the Christian tradition, vows are simply promises made to God. Whether undertaken out of penitence, gratitude or the desire for holiness, they serve to bind the one making the vow to do something which goes beyond what is required as a matter of ordinary moral obligation. They

are frequently found in non-Christian religions and in the OT (Gn. 28:20–22; Nu. 6:1–21; 1 Sa. 1:11; Ps. 132:2–5; Pr. 20:25; *etc.*), but appear less often in the NT (*cf.* Acts 18:18; 21:23–24), which is primarily interested in the consecration to God of the whole person (Rom. 12:1). Vows of celibacy became popular in the early church, and the rise of monasticism from the fourth century was accompanied by the distinction between 'precepts' (to be obeyed by all Christians) and 'evangelical counsels' (required as vows only of those undertaking the monastic life), and the development of the threefold cord of monastic commitment, the vows of poverty, chastity and obedience.

The Reformers criticized monastic vows on the grounds that, amongst other things, they implied a form of righteousness by works, imposed human obligations that were not demanded by Christ, and denied that only one common way of life was given to be followed by all Christians. As a result, the role of vows in the Protestant churches has been greatly diminished.

Yet John Calvin* could also find a more positive role for the practice of vowing (*Institutes*, IV.xiii). Seeing all vows as summed up in the baptismal vow to yield to God's commandments, he regarded them as a valuable tool of personal spiritual discipline,* and laid down rules for their use. This suggests the possibility of a healthier appreciation of their worth. Handled discerningly and with imagination, vows can be a God-given resource to strengthen resolve and enable one to rise above immediate circumstances, and to restore continuity to lives fractured by the pressures of a disorienting world. Far from being a constraint on freedom, they can (so long as ill-considered vows are avoided) fulfil freedom through being an exercise of it. And as a form of participation in Christian discipleship, rather than of supererogatory works, they may assist in expressing a grateful response to God's covenant faithfulness shown in Jesus Christ.

R.J.So.

PROPAGANDA has two distinct meanings: 1. The *organized dissemination of information and ideas*, usually by governments, institutions or agencies, *to persuade* the recipients of the truth of their propositions and beliefs. This is done by the use of all and any media – and not solely through words, but also via symbols and non-verbal sounds. In this sense propaganda, its aims and activity can be said to be *neutral* though *not* value-free. Propaganda has always been a constant human and social activity in history and should not be assumed to be solely a modern activity or restricted to forms of mass media. Preaching, evangelism* and mission as well as advertising,* health education or broadcasting (see Media*) can be propaganda. In this neutral, descriptive sense, churches and other agencies have seen no need to be embarrassed or ashamed of being involved in propaganda (*e.g.* reflected in the name of the mission agency, the United Society for the Propagation of the Gospel), and the NT Gospels are propaganda tools.

2. The second (and popular) understanding is that propaganda is by definition deceptive – containing half-truths, or even deliberate and calculated outright lies dressed up in such a way that they should be believed as truths. This is an abuse of human dignity.

For propagandists (evangelist, teacher, artist, political campaigner, *etc.*), ethical constraints govern their activity which the Christian might see derived from, among other places, Paul's criteria for his mission as described in 2 Cor. 4:2–3: 'we have renounced secret and shameful ways; we do not use deception, nor do we distort the word of God. On the contrary, by setting forth the truth plainly we commend ourselves to every [person's] conscience in the sight of God.' By such criteria, human communication should be marked by its openness, never wittingly deceiving or disguising uncomfortable truths. And the judge of the means and truthfulness of the communication is 'every person', not just the consciences of the propagators and their circle – *e.g.* not just Christians when it comes to the church's mission. The consideration and integrity of the recipient are vital ethical constraints on all communication.

For the recipient, it is irresponsible to dismiss discrete items of communication as 'propaganda' (*i.e.* in sense 2, above). In doing so the recipient is not rendered immune from its message, but rather is most likely its easy prey. Sophisticated propaganda (as much propaganda is) needs to be met by a greater understanding of the tools and practices of propaganda, and with discernment – to distinguish truth from half-truth and lies. Because propaganda is effective, and can often be deceptive and manipulative, the Christian citizen has a duty to work for an open society which provides democratic controls and legal protection against excesses.

See also: Brainwashing; Manipulation.

T.D.

PROPERTY. The right to private property is affirmed in the Universal Declaration of Human Rights (Article 17).

The modern Western concept is based on outright ownership by an individual or corporate body. Variations such as leasehold are often seen as cramping personal freedom. It is ownership of the capital of a company that carries weight, not the interests of its non-shareholding workers. However, rights over property are limited by restraints such as planning law. There are calls for companies to be subject to 'social' audits. Nevertheless the slogan 'Taxation is theft' (because it alienates personal property) rings bells with modern men and women.

Property includes fixed assets such as land and movable possessions, and also 'intellectual' property, such as copyright.*

In the church

Catholic writers call property a 'natural right' but maintain that it is not 'absolute and untouchable' (John Paul II, *Laborem Exercens* [ET, *On Human Work*, London, 1981]; see Papal Encyclicals*). This tradition goes back through the schoolmen to the Fathers, who called private property a necessary evil in a fallen world. Even if owned personally it should be used for the common benefit. Pierre-Joseph Proudhon's (1809–65) adage, 'Property is theft', could almost represent the views of Pelagius (*fl. c.* 383–424), who in this was orthodox.

Modern concepts of property differ from those held in Christian tradition, and in other times and societies. 'The earth is the LORD's, and everything in it' (Ps. 24:1). That was applied in the institution of the Jubilee* (Lv. 25:13ff., but *cf.* 1 Ki. 21:1–7), in which the land reverted to those to whom God had originally granted it. Movable property also was God's gift: 'Everything comes from you, and we have given you only what comes from your hand' (1 Ch. 29:14). Paul calls love of silver the root of evil (1 Tim. 6:10). Jesus denounced the complacency and acquisitiveness of the rich (*e.g.* Lk. 6:24; 12:13–34; 16:13, 19, 25; *cf.* 18:22–25). Luke also records a positive use of riches (Lk. 8:3; *cf.* 16:9 – to win friends using amoral 'Mammon').

The 'communism' of Acts 2 represents a willingness to expend property for common benefit, not enforced common ownership* (Acts 2:44–45; 4:32–37; 5:4). The term 'communism' with its modern overtones is misleading, as is the allegation that 'the experiment soon ceased'. It characterized the Christian attitude to property as late as the last pagan Emperor Julian (d. 363), who complained about it! That approach led the Fathers to such statements as 'whatever exceeds the consumer's needs is held violently' (Ambrose,* quoted favourably by Thomas Aquinas*). Some Fathers interpreted literally the command to 'sell your possessions and give to the poor' (Lk. 12:33). Others took it to mean giving up wealth-dominated attitudes. Thus Augustine* wrote, 'Greed is not something wrong with gold; the fault is in a man who perversely loves gold and for its sake abandons justice' (City of God XII.8, tr. H. Bettenson, Harmondsworth, 1970, p. 480). Some early Christian leaders applied Lk. 16:9 literally; Patrick (c. 389–c. 461) established gift-friendships for the gospel's sake with what he received, while maintaining personal poverty. The ideal of evangelical poverty inspired the religious orders – notably the Franciscans, whose challenge to the wealth of the contemporary church earned persecution.

At the Reformation some Anabaptists attempted to impose common ownership (cf. The Book of Common Prayer, Article 38). During the Commonwealth the Levellers spoke of wealth deriving from sin, and sought to limit property and income. However, most attempts to copy the early church have been voluntary. Luther* warned against the corruption of wealth. Calvin* took a more positive line, saying, 'Look not for any prosperity apart from the blessing of God' (Institutes III.vii.8). He likened all possessions to deposits entrusted to us in order to be used for the good of our neighbour. Rapid social change in the 17th century created tensions for Christian moralists. Richard Baxter* warned about wealth leading to idleness and temptation, but also said it was wrong to take a less productive action if God showed a legitimate way of increasing wealth. Puritan capitalism* suffered the same vicious circle as monasticism; disciplined work and limited consumption (see Puritan Ethics*) led to the accumulation of property. The dominant theological attitude to property became stewardship.*

Wider society

Theories of 'primitive communism' in human social development are over-simplifications. There is no evidence for a society in which all had equal claims on everything. A truer picture is that personal goods (e.g. weapons) are owned individually, while complex networks of rights and obligations govern use and control of 'capital' goods, like cattle. The encounter between Western notions of individual ownership and such cultures has often been tragic (J. Beattie, Other Cultures, London, 1964, pp. 190–195). Lacking such networks, modern attempts at communes often fail because what everyone owns no-one maintains.

As means of production became larger and employed many people, the sense that it was immoral for them to be in private hands led to various political programmes, such as State ownership or employee shares.

Possessions have emotional and symbolic as well as economic significance, expressing success, relationship and identity: a house in a particular area or a brand of car conveys a person's status; an exchange of gifts is in some cultures a sign of mutual obligation, not bribery; an heirloom represents family memories.

See also: COMMUNISM; POVERTY; WEALTH.

Bibliography
R. Mullin, The Wealth of Christians (Exeter, 1983); D. L. Munby, Christianity and Economic Problems (London, 1956); M. Weber, The Protestant Ethic and the Spirit of Capitalism (1904–05; ET, London, 1930).

G.S.F.

PROPHECY, OLD TESTAMENT.
Prophets and prophetesses (hereafter simply termed 'prophets') are God's spokespersons (cf. Ex. 7:1). Under the inspiration of the Holy Spirit* they give voice to the invisible God's ethical rule (2 Pet. 1:21). Moreover, God accomplishes his will on earth through their powerful words (Is. 55:10–11; Je. 1:9–10).

Old Testament prophecy and the Christian church

In the OT, the Holy Spirit sovereignly came upon a few, select prophets (cf. 1 Sa. 10:6; Ezk. 11:5; Ho. 9:7; Joel 3:1–2), such as Moses. Moses, however, wished that God would put his Spirit on all his people (Nu. 11:16–30), and Joel later prophesied that someday God would do just that (Joel 2:28–32). The ascended Jesus Christ fulfilled Joel's prophecy at Pentecost (Acts 2:1–36). While there is a unique gift of prophecy in the NT church (*cf.* 1 Cor. 12:10), within the broad definition of prophecy all Christians are prophets because, empowered by the Holy Spirit, they represent to the world God's revealed, saving will (Acts 1:8).

Old Testament prophecy and God's covenants

God's covenants* with Israel constitute the basis for OT prophecy. Indeed, he mediated those covenants through prophets: through Abraham, his promise to give Abraham an innumerable seed and the land of Canaan (*cf.* Gn. 15:1–21; 22:17); through Moses, his law (*cf.* Ex. 20:18–21; Dt. 5:22–33; 34:10); through Nathan, his covenant to give David an eternal seed, throne and kingdom (2 Sa. 7:8–17); and through Jesus* Christ, who as Son of God is even more than a prophet like Moses (*cf.* Dt. 18:15; 34:10; Jn. 1:21–22; 6:14; 7:40–41; Acts 3:17–26), the new covenant (*cf.* Is. 42:6; Je. 31:31–34; Ezk. 36:26–27; 2 Cor. 3:1–18; Heb. 7 – 8).

Prophecy and authority

All prophets, who are Moses' successors, speak with God's authority (Dt. 18:17–19). Nevertheless, other OT prophets are not equal to Moses. In contrast to them, God spoke to Moses directly 'face to face', not indirectly in 'visions and dreams', and 'clearly', not 'in riddles'. If there be any tension in our understanding between the law of Moses and the prophets, priority must be given to Moses (Nu. 12:1–15). Moreover, if there be any tension in our understanding between the OT and the NT, priority must be given to the latter, for, whereas Moses was only a 'servant' in God's house, Jesus Christ is God's Son over his house (Heb. 3:6).

The message of the prophets

Prophetic oracles can be classified into many types. Here we consider three types that best give insight into their message. We conclude this section with some general observations on prophets and ethics.

Accusation oracles. God sent prophets like Hosea, Micah, Isaiah and Jeremiah from his heavenly court to the courts of Samaria and especially Jerusalem at the time he summoned the Assyrians (*c.* 750–650 BC) and the Babylonians (*c.* 605–586 BC) to take the holy land 'away' from his people and to exile them. To explain this disastrous turn of fortune, the Lord brought his people to trial through these messengers and, after accusing them of having broken the Mosaic covenant, he sentenced them to its curses, which included exile (Lv. 26:14–39; Dt. 28:15–68; Is. 1:2; Je. 2:9; Ho. 4:1; Mi. 1:2; 6:2).

Judgment oracles. The Lord's plenipotentiaries were filled with indignation against injustice (*e.g.* Mi. 2:1–5; 3:1–12). They delivered their oracles of doom against the greedy rich and/or powerful officials who exploited the defenceless. They saw the times in which they lived from the divine point of view, a very different thing from the relativism of the human viewpoint. Having seen God's holiness (*cf.* Is. 6:1–10), they were intolerant of idolatry and human hubris, and they were very sensitive to sin (see Sin and Salvation⑤). Whereas unenlightened humans have an incapacity to sense the depth of misery caused by moral failures, such as cheating in business and exploitation of the poor, enlightened prophets see it as a catastrophe, a death-blow to society, deserving God's righteous judgment.*

At the same time, it must be borne in mind that these patriots interceded for condemned peoples, even as Moses had (Ex. 32:31–32). Isaiah pleaded for Israel (Is. 6:11), moaned for Moab (Is. 15:5), and wept bitterly over Jerusalem (Is. 22:4). The Lord repeatedly had to tell Jeremiah to stop praying for the people (Je. 7:16; 11:14; 14:11). Jonah is faulted because he neither had compassion for Assyria nor sought its conversion. In the same vein, the Lord Jesus wept over Jerusalem (Mt. 23:37–39), and the church should join Paul in prayer for the conversion of ethnic Israel (Rom. 9:1–3), whose history has been tragic.

Salvation oracles. The prophets comforted the righteous remnant that survived the divine judgments through Assyria and Babylon (*cf.* Is. 1:9; Mi. 4:6–7; 5:7–9) with oracles of salvation. Whole sections of the major prophets are books of consolation (Is. 40 – 55; Je. 30 – 33; Ezk. 40 – 48). These consoling prophecies were based both on God's promises to Abraham that he would give his heirs who shared his faith an eternal seed and the Promised Land for ever (Gn. 12:1–3; 15:1–21; 17:1–22; 22:15–18; Mi. 7:20; Gal. 3:26–29; Eph. 2:12–13) and on his promise through

Moses that after the exile he would make a new covenant with Israel and Judah (Dt. 30:1–10; Heb. 8:7–13). This new covenant, effected through the blood of Jesus Christ (Lk. 22:20), did not alter the substance of the Ten Commandments (see Decalogue*) but changed its style (Je. 31:31–34). Instead of being written on tablets of stone, Christ, through the Holy Spirit, now writes the law on the hearts of his saints (2 Cor. 3:3, 6).

Prophets and ethics. Prophecy is always consistent with ethics. If God predicts judgment on a nation and it then repents, the judgment will not come to pass; on the other hand, if he predicts blessing on people who thereafter apostasize, the blessing will not happen (Je. 18:1–12). True prophets never contradict the equity of God's law.* Even if prophets perform signs and wonders,* if they do not preach God's righteous commandments, they are false and should be put to death in the OT and excommunicated from the church in the NT (Dt. 13:1–15; 1 Ki. 13:7–22; 1 Cor. 5:1–8). Finally, the prophet's personal conduct adorned the message. True prophets exposed false ones by the immoral behaviour of the latter (Je. 23:9–14; *cf.* 2 Tim. 3:6; 1 Ki. 22:24; *cf.* 1 Tim. 3:3; Tit. 1:7). Prophecy for profit is always suspect (Je. 6:13; Mi. 3:5, 11; *cf.* 1 Tim. 3:3; 1 Pet. 5:2).

Bibliography

C. E. Armerding and W. W. Gasque (eds.), *Dreams, Visions and Oracles: The Layman's Guide to Biblical Prophecy* (Grand Rapids, 1977); P. Fairbairn, *Prophecy and Prophetic Interpretation* (Grand Rapids, ²1976); R. B. Girdlestone, *The Grammar of Prophecy* (Grand Rapids, ²1955); C. F. H. Henry, *Personal Christian Ethics* (Grand Rapids, 1957), pp. 278–326; A. Hoekema, *The Bible and the Future* (Grand Rapids and Exeter, 1979); G. E. Ladd, 'Eschatology and Ethics', in *BCDE*; H. K. LaRondelle, *The Israel of God in Prophecy* (Berrien Springs, MI, 1983); J. Moltmann, *Theology of Hope: On the Ground and the Implications of a Christian Eschatology* (ET, London, 1967); E. J. Young, *My Servants the Prophets* (Grand Rapids, 1952).

B.K.W.

PROPORTION, DOCTRINE OF. This doctrine suggests that a judgment whether an action is good or evil can be determined by 'weighing' the positive results of the action against its negative results. If the proportion of good is greater than the proportion of evil, then the act may be considered good. This is an essentially teleological* method of moral judgment. Good and evil reside in the results of action rather than in the action itself. That contrasts with deontological* morality, which considers the rightness or wrong of the act itself, irrespective of its results.

Proportionalism is relevant to every area of moral decision-making in which it is useful to 'weigh', or 'measure', the relative goods and evils of a given course of action. For example, in the ethics of undercover police work, it might be asked whether the evil required by the lying and deceit of a 'sting operation' are greater or less than the good results of capturing a drug dealer. Proportionalism requires that all the results of a course of action be considered in their context and weighed against each other, rather than considered as discrete parts. In contrast, some Christians would simply say that all lying is prohibited, no matter what its context or result.

Nevertheless, in everyday life, proportionalism is probably the most usual method of moral judgment. Some common questions of proportion, in which various goods and evils are measured against each other, are: 'Should I work full-time or spend more time with my family?', 'Should divorce be legal or illegal?', 'Should I skip church in order to study for an examination?', 'Should the government increase spending on defence or on education?', 'Should my family stay in the city or move to the suburbs?', 'Should I buy a car or give the money to missions?'

The doctrine of proportion has received its most extensive expression in the ethics of war.* In the field of just-war theory,* the justifiability both of entering a war and of the tactics used in the war is largely determined on the basis of the doctrine of proportion. Thus, given the premise that killing and warfare may be justifiable in certain circumstances, the primary criterion for determining when they are justifiable is taken to be the proportional good of the war as a whole in relation to the evil of allowing an aggressor to go unchecked. Other just-war criteria (*e.g.* just cause, probability of success, legitimate authority) can be seen as ways of measuring and safeguarding the proportionality of the whole enterprise.

In the ethics of specific tactics of war (*jus in bello*), the doctrine of proportion is balanced with the principle of non-combatant immunity.

The proportional good of, for example, bombing a city, cannot be considered apart from the absolute prohibition of direct, intentional killing of non-combatants.

The doctrine of proportion has a number of telling weaknesses: 1. It is often difficult or impossible to calculate the outcome of a given course of action, especially in a matter as complex as war. 2. The proportion of various kinds of goods and evils are difficult or impossible to weigh against each other. How, for example, do you weigh the 'good' of a scientific experiment against the 'evil' of lying to the subjects of the experiment? 3. If a given good (*e.g.* national security) is given sufficient weight, it is possible to rationalize almost any action in terms of proportionality. 4. The moral meaning of a course of action cannot be measured in quantitative terms that give meaning to proportionality. Thus proportionality is essentially a subjective approach to ethics. 5. Morality is closely related to context, culture, story and an intricate web of symbolic meaning which vitiates the power of proportionality as a tool of moral analysis.

As long as individuals and groups continue to measure the relative goods and evils of their actions, proportionality will remain a significant means of ethical discourse. But proportionality should never be the sole criterion of action. It must be supplemented with and circumscribed by absolute principles of conduct. For Christians it must remain a tool of the wider imperative to love God and one's neighbour in all that one does.

B.T.A.

PROSELYTISM. The words 'proselyte' and 'proselytism' are derived from the Gk. *prosēlytos*. It is not found in classical Greek, but occurs over 70 times in the Septuagint, translating the Heb. *gēr*, a word which developed in meaning from referring simply to a non-Israelite choosing to live as a resident in Israel, to describing someone who voluntarily converted to the religion of Israel. It is in the context of the Greek and Roman empires that we encounter widespread use of the term 'proselyte', since vast numbers of non-Jews were attracted to the monotheism and high moral standards of the Jewish faith, many converting to Judaism, and many more stopping just short of final conversion. The term, therefore, originated within the area of Jewish witness to God, and is found in this context in the NT.

In time, proselytism became a general term for propagation of one's faith, while referring to someone as 'a proselyte' simply meant that he or she was a convert from one faith to any another. Religions were described as proselytizing if they gave high priority to trying to persuade people of other faiths or ideologies to join them instead, the term being mostly used to refer to Judaism, Islam, Buddhism and, most especially, to Christianity. This is a sensitive religious area, involving questions of theology, ethics, community life, evangelism,* mission* and conversion.* How then did it come about that in contemporary society proselytism has become a term for unethical behaviour?

The first negative use of the term 'proselytism' comes from the post-Enlightenment 18th century, reflecting the roots of the modern Western distaste for religious dogma. The word came to be associated with those who claim to have a monopoly on truth, and was linked to those who are actively, even aggressively, engaged in trying to win converts. None the less, it largely remained a term for high-profile, well-organized evangelism.

Since the Second World War, however, and in particular since the 1960s, there has been a further development in the use of this term. This can be seen in two definitions which have passed into common currency. The documents of Vatican II include: 'Proselytism is a corruption of Christian witness by appealing to hidden forms of coercion or by a style of propaganda unworthy of the gospel' (and see H. Croner, *More Stepping Stones to Jewish–Christian Relations*, Mahweh, NJ, 1985, pp. 50f.). The World Council of Churches states: 'Proselytism embraces whatever violates the right of the human person, Christian or non-Christian, to be free from . . . whatever . . . does not conform to the ways God draws free men to himself . . .' (*EcR* 24.1, 1971, p. 11). Proselytism is here used to describe the abuse of freedom,* and the distortion of the way in which God relates to people. So a new cluster of terms and concepts now comes to bear on any serious study of proselytism, *viz.* exploitation,* coercion (see Force*) and manipulation.*

There is clearly a need for a term to describe such unacceptable behaviour; however, the word 'proselytism' in its traditional sense of evangelism is still used by some, while others use it in this new way only to express unethical attitudes and actions. Two major ethical issues are involved here: 1. Is it, in principle, a violation of other people's rights (see Rights, Human*) if one seeks to persuade them to change their religious (or other) views, or is it only the methods which need to be monitored? 2. Is it acceptable for some people to use the term 'proselytism' when they simply mean 'evangelism', if they are none the less aware that this will lead others to infer that manipulative or coercive tactics are being employed?

Another fundamental issue involving the use of the term 'proselytism' by people opposed to evangelism is the presupposition that only some form of exploitation of people at a time of particular vulnerability could possibly explain someone abandoning their religious beliefs in favour of those of another community. This assumption must be challenged in light of the real and imagined fears of certain individuals and communities. Evangelism or mission can be linked with an image of cult-like activity involving recruitment through 'proselytism'. Such an image consists of a mixture of attitudes and practices: rejection of cultural diversity, authoritarianism, exclusivity, feelings of superiority, legalism,* brainwashing,* etc., each of which can be found in various new religious movements, but none of which can be assumed to be characteristic of all religious or even quasi-religious communities. They are certainly not manifestations of authentic Christianity.

It would also be true to say that a common image of 'proselytes', including people who become active Christians, is of marginalized people, alienated* from themselves and society, immature, and seeking only an escape from responsibility.* While such people do join certain religious groups, sociological research shows that this is not the norm. These people are often thoughtful, socially aware, and searching for a responsible integration of their lives with others and with their whole environment. Christians involved in evangelism, then, are not exploiters of the vulnerable, but people committed to helping others find the truth and love for which they are searching.

Any form of manipulative or coercive evangelism is to be rejected, but the intention to try to persuade someone of the truth of the gospel is not in itself a sign of arrogance or a desire to exploit. Christians must be alert to the distinctions between acceptable and unacceptable motives for evangelism, and between proper and improper methods, but the new and growing tendency to label all evangelism as proselytism, in the contemporary negative sense, must be resisted.

Bibliography

J. T. Richardson, 'The Active vs. Passive Convert: Paradigm Conflict in Conversion /Recruitment Research', *JSSR* 24.2, 1985, pp. 163–179; R. V. Travisano, 'Alternation and Conversion As Qualitatively Different Transformations', in G. Stone and H. Farberman (eds.), *Social Psychology Through Symbolic Interaction* (Waltham, MA, 1970), pp. 594–605.

W.R.

PROSPERITY, see PROPERTY.

PROSTITUTION. The term 'prostitution'
is used to identify sexual intercourse for non-affectional purposes, normally for financial gain. Male prostitutes exist, but are less common than female prostitutes.

The female prostitute sells her body to men for money. While some prostitutes work on an appointment basis, most solicit their clients in public places. The secular prostitute is socially inconspicuous and not openly valued in society.

In pagan religions, the 'cult prostitute' (*cf.* Dt. 23:17–18) was associated with processes of nature in linking the gods and goddesses with human fertility and the propagation of life. Worshippers of fertility deities used sexual intercourse with the sacred prostitute to achieve fertility of home, herd and crops.

Biblical injunctions against prostitution are uniform in denouncing the sins of fornication* and harlotry. Leviticus 21:9 warns that a daughter of a priest who becomes a harlot shall be burned; likewise stoning for harlotry was standard (Dt. 22:21). Daughters of Israel were prohibited from becoming prostitutes (Lv. 19:29). Neither female nor male prostitution (see 1 Ki. 15:12; 22:46) was to be tolerated in Israel.

The fertility cults were a much more serious spiritual threat to Israel than commercial prostitution. The gods Baal and Asherah were at the core of the fertility cults and were anathema to the OT writers (*cf.* Ho. 4:10–14). The chief function of fertility cults is sexual intercourse as a means of offering one's body to gain cultic ritual blessings.

The force of biblical prohibitions against prostitution is seen in the various ways harlotry and prostitution were used as negative similes or metaphors to heighten the awareness of sin, guilt and transgression against God. Playing the harlot became a frequently-used term of spiritual denunciation and judgment against Israel (see. Nu. 25:1–2 and Je. 3:6, RSV).

Jesus' open affiliation with tax collectors and prostitutes (Mt. 21:31–32) and his use of them as exemplars of the faithful were 'statements' about the radical faith required for subjects in God's kingdom. The worst of penitent sinners, including saved prostitutes, were the cornerstone of the kingdom.

Judaeo-Christian teachings hold high moral standards for sexual conduct (see Sexuality⑪). Promiscuous intercourse is not encouraged in the Bible as it was in Plato's *Phaedo*, which made ample room for 'the sober exercise of natural faculties and the moderate enjoyment of natural pleasures'. By sharp contrast, the Christian faith affirms the unity of body and spirit in Jesus Christ. Submitting to commercial or sacred prostitution is rejected by the Christian. The apostle Paul reminds the early Christians, 'your bodies are members of Christ' (1 Cor. 6:15) and 'you yourselves are God's temple' (1 Cor. 3:16). For Paul, the prostitute was a double evil: 'he who unites himself with a prostitute is one with her in body' because 'the two will become one flesh' (1 Cor. 12:16).

The church has been ambivalent about prostitution. Augustine* denounced it, denying baptism to children of prostitutes and excommunicating parents of prostitutes, but he was hesitant to prohibit the practice, fearing that without prostitution 'you will pollute all things with lust' (*De Ordine*, II.iv [12]). Thomas Aquinas* followed suit, declaring that prostitution is a lesser of two evils: some evils must be tolerated to prevent a greater evil.

In line with Augustine's 'permission' of prostitution, some argue for the legalizing of brothels and mandatory regular health checks for registered prostitutes. Such measures, already adopted in countries such as Germany and some States in the USA, are seen as a lesser evil than allowing uncontrolled prostitution. The legalizing of brothels could also be used to outlaw open, public soliciting in residential areas, and, it is urged, help to curb the spread of AIDS.*

A contrary position is maintained by those who argue that the State ought not to condone immorality or use tax-payers' money to do so.

Feminists* and others point out the injustice of fining prostitutes but not their clients. An increasing problem is the resort to prostitution among homeless young people (see Homelessness*) of both sexes, and among the very poor, in order to obtain money to support themselves. This is particularly so in Uganda, and is contributing significantly towards the rapid expansion of the problem of AIDS. Others resort to prostitution to feed their habit of drug* abuse.

Some therapists use paid surrogates to help clients with severe sexual difficulties (see Sexual Counselling and Therapy*). Biblical teaching on sexuality in general, and fornication* in particular, would clearly seem to rule out the use of such surrogates by Christian therapists.

The clear theological witness of the church is the prohibitive stance of the ancient biblical texts that rejects any form of prostitution, and is a witness to women (both mothers and daughters) of the integrity of the family and the need to conduct sexual life within the bonds of holy matrimony.

Bibliography
O. J. Baab, *IDB* 3, pp. 931–934; D. S. Bailey, *Sexual Offenders and Social Punishment* (London, 1956); V. L. Bullough, *Sexual Variance in Society and History* (Chicago, 1976); B. Harrop, *DPC*, p. 221; F. A. Marglin, *ER* 6, pp. 309–312; E. R. Moberly, *DPCC*, pp. 29–30; W. J. Woodhouse, *ERE* 10, pp. 404–409.

P.A.Mi.

PROTEST. The right of the citizen to protest against government and against those who hold the offices of power* in society* is a vital protection of personal and political liberty. Protest has an honourable history in Christianity. The word 'Protestantism' takes its root from protest – in this case the protest made by Martin Luther* against the corruption of the church of his time. 'Here I stand,' he proclaimed, as he stood against the institutional strength of the papacy, 'I can do no other.'

This important movement of protest against the established life of the institutional church can be found across the length of its history. Religion and social protest were often intertwined. From the Peasants' Revolt in medieval times, through the various Anabaptist movements of the 16th and 17th centuries into the dissenting tradition of the 17th and 18th centuries and the development of nonconformity in the 19th century, the church has experienced within its own life the power of protest against perceived abuse and injustice.

In the 20th century, the Christian contribution to protest movements has taken various forms. This has almost invariably been non-violent in character. Martin Luther King* welded together Gandhi's (1869–1948) commitment to non-violence* with an active understanding of the duty of Christians to resist racist (see Race*) injustice. In particular he drew on Reinhold Niebuhr* in finding a way of actively confronting the systems of power which fell short of actual violence.*

In more extreme circumstances, Christians have had to face the question of violence. Dietrich Bonhoeffer* participated in the attempt to kill Hitler (1889–1945) in 1944 but did so as one outside the church (see Tyrannicide*). This was not because he had lost his faith but rather because he saw such direct political action against the rulers of the State as belonging to the political rather than the ecclesiastical sphere.

In Southern Africa the churches have had to wrestle with the issue of violence over many decades. In Rhodesia / Zimbabwe the civil war against the illegal Smith regime taxed the church as to the position they needed to hold. Bishop Kenneth Skelton (1918–) was one of but a few leaders of the church who saw the issue of justice (see Justice and Peace[3]) with clarity and yet managed to hold the integrity of the gospel of peace. In South Africa itself the churches have supported the 'struggle' against apartheid,* identifying the evil of the violence done by the authorities to black people and the way in which this systematically created a climate within which violence was seen as the only legitimate response to violence. Attempts to develop the concept of the just war* to a just struggle against oppression indicate the real need for Christians in such circumstances to find meaningful boundaries to violent conduct (see Liberation Theology;* Rebellion*).

The inspiration of those who, in the name of Christ, have sought to resist abuse, corruption and oppression has been found in Jesus himself and in the liberation tradition of the OT. Jesus' own non-violent resistance to the decaying religious order of his day, which led to his own suffering and crucifixion, has helped many committed to this non-violent path of witness and resistance. In the struggle against oppression, the story of the Exodus has been a powerful motive in guiding those actively seeking to overthrow corrupt rulers.

Whilst abuse of power and the corruption of the church remain persistent features of human existence and Christian history, the need for, and commitment to, protest is bound to continue to be a significant part in the life of the church. Its form and its justification change with the changing needs of the human situation.

J.W.G.

PRUDENCE, see VIRTUE AND VIRTUES.

PSYCHIATRIC CARE, ETHICS OF.

The aim of psychiatric care is the treatment of mental illness (see Mental Health*), relief of symptoms, and restitution to coping adequately with the normal demands of life. This entails trying to reduce the risk of suicide,* working at improving disturbed relationships, and attempting to correct abnormal patterns of thinking and behaviour. An important consequence of depressive illness (see Depression*) may be complete loss of religious faith or at least loss of assurance of salvation; effective treatment usually restores this. The problem for Christians, however, lies in the conflicting intellectual bases, history and rationale of Christian theology and psychiatric practice.

Although many medieval monastic foundations treated the mentally ill as well as the physically ill (e.g. the Bethlem Royal Hospital in London, established 1247, and which gave rise to the word 'Bedlam'), those who developed a theory of mental illness as distinct from seeing it as sinfulness or demonization (see Demonic*) were often anti-clerical in their attitudes and opposed by the church. Many of the roots of modern psychiatry have also tended to be atheistic: Sigmund Freud* stated that belief in God was delusional; Ivan Pavlov (1849–1936) founded atheistic psychology in Russia on animal work; B. F. Skinner,* the proponent of operant conditioning, denied the existence of the soul; and, of course, drug treatment in our word 'pharmacology' is derived from *pharmakeia*, 'sorcery'. With such inauspicious parentage it is not surprising that the progeny also is suspect! The great majority of psychiatrists today, although they will not usually share the patients' religious beliefs, will not wish to explain away religious doubts* or guilt,* or view religion as delusion or shared fantasy; they are more likely to affirm faith* as something that is helpful to the individual and church membership as a cohesive social environment.

The other strain in the development of modern psychiatry is scientific rationalism, testing hypotheses by observation and deduction. Some have considered this approach unacceptable for investigating human beings, but the method has produced rich rewards for medicine. Part of the ethical problem here is the distinction some draw between the psychological and the spiritual: some psychiatrists may see the underlying cause of an individual's depression to be entirely psychological, *e.g.* following death of his or her mother in early childhood; while some theologians may consider it to be entirely spiritual, *i.e.* guilt following acknowledged misdemeanours. The truth is probably that different elements are important and may be contributory.

There are similarities and differences in the ways ministers of religion or psychiatrists carry out their work with the parishioner or patient. The individual with problems or symptoms may present a similar story to either the minister or psychiatrist but the approach of different professionals naturally varies. Moral understanding, absolution* and reconciliation* with God may be part of the aims of consultation with a priest or minister; psychological understanding, relief of symptoms and the ability to function at home and at work are sought from psychiatric consultation. Obviously these overlap to a considerable extent, and while it is important for each professional to maintain his or her distinctive professional role, co-operation between professionals – particularly when working with more disturbed people – can be very advantageous.

The methods of psychiatric treatment are sometimes considered to be controversial. Treatments may be divided into physical and psycho-social methods. Physical treatment includes the use of drugs* and other procedures such as electroconvulsive therapy (ECT), and there are misapprehensions about these. ECT involves the passage of electrical current across the brain of an anaesthetized patient in order to induce a fit or convulsion, identical in form to an epileptic fit; the fit is essential for effective treatment and a course may comprise five to eight treatments. Efficacy for certain major depressive states is extremely well validated and the procedure is safe. Temporary memory disturbance may occur but long-term side-effects are extremely rare.

ECT does not have any long-term effects on the patients or their personalities, or make them act differently; it simply restores them to their state before the illness supervened. Drug treatment is indicated for certain major illnesses such as schizophrenia, mania and depression where there is a probable chemical disturbance of the brain; patients do not become dependent upon such treatment. The prescription of minor tranquillizers, such as benzodiazepine drugs, to people in an unsatisfactory social situation, if prolonged beyond a few weeks, does carry a risk of dependence. There is no evidence that any of the presently available drugs take away the individual's ability to think, act or maintain his or her Christian faith.

This leads to the important issue of diagnosis, which is as essential within psychiatry as in physical medicine. A lot of confusion is engendered by discussing 'mental illness' as a collective term, when the range of disturbance and the type of treatment are so manifestly different between, for instance, chronic schizophrenia causing disability over decades, depression following bereavement,* and dementia* associated with chronic alcohol abuse (see Dependence*). Diagnosis is an essential element for consideration in the ethics of psychiatric care.

Another issue of relevance is that some psychiatric conditions may not be seen as morally neutral, *e.g.* alcoholism,* anorexia nervosa (see Eating Disorders*), various abnormalities of sexual preference, and deliberate self-harm by an overdose of drugs. In all such cases the patient will probably have been told, 'It's all your fault.' In one sense this may be true, but it is quite unhelpful for the sufferer in coping with it. The doctor will need to accept the patients in their present state unjudgmentally, and try to work with them in achieving a better pattern of life.

Psychiatrists do not advocate abrogation of responsibility* or deny the importance of self-control. They do try to understand and find causes for behaviour, but that does not imply that the behaviour is justified, nor does it remove the individual's responsibility for what he or she has done. It is a difficult judgment to determine to what extent an individual has control over his or her actions; a psychotic individual who carries out a violent act in response to an auditory hallucination, 'hearing a voice telling me to do it', is clearly not responsible for his or her action; neither is the phobic person who rushes out of the examination hall to be held wholly responsible for failing to complete the examination paper.

Lack of responsibility for one's actions may affect the individual's decision to receive treatment. In the rest of medicine the contract* starts with the patient requesting treatment; there is a civil right, sometimes exercised by Jehovah's Witnesses refusing blood transfusion, not to be compelled to receive treatment against one's will. But there is also a human right (see Rights, Human*), enshrined in the UK Mental Health Act (1983), for people who are mentally ill and in danger of harming themselves or other people to receive compulsory hospitalization* and treatment. The ethical and practical issue is to decide when these powers of compulsory detention and treatment should be used.

Psychotherapy implies treatment using the communication and relationship established between a patient and a skilled practitioner. It takes many different forms with widely diverse theoretical models. Two objections are sometimes raised: 1. that one person should change another's mind by persuasion, suggestion or the nature of their relationship (this places it in the same position as education or even religious conversion); and 2. that the therapist may be morally wrong or hold a different religious view than the patient and may impose these upon the latter. This has been particularly of concern for some methods of treatment (see Hypnosis*). Psychotherapy will not destroy a person's faith. However, if the religious views are a response to neurotic anxieties and doubts, successful therapy, by removing these conflicts, may result in the individual feeling no need for previous beliefs.

The ethical dilemmas in psychiatric care are numerous, and it is not possible in a short space to deal with them adequately. It is important in treatment for the psychiatrist to empathize, *i.e.* to use his or her capacity for human understanding in order to put himself or herself in the position of the patient and be able to understand what the patient is experiencing and how that person has arrived in this particular situation. The doctor ascertains what is the patient's understanding of morality and what is his or her world-view, and is not entitled to impose his or her own views upon the patient – nor would this achieve any long-lasting change in the attitudes and beliefs of the patient. Treatment should be directed to a specific condition of the individual and this should be validated by scientific research.

Bibliography
A. W. Clare, *Psychiatry in Dissent: Controversial Issues in Thought and Practice* (London, 1976); G. Davies, *Stress: The Challenge to Christian Caring* (Eastbourne, 1988); K. W. M. Fulford, *Moral Theory and Medical Practice* (Cambridge, 1989); M. G. Gelder *et al.*, *Oxford Textbook of Psychiatry* (Oxford, ²1989).

A.C.P.S.

PSYCHOANALYSIS is defined as: 1. a theory of mental life; 2. a method of treatment. Both were originated by Sigmund Freud,* and underwent correction and addition by him over a number of years. The term 'psychoanalysis' is also used to mean the research method by which the theory and treatment evolved.

The basic postulates of the theory are that mental activity is caused by biologically-based instincts. A large part of this activity is unconscious, but exercises a powerful influence on behaviour. Fantasies and wishes from early childhood, largely dominated by sexual and aggressive impulses, are 'forgotten' as they are resisted by a mechanism called repression (see Repression, Psychological*) because of the anxiety they would cause should they become conscious. They are observable in disguised form in, among other manifestations, slips of the tongue and pen, artistic creation and dreams.

The mind is conceived of as having three structures (the psychical apparatus): the id, the ego and the super-ego. These are not anatomical entities, but abstract concepts. The *id* is the repository of all that with which the infant is endowed at birth, and especially of the instincts. The *ego* gradually becomes differentiated from the id; it includes consciousness, and controls interaction with the outside world, including the capacity to think, form judgments, test reality, obtain insight and control mobility. It mediates between the demands of the id for immediate gratification, the strictures of the super-ego, and the requirements of the external world, seeking the maximum pleasure available in reality. Conflicts which arise between these competing elements are experienced as anxiety. Part of the ego remains unconscious, and this includes the mechanisms by which it defends itself against this anxiety, including repression, denial, projection, displacement and sublimation. In sleep, the ego is almost inactive, though it still exercises some censorship on the unconscious;* dreams* largely represent wish-fulfilment, disguised so as to avoid the censor.

The *super-ego* represents parental prohibitions and the young child's misperception of these, which become internalized (introjected); in males this process is closely connected with the need to repress the hostility felt towards the father for fear of his reprisal (castration), and the desire to replace him in possessing the mother, which Freud called the Oedipus complex. The severity of the super-ego represents the degree of harshness with which the Oedipal wishes have been repressed. It is largely unconscious, and manifests itself in guilty feelings. (For a discussion of the super-ego and conscience, see R. Markillie, 'Conscience and Guilt', in M. A. Jeeves, ed., *Behavioural Sciences: A Christian Perspective*, Leicester, 1984.) The satisfactory resolution of the Oedipal involves identifying with the father and renouncing the mother, so freeing the child to seek a love object of his own. (The corresponding process in the female, the Electra complex, was never fully elaborated by Freud. For discussion from a feminist perspective, see J. Mitchell, *Psychoanalysis and Feminism*, Harmondsworth, 1974.)

Instincts are somatic demands upon the mind. There is one primary drive, eros, concerned with sexual pleasure and self-preservation (though Freud later postulated a second destructive instinct, the death instinct; see *Complete Works 23: An Outline of Psychoanalysis*). The libido is a relatively fixed amount of emotional energy which powers the drives. It is capable of altering its aim, attaching itself to different objects (people) as well as to itself (narcissism), and obtaining pleasure from different bodily zones as the child develops. Gratification is obtained first through the mouth (the oral phase); then the anus (the anal phase); the phallus (Oedipal phase), then after a period of latency, and when earlier conflicts have been worked through afresh, in full genital satisfaction. The libido can, however, become fixated, creating problems in passing from one developmental phase to another, and regressing to an earlier stage in times of anxiety.

The aim of psychoanalysis as a treatment method is to make the unconscious conscious, so that mastery can be gained over it. It is largely used in the treatment of neurosis,* where conflict and the anxiety* caused is leading to painful symptoms. The patient is invited to free-associate,* and the process is assisted by dream interpretation. A stage will be reached when the reawakened wishes are transferred to the analyst; working though this transference* and its resolution is the continuing work of analysis, a process which usually requires a number of years, often on a daily basis.

Practitioners are required to undergo a training analysis; although many are medically qualified, Freud himself encouraged laymen to train and to practise.

Although psychoanalysis has been criticized from many perspectives, from its claims as a scientific discipline to its methodology, assumptions and metaphysical speculations, it has influenced most subsequent psychotherapies (see [12]) and provided insights which have profoundly influenced thought and culture in the 20th century.

Bibliography
P. Fonagy and A. Higgitt, *Personality Theory and Clinical Practice* (London, 1984); S. Freud, *The Complete Psychological Works of Sigmund Freud*, 24 vols. (ET, London and New York, 1953–74; repr. 1978–81); D. Stafford-Clark, *What Freud Really Said* (Harmondsworth, 1965).

J.R.G.

PSYCHOLOGY OF MORAL BEHAVIOUR, see MORAL BEHAVIOUR, PSYCHOLOGY OF.

PSYCHOLOGY OF RELIGION. Psychologists have played a major part in the study of religion by social scientists in the second half of this century (*e.g.* M. L. Lynn and D. L. Moberg, *Research in the Social Scientific Study of Religion*, London, 1989). Broadly speaking, they have concentrated on the roots and the fruits of religion. L. S. Hearnshaw (1907–91) identified four significant influences at the end of the 19th century which provided the basis for later psychological studies of religion (see *A Short History of British Psychology*, London, 1964, pp. 292–295). These influences were: 1. Francis Galton's (1822–1911) studies of the manifestations of religion (*e.g.* prayer); 2. studies of anthropologists, such as Sir James Frazer (1854–1941), of comparative religion and the origins of religion; 3. the writings of theologians, such as W. R. Inge (1860–1954), on mysticism and religious experience; and 4. the beginnings of the systematic psychology of religion, *e.g.* E. D. Starbuck's (1866–1947) *The Psychology of Religion* (New York, 1899; London, 1901). These culminated in the classic work by William James,* *The Varieties of Religious Experience* (1902).

There is today no single psychology of religion. At any particular time, the study of the psychology of religion seems to reflect current developments in mainline psychology.

Freud and Jung on religion

Despite the fact that the psychological theories of Sigmund Freud* and Carl Jung* are given little time in modern academic studies in psychology, their theories continue to fascinate us all. And, since in the popular mind psychology is still often seen as synonymous with Freud, it is not surprising that his views on religion continue to appeal to many and are widely quoted.

Freud wrote about primitive religion and developed religion. He saw the origins of religion in the psychological connection between his 'Oedipus complex' and 'totemism' as it existed in small primitive groups. Hence, the 'Oedipus complex' identifies the unconscious hostility that young men have to their fathers. The young men of a primal hoard were supposed to have killed their father in order to possess his wives. Thus, the 'Totem Feast was the commemoration of the fearful deed from which sprang man's sense of guilt* (the original sin) in which was the beginning at once of social organization, of religion and of ethical restriction' (from *Totem and Taboo*, London, 1919; quoted in R. H. Thouless, *Introduction to the Psychology of Religion*, London, 1971, p. 75). In *Moses and Monotheism* (1939), Freud developed his speculative theories about the origins of religion. However, with the development of more soundly-based anthropological knowledge, it became clear that many of the so-called 'facts' upon which Freud based his theories were incorrect, and consequently his views fell more and more into disrepute (*e.g.* see B. Malinowski, *Sex and Repression in Primitive Society*, London, 1927, and *The Foundations of Faith and Morals*, London, 1936).

Freud's books *The Future of an Illusion* (1927) and *Civilization and its Discontents* (1930) are about developed religion. It is important to note that in Freud's terminology an 'illusion' stands for any belief system which is based on human wishes. He was careful to

point out that such a basis does not necessarily imply that the system is false; nevertheless, as far as Christianity was concerned, he clearly believed that it was. He did not deny that religion had served a useful purpose in providing a sense of security for humanity in the face of a hostile environment, whilst at the same time providing an important reservoir for ethical standards as civilization had developed. He believed, however, that the time had come when such a basis could no longer usefully serve the needs of modern people, who must find some more rational grounds for living a civilized life.

Freud concluded that religion is an interim social neurosis,* which people must grow out of if they are to become mature, educated persons able to cope with reality. For this reason he emphasized how, in the past, religion had frequently offered a means of escape from the realities of life. Faced with the challenges and puzzles of the natural world and the restraints imposed upon individuals by organized society, religion, according to Freud, offered, on the one hand, an explanation of these puzzles and, on the other, an escape from the constraints. The idea of religion as a means of protection and escape is closely associated with Freud's view that the function of gods is that they are substitute ideal fathers. Religion became the projection of the child's relationship with the father, so that gods in all their different guises were simply magnified father-figures.

Jung, for a time a close collaborator of Freud, subsequently developed his own views within the psychoanalytic* tradition. During his association with Freud, he produced a small work which made it clear that his views on the significance of the father-figure were very similar to those of Freud. Soon, however, his views underwent considerable change. Jung suggested that all religions have their psychological roots in what he called the 'collective unconscious' of the human race. For Jung, religion is not a matter of theological concepts but primarily of experience, since it is only through experiences that concepts can be formulated. That did not mean that for Jung God was nothing but a psychic event in the unconscious. He was careful to point out that what exists in the human psyche, in his judgment, existed in reality.

Freud and Jung, as in matters of psychoanalysis, ultimately differed radically in their views of religion. Whilst for Freud, psychology pointed to religion as a neurosis which in time could be dispelled and the patient cured, for Jung religion is an essential activity of humanity, and the task of psychology is not to explain away religion but to try and understand how human nature reacts to situations normally described as religious. Summing up the difference between the Freudian and Jungian views, G. S. Spinks (1903–78) aptly wrote: 'For Freud religion was an obsessional neurosis, and at no time did he modify that judgment. For Jung it was the absence of religion that was the chief cause of adult psychological disorders. These two sentences indicate how great is the difference between their respective standpoints on religion' (*Psychology and Religion*, London, 1963, p. 102).

Other psychological views of religion

Since the Second World War, there have been several noteworthy attempts to offer new insights into religion through the eyes of psychology. Gordon Allport (1897–1967), in *The Individual and his Religion* (New York, 1960; London, 1951), traced how religion develops from childhood into adolescence and through into maturity. He emphasized how belief in God functions differently for different people at different times in their lives. A noteworthy feature of his approach was his attempt to substantiate his claims from empirical studies of religious belief and behaviour. In this same tradition are the contributions of Michael Argyle (1925–) in *Religious Behaviour*, and, in collaboration with B. Beit-Hallahmi (1943–), in *The Social Psychology of Religion*. These books constitute a mine of information, which summarizes empirical studies on social psychological aspects of religious behaviour.

The psychiatrist William Sargant (1907–88) speculated about the psychophysiological bases of religious experience and behaviour in *Battle for the Mind* and *The Mind Possessed,* attempting to link brainwashing* and religious conversion.* Suggestion and brainwashing, he said, both operate in large evangelistic meetings. He identified the effective ingredients at work intentionally or unintentionally in such campaigns. These included prior publicity, aimed at enhancing the prestige of the evangelist; a delivery with great fervour, conviction and authority at a crowded meeting; repetitive singing of emotional hymns and choruses; bright lights, massed choirs and stir-

ring music, often with a rhythmic beat and in a minor key. It was in such circumstances, argued Sargant, that physical and psychological stresses are skilfully applied to produce dramatic changes in emotional arousal when new beliefs can be implanted.

According to Sargant, these are less florid examples of what happens in the meetings of the snake-handling sects of the southern States of America. There, emotional exhaustion leads to heightened suggestibility when beliefs can most readily be absorbed.

No doubt we shall gradually gain increasing insight into the physiological processes underlying the implantation of beliefs. Whatever these turn out to be, they cannot of themselves tell us anything one way or the other about the truth or falsehood of resulting beliefs. Those have to be assessed in the light of the available and relevant evidence.

Skinner on religion

B. F. Skinner,* a distinguished behaviourist* psychologist, having achieved great success in the development of techniques for modifying behaviour, went on to speculate about how such techniques could be harnessed to shape the future of our society. He believed that similar principles, based on the effects of reward and punishment, could explain how the practice of religion functions psychologically. 'The religious agency', he said, 'is a special form of government under which "good" and "bad" become "pious" and "sinful". Contingencies involving positive and negative reinforcement, often of the most extreme sort, are codified – for example as commandments – maintained by specialists, usually with the support of ceremonies, rituals and stories' (*Beyond Freedom and Dignity*, p. 116). He argued that the good things, personified in a god, are reinforcing, whereas the threat of hell (see Heaven and Hell*) is an aversive stimulus, and these are used to shape behaviour. Underlying Skinner's approach is a reductionist* presupposition. He speaks of concepts of God being 'reduced to' what we find positively reinforcing.

The biology of God

Writing under the provocative title *The Biology of God*, Professor Alister Hardy (1896–1985) traced out his wider view of biology to encompass the records of human experience and studies of human behaviour. Believing that the major adaptations which distinguish the main diverging lines of animal evolution are essentially examples of what he calls 'behavioural selection,' he asks the question, 'To what extent have the traditions of religious belief and practice been ... biological instruments in the development of human culture?' (p. 61). His answer is that an important link between the biological system and the evolution of religion has been 'the process of building into the mind of man *a capacity for belief*' (p. 66), but he then quite explicitly says that 'theology and its doctrines, do not make up the real essence of religion' (p. 72).

Later in his book, he reaches the crux of his argument that, to understand how the idea of God arose, we should examine the similarities in the relationship between dog and man, and man and God (p. 165). He believes that 'the relationship of man to what he calls God is a biological one, in just the same sense that the association of the dog with man is a biological one. This is what I mean when I speak of the biology of God; *this* is what my book is about' (p. 169).

Professing that it is 'the spirit of Christianity that matters', Hardy has little time for the historical events of redemption history as recorded in Scripture, and has little difficulty in selecting suitable quotes from theologians to bolster his view. He concludes that 'the idea that Jesus proclaimed himself as God incarnate, and as the sole point of saving contact between God and man, is without historical foundation and represents a doctrine developed by the church' (pp. 222–223). However, one must reply that the crux of his own thesis is largely special pleading, as when he writes that 'the faithfulness, love and devotion of a dog for his master ... show us the same elements that make up the essentials of man's attitude to his personal God' (p. 169). Drawing such loose parallels will not suffice, and his theory is itself essentially without clear biological foundations, being a mixture of theological naîvety and highly speculative biology.

Evaluating psychological accounts of religion

The psychology of religion has, potentially, much to offer the Christian church. Wherever there are developments, *e.g.* in religious education* and in methods for the selection and training of clergy, it would be sensible to base judgments about the efficacy of these not on the deliberations of small committees but on evaluations carried out professionally by psychologists. With their aid, balanced assessments can be made of their short- and long-term effects. Likewise, systematic attempts to understand differences between the behaviours of religious and non-religious people can be undertaken.

Another contemporary issue susceptible to careful psychological study is the way in which some hallucinogenic drugs may raise religious awareness. Is this at all related to normal but similar non-drug-induced experiences reported by some religious people? The time has passed when psychology is viewed as necessarily a potential threat to religion. In itself it is neutral, and may be applied in ways which are either helpful or unhelpful. Any aspect of religious behaviour may, in principle, be investigated by psychologists. The study of conversion is a good example of this. To focus on the psychological aspects of conversion does not mean that one must either ignore or deny that, ultimately, the prime ingredient in any conversion experience is the truth gripping the mind of the hearer, rather than the mere stirring of the emotions. It is also clear that the concern of Scripture is with the God who initiates and overrules these conversion events.

The majority of psychologists recognize that to offer an explanation of religious behaviour, its origins and expressions, does not necessarily amount to an attempt to explain away these beliefs. Argyle states quite categorically: 'It does not follow that because a belief has psychological roots it is therefore false', and 'There needs to be no relation between a psychological basis for a belief and the truth of that belief' (*Seven Psychological Roots of Religion*, London, 1964, pp. 333–339). Whilst a person who is converted will frequently describe his or her experience in personal terms, talking of a new relationship with God in Jesus Christ, a non-Christian may always say that he or she finds that kind of language and explanation superfluous or that interpretation meaningless. No amount of arguing can produce incontestable proofs that the non-Christian is right or the Christian is wrong, or vice versa. At the same time, to regard the psychological account as in competition with the personal religious account is to make a category mistake (see M. A. Jeeves, *Psychology and Christianity*, pp. 140–144; D. Myers and M. A. Jeeves, *Psychology Through the Eyes of Faith*).

Bibliography

M. Argyle, *Religious Behaviour* (London, 1958); M. Argyle and B. Beit-Hallahmi, *The Social Psychology of Religion* (London, 1975); S. Freud, *Civilization and its Discontents* (1930; London, 1939); *idem*, *The Future of an Illusion* (1927; London, 1934); A. Hardy, *The Biology of God* (London, 1975); D. Hay, *Exploring Inner Space: Scientists and Religious Experience* (London, 1982); W. James, *The Varieties of Religious Experience* (1902; repr. Harmondsworth, 1983); M. A. Jeeves, *Psychology and Christianity: The View Both Ways* (Leicester, 1976); C. G. Jung, *Collected Works* 11: *Psychology and Religion* (London, 1958); *idem*, *Modern Man in Search of a Soul* (London, 1936); D. Myers and M. A. Jeeves, *Psychology Through the Eyes of Faith* (San Francisco, 1988); W. Sargant, *Battle for the Mind* (London and New York, 1957); *idem*, *The Mind Possessed* (London, 1973); B. F. Skinner, *Beyond Freedom and Dignity* (New York, 1971; London, 1972).

M.A.J.

PSYCHOPATHY. While the word may be taken broadly to mean any disease of the mind, it is usually taken to mean *psychopathic personality disorder*, defined in the English Mental Health Act (1983) as 'a persistent disorder or disability of mind (whether or not including significant impairment of intelligence) which results in abnormally aggressive or seriously irresponsible conduct on the part of the person concerned'. Earlier, labels were loosely used: psychopaths were spoken of as being creative, inadequate or hysterical (or histrionic). Sociopathy (or dyssocial personality) is a concept which stresses the antisocial aspect of psychopathic disorders: sometimes they are called *explosive*, to stress the impulsive character of such people, and the low tolerance of frustration.* The confidence trickster displays another variant of psychopathy.

Psychopathy has been much criticized (*e.g.* by B. Wootton) for vagueness and circularity of argument; yet a consensus exists. It has been much studied in medicine and the law. There is some genetic basis, close links with both familial disharmony (*cf.* M. Rutter: not simply broken homes) and the cycle of deprivation. Psychopathy carries a poor outlook; it is unlikely to respond to treatment. Christians see psychopathy as partly the result of struc-

tural sin – the effects of lawlessness both in the heart and in society – and they look both for prophylaxis by reform, and for the slow and patient learning of new, less delinquent patterns of behaviour.

Bibliography

R. Bluglass and P. Bowden, *Principles and Practice of Forensic Psychiatry* (Edinburgh, 1990); B. Wootton, *Social Science and Social Pathology* (London, 1960); M. Rutter and N. Madge, *Cycles of Disadvantage* (Oxford, 1976).

G.D.

PSYCHOSIS. The word 'psychosis' is used to mean a mental illness or psychiatric disorder of a severe kind, characterized by a loss of contact with reality. It usually involves disorders of perception (such as hallucinations, *e.g.* 'hearing voices'), or persistently held false beliefs not shared by the patient's cultural group ('delusions'); and some disorders of the *forms* of thought and speech. Schizophrenia and bipolar affective disorders (or manic-depressive disorder) are the two commonest functional psychoses.

Organic psychosis is seen in any feverish delirium, drug-induced disorders, alcoholism's *delirium tremens* with visual hallucinations, and other disturbances.

Antipsychotic drugs, such as phenothiazines, are usually effective in controlling psychotic symptoms, especially the above so-called positive symptoms. Negative psychotic symptoms, such as withdrawal and loss of motivation, are less responsive to medication.

Recognition of a psychosis depends on using some knowledge and experience. It may be a factor in some religious experiences in which such illness may exist as a treatable complication. To miss it is to court disaster in pastoral ministry.

See also: MENTAL HEALTH.

G.D.

PSYCHOTHERAPY, see CHARACTER; [10] PASTORAL CARE, COUNSELLING AND PSYCHOTHERAPY. [12]

PUNISHMENT is the intentional infliction of pain by a legal authority on persons who, capable of choice, have breached established standards of conduct. Under this broad definition, punishment may be imposed by parents, employers or private associations, as well as by the criminal justice* system. However, discussion here is limited to punishment for criminal activity.

1. Moral justifications for punishment

Moral issues are raised in considering the government's intentional use of pain to accomplish its purposes. Traditionally, justification for punishment has been found in its retributive and utilitarian purposes.

a. *Retributive justification* stems from the notion of desert: those who do wrong should suffer for doing so. The immediate benefit of the punishment (or the form of punishment) is less important than the fact that a penalty has been imposed.

Advocates of retribution* argue that it accomplishes several important purposes: 1. it helps define and reinforce community values; 2. it affirms individual responsibility* and freedom of choice;* and 3. it satisfies the desire for redress which results when law-abiding members of the community observe a lawbreaker. Fairness requires that those who have forgone ill-gotten gains by obeying the law should be vindicated when others reap the benefits of crime.*

Opponents argue that there are more productive ways to define and reinforce values,* such as by education. They have questioned whether humans are in fact free to choose in the way that retributive theory assumes. If an individual's moral character can be influenced by punishment imposed on others (an assumption made by those who argue that punishment helps establish values), then to that extent the individual is not a totally free moral agent. Finally, they question the feasibility of retribution on fairness grounds, since it is a practical impossibility to identify penalties for each lawbreaker which are identical to the sacrifices made by each citizen who has obeyed that particular law.

b. *Utilitarian justifications* (see Consequentialism*) typically take one of three forms: rehabilitation, deterrence or incapacitation. Rehabilitation is the theory that punishment can change offenders' personalities or circumstances so that their criminal behaviour is curtailed. Deterrence (see Deterrence, Nonnuclear*) is the theory that sufficiently severe punishment will reduce further crime by discouraging the offender being punished or other potential offenders. Incapacitation relies on the ability of certain punishments (such as prison) physically to prevent the offender from committing new crimes.

Critics of utilitarian theories make two fundamental objections: 1. Substantial criminological research raises questions about their efficacy with all offenders. In other words, rehabilitation, deterrence and incapacitation do not 'work' any better than other, less costly and less intrusive, sanctions. 2. It is unjust to treat criminal offenders as a means to a societal end. In fact, critics argue, it would be possible – although unjust – to defend punishment of *innocent* persons whom the public believes to be guilty under the deterrence argument.

c. *Hybrid justifications* have begun to emerge, which feature utilitarian theories limited by considerations of proportionality and desert. An example of this is a statute which limits judges to a relatively narrow range of sentencing options based on the seriousness of the offence and the offender's criminal history. The precise sentence within that range is determined by applying utilitarian theory. The judge's discretion is thereby restricted but not abolished.

2. Forms of punishment

It is possible to categorize punishments by the nature of the 'harm' inflicted on the offender: a. there are harms to the *body* of the offender: corporal punishment and execution; b. harms to the *property* of the offender: restitution,* fines, property forfeiture and restrictions on employment or licensing; c. harms to the *free movement* of the offender: imprisonment, probation, house arrest and prohibitions from associating with certain individuals or classes of individuals; and d. harms to the *reputation* of the offender: shaming and registration requirements for ex-offenders.

For the past 200 years, imprisonment and probation have been the dominant forms of punishment in Western nations. Although prisons* and jails had long been used to hold defendants prior to trial or punishment, it was not until the late 18th century that imprisonment itself began to be used as a means of punishment. Its appeal stemmed from the belief of reformers that prisons could be constructed and operated so as to produce rehabilitated offenders. The utilitarian justification of punishment as rehabilitative, then, led to the dominance of imprisonment over other possible sanctions as the 'standard currency' of punishment.

3. Biblical perspectives on punishment

The OT understanding of crime was that it violated shalom, defiling the right relationships that were to exist within a community and between the community and God. Those who administered justice were to seek to restore those relationships.

Restitution was an essential part of that response, and is found throughout the OT law (*e.g.* Ex. 22:5–6, 11–12) as well as in the NT (*e.g.* Lk. 19:8). The Heb. word for making restitution is *šillam* (pi'el form of *šālam*), which in the hiph'il is used as a denominative of *šālôm* (*cf.* 2 Sa. 10:19), indicating the close connection between compensatory justice and the well-being of society. Restitution restores shalom.

Western nations, with their division of civil and criminal justice systems, are at a disadvantage in attempting to infuse this notion of compensation into criminal sanctions, although courts have increasingly been using restitution orders to do so. For the most part, these are additions to sentences which would otherwise be imposed, and the N. American expression that criminals must 'pay their debt to society' continues to mean suffering the deprivation of imprisonment, not making compensation in any direct way.

In the past decade, a criminal justice reform movement has emerged on both sides of the Atlantic advocating 'restorative justice'. The central premise of this movement is that, since crime causes injuries, the purpose of criminal sanctions should be to repair those injuries. In that sense, this movement reflects the Heb. understanding that punishment should compensate.

See also: CAPITAL PUNISHMENT; JUVENILE DELINQUENCY; SENTENCING, PRISON.

Bibliography

K. Greenawalt, 'Punishment', in *ECJ*; H. L. A. Hart, *Punishment and Responsibility* (Oxford, 1968); J. Rawls, *A Theory of Justice* (Cambridge, MA, 1971; Oxford, 1972); D. Van Ness, *Crime and Its Victims* (Downers Grove, IL, 1986; Leicester, 1989); *idem*, 'Restorative Justice', in B. Galaway and J. Hudson (eds.), *Criminal Justice, Restitution and Reconciliation* (Monsey, NY, 1990); C. J. H. Wright, *Living as the People of God* (Leicester, 1983) = *An Eye for An Eye* (Downers Grove, IL, 1983).

D.W.V.N.

PURITAN ETHICS was grounded in the theology and historical circumstances of the Puritan movement. Puritans were the 'advanced' party of the Eng. Reformation who wanted to finish the work of reform begun during the reigns of Henry VIII (1509–47; b. 1491) and Edward VI (1547–53; b. 1537). Under Queen Elizabeth I (1558–1603; b. 1533) and her Stuart successors, James I (1603–25; b. 1566) and Charles I (1625–49; b. 1600), who chose a traditionalist course for the Church of England, Puritans in varying degrees became dissenters. They expounded a high Reformed theology, exalted Scripture over tradition* (especially for questions concerning the organization and functions of the church), and sought reform of the entire Eng. society. When monarchs and unfriendly bishops checked their efforts, the Puritans turned inward and mounted systematic efforts to sanctify the family* and encourage lives of private devotion. After 1630 and large-scale migrations to New England, Puritans in that part of the world joined their Eng. colleagues in trying to fashion society, church, and the self according to their understanding of the Bible.

The bridge between the Puritans' exalted view of God's saving grace* and their own ethical seriousness was a theology of covenant.* In their view, God had promised new life in the Holy Spirit to all who turned in faith to Christ. Believers, as recipients of this covenant of grace, now had the privilege and responsibility of reflecting God's glory in their own lives. The path to that end lay in following the precepts of Scripture, where God has set out with unique authority the conditions for entering into covenant and for living as a covenant-keeping people.

Puritan ethical reasoning grew out of this focused attention to Scripture. In the greatest work of Puritan moral casuistry,* William Ames' *Conscience with the Power and Cases Thereof* (Lat. 1632, Eng. 1639), Scripture references are cited as the ground for almost every major assertion and many of Ames' subpoints as well. But Puritan moral philosophy was also dependent upon currents of the time. Puritans became avid exponents of the logic of Peter Ramus (1515–72), a French Calvinist assassinated with other Protestants in the infamous St Bartholomew's Day massacre. Ramist 'method' offered an alternative to the Aristotelian syllogism by proposing a scheme that subdivided propositions into their simplest 'axioms'. The truth of these axioms (*e.g.* the basic building-blocks of scriptural interpretation, theology or morality) could then be grasped intuitively by attentive students. Puritans like William Ames (1576–1633) or the leading theologian, William Perkins (1558–1602), presented their major works as systems of subdivision and reconstituted conclusions, often complete with elaborate binary charts. With its stress on the human ability to grasp simple truths intuitively, this method of reasoning was a natural complement to Puritan spiritual theology, where the immediate activity of the Holy Spirit was held to impress the reality of faith upon the consciences of believers. As Ramists and Calvinists, Puritans like Ames promoted a transitional ethical system. With earlier Catholics and Protestants, they took human sinfulness with great seriousness and also presupposed the absolute authority of the Bible. But like the 'new moral philosophy' of the 18th century, Puritan ethics was voluntaristic* and affectional rather than intellectualist and rational. Jonathan Edwards,* who could be called the last of the Puritan ethicists, devoted his moral writings to defending the kind of voluntaristic and affectional, but also biblical and theocentric, moral philosophy that Ames and other Puritans had pioneered, but which became increasingly unfashionable in the optimistic age of the Enlightenment.*

In practice, Puritan morality developed into a full-scale system of rights (see Rights, Human*) and duties.* Puritans believed that God called people to their vocations so as to make all legitimate forms of work means of serving him. In this respect they helped to shape the Protestant work ethic. They held that sex was a good gift of God given to husbands and wives for enjoyment as well as for procreation. They felt that the family should constitute 'a little church' where God set out the boundaries and rewards as clearly as he did to Christian assemblies. Those boundaries assumed a domestic hierarchy, with husbands guiding the household, wives assisting as subordinates with their own spheres of activity, and children both encouraged by love and restrained by chastisement. Despite ambiguities between their emphasis on grace and their stress on covenant-keeping, Puritans promoted education* as a way of combining understanding of special biblical revelation and general natural revelation. The example of Oliver Cromwell (1599–1658), architect of England's

Puritan revolution, and John Winthrop (1588–1649), the leading early governor in Massachusetts, testified to the Puritans' development of political theories drawn in part from general precepts concerning justice of the OT (see Old Testament Ethics[8]) and in part from the application of sanctified common sense to the exigencies of rapidly changing social circumstances.

See also: SABBATH.

Bibliography

W. Ames, *Conscience with the Power and Cases Thereof* (1632; ET, 1639; Norwood, NJ, 1975); *idem*, *Technometry* (ET, Philadelphia, 1979); N. Fiering, *Moral Philosophy at Seventeenth-Century Harvard: A Discipline in Transition* (Chapel Hill, NC, 1981); C. Hill, *Society and Puritanism in Pre-Revolutionary England* (New York, ²1967; London, ²1969); J. T. Johnson, *A Society Ordained by God: English Puritan Marriage Doctrine in the First Half of the Seventeenth Century* (Nashville, TN, 1970); E. S. Morgan, *The Puritan Family: Religion and Domestic Relations in Seventeenth-Century New England* (New York, ²1966); J. Morgan, *Godly Learning: Puritan Attitudes towards Reason, Learning and Education, 1560–1640* (Cambridge, 1986); L. Ryken, *Worldly Saints: The Puritans as They Really Were* (Grand Rapids, 1986).

M.A.N.

PURITANS, PASTORAL COUNSELLING OF. The Puritans, who are caricatured today as wooden legalists, were in their own day more properly known as physicians of the soul. Puritanism may have assumed a formal shape in the process of struggling for reform of England's national church and in setting up 'holy commonwealths' in New England, but the heart of Puritanism was always the offer of comfort to the wounded heart. Puritanism emerged as a movement during the second half of the 16th century when a network of Cambridge fellows and London preachers joined to proclaim a distinct Christian message. That message stressed the perfection of God's law,* but even more the plenitude of his grace.* Puritan response to that message marked a new stage in the history of Protestantism. Perhaps because of their failure at winning ecclesiastical and political reform, perhaps as a complicated response to response to fresh biblical study or new structures in society, Puritans (for whatever reason) were marked by unusual sensitivity to the inward spiritual life. Because of that sensitivity, they were responsible for several innovations – e.g. maintaining spiritual journals, writing spiritual biographies of leading teachers, and outlining a morphology of steps towards conversion.* At the heart of Puritanism as a spiritual movement was its concern for the cure of souls.

A trio of notable Puritan mentors – Laurence Chaderton (c. 1538–1640), John Dod (c. 1549–1645), and Arthur Hildersam (d. 1632) – exemplified the best of Puritan pastoral care. Each was a student at Cambridge. Chaderton was the founding master of Emmanuel College (1584), long a centre of Puritan concern, and all maintained a wide network of connections with other Puritans. Comments from Dod's biographer suggest the character of their pastoral work. Dod opened his home after each of his two Sunday sermons, as well as once during the week, in order to counsel those burdened about the state of their souls. He also made it easy for individuals to talk privately with him in his church, which he used for pastoral study. Pastors like the Cambridge Puritans expected their forthright preaching of the law to sting the conscience, and they thought a person might well hang suspended for a long time (perhaps several years) between idolatrous fixation on the self and abandonment to God. But throughout, they also proclaimed the sovereign, free and loving power of divine grace.*

The result was a tide of spiritual influence extending over generations. Hildersam nurtured John Preston (1587–1628) in faith, and Preston in turn showed the anguished Emmanuel undergraduate Thomas Shepard (1605–49) how 'Christ is made wisdom, righteousness, sanctification, and redemption' (M. McGiffert, God's Plot, p. 45). Shepard, for his part, after migrating to the American colonies, was named minister of the church in Cambridge, Massachusetts, where he won enduring respect as a sensitive spiritual counsellor to several generations of Harvard undergraduates. Puritan pastoral care grew out of a profound grasp of human sinfulness, overmatched only by a sense of greater grace in Christ. It was a pastoral emphasis that flourished in the ministry of later English ministers like Richard Baxter,* that exerted a powerful influence in America from the time of John Cotton (1584–1652) to the age of Jonathan Edwards,* that lingered to shape the revival preaching of George Whitefield (1714–70), and that lies behind the ministry of at least a few contemporary pastors (e.g. D. M. Lloyd-Jones, Spiritual Depression: Its Causes and Cure, London and Grand Rapids, 1965).

Bibliography

W. Ames, Conscience with the Power and Cases Thereof (1632; ET, 1639; Norwood, NJ, 1975); R. Baxter, The Reformed Pastor (1656; Edinburgh, 1974); W. Haller, The Rise of Puritanism (New York, 1938); C. E. Hambrick-Stowe, The Practice of Piety: Puritan Devotional Disciplines in Seventeenth-Century New England (Chapel Hill, NC, 1982); P. Lewis, The Genius of Puritanism (Haywards Heath, 1977), pp. 63–135; M. McGiffert (ed.), God's Plot: The Paradoxes of Puritan Piety, Being the Autobiography and Journal of Thomas Shepard (Boston, MA, 1972).

M.A.N.

Q

QALY (quality-adjusted life years) is a mathematical concept for measuring the quality of life of defined illness states. As such, it is an ethically neutral academic exercise. However, it has been suggested that this valuation should be used as an instrument for guiding decisions in health-service resource allocation (see Health and Health Care*), and this raises profound ethical issues concerning the care of the sick and the stewardship* of resources.

The scale of values was developed from a series of interviews with a sample of persons which focused on two aspects of serious chronic illness: 1. distress, i.e. pain, dyspnoea, dysphagia, etc.; and 2. disability, i.e. loss of mobility and of independence. Neither of these aspects addresses a religious or Christian assessment of the nature of humankind, but both may be alleviated by medical or surgical interventions which may be costed.

The scale permits a year's experience of a particular disease state to be adjudicated as, say, 95% of the quality of a healthy year; alternatively the year's survival may be adjusted by a factor of .95. Incorporation into this formula of the required resources produces the 'cost per QALY', and so one year's medical care buys the equivalent of only .95 x one year's healthy life. Treatment can then be evaluated by dividing its cost by the number of QALYs (based on mean survival statistics) which it gains. Various treatments, each of which may be competing for limited resources, can thus be compared. The comparison may be used to enlighten discussions about the distribution of resources either for macro-allocative or for micro-allocative decisions.

The QALY concept is welcomed in so far as it is in tune with biblical teaching on stewardship,* for it forces us to tailor care to available resources. It should probably be applied globally and not just nationally. However, it is a utilitarian (see Consequentialism*) approach which risks placing too low a value on the individual, on the basis of accepting the maxim that 'the end justifies the means', and ultimately of favouring euthanasia* for the few that the majority may thrive.

See also: QUALITY OF LIFE.

Bibliography
S. Baldwin *et al.* (eds.), *Quality of Life: Perspectives and Policies* (London, 1994); A. J. Wing, *Quality Adjusted Life Years: A Christian Approach* (London, 1989).

A.J.W.

QUAKER ETHICS. The genesis of Quaker ethics comes from the public ministry of George Fox (1624–91). The early people gathered by Fox have been described as charismatic transformationists. They conjoined the Puritan desire to transform both church and society with a powerful expression of the Spirit breaking into the present. The light of Christ is present in every person (Jn. 1:9) and the Spirit of Christ is present in the community to take away hatred and pride, which provide the occasion for war. Christ is present today to teach his people the ways of justice, peace and righteousness.

For Quakers (also called 'Friends'), Christ enlists his people to fight in the Lamb's War, a metaphor found in Revelation. This war is an eternal, prophetic, evangelistic, social, economic and political struggle against evil in human history until God in mercy brings all to the peaceable kingdom promised by Isaiah. For Friends, however, the war is waged nonviolently in love. For the struggle, Christians need to be open to perfecting their lives by the Holy Spirit in the confidence that the Lord is at work in this thick night of darkness.

Quakers reject any 'two kingdoms' notion. For them there is only one kingdom, the same one for structures and governments as for persons. Thus, Quakers feel led to speak truth to those in power.

Quakers often appear to be naïve and overly optimistic, lacking a biblical realism about fallen humanity. Most of us, however, need more of their sense of expectancy that the Spirit might be able to do something with our witness. We need to imbibe their confidence in God's ultimate victory.

See also: NON-VIOLENCE.

Bibliography
H. Barbour and A. O. Roberts (eds.), *Early Quaker Writings* (Grand Rapids, 1973).

D.W.Br.

QUALITY OF LIFE. Decisions about whether life is worth living have focused on how to measure the quality of life. In a society where longevity is the norm and technology* is able to keep people alive, the quality as well as the quantity of life is an issue.

In the euthanasia* debate, the proponents argue that the quality of life may become so poor that life is not worth living. Examples are increasing, such as irreversible dependency, senile dementia,* some physically or mentally destructive wasting diseases, or just the loss of the capacities necessary for worthwhile existence. While individuals may not wish to live in such conditions, the fear is that those who know only this, and who are content, will become vulnerable in a society which disposes of people with such disabilities.

Technology's capacity to keep people 'alive' on life-support machines gives focus to how far we should go in keeping people alive, especially in a world of limited resources and relatively unlimited skills. Various attempts to define quality of life have been made, including QALY* (quality-adjusted life years). The focus has been on describing objectively measurable personal and relational skills, individual dignity, and the ability to interact in a meaningful way. Such criteria raise hard questions for life in the womb, as well as for people with handicaps and the senile. Subjective judgments about life-quality are no more reliable. Balancing individual preferences with society's standards will continue to be a tension.

See also: Ethics of Medical Care; [14] Life, Health and Death. [13]

Bibliography

A. Hopkins, *Measuring the Quality of Medical Care* (London, 1990); A. Hopkins and D. Costain (eds.), *Measuring the Outcomes of Medical Care* (London 1990).

E.D.C.

QUIETISM. In the Christian tradition, quietism has often referred to the mystical way proposed by Miguel de Molinos (1628–96), a Spanish monastic, who in his last years was imprisoned as a heretic by the papacy. He desired to do away with all human effort, even adoration of God in prayer, for he believed that God must do everything and humans should not attempt to co-operate. Mystics with a Lutheran orientation were often attracted to his writings because of their strong emphasis on *sola gratia* (grace alone).

Another historical expression of quietism was a legacy of the 16th-century Radical Reformation. The persecution was so severe that subsequent generations of Anabaptist groups developed a survival mentality in separatist communities. Later Mennonites were often referred to as *Stille im Lande* (the quiet in the land) because of their separatist stance. The same political connotation of the word probably accounts for John Wesley's* naming the quietism of the Moravians as a reason for his break with them.

Pastoral guidance in areas of spirituality* needs to discern the dangers of complete passivity, antinomian* outlooks on morality and the lack of compassionate concern for corporate structures and God's good creation. Positively, Christian spirituality needs the input of what is signified by our Lord's retreating to the wilderness in preparation for public ministry, *i.e.* the proper rhythm between the inward and outward journey.

D.W.Br.

R

RACE. Approaches to the concept of race may be divided into three broad types: 1. analytical; 2. folk; and 3. social.

1. In the *analytical* or scientific sense, race is defined by reference to genetic factors. Human groups are characterized by underlying genetic patterns, which produce genetic profiles of individuals and populations not necessarily related to physiological differences. According to the folk or everyday concept, however, race is defined principally by physical features (*e.g.* colour, body size, hair, nasal form, lip form, *etc.*), which demarcate races from one another. A variation on this is the ascription to groups of cultural characteristics (*e.g.* music, hairstyle, food, family customs, *etc.*).

2. '*Folk*' doctrines of race originated in their present form in the 19th century. The rise of modern biology and zoology produced taxonomies in the animal and plant kingdoms to differentiate between species and their related subgroups. By a process of transfer, similar attempts were made to classify human beings according to physical and biological criteria – hence the rise of a quasi-scientific understanding of race which recognized a single human species but proceeded to subdivide it taxonomically. The common categories in use today, *i.e.* Mongoloid, Negroid and Caucasian, derive from this approach. Darwinian evolutionary theory added further impetus by reinforcing the notion that biology supported the idea of a hierarchy of human types arranged according to successive stages of evolutionary advancement.

Whilst physiologically useful for simple identificatory purposes, such taxonomies amount to little more than sweeping generalizations. Borderline cases have to be categorized by an ever-increasingly complex system of subdivisions until the overall approach becomes severely undermined. Moreover, as modern genetics has shown, the basic underlying human genotype suggests that the differences are less striking than the similarities.

Nevertheless, physiological taxonomies have been used to construct a rigid doctrine of racial difference leading to notions of superiority. Assumptions within such a doctrine include: a. that variations in the physical appearance of peoples indicate distinctive racial types of a fixed and permanent kind; b. that these types develop markedly different cultures determined by biological differences; c. that history demonstrates the superiority of European races, especially in terms of intelligence; and d. that friction between nations or racial groups is natural and inevitable since it springs from biological sources.

It is not hard to see how these assumptions have been used to support philosophical and political theories of racial segregation and superiority. Nazism is the clearest 20th-century example, though the doctrine of apartheid* reflects similar beliefs.

3. A third approach sees race as a *socially-constructed* concept. According to this, 'science cannot give support to the idea that social characteristics and cultural forms are biologically programmed either in detail or in broad general sweep'; consequently, 'the sociologist can safely leave biology aside and concentrate on how race is socially constructed' (J. Richardson and J. Lambert, *The Sociology of Race*, p. 14).

Such a view holds that concepts of race are produced by societies who choose to attribute social meanings to physical and cultural variables. These meanings are not inherent within the variables themselves but are imposed upon them. As with all social phenomena, they are determined by wider forces such as history, ideology, class, power structures and religion. The social construction of race concepts is thus rooted in the nature of the society which produces them. This stands in stark contrast to the analytical and folk approaches, which seek to establish some kind of scientifically objective basis for racial differentiation.

Theology

Neither Scripture nor Christian theology knows anything of a hierarchy of races in the sense defined above. The weight of both is in the direction of unity (though not uniformity) and solidarity of individuals and groupings. A number of theological themes make this clear.

1. The image of God in creation. Although commentators have been historically divided as to the precise meaning of the *imago Dei*, Gn. 1:26–27 speaks of it as having been bestowed upon all humanity as created beings after God's likeness. Even the Fall* does not obliterate it (Gn. 9:6), though it does mar it. Moreover, humanity is created for solidarity in that Adam and Eve are made for mutual complementarity. They thus symbolize the human race. Together they are given the command to subdue the earth and to rule creation.* Together they are given the image of God.* Significantly the only human differentiation recognized in creation is based on gender, and even here it is differentiation which arises out of fundamental unity and involves inter-

dependence, not animosity.

2. Solidarity in sin. The unity of the human race in creation is mirrored by its unity in sin. This is signified not only by the picture of Adam and Eve expelled from the garden but also by the apostle Paul's teaching in the opening chapters of Romans. According to Ernst Käsemann (1906–), Rom. 1 expresses Paul's version of the Fall, making it clear that the whole of humankind is contaminated by sin. This is made explicit in the famous words of Rom. 3:23, 'all have sinned and fall short of the glory of God'. The unity of the human race is portrayed, therefore, even in its sinfulness and need of salvation (see Sin and Salvation⑤).

3. A universal kingdom. 'The Christian faith claims that it is a faith for all nations, a universal faith witnessing to a universal Kingdom' (Kenneth Leech, *Struggle in Babylon*, p. 196). Both the OT and NT are emphatic that God is Lord of all the nations.

a. *Old Testament.* The purpose of Israel's salvation was to witness to the universal power and love of God. The community of Israel was called to act as a paradigm community foreshadowing the coming kingdom of Yahweh (see Kingdom of God*) over all the world: 'It is too small a thing for you to be my servant to restore the tribes of Jacob and bring back those of Israel I have kept. I will also make you a light for the Gentiles, that you may bring my salvation to the ends of the earth' (Is. 49:6).

The election of Israel was thus not for ethnocentric purposes but for universal redemption. Its worship was envisaged as becoming the worship of the nations, not out of racial imperialism but so that others will see the glory of God and be drawn: 'I . . . am about to come and gather all nations and tongues, and they will come and see my glory' (Is. 66:18).

Israel's calling to servanthood (Is. 53) is consequently viewed as the opposite to racial superiority. The grace of God is given to his covenant* people not according to their race or any other quality, but solely out of divine love. In turn they are to mediate this to the world.

b. *New Testament.* When we turn to the NT we see the principle of universality radicalized in Christ. In the Gospels, he speaks out against racial particularism by attacking anti-Samaritan views (Lk. 9:54–55) and holding up the Samaritan as a model (Lk. 10:33). Moreover, his promise to the disciples immediately prior to the ascension emphasized that the Holy Spirit* would come upon them not for their sake alone but so that the gospel might be spread among the nations (Acts 1:8).

The experience of the early church revealed the existence of both racially superior assumptions among the Jewish Christians and the theological responses developed by the apostles to counter such assumptions.

Of decisive theological and ecclesiological significance is Peter's vision in Acts 10:9ff. Through this it became clear that Gentiles were to be brought within the saving purpose of God, thereby revealing the universality of the gospel. In Peter's words: 'I now realise how true it is that God does not show favouritism but accepts men from every nation who fear him and do what is right' (Acts 10:34–35).

Likewise, the pouring out of the Spirit on the day of Pentecost (Acts 2) showed that the power of God was for all. The symbolism of Babel reversed should not be overlooked.

In his epistles, Paul makes it clear that salvation in Christ is independent of all racial, gender or social divisions, and stands over and against them. Believers are justified solely on the basis of God's grace through faith. Having become members of Christ's body they are united and unified in him: 'You are all sons of God through faith in Christ Jesus, for all of you who were baptised into Christ have clothed yourselves with Christ. There is neither Jew nor Greek, slave nor free, male nor female, for you are all one in Christ Jesus' (Gal. 3:26–28). As this passage emphasizes, the essential solidarity of believers is symbolized in baptism. Just as baptism signifies the washing away of sin and the incorporation of believers into Christ, so it symbolizes their oneness in him. All who are baptized are thus one.

A similar line of argument can be found in Colossians. In the opening chapter, Paul grounds the unity of the church in the cosmic lordship of Christ: 'By him all things were created . . . He is before all things, and in him all things hold together. And he is the head of . . . the church' (Col. 1:16–18).

The logic of this is that Christ's unifying of creation through his death finds its paradigmatic expression in the church* and thus signifies the unifying purpose of God for the whole world. Consequently, in him 'there is no Greek or Jew, circumcised or uncircumcised, barbarian, Scythian, slave or free, but Christ is all and is in all' (Col. 3:11).

The letter to the Ephesians extends the Christological argument by giving a theological basis for the unity, not simply of the church, but of humanity and the entire created order. God's purpose is 'to bring all things in heaven and on earth together under one head, even Christ' (Eph. 1:10).

Attempts, therefore, to construct a doctrine of racial hierarchy or superiority fly in the face of NT teaching. The universality of the kingdom expressed in the OT is fulfilled in Christ. Believers possess a fundamental equality before God and one another which is an ontological equality: it is rooted in their new being in Christ (2 Cor. 5:17). Moreover, as the firstfruits of the kingdom, the church ontologically expresses the will of God for the whole of humanity in Christ. Racial equality, therefore, whilst beginning with the church, is God's will for the world and finds its grounding in his lordship over it.

4. The incarnation and Trinity. In his incarnation, Jesus* Christ embodied humanity in all its facets. In the incarnate Christ, all racial groupings find expression. He is the principle of solidarity-in-unity personified. For this reason, it is illegitimate to speak of humanity as composed of different races in an ontological sense. Phenomenologically, it may appear so, but underlying the appearances is the fact that, in terms of being, the human race possesses an essential oneness made explicit in the incarnate Christ.

From a trinitarian standpoint, moreover, the idea of diversity and differentiation within unity is fundamental. The relationship between the Persons of the Godhead offers a further paradigm which expresses ontological unity. Speaking of the Trinity, Leonardo Boff (1938–) has commented: 'The essential characteristic of each Person is to be *for* the others, *through* the others, *with* the others and *in* the others. They do not exist in themselves, for themselves: the 'in themselves' is 'for the others' (*Trinity and Society*, pp. 127–128). Consequently, the Trinity offers a model for human relationships which is distinctly anti-racist: 'The Trinity can be seen as the model for any just, egalitarian (while respecting differences) social organisation' (*ibid.*, p. 11). This is not to say (any more than in the paradigm of the incarnation) that the translation of this principle into programmatic or policy terms is straightforward. Rather, the purpose of both the incarnation and Trinity is to supply ontological models and theological insights into the structural values which should govern relationships between human groupings and individuals. They are not utopian programmes.

Conclusions

Four conclusions can be drawn. 1. Ideas of racial superiority and racial hierarchy run counter to biblical and theological teaching on the unity and solidarity of humanity. 2. Phenomenological differences between groupings are not ontologically grounded. 3. Models of humanity derived from the doctrines of God, Christ and the Trinity, whilst allowing for diversity, emphasize essential unity. 4. Race is thereby relativized.

Bibliography

L. Boff, *Trinity and Society* (ET, London and Maryknoll, NY, 1988); Church of England Board for Social Responsibility, *Theology and Racism* (London, 1985 and 1986); K. Leech, *Struggle in Babylon: Racism in the Cities and Churches of Britain* (London, 1988); J. Richardson and J. Lambert, *The Sociology of Race* (Ormskirk, 1985); P.V. Tobias, *The Meaning of Race* (Johannesburg, ²1972). See also *Racial Justice* (Birmingham, 1987–), journal published by Evangelical Christians for Racial Justice.

F.W.B.

RACIAL DISCRIMINATION, see DISCRIMINATION.

RACISM, see RACE.

RAMSEY, PAUL (1913–88), one of the leading Christian ethicists of this century, addressed some of the most pressing contemporary moral issues with a rigour which was faithful to the Christian tradition and which also respected the realities of practical action. His significance lies in his handling of several different disciplines, and the way he brought them together to probe the difficult dilemmas of the modern age.

Ramsey's understanding of ethics rests throughout on his view of God's covenant* love (see ②) as formative for all our moral responses. Christian ethics is the reasoned application of love to the practical dilemmas we face. His moral method was fashioned in the 1960s in response to the debate over situation ethics.* His book *Deeds and Rules in Christian Ethics* laid the foundation for a casuistry* which is not legalistic. Ramsey argues for exceptionless moral rules which have to be for-

mulated with care and applied flexibly to different situations. At the same time he was rethinking the just-war* tradition in relation to the problems posed by nuclear deterrence (see Deterrence, Nuclear*). Ramsey's analysis here combined the political realism of Augustine* and Reinhold Niebuhr* with a sharp moral analysis of what should never be done in warfare.

In the 1970s Ramsey turned to medical ethics. In *Fabricated Man*, *The Patient as Person* and *Ethics at the Edges of Life* he was one of the first Christian ethicists to tackle such questions as the nature of consent, the definition of death,* euthanasia* and genetic engineering.* His penetrating analyses remain among the most helpful and provocative writings in handling these difficult questions.

Bibliography

Deeds and Rules in Christian Ethics (London and Edinburgh, 1965; New York, 1967); *Ethics at the Edges of Life* (New Haven, CT, 1978); *Fabricated Man* (New Haven, CT, and London, 1970); *The Just War* (New York, 1968); *The Patient as Person* (New Haven, CT, and London, 1970); *War and the Christian Conscience* (Durham, NC, 1961).

D. Attwood, *Paul Ramsey's Political Ethics* (Lanham, MD, 1992); O. O'Donovan, 'Obituary', *Studies in Christian Ethics* 1.1, 1988, pp. 82–90.

D.J.E.A.

RAPE is forcible sexual intercourse without consent. Rape is usually physically violent; it is always an assault on the personhood of the victim. Rape desecrates a person created in God's image, physically, emotionally and spiritually. In rape the bodily integrity of the victim is despoiled, and the person is humiliated, overpowered and degraded, overwhelmed by feelings of helplessness and fear.*

Legally, rape is a crime which is defined variously from jurisdiction to jurisdiction. Whereas previously rape laws usually specified forced vaginal intercourse by a male on a female, today there are more comprehensive definitions which refer to forced penetration of a penis or any object of the vagina, mouth or anus against the will of the victim. Assault and battery are lesser forms of forced sexual contact. The inclusive definition is greatly to be preferred because it is gender-neutral and includes forced oral and anal sex.

Rape is fundamentally not about sex or love, but about power* and violence.* Using sex as a weapon, rape is an act of aggression, anger* and hatred* to prove that the rapist can dominate, often to counteract feelings of powerlessness in the perpetrator. There appear to be three basic patterns of rape: in power rape, rapists seek to possess and dominate; in anger rape, they set out to humiliate and harm; and in sadistic rape, rapists elicit satisfaction from tormenting and abusing the victim.

Rape and all forms of sexual violence are sinful. Not only is the victim sinned against, but the offender sins against himself or herself by violating trust* and destroying the possibility of relationship between neighbours. And, as the OT references make clear, rape is a sin against the community (Gn. 34:7; Jdg. 20:6; 2 Sa. 13:12). Fear, mistrust, hostility and alienation spread, creating havoc, tearing away at the integrity of the whole community. Rape is a sin against God because it is a violation of a person as God's image-bearer.

After rape, life is never the same. Humiliation, shame,* self-blame, anger,* fear, depression,* loss of confidence, low self-esteem,* nightmares and phobias are very typical. A victim's sense of trust in a safe environment is shattered. Victims need to know they will not be abandoned, that they are worthwhile persons not responsible for their plight. Since support is so very crucial in recovering from the trauma of rape, the process of recovery is severely hindered when the victim is not able to share the experience and seek support. Even with a community of support, recovery may be painful and long. Initially victims have to overcome the shock, denial and disbelief that such a horrendous thing can happen to them. When awareness sets in, feelings of fear, anger and depression need to be worked through. Then, hopefully, a person is able to move on with a sense of resolution about how to live on into the future with hope in the light of the reality of the experience.

Although men may also be the victims of rape, by far the greater number of victims are women and children. It is now becoming clearer that this greater violence against women and children is the extension of male dominance typical in patriarchal societies. Women and children have the subordinate status and thus become vulnerable targets for abuse* and exploitation.* The imbalance of power creates the potential for the abuse by the more powerful of the less powerful. Often male sexuality is portrayed as demanding, hostile, possessive, controlling and violent rather than as giving, loving, sharing, mutual and tender. The male is believed to have the prerogative to make sure his needs are met, even if by coercion (see Force*). Likewise the female is socialized to believe that she can get her needs met only by manipulation, and that sex is something done to her by a male. For both sexes mutuality and trust are replaced by manipulation and coercion. Today there is even an alarming tendency, apparent in hardcore pornography,* advertising* and some music, to eroticize violence. Acts of violence and abuse can be experienced as sexually arousing.

Confronting the scourge of sexual violence begins by recognizing some of the false myths that are still deeply rooted in our culture. One of the most pernicious is the belief that victims of rape 'ask for it', or at least encourage it. Women mean 'yes' even when they say 'no', it is said, because women prefer men who control them. Consequently, it is considered acceptable for a man to force sexual intercourse if the woman leads him on or arouses him sexually. This blaming of the victim wrongly assumes that men are not able to control themselves and are not responsible for their sexual feelings and behaviours. In working to eliminate sexual violence we need to emphasize the crucial importance of consent* and mutuality in all sexual interactions. Accepting the importance of consent also means recognizing the reality of 'acquaintance rape' (assault by someone known and trusted) and of 'marital rape'. Sexual activity is not right simply because the partners are married. At any stage or at any time in the sexual interaction a 'no' from either of the partners needs to be accepted. Even initial consent is not irreversible. People can and do have the right to change their minds, and their wishes deserve respect. If a person's 'no' at any stage of the interaction is not respected, the spectre of violence has entered in.

Since the late 1970s we have become increasingly aware of both the seriousness and scope of sexual violence. Sexual violence – from leering and other forms of sexual harassment* to wife-battering, child abuse and actual rape – have reached monstrous proportions to the point that many women feel no place is safe. Prosecution is frequently very difficult, with victims often feeling that they are on trial. Rape crisis centres have been set up in many places to offer support and advice. But even today many rapes remain unreported. Developing a just response to sexual violence – including compassion* and advocacy for the victims, and prosecution of and accountability* for the offenders, including repentance* and forgiveness,* as well as prevention – remains a high priority.

Bibliography
S. Brownmiller, *Against Our Will* (London and New York, 1975); M. M. Fortune, *Sexual Violence* (New York, 1983); J. Saward and W. Green, *Rape: My Story* (London, 1990).

J.H.O.

RATIONAL-EMOTIVE THERAPY (RET), see CHARACTER;10 ELLIS, ALBERT.

REALISM. Moral realism is the view that either moral values or moral truths, or both, exist independently of any created mind and, in some versions, independently of the divine mind. Such a view is to be contrasted with various forms of idealism* (the view that moral truths are mental or intellectual constructions), or with sociological variations of the idealistic theme (that they are the construction of a social group or culture).

Moral realists, with one proviso, cannot therefore be moral relativists. The independently existing values or truths provide the objective standard of rightness and wrongness. The proviso is that the moral truths which are held to exist are knowable by the human mind. But if the moral realist were also a sceptic, holding that there are moral truths but that they are unknowable by us, it would be possible to combine theoretical realism with practical relativism.*

If they are not sceptics, moral realists must give an account of how such truths are known. They cannot presumably be known through empirical enquiry, since empirical evidence is partial and changing while the moral truths are timeless and immutable. The classic answer is that they are known through conscience* or moral sense or some other moral intuitive faculty (see Intuitionism*). But what if the verdicts pronounced by different intuitions differ?

Moral realism provides one clear sense in which moralists have referred to 'absolute truths', absolute in the sense that they are not qualified or conditioned by anything that is contingent. So moral truths as conceived by the realist are necessary truths. It is only by positing such truths, the realist claims, that full justice can be done both to moral disagreement and to the seriousness of moral issues. (There is another sense in which moral realists need not be committed to propounding moral absolutes, in that the truths in question need not have an invariant or exceptionless character. There is no reason why among the moral truths there should not be 'Stealing is often wrong', for example.)

Theists who are moral realists are faced with the question of the relationship between the moral values and the moral character of God and his commands. Are the values independent of God, values which he must endorse, or are they his eternal creation? And if they are his creation, could he have willed the rightness of values other than those he has in fact willed?

Some, such as Augustine,* have solved this problem by identifying positive moral values with the character of God, and others, such as Thomas Aquinas* and John Calvin,* have stressed the inseparability of God's will from his moral character. But if moral values are to be identified with the divine character, what of negative moral values such as the wrongness of cruelty and deceit? For Augustine and others like him, since these values are essentially disvalues, deficiencies or privations, they are not to be identified with anything, least of all with any feature of the divine character. Scripture appears to content itself with the view that moral truths are not relative, and not human constructions. Whether moral truths are metaphysically necessary, or grounded in the will or nature of God, are questions that cannot be decided from the data of Scripture alone.

See also: OBJECTIVITY OF MORALS.

Bibliography
P. Helm (ed.), *Divine Commands and Morality* (Oxford and New York, 1981).

P.H.

REALITY THERAPY, see GLASSER, WILLIAM.

REALPOLITIK is a borrowed Ger. term which signifies politics, especially foreign policy, that concentrates on the concrete facts, the supposed 'realities', of political life rather than on ethical ideals. These 'facts' are that States will typically follow their self-interest, and that their means of doing so is through their power, especially their military power. The supposed corollary is that a State is both wise and prudent to adopt such policies.

The term is closely related to the Ger. *Machtpolitik*, which stresses and accents the use of force by States pursuing their objectives. The Fr. term *raison d'état* similarly accepts the overriding importance of State interests over other considerations. The principal modern manifestation of *Realpolitik* is the school of 'realism' in international relations.

Antecedents of such views are claimed as Thucydides' (471–400 BC) writing on the Peloponnesian war, Machiavelli's (1469–1527) studies of political manipulation, and in Karl von Clausewitz's (1780–1831) analysis of the relation of politics and military power in his famous *On War* (1833; ET, Harmondsworth, 1968; Princeton, NJ, 1976). However, the actual term *Realpolitik* became current in Ger. only in the 1850s and developed as a description of Bismarck's (1815–98) promotion of Ger. interests in the newly developed world of nation-states and nationalism.* Its Eng. use commences in the 20th century, as does that of its cognate terms.

At first glance *Realpolitik* appears inimical to Christian ethics, but it found a forceful exponent, and perhaps its most articulate proponent of any kind, in Reinhold Niebuhr.* Niebuhr lauded Machiavelli's desire 'to follow the truth of the matter rather than the imagination of it' and held that realism dealt honestly with the brutal facts of human behaviour and original sin.* It is perhaps not insignificant that Niebuhr is one of the few Christian theorists to command the attention of diplomats, politicians and international-relations theorists.

See also: GLOBAL ETHICS. 15

Bibliography

J. Herz, 'Political Realism Revisited', *ISQ* 25, 1981, pp. 182–241; D. McCann, *Christian Realism and Liberation Theology* (New York, 1981); H. Morgenthau, *Politics Among Nations* (New York, 1966); R. Niebuhr, *Christianity and Power Politics* (New York, 1940); idem, *Christian Realism and Political Problems* (New York, 1953); P. Ramsey, 'The Uses of Power', in *The Just War* (New York, 1968).

P.A.M.

REARMAMENT, MORAL, see MORAL REARMAMENT.

REASON AND RATIONALISM.

'Reason' in its narrowest sense is synonymous with the canons of deductive logic; more broadly, it is equivalent to what is reasonable either in terms of probability (*e.g.* 'It is reasonable to believe that the sun will rise tomorrow') or in terms of what a reasonable person believes. In this last case, reason is quite clearly culturally determined. Reason has directly influenced Christian ethics in each of these senses. Since no-one wishes to be unreasonable, the rhetorical effect of appealing to 'reason' should not be ignored.

Deductive reasoning has affected Christian ethics through the so-called practical 'syllogism', reasoning in which the conclusion is not a statement of what is the case (given the premises) but of what ought to be the case (*e.g.* 'I am a citizen; every citizen ought to pay his taxes; therefore, I ought to pay my taxes'). Such reasoning entered Christian ethics through Aristotle's* influence, and has been especially important both pastorally and in the development of casuistry,* both Roman Catholic and Protestant.

A more recent application of logic to ethics has been in the development of deontic (see Deontology*) logic, a form of modal logic in which obligation* is taken as the key concept. As it is impossible for a proposition to be both necessary and impossible, so it is impossible for a rule to be both obligatory and forbidden; as a proposition may be possible and not necessary, so a rule may be permissible and not obligatory, and so on.

Both applications of logic to ethics depend upon there being general statements of obligatoriness. Where there has been doubt about whether there are such statements, as in existentialist-inspired approaches to ethics (see Existentialist Ethics*) such as 'situationism' (see Situation Ethics*), then the influence of logic upon ethics has been minimal.

The estimation of probabilities is relevant to all forms of consequentialism* in ethics. For where ethical rightness depends solely upon the effects of an action, it is necessary to form an accurate estimate of those effects. But while there are important consequentialist elements in Christian ethics, and important consequentialist thinkers in its history (*e.g.* William Paley, 1743–1805), it is more characteristic of Christian ethics to inculcate actions which go against what is probable. On this view Christian ethics is an out-working of Christian faith, which is formed not by an estimate of probabilities but by reliance upon the divine promises and respect for divine commands which often cut across what seems likely or desirable. However, judgments of relative importance must be made in situations where moral principles conflict.

One major way in which reason has influenced Christian ethics is through views of human nature or human powers. Of the main models of human nature, two may be singled out for attention. Platonistically-inspired Christian thinkers have held that all human beings possess basic powers to intuit moral truths or principles which are metaphysically or ontologically objective and necessary. Sometimes, as with the Cambridge Platonists, the emphasis in this general outlook has been upon the status of the moral principles, while with others (e.g. Joseph Butler*), it has been upon the human capacity to discern, through the conscience,* a range of moral truths and obligations.

A very different estimate of human reason derives from the Enlightenment,* particularly from Immanuel Kant.* A basic principle of Kant's moral philosophy is that morality is autonomous, self-chosen or self-legislated in accordance with the principles of pure practical reason. At its mildest, this means that moral choices should not be coerced but should be unconstrainedly chosen; more strongly, that morality is a matter of free human decision taken in a cultural void.

While allowing, and even welcoming, the Kantian emphasis upon the need for an individual to internalize moral principles, Christian moral theology is understandably suspicious of any appeal to reason which dilutes the authority of Scripture on moral issues and which regards the tradition of Christian reasoning as of only historical or sociological importance. The Enlightenment's appeal to 'reason' has the appearance of objectivity, yet the canons of reason that it endorses reveal an anti-authoritarian bias characteristic of that culture. There is an inevitable and acceptable tension between the given moral principles of Scripture and changing human circumstances, and in the need to apply the one to the other. However, moral rationalism is invariably signalled when moral norms not derived from or at least endorsed by Scripture are elevated to a central place, and when the moral principles of Scripture and of traditional Christian teaching are assessed and found wanting when compared to these standards.

See also: CHRISTIAN MORAL REASONING; [18] OBJECTIVITY OF MORALS.

Bibliography
I. Kant, *Religion Within the Limits of Reason Alone* (1793; ET, New York and Evanston, IL, 1960); A. J. P. Kenny, *Will, Freedom and Power* (Oxford, 1976).

P.H.

REBELLION is the resistance to or defiance of any authority. It may turn into armed resistance to one's government or ruler, and it becomes revolution when executed by a significant proportion of the people in order to obtain a redistribution of power and a revision of the forms and direction of institutions in society.

If we accept that the pattern of human life under authority in family, society and nation has been established by God (Rom. 13:1), it appears as logical that rebellion is sinful (Rom. 13:2). This view became predominant in the Christendom situation of Europe and the Americas, where Catholic and Eastern Orthodox churches became established institutions in society, although Thomas Aquinas* allowed rebellion against State authorities who disobeyed natural law.* Within Protestantism, Calvinists made room for the possibility of rebellion against tyrannical governments (see Tyrannicide*) when it was clearly perceived that they were not performing their functions well (Rom. 13:3–7).

Events of our century have caused theologians and ethicists to revise the traditional position. New questions were faced by Christians who could not in good conscience obey the demands of political regimes hostile to the church, such as Nazism and Communism. During the two World Wars, Christians participated not only in war itself but also in armed or non-violent resistance movements against foreign armies occupying their countries. The rise of anti-colonial movements parallel to the flourishing of young churches in Asia and Africa, as well as the participation of Christians in movements that aimed to change unjust and oppressive social structures in Latin America, posed dramatically the issue of the legitimacy of rebellion, which became acute also in the effort to fight apartheid* in South Africa.

Within the ecumenical movement (see Ecumenical Ethics*), the theological search for answers reached its peak in a conference organized by the World Council of Churches (WCC) about 'Christians in the Technical and Social Revolutions of Our Time' (Geneva 1966). Here the teachings of Paul Lehmann (1906–) were very influential (see Contextual Ethics*). It was understood that unjust structures and oppression in society had a dehumanizing effect contrary to God's design, and that God's action in history was aimed at making life more human, *i.e.* humanization. Consequently Christians could not remain neutral, and were called to take part in the historical process of our century, in which revolution represented the cutting edge of humanization. This view provided the basis for the controversial WCC policy of using church-given funds to provide humanitarian help to revolutionary movements, especially in Africa.

This view and the 'theology of hope' of Jürgen Moltmann (1926–) were also influential in the development of theologies of liberation, in which history is conceived as 'a process of human liberation' which is achieved by human beings as a 'historical conquest', an unending process (see Liberation Theology*). For theologian Gustavo Gutiérrez (1928–), 'The goal is not only better living conditions, a radical change of structures, a social revolution; it is much more: the continuous creation, never ending, of a new way to be human, a permanent cultural revolution' (*A Theology of Liberation*, p. 21). Within this theological frame of reference, José Míguez Bonino (1924–) has formulated the ethical dilemma of the Christian in this thesis: 'In carrying out needed structural changes we encounter an inevitable tension between the human cost of their realization and the human cost of their postponement. The basic ethical criterion is the maximizing of universal possibilities and the minimizing of human costs' (*Towards a Christian Political Ethics*, p. 107). Míguez Bonino as well as Stephen Mott (1940–) believes that for Christians who accept a theology of 'just war'* (*i.e.* a guide to justify and limit warfare), it should not be impossible to develop a theology of 'just revolution', which would provide a guideline for ethical decisions. In face of situations where social change was inevitable, other theologians have stressed the responsibility of the Christian to fight against evil through non-violent means.

There is a growing consensus that in order to do justice to the NT material, it is not possible to overlook the eschatological and critical stance of Jesus and the apostles in face of political and religious authorities. In his central message about the kingdom of God,* Jesus was proclaiming a gospel that was more than just individualistic interior salvation. In his ministry that culminates in the cross,* Jesus gives us the example of using words (Lk. 13:32; Mt. 23) and actions (Jn. 2:13–17) to confront openly corrupt and inefficient religious and political authorities. However, he refused very clearly the Zealot way of violent rebellion in his command against the use of the sword (Mt. 26:52) and his message of peace (Jn. 14:27) and love for enemies (Mt. 5:38–48). The cross was to be not only the means for the redemption of human beings through Christ's atoning work (see Atonement*), but also an example of social behaviour for his followers (1 Pet. 2:20–24). The apparently conservative stance of Paul in Rom. 13:1–7 should be complemented by careful attention to his social behaviour and the teaching of other parts of Scripture such as Rev. 13.

Pacifists like André Trocmé (1901–71), and Anabaptist theologians such as John H. Yoder (1927–), have provided a good amount of exegetical work to support these views. They emphasize the fact that the example of Jesus is normative for the Christian today. They also insist that there are examples from the OT and history, such as those of Mohandas (Mahatma) Gandhi (1869–1948) and Martin Luther King,* which prove that it is possible to achieve significant social transformation through active non-violence.

See also: KAIROS DOCUMENT; NON-VIOLENCE.

Bibliography
J. Bennett (ed.), *Christian Social Ethics in a Changing World* (London and New York, 1966); G. Gutiérrez, *A Theology of Liberation* (ET, London and Maryknoll, NY, ²1988); J. Míguez Bonino, *Towards a Christian Political Ethics* (London and Philadelphia, 1983); S. C. Mott, *Biblical Ethics and Social Change* (New York and Oxford, 1982); A. Trocmé, *Jesus and the Nonviolent Revolution* (ET, Scottdale, PA, 1973); J. H. Yoder, *The Politics of Jesus* (Grand Rapids, 1972); *The Kairos Document* (Johannesburg and Grand Rapids, ²1986).

J.S.E.

RECONCILIATION is a concept which stems from the realm of human personal relationships. It is the renewing of warmth and trust after a period of hostility and conflict. The concept can be extended to refer to peacemaking between conflicting groups, communities, institutions or nations. It is closely related to forgiveness,* which is an important element in reconciliation, but the two are not identical. One person can forgive another and let the memory of an injury fade away; reconciliation involves the willingness of both sides to resume the risks of relating with each other once again.

In Jesus' parable, the prodigal son hoped that his father's hurt feelings would be sufficiently abated to allow him to creep back in to the household as a hired servant, but the father, of course, ran out to meet him and publicly celebrated the return of his son (Lk. 15:17–24). In another parable, Jesus portrays God as a debt-cancelling king (Mt. 18:23–26). These are pictures of salvation, but they carry a clearly articulated ethical implication. Those who are reconciled to God are to be people who forgive others. When relationships break down, those involved are to take initiatives and get the process of reconciliation underway (Mt. 18:15–16, 33).

In infancy, the process of establishing identity as a person includes testing the will of a parent to the point where parental anger* produces rebuke or punishment. Provided these reactions are swiftly followed by loving reassurance, the toddler feels secure to explore more widely in relationships and in the physical environment, taking ever bigger risks of rejection. The rapidly changing patterns of friendship in early schooldays allow the child to discover that conflict is inevitable. A choice in favour of one friend can mean losing the good will of another. A gang of peers may offer reconciliation to an individual on terms which cut across the adolescent's own values and goals. Such pressures may have to be robustly resisted in the interests of integrity and growth. In courtship, quarrels provide important milestones, as the couple learn to understand each other's negative feelings and to give and receive forgiveness.

Reconciliation after an incident of injury or conflict involves firstly clarification: the parties need to understand what has happened and how it looks on the other side; there needs to be honesty about the strength of anger or embarrassment involved. Then comes a point of commitment: free pardon is offered for the hurts, with all claims on the account relin-

quished; the pardon is accepted, with any appropriate restitution at least being offered. Resentment and guilt* are now presumed to cease and this is usually helped by the positive feelings which come from the renewed sense of love (see ⑫) and trust. In most situations hurts have been incurred on both sides and repentance* and forgiveness are mutual. Marital reconciliation, even where it seems obvious that one partner is the 'offender', is fragile and suspect unless forgiveness has been two-way.

Reconciliation is an important concept in Paul's understanding of why Jesus had to die. Romans 5:8–11 describes us as being in a war-type conflict with God, enemies in mortal danger of God's anger, but that is firmly set within the context of God's love (5:8). God demonstrates love, Christ dies for us, and we receive reconciliation. 2 Corinthians 5:14–21 has a similar stress on love (Christ's love, 5:14) and on God's initiative in reconciling us to himself. Yet reconciliation is also the evangelist's invitation (5:20); by definition it includes our response.

There has been fierce debate in this century about the significance here of the cross.* Have justice and punishment any relationship to the overwhelming mercy of God? There are important parallels in our pastoral and ethical thinking. In families, institutions and the State's legal system, anger, rebuke and punishment* indicate that an offender is taken seriously and valued as a responsible agent whose actions can damage others, or exert an influence over them by example or other means. Society's goals will be to reform the offender and deter others. Reformative ideals have dominated recent criminology, though popular calls for 'stiffer sentences' may presage a shift back towards deterrence. Thinkers such as C. S. Lewis* or R. C. Moberly (1845–1903) argue that a central concept of a 'just desert' is required to safeguard offenders against severity or manipulation.

Using a variety of images, NT writers describe the just desert for sin (see Sin and Salvation ⑤) as death and destruction, the opposite of an eternal life of loving dependence on God. God's reconciliation offers us a free pardon but in a way which does not undervalue us as responsible agents or trivialize the deep damage caused by our sin. In Christ, God himself has entered history and died on our behalf and in our place. The full horror of the effects of sin is revealed in the events of Jesus' death. There is nothing to do but to take the risk of accepting his pardon and come face to face with God in repentance and thankfulness.

Believers continue to be sinners, and regularly discover joy and energy for change in their lives through experiences of repentance and forgiveness. What if the sin is serious, though? The church has struggled down the centuries with her response to major sin in one of her members. Financial swindles, adultery, violence and other such things damage the trust between those who gather together to share communion. In the 3rd and 4th centuries a disciplinary period of exclusion from communion was followed by a rite of reconciliation which involved public confession* of sin. In the Middle Ages, perhaps partly because of the pastoral difficulties which public confession presents, the church moved into a system of private penance with increasing emphasis on an obligation to receive priestly absolution.* Fear that the practices of penance were undermining the pardoning grace of God became an issue in the 16th century. The Reformed churches returned to an emphasis on public discipline, based on withholding communion. They continued to find it sensitive to implement in practice. Protestant missionaries starting from scratch in new cultures have, however, often introduced discipline procedures for post-baptismal sin. Public traditions of reconciliation are more common in Africa than in Europe today.

Ephesians 2 presents the reconciliation of the cross as a motive for unity between Jewish and Gentile believers despite the colossal religious and social forces which separated them outside the church. In Col. 1:20–22 there is a glimpse of cosmic reintegration as every aspect of the universe is ultimately reconciled or brought into its right relationship with God. Such texts undergird the convictions of Christians who work towards breaking down barriers of prejudice and privilege centred on class, gender, race and religious practice, or who search for better patterns of caring for the environment.

Bibliography

D. W. Augsburger, *The Freedom of Forgiveness* (Chicago, 1988); J. Houston, *DPC*, pp. 233–234; S. B. Leas, *Leadership and Conflict* (Nashville, TN, 1982); R. P. Martin, *Reconciliation: A Study of Paul's Theology* (London and Atlanta, 1981); E. R. Moberly, *NDCE*, pp. 462–464; O. O'Donovan, *NDCE*,

p. 528; R. Rice-Oxley, *Forgiveness: The Way of Peace* (Bramcote, Nottingham, 1989); J. R. W. Stott, *The Cross of Christ* (Leicester and Downers Grove, IL, 1986).

V.M.S.

REDEMPTION, see COMMUNITY ETHICS; [16] SIN AND SALVATION. [5]

REDUCTIONISM is the programme of eliminating unnecessary entities in accordance with William of Ockham's (*c*. 1280/ 85–1349) dictum, 'Entities are not to be multiplied beyond necessity.' The motivation for this is not only ontological tidiness and parsimony, but the ambition to account for the manifold of experience in terms of one kind, or at least a very few kinds, of entity. This is the inspiration behind, say, materialism* or physicalism, or, at the other end of the metaphysical spectrum, the subjective idealism* of Bishop Berkeley (1685–1753).

Whether a proposal is considered to be reductionist or not depends upon one's original starting-point. In meta-ethics, all forms of non-cognitivism have generally been regarded as reductionist, since prima facie many ethical sentences are capable of having a truth value. But many non-cognitivists have accepted some version of non-naturalism as a premiss, and non-naturalism might be regarded as a form of anti-reductionism by the ethical naturalist.

In Christian ethics any attempt to demonstrate that ethical judgments are nothing but psychological statements (about preferences or feelings) or sociological statements (about group reactions and traditions) would be regarded as reductionist in intent. For such proposals would eliminate the objectivity usually ascribed to ethical principles by Christian theology.

In Christian normative ethics, reductionism is less easy to assess, though theories of mono-causal motivation, ascribing all action to, say, selfishness or sibling rivalry, would be regarded as such. Paul's statement that love is the fulfilling of the law (Rom. 13:10) may be said to be reductionist if one supposes that he is teaching that love supplants the law, but not if he is teaching that the law defines what love is.

P.H.

REHABILITATION OF OFFENDERS, see PUNISHMENT.

RELATIVISM is the idea that what is right and wrong, good and bad, true and false varies from time to time, place to place, and person to person. There are no absolute standards of truth or morality, but these depend on where, when, and who you are. Relativism stems from the fact of the variety of views in the world, particularly between different cultures. Cultural relativism suggests that what is viewed as right in one culture may be regarded as wrong in another. This leads to the notion that there are no absolute or universal standards of right and wrong, truth and falsity. These are always relative to a particular context, setting, time and place. For a society to function there must be tolerance to cope with the differences. Relativism has created doubt among various groups and cultures, as exposure to other cultures and their values has made people question the validity of their own values and view of truth.

In fact, relativism rests on a self-contradiction. The statement that 'everything is relative' is itself an absolute claim. Even if everything is relative, there is no way that we can express this as absolutely true, far less live it, without falling into contradiction and nonsense. The fact of different views does not in itself mean that there are no true or right values. The fact that different cultures, religions, moral and legal codes have all expressed rules about parent–children relationships, sexual behaviour, truth-telling, the sanctity of life, and what belongs to me or to my community and what does not, seems to point to universal, absolute standards. These may have different expressions in different cultures, but that does not affect their validity. Christians find in the fact of God's creation of the world and of humankind in his image (see Image of God*) that God's law is written in the very nature of the world and of humanity, and in conscience (Rom. 1 – 3). The very fact that we engage in moral discussion, recognizing what counts as a moral issue and as morally relevant, and that we use moral language which has agreed terms, reveals that there is a common view of what constitutes morality and an objective core to moral reflection. Without such a core, moral discourse and debate would be as impossible as the resolution of moral disagreement is held to be by the relativist. The validity of the view depends on an empirical analysis of alleged cultural variation, what common basis there is behind such variation, and the exploration of what the Catholic community has called natural law.* Any view which puts God as creator and law-giver at its

heart will deny the relativist thesis, believing that there are objective truths and values which can be known and which form the basis for moral discussion, debate, and the resolution of moral differences. Tolerance is inadequate, for it becomes an absolute, and it is fundamentally limited when confronted by intolerance.

Bibliography
D. Cook, *Dilemmas of Life* (Leicester, 1990); E. A. Westermark, *Ethical Relativity* (New York, 1937), ch. 5.

E.D.C.

RELIGION AS PROJECTION, see PSYCHOLOGY OF RELIGION.

RELIGIOUS EDUCATION. In the British context, where Religious Education (RE) is an element of the State-provided school curriculum, a number of difficult theological and ethical issues arise which do not do so in countries where RE is seen to be the responsibility of the churches.

In the UK, debates about RE usually centre on the legally required component of the school curriculum. In the literature this is carefully distinguished from education* which takes place within the church community. The crucial distinction made is between a form of education which can legitimately assume a faith context and seek to transmit that faith, and a form which has to be appropriate to the needs of all pupils who attend State-funded secular schools, whatever their own faith background. In this latter case it is usually argued that RE cannot legitimately assume the truth of, nor seek to transmit, any one religion. The 'professional' concerns of the 'secular' RE teacher working in the multi-faith context of schools are therefore contrasted with the 'confessional' concerns of those responsible for nurture and evangelism within the church.

For the Christian seeking to apply biblical theology to RE, a key challenge is to avoid either relativism* or syncretism as Christian truth is placed alongside 'truth' from other religions in the classroom. A related problem is that, in the cause of educational objectivity, religious faith will be treated as a purely private matter. The rationale for this is that in the public, secular arena of the school, only those beliefs and values which are shared by all rational beings should be promoted. It is argued that controversial or sectarian beliefs should not appear in schools, except as objects for dispassionate study and individual, private choice. The universal application of absolute Christian truth is thereby denied; it ceases to function as public truth.

In the professional literature on RE some unease has been expressed at this privatization of religious belief. However, most writers still want to treat RE as an autonomous, secular discipline, having aims which are independent of particular religious beliefs. The solution usually proffered is to allow religious faith a restricted role as the provider of theological illumination on previously established, objective educational ideals. The independent rationality of education must not, however, be compromised; theology, it is said, cannot legitimately adjudicate in educational decisions. Teachers are therefore encouraged to develop a personal theology which can support their practice as professional religious educators. This theology often turns out to be pluralist in character, emphasizing the tentative, even sceptical nature of 'rational' religious commitment and the subjectivist character of religious language. This is in direct contrast to the importance evangelical Christians place upon the truthfulness of the biblical revelation of God and his saving purpose in Christ.

This 'professional' approach is clearly not theologically neutral, and amounts to the imposition of a particular controversial framework. One possible response to this is to argue that RE can never be theologically value-free, and therefore to develop an alternative which is grounded in Christian thought. This is possible in Christian schools where distinctively Christian goals can be pursued. The difficulty is in State-funded schools, where a variety of theological persuasions, both Christian and non-Christian, will be represented amongst both staff and pupils.

The problem is one of political ethics and hinges on the question of the proper relation of the State to the promotion of religious belief. If, in a plural democracy, it is illegitimate for government to impose a particular religious framework, then it is clearly wrong for any particular theology to be assumed as the basis for RE. However, it seems difficult to see how this can be avoided if education cannot escape being theologically value-laden.

One way forward, if it is to succeed in being impartial, is to accept that RE can fulfil only a limited function. Appropriate aims might be to give young people an understanding of the importance of religion, to encourage them to interact with and learn from others of different religious persuasion and to reflect on their own religious commitments. This will fall short of the aspirations of the various faith communities wishing to transmit their beliefs through education. However, the motivation for participating in this limited process is that its aims are recognized to be of value in the education of future citizens. Restraints on the full expression of Christian truth can be accepted as long as others of different persuasions accept the same restraints. The required behaviour could be expressed in the form of a code of conduct governing the application of theology to RE.

Perhaps one of the most important principles that can be adopted as part of this code is to utilize non-prescriptive language. By this is meant that all truth claims and statements of worship should be 'grounded' in a specific religious tradition and should not assume assent from pupils or teachers. For example, any celebration of Divali should make it quite plain that this festival 'belongs' to Hindus. Those who are not Hindus are not then made to feel that they should 'own' the language of Divali. The crucial distinction is between learning about, and even from, another religion and actually participating in some sense in that religion. A Christian can then, with integrity, be an observer at, and teach about, acts of worship from another religion. This is, however, to be distinguished from participation in a multi-faith act of worship, a model which implicitly assumes that all participants are engaged in a common activity. To complement school RE, Christian churches should develop educational programmes which aim to pass on the truths of the faith to children. In the modern context it is inappropriate to expect schools to fulfil this confessional function.

Bibliography

J. Astley and D. Day, *Contours of Christian Education* (Southend-on-Sea, 1992); L. Francis and A. Thatcher, *Christian Perspectives For Education* (Leominster, 1990); M. Grimmitt, *Religious Education and Human Development* (Southend-on-Sea, 1987); B. V. Hill, *That They May Learn: Towards a Christian View of Education* (Exeter, 1990); J. Hull, *Mishmash: Religious Education In Multi-Cultural Britain* (Derby, 1991); M. Leicester and M. Taylor, *Ethics, Ethnicity and Education* (London, 1992); M. Palmer, *What Should We Teach?:*

Christians and Education in a Pluralist World (Geneva, 1991).

T.J.Co.

RELIGIOUS TOLERATION, see TOLERATION, RELIGIOUS.

REMARRIAGE. The Christian church has never spoken with one voice concerning the marriage* of a person who has a former partner still living, because it has not spoken with one voice about divorce.* In the early centuries, most Christians rejected divorce and remarriage (Tertullian* even forbidding second marriage after the death of a spouse), but by the 6th century the Eastern church was allowing such practices for a variety of causes. By contrast, the Western church held to the view that marriage was indissoluble, Augustine* believing that a valid marriage once made should not be dissolved. By the Middle Ages, the sacramental view of marriage was held to imply that a valid marriage could not be dissolved. The Catholic traditions within the church have held this view, sometimes together with procedures for annulment (see Nullity*) for dealing with marital breakdown.

The Continental Protestant Reformers rejected the sacramental concept of marriage and the doctrine of absolute indissolubility. They argued that the NT implies the permissibility of divorce with right of remarriage in certain circumstances. The Reformers in England inherited aspects both of Catholic and Protestant strands. If Archbishop Cranmer's (1489–1556) proposals for a revised Canon Law (*The Reformatio Legum Ecclesiasticarum*, 1553) had ever become law, they would have included provision of divorce for adultery,* malicious desertion,* prolonged absence without news, attempts against the partner's life and cruelty. Punishment for adultery was prescribed, but the innocent partner was allowed to remarry. In 17th-century England, a number of divorces procured by Special Act of Parliament were followed by remarriage in church.

The issue is important at a number of levels. 1. At the *exegetical* level, there is some unclarity concerning the meaning of the Synoptic divorce material in Mt. 19:3–12 and Mk. 10:2–12. Whilst second marriage is clearly presupposed in Dt. 24:1–4, referred to in these Synoptic texts (although in the Deuteronomic legislation, return to the first husband is forbidden for a wife divorced by a second husband – presumably to curb male cruelty), there is disagreement concerning Jesus' meaning. Is he forbidding all divorce? Is he calling all remarriage 'adultery'? Does the exceptive clause (except for the case of *porneia, i.e.* sexual sin) in Mt. 5:32 and 19:9 mean that in this one case a husband is free to separate from his wife? If so, may he marry another? Or is Jesus in these passages affirming both the divine ideal for the permanence of marriage, and also recognizing the effects of sin (hardness of heart)? Some believe that by 'divorce' Jesus means 'put away by separation without right of remarriage'. Others think that, since such separation was unknown in his day, and because Jesus is in fact discussing Dt. 24 in which right of remarriage is assumed, he would not have been understood to be saying something radically new without further explanation.

2. At the *hermeneutical* level, we have to decide how Jesus is actually wanting his teaching to be understood. Is he offering us a new law to replace the law of Moses (and if so, is he being unusually prescriptive)? Or is he reminding us of the demands of the kingdom,* and the sort of righteousness* which characterizes kingdom life? The exceptive clause in Matthew would then be the recognition of the need in the Matthean community for some legislation given that not all can live up to the demands of the kingdom in this life. We have to decide what to do with Jesus' reference to *porneia*, and the fact that in his discussion of marriage, the apostle Paul does not refer to it at all, but rather discusses desertion by an unbelieving partner (1 Cor. 7). Some have suggested that the Deuteronomic implication of cruelty, the Matthean reference to sexual sin, and Paul's words about desertion point to the sorts of serious situations in which divorce might be contemplated.

3. At the *moral* level, we need to decide whether the Scriptures allow divorce with right of remarriage at all, and if so in which circumstances. Those following the more Protestant traditions tend to argue that, though God's intention for marriage is permanence, it is not always wrong to break the marital covenant, though it can never be good to do so. There are situations in which sin so traps us that no ways open to us are good, and then, recognizing our need of forgiveness and mercy, we may decide to take a lesser-evil choice. Divorce is never the first, always the last, option. It can never take place without damage to

the partners (the OT word translated 'divorce' is related to that for cutting down trees and amputating limbs). If divorce is the right (though not a good) choice, the question of remarriage comes into focus. We cannot simply put all situations of divorce and all situations of possible remarriage into one moral category. Some marriages fail because of persistent cruelty and unfaithfulness; others because they should never have taken place at all; others for other reasons. Obligations to children or others must not be ignored. Some Christians take the view that there are circumstances in which second marriage while a former partner is still living can sometimes be a responsible choice, but only under the shadow of a broken covenant,* and only by seeking the grace of God for a new start.

4. The *pastoral* questions are thus not straightforward. Many marriages are broken through some personal inadequacy or need in one or both of the partners. It is not self-evident that a subsequent marriage will be any more successful without counselling help. A broken marriage raises the possibility of a calling to celibacy (see Singleness*). There are those, however, who testify to the blessing of God on a second marriage, and for whom the experience of grace in a new start has enabled a new marriage relationship to declare something of the divine covenant.

5. The *ecclesiastical* questions concerning church discipline, and the permissibility of solemnizing a second marriage in church, will depend on the approach taken to the biblical and moral questions. How should the church institutionalize its double task: a. to bear witness to the divine will for the permanence of marriage; and b. to the gospel of grace, forgiveness, and the fact that our sins do not simply accumulate against us? Some will allow second marriage in church in some circumstances: others believe that a 'service of blessing' following civil marriage is a more appropriate course.

See also: SEXUALITY. [11]

Bibliography

D. Atkinson, *To Have and to Hold* (London, 1979); Church Information Office, *Marriage and the Church's Task* (London, 1978); A. J. C. Cornes, *Divorce and Remarriage* (London, 1993); K. T. Kelly, *Divorce and Second Marriage* (London, 1992); A. R. Winnett, *Divorce and Remarriage in Anglicanism* (London, 1958).

D.J.A.

REPENTANCE. In the OT, two Heb. words express the idea of repentance: *nāham*, which came to mean 'to lament, grieve, be sorry, change one's mind'; and *šûb*, meaning 'to turn back, return'. The former is most often used of God, where it is said that he would 'repent of the evil' which he had thought to do to his people (*e.g.* see RSV, Je. 18:8; 26:3, 13, 19; Am. 7:3, 6), often in response to the people's changing of their wrong behaviour. The latter word usually refers to humankind being called to return to creaturely dependence on God. It is a term frequently used by the prophets to indicate a call for a total change in one's attitude towards sin and God in terms of turning away from sin to righteousness and entering into new fellowship with God (Is. 10:21–22; 30:15; Je. 3:14; 15:15–21; Ho. 6:1–3; 14:1–2).

In the Gospels, a key theme of Jesus' preaching was that of repentance. He underlined it at the beginning of his ministry (Mt. 4:17), and emphasized it near the close when he urged the disciples to give prominence to it in their preaching (Lk. 24:46–47). This emphasis had several key elements: 1. to feel *sorrow* for sin (*e.g.* when the lost son 'came to his senses' and said, 'I have sinned against heaven', Lk. 15:17–18; and when the tax collector prayed, 'God, have mercy on me, a sinner', Lk. 18:13); 2. to *turn away* from sin (*e.g.* Zacchaeus stopped his cheating, Lk. 19:8; and the rich man was to give up his attachment to material possessions, Mk. 10:21); 3. to *alter completely* the course and motivation of one's life. Repentance is to take hold of the *whole* person and all of life: it is not merely to affect one's mind; rather, positive change is to take place (see Mt. 3:8 and Mk. 10:21); 4. to *trust completely* in the grace* of God (as did the lost son as he made his way home to his father, Lk. 15:18–24, 32; and as did the tax collector in submitting himself to God's mercy, Lk. 18:13).

In the NT, repentance is closely connected with fear at the prospect of judgment (Mt. 3:10), desire to enter the kingdom of heaven (see Kingdom of God;* Mt. 3:2; 4:17; 18:3), receiving forgiveness of sins (Acts 2:38; 3:19; 5:31), and responding to the grace of God (Rom. 2:4).

Repentance is presented both as a gift of God and as the responsibility and duty of every person (*cf.* Acts 5:31 and 11:18 with Mt. 3:7ff., Acts 13:24 and 19:4). Certain facets of repentance highlight the human aspect, *e.g.* conversion* (Acts 3:19) and faith* (Acts 20:21), while others, *e.g.* forgiveness* of sins (Lk. 24:47), lay stress on blessings of which God alone is the author.

Repentance is something which affects the whole personality: the *intellect*, in that repentance involves a change of mind regarding a person's sin, involving recognition of guilt and helplessness before God; this leads to an *emotional* element, a change of feeling showing itself in sorrow for sin. (It is in fact possible to have a knowledge of sin without seeing it as something that dishonours God, but this sort of view leads only to a fear of punishment rather than to a desire to abandon sin.) True repentance necessarily involves a change in emotional attitude, a consciousness that sin has an effect on humankind and is an offence to God. Deep sorrow for sin (sometimes termed 'contrition') should be a strong impulse for turning away from sin. In the *will*, there is a change of purpose, an inward turning away from sin, and a desire to take responsibility for it and to seek God's forgiveness.

It seems clear, then, that repentance is at the heart of the Christian message, a foundation element in the presentation of the gospel (Heb. 6:1). Some have suggested that the early church began to consider whether it was possible for a person to turn in repentance to God on a number of occasions. Thus, for example, Peter is told by Jesus that he will 'turn again' (Lk. 22:32). Some see Heb. 6:4–5 as teaching that it is impossible to repent a second time (or even more times). But these verses may well be reacting to a form of Christianity that was lapsing into apathy and apostasy. However that may be, it is clear that *Christians* can repent and need to repent, as is made plain in 2 Cor. 7:9–10; 12:21; Jas. 5:19–20; 1 Jn. 1:8–2:2; Rev. 2:5, 16, 21–22; 3:3, 5, 16 (referring to individual Christians as well as to unfaithful churches).

In the pastoral ministry, repentance may be said to be an important factor to be presented by counsellors. This is especially so in the counselling approach represented by Jay Adams (see Biblical Counselling*), who places considerable emphasis on repentance, arguing that 'the task of the Christian counsellor is to call for repentance' (*The Christian Counselor's Manual*, p. 173). Adams' belief seems to be that as sin is often a key part of a counsellee's problem, part of effecting biblical change is to emphasize the vital role of repentance. Adams thinks that even for many Christian counsellors, the need for repentance is rarely suggested, but a glance at Roger Hurding's *Roots and Shoots* would not seem to bear this out (see pp. 327–328, 349, 366 and 395–396, and particularly the reference to Paul Tournier,* who aims to bring 'soul-healing' to those who seek help, part of which is repentance).

See also: SIN AND SALVATION. [5]

Bibliography
J. E. Adams, *The Christian Counselor's Manual* (Phillipsburg, 1973); *idem*, *How to Help People Change* (Grand Rapids, 1986), esp. ch. 17; B. H. DeMent, *ISBE* 4, ²1988, pp. 135–137; J. Goetzmann, *NIDNTT* 1, pp. 353–359; R. F. Hurding, *Roots and Shoots: A Guide to Counselling and Psychotherapy* (London, 1986) = *The Tree of Heaven* (Grand Rapids, 1988).

P.D.W.

R EPRESSION, POLITICAL. For the seventy-one years of its existence as a ruling political ideology, communism universally propagated atheism, often hand in hand with active political repression. During 1988–91, before the abolition of the Soviet Communist Party, Mikhail Sergeyevich Gorbachev (1931–   ) encouraged its active co-operation with religion and change ensued everywhere.

Lenin (1870–1924) quoted Marx* as his justification for persecuting religion, initiating a frontal attack against the clergy. Under Stalin (1879–1953) this became more systematic, including the destruction of thousands of churches, monasteries, mosques and synagogues. Only the Second World War brought respite. Stalin encouraged the reopening of churches to provide moral support at a time when catastrophe threatened.

At the end of the war, the Soviet Union acquired by conquest new areas beyond its Western borders, against which Stalin unleashed a wave of reprisals, as he did against the satellite States of Eastern and Central Europe. Catholic, Orthodox and Protestant leaders were brought to trial and invariably condemned, and some were executed. Only the German Democratic Republic escaped, where church leaders were required to aid the national rebuilding process.

The new communist regimes of China, North Korea, North Vietnam, Cambodia and eventually Cuba and (later) Ethiopia all considered religious persecution as a prerequisite to establishing a revolutionary political system.

However, once Stalin had died, the countries of the Soviet bloc began to evolve their own 'roads to socialism', which in practice meant an accommodation with religion. In 1956 the denunciation of Stalin by Nikita Sergeyevich Khrushchev (1894–1971) caused the release of many political prisoners and the worst days of persecution in many countries were over. The Soviet Union was an exception. Here Khrushchev closed many churches again. The imprisonment of those who resisted persecution sharpened an opposition movement in which Baptists were influential. Its key demand was for religious liberty, finally guaranteed under the new law of 1990.

Albania was the only country in world history to abolish all manifestations of religion (1967), but this policy was reversed in 1991. China and North Korea, too, have shown signs of greater flexibility.

In every communist country the campaign to eradicate religion failed utterly. In Poland, the growth of Catholicism, especially as a political force after the election in 1978 of Pope John Paul II (1920–) led to destabilization on a scale sufficient eventually to undermine the communist system in Eastern and Central Europe as a whole. In the Soviet Union from the 1960s there was a growing desire to discover a Christian ideal to replace the discredited morality of communism, and the Russian Orthodox Church eventually re-emerged to play a leading role in society.

There are many other areas of the world which practise forms of religious discrimination, especially those dominated by Islamic fundamentalism. Christian activity is restricted, though not illegal, in Israel. There are many countries where Christian motivation has led to political activity which has been persecuted by the regime: several countries of Latin America, Malawi and most significantly (until the recent changes) South Africa.

M.A.B.

REPRESSION, PSYCHOLOGICAL.
Repression is often considered to be the most basic of the defence mechanisms,* upon which all others are based. Theodore Lidz (1910–) defines it as 'the barring or banishment of memories, perceptions or feelings that would arouse the forbidden'. Unacceptable ideas, feelings, impulses or motives are pushed from consciousness to unconsciousness.*

Repression was one of the earliest Freudian concepts. Freud* distinguished between *primary repression* in which an 'instinctual impulse' is repressed, and *secondary repression* where indirect expressions of the instinct are unconscious. He examined in particular repression in connection with people exhibiting 'hysterical' symptoms. Memories had been repressed but their presence was revealed in subtle ways such as stammering. Freud would try to discover the original cause of the symptom. The patient would be encouraged to talk about it and consciously come to terms with it. The symptom would then disappear.

At times repression can become confused with the term 'inhibition'. Charles Rycroft (1914–) distinguishes between the two. He says that repression is like a dam continuously holding back the flow of a river, whereas inhibition resembles the periodic switching off of an electric light.

The person concerned is not aware consciously of the repressed material, but it continues to affect him or her. One very common form of repression is amnesia. This can occur when something terrible has happened. It is as if the memory wants to protect the person from the experience by 'forgetting' about it. It is pushed down into the unconscious. For instance, a person seriously injured as a child in an accident involving a Volvo car may have strange feelings of panic whenever he sees a Volvo. He cannot understand why he is anxious, because he has no recollection of the Volvo in the accident.

The repression of an experience may not always be complete, however. The experience may be revealed through dreams,* especially nightmares, or slips of the tongue. Psychoanalysts* explain the dreams as being the time when the 'ego' is asleep and repressions are partly lifted, so that the person is able once again to experience the memories.

Sometimes repression is only a temporary state. As other resources or methods of coping with the experience become available, the repression decreases and the memory returns to the consciousness. For instance, a girl who has been sexually abused by her father may bury the incident in her unconscious because she cannot deal with the trauma. Despite being in her unconsciousness, the memory affects her relationships, particularly with men, and the way she views herself. However, as she matures and is better equipped to deal with the trauma, the memory slowly returns to consciousness.

From a biblical viewpoint we can certainly

acknowledge the complexity of the human psyche, but certain points need to be made concerning the way repression has traditionally been dealt with. Repression can be of different things, such as an experience (*e.g.* sexual abuse*), or something of which the person is guilty (*e.g.* theft). Freud does not take this into account in his treatment of repression. We do not have to know ourselves exhaustively in order to be able to behave rightly.

Bibliography

J. N. Isbister, *Freud: An Introduction to His Life and Work* (Cambridge, 1985); T. Lidz, *The Person* (New York, 1968); C. Rycroft, *CDP*.

H.C.H.

REPRODUCTIVE TECHNOLOGIES.
Medicine is now able to afford hope to many thousands of couples who have been unsuccessful in their attempts to bear a child. Infertility (see Childlessness*), defined as a couple's failure to conceive after one year of unprotected intercourse, affects approximately one in seven married couples. While adoption* remains an option for some, the low numbers of available healthy children (*e.g.* 22,000 babies for two million prospective adoptive couples per year in the US) create a continued strong and growing demand for reproductive technologies.

The least controversial reproductive technologies are surgical repair of blocked or damaged Fallopian tubes, the surgical and medical treatment of endometriosis, and the careful administration of drugs designed to stimulate ovulation and to promote normal growth of the endometrium. Many, but by no means all, cases of infertility are treatable in these ways.

Artificial insemination (AI) is a common and inexpensive means of assisted reproduction, having been reported as early as the turn of the century. Concentrated semen is introduced into the female reproductive system artificially in the clinic. Other than the methods of obtaining and delivering the semen, there is nothing biologically unusual about any conception that might take place. Artificial insemination by husband (AIH) has been the least controversial, since the gametes involved belong to the couple themselves. It can be seen as the overcoming of a mere physical obstacle to the conception of the couple's own child.

Artificial insemination by donor (AID) has been more controversial, involving the sperm of another male, typically an anonymous sperm donor, so that any child conceived will be genetically linked only to its mother. This would be resorted to when the husband lacks viable sperm or when he carries the trait for a genetic disorder such as Huntington's chorea which he might pass on to any offspring. A compromise technique, heterologous artificial insemination, uses any available semen from the husband in conjunction with that of the donor for whatever psychological benefits there may be in the couple's believing that the child might after all be 'his'. Artificial insemination is often done using frozen, banked sperm, which is screened for disease and matched by physical characteristics of the donor and couple. Alternatively, husbands can have their semen frozen prior to undergoing a vasectomy to render them sterile, so that they can father a child later.

In vitro ('in glass') fertilization (IVF) is the process whereby a woman's egg, removed by laparoscopy, is fertilized with sperm in the laboratory. Typically, the ovaries are stimulated by a fertility drug, and then a few ova are removed and fertilized. The most promising zygote is then placed into the uterus, and hopefully it develops into a pregnancy and birth. In 1978 the first so-called 'test tube baby' was born with the assistance of British specialists Patrick Steptoe (1913–88) and Robert Edwards (1925–), and many thousands have been born since then. IVF technology has made possible other controversial techniques, including the production of human embryos in the laboratory for research purposes, the transfer of embryos into host mothers ('full surrogates'), the possibility of genetic manipulation* of embryos prior to implantation, and even the use of eggs from a miscarried or aborted female foetus. Many have found this latter proposal unacceptable on aesthetic grounds, on theological grounds as a denial of the dignity of the human body, and on the social grounds that any child born comes from the egg of a 'mother' who did not exist.

GIFT (gamete intra-Fallopian transfer) is the process of taking eggs from follicles stimulated to ripen by means of fertility drugs, and then introducing them, along with sperm, into the Fallopian tubes. This procedure is less technically difficult than IVF and simulates most closely the natural process of conception.

Surrogacy* is both a form of reproductive

technology and a social arrangement. Partial surrogacy involves impregnating a woman with the sperm of the husband of a childless couple. She then carries the child to term and delivers it to the couple. This is done for payment under contract in some countries, though this practice is illegal in Great Britain. Full surrogacy involves a woman undergoing pregnancy with another woman's egg, fertilized by that woman's husband.

A great number of ethical, legal, social and theological issues are raised by the new reproductive technologies. Some of the more salient questions include: Is it ethical to reproduce in a way that is not 'natural'? Does the use of a stranger's sperm, egg or uterus violate the integrity of marital child-begetting? Should children be told that they were conceived by means of donor sperm or *in vitro*? Is it ethical to perform research on human embryos, and if so, up to what point? What is to be done with embryos that are discarded in fertility treatment? What are the moral and social limits on possible genetic manipulation of human beings in embryo?

An early and outspoken critic of these technologies was Paul Ramsey,* a leading conservative Protestant ethicist at Princeton University. Ramsey was concerned, among other things, that to conceive an individual in experimental conditions, as in IVF, meant that the child would be exposed to risks that are impossible to estimate, and to do so without its consent. Other Protestants have also been cautious or critical. A straightforward denunciation of virtually all means of reproductive technology came from the Roman Catholic Congregation for the Doctrine of the Faith in the Vatican in 1987. The Congregation believes that the human dignity of the embryo and the essential connection of marital sexuality and reproduction rule out IVF, GIFT, AID and even AIH as morally acceptable options, leaving only drug and surgical therapies. Further, the Vatican urges all nations to outlaw such procedures.

Many Christian couples of various church traditions will wish to investigate reproductive technologies to help them overcome infertility. Infertility is an especially painful, emotional ordeal, involving as it does the incapacity of a couple to fulfil their love by having children to love and nurture. Its trauma is intensified by the fact that the investigation of its causes as well as the administration of treatment can take many months or even years,

and consume a great proportion of the couple's financial as well as emotional resources. Social pressures on couples to reproduce are significant, particularly in the church, and the reproach of 'barrenness', while perhaps not as powerful as it was in biblical times, is still a source of intense dismay. With this in mind, the motivation of Christian couples to seek medical assistance is quite understandable. It is hard to find moral fault with drug or surgical therapy, or with AIH or GIFT that uses the couple's own gametes. Arguably, even IVF is acceptable if the couple's own genetic material is used. The introduction of third-party material into the reproductive process, however, does seem to violate the 'one-flesh' nature of Christian marriage (Gn. 2:22–24; Eph. 5:28–31), and reproduction by such means seems to expose children to unknown emotional risk. Some also question the stewardship* aspects of devoting large sums of money to infertility treatment when other needs are so great. As adoption becomes more and more difficult, pressure will continue to grow for the moral acceptability of such reproductive technology.

See also: EMBRYOLOGY; EMBRYO TRANSFER.

Bibliography

H. Bouma III *et al.*, *Christian Faith, Health, and Medical Practice* (Grand Rapids, 1989); R. T. Hull, *Ethical Issues in the New Reproductive Technologies* (Belmont, CA, 1990); D. G. Jones, *Manufacturing Humans: The Challenge of the New Reproductive Technologies* (Leicester, 1987); O. O'Donovan, *Begotten or Made?* (Oxford, 1984); M. Warnock (chairperson), *Report of the Committee of Inquiry into Human Fertilisation and Embryology* (London, 1984).

D.B.F.

RERUM NOVARUM, see PAPAL ENCYCLICALS.

RESISTANCE MOVEMENTS, see REBELLION; VIOLENCE.

RESOURCE ALLOCATION, see HEALTH AND HEALTH CARE; QALY.

RESPONSIBILITY is a complex concept involving notions of accountability* and obligation.* Accountability looks back to some deed done or attitude held. Obligation looks forward to moral demands that need to be met in relationships. Responsibility has to do, therefore, with relationships, deeds and attitudes which may attract either praise or blame. Responsibility is usually discussed in secular literature in terms of either moral or legal discourse. In this article, moral responsibility will be examined in terms of 1. the presuppositions of responsibility, 2. the spheres of responsibility, 3. establishing responsibility, 4. the place of responsibility in a biblical model of obligation, 5. the significance of responsibility, and 6. the implications of responsibility for ministry.* It is also worth noting at the outset that, although responsibility is a biblical concept, one searches the standard dictionaries of the Bible in vain to find an article on it.

1. Responsibility appears to presuppose freedom.* The genuine moral agent, to be such, possesses either the liberty of indifference (the power to act without motive) or the liberty of spontaneity (the power to act in accord with one's nature). With regard to the former, a person is responsible for attitudes and actions if he or she could have done or could do otherwise in a moral situation. (A moral situation is one in which the language of praise and blame is appropriate. Falling asleep after a hard day's work at the office does not create a moral situation. Falling asleep on duty as a soldier does create one.) Those who argue for the latter concept of freedom contend that a person is responsible if his or her choice flows out of his or her desires, intentions and beliefs. On either view, some recognition of human freedom is required if the language of accountability and obligation is to have content. For example, on neither view would a person be held responsible if forced to rob a bank with a gun at the head, in the sense that the robber holding the gun would be held responsible.

2. Philosophically considered, both these positions on liberty (indifference and spontaneity) raise metaphysical questions about freedom and determinism (see Free Will and Determinism*) that lie beyond the scope of the present discussion. For example, the libertarian (believing that at least some human acts are uncaused) affirms moral responsibility. The soft determinist (believing that at least some human acts are self-caused) does also. But the hard determinist (who believes that all human acts are determined by antecedent conditions) denies moral responsibility. There is also debate amongst moral philosophers on

whether the concept of responsibility is better situated in a deontological* framework (an ethic of duty) or in a utilitarian one (an ethic of consequences; see Consequentialism*). Still further, there is debate whether a retributive theory of justice comports with the concept of responsibility better than a reformative one (see Punishment*). Theologically considered, pursuing the issue of freedom and determinism raises the sorts of question that Augustine* wrestled with in his debates with the Pelagians – debates continued by Martin Luther* with Erasmus (c. 1469–1536) and by John Wesley* with George Whitefield (1714–70).

3. Establishing the responsibility of the moral agent must, biblically speaking, take into the equation the knowledge, circumstances and physico-social maturity of the person on view. Knowledge brings or mitigates responsibility, in the sense of accountability and obligation, as the prophets and our Lord make plain (Am. 3:2; Lk. 12:41–48; Jn. 15:22). Likewise, physico-social maturity affects the question of responsibility, as God's words to the wilderness generation make clear (Dt. 1:34–40). There is an age of accountability or responsibility, according to the biblical witness (see, e.g., Dt. 1:39; Is. 7:16). Further, in a biblical ethic attitudes as well as actions are morally significant, as Jesus' view of adultery indicates (Mt. 5:27–30).

If responsibility is to be established along the lines of relationship, then analysis needs to recognize that the moral agent is involved in more than one sphere of responsibility. Traditionally, in Christian moral philosophy three spheres or fields of moral responsibility (in terms of both accountability and obligation) have been isolated: responsibility to God (e.g. worship), responsibility to neighbours (e.g. just dealings), and responsibility to oneself (e.g. to keep a clear conscience*). A fourth sphere of responsibility has come to the fore in the light of modern ecological concerns: namely, the environment* and its plight (i.e. the responsibility to be a wise steward* of the good earth). But since in this fourth field nature is not a moral agent, responsibility is a matter of obligation to God for creation,* rather than to nature itself. All four areas have rich biblical support, to look no further than the primal narratives of Genesis (Gn. 1 – 11). Strictly speaking, from a biblical perspective, responsibilities to others, to self and for nature are subsets of responsibility to God. Hence

David's sin with Bathsheba was not only against Uriah but also against God, and meant accountability to God (Ps. 51, on the traditional view).

4. The biblical presentation of the drama of salvation (and the canonical literature it has generated) is rich with insights for the Christian ethicist. There is a logic to biblical obligation. Broadly speaking, in the Scriptures, relationship (*i.e.* covenant*) brings with it responsibilities and rights. Reflection on relationships, as revealed in the order of redemption or found in the order of creation (see the book of Proverbs), requires wisdom. Wisdom distils the relevant, ethical principles underlying moral rules, which in their turn ought to inform specific moral actions in a given moral situation. For example, Paul calls upon children in his Ephesian letter to obey their parents (Eph. 6:1). This responsibility he bases on the moral rule, found in the Decalogue, about honouring parents (Eph. 6:2–3; Dt. 5:16). If this analysis were pursued, ultimately responsibility would be grounded upon the triune nature of the covenant God. The triune God is an intra-deically obligated being (*e.g.* the Son to the Father and vice versa). On this view, morality is dependent upon divine ontology.

5. The significance of the concept of responsibility is manifold. God is judge (see Judgment*). All humankind stands in relationship to him. Relationship brings responsibility and with responsibility comes accountability and obligation. Thus all in Adam are responsible for the conduct of their creaturehood to their creator and will appear before the great white throne of Revelation (Rom. 1:18–32; Rev. 14:6–7; 20:11–15). Those in Christ, as the adopted sons and daughters of the Father, will appear before the judgment seat of Christ to give an account to their redeemer (Rom. 14:10–12; 2 Cor. 5:6–10). Further, God too has his responsibilities, not in the sense of being accountable to his creatures, but in the sense of meeting the demands of relationship as creator. In other words, God is righteous. He is responsible for his world and for the sin in it – responsible, but not culpable. He would be culpable only if he left the problem of evil* unaddressed. The cross* of Christ is the Christian's guarantee that the universe's Lord is indeed righteous and responsible.

6. Christian ministry too needs to recognize that responsibilities flow from relationships. Preachers and counsellors, for example, ought

to be wary of appeals to abstractions like 'the Christian life'. Christians live their lives in varying networks of obligation and accountability. Some are male. Some are female. Some are mothers. Some are fathers. Some are married. Some are single. Moreover, configurations of responsibility may change over time. Some have aged parents to care for. Some no longer do. Sensitive ministry recognizes these relational facts. Making a relational inventory of a congregation or counsellee, therefore, is an important element in relevant ministry.

Bibliography
H. B. Acton (ed.), *The Philosophy of Punishment* (London, 1969); W. K. Frankena, *Ethics* (Englewood Cliffs, NJ, ²1973); A. F. Holmes, *Ethics: Approaching Moral Decisions* (Downers Grove, IL, and Leicester, 1984); H. Jonas, *The Imperative of Responsibility* (Chicago, 1984); H. Richard Niebuhr, *The Responsible Self* (New York and London, 1963).

G.A.C.

REST, see LEISURE; SABBATH.

RESTITUTION is the usual biblical punishment for theft* or damage to property.* The Heb. verb translated 'make restitution' (*šillēm*) literally means 'make whole, complete'. Thus the thief makes good the loss he has caused the owner.

Typically, double restitution is required. For example, if a thief is caught with a stolen animal, he must pay back double (Ex. 22:4, *cf.* 22:7, 9). In cases of loss caused by carelessness, single restitution is sufficient, *e.g.* damage to crops caused by grazing or fire, or the loss of a borrowed animal (Ex. 22:5–6, 12, 14). If the borrower is not to blame for the loss, no restitution is required (Ex. 22:13, 15).

The norm of double restitution for theft may be doubled when there is an attempt to hide the theft by killing or selling the animal (Ex. 22:1). On the other hand, voluntary confession of one's theft reduces the penalty to restitution of 120% (Lv. 6:5). The reduction in penalty in this case is probably to encourage confession. Zacchaeus, however, promised fourfold restitution to anyone he had cheated (Lk. 19:8).

Convicted thieves who could not make restitution could be sold as slaves to pay off their debt, *i.e.* they would lose their status as freemen (self-employed) and become employees for up to six years or until the year of jubilee* (Ex. 22:2, *cf.* 21:2–6). Imprisonment as a punishment was avoided in OT law, unlike ancient Egypt (Gn. 39 – 40). Nor were fines imposed to enrich the State: restitution on the other hand restores what has been lost to its owner and hopefully encourages neighbourliness between the offender and the offended party.

Bibliography

J. L. Saalschütz, *Das Mosaische Recht* (Berlin, 1853), pp. 554–561; G. J. Wenham, *The Book of Leviticus* (Grand Rapids, 1979), pp. 281–286.

G.J.W.

RESURRECTION as an ethical category is inseparably linked to the resurrection of Christ. In the first instance, our Lord's resurrection was not an individual act, but the introduction of a new world order, the onset of the new creation and the commencement of God's apocalyptic / eschatological design for the human race. By rising victorious from the grave, he triumphed over those powers which dominated the creation since the fall of Adam: sin, death and the law (Rom. 6 – 8; Col. 2:11–15). Having died to the old age, under the sway of 'the god of this age' (2 Cor. 4:4), he entered a new era in which he now lives to God by the power imparted by the Holy Spirit (Rom. 1:4; 2 Cor. 13:4), when he rose from the dead.

It is just the connection of the believer's resurrection with that of Christ which illumines the character of Christian existence as life from the dead. Because believers are in Christ, 'the firstfruits of those who have fallen asleep' (1 Cor. 15:20), the people of God have already tasted the powers of the age to come, so that even now they live in the power of the same Spirit who was instrumental in liberating Jesus from the grip of death.* The hour is not only coming, but now is, when the dead hear the voice of the Son of God and live (Jn. 5:25). Consequently, though there is the prospect that we will rise in the last day, we are alive even as we presently believe in the Christ who brings the victory of life over death (Jn. 11:24–27). The church* is thus the eschatological community, 'the avant-garde of the new creation in a hostile world, creating beachheads in this world of God's dawning new world and yearning for the day of God's visible lordship over his creation, the general resurrection of the dead' (J. C. Beker, *Paul the Apostle*, p. 155). In short, to be a Christian *is* to live the life of the resurrection, in anticipation of the day when God will bring to consummation the good work he has begun in his people (Phil. 1:6).

As the first to rise from the dead, Christ exchanged the 'likeness of sinful flesh' (Rom. 8:3, RSV) for the 'spiritual body' (1 Cor. 15:44–45), a transformation not for his sake only but ultimately for the purpose of bringing his people through the same process (Phil. 3:20–21). Yet even before the believer rises in 'his own turn' (1 Cor. 15:23), he or she has in principle died to sin and risen in newness of life, with the assurance that he or she will one day be united with Jesus in his bodily resurrection (Rom. 6:1–11; Phil. 3:21). Therefore, integral to the Christian's self-identification is his or her death to a former life. Again with Christ as the pattern, a grain of wheat must fall into the earth and die as the precondition of fruit-bearing (Jn. 12:24; 1 Cor. 15:35–50). To 'die' means not to cease to exist, but to undergo a metamorphosis, to put off one's prior form of existence and become something one was not before. Consequently, resurrection means an abandonment of the values and principles of the old creation and an awakening to a new world. It is in this sense that the seed falls into the earth and dies: there is a disintegration of a former mode of being in order that another may begin.

It is precisely the believer's death to sin (Rom. 6:10–11) which provides the fundamental perspective of what it means to live the life of the resurrection. In a number of notable passages, both biblical and extra-biblical, 'sin' assumes the meaning of apostasy (*e.g.* Ps. 51:5; Jn. 8:34; Rom. 2:12; 3:23; 5:12; Heb. 4:15; 10:26; 1 Pet. 2:22; 1 Jn. 3:4–9; Sirach 24:22; Wisdom of Solomon 14:29–31; 15:2). Moreover, Paul's use of the singular noun 'sin' throughout Rom. 5 – 8 intimates that sin is contemplated as a unified and coherent whole; along with death and the law, it stands for the old creation as that entity that is hostile to God and aligned with evil. Therefore, while individual sins occasion the wrath of God (Col. 3:5–7), they are all reducible to an inward disposition of rebellion against God, arising out of the worship of the creature (Rom. 1:18–32).

Since, then, 'sin' is apostasy, Paul can insist in Rom. 6:5–11 that the believer has died to sin, *i.e.* he has renounced his former condition of rebellion: his orientation is now to the new age and its ideals. Whereas previously one's loyalties and sympathies were with the old order, the inward person of the believer, renewed by the Holy Spirit (Rom. 12:2; Eph. 4:23; Col. 1:21–22), is henceforth aligned with the new creation (*e.g.* Rom. 8:5–7; Eph. 2:1–10; 4:22–24; Col. 3:9–10). Thus, those who have been made alive (Eph. 2:1), *i.e.* raised with Christ (Eph. 2:6; Col. 3:1), are now exhorted to set their minds on the things that are above, where the exalted Christ is enthroned, because their lives have become one with Christ's life in God (Col. 3:2–3). Accordingly, they are to 'put on' the virtues* befitting those who have been raised with Christ (Col. 3:12–17), bearing the fruit of the Spirit by whose power Jesus arose from the dead (Gal. 5:16–26).

However, until finally saved by the risen Christ (Rom. 4:25; 5:9–10), Christians, like their Lord, must labour and persevere amidst circumstances which are far from favourable, because 'the process of consummating the work of salvation is more like an obstacle course than a downhill ride to the finish-line. For the destiny of Christians does not go unchallenged in a world opposed to God's purposes. The powers of evil in the form of afflictions and trials threaten continuity in . . . salvation' (Gundry Volf, *Paul and Perseverance*, p. 81). Particularly in Pauline thought, it is the believer's own outer person ('body', 'flesh', 'members') which lends itself to the forces hostile to final salvation. However willing the spirit may be, the flesh* remains weak; and it is the flesh which constantly attempts to draw the renewed person in Christ back to the courses of idolatry and self-love (Rom. 7:14–25; Gal. 5:17).

Therefore, the experience of the resurrection power of Christ at the present time is a very real one (Jn. 11:24–27; Rom. 6:4–11; Phil. 3:10); Christ actually lives in his people (Gal. 2:20). But until his second coming, while old and new creations exist side by side, it is a power which, paradoxically, is complemented by simultaneous weakness (2 Cor. 4:7–12; 12:1–10). As such, the Christian reproduces Jesus' own experience of the Spirit, the one who was weak and then became strong (2 Cor. 13:4). In practical terms, then, to know Christ and the power of his resurrection is to imitate the example set by him, the one who was tested in all points as we are, yet without 'sin' (Heb. 4:15). As he always did what was pleasing to his Father (Ps. 40:8; Mt. 3:17; Jn. 8:29), refusing the solicitations of the devil to forsake his God (Mt. 4:1–11, par.), so his people exhibit the life of the resurrection when they side with the Spirit, determined to press on until they obtain the prize of the upward call of God in Christ Jesus (Phil. 3:12–16).

See also: CHRISTIAN MORAL REASONING;[18] HUMANITY.[4]

Bibliography

J. C. Beker, *Paul the Apostle: The Triumph of God in Life and Thought* (ET, Philadelphia, 1980; Edinburgh, 1989); J. D. G. Dunn, *Jesus and the Spirit* (London, 1975); R. B. Gaffin, *The Centrality of the Resurrection* (Grand Rapids, 1978); D. Garlington, 'Romans 7:24–25 and the Creation Theology of Paul', *TrinJ*, n.s. 11, 1990, pp. 197–235; D. Garlington and D. Macleod, *NDT*, pp. 582–585; J. M. Gundry Volf, *Paul and Perseverance: Staying in and Falling Away* (Louisville, KY, 1990); O. O'Donovan, *Resurrection and Moral Order* (Leicester and Grand Rapids, ²1994).

D.B.G.

RETIREMENT. Against the broad backcloth of human history and geography, retirement is a relatively unusual phenomenon. The idea of spending up to thirty years or so in a state of leisure (which is the common view of retirement) is still novel. As a way of life, it rarely comes up to expectations because people frequently have unrealistic hopes or fears about their own retirement. These usually derive from a false understanding of the place of work* in human life. Too easily, work is identified with, and limited to, paid employment. A better and more biblical definition of work might be 'all forms of purposeful activity'. Seen in that light, work is part of being human, of being a person created in God's image* (see *Laborem Exercens* in Papal Encyclicals*). In this sense a person will not cease from work until death, or a major illness, intervenes. Retirement will then be perceived not as marking the end of work but as a moment of discontinuity, when paid employment is replaced by other forms of activity.

Retirement brings many changes, which can result in anxiety* and stress,* both in anticipation of, and during the process of, retiring – even for those who start off with the positive attitude of Robert Browning's (1812–

89) Rabbi ben Ezra, 'Grow old along with me! The best is yet to be.' Often trauma in retirement is related to the sudden availability of choice in how time is to be used. For many people, retirement is their first opportunity to exercise control over how to spend their time. Steady paid employment, among other things, has provided for many a rigid context and shape to the use of time.

Retirement brings other new challenges. Many people confuse a person's worth with the role which he or she occupies at work. People and their families may thus suffer a diminution in self-esteem* when they sense a loss of status at retirement. Others may miss the responsibility and stimulus of their duties (though yet others may rejoice in release from drudgery). Most people will experience a big drop in income on retirement, and many will miss colleagues or customers at their work-place.

A combination of all or some of these can add up to an experience which has been compared to a bereavement.* Even if it is not felt so strongly, retirement is a major life event of the same order as entry to work, marriage or divorce. When it coincides, as sometimes happens, with moving house, children leaving home, the death or illness of a parent and, in some cases, personal ill-health (which often triggers early retirement), support and counselling are often called for. The provision of such help is a recent development; as has been observed, 'Many years went into preparing us for the world of work but nothing much is done to help us to leave it.'

Retirement has an impact on a person's spouse, whether the spouse goes out to work or not. For many couples, retirement brings stress, initially at least. The closer companionship of retirement creates new, if subtle, aspects in their relationship. Matters of communication, decisions over space in the home and friendships arise in a fresh way. Most couples find the need to reassess their marriages after one partner retires.

Adequate planning for retirement will include careful consideration of what is to replace the things from which satisfaction has been obtained during a working life. Too often, busy executives or those in vocational occupations have been so immersed in their daily work that they have barely had time to give to their families, let alone to activities which they can pursue in later life. Happiness in retirement seems to be related to purposeful activity. Those without it need to find it, and

will require time to reflect on what they wish to achieve. Retirement can be an opportunity to follow ideals and dreams which may have necessarily been subordinated to the practical demands of earning a living. Those who have difficulty in making choices can benefit from counselling or from the many books containing self-assessment exercises.

Much human unhappiness is caused because people are in paid employment which is not suited to their personal value system or motivation. It is common for people to feel at retirement that they have never been able to do anything really worthwhile in life. In many Western countries, there are many opportunities for adult education and training, so that, with good health, what may seem to have been lost opportunities can be redeemed in retirement.

See also: HUMAN DEVELOPMENT.

T.E.C.H.

RETRIBUTION is the doing of justice upon someone who has brought about injustice, usually through injuring another. Retribution is usually thought of in the context of criminal justice,* though it need not be limited to that sphere, as where by civil process someone is found liable to pay damages to someone. The roots of the word imply a 'giving back' or 'repayment'. Within criminal justice, retribution implies that not only is an act punished because it has been classed as a crime* or offence by law,* but the act has an element of wickedness in it.

Retribution may be confused with revenge,* particularly by someone seeking revenge. This is an error. As 'giving back' or 'repayment' implies, properly construed retribution matches the action with the consequences, the 'offence' with the 'punishment'.

The intention to exact retribution forms the connection between an individual and the imposed punishment* or obligation to make reparation. In most cases retribution is only one element or purpose of the actions of the civil authorities which it justifies. Thus in criminal justice, when retribution occurs through punishment, other purposes such as expiation and deterrence (see Deterrence, Non-nuclear*) may be simultaneously served, and the reformation of the offender may also be hoped for. An extreme retributive theory of punishment may, however, rank the purpose of making things unpleasant for an offender so highly as to lose sight of any purpose of reformation.

The doctrine of hell has over the years been attacked as being so unduly retributive as to be incredible (see Heaven and Hell*). This disregards clear teaching in the Bible itself in favour of a sentimental unwillingness to believe in the implacable hatred of evil* for good, and vice versa.

See also: JUSTICE AND PEACE. 3

Bibliography

W. Moberly, *The Ethics of Punishment* (London, 1968); O. O'Donovan, *Measure for Measure: Justice in Punishment and the Sentence of Death* (Bramcote, Nottingham, 1977).

F.L.

REVELATION. Christian theology has traditionally maintained that our knowledge of what is good and our sense of what is right is derived from God (see 1); to know what is good and right is equivalent to discovering God's will. This knowledge can therefore be reliably grounded only in God's self-disclosure or revelation. Even when human reason discovers ethical truths, these are themselves derived from that general revelation to which all humanity has access (*cf*. Rom. 1:18–20).

Although revelation has been regarded as the source of all knowledge of God and his purposes, the concept has been sharply criticized in recent years. Some contemporary theologians question the continuing significance of 'revelation' as a category, and others argue that the traditional concept of revelation does not make sense. Despite this criticism, many continue to maintain that the traditional understanding of revelation remains coherent, and that our knowledge of God depends upon his own unveiling or disclosure.

There is disagreement also about the locus of revelation; where is the self-disclosure of God to be found? The most intensive disclosure of God clearly lies in the person of Jesus* himself. The example and teaching of Jesus put before us a unique revelation of God's will for humanity.

Further, alongside this intensive unveiling of God in Christ, Christians have taken the Scriptures of the OT and NT to be the extensive revelation of God. In the Scriptures are to be found the moral precepts of Israel in the OT,

and the ethical vision of the kingdom of God* in the NT, together with the scriptural evaluation of humanity which is the presupposition of Christian pastoral practice.

The Roman Catholic and Orthodox traditions (see Roman Catholic Moral Theology;* Orthodox Ethics*) have understood the teaching of the church to be a continuing unfolding of this initial scriptural revelation. The churches of the Reformation (see Calvinistic Ethics;* Lutheran Ethics*), though, take the Scriptures to be supremely authoritative because they contain the once-for-all revelation of God's will for his people. For this reason they regard the Scriptures as a yardstick against which the teaching and life of the contemporary church and its members may be encouraged, criticized and reformed.

The contrast between revelation in words or propositions (such as the Bible may contain), and in person or event (as in the coming of Christ), has been the centre of one of the main debates over revelation in the 20th century. The Bible itself suggests that the disclosure of truths about God is to be found both in the words of Scripture (2 Tim. 3:16), and in the persons and events to which they bear witness (Jn. 5:39).

Biblical scholarship since the late 18th century has been concerned to uncover as much as possible about the historical circumstances of the Bible and its world. This has led to a renewed emphasis on the notion of progressive revelation, the idea that God's revelation of his purposes may be more complete and substantial at a later stage of the scriptural record than at an earlier one.

The self-disclosure of God in Scripture means, then, that the Scriptures contain guidance on individual moral questions and on matters of interpersonal relations (2 Tim. 3:16–17). The fact that this revelation comes to us through a particular culture and society means that in seeking guidance from Scripture on ethical and pastoral matters we must pay attention to the customs and culture of the biblical milieu. So, for instance, in interpreting what the NT has to say on divorce, we will need to know what concept of marriage was current in that time and culture if we are to avoid misunderstanding its message.

In interpreting the revelation of God's will in the OT, a theological distinction may have to be borne in mind between the full revelation of God's will in Christ and the preliminary revelation which prepared for and preceded it. So, while the apparent endorsement of ruthless warfare (see Holy War*) which we find in the opening books of the Bible may represent a revelation of God's will in the tribal society of early Israel, it will not be the final and normative revealing of his will as we find it in Christ.

The revelation we possess in Scripture undoubtedly calls for interpretation, but all distinctively Christian ethical thought and pastoral reflection must relate itself to the revelation of the divine will in Scripture.

Bibliography

G. C. Berkouwer, *General Revelation* (Grand Rapids, 1955); J. D. G. Dunn, *The Living Word* (London, 1987); P. Helm, *The Divine Revelation* (Westchester, IL, and London, 1982); J. I. Packer, 'Infallible Scripture and the Role of Hermeneutics', in D. A. Carson and J. A. Woodbridge (eds.), *Scripture and Truth* (Grand Rapids and Leicester, 1983).

W.A.S.

REVENGE is an inflamed and distorted desire that a wrong shall be punished. The putting right of the injury that constitutes the wrong is normally subordinated to the desire to inflict pain and suffering on the malefactor. The 'injury' may be real or imagined, and is usually suffered by the person seeking revenge, by his or her blood relative, or by some close associate. It may therefore be distinguished from retribution* and from vengeance. In revenge, the 'wronged party' often seeks personally to inflict what is conceived of as the 'punishment', and usually desires to be the instrument through which the process that leads to punishment is invoked. The early Jewish institution of 'the avenger of blood' (Dt. 19:4–13) is an instance where such a connection was lawful, but in modern societies an injured person 'taking the law into his own hands' is usually frowned on, while at the same time some mitigation of sentence may be justified in such a case.

It is virtually axiomatic that malice and passion invest revenge. In most cases there is a desire that the offender shall be made to suffer above and beyond the requirements of justice. Under such circumstances dispassionate inquiry into what actually is the case, or what actually happened, or whether there are two sides to the question, can become submerged and justice made secondary to the assuaging of outraged feelings by the person seeking revenge.

Such over-reaction makes for injustice rather than justice, but fallen human nature is prone to it. What is required is some standard to control the limits of acceptable 'revenge'. Therefore Dt. 19:21, while excluding pity for a false witness, also sets limits to the punishment: 'life for life, eye for eye, tooth for tooth, hand for hand, foot for foot'. This language was later interpreted by the rabbis and by Christian thinking as general indicators of the limits of appropriate punishment, rather than as its requirements. In the absolute, vengeance is a matter for God (Rom. 12:19). Within civil society it is a matter for the civil authority (*cf.* Criminal Justice*).

Unfettered 'revenge' is a perversion of the proper feeling that 'justice shall be done'. At its worst it can produce a society in which considerations of 'honour' foment and sustain a blood-feud. Even short of that stage, a desire to secure revenge inhibits Christian charity and makes impossible the 'turning of the other cheek' (*cf.* Mt. 5:38–48; Lk. 6:27–36).

F.L.

REVOLUTION, see Just-War Theory; Rebellion.

REWARD. Foundational to the biblical concept of reward is the *relationship* which humankind sustains to God. This is depicted variously as: 1. creator and image-bearer; 2. husband and wife or parent and child; 3. master and servant; and 4. employer and employee. The actual terminology of reward draws mostly from the last mentioned and connotes a kind of transaction. Yet the most prominent usages of 'reward' in the Bible occur in ethical rather than in commercial contexts. 'One reason for this is that the biblical writers viewed human life itself as inherently ethical; i.e., they saw an intrinsic correspondence between actions and their consequences, whether good or evil' (T. B. Dozeman, 'Reward', in *ISBE* 4, ²1988, p. 179).

However, even in the ethical contexts it is important that the imagery of transaction be balanced with the other pictures of the relation between God and his people. Particularly in light of the family and the master / servant metaphors, good gifts or 'rewards' bestowed by God are not to be conceived of as merited or earned, strictly speaking, whereby God is placed in debt. They are, rather, the outgrowth of God's love and a desire to sustain the household ties which bind him and his people together. It is true that according to the 'Deuteronomic theology' blessing and prosperity were promised as the reward of Israel's obedience (*e.g.* Lv. 26; Dt. 28). Nevertheless, life and nationhood were bestowed on Israel as the result of God's sovereign and gracious election; therefore, Israel's doing of the law (Lv. 18:5) is to be construed as perseverance, not achievement. It was perseverance* within a love relationship which would ensure continued life in the land under the blessing of God.

The most explicit statements of Jesus about reward are set within the master / servant relationship. This master / servant context underscores the fact that the labourer serves his master not for the sake of gain, but rather in order to please him (*cf.* 2 Tim. 2:4). The servant (slave) is the property of his Lord, and everything entrusted to him is ultimately the Lord's. It is, therefore, the servant's duty to be faithful to his wishes, however strange or incomprehensible they may seem. This means that the servant's reward is a token of the kindness of a sensitive master, who not only provides for the basic needs of those under him, but also wishes to encourage them in his service (*cf.* Mt. 20:1–16).

From one point of view, the reward of all Christians is the same, *i.e.* the eschatological kingdom of God* (*e.g.* Mt. 25:34). Expressed otherwise, the reward of the servants of God is final salvation (1 Pet. 1:9); the glory of the new heavens and new earth (Is. 65:17; Heb. 2:5–9; 2 Pet. 3:13; Rev. 21:1), commensurate with the revelation of the sons of God (Rom. 8:18–25); eternal life (Jn. 6:40; Gal. 6:8; Jas. 1:12); the crown of righteousness (2 Tim. 4:8); the sabbath rest (Heb. 4:1, 9); the inheritance of the promises (Heb. 6:10–12); the heavenly city of God (Heb. 11:10, 14–16; Rev. 21:1–4).

From a different perspective, however, we are led to believe that there is not to be a uniformity among Christians as regards the life of the age to come. In the words of Rev. 14:13, 'their deeds will follow them'. The very conversation between Jesus and Peter which occasioned the parable of the workers in the vineyard implies that the immediate disciples of Jesus are to assume a position of unique privilege, *i.e.* judging the twelve tribes of Israel (Mt. 19:28; Lk. 22:30). Jesus' parable of the talents (Mt. 25:14–30; Lk. 19:11–27) likewise presupposes that even among the faithful servants of God different levels of trust and consequent reward are to be reckoned with. Various degrees of prominence in the kingdom are also implied by Mt. 5:19; 20:26–27; Mk. 9:33–37; 10:35–45; 1 Cor. 3:12–15.

In the light of the connection between the servanthood of Christ and the aspirations of his disciples for the high places in the kingdom (Mk. 10:35–45; Lk. 22:28–30), it would seem to follow that one's ultimate standing in the eschatological kingdom hinges particularly on one's conformity to Christ in his humility* and suffering.* Because he was crucified 'outside the camp' (Heb. 13:13) as an apostate from God's covenant (Mt. 11:19 = Dt. 21:20), greatness in the kingdom entails a willingness to be identified with Jesus as the rejected one. As such, reward, in the teaching of Jesus, stands over against the mentality that rank is to be accorded to those who have distinguished themselves by outstanding fidelity to Israel or the traditions of specific groups within Israel, especially Pharisaic tradition (*e.g.* Mt. 6:1–18; Mk. 7:1–13). Thus, a paradox emerges from the pages of the Gospels: the degree of ultimate glory corresponds to the degree of servanthood, as evidenced by humility, obscurity and willingness to be despised and rejected by humankind.

It is particularly in view of suffering that reward is held before the Christian as an incentive to perseverance (Mt. 5:12) and unflagging zeal for Christ. In the parables of the second coming (Mt. 24:45 – 25:30), it is not only the dread of punishment but the prospect of hearing the master say, 'Well done, good and faithful servant' (Mt. 25:21, 23), which is meant to spur the servant on to vigilance and hard work until the end. Paul can exhort slaves to continue their present unrewarding service of their earthly masters, because they serve the Lord himself, and their reward will eventually come from him (Col. 3:22–25). Similarly, the epistle to the Hebrews reminds its jaded and discouraged readers that God is the rewarder of those who diligently seek him (Heb. 11:6). The reward is nothing less than the world to come (2:5–9), which has now been subjected to Christ. It is in Hebrews particularly that reward, perseverance and Christology are linked. That is to say, only in Christ can the latter-day people of God receive the reward held before Israel in the wilderness, *i.e.* of inheriting the promised land and entering the sabbath rest. Christians, therefore, are like

Christ, who himself has received the inheritance / reward of the sabbath rest (Heb. 1:3b), a name (1:4), a people (2:10–13), and the age to come (2:5–9), as a result of his endurance of suffering (2:9–10, 17–18; 4:15; 5:7–10).

To summarize, the people of God may anticipate a reward for their faithfulness. This reward is a recompense for labour and sacrifice, but it is not a 'wage' in the strict sense of the term: as the owner of his servants, God is not obligated to 'repay' anything (Lk. 17:7–10; 1 Cor. 9:18). For this reason, reward is never regarded as the goal of Christian behaviour, so that one serves for the sake of gain. In a very real sense, the reward of the labourer is his or her continued devotion to the affairs of his or her Lord.

Generally speaking, the believer's reward is the glory of the eschatological kingdom of God, which is not in any sense dependent on the length of the believer's service. At the same time, among those who inherit the kingdom there are to be various degrees of recognition, corresponding to each believer's conformity to the servanthood of Christ.

Bibliography

C. Blomberg, 'Degrees of Reward in the Kingdom of Heaven?' *JETS* 35, 1992, pp. 159–172; G. Bornkamm, 'Der Lohngedanke im Neuen Testament', in *Studien zu Antike und Christentum. Gesammelte Aufsätze 2,* (Münich, 1963), pp. 69–92; P. C. Böttger *et al., NIDNTT* 3, pp. 134–145; L. Morris, *The Biblical Doctrine of Judgment* (Grand Rapids and London, 1960); H. Preisker and E. Würthwein, *TDNT* 4, pp. 695–728; G. de Reu, 'The Concept of Reward in the Teaching of Jesus', *NovT* 8, 1966, pp. 202–222; K. Seybold, *TDOT* 3, pp. 23–33.

D.B.G.

RIGHT AND WRONG, see CHRISTIAN MORAL REASONING. [18]

RIGHTEOUSNESS. The biblical idea of righteousness is rooted in creation.* In Eden a family bond (or covenant*) was established between the creator and his creatures. Genesis 1 and 2 record God's pledge to bless, multiply and sustain the human beings made to hold fellowship with him and be the recipient of his fatherly care. It is loyalty to this relationship of mutual love (see [2]) and faithfulness which is called 'righteousness'. The Sinai covenant, with whose inception the terminology of righteousness becomes especially prominent, continues the creation emphasis on a relationship between God and his people, the outstanding metaphors for which are husband / wife and parent / child. It is within this family unit that the law* of God forms the 'house rules', the norm according to which the behaviour of Israel is to be measured. The adjective 'righteous' henceforth becomes the standard term to designate those who remain loyal to Yahweh's covenant and endeavour to do his will: it is they who love God and their neighbour as themselves (Dt. 6:5; Lv. 19:18; Mt. 22:37–40).

The NT inherits this conception of righteousness, but with a distinctively Christological emphasis. Romans 3:21 – 8:39 elaborates that God's justifying act has restored those 'in Christ' to their obligatory submission to the creator. But it is specifically Christ, the image of the invisible God (Col. 1:15) and God's new beginning (Rom. 5:12–19), who is to be obeyed (Phil. 2:12–13), because he himself was obedient to the Father (Phil. 2:8). Consequently, having put on Christ, it is to his image that believers are being conformed (Rom. 8:29; 13:14; Gal. 3:27; Eph. 4:24; Col. 3:10); it is to him they render the obedience of faith (Rom. 1:5; 16:26). Whereas once they were the slaves of sin (Jn. 8:34; Rom. 5:6–10; 6:17, 20–21; Eph. 2:1–3; Col. 3:5–7), they are now those in whose hearts the peace of Christ reigns (Col. 3:12–17). In short, it is 'in Christ' that they have become the righteousness of God (Rom. 5:16–19; 2 Cor. 5:21). Righteousness, then, entails the acceptance of one's identity as the image of God* and the consequent obligation of creaturely (covenantal) service, made possible by the gift of God's own righteousness in Christ (Rom. 1:17; 3:21–26; 5:17; 6:23).

In sum, righteousness is the Bible's compendious way of designating loyalty to a family relationship – the covenant – and the resultant behaviour appropriate to that relationship. Accordingly, righteousness has both a personal and an ethical dimension: it is love of family members, accompanied by conformity to a set of 'house rules' which govern the everyday life of the family. In NT terms, righteousness is specifically a commitment to Christ and his people, resulting in a determination to please both. Righteousness is thus the sum and substance of the Christian ethic and of Christian character.

In its distinctively biblical sense, righteousness has primary reference to the way in which Christians relate to one another in the common body of Christ, under his lordship and governed by his law (Gal. 6:2; 1 Cor. 9:21). The will of Christ for this new, righteous humanity is both concrete and practical. Righteousness regulates the relationships of husband and wife (Eph. 5:21–33; Col. 3:18–19), parent and child (Eph. 6:1–4; Col. 3:20–21), and master and servant (Eph. 6:5–9; Col. 3:22–24); it prohibits falsehood (Eph. 4:25), unjustified anger (Eph. 4:26–27), theft (Eph. 4:28), evil talk (Eph. 4:29), bitterness, malice and misrepresentation of others (Eph. 4:31); it must eventuate in kindness and forgiveness, modelled on the divine pattern (Eph. 4:32); and it can do none other than maintain the unity of the Spirit in the bond of peace (Eph. 4:3–16), because the renewed human spirit is clothed with love, meekness, forbearance and patience – the fruit of the Spirit (Gal. 5:22–24; Eph. 4:2–3).

It is love, most conspicuously, which binds all acts of righteousness together in perfect harmony (Col. 3:14) and thus distinguishes the people of Christ as a community of love, forgiveness and mutual service (Mt. 18:21–22; Jn. 13:12–17, 34–35; Eph. 4:2; 5:2; Col. 3:12–15; 1 Pet. 1:22). With Jesus as its Lord and example (Jn. 13:12–17), the church is depicted as the embodiment of ideal humanity, *i.e.* a family marked by love, peace and harmony. Because Christ has restored his people to their proper role as truly human beings, they must be servants one of another (Jn. 13:12–17; Gal. 5:13), in conformity to him who trod the path of sacrifice and self-denial.

Because righteousness and love are so closely allied, the restoration of offending Christians in 'a spirit of gentleness' occupies a place of particular importance (2 Cor. 2:5–11; Gal. 6:1–5; Eph. 4:31–32). Over against the circumcision party, whose 'own righteousness' (Rom. 10:3; Phil. 3:9) engendered an attitude of biting and devouring, self-conceit, envy and provocation of others (Gal. 5:15, 26), Paul required that his converts walk by the Spirit (Rom. 8:5–17; Gal. 5:25) and bear the fruit of the Spirit (Gal. 5:22–24) – pre-eminently love and its attendant attitudes (Gal. 5:13–14, 22–23). It is none other than love which fulfils the law (Rom. 13:8–10; Gal. 5:14), because the law was never intended to articulate a purely idealistic standard of behaviour apart from the well-being of those under it; rather,

its design was to create and sustain a community rooted and grounded in love (Eph. 3:17). Thus, the 'law of Christ' achieves its reason for existence when the people of God 'bear one another's burdens' (Gal. 6:2); and Paul is understandably anxious that 'righteous indignation' over sin be tempered by the realism of a still vulnerable human nature.

It is to the 'spiritual', those made 'righteous' through the work of Christ (Rom. 3:21 – 8:39; 1 Cor. 6:11; Gal. 3–4; Phil. 3:8–9; Tit. 3:5–7) who await 'the righteousness for which we hope' (Gal. 5:5), that Paul assigns the task of restoration through burden-bearing (Gal. 6:1–5). The 'burdens' (Gal. 6:2) are specifically the sin-burdens of the one who has fallen. These are to be borne in at least two ways: 1. by involving oneself in the difficulties – the 'burdens' – created by the sin; 2. by forbearing the person himself or herself, with the assurance that he or she is not rejected, either by Christ or by his body (2 Cor. 2:5–11).

The treatment of those who sin embodies the very genius of righteousness, inasmuch as it represents love going into action, the commitment of the members of Christ's family to one another, the fruit of the Spirit borne by those against whom there is no law (Gal. 5:23). To bear one another's burdens is to reflect God's own parental care (1 Pet. 5:7) as one fulfils 'the law of Christ', his demand for righteous living within the new covenant. In brief, righteousness *is* love, and love *is* righteousness.

Significantly, it is righteousness as the love and service of others which permits an application of the concept beyond the covenant community. Rather than growing weary in 'well-doing', Christians are, as opportunity is granted, to do 'good to *all people*' (Gal. 6:9–10). The terms 'well-doing' and 'good' in Paul's letters have specific reference to the creation ideal of service of God (Rom. 2:7, 10; 7:13–20; 15:2; 16:19). Thus, as he occupies a place in society, the believer is to extend the love of God to *all* who bear his image. 'The universal character of God's redemption corresponds to the universality of Christian social and ethical responsibility. If God's redemption in Christ is universal, the Christian community is obliged to disregard all ethnic, national, cultural, social, sexual and even religious distinctions within the human community. Since before God there is no partiality, there cannot be partiality in the Christian's attitude toward his fellow man' (H. D. Betz, *Galatians*, Philadelphia, 1979, p. 311).

It is this evangelistic and humanitarian purpose which compels the church to be salt and light to the present generation (Mt. 5:13–16; Phil. 2:14–16), blameless before a watching world (1 Cor. 6:9–11; Eph. 4:17–24; 5:3–20; Phil. 2:4; Jas. 1:26–27; 1 Pet. 1:13–21; 2:11–25), caring for the destitute (1 Tim. 5:3–8; Jas. 1:27), submissive to civil authority (Rom. 13:1–7; 1 Pet. 2:17), and prayerful for those in positions of responsibility (1 Tim. 2:1–4), that humanity outside of Christ may come to a knowledge of the truth (1 Tim. 2:4–6). With this great vision before him or her, the believer strives to maintain a conscience* devoid of offence before God and others (Acts 24:16), anticipating the time when justice rolls down like waters, and righteousness like an ever-flowing stream (Am. 5:24; Gal. 5:5), when the earth is filled with the knowledge of the Lord as the waters cover the sea (Is. 11:9).

Bibliography

V. P. Furnish, *Theology and Ethics in Paul* (Nashville, TN, 1968); D. B. Garlington, 'The Obedience of Faith in the Letter to the Romans': part 1 in *WTJ* 52, 1990, pp. 201–224; part 2 in *WTJ* 53, 1991, pp. 47–72; part 3 in *WTJ* 55, 1993, pp. 281–297; idem, 'Burden Bearing: The Recovery of Offending Christians (Galatians 6:1–5)', *TrinJ*, n.s. 12, 1991, pp. 151–183; E. Käsemann, '"The Righteousness of God" in Paul', in *New Testament Questions of Today* (ET, Philadelphia and London, 1969), pp. 168–182; B. Przybylski, *Righteousness in Matthew and His World of Thought* (Cambridge, 1980); J. Reumann, *Righteousness in the New Testament* (Philadelphia, 1982); J. A. Ziesler, *The Meaning of Righteousness in Paul: A Linguistic and Theological Enquiry* (Cambridge, 1972).

D.B.G.

RIGHTS, see NATURAL RIGHTS; RIGHTS, ANIMAL; RIGHTS, HUMAN.

RIGHTS, ANIMAL. The traditional concern for animal welfare has largely been superseded by a debate about 'animal rights'. Do animals have rights? What is meant by 'rights'? On what basis are rights defined? What kinds of duties do human beings have towards animals?

From those who in conscience are vegetarian or vegan, or who oppose factory farming or who sabotage hunts, to those who campaign for the abolition of animal acts in circuses, and the extremists who fire-bomb laboratories where animal experimentation and vivisection are carried out, the debate is now conducted on the premise that animals have rights which are not being respected and safeguarded.

For a long period of Christian history, the doctrine that human beings are made in the image of God,* and are 'to subdue' the earth and have dominion over it (Gn. 1:28), was understood to mean that animals and plants are there simply for the benefit of human beings. Thomas Aquinas,* for example, replied to objections against killing animals that 'there is no sin in using a thing for the purpose for which it is'. Plants, he argued, are there for animals, and animals for human beings to use for food. In 1967, the American historian Lynn White Jr blamed the worsening ecological crisis on 'the Christian axiom that nature has no reason for existence save to serve man' (an axiom which, we may judge, does not do justice to the biblical view that the natural order has value in itself because God created it). White described Western medieval Christianity as 'the most anthropocentric religion the world has ever seen'. None the less, he pointed to Francis of Assisi* as a Christian radical who tried to substitute the idea of the equality of all creatures, and he urged that St Francis be adopted as the patron saint of ecology, a suggestion adopted by the Pope in 1980. The historian Keith Thomas (1933–) illustrates from popular attitudes in the 16th century how human relations with domestic and other animals were often closer than official religion implied. Furthermore, the biblical traditions were much broader than the medieval interpretation of Genesis might indicate. Humane treatment of animals is illustrated in many parts of the OT. All animals are protected in the story of the ark (Gn. 6 – 8). God requires 'an accounting' for every animal that is killed for food, for all life belongs to him (Gn. 9:5). The Deuteronomic codes provide protection for straying oxen, sheep and asses (Dt. 22:1–4), as well as young birds in the nest (Dt. 22:6–7). The ox is not to be muzzled when it treads out grain (Dt. 25:4). The ox and the ass are to rest along with human beings on the sabbath (Ex. 20:10). The psalmist records God's provision of food and shelter for animals (Ps. 104), and the prophets look forward to a time when animals and human beings are together in a kingdom of peace (Is. 11:6–9). Hosea 2:18 implies that animals are part of God's covenant. The righteous man 'cares for the needs of his beast' (Pr. 12:10). The NT picks up some of these themes (Mt. 12:9–13; 1 Cor. 9:9–10), and adds to them God's provision for the birds of the air (Mt. 6:26) and his concern even for a sparrow (Mt. 10:29–31).

Clearly, therefore, the Bible cannot be used to support the case that human beings have no obligations towards animals. Indeed, the fact that Gn. 1 refers to God's creation of animals of all kinds, as well as of humans, shows that all have a place in God's interest and purpose, and therefore merit human respect and care. It is precisely because God is creator of all and because human beings are made in God's image that we should understand our 'dominion' in terms of stewardship,* creative care and responsibility, coupled with the accountability to God that stewardship implies, rather than exploitation and selfish use. There is a Christian duty towards the welfare of animals, whose life is God's gift and God's concern.

Since Jeremy Bentham,* however, the debate has more often been couched in terms of 'animal rights'. In 1789, he wrote: 'The day *may* come when the rest of the animal creation may acquire those rights which never could have been withholden from them but by the hand of tyranny' (*Introduction to the Principles of Morals and Legislation*, ch. 18, sec. 1). Bentham argued that it is the capacity for suffering which confers interests on a being, and entitles that being to equal consideration. Sentience then becomes the only defensible boundary of concern for the interests of others. This debate has gathered momentum since the 1970s. Contemporary utilitarian philosophers, such as Peter Singer (1946–), have taken Bentham's line to argue that the principle of equal consideration of interests, which gives him his moral basis for judging relationships between human beings, applies equally to non-human animals, beings which are as capable as humans of feeling pain. Just as racists violate the principle of equality by giving priority to the interests of members of their own race, so human 'speciesists' (such as Christians, whom Singer criticizes) 'do not accept that pain is as bad when it is felt by pigs or mice as when it is felt by humans' (*Practical Ethics*, p. 51). Others (*e.g.* T. Regan) regard 'being the subject of a life' as the appropriate basis of animal 'rights'.

Christians can agree with Singer and other animal-rights advocates that animals should not be caused pain without adequate reason (though of course the moral criteria for defining 'adequate' are disputed). This is partly because they are creatures for which God cares, and partly because, since humans are made in God's image, cruelty of any kind is also dehumanizing to persons. But the biblical perspectives, while requiring of us a concern for animal welfare, do display an unrepentant 'speciesism' in the sense that it is the human species alone which is said to be made in the image of God. However, they also demonstrate that human beings have an obligation before God for the care of, and a responsible attitude towards, all other living creatures. Some believe that such an obligation requires the abandonment of any use of animals for food, for sport or for pleasure, while others accept that such uses of animals can be consistent with respect for their status as creatures of God, provided that farming methods and slaughter for food are humane, and that play (*e.g.* horse-riding) and pleasure (*e.g.* keeping pets) do not cause animals pain or harm. Hard decisions need to be taken over some questions of animal population and pest control. Many would reject all vivisection (surgery on living animals) and any use of animals for experimentation, on the grounds that the medical benefits are meagre and that it dehumanizes the practitioners and denies the fundamental value of animals. Others do allow for some vivisection, testing of medication, and physiological animal research under strict conditions, arguing that animal suffering is minimal, and that these practices can be a responsible use of animals which can yield beneficial medical or veterinary knowledge unobtainable in any other way. Most argue against any experimental use of animals merely for testing cosmetics or developing non-essential goods.

It is much less clear whether Christian belief in animals' createdness, or humans' stewardly responsibilities towards the animal kingdom, should appropriately be discussed in the language of 'animal *rights*'. This is still a subject of considerable debate (*cf.* A. Linzey and T. Regan, *Animals and Christianity*; R. Griffiths, *The Human Use of Animals*).

Bibliography

S. R. Clark, *The Moral Status of Animals* (Oxford, 1977); R. Griffiths, *The Human Use of Animals* (Bramcote, Nottingham, 1982); A. Linzey and T. Regan (eds.), *Animals and*

Christianity (New York, 1988; London, 1989); M. Midgley, *Animals and Why They Matter* (Harmondsworth, 1983); P. Singer, *Practical Ethics* (Cambridge, 1979); K. Thomas, *Man and the Natural World* (Harmondsworth, 1983).

D.J.A.

RIGHTS, HUMAN. The term 'rights' is used in at least three ways and these ways are often confused with one another. The most basic use refers to 'legal rights', which are political arrangements in which certain interests, goods or choices are given guaranteed legal protection. A person has a right to free speech, or to walk on the street. In this sense any form of legal guarantee, or any positive form of legal status, may be regarded as a right.

The other uses of 'rights' usually refer to purported justifications for legal rights. One set of uses refers to general claims based variously on views of natural law,* justice or divine grace. If we say that tyranny violates rights, we are using the term in this sense. Another set of justifications treats rights as pre-legal moral entitlements. An example of this would be medical ethics predicated on the view that patients have an inherent right to veto decisions concerning their treatment. This latter use of rights is referred to as 'moral rights', ' natural rights',* 'inherent rights' or, in continental jurisprudence, 'subjective rights'.

Each of these three senses of rights can also include 'human rights'. A human right is usually held to be a right, legal or moral, which is possessed, or ought to be possessed, by all human beings or, at least, all human beings within a particular legal jurisdiction. The key feature is universality. People who believe in moral rights generally regard them as a type of human rights.

The more general justifications of legal rights often amount to little more than the claim that there are standards for the treatment of human beings which are higher than, and which properly shape, the content of human legislation. Many commentators point to Sophocles' formulation of Antigone's declaration to Creon that even he, a king, could not overcome 'God's eternal unwrit laws' as an early (*c.* 422 BC) example of such a 'right'. In this broad sense rights are certainly biblically rooted. God's demands for justice and peace, the stress on human beings as the *imago Dei* (see Image of God*), the call to love our neighbours as ourselves, the Ten Commandments, indeed the very idea of revealed law, can all be regarded as foundations for rights. However, the generality of these conceptions weakens their relation to rights, and they are more fruitfully discussed under separate headings such as 'natural law' or 'justice'.

Ethical reflection

The two aspects of rights which are of most direct concern for Christian ethical reflection are the notion of moral rights and the question of legally protected human rights.

There is growing agreement that the view of personal entitlement implied by the notions of moral, innate or natural rights (as distinct from natural law or duty) was not present in the ancient world, including the biblical world. It first developed in medieval canon law and was articulated philosophically by William of Ockham (1280/85–1349). Its influence spread, especially in the 17th century in the work of figures such as Hugo Grotius* and John Locke (1632–1704). The theory of natural right, particularly as embodied in a view of social contract,* became the focus of political reflection. The 18th-century declarations of rights, especially in France and the new world, were shaped by these views of natural right and the 'rights of man'. It was a major feature of Immanuel Kant's* thought and is a dominant theme in contemporary liberal legal and political thought, with noted exponents such as H. L. A. Hart (1907–92; see Devlin–Hart Debate*) and Ronald Dworkin (1931–).

Such theories postulate moral rights as virtually inviolate spheres of personal autonomy* and authority.* Consequently they emphasize individual freedom* and choice* and place great stress on the virtue of toleration.* They are now important in wider ethical discussion, especially in medical and sexual ethics. In these fields individual choice is often given privileged status and there is strong disapproval of externally imposed constraints. Such theories have also gained influence in Christian circles: this may be because they are incorrectly assumed to have a necessary connection with the widely approved stress on human rights in law.

Legal rights, human or otherwise, are complex things which have been subjected to bewildering detailed analysis in jurisprudence. One of the most influential classifications is that proposed by W. N. Hohfeld (1879–1918) who distinguished: 1. 'privileges' or 'liberties', such as the right one has to defend one's property; 2. 'claim rights', such as the right not to have something stolen; 3. 'powers', such as the right to sell or give property to another; and 4. 'immunities', such as a right not to be expropriated. These rights are inherent features of legal systems. Any system of laws, including biblical law, necessarily confers these types of rights on somebody and something.

The question whether the types of legal rights elaborated in the Pentateuch are human rights is debatable. One can point to the right of field workers to eat while harvesting (Dt. 23:25), limitations on slavery (Ex. 21:2; Lv. 25:10, 39–41), protection of female slaves (Ex. 21:7–11), provisions for the equitable distribution of land (Nu. 33:54; Lv. 25:14–18, 25–34), and the general theme of the subordination of rulers to law (1 Sa. 22:17; 2 Sa. 11 – 12). These were rights held generally by the Israelites but not equally applicable to women or to aliens. However, there are indications that the eventual goal was to universalize God's law so that it would *become* clearly applicable to all humans, a theme developed in the NT. Certainly they were akin to legal human rights.

Protection

One of the major current and effective ways of trying to protect human rights in law is by means of constitutional charters or bills of rights. As the constitution is law that binds the government itself, this gives rights a solid basis. Indeed this stress on charters has become so common that it is sometimes equated with protection of human rights. This would be a mistake, since there are a variety of possible means to give legal protection to human life and each can be regarded as a type of human-rights law. Decentralization of power, representative government, separation of governmental powers between executive, legislative and judicial functions, ombudsmen, common-law provisions, international treaties and other political mechanisms can stand alongside of, or substitute for, bills of rights as means of legal protection.

When understood in this way, the protection of human rights in the modern world draws on a wide variety of influences and has a long history. The *Magna Carta* (1215) stands in this tradition, not because it tried to guarantee rights to the whole population (which it did not), but because it was a step in limiting the power of the king. Parallel provisions occurred

at this time in other parts of Europe, notably León and Hungary. Similarly the Bill of Rights (1689) gave protection not by guaranteeing rights to the population but by elevating Parliament over the Crown while, in turn, Parliament, and therefore the Crown, were beholden to the population by election. The first instance of a constitution naming and protecting certain individual human rights seems to have been the 1776 Virginia declaration of rights. Similar provisions were enacted by other N. American States and, though only in the form of a manifesto, by the French National Assembly in 1789. The first ten amendments to the US Constitution (the 'Bill of Rights') and the French Constitution of 1791 were the first national human-rights charters. Their example was followed throughout Europe in the 19th century, and throughout the world in the 20th century.

Another major feature of modern human-rights protection is international law. The operative principle here is that States commit themselves by treaty to treat their own citizens in a protective way. The legal power of the treaty helps to shape domestic law, and there is the possibility of international review and repercussions if a State violates its commitment.

The earliest European examples of such arrangements are probably the post-Reformation treaties that guaranteed religious freedom to minority religious groups. Grotius and Emerich de Vattel (1714–67), the principal theorists of international law, both made provision for international protection of rights. This helped shape the 19th-century conventions on slavery, the turn-of-the-century Hague and Geneva Conventions on conduct during warfare, the labour standards formulated by the International Labour Organization (1919), and the largely impotent charter of the post-First World War League of Nations.

In the Second World War, the protection of human rights became a rallying point for the Allied powers and, hence, became a key feature in the formation of the United Nations. This produced the 1948 Universal Declaration of Human Rights and Fundamental Freedoms, which in turn acquired legal status in the form of the International Covenant on Economic, Social and Cultural Rights (1966) and International Covenant on Civil and Political Rights (1966). Subsequently, there have been regional treaties along similar lines. These are the European Convention for the Protection of Human Rights and Fundamental Freedoms (1950), the American Convention on Human Rights (1969), and the African Convention on Human and Peoples' Rights (1981). At present the European system is the most developed and active.

The rights which are protected by international law, by charters and by other means, include a group of what are often called 'civil and political', 'freedom', or 'negative' rights. These typically involve freedom from discrimination;* rights to life, liberty and security of the person; freedom from torture* or cruel punishment; the right to legal personality and a fair trial; freedom of movement and residence; the right to asylum, to a nationality, to marry and found a family, to property; freedom of religion, thought, conscience, opinion and expression; the right to take part in the government of one's country and to equal access to public services. The rights on this list are supported by most human-rights advocates.

Another group of rights includes what are called 'economic, social and cultural' or, sometimes, 'positive' rights. These include the right to social security; the right to work and to rest; the right to a standard of living adequate for health and well-being; the right to education, and the right to participate in the cultural life of the community. This second group of rights has drawn criticism on the grounds that it does not limit government actions but calls for specific government achievements. Such achievement could, in principle, not be possible, and therefore not universal, or else its pursuit could involve trespasses against 'negative' rights.

Christian attitudes

Christian attitudes towards human rights have usually been positive, though this may be because they are vague about what could be meant by such rights. In the case of theories of moral rights some criticism is called for, since these theories seem to place not a divine call but a purported human attribute, sometimes even human autonomy, as an important feature of, and even as the very foundation of, moral reflection. Furthermore, such rights stress what people should have *done to* them rather than what they should *do*. Hence a stress on moral rights tends to put human self-interest at the centre of ethics. This, in turn, neglects the fact that, *contra* Cain, we are called by God to be our 'brother's keeper'. In

particular, it loses the biblical call to surrender ourselves and our 'rights' as exemplified by Jesus, who, 'being in very nature God, did not consider equality with God something to be grasped, but made himself nothing, taking the very nature of a servant' (Phil. 2:6–7). Even so, some Christians, notably Jacques Maritain (1882–1973) and, currently, John Finnis (1940–), have developed a persuasive case for moral rights by weaving a close relation between natural law and natural right.

Except for an occasional reiteration of concerns about 'social' rights, there has been comparatively little dispute among Christians over legal rights. Occasionally a question is raised about the propriety of humans asserting rights, but, while we should be careful about inflated claims, this criticism is more properly directed toward the issue of moral rights. The most common position is that, as human beings are made in God's image, they are valuable and should be protected. While this is undoubtedly true, it gives little legal guidance about what rights are, how rights relate to other normative considerations of the political order, and how conflicts between rights should be judged. As Maritain noted in his work on the United Nations Declaration of Human Rights, legal rights (and perhaps also moral rights) always conflict. We are faced not with one person with a right but with many people with many plausible claims to rights, such as a woman's right to control her own body and an unborn child's right to life, or one person's right to security of property and another person's right to shelter. In this case, a more fruitful line of inquiry might be one that tries to derive rights from a Christian view of the social order, human vocation and God's requirements of justice. Hence rights would lose their quasi-absolute status and be subject to a view of just relations. In either position the root of human rights would be not intrinsic human merit but divine grace extended to all. In this case legal human rights could be seen as an authentic expression of the gospel.

See also: JUSTICE AND PEACE. ③

Bibliography

M. Cranston, *What are Human Rights?* (New York, 1962); J. M. Finnis, *Natural Law and Natural Rights* (Oxford, 1980); S. Greidanus, 'Human Rights in Biblical Perspective', *CTJ* 19, 1984, pp. 5–31; D. Hollenbach, *Claims in Conflict: Retrieving and Renewing the Catholic Human Rights Tradition* (New York, 1979); H. Lauterpacht, *International Law and Human Rights* (London, 1950); J. Lissner and A. Sovik (eds.), *A Lutheran Reader on Human Rights* (Geneva, 1977); J. Maritain, *The Rights of Man and Natural Law* (ET, New York, 1963); P. Marshall, *Human Rights Theories in Christian Perspective* (Toronto, 1983); P. Sieghart, *The Lawful Rights of Mankind* (Oxford, 1987); R. Tuck, *Natural Rights Theories* (Cambridge, 1978); C. J. H. Wright, *Human Rights: A Study in Biblical Themes* (Bramcote, Nottingham, 1979).

P.A.M.

RIGHTS, TYPES OF, see JUSTICE AND PEACE. ③

RIGORISM. In general, rigorism means extreme strictness in ethical matters. In particular, it is the view in casuistry* that if there is any doubt whether a particular action is my duty or not, I should follow the more rigorous line, even if it is highly probable that I have no need to. The view is also known as 'tutiorism', because I should thus be taking the safer (Lat. *tutior*) course.

It seems that a rigorist will not run much risk of doing wrong. But it has been widely felt that the view is mistaken for all that. 1. Surely I cannot be expected to do something if it is far more likely than not that I am under no obligation to do it. 2. It makes the Christian life seem intolerably bleak, for the natural result of rigorism is the attitude that if I have even the slightest doubts about the rightness of an action, I am to take the course I find less enjoyable. 3. It is clearly a bad guide where the choice is not between a pleasant course and a possible moral duty* but between two possible moral duties. It is by no means clear that the more rigorous line will here necessarily be the right one. 4. It has been urged that rigorism is psychologically and doctrinally objectionable, encouraging unnecessary scruples (see Conscience;* Scrupulosity*) and leading almost inevitably to an attempt at justification* by works.

Bibliography

K. E. Kirk, *Some Principles of Moral Theology* (London, 1920), ch. 8, §4.

R.L.S.

ROGERS, CARL (1902–87). Carl Ransom Rogers is probably the best-known and most influential proponent of the person-centred approach within humanistic psychology* (see Client-centred Counselling*). Born in Illinois in the US, Rogers grew up within a close-knit family that was committed to hard work and a conservative, even fundamentalist, Christian perspective. It is interesting to note that, in contrast to his parents' excluding and sin-conscious views, the adult Rogers emphasized openness to others, and the humanist* belief that each person possesses all the inner resources needed for growth into maturity.

At the University of Wisconsin, through his involvement with Christian students of a more liberal persuasion, he rejected his parents' conservatism, choosing, in turn, to give up agriculture, read history and then proceed to the Union Theological Seminary to study for the ordained ministry. The latter route became incompatible with his free-thinking views and he transferred to Teachers College, Columbia University, where he received his MA in psychology in 1928. Following initial work in child guidance, from 1940, when he became professor of psychology at Ohio State University, Rogers pursued a successful career as both academic psychologist and therapist. His later years were spent as a resident fellow at the Center for Studies of the Person at La Jolla, California.

Rogers' subsequent views were shaped by a wide range of influences from his earlier years in clinical and academic work: positively, the teachings of John Dewey (1859–1952), the educational philosopher, who stressed that learning and growth take place through the dynamic of experience; more negatively, the behaviourist* emphasis of Teachers College, following Eduard Thorndike (1874–1949); and the eclectic brand of Freudianism of the Institute of Child Guidance of New York during his internship. Seeking to resolve the conflict between the scientific and the clinical, the objective and subjective, in the last two approaches, he gradually developed the 'both/and' quality of his 'third-force' personalism.

Rogers was always true to the experimental and experiential emphases of Dewey's pragmatism,* modifying his therapeutic approaches from the non-directiveness of the 1940s, through the client-centredness of the 50s, the person-centredness (stressing change in client, therapist and significant others) of the 60s, to the more mystical and transpersonal views of the 70s and 80s. Here we see a movement from the intrapersonal through the interpersonal to the transpersonal. Within the broad sweep of his productive life, Rogers' cardinal influence on the counselling movement, his research on the core conditions for the effective therapist (genuineness, accurate empathy* and unconditional positive regard), and his commitment to group work and community change are worthy of note.

Bibliography

Counseling and Psychotherapy (Boston, MA, 1942); *On Becoming a Person* (Boston, MA, 1961; London, ²1967); 'A Theory of Therapy, Personality and Interpersonal Relations', in S. Koch (ed.), *Psychology: A Study of a Science*, vol. 3 (New York, 1959); *A Way of Being* (Boston, MA, 1980).

R. F. Hurding, *Roots and Shoots: A Guide to Counselling and Psychotherapy* (London, 1986) = *The Tree of Heaven* (Grand Rapids, 1988); S. L. Jones and R. E. Butman, *Modern Psychotherapies: A Comprehensive Christian Appraisal* (Downers Grove, IL, 1991); R. Nelson-Jones, *The Theory and Practice of Counselling Psychology* (London and New York, 1982); H. A. Van Belle, *The Basic Intent and Therapeutic Approach of Carl R. Rogers* (Toronto, 1980).

R.F.H.

ROMAN CATHOLIC MORAL THEOLOGY. Though inevitably there are many continuities with the past, the present shape of Roman Catholic moral theology largely stems from the work of the Second Vatican Council* (1962–65). Prior to this point, underlying principles were obscured by a heavily legalistic framework of detailed case law (casuistry*), often justified solely by appeal to the teaching authority of the Church (the *magisterium*) and reinforced by the conviction that the primary use of moral theology was in providing manuals for confessors (*i.e.* for priests who hear confessions). In effecting this change, Bernard Häring (1912–) played a major role particularly through his widely disseminated 1954 work *The Law of Christ* (which went through seven editions and was translated from the original Ger. into many other languages).

Most notable of the changes was a renewed concern with Scripture. Though Häring's chosen title may sound legalistic, there is a significant change of emphasis, with the law* now understood as the law of the Spirit giving life in Christ, the need for conversion* stressed, and the call to perfection seen as a summons to all Christians and not just a monastic élite. By the time of his second major work, *Free and Faithful in Christ*, the transition is complete: law has become entirely secondary to a relationship with Christ. The extent of the change is also well illustrated by the way in which the Roman Catholic theologian John Mahoney (1931–) can give a largely negative verdict on the history of his own church's tradition in *The Making of Moral Theology*. The failure of Vatican II's reforms of the practice of confession* (now known as the sacrament of reconciliation) has still further distanced moral theology (see Christian Moral Reasoning[18]) from its traditional context.

None the less, continuities remain. Though Vatican II's unqualified endorsement of freedom of conscience (in *Dignitatis Humanae*) was new, the stress on conscience* as such was not. It is viewed as a rational faculty given to us by God through which the universal natural law* ordained by him may be made known to us. As such it is seen as the basis of all morality, with Scripture there to summon us to a higher level, not to contradict it. But even here there are differences, with the stress now much less on 'law' and much more on 'natural', on the proper fulfilment of the capacities which have been given to us by the creator. This is seen not only in the writings of professional theologians (*e.g.* Josef Fuchs, 1912–), but also in the encyclicals of John Paul II (1978– ; b. 1920), who has been much influenced by philosophical phenomenology (as in his book *The Acting Person*, Dordrecht, 1979). With this has also gone a return to a more traditional concern, an analysis of human character (see [10]) and its appropriate virtues,* a feature which is also prominent in some recent Protestant writing (*e.g.* Stanley Hauerwas, 1940–). Added impetus to the move away from a morality of individual acts to that of character traits has been given by the very influential writings of the philosopher Alasdair MacIntyre (1929– ; see Philosophical Ethics*), himself a convert to Rome.

Widespread disobedience of Paul VI's encyclical on contraception, *Humanae Vitae** (1968; see Papal Encyclicals*), provides a salutary warning that the Roman communion is no longer the monolithic church it once was. This is well illustrated by contemporary writing in the US, where, of the country's three leading moral theologians, Richard McCormick (1922–) tries to occupy a mediating position between Germain Grisez (1929– ; normally supportive of the *magisterium*) and Charles Curran (1934– ; frequently critical). Curran has for instance defended the morality of homosexual* acts in the context of a loving relationship; he has also argued for public funding for abortion* (though himself opposed to abortion, he believes the status of the foetus too uncertain to justify precluding others from exercising a free choice). Critics have also maintained that the way in which he applies the technical term 'proportionate reason' is at times indistinguishable from secular utilitarianism (see Consequentialism*). It is therefore perhaps not surprising that he has incurred censure from the Vatican.

So too, though for very different reasons, did the five priests who joined the Sandanista government upon the overthrow of the Somoza dictatorship in Nicaragua in 1979. The poet and priest Ernesto Cardenal (1925–) had been particularly active in supporting the guerillas, but this would be untypical of liberation theology* as a whole. This movement had its origins in the second conference of Latin American bishops held at Medellín in Mexico in 1968. Through encouragement of what are known as 'base ecclesial communities' (groups of fifteen to twenty families meeting for Bible study and discussion of social issues), it has sought to make the poor more aware of their rights. In attempting to achieve this, the non-violent civil disobedience of the assassinated Archbishop Romero (1917–80) of El Salvador would be much more characteristic than what happened in Nicaragua.

While the Vatican has at times been highly critical of liberation theology (see Vatican Statements*), it would be quite wrong to suggest that its stance on social issues as a whole is conservative. Thus in marked contrast to the *Syllabus Errorum* (1864) of Pius IX (1846–78; b. 1792), which condemned among other things liberalism, socialism and democracy, modern papal encyclicals have demonstrated a marked concern for workers' conditions and their rights. In John XXIII's* *Mater et Magistra* (1961) attention is focused on farm labourers, and the *Populorum Progressio* (1967) of Paul VI (1963–78; b. 1897) focused on the plight of the Third World, while John

Paul II's *Laborem Exercens* (1981; see Papal Encyclicals*) seeks by appeals to both Genesis and natural law to give a new dignity to work. The National Conference of Catholic Bishops of the US has also been prominent in pronouncing upon social issues, as in the Bishops' pastoral letter on *The Challenge of Peace* (Washington, DC, and London, 1983) or on *Economic Justice for All*.

Bibliography

C. E. Curran, *Transition and Tradition in Moral Theology* (London and Notre Dame, IN, 1979); J. M. Finnis *et al.*, *Nuclear Deterrence, Morality and Realism* (Oxford, 1987); R. P. Hamel and K. R. Himes (eds.), *Introduction to Christian Ethics* (New York, 1989); B. Häring, *Free and Faithful in Christ*, 3 vols. (ET, Slough and New York, 1978–81); A. T. Hennelly (ed.), *Liberation Theology: A Documentary History* (New York, 1990); A. MacIntyre, *After Virtue* (Notre Dame, IN, ²1984; London, ²1985); *idem*, *Three Rival Versions of Moral Enquiry* (London, 1990); J. Mahoney, *The Making of Moral Theology* (Oxford, 1987); National Conference of Catholic Bishops, *Economic Justice for All: Pastoral Letter on Catholic Social Teaching and the US Economy* (Washington, DC, 1986); R. Schnackenberg, *The Moral Teaching of the New Testament* (ET, New York, 1967; London, ²1975).

D.W.Bro.

ROUSSEAU, JEAN-JACQUES, see GLOBAL ETHICS. 15

RULES specify particular actions as obligatory, permissible or forbidden. They take an imperative form, and may be sanctioned by the forces of law, society or religion. As such they comprise a very widespread form of ethical discourse. But the importance attached to rules varies from one ethical approach or system to another. A deontological* approach to ethics puts a strong emphasis on rules and tends to regard them as absolute. A consequentialist* approach puts less emphasis on rules and believes there may be situations where it is right to break them if a calculation of likely consequences points in that direction.

Christian ethics, in all its variety, cannot be said to have adopted either approach consistently. But in general it has given considerable prominence to rules. In the OT the great profusion of statements which take the form of divine commands (613 in all in the Mosaic law) is very striking. The Ten Commandments (see Decalogue*) have often played a central role in the church's moral teaching. The NT re-evaluates the place of law* in the life of the Christian but still lays down many constraints on human behaviour. Paul's first letter to the church at Corinth includes rule-type statements on a wide range of moral issues.

There are definite merits in an ethical approach which emphasizes rules strongly. Rules provide invaluable signposts in the complexity and uncertainty which often characterize the moral life. Well-established rules reflect the tried and tested wisdom of past generations; they are the distillation of human experience, often giving an authoritative witness to what does and does not make for human well-being. The persistence of these rules illustrates the need for consistency and stability in human relationships. For rules to play a constructive role in people's lives, they require both intellectual assent (so that an individual or group can see the purpose of the rule) and emotional reinforcement (so that the individual or group is deterred from breaking the rule where human weakness or unusual circumstances represent a temptation to do so). Appeal to a rule can then remove some of the burden from the decision-making process.

There are some rules which appear to hold good for every type of situation. The prohibition of rape* is an example. Rape forces another person into the most intimate of physical behaviour against his or her will. It invariably humiliates, hurts and damages the victim, mentally and physically. It violates human dignity at a very deep level. Most of the rules which are strong candidates for being accorded absolute status share this concern with protecting human dignity.

However, a rule-centred approach also has its limitations. 1. Too much emphasis on a rule can distract attention from the principle or value which the rule is designed to safeguard. Principles (such as respect for human dignity) are more fundamental. Jesus summed up 'the Law and the Prophets' in the two commandments to love God and love one's neighbour (Mt. 22:37–40). These commandments are better described as principles, denoting a quality which should be present across a whole range of different actions, rather than rules. He criticized the scribes and Pharisees for concentrating on legal minutiae to the neglect of 'the more important matters of the law – justice, mercy and faithfulness' (Mt. 23:23). In situations for which no existing rule lies ready at hand, turning to principles such as these for guidance is especially important.

2. Many rules display a cultural relativity. Rules whose validity seems obvious to one generation or ethnic group are often held in light regard by another. This is not just a matter of 'higher' or 'lower' standards, though it would be illusory to pretend that all different cultures are on the same moral plane. But social, economic and demographic factors all help to explain why some rules make sense at certain times and places and not at others.

3. Rules may sometimes come into conflict. For instance, in some extreme situations there may be an unavoidable clash between the duties to tell the truth* and to preserve life (as, e.g., in the case of Rahab and the Israelite spies, Jos. 2:1–7). Decisions then have to be made about which is the higher claim. A rule-centred approach cannot escape from the responsibility that human beings have to rank their moral priorities.

There would thus seem to be a proper balance to be observed in the Christian attitude to rules. They provide structure and direction in the moral life and can protect us from our propensity to sinfulness and self-deception. But they do not penetrate to the heart of Christ's moral challenge, and if we resort to them too readily, we run the risk of ignoring complexity and evading responsibility.*

See also: LEGALISM.

Bibliography

J. A. Baker, *The Foolishness of God* (London, 1975); C. E. Curran, *New Perspectives in Moral Theology* (Notre Dame, IN, 1976); J. Fletcher, *Situation Ethics* (Philadelphia and London, 1966); R. Higginson, *Dilemmas: A Christian Approach to Moral Decision-making* (London and Louisville, KY, 1988); G. H. Outka and P. Ramsey, *Norm and Context in Christian Ethics* (London and New York, 1968); L. Smedes, *Mere Morality* (Grand Rapids and Tring, 1983).

R.A.Hig.

S

SABBATH. The word 'sabbath' derives from a Heb. root (*šābat*) meaning 'cease' or 'rest'. The sabbath day was instituted in OT times to mark the end of the six-day working week. On it no work was to be done, and special religious rites were to be observed.

The Ten Commandments (see Decalogue*), as they appear in Exodus and Deuteronomy, give two reasons for observing the sabbath, reflecting the biblical doctrines of redemption (see Sin and Salvation⑤) and creation* respectively.

In Dt. 5:12, God's people are told to keep the sabbath day holy as a reminder of their redemption from slavery in Egypt. It provided an opportunity for joyful corporate worship (Lv. 23:3; Is. 58:13), marked ceremonially by the replacing of the show-bread in the tabernacle and by an offering of lambs, drink and grain (Lv. 24:5–8; Nu. 28:9–10). The sabbath was a 'sign' of the everlasting covenant* made by the redeemer with his people (Ex. 31:12–17; Ezk. 20:12).

In Ex. 20:8–11, God's role as creator is highlighted. People should keep the sabbath day holy, demands the fourth commandment, because the Lord rested on the seventh day after his work of creation (Gn. 2:2–3).

This instruction to follow the Lord's example brings into play the most powerful motivating factor in biblical ethics – the appeal to imitate God. It is reinforced by an even more daring anthropomorphism in Ex. 31:17, where sabbath observance is backed by the astonishing statement that the Lord paused to 'get his breath back' (Heb. *wayyinnāpaš*) on the seventh day.

In this 'creation' sense, the OT's development of the sabbath principle is the obverse of its teaching about work.* Just as work does not always involve energetic activity, so sabbath rest does not necessarily imply enforced inactivity. And as work (in its biblical sense) means more than wage-earning, so the sabbath principle embraces children, the unemployed and the retired, as well as those in paid employment.

Change is the keynote. If work describes a person's major occupation, sabbath is the counter-balancing minor element in life. So when they were travelling through the desert, the Israelites were told to stay in their tents on the sabbath day and collect no manna, because that was the only change possible in their nomadic lifestyle (Ex. 16:22–30). In more settled times, the applications of the sabbath principle naturally developed in step with changes in occupation. The farmer must stop his ploughing or harvesting, even if conditions are ideal (Ex. 34:21); and the salesman must put his samples away on the sabbath day (Je. 17:27). The specific applications vary, but the general principle (that people need appropriate minors to balance their majors) remains constantly valid.

The law's provision for a sabbatical (seventh) year, when the land was to lie fallow (Lv. 25:1–7), is an extension of the same creation principle. So is the year of jubilee* (after 'seven times seven years'), which was marked by an amnesty for slaves, debtors and the dispossessed (Lv. 25:8ff.). The humanitarian emphasis which has such a high profile in this legislation was a feature of all sabbath law (*cf.* Dt. 5:14; Lv. 25:6–7).

In contrast to the rest of the Decalogue, the sabbath commandment is not restated in the NT. Jesus attended synagogue worship on the sabbath day (Lk. 4:16), but clashed with the Pharisees' use of the Mishnah to submerge the sabbatical principle in a deluge of by-laws. He was especially critical of their legalistic insistence on the observance of specific minutiae which robbed the principle of its humanitarian character (*e.g.* Mt. 12:9–14). As Lord of the sabbath, he insisted that observance of the seventh day was meant for human refreshment and mutual care (Mk. 2:27–28).

Paul echoed Jesus (as well as the OT prophets; *cf.* Is. 1:13; Am. 8:5) in condemning the kind of ceremonial sabbath observances which turned people away from God's intention and from the freedom of the gospel (Col. 2:13–17). According to Hebrews, the Christian fulfilment of the sabbath principle is not to be found in rules and regulations, but in God's rest which consists of eternal life in Christ (Heb. 4:1–11).

The twin themes of creation and redemption, which thread their way through the Bible's teaching on the sabbath, reappear (often interwoven) in its application to contemporary Christian and secular social lifestyles. Some, highlighting the redemption motif, see the sabbath – transferred (except in the case of Seventh Day Adventists) from Saturday to Sunday* – as primarily a day of worship for God's people. Others, stressing its status as a creation ordinance, use the sabbath principle as a God-given indicator of humankind's need for regular change, as a corrective to any tendency to deify work, and as a platform from which to construct a Christian understanding of leisure.*

Bibliography

R. T. Beckwith and W. Stott, *This is the Day* (London, 1978); D. A. Carson (ed.), *From Sabbath to Lord's Day* (Grand Rapids, 1982); W. Rordorf, *Sunday* (ET, London, 1968).

D.H.F.

SACRAMENTAL HEALING. A sacrament is an outward and visible sign of an inward and spiritual grace. Sacramental healing refers to the use of such signs in the context of prayer for healing.

1. Laying on of hands

In the OT, the laying on of hands is predominantly a sign of the transfer of guilt* from the sinner to a sacrificial victim (*e.g.* Lv. 16:21). It is also a sign of blessing* (*e.g.* Gn. 48:13–20), authority* (*e.g.* Nu. 27:23) and power* (*e.g.* Dt. 34:9) being imparted from one person to another. These are the aspects which come to the fore in the NT (see below and Acts 6:6; 13:3).

Highlighting the comforting power of touch,* Jesus laid his hands on people in response to requests for the blessing of children (*e.g.* Mt. 19:13–15) and for healing* of the sick (Mt. 9:18; Mk. 5:23; 7:32), an action which also accompanied other miracles of healing (Mk. 6:5; 7:33; 8:23–25; Lk. 4:40; 13:13). In the disputed ending to Mark's Gospel, Jesus says that his disciples 'will place their hands on sick people, and they will get well' (Mk. 16:18). In Acts, the laying on of hands is described in connection with the receiving of the Holy Spirit* and his gifts, including the blessing of healing from physical illness (Acts 8:17; 9:17; 19:6; 28:8; 1 Tim. 4:14; 2 Tim. 1:6).

The prayer of the early church recorded in Acts 4:30 is significant: 'Stretch out *your* hand to heal and perform miraculous signs and wonders through the name of your holy servant Jesus.' It is *God* who heals, using those who minister, not the other way round. Though it can be misinterpreted as a magical act, laying on of hands should be seen rather as an expression both of compassionate identification with the sick person and also of faith* that the prayers which accompany it are being heard by a trustworthy God.

2. Anointing with oil

In Bible times, oil was used for its medical and cosmetic properties, as illustrated in the parable of the good Samaritan (Lk. 10:34). It also had religious significance. Places, objects and people (notably priests, kings and prophets) were anointed to show that they belonged exclusively to God (*e.g.* Lv. 8:10–12). Anointing symbolizes the bestowal of the Holy Spirit with the implication that the one so anointed is set apart and empowered to serve God (1 Sa. 16:13; Is. 61:1; Acts 10:38; 2 Cor. 1:21–22).

Mark's Gospel indicates that the disciples of Jesus 'drove out many demons and anointed many sick people with oil and healed them' (Mk. 6:13). The only other specific reference to this practice is in Jas. 5:14. Commentators differ as to whether Mark and James have in mind a 'ritual' or a 'remedial' anointing. The latter is suggested by the fact that the Gk. word for 'ordinary' anointing, *aleiphō*, is used rather than the ceremonial word, *chriō*. But this is far from conclusive. Either way, the emphasis is on the 'prayer offered in faith' (Jas. 5:15). As with the laying on of hands, anointing with oil should be seen as the outward expression of faith that God will anoint with the Holy Spirit those who are brought to him in faithful prayer.

In episcopal churches, the oil used (usually olive) is normally that which has been blessed by the bishops during the eucharist on Maundy Thursday. This emphasizes the solidarity of the church as a whole with the sick individual (*cf.* 1 Cor. 12:26). The oil is applied to the forehead (and sometimes the hands) in the form of the cross.

Within the Roman Catholic Church, anointing with oil became the sacrament of extreme unction or the last rites, concentrating on the forgiveness of sins as a preparation for death. This policy was changed by the Second Vatican Council.* Now known as 'the anointing of the sick', the rite is no longer restricted to those in danger of imminent death, but is seen as appropriate for the strengthening and healing of all with serious illness.

3. Holy Communion

Many cite Holy Communion as an environment within which prayer for healing is especially effective. Just as the person who participates in the Holy Communion 'without recognising the body of the Lord eats and drinks judgment on himself' (1 Cor. 11:29) through weakness, sickness and even death (11:30), so taking part properly should be an avenue for strength, health and life. Christ is specially present when his people recall his death in the service of Holy Communion, and his presence above all can bring healing of all kinds.

Apart from anything else, true participation in Holy Communion demands prior examination of an individual's spiritual state (1 Cor. 11:28). Since much physical and mental ill-health flows from spiritual malaise, restoration of this primary relationship with God can be expected to lead to improved physical and mental health too.

Where they help people to become more aware of the spiritual realities they signify, other sacramental acts may also be associated with physical, mental and spiritual healing. In addition to the eucharist and anointing, examples from penance, baptism, marriage and ordination have been cited.

Bibliography

R. East, *Heal the Sick* (London, 1987); F. S. MacNutt, *Healing* (Altamonte Springs, FL, ²1988; London, ²1989); M. Maddocks, *The Christian Healing Ministry* (New York and London, ²1990); J. Wilkinson, *Health and Healing* (Edinburgh, 1980).

D.A.S.

SADOMASOCHISM, see SEXUAL DEVIATION.

SALVATION, see SIN AND SALVATION. 5

SANCTIFICATION. The theological term 'sanctification' most literally means 'to make holy'. Defined more fully, it is used to convey the following distinct yet related ideas: 1. the process of setting apart as holy some thing or person; 2. the process of making someone free from sin(s); 3. the process of eliminating evil dispositions and practices ('the works of the flesh' or vices); and 4. producing godly graces and actions ('the fruit of the Spirit' or virtues) in a person or community. So defined, sanctification as a *process* is distinguished from holiness as the *state* to be attained and moral goodness as the *quality* of that state. Sanctification is a gracious work of the Holy Spirit* of God in freeing sinners from the guilt* and domination of sin (see Sin and Salvation 5), in calling them to strive for a Christlike character, and in dedicating them to loving service to God and their neighbour. These three themes are stressed in the NT.

1. The process of sanctification is made possible by, and draws its quality of moral purity from, the fully achieved holiness of Jesus Christ in his life of obedience to his Father (1 Cor. 1:30; Eph. 5:26; Heb. 2:11; 2 Pet. 1:9). The book of Hebrews particularly emphasizes the life and death of Jesus as at once the fulfilment and the abolition of ritual purification under the old covenant. Just as the OT required that an unblemished animal should be dedicated in sacrifice to purge the pollution of sin, so the writer of Hebrews insists that God's righteousness* demands that sinners be cleansed from the defilement of personal sin through the once-for-all sacrifice of Jesus on the cross* (Heb. 9:11–14; 10:10–14, 19–22; 12:14; *cf.* Rom. 12:1).

2. While the process of sanctification is initiated by the grace* of God, and cannot be sustained without it, nevertheless, the presence and power of the Holy Spirit does not operate apart from the believer's own moral striving: 'putting to death' selfish dispositions and practices (Gal. 5:16–21; Eph. 4:22–28; Col. 3:5–9); and cultivating the graces of Christ (Gal. 5:22–26; Col. 1:10–14; Rom. 6:19–22; 2 Cor. 7:1).

3. These two necessary conditions, divine grace and human responsibility, are famously described in these words of the apostle Paul: 'Continue to work out your salvation with fear and trembling, for it is God who works in you to will and to act according to his good purpose' (Phil. 2:12–13; *cf.* Col. 3:9–10; 2 Thes. 2:13–15; 1 Pet 1:2). The divine grace always brings responsibility to love God and serve our neighbour (*cf.* 1 Pet. 2:12).

In developing the NT teaching on sanctification, Christian theologians and moralists have largely agreed on the importance of the following points:

1. Sanctification is most profoundly a matter of a person or community being set apart by God, prepared by God and possessed by God for his delight and holy use. A settled awareness of this essential truth has served

historically to combat various unbiblical interpretations. Given this understanding, becoming holy cannot be identified just with forsaking known sin and observing morally correct behaviour, or with practices that discipline body and soul, or with service to the neighbour, or even with individual devotion to God. This is because, whilst each may be attempted *apart* from the grace of God, each is an *indispensable* way of responding to the presence and power of the Holy Spirit of God.

2. If sanctification is not just a matter of individual *moral development*, neither is it merely a matter of *individual* moral development. The NT never once refers to a single saint, though it often refers to all baptized and believing Christians as 'saints' or as 'holy' people (Rom. 1:7; 16:2, 15; 1 Cor. 1:2; Eph. 1:1; Phil. 1:1; *cf.* Tit. 2:14; 1 Pet. 2:9). The 'sanctified' are all baptized believers who have been 'justified in the name of the Lord Jesus Christ and by the Spirit of our God', regardless of the differing degrees of holiness each may have attained (1 Cor. 6:11).

3. For the most part, sanctification has not been thought to result in faultlessness in this life. Allowance has been made for lapses into sin through ignorance, neglect or even deliberate transgression. The remedy for postbaptismal sinning is sincere repentance, confession and forgiveness (Lk. 15) and a renewed personal love for Christ. Knowing their proclivity to sin, the tenacity of anxious self-interest, and the habitual allure of sex, power and possessions, wise Christians have recognized the importance of following their Lord and his apostles in practising spiritual disciplines that combat and eliminate these evil tendencies. If mortification* of sin may be thought of as the negative side of the believer's responsibility and the cultivation of Christlike graces the positive side, then both require the faithful practice of 'disciplines of abstinence' like solitude, fasting,* chastity* and sacrifice, and 'disciplines of engagement' like study, worship, prayer* and fellowship* (*cf.* Dallas Willard, *The Spirit of the Disciplines*, San Francisco, 1988, ch. 9).

Genuine sanctification does not produce defensive, sanctimonious personalities whose natural humour, gifts or talents have been sublimated or denied expression. The presence of God frees, empowers and makes more sensitive and loving the exercise of just those distinctive qualities that constitute each unique personality, and amiably modifies and makes endearing many idiosyncrasies of personality. The power of the Holy Spirit of God is present as the 'Comforter', the one whose task it is to encourage Christians everywhere and at all times to 'live a life worthy of the Lord ... [to] please him in every way: bearing fruit in every good work, ... [having] great endurance and patience, and joyfully giving thanks to the Father', until they all come 'to share in the inheritance of the saints in the kingdom of light' (Col. 1:10–12).

M.A.R.

SANCTIONS, see ECONOMIC SANCTIONS.

SANCTIONS, PENAL, see PUNISHMENT; SENTENCING, PRISON.

SANCTITY OF HUMAN LIFE. Though never used as such in Scripture, this phrase is best understood as referring to the particular respect which is owed to human life as the gift of God (Acts 17:25), as created in his image (see Image of God;* Gn. 1:26–27) and as subject to the laws of the covenants* with Noah and with Moses (Gn. 9:5–6; Ex. 20:13). Everyone has a duty to conserve and respect human life (Gn. 9:5; 4:8–10, 15), and to accept responsibility for the life of their fellow humans (Gn. 4:9; Dt. 21:1–9).

The phrase 'sanctity of human life' is often used incorrectly or ambiguously to imply a duty to save life at all costs, a notion nowhere evinced in Scripture – which emphasizes the inevitability of natural death (Heb. 9:27), and carefully restricts instances in which human life can be taken (*e.g.* judicially, *cf.* Gn. 9:6). Outside of these instances, innocent human beings do have an absolute right not to be deliberately killed (e.g. non-combatants in wartime). Exceptions are rare and very debatable, *e.g.* the situation of 'tragic choice', and its extensions into areas where extreme economic or social pressures could force choices to be made between innocent lives. The duty to conserve life extends to the means of its conservation, *e.g.* clothing, food and warmth (Lv. 19:16b; Dt. 24:6, 12–13) and to special care for the disabled or disadvantaged (Lv. 19:14, 33–34). Even killing intended to bring about God's purposes was condemned (Ho. 1:4; *cf.* 2 Ki. 9:1–10). Hence care for lives includes the motives of the heart (Mt. 5:21–26), not simply outward actions.

God's sovereignty over human life must not be usurped. Human life is sacred because it is precious to God (Ps. 116:15), and because God took human nature at the incarnation (Jn. 1:1, 14), thus demonstrating the value he places upon it. Human life can therefore never become disposable for reasons of utility. Though it has been argued that in 'tragic choice', where both cannot be saved, one life may be sacrificed for the sake of another (*e.g.* Is. 43:4; Jon. 1:14), this is a claim which is vanishingly applicable in practice and too easily used as a justification for dubious choice.

See also: ETHICS OF MEDICAL CARE;14 LIFE, HEALTH AND DEATH.13

D.W.V.

SARTRE, JEAN-PAUL (1905–80) is the best-known existentialist philosopher. Cousin of Albert Schweitzer (1875–1965), he studied psychology and philosophy at the Ecole Normale Supérieure. Multi-talented (teacher, novelist, dramatist, essayist, biographer, literary critic and political activist), he is one of the most influential thinkers of the 20th century. He was awarded, but did not accept, the Nobel Prize for Literature in 1964.

A resolute atheist, he was influenced by Edmund Husserl's (1859–1938) phenomenology and his concept of intentionality, and by the existentialist ontology of Martin Heidegger (1889–1976). In his key work *Being and Nothingness* (1943; ET, London, 1957), he argues that the individual consciousness (*pour-soi*, 'for itself') is a nothingness at the heart of being (*en-soi*, 'in itself') and is condemned to be free, to choose itself *in the world*. No objective moral (see Objectivity of Morals*) or other norms from revelation,* reason* or convention bind the individual, who is the autonomous source of all moral values. Moral choices are relative and indifferent, but always undertaken in situation. Although sometimes misunderstood by 'café existentialists' as advocating moral libertinism, he is, in fact, concerned with authentic moral action – the discovery and continual exercising of one's freedom. This ethical stance emphasizes choice, undertaken in anxiety, individual moral responsibility and constant self-projection, and the virtues of honesty, sincerity and courage. Those who conceal this basic moral freedom are guilty of *mauvaise foi* ('bad faith').

In *Being and Nothingness*, relationships (*pour-autrui*, 'for others') mean conflict as the individual seeks to subject the freedom of the other to his (or her) purposes. However, in *Existentialism and Humanism* (1945; ET, London, 1948), Sartre states that man is what he makes himself and that each man in choosing his values chooses for all men. In realizing his own freedom he recognizes it in others. Reciprocal freedom, respecting the existential freedom of the other, undergirds Sartre's view of 'engagement': commitment to moral action and to a great moral project. Values are developed in situation and in action. The fact that *Cahiers sur la Morale* (written in 1947–48, and published in Paris in 1983) was unfinished, however, is testimony to his difficulty in elaborating an existentialist ethics. His moral position lacks precision; however, as his political interests intensified, his championing of classic liberal / Left causes of political action, such as the rejection of racism and colonialism,* confirmed the existence of recognizably humanist moral norms already evident in his wartime writings.

Later attempts to correlate existentialism and Marxism (see *The Problem of Method* [1957; ET, London, 1963] and *Critique of Dialectical Reason* [1960; ET, London, ²1976]) depict scarcity as the foundation of conflict in human society and reflect his concern to liberate groups of people from passive 'seriality' to radical, practical freedom.

See also: EXISTENTIALIST ETHICS; HISTORY OF CHRISTIAN ETHICS.6

J.H.G.

SATAN. That Satan is understood by the biblical writers as a *personal* being, rather than a force of principle, seems to be implied by: 1. the personal attributes attributed to him, such as intelligence (2 Cor. 2:11; Eph. 6:11) and will and intention (Lk. 22:31; 1 Pet. 5:8; Rev. 12:9ff.; 20:3, 7–8); 2. the accounts of his encounters with both God (Jb. 1 – 2) and Jesus (Mt. 4:1–11); and 3. the way in which his name is juxtaposed with that of Christ (2 Cor. 6:15) or of God (Jas. 4:7). Little reference is made in the Bible to Satan's origin, although Jn. 8:44 ('not holding to the truth') seems to presuppose a 'fall'. Certainly any notion of an absolute cosmological dualism* is excluded by the Bible's consistent monotheism, its frequent affirmation of God's sovereignty even over forces of evil, and its confidence in the decisive defeat of Satan as both past event and future certainty.

In the OT, the supernatural *śāṭān* of 1 Ch. 21:1, Jb. 1:6ff., and Zc. 3:1, bears already some of the features of an adversary of both God and humanity. His hostility towards humankind is understood primarily in moral terms, as the accuser and tempter of the righteous, although in Job he is also a physical tormentor. In the NT, however, his fundamentally evil character is more clearly delineated, and a consciousness of his present power is also pervasive. Not only is he prince of demons (Lk. 11:15–18, and par.) and served by a retinue of evil angels (Mt. 25:41; Rev. 12:7), but also ruler of the world (Jn. 12:31; 14:30; 16:11), its god (2 Cor. 4:4), and the one in whom it 'lies' (1 Jn. 5:19; *cf.* also Mt. 4:9, and par.). Nevertheless, consistent with OT perceptions, his power over the human race is understood in primarily moral terms, and consists in the fact that he inspires the wickedness of sinful humanity (Eph. 2:2) and keeps it from apprehending the gospel (2 Cor. 4:4). He is widely identified in the NT as the serpent whose seduction of Eve precipitated the primal sin (Gn. 3:1–6, 14–15; *cf.* Rev. 12:9; Jn. 8:44; 2 Cor. 11:3–15), and numerous allusions are made to his ongoing work of temptation. He is also the destroyer, or murderer (Jn. 8:44; 1 Cor. 5:5; Rev. 9:11); death is the consequence of sin (Gn. 3:16–19; Rom. 6:23), but it is Satan who has 'the power of death' (Heb. 2:14) and is thus in some sense executor of sin's penalty. He is moreover portrayed as the 'accuser' (Rev. 12:10; *cf.* Jb. 1 – 2; Zc. 3:1), demanding the condemnation of those whom he seduces. Humanity is therefore victim of a satanic tyranny (1 Jn. 5:19; *cf.* Eph. 2:2) which both inspires human rebellion and insists upon the imposition of its consequence. Nevertheless Satan's inspiration of human wickedness does not mitigate people's responsibility for their sins, for it is in those very sins that the source of his tyranny lies. Thus such texts as Jn. 8:44 and Eph. 2:2–5, while affirming his domination of sinful human beings, simultaneously assume their responsibility, and consequent guilt, for their transgressions.

In the thought of the NT writers, therefore, the death of Christ brings about the defeat of Satan, and indeed of all the powers of evil, precisely by dealing with that sin which they exploit. In NT thought, the essence of Christ's work (see Atonement*) lies in the fact that it takes away sins (*cf.*, *e.g.*, the summary credal formula of 1 Cor. 15:3ff.). The destruction of

Satan's dominion is a necessary consequence of the cross* but not its primary focus: it is the removal of sins and the consequent emasculation of death (1 Cor. 15:55–57) that destroys him (Heb. 2:14–15). Thus in both Col. 1:13–14 and Gal. 1:4 the redemption of believers from the present evil age, the dominion of darkness, is associated with the forgiveness of their sins. In Revelation the conquest of the accuser, Satan, is achieved by the blood of the Lamb, which has freed the Christian from sins (Rev. 12:11; *cf.* 1:5), and in 1 John the reason for the appearance of the Son of God is the destruction of Satan's 'works', which may equally be understood as the removal of sins (1 Jn. 3:5, 8). Moreover, in Col. 2:13–15 the 'principalities and powers' are similarly disarmed of such authority as they formerly held by the forgiveness of trespasses through the cancellation of the 'bond'. The gospel accordingly addresses people first and foremost as sinners rather than as victims of Satan.

It does, however, liberate them from Satan's tyranny. Paul exhorts his readers not to give him opportunity (Eph. 4:27; *cf.* 1 Cor. 7:5; 2 Cor. 2:11), thereby implying that Satan has only such power over them as is freely conceded to him. This does not mean that he is unable to attack them; he makes war on the church (Rev. 12:13–17), both seeking to seduce it and inspiring persecution which may bring about the suffering and even death of its members (Rev. 2:10; 11:7; 13:7). What it does mean is that believers can maintain their faithfulness to God despite these assaults, resisting temptations (Jas. 4:7), both moral and doctrinal (*cf.* 1 Tim. 4:1; 1 Jn. 4:1–6), because of the divine resources now available to them (Eph. 6:10–20). Moreover, they have the confidence that the war he wages upon them is of limited duration (Rom. 16:20). As is the case with the world, Satan's judgment has already taken place at the cross (Jn. 16:11; *cf.* 12:31) and awaits only its final realization (Rev. 20:7–10).

See also: Deliverance Ministry; Demonic, the.

Bibliography

M. Green, *I Believe in Satan's Downfall* (London and Grand Rapids, 1981); E. Langton, *Essentials of Demonology* (London, 1949); *idem*, *Satan, a Portrait* (London, 1945); F. S. Leahy, *Satan Cast Out: A Study in*

Biblical Demonology (Edinburgh, 1975); B. Noack, *Satanás und Sotería: Untersuchungen zur Neutestamentlichen Dämonologie* (Kobenhavn, 1948); J. B. Russell, *Satan: The Early Christian Tradition* (Ithaca, NY, and London, 1981).

K.F.

SCEPTICISM in morality is an attitude of doubt about whether there are any moral truths or, more typically, the view that no moral truths can be known for certain. Such scepticism must be distinguished from the possession of a critical attitude to moral issues.

Moral scepticism may be part of a more general, chronic scepticism. It might be claimed that because there is the possibility of doubt or deception, no truths, and therefore no moral truths, may be known. Moral scepticism may, alternatively, rest on grounds that are characteristically moral, having to do with human sin or failure. More secular versions of moral scepticism rely upon moral diversity among different cultures or within one culture. So it is asserted that the fact of cultural pluralism entails that the grounds for holding one moral opinion are no better or worse than the grounds for holding any other. An attempt to rebut such positions can be made by invoking natural law* or natural reason, and by claiming that in fact there is a remarkable convergence on moral questions across different cultures.

A practical moral scepticism may arise from the sheer complexity of situations in which moral questions arise, and from the experience of facing conflicting moral principles.

Scripture teaches that there is a knowledge of moral truth which a person can possess independently of revelation (*cf.* Rom. 2:14–15), but Scripture itself both fills out the content of such natural morality and provides a context in which it is made intelligible and applicable.

See also: RELATIVISM.

P.H.

SCHAEFFER, FRANCIS (1912–84). Born in Philadelphia, USA, Francis August Schaeffer was essentially a practical, not just a theoretical, apologist. He felt keenly the 'lostness' of modern man. In his view the post-Christian West had been driven inexorably towards the logical conclusions of the 18th-century Enlightenment* philosophy. Having sown the wind of naturalism, by the second half of the 20th century it was reaping the whirlwind of meaninglessness and moral relativism.*

The church, he felt, had done little to address this situation: instead of providing 'honest answers to honest questions' it had retreated into either existential irrationalism or pietistic anti-intellectualism.

Starting in 1955, within the context of his own home in Switzerland, he attempted to address these issues. The work of L'Abri Fellowship was the result. People from a wide range of backgrounds and, in due course, from many parts of the world, came to 'The Shelter' looking for answers. What lay at the centre of their discussion was the Bible. Schaeffer believed that the Bible was the only 'world-view' which could adequately explain the phenomena of human experience; in particular, what he called 'The Form of the Universe' and 'The Mannishness of Man'.

In this sense he was a presuppositionalist. Nevertheless, unlike some presuppositionalists, he affirmed an area of 'common ground' with the non-Christian, since every individual is in fact made in the image of God* and lives within a created universe. All truth, therefore, is God's truth; hence the Christian has a responsibility as much to persuade as to proclaim.

In 1977 Schaeffer's *How Should We Then Live?* (film and book) influenced the beginnings of the evangelical involvement in the pro-life campaign in the US. This influence was considerably extended two years later through a similar film series and book made in conjunction with C. Everett Koop (later Surgeon General of the USA) entitled *Whatever Happened to the Human Race?*

Francis Schaeffer was ordained as a Presbyterian minister. However, his work within the L'Abri Fellowship in Huemoz, Switzerland, was interdenominational, and his twenty-three books made an impact upon evangelical life and thought throughout the world. He died in Rochester, Minnesota, in 1984.

Bibliography

Complete Works, 5 vols. (Westchester, IL, ²1985).

L. T. Dennis, *Francis A. Schaeffer: Portraits of the Man and His Work* (Westchester, IL, 1986); R. W. Ruegsegger (ed.), *Reflections on Francis Schaeffer* (Grand Rapids, 1986).

R.C.M.

SCHLEIERMACHER, F. D. E. (1768–
1834). A German Protestant theologian,
often termed the 'Father of Protestant
Liberalism', Friedrich Daniel Ernst Schleiermacher opened a new era of theology with his
Speeches on Religion to Its Cultured Despisers
(1799; ET, London, 1894) and *The Christian
Faith* (1821–22).

Schleiermacher grounded religion in feeling
(*Gefuhl*) rather than in metaphysics, ethics or
traditional sources of authority. Religion is 'the
consciousness of being absolutely dependent,
or, which is the same thing, of being in relation
with God', the 'Whence' of our religious self-
consciousness (*The Christian Faith*, sec. 4).
This religious consciousness is at least latent in
every individual, waiting to be awakened (*e.g.*
through preaching) and expressed in some
definite form ('positive religion'). The best expression of this consciousness is Christianity.
Christian doctrines are verbal descriptions of
the religious self-consciousness found in Jesus
Christ (who possessed the full potency of God-
consciousness) and in the community to which
Christ has communicated this God-consciousness. Accordingly, traditional doctrines are
evaluated and redefined in light of what is found
in the religious self-consciousness. Thus, 'sin' is
resistance to God-consciousness; 'salvation' involves the awakening and 'steady flame' of
God-consciousness; the 'Holy Spirit' is the
common spirit of the church through which
salvation is mediated. The final aim of Christian theology is the cure of souls (practical
theology; see 7); not surprising, since religion's awareness of the interconnectedness of
all reality in its dependence on God means that
religion is essentially ethical in intent.

Schleiermacher was not only a product of
the Romantic period, but was also influenced
by objective idealism* (being a renowned
scholar and translator of Plato*), by Immanuel
Kant's* critical transcendental philosophy, by
a Reformed heritage (being the fourth in a line
of Reformed pastors) and by pietism* (having
been educated at Moravian Brethren schools).
He held significant university posts at Halle
and Berlin, and preached extensively throughout his career. Schleiermacher raised the status
of practical (pastoral) theology as a serious
discipline in its own right. He saw its task as
'stabilizing and advancing the community'. He
influenced a generation of Protestant theologians, including Albrecht Ritschl (1822–89),
Adolf Harnack (1851–1930) and Ernst
Troeltsch (1865–1923).

Bibliography

Brief Outline on the Study of Theology (ET,
Richmond, VA, 1966); *The Christian Faith*
(ET, Edinburgh and Philadelphia, 1928).

R. R. Niebuhr, *Schleiermacher on Christ
and Religion* (New York and London, 1964);
M. Redeker, *Schleiermacher* (Philadelphia,
1973); R. Roberts, 'The Feeling of Absolute
Dependence', *JR* 57.3, 1977, pp. 252–266; C.
Welch, *Protestant Thought in the Nineteenth
Century, Vol. 1: 1799– 1870* (New Haven,
CT, 1972).

D.L.O.

SCIENCE. The past three decades have
seen a revolution in our understanding of
the nature and operation of science. Prior to
the 1960s, science was generally conceived as a
rigorously rational, rigidly objective empirical
investigation of a material reality which was
fundamentally independent of human beings.
The rationality, objectivity and empirical
foundation of the investigation gave scientific
results their presumed reliability and cognitive
legitimacy – indeed, accepting the results of
science was often held to be intellectually
obligatory, and accepting anything not
verifiable by scientific processes was often
alleged to be intellectually vicious. The requisite rigour and rigidity were to be preserved
within science by adherence to a strictly defined, rule-governed method – the 'scientific
method'. The rules themselves were to be pat-
terned after those of 20th-century symbolic
logic. Although those advocating this picture
of science (*e.g.* positivists) were unable
satisfactorily to specify all the necessary 'rules'
of the scientific method, the overall idea
(roughly descended from 17th-century roots)
was that only what could be elicited from
observable empirical data was properly scientific and hence rationally legitimate.

Had the positivists (and others) been correct
in their contentions both that science was essentially logical construction upon pure empirical
data, and that any beliefs not arrived at in this
way were rationally illegitimate, then religious
beliefs – most of which cannot be directly
substantiated in this way – would have largely
lost any claim to rational acceptability. That
produced real anguish for many Christians who
had some sort of stake in science. However,
shortly after the middle of the century, it began
to be increasingly clear that the positivists' inability to specify successfully the 'rules' of
science was a consequence of deeper problems

in their view. In the light of both philosophical and historical studies (*e.g.* by S. Toulmin, 1922– ; Thomas Kuhn, 1922– ; and Michael Polanyi, 1891–1976), it has become evident that neither of the above contentions is correct. For a number of such reasons, positivism experienced a more or less total collapse within philosophy generally and philosophy of science in particular.

Indeed, there are formal reasons why science, no matter what sort of persons engaged in it, could not be conducted as mere logical, rule-governed construction upon empirical data. Data, no matter in what quantity or how complete, do not logically dictate scientific theory. There are always in principle innumerable distinct theories that can account for any given body of data (whether we can think of such theories or not). That means that scientific theories are never rigorously proven by empirical data. For reasons partially connected to this point, scientific theories cannot logically be conclusively disproven by empirical data either, contrary to one currently popular view. Consequently, in evaluating and accepting scientific theories we cannot, even in principle, avoid employing non-empirical considerations and principles in such evaluating and accepting. That employment is often nearly unconscious, and it is currently a matter of dispute just what all those principles might be, and what (if anything) might distinguish scientifically legitimate non-empirical principles (*e.g.* simplicity, predictive power, fruitfulness) from illegitimate ones. But it is indicative of the substantial departure from positivist views that virtually no contemporary philosophers of science deny that factors which are economic, social, psychological and even in some broad sense 'philosophical' play an ineradicable role in the very fabric and processes of science.

Although there is no current dominant philosophical 'orthodoxy' concerning the nature and operation of science, several broad themes are generally accepted. It is now widely believed that scientific rationality is not *sui generis*, but that it is of the same overall structure as human rationality more generally (although there is less than total clarity concerning what that structure is). Since humans are integral beings, reasoning, theorizing, evaluating and even perceiving involve multiple aspects of one's self – in some cases even one's deep world-view commitments. This broader self-involvement in one's 'scientific' activities, is, on this view, neither avoidable nor regrettable; it is simply the way human persons – who are not computers – work, and thus science, being a human pursuit, must reflect this integral character as well.

Further, it seems increasingly clear that science must be seen as at least partially embedded in wider world-view contexts, and that at least some of the indispensable non-empirical factors operating within science are drawn from those wider contexts. Given the broad variety of world-views and the alternative possibilities for shaping the larger contours of science, it is not surprising that the world-view factors drawn upon have differed across times and cultures, and that the resultant contours of science have varied as well. Historically, there simply does not seem to be any such thing as 'the' scientific method, or any inviolate, canonical set of rules definitive of science. Over the centuries, and even over recent decades, there have been deep changes within the scientific community itself concerning such key philosophical issues as what sorts of theories are or are not acceptable, over the permissibility or impermissibility of theoretical hypotheses, over the extent and types of teleological* considerations admissible, over the types and scope of causal principles required, over the criteria for what does or does not constitute adequate explanation, over what external constraints scientific theories can be properly subjected to, and so forth. In any case, there is currently no known unchangeable and workable set of *rules* for science and no visible prospect of such.

It is also widely (but not universally) believed that scientists typically work within the framework of an active, integrated package of assumptions, commitments, methodological prescriptions, values and conceptual grids that affects theorizing, evaluations, and possibly even perception in varying and disputed degrees. These paradigms, as such packages are sometimes called, shape the resulting science, and are held with surprising tenacity, sometimes even in the face of seemingly devastatingly contrary data, until overthown by some more successful paradigm. The conceptual changes involved in such overthrows are sometimes quite abrupt and substantial, and the progress of science is now seen not as the smooth, ongoing accumulation of new layers of knowledge on the already-existing structure of science, but as sometimes involving the demolition of the old structure and the 'revolutionary' reconstruction of a different structure along new lines, down to the very conceptual foundations of science.

Science is thus a delicate, complicated, historically shifting interplay among theories, data, nature, and a host of sometimes un-articulated, non-empirical principles shaping our thinking, evaluating, constructing, perceiving and theorizing. There are, however, still disputes over the types of principle, the types of role they play, and how they play them.

Some of the recent shifts have strengthened the suspicions of some philosophers of science that science is not capable of producing theoretical truth, but has perhaps, *e.g.*, only predictive power. The history of science is in significant part the history of overturned theories, and some (anti-realists) have asked why we might think that our own favoured theories should be immune to that historical pattern – which is what claiming that our own theories constitute truth would imply. Thus, although there is a substantial body (perhaps a majority) of scientists and philo-sophers of science who maintain that in many areas and to significant degrees, science does provide access to hidden – indeed unobserv-able – facets of nature, there is an increased modesty in the claims made for science.

The above profound shifts have put a very different face on Christianity/science issues. Previously, it seemed that Christianity, if not flatly counter-rational, either had to maintain a precarious existence within gaps in the scien-tific picture of reality, ever at risk from new scientific advances, or else had to operate wholly within an isolated 'spiritual' realm, pro-tected from any possible threat from science, but also rendered irrelevant to significant areas of human life by the very isolation which pro-tected it. Of course, if science does not generate proofs for its theoretical results, then those results cannot be advanced as conclusive disproofs of religion. And, should anti-realists turn out to be correct, the theoretical products of science could make no claim to truth at all, and thus could not even in principle constitute disconfirmation of the truth of theological principles. But more importantly, with science now seen as at least partially embedded in a wider conceptual context and as inescapably drawing resources from that wider context, even many secular thinkers now admit that there are no compelling reasons for thinking that Christian thought cannot provide such a context, and a perfectly legitimate one. Indeed,

it has been argued by some historians of science that the Christian intellectual context of the 16th and 17th centuries was indispensable for the initial rise of modern science. For instance, the Christian position that the cosmos is a freely constructed creation of a rational Person might explain why it is that although investiga-tion of the world must be empirical (since God was *free* in deciding what and how to create, we must actually look in order to see what he in fact chose to do), there is hope that that in-vestigation can produce genuine understand-ing (it was created according to *consistent* principles by a *rational* Person who also created the cognitive faculties we employ in such investigation).

But the point goes even deeper. Within the newer picture of science, it is in principle ra-tionally permissible for Christians to assess scientific theories in part on grounds of whether or not such theories conflict with well-grounded theological principles. Even some secular philosophers of science now admit that. Granted that we live in a deliberately created cosmos it need not be surprising that truth should exhibit that sort of unity and interconnectedness. (Given the philosophical and theological difficulties that beset older conceptions of science, and given the pos-sibilities for Christian appropriation opened up by the newer conceptions of science, it is ironic that the currently most visible promoters of the idea of a distinctive Christian voice within science – creationists – are largely committed to a nearly positivist philosophy of science, merely taking Scripture as an addi-tional, authoritative source of objective em-pirical data.)

Among the principles presently imported even into secular science practice from the wider world-view context are also a variety of normative principles reflecting traditional Christian virtues.* Good science demands honesty, integrity, patience, perseverance and a number of other such virtues. Indeed, it may be revealing that the creation* *forces* those vir-tues upon us in science. Those who are dishonest with experiment, who let ego over-ride data, or who admit inconsistency into theorizing, generally produce pseudoscience at best.

Responsible use of the results of scientific investigation, and morally legitimate use of the power that scientific and technological know-ledge brings, also demand virtues – virtues that humans are not always particularly good at exercising. From science have arisen instruments of healing and life. And from it have arisen instruments of enslavement and death. It is a disputed question whether science and technology* are inherently neutral and only our uses and misuses have moral significance, or whether science and technology merely by their very existence subtly alter our intellectual and moral landscapes in morally non-neutral ways. But in either case, the sometimes awesome potentials born of science place upon the scientist a particular responsibility for faithful vigilance in ensuring that his or her scientific work fits within, and is of a piece with, a wider Christian commitment.

In any case, some of the fears that so long haunted many educated Christians – *e.g.* that science had, if not disproved Christianity, at least rendered it intellectually disreputable – seem now to have been based not on genuine science/Christianity incompatibility, but rather either upon philosophical confusion or upon perfectly ordinary world-view conflicts, with a metaphysics-laced science merely serving as convenient vehicle. For instance, in some of those disputes science has been commandeered as an agent of the philosophical materialism and naturalism within which various secular thinkers have embedded it.

Being a faithful Christian in science and in the face of a secularized science in an overwhelmingly secularized society is sometimes no easy thing. But science, as the cognitive exploration of a creation which is the vehicle of 'general revelation', can play a positive role in the life of the church. It can open that creation up to us in such a way that we may, as Johann Kepler (1571–1630) phrased it, think the creator's thoughts after him. Sometimes science can also provide clues to the proper interpretation of passages of Scripture (*e.g.* telling us that scriptural talk of the earth's immovability is not to be taken literally). Discovering when, where and how to let theology inform science, and when, where and how to let science inform theology, is also no easy thing. But the voice which speaks to us through Scripture and through creation (and sometimes perhaps in other ways as well) is finally one voice, and we must learn to see the wholeness of the picture revealed.

A dialogue must therefore take place between our interpretation of God's creation* (science) and our interpretation of God's Word – something perhaps like the often-described reciprocal interplay within science

between theory and data – and we may well get the content of neither part of the dialogue right if we ignore the other part. Exactly how to shape that dialogue is not currently obvious, but probably must be discovered in the doing of it, just as the proper process of science itself was and must continue to be discovered in the doing of science. There are probably no iron-clad rules for this dialogue and no convenient a priori short cuts, just as there seem to be none within science itself. Wisdom and sensitivity are demanded. But the creation is God's handiwork, and he declared it good. We need not fear it. Neither need we fear what a faithfully conducted science may tell us about it.

Bibliography

T. Kuhn, *The Structure of Scientific Revolutions* (Chicago, 1962); D. L. Ratzsch, *Philosophy of Science* (Downers Grove, IL, and Leicester, 1986); C. A. Russell, *Crosscurrents: Interactions between Science and Faith* (Leicester and Grand Rapids, 1985)

D.R.

SCRUPULOSITY. Whilst a healthy conscience* has a valuable place in a person's moral life, there are occasions when it may be unreasonably demanding, resulting in an excessive fear of committing an offence, particularly over small details rather than major issues of moral concern.

Such scruples appear to be associated with a variety of situations, though the precise cause is still uncertain. For example, they may be caused by an inadequate theology which focuses attention on a harsh view of law.* In practice such a theology may result in a fear* in which God's every claim is viewed as a threat, and every moral decision is thought to be fraught with the danger of losing salvation. Such anxiety* may also be the result of harsh parenting and teaching.

There are times in our lives when we face temporary crises, as at puberty or in mid-life, or at times of conversion* and renewal. Such times can result in a disorientation and a scrupulous attention to the details of life.

More serious are cases of obsessive neurotic* scrupulosity, which result from an inability to integrate certain basic drives and values of life into the personality. The result is a fixation on a legality which issues in taboos.* Some form of psychotherapy is sometimes needed to deal with such scrupulosity.

Bibliography

B. Häring, *Free and Faithful in Christ*, vol. 1 (ET, Slough and New York, 1978); W. M. Nolan, *DPCC*, p. 1120.

C.A.B.

S ECOND VATICAN COUNCIL (1962–65). In Roman Catholic reckoning, the twentieth ecumenical ('universal') council of the Church, and the second to be held at the Vatican. It was convened by Pope John XXIII* in order to 'update' the Roman Church (the famous process of *aggiornamento*), and continued into the reign of his more conservative successor Pope Paul VI (1963–78; b. 1897) to whom fell the arduous task of implementing its decrees.

Though not intended to be radical, the Second Vatican Council soon became a rallying point for all the most liberal forces inside the Roman Church, who used its authority to further their own aims. In the process, the real teaching of the Council became obscured, and the Roman Curia has since attempted, with varying degrees of success, to move the Church back to a more conservative stance without derogating from the Council's decrees or intentions.

The Council convened in nine separate sessions and produced a total of sixteen documents, of which four are 'constitutions', three 'declarations' and nine 'decrees'. The *constitutions* deal with the liturgy (4 December 1963), the doctrine of the church (21 November 1964), divine revelation (18 November 1965), and the place of the church in the modern world (7 December 1965). It is in the last of these constitutions, *Gaudium et Spes*, that the social teaching of the Council is most fully developed. The Roman Catholic Church committed itself to a search for human progress and dignity which might be shared with non-believers, though it restated its conviction that only in Christ could true human fulfilment be found.

In *Gaudium et Spes*, the Council laid great emphasis on the freedom and dignity of the individual, as one created in the image and likeness of God (see Image of God*). It stressed the need for individuals to work in community, and advocated the struggle for social justice and human community as part of God's will. It also laid great stress on the fundamental importance of marriage* and the family,* establishing the basis for subsequent pronouncements against artificial means of birth control.* In its statements about economic and social affairs, the Council advocated the responsible use of private property,* and the co-ordinated development of individual cultural resources for the benefit of the entire human race. Finally, it also advocated a new international order* in which war would be effectively outlawed.

The three *declarations* advocated more effective efforts at Christian education (28 October 1965), closer relations with non-Christians (28 October 1965), and religious freedom (7 December 1965). The *decrees* covered a wide range of topics, including the means of social communication (4 December 1963), the Catholic churches of the Eastern rite (21 November 1964), ecumenism (21 November 1964), the pastoral role of the bishops (28 October 1965), the renewal of the religious life (28 October 1965), the priesthood (28 October 1965 and 7 December 1965), the laity (18 November 1965), and missionary work (7 December 1965). The general tone of all these documents was more relaxed and open to new ideas than had been the custom in the years preceding the Council, and many of them were highly influential in the revolution which subsequently entered Catholic thinking on many of these topics.

The reception of the Council in the Church is still far from complete, and it is too early to say what its long-term impact will be. However, it seems certain that the Roman Catholic Church will never again be as isolated from other Christian bodies or from secular thought and life as it was before 1962. It also seems probable that the Church will in future manifest an inner pluralism, even in matters of faith and morals, which was previously excluded, though it remains uncertain whether the present trend towards conservatism at the centre, reinforced by the pronouncements of Pope John Paul II (1978– ; b. 1920) will continue to have the upper hand indefinitely.

Bibliography

The Lat. text of the conciliar documents is available in *Conciliorum Oecumenicorum Decreta* (Bologna, 1973); ETs in A. Flannery (ed.), *Vatican Council II: The Conciliar and Post-Conciliar Documents* (Dublin, 1975). See also X. Rynne, *Letters from Vatican City* (London, 1963); *The Second Session* (London, 1963); *The Third Session* (London, 1964); *The Fourth Session* (London, 1965).

G.L.B.

S ECRECY. While there is a general obligation to tell the truth,* there is not a similar obligation to tell the whole truth even when requested to do so. A person may deliberately refrain from telling the truth, *e.g.* because it would be too painful to do so, or because he or she is under an obligation not to do so, or because the truth concerns a private matter. Such discretion, and respect for others' discretion, and the secrecy upon which it rests, is an important aspect of human privacy* and of that reserve and decency which are not only important features of civilized society but also conditions for the development of self-identity and self-knowledge.

It would appear to be impossible to enjoy privacy without secrecy; and even if one chooses to disclose in confidence the details of one's private life to another, to that extent one's life is less private than it was. The alarming consequences of threats to such privacy in a totalitarian State have been vividly depicted by George Orwell (1903–50) in his novel *Nineteen-Eighty-four*.

Two problems arise, however, where such a right to secrecy is upheld. Where less than the whole truth is spoken, there is the possibility of deception, even where there is no intention to deceive, for there may be the belief or expectation that the whole truth *is* being spoken. More controversially, it has been argued that in certain circumstances it is permissible to deceive by equivocating over the meaning of a word or words in order to conceal the truth, when to tell the truth would be incriminating or embarrassing. Blaise Pascal (1623–62) in his *Provincial Letters* (1657) famously castigates the Jesuit practice of *directing the intention* in a particular way in order, by equivocation, to avoid the moral consequences of a sentence's plain meaning. Such practices are deplorable because they are transparently devised to avoid moral principles.

The right to privacy which underlies the right not to tell the whole truth is grounded in ideals of human individuality and personality and, more recently, in the liberal ideal of non-interference. The dilemmas that this right may raise have more recently been made more complex and acute by legislation in Western liberal democracies. A person may have a legal right to see his or her own medical records, and there is developing a more general legal right (*e.g.* in the USA, the Freedom of Information Act) to freedom of information held by government agencies and departments previously decreed to be secret.

There is thus a growing tension between an individual's right to privacy (*e.g.* through the secret ballot, and the illegality of certain sorts of surveillance) and his or her right to information. Many would argue that the State has a duty to its citizens which may entail secrecy over matters which have important public consequences. The issue of industrial secrecy, on either commercial or strategic grounds, is also assuming greater importance.

To the keeping of some secrets there is a strongly conventional aspect, as when euphemisms and circumlocutions are used, *e.g.* in concealing from patients the true nature of their illness by the use of medical terminology. In situations where the intention is not to help someone else but to hide the moral character of the speaker, the effect of secrecy is to promote hypocrisy,* for the speaker knowingly gives false information in order to present himself or herself in a better light.

The rightness or otherwise of belonging to secret societies, such as the Freemasons, has been debated among Christians. Given the right of individuals not to have information about themselves disclosed, there can be no objection to groups of individuals, whether these are married couples, extended families or clubs, sharing secrets. The difficulties arise over the possible deception that membership of such a society may involve a person in, and in what may be the politically subversive activities of such groups. The same considerations apply to membership of a State secret service.

In Scripture certain types of secrecy are commended, *e.g.* of prayer* (Mt. 6:5–6) and the giving* of alms (Mt. 6:1–4), and the dangers of speaking ill-advisedly are warned against (*e.g.* Pr. 29:11). Warnings are given not to pry into matters which are known to God alone (Dt. 29:29). The Christian's attitude to secrecy and privacy is ultimately governed by his or her knowledge that God knows the secrets of hearts, so that while it is possible both to practice and to suffer from the deception that the ability to keep secrets confers, no deception can be practised against God.

See also: CONFIDENTIALITY.

Bibliography

S. Bok, *Secrets: On the Ethics of Concealment and Revelation* (New York, 1983; Oxford, 1984).

P.H.

SECULARIZATION is a complex and controversial term that refers to the changing relationship between religion and society.* Its earliest and perhaps most familiar usage dates from the Peace of Westphalia (1648), referring to the transfer of ecclesiastical property into princely hands. The institutional church* thus lost temporal power, and such waning of influence is often taken to be at the heart of secularization. So, for example, Bryan Wilson (1926–) defines secularization as the process in which religious institutions, actions and consciousness lose their social significance.

Modernity and religious decline

The strong version of the secularization thesis posits a direct correlation between the coming of modernity (see Modernity and Postmodernity*) and the decline of religion. This has many varieties and nuances, however, and there is often confusion between them. For instance, secularization as the loss of institutional church power or influence may be conflated with a more subjective secularization of consciousness.

The extent of secularization is also disputed. Some make strict qualifications about what exactly the term refers to; others point to the palpable persistence of religion and dismiss the whole concept of secularization as a 'myth'.

1. Take the case of secularization as loss of temporal power. No doubt institutional churches have become socially marginal in the modern world; the religious monopolies of medieval times have indeed crumbled. Note that this definition also locates the initial secularization patterns in Europe, on which other secularization patterns – such as those in N. America – are contingent. Nowhere is the loss of temporal power more clearly seen than in the sundering of church and State,* although it must be noted that this occurred in different ways. France abolished the connection via revolution (see Violence*); the USA avoided such collusion from the start; while other countries have operated with varying mixes of national and free churches. As David Martin (1929–) clearly shows, the patterns are different again in countries such as those of the Pacific rim or Latin America where Christianity is currently in the ascendant.

The process of the demonopolization and marginalization of religion has left in its wake uncertainties about the role of the institutional churches: should they accept a new position that concentrates on private devotion and perhaps overseas mission; should they try to regain lost influence through civic activity or industrial mission, as did the social gospel* movement; or should they build new communities of commitment, modelled perhaps on Latin American experience, that stand against the *status quo*? These responses, too, vary with time and place.

2. Secularization may also be viewed on a broader, societal plane. Max Weber's (1864–1920) gloomy prognosis of a 'disenchanted' world places the discussion at this level. While he noted that certain historical trends seemed traceable at least in part to religious impulses (see *The Protestant Ethic and the Spirit of Capitalism*, 1904–05), the irony of the modern world is that the spheres of religion and society have diverged so much that religion can no longer either legitimate or challenge the world. The reason is that both have become subject to rationalization, obviating any need for a transcendent reference. The calculating mentality, typical of capitalism* and bureaucracy,* lay behind secularization as disenchantment.

Weber himself thought that individuals would continue to seek meaning and purpose in religion but that this would lead to religion becoming a merely private affair, cut off from the daily realities of public life, where calculability held sway. He also predicted that conflicts would occur between 'church' and 'sect' over appropriate ways of relating to 'the world'. Indeed, this has actually come to be another way in which secularization is defined, as 'worldliness' within the church. The more 'church-like' the religiosity, the more it accommodates to the world through its social inclusiveness. The more 'sect-like', on the other hand, the greater the emphasis on doctrinal purity and ethical discipline. But an unanticipated consequence of the sectarian stance is, paradoxically, worldly success, which may in turn blunt the religious cutting edge.

A contemporary follower of Weber, Peter Berger (1929–), takes further the idea that, in effect, Christianity has been its own gravedigger. The rationality of the Western world has religious roots, but is corrosive of the very contexts that might foster religion. So Berger sees the growth of pluralism,* the divide between religious and secular outlooks in everyday life, and the weakening of, Christian-based assumptions about the human condition, once taken for granted, as results of this rationalization process.

Further consequences follow, which relate back to the first definition of secularization. Religious institutions tend to operate more and more like economic ones, competing with each other in a market-place. As 'consumers' are obliged to choose between them, personal preference rather than some concept of revealed truth becomes the criterion. Berger speaks of this as the 'heretical imperative'. In the wider world, meanwhile, people know less who they are, while their lives are dominated by big bureaucratic organizations. They have 'homeless minds', whose unfulfilled quest for meaning and identity in the face of suffering and death is a chronic condition of modern life.

The Weberian account of secularization pictures modern society creating for itself an 'iron cage' from which there appeared to be little chance of escape, and much of Berger's work follows fairly faithfully in this vein. It should be noted that Berger's own stance is ambiguous here. On the one hand, he argues that religion can be studied while bracketing belief (he calls this 'methodological atheism'). On the other, his work seems to depend on a Schleiermacherian* world-view which he insists is not closed to 'a rumour of angels'. But this has not obviated 'iron cage' readings of his secularization thesis.

Weberian accounts may seem to offer little hope for the persistence of religion in modern society, but not all studies of secularization are equally pessimistic. Richard Fenn and Daniele Hervieu-Leger, for instance, accept the relatively marginal place of religion but see simultaneously its 'paradoxical revival'. Fenn examines the ways that the public language of modern societies reduces authoritative declarations to assertions of personal opinion, making it hard to take 'religious' utterances seriously. But he argues that religion thus becomes more controversial, as a vehicle for expressing 'how things really are', which is systematically denied within education or bureaucratic administration. The boundary between the sacred and the secular then becomes a matter for active struggle – for instance over abortion* or religious education* in schools – not simply a bow to the supposedly inevitable. Hervieu-Leger takes a different tack, suggesting that the very erosion of established beliefs characteristic of modernity, such as the authority of science, creates space for new religious formations. Christianity may grasp opportunities thus presented, if they are recognized.

The concept of secularization

The concept of secularization has had a curious career. Not only has it been used within historical sociology as a tool for understanding the religion/society relationship, but also as a polemical weapon. As such, it sometimes refers to the secularizing activities of anti-clerical or atheistic groups such as rationalists or humanists who wish to rid the world of religion. But, ironically, it has also been harnessed polemically by certain theologians (e.g. J. A. T. Robinson, 1919–83; Harvey Cox, 1929– ; and R. Gregor Smith, 1913–68), who insisted that secularization expressed Christian truth. Taking a cue from Dietrich Bonhoeffer* regarding 'religionless Christianity', they turned a proper Christian concern with the affairs of 'this world' into a pretext for preoccupation with purely temporal human life. This is so-called secular theology.

Not surprisingly, the concept of secularization has often retained one or other of such connotations within historical sociology. When these are left implicit, the analytical waters are muddied even further. And for a long time some sociologists assumed simplistically that religion, as part of the old order of feudalism and traditional society, would not survive modernity. Secularization studies seemed to confirm that religion in general and Christianity in particular had a merely residual existence.

For Emile Durkheim,* as an example, religious symbolism was changing as industrial society evolved out of pre-industrial society. He noted the growing differentiation between religious and other social institutions but predicted that new social forms of religion would emerge, more appropriate, as he saw it, to the new social circumstances. For Karl Marx* and Friedrich Engels (1820–95), however, religion was hopelessly bound up with the dynamics of capitalist society, to which it lent ideological justification or from which it offered temporary solace. They expected religion's demise along with that of capitalism.

At the same time, each of the above approaches, which have often been dismissed as quite alien to a Christian viewpoint, may help to throw light on the prospects for religion at the turn of the 20th century. The Durkheimian perspective allows the possibility for religious – though not necessarily Christian –

vitality, particularly in the quest for 'belonging' in an apparently impersonal world. The emergence of 'civil religion' would be an example of this. And from what James A. Beckford (1942–86) calls the contemporary 'quasi-Marxist' perspective comes the insight that some spiritual emphases within new social movements – such as feminism* or the Greens (see Environment*) – may signal a revival of concern with religious matters.

From a Christian perspective, such a concern with religion as a 'cultural resource' rather than merely as an institution may help to locate the specific activities and role of the churches in the late modern period. It deflects attention from the idea that the demonopolization and marginality of the institutional churches somehow spell either the loss of religion *per se* or the redundancy or futility of Christian mission and Christian hope in the present day. For secularization has all too often been taken, negatively, as the 'last word' on religion in modern society, with the implication that it simply will not be a major issue in the future. This perspective reminds us that religion is a perennial and significant feature of human society.

Religion and society

It seems likely that, whatever the shortcomings of the concept, secularization will continue to be used to signal some interesting and important aspects of the relationship between religion and society in the modern world. While it certainly should not be accorded pride of place, it does retain some utility for contextualizing Christian practice.

1. It focuses attention on the peculiar condition of modernity and the place of Christianity in a world of bureaucratic organizations, economic calculation and nation-states. Such taken-for-granted realities, along with their legitimations, may often contrast and even conflict with properly Christian priorities and practices. Secularization as a historical concept reminds us that modernity itself is in flux, and that therefore the intellectual engagement with the issue of religion in contemporary society is an ongoing necessity. At the same time it may prove less than helpful for understanding some aspects of modernity, such as its global reach. Secularization in non-Western contexts or non-Christian cultures may be a very different phenomenon.

2. Secularization studies help draw attention to the perennial ambiguity of the Christian stance of being 'in but not of the world'. The perils of identification and accommodation, seen as negligent or wilful compromise with the world, must be set alongside the biblical mandate to work within the creation,* opening further its potential, which is reinforced by Jesus' sending disciples into the world, even as God sent him. Secularization within the Christian community may be seen as tacit and practical acceptance of the view that Christianity does indeed have little relevance for modern life, or, to put it the other way round, that Jesus is Lord of only a narrow, private segment of individual existence. Secularization studies may thus offer a challenge to the authenticity of Christian commitment.

3. Secularization studies may highlight new aspects of opportunity for Christian mission. The social marginality of Christian churches in the West, for instance, may be a strength, both in the sense that they are less associated with – and thus perhaps less tainted by – established political power, and that the central institutions of modernity, by eroding certain kinds of belief, have created new space for religious alternatives. The question then is how to present historic Christian commitment with integrity and contemporaneity but without the superfluous cultural baggage of earlier times.

Bibliography

J. A. Beckford, *Religion and Advanced Industrial Society* (London, 1989); P. L. Berger, *The Sacred Canopy* (New York, 1967) = *The Social Reality of Religion* (London, 1969); R. Fenn, *Liturgies and Trials* (London, 1981); D. Hervieu-Leger, *Vers un nouveau Christianisme?* (Paris, 1986); D. Lyon, 'Rethinking Secularization: Retrospect and Prospect', *RRR* 26.3, 1985; *idem*, 'Secularization: The Fate of Faith in Modern Society?', *Them* 10.1, 1984, pp. 14–22; *idem*, *The Steeple's Shadow: On the Myths and Realities of Secularization* (London, 1985); M. A. Noll, *A History of Christianity in the United States and Canada* (Grand Rapids, 1992); M. Weber, *The Protestant Ethic and the Spirit of Capitalism* (1904–05; ET, London, 1930); B. Wilson, *Religion in Sociological Perspective* (London, 1982).

D.A.L.

SECURITY. The term 'security' is used in international relations to refer to the ability of a nation to protect itself against external and internal threats. At times States try to maintain their independence by force of arms while often they rely on co-operation. Because the current level of arms development (see Armaments*) makes the use of military force a risky form of security, nations have begun to rely on economic power and democratic processes to ensure stability.

The present world situation consisting of a number of States* existing in relatively unstable equilibrium began in the 17th century. Before that time, most scholars and rulers believed in a universal empire. This concept began in ancient Rome, which included most of the political world known to its inhabitants. The task of keeping the peace in such a situation was considered to be an internal problem. In reality, security was never very complete or long-lasting. After the fall of Rome, the papacy and the Holy Roman Empire kept the ideal of universal empire alive during the Middle Ages. A basis for this was found in Stoic* philosophy which stressed a natural law* that culminated in a society of nations. However, in reality the two institutions quarrelled with each other and struggled against rising dynastic States such as France, England and Spain. The Protestant Reformation of the 16th century led to a series of conflicts which were settled by the Peace of Westphalia (1648). This treaty established a new basis for international security by allowing rulers to decide all important matters within their own territory. Princes could have different views of religion (Catholic, Lutheran or Reformed) and could enforce them on their subjects.

These States usually operated according to the principle of the balance of power. When one State was too strong, others would ally against it to maintain their own security. This system was reinforced by peace settlements such as the Congress of Vienna (1815). Following this treaty, the major powers of Europe worked together during the 19th century in an attempt to contain international conflict, but the First World War (1914–18) brought an end to this era and gave those who stressed a universal approach a new importance. The idea of collective security resulted in the proposal by President Woodrow Wilson (1856–1924) for a League of Nations (established 1920). The League was based on the theory that a war affecting any member nation was to be met by the collective action of the world community. However, it was left to the few powerful States who were represented on the League Council to recommend the measures to be taken against the aggressor.

Frequent deadlock in this group made it impossible for the League to act. Also, security was defined as the maintenance of the *status quo*, but because social and political conditions are constantly changing this proved to be an impossible task.

After the Second World War (1939–45) another type of solution was tried. The Charter of the United Nations (UN) frankly recognized the responsibility of the five leading victorious powers – the US, the USSR, Great Britain, France and China – for maintaining peace. They made up the UN Security Council along with elected members representing various parts of the world. The 'big five' could veto any action of the Council which thus could only act with their unanimous consent. This flaw, when coupled with the Cold War animosity between the US and the USSR, led to many failures by the UN to stop aggression and provide for the security of smaller States.

In addition to work through the UN, the USA, in an attempt to counter the spread of communism and provide for its own security, formed a series of international alliances such as the North Atlantic Treaty Organization (NATO). To meet this threat, the Soviet Union organized its European client States into the Warsaw Pact. This restored much of the old power network of States which was supposed to be replaced by the UN. With the fall of communism these tensions have eased, and the UN has been able to operate in Kuwait, Cambodia, Somalia and Bosnia to try to keep the peace and to confront aggression.

Maintaining national security in a nuclear world raises a number of moral issues. 1. There is the problem of cost: with so much of the gross national product having to be devoted to armaments and the payment of the armed forces, economies can be put under severe strain and social development is in consequence retarded. 2. There is the problem of 'overkill', the amassing of weaponry many times more powerful than is needed to provide adequate defence. 3. There is, paradoxically, a serious element of insecurity as smaller nations seek to develop their own nuclear weapons, with the consequent danger of their use outside the bounds of international constraint which have operated since 1945.

From a Christian perspective, it needs to be recognized that the pursuit of security becomes idolatrous if it is sought outside of trust in God (*cf.* Is. 30:1–5, 15–17).

See also: INTERNATIONAL ORDER.

Bibliography

I. L. Claude, Jr., *Swords into Plowshares: The Problems and Progress of International Organization* (New York, ⁴1971); C. W. Kegley (ed.), *The Long Postwar Peace* (New York, 1991); P. Kennedy, *The Rise and Fall of the Great Powers: Economic Change and Military Conflict from 1500 to 2000* (New York, 1987; London, 1988).

R.G.C.

SEGREGATION, RACIAL, see
APARTHEID.

SELF. The concept of the 'self' in modern philosophy can be traced back as far as René Descartes (1596–1650), who introduced the concept of the self as a spiritual substance. John Locke (1632–1704) disputed this concept and suggested that the existence of the self depends on consciousness of oneself continuing in the present the same as in the past. This self is the seat of personal identity as distinct from the soul or spiritual substance.

David Hume* found it impossible to intuit a permanent self by an analysis of consciousness. The self had subjective validity only as an inference drawn from experience, though he admitted that the self was always more than the experience of the self at any one time. Immanuel Kant* restricted the status of the self to the phenomenal realm of experience. The self is something which persons are called upon to realize and bring into existence through response to duty* and freedom.* In this conscious ethical action, the true self comes to know itself. J. G. Fichte (1762–1814), followed by G. W. F. Hegel (1770–1831), developed an ideal concept of the self through a dialectical process by which an absolute subject emerges which guarantees the unity of the self in the face of the antithetical principles of existence. William James* suggested a psychological approach to the self as the functional centre of the person who is known by others as this person, and thus who knows himself or herself through these many 'social selves'. Psychology, concluded James, has little use for a concept of the self as an entity.

Modern psychology at first tended to reject a concept of the self as inaccessible to empirical study and thus not formalizable in psychological theories. The banishment of the self was most pronounced in the work of B. F. Skinner* (*Science and Human Behaviour*) and the development of behaviourism.* At the same time, in the more recent work in the neo-Freudian analytic school of ego psychology represented by the British object-relations psychology (see Klein, Melanie;* Lake, Frank*), there is renewed interest in the self (H. Guntrip, *Psychoanalytic Theory, Therapy, and the Self*, New York, 1971). This is also true in the so-called third-force psychologies: humanistic psychology,* existential psychology* and phenomenology. In these movements the self is considered to be not only driven by urges or outside stimuli, but moved by meanings and values.

Social psychologists gave attention to self-conception variables in their theories about interpersonal attraction and conformity behaviours, but with little concern for the concept of a self lying behind the socially formed identity of the person. Theorists and researchers have thus far considered the self almost entirely as a phenomenon of self-consciousness. Carl Rogers* (*On Becoming a Person*) was one of the first clinicians to attempt extensive research on self-conceptions and described the self as an organized configuration of perceptions which are admissible to awareness. While there is continued interest in the phenomenon of the self in both philosophical and psychological literature, there is little agreement as to the existence of a self beyond the variables of self-perception.

Moral philosophers and ethicists are generally committed to the concept of a self that has continuity over time as a basis for attributing moral responsibility.* Many assert that it is illogical to hold a person morally responsible for an act unless that act is freely performed by the person. In this respect, Kant at least provided a basis for considering the self as a moral agent accountable to the categorical imperative* of willing the good as an ethical duty for all persons in all situations. J. Macmurray (*The Self as Agent*, London, 1957) argued that selfhood is derivative of personal agency in positive interaction with other persons.

The Christian faith requires the concept of the self in much the same way as does moral philosophy. God (see ①) is viewed as the judge of all humankind who holds persons responsible for their actions. The continued identity of the self as originally created by God, fallen into sin, restored through divine forgiveness* based on the atonement* of Christ, and destined to inherit eternal life through resurrection,* is essential to Christian faith. Created in the image of God,* who is considered to be the quintessence of personal being, humans are held to be inherently personal. Violation of this personal being that is unique to each individual carries with it severe consequences in the biblical literature (*cf.* Gn. 9:6; Mt. 18:6). Some Christian theorists adopt a functional view of the self and deny that the self is an internal organ of identity, maintaining that it is only a 'theory which persons have about themselves' (J. I. McFadyen, *The Call to Personhood*, Cambridge and New York, 1990). This concept, however, appears to undercut the biblical emphasis on the self as an essential and not merely a functional attribute of personal existence.

The Bible rarely uses the word 'self' in the sense of self-life. In the NT, the major instance is the phrase 'deny yourself' (*cf.* Mt. 16:24; Mk. 8:34; Lk. 9:23). These three passages refer to the same incident in which Jesus reminds his disciples that, following his own devotion to the service of God, they too must be willing to turn away from the kind of self-preoccupation that leads to loss of life, and invest themselves in daily commitment to God's sovereign will and thus 'gain' their life. The 'old self' (Rom. 6:6; sometimes called 'flesh' by Paul, Rom. 7:18, RSV), is devoted to self-interest, while the 'new self' (Eph. 4:24; Col. 3:10, sometimes spoken of as being 'raised with Christ', Eph. 2:5–6), is devoted to self-fulfilment and realization of one's deepest longings and eternal joy through the indwelling Holy Spirit.* In the vocabulary of the NT, self can mean (negatively) the egocentric self-life, but it can also mean (positively) the person's soul or spirit which is of inestimable value both to God and therefore to oneself (D. K. Clark, 'Interpreting the Biblical Words for Self', *JPT* 18.4, 1990, pp. 309–317). We are to love God with all of our heart, soul, strength and mind, and to love our neighbour as ourselves (Mt. 22:39).

Without a sense of the value of the self as an intrinsic quality of personal life created by God, and sustained by God even through times of spiritual and moral defection due to sin, there would be no basis for moral responsibility and spiritual freedom to love either God or the neighbour. While sin is viewed as vitiating the entire self so that all moral and religious motives and actions are corrupted (Rom. 3:9–20), each person is still considered responsible for immoral and unlawful actions. While psychological ambivalence is confessed

by Paul, he can still claim a love for the law of God in the depths of his 'inmost self' (Rom. 7:22, RSV). From this we can conclude that the self that God created within each person has been endowed with a capacity to love God as well as itself, and that sin does not utterly destroy the self. It is the failure of the self to overcome the destructive and disabling consequences of sin that renders it powerless unless renewed by God's grace. The 'new self' which is renewed through Jesus Christ in the power of the Holy Spirit is not a replacement for the self, but a renewing of the self that God gave to each person and that God loves in each person.

See also: PERSONALITY.

Bibliography
R. S. Anderson, *On Being Human* (Grand Rapids, 1982); A. Castell, *The Self in Philosophy* (New York, 1957); W. James, *Principles of Psychology*, vol. 1 (New York, 1890); B. Lee (ed.), *Psychological Theories of the Self* (New York and London, 1982); C. R. Rogers, *On Becoming a Person* (Boston, MA, 1961); London, ²1967); B. F. Skinner, *Science and Human Behavior* (New York, 1953).

R.S.A.

SELF-ACCEPTANCE, see SELF-ESTEEM.

SELF-ACTUALIZATION. The term 'self-actualization' was first coined by Kurt Goldstein (1878–1965) while working in New York in the 1940s, and following his study of brain-damaged men in Germany during and after the First World War. He concluded that, in the healthy state, people are driven by a single motivational force towards self-actualization, or self-realization, the fulfilment of the 'definite potentialities ... of the organism' (*Human Nature in the Light of Psychopathology*, p. 146). The notion of an intrinsic principle urging the individual towards a sense of completeness was taken up and popularized by Abraham Maslow,* although similar concepts were widely accepted amongst humanistic psychologists* of the time. Maslow wrote that the process of self-actualization is an 'ongoing [one] of potentials, capacities and talents' which incorporates 'an unceasing trend toward unity, integration or synergy within the person' (*Toward a Psychology of Being*, p. 25). Growth towards self-actualization is seen, within the humanistic framework, as the legitimate aim of counselling and psychotherapy and, indeed, as the ultimate motivating principle of all human life. Broadly, this process and goal can be compared with Carl Jung's* 'individuation', Viktor Frankl's* 'will to meaning', and Carl Rogers'* idealized picture of the 'fully functioning person'.

After the Second World War, Maslow, through observing the characteristics of admired colleagues and through extensive studies of students, other contemporaries and historic figures, began to formulate the characteristics of the self-actualized person. These include: a clear insight into and appreciation of life's realities; a developed acceptance* of self, others and the natural order; increased independence, spontaneity and creativity; a resistance to the dictates of culture;* a greater compassion and enjoyment of deeper relationships; and the presence of more frequent 'peak experiences' – mystical events, such as falling in love, appreciating a great piece of music or poetry, and gaining inspirational insight.

These idealistic notions of self-realization were tempered in Maslow's thinking by his acknowledgment that fundamental human needs (for food, drink, sleep, shelter and clothing) must first be met before there can be a response to the goal of personal fulfilment. Further, he was aware that growth towards self-actualization (marked by Being-love or B-love) can be readily thwarted by the counter-pull of human selfishness (Deficiency-love or D-love). In his later thought, Maslow began to see the limitations of the individual's quest for self-realization, postulating the need for 'the transcendent and transpersonal', for 'something "bigger than we are"' (*Toward a Psychology of Being*, pp. iii–iv).

Bibliography

K. Goldstein, *Human Nature in the Light of Psychopathology* (Cambridge, MA, 1940); A. H. Maslow, *Towards a Psychology of Being* (New York, ²1968); *idem*, Motivation and Personality (New York, ²1970); P. C. Vitz, *Psychology as Religion: The Cult of Self Worship* (Grand Rapids, 1977; Tring, ²1981); J. A. Walter, *All You Love is Need* (London, 1985) = *Need: The New Religion* (Downers Grove, IL, 1985).

R.F.H.

S ELF-DENIAL involves the disciplined refusal to gratify appetites or to give in to inclinations. In the NT it denotes something more radical – the renunciation of *self*, resulting from baptism into Christ's crucifixion (Rom. 6:3–6). This is a requirement for discipleship (Mt. 16:24, and par.) and an aspect of ongoing sanctification* (along with mortification* of the flesh or 'cross-bearing'). It is more than merely a renunciation of sins or a sinful element within us; it is the death of our selfish ego. The concupiscence* that resulted from the Fall* has established a loyalty to self that must be renounced.

The NT idea of self-denial is not merely negative. It allows one to find a new identity in Christ (2 Cor. 5:15; Gal. 2:20; Col. 3:3). Ironically, such abnegation results in the fulfilment of one's life as God meant it to be experienced (Mt. 16:25). Self-denial makes possible unreserved dedication to Christ and, therefore, to others. Accordingly, self-denial has the happy effect of promoting Christian fellowship (see Phil. 2:1–7).

Through the lifelong exercise of daily acts of self-denial we cultivate a habitual self-denial or a total unselfishness.

In practising self-denial one must avoid extremes that have the opposite effect of calling attention to self. Self-denial must not be confused with self-hatred, which can have disastrous effects when projected on to others. Furthermore, self-denial must not be thought of as meritorious towards salvation.

Self-denial is an essential component of the Christian life, and it is timely in an age of consumerism, consumption, gratification of every desire and addictions. It can yield positive social benefits for those who are the victims of others' over-consumption.

See also: ASCETICISM; DISCIPLINE.

Bibliography

E. Brunner, *The Divine Imperative* (ET, London and New York, 1937); J. Calvin, *The Institutes of the Christian Religion*, LCC 20–21, III.7 and 8; R. H. Ramey, Jr, and B. C. Johnson, *Living the Christian Life* (Louisville, KY, 1992); H. Schlier, TDNT 1, pp. 469–471.

D.L.O.

S ELF-ESTEEM, or self-acceptance, is not some sort of scale with which we assess our value, nor is it something external to ourselves. It is an essential part of our very being.

The self* is the inner core of personality;* the almost indefinable centre from which one's basic being radiates. From this focus one is able to say 'I am' (echoing the words of our creator). This 'I am' means that one can exist as a person independently of other people's affirmation and approval or opinions, though inter-dependence in living contact is an essential part of the enjoyment of 'I am'. The self is about being', not about 'doing'. The self is not found by achieving status through good or important activities, wealth, beauty, intellect or heroics of various sorts. These things will vanish away in due course but the self remains. Much of our busyness or 'playing to the gallery' shields us from the difficulty of finding ourselves. That search requires space and the opportunity for quiet reflection. It is sometimes painful to face the dark areas which we have hidden away, denied or called by some other name, because we find them unpleasant and frightening (see Repression, Psychological*).

The sense of self grows gradually within the parent–infant relationship where there is an atmosphere of unconditional love (see ②) and acceptance.* Such an infant is on the receiving end of fairly consistent love and gradually ab-sorbs the life-giving qualities of that love which can also contain and manage the negatives. No experience of parenting (see Parenthood, Parenting*) is perfect, but hopefully the child receives enough love to take into itself a sense of secure identity and selfhood which becomes its own. This child begins gradually to ex-perience himself or herself as a valuable person in his or her own right. This is self-esteem: the ability to be at home within oneself; not needing to seek endless distractions or affirma-tion. On every level, we learn to love only because we have first been loved (1 Jn. 4:19). However, the world is not a perfect place in which to grow up, and the emerging personal-ity can and does have many hard encounters which can badly damage a self which is fragile and uncertain about its identity. Many people struggle throughout their lives with the debilitating effects of this damage to the self. It creates low self-esteem because these people have taken into themselves the message that they are not adequately loved. They are im-paired in their ability to be comfortable within themselves, always needing approval and reassurance from outside. They are unsure about decision-making and activities which they would like to pursue. They may have a constant need to prove themselves to be better than others, or they may display a compulsive striving for power. Their overriding need to please people and to be liked interferes with

their ability to love spontaneously and openly; their ability to accept themselves is also severely hampered. Self-esteem has nothing to do with having an exaggerated idea of one's own importance. That is egocentricity and is often a compensatory device for a low self-esteem (see Rom. 12:3).

The quest to discover one's true core of per-sonality is of primary importance. It is a lifetime's journey. The Christian mystics have often described the self as 'the summit of the soul' (Julian of Norwich, c. 1342–1420; John of the Cross, 1542–91; Teresa of Avila, 1515–82), the place where God dwells within us. It is only in our own centre of 'being' that we can 'be still and know that I am ...' (Ps. 46:10). Carl Jung,* with his characteristic verbal impreci-sion, has sometimes called the self 'God' and thereby caused much confusion. More harm and confusion have been caused by the erro-neous impression that such Bible verses as 'not I ... but Christ' (Gal. 2:20, RSV) and concepts such as 'dying to self', imply the necessity to ex-punge the self and replace it with someone or some concept which is foreign to one's essential being. Paul is the main exponent of this theme, but he is referring not to the vital inner core of self but to egocentricity. Indeed, he makes frequent reference to the vital inner self (e.g. Eph. 3:16–17), mostly described as 'the heart'. Egocentricity consists of the accretions to the self which are caused by sin and need in this existence. It is they which are consciously concerned with self-esteem. On the other hand, the self-esteem which arises from the self is unselfconscious and natural. Self-esteem is not the same as the self, but is inseparable from it. When one is centred in the self, esteem for and acceptance of it are natural consequences.

Bibliography
C. Bryant, *The River Within* (London, 1978); J. and A. McGrath, *The Dilemma of Self-esteem: The Cross and Christian Con-fidence* (Wheaton, IL, and Cambridge, 1992); J. Sturt, 'Low Self-esteem', in *CC*, 1993, 3.2, pp. 37–42, and 3.3, pp. 2–7. S. Verney, *Water into Wine* (London, 1985).

M.C.-J.

SELF-EXPRESSION, see SELF.

SELF-LOVE, see LOVE; ② SELF-ESTEEM.

SELF-POISONING may be defined as in-tentional self-harm by the ingestion, inhalation, injection or introduction by other means of a toxic substance, which may lead to death. The phenomenon accounts for the vast majority of parasuicides (intentional self-harm not ending in death). Many such episodes are not accompanied by the intention of actually producing death. In the Western world, the phenomenon has become one of major importance, not only in terms of human suffering, but also in terms of economic consequences and health-services issues. Many (probably the vast majority) of such incidents do not come into contact with official services.

According to R. F. W. Diekstra in 'Suicide and Parasuicide', the different motives behind such incidents can be categorized as follows: cessation (stopping conscious experience for ever), interruption (to interrupt conscious experience for a while, or 'time out'), and appeal (for help from others). Depression,* accompanied by many interpersonal conflicts, is common in suicide-attempters, as also are poor employment records, alcohol (see Alcoholism*) and drug* abuse, and a family history of self-harm. The problem is to distinguish serious episodes from less serious ones, bearing in mind that anyone having carried out a parasuicide attempt is much more likely to end his or her life by actual suicide (10% to 14%). The high-risk group (see Suicide*) is often identified by routine screening, and individuals in need of treatment are thereby referred on for appropriate psychiatric help. Screening usually takes place in the context of hospital acute admission wards specifically designed for such individuals, and it has been shown in a 1977 study that up to 20% of acute medical admissions are for parasuicide (see H. J. Mollier, 'Compliance'). Since, however, such individuals rarely remain in hospital for long periods of time, parasuicide does not take up one fifth of medical resources.

A number of important ethical issues can be identified. One is the ready availability of highly toxic chemicals which are often prescribed for psychiatric purposes. The commonest poisons employed have been barbiturate drugs, tricyclic and other anti-depressants, and easily-obtained analgesics such as aspirin and paracetamol. Fortunately, dangerous psychotropic medications are now being replaced by less toxic but equally effective ones. On the one hand, antidepressants, for example, have probably been over-prescribed in ineffective doses for conditions where adequate counselling and psychotherapy (see 12) could have been helpful. From a clinical standpoint, the latter are more appealing than chemotherapy, particularly in a context of maladjustment to situational stress.* On the other hand, depressive disorder is often under-treated with ineffective doses of antidepressants.

The question of the explanation of the rise in self-poisoning remains largely a matter of conjecture, but depressive disorders (and the rise in the rate of self-poisoning) may be due to maladjustment to the excessive materialism of the age with its almost total lack of spiritual values.

Pastoral issues are obviously of great importance, and the average congregation will produce episodes of intentional self-harm from time to time. Many may not have come into contact with official services. Because of the general risks of later *actual* suicide, it is therefore wise to obtain a medical (psychiatric) opinion and press the need for treatment if necessary. The approach pastorally will obviously depend on the motive. As in the case of suicide, the act is morally wrong, although the question of 'blame' in an individual with depressed mood is an unclear one. The desire for 'time out' may be understandable in the context of situational stress, but it is highly dangerous. Appropriate help will seek to resolve conflicts. Where the motive was actual suicide, there is often incredulity on reflection by the individual that he or she has been involved in such an episode, and also feelings of shame* and guilt.* Provided they are not excessive, the latter can be helpful in planning more realistic future courses of action to deal with unsatisfying lifestyles.

Attention-seeking behaviour can be difficult to cope with, even by caring professionals, especially in the repeated overdoser. However, pastoral counsel should primarily seek to help with the situational stress.

Bibliography

R. F. W. Diekstra, 'Suicide and Parasuicide: A Global Perspective', in S. A. Montgomery and N. L. M. Goeting (eds.), *Suicide and Attempted Suicide* (Southampton, 1991); R. F. W. Diekstra and K. Hawton (eds.), *Suicide in Adolescence* (Dordrecht, 1987); K. Hawton, 'Repetition and Suicide Following Attempted Suicide', in S. A. Montgomery and N. L. M. Goeting (eds.), *Suicide and Attempted Suicide* (Southampton, 1991); H. J. Mollier, 'Compliance', in N. Kreitman and S. Platt (eds.), *Current Research on Suicide and Parasuicide* (Edinburgh, 1989), pp. 164–172.

B.H.

SELF-WORTH, see Self-esteem.

S ENTENCING, PRISON. The sentence is the order of a court of criminal jurisdiction imposed as the sanction for wrongdoing of a criminal nature (see Crime*), *i.e.* in proceedings brought against an individual in the name of the State or the people (in Eng. law in the name of the monarch) to ensure good order. It is distinguishable from the orders or judgments of courts of civil jurisdiction, whose sanctions consist of awards, *e.g.* of damages, or other orders intended to do justice in disputes between individuals.

In the US, the philosophy of prison sentencing has undergone three stages of evolution. Retribution* was replaced by deterrence (see Deterrence, Non-nuclear*) as the primary motivation for punishment of crime in the Enlightenment period of the late 18th and early 19th centuries. As a result, imprisonment instead of corporal punishment became the main means of punishment. In the late 19th and early 20th centuries, rationalism declined and individualized rehabilitative programmes arose. These included education, casework and psychotherapy, designed to combat mental, emotional and social deficiencies believed to be the major causes of criminal activities. This led to an institution of the indeterminate sentence, which consists of a set minimum and maximum length of sentence for a particular offence. The goal of the indeterminate sentence was to offer an incentive for rehabilitation. At present, however, an alarming increase in the rate of crime has led to disillusionment with the rehabilitative model, and several States have returned to more severe mandatory sentencing laws.

After conviction in the US, the judge passes a sentence whose limits are usually delineated by laws concerning the crime. The judge may, however, employ personal judgment in determining the severity of a specific punishment. Indeterminate sentencing is characterized by opportunities for parole or probation. Parole is the partial recovery of freedom after serving the minimum sentence – a normal civilian life under supervision of a parole board, as long as the prisoner's behaviour is exemplary. Probation, like parole, is a conditional and supervised sentence, and it may be substituted for a prison sentence. Indeterminate sentencing, with its corollaries of parole and probation, is currently under much criticism. Critics believe it has resulted in over-lenient punishments that do not effectively deter crime. One of the results of this criticism is the 1984 federal legislation mandating standard prison sentences for federal crimes.

Amongst the sentencing powers possessed by the UK courts, the ordering of a period of imprisonment or other similar restriction of liberty, *e.g.* detention in a young offenders' institution, figures prominently. The aim of 19th-century prison reformers to utilize imprisonment as providing an opportunity for reformation through education has in practice been undermined by the pressures created by increasing criminal activity, with the consequent incarceration of more convicted offenders and the inability of the prison system to do much more than contain offenders and punish them by simple loss of liberty (see Punishment*).

The high cost of detaining people in prison, together with its unproductive nature (apart from simple containment), has led to a widening of sentencing powers, as embodied in the UK in the Powers of Criminal Courts Act (1983) which permits a variety of other sanctions. The powers of the courts to commit younger offenders to prison have also been periodically under review in a succession of statutory provisions governing both the nature of the institution to which commitment is made, and the essential prerequisites to be considered as qualification for commitment. In this last regard the present criteria are contained in sections 1–4 of the Criminal Justice Act (1991), but it is a matter which for younger and older offenders alike will probably be kept under continuing review and amendment from time to time. The 1991 statute obliges the court to consider whether a prison sentence is necessary because of the seriousness of the offence or the need to protect the public. The sentencing procedure is so prescribed as to focus the court's attention on these criteria, making it obligatory for the reasons to be stated in open court.

The prevailing approach in the UK, as embodied in statutory provisions and the judgments of the courts, is that imprisonment is either a sentence of last resort, to be applied when all else has failed, or only to be used in those cases where the offence causes such outrage and is of such a degree of seriousness that imprisonment can be regarded as the only means of expressing public disapproval or of achieving public protection. The present state of Eng. penal law permits some sentences (those of no more than two years' duration) to be suspended for no more than two years. In such cases the suspended sentence may be invoked if the defendant re-offends within the time limit of the suspension. Alternative methods of restricting the offender's liberty but in a more constructive manner are exemplified by the community service order (not exceeding 240 hours of work performed by instalments), and the probation order with a provision for attendance at a day activity centre (again by instalments, not aggregating more than 60 days).

The period of a sentence for which a prisoner remains in detention may be reduced under the Prison Regulations by remission for good conduct (a fixed fraction of the sentence) or by parole, a discretionary system whereby a prisoner is released upon licence under supervision and remains thereafter at liberty subject to the terms of his or her licence. Breach of those terms within the unexpired balance of the sentence renders him or her liable to recall to serve the remainder of the sentence.

A record of the sentence is maintained at the Criminal Records Office. There are statutory rules under the Rehabilitation of Offenders Act, 1974, whereby after a passage of time old convictions become 'spent' and the offender is entitled by statute to have his or her character assessed free from their taint.

In addition to these sanctions for the breach of the criminal law, Eng. courts have a power to imprison for contempt of the court. This power, the exercise of which is subject to statutory rules, exists to sustain the authority of the court in regulating its proceedings and for the purpose of ensuring that the court's orders are obeyed, *e.g.* so that the relief granted to one litigant is not rendered nugatory by the high-handedness of his or her opponent. Such a sentence may be for a specific period of time as a punishment for disobedience, or it may be for the purpose of enforcing compliance with an order or judgment, in which case the contemner may 'purge' his or her contempt by compliance and apology.

See also: CRIMINAL JUSTICE; PRISON AND PRISON REFORM.

R.J.T.

SERMON ON THE MOUNT. The title was first used by Augustine.* The 'Sermon on the Mount' comprises chs. 5 – 7 of Matthew's Gospel. Luke's so-called 'Sermon on the Plain' (Lk. 6:20–49) contains many parallels, though it is much shorter.

It would be hard to exaggerate the influence that the Sermon on the Mount has had in forming moral attitudes and political programmes, both inside and outside the church. The Beatitudes* (Mt. 5:3–12), the Lord's Prayer (6:9–13) and the 'golden rule'* (7:12) are probably the best-known sections. Both Leo Tolstoy* and Mohandas (Mahatma) Gandhi (1869–1948) acknowledged the Sermon's enormous effect in shaping their social philosophies.

Nevertheless, commentators have always found difficulties in applying this major piece of Jesus' teaching to their contemporary ethical and pastoral issues. The main problem is highlighted by the Sermon's most obvious characteristic – the extreme and radical nature of its demands.

The result has been a broad spectrum of interpretation. At one end we find Anabaptists* and Mennonites (see Mennonite Ethics*) for whom the Sermon's imperatives are absolute. They conclude that taking oaths (Mt. 5:33–37), using violence* (5:38–42) and serving on the judiciary (7:1–2) are forbidden to Christians.

At the other extreme stand those who (like some modern Lutherans) understand Jesus' purpose quite differently. The Lord makes impossibly high demands in the Sermon on the Mount, they maintain, in order to impel his listeners to seek God's merciful forgiveness* when their complete inability to live lives that are pleasing to him is exposed.

Mediating positions attempt to restrict the application of Jesus' demands to certain times, people or circumstances. Five are particularly worth noticing.

1. *Albert Schweitzer* (1875–1965) described the Sermon as an 'interim ethic',* a set of emergency rules for those who lived in the 'end times' before God's kingdom (see Kingdom of God*) was fully manifested. Jesus expected those times to be short. He was mistaken, so Christians today are exempt from taking his demands at face value. The Sermon simply does not apply to 'settled' life.

2. *Dispensationalism* explains the relationship between the Sermon and the kingdom a little differently. Jesus' teaching, dispensationalists say, will apply fully only when the kingdom has fully come. So Christians today can anticipate that time only by observing the principles which the Sermon's demands express.

3. Traditionally (looking back to Thomas Aquinas*), the *Roman Catholic Church* has detected a double standard in the Sermon on the Mount. Some of its precepts are binding on all Christians, but others express 'evangelical counsels' which apply only to the spiritual élite who are called to take monastic vows.

4. In developing his theory of the 'two realms', *Martin Luther** distinguished between personal relationships and social obligations. He restricted the Sermon on the Mount's application to the former (so while a Christian man must never use force to resolve a personal conflict, he may fight in a war with a clear conscience if the State conscripts him).

5. Finally, and more radically, many commentators prefer to restrict the application of the Sermon's imperatives to Christian attitudes. Jesus did not intend to legislate, they say. He expressed his teaching in the shape of rules and regulations (and used hyperbole) to add weight and urgency to his teaching. His listeners, used to rabbinic Haggadah, would quickly realize that he was illustrating values (like honesty), not specifying rules (like 'You shall not swear oaths').

To find one's way through this interpretative maze, it is necessary to answer two key questions, each of which conceals a theological and ethical tension.

1. *What is the relationship between the Sermon on the Mount and the Old Testament law?* The Sermon's setting (a new Moses delivering a new law* from a new Sinai) certainly suggests continuity (*cf.* Mt. 5:17–18), while the 'antithesis formula' ('It has been said . . . But I tell you') may suggest something more radical than a break with the law's acknowledged teachers. Jesus' claim to 'fulfil' the law helps to resolve the tension. He brings out the law's full meaning by highlighting the inward attitudes which underlie behaviour and by exposing hypocritical motives. The resulting 'righteousness'* which 'surpasses that of the Pharisees' (Mt. 5:20) virtually defies codification.

2. *What is the relationship between the Sermon on the Mount and Jesus' teaching about the kingdom of God?* The latter certainly pervades the sermon, just as it frames the whole of Jesus' ethical teaching (see New Testament Ethics[9]). It seems that Jesus taught both the presence and the future imminence of God's rule. The kingdom's presence (especially in Jesus' own person) highlights the urgency of his demands as well as promising royal resources

to meet them; while its imminence explains why total obedience (especially to Mt. 5:48) will lie beyond the Christian's reach until the 'not yet' becomes 'now' and the tension is resolved.

Bibliography

H. D. Betz, *Essays on the Sermon on the Mount* (Philadelphia, 1985); R. A. Guelich, *The Sermon on the Mount: A Foundation for Understanding* (Waco, TX, 1982); W. S. Kissinger, *The Sermon on the Mount: A History of Interpretation and Bibliography* (Metuchen, NJ, 1975).

D.H.F.

SEX, see SEXUALITY. [11]

SEX CHANGE, see TRANSSEXUALISM.

SEX DISCRIMINATION, see DISCRIMINATION; SEXISM.

SEXISM comprises attitudes or actions which discriminate against women or men on the grounds of gender. In common usage it refers to discrimination against women, but it properly applies to both sexes. The term is coming to be applied also to discrimination against homosexual men and women.

The Scriptures clearly reject actions such as rape* or assault, and attitudes such as lust* or coveting. They teach that both men and women are 'made in the image of God'* (Gn. 1:26), and that in Christ 'there is neither male nor female' (Gal. 3:28). Jesus treated women and men alike with full seriousness, with no suggestion of discrimination. The early churches were noteworthy for the active participation of both sexes, although leadership was largely in men's hands. The Christian tradition has therefore a long record of opposition to the explicit oppression of women, *e.g.* as seen in the abolition of purdah, widow-burning and foot-binding. Women have commonly formed the majority of local-church members, finding that faith in Christ yields positive self-worth and gives meaning to life.

Yet the Christian tradition has also tolerated and legitimized social, cultural and legal practices which favour men, *e.g.* denying married women the right to own property, tolerating lower wage rates for women, or excluding women from holding many church offices. Some feminists argue that the overwhelmingly male imagery entailed in Christian belief and ministry renders Christianity at worst patriarchal and at best paternalistic. Such questioning has raised the charge of sexism against the Christian faith in recent decades.

All Christians agree that there are distinctive aspects of being male or female, and that women and men alike are both eligible for, and need, salvation in Christ. There are differences in how these distinctive aspects work out in practice. Some interpret 1 Tim. 2:11–14 and 1 Cor. 11:1–16 as implying that these differences presuppose a 'creation order' in which the male role is to lead, the female to follow. In this view the equality of men and women in the sight of God is affirmed, but in both society and church their roles are limited (usually expressed in restricting leadership to men, and preferring home-maker lifestyles for women). Others interpret such subordination of women to the effects of sin (the 'curse' of Gn. 3:16). This is done away with in Christ (Gal. 3:26–29), and will not be part of the new creation: therefore such restrictions have no part in the body of Christ, though the distinctive contributions of each Christian need to be affirmed and received. While under both views sexist attitudes often remain in practice, many women find they are unable to live in communities where the first position is taken, since it questions their human and Christian identity.

Sexism has a particular focus in language. Some tongues possess gender-inclusive pronouns or words for men and women, some use gender as a grammar-marker only, while others (including Eng.) lack gender-inclusive terms. Until recently 'man' functioned in Eng. to refer both to males and to human beings in general. Most Christian traditions have moved to avoid such double usage in their public language of prayer, most commonly by employing plural pronouns or rephrasing. The Scriptures, however, contain a number of places where gender-specific language is used in a generic way: how to translate these remains an issue, although such translations have been made (e.g. the New Revised Standard Version, 1990). Most would distinguish between a 'conservative' policy in regard to Scripture translation, and a 'progressive' policy in regard to the use of the Scriptures in prayer, liturgy or preaching. Particular problems arise with the Psalter, used as the basis of daily prayer in many traditions; here the line between translation and use becomes transparent.

The central theological issue concerns language about God (see ①). The biblical data portrays God in both masculine and feminine terms, but masculine terms, metaphors and images predominate. The best known is the naming of God as Father. This is never an absolute naming, in which God would be identified as 'Father' (which is patriarchy); it is rather relational (God as the Father of Israel's king, and the Father of Jesus Christ). Maternal verbs and adjectives are used of God, but less frequently than 'father' terms, and the noun 'mother' is never used of God (cf. Is. 66:13). The personal revelation of God occurs through Jesus, a male who confessed himself to be 'Lord' and 'Son of God'. God is identified in Christian theology in the naming 'Father, Son and Holy Spirit'. Although the doctrine of the Trinity was formulated to avoid any literal understanding of divine imagery, and functions so as to undermine hierarchical notions of God and human society, this naming involves inescapably male terminology.

Some therefore see the Christian tradition, and the Scriptures from which it is formed, as themselves sexist, legitimizing male superiority by imaging God in male ways. Others regard the preponderance of male imagery as reflecting cultural relativities; others again as formed against the background of the sinful state of male domination since the Fall.* These latter positions allow for the correction of perceived male bias by emphasizing the distinctive roles of male and female but affirming equality of essence and opportunity for ministry.* More conservative Christians see the male priority in the Scriptures as continuing to reflect the asymmetrical nature of reality, the irreducible distinctiveness of masculine and feminine aspects of human nature. Each position would reject the charge of encouraging or undergirding sexist attitudes, while conceding that no tradition has yet grown beyond sexism. All Christians face the challenge of sexism in the way they form and express personal attitudes through their ethos, liturgical traditions, styles of biblical exegesis, and ministry structures (both formal and informal).

See also: FEMINISM; HEADSHIP.

Bibliography

D. G. Bloesch, *The Battle for the Trinity* (Ann Arbor, MI, 1985); S. Clark, *Man and Woman in Christ* (Ann Arbor, MI, 1980); M. Hayter, *The New Eve in Christ* (London,

1987); K. Keay (ed.), *Men, Women and God* (London, 1987); C. H. Sherlock, *God in the Inside* (Melbourne, 1991); P. Trible, *God and the Rhetoric of Sexuality* (Philadelphia, 1978); B. Wren, *What Language Shall I Borrow?* (London and New York, 1989).

C.H.S.

SEXUAL ABUSE, see ABUSE.

SEXUAL ADDICTION. Nowadays, it is increasingly recognized that much sexual behaviour stems from emotional pain (see Clinical Theology*) rather than emotional desire. The major paradigm for this is sexual addiction. In addictions generally, the addict is involved in a dysfunctional relationship with a mood-altering substance or activity. For the sexual addict, sex is the activity chosen to mask or to 'medicate' emotional pain. As in other addictions, such attempts are self-defeating. The underlying pain is avoided rather than dealt with, and there is only temporary relief rather than long-term resolution. The addict gets caught in a downward spiral of increasing involvement in sexual activity, which he or she is powerless to control. The addict experiences increasing pain and shame* and loneliness.* This may damage family relationships, compromise the person's own sense of values, and risk the loss of job and other negative social consequences. The renewed pain leads to renewed attempts to escape pain through sexual acting-out. Thus, the addict's life becomes one of unmanageability and desperation.

The pioneeering work of P. Carnes (1944–) describes both the addictive process and steps towards recovery. Carnes refers to three levels of addiction, characterized by behaviour that is increasingly intrusive and unacceptable to social norms. The first level involves such activities as pornography,* masturbation,* promiscuous relationships, and sex with prostitutes. The second level includes exhibitionism, voyeurism and obscene phone-calls. Rape,* incest,* and child-molestation (see Abuse*) are characteristic of the third level. Not all persons who engage in these activities are sex addicts, but only those for whom the behaviour is compulsive.

Addicts typically have a very low sense of self-esteem,* and find it hard to believe that anyone would love them for themselves. Many were sexually or emotionally abused as children, and grew up in a dysfunctional family. All addictions thrive on isolation, and an important part of the healing process is to break through the isolation and denial. The fellowship provided by a caring support-group brings addicts out of isolation. They can work through the unresolved pain and shame stemming from their family of origin. Addicts can learn new beliefs and new coping behaviours. In therapy and in twelve-step programmes, they can get help to heal the past, restore self-esteem, and rebuild healthy values and healthy relationships.

As in other addictions, it is important for other family members to receive help. The co-addict or codependant has structured his or her own life around the addict, and has experienced similar unmanageability. For instance, the spouse of a sexual addict may have attempted to control or conceal the partner's behaviour, but without success. It is important for co-addicts to deal with their own pain and damaged self-esteem, and to learn new and more functional ways of coping with life.

Likewise, the children of a sex addict are inevitably growing up in a home that is dysfunctional. Even if no sexual abuse is involved, their self-esteem and ability to form healthy relationships may be affected. All who are affected directly or indirectly by sexual addiction can benefit from suitable therapeutic help.

See also: SEXUAL DEVIATION.

Bibliography
Hope and Recovery: A 12-step Guide for Healing for Compulsive Sexual Behaviour (Minneapolis, MN, 1987); P. Carnes, *Don't Call it Love* (London and New York, 1991); R. Earle and G. Crow, *Lonely All the Time* (London and New York, 1989); B. L. Robinson and R. L. Robinson, *If my Dad's a Sexaholic, What Does that Make Me?* (Minneapolis, MN, 1991).

E.R.M.

SEXUAL COUNSELLING AND THERAPY. In a society apparently obsessed by sex, sexual activity remains a source of misery to many. Earlier this century, psychoanalysis* was the main way of helping people with sexual difficulties. After the Second World War, the research by A. C. Kinsey (1894–1956) into human sexual behaviour (see Kinsey Reports*) was quickly followed by the work of William Masters (1915–) and Virginia Johnson (1925–) on human sexual responses. This led to the latter's programme for the treatment of sexual difficulties, which is predominantly behaviourist* in approach. Various forms of sex therapy are now available in the USA, and in Britain through National Health Service clinics, the Family Planning Association, Relate Marriage Guidance, and individual counsellors or therapists.

With its concern for marriage* and broken lives, the church needs to be involved in this area. Yet few Christian books on marriage mention sexual difficulties or therapy; most imply that sex will be exhilarating and easy, compounding the pain of those whose experience is otherwise. Some negative aspects of the Christian tradition concerning sexuality (see 11) have exacerbated the problems for some people.

Sexual difficulties include insufficient sexual interest or enjoyment, or pain or a lack of feeling, as well as the particular problems of impotence or premature ejaculation in men, and vaginismus or lack of orgasm in women. Sex therapy aims to relieve the actual difficulty, setting a limited contract* with specific goals for each couple, who ideally are treated together. It begins with history-taking, and involves a learning process, moving from touch and communication, towards genital contact and eventually coitus. Gradually the couple are weaned off the therapist's control, and arrangements are made for follow-up. Success rates are usually good, especially with highly motivated clients. Sex therapy can play a helpful role in building up marriages and preventing divorce.*

No form of therapy or counselling (see Pastoral Care, Counselling and Psychotherapy 12) is value-free, and Christians are often anxious about the values of secular counselling. The Christian ethic of sexuality, the priority of the person, the need for appropriate professionalism, and a commitment to all therapy as part of God's redeeming of creation, are all important considerations for Christians involved in sexual counselling and therapy.

Some may question the use of a therapist at all: is it right to admit someone else into the heart of a marriage? However, the intention* of healing the pain, and the probable consequence (see Consequentialism*) of a better marriage relationship, suggest that appropriate therapy is perfectly acceptable. Others object to the temporary ban on sexual intercourse, which is usually part of sexual therapy, while the couple learn to take pleasure

in touch and other non-coital sexual stimulation. Obviously, a traditional ethic of sexual expression only within intercourse with the intention of *procreation* (Gn. 1:28) will have problems here. However, the alternative emphasis on the *relational* aspect of sexual expression (Gn. 2:18, 23–25) will encourage such expressions of mutual love. Some therapy includes the use of the imagination, sexual fantasy or erotic literature. Where are lines to be drawn between therapy, healthy interest and pornography*? The recent development of various sex education videos (*e.g.* The Lovers' Guide) has proved helpful for some counsellors and clergy in their work with couples, while others find such videos too explicit.

Increasing numbers of Christians are taking the view that the main tasks and techniques used in therapy can be justified within the ethic of sex as God-given and the need to alleviate suffering. However, careful pastoral sensitivity is needed with clients whose moral or spiritual upbringing and beliefs lead them to consider some of the techniques dirty or sinful. Good therapists do not seek to alter a client's value-system, but it may be appropriate to work with values which seem to contribute to dysfunction. Christian clients worried about suggested techniques may benefit from support and discussion with their minister or pastor while therapy is being undertaken.

A further issue for Christian therapists is whether to treat only married couples, or whether their work may include other heterosexual couples and homosexual couples. The development of 'safer sex' techniques, following the spread of HIV infection and AIDS-related illnesses, will also impinge on sexual counsellors. A wider ethical issue here is the extent to which Christians can expect their ethics to be shared by the rest of the world.

Some secular therapists use sexual surrogate* partners in the treatment of single people with sexual difficulties. In the USA large sums of money are involved in sex clinics using surrogate prostitutes. The traditional Christian teaching that sex is for marriage will not permit the use of surrogates. This places a particular obligation on the church to provide pastoral care to single people with sexual difficulties. Confession,* healing of memories (see Inner Healing*) and especially the provision of a loving environment, can all contribute towards personal wholeness.

Although sex therapists have no universal code of professional practice, most agree that sexual activity between therapist and client, or observation of clients making love by the therapist, should be avoided. Any genital examination should be undertaken only by a doctor. There is clearly wide scope for abuse of the therapist's power in this area. Given the lack of statutory controls, a careful check on a therapist's professional training and accreditation* is recommended.

Christians may be involved in sex therapy at various levels. Christian marriages are not immune to sexual difficulties; therapy can sometimes offer the opportunity for healing and recovering the God-given joy of sex. Clergy have many opportunities with couples in marriage preparation and later support, while Christian counsellors and therapists can be involved in the profession itself. William Masters, one of the pioneers of sex therapy and research, invited theological contribution to the ethical debate. The church still has much to offer by way of a response. Sex therapy does not have all its ethics worked out satisfactorily as yet. Christian people must not only press ethical questions, but also contribute towards the process.

Bibliography

J. Bancroft, *Human Sexuality and its Problems* (Edinburgh and New York, ²1989); R. A. Burridge, *Sex Therapy: Some Ethical Considerations* (Bramcote, Nottingham, 1985); D. Jehu, *Sexual Dysfunction: A Behavioural Approach to Causation, Assessment and Treatment* (Chichester, 1979); H. S. Kaplan, *The New Sex Therapy* (London, 1974); U. Kroll, *Sexual Counselling* (London, 1980); W. H. Masters *et al.* (eds.), *Ethical Issues in Sex Therapy and Research* (Boston, MA, 1977); E. and G. Wheat, *Intended for Pleasure: Sex Technique and Sexual Fulfilment in Christian Marriage* (London, 1979).

R.A.B.

SEXUAL DEVIATION. In the late 20th century there is much controversy about what aspects of sexuality (see ⑪) should be regarded as normative, together with a reluctance to use such labels as 'deviant' or 'abnormal'. Christians need to be aware of this debate, together with its merits and demerits. Positive concerns are an increasingly nuanced understanding of ethics; a willingness to learn from the insights of psychology; and a desire to respond with greater compassion to persons involved in unusual sexual behaviour. Some

disadvantages are an underlying philosophy of relativism;* an emphasis on self-expression that may discount or disregard the needs of others; a resulting shallowness or instability in relationships; and an inadequate recognition of how much sexual behaviour is an expression of emotional pain, rather than emotional fulfilment. Thus, Christians are called both to learn from the contemporary debate, and to challenge its presuppositions.

The normative biblical model for sexual behaviour is the model of heterosexual marriage:* a mutually faithful, lifelong commitment between two adult persons of the opposite sex. This provides an opportunity not only for sexual expression, but for growth in mutual trust,* good communication, an ability to negotiate differences, and the emotional and spiritual growth of both partners. In addition, a long-term loving relationship gives the needed stability of environment for raising children (see Family*).

However, whether or not one chooses to use the term 'deviation', it has to be admitted that much of human sexuality falls short of the ideal. This can be true of marriage itself, which may be disrupted by adultery,* physical abusiveness (see Abuse*), or unresolved hurts and expectations from childhood. Typically, it is not incompatibility that disrupts a marriage, but the inability to *negotiate* the incompatibility that is inevitably present in any relationship.

Other expressions of sexual behaviour also fall short of the basic model. These include premarital sex; sex for pay (prostitution*); the sexual expression of anger and hate towards women (rape*); sexual involvement with children (incest,* paedophilia*); sexual obsession with an inanimate object or one part of the body (fetishism); sexual arousal through cross-dressing (transvestism*); erotic subjugation and submission (sado-masochism); exposing oneself (exhibitionism); and watching the sexual activity of others (voyeurism). There is also increasing recognition of sexual addiction,* where compulsive sexual behaviour of any kind stems from underlying emotional pain (see Clinical Theology*) and shame.* As in alcoholism* or other addictions, the addict is attempting to medicate his or her emotional pain through the addictive behaviour. This results in a downward spiral of increasing involvement in sexual activity, which the addict is powerless to control; increasing unmanageability and shame and negative social consequences; and even further sexual acting-out, in a futile attempt to escape from the emotional pain. Help for such persons is available in addiction treatment programmes.

There is also current controversy about the status of homosexuality.* Traditionally regarded as a sexual deviation, some now wish to regard it as a legitimate sexual variant. A mediating position between these two viewpoints is offered in *Homosexuality: A New Christian Ethic*, where same-sex love is seen as a legitimate developmental drive. However, as a pre-adult developmental drive, it is inappropriate for this need to be met sexually. This reframing of the traditional Christian distinction between the homosexual condition and homosexual acts is based on the view that the homosexual – whether male or female – has experienced some early difficulty in the relationship with the same-sex parent. Typically, there was short-term or long-term separation, or the parent was emotionally unavailable. As a result, an unmet need for same-sex love carries over into adult life, together with a half-hidden sense of hurt or grievance towards members of the same sex. In terms of psychological development, a male homosexual is like a boy still looking for his father's love. The lesbian is like a girl still looking for her mother's love.

Traditional counselling often pressured homosexuals into dating or marriage prematurely. The alternative given in *Homosexuality: A New Christian Ethic* is gender-affirmative or reparative therapy. A same-sex therapist works with the homosexual, to help resolve same-sex hurts from the past, and to provide healthy, non-sexual fulfilment of legitimate same-sex developmental needs. Building a more secure masculine or feminine identity is the path towards heterosexuality, for those homosexuals who are motivated to change.

In responding to different expressions of sexual behaviour, Christians need to maintain a biblical balance of both ethical seriousness and constructive compassion;* to repent of hostility and complacent self-righteousness; and to seek to respond to the complexities of sin (see Sin and Salvation⑤) and suffering* that together lead human sexuality to fall short of God's best purposes.

Bibliography

Homosexuality: W. Consiglio, *Homosexual No More* (Wheaton, IL, 1991); E. R. Moberley, *Homosexuality: A New Christian Ethic* (Cambridge, 1983).

Incest (female): J. Frank, *A Door of Hope* (San Bernardino, CA, 1987); M. Hancock and K. B. Mains, *Child Sexual Abuse* (Wheaton, IL, 1987; Crowborough, 1988).

Incest (male): M. Hunter, *Abused Boys* (Lexington, MA, 1990); M. Lew, *Victims No Longer* (London and New York, 1990).

Rape: C. Walters, *Invisible Wounds* (Portland, OR, 1987); R. Warshaw, *I Never Called it Rape* (London and New York, 1988).

Sexual Addiction: P. Carnes, *Out of the Shadows* (Minneapolis, MN, 1983); *idem*, *Contrary to Love* (Minneapolis, MN, 1989); *idem*, *Don't Call it Love* (London and New York, 1991).

E.R.M.

SEXUAL HARASSMENT is a sexual advance or demand for sexual favours, or conduct of a sexual and coercive nature, directed at someone who does not welcome it. It includes the following range of behaviours: sexual jokes; offensive telephone calls; displays of obscene or pornographic* photographs, pictures, posters, reading matter or objects; sexual propositions or persistent unwelcome requests for dates; persistent staring; physical contact such as patting, pinching or touching in a sexual way, or unnecessary familiarity such as deliberately brushing against a person or putting an arm around another person's body at work; unwelcome and uncalled for remarks or insinuations about a person's sex or private life; suggestive comments about a person's appearance or body; offensive comments, leering, wolf-whistles, cat-calls, obscene gestures; indecent exposure; sexual assault and rape.* It does not include friendships (sexual or otherwise) where both people consent.

Both men and women may engage in sexual harassment, although it is most often practised by men, and directed at women. While sexual harassment is generally thought of as occurring in the workplace, it also commonly occurs in other contexts within the community, including teacher–student relationships, shops, social situations and in the home.

Sexual harassment depends on the idea that one person has the right to impose his sexuality on another, regardless of that other person's wishes. It is inherently violent, and in all its forms debases and dehumanizes the victim and asserts the dominance of the attacker. It can inflict physical and/or psychological, emotional and spiritual injury.

Sexual harassment is an issue for the Christian church. Far from being a sanctuary, the church has systematic factors within its established traditions, theology and practice which provide a context in which sexual harassment is, if not accepted, at least hidden.

Some ideas based in the Scriptures have sometimes been interpreted as legitimating sexual harassment. It is important to distinguish between what is recorded as having occurred in the history of Israel, and what was commanded by God. Thus women and children are recorded as being considered to be the property of men (Nu. 31:9; 1 Sa. 30:22; 1 Ki. 20:3, 5, 7; Jb. 42:12–13); sexual violation of a woman violates the property rights of the man to whom she belongs (Gn. 34; Jdg. 19:11–30; 2 Sa. 13; 16:22; Ezk. 18:6, 11, 15); and women may be taken by force (Jdg. 21:21–23). It is of the utmost importance to note that these actions are not explicitly condoned by God.

Furthermore, some passages have been interpreted in such a way as to provide a context for legitimation of sexual harassment. These include the idea that woman is created primarily to serve man and meet his needs (Gn. 2:15 – 3:20; Eph. 5:22–24; Col. 3:18); laws providing for the protection of women and children being interpreted as a licence for power (Ex. 20:17; Dt. 5:21; 21:11–13); and apparent double standards of sexual behaviour for men and women (Ex. 22:16–17; Nu. 5:11–31; Dt. 22:21, 28–29; 1 Sa. 1:2; 25:42–44; 1 Ki. 11:3).

However, such interpretations are shown to be unacceptable in the light of the overwhelming message of Scripture because: 1. both woman and man are created by God in the divine image (see Image of God*), and therefore have equal value (Gn. 1:26–27); 2. relationships, including marriage, should be characterized by mutual submission, love and justice (Mk. 12:31; Eph. 5:21, 22–33; Col. 3:18 – 4:1); 3. God himself shows compassionate partiality towards the marginalized, outcasts, and the powerless, including women (Is. 3:14–15; Mt. 15:21–28; 7:24–30; Lk. 7:36–50; 8:43–48); 4. women are treated as persons in their own right and worthy of sincere human relationships that are not of a sexual nature (Mt. 15:21–28; 26:6–13; Mk. 7:24–39; 14:3–9; Lk. 7:36–50; 10:38–42; Jn. 4:7–42; 11:20–33; 12:1–8); 5. women should be treated with purity (1 Tim. 5:2–3);

6. women who are victims of sexual violence should not be doubly victimized by the response they receive (Lk. 7:37–47; Jn. 4:7–42; 8:3–8); and 7. sexual impurity is avoidable and is condemned (Ex. 20:14, 17; Dt. 27:20–23; 2 Sa. 13:1–19; Je. 7:9; Mt. 5:27–28; 1 Cor. 5:1–5; 6:9–20; Col. 3:5; 1 Pet. 4:3).

The most important response for the Christian church to make to the occurrence of sexual harassment is to acknowledge its existence. Sexual harassment in all its forms is present in the community and within the church. Indeed, a number of kinds of sexual abuse appear to be more common in the conservative Christian environment than in the population at large. The emphasis on the traditional role of women in home and church creates a submissiveness which limits complaint and gives men, and all those in positions of power, the security to pursue inappropriate and illegal behaviour.

Action which can be taken to prevent sexual harassment includes provision of an environment which is free of the power imbalances which make sexual harassment possible; encouraging relationships in which people value each other as persons in their own right; discouraging attitudes towards people as (sexual) objects; education on the unacceptability of behaviour which constitutes sexual harassment; and provision of counselling and other support mechanisms for those with problems in this area.

It is important to be prepared to respond appropriately to the victims of sexual harassment, with compassion, recognizing that they are victims. Feelings that need to be dealt with may include anger, guilt, conflicting loyalties, powerlessness and vulnerability. There may also be physical or other injury. Some victims may need a very high level of support in order to recover from their experience. An appropriate response must also be made to the perpetrator, who in some cases will have many of the same feelings. The perpetrator must be held accountable for his or her actions, but will probably also need support and counselling.

Particular dilemmas arise when allegations of sexual harassment are made within a Christian organization. They include the extent to which confidentiality* should be maintained; whether civil authorities should be informed where law-breaking has occurred; whether action should be taken which may damage the ministry of the organization in order to prevent further occurrences; and what steps should be taken to prevent a recurrence, particularly where this impacts on families.

See also: ABUSE; LUST.

Bibliography
J. and P. Alsdurf, *Battered into Submission: The Tragedy of Wife Abuse in the Christian Home* (Downers Grove, IL, 1989); L. W. Carlson, *Child Sexual Abuse: A Handbook for Clergy and Church Members* (Valley Forge, PN, 1988); Casa House, *A Pastoral Report to the Churches on Sexual Violence against Women and Children of the Church Community* (Melbourne, 1990); R. Clarke, *Pastoral Care of Battered Women* (Philadelphia, 1986); L. W. Countryman, *Dirt, Greed and Sex: Sexual Ethics in the New Testament and their Implications for Today* (Philadelphia, 1988; London, 1989); M. M. Fortune, *Sexual Violence: The Unmentionable Sin* (New York, 1983); P. Rutter, *Sex in the Forbidden Zone* (London, 1990); E. D. Wilson, *A Silence to be Broken: Hope for those Caught in the Web of Child Abuse* (Leicester, 1986).

R.J.W.

SHAFTESBURY, LORD. Anthony Ashley Cooper, seventh Earl of Shaftesbury (1801–85), was one of the most energetic social reformers in 19th-century England. He was educated at Harrow School and Christ Church, Oxford, where he gained his degree. Converted to evangelical faith in the mid-1820s, he entered Parliament in 1826 and held minor office in 1828–30 and 1834–35.

Shaftesbury made his mark in politics by championing Protestant causes against perceived Catholic threats and by leading humanitarian campaigns. He is best known for demanding statutory restrictions on the hours worked in factories. In 1833 he carried a Bill limiting children's employment to ten hours a day. Subsequently, in 1842, he carried a measure prohibiting underground work in mines by women and children. He diligently enforced sanitary reforms in London, and helped ensure acceptable conditions in lodging houses and mental asylums. He was patron of many voluntary societies, such as the Ragged School Union, which gave free education to the poorest children. He called for State-enforced Sunday observance and, in his later years, was prepared to criticize the aggressive foreign policy of his own Conservative Party. Shaftesbury believed that paternalism by the rich should create a response of deference among the poor. The nation was corporately responsible to God for the well-being of its citizens. As the leading evangelical Anglican layman of his day, he aimed, as he wrote in 1825, 'to found a policy upon the Bible'.

Bibliography
G. B. A. M. Finlayson, *The Seventh Earl of Shaftesbury* (London, 1981).

D.W.Be.

SHALOM, see JUSTICE AND PEACE;[3] LIFE, HEALTH AND DEATH;[13] PEACE.

SHAME is a state of mind, or more accurately a state of feeling (or affect), which follows when a person realizes that there has been a failure to live up to ideals or expectations. It may be induced very early in an infant whose mother makes the child feel bad or unworthy: 'You ought to be ashamed of yourself!' It can also be implied by a look or word of disapproval used by a person in authority.

Sigmund Freud* may have been influenced by his own Jewish antecedents (with the close link in the OT between shame and nakedness) when he said it was the visibility of genitals, or their evident deficiency, which provoked shame. Other psychoanalysts saw it differently: Alfred Adler* saw shame as linked to any sense of inferiority. Erik Erikson,* an influential neo-Freudian, saw it as part of his stages of identity crises. He related it to the stage of toilet-training, where there is conflict between autonomy* versus shame and doubt.

In these psychoanalytical terms perhaps the most important idea was that shame arises from tension between ego and ego ideal. Guilt,* by contrast, arises from tension between ego and super-ego.

Shame is recognized by the facial expression, by the hanging head, or by blushing and by lowered eyes. It is often a component of shyness in social relationships, and embarrassment (shame before an audience) is closely linked. Yet to say that shame is visual and public, and guilt private and personal, is too simple. Nor is it true to say that guilt is about acts and shame about the self:* we may be ashamed of our acts, and we may also be ashamed of ourselves.

Shame may be felt in relation to letting the side down: the side may be our family, religious, national or ethnic group. To feel profoundly ashamed may have far-reaching effects, not all of them negative. It may make us reassess ourselves and construe our lives differently. It may be a powerful tool which, by way of the conscience,* enables us to grow morally and spiritually. It may help us to know ourselves better, realizing 'the depths of inbred sin', and prevent a facile hypocrisy* which deals with shame by pretending it does not matter.

Great interest has developed in the role of shame in many prevalent problems such as addictions (see Dependence*), eating disorders,* and physical and sexual abuse.* In all these, anger, fear, disgust and distress may play a vital part, but it is shame which has a central, organizing role. These disorders are hard to help and time-consuming to treat, with poor results for much work done.

It is the shame induced by parents that has had a key role in many disorders in addition to the above: self-esteem* is nowhere so low as when such powerful figures exercise a belittling, diminishing role. To distinguish between deserved and justified shame, and that put upon us by others (in power over us) is very important to well-being. 'Being put in the wrong' is often as much to do with inappropriate shame as with guilt being wrongly imputed.

Shaming can be used therapeutically as part of aversion therapy. This is done by agreement with the patient or client who wants to change a behaviour pattern which is wrong or unacceptable.

It is not fanciful to see the use of shame in the Bible as similarly intended to be aversive. The distinctive feature of proper shame (as with proper guilt) is that it is always related to the truth and to the demands of God's law,* both in the letter and the spirit. Thus conscience becomes a point at which the truth of the gospel enters, and a sense of need is created as part of a conviction of sin (which will include a sense of shame as well as a sense of guilt).

This is to recognize a due sense of shame as a necessary step which leads to repentance,* forgiveness* and new life – followed by a new lifestyle. Regrettably, Christian groups and families may create shame about things that are morally indifferent, and can inhibit growth and development by so doing.

Bibliography

E. H. Erikson, *Childhood and Society* (New York, 1963; Harmondsworth, ²1965); G. Kaufman, *The Psychology of Shame* (New York, 1989); G. Piers and M. B. Singer, *Shame and Guilt* (New York, 1971).

G.D.

SHEPHERDING MOVEMENT. This

movement is particularly, though not exclusively, associated with the so-called house churches of the charismatic movement. As a reaction against the low level of commitment, lack of real community, and easy-going individualism of more traditional churches, the shepherding movement has sought to bring about a 'whole-of-life' discipleship among house-church members.

To grow into spiritual maturity all Christians must be shepherded. Each church member is accountable to a house-group leader whose task is to encourage spiritual growth, exercise of gifts, and responsible church membership. Group leaders are in turn accountable to the elders of the church.

A key concept is 'covering'. Any important decision must be 'covered' or sanctioned by house-group leaders, elders or the pastor. Examples are change of employment, moving house and marriage, but sometimes even a doctor's appointment has to be 'covered' (J. Barrs, *Freedom and Discipleship*, p. 47).

Shepherding and covering seem to have been taught by Watchman Nee (1903–72), leader of the Little Flock churches in China in the 1920s and 30s. Much more recently they have received considerable emphasis in the USA, in the teaching of such charismatic leaders as Bob Mumford (1930–), Derek Prince (1915–) Charles Simpson (1937–), Don Basham (1926–) and Ern Baxter (1914–).

Despite its laudable aim, the shepherding movement can lead to a dependence on leaders which promotes spiritual immaturity, discourages the examination of Scripture for oneself (*cf.* Acts 17:11), and effectively denies the priesthood of all believers. There is also the danger that fallible, human counsel is surrounded with such an aura of authority that it is virtually equated with the will of God. When this happens, the door is open for every kind of manipulation (see R. Peacock, *The Shepherd and the Shepherds*, p. 126).

Bibliography

J. Barrs, *Freedom and Discipleship* (Leicester, 1983); J. C. Ortiz, *Disciple* (London, 1976); R. Peacock, *The Shepherd and the Shepherds* (Eastbourne, 1988).

D.P.K.

SICK, CARE OF. The term 'care of the sick' may not seem to need defining, but a little reflection on the meaning of the two key words will be beneficial while considering the biblical guidelines that Christians will want to follow. The word 'sick' to most people immediately conveys a picture of a physical or mental disorder, restricted to body or mind. However, the biblical view of humanity is that each person is an inseparable whole of body, soul (or mind) and spirit (e.g. 1 Thes. 5:23), and the reductionism* which leads the West to see separate elements is not Christian.

Thus, the word 'sick' may unhelpfully narrow the perspective. The word 'health' means much more than the opposite of 'sickness', with roots linked to concepts of wholeness and holiness. 'Health' is hard to define. If we use Jürgen Moltmann's (1926–) definition of health as 'the strength to be human', we are led straight to the basic question, 'What is meant by "human"?' (see Humanity④).

Christians answer that question in terms of relationships: with God, with others, with self* and with the environment.* There cannot be full health if any of these relationships is impaired. While always encouraging the broadest of outlooks, the definition also covers narrower models of 'sickness'. Much physical ill-health involves impaired relationships of one part of the body with another, or disease caused by an invading micro-organism may represent a breakdown of the relationship with the environment. Similarly, mental illness (see Mental Health*) includes a breakdown of relationships with others or with self.

Whilst Christian healthcare will sometimes have to be content with limited solutions, it should always keep the whole-person concept in mind. The popularity of complementary medicines (which may or may not be 'holistic') illustrates the fact that patients believe that conventional Western medicine often ignores many of their real needs. Christians should be in the forefront of applying medicine which is rational and objectively based in the context of a loving, caring relationship with the whole person.

From the definition of health as 'the strength to be human', it follows that health promotion is more than the prevention of sickness, but at the more limited physical level prevention is of course 'better than cure'. Christians always want to prevent sickness, e.g. by advocating the practice of good hygiene (cf. Dt. 23:12–13), yet they would also want to insist that if biblical guidelines for behaviour were observed, much sickness would be prevented and better health promoted. Obvious examples occur in the area of sexuality (see ⑪; cf. 1 Cor. 6:13; 1 Thes. 4:3).

'Care'* is a word that causes few problems. It must, however, be distinguished from 'cure'. Cure of physical or mental disease is sometimes possible, but when it is not, care continues. The Christian never says, 'There is nothing more I can do for you', but seeks to continue to care creatively. The hospice* movement (which was initially Christian) has illustrated this powerfully in the case of care for patients with terminal cancer. There is a famous motto which sums up care: 'To cure sometimes, to relieve often, to comfort always' (folk-saying, c. 15th century, inscribed on the statue of Dr Edward Livingstone Trudeau, 1848–1915, at Saramac Lake, New York). The exhortation to care is both implicit in the compassion* required by 'Love your neighbour as yourself' (e.g. Mk. 12:31, quoting Lv. 19:18), and occasionally explicit in command, e.g. as in Lk. 9:2, which has been used as a foundation text for a number of medical missions: 'He sent them out to preach the kingdom of God and to heal the sick.' The healing professions have always attracted Christians, who have sought to follow the Lord in acts of humble service. (The logo of the International Christian Medical and Dental Association, for instance, is the towel and basin of Jn. 13.) Christians have also realized that such service may give opportunity for sharing the gospel.

The early church in Britain pioneered caring for the sick, and its 'hospices' (in the original sense of places for rest and recovery) led to the development of most of the early hospitals. Levitical concepts may well have inspired some early Western public-health initiatives, and a Christian global view led to an impressive commitment to worldwide medical mission.

Health care in much of the developing world today still depends on Christians. The late 20th century brings new challenges, not just in fighting new diseases like AIDS* but in the need to develop health care in the context of much wider social issues like poverty,* famine and the 'North–South'* imbalance. The definition of health in terms of relationships is clearly relevant here.

Luke was a doctor, and the parable of the good Samaritan (Lk. 10:25–37) provides a model of care which remains helpful no matter how restricted finite resources may seem. The

Samaritan demonstrated care which was compassionate (10:33), costly in its commitment (10:34–35a) and continuing (10:35b).

These principles still guide Christians in the medical and caring professions to care for the sick as they seek further to make their patients truly healthy and truly whole in Christ.

See also: ETHICS OF MEDICAL CARE; [14] HEALTH AND HEALTH CARE.

Bibliography
A. Fergusson (ed.), *Health: The Strength to be Human* (Leicester, 1993); B. Palmer (ed.), *Medicine and the Bible* (Exeter, 1986).

D.A.N.F.

SIGNS AND WONDERS. The term 'signs and wonders' occurs eighteen times in the OT and sixteen in the NT, mainly in connection with Moses and Jesus. Under Moses, the liberation of Israel from bondage in Egypt and the journey to the Promised Land modelled the much greater redemptive act which took place in and through Jesus (Jn. 1:6–17; Heb. 3:3–6), *i.e.* the coming of the kingdom of God.

Jesus came preaching and practising the presence of the kingdom of God* (*e.g.* Lk. 4:17–21; 11:20; *cf.* Mt. 10:2–7; 13:1–52) with all its ramifications – spiritual, social and physical. Here, in and through Jesus, God's final destiny for humankind and for the whole creation begins: a reconciliation and a renewal which will reverse the effects of the Fall* and restore men and women and their world to a condition of peace and prosperity as in the beginning (Gn. 1:31; Rom. 8:19–23; Col. 1:19–20; Rev. 21:1, 5; 22:1–5).

In John's Gospel, Jesus' mighty works are called *signs*, in order to point us beyond the miracle to its meaning. Signs are significant. They reveal in an extraordinary way something about God: not only his power, but also his kingdom and his plan of salvation. Such signs are meant to evoke *wonder*: *i.e.* not merely astonishment but praise to God and the humble enquiry, 'What is God saying to others and to me in this sign?'

If such faith is absent, the miraculous will not be significant, only fascinating or even irritating. The demand for signs was not accepted by Jesus (Mt. 16:1–4) or admired by Paul (1 Cor. 1:22). The clamour for a sign, with which Jesus was at times confronted, indicated not faith but unbelief and tended to subordinate Jesus to his performance of mighty works. Jesus himself was and is the great sign in his person and self-revelation (Jn. 6:30–35; *cf.* Mt. 12:40) and in his death and resurrection (Jn. 6:51–54). Although God accredited him with 'miracles, wonders and signs' (Acts 2:22), these were of no value where they did not meet with faith. To be blind to Jesus in his own person was to render oneself unable to know or do the works God required (Jn. 6:28–30). Divorced from Jesus, signs and wonders in the NT are seen as inadequate and deceiving (Mt. 24:24; Acts 4:29–30; 2 Thes. 2:9–10).

Yet Jesus and his mighty works belong together (Mt. 11:4–6; Jn. 14: 9–11). They announce and inaugurate a new age (Jn. 14:12–14). If there is a sign-hunger in the Gospels which is condemned, there is a sign-presence in Acts which is celebrated (Acts 2:19, 22, 43; 4:30; 5:12; 6:8; 7:36; 14:3; 15:12; *cf.* Rom. 15:19; 2 Cor. 12:12; Heb. 2:4). Indeed the church herself becomes a sign in her existence and character (*e.g.* Mt. 16:18; Acts 2:41, 47; 6:7; 1 Thes. 1:1, 8–10) as well as in her gifts (*e.g.* Rom. 12:3–8; 1 Cor. 12:7–11; 1 Pet. 4:10–11).

However, the servant role of the church is never spoiled or compromised by such miraculous power. Signs and wonders signify the sovereign activity of the risen Lord. They are never 'possessed' by his servants and never 'on tap'. They inspire awe among believers as much as wonder in those around (Acts 2:43). The church cannot perform them at will, but must pray (Acts 4:30–31). Miraculous activity occurs in generous bursts at some times (Acts 5:12–16; 19:11–12) and selectively at others (Acts 9:32–42). Sometimes the most greatly used of Christ's servants have to wait for power to do mighty works in his name (Acts 16:18), and sometimes they wait in vain (2 Cor. 12:7–10; 2 Tim. 4:20). The faith-formula of Jesus ('If you have faith . . . nothing will be impossible', Mt. 17:20; *cf.* 9:29; Jn. 14:12–13) is not a reference simply to a human decision but to a divine movement in which believers are taken up in co-operation by God. Such faith is first *given* and only then *exercised* with insight and entire confidence (*e.g.* Acts 3:16; 9:34, 40; 14:8–10).

In recent years 'signs and wonders' have been put back on the theological and pastoral agenda by the contention of John Wimber (1937–) and C. Peter Wagner (1930–), among others, that the kingdom of God advances in history through proclamation *and* the manifestation of miracles in combination. The movement which they represent, popularly known as 'power evangelism', challenges the world-view of many Western Christians who have accepted the Enlightenment* assumption that in a closed universe miracles cannot occur. It also calls into question the assumption, held by both dispensationalists and many in the Reformed tradition, that miracles were confined to the apostolic age and are not to be expected today.

Advocates of power evangelism have drawn attention to texts too easily passed over (*e.g.* Mt. 12:28; Lk. 7:21–22; Jn. 14:11–12), and to the supernatural conflict in which the church is called to engage. However, they have been criticized for overlooking the fact that signs and wonders also occur in non-Christian religions; for being insufficiently aware of the dangers of suggestibility and manipulation; and for failing to appreciate that heightened expectations of physical healing* which are not met can lead to disappointment, which in turn can easily lead to despair and even loss of faith.

In the continuing debate it is important to recognize that the old order of creation* (Gn. 1:31; 8:20–22) and the new of the kingdom of God (Lk. 4:40–43; 11:20) are both of God and that the two need to be held together in a balanced theology. Extremes of both an under-realized eschatology and an over-realized eschatology should be avoided: the old order continues, and though the kingdom of God has truly come in Jesus, it has yet to come in its fullness, renewing the whole creation (Rom. 8:20–21; Rev. 21:1–5).

Miracles are always *possible* because God is always sovereign in the universe he sustains and never a prisoner of his own laws. Miracles are always *serious* because they are breaches of a general and covenanted order which maintains stability in creation (Gn. 8:20–22). Miracles are always *significant* because they are signs of the kingdom of God which is here to stay (Mk. 16:17–20). They are never ordinary because we are not yet in the new earth (2 Pet. 3:13; Rev. 21:1) and such powers most properly belong to that glorious future. They are extraordinary signs of the kingdom of God, singular events which proclaim far and wide that our sins and our sicknesses are not the last word, that our disturbed planet and our dying race are not locked into a situation from which there is no escape. They point to a day when the dwelling of God shall be with humankind, when 'There will be no more death or mourning or crying or pain, for the old order of things has passed away' (Rev. 21:4).

Bibliography

D. Bridge, *Signs and Wonders Today* (Leicester, 1985); *idem*, *Power Evangelism and the Word of God* (Eastbourne, 1987); C. Brown, *That You May Believe: Miracles and Faith Then and Now* (Exeter and Grand Rapids, 1986); R. Gardner, *Healing Miracles* (London, 1986); D. M. Lloyd-Jones, *Prove All Things* (Eastbourne, 1985); L. B. Smedes, *Ministry and the Miraculous* (Pasadena, CA, 1987); J. Wimber, *Power Evangelism: Signs and Wonders Today* (London, 1985; San Francisco, 1986).

P.H.L.

SIMEON, CHARLES (1759–1836). Simeon was a deeply loyal and convinced Anglican. His ministry, more than that of any other person, inspired many evangelicals to remain within and contribute to the life of the national established church.

As an undergraduate, Simeon experienced a profound conversion* to Christ, the culmination of a conscientious attempt to prepare himself for compulsory attendance at Holy Communion at King's College, Cambridge. In 1782 when only twenty-three years of age he was appointed Vicar of Holy Trinity, Cambridge, where for the next fifty-four years he exercised a ministry of preaching and pastoral care, remarkable both for the opposition which it provoked and for the strategic importance of its influence and effectiveness amongst students. In his preaching Simeon sought 'to humble the sinner, to exalt the Saviour, and to promote holiness', and taught the same in the sermon classes and conversation parties which he held for undergraduates preparing for ordination.

Throughout his demanding ministry Simeon consecrated himself to the discipline of personal prayer, study, correspondence and the spiritual counsel of others. But he never lost his zest for life, his love for horses and fine clothes or his appetite for good food. His immense energy and zeal for evangelism contributed greatly to the founding of the Church Missionary Society in 1799 and the active support of countless other endeavours. Shrewdly, he used his considerable wealth to purchase the legal right to appoint evangelical clergy to many parishes around the country and thus ensure there a faithful biblical ministry.

Bibliography
Let Wisdom Judge, with Introduction by A. Pollard, ed. (London, 1959).
H. E. Hopkins, *Charles Simeon of Cambridge* (London, 1977); A. Pollard and M. Hennell (eds.), *Charles Simeon (1759–1836)* (London, 1959).

R.A.Hin.

SIMONS, MENNO, see MENNO SIMONS.

SIN, see ORIGINAL SIN; SIN AND SALVATION. ⑤

SIN, STRUCTURAL, see LIBERATION THEOLOGY.

SINGLENESS. Most people have a period in their lives when they live as single adults, increasingly independent of their parents but not covenanted to a marriage partner. Marriages* which end with the death of one partner leave the other partner with a period of singleness again at the end of life. In many countries the steadily increasing divorce* rate means there is a growing body of people of all ages who are no longer married, and many of these are caring for children (see Single Parents*). In most modern societies it is feasible for single people to live in their own home or to share with other singles. Households that do not contain a married couple are a sizeable minority within the community and are well represented in most churches.

The term 'single person' is often narrowed down to mean someone who possibly or probably will never marry. Some are conscious that, within the limits of their circumstances, they have made a choice and prefer to be single rather than to be married or actively searching for a partner. Others feel that they have had no scope for choice. There may be physical or emotional factors, or unpromising social or economic circumstances which are constraining them to be single. The way people view their single state is likely to change at various stages in life. A person who at one time feels that singleness is a frustrating handicap may at another stage be glad of the opportunities of the single lifestyle and positively aware of choices which have contributed to it. There are relatively few situations in which some form of marriage is completely ruled out as a future possibility for a single person.

Singleness as pathology or privilege?

A key issue for Christian theology is what emphasis to give to singleness in relation to the state of marriage. Is it to be treated as pathological: something abnormal that requires either a cure or at least the alleviation of pain? Or should we emphasize it as a privilege: the special vocation* of the truly devoted follower of Christ? The middle way is to view singleness and marriage as parallel states, each having their own particular joys and sorrows. Single people are a minority, but not an abnormal, group. Most churches pay lip-service to the third view but find it a difficult emphasis to maintain in practice.

Biblical themes

Creation and fall. Genesis 1 and 2 affirm that sexuality (see ⑪) is a fundamental aspect of humanity, created by God and very good. 'It is not good for the man to be alone' (Gn. 2:18). This statement from the mouth of God introduces the story which climaxes in the description of marriage as a one-flesh union (Gn. 2:24). Although the primary focus here is on the marriage of Adam and Eve, they also represent the start of the human community with family,* and friendship,* communication and co-operation. Where marriage is a secure institution in society, single people can have support and loving relationships within the extended family and the community. They are not alone in an absolute sense.

With the entry of sin comes death and the disruption of relationships between the sexes. Widowhood,* divorce and much painful singleness can be related back to the effects of the Fall.*

The Old Testament covenant. In the OT covenant* there is no clear revelation about an afterlife. A sense of continuity and the concept of God's future blessing are linked to one's children. To be barren was therefore a great tragedy. In Israel's patriarchal structure, single people would remain in the extended family for protection and their livelihood. Two examples of singleness are Jeremiah, who has no wife (Je. 16:2), and Ezekiel, whose wife dies (Ezk. 24:18). These painful experiences are used by God to help the prophets communicate how much God suffers because of his burning love for his people (Je. 18:13–15; Ezk. 24:13, 24). The overall OT view, still prominent in Judaism, is that to marry and bear children is a sacred duty. To refuse to do so is irresponsible.

To be unable to do so is tragic (1 Sa. 1:5–8; Pr. 30:16; Is. 49:21).

The incarnation and resurrection. It becomes even more notable, therefore, that the central figure of the NT is a single man. Jesus is the model of perfect humanity. He is complete and whole as a single person. The Gospels give concrete examples of the way he relates to his family, to his friends, and to individuals both male and female.

Two passages in Matthew indicate Jesus' thinking about singleness and marriage. Mt. 22:30 gives the future perspective. The marriage bond is limited in significance to this life. It does not carry on into the resurrection.*

In Mt. 19:1–11 Jesus endorses marital permanence on the basis of Gn. 2:24. The disciples protest that it might be better to be unmarried, and the passage is rounded off with a statement about three categories of eunuch (Mt. 19:12). Commentators usually see this as a vivid way of referring to celibate singleness. One can be single for congenital reasons or as a result of social circumstances, but there is a category of those who choose or accept it because of the kingdom* of heaven.

Life in the redeemed community. Strikingly similar themes emerge in Paul's discussion of singleness versus marriage in 1 Cor. 7. Some Corinthian Christians seem to have held the view that sexual intercourse hindered spiritual growth and should be avoided by Christians. Paul's response is long and careful. He affirms that marriage is a good gift and partners should not deny each other sexually. But he also states that singleness is a charismatic gift; it comes from God's grace (1 Cor. 7:7). It is his preferred gift and he would like all his readers to have it, but in so far as they have scope for choice, they should be realistic about their sexual needs (7:9). Later in the chapter he makes it plain that it is not freedom from sexual intercourse which makes singleness attractive to him, but freedom from anxiety and freedom for undivided devotion to, and service for, the Lord (7:32–35).

So the Christian perspective on the biblical material is that, while the first created human beings, Adam and Eve, were a married couple, in the new creation the second Adam, Jesus Christ, was a single man. Singleness and marriage are parallel routes for loving and serving in the world and preparing us for life in the resurrection community. They are gifts from God to be accepted or to be chosen within the scope he gives us for choice. There is no essential problem about being single but a variety of difficulties typically occur.

Pastoral considerations

Identity and self-worth. Low self-worth (see Self-esteem*) is a frequent problem of single people. The causes may be external. In many cultures the colloquial terms for single people convey disrespect. Customs which require balanced numbers at dinner parties, anxious comments of parents and friends, and clumsy attempts at match-making all serve to make single people feel second rate. The celibate single person may be labelled immature or abnormal (see Discrimination*). Modern Western society has seen such attitudes rapidly changing. The single lifestyle is given a new positive value. It stands for freedom to pursue a career, to be mobile and financially successful. But it is also seen as the freedom to pursue a variety of sexual relationships, unencumbered by commitment and child-rearing.

As well as the external pressures, singles often have a low self-image because of emotional deprivation. They may be conscious that they lack a special person in their life, who would give them top priority in a time of need; friends or relatives who affirm, admire and encourage; anyone who touches them in a loving way; the presence of a familiar person in their home; someone to laugh with and help them relax from the pressures of work; and contact with children.

None of these is exclusively a problem for single people; all may occur at times in marriage. Also, once any one of these needs is identified, there are many ways in which it can be alleviated or met. If singleness is accepted as a parallel way towards the goal of maturity and love in the kingdom of God, then its particular gift is for a wider number of relationships. Singles need to take time to cultivate a range of friendships with other singles, with couples, and with children. They need, like Jesus, to have a smaller circle of close friends with whom they can share intimacy and feel accepted as they really are (see Acceptance*).

It is helpful if pastors and preachers use language and examples which affirm the lifestyles of single people and build their confidence. The concern to strengthen Christian marriages has sometimes led to an unnecessary neglect of single people. Structures should be examined to see if they are preventing singles from exercising their spiritual gifts. For some individuals, low self-worth may be linked with a measure of depression* which makes it hard for them to take initiatives in friendship. Specific care or counselling may be needed to integrate them into the fellowship.

Solitude or loneliness. There has been a tendency this century to assume that intimate relationships are the chief source of human happiness. Recently the psychiatrist Anthony Storr (1920–) has argued that much human pleasure and fulfilment come from solitude. Scientific discovery and artistic creativity thrive in it. A deep prayer life needs space and time alone with God. Jesus regularly withdrew from crowded places to pray. The single life holds greater potential for solitude.

Solitude becomes loneliness* if it is experienced as distressing. When someone feels lonely, prayer becomes difficult and creativity declines. In pastoral oversight it is presumptuous to assume that solitary people are lonely. Nevertheless, when a relationship of warmth is established, underlying feelings of loneliness, perhaps deeply buried, may emerge into consciousness and be acknowledged.

Sexuality and celibacy. It is hard to reconcile a theology of singleness as a gift from God with an experience of singleness as the lack or loss of a genital sexual relationship. In the early and medieval church there was a tendency to see celibacy as a higher, more spiritual calling than marriage. This was thoroughly intertwined with the idea that in a fallen world, sexual intercourse inevitably involves a measure of sinful lust, drawing a person away from communion with God. The celibate was someone set free for pure, undivided devotion to the Lord.

The Reformers argued vigorously against marriage as a second-class gift and tried to root out the pressure which was being exerted in favour of celibacy. But they still tended to view sexuality with some suspicion, retaining the emphasis on marriage as a remedy against incontinence. John Calvin* urges 'dignity, measure, modesty not wantonness' in the mutal behaviour of husband and wife (*Institutes* II.viii.44).

Today we have become very sensitive to the dangers of dualistic thinking in the area of sexuality. Spiritual maturity involves an integration of thought and emotion, and of bodily impulses. We worship and pray bodily. Psychology has shown the importance of physical touch* and eye contact in the growth of our ability to love, and it has warned of the dangers to the personality when sexual needs are denied.

Some therefore question whether, in an age of effective contraception, celibacy should be required for single Christians. Jesus and his apostles spoke of the sinfulness of sexual immorality (Gk. *porneia*). But would they have applied the term to loving, responsible relationships today?

It is relevant to observe how Paul's teaching on singleness and marriage in 1 Cor. 7 follows the most detailed NT discussion of *porneia* in 1 Cor. 6:9–20. The context is that of married men visiting prostitutes, but his arguments have more universal application. He looks back to creation to establish that sexuality (see 11) is so intimately established in the personality that even the most casual act of intercourse establishes the one-flesh bond which God intended to be permanent. He looks forward to the resurrection to emphasize that the body is of eternal significance. Then he stresses the incongruity of someone who is redeemed by Christ, lived in by the Holy Spirit and a member of Christ's church using his or her own body for sexual gratification outside the covenant of marriage (see Chastity*).

For those who follow a Christian path of celibacy, maturity involves accepting, not denying, sexual feelings and needs. Fantasies and acts of comfort or self-gratification should not be regarded with excessive guilt or fear (see Masturbation*). They often provide clues towards needs which can be met in other ways. A wise and gentle self-discipline is needed to avoid unhelpful habits.

The Catholic writer Donald Goergen (1943–) distinguishes genital sexuality, unfulfilled in the celibate, from affective sexuality which can be fully expressed through compassion, tenderness and affection in relationships. His description perhaps needs to be augmented with the aspect of sexuality as a source of energy and fun. Accepting and celebrating the existence of this potential is part of the process of becoming a channel for God's love in the world.

In the process there will be times when the pain of unfulfilled genitality becomes particularly acute for the single person. A woman in mid-life may suddenly realize that the opportunities for motherhood have passed, and she may find she needs to grieve that loss. Often the pain is magnified rather than comforted by the feelings of family members and married friends. Such sympathetic feelings have led to the current trend to encourage full genital activity among the mentally handicapped in residential care. Jean Vanier (1928–), in his L'Arche communities, however, seeks to demonstrate that compassion is compatible with the celibate way.

Glib sermons from married people on the gift of singleness nearly always stir painful wounds and produce angry reactions. A variety of testimonies and role models can be more effective in helping the whole community understand the way of singleness with its supreme model, Christ the unique and single Son of God.

See also: WIDOWHOOD, WIDOWERHOOD.

Bibliography

M. Evening, *Who Walk Alone* (London, 1974); D. Gillett *et al.*, *A Place in the Family* (Bramcote, Nottingham, 1981); D. Goergen, *The Sexual Celibate* (New York, 1974; London, 1976); M. Israel, *Living Alone* (London, 1982); A. Storr, *Solitude* (New York, 1988; London, 1989); P. Tovey, 'An Unwanted Gift?', *Th* 759, 1990; J. Vanier, *Man and Woman He Made Them* (Paris and Montreal, 1984; London, 1985); I. J. Yoder, 'Where is My Family?' and B. Yoder, 'Holy Loneliness', in B. and I. J. Yoder (eds.), *Single Voices* (Scottdale, PA, and Kitchener, Ontario, 1982).

V.M.S.

SINGLE PARENTS. Single parenthood is a complex phenomenon, despite the fact that the term is often used by politicians and the media as a blanket description (often with pejorative overtones). Single parents can be young girls who have an unplanned pregnancy, women who want a child but not a partner, a parent deserted or divorced by a spouse, former cohabitees (see Cohabitation*), or widows or widowers (see Widowhood, Widowerhood*) left to care for young children. Sometimes a person becomes a single parent in all but name, because of the other partner's inability, physical or mental, to share in caring for the children.

By far the majority of single parents are women (90%). Many single mothers receive no financial support from the father(s) of their children. (The Child Support Agency, a British government body, in 1993 cited a 1989 survey which revealed that only 30% of all lone mothers received regular child maintenance.) Prevented from earning an adequate salary because of the need to care for children, these mothers are dependent upon welfare payments from the State. The rules governing the receipt of such payments permit only a small extra amount to be earned, with the result that single parents are frequently caught in a poverty trap. Affordable nursery care provided by local authorities is often not available, and private nursery fees are frequently too high to be met out of a low (subsistence) income. Thus, even when there is a desire to work or to retrain, it is often impossible to fulfil it.

Social and cultural changes in the years since the Second World War seem to have contributed to the development of the phenomenon described as single parenthood. Greater social mobility has tended to diminish support available from the wider family. The loss of the stigma once attached to illegitimacy means that there is less social pressure on single women to marry should they become pregnant. The increase in divorce (from 25,000 in 1961 to 150,000 in 1989) and in the practice of cohabitation (often not lasting) also helps to make single parenthood a marked feature of Western societies.

There is little if any direct teaching in Scripture on single parenthood, for the obvious reason that premarital sexual intercourse is strongly forbidden (see Fornication*). Yet there is significant material to provide guidance for the church today. Hagar, in effect a single mother, returned to Abraham's household on the instruction of the angel of the Lord (Gn. 16:9), there to bear his child Ishmael. According to the law, a slave wife could claim her freedom if her husband withheld her food, clothing and conjugal rights (Ex. 21:10–11). Widows, along with the poor and aliens, were allowed to glean at harvest time (Dt. 24:19–22); *cf.* Ru. 2:2–3, 6–7). Widows are not to be taken advantage of (Ex. 22:22–23), because God is the protector and vindicator of the widow and the fatherless (Dt. 10:18; Ps. 68:5) and concerned for their plight (Acts 4:34; *cf.* 6:1–3).

Since single parents of whatever kind are often poor and vulnerable (especially single mothers), it follows that God desires that they receive justice (see Dt. 27:19). However, political debate continues as to the best ways of helping single parents. Welfare politics reflect conflicting philosophies. Some, recognizing the special needs of single parents, see welfare payments as a positive means of alleviating poverty and as enabling single parents to care for their children without having to work outside the home. Others, dismayed at the increasing breakdown in family life, the huge cost to the State of supporting one-parent families (£4.3 billion in the UK in 1990–91), and the creation of a culture of permanent dependency, argue that benefits should be reduced and given only to those who are prepared to retrain or to work while their children are cared for in nurseries. (In some States in the USA, welfare is now being switched to 'workfare'.) It is also argued that fathers should be forced to pay maintenance, even if it is necessary to deduct this at source from their wages (as in Australia).

Even if the financial needs of single parents are adequately provided for, other needs remain, of which individual Christians and churches need to be aware. Single parents need wholesome friendship because they often suffer from a sense of isolation and loneliness.* Many get into financial difficulty and require debt counselling. Left alone to bring up children, they often lack support of a practical kind and are often cut off from any meaningful social life of their own. The church, as God's extended family, can provide a caring community to support single parents and perhaps also significant adults to fill gaps in some children's lives. The church is certainly called to care rather than to condemn and, by understanding, compassion and love, to demonstrate the nature of true religion (Jas. 1:27). In the church community, single parents ought to be able to find healing for their hurts through the gospel, and a loving acceptance which models the grace of God revealed in Christ.

Bibliography

S. Bradshaw and J. Millar, *Lone Families in the UK* (London, 1991); L. Burgess, *One Parent Families: Policy Options for the 1990s* (York, 1993); D. Uttings, *Crime and the Family* (London, 1993).

V.G.

S ITUATION ETHICS. Joseph Fletcher,* an American Episcopalian moralist, coined the phrase 'situation ethics'. In response to the alleged failures of legalism and antinomianism (see Law*), Fletcher argued for a middle way which entered into every situation fully armed with the precepts and lessons of the past, but willing to set those aside, if love were better served.

Fletcher propounded the four presupposi-

tions and six key propositions of situationalism. The presuppositions were pragmatism,* relativism,* positivism and personalism. Fletcher's strategy was pragmatic. His tactics were relativistic. He posited *agapē* love (see 2) by faith and put people before principles in decision-making. With its roots in existentialism and stressing the freedom and autonomy of the individual, Fletcher put *agapē* love at the centre of situationalism. This self-giving love is carefully defined. Love only is always good. Love is the only norm.* Love and justice are the same, for justice is love distributed. Love is not liking. Only the end of love justifies the means. Love decides there and then in each situation.

Fletcher presented his view by the extensive use of hard cases. He claimed to show that the application of the law or the refusal to use *agapē* love led to disaster. He argued that the rightness of actions is judged in relation to the situations in which actions take place. What is the loving thing needs to be calculated in terms of the intention of the doer and the resulting loving consequences. These results are what justifies an action as good.

Initially, this view was seized upon as part of the freedom of the 1960s with its rejection of traditional values by Bishop John A. T. Robinson (1919–83). But closer scrutiny led to serious doubts about the validity and integrity of situation ethics. It seems oddly legalistic with its universal application of one rule on the basis of four presuppositions and by means of six propositions. Situationalism derives its force from hard, exceptional cases which are never a sound basis for making general rules or laws. It never adequately defines what constitutes a situation or at what point the final calculation of consequences takes place, far less giving a clear unit for calculation or a means of calculating. Many rejected the consequentialism* of the view, stressing the importance of motives as well as the nature of the act as having moral significance. Fletcher ends up calling 'good' what is in reality evil. His attempts to justify such things as adultery seem to point to an over-optimistic view of human nature and of the world. Living in a fallen world means that sometimes we are faced with a choice between evils. Fletcher exaggerates the capacity of human beings to know enough in order to make the kind of choices necessary to be morally correct, and he fails to see that love can be the fulfilling of the law (Mt. 22:36ff.; Rom. 13:10).

Bibliography

J. Fletcher, *Moral Responsibility: Situation Ethics at Work* (Philadelphia and London, 1967); *idem, Situation Ethics: The New Morality* (Philadelphia and London, 1966); J. Macquarrie, *Three Issues in Ethics* (London, 1970); P. Ramsey, *Deeds and Rules in Christian Ethics* (London and Edinburgh, 1965; New York, 1967).

E.D.C.

SKINNER, B. F. (1904–90). A leading American psychologist, Burrhus Frederick Skinner championed the ideas of behaviourism* and psychological engineering. From the foundation of scientific psychology, Skinner suggested a value structure that could be used to guide his behavioural technology. He discussed the behavioural management of an entire society in *Beyond Freedom and Dignity* (1971) and his utopian novel *Walden Two* (1948).

Skinner did not think that the values behind behaviour were derived from a supernatural being or from some built-in motivation towards the good. Our concept of the good, he argued, was a product of the reinforcing environment. Whatever a person preferred or found reinforcing was to be considered valuable, because those things obviously allowed humanity to survive. Thus, for Skinner, the ultimate value was the survival of the human race. However, this method of looking at what has worked for society's survival involves using a hidden value* system to measure what has 'worked'.

In contrast to Skinner's ethic, the Christian has a solid basis for assigning worth to a particular behaviour or direction in science, because the Bible contains both ethical absolutes and general principles that can guide behaviour. The Christian ethic is anchored firmly in the unchanging nature of a God (see ①) of perfect love (see ②) and justice (see Justice and Peace③). The Christian view of change in society also offers a superior motivation to Skinner's reinforcement theory. Since human beings are free persons, they are challenged by God to do right. Christians also have hope for a better world, not because the environment will change its reinforcements, but because people can experience a spiritual rebirth that has a deep impact on the self-centredness of human nature.

Bibliography

Beyond Freedom and Dignity (New York,

1971; London, 1972); *Walden Two* (New York, 1948).

M. P. Cosgrove, *B. F. Skinner's Behaviourism: An Analysis* (Grand Rapids, 1982); F. A. Schaeffer, *Back to Freedom and Dignity* (Downers Grove, IL, 1972).

M.P.C.

SLANDER, see SPEECH AND THE TONGUE.

SLAVERY is a form of servitude which involves the ownership of a person or persons as property by another or others. Unlike serfdom, slavery reduces the human to the level of chattel or personal property, and thereby denies basic human rights (see Rights, Human*). Unlike contractual indentured servitude, slavery is, barring the unforeseen, frequently a lifelong, permanent condition of being the property of another.

The origins of slavery are obscured in the mists of antiquity, but it appears that virtually all ancient societies practised slavery in some form or another. In ancient Israel, the law permitted the Hebrews to purchase slaves from foreigners (Lv. 25:44–46), and allowed a convicted thief unable to pay his fines and damages to make restitution by serving for a period as a slave (Ex. 22:3b). Apparently the more labour-intensive societies, those involved in large-scale enterprises such as mining and agribusiness, turned most often to slave labour, or, as Aristotle called them, 'living tools'.

The Greeks made slavery a major foundation of their economy, not only in their large-scale buying and selling of conquered peoples (the island of Delos was equipped to process 10,000 slaves for the market each week), but in their use of slave labour as a type of individual retirement account. The Gk. worker would often purchase slaves – at varying prices, but roughly equivalent to the cost of a modern automobile – to be hired out when the worker could no longer work them himself. In this way, Graeco-Roman slavery became more intricately interwoven into society. It was not only a practice of the wealthy landowner or mining magnate, but also a common resort among the middle-income population.

Slavery grew so pervasively in Graeco-Roman society that the customary stigma attached to it became confused when 'white-collar' jobs were held by slaves. The management of the Athenian silver mines was in the hands of a slave in the 5th century BC, while most ships' captains in the Roman navy were slaves owned by the Emperor. Farm managers frequently were slaves, as were many of the chief executive officers of the primitive banks of the age. Even though the Roman government made slavery in the mines (*damnatio ad metallum*) a useful substitute for capital punishment, slavery was not always so harsh. The need for freedom could often be more than balanced by the power of the position that the slave held. As a result, the Christian community did not call for the abolition of slavery, but rather for the fair treatment of slaves. In fact, the early church partook in the social order of the day, slavery and all. The late Roman saint Martin of Tours (*c.* 335 – *c.* 400) was counted an ascetic, in part because he contented himself with only one domestic slave. By the 6th century AD, the condition of *servitium*, or being a slave owned by the church, was common.

The spread of serfdom in the Middle Ages greatly reduced the incidence of slavery in Europe, though the Vikings carried on a brisk trade in slaves, notably Irish, with the Middle East, and Arab slave emporiums flourished in Africa. It was with the Age of Exploration, however, that a type of renaissance of slavery took place. Enslavement of the native American population soon faltered, only to be augmented by the importation of large numbers of African slaves, and the *encomiendas* of the Latin south, as well as the plantations of the US, provided a robust market. These systems were not mitigated by slaves being placed in high social positions, and they carried the added complication of racial and ethnic differences between the masters and their mestizo and African slaves. The brutality of these systems provoked a Christian call for abolition (see Wilberforce, William*), echoed in the Enlightenment* enunciation of the 'rights of man', which bore fruit in the early 19th century, first in the UK, and then, by treaty at the Congress of Vienna (1814–15), more widely in Europe. American slavery ceased only with the independence struggles in Latin America and by means of devastating civil war in the US.

Slavery has not vanished in the 20th century but has assumed different forms, such as the notorious work camps of Siberia, so graphically described by Alexander Solzhenitsyn (1918–), and the slave-labour of children in some of the under-developed countries of the world.

Slavery is rightly criticized as dehumanizing to both slave and owner, as open to all kinds of abuse, and as frequently promoting racism and sexism. Yet, for the Christian, it provides a suggestive metaphor of willing, loving submission to God (Rom. 1:1; Phil. 1:1), 'whose service is perfect freedom' (*BCP*, second collect for Morning Prayer; *cf.* Rom. 6:17–18).

Bibliography
D. B. Davis, *The Problem of Slavery in Western Culture* (Ithaca, NY, 1966); M.I. Finley (ed.), *Slavery in Classical Antiquity* (Cambridge, 1960); C. Mossé, *The Ancient World at Work* (ET, New York, 1969); R. Sawyer, *Slavery in the Twentieth Century* (London, 1986); R. Winks (ed.), *Slavery: A Comparative Perspective* (New York, 1972).

B.W.R.

SOCIAL CONTEXT OF PASTORAL CARE, see PRACTICAL AND PASTORAL THEOLOGY.�7

S OCIAL CONTRACT. What makes political authority legitimate in society? One answer is an appeal to social contract. Political society should be understood in terms of a contract, or contracts, to secure the network of rights (see Rights, Human*) and obligations required for the viability of proper social life.

Sometimes a distinction has been drawn between governmental contract and social contract. The former deals with the question of specifically governmental authority, the latter with the very being of society. But the phrase 'social contract' typically covers both. It embraces several diverse ideas.

The origin of the idea in the Christian era can be traced back to the Middle Ages, when it developed out of a concern to demarcate and delimit the rights of monarchs in relation to people. There is something like a contract here between ruler and ruled. Therefore obedience was not unconditional but dependent on the mutual performance of duty. This notion had important consequences in the development of social and political thought after the Reformation, particularly in Calvinism. For example, Samuel Rutherford (1600–61), among others, argued in his *Lex Rex: A Dispute for the Just Prerogative of King and People* (1644), on the basis of Dt. 17:14–20, that both king and people are parties to a covenant* under God.

Because the relationship was contractual, rebellion* was justified and even mandatory in circumstances where the ruler violated its provisions. The political issues that generated such a development typically concerned the question of enforcement and liberty in religion which characterized the novel European social scene. In medieval and 16th-century thought, however, talk of anything like contract was rooted in belief that God is sovereign and that rulers, like the ruled, are accountable to him. In the golden age of contract theory, the 17th and 18th centuries, this belief sometimes became marginalized in the formation of social and political theory.

While they differed in their religious beliefs, three figures contributed particularly to the theory of social contract at this time. Thomas Hobbes (1588–1679) argued that in the pre-political situation – the 'state of nature' – strife and competition held sway. Political society is the necessary response in which people agree to transfer their rights to the ruler in return for protection. In the work of Hobbes, social contract functions to uphold authority in an absolutist form (although Hobbes holds that subjects' rights of self-defence are retained), and he brings together in one move the agreement to live socially and the agreement to live under such government.

John Locke (1632–1704) envisaged a more amicable state of nature, but also believed that the adjudication of conflicting claims was necessary. The transfer of individual rights here is far more limited and designed to protect liberty and property as well as life. Locke's scheme functioned to justify resistance rather than sovereign power.

Finally, Jean-Jacques Rousseau (1712–78) differed again. For Rousseau the state of nature was not one of Hobbesian conflict but, unlike Locke, he conceived of the emergence of civilized society as a degeneration, a welding of chains binding the man born free. Rousseau proposed a political theory of the general will whereby the collective will of citizens, equally represented, prevailed. His principal essay setting this out is actually titled *The Social Contract* (1762).

In social-contract theory, the pre-political state of nature could be conceived either as a literal, historical state or as a kind of theoretical construct designed to show the logic of obligation. The classic texts are differently interpreted on this score. But in the modern revival of social-contract theory, it is clear that no historical pre-political state of nature is involved. This revival, after a long period of decline since Rousseau, has centred on the work of John Rawls (1921–), particularly *A Theory of Justice* (Cambridge, MA, 1971; Oxford, 1972). Admittedly, it has been argued that Rawls' theory is not a *bona fide* social-contract theory at all. Rawls' chief concern is the principle of social justice, which he works out with reference to a theoretical state of fairness (not state of nature). This gives him notions of self-interest, rationality and equality to ground his detailed theory. Rawls' thought has developed over the years and his work still evokes much debate.

There are at least three reasons for theological engagement with the notion of social contract: 1. It flowered at a period of crucial political transition largely produced by the social force of the Reformation. At a time when we need to scrutinize the religious roots of our social institutions, its study is important. 2. The secular democratic liberalism which has succeeded Christendom is the subject of much debate and some disaffection today. A theological attempt at social and political theory will profit from reflection on social contract. 3. Both stability and justice seem to require a structured set of social rights and obligations, and the broad idea of contract appears to be an attempt to provide the same thing. But of course any use we make of it must be integrated into the paramount theological conviction that both social existence and governmental authority derive from the will of God.

Bibliography

M. Lessnoff, *Social Contract* (London, 1986); *idem* (ed.), *Social Contract Theory* (Oxford, 1990); J. B. Torrance, 'The Covenant Concept in Scottish Theology and Politics and its Legacy', *SJT* 34, 1981, pp. 225–243.

S.N.W.

SOCIAL ETHICS. The term 'social ethics' is misleading because all Christian ethics is social ethics, given that fundamental to the Christian understanding of humanity (see 4) is that we live in relationship with God and our neighbour. Nevertheless, the term is helpful in distinguishing ethical concern with processes and structures in society* and in the international order* from more individual and interpersonal ethical issues. The field of social ethics is thus typically concerned with issues of war* and peace, social justice in the political and economic order and between the sexes, business ethics (see Economic Ethics[17]) and medical ethics (see Ethics of Medical Care[14]).

For much of church history, mainstream Christian social ethics has legitimated a static and status view of society. This held that the institutions of society are a given, and that this life is a 'vale of tears' to be endured, in whatever calling one was born, for the sake of inheriting the blessings of the life to come. The major revolutions of the 18th century – the Industrial Revolution, the American War of Independence and the French Revolution of 1789 – called this view into question by suggesting possibilities of social transformation that had previously been agitated for only by apocalyptic and millenarian movements within Christianity. Today, the challenge of these secular revolutions and their legacies sets much of the agenda of Christian social ethics.

The major methodological debate within Christian social ethics is whether the Christian faith adds any distinctive material content to a social ethic. The claim for distinctiveness is opposed on the ground that Jesus did not have a social ethic and is to be 'regarded as normative [only] because he is believed to have experienced what it is to be human in the fullest way and at the deepest level' (S. Hauerwas, *A Community of Character*, p. 39). Catholic social ethics has traditionally identified with this position in its espousal of a universal natural law* open to the eye of reason. Taking a different view are the approaches which base their ethics on either the person of Jesus* and his teaching about the kingdom of God,* or his story, or by way of analogy from the community life of the early church, or from the values fostered by worshipping Christian communities. Protestant social ethics is usually identified with these approaches because of an interpretation of the Fall,* which is held to have so distorted creation* that it is now impossible to read off moral obligations from nature. A middle position in the debate claims that the Bible provides only general moral principles, 'middle axioms' (see Axiom*), which point out the direction for moral action, and which need to be interpreted in the light of the flawed nature of the whole of human existence.

Recent scholarship sheds some light on this debate by identifying three ideological strands of thought within the NT. 1. The first strand, which is seen as the origin of early activist Christian utopianism, provides biblical warrant for the kind of perfectionist* ethic that seeks to construct a just social order on the lines of the kingdom of God proclaimed by Jesus (Mt. 5:38–39; Acts 4:32). 2. A second strand, which is the predominant ideological type in the NT, is held to underlie the subversive anticipation of an ideal new order that God is to inaugurate. It provides biblical warrant for a realist* ethic which, in pointing forward to the kingdom, none the less recognizes that, because of the pervasiveness of sin (see Sin and Salvation[5]), it is never fully possible to realize its standards in the processes and structures of society (Mt. 19:8–9, contrast Mk. 10:1–12; 1 Cor. 4:8–9; 7). 3. The third ideological strand is held to have come close to legitimating the then-existing social order, perhaps because there was no possibility that it could be overthrown, or because its stability helped forward the cause of evangelism, the primary function of the Christian community. This strand provides support for the view that evangelism is the distinctive contribution that the church can make towards building a better world; as Augustine* put it, the first duty to our neighbour is to 'seize him for Christ' (Rom. 13:1–4; 1 Cor. 1:20–24; Col. 3:22–25). Since it is difficult to dissociate any of these three strands from Jesus or Paul, or indeed from the rest of the NT, a Christian social ethic which takes the NT seriously must take all of them into consideration.

In addition to taking the Scriptures seriously, Christian social ethics needs to take the situation seriously by calling on secular expertise. One implication of this interdisciplinary approach, with its reliance on the contestable data of the social sciences, is that, while the solutions proposed in Christian social ethics may be treated as authoritative, they should never be regarded as infallible.

See also: CHRISTIAN MORAL REASONING; COMMUNITY ETHICS.[16]

Bibliography

J. L. Allen, 'Social Ethics' in *NDCE*, pp. 592–593; J. M. Finnis, *Natural Law and Natural Rights* (Oxford, 1980); R. Gill, *Christian Ethics in Secular Worlds* (Edinburgh, 1991); S. Hauerwas, *A Community of Character* (Notre Dame, IN, 1981); J. Mahoney, *The Making of Moral Theology* (Oxford, 1987); C. Rowland, *Christian Origins* (London, 1985).

C.Y.

SOCIAL GOSPEL. The term 'social gospel' originally referred to formulations of the gospel made by Christians in N. America in situations of great poverty and deprivation in the 19th century, *e.g.* Walter Rauschenbusch (1861–1918). These formulations stressed the compassion of Jesus.

Some evangelicals perceived these views to be reductionist in Christology, because they focused only on Jesus' example of a ministry of good works, were imbued with evolutionary optimism that God's will for human harmony would come through human action and historical progress, and implied that humanity would through its own efforts bring in God's kingdom of justice and peace. Many evangelicals therefore began to use the term 'social gospel' as a means of labelling as unorthodox any views which highlighted the social dimension of the gospel.

The First World War dashed many of the hopes of the old social-gospel movement. A strong theological reaction developed, expressed by Reinhold Niebuhr,* Karl Barth* and Hendrik Kraemer (1888–1965). They pointed out the discontinuity between God's will and the strivings of sinful humanity; they criticized the over-emphasis on the present experience of God's kingdom. Niebuhr pointed out the unpracticality of the Sermon on the Mount,* and Barth emphasized the transcendent rule of God. Their position also had a weakness in tending to render the Christian faith so discontinuous with human history that it made no practical contribution to issues of poverty* and injustice (see Justice and Peace[3]).

Similar reaction took place in the evangelical missionary movement. According to the personal testimony of the late Bishop Stephen Neill (1900–84), whether the gospel had a social dimension was the issue that caused the divisions in the early 20th century between the student missionary movements that derived their origin from the Edinburgh Missionary Conference of 1910. Those who denied that the gospel had a social dimension claimed that their view represented the true, biblical view.

In actual fact, the origins of the 19th-century missionary movement lay in social concern. In particular, following the abolition of the slave (see Slavery*) trade, there was a major concern to repay the debt owed to Africa for the centuries of exploitation through the slave trade. This was a mainspring of the British missionary movement. The need to engage in economic and political as well as religious activity, in order to repay that debt, also gave rise to the birth of the second British Empire. Exeter Hall, a centre for societies with evangelical missionary concern, 'believed that the power of Great Britain should be used to guard the welfare of backward peoples, to protect them from exploitation and to guide them in the Christian way' (James Morris, *Heaven's Command*, Harmondsworth, 1979, p. 37). 'For many Victorian Englishmen, the instinct of empire was first to be rationalized as a call to Christian duty' (*ibid.*).

Particularly since the Berlin Congress on Evangelism in 1966, there has been a recovery among evangelicals of an understanding that the gospel of Jesus Christ has inescapable social dimensions. This was most publicly expressed in the Lausanne Covenant* of 1974, in paragraph 5 on the mission of the church.

The issues are as follows: some claim that the gospel is about certain beliefs about Jesus Christ and the need to believe in him in order to experience eternal life, which consists in the forgiveness of sins and the assurance of resurrection life after death. These benefits can be experienced only by the individual. Converted individuals will as a matter of witness and obedience show love to their neighbours, but such love is not constitutive of the gospel. That would be to substitute works for faith.

Others claim that while the gospel includes forgiveness and everlasting life, its focus is not on benefits to individuals but on the lordship of Christ. This lordship is expressed through his current rule (the kingdom of God*) which embraces all of life. This rule brings new relationships with God whereby people are forgiven by God and receive a new status as his sons and daughters; people are brought into new relationships with each other of mutual forgiveness (Jew and Greek, slave and free, male and female, Gal. 3:28), and into new relationships with the natural order over which they were appointed to have dominion and stewardship (Gn. 1:27–28). The fulfilment of this rule in the new heavens and new earth at the return of Christ will include the transformation of all these relationships (Rev. 21:2–4, 24–27).

Underlying the disagreement (as with many theological disagreements) are presuppositions about the nature of humanity (see [4]; see also Image of God*) and the Fall.* Is humanity in relation to God essentially constituted of individuals or is it constituted of persons in-community? Was the Fall therefore fundamentally a sundering only of the relationship between people and God which sundered other relationships *as a consequence*, or was it a sundering of a relationship with God with the sundering of other relationships as an expression or dimension of that sundering?

A series of international conferences between 1966 and 1983 saw developments in evangelical theological reflection, especially from Christians in the Third World grappling with the issues of Christian encounter with hunger* and poverty.* They point to the following theological categories: that the gospel is the gospel of the kingdom of God, both present and yet to come; that the gospel is addressed to people in communities, and that people are 'persons in relationships', not isolated individuals; that the cross* breaks down barriers between people in hostile groups; that the gospel creates a new human community, the church (Eph. 3:1–10); that it is the gospel of grace and of free forgiveness through the cross that imparts to poor people dignity, status and hope and that overcomes the barriers between hostile groups; and that love of the neighbour, especially the poor, is a distinctive aspect of Christianity in the world of religions.

Holders of such views claim to differ from 19th-century expressions of the social gospel because they do not reduce the divinity of the person of Christ, they do not have an evolutionary optimism, and they make the cross of Christ central in their exposition of Christianity. They differ from some expressions of socially concerned Christianity in this century which revised evolutionary optimism (such as liberation theology*), in that they move beyond the identification of the poor as victims to their experience of victory now in Christ. They claim that they differ from the first views expressed because the social dimensions of the gospel are implicit and intrinsic to the proclamation and demonstration of the gospel. Thus, properly understood, they would seek to rehabilitate the term, claiming that the gospel is a social, as well as a personal and religious, gospel.

Bibliography

T. Chester, *Awakening to a World of Need: The Recovery of Evangelical Social Concern* (Leicester, 1993); R. T. Handy (ed.), *The Social Gospel in America 1870–1920* (New York, 1966); D. O. Moberg, *The Great Reversal* (Philadelphia, 1972; London, 1973); R. Padilla and C. Sugden (eds.), *Texts on Evangelical Social Ethics 1974–83*, vols. 1–3 (Bramcote, Nottingham, 1985–87); C. Sugden, 'Evangelicals and Wholistic Evangelism', in V. Samuel and A. Hauser (eds.), *Proclaiming Christ in Christ's Way* (Oxford, 1989).

C.M.N.S.

SOCIALISM. The term 'socialism' refers to a varied group of political movements and theories. This political group shares collectivist ideals and a dislike for the unequal resources and power relationships that exist in capitalist* free-market and developing economies. It also agrees that economic relationships and production are fundamental to how a society functions, so that any changes need to focus on these elements. Beyond this the group differs widely in its views on the desirable extent of State ownership of production, the extent of redistribution of income, and the means which are acceptable to bring about changes.

Socialist ideas and agitation began in England and France in the first half of the 19th century. Socialism was offered as a solution to the large-scale poverty existing at the time, which was thought to have been brought about by the introduction of the factory system of industrial production and the increased reliance on wages, even in handicraft industries. Most of the early socialists were middle-class reformers and philanthropists who thought that there was a need to go beyond charitable works in order to better the lot of the poor.

The theorists include Robert Owen (1771–1858), Pierre-Joseph Proudhon (1809–65), Henri de Saint-Simon (1760–1825) in the first half of the 19th century, and in the latter half, Karl Marx* and Friedrich Engels (1820–95). Marx and Engels criticized the early socialists as utopian idealists and offered a more schematic theory. According to them, the basic problem was in the system of social production in which the two major classes have opposing interests because of their different relationship to the means of production: they are either owners of the means of production, or wage labourers. The class struggle was to be the basis of socialism, and socialism was to be identified with the working class in its fight to overthrow exploitation* and oppression. Exploitation was defined by virtue of the working class failing to receive recompense from their labour equal to the whole of their product. The overthrow of the capitalists would usher in a new period of popular self-government in which there would be no domination of man by man.

The ideas of socialism later became institutionalized in a number of different ways in Europe. On the one hand, in Britain these ideas were taken up by labour unions and then the Labour Party. The period 1870–1914 saw an increase in the State's control and administration over mass schooling, social insurance, public health, sewerage and electricity. This strand of socialism has continued into the 20th century and is now the foundation of the socialist democratic political parties existing in many European countries. On the other hand, communism,* under which economic matters became totally planned by the central government, was a further outcome in Eastern Europe following the Russian Revolution based on the ideas of Marx, as interpreted by Lenin (1870–1924). There is a range of other opinions and political representations which lie between these two poles. Since the 1970s socialist doctrine has entered a period of diversity not unlike the era of its origins in the first half of the 19th century. The socialist democratic parties have been challenged by their more left-wing elements. At the same time, the collapse of the planned economies of the Eastern bloc has removed the argument that more and more central control and economic planning can work effectively; but how and whether these economies can and should change to become viable again is by no means clear.

Socialist ideas can be evaluated by seeing how they match up to scriptural principles. Over the last two decades, people motivated by socialist ideas have helped to bring about many improvements in European countries. Socialism has helped us see that the market system may not always be the most effective way of allocating resources in the areas of health, education and religious life. Clearly underlying many socialist ideas is a faith that social engineering alone will solve society's problems. For Christians, such a faith is naïve and does not take into account the inherent sinfulness of men and women. Donald Hay in *Economics Today* evaluates socialist ideas against scriptural principles under a number of headings: the role of the State, public ownership of productive assets, planning to replace or supplement markets, restrictions on economic freedom, the organization of work and policies to promote equality. He concludes that a communist system is definitely incompatible with biblical criteria, but that a social democratic system may not be. Planned economies clearly do prevent individuals from exercising personal stewardship. In the area of work, socialist ideas of work, as a co-operative activity, are close to biblical principles. Similarly, some socialist ideas about the redistribution of income accord well with biblical notions that institutional structures should be trying to avoid people getting locked into poverty,* whilst relieving its worst effects when they are found.

Bibliography

R. H. S. Crossman (ed.), *New Fabian Essays* (London, 1972); D. A. Hay, *Economics Today* (Leicester, 1989); S. Holland, *The Socialist Challenge* (London, 1975); K. Marx and F. Engels, *The Communist Manifesto* (1848), ET in D. McLellan (ed.), *Karl Marx: Selected Writings* (Oxford, 1977).

S.D.

SOCIETY is an abstract concept referring to the system of interrelationships connecting individuals who share a common culture.* Debate over the nature of, and changes within, society is central to sociology and other social sciences. Though society once meant fellowship or companionship, it is just these things that are often supposed to be missing from modern society. On the other hand, without some concept of society, it seems we are left with naked individualism.* Thus both philosophical and practical, pastoral questions are raised by the consideration of society.

Society, as used in social science, is generally equivalent to the boundaries of nation-states. Thus we speak of 'Malaysian society' or 'Icelandic society', but this could be misleading, say, in the case of 'Palestinian society', 'Canadian society' or 'Nigerian society' where boundaries are disputed or common culture is absent. This confusion is very revealing, because it shows, for example, that societies are not self-contained but heavily influenced by others, and that they often tend to be culturally and ethnically diverse. In other words, societies should not be thought of as free-standing, coherent entities, but both as part of larger wholes and as internally divided.

Within sociology, society has been contrasted with community. Ferdinand Tönnies' (1855–1936) classic *Gemeinschaft und Gesellschaft* (1887; ET, *Community and*

Association, London, 1955) suggested that while traditional societies had been characterized by relatively close-knit, face-to-face relations, often based on kinship, modern ones evidenced new kinds of impersonal, contractual relations, lacking a sense of belonging. This kind of perspective implies that authentic social life takes place only in small-scale and local settings. Personal identification with an entity like the nation-state is rendered problematic.

Perhaps the most common dualism,* however, counterposes society and individual. While each has some commonsense resonance, the individual turns out to be as abstract a concept as society. Early sociologists rejected the liberal focus on individuals – *e.g.* as seen in Adam Smith's (1723–90) *The Wealth of Nations* (1776) – with the view that individual action can be scientifically explained in terms of society. This supposed 'social whole' was a primary datum of 'social science'. This problem, though originating with Auguste Comte (1798–1857) and mediated by Emile Durkheim,* is still, arguably, at the centre of sociological debate.

Various solutions have been sought, more recently in notions of a *duality* of social structure and social action, or linguistic formulae (*narratives*) that would dissolve sociology in history. Rather than comment on the relative merits of what may seem like arcane controversy, a more fruitful endeavour may be to consider some Christian criteria relating to society. However, this term itself is called in question, not only because of its reductionist* use in some sociology, but also because society refers to no coherent reality except perhaps the nation-state.

The following comments set the stage for some Christian thinking about society, at a less theoretical level, but in a manner intended to stimulate Christian sociological investigations as well as general social thinking none the less.

1. Biblical accounts know nothing of society, or for that matter of individuals, in the Western sense. But they do have much to say about the social dimension of human life. Human beings are made in the image* of a God who is three persons; sociality is ontological. This has important implications. It suggests that thinking of individuals as social 'atoms' is inappropriate; we are all bound to each other. Furthermore, our lack of consistency and wholeness in social relations may be transcendentally located in the ruptured relations between God and humanity (see ④). Personhood, in this view, is essentially relational.

2. Sociality, however expressed, is more significant than 'society'. People relate to each other in various ways within biblical narratives: children with parents; friends, enemies and spouses with each other; wage-labourers with owners; citizens with government officials; soldiers with commanders; *etc.* Different levels of sociality are evident here, each carrying appropriate responsibilities and expectations. Social institutions also appear, from the monarchy to marriage, from priesthood to patriarchy. None is eternal; some exist only due to human hardness of heart (*cf.* Mt. 19:8) and are destined for dismantling. But each sphere of social life is accountable in its way to God, and also bears relation to the rest of creation.

3. In the NT, the church* itself becomes a sign of alternative social relations. A product of Christ's reconciliation,* the church itself acts as agent of reconciliation. Where ethnic, gender, class and religious barriers once stood, now diversity in unity obtains. This further relativizes the *status quo* of dominant social relations and simultaneously points forward to future fulfilment of the God–people–land triad. None the less, this 'new people' of God is mandated to be salt and light in the contemporary world, demonstrating the way of Jesus and influencing social relations through authentic commitment to neighbour-love, justice, freedom and hope.

See also: HUMANITY.④

Bibliography

J. M. Houston, 'Spiritual Life Today: An Appropriate Spirituality for a Post-modern World', in M. Eden and D. F. Wells (eds.), *The Gospel in the Modern World* (Leicester, 1991); D. Lyon, *Sociology and the Human Image* (Leicester, 1983); C. J. W. Wright, *Living as the People of God* (Leicester, 1983) = *An Eye for an Eye* (Downers Grove, IL, 1983).

D.A.L.

SOCIOBIOLOGY is a reductionist* theory, devised by Edward O. Wilson (1929–), which explains animal and human social behaviour in terms of Darwinian evolution. Critics have replied that human beings are more than just animals, and that human behaviour is determined partly by culture* and by free will as well as by genetics.

According to Wilson and his followers, the elements between which natural selection discriminates are genes, which are the units of inheritance and the biological basis of behaviour. The popularizer of sociobiology, Richard Dawkins (1941–), has said that for genes to survive they must be selfish, by which he means that individuals bearing those genes tend to behave in ways which enable them to live in a competitive world long enough to reproduce themselves and thereby ensure the survival of the genes.

The immediate objection to this theory is the continued existence amongst humans and other animals of anti-evolutionary phenomena such as unselfishness and homosexuality. Sociobiologists have tried to show that such traits may actually help the gene to survive since, for example, the sacrifice of one individual may benefit a relative who shares the same genes, but some kinds of unselfishness (e.g. self-sacrifice for a non-relative, cf. Jn. 15:13) cannot be explained in such ways.

Wilson explains the origin of both religion and ethics in terms of sociobiology. Moral codes may be criticized by biological criteria: e.g. Wilson rejects Catholic teaching on natural law.* He claims that certain ethical principles can be deduced from biology, but critics have accused him of illegitimately seeking to derive 'ought' from 'is'.

Bibliography

R. Dawkins, *The Selfish Gene* (Oxford, 1976); M. Ruse, *Sociobiology: Sense or Nonsense?* (Dordrecht, ²1985); P. Singer, *The Expanding Circle: Ethics and Sociobiology* (Oxford, 1981); E. O. Wilson, *Sociobiology: The New Synthesis* (Cambridge, MA, 1975).

C.E.H.

SOCIOLOGY OF ETHICS. Ethics is concerned with the formation of value* judgments and principles of conduct. The sociology of ethics refers to the social correlates of these principles, both in formal ethical deliberation and in everyday life. It is based on the theoretical and empirical analysis of culture, morality, values, attitudes and social behaviour. As Emile Durkheim* wrote: 'Moral facts are phenomena like others: they consist of rules of action recognizable by certain distinctive characteristics. It must, then, be possible to observe them, describe them, classify them and look for the laws explaining them' (*The Division of Labor in Society*, 1893; New York, 1964, p. 32).

In functionalist theories of society, the significance of ethics comes from the need for a common system of culture* and values to provide social cohesion and stability. Conflict over the basic norms of society is seen as a prelude to social disintegration, and social groups which deviate from the norm are seen as marginal to or even threatening to the social order. Although a version of this theory lies behind many popular views of moral and cultural decline, it fails to explain apparently endemic conflicts in modern society, or how such societies continue to survive in the absence of any overarching cosmology or 'sacred canopy' of religion. Alternatives to functionalism stress that material factors like economic necessity, legal compulsion and force are more important sources of social cohesion. The Marxist view of culture and morality, for example, sees it as a site of an unequal class struggle and does not assume that a value consensus exists. Both functionalist and Marxist theories have been partly superseded by theories which interpret ethical variety in terms of the irreducible pluralism* of modern life.

The extent of agreement and disagreement in core beliefs and values has been mapped in a number of national and international surveys. For example, the annual British Social Attitudes Survey by the Social and Community Planning Research group has identified issues on which agreement is relatively high and issues on which there is disagreement, whether structured or diffuse. On economic issues like wealth distribution and public spending, there is divergence between classes: the working class is most in favour of redistribution, while the petty bourgeoisie and salaried employees are the least in favour. However, with this topic, as with most others, there is almost as much dissensus within each class as between each class. Only in the area of sexual morality is there clear evidence of polarization of values. Questions on homosexuality, for example, show a majority (59%) who believe that homosexual relations are always wrong but a second, smaller cluster (15%) at the other extreme who believe that homosexual relations are not at all wrong. The social bases of consensus or disagreement are complex. Class, education and gender all play a part, and people may revert to more traditional values as they age. Religious belief correlates with stricter, less permissive interpretations of right and wrong in matters of public as well as private life (see Sociology of Religion*).

One definite conclusion which can be drawn is that the areas of greatest divergence are those least likely to be central to current political debates. But differences of religion, ethnicity* and regional identity can and do correspond with major political cleavages in other countries and contexts.

Normative frameworks can be organized in different ways with different consequences for society. In small-scale societies they are likely to have a traditional character, taking the form of mores and folk-ways which set prescriptive standards and maintain society by regulating individual behaviour. Some cultures, on the other hand, depend on a general theory, religious or non-religious, which is codified in texts and systems of law and regulation. Modern societies, in contrast, tend to have an ethos of pluralism and reject the possibility of a transcendental theory of values. Hence there is a tendency towards pragmatism* in ethical discourse, or even a rejection of ethical discussion as irrational. Codes of 'professional ethics'* (especially in the younger professions) illustrate this: they have been created mainly in response to the need to regulate competition, control recruitment, and present a good face to clients, not as the articulation of a general moral theory.

The sociology of ethics has not been as salient in Christian ethical discourse as problems of the relationship between theology and ethics. Yet from the pastoral and apologetic point of view there is a compelling need for a 'communicative ethics' (such as the theory developed by Jürgen Habermas, 1929–), which takes full account of the normative structures which condition the social interaction between participants in discourse. The social dimension is, indeed, unavoidable in the pastoral context, where the bases of ethical agreement and disagreement have become progressively more complex. The public role for Christian ethics in this situation is to counsel with authority, neither adopting the non-directive dialogue model, nor relying on appeal to the church's own political authority, but by argument, persuasion and the exposition of Scripture. In this endeavour, Christian ethics will find that its ability to speak with authority will depend on the church's own nature as a social and ethical community.

Bibliography

J. Habermas, *Moral Consciousness and Communicative Action* (ET, Cambridge and Cambridge, MA, 1990); S. Harding *et al.*, *Contrasting Values in Western Europe* (London, 1986); R. Jowell *et al.*, *British Social Attitudes Survey: the 8th report* (Aldershot, 1991); M. Ossowska, *The Social Determinants of Moral Ideas* (London, 1971).

H.H.D.

SOCIOLOGY OF RELIGION. Although informal explanations about how religion operates sociologically occurred over an extended period, at least two conditions seemed necessary for sociology of religion to emerge as an intellectual endeavour. 1. Scholars other than theologians and religionists took on the task of explaining religion systematically: and 2. there was an underlying commitment to the idea of secularization* and the presumed demise of religion, with its likely replacement by science as a metaphysical system. Post-Enlightenment thinkers such as Henri de Saint-Simon (1760–1825) and Auguste Comte (1798–1857) were the immediate precursors of sociology of religion. Both men sought to explain away traditional religious beliefs and expressions, while establishing social science as the final arbiter among persisting humanistic religious notions.

The two giants in classical sociology of religion, Emile Durkheim* and Max Weber (1864–1920), both took religion seriously as an enduring sociological element, as well as constructing theoretical systems in sociology of which the sociology of religion was an integral part. Durkheim argued for the functional necessity of religion within society. Societies have both distinctively profane and sacred aspects, with religion being the basis of all social institutions but also little other than a society worshipping itself. While religion has probably been transformed within modern societies whose organic solidarity is derived from the division of labour, religion also is functionally irreplaceable in the modern world (*cf.* Durkheim, *The Elementary Forms of the Religious Life*, ET, London, 1915).

Weber's sociology of religion was considerably different from and more 'modern' than Durkheim's. Trained as an historical economist, Weber is best known for the two essays published as *The Protestant Ethic and the Spirit of Capitalism* (1904–05). There he argued that modern rational capitalism developed because of the characteristics it shared in 'elective affinity' with rational

Calvinistic beliefs (see Calvinistic Ethics*) about working hard to the glory of God and living an ascetic lifestyle as a means to confirming one's election. (Parenthetically, the ghost of Karl Marx's historical materialism probably served as a stimulus for Weber's analysis.) In subsequent studies, Weber extended his historically comparative theses beyond Western Protestantism and also added a wide variety of still-essential concepts to the field – theodicy, charisma and its routinization, and church and sect, to name several.

If sociology of religion was well established by the First World War, it then wandered erratically for the next half-century, particularly because of its declining significance within either religious studies or secular sociology. Those interested in religion *qua* religion had little time for the purposes or methodologies of social science, and mainstream sociology in Britain, N. America and the Continent assumed that religion was inevitably waning and so not worth pursuing as a subject of either popular practice or academic investigation. The long-term result was tragic, as sociology of religion slipped to the periphery of social-scientific study, a situation which continues today despite efforts by the current generation to restore its import.

What happened in the meantime is that several topic areas have received widespread attention from groups of scholars, often in the tradition of either Durkheim or Weber.

1. The first is the multi-faceted concept of *secularization*. As the West moved into the modern era, sociological verities such as industrialization,* urbanization* and the rise of science* presupposed the parallel process of the demise of the sacred – really a fuller articulation of Weber's Protestant-ethic thesis. Scholars including David Martin (1929–), Karel Dobbelaere, Thomas Luckmann (1927–), Peter Berger (1929–), and others have attempted to explain secularization as both a product and a carrier of the modern ethos. Recently, a reassessment of the underlying ideology and presuppositions has begun, and the controversy over secularization continues.

2. A second topic of interest in the past 30 years has been *civil religion* and the quest to understand societies' penchant to attribute theological meaning to their own history, tradition and place in the world. Taking a Durkheimian approach to religion, Robert Bellah (1927–) rekindled the debate over civil religion in the mid-1960s. Recent events in the Middle East, Eastern Europe, and the former Soviet Union have extended this discussion far beyond its earlier N. American context.

3. A third area of interest pursued by Bryan Wilson (1926–) and others has been the explanation of ongoing *religious organizational forms*, especially the concept of the sect. Based on Weber, Ernst Troeltsch (1865–1923), and H. Richard Niebuhr,* these studies attempt to explain organizational tensions between religion and its cultural milieux. The emergence of new religious movements (formerly called cults) also stimulates these analyses.

4. A final topic of widespread interest has been the growth of *fundamentalist, evangelical and neo-pentecostal religious forms* during the final third of the 20th century. Frequently, these forms emphasize religious experience as opposed to mere belief or organizational affiliation. Fundamentalisms both within and outside Christianity and the rapid proliferation of charismatic Protestant groups in the southern hemisphere were challenged early on as mere products of the media, but subsequent evidence suggests that something deeper is occurring. These upsurges of religious activity also have challenged the accepted secularization model.

Since the 1970s, interest in the sociology of religion has grown, both in Britain and in N. America. A persisting problem, however, has been the fragmented quality of the analyses and the difficulty of integrating the academic activity back into the mainstream of theoretically sociological explanation. On its own terms, the study of religion has benefited from this recent activity, and the prospects are encouraging that similar strides can be accomplished within sociology.

Bibliography
W. Davis, *ER* 13, pp. 393–401; R. O'Toole, *Religion: Classic Sociological Approaches* (Toronto, 1984); R. Robertson, *A Sociological Interpretation of Religion* (Oxford, 1970); R. J. Wuthnow, *HS*, pp. 473–509.

J.A.M.

SPEECH AND THE TONGUE. The importance of speech is rooted, for the Christian, in the nature and activity of God. He is the great communicator. With delicate economy, the Gospel-writers record how the Father spoke directly to the Son (Mt. 3:17; 17:5), and how the Son conversed with the Father in prayer (Lk. 22:41–42).

Moreover, both the OT and the NT stress the vital role of words in God's self-revelation. God uses words to teach his truth and to proclaim his values. He commands, counsels, promises, warns and appeals. In OT times, he spoke through the prophets (who were both 'seers', hearing his word, and 'spokesmen', proclaiming it). With the coming of Christ, the Word *par excellence*, he spoke decisively and conclusively in his Son (Heb. 1:1–2; Jn. 1:18).

Men and women, made in God's image,* are born to be communicators too. That is why one of the prophesied Messiah's roles was to make the stammerer speak distinctly, a speech therapist's role which Jesus filled in several of his miracles (Is. 32:4; Mt. 9:32–33).

Translated into socio-political terms, freedom of speech is a vital Christian value, as well as a human right enshrined in the First Amendment to the Constitution of the USA. The boldness (*parrēsia*) for which Paul longed as an evangelist (Eph. 6:19–20) was the democratic right, enjoyed by every ancient Gk. citizen, to speak his mind freely (see Rights, Human*).

In several striking metaphors and similes, the Bible highlights the immense power of the spoken word. Words are weapons – spears, swords and arrows (Pss. 57:4; 64:3; Je. 9:8). The tongue is like a bit in the horse's mouth, a rudder at the stern of a ship, or a small spark that sets a forest ablaze; its influence is out of all proportion to its size (Jas. 3:2–12).

It is in the world of ideas that the tongue is at its most influential. The book of Proverbs brings that out with particular force. Words shape convictions and change attitudes (Pr. 10:21; 18:8). Indeed, this is the sphere of human experience in which God's Word is especially active, as it penetrates to the level of thoughts and intentions (Heb. 4:12). Modern Christians need no persuading of the power of propaganda* and the influence of the media.*

Like any other source of power, the faculty of speech may be used positively or abused disastrously. The Bible, reflected by all Christian tradition, lists four areas of life where ethical checks must be applied.

1. Words should express *truth*.* Any human community relies for its health on its members' honesty* when they communicate with one another (Eph. 4:25). Truthful speech goes hand in hand with love, Christianity's prime virtue, in enhancing corporate growth (2 Cor. 6:7; Eph. 4:15). Conversely, denying or disguising the truth by lies and deceit is a recipe for social destruction (Pr. 28:24).

2. Words should help towards genuine *self-understanding*. The obverse, self-deception, is often stimulated by flattery (Pr. 26:28; Rom. 16:17–18) and leads its victim into hypocrisy,* when tongue and mind are at variance (Pr. 26:23; 1 Jn. 3:18). An honest, loving rebuke is often the best antidote (Pr. 17:10; 28:23).

3. Words should be used to build good *human relationships*. Wisdom* and justice* find a powerful ally in the tongue (Ps. 37:30), while a well-chosen message can bring strength, healing and encouragement to life's casualties (Is. 50:4; Jb. 4:4; Heb. 13:22). Used wrongly, on the other hand, words can wreck relationships by feeding malice, ruining reputations and exposing other people to ridicule (Rom. 1:29–30; 3:8; see Libel*).

4. Words should be used to build good *relationships between people and God*. People cannot hear God's reconciling gospel without a preacher and – once evangelized – it is their verbal testimony which seals their salvation (Rom. 10:8–17). Faith is fed by words, too, and expressed in praise and thanksgiving (Lk. 24:27, 32; Ps. 51:14–15). The Bible highlights open criticism of God ('murmuring') as a particularly dangerous way of using the tongue, because it erodes faith and stifles praise (Nu. 14:11; 1 Cor. 10:9–10).

It is, however, in expressing love and praise for God that the weakness of language is exposed. The believer's joy sometimes defies ordinary words (1 Pet. 1:8). Inspired by the Holy Spirit, many Christians today, as in Bible times, express their praise in sounds which are not immediately recognized by their hearers as known words (1 Cor. 14:2; see Holy Spirit*), and which require interpretation.

The practice of silent meditation, too, has deep roots in the Christian tradition. Some link it with the awed silence in heaven described in Rev. 8:1 (*cf.* Hab. 2:20). The monastic tradition especially, following Benedict's Rule, has made much of the virtue of silence in contemplative prayer and praise. Earlier, Gregory of Nazianzus (329–389) wrote, 'To speak of God is an exercise of great value, but there is one which is worth much more, namely to purify one's soul before God in silence' (*Orations*, xxvi).

D.H.F.

SPINOZA, BENEDICT DE, see HISTORY OF CHRISTIAN ETHICS. [6]

S PIRITUAL DIRECTION, a seeking of the Holy Spirit's leading in a Christian's life, refers to the biblical teaching that Christians are pilgrims journeying towards a particular goal, their heavenly home (Heb. 11:13–16). It is the Spirit who guides them, so that their journey is not aimless but involves growing maturity according to God's purpose. However, the Spirit normally gives this growth not in isolation but within the Christian community; Christians need one another's help in finding spiritual direction.

Since the Spirit is the only true director, some think it is best to avoid using the term 'spiritual director' of any human helper, since it has connotations of domination and blind obedience; 'guide' or 'soul friend' is preferable. Spiritual direction occurs when two (or more) Christians meet to discern the Spirit's direction in the life of one of them. The guide asks questions, listens and suggests possible directions, but finally leaves it to the disciple to find how the Spirit is leading.

Spiritual direction is concerned with the whole of life: with relationships, moral problems, and even social and political issues, as well as with the devotional life. The guide encourages growth in prayer,* but also helps the individual to reflect on God's work in the everyday world. This is not the same as pastoral counselling (see Pastoral Care, Counselling and Psychotherapy⎡12⎤), though there is an overlap. If there is a problem inhibiting Christian growth, it will probably be discussed, but the aim of spiritual direction is healthy growth rather than problem-solving.

Biblical examples of spiritual direction include Moses and Joshua, Eli and Samuel, Elijah and Elisha, Paul and Timothy and, above all, Jesus and his disciples. John 4:1–26 and 21:15–23 give examples of Jesus' pattern in this ministry; he describes its principles in Jn. 10:1–18. The command 'encourage one another and build each other up' (1 Thes. 5:11) gives a biblical justification for spiritual direction (cf. Eph. 4:15–16).

The early Fathers affirmed its value within the church. Basil of Caesarea (c. 329–79; also called Basil the Great) writes, 'God the Creator arranged things so that we need each other.' When, in the 3rd and 4th centuries, many Christians devoted themselves to prayer and spiritual warfare in the deserts, they realized the dangers of excessive individualism* in their solitary lives. A system of spiritual direction was organized for the first time, in which the young monks put themselves under the guidance of an *abba* ('father') of a small group. This pattern was taken up by both Eastern Orthodox and Catholic tradition and, after the Reformation, by Protestants who, while wary of sacerdotalism, saw the value of mutual encouragement.

Spiritual direction is not, therefore, restricted to one tradition. Protestants may be more likely to look to a soul friend, Pentecostals to a group whose members are accountable to each other, and Catholics to a priest who has received specialized training. They all affirm the same principle, that the Christian life is not a solitary walk or a private mystical trip. Christians need each other, not only at points of crisis, but also for normal, regular discernment of what God is doing. Spiritual direction may be sought from a man or woman, or even a group of people, but indispensable qualities are required: they must be Christian pilgrims themselves, humbly receiving guidance from others. They need to have experience and, if possible, training in Bible knowledge, different aspects of prayer, and psychology. Above all, they need to be the Spirit's ministers, not encouraging an unhealthy dependence on themselves, but enabling the disciple to recognize and follow the Spirit's leading.

See also: CONFESSION.

Bibliography
G. Jeff, *Spiritual Direction for Every Christian* (London, 1987); K. Leech, *Soul Friend* (London, 1977); A. Long, *Approaches to Spiritual Direction* (Bramcote, Nottingham, 1984); M. Thornton, *Spiritual Direction* (London, 1984).

C.J.H.H.

SPIRITUAL DISCIPLINES, see DISCIPLINES, SPIRITUAL.

SPIRITUAL HEALING, see HEALING; INNER HEALING.

S PIRITUALITY. The term 'spirituality' is notoriously difficult to define. It has a secular use (to describe a longing for something beyond the merely material), and a general religious use, but in Christian terms it is best used to mean simply 'living as a Christian'. It describes the whole of the lives of those who have responded to God's gracious call to live in fellowship with him.

The noun 'spirituality' does not occur in the Bible. In its Lat. form *spiritualitas*, it is first found in a 5th-century letter wrongly attributed to Jerome (*c*. 342–420), where its use is close to what Paul means by 'spiritual' (*pneumatikos*). Christians, because of their new birth, are 'led by the Spirit' (Rom. 8:14) and 'live by the Spirit' (Gal. 5:25). The word therefore refers, not to the human spirit, but to the Holy Spirit.

Paul defines true spirituality in 1 Cor. 2:13–16. His opponents claim a higher spirituality, whose marks are superior wisdom and speech, and divisive self-concern. Paul insists that the essence of true spirituality is a genuine love for others (1 Cor. 13).

'Spirituality' describes specifically the life of the *Christian*. It is the life of grace,* which begins with God the Father, who calls the sinner to himself, who has made a relationship with himself possible through the death of his Son, and who initiates and sustains that relationship through the Spirit.

Spirituality includes the life of the whole person (and not just of a supposedly 'spiritual' part). It is contrasted, not with the active elements of the Christian life, but with the carnal life of the natural man. Perhaps it is inevitable that popular usage often emphasizes the devotional aspects of spirituality, but these are of little worth, or dangerous, when they do not lead to a life of obedience and service (Is. 1:11–17). Writers like Richard Lovelace (1930–), Gerard Hughes and Charles Elliott (1939–) stress concern for social justice as a vital part of Christian spirituality (see Justice and Peace③).

There are essentials in spirituality which are the same for all Christians, both in the aim (being 'conformed to the likeness of [God's] Son', Rom. 8:29), and in the means (Bible study and meditation, prayer, the sacraments, fasting, self-examination, attendance at public worship, and service in the world). This does not mean that there is one uniform spirituality for all Christians. The spiritual life is a matter not only of theology, but also of temperament* and background. It is the duty of all Christians to find a personal spirituality which is biblical, but which is also faithful to God's particular plan for them as unique individuals (see Disciplines, Spiritual*).

A recent development has been a breaking down of the barriers between traditions, whether evangelical, Catholic or Orthodox. Some evangelicals realize that, in reacting against extreme sacramentalism, they have lost a biblical understanding of the material world as sacramental, which they now want to recover. Catholics, on the other hand, are anxious to restore Bible study to the centre of their lives. Some Catholics are also becoming aware of the riches of Puritan and pietist spirituality. Behind this lies a recognition of the poverty of much modern spirituality, and a humility which rejoices in the truth wherever it is found and however unfamiliar may be its garb.

Some Christians urge a return to the evangelical spirituality of the past, particularly that of Puritans like John Owen (1616–83), Richard Baxter* and Jonathan Edwards.* Others put their hope in modern pentecostal teaching. This becomes more feasible when Pentecostals no longer emphasize spiritual gifts (especially tongues) as the mark of spirituality, or a 'second blessing' as an essential for spiritual growth, but stress rather the living God acting powerfully in the life of an individual or a church.

The Catholic teaching on the rosary or devotion to Mary, and the interest in non-Christian mysticism shown by modern Catholic writers like Thomas Merton (1915–68), Anthony de Mello (1931–) and William Johnston (1925–), have not generally been accepted by evangelicals; neither has some Orthodox use of icons.

However, many Christians find in modern Catholic writings a biblical stress on silence, solitude and receptivity which redresses a weakness in much evangelical spirituality, with its over-emphasis on activity. Through meditation, Christians have learned to reflect on God's words, using imagination as well as reason, so that Scripture penetrates more deeply from mind to heart. There has been a rediscovery of retreats, spiritual direction,* and many different aids to the devotional life.

The aim of true spirituality is that the Christian will become increasingly like Jesus. It can never be a selfish, introverted egoism,* or simply a journey of self-discovery. The spiritual person will be marked by a growing awareness of others' needs, and a willingness to work sacrificially to meet them. The church has always recognized the first duty of Christians to follow the contemplative example of Mary, but not at the expense of the active example of Martha (Lk. 10:38–42). One who has sat at Jesus' feet will inevitably be driven out into the world to serve him.

Spirituality is not a technique to be mastered: it is a response to God. 'We love because he first loved us' (1 Jn. 4:19). 'We come to God by love, not by navigation' (Augustine). Spirituality seen as a mastering of technique is incompatible with spirituality rightly understood as a life of dependence on God. If spirituality is an exercise, it can be mastered with reasonable competence by its practitioner. True spirituality always arises from incompetence, the state of total dependence and helplessness of the creature before the creator.

Bibliography

R. F. Lovelace, *Dynamics of Spiritual Life* (Exeter and Downers Grove, IL, 1979); J. I. Packer, *Among God's Giants: The Puritan Vision of the Christian Life* (Eastbourne, 1991) = *Quest for Godliness* (Westchester, IL, 1991); P. Toon (ed.), *Guidebook to the Spiritual Life* (Basingstoke, 1988); S. Tugwell, *Ways of Imperfection* (London, 1984); G. S. Wakefield (ed.), *DCS*.

C.J.H.H.

SPIRITUAL WARFARE, see
DELIVERANCE MINISTRY; DEMONIC, THE.

S**PORT** may be defined as a way of using time in a combination of physical and mental skills, usually in a competitive way. Such a definition includes both professional and amateur sport, since it does not restrict sport to leisure* time and covers both the more obvious 'sports' such as soccer, cricket, Rugby, athletics, *etc.*, as well as chess or clay-pigeon shooting. There will inevitably be arguments over some activities, *e.g.* field sports or boxing. Others, *e.g.* synchronized swimming or rhythmic gymnastics, raise the question of where sport ends and art begins.

Play* is a gift from God, and is as normal a part of a person's life as eating or sleeping. As God's image-bearers humanity has play woven into its fabric.

In Scripture, play is an anticipated social activity of God's people. It is basic to the advice offered in the book of Ecclesiastes, pervasive in the sexuality of the Song of Songs, and apparent in the Israelite practices of festival, feasting, dancing and hospitality. It is part of the anticipated consummation of the kingdom of God:* 'the city streets will be filled with boys and girls playing there' (Zc. 8:5).

In the NT, there is no hesitation over applying analogies drawn from sport to the Christian life. Paul advises Timothy that physical training is valuable but not as valuable as training in godliness (1 Tim. 4:8). His comparison of ministry and training for 'the games' (presumably the Olympic games) allows him to affirm both boxing (or perhaps wrestling) and running (1 Cor. 9:24–27). He certainly has a victory ceremony in mind when he writes to the Philippians (Phil. 3:12–14). The writer to the Hebrews, exhorting his readers to follow in the footsteps of the great OT saints, urges them to run unentangled by sin, perseveringly and purposefully with their eyes fixed upon Jesus (Heb. 12:1–3).

Yet sport, like every other human activity, is not immune from the operation of sin. It can become a substitute religion (*e.g.* 'Some say God, we say Shankley' [the Liverpool manager], proclaimed one banner at the Liverpool–Arsenal soccer cup final in 1971), idolatrous in its claims on the lives of participants and spectators. Sport can also engender a 'win at all costs' mentality (especially when large sums of money or national pride are involved), resulting in the use of performance-enhancing steroids in athletics or violent play in Rugby football and soccer. It is also used as an instrument of politics, *e.g.* by Adolf Hitler (1889–1945) to prove Aryan supremacy in the Berlin Olympics of 1936, or (more controversially, perhaps) as a means of 'social engineering', *e.g.* in the provision of leisure centres in areas of high unemployment and social unrest (such as Belfast and Liverpool). Commercial sponsorship of sport also raises issues such as the timing of events to suit prime-time television, and the multiplying of competitions to gain more advertising* revenue. Moreover, the macho image of much modern sport can tend to make some women feel that sport is not for them, or cause them to regard it as a bastion of sexism.*

The individual Christian sportsman or sportswoman will face the challenge of competing Christianly in a largely un-Christian environment. It will not always be enough to say that he or she will 'compete fairly within the rules'. Interpretation of rules varies from one country to another, as does the concept of fair play. Certain sports will present particular challenges. Gambling* is associated with many sports, but in horse-racing and greyhound-racing, especially, the Christian sportsman or sportswoman will have to face the implications of this pervasive practice. The danger of permanent injury, even death, is present in many sports. Boxing carries with it the risk of brain damage, and has been criticized because the goal of the contest is to cause physical damage to one's opponent. The Bible teaches that the body is the temple of the Holy Spirit (1 Cor. 6:19), and there is an irony in the fact that sport requires physical fitness yet carries with it the risk of bodily impairment.

One implication of the positive view of sport is to be seen in the development of sports ministry. The world of sport is regarded as one that merits the attention of Christian ministry. Those who play sport at high level, attaining fame and fortune thereby, have many opportunities to present themselves and be presented as Christian role models. Their evangelistic impact may be much greater than that of 'traditional' missionaries, since they will often transcend cultural and linguistic barriers. While many societies in the world are closed to the propagation of the gospel, they are open to sport. Thus the modern itinerant evangelist can say, 'With a football and Bible, I can go anywhere and guarantee a crowd.'

Sports ministry also has implications for the local church. Sport and leisure/play provide an obvious way of contacting the local community. The development of sports centres in churches (especially in the US) and the emergence of church football teams and coaching classes (as in the UK) are examples of such activity.

Sport occupies an increasingly important place in national and international life. Christians are called to witness to God's creativity, love and redemption wherever they are found, and that will include the world of sport. Part of that witness will involve evangelism,* but there will also be a prophetic role concerning the standards and values enshrined in sport. The Christian must compete but he or she must do so with 'the mind of Christ' (1 Cor. 2:16; *cf.* Phil. 2:5ff.).

Bibliography

P. Ballantine, *Sport: The Opiate of the People?* (Bramcote, Nottingham, 1988); G. Baum and J. Coleman (eds.), *Sport* (*Concilium* 205, October 1989); L. Browne, *Sport and Recreation, and Evangelism in the Local Church* (Bramcote, Nottingham, 1991); R. W. Coles, 'Football as a "Surrogate Religion"', in M. Hill (ed.), *A Sociological Yearbook of Religion in Britain*, No. 8 (London, 1975); R. K. Johnston, *The Christian at Play* (Grand Rapids, 1983).

A.R.W.D.

SPURGEON, CHARLES HADDON
(1834–92), was born on 19 June 1834, of Independent (Congregational) stock at Kelvedon in the Eng. county of Essex, converted in a Primitive Methodist chapel in Colchester on 6 January 1850, and baptized by immersion in May of the same year. He became a Baptist pastor at Waterbeach, a village six miles from Cambridge, in October 1851, some four months after his seventeenth birthday. At the age of nineteen, he entered the pastorate of the New Park Street (Particular, *i.e.* Calvinistic) Baptist Church, Southwark, London, in February 1854. Soon the declining congregation so increased that it had to worship first in large public halls and then in the purpose-built Metropolitan Tabernacle at the Elephant and Castle. Under Spurgeon's ministry the membership grew to over 5,000, Spurgeon remaining the pastor despite increasing bouts of illness until his death on 31 January 1892 at Mentone in the south of France.

Though remembered primarily as a preacher whose magnificent voice could carry to every corner of the Metropolitan Tabernacle and whose weekly printed sermons were avidly read in all parts of the English-speaking world, Spurgeon was also a man of deep social concern. Well acquainted with the sufferings of both the rural and urban poor, he insisted that practical sympathy is the duty of every Christian. He would permit no escape into other-worldliness, for 'religion must be intended for this life; the duties of it cannot be practised, unless they are practised here' (New Park Street Pulpit, 1858, p. 253). He also deplored any tendency to divide the secular from the sacred and to neglect the former to concentrate upon the latter.

Under his leadership his church became a hive of social ministries, ranging from the staffing of Ragged Schools to the support of the Stockwell Orphanage (1867), and the provision of evening classes in commercial subjects to improve education. A convinced though not uncritical Liberal in politics, Spurgeon opposed slavery in the US and, though not a pacifist, he frequently emphasized the horrors of war in the heyday of British imperialism.

Bibliography

D. P. Kingdon, 'The Social Concern of C. H. Spurgeon', in T. Curnow *et al.*, *A Marvellous Ministry* (Ligonier, PA, 1993).

D.P.K.

STATE, THE.

Christian faith and experience have in the main taken a positive approach towards the State and political authority, despite the events of the earliest years of Christianity.

Jesus himself, born in Bethlehem because of a decree of Caesar Augustus that all the world should be enrolled for taxation purposes (Lk. 2:1–7), was a member of the Jewish people at a time when they were under Roman occupation. His public ministry ended in crucifixion – an order made by the Roman Governor, Pontius Pilate, and carried out by Roman soldiers (Jn. 19:12–24).

The early years of the Christian church were continually interrupted by persecution conducted by the civil authorities. Early documents record the heroic martyrdom of such as Polycarp (c. 69–c. 155) at the hands of the Roman government. Yet, with rare exceptions throughout, the church maintained a stance of living peacefully under the law and of continuing to pray for the authorities. That the church refused to recognize the imperial cult in no way undermined its sense of obligation to live peacefully within the law and in due respect of those in authority (1 Pet. 2:13–17). The historical circumstances of the church changed dramatically when Constantine* became emperor in 314, following the victory at the battle of the Milvian Bridge. Suddenly the church found itself living under the rule of a Christian emperor keen to further the interests of the church. The subsequent and long involvement of the established church with those in political authority* has its roots in these events.

Theologically, however, the foundation for the positive approach taken by the church towards the State is located in some crucial aspects of Christian belief.

1. The Christian conviction that all human life is created by God in God's image* helps in the affirmation of all aspects of what it means to be human. Traditionally, the church has interpreted the Genesis stories of creation as affirming the social and communal aspect of human life as God-given. The institution of marriage and the establishment of procedures for expressing the life of the wider community or society* are seen as part of what God gave to humanity for our benefit.

Thus, in principle, systems of government* and its associated organization in the State are recognized as a good in human life. This is not to suggest that every particular expression of this is to be welcomed, but rather that the principle of social organization is recognized as good for us. It is up to us to ensure that the actual order of government and of the State helps and encourages the development of our community life and is respectful of its origins in the gifts of God.

2. Throughout the biblical story there is a basic recognition that political authority is included in the good purposes of God. Thus social systems are established for the government of Israel, and due recognition is made of good rulers of other nations. Cyrus, King of Persia, is recognized as an instrument of the good purposes of God. He was the ruler who initiated the return of the people of Israel from exile. Although there is hesitancy in the OT about the institution of kingship (1 Sa. 8) because of the possibilities of the abuses of excessive power* in the hands of one person, nevertheless God used the period of the kings, and out of it was born the Messianic hope of a true and perfect son of David who would bring peace and justice to the people (Is. 9:1–7).

3. Jesus recognized the legitimacy of the political role and task. His famous reply to the question about taxes, 'Give to Caesar what is Caesar's, and to God what is God's' (Mt. 20:15–22), is a clear command that, whatever the people may think about the government, they should pay their taxes. At his trial, Jesus debated with Pilate the whole business of authority. He did not question Pilate's right to act. He did tell Pilate that the power he possessed belonged to God (Jn. 19:11). No-one wields power without the consent of God. Whether a person wields it for justice (see Justice and Peace③) and truth or for political self-protection is a decision that he or she must make. Pilate failed the test of justice and truth,* but there is no suggestion that he should not have had the power to decide.

4. The reflections of the early apostles are all affirmative of the duties of Christians towards those in authority. The apostle Paul's famous affirmation that governing authority is from God (Rom. 13:1–7) is a clear theological undergirding of the need for Christians to behave as law-abiding and peace-loving citizens. There is no suggestion that this provides any justification for those in authority to abuse their power. The whole thrust of the argument is to suggest that power comes from God and that those who wield it are, by implication, accountable to God.

5. The actual experience we have of the way

power is exercised through State machinery may be far distant from any sense of its origin in and obligation to God. In the NT, there are plenty of examples of the corruption of power. Paul himself used his rights as a citizen to appeal to Rome for justice (Acts 25:11–12). He did not receive justice; he was innocent, and yet in the end he was executed. The legal system failed to deliver justice.

Our experience of the State is mixed. The gift of God in the ordering of our social life in peace and freedom is corruptible into the abuse of power by those who control the organs of civic life. The Bible recognizes this ambivalence about power, and passages such as Rev. 17 remind us of the experience of the early Christians in the abuse of power in the Roman Empire. Christians have therefore always tempered their respect for the State with caution about the dilemma concerning its use, and potential abuse, of power.

This is the tension with which Christians have had to live from the outset. On the one hand, they recognize the need for social order and its roots in God our creator. On the other hand, much experience at the hands of those who use power in society has been bad. The church is persecuted; people are denied justice; tyrants gather power to themselves and abuse it.

Christians have tried to resolve this tension by one of two extremes. 1. One approach is pursued by those who might benefit by attachment to political power. This is to baptize power and leave Christians with no right of critical comment or protest. Since power is from God, we are bound to accept the actual exercise of power as it is. Kings are given a divine right, and rulers exempted from critical scrutiny. 2. The other way of escape from the tension is to refuse to accept that God is behind the fact of political power. This is to assign the State to a fallen world and to sinful humanity. The need for politics,* laws and the State is rooted in sin and corruption. We cannot expect any real good to come by this route. If extreme Erastianism symbolizes the first approach, then extreme Anabaptism* and sectarianism symbolizes the second.

There is a rich tradition of Christian reflection about the nature and purpose of the State. Important contributions to this have been made by Augustine,* Thomas Aquinas,* Martin Luther* (see also Lutheran Ethics*), John Calvin* (see also Calvinist Ethics*), Abraham Kuyper* and Reinhold Niehbuhr.*

The heart and mainstream of the Christian church have accepted the need to live with the tension between the statement of faith in the power of God and the reality of the abuse of power in human life. The church has adopted different tactics in different situations as a result. In places where it is clear that there is a real measure of accountability in the use of power by the State, the church has often adopted a position of 'critical solidarity' with the State. It has been ready to work alongside the authorities whilst maintaining its right of critical comment. In the contemporary world, the church has affirmed the positive value of democratic institutions of government.

In situations of the abuse of political power by the institutions of the State, the church has identified itself with opposition movements. In so doing, it has continued to pray for those who carry power but shared in the call for radical change. Situations of tyrannical rule and sectarian and racist abuses of power are particular examples of this in our world.

In situations when the church itself has been persecuted and crushed, the predominant witness to the future has taken the shape of seeking tactics of survival. To keep the flame of faith alive through secret worship and prayer is itself an act of defiance of the abuses of power.

Sadly, there are those Christian churches which have taken to none of these paths, but have remained silent and collusive with the abuses of power and themselves shared in disobedience to the purposes of God. Churches have supported tyranny out of fear and self-interest and have baptized racist and sectarian philosophies.

The growing power of the State in the 20th century has added a very sharp edge to the way Christians respond to it. On the negative side, we have witnessed in various parts of the world the huge power of the modern machinery of the State wielded to commit genocide, to crush opposition by terror, and to threaten many of the fundamentals of genuinely human life. On the positive side, we have seen endeavours at using the power and structure of the State to assist in the development of human life by the provision of crucial services and systems of support to people in need. Yet, the question of the boundaries of State power and usefulness are raised in this positive context as well as by the awfulness of some of our recent experience.

In other words, the tension remains between vision and reality, possibility and reality. The Christian gospel gives us a way of understanding this theologically, and requires us to work out our own responses in the light of the needs we face today. Indeed, one of the most urgent questions of our time is how the church can play a part in helping the State to recognize the origins and sources of power, and so to see them as existing for the purposes of human well-being and flourishing. The dreadful things which have happened in our own age in the name and power of the State make the issue inescapable for all Christians who are concerned for the integrity of our witness to the truth as it is in Jesus.

Bibliography

O. Cullmann, *The State in the New Testament* (ET, New York, 1956; London, 1957); H. A. Deane, *The Political and Social Ideas of St. Augustine* (New York and London, 1963); T. G. Sanders, *Protestant Concepts of Church and State* (New York, 1964); L. Verduin, *The Reformers and their Stepchildren* (Exeter, 1964); P. S. Watson, *The State as a Servant of God: A Study of its Nature and Tasks* (London, 1946).

J.W.G.

STATEMENT OF CONCERNED EVANGELICALS, see EVANGELICAL WITNESS IN SOUTH AFRICA.

STEALING, see THEFT.

STERILIZATION is the permanent loss of reproductive capacity. In women it is accomplished by tubal ligation, the tying off and severing of the Fallopian tubes. Male sterilization ordinarily is by means of bilateral vasectomy, in which the sperm ducts are severed, so that sperm will no longer be present in the otherwise normal ejaculate. Hysterectomy, the surgical removal of the uterus, has been used for sterilization but is now seen as far too expensive and medically risky. Sterilization is generally considered to be irreversible, although there is some possibility that reproductive capacity can be restored in certain cases, particularly after vasectomy.

Sterilization has been performed not only for contraceptive but also for therapeutic, eugenic, social and punitive reasons. *Therapeutic* sterilization is performed when the woman's life or health is threatened by future pregnancy, as for example the removal of a damaged uterus. *Eugenic* sterilization has been advocated and performed to prevent reproduction

by those considered to have an inheritable defect. Its supporters frequently justify sterilization without the consent, or even the knowledge, of the individuals to be so sterilized.

Social sterilization is compulsory sterilization in the interests of society. It has been advocated for mothers on State benefits, those deemed incapable of properly raising children, epileptics, and those who engage in 'perverted' sexual practices. Notably, the targets of this activity are often the economically disadvantaged and the non-white. *Punitive* sterilization, such as castration, has sometimes been advocated for sex criminals and has been legally permitted for third-time offenders of certain sorts of felonies such as larceny. In the USA, individual States may still allow punitive sterilization, although federal courts have rejected involuntary sterilization in facilities receiving federal funds.

Contraceptive sterilization is preferred by many over the available, temporary contraceptive alternatives for a variety of reasons, including the near absence of side-effects, the gain in spontaneity in sexual relations, lower costs, as well as its almost total reliability. Both Orthodox and Conservative Judaism have opposed such sterilization as contrary to nature and to the divine decree to reproduce (Gn. 1:28). Reform Judaism, however, resembles Protestant thought in this regard. Eastern Orthodoxy has paid scant attention to the topic, but its position on the importance of the transmission of life and its opposition to abortion* and contraception (see Birth Control*) seem at least to imply a negative judgment on all but therapeutic sterilization.

Offical Roman Catholicism accepts only therapeutic sterilization. Under the principle of totality, mutilation is permissible only to save the entire organism, and not directly to prevent reproduction. Some Catholic scholars have demurred from this nearly absolute ban on sterilization, joining Protestant ethicists such as Karl Barth,* Helmut Thielicke* and Paul Ramsey* in accepting voluntary sterilization as permissible in many cases. The Protestant case has been based on the view that sexual activity in marriage is unitive as well as for the purpose of reproduction (although deliberate childlessness typically is not accepted). Sterilization is permitted for therapeutic reasons, to prevent genetically impaired offspring, and in cases in which a couple have already borne all of the children they find they can raise properly.

Many religious ethicists have opposed involuntary sterilization for the indications mentioned above, with exceptions such as Joseph Fletcher.* Many feminist writers have vigorously opposed involuntary sterilization of women, although they welcome access to the procedure for women as part of the needed control that women are to have over their own lives.

Many Christian couples today are availing themselves of sterilization as a method of family planning when they have borne the number of children they believe they can parent responsibly. While the Bible does not prohibit the practice, it should be used advisedly, conscious of the need for full consent from both partners, for prayerful consideration of possible future changes of heart and indeed of the possibility of the death of a partner or of divorce, followed by remarriage with the possible desire for more children. In a stable Christian home, and on the basis of an open, communicative relationship, sterilization can free a couple from fear of unplanned pregnancy and can give spontaneity to their sexual lives. Christians must, however, consider very carefully the dangers of possible policies to promote compulsory sterilization and must make their voices heard on behalf of the poor and powerless in society.

Bibliography

D. Kevles, *In the Name of Eugenics: Genetics and the Uses of Human Heredity* (New York, 1985); S. E. Lammers and A. Verhey (eds.), *On Moral Medicine: Theological Perspectives in Medical Ethics* (Grand Rapids, 1987); R. A. McCormick, *How Brave a New World? Dilemmas in Bioethics* (Washington, DC, and London, 1981); J. T. Noonan, *Contraception: A History of Its Treatment by the Catholic Theologians and Canonists* (Cambridge, MA, and London, 21986); W. O. Spritzer and C. L. Saylor, *Birth Control and the Christian: A Protestant Symposium on the Control of Human Reproduction* (Wheaton, IL, 1964); H. Thielicke, *The Ethics of Sex* (ET, New York and London, 1964).

D.B.F.

STEWARDSHIP. The principle of stewardship is closely linked to the concept of grace.* Everything comes from God as a gift and is to be administered faithfully on his behalf. There is thus both stewardship of the earth and stewardship of the gospel (*cf.* J. Goetzmann, in *NIDNTT* 2, pp. 253–256); stewardship of personal resources of time, money* and talents, and stewardship of the resources of church and society. Along with questions of mission strategy and support there are issues of personal and corporate lifestyle, just wages (see Wage*) and fair prices, poverty* and wealth, all related to explicit or implicit theologies of the kingdom* of God, work* and nature (*cf.* 'The Oxford Declaration on Christian Faith and Economics', *Tr* 7.2, 1990, pp. 1–8).

Despite, or perhaps because of, the wide potential application of the principle of stewardship, it has often been overlooked (most books on Christian ethics omit it) or restricted in application. This has far-reaching consequences. For while the principle does not provide detailed answers to practical questions, to abandon the concept is to run the risk of forgetting grace and gratitude and changing one's basic outlook from 'stewardship' to 'ownership'.

In the economic sphere such a shift tends to restrict stewardship to the use and disposal of wealth and ignores the way it is acquired. Some (*cf.* R. Mullin, *The Wealth of Christians*, Exeter, 1983) would say that this shows that *voluntary* poverty is a far more Christian concept than stewardship, which, historically, produced capitalism.* It could just as well be argued that the problem is a partial understanding of stewardship: wealth is derived from the finite resources of the planet, so stewardship must be just as concerned with issues of ecological (see Environment*) and political exploitation,* and with seeking what the World Council of Churches has called 'a just, participatory and sustainable society' that respects the integrity of creation. 'Dominion' (Gn. 1:28) must no longer be misunderstood as domination. As awareness of the consequences of consuming non-renewable resources or of permanently affecting the ecological balance increases, so does accountability, both to God and to our neighbour, of this and of future generations.

Partial understandings of stewardship can also be found in the church context. The focus of congregational stewardship campaigns on the giving of time, talents and money can lead to legalistic activism, and the weight that is often put on the fund-raising aspect raises further issues. Overlooking the wider meaning of stewardship of the household of God as the faithful handing on of the gospel through the Spirit-endowed ministry of the whole congregation (1 Cor. 4:1; 1 Pet. 4:10) risks making money an end rather than a means. Although placing a cash value on commitment could be salutary for members of endowed or State-supported congregations, and could underline their responsibility for regular, proportionate, cheerful and generous giving for inter-church aid (*cf.* 1 Cor. 16:2; 2 Cor. 9:6–15), a number of questions need to be faced, including: Are secular methods of fund-raising or professional fund-raisers appropriate? Would financial success indicate spiritual health? How relevant would the OT tithe be? Should such a standard be a starting-point or a goal? Would the approach adopted produce feelings of guilt* or self-satisfaction?

Moving towards a fuller understanding of stewardship, further questions would arise. Could the giving of money be a way to avoid more costly commitment? Might the gift of a proportion of one's income be misinterpreted as complete freedom to dispose of the rest as one pleased, or as a bargain with God that ensured one's financial success? To what extent should energies be devoted to church projects? Would maintenance swallow up mission? To what degree might mission be to join with others to campaign, for example, to save the planet or to alleviate the consequences of mass unemployment?*

Saving the planet and responding to unemployment are both complex issues that require the exercise of the wisdom* that is implied in faithful and accountable stewardship, and the latter topic raises other aspects of the matter, under what might be called the stewardship of human resources.

There would be questions about causes as well as consequences. What are the causes of mass unemployment? Do they stem from un-biblical assessments of human activity solely in terms of profit or economic worth? Has technological* change in industry been pursued without a respect for human values? Are the two incompatible or can new practices be humanized? Will the proposed solutions to unemployment reduce or enhance human resources? This is as much a qualitative as a quantitative matter, that includes questions like 'Will these measures produce dependency or encourage self-respect?' There is also the inescapable question that underlies the fact that stewardship in church and society cannot be separated: 'What sort of relation should there be between personal or non-governmental charity (including that offered by individual church members and congregations) and statutory provision funded by general taxation?'

In more general terms, which apply just as much to questions of environmental stewardship, one would want to ask if change was best achieved by encouraging voluntary action (even if motivated by enlightened self-interest) or by legislation. What balance between the two should there be in society? And to what extent can or should the church, aware of the power of example, commend or impose a simple lifestyle on itself and its members? If there is no absolute or universal standard of simplicity or voluntary poverty, how is one to find a standard that is realistic without being legalistic?

Bibliography

P. Abrecht (ed.), *Faith, Science and the Future* (Geneva, 1978); R. Attfield, *The Ethics of Environmental Concern* (Oxford, 1983); H. Brattgard, *God's Stewards* (Augsburg, MN, 1963); D. J. Hall, *Imaging God: Dominion as Stewardship* (Grand Rapids, 1986); *idem, The Steward: A Biblical Symbol Come of Age* (Grand Rapids, [2]1990); J. Mark, *The Question of Christian Stewardship* (London, 1964); R. J. Sider (ed.), *Lifestyle in the Eighties: An Evangelical Commitment to Simple Lifestyle* (Exeter and Philadelphia, 1982); *idem, Evangelicals and Development: Towards a Theology of Social Change* (Exeter, 1981); C. Sugden (ed.), *The Church in Response to Human Need* (Exeter, 1987); *idem, Radical Discipleship* (London, 1981); T. K. Thompson (ed.), *Stewardship in Contemporary Theology* (New York, 1960); World Council of Churches, *Faith and Science in an Unjust World*, 2 vols. (Geneva, 1980).

P.N.H.

STOCK MARKET. The organization of the stock markets around the world is very complex, but their principal purposes and functions are fairly simple. There are institutional markets (*e.g.* the London Stock Exchange, the New York Stock Exchange) where the buying and selling of publicly traded securities and debt instruments take place under supervised rules and regulations. Both individuals and institutions trade in these organized and regulated markets. The market is also thought of as those individuals and institutions that trade securities and participate in the private placement of securities. So owners of stocks and bonds speak of 'being in the stock market', and those who earn their living as brokers, agents and traders speak of 'working in the stock markets'.

The organized stock markets around the world have been established for a number of purposes: 1. to provide a definitive place where buyers and sellers of stock can easily locate one another; 2. to establish a set of governing rules to regulate the trading transaction so that principles of equity may prevail between traders; 3. to establish procedures for the transfer of securities and moneys and the legal registration of the securities transactions following the trades; 4. to provide a market that will foster a high level of liquidity for the holders of securities; 5. to produce a forum where reliable information can inform the market; and 6. to promote the efficient financial markets.

The sinful human nature is ever present and frequently at work, however, and thus all efforts to achieve equity and justice in the market-place will be imperfect. But there is more good than ill wrought by the organized stock markets. For example, while some people will always try to gain unfair advantages in a financial arena through such things as the use of inside information (see Insider Dealing*) or the filing of misleading financial statements, the majority of the system's users will not let such behaviour go unchecked, lest it destroy the underlying confidence in the system so necessary for it to perform its function. The many vital services provided by the stock market, as outlined in the preceding paragraph, are so basic to the financial well-being of the general community that the prudential self-interest of the majority, if not their ethical sensitivity, will cause the majority to police the markets. The stock markets are, to date, the best-known institutions to service the capital needs of industry. They enhance the flow of capital, and the assembly of capital, for the purpose of creating and sustaining the economic processes that are necessary to carry out the work mandates God gave to humankind (Gn. 1:26–30).

See also: ECONOMIC ETHICS. 17

R.C.C.

S TOICISM, a tradition of Hellenistic and Roman thought that influenced Christian ethics, especially among the Fathers. Its founder Zeno (d. 263 BC) taught in a colonnade (*stoa*) in Athens. Later teachers included Cleanthes (d. 232 BC), Chrysippus (d. 207 BC), Panaetius (d. 109 BC), Posidonius (d. *c.* 50 BC) and Seneca (*c.* 4 BC–AD 65). Romanized Stoicism appealed to prominent figures like Cicero (106–43 BC) and the emperor Marcus Aurelius (121–180 AD).

Stoics believed that all reality was material, and that the cosmos was suffused with a directive spirit or *logos* (reason), which was itself refined matter and corresponded to deity, fate or providence. In this pantheistic materialism, the human being was a microcosm of the whole, with a subtly material *logos* or soul governing bodily life. Virtue* was the only good, and consisted in living according to reality or nature, *i.e.* being directed by one's *logos* in conformity with the universal principle of rational order. Chance had no place in this system with its cyclical destruction and regeneration of the world.

Stoic ethics stressed the rationality of virtue and disparaged emotions. The virtuous person remained undisturbed by external circumstances or experiences, focusing on inner dispositions which were within one's own control. Evil, which was vice, had its roots in passions, and virtue was 'passionlessness' (Gk. *apatheia*). External or physical factors such as wealth, sickness, solitude and fame were matters of indifference (*adiaphora*). From such emphases derives the use of 'stoical' to characterize exemplary self-control or endurance.

Stoicism made a deeper impression on patristic ethics* than any other non-Judaeo-Christian tradition (aided by apocryphal correspondence, accepted from the time of Jerome [*c.* 342–420] onwards, between Seneca and Paul). Tertullian* and others wrote on patience; the ideal of *apatheia* enjoyed immense vogue in ascetic theory from Clement of Alexandria (*c.* 150–*c.* 215) onwards; Ambrose* named Panaetius and Cicero as reliable guides and discussed the four cardinal Stoic virtues of prudence, justice, fortitude and temperance; and the place of conscience* and arguments from natural law* and the natural order in Christian ethics were significantly advanced.

Criticisms of Stoicism (quite apart from its patently untenable metaphysics) fastened especially on its tendency to fatalism. Lactantius (*c.* 240–*c.* 320) condemned its dismissal of the emotions, and Augustine* faulted its rejection of both fear and pity in moral behaviour.

Stoicism continued to influence Christian thought during the Middle Ages, even in unlikely combination with Augustinianism. It experienced a revival in the Renaissance and early modern Europe, through Erasmus (*c.* 1469–1536) and other humanists and among Anglicans like Joseph Hall (1574–1656), especially those with deist inclinations. John Calvin's* first work was a commentary on Seneca's *On Clemency*, and he remained indebted to Stoicism, *e.g.* on natural law, while sharply critical of it in other important aspects.

Bibliography

M. L. Colish, *The Stoic Tradition from Antiquity to the Early Middle Ages*, 2 vols. (Leiden, 1985); C. B. Schmitt *et al.* (eds.), *The Cambridge History of Renaissance Philosophy* (Cambridge, 1988), pp. 360–374; M. Spanneut, *Le Stoïcisme des pères de l'église ... à Clément d'Alexandrie* (Paris, 1957); R. W. Wenley, *Stoicism and its Influence* (New York, 1963); L. Zanta, *La Renaissance du Stoicisme au XVIᵉ siècle* (Paris, 1914).

D.F.W.

STRESS is the human reaction to change. Since Hans Selye (1907–82) first described *le stresse* almost fifty years ago, books on the subject have multiplied, and stress has become all-inclusive. Selye described 'dys-stress' with its harmful results in suffering, pain or disease, while 'eustress' was his word for challenging pressures which may be good and pleasant.

The term 'stress' is used in two distinct ways: 1. to describe the *causes*, *i.e.* stressors which are outside pressures associated with change; and 2. to describe the *results* of internal and external pressures, as in saying, 'I feel all stressed up'.

Research has clarified the causes of stress by the study of life events, measured in Life Change Units (LCUs). Thus, the loss of a spouse or a child by death has the maximum of 100 LCUs, divorce 73, and a holiday 13. In more recent years, the emphasis has been on the meaning of life events. The changes often involve loss – *e.g.* by death, retirement, redundancy or a broken relationship. However, events like promotion, marriage, the birth of a child or any personal success may also be stressful. Our coping abilities may decide whether changes result in a stress-related breakdown, or in a happy issue out of all the troubles. A breakdown may be diagnosed as an adjustment disorder.

Personality* type is relevant: *e.g.* the ambitious and the worriers are at high risk of physical illness. People who are competitive, ambitious to succeed quickly, punctual and cynical may develop early coronary thrombosis. No radical change in personality structure is possible, although Christian conversion* and new life gives new motivation, new direction and new status. Growth in grace* may also aid in self-knowledge, and lead to modifying some traits and learning new patterns of living.

The results of harmful stress include anxiety* in its many forms. Symptoms of depression,* as in grief reactions (see Bereavement*), may follow any loss. Prolonged harmful pressures lead to stress-related disorders like high blood pressure, thyroid problems, neurodermatitis, colitis and peptic ulcer. New knowledge about the immune system has shown how complex such diseases are. Trigger factors, vulnerability and genetic factors all play a part in determining the onset, course and recovery from such disorders.

'Burn-out' has been the name given to the condition where a person has lost his or her usual ability to respond with zest or idealism to the needs of work or vocation. Fatigue and frustration follows when the expected rewards do not come after prolonged and devoted effort. Such burn-out may be more common in professions and business posts with a strong vocational element.

'Post-traumatic stress disorder' (PTSD) may follow an experience such as assault, rape* or major life-threatening accident. It may be a close relative or the home, not the person himself or herself, that has been threatened, hurt or damaged. There may be distressing recall (flashbacks) or dreams, and avoidance of any reminder of the trauma. It may cause both over-arousal and also emotional numbness. Anything that reminds one of the painful incident may be avoided. PTSD is now recognized in law. Treatment is partly by behaviour therapy (see Behaviourism*), and the relief of anxiety and depression by medication.

No-one is exempt from stress, and Christians are often subject to extra pressure because of high expectations. The obsessional workaholic, compelled to work seven days a week, needs reminding that God has ordained a period of rest in the sabbath* principle. We should seek regular rest, both daily and weekly, and holidays or retreats. Time off to relax and to enjoy recreation and refreshment is a self-evident human need. Some churches may encourage overwork, but exhorting people to 'burn out for God' may be unwise.

Some relaxation techniques have been criticized, but honourable and practised Christian methods of meditation are available. They are helps to 'Be still, and know that I am God' (Ps. 46:10). This aspect of coping with stress is passive. The active mode is shown in assertiveness training; at best this is a method of insisting quietly on one's rights as a human being without aggression or violent arousal. Thus a quietly assertive refusal may be needed if a local leader (e.g. by 'heavy shepherding'; see Shepherding Movement*) seeks to impose his will inappropriately, and invades the integrity of the personality. Such skills applied with wisdom may enable us to be active in working out our salvation (cf. Phil. 2:12).

Our beliefs determine the way we see and react to life events. Learned helplessness or hopelessness may often follow loss and change. Some families foster a pattern of feeling unworthy or being unable to cope. True Christian teaching promotes the courage which is the ultimate answer to stressful pressures. To 'be of good courage' requires practical outworking of our beliefs in God's love for us, and the support that all loving relationships provide. The role of hope* and a truer perspective helps us to transform our understanding of the meaning of life's events.

The denial of sadness, depression or illness is usually best avoided, although sometimes denial may have positive value. Thus, someone who has had a serious heart attack may choose not to look at the dark side, and may summon up the resources to recover. We should also argue with ourselves as the words of the psalmist suggest: 'Why are you downcast, O my soul?' (Pss. 42:5, 11; 43:5). The process of thus looking at the pattern of thoughts is part of the modern emphasis on cognitive therapy.* By seeing how we may 'generalize' or 'catastrophize' in any given situation, we may learn to alter such a pattern. Thus we may have to say: 'I made a mess of that today', instead of saying: 'I am a total failure'. Such therapy fits in with being 'transformed by the renewing of your mind' (Rom. 12:2).

Bibliography

G. Davies, *Stress: The Challenge to Christian Caring* (Eastbourne, 1988); M. F. Foyle, *Honourably Wounded: Stress among Christian Workers* (Bromley, 1987) = *Overcoming Missionary Stress* (Wheaton, IL, 1988); H. J. Freudenberg, *Burnout* (London and Garden City, NY, 1985); D. Meichenbaum, *Stress Inoculation Training* (Oxford and New York, 1985).

G.D.

STRIKES. A strike results when employees decide to withdraw their labour until some grievance over pay, working conditions, *etc.*, is remedied.

An employer dissatisfied with an employee may simply terminate the employment and look for a replacement. Employees are frequently easily replaced, especially the less skilled ones. Unskilled labour is the least paid and also the most subject to exploitation, and a worker who is underpaid or in some way victimized is unlikely to have any redress of his or her own.

With the coming of industrialization, trade unions* sprang up to protect individuals against exploitation through the organization of labour. If an employee is underpaid, or provided with bad or unsafe working conditions, the union will seek to respond, once negotiations with the employer are unable to produce a satisfactory improvement, by going on strike, *i.e.* depriving the employer of his entire work force, thus causing him economic damage until he comes to settlement terms. For a strike to be successful, its organizers need to ensure that no-one else will do the work normally done by the strikers, and that the wages lost by the strikers are made good as far as possible by payments from the union funds. Transport workers must be dissuaded from taking supplies into or out of the work place (see Picketing*), and every effort needs to be made to ensure that the employer receives no support or benefit from any person who could supply alternative labour. The purpose is to close down the employer's operation completely, and to persuade him that greater economic damage will be done to him if he does not accede to the requirements of the trade union than if he does accede.

Strikes might also take place where one worker (frequently in practice a trade-union activist) is dismissed by an employer in circumstances felt by his fellow employees to constitute victimization. It is generally important at the end of the strike to ensure that settlement terms with the employer guarantee the reinstatement of the strikers without victimization. Ideally, the strikers seek to obtain support from other workers by gaining recognition that their cause is a just one and that it is in the interests of all workers to support it. Anyone who seeks to break the strike by continuing to work for the employer risks having the benefit of his trade-union membership withdrawn, as well as having social opprobrium heaped upon him by his peers. The latter is a forceful consideration where a whole community is largely dependent on a single employer for its livelihood.

Where a strike is called and organized by a trade union in accordance with the procedures in its rules, the strike is viewed as 'official'; a spontaneous local withdrawal of labour is frequently dubbed 'unofficial'. Originally, the distinction mattered only in order to determine whether or not the strikers received financial support from the union during the strike, but now the position at law of the strikers and their leaders may also be determined by whether or not the strike is 'official'.

In British common law, the legal analysis of a strike is that anyone is entitled to withdraw his or her labour (though the employer is entitled to dismiss him or her for breach of contract without notice or compensation), but that employee may not induce others to do likewise. Originally, therefore, strike-organizers (generally the trade unions) were liable to an action for substantial damages by the employer for any economic losses incurred by him. Following a celebrated case early in the 20th century, statutory immunity against such actions for damages was granted in the UK for most strikes officially organized by unions. This immunity was thought by many to have been abused, and it has gradually been reduced in scope. It was also felt that many strikes were called or instigated by union leaders for their own political ends, without real support from the workers themselves. Immunity from damages is now given only to those strikes which are approved in advance in a secret ballot of the workers concerned, and only employees directly affected by the dispute may take part.

For some Christians, the moral dilemma centres around the apostolic injunction that slaves should obey their masters (Eph. 6:5; 1 Pet. 2:18; etc.), which, they believe, obliges them to go on working for their employers no matter how unjust the conditions. On the other hand, both OT and NT teach clearly that God is the defender of the poor and the exploited. Even if a Christian is prepared to work for an employer who treats his employees unfairly,

should he or she be prepared to assist that unfairness by breaking the solidarity upon which organized labour depends for its effectiveness?

Whilst normally directed at one employer, strikes (especially by workers in key sections of a national economy) have been used increasingly during the 20th century as political weapons against unpopular governments, so that at times it is hard to draw the distinction between a strike and a nascent revolution. The moral rightness of such action tends to be judged according to the perceived morality of the government concerned. The miners' strike in the UK in 1984–85, which was seen at least in part as a challenge to the democratically elected government, was generally felt to be a mischievous act; whereas strikes by the Solidarity union in Poland during the 1980s and by the miners in Romania in 1989–90, which hastened the downfall of the Communist regimes in those countries, were largely considered to be justified. In South Africa, strikes formed part of the strategy of those opposed to apartheid* and, together with external sanctions, hastened the end of minority white rule.

In the 19th and early 20th centuries, strikes were largely born of poverty, and undoubtedly advanced the cause of the working class through labour solidarity. Subsequently, comparatively small groups of workers in key sections of the economy have obtained wages and conditions which may be thought to be high rewards for relatively safe and routine jobs, because they have exploited the likely severe economic damage which would be suffered by their employers by even a fairly short withdrawal of labour.

Sometimes the harm done by strikes is not to the employer but to third parties. Wherever the government or a public monopoly is the employer, the true sufferer is the general public – whether the public as a whole or just one vulnerable section.

When a strike manifests a genuine feeling of grievance on the part of the strikers, a small picket-line will normally suffice to achieve the necessary support. However, strike-organizers with a fervent belief in their cause have at times resorted to violence or intimidation in order to force others to join a strike against their true will, on the basis that the end justifies the means (see Ends and Means*).

See also: Industrial Relations.

D.P.N.

SUAREZ, FRANCISCO DE (1548–1617). A native of Granada, Spain, Suarez became the principal exponent of Jesuit doctrine and the most prominent Scholastic theologian since Thomas Aquinas.* While much of his work was on metaphysical topics, he is none the less one of the main authors of Roman Catholic moral theology.* He saw the essence of mortal sin as loving a creature more than God (Rom. 1:25), explored the extent of a fallen person's weakness in obeying the moral law, and concluded that God gives sufficient grace to achieve conduct congruent with one's own will. The crux of the moral life is thus the intent of the will and its love.

In *On Laws and God the Lawgiver* (1612), Suarez follows Francis de Vitoria* in holding that governmental authority rests with the people themselves and is to be for the common good. The State therefore results from a social contract* to which the people consent, and they individually possess natural rights* to life, liberty and property. He therefore rejected the divine right of kings. Slavery and tyranny alike are contrary to natural law,* although the civil society remains subject to the church.

In *The Three Theological Virtues* (1622), his discussion of love includes a systematic development of just-war theory.* But whereas Vitoria emphasized practical issues in war against the Indians, Suarez concentrates more on justifying and integrating the premises. In particular, the law of nations, which Aquinas regarded as a universally applicable inference from natural law, is found to be grounded in universal custom. It is in harmony with, and may result from reflections on, natural law, but even universal custom is somewhat liable to change. In contrast to civil law, it is not promulgated in written form, but neither is it as changeable as civil law. The law of nations therefore falls in between natural and civil law in regard to its changeability and moral basis. Suarez's work in this regard deeply influenced Hugo Grotius,* the distinguished Dutch exponent of international law.

A.F.H.

SUBJECTIVISM may refer either to an epistemological theory (concerning how we know) or to an ethical theory. The epistemological theory puts the subject's consciousness at the centre of any claim to know. Descartes (1596–1650) with his famous dictum *cogito ergo sum* ('I think, therefore I am') is the great exemplar of this position. Some go further and suggest that there is no reality apart from consciousness (various forms of idealism*). Bishop Berkeley (1685–1753) was one major Western thinker who took epistemological subjectivism to its logical conclusion ('To be is to be perceived').

As an ethical theory, subjectivism needs to be distinguished from a number of competing theories on the nature of the good. *Objectivism* claims that the good is a moral fact determined either empirically (naturalistic objectivism) or intuitively (non-naturalistic objectivism). Objectivist theories claim that ethical discourse is informative (either true or false). *Prescriptivism*, on the other hand, argues that language about the good is really about the direction an action should take. Yet another theory, *emotivism*, maintains that language apparently about the good is in reality the ventilation of feelings. Both prescriptivism and emotivism claim that ethical discourse is non-cognitive or non-information-bearing (neither true nor false).

In contradistinction to both prescriptivism and emotivism, but in agreement with objectivism, subjectivism contends that language about the good is information-bearing. However, the subjectivist contends that ethical discourse is descriptive of the speaker's likes or dislikes, approvals or disapprovals, but not of moral facts, or of a moral order independent of human moral feelings. Hence ethical subjectivism is sometimes referred to as ethical relativism, since it affirms that the individual (or society, as we shall see) is the source of moral valuation.

The differences between these theories are easily illustrated. Suppose Fred is arrested for robbing a bank and is brought to trial. In sentencing Fred the judge tells the court, and especially Fred, 'Stealing is wrong.' The objectivist would claim that 'Stealing is wrong' is a statement about the moral order. It is a fact, just like the fact that water boils at a certain temperature. (Objectivists differ over how the fact that stealing is wrong is to be established.) The prescriptivist would maintain, however, that the judge is really saying, 'Do not steal!' He is giving moral directions. The emotivist would contend that the judge is merely expressing his feelings about stealing ('Boo for stealing!'). The subjectivist would say that the judge is stating his likes and dislikes. In effect he is saying he dislikes stealing.

In the above illustration the subjectivist would claim, as would the objectivist, that the judge is giving the court information in stating that stealing is wrong. However, whereas the objectivist would claim that the information so given is about a moral fact or order, the subjectivist would claim that the judge is giving information about his own feeling states or attitudes. The subjectivist view admits of further refinement. Some subjectivists might claim that the judge is speaking of his own likes and dislikes ('I dislike stealing'). Others might argue that the judge is stating his society's likes and dislikes ('We dislike stealing').

From a philosophical perspective a great difficulty with subjectivist theories, whether individualistic or societal, is that moral subjects act as though they are making claims beyond the mere statement of their likes and dislikes, when arguing for the rightness or wrongness of a moral action (e.g. in claiming that it was wrong of Fred to rob the bank). If contradicted, we do not usually say, 'Well, I dislike stealing.' Instead, we offer reasons for regarding Fred as in the wrong, difficult though it may be to tease out the logic of such judgments.

Amongst Christian moral thinkers this century, the great advocate for objectivism in ethics and the great opponent of subjectivism in any form was C. S. Lewis.* Lewis labelled subjectivism 'poison'. According to Lewis, right and wrong are as objective as the existence of the sun. Moreover, he argued that moral objectivism is the classical position of humankind, whether the culture on view is Greek, Roman, Christian, Hindu or Buddhist. On his view, unless modern people return to a belief in objective value then humankind will perish (see Objectivity of Morals*). However, such a return need not be a return to a detailed Christian ethic. Rather, it would be a return to an older ethic that Christianity itself presupposes. According to Lewis, the Scriptures show that our knowledge of this older moral law has not been depraved to the same degree as our power to fulfil it. There is abundant biblical evidence to support Lewis' assertion (e.g. Mt. 5:16; 7:11; Rom. 1:32; 2:14–16; 1 Pet. 3:16).

The subjectivist position raises interesting questions about God's relation to the good. If the good is the moral agent's likes and dislikes, then is the good ultimately God's likes and dislikes? The classic presentation of the dilemma this suggestion raises is found in Plato.* In the Euthyphro, the question takes the form: 'Is the good what the gods will or do the gods will in accord with the good?' Put into subjectivist guise: 'Is the good what the gods like or do the gods like in accord with the good?' If the former, is the good arbitrary? If the latter, is the good greater than the gods? For the Christian theist the dilemma is acute. How can anything be greater than God in the sense that God himself wills in accord with it?

However, the Christian's God is no lonely monad. Instead the God (see 1) of biblical disclosure enjoys the richness of trinitarian life as Father, Son and Holy Spirit. On a trinitarian view God arguably neither creates nor obeys the good. Rather, the good is grounded on his own intra-trinitarian relations (as C. S. Lewis himself argued). To suggest that the good limits God (and thus threatens his omnipotence) because God is not free to be evil is as sensible as suggesting that rationality limits God because he is not free to be irrational. In other words God has a nature. A Christian resolution of the Euthyphro dilemma is best developed along specifically trinitarian lines. Moreover, it is within a trinitarian conceptuality that the traditional polarity represented by objectivist and subjectivist theories finds a higher synthesis.

See also: PHILOSOPHICAL ETHICS.

Bibliography
C. S. Lewis, 'On Ethics', and 'The Poison of Subjectivism', in W. Hooper (ed.), Christian Reflections (London, 1967); idem, The Abolition of Man (London, 1943); W. H. Halverson, A Concise Introduction To Philosophy (New York, ²1972); J. Mackie, 'A Refutation of Morals', in P. Y. Windt (ed.), An Introduction to Philosophy: Ideas In Conflict (St Paul, MN, 1982), pp. 268–275.

G.A.C.

SUBMISSION AND SUBORDINATION.
Authority-structures are universal in human societies, and the issues of freedom and submission are constant themes in human ethical discourse. They figure also in the Bible and Christian tradition, where two streams of interpretation are distinguishable.

The subordinationist approach
This approach emphasizes the God-givenness of human authority-structures, and the consequent Christian duty to submit and obey. Central texts in this approach are Rom. 13:1–7 and 1 Pet. 2:13–17. The same view is applied within the family sphere, so that the obedient

submission of children to parents, and wives to husbands, is emphasized (Eph. 5:22 – 6:4; Col. 3:18–21). The language of 'headship' is interpreted to indicate a hierarchy of authority, which starts within God himself and is then reflected in human relationships and in the relationship between Christ and the church (1 Cor. 11:3; Eph. 4:15–16; 5:23–24). Just as the Son submits to the Father (1 Cor. 15:28), so the church submits to Christ, wives submit to their husbands, and all of us submit to secular authorities ordained by God.

Difficulties arise with this approach when we try to determine the effects of both the Fall* and redemption (see Sin and Salvation[5]). What difference does it make if governments do *not* punish the wicked and reward the good (Rom. 13:4; 1 Pet. 2:14), but do the reverse – or if a husband maltreats his wife and children? Is obedient submission still required? Similarly, what difference does it make to believe that 'this world in its present form is passing away' (1 Cor. 7:31), that a new creation is taking place (2 Cor. 5:17), and that we are citizens of heaven (Phil. 3:20)? Does this to any extent challenge the hierarchies of the present order right now?

The revolutionist approach

The Anabaptist* tradition illustrates the second approach, in which the new world is seen as intruding with revolutionary effect into the present age. In contrast to the Catholic Church, which saw itself as wielding secular power directly over its subjects, and in contrast also to the Reformers, who relied upon the support of secular power, the early Anabaptists saw themselves as a gathering of the new age, from which the hierarchies of secular government were banished. Here central texts were Mt. 23:8–12 and Mk. 10:42–45. Naturally, they were regarded as a threat to civilized order, and were persecuted.

Generally Anabaptist churches have survived by compromising on the 'revolutionist' principle. Hierarchies within the churches have been avoided, so that believers are thought to submit only to Christ through the Spirit. But outside the church, the God-given legitimacy of secular power has increasingly been affirmed. Within Anabaptist churches, too, the authority of the husband in marriage has often been retained, although women have risen to positions of leadership more easily in Anabaptist churches than in churches with hierarchical orders of government.

Two streams in the Bible

The subordinationist and the revolutionist approaches represent parallel streams in the Bible, so that we are called to make a nuanced judgment, rather than to a simple prooftext affirmation of one approach or the other.

In the first place, 'submission' is different from 'obedience'. The Paul who wrote Rom. 13:1 had not obeyed when the Jewish authorities tried to stop him preaching (1 Thes. 2:14–16). 'We must obey God rather than men' (Acts 5:29) is the presupposition of all authentic Christian relating to the world. Against this background, 'submission' is the recognition of the sovereignty of God over all the affairs of this world and over our own individual involvement in it. So, while he refused to stop preaching, Paul submitted to the imprisonment he received as a result.

Similarly, Paul exploded slavery* by telling Christian slaves that they serve God and *not* men (Eph. 6:7; Col. 3:23), and masters that they too are slaves, and brothers in Christ to their slaves (Eph. 6:9; Col. 4:1; Phm. 16). But at the same time he did not start a social revolution, but urged slaves to see their slavery as God's calling (1 Cor. 7:17). The new relationship must be expressed within the old institution: slaves 'who have believing masters are not to show less respect for them because they are brothers. Instead, they are to serve them even better' (1 Tim. 6:2).

Likewise, marriage is affirmed and the word 'submission' (but not 'obedience') used of the wife's attitude to her husband, even though Paul also writes that in Christ, 'there is neither Jew nor Greek, slave nor free, male nor female' (Gal. 3:28). In fact Paul grants both husband and wife authority over each other in 1 Cor. 7:4. The 'headship' language in 1 Cor. 11:3 and Eph. 5:23 should probably therefore not be interpreted as signalling hierarchical authority and patriarchy, but intimacy, union and responsibility; and 'submission' should be understood as self-giving in love, rather than recognition of status.

Finally, the Holy Spirit's direct supervision of the church is clearly taught (1 Cor. 12); but, with no sense of incompatibility, we also find the appointment of an 'official' leadership, to which believers are urged to 'submit' (1 Cor. 14:37; Heb. 13:17).

See also: SEXUALITY.[11]

Bibliography

J. Dominian, *Authority* (London, 1976); J. B. Hurley, *Man and Woman in Biblical Perspective* (Leicester and Grand Rapids, 1981).

S.M.

SUBSTANCE ABUSE, see DRUGS.

SUFFERING. The term 'suffering' is closely allied to the concepts of evil* and pain.* Although the verb 'suffer' can be used either in the sense of 'undergo' and 'endure' or in the sense of 'allow' and 'tolerate', the noun 'suffering' is usually linked with the former meaning. Suffering is the experience of anguish or misery in which sentient beings are aware of the deprivation of their intent or function. For humankind, suffering, with its biological, psychological and ontological elements, may be the outcome of moral evil,* where human sin (see Sin and Salvation⑤) and folly lead to affliction (injustice, exploitation,* greed, war,* violence,* rape,* desertion, disease related to wrong behaviour), or of natural evil (drought, floods, earthquakes, accident, illness and death that are unrelated to human culpability). Suffering, as a state of mind, may also relate to circumstances of place, possessions and people rather than to the problem of evil. Although suffering may be due to unrelieved pain, not all pain, as a physical sensation, necessarily entails suffering.

1. Suffering in the Bible

Although the Bible presents no clearly argued theodicy,* defending the nature of God in the face of the reality of evil, it declares a close connection between the Fall* of humankind (with a fall of certain angels hinted at) and the advent of suffering: human sin is linked with the misery of alienation* from a holy God (Gn. 3:1–13; 6:5–7), discord and enmity amongst fellow beings (Gn. 3:15; 4:1–16) and adversity and affliction in the subduing of the created order (Gn. 3:17–19; Ec. 5:16–17). More broadly in the OT, God is seen to send both good and evil, healing* and suffering (Jb. 2:10; 5:18; Am. 3:6; Hab. 3:5): there is no dualistic* opposition between equal forces of light and darkness, for God is sovereign and even his enemies are subject to his will.

The significance of suffering is at its clearest where it is the outcome of disobedience – at both the individual level (Pss. 38; 51; Pr. 26:27) and the corporate (Is. 1:2–9; Am. 1 – 3). We also see the repercussions of moral evil in the lives of those who are not directly implicated: Moses (Nu. 11:11), Elijah (1 Ki. 19), Jeremiah (Je. 15:10; 18:18) and Hosea (Ho. 1 – 3) are examples of those who suffer as a result of other people's rebellions. Similarly, and as a paradigm of innocent suffering, both moral evil and natural disaster are unleashed on Job, the Lord's servant who 'was blameless and upright' (Jb. 1:1 – 2:10). Job, sorely tested by personal grief, dispossession and disfiguring illness, finds his suffering the path to submission before, and a new relationship with, an all-powerful and sovereign God (Jb. 38:1 – 42:6).

The mystery of the suffering of the innocent is at its starkest in the 'Servant Songs' of Isaiah (Is. 42:1–4; 49:1–6; 50:4–9; 52:13 – 53:12; see also Is. 41:8–10; 43:10; 44:1–5, 21; 45:4; 48:20; 50:10; 54:17; 61:1–3). In this range of passages the 'Suffering Servant' is, variously, the prophet, Israel – the people of God – and, supremely, the Messiah. Here we see the profoundest dimension of suffering, for it is the Messianic Servant who suffers and dies: 'despised and rejected by men, a man of sorrows, and familiar with suffering', he is 'led like a lamb to the slaughter' (Is. 53:3, 7). Suffering is here revealed as uniquely redemptive, since it is said of the promised one: 'the Lord has laid on him the iniquity of us all' (Is. 53:6).

In the NT, we find the same perspectives on suffering expressed through *paschō* (suffer, endure), *pathēma* (suffering, affliction, misfortune), and allied words, as well as more generally in and through the passion of Christ and the sufferings of the people of God. We see that suffering, and even death,* can be the result of individual and collective sin (Acts 5:1–10; Rom. 1:21–27; 1 Pet. 2:20; 3:17; 4:15); that suffering is not inevitably linked, though, with personal (Jn. 9:1–3) or corporate guilt (Lk. 13:1–5); and indeed that those who are forgiven and faithful are not exempt from suffering (Acts 9:15–16; Phil. 1:29–30; 1 Pet. 4:16, 19).

The theme of the 'Suffering Servant' echoes throughout the NT: affliction is foretold even in Christ's infancy (Lk. 2:34–35); the public ministry of Jesus is riven with misunderstanding, opposition and rejection (Mt. 16:1; 22:15; Mk. 3:22; Lk. 4:24–30; Jn. 6:66; 9:28–29; 10:31; 11:53); from Peter's declaration of Christ's Messiahship onwards, the Lord predicts his coming passion repeatedly (Mk. 8:31; 9:12, 31; 10:32–34, 45; see also Lk. 9:31, 51); and, following his crucifixion and resurrection, the fact of his suffering and death is alluded to time and again within the story of the early church (Acts 2:23; 3:13, 18; 4:10; 7:52; 10:39), while the theology of the cross* is further unfolded (Acts 8:32–35; Rom. 3:25; 5:6–8; 6:2, 8–10; 8:3, 32; 1 Cor. 1:18 – 2:5; 2 Cor. 5:21; Gal. 3:13; Eph. 1:7; 5:2; Heb. 2:9–18; 13:11–12; 1 Pet. 2:24; 3:18; 1 Jn. 2:2; 4:10).

Although the weight of biblical teaching on the cross centres on the atonement,* there is another important strand which closely links the sufferings of Christ with the sufferings of his people: their identification with him leads to insult and persecution (Jn. 15:18 – 16:4; 1 Pet. 4:12–19); conversely, his identification with them leads to solace and encouragement (Rom. 8:17; 2 Cor. 1:5, 8–10; Heb. 2:18; 4:14–16; 12:2–4). In following the example of the suffering Christ (Mk. 8:34–38; Heb. 13:12–13; 1 Pet. 2:21), the church experiences a fellowship in adversity (Phil. 1:29–30; Col. 1:24; 1 Thes. 2:14; 2 Tim. 1:8; Heb. 10:34), growth in maturity (Rom. 5:3–5; Jas. 1:2–4), and the hope of glory (1 Pet. 4:13; 5:1, 10), when all suffering shall cease (Rev. 7:14–17; 21:1–4).

2. Suffering and the church

The people of God, as well as being prey to the affliction and adversity of a fallen world, have always been subject to disgrace and persecution when their obedience to Christ comes into conflict with the prevailing culture.* Throughout history, pastoral care (see Pastoral Care, Counselling and Psychotherapy[12]) has sought to offer solace to others within the whole gamut of suffering, including, for instance, through the letters of Cyprian (c. 200–58), Bishop of Carthage, written to encourage the faithful during the Decian persecution; the consoling *Letter to a Young Widow* by John Chrysostom;* Gregory the Great's (see Gregory I*) *Moral Reflections on Job*; the *Fourteen Comforts for the Weary and Heavy Laden* (c. 1519) by Martin Luther;* and Jeremy Taylor's* *The Rule and Exercise of Holy Dying* (1651). There is also much rich counsel for suffering believers in such Puritan writers as Thomas Watson (d. c. 1686) in *A Divine Cordial* (1663), and Richard Sibbes (1577–1635) in *The Mute Christian under the Smarting Rod*, and in Samuel Rutherford's (1660–61) *Letters* (repr. Edinburgh, 1984).

The problem of evil, and thereby suffering, has been considered philosophically by many since the 17th century. Of particular influence are two Protestant thinkers. Gottfried von Leibniz (1646–1716), who first coined the term 'theodicy', declared that God, who had created the best of possible worlds and had ordained human freedom, could still bring good out of the resulting evil. F. D. E. Schleiermacher* argued that sin and suffering, for which God is ultimately responsible, are inevitable consequences of humanity's growth towards 'God-consciousness'.

The 20th century has witnessed a volume of human misery and suffering of unprecedented proportions – through two world wars, the increasing sophistication of weapons of intimidation and destruction, and the advent of natural disasters on a scale enhanced by the population explosion. In the face of this enormity, philosophers and theologians have continued to grapple with the enigma of evil and suffering. Noteworthy in the tradition of philosophical theodicy are John Hick (1922–), whose 'soul-making' approach looks to Irenaeus (c. 130–c. 200) and sees the eventual resolution of evil and adversity in the perfectibility of human nature in the 'likeness' of God; and Alvin Plantinga (1932–), whose 'free-will defence', influenced by Augustine,* postulates that an omnipotent and wholly good God, in creating human choice, inevitably permits evil and suffering.

The two world wars in particular have stimulated theological reflection on the cross in the face of inordinate human suffering. P. T. Forsyth (1848–1921), seeking to justify God in the context of the First World War, rejected the remoteness of traditional philosophy and offered a Christocentric approach in which 'the only theodicy is that which redeems'. It is the impossible suffering and degradation of the Holocaust that have raised the profoundest questions about human evil and a God of love. Dorothee Soelle (1929–) criticizes passivity in relation to suffering as 'Christian masochism' and urges a social response to sufferers which expresses solidarity with the suffering Christ. Jürgen Moltmann (1926–) centres his theodicy in a theology of the cross, the identification of the trinitarian God with suffering humanity and the eschatological hope of triumph over all evil. Kenneth Surin (1948–), in the light of the horrors of Auschwitz, declares a 'rupture' of language and the need for unbelief, as well as belief, in relation to God's apparent inaction; the only legitimate response to such unspeakable suffering, he adds, is that of 'penance and conversion'.

Bibliography

D. Bonhoeffer, *Letters and Papers from Prison* (ET, London, ⁴1971); D. A. Carson, *How Long, O Lord?* (Grand Rapids, 1990; or Leicester, 1991); P. T. Forsyth, *The Justification of God: Lectures for War-Time on a Christian Theodicy* (London, 1916); S. Hauerwas, *Suffering Presence: Theological Reflections on Medicine, the Mentally Handicapped, and the Church* (Edinburgh and Notre Dame, IN, 1986); J. Hick, *Evil and the God of Love* (London, ²1977); M. Israel, *The Pain that Heals* (London, 1981); C. S. Lewis, *The Problem of Pain* (London, 1948); J. Moltmann, *The Crucified God* (ET, London, 1974); A. C. Plantinga, *God, Freedom, and Evil* (Grand Rapids, 1974); D. Soelle, *Suffering* (London and Philadelphia, 1975); M. Spufford, *Celebration* (Glasgow, 1989); K. Surin, *Theology and the Problem of Evil* (Oxford and New York, 1986); P. Tournier, *Creative Suffering* (ET, London and San Francisco, 1982); J. Walsh and E. P. G. Walsh, *Divine Providence and Human Suffering: The Message of the Fathers of the Church*, vol. 17 (Wilmington, DE, 1985); E. Wiesel, *Night* (New York, 1960; London, 1972).

R.F.H.

SUICIDE, the intentional taking of his or her own life by the person involved, raises a number of ethical and pastoral issues.

Theological perspectives

There is little in the Bible concerning the morality of suicide. Indeed, the word 'suicide' (self-murder) does not appear. There certainly are examples (without comment on the moral nature of the act) as in the cases of Saul and his armour-bearer (1 Sa. 31:4–5), Ahithophel (2 Sa. 17:23) and Zimri (1 Ki. 16:18). In the NT, the only example is that of Judas Iscariot (Mt. 27:5). The death of Samson (Jdg. 16:28–31) may possibly be seen as a heroic suicide, although it is possible that Samson did not primarily will his own death, but accepted it as the unavoidable consequence of his actions.

The early church, however, soon came to regard suicide as akin to murder (murder of oneself) and therefore as prohibited under the sixth commandment. Early Christian thought was crystallized in Augustine's* *City of God* (413–26). His main argument was that suicide is a form of homicide from which the likelihood of repentance is small: 'Nay, the law, rightly interpreted, even prohibits suicide, where it says "thou shalt not kill"'. However, later writers, such as John Donne (1571/2–1631) in *Biathanatos* (pub. 1644), challenged the Augustinian view as a human placing of limits upon the grace* of God.

Considered Christian opinion is that suicide is morally wrong. In the Westminster Larger Catechism, the answer to question 136 begins thus: 'The Sins Forbidden in the Sixth Commandment *are all taking away the Life of ourselves* ...' The Judaeo-Christian tradition is thus that only God in his sovereignty has the right to give and take away life. Suicide therefore is seen as a challenge to the sovereignty of God. However, the question of responsibility* and culpability remains, especially since major mental illness (see Mental Health*) or stress reactions indistinguishable from the same are usually present in the individual suicide.

The phenomenon

Suicide – and its associate, parasuicide (intentional self-harm not ending in death) – have leapt to the fore as highly significant causes of mortality and morbidity in all age groups in Western society. A World Health Organization estimate of 300,000–400,000 annually throughout the world (*World Health Statistics Annual*, Geneva, 1987) is an admitted underestimate because of the reluctance of admission of suicide as a cause of death and the lack of registration of suicides in the vast majority of countries. In the northern countries of Europe and in those countries populated largely with their progeny, *e.g.* Canada, the USA and Australia, rates are highest; and in the younger age group (15–35 years), suicide is one of the most important single causes of death. Rates of suicide are apparently highest in countries such as the former West Germany, France, Switzerland and Japan, and lowest in countries such as Egypt. Arabic countries in general have low rates, whereas Asian countries come towards the middle of the range. There is much evidence which supports the finding that particularly at risk are males who are older, isolated (*e.g.* divorced, widowed or bereaved) and with an underlying alcohol problem (see Alcoholism*). However, studies have shown in general that parasuicide of any kind is a significant associate of eventual suicide. Of those making a non-fatal attempt at suicide, 10%–14% will die as a result of a subsequent attempt (M. Van Egmond and R. F. W. Diekstra, 'The Predictability of Suicidal Behaviour'). Other factors associated with a rising suicide-rate include unemployment, an ageing population, women working, increase in divorce-rate, major mental illness, increase in homicide-rate and percentage-change in church membership. The latter probably reflects changing moral values and a decrease in social integration (R. F. W. Diekstra and B. Mortiz, 'Suicidal Behaviour among Adolescents').

When a suicide occurs, the reverberations in terms of impact on family and society are enormous, and vary from catastrophic bereavement* reactions associated with unanswered questions in close family and loved ones, to the 'modelling' phenomenon when a media star commits suicide and there are associated attempts throughout the world. Various writers (e.g. E. Durkheim, Suicide) have demonstrated the complex motives for suicide such as avoidance of shame* or painful death, revenge, desire for oblivion and religious motives. The latter may range from suttee (widow-burning) in India to mass suicides associated with extremist Christian cults, such as that of the members of the People's Temple in Guyana in 1978, many of whom committed suicide to enter directly into a 'new world'.

Pastoral problems

The phases of bereavement reactions are exaggerated when a suicide occurs, and have been divided into denial, hostility/anger,* depression,* prolonged grief and delay (see 'Bereavement', in M. Gelder et al., Oxford Textbook of Psychiatry). Sudden death is always difficult to come to terms with, and the more sudden and unexpected, the greater the denial which may be seen in the bereaved. This may vary from perplexity and the individual expressing an inability to believe what has happened, or a refusal to accept reality, to repression of the information, and occasionally a 'fugue'-like state with loss of memory. In such a fugue, the mental state of the individual may seem to be characterized by not knowing what has happened, and apparent lack of orientation.

Denial in its milder forms is best dealt with by simple support and non-intervention in the sense of trying to produce explanations and understandings of what has happened. From a Christian point of view this is particularly difficult; but to help in a practical way with arrangements and 'being there' is of much greater value than succumbing to pressures to offer facile answers to unanswered questions. Occasionally when a more serious reaction such as a fugue occurs, the patient may need hospitalization for safety.

Anger and hostility are commonly directed towards the people involved, such as professionals (i.e. doctors and nurses) or persons last in contact with the individual. Simple support and acceptance are what is needed. Bereavement reactions in terms of depression are often indistinguishable from major depressive illness except that the sense of loss may be greater in the case of suicide. Unanswerable questions such as the 'fate' of the dead become more pertinent and, as in normal bereavement, exhortations to rest in the sovereignty of God are the most helpful approach. Sleeplessness can be a major problem, and simple night sedation for a very brief period of time may be helpful. Delayed bereavement reaction or a prolonged bereavement reaction needs referral to a Christian counsellor to encourage coming to terms with the loss.

A family history of suicide is particularly important when assessing a living client, and it is essential information to obtain when determining the risk of such an individual taking his or her own life.

Bibliography

G. L. and G. C. Carr, After the Storm: Hope in the Wake of Suicide (Leicester, 1990) = The Fierce Goodbye (Downers Grove, IL, 1990); R. F. W. Diekstra and B. Mortiz, 'Suicidal Behaviour among Adolescents', in R. F. W. Diekstra and K. Hawton (eds.), Suicide in Adolescence (Dordrecht, 1987); E. Durkheim, Suicide: A Study in Sociology (ET, Glencoe, IL, 1951); M. Gelder et al., 'Bereavement', in Oxford Textbook of Psychiatry (Oxford, ²1989); M. Van Egmond and R. F. W. Diekstra, 'The Predictability of Suicidal Behaviour', in R. F. W. Diekstra et al., Suicide Prevention: The Role of Attitude and Imitation (Leiden, 1989).

B.H.

SUNDAY. Direct biblical evidence for Sunday observance is scanty. The earliest NT reference to any regular Christian activity on the first day of the week is in 1 Corinthians, where Paul asks church members to set aside money for the poor every Sunday (16:1–4).

The implication is that special church meetings took place on that day which would facilitate collections.

Luke gives a more detailed account of a church Sunday meeting in Acts, where he describes the all-night service at Troas (20:7–12). Paul preached, and the focal point of worship was the breaking of bread – a semi-technical term for eating the Lord's Supper and (probably) sharing in the fellowship of the 'love feast' (*cf.* 1 Cor. 11:17–34).

The only other reference to Sunday in the NT is also the only one which refers to it as 'the Lord's Day'. In Rev. 1:10, John explains how he was told to write letters to seven Asian churches while at worship on a Sunday. Some commentators believe he is referring to a special occasion (Easter, perhaps, or the Day of Judgment), but it is more likely that 'the *Lord's* Day' refers to the day of the week when Christians met regularly to express their commitment to Jesus as Lord. There may even be a verbal allusion to the centrality of the Lord's Supper in early Sunday worship, because the adjective (Gk. *kyriakos*) recurs only in that context in the rest of the NT (1 Cor. 11:20).

Do these scattered references support the conclusion that, even in the church's earliest days, Sunday was well on the way towards becoming a Christian replacement for the Jewish sabbath?*

No direct verbal link is made between sabbath and Sunday in the NT, but the allusions to worship, teaching and giving on the first day of the week are clear reflections of major sabbath activities. The transfer of Jewish Christians' attention from Saturday to Sunday as a special day of worship would have been eased by the fact that Christ's resurrection and the giving of the Holy Spirit both took place on the first day of the week. It is, however, extremely unlikely that Sunday and sabbath were ever identified in the minds of early Christians. Apart from Jesus' criticisms of contemporary sabbath observance, and Paul's ambivalence towards the keeping of any special days (*cf.* Rom. 14:5–9; Gal. 4:8–11), it would have been socially impossible for the first Christians to have kept Sunday as a day of rest.

Most early patristic writers testify to a distinction between sabbath and Sunday. Sunday soon became established as a day of worship, but not as a day of rest. The sabbath principle was spiritualized. The injunction to abstain from work on the seventh day was transformed into a command to abstain from all sinful acts on any day of the week.

In 321, the Roman Emperor Constantine* forbade most kinds of work on Sundays. That gave historical impetus to a much closer linkage between Sunday and sabbath observance, an identification which was expressed with particular force and clarity by Thomas Aquinas,* the Westminister Confession (1648), and the Lord's Day Observance Society (founded 1831). Sabbatarianism was backed by legal sanctions both in Britain (where an Act of Parliament passed in the time of Charles II [1660–85; b. 1630] required church attendance and banned 'worldly labour') and in the USA (where the 'blue laws' restricted Sunday trading). The command to rest was usually interpreted as a veto on all forms of recreational activity as well as paid work.

Both Martin Luther* and John Calvin* registered strong protests against strict sabbatarianism. Distinguishing between the Bible's ceremonial and moral laws, they rejected 'superstitious observance of days' (Calvin), while supporting the provision of a weekly day of rest on humanitarian grounds.

The contemporary debate about Sunday trading in Britain throws the relationship between sabbath and Sunday into particularly sharp focus. While denying the total identification of the two, those who want to see a conservative revision of the Shops Act (1950) advocate the retention of sabbatical restrictions on Sundays. The sabbath, they argue, is a creation ordinance which may properly be the object of legislation because its provisions apply to all people. Restrictions on Sunday trade protect workers' rights to a day off and families' freedom to enjoy quality leisure time together. Their opponents fight for a total repeal of the law on the grounds that sabbatical restrictions in a secular, pluralistic society are undemocratic and legalistic. Neither side wishes to restrict opportunities for Christians to worship together on Sundays, but there is disagreement about the churches' right to expect freedom from competition at service times.

Bibliography
R. T. Beckwith and W. Stott, *This is the Day* (London, 1978); D. A. Carson (ed.), *From Sabbath to Lord's Day* (Grand Rapids, 1982); W. Rordorf, *Sunday* (ET, London, 1968).

D.H.F.

SUPER-EGO, see PERSONALITY; PSYCHOANALYSIS; UNCONSCIOUS.

SUPERVISION (*i.e.* supervision in the helping professions) developed from three main traditions: 1. the responsibility given to supervisors in social-welfare agencies to ensure a good service for clients and the best use of resources in line with agency policy; 2. the training and supervision of analysts; and 3. consultancy in mental-health specialties, involving work with an individual or a group of staff, possibly from another profession, for a limited period, on specific problems of administration, programme planning or individual treatment. The model adopted varies according to the setting, the supervisor's style and training and whether managerial responsibility is carried.

The roles of supervisor and consultant are not always clearly distinguished but, in general, supervision implies some shared accountability, while consultancy does not. A consultant may be engaged as an expert in a specific area or in order to provide clarification, analysis and objectivity.

Whatever model is used, all concerned need to agree as to the lines of accountability,* goals and methods to be adopted, the time, place and duration of sessions, and opportunities for review. This is sometimes formalized in a contract.* The establishment of mutual trust is essential. All parties, including the client, need to understand the circumstances under which information will be divulged and to whom, especially if the supervisor has knowledge of the client in other contexts.

Supervised practice or practice teaching is the main forum in which students of the helping professions integrate theory with practice, learn to work within the constraints of the setting, develop professional discipline, establish good relationships with colleagues, and manage a case-load. The supervisor is often taken as a role model, and exerts a powerful influence. Where training is split between an educational institution and a placement agency, the supervisor will be accountable to the institution for teaching and assessment, but to the agency for the welfare of the students' clients. Skill is needed in handling this network of relationships without collusion and without over-identification with one or other of what can be competing interests.

Supervision helps newly qualified staff to move from the role of student to that of independent practitioner. It also ensures the continued use of knowledge and skill already acquired, and provides a safe framework to try new methods. Workers' attitudes to continued learning will be greatly influenced by the provision made for supervision in their first job. If it is regarded or used as a tool of managerial control, or as implying lack of confidence in the worker, its usefulness will be undermined.

The element of support in supervision is an important one. Receiving care makes it easier to care for others. Hearing about suffering* is painful, and it is hard to bear the weight of others' powerful emotions. In addition to anxiety over progress, and feelings of guilt* if clients are disliked or finish prematurely, the worker often carries some of the client's feelings of helplessness and depression.* The supervisor can give recognition to this, help to provide some perspective on the experience, and identify what is going on in the interaction, so that more accurate assessment and better treatment plans can be made.

Supervision will help to identify learning patterns, recurring themes, gaps in knowledge, and the extent and balance of the workload. It can also help identify responses arising from the worker's past, areas of vulnerability which may be affecting judgment, and help detect signs of 'burnout' (see Stress*).

Experienced workers also recognize their continuing need of supervision, and frequently seek it from one of their peer group whom they respect; they may give as well as receive it. Church leaders, especially those who counsel in isolation, find similar arrangements helpful.

Where individual supervision is not available, the use of a group with an outside consultant, or peer-group supervision, can be helpful. This requires careful selection and a capacity to handle group dynamics. Where the group consists of members of a working team, additional dynamics will be operating.

The skills required in supervision are similar to those needed in counselling, but differently applied. The focus is still the clients' welfare, but this will be achieved through developing the skills of the worker; this requires willingness to share and a commitment to teach. While supervision should be a positive and probably therapeutic experience, temptations to engage in therapy have to be resisted. The primary task is educational, or enabling objectivity. Supervisors need confidence in their own practice, clarity about their limits of competence, ability to mobilize other resources, and a wish to develop their own learning.

The need of supervisors for training opportunities in their new role is becoming more generally recognized, and the provision made is increasing.

See also: CONFIDENTIALITY.

Bibliography

J. S. Atherton, *Professional Supervision in Group Care* (London, 1986); C. Caplan, *Principles of Preventative Psychiatry* (London and New York, 1964); P. Hawkins and R. Shohet, *Supervision in the Helping Professions* (Buckingham, 1989); J. Mattison, *The Reflection Process in Casework Supervision* (London, 1975); H. F. Searles, 'Problems of Psycho-Analysis Supervision', in *Collected Papers on Schizophrenia and Other Subjects* (London, 1965); J. Westheimer, *The Practice of Supervision in Social Work* (East Grinstead, 1977).

J.R.G.

SURROGATE MOTHERHOOD is the bearing of a child by a woman for another couple. In partial surrogacy, a woman agrees to be inseminated artificially by the husband of a childless couple in order to provide for the couple a child who will be genetically related to the husband, if not the wife. This is performed if the wife is infertile (see Childlessness*). Full, or gestational, surrogacy is the procedure of transferring an egg fertilized in the laboratory (*in vitro* fertilization) to a woman who then carries it to term and delivers the baby to the couple. The surrogate mother is typically engaged by an agency, which for a fee arranges a contract between the couple and the mother (though this practice is illegal in the UK). The contract stipulates that the surrogate will abstain from intercourse that might pre-empt the artificial insemination by the husband of the couple and take certain precautions in pregnancy to safeguard the welfare of the baby. Importantly, it requires her to surrender the child-to-be-conceived when it eventually is born. Not surprisingly, in view of the fact that substantial sums of money are often paid by the couple and received by the surrogate, couples tend to be from the upper middle class and surrogates from lower classes.

Surrogate motherhood has been the subject of substantial dispute by lawyers, the courts and legislatures, feminists and philosophers, as well as the public. Legal quandaries have appeared when surrogates have refused to relinquish the child, as in the famous New Jersey case of 'Baby M', and in cases in which the child has been born with congenital difficulties and has been rejected both by the couple and by the surrogate.

While it is understandable for a childless couple to desire to have borne for them a child who is genetically related to at least one of them, very serious concerns persist. It is seen as dehumanizing to treat a woman, in her intimate and sacred role as mother, as an incubator, committed even before conception to give up the child, usually for payment of a fee. Surrogacy demeans the birth mother's status as a person by reducing her to a reproductive appliance, and it deliberately breaks the relationship between birth mother and child, with financial gain often being the main consideration. There is a substantial question of financial exploitation of poor but fertile women who are induced to 'sell' their reproductive potential. Surrogacy has even been regarded by some as analogous to prostitution, in that it rents the use of sexual-reproductive organs. Perhaps most importantly, it creates unknown emotional and psychological risks for any child born in this manner. Although an instance of surrogate mothering is recorded in Scripture, in the story of Abraham, Sarah and Hagar, this is hardly an endorsement of the arrangement (Gn. 16). The Vatican has categorically rejected surrogacy as a morally legitimate mode of reproduction and has called on governments to outlaw the practice. Other Christians also have for the most part rejected surrogacy as an illegitimate intrusion into the 'one-flesh' nature of marital child-begetting, although not all have favoured using the criminal law to suppress surrogate arrangements.

See also: PARENTHOOD, PARENTING; REPRODUCTIVE TECHNOLOGIES.

Bibliography

R. T. Hull, *Ethical Issues in the New Reproductive Technologies* (Belmont, CA, 1990); D. G. Jones, *Manufacturing Humans: The Challenge of the New Reproductive Technologies* (Leicester, 1987); H. T. Krimmel, 'The Case Against Surrogate Parenting', *Hastings Center Report* 13.5, 1983; O. O'Donovan, *Begotten or Made?* (Oxford, 1984); P. Ramsey, *Fabricated Man* (New Haven, CT, and London, 1970); M. Warnock (chairperson), *Report of the Committee of Inquiry into Human Fertilisation and Embryology* (London, 1984).

D.B.F.

SWEARING, see OATH.

T

TABOO. A powerful prohibition, cultural or individualistic, leading to strict avoidance of the forbidden act, object, person or place. Avoidance is maintained by fear of a particular punishment or by dread of some unspecified catastrophe that defies reason, logic and conscious analysis. In time the subject of a taboo becomes detached from daily life, being considered either too sacred for ordinary people to associate with or alternatively so cursed that it will inevitably bring evil on anyone breaking it. Strong power is attributed to the object of the taboo, often, although not always, ascribed to malevolent spirits. The catastrophic consequences of breaking a taboo are sometimes held to extend to the relatives or whole community of the transgressor, providing a powerful incentive to its observance and the likelihood of human punishment.

Death and sexual and reproductive activity are the most widely found subjects of taboo, with incest being an almost universal one. Relative rather than absolute taboos exist, as in contemporary British society where excretory functions are taboo in polite company, although they become acceptable as swearwords and in comedy. Psychoanalysts consider that individual taboos arise from external prohibitions regarding sexuality clashing with unconscious internal affections, the conflict being partially resolved by the imposition of personal taboos which frequently become detached from the original object or situation and take on a pathological form. Behaviourists* view the same manifestation as learned habits, and treat them more directly.

Originally protective in intent, taboos become restrictive, tending to exclude people from places and relationships.

R.F.

TARIFFS, see INTERNATIONAL TRADE.

TAWNEY, R. H. (1880–1962). The 1920s produced some remarkable intellectual leaders for the church at a time of social unrest and of deep challenge to the inherited culture of Christendom in England. Richard Henry Tawney was a contemporary of William Temple* at school and university. They became life-long friends and formed part of a group of theological, ethical, social and political thinkers whose influence upon both church and politics in the 1920s is incalculable.

Tawney was a socialist and a Christian. He found deep connections between his sense of the corporate life of the church and his political conviction about the collective life of the people. In the ten years between 1921 and 1931 he produced his three major books: *The Acquisitive Society* (London, 1921), *Religion and the Rise of Capitalism* (London, 1926), and *Equality* (London, 1931). In these he set out his vision of a just and workable society rooted in values which for him arose out of the gospel.

If Temple was a statesman in the church, Tawney's life was to be found more in the political realm (see Politics*). He was the author of crucial Labour Party policies on education and wrote the 1929 Labour manifesto. In 1918 he played a large part in writing the Archbishop's report 'Christianity and Industrial Problems' and was a member of the Royal Commission on the Mines in 1920, which recommended the nationalization of the industry.

Tawney's thinking shaped the intellectual culture of the British Labour Party in the 20th century and played a crucial role in shaping one of the church's approaches to social questions. No account of the life of the church in Britain in the 1920s is complete without substantial reference to him.

Bibliography

J. R. Atherton, *Moral and Theological Aspects of the Work of R. H. Tawney*, MA thesis (Manchester, 1974); A. Hastings, *A History of English Christianity, 1920–1985* (London, 1986); R. Terrill, *R. H. Tawney and his Times* (Cambridge, MA, 1973; London, 1974).

J.W.G.

TAXATION has been defined as 'that part of the revenue of a State obtained by compulsory dues or charges upon its subjects'. Taxes can be further classified in various ways, but, for the purposes of this article, division into direct and indirect taxes will suffice. Direct taxes are those levied on the citizen's income or capital. Prime examples of these are income tax, capital gains tax and inheritance taxes. Indirect taxes, broadly, are those attached to the prices people pay for goods and services.

Historical and biblical background

When taxes were first levied is unknown. We may assume that as the family gave place to the tribe, and the tribe to the city or area as the local political or social unit, the chosen leader or king demanded some kind of payment (presumably in kind) for providing rule and protection. Certainly in Palestine by the time of Samuel (*c.* 1100 BC) the position was clear, as was the going rate. A king was expected to demand one tenth of a subject's grain, vintage and flocks annually (1 Sa. 8:15–17).

By NT times the Romans had built up an elaborate and onerous system of imperial and local taxation, extending over virtually the whole of the Mediterranean world into which the church was to penetrate. It was against this background that Jesus made his well-known reply about the tribute money, 'Give to Caesar what is Caesar's, and to God what is God's' (Mt. 22:21), and Paul, a generation later, gave the directions contained in Rom. 13:1–7 to the church in that city. It may be assumed that by the 50s and 60s of the 1st century, the churches contained a growing number of people who found themselves required to pay taxes to fund a series of dissolute and persecuting emperors. Qualms of conscience, as they saw the end to which their money was being put, may have tempted them to consider refusing payment, so putting themselves on a collision course with the authorities. Perhaps they canvassed the question with Paul, and the Romans passage may be his reply.

Whatever the circumstances, Paul's advice is clear. Government is a divine appointment for the good of society. The 'governing authorities' in Rome are 'God's servants', a phrase he uses three times. Their God-given ministry of governing is to be financed. Christians should therefore pay the taxes demanded of them with a good conscience, and not merely as a duty. Governments are to be not only prayed for (1 Tim. 2:1–2) but paid for!

That the taxes 'owed' in Paul's phrase (the same word is used in the context of Mt. 18:32) had to be ones lawfully due had come to be accepted in England by the later Middle Ages. The refusal of John Hampden (*c.* 1595–1643), a devout Puritan, to pay the ship money levied by the Crown in 1636 without the consent of Parliament, rested on this principle. During the ensuing Civil War, both king and Parliament claimed to be the lawful taxing authority, leaving the citizen with the unenviable task of deciding whether to meet the demands of either or both.

Since 1689 the matter has been beyond doubt, and in Britain today taxes are imposed annually by Parliament. The mechanics of assessment and collection, regarding both subject and quantum, are supervised by tribunals and the courts. A continually growing body of judicial precedents exists to safeguard the interests of both the Crown and the citizen. A comparable situation exists in many other countries.

Ethical considerations

Taxation exists to raise revenue. Paul gives no support to Christian citizens who might be minded to hold back part of their tax liability because they disapprove of the way in which the government might spend the money (as some people did during the nuclear-weapon debates) or because they doubt its fairness (as did some during the time of the community charge or 'poll tax' in the UK). In happier days than Paul's, Christians nowadays are free to pursue their objections by political means. Short of refusing payment, they are in no way inhibited from resisting or criticizing what they conceive to be an attempt to levy an unjust tax, or, once the tax has become payable, from seeking to get the law changed thereafter.

Direct taxes as a group are, or have been made, the subject of 'social engineering'. Thus income tax at the top of the scale can be kept down in the interests of the wealthy, or raised to promote, in theory at least, a broader spread of wealth throughout society. There is some evidence, however, of a correlation between low taxation and low tax avoidance, and of a marked growth of the 'tax-avoidance industry' when direct taxes are high. High taxation is also claimed to discourage the once highly regarded Puritan virtues of thrift and enterprise (see Puritan Ethics*).

Every citizen is entitled to arrange his or her affairs so as to pay as little tax as possible, but courts today tend to look more and more closely at the many proposed ways of doing so. The line between avoidance (which is legal) and tax evasion (which is a crime) can be a very narrow one.

Indirect taxation brings its own problems. Thus, for instance, to the State a tax on beer is a valuable source of income; to a publican an increase brings the threat of higher prices and less trade; to the temperance worker it holds the prospect that beer-drinking may decline. A tax on tobacco is welcomed by the doctors, but feared by employees in the industry. A tax on betting may discourage gambling, but put the bloodstock industry in peril.

Increased import duties (at the behest perhaps of the EU) may raise prices to levels citizens cannot afford. They may also impoverish Third World producers. Higher export duties may deprive factory workers of their jobs. Value-added tax strikes rich and poor alike; without adequate exemptions it represents a continuing threat to those able to afford only the bare necessities of life.

J.C.D.

TAX EVASION, see TAXATION.

TAYLOR, JEREMY (1613–67). An Anglican bishop and voluminous writer of devotional literature, Taylor was born and educated at Cambridge and quite early became a protégé of William Laud (1573–1645), who found a place for him at All Souls, Oxford, and as his chaplain. Later, during the English Civil War, he became chaplain to Charles I (1625–49; b. 1600). He suffered sequestration and imprisonment after the war but found refuge during the Commonwealth on the estates of Lord Carbery in Wales. It was here that he composed most of his writings.

The Rule and Exercise of Holy Living (1650), which had gone through fourteen editions by 1686, and *The Rule and Exercise of Holy Dying* (1651), which had twenty-one editions by 1710, were by far his most popular and influential works, enjoying a largely uncritical use even into the 20th century. *Ductor Dubitantium* (1660), a work of casuistry* intended as a guide for clergy in their pastoral responsibilities, never received the attention appropriate to what he considered to be his *magnum opus*.

His *Unam Necessarium* (1655), on repentance,* evoked widespread charges of Pelagianism, including those by four contemporary bishops. At the Restoration he was given neither English preferment nor any role in the 1662 revision of the Prayer Book, despite his close association with Laud and Charles, his loyalty and suffering under the Commonwealth, and his incomparable talent in composing prayers and religious prose. It has been suggested that his second wife, perhaps the natural child of Charles, was the cause of his exile to Ireland in 1658; but more probably it was because that age was more critical of his

theology than was the subsequent Restoration period with its more romantic viewpoint.

Samuel Taylor Coleridge's (1772–1834) dictum best sums up the inadequacy of Taylor's theology: 'In short, Socinianism is as inevitable a deduction from Taylor's scheme as Deism or Atheism is from Socinianism.' Yet Coleridge makes no mention of the contrasting doctrine found in Taylor's prayers, which is not open to the criticism legitimately levelled against his other works.

It could not be said of Taylor that he was unacquainted with grief. He experienced the beheading of the archbishop and the king, to each of whom he had been chaplain. He buried his first wife and five sons. He was impoverished and several times imprisoned for his writings during the Commonwealth. With the Restoration of the monarchy he was made Bishop of Down and Connor (1660), in a most difficult part of Ireland where the sentiments of his previous *Liberty of Prophesying* (1647), a pioneering work on religious toleration, seemed to have no role in his disagreeable relations with both Presbyterians and Roman Catholics in his diocese.

Taylor's popularity over the centuries is due more to his literary genius than to his theology, which does not possess the quality of that of his predecessors, Richard Hooker,* Lancelot Andrewes (1555–1626), John Donne (1571/2–1631), or George Herbert (1593–1633). Coleridge, one of his severest doctrinal critics, nevertheless ranks him with William Shakespeare (1564–1616) and John Milton (1608–74) in literary gifts.

Bibliography
Works, ed. C. P. Eden, 10 vols. (London, 1847–54); *Works*, ed. R. Heber, 15 vols. (London, 1828).

C. F. Allison, *The Rise of Moralism: The Proclamation of the Gospel from Hooker to Baxter* (Wilton, CT, 1965; London, 1966); C. J. Stranks, *The Life and Writings of Jeremy Taylor* (London, 1952).

C.F.A.

TECHNOLOGY is understood in at least three ways: 1. as actual objects, such as computers; 2. as processes, *i.e.* the way things get done, such as assembly lines or coalmining; and 3. as specialized knowledge about what people do. Because each definition refers to human activity – the production of objects, involvement in processes and knowing about things – technology may be thought of as an aspect of cultural life. Thus from a biblical perspective technology may be thought of as a human response to the divine mandate responsibly to open up the potential of the creation (Gn. 1:26–28).

A biblical framework

Locating technology within a biblical framework reveals its different facets. In terms of creation,* technology as a means of fulfilling the cultural mandate should be seen positively. It is a calling to be pursued within the rubric of reflecting God's character and attitude to the world. He sustains the creation out of love in faithfulness and justice (see Justice and Peace ③). Even after the covenant* is broken, Tubal-Cain, as a kind of proto-technologist (Gn. 4:22), continues this creation-caring task.

The rupture of relationships consequent on sin's entry into the created environment* affects technology no less than other areas. Not only are tools used destructively as weapons, but an element of transferred trust is also present, later to be denounced by prophetic woes on those who *rely on* their chariots and spears (Is. 31:1–3). The story of the tower of Babel (Gn. 11:1–9) represents a particularly low point in technological history, where the whole project is both breathtaking in conception and idolatrous in intention.

Misdirected and idolatrous technology is not the whole story, however. Redemption (see Sin and Salvation ⑤) in both OT and NT has implications for doing technology. OT law (see Old Testament Ethics ⑧), given to indicate what redemption means for everyday life, recalls God's people to a concern with the proper purposes and limits of technology. For instance, building design had to incorporate safety features (see Dt. 22:8). The NT, while urging that the activities of everyday life (presumably including technological ones) be done wholeheartedly, as to the Lord (Col. 3:23), also echoes earlier promises of a future state where technology is transformed from the destructive to the socially useful. Swords to ploughshares and spears to pruning hooks (Mi. 4:3) may be seen as a technological goal.

History

From earliest times, human beings have made and used tools, for hunting and cooking, for fighting and for transport. Different eras of history are often distinguished by technological change, *e.g.* the Bronze Age and the Iron Age. Only in the modern world, however, has technology, along with science,* become a major social institution in its own right. In Europe the Renaissance played a part in this, as did Puritanism (see Puritan Ethics*). The humanism* of the former stressed limitless human capacities, while Christianity, particularly via figures such as Robert Boyle (1627–92) and Isaac Newton (1642–1727), emphasized diligent worldly labour (see Work*), bringing glory to God through discovering his wisdom* revealed in creation.

In the work of Francis Bacon (1561–1626) these two motifs are fused, for instance in his *New Atlantis* (1627). Biblical language concerning science and technology as a means of extending God's care and resisting the effects of sin is mixed with the humanistic hope that human progress is assured through the scientific and technological exploitation of nature. Nature is portrayed as female, and the human mind, gaining mastery over her, as male, a fact that has not escaped contemporary feminists and ecologists, who understandably connect Bacon's Christian comments with this dominative approach.

There is little doubt that in the modern era, despite some outstanding individual examples to the contrary, and despite the authentic social benefits accruing through such development, technological activity in general has been cut off from religious and often ethical concerns. The Machiavellian approach lying behind this sees technology only as a means to the end of wealth-creation and as justified by its contribution to the common good, and underplays themes like stewardship* of nature or economic justice and fairness.

Since at least Victorian times, technological advancement has been solidly identified with human progress, on both sides of the Atlantic. It is at once a political aspiration, to apply science and technology to all areas of life, and a means of explaining social change. Undoubtedly much drudgery and pain have been reduced through technological development, and the quality of life, as measured by material comforts and security, has improved dramatically. In its strongest utopian versions, however, technology would ensure the eventual abolition of scarcity and human conflict, beliefs that have reappeared in the late 20th century in programmes such as the 'green revolution' (to increase especially Third World crop yields) or space weaponry (the so-called defensive shield).

Technology's political role in the modern world also means that it has attracted criticism. For instance, technological advancement has enabled the 20th century to witness proportionately more war-deaths than ever before in human history. Under the guise of 'aid' to the 'less developed' parts of the world, technologically advanced societies often create new forms of dependency through 'technology transfer' programmes, which tend to tie recipients to donors. The dangers of over-reliance on technology or of permitting its unrestricted growth have been repeatedly questioned by humanists such as Aldous Huxley (1894–1963), Jeremy Rifkin (1945–) or Theodore Roszak (1933–), by neo-Marxists such as Herbert Marcuse (1898–1979) or Jürgen Habermas (1929–), and by Christians such as Jacques Ellul,* George Grant (1918–88) or C. S. Lewis.*

Technology today

Today technology is more central than ever to social, political and economic life. Two features mark it out from earlier times: 1. technology is science-based, depending not upon eccentric backyard tinkering but upon expensive research programmes sponsored by government and industry; and 2. it is ubiquitous and expands at an accelerating pace. So people in the advanced societies both depend upon (and enjoy the benefits of) plastic cards for shopping, upon cars, trains and planes for travel, and upon phones, satellites and TV for communication, and simultaneously understand very little about where these things came from or how they work.

Culturally, technology expresses some significant features of modernity. For some, it speaks of a certain control over a hostile environment, the ability to wrest from the earth the raw materials for continued human existence, and the celebration of the power of human intellect. For others, the connotations are less positive. The focus on means to the downgrading of ends, the emphasis on technique, the quest for a 'technological fix' – often to solve other problems caused by the development of new technologies – and the sense that political life is increasingly the domain of 'technocrats' are all examples of this. An area such as genetic engineering,* if severed from ethical constraint, would also express this focus, with antisocial if not inhuman results. The belief in human autonomy and power, manifest in technological development,

may be thought of as *technicism*.

In terms of the biblical framework outlined above, positive attitudes to technology may be related to the cultural mandate, though without a strong sense of the potential for misdirection this easily slips into hubris. Such hubris may be expressed as technicism, opposition to which draws on the broken-covenant theme. Lacking any reference to redemption, however, this oppositional stance frequently lapses into sheer technological pessimism. In this view, technology can be neither tamed nor transformed. The biblical viewpoint, significantly, stresses the salience of all three features – creation, broken covenant and redemption – in interpreting technological activity.

The main approaches to the social and ethical study of technology may be found on a spectrum between technological determinism and social construction. The former extreme views technology as a self-augmenting process, running according to its own inner logic, with the social aspects seen as mere effects of causal technology. The latter denies any independent role to technology, insisting instead that technological development may be explained in terms of the political, economic and cultural contexts in which it is rooted. In between are softer positions which admit to some relatively independent social or technological factors.

Ethical issues

Answers to two important ethical questions – Is technology neutral? and, Can technology be controlled? – relate in different ways to the above spectrum. For instance, some technological determinists believe that technology is neutral; everything depends on *how* it is applied. Those accepting that technology is socially shaped, such as some Marxists, would point to the value-ladenness of technology. Some analysts would follow the line that because technology is a social construction it can also be controlled and reconstructed. Others, such as Langdon Winner, say technology is a human creation but it has also got out of control.

It is hard to see how the technological neutrality position could be maintained from a Christian perspective; everything in a theistic universe is necessarily value-laden. More particularly, technology, whether as artefacts, technique or technical knowledge, is the product of purposive human activity. Biblically, it seems clear that technology should be done for the purposes of creation-care and human benefit and within the limits of the demands for justice and love (see ②). Technology not fulfilling these criteria should be the object of prophetic critique and positive alternative proposals.

Following from this, the quest for responsible technology is paramount, though exceedingly difficult. Human beings have no right to abrogate the duty to try to control and direct technology. True, existing technological conditions and consequences now act as complex constraints on what is possible. Moreover, some well-meaning alterations of practice in a discrete area may even seem to contribute overall to the technological system of Babel, given its global and interdependent character. But the worse danger lies in wilful ignorance, quietism* or neglect. Courage is required to counter technological trends and to offer other ways that enhance the environment, maintain human skills, foster better communication or protect and empower the vulnerable, and so on.

The debate over technology will continue to be central to political life in the 21st century. Christian contributions to this debate become increasingly important in contexts where secularization* has eroded and excluded the sense that there are any real norms to guide technological development. Both critical awareness, as advocated by Ellul and his followers, and the transformative involvement encouraged by writings such as S. V. Monsma's (1936–) *Responsible Technology* seem compatible with biblical commitment and appropriate for these times.

Bibliography

J. Ellul, *The Technological System* (ET, New York, 1980); C. Mitcham, 'The religious and political origins of modern technology', in P. Durbin and F. Rapp (eds.), *Philosophy and Technology* (Dordrecht, 1983); S. V. Monsma (ed.), *Responsible Technology* (Grand Rapids, 1986); E. Schuurman, *Technology and the Future* (Toronto, 1980); L. Winner, *Autonomous Technology: Technics-out-of-control as a Theme of Political Thought* (Cambridge, MA, 1977).

D.A.L.

TELEOLOGY. Literally, teleology refers to ends and goals, so that in moral decision-making a variety of teleological theories share a common principle that actions are to be judged in the light of an end or goal. For such theories an action is morally good if it serves to achieve the goal, and morally bad if it prevents the goal being achieved. In contrast to deontological* accounts of ethics, the teleologist looks to the consequences of actions rather than to any intrinsic goodness or badness in an action.

When it comes to identifying the ends and goals that will provide us with the yardstick against which to make our judgments, we can look to subordinate goals, *e.g.* gaining a better quality of life for the elderly, or an ultimate goal such as the glory of God.

We use subordinate goals frequently, looking at the possible outcomes of our actions when deciding on the action to be taken. Paul clearly used such goals as criteria in dealing with issues such as eating meat offered to idols (1 Cor. 8). The difficulty in such cases lies in knowing whether a given action will in fact achieve the desired end.

The variety of teleological theories is evidence of the problem of establishing ultimate goals. Whilst a major teleological theory such as utilitarianism (see Consequentialism*) appeals to happiness,* a Christian teleology rests on the concept of God as the *summum bonum*, with ethics as a response to such a God.

See also: PHILOSOPHICAL ETHICS.

Bibliography

I. C. M. Fairweather and J. I. H. McDonald, *The Quest for Christian Ethics* (Edinburgh, 1984); O. O'Donovan, *Resurrection and Moral Order* (Leicester and Grand Rapids, ²1994).

C.A.B.

TEMPERAMENT. The sum of our individual characteristics, which tend to lead to particular ways of thinking, acting and feeling, may be called 'temperament'. It is closely related to personality,* but emphasizes those aspects which are constitutional, inborn and inherited. If we know someone's temperament we can predict the way he or she will react in a given situation, to some extent.

Types of temperament

The oldest view (which is still found in use) is attributed to Galen (130–200) and is based on the ancient notion of four humours in the body which were thought, by their effects, to produce a typical temperament. Thus the melancholic, choleric, sanguine and phlegmatic types were described. This approach is best abandoned, but it lingers in the way we think of temperament as physically based. William H. Sheldon's (1898–1977) influential books sought to show that *physique and temperament* were related (*e.g.* W. H. Sheldon and S. Stevens, *The Varieties of Temperament*, London, 1942). He divided people physically into mesomorphs (average build), ectomorphs (short and stout) and endomorphs (tall and thin). He sought to relate these physical characteristics to types of personality: his approach has not stood up to scientific scrutiny. Yet it persists, and it influenced the Ger. psychiatrist Ernst Kretschmer (1888–1964), who applied it to the idea that certain body types developed typical mental illnesses, a view that is not now accepted.

Carl Jung,* in his famous work *Psychological Types*, analysed many historical characters and offered his theory of *introversion and extroversion* to explain temperaments. He thought of them as thinking, feeling, sensation and intuitive subtypes of both his main categories. Jung thought that a person who was consciously extrovert might have an introverted life at the unconscious level. Hans Eysenck (1916–) spent a lifetime of research to show how he considered introversion and extroversion could be measured, and the results applied in the study of personality and psychiatric disorders.

In Eysenck's terms the stable extrovert is sanguine: sociable, outgoing, responsive, lively and a good leader. If he becomes unstable, the extrovert suffers because he becomes like the choleric person: impulsive, excitable, aggressive, restless and touchy. The introvert, if stable, is careful, thoughtful and controlled, reliable and calm (*i.e.* phlegmatic). If he becomes unstable, the introvert becomes unsociable, pessimistic, rigid, anxious and moody (*i.e.* melancholic).

Raymond B. Cattell (1905–) had earlier sought to measure *temperamental traits* and had used factor analysis extensively in his scientific study of personality; his views have not been put to as much use as Eysenck's, though they are in some ways similar. Traits themselves have been seen as those observed and consistent features of our behaviour as individuals which, when taken together, add up to a type of temperament.

Jung was careful to say that we were all on a continuum between the extremes of extroversion and introversion. This is borne out by Eysenck and others who have devised personality questionnaires which can be used to measure our traits and yield a score in terms of various factors (*e.g.* neuroticism,* extroversion and psychoticism*).

Understanding temperaments

In terms of personality, knowing enough about temperament may help us to diagnose and understand a person with personality problems (or, if psychiatrically ill, a personality disorder). Thus a psychopathic* personality disorder exists in someone whose temperament shows persistent asocial or antisocial tendencies to offend, and may suffer legal punishment. By the same token, a cyclothymic temperament may have many mood swings without necessarily having a bipolar or manic-depressive illness.

Intelligence and a spectrum of abilities is often clearly linked to temperament. These features may influence our experience of God's grace, and religious belief and experience generally. The classical view is that temperament does not change with the new birth and the new creation, but a person's inherent abilities are put to new use, and serve a new master. It may be easier for some than for others to learn to live in a way that produces an exemplary character. Yet each temperament requires its own discipline and has its own special besetting risks in terms of behaviour, temptation and fulfilment. This has long been known to counsellors and those involved in spiritual direction.* The approach to a rigid obsessional introvert will need to be quite different from that taken towards a devil-may-care extrovert.

Bibliography

H. J. Eysenck and M. W. Eysenck, *Personality and Individual Differences: A Natural Science Approach* (London, 1985); P. Fonaghy and A. Higgitt, *Personality Theory and Clinical Practice* (London, 1984); C. G. Jung, *Psychological Types* (London and Princeton, NJ, 1971).

G.D.

TEMPERANCE, properly understood, has always been thought a distinct virtue* of the Christian life. It is also named as one of the four Platonic cardinal virtues. The

Christian understanding of the role of temperance differs in significant ways from that of Plato.* For Plato, temperance functions to discipline inordinate appetites (*e.g.* food or drink) or passions (*e.g.* anger or lust) through the instruction of reason and the power of the will. For Paul and the other apostles, these natural powers prove insufficient due to the impairment of sin: the redemption of the Christ is required (Rom. 7 – 8; 2 Pet. 1:3–4). Temperance, or self-control, is at once a distinctive mark of the character of Jesus and a 'fruit of the Spirit' (Mt. 11:18–19; Gal. 5:22–25; Eph. 3:14–21; 1 Pet. 1:13–16).

While temperance in the sense of moderation and self-control is praised in the NT (*sōphrosynē*, 1 Tim. 2:9; *egkrateia*, Gal. 5:23; 2 Pet. 1:6), it is difficult practically to specify very precisely *all* the actions that embody this virtue, or *each* act that is intemperate. Clearly, forbidden actions like adultery or stealing cannot be indulged moderately: the same is true for evil passions like envy, lust or greed. And the highest expressions of love (*agapē*) are immoderate; the self-denials they often require, too, are intemperate. The identification of temperance with abstinence* in the use of alcohol (as in the temperance movement in the 19th century) has had the unfortunate effect of obscuring the sense of proportion and of moral discernment that is an essential feature of temperance. In view of these considerations, the traditional idea that temperance is a virtue having particular reference to pleasures of the senses is helpful. (*Cf.* Thomas Aquinas, *STh* 2a2ae 141–170.) To the degree that Christians find it difficult to control their desires for pleasure,* they need to recognize: 1. that the pleasures of the senses are gifts of God; 2. that over-indulgence can weaken their love for God and neighbour; and 3. that unlike abstinence, temperance requires them to practise a discerning self-discipline of their sensuous experience that the gracious power of the Holy Spirit will confirm and strengthen.

M.A.R.

TEMPLE, WILLIAM (1881–1944) was the son of a former Archbishop of Canterbury, Frederick Temple (1821–1902). He was one of the most influential leaders of the Christian church in the 20th century. After a distinguished academic career, he became Bishop of Manchester in 1921, and thereafter Archbishop of York in 1929 and Archbishop of Canterbury in 1942. His tragic death in

1944 robbed the church of one of its greatest archbishops, just at a time when he might have influenced the way the church shaped its life in the post-war era.

The years of Temple's episcopate were turbulent. The years following the Great War of 1914–18 saw economic and political instability, mass unemployment, the rise of the Labour movement, and the collapse of the old order. The church had been badly shaken by the experience of the World War. It was to be further challenged by both social unrest and change and by the rise of Fascism. Temple's capacity to understand the significance of these movements, to respond to them with clear and lasting theological insight, and to help the church begin the task of facing these challenges ecumenically and internationally, made him an ecclesiastical statesman of unrivalled vision and ability.

Temple's prolific writing revealed the intellectual status of the man. His *Christianity and Social Order* (Harmondsworth, 1942) brought a theological contribution to the growing body of political thought looking for a new order once the war was over. His *Readings in St John's Gospel* (London, 1939–40) reveal his pastoral insight, and his *Nature, Man and God* (London, 1934) his theological vision.

Bibliography

F. A. Iremonger, *William Temple, Archbishop of Canterbury* (London, 1948).

J.W.G.

TEMPTATION. The primary idea in the biblical term 'to tempt' is 'to test' or 'to put on trial'. Temptation is a test that comes to us every day of our lives, from different sources and with different purposes. God sometimes brings us into times of testing, which test our character, our maturity and the reality of our Christian claims, and sometimes into trials to refine us (Ps. 66:10) and strengthen us yet further (Rom. 5:3–5; 1 Pet. 5:10–11) even when, as in the cases of Abraham and Job, our integrity and stature already please and honour him (*e.g.* Gn. 22:1; Jb. 1:8). The tests of God in life may take us through experiences of persecution (1 Pet. 4:12), sickness (2 Cor. 12:7) and loss (Jb. 1:13–19; 2:7). In times of testing there is real danger of self-pity, anger,* unbelief and loss of opportunity (*e.g.* 2 Ki. 20:1–21; 2 Ch. 32:31). Such testing times, however, may lead us to our highest point in

honouring, serving and knowing God (Jas. 1:2–4).

More often we use the term 'temptation' to indicate seduction to sin, and here it is Satan* who figures prominently (1 Thes. 3:5; 1 Pet. 5:8), enticing us away from God, from faith in him, from his fellowship and standards, and from his direction for our lives; and seducing us into sin which grieves and dishonours our God. To ignore the part of Satan in temptation is to forget Scripture and to play into his hands (Mt. 4:3; 1 Pet. 5:8–10; *cf.* 2 Cor. 2:11). While Satan may seek to confuse us at the intellectual level with heresy, half-truths and ideological distortions (Mt. 4:6; 1 Cor. 7:5; Gal. 3:1; 1 Jn. 4:1–6), he also (and often more fatally) seeks to manipulate us at more hidden levels of our being: the levels of desire, impulse, instinct, prejudice and fear* (*cf.* Eph. 4:17–19; 5:3–14; 1 Pet. 4:3–6; 1 Jn. 2:13–17). He hates God and he hates humankind, which was made for God and in his image (Gn. 3:4–5; Jb. 1:9–11; 1 Jn. 3:8; Rev. 9:11 mg.; 12:10). He strives to keep fallen, rebellious people from being reconciled with God; and so to seal our eternal loss (2 Cor. 4:4). Hence he opposes the work of Christ at every stage. In all this, however, there are limits to his power, but no limits to our resources in God (Jn. 16:33; 1 Cor. 10:13; 1 Jn. 4:4; 5:18–20).

Temptation also comes from within (Mk. 7:20–23); 'self' ruthlessly pursues its own goals: 'the cravings of sinful man, the lust of his eyes and the boasting of what he has and does' (1 Jn. 2:16). But in so doing it falls foul of others who are in a similar state (Rom. 1:29–31; 3:10–18) and of Satan who adeptly manipulates the situation for our common destruction.

The Christian is not free from temptation in any of the above aspects: God tests, Satan entices and sin stirs in the heart. Consequently Christ warns his followers to 'Watch and pray' against temptation at all times (Mk. 14:38). Though the new birth has truly changed our identity, making us children of God (Jn. 1:10–13; Gal. 3:26 – 4:7), and though the Holy Spirit dwells within us at the centre of our being (Rom. 8:9–10), the total transformation of our lives, inner and outer, is as yet incomplete. We still have old tendencies to think or act or desire in independence from God and in correspondence with the world around us, and its priorities and standards (Eph. 4:22–25). Hence conscience* needs to be educated by the gospel (*cf.* Acts 24:16) and enlivened by the Holy Spirit (*cf.* Rom. 9:1). Personal responsibility* in resisting temptation to sin must also be accepted (Rom. 6:11–13), it being recognized that temptation is not sinful *per se* (Jas. 1:13–15; *cf.* Mt. 4:1–11).

Power to resist temptation is available through Christ our great High Priest, who prays for us constantly and effectively, and whose prayers in heaven protect and inspire our lives on earth both individually and collectively as his people (Lk. 22:31–32; Jn. 17:15–21; Heb. 2:18; 4:15; 7:25; *cf.* Rom. 8:33–34). On the basis of his decisive victory at the cross (Col. 2:15), Christ will have complete triumph in the final judgment (Rev. 20:3, 7, 10; 21:3–4, 26–27).

Today Christians in the Western world in particular face temptations which have been fuelled by modern philosophies such as nihilism* and relativism,* fashionable materialism and the sexual revolution. In our response to these we have been tempted further to reactionary extremes of worldliness* on the one hand and pietistic* withdrawal on the other. Our proper response to these temptations is one which is rooted in an understanding of biblical truth, a commitment to God's priorities, and a firm obedience to the Lord Jesus Christ's demands for purity of heart and integrity of life (Mt. 5:13–16).

Bibliography

D. Bonhoeffer, *Temptation* (ET, London, 1955); C. Durham, *Temptation* (Downers Grove, IL, 1984; London, 1985); O. Guinness, *The Gravedigger File* (Downers Grove, IL, and London, 1983); C. S. Lewis, *The Screwtape Letters* (London, 1942); J. Owen, *Of Temptation* (1658), in W. H. Goold (ed.), *The Works of John Owen*, vol. 6 (repr. London, 1965–66).

P.H.L.

TEN COMMANDMENTS, see DECALOGUE.

TERESA, MOTHER (1910–). Mother

Teresa of Calcutta, born in Skopje (then in Yugoslavia, now in Macedonia) and christened Ganxhe Agnes Bojaxhiu, was the daughter of a merchant who died young. His widow provided an outstanding example of hard work, compassion for the poor and sick, and a strong Roman Catholic faith. Committed to the life of the church from childhood,

Mother Teresa had an early vocation for missionary work in India: she joined the Loreto Sisters and sailed for Calcutta in 1928.

The work that was to bring her (unwanted) world fame and the 1979 Nobel Peace Prize began after many years spent teaching and supervising nuns. In 1946 she received a 'call within a call' and was permitted to leave the convent to serve 'the poorest of the poor'. In 1948, after nursing training, she began her work among the teeming poor and dying of Calcutta's slums, dressing in a sari and adopting a frugal lifestyle. The Missionaries of Charity, whose work is now world-wide, were instituted in 1950.

A strict traditionalist, her stance on ethical issues, notably abortion,* is firm and vocal. She has challenged many Western governments to consider their unacknowledged welfare failures: in 1968 Pope Paul VI (1963–78; b. 1897) invited her to open a House for the Destitute in Rome. Her ministry emphasizes the sacramental nature of suffering and the divine presence in every individual, however disadvantaged: to dress the wounds of a Calcutta beggar is to dress the wounds of Christ. Passages in her writings have implied that suffering has a redemptive function.

Bibliography
D. Porter, *Mother Teresa: The Early Years* (London, 1986).

D.R.L.P.

TERMINAL ILLNESS, see DEATH AND DYING; HOSPICE.

TERRORISM is the use of unpredictable violence,* often directed against innocent bystanders, in order to achieve political objectives by creating a climate of terror. It has to be distinguished from insurgency as a whole, including armed revolutionary movements, guerrilla movements and wars of liberation. Terrorism is one of the methods often used by insurgents. But it is worth noting that terror has also been used by governments and not only by forces of opposition. Some revolutionary forces, on the other hand, eschew the use of terror, or place substantial limits on terrorist action.

Terrorism is not simply a 20th-century phenomenon. Its history goes back before the French 'Reign of Terror' (1793–94), and also includes the Ku Klax Klan and anarchist groups in the 19th century. However, two features of modern times are probably key factors in the growth of terrorist activities from, say, 1945: 1. The technology of modern weapons, both guns and explosives, makes terrorism much easier to carry out. 2. Terrorists use the mass media to gain publicity for their activities and goals; violent acts are seen as a key way of gaining public impact for their cause.

The anatomy of terrorism is not easy to analyse. The use of terror by governments or occupying forces differs in many ways from its use by revolutionaries or anarchists. The aims and methods of such groups also vary considerably. For instance, the Baader-Meinhof gang of the former West Germany, the IRA in N. Ireland, and the Sendero Luminoso (the 'Shining Path') in Peru all differ from each other in a number of respects. The Baader-Meinhof gang were an anarchist (see Anarchy*) group with no simply defined cause. The Sendero Luminoso have succeeded in gaining control of substantial areas of Peru with their highly destructive revolutionary methods. The IRA have employed violent methods, perhaps in a somewhat more discriminating way, to try to promote the political reunification of Ireland. The three diverge in terms of ideology, aims and precise methods. All that they have in common is a readiness to use violence as an essential means.

It is not hard to arrive at a negative moral verdict on terrorism. There can certainly be no justification for it using just-war* criteria. There are several obvious reasons for this. Decisively, terrorism attacks civilians, those who play no part in the political issue allegedly being contested. The attempt to serve a political cause by creating a climate of fear and anxiety cannot be justified no matter how noble the cause. Such means cannot be the way of love or justice. The political reasoning of terrorist groups may also be questioned. It is hard to see how the violence employed can serve to create the conditions for the loyal and peaceable agreement which is necessary to a healthy political life. Terrorist violence, in other words, is counter-productive. Both reason and experience suggest that violence provokes further violence. Nor is it easy to point to historical examples of successful political regimes which have endured for long on such foundations, even if terror may sometimes seem effective in a certain limited way in the short term.

It is true that theologians have occasionally

lent support to terrorist methods. Most notably, theologians of liberation have been accused of doing so. As a generalization, this is an unfair accusation. Liberation theology* has a number of contrasting views on the question of violence. Its theologians range from the pacifism of Helder Camara (1909–), through the careful just-war approaches of Gustavo Gutiérrez (1928–) or José Míguez Bonino (1924–) (for instance), to the cynical pragmatism of Juan Luís Segundo (1925–), and the open participation of Camilo Torres (1929–66) in revolutionary acts. Torres gave up the priesthood to become a guerrilla, and died in combat. However, in none of these does one find any justification for the random violence of terrorism. Rather, there is a variety of ways of using arguments typical of various strands of just-war thought in order to arrive at a Christian outlook.

Of these, Segundo comes closest to offering grounds on which terrorism might be defended. He reasons that violence is endemic in society, in that all our socially defined relationships depend on violence in some sense. Violence must be considered on a continuum, and the absence of physical constraint does not necessarily mean the absence of violence. To this Segundo adds the claim that 'the end justifies the means'; that no action is inherently wrong but can only be considered in relation to its goal. Even on this basis, a terrorist would have to show how good could come from the evil and suffering caused. This would be hard to do, for reasons given above. Nevertheless, Segundo's two arguments must be rejected on Christian grounds. 1. To redefine the language of violence as he does blurs over important distinctions which must be kept clear. 2. Christian moral thought does not accept that actions can be justified simply by their effects. On the contrary, there are things that should never be done, including the random violence of terrorism.

Guerrilla wars, revolutions and wars of liberation do not always depend on terrorist methods. The moral criteria by which insurgency movements in general should be judged are essentially those of the just-war theory. For instance, the urgency and weight of the cause, in terms of injustice and suffering, have to be weighed against the destruction and disorder of revolution. Whether there is reasonable prospect of success, and of achieving a better state of affairs in the end, must be carefully considered. The methods of insurgency should also be judged by just-war criteria. It can never be finally ruled out that there may be a moral case to be made for a just revolution in some rare circumstances. But just-war theory offers no support for terrorism, whether on the part of government or on the part of groups of opposition.

Moral questions are often raised in connection with the combating of terrorism. Normal policing methods may be inadequate, and legal processes may seem to need adapting for various reasons. Moral judgments cannot be divorced from the technicalities, but two comments may safely be made. 1. It is always better to preserve normal methods wherever possible, to preserve civil rights and liberties. 2. A key point in struggles against insurgency is often the battle for the political loyalty of the population. The need is to win the 'hearts and minds' of the public, and counter-terrorism must always remember this. Nevertheless, terrorism challenges the social order in a particularly negative way, and exceptional methods may be needed in order to combat it.

Bibliography

J. Ellul, *Violence: Reflections from a Christian Perspective* (ET, New York, 1969; London, 1970); D. C. Rapoport and Y. Alexander (eds.), *The Morality of Terrorism: Religious and Secular Justifications* (Oxford, 1982); J. L. Segundo, *The Liberation of Theology* (ET, London and Maryknoll, NY, 1976); M. Taylor, *The Terrorist* (London, 1988); P. Wilkinson, *Terrorism and the Liberal State* (London, 1977).

D.J.E.A.

TERTULLIAN (*fl. c.* AD 196– *c.* AD 212). A native of Carthage in N. Africa, Tertullian became a Christian about AD 190. Nothing is known for certain about his background, although it is clear from his writings that he belonged to the upper classes. Over thirty of his books have come down to us, covering a wider range of subject matter than those of any other Christian writer before the time of Constantine.* The first major Christian writer to use Lat., Tertullian was responsible for inventing much of the theological vocabulary still used by Western Christian theologians. It is generally believed that he left the main body of the church shortly after AD 200, to join the sect of the Montanists, a millenarian body which practised the strictest form of ascetical* morality. However, there are important differences between Tertullian's writings and those of the Montanists, and Tertullian's moral rigidity was apparent long before he came into contact with that sect, so that the precise nature of his relationship to them remains uncertain. It is not known when he died, or in what circumstances.

Tertullian derived his ethical norms from a combination of the OT and Stoicism,* with a tinge of Montanism in his later works. His main belief was that God had called Christians to a life of holiness in imitation of the divine substance. He stressed that it was the duty of Christians to demonstrate that their righteousness was greater than that of the scribes and Pharisees, a command which he interpreted to mean that Christians should adhere more strictly to the precepts of the divine law. He referred to the gospel as a 'new law' (*nova lex*), and regarded the indulgence of the apostles towards such matters as the remarriage of widows as temporary concessions, to be withdrawn when the reign of the Paraclete began.

This reign, Tertullian believed, had come in his own time, and he interpreted the prophecies of Montanus as a sign of the imminence of the Parousia. Because of this, married couples were to live as single people. Among his arguments for this was one which stated that a pregnant woman would remain in that condition in eternity, should Christ return before she gave birth! Children were not to be baptized, because of the danger of losing their salvation through inadvertent post-baptismal sin. Tertullian believed that there could be no forgiveness for believers who had lapsed, and this governed his rigorous attitude towards those who took flight or recanted temporarily in times of persecution.

Tertullian extended his legal (see Legalism*) approach to every aspect of life, including matters of dress and behaviour. He wrote an entire treatise to demonstrate that Paul's command to women to cover their heads should apply to the unmarried as well as to the married, and he was also extremely censorious of Christians who attended the theatre or the public games. In a very real sense, he may be claimed as the ancestor of what has come to be called the 'Puritan' tradition of morality in the Western church.

Bibliography

T. Barnes, *Tertullian* (Oxford, 1975); G. L. Bray, *Holiness and the Will of God: Perspectives on the Theology of Tertullian* (London and Atlanta, 1979).

G.L.B.

TESTAMENT, see Wills.

TEST-TUBE BABIES, see Reproductive Technologies.

THEFT is the dishonest appropriation of property* belonging to another, with the intention of permanently depriving the owner of it, and against the owner's reasonable consent. Aggravated forms of theft include robbery (when accompanied by the threat or use of force), burglary (when the thief has entered a building as a trespasser), and fraud (when the property is obtained by deception). Many of the moral considerations which apply to theft also obtain in cases of blackmail, extortion, handling stolen goods, denying workers their just wages, charging usurious rates of interest, and the like.

What makes theft wrong?

In common with perhaps universal moral understanding, the biblical writings regard theft as wrong. It is condemned in the eighth commandment of the Decalogue (Ex. 20:15, though this may refer to the kidnapping of persons) and appears in other OT lists of sins or crimes (Lv. 19:11, 13; Je. 7:9; Ho. 4:2; *etc.*). In the NT theft is one of the evil designs that come out of the human heart (Mk. 7:21), and thieves are among those who will not inherit the kingdom of God* (1 Cor. 6:10). Aside from its often being an expression of covetousness* (Jos. 7:21; Mi. 2:2) or laziness (Eph. 4:28), Scripture condemns theft for being unloving (Rom. 13:9–10) and unjust (*cf.* Is. 10:2).

Behind these general concerns, however, may be discerned more specific reasons for the prohibition of theft:

1. Theft is an injustice with regard to property: where there is no property there can be no theft, and what makes theft wrong is in part what makes property right. The institution of property in general should be understood as a means to the stewardship* of the natural world and the well-being of all people through their engagement with material things; conversely, at this broad level, theft may be understood as a wrong against these goods. Similarly, private property, as a subordinate category of property

in general, may be defended as being (in most historical circumstances) a suitable means of realizing these social and ecological goals. Thus permitting theft would deny all the things which private property is argued to safeguard: it would make it impossible to enjoy the fruits of one's labour, deny the significant role which possessions may play in forming one's identity, hinder the proper use of the earth's riches, allow the exploitation of the weak by the strong, imperil peace and security, and so on.

2. Theft is an injustice with respect to fair dealings between people. It essentially involves dishonesty, whether this be in the form of deception, secrecy, breach of agreement, bafflement through complexity, covert manipulation of desires, or of other failures of truthfulness or impartiality between persons. Beyond that, it can cause fear, hatred, unhappiness, the desire for revenge, the breakdown of trust and security, the need for expenditure on law and order, and a general deterioration in the common welfare.

Is theft ever justified?

For these reasons, all theft in the sense defined above is wrong. Nevertheless, the subordination of property rights to the prior demands of stewardship and human well-being suggests that there may be circumstances in which expropriating the property of others may be justified. In contrast with the classical Roman law idea of ownership as complete and final control over a thing and the modern capitalist notion of 'absolute' property rights, this emphasis on the social purpose of property not only lays obligations upon property-owners but also confers rights on those in extreme necessity. Thus Thomas Aquinas* allowed that in a case of urgent need (*e.g.* if a person would otherwise die of starvation), the lack might legitimately be supplied from somebody else's surplus property. Such would not be an example of theft, but of justified expropriation, since the owner's refusal to consent to the appropriation could not be regarded as reasonable.

The vast majority of cases of theft could not be justified by appeal to this principle, and it offers no support for a culture of theft. Nor should it be confused with the idea that property which is surplus to an owner's needs may thereby be rightfully stolen (one may not steal even from people who have no title to the thing stolen), or that neglecting to honour the social obligations inherent in one's property is itself a

form of theft (such a failure, while wrong [*cf.* 1 Jn. 3:17] is not theft, inasmuch as theft is an act of commission). In general, however, the prohibition of theft is rightly seen within the context of right ownership. This counsels contentment with what one possesses, yet also requires that one does not exploit others, but helps them to get what is properly theirs, in order that there may be a community in which under God the goods of each are maintained for the good of all.

See also: COPYRIGHT.

R.J.So.

THEOCRACY literally means 'rule by God'. The term is not found in the Bible but was coined by Josephus (*theokratia, Contra Apion* II.16.165) to describe rule in ancient Israel. He contrasted monarchies, oligarchies and republics to God's direct involvement in Israelite affairs. Josephus' view is ambiguous, since in the same place he describes Moses as 'our law-giver'. He thus confused God's role as the *ultimate source* of authority* with the (usually) human role as mediator of that authority. This confusion has plagued the term ever since.

In popular usage, 'theocracy' it has become a term of condemnation. The sociologist Karl Mannheim (1893–1947) thought that its major purpose was now to provide secularists with a word to condemn supposedly repressive, religiously-shaped societies and movements. Currently it is often used to stigmatize groups, such as Shiite Muslims or the Moral Majority, thought to be authoritarian and doctrinaire. More responsibly, G. W. F. Hegel (1770–1831) used it to describe ancient civilizations which had no distinction between the realms of religion and State. Scholars often apply it generally to States with a strong religious identity, to the union of church and State, to the exercise of political authority by a priesthood, or where a king (like James I, 1603–25; b. 1566) claims a divine authority or right. Some authors have distinguished between general theocracy (rule by divine will or law), royal theocracy (rule by a sacred king), hierocracy (rule by priests or prophets), and eschatological theocracy (anticipated rule by the divine). Regimes described in these terms have included ancient Israel, pharaonic Egypt, Islam, Japan, China, Tibet, certain phases of the papacy, Calvin's Geneva and New England Puritanism.

When the word is used in these loose senses, it is clear that OT Israel was a type of theocracy. Israel was covenanted as God's people and this shaped every dimension of their life. Yahweh was described as Israel's king, ruler and judge (Dt. 33:5; Is. 33:22), while Israel was God's army who fought God's wars (Ex. 7:4; Nu. 21:14). The patriarchs, priests, legislators, judges, kings and prophets all derived their authority from God and, in turn, God's relation with Israel is described by analogy to these offices (Ex. 19:6; Dt. 17:14–20; Jdg. 8:23; 1 Sa. 8:7; 2 Sa. 7:1–17). In the NT, the church can also be described as a theocracy. Christ is its head and the source of all its authority (Eph. 5:23–24), while leaders must always be leaders 'in the Lord' (1 Thes. 5:12). Both Paul and Peter stress the divine origin and foundation of political authority (Rom. 13:1–8; 1 Pet. 2:13–17).

If we use the term with more precision and accuracy, then many of the distinctions noted above break down. Societies where the source of political authority is held to be God, or God's revelation* or God's law,* include many more than those usually described as theocratic. God's sovereignty can be mediated and exercised not only by priests and kings, but by judges, prime ministers, elected legislators or the population itself. Many theories of democracy, such as that of John Locke (1632–1704), hold that the people exercise a political authority derived from God's ownership of their lives. A good number of Western constitutional democracies hold that their laws should reflect a divine or natural law. The American Declaration of Independence speaks of political authority ('rights') as being given by 'Nature's God'. The recent Canadian Constitution speaks of itself as founded on the 'supremacy of God'. It is quite possible to be a representative democracy and a so-called 'theocracy' at the same time.

If the term is used precisely, there are few instances of actual theocracies. Direct rule by God would seem to require something like continuing theophany, oracular command or 'divine' humans. Examples of continuing theophany can be found in the OT before the time of Noah (ending perhaps at Gn. 9:6). Examples of rule by 'divine' humans might be pharaonic Egypt, imperial Rome and imperial Japan.

As Jesus is both human and divine, the embryonic church* while he was on earth would have been an instance of genuine theocracy. This may also be the case when the Holy Spirit leads directly in the church today. But few people, including charismatics, believe that this is the only form of church rule, and most accept the need for some officially recognized mediation of the divine will.

As the term is subject to confusion and abuse, and as there is little indication that God desires a theocracy in the precise sense, then it would be better to describe both churches and States by their particular form of polity (e.g. monarchy, constitutional democracy, episcopal, congregational) and to drop, or severely restrict, the word 'theocracy' altogether.

Bibliography
J. C. Brauer, 'The Rule of the Saints in American Politics', *CH* 27, 1958, pp. 240–255; M. Fakhry, 'The Theocratic Idea of the State in Recent Controversies', *International Affairs* 30, 1954, pp. 450–462; R. J. S. Hoffman, 'Theocratic Heresy in Politics', *Thought* 24, 1949, pp. 389–394; H. Frankfort, *Kingship and the Gods: A Study of Ancient Near Eastern Religion* (Chicago, 1948); C. J. Friedrich, *Transcendent Justice: The Religious Dimensions of Constitutionalism* (Durham, NC, 1964); D. D. Wallace, *ER* 14, pp. 427–430.

P.A.M.

THEODICY. How can God be both good and almighty, when there is so much evil* in the world? The word 'theodicy', meaning 'justice of God', was coined by Gottfried von Leibniz (1646–1716) to refer to the work of defending the idea of a just God in the face of what seems contrary evidence. Leibniz himself argued that God, being perfectly good, must have created the best of all possible worlds; any alteration in this world (as a whole – past, present and future) for the better in one respect would entail making it worse in some other. This has not convinced many. It seems absurd to say that this world could not be improved in any way whatever. Indeed, the idea of a 'best possible world' may be as absurd as that of a 'largest possible number'; however great the good in the world, surely there could always be more of it? Moreover, this view seems to rule out human free will (see Free Will and Determinism*); our decisions must be controlled by God in order to produce this best possible world.

Others have sought to define 'good' or 'just' in terms of God's will. If 'just' means 'decreed by God', then by definition nothing God decrees can be unjust. But this means that atheists can never use the word 'just' meaningfully, as they do not believe there is a God to decree anything; and clearly they can and do. Moreover, it seems to imply that it simply happens to be the case that God has commanded love and forbidden murder; he could perfectly well have done the opposite, in which case love would have been a sin and murder virtuous.

The idea that all well-being and suffering are deserved, decisively rejected in the book of Job, has more plausibility in religions like Hinduism and Buddhism, which believe in reincarnation; might the good and evil we undergo, which has not been merited in this life, have been merited by what was done in a previous one? But even so it is hard to see how God could justly punish someone who is now good, or reward someone now evil, for deeds of which he or she has no knowledge whatever.

Some (most recently 'process' theologians, but also, earlier, some of the 'personal idealists' such as Hastings Rashdall, 1858–1924, and E. S. Brightman, 1884–1953) have suggested that God is in some way limited in power. This would certainly allow a full insistence on his goodness, but it is hard to see just what limits there could possibly be on God's power which would be relevant to the existence of evil.

The most usual form of theodicy among Christians has been the argument that God has allowed some evil (in a world itself overwhelmingly good) for the sake of a greater good that could not be achieved without it: specifically, in order to give those created in his image* freedom* to grow in love and goodness. The possibility of wrongdoing must be there if choice is to be genuine; and some evils must exist in the natural world as by-products of the laws of nature, and for the sake of qualities like love and compassion. It has become common to distinguish between 'Augustinian' views, which see evil as brought into a perfect world by the sin of Adam, and 'Irenaean', which see the world, including Adam, as created good but incomplete and requiring human progress (which the Fall hindered) for its perfection; but these are in practice agreed on the centrality of human responsibility* and the goodness of the divine purpose.

It has also been pointed out that, whatever God's reasons for allowing evil in the world, Christians believe he has not left the world to bear it alone, but has in the incarnation, and above all on the cross, shared its burden with his creation.

See also: PAIN.

Bibliography

E. S. Brightman, *A Philosophy of Religion* (London and New York, 1947); P. T. Geach, *Providence and Evil* (Cambridge and New York, 1977); J. Hick, *Evil and the God of Love* (London, 21977); G. W. von Leibniz, *Essais de Théodicée* (1710; ET, London, 1951); U. Sharma, 'Theodicy and the Doctrine of Karma', in W. Foy (ed.), *Man's Religious Quest* (London, 1978); C. W. S. Williams, 'The Cross', in *The Image of the City* (Oxford, 1958).

R.L.S.

THEOLOGICAL VIRTUES. Faith,* hope* and love (*agapē*, see [2]), three pre-eminent graces of the Christian life identified by the apostle Paul in 1 Cor. 13:13, came to be named the three 'theological' virtues* in contrast to the four Platonic or natural virtues of wisdom,* courage,* temperance* and justice (*The Republic*, Bk. 4). By the 14th century, the theological virtues were combined with the Platonic virtues and called the seven cardinal virtues. In Dante's *Divine Comedy*, each is richly described in opposition to the seven deadly sins.*

To describe a virtue as 'natural' is to say that it is humanly conceived and acquired (no matter how fundamental it may be for the moral ordering of a soul or a society). To describe a virtue as 'theological' is to say that its distinctive quality as a virtue is rooted in the character of God (see [1]) and that it has been revealed, and may be bestowed, by God alone. While all virtues are settled, strong, inner dispositions or tendencies, natural virtues may be acquired through self-discipline and training, and theological ones are gifts of God inseparable from the presence of Christ in the life of the redeemed. Augustine* concluded that since the natural virtues have no reference to God, they are not true virtues at all but 'splendid vices'. Thomas Aquinas,* on the other hand, separates the theological virtues from the natural virtues.

Following Paul, Christian thinkers have consistently extolled love as the supreme virtue. Leading 20th-century moral theologians have added richly to our understanding of the theological virtues by exploring the distinctive character and function of faith (K. Barth, *Church Dogmatics*, II, III), of hope (J. Moltmann, *Theology of Hope*, ET, London, 1967), as well as of *agapē* (A. Nygren, *Agape and Eros*, ET, London and Philadelphia, 1953; G. Outka, *Agape: An Ethical Analysis*, New Haven, CT, and London, 1972), in ordering the personal and social life of Christians in the kingdom of God.*

M.A.R.

THEONOMY refers generally to divine rule or the situation of being so ruled. While derived from Gk. terms for 'God' and 'law', it is of recent vintage (from the 19th-century Ger. *Theonomie*) and is employed in a variety of ways. It has more technical, general and particular uses.

Its more precise use in ethics claims that the ultimate source of authority* is God. In some versions it is akin to a 'divine command' theory of ethics, in which something is right or wrong simply because God has said so. This can be contrasted with an emphasis that ethical norms are inherent in the nature of things and, perhaps, that God is therefore also subject to such norms. William of Ockham (1280/5–1349) held that good and evil reflected God's will and that God could have willed that they be something entirely different. This emphasis on God's will, as distinct from God's reason, as the source of law* distances law from purported reasonableness. If authority is not authority by divine reason, it appears less likely to be in accord with human reason.* This makes it less likely that God's law would be discerned in the order of creation* or be congruent with human standards and perceptions. In turn, this tends to produce a greater reliance on revelation* and less on supplemental human reflection as a guide to conduct.

Theonomy in this sense is not accepted by all Christians. To some, especially Christians who stress the role of reason, it tends to lead to relativism* or divine capriciousness. In addition a supposed inability to go 'behind' the divine command, to find reasons for it, seems to preclude the possibility of developing general principles applicable to novel situations and, thus, potentially, could narrow the scope of divine command and law (*cf.* Rom. 2:14–15).

When theonomy is used in a broader sense, it is generally agreed to be a biblical concept. Both OT and NT proclaim God as the source of ethical norms. God was Israel's king, ruler and judge (Ex. 7:4; 19:6; Dt. 17:14–20; 33:5; Ps. 89:18; Is. 33:22). Jesus is the holder of all authority in heaven and earth, church and world (Rom. 13:1–3, esp. 13:1; Eph. 1:11; 5:23–24). While Israel's laws properly could and did vary with circumstances, their ultimate validity derived from God, who was the legal as well as the moral and practical sovereign.

In sociological literature the term 'theonomy' can be used in a fashion similar to 'theocracy'* and applied to societies where there is a divine, or semi-divine, ruler or where a church wields some political power. But if we distinguish God as the ultimate source of authority from the human mediators of that authority, then theonomy is in principle compatible with social forms as diverse as monarchy and democracy.

The expression 'Theonomists' is used in a particular way to refer to a movement, also called 'reconstructionism', influential in some evangelical and fundamentalist circles, especially in the US (see Christian Reconstruction Movement*). It stresses the continuing validity of OT law, except ceremonial law. This use of theonomy is a little unfortunate, as what is distinct about this movement is not its stress on the current validity of divine law (a stress common among Christians) but its claim that biblical law should be reimplemented with little allowance for changed historical circumstances.

Bibliography

G. L. Bahnsen, *Theonomy in Christian Ethics* (Phillipsburg, NJ, ²1984); W. S. Barker and W. R. Godfrey (eds.), *Theonomy: A Reformed Critique* (Grand Rapids, 1990); A. S. McGrade, *The Political Thought of William of Ockham* (Cambridge, 1974); O. O'Donovan, *Resurrection and Moral Order* (Leicester and Grand Rapids, ²1994); V. S. Poythress, *The Shadow of Christ in the Law of Moses* (Brentwood, TN, 1991).

P.A.M.

THERAPEUTIC COMMUNITY, see PRACTICAL AND PASTORAL THEOLOGY. [7]

THIRD-FORCE PSYCHOLOGY, see HUMANISTIC PSYCHOLOGY.

THIELICKE, HELMUT (1908–86), Ger. Lutheran theologian, was the author of a vast four-volume *Theological Ethics* (*TE*) over half of which has been translated into

English. A leading member of the Confessing Church, he won a considerable reputation as a popular preacher both during and after the Second World War. He is still best known in the English-speaking world for his memorable series of collected sermons, such as *The Waiting Father* (ET, Cambridge, 1960), on the parables of Jesus, and *The Prayer that Spans the World* (ET, Cambridge, 1965), on the Lord's Prayer. In 1954 he was appointed Professor of Systematic Theology at the University of Hamburg, where he lived and worked (more latterly as Professor Emeritus) till the end of his life. He also wrote a three-volume dogmatics, *The Evangelical Faith* (ET, Grand Rapids and Edinburgh, 1974–82).

Thielicke's TE is a comprehensive restatement of ethics from within the Lutheran tradition (see Lutheran Ethics*), the outcome of a self-set task of 'declining the doctrine of justification through all the case forms in which it appears within the grammar of our existence' (vol. 1, *Foundations*, ET, Philadelphia, 1966, and London, 1968, p. 14). After the opening volume, in which he lays his theological foundations with great care, he discusses in detail questions of politics, economics, sex, art and law.

Justification* for Thielicke signifies that the Christian stands no longer under the dictatorship of a legalistic 'You ought', but in the magnetic field of Christian freedom, under the empowering of the 'You may'. He or she lives under the gospel rather than under the law.* But the law still has regulative significance, in reminding one of the ways in which obedience may be exercised; the freedom which the Spirit brings is no caprice.

Fundamental to Thielicke's presentation of 'evangelical' ethics is the view that, as Christians, we stand in a field of tension between two aeons: the present world, which is one day to pass away; and the coming world, which will replace it and already makes inroads upon it. Christians are called out of their old lives into a new existence, notably by the very radical demands of the Sermon on the Mount.* But they still have to live in a far-from-perfect world with all the circumscriptions on action that it brings. They thus stand in a relationship both of continuity and discontinuity to the present era.

Thielicke explores this tension in two main ways, both characteristically Lutheran.

1. He uses the concepts of the *two kingdoms* and the *orders of creation*. God enacts his will in a different way in the sphere of the orders (*e.g.* the family, or the State) than he does in the sphere of redemption. The motive for Christian action should always be one of love, (see [2]) but this may sometimes be allied to force where, *e.g.*, it is necessary to discipline errant children, or take punitive action on the criminal. Thielicke links this to what he calls the Noachic ordinance in Gn. 9, whereby God 'condescends' to the fallen state of the world, tolerates the laws of conflict by which human beings live in the world, and makes use of force in order to restrain force. This emphasis gives Thielicke's social ethics a rather conservative hue.

2. He also explores this tension in terms of *borderline situations*. These are situations which illustrate the tensions of the fallen world most starkly, because they throw up dilemmas where it seems impossible to avoid sinful action. Thielicke gives some fascinating examples from the Nazi era, where those who resisted Nazism often resorted to devious means, and prisoners in concentration camps or doctors in mental institutions faced the quandary of whether to sacrifice some innocent people in the hope of saving others. Martin Luther's* understanding of the Christian as *simul justus et peccator* ('at the same time a justified man and a sinner'), and his advice in a letter to Philip Melanchthon (1497–1560), 'Sin boldly, but believe and rejoice in Christ even more boldly,' are central to Thielicke's approach here. The Christian should acknowledge the sinfulness which attaches to whatever option is undertaken, but nevertheless feel emboldened to act, confessing his or her sin, and secure in the promise of God's forgiveness.

Thielicke's attempt to provide a theological underpinning to ethical action is not without its problems, but it is certainly a distinctive approach, worthy of thoughtful study. His exploration of detailed areas of life appears more dated in contrast. *The Ethics of Sex*, where he emphasized the cruciality of the creative power of *agapē* for the outworking of the *erōs* relationship, and made influential contributions to discussion of homosexuality* and artificial insemination (see Reproductive Technologies*), is the volume which has attracted most interest.

Bibliography

The Ethics of Sex (ET, London and New York, 1964); *Theological Ethics*: vol. 1,

Foundations (abridged ET, Philadelphia, 1966; London, 1968); vol. 2, *Politics* (abridged ET, Philadelphia and London, 1969); and 3-vol. ed., including vol. 3, *Sex* (Grand Rapids, 1978).

R. Higginson, *The Contribution of Helmut Thielicke to Theological Ethics* (Manchester, 1982).

R.A.Hig.

THIRD WORLD AID. 'The Third World' is the term generally used to denote those countries listed by the World Bank as low-income and middle-income countries (otherwise known as the 'developing countries'). Following the World Evangelical Fellowship conference at Wheaton, IL, in 1983, prominent Third World theologians promoted the alternative term 'Two Thirds World', emphasizing a majority in terms of population, rather than inferiority in economic league tables. The same conference produced the concept of 'transformation' as a Christian, holistic alternative to development (see Economic Development*).

Willy Brandt (see Brandt Report*) identified twenty-nine least-developed countries particularly clustered in two poverty belts: across sub-Saharan Africa, and from the Yemen and Afghanistan eastwards through Central and Eastern Asia. In these countries average gross domestic product (GDP) per capita (at 1970 prices) was less than \$100; manufacturing accounted for less than 20% of GDP, and less than 20% of adults are literate. In addition, many of these countries face severe ecological problems, compounded by rapid population growth. Historically, much of the Third World has a recent colonial past, and present economic structures reflect the exploitative policies of the colonial powers (see Colonialism*).

Factors contributing to Third World poverty include the increasingly high levels of indebtedness of many countries (Africa's current debt is equivalent to 90% of the continent's gross national product [GNP], and debt servicing accounts for 30% of total export earnings). Another factor is the imbalance in the terms of trade (see International Trade*), where powerful industrial nations are able to ensure a rising standard of living for their citizens through manipulation of export prices, whilst the developing countries can only 'take what they can get' for their primary products. The pur-chasing power of their exports has been declining by about 2% each year since 1950. The Church of England's Board of Social Responsibility suggests that 'no more powerful mechanism (except perhaps slavery) . . . for transferring wealth from the poor to the rich has ever been invented . . .'

Third World Aid is essentially a post-colonial phenomenon, originally set in motion by the Bretton Woods (USA) conference in 1944, which led to the formation of the World Bank and the International Monetary Fund (L. Pearson, *Partners in Development*, p. 208). It has been characterized by a number of phases. In the late 1950s and 1960s the emphasis was on major industrial projects, modernization and 'trickle-down' development theories. This strategy was fired by both moral and political imperatives (the latter increasingly reflected Cold War alignments). In the 1970s the emphasis shifted to meeting basic needs (as underlined by the British Goverment's White Paper, 1975: *The Changing Emphasis in British Aid Policies: More Help to the Poorest*). The 1980s saw a shift towards new assumptions about market forces, and the growth of private initiatives (*e.g.* Band Aid) which tended to overshadow the 'collective moral response of the governments' (R. C. Riddell, *Foreign Aid Reconsidered*, pp. 6–11). In the 1990s official aid is becoming both more hard-nosed and more idealistic, governed by notions of 'conditionality', structural adjustment (particularly in Russia and Eastern Europe) and the tying of aid to notions of 'good government', including acceptance of respect for human rights (see Rights, Human*) and the growth of domestic processes.

Aid has generally been administered through a range of different agencies, categorized as 'multilateral' (UN agencies, World Bank, EU, *etc.*), 'bilateral' (government to government, *e.g.* the UK's Overseas Development Administration), and non-government (private and voluntary) organizations. The last include both secular and religious agencies. Amongst them are many distinctly evangelical organizations (Tear Fund, World Vision, Christian Outreach, *etc.*, as well as the many missionary societies), often working in partnership with local churches and organizations overseas.

Over the decades the moral imperative for aid has shifted from issues of *charity* to those of *justice*. There are strong biblical imperatives for both justice (see Justice and Peace[3]) and compassion* (*e.g.* see Dt. 16:20, and the teaching on the jubilee* in Lv. 25:8–54, which provides a very persuasive argument for a debt moratorium for poorer nations). Jesus' special regard for the poor (*e.g.* Lk. 4:18) provided a basis for social concern in the NT church. This is reflected for instance in Jas. 2:5–17. Paul's campaign to encourage the new churches in Greece, Macedonia and Asia to collect aid for the relief of the poorer brethren in Jerusalem and Judaea (then very much the 'third world' of the Roman Empire) provides a scriptural model for Christian involvement in Third World aid today (Rom. 15:25–29; 1 Cor. 16:1–4; 2 Cor. 1:16–17; 8:9).

See also: GLOBAL ETHICS. [15]

Bibliography
W. Brandt *et al.*, *North–South: A Programme for Survival* (London and Cambridge, MA, 1980); General Synod of the Church of England, *Let Justice Flow: A Contribution to the Debate about Development* (London, 1986); D. Hay, 'The International Socio-Economic Political Order and our Lifestyle', in R. Sider (ed.), *Lifestyle in the Eighties: An Evangelical Commitment to Simple Lifestyle* (Exeter and Philadelphia, 1982), pp. 84–128; P. Mosley, *Overseas Aid: Its Defence and Reform* (Brighton, 1987); L. Pearson *et al.*, *Partners in Development: Report of the Commission on International Development* (New York, 1969); R. C. Riddell, *Foreign Aid Reconsidered* (London, 1987); J. R. W. Stott, *Issues Facing Christians Today* (Basingstoke, ²1990) = *Involvement* (Old Tappan, NJ, ²1990); United Nations, *African Debt: The Case for Debt Relief* (New York, 1991).

I.R.W.

THOMAS AQUINAS (*c.* 1224–74), Dominican theologian, whose writings represent the greatest achievement of the mendicant movement in the 13th century. At that time the Western church was challenged from without by the expansion of the Islamic world and more especially by the Aristotelian worldview; from within, the church faced the increasing tension caused by the wealth of the papacy and the increasing urbanization* of society. The mendicant movements, most notably the Dominicans and the Franciscans, replaced Benedictine* monasticism* as the dominant spiritual power in the church. The Dominicans were primarily preachers, and Aquinas spent his life in Paris, Naples and other university centres teaching and writing for Dominican students.

Through contact with the Arabs, Western Europe had become aware of the writings of Aristotle.* These writings offered the West a far more powerful body of scientific knowledge than Europe had known up to that time. However, this science denied certain basic Christian beliefs, for Aristotle, at least as interpreted by some of his commentators, held that the world was eternal and the human soul mortal. A great debate ensued. Augustinians rejected Aristotle, but the Averroists or 'radical Aristotelians', went so far as to claim that to philosophize one must agree with Aristotle. In Aquinas' writings one finds a revised Aristotelianism in which he employs Aristotle's principles, even while revising or rejecting his conclusions. Using an Aristotelian methodology in theology was a radical innovation, which was challenged by Aquinas' contemporaries and is still condemned by some today.

For Aquinas, sacred theology is founded on Scripture, *i.e.* the canonical books, but because of the weakness of the human intellect it makes use of human reason* to clarify divine teaching. 'Grace does not destroy nature, but perfects it.' Natural reason serves faith. This can be seen when considering the question of the existence of God. For the theologian the issue is not whether God exists, but whether a proof of his existence is possible. Philosophers have shown that there is a first mover, a first efficient cause, *etc*. The theologian recognizes that these descriptions can apply to God alone, inadequate though they be.

Aquinas made an immense contribution to moral theology (see Christian Moral Reasoning [18]) by providing a comprehensive account of the moral life which drew on both the ancient philosophical tradition and the Gk. and Lat. Fathers. For him the goal of human life is happiness,* and happiness is found in the vision of God. This vision is not acquired by human effort, but rather through grace* and only in the future life. To attain this end, persons must act rightly. Aquinas analyses the nature and conditions of these actions, the role of the emotions and dispositions. Those dispositions that tend to good actions are virtues (see Virtue and Virtues*) and those which tend to bad actions are vices.*

Humankind is fallen (see Fall*). The essence of original sin* is that the will* of human beings is no longer subjected to God. From this disorder in the will follows disorder in all the other powers of the soul. This disorder is found mainly in 'concupiscence',* the disorder of desire which affects not only the appetites but also clouds and upsets reason.

Had humankind not fallen, the natural law,* which is an impression of the eternal law within us, would have sufficed for virtue, but now divine law as found in revelation* is necessary. The old law of the OT and the gospel of grace are the two forms of divine law.

Aquinas organizes the life under grace according to the theological and cardinal virtues. The theological virtues (see Theological Virtues*) of faith, hope and love are treated first, because through them persons are related directly to God. In this context the cardinal virtues – prudence, justice, fortitude and temperance* – are considered, for it is the relationship to God that provides the context for all other human actions and relationships to others.

In the discussion of each virtue, Aquinas also presents the corresponding gifts of the Spirit, vices opposed to the virtue and commands related to the virtue. Thus faith is a knowledge of God whose content is accepted because it is from God. This content is summarized in the Apostles' Creed. Faith's inner act is to believe; its outer act is to confess. From faith flow wisdom* and understanding as gifts of the Spirit. Among the vices opposed to faith are heresy, apostasy and blasphemy.* The other virtues are treated in similar fashion.

After treating human life, Aquinas discusses the work of Christ and the church. He agrees with those who say that the incarnation was ordered by God as a remedy for sin, so that the nature that was created good might be restored and perfected in the vision of God.

See also: REBELLION; HISTORY OF CHRISTIAN ETHICS; 6 THOMIST ETHICS.

Bibliography
Summa Contra Gentiles (ET, Notre Dame, IN, 1975); Summa Theologiae (ET, 60 vols. and Index, London and New York, 1964–81). F. Copleston, Aquinas (Harmondsworth, 1955).

A.G.V.

THOMIST ETHICS, the ethical tradition that has its origin in the moral thought of Thomas Aquinas.* While Aquinas treated moral issues in a number of his works, the most important of which is the entire second part of the Summa Theologiae, he usually discussed them in a theological context, where moral good and evil* are viewed in relation to the divine law* revealed in Scripture. Thomist ethics is the work of followers who use Aquinas' principles to confront other ethical traditions and current moral issues.

For Aquinas, ethics is concerned with human actions, but only those actions for which one is answerable or responsible, not the fortuitous and the unintended. Every action is done for some purpose, and such an end has the character of good. The good is desirable; it is sought because in some way it will fulfil the agent.

The directives or rules* that guide such actions are held to arise from human nature. Just as first principles, such as the law of non-contradiction, guide our theorizing, so precepts of practical reason,* such as 'The good is to be done, and evil avoided', guide our moral reasoning. Right reason is the criterion of ethical judgment. While Aquinas' ethics is often described as a natural-law* theory, it is perhaps better to describe it as an ethics in which right reason is the proximate standard and the eternal law of God the ultimate standard for action.

By their nature, humans are inclined to preserve their life, to reproduce, and to attain the good of reason, which is to know God and live in society. Human acts are good or bad depending on whether they attain or fail to attain these ends. Among ends there is an order, but the ultimate human goal is loving union with God in the beatific vision.

Bibliography
R. McInery, Ethica Thomistica (Washington, DC, 1982); J. Maritain, Moral Philosophy (ET, New York and London, 1964).

A.G.V.

THURNEYSEN, EDUARD (1888–1974). Swiss theologian and friend of Karl Barth,* Thurneysen wrote a major treatise on pastoral theology (see Practical and Pastoral Theology 7) from a Barthian perspective. A Theology of Pastoral Care (ET, Richmond, VA, 1962) argues that pastoral care exists within the church as the communication of the Word of God to individuals. Practical theology, alongside historical and systematic theology, is the doctrine of human proclamation which serves the divine Word, and of the human acceptance which is effected by this Word. Pastoral care is thus preaching in the broadest sense, though in a private form, accompanying the sermon and the sacraments as one of the signs by which the community of faith is established. The nature and form of pastoral care must therefore be a 'conversation' which leads from the Word of God, and on into its proclamation in the church, for the sanctification* and discipline* of individuals in the totality of their personalities. It is a listening and a responding to the Word of God as established by the incarnation of Christ, and a listening to the man who can come to understand his life in the light of Christ. Psychological, ethical and social dimensions of life must be placed under the judgment of the Word, though all these 'auxiliary tools' must be used in the evaluation of personal need. The centre of pastoral care is the communication of the forgiveness* of sins, a gift which is given through the Holy Spirit* and prayer.

Although providing a clearer theological foundation for pastoral care than some of his American contemporaries (such as Seward Hiltner*), Thurneysen has been criticized for too restrictive a view of the nature of pastoral ministry, and too limited a use of the human sciences.

See also: PASTORAL CARE, COUNSELLING AND PSYCHOTHERAPY. [12]

D.J.A.

TIME MANAGEMENT. Time is God's creation and God's gift. From this derive human responsibility and the measure of ultimate values. Like OT leaders who learned to manage their God-given lives and responsibilities (Gn. 41:37ff.; Ex. 18:17ff.; 1 Ki. 3:5ff.; Ne. 4:15ff.), Jesus lived consciously dependent on the Father's providential ordering of his time (Mt. 26:18; Jn. 2:4). Christians live in the 'last times', the era of the Spirit. Time has a divine purpose, affirmed in daily prayer (Ps. 90:12; Mt. 6:10) and discipleship (Eph. 5:15–16; 1 Pet. 4:7–10).

Time management can encourage discipleship, maturity and personal effectiveness. Time is a finite resource, given equally to every person. To take control of time can help one to take control of the whole self. There are skills which can be learned and procedures which can be followed in the management of time. Authors of materials on time management are not consistent in the vocabulary they use, though there is broad agreement on the issues that need attention. These include: 1. clarification of personal values and goals; 2. study of one's current use of time, leading to decisions about planning; and 3. development of skills with people, and skills in handling practical tasks.

There are fundamental beliefs that shape the way people direct their lives (both inside and outside of work). *Goals* are specific, measurable and achievable tasks towards which someone can work during an agreed time period. The priority any individual assigns to particular goals, and the manner in which these goals are accomplished, will vary according to how a person is motivated. The institutional setting will affect the extent to which personal goals are totally realizable, and also impose expectations regarding what those goals should be.

A 'log' of how time is used over a two-week period gives the raw material for *analysis* into suitable categories (meetings, reading, phone calls) and for evaluation (goals fulfilled, or time wasted by one's own indiscipline, unexpected visits by others, *etc.*).

Knowing when an individual works best, and knowing what tasks have priority, are the two keys to *good planning*. Important tasks should occupy the best working times. Some time can be reserved for callers and to react to events. Urgent (but unimportant) tasks and lesser priorities can be eliminated, delegated or done quickly in small remnants of time.

Team-building and leadership training both maximize other people's effectiveness. Delegating authority to others (but still keeping in touch) saves time, but takes time to set up in the first instance.

Time is saved by good communication with people (secretary, and telephone and personal callers), efficient use of office systems (files, dictaphone, agenda-planning), and forward planning in the short term, medium term and long term (5 to 10 years). In-service training or annual job appraisal affords obvious opportunities to introduce questions of time management rather than waiting for a crisis of ill health or overwork.

Implementing ideas about time management may create problems for which a clear understanding of human nature is needed. Guilt* about the past and fear of the future can be transformed. Idealism* and individualism,* as well as personal insecurity about delegation or fear of competition, can be checked and eased by a new appreciation of the corporateness of humankind 'in Christ'.

Above all, time management can be prey to all the dangers of the Protestant work ethic. Only with the complementary emphasis on leisure,* joy* and celebration can people learn to manage time to the glory of Almighty God.

Jesus had clear priorities, but also time for people. He gave himself to the crowds, yet also trained a small group of future leaders, delegating responsibility to them. His priority of time alone with God became his recipe for others (Lk. 10:38–42) so that in the crisis he knew where his ultimate values and priorities lay (Lk. 22:42).

Jesus can serve as our model in time management so long as we also recall his patience with the disciples' failures, realize that his kingdom is still 'not yet', remember that within the security of his care he was also uncomfortably critical of people's wrong attitudes and actions, and recognize that (even with others' help) we do not enjoy his unclouded communion with the Father.

Bibliography

D. Cormack, *Seconds Away* (Eastbourne, ²1989); P. F. Drucker, *Managing for Results* (New York and London, 1964); Ted W. Engstrom and R. A. Mackenzie, *Managing Your Time* (Grand Rapids, ²1988); E. Gibbs, *Followed or Pushed?* (Bromley, 1987); C. B. Handy, *Understanding Organisations* (Harmondsworth, ²1985); M. E. Haynes, *Effective Meeting Skills* (London, 1988); J. Noon, *'A' Time* (Wokingham, 1985).

G.O.S.

TIME, USE OF, see COMMUNITY ETHICS. [16]

TITHE, TITHING, see GIVING.

TOLERATION, RELIGIOUS, is the granting of freedom of belief or practice to those who dissent from the official religion. As a form of public policy, it may be distinguished from tolerance, which is the personal and communal virtue of putting up with something of which one disapproves.

For most of its history, the Christian church has been unsympathetic to a doctrine of general toleration, being more mindful of its obligations to the truth than of upholding the rights of error. Thus Augustine* defended the pastoral use of coercion for the sake of the salvation of souls, like a medicine administered to an unwilling patient; Thomas Aquinas* argued that the rites of unbelievers and Jews should not be tolerated, except for a greater good, and that heretics and apostates should be constrained both for their own sake and for the protection of others; and John Calvin* maintained that the appointed end of civil authority included protection of the outward worship of God and the defence of sound doctrine and the standing of the church.

The logic of intolerance is perhaps most clearly portrayed in the pre-Vatican II Roman Catholic doctrine of the 'double standard'. According to this, when Catholics are in a majority, religious error ought to be suppressed; but when they are in a minority, it should be tolerated as the lesser evil. This is not a hypocritical position: it reflects the thought that, since the Christian church has been given revelation of God's truth and of the means to salvation, it has the right, and indeed the responsibility, to use any appropriate method to spread the Christian faith. And to the extent that the issue of eternal salvation was perceived to be at stake, it is clear why appeals to love or the attractions of civil peace were thought inadequate objections to intolerance.

Against this, cogent arguments for toleration have been broadly of two kinds.

1. The first argument questions what it means to be in full possession of the truth. This line of thought may refer to the idea that we are continually growing in our understanding of truth (*cf.* Jn. 16:13); that insights may be given to anybody in the community (*cf.* Acts 2:17–18); that God is greater than any human thoughts about him (*cf.* Is. 55:9); or that truth will always benefit from free investigation (John Milton, 1608–74). More sceptically, it may claim that certainty in religious questions is impossible to achieve (Sebastian Castellio, 1515–63).

2. The defence of toleration does not, however, require any concession to scepticism or religious uncertainty. Even if one were to accept that it is possible to be in full possession of the truth, it may still be invalid to deduce that suppression of dissent is justified. This second approach in favour of toleration may appeal to the idea that respect is due to the weaker conscience (*cf.* Rom. 14:1–23; 1 Cor. 8:1–13; 10:14–33); that assent to religious truth is a matter of the free will, and faith cannot and should not be secured through force (*e.g.* Tertullian*); that human beings are created intelligent and free, and it is consonant with their dignity that they should not be coerced (the Second Vatican Council*); or, finally, that

individuals have the right to follow their conscience (some contemporary Catholic writers).

A declared policy of toleration falls short of a commitment to full religious freedom, and tolerance is only one of the virtues necessary for participation in a free society. The post-Reformation predicament of whether to breach religious uniformity in the name of tolerance has given way to the liberal project of establishing a pluralist State which essays a strict neutrality between all religions and world-views. Consequently, the problem of holding together a diversity of beliefs within some shared framework of common values has become one of the chief practical and theoretical questions of modern plural societies. On the one hand it is doubtful to what extent a public policy of State neutrality can be adopted without either implicitly favouring some religions or else discriminating against all religion as such; on the other hand, for States whose substantive public moral and religious commitments are acknowledged, there remains the task of recognizing those religious groups whose presence should be not merely tolerated but also, in public legislation and general social ethos, welcomed and respected.

Serious Christian theological discussion of this will be rooted in an understanding of the relations of church and political authority. It should be suspicious of taking as its primary theological model the idea of the church as one voluntary association of like-minded believers amongst others, all subjected to an autonomous secular State: such an approach constantly runs the danger of divinizing the State and subordinating all other associations to its needs. The political realm is fundamentally incapable of achieving of itself an eschatological peace, and is constituted in the first place purely by the willingness of people to live together. It is within this that the church should seek to witness to the justice and peace of the kingdom,* recognizing and prompting the freedom of all to be messengers of a word of truth.

See also: DEVLIN–HART DEBATE; RIGHTS, HUMAN.

R.J.So.

TOLSTOY, LEO (1828–1910), Russian novelist and philosopher. Tolstoy's thought is complex and at times self-contradictory. It cannot be condensed into a neat 'system', and he cannot be said to have founded a new religion. Tolstoy once claimed: 'There is neither a Tolstoyan sect nor a Tolstoyan teaching.' Instead, Tolstoy believed that the plain teaching of Jesus had been forced into the background by the early church, and that such concepts as the deity of Christ and the Trinity had no place in true Christianity. He reduced Christianity to a few precepts distilled from the Sermon on the Mount: the prohibitions on anger, adultery, swearing and resisting evil, and also the command to love one's enemies. (Tolstoy differed so much from the theology of the Russian Orthodox Church that in 1901 he was excommunicated.)

The principle of non-violence* became a dominant theme in his teaching. For Tolstoy, war* could never be 'just'. Furthermore, any kind of violence to the individual soul or conscience was un-Christian. Thus Tolstoy rejected (in theory at any rate) compulsory military service, traditional forms of education, art-forms which lacked genuine human 'feeling', the whole system of civil and criminal law, government, and private property. His principles led him to champion the cause of the radical religious sect known as the Dukhobors.

Influenced by Jean-Jacques Rousseau (1712–78), Tolstoy believed that within human nature lies the spiritual strength which enables men and women to live as they should. He himself tried the 'back to nature' formula, although his quest for peasant simplicity coexisted uncomfortably with his material and social privileges.

Bibliography

Major works available in ET include: *Anna Karenina* (1877), *A Confession* (1879–82). *The Kingdom of God is Within You* (1893), *Resurrection* (1899), *War and Peace* (1860) and *What I Believe* (1885).

H. Gifford, *Tolstoy* (Oxford, 1982); E. B. Greenwood, 'Tolstoy and Religion', in M. Jones (ed.), *New Essays on Tolstoy* (Cambridge, 1978); H. Troyat, *Tolstoy* (New York, 1978); A. N. Wilson, *Tolstoy* (London, 1988).

M.J.D.

TONGUE, see SPEECH AND THE TONGUE.

TORTURE. The Declaration of Tokyo (1975), drawn up by representatives of the medical profession (see Medical Codes of Practice*), defines torture as 'the deliberate, systematic or wanton infliction of physical or mental suffering by one or more persons acting alone or on the orders of any authority, to force another person to yield information, to make a confession, or for any other reason'.

Some have defended the torturing of a suspect in order to gain information which will benefit the community (*e.g.* extracting information about planned explosions from a terrorist). Augustine,* starting from the premise that the State can never be perfectly just, allowed (somewhat reluctantly) that torture could be used to obtain information from accused persons and witnesses as 'a grim necessity of criminal justice' (Herbert A. Deane, *The Political and Social Ideas of St Augustine*, New York and London, 1963, p. 302). The judge who sanctions the use of torture is not guilty of sin but, says Augustine, 'Were he to recognize the misery of these necessities, and shrink from his own implication in that misery . . . had he any piety about him, he would cry to God, "From my necessities deliver Thou me"' (*City of God*, XIX.6). However, it is clear that Augustine was against the use of torture in any investigation or trial in which the church was involved, particularly in proceedings against the Donatists. This rejection of torture in such circumstances was not followed later by officials of the Inquisition.* They freely used torture against persons suspected of heresy. (In 1252, Pope Innocent IV's bull *Ad extirpanda* allowed the use of torture in order to break the resistance of the accused.)

From a legal point of view, nearly all nations in the world regard torture as a criminal offence. For example, in the UK, the criminal law treats torture as an offence against the person. Section 134 of the Criminal Justice Act (1988) states that if, in the UK or elsewhere, a public official or person acting in an official capacity, whatever his (or her) nationality, intentionally inflicts severe pain or suffering on another person in the performance or purported performance of his official duties, he is guilty of an offence and, if indicted, is liable on conviction to imprisonment for life or for any shorter term. For the purposes of this Act, Section 134(3), it is immaterial whether that pain or suffering is physical or mental and whether it is caused by an act or an omission. (See *Halsbury's Laws of England*, vol. 11 (1) *Criminal Law, Evidence and Procedure*, London, [4]1990, para. 504, p. 378.)

Given the many incidents of torture by government officials in different parts of the world, catalogued by the Annual Reports of Amnesty International, the criminal justice system in the UK starts at the right place. The Act also states that any person, whatever his nationality, not being a public official or person acting in an official capacity, is guilty of an offence if: 1. in the UK or elsewhere he intentionally inflicts severe pain or suffering on another at the instigation of, or with the consent or acquiescence of, a public official or of a person acting in an official capacity; and if 2. that official or other person is performing or purporting to perform his official duties when he instigates the commission of the offence or consents to or acquiesces in it. That person, if indicted, is liable on conviction to imprisonment for life or for any shorter term. Such a clearly stated point of law would seem to prevent torturers from claiming that they were acting under orders. However, the UK Criminal Justice Act also states that it is a defence for a person who is charged with an offence under the above provision in respect of any conduct to prove that he had lawful authority, justification or excuse for the conduct.

In the NT, there are two Gk. words that approximate to the sense of torture.

1. *Typtō* is used fifteen times to mean 'beat, strike, wound, injure, torture' (*e.g.* Mt. 24:49; 27:30; Acts 21:32). Torture is not only physical, however, and according to 1 Cor. 8:12, people's consciences can be tortured: 'By . . . injuring [your brothers'] weak consciences, it would be Christ against whom you have sinned' (JB).

2. *Basanos* (and the related verb *basanizō*) is used firstly in the sense of 'pain, agony, distress, outrage, torment'. For example, in Mt. 4:24, those suffering from diseases and 'painful complaints' were brought to Jesus (*cf.* Mt. 8:6). In 2 Pet. 2:8, the soul of Lot is 'tormented' by the lawless deeds of Sodom.

Secondly, *basanos* is used to describe the torment or torture of devils or demons (Mt. 8:29; Mk. 5:7; Lk. 8:28).

Thirdly, *basanos* is used to describe the torment or torture experienced in Hades, hell or Sheol (see Heaven and Hell*). 'Sheol' means the state of death (Ps. 6:5; *cf.* 18:5), and the resting-place of all people (1 Sa. 2:6; Jb. 21:13) consciously existing after death (Is. 14:9). There the wicked receive punishment (Nu. 16:30; Dt. 32:22; Ps. 9:17). They are put to shame and silenced in Sheol (Ps. 31:17). Jesus alluded to Isaiah's use of Sheol

(Is. 14:13–15) in pronouncing judgment on Capernaum in Mt. 11:23, where 'Hades' (Gk. *hadēs*) translates Heb. *šᵉ'ôl* (Sheol), meaning the place of continuing existence and judgment. His teaching in Lk. 16:19–31 seems to reflect accurately the OT concept of Sheol, as a place of conscious existence after death, one side of which is occupied by the suffering, unrighteous dead, who are separated from the righteous dead enjoying their reward: 'In his *torment* in Hades [the rich man] looked up and saw Abraham a long way off with Lazarus in his bosom'; and 'Give [my brothers] warning so that they do not come to this place of *torment* too' (Lk. 16:23, 28, JB).

In Rev. 14:10–11, the EVV avoid the possible translation 'tortured' in favour of 'tormented', presumably to guard against the idea that the impenitent are tortured rather than 'righteously punished' for ever and ever. According to John Sweet (1927– ; see *Revelation,* London, 1979, p. 227), the language is liturgical, standing in terrible contrast with the ceaseless worship of heaven. At death, the supreme torment of those who worship the beast (14:9) is to see the glory of the Most High against whom they have sinned. 'If Satan symbolises freedom to sin and its consequences, this may be to say that the human drama is not an episode in the divine plan which can be simply transcended. If the blood of the Lamb's victory is eternal, so must be the smoke of Satan's defeat' (p. 292).

Torture is to be condemned as dehumanizing, both to its victims and its perpetrators. The end (*i.e.* extracting information) does not justify the means (see Ends and Means*). The use of torture seems incompatible with the biblical view of persons as created in the image of God* (*cf.* Jas. 2:9). This demands that people should be treated with respect, and that their vulnerability (*e.g.* as prisoners of war) should not be exploited (*cf.* Am. 1:13).

The Declaration of Tokyo states: 'The doctor shall not countenance, condone or participate in the practice of torture or other forms of cruel, inhuman or degrading procedures, whatever the offence of which the victim of such procedures is suspected, accused or guilty, and whatever the victim's beliefs or motives, and in all situations, including armed conflict and civil strife.' This stands not only for doctors, but also for Christians in general.

J.M.S.

TOTAL DEPRAVITY, see ORIGINAL SIN.

TOUCH. The various uses of the word 'touch', or 'touching', convey a sense of communication. Physical contact is brought about so as to convey a message of some sort. This may include the desire to underline or accentuate a message.

One can thus describe touch as a distinctive mode or representation of a system of thought, often embedded in the way we verbalize. We make distinctions in our everyday experience in terms of kinesthetic sense. For instance, when we distinguish between various locations of pressure (hard or soft), extent (big or small), texture (rough or smooth), weight (light or heavy), or temperature or duration or shape, we are making distinctions in terms of our sense of touch.

Many of our everyday words and phrases are based on our tactile senses. We often use them without noting their origin, *e.g.* 'warmhearted', or 'firm foundation'.

This means of communication is subject to abuse. It forms part of the total expression of humanity's fallen nature, and can be, and is, in that sense, often perverted. In instances of sensory deprivation or sensory abuse, touching has become associated with negative, painful feelings. Such simple actions as a touch on the shoulder, head or hair, may be ensconced in a frame of reference or notion which immediately elicits discomfort for the person who is touched. Thus touching remains an area of necessity for only some people.

Touching, however, can be a reflection of the fact that the person touching or being touched is in a state of comfort with himself or herself and with others, and that he or she is able to identify with his or her own gender. As a conveyer of information, touching is an action which is best understood in terms of a relationship, and it can either initiate or intensify the relationship. This seems so basic, and yet it is an element which in some family settings is almost entirely lacking. Touching can convey a message of love or affection. Similarly, it can convey pain or distress. An episode of physical contact can underline or accentuate a message (*e.g.* acceptance, Lk. 15:20), and can be a strong means of focusing attention on the other person. Again, many of these elements are lacking in many of our family settings, due to the lack of the experience of touch.

A touch may make it possible for help to be sought and given. It can bring about a situation where there is a reaching out and asking, 'What do you think?' or 'Where are you at this time?'

In such circumstances it can become a strong vehicle of encouragement or comfort, saying in effect, 'You are here, you are worth touching. I am comfortable with you, you have worth.' Similarly, various forms of touching are known to convey messages of enthusiasm or joy.

It has been suggested by some commentators that our Lord's action in touching the leprous man (Lk. 5:13) reflected a desire to let love and pity have preference over ceremonial laws. As his touching of the leper reflected his love and pity, so his touching of the infants (Lk. 18:15) is a reflection of the attachment he wished to express towards them.

Our Lord seems to communicate the wholeness he brings about by the action of touching, and underlines the fact that by touching those he cured – or by allowing himself to be touched by the ritually unclean – the source of healing virtue lies in his own person (Mk. 5:28; 7:33). The touching of the blind man from Bethsaida shows our Lord's deep compassion and willingness to heal (Mk. 8:22–25), and the word that is used here in Mk. 8:22 is used of touching as a means of conveying divine blessing (cf. Mk. 10:13). When our Lord washes the disciples' feet in Jn. 13, it is part of a visual-tactile activity which underlines the unity and identification between our Lord and his disciples (Jn. 13:8–15).

Thus the activity of touching, in spite of its obvious susceptibility to abuse, needs to be carefully examined and introduced, not only as an aid to the message of identification and acceptance, but also as part and parcel of the evangelical ministry of restoration and renewal.

See also: SACRAMENTAL HEALING.

F.S.

TOURNIER, PAUL (1898–1986), a Swiss physician who grew up as a lonely orphan, and achieved world-wide fame as an author and Christian counsellor. His career as a general practitioner took an unexpected turn in 1932 when he became involved with the Oxford Group (see Moral Rearmament*) in Geneva. The experience stimulated a new interest in spirituality* and a deeper awareness of human needs. Soon, Tournier was spending increasing time listening to the problems of his patients, and less time in routine medical consultation. Friends discouraged him from the formal study of psychiatry: instead he developed his own counselling skills and in 1940 published *The Healing of Persons* (ET, London, 1966).

Like the books that followed, Tournier's first volume was not systematic or clearly organized. He called it 'a collection of experiences and thoughts', interwoven with stories of the real people who came to him for counsel. His purpose was to demonstrate the close relationship between personal and physical problems and to show that problems are best solved when people submit themselves to a sovereign God. Tournier was a pioneer in developing the now-accepted belief that psychological, physical and spiritual issues are interrelated and must all be treated in counselling. He termed this 'the medicine of the whole person'.

Tournier was an early leader in Christian counselling. His work and his life demonstrated a dedication to science, a genuine concern about people, an unwavering submission to God, and a desire to help individuals find practical guidelines for what he called 'the adventure of living'.

Bibliography
The Gift of Feeling (ET, London, 1982); *Guilt and Grace* (ET, Crowborough, ²1987).

G.R.C.

TRADE. The term 'trade' is used by economists to refer to any form of exchange between parties. This includes bartering, as well as more conventional exchanges, such as an individual purchasing goods from a shop, a firm buying raw materials from another firm, a company renting an office from a government department, or a multinational* company in one country borrowing funds from a bank in another.

In standard economic models of trade or exchange, it is generally assumed that each party to a trade enters into it voluntarily, and does so primarily in order to promote its own self-interest. In combination with a number of other conditions (some very stringent), it can be demonstrated that such exchanges generate material benefits for at least one of the parties (if not all), and that none of them loses.

Though self-interest is often the motive, it is not always so. Two classes of exception may be distinguished.

1. One party or more may be motivated by selflessness or self-giving. In such cases, the

economic outcome may well be different from that deduced in standard economic models. (For example, a selfless farmer, after a poor harvest, might sell his produce at the usual price, rather than the higher [probably exploitative] price that the 'market' would induce where supply is short. The consequence, however, is that all his produce is bought up by those at the front of the queue, with everyone else getting none. By contrast, the 'market outcome' tends to limit the amount purchased by any one person, because the higher price means they cannot afford much, and so the reduced supply is spread more widely.) Essentially, if some market participants do not 'play by the rules' of self-interest, then distortions arise in the allocation of resources, such that the overall benefits from trade are less than they would otherwise be. This in turn raises the question whether there is some kind of tension between what is economically efficient and what is ethically desirable.

2. Parties to some trades may participate involuntarily. A starving man who spends his money on exorbitantly-priced food is not, in any meaningful sense, a voluntary or free agent. Indeed, if he were, he would use his freedom to negotiate a better price. This is, then, an example of the more general problem of 'monopoly power', whereby an imbalance of power between parties enables the one to exploit the weakness of the other. Involuntary trade may be seen to arise either from lack of knowledge (a special case of 'involuntary'), or from lack of choice, which is essentially an imbalance in the initial distribution of resources between the parties.

To the extent that the motive of self-interest is true, however, a number of issues arise in terms of Christian ethics. Some of these issues are intertwined with questions concerning profit,* and at least three strands of scriptural teaching are relevant.

1. The notion of 'gain' from business or entrepreneurial endeavours receives endorsement in Scripture (Lv. 25:45; Pr. 31:10–14). On occasions, this gain is attributed specifically to God's blessing on an individual, family or nation (e.g. 1 Ki. 3:10–14). Whilst the modern notion of profit is not identical with 'gain' (since 'profit' relies on a set of accounting concepts and measures), there are sufficient similarities for the modern business person to draw encouragement from the business success of, say, the woman praised in Pr. 31.

2. Dishonest and oppressive trading behaviour is strongly condemned (Lv. 19:35–36; Am. 8:4–6). Whilst the Christian Reconstructionism* school in the USA, led by Gary North (1941– ; see Honest Money) interprets the contemporary significance of these strictures largely in terms of fraudulent money* (and thus the need for a non-inflationary supply of money), one may equally recognize a general injunction not to oppress the weaker party in any way (e.g. late payment of bills; misleading advertising*).

3. The command to 'love your neighbour as yourself' (Lv. 19:18; Lk. 10:27) may appear to conflict with the notion of 'gain'. It is difficult to think of a successful modern business whose profit does not derive in some way from 'buying cheap and selling dear'. Ideally, the successful business thrives by 'adding value', i.e. combining a set of resources and inputs in such a manner, and with such skill and effort, that the customer is willing to reward the producer by paying a price that more than covers the costs. The problem is: How much 'more than'? A customer may be willing to pay a price that is three times the full costs of production and supply, but is such a producer not exploiting rather than loving his neighbour? The underlying issue in such cases, where the producer enjoys some degree of monopoly power, is how to decide on a fair or just profit. There are similarities with the 'just price'* debates.

The danger that the powerful might exploit the weak through trade (because of some combination of monopoly power with its unjust use) has given rise to various strategies to limit or prevent such exploitation by the regulation and restriction of trade.

1. On the radical left, the tendency of those who own financial capital to use it exploitatively is seen as endemic and irreversible. Thus there is a call for private ownership of capital to be banned, to be replaced by some form of communal or social ownership (with or without a major role for the State in such ownership). This strategy, however, raises the question whether the exploitative side of fallen human nature might not reappear, perhaps in a new guise, under the new regime.

2. A second strategy, favoured by the political right, and including evangelical Christians such as Brian Griffiths (1942– ; see The Creation of Wealth, ch. 4), is to work tirelessly to attack and remove monopoly* power; the forces of competition would then prevent exploitative behaviour, even if some business people wished otherwise. One problem here is

that the underlying immorality of oppression has not been challenged. A second problem is that capitalism* seems to have an unavoidable tendency to produce clear 'winners' who, once successful, seek to keep hold of their hard-won degree of monopoly power. Thus, in practice, a contest is set up between regulator and business, in which each seeks to outmanoeuvre the other, and to which there is no end.

(A 'middle-way' variant on this second strategy is to encourage regulation by parties themselves, *e.g.* trade and consumer associations, which aim to maintain high standards and to highlight fraudulent behaviour.)

3. A third strategy (see Economic Ethics ⟦17⟧) is to develop structures of ownership which (negatively) automatically limit the likelihood of any one trader achieving the dominance of monopoly power, and which (positively) encourage trading behaviour whereby the interests of the customer, worker, business, families and local community are seen not as opposed, but as mutually reinforcing (see G. W. Goyder, 1908– , in *The Just Enterprise*). It can be argued that the OT, in particular, specifically developed a pattern of structures and behaviour in which, under God, this communality of interests, far from being idealistic, was reality.

See also: INTERNATIONAL TRADE.

Bibliography

G. W. Goyder, *The Just Enterprise* (London, 1987); B. Griffiths, *The Creation of Wealth* (London, 1984); G. North, *Honest Money: The Biblical Blueprint for Money and Banking* (Nashville, TN, 1986).

A.J.H.

TRADE UNIONS. Craftsmen's guilds existed in ancient history and flourished in medieval times among the artisan class. They had two functions: 1. through apprenticeship, a craft was passed down through the generations, and high standards were maintained; and 2. by regulating entry to the craft to those approved by existing masters, the artisans ensured that the demand for their work was kept so far as possible in balance with the available supply of their skills. Through establishing the terms on which members should agree to work, the guild endeavoured to protect its members from exploitation. Whilst not springing from them, the modern trade-union movement assumed certain characteristics of the ancient guilds. Some unions recruited exclusively members with a particular skill, jealously guarding wage* differentials and privileged positions over those perceived to have less or no such skill. Others recruited more generally, seeking widespread improvement of conditions among those workers whose lack of particular skills meant that they provided a pool of general labour for a wide variety of industries.

Many early trade unions in Great Britain were linked with nonconformist denominations, branch meetings frequently being held on chapel premises. Elsewhere (and subsequently in Britain) unions were an integral part of the socialist idea, and played an essential role in the enfranchisement of the working classes. Primarily, their purpose is to secure adequate wages and working conditions for their members. In the last analysis this may have to be achieved by strikes,* but, as trade unions have matured and gained respectability, many large employers find it preferable to negotiate all changes in working practices and conditions with a union representative, whose salary and office accommodation may often be funded in whole or part by the employer.

The trade-union movement and its associated organizations of the political left are entitled to much of the credit for the introduction of modern welfare benefits (see Welfare State*), such as health care, subsistence payments to the unemployed, and education. Before the State assumed wide responsibility for these, trade unions themselves, through the subscriptions of members, made impressive provision for their members and families. Union funds, raised by small weekly contributions from the members, provided payments for those on strike or locked out, thus preventing them being forced back to work through starvation. They also financed education classes at a time when most working-class people received only the most elementary State education (or no education at all). Sanatoriums and convalescent homes were built and run for members, especially by unions in industries where disease or injury due to hazardous working-conditions were at one time considered an almost inevitable concomitant of the job. Such conditions themselves were gradually ameliorated by the unions through a combination of direct action against employers, political lobbying and taking legal actions for damages through the courts on

857

behalf of injured members. The latter service remains an important part of the benefits provided for members by modern unions, as does the provision of pensions which are funded by separate contributions and supplement those provided by the State or employer. Many unions also sponsor British Members of Parliament, ensuring a direct political voice in issues affecting their members. In the US, unions often organize or support political committees to lobby law-makers.

Because the effectiveness of organized labour depends largely on the solidarity of action taken by the workforce, unions have sought to ensure that all employees at a particular workplace are members of a single union. This can be to an employer's advantage, as all terms of employment can be negotiated with the same union, and rivalry over status between groups of workers is largely avoided. This may result in problems of conscience for individual workers, whose employment may be dependent upon joining a union, some of whose policies may be inimical to them. Unions seek to justify forcing an employer to operate such a 'closed-shop' policy, on the basis that it is unfair that individuals should benefit from wages and conditions negotiated by the union for the whole workplace whilst not contributing financially to it as their fellow workers have.

As the potential strength of organized labour became apparent, many ambitious people saw trade-union office as a route to personal power. Whilst many used this for the general good, others have appeared to exploit their office, leading to a shift of public opinion against trade unions which were believed to have become too powerful. In most Western countries, legislation now exists to prevent the abuse of such power, and to confine unions to a suitable position within the checks and balances of a modern democracy.

See also: EMPLOYERS' CONFEDERATIONS; INDUSTRIAL RELATIONS.

D.P.N.

TRADITION. Any group that lasts for a long time develops traditions: customs, beliefs or habits of thought, some of which are deliberately passed down and some of which are taken largely for granted. In the NT, the word translated 'tradition' (*paradosis*), or the verb from which it is derived (*paradidōmi*), is used of Jewish traditions, either found in the Scriptures (Acts 6:14) or developed separately (Mk. 7:3–13). Jesus, unlike the Pharisees, rejected the authority of the latter, the 'oral Torah'. It is also used of Christian traditions current in the church before the NT itself was composed (*e.g.* 1 Cor. 11:2; 2 Thes. 2:15; Jude 3) and of purely human traditions threatening to corrupt the gospel (Col. 2:8).

The main body of Christian 'traditions' (in the third of these senses) was embodied in the NT. For example, remarkably few sayings ascribed to Christ which have any likelihood of being authentic are to be found outside its pages. Nevertheless, a variety of traditional customs developed in the church as time went on, and tended to be regarded as almost part of the essential core of the church's life: examples might be the creeds, the threefold ministry, and the sign of the cross. A fourth sense of the word therefore became important: 'tradition' meaning a practice common among Christians but not authorized by Scripture. Such practices were justified (if they were questioned at all) by an appeal to the authority of tradition, and this was also used later on to justify not only customs but actual doctrines which did not seem to be supported by Scripture: *e.g.* about the number of the sacraments, the invocation of saints, or the nature of the eucharist. The Reformers strongly rejected the idea that tradition could be regarded as an authority parallel to the Bible, while at the same time denying that their opponents could in fact produce genuine chains of tradition back to apostolic times in support of their beliefs.

An alternative defence of tradition as authoritative, adopted for instance by John Henry Newman (1801–90), sees it less as a method of access to apostolic teaching independent of Scripture than as the continuing life and thought of the church developing under the guidance of the Holy Spirit. The difficulty, naturally, is to know which developments are of divine origin and which of human. 'The history of Development can only tell us what has been, not what ought to be . . . [It] will afford as good a justification for the revolt from Papal authority in the sixteenth century as for its rise and growth in the third or fourth' (G. Salmon, *The Infallibility of the Church*, Lecture XX). Recent Roman Catholic thought, however, has tended to see tradition as repeating biblical teaching in another form, not as a supplement to it, pointing out that even the Council of Trent refrained from claiming the latter function for it.

Ethical traditions have grown up in all movements and denominations. It is often the case that a Christian's attitude, *e.g.* to divorce* or to the drinking of alcohol,* will have sprung originally from his or her particular tradition, although it may be defended by appeal, not to that tradition, but to social effects or the teaching of the Bible. Traditions may well embody the experience and wisdom of generations of Christian believers, and deserve respect; they may pass on understanding that one would not have reached by oneself. But they can also be influenced by the world and by temporary fashions, or the unrecognized self-interest of those who pass them on. A tradition may, moreover, be taken for granted with hardly any questioning, even when it seems indefensible to those outside the tradition: one example would be the tradition of supporting apartheid,* which until recently was normal in the Dutch Reformed churches of South Africa. Traditions, therefore, however useful, need to be kept under constant scrutiny.

Bibliography

Y. Congar, *Tradition and Traditions* (ET, London, 1966); G. Salmon, *The Infallibility of the Church* (London, 1888); World Council of Churches (Faith and Order Commission), *The Old and the New in the Churches* (London, 1961).

R.L.S.

TRANSACTIONAL ANALYSIS (TA) was first developed in 1958 by Eric Berne (1910–70), a Canadian psychiatrist who also trained as a psychoanalyst at the New York Psychoanalytic Institute. Berne saw TA as a 'systematic phenomenology' (see Existential Psychologies*) which regarded a person's subjective experience as of greater importance than the application of presupposition and interpretation. Acknowledged influences on Berne included the research of the neurosurgeon Wilder Penfield (1891–1976), who established that early, formerly hidden experiences can be relieved in response to certain stimuli, and the 'ego state' psychology of Paul Federn (1871–1950), a patriarch of Viennese psychoanalysis,* and his Italian pupil, Eduardo Weiss.

Under the aegis of Berne and, initially, with strong behaviourist* influence, the San Francisco Social Psychiatry Seminar was set up in 1958 to explore the place of TA within mental health.* In 1965, the International Transactional Analysis Association was founded and, throughout the 1960s and early 70s, the publication of Berne's prolific writing spread and popularized the concepts of TA worldwide. Although courses in TA were introduced for mature students through the University of Leicester in the early 1960s, it was not until the 70s that this system become part of the so-called 'new therapies' in Britain. In 1974, the first annual conference of the Institute for Transactional Analysis, a professional body set up to encourage standardization and an ethical code of practice in the UK, was held at Heythrop College in London.

Berne's central contribution to TA is his developed thinking on ego states, units of 'experienced reality of a person's mental and bodily ego' which are seen in relation to the time-span of their development and existence. Amongst the great number of ego states present in the psyche, Berne recognized three main categories: the Parent (subdivided into the Controlling Parent and the Nurturing Parent), in which there is internalization of significant, formative figures; the Adult, concerned with present reality; and the Child (the Free Child and the Adapted Child), containing relics of past experience.

In his work of child development, Berne, using his terminology of 'OK-ness' to denote human worth, looked to the object-relations theory of Melanie Klein* and postulated three 'not-OK' 'positions' for the psyche: 'I'm OK – you're not OK' (paranoid); 'I'm not OK – you're OK' (depressive); and 'I'm not OK – you're not OK' (schizoid). His own, non-Kleinian, fourth position of 'I'm OK – you're OK' implies both the presupposition of humanistic psychology* of an innate drive towards health* and self-actualization,* and his argument that this 'OK-ness' can be existentially maintained through the modification of and adjustment to the restrictions of heredity and upbringing. Berne also readily conceded that human destructiveness frequently pushes the individual into 'not-OK' positions. Consequent loss of well-being may come about through 'contamination' of the Adult ego state by the Parent (as in the ingraining of prejudice), or by the Child (as with the development of phobias). An important ingredient in the genesis of psychological ill health is Berne's notion of the 'script', a far-reaching stance formed in childhood and moulded by interaction with parents and other significant figures. The script of early childhood, 'I must never get close to people', may be reinforced later by the parental 'counterscript', 'Work hard'. The term 'racket system' was coined by Richard Erskine and Marilyn Zalcman, in 1979, to refer to the repetitive pattern of feelings, thoughts and behaviours that express the maladjustments of the 'life-script'. Within this pattern, 'transactions', small units of stimulus and response between the ego states of one person and another, and 'games', series of transactions with ulterior motives, are played out.

The ultimate aim of TA is to help the client towards 'autonomy', a well-functioning state marked by awareness, spontaneity and intimacy. The person in need may be helped towards this 'script-free' state through brief or long-term psychotherapy, where contracts are made for clearly circumscribed goals. Transactional Analysis seeks to offer a therapeutic relationship that is 'game-free' and of mutual respect ('I'm OK – you're OK'), and can be adapted, through individual, group* or family therapy* to a wide range of clients, including those with personality disorders, the mentally handicapped (see Learning Disabilities*) and people suffering from a range of neuroses* and psychoses.* Strategies and techniques include the exploration and enactment of transactions and games, and the use of transference* interpretation, to achieve 'decontamination' of the Adult from baleful Parent and Child influences. More fundamentally, 'Redecision' therapy aims to allow a re-experiencing of past hurts in order to achieve restructuring of the Child ego state, and 'reparenting' (at its most radical, in the community-based work of Jacqui Schiff [1934–] amongst schizophrenics) seeks to help the client regress to earliest childhood and then, supported by the new 'parent', progress freshly through the development cycle, thus forming a new Parent ego state.

The functional model of Berne's ego states has attracted many Christian counsellors, including, *e.g.*, Jean Morrison (née Grigor) of Edinburgh, who use the structural concepts and strategies of TA without adhering to its humanistic basis. Thomas Oden (1931–), the American theologian (see Pastoral Care, Counselling and Psychotherapy[7]), in his *Game Free*, gives a valuable critique of TA from a Christian standpoint.

Bibliography

E. Berne, *Transactional Analysis in Psychotherapy: A Systematic Individual and Social Psychiatry* (New York, 1961; London, 1975); *idem*, *What Do You Say After You Say Hello? The Psychology of Human Destiny* (London, 1974; New York, [2]1984); P. Clarkson and M. Gilbert, 'Transactional Analysis', in W. Dryden (ed.), *Individual Therapy: A Handbook* (Milton Keynes and Bristol, PA, 1990); R. G. Erskine and M. J. Zalcman, 'The Racket System: A Model for Racket Analysis', *Transactional Analysis Journal*, 9.1, 1979, pp. 51–59; J. C. Morrison, *A Tool for Christians: Book 1* (Edinburgh, [3]1987), *Book 2* (Edinburgh, 1983); T. C. Oden, *Game Free: A Guide to the Meaning of Intimacy* (New York, 1974); W. Penfield, 'Memory Mechanisms', *Archives of Neurology and Psychiatry* 67, 1952, pp. 178–198; J. L. Schiff *et al.*, *Cathexis Reader: Transactional Analysis Treatment of Psychosis* (New York, 1975).

R.F.H.

TRANSFERENCE. The term 'transference' has several definitions:

1. Transference was a term used by Sigmund Freud* to describe the feelings and perceptions which his patients attached to him, which properly belonged to parents and other important figures in early life. First observed in patients with hysteria and regarded as unhelpful, Freud came to regard recognition and interpretation of the transference as the primary diagnostic and treatment tool of psychoanalysis.* He believed that powerful sexual and aggressive drives gave rise to wishes, attitudes, phantasies and emotions which the patient had repressed because of the anxiety* they would provoke if allowed into consciousness. The major work of analysis was to identify the repressed material and its origins. The patient could then be helped to separate past from present reality, and give up the symptoms the repression had produced. Both strong, loving feelings (positive transference) and hostile feelings (negative transference) had to be traced to their origins for the work to proceed. Freud regarded any other approach as superficial and any relief it gave as temporary.

Other analysts differed in their views of the origin and place in treatment of the transference phenomena. The object-relations school, following Ronald Fairbairn (1890–1964), rejected instinct theory and emphasized the repetition of early relationships, while Melanie Klein* traced the repressed material to infancy when a baby was relating, not to whole people, but to part-objects (*e.g.*

the mother's breast). Rosemary Gordon described in 1968 the change aimed at in treatment as resembling one from the I–It to the I–Thou relationships of Martin Buber (1878–1965). Franz Alexander thought that transference should be recognized, but controlled and used flexibly, treatment being effected by providing a corrective emotional experience. Heinz Kohut (1913–81), concerned with the struggle to develop the self,* sees analysis of the transference as an aid to maturity.

2. Transference is also used to describe the repetition of any former and unmodified reaction. Such material, more accessible to consciousness, frequently emerges in psychotherapy and counselling. Some positive transference must exist for treatment to proceed, but both positive and negative provide insights into areas of distortion; the way of handling them, however, will vary according to the client's needs, the nature of the contract,* and the worker's skills. For some, the intense feelings from a developing transference might be too frightening, but they may be helped by the consistent benign authority of the counsellor who remains undamaged and refuses to react as expected. Others can be helped by being made aware of some of the connections between past and present or between those inside and those outside the counselling relationship. Control of transference can be achieved by regulating the frequency of meetings, the topics discussed and the degree of dependency, and by establishing the counsellor as a real person.

3. Transference is a universal phenomenon which occurs in all relationships and experiences. 'All perception of the external world is governed by the transference of attitudes and feelings from various parts of our personalities' (J. Sullivan, *Relationship in Casework*, p. 26). The degree, intensity and amount of distortion distinguish the pathological from the normal. Patterns of interaction between analyst and client are increasingly being seen as crucial to treatment. This in turn has led to increasing awareness of *counter-transference*, a term used of the feelings produced in the therapist: a. by the client, and especially the client's transference; and b. by the total therapeutic encounter. Training analysis, personal therapy and supervised practice (see Supervision*) provide opportunities for identifying biases which might hinder treatment.

Since all authority figures are likely to be objects of transference, church leaders need to be able to recognize this, and so avoid either colluding with a strongly positive, or responding defensively to a negative, transference. Support groups help leaders identify the difference between attitudes which have a basis in reality and those correctly ascribed to transference. Considerable opportunities exist for helping people even with quite damaged personalities by providing stable parental figures who encourage growth.

Because God is the ultimate and all-powerful authority figure, he is inevitably the object of transference, being perceived as, for instance, rejecting, hostile, indulgent, or arbitrary. Preachers especially need to identify and correct their own projections.

Bibliography

S. Freud, *A General Introduction to Psychoanalysis* (1916; ET, New York, 1920; London, 1922); J. W. Jones, *Contemporary Psychoanalysis and Religion: Transference and Transcendence* (New Haven, CT, 1991); R. S. Lee, *Principles of Pastoral Counselling* (London, 1968); J. Mattinson, *The Reflection Process in Casework Supervision* (Tavistock Institute of Marital Studies; London, 1975); J. Sullivan and E. Irvine in *Relationship in Casework* (Association of Psychiatric Social Workers; London, 1963).

J.R.G.

TRANSPERSONALISM, see PASTORAL CARE, COUNSELLING AND PSYCHOTHERAPY. [12]

TRANSPLANT SURGERY nowadays abounds with ethical issues. The 20th century has seen the evolution of many successful techniques, most dramatized by their life-saving potential, which have posed a series of hotly debated questions. Ethical problems arise from tissue donation and reception, from attitudes to the dead body (see Cannibalism*) and to organs removed for transplantation, and from the scarcity of organs and the prospect of the use of animal grafts.

1. Blood and bone marrow

The first organ transplant procedure to become part of the routine of modern medicine was the *transfusion of blood*. In most cultures donation of blood is regarded as a free gift – a good act, demonstrating love of neighbour. In some countries the donor is paid for his or her blood, thus changing the gift relationship to a commercial transaction. Donors motivated by financial gain are more likely to donate blood which carries disease, but it is thought that nearly all infected carriers can be identified by screening.

Jehovah's Witnesses quote biblical teaching (*e.g.* Lv. 17:11–14) to support their rigid stance against blood transfusion. Adult members of this sect may therefore refuse life-saving treatment, but occasionally their views may be overruled by a court if a child's life is at stake.

Blood transfusion was made safe by the definition of blood groups, and, since there are few blood groups, it is possible to store blood, selecting the appropriate blood group 'off the shelf' when the need arises.

Blood regenerates, and so the donor suffers no permanent loss. This is also true of *bone-marrow transplantation*. However, the immunological barriers are more difficult to overcome, and for both bone-marrow and solid-organ transplantation, tissue-typing of the donor and recipient is required to obtain a good match. The availability of the right tissue thus determines if and when a transplant can be carried out. Bone-marrow transplants are obtained from living volunteer donors and it has been necessary to recruit and type a very large number, calling them forward when a patient presents with their particular tissue type.

2. Organs

Transplantation of solid, non-regenerating organs raises other ethical debates. They must be obtained either from live volunteer donors or from the cadavers of those who have recently died (Human Tissue Act, 1961). *Live donation* carries the risk of the operation, namely the minimal hazard of modern anaesthesia which the donor must be willing to undergo. Live donation is possible only in the case of a paired organ, the kidney (although there are a few examples of liver segments from live donors being transplanted). Mortality after donating a kidney is not increased, but some immediate morbidity is incurred and there may be a long-term increased risk of hypertension. Recent debates at the level of international societies of transplant surgeons have effectively outlawed the paid inducement of donors, and this recently became illegal in the UK (Human Organ Transplants Act, 1989), although it still continues in some Third-World countries. So difficult is it to be certain of the motivation of donors that in the UK it is now possible to use only live donors whose family relationship can be proved, usually with typing to establish genetic links.

Cadaveric donation poses a potential conflict of interest between the care of the dying patient (see Death and Dying*) and his or her preservation on behalf of potential recipients. Conflict is effectively resolved by keeping the transplant surgical team out of the picture until the death of the patient is no longer in doubt. The cadaver represents the only source of supply of unpaired solid human organs such as the liver, heart and pancreas.

Diagnosis of death has been clarified by the wide acceptance of the criteria and physical signs of brain-stem death (see Brain Death*), which, when repeated after a proper interval, define a condition of irreversible destruction of the brain beyond which there is inevitable cessation of all bodily function over a time-scale of no more than a few days, whatever resuscitative measures are taken. In practical terms these patients are, for their own sakes, already being nursed in an intensive care* ward or intensive therapy unit (ITU) on ventilators and other life-supporting equipment and drugs. They should be distinguished from patients in the persistent vegetative state (see Coma*) who require no more than tube feedings and regular nursing care and are in a totally different physiological state.

There are two other classes of cadaveric donors whose use has been advocated: the *asystolic donor*, *i.e.* someone who dies when his or her heart stops beating but who is at no time admitted to an ITU and whose organs must be removed with speed if transplantation is to be successful; and the *electively ventilated donor*, *i.e.* someone transferred to an ITU at the time of death solely for the purpose of organ retrieval. Very careful organization is essential if the dignity of the dying person is to be preserved in these situations. Expeditious speed in moving the body must not become unseemly haste. Elective ventilation requires adequate ITU facilities. Most of these donors have sudden cerebro-vascular accidents, but some, notably those dying of brain tumours, will be able to discuss organ donation before their illnesses reach the terminal stages. As organ transplantation becomes more widely accepted as a regular surgical procedure, and provided confidence in the medical profession is retained, then these rather strange-sounding approaches will become routine practice. Here an ethical starting-point in Christian tradition is respect for the dead body.

Organ retrieval from the cadaver does not seem to cause offence to any particular religious point of view. Even those religions which regard the dead body as unclean seem prepared to adjust their practices in the light of the higher claims of saving life. However, culturally determined attitudes may require re-educating. Publicity leading to domestic discussion around the signing of donor cards or the annotation of driving licences has been a favoured approach. Some countries have legislation which presumes consent when objection has not been recorded ('opting out'), and there is a broadly based view that such legislation would be acceptable in the UK. It would remove the requirement for medical teams to discuss donation with grief-stricken relatives, and evidence from other countries suggests that it would increase the availability of organs for transplantation. At the present time the doctor working in Britain must establish that the family or next of kin did not know of any objection which had been expressed by the deceased or, if his or her attitudes were not known, that the family have no objection to the regular practice of organ retrieval for transplantation. Many families, saddened by recent bereavement, have found some solace in the fact that, by including within the donation all solid organs and the corneas of the eyes, as many as six or seven patients can receive new life or new sight by transplantation from the body of their relative.

The human organ removed for transplantation is a precious resource. To whom does it belong? Most surgeons would now concur with the view that it belongs to the community. To whom should it be allocated? To the patient who needs it most desperately, perhaps driven to the brink of suicide by the rigours of dialysis? To the patient who will be least likely to reject it, *i.e.* the one with the closest tissue type? To the patient who occupies a place on a dialysis programme, demanding an excessive share in scarce treatment resources, and possibly keeping others from such treatment? These questions emphasize the inestimable value of the organ ready for transplantation. Ethical answers in each individual case will come from a standpoint of responsible stewardship.*

The main problem in transplant surgery is the *shortage* of donor organs. World-wide, there are nearly half a million patients on dialysis, all possible candidates for a kidney transplant. Larger numbers die of heart disease, and the indications for cardiac transplantation are widening. Some com-munities have resolved the ethical issues by deciding not to have heart-transplant programmes, either because of their huge cost or because of the shortage of organs, which means that however much money is put into the programme there will always be a majority of patients for whom no graft will be available at the time it is needed.

Some experimenters think that xenografting – the use of organs from a different species – could solve the problem of organ supply. When the necessary immunological breakthrough is made, ethical questions will be posed. It will be better if they are answered before the scientific advance occurs. The chimpanzee is closest to the human in immunological terms, but is at present expensive and difficult to breed in captivity. Baboon-kidney grafting to humans has been done, but the organs lasted for a short time only. The pig is a possible source of organs which approximate to humans physiologically and can be bred to any size. Animal rights (see Rights, Animal*) activists are opposed, but the basis for their opposition seems to lie more in sentiment than in logic based on the creation ordinance (see Gn. 1:26–27). A reasoned and reasonable ethical stance is required before xenotransplantation becomes an emotionally charged issue.

Bibliography

Conference of Medical Royal Colleges, 'Diagnosis of Brain Death', *BMJ* 1976, 2, pp. 1187–1188; C. M. Kjellstrand and J. B. Dosseter, *Ethical Problems in Dialysis and Transplantation* (Dordrecht, 1992); C. Pallis, 'Death', in *Encyclopaedia Britannica* (Chicago, 131986), pp. 1030–1042; R. M. Titmuss, *The Gift Relationship* (London, 1970); Working Party of United Kingdom Health Departments, *Cadaveric Organs for Transplantation: A Code of Practice* (London, 1983).

A.J.W.

TRANSSEXUALISM. Transsexuals are men or women who are normal according to physiological criteria, but who experience themselves as members of the opposite sex. This sense of being 'trapped in the wrong body' may result in a demand for hormonal and surgical interventions to modify their appearance and sexual characteristics. This is commonly known as gender reassignment or – more colloquially – as a sex-change.

Transsexualism is a relatively rare condition, involving more men than women. It must be distinguished from three other conditions: transvestism,* which involves cross-dressing for erotic stimulation, such a man being typically heterosexual and not seeking a sex-change; the physiological intersexes (or hermaphroditism), involving a variety of conditions where genetic or hormonal abnormalities result in people possessing some physical characteristics of the opposite sex; and homosexuality,* in which individuals experience attraction and ambivalence towards members of the same sex, but typically have little or no sense of cross-gender identity.

The recognition of transsexualism as a specific condition is relatively recent. It is common to date such recognition back to 1952, when the widely publicized sex-change of former American GI Christine Jorgensen took place. However, there is evidence to suggest that transsexualism has occurred within a variety of cultures and in earlier centuries.

R. J. Stoller (1924–) in *The Transsexual Experiment* hypothesized that male-to-female transsexualism arises from early imprinting and non-conflictual learning, as the young boy develops an unusually close relationship to his mother. By contrast, Elizabeth Moberly believes that transsexualism in both sexes has a traumatic origin (see *Homosexuality: A New Christian Ethic*). It is thought to stem from the early breakdown of the child's relationship to the same-sex parent, thereby disrupting the normal process of developing a same-sex identity. The young child disidentifies from the same-sex parent, who was absent or emotionally unavailable. The apparent sense of cross-gender identity is then interpreted as a radical absence of same-sex identity. A massive unmet need for same-sex love carries over into adult life, together with a half-hidden sense of hurt or grievance towards members of the same sex. The male-to-female transsexual is like a very young boy who is still looking for his father's love. The female-to-male transsexual is like a very young girl who is still looking for her mother's love. The primary ethical and psychological problem of sex-change surgery is that it leaves the 'wounded child' unhealed.

On this view, transsexualism is the extreme end of the homosexual spectrum. In most homosexuals, the sense of same-sex identity is viable, even though incomplete. In transsexuals, the disruption of the parent–child relationship took place so early that there is no viable sense of same-sex identity. Ethically and psychologically, transsexualism is comparable to homosexuality. Therapy for motivated transsexuals is also comparable. As the originator of gender-affirmative or reparative therapy, Moberly recommends that transsexuals and homosexuals alike should work with a same-sex therapist and focus on same-sex issues. Same-sex hurts from the past need to be resolved; and legitimate needs for same-sex bonding and affirmation can receive healthy fulfilment without sexual acting-out. In this way, a stable same-sex identity may be reconstructed.

Bibliography

E. R. Moberly, *Homosexuality: A New Christian Ethic* (Cambridge, 1983); *idem*, *Psychogenesis* (London and Boston, MA, 1983); R. J. Stoller, *The Transsexual Experiment* (London, 1975).

E.R.M.

TRANSVESTISM.

The transvestite achieves sexual arousal by wearing clothes generally assumed to be more appropriate to the opposite sex. Anxiety and depression about the subject's gender role may be relieved by cross-dressing, but transvestism is to be clearly distinguished from transsexualism* (where a sex-change operation is sought, to compensate for a persistent conviction that the person concerned is trapped within a body which seems anatomically alien to him or to her).

Typically, transvestites are heterosexual males who do not engage in homosexual* behaviour. Their condition should not be confused with the cross-dressing of 'drag' performers in the entertainment business.

P.A.M.

TRIAGE.

Healthcare provision and delivery face a crisis of ever-growing demand and limited resources. Some means of allocating limited resources is necessary to decide which patients should receive priority in treatment and which treatments should be offered. In war situations, the system of triage developed when there was a need to categorize large numbers of patients quickly. Emergency settings, like war and disaster, force doctors to make hard decisions between patients. Usually, this involves distinguishing between those who have no real hope of survival even if treated immediately, those who are only slightly injured and will survive anyway, and those who are given priority in treatment on the grounds that they will survive only if they are treated immediately.

Everyday medicine is in fact making these kinds of decisions largely on a utilitarian basis (see Consequentialism*). With the growth of technology, the number of elderly people, conflict between preventive and curative medicine, and the expectation that medicine will provide 'a pill for every ill', new attention has focused on resource allocation at both the micro and macro levels (see Health and Health Care*). Individual doctors, as well as governments and healthcare authorities, are reviewing their practice by both medical and professional, as well as financial, audit, in order to seek better value for money. Strategies to respond to the problem will include how best to develop resources and better management, and how to educate the public to take more responsibility for health, especially through exercise and healthy-eating programmes. Particular attempts to measure scales of outcomes and different healthcare delivery systems are fraught with problems. The use of QALY* (quality adjusted life years) to decide between patients and treatments has been shown to favour the fit and young rather than the sick and elderly. What is more important is the moral criteria that are used.

Treating according to need means having to define what is necessary. While this is clear at the extremes of life and death, ordinary and extraordinary treatments, it may confuse needs with wants, and requires a clear account of what human beings require to survive and flourish. Treating according to merit means deciding what different people deserve. This might lead to discrimination against those with self-inflicted illnesses as a result of smoking, sexual activity or risky lifestyles and hobbies. It might also involve some measure of social worth in terms of past or future contribution to society. This utilitarian approach clashes with traditional medical ethics which sees alleviation of pain as primary. Treating according to ability to pay means that health care would be available only to the rich and that the poor would suffer, as they do in the USA where 37 million people are without health insurance and a further 14 million are under-insured. Treating people equally involves no unwarranted discrimination. In practice, it comes to 'first come, first served', which is what usually happens in emergency rooms and casualty departments. This has led some moralists, following Paul Ramsey,* to argue that we ought to draw lots or randomize treatments. He argues that only thus will equality of opportunity, justice and fairness be achieved. This is the way to avoid reducing people simply to the roles they play in society, and protects those who have no apparently signficant societal function. Many argue that there is a right to treatment, but where this right is grounded, and whose responsibility is involved, is less clear, especially if we look at the state of the nations world-wide. Where the State is the main or sole provider of health care through general or specific taxation, there may be a clear claim on the part of citizens for health care. This rests on a contract notion of medicine and sits uneasily with a more covenant-based approach to healthcare provision.

Medicine is rooted in loving service which responds to the needs of others and acts justly, treating everyone fairly and appropriately. Societies need to work for an agreed moral framework, factual basis, medical audit and strategies to match resources with needs (see also Medical Codes of Practice*). Christians will stress responsibility for the vulnerable and needy, neighbour love which responds to everyone in need, God's desire and will for shalom and wholeness for human beings, Christ's example of healing in response to need, and a perspective on life and death which is not selfish and does not seek to avoid death at all costs. These values will challenge the prevailing cultural norms of health and fear of death, which may help alleviate the demands for ever more health care.

See also: ETHICS OF MEDICAL CARE. 14

Bibliography

S. E. Lammers and A. Verhey (eds.), On Moral Medicine: Theological Perspectives in Medical Ethics (Grand Rapids, 1987); P. Ramsey, The Patient as Person (New Haven, CT, and London, 1970).

E.D.C.

TRIAL MARRIAGE, see COHABITATION.

TRINITY, see GOD; 1 HUMANITY. 4

TROTH, see MARRIAGE.

TRUST. The concept of trust has at least three perspectives: psychological, moral and theological.

Psychological perspectives

Fundamental to psychological interpretations of trust is that it is a *relational* concept (*i.e.* it is defined first and foremost by reference to relationships between persons). Other usages such as 'You can trust this map to be accurate' are metaphorical and derivative from the basic idea of trust as a relational quality.

Developmental psychologists such as Erik Erikson,* D. W. Winnicott* and John Bowlby 1907–90) have emphasized the crucial importance of the first months of infancy to the formation of trust. It is at this time that infants learn to trust their mothers for sustenance, both physical and emotional. When this happens, positive bonding takes place and security develops. Conversely, infants who find their parents to be untrustworthy in supplying their needs may fail to develop adequate bonds, thus engendering a persistent inability to trust others later in life. All this takes place at the unconscious level and therefore may go unperceived until a life crisis occurs.

A further outcome, according to this school, is likely to be a basic lack of trust in oneself, since learning to trust in one's mother and in return receiving affection provide the foundation for trust in one's own abilities and judgment. Such an outcome inevitably weakens the capacity to move on to the next stage in the developmental cycle. Trust is therefore foundational to human growth and development.

Moral perspectives

Implicit within the idea of trust as a relational concept is the notion of reciprocity. The effective operation of trust between persons requires that both parties be willing to trust each other, since one-sided trust is unstable. A reciprocal relationship is thus created.

Out of reciprocity arises moral obligation. The bond of trust creates (and is dependent upon) a sense of two-way fairness which governs the relationship. For fairness to be maintained, both parties must recognize that an obligation is laid upon them to act according to the fairness criterion. Once this is introduced, trust passes from being a psychological to a moral phenomenon.

In moral debate, a division exists at this point between those who hold that the maintenance of obligation* (and thereby trust) requires objective moral rules or criteria to determine right and wrong, and those who argue that subjective commitment to recipro-city is adequate. Those who adhere to the first view advocate specific moral norms or frameworks to govern actions in detail. Those who advocate the second rely upon the application of very general requirements (*e.g.* 'Act fairly in all things') to situations by means of moral intuition.* From the point of view of trust, the essential difference is that 'objectivists' (see Objectivity of Morals*) identify a need for subjective trust to be supported by moral structures (rules or norms) while, on the other hand, 'subjectivists'* reckon trust to be self-sufficient as a structure in itself.

Theological perspectives

The key category in a theological understanding of trust is that of covenant.* Biblical covenants are modelled on contemporary Near-Eastern political covenants viewed as agreements between parties involving reciprocal promises and obligations. This is so whether speaking of covenants between human beings, between God and individuals, or between God and his people. It is encapsulated in the covenant formula, 'I shall be your God and you shall be my people.'

Consequently, trust and faith are closely linked and frequently synonymous. Two paradigm figures are Abraham and Jesus. Abraham received the covenant of God, the essence of which was that he was called to exercise faith (trust) in response to the word of God by leaving his home and travelling to an unknown country which God promised would belong to his descendants. Abraham thereby came to serve as the paradigm case for OT and NT alike (*cf.* Heb. 11:8–12).

When we observe the life of Jesus we see an even more profound trust at work. The Son is called by the Father to a ministry which leads to suffering and death. Yet in the garden of Gethsemane and subsequently on the cross itself, the Son trusts the Father that obedience to his will leads to glory (Jn. 17).

In recent years, theological and psychological perspectives have been brought together by faith developmentalists such as James Fowler (1940– ; see Faith Development*). Following Erikson, Fowler argues that there exists a close relationship between the development of the capacity to trust one's mother in childhood and the ability to trust God. The reason for this is that to all intents and purposes, a mother is as a god to the infant. The child who discovers his or her mother to be loving, trustworthy and present in times of need will more readily develop an image of God which is likewise loving and trustworthy. This is not to say that Fowler holds the classical Freudian view that religious beliefs are no more than projections out of the human psyche. Rather, it is that the images of the divine which lie deep within the subconscious are shaped by the relational experience of the earliest weeks, months and years. Indeed, Fowler uses the metaphor of covenant to bridge psychological and theological perspectives on faith.

Erikson goes further in holding that human experiences of the numinous are similarly conditioned by the infant–parent bond. In sacred rites, the numinous involves a sense of looking at, or being looked upon, which is tinged with awe. According to Erikson, this characteristic governs the relationship between mother and baby and makes trust more than sentimental. Trust can thus be seen to be a multiple concept which cannot adequately be understood from one perspective alone.

Bibliography

E. Erikson, *Childhood and Society* (New York, ²1963; Harmondsworth, ²1965); J. W. Fowler, *Stages of Faith: The Psychology of Human Development and the Quest for Meaning* (San Francisco, 1981); M. Jacobs, *Towards the Fullness of Christ: Pastoral Care and Christian Maturity* (London, 1988).

F.W.B.

TRUTH. Many philosophical and ethical issues arise over 'truth'. This article looks briefly at just one or two of those philosophical issues before turning to the ethical field.

Philosophers have long debated the nature of truth. Is a statement true because it corresponds to a specific fact, or because it coheres with our whole system of knowledge? Should we look on truth in a pragmatic way (*i.e.* what works is true) or in a subjective way (*i.e.* truth for me will not necessarily be truth for you)?

Existentialism has stressed the subjective nature of truth: truth is personal, something I appropriate for myself, my experience of encounter. Such a view needs to be balanced with an understanding of truth as objective: a truth will be true even if no-one believes it (*e.g.* 'The earth is a sphere', uttered in the days when everyone thought it was flat); the truth we appropriate to ourselves subjectively is in itself objective.

Acceptance of the objectivity of truth precludes relativism* and pluralism.* Though we may readily accept that another philosophy or religion contains many things that are true, if at any point it contradicts the claims of, say, Christianity, then either it or Christianity must necessarily be false at that point. God (see ①) cannot, for instance, be both one and many; if he is one, he is not many, and polytheistic religions are false at that point.

If we are concerned for truth we must be prepared to stick to it, even against the current cultural tide, though always ensuring we do so 'in love' (Eph. 4:15).

In the Bible, truth is rooted in the being and nature of God himself. Not only is he true in all his ways (Rev. 15:3), but he *is* truth (Is. 65:16); references to 'the true God' or 'God of truth' (*e.g.* Jn. 17:3) are not simply contrasting him with false gods; they are claiming that his nature is truth (*cf.* Jn. 14:6; 15:26). God's truth is closely linked with his righteousness;* it ensures his faithfulness and trustworthiness. So far from being a theoretical concept, truth in the Bible is personal and practical. We are called to live the truth as well as to tell it; we do truth as well as know it (Jn. 3:21); truth is moral as well as factual.

By contrast with God, Satan* is 'a liar and the father of lies' (Jn. 8:44). Falsehood is something God detests (Pr. 12:22); the sin of deliberate deception was viewed especially severely (Achan at the beginning of the possession of the Promised Land, Jos. 7; Ananias and Sapphira at the beginning of the early church, Acts 5:1–11); Christians must get rid of all falsehood (Eph. 4:25); liars are specifically mentioned in Rev. 21:8 as destined for the fiery lake.

Those who live and speak the truth demonstrate the character of God, and enable trusting relationships to be built up, without which life in community would be impossible. Falsehood, by contrast, alienates a person from God, destroys relationships and community, and dehumanizes the person practising it.

As in many areas (*e.g.* love of our neighbour) most Christians have to accept that perfection in the area of truth is still largely beyond our grasp. Transparent honesty* and total trustworthiness are hard to attain; not every promise can be kept; elements of pretence ('keeping up appearances') and self-deception are hard to eradicate. In these areas we need to aim at the highest goals while viewing realistically our own humanness and sinfulness, and humbly accepting God's mercy and grace.

Whether or not Christians should ever lie has been widely debated (see Norms*). Some, such as Augustine* and John Wesley,* have stated that in no circumstances should a Christian ever deliberately tell a lie. Others (*e.g.* Martin Luther* and Dietrich Bonhoeffer*) have argued that there are exceptions when falsehood is permissible.

Some of these exceptions may be relatively trivial in that they contain no serious intent to deceive, *e.g.* if we are teasing someone, telling a joke or a story, or giving a conventional reply to a conventional greeting ('How are you?' 'Fine, thanks'). But others are far from trivial. Was it right for Christians who were hiding Jews from the Gestapo in the Second World War to say there were none in the house? Should we tell the truth to a terminally ill person when the doctors and the family have forbidden it? Should a Christian doctor prescribe a placebo? What should we say to our children about Father Christmas? Does honesty demand that we say exactly what we think to someone we find objectionable?

Those who feel there may be justification for telling a lie in exceptional circumstances point to a few Bible passages where a greater or lesser degree of deceit seems to have been used without being condemned: the Hebrew midwives (Ex. 1:19), Rahab (Jos. 2:4–6; *cf.* Heb. 11:31), Jael and Sisera (Jdg. 4:18–21), Samuel at Bethlehem (1 Sa. 16:2), the lying spirit (1 Ki. 22:19–23), Elisha at Dothan (2 Ki. 6:19), concealing the fact that we are fasting (Mt. 6:17–18), and Jesus acting as if he were going further (Lk. 24:28).

The existence of these passages can be taken as indicating that the Bible does not set before us an unbreakable principle which asserts that the claims of truthfulness must override all other claims, such as those of love or Christlikeness. But at the same time the fact that there are so few such passages, and that the teaching on truthfulness is so strong, should prevent us from claiming that the Bible readily sanctions lies. If lying is permitted it is only in the most exceptional circumstances and for the very best of reasons.

In a society where deceit and falsehood have apparently become an essential part of personal living, trade and industry, advertising, politics and international relationships, Christians are called to demonstrate, in life and word, truth that reflects the nature of God himself.

Bibliography

S. Bok, *Living: Moral Choice in Public and Private Life* (Hassocks, 1978; New York, 1979); H. Thielicke, *TE* 1 (ET, Philadelphia, 1966; London, 1968), pp. 520–566; A. C. Thiselton, *NIDNTT* 3, pp. 874–902.

P.A.H.

TWO CITIES, TWO KINGDOMS, see AUGUSTINE; LUTHERAN ETHICS; THIELICKE, HELMUT.

TYRANNICIDE is the killing of a tyrant. It presents three difficulties: Who is a tyrant? Is such killing justified? Who decides? The earlier Gk. notion of *tyrannos* was not necessarily negative: it referred to a seizer of power. What followed was what mattered. Gradually, probably stimulated by the actual behaviour of tyrants, it meant one who pursued his own, rather than official, ends.

Plato,* Aristotle* and Cicero (106–43 BC) justified tyrannicide, while Ehud (Jdg. 3:15–30) and Jehu (2 Ki. 9:21–37) seem to provide biblical precedents. The NT seems more quiescent, but possible grounds could be found in the apostles' call to 'obey God rather than men' (Acts 5:29, also 4:19) coupled with a view that Paul (Rom. 13:1–8) is justifying the basic office of ruling, not any particular ruler.

Christian theology generally has accepted a need and duty to oppose, and perhaps kill, tyrants. Thomas Aquinas* and, later, Francisco de Vitoria, Francisco de Suarez* and John Calvin* thought that lower officials could do so, basically for grounds similar to those of a just war.* Juan Mariana (1536–1624), John Knox (*c.* 1513–72), Huguenot writers, and perhaps Martin Luther,* thought even private citizens could do so, a view subsequently repudiated by the Jesuits. In Protestantism, especially Calvinism, tyrannicide was a live problem, and the execution of Charles I (1625–49; b. 1600) a possible instance.

Tyrannicide involves not only the legitimacy of a ruler but the complex question of the legitimacy of an opponent. The anarchic idea that any individual Christian (or congregation) should decide simply to 'obey God rather than man' manifests more Western individualism than biblical insight. Furthermore, the growth of representative government and division of political powers now provide a variety of means to oppose tyranny. However, as Hitler's constitutional but tyrannical regime shows, tyrannicide will always be an option (see Bonhoeffer, Dietrich*).

Bibliography
L. Rasmussen, *Dietrich Bonhoeffer: Reality and Resistance* (Nashville, TN, 1972); L. Strauss, *On Tyranny* (New York, 1963); M. Walzer, *Obligations* (Cambridge, MA, 1970).

P.A.M.

U

UNCONSCIOUS, THE.

Freudian theory (see Freud, Sigmund*) postulates a topography of the mind which has three dimensions: unconscious, preconscious and conscious. The unconscious contains the id, thoughts and feelings which were once conscious but have been repressed, the defensive part of the ego, and the super-ego. It is dynamic, seeking gratification, and can shift and change.

The unconscious is characterized by a primary process in which there is no organization or co-ordination between the drives seeking gratification. Opposites and contradictions exist side by side, and it is timeless. It is most accessible in dreams, when the secondary process which characterizes the ego is partially suspended in disguised or symbolic form. Not directly observable, its existence can be inferred from normal behaviour, lapses of speech and memory, 'mistakes' in behaviour and seemingly chance actions.

The unconscious remains so through the ego defence of repression (see Repression, Psychological*), which it is the aim of analysis (see Psychoanalysis*) to undo. Too great a spontaneous relaxation of resistances can lead to psychosis.*

The preconscious is more accessible than the unconscious and is capable of becoming conscious; it is the storehouse of memory. A large part of the ego is preconscious; it is also connected with speech residues.

Carl Jung* called the unconscious and preconscious the 'personal unconscious', distinguishing it from the 'collective unconscious'. This he considered resulted from inherited brain structure, a component shared by the human race, noting that symbols and complexes kept recurring throughout the history of civilization.

See also: CHARACTER. [10]

Bibliography
S. Freud, *The Ego and the Id* (1923), in *The Complete Psychological Works of Sigmund Freud*, vol. 19 (London, 1964); J. Jacobi, *The Psychology of C. G. Jung* (London, 1942).

J.R.G.

UNEMPLOYMENT.

The experience of unemployment is typically painful. The person made redundant, or released from work, may initially experience shock ('I can't believe that this has happened'). There may be a phase of denial, as the person behaves as if he or she is on holiday or vacation, believing that there will not be too much difficulty in finding another job. There may follow a period of active search, during which he or she may discover that it is extremely hard to get a job. Often there is then a prolonged period of despair, characterized by a sense of personal failure, isolation and purposelessness. If out of work for a long time, the person may become resigned to unemployment, passively accepting his or her fate and suffering a degree of emotional and physical decline.

It is important to stress variations in the experience of unemployment. Some will find it easier to adjust to the stigma of unemployment than others, *e.g.* the 58-year-old man who can claim that he has taken early retirement. In areas of high unemployment, the stigma will be less than in places where the individual feels that he or she is the only one out of work. In some areas, the young will be unemployed as they switch from one job to another, exploring the labour market till they find a path that suits them. They will feel very different from youngsters who are long-term unemployed and see no job on the horizon. Unemployment will feel different again for those who have been out of the labour market, *e.g.* full-time mothers, who might have looked for a job if unemployment was lower but are not doing so because unemployment is so high.

Various explanations are typically advanced during periods of high unemployment. The monetarist* will frequently argue that lax control of the money supply has led to inflation, and that the attempt to squeeze out inflation by tighter money control inevitably produces unemployment. If a country had persistently high unemployment but low inflation, the monetarist would blame this on inefficiencies in the market-place arising from a lack of competition. Keynesians, who follow the economic thought of John Maynard Keynes (1883–1946), argue that behaviour in the real economy (*i.e.* everyday economic life) determines money supply, not the other way round. They tend to focus on the role of government as the cause of unemployment: by spending less or raising taxes, government may reduce the demand for goods and services, which then puts people out of work. Appropriate fiscal policy can reduce unemployment.

Others focus on long-term structural changes in the economy: the decline of old industries, like coal-mining in Britain, which leads to unemployment; the emergence of new exporters whose competitive advantage forces old producers to rationalize by shedding labour (*e.g.* the effects of the Japanese car industry); the effects of new technologies which may reduce employment in some activities and increase jobs in others, causing unemployment while the economy adjusts. Marxists will point to the underlying conflict between labour and capital, which leads to inefficiencies and so eventually to unemployment. The prime loyalty of employees may tend to be towards the people they work with rather than the employer they work for, and this may be a prime cause of inefficiency. It may be most helpful to look for insights in all these approaches, rather than to focus on one.

A number of theological insights are relevant to unemployment.

1. The first is the biblical view that human worth does not depend on work.* In Gn. 1:27–28 men and women are created in God's image* before they are given their work. They are given a great job to do because they have been made great in the first place. Their worth precedes their work. This challenges the contemporary view that a person's worth is closely linked to his or her job – a view which leaves many unemployed feeling worth-less.

2. Genesis 1:28 defines work in terms of mastering the world. Work is anything that involves mastering a law of nature – be it the laws of a musical instrument or a word processor or whatever. This breath-takingly broad definition of work means that work need not be equated with a job. You can be at work whether you have paid employment or not. This challenges society to broaden its view of work and to provide unconventional forms of employment for those who are not in traditional jobs.

3. The OT jubilee* principle enshrines the notion of equal access to the source of income (land, in the case of ancient Israel). A modern application would be roughly equal access to paid jobs, which is the prime source of income for most people today. This would argue for the development of various forms of job-sharing.

The church should respond to unemployment by developing proposals for how these theological insights can be concretely applied; by working with the unemployed where possible to form mutual support groups, and to develop training and job creation projects; and by providing sensitive pastoral support for individuals who are out of work.

Bibliography

C. B. Handy, *The Future of Work* (Oxford, 1984); M. Moynagh, *Making Unemployment Work* (Tring, 1985); L. Ryken, *Work and Leisure in Christian Perspective* (Portland, OR, 1987; Leicester, 1989); J. A. Walter, *Hope on the Dole* (London, 1985).

M.M.

URBANIZATION is the process of the development of towns and cities (see City*), and the term includes the social consequences of an increase in the proportion of a country's population living in urban centres.

Since they first appeared around 3500 BC, cities have played an important role as a focus for trade, military and religious organization, and culture;* and at each stage in the history of human societies the character of urban life has profoundly influenced ideas about human nature and civilization. The city is one of the sources of biblical metaphor, serving as a symbol of humanity's pride in its own achievements (as in the Babel story, Gn. 11:1–9) and as a symbol of heaven (the city of God, the new Jerusalem, Rev. 21:2). Urbanization still attracts contrasting evaluations: those which see cities as a focus of civilization, opportunity and creativity, and those which emphasize the diversity of urban cultures, and point to the evidence the destructive effects of social anonymity, crowding, pollution or the concentration of social problems. There have been numerous, but not entirely successful, attempts to link urbanization with secularization* and the disintegration of religious tradition.

Pre-industrial cities were a way of life for only a very small minority of the population, a fact which sets them apart from the modern urban environment, which is home for 60% to 90% of the population in industrialized countries. The social aspects of urbanization vary according to the speed of change, the extent to which developments are planned, and changes in the pattern of economic production. In Europe and N. America, the growth of modern cities has paralleled industrialization over nearly 200 years. Patterns of urban life therefore reflect the long history of competition between social groups for scarce resources, and spatial organization can be represented as a pattern of human ecological specialization developed in response to successive movements of populations in search of work, housing and urban amenities. Urbanization in the industrialized countries has been regulated partly by market competition of land and housing, and partly by political means. Early theories of urban life (*e.g.* L. Wirth, 'Urbanism as a Way of Life', *AJS* 44, 1938, pp. 1–24) held that the size, density and heterogeneity of urban populations consistently lead to the loss of primary relationships, weakening of social control, and the tendency for urban dwellers to behave instrumentally towards each other. More recent theories deny these universal claims, emphasize the diversity of urban cultures, and point to the evidence that urban life may actually promote close personal and community ties. In this view, the negative consequences of urbanization are attributed to the perpetual restructuring of industrial and economic activity, leading to patterns of disruption, decline and expansion. Questions of planning, power and political control over the created environment* then become central.

While the Christian churches have, on the whole, been concerned to maintain a presence in areas which suffer most from the problems of urbanization, they also have to contend with these same problems: shifting populations, disruption of communities, inappropriate buildings and high costs. The 'suburbanization' of religion has been a predictable consequence.

A pattern of specialist urban ministries (*e.g.* university settlements, family and youth projects, community work, *etc.*) has developed in response to the missionary and social challenges of the inner cities. The 1985 Archbishop's Commission on Urban Priority Areas highlighted the increase in poverty* and related urban problems and proposed a strategy for action. This has been an important symbol of the church's commitment, and a means for promoting Christian social involvement, although the practical results have been small in relation to the needs.

Contemporary Christian theology and practice have to be worked out in the context of urban society. 'Inner-city' problems in themselves do not necessarily pose peculiar challenges, but they are highly symptomatic of the political, economic and social processes which generate poverty and injustice. The urban context has, however, proved to be unusually fertile for a number of developments, including ecumenical co-operation, the establishment of black-led churches, new concepts of urban mission, and innovative approaches in community work.

The problems of the inner cities in the developed countries do not have direct parallels elsewhere. The much shorter history of Third World urbanization is one of largely unplanned, rapid expansion through migration of populations from rural areas, creating a fringe of squatter zones where housing is illegal and living conditions are extremely poor. The most urgent political and ethical issue is justice for the urban poor and the struggle for fundamental human rights.

The meaning of cities, whether old or new, is that they are humanity's greatest creation and at the same time an attempt to create a home independent of God. The urban world may have rejected God, but the gospel message is that God has not rejected those who dwell in it.

Bibliography

Archbishop of Canterbury's Commission on Urban Priority Areas, *Faith in the City* (London, 1985); J. Ellul, *The Meaning of the City* (ET, Grand Rapids, 1970); A. Gilbert *et al.*, *Cities, Poverty and Development: Urbanization in the Third World* (Oxford, 1982); D. Harvey, *Consciousness and the Urban Experience: Studies in the History and Theory of Capitalist Urbanization* (Oxford, 1985); D. Sheppard, *Built as a City: God and the Urban World Today* (London, 1975).

H.H.D.

USURY, see ECONOMIC ETHICS; [17] INTEREST.

UTILITARIANISM, see
CONSEQUENTIALISM.

UTOPIANISM, see SOCIAL ETHICS.

V

VALUES, VALUE JUDGMENTS.

The terms 'values' and 'value judgments' are now widely used, though often without clear meaning, in both popular and more learned discourse. *Webster's New World Dictionary* (1970) defines 'values' as 'the social principles, goals, or standards held or accepted by an individual, class, society, etc.', and 'value judgments' as any 'estimate made of the worth, goodness, etc. of a person, action, event, or the like, esp. when making such judgment is improper or undesirable'. Prior to the late 19th century, 'value' meant the worth of persons or things; 'valuation' an estimate of their worth, primarily their economic worth. The development of general 'theories of value' and the use of these terms in aesthetics, jurisprudence,* historiography, pedagogy and even in ethics was a late 19th-century, largely continental European, development. Important philosophers like John Dewey (1859–1952) and R. B. Perry (1876–1957), among others, popularized their use in America, whereas British contemporaries like G. E. Moore (1873–1958) and W. D. Ross (1877–1940) continued to use the traditional terms 'right' and 'good'.

Various distinctions can be made in the use of the term 'values': 1. It functions most often in a *concrete sense* when we speak of someone's values or of 'Christian values', or when we distinguish 'material values' like cars or property from 'spiritual values' like knowledge of God. And if we were to value knowledge of God over acquiring property, then we would have made a comparative 'value judgment', to the effect that knowing God is better than acquiring property. 2. Some of a person's values may be *moral*, others *non-moral*. The sorts of things that are morally good or bad are persons or qualities of persons such as traits of character (virtues* and vices*), intentions,* dispositions, emotions and motives,* while things such as property, or experiences such as knowledge, may be non-morally good or bad. 3. Material possessions such as money or property may have only *utility* value, *i.e.* usefulness for some other purpose, like buying a painting. The painting may then have *in-*

herent and not just utility value for its owner. The enjoyment one receives from contemplating it is itself good. This experience may also have *contributory* value, *i.e.* it may be an important part of the *final* values, moral and non-moral, that together constitute the best life. In a Christian ethic, God may properly be thought to have value in each of these senses where it is understood that, strictly speaking, only God – Father, Son and Holy Spirit – has *intrinsic* value ('God *is* love', 1 Jn. 4:16), and that every other thing or person, their properties and relations, have value, moral and non-moral, only in relation to him.

Historically, there have been two principal approaches to the vexed issue of the definition of 'value(s)': the objective (see Objectivity of Morals*), and the subjective (see Subjectivism*). For objectivists like Plato* and G. E. Moore, values are intrinsic properties of things independent of our knowing, believing or valuing. Objectivists differ on how such objective values are apprehended. For subjectivists like R. B. Perry, a value is 'any object of interest', anything desired. The objectivist argues that values are *discovered* by us just as facts are, whereas the subjectivist maintains that they are *chosen* and that the principal difference between facts and values is that facts are discovered and values are chosen or assigned. If a drunken driver's car crashes, killing a family, that is a fact. Readers of the newspaper account say, 'That's reprehensible.' They have chosen or assigned a negative moral value to the driver's action. Orthodox Christianity has supported – and must support – the objectivist view for, in the first instance, God 'does not decide that love shall be good and hatred bad, so that if He had chosen otherwise it would have been so . . . Hatred is fundamentally perverse, not because God says so but because it could not be otherwise. What God makes is not values but a world of facts in which we can discover values' (Helen Oppenheimer, *The Hope of Happiness*, London, 1983, pp. 54f.). Our choices neither add values to the world nor remove values from it, though they can, and everywhere do, either cultivate, weaken or ignore them. To deny that we choose values is not to deny that we choose how to live, or what to do. A large part of what we find ourselves doing morally is not just making choices to do or not do what is absolutely commanded or forbidden, but also evaluating our own or others' actions, their motives and consequences, as good or bad, better or worse. 'In all this, it is more accurate to say that people shape their *lives* by their positive and negative choices than to say that they shape their *values*' (*ibid.*, p. 57).

Christian ethics understands God to be the objective, unitary ground of all moral values and Christ to be the perfect moral exemplar of those values, both in the sense that 1. as the man Jesus he alone fully discerned and fully realized these values in his perfect life and obedient death; and that 2. only by accepting reconciliation with God, effected by this perfect obedience, can anyone progressively realize in his or her life all values as forms of the love of God.

Webster's definition of 'value judgments' cited earlier ends with the observation that the term is especially associated with 'improper or undesirable' judgments. Knowing the inveterate and seemingly ineradicable human tendency to bad pride and moral complacency, biblical writers indicate why judgments of value are 'improper' or 'undesirable' in a strong moral sense. 1. Ultimate or final moral judgments about the character or action of other people are forbidden, for only God in the perfection of his knowledge and goodness can wisely make such judgments (Mt. 7:1; Rom. 2:16; 14:10–12; 2 Tim. 4:1; Jas. 4:12). 2. Judgments that multiply or magnify the evils in others while minimizing or ignoring evils in ourselves, or that scrupulously specify minor moral obligations like tithing herbs while neglecting major ones like justice, mercy and faithfulness, are condemned as dishonest and unjust (Mt. 7:3–5; 23:23–24; 1 Tim. 5:24–25; Jas. 3:13–17). 3. While Christians should welcome moral evaluation of their actions and character, the good judgments or the bad judgments of others should never be accepted uncritically (Pr. 1; 19:20, 25, 27; 1 Cor. 10:15; Eph. 4:15, 25; Jas. 1:9). The former could be mistaken, ironic or mere flattery, and the latter could be motivated by bad passions like anger, envy or jealousy that share a common carelessness for truth or justice (Pr. 15:20–32; Mt. 27:18; Acts 13:45; 1 Pet. 2:1).

M.A.R.

VATICAN II, see SECOND VATICAN COUNCIL.

VATICAN STATEMENTS. Three subjects on which Vatican statements of particular importance have been issued are euthanasia, liberation theology and sexual ethics. Such statements are issued by one or other of the eleven Vatican-based Congregations of the Curia of the Catholic Church, which do not act on their own authority but on the delegated authority of the Pope.

Euthanasia

In 1940, the Roman Catholic Church officially condemned euthanasia* or 'mercy killing' (see *Acta Apostolicae Sedis* 32). This is understood as the direct inducement of death, painlessly, for persons incurably diseased, mentally deficient or suffering from intractable pain. It is not to be identified or equated with the refusal or withdrawal of artificial / mechanical life-support systems, or with the administration of pain-relieving drugs which also shorten life.

Euthanasia is seen as intrinsically evil, since it violates a human being's primary and natural right to life and constitutes a sin against the fifth commandment: 'You shall not murder' (Ex. 20:13). Furthermore, it transgresses the supreme authority and dominion of God, the author of human life (see Sanctity of Human Life*).

Liberation theology

The Vatican Congregation for the Doctrine of the Faith has issued two statements ('instructions') on liberation theology.* The *Instruction on Certain Aspects of the Theology of Liberation* (6 August 1984) sees liberation from sin as primary, and freedom from oppression in other spheres as stemming from it. 'Liberation is first and foremost liberation from the radical slavery of sin. Its end and its goal is the freedom of the children of God. As a logical consequence, it calls for freedom from many different kinds of slavery in the cultural, economic, social and political spheres, all of which derive ultimately from sin, and so often prevent people from living in a manner befitting their dignity' (Introduction).

The same Congregation issued an *Instruction on Christian Freedom and Liberation* (22 March 1986). This takes a more nuanced position. It recognizes several forms of liberation theology, while stressing the church's determination to identify with the poor and the oppressed. However, it criticizes the liberationists' use of the Exodus as exclusively a model of political liberation. 'The major and fundamental event of the Exodus . . . has a meaning which is both religious and political. God sets his People free and gives them descendants, a land and a law, but within a Covenant and for a Covenant. One cannot therefore isolate the political aspect for its own sake; it has to be considered in the light of a plan of a religious nature within which it is integrated' (44).

Sexual ethics

Many statements from the Vatican have been issued over the years on the subject of sexual ethics (*e.g. Persona Humana,* the Declaration on Certain Questions Concerning Sexual Ethics, 1975; Letter to Bishops on the Pastoral Care of Homosexual Persons, 1986).

In current Vatican teaching, sexual intercourse is regarded as both unitive and pro-creative. The bodily intimacy which the sexual act involves is seen as demanding exclusivity. All genital sexual expressions must take place within marriage,* where alone they can play their due part in the enrichment of both spouses.

Every genital act must by its very nature be open to the possibility of bringing a new life into being. This premise is used to condemn masturbation,* homogenital acts (see Homosexuality*) and the use of contraceptives, but not the so-called 'safe period' or rhythm method of avoiding conception. It is claimed that these prohibitions are immutable laws inscribed in the constitutive elements of human nature.

See also: PAPAL ENCYCLICALS.

P.T.

VEGETARIANISM. Refraining from eating meat is a practice found only occasionally in the ancient world (*e.g.* among the Pythagoreans), and the Bible never condemns it. Nevertheless, killing animals for food is regarded as acceptable throughout nearly all of Scripture: Jesus ate fish (Lk. 24:42–43), and there is no reason to doubt that he ate meat (*cf.* Mt. 11:19); moreover, a recurrent NT theme stresses the ritual purity of all foods (Mk. 7:15; Acts 10:9–16; 1 Tim. 4:4; *etc.*).

However, though they provide no basis for an outright rejection of meat-eating, there is a tension in the biblical writings. In paradise human beings were vegetarians (Gn. 1:29), and the permission to eat meat was given only at the time of the Noachic covenant (Gn. 9:2–4). Yet even then the prohibition against consuming the lifeblood indicates that animals belong finally to God and are not simply at human disposal: meat-eating is the result of

divine forbearance and, while permitted, should be undertaken with a sense of responsibility for creation.

There is a variety of positive reasons for not eating meat: as a protest against cruel, intensive farming methods (see Battery Farming*) and inhumane forms of slaughter, as a rejection of inefficient uses of cereal grains, and (arguably) as part of a healthier diet. Whether or not the language of animal rights (see Rights, Animal*) is justified, human responsibility towards animals as part of the stewardship* of creation also suggests that blithe assumptions about treating them instrumentally as a means to human benefit should be reconsidered. Above all, in its attention to the prophetic vision of a time when 'the lion will eat straw like the ox' (Is. 65:25; *cf.* 11:6–9; Ho. 2:18), the practice of refraining from meat bears witness to the future harmony of human beings and animals in a redeemed creation.

R.J.So.

VICE. The term 'vice' and its opposite term, 'virtue',* are both archaic (though it may well be asked if suitable terms have replaced them in contemporary moral discourse). In present Eng. usage, 'vice' does not always denote great wickedness or depravity, *e.g.* when someone says, 'A fondness for chocolates is her only vice.' The strong sense of wickedness or depraved conduct is conveyed, for instance, in 'vice squad' (a police unit assigned to the control of prostitution, gambling or drugs). While these two uses differ in the degree of moral failure conveyed, they share a feature that is essential to many uses of the term, namely, it denotes something *habitual.* Virtues and vices are habitual inner tendencies, or dispositions, to perform morally good or bad acts. In contemporary usage, vices are more firmly connected than are virtues with the idea of habit* (vices are bad habits), while they are less solidly identified than are virtues with the concept of an inner tendency to act rather than the acts themselves.

In traditional moral theology (see Christian Moral Reasoning [18]), vice and vices have functioned as synonyms for sin and sins. For example, given the definition just provided, the seven deadly sins* – pride, envy, wrath, sloth, avarice, lust and gluttony – are clearly vices. Each names bad or sinful habitual dispositions rather than wrong actions or behaviour. While Protestant moralists do use the terms 'virtue(s)' and 'vice(s)', they have thought that Roman Catholic moral theologians (see Roman Catholic Moral Theology*) generally give too large a place to human effort and too small a place to God's grace* in eliminating vice and achieving virtue. However, Protestant, and perhaps especially evangelical, moralists may well profit from the acute descriptions of individual vices and their unity provided by the rich tradition of Catholic moral theology. The great advantage of that tradition lies in its clear understanding that sin or vice must not be confused with sins or vices.

The great pagan philosophers of antiquity understood vice as a tendency to do what is evil and equally as a disposition not to do what is good. And, if virtue is developed by education and self-discipline, vice may be overcome by the same means. Persons of base character have either been denied the proper training and discipline of parents and teachers or they have refused to accept it. They have failed to shape a good character for themselves by way of moral reflection, self-knowledge and self-discipline. The description of vice given by Plutarch (AD 46–120) in his *Moralia* is typical: the impulses and passions of base persons are not controlled by reason, so their souls become disordered, anxious and discontented.

Christian philosophers generally did not wholly reject the pagan philosophers' account of vice, but they understood it to be a more serious matter than a disordered soul due to defective education. Vice is *sin*: rejection of the good that is God; transgression of his law (Rom. 3:9–20). According to Augustine,* the pagan prescriptions for preventing or eliminating vice by education and self-discipline fail to understand the humanly intractable character of all vices as occasioned by sin, *i.e.* the perverse delight of sinners in rejecting God and his goodness (see Sin and Salvation 15). The reversal of vice requires a repentant acceptance of the gracious reconciliation with God effected in the atoning (see Atonement*) death of Christ.

While Christian theologians have generally accepted the clear teachings of the Scriptures that human beings are sinners, they have differed on the nature of sin or vice. For example, Augustine sees sin or vice not as consisting in a natural drive to satisfy various desires in defiance of the will of God (as does Abelard*), but as a sheerly perverse desire to disobey God. On the other hand, both agree that vice is not to be identified with actions but with the mo-

ment one intends to act. If someone decides to steal something, then the moment he or she intends to do this, vice is present, and this is true even if they subsequently fail to do, or are prevented from doing, what they had intended. Joseph Butler* also denies that anyone loves sin for its own sake. Rather, all vice is a consequence of self-deception, a blindness about what is really just and benevolent. Vice 'is false selfishness alone' (*Fifteen Sermons upon Human Nature*, 1726). Here, too, vice is not to be identified with particularly heinous acts but with that self-deception that enables a person to do such evil acts in a self-righteous manner.

See also: CHARACTER. 10

M.A.R.

VIOLENCE. Defining violence is a very complex task, and its resolution will determine to a large extent any ethical analysis and prescription which follow. It might be defined as 'intentional, forceful action that causes unwelcome physical injury to another human being'. To this some would add actions that 'compel or prevent another's action against his or her will', whether or not physical injury results.

The Lat. etymological roots of 'violence' call attention more to the psychological and physical condition of the violent agent (vehemence, impetuosity, great agitation) than to his or her effects on others. However, violent dancing, wood-chopping or yodelling do not, in and of themselves, pose any particular ethical or pastoral questions because they do not inflict injury on the self or others. Nevertheless, our definition should retain some of this etymological flavour, since to include all instances of compulsion or force,* no matter how slow, subtle or indirect, is too broad and inclusive to be helpful. Violence is forceful.

We may set aside most of what appears to be violence in sports and games. To the extent that it falls within rules accepted by all participants (and is thus not 'unwelcome' in the terms of our opening definition), and inasmuch as any injury is accidental rather than intentional, even very rough play on the Rugby or football field is not an ethical issue. Of course, illegal, 'dirty' play, intending to injure an opponent, is as unacceptable in sports as anywhere else. More problematic is athletic competition such as boxing which, while bounded by agreed-upon rules (*e.g.* no blows below the belt or after the round ends), intends at least temporary physical injury to the opponent (and seriously risks permanent injury).

Finally, we should note the broader issue of intentionality (see Intention*). It is unacceptable violence for someone deliberately to slam his car into mine and injure me. But if someone is drunk and drives into me, or is haphazard in aircraft maintenance, leading to my injury in a plane crash, I experience a 'violent' injury but it is accidental and not intended. For such cases, the primary ethical problem is irresponsibility. The resultant experience of serious injury is tragic but unintended and, therefore, not morally equivalent to violence.

1. Categories of violence

With these preliminary qualifications in mind, we may proceed to map out the problem of violence in relation to four sets of criteria.

a. Individual and corporate violence. Violence occurs among individuals in the familiar forms of assault, battery, murder, rape, spousal and child abuse, *etc.* Self-defence, counter-attacking the assailant of a neighbour, and the physical punishment or discipline of children are some of the individual cases that require more careful attention. Violence occurs on a corporate scale in gang fights and family feuds, and in institutional forms such as police forces and armies. The ethical analysis of corporate violence must include questions of how moral responsibility is shared variously among all concerned, from the 'trigger finger' to the leaders, from the agents of violence to those enjoying their protection, from the inventor and manufacturer of a weapon to its user.

b. Overt and covert violence. Overt violence is not difficult to identify, and such phenomena constitute the essence of violence. However, it is often argued that violence can be expressed in covert ways which are as coercive, manipulative, harmful and dehumanizing as their overt counterparts. Verbal attacks may hurt as much as physical abuse; seducing an alcohol-drugged date may be *de facto* rape; inheritance-tax laws may have as violent an impact on a surviving spouse as a band of outlaws stealing property. Subliminal propaganda, hypnosis, advertising, ecclesiastical shunning, market monopolies, union strikes, State laws and even the subtle grip of tradition may be violence wearing a velvet glove. Having noted these possibilities, however, it is best to concentrate primary ethical analysis on the overt forms of violence, and then direct a derivative moral scrutiny toward possible covert substitutes. To collapse this distinction between overt and covert violence risks the loss of precise, focused responses to contemporary violence by casting the net so wide that almost anything can be included.

c. Legal and illegal violence. Forceful, violent actions upon others by police, armed forces, athletic competitors and parents are different from mob, mugger or terrorist* violence in that they are explicitly permitted by the laws governing a given social body. Violence that exceeds the limits permitted by law is then called brutality or abuse. The same action that is carried out by a legally recognized authority and is designated 'force' may be rejected as 'violence' or 'terrorism' when performed by those without legally recognized rights to do so. Difficulties arise when one group's law allows what another group rejects. The revolt of Britain's American colonies, the current Northern Irish IRA-led revolt against the British, the American invasion of Grenada and Panama, Iraq's invasion of Kuwait, the Basque revolt against Spain, and countless other examples raise issues of law and violence.

d. Just and unjust, moral and immoral violence. Ultimately, the law cannot decide all issues of appropriate violence or force. Nazi Germany is only one example, but the best known, of many societies in which terrible violence was entirely legal and yet unjust and immoral. The higher and more profound criteria in our evaluation of violence are those of ethics: the criteria of justice, rightness and goodness. Our laws (and, more broadly, our customs and traditions) concerning violence need continual revision so that they may approximate ever more closely to standards of justice and goodness. While it is a tempting strategy, it is finally misleading to restrict the term 'violence' to unethical or illegal force (and use 'force' for what we approve). A police team clearing a building of terrorists is employing violence; whether it is right or not is a separate question, not to be decided in advance through labelling.

For Christians, the good, the right and the just (for questions of violence as all else) are to be found in the character and will of God, who has revealed himself in Jesus* Christ and Scripture (see Revelation*). The Word of God is given to the people of God (see Church*), who are assisted by the indwelling Spirit of God (see Holy Spirit*) in the ethical tasks of discernment and implementation. Christian ethics seeks a clear understanding of, and faithful obedience to, the Word of God regarding violence in our time and place. The constancy and reliability of God's character, on the one hand, and the obvious historical and cultural variety throughout biblical and ecclesiastical history (regarding violence and the people of God), on the other, must inform our ethical study. Having carried out Christian ethical research, our task becomes that of faithfully making our presence felt in the broader multicultural consensus governing our society.

2. The origin and character of violence

How are we to account for violence in human experience? Arguments can be made that violence is a necessary and perhaps even a beneficial attribute of human life. The glorification of violence in the form of personal prowess (the hunter and warrior) and military conquest appears virtually everywhere in human history and mythology. This is because of the social and economic benefits of victory as well as the alleged value of such character traits as courage and bravery cultivated in violent conflict. Charles Darwin's* theory of evolution seemed to provide a scientific basis for understanding violence as an entirely natural, beneficial, progressive competition in which the fittest survive and the weak are eliminated. Humans are violent because of both genetic endowment and their learned behaviour.

Of course, those injured by the violence of others have left their own sad lament across time and space. Many would argue that at this stage in our evolution, humanity should rise above violent, predatory struggle (necessary as it was in earlier eras) to a benevolent, rational, non-violent planning and co-operation. Others argue that some final stage of revolutionary violence might be yet necessary to overthrow the last vestiges of oppression before a more just and peaceful era of co-operation can emerge. In any case, violence appears to be a normal and necessary condition of human existence with both beneficial and tragic consequences.

3. Violence in Scripture

In contrast to such views, the Bible portrays violence as fundamentally abnormal and pathological. Neither the original creation of Gn. 1 – 2 nor the eventual new creation of Rev. 21 – 22 has any place for violence. Violence results from and manifests sin, the revolt against the creator. Thus, the Fall* into sin (Gn. 3) leads directly to Adam and Eve's mutual alienation and to Cain's murder of Abel (Gn. 4). Murder is followed by kidnapping, rape, warfare and even the institutional State violence of slavery and economic co-option (supervised by Joseph) in Genesis alone. Violence is a sin and the result of sin. It is identified and condemned as such in many different forms and settings throughout the OT and NT. Separated from the authority and guidance of God, human desires become distorted and selfish, and aggressive energy can be misdirected into violent attacks on others. Violence is, thus, common in a sinful world but abnormal relative to God's original and ultimate character and purposes.

There are five main lines of response to violence in the Bible. a. Certain acts of violence are *prohibited* by law (*e.g.* 'You shall not murder'). b. Violence is *contained* by law (*e.g.* the *lex talionis*, [only] 'an eye for an eye') and political-social organization (*e.g.* a legal and penal system). c. Violence is met with *counterforce* (*e.g.* Israel is commanded to fight against the Philistines; the apocalyptic armies of God smash the armies of the Antichrist and the beast at Armageddon). d. Violence is *replaced* by creative, non-violent alternatives (*e.g.* Gideon's candles, clay pots and trumpets; Jesus' teaching on negotiation and reconciliation). e. Violence is *absorbed* with patient suffering and forgiving love (*e.g.* 'turning the other cheek', Jesus' death on the cross).

The Bible reveals a historical progression in its word on violence as on other matters. The fact that violence is not part of God's creation and not part of the New Jerusalem is of considerable importance. Violence is a result of the chaos, alienation* and pride* of the Fall. It is fundamentally the work of the Evil One (see Satan*). To the extent that the Bible countenances the people of God participating in violence, it appears to be limited in the OT by the particular circumstances of Israel in its geographic and national vocation as God's chosen witness in the ancient world. God chose to enter an epoch filled with tribal warfare and violence; Israel, God's chosen vehicle for this historical presence, participates in warfare, kingship, polygamy and other phenomena that are not representative of God's original or final purposes for humankind. In comparison to contemporary practice, such participation is limited, qualified, even elevated and improved by the God of Israel. But it remains a difficult matter, understandable only in light of God's loving refusal to abandon fallen humanity sunk far below the creator's intentions.

In the NT the people of God are diffused as aliens, pilgrims and ambassadors among the nations of the world. Their primary citizenship is in the coming kingdom of God* in which swords will at last be beaten into ploughshares. With the teaching and example of Jesus Christ fully exhibiting God's will in a violent world, the NT call to peace-making, patient suffering even for an unjust cause, non-retaliation, and a general strategy of overcoming evil with good dominates the text. Christian 'warfare' is carried out by means of spiritual 'weapons' such as faith, prayer and the gospel. Secondary motifs in the NT remind us that some of the people of God may find themselves in military or police posts (e.g. Cornelius), that God intends to use those who bear the sword to punish evil and protect the good (e.g. Rom. 13:3–5), and that a violent end awaits Satan and his cohorts at the end of our history (Rev. 19:11–15; 20:1–10). One of the challenges of the NT is that its counsel to non-retaliation is addressed to the reader and does not clearly direct the reader's response to violence against third parties, especially the weak.

4. The Christian tradition

Historically, our Christian forebears have interpreted the call of God and the teaching of Scripture in several different ways, which might be summarized as follows. At one extreme is the Christian 'crusade'. From Constantine* to the Crusades and on into our century, inspired by Israel's wars of conquest in the Promised Land (and perhaps as well by a highly literal anticipation of the conflict of Armageddon), some Christians would take up arms in a pro-active attempt to conquer in the name of Christ. On a smaller scale, individuals and groups may still share this aggressive willingness to employ violence in the name of Christ (e.g. the Ku Klux Klan).

At the other extreme, various Amish and Mennonite (see Mennonite Ethics*) groups are the best-known proponents of complete non-resistance to violence (see Non-violence*) and evil. On this view, since Jesus inaugurated the new covenant, Christians are called to be 'in the world' but radically 'not of' the world. This implies a total refusal to use the weapons of violence, even if suffering and death result. A third tradition might be summarized as 'pacifism'* or 'non-violent resistance' as exemplified in some Mennonite groups, Quakers, Martin Luther King* and the Southern Christian Leadership Conference, and the Catholic Worker Movement. In common with the 'non-resistance' tradition, the pacifists reject all recourse to violence against human beings. But in contrast to the non-resistance tradition, pacifists would find alternative ways actively to make peace and stop violence. This might include public demonstrations, strikes and work stoppages, and destruction of property.

Finally, the dominant tradition in Christian history is that of the 'just use' of force or violence (see Just-War Theory*). Provided it is limited in scope and duration, precisely targeted at the enemy and will not harm the innocent, and is undertaken for a principled, just cause, Christians may use violent means. Thus, police force to maintain law and order, armed force to protect national boundaries and populations, and personal self-defence against an attacker would all be possible. In some versions of this tradition (typically the Reformed rather than the Lutheran approach), violence may be justified even in a revolt (see Rebellion*) against the government if the latter is clearly not fulfilling the norms of Rom. 13 as a promoter of good and punisher of evil. In any case, the non-violence of the NT is understood to apply to personal relations, the realm of the church, or perhaps to stand as the ultimate ethical judging of our provisional, relative efforts.

5. A Christian ethic of violence

Neither the 'crusade' nor the 'non-resistance' ('quietist') extremes will be persuasive to most Christians today. In our violent world, the most compelling general stance from both biblical and practical standpoints will be that of active peace-making and a commitment to non-violent ways of resisting violence and evil. Violence tends to beget more violence; there has not appeared any war to end all wars. Christians should follow their Lord in bearing the cross* and trying to break the cycle of violence. More than passive suffering, Christians will search for creative and redemptive ways of mitigating conditions (social, economic, psychological, religious) which provoke or encourage anger, pride, envy and violence. They may help the potentially violent to discover non-violent ways of expression.

They can often defuse rage with a caring, empathetic listening ear.

Christians can protect and honour life with their actions as well as their words. This will no doubt require a 'no' to epidemic abortion on demand, the abuse of the young, the weak and the aged, gang violence, police brutality and all other forms of excessive force in our world, as well as to the popular media which glorify violence. Saying 'no' may need to be accompanied by demonstrations, strikes, political campaigns and legislative reform efforts. Still more important is the Christian 'yes', expressed in words celebrating the goodness of life, health and peace, and in actions which create safe places for the threatened, and healing places for both the victim and the violent.

While an aggressive, creative peace-making is the basic Christian stance towards violence in all of its forms today, it cannot be denied that Christians may find themselves drawn into the web of violence in ways which appear not to allow a non-violent response. This is particularly true when we find ourselves the observers of violence against the weak. While it is laudable to decide for oneself to suffer without retaliation, it is not so obviously laudable to watch the strong beat up the weak without intervening, whether at a small, interpersonal level or a broader social level (*e.g.* Iraq invading Kuwait, neo-Nazis attacking minorities). Even in the NT the evidence suggests that God is present and active amid the violence and failure of society at large, and not just within the church.

The crucial requirements for Christian participation in violence (be it as a member of the police or armed forces, or in subduing a mugger, or in revolting against an illegitimate regime) are: a. a thorough search for peaceful, non-violent alternatives; b. a prayerful quest for guidance from God; c. a conscientious reflection and decision in a group of Christians (both moral discernment and authority are promised to the Christian koinonia [see Fellowship*], not to the autonomous individual); d. a careful attempt to use limited, proportionate means and only because of a just cause; and e. a vigilant effort not to justify violence or force as 'Christian' (even though we pray that God is guiding, we should not claim divine approval and thus undermine the Christian witness in the world).

Specific cases of violence are legion. Consider a. a woman with an unwanted pregnancy as a result of being raped, b. the democratic revolutionary underground in an authoritarian, oppressive nation, c. a policeman confronted with a gun-waving drunk in a busy shopping mall, and d. an elderly man being kept alive in constant pain on artificial life-support machines. In each case the appeal of some form of violence (against the foetus, the dictators, the gunman, the self) is strong. There are no easy answers, but if Christians carry out their search for the will of God in the context of Scripture, prayer and community, if they make a whole-hearted effort to find a non-violent, peaceful response, and if they resort to violent means only under the strictly limited conditions described above, then their likelihood of sowing peace in a violent world will be greatly increased.

Bibliography

S. Brownmiller, *Against Our Will: Men, Women and Rape* (London and New York, 1975); N. F. Chase, *A Child is Being Beaten: Violence Against Children, an American Tragedy* (New York, 1975); J. Ellul, *Violence: Reflections from a Christian Perspective* (ET, New York, 1969; London, 1970); O. Guinness, *Violence: A Study of Contemporary Attitudes* (Downers Grove, IL, 1974); M. Hengel, *Victory Over Violence* (ET, Philadelphia, 1973; London, 1975); K. Kaunda, *The Riddle of Violence* (San Francisco, 1980); W. Laqueur, *Terrorism* (Boston, MA, and London, 1977); M. Lind, *Yahweh is a Warrior: The Theology of Warfare in Ancient Israel* (Scottdale, PA, 1980); K. Lorenz, *On Aggression* (New York and London, 1966); R. J. Sider, *Christ and Violence* (Scottdale, PA, 1979; Tring, 1980); G. Sorel, *Reflections on Violence* (New York, 1950); P. Tournier, *The Violence Within* (ET, San Francisco, 1978) = *The Violence Inside* (London, 1978); E. van den Haag, *Political Violence and Civil Disobedience* (New York, 1972); M. Walzer, *Just and Unjust Wars* (New York, 1977; Harmondsworth, 1980); J. H. Yoder, *The Politics of Jesus* (Grand Rapids, 1972).

D.W.G.

VIRGINITY is a term that can be applied to the condition of either a man or a woman who has not yet engaged in sexual intercourse. Sociological studies reveal widely varying attitudes to it. Male virginity has rarely been prized among men. Adolescent boys have a tendency to engage in heterosexual intercourse to boost their status within their male group. On the other hand, virginity in women up to the point of marriage has been highly valued in established societies and property-owning classes, where a promiscuous bride could be a threat to the male lineage and the inheritance of wealth. In poorer social groups virginity was considered less important than solid evidence of fecundity. In rural areas of Europe up to the 18th and 19th centuries, courtship included night-visiting in the girl's sleeping-quarters, and marriage did not take place until a pregnancy was established.

References to virginity in the Pentateuch presuppose a patriarchal structure in which the premarital virginity of a woman directly reflects on the honour of her father or husband. Passages such as Dt. 22:13–29 legislate for disputes in the light of such values, including producing physical evidence of the bride's virginity. Bearing in mind how Jesus viewed the divorce provision in Deuteronomy (Mk. 10:3–5), Christian ethics does not assume that such background assumptions are to be taken as norms. When we look to the NT, however, we find little that addresses the subject of virginity directly.

In 2 Cor. 11:2 Paul uses the language of purity to describe a virgin presented to her husband. L. W. Countryman (1941–) has raised an important debate over concepts of cleanness or purity in relation to sexuality (see [11]) in Scripture. Since sexual feelings are so strong and often bewildering in adolescence,* it is very easy for heavy-handed warnings against impurity to become associated with a tendency towards anxiety* and guilt* about any kind of sexual arousal. It is clear, however, in 2 Cor. 11:3 that the purity the apostle is emphasizing is an undivided devotion, a faithful advance commitment to a future life partner.

Along with many other Protestant theologians since the 1960s, Countryman wants to go further than merely dissociating virginity from an emotive or ritual association with cleanliness. His emphasis on the relational aspects of sexual intercourse leads to the conclusion that within the context of modern Western culture, losing virginity in a temporary relationship is not necessarily damaging, and may be commendable if it contributes towards maturity in an eventual marriage union. This position does not do justice to the strength of Paul's arguments in 1 Cor. 6 and 7.

Lewis Smedes (1921–) points out that there we find more than a morality of caution, and concern about the risks of pregnancy and sexually transmitted disease. It is also more than a morality of personal relationships where the consequences for each other's physical and emotional needs are calculated. Paul's arguments are based on sexual intercourse having universal moral significance as a life-uniting act – becoming one flesh (Gn. 2:24). A sexual union outside the context of a life-union of marriage is a sin regardless of the consequences to others. It is an offence against one's own God-given integrity of body and soul. The body is saying, 'I love you and want to have a life-union with you', while the heart is saying, 'I don't.'

In this traditional Christian understanding of sexual union, virginity in both men and women is valued as something precious, to be protected so that it can be offered as a gift in the self-giving of a life-union. For those who for various reasons do not choose or find a partner, lifelong virginity can be embraced as a commitment to integrity and faithfulness in love which will have a wider fulfilment in the future life in the kingdom of God.* For some it is a choice to follow in the footsteps of Jesus or to respond to the apostle Paul's challenge to live in undivided devotion to the Lord (see 1 Cor. 7:34).

It is pastorally important, however, that such theological views do not prevent virgins from owning the pain and frustration being experienced in the present, or from examining some of the psychological motivations which may be limiting their freedom of choice.

If Jesus has provided a role model for male virginity, the model of Mary his mother is more complex. In the church in the early 4th century, ascetic* ideals in relation to sexuality became increasingly widespread. Mary began to be offered as a role model of continence, being presented by such Church Fathers as Jerome (c. 342–420) as a perpetual virgin. (See his *Against Helvidius* [AD 383] concerning the perpetual virginity of the blessed virgin.) Many women today note the danger of using Mary as a symbol of desexualized motherhood. Protestant theology, however, has not accepted a doctrine of her permanent virginity. All churches can unite to affirm the significance of the teenage virgin who responded to an amazing message from God and trusted it, despite the obvious risks of pain and rejection it brought into her life.

See also: FORNICATION; SINGLENESS.

Bibliography

J. Bancroft, *Human Sexuality and its Problems* (Edinburgh and New York, ²1989); L. W. Countryman, *Dirt, Greed and Sex* (Philadelphia, 1988; London, 1987); J. Dominian, *Sexual Integrity* (London, 1987); D. J. Goergen, *DPCC*, pp. 133–135; L. Smedes, *Sex in the Real World* (Grand Rapids, 1976; Tring, 1979).

V.M.S.

VIRTUE, VIRTUES. The word 'virtue' comes from the Lat. *vir*, meaning 'man'; virtue was originally the quality of manliness. The sexist overtone has been lost, but the idea remains that a virtue is a quality marking someone's success as a person; to have the virtues is to be self-actualized, well adapted, fully functioning, and to be a good specimen of the human kind.

A virtue can be defined as any one of a set of interdependent traits which, as a set, adapt a person for living an ideally human life and express the proper human potential. Two closely related issues are in view: what kind of setting it is that one has to live in, and what kind of a being one is. For Aristotle,* the setting is the city-state and the person is an acting, happiness-seeking rational agent. For the Stoic,* the setting is a law-governed nature (universe) over which no control is possible, and the person is a frustration-shunning mind who does have control over his or her thoughts and desires.

In the Christian view, an ideally human life is one lived in the kingdom of God.* The Christian virtues are thus traits that fit a person for life in that kingdom. The Christian life is also to be lived in our present fallen state and world, in which we see unclearly and face many temptations and oppositions; several of the Christian virtues fit us especially to survive spiritually in this context. Since the proper human potential is to be a child of God, the Christian virtues, taken as a set, are the actualization of a personality characteristic of a child of God.

It is clear from our definition that virtues are not just dispositions to *behave* properly; they embody a person's philosophy of life (self-understanding and understanding of the natural and social world) and determine his or her concerns, desires, emotions and perceptions of virtually everything, as well as his or her actions. Virtues will vary in structure according to the philosophy of life to which they belong; thus the Christian virtues will be quite distinct, in important ways, from their non-Christian counterparts (see Character⑩).

The seven cardinal virtues of medieval Christian tradition are wisdom, fortitude, temperance and justice (adapted from the pagan cardinal virtues of antiquity), along with faith, hope and love (the so-called theological virtues). But many other virtues are commended in the NT: *e.g.* joy (Rom. 5:2, 3, 11), obedience (1 Pet. 1:2), holiness (1 Pet. 1:15–16), purity (2 Cor. 6:6), tenderheartedness (Eph. 4:32, RSV and NEB), contentment (Phil. 4:11–12), peace (Phil. 4:7), compassion (Col. 3:12), gratitude (1 Thes. 5:18), kindness (2 Cor. 6:6), hospitality (Rom. 12:13), gentleness (1 Tim. 6:11), generosity (2 Cor. 9:11, 13), peaceableness (Rom. 12:18), truthfulness (Eph. 4:15, 25), humility* (Phil. 2:3), fear of God (2 Cor. 5:11), confidence (2 Cor. 5:6, 8), meekness (Jas. 1:21, RSV), forgiveness (Col. 3:13), patience (1 Cor. 13:4), forbearance (Phil. 4:5, RSV), self-control (Gal. 5:23), perseverance (Rom. 5:3–4), courage (Phil 1:20). If full blessedness consists in loving God with one's whole heart and one's neighbour as oneself, then the powers and dispositions that go by the above names are the personality-conditions for approximating to that blessedness in this present troubled life, and becoming ready to enjoy it fully in the next.

The implications of the virtues for pastoral work are enormous. As an ethicist, the pastor is more than an exhorter of the congregation to good 'behaviour', more than an adviser in situations of ethical crisis, and more than a facilitator of social service projects or structural social change. He or she is a spiritual guide (see Spiritual Direction*), a shaper of personalities, a nurturer of hearts, a therapist of souls in the interest of God's kingdom. An understanding of the Christian virtues is vital for the pastor's ability to minister. Alongside close study of NT psychology (*i.e.* spirituality*), the pastor's preaching and counselling ministry will relate personal needs to the growth of Christian virtues. He or she needs to be well acquainted with the spiritual disciplines and congregational activities by which the Christian virtues are cultivated. To this end he or she is aided by the classic Christian writings on the virtues, and on the lives of Christian saints.

See also: THEOLOGICAL VIRTUES.

Bibliography

P. French *et al.* (eds.), *Ethical Theory: Character and Virtue* (Notre Dame, IN, 1988); P. T. Geach, *The Virtues* (Cambridge and New York, 1977); D. L. Jeffrey (ed.), *A Burning and a Shining Light: English Spirituality in the Age of Wesley* (Grand Rapids, 1987); J. Pieper, *The Four Cardinal Virtues* (Notre Dame, IN, 1966); R. C. Roberts, *Spirituality and Human Emotion* (Grand Rapids, 1983); J. E. Smith (ed.), *The Works of Jonathan Edwards, vol. 2: Religious Affections* (New Haven, CT, 1959).

R.C.R.

VITORIA, FRANCISCO DE (*c.* 1485– *c.* 1546). Spanish jurist and Dominican theologian, Vitoria has been called the father of modern international law. Building on the natural-law* teaching of Thomas Aquinas,* he argued that only in an organized society can people, being by nature social animals, achieve a full life. The political power inherent in a society is given by God for the common good, so that the form of government and the particular individuals who are to exercise authority are left to the full determination of the people. Not only separate States, but the world as a whole, may be seen as empowered to create just laws fitting for all persons. International law thereby rests on the law of nations (*lex gentium*) derived from natural law.

Vitoria's two contributions *On the Indians* in his 'Relectiones' (conferences given between 1527 and 1540) inquire on this basis into the rights of the Spanish to have dominion over the New World, and into the morality of their war against the Indians. He argues that the Indians are rational beings of sound mind who legally owned their property before the arrival of the Spaniards, and that this claim is unaffected by either their unbelief or any other mortal sins. Since neither the emperor nor the pope has been granted power over the whole world, neither of them has the right to seize their possessions or otherwise punish them. The Spaniards have the right to travel, trade and preach the gospel; they may defend themselves against attack, but may not make war to extend the empire, either for personal glory or gain, or to force conversion to Christianity. In this analysis, Vitoria develops detailed applications of just-war* rules.

A.F.H.

VIVISECTION, see RIGHTS, ANIMAL.

VOCATION refers to God's call to men and women to serve him. The Reformers taught that a person might have several 'callings' in his work,* at home, in the church,* and so on. It is God's call in relation to work that has proved particularly difficult to express theologically. How does God's call to serve him (vocation) relate to the totality of one's work? One can discern perhaps five models.

1. *Vocation is outside of work.* This was basically the medieval view, which saw priestly and monastic work as being 'sanctified' and of more value than secular work. It is expressed in the church today, *e.g.* when an accountant justifies his job as providing an income to support those in paid Christian employment, or when he says that his real work for the Lord is what he does in the church as a youth leader. Vocation is seen to be outside of secular work. The strength of this view is that it reflects a high doctrine of the church; its weakness is that it has a low doctrine of creation.* It underestimates the extent to which God is at work in the world.

2. Martin Luther* and other Reformers reacted against this and developed a doctrine that comes close to saying that *vocation equals work.* Men and women are co-creators with God. Through work we continue and take forward the process of creation begun by God. In his desire to affirm the value of work, Luther at times implies that all the work we do is God's work. This reflects a positive doctrine of creation. A weakness is that insufficient attention is given to the Fall.* Not all of every job is an extension of God's creativity. Jobs which destroy the environment* are in a different category altogether.

3. The 20th-century Swiss theologian Karl Barth's* view can be summarized as *vocation within work.* He recognized that aspects of work are 'fallen', and so are not in line with God's will. The Christian fulfils his or her vocation as he or she does God's will within the job. This gets a better balance between the doctrines of creation and the Fall. But it is rather passive. It does not do much to encourage people to combat evil at work.

4. Another approach, therefore, would be to say that *vocation reforms work.* This would be the view of Christians committed to the 'social gospel'. Christians are called to be 'salt and light'. We are to challenge evil wherever we find it, including the work-place. This is a more dynamic view than Barth's, but does it overestimate the degree to which individuals

can produce change at work? How much control do individuals (even boards of directors) have over their organizations?

5. A fifth view is associated with the French professor of law and political science, Jacques Ellul.* He argued that work is so contaminated by the Fall that no meaningful reform is possible. Organizations have their own dynamics, their own inherent laws, which make significant change impossible. For a work-place to reflect Christian values, so much change would be necessary that it would be impracticable within the modern, technological system. Christians should point to how 'fallen' work is, to God's judgment of work at the end of history, and to humanity's need of God if it is to avoid judgment. So *vocation judges work*. This view is realistic about the complexities of the modern world, but is it too pessimistic about the scope for change?

Perhaps each of these models contains insights which we should hold together if we want a rounded doctrine of vocation.

Bibliography

K. Barth, *CD* III/4; J. Ellul, *The Ethics of Freedom* (London, 1976), pp. 447ff.; L. Ryken, *Work and Leisure in Christian Perspective* (Portland, OR, 1987; Leicester, 1989); J. Zylstra (ed.), *Labour of Love: Essays on Work* (Toronto, 1980).

M.M.

VOLUNTARISM properly refers to any theory giving pre-eminence to the exercise of the will,* usually at the expense of reason.* Applied to humankind, it has been associated with many including Thomas Hobbes (1588–1679), David Hume,* and William James* in *The Will to Believe*. Some accounts of ethics regard the whole of morality as a creation of the human will, making '*x* is right' indistinguishable from 'I choose *x*'. In popular usage the term has also been substituted for 'voluntaryism', *i.e.* the reliance of churches, schools, trade unions, *etc.*, for membership or finance on voluntary offering rather than on say, State taxation (*e.g.* the church tax in Germany).

Applied to God, it has been attributed in varying degree to many theologians. To infer 'rightness' solely from God's having so willed and declared it, as did, *e.g.*, John Duns Scotus (1265–1308) and William of Ockham (1280/5–1349), preserves God's freedom to command, stresses the limits of human reason

and demands unquestioning obedience (as of Abraham in Gn. 22:1–19).

Nevertheless, what God wills is consistent with his whole character, and creation also reflects that character, hence his will is in measure accessible to human understanding (*cf.* Ps. 32:8–9; according to Heb. 11:19 even Abraham tried to understand). There therefore remains a place for moral argument from consequences (see Consequentialism*), from the pattern of creation ('natural law'*) and from the nature of God himself. Seemingly arbitrary divine requirements may then serve as simple tests of obedience, arise when morally neutral situations require a decision, or else rest on aspects of divine wisdom hidden from us.

See also: PHILOSOPHICAL ETHICS.

Bibliography

W. James, *The Will to Believe and Other Essays in Popular Philosophy* (1897; Cambridge, MA, and London, 1979); J. L. Mackie, *Ethics: Inventing Right and Wrong* (Harmondsworth, 1977).

F.V.W.

VOWS, see PROMISES.

VOYEURISM, see SEXUAL ADDICTION; SEXUAL DEVIATION.

WAGE. A wage exists where a person is hired as an employee by another party (*i.e.* the employer), with the latter paying a wage to the former as remuneration for the service (*i.e.* work) rendered. Many of the ethical issues revolve around the general question of what is a fair or just wage, *i.e.* its level.

Although employer-based arrangements (explicit or implicit) are the norm in Western or industrialized economies, other patterns of work and reward are possible. In a subsistence agrarian setting, for instance, if each family group owns its own piece of land, and is basically self-sufficient, then no 'wage', as such, will be paid to any family member. All share from the common pool of crops and animals. (The nature of the sharing depends on the 'system' adopted. The ethical principles operating here would in general have little or nothing to do with wages, *e.g.* so long as every one receives sufficient food at mealtimes, then no other distributive issues would arise, except in the longer term.) Western cases of non-monetary payment include, for instance, ad hoc arrangements in areas of high unemployment (*e.g.* 'I'll paint your house, if you repair my car').

Since the economic setting of the OT is, for the most part, precisely such a subsistence agrarian one, then it is not surprising that the OT says relatively little about wages (compared to, *e.g.,* interest* and debt*). Apart from land owner-workers, there were two other main categories of worker: the slaves (who, by definition, received no wage); and the hired servants. For the latter, 'wage labour was a social safeguard (Dt. 24:15) for those who had lost possession of their land until the Jubilee' (D. A. Hay, *Economics Today,* p. 74; and see Jubilee*). The OT law says very little about the level of wages, other than the injunction not to oppress or rob one's neighbour (Lv. 19:13a). The chief command is that the wage must be paid at the end of the working day, and not held back overnight (Lv. 19:13b; Dt. 24:14–15). This is reiterated in the NT by Jas. 5:4. (A modern-day example of an equivalent practice is the routinely late payment of bills to small sub-contractors by some more powerful companies.) In the OT prophets, the absence of due wages is thus seen as evidence of injustice and woe (Zc. 8:10; Je. 22:13). The NT encourages people to be content with their wages (Lk. 3:14), and restates the principle that the labourer is worthy of his hire (Lk. 10:7; 1 Cor. 9:7), but gives no further guidance on the appropriate level of wage. (Few commentators would regard Jesus' parable of the vineyard workers in Mt. 20:1–16 as, in context, saying anything about the ethics of wages in an economic setting.)

Regarding the modern Western economic setting, therefore, the Scriptures teach the general principle not to oppress an employee, but do not appear to give any guidance that is more specific. (Whether the overall biblical teaching on economics compels one to seek an entirely different system of ownership and allocation from the current Western system, is beyond the scope of this article; see Economic Ethics. [17])

In a Western or industrialized context, the ethical issues concerning wages include the following: 1. Should a *minimum* wage be in some way enforced, in order to protect weak workers? If so, how should the minimum be determined? 2. Should *excessive* wages be in some way curbed (on the grounds that such wages cause other people either to have lower wages, and/or to become jobless? 3. In what circumstances, if any, is it appropriate for employees who believe their wages are oppressively low to take industrial action (see Strikes*)? 4. What links should there be between variations in work done and variations in wages paid? Is performance-related pay justified? 5. Within a capitalist* system, should the relative amounts paid out in wages compared to profit* be in some way regulated?

The first two issues are closely related, since both revolve around the question of oppression. A 'free-market' response to both issues is to ensure that all participants in the employment 'market' participate on an equal basis, in the sense that no-one, in their economic behaviour, receives protection from the law (other than the enforcement of property rights, *i.e.* no stealing). The underlying argument here is that the economic outcomes generated by free markets cannot be bettered (see Trade*).

With regard to the labour market, then, such a view rules out any minimum-wage protection, since such protection (if it makes any impact at all) can only force wages higher than they would otherwise be, with the consequence that employers can no longer afford to employ some of their staff. To the criticism that such a free-for-all might produce starvation wages, the response would be that a tax-funded safety net (special payments to the poorest) is the best solution, since it is paid for by the many, rather than by the few who by minimum-wage legislation are forced into unemployment.

A free-market perspective would also disallow any right to strike, on similar grounds: a successful strike can raise one group's wages only at the expense of someone else (who does not enjoy protection under the law); thus the only fair solution is to allow employers to pay the wage that reflects the value of the work done by each individual.

These market-based approaches, however, depend critically on the assumption that markets work in the manner indicated by the textbooks. However, since the necessary conditions for this assumption do not in general obtain, it is not possible to resolve the ethical issues simply by an appeal to 'the market'.

In this light, the biblical injunction to treat others fairly, not oppressively, takes on renewed importance. For employers, who in general enjoy some discretion over the level of wages they pay, there appears to be no short-cut (market) solution to the question of what is the appropriate wage. They must, using their conscience, and their awareness of the social conditions of their staff and the wider community, work out for themselves what is a fair wage.

Two papal encyclicals* have specifically addressed the question of a just wage. In *Rerum Novarum* (1891), Pope Leo XIII (1878–1903; b. 1810) expounds the principle of a just living wage. This is explored more recently by John Paul II (1978– ; b. 1920) in *Laborem Exercens* (1981), which sees remuneration as a means whereby ordinary people can have access to products and services which ought to be enjoyed by all. Thus, just remuneration (for an adult who is responsible for a family) is that which 'will suffice for establishing and properly maintaining a family and for providing security for its future' (p. 69).

A final question concerns regulation and legislation. If the community, and in particular the ruling authorities (with their particular responsibility to ensure justice, *e.g.* Ps. 72:1–14), believe that any employer is acting oppressively, then action of some kind must be taken to stop the oppression. (Some would argue that that should include legislation to allow workers to protect themselves through industrial action.)

By the same reasoning, workers who have the power to influence their own level of wages have an equivalent responsibility to decide what is a fair wage. If they push for wages which are excessive, and thus result in oppression for others in the community, then action must again be taken to curtail this.

See also: INDUSTRIAL RELATIONS; TRADE UNIONS.

Bibliography

D. A. Hay, *Economics Today: A Christian Critique* (Leicester, 1989); Pope John Paul II, *Laborem Exercens* (ET, *On Human Work*, London, 1981).

A.J.H.

WAR presents the Christian with an obvious question. Can a Christian ever participate in warfare, or support it? Answering this question means considering whether a Christian may ever use force, even for good ends. Our attitude to war is also inextricably linked to our view of politics.* Christians have offered many different answers, which have varied for theological and political reasons. For most of its history, the church's view has been that it may be a proper duty for the Christian to fight for justice (see Justice and Peace 3) out of a loving concern for the neighbour. Pacifism* has been a significant minority view, except in the early centuries of Christianity, when it was church teaching that Christians should not fight or shed blood.

The Bible does not settle this question, though it has a great deal to tell us about the way in which we should be pacifist or non-pacifist. The OT differs markedly in tone from the NT. Whereas the OT sees God fighting for Israel, and commanding them to fight, the NT presents Jesus as the bringer of peace. While the distinction can be exaggerated, it is none the less a real one. When all the work of examining key texts is done (perhaps pre-eminently Mt. 5:38–45 and Rom. 13:1–5), the central debate turns on our understanding of Christ's place in God's plan of redemption. Does the example of Christ's suffering love mean that Christians should not use power* and coercion for good ends? Specifically, does Christ's death for the salvation of our lives absolutely forbid the Christian to take human life? And does the Christian's allegiance to Christ's kingdom (see Kingdom of God*) draw him or her out of the business of earthly kingdoms, or lead to involvement with them? There are many varieties of pacifism, but the main line of pacifist answers to these questions is straightforward.

Non-pacifist (just-war*) thought is first to be seen as an alternative way of answering these questions. Following Ambrose* and Augustine,* this tradition holds that the Christian may have a duty to use force to protect others. Like pacifism, it believes that Christ's death sanctifies human life, but it considers that life may be taken in order to protect or defend the lives of others. Just-war thought also refuses to see political concerns as ultimate, but sees them as related to divine realities. There is a relationship between the two cities, between the two kingdoms, between human justice and divine righteousness. Christ's transforming lordship over kings and presidents is partly mediated through Christian life and witness. The just-war tradition does not glorify war, or see it as other than tragic, but accepts the duty to strive for justice on earth even by means of war if necessary.

War may be thought of as a prism through which important aspects of politics can be viewed. Just-war theory is not only about war, but also offers a Christian perspective on power, on political obligation, on justice and peace, among other things. In this sense, the theory can never be irrelevant, though it cannot simply provide answers to new problems without deep and careful thought. The second half of the 20th century has produced new weaponry; it has also seen new attitudes to war. These new attitudes lay heavy stress on war as a battle of wills, in which threat, counter-threat and bluff assume exaggerated importance. These threats are often directed at large civilian populations, so that there is an in-built terrorist mentality in our planning for security* and defence.*

Just-war thought brings to these questions a moral framework which is articulated in relation to political and military realities. A code of morality is not made in the abstract, but in analysis of the purposes of politics and warfare. The basic concerns of politics are seen as an ordered peace and justice. War may need to be entered in order to protect a good social fabric within which we may live in safety and security. By the same token, the concern for justice and for human life places substantial moral limits on resort to war (*jus ad bellum*) and the conduct of war (*jus in bello*).

Resort to war: *jus ad bellum*

The just-war tradition, as it has been developed over several hundred years in association with Christian influence (see Thomas Aquinas,* Vitoria,* Suarez* and Grotius*), offers ways of assessing imponderable decisions and issues which arise in politics. It recognizes that there may be a tension between justice and peace; a certain injustice may warrant resort to war, or perhaps the potential costs of war and concern for peace may require that some injustice be left unremedied. Resort to war can be justified only when it seems that war may offer at least reasonable prospects of leading to a better state of affairs than would otherwise prevail. To help estimate this, four criteria of *jus ad bellum* are conventionally stated as follows: 1. that resort to war should be taken only by legitimate authority; 2. that there should be a just cause for resort to war; 3. that the overall aim or intention is right, *i.e.* to bring about a better justice; and 4. that war should be a last resort,

after all other reasonable avenues have been explored. It is important to notice that all of these criteria are intended as aids to thinking out the basic issue, which is that war should do more good than harm. The principles of justice and political reason are essential to this assessment. In politics one cannot ask for watertight assurances on all these points, but one can ask for clear and dispassionate thought and an attempt to sift motives and intentions.

In this century two further considerations have often come to dominate discussion of *jus ad bellum*, namely the prohibition of aggression, and the greatly increased costs (human, environmental and economic) of modern war. It is commonly argued that the only just cause for war is that of defence against aggression. While it is hard to see how an openly aggressive act could be justified, there are at least two major questions against this as a leading principle. In the first place, the history of nations is too varied to make this distinction wholly satisfactory. Is intervention in another State groaning under horrible tyranny (*e.g.* Amin's Uganda and Saddam Hussein's Iraq) to be classed as aggression? When one State makes a pre-emptive strike to foil another's obviously aggressive intent, perhaps in a time of continuing tension (*e.g.* Israel and neighbouring Arab nations), who is the aggressor? Such ambiguities make this distinction less useful than it may appear. In the second place, the distinction may suggest that the defender can do no wrong, and the aggressor no right. Such an assumption is much too simplistic, both morally and politically. Things are rarely so clear-cut; it is quite possible to pursue a just cause in an unjust way.

The destructive weapons that are available in contemporary warfare undoubtedly count against the possibility of a justified resort to war. The fear of the scale of destruction rightly inhibits nations from war. However, this fear is sometimes sentimentally attached to the secular conviction that human life is the only ultimate value, and that nothing can justify the giving up of one's life for political causes. These beliefs can be attached to a nominal allegiance to just-war principles, which are then applied in a rigidly rigorous way in order to disqualify almost any resort to war on one ground or another. Such use of the just-war traditions amounts in effect to a crypto-pacifism.

A classic problem for determining *jus ad bellum* is that both the enemy nations usually claim that they have a just cause. Of course, there are instances when a disinterested observer could easily adjudicate between competing claims. But it is also common enough for enemies to have reasonable grounds to claim that justice is on their side. This undeniable fact does not mean that the just-war theory is useless at this point. It is an acknowledgment that politics is full of such ambiguities. The just-war tradition does not claim that it can resolve all claims and counter-claims about justice, or about political values and decisions. What it can do is provide a framework of thought within which they can be considered and assessed.

The conduct of war: *jus in bello*

Just-war theory places definite moral limits on the conduct of war, independently of the rights and wrongs of the decision to go to war. These limits are expressed as the tests of discrimination and proportion.* The principle of discrimination specifies that it can never be justified deliberately and directly to attack non-combatants. The principle of proportion is more general in scope, for it requires that the likely costs of military action should be outweighed by the prospective gains.

The principle of discrimination has been widely questioned and dismissed in the modern age, especially during and since the Second World War. The questions run in three related directions. It is argued: 1. that it is impossible in modern war to distinguish between combatant and non-combatant; 2. that it is morally indifferent whether someone is killed directly or indirectly, and since non-combatants inevitably are killed in modern warfare, then warfare is inevitably immoral; and 3. that the only important thing in war, both morally and politically, is to win, and that to fight by moral rules is to fight with one hand tied behind one's back. These objections have gained wide-spread credence in an age of nuclear weapons and nuclear deterrence (see Deterrence, Nuclear*). They have been decisively answered by Paul Ramsey* and others, but their answers can barely be sketched in this article.

First, it can easily be shown that there are non-combatants, including (among many others) children, the sick and the elderly. It is possible to draw a distinction between those who work to maintain the fabric of society, and those who contribute directly to the war effort. War ought not to be thought of as a total contest between two societies, but as a battle between rival armed forces. The fact that there are civilians who may be classed as combatants (*e.g.* workers in arms factories), and other grey areas, does not invalidate the distinction. Secondly, the morality of combat cannot be determined by consequences alone. There is a vital moral difference between killing someone accidentally, and killing him or her deliberately, a distinction easily recognized, and enshrined in the law. The apparent loss of this moral distinction in our time has gravely affected our moral confidence. As G. E. M. Anscombe put it: '[People] become convinced that a number of things are wicked which are not; hence, seeing no way of avoiding "wickedness", they set no limits to it' ('War and Murder', in Walter Stein, ed., *Nuclear Weapons and Christian Conscience*, London, 1961, p. 56). Thirdly, it must be maintained that the cause of justice cannot be served by actions which are themselves unjust. One cannot claim to be fighting against oppression, and oneself oppress those who are innocent. Finally, in order to uphold just-war theory at this point, one has to wrestle with the intractable questions of nuclear deterrence. Does the principle of discrimination effectively prohibit all possession and use of nuclear weapons? The just-war tradition has to be made relevant to this issue, as it undoubtedly can be.

The principle of proportion is less controversial. The principle that the gains of action should outweigh the costs follows from the pragmatic argument at the root of the tradition. It includes both the requirement that only minimum force* should ever be used, and the prohibition of excessive violence* and destruction. But it goes wider than those points. Costs and gains have to be reckoned sometimes widely, sometimes narrowly, but nothing is automatically excluded. Actions which might appear proportionate in merely military terms might be quite disproportionate in political terms (one thinks of counter-terrorist action) and vice versa.

Conscience* and conscientious objection

The right to conscientious objection is rightly recognized by many nations. It is generally confined to pacifists who object in conscience to any participation in war. This leaves out those who might be prepared to fight in some wars, but might wish to object to some particular wars. In a democratic society, it would obviously be desirable for a right of selective conscientious objection to be recognized. But there are real difficulties about this. Clearly, members of the armed forces have to be under clear political control, and must obey orders. The only exception to this is that they have a duty to disobey orders which clearly and flagrantly break the laws of war (*e.g.* orders to commit atrocities). More worryingly, if a country in time of national emergency needs all its available workforce for purposes of war, intolerable strains might be imposed if anyone with a reasonable political disagreement was allowed the right of selective conscientious objection. In an emergency, a nation may need to call on the loyalty of a whole people, in spite of specific disagreements. This difficulty probably means that Christians should be ready to press for the right only to object selectively to wars fought with weapons of mass destruction, especially nuclear weapons. There is need for continuing discussion of this, so that Christians and others may point the way back from war fought with such weapons. For this, the just-war tradition will prove to be of continuing significance.

Bibliography

D. Atkinson, *Peace in Our Time?* (Leicester, 1985); R. H. Bainton, *Christian Attitudes toward War and Peace* (Nashville, TN, 1960) = *Christian Attitudes to War and Peace* (London, 1961); O. R. Barclay (ed.), *Pacifism and War* (Leicester, 1984); R. Harries, *Christianity and War in a Nuclear Age* (London, 1986); B. Paskins and M. Dockrill, *The Ethics of War* (Minneapolis, MN, 1979); P. Ramsey, *War and the Christian Conscience* (Durham, NC, 1961); *idem*, *The Just War* (New York, 1968); H. Thielicke, *TE* 1; M. Walzer, *Just and Unjust Wars* (New York, 1977; Harmondsworth, 1980).

D.J.E.A.

WARFARE, SPIRITUAL, see DELIVERANCE MINISTRY; DEMONIC, THE.

WASTE. From a purely economic perspective, waste might be anything from an inefficient use of resources to the unavoidable by-product of producing something valuable. It becomes a moral issue when viewed in the context of a set of values which imply obligations in the use of the material creation.

Christian values with respect to creation* include the following:

1. Humanity is to steward (see Steward-

ship*), manage, subdue and bring creation to its fulfilment in accountability (see Responsibility*) to the ultimate 'owner', God. God is concerned for the well-being of the whole creation. He knows when a sparrow falls to the ground (Mt. 10:29); he commanded Noah to take a male and a female of every kind of animal to keep them alive (Gn. 6:19–20).

To 'waste' the resources of creation includes failing to use them for tasks which are according to the will of God. God's will is that all members of humanity be stewards and have enough to live by. His purpose for Israel (and so for all people) was that there be no poor among them (Dt. 15:4). Proverbs says, 'Unused fields could yield plenty of food for the poor, but unjust men keep them from being farmed' (Pr. 13:23, GNB). Such fields are a waste of the productive capacity of creation.

The philosophy of the ultimate rights of private ownership would allow people to dispose of and even waste resources as they see fit. However, the laws of gleaning show that those with resources are expected to leave some of their produce for the poor (Lv. 23:22). The parable of the talents shows that those who reap the benefits of their industry do not simply keep the results, but are given extra responsibility (Mt. 25:14ff.). The rich women of Israel were condemned by Amos (Am. 4:1–3), and the rich man was condemned in Jesus' parable for feasting while others hungered (Lk. 16:19–31). Waste is therefore especially a moral issue in the context of the misuse of resources which should be available for the good of the whole community. Paul counsels that 'if we have food and clothes, that should be enough for us' (1 Tim. 6:8, GNB).

2. A second value with respect to creation is to refrain from extracting every last ounce of work* or productivity from it. The concept of the sabbath* in Scripture is the concept that human beings should be like God, displaying their mastery over creation and work, not being mastered by them. Thus to waste is not to fail to maximize the profitability or usefulness of resources; the opposite of waste is not absolute efficiency but proper use with respect to the need to sustain the humanity and the community of human society by resting and by caring for the poor.

In contrast to biblical views, much current economic thought sees land* and material resources as commodities, without any value until they are processed. The earth consists of raw materials waiting to be converted into something useful. Creation is merely a resource whose value comes only through being changed into marketable products. Until it is processed, it lies waste. This degrades the whole creation, which provides all the sun and rain from the hand of the good creator, to the level of a 'free good'. By contrast, the book of Job shows that creation is not anthropocentric, and does not have to justify its existence with relation to humanity (Jb. 41).

We need a reason to value nature in, and of, itself; yet not in such a way that nature exercises a tyranny over us so that we cannot get on with the business of living.

We need to understand what nature is and who we are. The Bible holds that nature belongs to God and that men and women together are his image,* stewards, caretakers and managers of the non-human creation on behalf of the 'absentee' landlord. The bodily resurrection of Jesus Christ is also a most powerful statement of the goodness of creation, because it demonstrates that creation is so good that God intends to restore it to wholeness.

This biblical Christian view is to be contrasted with dualistic* views (some of which claim to be Christian), which would exalt the 'spiritual' to the detriment of the material, and thus deprive our relation to the material creation of any moral evaluation.

It is also a distortion of this biblical view to regard it as giving humanity unbridled dominion over nature to use it without regard to the consequences.

3. A third value follows from humanity's stewardship and care for the proper availability of the fruits of creation to all. That is the concern that the creation is not despoiled. This can happen in many ways. In the first centuries of the Common Era, the rich fertile lands of N. Africa were over-cropped so that they became desert. In this generation, the rain forests are being depleted (see Deforestation*), hazardous emissions from fossil fuels are destroying the quality of the air people breathe, other emissions are destroying the ozone layer, and the disposal of radioactive by-products from nuclear reactors is proving hard to control (see Environment*).

A number of biblical passages speak of God's displeasure at the spoiling of the created order: 'I brought them into a fertile land to enjoy its harvest and its other good things. But instead they ruined my land; they defiled the country I had given them' (Je. 2:7, GNB).

Ezekiel uses a farming metaphor in condemning the behaviour of Israel's priests: 'Some of you are not satisfied with eating the best grass; you even trample down what you don't eat! You drink the clear water and muddy what you don't drink' (Ezk. 34:18, GNB). Isaiah speaks of the way God's people have defiled the earth (Is. 24:5).

Different cultures demonstrate many ways to combat waste. Organic kitchen waste can be recycled to provide gardening compost, or in other cultures it is put out in tips and scavenged by the poor. In India, Mexico and the Philippines a healthy recycling industry takes place among poor communities who work over refuse tips or dumps. Paper may be recycled to save trees in the West, while campaigns are mounted in Nepal against the tourist hotels which ravage hillsides for firewood. Alternative sources of energy may be explored; water can be conserved; people can use sales of second-hand clothing and goods; and public transportation can be preferred to private cars.

See also: COMMUNITY ETHICS; [16] ECONOMIC ETHICS. [17]

Bibliography

J. V. Taylor, *Enough is Enough* (London, 1975; Minneapolis, MN, 1977); J. A. Walter, *The Human Home: The Myth of the Sacred Environment* (Tring, 1982); C. de Witt (ed.), *The Environment and the Christian* (Grand Rapids, 1991).

C.M.N.S.

WEALTH, see STEWARDSHIP.

WEAPONS TECHNOLOGY, see ARMAMENTS.

WELFARE STATE, THE. The report *Social Insurance and Allied Services,* published by the British Government in 1942 and written in the main by William H. Beveridge (1879–1963), marks the pivotal point in the 20th-century British development of the Welfare State. Before the State lay the struggle to find principles and processes for an urban industrial society (see Industrialization*) in order to make adequate provision for the needs of multitudes of its people, who were threatened with poverty, disease, lack of educational opportunity and poor housing. Earlier in the century, the Liberal Government of 1906 had started establishing certain services for education and pensions on the basis of universal contributions or out of public revenues. Throughout the early part of the 20th century, the rise of the Labour movement had created a momentum for seeking collective solutions to these large-scale problems – seen especially during the inter-war years of the slump and economic depression. Paralleling this was the work of many distinguished church leaders and thinkers – e.g. R. H. Tawney,* William Temple* (who became Archbishop of Canterbury in the year of the publication of the Beveridge report), and J. H. Oldham (1874–1969) – who wrestled with the demands of Christian faith as it was confronted with the problems outlined above.

The principles set out in the Beveridge Report were both simple and widely attractive. Its framers believed that a system of universal contributions through a national insurance scheme would provide the resources for every person to have certain basic requirements met at the point of need. The expense of providing health* care, a universal State pension and unemployment benefit would be met out of the (legislated) contributions made by all. Everyone would be committed to the scheme, because all would be potential beneficiaries. By similar universal provision, the basic educational opportunities needed in a progressive society could be found for all children, irrespective of their family's financial situation. Accordingly, there is in the report a commitment to a basic equality* of opportunity, enshrined in universal public provision of essential services.

The Beveridge Report was timely. Its arrival came at a moment, in the midst of a terrible war, when the State* was having to organize services on a national and universal scale. It was also having to develop its own internal structures to meet the massive challenge of defeating Adolf Hitler (1889–1945). These developed structures could be turned to peaceful purposes once the war was over, and this would be acceptable to a people who had learned the necessity of large contributions to meet the challenge of war. Could not the challenge of poverty,* education,* housing and health be met by similar large-scale, centrally organized national effort? The election of a Labour Government in 1945, with a massive majority, provided the political basis for a major development of welfare services, on the lines set out by Beveridge. Thus the

National Health Service was born, National Insurance developed, pensions extended, educational opportunities widened, and public housing greatly extended. These possibilities were enhanced by the economic theory of the time in the work of J. M. Keynes (1883–1946), who saw the management of public finances and public investment as a way of dealing with the cycle of growth and recession which had been such a curse before the Second World War. So Keynes, Beveridge, Labour politics and postwar popular expectation fed the establishment of the Welfare State.

All of this went well for two decades. However, the cost of maintaining public services, and their seemingly unquenchable need for more and more resources, together with the changing public expectation of a society growing ever more prosperous, began to bring major questions to the surface. Apart from anything else, it was clear that however good the Welfare State was, it had not abolished poverty and need. Furthermore, irrespective of political affiliation, governments could not meet the increasing demands on the public purse represented by its burgeoning services. Thus in the late 1960s and 70s more and more people began to question the basis on which it had been established. Influential philosophers, such as Friedrich von Hayek (1899–1992) and latterly Robert Nozick (1938–), have questioned the moral legitimacy of the large and pervasive State.

At the end of the 20th century, some questions remain unanswered. What ought to be provided on a universal and public basis, and what should be targeted to particular groups? What are the respective roles of the State, the voluntary sector and the private sector in meeting welfare needs? How can we more effectively provide the necessary help for those in need without fracturing the foundations of both the economy and a free society?

Christians, building on the long tradition of both practical and theological work in support of the vulnerable, will want to share in their debate and help it to be rooted in spiritual and moral values which offer hope to the poor.

Bibliography

W. H. Beveridge (chairman), Social Insurance and Allied Services (London, 1942); Church of England Board for Social Responsibility, Not Just for the Poor: Christian Perspectives on the Welfare State (London, 1986); K. Coates and R. Silburn, Poverty: The

Forgotten Englishman (Harmondsworth, 1970); D. B. Forester, *Christianity and the Future of Welfare* (London, 1970).

J.W.G.

WESLEY, JOHN AND CHARLES.

The Wesley brothers, John (1703–91) and Charles (1709–88), were born in the rectory of Epworth, Lincolnshire, the fifteenth and eighteenth children of Samuel and Susannah. Together they gave leadership to the 18th-century Evangelical Revival and to the people called Methodists.

As a boy, John was educated at the Charterhouse, London, before attending Christ Church, Oxford, completing his BA in 1724 and his MA in 1727. Later that year he left Oxford to serve as his father's curate, being ordained presbyter in 1728.

Charles left Epworth for Westminster School in London before his ninth birthday, and then followed John to Christ Church, Oxford, in 1726, completing both a BA and MA by 1733. At this time Charles was a scholar and poet with no intention to enter holy orders.

In 1729 John returned to Oxford and soon became the spiritual leader of a small group of students his brother Charles had gathered together. This band became known as the 'Holy Club' or 'Methodists', because of their disciplined method of Christian living. As the group grew and evolved, their study of the Lat. classics and the Gk. NT expanded to include numerous theological and devotional works, fasting on Wednesdays and Fridays, weekly reception of the Sacrament, and regular visits to the poor, sick and imprisoned. Devotion, discipline and social involvement were central to Methodist spirituality from the 1730s onward.

In May of 1738, after their return from a brief mission to America, first Charles and then his brother John had evangelical experiences that warmed their hearts and confirmed their sense of mission – which was both personal (to save one's own soul) and corporate (to save as many others as possible), both spiritual and social (caring for the mind and the body, as well as for the soul). As pulpits closed to their message of salvation by faith alone, the Wesleys went into the open fields to preach to the labouring masses. Charles, one of England's greatest hymnwriters, gave poetic voice to the evangelical doctrines both brothers proclaimed.

The theological foundation for the Wesleys' mission was the universal love and grace of God. They believed that everyone could be saved, that everyone must be saved, that everyone could be saved now, and that everyone can be saved to the uttermost. Although John and Charles differed in their understanding of sanctifying grace (see Sanctification*), they joined in the mission 'to spread scriptural holiness across the land'. This holiness or 'Christian perfection' was understood as the ultimate goal of every believer as the Holy Spirit inspired each one to love God and neighbour. Love for God was expressed in worship, prayer and praise. Love for neighbour could take many forms: for those who were lost, it meant 'offering them Christ'. Love for the poor meant homes for widows and orphans, free health clinics, home visits to supply prayer, food, clothing and coal for heat. It also meant schools, Sunday Schools, no-interest loan funds and employment in cottage industries.

Methodism was a revival of evangelical witness, pastoral care, social involvement and spiritual nurture through a structure of small groups ('class meetings'), local leaders, and travelling preachers. Its real genius was the ability to enlist, develop and utilize the spiritual talents of lay men and women who were willing to 'believe, love, and obey' God.

Bibliography
H. Lindström, *John Wesley and Sanctification* (London, 1946); M. Schmidt, *John Wesley: A Theological Biography*, 2 vols. in 3 (London and Nashville, TN, 1962–73); R. G. Tuttle, *John Wesley: His Life and Theology* (Grand Rapids, 1978); F. Whaling (ed.), *John Wesley and Charles Wesley: Selected Writings and Hymns* (New York, 1981).

T.R.A.

WHOLENESS, see PEACE; SIN AND SALVATION. ⑤

WIDOWHOOD, WIDOWERHOOD.

The terms 'widow' and 'widower' apply, respectively, to a woman or man whose marriage* partner has died and who has not remarried.

Study of biblical ethics indicates that God constantly saves those who are helpless (like widows in biblical times), giving them homes and security. OT stories reveal God as being one who sees his friends in distress and rescues them. God's people are expected to do what

God does. Thus, the OT's frequent call to God's people to 'Remember Egypt!' (*cf.* Dt. 10:18–19) is a challenge to be like God – and to rescue those who are helpless, as God once saved his people from Egyptian oppression.

In the OT, Hebrew culture was based on a sense of community – each man belonged to his brother and eventually through him to the nation. Emphasis is given to the importance of justice – which reflects the ideal that all should receive their due. The concept of mercy recognizes the bonding between human beings, and responds by offering assistance, loyalty and empathetic concern for those who are oppressed. God's righteousness,* justice and mercy are linked with God's concern that the oppressed should be vindicated. A widow lacked her husband, the person vital to her well-being who would protect and provide for her. It was hard for her to survive, even at sub-sistence level. She was open to exploitation* and to being denied her most basic rights. This led to the teaching in Dt. 25:5ff. that the dead husband's brother was to rescue a widow by taking her into his home with the rights of a wife. Permanent widowhood was, thus, seen as shameful (Is. 54:4). Their vulnerability made widows the object of a special call for protection (Ex. 22:22).

NT teaching (1 Tim. 5:3–16) limits the pro-vision given by the church to widows over 60 years of age, who conformed to certain ex-pectations, and who had no supportive children or grandchildren.

In the biblical period, patriarchy was the norm: women belonged to their husbands. Such ownership was reflected in English law until 1882, when the Married Woman's Prop-erty Act changed old laws in which a woman's property had transferred automatically to her husband on marriage. A further Act in 1938 gave the wife some claims on her dead hus-band's estate. Since 1925, the State has pro-vided life-long widows' pensions plus provi-sion for dependent children. Similarly, the US also did not begin to recognize the property rights of women until the 20th century.

The rise of feminism* and the equal-opportunities movement has shaken age-old assumptions that women must be cared for by men and that a man can 'own' a woman. Therefore, the underlying principle of 'Remember Egypt!' must be examined and reapplied to today's shifting cultural norms, and it may now sometimes apply to widowers rather than widows. It is increasingly cultur-ally acceptable for fathers to be the primary care-givers for children. Thus, widowers may require further support at the level of Social Service provision and at the level of emotional support, should they quit work to rear their children or require leave of absence to care for children who are sick or during school holidays.

Those who have lost a partner through death call for careful pastoral support, especially in the period of six weeks to six months after the death and on significant anniversaries. They may need help in coming to terms with their loss themselves, and also in working it through with their bereaved children. Bereavement* services have a vital role to play in this. The normal stages of loss must be worked through, and empathetic listening can help a great deal. There is a need to separate from the dead person and from his or her status and role; there is a transition to be undergone from confusion and uncertainty to being able to discover and accept a new status (being partnerless) and finally reincorporation into the community. It is realistic to allow up to two years or even longer for this. A wife who is pregnant when her husband dies is usually unable to work through her grief at the same time as carrying a new life. She can be expected to go through a delayed bereavement reaction some time after giving birth. Her reactions are likely to appear inappropriate unless anti-cipated and accepted as normal in one who is pregnant.

A.J.T.

WILBERFORCE, WILLIAM (1759–1833), evangelical politician and oppo-nent of the slave trade, was educated at his native Hull and at St John's College, Cam-bridge, and from 1784 sat as MP for Yorkshire.

Converted under the influence of Isaac Milner (1750–1820), he launched a campaign to urge magistrates to enforce the law more rigorously against blasphemy and drunken-ness. His book *A Practical View* recommended the gentlemen of England to consider whether their common addiction to gaming and theatre-going was compatible with the NT. If not, they should turn from their negligence to 'vital Christianity'.

Like many of his contemporaries, Wilber-force was swayed by Enlightenment* thinkers to recognize the wickedness of the slave* trade. Unlike others, he was driven by his sense of

Christian responsiblity to seek its abolition. From 1789 onwards he regularly called on the House of Commons to restrict the trade, but he was stoutly opposed by the W. India merchants. Only in 1807 was abolition of the trade achieved. Wilberforce continued to press for enforcement of the measure and for its adoption by other countries. He also concerned himself with improving the conditions of slaves in British territories, eventually reaching the conclusion that slavery itself must be extinguished. Although he retired from Parliament in 1825, he was overjoyed to learn on his deathbed in 1833 that the slaves were to be free.

Wilberforce used his political position to promote the Christian faith, *e.g.* by campaigning for the opening of British India to missionaries. He was a man of great charm, who dedicated himself to moral reform.

See also: CLAPHAM SECT.

Bibliography
A Practical View of the Prevailing Religious System of Professed Christians (London, 1797).
J. Pollock, *Wilberforce* (London, 1977).
D.W.Be.

WILL, HUMAN. The concept of 'will', or volition, expresses the ability of a rational being to want something, and this is the power that moves a person to choose things and perform actions. 'Motivation' is a wider concept, because it includes instincts and subconscious desires, while 'will' refers to conscious purposes and desires that can be articulated. Because of its crucial importance for morality, the will has been the subject of much discussion; and well before the extra problems introduced by the development of modern psychology (including the attempt to eliminate 'will' altogether), the subject was fraught with error and confusion.

The Bible, although it lacks a systematic theory, presents a unified view of the human agent, *i.e.* no radical separation is made between intellect, will and emotion. This is especially evident in the common use of 'heart' and 'mind', which are overlapping categories, and stresses that it is the whole person which relates to the world, to other people and to God.

From the long history of Western moral thought, we may summarize two fatal developments in theory about the will: 1. making the will the sole agent of human choice* and action; and 2. the separation of will from reason* and affection. These developments were influenced by both philosophical and theological factors. It is a simpler and more economical explanation of human action to say that the intellect (through reason or conscience*) thinks about what should be done, and then that it is the task of the will to decide and execute. This was attractive to theologians also, because it offers a ready explanation for sin: wrong action and sin are a result of the will not wanting to obey what reason knows should be done.

The model of a process of action which puts intellect (conscience) and will (choice) in sequence reinforces the separation by making deliberation purely rational, with the will the faculty of decision. For many thinkers the element of freedom in action is a function of the will alone, which means, within this model, that a defence of the 'freedom of the will' amounts to little more than a defence of the freedom to be irrational (evident in much 20th-century thought). Further fracturing of the human agent occurred with the rise of the Cartesian view of the soul, where emotions* are given a physicalist explanation separate from the intellect.

This view of the split psyche has profoundly affected Western thought, in theology as well as in philosophy and psychology. Note that when Immanuel Kant* redefined the will by reuniting it with rationality, he cemented further its separation from desire and affection. When rationality came under attack (in the last two centuries), the will then became, in much secular thought, the unfettered power for control and self-expression. Where the moral tradition maintained an emphasis on the human ability to know moral obligation (through reason or revelation), the dominant model usually remained a soul divided into tight compartments (often known as 'faculty psychology').

Mindful of these errors in our tradition, we may attempt a summary of the doctrine of will in line with Scripture, Augustine* and Thomas Aquinas.* (The Protestant Reformers unfortunately inherited a view which had already split intellect from will and thereby restricted freedom of choice to the will.)

It is fair to note that awareness of the fallenness of humankind and the loss of orientation to God meant that there is a certain 'voluntarism'* (emphasis on the centrality of the will) in Christian thought not found in classical ethical theory (*e.g.* in Aristotle, although this has been exaggerated by A. Dihle and others). Yet if we recognize that actions are the result of the whole personality, then Christian focus on the will has primarily a theological and spiritual purpose, and supplements, rather than contradicts, a theory of practical reason. Though the will becomes of central importance to Augustine, he in no way separated it from intellect and emotion, as is borne out by his use of the relation of the powers of the soul as an analogy of the distinctions within the unity of the Trinity.

It is in Thomas Aquinas' *Summa Theologiae* that we have the only fully theological view of the human will deftly combined with an Aristotelian account of practical reason (*STh* 1a and 1a2ae). The will is the 'rational appetite', *i.e.* the desire for actions and states of affairs that require an understanding of purpose. For instance, when we take a trip, we do so in order to see a friend, conduct business, take a holiday, *etc.*: our mind sees the connection between actions and purpose. Even actions such as eating and sleeping, which have a built-in purpose based on bodily needs, become part of our overall system of desires and purposes and choices.

Thus the human will can be defined as the ensemble of purposes and desires which shape a person's character, choices and actions. For both Augustine and Aquinas (and we might include others such as Jonathan Edwards*), the will is by its nature shaped by the mind's understanding of what is good; thus the intellect is part of the definition of the will. The will also includes emotion, because the person desires what he wants and takes delight when he achieves it. Not every action we choose is delightful in itself, of course: when we undergo painful medical treatment we must endure it, but we choose it because we hope thereby to be able to rejoice in the gift of good health.

The effect of sin is to bring disorder to the harmony and function of the entire person (not the will alone), so that with darkened understanding and contrary affections, false goals and desires dominate the human will. Hence the importance of grace* is to restore to us a sound mind and heart so that we can know and love what we should know and love, and be able to choose and execute our actions without a divided will or contrary affections. By having a will directed to God above all (which is impossible without grace), we are able to see and love what is our true and final Good; it is only then that all of the other good purposes of this life take their proper place within a soul reordered by the transforming power of the Holy Spirit.*

Bibliography

R. Baumgaertel and J. Behm, *TDNT* 3, pp. 605–614; V. J. Bourke, *Will in Western Thought: An Historico-Critical Survey* (New York, 1964); A. Dihle, *The Theory of Will in Classical Antiquity* (Berkeley, CA, and London, 1982); E. Jacob *et al.*, *TDNT* 9, pp. 608–656; A. J. P. Kenny, *The Metaphysics of Mind* (Oxford, 1989).

D.A.W.

WILLS. Our 'last will and testament' is our last act of stewardship* over what God has entrusted to us on this earth. If we accept that we have been entrusted personally to a greater or lesser extent with responsibility* during our lifetime for property and for people, then a will gives us power to choose how to dispose of those responsibilities after our death. Societies have always recognized the importance and moral force of 'death-bed' wishes, and in our Western society a will is a formal and binding way of expressing those wishes. A will is a written document by which testators can appoint executors to administer their estate, and can dispose of all their individual property and other property over which they have power, and of their powers of guardianship over any infant children, and can give directions, conditions and restrictions on the use and disposal of their property. From an ethical point of view, two issues arise: 1. why people should make a will, and 2. what people should do with their property.

From a legal point of view, if a person chooses *not* to make a will, then the rules of intestacy apply to implement what society considers to be a reasonable distribution of the estate, and the criteria used are based on the family* being the primary unit in society and providing our primary relationships and responsibilities (*cf.* 1 Tim. 5:8). This is a view which in the Western world goes back to Roman law and the importance of the family group as an economic and social unit. However, society's criteria may be too rigid to meet our changing social structure fairly. In our modern world, where the wider family often has less cohesion and sense of interdependence, where members of the nuclear family are often more socially and financially independent of each other, and where family groups may split and separate, then the rigid provision made by the intestacy rules may not always be appropriate. In addition, apart from the importance of other relationships outside the family, there is a growing awareness of needs beyond the individual, and a growing involvement in the local community, in national concerns and in global needs. There is a bewildering array of charities seeking our support both during our lifetime and after our death; and, for the Christian, there is the desire to support the spread of the gospel. The choice, therefore, when considering a will, is whether to allow society to implement its rules or whether to make the decisions for oneself. The general thrust of Christian teaching is that we should make our own decisions, using our own criteria, and not accept the world's criteria without question.

If a person does choose to make a will, then the freedom of choice, of testation, is limited by various legal considerations. These include, in the UK, a rigid observance of the formalities laid down by the Wills Act 1837, the impact of taxation on an estate, and the responsibilities imposed by the Inheritance (Provision for Family and Dependants) Act 1975. Society still requires that testators should be responsible for those who are financially dependent on them, and also requires that wealthier testators should contribute some of their wealth to the community by way of taxation on death. The Christian has to move with integrity within the framework of the law, and make decisions and choices within the limitations that society has imposed. It is true that 'we brought nothing into this world and we take nothing out', but in the interim we have played our part in a continuing cycle of human interaction in a material world which has created responsibilities, and we should be concerned to ensure that the people and the causes for which we care are appropriately provided for. The key word is 'appropriate', and each individual will decide differently, balancing competing needs and assessing different assets, aware that land, houses, businesses, money and chattels all have different characters and uses and may need to be disposed of separately, particularly if there is any element of heirloom or moral obligation to pass particular assets on to the next generation. (Wills can be and have been abused and used as means of revenge, retribu-

tion and moral blackmail, and this has no place in the Christian ethic!) Making a will puts our attitude to our material possessions in perspective, and Christians need to learn not to be possessive but to enjoy both the reality of giving now and the prospect of giving after death.

Bibliography
R. H. Helmholz, *Canon Law and the Law of England* (London, 1987); C. H. Sherrin, *Williams' Law Relating to Wills*, 2 vols. (London, ⁵1980).

J.K.C.

WINNICOTT, D. W. (1896–1971).

Working within a psychoanalytic* frame of reference, Winnicott's work focuses on theories of the emotional development of children, and has been significant not only for the psychology of growth and of motherhood, but also for the psychology of religion.* His early papers, which document his work, are published in *Through Paediatrics to Psychoanalysis*. His work from 1957 to 1963 is collected in the volume *The Maturational Processes and the Facilitating Environment*. He wrote of the 'true self' and the 'false self': the latter, often presented to the external world, is a defensive shield protecting the true ego within. The weak ego of the small child needs an environment which is 'facilitating' (*i.e.* providing the warmth and security needed: what Winnicott called in his famous phrase 'goodenough mothering'), for adequate individual development.

One important contribution is the theory that children grow into independence by means of transitional stages. In his paper 'Transitional Objects and Transitional Phenomena', Winnicott noted that the baby's transitional objects (the sucked thumb, the cuddly blanket, the teddy bear) represent an experience of reality between the inner world of the child and the external world. This kind of intermediate reality is found also in art, dreams, creative work and religion. Transitional objects mediate between two worlds, as do, *e.g.*, the sound of a symphony, and the elements in the sacrament of Holy Communion.

Some psychologists of religion (*e.g.* Heije Faber, Fraser Watts and Mark Williams) have built on Winnicott's approach to suggest that God is to be found not wholly in a person's inner world, or wholly in the world of external reality, but in the transitions, 'outside, inside, at the border'.

Bibliography

The Maturational Processes and the Facilitating Environment (London and New York, 1965); *Playing and Reality* (Harmondsworth, 1971); *Through Paediatrics to Psychoanalysis* (London and New York, 1958).

H. Faber, *Psychology of Religion* (ET, London, 1972); F. Watts and M. Williams, *The Psychology of Religious Knowing* (Cambridge, 1988).

D.J.A.

WISDOM is popularly distinguished from knowledge because it is instinctively recognized that whereas knowledge can fuel pride (*cf.* 1 Cor. 8:1), wisdom applies knowledge and experience to life with a view to living it wholesomely and harmoniously. Most cultures, ancient and modern, have their wisdom traditions, because humans have always been concerned to get the most out of life.

The wisdom literature of the Bible, principally represented by the books of Job, Proverbs and Ecclesiastes (but *cf.* also Ps. 19), employs various kinds (genres) of expression, *e.g.* the proverb, riddle, narrative, poetry and even law. Regardless of the form of expression, however, 'wisdom' discussions, whether in Israel or in the ancient Near East, generally centred around certain basic concerns.

Basic issues in wisdom literature

1. 'Profit'. Put simply, wisdom literature seeks to find some kind of reward or profit in life which can make one's life better. What sorts of accumulation does life offer so that the end of one's life is better than the beginning? What is it that truly enriches human life? When one looks back on life, what is there that is 'left over' from the course of life that makes one say, 'It was worth it'?

The word 'profit' usually serves as an adequate label for this aspect of wisdom texts. Thus we can say that wisdom literature concerns itself with the question of how one can gain a 'profit' in the course of this life (*e.g.* Pr. 3:13–18).

2. Orientation towards this world. The focus of wisdom literature is earthly life. Not that it never discusses the eternal values; it is rather that everything it discusses is viewed in terms of its meaning for the present life.

3. Universal scope. Wisdom literature does not seek to answer specific historical or social questions about particular groups of people. It wants to know what is true for all people at all times. How can all persons profit in this life (*e.g.* Pr. 3:3–4)?

4. Quest for knowledge. Another basic issue is the necessity of a quest. The truth about this life and how it is to be lived is there for those who seek it. One must apply oneself to wisdom; or, as Proverbs puts it in NASB: 'Wisdom shouts in the street' (Pr. 1:20) and one must go out to meet her. One must 'seek her as silver' (2:4); make one's ear 'attentive' to her (2:2); and cry out to her for understanding (2:3). The watchword of those who would be wise is, 'Seek and ye shall find' (*e.g.* Pr. 8:34–36).

5. Creation theology. Briefly stated, creation* theology entails the acceptance of and understanding of the world created by God as a harmonious whole and sovereignly ordered so that in it all things have their proper time and place. Moreover, it entails the assumption that the orderliness in creation is observable and that, if men and women seek and find their own relationship to this created order, it will provide the key to the profit of their lives. Within such a construct, wisdom is understood as the concerted effort of the successive generations to seek out and articulate the contours of God's created order and to find humanity's place in nature (*e.g.* Jb. 26:7–14; Pr. 8:22–31).

To a large extent, biblical wisdom literature shared many of the above issues with the ancient Near Eastern wisdom traditions. We even find that, on occasion, the biblical historian compared the wisdom of Israel with the wisdom of the ancient Near East (*cf.* 1 Ki. 4:30). Besides the similarities, however, there were fundamental differences between the wisdom of Israel and that of the ancient Near East.

Distinctive features of Israel's wisdom

The primary differences in Israel's wisdom literature can be directly attributed to the influence of the covenant* concept.

1. The most prominent feature of Israelite wisdom was the way in which it succeeded in integrating obedience to the covenant with the goal of universal wisdom. If the general wisdom traditions had as their goal the skill of getting along well in this life, Israelite wisdom, without rejecting this goal, was able to construe it as obedience to the will of the covenant God. God's Torah, *e.g.* in Dt. 4:6, is identified

as Israel's 'wisdom' in distinction from the wisdom of the nations around them. Such is also the meaning of the oft-repeated phrase 'the fear of the LORD is the beginning of wisdom' (Pr. 9:10). All wisdom comes out of the attitude of the fear of the Lord, the covenant God.

2. Another fundamental difference, again due to the influence of the covenant concept, was the way in which biblical wisdom altered one's understanding of 'creation theology'. God created the universe as a harmonious whole and sovereignly ordered it so that all things have their proper time and place (see Ec. 3:1–8). This orderliness in creation is observable, and by seeking it out one could learn to live well. But on this point there is also a distinction: for the Bible, the world order did not tell the whole story, nor did it tell its own story. Creation was not wisdom's only dictum. The creator God was also the covenant God. What he had painted in the universe he had written in the Torah. Both the universe and the Torah, then, show the way in which a wise person should go (cf. Ps. 19).

3. A third difference in biblical wisdom is also concerned with 'creation theology'. If left unchecked, creation theology tends to diminish the personal involvement of God with his creation. Looking at it technically, we could say it tends towards a deistic view of the world, i.e. the belief that the creator formed the universe, subjected it to certain observable laws, and then left humankind to discover itself and its God as it seeks to discover the laws of nature. There is little doubt that the ancient Near Eastern Wisdom traditions largely succumbed to this tendency.

A good case can be made that one of the main purposes of the book of Job is the warning lest wisdom's creation theology in some way eclipse the sovereign will of the covenant God. Job's problem, and that of his friends, is the assumption that they can subject God to scrutiny on the basis of the observable data of creation. Both Job and his friends, all wise men, use the created order to ensnare the creator. However fitting this may have been for the wisdom traditions of the ancient Near East, the God of the covenant could not be thus treated. Job learned, at the end of the book, as God spoke to him from the whirlwind, that God is 'too wonderful', and Job thus acknowledged: 'Surely I spoke of things I did not understand, things too wonderful for me to know' (Jb. 42:3).

Wisdom in the New Testament

In Christ, God's wisdom becomes incarnate. The wisdom he exhibits in his teachings evokes astonishment (Mk. 6:2–3) but seldom repentance (Mt. 12:41–42). Though the created order is invested with wisdom (cf. Rom. 1:20), the world does not know Christ, the wisdom of God (1 Cor. 1:21, 24). The cross both reverses and judges human wisdom (1 Cor. 1:23–25), and it remains foolishness until God causes the light of the gospel to shine in the heart (2 Cor. 4:6). For both Paul and James, divine wisdom stands in contrast to human wisdom in terms of both origin and nature (1 Cor. 1:18–20; Jas. 3:13–17). For believers, however, wisdom is found in Christ (Col. 2:3; cf. 1 Cor. 1:30) and granted in answer to prayer, especially (it would seem) to enable them to discern God's purpose in times of testing (Jas. 1:5).

Contemporary debate

There is considerable debate about the role that wisdom should play in decision-making. Against the traditional evangelical view that tends to downplay wisdom by emphasizing the guidance of God through Scripture, providence and inward impressions, Garry Friesen (1947–) and others stress the role of wisdom in the making of decisions, and (more controversially) deny that the Bible teaches that God has 'an ideal, detailed life-plan for each person' (Decision Making and the Will of God, p. 151).

See also: OLD TESTAMENT ETHICS. [8]

Bibliography

G. Friesen and J. R. Maxson, Decision Making and the Will of God: A Biblical Alternative to the Traditional View (Portland, OR, 1983); D. Kidner, Wisdom to Live By (Leicester, 1985) = The Wisdom of Proverbs, Job and Ecclesiastes (Downers Grove, IL, 1985).

J.H.S.

WITTGENSTEIN, LUDWIG (1899–1951).

To try to summarize Wittgenstein's philosophical thought is almost thereby to distort and to betray it. He did not propound a system of ethics. In his earliest work, especially in the Tractatus Logico-Philosophicus (Ger., 1921), he attempted to explore the limits of thought and language by examining the nature of propositions and of logical necessity. Value, he concluded, cannot be meaningfully articulated within a calculus of descriptive propositions. Propositions can only describe states of affairs which may or may not be the case in the world, and may also elucidate logical relations as tautologies or analytical statements. But 'it is clear that ethics cannot be put into words' (*Tractatus* 6.421).

This conclusion, however, held a different significance for the early Wittgenstein from that which it held for Bertrand Russell (1872–1970). Whereas for Russell the descriptive propositions of natural science expressed all that was important and communicable, Wittgenstein believed that ethical value, like 'the mystical', was simply too profound to be caught in the net of descriptive language which applied to the physical world. Value could only become 'manifest'. For descriptive propositions concern what might or might not be the case, whereas ultimate value cannot be called into question as in principle true or false. With more than an echo of Immanuel Kant,* Wittgenstein cannot include ethics among the subject-matter of *contingent* propositions. Hence he writes: 'If there is any value that does have value, it must be outside the sphere of what happens and is the case. For all that happens and is the case is accidental . . . So it is impossible for there to be propositions of ethics. Propositions can express nothing that is higher' (*Tractatus* 6.41 and 6.42). This leads on to Wittgenstein's final statement that 'What we cannot speak about we must pass over in silence' (*Tractatus* 7).

During the so-called middle period, from 1929 to 1932, Wittgenstein's mode of approach began to change. In 1929, the year of his 'Lecture on Ethics', he wrote in what has now been published under the title *Culture and Value*: 'What is good is also divine . . . Only something supernatural can express the Supernatural . . . The good is outside the space of facts' (*Culture and Value*, 3e). But by the period of *The Blue Book* (1933–35), Wittgenstein has come to replace the model of language as a general system of propositions for that of operative procedures in given situations. Ethical discourse is now to be understood as depending for its currency on a network of attitudes and responsibilities adopted and shared by speakers within a specific context of life and culture. Towards the end of his life in 1950 Wittgenstein assessed the 'seriousness' of a speaker's ethical concerns by 'the difference they make at various points in your life . . .

Practice [his italics] gives the words their sense' (*Culture and Value*, 85e).

Although his ethics are far more complex, here lies Wittgenstein's greatest challenge to ethics and pastoral theology (see ⑦). Human life and action give 'backing' to the language of evaluation, of belief, and of responsibility, by its interwovenness with language. For example, I can say of pain: 'Oh, I feel it strongly – oh, now it has gone off'; but can I say the same of love? Wittgenstein writes: 'Love is put to the test, pain not' (*Zettel*, sec. 504). What does it mean to repent? He writes: 'Only someone who can reflect on the past can repent' (*Zettel*, sec. 519). Wittgenstein observes: '"I believe . . ." throws light on my state. Conclusions about my conduct can be drawn from this expression . . . My own relation to my words is wholly different from other people's' (*Philosophical Investigations*, vol. 2, pp. 191–192e). In this sense, '*Life* can educate one to believe in God' (*Culture and Value*, 86e). In post-Wittgensteinian philosophy of language it would be said that certain ethical and religious utterances would draw their operative currency from their self-involving implications for the life of the speaker, or for given human agents or traditions of belief and action. Pastoral theology similarly addresses the issue of this need for a match between speech and life in given patterns of situations.

Bibliography

Culture and Value (Oxford, ²1980); 'A Lecture on Ethics' (1929), *Philosophical Review* 74, 1965, pp. 3–26; *Lectures and Conversations on Aesthetics, Psychology, and Religious Belief* (Oxford, 1966); *Philosophical Investigations* (Oxford, ³1968); *Tractatus Logico-Philosophicus* (London, 1961); *Zettel* (Oxford, 1967).

C. Barrett, *Wittgenstein on Ethics and Religious Beliefs* (Oxford, 1991); A. P. Griffiths, 'Wittgenstein, Schopenhauer, and Ethics', in *Royal Institute of Philosophy Lectures, 7: Understanding Wittgenstein* (London, 1974), pp. 96–116; R. Rhees, 'Some Developments in Wittgenstein's View of Ethics', in *Discussions of Wittgenstein* (London, 1970), pp. 94–103.

A.C.T.

WOMEN, ORDINATION OF, see MINISTRY.

WOMEN'S RIGHTS, see FEMINISM.

WORK is commonly understood as human activity designed to accomplish something that is needed as distinct from activity that is satisfying in itself. The latter is usually regarded as play,* while the absence of activity is usually regarded as rest. If we consider that work, whether paid or unpaid, consumes most of the waking hours of most people, it has received comparatively little focused attention in theological circles. This is doubly regrettable since work has had an unusual significance in the Christian faith and, through this faith, has acquired an unusual significance in the modern world.

1. Work in the Bible

In the OT the context of work is provided by the 'cultural mandate' wherein humankind, as the image of God,* is made and called to cultivate and keep the world that God has made (Gn. 1:26, 28; 9:7). Human beings are responsible for the world and are to shape human culture* and history. Hence explicit attention is paid to human work (Gn. 4:17, 20–22; 9:20). Even God is described as one who makes, forms, builds and plants. The creator's blessing* enables us to grow up and grow into human culture. Culture is both a gift of God and the fruit of human activity. While the mandate originally addressed arable farming and husbandry, it applies to everything that can be 'cultivated' and 'kept', everything with which humans have been entrusted. Hence it involves all aspects of human civilization, including the sciences, social affairs, arts, literature and education.* This implies that intellectual and other mental effort should not be excluded from work, and it implies equally that manual and physical labour should not be regarded as a lower form of activity. While some tasks may in context be more urgent than others, there is no biblical basis for a hierarchy of types of work.

This positive theme continues in the NT. Jesus' parables are suffused with the everyday world of work. Paul condemned idleness (2 Thes. 3:6) and exhorted Christians to useful activity (Eph. 4:28). He criticized the Thessalonians who had abandoned work in eschatological hope (1 Thes. 5:12). He used the same terms to refer to both his apostolic service and the labour by which he earned a living (1 Cor. 4:12; 15:10; Phil. 2:16; Col. 1:29). The 'new nature' created in God's likeness is to do manual work (2 Thes. 3:10).

But while work is treated with great honour in Scripture, it is never idealized. Human work became corrupted and perverted in the Fall. The alienation* between human beings and God, between fellow humans, and between human beings and the rest of creation makes labour a source of pain* and suffering.* The curse means that work is degraded to sweat and toil (Gn. 3:17–19). Sin also makes work a source of danger. In the song of Lamech (Gn. 4:23–24) ironworking has produced weapons designed to exercise power.* The tower of Babel, the pinnacle of human labour, shows a human community destroying itself as it tries to go beyond human limitations by putting its own achievements in competition with God (Gn. 11:1–9).

Work is conditioned not only by the effects of sin but also by the created limits to human achievement. Work is not the means of salvation: it cannot mediate between God and humankind, it cannot eradicate sin and it cannot produce a new creation. Salvation is a gift, not the fruit of labour. Our lives are in God's hands, not ours. Hence Jesus told us to consider the birds, who do not sow or reap, and the lilies, who do not toil or spin (Mt. 6:26–28).

There is no basis in Scripture for limiting our calling solely to work. The human calling also involves play,* friendship, worship and rest (see Sabbath*). Israel's life was a rhythm of work and rest. Rest is in turn tied to trust in God, so that it is an image of salvation (Lv. 25:10–24; Ps. 95:7b–11; Heb. 3:7 – 4:11). Jesus promised rest, as well as work, to those who come to him.

Despite the effects of sin, work retains its place in redemption. Isaiah prophesies building, planting and enjoying the fruits of one's labours (Is. 65:21–22). Swords and spears are not merely cast away but become ploughshares and pruning hooks (Mi. 4:3).

The portrayal of work in Genesis is in sharp contrast to much religious speculation on the subject. Many myths viewed the things of human culture as produced by the gods and then given to humans, or as stolen from a hostile divinity (in the Promethean myth), or as a hostile nature (in the modern age). The NT also stands in sharp relief to the surrounding Hellenistic culture. Gk. and Roman theorists viewed work as necessary and therefore unfree, and hence lower than the more intrinsically human life of the mind or of politics. Work was 'un-leisure', a necessary but demeaning substratum on which genuinely human activities could be based.

2. Work in Christian tradition

A biblical view of work, as an essential though partial element of the divine calling which has now been marred by sin but which can be restored by God, continued in the post-apostolic period. However, the Church Fathers gradually began to draw more heavily on Gk. and Roman motifs. While the church continued to affirm everyday work and never accepted the idea that it was less than human, a view developed in which it was seen as a second-order activity, subservient to pious duties. By the early part of the 4th century Eusebius of Caesarea's (c. 265–c. 339) doctrine of the two lives distinguished a perfect form 'beyond common human living' from a secondary form which allowed for 'farming, for trade, and the other more secular interests'. Augustine* praised farmers, craftsmen and even merchants, but he still tended to treat these activities as less than contemplation: 'The one is loved, the other endured.' For Thomas Aquinas* 'the life of contemplation' was still 'better than the life of action'. While there were exceptions to this trend, it has continued to influence much of Roman Catholicism, Orthodoxy and, to a lesser extent, Protestantism.

A shift from this depreciation of 'secular' work took place in the Reformation, notably with Martin Luther.* He described everyday work as a *Beruf*, a 'calling', a term hitherto restricted to monastic or clerical positions. Such work was on a spiritual par with priestly duties. This theme was further developed by John Calvin,* who emphasized that the 'talents' of Mt. 25:14–30 included all human effort and abilities. He stressed the utility of work and on this basis developed a view of the division of labour as a sign of the fellowship and solidarity of humanity under God.

This Protestant rediscovery of a biblical view of work has been credited or blamed as a major factor in shaping the modern age. The sociologist Max Weber (1864–1920), in a famous work of social science, emphasized the unique 'this-worldly' focus of the Protestant ethic of vocation* and maintained that this ethic was one of the major causes of modern capitalism (*i.e.* industrialism). Ernst Troeltsch (1865–1923) held similar views, while R. H. Tawney* stressed that it was the *corruption* of the authentic Reformation view that produced a so-called 'Protestant ethic'.

3. Work in contemporary society

Whatever the merits of Weber's views, which remain hotly debated, the modern world is characterized by an unparalleled stress on work. In economics the labour theory of value – which appeared with John Locke (1632–1704), was refined by Adam Smith (1723–90) and David Ricardo (1772–1823), and reached its apogee in Karl Marx* – ascribed to work everything that is of value in human life. Work has now acquired a secular doctrine of salvation on both a personal and social level. For Marx, world history was 'nothing but the creation of man by labour' which would usher in a 'realm of freedom' (communism) 'where labour . . . determined by . . . mundane considerations ceases'. Similar themes can be garnered from more capitalist writings, especially those of John Maynard Keynes (1883–1946). In each case human fulfilment is seen as an escape from work and necessity, but the means to this fulfilment is still human work and achievement. At a personal level this is manifest as a drive to work in order to increase wealth in order to achieve leisure. At a social, economic and political level it is manifested as a policy of increased production and productivity in the hope that plenty will produce peace and freedom. Consequently, work is usually considered in terms of its consequences for the production and distribution of commodities, and all too rarely as an activity in its own right. Thus the modern world combines a rejection of God's good gift of work with an idolization that gives it a significance it cannot bear.

Neither the Bible nor Christian reflection provides us with a set of rules to respond to this situation. Instead they orient us to the proper place of work in human life. The ancient rejection of work and the modern ambiguous infatuation with it can both be seen as miscasting its role within the creation. Work should not be despised as a burden and barrier to human fulfilment, nor should it be idolized as the centre of human life or the means to personal and social fulfilment. At a personal level we must avoid the semi-gnosticism which treats work as unimportant, secondary or irrelevant to the kingdom of God.* We must also stress that, without the discipline, achievement and means of service provided by honest labour, human life can disintegrate. At the same time we need to criticize the rejection of grace* implied in a focus on work at the cost of neighbourliness, family life, play or rest. Every aspect of human life is a calling, and rest is a gift of God as valuable as any human achievement.

At a social level we should acknowledge that there is no intrinsic merit to longer working hours, while rejecting the view that the elimination of work and the increase of leisure* is a key to human freedom. Coupled with these is the great need to alleviate unemployment* and to help make work available to all. At the same time we should not overvalue work and production or give them a priority over other aspects of existence. The value of work must be weighed together with other needs such as family* life and environmental* protection. Work must be cherished not only for what it produces but also for what it is. It is carried out by creatures made in the image of God and must be an act of genuine responsibility.* This requires an emphasis not on income as a compensation for work (though people need to be sustained in and by it) but on the work process itself. Here there is a subjective side which requires a sense of vocation that sees work as the use of one's gifts in service to others. There is also an objective side in that work situations and jobs must be structured so as to allow and encourage human fulfilment and service. This calls for a concentration on good work and a rejection of the notion that labour can be treated as a commodity which can be bought or sold. Though work will not be perfected and its pain will not disappear, we are called to renew it as much as is possible.

The renewal of work is a communal and personal responsibility rooted in trust. Genuine work is not the basis of our security but can take place when we know that our needs can be met by God. We work not in order to be accepted but because we have already been accepted in grace.

See also: SIN AND SALVATION. [5]

Bibliography

G. Agnell, Work, Toil and Sustenance (Lund, 1976); L. Hardy, The Fabric of this World (Grand Rapids, 1990); John Paul II, Laborem Exercens (ET, On Human Work, London, 1981); P. Marshall, 'Calling, Work and Rest', in M. Noll and D. Wells (eds.), Christian Faith and Practice in the Modern World (Grand Rapids, 1988); P. Marshall et al., Labour of Love: Essays on Work (Toronto, 1980); J. Moltmann, On Human Dignity (ET, London and Philadelphia, 1984); J. O. Nelson (ed.), Work and Vocation (New York, 1954); A. Richardson, The Biblical Doctrine of Work (London, 1952); E. F. Schumacher, Good Work (London, 1979); M. Weber, The Protestant Ethic and the Spirit of Capitalism (1904–05; ET, London, 1930); C. Westermann, 'Work Civilization and Culture in the Bible', in G. Baum (ed.), Work and Religion (New York, 1980).

P.A.M.

WORLD COUNCIL OF CHURCHES, see ECUMENICAL ETHICS.

WORLD ECONOMIC ORDER, see GLOBAL ETHICS. [15]

WORLD HUNGER, see HUNGER, WORLD.

WORLD, THE. Although it is often used loosely to refer to everything that has been created, the term 'the world' in Christian theological and ethical discussion designates principally the entirety of the structures within which human existence takes place, and, more specifically, the various dimensions of human intellectual, cultural, social and political activity. Since the world is fallen, the term is frequently used to refer to that which is opposed to God, with a set of overlapping meanings which may range from the totality of unredeemed human structures and patterns of life and thought, subject to the rebellious principalities and powers, to sinful humankind as a whole.

The Bible and the world

The notion of the world as a self-subsistent entity is alien to the biblical writers. The OT refers to the universe as 'the heavens and the earth' (e.g. Gn. 1:1) or 'all things' (e.g. Ps. 8:6, RSV; Je. 10:16), but always with the implication that it owes its origins and continued existence to the sovereign power of Yahweh (e.g. Ps. 89:11; Is. 66:1). In the NT the term principally used for the world (kosmos) sometimes refers to the created universe (e.g. Acts 17:24), the inhabited world (Mt. 4:8), or the arena of human life (1 Tim. 6:7). However, in its theologically most significant sense it bears a range of meanings which focus on the world as the whole created order whose orientation derives from the response to God of human beings, who stand at its head: frequently, therefore, it may simply refer to humankind (Jn. 1:10, 'the world did not recognise him'). Because human response to God is one of disobedience, the orientation of the world is one of hostility to God: it has become '*this* world' (*e.g.* Jn. 9:39; 1 Cor. 3:19) and is subject to divine judgment (Rom. 3:19). The Johannine writings indicate that the *kosmos* is ruled by the prince of this world (Jn. 12:31); while the Pauline writings virtually identify it with the present aeon, in bondage to elemental powers (Col. 2:8), to which the Christian is crucified (Gal. 6:14) – indeed, the word is never here used to describe the coming world.

Despite its rebelliousness, the world is not intrinsically evil: it is the object of God's love (Jn. 3:16) and of his salvific plan of reconciliation to himself through Christ (Jn. 1:29; 2 Cor. 5:19). Christ has conquered the world (Jn. 16:33), and through his work its ruler has been judged (Jn. 16:11). Those who believe have overcome the world (1 Jn. 5:4–5), are sent into the world (Mt. 5:14; Mk. 16:15), and are to live in the world (Jn. 17:11). They are, however, not 'of the world' (Jn. 17:16), and are commanded not to love the world or the things in the world. The form of the world is passing away (1 Cor. 7:31), and is giving way to the time described by the writer of Revelation, when 'the kingdom of the world has become the kingdom of our Lord and of his Christ, and he will reign for ever and ever' (Rev. 11:15).

The biblical writings convey, then, a powerful sense of the fallenness of the world, and of human beings entangled in this. Yet Scripture never goes so far as to deny the fundamental goodness of the world. Even if the present world-order is to pass away, redemption is not ultimately *from* the world but *of* the world. From this derives the tension which has characterized all Christian thought, between that in the world which must be rejected, and that which must be affirmed. Simply to state that Christians should be 'in the world but not of the world' does not solve this problem, but merely names it.

The world in Christian theology

The variety of theological positions offered in response to this resist any simple classification. Yet some of the more prominent tendencies can be illustrated, each of which, as is to be expected, has implications not only in respect of ethics and pastoral practice, but also with regard to spirituality,* the relations between church* and world, and between revelation* and reason,* as well as the major *loci* of traditional Christian theology.

1. World-rejecting approaches emphasize that Christians should not be of the world. In relation to these, a broad distinction should be drawn between a. discipline of the body and bodily desires through ascetic* or self-denying practices, and b. rejection of the world and its institutions. These two are sometimes found together: Tertullian,* for example, while not counselling complete separation from worldly affairs, was a firm moral rigorist, and shunned the political, military, philosophical and artistic life of the Roman world as belonging to the devil. Again, the monastic (see Monasticism*) tradition combines ascetic discipline with separation from the world; though here, as often amongst those emphasizing world-renunciation, the pursuit of holiness* is frequently understood in terms of greater service of the world, and the fundamental impulse is not retreat from the world but the quest for a renewed humanity, displaying the fullness of life in Christ. Many Christian groups have, however, stressed world-renunciation without any especial commitment to ascetic practice. From the Reformation period onwards Mennonites,* and Anabaptists* in general, have affirmed the peaceable church community in opposition to the coercive structures of the State, including war, the law, and sometimes the economic profit-system: by its life and very existence, the church as a believers' community is called to show the world its worldliness.

Although the world-denying strain in Christian history has often been a response to worldliness* and compromise* within the church, it is more than a mere reaction. It leans towards clear distinctions between Christians and non-Christians (or between different classes of Christians), an acceptance of the sole authority of Christ, and a rejection of non-Christian culture* as evil. These may be reinforced through emphatic spiritual and moral discipline, or varying degrees of physical (or other) separation from what is perceived to be the world, or both. Correspondingly, this range of positions has affinities with strong contrasts between revelation and reason, Christian and non-Christian moral practice, salvation history and secular history, eschatological promise and present reality, and, at the extreme, between God as redeemer and God as creator.

2. World-affirming approaches, by contrast, emphasize God's activity and human responsibility in the world beyond the church. An example is 19th-century culture-Protestantism, from F. D. E. Schleiermacher's* 'speeches' on religion to its 'cultured despisers', through Albrecht Ritschl's (1822–89) inclusion of political and social relations in the community of the kingdom of Christ (see Kingdom of God*), to the N. American social gospel* programme. This last movement focused on the prior importance of social salvation to individual salvation, locating the redemption of the social order in a story of the universal evolutionary progress of the world towards the ethical ideals of the kingdom. Perhaps the most explicit embracing of the world, however, is found in the 'theology of secularity' of the 1960s. This claimed inspiration from Dietrich Bonhoeffer's* tentative explorations of 'religionless Christianity', according to which the correct Christian response to the modern world's 'coming of age' should be not condemnation of its aspirations to autonomy,* but recognition of the presence of the crucified Christ in its very secularity and godlessness.

The attractiveness of such world-affirming positions frequently stems from perceptions of the church's insularity and irrelevance to its cultural context. By contrast with the world-denying tendency, their stress on Christ as saviour of the world and not just of a few, and on the work of the Holy Spirit* beyond the boundaries of the church, often leads them to a celebration of the life of the world. While different world-affirming approaches may disagree, their general tenor is usually towards highlighting the continuity (or even identity) of salvation history and the history of human progress, of Christian ethics and the best in secular ethics, as well as towards a high evaluation of nature in relation to grace* and of reason in relation to revelation.

3. Mixed approaches to the world, as they might non-technically be called, have characterized the mainstream of the Western Christian tradition. Augustine* allowed that the heavenly city should use the temporal institutions of the earthly city, but argued that the earthly city was itself destined for destruction. Thomas Aquinas'* theorization of medieval civilization recognized the intrinsic value of life in the world, but also limited its scope: the natural institutions of society are incorporated into a unified Christian order, thereby allowing the reach of Christian ethics

to extend beyond the church, but are subordinated as a preparatory stage for the higher life of grace. The same mixed approach to the world is found in Martin Luther's* contrast between the kingdom of the world, *i.e.* the temporal realm, and the spiritual kingdom, which corresponds to the order of salvation: the former, though marred by the Fall, is not simply the kingdom of Satan,* but rather relates to God's government of the world through the sword of the secular governments.* Calvinism (see Calvinistic Ethics*) again, while allowing in principle a more joyful acceptance of the world, yet cultivates a deep spiritual detachment from it.

These approaches do not admit of ready generalization, but they tend towards an acceptance of the propriety of Christian influence, or even control, beyond the institutional church, together with a certain scepticism about the extent to which it can be achieved. The universal scope of God's work in the world may be acknowledged, but also a recognition of the higher calling of the church. By combining in different ways attachment to the world with distance from it, they make clear the nature of the world as both created and fallen.

Towards a theology of the world

By way of positive recommendation for a theology of the world, the following points might be suggested.

1. The world is a theologically-constructed concept, *i.e.* its meaning is determined by theological requirements, not by everyday or non-theological usage of the term. By treating social, political and cultural activity in terms of a unified totality rather than its constituent parts, a theology of the world makes clear that the structures of human existence as a whole are of theological significance. Moreover, by connecting the world with the desires, attitudes and behaviour that constitute worldliness, it shows that theological concern extends beyond an external understanding of those structures.

2. The most perspicuous feature of the world in the NT is its fallenness. Nevertheless, a rounded Christian view will place NT negativity about the world in the context of the OT affirmation of creation. Consequently, a rejection of worldliness should be understood as a refusal not of desire or of material goods or of social or political forms, but of their distorted images. Likewise, the kingdom is at

once a denial of the fallen world and an affirmation of a renewed and transformed creation.

3. In view of this, the church, as the sign of the kingdom, is called both to cultivate a distinctiveness that points to the world's future, and to live and work in the world's present. It is to be light, showing the life of the kingdom to the world, and salt, permeating the world. Thus, while the values of the kingdom should be present most evidently in the church, they will also be reflected beyond the church.

4. The church's first commitment is fidelity to Christ, not relevance to the world; with Karl Rahner (1904–84), it is not in the first place 'an organization for a better world'. Christian social and political engagement therefore starts with criticism of the life and structures of the church before it can presume to address the world. Recognizing the force of the world's own view of the church, this criticism will also include judgment of worldliness in the church, since without undergoing this it will be in no position to show the worldliness of the world.

5. The second commitment of the church, flowing from its faithfulness to Christ just as mission flows from worship, is to work in the world, with the world, for the sake of the world. Because Christ is Lord of all, the world is not 'foreign territory' (Bonhoeffer): the world *is* the church's agenda, even if it does not wholly *set* that agenda. This cannot, however, allow unqualified identification with any particular human project; indeed, at times the church's affirmation of the world may have to take the form of rejection of the world's understanding of its own needs.

6. Finally, even if world-renunciation is ultimately ordered to world-affirmation, the world is still in the grip of hostile powers. Although Christian theology rightly talks about redemption *of* the world, the contrast with the future is so marked that Scripture regards the world to come as a new world. But even that world is not the final object of the Christian hope; Christ 'does not direct attention away from this world to another; but from all worlds . . . to the One who creates all worlds' (H. Richard Niebuhr, *Christ and Culture*, p. 28).

Discerning worldliness

The art of Christian living in relation to the world is a matter of learning a Christian practical wisdom* that is at once fully discerning of worldliness and yet critically engaged in the life of the world. The roots of this practical wisdom lie in the discipline of listening to Scripture. This should be conceived as an enterprise that is primarily communal rather than individual in nature, understands the Christian tradition as a tradition of interpreting Scripture, seeks to unmask ideological misinterpretation, and is grounded in worship, guarded by obedience, and guided by the Spirit.

The fruit of this wisdom will be a discernment that conquers the world. Worldliness is identified in the NT in a number of ways: as 'the desire of the flesh, the desire of the eyes, the pride of riches' (1 Jn. 2:16, NRSV); as bitter envy, selfish ambition and the like, contrasted with peaceableness, gentleness, sincerity, *etc.* (Jas. 3:13 – 4:6); as following deceptive human philosophies and legalistic regulations (Col. 2:8, 20–23); *etc.* Its core might be characterized in terms of pride,* covetousness,* the idolatrous worship of something other than God, the autonomous following of self-chosen ends, or an uncritical and unspiritual conformity to the standards of society beyond the church. Such worldliness is of course a matter of much more than 'microethical' details of personal behaviour (*e.g.* the alleged impropriety of smoking, drinking and dancing), and will extend to the deepest themes of modern culture. It will be conquered only by those who believe that Jesus is the Son of God (1 Jn. 5:4–5), set their minds on things above (Col. 3:2), and refuse the schizophrenic love of both God and world (Jas. 4:4).

Yet this wisdom will also love the world, and sacrifice itself to be incarnate in the world (Jn. 3:16). A discerning worldliness will not take the form of a Christian secularism, but will be rooted in Christian distinctiveness. It will recognize value in the structures of the world, while at the same time pointing to their fulfilment in Christ. And with Bonhoeffer it will follow not 'the shallow and banal thisworldliness of the enlightened, the busy, the comfortable, or the lascivious, but the profound this-worldliness, characterized by discipline and the constant knowledge of death and resurrection', and will reckon with Bonhoeffer's claim that 'a genuine worldliness is possible solely and exclusively on the basis of the proclamation of the cross of Jesus Christ' (*Ethics*, ET, London, 1955, p. 263).

Bibliography

D. Bonhoeffer, *Letters and Papers from*

Prison (ET, London, ²1971); D. J. Bosch, *Transforming Mission* (Maryknoll, NY, 1991); K. E. Kirk, *The Vision of God* (London and New York, 1931); R. A. Muller, *ISBE* 4, pp. 1112–1116; H. R. Niebuhr, *Christ and Culture* (New York, 1951; London, 1952); O. O'Donovan, *Resurrection and Moral Order* (Leicester and Grand Rapids, ²1994); K. Rahner (ed.), *Sacramentum Mundi* 1 (New York, 1968), pp. 346–357; H. Sasse, *TDNT* 3, pp. 867–898; E. Troeltsch, *The Social Teaching of the Christian Churches*, 2 vols. (ET, London and New York, 1931); J. H. Yoder, *The Christian Witness to the State* (Newton, KS, 1964).

R.J.So.

WORLDLINESS. There is no actual equivalent biblical word for 'worldliness', as the concept is based on the command 'Do not love the world' (1 Jn. 2:15; see 2 Tim. 4:10). The term 'the world',* however, appears frequently in Scripture, with three distinct meanings. Sometimes it refers to the whole created order (Jn. 1:10); sometimes to humanity, which 'God so loved' (Jn. 3:16); and sometimes to the system of human thought and society organized without recognition of God and often in opposition to his will (1 Cor. 1:21; 1 Jn. 2:16).

Worldliness is that attitude to the world (*i.e.* the third of these senses) that makes the world a rival to the love and service of God, because the world, in this sense, is deeply corrupted by sin and is described as 'under the control of the evil one' (1 Jn. 5:19).

The classical statements come mostly in 1 John. Thus in 1 Jn. 2:15–17 we are warned not to 'love the world or anything in the world. If anyone loves the world, the love of the Father is not in him' (see also 1 Jn. 3:1; 4:5; 5:4, 19). Jesus prayed that his disciples would be kept from being 'of the world' while they remained 'in the world' (Jn. 17:11, 14, 18).

Worldliness therefore can be defined as giving service and loyalty to created things rather than to God, *i.e.* loving them, in the strong sense of giving them priority (Rom. 1:25). It involves being diverted from the exclusive love and loyalty that are due to God alone by the attitudes, priorities and practices of our culture. Instead, we are to 'overcome the world' (Jn. 16:33; 1 Jn. 5:4; Rom. 12:2).

These emphases have often been translated into practice in terms of having as little to do with normal life as possible. The 'spiritual' life has then been seen in terms of celibacy, poverty and the monastic life. In Protestant circles it has sometimes been translated into a set of rules about things that one should not do. It has meant to some that they should not play any part in politics* or social and cultural life except within the church. It has seemed to encourage a negative asceticism.*

There are, however, two major qualifications of this basic contrast between the world and a Christian outlook:

1. The Bible teaches that we are to regard the created order and the social and cultural order as containing elements which are good and a cause for thanksgiving to God. They are not as bad as they could be, and God in his goodness restrains evil so that secular powers are to be obeyed and supported (Rom. 13:1–7), and we are to give our minds to all that is good and wholesome in our society (Phil. 4:8–9). Marriage and food are to be received with thanksgiving (1 Tim. 4:1–4), and it is God 'who richly provides us with everything for our enjoyment' (1 Tim. 6:17).

It was a rediscovery of these truths at the Protestant Reformation that undermined the then generally accepted negative asceticism. Whereas to have a vocation* had been seen exclusively in terms of a celibate life, for instance, the concept was now enthusiastically transferred to all wholesome occupations. Priests and nuns were encouraged to marry; money was seen as a good thing to share, rather than something in itself corrupt; and social life was to be reformed and not shunned. The thinking of the Reformers, particularly John Calvin,* has continually maintained a positive emphasis in some circles, especially in Holland.

The pietist movements of the last 300 years, however, have tended to push Protestants back to a much more negative stance, but there has been a recovery of a positive attitude in evangelical circles in the second half of the 20th century, led by writers such as Francis Schaeffer,* H. R. Rookmaaker (1922–72), J. N. D. Anderson (1908–) and John Stott (1921–).

2. If we take a positive attitude to all the truly good things in life, we are warned that we must be aware of the subtle influences of the world on our thinking and living. We are sinful, and good things can become a temptation to covetousness,* which is 'idolatry' (Col. 3:5), and the thinking of a godless society can easily infect us. Therefore we are warned: 'Don't let the world around you squeeze you into its own mould, but let God remould your

minds from within' (Rom. 12:2, JBP). The pietists were right when they stressed that a living faith and love for God are essential to keep us from being subtly infected by evil.*

Christians therefore have to combine resistance to every kind of evil (1 Thes. 5:22) with insisting that God wants us to enjoy all the good that he has given us, even when, as so often, it presents itself mixed up with evil in this fallen world.

Bibliography

J. N. D. Anderson, *Into the World: The Needs and Limits of Christian Involvement* (London, 1968); P. Helm, *The Callings* (Edinburgh, 1987); H. R. Rookmaaker, *The Creative Gift* (London and Westchester, IL, 1981); *idem, Modern Art and the Death of a Culture* (1970; Westchester, IL, and Leicester, ²1994); F. A. Schaeffer, *Escape from Reason* (London and Downers Grove, IL, 1968); *idem, The God Who is There* (London and Chicago, 1968); J. R. W. Stott, *Issues Facing Christians Today* (Basingstoke, ²1990) = *Involvement* (Old Tappan, NJ, ²1990); *idem* and R. T. Coote (eds.), *Down to Earth: Studies in Christianity and Culture* (Grand Rapids, 1980; London, 1981); A. N. Triton, *Whose World?* (London, 1970).

O.R.B.

Z

ZEAL, ZEALOT. In Scripture, the Heb. and Gk. words sometimes translated 'zeal' can have two main meanings, depending on whether the motive for the zeal is good or bad: if good, zeal means an eager, positive enthusiasm and striving for an idea or a cause; in a bad sense, zeal has a wrong goal and means jealousy or envy (see Jealousy and Envy*).

In the OT, the noun *qin'â* is mostly used in a good sense to speak of God's jealousy, *i.e.* zeal. God is jealous for his people Israel, both to protect them, and to judge them when they are unfaithful (Is. 59:17; Ezk. 16:38). His zeal is shown both as mercy to those who fear him (*e.g.* Is. 63:15), and also as being against wrongdoers, to punish them (*e.g.* Dt. 29:20, 'zeal' indicating God's wrath).

In the NT, the noun *zēlos* (which with two exceptions translates *qin'â* in the LXX) can

be either negative or positive. Negatively, jealousy and envy can undermine the life of a church (Jas. 3:14, 16). Jealousy belongs to the sinful nature and is to be rejected (Gal. 5:20). There is also a wrong zeal for the law. Paul was zealous for the Jewish traditions, and this zeal for God, found also in the Jewish people (Acts 22:3), causes him to persecute the church (Phil. 3:6). As he reflected after his conversion, he realized he had acted with unenlightened zeal, as did the Israelites with their zeal for God (Rom. 10:2–4).

But zeal is also presented in a positive way. Christ himself is described as someone whose zeal for the house of God consumed him (Jn. 2:17, where Ps. 69:9 is quoted, probably being taken as a Messianic prophecy describing Jesus' motivation for his action of cleansing the Temple). In 2 Cor. 11:2, Paul describes himself as 'jealous . . . with a godly jealousy' for his converts, maybe indicating the dual functions of the word. Positive zeal for the welfare of others is commended (2 Cor. 7:7; 9:2). Paul specifically states the positive side of being zealous in Gal. 4:18 as he commends missionary zeal, while noting in verse 17 how it is possible to be zealous in the wrong way. Further, the Corinthians are encouraged 'eagerly [to] desire' the gifts of the Holy Spirit, especially the gifts that build up the church (1 Cor. 12:31; 14:12), this zeal being seen in the context of love (1 Cor. 13:4), without which it is nothing. The believer is also to be eager to do good (Tit. 2:14; 1 Pet. 3:13).

The term 'Zealot' has generally been used to refer to those who took part in Jewish resistance to the Roman rule of Palestine, from the time of Judas of Galilee (AD 6; see Acts 5:37) through to the war with Rome (AD 66–70), although not all would be happy with identifying the 'Zealots' as a specific rebel group until this war began. However, the notion of being willing both to use violence* and to suffer injury and even martyrdom for the sake of the Torah was prevalent throughout the 1st century. We may note that Paul describes himself as having been a religious zealot (Acts 22:3; Gal. 1:14), and the members of the church at Jerusalem are described as all 'zealous for the law' (Acts 21:20). They were all Zealots for the tradition without being revolutionaries. Simon the Zealot is named as one of Jesus' disciples, although this may be a nickname given to him rather than indicating that he was a member of the Zealot party.

Some scholars have suggested that Jesus had

strong links with the Zealots, and that he had some sympathy for their aims. For example, he was executed by a Roman governor on a charge of being a political rebel ('king of the Jews', Mt. 22:37). Also, Jesus' entry into Jerusalem is seen by some as having royal overtones, followed by his act of cleansing the Temple in a violent manner. Further, Jesus seemed to mix with common, poor people, he criticized the wealthy, and came into conflict with powerful religious leaders – all aspects of which Zealots would have approved.

It is likely, however, that these factors are pressed too far. It is doubtful whether the Romans saw Jesus and his disciples as a military threat. Although they executed him, it does not follow that they perceived him as a supporter of armed resistance. Also, Jesus did not support non-payment of Roman taxes (Mt. 22:15–22), and his commands to love enemies and not to resist evil people (Mt. 5:38–48) were hardly in keeping with Zealot attitudes. It is also probably more accurate to see Jesus' entry into Jerusalem and his subsequent action in the Temple as prophetic signs rather than acts of revolution. Jesus declared his kingdom (see Kingdom of God*) to be not of this world, and that it could not be brought in by politics and violence (Jn. 18:36–37). Thus Jesus' overall attitude, actions and teachings all tell against his being sympathetic to, or a supporter of, the Zealots.

Bibliography

E. Bammel and C. F. D. Moule (eds.), *Jesus and the Politics of his Day* (Cambridge and New York, 1984); S. G. F. Brandon, *Jesus and the Zealots: A Study of the Political Factors in Primitive Christianity* (Manchester, 1967); H.-C. Hahn, *NIDNTT* 3, pp. 1166–1168; M. Hengel, *The Zealots* (ET, Edinburgh, 1989).

P.D.W.

INDEX OF NAMES

Index of Names

Page references to articles are denoted by **bold type**.